Praise for *The Unicode Standard, Version 5.0*

"The world is a global village, trade crosses language barriers, and yet every one of us likes to feel comfortable within their own mother tongue. Unicode enabled us to give the local sense to every one of our users, while connecting the world of trade—which is the reason we will support Unicode in all of our products."

—**Shai Agassi**, Member
SAP Executive Board

"The W3C was founded to develop common protocols to lead the evolution of the World Wide Web. The path W3C follows to making text on the Web truly global is Unicode. Unicode is fundamental to the work of the W3C; it is a component of W3C Specifications, from the early days of HTML, to the growing XML Family of specifications and beyond."

—**Sir Tim Berners-Lee**, KBE
Web Inventor and Director of the World Wide Web Consortium (W3C)

"The IETF has made the Unicode-compatible UTF-8 format of ISO 10646 the basis for its preferred default character encoding for internationalization of Internet application protocols, so I am delighted to see the official release of Unicode 5.0."

—**Brian E. Carpenter**, Chair, Internet Engineering Task Force
Distinguished Engineer, Internet Standards & Technology, IBM

"Google's objective is to organize the world's information and to make it accessible. Unicode plays a central role in this effort because it is the principal means by which content in every language can be represented in a form that can be processed by software. As Unicode extends its coverage of the world's languages, it helps Google accomplish its mission."

—**Vint Cerf**, Chief Internet Evangelist
Google, Inc.

"Unicode Standard Version 5.0 is a great milestone for the Unicode Standard, which has been critical to computing since it was first published in 1991. With extended script and character support, this new version will help us bridge the digital divide by enabling more people to access computing in the language they use every day. The comprehensive set of mathematics symbols simplifies support for technical documents in business software. For more than a decade, Unicode has been a foundation for many Microsoft products and technologies: Unicode Standard Version 5.0 will help us deliver important new benefits to users."

—**Bill Gates**, Chairman
Microsoft Corporation

"Unicode transformed characters from being a random collection of bits to things of meaning. Without Unicode, Java wouldn't be Java, and the Internet would have a harder time connecting the people of the world."

—**James Gosling**, Inventor of Java
Sun Microsystems, Inc.

"In the Directorate-General for Translation of the European Commission, the databases for internal document management and the interfaces of software applications and hardware equipment—including keyboards—have been built around Unicode, allowing representation of alphabets of all languages. Therefore, introducing languages using Cyrillic characters, or any other character set recognised by Unicode, is no problem."

—**Tytti Granqvist**, Coordinator for External Communication
Directorate-General for Translation of the European Commission

"Because the character primitive in Java is Unicode, the global market readiness of internationalized Java applications depends on the features and coverage of the scripts that Unicode provides. As a member of the Java community, I greatly welcome Unicode 5.0. Developers will find it easy to implement—the standard is far more thoroughly explained than ever before. Computer users in global markets will also appreciate its larger coverage of scripts."

—**Kazuhiro Kazama**, Senior Research Engineer
Nippon Telegraph and Telephone Corporation, Japan

"The development of Unicode has underscored the Internet's truly global character. The recorded history of every nation and culture can travel in its natural form across Cyberspace for the use of anyone, anywhere. Through the power of Unicode, a worldwide audience is finally able to share in the breadth of human creativity."

—**Brendan Kehoe**
Zen and the Art of the Internet

"Hard copy versions of the Unicode Standard have been among the most crucial and most heavily used reference books in my personal library for years. Unicode allows me to celebrate the fact that computer science is a vast worldwide collaboration. And Unicode is perhaps the best tool I know to help bring understanding between people of different cultures."

—**Donald E. Knuth**, Professor Emeritus of The Art of Computer Programming
Stanford University

"Our innate desire to communicate defines us, both as individuals and as a species. Operating systems such as Solaris 10 use Unicode to enable humans to communicate across the Internet, and to bridge the digital divide."

—**Tim Marsland**, Software CTO, VP/Fellow
Sun Microsystems, Inc.

"Unicode, as an enabler to support multiple languages and locales across multiple platforms without re-engineering, is a solid foundation for e-business in a global economy. IBM's implementation of Unicode support across our product lines echoes our overall commitment to the importance of open standards in the evolving global marketplace."

—**Steve Mills**, General Manager Solutions and Strategy
IBM Software Group

"XML software tools are well internationalized, thanks to XML's adoption of Unicode. The addition of JIS X 0213 characters to Unicode 5.0 provides the characters required by the Japanese e-government."

—**Makoto Murata**, Research Specialist
Tokyo Research Lab, IBM Japan, Ltd.

"Unicode marks the most significant advance in writing systems since the Phoenicians."

—**James J. O'Donnell**, Provost,
Georgetown University

"I applaud the efforts of the Unicode community, ensuring computers worldwide work seamlessly in everyone's language."

—**Larry Page**, co-founder
Google, Inc.

"Unicode and its companion ISO/IEC 10646 overcome the limitations and confusion of all earlier character coding standards. They enable every nation and community to write its own language with computers. They ensure a firm foundation for reliable and efficient interchange of text worldwide."

—**Hugh McGregor Ross**
First editor of ISO/IEC 10646

"Apple has been supporting Unicode since the beginning. We're thrilled to see the growing adoption of the Unicode and welcome Unicode 5.0 as a new milestone in the definition of the standard."

—**Bertrand Serlet**, Senior Vice President of Software Engineering
Apple, Inc.

"Unicode is arguably the most widely adopted software standard in the world, reaching into any program, application, or system that displays text. Though starting from a high point, Unicode 5.0 manages to increase quality yet again, which will continue to expand adoption and support integration."

—**Richard Mark Soley**, Ph.D., Chairman and CEO
Object Management Group

"If you are a programmer working in 2006 and you don't know the basics of characters, character sets, encodings, and Unicode, and I catch you, I'm going to punish you by making you peel onions for six months in a submarine."

—**Joel Spolsky**
Joel on Software

"The Java™ programming language was designed to be a portable, platform-independent programming language for the World Wide Web—not the ASCII Web or the ISO-Latin-1 Web, but for the entire world. It was for this reason that Java's designers broke out of the 8-bit straitjacket and based the character and string datatypes firmly on Unicode, the character encoding standard designed to support all the world's languages for truly international communication and commerce. Version 5.0 of the Unicode Standard is the most comprehensive and thoroughly documented version yet."

—**Guy L. Steele Jr.**, Sun Fellow
Sun Microsystems, Inc.

"Justsystems was the first vendor in Japan to implement the Unicode architecture in word processing software. Thus for over a decade Japanese computer users have enjoyed the benefits of Unicode, especially the CJK Unified Ideographs. We are now aggressively launching our new technology 'xfy' on XML and Java—thanks to Unicode, it is already internationalized! Justsystems appreciates the Unicode philosophy and architecture of universality, and welcomes the publication of Version 5.0."

—**Kazunori Ukigawa**, President and CEO
Justsystems Corp.

"Modern programs must handle Unicode—Python has excellent support for Unicode, and will keep getting better."

—**Guido van Rossum**
Inventor of Python

"Unicode is marvellous. It makes it possible for phoneticians throughout the world to use all manner of phonetic symbols in their work and display them on computer screens in the certainty that they will not now be garbled or turned into wingdings (as once used to happen all too often). All alphabetic phonetic symbols officially recognized by the International Phonetic Association are now included in the Unicode Standard."

—**John Wells**, President
International Phonetic Association

***

For additional acclaim, see http://www.unicode.org/press/quotations.html.

THE Unicode STANDARD 5.0

THE Unicode STANDARD 5.0

THE UNICODE CONSORTIUM

Edited by
Julie D. Allen, Joe Becker, Richard Cook, Mark Davis, Michael Everson, Asmus Freytag, John H. Jenkins, Mike Ksar, Rick McGowan, Lisa Moore, Eric Muller, Markus Scherer, Michel Suignard, and Ken Whistler

Addison-Wesley

Upper Saddle River, NJ • Boston • Indianapolis • San Francisco
New York • Toronto • Montreal • London • Munich • Paris • Madrid
Capetown • Sydney • Tokyo • Singapore • Mexico City

Dai Kan-Wa Jiten, used as the source of reference Kanji codes, was written by Tetsuji Morohashi and published by Taishukan Shoten.

Cover and CD-ROM label design: Steve Mehallo, www.mehallo.com

Library of Congress Cataloging-in-Publication Data

The Unicode Standard / the Unicode Consortium ; edited by Julie D. Allen ... [et al.]. — Version 5.0.
p. cm.
Includes bibliographical references and index.
ISBN 0-321-48091-0 (hardcover : alk. paper)
1. Unicode (Computer character set) I. Allen, Julie D.
II. Unicode Consortium.
QA268.U545 2007
005.7'22—dc22

2006023526

Pearson Education, Inc.
Rights and Contracts Department
75 Arlington Street, Suite 300
Boston, MA 02116
Fax: (617) 848-7047

ISBN 0-321-48091-0
Text printed in the United States on recycled paper at Courier in Westford, Massachusetts.
First printing, October 2006

Contents

Figures

Tables

Foreword

Without much fanfare, Unicode has completely transformed the foundation of software and communications over the past decade. Whenever you read or write anything on a computer, you're using Unicode. Whenever you search on Google, Yahoo!, MSN, Wikipedia, or many other Web sites, you're using Unicode. Unicode 5.0 marks a major milestone in providing people everywhere the ability to use their own languages on computers.

We began Unicode with a simple goal: to unify the many hundreds of conflicting ways to encode characters, replacing them with a single, universal standard. Those existing legacy character encodings were both incomplete and inconsistent: Two encodings could use the same internal codes for two different characters and use different internal codes for the same characters; none of the encodings handled any more than a small fraction of the world's languages. Whenever textual data was converted between different programs or platforms, there was a substantial risk of corruption. Programs were hard-coded to support particular encodings, making development of international versions expensive, testing a nightmare, and support costs prohibitive. As a result, product launches in foreign markets were expensive and late—unsatisfactory both for companies and their customers. Developing countries were especially hard-hit; it was not feasible to support smaller markets. Technical fields such as mathematics were also disadvantaged; they were forced to use special fonts to represent arbitrary characters, but when those fonts were unavailable, the content became garbled.

Unicode changed that situation radically. Now, for all text, programs only need to use a single representation—one that supports all the world's languages. Programs could be easily structured with all translatable material separated from the program code and put into a single representation, providing the basis for rapid deployment in multiple languages. Thus, multiple-language versions of a program can be developed almost simultaneously at a much smaller incremental cost, even for complex programs like Microsoft Office or OpenOffice.

The assignment of characters is only a small fraction of what the Unicode Standard and its associated specifications provide. They give programmers extensive descriptions and a vast amount of data about how characters *function*: how to form words and break lines; how to sort text in different languages; how to format numbers, dates, times, and other elements appropriate to different languages; how to display languages whose written form flows from right to left, such as Arabic and Hebrew, or whose written form splits, combines, and reorders, such as languages of South Asia; and how to deal with security concerns regarding the many "look-alike" characters from alphabets around the world. Without the properties, algorithms, and other specifications in the Unicode Standard and its associated specifications, interoperability between different implementations would be impossible.

With the rise of the Web, a single representation for text became absolutely vital for seamless global communication. Thus the textual content of HTML and XML is defined in terms of Unicode—every program handling XML must use Unicode internally. The search engines all use Unicode for good reason; even if a Web page is in a legacy character encoding, the only effective way to index that page for searching is to translate it into the lingua franca, Unicode. All of the text on the Web thus can be stored, searched, and matched with the same program code. Since all of the search engines translate Web pages into Unicode, the most reliable way to have pages searched is to have them be in Unicode in the first place.

This edition of *The Unicode Standard, Version 5.0*, supersedes and obsoletes all previous versions of the standard. The book is smaller in size, less expensive, and yet has hundreds of pages of new material and hundreds more of revised material. Like any human enterprise, Unicode is not without its flaws, of course. This book will help you work around some of the "gotchas" introduced into Unicode over the course of its development. Importantly, it will help you to understand which features may change in the future, and which cannot, so that you can appropriately optimize your implementations. You will also find a wealth of other information on the Unicode Web site (www.unicode.org). If you are interested in having a voice in determining directions for future development of Unicode, or want to follow closely the ongoing work, you will find information there on joining the Consortium.

What you have in your hands is the culmination of many years of experience from experts around the globe. I am sure you will find it very useful.

Mark Davis, Ph.D.
President
The Unicode Consortium

Preface

This book, *The Unicode Standard, Version 5.0*, together with the Unicode Character Database, is the authoritative source of information on Version 5.0 of the Unicode character encoding standard.

Version 5.0 of the standard is a significant departure from prior versions. It lays out much clearer requirements for supporting Unicode and provides more explicit guidance for implementers to quickly embrace the proliferation of new growth technologies and emerging markets while at the same time meeting users' needs for secure, robust software.

Why Buy This Book

In a major enhancement, Version 5.0 of the Unicode Standard is now available in a smaller, more convenient size while including much more textual content. Most notably, for the first time the book includes *all* of the Unicode Standard Annexes, which provide specifications for vital processes such as text normalization, bidirectional handling, and identifier parsing.

Version 5.0 contains the knowledge gained from many years of worldwide implementation experience and has been enhanced significantly: the text incorporates 15 years of user feedback, provides thorough answers to the many questions users of Unicode have raised, and is much more accessible—with greatly improved figures and tables, and with the text revised for clarity.

- Four-fifths of the figures are new.
- Two-thirds of the definitions are new.
- One-half of the Unicode Standard Annexes are new.
- One-third of the conformance clauses are new.
- One-fourth of the tables are new.

In addition, the text of Version 5.0 reflects advances in the computer implementation of writing systems. It substantially improves the descriptions of rendering Indic scripts to meet the demands of this area of growing market importance—Unicode-based implementations are supported by the government of India, and this book explains how to build them. Version 5.0 also highlights the newly established core CJK subset of characters, IICore, which is critical for rendering and interoperability in the East Asian market.

In short, *The Unicode Standard, Version 5.0*, enables developers to implement quickly the latest advances for worldwide software users while opening new opportunities in high-growth markets. The changes from Versions 3.0 and 4.0 to Version 5.0 are major and important—this is the one book all Unicode implementers must have.

Why Upgrade to Version 5.0

Version 5.0 of the Unicode Standard brings significant improvements beyond Versions 3.0 and 4.0. The industry has noticed and is quickly moving to Version 5.0—Windows Vista runs on 5.0; ICU, Google, and Yahoo! all have plans to upgrade to 5.0. Internet and W3C protocols are built on Unicode and are continually adapting to the latest versions. The International Standard ISO/IEC 10646 is also synchronized with Version 5.0.

This latest version of the Unicode Standard is the basis for Unicode security mechanisms, the Unicode collation algorithm, the locale data provided by the Common Locale Data Repository, and support for Unicode in regular expressions. Improved expression of the Unicode encoding model makes it much clearer how implementers need to support the representation of Unicode text in UTF-8 and other encoding forms. Character properties have been systematized and greatly extended to help implementers in support of Unicode text processing. The standard has also established principles of stability for casefolding and identifiers, crucial for interoperability and backward compatibility for formal language use and in other contexts that depend on exact usage and matching of identifiers.

Version 5.0 delivers a stable, practical character processing model in sync with today's information technology needs. Unicode now offers:

- Round-trip compatibility with the Chinese standards GB18030 and HKSCS
- The specification of the newly established core CJK subset of characters, IICore
- Refinements to casing and bidirectional behavior to meet industry requirements
- Improved Indic rendering guidelines
- Better guidance on the handling of combining characters, Unicode strings, variation selectors, line breaking, and segmentation

Implementers who want to keep pace with the industry and take advantage of a stable foundation for security, to align with the latest collation and locale data definitions, and, most importantly, to expand their market reach need to upgrade to Version 5.0 as soon as possible.

Detailed Change Information. See *Appendix D, Changes from Previous Versions*, for detailed information about the changes from previous versions of the standard, including character counts, stability guarantees, and updates to the Unicode Character Database and Unicode Standard Annexes.

Version 5.0 of the Unicode Standard corresponds to ISO/IEC 10646:2003 plus Amendments 1 and 2 to that standard and four characters to support Sindhi from Amendment 3.

Organization of This Book

This book and the Unicode Character Database define Version 5.0 of the Unicode Standard. The book gives the general principles, requirements for conformance, guidelines for implementers, character code charts and names, and the Unicode Standard Annexes.

Concepts, Architecture, Conformance, and Guidelines. The first five chapters of Version 5.0 introduce the Unicode Standard and provide the fundamental information needed to produce a conforming implementation. Basic text processing, working with combining marks, and encoding forms are all described. A special chapter on implementation guidelines answers many common questions that arise when implementing Unicode.

> *Chapter 1* introduces the standard's basic concepts, design basis, and coverage and discusses basic text handling requirements.
>
> *Chapter 2* sets forth the fundamental principles underlying the Unicode Standard and covers specific topics such as text processes, overall character properties, and the use of combining marks.
>
> *Chapter 3* constitutes the formal statement of conformance. This chapter also presents the normative algorithms for three processes: the canonical ordering of combining marks, the encoding of Korean Hangul syllables by conjoining *jamo*, and default casing.
>
> *Chapter 4* describes character properties in detail, both normative (required) and informative. Tables giving additional character property information appear in the Unicode Character Database.
>
> *Chapter 5* discusses implementation issues, including compression, strategies for dealing with unknown and unsupported characters, and transcoding to other standards.

Character Block Descriptions. *Chapters 6 through 16* contain the character block descriptions that give basic information about each script or group of symbols and may discuss specific characters or pertinent layout information. Some of this information is required to produce conformant implementations of these scripts and other collections of characters.

Code Charts. *Chapter 17* gives the code charts and the Character Names List. The code charts contain the normative character encoding assignments, and the names list contains normative information as well as useful cross references and informational notes.

Han Radical-Stroke Index. *Chapter 18* provides a Han radical-stroke index for the IICore subset of CJK ideographs. This index aids in locating specific, common ideographs encoded in the Unicode Standard.

Appendices. The appendices contain detailed background information on important topics regarding the history of the Unicode Standard and its relationship to ISO/IEC 10646.

> *Appendix A* documents the notational conventions used by the standard.
>
> *Appendix B* provides abstracts of Unicode Technical Reports and lists other important Unicode resources.
>
> *Appendix C* details the relationship between the Unicode Standard and ISO/IEC 10646.
>
> *Appendix D* lists the changes to the Unicode Standard since Version 4.0.

Appendix E describes the history of Han unification in the Unicode Standard.

Appendix F reproduces the text of the policies of the Unicode Consortium regarding character encoding stability.

Glossary, References, and Indices. The appendices are followed by a glossary of terms, a bibliography, and two indices: an index to Unicode characters and an index to the text of the book.

Unicode Standard Annexes

The Unicode Standard Annexes are printed in the back of this book, following the indices. These annexes form an integral part of the Unicode Standard. Conformance to a version of the Unicode Standard includes conformance to its Unicode Standard Annexes.

Unicode Standard Annex #9, "The Bidirectional Algorithm," describes specifications for the positioning of characters in mixed-directional text, such as Arabic or Hebrew.

Unicode Standard Annex #11, "East Asian Width," presents the specification of an informative property for Unicode characters that is useful when interoperating with East Asian legacy character sets.

Unicode Standard Annex #14, "Line Breaking Properties," presents the specification of line breaking properties for Unicode characters.

Unicode Standard Annex #15, "Unicode Normalization Forms," describes specifications for four normalized forms of Unicode text.

Unicode Standard Annex #24, "Script Names," specifies an assignment of script names to all Unicode code points.

Unicode Standard Annex #29, "Text Boundaries," describes guidelines for determining default boundaries between certain significant text elements: grapheme clusters ("user-perceived characters"), words, and sentences.

Unicode Standard Annex #31, "Identifier and Pattern Syntax," describes specifications for recommended defaults for the use of Unicode in the definitions of identifiers and in pattern-based syntax.

Unicode Standard Annex #34, "Unicode Named Character Sequences," defines the concept of a Unicode named character sequence and a set of rules constraining possible names applied to character sequences.

Unicode Standard Annex #41, "Common References for Unicode Standard Annexes," contains the listing of references shared by other Unicode Standard Annexes.

The 5.0.0 version of each UAX is included on the CD-ROM. All versions, including the most up-to-date versons of all Unicode Standard Annexes, are available on the Unicode Web site:

http://www.unicode.org/reports/

The Unicode Character Database

The Unicode Character Database (UCD) is a collection of data files containing character code points, character names, and character property data. It is described more fully in *Section 4.1, Unicode Character Database.* All versions, including the most up-to-date version of the Unicode Character Database, are found on the Unicode Web site:

http://www.unicode.org/ucd/

The files for Version 5.0.0 of the Unicode Character Database are also supplied on the CD-ROM that accompanies this book.

Information on versioning and on all versions of the Unicode Standard can be found on the Unicode Web site:

http://www.unicode.org/versions/

Unicode Technical Standards and Unicode Technical Reports

Unicode Technical Reports and Unicode Technical Standards are separate publications and do not form part of the Unicode Standard.

All versions of all Unicode Technical Reports and Unicode Technical Standards are available on the Unicode Web site:

http://www.unicode.org/reports/

The latest available version of each document at the time of publication is included on the CD-ROM. See *Appendix B, Unicode Publications and Resources*, for a summary overview of important Unicode Technical Standards and Unicode Technical Reports.

On the CD-ROM

The CD-ROM contains additional information, such as sample code, which is maintained on the Unicode FTP site:

ftp.unicode.org

It is also available via HTTP:

http://www.unicode.org/Public/

For the contents of the CD-ROM, see its ReadMe.txt file.

Updates and Errata

Reports of errors in the Unicode Standard, including the Unicode Character Database and the Unicode Standard Annexes, may be reported using the online reporting form:

http://www.unicode.org/reporting.html

A list of known errata is maintained on the Unicode Web site:

http://www.unicode.org/errata/

Any currently listed errata will be fixed in subsequent versions of the standard.

Acknowledgments

The production of *The Unicode Standard, Version 5.0*, is due to the dedication of many people over several years. We would like to acknowledge the following individuals, whose major contributions were central to the design, authorship, and review of this book.

Julie D. Allen was responsible for the editing of the book. As Senior Editor and Project Manager, she contributed to the rewriting of many of the script descriptions and managed the general project schedule for the completion of the book. Julie led the updating of the glossary and the coordination with the publisher, graphic artist, and other contributors.

Joe Becker created the original Unicode prospectus and continued as contributing editor for this version.

Richard Cook contributed to maintaining and updating the Unihan database and its documentation. He also served as a Unicode Consortium representative to the IRG.

Mark Davis was essential to the development of Version 5.0. Mark led many aspects of overall design of the Unicode Standard. He contributed significant revisions and enhancements to the statement of conformance, casing behavior, the stability of programmatic identifiers, text boundaries, bidirectional behavior, implementation guidelines, normalization, and the addition of properties to the Unicode Character Database. Mark is the author of three of the Unicode Standard Annexes, is a co-author of two others, and was a major contributor in defining Unicode security mechanisms.

Michael Everson was the driving force behind encoding many of the minority and historic scripts that were added in Version 5.0 and was a major contributor to their script descriptions. These scripts include Balinese, Coptic, Glagolitic, N'Ko, New Tai Lue, Old Persian, Phoenician, and Sumero-Akkadian Cuneiform. Michael provided many of the fonts used in this standard and extensively reviewed code charts, character names, and annotations.

Asmus Freytag made significant contributions to the general structure and property chapters, and continued his focus on symbols. He led the updates to punctuation, symbols, and special areas and format characters, and he also made contributions to European alphabetic scripts, bidirectional behavior, and line breaking properties. He designed a number of additional figures and suggested improvements to many others. Asmus drove the effort to define the Unicode character property model, was the author of two Unicode Standard Annexes, and is a co-author of one other. He was instrumental in incorporating the annexes into the book. He also created custom formatting software, negotiated font donations, and produced the code charts.

John H. Jenkins, as Unicode Consortium representative to the IRG, contributed to the maintenance and extension of the Unihan database, extended the Han radical-stroke index to the ideographic content of the standard, and prepared the radical-stroke index of the IICore Han subset. John was also responsible for maintaining the Han cross-reference tables and contributed fonts for KangXi and CJK radicals.

Mike Ksar, as Convener of JTC1/SC2/WG2 and SC2 liaison, led the effort to synchronize Version 5.0 and ISO/IEC 10646:2003 Amendments 1 and 2. He contributed to Middle Eastern scripts, *Appendix C*, and he thoroughly reviewed all of the newly added scripts and ensured they were well documented in both standards.

Rick McGowan coordinated the work to encode new scripts and contributed to the editing of many of the new script descriptions. He revised or drew more than 100 figures in the book and was responsible for mastering and producing the CD-ROM.

Lisa Moore, as Chair of the Unicode Technical Committee, oversaw the content of Version 5.0. She edited the Kharoshthi description, rewrote *Appendix D* and much of the front matter, and contributed to the general editing of the text.

Eric Muller thoroughly reviewed all chapters of the book, making many improvements in the clarity and consistency of the text. He contributed to the validation of Unihan data and provided critical PDF expertise.

Markus Scherer thoroughly reviewed the general structure and conformance chapters of Unicode Version 5.0, contributed significant updates to the implementation guidelines found in the standard, and provided a painstakingly thorough verification of properties.

Michel Suignard was a leader in the synchronization of Unicode and ISO/IEC 10646 through his role as Project Editor for 10646. He was responsible for editing ISO/IEC 10646: 2003, Amendments 1 and 2, and thus provided the foundation for the seamless coordination with the publication of Unicode Versions 4.1 and 5.0. Michel added IRG sources to Unihan and was a major contributor in defining Unicode security mechanisms.

Ken Whistler was the managing editor of Version 5.0. He led the effort to redesign the book to a smaller size while including expanded script descriptions and all of the Unicode Standard Annexes. He had responsibility for all aspects of production and verified the accuracy and quality of all updates to the text. Ken meticulously updated the Unicode Character Database, adding all of the new characters and some of their properties. He also maintained the Character Names List and supplied many of the annotations. Ken led the rewriting of the parts of the general structure and conformance chapters related to combining classes and the application of combining marks, as well as the renumbering of conformance clauses and definitions.

***

Fonts were essential for the production of this book. Asmus Freytag worked to acquire and organize the font collection with support from Michael Everson, further developing the original collection of fonts for Unicode 2.0 assembled by John Jenkins. In addition to the individuals mentioned previously, and the companies and organizations named in the colophon, fonts were contributed by Patrick Andries (Tifinagh), Cora Chang (Braille), Oliver Corff (Yi), Anton Dumbadze and Irakli Garibashvili (Georgian), Andrew Glass (Kharoshthi), Yannis Haralambous (Greek, Syriac, and Thai), George Kiraz (Syriac), Svante Lagman (Runic), Raymond Mercier (Greek zero), Stephen Morey and Michael Everson (Tai Le), Paul Nelson and Sarmad Hussain (Syriac and Sindhi/Urdu numbers), David Perry and James Kass (Greek musical symbols), Peter Martin (Phonetic Additions), Hector Santos (Philippine scripts), Yayasan Bali Simbar (Balinese), Ngakham Southichack (Lao), Michael Stone (Armenian), Steve Tinney and Michael Everson (Cuneiform), Dirk VanDamme (Coptic), Al Webster (Cherokee), Andrew West (Phags-pa), and K. Yarang, J. R. Pandhak, Y. Lawoti, and Y. P. Yakwa (Limbu).

Michael Everson (Evertype) provided fonts for Canadian Syllabics, Osmanya, many historic scripts (including Kharoshthi, Linear B, Ogham, and Old Persian), symbols, and Latin, Greek, and Cyrillic characters. John M. Fiscella (Production First Software) designed fonts for symbols and many of the alphabetic scripts. Yang Song Jin of the Pyongyang Informatics Centre (DPR of Korea) provided the CJK compatibility symbols. Thomas Milo (DecoType) designed the Arabic font. SIL contributed several fonts designed by Jonathan Kew (Arabic Additions), Peter Martin (Phonetic Additions), as well as Victor Gaultney (New Tai Lue). The fonts for CJK Extensions A and B were provided by Beijing Zhong Yi (Zheng Code) Electronics Company. Extension A was designed by Technical Supervisor Zheng Long and Hua Weicang. Asmus Freytag created many individual glyphs for symbols or special characters.

Critical comments and work on fonts are due to Heidi Jenkins, Dr. Virach Sornlertlamvanich (Thai), Dr. Sarmad Hussain (Urdu), Roozbeh Pournader (Farsi), Barbara Beeton and Patrick Ion (Mathematical Symbols), and many others. Many individuals and organizations provided additional fonts used during the development of Version 5.0.

New figures enhanced the text significantly. Grenfel (1921), Austin (1973), and Allen (1931) were used as sources to draw the large figure for Greek editorial marks. Parisian Schola Cantorum and Hymns of Faith were the sources used for Arabic musical passages. The Kharoshthi map in *Figure 10-5* was adapted from Glass (2000).

Steve Mehallo designed the cover for the book. He also updated existing chapter divider artwork and designed additional new artwork for Version 5.0. Kamal Mansour was instrumental in the graphic design process and continued his longstanding support in coordinating the cover design of this book. Monotype Imaging generously sponsored the cost of the cover design, the CD-ROM design, and updates to the chapter divider artwork for Version 5.0.

The development of this book would not have been possible without the support of the office staff of Unicode, Inc., and the work of Mike Kernaghan, as operational manager of the Unicode office. We thank Magda Danish, who helped with Version 5.0 in countless ways, including assistance in editing of the Unicode Standard Annexes, painstaking proofing of Pinyin data for the Unihan database, and additions and corrections for the technical references. We also thank Sarasvati, who minded the mailing lists. We especially wish to thank Microsoft for its generous support in providing office space.

The text, code charts, and data were reviewed critically by experts. The Editorial Committee appreciates the expert contributions and feedback provided for specific scripts: Barbara Beeton (mathematical symbols), Peter Constable (New Tai Lue and phonetic extensions), Roozbeh Pournader (Arabic), Lorna Priest (Cyrillic), Andrew West (Phags-pa, Mongolian and Yi), and the members of the International Forum for Information Technology in Tamil, INFITT (Tamil), in addition to Kent Karlsson and many others. Thomas Bishop checked the data for CJK ideographs and contributed stroke data for sorting the radical-stroke index. We also wish to acknowledge the inestimable contribution by Patrick Andries for the French translation of the character chart annotations for Unicode 4.1, along with help from François Yergeau, Alain LaBonté, Jacques André, and other reviewers.

A number of individuals contributed to the better representation of Indic scripts in Version 5.0: Stefan Baums (Devanagari), Gihan Dias (Sinhala), Naga Ganesan (Malayalam), Manoj Jain (improvement of the overall Indic text), Gautam Sengupta (Bengali), Sukhjinder Sidhu (Gurmukhi), K. G. Sulochana (Malayalam), and Om Vikas (improvement of the overall Indic text). New characters were added, script descriptions were improved, many annotations were added, and a systematization of the approach to encoding was established.

The work to develop and verify the consistency of many of the character properties and algorithms was a significant contribution to Version 5.0. An important role in this effort was played by the International Components for Unicode (ICU) team, including the following individuals: Min Cui, Mark Davis, John Emmons, Doug Felt, Deborah Goldsmith, Andy Heninger, Qian Jing, Yan Xuan Liang, Alan Liu, Steven Loomis, Eric Mader, George Rhoten, Markus Scherer, Bei Shu, William Sullivan, Raghuram Viswanadha, and Vladimir Weinstein. In addition, Kent Karlsson carefully reviewed properties.

The growth of the synchronized character repertoires of the Unicode Standard and International Standard ISO/IEC 10646 reflects a worldwide effort conducted over a number of years. For Version 5.0, a number of universities and research institutes contributed many excellent proposals for the encoding of minority and historic scripts. The Script Encoding Initiative, University of California at Berkeley, led by Deborah Anderson with the assistance of Rick McGowan, secured funding and created proposals for many historic and minority scripts. Major funders of this effort include the National Endowment for the Humanities, the N'Ko Institute of America and Mamady Doumbouya, the Society of Biblical Literature, Association Manden, and UNESCO (Communication & Information Sector, Initiative B@bel). Other universities and research institutes to which the Unicode Consortium is much indebted include Thesaurus Linguae Graecae Project, University of California, Irvine, the Initiative for Cuneiform Encoding (ICE), Johns Hopkins University, and the International Association for Coptic Studies.

With Version 5.0, the Unicode Standard encodes all of the major modern scripts and a significant number of historic and minority scripts. We express deep appreciation to the following experts who shared their specialized knowledge to bring about this achievement:

- For Arabic additions: Jonathan Kew, Michael Everson, and Roozbeh Pournader.
- For Balinese: Michael Everson, Made Suatjana, also thanks are due to Ida Bagus Adi Sudewa, I Nyoman Suarka, Donny Harimurti, Tudy Harimurti, and Nyoman Sugiarta. Unicode gratefully acknowledges support from UNESCO, the National Endowment for the Humanities, and the Yayasan Bali Galang (Bright Bali Foundation), which organized the technical discussion sessions in Bali.
- For Buginese: Michael Everson.
- For CJK ideographs, symbol, and mark additions: China National Information Technology Standardization Technical Committee, Christopher Cullen, Deborah Goldsmith, John Jenkins, Eric Muller, Michel Suignard, and Andrew West.
- For Coptic: Michael Everson, Gerald Browne, Stephen Emmel, and the International Association for Coptic Studies.
- For Cyrillic additions: Lorna Priest.
- For Ethiopic additions: Daniel Yacob.
- For Georgian additions: Michael Everson, Georgian State Department of Information Technology, David Tarkhan-Mouravi (Chair), and Jost Gippert.
- For Glagolitic: Michael Everson and Ralph Cleminson.
- For Greek: Maria Pantelia, Deborah Anderson, Nick Nicholas, and Richard Peevers.
- For Hebrew additions: Peter Constable, Michael Everson, Peter Kirk, and Mark Shoulson.
- For Indic additions: Government of India, Ministry of Information Technology, Om Vikas and Manoj Jain, INFITT, Michael Kaplan, and Peter Constable.
- For Kannada and Devanagari additions: Michael Everson.
- For Kharoshthi: Andrew Glass, Stefan Baums, and Richard Salomon.
- For Latin additions: Peter Constable, Mark Davis, Michael Everson, Chris Harvey, Jonathan Kew, and Lorna Priest.
- For Mongolian: Andrew West.
- For New Tai Lue: China National Information Technology Standardization Technical Committee and Michael Everson.
- For N'Ko: Michael Everson, Mamadi Doumbouya, Mamadi Baba Diané, and Karamo Kaba Jammeh. Unicode gratefully acknowledges support from UNESCO Initiative B@bel, N'Ko Institute of America and Mamady Doumbouya, and Association Manden.
- For Old Persian: Michael Everson.

- For Phags-pa: China National Information Technology Standardization Technical Committee, Mongolian Agency for Standardization and Metrology, Andrew West, and Chris Fynn.
- For Phoenician: Michael Everson.
- For phonetic extensions: Peter Constable, Mark Davis, Michael Everson, and Lorna Priest.
- For Sumero-Akkadian Cuneiform: Michael Everson, Karljürgen Feuerherm, Steve Tinney, Madeleine Fitzgerald, and Cale Johnson. This script addition was aided in part by funds made available to participants by Johns Hopkins University through the Initiative for Cuneiform Encoding, by the National Science Foundation through the Digital Hammurabi Project, by the Society of Biblical Literature, and by the Script Encoding Initiative, University of California Berkeley. Special thanks are due to Dean Snyder and Jerrold S. Cooper of Johns Hopkins University for their leading roles in organizing and hosting two ICE conferences that were crucial to progress on the encoding.
- For Syloti Nagri: Peter Constable, James Lloyd-Williams and Sue Lloyd-Williams, Shamsul Islam Chowdhury, Asaddar Ali, Mohammed Sadique, and Matiar Rahman.
- For symbol additions: Asmus Freytag, Barbara Beeton, Michael Everson, Murray Sargent, and Andreas Stoetzner.
- For Tifinagh: Patrick Andries, François Yergeau, and Alain LaBonté.
- For Unihan: Dr. George Bell, Joy Zhao Rouxer, and Steve Mann for donation to the Unihan Database of the complete electronic data from their book *Quick and Easy Index of Chinese Characters* (formerly *Alphanumeric Identification of Chinese Characters*), and many contributions by Ken Lunde.

The technical content of the Unicode Standard is determined by the Unicode Technical Committee (UTC), which was chaired during the development of Version 5.0 by Lisa Moore, was vice-chaired by Cathy Wissink and Eric Muller, and had Rick McGowan as recording secretary. Contributors to the work of the UTC include representatives of Full, Institutional, Supporting, and Associate Members, Individual Members, and Unicode Officers, as well as invited experts and liaisons. Version 5.0 would not have been possible without the creative work and critical thinking over the past three years by all member representatives: Mujahid Agha (Pakistan, NLA), Joan Aliprand (formerly of RLG), Deborah Anderson (UC Berkeley, Department of Linguistics), Rick Andrews (VeriSign), Takeshi Asano (Sun), Andreas Bäß (Denic), Christopher Chapman (Monotype Imaging), Daniel Chen (IBM), Steve Cohen (Basis), Peter Constable (Microsoft), Richard Cook (UC Berkeley, Department of Linguistics), Mark Davis (Google, formerly of IBM), Sabine Dolderer (Denic), Attash Durrani (Pakistan, NLA), Peter Edberg (Apple), Asmus Freytag (for Basis Technology), Deborah Goldsmith (Apple), Geoffry Greve (Monotype Imaging), Hideki Hiura (Justsystem, formerly of Sun), Takahiro Imai (formerly of Peoplesoft), Manoj Kumar Jain (India, MIT), John Jenkins (Apple), Bob Jung (Google), Susan Kline (HP), Tatsuo

Kobayashi (Justsystem), Gary Krall (VeriSign), Hirobumi Kurosu (formerly of PeopleSoft), Swaran Lata (India, MIT), Ken Lunde (Adobe), Ian Macleod (Sybase), Kamal Mansour (Monotype Imaging), Benson Margulies (Basis), Shinobu Matsuzuka (Sun), Matthias Mittelstein (SAP), Lisa Moore (IBM), Nobuyoshi Mori (SAP), Eric Muller (Adobe), Mihai Nita (Adobe), Sandra Martin O'Donnell (formerly of Compaq, HP), Dave Opstad (Monotype Imaging), Pierre Ouédraogo (Agence Intergouvernementale de la Francophonie), Shripad Patki (Sun), Addison Phillips (Yahoo!), Toby Phipps (formerly of Peoplesoft), Gabriel Plumlee (formerly of Peoplesoft), Erik van der Poel (Google), Wendy Rannenberg (Compaq, then HP), Mike Van Riper (VeriSign), Lynn Ruggles (HP), Marcos Sanz (Denic), Murray Sargent (Microsoft), Bernhard Schilling (SAP), Karen Smith-Yoshimura (RLG), Michel Suignard (Microsoft), Ienup Sung (Sun), Tex Texin (Yahoo!), V. S. Umamaheswaran (IBM), Om Vikas (India, MIT), Ken Whistler (Sybase), Cathy Wissink (Microsoft), Jianping Yang (Oracle), Michael Yau (Oracle), and Weiran Zhang (Oracle).

Other members and experts who have contributed to the work of the Unicode Technical Committee include Mati Allouche, Harald Alvestrand, Barbara Beeton, Peter Constable, James Do, Martin Dürst, Behdad Esfahbod, Patrik Fältström, John M. Fiscella, Paul Hoffman, Michael Kaplan, Jonathan Kew, Kamal Mansour, Thomas Milo, Paul Nelson, Nick Nicholas, Roozbeh Pournader, Jonathan Rosenne, and Zhang Zhoucai.

The Unicode Technical Committee has worked closely with Technical Committee L2 of the InterNational Committee for Information Technology Standards (INCITS). We appreciate the cooperation of Chairs Cathy Wissink and Eric Muller, and Vice-Chair Lisa Moore. Rick McGowan efficiently maintained the Web-based archive of L2 documents so crucial to the development of Version 5.0.

The Unicode Consortium continues to maintain mutually beneficial relationships with international standards organizations. We appreciate the efforts and support of the members of ISO/IEC JTC1/SC2/WG2 and the members of the Ideographic Rapporteur Group toward the common goal of keeping both standards synchronized. We would particularly like to thank the Convener of WG2, Mike Ksar; the Rapporteur of the IRG, Dr. Lu Qin, and its former Rapporteur, Zhang Zhoucai; and the Editors and Contributing Editors of WG2, Michel Suignard, Asmus Freytag, Michael Everson, and Ken Whistler. We also thank Asmus Freytag for his effective representation of the Unicode Consortium at WG2 meetings. We would like to thank the collation ad hoc members of ISO/IEC JTC1/SC2, especially Alain LaBonté and Ken Whistler, for their work with the Consortium on a common collation definition.

During the development of Version 5.0, we benefited greatly from close collaboration with the Internationalization Working Group of the W3C. We appreciate its many contributions and especially wish to thank Martin Dürst, Richard Ishida, Addison Phillips, Felix Sasaki, Tex Texin, Misha Wolf, and François Yergeau for timely and thorough review of and improvements to new proposals.

The IETF has contributed greatly to the adoption of Unicode in worldwide Internet applications. We appreciate its efforts and effective collaboration with the Consortium, and we would particularly like to thank Harald Alvestrand, Patrik Fältström, and Paul Hoffman for their efforts to help us improve the stability of the standard.

The support of member companies has been crucial to *The Unicode Standard, Version 5.0.* Adobe Systems, Inc., generously supplied the license for the Minion fonts, Adobe® Framemaker® 7.2, and Adobe® Creative Suite 2 Premium, which were used to create the text and graphics of this book. In addition, particular thanks for facilities, equipment, and resources are owed to Apple Computer, Inc., Microsoft Corporation, and Monotype Imaging. PdfLib GmbH donated PDFlib+PDI 6.0.3 for Microsoft Windows and PDFlib TET (Text Extraction Toolkit) 2.1.0 for Microsoft Windows, plus custom-built software for post-production processing of PDFs for the code charts and the Unicode Standard Annexes.

The Unicode Standard, Version 5.0, would not have been possible without those who made important contributions to earlier versions: Glenn Adams, Joan Aliprand, Avery Bishop, Lori Brownell, Lee Collins, Andy Daniels, Burwell Davis, Bill English, Edwin Hart, Masami Hasegawa, Lloyd Honomichl, Liao Huan-Mei, Eric Mader, Dave Opstad, Hugh McGregor Ross, Isai Scheinberg, Ed Smura, Alan Tucker, Bill Tuthill, and J. G. Van Stee.

While we gratefully acknowledge the contributions of all persons named in this section, any errors or omissions in this work are the responsibility of the Unicode Consortium.

Unicode Consortium Members

While Version 5.0 of the Unicode Standard was under development, the following companies and governments were members of Unicode. Some members changed their level of membership during this time period and are listed twice.

Full Members

Adobe Systems, Inc.
Agence Intergouvernementale de la Francophonie
Apple Computer, Inc.
Basis Technology Corporation
Denic e.G.
Google, Inc.
Hewlett-Packard Company
IBM Corporation
India, Ministry of Information Technology
Justsystem Corporation
Microsoft Corporation
Monotype Imaging
Oracle Corporation
Pakistan, National Language Authority
Peoplesoft
RLG
SAP AG
Sun Microsystems, Inc.
Sybase, Inc.
VeriSign, Inc.
Yahoo! Inc.

Institutional Members

India, Ministry of Information Technology
Pakistan, National Language Authority
The University of California at Berkeley

Current Supporting Members

Basis Technology Corporation
Monotype Imaging

Current Associate Members

Adams Globalization
AOL
Beijing Founder Electronic Company
Beijing Zhong Yi Electronics Co.
Bibliothèque universitaire des langues et civilisations
Booz, Allen & Hamilton, Inc.
The Church of Jesus Christ of Latter-day Saints
Columbia University
DecoType, Inc.
Edgenet, Inc.
Endeavor Information Systems, Inc.
Evertype
Ex Libris Ltd.
Google, Inc.
The Government of Tamil Nadu and Tamil Virtual University, India
Innovative Interfaces, Inc.
Language Analysis Systems, Inc.
LIB-IT GmbH Bibliotheks EDV-Systeme
The Library Corporation
Linotype Library GmbH
NCR Corporation
Nokia
OCLC, Inc.
The Perl Foundation
RLG
SAS Institute, Inc.
SIL International
SIRSI Corporation
Sony Ericsson
Symbian, Ltd.
Talis Information, Ltd.
United Bible Societies
Utilika Foundation
VeriSign, Inc.
Vernacular Inormation Society Project
VTLS, Inc.

Current Individual Members

James Agenbroad, Matthew Y. Ahn, Harald Alvestrand, Lloyd Anderson, Patrick Andries, Scott Atwood, Charles W. Bishop, Philip Blair, Bert Blodau, Anthony Bova, Kevin Brown, Pierre Cadieux, John Cain, Christian Carey, Marco Cimarosti, John Clay, John Cowan, Mark Crispin, Paul Deuter, Martin Dürst, Patrick Durusau, David W. Edwards, Yutaka Emura, Doug Ewell, James M. Farrow, John Fay, Allen Fisher, Naga Ganesan, Richard A. Gard, Debbie Garside, Thomas Gewecke, Daniel Goldschmidt, Adam Goode, Jennifer Goodman, Kenneth Gorman, Tim Greenwood, William Hall, Martin Heijdra, Andrew Hodgson, Paul Hoffman, Robert Hoshide, John Hudson, Charles Husbands, Laurențiu Iancu, Anne Ingram, Reto Jeger, Michael Johnson, Simon Josefsson, Bohdan Kantor, Kent Karlsson, Cary Karp, James Kass, Wolfgang Keber, Brendan Kehoe, Daphne Khoury, Erkki I. Kolehmainen, Alain LaBonté, Julie Maitra, Yuko Miyata, Ben Monroe, Tag Young Moon, K. S. Nagarajan, Htoo Myint Naung, Andrew Neilson, Sandra O'Donnell, Karl Pentzlin, Åke Persson, Ghulam Quader, Omar Rabbolini, Jason Reed, Arthur Reutenauer, Charles Riley, Richard Rosenbaum, Jonathan Rosenne, Christopher Scholten, Ron Schwartz, Sukhjinder Sidhu, Javier Sola, Andreas Stötzner, Ferdinand Susi, Paul Timperman, Benjamin Titze, Herbert E. Unger, Jr., Andrew West, Grace Wiersma, Mark Wilson, Arnold Winkler, Joan M. Winters, Richard Wordingham, Daniel Yacob, François Yergeau, Foster Zhang.

Unicode Consortium Liaison Members

Center of Computer and Information Development (CCID), Beijing
CEN/ISSS Cultural Diversity Focus Group (CDFG)
Free Standards Group Open Internationalization Initiative (OpenI18n.org)
High Council of Informatics (HCI), Iran
Information and Communication Technology Agency of Sri Lanka (ICTA)
Institute for the Languages and Cultures of Asia and Africa (ILCAA)
International Forum for Information Technology in Tamil (INFITT)
International Telecommunication Union (ITU)
Internet Engineering Task Force (IETF)
ISO/IEC JTC1/SC2 and its working group WG2
ISO/TC 37/SC 2 Terminography and Lexicography
Linguistic Society of America (LSA)
National Endowment for the Humanities (NEH)
National Information Standards Organization (NISO)
NSAI/ICTSCC/SC4: Subcommittee for Irish standardization in the field of Codes, Character Sets, and Internationalization
Object Management Group (OMG)
Research Institute for the Languages of Finland (RILF)
Special Libraries Association (SLA)
Standard Norge
Swedish Standards Institute (SIS/TK 445)
Technical Committee on Information Technology (TCVN/TC1), Hanoi, Viet Nam
United Nations Group of Experts on Geographical Names (UNGEGN)
World Wide Web Consortium (W3C) I18N Core Working Group

Unicode Consortium Board of Directors

Current Members of the Board of Directors

Harald Tveit Alvestrand (Cisco Systems)
Lori Brownell (Microsoft Corporation)
Carl Hoffman (Basis Technology)
Tatsuo L. Kobayashi (Justsystem Corportation)
Marypat Meuli (Microsoft Corporation)
David R. Richards (RLG)
William J. Sullivan (IBM Corporation)
Celia Vigil (Apple Computer, Inc.)

Former Members of the Board of Directors

Jerry Barber (Aldus Corporation)
Wayne R. Boyle (NCR Corporation)
Janet Buschert (Hewlett-Packard Company)
Brian E. Carpenter (IBM Corporation & Internet Architecture Board)
Robert M. Carr (Go Corporation)
Kevin Cavanaugh (Lotus Development Corporation)
John Gage (Sun Microsystems, Inc.)
Paul Hegarty (NeXT Software, Inc.)
Gary C. Hendrix (Symantec Corporation)
Richard J. Holleman (IBM Corporation)
Charles Irby (Metaphor, Inc.)
Jay E. Israel (Novell, Inc.)
Mike Ksar (Microsoft Corporation)
Ilene H. Lang (Digital Equipment Corporation)
Paul Maritz (Microsoft Corporation)
Susan Pond Mills (IBM Corporation)
Elizabeth G. Nichols (IBM Corporation)
Stephen P. Oksala (Unisys Corporation)
Mike Potel (Taligent, Inc.)
Chris Pratley (Microsoft Corporation)
Wendy Rannenberg (Compaq Computer Corporation)
Franz G. Rau (Microsoft Corporation)
Betrand Serlet (Apple Computer, Inc.)
Rick Spitz (Apple Computer, Inc.)
Lawrence Tesler (Apple Computer, Inc.)
Guy "Bud" Tribble (NeXT Software, Inc.)
Kazuya Watanabe (Novell KK)
Gayn B. Winters (Digital Equipment Corporation)

CHAPTER 1

Chapter 1

Introduction

The Unicode Standard is the universal character encoding standard for written characters and text. It defines a consistent way of encoding multilingual text that enables the exchange of text data internationally and creates the foundation for global software. As the default encoding of HTML and XML, the Unicode Standard provides a sound underpinning for the World Wide Web and new methods of business in a networked world. Required in new Internet protocols and implemented in all modern operating systems and computer languages such as Java and C#, Unicode is the basis of software that must function all around the world.

With Unicode, the information technology industry has replaced proliferating character sets with data stability, global interoperability and data interchange, simplified software, and reduced development costs.

While taking the ASCII character set as its starting point, the Unicode Standard goes far beyond ASCII's limited ability to encode only the upper- and lowercase letters A through Z. It provides the capacity to encode all characters used for the written languages of the world—more than 1 million characters can be encoded. No escape sequence or control code is required to specify any character in any language. The Unicode character encoding treats alphabetic characters, ideographic characters, and symbols equivalently, which means they can be used in any mixture and with equal facility (see *Figure 1-1*).

The Unicode Standard specifies a numeric value (code point) and a name for each of its characters. In this respect, it is similar to other character encoding standards from ASCII onward. In addition to character codes and names, other information is crucial to ensure legible text: a character's case, directionality, and alphabetic properties must be well defined. The Unicode Standard defines these and other semantic values, and it includes application data such as case mapping tables and character property tables as part of the Unicode Character Database. Character properties define a character's identity and behavior; they ensure consistency in the processing and interchange of Unicode data. See *Section 4.1, Unicode Character Database.*

Unicode characters are represented in one of three encoding forms: a 32-bit form (UTF-32), a 16-bit form (UTF-16), and an 8-bit form (UTF-8). The 8-bit, byte-oriented form, UTF-8, has been designed for ease of use with existing ASCII-based systems.

The Unicode Standard, Version 5.0, is code-for-code identical with International Standard ISO/IEC 10646. Any implementation that is conformant to Unicode is therefore conformant to ISO/IEC 10646.

Figure 1-1. Wide ASCII

ASCII/8859-1 Text

A	0100 0001
S	0101 0011
C	0100 0011
I	0100 1001
I	0100 1001
/	0010 1111
8	0011 1000
8	0011 1000
5	0011 0101
9	0011 1001
-	0010 1101
1	0011 0001
	0010 0000
t	0111 0100
e	0110 0101
x	0111 1000
t	0111 0100

Unicode Text

A	0000 0000 0100 0001
S	0000 0000 0101 0011
C	0000 0000 0100 0011
I	0000 0000 0100 1001
I	0000 0000 0100 1001
	0000 0000 0010 0000
天	0101 1001 0010 1001
地	0101 0111 0011 0000
	0000 0000 0010 0000
س	0000 0110 0011 0011
ل	0000 0110 0100 0100
ا	0000 0110 0010 0111
م	0000 0110 0100 0101
	0000 0000 0010 0000
α	0000 0011 1011 0001
≰	0010 0010 0111 0000
γ	0000 0011 1011 0011

The Unicode Standard contains 1,114,112 code points, most of which are available for encoding of characters. The majority of the common characters used in the major languages of the world are encoded in the first 65,536 code points, also known as the Basic Multilingual Plane (BMP). The overall capacity for more than 1 million characters is more than sufficient for all known character encoding requirements, including full coverage of all minority and historic scripts of the world.

1.1 Coverage

The Unicode Standard, Version 5.0, contains 99,024 characters from the world's scripts. These characters are more than sufficient not only for modern communication in most languages, but also for the classical forms of many languages. The standard includes the European alphabetic scripts, Middle Eastern right-to-left scripts, and scripts of Asia, as well as many others. The unified Han subset contains 70,229 ideographic characters defined by national and industry standards of China, Japan, Korea, Taiwan, Vietnam, and Singapore.

In addition, the Unicode Standard includes punctuation marks, mathematical symbols, technical symbols, geometric shapes, and dingbats.

Many new scripts have been added between Version 4.0 and Version 5.0, including N'Ko, New Tai Lue, Buginese, Glagolitic, Coptic, Tifinagh, Syloti Nagri, Balinese, Phags-pa, Old Persian, Phoenician, Kharoshthi, and Sumero-Akkadian Cuneiform. Many other characters have been added, including significant extensions for the Arabic and Ethiopic scripts, as well as additions to complete the representation of Biblical Hebrew texts. Additional phonetic characters have been included to support phonetic transcriptions other than IPA. Overall character and code ranges are detailed in *Chapter 2, General Structure.*

Note, however, that the Unicode Standard does not encode idiosyncratic, personal, novel, or private-use characters, nor does it encode logos or graphics. Graphologies unrelated to text, such as dance notations, are likewise outside the scope of the Unicode Standard. Font variants are explicitly not encoded. The Unicode Standard reserves 6,400 code points in the BMP for private use, which may be used to assign codes to characters not included in the repertoire of the Unicode Standard. Another 131,068 private-use code points are available outside the BMP, should 6,400 prove insufficient for particular applications.

Standards Coverage

The Unicode Standard is a superset of all characters in widespread use today. It contains the characters from major international and national standards as well as prominent industry character sets. For example, Unicode incorporates the ISO/IEC 6937 and ISO/IEC 8859 families of standards, the SGML standard ISO/IEC 8879, and bibliographic standards such as ISO 5426. Important national standards contained within Unicode include ANSI Z39.64, KS X 1001, JIS X 0208, JIS X 0212, JIS X 0213, GB 2312, GB 18030, HKSCS, and CNS 11643. Industry code pages and character sets from Adobe, Apple, Fujitsu, Hewlett-Packard, IBM, Lotus, Microsoft, NEC, and Xerox are fully represented as well.

For a complete list of ISO and national standards used as sources, see *References.*

The Unicode Standard is fully conformant with the International Standard ISO/IEC 10646:2003, *Information Technology—Universal Multiple-Octet Coded Character Set (UCS)—Architecture and Basic Multilingual Plane, Supplementary Planes,* known as the Universal Character Set (UCS). For more information, see *Appendix C, Relationship to ISO/IEC 10646.*

New Characters

The Unicode Standard continues to respond to new and changing industry demands by encoding important new characters. As the universal character encoding scheme, the Unicode Standard also responds to scholarly needs. To preserve world cultural heritage, important archaic scripts are encoded as consensus about the encoding is developed.

1.2 Design Goals

The primary goal of the development effort for the Unicode Standard was to remedy two serious problems common to most multilingual computer programs. The first problem was the overloading of the font mechanism when encoding characters. Fonts have often been indiscriminately mapped to the same set of bytes. For example, the bytes 0x00 to 0xFF are often used for both characters and dingbats. The second major problem was the use of multiple, inconsistent character codes because of conflicting national and industry character standards. In Western European software environments, for example, one often finds confusion between the Windows Latin 1 code page 1252 and ISO/IEC 8859-1.

When the Unicode project began in 1988, the groups most affected by the lack of a consistent international character standard included publishers of scientific and mathematical software, newspaper and book publishers, bibliographic information services, and academic researchers. More recently, the computer industry has adopted an increasingly global outlook, building international software that can be easily adapted to meet the needs of particular locations and cultures. The explosive growth of the Internet has added to the demand for a character set standard that can be used all over the world.

The designers of the Unicode Standard envisioned a uniform method of character identification that would be more efficient and flexible than previous encoding systems. The new system would satisfy the needs of technical and multilingual computing and would encode a broad range of characters for professional-quality typesetting and desktop publishing worldwide.

The Unicode Standard was designed to be:

- *Universal.* The repertoire must be large enough to encompass all characters that are likely to be used in general text interchange, including those in major international, national, and industry character sets.
- *Efficient.* Plain text is simple to parse: software does not have to maintain state or look for special escape sequences, and character synchronization from any point in a character stream is quick and unambiguous. A fixed character code allows for efficient sorting, searching, display, and editing of text.
- *Unambiguous.* Any given Unicode code point always represents the same character.

Figure 1-2 demonstrates some of these features, contrasting the Unicode encoding with mixtures of single-byte character sets with escape sequences to shift the meanings of bytes in the ISO/IEC 2022 framework using multiple character encoding standards.

Figure 1-2. Unicode Compared to the 2022 Framework

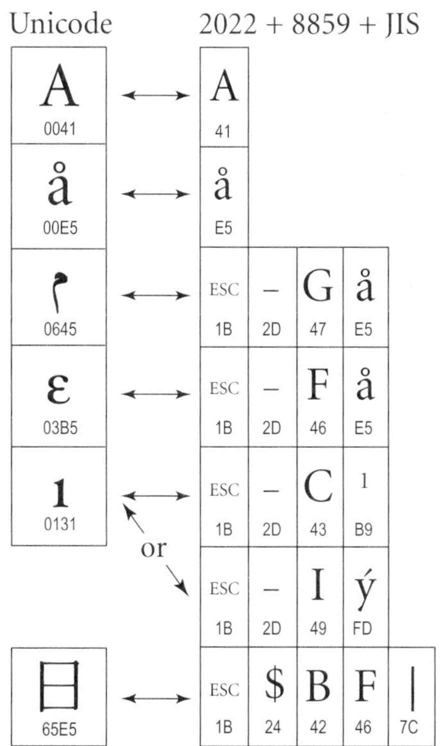

1.3 Text Handling

Computer text handling involves both encoding and processing. When a word processor user types in the letter "T" via a keyboard, the computer's system software receives a message that the user pressed a key combination for "T", which it encodes as U+0054. The word processor stores the number in memory and also passes it on to the display software responsible for putting the character on the screen. This display software, which may be a windows manager or part of the word processor itself, then uses the number as an index to find an image of a "T", which it draws on the monitor screen. The process continues as the user types in more characters.

The Unicode Standard directly addresses only the encoding and semantics of text and not any other actions performed on the text. In the preceding scenario, the word processor might check the typist's input after it has been encoded to look for misspelled words and then highlight any errors it finds. Alternatively, the word processor might insert line breaks when it counts a certain number of characters entered since the last line break. An important principle of the Unicode Standard is that the standard does not specify how to carry out these processes as long as the character encoding and decoding is performed properly and the character semantics are maintained.

The difference between identifying a character and rendering it on screen or paper is crucial to understanding the Unicode Standard's role in text processing. The character identified by a Unicode code point is an abstract entity, such as "LATIN CAPITAL LETTER A" or "BENGALI DIGIT FIVE". The mark made on screen or paper, called a glyph, is a visual representation of the character.

The Unicode Standard does not define glyph images. That is, the standard defines how characters are interpreted, not how glyphs are rendered. Ultimately, the software or hardware rendering engine of a computer is responsible for the appearance of the characters on the screen. The Unicode Standard does not specify the precise shape, size, or orientation of on-screen characters.

Text Elements

The successful encoding, processing, and interpretation of text requires appropriate definition of useful elements of text and the basic rules for interpreting text. The definition of text elements often changes depending on the process that handles the text. For example, when searching for a particular word or character written with the Latin script, one often wishes to ignore differences of case. However, correct spelling within a document requires case sensitivity.

The Unicode Standard does not define what is and is not a text element in different processes; instead, it defines elements called *encoded characters*. An encoded character is represented by a number from 0 to $10FFFF_{16}$, called a code point. A text element, in turn, is represented by a sequence of one or more encoded characters.

CHAPTER 2

Chapter 2

General Structure

This chapter describes the fundamental principles governing the design of the Unicode Standard and presents an informal overview of its main features. The chapter starts by placing the Unicode Standard in an architectural context by discussing the nature of text representation and text processing and its bearing on character encoding decisions. Next, the Unicode Design Principles are introduced—10 basic principles that convey the essence of the standard. The Unicode Design Principles serve as a tutorial framework for understanding the Unicode Standard.

The chapter then moves on to the Unicode character encoding model, introducing the concepts of character, code point, and encoding forms, and diagramming the relationships between them. This provides an explanation of the encoding forms UTF-8, UTF-16, and UTF-32 and some general guidelines regarding the circumstances under which one form would be preferable to another.

The sections on Unicode allocation then describe the overall structure of the Unicode codespace, showing a summary of the code charts and the locations of blocks of characters associated with different scripts or sets of symbols.

Next, the chapter discusses the issue of writing direction and introduces several special types of characters important for understanding the Unicode Standard. In particular, the use of combining characters, the byte order mark, and other special characters is explored in some detail.

The section on equivalent sequences and normalization describes the issue of multiple equivalent representations of Unicode text and explains how text can be transformed to use a unique and preferred representation for each character sequence.

Finally, there is an informal statement of the conformance requirements for the Unicode Standard. This informal statement, with a number of easy-to-understand examples, gives a general sense of what conformance to the Unicode Standard means. The rigorous, formal definition of conformance is given in the subsequent *Chapter 3, Conformance*.

2.1 Architectural Context

A character code standard such as the Unicode Standard enables the implementation of useful processes operating on textual data. The interesting end products are not the character codes but rather the text processes, because these directly serve the needs of a system's users. Character codes are like nuts and bolts—minor, but essential and ubiquitous components used in many different ways in the construction of computer software systems. No single design of a character set can be optimal for all uses, so the architecture of the Unicode Standard strikes a balance among several competing requirements.

Basic Text Processes

Most computer systems provide low-level functionality for a small number of basic text processes from which more sophisticated text-processing capabilities are built. The following text processes are supported by most computer systems to some degree:

- Rendering characters visible (including ligatures, contextual forms, and so on)
- Breaking lines while rendering (including hyphenation)
- Modifying appearance, such as point size, kerning, underlining, slant, and weight (light, demi, bold, and so on)
- Determining units such as "word" and "sentence"
- Interacting with users in processes such as selecting and highlighting text
- Accepting keyboard input and editing stored text through insertion and deletion
- Comparing text in operations such as in searching or determining the sort order of two strings
- Analyzing text content in operations such as spell-checking, hyphenation, and parsing morphology (that is, determining word roots, stems, and affixes)
- Treating text as bulk data for operations such as compressing and decompressing, truncating, transmitting, and receiving

Text Elements, Characters, and Text Processes

One of the more profound challenges in designing a character encoding stems from the fact that there is no universal set of fundamental units of text. Instead, the division of text into *text elements* necessarily varies by language and text process.

For example, in traditional German orthography, the letter combination "ck" is a text element for the process of hyphenation (where it appears as "k-k"), but not for the process of sorting. In Spanish, the combination "ll" may be a text element for the traditional process of sorting (where it is sorted between "l" and "m"), but not for the process of rendering. In English, the letters "A" and "a" are usually distinct text elements for the process of rendering, but generally not distinct for the process of searching text. The text elements in a given language depend upon the specific text process; a text element for spell-checking may have different boundaries from a text element for sorting purposes. For example, in the phrase "the quick brown fox," the sequence "fox" is a text element for the purpose of spell-checking.

In contrast, a character encoding standard provides a single set of fundamental units of encoding, to which it uniquely assigns numerical code points. These units, called *assigned characters*, are the smallest interpretable units of stored text. Text elements are then represented by a sequence of one or more characters.

Figure 2-1 illustrates the relationship between several different types of text elements and the characters that are used to represent those text elements. Unicode Standard Annex #29, "Text Boundaries," provides more details regarding the specifications of boundaries.

Figure 2-1. Text Elements and Characters

	Text Elements	Characters	
Composite:	Ç	Ç	
		C ◌̧	
Collation Unit:	ch	c h	(Slovak)
Syllable:	क्षि	क ◌् ष ि	
Word:	cat	c a t	

The design of the character encoding must provide precisely the set of characters that allows programmers to design applications capable of implementing a variety of text processes in the desired languages. Therefore, the text elements encountered in most text processes are represented as sequences of character codes. See Unicode Standard Annex #29, "Text Boundaries," for detailed information on how to segment character strings into common types of text elements. Certain text elements correspond to what users perceive as single characters. These are called *grapheme clusters*.

Text Processes and Encoding

In the case of English text using an encoding scheme such as ASCII, the relationships between the encoding and the basic text processes built on it are seemingly straightforward: characters are generally rendered visible one by one in distinct rectangles from left to right in linear order. Thus one character code inside the computer corresponds to one logical character in a process such as simple English rendering.

When designing an international and multilingual text encoding such as the Unicode Standard, the relationship between the encoding and implementation of basic text processes must be considered explicitly, for several reasons:

- Many assumptions about character rendering that hold true for the English alphabet fail for other writing systems. Characters in these other writing systems are not necessarily rendered visible one by one in rectangles from left to right. In many cases, character positioning is quite complex and does not proceed in a linear fashion. See *Section 8.2, Arabic*, and *Section 9.1, Devanagari*, for detailed examples of this situation.
- It is not always obvious that one set of text characters is an optimal encoding for a given language. For example, two approaches exist for the encoding of accented characters commonly used in French or Swedish: ISO/IEC 8859 defines letters such as "ä" and "ö" as individual characters, whereas ISO 5426 represents them by composition with diacritics instead. In the Swedish language, both are considered distinct letters of the alphabet, following the letter "z". In French, the diaeresis on a vowel merely marks it as being pronounced in isolation. In practice, both approaches can be used to implement either language.
- No encoding can support all basic text processes equally well. As a result, some trade-offs are necessary. For example, following common practice, Unicode defines separate codes for uppercase and lowercase letters. This choice causes some text processes, such as rendering, to be carried out more easily, but other processes, such as comparison, to become more difficult. A different encoding design for English, such as case-shift control codes, would have the opposite effect. In designing a new encoding scheme for complex scripts, such trade-offs must be evaluated and decisions made explicitly, rather than unconsciously.

For these reasons, design of the Unicode Standard is not specific to the design of particular basic text-processing algorithms. Instead, it provides an encoding that can be used with a wide variety of algorithms. In particular, sorting and string comparison algorithms *cannot* assume that the assignment of Unicode character code numbers provides an alphabetical ordering for lexicographic string comparison. Culturally expected sorting orders require arbitrarily complex sorting algorithms. The expected sort sequence for the same characters differs across languages; thus, in general, no single acceptable lexicographic ordering exists. See Unicode Technical Standard #10, "Unicode Collation Algorithm," for the standard default mechanism for comparing Unicode strings.

Text processes supporting many languages are often more complex than they are for English. The character encoding design of the Unicode Standard strives to minimize this additional complexity, enabling modern computer systems to interchange, render, and manipulate text in a user's own script and language—and possibly in other languages as well.

Character Identity. Whenever Unicode makes statements about the default layout behavior of characters, it is in an attempt to ensure that users and implementers face no ambiguities as to which characters or character sequences to use for a given purpose. For bidirectional writing systems, this includes the specification of the sequence in which characters are to be encoded so as to correspond to a specific reading order when displayed. See *Section 2.10, Writing Direction*.

The actual layout in an implementation may differ in detail. A mathematical layout system, for example, will have many additional, domain-specific rules for layout, but a well-designed system leaves no ambiguities as to which character codes are to be used for a given aspect of the mathematical expression being encoded.

The purpose of defining Unicode default layout behavior is not to enforce a single and specific aesthetic layout for each script, but rather to encourage uniformity in encoding. In that way implementers of layout systems can rely on the fact that user would have chosen a particular character sequence for a given purpose, and users can rely on the fact that implementers will create a layout for a particular character sequence that matches the intent of the user to within the capabilities or technical limitations of the implementation.

In other words, the ideal is that two users who are familiar with the standard and who are presented with the same text would choose the same sequence of character codes to encode the text. In actual practice there are many limitations that mean this goal cannot always be realized.

2.2 Unicode Design Principles

The design of the Unicode Standard reflects the 10 fundamental principles stated in *Table 2-1*. Not all of these principles can be satisfied simultaneously. The design strikes a balance between maintaining consistency for the sake of simplicity and efficiency and maintaining compatibility for interchange with existing standards.

Table 2-1. The 10 Unicode Design Principles

Principle	Statement
Universality	The Unicode Standard provides a single, universal repertoire.
Efficiency	Unicode text is simple to parse and process.
Characters, not glyphs	The Unicode Standard encodes characters, not glyphs.
Semantics	Characters have well-defined semantics.
Plain text	Unicode characters represent plain text.
Logical order	The default for memory representation is logical order.
Unification	The Unicode Standard unifies duplicate characters within scripts across languages.
Dynamic composition	Accented forms can be dynamically composed.
Stability	Characters, once assigned, cannot be reassigned and key properties are immutable.
Convertibility	Accurate convertibility is guaranteed between the Unicode Standard and other widely accepted standards.

Universality

The Unicode Standard encodes a single, very large set of characters, encompassing all the characters needed for worldwide use. This single repertoire is intended to be universal in coverage, containing all the characters for textual representation in all modern writing systems, in most historic writing systems, and for symbols used in plain text.

The Unicode Standard is designed to meet the needs of diverse user communities within each language, serving business, educational, liturgical and scientific users, and covering the needs of both modern and historical texts.

Despite its aim of universality, the Unicode Standard considers the following to be outside its scope: writing systems for which insufficient information is available to enable reliable encoding of characters, writing systems that have not become standardized through use, and writing systems that are nontextual in nature.

Because the universal repertoire is known and well defined in the standard, it is possible to specify a rich set of character semantics. By relying on those character semantics, implementations can provide detailed support for complex operations on text in a portable way. See "Semantics" later in this section.

Efficiency

The Unicode Standard is designed to make efficient implementation possible. There are no escape characters or shift states in the Unicode character encoding model. Each character code has the same status as any other character code; all codes are equally accessible.

All Unicode encoding forms are self-synchronizing and non-overlapping. This makes randomly accessing and searching inside streams of characters efficient.

By convention, characters of a script are grouped together as far as is practical. Not only is this practice convenient for looking up characters in the code charts, but it makes implementations more compact and compression methods more efficient. The common punctuation characters are shared.

Format characters are given specific and unambiguous functions in the Unicode Standard. This design simplifies the support of subsets. To keep implementations simple and efficient, stateful controls and format characters are avoided wherever possible.

Characters, Not Glyphs

The Unicode Standard draws a distinction between *characters* and *glyphs*. Characters are the abstract representations of the smallest components of written language that have semantic value. They represent primarily, but not exclusively, the letters, punctuation, and other signs that constitute natural language text and technical notation. The letters used in natural language text are grouped into scripts—sets of letters that are used together in writing languages. Letters in different scripts, even when they correspond either semantically or graphically, are represented in Unicode by distinct characters. This is true even in those instances where they correspond in semantics, pronunciation, or appearance.

Characters are represented by code points that reside only in a memory representation, as strings in memory, on disk, or in data transmission. The Unicode Standard deals only with character codes.

Glyphs represent the shapes that characters can have when they are rendered or displayed. In contrast to characters, glyphs appear on the screen or paper as particular representations of one or more characters. A repertoire of glyphs makes up a font. Glyph shape and methods of identifying and selecting glyphs are the responsibility of individual font vendors and of appropriate standards and are not part of the Unicode Standard.

Various relationships may exist between character and glyph: a single glyph may correspond to a single character or to a number of characters, or multiple glyphs may result from a single character. The distinction between characters and glyphs is illustrated in *Figure 2-2*.

Figure 2-2. Characters Versus Glyphs

Glyphs	Unicode Characters
A A A A A A A A A	U+0041 LATIN CAPITAL LETTER A
a a a a a a a a a	U+0061 LATIN SMALL LETTER A
п *п* *ū*	U+043F CYRILLIC SMALL LETTER PE
ه ـه هـ ـهـ	U+0647 ARABIC LETTER HEH
fi fi	U+0066 LATIN SMALL LETTER F + U+0069 LATIN SMALL LETTER I

Even the letter "a" has a wide variety of glyphs that can represent it. A lowercase Cyrillic "п" also has a variety of glyphs; the second glyph for U+043F CYRILLIC SMALL LETTER PE shown in *Figure 2-2* is customary for italic in Russia, while the third is customary for italic in Serbia. Arabic letters are displayed with different glyphs, depending on their position in a word; the glyphs in *Figure 2-2* show independent, final, initial, and medial forms. Sequences such as "fi" may be displayed with two independent glyphs or with a ligature glyph.

What the user thinks of as a single character—which may or may not be represented by a single glyph—may be represented in the Unicode Standard as multiple code points. See *Table 2-2* for additional examples.

For certain scripts, such as Arabic and the various Indic scripts, the number of glyphs needed to display a given script may be significantly larger than the number of characters encoding the basic units of that script. The number of glyphs may also depend on the orthographic style supported by the font. For example, an Arabic font intended to support

Table 2-2. User-Perceived Characters with Multiple Code Points

Character	Code Points	Linguistic Usage
ch	0063 0068	Slovak, traditional Spanish
tʰ	0074 02B0	Native American languages
x̣	0078 0323	
ƛ̓	019B 0313	
ą́	00E1 0328	Lithuanian
i̇́	0069 0307 0301	
ト゚	30C8 309A	Ainu (in kana transcription)

the *Nastaliq* style of Arabic script may possess many thousands of glyphs. However, the character encoding employs the same few dozen letters regardless of the font style used to depict the character data in context.

A font and its associated rendering process define an arbitrary mapping from Unicode characters to glyphs. Some of the glyphs in a font may be independent forms for individual characters; others may be rendering forms that do not directly correspond to any single character.

Text rendering requires that characters in memory be mapped to glyphs. The final appearance of rendered text may depend on context (neighboring characters in the memory representation), variations in typographic design of the fonts used, and formatting information (point size, superscript, subscript, and so on). The results on screen or paper can differ considerably from the prototypical shape of a letter or character, as shown in *Figure 2-3*.

For the Latin script, this relationship between character code sequence and glyph is relatively simple and well known; for several other scripts, it is documented in this standard. However, in all cases, fine typography requires a more elaborate set of rules than given here. The Unicode Standard documents the default relationship between character sequences and glyphic appearance for the purpose of ensuring that the same text content can be stored with the same, and therefore interchangeable, sequence of character codes.

Semantics

Characters have well-defined semantics. These semantics are defined by explicitly assigned character properties, rather than implied through the character name or the position of a character in the code tables (see *Section 3.5, Properties*). The Unicode Character Database provides machine-readable character property tables for use in implementations of parsing, sorting, and other algorithms requiring semantic knowledge about the code points.

Figure 2-3. Unicode Character Code to Rendered Glyphs

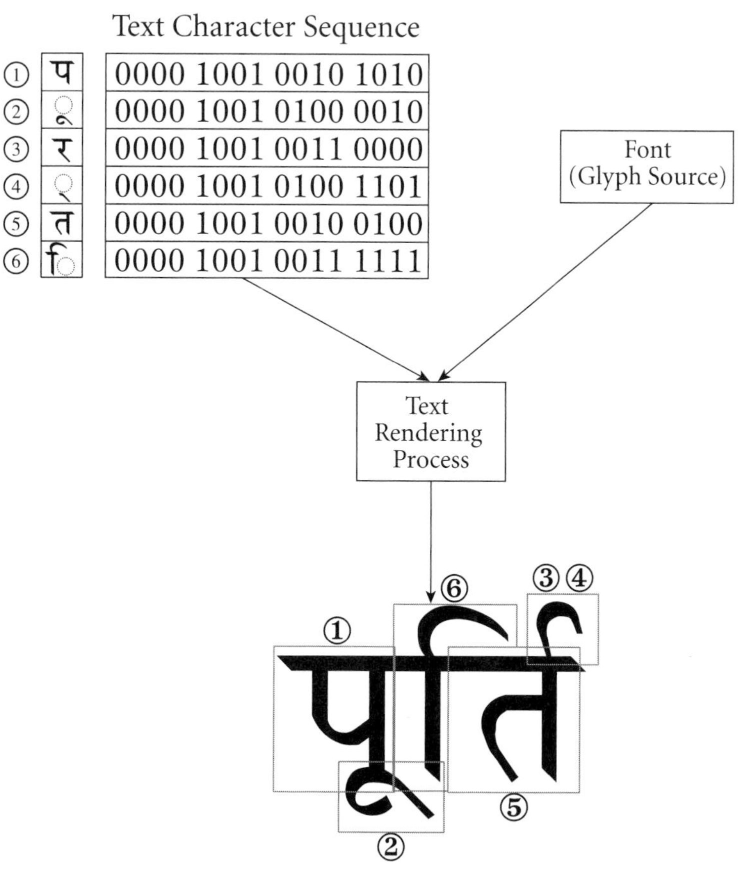

These properties are supplemented by the description of script and character behavior in this standard. See also Unicode Technical Report #23, "The Unicode Character Property Model."

The Unicode Standard identifies more than 50 different character properties, including numeric, casing, combination, and directionality properties (see *Chapter 4, Character Properties*). Additional properties may be defined as needed from time to time. Where characters are used in different ways in different languages, the relevant properties are normally defined outside the Unicode Standard. For example, Unicode Technical Standard #10, "Unicode Collation Algorithm," defines a set of default collation weights that can be used with a standard algorithm. Tailorings for each language are provided in the Common Locale Data Repository (CLDR); see *Section B.6, Other Unicode Online Resources*.

The Unicode Standard, by supplying a universal repertoire associated with well-defined character semantics, does not require the *code set independent* model of internationalization and text handling. That model abstracts away string handling as manipulation of byte streams of unknown semantics to protect implementations from the details of hundreds of different character encodings and selectively late-binds locale-specific character properties to characters. Of course, it is always possible for code set independent implementations to retain their model and to treat Unicode characters as just another character set in that context. It is not at all unusual for Unix implementations to simply add UTF-8 as another character set, parallel to all the other character sets they support. By contrast, the Unicode approach—because it is associated with a universal repertoire—assumes that characters and their properties are inherently and inextricably associated. If an internationalized application can be structured to work directly in terms of Unicode characters, all levels of the implementation can reliably and efficiently access character storage and be assured of the universal applicability of character property semantics.

Plain Text

Plain text is a pure sequence of character codes; plain Unicode-encoded text is therefore a sequence of Unicode character codes. In contrast, *styled text,* also known as *rich text,* is any text representation consisting of plain text plus added information such as a language identifier, font size, color, hypertext links, and so on. For example, the text of this book, a multifont text as formatted by a book editing system, is rich text.

The simplicity of plain text gives it a natural role as a major structural element of rich text. SGML, RTF, HTML, XML, and TEX are examples of rich text fully represented as plain text streams, interspersing plain text data with sequences of characters that represent the additional data structures. They use special conventions embedded within the plain text file, such as "<p>", to distinguish the markup or *tags* from the "real" content. Many popular word processing packages rely on a buffer of plain text to represent the content and implement links to a parallel store of formatting data.

The relative functional roles of both plain text and rich text are well established:

- Plain text is the underlying content stream to which formatting can be applied.
- Rich text carries complex formatting information as well as text context.
- Plain text is public, standardized, and universally readable.
- Rich text representation may be implementation-specific or proprietary.

Although some rich text formats have been standardized or made public, the majority of rich text designs are vehicles for particular implementations and are not necessarily readable by other implementations. Given that rich text equals plain text plus added information, the extra information in rich text can always be stripped away to reveal the "pure" text underneath. This operation is often employed, for example, in word processing systems that use both their own private rich text format and plain text file format as a universal, if limited, means of exchange. Thus, by default, plain text represents the basic, interchangeable content of text.

Plain text represents character content only, not its appearance. It can be displayed in a varity of ways and requires a rendering process to make it visible with a particular appearance.

If the same plain text sequence is given to disparate rendering processes, there is no expectation that rendered text in each instance should have the same appearance. Instead, the disparate rendering processes are simply required to make the text legible according to the intended reading. This legibility criterion constrains the range of possible appearances. The relationship between appearance and content of plain text may be summarized as follows:

> *Plain text must contain enough information to permit the text to be rendered legibly, and nothing more.*

The Unicode Standard encodes plain text. The distinction between plain text and other forms of data in the same data stream is the function of a higher-level protocol and is not specified by the Unicode Standard itself.

Logical Order

The order in which Unicode text is stored in the memory representation is called *logical order.* This order roughly corresponds to the order in which text is typed in via the keyboard; it also roughly corresponds to phonetic order. For decimal numbers, the logical order consistently corresponds to the most significant digit first, which is the order expected by number-parsing software.

When displayed, this logical order often corresponds to a simple linear progression of characters in one direction, such as from left to right, right to left, or top to bottom. In other circumstances, text is displayed or printed in an order that differs from a single linear progression. Some of the clearest examples are situations where a right-to-left script (such as Arabic or Hebrew) is mixed with a left-to-right script (such as Latin or Greek). For example, when the text in *Figure 2-4* is ordered for display, the glyph that represents the first character of the English text appears at the left. The logical start character of the Hebrew text, however, is represented by the Hebrew glyph closest to the right margin. The succeeding Hebrew glyphs are laid out to the left.

Figure 2-4. Bidirectional Ordering

In logical order, numbers are encoded with most significant digit first, but are displayed in different writing directions. As shown in *Figure 2-5* these writing directions do not always correspond to the writing direction of the surrounding text. The first example shows N'Ko, a right-to-left script with digits that also render right to left. Examples 2 and 3 show Hebrew and Arabic, in which the numbers are rendered left to right, resulting in bidirectional layout. In left-to-right scripts, such as Latin and Hiragana and Katakana (for Japanese), numbers follow the predominant left-to-right direction of the script, as shown in Examples 4 and 5. When Japanese is laid out vertically, numbers are either laid out vertically or may be rotated clockwise 90 degrees to follow the layout direction of the lines, as shown in Example 6.

Figure 2-5. Writing Direction and Numbers

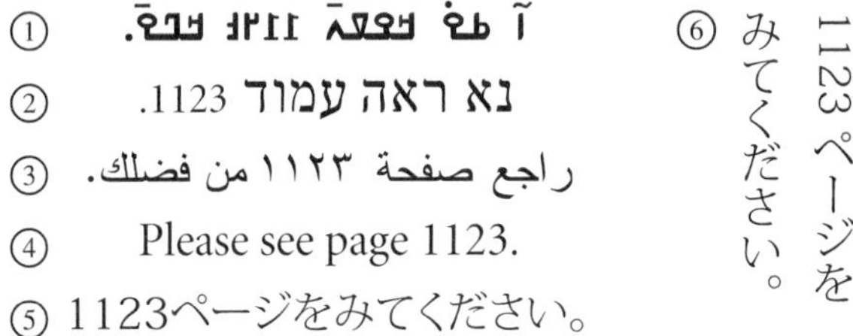

The Unicode Standard precisely defines the conversion of Unicode text from logical order to the order of readable (displayed) text so as to ensure consistent legibility. Properties of directionality inherent in characters generally determine the correct display order of text. The Unicode Bidirectional Algorithm specifies how these properties are used to resolve directional interactions when characters of right-to-left and left-to-right directionality are mixed. (See Unicode Standard Annex #9, "The Bidirectional Algorithm.") However, when characters of different directionality are mixed, inherent directionality alone is occasionally insufficient to render plain text legibly. The Unicode Standard therefore includes characters to explicitly specify changes in direction when necessary. The Bidirectional Algorithm uses these directional layout control characters together with the inherent directional properties of characters to exert exact control over the display ordering for legible interchange. By requiring the use of this algorithm, the Unicode Standard ensures that plain text used for simple items like file names or labels can always be correctly ordered for display.

Besides mixing runs of differing overall text direction, there are many other cases where the logical order does not correspond to a linear progression of characters. Combining characters (such as accents) are stored following the base character to which they apply, but are positioned relative to that base character and thus do not follow a simple linear progression in the final rendered text. For example, the Latin letter "ẋ̣" is stored as "x" followed by combining "◌̣"; the accent appears below, not to the right of the base. This position with respect to the base holds even where the overall text progression is from top to bottom—for example, with "x̣" appearing upright within a vertical Japanese line. Characters may also combine into ligatures or conjuncts or otherwise change positions of their components radically, as shown in *Figure 2-3* and *Figure 2-20*.

There is one particular exception to the usual practice of logical order paralleling phonetic order. With the Thai and Lao scripts, users traditionally type in visual order rather than phonetic order, resulting in some vowel letters being stored ahead of consonants, even though they are pronounced after them.

Unification

The Unicode Standard avoids duplicate encoding of characters by unifying them within scripts across language. Common letters are given one code each, regardless of language, as are common Chinese/Japanese/Korean (CJK) ideographs. (See *Section 12.1, Han.*)

Punctuation marks, symbols, and diacritics are handled in a similar manner as letters. If they can be clearly identified with a particular script, they are encoded once for that script and are unified across any languages that may use that script. See, for example, U+1362 ETHIOPIC FULL STOP, U+060F ARABIC SIGN MISRA, and U+0592 HEBREW ACCENT SEGOL. However, some punctuation or diacritic marks may be shared in common across a number of scripts—the obvious example being Western-style punctuation characters, which are often recently added to the writing systems of scripts other than Latin. In such cases, characters are encoded only once and are intended for use with multiple scripts. Common symbols are also encoded only once and are not associated with any script in particular.

It is quite normal for many characters to have different usages, such as *comma* "," for either thousands-separator (English) or decimal-separator (French). The Unicode Standard avoids duplication of characters due to specific usage in different languages; rather, it duplicates characters *only* to support compatibility with base standards. Avoidance of duplicate encoding of characters is important to avoid visual ambiguity.

There are a few notable instances in the standard where visual ambiguity between different characters is tolerated, however. For example, in most fonts there is little or no distinction visible between Latin "o", Cyrillic "o", and Greek "o" (*omicron*). These are not unified because they are characters from three different scripts, and many legacy character encodings distinguish between them. As another example, there are three characters whose glyph is the same uppercase barred D shape, but they correspond to three distinct lowercase forms. Unifying these uppercase characters would have resulted in unnecessary complications for case mapping.

The Unicode Standard does not attempt to encode features such as language, font, size, positioning, glyphs, and so forth. For example, it does not preserve language as a part of character encoding: just as French *i grec*, German *ypsilon*, and English *wye* are all represented by the same character code, U+0057 "Y", so too are Chinese *zi*, Japanese *ji*, and Korean *ja* all represented as the same character code, U+5B57 字.

In determining whether to unify variant CJK ideograph forms across standards, the Unicode Standard follows the principles described in *Section 12.1, Han*. Where these principles determine that two forms constitute a trivial difference, the Unicode Standard assigns a single code. Just as for the Latin and other scripts, typeface distinctions or local preferences in glyph shapes alone are not sufficient grounds for disunification of a character. *Figure 2-6* illustrates the well-known example of the CJK ideograph for "bone," which shows significant shape differences from typeface to typeface, with some forms preferred in China and some in Japan. All of these forms are considered to be the same *character*, encoded at U+9AA8 in the Unicode Standard.

Figure 2-6. Typeface Variation for the Bone Character

Many characters in the Unicode Standard could have been unified with existing visually similar Unicode characters or could have been omitted in favor of some other Unicode mechanism for maintaining the kinds of text distinctions for which they were intended. However, considerations of interoperability with other standards and systems often require that such compatibility characters be included in the Unicode Standard. See *Section 2.3, Compatibility Characters*. In particular, whenever font style, size, positioning or precise glyph shape carry a specific meaning and are used in distinction to the ordinary character—for example, in phonetic or mathematical notation—the characters are not unified.

Dynamic Composition

The Unicode Standard allows for the dynamic composition of accented forms and Hangul syllables. Combining characters used to create composite forms are productive. Because the process of character composition is open-ended, new forms with modifying marks may be created from a combination of base characters followed by combining characters. For example, the diaeresis "¨" may be combined with all vowels and a number of consonants in languages using the Latin script and several other scripts, as shown in *Figure 2-7*.

Figure 2-7. Dynamic Composition

Equivalent Sequences. Some text elements can be encoded either as static precomposed forms or by dynamic composition. Common precomposed forms such as U+00DC "Ü" LATIN CAPITAL LETTER U WITH DIAERESIS are included for compatibility with current standards. For static precomposed forms, the standard provides a mapping to an equivalent dynamically composed sequence of characters. (See also *Section 3.7, Decomposition.*) Thus different sequences of Unicode characters are considered equivalent. A precomposed character may be represented as an equivalent composed character sequence (see *Section 2.12, Equivalent Sequences and Normalization*).

Stability

Certain aspects of the Unicode Standard must be absolutely stable between versions, so that implementers and users can be guaranteed that text data, once encoded, retains the same meaning. Most importantly, this means that once Unicode characters are assigned, their code point assignments cannot be changed, nor can characters be removed.

Characters are retained in the standard, so that previously conforming data stay conformant in future versions of the standard. Sometimes characters are deprecated—that is, their use in new documents is discouraged. Usually, this is because the characters were found not to be needed, and their continued use would merely result in duplicate ways of encoding the same information. While implementations should continue to recognize such characters when they are encountered, spell-checkers or editors could warn users of their presence and suggest replacements.

Unicode character names are also never changed, so that they can be used as identifiers that are valid across versions. See *Section 4.8, Name—Normative.*

Similar stability guarantees exist for certain important properties. For example, the decompositions are kept stable, so that it is possible to normalize a Unicode text once and have it remain normalized in all future versions.

For a list of stability policies for the Unicode Standard, see *Appendix F, Unicode Encoding Stability Policies.*

Convertibility

Character identity is preserved for interchange with a number of different base standards, including national, international, and vendor standards. Where variant forms (or even the same form) are given separate codes within one base standard, they are also kept separate within the Unicode Standard. This choice guarantees the existence of a mapping between the Unicode Standard and base standards.

Accurate convertibility is guaranteed between the Unicode Standard and other standards in wide usage as of May 1993. Characters have also been added to allow convertibility to several important East Asian character sets created after that date—for example, GB 18030. In general, a single code point in another standard will correspond to a single code point in the Unicode Standard. Sometimes, however, a single code point in another standard corresponds to a sequence of code points in the Unicode Standard, or vice versa. Conversion between Unicode text and text in other character codes must, in general, be done by explicit table-mapping processes. (See also *Section 5.1, Transcoding to Other Standards.*)

2.3 Compatibility Characters

Compatibility Variants

Conceptually, compatibility characters are those that would not have been encoded except for compatibility and round-trip convertibility with other standards. They are variants of characters that already have encodings as *normal* (that is, non-compatibility) characters in the Unicode Standard; as such, they are more properly referred to as *compatibility variants.* Examples of compatibility variants in this sense include all of the glyph variants in the Compatibility and Specials Area: halfwidth or fullwidth characters from East Asian character encoding standards, Arabic contextual form glyphs from preexisting Arabic code pages, Arabic ligatures and ligatures from other scripts, and so on. Other examples include CJK compatibility ideographs, which are generally duplicates of a unified Han ideograph, and legacy alternate format characters such as U+206C INHIBIT ARABIC FORM SHAPING.

The fact that a character can be considered a compatibility variant does not mean that the character is deprecated in the standard. The use of many compatibility variants in general interchange is unproblematic. Some, however, such as Arabic contextual forms or vertical forms, can lead to problems when used in general interchange. In identifiers, compatibility variants should be avoided because of their visual similarity with regular characters. (See Unicode Technical Report #36, "Unicode Security Considerations.")

The Compatibility and Specials Area contains a large number of compatibility characters, but the Unicode Standard also contains many compatibility characters that do not appear in that area. These include examples such as U+2163 "IV" ROMAN NUMERAL FOUR, U+2007 FIGURE SPACE, and U+00B2 "^{2}" SUPERSCRIPT TWO. There is no formal listing of all compatibility characters in the Unicode Standard.

Compatibility Decomposable Characters

There is a second, narrow sense of the term "compatibility character" in the Unicode Standard, corresponding to the notion of a *compatibility decomposable* introduced in *Section 2.2, Unicode Design Principles.* This sense is strictly defined as any Unicode character whose compatibility decomposition is not identical to its canonical decomposition. (See definition D66 in *Section 3.7, Decomposition.*) Because a compatibility character in this narrow sense must also be a composite character, it may also be unambiguously referred to as a compatibility composite character, or *compatibility composite* for short. The compatibility decomposable characters are precisely defined in the Unicode Character Database. Because of their use in normalization, their compatibility decompositions are stable and cannot be changed.

Compatibility decomposable characters and compatibility characters are two distinct concepts, even though the two sets of characters overlap. Not all compatibility characters have decomposition mappings. For example, the deprecated alternate format characters do not have any distinct decomposition, and CJK compatibility ideographs have canonical decomposition mappings rather than compatibility decomposition mappings.

Some compatibility decomposable characters are widely used characters serving essential functions. The *no-break space* is one example. A large number of compatibility decomposable characters are really distinct symbols used in specialized notations, whether phonetic or mathematical. They are therefore not compatibility variants in the strict sense. Rather, their compatibility mappings express their historical derivation from styled forms of standard letters. In these and similar cases, such as fixed-width space characters, the compatibility decompositions define possible fallback representations.

Mapping Compatibility Characters

Identifying one character as a compatibility variant of another character usually implies that the first can be remapped to the second without the loss of any textual information other than formatting and layout. However, such remapping cannot always take place because many of the compatibility characters are included in the standard precisely to allow systems to maintain one-to-one mappings to other existing character encoding standards and code pages. In such cases, a remapping would lose information that is important to maintaining some distinction in the original encoding. By definition, a compatibility decomposable character decomposes into a compatibly equivalent character or character sequence. Even in such cases, an implementation must proceed with due caution—replacing one with the other may change not only formatting information, but also other textual distinctions on which some other process may depend.

In many cases there exists a visual relationship between a compatibility composition and a standard character that is akin to a font style or directionality difference. Replacing such characters with unstyled characters could affect the meaning of the text. Replacing them with rich text would preserve the meaning for a human reader, but could cause some programs that depend on the distinction to behave unpredictably. This issue particularly affects compatibility characters used in mathematical notation.

In some usage domains (for example, network identifiers), it may be acceptable to prohibit the use of compatibility variants or to remap them consistently. In fact, in such cases, further sets of characters may be restricted in a similar way to compatibility variants. For more information and an introduction to the concept of "confusable" characters, see Unicode Technical Standard #39, "Unicode Security Mechanisms."

2.4 Code Points and Characters

On a computer, abstract characters are encoded internally as numbers. To create a complete character encoding, it is necessary to define the list of all characters to be encoded and to establish systematic rules for how the numbers represent the characters.

The range of integers used to code the abstract characters is called the *codespace.* A particular integer in this set is called a *code point.* When an abstract character is mapped or *assigned* to a particular code point in the codespace, it is then referred to as an *encoded character.*

In the Unicode Standard, the codespace consists of the integers from 0 to $10FFFF_{16}$, comprising 1,114,112 code points available for assigning the repertoire of abstract characters.

There are constraints on how the codespace is organized, and particular areas of the codespace have been set aside for encoding of certain kinds of abstract characters or for other uses in the standard. For more on the *allocation* of the Unicode codespace, see *Section 2.8, Unicode Allocation.*

Figure 2-8 illustrates the relationship between abstract characters and code points, which together constitute encoded characters. Note that some abstract characters may be associated with multiple, separately encoded characters (that is, be encoded "twice"). In other instances, an abstract character may be represented by a sequence of two (or more) other encoded characters. The solid arrows connect encoded characters with the abstract characters that they represent and encode.

Figure 2-8. Codespace and Encoded Characters

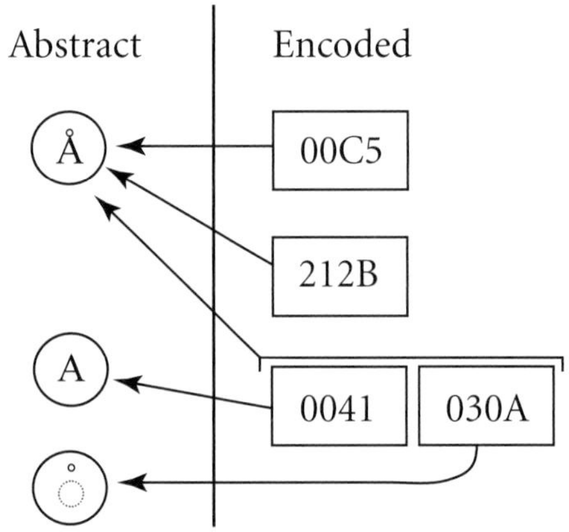

When referring to code points in the Unicode Standard, the usual practice is to refer to them by their numeric value expressed in hexadecimal, with a "U+" prefix. (See *Appendix A, Notational Conventions.*) Encoded characters can also be referred to by their code points only. To prevent ambiguity, the official Unicode name of the character is often added; this clearly identifies the abstract character that is encoded. For example:

U+0061 LATIN SMALL LETTER A

U+10330 GOTHIC LETTER AHSA

U+201DF CJK UNIFIED IDEOGRAPH-201DF

Such citations refer only to the encoded character per se, associating the code point (as an integral value) with the abstract character that is encoded.

Types of Code Points

There are many ways to categorize code points. *Table 2-3* illustrates some of the categorizations and basic terminology used in the Unicode Standard.

Not all assigned code points represent abstract characters; only Graphic, Format, Control and Private-use do. Surrogates and Noncharacters are assigned code points but are not assigned to abstract characters. Reserved code points are assignable: any may be assigned in a future version of the standard. The General Category provides a finer breakdown of

Table 2-3. Types of Code Points

<table>
<tr><th>Basic Type</th><th>Brief Description</th><th>General Category</th><th>Character Status</th><th>Code Point Status</th></tr>
<tr><td>Graphic</td><td>Letter, mark, number, punctuation, symbol, and spaces</td><td>L, M, N, P, S, Zs</td><td rowspan="4">Assigned to abstract character</td><td rowspan="6">Designated (assigned) code point</td></tr>
<tr><td>Format</td><td>Invisible but affects neighboring characters; includes line/paragraph separators</td><td>Cf, Zl, Zp</td></tr>
<tr><td>Control</td><td>Usage defined by protocols or standards outside the Unicode Standard</td><td>Cc</td></tr>
<tr><td>Private-use</td><td>Usage defined by private agreement outside the Unicode Standard</td><td>Co</td></tr>
<tr><td>Surrogate</td><td>Permanently reserved for UTF-16; restricted interchange</td><td>Cs</td><td rowspan="3">Not assigned to abstract character</td></tr>
<tr><td>Noncharacter</td><td>Permanently reserved for internal usage; restricted interchange</td><td rowspan="2">Cn</td></tr>
<tr><td>Reserved</td><td>Reserved for future assignment; restricted interchange</td><td>Undesignated (unassigned) code point</td></tr>
</table>

Graphic characters and also distinguishes between the other basic types (except between Noncharacter and Reserved). Other properties defined in the Unicode Character Database provide for different categorizations of Unicode code points.

Control Codes. Sixty-five code points (U+0000..U+001F and U+007F..U+009F) are reserved specifically as control codes, for compatibility with the C0 and C1 control codes of the ISO/IEC 2022 framework. A few of these control codes are given specific interpretations by the Unicode Standard. (See *Section 16.1, Control Codes.*)

Noncharacters. Sixty-six code points are not used to encode characters. Noncharacters consist of U+FDD0..U+FDEF and any code point ending in the value FFFE$_{16}$ or FFFF$_{16}$—that is, U+FFFE, U+FFFF, U+1FFFE, U+1FFFF, ... U+10FFFE, U+10FFFF. (See *Section 16.7, Noncharacters.*)

Private Use. Three ranges of code points have been set aside for private use. Characters in these areas will never be defined by the Unicode Standard. These code points can be freely used for characters of any purpose, but successful interchange requires an agreement between sender and receiver on their interpretation. (See *Section 16.5, Private-Use Characters.*)

Surrogates. Some 2,048 code points have been allocated as surrogate code points, which are used in the UTF-16 encoding form. (See *Section 16.6, Surrogates Area.*)

Restricted Interchange. Code points that are not assigned to abstract characters are subject to restrictions in interchange.

- Surrogate code points cannot be conformantly interchanged using Unicode encoding forms. They do not correspond to Unicode scalar values and thus do not have well-formed representations in any Unicode encoding form. (See *Section 3.8, Surrogates.*)
- Noncharacter code points are reserved for internal use, such as for sentinel values. They should never be interchanged. They do, however, have well-formed representations in Unicode encoding forms and survive conversions between encoding forms. This allows sentinel values to be preserved internally across Unicode encoding forms, even though they are not designed to be used in open interchange.
- All implementations need to preserve reserved code points because they may originate in implementations that use a *future* version of the Unicode Standard. For example, suppose that one person is using a Unicode 5.0 system and a second person is using a Unicode 3.2 system. The first person sends the second person a document containing some code points newly assigned in Unicode 5.0; these code points were unassigned in Unicode 3.2. The second person may edit the document, not changing the reserved codes, and send it on. In that case the second person is interchanging what are, as far as the second person knows, reserved code points.

Code Point Semantics. The semantics of most code points are established by this standard; the exceptions are Controls, Private-use, and Noncharacters. Control codes generally have semantics determined by other standards or protocols (such as ISO/IEC 6429), but there are a small number of control codes for which the Unicode Standard specifies particular semantics. See *Table 16-1* in *Section 16.1, Control Codes*, for the exact list of those control codes. The semantics of private-use characters are outside the scope of the Unicode Standard; their use is determined by private agreement, as, for example, between vendors. Noncharacters have semantics in internal use only.

2.5 Encoding Forms

Computers handle numbers not simply as abstract mathematical objects, but as combinations of fixed-size units like bytes and 32-bit words. A character encoding model must take this fact into account when determining how to associate numbers with the characters.

Actual implementations in computer systems represent integers in specific *code units* of particular size—usually 8-bit (= byte), 16-bit, or 32-bit. In the Unicode character encoding model, precisely defined *encoding forms* specify how each integer (code point) for a Unicode character is to be expressed as a sequence of one or more code units. The Unicode Standard provides three distinct encoding forms for Unicode characters, using 8-bit, 16-bit, and 32-bit units. These are named UTF-8, UTF-16, and UTF-32, respectively. The

"UTF" is a carryover from earlier terminology meaning Unicode (or UCS) Transformation Format. Each of these three encoding forms is an equally legitimate mechanism for representing Unicode characters; each has advantages in different environments.

All three encoding forms can be used to represent the full range of encoded characters in the Unicode Standard; they are thus fully interoperable for implementations that may choose different encoding forms for various reasons. Each of the three Unicode encoding forms can be efficiently transformed into either of the other two without any loss of data.

Non-overlap. Each of the Unicode encoding forms is designed with the principle of non-overlap in mind. *Figure 2-9* presents an example of an encoding where overlap is permitted. In this encoding (Windows code page 932), characters are formed from either one or two code bytes. Whether a sequence is one or two bytes in length depends on the first byte, so that the values for lead bytes (of a two-byte sequence) and single bytes are disjoint. However, single-byte values and trail-byte values can overlap. That means that when someone searches for the character "D", for example, he or she might find it either (mistakenly) as the trail byte of a two-byte sequence or as a single, independent byte. To find out which alternative is correct, a program must look backward through text.

Figure 2-9. Overlap in Legacy Mixed-Width Encodings

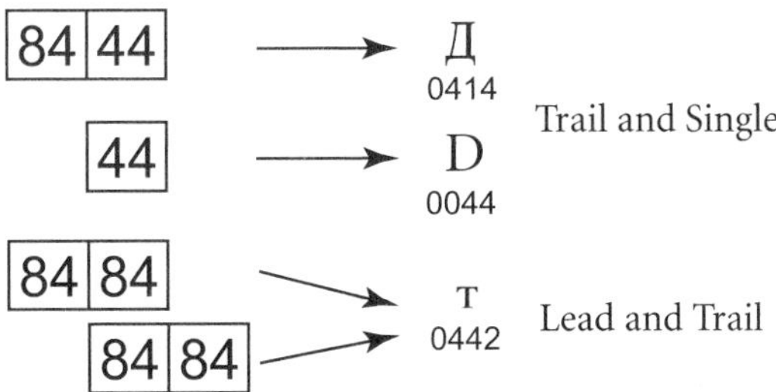

The situation is made more complex by the fact that lead and trail bytes can also overlap, as shown in the second part of *Figure 2-9*. This means that the backward scan has to repeat until it hits the start of the text or hits a sequence that could not exist as a pair as shown in *Figure 2-10*. This is not only inefficient, but also extremely error-prone: corruption of one byte can cause entire lines of text to be corrupted.

Figure 2-10. Boundaries and Interpretation

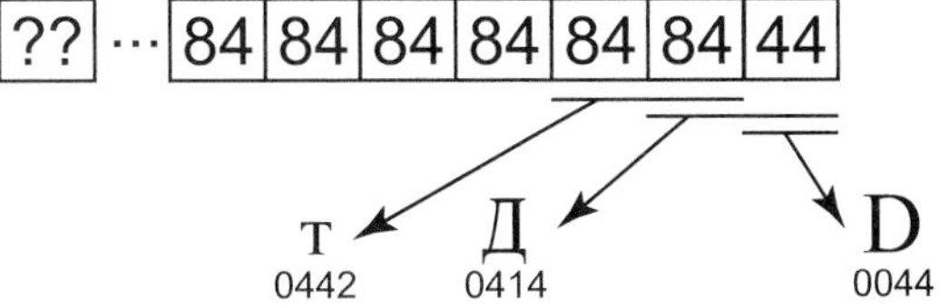

The Unicode encoding forms avoid this problem, because *none* of the ranges of values for the lead, trail, or single code units in any of those encoding forms overlap.

Non-overlap makes all of the Unicode encoding forms well behaved for searching and comparison. When searching for a particular character, there will never be a mismatch against some code unit sequence that represents just part of another character. The fact that all Unicode encoding forms observe this principle of non-overlap distinguishes them from many legacy East Asian multibyte character encodings, for which overlap of code unit sequences may be a significant problem for implementations.

Another aspect of non-overlap in the Unicode encoding forms is that all Unicode characters have determinate boundaries when expressed in any of the encoding forms. That is, the edges of code unit sequences representing a character are easily determined by local examination of code units; there is never any need to scan back indefinitely in Unicode text to correctly determine a character boundary. This property of the encoding forms has sometimes been referred to as *self-synchronization*. This property has another very important implication: corruption of a single code unit corrupts *only* a single character; none of the surrounding characters are affected.

For example, when randomly accessing a string, a program can find the boundary of a character with limited backup. In UTF-16, if a pointer points to a leading surrogate, a single backup is required. In UTF-8, if a pointer points to a byte starting with 10xxxxxx (in binary), one to three backups are required to find the beginning of the character.

Conformance. The Unicode Consortium fully endorses the use of any of the three Unicode encoding forms as a conformant way of implementing the Unicode Standard. It is important not to fall into the trap of trying to distinguish "UTF-8 *versus* Unicode," for example. UTF-8, UTF-16, and UTF-32 are *all* equally valid and conformant ways of implementing the encoded characters of the Unicode Standard.

Examples. *Figure 2-11* shows the three Unicode encoding forms, including how they are related to Unicode code points.

Figure 2-11. Unicode Encoding Forms

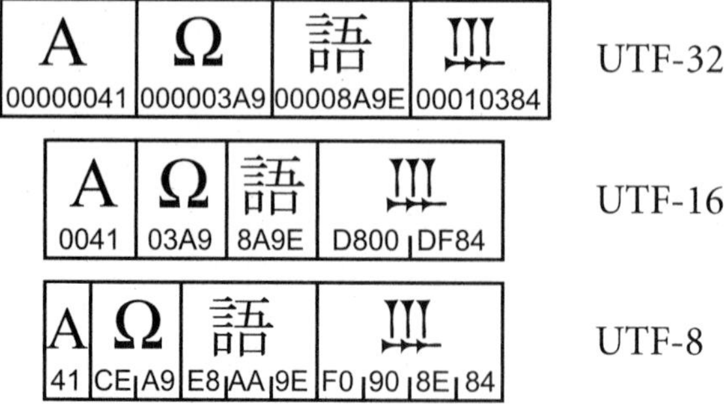

In *Figure 2-11*, the UTF-32 line shows that each example character can be expressed with one 32-bit code unit. Those code units have the same values as the code point for the character. For UTF-16, most characters can be expressed with one 16-bit code unit, whose value is the same as the code point for the character, but characters with high code point values require a pair of 16-bit surrogate code units instead. In UTF-8, a character may be expressed with one, two, three, or four bytes, and the relationship between those byte values and the code point value is more complex.

UTF-8, UTF-16, and UTF-32 are further described in the subsections that follow. See each subsection for a general overview of how each encoding form is structured and the general benefits or drawbacks of each encoding form for particular purposes. For the detailed formal definition of the encoding forms and conformance requirements, see *Section 3.9, Unicode Encoding Forms.*

UTF-32

UTF-32 is the simplest Unicode encoding form. Each Unicode code point is represented directly by a single 32-bit code unit. Because of this, UTF-32 has a one-to-one relationship between encoded character and code unit; it is a fixed-width character encoding form. This makes UTF-32 an ideal form for APIs that pass single character values.

As for all of the Unicode encoding forms, UTF-32 is restricted to representation of code points in the range 0..$10FFFF_{16}$—that is, the Unicode codespace. This guarantees interoperability with the UTF-16 and UTF-8 encoding forms.

Fixed Width. The value of each UTF-32 code unit corresponds exactly to the Unicode code point value. This situation differs significantly from that for UTF-16 and especially UTF-8, where the code unit values often change unrecognizably from the code point value. For example, U+10000 is represented as <00010000> in UTF-32 and as <F0 90 80 80> in UTF-8. For UTF-32, it is trivial to determine a Unicode character from its UTF-32 code unit representation. In contrast, UTF-16 and UTF-8 representations often require doing a code unit conversion before the character can be identified in the Unicode code charts.

Preferred Usage. UTF-32 may be a preferred encoding form where memory or disk storage space for characters is not a particular concern, but where fixed-width, single code unit access to characters is desired. UTF-32 is also a preferred encoding form for processing characters on most Unix platforms.

UTF-16

In the UTF-16 encoding form, code points in the range U+0000..U+FFFF are represented as a single 16-bit code unit; code points in the supplementary planes, in the range U+10000..U+10FFFF, are represented as pairs of 16-bit code units. These pairs of special code units are known as *surrogate pairs*. The values of the code units used for surrogate pairs are completely disjunct from the code units used for the single code unit representations, thus maintaining non-overlap for all code point representations in UTF-16. For the formal definition of surrogates, see *Section 3.8, Surrogates.*

Optimized for BMP. UTF-16 optimizes the representation of characters in the Basic Multilingual Plane (BMP)—that is, the range U+0000..U+FFFF. For that range, which contains the vast majority of common-use characters for all modern scripts of the world, each character requires only one 16-bit code unit, thus requiring just half the memory or storage of the UTF-32 encoding form. For the BMP, UTF-16 can effectively be treated as if it were a fixed-width encoding form.

Supplementary Characters and Surrogates. For supplementary characters, UTF-16 requires two 16-bit code units. The distinction between characters represented with one versus two 16-bit code units means that formally UTF-16 is a variable-width encoding form. That fact can create implementation difficulties if it is not carefully taken into account; UTF-16 is somewhat more complicated to handle than UTF-32.

Preferred Usage. UTF-16 may be a preferred encoding form in many environments that need to balance efficient access to characters with economical use of storage. It is reasonably compact, and all the common, heavily used characters fit into a single 16-bit code unit.

Origin. UTF-16 is the historical descendant of the earliest form of Unicode, which was originally designed to use a fixed-width, 16-bit encoding form exclusively. The surrogates were added to provide an encoding form for the supplementary characters at code points past U+FFFF. The design of the surrogates made them a simple and efficient extension mechanism that works well with older Unicode implementations and that avoids many of the problems of other variable-width character encodings. See *Section 5.4, Handling Surrogate Pairs in UTF-16*, for more information about surrogates and their processing.

Collation. For the purpose of sorting text, binary order for data represented in the UTF-16 encoding form is not the same as code point order. This means that a slightly different comparison implementation is needed for code point order. For more information, see *Section 5.17, Binary Order*.

UTF-8

To meet the requirements of byte-oriented, ASCII-based systems, a third encoding form is specified by the Unicode Standard: UTF-8. This variable-width encoding form preserves ASCII transparency by making use of 8-bit code units.

Byte-Oriented. Much existing software and practice in information technology have long depended on character data being represented as a sequence of bytes. Furthermore, many of the protocols depend not only on ASCII values being invariant, but must make use of or avoid special byte values that may have associated control functions. The easiest way to adapt Unicode implementations to such a situation is to make use of an encoding form that is already defined in terms of 8-bit code units and that represents all Unicode characters while not disturbing or reusing any ASCII or C0 control code value. That is the function of UTF-8.

Variable Width. UTF-8 is a variable-width encoding form, using 8-bit code units, in which the high bits of each code unit indicate the part of the code unit sequence to which each byte belongs. A range of 8-bit code unit values is reserved for the first, or *leading*, element of a UTF-8 code unit sequences, and a completely disjunct range of 8-bit code unit values is reserved for the subsequent, or *trailing*, elements of such sequences; this convention preserves non-overlap for UTF-8. *Table 3-6* on page 103 shows how the bits in a Unicode code point are distributed among the bytes in the UTF-8 encoding form. See *Section 3.9, Unicode Encoding Forms*, for the full, formal definition of UTF-8.

ASCII Transparency. The UTF-8 encoding form maintains transparency for all of the ASCII code points (0x00..0x7F). That means Unicode code points U+0000..U+007F are converted to single bytes 0x00..0x7F in UTF-8 and are thus indistinguishable from ASCII itself. Furthermore, the values 0x00..0x7F do not appear in any byte for the representation of any other Unicode code point, so that there can be no ambiguity. Beyond the ASCII range of Unicode, many of the non-ideographic scripts are represented by two bytes per code point in UTF-8; all non-surrogate code points between U+0800 and U+FFFF are represented by three bytes; and supplementary code points above U+FFFF require four bytes.

Preferred Usage. UTF-8 is typically the preferred encoding form for HTML and similar protocols, particularly for the Internet. The ASCII transparency helps migration. UTF-8 also has the advantage that it is already inherently byte-serialized, as for most existing 8-bit character sets; strings of UTF-8 work easily with C or other programming languages, and many existing APIs that work for typical Asian multibyte character sets adapt to UTF-8 as well with little or no change required.

Self-synchronizing. In environments where 8-bit character processing is required for one reason or another, UTF-8 has the following attractive features as compared to other multibyte encodings:

- The first byte of a UTF-8 code unit sequence indicates the number of bytes to follow in a multibyte sequence. This allows for very efficient forward parsing.
- It is efficient to find the start of a character when beginning from an arbitrary location in a byte stream of UTF-8. Programs need to search at most four bytes backward, and usually much less. It is a simple task to recognize an initial byte, because initial bytes are constrained to a fixed range of values.
- As with the other encoding forms, there is no overlap of byte values.

Comparison of the Advantages of UTF-32, UTF-16, and UTF-8

On the face of it, UTF-32 would seem to be the obvious choice of Unicode encoding forms for an internal processing code because it is a fixed-width encoding form. It can be conformantly bound to the C and C++ wchar_t, which means that such programming languages may offer built-in support and ready-made string APIs that programmers can take advantage of. However, UTF-16 has many countervailing advantages that may lead implementers to choose it instead as an internal processing code.

While all three encoding forms need at most 4 bytes (or 32 bits) of data for each character, in practice UTF-32 in almost all cases for real data sets occupies twice the storage that UTF-

16 requires. Therefore, a common strategy is to have internal string storage use UTF-16 or UTF-8 but to use UTF-32 when manipulating individual characters.

UTF-32 Versus UTF-16. On average, more than 99 percent of all UTF-16 data is expressed using single code units. This includes nearly all of the typical characters that software needs to handle with special operations on text—for example, format control characters. As a consequence, most text scanning operations do not need to unpack UTF-16 surrogate pairs at all, but rather can safely treat them as an opaque part of a character string.

For many operations, UTF-16 is as easy to handle as UTF-32, and the performance of UTF-16 as a processing code tends to be quite good. UTF-16 is the internal processing code of choice for a majority of implementations supporting Unicode. Other than for Unix platforms, UTF-16 provides the right mix of compact size with the ability to handle the occasional character outside the BMP.

UTF-32 has somewhat of an advantage when it comes to simplicity of software coding design and maintenance. Because the character handling is fixed width, UTF-32 processing does not require maintaining branches in the software to test and process the double code unit elements required for supplementary characters by UTF-16. Conversely, 32-bit indices into large tables are not particularly memory efficient. To avoid the large memory penalties of such indices, Unicode tables are often handled as multistage tables (see "Multistage Tables" in *Section 5.1, Transcoding to Other Standards*). In such cases, the 32-bit code point values are sliced into smaller ranges to permit segmented access to the tables. This is true even in typical UTF-32 implementations.

The performance of UTF-32 as a processing code may actually be worse than the performance of UTF-16 for the same data, because the additional memory overhead means that cache limits will be exceeded more often and memory paging will occur more frequently. For systems with processor designs that impose penalties for 16-bit aligned access but have very large memories, this effect may be less noticeable.

Characters Versus Code Points. In any event, Unicode code points do *not* necessarily match user expectations for "characters." For example, the following are not represented by a single code point: a combining character sequence such as <g, acute>; a conjoining jamo sequence for Korean; or the Devanagari conjunct "ksha." Because some Unicode text processing must be aware of and handle such sequences of characters as text elements, the fixed-width encoding form advantage of UTF-32 is somewhat offset by the inherently variable-width nature of processing text elements. See Unicode Technical Standard #18, "Unicode Regular Expression Guidelines," for an example where commonly implemented processes deal with inherently variable-width text elements owing to user expectations of the identity of a "character."

UTF-8. UTF-8 is reasonably compact in terms of the number of bytes used. It is really only at a significant size disadvantage when used for East Asian implementations such as Chinese, Japanese, and Korean, which use Han ideographs or Hangul syllables requiring three-byte code unit sequences in UTF-8. UTF-8 is also significantly less efficient in terms of processing than the other encoding forms.

Binary Sorting. A binary sort of UTF-8 strings gives the same ordering as a binary sort of Unicode code points. This is obviously the same order as for a binary sort of UTF-32 strings.

All three encoding forms give the same results for binary string comparisons or string sorting when dealing only with BMP characters (in the range U+0000..U+FFFF). However, when dealing with supplementary characters (in the range U+10000..U+10FFFF), UTF-16 binary order does not match Unicode code point order. This can lead to complications when trying to interoperate with binary sorted lists—for example, between UTF-16 systems and UTF-8 or UTF-32 systems. However, for data that is sorted according to the conventions of a specific language or locale rather than using binary order, data will be ordered the same, regardless of the encoding form.

2.6 Encoding Schemes

The discussion of Unicode encoding forms in the previous section was concerned with the machine representation of Unicode code units. Each code unit is represented in a computer simply as a numeric data type; just as for other numeric types, the exact way the bits are laid out internally is irrelevant to most processing. However, interchange of textual data, particularly between computers of different architectural types, requires consideration of the exact ordering of the bits and bytes involved in numeric representation. Integral data, including character data, is *serialized* for open interchange into well-defined sequences of bytes. This process of *byte serialization* allows all applications to correctly interpret exchanged data and to accurately reconstruct numeric values (and thereby character values) from it. In the Unicode Standard, the specifications of the distinct types of byte serializations to be used with Unicode data are known as Unicode *encoding schemes.*

Byte Order. Modern computer architectures differ in *ordering* in terms of whether the most significant byte or the least significant byte of a large numeric data type comes first in internal representation. These sequences are known as "big-endian" and "little-endian" orders, respectively. For the Unicode 16- and 32-bit encoding forms (UTF-16 and UTF-32), the specification of a byte serialization must take into account the big-endian or little-endian architecture of the system on which the data is represented, so that when the data is byte serialized for interchange it will be well defined.

A *character encoding scheme* consists of a specified character encoding form plus a specification of how the code units are serialized into bytes. The Unicode Standard also specifies the use of an initial *byte order mark* (BOM) to explicitly differentiate big-endian or little-endian data in some of the Unicode encoding schemes. (See the "Byte Order Mark" subsection in *Section 16.8, Specials.*)

When a higher-level protocol supplies mechanisms for handling the endianness of integral data types, it is not necessary to use Unicode encoding schemes or the byte order mark. In those cases Unicode text is simply a sequence of integral data types.

For UTF-8, the encoding scheme consists merely of the UTF-8 code units (= bytes) in sequence. Hence, there is no issue of big- versus little-endian byte order for data represented in UTF-8. However, for 16-bit and 32-bit encoding forms, byte serialization must break up the code units into two or four bytes, respectively, and the order of those bytes must be clearly defined. Because of this, and because of the rules for the use of the byte order mark, the three encoding forms of the Unicode Standard result in a total of seven Unicode encoding schemes, as shown in *Table 2-4*.

Table 2-4. The Seven Unicode Encoding Schemes

Encoding Scheme	Endian Order	BOM Allowed?
UTF-8	N/A	yes
UTF-16	Big-endian or little-endian	yes
UTF-16BE	Big-endian	no
UTF-16LE	Little-endian	no
UTF-32	Big-endian or little-endian	yes
UTF-32BE	Big-endian	no
UTF-32LE	Little-endian	no

The endian order entry for UTF-8 in *Table 2-4* is marked N/A because UTF-8 code units are 8 bits in size, and the usual machine issues of endian order for larger code units do not apply. The serialized order of the bytes must not depart from the order defined by the UTF-8 encoding form. Use of a BOM is neither required nor recommended for UTF-8, but may be encountered in contexts where UTF-8 data is converted from other encoding forms that use a BOM or where the BOM is used as a UTF-8 signature. See the "Byte Order Mark" subsection in *Section 16.8, Specials*, for more information.

Encoding Scheme Versus Encoding Form. Note that some of the Unicode encoding schemes have the same labels as the three Unicode encoding forms. This could cause confusion, so it is important to keep the context clear when using these terms: character encoding *forms* refer to integral data units in memory or in APIs, and byte order is irrelevant; character encoding *schemes* refer to byte-serialized data, as for streaming I/O or in file storage, and byte order *must* be specified or determinable.

The Internet Assigned Numbers Authority (IANA) maintains a registry of *charset names* used on the Internet. Those charset names are very close in meaning to the Unicode character encoding model's concept of character encoding schemes, and all of the Unicode character encoding schemes are, in fact, registered as *charsets*. While the two concepts are quite close and the names used are identical, some important differences may arise in terms of the requirements for each, particularly when it comes to handling of the byte order mark. Exercise due caution when equating the two.

Examples. *Figure 2-12* illustrates the Unicode character encoding schemes, showing how each is derived from one of the encoding forms by serialization of bytes.

In *Figure 2-12*, the code units used to express each example character have been serialized into sequences of bytes. This figure should be compared with *Figure 2-11*, which shows the

Figure 2-12. Unicode Encoding Schemes

	A	Ω	語	𐎄
UTF-32BE	00 00 00 41	00 00 03 A9	00 00 8A 9E	00 01 03 84
UTF-32LE	41 00 00 00	A9 03 00 00	9E 8A 00 00	84 03 01 00
UTF-16BE	00 41	03 A9	8A 9E	D8 00 DF 84
UTF-16LE	41 00	A9 03	9E 8A	00 D8 84 DF
UTF-8	41	CE A9	E8 AA 9E	F0 90 8E 84

same characters before serialization into sequences of bytes. The "BE" lines show serialization in big-endian order, whereas the "LE" lines show the bytes reversed into little-endian order. For UTF-8, the code unit is just an 8-bit byte, so that there is no distinction between big-endian and little-endian order. UTF-32 and UTF-16 encoding schemes using the byte order mark are not shown in *Figure 2-12*, to keep the basic picture regarding serialization of bytes clearer.

For the detailed formal definition of the Unicode encoding schemes and conformance requirements, see *Section 3.10, Unicode Encoding Schemes*. For further general discussion about character encoding forms and character encoding schemes, both for the Unicode Standard and as applied to other character encoding standards, see Unicode Technical Report #17, "Character Encoding Model." For information about charsets and character conversion, see Unicode Technical Standard #22, "Character Mapping Markup Language (CharMapML)."

2.7 Unicode Strings

A Unicode string data type is simply an ordered sequence of code units. Thus a Unicode 8-bit string is an ordered sequence of 8-bit code units, a Unicode 16-bit string is an ordered sequence of 16-bit code units, and a Unicode 32-bit string is an ordered sequence of 32-bit code units.

Depending on the programming environment, a Unicode string may or may not be required to be in the corresponding Unicode encoding form. For example, strings in Java,

C#, or ECMAScript are Unicode 16-bit strings, but are not necessarily well-formed UTF-16 sequences. In normal processing, it can be far more efficient to allow such strings to contain code unit sequences that are not well-formed UTF-16—that is, isolated surrogates. Because strings are such a fundamental component of every program, checking for isolated surrogates in every operation that modifies strings can create significant overhead, especially because supplementary characters are extremely rare as a percentage of overall text in programs worldwide.

It is straightforward to design basic string manipulation libraries that handle isolated surrogates in a consistent and straightforward manner. They cannot ever be interpreted as abstract characters, but they can be internally handled the same way as noncharacters where they occur. Typically they occur only ephemerally, such as in dealing with keyboard events. While an ideal protocol would allow keyboard events to contain complete strings, many allow only a single UTF-16 code unit per event. As a sequence of events is transmitted to the application, a string that is being built up by the application in response to those events may contain isolated surrogates at any particular point in time.

Whenever such strings are specified to be in a particular Unicode encoding form—even one with the same code unit size—the string must not violate the requirements of that encoding form. For example, isolated surrogates in a Unicode 16-bit string are not allowed when that string is specified to be *well-formed* UTF-16. (See *Section 3.9, Unicode Encoding Forms*.) A number of techniques are available for dealing with an isolated surrogate, such as omitting it, converting it into U+FFFD REPLACEMENT CHARACTER to produce well-formed UTF-16, or simply halting the processing of the string with an error. For more information on this topic, see Unicode Technical Standard #22, "Character Mapping Markup Language (CharMapML)."

2.8 Unicode Allocation

For convenience, the encoded characters of the Unicode Standard are grouped by linguistic and functional categories, such as script or writing system. For practical reasons, there are occasional departures from this general principle, as when punctuation associated with the ASCII standard is kept together with other ASCII characters in the range U+0020..U+007E rather than being grouped with other sets of general punctuation characters. By and large, however, the code charts are arranged so that related characters can be found near each other in the charts.

Grouping encoded characters by script or other functional categories offers the additional benefit of supporting various space-saving techniques in actual implementations, as for building tables or fonts.

For more information on writing systems, see *Section 6.1, Writing Systems*.

Planes

The Unicode codespace consists of the single range of numeric values from 0 to $10FFFF_{16}$, but in practice it has proven convenient to think of the codespace as divided up into *planes* of characters—each plane consisting of 64K code points. Because of these numeric conventions, the Basic Multilingual Plane is occasionally referred to as *Plane 0*. The last four hexadecimal digits in each code point indicate a character's position inside a plane. The remaining digits indicate the plane. For example, U+23456 CJK UNIFIED IDEOGRAPH-23456 is found at location 3456_{16} in Plane 2.

Basic Multilingual Plane. The Basic Multilingual Plane (BMP, or Plane 0) contains the common-use characters for all the modern scripts of the world as well as many historical and rare characters. By far the majority of all Unicode characters for almost all textual data can be found in the BMP.

Supplementary Multilingual Plane. The Supplementary Multilingual Plane (SMP, or Plane 1) is dedicated to the encoding of lesser-used historic scripts, special-purpose invented scripts, and special notational systems, which either could not be fit into the BMP or would see very infrequent usage. Examples of each type include Gothic, Shavian, and musical symbols, respectively. A number of major and minor historic scripts do not yet have their characters encoded in the Unicode Standard, and many of those will eventually be allocated in the SMP.

Supplementary Ideographic Plane. The Supplementary Ideographic Plane (SIP, or Plane 2) is intended as an additional allocation area for those CJK characters that could not be fit in the blocks set aside for more common CJK characters in the BMP. While there are a small number of common-use CJK characters in the SIP (for example, for Cantonese usage), the vast majority of Plane 2 characters are extremely rare or of historical interest only.

Supplementary Special-purpose Plane. The Supplementary Special-purpose Plane (SSP, or Plane 14) is the spillover allocation area for format control characters that do not fit into the small allocation areas for format control characters in the BMP.

Private Use Planes. The two Private Use Planes (Planes 15 and 16) are allocated, in their entirety, for private use. Those two planes contain a total of 131,068 characters to supplement the 6,400 private-use characters located in the BMP.

Allocation Areas and Character Blocks

Allocation Areas. The Unicode Standard does not have any normatively defined concept of *areas* or *zones* for the BMP (or other planes), but it is often handy to refer to the allocation areas of the BMP by the general types of the characters they include. These areas are merely a rough organizational device and do not restrict the types of characters that may end up being allocated in them. The description and ranges of areas may change from version to version of the standard as more new scripts, symbols, and other characters are encoded in previously reserved ranges.

Blocks. The various allocation areas are, in turn, divided up into character *blocks*, which are normatively defined, and which are used to structure the actual charts in *Chapter 17, Code Charts.* For a complete listing of the normative character blocks in the Unicode Standard, see Blocks.txt in the Unicode Character Database.

The normative status of character blocks should not, however, be taken as indicating that they define significant sets of characters. For the most part, the character blocks serve only as ranges to divide up the code charts and do not necessarily imply anything else about the types of characters found in the block. Block identity cannot be taken as a reliable guide to the source, use, or properties of characters, for example, and it cannot be reliably used alone to process characters. In particular:

- Blocks are simply ranges, and many contain reserved code points.
- Characters used in a single writing system may be found in several different blocks. For example, characters used for letters for Latin-based writing systems are found in at least 12 different blocks: Basic Latin, Latin-1 Supplement, Latin Extended-A, Latin Extended-B, Latin Extended-C, IPA Extensions, Phonetic Extensions, Phonetic Extensions Supplement, Latin Extended Additional, Spacing Modifier Letters, Combining Diacritical Marks, and Combining Diacritical Marks Supplement.
- Characters in a block may be used with different writing systems. For example, the *danda* character is encoded in the Devanagari block but is used with numerous other scripts; Arabic combining marks in the Arabic block are used with the Syriac script; and so on.
- Block definitions are not at all exclusive. For instance, many mathematical operator characters are not encoded in the Mathematical Operators block—and are not even in any block containing "Mathematical" in its name; many currency symbols are not found in the Currency Symbols block, and so on.

For reliable specification of the properties of characters, one should instead turn to the detailed, character-by-character property assignments available in the Unicode Character Database. See also *Chapter 4, Character Properties.* For further discussion of the relationship between Unicode character blocks and significant property assignments and sets of characters, see Unicode Standard Annex #24, "Script Names," and Unicode Technical Standard #18, "Unicode Regular Expression Guidelines."

Allocation Order. The allocation order of various scripts and other groups of characters reflects the historical evolution of the Unicode Standard. While there is a certain geographic sense to the ordering of the allocation areas for the scripts, this is only a very loose correlation. The empty spaces will be filled with future script encodings on a space-available basis. The relevant character encoding committees follow an organized roadmap to help them decide where to encode new scripts within the available space. Until the characters for a script are actually standardized, however, there are no absolute guarantees where future allocations will occur. In general, implementations should not make assumptions about where future scripts may be encoded based on the identity of neighboring blocks of characters already encoded.

Assignment of Code Points

Code points in the Unicode Standard are assigned using the following guidelines:

- Where there is a single accepted standard for a script, the Unicode Standard generally follows it for the relative order of characters within that script.
- The first 256 codes follow precisely the arrangement of ISO/IEC 8859-1 (Latin 1), of which 7-bit ASCII (ISO/IEC 646 IRV) accounts for the first 128 code positions.
- Characters with common characteristics are located together contiguously. For example, the primary Arabic character block was modeled after ISO/IEC 8859-6. The Arabic script characters used in Persian, Urdu, and other languages, but not included in ISO/IEC 8859-6, are allocated after the primary Arabic character block. Right-to-left scripts are grouped together.
- To the extent possible, scripts are allocated so as not to cross 128-code-point boundaries (that is, they fit in ranges nn00..nn7F or nn80..nnFF). For supplementary characters, an additional constraint not to cross 1,024-code-point boundaries is applied (that is, scripts fit in ranges nn000..nn3FF, nn400..nn7FF, nn800..nnBFF, or nnC00..nnFFF). Such constraints enable better optimizations for tasks such as building tables for access to character properties.
- Codes that represent letters, punctuation, symbols, and diacritics that are generally shared by multiple languages or scripts are grouped together in several locations.
- The Unicode Standard does not correlate character code allocation with language-dependent collation or case. For more information on collation order, see Unicode Technical Standard #10, "Unicode Collation Algorithm."
- Unified CJK ideographs are laid out in three sections, each of which is arranged according to the Han ideograph arrangement defined in *Section 12.1, Han*. This ordering is roughly based on a radical-stroke count order.

2.9 Details of Allocation

This section provides a more detailed summary of the way characters are allocated in the Unicode Standard. *Figure 2-13* gives an overall picture of the allocation areas of the Unicode Standard, with an emphasis on the identities of the planes. The following subsections discuss the allocation details for specific planes.

Figure 2-13. Unicode Allocation

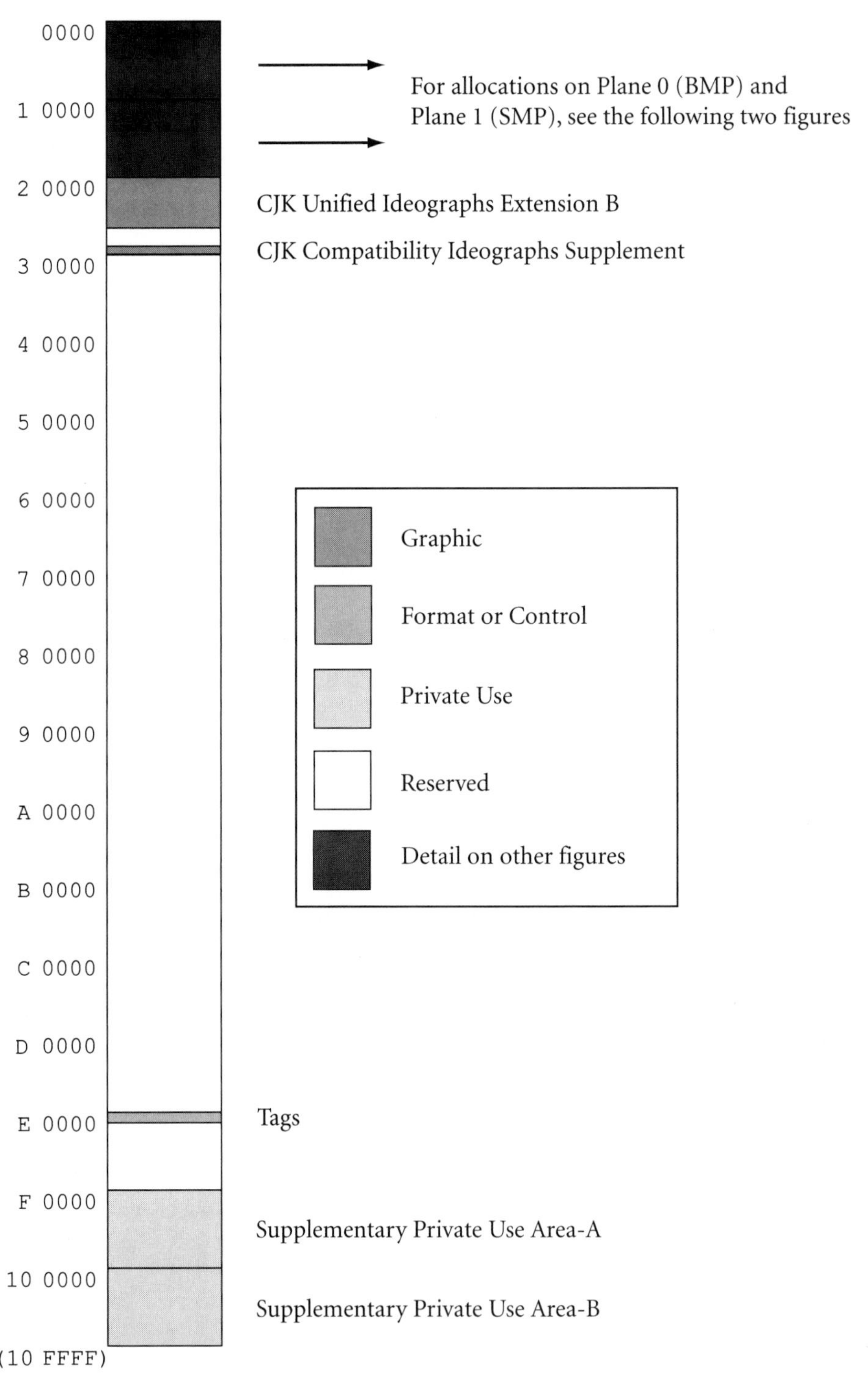

Plane 0 (BMP)

Figure 2-14 shows the BMP in an expanded format to illustrate the allocation substructure of that plane in more detail. The following text describes the allocation areas on the BMP in order of their location on the BMP.

General Scripts Area. The General Scripts Area contains a large number of modern-use scripts of the world, including Latin, Greek, Cyrillic, Arabic, and so on. This area is shown in expanded form in *Figure 2-14*. The order of the various scripts can serve as a guide to the relative positions where these scripts are found in the code charts. Most of the characters encoded in this area are graphic characters, but all 65 C0 and C1 control codes are also located here because the first two character blocks in the Unicode Standard are organized for exact compatibility with the ASCII and ISO/IEC 8859-1 standards.

Symbols Area. The Symbols Area contains all kinds of symbols, including many characters for use in mathematical notation. It also contains symbols for punctuation as well as most of the important format control characters.

Supplementary General Scripts Area. This area contains scripts or extensions to scripts that did not fit in the General Scripts Area itself. Currently it contains the Glagolitic, Coptic, and Tifinagh scripts, plus extensions for the Georgian and Ethiopic scripts.

CJK Miscellaneous Area. The CJK Miscellaneous Area contains some East Asian scripts, such as Hiragana and Katakana for Japanese, punctuation typically used with East Asian scripts, lists of CJK radical symbols, and a large number of East Asian compatibility characters.

CJKV Ideographs Area. This area contains all the unified Han ideographs in the BMP. It is subdivided into a block for the Unified Repertoire and Ordering (the initial block of 20,902 unified Han ideographs plus 22 later additions) and another block containing Extension A (an additional 6,582 unified Han ideographs).

Asian Scripts Area. The Asian Scripts Area currently contains the Yi, Syloti Nagri, and Phags-pa scripts, plus 11,172 Hangul syllables for Korean.

Surrogates Area. The Surrogates Area contains *only* surrogate code points and *no* encoded characters. See *Section 16.6, Surrogates Area*, for more details.

Private Use Area. The Private Use Area in the BMP contains 6,400 private-use characters.

Compatibility and Specials Area. This area contains many compatibility variants of characters from widely used corporate and national standards that have other representations in the Unicode Standard. For example, it contains Arabic presentation forms, whereas the basic characters for the Arabic script are located in the General Scripts Area. The Compatibility and Specials Area also contains a few important format control characters and other special characters. See *Section 16.8, Specials*, for more details.

Plane 1

Figure 2-15 shows Plane 1 in expanded format to illustrate the allocation substructure of that plane in more detail.

Figure 2-14. Allocation on the BMP

Figure 2-15. Allocation on Plane 1

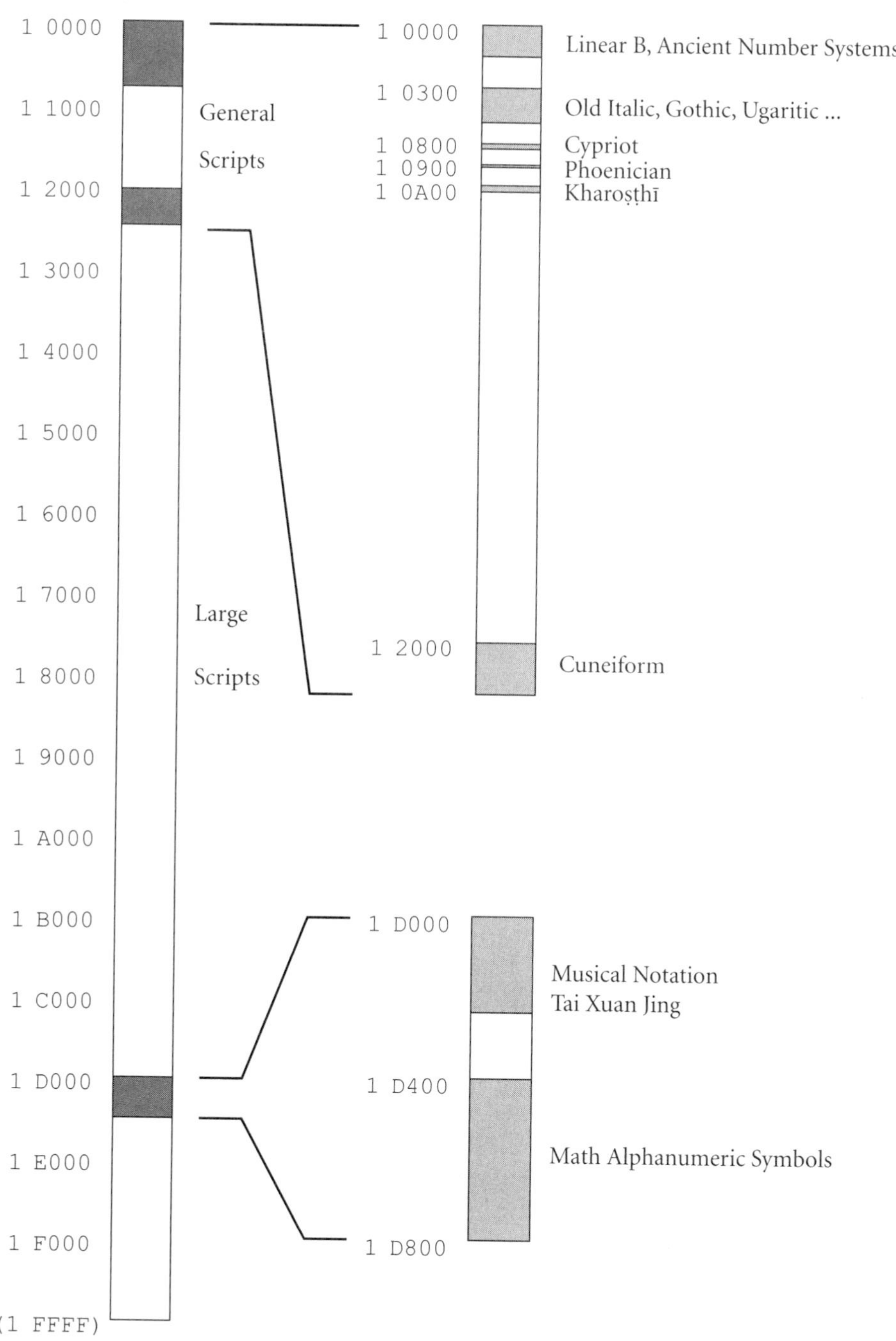

Plane 1 currently has three allocation areas: a General Scripts Area at the beginning of the plane, containing various small historic scripts; a Large Historic Scripts Area, currently containing Sumero-Akkadian Cuneiform; and a Notational Systems Area, which currently contains sets of musical symbols, alphanumeric symbols for mathematics, and a system of divination symbols similar to those used for the *Yijing*.

Plane 2

Plane 2 consists primarily of one big area, starting from the first code point in the plane, that is dedicated to encoding additional unified CJK characters. A much smaller area, toward the end of the plane, is dedicated to additional CJK compatibility ideographic characters—which are basically just duplicated character encodings required for round-trip conversion to various existing legacy East Asian character sets. The CJK compatibility ideographic characters in Plane 2 are currently all dedicated to round-trip conversion for the CNS standard and are intended to supplement the CJK compatibility ideographic characters in the BMP, a smaller number of characters dedicated to round-trip conversion for various Korean, Chinese, and Japanese standards.

Other Planes

The first 4,096 code positions on Plane 14 form an area set aside for special characters that have the Default_Ignorable property. A small number of language tag characters, plus some supplementary variation selection characters, have been allocated there. All remaining code positions on Plane 14 are reserved for future allocation of other special-purpose characters.

Plane 15 and Plane 16 are allocated, in their entirety, for private use. Those two planes contain a total of 131,068 characters, to supplement the 6,400 private-use characters located in the BMP.

All other planes are reserved; there are no characters assigned in them. The last two code positions of *all* planes are permanently set aside as noncharacters. (See *Section 2.13, Special Characters and Noncharacters*).

2.10 Writing Direction

Individual writing systems have different conventions for arranging characters into lines on a page or screen. Such conventions are referred to as a script's *directionality*. For example, in the Latin script, characters are arranged horizontally from left to right to form lines, and lines are arranged from top to bottom, as shown in the first example of *Figure 2-16*.

Bidirectional. In most Semitic scripts such as Hebrew and Arabic, characters are arranged from right to left into lines, although digits run the other way, making the scripts inherently bidirectional, as shown in the second example in *Figure 2-16*. In addition, left-to-right and right-to-left scripts are frequently used together. In all such cases, arranging characters into

Figure 2-16. Writing Directions

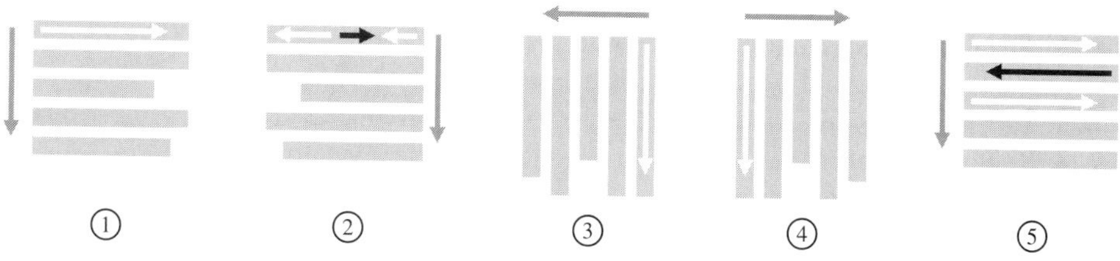

lines becomes more complex. The Unicode Standard defines an algorithm to determine the layout of a line, based on the inherent directionality of each character, and supplemented by a small set of directional controls. See Unicode Standard Annex #9, "The Bidirectional Algorithm," for more information.

Vertical. East Asian scripts are frequently written in vertical lines in which characters are arranged from top to bottom. Lines are arranged from right to left, as shown in the third example in *Figure 2-16*. Such scripts may also be written horizontally, from left to right. Most East Asian characters have the same shape and orientation when displayed horizontally or vertically, but many punctuation characters change their shape when displayed vertically. In a vertical context, letters and words from other scripts are generally rotated through 90-degree angles so that they, too, read from top to bottom.

In contrast to the bidirectional case, the choice to lay out text either vertically or horizontally is treated as a formatting style. Therefore, the Unicode Standard does not provide directionality controls to specify that choice.

Mongolian is usually written from top to bottom, with lines arranged from left to right, as shown in the fourth example. When Mongolian is written horizontally, the characters are rotated.

Boustrophedon. Early Greek used a system called *boustrophedon* (literally, "ox-turning"). In boustrophedon writing, characters are arranged into horizontal lines, but the individual lines alternate between right to left and left to right, the way an ox goes back and forth when plowing a field, as shown in the fifth example. The letter images are mirrored in accordance with the direction of each individual line.

Other Historical Directionalities. Other script directionalities are found in historical writing systems. For example, some ancient Numidian texts are written from bottom to top, and Egyptian hieroglyphics can be written with varying directions for individual lines.

The historical directionalities are of interest almost exclusively to scholars intent on reproducing the exact visual content of ancient texts. The Unicode Standard does not provide direct support for them. Fixed texts can, however, be written in boustrophedon or in other directional conventions by using hard line breaks and directionality overrides or the equivalent markup.

2.11 Combining Characters

Combining Characters. Characters intended to be positioned relative to an associated base character are depicted in the character code charts above, below, or through a dotted circle. When rendered, the glyphs that depict these characters are intended to be positioned relative to the glyph depicting the preceding base character in some combination. The Unicode Standard distinguishes two types of combining characters: spacing and nonspacing. Nonspacing combining characters do not occupy a spacing position by themselves. Nevertheless, the combination of a base character and a nonspacing character may have a different advance width than the base character by itself. For example, an " î " may be slightly wider than a plain "i". The spacing or nonspacing properties of a combining character are defined in the Unicode Character Database.

All combining characters can be applied to any base character and can, in principle, be used with any script. As with other characters, the allocation of a combining character to one block or another identifies only its primary usage; it is not intended to define or limit the range of characters to which it may be applied. *In the Unicode Standard, all sequences of character codes are permitted.*

This does not create an obligation on implementations to support all possible combinations equally well. Thus, while application of an Arabic annotation mark to a Han character or a Devanagari consonant is permitted, it is unlikely to be supported well in rendering or to make much sense.

Diacritics. Diacritics are the principal class of nonspacing combining characters used with the Latin, Greek, and Cyrillic scripts and their relatives. In the Unicode Standard, the term "diacritic" is defined very broadly to include accents as well as other nonspacing marks.

Symbol Diacritics. Some diacritical marks are applied primarily to symbols. These combining marks are allocated in the Combining Diacritical Marks for Symbols block, to distinguish them from diacritic marks applied primarily to letters.

Enclosing Combining Marks. *Figure 2-17* shows examples of combining enclosing marks for symbols. The combination of an enclosing mark with a base character has the appearance of a symbol. As discussed in "Properties" later in this section, it is best to limit the use of combining enclosing marks to characters that encode symbols. A few symbol characters are intended primarily for use with enclosing combining marks. For example, U+2139 INFORMATION SOURCE is a symbol intended for use with U+20DD COMBINING ENCLOSING CIRCLE or U+20E2 COMBINING ENCLOSING SCREEN. U+2621 CAUTION SIGN is a winding road symbol that can be used in combination with U+20E4 COMBINING ENCLOSING UPWARD POINTING TRIANGLE or U+20DF COMBINING ENCLOSING DIAMOND.

Script-Specific Combining Characters. Some scripts, such as Hebrew, Arabic, and the scripts of India and Southeast Asia, have both spacing and nonspacing combining characters specific to those scripts. Many of these combining characters encode vowel letters. As such, they are not generally referred to as diacritics, but may have script-specific terminology such as *harakat* (Arabic) or *matra* (Devanagari). See *Section 7.9, Combining Marks.*

Figure 2-17. Combining Enclosing Marks for Symbols

① 26A1 + 20E4 → ③ 2139 + 20DD →
② 2615 + 20E0 → ④ 2621 + 20DF →

Sequence of Base Characters and Diacritics

In the Unicode Standard, all combining characters are to be used in sequence following the base characters to which they apply. The sequence of Unicode characters <U+0061 “a” LATIN SMALL LETTER A, U+0308 “◌̈” COMBINING DIAERESIS, U+0075 “u” LATIN SMALL LETTER U> unambiguously represents “äu” and not “aü”, as shown in *Figure 2-18*.

Figure 2-18. Sequence of Base Characters and Diacritics

a + ◌̈ + u → äu (*not* aü)
0061 0308 0075

Ordering. The ordering convention used by the Unicode Standard—placing combining marks after the base character to which they apply—is consistent with the logical order of combining characters in Semitic and Indic scripts, the great majority of which (logically or phonetically) follow the base characters with respect to which they are positioned. This convention also conforms to the way modern font technology handles the rendering of nonspacing graphical forms (glyphs) so that mapping from character memory representation order to font rendering order is simplified. It is different from the convention used in the bibliographic standard ISO 5426.

Properties. A sequence of a base character plus one or more combining characters generally has the same properties as the base character. For example, “A” followed by “ˆ” has the same properties as “Â”. For this reason, most Unicode algorithms ensure that such sequences behave the same way as the corresponding base character. However, when the combining character is an enclosing combining mark—in other words, when its General_Category value is Me—the resulting sequence has the appearance of a symbol. In *Figure 2-19*, enclosing the *exclamation mark* with U+20E4 COMBINING ENCLOSING UPWARD POINTING TRIANGLE produces a sequence that looks like U+26A0 WARNING SIGN.

Figure 2-19. Properties and Combining Sequences

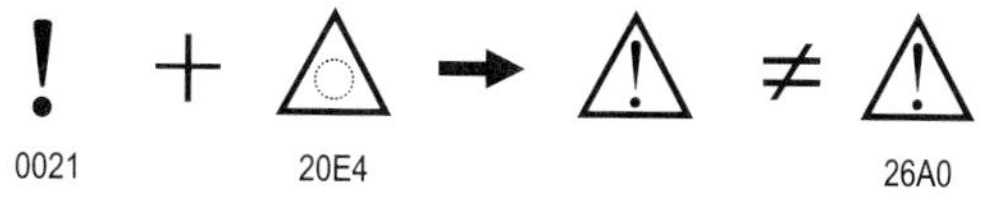

! + △ → ⚠ ≠ ⚠
0021 20E4 26A0

Because the properties of U+0021 EXCLAMATION MARK are that of a punctuation character, they are different from those of U+26A0 WARNING SIGN. For example, the two will behave differently for line breaking. To avoid unexpected results, it is best to limit the use of combining enclosing marks to characters that encode symbols. For that reason, the *warning sign* is separately encoded as a miscellaneous symbol in the Unicode Standard and does not have a decomposition.

Indic Vowel Signs. Some Indic vowel signs are rendered to the left of a consonant letter or consonant cluster, even though their logical order in the Unicode encoding follows the consonant letter. In the charts, these vowels are depicted to the left of dotted circles (see *Figure 2-20*). The coding of these vowels in pronunciation order and not in visual order is consistent with the ISCII standard.

Figure 2-20. Reordered Indic Vowel Signs

फ + ि → फि

092B 093F

Multiple Combining Characters

In some instances, more than one diacritical mark is applied to a single base character (see *Figure 2-21*). The Unicode Standard does not restrict the number of combining characters that may follow a base character. The following discussion summarizes the default treatment of multiple combining characters. (For the formal algorithm, see *Section 3.11, Canonical Ordering Behavior.*)

Figure 2-21. Stacking Sequences

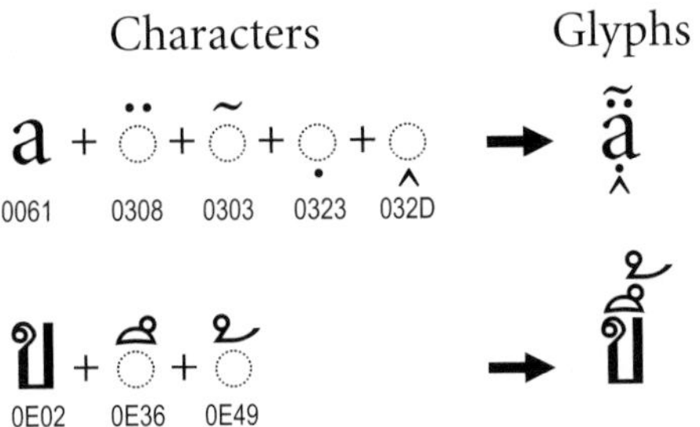

If the combining characters can interact typographically—for example, U+0304 COMBINING MACRON and U+0308 COMBINING DIAERESIS—then the order of graphic display is determined by the order of coded characters (see *Table 2-5*). By default, the diacritics or other combining characters are positioned from the base character's glyph outward. Combining characters placed above a base character will be stacked vertically, starting with the first encountered in the logical store and continuing for as many marks above as are required by the character codes following the base character. For combining characters placed below a base character, the situation is reversed, with the combining characters starting from the base character and stacking downward.

When combining characters do not interact typographically, the relative ordering of contiguous combining marks cannot result in any visual distinction and thus is insignificant.

Table 2-5. Interaction of Combining Characters

Glyph	Equivalent Sequences
ã	LATIN SMALL LETTER A WITH TILDE LATIN SMALL LETTER A + COMBINING TILDE
ȧ	LATIN SMALL LETTER A WITH DOT ABOVE LATIN SMALL LETTER A + COMBINING DOT ABOVE
ạ̃	LATIN SMALL LETTER A WITH TILDE + COMBINING DOT BELOW LATIN SMALL LETTER A + COMBINING TILDE + COMBINING DOT BELOW LATIN SMALL LETTER A WITH DOT BELOW + COMBINING TILDE LATIN SMALL LETTER A + COMBINING DOT BELOW + COMBINING TILDE
ạ̇	LATIN SMALL LETTER A WITH DOT BELOW + COMBINING DOT ABOVE LATIN SMALL LETTER A + COMBINING DOT BELOW + COMBINING DOT ABOVE LATIN SMALL LETTER A WITH DOT ABOVE + COMBINING DOT BELOW LATIN SMALL LETTER A + COMBINING DOT ABOVE + COMBINING DOT BELOW
ấ	LATIN SMALL LETTER A WITH CIRCUMFLEX AND ACUTE LATIN SMALL LETTER A WITH CIRCUMFLEX + COMBINING ACUTE LATIN SMALL LETTER A + COMBINING CIRCUMFLEX + COMBINING ACUTE
á̂	LATIN SMALL LETTER A ACUTE + COMBINING CIRCUMFLEX LATIN SMALL LETTER A + COMBINING ACUTE + COMBINING CIRCUMFLEX

Another example of multiple combining characters above the base character can be found in Thai, where a consonant letter can have above it one of the vowels U+0E34 through U+0E37 and, above that, one of four tone marks U+0E48 through U+0E4B. The order of character codes that produces this graphic display is *base consonant character + vowel character + tone mark character*, as shown in *Figure 2-21*.

Many combining characters have specific typographical traditions that provide detailed rules for the expected rendering. These rules override the default stacking behavior. For example, certain combinations of combining marks are sometimes positioned horizontally rather than stacking or by ligature with an adjacent nonspacing mark (see *Table 2-6*). When positioned horizontally, the order of codes is reflected by positioning in the predominant direction of the script with which the codes are used. For example, in a left-to-right script, horizontal accents would be coded from left to right. In *Table 2-6*, the top example is correct and the bottom example is incorrect.

Such override behavior is associated with specific scripts or alphabets. For example, when used with the Greek script, the "breathing marks" U+0313 COMBINING COMMA ABOVE (*psili*) and U+0314 COMBINING REVERSED COMMA ABOVE (*dasia*) require that, when used together with a following acute or grave accent, they be rendered side-by-side rather than the accent marks being stacked above the breathing marks. The order of codes here is *base character code + breathing mark code + accent mark code.* This example demonstrates the script-dependent or writing-system-dependent nature of rendering combining diacritical marks.

Table 2-6. Nondefault Stacking

ἄ	GREEK SMALL LETTER ALPHA + COMBINING COMMA ABOVE (psili) + COMBINING ACUTE ACCENT (oxia)	This is correct
ά̓	GREEK SMALL LETTER ALPHA + COMBINING ACUTE ACCENT (oxia) + COMBINING COMMA ABOVE (psili)	This is incorrect

For additional examples of script-specific departure from default stacking of sequences of combining marks, see the discussion of positioning of multiple points and marks in *Section 8.1, Hebrew*, or the discussion of nondefault placement of Arabic vowel marks accompanying *Figure 8-5* in *Section 8.2, Arabic.*

The Unicode Standard specifies default stacking behavior to offer guidance about which character codes are to be used in which order to represent the text, so that texts containing multiple combining marks can be interchanged reliably. The Unicode Standard does not aim to regulate or restrict typographical tradition.

Ligated Multiple Base Characters

When the glyphs representing two base characters merge to form a ligature, the combining characters must be rendered correctly in relation to the ligated glyph (see *Figure 2-22*). Internally, the software must distinguish between the nonspacing marks that apply to positions relative to the first part of the ligature glyph and those that apply to the second part. (For a discussion of general methods of positioning nonspacing marks, see *Section 5.12, Strategies for Handling Nonspacing Marks.*)

For more information, see "Application of Combining Marks" in *Section 3.11, Canonical Ordering Behavior.*

Ligated base characters with multiple combining marks do not commonly occur in most scripts. However, in some scripts, such as Arabic, this situation occurs quite often when

Figure 2-22. Ligated Multiple Base Characters

f + ◌̃ + i + ◌̣ → f̃ị

0066 0303 0069 0323

vowel marks are used. It arises because of the large number of ligatures in Arabic, where each element of a ligature is a consonant, which in turn can have a vowel mark attached to it. Ligatures can even occur with three or more characters merging; vowel marks may be attached to each part.

Exhibiting Nonspacing Marks in Isolation

Nonspacing combining marks used by the Unicode Standard may be exhibited in apparent isolation by applying them to U+00A0 NO-BREAK SPACE. This convention might be employed, for example, when talking about the combining mark itself as a mark, rather than using it in its normal way in text (that is, applied as an accent to a base letter or in other combinations).

Prior to Version 4.1 of the Unicode Standard, the standard recommended the use of U+0020 SPACE for display of isolated combining marks. This practice is no longer recommended because of potential conflicts with the handling of sequences of U+0020 SPACE characters in such contexts as XML. For additional ways of displaying some diacritical marks, see "Spacing Clones of Diacritics" in *Section 7.9, Combining Marks.*

"Characters" and Grapheme Clusters

End users have various concepts about what constitutes a letter or "character" in the writing system for their language or languages. The precise scope of these end-user "characters" depends on the particular written language and the orthography it uses. In addition to the many instances of accented letters, they may extend to digraphs such as Slovak "ch", trigraphs or longer combinations, and sequences using spacing letter modifiers, such as "k^w". Such concepts are often important for processes such as collation, for the definition of characters in regular expressions, and for counting "character" positions within text. In instances such as these, what the user thinks of as a character may affect how the collation or regular expression will be defined or how the "characters" will be counted. Words and other higher-level text elements generally do not split within elements that a user thinks of as a character, even when the Unicode representation of them may consist of a sequence of encoded characters.

The variety of these end-user-perceived characters is quite great—particularly for digraphs, ligatures, or syllabic units. Furthermore, it depends on the particular language and writing system that may be involved. Despite this variety, however, the core concept "characters that should be kept together" can be defined for the Unicode Standard in a language-independent way. This core concept is known as a *grapheme cluster*, and it consists of any combining character sequence that contains only *nonspacing* combining marks or any sequence of characters that constitutes a Hangul syllable (possibly followed by one or more nonspacing marks). An implementation operating on such a cluster would almost never want to break between its elements for rendering, editing, or other such text processes; the grapheme cluster is treated as a single unit. Unicode Standard Annex #29, "Text Boundaries," provides a complete formal definition of a grapheme cluster and discusses its application in the context of editing and other text processes. Implementations also may tailor the definition of a grapheme cluster, so that under limited circumstances, particular to one written language or another, the grapheme cluster may more closely pertain to what end users think of as "characters" for that language.

2.12 Equivalent Sequences and Normalization

In cases involving two or more sequences considered to be equivalent, the Unicode Standard does not prescribe one particular sequence as being the *correct* one; instead, each sequence is merely equivalent to the others. *Figure 2-23* illustrates the two major forms of equivalent sequences formally defined by the Unicode Standard. In the first example, the sequences are canonically equivalent. Both sequences should display and be interpreted the same way. The second and third examples illustrate different compatibility sequences. Compatible-equivalent sequences may have format differences in display and may be interpreted differently in some contexts.

Figure 2-23. Equivalent Sequences

① B + Ä ≡ B + A + ◌̈
0042 00C4 0042 0041 0308

② Ǉ + A ≈ L + J + A
01C7 0041 004C 004A 0041

③ 2 + ¼ ≈ 2 + 1 + ⁄ + 4
0032 00BC 0032 0031 2044 0034

If an application or user attempts to distinguish between *canonically* equivalent sequences, as shown in the first example in *Figure 2-23*, there is no guarantee that other applications would recognize the same distinctions. To prevent the introduction of interoperability problems between applications, such distinctions must be avoided wherever possible. Making distinctions between compatibly equivalent sequences is less problematical. However, in restricted contexts, such as the use of identifiers, avoiding compatibly equivalent sequences reduces possible security issues. See Unicode Technical Report #36, "Unicode Security Considerations."

Normalization. Where a unique representation is required, a normalized form of Unicode text can be used to eliminate unwanted distinctions. The Unicode Standard defines four normalization forms: Normalization Form D (NFD), Normalization Form KD (NFKD), Normalization Form C (NFC), and Normalization Form KC (NFKC). Roughly speaking, NFD and NFKD decompose characters where possible, while NFC and NFKC compose characters where possible. For more information, see Unicode Standard Annex #15, "Unicode Normalization Forms," and *Section 5.6, Normalization*.

A key part of normalization is to provide a unique canonical order for visually nondistinct sequences of combining characters. *Figure 2-24* shows the effect of canonical ordering for multiple combining marks applied to the same base character.

Figure 2-24. Canonical Ordering

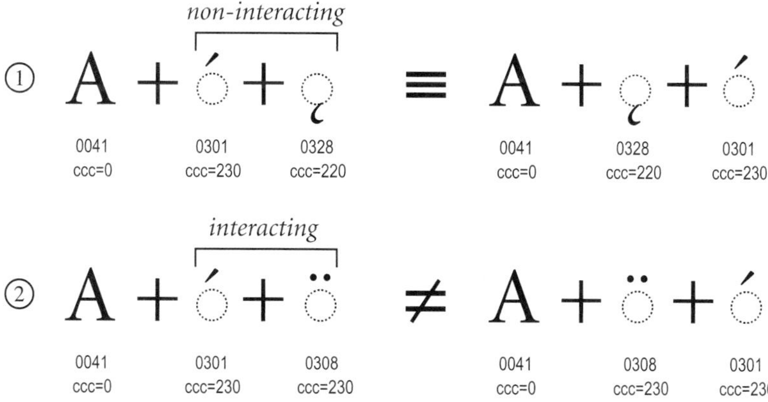

In the first row of *Figure 2-24*, the two sequences are visually nondistinct and, therefore, equivalent. The sequence on the right has been put into canonical order by reordering in ascending order of the Canonical_Combining_Class (ccc) values. The ccc values are shown below each character. The second row of *Figure 2-24* shows an example where combining marks interact typographically—the two sequences have different stacking order, and the order of combining marks is significant. Because the two combining marks have been given the same combining class, their ordering is retained under canonical reordering. Thus the two sequences in the second row are not equivalent.

Decompositions. Precomposed characters are formally known as decomposables, because they have decompositions to one or more *other* characters. There are two types of decompositions:

- *Canonical.* The character and its decomposition should be treated as essentially equivalent.
- *Compatibility.* The decomposition may remove some information (typically formatting information) that is important to preserve in particular contexts.

Types of Decomposables. Conceptually, a decomposition implies reducing a character to an equivalent sequence of constituent parts, such as mapping an accented character to a base character followed by a combining accent. The vast majority of nontrivial decompositions are indeed a mapping from a character code to a character sequence. However, in a small number of exceptional cases, there is a mapping from one character to another character, such as the mapping from *ohm* to *capital omega*. Finally, there are the "trivial" decompositions, which are simply a mapping of a character to itself. They are really an indication that a character cannot be decomposed, but are defined so that all characters formally have a decomposition. The definition of *decomposable* is written to encompass only the nontrivial types of decompositions; therefore these characters are considered *nondecomposable.*

In summary, three types of characters are distinguished based on their decomposition behavior:

- *Canonical decomposable.* A character that is not identical to its canonical decomposition.
- *Compatibility decomposable.* A character whose compatibility decomposition is not identical to its canonical decomposition.
- *Nondecomposable.* A character that is identical to both its canonical decomposition and its compatibility decomposition. In other words, the character has trivial decompositions (decompositions to itself). Loosely speaking, these characters are said to have "no decomposition," even though, for completeness, the algorithm that defines decomposition maps such characters to themselves.

Because of the way decompositions are defined, a character cannot have a nontrivial canonical decomposition while having a trivial compatibility decomposition. Characters with a trivial compatibility decomposition are therefore always nondecomposables.

Examples. *Figure 2-25* illustrates these three types. The solid arrows indicate canonical decompositions and the dotted arrows indicate compatibility decompositions. Compatibility decompositions that are redundant because they are identical to the canonical decompositions are not shown. The figure illustrates two important points:

- Decompositions may be to single characters *or* to sequences of characters. Decompositions to a single character, also known as *singleton decompositions*, are seen for the *ohm sign* and the *halfwidth katakana ka* in *Figure 2-25*. Because of examples like these, decomposable characters in Unicode do not always consist of obvious, separate parts; one can know their status only by examining the data tables for the standard.
- A very small number of characters are both canonical and compatibility decomposable. The example shown in *Figure 2-25* is for the Greek hooked upsilon symbol with an acute accent. It has a canonical decomposition to one sequence and a compatibility decomposition to a different sequence.

For more precise definitions of these terms, see *Chapter 3, Conformance.*

Figure 2-25. Types of Decomposables

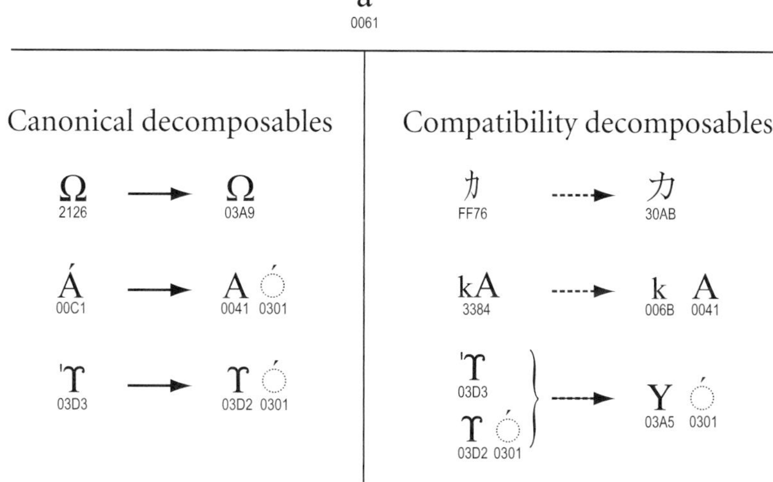

2.13 Special Characters and Noncharacters

The Unicode Standard includes a small number of important characters with special behavior; some of them are introduced in this section. It is important that implementations treat these characters properly. For a list of these and similar characters, see *Section 4.12, Characters with Unusual Properties*; for more information about such characters, see *Section 16.1, Control Codes*; *Section 16.2, Layout Controls*; *Section 16.7, Noncharacters*; and *Section 16.8, Specials.*

Special Noncharacter Code Points

The Unicode Standard contains a number of code points that are intentionally *not* used to represent assigned characters. These code points are known as *noncharacters.* They are permanently reserved for internal use and should never be used for open interchange of Unicode text. For more information on noncharacters, see *Section 16.7, Noncharacters.*

Byte Order Mark (BOM)

The UTF-16 and UTF-32 encoding forms of Unicode plain text are sensitive to the byte ordering that is used when serializing text into a sequence of bytes, such as when writing data to a file or transferring data across a network. Some processors place the least significant byte in the initial position; others place the most significant byte in the initial position. Ideally, all implementations of the Unicode Standard would follow only one set of byte order rules, but this scheme would force one class of processors to swap the byte order on reading and writing plain text files, even when the file never leaves the system on which it was created.

To have an efficient way to indicate which byte order is used in a text, the Unicode Standard contains two code points, U+FEFF ZERO WIDTH NO-BREAK SPACE (*byte order mark*) and U+FFFE (a noncharacter), which are the byte-ordered mirror images of each other. When a BOM is received with the opposite byte order, it will be recognized as a noncharacter and can therefore be used to detect the intended byte order of the text. The BOM is not a control character that selects the byte order of the text; rather, its function is to allow recipients to determine which byte ordering is used in a file.

Unicode Signature. An initial BOM may also serve as an implicit marker to identify a file as containing Unicode text. For UTF-16, the sequence FE_{16} FF_{16} (or its byte-reversed counterpart, FF_{16} FE_{16}) is exceedingly rare at the outset of text files that use other character encodings. The corresponding UTF-8 BOM sequence, EF_{16} BB_{16} BF_{16}, is also exceedingly rare. In either case, it is therefore unlikely to be confused with real text data. The same is true for both single-byte and multibyte encodings.

Data streams (or files) that begin with the U+FEFF byte order mark are likely to contain Unicode characters. It is recommended that applications sending or receiving untyped data streams of coded characters use this signature. If other signaling methods are used, signatures should not be employed.

Conformance to the Unicode Standard does not requires the use of the BOM as such a signature. See *Section 16.8, Specials*, for more information on the byte order mark and its use as an encoding signature.

Layout and Format Control Characters

The Unicode Standard defines several characters that are used to control joining behavior, bidirectional ordering control, and alternative formats for display. Their specific use in layout and formatting is described in *Section 16.2, Layout Controls.*

The Replacement Character

U+FFFD REPLACEMENT CHARACTER is the general substitute character in the Unicode Standard. It can be substituted for any "unknown" character in another encoding that cannot be mapped in terms of known Unicode characters (see *Section 5.3, Unknown and Missing Characters*, and *Section 16.8, Specials*).

Control Codes

In addition to the special characters defined in the Unicode Standard for a number of purposes, the standard incorporates the legacy control codes for compatibility with the ISO/IEC 2022 framework, ASCII, and the various protocols that make use of control codes. Rather than simply being defined as byte values, however, the legacy control codes are assigned to Unicode code points: U+0000..U+001F, U+007F..U+009F. Those code points for control codes must be represented consistently with the various Unicode encoding forms when they are used with other Unicode characters. For more information on control codes, see *Section 16.1, Control Codes.*

2.14 Conforming to the Unicode Standard

Conformance requirements are a set of unambiguous criteria to which a conformant implementation of a standard must adhere, so that it can interoperate with other conformant implementations. The universal scope of the Unicode Standard complicates the task of rigorously defining such conformance requirements for all aspects of the standard. Making conformance requirements overly confining runs the risk of unnecessarily restricting the breadth of text operations that can be implemented with the Unicode Standard or of limiting them to a one-size-fits-all lowest common denominator. In many cases, therefore, the conformance requirements deliberately cover only minimal requirements, falling far short of providing a complete description of the behavior of an implementation. Nevertheless, there are many core aspects of the standard for which a precise and exhaustive definition of conformant behavior is possible.

This section gives examples of both conformant and nonconformant implementation behavior, illustrating key aspects of the formal statement of conformance requirements found in *Chapter 3, Conformance.*

Characteristics of Conformant Implementations

An implementation that conforms to the Unicode Standard has the following characteristics:

It treats characters according to the specified Unicode encoding form.

- The byte sequence <20 20> is interpreted as U+2020 '†' DAGGER in the UTF-16 encoding form.
- The same byte sequence <20 20> is interpreted as the sequence of two spaces, <U+0020, U+0020>, in the UTF-8 encoding form.

It interprets characters according to the identities, properties, and rules defined for them in this standard.

- U+2423 is '␣' OPEN BOX, *not* 'ぃ' *hiragana small i* (which is the meaning of the bytes 2423_{16} in JIS).
- U+00F4 'ô' is equivalent to U+006F 'o' followed by U+0302 '◌̂', but *not equivalent to* U+0302 followed by U+006F.
- U+05D0 'א' followed by U+05D1 'ב' looks like 'אב', *not* 'בא' when displayed.

When an implementation supports the display of Arabic, Hebrew, or other right-to-left characters and displays those characters, they must be ordered according to the Bidirectional Algorithm described in Unicode Standard Annex #9, "The Bidirectional Algorithm."

When an implementation supports Arabic, Devanagari, or other scripts with complex shaping for their characters and displays those characters, at a minimum the characters are shaped according to the relevant block descriptions. (More sophisticated shaping can be used if available.)

Unacceptable Behavior

It is unacceptable for a conforming implementation:

To use unassigned codes.

- U+2073 is unassigned and not usable for '^{3}' (*superscript 3*) or any other character.

To corrupt unsupported characters.

- U+03A1 "P" GREEK CAPITAL LETTER RHO should not be changed to U+00A1 (first byte dropped), U+0050 (mapped to Latin letter *P*), U+A103 (bytes reversed), or anything other than U+03A1.

To remove or alter uninterpreted code points in text that purports to be unmodified.

- U+2029 is PARAGRAPH SEPARATOR and should not be dropped by applications that do not support it.

Acceptable Behavior

It is acceptable for a conforming implementation:

To support only a subset of the Unicode characters.

- An application might not provide mathematical symbols or the Thai script, for example.

To transform data knowingly.

- Uppercase conversion: 'a' transformed to 'A'
- Romaji to kana: 'kyo' transformed to きょ
- Decomposition: U+247D '(10)' decomposed to <U+0028, U+0031, U+0030, U+0029>

To build higher-level protocols on the character set.

- Examples are defining a file format for compression of characters or for use with rich text.

To define private-use characters.

- Examples of characters that might be defined for private use include additional ideographic characters (*gaiji*) or existing corporate logo characters.

To not support the Bidirectional Algorithm or character shaping in implementations that do not support complex scripts, such as Arabic and Devanagari.

To not support the Bidirectional Algorithm or character shaping in implementations that do not display characters, as, for example, on servers or in programs that simply parse or transcode text, such as an XML parser.

Code conversion between other character encodings and the Unicode Standard will be considered conformant if the conversion is accurate in both directions.

Supported Subsets

The Unicode Standard does not require that an application be capable of interpreting and rendering all Unicode characters so as to be conformant. Many systems will have fonts for only some scripts, but not for others; sorting and other text-processing rules may be implemented for only a limited set of languages. As a result, an implementation is able to interpret a subset of characters.

The Unicode Standard provides no formalized method for identifying an implemented subset. Furthermore, such a subset is typically different for different aspects of an implementation. For example, an application may be able to read, write, and store any Unicode character and to sort one subset according to the rules of one or more languages (and the rest arbitrarily), but has access to fonts for only a single script. The same implementation may be able to render additional scripts as soon as additional fonts are installed in its environment. Therefore, the subset of interpretable characters is typically not a static concept.

CHAPTER 3

Chapter 3

Conformance

This chapter defines conformance to the Unicode Standard in terms of the principles and encoding architecture it embodies. The first section defines the format for referencing the Unicode Standard and Unicode properties. The second section consists of the conformance clauses, followed by sections that define more precisely the technical terms used in those clauses. The remaining sections contain the formal algorithms that are part of conformance and referenced by the conformance clause. Additional definitions and algorithms that are part of this standard can be found in the Unicode Standard Annexes listed at the end of *Section 3.2, Conformance Requirements.*

In this chapter, conformance clauses are identified with the letter *C*. Definitions are identified with the letter *D*. Bulleted items are explanatory comments regarding definitions or subclauses.

The numbering of clauses and definitions has been changed from that of prior versions of *The Unicode Standard*. This change was necessitated by the addition of a substantial number of new definitions that did not fit well into the prior numbering scheme. A cross-reference table enabling the matching of a clause or definition between Version 5.0 and earlier versions of the standard is available in *Section D.3, Clause and Definition Numbering Changes.*

For information on implementing best practices, see *Chapter 5, Implementation Guidelines.*

3.1 Versions of the Unicode Standard

For most character encodings, the character repertoire is fixed (and often small). Once the repertoire is decided upon, it is never changed. Addition of a new abstract character to a given repertoire creates a new repertoire, which will be treated either as an update of the existing character encoding or as a completely new character encoding.

For the Unicode Standard, by contrast, the repertoire is inherently open. Because Unicode is a universal encoding, any abstract character that could ever be encoded is a potential candidate to be encoded, regardless of whether the character is currently known.

Each new version of the Unicode Standard supersedes the previous one, but implementations—and, more significantly, data—are not updated instantly. In general, major and minor version changes include new characters, which do not create particular problems with old data. The Unicode Technical Committee will neither remove nor move characters. Characters may be *deprecated*, but this does not remove them from the standard or from existing data. The code point for a deprecated character will never be reassigned to a different character, but the use of a deprecated character is strongly discouraged. Generally these rules make the encoded characters of a new version backward-compatible with previous versions.

Implementations should be prepared to be forward-compatible with respect to Unicode versions. That is, they should accept text that may be expressed in future versions of this standard, recognizing that new characters may be assigned in those versions. Thus they should handle incoming unassigned code points as they do unsupported characters. (See *Section 5.3, Unknown and Missing Characters.*)

A version change may also involve changes to the properties of existing characters. When this situation occurs, modifications are made to the Unicode Character Database and a new update version is issued for the standard. Changes to the data files may alter program behavior that depends on them. However, such changes to properties and to data files are never made lightly. They are made only after careful deliberation by the Unicode Technical Committee has determined that there is an error, inconsistency, or other serious problem in the property assignments.

Stability

Each version of the Unicode Standard, once published, is absolutely stable and will *never* change. Implementations or specifications that refer to a specific version of the Unicode Standard can rely upon this stability. When implementations or specifications are upgraded to a future version of the Unicode Standard, then changes to them may be necessary. Note that even errata and corrigenda do not formally change the text of a published version; see "Errata and Corrigenda" later in this section.

Some features of the Unicode Standard are guaranteed to be stable *across* versions. These include the names and code positions of characters, their decompositions, and several other character properties for which stability is important to implementations. See also "Stability of Properties" in *Section 3.5, Properties.* The formal statement of such stability guarantees is contained in the policies on character encoding stability found on the Unicode Web site. See the subsection "Policies" in *Section B.6, Other Unicode Online Resources. Appendix F, Unicode Encoding Stability Policies*, presents a copy of these policies in effect at the time of this publication. See also the discussion of backward compatibility in Unicode Standard Annex #31, "Identifier and Pattern Syntax," and the subsection "Interacting with Downlevel Systems" in *Section 5.3, Unknown and Missing Characters.*

Version Numbering

Version numbers for the Unicode Standard consist of three fields, denoting the major version, the minor version, and the update version, respectively. For example, "Unicode 3.1.1" indicates major version 3 of the Unicode Standard, minor version 1 of Unicode 3, and update version 1 of minor version Unicode 3.1.

Formally, each new version of the Unicode Standard supersedes all earlier versions. However, because of the differences in the ways major, minor, and update versions are documented, minor and update versions generally do not obsolete all of the documentation of the immediately prior versions of the standard.

Additional information on the current and past versions of the Unicode Standard can be found on the Unicode Web site. See the subsection "Versions" in *Section B.6, Other Unicode Online Resources*. The online document contains the precise list of contributing files from the Unicode Character Database and the Unicode Standard Annexes, which are formally part of each version of the Unicode Standard.

The differences between major, minor, and update versions are as follows:

Major Version. A major version represents significant additions to the standard, including but not limited to major additions to the repertoire of encoded characters. A major version is published as a book, together with associated updates to Unicode Standard Annexes and the Unicode Character Database.

A major version consolidates all errata and corrigenda to data. The publication of the book for a major version supersedes any prior documentation for major, minor, and update versions.

Minor Version. A minor version also represents significant additions to the standard. It may include small or large additions to the repertoire of encoded characters or other significant normative changes. A minor version is published only online and is not published as a book. Prior to Unicode 4.1, a minor version was published as a Unicode Standard Annex (or as a Unicode Technical Report for the very earliest minor versions). Starting with Unicode 4.1, minor versions are published as stable version pages online. A minor version is also associated with an update to the Unicode Character Database and updates to the UAXes.

A minor version incorporates selected errata as appropriate. The documentation for a minor version does not stand alone, but rather amends the documentation of the prior version.

Update Version. An update version represents relatively small changes to the standard, focusing on updates to the data files of the Unicode Character Database. An update version never involves any additions to character repertoire. It is published only online. Starting with Unicode 3.0.1, update versions are published as stable version pages online. Prior to that version, update versions were simply documented with the list of relevant data file changes to the Unicode Character Database.

An update version incorporates selected errata, primarily for the data files. The documentation for an update version does not stand alone, but rather amends the prior version.

Errata and Corrigenda

From time to time it may be necessary to publish errata or corrigenda to the Unicode Standard. Such errata and corrigenda will be published on the Unicode Web site. See *Section B.6, Other Unicode Online Resources*, for information on how to report errors in the standard.

Errata. Errata correct errors in the text or other informative material, such as the representative glyphs in the code charts. See the subsection "Updates and Errata" in *Section B.6, Other Unicode Online Resources*. Whenever a new major version of the standard is published, all errata up to that point are incorporated into the text.

Corrigenda. Occasionally errors may be important enough that a corrigendum is issued prior to the next version of the Unicode Standard. Such a corrigendum does not change the contents of the previous version. Instead, it provides a mechanism for an implementation, protocol, or other standard to cite the previous version of the Unicode Standard with the corrigendum applied. If a citation does not specifically mention the corrigendum, the corrigendum does not apply. For more information on citing corrigenda, see "Versions" in *Section B.6, Other Unicode Online Resources*.

References to the Unicode Standard

The documents associated with the major, minor, and update versions are called the major reference, minor reference, and update reference, respectively. For example, consider Unicode Version 3.1.1. The major reference for that version is *The Unicode Standard, Version 3.0* (ISBN 0-201-61633-5). The minor reference is Unicode Standard Annex #27, "The Unicode Standard, Version 3.1." The update reference is Unicode Version 3.1.1. The exact list of contributory files, Unicode Standard Annexes, and Unicode Character Database files can be found at Enumerated Version 3.1.1.

The reference for *this* version, Version 5.0.0, of the Unicode Standard, is

> The Unicode Consortium. The Unicode Standard, Version 5.0.0, defined by: *The Unicode Standard, Version 5.0* (Boston, MA: Addison-Wesley, 2007. ISBN 0-321-48091-0)

References to an update or minor version include a reference to both the major version and the documents modifying it. For the standard citation format for other versions of the Unicode Standard, see "Versions" in *Section B.6, Other Unicode Online Resources*.

Precision in Version Citation

Because Unicode has an open repertoire with relatively frequent updates, it is important not to over-specify the version number. Wherever the precise behavior of all Unicode characters needs to be cited, the full three-field version number should be used, as in the first example below. However, trailing zeros are often omitted, as in the second example. In such a case, writing 3.1 is in all respects equivalent to writing 3.1.0.

1. The Unicode Standard, Version 3.1.1
2. The Unicode Standard, Version 3.1
3. The Unicode Standard, Version 3.0 or later
4. The Unicode Standard

Where some basic level of content is all that is important, phrasing such as in the third example can be used. Where the important information is simply the overall architecture and semantics of the Unicode Standard, the version can be omitted entirely, as in example 4.

References to Unicode Character Properties

Properties and property values have defined names and abbreviations, such as

> Property: General_Category (gc)
>
> Property Value: Uppercase_Letter (Lu)

To reference a given property and property value, these aliases are used, as in this example:

> The property value Uppercase_Letter from the General_Category property, as specified in Version 5.0.0 of the Unicode Standard.

Then cite that version of the standard, using the standard citation format that is provided for each version of the Unicode Standard.

When referencing multi-word properties or property values, it is permissible to omit the underscores in these aliases or to replace them by spaces.

When referencing a Unicode character property, it is customary to prepend the word "Unicode" to the name of the property, unless it is clear from context that the Unicode Standard is the source of the specification.

References to Unicode Algorithms

A reference to a Unicode algorithm must specify the name of the algorithm or its abbreviation, followed by the version of the Unicode Standard, as in this example:

> The Unicode Bidirectional Algorithm, as specified in Version 4.1.0 of the Unicode Standard.
>
> See Unicode Standard Annex #9, "The Bidirectional Algorithm," (http://www.unicode.org/reports/tr9/tr9-15.html)

Where algorithms allow tailoring, the reference must state whether any such tailorings were applied or are applicable. For algorithms contained in a Unicode Standard Annex, the document itself and its location on the Unicode Web site may be cited as the location of the specification.

When referencing a Unicode algorithm it is customary to prepend the word "Unicode" to the name of the algorithm, unless it is clear from the context that the Unicode Standard is the source of the specification.

Omitting a version number when referencing a Unicode algorithm may be appropriate when such a reference is meant as a generic reference to the overall algorithm. Such a generic reference may also be employed in the sense of latest available version of the algorithm. However, for specific and detailed conformance claims for Unicode algorithms, generic references are generally not sufficient, and a full version number must accompany the reference.

3.2 Conformance Requirements

This section presents the clauses specifying the formal conformance requirements for processes implementing Version 5.0 of the Unicode Standard. A few of these clauses have been revised from Version 4.0 of the Unicode Standard. The revisions do not change the fundamental substance of the conformance requirements previously set forth, but rather are reformulated to clarify their applicability to Unicode algorithms and tailoring. The definitions that these clauses—particularly conformance clause C4—depend on have been extended to cover additional aspects of properties and algorithms.

In addition to the specifications printed in this book, the Unicode Standard, Version 5.0, includes a number of Unicode Standard Annexes (UAXes) and the Unicode Character Database. Both are available only electronically, either on the CD-ROM or on the Unicode Web site. At the end of this section there is a list of those annexes that are considered an integral part of the Unicode Standard, Version 5.0.0, and therefore covered by these conformance requirements.

The Unicode Character Database contains an extensive specification of normative and informative character properties completing the formal definition of the Unicode Standard. See *Chapter 4, Character Properties*, for more information.

Not all conformance requirements are relevant to all implementations at all times because implementations may not support the particular characters or operations for which a given conformance requirement may be relevant. See *Section 2.14, Conforming to the Unicode Standard*, for more information.

In this section, conformance clauses are identified with the letter *C*.

The numbering of clauses has been changed from that of prior versions of *The Unicode Standard*. A cross-reference table enabling the matching of a clause between Version 5.0 and earlier versions of the standard is available in *Section D.3, Clause and Definition Numbering Changes.*

Code Points Unassigned to Abstract Characters

C1 *A process shall not interpret a high-surrogate code point or a low-surrogate code point as an abstract character.*

- The high-surrogate and low-surrogate code points are designated for surrogate code units in the UTF-16 character encoding form. They are unassigned to any abstract character.

C2 *A process shall not interpret a noncharacter code point as an abstract character.*

- The noncharacter code points may be used internally, such as for sentinel values or delimiters, but should not be exchanged publicly.

C3 *A process shall not interpret an unassigned code point as an abstract character.*

- This clause does not preclude the assignment of certain generic semantics to unassigned code points (for example, rendering with a glyph to indicate the position within a character block) that allow for graceful behavior in the presence of code points that are outside a supported subset.
- Unassigned code points may have default property values. (See D26.)
- Code points whose use has not yet been designated may be assigned to abstract characters in future versions of the standard. Because of this fact, due care in the handling of generic semantics for such code points is likely to provide better robustness for implementations that may encounter data based on future versions of the standard.

Interpretation

C4 *A process shall interpret a coded character sequence according to the character semantics established by this standard, if that process does interpret that coded character sequence.*

- This restriction does not preclude internal transformations that are never visible external to the process.

C5 *A process shall not assume that it is required to interpret any particular coded character sequence.*

- Processes that interpret only a subset of Unicode characters are allowed; there is no blanket requirement to interpret *all* Unicode characters.
- Any means for specifying a subset of characters that a process can interpret is outside the scope of this standard.
- The semantics of a private-use code point is outside the scope of this standard.
- Although these clauses are not intended to preclude enumerations or specifications of the characters that a process or system is able to interpret, they do separate supported subset enumerations from the question of conformance. In actuality, any system may occasionally receive an unfamiliar character code that it is unable to interpret.

C6 *A process shall not assume that the interpretations of two canonical-equivalent character sequences are distinct.*

- The implications of this conformance clause are twofold. First, a process is never required to give different interpretations to two different, but canonical-equivalent character sequences. Second, no process can assume that another process will make a distinction between two different, but canonical-equivalent character sequences.

- Ideally, an implementation would always interpret two canonical-equivalent character sequences identically. There are practical circumstances under which implementations may reasonably distinguish them.
- Even processes that normally do not distinguish between canonical-equivalent character sequences can have reasonable exception behavior. Some examples of this behavior include graceful fallback processing by processes unable to support correct positioning of nonspacing marks; "Show Hidden Text" modes that reveal memory representation structure; and the choice of ignoring collating behavior of combining sequences that are not part of the repertoire of a specified language (see *Section 5.12, Strategies for Handling Nonspacing Marks*).

Modification

C7 *When a process purports not to modify the interpretation of a valid coded character sequence, it shall make no change to that coded character sequence other than the possible replacement of character sequences by their canonical-equivalent sequences or the deletion of* noncharacter *code points.*

- Replacement of a character sequence by a compatibility-equivalent sequence *does* modify the interpretation of the text.
- Replacement or deletion of a character sequence that the process cannot or does not interpret *does* modify the interpretation of the text.
- Changing the bit or byte ordering of a character sequence when transforming it between different machine architectures does not modify the interpretation of the text.
- Changing a valid coded character sequence from one Unicode character encoding form to another does not modify the interpretation of the text.
- Changing the byte serialization of a code unit sequence from one Unicode character encoding scheme to another does not modify the interpretation of the text.
- If a noncharacter that does not have a specific internal use is unexpectedly encountered in processing, an implementation may signal an error or delete or ignore the noncharacter. If these options are not taken, the noncharacter should be treated as an unassigned code point. For example, an API that returned a character property value for a noncharacter would return the same value as the default value for an unassigned code point.
- All processes and higher-level protocols are required to abide by conformance clause C7 at a minimum. However, higher-level protocols may define additional equivalences that do not constitute modifications under that protocol.

For example, a higher-level protocol may allow a sequence of spaces to be replaced by a single space.

Character Encoding Forms

C8 *When a process interprets a code unit sequence which purports to be in a Unicode character encoding form, it shall interpret that code unit sequence according to the corresponding code point sequence.*

- The specification of the code unit sequences for UTF-8 is given in D92.
- The specification of the code unit sequences for UTF-16 is given in D91.
- The specification of the code unit sequences for UTF-32 is given in D90.

C9 *When a process generates a code unit sequence which purports to be in a Unicode character encoding form, it shall not emit ill-formed code unit sequences.*

- The definition of each Unicode character encoding form specifies the ill-formed code unit sequences in the character encoding form. For example, the definition of UTF-8 (D92) specifies that code unit sequences such as <C0 AF> are ill-formed.

C10 *When a process interprets a code unit sequence which purports to be in a Unicode character encoding form, it shall treat ill-formed code unit sequences as an error condition and shall not interpret such sequences as characters.*

- For example, in UTF-8 every code unit of the form $110xxxx_2$ *must* be followed by a code unit of the form $10xxxxxx_2$. A sequence such as $110xxxxx_2$ $0xxxxxxx_2$ is ill-formed and must never be generated. When faced with this ill-formed code unit sequence while transforming or interpreting text, a conformant process must treat the first code unit $110xxxxx_2$ as an illegally terminated code unit sequence—for example, by signaling an error, filtering the code unit out, or representing the code unit with a marker such as U+FFFD REPLACEMENT CHARACTER.
- Conformant processes cannot interpret ill-formed code unit sequences. However, the conformance clauses do not prevent processes from operating on code unit sequences that do not purport to be in a Unicode character encoding form. For example, for performance reasons a low-level string operation may simply operate directly on code units, without interpreting them as characters. See, especially, the discussion under definition D89.
- Utility programs are not prevented from operating on "mangled" text. For example, a UTF-8 file could have had CRLF sequences introduced at every 80 bytes by a bad mailer program. This could result in some UTF-8 byte sequences being interrupted by CRLFs, producing illegal byte sequences. This mangled text is no longer UTF-8. It is permissible for a conformant program to repair such text, recognizing that the mangled text was originally well-formed UTF-8

byte sequences. However, such repair of mangled data is a special case, and it must not be used in circumstances where it would cause security problems.

Character Encoding Schemes

C11 *When a process interprets a byte sequence which purports to be in a Unicode character encoding scheme, it shall interpret that byte sequence according to the byte order and specifications for the use of the byte order mark established by this standard for that character encoding scheme.*

- Machine architectures differ in *ordering* in terms of whether the most significant byte or the least significant byte comes first. These sequences are known as "big-endian" and "little-endian" orders, respectively.
- For example, when using UTF-16LE, pairs of bytes are interpreted as UTF-16 code units using the little-endian byte order convention, and any initial <FF FE> sequence is interpreted as U+FEFF ZERO WIDTH NO-BREAK SPACE (part of the text), rather than as a byte order mark (not part of the text). (See D97.)

Bidirectional Text

C12 *A process that displays text containing supported right-to-left characters or embedding codes shall display all visible representations of characters (excluding format characters) in the same order as if the Bidirectional Algorithm had been applied to the text, unless tailored by a higher-level protocol as permitted by the specification.*

- The Bidirectional Algorithm is specified in Unicode Standard Annex #9, "The Bidirectional Algorithm."

Normalization Forms

C13 *A process that produces Unicode text that purports to be in a Normalization Form shall do so in accordance with the specifications in Unicode Standard Annex #15, "Unicode Normalization Forms."*

C14 *A process that tests Unicode text to determine whether it is in a Normalization Form shall do so in accordance with the specifications in Unicode Standard Annex #15, "Unicode Normalization Forms."*

C15 *A process that purports to transform text into a Normalization Form must be able to produce the results of the conformance test specified in Unicode Standard Annex #15, "Unicode Normalization Forms."*

- This means that when a process uses the input specified in the conformance test, its output must match the expected output of the test.

Normative References

C16 *Normative references to the Unicode Standard itself, to property aliases, to property value aliases, or to Unicode algorithms shall follow the formats specified in Section 3.1, Versions of the Unicode Standard.*

C17 *Higher-level protocols shall not make normative references to provisional properties.*

- Higher-level protocols may make normative references to informative properties.

Unicode Algorithms

C18 *If a process purports to implement a Unicode algorithm, it shall conform to the specification of that algorithm in the standard, including any tailoring by a higher-level protocol as permitted by the specification.*

- The term *Unicode algorithm* is defined at D17.
- An implementation claiming conformance to a Unicode algorithm need only guarantee that it produces the same results as those specified in the logical description of the process; it is not required to follow the actual described procedure in detail. This allows room for alternative strategies and optimizations in implementation.

C19 *The specification of an algorithm may prohibit or limit tailoring by a higher-level protocol. If a process that purports to implement a Unicode algorithm applies a tailoring, that fact must be disclosed.*

- For example, the algorithms for normalization and canonical ordering are not tailorable. The Bidirectional Algorithm allows some tailoring by higher-level protocols. The Unicode Default Case algorithms may be tailored without limitation.

Default Casing Algorithms

C20 *An implementation that purports to support Default Case Conversion, Default Case Detection, or Default Caseless Matching shall do so in accordance with the definitions and specifications in Section 3.13, Default Case Algorithms.*

- A conformant implementation may perform casing operations that are different from the default algorithms, perhaps tailored to a particular orthography, so long as the fact that a tailoring is applied is disclosed.

Unicode Standard Annexes

The following standard annexes are approved and considered part of Version 5.0 of the Unicode Standard. These annexes may contain either normative or informative material, or both. Any reference to Version 5.0 of the standard automatically includes these standard annexes.

- UAX #9: The Bidirectional Algorithm, Version 5.0.0
- UAX #11: East Asian Width, Version 5.0.0
- UAX #14: Line Breaking Properties, Version 5.0.0
- UAX #15: Unicode Normalization Forms, Version 5.0.0
- UAX #24: Script Names, Version 5.0.0
- UAX #29: Text Boundaries, Version 5.0.0
- UAX #31: Identifier and Pattern Syntax, Version 5.0.0
- UAX #34: Unicode Named Character Sequences, Version 5.0.0

Conformance to the Unicode Standard requires conformance to the specifications contained in these annexes, as detailed in the conformance clauses listed earlier in this section.

3.3 Semantics

Definitions

This and the following sections more precisely define the terms that are used in the conformance clauses.

The numbering of definitions has been changed from that of prior versions of *The Unicode Standard.* A cross-reference table enabling the matching of a definition between Version 5.0 and earlier versions of the standard is available in *Section D.3, Clause and Definition Numbering Changes.*

Character Identity and Semantics

D1 *Normative behavior:* The normative behaviors of the Unicode Standard consist of the following list or any other behaviors specified in the conformance clauses:

- Character combination
- Canonical decomposition
- Compatibility decomposition
- Canonical ordering behavior
- Bidirectional behavior, as specified in the Unicode Bidirectional Algorithm (see Unicode Standard Annex #9, "The Bidirectional Algorithm")

- Conjoining jamo behavior, as specified in *Section 3.12, Conjoining Jamo Behavior*
- Variation selection, as specified in *Section 16.4, Variation Selectors*
- Normalization, as specified in Unicode Standard Annex #15, "Unicode Normalization Forms"
- Default casing, as specified in *Section 3.13, Default Case Algorithms*

D2 *Character identity:* The identity of a character is established by its character name and representative glyph in *Chapter 17, Code Charts.*

- A character may have a broader range of use than the most literal interpretation of its name might indicate; the coded representation, name, and representative glyph need to be assessed in context when establishing the identity of a character. For example, U+002E FULL STOP can represent a sentence period, an abbreviation period, a decimal number separator in English, a thousands number separator in German, and so on. The character name itself is unique, but may be misleading. See "Character Names" in *Section 17.1, Character Names List.*
- Consistency with the representative glyph does not require that the images be identical or even graphically similar; rather, it means that both images are generally recognized to be representations of the same character. Representing the character U+0061 LATIN SMALL LETTER A by the glyph "X" would violate its character identity.

D3 *Character semantics:* The semantics of a character are determined by its identity, normative properties, and behavior.

- Some normative behavior is default behavior; this behavior can be overridden by higher-level protocols. However, in the absence of such protocols, the behavior must be observed so as to follow the character semantics.
- The character combination properties and the canonical ordering behavior cannot be overridden by higher-level protocols. The purpose of this constraint is to guarantee that the order of combining marks in text and the results of normalization are predictable.

D4 *Character name:* A unique string used to identify each abstract character encoded in the standard.

- The character names in the Unicode Standard match those of the English edition of ISO/IEC 10646.
- Character names are immutable and cannot be overridden; they are stable identifiers. For more information, see *Section 4.8, Name—Normative.*
- The name of a Unicode character is also formally a character property in the Unicode Character Database. Its long property alias is "Name" and its short

property alias is “na”. Its value is the unique string label associated with the encoded character.

D5 *Character name alias:* An additional unique string identifier, other than the character name, associated with an encoded character in the standard.

- Character name aliases are assigned when there is a serious clerical defect with a character name, such that the character name itself may be misleading regarding the identity of the character. A character name alias constitutes an alternate identifier for the character.
- Character name aliases are unique within the common namespace shared by character names, character name aliases, and named character sequences.
- Character name aliases are a formal, normative part of the standard and should be distinguished from the informative, editorial aliases provided in the code charts. See *Section 17.1, Character Names List,* for the notational conventions used to distinguish the two.

D6 *Namespace:* A set of names together with name matching rules, so that all names are distinct under the matching rules.

- Within a given namespace all names must be unique, although the same name may be used with a different meaning in a different namespace.
- Character names, character name aliases, and named character sequences share a single namespace in the Unicode Standard.

3.4 Characters and Encoding

D7 *Abstract character:* A unit of information used for the organization, control, or representation of textual data.

- When representing data, the nature of that data is generally symbolic as opposed to some other kind of data (for example, aural or visual). Examples of such symbolic data include letters, ideographs, digits, punctuation, technical symbols, and dingbats.
- An abstract character has no concrete form and should not be confused with a *glyph.*
- An abstract character does not necessarily correspond to what a user thinks of as a “character” and should not be confused with a *grapheme.*
- The abstract characters encoded by the Unicode Standard are known as Unicode abstract characters.
- Abstract characters not directly encoded by the Unicode Standard can often be represented by the use of combining character sequences.

D8 *Abstract character sequence:* An ordered sequence of one or more abstract characters.

D9 *Unicode codespace:* A range of integers from 0 to $10FFFF_{16}$.

- This particular range is defined for the codespace in the Unicode Standard. Other character encoding standards may use other codespaces.

D10 *Code point:* Any value in the Unicode codespace.

- A code point is also known as a *code position*.
- See D77 for the definition of *code unit*.

D11 *Encoded character:* An association (or mapping) between an abstract character and a code point.

- An encoded character is also referred to as a *coded character*.
- While an encoded character is formally defined in terms of the mapping between an abstract character and a code point, informally it can be thought of as an abstract character taken together with its assigned code point.
- Occasionally, for compatibility with other standards, a single abstract character may correspond to more than one code point—for example, "Å" corresponds both to U+00C5 Å LATIN CAPITAL LETTER A WITH RING ABOVE and to U+212B Å ANGSTROM SIGN.
- A single abstract character may also be *represented* by a sequence of code points—for example, *latin capital letter g with acute* may be represented by the sequence <U+0047 LATIN CAPITAL LETTER G, U+0301 COMBINING ACUTE ACCENT>, rather than being mapped to a single code point.

D12 *Coded character sequence:* An ordered sequence of one or more code points.

- A coded character sequence is also known as a *coded character representation*.
- Normally a coded character sequence consists of a sequence of encoded characters, but it may also include noncharacters or reserved code points.
- Internally, a process may choose to make use of noncharacter code points in its coded character sequences. However, such noncharacter code points may not be interpreted as abstract characters (see conformance clause C2), and their removal by a conformant process does not constitute modification of interpretation of the coded character sequence (see conformance clause C7).
- Reserved code points are included in coded character sequences, so that the conformance requirements regarding interpretation and modification are properly defined when a Unicode-conformant implementation encounters coded character sequences produced under a future version of the standard.

Unless specified otherwise for clarity, in the text of the Unicode Standard the term *character* alone designates an encoded character. Similarly, the term *character sequence* alone designates a coded character sequence.

D13 *Deprecated character:* A coded character whose use is strongly discouraged. Such characters are retained in the standard, but should not be used.

- Deprecated characters are retained in the standard so that previously conforming data stay conformant in future versions of the standard. Deprecated characters should not be confused with obsolete characters, which are historical. Obsolete characters do not occur in modern text, but they are not deprecated; their use is not discouraged.

D14 *Noncharacter:* A code point that is permanently reserved for internal use and that should never be interchanged. Noncharacters consist of the values U+*n*FFFE and U+*n*FFFF (where n is from 0 to 10_{16}) and the values U+FDD0..U+FDEF.

- For more information, see *Section 16.7, Noncharacters.*
- These code points are permanently reserved as noncharacters.

D15 *Reserved code point:* Any code point of the Unicode Standard that is reserved for future assignment. Also known as an *unassigned code point.*

- Surrogate code points and noncharacters are considered assigned code points, but not assigned characters.
- For a summary classification of reserved and other types of code points, see *Table 2-3.*

In general, a conforming process may indicate the presence of a code point whose use has not been designated (for example, by showing a missing glyph in rendering or by signaling an appropriate error in a streaming protocol), even though it is forbidden by the standard from *interpreting* that code point as an abstract character.

D16 *Higher-level protocol:* Any agreement on the interpretation of Unicode characters that extends beyond the scope of this standard.

- Such an agreement need not be formally announced in data; it may be implicit in the context.
- The specification of some Unicode algorithms may limit the scope of what a conformant higher-level protocol may do.

D17 *Unicode algorithm:* The logical description of a process used to achieve a specified result involving Unicode characters.

- This definition, as used in the Unicode Standard and other publications of the Unicode Consortium, is intentionally broad so as to allow precise logical description of required results, without constraining implementations to follow the precise steps of that logical description.

D18 *Named Unicode algorithm:* A Unicode algorithm that is specified in the Unicode Standard or in other standards published by the Unicode Consortium and that is given an explicit name for ease of reference.

- Named Unicode algorithms are cited in titlecase in the Unicode Standard.
- When referenced outside the context of the Unicode Standard, it is customary to prepend the word "Unicode" to the name of the algorithm.

Table 3-1 lists the named Unicode algorithms and indicates the locations of their specifications. Details regarding conformance to these algorithms and any restrictions they place on the scope of allowable tailoring by higher-level protocols can be found in the specifications. In some cases, a named Unicode algorithm is provided for information only.

Table 3-1. Named Unicode Algorithms

Name	Description
Canonical Ordering	*Section 3.11*
Hangul Syllable Boundary Determination	*Section 3.12*
Hangul Syllable Composition	*Section 3.12*
Hangul Syllable Decomposition	*Section 3.12*
Hangul Syllable Name Generation	*Section 3.12*
Default Case Conversion	*Section 3.13*
Default Case Detection	*Section 3.13*
Default Caseless Matching	*Section 3.13* and *Section 5.18*
Bidirectional Algorithm	UAX #9
Line Breaking Algorithm	UAX #14
Normalization Algorithm	UAX #15
Grapheme Cluster Boundary Determination	UAX #29
Word Boundary Determination	UAX #29
Sentence Boundary Determination	UAX #29
Default Identifier Determination	UAX #31
Alternative Identifier Determination	UAX #31
Pattern Syntax Determination	UAX #31
Identifier Normalization	UAX #31
Identifier Case Folding	UAX #31
Standard Compression Scheme for Unicode (SCSU)	UTS #6
Collation Algorithm (UCA)	UTS #10

3.5 Properties

The Unicode Standard specifies many different types of character properties. This section provides the basic definitions related to character properties.

The actual values of Unicode character properties are specified in the Unicode Character Database. See *Section 4.1, Unicode Character Database*, for an overview of those data files. *Chapter 4, Character Properties*, contains more detailed descriptions of some particular, important character properties. Additional properties that are specific to particular characters (such as the definition and use of the *right-to-left override* character or *zero width space*) are discussed in the relevant sections of this standard.

The interpretation of some properties (such as the case of a character) is independent of context, whereas the interpretation of other properties (such as directionality) is applicable to a character sequence as a whole, rather than to the individual characters that compose the sequence.

Types of Properties

D19 *Property:* A named attribute of an entity in the Unicode Standard, associated with a defined set of values.

D20 *Code point property:* A property of code points.

- Code point properties refer to attributes of code points per se, based on architectural considerations of this standard, irrespective of any particular encoded character.
- Thus the Surrogate property and the Noncharacter property are code point properties.

D21 *Abstract character property:* A property of abstract characters.

- Abstract character properties refer to attributes of abstract characters per se, based on their independent existence as elements of writing systems or other notational systems, irrespective of their encoding in the Unicode Standard.
- Thus the Alphabetic property, the Punctuation property, the Hex_Digit property, the Numeric_Value property, and so on are properties of abstract characters and are associated with those characters whether encoded in the Unicode Standard or in any other character encoding—or even prior to their being encoded in any character encoding standard.

D22 *Encoded character property:* A property of encoded characters in the Unicode Standard.

- For each encoded character property there is a mapping from every code point to some value in the set of values associated with that property.

Encoded character properties are defined this way to facilitate the implementation of character property APIs based on the Unicode Character Database. Typically, an API will take a property and a code point as input, and will return a value for that property as output, interpreting it as the "character property" for the "character" encoded at that code point. However, to be useful, such APIs must return meaningful values for unassigned code points, as well as for encoded characters.

In some instances an encoded character property in the Unicode Standard is exactly equivalent to a code point property. For example, the Pattern_Syntax property simply defines a range of code points that are reserved for pattern syntax. (See Unicode Standard Annex #31, "Identifier and Pattern Syntax.")

In other instances, an encoded character property directly reflects an abstract character property, but extends the domain of the property to include all code points, including unassigned code points. For Boolean properties, such as the Hex_Digit property, typically an encoded character property will be true for the encoded characters with that abstract character property and will be false for all other code points, including unassigned code points, noncharacters, private-use characters, and encoded characters for which the abstract character property is inapplicable or irrelevant.

However, in many instances, an encoded character property is semantically complex and may telescope together values associated with a number of abstract character properties and/or code point properties. The General_Category property is an example—it contains values associated with several abstract character properties (such as Letter, Punctuation, and Symbol) as well as code point properties (such as \p{gc=Cs} for the Surrogate code point property).

In the text of this standard the terms "Unicode character property," "character property," and "property" without qualifier generally refer to an encoded character property, unless otherwise indicated.

A list of the encoded character properties formally considered to be a part of the Unicode Standard can be found in PropertyAliases.txt in the Unicode Character Database. See also "Property Aliases" later in this section.

Property Values

D23 *Property value:* One of the set of values associated with an encoded character property.

- For example, the East_Asian_Width [EAW] property has the possible values "Narrow", "Neutral", "Wide", "Ambiguous", and "Unassigned".

A list of the values associated with encoded character properties in the Unicode Standard can be found in PropertyValueAliases.txt in the Unicode Character Database. See also "Property Aliases" later in this section.

D24 *Explicit property value:* A value for an encoded character property that is explicitly associated with a code point in one of the data files of the Unicode Character Database.

D25 *Implicit property value:* A value for an encoded character property that is given by a generic rule or by an "otherwise" clause in one of the data files of the Unicode Character Database.

- Implicit property values are used to avoid having to explicitly list values for more than 1 million code points (most of them unassigned) for every property.

D26 *Default property value:* The value (or in some cases small set of values) of a property associated with unassigned code points or with encoded characters for which the property is irrelevant.

- For example, for most Boolean properties, "false" is the default property value. In such cases, the default property value used for unassigned code points may be the same value that is used for many assigned characters as well.
- Some properties, particularly enumerated properties, specify a particular, unique value as their default value. For example, "XX" is the default property value for the Line_Break property.
- A default property value is typically defined implicitly, to avoid having to repeat long lists of unassigned code points.
- In the case of some properties with arbitrary string values, the default property value is an implied null value. For example, the fact that there is no Unicode character name for unassigned code points is equivalent to saying that the default property value for the Name property for an unassigned code point is a null string.
- In some instances, an encoded character property may have multiple default values. For example, the Bidi_Class property defines a range of unassigned code points as having the "R" value, another range of unassigned code points as having the "AL" value, and the otherwise case as having the "L" value.

Classification of Properties by Their Values

D27 *Enumerated property:* A property with a small set of named values.

- As characters are added to the Unicode Standard, the set of values may need to be extended in the future, but enumerated properties have a relatively fixed set of possible values.

D28 *Closed enumeration:* An enumerated property for which the set of values is closed and will not be extended for future versions of the Unicode Standard.

- Currently, the General Category is the only closed enumeration, except for the Boolean properties.

D29 *Boolean property:* A closed enumerated property whose set of values is limited to "true" and "false".

- The presence or absence of the property is the essential information.

D30 *Numeric property:* A numeric property is a property whose value is a number that can take on any integer or real value.

- An example is the Numeric_Value property. There is no implied limit to the number of possible distinct values for the property, except the limitations on representing integers or real numbers in computers.

D31 *String-valued property:* A property whose value is a string.

- The Canonical_Decomposition property is a string-valued property.

D32 *Catalog property:* A property that is an enumerated property, typically unrelated to an algorithm, that may be extended in each successive version of the Unicode Standard.

- Examples are the Age and Block properties. Additional values for both may be added each time a new version of the Unicode Standard adds new characters or blocks.

Normative and Informative Properties

Unicode character properties are divided into those that are normative and those that are informative.

D33 *Normative property:* A Unicode character property used in the specification of the standard.

Specification that a character property is *normative* means that implementations which claim conformance to a particular version of the Unicode Standard and which make use of that particular property must follow the specifications of the standard for that property for the implementation to be conformant. For example, the directionality property (bidirectional character type) is required for conformance whenever rendering text that requires bidirectional layout, such as Arabic or Hebrew.

Whenever a normative process depends on a property in a specified way, that property is designated as normative.

The fact that a given Unicode character property is normative does *not* mean that the values of the property will never change for particular characters. Corrections and extensions to the standard in the future may require minor changes to normative values, even though the Unicode Technical Committee strives to minimize such changes. See also "Stability of Properties" later in this section.

Some of the normative Unicode algorithms depend critically on particular property values for their behavior. Normalization, for example, defines an aspect of textual interoperability that many applications rely on to be absolutely stable. As a result, some of the normative properties disallow any kind of overriding by higher-level protocols. Thus the decomposition of Unicode characters is both normative and *not overridable*; no higher-level protocol may override these values, because to do so would result in non-interoperable results for the normalization of Unicode text. Other normative properties, such as case mapping, are *overridable* by higher-level protocols, because their intent is to provide a common basis for behavior. Nevertheless, they may require tailoring for particular local cultural conventions or particular implementations.

Some important normative character properties of the Unicode Standard are listed in *Table 3-2*, with an indication of which sections in the standard provide a general description of the properties and their use. Other normative properties are documented in the Unicode Character Database. In all cases, the Unicode Character Database provides the definitive list of character properties and the exact list of property value assignments for each version of the standard. A list of additional special character properties can be found in *Section 4.12, Characters with Unusual Properties.*

Table 3-2. Normative Character Properties

Property	Description
Bidi_Class (directionality)	UAX #9 and *Section 4.4*
Bidi_Mirrored	*Section 4.7* and UAX #9
Block	*Chapter 17*
Canonical_Combining_Class	*Section 3.11*, *Section 4.3*, and UAX #15
Case-related properties	*Section 3.13*, *Section 4.2*, and *Chapter 17*
Composition_Exclusion	UAX #15
Decomposition_Mapping	*Chapter 3*, *Chapter 17*, and UAX #15
Default_Ignorable_Code_Point	*Section 5.20*
Deprecated	*Section 3.1*
General_Category	*Section 4.5*
Hangul_Syllable_Type	*Section 3.12* and UAX #29
Jamo_Short_Name	*Section 3.12*
Joining_Type and Joining_Group	*Section 8.2*
Name	*Chapter 17*
Noncharacter_Code_Point	*Section 16.7*
Numeric_Value	*Section 4.6*
White_Space	UCD.html

D34 *Overridable property:* A normative property whose values may be overridden by conformant higher-level protocols.

- For example, the Canonical_Decomposition property is not overridable. The Uppercase property can be overridden.

D35 *Informative property:* A Unicode character property whose values are provided for information only.

A conformant implementation of the Unicode Standard is free to use or change informative property values as it may require, while remaining conformant to the standard. An implementer always has the option of establishing a protocol to convey the fact that informative properties are being used in distinct ways.

Informative properties capture expert implementation experience. When an informative property is explicitly specified in the Unicode Character Database, its use is strongly recommended for implementations to encourage comparable behavior between implementations. Note that it is possible for an informative property in one version of the Unicode Standard to become a normative property in a subsequent version of the standard if its use starts to acquire conformance implications in some part of the standard.

Table 3-3 provides a partial list of the more important informative character properties. For a complete listing, see the Unicode Character Database.

Table 3-3. Informative Character Properties

Property	Description
Dash	*Section 6.2* and *Table 6-3*
East_Asian_Width	*Section 12.4* and UAX #11
Letter-related properties	*Section 4.10*
Line_Break	*Section 16.1*, *Section 16.2*, and UAX #14
Mathematical	*Section 15.4*
Script	UAX #24
Space	*Section 6.2* and *Table 6-2*
Unicode_1_Name	*Section 4.9*

D36 *Provisional property:* A Unicode character property whose values are unapproved and tentative, and which may be incomplete or otherwise not in a usable state.

- Provisional properties may be removed from future versions of the standard, without prior notice.

Some of the information provided about characters in the Unicode Character Database constitutes provisional data. This data may capture partial or preliminary information. It may contain errors or omissions, or otherwise not be ready for systematic use; however, it is included in the data files for distribution partly to encourage review and improvement of the information. For example, a number of the tags in the Unihan.txt file provide provisional property values of various sorts about Han characters.

The data files of the Unicode Character Database may also contain various annotations and comments about characters, and those annotations and comments should be considered provisional. Implementations should not attempt to parse annotations and comments out of the data files and treat them as informative character properties per se.

Context Dependence

D37 *Context-dependent property:* A property that applies to a code point in the context of a longer code point sequence.

- For example, the lowercase mapping of a Greek sigma depends on the context of the surrounding characters.

D38 *Context-independent property:* A property that is not context dependent; it applies to a code point in isolation.

Stability of Properties

D39 *Stable transformation:* A transformation *T* on a property *P* is stable with respect to an algorithm *A* if the result of the algorithm on the transformed property *A*(*T*(*P*)) is the same as the original result *A*(*P*) for all code points.

D40 *Stable property:* A property is stable with respect to a particular algorithm or process as long as possible changes in the assignment of property values are restricted in such a manner that the result of the algorithm on the property continues to be the same as the original result for all previously assigned code points.

- For example, while the absolute values of the canonical combining classes are *not* guaranteed to be the same between versions of the Unicode Standard, their relative values will be maintained. As a result, the Canonical Combining Class, while not immutable, is a stable property with respect to the Normalization Forms as defined in Unicode Standard Annex #15, "Unicode Normalization Forms."
- As new characters are assigned to previously unassigned code points, the replacement of any default values for these code points with actual property values must maintain stability.

D41 *Fixed property:* A property whose values (other than a default value), once associated with a specific code point, are fixed and will not be changed, except to correct obvious or clerical errors.

- For a fixed property, any default values can be replaced without restriction by actual property values as new characters are assigned to previously unassigned code points. Examples of fixed properties include Age and Hangul_Syllable_Type.
- Designating a property as fixed does not imply stability or immutability (see "Stability" in *Section 3.1, Versions of the Unicode Standard*). While the age of a character, for example, is established by the version of the Unicode Standard to which it was added, errors in the published listing of the property value could be corrected. For some other properties, explicit stability guarantees prohibit the correction even of such errors.

D42 *Immutable property:* A fixed property that is also subject to a stability guarantee preventing *any* change in the published listing of property values other than assignment of new values to formerly unassigned code points.

- An immutable property is trivially stable with respect to *all* algorithms.
- An example of an immutable property is the Unicode character name itself. Because character names are values of an immutable property, misspellings and incorrect names will *never* be corrected clerically. Any errata will be noted in a comment in the character names list and, where needed, an informative character name alias will be provided.

- When an encoded character property representing a code point property is immutable, none of its values can ever change. This follows from the fact that the code points themselves do not change, and the status of the property is unaffected by whether a particular abstract character is encoded at a code point later. An example of such a property is the Pattern_Syntax property; all values of that property are unchangeable for all code points, forever.
- In the more typical case of an immutable property, the values for existing encoded characters cannot change, but when a new character is encoded, the formerly unassigned code point changes from having a default value for the property to having one of its nondefault values. Once that nondefault value is published, it can no longer be changed.

D43 *Stabilized property:* A property that is neither extended to new characters nor maintained in any other manner, but that is retained in the Unicode Character Database.

- A stabilized property is also a fixed property.

D44 *Deprecated property:* A property whose use by implementations is discouraged.

- One of the reasons a property may be deprecated is because a different combination of properties better expresses the intended semantics.
- Where sufficiently widespread legacy support exists for the deprecated property, not all implementations may be able to discontinue the use of the deprecated property. In such a case, a deprecated property may be extended to new characters so as to maintain it in a usable and consistent state.

Informative or normative properties in the standard will not be removed even when they are supplanted by other properties or are no longer useful. However, they may be stabilized and/or deprecated.

For a list of stability policies related to character properties, see *Appendix F, Unicode Encoding Stability Policies.*

Simple and Derived Properties

D45 *Simple property:* A Unicode character property whose values are specified directly in the Unicode Character Database (or elsewhere in the standard) and whose values cannot be derived from other simple properties.

D46 *Derived property:* A Unicode character property whose values are algorithmically derived from some combination of simple properties.

The Unicode Character Database lists a number of derived properties explicitly. Even though these values can be derived, they are provided as lists because the derivation may not be trivial and because explicit lists are easier to understand, reference, and implement. Good examples of derived properties include the ID_Start and ID_Continue properties, which can be used to specify a formal identifier syntax for Unicode characters. The details of how derived properties are computed can be found in the documentation for the Unicode Character Database.

Property Aliases

To enable normative references to Unicode character properties, formal aliases for properties and for property values are defined as part of the Unicode Character Database.

D47 *Property alias:* A unique identifier for a particular Unicode character property.

- The identifiers used for property aliases contain only ASCII alphanumeric characters or the underscore character.
- Short and long forms for each property alias are defined. The short forms are typically just two or three characters long to facilitate their use as attributes for tags in markup languages. For example, "General_Category" is the long form and "gc" is the short form of the property alias for the General Category property.
- Property aliases are defined in the file PropertyAliases.txt in the Unicode Character Database.
- Property aliases of normative properties are themselves normative.

D48 *Property value alias:* A unique identifier for a particular enumerated value for a particular Unicode character property.

- The identifiers used for property value aliases contain only ASCII alphanumeric characters or the underscore character, or have the special value "n/a".
- Short and long forms for property value aliases are defined. For example, "Currency_Symbol" is the long form and "Sc" is the short form of the property value alias for the currency symbol value of the General Category property.
- Property value aliases are defined in the file PropertyValueAliases.txt in the Unicode Character Database.
- Property value aliases are unique identifiers only in the context of the particular property with which they are associated. The same identifier string might be associated with an entirely different value for a different property. The combination of a property alias and a property value alias is, however, guaranteed to be unique.
- Property value aliases referring to values of normative properties are themselves normative.

The property aliases and property value aliases can be used, for example, in XML formats of property data, for regular-expression property tests, and in other programmatic textual descriptions of Unicode property data. Thus "gc=Lu" is a formal way of specifying that the General Category of a character (using the property alias "gc") has the value of being an uppercase letter (using the property value alias "Lu").

Private Use

D49 *Private-use code point:* Code points in the ranges U+E000..U+F8FF, U+F0000..U+FFFFD, and U+100000..U+10FFFD.

- Private-use code points are considered to be assigned characters, but the abstract characters associated with them have no interpretation specified by this standard. They can be given any interpretation by conformant processes.
- Private-use code points may be given default property values, but these default values are overridable by higher-level protocols that give those private-use code points a specific interpretation.

3.6 Combination

D50 *Graphic character:* A character with the General Category of Letter (L), Combining Mark (M), Number (N), Punctuation (P), Symbol (S), or Space Separator (Zs).

- Graphic characters specifically exclude the line and paragraph separators (Zl, Zp), as well as the characters with the General Category of Other (Cn, Cs, Cc, Cf).
- The interpretation of private-use characters (Co) as graphic characters or not is determined by the implementation.
- For more information, see *Chapter 2, General Structure*, especially *Section 2.4, Code Points and Characters*, and *Table 2-3*.

D51 *Base character:* Any graphic character except for those with the General Category of Combining Mark (M).

- Most Unicode characters are base characters. In terms of General Category values, a base character is any code point that has one of the following categories: Letter (L), Number (N), Punctuation (P), Symbol (S), or Space Separator (Zs).
- Base characters do not include control characters or format controls.
- Base characters are independent graphic characters, but this does not preclude the presentation of base characters from adopting different contextual forms or participating in ligatures.
- The interpretation of private-use characters (Co) as base characters or not is determined by the implementation. However, the default interpretation of private-use characters should be as base characters, in the absence of other information.

D52 *Combining character:* A character with the General Category of Combining Mark (M).

- Combining characters consist of all characters with the General Category values of Spacing Combining Mark (Mc), Nonspacing Mark (Mn), and Enclosing Mark (Me).
- All characters with non-zero canonical combining class are combining characters, but the reverse is not the case: there are combining characters with a zero canonical combining class.
- The interpretation of private-use characters (Co) as combining characters or not is determined by the implementation.
- These characters are not normally used in isolation unless they are being described. They include such characters as accents, diacritics, Hebrew points, Arabic vowel signs, and Indic matras.
- The graphic positioning of a combining character depends on the last preceding base character, unless they are separated by a character that is neither a combining character nor either ZERO WIDTH JOINER or ZERO WIDTH NON-JOINER. The combining character is said to *apply* to that base character.
- There may be no such base character, such as when a combining character is at the start of text or follows a control or format character—for example, a carriage return, tab, or RIGHT-LEFT MARK. In such cases, the combining characters are called *isolated combining characters*.
- With isolated combining characters or when a process is unable to perform graphical combination, a process may present a combining character without graphical combination; that is, it may present it as if it were a base character.
- The representative images of combining characters are depicted with a dotted circle in the code charts. When presented in graphical combination with a preceding base character, that base character is intended to appear in the position occupied by the dotted circle.

D53 *Nonspacing mark:* A combining character with the General Category of Nonspacing Mark (Mn) or Enclosing Mark (Me).

- The position of a nonspacing mark in presentation depends on its base character. It generally does not consume space along the visual baseline in and of itself.
- Such characters may be large enough to affect the placement of their base character relative to preceding and succeeding base characters. For example, a circumflex applied to an "i" may affect spacing ("î"), as might the character U+20DD COMBINING ENCLOSING CIRCLE.

D54 *Enclosing mark:* A nonspacing mark with the General Category of Enclosing Mark (Me).

- Enclosing marks are a subclass of nonspacing marks that surround a base character, rather than merely being placed over, under, or through it.

D55 *Spacing mark:* A combining character that is not a nonspacing mark.

- Examples include U+093F DEVANAGARI VOWEL SIGN I. In general, the behavior of spacing marks does not differ greatly from that of base characters.
- Spacing marks such as U+0BCA TAMIL VOWEL SIGN O may appear on both sides of a base character, but are not enclosing marks.

D56 *Combining character sequence:* A maximal character sequence consisting of either a base character followed by a sequence of one or more characters where each is a combining character, ZERO WIDTH JOINER, or ZERO WIDTH NON-JOINER; or a sequence of one or more characters where each is a combining character, ZERO WIDTH JOINER, or ZERO WIDTH NON-JOINER.

- When identifying a combining character sequence in Unicode text, the definition of the combining character sequence is applied maximally. For example, in the sequence <c, dot-below, caron, acute, a>, the entire sequence <c, dot-below, caron, acute> is identified as the combining character sequence, rather than the alternative of identifying <c, dot-below> as a combining character sequence followed by a separate (defective) combining character sequence <caron, acute>.

D57 *Defective combining character sequence:* A combining character sequence that does not start with a base character.

- Defective combining character sequences occur when a sequence of combining characters appears at the start of a string or follows a control or format character. Such sequences are defective from the point of view of handling of combining marks, but are not *ill-formed.* (See D84.)

D58 *Grapheme base:* A character with the property Grapheme_Base, or any standard Korean syllable block.

- Characters with the property Grapheme_Base include all base characters plus most spacing marks.
- The concept of a grapheme base is introduced to simplify discussion of the graphical application of nonspacing marks to other elements of text. A grapheme base may consist of a spacing (combining) mark, which distinguishes it from a base character per se. A grapheme base may also itself consist of a sequence of characters, in the case of the standard Korean syllable block.
- For the definition of standard Korean syllable block, see D117 in *Section 3.12, Conjoining Jamo Behavior.*

D59 *Grapheme extender:* A character with the property Grapheme_Extend.

- Grapheme extender characters consist of all nonspacing marks, ZERO WIDTH JOINER, ZERO WIDTH NON-JOINER, and a small number of spacing marks.

- A grapheme extender can be conceived of primarily as the kind of nonspacing graphical mark that is applied above or below another spacing character.
- ZERO WIDTH JOINER and ZERO WIDTH NON-JOINER are formally defined to be grapheme extenders so that their presence does not break up a sequence of other grapheme extenders.
- The small number of spacing marks that have the property Grapheme_Extend are all the second parts of a two-part combining mark.

D60 *Grapheme cluster:* A maximal character sequence consisting of a grapheme base followed by zero or more grapheme extenders or, alternatively, the sequence <CR, LF>.

- The grapheme cluster represents a horizontally segmentable unit of text, consisting of some grapheme base (which may consist of a Korean syllable) together with any number of nonspacing marks applied to it.
- A grapheme cluster is similar, but not identical to a combining character sequence. A combining character sequence starts with a *base* character and extends across any subsequent sequence of combining marks, *nonspacing* or *spacing*. A combining character sequence is most directly relevant to processing issues related to normalization, comparison, and searching.
- A grapheme cluster starts with a *grapheme base* and extends across any subsequent sequence of *nonspacing* marks. A grapheme cluster is most directly relevant to text rendering and such processes as cursor placement and text selection in editing.
- In most processing using character properties, a grapheme behaves as if it were a single character cluster with the same properties as the grapheme base. For example, <x, macron> behaves in line breaking or bidirectional layout as if it were the character x.
- For many processes, a grapheme cluster behaves as if it were a single character with the same properties as its base character. Effectively, nonspacing marks apply graphically to the base character but do not change the properties of the base character.

D61 *Extended grapheme cluster:* The text between grapheme cluster boundaries as specified by Unicode Standard Annex #29, "Text Boundaries."

- Extended grapheme clusters are either a grapheme cluster, a single character such as a control character, or the sequence <CR, LF>. They do not have linguistic significance, but are used to break up a string of text into units for processing.

3.7 Decomposition

D62 *Decomposition mapping:* A mapping from a character to a sequence of one or more characters that is a canonical or compatibility equivalent, and that is listed in the character names list or described in *Section 3.12, Conjoining Jamo Behavior.*

- Each character has at most one decomposition mapping. The mappings in *Section 3.12, Conjoining Jamo Behavior*, are canonical mappings. The mappings in the character names list are identified as either canonical or compatibility mappings (see *Section 17.1, Character Names List*).

D63 *Decomposable character:* A character that is equivalent to a sequence of one or more other characters, according to the decomposition mappings found in the Unicode Character Database, and those described in *Section 3.12, Conjoining Jamo Behavior.*

- A decomposable character is also referred to as a *precomposed* character or *composite* character.
- The decomposition mappings from the Unicode Character Database are also given in *Section 17.1, Character Names List.*

D64 *Decomposition:* A sequence of one or more characters that is equivalent to a decomposable character. A full decomposition of a character sequence results from decomposing each of the characters in the sequence until no characters can be further decomposed.

Compatibility Decomposition

D65 *Compatibility decomposition:* The decomposition of a character that results from recursively applying *both* the compatibility mappings *and* the canonical mappings found in the Unicode Character Database, and those described in *Section 3.12, Conjoining Jamo Behavior*, until no characters can be further decomposed, and then reordering nonspacing marks according to *Section 3.11, Canonical Ordering Behavior.*

- The decomposition mappings from the Unicode Character Database are also given in *Section 17.1, Character Names List.*
- Some compatibility decompositions remove formatting information.

D66 *Compatibility decomposable character:* A character whose compatibility decomposition is not identical to its canonical decomposition. It may also be known as a *compatibility precomposed* character or a *compatibility composite* character.

- For example, U+00B5 MICRO SIGN has no canonical decomposition mapping, so its canonical decomposition is the same as the character itself. It has a compatibility decomposition to U+03BC GREEK SMALL LETTER MU. Because MICRO sign has a compatibility decomposition that is not equal to its canonical decomposition, it is a compatibility decomposable character.

- For example, U+03D3 greek upsilon with acute and hook symbol canonically decomposes to the sequence <U+03D2 greek upsilon with hook symbol, U+0301 combining acute accent>. That sequence has a compatibility decomposition of <U+03A5 greek capital letter upsilon, U+0301 combining acute accent>. Because greek upsilon with acute and hook symbol has a compatibility decomposition that is not equal to its canonical decomposition, it is a compatibility decomposable character.
- This term should not be confused with the term "compatibility character," which is discussed in *Section 2.3, Compatibility Characters.*
- Many compatibility decomposable characters are included in the Unicode Standard solely to represent distinctions in other base standards. They support transmission and processing of legacy data. Their use is discouraged other than for legacy data or other special circumstances.
- Some widely used and indispensable characters, such as NBSP, are compatibility decomposable characters for historical reasons. Their use is not discouraged.
- A large number of compatibility decomposable characters are used in phonetic and mathematical notation, where their use is not discouraged.
- For historical reasons, some characters that might have been given a compatibility decomposition were not, in fact, decomposed. Stability of normalization prevents adding decompositions in the future.
- Replacing a compatibility decomposable character by its compatibility decomposition may lose round-trip convertibility with a base standard.

D67 *Compatibility equivalent:* Two character sequences are said to be compatibility equivalents if their full compatibility decompositions are identical.

Canonical Decomposition

D68 *Canonical decomposition:* The decomposition of a character that results from recursively applying the canonical mappings found in the Unicode Character Database and those described in *Section 3.12, Conjoining Jamo Behavior*, until no characters can be further decomposed, and then reordering nonspacing marks according to *Section 3.11, Canonical Ordering Behavior.*

- The decomposition mappings from the Unicode Character Database are also printed in *Section 17.1, Character Names List.*
- A canonical decomposition does not remove formatting information.

D69 *Canonical decomposable character:* A character that is not identical to its canonical decomposition. It may also be known as a *canonical precomposed* character or a *canonical composite* character.

- For example, U+00E0 LATIN SMALL LETTER A WITH GRAVE is a canonical decomposable character because its canonical decomposition is to the sequence <U+0061 LATIN SMALL LETTER A, U+0300 COMBINING GRAVE ACCENT>. U+212A KELVIN SIGN is a canonical decomposable character because its canonical decomposition is to U+004B LATIN CAPITAL LETTER K.

D70 *Canonical equivalent:* Two character sequences are said to be canonical equivalents if their full canonical decompositions are identical.

- For example, the sequences <*o, combining-diaeresis*> and <*ö*> are canonical equivalents. Canonical equivalence is a Unicode property. It should not be confused with language-specific collation or matching, which may add other equivalencies. For example, in Swedish, *ö* is treated as a completely different letter from *o* and is collated after *z*. In German, *ö* is weakly equivalent to *oe* and is collated with *oe*. In English, *ö* is just an *o* with a diacritic that indicates that it is pronounced separately from the previous letter (as in *coöperate*) and is collated with *o*.
- By definition, all canonical-equivalent sequences are also compatibility-equivalent sequences.

For information on the use of decomposition in normalization, see Unicode Standard Annex #15, "Unicode Normalization Forms."

3.8 Surrogates

D71 *High-surrogate code point:* A Unicode code point in the range U+D800 to U+DBFF.

D72 *High-surrogate code unit:* A 16-bit code unit in the range $D800_{16}$ to $DBFF_{16}$, used in UTF-16 as the leading code unit of a surrogate pair.

D73 *Low-surrogate code point:* A Unicode code point in the range U+DC00 to U+DFFF.

D74 *Low-surrogate code unit:* A 16-bit code unit in the range $DC00_{16}$ to $DFFF_{16}$, used in UTF-16 as the trailing code unit of a surrogate pair.

- High-surrogate and low-surrogate code points are designated only for that use.
- High-surrogate and low-surrogate code units are used *only* in the context of the UTF-16 character encoding form.

D75 *Surrogate pair:* A representation for a single abstract character that consists of a sequence of two 16-bit code units, where the first value of the pair is a high-surrogate code unit and the second value is a low-surrogate code unit.

- Surrogate pairs are used only in UTF-16. (See *Section 3.9, Unicode Encoding Forms.*)
- Isolated surrogate code units have no interpretation on their own. Certain other isolated code units in other encoding forms also have no interpretation on their own. For example, the isolated byte 80_{16} has no interpretation in UTF-8; it can be used *only* as part of a multibyte sequence. (See *Table 3-7.*)
- Sometimes high-surrogate code units are referred to as *leading surrogates*. Low-surrogate code units are then referred to as *trailing surrogates*. This is analogous to usage in UTF-8, which has *leading bytes* and *trailing bytes*.
- For more information, see *Section 16.6, Surrogates Area*, and *Section 5.4, Handling Surrogate Pairs in UTF-16.*

3.9 Unicode Encoding Forms

The Unicode Standard supports three character encoding forms: UTF-32, UTF-16, and UTF-8. Each encoding form maps the Unicode code points U+0000..U+D7FF and U+E000..U+10FFFF to unique code unit sequences. The size of the code unit is specified for each encoding form. This section presents the formal definition of each of these encoding forms.

D76 *Unicode scalar value:* Any Unicode code point except high-surrogate and low-surrogate code points.

- As a result of this definition, the set of Unicode scalar values consists of the ranges 0 to $D7FF_{16}$ and $E000_{16}$ to $10FFFF_{16}$, inclusive.

D77 *Code unit:* The minimal bit combination that can represent a unit of encoded text for processing or interchange.

- Code units are particular units of computer storage. Other character encoding standards typically use code units defined as 8-bit units—that is, *octets*. The Unicode Standard uses 8-bit code units in the UTF-8 encoding form, 16-bit code units in the UTF-16 encoding form, and 32-bit code units in the UTF-32 encoding form.
- A code unit is also referred to as a *code value* in the information industry.
- In the Unicode Standard, specific values of some code units cannot be used to represent an encoded character in isolation. This restriction applies to isolated surrogate code units in UTF-16 and to the bytes 80–FF in UTF-8. Similar restrictions apply for the implementations of other character encoding standards; for example, the bytes 81–9F, E0–FC in SJIS (Shift-JIS) cannot represent an encoded character by themselves.

- For information on use of `wchar_t` or other programming language types to represent Unicode code units, see "ANSI/ISO C wchar_t" in *Section 5.2, Programming Languages and Data Types.*

D78 *Code unit sequence:* An ordered sequence of one or more code units.

- When the code unit is an 8-bit unit, a code unit sequence may also be referred to as a *byte sequence.*
- A code unit sequence may consist of a single code unit.
- In the context of programming languages, the *value* of a *string* data type basically consists of a code unit sequence. Informally, a code unit sequence is itself just referred to as a *string*, and a *byte sequence* is referred to as a *byte string*. Care must be taken in making this terminological equivalence, however, because the formally defined concept of a string may have additional requirements or complications in programming languages. For example, a *string* is defined as a *pointer to char* in the C language and is conventionally terminated with a NULL character. In object-oriented languages, a *string* is a complex object, with associated methods, and its value may or may not consist of merely a code unit sequence.
- Depending on the structure of a character encoding standard, it may be necessary to use a code unit sequence (of more than one unit) to represent a single encoded character. For example, the code unit in SJIS is a byte: encoded characters such as "a" can be represented with a single byte in SJIS, whereas ideographs require a sequence of two code units. The Unicode Standard also makes use of code unit sequences whose length is greater than one code unit.

D79 A *Unicode encoding form* assigns each Unicode scalar value to a unique code unit sequence.

- For historical reasons, the Unicode encoding forms are also referred to as *Unicode* (or *UCS*) *transformation formats* (UTF). That term is actually ambiguous between its usage for encoding forms and encoding schemes.
- The mapping of the set of Unicode scalar values to the set of code unit sequences for a Unicode encoding form is *one-to-one.* This property guarantees that a reverse mapping can always be derived. Given the mapping of any Unicode scalar value to a particular code unit sequence for a given encoding form, one can derive the original Unicode scalar value unambiguously from that code unit sequence.
- The mapping of the set of Unicode scalar values to the set of code unit sequences for a Unicode encoding form is not *onto.* In other words, for any given encoding form, there exist code unit sequences that have no associated Unicode scalar value.
- To ensure that the mapping for a Unicode encoding form is one-to-one, *all* Unicode scalar values, including those corresponding to noncharacter code

points and unassigned code points, must be mapped to unique code unit sequences. Note that this requirement does not extend to high-surrogate and low-surrogate code points, which are excluded by definition from the set of Unicode scalar values.

D80 *Unicode string:* A code unit sequence containing code units of a particular Unicode encoding form.

- In the rawest form, Unicode strings may be implemented simply as arrays of the appropriate integral data type, consisting of a sequence of code units lined up one immediately after the other.
- A single Unicode string must contain only code units from a single Unicode encoding form. It is not permissible to mix forms within a string.

D81 *Unicode 8-bit string:* A Unicode string containing only UTF-8 code units.

D82 *Unicode 16-bit string:* A Unicode string containing only UTF-16 code units.

D83 *Unicode 32-bit string:* A Unicode string containing only UTF-32 code units.

D84 *Ill-formed:* A Unicode code unit sequence that purports to be in a Unicode encoding form is called *ill-formed* if and only if it does *not* follow the specification of that Unicode encoding form.

- Any code unit sequence that would correspond to a code point outside the defined range of Unicode scalar values would, for example, be ill-formed.
- UTF-8 has some strong constraints on the possible byte ranges for leading and trailing bytes. A violation of those constraints would produce a code unit sequence that could not be mapped to a Unicode scalar value, resulting in an ill-formed code unit sequence.

D85 *Well-formed:* A Unicode code unit sequence that purports to be in a Unicode encoding form is called *well-formed* if and only if it *does* follow the specification of that Unicode encoding form.

- A Unicode code unit sequence that consists entirely of a sequence of well-formed Unicode code unit sequences (all of the same Unicode encoding form) is itself a well-formed Unicode code unit sequence.

D86 *Well-formed UTF-8 code unit sequence:* A well-formed Unicode code unit sequence of UTF-8 code units.

D87 *Well-formed UTF-16 code unit sequence:* A well-formed Unicode code unit sequence of UTF-16 code units.

D88 *Well-formed UTF-32 code unit sequence:* A well-formed Unicode code unit sequence of UTF-32 code units.

D89 *In a Unicode encoding form:* A Unicode string is said to be *in* a particular Unicode encoding form if and only if it consists of a well-formed Unicode code unit sequence of that Unicode encoding form.

- A Unicode string consisting of a well-formed UTF-8 code unit sequence is said to be *in UTF-8*. Such a Unicode string is referred to as a *valid UTF-8 string*, or a *UTF-8 string* for short.
- A Unicode string consisting of a well-formed UTF-16 code unit sequence is said to be *in UTF-16*. Such a Unicode string is referred to as a *valid UTF-16 string*, or a *UTF-16 string* for short.
- A Unicode string consisting of a well-formed UTF-32 code unit sequence is said to be *in UTF-32*. Such a Unicode string is referred to as a *valid UTF-32 string*, or a *UTF-32 string* for short.

Unicode strings need not contain well-formed code unit sequences under all conditions. This is equivalent to saying that a particular Unicode string need not be *in* a Unicode encoding form.

- For example, it is perfectly reasonable to talk about an operation that takes the two Unicode 16-bit strings, <004D D800> and <DF02 004D>, each of which contains an ill-formed UTF-16 code unit sequence, and concatenates them to form another Unicode string <004D D800 DF02 004D>, which contains a well-formed UTF-16 code unit sequence. The first two Unicode strings are not *in* UTF-16, but the resultant Unicode string is.
- As another example, the code unit sequence <C0 80 61 F3> is a Unicode 8-bit string, but does not consist of a well-formed UTF-8 code unit sequence. That code unit sequence could not result from the specification of the UTF-8 encoding form and is thus ill-formed. (The same code unit sequence could, of course, be well-formed in the context of some other character encoding standard using 8-bit code units, such as ISO/IEC 8859-1, or vendor code pages.)

If a Unicode string *purports* to be *in* a Unicode encoding form, then it must contain only a well-formed code unit sequence. If there is an ill-formed code unit sequence in a source Unicode string, then a conformant process that verifies that the Unicode string is in a Unicode encoding form must reject the ill-formed code unit sequence. (See conformance clause C9.) For more information, see *Section 2.7, Unicode Strings*.

Table 3-4 gives examples that summarize the three Unicode encoding forms.

Table 3-4. Examples of Unicode Encoding Forms

Code Point	Encoding Form	Code Unit Sequence
U+004D	UTF-32	0000004D
	UTF-16	004D
	UTF-8	4D

Table 3-4. Examples of Unicode Encoding Forms (Continued)

Code Point	Encoding Form	Code Unit Sequence
U+0430	UTF-32	00000430
	UTF-16	0430
	UTF-8	D0 B0
U+4E8C	UTF-32	00004E8C
	UTF-16	4E8C
	UTF-8	E4 BA 8C
U+10302	UTF-32	00010302
	UTF-16	D800 DF02
	UTF-8	F0 90 8C 82

UTF-32

D90 *UTF-32 encoding form:* The Unicode encoding form that assigns each Unicode scalar value to a single unsigned 32-bit code unit with the same numeric value as the Unicode scalar value.

- In UTF-32, the code point sequence <004D, 0430, 4E8C, 10302> is represented as <0000004D 00000430 00004E8C 00010302>.
- Because surrogate code points are not included in the set of Unicode scalar values, UTF-32 code units in the range $0000D800_{16}$..$0000DFFF_{16}$ are ill-formed.
- Any UTF-32 code unit greater than $0010FFFF_{16}$ is ill-formed.

For a discussion of the relationship between UTF-32 and UCS-4 encoding form defined in ISO/IEC 10646, see *Section C.2, Encoding Forms in ISO/IEC 10646.*

UTF-16

D91 *UTF-16 encoding form:* The Unicode encoding form that assigns each Unicode scalar value in the ranges U+0000..U+D7FF and U+E000..U+FFFF to a single unsigned 16-bit code unit with the same numeric value as the Unicode scalar value, and that assigns each Unicode scalar value in the range U+10000..U+10FFFF to a surrogate pair, according to *Table 3-5*.

- In UTF-16, the code point sequence <004D, 0430, 4E8C, 10302> is represented as <004D 0430 4E8C D800 DF02>, where <D800 DF02> corresponds to U+10302.
- Because surrogate code points are not Unicode scalar values, isolated UTF-16 code units in the range $D800_{16}$..$DFFF_{16}$ are ill-formed.

Table 3-5 specifies the bit distribution for the UTF-16 encoding form. Note that for Unicode scalar values equal to or greater than U+10000, UTF-16 uses surrogate pairs. Calculation of the surrogate pair values involves subtraction of 10000_{16}, to account for the starting offset to the scalar value. ISO/IEC 10646 specifies an equivalent UTF-16 encoding form. For details, see *Section C.3, UCS Transformation Formats.*

Table 3-5. UTF-16 Bit Distribution

Scalar Value	UTF-16
xxxxxxxxxxxxxxxx	xxxxxxxxxxxxxxxx
000uuuuuxxxxxxxxxxxxxxxx	110110wwwwxxxxxx 110111xxxxxxxxxx

Note: wwww = uuuuu - 1

UTF-8

D92 *UTF-8 encoding form:* The Unicode encoding form that assigns each Unicode scalar value to an unsigned byte sequence of one to four bytes in length, as specified in *Table 3-6.*

- In UTF-8, the code point sequence <004D, 0430, 4E8C, 10302> is represented as <4D D0 B0 E4 BA 8C F0 90 8C 82>, where <4D> corresponds to U+004D, <D0 B0> corresponds to U+0430, <E4 BA 8C> corresponds to U+4E8C, and <F0 90 8C 82> corresponds to U+10302.
- Any UTF-8 byte sequence that does not match the patterns listed in *Table 3-7* is ill-formed.
- Before the Unicode Standard, Version 3.1, the problematic "non-shortest form" byte sequences in UTF-8 were those where BMP characters could be represented in more than one way. These sequences are ill-formed, because they are not allowed by *Table 3-7.*
- Because surrogate code points are not Unicode scalar values, any UTF-8 byte sequence that would otherwise map to code points D800..DFFF is ill-formed.

Table 3-6 specifies the bit distribution for the UTF-8 encoding form, showing the ranges of Unicode scalar values corresponding to one-, two-, three-, and four-byte sequences. For a discussion of the difference in the formulation of UTF-8 in ISO/IEC 10646, see *Section C.3, UCS Transformation Formats.*

Table 3-6. UTF-8 Bit Distribution

Scalar Value	First Byte	Second Byte	Third Byte	Fourth Byte
00000000 0xxxxxxx	0xxxxxxx			
00000yyy yyxxxxxx	110yyyyy	10xxxxxx		
zzzzyyyy yyxxxxxx	1110zzzz	10yyyyyy	10xxxxxx	
000uuuuu zzzzyyyy yyxxxxxx	11110uuu	10uuzzzz	10yyyyyy	10xxxxxx

Table 3-7 lists all of the byte sequences that are well-formed in UTF-8. A range of byte values such as A0..BF indicates that any byte from A0 to BF (inclusive) is well-formed in that position. Any byte value outside of the ranges listed is ill-formed. For example:

- The byte sequence <C0 AF> is *ill-formed*, because C0 is not well-formed in the "First Byte" column.
- The byte sequence <E0 9F 80> is *ill-formed*, because in the row where E0 is well-formed as a first byte, 9F is not well-formed as a second byte.
- The byte sequence <F4 80 83 92> is *well-formed*, because every byte in that sequence matches a byte range in a row of the table (the last row).

Table 3-7. Well-Formed UTF-8 Byte Sequences

Code Points	First Byte	Second Byte	Third Byte	Fourth Byte
U+0000..U+007F	00..7F			
U+0080..U+07FF	C2..DF	80..BF		
U+0800..U+0FFF	E0	***A0***..BF	80..BF	
U+1000..U+CFFF	E1..EC	80..BF	80..BF	
U+D000..U+D7FF	ED	80..***9F***	80..BF	
U+E000..U+FFFF	EE..EF	80..BF	80..BF	
U+10000..U+3FFFF	F0	***90***..BF	80..BF	80..BF
U+40000..U+FFFFF	F1..F3	80..BF	80..BF	80..BF
U+100000..U+10FFFF	F4	80..***8F***	80..BF	80..BF

In *Table 3-7*, cases where a trailing byte range is not 80..BF are shown in bold italic to draw attention to them. These exceptions to the general pattern occur only in the second byte of a sequence.

As a consequence of the well-formedness conditions specified in *Table 3-7*, the following byte values are disallowed in UTF-8: C0–C1, F5–FF.

Encoding Form Conversion

D93 *Encoding form conversion:* A conversion defined directly between the code unit sequences of one Unicode encoding form and the code unit sequences of another Unicode encoding form.

- In implementations of the Unicode Standard, a typical API will logically convert the input code unit sequence into Unicode scalar values (code points) and then convert those Unicode scalar values into the output code unit sequence. Proper analysis of the encoding forms makes it possible to convert the code units directly, thereby obtaining the same results but with a more efficient process.
- A conformant encoding form conversion will treat any ill-formed code unit sequence as an error condition. (See conformance clause C10.) This guarantees that it will neither interpret nor emit an ill-formed code unit sequence. Any

implementation of encoding form conversion must take this requirement into account, because an encoding form conversion implicitly involves a verification that the Unicode strings being converted do, in fact, contain well-formed code unit sequences.

3.10 Unicode Encoding Schemes

D94 *Unicode encoding scheme:* A specified byte serialization for a Unicode encoding form, including the specification of the handling of a byte order mark (BOM), if allowed.

- For historical reasons, the Unicode encoding schemes are also referred to as *Unicode* (or *UCS*) *transformation formats* (UTF). That term is, however, ambiguous between its usage for encoding forms and encoding schemes.

The Unicode Standard supports seven encoding schemes. This section presents the formal definition of each of these encoding schemes.

D95 *UTF-8 encoding scheme:* The Unicode encoding scheme that serializes a UTF-8 code unit sequence in exactly the same order as the code unit sequence itself.

- In the UTF-8 encoding scheme, the UTF-8 code unit sequence <4D D0 B0 E4 BA 8C F0 90 8C 82> is serialized as <4D D0 B0 E4 BA 8C F0 90 8C 82>.

- Because the UTF-8 encoding form already deals in ordered byte sequences, the UTF-8 encoding scheme is trivial. The byte ordering is already obvious and completely defined by the UTF-8 code unit sequence itself. The UTF-8 encoding scheme is defined merely for completeness of the Unicode character encoding model.

- While there is obviously no need for a byte order signature when using UTF-8, there are occasions when processes convert UTF-16 or UTF-32 data containing a byte order mark into UTF-8. When represented in UTF-8, the byte order mark turns into the byte sequence <EF BB BF>. Its usage at the beginning of a UTF-8 data stream is neither required nor recommended by the Unicode Standard, but its presence does not affect conformance to the UTF-8 encoding scheme. Identification of the <EF BB BF> byte sequence at the beginning of a data stream can, however, be taken as a near-certain indication that the data stream is using the UTF-8 encoding scheme.

D96 *UTF-16BE encoding scheme:* The Unicode encoding scheme that serializes a UTF-16 code unit sequence as a byte sequence in big-endian format.

- In UTF-16BE, the UTF-16 code unit sequence <004D 0430 4E8C D800 DF02> is serialized as <00 4D 04 30 4E 8C D8 00 DF 02>.

- In UTF-16BE, an initial byte sequence <FE FF> is interpreted as U+FEFF ZERO WIDTH NO-BREAK SPACE.

D97 *UTF-16LE encoding scheme:* The Unicode encoding scheme that serializes a UTF-16 code unit sequence as a byte sequence in little-endian format.

- In UTF-16LE, the UTF-16 code unit sequence <004D 0430 4E8C D800 DF02> is serialized as <4D 00 30 04 8C 4E 00 D8 02 DF>.
- In UTF-16LE, an initial byte sequence <FF FE> is interpreted as U+FEFF ZERO WIDTH NO-BREAK SPACE.

D98 *UTF-16 encoding scheme:* The Unicode encoding scheme that serializes a UTF-16 code unit sequence as a byte sequence in either big-endian or little-endian format.

- In the UTF-16 encoding scheme, the UTF-16 code unit sequence <004D 0430 4E8C D800 DF02> is serialized as <FE FF 00 4D 04 30 4E 8C D8 00 DF 02> or <FF FE 4D 00 30 04 8C 4E 00 D8 02 DF> or <00 4D 04 30 4E 8C D8 00 DF 02>.
- In the UTF-16 encoding scheme, an initial byte sequence corresponding to U+FEFF is interpreted as a byte order mark; it is used to distinguish between the two byte orders. An initial byte sequence <FE FF> indicates big-endian order, and an initial byte sequence <FF FE> indicates little-endian order. The BOM is not considered part of the content of the text.
- The UTF-16 encoding scheme may or may not begin with a BOM. However, when there is no BOM, and in the absence of a higher-level protocol, the byte order of the UTF-16 encoding scheme is big-endian.

Table 3-8 gives examples that summarize the three Unicode encoding schemes for the UTF-16 encoding form.

Table 3-8. Summary of UTF-16BE, UTF-16LE, and UTF-16

Code Unit Sequence	Encoding Scheme	Byte Sequence(s)
004D	UTF-16BE	00 4D
	UTF-16LE	4D 00
	UTF-16	FE FF 00 4D FF FE 4D 00 00 4D
0430	UTF-16BE	04 30
	UTF-16LE	30 04
	UTF-16	FE FF 04 30 FF FE 30 04 04 30
4E8C	UTF-16BE	4E 8C
	UTF-16LE	8C 4E
	UTF-16	FE FF 4E 8C FF FE 8C 4E 4E 8C

Table 3-8. Summary of UTF-16BE, UTF-16LE, and UTF-16 (Continued)

Code Unit Sequence	Encoding Scheme	Byte Sequence(s)
D800 DF02	UTF-16BE	D8 00 DF 02
	UTF-16LE	00 D8 02 DF
	UTF-16	FE FF D8 00 DF 02 FF FE 00 D8 02 DF D8 00 DF 02

D99 *UTF-32BE encoding scheme:* The Unicode encoding scheme that serializes a UTF-32 code unit sequence as a byte sequence in big-endian format.

- In UTF-32BE, the UTF-32 code unit sequence <0000004D 00000430 00004E8C 00010302> is serialized as <00 00 00 4D 00 00 04 30 00 00 4E 8C 00 01 03 02>.
- In UTF-32BE, an initial byte sequence <00 00 FE FF> is interpreted as U+FEFF ZERO WIDTH NO-BREAK SPACE.

D100 *UTF-32LE encoding scheme:* The Unicode encoding scheme that serializes a UTF-32 code unit sequence as a byte sequence in little-endian format.

- In UTF-32LE, the UTF-32 code unit sequence <0000004D 00000430 00004E8C 00010302> is serialized as <4D 00 00 00 30 04 00 00 8C 4E 00 00 02 03 01 00>.
- In UTF-32LE, an initial byte sequence <FF FE 00 00> is interpreted as U+FEFF ZERO WIDTH NO-BREAK SPACE.

D101 *UTF-32 encoding scheme:* The Unicode encoding scheme that serializes a UTF-32 code unit sequence as a byte sequence in either big-endian or little-endian format.

- In the UTF-32 encoding scheme, the UTF-32 code unit sequence <0000004D 00000430 00004E8C 00010302> is serialized as <00 00 FE FF 00 00 00 4D 00 00 04 30 00 00 4E 8C 00 01 03 02> or <FF FE 00 00 4D 00 00 00 30 04 00 00 8C 4E 00 00 02 03 01 00> or <00 00 00 4D 00 00 04 30 00 00 4E 8C 00 01 03 02>.
- In the UTF-32 encoding scheme, an initial byte sequence corresponding to U+FEFF is interpreted as a byte order mark; it is used to distinguish between the two byte orders. An initial byte sequence <00 00 FE FF> indicates big-endian order, and an initial byte sequence <FF FE 00 00> indicates little-endian order. The BOM is not considered part of the content of the text.
- The UTF-32 encoding scheme may or may not begin with a BOM. However, when there is no BOM, and in the absence of a higher-level protocol, the byte order of the UTF-32 encoding scheme is big-endian.

Table 3-9 gives examples that summarize the three Unicode encoding schemes for the UTF-32 encoding form.

The terms *UTF-8*, *UTF-16*, and *UTF-32*, when used unqualified, are ambiguous between their sense as Unicode encoding forms or Unicode encoding schemes. For UTF-8, this ambiguity is usually innocuous, because the UTF-8 encoding scheme is trivially derived

Table 3-9. Summary of UTF-32BE, UTF-32LE, and UTF-32

Code Unit Sequence	Encoding Scheme	Byte Sequence(s)
0000004D	UTF-32BE	00 00 00 4D
	UTF-32LE	4D 00 00 00
	UTF-32	00 00 FE FF 00 00 00 4D FF FE 00 00 4D 00 00 00 00 00 00 4D
00000430	UTF-32BE	00 00 04 30
	UTF-32LE	30 04 00 00
	UTF-32	00 00 FE FF 00 00 04 30 FF FE 00 00 30 04 00 00 00 00 04 30
00004E8C	UTF-32BE	00 00 4E 8C
	UTF-32LE	8C 4E 00 00
	UTF-32	00 00 FE FF 00 00 4E 8C FF FE 00 00 8C 4E 00 00 00 00 4E 8C
00010302	UTF-32BE	00 01 03 02
	UTF-32LE	02 03 01 00
	UTF-32	00 00 FE FF 00 01 03 02 FF FE 00 00 02 03 01 00 00 01 03 02

from the byte sequences defined for the UTF-8 encoding form. However, for UTF-16 and UTF-32, the ambiguity is more problematical. As encoding forms, UTF-16 and UTF-32 refer to code units in memory; there is no associated byte orientation, and a BOM is never used. As encoding schemes, UTF-16 and UTF-32 refer to serialized bytes, as for streaming data or in files; they may have either byte orientation, and a BOM may be present.

When the usage of the short terms "UTF-16" or "UTF-32" might be misinterpreted, and where a distinction between their use as referring to Unicode encoding forms or to Unicode encoding schemes is important, the full terms, as defined in this chapter of the Unicode Standard, should be used. For example, use *UTF-16 encoding form* or *UTF-16 encoding scheme.* These terms may also be abbreviated to *UTF-16 CEF* or *UTF-16 CES*, respectively.

When converting between different encoding schemes, extreme care must be taken in handling any initial byte order marks. For example, if one converted a UTF-16 byte serialization with an initial byte order mark to a UTF-8 byte serialization, thereby converting the byte order mark to <EF BB BF> in the UTF-8 form, the <EF BB BF> would now be ambiguous as to its status as a byte order mark (from its source) or as an initial *zero width no-break space.* If the UTF-8 byte serialization were then converted to UTF-16BE and the initial <EF BB BF> were converted to <FE FF>, the interpretation of the U+FEFF character would have been modified by the conversion. This would be nonconformant behavior according to conformance clause C7, because the change between byte serializations would have resulted in modification of the interpretation of the text. This is one reason why the use of the initial byte sequence <EF BB BF> as a signature on UTF-8 byte sequences is not recommended by the Unicode Standard.

3.11 Canonical Ordering Behavior

This section provides a formal statement of canonical ordering behavior, which determines, for the purposes of interpretation, which combining character sequences are to be considered equivalent. A precise definition of equivalence is required so that text containing combining character sequences can be created and interchanged in a predictable way.

When combining sequences contain multiple combining characters, different sequences can contain the same characters, but in a different order. Under certain circumstances two such sequences may be equivalent, even though they differ in the order of the combining characters.

Canonical ordering is a process of specifying a defined order for sequences of combining marks, whereby it is possible to determine definitively which sequences are equivalent and which are not.

Canonical ordering behavior—and more specifically, *canonical ordering*—is a required part of the normative specification of *normalization* for the Unicode Standard. See Unicode Standard Annex #15, "Unicode Normalization Forms."

Canonical ordering is also a required part of the separate specification, Unicode Technical Standard #10, "Unicode Collation Algorithm."

Application of Combining Marks

A number of principles in the Unicode Standard relate to the application of combining marks. These principles are listed in this section, with an indication of which are considered to be normative and which are considered to be guidelines.

In particular, guidelines for rendering of combining marks in conjunction with other characers should be considered as appropriate for defining default rendering behavior, in the absence of more specific information about rendering. It is often the case that combining marks in complex scripts or even particular, general-use nonspacing marks will have rendering requirements that depart significantly from the general guidelines. Rendering processes should, as appropriate, make use of available information about specific typographic practices and conventions so as to produce best rendering of text.

To help in the clarification of the principles regarding the application of combining marks, a distinction is made between *dependence* and *graphical application*.

D102 *Dependence:* A combining mark is said to *depend* on its associated base character.

- The associated base character is the base character in the combining character sequence that a combining mark is part of.

- A combining mark in a defective combining character sequence has no associated base character and thus cannot be said to depend on any particular base character. This is one of the reasons why fallback processing is required for defective combining character sequences.
- Dependence concerns *all* combining marks, including spacing marks and combining marks that have no visible display.

D103 *Graphical application:* A nonspacing mark is said to *apply* to its associated grapheme base.

- The associated grapheme base is the grapheme base in the grapheme cluster that a nonspacing mark is part of.
- A nonspacing mark in a defective combining character sequence is not part of a grapheme cluster and is subject to the same kinds of fallback processing as for any defective combining character sequence.
- Graphic application concerns visual rendering issues and thus is an issue for nonspacing marks that have visible glyphs. Those glyphs interact, in rendering, with their grapheme base.

Throughout the text of the standard, whenever the situation is clear, discussion of combining marks often simply talks about combining marks "applying" to their base. In the prototypical case of a nonspacing accent mark applying to a single base character letter, this simplification is not problematical, because the nonspacing mark both depends (notionally) on its base character and simultaneously applies (graphically) to its grapheme base, affecting its display. The finer distinctions are needed when dealing with the edge cases, such as combining marks that have no display glyph, graphical application of nonspacing marks to Korean syllables, and the behavior of spacing combining marks.

The distinction made here between notional dependence and graphical application does not preclude spacing marks or even sequences of base characters from having effects on neighboring characters in rendering. Thus spacing forms of dependent vowels (*matras*) in Indic scripts may trigger particular kinds of conjunct formation or may be repositioned in ways that influence the rendering of other characters. (See *Chapter 9, South Asian Scripts-I*, for many examples.) Similarly, sequences of base characters may form ligatures in rendering. (See "Cursive Connection and Ligatures" in *Section 16.2, Layout Controls*.)

The following listing specifies the principles regarding application of combining marks. Many of these principles are illustrated in *Section 2.11, Combining Characters*, and *Section 7.9, Combining Marks*.

P1 ***[Normative] Combining character order: Combining characters follow the base character on which they depend.***

- This principle follows from the definition of a combining character sequence.

- Thus the character sequence <U+0061 "a" LATIN SMALL LETTER A, U+0308 "◌̈" COMBINING DIAERESIS, U+0075 "u" LATIN SMALL LETTER U> is unambiguously interpreted (and displayed) as "äu", not "aü". See *Figure 2-18*.

P2 ***[Guideline] Inside-out application. Nonspacing marks with the same combining class are generally positioned graphically outward from the grapheme base to which they apply.***

- The most numerous and important instances of this principle involve nonspacing marks applied either directly above or below a grapheme base. See *Figure 2-21*.
- In a sequence of two nonspacing marks above a grapheme base, the first nonspacing mark is placed directly above the grapheme base, and the second is then placed above the first nonspacing mark.
- In a sequence of two nonspacing marks below a grapheme base, the first nonspacing mark is placed directly below the grapheme base, and the second is then placed below the first nonspacing mark.
- This rendering behavior for nonspacing marks can be generalized to sequences of any length, although practical considerations usually limit such sequences to no more than two or three marks above and/or below a grapheme base.
- The principle of inside-out application is also referred to as *default stacking behavior* for nonspacing marks.

P3 ***[Guideline] Side-by-side application. Notwithstanding the principle of inside-out application, some specific nonspacing marks may override the default stacking behavior and are positioned side-by-side over (or under) a grapheme base, rather than stacking vertically.***

- Such side-by-side positioning may reflect language-specific orthographic rules, such as for Vietnamese diacritics and tone marks or for polytonic Greek breathing and accent marks. See *Table 2-6*.
- When positioned side-by-side, the visual rendering order of a sequence of nonspacing marks reflects the dominant order of the script with which they are used. Thus, in Greek, the first nonspacing mark in such a sequence will be positioned to the left side above a grapheme base, and the second to the right side above the grapheme base. In Hebrew, the opposite positioning is used for side-by-side placement.

P4 ***[Guideline] Traditional typographical behavior will sometimes override the default placement or rendering of nonspacing marks.***

- Because of typographical conflict with the descender of a base character, a combining comma below placed on a lowercase "g" is traditionally rendered as if it were an inverted comma above. See *Figure 7-1*.

- Because of typographical conflict with the ascender of a base chracter, a combining háček (caron) is traditionally rendered as an apostrophe when placed, for example, on a lowercase "d". See *Figure 7-1.*

- The relative placement of vowel marks in Arabic cannot be predicted by default stacking behavior alone, but depends on traditional rules of Arabic typography. See *Figure 8-5.*

P5 ***[Normative] Nondistinct order. Nonspacing marks with different, non-zero combining classes may occur in different orders without affecting either the visual display of a combining character sequence or the interpretation of that sequence.***

- For example, if one nonspacing mark occurs above a grapheme base and another nonspacing mark occurs below it, they will have distinct combining classes. The order in which they occur in the combining character sequence does not matter for the display or interpretation of the resulting grapheme cluster.

- Inserting a *combining grapheme joiner* between two combining marks with nondistinct order prevents their canonical reordering. For more information, see "Combining Grapheme Joiner" in *Section 16.2, Layout Controls.*

- The introduction of the combining class for characters and its use in canonical ordering in the standard is to precisely define canonical equivalence and thereby clarify exactly which such alternate sequences must be considered as identical for display and interpretation. See *Figure 2-24.*

- In cases of nondistinct order, the order of combining marks has no linguistic significance. The order does not reflect how "closely bound" they are to the base. After canonical reordering, the order may no longer reflect the typed-in sequence. Rendering systems should be prepared to deal with common typed-in sequences and with canonically reordered sequences. See *Table 5-3.*

P6 ***[Guideline] Enclosing marks surround their grapheme base and any intervening nonspacing marks.***

- This implies that enclosing marks successively surround previous enclosing marks. See *Figure 3-1.*

Figure 3-1. Enclosing Marks

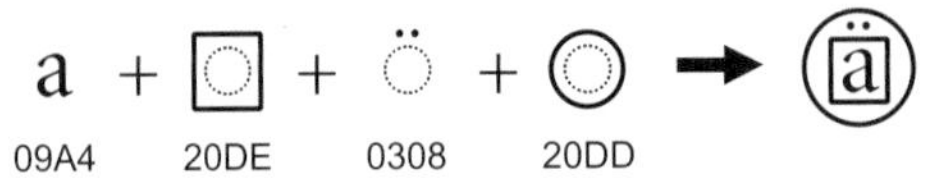

a + ⃞ + ̈ + ⃝ → ⓐ̈

09A4 20DE 0308 20DD

- Dynamic application of enclosing marks—particularly sequences of enclosing marks—is beyond the capability of most fonts and simple rendering processes. It is not unexpected to find fallback rendering in cases such as that illustrated in *Figure 3-1.*

P7 ***[Guideline] Double diacritic nonspacing marks, such as U+0360 COMBINING DOUBLE TILDE, apply to their grapheme base, but are intended to be rendered with glyphs that encompass a following grapheme base as well.***

Because such double diacritic display spans combinations of elements that would otherwise be considered grapheme clusters, the support of double diacritics in rendering may involve special handling for cursor placement and text selection. See *Figure 7-8* for an example.

P8 ***[Guideline] When double diacritic nonspacing marks interact with normal nonspacing marks in a grapheme cluster, they "float" to the outermost layer of the stack of rendered marks (either above or below).***

- This behavior can be conceived of as a kind of looser binding of such double diacritics to their bases. In effect, all other nonspacing marks are applied first, and then the double diacritic will span the resulting stacks. See *Figure 7-9* for an example.
- Double diacritic nonspacing marks are also given a very high combining class, so that in canonical order they appear at or near the end of any combining character sequence. *Figure 7-10* shows an example of the use of CGJ to block this reordering.
- The interaction of enclosing marks and double diacritics is not well defined graphically. It is unlikely that most fonts or rendering processes could handle combinations of these marks felicitously. It is not recommended to use combinations of these together in the same grapheme cluster.

P9 ***[Guideline] When a nonspacing mark is applied to the letters*** i ***and*** j ***or any other character with the Soft_Dotted property, the inherent dot on the base character is suppressed in display.***

- See *Figure 7-2* for an example.
- For languages such as Lithuanian, in which both a dot and an accent must be displayed, use U+0307 COMBINING DOT ABOVE. For guidelines in handling this situation in case mapping, see *Section 5.18, Case Mappings*.

Combining Marks and Korean Syllables. When a grapheme cluster comprises a Korean syllable, a combining mark applies to that entire syllable. For example, in the following sequence the *grave* is applied to the entire Korean syllable, not just to the last jamo:

U+1100 ᄀ *choseong kiyeok* + U+1161 ᅡ *jungseong a* + U+0300 ◌̀ *grave* →
가̀

If the combining mark in question is an *enclosing* combining mark, then it would enclose the entire Korean syllable, rather than the last jamo in it:

U+1100 ᄀ *choseong kiyeok* + U+1161 ᅡ *jungseong a* + U+20DD ◌⃝ *enclosing circle* → 가⃝

This treatment of the application of combining marks with respect to Korean syllables follows from the implications of canonical equivalence. It should be noted, however, that older implementations may have supported the application of an enclosing combining mark to an entire Indic consonant conjunct or to a sequence of grapheme clusters linked together by combining grapheme joiners. Such an approach has a number of technical problems and leads to interoperability defects, so it is strongly recommended that implementations do not follow it.

For more information on the recommended use of the combining grapheme joiner, see the subsection "Combining Grapheme Joiner" in *Section 16.2, Layout Controls*. For more discussion regarding the application of combining marks in general, see *Section 7.9, Combining Marks*.

Combining Classes

Each character in the Unicode Standard has a combining class associated with it. The combining class is a numerical value used by the Canonical Ordering Algorithm to determine which sequences of combining marks are to be considered canonically equivalent and which are not. Canonical equivalence is the criterion used to determine whether two alternate sequences are considered identical for interpretation.

D104 *Combining class:* A numeric value in the range 0..255 given to each Unicode code point, formally defined as the property Canonical_Combining_Class.

- The combining class for each encoded character in the standard is specified in the file UnicodeData.txt in the Unicode Character Database. Any code point not listed in that data file defaults to \p{Canonical_Combining_Class = 0} (or \p{ccc = 0} for short).
- An extracted listing of combining classes, sorted by numeric value, is provided in the file DerivedCombiningClass.txt in the Unicode Character Database.
- Only combining marks have a combining class other than zero. Almost all combining marks with a class other than zero are also nonspacing marks, with a few exceptions. Also, not all nonspacing marks have a non-zero combining class. Thus, while the correlation between ^\p{ccc=0] and \p{gc=Mn} is close, it is not exact, and implementations should not depend on the two concepts being identical.

D105 *Fixed position class:* A subset of the range of numeric values for combining classes—specifically, any value in the range 10..199.

- Fixed position classes are assigned to a small number of Hebrew, Arabic, Syriac, Telugu, Thai, Lao, and Tibetan combining marks whose positions were conceived of as occurring in a fixed position with respect to their grapheme base, regardless of any other combining mark that might also apply to the grapheme base.

- Not all Arabic vowel points or Indic matras are given fixed position classes. The existence of fixed position classes in the standard is an historical artifact of an earlier stage in its development, prior to the formal standardization of the Unicode Normalization Forms.

D106 *Typographic interaction:* Graphical application of one nonspacing mark in a position relative to a grapheme base that is already occupied by another nonspacing mark, so that some rendering adjustment must be done (such as default stacking or side-by-side placement) to avoid illegible overprinting or crashing of glyphs.

The assignment of combining class values for Unicode characters was originally done with the goal in mind of defining distinct numeric values for each group of nonspacing marks that would typographically interact. Thus all generic nonspacing marks above are given the value \p{ccc=230}, while all generic nonspacing marks below are given the value \p{ccc=220}. Smaller numbers of nonspacing marks that tend to sit on one "shoulder" or another of a grapheme base, or that may actually be attached to the grapheme base itself when applied, have their own combining classes.

When assigned this way, canonical ordering assures that, in general, alternate sequences of combining characters that typographically interact will not be canonically equivalent, whereas alternate sequences of combining characters that do *not* typographically interact *will* be canonically equivalent.

This is roughly correct for the normal cases of detached, generic nonspacing marks placed above and below base letters. However, the ramifications of complex rendering for many scripts ensure that there are always some edge cases involving typographic interaction between combining marks of distinct combining classes. This has turned out to be particularly true for some of the fixed position classes for Hebrew and Arabic, for which a distinct combining class is no guarantee that there will be no typographic interaction for rendering.

Because of these considerations, particular combining class values should be taken only as a guideline regarding issues of typographic interaction of combining marks.

The only *normative* use of combining class values is as input to the Canonical Ordering Algorithm, where they are used to normatively distinguish between sequences of combining marks that are canonically equivalent and those that are not.

Canonical Ordering

The canonical ordering of a decomposed character sequence results from a sorting process that acts on each sequence of combining characters according to their combining class. The canonical order of character sequences does *not* imply any kind of linguistic correctness or linguistic preference for ordering of combining marks in sequences. See the information on rendering combining marks in *Section 5.13, Rendering Nonspacing Marks*, for more information. Characters with combining class zero are never reordered relative to other characters, so the amount of work in the algorithm depends on the number of non-class-zero characters in a row. An implementation of this algorithm will be extremely fast for typical text.

The algorithm described here represents a logical description of the process. Optimized algorithms can be used in implementations as long as they are equivalent—that is, as long as they produce the same result. This algorithm is not tailorable; higher-level protocols shall not specify different results.

More explicitly, the canonical ordering of a decomposed character sequence D results from the following algorithm.

R1 ***For each character x in D, let p(x) be the combining class of x.***

R2 ***Whenever any pair (A, B) of adjacent characters in D is such that $p(B) \neq 0$ & $p(A) > p(B)$, exchange those characters.***

R3 ***Repeat R2 until no exchanges can be made among any of the characters in D.***

Sample combining classes for this discussion are listed in *Table 3-10*.

Table 3-10. Sample Combining Classes

Combining Class	Abbreviation	Code	Unicode Name
0	a	U+0061	LATIN SMALL LETTER A
220	underdot	U+0323	COMBINING DOT BELOW
230	diaeresis	U+0308	COMBINING DIAERESIS
230	breve	U+0306	COMBINING BREVE
0	a-underdot	U+1EA1	LATIN SMALL LETTER A WITH DOT BELOW
0	a-diaeresis	U+00E4	LATIN SMALL LETTER A WITH DIAERESIS
0	a-breve	U+0103	LATIN SMALL LETTER A WITH BREVE

Because *underdot* has a lower combining class than *diaeresis*, the algorithm will return the *a*, then the *underdot*, then the *diaeresis*. The sequence *a* + *underdot* + *diaeresis* is already in the final order, so it is not rearranged by the algorithm. The sequence in the opposite order, *a* + *diaeresis* + *underdot*, is rearranged by the algorithm.

a + *underdot* + *diaeresis* → *a* + *underdot* + *diaeresis*

a + *diaeresis* + *underdot* → *a* + *underdot* + *diaeresis*

However, because *diaeresis* and *breve* have the same combining class (because they interact typographically), they are not rearranged.

a + *breve* + *diaeresis* ↛ *a* + *diaeresis* + *breve*

a + *diaeresis* + *breve* ↛ *a* + *breve* + *diaeresis*

Applying the algorithm gives the results shown in *Table 3-11*.

Table 3-11. Canonical Ordering Results

Original	Decompose	Sort	Result
a-diaeresis + underdot	a + diaeresis + underdot	a + underdot + diaeresis	a + underdot + diaeresis
a + diaeresis + underdot		a + underdot + diaeresis	a + underdot + diaeresis
a + underdot + diaeresis			a + underdot + diaeresis
a-underdot + diaeresis	a + underdot + diaeresis		a + underdot + diaeresis
a-diaeresis + breve	a + diaeresis + breve		a + diaeresis + breve
a + diaeresis + breve			a + diaeresis + breve
a + breve + diaeresis			a + breve + diaeresis
a-breve + diaeresis	a + breve + diaeresis		a + breve + diaeresis

3.12 Conjoining Jamo Behavior

The Unicode Standard contains both a large set of precomposed modern Hangul syllables and a set of conjoining Hangul jamo, which can be used to encode archaic Korean syllable blocks as well as modern Korean syllable blocks. This section describes how to

- Determine the syllable boundaries in a sequence of conjoining jamo characters.
- Compose jamo characters into precomposed Hangul syllables.
- Determine the canonical decomposition of precomposed Hangul syllables.
- Algorithmically determine the names of precomposed Hangul syllables.

For more information, see the "Hangul Syllables" and "Hangul Jamo" subsections in *Section 12.6, Hangul.* Hangul syllables are a special case of grapheme clusters.

Definitions

The following definitions use the Hangul_Syllable_Type property, which is defined in the UCD file HangulSyllableType.txt.

D107 *Leading consonant:* A character with the Hangul_Syllable_Type property value Leading_Jamo. Abbreviated as *L*.

- When not occurring in clusters, the term *leading consonant* is equivalent to *syllable-initial character.*

D108 *Choseong:* A sequence of one or more leading consonants.

- In Modern Korean, a *choseong* consists of a single jamo. In Old Korean, a sequence of more than one leading consonant may occur.
- Equivalent to *syllable-initial cluster.*

D109 *Choseong filler:* U+115F HANGUL CHOSEONG FILLER. Abbreviated as L_f.

- A *choseong filler* stands in for a missing choseong to make a well-formed Korean syllable.

D110 *Vowel:* A character with the Hangul_Syllable_Type property value Vowel_Jamo. Abbreviated as *V*.

- When not occurring in clusters, the term *vowel* is equivalent to *syllable-peak character*.

D111 *Jungseong:* A sequence of one or more vowels.

- In Modern Korean, a *jungseong* consists of a single jamo. In Old Korean, a sequence of more than one vowel may occur.
- Equivalent to *syllable-peak cluster*.

D112 *Jungseong filler:* U+1160 HANGUL JUNGSEONG FILLER. Abbreviated as V_f.

- A *jungseong filler* stands in for a missing jungseong to make a well-formed Korean syllable.

D113 *Trailing consonant:* A character with the Hangul_Syllable_Type property value Trailing_Jamo. Abbreviated as *T*.

- When not occurring in clusters, the term *trailing consonant* is equivalent to *syllable-final character*.

D114 *Jongseong:* A sequence of one or more trailing consonants.

- In Modern Korean, a *jongseong* consists of a single jamo. In Old Korean, a sequence of more than one trailing consonant may occur.
- Equivalent to *syllable-final cluster*.

D115 *LV_Syllable:* A character with Hangul_Syllable_Type property value LV_Syllable. Abbreviated as *LV*.

- An LV_Syllable is canonically equivalent to a sequence of the form <*L V*>.

D116 *LVT_Syllable:* A character with Hangul_Syllable_Type property value LVT_Syllable. Abbreviated as *LVT*.

- An LVT_Syllable is canonically equivalent to a sequence of the form <*L V T*>.

D117 *Precomposed Hangul syllable:* A character that is either an LV_Syllable or an LVT_Syllable.

D118 *Syllable block:* A sequence of Korean characters that should be grouped into a single square cell for display.

- This is different from a precomposed Hangul syllable and is meant to include sequences needed for the representation of Old Korean syllables.
- A syllable block may contain a precomposed Hangul syllable *plus* other characters.

Hangul Syllable Boundary Determination

In rendering, a sequence of jamos is displayed as a series of syllable blocks. The following rules specify how to divide up an arbitrary sequence of jamos (including nonstandard sequences) into these syllable blocks.

The precomposed Hangul syllables are of two types: *LV* or *LVT*. In determining the syllable boundaries, the *LV* behave as if they were a sequence of jamo *L V*, and the *LVT* behave as if they were a sequence of jamo *L V T*.

Within any sequence of characters, a syllable break never occurs between the pairs of characters shown in *Table 3-12*. In *Table 3-12* non-opportunities for syllable breaks are shown by "×". Combining marks are shown by the symbol *M*.

In all cases other than those shown in *Table 3-12*, a syllable break occurs before and after any jamo or precomposed Hangul syllable. As for other characters, any combining mark between two conjoining jamos prevents the jamos from forming a syllable block.

Table 3-12. Hangul Syllable No-Break Rules

Do Not Break Between		Examples
L	L, V, or precomposed Hangul syllable	L × L L × V L × LV L × LVT
V or LV	V or T	V × V V × T LV × V LV × T
T or LVT	T	T × T LVT × T
Jamo or precomposed Hangul syllable	Combining marks	L × M V × M T × M LV × M LVT × M

Even in Normalization Form NFC, a syllable block may contain a precomposed Hangul syllable in the middle. An example is *L LVT T*. Each well-formed modern Hangul syllable, however, can be represented in the form *L V T?* (that is one *L*, one *V* and optionally one *T*) and consists of a single encoded character in NFC.

For information on the behavior of Hangul compatibility jamo in syllables, see *Section 12.6, Hangul.*

Standard Korean Syllables

D119 Standard Korean syllable block: A sequence of one or more *L* followed by a sequence of one or more *V* and a sequence of zero or more *T*, or any other sequence that is canonically equivalent.

- All precomposed Hangul syllables, which have the form *LV* or *LVT*, are standard Korean syllable blocks.
- Alternatively, a standard Korean syllable block may be expressed as a sequence of a choseong and a jungseong, optionally followed by a jongseong.
- A choseong filler may substitute for a missing leading consonant, and a jungseong filler may substitute for a missing vowel.

Using regular expression notation, a canonically decomposed standard Korean syllable block is of the following form:

*L+ V+ T**

Arbitrary standard Korean syllable blocks have a somewhat more complex form because they include any canonically equivalent sequence, thus including precomposed Korean syllables. The regular expressions for them have the following form:

(L+ V+ T) | (L* LV V* T*) | (L* LVT T*)*

All standard Korean syllable blocks (without fillers) of the form <*L V T*> or <*L V*> have equivalent, single-character precomposed forms. Such syllables cover the requirements of modern Korean, but do not provide for syllables that are used in Old Korean.

Using canonically decomposed text may facilitate further processing such as searching and sorting when dealing with Old Korean data, because the text then consists only of sequences of jamos *(L+ V+ T*)*, and not mixtures of precomposed Hangul syllables and jamos.

Transforming into Standard Korean Syllables. A sequence of jamos that do not all match the regular expression for a standard Korean syllable block can be transformed into a sequence of standard Korean syllable blocks by the correct insertion of choseong fillers and jungseong fillers. This transformation of a string of text into standard Korean syllables is performed by determining the syllable breaks as explained in the earlier subsection "Hangul Syllable Boundaries," then inserting one or two fillers as necessary to transform each syllable into a standard Korean syllable. Thus

L [^V] → L V_f [^V]

[^L] V → [^L] L_f V

[^V] T → [^V] L_f V_f T

where [^X] indicates a character that is not X, or the absence of a character.

Examples. In *Table 3-13*, the first row shows syllable breaks in a standard sequence, the second row shows syllable breaks in a nonstandard sequence, and the third row shows how the sequence in the second row could be transformed into standard form by inserting fillers into each syllable. Syllable breaks are shown by *middle dots* "·".

Table 3-13. Korean Syllable Break Examples

No.	Sequence		Sequence with Syllable Breaks Marked
1	$LVTLVLVLV_fL_fVL_fV_fT$	→	$LVT \cdot LV \cdot LV \cdot LV_f \cdot L_fV \cdot L_fV_fT$
2	LLTTVVTTVVLLVV	→	LL · TT · VVTT · VV · LLVV
3	LLTTVVTTVVLLVV	→	$LLV_f \cdot L_fV_fTT \cdot L_fVVTT \cdot L_fVV \cdot LLVV$

Hangul Syllable Composition

The following algorithm describes how to take a sequence of canonically decomposed characters D and compose Hangul syllables. Hangul composition and decomposition are summarized here, but for a more complete description, implementers must consult Unicode Standard Annex #15, "Unicode Normalization Forms." Note that, like other non-jamo characters, any combining mark between two conjoining jamos prevents the jamos from composing.

First, define the following constants:

```
SBase  = AC00₁₆
LBase  = 1100₁₆
VBase  = 1161₁₆
TBase  = 11A7₁₆
SCount = 11172
LCount = 19
VCount = 21
TCount = 28
NCount = VCount * TCount
```

1. Iterate through the sequence of characters in D, performing steps 2 through 5.

2. Let *i* represent the current position in the sequence D. Compute the following indices, which represent the ordinal number (zero-based) for each of the components of a syllable, and the index *j*, which represents the index of the last character in the syllable.

```
LIndex = D[i]   - LBase
VIndex = D[i+1] - VBase
TIndex = D[i+2] - TBase
j      = i + 2
```

3. If either of the first two characters is out of bounds (*LIndex* < 0 OR *LIndex* ≥ *LCount* OR *VIndex* < 0 OR *VIndex* ≥ *VCount*), then increment *i*, return to step 2, and continue from there.

4. If the third character is out of bounds ($TIndex \le 0$ or $TIndex \ge TCount$), then it is not part of the syllable. Reset the following:

```
TIndex = 0
j      = i + 1
```

5. Replace the characters D[i] through D[j] by the Hangul syllable S, and set i to be $j + 1$.

```
S      = (LIndex * VCount + VIndex) * TCount + TIndex + SBase
```

Example. The first three characters are

U+1111	ᄑ	HANGUL CHOSEONG PHIEUPH
U+1171	ᅱ	HANGUL JUNGSEONG WI
U+11B6	ᆶ	HANGUL JONGSEONG RIEUL-HIEUH

Compute the following indices:

```
LIndex = 17
VIndex = 16
TIndex = 15
```

Replace the three characters as follows:

```
S      = [(17 * 21) + 16] * 28 + 15 + SBase
```
$= \text{D4DB}_{16}$

= 퓛

Hangul Syllable Decomposition

The following algorithm describes the reverse mapping—how to take Hangul syllable S and derive the canonical decomposition D. This normative mapping for these characters is equivalent to the canonical mapping in the character charts for other characters.

1. Compute the index of the syllable:

```
SIndex = S - SBase
```

2. If $SIndex$ is in the range ($0 \le SIndex < SCount$), then compute the components as follows:

```
L      = LBase + SIndex / NCount
V      = VBase + (SIndex % NCount) / TCount
T      = TBase + SIndex % TCount
```

The operators "/" and "%" are as defined in *Table A-3* in *Appendix A, Notational Conventions.*

3. If $T = TBase$, then there is no trailing character, so replace S by the sequence *L V*. Otherwise, there is a trailing character, so replace S by the sequence *L V T*.

Example. Compute the components:

```
L      = LBase + 17
V      = VBase + 16
T      = TBase + 15
```

and replace the syllable by the sequence of components:

$D4DB_{16} \rightarrow 1111_{16}, 1171_{16}, 11B6_{16}$

Hangul Syllable Name Generation

The character names for Hangul syllables are derived from the decomposition by starting with the string HANGUL SYLLABLE, and appending the short name of each decomposition component in order. (See *Chapter 17, Code Charts*, and Jamo.txt in the Unicode Character Database.) For example, for U+D4DB, derive the decomposition, as shown in the preceding example. It produces the following three-character sequence:

U+1111 HANGUL CHOSEONG PHIEUPH (P)
U+1171 HANGUL JUNGSEONG WI (WI)
U+11B6 HANGUL JONGSEONG RIEUL-HIEUH (LH)

The character name for U+D4DB is then generated as HANGUL SYLLABLE PWILH, using the short name as shown in parentheses above. This character name is a normative property of the character.

3.13 Default Case Algorithms

This section specifies the default algorithms for case conversion, case detection, and caseless matching. For information about the data sources for case mapping, see *Section 4.2, Case—Normative*. For a general discussion of case mapping operations, see *Section 5.18, Case Mappings*.

The default casing operations are to be used in the absence of tailoring for particular languages and environments. Where a particular environment (such as a Turkish locale) requires tailoring, that can be done without violating conformance.

All of these specifications are *logical* specifications. Particular implementations can optimize the processes as long as they provide the same results.

Definitions

The full case mappings for Unicode characters are obtained by using the mappings from SpecialCasing.txt *plus* the mappings from UnicodeData.txt, excluding any of the latter mappings that would conflict. Any character that does not have a mapping in these files is considered to map to itself. The full case mappings of a character C are referred to as Lowercase_Mapping(C), Titlecase_Mapping(C), and Uppercase_Mapping(C). The full case folding of a character C is referred to as Case_Folding(C).

Detection of case and case mapping requires more than just the General_Category values (Lu, Lt, Ll). The following definitions are used:

D120 A character C is defined to be *cased* if and only if C has the Lowercase or Uppercase property or has a General_Category value of Titlecase_Letter.

- The Uppercase and Lowercase property values are specified in the data file DerivedCoreProperties.txt in the Unicode Character Database.

D121 A character C is defined to be *case-ignorable* if C has the value MidLetter for the Word_Break property or its General_Category is one of Nonspacing_Mark (Mn), Enclosing_Mark (Me), Format (Cf), Modifier_Letter (Lm), or Modifier_Symbol (Sk).

- The Word_Break property is defined in Unicode Standard Annex #29, "Text Boundaries."

D122 *Case-ignorable sequence*: A sequence of zero or more case-ignorable characters.

D123 A character C is in a particular *casing context* for context-dependent matching if and only if it matches the corresponding specification in *Table 3-14.*

Table 3-14. Context Specification for Casing

Context	**Description**	**Regular Expressions**	
Final_Sigma	C is preceded by a sequence consisting of a cased letter and a case-ignorable sequence, and C is not followed by a sequence consisting of a case ignorable sequence and then a cased letter.	Before C	\p{cased} (\p{case-ignorable})*
		After C	! ((\p{case-ignorable})* \p{cased})
After_Soft_Dotted	There is a Soft_Dotted character before C, with no intervening character of combining class 0 or 230 (Above).	Before C	[\p{Soft_Dotted}] ([^\p{ccc=230} \p{ccc=0}])*
More_Above	C is followed by a character of combining class 230 (Above) with no intervening character of combining class 0 or 230 (Above).	After C	[^\p{ccc=0}]* [\p{ccc=230}]
Before_Dot	C is followed by COMBINING DOT ABOVE (U+0307). Any sequence of characters with a combining class that is neither 0 nor 230 may intervene between the current character and the combining dot above.	After C	([^\p{ccc=230} \p{ccc=0}])* [\u0307]
After_I	There is an uppercase I before C, and there is no intervening combining character class 230 (Above) or 0.	Before C	[I] ([^\p{ccc=230} \p{ccc=0}])*

In *Table 3-14*, a description of each context is followed by the equivalent regular expression(s) describing the context before C, the context after C, or both. The regular expressions use the syntax of Unicode Technical Standard #18, "Unicode Regular Expressions," with one addition: "!" means that the expression does not match. All of the regular expressions are case-sensitive.

Default Case Conversion

The following specify the default case conversion operations for Unicode strings, in the absence of tailoring. In each instance, there are two variants: simple case conversion and full case conversion. In the full case conversion, the context-dependent mappings based on the casing context mentioned earlier must be used.

For a string X:

R1 ***toUppercase(X): Map each character C in X to Uppercase_Mapping(C).***

R2 ***toLowercase(X): Map each character C in X to Lowercase_Mapping(C).***

R3 ***toTitlecase(X): Find the word boundaries in X according to Unicode Standard Annex #29, "Text Boundaries." For each word boundary, find the first cased character F following the word boundary. If F exists, map F to Titlecase_Mapping(F); then map all characters C between F and the following word boundary to Lowercase_Mapping(C).***

R4 ***toCasefold(X): Map each character C in X to Case_Folding(C).***

Default Case Detection

The casing status of the string can be determined in accordance with the casing operations defined earlier. The following definitions provide a specification for determining this status. These definitions assume that X and Y are strings and that Y equals toNFD(X). When case conversion is applied to a string that is decomposed (normalized to NFD), applying the case conversion character by character does not affect the normalization. Therefore, the following are specified in terms of Normalization Form NFD.

D124 isLowercase(X): isLowercase(X) is true when toLowercase(Y) = Y.

- For example, isLowercase("combining mark") is true, and isLowercase("Combining mark") is false.

D125 isUppercase(X): isUppercase(X) is true when toUppercase(Y) = Y.

- For example, isUppercase("COMBINING MARK") is true, and isUppercase("Combining mark") is false.

D126 isTitlecase(X): isTitlecase(X) is true when toTitlecase(Y) = Y.

- For example, isTitlecase("Combining Mark") is true, and isTitlecase("Combining mark") is false.

D127 isCasefolded(X): isCasefolded(X) is true when toCasefold(Y) = Y.

- For example, isCasefolded("heiss") is true, and isCasefolded("heiß") is false.

Uncased characters do not affect the results of casing detection operations such as isLowercase. Thus a space or a number added to a string does not affect the results. There is a degenerate case, such as "123", where the string contains no cased letters and thus isLowercase("123") evaluates as true. In many situations it may be appropriate for implementations to also test whether there are any cased characters in the strings. This is accomplished by testing for (isLowercase(X) AND isCased(X)), using the following definition (D128).

D128 isCased(X): isCased(X) when isLowercase(X) is false, or isUppercase(X) is false, or isTitlecase(X) is false.

- Any string that is not isCased consists entirely of characters that do not case map to themselves.
- For example, isCased("abc") is true, and isCased("123") is false.

The examples in *Table 3-15* show that these conditions are not mutually exclusive. "A2" is both uppercase and titlecase; "3" is uncased, so it is lowercase, uppercase, and titlecase.

Table 3-15. Case Detection Examples

Case	Letter	Name	Alphanumeric	Digit
Lowercase	a	john smith	a2	3
Uppercase	A	JOHN SMITH	A2	3
Titlecase	A	John Smith	A2	3

Default Caseless Matching

Default caseless (or case-insensitive) matching is specified by the following:

D129 A string X is a caseless match for a string Y if and only if:
toCasefold(X) = toCasefold(Y)

Caseless matching should also use normalization, which means using one of the following operations:

D130 A string X is a canonical caseless match for a string Y if and only if:
NFD(toCasefold(NFD(X))) = NFD(toCasefold(NFD(Y)))

D131 A string X is a compatibility caseless match for a string Y if and only if:
NFKD(toCasefold(NFKD(toCasefold(NFD(X))))) =
NFKD(toCasefold(NFKD(toCasefold(NFD(Y)))))

The invocations of normalization before case folding in the preceding definitions are to catch very infrequent edge cases. Normalization is not required before case folding, except for the character U+0345 ͅ COMBINING GREEK YPOGEGRAMMENI and any characters that have it as part of their decomposition, such as U+1FC3 ῃ GREEK SMALL LETTER ETA WITH YPOGEGRAMMENI.

In practice, optimized versions of implementations can catch these special cases, thereby avoiding an extra normalization.

CHAPTER 4

Chapter 4

Character Properties

> ### *Disclaimer*
>
> The content of all character property tables has been verified as far as possible by the Unicode Consortium. However, in case of conflict, the most authoritative version of the information for Version 5.0.0 is that supplied in the Unicode Character Database on the Unicode Web site. *The contents of all the tables in this chapter may be superseded or augmented by information in future versions of the Unicode Standard.*

The Unicode Standard associates a rich set of semantics with characters and, in some instances, with code points. The support of character semantics is required for conformance; see *Section 3.2, Conformance Requirements*. Where character semantics can be expressed formally, they are provided as machine-readable lists of character properties in the Unicode Character Database (UCD). This chapter gives an overview of character properties, their status and attributes, followed by an overview of the UCD and more detailed notes on some important character properties. For a further discussion of character properties, see Unicode Technical Report #23, "Unicode Character Property Model."

Status and Attributes. Character properties may be normative or informative. Normative properties are those required for conformance. The following sections discuss important properties identified by their status. Many Unicode character properties can be overridden by implementations as needed. *Section 3.2, Conformance Requirements*, specifies when such overrides must be documented. A few properties, such as Noncharacter_Code_Point, may not be overridden. See *Section 3.5, Properties*, for the formal discussion of the status and attributes of properties.

Consistency of Properties. The Unicode Standard is the product of many compromises. It has to strike a balance between uniformity of treatment for similar characters and compatibility with existing practice for characters inherited from legacy encodings. Because of this balancing act, one can expect a certain number of anomalies in character properties. For example, some pairs of characters might have been treated as canonical equivalents but are left unequivalent for compatibility with legacy differences. This situation pertains to U+00B5 µ MICRO SIGN and U+03BC μ GREEK SMALL LETTER MU, as well as to certain Korean jamo.

In addition, some characters might have had properties differing in some ways from those assigned in this standard, but those properties are left as is for compatibility with existing practice. This situation can be seen with the halfwidth voicing marks for Japanese (U+FF9E HALFWIDTH KATAKANA VOICED SOUND MARK and U+FF9F HALFWIDTH KATAKANA SEMI-VOICED SOUND MARK), which might have been better analyzed as spacing combining marks, and with the conjoining Hangul jamo, which might have been better analyzed as an initial base character followed by formally combining medial and final characters. In the interest of efficiency and uniformity in algorithms, implementations may take advantage of such reanalyses of character properties, as long as this does not conflict with the conformance requirements with respect to normative properties. See *Section 3.5, Properties*; *Section 3.2, Conformance Requirements*; and *Section 3.3, Semantics*, for more information.

4.1 Unicode Character Database

The Unicode Character Database (UCD) consists of a set of files that define the Unicode character properties and internal mappings. For each property, the files determine the assignment of property values to each code point. The UCD also supplies recommended property aliases and property value aliases for textual parsing and display in environments such as regular expressions.

The properties include the following:

- Name
- General Category (basic partition into letters, numbers, symbols, punctuation, and so on)
- Other important general characteristics (whitespace, dash, ideographic, alphabetic, noncharacter, deprecated, and so on)
- Display-related properties (bidirectional class, shaping, mirroring, width, and so on)
- Casing (upper, lower, title, folding—both simple and full)
- Numeric values and types
- Script and Block
- Normalization properties (decompositions, decomposition type, canonical combining class, composition exclusions, and so on)
- Age (version of the standard in which the code point was first designated)
- Boundaries (grapheme cluster, word, line, and sentence)
- Standardized variants

See the Unicode Character Database for more details on the character properties, their distribution across files, and the file formats.

Unihan Database. In addition, a large number of properties specific to CJK ideographs are defined in the Unicode Character Database. These properties include source information, radical and stroke counts, phonetic values, meanings, and mappings to many East Asian standards. These properties are documented in the file Unihan.txt, also known as the *Unihan Database*. For a complete description of the properties in the Unihan Database, see the documentation file Unihan.html in the Unicode Character Database. (See also "Online Unihan Database" in *Section B.6, Other Unicode Online Resources*.)

Many properties apply to both ideographs and other characters. These are not specified in the Unihan Database.

Stability. While the Unicode Consortium strives to minimize changes to character property data, occasionally character properties must be updated. When this situation occurs, a new version of the Unicode Character Database is created, containing updated data files. Data file changes are associated with specific, numbered versions of the standard; character properties are never silently corrected between official versions.

Each version of the Unicode Character Database, once published, is absolutely stable and will never change. Implementations or specifications that refer to a specific version of the UCD can rely upon this stability. Detailed policies on character encoding stability as they relate to properties are found in *Appendix F, Unicode Encoding Stability Policies*. See the subsection "Policies" in *Section B.6, Other Unicode Online Resources*. See also the discussion of versioning and stability in *Section 3.1, Versions of the Unicode Standard*.

Aliases. Character properties and their values are given formal aliases to make it easier to refer to them consistently in specifications and in implementations, such as regular expressions, which may use them. These aliases are listed exhaustively in the Unicode Character Database, in the data files PropertyAliases.txt and PropertyValueAliases.txt.

Many of the aliases have both a long form and a short form. For example, the General Category has a long alias "General_Category" and a short alias "gc". The long alias is more comprehensible and is usually used in the text of the standard when referring to a particular character property. The short alias is more appropriate for use in regular expressions and other algorithmic contexts.

In comparing aliases programmatically, loose matching is appropriate. That entails ignoring case differences and any whitespace, underscore, and hyphen characters. For example, "GeneralCategory", "general_category", and "GENERAL-CATEGORY" would all be considered equivalent property aliases. See UCD.html in the Unicode Character Database for further discussion of property and property value matching.

For each character property whose values are not purely numeric, the Unicode Character Database provides a list of value aliases. For example, one of the values of the Line_Break property is given the long alias "Open_Punctuation" and the short alias "OP".

Property aliases and property value aliases can be combined in regular expressions that pick out a particular value of a particular property. For example, "\p{lb=OP}" means the Open_Punctuation value of the Line_Break property, and "\p{gc=Lu}" means the Uppercase_Letter value of the General_Category property.

Property aliases define a namespace. No two character properties have the same alias. For each property, the set of corresponding property value aliases constitutes its own namespace. No constraint prevents property value aliases for *different* properties from having the same property value alias. Thus "B" is the short alias for the Paragraph_Separator value of the Bidi_Class property; "B" is also the short alias for the Below value of the Canonical_Combining_Class property. However, because of the namespace restrictions, any combination of a property alias plus an appropriate property value alias is guaranteed to constitute a unique string, as in "\p{bc=B}" versus "\p{ccc=B}".

For a recommended use of property and property value aliases, see Unicode Technical Standard #18, "Unicode Regular Expressions." Aliases are also used for normatively referencing properties, as described in *Section 3.1, Versions of the Unicode Standard.*

CD-ROM and Online Availability. A copy of the 5.0.0 version of the UCD is provided on the CD-ROM. All versions of the UCD are available online on the Unicode Web site. See the subsections "Online Unicode Character Database" and "Online Unihan Database" in *Section B.6, Other Unicode Online Resources.*

4.2 Case—Normative

Case is a normative property of characters in certain alphabets whereby characters are considered to be variants of a single letter. These variants, which may differ markedly in shape and size, are called the *uppercase* letter (also known as *capital* or *majuscule*) and the *lowercase* letter (also known as *small* or *minuscule*). The uppercase letter is generally larger than the lowercase letter.

Because of the inclusion of certain composite characters for compatibility, such as U+01F1 LATIN CAPITAL LETTER DZ, a third case, called *titlecase*, is used where the first character of a word must be capitalized. An example of such a character is U+01F2 LATIN CAPITAL LETTER D WITH SMALL LETTER Z. The three case forms are UPPERCASE, Titlecase, and lowercase.

For those scripts that have case (Latin, Greek, Coptic, Cyrillic, Glagolitic, Armenian, Deseret, and archaic Georgian), uppercase characters typically contain the word *capital* in their names. Lowercase characters typically contain the word *small*. However, this is not a reliable guide. The word *small* in the names of characters from scripts other than those just listed has nothing to do with case. There are other exceptions as well, such as small capital letters that are not formally uppercase. Some Greek characters with *capital* in their names are actually titlecase. (Note that while the archaic Georgian script contained upper- and lowercase pairs, they are not used in modern Georgian. See *Section 7.7, Georgian.*) The authoritative source for case of Unicode characters is the specification of lowercase, uppercase, and titlecase properties in the Unicode Character Database.

Case Mapping

The default case mapping tables defined in the Unicode Standard are normative, but may be overridden to match user or implementation requirements. The Unicode Character Database contains five files with case mapping information, as shown in *Table 4-1*. Full case mappings for Unicode characters are obtained by using the basic mappings from UnicodeData.txt and extending or overriding them where necessary with the mappings from SpecialCasing.txt. Full case mappings may depend on the context surrounding the character in the original string.

Some characters have a "best" single-character mapping in UnicodeData.txt as well as a full mapping in SpecialCasing.txt. Any character that does not have a mapping in these files is considered to map to itself. For more information on case mappings, see *Section 5.18, Case Mappings*.

Table 4-1. Sources for Case Mapping Information

File Name	Description
UnicodeData.txt	Contains the case mappings that map to a single character. These do not increase the length of strings, nor do they contain context-dependent mappings.
SpecialCasing.txt	Contains additional case mappings that map to more than one character, such as "ß" to "SS". Also contains context-dependent mappings, with flags to distinguish them from the normal mappings, as well as some locale-dependent mappings.
CaseFolding.txt	Contains data for performing locale-independent case folding, as described in "Caseless Matching," in *Section 5.18, Case Mappings*.
DerivedCoreProperties.txt	Contains definitions of the properties Lowercase and Uppercase.
PropList.txt	Contains the definition of the property Soft_Dotted.

The single-character mappings in UnicodeData.txt are insufficient for languages such as German. Therefore, only legacy implementations that cannot handle case mappings that increase string lengths should use UnicodeData.txt case mappings alone.

A set of charts that show the latest case mappings is also available on the Unicode Web site. See "Charts" in *Section B.6, Other Unicode Online Resources*.

4.3 Combining Classes—Normative

Each combining character has a normative canonical *combining class*. This class is used with the Canonical Ordering Algorithm to determine which combining characters interact typographically and to determine how the canonical ordering of sequences of combining characters takes place. Class *zero* combining characters act like base letters for the purpose of determining canonical order. Combining characters with non-zero classes participate in reordering for the purpose of determining the canonical order of sequences of characters. (See *Section 3.11, Canonical Ordering Behavior*, for a description of the algorithm.)

The list of combining characters and their canonical combining class appears in the Unicode Character Database. Most combining characters are nonspacing.

The canonical order of character sequences does *not* imply any kind of linguistic correctness or linguistic preference for ordering of combining marks in sequences. For more information on rendering combining marks, see *Section 5.13, Rendering Nonspacing Marks*.

Class zero combining marks are never reordered by the Canonical Ordering Algorithm. Except for class zero, the exact numerical values of the combining classes are of no importance in canonical equivalence, although the relative magnitude of the classes is significant. For example, it is crucial that the combining class of the cedilla be lower than the combining class of the dot below, although their exact values of 202 and 220 are not important for implementations.

Certain classes tend to correspond with particular rendering positions relative to the base character, as shown in *Figure 4-1*.

Figure 4-1. Positions of Common Combining Marks

Reordrant, Split, and Subjoined Combining Marks

In some scripts, the rendering of combining marks is notably complex. This is true in particular of the Brahmi-derived scripts of South and Southeast Asia, whose vowels are often encoded as class zero combining marks in the Unicode Standard, known as *matras* for the Indic scripts.

In the case of simple combining marks, as for the accent marks of the Latin script, the normative Unicode combining class of that combining mark typically corresponds to its positional placement with regard to a base letter, as described earlier. However, in the case of the combining marks representing vowels (and sometimes consonants) in the Brahmi-derived scripts, all of the combining marks are given the normative combining class of zero, regardless of their positional placement within an *aksara*. The placement and rendering of a class zero combining mark cannot be derived from its combining class alone, but rather depends on having more information about the particulars of the script involved. In some instances, the position may migrate in different historical periods for a script or may even differ depending on font style.

Such matters are not treated as normative character properties in the Unicode Standard, because they are more properly considered properties of the glyphs and fonts used for rendering. However, to assist implementers, earlier versions of the Unicode Standard did subcategorize some class zero combining marks, pointing out significant types that need to be handled consistently. That earlier subcategorization is extended and refined in this section.

Reordrant Class Zero Combining Marks. In many instances in Indic scripts, a vowel is represented in logical order *after* the consonant of a syllable, but is displayed *before* (to the left of) the consonant when rendered. Such combining marks are termed *reordrant* to reflect their visual reordering to the left of a consonant (or, in some instances, a consonant cluster). Special handling is required for selection and editing of these marks. In particular, the possibility that the combining mark may be reordered left past a cluster, and not simply past the immediate preceding character in the backing store, requires attention to the details for each script involved.

The *visual* reordering of these reordrant class zero combining marks has nothing to do with the reordering of combining character sequences in the Canonical Ordering Algorithm. All of these marks are *class zero* and thus are *never* reordered by the Canonical Ordering Algorithm or during normalization. The reordering is purely a presentational issue for *glyphs* during rendering of text.

Table 4-2 lists reordrant class zero combining marks in the Unicode Standard.

Table 4-2. Class Zero Combining Marks—Reordrant

Script	Code Points
Devanagari	093F
Bengali	09BF, 09C7, 09C8
Gurmukhi	0A3F
Gujarati	0ABF
Oriya	0B47
Tamil	0BC6, 0BC7, 0BC8
Malayalam	0D46, 0D47, 0D48
Sinhala	0DD9, 0DDA, 0DDB
Myanmar	1031
Khmer	17C1, 17C2, 17C3
Balinese	1B3E, 1B3F
Buginese	1A19, 1A1B

In addition, there are historically related vowel characters in the Thai and Lao scripts that, for legacy reasons, are not treated as combining marks. Instead, for Thai and Lao, these vowels are represented in the backing store in visual order and require no reordering for rendering. The trade-off is that they have to be rearranged logically for searching and sorting. Because of that processing requirement, these characters are given a formal character property assignment, the Logical_Order_Exception property, as listed in *Table 4-3*. See PropList.txt in the Unicode Character Database.

Table 4-3. Thai and Lao Logical Order Exceptions

Script	Code Points
Thai	0E40..0E44
Lao	0EC0..0EC4

Split Class Zero Combining Marks. In addition to the reordrant class zero combining marks, there are a number of class zero combining marks whose representative glyph typically consists of two parts, which are split into different positions with respect to the consonant (or consonant cluster) in an aksara. Sometimes these glyphic pieces are rendered both to the left and the right of a consonant. Sometimes one piece is rendered above or below the consonant and the other piece is rendered to the left or the right. Particularly in the instances where some piece of the glyph is rendered to the left of the consonant, these split class zero combining marks pose similar implementation problems as for the reordrant marks.

Table 4-4 lists split class zero combining marks in the Unicode Standard, subgrouped by positional patterns.

Table 4-4. Class Zero Combining Marks—Split

Glyph Positions	Script	Code Points
Left and right	Bengali	09CB, 09CC
	Oriya	0B4B
	Tamil	0BCA, 0BCB, 0BCC
	Malayalam	0D4A, 0D4B, 0D4C
	Sinhala	0DDC, 0DDE
	Khmer	17C0, 17C4, 17C5
	Balinese	1B40, 1B41
Left and top	Oriya	0B48
	Sinhala	0DDA
	Khmer	17BE
Left, top, and right	Oriya	0B4C
	Sinhala	0DDD
	Khmer	17BF
Top and right	Oriya	0B57
	Kannada	0CC0, 0CC7, 0CC8, 0CCA, 0CCB
	Limbu	1925, 1926
	Balinese	1B43
Top and bottom	Telugu	0C48
	Tibetan	0F73, 0F76, 0F77, 0F78, 0F79, 0F81
	Balinese	1B3C
Top, bottom, and right	Balinese	1B3D
Bottom and right	Balinese	1B3B

One should pay very careful attention to all split class zero combining marks in implementations. Not only do they pose issues for rendering and editing, but they also often have canonical equivalences defined involving the separate pieces, when those pieces are also encoded as characters. As a consequence, the split combining marks may constitute exceptional cases under normalization. Some of the Tibetan split combining marks are discouraged from use.

The split vowels also pose difficult problems for understanding the standard, as the *phonological* status of the vowel phonemes, the *encoding* status of the characters (including any canonical equivalences), and the *graphical* status of the glyphs are easily confused, both for native users of the script and for engineers working on implementations of the standard.

Subjoined Class Zero Combining Marks. Brahmi-derived scripts that are not represented in the Unicode Standard with a virama may have class zero combining marks to represent subjoined forms of consonants. These correspond graphologically to what would be represented by a sequence of virama + consonant in other related scripts. The subjoined consonants do not pose particular rendering problems, at least not in comparison to other combining marks, but they should be noted as constituting an exception to the normal pattern in Brahmi-derived scripts of consonants being represented with base letters. This exception needs to be taken into account when doing linguistic processing or searching and sorting.

Table 4-5 lists subjoined class zero combining marks in the Unicode Standard.

Table 4-5. Class Zero Combining Marks—Subjoined

Script	Code Points
Tibetan	0F90..0F97, 0F99..0FBC
Limbu	1929, 192A, 192B

These Limbu consonants, while logically considered subjoined combining marks, are rendered mostly at the lower right of a base letter, rather than directly beneath them.

Strikethrough Class Zero Combining Marks. The Kharoshthi script is unique in having some class zero combining marks for vowels that are struck through a consonant, rather than being placed in a position around the consonant. These are also called out in *Table 4-6* specifically as a warning that they may involve particular problems for implementations.

Table 4-6. Class Zero Combining Marks—Strikethrough

Script	Code Points
Kharoshthi	10A01, 10A06

4.4 Directionality—Normative

Directional behavior is interpreted according to the Unicode Bidirectional Algorithm (see Unicode Standard Annex #9, "The Bidirectional Algorithm"). For this purpose, all characters of the Unicode Standard possess a normative *directional* type. The directional types left-to-right and right-to-left are called *strong types*, and characters of these types are called strong directional characters. Left-to-right types include most alphabetic and syllabic characters as well as all Han ideographic characters. Right-to-left types include Arabic, Hebrew, Phoenician, Syriac, Thaana, N'Ko, and Kharoshthi, and most punctuation specific to those scripts. In addition, the Unicode Bidirectional Algorithm uses *weak types* and *neutrals*. Interpretation of directional properties according to the Unicode Bidirectional Algorithm is needed for layout of right-to-left scripts such as Arabic and Hebrew.

For the directional types of Unicode characters, see the Unicode Character Database.

4.5 General Category—Normative

The Unicode Character Database defines a *General Category* for all Unicode code points. This General Category constitutes a partition of the code points into several major classes, such as letters, punctuation, and symbols, and further subclasses for each of the major classes.

Each Unicode code point is assigned a General Category value. Each value of the General Category is defined as a two-letter abbreviation, where the first letter gives information about a major class and the second letter designates a subclass of that major class. In each class, the subclass "other" merely collects the remaining characters of the major class. For example, the subclass "No" (Number, other) includes all characters of the Number class that are not a decimal digit or letter. These characters may have little in common besides their membership in the same major class.

Table 4-7 enumerates the General Category values, giving a short description of each value. See *Table 2-3* for the relationship between General Category values and basic types of code points.

A common use of the General Category of a Unicode character is to assist in determination of boundaries in text, as in Unicode Standard Annex #29, "Text Boundaries." Other common uses include determining language identifiers for programming, scripting, and markup, as in Unicode Standard Annex #31, "Identifier and Pattern Syntax," and in regular expression languages such as Perl. For more information, see Unicode Technical Standard #18, "Unicode Regular Expression Guidelines."

This property is also used to support common APIs such as `isDigit()`. Common functions such as `isLetter()` and `isUppercase()` do not extend well to the larger and more complex repertoire of Unicode. While it is possible to naively extend these functions to Unicode using the General Category and other properties, they will not work for the entire

Table 4-7. General Category

Lu	=	Letter, uppercase
Ll	=	Letter, lowercase
Lt	=	Letter, titlecase
Lm	=	Letter, modifier
Lo	=	Letter, other
Mn	=	Mark, nonspacing
Mc	=	Mark, spacing combining
Me	=	Mark, enclosing
Nd	=	Number, decimal digit
Nl	=	Number, letter
No	=	Number, other
Pc	=	Punctuation, connector
Pd	=	Punctuation, dash
Ps	=	Punctuation, open
Pe	=	Punctuation, close
Pi	=	Punctuation, initial quote (may behave like Ps or Pe depending on usage)
Pf	=	Punctuation, final quote (may behave like Ps or Pe depending on usage)
Po	=	Punctuation, other
Sm	=	Symbol, math
Sc	=	Symbol, currency
Sk	=	Symbol, modifier
So	=	Symbol, other
Zs	=	Separator, space
Zl	=	Separator, line
Zp	=	Separator, paragraph
Cc	=	Other, control
Cf	=	Other, format
Cs	=	Other, surrogate
Co	=	Other, private use
Cn	=	Other, not assigned (including noncharacters)

range of Unicode characters and range of tasks for which people use them. For more appropriate approaches, see Unicode Standard Annex #31, "Identifier and Pattern Syntax"; Unicode Standard Annex #29, "Text Boundaries"; *Section 5.18, Case Mappings*; and *Section 4.10, Letters, Alphabetic, and Ideographic.*

4.6 Numeric Value—Normative

Numeric value is a normative property of characters that represent *numbers*. This group includes characters such as fractions, subscripts, superscripts, Roman numerals, currency numerators, encircled numbers, and script-specific digits. In many traditional numbering systems, letters are used with a numeric value. Examples include Greek and Hebrew letters as well as Latin letters used in outlines (II.A.1.b). These special cases are not included here as numbers to prevent simplistic parsers from treating these letters numerically by mistake.

Decimal digits form a large subcategory of numbers consisting of those digits that can be used to form decimal-radix numbers. They include script-specific digits, but exclude characters such as Roman numerals and Greek acrophonic numerals. (Note that <1, 5> = 15 = fifteen, but <I, V> = IV = four.) Decimal digits also exclude the compatibility subscript or superscript digits to prevent simplistic parsers from misinterpreting their values in context. Numbers other than decimal digits can be used in numerical expressions and may be interpreted by a numeric parser, but it is up to the implementation to determine such specialized uses.

The Unicode Standard assigns distinct codes to the particular digits that are specific to a given script. Examples are the digits used with the Arabic script, Chinese numbers, or those of the Indic scripts. For naming conventions relevant to Arabic digits, see the introduction to *Section 8.2, Arabic*.

The Unicode Character Database gives the numeric values of Unicode characters that normally represent numbers.

Ideographic Numeric Values

CJK ideographs also may have numeric values. The primary numeric ideographs are shown in *Table 4-8*. When used to represent numbers in decimal notation, zero is represented by U+3007. Otherwise, zero is represented by U+96F6.

Table 4-8. Primary Numeric Ideographs

Code Point	Value
U+96F6	0
U+4E00	1
U+4E8C	2
U+4E09	3
U+56DB	4
U+4E94	5
U+516D	6
U+4E03	7
U+516B	8
U+4E5D	9
U+5341	10
U+767E	100
U+5343	1,000
U+4E07	10,000
U+5104	100,000,000 (10,000 × 10,000)
U+4EBF	100,000,000 (10,000 × 10,000)
U+5146	1,000,000,000,000 (10,000 × 10,000 × 10,000)

Ideographic accounting numbers are commonly used on checks and other financial instruments to minimize the possibilities of misinterpretation or fraud in the representation of numerical values. The set of accounting numbers varies somewhat between Japanese, Chinese, and Korean usage. *Table 4-9* gives a fairly complete listing of the known accounting characters. Some of these characters are ideographs with other meanings pressed into service as accounting numbers; others are used only as accounting numbers.

Table 4-9. Ideographs Used as Accounting Numbers

Number	Multiple Uses	Accounting Use Only
1	U+58F9, U+58F1	U+5F0C
2		U+8CAE, U+8CB3, U+8D30, U+5F10, U+5F0D
3	U+53C3, U+53C2	U+53C1, U+5F0E
4	U+8086	
5	U+4F0D	
6	U+9678, U+9646	
7	U+67D2	
8	U+634C	
9	U+7396	
10	U+62FE	
100	U+964C	U+4F70
1,000	U+4EDF	
10,000	U+842C	

In Japan, U+67D2 is also pronounced *urusi*, meaning "lacquer," and is treated as a variant of the standard character for "lacquer," U+6F06.

The Unicode Character Database gives the most up-to-date and complete listing of primary numeric ideographs and ideographs used as accounting numbers, including those for CJK repertoire extensions beyond the Unified Repertoire and Ordering.

4.7 Bidi Mirrored—Normative

Bidi Mirrored is a normative property of characters such as parentheses, whose images are mirrored horizontally in text that is laid out from right to left. For example, U+0028 LEFT PARENTHESIS is interpreted as *opening parenthesis*; in a left-to-right context it will appear as "(", while in a right-to-left context it will appear as the mirrored glyph ")".

Paired delimiters are mirrored even when they are used in unusual ways, as, for example, in the mathematical expressions [a,b) or]a,b[. If any of these expression is displayed from right to left, then the mirrored glyphs are used. Because of the difficulty in interpreting such expressions, authors of bidirectional text need to make sure that readers can determine the desired directionality of the text from context.

For some mathematical symbols, the "mirrored" form is not an exact mirror image. For example, the direction of the circular arrow in U+2232 CLOCKWISE CONTOUR INTEGRAL reflects the direction of the integration in coordinate space, not the text direction. In a right-to-left context, the integral sign would be mirrored, but the circular arrow would retain its direction. In a similar manner, the bidi-mirrored form of U+221B CUBE ROOT would be composed of a mirrored radix symbol with a non-mirrored digit "3". For more information, see Unicode Technical Report #25, "Unicode Support for Mathematics."

The list of mirrored characters appears in the Unicode Character Database. Note that mirroring is not limited to paired characters, but that any character with the mirrored property will need two mirrored glyphs—for example, U+222B INTEGRAL. This requirement is necessary to render the character properly in a bidirectional context. It is the default behavior in Unicode text. (For more information, see the "Semantics of Paired Punctuation" subsection in *Section 6.2, General Punctuation.*)

This property is not to be confused with the related *Bidi Mirroring Glyph* property, an informative property, that can assist in rendering mirrored characters in a right-to-left context. For more information, see BidiMirroring.txt in the Unicode Character Database.

4.8 Name—Normative

All Unicode characters have unique names that serve as formal, unique identifiers for each character. Unicode character names contain only uppercase Latin letters A through Z, digits, space, and hyphen-minus; this convention makes it easy to generate computer-language identifiers automatically from the names. (See UAX #34, "Unicode Named Character Sequences," for more information on the character name syntax.) The character names in the Unicode Standard are identical to those of the English-language edition of ISO/IEC 10646.

Where possible, character names are derived from existing conventional names of a character or symbol in English, but in many cases the character names nevertheless differ from traditional names widely used by relevant user communities. The character names of symbols and punctuation characters often describe the shape, rather than the function because these characters are used in many different contexts.

Character names are listed in *Chapter 17, Code Charts.*

Ideographs and Hangul Syllables. Names for ideographs and Hangul syllables are derived algorithmically. Unified CJK ideographs are named CJK UNIFIED IDEOGRAPH-*x*, where *x* is replaced with the hexadecimal Unicode code point—for example, CJK UNIFIED IDEOGRAPH-4E00. Similarly, compatibility CJK ideographs are named "CJK COMPATIBILITY IDEOGRAPH-*x*". The names of Hangul syllables are generated as described in "Hangul Syllable Names" in *Section 3.12, Conjoining Jamo Behavior.*

Control Codes. In the Unicode Standard, all control codes (characters with General Category=Cc) have been given the special value <control> instead of a unique character name. However, for control characters, the values of the informative Unicode 1.0 name property match the names of control functions from ISO/IEC 6429. (See *Section 4.9, Unicode 1.0 Names.*) ISO/IEC 10646 does not define names for control codes.

Named Character Sequences. In some instances, character sequences are given a normative name in the Unicode Standard. These characters are from the same namespace as character names and are unique. For details, see Unicode Standard Annex #34, "Unicode Named Character Sequences." Named character sequences are not listed in *Chapter 17, Code Charts*.

Stability. Once assigned, a character name is immutable. It will never be changed in subsequent versions of the Unicode Standard. Implementers and users can rely on the fact that a character name uniquely represents a given character. The same is true for named character sequences.

Character Name Aliases. Sometimes errors in a character name are discovered after publication. Because character names are immutable, such errors are not corrected by changing the names. However, in some instances, the Unicode Standard publishes a corrected name as a normative *character name alias*. Character name aliases are themselves immutable once published and are also guaranteed to be unique in the namespace for character names. A character may have more than one normative character name alias.

A normative character name alias is different from the informative aliases listed in *Chapter 17, Code Charts*. Informative aliases merely point out other common names in use for a given character. They are not immutable, are not guaranteed to be unique, and therefore cannot serve as an identifier for a character. Their main purpose is to help readers of the standard to locate particular characters.

User Interfaces. A list of Unicode character names may not always be the most appropriate set of choices to present to a user in a user interface. Many common characters do not have a single name for all English-speaking user communities and, of course, their native name in another language is likely to be different altogether. The names of many characters in the Unicode Standard are based on specific Latin transcription of the sounds they represent. There are often competing transcription schemes. For all these reasons, it can be more effective for a user interface to use names that were translated or otherwise adjusted to meet the expectations of the targeted user community. By also listing the formal character name, a user interface could ensure that users can unambiguously refer to the character by the name documented in the Unicode Standard.

Character Name Matching. Character names are constructed so that they can easily be transposed into identifiers in another context, such as a computer language. In matching identifiers constructed from character names, it is possible to ignore case, whitespace, and all medial hyphens except the hyphen in U+1180 HANGUL JUNGSEONG O-E and still result in a unique match. For example, "ZERO WIDTH SPACE" is equivalent to "zero-width-space" or "ZeroWidthSpace", but "CHARACTER -A" is not equivalent to "CHARACTER A" because the hyphen is not medial.

Because Unicode character names do not contain an underscore ("_"), a common strategy is to replace the hyphen, the space, or both by "_" when constructing an identifier from a character name.

4.9 Unicode 1.0 Names

The *Unicode 1.0 character name* is an informative property of the characters defined in Version 1.0 of the Unicode Standard. The names of Unicode characters were changed in the process of merging the standard with ISO/IEC 10646. The Version 1.0 character names can be obtained from the Unicode Character Database. Where the Version 1.0 character name provides additional useful information, it is listed in *Chapter 17, Code Charts*. For example, U+00B6 PILCROW SIGN has its Version 1.0 name, PARAGRAPH SIGN, listed for clarity.

The status of the Version 1.0 character names in the case of control codes differs from that for other characters. *The Unicode Standard, Version 1.0,* gave names to the C0 control codes, U+0000..U+001F, U+007F, based on then-current practice for reference to ASCII control codes. Unicode 1.0 gave no names to the C1 control codes, U+0080..U+009F. Currently, the Unicode 1.0 character name property defined in the Unicode Character Database has been updated for the control codes to reflect the ISO/IEC 6429 standard names for control functions. Those names can be seen as annotations in *Chapter 17, Code Charts*. In a few instances, because of updates to ISO/IEC 6429, those names may differ from the names that actually occurred in Unicode 1.0. For example, the Unicode 1.0 name of U+0009 was HORIZONTAL TABULATION, but the ISO/IEC 6429 name for this function is CHARACTER TABULATION, and the commonly used alias is, of course, merely *tab*.

4.10 Letters, Alphabetic, and Ideographic

Letters and Syllables. The concept of a letter is used in many contexts. Computer language standards often characterize identifiers as consisting of letters, syllables, ideographs, and digits, but do not specify exactly what a "letter," "syllable," "ideograph," or "digit" is, leaving the definitions implicitly either to a character encoding standard or to a locale specification. The large scope of the Unicode Standard means that it includes many writing systems for which these distinctions are not as self-evident as they may once have been for systems designed to work primarily for Western European languages and Japanese. In particular, while the Unicode Standard includes various "alphabets" and "syllabaries," it also includes writing systems that fall somewhere in between. As a result, no attempt is made to draw a sharp property distinction between letters and syllables.

Alphabetic. The alphabetic property is an informative property of the primary units of alphabets and/or syllabaries, whether combining or noncombining. Included in this group would be composite characters that are canonical equivalents to a combining character sequence of an alphabetic base character plus one or more combining characters; letter digraphs; contextual variants of alphabetic characters; ligatures of alphabetic characters; contextual variants of ligatures; modifier letters; letterlike symbols that are compatibility equivalents of single alphabetic letters; and miscellaneous letter elements. Notably, U+00AA FEMININE ORDINAL INDICATOR and U+00BA MASCULINE ORDINAL INDICATOR are simply abbreviatory forms involving a Latin letter and should be considered alphabetic rather than nonalphabetic symbols.

Ideographic. The ideographic property is an informative property defined in the Unicode Character Database. The ideographic property is used, for example, in determining line breaking behavior. Characters with the ideographic property include Unified CJK Ideographs, CJK Compatibility Ideographs, and characters from other blocks—for example, U+3007 IDEOGRAPHIC NUMBER ZERO and U+3006 IDEOGRAPHIC CLOSING MARK. For more information about Han ideographs, see *Section 12.1, Han*. For more about ideographs and logosyllabaries in general, see *Section 6.1, Writing Systems*.

4.11 Properties Related to Text Boundaries

The determination of text boundaries, such as word breaks or line breaks, involves contextual analysis of potential break points and the characters that surround them. Such an analysis is based on the classification of all Unicode characters by their default interaction with each particular type of text boundary. For example, the Line_Break property defines the default behavior of Unicode characters with respect to line breaking.

A number of characters have special behavior in the context of determining text boundaries. These characters are described in more detail in the subsection on "Line and Word Breaking" in *Section 16.2, Layout Controls*. For more information about text boundaries and these characters, see Unicode Standard Annex #14, "Line Breaking Properties," and Unicode Standard Annex #29, "Text Boundaries."

4.12 Characters with Unusual Properties

The behavior of most characters does not require special attention in this standard. However, the characters in *Table 4-10* exhibit special behavior. Many other characters behave in special ways but are not noted here, either because they do not affect surrounding text in the same way or because their use is intended for well-defined contexts. Examples include the compatibility characters for block drawing, the symbol pieces for large mathematical operators, and many punctuation symbols that need special handling in certain circumstances. Such characters are more fully described in the following chapters.

Table 4-10. Unusual Properties

Function	Description	Code Point and Name
Fraction formatting	*Section 6.2*	2044 FRACTION SLASH
Special behavior with nonspacing marks	*Section 2.11*, *Section 6.2*, and *Section 16.2*	0020 SPACE 00A0 NO-BREAK SPACE
Double nonspacing marks	*Section 7.9*	035C COMBINING DOUBLE BREVE BELOW 035D COMBINING DOUBLE BREVE 035E COMBINING DOUBLE MACRON 035F COMBINING DOUBLE MACRON BELOW 0360 COMBINING DOUBLE TILDE 0361 COMBINING DOUBLE INVERTED BREVE 0362 COMBINING DOUBLE RIGHTWARDS ARROW BELOW
Combining half marks	*Section 7.9*	FE20 COMBINING LIGATURE LEFT HALF FE21 COMBINING LIGATURE RIGHT HALF FE22 COMBINING DOUBLE TILDE LEFT HALF FE23 COMBINING DOUBLE TILDE RIGHT HALF
Cursive joining and ligation control	*Section 16.2*	200C ZERO WIDTH NON-JOINER 200D ZERO WIDTH JOINER
Collation weighting and sequence interpretation	*Section 16.2*	034F COMBINING GRAPHEME JOINER
Bidirectional ordering	*Section 16.2*	200E LEFT-TO-RIGHT MARK 200F RIGHT-TO-LEFT MARK 202A LEFT-TO-RIGHT EMBEDDING 202B RIGHT-TO-LEFT EMBEDDING 202C POP DIRECTIONAL FORMATTING 202D LEFT-TO-RIGHT OVERRIDE 202E RIGHT-TO-LEFT OVERRIDE
Mathematical expression formatting	*Section 15.5*	2061 FUNCTION APPLICATION 2062 INVISIBLE TIMES 2063 INVISIBLE SEPARATOR
Deprecated alternate formatting	*Section 16.3*	206A INHIBIT SYMMETRIC SWAPPING 206B ACTIVATE SYMMETRIC SWAPPING 206C INHIBIT ARABIC FORM SHAPING 206D ACTIVATE ARABIC FORM SHAPING 206E NATIONAL DIGIT SHAPES 206F NOMINAL DIGIT SHAPES
Prefixed format control	*Section 8.2* and *Section 8.3*	0600 ARABIC NUMBER SIGN 0601 ARABIC SIGN SANAH 0602 ARABIC FOOTNOTE MARKER 0603 ARABIC SIGN SAFHA 06DD ARABIC END OF AYAH 070F SYRIAC ABBREVIATION MARK

Table 4-10. Unusual Properties (Continued)

Function	Description	Code Point and Name
Brahmi-derived script dead-character formation	*Chapter 9*, *Chapter 10*, and *Chapter 11*	094D DEVANAGARI SIGN VIRAMA 09CD BENGALI SIGN VIRAMA 0A4D GURMUKHI SIGN VIRAMA 0ACD GUJARATI SIGN VIRAMA 0B4D ORIYA SIGN VIRAMA 0BCD TAMIL SIGN VIRAMA 0C4D TELUGU SIGN VIRAMA 0CCD KANNADA SIGN VIRAMA 0D4D MALAYALAM SIGN VIRAMA 0DCA SINHALA SIGN AL-LAKUNA 0E3A THAI CHARACTER PHINTHU 1039 MYANMAR SIGN VIRAMA 1714 TAGALOG SIGN VIRAMA 1734 HANUNOO SIGN PAMUDPOD 17D2 KHMER SIGN COENG 1B44 BALINESE ADEG ADEG A806 SYLOTI NAGRI SIGN HASANTA 10A3F KHAROSHTHI VIRAMA
Historical viramas with other functions	*Section 10.2* and *Section 10.4*	0F84 TIBETAN MARK HALANTA 193B LIMBU SIGN SA-I
Mongolian variation selectors	*Section 13.2*	180B MONGOLIAN FREE VARIATION SELECTOR ONE 180C MONGOLIAN FREE VARIATION SELECTOR TWO 180D MONGOLIAN FREE VARIATION SELECTOR THREE 180E MONGOLIAN VOWEL SEPARATOR
Generic variation selectors	*Section 16.4*	FE00..FE0F VARIATION SELECTOR-1..VARIATION SELECTOR-16 E0100..E01EF VARIATION SELECTOR-17..VARIATION SELECTOR-256
Tag characters	*Section 16.9*	E0001 LANGUAGE TAG E0020..E007F LANGUAGE TAG SPACE..CANCEL TAG
Ideographic variation indication	*Section 6.2*	303E IDEOGRAPHIC VARIATION INDICATOR
Ideographic description	*Section 12.2*	2FF0..2FFB IDEOGRAPHIC DESCRIPTION CHARACTER LEFT TO RIGHT..IDEOGRAPHIC DESCRIPTION CHARACTER OVERLAID
Interlinear annotation	*Section 16.8*	FFF9 INTERLINEAR ANNOTATION ANCHOR FFFA INTERLINEAR ANNOTATION SEPARATOR FFFB INTERLINEAR ANNOTATION TERMINATOR
Object replacement	*Section 16.8*	FFFC OBJECT REPLACEMENT CHARACTER
Code conversion fallback	*Section 16.8*	FFFD REPLACEMENT CHARACTER

Table 4-10. Unusual Properties (Continued)

Function	Description	Code Point and Name
Musical format control	*Section 15.11*	1D173 MUSICAL SYMBOL BEGIN BEAM 1D174 MUSICAL SYMBOL END BEAM 1D175 MUSICAL SYMBOL BEGIN TIE 1D176 MUSICAL SYMBOL END TIE 1D177 MUSICAL SYMBOL BEGIN SLUR 1D178 MUSICAL SYMBOL END SLUR 1D179 MUSICAL SYMBOL BEGIN PHRASE 1D17A MUSICAL SYMBOL END PHRASE
Line break controls	*Section 16.2*	00AD SOFT HYPHEN 200B ZERO WIDTH SPACE 2060 WORD JOINER
Byte order signature	*Section 16.8*	FEFF ZERO WIDTH NO-BREAK SPACE

CHAPTER

5

Chapter 5

Implementation Guidelines

It is possible to implement a substantial subset of the Unicode Standard as "wide ASCII" with little change to existing programming practice. However, the Unicode Standard also provides for languages and writing systems that have more complex behavior than English does. Whether one is implementing a new operating system from the ground up or enhancing existing programming environments or applications, it is necessary to examine many aspects of current programming practice and conventions to deal with this more complex behavior.

This chapter covers a series of short, self-contained topics that are useful for implementers. The information and examples presented here are meant to help implementers understand and apply the design and features of the Unicode Standard. That is, they are meant to promote good practice in implementations conforming to the Unicode Standard.

These recommended guidelines are not normative and are not binding on the implementer, but are intended to represent best practice. When implementing the Unicode Standard, it is important to look not only at the letter of the conformance rules, but also at their spirit. Many of the following guidelines have been created specifically to assist people who run into issues with conformant implementations, while reflecting the requirements of actual usage.

5.1 Transcoding to Other Standards

The Unicode Standard exists in a world of other text and character encoding standards—some private, some national, some international. A major strength of the Unicode Standard is the number of other important standards that it incorporates. In many cases, the Unicode Standard included duplicate characters to guarantee round-trip transcoding to established and widely used standards.

Issues

Conversion of characters between standards is not always a straightforward proposition. Many characters have mixed semantics in one standard and may correspond to more than one character in another. Sometimes standards give duplicate encodings for the same character; at other times the interpretation of a whole set of characters may depend on the application. Finally, there are subtle differences in what a standard may consider a character.

For these reasons, mapping tables are usually required to map between the Unicode Standard and another standard. Mapping tables need to be used consistently for text data exchange to avoid modification and loss of text data. For details, see Unicode Technical Standard #22, "Character Mapping Markup Language (CharMapML)." By contrast, conversions between different Unicode encoding forms are fast, lossless permutations.

The Unicode Standard can be used as a pivot to transcode among n different standards. This process, which is sometimes called *triangulation*, reduces the number of mapping tables that an implementation needs from $O(n^2)$ to $O(n)$.

Multistage Tables

Tables require space. Even small character sets often map to characters from several different blocks in the Unicode Standard and thus may contain up to 64K entries (for the BMP) or 1,088K entries (for the entire codespace) in at least one direction. Several techniques exist to reduce the memory space requirements for mapping tables. These techniques apply not only to transcoding tables, but also to many other tables needed to implement the Unicode Standard, including character property data, case mapping, collation tables, and glyph selection tables.

Flat Tables. If diskspace is not at issue, virtual memory architectures yield acceptable working set sizes even for flat tables because the frequency of usage among characters differs widely. Even small character sets contain many infrequently used characters. In addition, data intended to be mapped into a given character set generally does not contain characters from all blocks of the Unicode Standard (usually, only a few blocks at a time need to be transcoded to a given character set). This situation leaves certain sections of the mapping tables unused—and therefore paged to disk. The effect is most pronounced for large tables mapping from the Unicode Standard to other character sets, which have large sections simply containing mappings to the default character, or the "unmappable character" entry.

Ranges. It may be tempting to "optimize" these tables for space by providing elaborate provisions for nested ranges or similar devices. This practice leads to unnecessary performance costs on modern, highly pipelined processor architectures because of branch penalties. A faster solution is to use an *optimized two-stage table*, which can be coded without any test or branch instructions. Hash tables can also be used for space optimization, although they are not as fast as multistage tables.

Two-Stage Tables. Two-stage tables are a commonly employed mechanism to reduce table size (see *Figure 5-1*). They use an array of pointers and a default value. If a pointer is `NULL`, the value returned by a lookup operation in the table is the default value. Otherwise, the pointer references a block of values used for the second stage of the lookup. For BMP characters, it is quite efficient to organize such two-stage tables in terms of high byte and low byte values. The first stage is an array of 256 pointers, and each of the secondary blocks contains 256 values indexed by the low byte in the code point. For supplementary characters, it is often advisable to structure the pointers and second-stage arrays somewhat differently, so as to take best advantage of the very sparse distribution of supplementary characters in the remaining codespace.

Figure 5-1. Two-Stage Tables

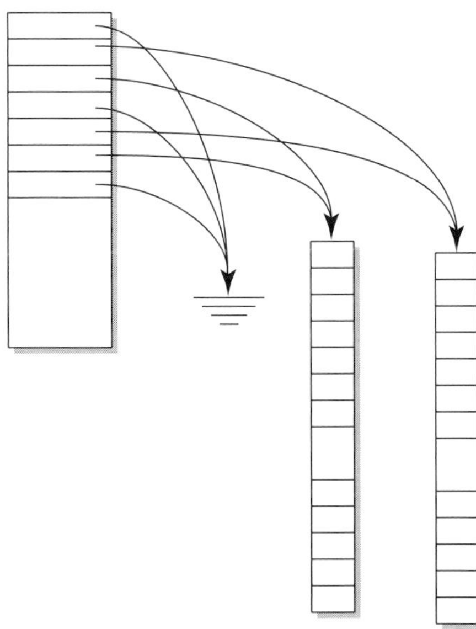

Optimized Two-Stage Table. Wherever any blocks are identical, the pointers just point to the same block. For transcoding tables, this case occurs generally for a block containing only mappings to the default or "unmappable" character. Instead of using `NULL` pointers and a default value, one "shared" block of default entries is created. This block is pointed to by all first-stage table entries, for which no character value can be mapped. By avoiding tests and branches, this strategy provides access time that approaches the simple array access, but at a great savings in storage.

Multistage Table Tuning. Given a table of arbitrary size and content, it is a relatively simple matter to write a small utility that can calculate the optimal number of stages and their width for a multistage table. Tuning the number of stages and the width of their arrays of index pointers can result in various trade-offs of table size versus average access time.

5.2 Programming Languages and Data Types

Programming languages provide for the representation and handling of characters and strings via data types, data constants (literals), and methods. Explicit support for Unicode helps with the development of multilingual applications. In some programming languages, strings are expressed as sequences (arrays) of primitive types, exactly corresponding to sequences of code units of one of the Unicode encoding forms. In other languages, strings are objects, but indexing into strings follows the semantics of addressing code units of a particular encoding form.

Data types for "characters" generally hold just a single Unicode code point value for low-level processing and lookup of character property values. When a primitive data type is used for single-code point values, a *signed* integer type can be useful; negative values can hold "sentinel" values like end-of-string or end-of-file, which can be easily distinguished from Unicode code point values. However, in most APIs, string types should be used to accommodate user-perceived characters, which may require sequences of code points.

Unicode Data Types for C

ISO/IEC Technical Report 19769, *Extensions for the programming language C to support new character types*, defines data types for the three Unicode encoding forms (UTF-8, UTF-16, and UTF-32), syntax for Unicode string and character literals, and methods for the conversion between the Unicode encoding forms. No other methods are specified.

Unicode strings are encoded as arrays of primitive types as usual. For UTF-8, UTF-16, and UTF-32, the basic types are `char`, `char16_t`, and `char32_t`, respectively. The ISO Technical Report assumes that `char` is at least 8 bits wide for use with UTF-8. While `char` and `wchar_t` may be signed or unsigned types, the new `char16_t` and `char32_t` types are defined to be unsigned integer types.

Unlike the specification in the `wchar_t` programming model, the Unicode data types do not require that a single string base unit alone (especially `char` or `char16_t`) must be able to store any one character (code point).

UTF-16 string and character literals are written with a lowercase `u` as a prefix, similar to the `L` prefix for `wchar_t` literals. UTF-32 literals are written with an uppercase `U` as a prefix. Characters outside the basic character set are available for use in string literals through the `\uhhhh` and `\Uhhhhhhhh` escape sequences.

These types and semantics are available in a compiler if the `<uchar.h>` header is present and defines the `__STDC_UTF_16__` (for `char16_t`) and `__STDC_UTF_32__` (for `char32_t`) macros.

Because Technical Report 19769 was not available when UTF-16 was first introduced, many implementations have been supporting a 16-bit `wchar_t` to contain UTF-16 code units. Such usage is not conformant to the C standard, because supplementary characters require use of pairs of `wchar_t` units in this case.

ANSI/ISO C wchar_t. With the `wchar_t` wide character type, ANSI/ISO C provides for inclusion of fixed-width, wide characters. ANSI/ISO C leaves the semantics of the wide character set to the specific implementation but requires that the characters from the portable C execution set correspond to their wide character equivalents by zero extension. The Unicode characters in the ASCII range U+0020 to U+007E satisfy these conditions. Thus, if an implementation uses ASCII to code the portable C execution set, the use of the Unicode character set for the `wchar_t` type, in either UTF-16 or UTF-32 form, fulfills the requirement.

The width of `wchar_t` is compiler-specific and can be as small as 8 bits. Consequently, programs that need to be portable across any C or C++ compiler should not use `wchar_t` for storing Unicode text. The `wchar_t` type is intended for storing compiler-defined wide characters, which may be Unicode characters in some compilers. However, programmers who want a UTF-16 implementation can use a macro or typedef (for example, `UNICHAR`) that can be compiled as `unsigned short` or `wchar_t` depending on the target compiler and platform. Other programmers who want a UTF-32 implementation can use a macro or typedef that might be compiled as `unsigned int` or `wchar_t`, depending on the target compiler and platform. This choice enables correct compilation on different platforms and compilers. Where a 16-bit implementation of `wchar_t` is guaranteed, such macros or typedefs may be predefined (for example, `TCHAR` on the Win32 API).

On systems where the native character type or `wchar_t` is implemented as a 32-bit quantity, an implementation may use the UTF-32 form to represent Unicode characters.

A limitation of the ISO/ANSI C model is its assumption that characters can always be processed in isolation. Implementations that choose to go beyond the ISO/ANSI C model may find it useful to mix widths within their APIs. For example, an implementation may have a 32-bit `wchar_t` and process strings in any of the UTF-8, UTF-16, or UTF-32 forms. Another implementation may have a 16-bit `wchar_t` and process strings as UTF-8 or UTF-16, but have additional APIs that process individual characters as UTF-32 or deal with pairs of UTF-16 code units.

5.3 Unknown and Missing Characters

This section briefly discusses how users or implementers might deal with characters that are not supported or that, although supported, are unavailable for legible rendering.

Reserved and Private-Use Character Codes

There are two classes of code points that even a "complete" implementation of the Unicode Standard cannot necessarily interpret correctly:

- Code points that are reserved
- Code points in the Private Use Area for which no private agreement exists

An implementation should not attempt to interpret such code points. However, in practice, applications must deal with unassigned code points or private-use characters. This may occur, for example, when the application is handling text that originated on a system implementing a later release of the Unicode Standard, with additional assigned characters.

Options for rendering such unknown code points include printing the code point as four to six hexadecimal digits, printing a black or white box, using appropriate glyphs such as for reserved and for private use, or simply displaying nothing. An implementation should not blindly delete such characters, nor should it unintentionally transform them into something else.

Interpretable but Unrenderable Characters

An implementation may receive a code point that is assigned to a character in the Unicode character encoding, but be unable to render it because it lacks a font for the code point or is otherwise incapable of rendering it appropriately.

In this case, an implementation might be able to provide limited feedback to the user's queries, such as being able to sort the data properly, show its script, or otherwise display the code point in a default manner. An implementation can distinguish between unrenderable (but assigned) code points and unassigned code points by printing the former with distinctive glyphs that give some general indication of their type, such as [L], [Я], [Θ], [◌̌], [か], [த], [ش], [क], [ש], [가], [漢], and so on.

Default Property Values

To work properly in implementations, unassigned code points must be given default property values as if they were characters, because various algorithms require property values to be assigned to every code point before they can function at all. These default values are not uniform across all unassigned code points, because certain ranges of code points need different values to maximize compatibility with expected future assignments. For information on the default values for each property, see its description in the Unicode Character Database.

Except where indicated, the default values are not normative—conformant implementations can use other values.

Default Ignorable Code Points

Normally, code points outside the repertoire of supported characters would be displayed with a fallback glyph, such as a black box. However, format and control characters must not have visible glyphs (although they may have an effect on other characters in display). These characters are also ignored except with respect to specific, defined processes; for example, ZERO WIDTH NON-JOINER is ignored by default in collation. To allow a greater degree of compatibility across versions of the standard, the ranges U+2060..U+206F, U+FFF0..U+FFFB, and U+E0000..U+E0FFF are reserved for format and control characters (General Category = Cf). Unassigned code points in these ranges should be ignored in processing and display. For more information, see *Section 5.20, Default Ignorable Code Points.*

Interacting with Downlevel Systems

Versions of the Unicode Standard after Unicode 2.0 are strict supersets of Unicode 2.0 and all intervening versions. The Derived Age property tracks the version of the standard at which a particular character was added to the standard. This information can be particularly helpful in some interactions with downlevel systems. If the protocol used for communication between the systems provides for an announcement of the Unicode version on each one, an uplevel system can predict which recently added characters will appear as unassigned characters to the downlevel system.

5.4 Handling Surrogate Pairs in UTF-16

The method used by UTF-16 to address the 1,048,576 supplementary code points that cannot be represented by a single 16-bit value is called *surrogate pairs*. A surrogate pair consists of a high-surrogate code unit (leading surrogate) followed by a low-surrogate code unit (trailing surrogate), as described in the specifications in *Section 3.8, Surrogates*, and the UTF-16 portion of *Section 3.9, Unicode Encoding Forms*.

In well-formed UTF-16, a trailing surrogate can be preceded only by a leading surrogate and not by another trailing surrogate, a non-surrogate, or the start of text. A leading surrogate can be followed only by a trailing surrogate and not by another leading surrogate, a non-surrogate, or the end of text. Maintaining the well-formedness of a UTF-16 code sequence or accessing characters within a UTF-16 code sequence therefore puts additional requirements on some text processes. Surrogate pairs are designed to minimize this impact.

Leading surrogates and trailing surrogates are assigned to disjoint ranges of code units. In UTF-16, non-surrogate code points can never be represented with code unit values in those ranges. Because the ranges are disjoint, each code unit in well-formed UTF-16 must meet one of only three possible conditions:

- A single non-surrogate code unit, representing a code point between 0 and $D7FF_{16}$ or between $E000_{16}$ and $FFFF_{16}$
- A leading surrogate, representing the first part of a surrogate pair
- A trailing surrogate, representing the second part of a surrogate pair

By accessing at most two code units, a process using the UTF-16 encoding form can therefore interpret any Unicode character. Determining character boundaries requires at most scanning one preceding or one following code unit without regard to any other context.

As long as an implementation does not remove either of a pair of surrogate code units or incorrectly insert another character between them, the integrity of the data is maintained. Moreover, even if the data becomes corrupted, the corruption remains localized, unlike with some other multibyte encodings such as Shift-JIS or EUC. Corrupting a single UTF-16 code unit affects only a single character. Because of non-overlap (see *Section 2.5, Encoding Forms*), this kind of error does not propagate throughout the rest of the text.

UTF-16 enjoys a beneficial frequency distribution in that, for the majority of all text data, surrogate pairs will be very rare; non-surrogate code points, by contrast, will be very common. Not only does this help to limit the performance penalty incurred when handling a variable-width encoding, but it also allows many processes either to take no specific action for surrogates or to handle surrogate pairs with existing mechanisms that are already needed to handle character sequences.

Implementations should fully support surrogate pairs in processing UTF-16 text. Without surrogate support, an implementation would not interpret any supplementary characters or guarantee the integrity of surrogate pairs. This might apply, for example, to an older implementation, conformant to Unicode Version 1.1 or earlier, before UTF-16 was defined. Support for supplementary characters is important because a significant number of them are relevant for modern use, despite their low frequency.

The individual *components* of implementations may have different levels of support for surrogates, as long as those components are assembled and communicate correctly. Low-level string processing, where a Unicode string is not interpreted but is handled simply as an array of code units, may ignore surrogate pairs. With such strings, for example, a truncation operation with an arbitrary offset might break a surrogate pair. (For further discussion, see *Section 2.7, Unicode Strings.*) For performance in string operations, such behavior is reasonable at a low level, but it requires higher-level processes to ensure that offsets are on character boundaries so as to guarantee the integrity of surrogate pairs.

Strategies for Surrogate Pair Support. Many implementations that handle advanced features of the Unicode Standard can easily be modified to support surrogate pairs in UTF-16. For example:

- Text collation can be handled by treating those surrogate pairs as "grouped characters," such as is done for "ij" in Dutch or "ch" in Slovak.
- Text entry can be handled by having a keyboard generate two Unicode code points with a single keypress, much as an ENTER key can generate CRLF or an Arabic keyboard can have a "*lam-alef*" key that generates a sequence of two characters, *lam* and *alef.*
- Truncation can be handled with the same mechanism as used to keep combining marks with base characters. For more information, see Unicode Standard Annex #29, "Text Boundaries."

Users are prevented from damaging the text if a text editor keeps *insertion points* (also known as *carets*) on character boundaries.

Implementations using UTF-8 and Unicode 8-bit strings necessitate similar considerations. The main difference from handling UTF-16 is that in the UTF-8 case the only characters that are represented with single code units (single bytes) in UTF-8 are the ASCII characters, U+0000..U+007F. Characters represented with multibyte sequences are very common in UTF-8, unlike surrogate pairs in UTF-16, which are rather uncommon. This difference in frequency may result in different strategies for handling the multibyte sequences in UTF-8.

5.5 Handling Numbers

There are many sets of characters that represent decimal digits in different scripts. Systems that interpret those characters numerically should provide the correct numerical values. For example, the sequence <U+0968 DEVANAGARI DIGIT TWO, U+0966 DEVANAGARI DIGIT ZERO> when numerically interpreted has the value *twenty.*

When converting binary numerical values to a visual form, digits can be chosen from different scripts. For example, the value *twenty* can be represented either by <U+0032 DIGIT TWO, U+0030 DIGIT ZERO> or by <U+0968 DEVANAGARI DIGIT TWO, U+0966 DEVANAGARI DIGIT ZERO> or by <U+0662 ARABIC-INDIC DIGIT TWO, U+0660 ARABIC-INDIC DIGIT ZERO>. It is recommended that systems allow users to choose the format of the resulting digits by replacing the appropriate occurrence of U+0030 DIGIT ZERO with U+0660 ARABIC-INDIC DIGIT ZERO, and so on. (See *Chapter 4, Character Properties,* for the information needed to implement formatting and scanning numerical values.)

Fullwidth variants of the ASCII digits are simply compatibility variants of regular digits and should be treated as regular Western digits.

The Roman numerals, Greek acrophonic numerals, and East Asian ideographic numerals are decimal numeral writing systems, but they are not formally decimal radix digit systems. That is, it is not possible to do a one-to-one transcoding to forms such as 123456.789. Such systems are appropriate only for positive integer writing.

Sumero-Akkadian numerals were used for sexagesimal systems. There was no symbol for zero, but by Babylonian times, a place value system was in use. Thus the exact value of a digit depended on its position in a number. There was also ambiguity in numerical representation, because a symbol such as U+12079 CUNEIFORM SIGN DISH could represent either 1 or 1×60 or $1 \times (60 \times 60)$, depending on the context. A numerical expression might also be interpreted as a sexigesimal fraction. So the sequence <1, 10, 5> might be evaluated as $1 \times 60 + 10 + 5 = 75$ or $1 \times 60 \times 60 + 10 + 5 = 3615$ or $1 + (10 + 5)/60 = 1.25$. Many other complications arise in Cuneiform numeral systems, and they clearly require special processing distinct from that used for modern decimal radix systems.

It is also possible to write numbers in two ways with CJK ideographic digits. For example, *Figure 5-2* shows how the number 1,234 can be written.

Figure 5-2. CJK Ideographic Numbers

一千二百三十四

or

一二三四

Supporting these ideographic digits for numerical parsing means that implementations must be smart about distinguishing between these two cases.

Digits often occur in situations where they need to be parsed, but are not part of numbers. One such example is alphanumeric identifiers (see Unicode Standard Annex #31, "Identifier and Pattern Syntax").

Only in higher-level protocols, such as when implementing a full mathematical formula parser, do considerations such as superscripting and subscripting of digits become crucial for numerical interpretation.

5.6 Normalization

Alternative Spellings. The Unicode Standard contains explicit codes for the most frequently used accented characters. These characters can also be composed; in the case of accented letters, characters can be composed from a base character and nonspacing mark(s).

The Unicode Standard provides decompositions for characters that can be composed using a base character plus one or more nonspacing marks. Implementations that are "liberal" in what they accept but "conservative" in what they issue will have the fewest compatibility problems.

The decomposition mappings are specific to a particular version of the Unicode Standard. Further decomposition mappings may be added to the standard for new characters encoded in the future; however, no existing decomposition mapping for a currently encoded character will ever be removed, nor will a decomposition mapping be added for a currently encoded character. This follows from the stability guarantees for normalization. See *Appendix F, Unicode Encoding Stability Policies*, for more information.

Normalization. Systems may normalize Unicode-encoded text to one particular sequence, such as normalizing composite character sequences into precomposed characters, or vice versa (see *Figure 5-3*).

Figure 5-3. Normalization

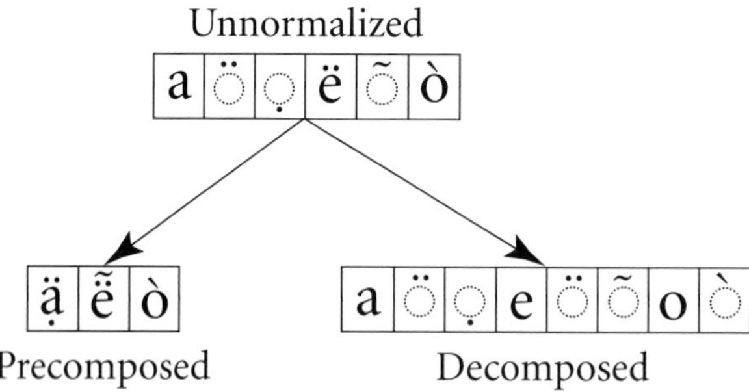

Compared to the number of *possible* combinations, only a relatively small number of precomposed base character plus nonspacing marks have independent Unicode character values. Most existed in dominant standards.

Systems that cannot handle nonspacing marks can normalize to precomposed characters; this option can accommodate most modern Latin-based languages. Such systems can use fallback rendering techniques to at least visually indicate combinations that they cannot handle (see the "Fallback Rendering" subsection of *Section 5.13, Rendering Nonspacing Marks*).

In systems that *can* handle nonspacing marks, it may be useful to normalize so as to eliminate precomposed characters. This approach allows such systems to have a homogeneous representation of composed characters and maintain a consistent treatment of such characters. However, in most cases, it does not require too much extra work to support mixed forms, which is the simpler route.

The standard forms for normalization are defined in Unicode Standard Annex #15, "Unicode Normalization Forms." For further information, see *Chapter 3, Conformance*; "Equivalent Sequences" in *Section 2.2, Unicode Design Principles*; and *Section 2.11, Combining Characters.*

5.7 Compression

Using the Unicode character encoding may increase the amount of storage or memory space dedicated to the text portion of files. Compressing Unicode-encoded files or strings can therefore be an attractive option if the text portion is a large part of the volume of data compared to binary and numeric data, and if the processing overhead of the compression and decompression is acceptable.

Compression always constitutes a higher-level protocol and makes interchange dependent on knowledge of the compression method employed. For a detailed discussion of compression and a standard compression scheme for Unicode, see Unicode Technical Standard #6, "A Standard Compression Scheme for Unicode."

Encoding forms defined in *Section 2.5, Encoding Forms*, have different storage characteristics. For example, as long as text contains only characters from the Basic Latin (ASCII) block, it occupies the same amount of space whether it is encoded with the UTF-8 or ASCII codes. Conversely, text consisting of CJK ideographs encoded with UTF-8 will require more space than equivalent text encoded with UTF-16.

For processing rather than storage, the Unicode encoding form is usually selected for easy interoperability with existing APIs. Where there is a choice, the trade-off between decoding complexity (high for UTF-8, low for UTF-16, trivial for UTF-32) and memory and cache bandwidth (high for UTF-32, low for UTF-8 or UTF-16) should be considered.

5.8 Newline Guidelines

Newlines are represented on different platforms by carriage return (CR), line feed (LF), CRLF, or next line (NEL). Not only are newlines represented by different characters on different platforms, but they also have ambiguous behavior even on the same platform. These characters are often transcoded directly into the corresponding Unicode code points when a character set is transcoded; this means that even programs handling pure Unicode have to deal with the problems. Especially with the advent of the Web, where text on a single machine can arise from many sources, this causes a significant problem.

Newline characters are used to explicitly indicate line boundaries. For more information, see Unicode Standard Annex #14, "Line Breaking Properties." Newlines are also handled specially in the context of regular expressions. For information, see Unicode Technical Standard #18, "Unicode Regular Expression Guidelines." For the use of these characters in markup languages, see Unicode Technical Report #20, "Unicode in XML and Other Markup Languages."

Definitions

Table 5-1 provides hexadecimal values for the acronyms used in these guidelines.

Table 5-1. Hex Values for Acronyms

Acronym	Name	Unicode	ASCII	EBCDIC	
CR	carriage return	000D	0D	0D	0D
LF	line feed	000A	0A	25	15
CRLF	carriage return and line feed	<000D 000A>	<0D 0A>	<0D 25>	<0D 15>
NEL	next line	0085	85	15	25
VT	vertical tab	000B	0B	0B	0B
FF	form feed	000C	0C	0C	0C
LS	line separator	2028	n/a	n/a	n/a
PS	paragraph separator	2029	n/a	n/a	n/a

The acronyms shown in *Table 5-1* correspond to characters or sequences of characters. The name column shows the usual names used to refer to the characters in question, whereas the other columns show the Unicode, ASCII, and EBCDIC encoded values for the characters.

Encoding. Except for LS and PS, the newline characters discussed here are encoded as control codes. Many control codes were originally designed for device control but, together with TAB, the newline characters are commonly used as part of plain text. For more information on how Unicode encodes control codes, see *Section 16.1, Control Codes.*

Notation. This discussion of newline guidelines uses lowercase when referring to functions having to do with line determination, but uses the acronyms when referring to the actual characters involved. Keys on keyboards are indicated in all caps. For example:

> The line separator may be expressed by LS in Unicode text or CR on some platforms. It may be entered into text with the SHIFT-RETURN key.

EBCDIC. *Table 5-1* shows the two mappings of LF and NEL used by EBCDIC systems. The first EBCDIC column shows the default control code mapping of these characters, which is used in most EBCDIC environments. The second column shows the z/OS Unix System Services (Open Edition) mapping of LF and NEL. That mapping arises from the use of the LF character for the newline function in C programs and in Unix environments, while text files on z/OS traditionally use NEL for the newline function.

NEL (next line) is not actually defined in 7-bit ASCII. It is defined in the ISO control function standard, ISO 6429, as a C1 control function. However, the 0x85 mapping shown in the ASCII column in *Table 5-1* is the usual way that this C1 control function is mapped in ASCII-based character encodings.

Newline Function. The acronym *NLF* (*newline function*) stands for the generic control function for indication of a new line break. It may be represented by different characters, depending on the platform, as shown in *Table 5-2*.

Table 5-2. NLF Platform Correlations

Platform	NLF Value
MacOS 9.x and earlier	CR
MacOS X	LF
Unix	LF
Windows	CRLF
EBCDIC-based OS	NEL

Line Separator and Paragraph Separator

A paragraph separator—independent of how it is encoded—is used to indicate a separation between paragraphs. A line separator indicates where a line break alone should occur, typically within a paragraph. For example:

> This is a paragraph with a line separator at this point,
> causing the word "causing" to appear on a different line, but not causing the typical paragraph indentation, sentence breaking, line spacing, or change in flush (right, center, or left paragraphs).

For comparison, line separators basically correspond to HTML <BR>, and paragraph separators to older usage of HTML <P> (modern HTML delimits paragraphs by enclosing them in <P>...</P>). In word processors, paragraph separators are usually entered using a keyboard RETURN or ENTER; line separators are usually entered using a modified RETURN or ENTER, such as SHIFT-ENTER.

A record separator is used to separate records. For example, when exchanging tabular data, a common format is to tab-separate the cells and to use a CRLF at the end of a line of cells. This function is not precisely the same as line separation, but the same characters are often used.

Traditionally, *NLF* started out as a line separator (and sometimes record separator). It is still used as a line separator in simple text editors such as program editors. As platforms and programs started to handle word processing with automatic line-wrap, these characters were reinterpreted to stand for paragraph separators. For example, even such simple programs as the Windows Notepad program and the Mac SimpleText program interpret their platform's *NLF* as a paragraph separator, not a line separator.

Once *NLF* was reinterpreted to stand for a paragraph separator, in some cases another control character was pressed into service as a line separator. For example, vertical tabulation VT is used in Microsoft Word. However, the choice of character for line separator is even less standardized than the choice of character for *NLF*.

Many Internet protocols and a lot of existing text treat *NLF* as a line separator, so an implementer cannot simply treat *NLF* as a paragraph separator in all circumstances.

Recommendations

The Unicode Standard defines two unambiguous separator characters: U+2029 PARAGRAPH SEPARATOR (PS) and U+2028 LINE SEPARATOR (LS). In Unicode text, the PS and LS characters should be used wherever the desired function is unambiguous. Otherwise, the following recommendations specify how to cope with an *NLF* when converting from other character sets to Unicode, when interpreting characters in text, and when converting from Unicode to other character sets.

Note that even if an implementer knows which characters represent *NLF* on a particular platform, CR, LF, CRLF, and NEL should be treated the same on input and in interpretation. Only on output is it necessary to distinguish between them.

Converting from Other Character Code Sets

R1 If the exact usage of any NLF is known, convert it to LS or PS.

R1a If the exact usage of any NLF is unknown, remap it to the platform NLF.

Recommendation R1a does not really help in interpreting Unicode text unless the implementer is the *only* source of that text, because another implementer may have left in LF, CR, CRLF, or NEL.

Interpreting Characters in Text

R2 Always interpret PS as paragraph separator and LS as line separator.

R2a In word processing, interpret any NLF the same as PS.

R2b In simple text editors, interpret any NLF the same as LS.

In line breaking, both PS and LS terminate a line; therefore, the Unicode Line Breaking Algorithm in Unicode Standard Annex #14, "Line Breaking Properties," is defined such that any NLF causes a line break.

R2c In parsing, choose the safest interpretation.

For example, in recommendation R2c an implementer dealing with sentence break heuristics would reason in the following way that it is safer to interpret any *NLF* as LS:

- Suppose an *NLF* were interpreted as LS, when it was meant to be PS. Because most paragraphs are terminated with punctuation anyway, this would cause misidentification of sentence boundaries in only a few cases.
- Suppose an *NLF* were interpreted as PS, when it was meant to be LS. In this case, line breaks would cause sentence breaks, which would result in significant problems with the sentence break heuristics.

Converting to Other Character Code Sets

R3 ***If the intended target is known, map NLF, LS, and PS depending on the target conventions.***

For example, when mapping to Microsoft Word's internal conventions for documents, LS would be mapped to VT, and PS and any *NLF* would be mapped to CRLF.

R3a ***If the intended target is unknown, map NLF, LS, and PS to the platform newline convention (CR, LF, CRLF, or NEL).***

In Java, for example, this is done by mapping to a string `nlf`, defined as follows:

```
String nlf = System.getProperties("line.separator");
```

Input and Output

R4 ***A `readline` function should stop at NLF, LS, FF, or PS. In the typical implementation, it does not include the NLF, LS, PS, or FF that caused it to stop.***

Because the separator is lost, the use of such a `readline` function is limited to text processing, where there is no difference among the types of separators.

R4a ***A `writeline` (or `newline`) function should convert NLF, LS, and PS according to the recommendations R3 and R3a.***

In C, `gets` is defined to terminate at a newline and replaces the newline with `'\0'`, while `fgets` is defined to terminate at a newline and includes the newline in the array into which it copies the data. C implementations interpret `'\n'` either as LF or as the underlying platform newline *NLF*, depending on where it occurs. EBCDIC C compilers substitute the relevant codes, based on the EBCDIC execution set.

Page Separator

FF is commonly used as a page separator, and it should be interpreted that way in text. When displaying on the screen, it causes the text after the separator to be forced to the next page. It is interpreted in the same way as the LS for line breaking, in parsing, or in input segmentation such as `readline`. FF does not interrupt a paragraph, as paragraphs can and do span page boundaries.

5.9 Regular Expressions

Byte-oriented regular expression engines require extensions to handle Unicode successfully. The following issues are involved in such extensions:

- Unicode is a large character set—regular expression engines that are adapted to handle only small character sets may not scale well.
- Unicode encompasses a wide variety of languages that can have very different characteristics than English or other Western European text.

For detailed information on the requirements of Unicode regular expressions, see Unicode Technical Standard #18, "Unicode Regular Expression Guidelines."

5.10 Language Information in Plain Text

Requirements for Language Tagging

The requirement for language information embedded in plain text data is often overstated. Many commonplace operations such as collation seldom require this extra information. In collation, for example, foreign language text is generally collated as if it were *not* in a foreign language. (See Unicode Technical Standard #10, "Unicode Collation Algorithm," for more information.) For example, an index in an English book would not sort the Slovak word "chlieb" after "czar," where it would be collated in Slovak, nor would an English atlas put the Swedish city of Örebro after Zanzibar, where it would appear in Swedish.

Text to speech is also an area where the case for embedded language information is overstated. Although language information may be useful in performing text-to-speech operations, modern software for doing acceptable text-to-speech must be so sophisticated in performing grammatical analysis of text that the extra work in determining the language is not significant in practice.

Language information can be useful in certain operations, such as spell-checking or hyphenating a mixed-language document. It is also useful in choosing the default font for a run of unstyled text; for example, the ellipsis character may have a very different appearance in Japanese fonts than in European fonts. Modern font and layout technologies produce different results based on language information. For example, the angle of the acute accent may be different for French and Polish.

Language Tags and Han Unification

A common misunderstanding about Unicode Han unification is the mistaken belief that Han characters cannot be rendered properly without language information. This idea might lead an implementer to conclude that language information must always be added to plain text using the tags. However, this implication is incorrect. The goal and methods of

Han unification were to ensure that the text remained legible. Although font, size, width, and other format specifications need to be added to produce precisely the same appearance on the source and target machines, plain text remains legible in the absence of these specifications.

There should never be any confusion in Unicode, because the distinctions between the unified characters are all within the range of stylistic variations that exist in each country. No unification in Unicode should make it impossible for a reader to identify a character if it appears in a different font. Where precise font information is important, it is best conveyed in a rich text format.

Typical Scenarios. The following e-mail scenarios illustrate that the need for language information with Han characters is often overstated:

- Scenario 1. A Japanese user sends out untagged Japanese text. Readers are Japanese (with Japanese fonts). Readers see no differences from what they expect.
- Scenario 2. A Japanese user sends out an untagged mixture of Japanese and Chinese text. Readers are Japanese (with Japanese fonts) and Chinese (with Chinese fonts). Readers see the mixed text with only one font, but the text is still legible. Readers recognize the difference between the languages by the content.
- Scenario 3. A Japanese user sends out a mixture of Japanese and Chinese text. Text is marked with font, size, width, and so on, because the exact format is important. Readers have the fonts and other display support. Readers see the mixed text with different fonts for different languages. They recognize the difference between the languages by the content, and see the text with glyphs that are more typical for the particular language.

It is common even in printed matter to render passages of foreign language text in native-language fonts, just for familiarity. For example, Chinese text in a Japanese document is commonly rendered in a Japanese font.

5.11 Editing and Selection

Consistent Text Elements

As far as a user is concerned, the underlying representation of text is not a material concern, but it is important that an editing interface present a uniform implementation of what the user thinks of as characters. (See "'Characters' and Grapheme Clusters" in *Section 2.11, Combining Characters.*) The user expects them to behave as units in terms of mouse selection, arrow key movement, backspacing, and so on. For example, when such behavior is implemented, and an accented letter is represented by a sequence of base character plus a nonspacing combining mark, using the right arrow key would logically skip from the start of the base character to the end of the last nonspacing character.

In some cases, editing a user-perceived "character" or visual cluster element by element may be the preferred way. For example, a system might have the *backspace* key delete by using the underlying code point, while the *delete* key could delete an entire cluster. Moreover, because of the way keyboards and input method editors are implemented, there often may not be a one-to-one relationship between what the user thinks of as a character and the key or key sequence used to input it.

Three types of boundaries are generally useful in editing and selecting within words: cluster boundaries, stacked boundaries and atomic character boundaries.

Cluster Boundaries. Arbitrarily defined cluster boundaries may occur in scripts such as Devanagari, for which selection may be defined as applying to syllables or parts of syllables. In such cases, combining character sequences such as *ka* + *vowel sign a* or conjunct clusters such as *ka* + *halant* + *ta* are selected as a single unit. (See *Figure 5-4.*)

Figure 5-4. Consistent Character Boundaries

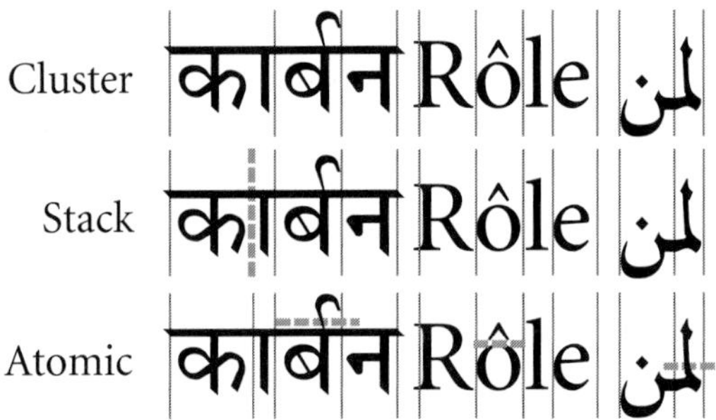

Stacked Boundaries. Stacked boundaries are generally somewhat finer than cluster boundaries. Free-standing elements (such as *vowel sign a* in Devanagari) can be independently selected, but any elements that "stack" (including vertical ligatures such as Arabic *lam* + *meem* in *Figure 5-4*) can be selected only as a single unit. Stacked boundaries treat default grapheme clusters as single entities, much like composite characters. (See Unicode Standard Annex #29, "Text Boundaries," for the definition of default grapheme clusters and for a discussion of how grapheme clusters can be tailored to meet the needs of defining arbitrary cluster boundaries.)

Atomic Character Boundaries. The use of atomic character boundaries is closest to selection of individual Unicode characters. However, most modern systems indicate selection with some sort of rectangular highlighting. This approach places restrictions on the consistency of editing because some sequences of characters do not linearly progress from the start of the line. When characters stack, two mechanisms are used to visually indicate partial selection: linear and nonlinear boundaries.

Linear Boundaries. Use of linear boundaries treats the entire width of the resultant glyph as belonging to the first character of the sequence, and the remaining characters in the backing-store representation as having no width and being visually afterward.

This option is the simplest mechanism. The advantage of this system is that it requires very little additional implementation work. The disadvantage is that it is never easy to select narrow characters, let alone a zero-width character. Mechanically, it requires the user to select just to the right of the nonspacing mark and drag just to the left. It also does not allow the selection of individual nonspacing marks if more than one is present.

Nonlinear Boundaries. Use of nonlinear boundaries divides any stacked element into parts. For example, picking a point halfway across a *lam* + *meem* ligature can represent the division between the characters. One can either allow highlighting with multiple rectangles or use another method such as coloring the individual characters.

With more work, a precomposed character can behave in deletion as if it were a composed character sequence with atomic character boundaries. This procedure involves deriving the character's decomposition on the fly to get the components to be used in simulation. For example, deletion occurs by decomposing, removing the last character, then recomposing (if more than one character remains). However, this technique does not work in general editing and selection.

In most editing systems, the code point is the smallest addressable item, so the selection and assignment of properties (such as font, color, letterspacing, and so on) cannot be done on any finer basis than the code point. Thus the accent on an "e" could not be colored differently than the base in a precomposed character, although it could be colored differently if the text were stored internally in a decomposed form.

Just as there is no single notion of text element, so there is no single notion of editing character boundaries. At different times, users may want different degrees of granularity in the editing process. Two methods suggest themselves. First, the user may set a global preference for the character boundaries. Second, the user may have alternative command mechanisms, such as Shift-Delete, which give more (or less) fine control than the default mode.

5.12 Strategies for Handling Nonspacing Marks

By following these guidelines, a programmer should be able to implement systems and routines that provide for the effective and efficient use of nonspacing marks in a wide variety of applications and systems. The programmer also has the choice between minimal techniques that apply to the vast majority of existing systems and more sophisticated techniques that apply to more demanding situations, such as higher-end desktop publishing.

In this section and the following section, the terms *nonspacing mark* and *combining character* are used interchangeably. The terms *diacritic, accent, stress mark, Hebrew point, Arabic vowel*, and others are sometimes used instead of *nonspacing mark*. (They refer to particular types of nonspacing marks.) Properly speaking, a nonspacing mark is any combining character that does not add space along the writing direction. For a formal definition of nonspacing mark, see *Section 3.6, Combination.*

A relatively small number of implementation features are needed to support nonspacing marks. Different levels of implementation are also possible. A minimal system yields good results and is relatively simple to implement. Most of the features required by such a system are simply modifications of existing software.

As nonspacing marks are required for a number of writing systems, such as Arabic, Hebrew, and those of South Asia, many vendors already have systems capable of dealing with these characters and can use their experience to produce general-purpose software for handling these characters in the Unicode Standard.

Rendering. Composite character sequences can be rendered effectively by means of a fairly simple mechanism. In simple character rendering, a nonspacing combining mark has a zero advance width, and a composite character sequence will have the same width as the base character.

Wherever a sequence of base character plus one or more nonspacing marks occurs, the glyphs for the nonspacing marks can be positioned relative to the base. The ligature mechanisms in the fonts can also substitute a glyph representing the combined form. In some cases the width of the base should change because of an applied accent, such as with "î". The ligature or contextual form mechanisms in the font can be used to change the width of the base in cases where this is required.

Other Processes. Correct multilingual comparison routines must already be able to compare a sequence of characters as one character, or one character as if it were a sequence. Such routines can also handle combining character sequences when supplied with the appropriate data. When searching strings, remember to check for additional nonspacing marks in the target string that may affect the interpretation of the last matching character.

Line breaking algorithms generally use state machines for determining word breaks. Such algorithms can be easily adapted to prevent separation of nonspacing marks from base characters. (See also the discussion in *Section 5.6, Normalization*. For details in particular contexts, see Unicode Technical Standard #10, "Unicode Collation Algorithm"; Unicode Standard Annex #14, "Line Breaking Properties"; and Unicode Standard Annex #29, "Text Boundaries.")

Keyboard Input

A common implementation for the input of combining character sequences is the use of *dead keys*. These keys match the mechanics used by typewriters to generate such sequences through overtyping the base character after the nonspacing mark. In computer implementations, keyboards enter a special state when a dead key is pressed for the accent and emit a precomposed character only when one of a limited number of "legal" base characters is entered. It is straightforward to adapt such a system to emit combining character sequences or precomposed characters as needed.

Typists, especially in the Latin script, are trained on systems that work using dead keys. However, many scripts in the Unicode Standard (including the Latin script) may be implemented according to the handwriting sequence, in which users type the base character first, *followed* by the accents or other nonspacing marks (see *Figure 5-5*).

Figure 5-5. Dead Keys Versus Handwriting Sequence

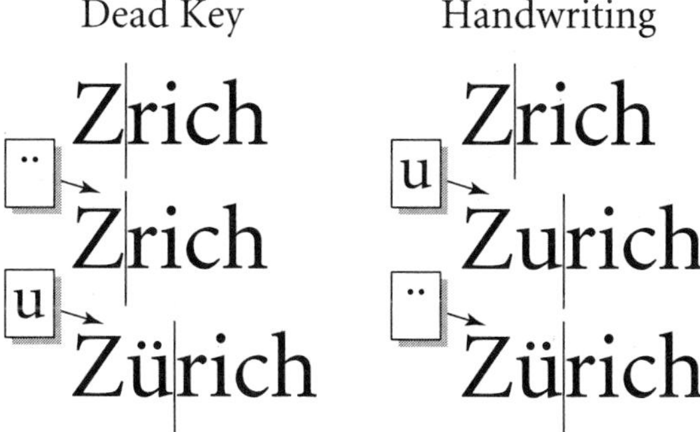

In the case of handwriting sequence, each keystroke produces a distinct, natural change on the screen; there are no hidden states. To add an accent to any existing character, the user positions the insertion point (*caret*) after the character and types the accent.

Truncation

There are two types of truncation: truncation by character count and truncation by displayed width. Truncation by character count can entail loss (be lossy) or be lossless.

Truncation by character count is used where, due to storage restrictions, a limited number of characters can be entered into a field; it is also used where text is broken into buffers for transmission and other purposes. The latter case can be lossless if buffers are recombined seamlessly before processing or if lookahead is performed for possible combining character sequences straddling buffers.

When fitting data into a field of limited storage length, some information will be lost. The preferred position for truncating text in that situation is on a grapheme cluster boundary. As *Figure 5-6* shows, such truncation can mean truncating at an earlier point than the last character that would have fit within the physical storage limitation. (See Unicode Standard Annex #29, "Text Boundaries.")

Truncation by displayed width is used for visual display in a narrow field. In this case, truncation occurs on the basis of the width of the resulting string rather than on the basis of a character count. In simple systems, it is easiest to truncate by width, starting from the end and working backward by subtracting character widths as one goes. Because a trailing nonspacing mark does not contribute to the measurement of the string, the result will not separate nonspacing marks from their base characters.

If the textual environment is more sophisticated, the widths of characters may depend on their context, due to effects such as kerning, ligatures, or contextual formation. For such

Figure 5-6. Truncating Grapheme Clusters

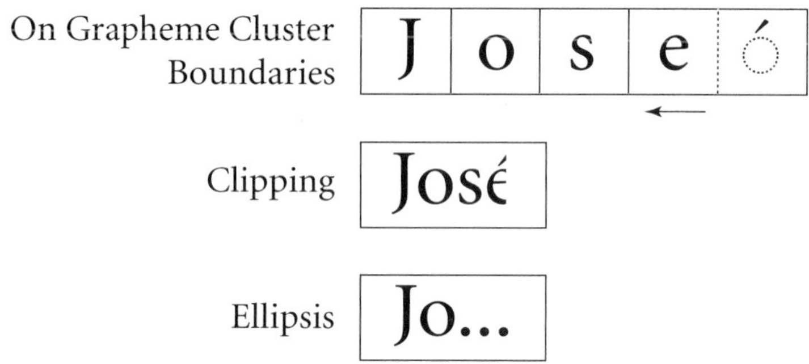

systems, the width of a precomposed character, such as an "ï", may be different than the width of a narrow base character alone. To handle these cases, a final check should be made on any truncation result derived from successive subtractions.

A different option is simply to clip the characters graphically. Unfortunately, this may result in clipping off part of a character, which can be visually confusing. Also, if the clipping occurs between characters, it may not give any visual feedback that characters are being omitted. A graphic or ellipsis can be used to give this visual feedback.

5.13 Rendering Nonspacing Marks

This discussion assumes the use of proportional fonts, where the widths of individual characters can vary. Various techniques can be used with monospaced fonts. In general, however, it is possible to get only a semblance of a correct rendering for most scripts in such fonts.

When rendering a sequence consisting of more than one nonspacing mark, the nonspacing marks should, by default, be stacked outward from the base character. That is, if two nonspacing marks appear over a base character, then the first nonspacing mark should appear on top of the base character, and the second nonspacing mark should appear on top of the first. If two nonspacing marks appear under a base character, then the first nonspacing mark should appear beneath the base character, and the second nonspacing mark should appear below the first (see *Section 2.11, Combining Characters*). This default treatment of multiple, potentially interacting nonspacing marks is known as the inside-out rule (see *Figure 5-7*).

This default behavior may be altered based on typographic preferences or on knowledge of the specific orthographic treatment to be given to multiple nonspacing marks in the context of a particular writing system. For example, in the modern Vietnamese writing system, an acute or grave accent (serving as a tone mark) may be positioned slightly to one side of a circumflex accent rather than directly above it. If the text to be displayed is known to

Figure 5-7. Inside-Out Rule

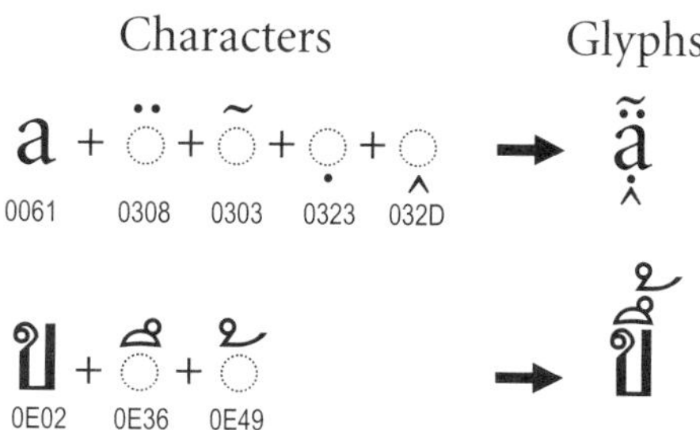

employ a different typographic convention (either implicitly through knowledge of the language of the text or explicitly through rich text-style bindings), then an alternative positioning may be given to multiple nonspacing marks instead of that specified by the default inside-out rule.

Fallback Rendering. Several methods are available to deal with an unknown composed character sequence that is outside of a fixed, renderable set (see *Figure 5-8*). One method (*Show Hidden*) indicates the inability to draw the sequence by drawing the base character first and then rendering the nonspacing mark as an individual unit, with the nonspacing mark positioned on a dotted circle. (This convention is used in *Chapter 17, Code Charts*.)

Figure 5-8. Fallback Rendering

Another method (*Simple Overlap*) uses a default fixed position for an overlapping zero-width nonspacing mark. This position is generally high enough to make sure that the mark does not collide with capital letters. This will mean that this mark is placed too high above many lowercase letters. For example, the default positioning of a circumflex can be above the ascent, which will place it above capital letters. Even though the result will not be particularly attractive for letters such as *g-circumflex*, the result should generally be recognizable in the case of single nonspacing marks.

In a degenerate case, a nonspacing mark occurs as the first character in the text or is separated from its base character by a *line separator*, *paragraph separator*, or other format character that causes a positional separation. This result is called a defective combining character sequence (see *Section 3.6, Combination*). Defective combining character sequences should be rendered as if they had a *no-break space* as a base character. (See *Section 7.9, Combining Marks*.)

Bidirectional Positioning. In bidirectional text, the nonspacing marks are reordered *with* their base characters; that is, they visually apply to the same base character after the algorithm is used (see *Figure 5-9*). There are a few ways to accomplish this positioning.

Figure 5-9. Bidirectional Placement

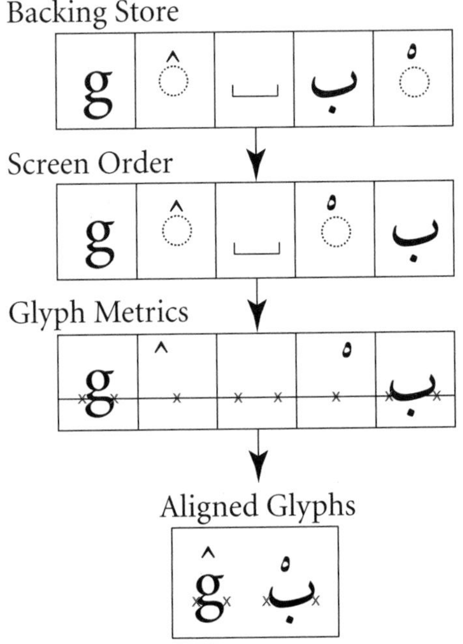

The simplest method is similar to the *Simple Overlap* fallback method. In the Bidirectional Algorithm, combining marks take the level of their base character. In that case, Arabic and Hebrew nonspacing marks would come to the left of their base characters. The font is designed so that instead of overlapping to the left, the Arabic and Hebrew nonspacing marks overlap to the right. In *Figure 5-9*, the "glyph metrics" line shows the pen start and end for each glyph with such a design. After aligning the start and end points, the final result shows each nonspacing mark attached to the corresponding base letter. More sophisticated rendering could then apply the positioning methods outlined in the next section.

Some rendering software may require keeping the nonspacing mark glyphs consistently ordered to the right of the base character glyphs. In that case, a second pass can be done after producing the "screen order" to put the odd-level nonspacing marks on the right of their base characters. As the levels of nonspacing marks will be the same as their base characters, this pass can swap the order of nonspacing mark glyphs and base character glyphs in right-to-left (odd) levels. (See Unicode Standard Annex #9, "The Bidirectional Algorithm.")

Justification. Typically, full justification of text adds extra space at space characters so as to widen a line; however, if there are too few (or no) space characters, some systems add extra letterspacing between characters (see *Figure 5-10*). This process needs to be modified if zero-width nonspacing marks are present in the text. Otherwise, if extra justifying space is added after the base character, it can have the effect of visually separating the nonspacing mark from its base.

Figure 5-10. Justification

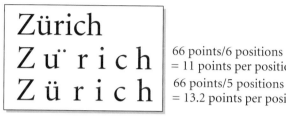

66 points/6 positions
= 11 points per position
66 points/5 positions
= 13.2 points per position

Because nonspacing marks always follow their base character, proper justification adds letterspacing between characters only if the second character is a base character.

Canonical Equivalence

Canonical equivalence must be taken into account in rendering multiple accents, so that any two canonically equivalent sequences display as the same. This is particularly important when the canonical order is not the customary keyboarding order, which happens in Arabic with vowel signs or in Hebrew with points. In those cases, a rendering system may be presented with either the typical typing order or the canonical order resulting from normalization, as shown in *Table 5-3*.

Table 5-3. Typing Order Differing from Canonical Order

Typical Typing Order	Canonical Order
U+0631 ر ARABIC LETTER REH + U+0651 ◌ّ ARABIC SHADDA + U+064B ◌ً ARABIC FATHATAN	U+0631 ر ARABIC LETTER REH + U+064B ◌ً ARABIC FATHATAN + U+0651 ◌ّ ARABIC SHADDA

With a restricted repertoire of nonspacing mark sequences, such as those required for Arabic, a ligature mechanism can be used to get the right appearance, as described earlier. When a fallback mechanism for placing accents based on their combining class is employed, the system should logically reorder the marks before applying the mechanism.

Rendering systems should handle *any* of the canonically equivalent orders of combining marks. This is not a performance issue: the amount of time necessary to reorder combining marks is insignificant compared to the time necessary to carry out other work required for rendering.

A rendering system can reorder the marks internally if necessary, as long as the resulting sequence is canonically equivalent. In particular, any permutation of the non-zero combining class values can be used for a canonical-equivalent internal ordering. For example, a rendering system could internally permute weights to have U+0651 ARABIC SHADDA precede all vowel signs. This would use the remapping shown in *Table 5-4*.

Table 5-4. Permuting Combining Class Weights

Combining Class		Internal Weight
27	→	33
28	→	27
29	→	28
30	→	29
31	→	30
32	→	31
33	→	32

Only non-zero combining class values can be changed, and they can be permuted *only*, not combined or split. This can be restated as follows:

- Two characters that have the same combining class values cannot be given distinct internal weights.
- Two characters that have distinct combining class values cannot be given the same internal weight.
- Characters with a combining class of zero must be given an internal weight of zero.

Positioning Methods

A number of methods are available to position nonspacing marks so that they are in the correct location relative to the base character and previous nonspacing marks.

Positioning with Ligatures. A fixed set of combining character sequences can be rendered effectively by means of fairly simple substitution (see *Figure 5-11*). Wherever the glyphs representing a sequence of <base character, nonspacing mark> occur, a glyph representing the combined form is substituted. Because the nonspacing mark has a zero advance width, the composed character sequence will automatically have the same width as the base character. More sophisticated text rendering systems may take additional measures to account for those cases where the composed character sequence kerns differently or has a slightly different advance width than the base character.

Positioning with ligatures is perhaps the simplest method of supporting nonspacing marks. Whenever there is a small, fixed set, such as those corresponding to the precomposed characters of ISO/IEC 8859-1 (Latin-1), this method is straightforward to apply. Because the composed character sequence almost always has the same width as the base character, ren-

Figure 5-11. Positioning with Ligatures

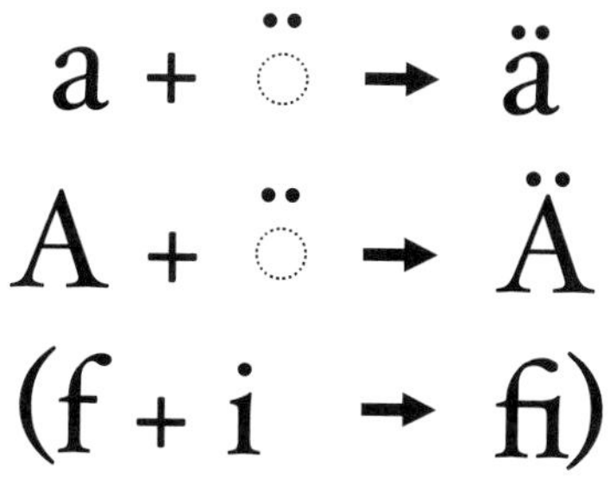

a + ◌̈ → ä

A + ◌̈ → Ä

(f + i → ﬁ)

dering, measurement, and editing of these characters are much easier than for the general case of ligatures.

If a combining character sequence does not form a ligature, then either positioning with contextual forms or positioning with enhanced kerning can be applied. If they are not available, then a fallback method can be used.

Positioning with Contextual Forms. A more general method of dealing with positioning of nonspacing marks is to use contextual formation (see *Figure 5-12*). In this case for Devanagari, a consonant RA is rendered with a nonspacing glyph (*reph*) positioned above a base consonant. (See "Rendering Devanagari" in *Section 9.1, Devanagari.*) Depending on the position of the stem for the corresponding base consonant glyph, a contextual choice is made between *reph* glyphs with different side bearings, so that the tip of the *reph* will be placed correctly with respect to the base consonant's stem. Base glyphs generally fall into a fairly small number of classes, depending on their general shape and width, so a corresponding number of contextually distinct glyphs for the nonspacing mark suffice to produce correct rendering.

Figure 5-12. Positioning with Contextual Forms

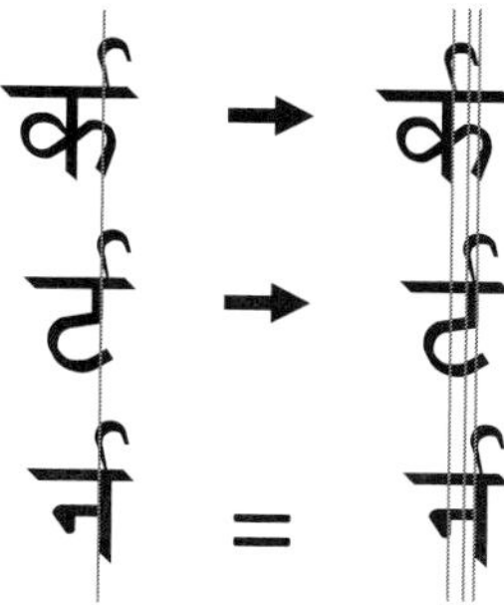

In general cases, a number of different heights of glyphs can be chosen to allow stacking of glyphs, at least for a few deep. (When these bounds are exceeded, then the fallback methods can be used.) This method can be combined with the ligature method so that in specific cases ligatures can be used to produce fine variations in position and shape.

Positioning with Enhanced Kerning. A third technique for positioning diacritics is an extension of the normal process of kerning to be both horizontal and vertical (see *Figure 5-13*). Typically, kerning maps from pairs of glyphs to a positioning offset. For example, in the word "To" the "o" should nest slightly under the "T". An extension of this system maps to both a *vertical* and a *horizontal* offset, allowing glyphs to be positioned arbitrarily.

Figure 5-13. Positioning with Enhanced Kerning

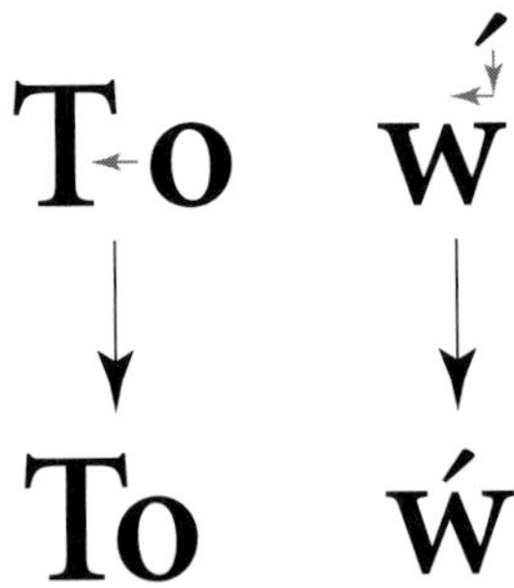

For effective use in the general case, the kerning process must be extended to handle more than simple kerning pairs, as multiple diacritics may occur after a base letter.

Positioning with enhanced kerning can be combined with the ligature method so that in specific cases ligatures can be used to produce fine variations in position and shape.

5.14 Locating Text Element Boundaries

A string of Unicode-encoded text often needs to be broken up into text elements programmatically. Common examples of text elements include what users think of as characters, words, lines, and sentences. The precise determination of text elements may vary according to locale, even as to what constitutes a "character." The goal of matching user perceptions cannot always be met, because the text alone does not always contain enough information to decide boundaries unambiguously. For example, the *period* (U+002E FULL STOP) is used ambiguously—sometimes for end-of-sentence purposes, sometimes for abbreviations, and sometimes for numbers. In most cases, however, programmatic text boundaries can match user perceptions quite closely, or at least not surprise the user.

Rather than concentrate on algorithmically searching for text elements themselves, a simpler computation looks instead at detecting the *boundaries* between those text elements. A precise definition of the default Unicode mechanisms for determining such text element boundaries are found in Unicode Standard Annex #14, "Line Breaking Properties," and in Unicode Standard Annex #29, "Text Boundaries."

5.15 Identifiers

A common task facing an implementer of the Unicode Standard is the provision of a parsing and/or lexing engine for identifiers. To assist in the standard treatment of identifiers in Unicode character-based parsers, a set of guidelines is provided in Unicode Standard Annex #31, "Identifier and Pattern Syntax," as a recommended default for the definition of identifier syntax. That document provides details regarding the syntax and conformance considerations. Associated data files defining the character properties referred to by the identifier syntax can be found in the Unicode Character Database.

5.16 Sorting and Searching

Sorting and searching overlap in that both implement degrees of *equivalence* of terms to be compared. In the case of searching, equivalence defines when terms match (for example, it determines when case distinctions are meaningful). In the case of sorting, equivalence affects the proximity of terms in a sorted list. These determinations of equivalence often depend on the application and language, but for an implementation supporting the Unicode Standard, sorting and searching must always take into account the Unicode character equivalence and canonical ordering defined in *Chapter 3, Conformance*.

Culturally Expected Sorting and Searching

Sort orders vary from culture to culture, and many specific applications require variations. Sort order can be by word or sentence, case-sensitive or case-insensitive, ignoring accents or not. It can also be either phonetic or based on the appearance of the character, such as ordering by stroke and radical for East Asian ideographs. Phonetic sorting of Han characters requires use of either a lookup dictionary of words or special programs to maintain an associated phonetic spelling for the words in the text.

Languages vary not only regarding which types of sorts to use (and in which order they are to be applied), but also in what constitutes a fundamental element for sorting. For example, Swedish treats U+00C4 LATIN CAPITAL LETTER A WITH DIAERESIS as an individual letter, sorting it after *z* in the alphabet; German, however, sorts it either like *ae* or like other accented forms of *ä* following *a*. Spanish traditionally sorted the digraph *ll* as if it were a letter between *l* and *m*. Examples from other languages (and scripts) abound.

As a result, it is not possible either to arrange characters in an encoding such that simple binary string comparison produces the desired collation order or to provide single-level sort-weight tables. The latter implies that character encoding details have only an indirect influence on culturally expected sorting.

Unicode Technical Standard #10, "Unicode Collation Algorithm" (UCA), describes the issues involved in culturally appropriate sorting and searching, and provides a specification for how to compare two Unicode strings while remaining conformant to the requirements of the Unicode Standard. The UCA also supplies the Default Unicode Collation Element Table as the data specifiying the default collation order. Searching algorithms, whether brute-force or sublinear, can be adapted to provide language-sensitive searching as described in the UCA.

Language-Insensitive Sorting

In some circumstances, an application may need to do language-insensitive sorting—that is, sorting of textual data without consideration of language-specific cultural expectations about how strings should be ordered. For example, a temporary index may need only to be in *some* well-defined order, but the exact details of the order may not matter or be visible to users. However, even in these circumstances, implementers should be aware of some issues.

First, some subtle differences arise in binary ordering between the three Unicode encoding forms. Implementations that need to do only binary comparisons between Unicode strings still need to take this issue into account so as not to create interoperability problems between applications using different encoding forms. See *Section 5.17, Binary Order*, for further discussion.

Many applications of sorting or searching need to be case-insensitive, even while not caring about language-specific differences in ordering. This is the result of the design of protocols that may be very old but that are still of great current relevance. Traditionally, implementations did case-insensitive comparison by effectively mapping both strings to uppercase before doing a binary comparison. This approach is, however, not more generally extensible to the full repertoire of the Unicode Standard. The correct approach to case-insensitive comparison is to make use of case folding, as described in *Section 5.18, Case Mappings*.

Searching

Searching is subject to many of the same issues as comparison. Other features are often added, such as only matching words (that is, where a word boundary appears on each side of the match). One technique is to code a fast search for a weak match. When a candidate is found, additional tests can be made for other criteria (such as matching diacriticals, word match, case match, and so on).

When searching strings, it is necessary to check for trailing nonspacing marks in the target string that may affect the interpretation of the last matching character. That is, a search for "San Jose" may find a match in the string "Visiting San José, Costa Rica, is a...". If an exact (diacritic) match is desired, then this match should be rejected. If a weak match is sought, then the match should be accepted, but any trailing nonspacing marks should be included when returning the location and length of the target substring. The mechanisms discussed in Unicode Standard Annex #29, "Text Boundaries," can be used for this purpose.

One important application of weak equivalence is case-insensitive searching. Many traditional implementations map both the search string and the target text to uppercase. However, case mappings are language-dependent and *not* unambiguous. The preferred method of implementing case insensitivity is described in *Section 5.18, Case Mappings.*

A related issue can arise because of inaccurate mappings from external character sets. To deal with this problem, characters that are easily confused by users can be kept in a weak equivalency class (đ *d-bar,* ð *eth,* Đ *capital d-bar,* Đ *capital eth*). This approach tends to do a better job of meeting users' expectations when searching for named files or other objects.

Sublinear Searching

International searching is clearly possible using the information in the collation, just by using brute force. However, this tactic requires an $O(m^*n)$ algorithm in the worst case and an $O(m)$ algorithm in common cases, where n is the number of characters in the pattern that is being searched for and m is the number of characters in the target to be searched.

A number of algorithms allow for fast searching of simple text, using sublinear algorithms. These algorithms have only $O(m/n)$ complexity in common cases by skipping over characters in the target. Several implementers have adapted one of these algorithms to search text pre-transformed according to a collation algorithm, which allows for fast searching with native-language matching (see *Figure 5-14*).

Figure 5-14. Sublinear Searching

```
T h e _ q u i c k _ b r o w n ...
q u i c k
  q u i c k
    q u i c k
      q u i c k
        q u i c k
```

The main problems with adapting a language-aware collation algorithm for sublinear searching relate to multiple mappings and ignorables. Additionally, sublinear algorithms precompute tables of information. Mechanisms like the two-stage tables shown in *Figure 5-1* are efficient tools in reducing memory requirements.

5.17 Binary Order

When comparing text that is visible to end users, a correct linguistic sort should be used, as described in *Section 5.16, Sorting and Searching.* However, in many circumstances the only requirement is for a fast, well-defined ordering. In such cases, a binary ordering can be used.

Not all encoding forms of Unicode have the same binary order. UTF-8 and UTF-32 data, and UTF-16 data containing only BMP characters, sort in code point order, whereas UTF-16 data containing a mix of BMP and supplementary characters does not. This is because supplementary characters are encoded in UTF-16 with pairs of surrogate code units that have lower values ($D800_{16}..DFFF_{16}$) than some BMP code points.

Furthermore, when UTF-16 or UTF-32 data is serialized using one of the Unicode encoding schemes and compared byte-by-byte, the resulting byte sequences may or may not have the same binary ordering, because swapping the order of bytes will affect the overall ordering of the data. Due to these factors, text in the UTF-16BE, UTF-16LE, and UTF-32LE encoding schemes does not sort in code point order.

In general, the default binary sorting order for Unicode text should be code point order. However, it may be necessary to match the code unit ordering of a particular encoding form (or the byte ordering of a particular encoding scheme) so as to duplicate the ordering used in a different application.

Some sample routines are provided here for sorting one encoding form in the binary order of another encoding form.

UTF-8 in UTF-16 Order

The following comparison function for UTF-8 yields the same results as UTF-16 binary comparison. In the code, notice that it is necessary to do extra work only once per string, not once per byte. That work can consist of simply remapping through a small array; there are no extra conditional branches that could slow down the processing.

```
int strcmp8like16(unsigned char* a, unsigned char* b) {
  while (true) {
    int ac = *a++;
    int bc = *b++;
    if (ac != bc) return rotate[ac] - rotate[bc];
    if (ac == 0) return 0;
  }
}

static char rotate[256] =
  {0x00, ...,                                        0x0F,
   0x10, ...,                                        0x2F,
      .                                                .
      .                                                .
      .                                                .
```

```
  0xD0, ...,                                                  0xDF,
  0xE0, ...,                                    0xED, 0xF0, 0xF1,
  0xF2, 0xF3, 0xF4, 0xEE, 0xEF, 0xF5, ...,                    0xFF};
```

The rotate array is formed by taking an array of 256 bytes from 0x00 to 0xFF, and rotating 0xEE and 0xEF to a position after the bytes 0xF0..0xF4. These rotated values are shown in boldface. When this rotation is performed on the initial bytes of UTF-8, it has the effect of making code points U+10000..U+10FFFF sort below U+E000..U+FFFF, thus mimicking the ordering of UTF-16.

UTF-16 in UTF-8 Order

The following code can be used to sort UTF-16 in code point order. As in the routine for sorting UTF-8 in UTF-16 order, the extra cost is incurred once per function call, not once per character.

```
int strcmp16like8(Unichar* a, Unichar* b) {
  while (true) {
    int ac = *a++;
    int bc = *b++;
    if (ac != bc) {
      return (Unichar)(ac + utf16Fixup[ac>>11]) -
             (Unichar)(bc + utf16Fixup[bc>>11]);
    }
    if (ac == 0) return 0;
  }
}
static const Unichar utf16Fixup[32]={
  0, 0, 0, 0, 0, 0, 0, 0,
  0, 0, 0, 0, 0, 0, 0, 0,
  0, 0, 0, 0, 0, 0, 0, 0,
  0, 0, 0, 0x2000, 0xf800, 0xf800, 0xf800, 0xf800
};
```

This code uses `Unichar` as an unsigned 16-bit integral type. The construction of the `utf16Fixup` array is based on the following concept. The range of UTF-16 values is divided up into thirty-two 2K chunks. The 28th chunk corresponds to the values 0xD800..0xDFFF—that is, the surrogate code units. The 29th through 32nd chunks correspond to the values 0xE000..0xFFFF. The addition of 0x2000 to the surrogate code units rotates them up to the range 0xF800..0xFFFF. Adding 0xF800 to the values 0xE000..0xFFFF and ignoring the unsigned integer overflow rotates them down to the range 0xD800..0xF7FF. Calculating the final difference for the return from the rotated values produces the same result as basing the comparison on code points, rather than the UTF-16 code units. The use of the hack of unsigned integer overflow on addition avoids the need for a conditional test to accomplish the rotation of values.

Note that this mechanism works correctly only on well-formed UTF-16 text. A modified algorithm must be used to operate on 16-bit Unicode strings that could contain isolated surrogates.

5.18 Case Mappings

Case is a normative property of characters in specific alphabets such as Latin, Greek, Cyrillic, Armenian, and archaic Georgian, whereby characters are considered to be variants of a single letter. These variants, which may differ markedly in shape and size, are called the uppercase letter (also known as capital or majuscule) and the lowercase letter (also known as small or minuscule). The uppercase letter is generally larger than the lowercase letter. Alphabets with case differences are called *bicameral*; those without are called *unicameral*. For example, the archaic Georgian script contained upper- and lowercase pairs, but they are not used in modern Georgian. See *Section 7.7, Georgian*, for more information.

The case mappings in the Unicode Character Database (UCD) are normative. This follows from their use in defining the case foldings in CaseFolding.txt and from the use of case foldings to define case-insensitive identifiers in Unicode Standard Annex #31, "Identifier and Pattern Syntax." However, the normative status of case mappings does not preclude the adaptation of case mapping processes to local conventions, as discussed below. See also the Common Locale Data Repository (CLDR), in *Section B.6, Other Unicode Online Resources*, for extensive data regarding local and language-specific casing conventions.

Titlecasing

Titlecasing refers to a casing practice wherein the first letter of a word is an uppercase letter and the rest of the letters are lowercase. This typically applies, for example, to initial words of sentences and to proper nouns. Depending on the language and orthographic practice, this convention may apply to other words as well, as for common nouns in German.

Titlecasing also applies to entire strings, as in instances of headings or titles of documents, for which multiple words are titlecased. The choice of which words to titlecase in headings and titles is dependent on language and local conventions. For example, "The Merry Wives of Windsor" is the appropriate titlecasing of that play's name in English, with the word "of" not titlecased. In German, however, the title is "Die lustigen Weiber von Windsor," and both "lustigen" and "von" are not titlecased. In French even fewer words are titlecased: "Les joyeuses commères de Windsor."

Moreover, the determination of what actually constitutes a word is language dependent, and this can influence which letter or letters of a "word" are uppercased when titlecasing strings. For example *l'arbre* is considered two words in French, whereas *can't* is considered one word in English.

The need for a normative Titlecase_Mapping property in the Unicode Standard derives from the fact that the standard contains certain digraph characters for compatibility. These digraph compatibility characters, such as U+01F3 "dz" LATIN SMALL LETTER DZ, require one form when being uppercased, U+01F1 "DZ" LATIN CAPITAL LETTER DZ, and another form when being titlecased, U+01F2 "Dz" LATIN CAPITAL LETTER D WITH SMALL LETTER Z. The latter form is informally referred to as a *titlecase character*, because it is mixed case, with the first letter uppercase. Most characters in the standard have identical values for their Titlecase_Mapping and Uppercase_Mapping; however, the two values are distinguished for these few digraph compatibility characters.

Complications for Case Mapping

A number of complications to case mappings occur once the repertoire of characters is expanded beyond ASCII.

Case mappings may produce strings of different lengths than the original. For example, the German character U+00DF ß LATIN SMALL LETTER SHARP S expands when uppercased to the sequence of two characters "SS". This also occurs where there is no precomposed character corresponding to a case mapping, such as with U+0149 ŉ LATIN SMALL LETTER N PRECEDED BY APOSTROPHE. The maximum string expansion as a result of case mapping in Unicode 5.0 is three. For example, uppercasing U+0390 ΐ GREEK SMALL LETTER IOTA WITH DIALYTIKA AND TONOS results in three characters.

The lengths of case-mapped strings may also differ from their originals depending on the Unicode encoding form. For example, the Turkish strings "topkapı" (with a *dotless i*) and "TOPKAPI" have the same number of characters and are the same length in UTF-16 and UTF-32; however, in UTF-8, the representation of the uppercase form takes only seven bytes, whereas the lowercase form takes eight bytes. By comparison, the German strings "heiß" and "HEISS" have a different number of characters and differ in length in UTF-16 and UTF-32, but in UTF-8 both strings are encoded using the same number of bytes.

Some characters require special handling, such as U+0345 COMBINING GREEK YPOGEGRAMMENI (*iota subscript*). As discussed in *Section 7.2, Greek*, the iota-subscript characters used to represent ancient text can be viewed as having special case mappings. Normally, the uppercase and lowercase forms of alpha-iota-subscript will map back and forth. In some instances, uppercase words should be transformed into their older spellings by removing accents and changing the iota subscript into a capital iota (and perhaps even removing spaces).

Characters may also have different case mappings, depending on the context. For example, U+03A3 "Σ" GREEK CAPITAL LETTER SIGMA lowercases to U+03C3 "σ" GREEK SMALL LETTER SIGMA if it is followed by another letter, but lowercases to U+03C2 "ς" GREEK SMALL LETTER FINAL SIGMA if it is not.

Characters may have case mappings that depend on the locale. The principal example is Turkish, where U+0131 "ı" LATIN SMALL LETTER DOTLESS I maps to U+0049 "I" LATIN

CAPITAL LETTER I and U+0069 "i" LATIN SMALL LETTER I maps to U+0130 " İ " LATIN CAPITAL LETTER I WITH DOT ABOVE.

Figure 5-15 shows the case mappings for these characters and canonically equivalent sequences. A mapping with a double-sided arrow round-trips—that is, the opposite case mapping results in the original sequence. A mapping with a single-sided arrow does not round-trip.

Figure 5-15. Case Mapping for Turkish I

Uppercase Mapping

Normal			Turkish		
i 0069	↔	I 0049	i 0069	↔	İ 0130
ı 0131	→	I 0049	ı 0131	↔	I 0049
i + ◌̇ 0069 0307	↔	I + ◌̇ 0049 0307	i + ◌̇ 0069 0307	↔	İ + ◌̇ 0130 0307

Lowercase Mapping

Normal			Turkish		
I 0049	↔	i 0069	I 0049	↔	ı 0131
İ 0130	→	i + ◌̇ 0069 0307	İ 0130	↔	i 0069
I + ◌̇ 0049 0307	↔	i + ◌̇ 0069 0307	I + ◌̇ 0049 0307	→	i 0069

Because many characters are really caseless (most of the IPA block, for example) and have no matching uppercase, the process of uppercasing a string does *not* mean that it will no longer contain any lowercase letters.

Case mappings may occasionally depend on the context surrounding a character in the original string. Such context-sensitive case mappings are not numerous, but where they occur, consideration of context is required for correct case operations. Because only a few context-sensitive case mappings exist, and because they involve only a very few characters, implementations may choose to hard-code the treatment of these characters for casing operations rather than using data-driven code based on the Unicode Character Database. However, if this approach is taken, each time the implementation is upgraded to a new version of the Unicode Standard, hard-coded casing operations should be checked for consistency with the updated data. See SpecialCasing.txt in the Unicode Character Database for details of context-sensitive case mappings.

Reversibility

No casing operations are reversible. For example:

> `toUpperCase(toLowerCase(`"John Brown"`))` → "JOHN BROWN"
>
> `toLowerCase(toUpperCase(`"John Brown"`))` → "john brown"

There are even single words like *vederLa* in Italian or the name *McGowan* in English, which are neither upper-, lower-, nor titlecase. This format is sometimes called *inner-caps*—or more informally *camelcase*—and it is often used in programming and in Web names. Once the string "McGowan" has been uppercased, lowercased, or titlecased, the original cannot be recovered by applying another uppercase, lowercase, or titlecase operation. There are also single characters that do not have reversible mappings, such as the Greek sigmas.

For word processors that use a single command-key sequence to toggle the selection through different casings, it is recommended to save the original string and return to it via the sequence of keys. The user interface would produce the following results in response to a series of command keys. In the following example, notice that the original string is restored every fourth time.

1. The quick brown
2. THE QUICK BROWN
3. the quick brown
4. The Quick Brown
5. The quick brown (repeating from here on)

Uppercase, titlecase, and lowercase can be represented in a word processor by using a character style. Removing the character style restores the text to its original state. However, if this approach is taken, any spell-checking software needs to be aware of the case style so that it can check the spelling against the actual appearance.

Caseless Matching

Caseless matching is implemented using *case folding*, which is the process of mapping strings to a canonical form where case differences are erased. Case folding allows for fast caseless matches in lookups because only binary comparison is required. It is more than just conversion to lowercase. For example, it correctly handles cases such as the Greek sigma, so that "όσος" and "ΌΣΟΣ" will match.

Normally, the original source string is not replaced by the folded string because that substitution may erase important information. For example, the name "Marco di Silva" would be folded to "marco di silva," losing the information regarding which letters are capitalized. Typically, the original string is stored along with a case-folded version for fast comparisons.

The CaseFolding.txt file in the Unicode Character Database is used to perform locale-independent case folding. This file is generated from the case mappings in the Unicode Character Database, using both the single-character mappings and the multicharacter mappings. It folds all characters having different case forms together into a common form. To compare two strings for caseless matching, one can fold each string using this data and then use a binary comparison.

Case folding logically involves a set of equivalence classes constructed from the Unicode Character Database case mappings as follows.

For each character X in Unicode, apply the following rules in order:

R1 ***If X is already in an equivalence class, continue to the next character. Otherwise, form a new equivalence class and add X.***

R2 ***Add any other character that uppercases, lowercases, or titlecases to anything in the equivalence class.***

R3 ***Add any other characters to which anything in the equivalence class uppercases, lowercases, or titlecases.***

R4 ***Repeat R2 and R3 until nothing further is added.***

R5 ***From each class, one representative element (a single lowercase letter where possible) is chosen to be the common form.***

Each equivalence class is completely disjoint from all the others, and every Unicode character is in one equivalence class. CaseFolding.txt thus contains the mappings from other characters in the equivalence classes to their common forms. As an exception, the case foldings for dotless i and dotted I do not follow the derivation algorithm for all other case foldings. Instead, their case foldings are hard-coded in the derivation for best default matching behavior. Additional, alternate case foldings for these characters that can be used for Turkic languages. However, the use of these alternate case foldings does not maintain canonical equivalence, and it is often undesirable to have alternate behavior for caseless matching. In addition, language information is often not available where caseless matching is applied.

The Unicode case folding algorithm is defined to be simpler and more efficient than case mappings. It is context-insensitive and language-independent (except for the optional, alternate Turkic case foldings). As a result, there are a few rare cases where a caseless match does not match pairs of strings as expected; the most notable instance of this is for Lithuanian. In Lithuanian typography for dictionary use, an "i" retains its dot when a grave, acute, or tilde accent is placed above it. This convention is represented in Unicode by using an explicit combining dot above, occurring in sequence between the "i" and the respective accent. (See *Figure 7-2.*) When case folded using the default case folding algorithm, strings containing these sequences will still contain the combining dot above. In the unusual situation where case folding needs to be tailored to provide for these special Lithuanian dictionary requirements, strings can be preprocessed to remove any combining dot above characters occurring between an "i" and a subsequent accent, so that the folded strings will match correctly.

For more information on character foldings, see Unicode Technical Report #30, "Character Foldings."

Where case distinctions are not important, other distinctions between Unicode characters (in particular, compatibility distinctions) are generally ignored as well. In such circumstances, text can be normalized to Normalization Form KC or KD after case folding, thereby producing a normalized form that erases both compatibility distinctions and case distinctions. However, such normalization should generally be done only on a restricted repertoire, such as identifiers (alphanumerics). See Unicode Standard Annex #15, "Unicode Normalization Forms," and Unicode Standard Annex #31, "Identifier and Pattern Syntax," for more information. For a summary, see "Equivalent Sequences" in *Section 2.2, Unicode Design Principles.*

Caseless matching is only an approximation of the language-specific rules governing the strength of comparisons. Language-specific case matching can be derived from the collation data for the language, where only the first- and second-level differences are used. For more information, see Unicode Technical Standard #10, "Unicode Collation Algorithm."

In most environments, such as in file systems, text is not and cannot be tagged with language information. In such cases, the language-specific mappings *must not* be used. Otherwise, data structures such as B-trees might be built based on one set of case foldings and used based on a different set of case foldings. This discrepancy would cause those data structures to become corrupt. For such environments, a constant, language-independent, default case folding is required.

Stability. The definition of case folding is guaranteed to be stable, in that any string of characters case folded according to these rules will remain case folded in Version 5.0 or later of the Unicode Standard. To achieve this stability, no new lowercase character will be added to the Unicode Standard as a casing pair of an existing upper- or titlecase character that has no lowercase pair

Normalization

Casing operations as defined in *Section 3.13, Default Case Algorithms*, preserve canonical equivalence, but are not guaranteed to preserve Normalization Forms. That is, some strings in a particular Normalization Form (for example, NFC) will no longer be in that form after the casing operation is performed. Consider the strings shown in the example in *Table 5-5*.

Table 5-5. Casing and Normalization in Strings

Original (NFC)	ǰ◌̣	<U+01F0 LATIN SMALL LETTER J WITH CARON, U+0323 COMBINING DOT BELOW>
Uppercased	J◌̌◌̣	<U+004A LATIN CAPITAL LETTER J, U+030C COMBINING CARON, U+0323 COMBINING DOT BELOW>
Uppercased NFC	J◌̣◌̌	<U+004A LATIN CAPITAL LETTER J, U+0323 COMBINING DOT BELOW, U+030C COMBINING CARON>

The original string is in NFC format. When uppercased, the *small j with caron* turns into an *uppercase J* with a separate *caron*. If followed by a combining mark below, that sequence is not in a normalized form. The combining marks have to be put in canonical order for the sequence to be normalized.

If text in a particular system is to be consistently normalized to a particular form such as NFC, then the casing operators should be modified to normalize after performing their core function. The actual process can be optimized; there are only a few instances where a casing operation causes a string to become denormalized. If a system specifically checks for those instances, then normalization can be avoided where not needed.

Normalization also interacts with case folding. For any string `X`, let `Q(X) = NFC(toCasefold(NFD(X)))`. In other words, `Q(X)` is the result of normalizing `X`, then case folding the result, then putting the result into NFC format. Because of the way normalization and case folding are defined, `Q(Q(X)) = Q(X)`. Repeatedly applying `Q` does not change the result; case folding is *closed* under canonical normalization for either Normalization Form NFC or NFD.

Case folding is not, however, closed under compatibility normalization for either Normalization Form NFKD or NFKC. That is, given `R(X) = NFKC(toCasefold(NFD(X)))`, there are some strings such that `R(R(X)) ≠ R(X)`. FC_NFKC_Closure, a derived property, contains the additional mappings that can be used to produce a compatibility-closed case folding. This set of mappings is found in DerivedNormalizationProps.txt in the Unicode Character Database.

5.19 Unicode Security

It is sometimes claimed that the Unicode Standard poses new security issues. Some of these claims revolve around unique features of the Unicode Standard, such as its encoding forms. Others have to do with generic issues, such as character spoofing, which also apply to any other character encoding, but which are seen as more severe threats when considered from the point of view of the Unicode Standard.

This section examines some of these issues and makes some implementation recommendations that should help in designing secure applications using the Unicode Standard.

Alternate Encodings. A basic security issue arises whenever there are alternate encodings for the "same" character. In such circumstances, it is always possible for security-conscious modules to make different assumptions about the representation of text. This conceivably can result in situations where a security watchdog module of some sort is screening for prohibited text or characters, but misses the same characters represented in an alternative form. If a subsequent processing module then treats the alternative form as if it were what the security watchdog was attempting to prohibit, one potentially has a situation where a hostile outside process can circumvent the security software. Whether such circumvention can be exploited in any way depends entirely on the system in question.

Some earlier versions of the Unicode Standard included enough leniency in the definition of the UTF-8 encoding form, particularly regarding the so-called *non-shortest form*, to raise questions about the security of applications using UTF-8 strings. However, the conformance requirements on UTF-8 and other encoding forms in the Unicode Standard have been tightened so that no encoding form now allows any sort of alternate representation, including non-shortest form UTF-8. Each Unicode code point has a single, unique encoding in any particular Unicode encoding form. Properly coded applications should not be subject to attacks on the basis of code points having multiple encodings in UTF-8 (or UTF-16).

However, another level of alternate representation has raised other security questions: the canonical equivalences between precomposed characters and combining character sequences that represent the same abstract characters. This is a different kind of alternate representation problem—not one of the encoding forms per se, but one of visually identical characters having two distinct representations (one as a single encoded character and one as a sequence of base form plus combining mark, for example). The issue here is different from that for alternate encodings in UTF-8. Canonically equivalent representations for the "same" string are perfectly valid and expected in Unicode. The conformance requirement, however, is that conforming implementations cannot be *required* to make an interpretation distinction between canonically equivalent representations. The way for a security-conscious application to guarantee this is to carefully observe the normalization specifications (see Unicode Standard Annex #15, "Unicode Normalization Forms") so that data is handled consistently in a normalized form.

Spoofing. Another security issue is *spoofing*, meaning the deliberate misspelling of a domain name, or user name, or other string in a form designed to trick unwary users into interacting with a hostile Web site as if it was a trusted site (or user). In this case, the confusion is not at the level of the software process handling the code points, but rather in the human end users, who see one character but mistake it for another, and who then can be fooled into doing something that will breach security or otherwise result in unintended results.

To be effective, spoofing does not require an exact visual match—for example, using the digit "1" instead of the letter "l". The Unicode Standard contains many *confusables*—that is, characters whose glyphs, due to historical derivation or sheer coincidence, resemble each other more or less closely. Certain security-sensitive applications or systems may be vulnerable due to possible misinterpretation of these confusables by their users.

Many legacy character sets, including ISO/IEC 8859-1 or even ASCII, also contain confusables, albeit usually far fewer of them than in the Unicode Standard simply because of the sheer scale of Unicode. The legacy character sets all carry the same type of risks when it comes to spoofing, so there is nothing unique or inadequate about Unicode in this regard. Similar steps will be needed in system design to assure integrity and to lessen the potential for security risks, no matter which character encoding is used.

The Unicode Standard encodes characters, not glyphs, and it is impractical for many reasons to try to avoid spoofing by simply assigning a single character code for every possible confusable glyph among all the world's writing systems. By unifying an encoding based strictly on appearance, many common text-processing tasks would become convoluted or impossible. For example, Latin B and Greek Beta B look the same in most fonts, but lowercase to two different letters, Latin b and Greek beta β, which have very distinct appearances. A simplistic fix to the confusability of Latin B and Greek Beta would result in great difficulties in processing Latin and Greek data, and in many cases in data corruptions as well.

Because all character encodings inherently have instances of characters that might be confused with one another under some conditions, and because the use of different fonts to display characters might even introduce confusions between characters that the designers of character encodings could not prevent, character spoofing must be addressed by other means. Systems or applications that are security-conscious can test explicitly for known spoofings, such as "MICROS0FT," "A0L," or the like (substituting the digit "0" for the letter "O"). Unicode-based systems can provide visual clues so that users can ensure that labels, such as domain names, are within a single script to prevent cross-script spoofing. However, provision of such clues is clearly the responsibility of the system or application, rather than being a security condition that could be met by somehow choosing a "secure" character encoding that was not subject to spoofing. No such character encoding exists.

Unicode Standard Annex #24, "Script Names," presents a classification of Unicode characters by script. By using such a classification, a program can check that labels consist only of characters from a given script or characters that are expected to be used with more than one script (such as the "COMMON" or "INHERITED" script names defined in Unicode Standard Annex #24, "Script Names"). Because cross-script names may be legitimate, the best method of alerting a user might be to highlight any unexpected boundaries between scripts and let the user determine the legitimacy of such a string explicitly.

For further discussion of security issues, see Unicode Technical Report #36, "Unicode Security Considerations," and Unicode Technical Standard #39, "Unicode Security Mechanisms."

5.20 Default Ignorable Code Points

Default ignorable code points are those that should be ignored by default in rendering unless explicitly supported. They have no visible glyph or advance width in and of themselves, although they may affect the display, positioning, or adornment of adjacent or surrounding characters. Some default ignorable code points are assigned characters, while others are reserved for future assignment.

The default ignorable code points are listed in DerivedCoreProperties.txt in the Unicode Character Database with the property Default_Ignorable_Code_Points. Examples of such characters include U+2060 WORD JOINER, U+00AD SOFT HYPHEN, and U+200F RIGHT-TO-LEFT MARK.

An implementation should ignore default ignorable characters in rendering whenever it does *not* support the characters.

This can be contrasted with the situation for non-default ignorable characters. If an implementation does not support U+0915 क DEVANAGARI LETTER KA, for example, it should not ignore it in rendering. Displaying *nothing* would give the user the impression that it does not occur in the text at all. The recommendation in that case is to display a "last-resort" glyph or a visible "missing glyph" box. See *Section 5.3, Unknown and Missing Characters,* for more information.

With default ignorable characters, such as U+200D [ZWJ] ZERO WIDTH JOINER, the situation is different. If the program does not support that character, the best practice is to ignore it completely without displaying a last-resort glyph or a visible box because the normal display of the character is invisible—its effects are on other characters. Because the character is not supported, those effects cannot be shown.

Other characters will have other effects on adjacent characters. For example:

- U+2060 [WJ] WORD JOINER does not produce a visible change in the appearance of surrounding characters; instead, its only effect is to indicate that there should be no line break at that point.
- U+2061 [f()] FUNCTION APPLICATION has no effect on the text display and is used only in internal mathematical expression processing.
- U+00AD [SHY] SOFT HYPHEN has a null default appearance in the middle of a line: the appearance of "ther[SHY]apist" is simply "therapist"—no visible glyph. In line break processing, it indicates a possible intraword break. At any intraword break that is used for a line break—whether resulting from this character or by some automatic process—a hyphen glyph (perhaps with spelling changes) or some other indication can be shown, depending on language and context.

This does *not* imply that default ignorable code points must always be invisible. An implementation can, for example, show a visible glyph on request, such as in a "Show Hidden" mode. A particular use of a "Show Hidden" mode is to show a visible indication of "misplaced" or "ineffectual" formatting codes. For example, this would include two adjacent U+200D [ZWJ] ZERO WIDTH JOINER characters, where the extra character has no effect.

The default ignorable *unassigned* code points lie in particular designated ranges. These ranges are designed and reserved for future default ignorable characters, so as to allow forward compatibility. All implementations should ignore all unassigned default ignorable code points in all rendering. Any new default ignorable characters should be assigned in those ranges, permitting existing programs to ignore them until they are supported in some future version of the program.

Some other characters have no visible glyphs—the whitespace characters. They typically have advance width, however. The line separation characters, such as the carriage return, do not clearly exhibit this advance width because they are always at the end of a line, but most implementations give them a visible advance width when they are selected.

Stateful Format Controls. There are a small number of *paired stateful controls.* These characters are used in pairs, with an initiating character (or sequence) and a terminating character. Even when these characters are ignored, complications can arise due to their paired nature. When text is deleted, these characters can become unpaired. To avoid this problem, any unpaired characters should be moved outside of the deletion so that the pairing is maintained. When text is copied or extracted, unpaired characters may also require the addition of the appropriate pairs to the copied text to maintain the pairing.

The paired stateful controls are listed in *Table 5-6.*

Table 5-6. Paired Stateful Controls

Characters	Documentation
Bidi Overrides and Embeddings	*Section 16.2, Layout Controls*; UAX #9
Deprecated Format Characters	*Section 16.3, Deprecated Format Characters*
Annotation Characters	*Section 16.8, Specials*
Tag Characters	*Section 16.9, Tag Characters*

The bidirectional overrides and embeddings and the annotation characters are more robust because their behavior terminates at paragraphs. The tag characters, by contrast, are particularly fragile. See *Section 5.10, Language Information in Plain Text*, for more information.

Some other characters have a scope of influence over the behavior or rendering of neighboring characters. These include the *fraction slash* and the *arabic end of ayah.* However, because these characters are not paired, they do not give rise to the same issues with unaware text modifications.

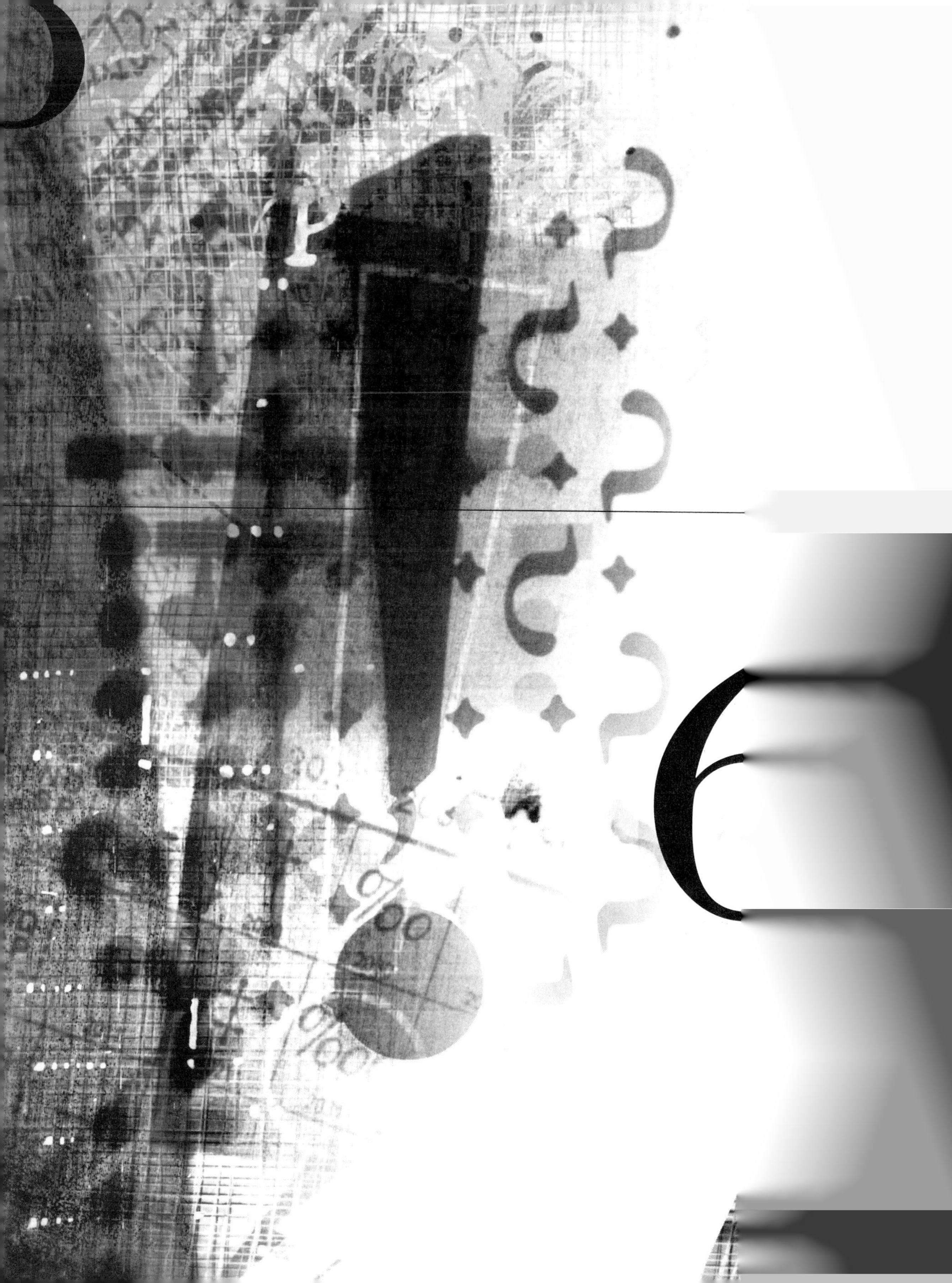

Chapter 6

Writing Systems and Punctuation

This chapter begins the portion of the Unicode Standard devoted to the detailed description of each script or other related group of Unicode characters. Each of the subsequent chapters presents a historically or geographically related group of scripts. This chapter presents a general introduction to writing systems, explains how they can be used to classify scripts, and then presents a detailed discussion of punctuation characters that are shared across scripts.

Scripts and Blocks. The codespace of the Unicode Standard is divided into subparts called *blocks*. Character blocks generally contain characters from a single script, and in many cases, a script is fully represented in its character block; however, some scripts are encoded using several blocks, which are not always adjacent. Discussion of scripts and other groups of characters are structured by character blocks. Corresponding subsection headers identify each block and its associated range of Unicode code points. The code charts in *Chapter 17, Code Charts*, are also organized by character blocks.

Scripts and Writing Systems. There are many different kinds of writing systems in the world. Their variety poses some significant issues for character encoding in the Unicode Standard as well as for implementers of the standard. Those who first approach the Unicode Standard without a background in writing systems may find the huge list of scripts bewilderingly complex. Therefore, before considering the script descriptions in detail, this chapter first presents a brief introduction to the types of writing systems. That introduction explains basic terminology about scripts and character types that will be used again and again when discussing particular scripts.

Punctuation. The rest of this chapter deals with a special case: punctuation marks, which tend to be scattered about in different blocks and which may be used in common by many scripts. Punctuation characters occur in several widely separated places in the character blocks, including Basic Latin, Latin-1 Supplement, General Punctuation, and CJK Symbols and Punctuation. There are also occasional punctuation characters in character blocks for specific scripts.

Most punctuation characters are intended for common usage with any script, although some of them are script-specific. Some scripts use both common and script-specific punctuation characters, usually as the result of recent adoption of standard Western punctuation marks. While punctuation characters vary in details of appearance and function between different languages and scripts, their overall purpose is shared: They serve to separate or otherwise organize units of text, such as sentences and phrases, thereby helping to clarify the meaning of the text. Certain punctuation characters also occur in mathematical and scientific formulae.

6.1 Writing Systems

This section presents a brief introduction to writing systems. It describes the different kinds of writing systems and relates them to the encoded scripts found in the Unicode Standard. This framework may help to make the variety of scripts, modern and historic, a little less daunting. The terminology used here follows that developed by Peter T. Daniels, a leading expert on writing systems of the world.

The term *writing system* has two mutually exclusive meanings in this standard. As used in this section, "writing system" refers to a way that families of scripts may be classified by how they represent the sounds or words of human language. For example, the writing system of the Latin script is alphabetic. In other places in the standard, "writing system" refers to the way a particular *language* is written. For example, the modern Japanese writing system uses four scripts: Han ideographs, Hiragana, Katakana and Latin (Romaji).

Alphabets. A writing system that consists of letters for the writing of both consonants and vowels is called an *alphabet.* The term "alphabet" is derived from the first two letters of the Greek script: *alpha, beta.* Consonants and vowels have equal status as letters in such a system. The Latin alphabet is the most widespread and well-known example of an alphabet, having been adapted for use in writing thousands of languages.

The correspondence between letters and sounds may be either more or less exact. Many alphabets do not exhibit a one-to-one correspondence between distinct sounds and letters or groups of letters used to represent them; often this is an indication of original spellings that were not changed as the language changed. Not only are many sounds represented by letter combinations, such as "th" in English, but the language may have evolved since the writing conventions were settled. Examples range from cases such as Italian or Finnish, where the match between letter and sound is rather close, to English, which has notoriously complex and arbitrary spelling.

Phonetic alphabets, in contrast, are used specifically for the precise transcription of the sounds of languages. The best known of these alphabets is the *International Phonetic Alphabet,* an adaptation and extension of the Latin alphabet by the addition of new letters and marks for specific sounds and modifications of sounds. Unlike normal alphabets, the intent of phonetic alphabets is that their letters exactly represent sounds. Phonetic alphabets are not used as general-purpose writing systems per se, but it is not uncommon for a formerly unwritten language to have an alphabet developed for it based on a phonetic alphabet.

Abjads. A writing system in which only consonants are indicated is an *abjad.* The main letters are all consonants (or long vowels), with other vowels either left out entirely or optionally indicated with the use of secondary marks on the consonants. The Phoenician script is a prototypical abjad; a better-known example is the Arabic writing system. The term "abjad" is derived from the first four letters of the traditional order of the Arabic script: *alef, beh, jeem, dal*. Abjads are often, although not exclusively, associated with Semitic languages, which have word structures particularly well suited to the use of consonantal writing. Some abjads allow consonant letters to mark long vowels, as the use of *waw* and *yeh* in Arabic for /u:/ or /i:/.

Hebrew and Arabic are typically written without any vowel marking at all. The vowels, when they do occur in writing, are referred to as *points* or *harakat*, and are indicated by the use of diacritic dots and other marks placed above and below the consonantal letters.

Syllabaries. In a *syllabary*, each symbol of the system typically represents both a consonant and a vowel, or in some instances more than one consonant and a vowel. One of the best-known examples of a syllabary is Hiragana, used for Japanese, in which the units of the system represent the syllables *ka, ki, ku, ke, ko, sa, si, su, se, so*, and so on. In general parlance, the elements of a syllabary are not called *letters*, but rather *syllables*. This can lead to some confusion, however, because letters of alphabets and units of other writing systems are also used, singly or in combinations, to write syllables of languages. So in a broad sense, the term "letter" can be used to refer to the syllables of a syllabary.

In syllabaries such as Cherokee, Hiragana, Katakana, and Yi, each symbol has a unique shape, with no particular shape relation to any of the consonant(s) or vowels of the syllables. In other cases, however, the syllabic symbols of a syllabary are not atomic; they can be built up out of parts that have a consistent relationship to the phonological parts of the syllable. The best example of this is the Hangul writing system for Korean. Each Hangul syllable is made up of a part for the initial consonant (or consonant cluster), a part for the vowel (or diphthong), and an optional part for the final consonant (or consonant cluster). The relationship between the sounds and the graphic parts to represent them is systematic enough for Korean that the graphic parts collectively are known as *jamos* and constitute a kind of alphabet on their own.

The jamos of the Hangul writing system have another characteristic: their shapes are not completely arbitrary, but were devised with intentionally iconic shapes relating them to articulatory features of the sounds they represent in Korean. The Hangul writing system has thus also been classified as a *featural syllabary.*

Abugidas. *Abugidas* represent a kind of blend of syllabic and alphabetic characteristics in a writing system. The Ethiopic script is an abugida. The term "abugida" is derived from the first four letters of the letters of the Ethiopic script in the Semitic order: *alf, bet, gaml, dant*. The order of vowels (-ä -u -i -a) is that of the traditional vowel order in the first four columns of the Ethiopic syllable chart. Historically, abugidas spread across South Asia and were adapted by many languages, often of phonologically very different types.

This process has also resulted in many extensions, innovations, and/or simplifications of the original patterns. The best-known example of an abugida is the Devanagari script, used in modern times to write Hindi and many other Indian languages, and used classically to write Sanskrit. See *Section 9.1, Devanagari*, for a detailed description of how Devanagari works and is rendered.

In an abugida, each consonant letter carries an inherent vowel, usually /a/. There are also vowel letters, often distinguished between a set of independent vowel letters, which occur on their own, and dependent vowel letters, or *matras*, which are subordinate to consonant letters. When a dependent vowel letter follows a consonant letter, the vowel overrides the inherent vowel of the consonant. This is shown schematically in *Figure 6-1*.

Figure 6-1. Overriding Inherent Vowels

ka + i → ki   ka + e → ke

ka + u → ku   ka + o → ko

Abugidas also typically contain a special element usually referred to as a *halant*, *virama*, or *killer*, which, when applied to a consonant letter with its inherent vowel, has the effect of *removing* the inherent vowel, resulting in a bare consonant sound.

Because of legacy practice, three distinct approaches have been taken in the Unicode Standard for the encoding of abugidas: the Devanagari model, the Tibetan model, and the Thai model. The Devanagari model, used for most abugidas, encodes an explicit virama character and represents text in its logical order. The Thai model departs from the Devanagari model in that it represents text in its visual display order, based on the typewriter legacy, rather than in logical order. The Tibetan model avoids an explicit virama, instead encoding a sequence of *subjoined consonants* to represent consonants occurring in clusters in a syllable.

The Ethiopic script is traditionally analyzed as an abugida, because the base character for each consonantal series is understood as having an inherent vowel. However, Ethiopic lacks some of the typical features of Brahmi-derived scripts, such as halants and matras. Historically, it was derived from early Semitic scripts and in its earliest form was an abjad. In its traditional presentation and its encoding in the Unicode Standard, it is now treated more like a syllabary.

Logosyllabaries. The final major category of writing system is known as the *logosyllabary*. In a logosyllabary, the units of the writing system are used primarily to write words and/or morphemes of words, with some subsidiary usage to represent syllabic sounds per se.

The best example of a logosyllabary is the Han script, used for writing Chinese and borrowed by a number of other East Asian languages for use as part of their writing systems. The term for a unit of the Han script is *hànzì* 漢字 in Chinese, *kanji* 漢字 in Japanese, and *hanja* 漢字 in Korean. In many instances this unit also constitutes a word, but more typically, two or more units together are used to write a word.

This unit has variously been referred to as an *ideograph* ("idea writing"), a *logograph* ("word writing"), or a *sinogram*, as well as other terms. No single English term is completely satisfactory or uncontroversial. In this standard, *CJK ideograph* is used because it is a widely understood term.

There are a number of other historical examples of logosyllabaries, such as Tangut, many of which may eventually be encoded in the Unicode Standard. They vary in the degree to which they combine logographic writing principles, where the symbols stand for morphemes or entire words, and syllabic writing principles, where the symbols come to represent syllables per se, divorced from their meaning as morphemes or words. In some notable instances, as for Sumero-Akkadian cuneiform, a logosyllabary may evolve through time into a syllabary or alphabet by shedding its use of logographs. In other instances, as for the Han script, the use of logographic characters is very well entrenched and persistent. However, even for the Han script a small number of characters are used purely to represent syllabic sounds, so as to be able to represent such things as foreign personal names and place names.

The classification of a writing system is often somewhat blurred by complications in the exact ways in which it matches up written elements to the phonemes or syllables of a language. For example, although Hiragana is classified as a syllabary, it does not always have an exact match between syllables and written elements. Syllables with long vowels are not written with a single element, but rather with a sequence of elements. Thus the syllable with a long vowel *kū* is written with two separate Hiragana symbols, {ku}+{u}. Because of these kinds of complications, one must always be careful not to assume too much about the structure of a writing system from its nominal classification.

Typology of Scripts in the Unicode Standard. *Table 6-1* lists all of the scripts currently encoded in the Unicode Standard, showing the writing system type for each. The list is an approximate guide, rather than a definitive classification, because of the mix of features seen in many scripts. The writing systems for some languages may be quite complex, mixing more than one type of script together in a composite system. Japanese is the best example; it mixes a logosyllabary (Han), two syllabaries (Hiragana and Katakana), and one alphabet (Latin, for *romaji*).

Table 6-1. Typology of Scripts in the Unicode Standard

Alphabets	Latin, Greek, Cyrillic, Armenian, Thaana, Georgian, Ogham, Runic, Mongolian, Glagolitic, Coptic, Tifinagh, Old Italic, Gothic, Ugaritic, Old Persian, Deseret, Shavian, Osmanya, N'Ko
Abjads	Hebrew, Arabic, Syriac, Phoenician
Abugidas	Devanagari, Bengali, Gurmukhi, Gujarati, Oriya, Tamil, Telugu, Kannada, Malayalam, Sinhala, Thai, Lao, Tibetan, Myanmar, Tagalog, Hanunóo, Buhid, Tagbanwa, Khmer, Limbu, Tai Le, New Tai Lue, Buginese, Syloti Nagri, Kharoshthi, Balinese, Phags-pa
Logosyllabaries	Han, Sumero-Akkadian
Simple Syllabaries	Cherokee, Hiragana, Katakana, Bopomofo, Yi, Linear B, Cypriot, Ethiopic, Canadian Aboriginal Syllabics
Featural Syllabaries	Hangul

Notational Systems. In addition to scripts for written natural languages, there are notational systems for other kinds of information. Some of these more closely resemble text than others. The Unicode Standard encodes symbols for use with mathematical notation, Western and Byzantine musical notation, and Braille, as well as symbols for use in divination, such as the Yijing hexagrams. Notational systems can be classified by how closely they resemble text. Even notational systems that do not fully resemble text may have symbols used in text. In the case of musical notation, for example, while the full notation is two-dimensional, many of the encoded symbols are frequently referenced in texts about music and musical notation.

6.2 General Punctuation

Punctuation characters—for example, U+002C COMMA and U+2022 BULLET—are encoded only once, rather than being encoded again and again for particular scripts; such general-purpose punctuation may be used for any script or mixture of scripts. In contrast, punctuation principally used with a specific script is found in the block corresponding to that script, such as U+058A ARMENIAN HYPHEN, U+061B "؛" ARABIC SEMICOLON, or the punctuation used with CJK ideographs in the CJK Symbols and Punctuation block. Script-specific punctuation characters may be unique in function, have different directionality, or be distinct in appearance or usage from their generic counterparts.

Punctuation intended for use with several related scripts is often encoded with the principal script for the group. For example, U+1735 PHILIPPINE SINGLE PUNCTUATION is encoded in a single location in the Hanunóo block, but it is intended for use with all four of the Philippine scripts.

Use and Interpretation. The use and interpretation of punctuation characters can be heavily context dependent. For example, U+002E FULL STOP can be used as sentence-ending punctuation, an abbreviation indicator, a decimal point, and so on.

Many Unicode algorithms, such as the Bidirectional Algorithm and Line Breaking Algorithm, both of which treat numeric punctuation differently from text punctuation, resolve the status of any ambiguous punctuation mark depending on whether it is part of a number context.

Legacy character encoding standards commonly include generic characters for punctuation instead of the more precisely specified characters used in printing. Examples include the single and double quotes, period, dash, and space. The Unicode Standard includes these generic characters, but also encodes the unambiguous characters independently: various forms of quotation marks, em dash, en dash, minus, hyphen, em space, en space, hair space, zero width space, and so on.

Rendering. Punctuation characters vary in appearance with the font style, just like the surrounding text characters. In some cases, where used in the context of a particular script, a specific glyph style is preferred. For example, U+002E FULL STOP should appear square when used with Armenian, but is typically circular when used with Latin. For mixed Latin/ Armenian text, two fonts (or one font allowing for context-dependent glyph variation) may need to be used to render the character faithfully.

Writing Direction. Punctuation characters shared across scripts have no inherent directionality. In a bidirectional context, their display direction is resolved according to the rules in Unicode Standard Annex #9, "The Bidirectional Algorithm." Certain script-specific punctuation marks have an inherent directionality that matches the writing direction of the script. For an example, see "Dandas" later in this section. The image of certain paired punctuation marks, specifically those that are brackets, is mirrored when the character is part of a right-to-left directional run (see *Section 4.7, Bidi Mirrored—Normative*). Mirroring ensures that the opening and closing semantics of the character remains independent of the writing direction. The same is generally not true for other punctuation marks even when their image is not bilaterally symmetric, such as *slash* or the *curly quotes*. See also "Paired Punctuation" later in this section.

In vertical writing, many punctuation characters have special vertical glyphs. Normally, fonts contain both the horizontal and vertical glyphs, and the selection of the appropriate glyph is based on the text orientation in effect at rendering time. However, see "CJK Compatibility Forms: Vertical Forms" later in this section.

Figure 6-2 shows a set of three common shapes used for *ideographic comma* and *ideographic full stop*. The first shape in each row is that used for horizontal text, the last shape is that for vertical text. The centered form may be used with both horizontal and vertical text. See also *Figure 6-4* for an example of vertical and horizontal forms for quotation marks.

Figure 6-2. Forms of CJK Punctuation

Horizontal	Centered	Vertical
、	、	、
。	。	。

Layout Controls. A number of characters in the blocks described in this section are not graphic punctuation characters, but rather affect the operation of layout algorithms. For a description of those characters, see *Section 16.2, Layout Controls*.

Encoding Characters with Multiple Semantic Values. Some of the punctuation characters in the ASCII range (U+0020..U+007F) have multiple uses, either through ambiguity in the original standards or through accumulated reinterpretations of a limited code set. For example, 27_{16} is defined in ANSI X3.4 as *apostrophe* (*closing single quotation mark; acute accent*), and $2D_{16}$ is defined as *hyphen-minus*. In general, the Unicode Standard provides the same interpretation for the equivalent code points, without adding to or subtracting from their semantics. The Unicode Standard supplies *unambiguous* codes elsewhere for the most useful particular interpretations of these ASCII values; the corresponding unambiguous characters are cross-referenced in the character names list for this block. For more information, see "Apostrophes," "Space Characters," and "Dashes and Hyphens" later in this section.

Blocks Devoted to Punctuation

For compatibility with widely used legacy character sets, the Basic Latin (ASCII) block (U+0000..U+007F) and the Latin-1 Supplement block (U+0080..U+00FF) contain several of the most common punctuation signs. They are isolated from the larger body of Unicode punctuation, signs, and symbols only because their relative code locations within ASCII and Latin-1 are so widely used in standards and software. The Unicode Standard has a number of blocks devoted specifically to encoding collections of punctuation characters.

The General Punctuation block (U+2000..U+206F) contains the most common punctuation characters widely used in Latin typography, as well as a few specialized punctuation marks and a large number of format control characters. All of these punctuation characters are intended for generic use, and in principle they could be used with any script.

The Supplemental Punctuation block (U+2E00..U+2E7F) is devoted to less commonly encountered punctuation marks, including those used in specialized notational systems or occurring primarily in ancient manuscript traditions.

The CJK Symbols and Punctuation block (U+3000..U+303F) has the most commonly occurring punctuation specific to East Asian typography—that is, typography involving the rendering of text with CJK ideographs.

The Vertical Forms block (U+FE10..U+FE1F), the CJK Compatibility Forms block (U+FE30..U+FE4F), the Small Form Variants block (U+FE50..U+FE6F), and the Halfwidth and Fullwidth Forms block (U+FF00..U+FFEF) contain many compatibility characters for punctuation marks, encoded for compatibility with a number of East Asian character encoding standards. Their primary use is for round-trip mapping with those legacy standards. For vertical text, the regular punctuation characters are used instead, with alternate glyphs for vertical layout supplied by the font.

The punctuation characters in these various blocks are discussed below in terms of their general types.

Format Control Characters

Format control characters are special characters that have no visible glyph of their own, but that affect the display of characters to which they are adjacent, or that have other specialized functions such as serving as invisible anchor points in text. All format control characters have General_Category=Cf. A significant number of format control characters are encoded in the General Punctuation block, but their descriptions are found in other sections.

Cursive joining controls, as well as U+200B ZERO WIDTH SPACE, U+2028 LINE SEPARATOR, U+2029 PARAGRAPH SEPARATOR, and U+2060 WORD JOINER, are described in *Section 16.2, Layout Controls*. Bidirectional ordering controls are also discussed in *Section 16.2, Layout Controls*, but their detailed use is specified in Unicode Standard Annex #9, "The Bidirectional Algorithm."

Invisible operators are explained in *Section 15.5, Invisible Mathematical Operators*. Deprecated format characters related to obsolete models of Arabic text processing are described in *Section 16.3, Deprecated Format Characters*.

The reserved code points U+2064..U+2069 and U+FFF0..U+FFF8, as well as any reserved code points in the range U+E0000..U+E0FFF, are reserved for the possible future encoding of other format control characters. Because of this, they are treated as default ignorable code points. For more information, see *Section 5.20, Default Ignorable Code Points*.

Space Characters

The most commonly used space character is U+0020 SPACE. Also often used is its non-breaking counterpart, U+00A0 NO-BREAK SPACE. These two characters have the same width, but behave differently for line breaking. For more information, see Unicode Standard Annex #14, "Line Breaking." U+00A0 NO-BREAK SPACE behaves like a numeric separator for the purposes of bidirectional layout. (See Unicode Standard Annex #9, "The Bidirectional Algorithm," for a detailed discussion of the Unicode Bidirectional Algorithm.) In ideographic text, U+3000 IDEOGRAPHIC SPACE is commonly used because its width matches that of the ideographs.

The main difference among other space characters is their width. U+2000..U+2006 are standard quad widths used in typography. U+2007 FIGURE SPACE has a fixed width, known as *tabular width*, which is the same width as digits used in tables. U+2008 PUNCTUATION SPACE is a space defined to be the same width as a period. U+2009 THIN SPACE and U+200A HAIR SPACE are successively smaller-width spaces used for narrow word gaps and for justification of type. The fixed-width space characters (U+2000..U+200A) are derived from conventional (hot lead) typography. Algorithmic kerning and justification in computerized typography do not use these characters. However, where they are used (for example, in typesetting mathematical formulae), their width is generally font-specified, and they typically do not expand during justification. The exception is U+2009 THIN SPACE, which sometimes gets adjusted.

In addition to the various fixed-width space characters, there are a few script-specific space characters in the Unicode Standard. U+1680 OGHAM SPACE MARK is unusual in that it is generally rendered with a visible horizontal line, rather than being blank.

Space characters with special behavior in word or line breaking are described in "Line and Word Breaking" in *Section 16.2, Layout Controls*, and Unicode Standard Annex #14, "Line Breaking."

U+00A0 NO-BREAK SPACE has an additional, important function in the Unicode Standard. It may serve as the base character for displaying a nonspacing combining mark in apparent isolation. Versions of the standard prior to Version 4.1 indicated that U+0020 SPACE could also be used for this function, but SPACE is no longer recommended, because of potential interactions with the handling of SPACE in XML and other markup languages. See *Section 2.11, Combining Characters*, for further discussion.

Space characters are found in several character blocks in the Unicode Standard. The list of space characters appears in *Table 6-2.*

Table 6-2. Unicode Space Characters

Code	Name
U+0020	SPACE
U+00A0	NO-BREAK SPACE
U+1680	OGHAM SPACE MARK
U+180E	MONGOLIAN VOWEL SEPARATOR
U+2000	EN QUAD
U+2001	EM QUAD
U+2002	EN SPACE
U+2003	EM SPACE
U+2004	THREE-PER-EM SPACE
U+2005	FOUR-PER-EM SPACE
U+2006	SIX-PER-EM SPACE
U+2007	FIGURE SPACE
U+2008	PUNCTUATION SPACE
U+2009	THIN SPACE
U+200A	HAIR SPACE
U+202F	NARROW NO-BREAK SPACE
U+205F	MEDIUM MATHEMATICAL SPACE
U+3000	IDEOGRAPHIC SPACE

The space characters in the Unicode Standard can be identified by their General Category, [gc=Zs], in the Unicode Character Database. One exceptional "space" character is U+200B ZERO WIDTH SPACE. This character, although called a "space" in its name, does not actually have any width or visible glyph in display. It functions primarily to indicate word boundaries in writing systems that do not actually use orthographic spaces to separate words in text. It is given the General Category [gc=Cf] and is treated as a format control character, rather than as a space character, in implementations. Further discussion of U+200B ZERO WIDTH SPACE, as well as other zero-width characters with special properties, can be found in *Section 16.2, Layout Controls.*

Dashes and Hyphens

Because of its prevalence in legacy encodings, U+002D HYPHEN-MINUS is the most common of the dash characters used to represent a hyphen. It has ambiguous semantic value and is rendered with an average width. U+2010 HYPHEN represents the hyphen as found in words such as "left-to-right." It is rendered with a narrow width. When typesetting text, U+2010 HYPHEN is preferred over U+002D HYPHEN-MINUS. U+2011 NON-BREAKING HYPHEN has the same semantic value as U+2010 HYPHEN, but should not be broken across lines.

U+2012 FIGURE DASH has the same (ambiguous) semantic as the U+002D HYPHEN-MINUS, but has the same width as digits (if they are monospaced). U+2013 EN DASH is used to indicate a range of values, such as 1973–1984, although in some languages *hyphen* is used for that purpose. The *en dash* should be distinguished from the U+2212 MINUS SIGN, which is an arithmetic operator. Although it is not preferred in mathematical typesetting, typographers sometimes use U+2013 EN DASH to represent the *minus sign*, particularly a *unary minus*. When interpreting formulas, U+002D HYPHEN-MINUS, U+2012 FIGURE DASH, and U+2212 MINUS SIGN should each be taken as indicating a *minus sign*, as in "x = a - b", unless a higher-level protocol precisely defines which of these characters serves that function.

U+2014 EM DASH is used to make a break—like this—in the flow of a sentence. (Some typographers prefer to use U+2013 EN DASH set off with spaces – like this – to make the same kind of break.) Like many other conventions for punctuation characters, such usage may depend on language. This kind of dash is commonly represented with a typewriter as a double hyphen. In older mathematical typography, U+2014 EM DASH may also used to indicate a *binary minus sign*. U+2015 HORIZONTAL BAR is used to introduce quoted text in some typographic styles.

Dashes and hyphen characters may also be found in other character blocks in the Unicode Standard. A list of dash and hyphen characters appears in *Table 6-3*. For a description of the line breaking behavior of dashes and hyphens, see Unicode Standard Annex #14, "Line Breaking Properties."

Table 6-3. Unicode Dash Characters

Code	Name
U+002D	HYPHEN-MINUS
U+007E	TILDE (when used as *swung dash*)
U+058A	ARMENIAN HYPHEN
U+05BE	HEBREW PUNCTUATION MAQAF
U+1806	MONGOLIAN TODO SOFT HYPHEN
U+2010	HYPHEN
U+2011	NON-BREAKING HYPHEN
U+2012	FIGURE DASH
U+2013	EN DASH
U+2014	EM DASH
U+2015	HORIZONTAL BAR (= *quotation dash*)
U+2053	SWUNG DASH
U+207B	SUPERSCRIPT MINUS
U+208B	SUBSCRIPT MINUS
U+2212	MINUS SIGN
U+2E17	DOUBLE OBLIQUE HYPHEN
U+301C	WAVE DASH
U+3030	WAVY DASH
U+30A0	KATAKANA-HIRAGANA DOUBLE HYPHEN
U+FE31	PRESENTATION FORM FOR VERTICAL EM DASH
U+FE32	PRESENTATION FORM FOR VERTICAL EN DASH
U+FE58	SMALL EM DASH
U+FE63	SMALL HYPHEN-MINUS
U+FF0D	FULLWIDTH HYPHEN-MINUS

Soft Hyphen. Despite its name, U+00AD SOFT HYPHEN is not a hyphen, but rather an invisible format character used to indicate optional intraword breaks. As described in

Section 16.2, Layout Controls, its effect on the appearance of the text depends on the language and script used.

Tilde. Although several shapes are commonly used to render U+007E "~" TILDE, modern fonts generally render it with a center line glyph, as shown here and in the code charts. However, it may also appear as a raised, spacing tilde, serving as a spacing clone of U+0303 "◌̃" COMBINING TILDE (see "Spacing Clones of Diacritics" in *Section 7.1, Latin*). This is a form common in older implementations, particularly for terminal emulation and typewriter-style fonts.

Some of the common uses of a tilde include indication of alternation, an approximate value, or, in some notational systems, indication of a logical negation. In the latter context, it is really being used as a shape-based substitute character for the more precise U+00AC "¬" NOT SIGN. A tilde is also used in dictionaries to repeat the defined term in examples. In that usage, as well as when used as punctuation to indicate alternation, it is more appropriately represented by a wider form, encoded as U+2053 "⁓" SWUNG DASH. U+02DC "˜" SMALL TILDE is a modifier letter encoded explicitly as the spacing form of the combining tilde as a diacritic. For mathematical usage, U+223C "∼" TILDE OPERATOR should be used to unambiguously encode the operator.

Paired Punctuation

Mirroring of Paired Punctuation. Paired punctuation marks such as parentheses (U+0028, U+0029), square brackets (U+005B, U+005D), and braces (U+007B, U+007D) are interpreted semantically rather than graphically in the context of bidirectional or vertical texts; that is, the orientation of these characters toward the enclosed text is maintained by the software, independent of the writing direction. In a bidirectional context, the glyphs are adjusted as described in Unicode Standard Annex #9, "The Bidirectional Algorithm." (See also *Section 4.7, Bidi Mirrored—Normative.*) During display, the software must ensure that the rendered glyph is the correct one in the context of bidirectional or vertical texts.

Paired punctuation marks containing the qualifier "LEFT" in their name are taken to denote *opening*; characters whose name contains the qualifier "RIGHT" are taken to denote *closing*. For example, U+0028 LEFT PARENTHESIS and U+0029 RIGHT PARENTHESIS are interpreted as opening and closing parentheses, respectively. In a right-to-left directional run, U+0028 is rendered as ")". In a left-to-right run, the same character is rendered as "(". In some mathematical usage, brackets may not be paired, or may be deliberately used in the reversed sense, such as]a,b[. Mirroring assures that in a right-to-left environment, such specialized mathematical text continues to read]b,a[and not [b, a]. See also "Language-Based Usage of Quotation Marks" later in this section.

Quotation Marks and Brackets. Like brackets, quotation marks occur in pairs, with some overlap in usage and semantics between these two types of punctuation marks. For example, some of the CJK quotation marks resemble brackets in appearance, and they are often used when brackets would be used in non-CJK text. Similarly, both single and double *guillemets* may be treated more like brackets than quotation marks.

Some of the editing marks used in annotated editions of scholarly texts exhibit features of both quotation marks and brackets. The particular convention employed by the editors determines whether editing marks are used in pairs, which editing marks form a pair, and which is the opening character. Unlike brackets, quotation marks are not mirrored in a bidirectional context.

Horizontal brackets—for example, those used in annotating mathematical expressions—are not paired punctuation, even though the set includes both top and bottom brackets. See "Horizontal Brackets" in *Section 15.6, Technical Symbols*, for more information.

Language-Based Usage of Quotation Marks

U+0022 QUOTATION MARK is the most commonly used character for quotation mark. However, it has ambiguous semantics and direction. Most keyboard layouts support only U+0022 QUOTATION MARK, therefore word processors commonly offer a facility for automatically converting the U+0022 QUOTATION MARK to a contextually selected curly quote glyph.

European Usage. The use of quotation marks differs systematically by language and by medium. In European typography, it is common to use *guillemets* (single or double angle quotation marks) for books and, except for some languages, curly quotation marks in office automation. Single guillemets may be used for quotes inside quotes. The following description does not attempt to be complete, but intends to document a range of known usages of quotation mark characters. Some of these usages are also illustrated in *Figure 6-3*. In this section, the words *single* and *double* are omitted from character names where there is no conflict or both are meant.

Dutch, English, Italian, Portugese, Spanish, and Turkish use a *left quotation mark* and a *right quotation mark* for opening and closing quotations, respectively. It is typical to alternate single and double quotes for quotes within quotes. Whether single or double quotes are used for the outer quotes depends on local and stylistic conventions.

Czech, German, and Slovak use the low-9 style of quotation mark for opening instead of the standard open quotes. They employ the *left quotation mark* style of quotation mark for closing instead of the more common *right quotation mark* forms. When guillemets are used in German books, they point to the quoted text. This style is the inverse of French usage.

Danish, Finnish, Norwegian, and Swedish use the same *right quotation mark* character for both the opening and closing quotation character. This usage is employed both for office automation purposes and for books. Books sometimes use the guillemet, U+00BB RIGHT-POINTING DOUBLE ANGLE QUOTATION MARK, for both opening and closing.

Hungarian and Polish usage of quotation marks is similar to the Scandinavian usage, except that they use low double quotes for opening quotations. Presumably, these languages avoid the low single quote so as to prevent confusion with the comma.

French, Greek, Russian, and Slovenian, among others, use the guillemets, but Slovenian usage is the same as German usage in their direction. Of these languages, at least French inserts space between text and quotation marks. In the French case, U+00A0 NO-BREAK SPACE can be used for the space that is enclosed between quotation mark and text; this choice helps line breaking algorithms.

Figure 6-3. European Quotation Marks

Single right quote = apostrophe

‘quote’ don’t

Usage depends on language

“English” « French »

„German“ »Slovenian«

”Swedish” »Swedish books»

East Asian Usage. The glyph for each quotation mark character for an Asian character set occupies predominantly a single quadrant of the character cell. The quadrant used depends on whether the character is opening or closing and whether the glyph is for use with horizontal or vertical text.

The pairs of quotation characters are listed in *Table 6-4*.

Table 6-4. East Asian Quotation Marks

Style	Opening	Closing
Corner bracket	300C	300D
White corner bracket	300E	300F
Double prime	301D	301F

Glyph Variation. The glyphs for “double-prime” quotation marks consist of a pair of wedges, slanted either forward or backward, with the tips of the wedges pointing either up or down. In a pair of double-prime quotes, the closing and the opening character of the pair slant in opposite directions. Two common variations exist, as shown in *Figure 6-4*. To confuse matters more, another form of double-prime quotation marks is used with Western-style horizontal text, in addition to the curly single or double quotes.

Three pairs of quotation marks are used with Western-style horizontal text, as shown in *Table 6-5*.

Overloaded Character Codes. The character codes for standard quotes can refer to regular narrow quotes from a Latin font used with Latin text as well as to wide quotes from an Asian font used with other wide characters. This situation can be handled with some suc-

Figure 6-4. Asian Quotation Marks

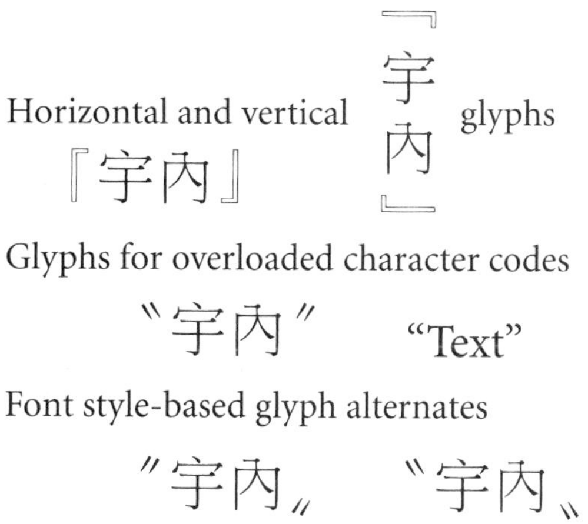

Horizontal and vertical glyphs

『宇內』 ﹃宇內﹄

Glyphs for overloaded character codes

〝宇內〞 “Text”

Font style-based glyph alternates

〞宇內〟 〝宇內〟

Table 6-5. Opening and Closing Forms

Style	Opening	Closing	Comment
Single	2018	2019	Rendered as “wide” character
Double	201C	201D	Rendered as “wide” character
Double prime	301D	301E	

cess where the text is marked up with language tags. For more information on narrow and wide characters, see Unicode Standard Annex #11, “East Asian Width.”

Consequences for Semantics. The semantics of U+00AB, U+00BB (double guillemets), and U+201D RIGHT DOUBLE QUOTATION MARK are context dependent. The semantics of U+201A and U+201B LOW-9 QUOTATION MARKS are always opening; this usage is distinct from the usage of U+301F LOW DOUBLE PRIME QUOTATION MARK, which is unambiguously closing. All other quotation marks may represent opening or closing quotation marks depending on the usage.

Apostrophes

U+0027 APOSTROPHE is the most commonly used character for apostrophe. For historical reasons, U+0027 is a particularly overloaded character. In ASCII, it is used to represent a punctuation mark (such as right single quotation mark, left single quotation mark, apostrophe punctuation, vertical line, or prime) or a modifier letter (such as apostrophe modifier or acute accent). Punctuation marks generally break words; modifier letters generally are considered part of a word.

When text is set, U+2019 RIGHT SINGLE QUOTATION MARK is preferred as apostrophe, but only U+0027 is present on keyboards. Word processors commonly offer a facility for automatically converting the U+0027 APOSTROPHE to a contextually selected curly quotation glyph. In these systems, a U+0027 in the data stream is always represented as a straight vertical line and can never represent a curly apostrophe or a right quotation mark.

Letter Apostrophe. U+02BC MODIFIER LETTER APOSTROPHE is preferred where the apostrophe is to represent a modifier letter (for example, in transliterations to indicate a glottal stop). In the latter case, it is also referred to as a *letter apostrophe*.

Punctuation Apostrophe. U+2019 RIGHT SINGLE QUOTATION MARK is preferred where the character is to represent a punctuation mark, as for contractions: "*We've been here before.*" In this latter case, U+2019 is also referred to as a *punctuation apostrophe*.

An implementation cannot assume that users' text always adheres to the distinction between these characters. The text may come from different sources, including mapping from other character sets that do not make this distinction between the letter apostrophe and the punctuation apostrophe/right single quotation mark. In that case, *all* of them will generally be represented by U+2019.

The semantics of U+2019 are therefore context dependent. For example, if surrounded by letters or digits on both sides, it behaves as an in-text punctuation character and does not separate words or lines.

Other Punctuation

Hyphenation Point. U+2027 HYPHENATION POINT is a raised dot used to indicate correct word breaking, as in dic‧tion‧ar‧ies. It is a punctuation mark, to be distinguished from U+00B7 MIDDLE DOT, which has multiple semantics.

Fraction Slash. U+2044 FRACTION SLASH is used between digits to form numeric fractions, such as 2/3 and 3/9. The standard form of a fraction built using the fraction slash is defined as follows: any sequence of one or more decimal digits (General Category = Nd), followed by the fraction slash, followed by any sequence of one or more decimal digits. Such a fraction should be displayed as a unit, such as ¾ or $\frac{3}{4}$. The precise choice of display can depend on additional formatting information.

If the displaying software is incapable of mapping the fraction to a unit, then it can also be displayed as a simple linear sequence as a fallback (for example, 3/4). If the fraction is to be separated from a previous number, then a space can be used, choosing the appropriate width (normal, thin, zero width, and so on). For example, 1 + THIN SPACE + 3 + FRACTION SLASH + 4 is displayed as 1¾.

Spacing Overscores and Underscores. U+203E OVERLINE is the above-the-line counterpart to U+005F LOW LINE. It is a spacing character, not to be confused with U+0305 COMBINING OVERLINE. As with all overscores and underscores, a sequence of these characters should connect in an unbroken line. The overscoring characters also must be distinguished from U+0304 COMBINING MACRON, which does not connect horizontally in this way.

Doubled Punctuation. Several doubled punctuation characters that have compatibility decompositions into a sequence of two punctuation marks are also encoded as single characters: U+203C DOUBLE EXCLAMATION MARK, U+2048 QUESTION EXCLAMATION MARK, and U+2049 EXCLAMATION QUESTION MARK. These doubled punctuation marks are included as an implementation convenience for East Asian and Mongolian text, when rendered vertically.

Period or Full Stop. The *period*, or U+002E FULL STOP, can be circular or square in appearance, depending on the font or script. The hollow circle period used in East Asian texts is separately encoded as U+3002 IDEOGRAPHIC FULL STOP. Likewise, Armenian, Arabic, Ethiopic, and several other script-specific periods are coded separately because of their significantly different appearance.

In contrast, the various functions of the period, such as its use as sentence-ending punctuation, an abbreviation mark, or a decimal point, are not separately encoded. The specific semantic therefore depends on context.

In old-style numerals, where numbers vary in placement above and below the baseline, a decimal or thousands separator may be displayed with a dot that is raised above the baseline. Because it would be inadvisable to have a stylistic variation between old-style and new-style numerals that actually changes the underlying representation of text, the Unicode Standard considers this raised dot to be merely a glyphic variant of U+002E "." FULL STOP. For other characters in this range that have alternative glyphs, the Unicode character is displayed with the basic or most common glyph; rendering software may present any other graphical form of that character.

Ellipsis. The omission of text is often indicated by a sequence of three dots "...", a punctuation convention called *ellipsis*. Typographic traditions vary in how they lay out these dots. In some cases the dots are closely spaced; in other cases the dots are spaced farther apart. U+2026 HORIZONTAL ELLIPSIS is the ordinary Unicode character intended for the representation of an ellipsis in text and typically shows the dots separated with a moderate degree of spacing. A sequence of three U+002E FULL STOP characters can also be used to indicate an ellipsis, in which case the space between the dots will depend on the font used for rendering. For example, in a monowidth font, a sequence of three *full stops* will be wider than the *horizontal ellipsis*, but in a typical proportional font, a *full stop* is very narrow and a sequence of three of them will be more tightly spaced than the the dots in *horizontal ellipsis*.

Conventions that use four dots for an ellipsis in certain grammatical contexts should represent them either as a sequence of <full stop, horizontal ellipsis> or <horizontal ellipsis, full stop> or simply as a sequence of four *full stop* characters, depending on the requirements of those conventions.

In East Asian typographic traditions, particularly in Japan, an ellipsis is raised to the center line of text. This effect requires the use of a Japanese-specific font, or at least a specific glyph for the *horizontal ellipsis* character.

Vertical Ellipsis. When text is laid out vertically, the ellipsis is normally oriented so that the dots run from top to bottom. Most commonly, an East Asian font will contain a vertically oriented glyph variant of U+2026 for use in vertical text layout. U+FE19 PRESENTATION FORM FOR VERTICAL HORIZONTAL ELLIPSIS is a compatibility character for use in mapping to the GB 18030 standard; it would not usually be used for an ellipsis except in systems that cannot handle the contextual choice of glyph variants for vertical rendering. U+22EE VERTICAL ELLIPSIS and U+22EF MIDLINE HORIZONTAL ELLIPSIS are part of a set of special ellipsis characters used for row or column elision in matrix notation. Their use is restricted to mathematical contexts; they should not be used as glyph variants of the ordinary punctuation ellipsis for East Asian typography.

U+205D TRICOLON has a superficial resemblance to a *vertical ellipsis*, but is part of a set of dot delimiter punctuation marks for various manuscript traditions. As for the *colon*, the dots in the *tricolon* are always oriented vertically.

Leader Dots. Leader dots are typically seen in contexts such as a table of contents or in indices, where they represent a kind of style line, guiding the eye from an entry in the table to its associated page number. Usually leader dots are generated automatically by page formatting software and do not require the use of encoded characters. However, there are occasional plain text contexts in which a string of leader dots is represented as a sequence of characters. U+2024 ONE DOT LEADER and U+2025 TWO DOT LEADER are intended for such usage. U+2026 HORIZONTAL ELLIPSIS can also serve as a three-dot version of leader dots. These leader dot characters can be used to control, to a certain extent, the spacing of leader dots based on font design, in contexts where a simple sequence of *full stops* will not suffice.

U+2024 ONE DOT LEADER also serves as a "semicolon" punctuation in Armenian, where it is distinguished from U+002E FULL STOP. See *Section 7.6, Armenian.*

Other Basic Latin Punctuation Marks. The interword punctuation marks encoded in the Basic Latin block are used for a variety of other purposes. This can complicate the tasks of parsers trying to determine sentence boundaries. As noted later in this section, some can be used as numeric separators. Both *period* and U+003A ":" COLON can be used to mark abbreviations as in "etc." or as in the Swedish abbreviation "S:ta" for "Sankta". U+0021 "!" EXCLAMATION MARK is used as a mathematical operator (*factorial*). U+003F "?" QUESTION MARK is often used as a substitution character when mapping Unicode characters to other character sets where they do not have a representation. This practice can lead to unexpected results when the converted data are file names from a file system that supports "?" as a wildcard character. U+003B ";" SEMICOLON is the preferred representation for the Greek question mark. (U+037E ";" GREEK QUESTION MARK is canonically equivalent to U+003B, so all normalized data will use the *semicolon*.)

Bullets. U+2022 BULLET is the typical character for a bullet. Within the general punctuation, several alternative forms for bullets are separately encoded: U+2023 TRIANGULAR BULLET, U+204C BLACK LEFTWARDS BULLET, and so on. U+00B7 MIDDLE DOT also often functions as a small bullet. Bullets mark the head of specially formatted paragraphs, often occurring in lists, and may use arbitrary graphics or dingbat forms as well as more conventional bullet forms. U+261E WHITE RIGHT POINTING INDEX, for example, is often used to highlight a note in text, as a kind of gaudy bullet.

Paragraph Marks. U+00A7 SECTION SIGN and U+00B6 PILCROW SIGN are often used as visible indications of sections or paragraphs of text, in editorial markup, to show format modes, and so on. Which character indicates sections and which character indicates paragraphs may vary by convention. U+204B REVERSED PILCROW SIGN is a fairly common alternate representation of the paragraph mark.

Numeric Separators. Any of the characters U+002C COMMA, U+002E FULL STOP, and the Arabic characters U+060C, U+066B, or U+066C (and possibly others) can be used as numeric separator characters, depending on the locale and user customizations.

Commercial Minus. U+2052 ⁒ COMMERCIAL MINUS SIGN is used in commercial or tax-related forms or publications in several European countries, including Germany and Scandinavia. The string "./." is used as a fallback representation for this character.

The symbol may also appear as a marginal note in letters, denoting enclosures. One variation replaces the top dot with a digit indicating the number of enclosures.

An additional usage of the sign appears in the Uralic Phonetic Alphabet (UPA), where it marks a structurally related borrowed element of different pronunciation. In Finland and a number of other European countries, the dingbats ⁒ and ✓ are always used for "correct" and "incorrect," respectively, in marking a student's paper. This contrasts with American practice, for example, where ✓ and ✗ might be used for "correct" and "incorrect," respectively, in the same context.

At Sign. U+0040 COMMERCIAL AT has acquired a prominent modern use as part of the syntax for e-mail addresses. As a result, users in practically every language community suddenly needed to use and refer to this character. Consequently, many colorful names have been invented for this character. Some of these contain references to animals or even pastries. *Table* 6-6 gives a sample.

Table 6-6. Names for the @

Language	Name and Comments
Chinese	= xiao laoshu (means "little mouse" in Mandarin Chinese), laoshu hao (means "mouse mark" in Mandarin Chinese)
Danish	= grishale, snabel-a (common, humorous slang)
Dutch	= apenstaartje (common, humorous slang)
Finnish	= ät, ät-merkki (Finnish standard) = kissanhäntä, miukumauku (common, humorous slang)
French	= arobase, arrobe, escargot, a crolle (common, humorous slang)
German	= Klammeraffe
Hebrew	= shtrudl ("Strudel", modern Hebrew) = krukhit (more formal Hebrew)
Hungarian	= kukac (common, humorous slang)
Italian	= chiocciola
Polish	= atka, małpa, małpka (common, humorous slang)
Portuguese	= arroba
Russian	= sobachka (common, humorous slang)
Slovenian	= afna (common, humorous slang)
Spanish	= arroba
Swedish	= snabel-a, kanelbulle (common, humorous slang)

Archaic Punctuation and Editorial Marks

Archaic Punctuation. Many archaic scripts use punctuation marks consisting of a set of multiple dots, such as U+2056 THREE DOT PUNCTUATION. The semantics of these marks can vary by script, and some of them are also used for special conventions, such as the use of U+205E VERTICAL FOUR DOTS in modern dictionaries. U+205B FOUR DOT MARK and U+205C DOTTED CROSS were used by scribes in the margin to highlight a piece of text.

These kinds of punctuation marks commonly occur in ancient scripts. Their specific function may be different in each script. However, encoding only a single set in the Unicode Standard simplifies the task of deciding which character to use for a given mark.

There are some exceptions to this general rule. Archaic scripts with script-specific punctuation include Runic, Aegean Numbers, and Cuneiform. In particular, the appearance of punctuation written in the Cuneiform style is sufficiently different that no unification was attempted.

Editorial Marks. The Greek text of the New Testament exists in a large number of manuscripts with many textual variants. The most widely used critical edition of the New Testament, the Nestle-Aland edition published by the United Bible Societies (UBS), introduced a set of editorial characters that are regularly used in a number of journals and other publications. As a result, these editorial marks have become the recognized method of annotating the New Testament.

U+2E00 RIGHT ANGLE SUBSTITUTION MARKER is placed at the start of a single word when that word is replaced by one or more different words in some manuscripts. These alternative readings are given in the *apparatus criticus.* If there is a second alternative reading in one verse, U+2E01 RIGHT ANGLE DOTTED SUBSTITUTION MARKER is used instead.

U+2E02 LEFT SUBSTITUTION BRACKET is placed at the start of a sequence of words where an alternative reading is given in the *apparatus criticus.* This bracket is used together with the U+2E03 RIGHT SUBSTITUTION BRACKET. If there is a second alternative reading in one verse, the dotted forms at U+2E04 and U+2E05 are used instead.

U+2E06 RAISED INTERPOLATION MARKER is placed at a point in the text where another version has additional text. This additional text is given in the *apparatus criticus.* If there is a second piece of interpolated text in one verse, the dotted form U+2E07 RAISED DOTTED INTERPOLATION MARKER is used instead.

U+2E08 DOTTED TRANSPOSITION MARKER is placed at the start of a word or verse that has been transposed. The transposition is explained in the *apparatus criticus.* When the words are preserved in different order in some manuscripts, U+2E09 LEFT TRANSPOSITION BRACKET is used. The end of such a sequence of words is marked by U+2E0A RIGHT TRANSPOSITION BRACKET.

The characters U+2E0B RAISED SQUARE and U+2E0C LEFT RAISED OMISSION BRACKET are conventionally used in pairs to bracket text, with RAISED SQUARE marking the start of a passage of omitted text and LEFT RAISED OMISSION BRACKET marking its end. In other editorial traditions, U+2E0C LEFT RAISED OMISSION BRACKET may be paired with U+2E0D RIGHT

RAISED OMISSION BRACKET. Depending on the conventions used, either may act as the starting or ending bracket.

Two other bracket characters, U+2E1C LEFT LOW PARAPHRASE BRACKET and U+2E1D RIGHT LOW PARAPHRASE BRACKET, have particular usage in the N'Ko script, but also may be used for general editorial punctuation.

Ancient Greek Editorial Marks. Ancient Greek scribes generally wrote in continuous uppercase letters without separating letters into words. On occasion, the scribe added punctuation to indicate the end of a sentence or a change of speaker or to separate words. Editorial and punctuation characters appear abundantly in surviving papyri and have been rendered in modern typography when possible, often exhibiting considerable glyphic variation. A number of these editorial marks are encoded in the range U+2E0E..U+2E16.

The punctuation used in Greek manuscripts can be divided into two categories: marginal or semi-marginal characters that mark the end of a section of text (for example, *coronis*, *paragraphos*), and characters that are mixed in with the text to mark pauses, end of sense, or separation between words (for example, *stigme*, *hypodiastole*). The *hypodiastole* is used in contrast with *comma* and is not a glyph variant of it.

A number of editorial characters are attributed to and named after Aristarchos of Samothrace (circa 216–144 BCE), fifth head of the Library at Alexandria. Aristarchos provided a major edition of the works of Homer, which forms the basis for modern editions.

A variety of Ancient Greek editorial marks are shown in the text of *Figure 6-5*, including the *editorial coronis* and *upwards ancora* on the left. On the right are illustrated the *dotted obelos*, *capital dotted lunate sigma symbol*, *capital reversed lunate sigma symbol*, and a glyph variant of the *downards ancora*. The numbers on the left indicate text lines. A *paragraphos* appears below the start of line 12. The opening brackets "[" indicate fragments, where text is illegible or missing in the original. These examples are slightly adapted and embellished from editions of the *Oxyrhynchus Papyri* and Homer's *Iliad*.

Figure 6-5. Examples of Ancient Greek Editorial Marks

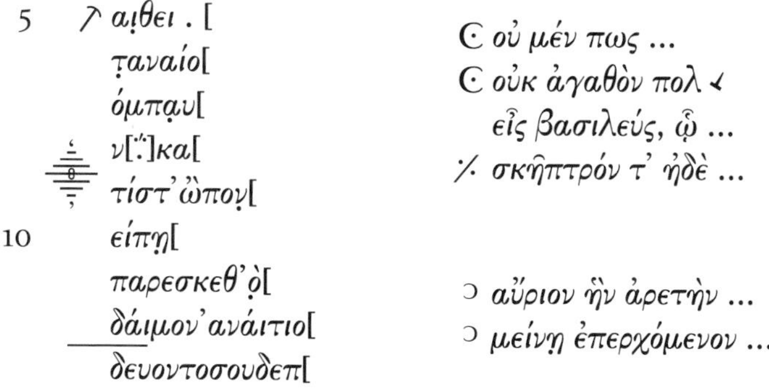

U+2E0F PARAGRAPHOS is placed at the beginning of the line but may refer to a break in the text at any point in the line. The *paragraphos* should be a horizontal line, generally stretching under the first few letters of the line it refers to, and possibly extending into the margin. It should be given a no-space line of its own and does not itself constitute a line or paragraph break point for the rest of the text. Examples of the *paragraphos*, *forked paragraphos*, and *reversed forked paragraphos* are illustrated in *Figure 6-6.*

Figure 6-6. Use of Greek Paragraphos

δαιμονα... δαιμονα... δαιμονα...

δευοντοσου... δευοντοσου... δευοντοσου...

Double Oblique Hyphen. U+2E17 "⸗" DOUBLE OBLIQUE HYPHEN is used in ancient Near Eastern linguistics to indicate certain morphological boundaries while continuing to use the ordinary hyphen to indicate other boundaries. This symbol is also semantically distinct from U+003D "=" EQUALS SIGN. Fraktur fonts use an oblique glyph of similar appearance for the hyphen, but that is merely a font variation of U+002D HYPHEN-MINUS or U+2010 HYPHEN, not the distinctly encoded DOUBLE OBLIQUE HYPHEN.

Indic Punctuation

Dandas. Dandas are phrase-ending punctuation common to the scripts of South and South East Asia. The Devanagari *danda* and *double danda* characters are intended for generic use across the scripts of India. They are also occasionally used in Latin transliteration of traditional texts from Indic scripts.

There are minor visual differences in the appearance of the dandas, which may require script-specific fonts or a font that can provide glyph alternates based on script environment. See *Chapter 9, South Asian Scripts-I*, for a list of scripts in question. For the four Philippine scripts, the analogues to the dandas are encoded once in Hanunóo and shared across all four scripts. The other Brahmi-derived scripts have separately encoded equivalents for the danda and double danda. See *Chapter 10, South Asian Scripts-II*, and *Chapter 11, Southeast Asian Scripts.*

The Bidirectional Class of the dandas matches that for the scripts they are intended for. Kharoshthi, which is written from right to left, has Bidirectional Class R for U+10A56 KHAROSHTHI PUNCTUATION DANDA. For more on bidirectional classes, see Unicode Standard Annex #9, "The Bidirectional Algorithm."

Note that the name of the danda in Hindi is *viram*, while the different Unicode character named *virama* is called *halant* in Hindi. If this distinction is not kept in mind, it can lead to confusion as to which character is meant.

CJK Punctuation

CJK Punctuation comprises punctuation marks and symbols used by writing systems that employ Han ideographs. Most of these characters are found in East Asian standards. Typical for many of these wide punctuation characters is that the actual image occupies only the left or the right half of the normal square character cell. The extra whitespace is frequently removed in a kerning step during layout, as shown in *Figure 6-7*. Unlike ordinary kerning, which uses tables supplied by the font, the character space adjustment of wide punctuation characters is based on their character code.

Figure 6-7. CJK Parentheses

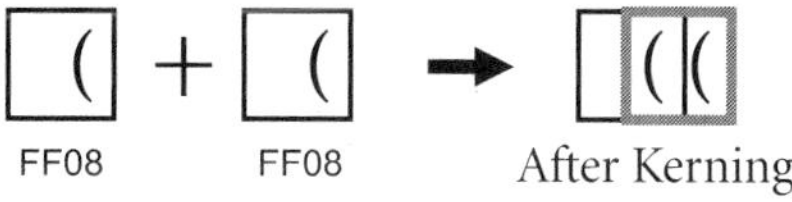

U+3000 IDEOGRAPHIC SPACE is provided for compatibility with legacy character sets. It is a fixed-width wide space appropriate for use with an ideographic font. For more information about wide characters, see Unicode Standard Annex #11, "East Asian Width."

U+301C WAVE DASH and U+3030 WAVY DASH are special forms of dashes found in East Asian character standards. (For a list of other space and dash characters in the Unicode Standard, see *Table 6-2* and *Table 6-3*.)

U+3037 IDEOGRAPHIC TELEGRAPH LINE FEED SEPARATOR SYMBOL is a visible indicator of the line feed separator symbol used in the Chinese telegraphic code. It is comparable to the pictures of control codes found in the Control Pictures block.

U+3005 IDEOGRAPHIC ITERATION MARK is used to stand for the second of a pair of identical ideographs occurring in adjacent positions within a document.

U+3006 IDEOGRAPHIC CLOSING MARK is used frequently on signs to indicate that a store or booth is closed for business. The Japanese pronunciation is *shime*, most often encountered in the compound *shime-kiri*.

The U+3008 and U+3009 angle brackets are unambiguously wide, as are other bracket characters in this block, such as double angle brackets, tortoise shell brackets, and white square brackets. Where mathematical and other non-CJK contexts use brackets of similar shape, the Unicode Standard encodes them separately.

U+3012 POSTAL MARK is used in Japanese addresses immediately preceding the numerical postal code. It is also used on forms and applications to indicate the blank space in which a postal code is to be entered. U+3020 POSTAL MARK FACE and U+3036 CIRCLED POSTAL MARK are properly glyphic variants of U+3012 and are included for compatibility.

U+3031 VERTICAL KANA REPEAT MARK and U+3032 VERTICAL KANA REPEAT WITH VOICED SOUND MARK are used only in *vertically written* Japanese to repeat pairs of kana characters occurring immediately prior in a document. The voiced variety U+3032 is used in cases where the repeated kana are to be voiced. For instance, a repetitive phrase like *toki-doki* could be expressed as <U+3068, U+304D, U+3032> in vertical writing. Both of these characters are intended to be represented by "double-height" glyphs requiring two ideographic "cells" to print; this intention also explains the existence in source standards of the characters representing the top and bottom halves of these characters (that is, the characters U+3033, U+3034, and U+3035). In horizontal writing, similar characters are used, and they are separately encoded. In Hiragana, the equivalent repeat marks are encoded at U+309D and U+309E; in Katakana, they are U+30FD and U+30FE.

Sesame Dots. U+FE45 SESAME DOT and U+FE46 WHITE SESAME DOT are used in vertical text, where a series of sesame dots may appear beside the main text, as a sidelining to provide visual emphasis. In this respect, their usage is similar to such characters as U+FE34 PRESENTATION FORM FOR VERTICAL WAVY LOW LINE, which are also used for sidelining vertical text for emphasis. Despite being encoded in the block for CJK compatibility forms, the sesame dots are not compatibility characters. They are in general typographic use and are found in the Japanese standard, JIS X 0213.

U+FE45 SESAME DOT is historically related to U+3001 IDEOGRAPHIC COMMA, but is not simply a vertical form variant of it. The function of an *ideographic comma* in connected text is distinct from that of a *sesame dot*.

Unknown or Unavailable Ideographs

U+3013 GETA MARK is used to indicate the presence of, or to hold a place for, an ideograph that is not available when a document is printed. It has no other use. Its name comes from its resemblance to the mark left by traditional Japanese sandals (*geta*). A variety of light and heavy glyphic variants occur.

U+303E IDEOGRAPHIC VARIATION INDICATOR is a graphic character that is to be rendered visibly. It alerts the user that the intended character is similar to, but not equal to, the character that follows. Its use is similar to the existing character U+3013 GETA MARK. A GETA MARK substitutes for the unknown or unavailable character, but does not identify it. The IDEOGRAPHIC VARIATION INDICATOR is the head of a two-character sequence that gives some indication about the intended glyph or intended character. Ultimately, the IDEOGRAPHIC VARIATION INDICATOR and the character following it are intended to be replaced by the correct character, once it has been identified or a font resource or input resource has been provided for it.

U+303F IDEOGRAPHIC HALF FILL SPACE is a visible indicator of a display cell filler used when ideographic characters have been split during display on systems using a double-byte character encoding. It is included in the Unicode Standard for compatibility.

See also "Ideographic Description Sequences" in *Section 12.1, Han*.

CJK Compatibility Forms

Vertical Forms. CJK vertical forms are compatibility characters encoded for compatibility with legacy implementations that encode these characters explicitly when Chinese text is being set in vertical rather than horizontal lines. The preferred Unicode approach to representation of such text is to simply use the nominal characters that correspond to these vertical variants. Then, at display time, the appropriate glyph is selected according to the line orientation.

The Unicode Standard contains two blocks devoted primarily to these CJK vertical forms. The CJK Vertical Forms block, U+FE10..U+FE1F, contains compatibility characters needed for round-trip mapping to the Chinese standard, GB 18030. The CJK Compatibility Forms block, U+FE30..U+FE4F, contains forms found in the Chinese standard, CNS 11643.

Styled Overscores and Underscores. The CJK Compatibility Forms block also contains a number of compatibility characters from CNS 11643, which consist of different styles of overscores or underscores. They were intended, in the Chinese standard, for the representation of various types of overlining or underlining, for emphasis of text when laid out *horizontally.* Except for round-trip mapping with legacy character encodings, the use of these characters is discouraged; use of styles is the preferred way to handle such effects in modern text rendering.

Small Form Variants. CNS 11643 also contains a number of small variants of ASCII punctuation characters. The Unicode Standard encodes those variants as compatibility characters in the Small Form Variants block, U+FE50..U+FE6F. Those characters, while construed as fullwidth characters, are nevertheless depicted using small forms that are set in a fullwidth display cell. (See the discussion in *Section 12.4, Hiragana and Katakana.*) These characters are provided for compatibility with legacy implementations.

Two small form variants from CNS 11643/plane 1 were unified with other characters outside the ASCII block: 2131_{16} was unified with U+00B7 MIDDLE DOT, and 2261_{16} was unified with U+2215 DIVISION SLASH.

Fullwidth and Halfwidth Variants. For compatibility with East Asian legacy character sets, the Unicode Standard encodes fullwidth variants of ASCII punctuation and halfwidth variants of CJK punctuation. See *Section 12.5, Halfwidth and Fullwidth Forms*, for more information.

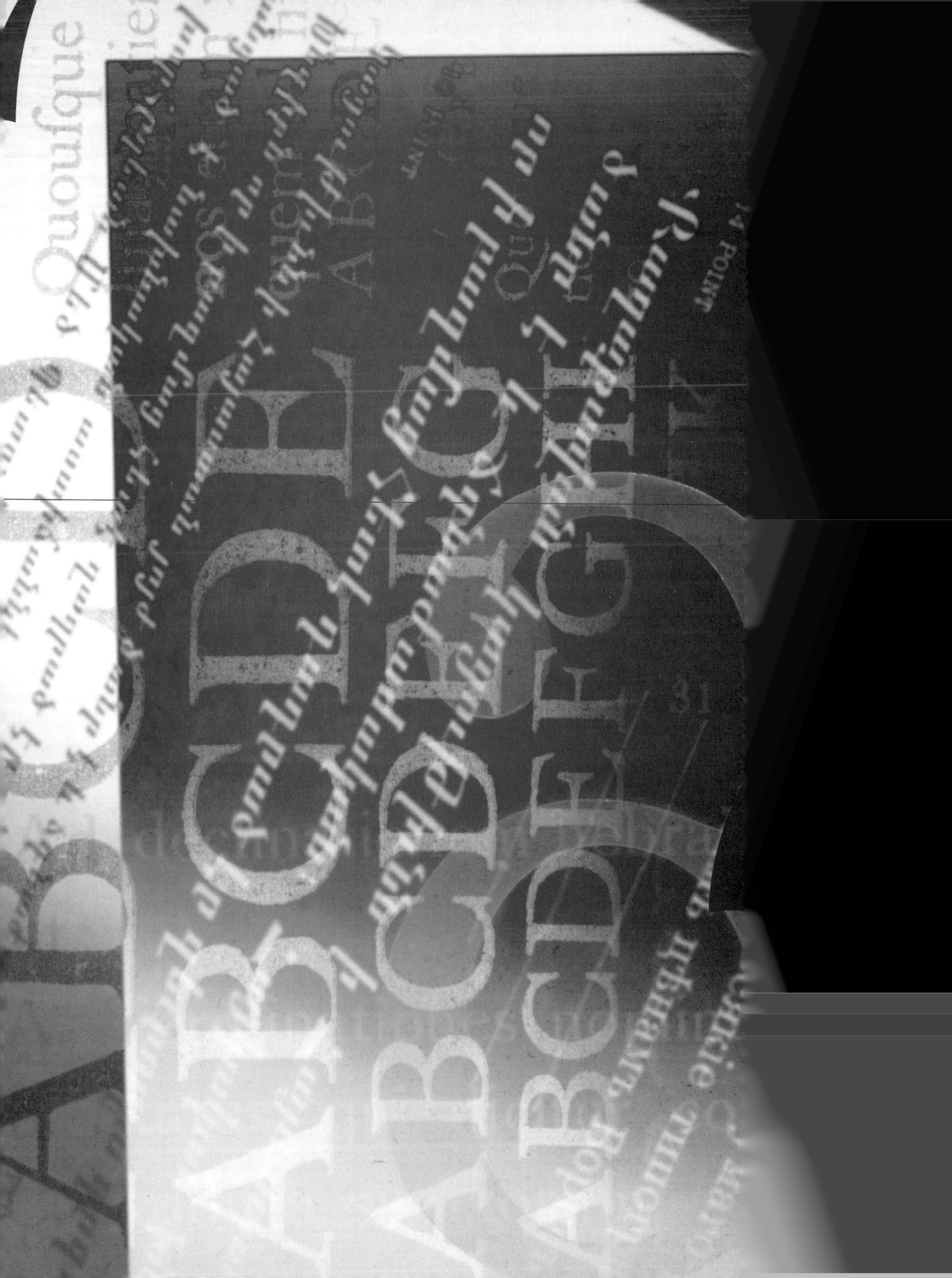

Chapter 7

European Alphabetic Scripts

Modern European alphabetic scripts are derived from or influenced by the Greek script, which itself was an adaptation of the Phoenician alphabet. A Greek innovation was writing the letters from left to right, which is the writing direction for all the scripts derived from or inspired by Greek.

The European alphabetic scripts and additional characters described in this chapter are

Latin	*Cyrillic*	*Georgian*
Greek	*Glagolitic*	*Modifier letters*
Coptic	*Armenian*	*Combining marks*

The European scripts are all written from left to right. Many have separate lowercase and uppercase forms of the alphabet. Spaces are used to separate words. Accents and diacritical marks are used to indicate phonetic features and to extend the use of base scripts to additional languages. Some of these modification marks have evolved into small free-standing signs that can be treated as characters in their own right.

The Latin script is used to write or transliterate texts in a wide variety of languages. The International Phonetic Alphabet (IPA) is an extension of the Latin alphabet, enabling it to represent the phonetics of all languages. Other Latin phonetic extensions are used for the Uralic Phonetic Alphabet.

The Latin alphabet is derived from the alphabet used by the Etruscans, who had adopted a Western variant of the classical Greek alphabet (*Section 14.2, Old Italic*). Originally it contained only 24 capital letters. The modern Latin alphabet as it is found in the Basic Latin block owes its appearance to innovations of scribes during the Middle Ages and practices of the early Renaissance printers.

The Cyrillic script was developed in the ninth century and is also based on Greek. Like Latin, Cyrillic is used to write or transliterate texts in many languages. The Georgian and Armenian scripts were devised in the fifth century and are influenced by Greek. Modern Georgian does not have separate uppercase and lowercase forms.

The Coptic script was the last stage in the development of Egyptian writing. It represented the adaptation of the Greek alphabet to writing Egyptian, with the retention of forms from Demotic for sounds not adequately represented by Greek letters. Although primarily used in Egypt from the fourth to the tenth century, it is described in this chapter because of its close relationship to the Greek script.

Glagolitic is an early Slavic script related in some ways to both the Greek and the Cyrillic scripts. It was widely used in the Balkans but gradually died out, surviving the longest in Croatia. Like Coptic, however, it still has some modern use in liturgical contexts.

This chapter also describes modifier letters and combining marks used with the Latin script and other scripts.

The block descriptions for other archaic European alphabetic scripts, such as Gothic, Ogham, Old Italic, and Runic, can be found in *Chapter 14, Archaic Scripts.*

7.1 Latin

The Latin script was derived from the Greek script. Today it is used to write a wide variety of languages all over the world. In the process of adapting it to other languages, numerous extensions have been devised. The most common is the addition of diacritical marks. Furthermore, the creation of digraphs, inverse or reverse forms, and outright new characters have all been used to extend the Latin script.

The Latin script is written in linear sequence from left to right. Spaces are used to separate words and provide the primary line breaking opportunities. Hyphens are used where lines are broken in the middle of a word. (For more information, see Unicode Standard Annex #14, "Line Breaking Properties.") Latin letters come in uppercase and lowercase pairs.

Languages. Some indication of language or other usage is given for many characters within the names lists accompanying the character charts.

Diacritical Marks. Speakers of different languages treat the addition of a diacritical mark to a base letter differently. In some languages, the combination is treated as a letter in the alphabet for the language. In others, such as English, the same words can often be spelled with and without the diacritical mark without implying any difference. Most languages that use the Latin script treat letters with diacritical marks as variations of the base letter, but do not accord the combination the full status of an independent letter in the alphabet. Widely used accented character combinations are provided as single characters to accommodate interoperation with pervasive practice in legacy encodings. Combining diacritical marks can express these and all other accented letters as combining character sequences.

In the Unicode Standard, all diacritical marks are encoded in sequence *after the base characters to which they apply.* For more details, see the subsection "Combining Diacritical Marks" in *Section 7.9, Combining Marks*, and also *Section 2.11, Combining Characters.*

Alternative Glyphs. Some characters have alternative representations, although they have a common semantic. In such cases, a preferred glyph is chosen to represent the character in the code charts, even though it may not be the form used under all circumstances. Some

Latin examples to illustrate this point are provided in *Figure 7-1* and discussed in the text that follows.

Figure 7-1. Alternative Glyphs in Latin

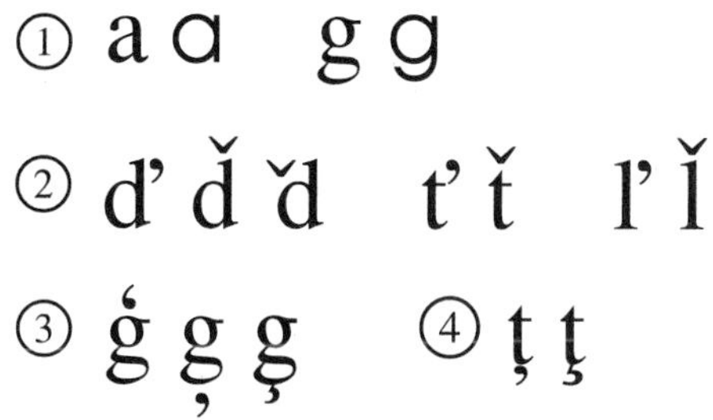

Common typographical variations of basic Latin letters include the open- and closed-loop forms of the lowercase letters "a" and "g", as shown in the first example in *Figure 7-1*. In ordinary Latin text, such distinctions are merely glyphic alternates for the same characters; however, phonetic transcription systems, such as IPA and Pinyin, often make systematic distinctions between these forms.

Variations in Diacritical Marks. The shape and placement of diacritical marks can be subject to considerable variation that might surprise a reader unfamiliar with such distinctions. For example, when Czech is typeset, U+010F LATIN SMALL LETTER D WITH CARON and U+0165 LATIN SMALL LETTER T WITH CARON are often rendered by glyphs with an apostrophe instead of with a caron, commonly known as a háček. See the second example in *Figure 7-1*. In Slovak, this use also applies to U+013E LATIN SMALL LETTER L WITH CARON and U+013D LATIN CAPITAL LETTER L WITH CARON. The use of an apostrophe can avoid some line crashes over the ascenders of those letters and so result in better typography. In typewritten or handwritten documents, or in didactic and pedagogical material, glyphs with háčeks are preferred.

A similar situation can be seen with the Latvian letter U+0123 LATIN SMALL LETTER G WITH CEDILLA, as shown in example 3 in *Figure 7-1*. In good Latvian typography, this character is always shown with a rotated comma *over* the g, rather than a cedilla below the g, because of the typographical design and layout issues resulting from trying to place a cedilla below the descender loop of the *g*. Poor Latvian fonts may substitute an acute accent for the rotated comma, and handwritten or other printed forms may actually show the cedilla below the *g*. The uppercase form of the letter is always shown with a cedilla, as the rounded bottom of the *G* poses no problems for attachment of the cedilla.

Other Latvian letters with a cedilla below (U+0137 LATIN SMALL LETTER K WITH CEDILLA, U+0146 LATIN SMALL LETTER N WITH CEDILLA, and U+0157 LATIN SMALL LETTER R WITH CEDILLA) always prefer a glyph with a floating comma below, as there is no proper attachment point for a cedilla at the bottom of the base form.

In Turkish and Romanian, a cedilla and a comma below sometimes replace one another depending on the font style, as shown in example 4 in *Figure 7-1*. The form with the cedilla is preferred in Turkish, and the form with the comma below is preferred in Romanian. The characters with explicit commas below are provided to permit the distinction from characters with a cedilla. Legacy encodings for these characters contain only a single form of each of these characters. ISO/IEC 8859-2 maps these to the form with the cedilla, while ISO/IEC 8859-16 maps them to the form with the comma below. Migrating Romanian 8-bit data to Unicode should be done with care.

In general, characters with cedillas or ogoneks below are subject to variable typographical usage, depending on the availability and quality of fonts used, the technology, and the geographic area. Various hooks, commas, and squiggles may be substituted for the nominal forms of these diacritics below, and even the directions of the hooks may be reversed. Implementers should become familiar with particular typographical traditions before assuming that characters are missing or are wrongly represented in the code charts in the Unicode Standard.

Exceptional Case Pairs. The characters U+0130 LATIN CAPITAL LETTER I WITH DOT ABOVE and U+0131 LATIN SMALL LETTER DOTLESS I (used primarily in Turkish) are assumed to take ASCII "i" and "I", respectively, as their case alternates. This mapping makes the corresponding reverse mapping language-specific; mapping in both directions requires special attention from the implementer (see *Section 5.18, Case Mappings*).

***Diacritics on* i *and* j.** A dotted (normal) *i* or *j* followed by a nonspacing mark above loses the dot in rendering. Thus, in the word *naïve*, the *ï* could be spelled with *i* + *diaeresis*. A *dotted-i* is not equivalent to a Turkish *dotless-i* + *overdot*, nor are other cases of accented *dotted-i* equivalent to accented *dotless-i* (for example, i + ̈ ≠ ı + ̈). The same pattern is used for *j*. *Dotless-j* is used in the *Landsmålsalfabet*, where it does not have a case pair.

To express the forms sometimes used in the Baltic (where the dot is retained under a top accent in dictionaries), use *i* + *overdot* + *accent* (see *Figure 7-2*).

Figure 7-2. Diacritics on *i* and *j*

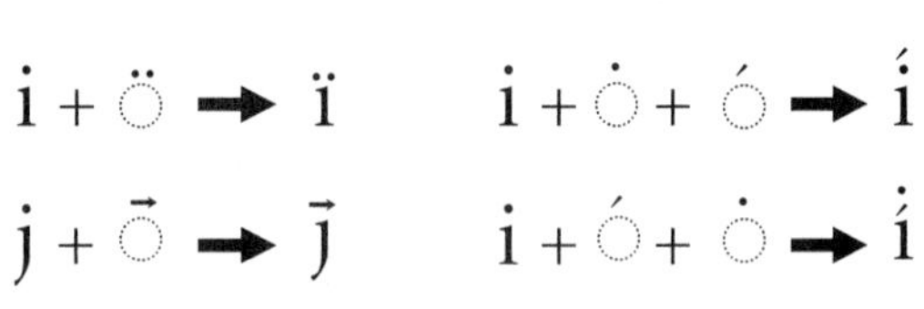

i + ◌̈ → ï   i + ◌̇ + ◌́ → i̇́

j + ◌⃗ → ȷ⃗   i + ◌́ + ◌̇ → í̇

All characters that use their dot in this manner have the Soft_Dotted property in Unicode.

Vietnamese. In the modern Vietnamese alphabet, there are 12 vowel letters and 5 tone marks (see *Figure 7-3*). Normalization Form C represents the combination of vowel letter and tone mark as a single unit—for example, U+1EA8 Ẩ LATIN CAPITAL LETTER A WITH CIRCUMFLEX AND HOOK ABOVE. Normalization Form D decomposes this combination into the combining sequence, such as <U+0041, U+0302, U+0309>. Some widely used implementations prefer storing the vowel letter and the tone mark separately.

Figure 7-3. Vietnamese Letters and Tone Marks

a ă â e ê i o ô ơ u ư y

The Vietnamese vowels and other letters are found in the Basic Latin, Latin-1 Supplement, and Latin Extended-A blocks. Additional precomposed vowels and tone marks are found in the Latin Extended Additional block.

The characters U+0300 COMBINING GRAVE ACCENT, U+0309 COMBINING HOOK ABOVE, U+0303 COMBINING TILDE, U+0301 COMBINING ACUTE ACCENT, and U+0323 COMBINING DOT BELOW should be used in representing the Vietnamese tone marks. The characters U+0340 COMBINING GRAVE TONE MARK and U+0341 COMBINING ACUTE TONE MARK are deprecated and should not be used.

Standards. Unicode follows ISO/IEC 8859-1 in the layout of Latin letters up to U+00FF. ISO/IEC 8859-1, in turn, is based on older standards—among others, ASCII (ANSI X3.4), which is identical to ISO/IEC 646:1991-IRV. Like ASCII, ISO/IEC 8859-1 contains Latin letters, punctuation signs, and mathematical symbols. These additional characters are widely used with scripts other than Latin. The descriptions of these characters are found in *Chapter 6, Writing Systems and Punctuation*, and *Chapter 15, Symbols*.

The Latin Extended-A block includes characters contained in ISO/IEC 8859—Part 2. *Latin alphabet No. 2*, Part 3. *Latin alphabet No. 3*, Part 4. *Latin alphabet No. 4*, and Part 9. *Latin alphabet No. 5*. Many of the other graphic characters contained in these standards, such as punctuation, signs, symbols, and diacritical marks, are already encoded in the Latin-1 Supplement block. Other characters from these parts of ISO/IEC 8859 are encoded in other blocks, primarily in the Spacing Modifier Letters block (U+02B0..U+02FF) and in the character blocks starting at and following the General Punctuation block. The Latin Extended-A block also covers additional characters from ISO/IEC 6937.

The Latin Extended-B block covers, among others, characters in ISO 6438 Documentation—African coded character set for bibliographic information interchange, *Pinyin* Latin transcription characters from the People's Republic of China national standard GB 2312 and from the Japanese national standard JIS X 0212, and Sami characters from ISO/IEC 8859 Part 10. *Latin alphabet No. 6*.

The characters in the IPA block are taken from the 1989 revision of the International Phonetic Alphabet, published by the International Phonetic Association. Extensions from later IPA sources have also been added.

Related Characters. For other Latin-derived characters, see Letterlike Symbols (U+2100..U+214F), Currency Symbols (U+20A0..U+20CF), Number Forms

(U+2150..U+218F), Enclosed Alphanumerics (U+2460..U+24FF), CJK Compatibility (U+3300..U+33FF), Fullwidth Forms (U+FF21..U+FF5A), and Mathematical Alphanumeric Symbols (U+1D400..U+1D7FF).

Letters of Basic Latin: U+0041–U+007A

Only a small fraction of the languages written with the Latin script can be written entirely with the basic set of 26 uppercase and 26 lowercase Latin letters contained in this block. The 26 basic letter pairs form the core of the alphabets used by all the other languages that use the Latin script. A stream of text using one of these alphabets would therefore intermix characters from the Basic Latin block and other Latin blocks.

Occasionally a few of the basic letter pairs are not used to write a language. For example, Italian does not use "j" or "w".

Letters of the Latin-1 Supplement: U+00C0–U+00FF

The Latin-1 supplement extends the basic 26 letter pairs of ASCII by providing additional letters for the major languages of Europe listed in the next paragraph.

Languages. The languages supported by the Latin-1 supplement include Catalan, Danish, Dutch, Faroese, Finnish, Flemish, German, Icelandic, Irish, Italian, Norwegian, Portuguese, Spanish, and Swedish.

Ordinals. U+00AA FEMININE ORDINAL INDICATOR and U+00BA MASCULINE ORDINAL INDICATOR can be depicted with an underscore, but many modern fonts show them as superscripted Latin letters with no underscore. In sorting and searching, these characters should be treated as weakly equivalent to their Latin character equivalents.

Latin Extended-A: U+0100–U+017F

The Latin Extended-A block contains a collection of letters that, when added to the letters contained in the Basic Latin and Latin-1 Supplement blocks, allow for the representation of most European languages that employ the Latin script. Many other languages can also be written with the characters in this block. Most of these characters are equivalent to precomposed combinations of base character forms and combining diacritical marks. These combinations may also be represented by means of composed character sequences. See *Section 2.11, Combining Characters*, and *Section 7.9, Combining Marks*.

Compatibility Digraphs. The Latin Extended-A block contains five compatibility digraphs, encoded for compatibility with ISO/IEC 6937:1984. Two of these characters, U+0140 LATIN SMALL LETTER L WITH MIDDLE DOT and its uppercase version, were originally encoded in ISO/IEC 6937 for support of Catalan. In current conventions, the representation of this digraphic sequence in Catalan simply uses a sequence of an ordinary "l" and U+00B7 MIDDLE DOT.

Another pair of characters, U+0133 LATIN SMALL LIGATURE IJ and its uppercase version, was provided to support the digraph "ij" in Dutch, often termed a "ligature" in discussions of Dutch orthography. When adding intercharacter spacing for line justification, the "ij" is kept as a unit, and the space between the *i* and *j* does not increase. In titlecasing, both the *i* and the *j* are uppercased, as in the word "IJsselmeer." Using a single code point might simplify software support for such features; however, because a vast amount of Dutch data is encoded without this digraph character, under most circumstances one will encounter an <i, j> sequence.

Finally, U+0149 LATIN SMALL LETTER N PRECEDED BY APOSTROPHE was encoded for use in Afrikaans. However, in nearly all cases it is better represented simply by a sequence of an apostrophe followed by "n".

Languages. Most languages supported by this block also require the concurrent use of characters contained in the Basic Latin and Latin-1 Supplement blocks. When combined with these two blocks, the Latin Extended-A block supports Afrikaans, Basque, Breton, Croatian, Czech, Esperanto, Estonian, French, Frisian, Greenlandic, Hungarian, Latin, Latvian, Lithuanian, Maltese, Polish, Provençal, Rhaeto-Romanic, Romanian, Romany, Sámi, Slovak, Slovenian, Sorbian, Turkish, Welsh, and many others.

Latin Extended-B: U+0180–U+024F

The Latin Extended-B block contains letterforms used to extend Latin scripts to represent additional languages. It also contains phonetic symbols not included in the International Phonetic Alphabet (see the IPA Extensions block, U+0250..U+02AF).

Arrangement. The characters are arranged in a nominal alphabetical order, followed by a small collection of Latinate forms. Uppercase and lowercase pairs are placed together where possible, but in many instances the other case form is encoded at some distant location and so is cross-referenced. Variations on the same base letter are arranged in the following order: turned, inverted, hook attachment, stroke extension or modification, different style, small cap, modified basic form, ligature, and Greek derived.

Croatian Digraphs Matching Serbian Cyrillic Letters. Serbo-Croatian is a single language with paired alphabets: a Latin script (Croatian) and a Cyrillic script (Serbian). A set of compatibility digraph codes is provided for one-to-one transliteration. There are two potential uppercase forms for each digraph, depending on whether only the initial letter is to be capitalized (titlecase) or both (all uppercase). The Unicode Standard offers both forms so that software can convert one form to the other without changing font sets. The appropriate cross references are given for the lowercase letters.

Pinyin Diacritic–Vowel Combinations. The Chinese standard GB 2312, the Japanese standard JIS X 0212, and some other standards include codes for Pinyin, which is used for Latin transcription of Mandarin Chinese. Most of the letters used in Pinyin romanization are already covered in the preceding Latin blocks. The group of 16 characters provided here completes the Pinyin character set specified in GB 2312 and JIS X 0212.

Case Pairs. A number of characters in this block are uppercase forms of characters whose lowercase forms are part of some other grouping. Many of these characters came from the International Phonetic Alphabet; they acquired uppercase forms when they were adopted into Latin script-based writing systems. Occasionally, however, *alternative* uppercase forms arose in this process. In some instances, research has shown that alternative uppercase forms are merely variants of the same character. If so, such variants are assigned a single Unicode code point, as is the case of U+01B7 LATIN CAPITAL LETTER EZH. But when research has shown that two uppercase forms are actually used in different ways, then they are given different codes; such is the case for U+018E LATIN CAPITAL LETTER REVERSED E and U+018F LATIN CAPITAL LETTER SCHWA. In this instance, the shared lowercase form is copied to enable unique case-pair mappings: U+01DD LATIN SMALL LETTER TURNED E is a copy of U+0259 LATIN SMALL LETTER SCHWA.

For historical reasons, the names of some case pairs differ. For example, U+018E LATIN CAPITAL LETTER REVERSED E is the uppercase of U+01DD LATIN SMALL LETTER TURNED E—not of U+0258 LATIN SMALL LETTER REVERSED E. For default case mappings of Unicode characters, see *Section 4.2, Case—Normative.*

Caseless Letters. A number of letters used with the Latin script are caseless—for example, the caseless *glottal stop* at U+0294 and U+01BB LATIN LETTER TWO WITH STROKE, and the various letters denoting click sounds. Caseless letters retain their shape when uppercased. When titlecasing words, they may also act transparently; that is, if they occur in the leading position, the next following cased letter may be uppercased instead.

Over the last several centuries, the trend in typographical development for the Latin script has tended to favor the eventual introduction of case pairs. See the following discussion of the glottal stop. The Unicode Standard may encode additional uppercase characters in such instances. However, for reasons of stability, the Standard will never add a new lowercase form for an existing uppercase character. See also "Caseless Matching" in *Section 5.18, Case Mappings.*

Glottal Stop. There are two patterns of usage for the *glottal stop* in the Unicode Standard. U+0294 ʔ LATIN LETTER GLOTTAL STOP is a caseless letter used in IPA. It is also widely seen in language orthographies based on IPA or Americanist phonetic usage, in those instances where no casing is apparent for *glottal stop*. Such orthographies may avoid casing for *glottal stop* to the extent that when titlecasing strings, a word with an initial *glottal stop* may have its second letter uppercased instead of the first letter.

In a small number of orthographies for languages of northwestern Canada, and in particular, for Chipewyan, Dogrib, and Slavey, case pairs have been introduced for *glottal stop*. For these orthographies, the cased *glottal stop* characters should be used: U+0241 Ɂ LATIN CAPITAL LETTER GLOTTAL STOP and U+0242 ɂ LATIN SMALL LETTER GLOTTAL STOP.

The glyphs for the *glottal stop* are somewhat variable and overlap to a certain extent. The glyph shown in the code charts for U+0294 ʔ LATIN LETTER GLOTTAL STOP is a cap-height form as specified in IPA, but the same character is often shown with a glyph that resembles the top half of a question mark and that may or may not be cap height. U+0241 Ɂ LATIN CAPITAL LETTER GLOTTAL STOP, while shown with a larger glyph in the code charts, often appears identical to U+0294. U+0242 ɂ LATIN SMALL LETTER GLOTTAL STOP is a small form of U+0241.

Various small, raised hook- or comma-shaped characters are often substituted for a *glottal stop*—for instance, U+02BC ʼ MODIFIER LETTER APOSTROPHE, U+02BB ʻ MODIFIER LETTER TURNED COMMA, U+02C0 ˀ MODIFIER LETTER GLOTTAL STOP, or U+02BE ʾ MODIFIER LETTER RIGHT HALF RING. U+02BB, in particular, is used in Hawaiian orthography as the *ʻokina*.

IPA Extensions: U+0250–U+02AF

The IPA Extensions block contains primarily the unique symbols of the International Phonetic Alphabet, which is a standard system for indicating specific speech sounds. The IPA was first introduced in 1886 and has undergone occasional revisions of content and usage since that time. The Unicode Standard covers all single symbols and all diacritics in the last published IPA revision (1989) as well as a few symbols in former IPA usage that are no longer currently sanctioned. A few symbols have been added to this block that are part of the transcriptional practices of Sinologists, Americanists, and other linguists. Some of these practices have usages independent of the IPA and may use characters from other Latin blocks rather than IPA forms. Note also that a few nonstandard or obsolete phonetic symbols are encoded in the Latin Extended-B block.

An essential feature of IPA is the use of combining diacritical marks. IPA diacritical mark characters are coded in the Combining Diacritical Marks block, U+0300..U+036F. In IPA, diacritical marks can be freely applied to base form letters to indicate the fine degrees of phonetic differentiation required for precise recording of different languages.

Standards. The International Phonetic Association standard considers IPA to be a separate alphabet, so it includes the entire Latin lowercase alphabet *a–z*, a number of extended Latin letters such as U+0153 œ LATIN SMALL LIGATURE OE, and a few Greek letters and other symbols as separate and distinct characters. In contrast, the Unicode Standard does not duplicate either the Latin lowercase letters *a–z* or other Latin or Greek letters in encoding IPA. Unlike other character standards referenced by the Unicode Standard, IPA constitutes an extended alphabet and phonetic transcriptional standard, rather than a character encoding standard.

Unifications. The IPA characters are unified as much as possible with other letters, albeit not with nonletter symbols such as U+222B ∫ INTEGRAL. The IPA characters have also been adopted into the Latin-based alphabets of many written languages, such as some used in Africa. It is futile to attempt to distinguish a transcription from an actual alphabet in such cases. Therefore, many IPA characters are found outside the IPA Extensions block. IPA characters that are not found in the IPA Extensions block are listed as cross references at the beginning of the character names list for this block.

IPA Alternates. In a few cases IPA practice has, over time, produced alternate forms, such as U+0269 LATIN SMALL LETTER IOTA "ɩ" versus U+026A LATIN LETTER SMALL CAPITAL I "ɪ." The Unicode Standard provides separate encodings for the two forms because they are used in a meaningfully distinct fashion.

Case Pairs. IPA does not sanction case distinctions; in effect, its phonetic symbols are all lowercase. When IPA symbols are adopted into a particular alphabet and used by a given written language (as has occurred, for example, in Africa), they acquire uppercase forms. Because these uppercase forms are not themselves IPA symbols, they are generally encoded in the Latin Extended-B block (or other Latin extension blocks) and are cross-referenced with the IPA names list.

Typographic Variants. IPA includes typographic variants of certain Latin and Greek letters that would ordinarily be considered variations of font style rather than of character identity, such as SMALL CAPITAL letterforms. Examples include a typographic variant of the Greek letter *phi* ɸ and the borrowed letter Greek *iota* ι, which has a unique Latin uppercase form. These forms are encoded as separate characters in the Unicode Standard because they have distinct semantics in plain text.

Affricate Digraph Ligatures. IPA officially sanctions six digraph ligatures used in transcription of coronal affricates. These are encoded at U+02A3..U+02A8. The IPA digraph ligatures are explicitly defined in IPA and have possible semantic values that make them not simply rendering forms. For example, while U+02A6 LATIN SMALL LETTER TS DIGRAPH is a transcription for the sounds that could also be transcribed in IPA as "ts" <U+0074, U+0073>, the choice of the digraph ligature may be the result of a deliberate distinction made by the transcriber regarding the systematic phonetic status of the affricate. The choice of whether to ligate cannot be left to rendering software based on the font available. This ligature also differs in typographical design from the "ts" ligature found in some old-style fonts.

Arrangement. The IPA Extensions block is arranged in approximate alphabetical order according to the Latin letter that is graphically most similar to each symbol. This order has nothing to do with a phonetic arrangement of the IPA letters.

Phonetic Extensions: U+1D00–U+1DBF

Most of the characters in the first of the two adjacent blocks comprising the phonetic extensions are used in the Uralic Phonetic Alphabet (UPA; also called Finno-Ugric Transcription, FUT), a highly specialized system that has been used by Uralicists globally for more than 100 years. Originally, it was chiefly used in Finland, Hungary, Estonia, Germany, Norway, Sweden, and Russia, but it is now known and used worldwide, including in North America and Japan. Uralic linguistic description, which treats the phonetics, phonology, and etymology of Uralic languages, is also used by other branches of linguistics, such as Indo-European, Turkic, and Altaic studies, as well as by other sciences, such as archaeology.

A very large body of descriptive texts, grammars, dictionaries, and chrestomathies exists, and continues to be produced, using this system.

The UPA makes use of approximately 258 characters, some of which are encoded in the Phonetic Extensions block; others are encoded in the other Latin blocks and in the Greek and Cyrillic blocks. The UPA takes full advantage of combining characters. It is not uncommon to find a base letter with three diacritics above and two below.

Typographic Features of the UPA. Small capitalization in the UPA means voicelessness of a normally voiced sound. Small capitalization is also used to indicate certain either voiceless or half-voiced consonants. Superscripting indicates very short schwa vowels or transition vowels, or in general very short sounds. Subscripting indicates co-articulation caused by the preceding or following sound. Rotation (turned letters) indicates reduction; sideways (that is, 90 degrees counterclockwise) rotation is used where turning (180 degrees) might result in an ambiguous representation.

UPA phonetic material is generally represented with italic glyphs, so as to separate it from the surrounding text.

Other Phonetic Extensions. The remaining characters in the phonetics extension range U+1D6C..U+1DFF are derived from a wide variety of sources, including many technical orthographies developed by SIL linguists, as well as older historic sources.

All attested phonetic characters showing struckthrough tildes, struckthrough bars, and retroflex or palatal hooks attached to the basic letter have been separately encoded here. Although separate combining marks exist in the Unicode Standard for overstruck diacritics and attached retroflex or palatal hooks, earlier encoded IPA letters such as U+0268 LATIN SMALL LETTER I WITH STROKE and U+026D LATIN SMALL LETTER L WITH RETROFLEX HOOK have never been been given decomposition mappings in the standard. For consistency, all newly encoded characters are handled analogously to the existing, more common characters of this type and are not given decomposition mappings. Because these characters do not have decompositions, they require special handling in some circumstances. See the discussion of single-script confusables in Unicode Technical Standard #39, "Unicode Security Mechanisms."

The Phonetic Extensions Supplement block also contains 37 superscript modifier letters. These complement the much more commonly used superscript modifier letters found in the Spacing Modifer Letters block.

U+1D77 LATIN SMALL LETTER TURNED G and U+1D78 MODIFIER LETTER CYRILLIC EN are used in Caucasian linguistics. U+1D79 LATIN SMALL LETTER INSULAR G is used in older Irish phonetic notation. It is to be distinguished from a Gaelic style glyph for U+0067 LATIN SMALL LETTER G.

Digraph for th. U+1D7A LATIN SMALL LETTER TH WITH STRIKETHROUGH is a digraphic notation commonly found in some English-language dictionaries, representing the voiceless (inter)dental fricative, as in *th*in. While this character is clearly a digraph, the obligatory strikethrough across two letters distinguishes it from a "th" digraph per se, and there is no mechanism involving combining marks that can easily be used to represent it. A common alternative glyphic form for U+1D7A uses a horizontal bar to strike through the two letters, instead of a diagonal stroke.

Latin Extended Additional: U+1E00–U+1EFF

The characters in this block constitute a number of precomposed combinations of Latin letters with one or more general diacritical marks. With the exception of U+1E9A LATIN

SMALL LETTER A WITH RIGHT HALF RING, each of the characters contained in this block is a canonical decomposable character and may alternatively be represented with a base letter followed by one or more general diacritical mark characters found in the Combining Diacritical Marks block.

Vietnamese Vowel Plus Tone Mark Combinations. A portion of this block (U+1EA0..U+1EF9) comprises vowel letters of the modern Vietnamese alphabet (*quốc ngữ*) combined with a diacritic mark that denotes the phonemic tone that applies to the syllable.

Latin Extended-C: U+2C60–U+2C7F

This small block of additional Latin characters contains orthographic Latin additions for minority languages, a few historic Latin letters, and further extensions for phonetic notations.

Uighur. The Latin orthography for the Uighur language was influenced by widespread conventions for extension of the Cyrillic script for representing Central Asian languages. In particular, a number of Latin characters were extended with a Cyrillic-style descender diacritic to create new letters for use with Uighur.

Claudian Letters. The Roman emperor Claudius invented three additional letters for use with the Latin script. Those letters saw limited usage during his reign, but were abandoned soon afterward. The *half h* letter is encoded in this block. The other two letters are encoded in other blocks: U+2132 TURNED CAPITAL F and U+2183 ROMAN NUMERAL REVERSED ONE HUNDRED (unified with the Claudian letter *reversed c*). Claudian letters in inscriptions are uppercase only, but may be transcribed by scholars in lowercase.

Latin Extended-D: U+A720–U+A7FF

This block is intended for further encoding of historic letters for the Latin script and other rare phonetic and orthographic extensions to the script. For Unicode 5.0, it contains only two modifier tone letters for use with UPA.

Latin Ligatures: U+FB00–U+FB06

This range in the Alphabetic Presentation Forms block (U+FB00..U+FB4F) contains several common Latin ligatures, which occur in legacy encodings. Whether to use a Latin ligature is a matter of typographical style as well as a result of the orthographical rules of the language. Some languages prohibit ligatures across word boundaries. In these cases, it is preferable for the implementations to use unligated characters in the backing store and provide out-of-band information to the display layer where ligatures may be placed.

Some format controls in the Unicode Standard can affect the formation of ligatures. See "Controlling Ligatures" in *Section 16.2, Layout Controls*.

7.2 Greek

Greek: U+0370–U+03FF

The Greek script is used for writing the Greek language. The Greek script had a strong influence on the development of the Latin, Cyrillic, and Coptic scripts.

The Greek script is written in linear sequence from left to right with the frequent use of nonspacing marks. There are two styles of such use: monotonic, which uses a single mark called *tonos*, and polytonic, which uses multiple marks. Greek letters come in uppercase and lowercase pairs. Spaces are used to separate words and provide the primary line breaking opportunities. Archaic Greek texts do not use spaces.

Standards. The Unicode encoding of Greek is based on ISO/IEC 8859-7, which is equivalent to the Greek national standard ELOT 928, designed for monotonic Greek. The Unicode Standard encodes Greek characters in the same relative positions as in ISO/IEC 8859-7. A number of variant and archaic characters are taken from the bibliographic standard ISO 5428.

Polytonic Greek. Polytonic Greek, used for ancient Greek (classical and Byzantine) and occasionally for modern Greek, may be encoded using either combining character sequences or precomposed base plus diacritic combinations. For the latter, see the following subsection, "Greek Extended: U+1F00–U+1FFF."

Nonspacing Marks. Several nonspacing marks commonly used with the Greek script are found in the Combining Diacritical Marks range (see *Table 7-1*).

Table 7-1. Nonspacing Marks Used with Greek

Code	Name	Alternative Names
U+0300	COMBINING GRAVE ACCENT	*varia*
U+0301	COMBINING ACUTE ACCENT	*tonos, oxia*
U+0304	COMBINING MACRON	
U+0306	COMBINING BREVE	
U+0308	COMBINING DIAERESIS	*dialytika*
U+0313	COMBINING COMMA ABOVE	*psili, smooth breathing mark*
U+0314	COMBINING REVERSED COMMA ABOVE	*dasia, rough breathing mark*
U+0342	COMBINING GREEK PERISPOMENI	*circumflex, tilde, inverted breve*
U+0343	COMBINING GREEK KORONIS	*comma above*
U+0345	COMBINING GREEK YPOGEGRAMMENI	*iota subscript*

Because the characters in the Combining Diacritical Marks block are encoded by shape, not by meaning, they are appropriate for use in Greek where applicable. The character U+0344 COMBINING GREEK DIALYTIKA TONOS should not be used. The combination of *dialytika* plus *tonos* is instead represented by the sequence <U+0308 COMBINING DIAERESIS, U+0301 COMBINING ACUTE ACCENT>.

Multiple nonspacing marks applied to the same baseform character are encoded in inside-out sequence. See the general rules for applying nonspacing marks in *Section 2.11, Combining Characters.*

The basic Greek accent written in modern Greek is called *tonos*. It is represented by an acute accent (U+0301). The shape that the acute accent takes over Greek letters is generally steeper than that shown over Latin letters in Western European typographic traditions, and in earlier editions of this standard was mistakenly shown as a vertical line over the vowel. Polytonic Greek has several contrastive accents, and the accent, or *tonos*, written with an acute accent is referred to as *oxia*, in contrast to the *varia*, which is written with a grave accent.

U+0342 COMBINING GREEK PERISPOMENI may appear as a circumflex ◌̂, an inverted breve ◌̑, a tilde ◌̃, or occasionally a macron ◌̄. Because of this variation in form, the *perispomeni* was encoded distinctly from U+0303 COMBINING TILDE.

U+0313 COMBINING COMMA ABOVE and U+0343 COMBINING GREEK KORONIS both take the form of a raised comma over a baseform letter. U+0343 COMBINING GREEK KORONIS was included for compatibility reasons; U+0313 COMBINING COMMA ABOVE is the preferred form for general use. Greek uses guillemets for quotation marks; for Ancient Greek, the quotations tend to follow local publishing practice. Because of the possibility of confusion between smooth breathing marks and curly single quotation marks, the latter are best avoided where possible. When either breathing mark is followed by an acute or grave accent, the pair is rendered side-by-side rather than vertically stacked.

Accents are typically written above their base letter in an all-lowercase or all-uppercase word; they may also be omitted from an all-uppercase word. However, in a titlecase word, accents applied to the first letter are commonly written to the left of that letter. This is a matter of presentation only—the internal representation is still the base letter followed by the combining marks. It is *not* the stand-alone version of the accents, which occur before the base letter in the text stream.

Iota. The nonspacing mark *ypogegrammeni* (also known as *iota subscript* in English) can be applied to the vowels *alpha*, *eta*, and *omega* to represent historic diphthongs. This mark appears as a small *iota* below the vowel. When applied to a single uppercase vowel, the iota does not appear as a subscript, but is instead normally rendered as a regular lowercase iota to the right of the uppercase vowel. This form of the iota is called *prosgegrammeni* (also known as *iota adscript* in English). In completely uppercased words, the iota subscript should be replaced by a capital iota following the vowel. Precomposed characters that contain iota subscript or iota adscript also have special mappings. (See *Section 5.18, Case Mappings.*) Archaic representations of Greek words, which did not have lowercase or accents, use the Greek capital letter iota following the vowel for these diphthongs. Such archaic representations require special case mapping, which may not be automatically derivable.

Variant Letterforms. U+03A5 GREEK CAPITAL LETTER UPSILON has two common forms: one looks essentially like the Latin capital Y, and the other has two symmetric upper branches that curl like rams' horns, "ϒ". The Y-form glyph has been chosen consistently for use in the code charts, both for monotonic and polytonic Greek. For mathematical usage, the rams' horn form of the glyph is required to distinguish it from the *Latin Y*. A third form is also encoded as U+03D2 GREEK UPSILON WITH HOOK SYMBOL (see *Figure 7-4*). The precomposed characters U+03D3 GREEK UPSILON WITH ACUTE AND HOOK SYMBOL and U+03D4 GREEK UPSILON WITH DIAERESIS AND HOOK SYMBOL should not normally be needed, except where necessary for backward compatibility for legacy character sets.

Figure 7-4. Variations in Greek Capital Letter Upsilon

Y ϒ ϒ

Variant forms of several other Greek letters are encoded as separate characters in this block. Often (but not always), they represent different forms taken on by the character when it appears in the final position of a word. Examples include U+03C2 GREEK SMALL LETTER FINAL SIGMA used in a final position and U+03D0 GREEK BETA SYMBOL, which is the form that U+03B2 GREEK SMALL LETTER BETA would take on in a medial or final position.

Of these variant letterforms, only *final sigma* should be used in encoding standard Greek text to indicate a final sigma. It is also encoded in ISO/IEC 8859-7 and ISO 5428 for this purpose. Because use of the final sigma is a matter of spelling convention, software should not automatically substitute a final form for a nominal form at the end of a word. However, when performing lowercasing, the final form needs to be generated based on the context. See *Section 3.13, Default Case Algorithms*.

In contrast, U+03D0 GREEK BETA SYMBOL, U+03D1 GREEK THETA SYMBOL, U+03D2 GREEK UPSILON WITH HOOK SYMBOL, U+03D5 GREEK PHI SYMBOL, U+03F0 GREEK KAPPA SYMBOL, U+03F1 GREEK RHO SYMBOL, U+03F4 GREEK CAPITAL THETA SYMBOL, U+03F5 GREEK LUNATE EPSILON SYMBOL, and U+03F6 GREEK REVERSED LUNATE EPSILON SYMBOL should be used only in mathematical formulas—never in Greek text. If positional or other shape differences are desired for these characters, they should be implemented by a font or rendering engine.

Representative Glyphs for Greek Phi. Starting with *The Unicode Standard, Version 3.0*, and the concurrent second edition of ISO/IEC 10646-1, the representative glyphs for U+03C6 φ GREEK SMALL LETTER PHI and U+03D5 ϕ GREEK PHI SYMBOL were swapped compared to earlier versions. In ordinary Greek text, the character U+03C6 is used exclusively, although this character has considerable glyphic variation, sometimes represented with a glyph more like the representative glyph shown for U+03C6 φ (the "loopy" form) and less often with a glyph more like the representative glyph shown for U+03D5 ϕ (the "straight" form).

For mathematical and technical use, the straight form of the small phi is an important symbol and needs to be consistently distinguishable from the loopy form. The straight-form phi glyph is used as the representative glyph for the symbol phi at U+03D5 to satisfy this distinction.

The representative glyphs were reversed in versions of the Unicode Standard prior to Unicode 3.0. This resulted in the problem that the character explicitly identified as the mathematical symbol did not have the straight form of the character that is the preferred glyph for that use. Furthermore, it made it unnecessarily difficult for general-purpose fonts supporting ordinary Greek text to add support for Greek letters used as mathematical symbols. This resulted from the fact that many of those fonts already used the loopy-form glyph for U+03C6, as preferred for Greek body text; to support the phi symbol as well, they would have had to disrupt glyph choices already optimized for Greek text.

When mapping symbol sets or SGML entities to the Unicode Standard, it is important to make sure that codes or entities that require the straight form of the phi symbol be mapped to U+03D5 and not to U+03C6. Mapping to the latter should be reserved for codes or entities that represent the small phi as used in ordinary Greek text.

Fonts used primarily for Greek text may use either glyph form for U+03C6, but fonts that also intend to support technical use of the Greek letters should use the loopy form to ensure appropriate contrast with the straight form used for U+03D5.

Greek Letters as Symbols. The use of Greek letters for mathematical variables and operators is well established. Characters from the Greek block may be used for these symbols.

For compatibility purposes, a few Greek letters are separately encoded as symbols in other character blocks. Examples include U+00B5 µ MICRO SIGN in the Latin-1 Supplement character block and U+2126 Ω OHM SIGN in the Letterlike Symbols character block. The *ohm sign* is canonically equivalent to the *capital omega*, and normalization would remove any distinction. Its use is therefore discouraged in favor of *capital omega*. The same equivalence does not exist between *micro sign* and *mu*, and use of either character as a micro sign is common. For Greek text, only the *mu* should be used.

Symbols Versus Numbers. The characters *stigma*, *koppa*, and *sampi* are used only as numerals, whereas *archaic koppa* and *digamma* are used only as letters.

Compatibility Punctuation. Two specific modern Greek punctuation marks are encoded in the Greek and Coptic block: U+037E ";" GREEK QUESTION MARK and U+0387 "·" GREEK ANO TELEIA. The *Greek question mark* (or *erotimatiko*) has the shape of a semicolon, but functions as a question mark in the Greek script. The *ano teleia* has the shape of a middle dot, but functions as a semicolon in the Greek script.

These two compatibility punctuation characters have canonical equivalences to U+003B SEMICOLON and U+00B7 MIDDLE DOT, respectively; as a result, normalized Greek text will lose any distinctions between the Greek compatibility punctuation characters and the common punctuation marks. Furthermore, ISO/IEC 8859-7 and most vendor code pages for Greek simply make use of semicolon and middle dot for the punctuation in question. Therefore, use of U+037E and U+0387 is not necessary for interoperating with legacy Greek data, and their use is not generally encouraged for representation of Greek punctuation.

Historic Letters. Historic Greek letters have been retained from ISO 5428.

Coptic-Unique Letters. In the Unicode Standard prior to Version 4.1, the Coptic script was regarded primarily as a stylistic variant of the Greek alphabet. The letters unique to Coptic were encoded in a separate range at the end of the Greek character block. Those characters were to be used together with the basic Greek characters to represent the complete Coptic alphabet. Coptic text was supposed to be rendered with a font using the Coptic style of depicting the characters it shared with the Greek alphabet. Texts that mixed Greek and Coptic languages using that encoding model could be rendered only by associating an appropriate font by language.

The Unicode Technical Committee and ISO/IEC JTC1/SC2 determined that Coptic is better handled as a separate script. Starting with Unicode 4.1, a new Coptic block added all the letters formerly unified with Greek characters as separate Coptic characters. (See *Section 7.3, Coptic.*) Implementations that supported Coptic under the previous encoding model may, therefore, need to be modified. Coptic fonts may need to continue to support the display of both the Coptic and corresponding Greek character with the same shape to facilitate their use with older documents.

Related Characters. For math symbols, see *Section 15.4, Mathematical Symbols.* For additional punctuation to be used with this script, see C0 Controls and ASCII Punctuation (U+0000..U+007F).

Greek Extended: U+1F00–U+1FFF

The characters in this block constitute a number of precomposed combinations of Greek letters with one or more general diacritical marks; in addition, a number of spacing forms of Greek diacritical marks are provided here. In particular, these characters can be used for the representation of polytonic Greek texts without the use of combining marks. Because they do not cover all possible combinations in use, some combining sequences may be required for a given text.

Each of the letters contained in this block may be alternatively represented with a base letter from the Greek block followed by one or more general diacritical mark characters found in the Combining Diacritical Marks block.

Spacing Diacritics. Sixteen additional spacing diacritic marks are provided in this character block for use in the representation of polytonic Greek texts. Each has an alternative representation for use with systems that support nonspacing marks. The nonspacing alternatives appear in *Table 7-2.* The spacing forms are meant for keyboards and pedagogical use and are not to be used in the representation of titlecase words. The compatibility decompositions of these spacing forms consist of the sequence U+0020 SPACE followed by the nonspacing form equivalents shown in *Table 7-2.*

Table 7-2. Greek Spacing and Nonspacing Pairs

Spacing Form	Nonspacing Form
1FBD GREEK KORONIS	0313 COMBINING COMMA ABOVE
037A GREEK YPOGEGRAMMENI	0345 COMBINING GREEK YPOGEGRAMMENI
1FBF GREEK PSILI	0313 COMBINING COMMA ABOVE
1FC0 GREEK PERISPOMENI	0342 COMBINING GREEK PERISPOMENI

Table 7-2. Greek Spacing and Nonspacing Pairs (Continued)

Spacing Form	Nonspacing Form
1FC1 GREEK DIALYTIKA AND PERISPOMENI	0308 COMBINING DIAERESIS + 0342 COMBINING GREEK PERISPOMENI
1FCD GREEK PSILI AND VARIA	0313 COMBINING COMMA ABOVE + 0300 COMBINING GRAVE ACCENT
1FCE GREEK PSILI AND OXIA	0313 COMBINING COMMA ABOVE + 0301 COMBINING ACUTE ACCENT
1FCF GREEK PSILI AND PERISPOMENI	0313 COMBINING COMMA ABOVE + 0342 COMBINING GREEK PERISPOMENI
1FDD GREEK DASIA AND VARIA	0314 COMBINING REVERSED COMMA ABOVE + 0300 COMBINING GRAVE ACCENT
1FDE GREEK DASIA AND OXIA	0314 COMBINING REVERSED COMMA ABOVE + 0301 COMBINING ACUTE ACCENT
1FDF GREEK DASIA AND PERISPOMENI	0314 COMBINING REVERSED COMMA ABOVE + 0342 COMBINING GREEK PERISPOMENI
1FED GREEK DIALYTIKA AND VARIA	0308 COMBINING DIAERESIS + 0300 COMBINING GRAVE ACCENT
1FEE GREEK DIALYTIKA AND OXIA	0308 COMBINING DIAERESIS + 0301 COMBINING ACUTE ACCENT
1FEF GREEK VARIA	0300 COMBINING GRAVE ACCENT
1FFD GREEK OXIA	0301 COMBINING ACUTE ACCENT
1FFE GREEK DASIA	0314 COMBINING REVERSED COMMA ABOVE

Ancient Greek Numbers: U+10140–U+1018F

Ancient Greeks primarily used letters of the Greek alphabet to represent numbers. However, some extensions to this usage required quite a few nonalphabetic symbols or symbols derived from letters. Those symbols are encoded in the Ancient Greek Numbers block.

Acrophonic Numerals. Greek acrophonic numerals are found primarily in ancient inscriptions from Attica and other Greek regions. *Acrophonic* means that the character used to represent each number is the initial letter of the word by which the number is called—for instance, H for "HECATON" = 100.

The Attic acrophonic system, named for the greater geographic area that includes the city of Athens, is the most common and well documented. The characters in the Ancient Greek Numbers block cover the Attic acrophonic numeral system as well as non-Attic characters that cannot be considered glyph variants of the Attic acrophonic repertoire. They are the standard symbols used to represent weight or cost, and they appear consistently in modern editions and scholarly studies of Greek inscriptions. Uppercase Greek letters from the Greek block are also used for acrophonic numerals.

The Greek acrophonic number system is similar to the Roman one in that it does not use decimal position, does not require a placeholder for zero, and has special symbols for 5, 50, 500, and so on. The system is language specific because of the acrophonic principle. In some cases the same symbol represents different values in different geographic regions. The symbols are also differentiated by the unit of measurement—for example, talents versus staters.

Other Numerical Symbols. Other numerical symbols encoded in the range U+10175..U+1018A appear in a large number of ancient papyri. The standard symbols used for the representation of numbers, fractions, weights, and measures, they have consistently been used in modern editions of Greek papyri as well as various publications related to the study and interpretation of ancient documents. Several of these characters have considerable glyphic variation. Some of these glyph variants are similar in appearance to other characters.

Symbol for Zero. U+1018A GREEK ZERO SIGN occurs whenever a sexagesimal notation is used in historical astronomical texts to record degrees, minutes and seconds, or hours, minutes and seconds. The most common form of zero in the papyri is a small circle with a horizontal stroke above it, but many variations exist. These are taken to be scribal variations and are considered glyph variants.

7.3 Coptic

Coptic: U+2C80–U+2CFF

The Coptic script is the final stage in the development of the Egyptian writing system. Coptic was subject to strong Greek influences because Greek was more identified with the Christian tradition, and the written demotic Egyptian no longer matched the spoken language. The Coptic script was based on the Greek uncial alphabets with several Coptic additional letters unique to Coptic. The Coptic language died out in the fourteenth century, but it is maintained as a liturgical language by Coptic Christians. Coptic is written from left to right in linear sequence; in modern use, spaces are used to separate words and provide the primary line breaking opportunities.

Prior to Version 4.1, the Unicode Standard treated Coptic as a stylistic variant of Greek. Seven letters unique to Coptic (14 characters with the case pairs) were encoded in the Greek and Coptic block. In addition to these 14 characters, Version 4.1 added a Coptic block containing the remaining characters needed for basic Coptic text processing. This block also includes standard logotypes used in Coptic text as well as characters for Old Coptic and Nubian.

Development of the Coptic Script. The best-known Coptic dialects are Sahidic and Bohairic. Coptic scholarship recognizes a number of other dialects that use additional characters. The repertoires of Sahidic and Bohairic reflect efforts to standardize the writing of Coptic, but attempts to write the Egyptian language with the Greek script preceded that standardization by several centuries. During the initial period of writing, a number of different solutions to the problem of representing non-Greek sounds were made, mostly by borrowing letters from Demotic writing. These early efforts are grouped by Copticists under the general heading of Old Coptic.

Casing. Coptic is considered a bicameral script. Historically, it was caseless, but it has acquired case through the typographic developments of the last centuries. Already in Old Coptic manuscripts, letters could be written larger, particularly at the beginning of paragraphs, although the capital letters tend to have the most distinctive shapes in the Bohairic tradition. To facilitate scholarly and other modern casing operations, Coptic has been encoded as a bicameral script, including uniquely Old Coptic characters.

Bohairic Coptic uses only a subset of the letters in the Coptic repertoire. A Sahidic font style is used for the code charts.

Characters for Cryptogrammic Use. U+2CB7 COPTIC SMALL LETTER CRYPTOGRAMMIC EIE and U+2CBD COPTIC SMALL LETTER CRYPTOGRAMMIC NI are characters for cryptogrammic use. A common Coptic substitution alphabet that was used to encrypt texts had the disadvantageous feature whereby three of the letters (*eie*, *ni*, and *fi*) were substituted by themselves. However, because *eie* and *ni* are two of the highest-frequency characters in Coptic, Copts felt that the encryption was not strong enough, so they replaced those letters with these cryptogrammic ones. Copticists preserve this substitution in modern editions of these texts and do not consider them to be glyph variants of the original letters.

U+2CC0 COPTIC CAPITAL LETTER SAMPI has a numeric value of 900 and corresponds to U+03E0 GREEK LETTER SAMPI. It is not found in abecedaria, but is used in cryptogrammic contexts as a letter.

Crossed Shei. U+2CC3 ⳃ COPTIC SMALL LETTER CROSSED SHEI is found in Dialect I of Old Coptic, where it represents a sound /ç/. It is found alongside U+03E3 ϣ COPTIC SMALL LETTER SHEI, which represents /ʃ/. The diacritic is not productive.

Abbreviations. Abbreviations are indicated by overlining several characters. This is done by following each character with U+0305 COMBINING OVERLINE.

Combining Diacritical Marks. Bohairic text uses a mark called *jinkim* to represent syllabic consonants, which is indicated by either U+0307 COMBINING DOT ABOVE or U+0300 COMBINING GRAVE ACCENT. Other dialects, including Sahidic, use U+0305 COMBINING MACRON for the same purpose. A number of other generic diacritical marks are used with Coptic.

Punctuation. Coptic texts use common punctuation, including *colon*, *full stop*, *semicolon* (functioning, as in Greek, as a question mark), and *middle dot*. Quotation marks are found in edited texts. In addition, Coptic-specific punctuation occurs: U+2CFE COPTIC FULL STOP and U+2CFF COPTIC MORPHOLOGICAL DIVIDER. Several other historic forms of punctuation are known only from Old Nubian texts.

Numerical Use of Letters. Numerals are indicated with letters of the alphabet, as in Greek. Sometimes the numerical use is indicated specifically by marking a line above, represented with U+0305 COMBINING OVERLINE. U+0375 GREEK LOWER NUMERAL SIGN or U+033F COMBINING DOUBLE OVERLINE can be used to indicate multiples of 1,000, as shown in *Figure 7-5*.

Figure 7-5. Coptic Numerals

Coptic	Value
ⲁ	1
ⲁ͵ or ⲁ̿	1,000
ⲁ͵ⲱ̅ⲡ̅ⲏ̅	1,888

U+0374 GREEK NUMERAL SIGN is used to indicate fractions. For example, ⲅʹ indicates the fractional value 1/3. There is, however, a special symbol for 1/2: U+2CFD COPTIC FRACTION ONE HALF.

7.4 Cyrillic

Cyrillic: U+0400–U+04FF

The Cyrillic script is one of several scripts that were derived from the Greek script. Cyrillic has traditionally been used for writing various Slavic languages, among which Russian is predominant. In the nineteenth and early twentieth centuries, Cyrillic was extended to write the non-Slavic minority languages of Russia and neighboring countries.

The Cyrillic script is written in linear sequence from left to right with the occasional use of nonspacing marks. Cyrillic letters have uppercase and lowercase pairs. Spaces are used to separate words and provide the primary line breaking opportunities.

Standards. The Cyrillic block of the Unicode Standard is based on ISO/IEC 8859-5. The Unicode Standard encodes Cyrillic characters in the same relative positions as in ISO/IEC 8859-5.

Historic Letterforms. The historic form of the Cyrillic alphabet is treated as a font style variation of modern Cyrillic because the historic forms are relatively close to the modern appearance, and because some of them are still in modern use in languages other than Russian (for example, U+0406 "I"CYRILLIC CAPITAL LETTER BYELORUSSIAN-UKRAINIAN I is used in modern Ukrainian and Byelorussian, and is encoded amidst other modern Cyrillic extensions). Some of the historic letterforms were used in modern typefaces in Russian and Bulgarian. Prior to 1917, Russian made use of *yat*, *fita*, and *izhitsa*; prior to 1945, Bulgaria made use of these three as well as *big yus*.

Extended Cyrillic. These letters are used in alphabets for Turkic languages such as Azerbaijani, Bashkir, Kazakh, and Tatar; for Caucasian languages such as Abkhasian, Avar, and Chechen; and for Uralic languages such as Mari, Khanty, and Kildin Sami. The orthographies of some of these languages have often been revised in the past; some of them have switched from Arabic to Latin to Cyrillic, and back again. Azerbaijani, for instance, is now officially using a Turkish-based Latin script.

Palochka. U+04C0 "Ӏ" CYRILLIC LETTER PALOCHKA is used in Cyrillic orthographies for a number of Caucasian languages, such as Adyghe, Avar, Chechen, and Kabardian. The name *palochka* itself is based on the Russian word for "stick," referring to the shape of the letter. The glyph for *palochka* is usually indistinguishable from an uppercase Latin "I" or U+0406 "І" CYRILLIC CAPITAL LETTER BYELORUSSIAN-UKRAINIAN I; however, in some serifed fonts it may be displayed without serifs to make it more visually distinct.

In use, *palochka* typically modifies the reading of a preceding letter, indicating that it is an ejective. The *palochka* is generally caseless and should retain its form even in lowercased Cyrillic text. However, there is some evidence of distinctive lowercase forms; for those instances, U+04CF CYRILLIC SMALL LETTER PALOCHKA may be used.

Glagolitic. The history of the creation of the Slavic scripts and their relationship has been lost. The Unicode Standard regards Glagolitic as a *separate* script from Cyrillic, not as a font change from Cyrillic. This position is taken primarily because Glagolitic appears unrecognizably different from Cyrillic, and secondarily because Glagolitic has not grown to match the expansion of Cyrillic. See *Section 7.5, Glagolitic.*

Cyrillic Supplement: U+0500–U+052F

Komi. The characters in the range U+0500..U+050F are found in ISO 10754; they were used in Komi Cyrillic orthography from 1919 to about 1940. These letters use glyphs that differ structurally from other characters in the Unicode Standard that represent similar sounds—namely, Serbian *љ* and *њ*, which are ligatures of the base letters *л* and *н* with a palatalizing soft sign *ь*. The Molodtsov orthography made use of a different kind of palatalization hook for Komi *ԉ*, *ԋ*, *ԏ*, *ԁ*, and so on.

7.5 Glagolitic

Glagolitic: U+2C00–U+2C5F

Glagolitic, from the Slavic root *glagol*, meaning "word," is an alphabet considered to have been devised by Saint Cyril in or around 862 CE for his translation of the Scriptures and liturgical books into Slavonic. The relatively few Glagolitic inscriptions and manuscripts that survive from this early period are of great philological importance. Glagolitic was eventually supplanted by the alphabet now known as Cyrillic.

Like Cyrillic, the Glagolitic script is written in linear sequence from left to right with no contextual modification of the letterforms. Spaces are used to separate words and provide the primary line breaking opportunities.

In parts of Croatia where a vernacular liturgy was used, Glagolitic continued in use until modern times: the last Glagolitic missal was printed in Rome in 1893 with a second edition in 1905. In these areas Glagolitic is still occasionally used as a decorative alphabet.

Glyph Forms. Glagolitic exists in two styles, known as round and square. Round Glagolitic is the original style and more geographically widespread, although surviving examples are less numerous. Square Glagolitic (and the cursive style derived from it) was used in Croatia from the thirteenth century. There are a few documents written in a style intermediate between the two. The letterforms used in the charts are round Glagolitic. Several of the letters have variant glyph forms, which are not encoded separately.

Ordering. The ordering of the Glagolitic alphabet is largely derived from that of the Greek alphabet, although nearly half the Glagolitic characters have no equivalent in Greek and not every Greek letter has its equivalent in Glagolitic.

Punctuation and Diacritics. Glagolitic texts use common punctuation, including *comma*, *full stop*, *semicolon* (functioning, as in Greek, as a question mark), and *middle dot*. In addition, several forms of multiple-dot, archaic punctuation occur, including U+2056 THREE DOT PUNCTUATION, U+2058 FOUR DOT PUNCTUATION, and U+2059 FIVE DOT PUNCTUATION. Quotation marks are found in edited texts. Glagolitic also used numerous diacritical marks, many of them shared in common with Cyrillic.

Numerical Use of Letters. Glagolitic letters have inherent numerical values. A letter may be rendered with a line above or a tilde above to indicate the numeric usage explicitly. Alternatively, U+00B7 MIDDLE DOT may be used, flanking a letter on both sides, to indicate numeric usage of the letter.

7.6 Armenian

Armenian: U+0530–U+058F

The Armenian script is used primarily for writing the Armenian language. It is written from left to right. Armenian letters have uppercase and lowercase pairs. Spaces are used to separate words and provide the primary line breaking opportunities.

The Armenian script was devised about 406 CE by Mesrop Maštoc‘ to give Armenians access to Christian scriptural and liturgical texts, which were otherwise available only in Greek and Syriac. The script has been used to write Classical or *Grabar* Armenian, Middle Armenian, and both of the literary dialects of Modern Armenian: East and West Armenian.

Orthography. Mesrop's original alphabet contained 30 consonants and 6 vowels in the following ranges:

U+0531..U+0554 Ա..Ք *Ayb* to *K‘ē*

U+0561..U+0584 ա..ք *ayb* to *k‘ē*

Armenian spelling was consistent during the *Grabar* period, from the fifth to the tenth centuries CE; pronunciation began to change in the eleventh century. In the twelfth century, the letters *ō* and *fē* were added to the alphabet to represent the diphthong [aw] (previously written աւ *aw*) and the foreign sound [f], respectively. The Soviet Armenian government implemented orthographic reform in 1922 and again in 1940, creating a difference between the traditional Mesropian orthography and what is known as Reformed orthography. The 1922 reform limited the use of *w* to the digraph *ow* (or *u*) and treated this digraph as a single letter of the alphabet.

User Community. The Mesropian orthography is presently used by West Armenian speakers who live in the diaspora and, rarely, by East Armenian speakers whose origins are in Armenia but who live in the diaspora. The Reformed orthography is used by East Armenian speakers living in the Republic of Armenia and, occasionally, by West Armenian speakers who live in countries formerly under the influence of the former Soviet Union. Spell-checkers and other linguistic tools need to take the differences between these orthographies into account, just as they do for British and American English.

Punctuation. Armenian makes use of a number of punctuation marks also used in other European scripts. Armenian words are delimited with spaces and may terminate on either a space or a punctuation mark. U+0589 ։ ARMENIAN FULL STOP, called *verǰakēt* in Armenian, is used to end sentences. A shorter stop functioning like the semicolon (like the *ano teleia* in Greek, but normally placed on the baseline like U+002E FULL STOP) is called *miǰakēt*; it is represented by U+2024 . ONE DOT LEADER. U+055D ՝ ARMENIAN COMMA is actually used more as a kind of colon than as a comma; it combines the functionality of both elision and pause. Its Armenian name is *bowt'*.

In Armenian it is possible to differentiate between word-joining and word-splitting hyphens. To join words, the *miowt'jan gic* - is used; it can be represented by either U+002D HYPHEN-MINUS or U+2010 ‐ HYPHEN. At the end of the line, to split words across lines, the *ent'amna* U+058A ֊ ARMENIAN HYPHEN may also be used. This character has a curved shape in some fonts, but a hyphen-like shape in others. Both the word-joiner and the word-splitter can also break at word boundaries, but the two characters have different semantics.

Several other punctuation marks are unique to Armenian, and these function differently from other kinds of marks. The tonal punctuation marks (U+055B ARMENIAN EMPHASIS MARK, U+055C ARMENIAN EXCLAMATION MARK, and U+055E ARMENIAN QUESTION MARK) are placed directly above and slightly to the right of the vowel whose sound is modified, instead of at the end of the sentence, as European punctuation marks are. Because of the mechanical limitations of some printing technologies, these punctuation marks have often been typographically rendered as spacing glyphs above and to the right of the modified vowel, but this practice is not recommended. Depending on the font, the kerning sometimes presents them as half-spacing glyphs, which is somewhat more acceptable.

The placement of the Armenian tonal mark can be used to distinguish between different questions.

U+055F ARMENIAN ABBREVIATION MARK, or *patiw*, is one of four abbreviation marks found in manuscripts to abbreviate common words such as God, Jesus, Christos, Lord, Saint, and so on. It is placed above the abbreviated word and spans all of its letters.

Preferred Characters. The apostrophe at U+055A has the same shape and function as the Latin apostrophe at U+2019, which is preferred. There is no left half ring in Armenian.

Unicode character U+0559 is not used. It appears that this character is a duplicate character, which was encoded to represent U+02BB MODIFIER LETTER TURNED COMMA, used in Armenian transliteration. U+02BB is preferred for this purpose.

Ligatures. Five Armenian ligatures are encoded in the Alphabetic Presentation Forms block in the range U+FB13..U+FB17. These shapes (along with others) are typically found in handwriting and in traditional fonts that mimic the manuscript ligatures. Of these, the *men-now* ligature is the one most useful for both traditional and modern fonts.

7.7 Georgian

Georgian: U+10A0–U+10FF, U+2D00–U+2D2F

The Georgian script is used primarily for writing the Georgian language and its dialects. It is also used for the Svan and Mingrelian languages and in the past was used for Abkhaz and other languages of the Caucasus. It is written from left to right. Spaces are used to separate words and provide the primary line breaking opportunities.

Script Forms. The script name "Georgian" in the Unicode Standard is used for what are really two closely related scripts. The original Georgian writing system was an inscriptional form called *Asomtavruli*, from which a manuscript form called *Nuskhuri* was derived. Together these forms are categorized as *Khutsuri* (ecclesiastical), in which *Asomtavruli* is used as the uppercase and *Nuskhuri* as the lowercase. This development of a bicameral script parallels the evolution of the Latin alphabet, in which the original linear monumental style became the uppercase and manuscript styles of the same alphabet became the lowercase. The *Khutsuri* script is still used for liturgical purposes, but was replaced, through a history now uncertain, by an alphabet called *Mkhedruli* (military), which is now the form used for nearly all modern Georgian writing.

Both the *Mkhedruli* alphabet and the *Asomtavruli* inscriptional form are encoded in the Georgian block. The *Nuskhuri* script form is encoded in the Georgian Supplement block.

Case Forms. The Georgian *Mkhedruli* alphabet is fundamentally caseless. The scholar Akaki Shanidze attempted to introduce a casing practice for Georgian in the 1950s, but this system failed to gain popularity. In his typographic departure, he used the *Asomtavruli* forms to represent uppercase letters, alongside "lowercase" *Mkhedruli*. This practice is anomalous—the Unicode Standard instead provides case mappings between the two *Khutsuri* forms: *Asomtavruli* and *Nuskhuri*.

Mtavruli Style. *Mtavruli* is a particular style of *Mkhedruli* in which the distinction between letters with ascenders and descenders is not maintained. All letters appear with an equal height standing on the baseline; *Mtavruli*-style letters are never used as capitals. A word is always entirely presented in *Mtavruli* or not. *Mtavruli* is a font style, similar to SMALL CAPS in the Latin script.

Figure 7-6 illustrates the various forms of Georgian and its case usage discussed in the text, using Akaki Shanidze's name.

Figure 7-6. Georgian Scripts and Casing

Asomtavruli majuscule	ႠႩႠႩႨ ႸႠႬႨႻႤ
Nuskhuri minuscule	ⴀⴉⴀⴉⴈ ⴘⴀⴌⴈⴛⴄ
Casing Khutsuri	Ⴀⴉⴀⴉⴈ Ⴘⴀⴌⴈⴛⴄ
Mkhedruli	აკაკი შანიძე
Mtavruli style	ᲐᲙᲐᲙᲘ ᲨᲐᲜᲘᲫᲔ
Shanidze's orthography	Ⴀკაკი Ⴘანიძე

Georgian Paragraph Separator. The Georgian paragraph separator has a distinct representation, so it has been separately encoded as U+10FB. It visually marks a paragraph end, but it must be followed by a newline character to cause a paragraph termination, as described in *Section 5.8, Newline Guidelines.*

Other Punctuation. For the Georgian full stop, use U+0589 ARMENIAN FULL STOP or U+002E FULL STOP.

For additional punctuation to be used with this script, see C0 Controls and ASCII Punctuation (U+0000..U+007F) and General Punctuation (U+2000..U+206F).

7.8 Modifier Letters

Spacing Modifier Letters: U+02B0–U+02FF

Modifier letters are an assorted collection of small signs that are generally used to indicate modifications of a preceding letter. A few may modify the following letter, and some may serve as independent letters. These signs are distinguished from diacritical marks in that modifier letters are treated as free-standing spacing characters. They are distinguished from similar- or identical-appearing punctuation or symbols by the fact that the members of this block are considered to be letter characters that do not break up a word. They mostly have the Alphabetic character property (see *Section 4.10, Letters, Alphabetic, and Ideographic*). The majority of these signs are phonetic modifiers, including the characters required for coverage of the International Phonetic Alphabet.

Phonetic Usage. Modifier letters have relatively well-defined phonetic interpretations. Their usage generally indicates a specific articulatory modification of a sound represented by another letter or intended to convey a particular level of stress or tone. In phonetic usage, the modifier letters are sometimes called "diacritics," which is correct in the logical sense that they are modifiers of the preceding letter. However, in the Unicode Standard, the term "diacritical marks" refers specifically to nonspacing marks, whereas the codes in this block specify *spacing characters*. For this reason, many of the modifier letters in this block correspond to separate diacritical mark codes, which are cross-referenced in *Chapter 17, Code Charts*.

Encoding Principles. This block includes characters that may have different semantic values attributed to them in different contexts. It also includes multiple characters that may represent the same semantic values—there is no necessary one-to-one relationship. The intention of the Unicode encoding is not to resolve the variations in usage, but merely to supply implementers with a set of useful forms from which to choose. The list of usages given for each modifier letter should not be considered exhaustive. For example, the glottal stop (Arabic *hamza*) in Latin transliteration has been variously represented by the characters U+02BC MODIFIER LETTER APOSTROPHE, U+02BE MODIFIER LETTER RIGHT HALF RING, and U+02C0 MODIFIER LETTER GLOTTAL STOP. Conversely, an apostrophe can have several uses; for a list, see the entry for U+02BC MODIFIER LETTER APOSTROPHE in the character names list. There are also instances where an IPA modifier letter is explicitly equated in semantic value to an IPA nonspacing diacritic form.

Latin Superscripts. Graphically, some of the phonetic modifier signs are raised or superscripted, some are lowered or subscripted, and some are vertically centered. Only those particular forms that have specific usage in IPA, UPA, or other major phonetic systems are encoded.

Spacing Clones of Diacritics. Some corporate standards explicitly specify spacing and nonspacing forms of combining diacritical marks, and the Unicode Standard provides matching codes for these interpretations when practical. A number of the spacing forms are covered in the Basic Latin and Latin-1 Supplement blocks. The six common European diacritics that do not have encodings there are encoded as spacing characters. These forms can have multiple semantics, such as U+02D9 DOT ABOVE, which is used as an indicator of the Mandarin Chinese fifth (neutral) tone.

Rhotic Hook. U+02DE MODIFIER LETTER RHOTIC HOOK is defined in IPA as a free-standing modifier letter. In common usage, it is treated as a ligated hook on a baseform letter. Hence U+0259 LATIN SMALL LETTER SCHWA + U+02DE MODIFIER LETTER RHOTIC HOOK may be treated as equivalent to U+025A LATIN SMALL LETTER SCHWA WITH HOOK.

Tone Letters. U+02E5..U+02E9 comprises a set of basic tone letters defined in IPA and commonly used in detailed tone transcriptions of African and other languages. Each tone letter refers to one of five distinguishable tone levels. To represent contour tones, the tone letters are used in combinations. The rendering of contour tones follows a regular set of ligation rules that results in a graphic image of the contour (see *Figure 7-7*).

For example, the sequence "1 + 5" in the first row of *Figure 7-7* indicates the sequence of the lowest tone letter, U+02E9 MODIFIER LETTER EXTRA-LOW TONE BAR, followed by the highest tone letter, U+02E5 MODIFIER LETTER EXTRA-HIGH TONE BAR. In that sequence, the tone letter is drawn with a ligation from the iconic position of the low tone to that of the high tone to indicate the sharp rising contour. A sequence of three tone letters may also be ligated, as shown in the last row of *Figure 7-7*, to indicate a low rising-falling contour tone.

Figure 7-7. Tone Letters

1 + 5	→	˩˥ (rising contour)
5 + 1	→	˥˩ (falling contour)
3 + 5	→	˧˥ (high rising contour)
1 + 3	→	˩˧ (low rising contour)
1 + 3 + 1	→	˩˧˩ (rising-falling contour)

Modifier Tone Letters: U+A700–U+A71F

The Modifier Tone Letters block contains modifier letters used in various schemes for marking tones. These supplement the more commonly used tone marks and tone letters found in the Spacing Modifier Letters block (U+02B0..U+02FF).

The characters in the range U+A700..U+A707 are corner tone marks used in the transcription of Chinese. They were invented by Bridgman and Wells Williams in the 1830s. They have little current use, but are seen in a number of old Chinese sources.

The tone letters in the range U+A708..U+A716 complement the basic set of IPA tone letters (U+02E5..U+02E9) and are used in the representation of Chinese tones for the most part. The dotted tone letters are used to represent short ("stopped") tones. The left-stem tone letters are mirror images of the IPA tone letters; like those tone letters, they can be ligated in sequences of two or three tone letters to represent contour tones. Left-stem versus right-stem tone letters are sometimes used contrastively to distinguish between tonemic and tonetic transcription or to show the effects of tonal sandhi.

The modifier letters in the range U+A717..U+A71A indicate tones in a particular orthography for Chinantec, an Oto-Manguean language of Mexico. These tone marks are also spacing modifier letters and are not meant to be placed over other letters.

7.9 Combining Marks

Combining marks are a special class of characters in the Unicode Standard that are intended to combine with a preceding character, called their *base*. They have a formal syntactic relationship—or *dependence*—on their base, as defined by the standard. This relationship is relevant to the definition of combining character sequences, canonical reordering, and the Unicode Normalization Algorithm. For formal definitions, see *Section 3.6, Combination*.

Combining marks usually have a visible glyphic form, but some of them are invisible. When visible, a combining mark may interact graphically with neighboring characters in various ways. Visible combining marks are divided roughly into two types: nonspacing marks and spacing marks. In rendering, the nonspacing marks generally have no baseline advance of their own, but instead are said to *apply* to their *grapheme base*. Spacing marks behave more like separate letters, but in some scripts they may have complex graphical interactions with other characters. For an extended discussion of the principles for the application of combining marks, see *Section 3.11, Canonical Ordering Behavior.*

Nonspacing marks come in two types: diacritic and other. The diacritics are exemplified by such familiar marks as the *acute accent* or the *macron*, which are applied to letters of the Latin script (or similar scripts). They tend to indicate a change in pronunciation or a particular tone or stress. They may also be used to derive new letters. However, in some scripts, such as Arabic and Hebrew, other kinds of nonspacing marks, such as *vowel points*, represent separate sounds in their own right and are not considered diacritics.

Sequence of Base Letters and Combining Marks. In the Unicode character encoding, all combining marks are encoded *after* their base character. For example, the Unicode character sequence U+0061 "a" LATIN SMALL LETTER A, U+0308 "◌̈" COMBINING DIAERESIS, U+0075 "u" LATIN SMALL LETTER U unambiguously encodes "äu", *not* "aü", as shown in *Figure 2-18*.

The Unicode Standard convention is consistent with the logical order of other nonspacing marks in Semitic and Indic scripts, the great majority of which follow the base characters with respect to which they are positioned. This convention is also in line with the way modern font technology handles the rendering of nonspacing glyphic forms, so that mapping from character memory representation to rendered glyphs is simplified. (For more information on the formal behavior of combining marks, see *Section 2.11, Combining Characters*, and *Section 3.11, Canonical Ordering Behavior*.)

Multiple Semantics. Because nonspacing combining marks have such a wide variety of applications, they may have multiple semantic values. For example, U+0308 = *diaeresis* = *trema* = *umlaut* = *double derivative*. Such multiple functions for a single combining mark are not separately encoded in the standard.

Glyphic Variation. When rendered in the context of a language or script, like ordinary letters, combining marks may be subjected to systematic stylistic variation, as discussed in *Section 7.1, Latin*. For example, when used in Polish, U+0301 COMBINING ACUTE ACCENT appears at a steeper angle than when it is used in French. When it is used for Greek (as *oxia*), it can appear nearly upright. U+030C COMBINING CARON is commonly rendered as an apostrophe when used with certain letterforms. U+0326 COMBINING COMMA BELOW is sometimes rendered as a *turned comma above* on a lowercase "g" to avoid conflict with the descender. In many fonts, there is no clear distinction made between U+0326 COMBINING COMMA BELOW and U+0327 COMBINING CEDILLA.

Combining accents above the base glyph are usually adjusted in height for use with uppercase versus lowercase forms. In the absence of specific font protocols, combining marks are often designed as if they were applied to typical base characters in the same font. However, this will result in suboptimal appearance in rendering and may cause security problems. See Unicode Technical Report #36, "Unicode Security Considerations."

For more information, see *Section 5.13, Rendering Nonspacing Marks.*

Marks as Spacing Characters. By convention, combining marks may be exhibited in (apparent) isolation by applying them to to U+00A0 NO-BREAK SPACE. This approach might be taken, for example, when referring to the diacritical mark itself as a mark, rather than using it in its normal way in text. Prior to Version 4.1 of the Unicode Standard, the standard also recommended the use of U+0020 SPACE for display of isolated combining marks. This is no longer recommended, however, because of potential conflicts with the handling of sequences of U+0020 SPACE characters in such contexts as XML.

In charts and illustrations in this standard, the combining nature of these marks is illustrated by applying them to a dotted circle, as shown in the examples throughout this standard.

In a bidirectional context, using any character with neutral directionality (that is, with a Bidirectional Class of ON, CS, and so on) as a base character, including U+00A0 NO-BREAK SPACE, a dotted circle, or any other symbol, can lead to unintended separation of the base character from certain types of combining marks during bidirectional ordering. The result is that the combining mark will be graphically applied to something other than the correct base. This affects spacing combining marks (that is, with a General Category of Mc) but not nonspacing combining marks. The unintended separation can be prevented by bracketing the combining character sequence with RLM or LRM characters as appropriate. For more details on bidirectional reordering, see Unicode Standard Annex #9, "The Bidirectional Algorithm."

Spacing Clones of Diacritical Marks. The Unicode Standard separately encodes clones of many common European diacritical marks, primarily for compatibility with existing character set standards. These cloned accents and diacritics are *spacing* characters and can be used to display the mark in isolation, without application to a NO-BREAK SPACE. They are cross-referenced to the corresponding combining mark in the names list in *Chapter 17, Code Charts*. For example, U+02D8 BREVE is cross-referenced to U+0306 COMBINING BREVE. Most of these spacing clones also have compatibility decomposition mappings involving U+0020 SPACE, but implementers should be cautious in making use of those decomposition mappings because of the complications that can arise from replacing a spacing character with a SPACE + combining mark sequence.

Relationship to ISO/IEC 8859-1. ISO/IEC 8859-1 contains eight characters that are ambiguous regarding whether they denote combining characters or separate spacing characters. In the Unicode Standard, the corresponding code points (U+005E ^ CIRCUMFLEX ACCENT, U+005F _ LOW LINE, U+0060 ` GRAVE ACCENT, U+007E ~ TILDE, U+00A8 ¨ DIAERESIS, U+00AF ¯ MACRON, U+00B4 ´ ACUTE ACCENT, and U+00B8 ¸ CEDILLA) are used only as spacing characters. The Unicode Standard provides unambiguous combining characters in the Combining Diacritical Marks block, which can be used to represent accented Latin letters by means of composed character sequences. U+00B0 ° DEGREE SIGN is also occasionally used ambiguously by implementations of ISO/IEC 8859-1 to denote a spacing form of a diacritic ring above a letter; in the Unicode Standard, that spacing diacritical mark is denoted unambiguously by U+02DA ˚ RING ABOVE. U+007E "~" TILDE is ambiguous between usage as a spacing form of a diacritic and as an operator or other punctuation; it is generally rendered with a center line glyph, rather than as a diacritic raised tilde. The spacing form of the diacritic tilde is denoted unambiguously by U+02DC " ˜ " SMALL TILDE.

Diacritics Positioned Over Two Base Characters. IPA, pronunciation systems, some transliteration systems, and a few languages such as Tagalog use diacritics that are applied to a sequence of two letters. In rendering, these marks of unusual size appear as wide diacritics spanning across the top (or bottom) of the two base characters. The Unicode Standard contains a set of double-diacritic combining marks to represent such forms. Like all other combining nonspacing marks, these marks apply to the previous base character, but they are intended to hang over the following letter as well. For example, the character U+0360 COMBINING DOUBLE TILDE is intended to be displayed as depicted in *Figure 7-8*.

Figure 7-8. Double Diacritics

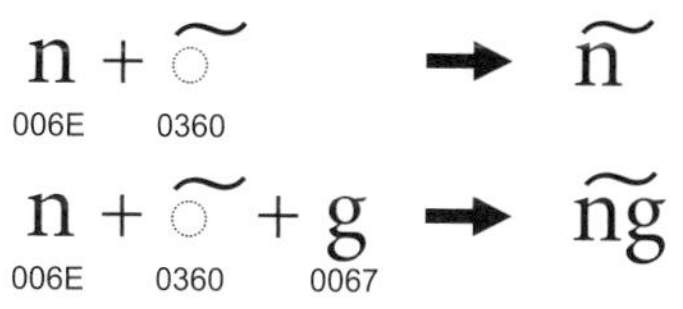

n + ◌͠ → n͠
006E 0360

n + ◌͠ + g → n͠g
006E 0360 0067

These double-diacritic marks have a very high combining class—higher than all other nonspacing marks except U+0345 *iota subscript*—and so always are at or near the end of a combining character sequence when canonically reordered. In rendering, the double diacritic will float above other diacritics above (or below other diacritics below)—excluding surrounding diacritics—as shown in *Figure 7-9*.

Figure 7-9. Positioning of Double Diacritics

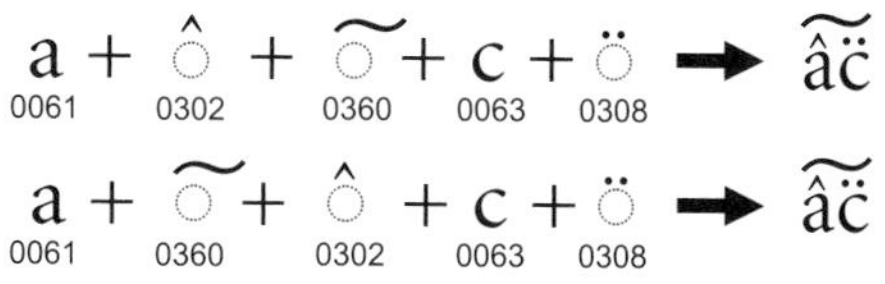

a + ◌̂ + ◌͠ + c + ◌̈ → â͠c̈
0061 0302 0360 0063 0308

a + ◌͠ + ◌̂ + c + ◌̈ → â͠c̈
0061 0360 0302 0063 0308

In *Figure 7-9*, the first line shows a combining character sequence in canonical order, with the double-diacritic tilde following a circumflex accent. The second line shows an alternative order of the two combining marks that is canonically equivalent to the first line. Because of this canonical equivalence, the two sequences should display identically, with the double diacritic floating above the other diacritics applied to single base characters.

Occasionally one runs across orthographic conventions that use a dot, an acute accent, or other simple diacritic *above* a *ligature tie*—that is, U+0361 COMBINING DOUBLE INVERTED BREVE. Because of the considerations of canonical order just discussed, one cannot represent such text simply by putting a *combining dot above* or *combining acute* directly after U+0361 in the text. Instead, the recommended way of representing such text is to place U+034F COMBINING GRAPHEME JOINER (CGJ) between the *ligature tie* and the combining mark that follows it, as shown in *Figure 7-10*.

Figure 7-10. Use of CGJ with Double Diacritics

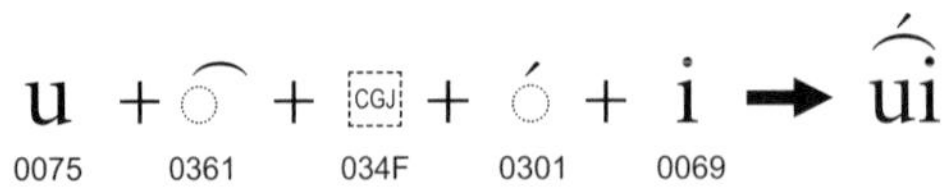

u + ◌͡ + CGJ + ◌́ + i → ú͡i

0075 0361 034F 0301 0069

Because CGJ has a combining class of zero, it blocks reordering of the double diacritic to follow the second combining mark in canonical order. The sequence of <CGJ, acute> is then rendered with default stacking, placing it centered above the *ligature tie*. This convention can be used to create similar effects with combining marks above other double diacritics (or below double diacritics that render below base characters).

For more information on the combining grapheme joiner, see "Combining Grapheme Joiner" in *Section 16.2, Layout Controls.*

Combining Marks with Ligatures. According to *Section 3.11, Canonical Ordering Behavior*, for a simple combining sequence such as <i , ◌̂> , the nonspacing mark ◌̂ both *applies* to and *depends* on the base character *i*. If the *i* is preceded by a character that can ligate with it, additional considerations apply.

Figure 7-11 shows typical examples of the interaction of combining marks with ligatures. The sequence <f , i, ◌̂> is canonically equivalent to <f, î>. This implies that both sequences should be rendered identically, if possible. The precise way in which the sequence is rendered depends on whether the *f* and *i* of the first sequence ligate. If so, the result of applying ◌̂ should be the same as ligating an *f* with an *î*. The precise choice of appearance depends on whatever typographical rules are established for this case, as illustrated in the first example of *Figure 7-11*. Note that the two characters *f* and *î* may not ligate, even if the sequence <f , i> does.

Figure 7-11. Interaction of Combining Marks with Ligatures

① f + i + ◌̂ ≡ f + î → fî, fî, fî

② f + ◌̃ + i + ◌̂ → f̃î, f̃î

③ f + ◌̂ + i + ◌̃ → f̂ĩ, f̂ĩ

④ f + ◌̃ + i + ◌̂ ≢ f + ◌̂ + i + ◌̃

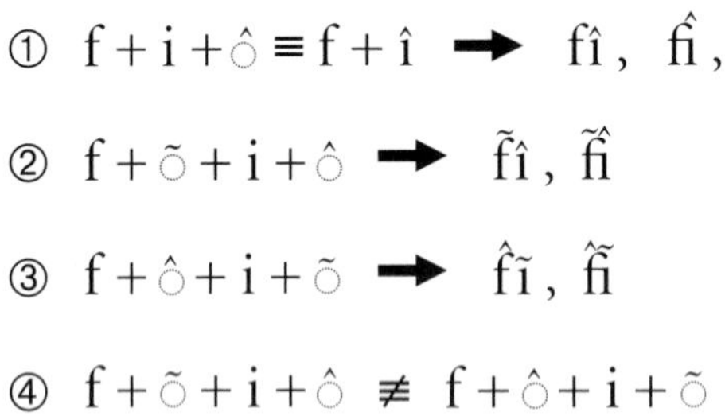

The second and third examples show that by default the sequence <f , ◌̃ , i , ◌̂> is visually distinguished from the sequence <f, ◌̂, i, ◌̃> by the relative placement of the accents. This is true whether or not the <f, ◌̃> and the <i, ◌̂> ligate. Example 4 shows that the two sequences are not canonically equivalent.

In some writing systems, established typographical rules further define the placement of combining marks with respect to ligatures. As long as the rendering correctly reflects the identity of the character sequence containing the marks, the Unicode Standard does not prescribe such fine typographical details.

Compatibility characters such as the *fi-ligature* are not canonically equivalent to the sequence of characters in their compatibility decompositions. Therefore, sequences like <fi-ligature, ◌> may legitimately differ in visual representation from <f, i, ◌>, just as the visual appearance of other compatibility characters may be different from that of the sequence of characters in their compatibility decompositions. By default, a compatibility character such as *fi-ligature* is treated as a single base glyph.

Combining Diacritical Marks: U+0300–U+036F

The combining diacritical marks in this block are intended for general use with any script. Diacritical marks specific to a particular script are encoded with that script. Diacritical marks that are primarily used with symbols are defined in the Combining Diacritical Marks for Symbols character block (U+20D0..U+20FF).

Standards. The combining diacritical marks are derived from a variety of sources, including IPA, ISO 5426, and ISO 6937.

Underlining and Overlining. The characters U+0332 COMBINING LOW LINE, U+0333 COMBINING DOUBLE LOW LINE, U+0305 COMBINING OVERLINE, and U+033F COMBINING DOUBLE OVERLINE are intended to connect on the left and right. Thus, when used in combination, they could have the effect of continuous lines above or below a sequence of characters. However, because of their interaction with other combining marks and other layout considerations such as intercharacter spacing, their use for underlining or overlining of text is discouraged in favor of using styled text.

Combining Diacritical Marks Supplement: U+1DC0–U+1DFF

This block is the supplement to the Combining Diacritical Marks block in the range U+0300..U+036F. It contains lesser-used combining diacritical marks.

U+1DC0 COMBINING DOTTED GRAVE ACCENT and U+1DC1 COMBINING DOTTED ACUTE ACCENT are marks occasionally seen in some Greek texts. They are variant representations of the accent combinations *dialytika varia* and *dialytika oxia*, respectively. They are, however, encoded separately because they cannot be reliably formed by regular stacking rules involving U+0308 COMBINING DIAERESIS and U+0300 COMBINING GRAVE ACCENT or U+0301 COMBINING ACUTE ACCENT.

U+1DC3 COMBINING SUSPENSION MARK is a combining mark specifically used in Glagolitic. It is not to be confused with a combining breve.

Combining Marks for Symbols: U+20D0–U+20FF

The combining marks in this block are generally applied to mathematical or technical symbols. They can be used to extend the range of the symbol set. For example, U+20D2 ◌⃒ COMBINING LONG VERTICAL LINE OVERLAY can be used to express negation, as shown in

Figure 7-12. Its presentation may change in those circumstances—changing its length or slant, for example. That is, U+2261 ≡ IDENTICAL TO followed by U+20D2 is equivalent to U+2262 ≢ NOT IDENTICAL TO. In this case, there is a precomposed form for the negated symbol. However, this statement does not always hold true, and U+20D2 can be used with other symbols to form the negation. For example, U+2258 CORRESPONDS TO followed by U+20D2 can be used to express *does not correspond to*, without requiring that a precomposed form be part of the Unicode Standard.

Figure 7-12. Use of Vertical Line Overlay for Negation

Other nonspacing characters are used in mathematical expressions. For example, a U+0304 COMBINING MACRON is commonly used in propositional logic to indicate logical negation.

Enclosing Marks. These nonspacing characters are supplied for compatibility with existing standards, allowing individual base characters to be enclosed in several ways. For example, U+2460 ① CIRCLED DIGIT ONE can be expressed as U+0031 DIGIT ONE "1" + U+20DD ◌⃝ COMBINING ENCLOSING CIRCLE. For additional examples, see *Figure 2-17*.

The combining enclosing marks surround their grapheme base and any intervening nonspacing marks. These marks are intended for application to free-standing symbols. See "Application of Combining Marks" in *Section 3.11, Canonical Ordering Behavior*.

Users should be cautious when applying combining enclosing marks to other than free-standing symbols—for example, when using a combining enclosing circle to apply to a letter or a digit. Most implementations assume that application of any nonspacing mark will not change the character properties of a base character. This means that even though the intent might be to create a circled symbol (General_Category=So), most software will continue to treat the base character as an alphabetic letter or a numeric digit. Note that there is no *canonical* equivalence between a symbolic character such as U+24B6 CIRCLED LATIN CAPITAL LETTER A and the sequence <U+0041 LATIN CAPITAL LETTER A, U+20DD COMBINING ENCLOSING CIRCLE>, partly because of this difference in treatment of properties.

Combining Half Marks: U+FE20–U+FE2F

This block consists of a number of presentation form (glyph) encodings that may be used to visually encode certain combining marks that apply to multiple base letterforms. These characters are intended to facilitate the support of such marks in legacy implementations.

Unlike other compatibility characters, these half marks do not correspond directly to a single character or a sequence of characters; rather, a discontiguous sequence of the combining half marks corresponds to a single combining mark, as depicted in *Figure 7-13*. The preferred forms are the double diacritics, such as U+0360 COMBINING DOUBLE TILDE.

Figure 7-13. Double Diacritics and Half Marks

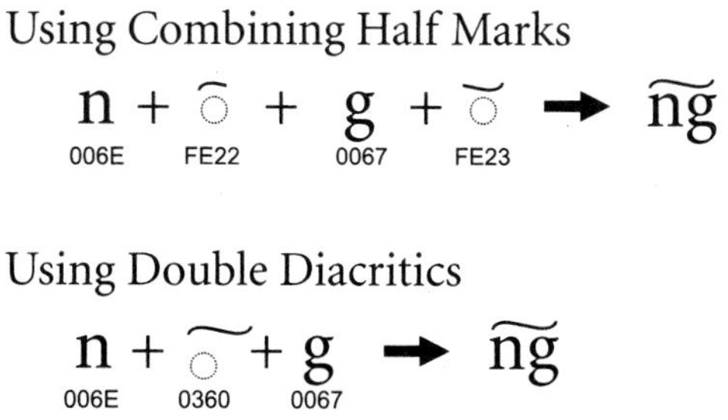

Using Combining Half Marks

n + ◌︢ + g + ◌︣ → n︢g︣

006E FE22 0067 FE23

Using Double Diacritics

n + ◌͠ + g → n͠g

006E 0360 0067

Combining Marks in Other Blocks

In addition to the blocks of characters in the standard specifically set aside for combining marks, many combining marks are associated with particular scripts or occasionally with groups of scripts. Thus the Arabic block contains a large collection of combining marks used to indicate vowelling of Arabic text as well as another collection of combining marks used in annotation of Koranic text. Such marks are mostly intended for use with the Arabic script, but in some instances other scripts, such as Syriac, may use them as well.

Nearly every Indic script has its own collection of combining marks, notably including sets of combining marks to represent dependent vowels, or *matras*.

In some instances a combining mark encoded specifically for a given script, and located in the code chart for that script, may look very similar to a diacritical mark from one of the blocks dedicated to generic combining marks. In such cases, a variety of reasons, including rendering behavior in context or patterning considerations, may have led to separate encoding. The general principle is that if a correctly identified script-specific combining mark of the appropriate shape is available, that character is intended for use with that script, in lieu of a generic combining mark that might look similar. If a combining mark of the appropriate shape is not available in the relevant script block or blocks, then one should make use of whichever generic combining mark best suits the intended purpose.

For example, in representing Syriac text, to indicate a dot above a letter that was identified as a *qushshaya*, one would use U+0741 SYRIAC QUSHSHAYA rather than the generic U+0307 COMBINING DOT ABOVE . When attempting to represent a *hamza* above a Syriac letter, one would use U+0654 ARABIC HAMZA ABOVE, which is intended for both Arabic and Syriac, because there is no specifically Syriac *hamza* combining mark. However, if marking up Syriac text with diacritics such as a macron to indicate length or some other feature, one would then make use of U+0304 COMBINING MACRON from the generic block of combining diacritical marks.

CHAPTER

8

Chapter 8

Middle Eastern Scripts

The scripts in this chapter have a common origin in the ancient Phoenician alphabet. They include

Hebrew	*Syriac*
Arabic	*Thaana*

The Hebrew script is used in Israel and for languages of the Diaspora. The Arabic script is used to write many languages throughout the Middle East, North Africa, and certain parts of Asia. The Syriac script is used to write a number of Middle Eastern languages. These three also function as major liturgical scripts, used worldwide by various religious groups. The Thaana script is used to write Dhivehi, the language of the Republic of Maldives, an island nation in the middle of the Indian Ocean.

The Middle Eastern scripts are mostly abjads, with small character sets. Words are demarcated by spaces. Except for Thaana, these scripts include a number of distinctive punctuation marks. In addition, the Arabic script includes traditional forms for digits, called "Arabic-Indic digits" in the Unicode Standard.

Text in these scripts is written from right to left. Implementations of these scripts must conform to the Unicode Bidirectional Algorithm (see Unicode Standard Annex #9, "The Bidirectional Algorithm"). For more information about writing direction, see *Section 2.10, Writing Direction*. There are also special security considerations that apply to bidirectional scripts, especially with regard to their use in identifiers. For more information about these issues, see Unicode Technical Report #36, "Unicode Security Considerations."

Arabic and Syriac are cursive scripts even when typeset, unlike Hebrew and Thaana, where letters are unconnected. Most letters in Arabic and Syriac assume different forms depending on their position in a word. Shaping rules for the rendering of text are specified in *Section 8.2, Arabic*, and *Section 8.3, Syriac*. Shaping rules are not required for Hebrew because only five letters have position-dependent final forms, and these forms are separately encoded.

Historically, Middle Eastern scripts did not write short vowels. Nowadays, short vowels are represented by marks positioned above or below a consonantal letter. Vowels and other marks of pronunciation ("vocalization") are encoded as combining characters, so support for vocalized text necessitates use of composed character sequences. Yiddish, Syriac, and

Thaana are normally written with vocalization; Hebrew and Arabic are usually written unvocalized.

8.1 Hebrew

Hebrew: U+0590–U+05FF

The Hebrew script is used for writing the Hebrew language as well as Yiddish, Judezmo (Ladino), and a number of other languages. Vowels and various other marks are written as *points,* which are applied to consonantal base letters; these marks are usually omitted in Hebrew, except for liturgical texts and other special applications. Five Hebrew letters assume a different graphic form when they occur last in a word.

Directionality. The Hebrew script is written from right to left. Conformant implementations of Hebrew script must use the Unicode Bidirectional Algorithm (see Unicode Standard Annex #9, "The Bidirectional Algorithm").

Cursive. The Unicode Standard uses the term *cursive* to refer to writing where the letters of a word are connected. A handwritten form of Hebrew is known as cursive, but its rounded letters are generally unconnected, so the Unicode definition does not apply. Fonts based on cursive Hebrew exist. They are used not only to show examples of Hebrew handwriting, but also for display purposes.

Standards. ISO/IEC 8859-8—Part 8. *Latin/Hebrew Alphabet.* The Unicode Standard encodes the Hebrew alphabetic characters in the same relative positions as in ISO/IEC 8859-8; however, there are no points or Hebrew punctuation characters in that ISO standard.

Vowels and Other Marks of Pronunciation. These combining marks, generically called *points* in the context of Hebrew, indicate vowels or other modifications of consonantal letters. General rules for applying combining marks are given in *Section 2.11, Combining Characters,* and *Section 3.11, Canonical Ordering Behavior.* Additional Hebrew-specific behavior is described below.

Hebrew points can be separated into four classes: *dagesh, shin dot* and *sin dot,* vowels, and other marks of punctuation.

Dagesh, U+05BC HEBREW POINT DAGESH OR MAPIQ, has the form of a dot that appears inside the letter that it affects. It is not a vowel but rather a diacritic that affects the pronunciation of a consonant. The same base consonant can also have a vowel and/or other diacritics. *Dagesh* is the only element that goes inside a letter.

The dotted Hebrew consonant *shin* is explicitly encoded as the sequence U+05E9 HEBREW LETTER SHIN followed by U+05C1 HEBREW POINT SHIN DOT. The *shin dot* is positioned on the upper-right side of the undotted base letter. Similarly, the dotted consonant *sin* is explicitly encoded as the sequence U+05E9 HEBREW LETTER SHIN followed by U+05C2 HEBREW POINT SIN DOT. The *sin dot* is positioned on the upper-left side of the base letter.

The two dots are mutually exclusive. The base letter *shin* can also have a *dagesh*, a vowel, and other diacritics. The two dots are not used with any other base character.

Vowels all appear below the base character that they affect, except for *holam*, U+05B9 HEBREW POINT HOLAM, which appears above left. The following points represent vowels: U+05B0..U+05B9, U+05BB.

The remaining three points are *marks of pronunciation*: U+05BD HEBREW POINT METEG, U+05BF HEBREW POINT RAFE, and U+FB1E HEBREW POINT JUDEO-SPANISH VARIKA. *Meteg*, also known as *siluq*, goes below the base character; *rafe* and *varika* go above it. The varika, used in Judezmo, is a glyphic variant of *rafe*.

Shin and Sin. Separate characters for the dotted letters *shin* and *sin* are not included in this block. When it is necessary to distinguish between the two forms, they should be encoded as U+05E9 HEBREW LETTER SHIN followed by the appropriate dot, either U+05C1 HEBREW POINT SHIN DOT or U+05C2 HEBREW POINT SIN DOT. (See preceding discussion.) This practice is consistent with Israeli standard encoding.

Final (Contextual Variant) Letterforms. Variant forms of five Hebrew letters are encoded as separate characters in this block, as in Hebrew standards including ISO/IEC 8859-8. These variant forms are generally used in place of the nominal letterforms at the end of words. Certain words, however, are spelled with nominal rather than final forms, particularly names and foreign borrowings in Hebrew and some words in Yiddish. Because final form usage is a matter of spelling convention, software should not automatically substitute final forms for nominal forms at the end of words. The positional variants should be coded directly and rendered one-to-one via their own glyphs—that is, without contextual analysis.

Yiddish Digraphs. The digraphs are considered to be independent characters in Yiddish. The Unicode Standard has included them as separate characters so as to distinguish certain letter combinations in Yiddish text—for example, to distinguish the digraph *double vav* from an occurrence of a consonantal *vav* followed by a vocalic *vav*. The use of digraphs is consistent with standard Yiddish orthography. Other letters of the Yiddish alphabet, such as *pasekh alef*, can be composed from other characters, although alphabetic presentation forms are also encoded.

Punctuation. Most punctuation marks used with the Hebrew script are not given independent codes (that is, they are unified with Latin punctuation) except for the few cases where the mark has a unique form in Hebrew—namely, U+05BE HEBREW PUNCTUATION MAQAF, U+05C0 HEBREW PUNCTUATION PASEQ (also known as *legarmeh*), U+05C3 HEBREW PUNCTUATION SOF PASUQ, U+05F3 HEBREW PUNCTUATION GERESH, and U+05F4 HEBREW PUNCTUATION GERSHAYIM. For paired punctuation such as parentheses, the glyphs chosen to represent U+0028 LEFT PARENTHESIS and U+0029 RIGHT PARENTHESIS will depend on the direction of the rendered text. See *Section 4.7, Bidi Mirrored—Normative*, for more information. For additional punctuation to be used with the Hebrew script, see *Section 6.2, General Punctuation*.

Cantillation Marks. Cantillation marks are used in publishing liturgical texts, including the Bible. There are various historical schools of cantillation marking; the set of marks included in the Unicode Standard follows the Israeli standard SI 1311.2.

Positioning. Marks may combine with vowels and other points, and complex typographic rules dictate how to position these combinations.

The vertical placement (meaning above, below, or inside) of points and marks is very well defined. The horizontal placement (meaning left, right, or center) of points is also very well defined. The horizontal placement of marks, by contrast, is not well defined, and convention allows for the different placement of marks relative to their base character.

When points and marks are located below the same base letter, the point always comes first (on the right) and the mark after it (on the left), except for the marks *yetiv*, U+059A HEBREW ACCENT YETIV, and *dehi*, U+05AD HEBREW ACCENT DEHI. These two marks come first (on the right) and are followed (on the left) by the point.

These rules are followed when points and marks are located above the same base letter:

- If the point is *holam*, all cantillation marks precede it (on the right) except *pashta*, U+0599 HEBREW ACCENT PASHTA.
- *Pashta* always follows (goes to the left of) points.
- *Holam* on a *sin* consonant (*shin* base + *sin dot*) follows (goes to the left of) the *sin dot*. However, the two combining marks are sometimes rendered as a single assimilated dot.
- *Shin dot* and *sin dot* are generally represented closer vertically to the base letter than other points and marks that go above it.

Meteg. *Meteg*, U+05BD HEBREW POINT METEG, frequently co-occurs with vowel points below the consonant. Typically, *meteg* is placed to the left of the vowel, although in some manuscripts and printed texts it is positioned to the right of the vowel. The difference in positioning is not known to have any semantic significance; nevertheless, some authors wish to retain the positioning found in source documents.

The alternate *vowel-meteg* ordering can be represented in terms of alternate ordering of characters in encoded representation. However, because of the fixed-position canonical combining classes to which *meteg* and vowel points are assigned, differences in ordering of such characters are not preserved under normalization. The *combining grapheme joiner* can be used within a *vowel-meteg* sequence to preserve an ordering distinction under normalization. For more information, see the description of U+034F COMBINING GRAPHEME JOINER in *Section 16.2, Layout Controls*.

For example, to display *meteg* to the left of (after, for a right-to-left script) the vowel point *sheva*, U+05B0 HEBREW POINT SHEVA, the sequence of *meteg* following *sheva* can be used:

<sheva, meteg>

Because these marks are canonically ordered, this sequence is preserved under normalization. Then, to display *meteg* to the right of the *sheva*, the sequence with *meteg* preceding *sheva* with an intervening CGJ can be used:

<meteg, CGJ, sheva>

A further complication arises for combinations of *meteg* with *hataf* vowels: U+05B1 HEBREW POINT HATAF SEGOL, U+05B2 HEBREW POINT HATAF PATAH, and U+05B3 HEBREW POINT HATAF QAMATS. These vowel points have two side-by-side components. *Meteg* can be placed to the left or the right of a *hataf* vowel, but it also is often placed between the two components of the *hataf* vowel. A three-way positioning distinction is needed for such cases.

The *combining grapheme joiner* can be used to preserve an ordering that places *meteg* to the right of a *hataf* vowel, as described for combinations of *meteg* with non-*hataf* vowels, such as *sheva*.

Placement of *meteg* between the components of a *hataf* vowel can be conceptualized as a ligature of the *hataf* vowel and a nominally positioned *meteg*. With this in mind, the ligation-control functionality of U+200D ZERO WIDTH JOINER and U+200C ZERO WIDTH NON-JOINER can be used as a mechanism to control the visual distinction between a nominally positioned *meteg* to the left of a *hataf* vowel versus the medially positioned *meteg* within the *hataf* vowel. That is, *zero width joiner* can be used to request explicitly a medially positioned *meteg*, and *zero width non-joiner* can be used to request explicitly a left-positioned *meteg*. Just as different font implementations may or may not display an "fi" ligature by default, different font implementations may or may not display *meteg* in a medial position when combined with *hataf* vowels by default. As a result, authors who want to ensure left-position versus medial-position display of *meteg* with *hataf* vowels across all font implementations may use joiner characters to distinguish these cases.

Thus the following encoded representations can be used for different positioning of *meteg* with a *hataf* vowel, such as *hataf patah*:

left-positioned *meteg*: <hataf patah, ZWNJ, meteg>

medially positioned *meteg*: <hataf patah, ZWJ, meteg>

right-positioned *meteg*: <meteg, CGJ, hataf patah>

In no case is use of ZWNJ, ZWJ, or CGJ *required* for representation of *meteg*. These recommendations are simply provided for interoperability in those instances where authors wish to preserve specific positional information regarding the layout of a *meteg* in text.

Atnah Hafukh and Qamats Qatan. In some older versions of Biblical text, a distinction is made between the accents U+05A2 HEBREW ACCENT ATNAH HAFUKH and U+05AA HEBREW ACCENT YERAH BEN YOMO. Many editions from the last few centuries do not retain this distinction, using only *yerah ben yomo*, but some users in recent decades have begun to reintroduce this distinction. Similarly, a number of publishers of Biblical or other religious texts have introduced a typographic distinction for the vowel point *qamats* corresponding to two different readings. The original letterform used for one reading is referred to as *qamats* or *qamats gadol*; the new letterform for the other reading is *qamats qatan*. Not all users of Biblical Hebrew use *atnah hafukh* and *qamats qatan*. If the distinction between accents *atnah hafukh* and *yerah ben yomo* is not made, then only U+05AA HEBREW ACCENT YERAH BEN YOMO is used. If the distinction between vowels *qamats gadol* and *qamats qatan* is not made, then only U+05B8 HEBREW POINT QAMATS is used. Implementations that support Hebrew accents and vowel points may not necessarily support the special-usage characters U+05A2 HEBREW ACCENT ATNAH HAFUKH and U+05C7 HEBREW POINT QAMATS QATAN.

Holam Male and Holam Haser. The vowel point *holam* represents the vowel phoneme /o/. The consonant letter *vav* represents the consonant phoneme /w/, but in some words is used to represent a vowel, /o/. When the point *holam* is used on *vav*, the combination usually represents the vowel /o/, but in a very small number of cases represents the consonant-vowel combination /wo/. A typographic distinction is made between these two in many versions of Biblical text. In most cases, in which *vav* + *holam* together represents the vowel /o/, the point *holam* is centered above the *vav* and referred to as *holam male*. In the less frequent cases, in which the *vav* represents the consonant /w/, some versions show the point *holam* positioned above left. This is referred to as *holam haser*. The character U+05BA HEBREW POINT HOLAM HASER FOR VAV is intended for use as *holam haser* only in those cases where a distinction is needed. When the distinction is made, the character U+05B9 HEBREW POINT HOLAM is used to represent the point *holam male on vav*. U+05BA HEBREW POINT HOLAM HASER FOR VAV is intended for use only on *vav*; results of combining this character with other base characters are not defined. Not all users distinguish between the two forms of *holam*, and not all implementations can be assumed to support U+05BA HEBREW POINT HOLAM HASER FOR VAV.

Puncta Extraordinaria. In the Hebrew Bible, dots are written in various places above or below the base letters that are distinct from the vowel points and accents. These dots are referred to by scholars as *puncta extraordinaria*, and there are two kinds. The *upper punctum*, the more common of the two, has been encoded since Unicode 2.0 as U+05C4 HEBREW MARK UPPER DOT. The *lower punctum* is used in only one verse of the Bible, Psalm 27:13, and is encoded as U+05C5 HEBREW MARK LOWER DOT. The *puncta* generally differ in appearance from dots that occur above letters used to represent numbers; the number dots should be represented using U+0307 COMBINING DOT ABOVE and U+0308 COMBINING DIAERESIS.

Nun Hafukha. The *nun hafukha* is a special symbol that appears to have been used for scribal annotations, although its exact functions are uncertain. It is used a total of nine times in the Hebrew Bible, although not all versions include it, and there are variations in the exact locations in which it is used. There is also variation in the glyph used: it often has the appearance of a rotated or reversed *nun* and is very often called *inverted nun*; it may also appear similar to a *half tet* or have some other form.

Currency Symbol. The NEW SHEQEL SIGN (U+20AA) is encoded in the currency block.

Alphabetic Presentation Forms: U+FB1D–U+FB4F

The Hebrew characters in this block are chiefly of two types: variants of letters and marks encoded in the main Hebrew block, and precomposed combinations of a Hebrew letter or digraph with one or more vowels or pronunciation marks. This block contains all of the vocalized letters of the Yiddish alphabet. The *alef lamed* ligature and a Hebrew variant of the plus sign are included as well. The Hebrew plus sign variant, U+FB29 HEBREW LETTER ALTERNATIVE PLUS SIGN, is used more often in handwriting than in print, but it does occur in school textbooks. It is used by those who wish to avoid cross symbols, which can have religious and historical connotations.

U+FB20 HEBREW LETTER ALTERNATIVE AYIN is an alternative form of *ayin* that may replace the basic form U+05E2 HEBREW LETTER AYIN when there is a diacritical mark below it. The basic form of *ayin* is often designed with a descender, which can interfere with a mark below the letter. U+FB20 is encoded for compatibility with implementations that substitute the alternative form in the character data, as opposed to using a substitute glyph at rendering time.

Use of Wide Letters. Wide letterforms are used in handwriting and in print to achieve even margins. The wide-form letters in the Unicode Standard are those that are most commonly "stretched" in justification. If Hebrew text is to be rendered with even margins, justification should be left to the text-formatting software.

These alphabetic presentation forms are included for compatibility purposes. For the preferred encoding, see the Hebrew presentation forms, U+FB1D..U+FB4F.

For letterlike symbols, see U+2135..U+2138.

8.2 Arabic

Arabic: U+0600–U+06FF

The Arabic script is used for writing the Arabic language and has been extended to represent a number of other languages, such as Persian, Urdu, Pashto, Sindhi, and Kurdish, as well as many African languages. Urdu is often written with the ornate Nastaliq script variety. Some languages, such as Indonesian/Malay, Turkish, and Ingush, formerly used the Arabic script but now employ the Latin or Cyrillic scripts.

The Arabic script is cursive, even in its printed form (see *Figure 8-1*). As a result, the same letter may be written in different forms depending on how it joins with its neighbors. Vowels and various other marks may be written as combining marks called *harakat*, which are applied to consonantal base letters. In normal writing, however, these harakat are omitted.

Directionality. The Arabic script is written from right to left. Conformant implementations of Arabic script must use the Unicode Bidirectional Algorithm to reorder the memory representation for display (see Unicode Standard Annex #9, "The Bidirectional Algorithm").

Figure 8-1. Directionality and Cursive Connection

Memory representation:	ه ه ه ␣ ه
After reordering:	ه ␣ ه ه ه
After joining:	ه ␣ ههه

Standards. ISO/IEC 8859-6—Part 6. *Latin/Arabic Alphabet.* The Unicode Standard encodes the basic Arabic characters in the same relative positions as in ISO/IEC 8859-6. ISO/IEC 8859-6, in turn, is based on ECMA-114, which was based on ASMO 449.

Encoding Principles. The basic set of Arabic letters is well defined. Each letter receives only one Unicode character value in the basic Arabic block, no matter how many different contextual appearances it may exhibit in text. Each Arabic letter in the Unicode Standard may be said to represent the inherent semantic identity of the letter. A word is spelled as a sequence of these letters. The representative glyph shown in the Unicode character chart for an Arabic letter is usually the form of the letter when standing by itself. It is simply used to distinguish and identify the character in the code charts and does not restrict the glyphs used to represent it.

Punctuation. Most punctuation marks used with the Arabic script are not given independent codes (that is, they are unified with Latin punctuation), except for the few cases where the mark has a significantly different appearance in Arabic—namely, U+060C ARABIC COMMA, U+061B ARABIC SEMICOLON, U+061E ARABIC TRIPLE DOT PUNCTUATION MARK, U+061F ARABIC QUESTION MARK, and U+066A ARABIC PERCENT SIGN. For paired punctuation such as parentheses, the glyphs chosen to represent U+0028 LEFT PARENTHESIS and U+0029 RIGHT PARENTHESIS will depend on the direction of the rendered text.

The Non-joiner and the Joiner. The Unicode Standard provides two user-selectable formatting codes: U+200C ZERO WIDTH NON-JOINER and U+200D ZERO WIDTH JOINER (see *Figure 8-2*, *Figure 8-3*, and *Figure 8-4*). The use of a non-joiner between two letters prevents those letters from forming a cursive connection with each other when rendered. Examples include the Persian plural suffix, some Persian proper names, and Ottoman Turkish vowels. The use of a joiner adjacent to a suitable letter permits that letter to form a cursive connection without a visible neighbor. This provides a simple way to encode some special cases, such as exhibiting a connecting form in isolation. For further discussion of joiners and non-joiners, see *Section 16.2, Layout Controls*.

Harakat (Vowel) Nonspacing Marks. *Harakat* are marks that indicate vowels or other modifications of consonant letters. The code charts depict a character in the harakat range in relation to a dashed circle, indicating that this character is intended to be applied via some process *to the character that precedes it* in the text stream (that is, the base character).

Figure 8-2. Using a Joiner

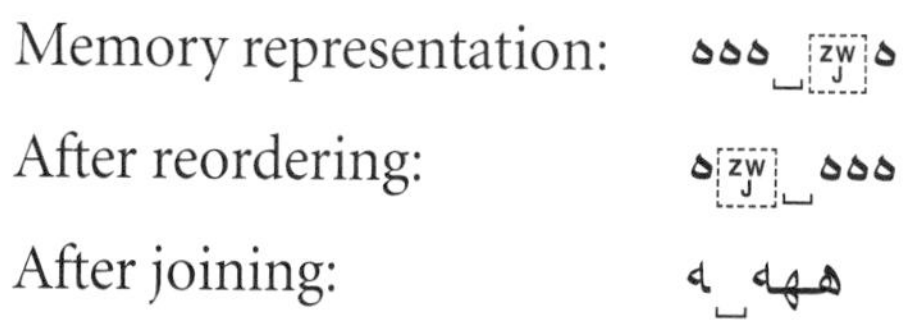

Memory representation:

After reordering:

After joining:

Figure 8-3. Using a Non-joiner

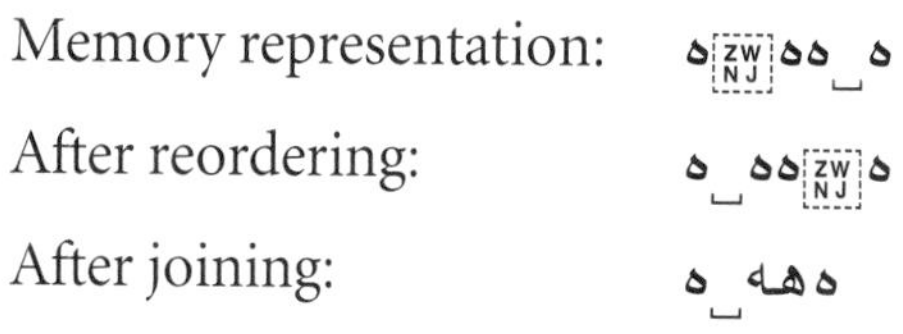

Memory representation:

After reordering:

After joining:

Figure 8-4. Combinations of Joiners and Non-joiners

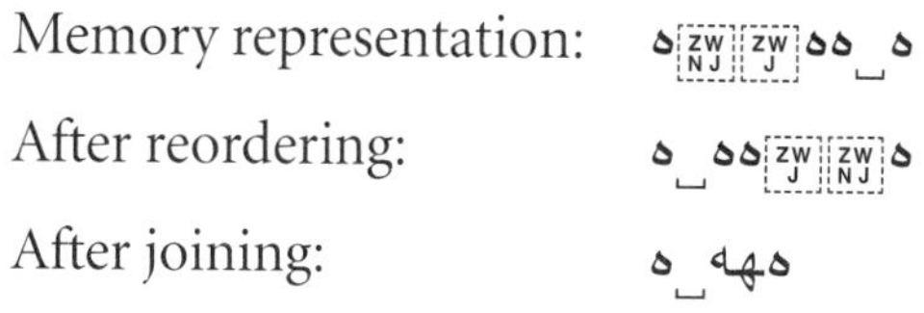

Memory representation:

After reordering:

After joining:

General rules for applying nonspacing marks are given in *Section 7.9, Combining Marks.* The few marks that are placed after (to the left of) the base character are treated as ordinary spacing characters in the Unicode Standard. The Unicode Standard does not specify a sequence order in case of multiple harakat applied to the same Arabic base character, as there is no possible ambiguity of interpretation. For more information about the canonical ordering of nonspacing marks, see *Section 2.11, Combining Characters,* and *Section 3.11, Canonical Ordering Behavior.*

The placement and rendering of vowel and other marks in Arabic strongly depends on the typographical environment or even the typographical style. For example, in *Chapter 17, Code Charts*, the default position of U+0651 ◌ّ ARABIC SHADDA is with the glyph placed above the base character, whereas for U+064D ◌ٍ ARABIC KASRATAN the glyph is placed below the base character, as shown in the first example in *Figure 8-5*. However, computer fonts often follow an approach that originated in metal typesetting and combine the *kasratan* with *shadda* in a ligature placed above the text, as shown in the second example in *Figure 8-5.*

Arabic-Indic Digits. The names for the forms of decimal digits vary widely across different languages. The decimal numbering system originated in India (Devanagari ०१२३...) and was subsequently adopted in the Arabic world with a different appearance (Arabic ٠١٢٣...). The Europeans adopted decimal numbers from the Arabic world, although

Figure 8-5. Placement of Harakat

once again the forms of the digits changed greatly (European 0123…). The European forms were later adopted widely around the world and are used even in many Arabic-speaking countries in North Africa. In each case, the interpretation of decimal numbers remained the same. However, the forms of the digits changed to such a degree that they are no longer recognizably the same characters. Because of the origin of these characters, the European decimal numbers are widely known as "Arabic numerals" or "Hindi-Arabic numerals," whereas the decimal numbers in use in the Arabic world are widely known there as "Hindi numbers."

The Unicode Standard includes *Indic* digits (including forms used with different Indic scripts), *Arabic* digits (with forms used in most of the Arabic world), and *European* digits (now used internationally). Because of this decision, the traditional names could not be retained without confusion. In addition, there are two main variants of the Arabic digits: those used in Iran, Pakistan, and Afghanistan (here called *Eastern Arabic-Indic*) and those used in other parts of the Arabic world. In summary, the Unicode Standard uses the names shown in *Table 8-1*.

Table 8-1. Arabic Digit Names

Name	Code Points	Forms
European	U+0030..U+0039	0123456789
Arabic-Indic	U+0660..U+0669	٠١٢٣٤٥٦٧٨٩
Eastern Arabic-Indic	U+06F0..U+06F9	۰۱۲۳۴۵۶۷۸۹
Indic (Devanagari)	U+0966..U+096F	०१२३४५६७८९

There is substantial variation in usage of glyphs for the Eastern Arabic-Indic digits, especially for the digits four, five, six, and seven. *Table 8-2* illustrates this variation with some example glyphs for digits in languages of Iran, Pakistan, and India. While some usage of the Persian glyph for U+06F7 EXTENDED ARABIC-INDIC DIGIT SEVEN can be documented for Sindhi, the form shown in *Table 8-2* is predominant.

The Unicode Standard provides a single, complete sequence of digits for Persian, Sindhi, and Urdu to account for the differences in appearance and directional treatment when rendering them. (For a complete discussion of directional formatting of numbers in the Unicode Standard, see Unicode Standard Annex #9, "The Bidirectional Algorithm.")

Table 8-2. Glyph Variation in Eastern Arabic-Indic Digits

Code Point	Digit	Persian	Sindhi	Urdu
U+06F4	4	۴	۴	۴
U+06F5	5	۵	۵	۵
U+06F6	6	۶	۶	۶
U+06F7	7	۷	۷	۷

Extended Arabic Letters. Arabic script is used to write major languages, such as Persian and Urdu, but it has also been used to transcribe some lesser-used languages, such as Baluchi and Lahnda, which have little tradition of printed typography. As a result, the Unicode Standard encodes multiple forms of some Extended Arabic letters because the character forms and usages are not well documented for a number of languages. For additional extended Arabic letters, see the Arabic Supplement block, U+0750..U+077F.

Koranic Annotation Signs. These characters are used in the Koran to mark pronunciation and other annotation. The enclosing mark U+06DE is used to enclose a digit. When rendered, the digit appears in a smaller size.

Additional Vowel Marks. When the Arabic script is adopted as the writing system for a language other than Arabic, it is often necessary to represent vowel sounds or distinctions not made in Arabic. In some cases, conventions such as the addition of small dots above and/or below the standard Arabic *fatha*, *damma*, and *kasra* signs have been used.

Classical Arabic has only three canonical vowels (/a/, /i/, /u/), whereas languages such as Urdu and Persian include other contrasting vowels such as /o/ and /e/. For this reason, it is imperative that speakers of these languages be able to show the difference between /e/ and /i/ (U+0656 ARABIC SUBSCRIPT ALEF), and between /o/ and /u/ (U+0657 ARABIC INVERTED DAMMA). At the same time, the use of these two diacritics in Arabic is redundant, merely emphasizing that the underlying vowel is long.

Honorifics. Marks known as honorifics represent phrases expressing the status of a person and are in widespread use in the Arabic-script world. Most have a specifically religious meaning. In effect, these marks are combining characters at the word level, rather than being associated with a single base character. Depending on the letter shapes present in the name and the calligraphic style in use, the honorific mark may be applied to a letter somewhere in the middle of the name. The normalization algorithm does not move such word-level combining characters to the end of the word.

Date Separator. U+060D ARABIC DATE SEPARATOR is used in Pakistan and India between the numeric date and the month name when writing out a date. This sign is distinct from U+002F SOLIDUS, which is used, for example, as a separator in currency amounts.

Full Stop. U+061E ARABIC TRIPLE DOT PUNCTUATION MARK is encoded for traditional orthographic practice using the Arabic script to write African languages such as Hausa, Wolof, Fulani, and Mandinka. These languages use ARABIC TRIPLE DOT PUNCTUATION MARK as a full stop.

Currency Symbols. U+060B AFGHANI SIGN is a currency symbol used in Afghanistan. The symbol is derived from an abbreviation of the name of the currency, which has become a symbol in its own right. U+FDFC RIAL SIGN is a currency symbol used in Iran. Unlike the AFGHANI SIGN, U+FDFC RIAL SIGN is considered a compability character, encoded for compatibility with Iranian standards. Ordinarily in Persian "rial" is simply spelled out as the sequence of letters, <0631, 06CC, 0627, 0644>.

End of Ayah. U+06DD ARABIC END OF AYAH graphically encloses a sequence of zero or more digits (of General Category Nd) that follow it in the data stream. The enclosure terminates with any non-digit. For behavior of a similar prefixed formatting control, see the discussion of U+070F SYRIAC ABBREVIATION MARK in *Section 8.3, Syriac.*

Other Signs Spanning Numbers. Several other special signs are written in association with numbers in the Arabic script. U+0600 ARABIC NUMBER SIGN signals the beginning of a number; it is written below the digits of the number.

U+0601 ARABIC SIGN SANAH indicates a year (that is, as part of a date). This sign is rendered below the digits of the number it precedes. Its appearance is a vestigial form of the Arabic word for *year*, /sanatu/ (*seen noon teh-marbuta*), but it is now a sign in its own right and is widely used to mark a numeric year even in non-Arabic languages where the Arabic word would not be known. The use of the year sign is illustrated in *Figure 8-6*.

Figure 8-6. Arabic Year Sign

U+0602 ARABIC FOOTNOTE MARKER is another of these signs; it is used in the Arabic script in conjunction with the footnote number itself. It also precedes the digits in logical order and is written to extend underneath them.

Finally, U+0603 ARABIC SIGN SAFHA functions as a page sign, preceding and extending under a sequence of digits for a page number.

Like U+06DD ARABIC END OF AYAH, all of these signs can span multiple-digit numbers, rather than just a single digit. They are not formally considered *combining marks* in the sense used by the Unicode Standard, although they clearly interact graphically with the sequence of digits that follows them. They *precede* the sequence of digits that they span, rather than following a base character, as would be the case for a combining mark. Their General Category value is Cf (format control character). Unlike most other format control characters, however, they should be rendered with a visible glyph, even in circumstances where no suitable digit or sequence of digits follows them in logical order.

Poetic Verse Sign. U+060E ARABIC POETIC VERSE SIGN is a special symbol often used to mark the beginning of a poetic verse. Although it is similar to U+0602 ARABIC FOOTNOTE MARKER in appearance, the poetic sign is simply a symbol. In contrast, the footnote marker is a format control character that has complex rendering in conjunction with following digits. U+060F ARABIC SIGN MISRA is another symbol used in poetry.

Arabic Cursive Joining

Minimum Rendering Requirements. A rendering or display process must convert between the logical order in which characters are placed in the backing store and the visual (or physical) order required by the display device. See Unicode Standard Annex #9, "The Bidirectional Algorithm," for a description of the conversion between logical and visual orders.

The cursive nature of the Arabic script imposes special requirements on display or rendering processes that are not typically found in Latin script-based systems. At a minimum, a display process must select an appropriate glyph to depict each Arabic letter according to its immediate *joining* context; furthermore, it must substitute certain ligature glyphs for sequences of Arabic characters. The remainder of this section specifies a minimum set of rules that provide legible Arabic joining and ligature substitution behavior.

Joining Classes. Each Arabic letter must be depicted by one of a number of possible contextual glyph forms. The appropriate form is determined on the basis of its joining class and the joining class of adjacent characters. Each Arabic character falls into one of the classes shown in *Table 8-3*. (See ArabicShaping.txt in the Unicode Character Database for a complete list.) In this table, *right* and *left* refer to visual order. The characters of the right-joining class are exemplified in more detail in *Table 8-8*, and those of the dual-joining class are shown in *Table 8-7*. When characters do not join or cause joining (such as DAMMATAN), they are classified as transparent.

Table 8-3. Primary Arabic Joining Classes

Joining Class	Symbols	Members
Right-joining	R	ALEF, DAL, THAL, REH, ZAIN …
Left-joining	L	None
Dual-joining	D	BEH, TEH, THEH, JEEM …
Join-causing	C	ZERO WIDTH JOINER (200D) and TATWEEL (0640). These characters are distinguished from the dual-joining characters in that they do not change shape themselves.
Non-joining	U	ZERO WIDTH NON-JOINER (200C) and all spacing characters, except those explicitly mentioned as being one of the other joining classes, are non-joining. These include HAMZA (0621), HIGH HAMZA (0674), spaces, digits, punctuation, non-Arabic letters, and so on. Also, U+0600 ARABIC NUMBER SIGN..U+0603 ARABIC SIGN SAFHA and U+06DD ARABIC END OF AYAH.

Table 8-3. Primary Arabic Joining Classes (Continued)

Joining Class	Symbols	Members
Transparent	T	All nonspacing marks (General Category Mn or Me) and most format control characters (General Category Cf) are transparent to cursive joining. These include FATHATAN (064B) and other Arabic *harakat*, HAMZA BELOW (0655), SUPERSCRIPT ALEF (0670), combining Koranic annotation signs, and nonspacing marks from other scripts. Also U+070F SYRIAC ABBREVIATION MARK.

Table 8-4 defines derived superclasses of the primary Arabic joining classes; those superclasses are used in the cursive joining rules. In this table, *right* and *left* refer to visual order.

Table 8-4. Derived Arabic Joining Classes

Joining Class	Members
Right join-causing	Superset of dual-joining, left-joining, and join-causing
Left join-causing	Superset of dual-joining, right-joining, and join-causing

Joining Rules. The following rules describe the joining behavior of Arabic letters in terms of their display (visual) order. In other words, the positions of letterforms in the included examples are presented as they would appear on the screen *after* the Bidirectional Algorithm has reordered the characters of a line of text.

An implementation may choose to restate the following rules according to logical order so as to apply them *before* the Bidirectional Algorithm's reordering phase. In this case, the words *right* and *left* as used in this section would become *preceding* and *following*.

In the following rules, if X refers to a character, then various glyph types representing that character are referred to as shown in *Table 8-5*.

Table 8-5. Arabic Glyph Types

Glyph Types	Description
X_n	Nominal glyph form as it appears in the code charts
X_r	Right-joining glyph form (both right-joining and dual-joining characters may employ this form)
X_l	Left-joining glyph form (both left-joining and dual-joining characters may employ this form)
X_m	Dual-joining (medial) glyph form that joins on both left and right (only dual-joining characters employ this form)

R1 Transparent characters do not affect the joining behavior of base (spacing) characters. For example:

MEEM.N + SHADDA.N + LAM.N → MEEM.R + SHADDA.N + LAM.L

م + ◌ّ + ل → ـم + ◌ّ + ﻟ → لمّ

R2 A right-joining character X that has a right join-causing character on the right will adopt the form X_r. For example:

ALEF.N + TATWEEL.N → ALEF.R + TATWEEL.N

ا + ـ → ـا + ـ → ـا

R3 A left-joining character X that has a left join-causing character on the left will adopt the form X_l.

R4 A dual-joining character X that has a right join-causing character on the right and a left join-causing character on the left will adopt the form X_m. For example:

TATWEEL.N + MEEM.N + TATWEEL.N → TATWEEL.N + MEEM.M + TATWEEL.N

ـ + م + ـ → ـ + ـمـ + ـ → ـمـ

R5 A dual-joining character X that has a right join-causing character on the right and no left join-causing character on the left will adopt the form X_r. For example:

MEEM.N + TATWEEL.N → MEEM.R + TATWEEL.N

م + ـ → ـم + ـ → ـم

R6 A dual-joining character X that has a left join-causing character on the left and no right join-causing character on the right will adopt the form X_l. For example:

TATWEEL.N + MEEM.N → TATWEEL.N + MEEM.L

ـ + م → ـ + مـ → مـ

R7 If none of the preceding rules applies to a character X, then it will adopt the nominal form X_n.

As just noted, the ZERO WIDTH NON-JOINER may be used to prevent joining, as in the Persian plural suffix or Ottoman Turkish vowels.

Arabic Ligatures

Ligature Classes. Certain types of ligatures are obligatory in Arabic script regardless of font design. Many other optional ligatures are possible, depending on font design. Because they are optional, those ligatures are not covered in this discussion.

For the purpose of describing the obligatory Arabic ligatures, certain Unicode characters fall into the following classes (see *Table 8-7* and *Table 8-8* for a complete list):

Alef-types:	MADDA-ON-ALEF, HAMZA ON ALEF, ...
Lam-types:	LAM, LAM WITH SMALL V, LAM WITH DOT ABOVE, ...

These two classes are designated in the joining type tables as *ALEF* and *LAM*, respectively.

Ligature Rules. The following rules describe the formation of ligatures. They are applied after the preceding joining rules. As for the joining rules just discussed, the following rules describe ligature behavior of Arabic letters in terms of their display (visual) order.

In the ligature rules, if X and Y refer to characters, then various glyph types representing combinations of these characters are referred to as shown in *Table 8-6*.

Table 8-6. Arabic Ligature Notation

Symbol	Description
$(X.Y)_n$	Nominal ligature glyph form representing a combination of an X_r form and a Y_l form
$(X.Y)_r$	Right-joining ligature glyph form representing a combination of an X_r form and a Y_m form
$(X.Y)_l$	Left-joining ligature glyph form representing a combination of an X_m form and a Y_l form
$(X.Y)_m$	Dual-joining (medial) ligature glyph form representing a combination of an X_m form and a Y_m form

L1 ***Transparent characters do not affect the ligating behavior of base (nontransparent) characters. For example:***

ALEF.R + FATHA.N + LAM.L → LAM-ALEF.N + FATHA.N

L2 ***Any sequence with*** *$ALEF_r$* ***on the left and*** *LAM_m* ***on the right will form the ligature*** *$(LAM\text{-}ALEF)_r$*. ***For example:***

ﺎ + ﻠ → ﻼ (not ﻠﺎ)

L3 ***Any sequence with*** *$ALEF_r$* ***on the left and*** *LAM_l* ***on the right will form the ligature*** *$(LAM\text{-}ALEF)_n$*. ***For example:***

ﺎ + ﻟ → ﻻ (not ﻟﺎ)

Optional Features. Many other ligatures and contextual forms are optional, depending on the font and application. Some of these presentation forms are encoded in the ranges FB50..FDFB and FE70..FEFE. However, these forms should *not* be used in general interchange. Moreover, it is not expected that every Arabic font will contain all of these forms, nor that these forms will include all presentation forms used by every font.

More sophisticated rendering systems will use additional shaping and placement. For example, contextual placement of the nonspacing vowels such as *fatha* will provide better appearance. The justification of Arabic tends to stretch words instead of adding width to spaces. Basic stretching can be done by inserting *tatweel* between characters shaped by rules R2, R4, R5, R6, L2, and L3; the best places for inserting tatweel will depend on the font and rendering software. More powerful systems will choose different shapes for characters such as *kaf* to fill the space in justification.

Arabic Character Joining Groups. The Arabic characters with the joining class of dual-joining (formally, Joining_Type=Dual_Joining) and those with the joining class of right-joining (Joining_Type=Right_Joining) can each be subdivided into shaping groups, based on the behavior of their letter skeletons when shaped in context. The Unicode character property that specifies these groups is called Joining_Group.

The Joining_Type and Joining_Group values for all Arabic characters are explicitly specified in ArabicShaping.txt in the Unicode Character Database. For convenience in reference, the Joining_Type values are extracted and listed in DerivedJoiningType.txt and the Joining_Group values are extracted and listed in DerivedJoiningGroup.txt.

Table 8-7 exemplifies dual-joining Arabic characters and illustrates the forms taken by the letter skeletons in context. Dual-joining characters have four distinct forms, for isolated, final, medial, and initial contexts, respectively. The name for each joining group is based on the name of a representative letter that is used to illustrate the shaping behavior. Most extended Arabic characters are merely variations on these basic shapes, with additional or different diacritic marks applied above or below the letter skeletons. For instance, the BEH joining group applies not only to U+0628 ARABIC LETTER BEH, which has a single dot below the skeleton, but also to U+062A ARABIC LETTER TEH, which has two dots above the skeleton, and to U+062B ARABIC LETTER THEH, which has three dots above the skeleton, as well as to the Persian and Urdu letter U+067E ARABIC LETTER PEH, which has three dots below the skeleton. The joining groups in the table are organized by shape and not by standard Arabic alphabetical order.

Table 8-7. Dual-Joining Arabic Characters

Group	X_n	X_r	X_m	X_l	Notes
BEH	ب	ـب	ـبـ	بـ	Includes TEH and THEH.
NOON	ن	ـن	ـنـ	نـ	
YEH	ي	ـي	ـيـ	يـ	Includes ALEF MAKSURA.

Table 8-7. Dual-Joining Arabic Characters (Continued)

Group	X_n	X_r	X_m	X_l	Notes
HAH	ح	ـح	ـحـ	حـ	Includes KHAH and JEEM.
SEEN	س	ـس	ـسـ	سـ	Includes SHEEN.
SAD	ص	ـص	ـصـ	صـ	Includes DAD.
TAH	ط	ـط	ـطـ	طـ	Includes ZAH.
AIN	ع	ـع	ـعـ	عـ	Includes GHAIN.
FEH	ڡ	ـڡ	ـڡـ	ڡـ	
QAF	ٯ	ـٯ	ـٯـ	ٯـ	
MEEM	م	ـم	ـمـ	مـ	
HEH	ه	ـه	ـهـ	هـ	
KNOTTED HEH	ھ	ـھ	ـھـ	ھـ	
HEH GOAL	ہ	ـہ	ـہـ	ہـ	Excludes HAMZA ON HEH GOAL.
KAF	ك	ـك	ـكـ	كـ	
SWASH KAF	ڪ	ـڪ	ـڪـ	ڪـ	
GAF	گ	ـگ	ـگـ	گـ	
LAM	ل	ـل	ـلـ	لـ	

Table 8-8 exemplifies right-joining Arabic characters, illustrating the forms they take in context. Right-joining characters have only two distinct forms, for isolated and final contexts, respectively.

Table 8-8. Right-Joining Arabic Characters

Group	X_n	X_r	Notes
ALEF	ا	ـا	
WAW	و	ـو	
DAL	د	ـد	Includes THAL.
REH	ر	ـر	Includes ZAIN.
TEH MARBUTA	ة	ـة	Includes HAMZA ON HEH.
HAMZA ON HEH GOAL	ۂ	ـۂ	
YEH WITH TAIL	ݍ	ـݍ	
YEH BARREE	ے	ـے	

In some cases, characters occur only at the end of words in correct spelling; they are called *trailing characters*. Examples include TEH MARBUTA, ALEF MAKSURA, and DAMMATAN. When trailing characters are joining (such as TEH MARBUTA), they are classified as right-joining, even when similarly shaped characters are dual-joining.

In the case of U+0647 ARABIC LETTER HEH, the glyph ﻫ is shown in the code charts. This form is often used to reduce the chance of misidentifying *heh* as U+0665 ARABIC-INDIC DIGIT FIVE, which has a very similar shape. The isolate forms of U+0647 ARABIC LETTER HEH and U+06C1 ARABIC LETTER HEH GOAL both look like U+06D5 ARABIC LETTER AE.

Jawi. U+06BD ARABIC LETTER NOON WITH THREE DOTS ABOVE is used for Jawi, which is Malay written using the Arabic script. Malay users know the character as *Jawi Nya*. Contrary to what is suggested by its Unicode character name, U+06BD displays with the three dots *below* the letter when it is in the initial or medial position. This is done to avoid confusion with U+062B ARABIC LETTER THEH, which appears in words of Arabic origin, and which has the same base letter shapes in initial or medial position, but with three dots above in all positions.

Arabic Supplement: U+0750–U+077F

The Arabic Supplement block contains additional extended Arabic letters mainly for the languages used in Northern and Western Africa, such as Fulfulde, Hausa, Songhoy, and Wolof. In the second half of the twentieth century, the use of the Arabic script was actively promoted for these languages. Characters used for other languages are annotated in the character names list. Additional vowel marks used with these languages are found in the main Arabic block.

Marwari. U+076A ARABIC LETTER LAM WITH BAR is used to represent a flapped retroflexed lateral in the Marwari language in southern Pakistan. It has also been suggested for use in the Gawri language of northern Pakistan but it is unclear how widely it has been adopted there. Contextual shaping for this character is similar to that of U+0644 ARABIC LETTER LAM, including the requirement to form ligatures with ALEF and related characters.

Arabic Presentation Forms-A: U+FB50–U+FDFF

This block contains a list of presentation forms (glyphs) encoded as characters for compatibility. At the time of publication, there are no known implementations of all of these presentation forms. As with most other compatibility encodings, these characters have a preferred encoding that makes use of noncompatibility characters.

The presentation forms in this block consist of contextual (positional) variants of Extended Arabic letters, contextual variants of Arabic letter ligatures, spacing forms of Arabic diacritic combinations, contextual variants of certain Arabic letter/diacritic combinations, and Arabic phrase ligatures. The ligatures include a large set of presentation forms. However, the set of ligatures appropriate for any given Arabic font will generally not match this set precisely. Fonts will often include only a subset of these glyphs, and they may also include glyphs outside of this set. These glyphs are generally not accessible as characters and are used only by rendering engines.

Ornate Parentheses. The alternative, ornate forms of parentheses (U+FD3E ORNATE LEFT PARENTHESIS and U+FD3F ORNATE RIGHT PARENTHESIS) for use with the Arabic script are considered traditional Arabice punctuation, rather than compatibility characters. These ornate parentheses are exceptional in rendering in bidirectional text; for legacy reasons, they do not have the Bidi_Mirrored property. Thus, unlike other parentheses, they do not automatically mirror when rendered in a bidirectional context.

Arabic Presentation Forms-B: U+FE70–U+FEFF

This block contains additional Arabic presentation forms consisting of spacing or *tatweel* forms of Arabic diacritics, contextual variants of primary Arabic letters, and the obligatory LAM-ALEF ligature. They are included here for compatibility with preexisting standards and legacy implementations that use these forms as characters. They can be replaced by letters from the Arabic block (U+0600..U+06FF). Implementations can handle contextual glyph shaping by rendering rules when accessing glyphs from fonts, rather than by encoding contextual shapes as characters.

Spacing and Tatweel Forms of Arabic Diacritics. For compatibility with certain implementations, a set of spacing forms of the Arabic diacritics is provided here. The tatweel forms are combinations of the joining connector tatweel and a diacritic.

Zero Width No-Break Space. This character (U+FEFF), which is not an Arabic presentation form, is described in *Section 16.8, Specials*.

8.3 Syriac

Syriac: U+0700–U+074F

Syriac Language. The Syriac language belongs to the Aramaic branch of the Semitic family of languages. The earliest datable Syriac writing dates from the year 6 CE. Syriac is the active liturgical language of many communities in the Middle East (Syrian Orthodox, Assyrian, Maronite, Syrian Catholic, and Chaldaean) and Southeast India (Syro-Malabar and Syro-Malankara). It is also the native language of a considerable population in these communities.

Syriac is divided into two dialects. West Syriac is used by the Syrian Orthodox, Maronites, and Syrian Catholics. East Syriac is used by the Assyrians (that is, Ancient Church of the East) and Chaldaeans. The two dialects are very similar and have almost no differences in grammar and vocabulary. They differ in pronunciation and use different dialectal forms of the Syriac script.

Languages Using the Syriac Script. A number of modern languages and dialects employ the Syriac script in one form or another. They include the following:

1. *Literary Syriac.* The primary usage of Syriac script.
2. *Neo-Aramaic dialects.* The Syriac script is widely used for modern Aramaic languages, next to Hebrew, Cyrillic, and Latin. A number of Eastern Modern Aramaic dialects known as *Swadaya* (also called vernacular Syriac, modern Syriac, modern Assyrian, and so on, and spoken mostly by the Assyrians and Chaldaeans of Iraq, Turkey, and Iran) and the Central Aramaic dialect, *Turoyo* (spoken mostly by the Syrian Orthodox of the Tur Abdin region in southeast Turkey), belong to this category of languages.
3. *Garshuni* (Arabic written in the Syriac script). It is currently used for writing Arabic liturgical texts by Syriac-speaking Christians. Garshuni employs the Arabic set of vowels and overstrike marks.
4. *Christian Palestinian Aramaic* (also known as Palestinian Syriac). This dialect is no longer spoken.
5. *Other languages.* The Syriac script was used in various historical periods for writing Armenian and some Persian dialects. Syriac speakers employed it for

writing Arabic, Ottoman Turkish, and Malayalam. Six special characters used for Persian and Sogdian were added in Version 4.0 of the Unicode Standard.

Shaping. The Syriac script is cursive and has shaping rules that are similar to those for Arabic. The Unicode Standard does not include any presentation form characters for Syriac.

Directionality. The Syriac script is written from right to left. Conformant implementations of Syriac script must use the Unicode Bidirectional Algorithm (see Unicode Standard Annex #9, "The Bidirectional Algorithm").

Syriac Type Styles. Syriac texts employ several type styles. Because all type styles use the same Syriac characters, even though their shapes vary to some extent, the Unicode Standard encodes only a single Syriac script.

1. *Estrangela type style.* Estrangela (a word derived from Greek *strongulos,* meaning "rounded") is the oldest type style. Ancient manuscripts use this writing style exclusively. Estrangela is used today in West and East Syriac texts for writing headers, titles, and subtitles. It is the current standard in writing Syriac texts in Western scholarship.
2. *Serto or West Syriac type style.* This type style is the most cursive of all Syriac type styles. It emerged around the eighth century and is used today in West Syriac texts, Turoyo (Central Neo-Aramaic), and Garshuni.
3. *East Syriac type style.* Its early features appear as early as the sixth century; it developed into its own type style by the twelfth or thirteenth century. This type style is used today for writing East Syriac texts as well as Swadaya (Eastern Neo-Aramaic). It is also used today in West Syriac texts for headers, titles, and subtitles alongside the Estrangela type style.
4. *Christian Palestinian Aramaic.* Manuscripts of this dialect employ a script that is akin to Estrangela. It can be considered a subcategory of Estrangela.

The Unicode Standard provides for usage of the type styles mentioned above. It also accommodates letters and diacritics used in Neo-Aramaic, Christian Palestinian Aramaic, Garshuni, Persian, and Sogdian languages. *Examples are supplied in the Serto type style, except where otherwise noted.*

Character Names. Character names follow the East Syriac convention for naming the letters of the alphabet. Diacritical points use a descriptive naming—for example, SYRIAC DOT ABOVE.

Syriac Abbreviation Mark. U+070F SYRIAC ABBREVIATION MARK (SAM) is a zero-width formatting code that has no effect on the shaping process of Syriac characters. The SAM specifies the beginning point of a *Syriac abbreviation,* which is a line drawn horizontally above one or more characters, at the end of a word or of a group of characters followed by a character other than a Syriac letter or diacritic mark. A Syriac abbreviation may contain Syriac diacritics.

Ideally, the Syriac abbreviation is rendered by a line that has a dot at each end and the center, as shown in the examples. While not preferable, it has become acceptable for computers to render the Syriac abbreviation as a line without the dots. The line is acceptable for the presentation of Syriac in plain text, but the presence of dots is recommended in liturgical texts.

The Syriac abbreviation is used for letter numbers and contractions. A Syriac abbreviation generally extends from the last tall character in the word until the end of the word. A common exception to this rule is found with letter numbers that are preceded by a preposition character, as seen in *Figure 8-7*.

Figure 8-7. Syriac Abbreviation

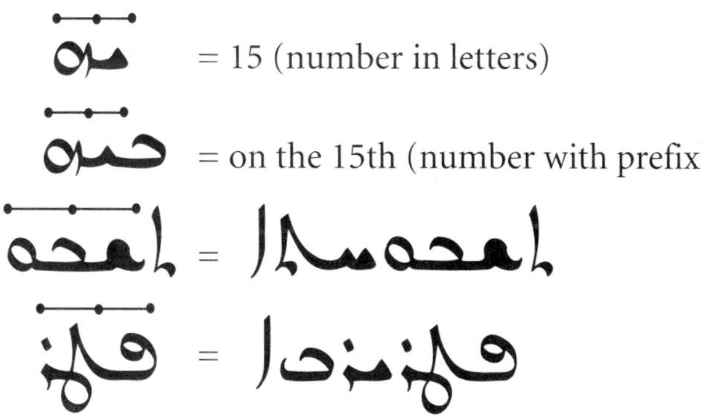

A SAM is placed before the character where the abbreviation begins. The Syriac abbreviation begins over the character following the SAM and continues until the end of the word. Use of the SAM is demonstrated in *Figure 8-8*.

Figure 8-8. Use of SAM

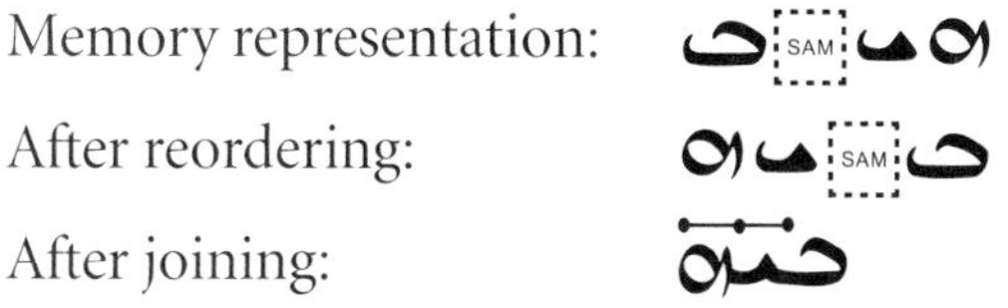

Memory representation: SAM

After reordering: SAM

After joining:

Note: Modern East Syriac texts employ a punctuation mark for contractions of this sort.

Ligatures and Combining Characters. Only one ligature is included in the Syriac block: U+071E SYRIAC LETTER YUDH HE. This combination is used as a unique character in the same manner as an "æ" ligature. A number of combining diacritics unique to Syriac are encoded, but combining characters from other blocks are also used, especially from the Arabic block.

Diacritic Marks and Vowels. The function of the diacritic marks varies. They indicate vowels (as in Arabic and Hebrew), mark grammatical attributes (for example, verb versus noun, interjection), or guide the reader in the pronunciation and/or reading of the given text.

> "The reader of the average Syriac manuscript or book is confronted with a bewildering profusion of points. They are large, of medium size and small, arranged singly or in twos and threes, placed above the word, below it, or upon the line."

There are two vocalization systems. The first, attributed to Jacob of Edessa (633–708 CE), utilizes letters derived from Greek that are placed above (or below) the characters they modify. The second is the more ancient dotted system, which employs dots in various shapes and locations to indicate vowels. East Syriac texts exclusively employ the dotted system, whereas West Syriac texts (especially later ones and in modern times) employ a mixture of the two systems.

Diacritic marks are nonspacing and are normally centered above or below the character. Exceptions to this rule follow:

1. U+0741 SYRIAC QUSHSHAYA and U+0742 SYRIAC RUKKAKHA are used only with the letters *beth*, *gamal* (in its Syriac and Garshuni forms), *dalath*, *kaph*, *pe*, and *taw*.
   - The *qushshaya* indicates that the letter is pronounced hard and unaspirated.
   - The *rukkakha* indicates that the letter is pronounced soft and aspirated. When the *rukkakha* is used in conjunction with the *dalath*, it is printed slightly to the right of the *dalath*'s dot below.
2. In Modern Syriac usage, when a word contains a *rish* and a *seyame*, the dot of the *rish* and the *seyame* are replaced by a *rish* with two dots above it.
3. The *feminine dot* is usually placed to the left of a final *taw*.

Punctuation. Most punctuation marks used with Syriac are found in the Latin-1 and Arabic blocks. The other marks are encoded in this block.

Digits. Modern Syriac employs European numerals, as does Hebrew. The ordering of digits follows the same scheme as in Hebrew.

Harklean Marks. The Harklean marks are used in the Harklean translation of the New Testament. U+070B SYRIAC HARKLEAN OBELUS and U+070D SYRIAC HARKLEAN ASTERISCUS mark the beginning of a phrase, word, or morpheme that has a marginal note. U+070C SYRIAC HARKLEAN METOBELUS marks the end of such sections.

Dalath and Rish. Prior to the development of pointing, early Syriac texts did not distinguish between a *dalath* and a *rish*, which are distinguished in later periods with a dot below the former and a dot above the latter. Unicode provides U+0716 SYRIAC LETTER DOTLESS DALATH RISH as an ambiguous character.

Semkath. Unlike other letters, the joining mechanism of *semkath* varies through the course of history from right-joining to dual-joining. It is necessary to enter a U+200C ZERO WIDTH NON-JOINER character after the *semkath* to obtain the right-joining form where required. Two common variants of this character exist: U+0723 SYRIAC LETTER SEMKATH and U+0724 SYRIAC LETTER FINAL SEMKATH. They occur interchangeably in the same document, similar to the case of Greek sigma.

Vowel Marks. The so-called Greek vowels may be used above or below letters. As West Syriac texts employ a mixture of the Greek and dotted systems, both versions are accounted for here.

Miscellaneous Diacritics. Miscellaneous general diacritics are used in Syriac text. Their usage is explained in *Table 8-9*.

Table 8-9. Miscellaneous Syriac Diacritic Use

Code Points	Use
U+0303, U+0330	These are used in Swadaya to indicate letters not found in Syriac.
U+0304, U+0320	These are used for various purposes ranging from phonological to grammatical to orthographic markers.
U+0307, U+0323	These points are used for various purposes—grammatical, phonological, and otherwise. They differ typographically and semantically from the *qushshaya*, *rukkakha* points, and the dotted vowel points.
U+0308	This is the plural marker. It is also used in Garshuni for the Arabic *teh marbuta*.
U+030A, U+0325	These are two other forms for the indication of *qushshaya* and *rukkakha*. They are used interchangeably with U+0741 SYRIAC QUSHSHAYA and U+0742 SYRIAC RUKKAKHA, especially in West Syriac grammar books.
U+0324	This diacritic mark is found in ancient manuscripts. It has a grammatical and phonological function.
U+032D	This is one of the *digit markers*.
U+032E	This is a mark used in late and modern East Syriac texts as well as in Swadaya to indicate a fricative *pe*.

Use of Characters of the Arabic Block. Syriac makes use of several characters from the Arabic block, including U+0640 ARABIC TATWEEL. Modern texts use U+060C ARABIC COMMA, U+061B ARABIC SEMICOLON, and U+061F ARABIC QUESTION MARK. The *shadda* (U+0651) is also used in the core part of literary Syriac on top of a *waw* in the word "O". Arabic *harakat* are used in Garshuni to indicate the corresponding Arabic vowels and diacritics.

Syriac Shaping

Minimum Rendering Requirements. Rendering requirements for Syriac are similar to those for Arabic. The remainder of this section specifies a minimum set of rules that provides legible Syriac joining and ligature substitution behavior.

Joining Classes. Each Syriac character is represented by a maximum of four possible contextual glyph forms. The form used is determined by its joining class and the joining class of the letter on each side. These classes are identical in behavior to those outlined for Arabic, with the addition of three extra classes that determine the behavior of final *alaphs*. See *Table 8-10*.

Table 8-10. Additional Syriac Joining Classes

Joining Class	Description
Afj	Final joining (alaph only)
Afn	Final non-joining *except* following dalath and rish (alaph only)
Afx	Final non-joining following dalath and rish (alaph only)

R1 ***An* alaph *that has a left-joining character to its right and a word breaking character to its left will take the form of*** A_{fj}.

ܐ + ܒ → ܐ + ܒ → ܒܐ

R2 ***An* alaph *that has a non-left-joining character to its right, except for a* dalath *or* rish, *and a word breaking character to its left will take the form of*** A_{fn}.

ܐ + ܗ → ܐ + ܗ → ܗܐ

R3 ***An* alaph *that has a* dalath *or* rish *to its right and a word breaking character to its left will take the form of*** A_{fx}.

ܐ + ܕ → ܐ + ܕ → ܕܐ

The above example is in the East Syriac font style.

Syriac Cursive Joining

Table 8-11, *Table 8-12*, and *Table 8-13* provide listings of how each character is shaped in the appropriate joining type. Syriac characters not shown are non-joining. These tables are in the Serto (West Syriac) font style, whereas the code charts in *Chapter 17, Code Charts*, are in the Estrangela font style. The shaping classes are included in ArabicShaping.txt in the Unicode Character Database.

Table 8-11. Dual-Joining Syriac Characters

Character	X_n	X_r	X_m	X_l
BETH	ܒ	‍ܒ	‍ܒ‍	ܒ‍
PERSIAN BHETH	ܭ	‍ܭ	‍ܭ‍	ܭ‍
GAMAL	ܓ	‍ܓ	‍ܓ‍	ܓ‍
GAMAL GARSHUNI	ܔ	‍ܔ	‍ܔ‍	ܔ‍
PERSIAN GHAMAL	ܮ	‍ܮ	‍ܮ‍	ܮ‍
HETH	ܚ	‍ܚ	‍ܚ‍	ܚ‍
TETH	ܛ	‍ܛ	‍ܛ‍	ܛ‍
TETH GARSHUNI	ܜ	‍ܜ	‍ܜ‍	ܜ‍
YUDH	ܝ	‍ܝ	‍ܝ‍	ܝ‍
KAPH	ܟ	‍ܟ	‍ܟ‍	ܟ‍
SOGDIAN KHAPH	ܯ	‍ܯ	‍ܯ‍	ܯ‍
LAMADH	ܠ	‍ܠ	‍ܠ‍	ܠ‍
MIM	ܡ	‍ܡ	‍ܡ‍	ܡ‍
NUN	ܢ	‍ܢ	‍ܢ‍	ܢ‍
SEMKATH	ܣ	‍ܣ	‍ܣ‍	ܣ‍
SEMKATH FINAL	ܤ	‍ܤ	‍ܤ‍	ܤ‍
E	ܥ	‍ܥ	‍ܥ‍	ܥ‍
PE	ܦ	‍ܦ	‍ܦ‍	ܦ‍
REVERSED PE	ܧ	‍ܧ	‍ܧ‍	ܧ‍
SOGDIAN FE	ݏ	‍ݏ	‍ݏ‍	ݏ‍
QAPH	ܩ	‍ܩ	‍ܩ‍	ܩ‍
SHIN	ܫ	‍ܫ	‍ܫ‍	ܫ‍

Table 8-12. Right-Joining Syriac Characters

Character	X_n	X_r
DALATH	ܕ	‍ܕ
DOTLESS DALATH RISH	ܖ	‍ܖ
PERSIAN DHALATH	ܯ	‍ܯ
HE	ܗ	‍ܗ
WAW	ܘ	‍ܘ
ZAIN	ܙ	‍ܙ
SOGDIAN ZHAIN	ݍ	‍ݍ
YUDH HE	ܞ	‍ܞ
SADHE	ܨ	‍ܨ
RISH	ܪ	‍ܪ
TAW	ܬ	‍ܬ

Table 8-13. Alaph-Joining Syriac Characters

Type Style	A_n	A_r	A_{fj}	A_{fn}	A_{fx}
Estrangela	ܐ	‍ܐ	‍ܐ	‍ܐ	‍ܐ
Serto (West Syriac)	ܐ	‍ܐ	‍ܐ	‍ܐ	‍ܐ
East Syriac	ܐ	‍ܐ	‍ܐ	‍ܐ	‍ܐ

Syriac Ligatures

Ligature Classes. As in other scripts, ligatures in Syriac vary depending on the font style. *Table 8-14* identifies the principal valid ligatures for each font style. When applicable, these ligatures are obligatory, unless denoted with an asterisk (*).

Table 8-14. Syriac Ligatures

Characters	Estrangela	Serto (West Syriac)	East Syriac	Sources
ALAPH LAMADH	N/A	Dual-joining	N/A	Beth Gazo
GAMAL LAMADH	N/A	Dual-joining*	N/A	Armalah
GAMAL E	N/A	Dual-joining*	N/A	Armalah
HE YUDH	N/A	N/A	Right-joining*	Qdom
YUDH TAW	N/A	Right-joining*	N/A	Armalah*
KAPH LAMADH	N/A	Dual-joining*	N/A	Shhimo
KAPH TAW	N/A	Right-joining*	N/A	Armalah
LAMADH SPACE ALAPH	N/A	Right-joining*	N/A	Nomocanon
LAMADH ALAPH	Right-joining*	Right-joining	Right-joining*	BFBS
LAMADH LAMADH	N/A	Dual-joining*	N/A	Shhimo
NUN ALAPH	N/A	Right-joining*	N/A	Shhimo
SEMAKATH TETH	N/A	Dual-joining*	N/A	Qurobo
SADHE NUN	Right-joining*	Right-joining*	Right-joining*	Mushhotho
RISH SEYAME	Right-joining	Right-joining	Right-joining	BFBS
TAW ALAPH	Right-joining*	N/A	Right-joining*	Qdom
TAW YUDH	N/A	N/A	Right-joining*	

8.4 Thaana

Thaana: U+0780–U+07BF

The Thaana script is used to write the modern Dhivehi language of the Republic of Maldives, a group of atolls in the Indian Ocean. Like the Arabic script, Thaana is written from right to left and uses vowel signs, but it is not cursive. The basic Thaana letters have been extended by a small set of dotted letters used to transcribe Arabic. The use of modified Thaana letters to write Arabic began in the middle of the twentieth century. Loan words from Arabic may be written in the Arabic script, although this custom is not very prevalent today. (See *Section 8.2, Arabic.*)

While Thaana's glyphs were borrowed in part from Arabic (letters *haa* through *vaavu* were based on the Arabic-Indic digits, for example), and while vowels and *sukun* are marked with combining characters as in Arabic, Thaana is properly considered an alphabet, rather than an abjad, because writing the vowels is obligatory.

Directionality. The Thaana script is written from right to left. Conformant implementations of Thaana script must use the Unicode Bidirectional Algorithm (see Unicode Standard Annex #9, "The Bidirectional Algorithm").

Vowels. Consonants are always written with either a vowel sign (U+07A6..U+07AF) or the null vowel sign (U+07B0 THAANA SUKUN). U+0787 THAANA LETTER ALIFU with the null vowel sign denotes a glottal stop. The placement of the Thaana vowel signs is shown in *Table 8-15.*

Table 8-15. Thaana Glyph Placement

Syllable	Display
tha	ތަ
thaa	ތާ
thi	ތި
thee	ތީ
thu	ތު
thoo	ތޫ
the	ތެ
they	ތޭ
tho	ތޮ
thoa	ތޯ
th	ތް

Numerals. Both European (U+0030..U+0039) and Arabic digits (U+0660..U+0669) are used. European numbers are used more commonly and have left-to-right display directionality in Thaana. Arabic numeric punctuation is used with digits, whether Arabic or European.

Punctuation. The Thaana script uses spaces between words. It makes use of a mixture of Arabic and European punctuation, though rules of usage are not clearly defined. Sentence-final punctuation is now generally shown with a single period (U+002E "." FULL STOP) but may also use a sequence of two periods (U+002E followed by U+002E). Phrases may be separated with a comma (usually U+060C ARABIC COMMA) or with a single period (U+002E). Colons, dashes, and double quotation marks are also used in the Thaana script. In addition, Thaana makes use of U+061F ARABIC QUESTION MARK and U+061B ARABIC SEMICOLON.

Character Names and Arrangement. The character names are based on the names used in the Republic of Maldives. The character name at U+0794, *yaa,* is found in some sources as *yaviyani,* but the former name is more common today. Characters are listed in Thaana alphabetical order from *haa* to *ttaa* for the Thaana letters, followed by the extended characters in Arabic alphabetical order from *hhaa* to *waavu.*

CHAPTER 9

Chapter 9

South Asian Scripts-I

The following South Asian scripts are described in this chapter:

Devanagari	*Gujarati*	*Telugu*
Bengali	*Oriya*	*Kannada*
Gurmukhi	*Tamil*	*Malayalam*

The scripts of South Asia share so many common features that a side-by-side comparison of a few will often reveal structural similarities even in the modern letterforms. With minor historical exceptions, they are written from left to right. They are all *abugidas* in which most symbols stand for a consonant plus an inherent vowel (usually the sound /a/). Word-initial vowels in many of these scripts have distinct symbols, and word-internal vowels are usually written by juxtaposing a vowel sign in the vicinity of the affected consonant. Absence of the inherent vowel, when that occurs, is frequently marked with a special sign. In the Unicode Standard, this sign is denoted by the Sanskrit word *virāma*. In some languages, another designation is preferred. In Hindi, for example, the word *hal* refers to the character itself, and *halant* refers to the consonant that has its inherent vowel suppressed; in Tamil, the word *puḷḷi* is used. The virama sign nominally serves to suppress the inherent vowel of the consonant to which it is applied; it is a combining character, with its shape varying from script to script.

Most of the scripts of South Asia, from north of the Himalayas to Sri Lanka in the south, from Pakistan in the west to the easternmost islands of Indonesia, are derived from the ancient Brahmi script. The oldest lengthy inscriptions of India, the edicts of Ashoka from the third century BCE, were written in two scripts, Kharoshthi and Brahmi. These are both ultimately of Semitic origin, probably deriving from Aramaic, which was an important administrative language of the Middle East at that time. Kharoshthi, written from right to left, was supplanted by Brahmi and its derivatives. The descendants of Brahmi spread with myriad changes throughout the subcontinent and outlying islands. There are said to be some 200 different scripts deriving from it. By the eleventh century, the modern script known as Devanagari was in ascendancy in India proper as the major script of Sanskrit literature.

The North Indian branch of scripts was, like Brahmi itself, chiefly used to write Indo-European languages such as Pali and Sanskrit, and eventually the Hindi, Bengali, and Gujarati languages, though it was also the source for scripts for non-Indo-European languages such as Tibetan, Mongolian, and Lepcha.

The South Indian scripts are also derived from Brahmi and, therefore, share many structural characteristics. These scripts were first used to write Pali and Sanskrit but were later adapted for use in writing non-Indo-European languages—namely, the languages of the Dravidian family of southern India and Sri Lanka. Because of their use for Dravidian languages, the South Indian scripts developed many characteristics that distinguish them from the North Indian scripts. South Indian scripts were also exported to southeast Asia and were the source of scripts such as Lanna and Myanmar, as well as the insular scripts of the Philippines and Indonesia.

The shapes of letters in the South Indian scripts took on a quite distinct look from the shapes of letters in the North Indian scripts. Some scholars suggest that this occurred because writing materials such as palm leaves encouraged changes in the way letters were written.

The major official scripts of India proper, including Devanagari, are documented in this chapter. They are all encoded according to a common plan, so that comparable characters are in the same order and relative location. This structural arrangement, which facilitates transliteration to some degree, is based on the Indian national standard (ISCII) encoding for these scripts and makes use of a virama.

While the arrangement of the encoding for the scripts of India is based on ISCII, this does not imply that the rendering behavior of South Indian scripts in particular is the same as that of Devanagari or other North Indian scripts. Implementations should ensure that adequate attention is given to the actual behavior of those scripts; they should not assume that they work just as Devanagari does. Each block description in this chapter describes the most important aspects of rendering for a particular script as well as unique behaviors it may have.

Many of the character names in this group of scripts represent the same sounds, and common naming conventions are used for the scripts of India.

9.1 Devanagari

Devanagari: U+0900–U+097F

The Devanagari script is used for writing classical Sanskrit and its modern historical derivative, Hindi. Extensions to the Sanskrit repertoire are used to write other related languages of India (such as Marathi) and of Nepal (Nepali). In addition, the Devanagari script is used to write the following languages: Awadhi, Bagheli, Bhatneri, Bhili, Bihari, Braj Bhasha, Chhattisgarhi, Garhwali, Gondi (Betul, Chhindwara, and Mandla dialects), Harauti, Ho, Jaipuri, Kachchhi, Kanauji, Konkani, Kului, Kumaoni, Kurku, Kurukh, Marwari, Mundari, Newari, Palpa, and Santali.

All other Indic scripts, as well as the Sinhala script of Sri Lanka, the Tibetan script, and the Southeast Asian scripts, are historically connected with the Devanagari script as descendants of the ancient Brahmi script. The entire family of scripts shares a large number of structural features.

The principles of the Indic scripts are covered in some detail in this introduction to the Devanagari script. The remaining introductions to the Indic scripts are abbreviated but highlight any differences from Devanagari where appropriate.

Standards. The Devanagari block of the Unicode Standard is based on ISCII-1988 (Indian Script Code for Information Interchange). The ISCII standard of 1988 differs from and is an update of earlier ISCII standards issued in 1983 and 1986.

The Unicode Standard encodes Devanagari characters in the same relative positions as those coded in positions A0–$F4_{16}$ in the ISCII-1988 standard. The same character code layout is followed for eight other Indic scripts in the Unicode Standard: Bengali, Gurmukhi, Gujarati, Oriya, Tamil, Telugu, Kannada, and Malayalam. This parallel code layout emphasizes the structural similarities of the Brahmi scripts and follows the stated intention of the Indian coding standards to enable one-to-one mappings between analogous coding positions in different scripts in the family. Sinhala, Tibetan, Thai, Lao, Khmer, Myanmar, and other scripts depart to a greater extent from the Devanagari structural pattern, so the Unicode Standard does not attempt to provide any direct mappings for these scripts to the Devanagari order.

In November 1991, at the time *The Unicode Standard, Version 1.0,* was published, the Bureau of Indian Standards published a new version of ISCII in Indian Standard (IS) 13194:1991. This new version partially modified the layout and repertoire of the ISCII-1988 standard. Because of these events, the Unicode Standard does not precisely follow the layout of the current version of ISCII. Nevertheless, the Unicode Standard remains a superset of the ISCII-1991 repertoire except for a number of new Vedic extension characters defined in IS 13194:1991 *Annex G—Extended Character Set for Vedic.* Modern, non-Vedic texts encoded with ISCII-1991 may be automatically converted to Unicode code points and back to their original encoding without loss of information.

Encoding Principles. The writing systems that employ Devanagari and other Indic scripts constitute abugidas—a cross between syllabic writing systems and alphabetic writing systems. The effective unit of these writing systems is the orthographic syllable, consisting of a consonant and vowel (CV) core and, optionally, one or more preceding consonants, with a canonical structure of (((C)C)C)V. The orthographic syllable need not correspond exactly with a phonological syllable, especially when a consonant cluster is involved, but the writing system is built on phonological principles and tends to correspond quite closely to pronunciation.

The orthographic syllable is built up of alphabetic pieces, the actual letters of the Devanagari script. These pieces consist of three distinct character types: consonant letters, independent vowels, and dependent vowel signs. In a text sequence, these characters are stored in logical (phonetic) order.

Principles of the Devanagari Script

Rendering Devanagari Characters. Devanagari characters, like characters from many other scripts, can combine or change shape depending on their context. A character's appearance is affected by its ordering with respect to other characters, the font used to render the character, and the application or system environment. These variables can cause the appearance of Devanagari characters to differ from their nominal glyphs (used in the code charts).

Additionally, a few Devanagari characters cause a change in the order of the displayed characters. This reordering is not commonly seen in non-Indic scripts and occurs independently of any bidirectional character reordering that might be required.

Consonant Letters. Each consonant letter represents a single consonantal sound but also has the peculiarity of having an *inherent vowel*, generally the short vowel /a/ in Devanagari and the other Indic scripts. Thus U+0915 DEVANAGARI LETTER KA represents not just /k/ but also /ka/. In the presence of a dependent vowel, however, the inherent vowel associated with a consonant letter is overridden by the dependent vowel.

Consonant letters may also be rendered as *half-forms*, which are presentation forms used to depict the initial consonant in consonant clusters. These half-forms do not have an inherent vowel. Their rendered forms in Devanagari often resemble the full consonant but are missing the vertical stem, which marks a syllabic core. (The stem glyph is graphically and historically related to the sign denoting the inherent /a/ vowel.)

Some Devanagari consonant letters have alternative presentation forms whose choice depends on neighboring consonants. This variability is especially notable for U+0930 DEVANAGARI LETTER RA, which has numerous different forms, both as the initial element and as the final element of a consonant cluster. Only the nominal forms, rather than the contextual alternatives, are depicted in the code chart.

The traditional Sanskrit/Devanagari alphabetic encoding order for consonants follows articulatory phonetic principles, starting with velar consonants and moving forward to bilabial consonants, followed by liquids and then fricatives. ISCII and the Unicode Standard both observe this traditional order.

Independent Vowel Letters. The independent vowels in Devanagari are letters that stand on their own. The writing system treats independent vowels as orthographic CV syllables in which the consonant is null. The independent vowel letters are used to write syllables that start with a vowel.

Dependent Vowel Signs (Matras). The dependent vowels serve as the common manner of writing noninherent vowels and are generally referred to as *vowel signs*, or as *matras* in Sanskrit. The dependent vowels do not stand alone; rather, they are visibly depicted in combination with a base letterform. A single consonant or a consonant cluster may have a dependent vowel applied to it to indicate the vowel quality of the syllable, when it is different from the inherent vowel. Explicit appearance of a dependent vowel in a syllable overrides the inherent vowel of a single consonant letter.

The greatest variation among different Indic scripts is found in the way that the dependent vowels are applied to base letterforms. Devanagari has a collection of nonspacing dependent vowel signs that may appear above or below a consonant letter, as well as spacing dependent vowel signs that may occur to the right or to the left of a consonant letter or consonant cluster. Other Indic scripts generally have one or more of these forms, but what is a nonspacing mark in one script may be a spacing mark in another. Also, some of the Indic scripts have single dependent vowels that are indicated by two or more glyph components—and those glyph components may *surround* a consonant letter both to the left and to the right or may occur both above and below it.

The Devanagari script has only one character denoting a left-side dependent vowel sign: U+093F DEVANAGARI VOWEL SIGN I. Other Indic scripts either have no such vowel signs (Telugu and Kannada) or include as many as three of these signs (Bengali, Tamil, and Malayalam).

Vowel Letters. Vowel letters are encoded atomically in Unicode, even if they can be analyzed visually as consisting of multiple parts. *Table 9-1* shows the letters that can be analyzed, the single code point that should be used to represent them in text, and the sequence of code points resulting from analysis that should not be used.

Table 9-1. Devanagari Vowel Letters

To Represent	Use	Do Not Use
ऄ	0904	<0905, 0946>
आ	0906	<0905, 093E>
ऊ	090A	<0909, 0941>
ऍ	090D	<090F, 0945>
ऎ	090E	<090F, 0946>
ऐ	0910	<090F, 0947>
ऑ	0911	<0905, 0949>
ऒ	0912	<0905, 094A>
ओ	0913	<0905, 094B>
औ	0914	<0905, 094C>

Virama (Halant). Devanagari employs a sign known in Sanskrit as the *virama* or vowel omission sign. In Hindi, it is called *hal* or *halant*, and that term is used in referring to the virama or to a consonant with its vowel suppressed by the virama. The terms are used interchangeably in this section.

The virama sign, U+094D DEVANAGARI SIGN VIRAMA, nominally serves to cancel (or kill) the inherent vowel of the consonant to which it is applied. When a consonant has lost its inherent vowel by the application of virama, it is known as a *dead consonant*; in contrast, a *live consonant* is one that retains its inherent vowel or is written with an explicit dependent vowel sign. In the Unicode Standard, a dead consonant is defined as a sequence consisting of a consonant letter followed by a virama. The default rendering for a dead consonant is to position the virama as a combining mark bound to the consonant letterform.

For example, if C_n denotes the nominal form of consonant C, and C_d denotes the dead consonant form, then a dead consonant is encoded as shown in *Figure 9-1*.

Figure 9-1. Dead Consonants in Devanagari

$$TA_n + VIRAMA_n \rightarrow TA_d$$

त + ◌् → त्

Consonant Conjuncts. The Indic scripts are noted for a large number of consonant conjunct forms that serve as orthographic abbreviations (ligatures) of two or more adjacent letterforms. This abbreviation takes place only in the context of a *consonant cluster.* An orthographic consonant cluster is defined as a sequence of characters that represents one or more dead consonants (denoted C_d) followed by a normal, live consonant letter (denoted C_l).

Under normal circumstances, a consonant cluster is depicted with a conjunct glyph if such a glyph is available in the current font. In the absence of a conjunct glyph, the one or more dead consonants that form part of the cluster are depicted using half-form glyphs. In the absence of half-form glyphs, the dead consonants are depicted using the nominal consonant forms combined with visible virama signs (see *Figure 9-2*).

Figure 9-2. Conjunct Formations in Devanagari

(1) $GA_d + DHA_l \rightarrow GA_h + DHA_n$

ग् + ध → ग्ध

(2) $KA_d + KA_l \rightarrow K.KA_n$

क् + क → क्क

(3) $KA_d + SSA_l \rightarrow K.SSA_n$

क् + ष → क्ष

(4) $RA_d + KA_l \rightarrow KA_l + RA_{sup}$

र् + क → र्क

A number of types of conjunct formations appear in these examples: (1) a half-form of GA in its combination with the full form of DHA; (2) a vertical conjunct K.KA; and (3) a fully ligated conjunct K.SSA, in which the components are no longer distinct. In example (4) in *Figure 9-2*, the dead consonant RA_d is depicted with the nonspacing combining mark RA_{sup} (*repha*).

A well-designed Indic script font may contain hundreds of conjunct glyphs, but they are not encoded as Unicode characters because they are the result of ligation of distinct letters.

Indic script rendering software must be able to map appropriate combinations of characters in context to the appropriate conjunct glyphs in fonts.

Explicit Virama (Halant). Normally a virama character serves to create dead consonants that are, in turn, combined with subsequent consonants to form conjuncts. This behavior usually results in a virama sign not being depicted visually. Occasionally, this default behavior is not desired when a dead consonant should be excluded from conjunct formation, in which case the virama sign is visibly rendered. To accomplish this goal, the Unicode Standard adopts the convention of placing the character U+200C ZERO WIDTH NON-JOINER immediately after the encoded dead consonant that is to be excluded from conjunct formation. In this case, the virama sign is always depicted as appropriate for the consonant to which it is attached.

For example, in *Figure 9-3*, the use of ZERO WIDTH NON-JOINER prevents the default formation of the conjunct form क्ष ($K.SSA_n$).

Figure 9-3. Preventing Conjunct Forms in Devanagari

$$KA_d + ZWNJ + SSA_l \rightarrow KA_d + SSA_n$$

क् + ZWNJ + ष → क्‌ष

Explicit Half-Consonants. When a dead consonant participates in forming a conjunct, the dead consonant form is often absorbed into the conjunct form, such that it is no longer distinctly visible. In other contexts, the dead consonant may remain visible as a *half-consonant form*. In general, a half-consonant form is distinguished from the nominal consonant form by the loss of its inherent vowel stem, a vertical stem appearing to the right side of the consonant form. In other cases, the vertical stem remains but some part of its right-side geometry is missing.

In certain cases, it is desirable to prevent a dead consonant from assuming full conjunct formation yet still not appear with an explicit virama. In these cases, the half-form of the consonant is used. To explicitly encode a half-consonant form, the Unicode Standard adopts the convention of placing the character U+200D ZERO WIDTH JOINER immediately after the encoded dead consonant. The ZERO WIDTH JOINER denotes a nonvisible letter that presents linking or cursive joining behavior on either side (that is, to the previous or following letter). Therefore, in the present context, the ZERO WIDTH JOINER may be considered to present a context to which a preceding dead consonant may join so as to create the half-form of the consonant.

For example, if C_h denotes the half-form glyph of consonant C, then a half-consonant form is represented as shown in *Figure 9-4*.

In the absence of the ZERO WIDTH JOINER, the sequence in *Figure 9-4* would normally produce the full conjunct form क्ष ($K.SSA_n$).

Figure 9-4. Half-Consonants in Devanagari

KA_d + ZWJ + SSA_l → KA_h + SSA_n

क् + ZWJ + ष → क्‍ष

This encoding of half-consonant forms also applies in the absence of a base letterform. That is, this technique may be used to encode independent half-forms, as shown in *Figure 9-5*.

Figure 9-5. Independent Half-Forms in Devanagari

GA_d + ZWJ → GA_h

ग् + ZWJ → ग्‍

Other Indic scripts have similar half-forms for the initial consonants of a conjunct. Some, such as Oriya, also have similar half-forms for the final consonants; those are represented as shown in *Figure 9-6*.

Figure 9-6. Half-Consonants in Oriya

KA_n + ZWJ + VIRAMA + TA_l → KA_l + TA_h

କ୍ + ZWJ + ◌୍ + ତ → କ‍୍ତ

In the absence of the ZERO WIDTH JOINER, the sequence in *Figure 9-6* would normally produce the full conjunct form କ୍ତ ($K.TA_n$).

Consonant Forms. In summary, each consonant may be encoded such that it denotes a live consonant, a dead consonant that may be absorbed into a conjunct, the half-form of a dead consonant, or a dead consonant with an overt halant that does not get absorbed into a conjunct (see *Figure 9-7*).

As the rendering of conjuncts and half-forms depends on the availability of glyphs in the font, the following fallback strategy should be employed:

- If the coded character sequence would normally render with a full conjunct, but such a conjunct is not available, the fallback rendering is to use half-forms. If those are not available, the fallback rendering should use an explicit (visible) virama.

Figure 9-7. Consonant Forms in Devanagari and Oriya

क + ष	→ कष	KA_l + SSA_n
क + ◌् + ष	→ क्ष	$K.SSA_n$
क + ◌् + ZWJ + ष	→ क्‍ष	KA_h + SSA_n
क + ◌् + ZWNJ + ष	→ क्‌ष	KA_d + SSA_n
କ + ◌୍ + ତ	→ କ୍ତ	$K.TA_n$
କ + ZWJ + ◌୍ + ତ	→ କ‍୍ତ	KA_n + TA_h
କ + ◌୍ + ZWNJ + ତ	→ କ୍‌ତ	KA_d + TA_n

- If the coded character sequence would normally render with a half-form (it contains a ZWJ), but half-forms are not available, the fallback rendering should use an explicit (visible) virama.

Rendering Devanagari

Rules for Rendering. This section provides more formal and detailed rules for minimal rendering of Devanagari as part of a plain text sequence. It describes the mapping between Unicode characters and the glyphs in a Devanagari font. It also describes the combining and ordering of those glyphs.

These rules provide minimal requirements for legibly rendering interchanged Devanagari text. As with any script, a more complex procedure can add rendering characteristics, depending on the font and application.

> *In a font that is capable of rendering Devanagari, the number of glyphs is greater than the number of Devanagari characters.*

Notation. In the next set of rules, the following notation applies:

C_n	Nominal glyph form of consonant C as it appears in the code charts.
C_l	A live consonant, depicted identically to C_n.
C_d	Glyph depicting the dead consonant form of consonant C.
C_h	Glyph depicting the half-consonant form of consonant C.
L_n	Nominal glyph form of a conjunct ligature consisting of two or more component consonants. A conjunct ligature composed of two consonants X and Y is also denoted $X.Y_n$.

RA_{sup} A nonspacing combining mark glyph form of U+0930 DEVANAGARI LETTER RA positioned above or attached to the upper part of a base glyph form. This form is also known as *repha*.

RA_{sub} A nonspacing combining mark glyph form of U+0930 DEVANAGARI LETTER RA positioned below or attached to the lower part of a base glyph form.

V_{vs} Glyph depicting the dependent vowel sign form of a vowel V.

$VIRAMA_n$ The nominal glyph form of the nonspacing combining mark depicting U+094D DEVANAGARI SIGN VIRAMA.

A virama character is not always depicted. When it is depicted, it adopts this nonspacing mark form.

Dead Consonant Rule. The following rule logically precedes the application of any other rule to form a dead consonant. Once formed, a dead consonant may be subject to other rules described next.

R1 ***When a consonant C_n precedes a $VIRAMA_n$, it is considered to be a dead consonant C_d. A consonant C_n that does not precede $VIRAMA_n$ is considered to be a live consonant C_l.***

$$TA_n + VIRAMA_n \rightarrow TA_d$$

त + ◌् → त्

Consonant RA Rules. The character U+0930 DEVANAGARI LETTER RA takes one of a number of visual forms depending on its context in a consonant cluster. By default, this letter is depicted with its nominal glyph form (as shown in the code charts). In some contexts, it is depicted using one of two nonspacing glyph forms that combine with a base letterform.

R2 ***If the dead consonant RA_d precedes a consonant, then it is replaced by the superscript nonspacing mark RA_{sup}, which is positioned so that it applies to the logically subsequent element in the memory representation.***

$$RA_d + KA_l \rightarrow KA_l + RA_{sup}$$ *Displayed Output*

र् + क → क + ◌र्‍ → र्क

$$RA^1_d + RA^2_d \rightarrow RA^2_d + RA^1_{sup}$$

र् + र् → र् + ◌र्‍ → र्र्

R3 ***If the superscript mark*** RA_{sup} ***is to be applied to a dead consonant and that dead consonant is combined with another consonant to form a conjunct ligature, then the mark is positioned so that it applies to the conjunct ligature form as a whole.***

$\mathsf{RA}_d + \mathsf{JA}_d + \mathsf{NYA}_l \rightarrow \mathsf{J.NYA}_n + \mathsf{RA}_{sup}$ *Displayed Output*

र् + ज् + ञ → ज्ञ + ◌र्‍ → र्ज्ञ

R4 ***If the superscript mark*** RA_{sup} ***is to be applied to a dead consonant that is subsequently replaced by its half-consonant form, then the mark is positioned so that it applies to the form that serves as the base of the consonant cluster.***

$\mathsf{RA}_d + \mathsf{GA}_d + \mathsf{GHA}_l \rightarrow \mathsf{GA}_h + \mathsf{GHA}_l + \mathsf{RA}_{sup}$ *Displayed Output*

र् + ग् + घ → ग‍ + घ + ◌र्‍ → र्ग्घ

R5 ***In conformance with the ISCII standard, the half-consonant form*** RRA_h ***is represented as eyelash-***RA***. This form of*** RA ***is commonly used in writing Marathi and Newari.***

$\mathsf{RRA}_n + \mathsf{VIRAMA}_n \rightarrow \mathsf{RRA}_h$

ऱ + ◌् → ऱ्‍

R5a ***For compatibility with*** The Unicode Standard, Version 2.0, ***if the dead consonant*** RA_d ***precedes*** ZERO WIDTH JOINER, ***then the half-consonant form*** RA_h, ***depicted as eyelash-***RA***, is used instead of*** RA_{sup}.

$\mathsf{RA}_d + \mathsf{ZWJ} \rightarrow \mathsf{RA}_h$

र् + ZWJ → ऱ्‍

R6 ***Except for the dead consonant*** RA_d***, when a dead consonant*** C_d ***precedes the live consonant*** RA_l***, then*** C_d ***is replaced with its nominal form*** C_n***, and*** RA ***is replaced by the subscript nonspacing mark*** RA_{sub}***, which is positioned so that it applies to*** C_n.

$\mathsf{TTHA}_d + \mathsf{RA}_l \rightarrow \mathsf{TTHA}_n + \mathsf{RA}_{sub}$ *Displayed Output*

ठ् + र → ठ + ◌्र → ठ्र

R7 ***For certain consonants, the mark*** RA_{sub} ***may graphically combine with the consonant to form a conjunct ligature form. These combinations, such as the one shown here, are further addressed by the ligature rules described shortly.***

$$\text{PHA}_d + \text{RA}_l \rightarrow \text{PHA}_n + \text{RA}_{sub} \quad \text{Displayed Output}$$

फ् + र → फ + ◌्र → फ्र

R8 ***If a dead consonant (other than*** RA_d***) precedes*** RA_d***, then the substitution of*** RA ***for*** RA_{sub} ***is performed as described above; however, the*** VIRAMA ***that formed*** RA_d ***remains so as to form a dead consonant conjunct form.***

$$\text{TA}_d + \text{RA}_d \rightarrow \text{TA}_n + \text{RA}_{sub} + \text{VIRAMA}_n \rightarrow \text{T.RA}_d$$

त् + र् → त + ◌्र + ◌् → त्र्

A dead consonant conjunct form that contains an absorbed RA_d ***may subsequently combine to form a multipart conjunct form.***

$$\text{T.RA}_d + \text{YA}_l \rightarrow \text{T.R.YA}_n$$

त्र् + य → त्र्य

Modifier Mark Rules. In addition to vowel signs, three other types of combining marks may be applied to a component of an orthographic syllable or to the syllable as a whole: *nukta*, *bindus*, and *svaras*.

R9 ***The nukta sign, which modifies a consonant form, is placed immediately after the consonant in the memory representation and is attached to that consonant in rendering. If the consonant represents a dead consonant, then*** NUKTA ***should precede*** VIRAMA ***in the memory representation.***

$$\text{KA}_n + \text{NUKTA}_n + \text{VIRAMA}_n \rightarrow \text{QA}_d$$

क + ◌़ + ◌् → क़्

R10 ***Other modifying marks, in particular bindus and svaras, apply to the orthographic syllable as a whole and should follow (in the memory representation) all other characters that constitute the syllable. The bindus should follow any vowel signs, and the svaras should come last. The relative placement of these marks is***

horizontal rather than vertical; the horizontal rendering order may vary according to typographic concerns.

$$\mathsf{KA}_n + \mathsf{AA}_{vs} + \mathsf{CANDRABINDU}_n$$

क + ◌ा + ◌ँ → काँ

Ligature Rules. Subsequent to the application of the rules just described, a set of rules governing ligature formation apply. The precise application of these rules depends on the availability of glyphs in the current font being used to display the text.

R11 ***If a dead consonant immediately precedes another dead consonant or a live consonant, then the first dead consonant may join the subsequent element to form a two-part conjunct ligature form.***

$$\mathsf{JA}_d + \mathsf{NYA}_l \rightarrow \mathsf{J.NYA}_n \qquad \mathsf{TTA}_d + \mathsf{TTHA}_l \rightarrow \mathsf{TT.TTHA}_n$$

ज् + ञ → ज्ञ   ट् + ठ → ट्ठ

R12 ***A conjunct ligature form can itself behave as a dead consonant and enter into further, more complex ligatures.***

$$\mathsf{SA}_d + \mathsf{TA}_d + \mathsf{RA}_n \rightarrow \mathsf{SA}_d + \mathsf{T.RA}_n \rightarrow \mathsf{S.T.RA}_n$$

स् + त् + र → स् + त्र → स्त्र

A conjunct ligature form can also produce a half-form.

$$\mathsf{K.SSA}_d + \mathsf{YA}_l \rightarrow \mathsf{K.SS}_h + \mathsf{YA}_n$$

क्ष् + य → क्ष्य

R13 ***If a nominal consonant or conjunct ligature form precedes*** RA_{sub} ***as a result of the application of rule R6, then the consonant or ligature form may join with*** RA_{sub} ***to form a multipart conjunct ligature (see rule R6 for more information).***

$$\mathsf{KA}_n + \mathsf{RA}_{sub} \rightarrow \mathsf{K.RA}_n \qquad \mathsf{PHA}_n + \mathsf{RA}_{sub} \rightarrow \mathsf{PH.RA}_n$$

क + ◌्र → क्र   फ + ◌्र → फ्र

R14 ***In some cases, other combining marks will combine with a base consonant, either attaching at a nonstandard location or changing shape. In minimal rendering, there are only two cases:*** RA_l ***with*** U_{VS} ***or*** UU_{VS}.

$RA_l + U_{VS} \rightarrow RU_n$ $\qquad$ $RA_l + UU_{VS} \rightarrow RUU_n$

र + ◌ु → रु $\qquad$ र + ◌ू → रू

Memory Representation and Rendering Order. The storage of plain text in Devanagari and all other Indic scripts generally follows phonetic order; that is, a CV syllable with a dependent vowel is always encoded as a consonant letter C followed by a vowel sign V in the memory representation. This order is employed by the ISCII standard and corresponds to both the phonetic order and the keying order of textual data (see *Figure 9-8*).

Figure 9-8. Rendering Order in Devanagari

Character Order				Glyph Order
KA_n	+	I_{VS}	→	$I_{VS} + KA_n$
क	+	ि◌	→	कि

Because Devanagari and other Indic scripts have some dependent vowels that must be depicted to the left side of their consonant letter, the software that renders the Indic scripts must be able to reorder elements in mapping from the logical (character) store to the presentational (glyph) rendering. For example, if C_n denotes the nominal form of consonant C, and V_{VS} denotes a left-side dependent vowel sign form of vowel V, then a reordering of glyphs with respect to encoded characters occurs as just shown.

R15 ***When the dependent vowel*** I_{VS} ***is used to override the inherent vowel of a syllable, it is always written to the extreme left of the orthographic syllable. If the orthographic syllable contains a consonant cluster, then this vowel is always depicted to the left of that cluster.***

$TA_d + RA_l + I_{VS} \rightarrow T.RA_n + I_{VS} \rightarrow I_{VS} + T.RA_d$

त् + र + ि◌ → त्र + ि◌ → त्रि

R16 ***The presence of an explicit virama (either caused by a ZWNJ or by the absence of a conjunct in the font) blocks this reordering, and the dependent vowel*** I_{vs} ***is rendered after the rightmost such explicit virama.***

$$TA_d + \text{ZWNJ} + RA_l + I_{vs} \rightarrow TA_d + I_{vs} + RA_l$$

त् + ZWNJ + र + ि → त्‌रि

Sample Half-Forms. *Table 9-2* shows examples of half-consonant forms that are commonly used with the Devanagari script. These forms are glyphs, not characters. They may be encoded explicitly using ZERO WIDTH JOINER as shown. In normal conjunct formation, they may be used spontaneously to depict a dead consonant in combination with subsequent consonant forms.

Table 9-2. Sample Devanagari Half-Forms

क	+	◌्	+	ZWJ	→	क्‍	न	+	◌्	+	ZWJ	→	न्‍
ख	+	◌्	+	ZWJ	→	ख्‍	प	+	◌्	+	ZWJ	→	प्‍
ग	+	◌्	+	ZWJ	→	ग्‍	फ	+	◌्	+	ZWJ	→	फ्‍
घ	+	◌्	+	ZWJ	→	घ्‍	ब	+	◌्	+	ZWJ	→	ब्‍
च	+	◌्	+	ZWJ	→	च्‍	भ	+	◌्	+	ZWJ	→	भ्‍
ज	+	◌्	+	ZWJ	→	ज्‍	म	+	◌्	+	ZWJ	→	म्‍
झ	+	◌्	+	ZWJ	→	झ्‍	य	+	◌्	+	ZWJ	→	य्‍
ञ	+	◌्	+	ZWJ	→	ञ्‍	ल	+	◌्	+	ZWJ	→	ल्‍
ण	+	◌्	+	ZWJ	→	ण्‍	व	+	◌्	+	ZWJ	→	व्‍
त	+	◌्	+	ZWJ	→	त्‍	श	+	◌्	+	ZWJ	→	श्‍
थ	+	◌्	+	ZWJ	→	थ्‍	ष	+	◌्	+	ZWJ	→	ष्‍
ध	+	◌्	+	ZWJ	→	ध्‍	स	+	◌्	+	ZWJ	→	स्‍

Sample Ligatures. *Table 9-3* shows examples of conjunct ligature forms that are commonly used with the Devanagari script. These forms are glyphs, not characters. Not every writing system that employs this script uses all of these forms; in particular, many of these forms are used only in writing Sanskrit texts. Furthermore, individual fonts may provide fewer or more ligature forms than are depicted here.

Table 9-3. Sample Devanagari Ligatures

क +	◌्	+	क →	क्क	ट +	◌्	+	ठ →	ट्ठ
क +	◌्	+	त →	क्त	ठ +	◌्	+	ठ →	ठ्ठ
क +	◌्	+	र →	क्र	ड +	◌्	+	ग →	ड्ग
क +	◌्	+	ष →	क्ष	ड +	◌्	+	ड →	ड्ड
ङ +	◌्	+	क →	ङ्क	ड +	◌्	+	ढ →	ड्ढ
ङ +	◌्	+	ख →	ङ्ख	त +	◌्	+	त →	त्त
ङ +	◌्	+	ग →	ङ्ग	त +	◌्	+	र →	त्र
ङ +	◌्	+	घ →	ङ्घ	न +	◌्	+	न →	न्न
ञ +	◌्	+	ज →	ञ्ज	फ +	◌्	+	र →	फ्र
ज +	◌्	+	ञ →	ज्ञ	श +	◌्	+	र →	श्र
द +	◌्	+	घ →	द्घ	ह +	◌्	+	म →	ह्म
द +	◌्	+	द →	द्द	ह +	◌्	+	य →	ह्य
द +	◌्	+	ध →	द्ध	ह +	◌्	+	ल →	ह्ल
द +	◌्	+	ब →	द्ब	ह +	◌्	+	व →	ह्व
द +	◌्	+	भ →	द्भ	ह +	◌ृ		→	हृ
द +	◌्	+	म →	द्म	र +	◌ु		→	रु
द +	◌्	+	य →	द्य	र +	◌ू		→	रू
द +	◌्	+	व →	द्व	र +	◌ृ		→	रृ
ट +	◌्	+	ट →	ट्ट	स +	◌्	+	त्र →	स्त्र

Sample Half-Ligature Forms. In addition to half-form glyphs of individual consonants, half-forms are used to depict conjunct ligature forms. A sample of such forms is shown in *Table 9-4*. These forms are glyphs, not characters. They may be encoded explicitly using ZERO WIDTH JOINER as shown. In normal conjunct formation, they may be used spontaneously to depict a conjunct ligature in combination with subsequent consonant forms.

Table 9-4. Sample Devanagari Half-Ligature Forms

क	+	्	+	ष	+	्	+	ZWJ	→	क्ष्‍
ज	+	्	+	ञ	+	्	+	ZWJ	→	ज्ञ्‍
त	+	्	+	त	+	्	+	ZWJ	→	त्त्‍
त	+	्	+	र	+	्	+	ZWJ	→	त्र्‍
श	+	्	+	र	+	्	+	ZWJ	→	श्र्‍

Language-Specific Allographs. In Marathi and some South Indian orthographies, variant glyphs are preferred for U+0932 DEVANAGARI LETTER LA and U+0936 DEVANAGARI LETTER SHA, as shown in *Figure 9-9*. Marathi also makes use of the "eyelash" form of the letter RA, as discussed in rule R5.

Figure 9-9. Marathi Allographs

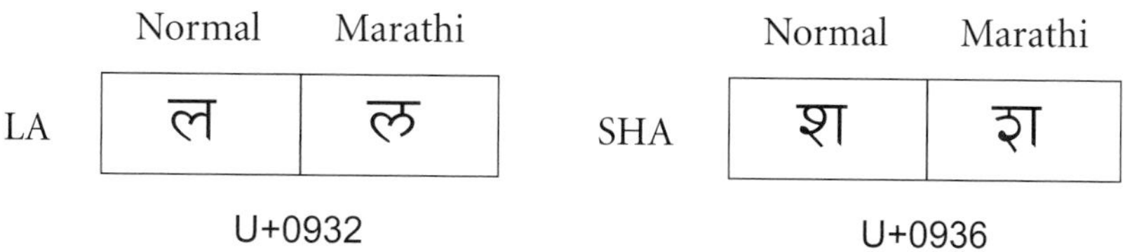

Combining Marks. Devanagari and other Indic scripts have a number of combining marks that could be considered diacritic. One class of these marks, known as bindus, is represented by U+0901 DEVANAGARI SIGN CANDRABINDU and U+0902 DEVANAGARI SIGN ANUSVARA. These marks indicate nasalization or final nasal closure of a syllable. U+093C DEVANAGARI SIGN NUKTA is a true diacritic. It is used to extend the basic set of consonant letters by modifying them (with a subscript dot in Devanagari) to create new letters. U+0951..U+0954 are a set of combining marks used in transcription of Sanskrit texts.

Digits. Each Indic script has a distinct set of digits appropriate to that script. These digits may or may not be used in ordinary text in that script. European digits have displaced the Indic script forms in modern usage in many of the scripts. Some Indic scripts—notably Tamil—lack a distinct digit for zero.

Punctuation and Symbols. U+0964 । DEVANAGARI DANDA is similar to a full stop. U+0965 ॥ DEVANAGARI DOUBLE DANDA marks the end of a verse in traditional texts. The term *danda* is from Sanskrit, and the punctuation mark is generally referred to as a *viram* instead in Hindi. Although the *danda* and *double danda* are encoded in the Devanagari block, the intent is that they be used as common punctuation for all the major scripts of India covered by this chapter. *Danda* and *double danda* punctuation marks are not separately encoded for

Bengali, Gujarati, and so on. However, analogous punctuation marks for other Brahmi-derived scripts *are* separately encoded, particularly for scripts used primarily outside of India.

Many modern languages written in the Devanagari script intersperse punctuation derived from the Latin script. Thus U+002C COMMA and U+002E FULL STOP are freely used in writing Hindi, and the *danda* is usually restricted to more traditional texts. However, the *danda* may be preserved when such traditional texts are transliterated into the Latin script.

U+0970 ° DEVANAGARI ABBREVIATION SIGN appears after letters or combinations of letters and marks the sequence as an abbreviation.

Encoding Structure. The Unicode Standard organizes the nine principal Indic scripts in blocks of 128 encoding points each. The first six columns in each script are isomorphic with the ISCII-1988 encoding, except that the last 11 positions (U+0955..U+095F in Devanagari, for example), which are unassigned or undefined in ISCII-1988, are used in the Unicode encoding.

The seventh column in each of these scripts, along with the last 11 positions in the sixth column, represent additional character assignments in the Unicode Standard that are matched across all nine scripts. For example, positions U+xx66..U+xx6F and U+xxE6.. U+xxEF code the Indic script digits for each script.

The eighth column for each script is reserved for script-specific additions that do not correspond from one Indic script to the next.

Other Languages. The characters U+097B DEVANAGARI LETTER GGA, U+097C DEVANAGARI LETTER JJA, U+097E DEVANAGARI LETTER DDDA, and U+097F DEVANAGARI LETTER BBA are used to write Sindhi implosive consonants. Previous versions of the Unicode Standard recommended representing those characters as a combination of the usual consonants with *nukta* and *anudatta*, but those combinations are no longer recommended. Konkani makes use of additional sounds that can be represented with combinations such as U+091A DEVANAGARI LETTER CA plus U+093C DEVANAGARI SIGN NUKTA and U+091F DEVANAGARI LETTER TTA plus U+0949 DEVANAGARI VOWEL SIGN CANDRA O.

9.2 Bengali

Bengali: U+0980–U+09FF

The Bengali script is a North Indian script closely related to Devanagari. It is used to write the Bengali language primarily in the West Bengal state and in the nation of Bangladesh. It is also used to write Assamese in Assam and a number of other minority languages, such as Bishnupriya Manipuri, Daphla, Garo, Hallam, Khasi, Mizo, Munda, Naga, Rian, and Santali, in northeastern India.

Virama (Hasant). The Bengali script uses the Unicode virama model to form conjunct consonants. In Bengali, the virama is known as *hasant*.

Vowel Letters. Vowel letters are encoded atomically in Unicode, even if they can be analyzed visually as consisting of multiple parts. *Table 9-5* shows the letters that can be analyzed, the single code point that should be used to represent them in text, and the sequence of code points resulting from analysis that should not be used.

Table 9-5. Bengali Vowel Letters

To Represent	Use	Do Not Use
আ	0986	<0985, 09BE>

Two-Part Vowel Signs. The Bengali script, along with a number of other Indic scripts, makes use of two-part vowel signs. In these vowels one-half of the vowel is placed on each side of a consonant letter or cluster—for example, U+09CB BENGALI VOWEL SIGN O and U+09CC BENGALI VOWEL SIGN AU. The vowel signs are coded in each case in the position in the charts isomorphic with the corresponding vowel in Devanagari. Hence U+09CC BENGALI VOWEL SIGN AU is isomorphic with U+094C DEVANAGARI VOWEL SIGN AU. To provide compatibility with existing implementations of the scripts that use two-part vowel signs, the Unicode Standard explicitly encodes the right half of these vowel signs. For example, U+09D7 BENGALI AU LENGTH MARK represents the right-half glyph component of U+09CC BENGALI VOWEL SIGN AU.

Special Characters. U+09F2..U+09F9 are a series of Bengali additions for writing currency and fractions.

Rendering Behavior. Like other Brahmic scripts in the Unicode Standard, Bengali uses the *hasant* to form conjunct characters. For example, U+0995 ক BENGALI LETTER KA + U+09CD ◌্ BENGALI SIGN VIRAMA + U+09B7 ষ BENGALI LETTER SSA yields the conjunct ক্ষ KSSA, which is pronounced *khya* in Assamese. For general principles regarding the rendering of the Bengali script, see the rules for rendering in *Section 9.1, Devanagari.*

Consonant-Vowel Ligatures. Some Bengali consonant plus vowel combinations have two distinct visual presentations. The first visual presentation is a traditional ligated form, in which the vowel combines with the consonant in a novel way. In the second presentation, the vowel is joined to the consonant but retains its nominal form, and the combination is not considered a ligature. These consonant-vowel combinations are illustrated in *Table 9-6.*

The ligature forms of these consonant-vowel combinations are traditional. They are used in handwriting and some printing. The "non-ligated" forms are more common; they are used in newspapers and are associated with modern typefaces. However, the traditional ligatures are preferred in some contexts.

No semantic distinctions are made in Bengali text on the basis of the two different presentations of these consonant-vowel combinations. However, some users consider it important that implementations support both forms and that the distinction be representable in plain text. This may be accomplished by using U+200D ZERO WIDTH JOINER and U+200C ZERO WIDTH NON-JOINER to influence ligature glyph selection. (See "Cursive Connection and Ligatures" in *Section 16.2, Layout Controls.*)

Table 9-6. Bengali Consonant-Vowel Combinations

	Code Points	Ligated	Non-ligated
gu	<0997, 09C1>	গু	গু
ru	<09B0, 09C1>	রু	রু
rū	<09B0, 09C2>	রূ	রূ
śu	<09B6, 09C1>	শু	শু
hu	<09B9, 09C1>	হু	হু
hṛ	<09B9, 09C3>	হৃ	হৃ

A given font implementation can choose whether to treat the ligature forms of the consonant-vowel combinations as the defaults for rendering. If the non-ligated form is the default, then ZWJ can be inserted to request a ligature, as shown in *Figure 9-10*.

Figure 9-10. Requesting Bengali Consonant-Vowel Ligature

গ + ◌ু → গু
0997 09C1

গ + ZWJ + ◌ু → গু
0997 200D 09C1

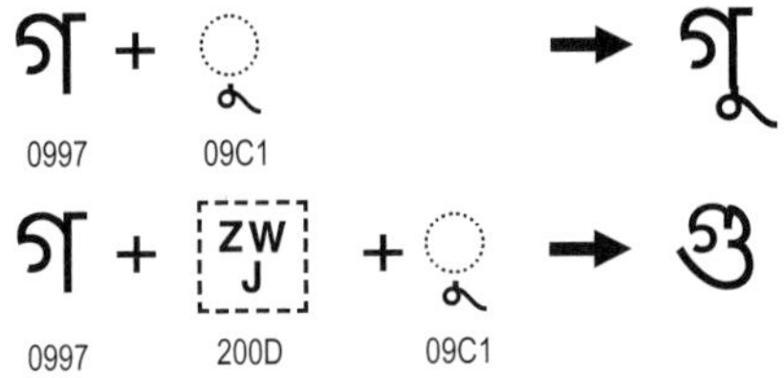

If the ligated form is the default for a given font implementation, then ZWNJ can be inserted to block a ligature, as shown in *Figure 9-11*.

Figure 9-11. Blocking Bengali Consonant-Vowel Ligature

গ + ◌ু → গু
0997 09C1

গ + ZWNJ + ◌ু → গু
0997 200C 09C1

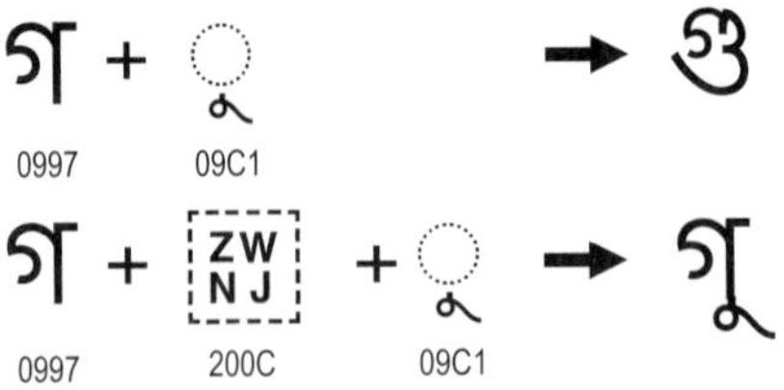

Khanda Ta. In Bengali, a dead consonant *ta* makes use of a special form, U+09CE BENGALI LETTER KHANDA TA. This form is used in all contexts except where it is immediately followed by one of the consonants: *ta*, *tha*, *na*, *ba*, *ma*, *ya*, or *ra*.

Khanda ta cannot bear a vowel matra or combine with a following consonant to form a conjunct *aksara*. It can form a conjunct *aksara* only with a preceding dead consonant *ra*, with the latter being displayed with a *repha* glyph placed on the *khanda ta*.

Versions of the Unicode Standard prior to Version 4.1 recommended that *khanda ta* be represented as the sequence <U+09A4 BENGALI LETTER TA, U+09CD BENGALI SIGN VIRAMA, U+200D ZERO WIDTH JOINER> in all circumstances. U+09CE BENGALI LETTER KHANDA TA should instead be used explicitly in newly generated text, but users are cautioned that instances of the older representation may exist.

The Bengali syllable *tta* illustrates the usage of *khanda ta* when followed by *ta*. The syllable *tta* is normally represented with the sequence <U+09A4 *ta*, U+09CD *hasant*, U+09A4 *ta*>. That sequence will normally be displayed using a single glyph *tta* ligature, as shown in the first example in *Figure 9-12*.

Figure 9-12. Bengali Syllable *tta*

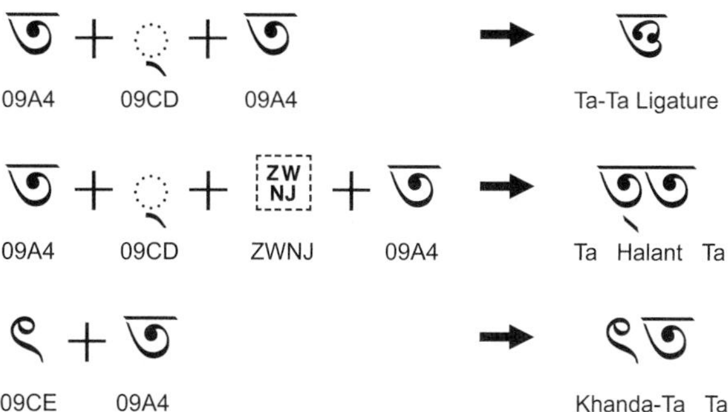

It is also possible for the sequence <*ta*, *hasant*, *ta*> to be displayed with a full *ta* glyph combined with a *hasant* glyph, followed by another full *ta* glyph ত্‌ত. The choice of form actually displayed depends on the display engine, based on the availability of glyphs in the font.

The Unicode Standard also provides an explicit way to show the *hasant* glyph. To do so, a ZERO WIDTH NON-JOINER is inserted after the *hasant*. That sequence is always displayed with the explicit *hasant*, as shown in the second example in *Figure 9-12*.

When the syllable *tta* is written with a *khanda ta*, however, the character U+09CE BENGALI LETTER KHANDA TA is used and no *hasant* is required, as *khanda ta* is already a dead consonant. The rendering of *khanda ta* is illustrated in the third example in *Figure 9-12*.

Ya-phalaa. *Ya-phalaa* (pronounced *jo-phola* in Bengali) is a presentation form of U+09AF য BENGALI LETTER YA. Represented by the sequence <U+09CD ◌্ BENGALI SIGN VIRAMA, U+09AF য BENGALI LETTER YA>, *ya-phalaa* has a special form ্য. When combined with U+09BE ◌া BENGALI VOWEL SIGN AA, it is used for transcribing [æ] as in the "a" in the English word "bat." *Ya-phalaa* can be applied to initial vowels as well:

অ্যা = <0985, 09CD, 09AF, 09BE> (*a- hasant ya -aa*)

এ্যা = <098F, 09CD, 09AF, 09BE> (*e- hasant ya -aa*)

If a candrabindu or other combining mark needs to be added in the sequence, it comes at the end of the sequence. For example:

অ্যাঁ = <0985, 09CD, 09AF, 09BE, 0981> (*a- hasant ya -aa candrabindu*)

Further examples:

অ + ◌্ + য + ◌া = অ্যা

এ + ◌্ + য + ◌া = এ্যা

ত + ◌্ + য + ◌া = ত্যা

Interaction of Repha aand Ya-phalaa. The formation of the *repha* form is defined in *Section 9.1, Devanagari*, "Rules for Rendering," R2. Basically, the *repha* is formed when a *ra* that has the inherent vowel killed by the *hasant* begins a syllable. This scenario is shown in the following example:

র + ◌্ + ম → র্ম as in কর্ম (karma)

The *ya-phalaa* is a post-base form of *ya* and is formed when the *ya* is the final consonant of a syllable cluster. In this case, the previous consonant retains its base shape and the *hasant* is combined with the following *ya*. This scenario is shown in the following example:

ক + ◌্ + য → ক্য as in বাক্য (bakyô)

An ambiguous situation is encountered when the combination of *ra* + *hasant* + *ya* is encountered:

র + ◌্ + য → র্য or র‍্য

To resolve the ambiguity with this combination, the Unicode Standard adopts the convention of placing the character U+200D ZERO WIDTH JOINER immediately after the *ra* to obtain the *ya-phalaa*. The *repha* form is rendered when no ZWJ is present, as shown in the following example:

র + ◌্ + য → র্য

09B0 09CD 09AF

র + ZWJ + ◌্ + য → র‍্য

09B0 200D 09CD 09AF

When the first character of the cluster is not a *ra*, the *ya-phalaa* is the normal rendering of a *ya*, and a ZWJ is not necessary but can be present. Such a convention would make it possible, for example, for input methods to consistently associate *ya-phalaa* with the sequence <ZWJ, *hasant*, *ya*>.

Punctuation. Danda and double danda marks as well as some other unified punctuation used with Bengali are found in the Devanagari block; see *Section 9.1, Devanagari.*

9.3 Gurmukhi

Gurmukhi: U+0A00–U+0A7F

The Gurmukhi script is a North Indian script used to write the Punjabi (or Panjabi) language of the Punjab state of India. Gurmukhi, which literally means "proceeding from the mouth of the Guru," is attributed to Angad, the second Sikh Guru (1504–1552 CE). It is derived from an older script called Landa and is closely related to Devanagari structurally. The script is closely associated with Sikhs and Sikhism, but it is used on an everyday basis in East Punjab. (West Punjab, now in Pakistan, uses the Arabic script.)

Encoding Principles. The Gurmukhi block is based on ISCII-1988, which makes it parallel to Devanagari. Gurmukhi, however, has a number of peculiarities described here.

The additional consonants (called *pairin bindi*; literally, "with a dot in the foot," in Punjabi) are primarily used to differentiate Urdu or Persian loan words. They include U+0A36 GURMUKHI LETTER SHA and U+0A33 GURMUKHI LETTER LLA, but do not include U+0A5C GURMUKHI LETTER RRA, which is genuinely Punjabi. For unification with the other scripts, ISCII-1991 considers *rra* to be equivalent to *dda+nukta*, but this decomposition is not considered in Unicode. At the same time, ISCII-1991 does not consider U+0A36 to be equivalent to <0A38, 0A3C>, or U+0A33 to be equivalent to <0A32, 0A3C>.

Two different marks can be associated with U+0902 DEVANAGARI SIGN ANUSVARA: U+0A02 GURMUKHI SIGN BINDI and U+0A70 GURMUKHI TIPPI. Present practice is to use *bindi* only with the dependent and independent forms of the vowels *aa*, *ii*, *ee*, *ai*, *oo*, and *au*, and with the independent vowels *u* and *uu*; *tippi* is used in the other contexts. Older texts may depart from this requirement. ISCII-1991 uses only one encoding point for both marks.

U+0A71 GURMUKHI ADDAK is a special sign to indicate that the following consonant is geminate. ISCII-1991 does not have a specific code point for addak and encodes it as a cluster. For example, the word ਪੱਗ *pagg*, "turban," can be represented with the sequence <0A2A, 0A71, 0A17> (or <pa, addak, ga>) in Unicode, while in ISCII-1991 it would be <pa, ga, virama, ga>.

Punjabi does not have complex combinations of consonant sounds. Furthermore, the orthography is not strictly phonetic, and sometimes the inherent /a/ sound is not pronounced. For example, the word ਗੁਰਮੁਖੀ *gurmukhī* is represented with the sequence <0A17, 0A41, 0A30, 0A2E, 0A41, 0A16, 0A40>, which could be transliterated as *gura-*

mukhii; this lack of pronunciation is systematic at the end of a word. As a result, the virama sign is seldom used with the Gurmukhi script.

In older texts, such as the *Sri Guru Granth Sahib* (the Sikh holy book), one can find consonants modified by both U+0A4B gurmukhi vowel sign oo, rendered above the consonant, and U+0A41 gurmukhi vowel sign u, rendered below the consonant. Because of the combining classes of those characters, the sequences <C, 0A41, 0A4B> and <C, 0A4B, 0A41> are not canonically equivalent. To avoid ambiguity in representation, the second sequence, with U+0A4B before U+0A41, should be used in such cases. When a consonant is not present, the same sequence of vowels may be represented by attaching the dependent vowel sign *u* to the independent vowel letter U+0A13 gurmukhi letter oo: <0A13, 0A41>. More generally, when a consonant or independent vowel is modified by two vowel signs with one above and one below, the vowel sign above should occur first.

Vowel Letters. Vowel letters are encoded atomically in Unicode, even if they can be analyzed visually as consisting of multiple parts. *Table 9-7* shows the letters that can be analyzed, the single code point that should be used to represent them in text, and the sequence of code points resulting from analysis that should not be used.

Table 9-7. Gurmukhi Vowel Letters

To Represent	Use	Do Not Use
ਆ	0A06	<0A05, 0A3E>
ਇ	0A07	<0A72, 0A3F>
ਈ	0A08	<0A72, 0A40>
ਉ	0A09	<0A73, 0A41>
ਊ	0A0A	<0A73, 0A42>
ਏ	0A0F	<0A72, 0A47>
ਐ	0A10	<0A05, 0A48>
ਓ	0A13	<0A73, 0A4B>
ਔ	0A14	<0A05, 0A4C>

Ordering. U+0A73 gurmukhi ura and U+0A72 gurmukhi iri are the first and third "letters" of the Gurmukhi syllabary, respectively. They are used as bases or bearers for some of the independent vowels, while U+0A05 gurmukhi letter a is both the second "letter" and the base for the remaining independent vowels. As a result, the collation order for Gurmukhi is based on a seven-by-five grid:

- The first row is U+0A73 *ura*, U+0A05 *a*, U+0A72 *iri*, U+0A38 *sa*, U+0A39 *ha*.
- This row is followed by five main rows of consonants, grouped according to the point of articulation, as is traditional in all South and Southeast Asian scripts.

- The semiconsonants follow in the seventh row: U+0A2F *ya*, U+0A30 *ra*, U+0A32 *la*, U+0A35 *va*, U+0A5C *rra*.
- The letters with *nukta*, added later, are presented in a subsequent eighth row if needed.

Rendering Behavior. For general principles regarding the rendering of the Gurmukhi script, see the rules for rendering in *Section 9.1, Devanagari*. In many aspects, Gurmukhi is simpler than Devanagari. There are no half-consonants, no half-forms, no *repha* (upper form of U+0930 DEVANAGARI LETTER RA), and no real ligatures. Rules R2–R5, R11, and R14 do not apply. Conversely, the behavior for subscript RA (rules R6–R8 and R13) applies to U+0A39 GURMUKHI LETTER HA and U+0A35 GURMUKHI LETTER VA, which also have subjoined forms, called *pairin* in Punjabi. The subjoined form for RA is like a knot, while the subjoined HA and VA are written the same as the base form, without the top bar, but are reduced in size. As described in rule R13, they attach at the bottom of the base consonant, and will "push" down any attached vowel sign for U or UU. When U+0A2F GURMUKHI LETTER YA follows a dead consonant, it assumes a different form called *addha* in Punjabi, without the leftmost part, and the dead consonant returns to the nominal form, as shown in *Table 9-8*.

Table 9-8. Gurmukhi Conjuncts

ਮ	+	◌੍	+	ਹ	→	ਮ੍ਹ	(*mha*)	pairin ha
ਪ	+	◌੍	+	ਰ	→	ਪ੍ਰ	(*pra*)	pairin ra
ਦ	+	◌੍	+	ਵ	→	ਦ੍ਵ	(*dva*)	pairin va
ਦ	+	◌੍	+	ਯ	→	ਦ੍ਯ	(*dya*)	addha ya

Other letters behaved similarly in old inscriptions, as shown in *Table 9-9*.

Table 9-9. Additional Pairin and Addha Forms in Gurmukhi

ਸ	+	◌੍	+	ਗ	→	ਸ੍ਗ	(*sga*)	pairin ga
ਸ	+	◌੍	+	ਚ	→	ਸ੍ਚ	(*sca*)	pairin ca
ਸ	+	◌੍	+	ਟ	→	ਸ੍ਟ	(*stta*)	pairin tta
ਸ	+	◌੍	+	ਠ	→	ਸ੍ਠ	(*sttha*)	pairin ttha
ਸ	+	◌੍	+	ਤ	→	ਸ੍ਤ	(*sta*)	pairin ta
ਸ	+	◌੍	+	ਦ	→	ਸ੍ਦ	(*sda*)	pairin da
ਸ	+	◌੍	+	ਨ	→	ਸ੍ਨ	(*sna*)	pairin na
ਸ	+	◌੍	+	ਥ	→	ਸ੍ਥ	(*stha*)	pairin tha

Table 9-9. Additional Pairin and Addha Forms in Gurmukhi (Continued)

ਸ	+	◌੍	+	ਯ	→	ਸ੍ਯ	(*sya*)	pairin ya
ਸ	+	◌੍	+	ਥ	→	ਸ੍ਥ	(*stha*)	addha tha
ਸ	+	◌੍	+	ਮ	→	ਸ੍ਮ	(*sma*)	addha ma

Older texts also exhibit another feature that is not found in modern Gurmukhi—namely, the use of a half- or reduced form for the first consonant of a cluster, whereas the modern practice is to represent the second consonant in a half- or reduced form. Joiners can be used to request this older rendering, as shown in *Table 9-10*. The reduced form of an initial U+0A30 GURMUKHI LETTER RA is similar to the Devanagari superscript RA (*repha*), but this usage is rare, even in older texts.

Table 9-10. Use of Joiners in Gurmukhi

ਸ	+	◌੍	+	ਵ			→	ਸ੍ਵ	(*sva*)
ਰ	+	◌੍	+	ਵ			→	ਰ੍ਵ	(*rva*)
ਸ	+	◌੍	+	ZWJ	+	ਵ	→	ਸ੍‍ਵ	(*sva*)
ਰ	+	◌੍	+	ZWJ	+	ਵ	→	ਰ੍‍ਵ	(*rva*)
ਸ	+	◌੍	+	ZWNJ	+	ਵ	→	ਸ੍‌ਵ	(*sva*)
ਰ	+	◌੍	+	ZWNJ	+	ਵ	→	ਰ੍‌ਵ	(*rva*)

A rendering engine for Gurmukhi should make accommodations for the correct positioning of the combining marks (see *Section 5.13, Rendering Nonspacing Marks*, and particularly *Figure 5-12*). This is important, for example, in the correct centering of the marks above and below U+0A28 GURMUKHI LETTER NA and U+0A20 GURMUKHI LETTER TTHA, which are laterally symmetrical. It is also important to avoid collisions between the various upper marks, vowel signs, *bindi*, and/or *addak*.

Other Symbols. The religious symbol *khanda* sometimes used in Gurmukhi texts is encoded at U+262C ADI SHAKTI in the Miscellaneous Symbols block. U+0A74 GURMUKHI EK ONKAR, which is also a religious symbol, can have different presentation forms, which do not change its meaning. The font used in the code charts shows a highly stylized form; simpler forms look like the digit one, followed by a sign based on *ura*, along with a long upper tail.

Punctuation. Danda and double danda marks as well as some other unified punctuation used with Gurmukhi are found in the Devanagari block. See *Section 9.1, Devanagari*, for more information. Punjabi also uses Latin punctuation.

9.4 Gujarati

Gujarati: U+0A80–U+0AFF

The Gujarati script is a North Indian script closely related to Devanagari. It is most obviously distinguished from Devanagari by not having a horizontal bar for its letterforms, a characteristic of the older Kaithi script to which Gujarati is related. The Gujarati script is used to write the Gujarati language of the Gujarat state in India.

Vowel Letters. Vowel letters are encoded atomically in Unicode, even if they can be analyzed visually as consisting of multiple parts. *Table 9-11* shows the letters that can be analyzed, the single code point that should be used to represent them in text, and the sequence of code points resulting from analysis that should not be used.

Table 9-11. Gujarati Vowel Letters

To Represent	Use	Do Not Use
આ	0A86	<0A85, 0ABE>
ઍ	0A8D	<0A85, 0AC5>
એ	0A8F	<0A85, 0AC7>
ઐ	0A90	<0A85, 0AC8>
ઑ	0A91	<0A85, 0AC9>
ઓ	0A93	<0A85, 0ACB>
ઔ	0A94	<0A85, 0ACC>

Rendering Behavior. For rendering of the Gujarati script, see the rules for rendering in *Section 9.1, Devanagari*. Like other Brahmic scripts in the Unicode Standard, Gujarati uses the virama to form conjunct characters. The virama is informally called *khoḍo*, which means "lame" in Gujarati. Many conjunct characters, as in Devanagari, lose the vertical stroke; there are also vertical conjuncts. U+0AB0 GUJARATI LETTER RA takes special forms when it combines with other consonants, as shown in *Table 9-12*.

Table 9-12. Gujarati Conjuncts

ક	+	◌્	+	ષ	→	ક્ષ	(*kṣa*)
જ	+	◌્	+	ઞ	→	જ્ઞ	(*jña*)
ત	+	◌્	+	ય	→	ત્ય	(*tya*)

Table 9-12. Gujarati Conjuncts (Continued)

ટ	+	◌્	+	ટ	→	ટ્ટ	(*ṭṭa*)
ર	+	◌્	+	ક	→	ર્ક	(*rka*)
ક	+	◌્	+	ર	→	ક્ર	(*kra*)

Punctuation. Words in Gujarati are separated by spaces. Danda and double danda marks as well as some other unified punctuation used with Gujarati are found in the Devanagari block; see *Section 9.1, Devanagari.*

9.5 Oriya

Oriya: U+0B00–U+0B7F

The Oriya script is a North Indian script that is structurally similar to Devanagari, but with semicircular lines at the top of most letters instead of the straight horizontal bars of Devanagari. The actual shapes of the letters, particularly for vowel signs, show similarities to Tamil. The Oriya script is used to write the Oriya language of the Orissa state in India as well as minority languages such as Khondi and Santali.

Special Characters. U+0B57 ORIYA AU LENGTH MARK is provided as an encoding for the right side of the surroundrant vowel U+0B4C ORIYA VOWEL SIGN AU.

Vowel Letters. Vowel letters are encoded atomically in Unicode, even if they can be analyzed visually as consisting of multiple parts. *Table 9-13* shows the letters that can be analyzed, the single code point that should be used to represent them in text, and the sequence of code points resulting from analysis that should not be used.

Table 9-13. Oriya Vowel Letters

To Represent	Use	Do Not Use
ଆ	0B06	<0B05, 0B3E>
ଐ	0B10	<0B0F, 0B57>
ଔ	0B14	<0B13, 0B57>

Rendering Behavior. For rendering of the Oriya script, see the rules for rendering in *Section 9.1, Devanagari.* Like other Brahmic scripts in the Unicode Standard, Oriya uses the virama to suppress the inherent vowel. Oriya has a visible virama, often being a lengthening of a part of the base consonant:

କ + ◌୍ → କ୍ (*k*)

The virama is also used to form conjunct consonants, as shown in *Table 9-14*.

Table 9-14. Oriya Conjuncts

କ	+	◌୍	+	ଷ	→	କ୍ଷ	(*kṣa*)
କ	+	◌୍	+	ତ	→	କ୍ତ	(*kta*)
ତ	+	◌୍	+	କ	→	ତ୍କ	(*tka*)
ତ	+	◌୍	+	ଯ	→	ତ୍ଯ	(*tya*)

Consonant Forms. In the initial position in a cluster, RA is reduced and placed above the following consonant, while it is also reduced in the second position:

ର + ◌୍ + ପ → ର୍ପ (*rpa*)

ପ + ◌୍ + ର → ପ୍ର (*pra*)

Nasal and stop clusters may be written with conjuncts, or the anusvara may be used:

ଅ + ଙ + ◌୍ + କ → ଅଙ୍କ (*aṅka*)

ଅ + ◌ଂ + କ → ଅଂକ (*aṁka*)

Vowels. As with other scripts, some dependent vowels are rendered in front of their consonant, some appear after it, and some are placed above or below it. Some are rendered with parts both in front of and after their consonant. A few of the dependent vowels fuse with their consonants. See *Table 9-15*.

Table 9-15. Oriya Vowel Placement

କ	+	◌ା	→	କା	(*kā*)
କ	+	◌ି	→	କି	(*ki*)
କ	+	◌ୀ	→	କୀ	(*kī*)
କ	+	◌ୁ	→	କୁ	(*ku*)
କ	+	◌ୂ	→	କୂ	(*kū*)
କ	+	◌ୃ	→	କୃ	(*kṛ*)
କ	+	◌େ	→	କେ	(*ke*)
କ	+	◌ୈ	→	କୈ	(*kai*)
କ	+	◌ୋ	→	କୋ	(*ko*)
କ	+	◌ୌ	→	କୌ	(*kau*)

U+0B01 ORIYA SIGN CANDRABINDU is used for nasal vowels:

କ + ◌ଁ → କଁ (*kaṁ*)

Oriya VA and WA. These two letters are extensions to the basic Oriya alphabet. Because Sanskrit वन *vana* becomes Oriya ବନ *bana* in orthography and pronunciation, an extended letter U+0B35 ଵ ORIYA LETTER VA was devised by dotting U+0B2C ବ ORIYA LETTER BA for use in academic and technical text. For example, basic Oriya script cannot distinguish Sanskrit बव *bava* from बब *baba* or वव *vava*, but this distinction can be made with the modified version of *ba*. In some older sources, the glyph ଵ is sometimes found for *va*; in others, ଵ and ଵ have been shown, which in a more modern type style would be ଵ. The letter *va* is not in common use today.

In a consonant conjunct, subjoined U+0B2C ବ ORIYA LETTER BA is usually—but not always—pronounced [wa]:

U+0B15 କ *ka* + U+0B4D ◌୍ *virama* + U+0B2C ବ *ba* → କ୍ବ [kwa]

U+0B2E ମ *ma* + U+0B4D ◌୍ *virama* + U+0B2C ବ *ba* → ମ୍ବ [mba]

The extended Oriya letter U+0B71 ୱ ORIYA LETTER WA is sometimes used in Perso-Arabic or English loan words for [w]. It appears to have originally been devised as a ligature of ଓ *o* and ବ *ba*, but because ligatures of independent vowels and consonants are not normally used in Oriya, this letter has been encoded as a single character that does not have a decomposition. It is used initially in words or orthographic syllables to represent the foreign consonant; as a native semivowel, *virama* + *ba* is used because that is historically accurate. Glyph variants of *wa* are ୱ, ୱ, and ୱ.

Punctuation and Symbols. Danda and double danda marks as well as some other unified punctuation used with Oriya are found in the Devanagari block; see *Section 9.1, Devanagari*. The mark U+0B70 ORIYA ISSHAR is placed before names of persons who are deceased.

9.6 Tamil

Tamil: U+0B80–U+0BFF

The Tamil script is descended from the South Indian branch of Brahmi. It is used to write the Tamil language of the Tamil Nadu state in India as well as minority languages such as the Dravidian language Badaga and the Indo-European language Saurashtra. Tamil is also used in Sri Lanka, Singapore, and parts of Malaysia.

The Tamil script has fewer consonants than the other Indic scripts. When representing the "missing" consonants in transcriptions of languages such as Sanskrit or Saurashtra, superscript European digits are often used, so ப^2 = *pha*, ப^3 = *ba*, and ப^4 = *bha*. The characters U+00B2, U+00B3, and U+2074 can be used to preserve this distinction in plain text. The Tamil script also avoids the use conjunct consonant forms, although a few conventional conjuncts are used.

Virama (Puḷḷi). Because the Tamil encoding in the Unicode Standard is based on ISCII-1988 (Indian Script Code for Information Interchange), it makes use of the *abugida* model. An abugida treats the basic consonants as containing an inherent vowel, which can be canceled by the use of a visible mark, called a *virama* in Sanskrit. In most Brahmi-derived scripts, the placement of a virama between two consonants implies the deletion of the inherent vowel of the first consonant and causes a conjoined or subjoined consonant cluster. In those scripts, ZERO WIDTH NON-JOINER is used to display a visible virama, as shown previously in the Devangari example in *Figure 9-3*.

The situation is quite different for Tamil because the script uses very few consonant conjuncts. An orthographic cluster consisting of multiple consonants (represented by <C1, U+0BCD TAMIL SIGN VIRAMA, C2, ...>) is normally displayed with explicit viramas (which are called *puḷḷi* in Tamil). The conjuncts *kssa* and *shra* are traditionally displayed by conjunct ligatures, as illustrated for *kssa* in *Figure 9-13*, but nowadays tend to be displayed using an explicit *puḷḷi* as well.

Figure 9-13. Kssa Ligature in Tamil

க + ◌் + ஷ → க்ஷ *kṣa*

To explicitly display a *puḷḷi* for such sequences, ZERO WIDTH NON-JOINER can be inserted after the *puḷḷi* in the sequence of characters.

Rendering of the Tamil Script. The Tamil script is complex and requires special rules for rendering. The following discussion describes the most important features of Tamil rendering behavior. As with any script, a more complex procedure can add rendering characteristics, depending on the font and application.

> *In a font that is capable of rendering Tamil, the number of glyphs is greater than the number of Tamil characters.*

Tamil Vowels

Independent Versus Dependent Vowels. In the Tamil script, the dependent vowel signs are not equivalent to a sequence of of *virama + independent vowel*. For example:

ள + ◌ி ≠ ள + ◌் + இ

Left-Side Vowels. The Tamil vowels U+0BC6 ெ◌, U+0BC7 ே◌, and U+0BC8 ை◌ are reordered in front of the consonant to which they are applied. When occurring in a syllable, these vowels are rendered to the left side of their consonant, as shown in *Table 9-16*.

Two-Part Vowels. Tamil also has several vowels that consist of elements which flank the consonant to which they are applied. A sequence of two Unicode code points can be used to express equivalent spellings for these vowels, as shown in *Figure 9-14*.

Table 9-16. Tamil Vowel Reordering

Memory Representation		Display
க	◌ெ	கெ
க	◌ே	கே
க	◌ை	கை

Figure 9-14. Tamil Two-Part Vowels

◌ொ 0BCA ≡ ◌ெ + ◌ா 0BC6 + 0BBE

◌ோ 0BCB ≡ ◌ே + ◌ா 0BC7 + 0BBE

◌ௌ 0BCC ≡ ◌ெ + ◌ௗ 0BC6 + 0BD7

In these examples, the representation on the left, which is a single code point, is the preferred form and the form in common use for Tamil. Note that the ◌ௗ in the third example is *not* U+0BB3 TAMIL LETTER LLA; it is U+0BD7 TAMIL AU LENGTH MARK.

In the process of rendering, these two-part vowels are transformed into the two separate glyphs equivalent to those on the right, which are then subject to vowel reordering, as shown in *Table 9-17*.

Table 9-17. Tamil Vowel Splitting and Reordering

Memory Representation			Display
க	◌ொ		கொ
க	◌ெ	◌ா	கொ
க	◌ோ		கோ
க	◌ே	◌ா	கோ
க	◌ௌ		கௌ
க	◌ெ	◌ௗ	கௌ

Even in the case where a two-part vowel occurs with a conjunct consonant or consonant cluster, the left part of the vowel is reordered around the conjunct or cluster, as shown in *Figure 9-15*.

Figure 9-15. Vowel Reordering Around a Tamil Conjunct

க + ◌் + ஷ + ெ◌ + ா → க்ஷொ *kṣo*

For either left-side vowels or two-part vowels, the ordering of the elements is unambiguous: the consonant or consonant cluster occurs first in the memory representation, followed by the vowel.

Tamil Ligatures

A number of ligatures are conventionally used in Tamil. Most ligatures involve the shape taken by a consonant plus vowel sequence. A wide variety of modern Tamil words are written without a conjunct form, with a fully visible *puḷḷi*.

***Ligatures with Vowel* i.** The vowel signs *i* ◌ி and *ii* ◌ீ form ligatures with the consonant *tta* ட as shown in examples 1 and 2 of *Figure 9-16*. These vowels often change shape or position slightly so as to join cursively with other consonants, as shown in examples 3 and 4 of *Figure 9-16*.

Figure 9-16. Tamil Ligatures with *i*

① ட + ◌ி → டி *ṭi*

② ட + ◌ீ → டீ *ṭī*

③ ல + ◌ி → லி *li*

④ ல + ◌ீ → லீ *lī*

***Ligatures with Vowel* u.** The vowel signs *u* ◌ு and *uu* ◌ூ normally ligate with their consonant, as shown in *Table 9-18*. In the first column, the basic consonant is shown; the second column illustrates the ligation of that consonant with the *u* vowel sign; and the third column illustrates the ligation with the *uu* vowel sign.

Table 9-18. Tamil Ligatures with *u*

x	*x* + ◌ு	*x* + ◌ூ
க	கு	கூ
ங	ஙு	ஙூ
ச	சு	சூ
ஞ	ஞு	ஞூ

x	*x* + ◌ு	*x* + ◌ூ
ப	பு	பூ
ம	மு	மூ
ய	யு	யூ
ர	ரு	ரூ

Table 9-18. Tamil Ligatures with *u* (Continued)

x	*x* + ◌ு	*x* + ◌ூ
ட	டு	டூ
ண	ணு	ணூ
த	து	தூ
ந	நு	நூ
ன	னு	னூ

x	*x* + ◌ு	*x* + ◌ூ
ற	று	றூ
ல	லு	லூ
ள	ளு	ளூ
ழ	ழு	ழூ
வ	வு	வூ

With certain consonants, ஜ, ஷ, ஸ, ஹ, and the conjunct க்ஷ, the vowel signs *u* ◌ு and *uu* ◌ூ take a distinct spacing form, as shown in *Figure 9-17*.

Figure 9-17. Spacing Forms of Tamil *u*

ஜ + ◌ு → ஜு *ju*

ஜ + ◌ூ → ஜூ *jū*

***Ligatures with* ra.** Based on typographical preferences, the consonant *ra* ர may change shape to ா, when it ligates. Such change, if it occurs, will happen only when the ா form of U+0BB0 ர TAMIL LETTER RA would not be confused with the nominal form ா of U+0BBE TAMIL VOWEL SIGN AA (namely, when ர is combined with ◌், ◌ி, or ◌ீ). This change in shape is illustrated in *Figure 9-18*.

Figure 9-18. Tamil Ligatures with *ra*

ர + ◌் → ர் *r*

ர + ◌ி → ரி *ri*

ர + ◌ீ → ரீ *rī*

However, various governmental bodies mandate that the basic shape of the consonant *ra* ர should be used for these ligatures as well, especially in school textbooks. Media and literary publications in Malaysia and Singapore mostly use the unchanged form of *ra* ர.

Ligatures with* aa *in Traditional Tamil Orthography. In traditional Tamil orthography, the vowel sign *aa* ◌ா optionally ligates with ண, ன, or ற, as illustrated in *Figure 9-19.*

Figure 9-19. Tamil Ligatures with *aa*

ண	+ ◌ா	→	ணா	*ṇā*
ன	+ ◌ா	→	னா	*ṉā*
ற	+ ◌ா	→	றா	*ṟā*

These ligations also affect the right-hand part of two-part vowels, as shown in *Figure 9-20.*

Figure 9-20. Tamil Ligatures with *o*

ண	+ ெ◌ா	→	ணொ	*ṇo*
ண	+ ே◌ா	→	ணோ	*ṇō*
ன	+ ெ◌ா	→	னொ	*ṉo*
ன	+ ே◌ா	→	னோ	*ṉō*
ற	+ ெ◌ா	→	றொ	*ṟo*
ற	+ ே◌ா	→	றோ	*ṟō*

Ligatures with* ai *in Traditional Tamil Orthography. In traditional Tamil orthography, the left-side vowel sign *ai* ை◌ is also subject to a change in form. It is rendered as ൈ◌ when it occurs on the left side of ண, ன, ல, or ள, as illustrated in *Figure 9-21.*

Figure 9-21. Tamil Ligatures with *ai*

ண + ை◌ → ணை *ṇai*

ன + ை◌ → னை *ṉai*

ல + ை◌ → லை *lai*

ள + ை◌ → ளை *ḷai*

By contrast, in modern Tamil orthography, this vowel does not change its shape, as shown in *Figure 9-22*.

Figure 9-22. Vowel *ai* in Modern Tamil

ண + ை◌ → ணை *ṇai*

***Tamil* aytham.** The character U+0B83 TAMIL SIGN VISARGA is normally called *aytham* in Tamil. It is historically related to the *visarga* in other Indic scripts, but has become an ordinary spacing letter in Tamil. It is used to modify the sound of other consonants and, in particular, to represent the spelling of words borrowed into Tamil from English or other languages.

Punctuation. Danda and double danda marks as well as some other unified punctuation used with Tamil are found in the Devanagari block; see *Section 9.1, Devanagari*.

9.7 Telugu

Telugu: U+0C00–U+0C7F

The Telugu script is a South Indian script used to write the Telugu language of the Andhra Pradesh state in India as well as minority languages such as Gondi (Adilabad and Koi dialects) and Lambadi. The script is also used in Maharashtra, Orissa, Madhya Pradesh, and West Bengal. The Telugu script became distinct by the thirteenth century CE and shares ancestors with the Kannada script.

Vowel Letters. Vowel letters are encoded atomically in Unicode, even if they can be analyzed visually as consisting of multiple parts. *Table 9-19* shows the letters that can be analyzed, the single code point that should be used to represent them in text, and the sequence of code points resulting from analysis that should not be used.

Rendering Behavior. Telugu script rendering is similar to that of other Brahmic scripts in the Unicode Standard—in particular, the Tamil script. Unlike Tamil, however, the Telugu

Table 9-19. Telugu Vowel Letters

To Represent	Use	Do Not Use
ఓ	0C13	<0C12, 0C55>
ఔ	0C14	<0C12, 0C4C>

script writes conjunct characters with subscript letters. Many Telugu letters have a v-shaped headstroke, which is a structural mark corresponding to the horizontal bar in Devanagari and the arch in Oriya script. When a virama (called *virāmamu* in Telugu) or certain vowel signs are added to a letter with this headstroke, it is replaced:

> U+0C15 క *ka* + U+0C4D ◌్ *virama* + U+200C [ZWNJ] ZERO WIDTH NON-JOINER → క్‌ (*k*)
>
> U+0C15 క *ka* + U+0C3F ◌ి *vowel sign i* → కి (*ki*)

Telugu consonant clusters are most commonly represented by a subscripted, and often transformed, consonant glyph for the second element of the cluster:

> U+0C17 గ *ga* + U+0C4D ◌్ *virama* + U+0C17 గ *ga* → గ్గ (*gga*)
>
> U+0C15 క *ka* + U+0C4D ◌్ *virama* + U+0C15 క *ka* → క్క (*kka*)
>
> U+0C15 క *ka* + U+0C4D ◌్ *virama* + U+0C2F య *ya* → క్య (*kya*)
>
> U+0C15 క *ka* + U+0C4D ◌్ *virama* + U+0C37 ష *ssa* → క్ష (*kṣa*)

Special Characters. U+0C55 TELUGU LENGTH MARK is provided as an encoding for the second element of the vowel U+0C47 TELUGU VOWEL SIGN EE. U+0C56 TELUGU AI LENGTH MARK is provided as an encoding for the second element of the surroundrant vowel U+0C48 TELUGU VOWEL SIGN AI. The length marks are both nonspacing characters. For a detailed discussion of the use of two-part vowels, see “Two-Part Vowels” in *Section 9.6, Tamil.*

Punctuation. Danda and double danda are used primarily in the domain of religious texts to indicate the equivalent of a comma and full stop, respectively. The danda and double danda marks as well as some other unified punctuation used with Telugu are found in the Devanagari block; see *Section 9.1, Devanagari.*

9.8 Kannada

Kannada: U+0C80–U+0CFF

The Kannada script is a South Indian script. It is used to write the Kannada (or Kanarese) language of the Karnataka state in India and to write minority languages such as Tulu. The

Kannada language is also used in many parts of Tamil Nadu, Kerala, Andhra Pradesh, and Maharashtra. This script is very closely related to the Telugu script both in the shapes of the letters and in the behavior of conjunct consonants. The Kannada script also shares many features common to other Indic scripts. See *Section 9.1, Devanagari*, for further information.

The Unicode Standard follows the ISCII layout for encoding, which also reflects the traditional Kannada alphabetic order.

Principles of the Kannada Script

Like Devanagari and related scripts, the Kannada script employs a halant, which is also known as a virama or vowel omission sign, U+0CCD ◌್ KANNADA SIGN VIRAMA. The halant nominally serves to suppress the inherent vowel of the consonant to which it is applied. The halant functions as a combining character. When a consonant loses its inherent vowel by the application of halant, it is known as a dead consonant. The dead consonants are the presentation forms used to depict the consonants without an inherent vowel. Their rendered forms in Kannada resemble the full consonant with the vertical stem replaced by the halant sign, which marks a character core. The stem glyph is graphically and historically related to the sign denoting the inherent /a/ vowel, U+0C85 ಅ KANNADA LETTER A. In contrast, a live consonant is a consonant that retains its inherent vowel or is written with an explicit dependent vowel sign. The dead consonant is defined as a sequence consisting of a consonant letter followed by a halant. The default rendering for a dead consonant is to position the halant as a combining mark bound to the consonant letterform.

Vowel Letters. Vowel letters are encoded atomically in Unicode, even if they can be analyzed visually as consisting of multiple parts. *Table 9-20* shows the letters that can be analyzed, the single code point that should be used to represent them in text, and the sequence of code points resulting from analysis that should not be used.

Table 9-20. Kannada Vowel Letters

To Represent	Use	Do Not Use
ಔ	0C94	<0C92, 0CCC>

Consonant Conjuncts. Kannada is also noted for a large number of consonant conjunct forms that serve as ligatures of two or more adjacent forms. This use of ligatures takes place in the context of a consonant cluster. A written consonant cluster is defined as a sequence of characters that represent one or more dead consonants followed by a normal live consonant. A separate and unique glyph corresponds to each part of a Kannada consonant conjunct. Most of these glyphs resemble their original consonant forms—many without the implicit vowel sign, wherever applicable.

In Kannada, conjunct formation tends to be graphically regular, using the following pattern:

- The first consonant of the cluster is rendered with the implicit vowel or a different dependent vowel appearing as the terminal element of the cluster.

- The remaining consonants (consonants between the first consonant and the terminal vowel element) appear in conjunct consonant glyph forms in phonetic order. They are generally depicted directly below or to the lower right of the first consonant.

A Kannada script font contains the conjunct glyph components, but they are not encoded as separate Unicode characters because they are simply ligatures. Kannada script rendering software must be able to map appropriate combinations of characters in context to the appropriate conjunct glyphs in fonts.

> *In a font that is capable of rendering Kannada, the number of glyphs is greater than the number of encoded Kannada characters.*

Special Characters. U+0CD5 ◌ೕ KANNADA LENGTH MARK is provided as an encoding for the right side of the two-part vowel U+0CC7 ◌ೇ KANNADA VOWEL SIGN EE should it be necessary for processing. Likewise, U+0CD6 ◌ೖ KANNADA AI LENGTH MARK is provided as an encoding for the right side of the two-part vowel U+0CC8 ◌ೈ KANNADA VOWEL SIGN AI. The Kannada two-part vowels actually consist of a nonspacing element above the consonant letter and one or more spacing elements to the right of the consonant letter. These two length marks have no independent existence in the Kannada writing system and do not play any part as independent codes in the traditional collation order.

Kannada Letter LLLA. U+0CDE ೞ KANNADA LETTER FA is actually an obsolete Kannada letter that is transliterated in Dravidian scholarship as ẓ, ḻ, or ṛ. This form should have been named "LLLA", rather than "FA", so the name in this standard is simply a mistake. This letter has not been actively used in Kannada since the end of the tenth century. Collations should treat U+0CDE as following U+0CB3 KANNADA LETTER LLA.

Rendering Kannada

Plain text in Kannada is generally stored in phonetic order; that is, a *CV* syllable with a dependent vowel is always encoded as a consonant letter *C* followed by a vowel sign *V* in the memory representation. This order is employed by the ISCII standard and corresponds to the phonetic and keying order of textual data. Unlike in Devanagari and some other Indian scripts, all of the dependent vowels in Kannada are depicted to the right of their consonant letters. Hence there is no need to reorder the elements in mapping from the logical (character) store to the presentation (glyph) rendering, and vice versa.

If any invisible base is required for the display of dependent vowels without any consonant base, U+200C ZERO WIDTH NON-JOINER can be used. It can also be used to provide proper collation of the words containing dead consonants.

Explicit Virama (Halant). Normally, a halant character creates dead consonants, which in turn combine with subsequent consonants to form conjuncts. This behavior usually results in a halant sign not being depicted visually. Occasionally, this default behavior is not desired when a dead consonant should be excluded from conjunct formation, in which case the halant sign is visibly rendered. To accomplish this, U+200C ZERO WIDTH NON-JOINER is introduced immediately after the encoded dead consonant that is to be excluded from conjunct formation. See *Section 9.1, Devanagari*, for examples.

Consonant Clusters Involving RA. Whenever a consonant cluster is formed with the U+0CB0 ರ KANNADA LETTER RA as the first component of the consonant cluster, the letter *ra* is depicted with two different presentation forms: one as the initial element and the other as the final display element of the consonant cluster.

U+0CB0 ರ *ra* + U+0CCD ್ *halant* + U+0C95 ಕ *ka* → ರ್ಕ *rka*

U+0CB0 ರ *ra* + ZWJ + U+0CCD ್ *halant* + U+0C95 ಕ *ka* → ರ‍್ಕ *rka*

U+0C95 ಕ *ka* + U+0CCD ್ *halant* + U+0CB0 ರ *ra* → ಕ್ರ *kra*

Modifier Mark Rules. In addition to the vowel signs, one more types of combining marks may be applied to a component of a written syllable or the syllable as a whole. If the consonant represents a dead consonant, then the nukta should precede the halant in the memory representation. The nukta is represented by a double-dot mark, U+0CBC ಼ KANNADA SIGN NUKTA. Two such modified consonants are used in the Kannada language: one representing the syllable *za* and one representing the syllable *fa*.

Avagraha Sign. A spacing mark called U+0CBD ಽ KANNADA SIGN AVAGRAHA is used when rendering Sanskrit texts.

Punctuation. Danda and double danda marks as well as some other unified punctuation used with this script are found in the Devanagari block; see *Section 9.1, Devanagari*.

9.9 Malayalam

Malayalam: U+0D00–U+0D7F

The Malayalam script is a South Indian script used to write the Malayalam language of the Kerala state. Malayalam is a Dravidian language like Kannada, Tamil, and Telugu. Throughout its history, it has absorbed words from Tamil, Sanskrit, Arabic, and English.

Vowel Letters. Vowel letters are encoded atomically in Unicode, even if they can be analyzed visually as consisting of multiple parts. *Table 9-21* shows the letters that can be analyzed, the single code point that should be used to represent them in text, and the sequence of code points resulting from analysis that should not be used.

Rendering Behavior. The shapes of Malayalam letters closely resemble those of Tamil. Malayalam, however, has a very full and complex set of conjunct consonant forms. In the 1970s and 1980s, Malayalam underwent orthographic reform due to printing difficulties. The treatment of the combining vowel signs *u* and *uu* was simplified at this time. These vowel signs had previously been represented using special cluster graphemes where the vowel signs were fused beneath their consonants, but in the reformed orthography they are represented by spacing characters following their consonants. In *Table 9-22*, an initial con-

Table 9-21. Malayalam Vowel Letters

To Represent	Use	Do Not Use
ഈ	0D08	<0D07, 0D57>
ഊ	0D0A	<0D09, 0D57>
ഐ	0D10	<0D0E, 0D46>
ഓ	0D13	<0D12, 0D3E>
ഔ	0D14	<0D12, 0D57>

sonant plus the vowel sign yields a syllable. Both the older orthography and the newer orthography are shown on the right.

Table 9-22. Malayalam Orthographic Reform

Syllable		Older Orthography	Newer Orthography
ku	ക + ◌ു	കു	കു
gu	ഗ + ◌ു	ഗു	ഗു
chu	ഛ + ◌ു	ഛു	ഛു
ju	ജ + ◌ു	ജു	ജു
ṇu	ണ + ◌ു	ണു	ണു
tu	ത + ◌ു	തു	തു
nu	ന + ◌ു	നു	നു
bhu	ഭ + ◌ു	ഭു	ഭു
ru	ര + ◌ു	രു	രു
śu	ശ + ◌ു	ശു	ശു
hu	ഹ + ◌ു	ഹു	ഹു
kū	ക + ◌ൂ	കൂ	കൂ
gū	ഗ + ◌ൂ	ഗൂ	ഗൂ
chū	ഛ + ◌ൂ	ഛൂ	ഛൂ
jū	ജ + ◌ൂ	ജൂ	ജൂ
ṇū	ണ + ◌ൂ	ണൂ	ണൂ
tū	ത + ◌ൂ	തൂ	തൂ
nū	ന + ◌ൂ	നൂ	നൂ
bhū	ഭ + ◌ൂ	ഭൂ	ഭൂ

Table 9-22. Malayalam Orthographic Reform (Continued)

rū	ര + ◌ൂ	രൂ	രൂ
śū	ശ + ◌ൂ	ശൂ	ശൂ
hū	ഹ + ◌ൂ	ഹൂ	ഹൂ

Like other Brahmic scripts in the Unicode Standard, Malayalam uses the virama to form conjunct characters (see *Table 9-23*); this is known as *candrakala* in Malayalam. There are both horizontal and vertical conjuncts. The visible virama usually shows the suppression of the inherent vowel, but sometimes indicates a reduced schwa sound [ə], often called "half-u".

Table 9-23. Malayalam Conjuncts

ക	+	◌്	+	ഷ	→	ക്ഷ	(*kṣa*)
ക	+	◌്	+	ക	→	ക്ക	(*kka*)
ജ	+	◌്	+	ഞ	→	ജ്ഞ	(*jña*)
ട	+	◌്	+	ട	→	ട്ട	(*ṭṭa*)
പ	+	◌്	+	പ	→	പ്പ	(*ppa*)
ച	+	◌്	+	ഛ	→	ച്ഛ	(*ccha*)
ബ	+	◌്	+	ബ	→	ബ്ബ	(*bba*)
ന	+	◌്	+	യ	→	ന്യ	(*nya*)
പ	+	◌്	+	ര	→	പ്ര	(*pra*)
ര	+	◌്	+	പ	→	ർപ	(*rpa*)
ശ	+	◌്	+	വ	→	ശ്വ	(*śva*)

Five sonorant consonants merge with the virama when they appear in syllable-final position with no inherent vowel. A consonant when so merged is called *cillakṣaram* or *chillu*:

ൺ *ṇ*

ൻ *n*

ർ *r*

ൽ *l*

ൾ *ḷ*

It is important to note the use of the ZERO WIDTH JOINER and ZERO WIDTH NON-JOINER in these environments:

ന + ◌് + മ → ന്മ (*nma*)

ന + ◌് + ZWNJ + മ → ന്‌മ (*nma*)

ന + ◌് + ZWJ + മ → ൻമ (*nma*)

Special Characters. In modern times, the dominant practice is to write the dependent form of the *au* vowel using only "ൗ", which is placed on the right side of the consonant it modifies; such texts are represented in Unicode using U+0D57 MALAYALAM AU LENGTH MARK. In the past, this dependent form was written using both "ൌ" on the left side and "ൗ" on the right side; U+0D4C MALAYALAM VOWEL SIGN AU can be used for documents following this earlier tradition. This historical simplification started much earlier than the orthographic reforms mentioned above.

For a detailed discussion of the use of two-part vowels, see "Two-Part Vowels" in *Section 9.6, Tamil.*

Punctuation. Danda and double danda marks as well as some other unified punctuation used with Malayalam are found in the Devanagari block; see *Section 9.1, Devanagari.*

CHAPTER

10

Chapter 10

South Asian Scripts-II

This chapter documents scripts of South Asia aside from the major official scripts of India, which are documented in *Chapter 9, South Asian Scripts-I.*

The following South Asian scripts are described in this chapter:

Sinhala	*Phags-pa*	*Syloti Nagri*
Tibetan	*Limbu*	*Kharoshthi*

Sinhala has a virama-based model, but is not structurally mapped to ISCII.

Tibetan stands apart, using a subjoined consonant model for conjoined consonants, reflecting its somewhat different structure and usage.

Phags-pa is a historical script related to Tibetan that was created as the national script of the Mongol empire. Even though Phags-pa was used mostly in Eastern and Central Asia for writing text in the Mongolian and Chinese languages, it is discussed in this chapter because of its close historical connection to the Tibetan script.

The Limbu script makes use of an explicit encoding of syllable-final consonants.

Syloti Nagri is used to write the modern Sylheti language of northeast Bangladesh.

The oldest lengthy inscriptions of India, the edicts of Ashoka from the third century BCE, were written in two scripts, Kharoshthi and Brahmi. These are both ultimately of Semitic origin, probably deriving from Aramaic, which was an important administrative language of the Middle East at that time. Kharoshthi, which was written from right to left, was supplanted by Brahmi and its derivatives.

10.1 Sinhala

Sinhala: U+0D80–U+0DFF

The Sinhala script, also known as Sinhalese, is used to write the Sinhala language, the majority language of Sri Lanka. It is also used to write the Pali and Sanskrit languages. The script is a descendant of Brahmi and resembles the scripts of South India in form and structure.

Sinhala differs from other languages of the region in that it has a series of prenasalized stops that are distinguished from the combination of a nasal followed by a stop. In other words, both forms occur and are written differently—for example, අඬ <U+0D85, U+0DAC> *aňḍa* [a^{n}ɖa] "sound" versus අණ්ඩ <U+0D85, U+0DAB, U+0DCA, U+0DA9> *aṇḍa* [aɳɖa] "egg." In addition, Sinhala has separate distinct signs for both a short and a long low front vowel sounding similar to the initial vowel of the English word "apple," usually represented in IPA as U+00E6 æ LATIN SMALL LETTER AE (*ash*). The independent forms of these vowels are encoded at U+0D87 and U+0D88; the corresponding dependent forms are U+0DD0 and U+0DD1.

Because of these extra letters, the encoding for Sinhala does not precisely follow the pattern established for the other Indic scripts (for example, Devanagari). It does use the same general structure, making use of phonetic order, matra reordering, and use of the virama (U+0DCA SINHALA SIGN AL-LAKUNA) to indicate conjunct consonant clusters. Sinhala does not use half-forms in the Devanagari manner, but does use many ligatures.

Vowel Letters. Vowel letters are encoded atomically in Unicode, even if they can be analyzed visually as consisting of multiple parts. *Table 10-1* shows the letters that can be analyzed, the single code point that should be used to represent them in text, and the sequence of code points resulting from analysis that should not be used.

Table 10-1. Sinhala Vowel Letters

To Represent	Use	Do Not Use
ආ	0D86	<0D85, 0DCF>
ඇ	0D87	<0D85, 0DD0>
ඈ	0D88	<0D85, 0DD1>
ඌ	0D8C	<0D8B, 0DDF>
ඎ	0D8E	<0D8D, 0DD8>
ඐ	0D90	<0D8F, 0DDF>
ඒ	0D92	<0D91, 0DCA>
ඓ	0D93	<0D91, 0DD9>
ඖ	0D96	<0D94, 0DDF>

Other Letters for Tamil. The Sinhala script may also be used to write Tamil. In this case, some additional combinations may be required. Some letters, such as U+0DBB SINHALA LETTER RAYANNA and U+0DB1 SINHALA LETTER DANTAJA NAYANNA, may be modified by adding the equivalent of a nukta. There is, however, no nukta presently encoded in the Sinhala block.

Historical Symbols. Neither U+0DF4 ෴ SINHALA PUNCTUATION KUNDDALIYA nor the Sinhala numerals are in general use today, having been replaced by Western-style punctuation and Western digits. The *kunddaliya* was formerly used as a full stop or period. It is included for scholarly use. The Sinhala numerals are not presently encoded.

10.2 Tibetan

Tibetan: U+0F00–U+0FFF

The Tibetan script is used for writing Tibetan in several countries and regions throughout the Himalayas. Aside from Tibet itself, the script is used in Ladakh, Nepal, and northern areas of India bordering Tibet where large Tibetan-speaking populations now reside. The Tibetan script is also used in Bhutan to write Dzongkha, the official language of that country. In addition, Tibetan is used as the language of philosophy and liturgy by Buddhist traditions spread from Tibet into the Mongolian cultural area that encompasses Mongolia, Buriatia, Kalmykia, and Tuva.

The Tibetan scripting and grammatical systems were originally defined together in the sixth century by royal decree when the Tibetan King Songtsen Gampo sent 16 men to India to study Indian languages. One of those men, Thumi Sambhota, is credited with creating the Tibetan writing system upon his return, having studied various Indic scripts and grammars. The king's primary purpose was to bring Buddhism from India to Tibet. The new script system was therefore designed with compatibility extensions for Indic (principally Sanskrit) transliteration so that Buddhist texts could be represented properly. Because of this origin, over the last 1,500 years the Tibetan script has been widely used to represent Indic words, a number of which have been adopted into the Tibetan language retaining their original spelling.

A note on Latin transliteration: Tibetan spelling is traditional and does not generally reflect modern pronunciation. Throughout this section, Tibetan words are represented in italics when transcribed as spoken, followed at first occurrence by a parenthetical transliteration; in these transliterations, the presence of the *tsek* (tsheg) character is expressed with a hyphen.

Thumi Sambhota's original grammar treatise defined two script styles. The first, called *uchen* (dbu-can, "with head"), is a formal "inscriptional capitals" style said to be based on an old form of Devanagari. It is the script used in Tibetan xylograph books and the one used in the coding tables. The second style, called *u-mey* (dbu-med, or "headless"), is more cursive and said to be based on the Wartu script. Numerous styles of *u-mey* have evolved since then, including both formal calligraphic styles used in manuscripts and running handwriting styles. All Tibetan scripts follow the same lettering rules, though there is a slight difference in the way that certain compound stacks are formed in *uchen* and *u-mey.*

General Principles of the Tibetan Script. Tibetan grammar divides letters into consonants and vowels. There are 30 consonants, and each consonant is represented by a discrete written character. There are five vowel sounds, only four of which are represented by written marks. The four vowels that are explicitly represented in writing are each represented with a single mark that is applied above or below a consonant to indicate the application of that vowel to that consonant. The absence of one of the four marks implies that the first vowel sound (like a short "ah" in English) is present and is not modified to one of the four other possibilities. Three of the four marks are written above the consonants; one is written below.

Each word in Tibetan has a base or root consonant. The base consonant can be written singly or it can have other consonants added above or below it to make a vertically "stacked" letter. Tibetan grammar contains a very complete set of rules regarding letter gender, and these rules dictate which letters can be written in adjacent positions. The rules therefore dictate which combinations of consonants can be joined to make stacks. Any combination not allowed by the gender rules does not occur in native Tibetan words. However, when transcribing other languages (for example, Sanskrit, Chinese) into Tibetan, these rules do not operate. In certain instances other than transliteration, any consonant may be combined with any other subjoined consonant. Implementations should therefore be prepared to accept and display any combinations.

For example, the syllable *spyir* "general," pronounced [tʃíː], is a typical example of a Tibetan syllable that includes a stack comprising a head letter, two subscript letters, and a vowel sign. *Figure 10-1* shows the characters in the order in which they appear in the backing store.

Figure 10-1. Tibetan Syllable Structure

① U+0F66 TIBETAN LETTER SA
② U+0FA4 TIBETAN SUBJOINED LETTER PA
③ U+0FB1 TIBETAN SUBJOINED LETTER YA
④ U+0F72 TIBETAN VOWEL SIGN I
⑤ U+0F62 TIBETAN LETTER RA
⑥ U+0F0B TIBETAN MARK INTERSYLLABIC TSHEG

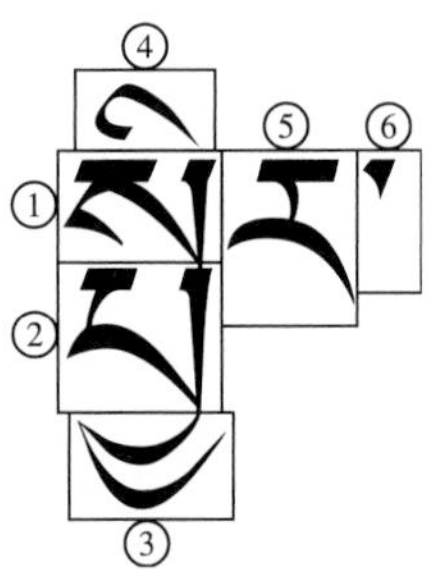

The model adopted to encode the Tibetan lettering set described above contains the following groups of items: Tibetan consonants, vowels, numerals, punctuation, ornamental signs and marks, and Tibetan-transliterated Sanskrit consonants and vowels. Each of these will be described in this section.

Both in this description and in Tibetan, the terms "subjoined" (-btags) and "head" (-mgo) are used in different senses. In the structural sense, they indicate specific slots defined in native Tibetan orthography. In spatial terms, they refer to the position in the stack; anything in the topmost position is "head," anything not in the topmost position is "subjoined." Unless explicitly qualified, the terms "subjoined" and "head" are used here in their spatial sense. For example, in a conjunct like "rka," the letter in the root slot is "KA." Because it is not the topmost letter of the stack, however, it is expressed with a subjoined character code, while "RA", which is structurally in the head slot, is expressed with a nominal character code. In a conjunct "kra," in which the root slot is also occupied with "KA", the "KA" is encoded with a nominal character code because it is in the topmost position in the stack.

The Tibetan script has its own system of formatting, and details of that system relevant to the characters encoded in this standard are explained herein. However, an increasing number of publications in Tibetan do not strictly adhere to this original formatting system. This change is due to the partial move from publishing on long, horizontal, loose-leaf folios, to publishing in vertically oriented, bound books. The Tibetan script also has a punctuation set designed to meet needs quite different from the punctuation that has evolved for Western scripts. With the appearance of Tibetan newspapers, magazines, school textbooks, and Western-style reference books in the last 20 or 30 years, Tibetans have begun using things like columns, indented blocks of text, Western-style headings, and footnotes. Some Western punctuation marks, including brackets, parentheses, and quotation marks, are becoming commonplace in these kinds of publication. With the introduction of more sophisticated electronic publishing systems, there is also a renaissance in the publication of voluminous religious and philosophical works in the traditional horizontal, loose-leaf format—many set in digital typefaces closely conforming to the proportions of traditional hand-lettered text.

Consonants. The system described here has been devised to encode the Tibetan system of writing consonants in both single and stacked forms.

All of the consonants are encoded a first time from U+0F40 through U+0F69. There are the basic Tibetan consonants and, in addition, six compound consonants used to represent the Indic consonants *gha*, *jha*, *d.ha*, *dha*, *bha*, and *ksh.a*. These codes are used to represent occurrences of either a stand-alone consonant or a consonant in the head position of a vertical stack. Glyphs generated from these codes will always sit in the normal position starting at and dropping down from the design baseline. All of the consonants are then encoded a second time. These second encodings from U+0F90 through U+0FB9 represent consonants in subjoined stack position.

To represent a single consonant in a text stream, one of the first "nominal" set of codes is placed. To represent a stack of consonants in the text stream, a "nominal" consonant code is followed directly by one or more of the subjoined consonant codes. The stack so formed continues for as long as subjoined consonant codes are contiguously placed.

This encoding method was chosen over an alternative method that would have involved a virama-based encoding, such as Devanagari. There were two main reasons for this choice. First, the virama is not normally used in the Tibetan writing system to create letter combinations. There is a virama in the Tibetan script, but only because of the need to represent Devanagari; called "srog-med", it is encoded at U+0F84 TIBETAN MARK HALANTA. The virama is never used in writing Tibetan words and can be—but almost never is—used as a substitute for stacking in writing Sanskrit mantras in the Tibetan script. Second, there is a prevalence of stacking in native Tibetan, and the model chosen specifically results in decreased data storage requirements. Furthermore, in languages other than Tibetan, there are many cases where stacks occur that do not appear in Tibetan-language texts; it is thus imperative to have a model that allows for any consonant to be stacked with any subjoined consonant(s). Thus a model for stack building was chosen that follows the Tibetan approach to creating letter combinations, but is not limited to a specific set of the possible combinations.

Vowels. Each of the four basic Tibetan vowel marks is coded as a separate entity. These code points are U+0F72, U+0F74, U+0F7A, and U+0F7C. For compatibility, a set of several compound vowels for Sanskrit transcription is also provided in the other code points between U+0F71 and U+0F7D. Most Tibetan users do not view these compound vowels as single characters, and their use is limited to Sanskrit words. It is acceptable for users to enter these compounds as a series of simpler elements and have software render them appropriately. Canonical equivalences are specified for all of these code points except U+0F77 and U+0F79. All vowel signs are nonspacing marks above or below a stack of consonants, sometimes on both sides.

A stand-alone consonant or a stack of consonants can have a vowel sign applied to it. In accordance with the rules of Tibetan writing, a code for a vowel sign applied to a consonant should always be placed after the bare consonant or the stack of consonants formed by the method just described.

All of the symbols and punctuation marks have straightforward encodings. Further information about many of them appears later in this section.

Coding Order. In general, the correct coding order for a stream of text will be the same as the order in which Tibetans spell and in which the characters of the text would be written by hand. For example, the correct coding order for the most complex Tibetan stack would be

head position consonant

first subjoined consonant

... (intermediate subjoined consonants, if any)

last subjoined consonant

subjoined vowel a-chung (U+0F71)

standard or compound vowel sign, or virama

Where used, the character U+0F39 TIBETAN MARK TSA -PHRU occurs immediately after the consonant it modifies.

Allographical Considerations. When consonants are combined to form a stack, one of them retains the status of being the principal consonant in the stack. The principal consonant always retains its stand-alone form. However, consonants placed in the "head" and "subjoined" positions to the main consonant sometimes retain their stand-alone forms and sometimes are given new, special forms. Because of this fact, certain consonants are given a further, special encoding treatment—namely, "wa" (U+0F5D), "ya" (U+0F61), and "ra" (U+0F62).

Head Position "ra". When the consonant "ra" is written in the "head" position (ra-mgo, pronounced *ra-go*) at the top of a stack in the normal Tibetan-defined lettering set, the shape of the consonant can change. This is called *ra-go* (ra-mgo). It can either be a full-form shape or the full-form shape but with the bottom stroke removed (looking like a short-stemmed letter "T"). This requirement of "ra" in the head position where the glyph representing it can change shape is correctly coded by using the stand-alone "ra" consonant (U+0F62) followed by the appropriate subjoined consonant(s). For example, in the normal Tibetan ra-mgo combinations, the "ra" in the head position is mostly written as the half-ra but in the case of "ra + subjoined nya" must be written as the full-form "ra". Thus the normal Tibetan ra-mgo combinations are correctly encoded with the normal "ra" consonant (U+0F62) because it can change shape as required. It is the responsibility of the font developer to provide the correct glyphs for representing the characters where the "ra" in the head position will change shape—for example, as in "ra + subjoined nya".

Full-Form "ra" in Head Position. Some instances of "ra" in the head position require that the consonant be represented as a full-form "ra" that never changes. This is *not* standard usage for the Tibetan language itself, but rather occurs in transliteration and transcription. Only in these cases should the character U+0F6A TIBETAN LETTER FIXED-FORM RA be used instead of U+0F62 TIBETAN LETTER RA. This "ra" will always be represented as a full-form "ra consonant" and will never change shape to the form where the lower stroke has been cut off. For example, the letter combination "ra + ya", when appearing in transliterated Sanskrit works, is correctly written with a full-form "ra" followed by either a modified subjoined "ya" form or a full-form subjoined "ya" form. Note that the fixed-form "ra" should be used *only* in combinations where "ra" would normally transform into a short form but the user specifically wants to prevent that change. For example, the combination "ra + subjoined nya" never requires the use of fixed-form "ra", because "ra" normally retains its full glyph form over "nya". It is the responsibility of the font developer to provide the appropriate glyphs to represent the encodings.

Subjoined Position "wa", "ya", and "ra". All three of these consonants can be written in subjoined position to the main consonant according to normal Tibetan grammar. In this position, *all* of them change to a new shape. The "wa" consonant when written in subjoined position is not a full "wa" letter any longer but is literally the bottom-right corner of the "wa" letter cut off and appended below it. For that reason, it is called a *wazur* (wa-zur, or "corner of a wa") or, less frequently but just as validly, *wa-ta* (wa-btags) to indicate that it is a subjoined "wa". The consonants "ya" and "ra" when in the subjoined position are called *ya-ta* (ya-btags) and *ra-ta* (ra-btags), respectively. To encode these subjoined consonants that follow the rules of normal Tibetan grammar, the shape-changed, subjoined forms U+0FAD TIBETAN SUBJOINED LETTER WA, U+0FB1 TIBETAN SUBJOINED LETTER YA, and U+0FB2 TIBETAN SUBJOINED LETTER RA should be used.

All three of these subjoined consonants also have full-form non-shape-changing counterparts for the needs of transliterated and transcribed text. For this purpose, the full subjoined consonants that do not change shape (encoded at U+0FBA, U+0FBB, and U+0FBC, respectively) are used where necessary. The combinations of "ra + ya" are a good example because they include instances of "ra" taking a short (ya-btags) form and "ra" taking a full-form subjoined "ya".

U+0FB0 TIBETAN SUBJOINED LETTER -A (*a-chung*) should be used only in the very rare cases where a full-sized subjoined a-chung letter is required. The small vowel lengthening a-chung encoded as U+0F71 TIBETAN VOWEL SIGN AA is *far* more frequently used in Tibetan text, and it is therefore recommended that implementations treat this character (rather than U+0FB0) as the normal subjoined a-chung.

Halanta (Srog-Med). Because two sets of consonants are encoded for Tibetan, with the second set providing explicit ligature formation, there is no need for a "dead character" in Tibetan. When a *halanta* (srog-med) is used in Tibetan, its purpose is to suppress the inherent vowel "a". If anything, the *halanta* should *prevent* any vowel or consonant from forming a ligature with the consonant preceding the *halanta*. In Tibetan text, this character should be displayed beneath the base character as a combining glyph and not used as a (purposeless) dead character.

Line Breaking Considerations. Tibetan text separates units called natively *tsek-bar* ("tsheg-bar"), an inexact translation of which is "syllable." *Tsek-bar* is literally the unit of text between *tseks* and is generally a consonant cluster with all of its prefixes, suffixes, and vowel signs. It is not a "syllable" in the English sense.

Tibetan script has only two break characters. The primary break character is the standard interword *tsek* (tsheg), which is encoded at U+0F0B. The second break character is the space. Space or *tsek* characters in a stream of Tibetan text are not always break characters and so need proper contextual handling.

The primary delimiter character in Tibetan text is the *tsek* (U+0F0B TIBETAN MARK INTERSYLLABIC TSHEG). In general, automatic line breaking processes may break after any occurrence of this *tsek*, except where it follows a U+0F44 TIBETAN LETTER NGA (with or without a vowel sign) and precedes a *shay* (U+0F0D), or where Tibetan grammatical rules do not permit a break. (Normally, *tsek* is not written before *shay* except after "nga". This type of tsek-after-nga is called "nga-phye-tsheg" and may be expressed by U+0F0B or by the special character U+0F0C, a nonbreaking form of *tsek*.) The Unicode names for these two types of *tsek* are misnomers, retained for compatibility. The standard *tsek* U+0F0B TIBETAN MARK INTERSYLLABIC TSHEG is always required to be a potentially breaking character, whereas the "nga-phye-tsheg" is always required to be a nonbreaking *tsek*. U+0F0C TIBETAN MARK DELIMITER TSHEG BSTAR is specifically not a "delimiter" and is not for general use.

There are no other break characters in Tibetan text. Unlike English, Tibetan has no system for hyphenating or otherwise breaking a word within the group of letters making up the word. Tibetan text formatting does not allow text to be broken within a word.

Whitespace appears in Tibetan text, although it should be represented by U+00A0 NO-BREAK SPACE instead of U+0020 SPACE. Tibetan text breaks lines after *tsek* instead of at whitespace.

Complete Tibetan text formatting is best handled by a formatter in the application and not just by the code stream. If the interword and nonbreaking *tseks* are properly employed as breaking and nonbreaking characters, respectively, and if all spaces are nonbreaking spaces, then any application will still wrap lines correctly on that basis, even though the breaks might be sometimes inelegant.

Tibetan Punctuation. The punctuation apparatus of Tibetan is relatively limited. The principal punctuation characters are the *tsek*; the *shay* (transliterated "shad"), which is a vertical stroke used to mark the end of a section of text; the space used sparingly as a space; and two of several variant forms of the *shay* that are used in specialized situations requiring a *shay*. There are also several other marks and signs but they are sparingly used.

The *shay* at U+0F0D marks the end of a piece of text called "tshig-grub". The mode of marking bears no commonality with English phrases or sentences and should not be described as a delimiter of phrases. In Tibetan grammatical terms, a *shay* is used to mark the end of an expression ("brjod-pa") and a complete expression. Two *shays* are used at the end of whole topics ("don-tshan"). Because some writers use the double *shay* with a different spacing than would be obtained by coding two adjacent occurrences of U+0F0D, the double *shay* has been coded at U+0F0E with the intent that it would have a larger spacing between component *shays* than if two *shays* were simply written together. However, most writers do not use an unusual spacing between the double *shay*, so the application should allow the user to write two U+0F0D codes one after the other. Additionally, font designers will have to decide whether to implement these *shays* with a larger than normal gap.

The U+0F11 *rin-chen-pung-shay* (rin-chen-spungs-shad) is a variant *shay* used in a specific "new-line" situation. Its use was not defined in the original grammars but Tibetan tradition gives it a highly defined use. The *drul-shay* ("sbrul-shad") is likewise not defined by the original grammars but has a highly defined use; it is used for separating sections of meaning that are equivalent to topics ("don-tshan") and subtopics. A *drul-shay* is usually surrounded on both sides by the equivalent of about three spaces (though no rule is specified). Hard spaces will be needed for these instances because the *drul-shay* should not appear at the beginning of a new line and the whole structure of spacing-plus-*shay* should not be broken up, if possible.

Tibetan texts use a *yig-go* ("head mark," yig-mgo) to indicate the beginning of the front of a folio, there being no other certain way, in the loose-leaf style of traditional Tibetan books, to tell which is the front of a page. The head mark can and does vary from text to text; there are many different ways to write it. The common type of head mark has been provided for with U+0F04 TIBETAN MARK INITIAL YIG MGO MDUN MA and its extension U+0F05 TIBETAN MARK CLOSING YIG MGO SGAB MA. An initial mark *yig-mgo* can be written alone or combined with as many as three closing marks following it. When the initial mark is written in combination with one or more closing marks, the individual parts of the whole must stay in proper registration with each other to appear authentic. Therefore, it is strongly recommended that font developers create precomposed ligature glyphs to represent the various combinations of these two characters. The less common head marks mainly appear in Nyingmapa and Bonpo literature. Three of these head marks have been provided for with U+0F01, U+0F02, and U+0F03; however, many others have not been encoded. Font developers will have to deal with the fact that many types of head marks in use in this literature have not been encoded, cannot be represented by a replacement that has been encoded, and will be required by some users.

Two characters, U+0F3C TIBETAN MARK ANG KHANG GYON and U+0F3D TIBETAN MARK ANG KHANG GYAS, are paired punctuation; they are typically used together to form a roof over one or more digits or words. In this case, kerning or special ligatures may be required for proper rendering. The right *ang khang* may also be used much as a single closing parenthesis is used in forming lists; again, special kerning may be required for proper rendering. The marks U+0F3E TIBETAN SIGN YAR TSHES and U+0F3F TIBETAN SIGN MAR TSHES are paired signs used to combine with digits; special glyphs or compositional metrics are required for their use.

A set of frequently occurring astrological and religious signs specific to Tibetan is encoded between U+0FBE and U+0FCF.

U+0F34, which means "et cetera" or "and so on," is used after the first few *tsek-bar* of a recurring phrase. U+0FBE (often three times) indicates a refrain.

U+0F36 and U+0FBF are used to indicate where text should be inserted within other text or as references to footnotes or marginal notes.

Other Characters. The Wheel of Dharma, which occurs sometimes in Tibetan texts, is encoded in the Miscellaneous Symbols block at U+2638.

Left-facing and right-facing *swastika* symbols are likewise used. They are found among the Chinese ideographs at U+534D ("yung-drung-chi-khor") and U+5350 ("yung-drung-nang-khor").

The marks U+0F35 TIBETAN MARK NGAS BZUNG NYI ZLA and U+0F37 TIBETAN MARK NGAS BZUNG SGOR RTAGS conceptually attach to a *tsek-bar* rather than to an individual character and function more like attributes than characters—for example, as underlining to mark or emphasize text. In Tibetan interspersed commentaries, they may be used to tag the *tsek-bar* belonging to the root text that is being commented on. The same thing is often accomplished by setting the *tsek-bar* belonging to the root text in large type and the commentary in small type. Correct placement of these glyphs may be problematic. If they are treated as normal combining marks, they can be entered into the text following the vowel signs in a stack; if used, their presence will need to be accounted for by searching algorithms, among other things.

Tibetan Half-Numbers. The half-number forms (U+0F2A..U+0F33) are peculiar to Tibetan, though other scripts (for example, Bengali) have similar fractional concepts. The value of each half-number is 0.5 less than the number within which it appears. These forms are used only in some traditional contexts and appear as the *last* digit of a multidigit number. For example, the sequence of digits "U+0F24 U+0F2C" represents the number 42.5 or forty-two and one-half.

Tibetan Transliteration and Transcription of Other Languages. Tibetan traditions are in place for transliterating other languages. Most commonly, Sanskrit has been the language being transliterated, although Chinese has become more common in modern times. Additionally, Mongolian has a transliterated form. There are even some conventions for transliterating English. One feature of Tibetan script/grammar is that it allows for totally accurate transliteration of Sanskrit. The basic Tibetan letterforms and punctuation marks contain most of what is needed, although a few extra things are required. With these additions, Sanskrit can be transliterated perfectly into Tibetan, and the Tibetan transliteration can be rendered backward perfectly into Sanskrit with no ambiguities or difficulties.

The six Sanskrit retroflex letters are interleaved among the other consonants.

The compound Sanskrit consonants are not included in normal Tibetan. They could be made using the method described earlier for Tibetan stacked consonants, generally by subjoining "ha". However, to maintain consistency in transliterated texts and for ease in transmission and searching, it is recommended that implementations of Sanskrit in the Tibetan script use the precomposed forms of aspirated letters (and U+0F69, "ka + reversed sha") whenever possible, rather than implementing these consonants as completely decomposed stacks. Implementations must ensure that decomposed stacks and precomposed forms are interpreted equivalently (see *Section 3.7, Decomposition*). The compound consonants are explicitly coded as follows: U+0F93 TIBETAN SUBJOINED LETTER GHA, U+0F9D TIBETAN SUBJOINED LETTER DDHA, U+0FA2 TIBETAN SUBJOINED LETTER DHA, U+0FA7 TIBETAN SUBJOINED LETTER BHA, U+0FAC TIBETAN SUBJOINED LETTER DZHA, and U+0FB9 TIBETAN SUBJOINED LETTER KSSA.

The vowel signs of Sanskrit not included in Tibetan are encoded with other vowel signs between U+0F70 and U+0F7D. U+0F7F TIBETAN SIGN RNAM BCAD (*nam chay*) is the visarga, and U+0F7E TIBETAN SIGN RJES SU NGA RO (*ngaro*) is the anusvara. See *Section 9.1, Devanagari*, for more information on these two characters.

The characters encoded in the range U+0F88..U+0F8B are used in transliterated text and are most commonly found in Kalachakra literature.

When the Tibetan script is used to transliterate Sanskrit, consonants are sometimes stacked in ways that are not allowed in native Tibetan stacks. Even complex forms of this stacking behavior are catered for properly by the method described earlier for coding Tibetan stacks.

Other Signs. U+0F09 TIBETAN MARK BSKUR YIG MGO is a list enumerator used at the beginning of administrative letters in Bhutan, as is the petition honorific U+0F0A TIBETAN MARK BKA- SHOG YIG MGO.

U+0F3A TIBETAN MARK GUG RTAGS GYON and U+0F3B TIBETAN MARK GUG RTAGS GYAS are paired punctuation marks (brackets).

The sign U+0F39 TIBETAN MARK TSA -PHRU (*tsa-'phru*, which is a lenition mark) is the ornamental flaglike mark that is an integral part of the three consonants U+0F59 TIBETAN LETTER TSA, U+0F5A TIBETAN LETTER TSHA, and U+0F5B TIBETAN LETTER DZA. Although those consonants are not decomposable, this mark has been abstracted and may by itself be applied to "pha" and other consonants to make new letters for use in transliteration and transcription of other languages. For example, in modern literary Tibetan, it is one of the ways used to transcribe the Chinese "fa" and "va" sounds not represented by the normal Tibetan consonants. *Tsa-'phru* is also used to represent *tsa*, *tsha*, and *dza* in abbreviations.

Traditional Text Formatting and Line Justification. Native Tibetan texts ("pecha") are written and printed using a justification system that is, strictly speaking, right-ragged but with an attempt to right-justify. Each page has a margin. That margin is usually demarcated with visible border lines required of a pecha. In modern times, when Tibetan text is produced in Western-style books, the margin lines may be dropped and an invisible margin used. When writing the text within the margins, an attempt is made to have the lines of text justified up to the right margin. To do so, writers keep an eye on the overall line length as they fill lines with text and try manually to justify to the right margin. Even then, a gap at the right margin often cannot be filled. If the gap is short, it will be left as is and the line will be said to be justified enough, even though by machine-justification standards the line is not truly flush on the right. If the gap is large, the intervening space will be filled with as many *tseks* as are required to justify the line. Again, the justification is not done perfectly in the way that English text might be perfectly right-justified; as long as the last *tsek* is more or less at the right margin, that will do. The net result is that of a right-justified, blocklike look to the text, but the actual lines are always a little right-ragged.

Justifying *tseks* are nearly always used to pad the end of a line when the preceding character is a *tsek*—in other words, when the end of a line arrives in the middle of tshig-grub (see the previous definition under "Tibetan Punctuation"). However, it is unusual for a line that ends at the end of a tshig-grub to have justifying *tseks* added to the *shay* at the end of the tshig-grub. That is, a sequence like that shown in the first line of *Figure 10-2* is not usually padded as in the second line of *Figure 10-2*, though it is allowable. In this case, instead of justifying the line with *tseks*, the space between *shays* is enlarged and/or the whitespace following the final *shay* is usually left as is. Padding is *never* applied following an actual space character. For example, given the existence of a space after a *shay*, a line such as the third line of *Figure 10-2* may not be written with the padding as shown because the final *shay* should have a space after it, and padding is never applied after spaces. The same rule applies where the final *consonant* of a tshig-grub that ends a line is a "ka" or "ga". In that case, the ending *shay* is dropped but a space is still required after the consonant and that space must not be padded. For example, the appearance shown in the fourth line of *Figure 10-2* is not acceptable.

Figure 10-2. Justifying Tibetan Tseks

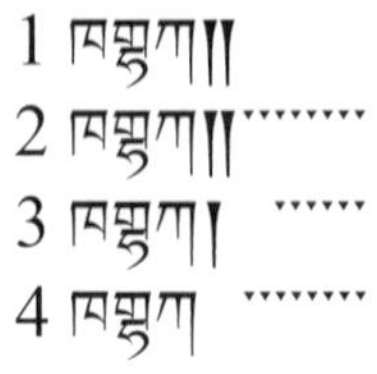

1 ཁཀྱག།།
2 ཁཀྱག།།་་་་་་་་་
3 ཁཀྱག། ་་་་་་་
4 ཁཀྱག ་་་་་་་་་

Tibetan text has two rules regarding the formatting of text at the beginning of a new line. There are severe constraints on which characters can start a new line, and the first rule is traditionally stated as follows: A *shay* of any description may never start a new line. Nothing except actual words of text can start a new line, with the only exception being a *go-yig* (yig-mgo) at the head of a front page or a *da-tshe* (zla-tshe, meaning "crescent moon"—for example, U+0F05) or one of its variations, which is effectively an "in-line" go-yig (yig-mgo), on any other line. One of two or three ornamental *shays* is also commonly used in short pieces of prose in place of the more formal *da-tshe*. This also means that a space may not start a new line in the flow of text. If there is a major break in a text, a new line might be indented.

A syllable (tsheg-bar) that comes at the end of a tshig-grub and that starts a new line must have the *shay* that would normally follow it replaced by a rin-chen-spungs-shad (U+0F11). The reason for this second rule is that the presence of the rin-chen-spungs-shad makes the end of tshig-grub more visible and hence makes the text easier to read.

In verse, the second *shay* following the first rin-chen-spungs-shad is sometimes replaced with a rin-chen-spungs-shad, though the practice is formally incorrect. It is a writer's trick done to make a particular scribing of a text more elegant. Although a moderately popular device, it does breaks the rule. Not only is rin-chen-spungs-shad used as the replacement for the *shay* but a whole class of "ornamental *shays*" are used for the same purpose. All are scribal variants on a rin-chen-spungs-shad, which is correctly written with three dots above it.

Tibetan Shorthand Abbreviations (bskungs-yig) and Limitations of the Encoding. A consonant functioning as the word base (ming-gzhi) is allowed to take only one vowel sign according to Tibetan grammar. The Tibetan shorthand writing technique called bskungs-yig does allow one or more words to be contracted into a single, very unusual combination of consonants and vowels. This construction frequently entails the application of more than one vowel sign to a single consonant or stack, and the composition of the stacks themselves can break the rules of normal Tibetan grammar. For this reason, vowel signs sometimes interact typographically, which accounts for their particular combining classes (see *Section 4.3, Combining Classes—Normative*).

The Unicode Standard accounts for plain text compounds of Tibetan that contain at most one base consonant, any number of subjoined consonants, followed by any number of vowel signs. This coverage constitutes the vast majority of Tibetan text. Rarely, stacks are seen that contain more than one such consonant-vowel combination in a vertical arrangement. These stacks are highly unusual and are considered beyond the scope of plain text rendering. They may be handled by higher-level mechanisms.

10.3 Phags-pa

Phags-pa: U+A840–U+A87F

The Phags-pa script is an historic script with some limited modern use. It bears some similarity to Tibetan and has no case distinctions. It is written vertically in columns running from left to right, like Mongolian. Units are often composed of several syllables and may be separated by whitespace.

The term *Phags-pa* is often written with an initial apostrophe: *'Phags-pa*. The Unicode Standard makes use of the alternative spelling without an initial apostrophe because apostrophes are not allowed in the normative character and block names.

History. The Phags-pa script was devised by the Tibetan lama Blo-gros rGyal-mtshan [lodoi jaltsan] (1235–1280 CE), commonly known by the title *Phags-pa Lama* ("exalted monk"), at the behest of Khubilai Khan (reigned 1260–1294) when he assumed leadership of the Mongol tribes in 1260. In 1269, the "new Mongolian script," as it was called, was promulgated by imperial edict for use as the national script of the Mongol empire, which from 1279 to 1368, as the Yuan dynasty, encompassed all of China.

The new script was not only intended to replace the Uighur-derived script that had been used to write Mongolian since the time of Genghis Khan (reigned 1206–1227), but was also intended to be used to write all the diverse languages spoken throughout the empire. Although the Phags-pa script never succeeded in replacing the earlier Mongolian script and had only very limited usage in writing languages other than Mongolian and Chinese, it was used quite extensively during the Yuan dynasty for a variety of purposes. There are many monumental inscriptions and manuscript copies of imperial edicts written in Mongolian or Chinese using the Phags-pa script. The script can also be found on a wide range of artifacts, including seals, official passes, coins, and banknotes. It was even used for engraving the inscriptions on Christian tombstones. A number of books are known to have been printed in the Phags-pa script, but all that has survived are some fragments from a printed edition of the Mongolian translation of a religious treatise by the Phags-pa Lama's uncle, Sakya Pandita. Of particular interest to scholars of Chinese historical linguistics is a rhyming dictionary of Chinese with phonetic readings for Chinese ideographs given in the Phags-pa script.

An ornate, pseudo-archaic "seal script" version of the Phags-pa script was developed specifically for engraving inscriptions on seals. The letters of the seal script form of Phags-pa mimic the labyrinthine strokes of Chinese seal script characters. A great many official seals and seal impressions from the Yuan dynasty are known. The seal script was also sometimes used for carving the title inscription on stone stelae, but never for writing ordinary running text.

Although the vast majority of extant Phags-pa texts and inscriptions from the thirteenth and fourteenth centuries are written in the Mongolian or Chinese languages, there are also examples of the script being used for writing Uighur, Tibetan, and Sanskrit, including two long Buddhist inscriptions in Sanskrit carved in 1345.

After the fall of the Yuan dynasty in 1368, the Phags-pa script was no longer used for writing Chinese or Mongolian. However, the script continued to be used on a limited scale in Tibet for special purposes such as engraving seals. By the late sixteenth century, a distinctive, stylized variety of Phags-pa script had developed in Tibet, and this Tibetan-style Phags-pa script, known as *hor-yig*, "Mongolian writing" in Tibetan, is still used today as a decorative script. In addition to being used for engraving seals, the Tibetan-style Phags-pa script is used for writing book titles on the covers of traditional style books, for architectural inscriptions such as those found on temple columns and doorways, and for calligraphic samplers.

Basic Structure. The Phags-pa script is based on Tibetan, but unlike any other Brahmic script Phags-pa is written vertically from top to bottom in columns advancing from left to right across the writing surface. This unusual directionality is borrowed from Mongolian, as is the way in which Phags-pa letters are ligated together along a vertical stem axis. In modern contexts, when embedded in horizontally oriented scripts, short sections of Phags-pa text may be laid out horizontally from left to right.

Despite the difference in directionality, the Phags-pa script fundamentally follows the Tibetan model of writing, and consonant letters have an inherent /a/ vowel sound. However, Phags-pa vowels are independent letters, not vowel signs as is the case with Tibetan, so they may start a syllable without being attached to a null consonant. Nevertheless, a null consonant (U+A85D PHAGS-PA LETTER A) is still needed to write an initial /a/ and is orthographically required before a diphthong or the semivowel U+A867 PHAGS-PA SUBJOINED LETTER WA. Only when writing Tibetan in the Phags-pa script is the null consonant required before an initial pure vowel sound.

Except for the *candrabindu* (which is discussed later in this section), Phags-pa letters read from top to bottom in logical order, so the vowel letters *i*, *e*, and *o* are placed below the preceding consonant—unlike in Tibetan, where they are placed above the consonant they modify.

Syllable Division. Text written in the Phags-pa script is broken into discrete syllabic units separated by whitespace. When used for writing Chinese, each Phags-pa syllabic unit corresponds to a single Han ideograph. For Mongolian and other polysyllabic languages, a single word is typically written as several syllabic units, each separated from each other by whitespace.

For example, the Mongolian word *tengri,* "heaven," which is written as a single ligated unit in the Mongolian script, is written as two separate syllabic units, *deng ri*, in the Phags-pa script. Syllable division does not necessarily correspond directly to grammatical structure. For instance, the Mongolian word *usun,* "water," is written *u sun* in the Phags-pa script, but its genitive form *usunu* is written *u su nu.*

Within a single syllabic unit, the Phags-pa letters are normally ligated together. Most letters ligate along a righthand stem axis, although reversed-form letters may instead ligate along a lefthand stem axis. The letter U+A861 PHAGS-PA LETTER O ligates along a central stem axis.

In traditional Phags-pa texts, normally no distinction is made between the whitespace used in between syllables belonging to the same word and the whitespace used in between syllables belonging to different words. Line breaks may occur between any syllable, regardless of word status. In contrast, in modern contexts, influenced by practices used in the processing of Mongolian text, U+202F NARROW NO-BREAK SPACE (NNBSP) may be used to separate syllables within a word, whereas U+0020 SPACE is used between words—and line breaking would be affected accordingly.

Candrabindu. U+A873 PHAGS-PA LETTER CANDRABINDU is used in writing Sanskrit mantras, where it represents a final nasal sound. However, although it represents the final sound in a syllable unit, it is always written as the first glyph in the sequence of letters, above the initial consonant or vowel of the syllable, but not ligated to the following letter. For example, *om* is written as a *candrabindu* followed by the letter *o*. To simplify cursor placement, text selection, and so on, the *candrabindu* is encoded in visual order rather than logical order. Thus *om* would be represented by the sequence <U+A873, U+A861>, rendered as shown in *Figure 10-3.*

Figure 10-3. Phags-pa Syllable Om

As the *candrabindu* is separated from the following letter, it does not take part in the shaping behavior of the syllable unit. Thus, in the syllable *om*, the letter *o* (U+A861) takes the isolate positional form.

Alternate Letters. Four alternate forms of the letters *ya, sha, ha,* and *fa* are encoded for use in writing Chinese under certain circumstances:

U+A86D PHAGS-PA LETTER ALTERNATE YA

U+A86E PHAGS-PA LETTER VOICELESS SHA

U+A86F PHAGS-PA LETTER VOICED HA

U+A870 PHAGS-PA LETTER ASPIRATED FA

These letters are used in the early-fourteenth-century Phags-pa rhyming dictionary of Chinese, *Menggu ziyun,* to represent historical phonetic differences between Chinese syllables that were no longer reflected in the contemporary Chinese language. This dictionary follows the standard phonetic classification of Chinese syllables into 36 initials, but as these had been defined many centuries previously, by the fourteenth century some of the initials had merged together or diverged into separate sounds. To distinguish historical phonetic characteristics, the dictionary uses two slightly different forms of the letters *ya, sha, ha,* and *fa.*

The historical phonetic values that U+A86E, U+A86F, and U+A870 represent are indicated by their character names, but this is not the case for U+A86D, so there may be some confusion as to when to use U+A857 PHAGS-PA LETTER YA and when to use U+A86D PHAGS-PA LETTER ALTERNATE YA. U+A857 is used to represent historic null initials, whereas U+A86D is used to represent historic palatal initials.

Numbers. There are no special characters for numbers in the Phags-pa script, so numbers are spelled out in full in the appropriate language.

Punctuation. The vast majority of traditional Phags-pa texts do not make use of any punctuation marks. However, some Mongolian inscriptions borrow the Mongolian punctuation marks U+1802 MONGOLIAN COMMA, U+1803 MONGOLIAN FULL STOP, and U+1805 MONGOLIAN FOUR DOTS.

Additionally, a small circle punctuation mark is used in some printed Phags-pa texts. This mark can be represented by U+3002 IDEOGRAPHIC FULL STOP, but for Phags-pa the *ideographic full stop* should be centered, not positioned to one side of the column. This follows traditional, historic practice for rendering the ideographic full stop in Chinese text, rather than more modern typography.

Tibetan Phags-pa texts also use head marks, U+A874 PHAGS-PA SINGLE HEAD MARK U+A875 PHAGS-PA DOUBLE HEAD MARK, to mark the start of an inscription, and *shad* marks, U+A876 PHAGS-PA MARK SHAD and U+A877 PHAGS-PA MARK DOUBLE SHAD, to mark the end of a section of text.

Positional Variants. The four vowel letters U+A85E PHAGS-PA LETTER I, U+A85F PHAGS-PA LETTER U, U+A860 PHAGS-PA LETTER E, and U+A861 PHAGS-PA LETTER O have different isolate, initial, medial, and final glyph forms depending on whether they are immediately preceded or followed by another Phags-pa letter (other than U+A873 PHAGS-PA LETTER CANDRABINDU, which does not affect the shaping of adjacent letters). The code charts show these four characters in their isolate form. The various positional forms of these letters are shown in *Table 10-2*.

Table 10-2. Phags-pa Positional Forms of I, U, E, and O

Letter	Isolate	Initial	Medial	Final
U+A85E PHAGS-PA LETTER I	ꡞ	ꡞ‍	‍ꡞ‍	‍ꡞ
U+A85F PHAGS-PA LETTER U	ꡟ	ꡟ‍	‍ꡟ‍	‍ꡟ
U+A860 PHAGS-PA LETTER E	ꡠ	ꡠ‍	‍ꡠ‍	‍ꡠ
U+A861 PHAGS-PA LETTER O	ꡡ	ꡡ‍	‍ꡡ‍	‍ꡡ

Consonant letters and the vowel letter U+A866 PHAGS-PA LETTER EE do not have distinct positional forms, although initial, medial, final, and isolate forms of these letters may be distinguished by the presence or absence of a stem extender that is used to ligate to the following letter.

The invisible format characters U+200D ZERO WIDTH JOINER (ZWJ) and U+200C ZERO WIDTH NON-JOINER (ZWNJ) may be used to override the expected shaping behavior, in the same way that they do for Mongolian and other scripts (see *Chapter 16, Special Areas and Format Characters*). For example, ZWJ may be used to select the initial, medial, or final form of a letter in isolation:

<U+200D, U+A861, U+200D> selects the medial form of the letter *o*

<U+200D, U+A861> selects the final form of the letter *o*

<U+A861, U+200D> selects the initial form of the letter *o*

Conversely, ZWNJ may be used to inhibit expected shaping. For example, the sequence <U+A85E, U+200C, U+A85F, U+200C, U+A860, U+200C, U+A861> selects the isolate forms of the letters *i*, *u*, *e*, and *o*.

Mirrored Variants. The four characters U+A869 PHAGS-PA LETTER TTA, U+A86A PHAGS-PA LETTER TTHA, U+A86B PHAGS-PA LETTER DDA, and U+A86C PHAGS-PA LETTER NNA are mirrored forms of the letters U+A848 PHAGS-PA LETTER TA, U+A849 PHAGS-PA LETTER THA, U+A84A PHAGS-PA LETTER DA, and U+A84B PHAGS-PA LETTER NA, respectively, and are used to represent the Sanskrit retroflex dental series of letters. Because these letters are mirrored, their stem axis is on the lefthand side rather than the righthand side, as is the case for all other consonant letters. This means that when the letters *tta*, *ttha*, *dda*, and *nna* occur at the start of a syllable unit, to correctly ligate with them any following letters normally take a mirrored glyph form. Because only a limited number of words use these letters, only the letters U+A856 PHAGS-PA LETTER SMALL A, U+A85C PHAGS-PA LETTER HA, U+A85E PHAGS-PA LETTER I, U+A85F PHAGS-PA LETTER U, U+A860 PHAGS-PA LETTER E, and U+A868 PHAGS-PA SUBJOINED LETTER YA are affected by this glyph mirroring behavior. The Sanskrit syllables that exhibit glyph mirroring after *tta*, *ttha*, *dda*, and *nna* are shown in *Table 10-3*.

Table 10-3. Contextual Glyph Mirroring in Phags-pa

Character	Syllables with Glyph Mirroring	Syllables without Glyph Mirroring
U+A856 PHAGS-PA LETTER SMALL A	*tthā*	*ttā, tthā*
U+A85E PHAGS-PA LETTER I	*tthi, nni*	*tthi*
U+A85F PHAGS-PA LETTER U	*nnu*	
U+A860 PHAGS-PA LETTER E	*tthe, dde, nne*	
U+A85C PHAGS-PA LETTER HA	*ddha*	
U+A868 PHAGS-PA SUBJOINED LETTER YA	*nnya*	

Glyph mirroring is not consistently applied to the letters U+A856 PHAGS-PA LETTER SMALL A and U+A85E PHAGS-PA LETTER I in the extant Sanskrit Phags-pa inscriptions. The letter *i* may occur both mirrored and unmirrored after the letter *ttha*, although it always occurs mirrored after the letter *nna*. *Small a* is not normally mirrored after the letters *tta* and *ttha* as its mirrored glyph is identical in shape to U+A85A PHAGS-PA LETTER SHA. Nevertheless, *small a* does sometimes occur in a mirrored form after the letter *ttha*, in which case context indicates that this is a mirrored letter *small a* and not the letter *sha*.

When any of the letters *small a*, *i*, *u*, *e*, *ha*, or *subjoined ya* immediately follow either *tta*, *ttha*, *dda*, or *nna* directly or another mirrored letter, then a mirrored glyph form of the letter should be selected automatically by the rendering system. Although *small a* is not normally mirrored in extant inscriptions, for consistency it is mirrored by default after *tta*, *ttha*, *dda*, and *nna* in the rendering model for Phags-pa.

To override the default mirroring behavior of the letters *small a*, *ha*, *i*, *u*, *e*, and *subjoined ya*, U+FE00 VARIATION SELECTOR-1 (VS1) may be applied to the appropriate character, as shown in *Table 10-4*. Note that only the variation sequences shown in *Table 10-4* are valid; any other sequence of a Phags-pa letter and VS1 is unspecified.

Table 10-4. Phags-pa Standardized Variants

Character Sequence	Description of Variant Appearance
<U+A856, U+FE00>	*phags-pa letter reversed shaping small a*
<U+A85C, U+FE00>	*phags-pa letter reversed shaping ha*
<U+A85E, U+FE00>	*phags-pa letter reversed shaping i*
<U+A85F, U+FE00>	*phags-pa letter reversed shaping u*
<U+A860, U+FE00>	*phags-pa letter reversed shaping e*
<U+A868, U+FE00>	*phags-pa letter reversed shaping ya*

In *Table 10-4*, "reversed shaping" means that the appearance of the character is reversed with respect to its expected appearance. Thus, if no mirroring would be expected for the character in the given context, applying VS1 would cause the rendering engine to select a mirrored glyph form. Similarly, if context would dictate glyph mirroring, application of VS1 would inhibit the expected glyph mirroring. This mechanism will typically be used to select a mirrored glyph for the letters *small a*, *ha*, *i*, *u*, *e*, or *subjoined ya* in isolation (for example, in discussion of the Phags-pa script) or to inhibit mirroring of the letters *small a* and *i* when they are not mirrored after the letters *tta* and *ttha*, as shown in *Figure 10-4*.

Figure 10-4. Phags-pa Reversed Shaping

The first example illustrates the normal shaping for the syllable *thi*. The second example shows the reversed shaping for *i* in that syllable and would be represented by a standardized variation sequence: <U+A849, U+A85E, U+FE00>. Example 3 illustrates the normal shaping for the Sanskrit syllable *tthi*, where the reversal of the glyph for the letter *i* is automatically conditioned by the lefthand stem placement of the Sanskrit letter *ttha*. Example 4 shows reversed shaping for *i* in the syllable *tthi* and would be represented by a standardized variation sequence: <U+A86A, U+A85E, U+FE00>.

10.4 Limbu

Limbu: U+1900–U+194F

The Limbu script is a Brahmic script primarily used to write the Limbu language. Limbu is a Tibeto-Burman language of the East Himalayish group and is spoken by about 200,000 persons mainly in eastern Nepal, but also in the neighboring Indian states of Sikkim and West Bengal (Darjeeling district). Its close relatives are the languages of the East Himalayish or "Kiranti" group in Eastern Nepal. Limbu is distantly related to the Lepcha (Róng) language of Sikkim and to Tibetan. Limbu was recognized as an official language in Sikkim in 1981.

The Nepali name *Limbu* is of uncertain origin. In Limbu, the Limbu call themselves *yakthuŋ*. Individual Limbus often take the surname "Subba," a Nepali term of Arabic origin meaning "headman." The Limbu script is often called "Sirijanga" after the Limbu culture-hero Sirijanga, who is credited with its invention. It is also sometimes called Kirat, *kirāta* being a Sanskrit term probably referring to some variety of non-Aryan hill-dwellers.

The oldest known writings in the Limbu script, most of which are held in the India Office Library, London, were collected in Darjeeling district in the 1850s. The modern script was developed beginning in 1925 in Kalimpong (Darjeeling district) in an effort to revive writing in Limbu, which had fallen into disuse. The encoding in the Unicode Standard supports the three versions of the Limbu script: the nineteenth-century script, found in manuscript documents; the early modern script, used in a few, mainly mimeographed, publications between 1928 and the 1970s; and the current script, used in Nepal and India (especially Sikkim) since the 1970s. There are significant differences, particularly between some of the glyphs required for the nineteenth-century and modern scripts.

Virtually all Limbu speakers are bilingual in Nepali, and far more Limbus are literate in Nepali than in Limbu. For this reason, many Limbu publications contain material both in Nepali and in Limbu, and in some cases Limbu appears in both the Limbu script and the Devanagari script. In some publications, literary coinages are glossed in Nepali or in English.

Consonants. Consonant letters and clusters represent syllable initial consonants and clusters followed by the inherent vowel, short open o ([ɔ]). Subjoined consonant letters are joined to the bottom of the consonant letters, extending to the right to indicate "medials" in syllable-initial consonant clusters. There are very few of these clusters in native Limbu words. The script provides for subjoined ◌ᤩ -ya, ◌ᤪ -ra, and ◌ᤫ -wa. Small letters are used to indicate syllable-final consonants. (See the following information on vowel length for further details.) The small letter consonants are found in the range U+1930..U+1938, corresponding to the syllable finals of native Limbu words. These letters are independent forms that, unlike the conjoined or half-letter forms of Indian scripts, may appear alone as word-final consonants (where Indian scripts use full consonant letters and a virama). The syllable finals are pronounced without a following vowel.

Limbu is a language with a well-defined syllable structure, in which syllable-initial stops are pronounced differently from finals. Syllable initials may be voiced following a vowel, whereas finals are never voiced but are pronounced unreleased with a simultaneous glottal closure, and geminated before a vowel. Therefore, the Limbu block encodes an explicit set of ten syllable-final consonants. These are called LIMBU SMALL LETTER KA, and so on.

Vowels. The Limbu vowel system has seven phonologically distinct timbres: [i, e, ɛ, a, ɔ, o, u]. The vowel [ɔ] functions as the inherent vowel in the modern Limbu script. To indicate a syllable with a vowel other than the inherent vowel, a *vowel sign* is added over, under, or to the right of the initial consonant letter or cluster. Although the vowel [ɔ] is the inherent vowel, the Limbu script has a combining vowel sign ◌ᤨ that may optionally be used to represent it. Many writers avoid using this sign because they consider it redundant.

Syllable-initial vowels are represented by a vowel-carrier character, U+1900 ᤀ LIMBU VOWEL-CARRIER LETTER, together with the appropriate vowel sign. Used without a following vowel sound, the vowel-carrier letter represents syllable-initial [ɔ], the inherent vowel. The initial consonant letters have been named *ka*, *kha*, and so on, in this encoding, although they are in fact pronounced ᤁ [kɔ], ᤂ [kʰɔ], and so on, and do not represent the Limbu syllables ᤁᤠ [ka], ᤂᤠ [kʰa], and so on. This is in keeping with the practice of educated Limbus in writing the letter-names in Devanagari. It would have been confusing to call the vowel-carrier letter A, however, so an artificial name is used in the Unicode Standard. The native name is ᤀᤶ [ɔm].

Vowel Length. Vowel length is phonologically distinctive in many contexts. Length in open syllables is indicated by writing U+193A ◌᤺ LIMBU SIGN KEMPHRENG, which looks like the diaeresis sign, over the initial consonant or cluster: ᤋ᤺ *tā*.

In closed syllables, two different methods are used to indicate vowel length. In the first method, vowel length is not indicated by *kemphreng*. The syllable-final consonant is written as a full form (that is, like a syllable-initial consonant), marked by U+193B ◌᤻ LIMBU SIGN SA-I: ᤐᤠᤏ᤻ *pān* "speech." This sign marks vowel length in addition to functioning as a virama by suppressing the inherent vowel of the syllable-final consonant. This method is widely used in Sikkim.

In the second method, which is in use in Nepal, vowel length is indicated by *kemphreng*, as for open syllables, and the syllable-final consonant appears in "small" form without *sa-i*: ᤐᤠ᤺ᤴ *pān* "speech." Writers who consistently follow this practice reserve the use of *sa-i* for syllable-final consonants that do not have small forms, regardless of the length of the syllable vowel: ᤏᤧᤛ᤻ᤛᤧ *nesse* "it lay," ᤗᤠ᤺ᤒ᤻ *lāb* "moon." Because almost all of the syllable finals that normally occur in native Limbu words have small forms, *sa-i* is used only for consonant combinations in loan words and for some indications of rapid speech.

U+193B ◌᤻ LIMBU SIGN SA-I is based on the Indic virama, but for a majority of current writers it has a different semantics because it indicates the length of the preceding vowel in addition to "killing" the inherent vowel of consonants functioning as syllable finals. It is therefore not suitable for use as a general virama as used in other Brahmic scripts in the Unicode Standard.

Glottalization. U+1939 LIMBU SIGN MUKPHRENG represents glottalization. *Mukphreng* never appears as a syllable initial. Although some linguists consider that word-final nasal consonants may be glottalized, this is never indicated in the script; *mukphreng* is not currently written after final consonants. No other syllable-final consonant clusters occur in Limbu.

Collating Order. There is no universally accepted alphabetical order for Limbu script. One ordering is based on the Limbu dictionary edited by Bairagi Kainla, with the addition of the obsolete letters, whose positions are not problematic. In Sikkim, a somewhat different order is used: the letter ᤏ *na* is placed before ᤋ *ta*, and the letter ᤄ *gha* is placed at the end of the alphabet.

Glyph Placement. The glyph positions for Limbu combining characters are summarized in *Table 10-5*.

Table 10-5. Positions of Limbu Combining Marks

Syllable	Glyphs	Code Point Sequence
ta	ᤋᤠ	190B 1920
ti	ᤋᤡ	190B 1921
tu	ᤋᤢ	190B 1922
tee	ᤋᤣ	190B 1923
tai	ᤋᤤ	190B 1924
too	ᤋᤥ	190B 1925
tau	ᤋᤦ	190B 1926
te	ᤋᤧ	190B 1927
to	ᤋᤨ	190B 1928
tya	ᤋᤩ	190B 1929
tra	ᤋᤪ	190B 192A
twa	ᤋᤫ	190B 192B
tak	ᤋᤰ	U+190B U+1930
taŋ	ᤋᤱ	U+190B U+1931
taṁ	ᤋᤲ	U+190B U+1932
tat	ᤋᤳ	U+190B U+1933
tan	ᤋᤴ	U+190B U+1934
tap	ᤋᤵ	U+190B U+1935
tam	ᤋᤶ	U+190B U+1936
tar	ᤋᤷ	U+190B U+1937
tal	ᤋᤸ	U+190B U+1938
tā	ᤋᤠ᤺	U+190B U+1920 U+193A
tī	ᤋᤡ᤺	U+190B U+1921 U+193A

Punctuation. The main punctuation mark used is the double vertical line, U+0965 DEVANAGARI DOUBLE DANDA. U+1945 ᥅ LIMBU QUESTION MARK and U+1944 ᥄ LIMBU EXCLAMATION MARK have shapes peculiar to Limbu, especially in Sikkimese typography. They are encoded in the Unicode Standard to facilitate the use of both Limbu and Devanagari scripts in the same documents. U+1940 ᥀ LIMBU SIGN LOO is used for the exclamatory particle *lo*. This particle is also often simply spelled out ᤗᤥ.

Digits. Limbu digits have distinctive forms and are assigned code points because Limbu and Devanagari (or Limbu and Arabic-Indic) numbers are often used in the same document.

10.5 Syloti Nagri

Syloti Nagri: U+A800–U+A82F

Syloti Nagri is a lesser-known Brahmi-derived script used for writing the Sylheti language. Sylheti is an Indo-European language spoken by some 5 million speakers in the Barak Valley region of northeast Bangladesh and southeast Assam in India. Worldwide there may be as many as 10 million speakers. Sylheti has commonly been regarded as a dialect of Bengali, with which it shares a high proportion of vocabulary.

The Syloti Nagri script has 27 consonant letters with an inherent vowel of /o/ and 5 independent vowel letters. There are 5 dependent vowel signs that are attached to a consonant letter. Unlike Devanagari, there are no vowel signs that appear to the left of their associated consonant.

Only two proper diacritics are encoded to support Syloti Nagri: *anusvara* and *hasanta*. Aside from its traditional Indic designation, *anusvara* can also be considered a final form for the sequence /-ng/, which does not have a base glyph in Syloti Nagri because it does not occur in other positions. *Anusvara* can also occur with the vowels U+A824 ◌ꠤ SYLOTI NAGRI VOWEL SIGN I and U+A826 ◌ꠦ SYLOTI NAGRI VOWEL SIGN E, creating a potential problem with the display of both items. It is recommended that *anusvara* always occur in sequence after any vowel signs, as a final character.

Virama and Conjuncts. Syloti Nagri is atypical of Indic scripts in use of the *virama* (*hasanta*) and conjuncts. Conjuncts are not strictly correlated with the phonology being represented. They are neither necessary in contexts involving a dead consonant, nor are they limited to such contexts. *Hasanta* was only recently introduced into the script and is used only in limited contexts. Conjuncts are not limited to sequences involving dead consonants but can be formed from pairs of characters of almost any type (consonant, independent vowel, dependent vowel) and can represent a wide variety of syllables. It is generally unnecessary to overtly indicate dead consonants with a conjunct or explicit *hasanta*. The only restriction is that an overtly rendered *hasanta* cannot occur in connection with the first element of a conjunct. The absence of *hasanta* does not imply a live consonant and has no bearing on the occurrence of conjuncts. Similarly, the absence of a conjunct does not imply a live consonant and has no bearing on the occurrence of *hasanta*.

Digits. There are no unique Syloti Nagri digits. When digits do appear in Syloti Nagri texts, they are generally Bengali forms. Any font designed to support Syloti Nagri should include the Bengali digits because there is no guarantee that they would otherwise exist in a user's computing environment. They should use the corresponding Bengali block code points, U+09E6..U+09EF.

Punctuation. With the advent of digital type and the modernization of the Syloti Nagri script, one can expect to find all of the traditional punctuation marks borrowed from the Latin typography: *period*, *comma*, *colon*, *semicolon*, *question mark*, and so on. In addition, the Devanagari *single danda* and *double danda* are used with great frequency.

Poetry Marks. Four native poetry marks are included in the Syloti Nagri block. The script also makes use of U+2055 ⁕ FLOWER PUNCTUATION MARK (in the General Punctuation block) as a poetry mark.

10.6 Kharoshthi

Kharoshthi: U+10A00–U+10A5F

The Kharoshthi script, properly spelled as Kharoṣṭhī, was used historically to write Gāndhārī and Sanskrit as well as various mixed dialects. Kharoshthi is an Indic script of the *abugida* type. However, unlike other Indic scripts, it is written from right to left. The Kharoshthi script was initially deciphered around the middle of the nineteenth century by James Prinsep and others who worked from short Greek and Kharoshthi inscriptions on the coins of the Indo-Greek and Indo-Scythian kings. The decipherment has been refined over the last 150 years as more material has come to light.

The Kharoshthi script is one of the two ancient writing systems of India. Unlike the pan-Indian Brāhmī script, Kharoshthi was confined to the northwest of India centered on the region of *Gandhāra* (modern northern Pakistan and eastern Afghanistan, as shown in *Figure 10-5*). Gandhara proper is shown on the map as the dark gray area near Peshawar. The lighter gray areas represent places where the Kharoshthi script was used and where manuscripts and inscriptions have been found.

The exact details of the origin of the Kharoshthi script remain obscure, but it is almost certainly related to Aramaic. The Kharoshthi script first appears in a fully developed form in the Aśokan inscriptions at Shahbazgarhi and Mansehra which have been dated to around 250 BCE. The script continued to be used in Gandhara and neighboring regions, sometimes alongside Brahmi, until around the third century CE, when it disappeared from its homeland. Kharoshthi was also used for official documents and epigraphs in the Central Asian cities of Khotan and Niya in the third and fourth centuries CE, and it appears to have survived in Kucha and neighboring areas along the Northern Silk Road until the seventh century. The Central Asian form of the script used during these later centuries is termed

Formal Kharoshthi and was used to write both Gandhari and Tocharian B. Representation of Kharoshthi in the Unicode code charts uses forms based on manuscripts of the first century CE.

Figure 10-5. Geographical Extent of the Kharoshthi Script

Directionality. Kharoshthi can be implemented using the rules of the Unicode Bidirectional Algorithm. Both letters and digits are written from right to left. Kharoshthi letters do not have positional variants.

Diacritic Marks and Vowels. All vowels other than *a* are written with diacritic marks in Kharoshthi. In addition, there are six vowel modifiers and three consonant modifiers that are written with combining diacritics. In general, only one combining vowel sign is applied to each syllable (*aksara*). However, there are some examples of two vowel signs on *aksaras* in the Kharoshthi of Central Asia.

Numerals. Kharoshthi employs a set of eight numeral signs unique to the script. Like the letters, the numerals are written from right to left. Numbers in Kharoshthi are based on an additive system. There is no zero, nor separate signs for the numbers five through nine. The number 1996, for example, would logically be represented as 1000 4 4 1 100 20 20 20 20 10 4 2 and would appear as shown in *Figure 10-6*. The numerals are encoded in the range U+10A40..U+10A47.

Figure 10-6. Kharoshthi Number 1996

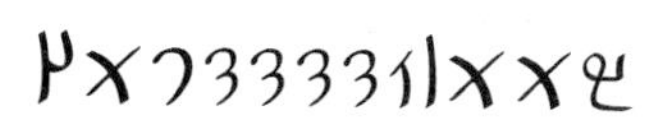

𐩇𐩃𐩃𐩀𐩆𐩅𐩅𐩅𐩅𐩄𐩃𐩁

Punctuation. Nine different punctuation marks are used in manuscripts and inscriptions. The punctuation marks are encoded in the range U+10A50..U+10A58.

Word Breaks, Line Breaks, and Hyphenation. Most Kharoshthi manuscripts are written as continuous text with no indication of word boundaries. Only a few examples are known where spaces have been used to separate words or verse quarters. Most scribes tried to finish a word before starting a new line. There are no examples of anything akin to hyphenation in Kharoshthi manuscripts. In cases where a word would not completely fit into a line, its continuation simply appears at the beginning of the next line. Modern scholarly practice uses spaces and hyphenation. When necessary, hyphenation should follow Sanskrit practice.

Sorting. There is an ancient ordering connected with Kharoshthi called *Arapacana*, named after the first five *aksaras*. However, there is no evidence that words were sorted in this order, and there is no record of the complete *Arapacana* sequence. In modern scholarly practice, Gandhari is sorted in much the same order as Sanskrit. Vowel length, even when marked, is ignored when sorting Kharoshthi.

Rendering Kharoshthi

Rendering requirements for Kharoshthi are similar to those for Devanagari. This section specifies a minimum set of combining rules that provide legible Kharoshthi diacritic and ligature substitution behavior.

All unmarked consonants include the inherent vowel *a*. Other vowels are indicated by one of the combining vowel diacritics. Some letters may take more than one diacritical mark. In these cases the preferred sequence is Letter + {Consonant Modifier} + {Vowel Sign} + {Vowel Modifier}. For example the Sanskrit word *parārdhyaiḥ* might be rendered in Kharoshthi script as **parārjaiḥ*, written from right to left, as shown in *Figure 10-7*.

Figure 10-7. Kharoshthi Rendering Example

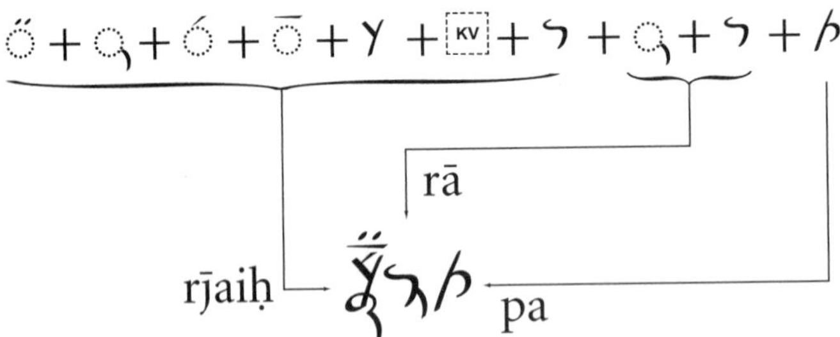

Combining Vowels. The various combining vowels attach to characters in different ways. A number of groupings have been determined on the basis of their visual types, such as horizontal or vertical, as shown in *Table 10-6*.

Table 10-6. Kharoshthi Vowel Signs

Type	Example	Group Members
Vowel sign i		
Horizontal	a + -i → i 𐨀 + 𐨁 → 𐨀𐨁	A, NA, HA
Vertical	tha + -i → thi 𐨠 + 𐨁 → 𐨠𐨁	THA, PA, PHA, MA, LA, SHA
Diagonal	ka + -i → ki 𐨐 + 𐨁 → 𐨐𐨁	All other letters
Vowel sign u		
Independent	ha + -u→ hu 𐨱 + 𐨂 → 𐨱𐨂	TTA, HA
Ligated	ma + -u → mu 𐨨 + 𐨂 → 𐨨𐨂	MA
Attached	a + -u → u 𐨀 + 𐨂 → 𐨀𐨂	All other letters
Vowel sign vocalic r		
Attached	a + -r̥ → r̥ 𐨀 + 𐨃 → 𐨀𐨃	A, KA, KKA, KHA, GA, GHA, CA, CHA, JA, TA, DA, DHA, NA, PA, PHA, BA, BHA, VA, SHA, SA
Independent	ma +-r̥ → mr̥ 𐨨 + 𐨃 → 𐨨𐨃	MA, HA
Vowel sign e		
Horizontal	a + -e → e 𐨀 + 𐨅 → 𐨀𐨅	A, NA, HA
Vertical	tha + -e → the 𐨠 + 𐨅 → 𐨠𐨅	THA, PA, PHA, LA, SSA
Ligated	da + -e→ de 𐨡 + 𐨅 → 𐨡𐨅	DA, MA
Diagonal	ka + -e→ ke 𐨐 + 𐨅 → 𐨐𐨅	All other letters
Vowel sign o		
Vertical	pa + -o → po 𐨤 + 𐨆 → 𐨤𐨆	PA, PHA, YA, SHA
Diagonal	a + -o→ o 𐨀 + 𐨆 → 𐨀𐨆	All other letters

Combining Vowel Modifiers. U+10A0C ◌𐨌 KHAROSHTHI VOWEL LENGTH MARK indicates equivalent long vowels and, when used in combination with -e and -o, indicates the diphthongs *–ai* and *–au.* U+10A0D ◌𐨍 KHAROSHTHI SIGN DOUBLE RING BELOW appears in some Central Asian documents, but its precise phonetic value has not yet been established. These two modifiers have been found only in manuscripts and inscriptions from the first century CE onward. U+10A0E ◌𐨎 KHAROSHTHI SIGN ANUSVARA indicates nasalization, and U+10A0F ◌𐨏 KHAROSHTHI SIGN VISARGA is generally used to indicate unvoiced syllable-final [h], but has a secondary use as a vowel length marker. *Visarga* is found only in Sanskritized forms of the language and is not known to occur in a single *aksara* with *anusvara.* The modifiers and the vowels they modify are given in *Table 10-7.*

Table 10-7. Kharoshthi Vowel Modifiers

Type	Example	Group Members
Vowel length mark	ma + ◌̄ → mā 𐨨 + ◌𐨌 → 𐨨𐨌	A, I, U, R, E, O
Double ring below	sa + ◌͚ → sa͚ 𐨯 + ◌𐨍 → 𐨯𐨍	A, U
Anusvara	a + -ṃ → aṃ 𐨀 + ◌𐨎 → 𐨀𐨎	A, I, U, R, E, O
Visarga	ka + -ḥ →kaḥ 𐨐 + ◌𐨏 → 𐨐𐨏	A, I, U, R, E, O

Combining Consonant Modifiers. U+10A38 ◌𐨸 KHAROSHTHI SIGN BAR ABOVE indicates various modified pronunciations depending on the consonants involved, such as nasalization or aspiration. U+10A39 ◌𐨹 KHAROSHTHI SIGN CAUDA indicates various modified pronunciations of consonants, particularly fricativization. The precise value of U+10A3A ◌𐨺 KHAROSHTHI SIGN DOT BELOW has not yet been determined. Usually only one consonant modifier can be applied to a single consonant. The resulting combined form may also combine with vowel diacritics, one of the vowel modifiers, or anusvara or visarga. The modifiers and the consonants they modify are given in *Table 10-8.*

Table 10-8. Kharoshthi Consonant Modifiers

Type	Example	Group Members
Bar above	ja + ◌̄ → j̄a 𐨗 + ◌𐨸 → 𐨗𐨸	GA, CA, JA, NA, MA, SHA, SSA, SA, HA
Cauda	ga + ◌́ → ǵa 𐨒 + ◌𐨹 → 𐨒𐨹	GA, JA, DDA, TA, DA, PA, YA, VA, SHA, SA
Dot below	ma + ◌̣ → ṃa 𐨨 + ◌𐨺 → 𐨨𐨺	MA, HA

Virama. The virama is used to indicate the suppression of the inherent vowel. The glyph for U+10A3F 𐨿 KHAROSHTHI VIRAMA shown in the code charts is arbitrary and is not actually rendered directly; the dotted box around the glyph indicates that special rendering is required. When not followed by a consonant, the virama causes the preceding consonant to be written as subscript to the left of the letter preceding it. If followed by another consonant, the virama will trigger a combined form consisting of two or more consonants. The resulting form may also be subject to combinations with the previously noted combining diacritics.

The virama can follow only a consonant or a consonant modifier. It cannot follow a space, a vowel, a vowel modifier, a number, a punctuation sign, or another virama. Examples of the use of the Kharoshthi virama are given in *Table 10-9*.

Table 10-9. Examples of Kharoshthi Virama

Type	**Example**
Pure virama	*dha* + *i* + *k* + VIRAMA → *dhik* 𐨢 + 𐨁 + 𐨐 + 𐨿 → 𐨢𐨁𐨐𐨿
Ligatures	*ka* + VIRAMA + *ṣa* → *kṣa* 𐨐 + 𐨿 + 𐨮 → 𐨐𐨿𐨮
Consonants with special combining forms	*sa* + VIRAMA + ya → *sya* 𐨯 + 𐨿 + 𐨩 → 𐨯𐨿𐨩
Consonants with full combined form	*ka* + VIRAMA + *ta* → *kta* 𐨐 + 𐨿 + 𐨟 → 𐨐𐨿𐨟

CHAPTER 11

Chapter 11

Southeast Asian Scripts

The following scripts are discussed in this chapter:

Thai	*Khmer*	*Philippine scripts*
Lao	*Tai Le*	*Buginese*
Myanmar	*New Tai Lue*	*Balinese*

The scripts of Southeast Asia are written from left to right; many use no interword spacing but use spaces or marks between phrases. They are mostly abugidas, but with various idiosyncrasies that distinguish them from the scripts of South Asia.

The four Philippine scripts included here operate on similar principles; each uses nonspacing vowel signs. In addition, the Tagalog script has a virama.

The term "Tai" refers to a family of languages spoken in Southeast Asia, including Thai, Lao, and Shan. This term is also part of the name of a number of scripts encoded in the Unicode Standard. The Tai Le script is used to write the language of the same name, which is spoken in south central Yunnan (China). The New Tai Lue script, also known as Xishuang Banna Dai, is unrelated to the Tai Le script, but is also used in south Yunnan.

Buginese and Balinese are scripts of Indonesia, and both are ultimately related to scripts of South Asia. Buginese is used in Sulawesi; Balinese is used on the island of Bali.

11.1 Thai

Thai: U+0E00–U+0E7F

The Thai script is used to write Thai and other Southeast Asian languages, such as Kuy, Lanna Tai, and Pali. It is a member of the Indic family of scripts descended from Brahmi. Thai modifies the original Brahmi letter shapes and extends the number of letters to accommodate features of the Thai language, including tone marks derived from superscript digits. At the same time, the Thai script lacks the conjunct consonant mechanism and independent vowel letters found in most other Brahmi-derived scripts. As in all scripts of this family, the predominant writing direction is from left to right.

Standards. Thai layout in the Unicode Standard is based on the Thai Industrial Standard 620-2529, and its updated version 620-2533.

Encoding Principles. In common with most Brahmi-derived scripts, each Thai consonant letter represents a syllable possessing an inherent vowel sound. For Thai, that inherent vowel is /o/ in the medial position and /a/ in the final position.

The consonants are divided into classes that historically represented distinct sounds, but in modern Thai indicate tonal differences. The inherent vowel and tone of a syllable are then modified by addition of vowel signs and tone marks attached to the base consonant letter. Some of the vowel signs and all of the tone marks are rendered in the script as diacritics attached above or below the base consonant. These combining signs and marks are encoded after the modified consonant in the memory representation.

Most of the Thai vowel signs are rendered by full letter-sized inline glyphs placed either before (that is, to the left of), after (to the right of), or *around* (on both sides of) the glyph for the base consonant letter. In the Thai encoding, the letter-sized glyphs that are placed before (left of) the base consonant letter, in full or partial representation of a vowel sign, are, in fact, encoded as separate characters that are typed and stored *before* the base consonant character. This encoding for left-side Thai vowel sign glyphs (and similarly in Lao) differs from the conventions for all other Indic scripts, which uniformly encode all vowels after the base consonant. The difference is necessitated by the encoding practice commonly employed with Thai character data as represented by the Thai Industrial Standard.

The glyph positions for Thai syllables are summarized in *Table 11-1*.

Table 11-1. Glyph Positions in Thai Syllables

Syllable	Glyphs	Code Point Sequence
ka	กะ	0E01 0E30
ka:	กา	0E01 0E32
ki	กิ	0E01 0E34
ki:	กี	0E01 0E35
ku	กุ	0E01 0E38
ku:	กู	0E01 0E39
ku'	กึ	0E01 0E36
ku':	กื	0E01 0E37
ke	เกะ	0E40 0E01 0E30
ke:	เก	0E40 0E01
kae	แกะ	0E41 0E01 0E30
kae:	แก	0E41 0E01
ko	โกะ	0E42 0E01 0E30

Table 11-1. Glyph Positions in Thai Syllables (Continued)

Syllable	Glyphs	Code Point Sequence
ko:	โก	0E42 0E01
ko'	เกาะ	0E40 0E01 0E32 0E30
ko':	กอ	0E01 0E2D
koe	เกอะ	0E40 0E01 0E2D 0E30
koe:	เกอ	0E40 0E01 0E2D
kia	เกีย	0E40 0E01 0E35 0E22
ku'a	เกือ	0E40 0E01 0E37 0E2D
kua	กัว	0E01 0E31 0E27
kaw	เกา	0E40 0E01 0E32
koe:y	เกย	0E40 0E01 0E22
kay	ไก	0E44 0E01
kay	ใก	0E43 0E01
kam	กำ	0E01 0E33
kri	กฤ	0E01 0E24

Rendering of Thai Combining Marks. The combining classes assigned to tone marks (107) and to other combining characters displayed above (0) do not fully account for their typographic interaction.

For the purpose of rendering, the Thai combining marks above (U+0E31, U+0E34..U+0E37, U+0E47..U+0E4E) should be displayed outward from the base character they modify, in the order in which they appear in the text. In particular, a sequence containing <U+0E48 THAI CHARACTER MAI EK, U+0E4D THAI CHARACTER NIKHAHIT> should be displayed with the *nikhahit* above the *mai ek*, and a sequence containing <U+0E4D THAI CHARACTER NIKHAHIT, U+0E48 THAI CHARACTER MAI EK> should be displayed with the *mai ek* above the *nikhahit*.

This does not preclude input processors from helping the user by pointing out or correcting typing mistakes, perhaps taking into account the language. For example, because the string <*mai ek, nikhahit*> is not useful for the Thai language and is likely a typing mistake, an input processor could reject it or correct it to <*nikhahit, mai ek*>.

When the character U+0E33 THAI CHARACTER SARA AM follows one or more tone marks (U+0E48..U+0E4B), the *nikhahit* that is part of the *sara am* should be displayed below those tone marks. In particular, a sequence containing <U+0E48 THAI CHARACTER MAI EK, U+0E33 THAI CHARACTER SARA AM> should be displayed with the *mai ek* above the *nikhahit*.

Thai Punctuation. Thai uses a variety of punctuation marks particular to this script. U+0E4F THAI CHARACTER FONGMAN is the Thai bullet, which is used to mark items in lists or appears at the beginning of a verse, sentence, paragraph, or other textual segment. U+0E46 THAI CHARACTER MAIYAMOK is used to mark repetition of preceding letters. U+0E2F THAI CHARACTER PAIYANNOI is used to indicate elision or abbreviation of letters; it is itself viewed as a kind of letter, however, and is used with considerable frequency because of its appearance in such words as the Thai name for Bangkok. *Paiyannoi* is also used in combination (U+0E2F U+0E25 U+0E2F) to create a construct called *paiyanyai*, which means "et cetera, and so forth." The Thai *paiyanyai* is comparable to its analogue in the Khmer script: U+17D8 KHMER SIGN BEYYAL.

U+0E5A THAI CHARACTER ANGKHANKHU is used to mark the end of a long segment of text. It can be combined with a following U+0E30 THAI CHARACTER SARA A to mark a larger segment of text; typically this usage can be seen at the end of a verse in poetry. U+0E5B THAI CHARACTER KHOMUT marks the end of a chapter or document, where it always follows the *angkhankhu* + *sara a* combination. The Thai *angkhankhu* and its combination with *sara a* to mark breaks in text have analogues in many other Brahmi-derived scripts. For example, they are closely related to U+17D4 KHMER SIGN KHAN and U+17D5 KHMER SIGN BARIYOOSAN, which are themselves ultimately related to the *danda* and *double danda* of Devanagari.

Thai words are not separated by spaces. Instead, text is laid out with spaces introduced at text segments where Western typography would typically make use of commas or periods. However, Latin-based punctuation such as comma, period, and colon are also used in text, particularly in conjunction with Latin letters or in formatting numbers, addresses, and so forth. If word boundary indications are desired—for example, for the use of automatic line layout algorithms—the character U+200B ZERO WIDTH SPACE should be used to place invisible marks for such breaks. The ZERO WIDTH SPACE can grow to have a visible width when justified. See *Figure 16-2*.

Thai Transcription of Pali and Sanskrit. The Thai script is frequently used to write Pali and Sanskrit. When so used, consonant clusters are represented by the explicit use of U+0E3A THAI CHARACTER PHINTHU (*virama*) to mark the removal of the inherent vowel. There is no conjoining behavior, unlike in other Indic scripts. U+0E4D THAI CHARACTER NIKHAHIT is the Pali *nigghahita* and Sanskrit *anusvara*. U+0E30 THAI CHARACTER SARA A is the Sanskrit *visarga*. U+0E24 THAI CHARACTER RU and U+0E26 THAI CHARACTER LU are vocalic /r/ and /l/, with U+0E45 THAI CHARACTER LAKKHANGYAO used to indicate their lengthening.

11.2 Lao

Lao: U+0E80–U+0EFF

The Lao language and script are closely related to Thai. The Unicode Standard encodes the characters of the Lao script in the same relative order as the Thai characters.

Encoding Principles. Lao contains fewer letters than Thai because by 1960 it was simplified to be fairly phonemic, whereas Thai maintains many etymological spellings that are homonyms. Unlike in Thai, Lao consonant letters are conceived of as simply representing the consonant sound, rather than a syllable with an inherent vowel. The vowel [a] is always represented explicitly with U+0EB0 LAO VOWEL SIGN A.

Punctuation. Regular word spacing is not used in Lao; spaces separate phrases or sentences instead.

Glyph Placement. The glyph placements for Lao syllables are summarized in *Table 11-2*.

Table 11-2. Glyph Positions in Lao Syllables

Syllable	Glyphs	Code Point Sequence
ka	ກະ	0E81 0EB0
ka:	ກາ	0E81 0EB2
ki	ກິ	0E81 0EB4
ki:	ກີ	0E81 0EB5
ku	ກຸ	0E81 0EB8
ku:	ກູ	0E81 0EB9
ku'	ກຶ	0E81 0EB6
ku':	ກື	0E81 0EB7
ke	ເກະ	0EC0 0E81 0EB0
ke:	ເກ	0EC0 0E81
kae	ແກະ	0EC1 0E81 0EB0
kae:	ແກ	0EC1 0E81
ko	ໂກະ	0EC2 0E81 0EB0
ko:	ໂກ	0EC2 0E81
ko'	ເກາະ	0EC0 0E81 0EB2 0EB0
ko':	ກໍ	0E81 0ECD
koe	ເກິ	0EC0 0E81 0EB4
koe:	ເກີ	0EC0 0E81 0EB5
kia	ເກັຽ ເກຢ	0EC0 0E81 0EB1 0EBD 0EC0 0E81 0EA2
ku'a	ເກືອ	0EC0 0E81 0EB7 0EAD
kua	ກົວ	0E81 0EBB 0EA7
kaw	ເກົາ	0EC0 0E81 0EBB 0EB2

Table 11-2. Glyph Positions in Lao Syllables (Continued)

Syllable	Glyphs	Code Point Sequence
koe:y	ເກີຽ ເກີຍ	0EC0 0E81 0EB5 0EBD 0EC0 0E81 0EB5 0EA2
kay	ໄກ	0EC4 0E81
kay	ໃກ	0EC3 0E81
kam	ກຳ	0E81 0EB3

Additional Letters. A few additional letters in Lao have no match in Thai:

U+0EBB LAO VOWEL SIGN MAI KON

U+0EBC LAO SEMIVOWEL SIGN LO

U+0EBD LAO SEMIVOWEL SIGN NYO

The preceding two semivowel signs are the last remnants of the system of subscript medials, which in Myanmar retains additional distinctions. Myanmar and Khmer include a full set of subscript consonant forms used for conjuncts. Thai no longer uses any of these forms; Lao has just the two.

Rendering of Lao Combining Marks. The combining classes assigned to tone marks (122) and to other combining characters displayed above (0) do not fully account for their typographic interaction.

For the purpose of rendering, the Lao combining marks above (U+0EB1, U+0EB4..U+0EB7, U+0EBB, U+0EC8..U+0ECD) should be displayed outward from the base character they modify, in the order in which they appear in the text. In particular, a sequence containing <U+0EC8 LAO TONE MAI EK, U+0ECD LAO NIGGAHITA> should be displayed with the *niggahita* above the *mai ek*, and a sequence containing <U+0ECD LAO NIGGAHITA, U+0EC8 LAO TONE MAI EK> should be displayed with the *mai ek* above the *niggahita.*

This does not preclude input processors from helping the user by pointing out or correcting typing mistakes, perhaps taking into account the language. For example, because the string <*mai ek, niggahita*> is not useful for the Lao language and is likely a typing mistake, an input processor could reject it or correct it to <*niggahita, mai ek*>.

When the character U+0EB3 LAO VOWEL SIGN AM follows one or more tone marks (U+0EC8..U+0ECB), the *niggahita* that is part of the *sara am* should be displayed below those tone marks. In particular, a sequence containing <U+0EC8 LAO TONE MAI EK, U+0EB3 LAO VOWEL SIGN AM> should be displayed with the *mai ek* above the *niggahita.*

Lao Aspirated Nasals. The Unicode character encoding includes two ligatures for Lao: U+0EDC LAO HO NO and U+0EDD LAO HO MO. They correspond to sequences of [h] plus [n] or [h] plus [m] without ligating. Their function in Lao is to provide versions of the [n] and [m] consonants with a different inherent tonal implication.

11.3 Myanmar

Myanmar: U+1000–U+109F

The Myanmar script is used to write Burmese, the majority language of Myanmar (formerly called Burma). Variations and extensions of the script are used to write other languages of the region, such as Shan and Mon, as well as Pali and Sanskrit. The Myanmar script was formerly known as the Burmese script, but the term "Myanmar" is now preferred.

The Myanmar writing system derives from a Brahmi-related script borrowed from South India in about the eighth century to write the Mon language. The first inscription in the Myanmar script dates from the eleventh century and uses an alphabet almost identical to that of the Mon inscriptions. Aside from rounding of the originally square characters, this script has remained largely unchanged to the present. It is said that the rounder forms were developed to permit writing on palm leaves without tearing the writing surface of the leaf.

Because of its Brahmi origins, the Myanmar script shares the structural features of its Indic relatives: consonant symbols include an inherent "a" vowel; various signs are attached to a consonant to indicate a different vowel; ligatures and conjuncts are used to indicate consonant clusters; and the overall writing direction is from left to right. Thus, despite great differences in appearance and detail, the Myanmar script follows the same basic principles as, for example, Devanagari.

Standards. There is not yet an official national standard for the encoding of Myanmar/Burmese. The current encoding was prepared with the consultation of experts from the Myanmar Information Technology Standardization Committee (MITSC) in Yangon (Rangoon). The MITSC, formed by the government in 1997, consists of experts from the Myanmar Computer Scientists' Association, Myanmar Language Commission, and Myanmar Historical Commission.

Encoding Principles. As with Indic scripts, the Myanmar encoding represents only the basic underlying characters; multiple glyphs and rendering transformations are required to assemble the final visual form for each syllable. Even some single characters, such as U+102C ◌ာ MYANMAR VOWEL SIGN AA, may assume variant forms (for example, ◌ါ) depending on the other characters with which they combine. Conversely, characters and combinations that may appear visually identical in some fonts, such as U+101D ဝ MYANMAR LETTER WA and U+1040 ၀ MYANMAR DIGIT ZERO, are distinguished by their underlying encoding.

Composite Characters. As is the case in many other scripts, some Myanmar letters or signs may be analyzed as composites of two or more other characters and are not encoded separately. The following are examples of Myanmar letters represented by combining character sequences:

myanmar vowel sign o

> U+1000 က *ka* + U+1031 ေ◌ *vowel sign e* + U+102C ◌ာ *vowel sign aa* → ကော *kō*

myanmar vowel sign au

> U+1000 က *ka* + U+1031 ေ◌ *vowel sign e* + U+102C ◌ာ *vowel sign aa* + U+1039 ◌္ *virama* + U+200C ZWNJ → ကော် *kau*

myanmar vowel sign ui

> U+1000 က *ka* + U+102F ◌ု *vowel sign u* + U+102D ◌ိ *vowel sign i* → ကို *kui*

Encoding Subranges. The basic consonants, independent vowels, and dependent vowel signs required for writing the Myanmar language are encoded at the beginning of the Myanmar range. Extensions of each of these categories for use in writing other languages, such as Pali and Sanskrit, are appended at the end of the range. In between these two sets lie the script-specific signs, punctuation, and digits.

Conjunct and Medial Consonants. As in other Indic-derived scripts, conjunction of two consonant letters is indicated by the insertion of a virama U+1039 ◌္ MYANMAR SIGN VIRAMA between them. It causes ligation or other rendered combination of the consonants, although the virama itself is not rendered visibly.

The conjunct form of U+1004 င MYANMAR LETTER NGA is rendered as a superscript sign called *kinzi*. *Kinzi* is encoded in logical order as a conjunct consonant *before* the syllable to which it applies; this is similar to the treatment of the Devanagari *ra*. (See *Section 9.1, Devanagari*, rule R2.) For example, *kinzi* applied to U+1000 က MYANMAR LETTER KA would be written via the following sequence:

> U+1004 င *nga* + U+1039 ◌္ *virama* + U+1000 က *ka* → င်္က *ṅka*

The Myanmar script traditionally distinguishes a set of subscript "medial" consonants: forms of *ya*, *ra*, *wa*, and *ha* that are considered to be modifiers of the syllable's vowel. Graphically, these medial consonants are sometimes written as subscripts, but sometimes, as in the case of *ra*, they surround the base consonant instead. In the Myanmar encoding, the medial consonants are treated as conjuncts; that is, they are coded using the virama. For example, the word *krwe* ကြွေ [kjwei] ("to drop off") would be written via the following sequence:

> U+1000 က *ka* + U+1039 ◌္ *virama* + U+101B ရ *ra* + U+1039 ◌္ *virama* + U+101D ဝ *wa* + U+1031 ေ◌ *vowel sign e* → ကြွေ *krwe*

Explicit Virama. The virama U+1039 ◌္ MYANMAR SIGN VIRAMA also participates in some common constructions where it appears as a *visible* sign, commonly termed *killer*. In this usage where it appears as a visible diacritic, U+1039 is followed by a U+200C ZERO WIDTH NON-JOINER, as with Devanagari (see *Figure 9-3*).

Ordering of Syllable Components. Dependent vowels and other signs are encoded after the consonant to which they apply, except for *kinzi*, which precedes the consonant. Characters occur in the relative order shown in *Table 11-3.*

Table 11-3. Myanmar Syllabic Structure

Name	Encoding	Example
kinzi	<U+1004, U+1039>	◌င်္
consonant	[U+1000..U+1021]	က
subscript consonant	<U+1039, [U+1000..U+1019, U+101C, U+101E, U+1020, U+1021]>	◌္က
medial ya	<U+1039, U+101A>	◌ျ
medial ra	<U+1039, U+101B>	◌ြ
medial wa	<U+1039, U+101D>	◌ွ
medial ha	<U+1039, U+101F>	◌ှ
vowel sign e	U+1031	ေ◌
vowel sign u, uu	[U+102F, U+1030]	◌ု, ◌ူ
vowel sign i, ii, ai	[U+102D, U+102E, U+1032]	◌ိ, ◌ီ, ◌ဲ
vowel sign aa	U+102C	◌ာ
anusvara	U+1036	◌ံ
atha (killer)	<U+1039, U+200C>	◌်
dot below	U+1037	◌့
visarga	U+1038	◌း

U+1031 ေ◌ MYANMAR VOWEL SIGN E is encoded *after* its consonant (as in the earlier example), although in visual presentation its glyph appears *before* (to the left of) the consonant form.

Spacing. Myanmar does not use any whitespace between words. If word boundary indications are desired—for example, for the use of automatic line layout algorithms—the character U+200B ZERO WIDTH SPACE should be used to place invisible marks for such breaks. The ZERO WIDTH SPACE can grow to have a visible width when justified.

11.4 Khmer

Khmer: U+1780–U+17FF

Khmer, also known as Cambodian, is the official language of the Kingdom of Cambodia. Mutually intelligible dialects are also spoken in northeastern Thailand and in the Mekong Delta region of Vietnam. Although Khmer is not an Indo-European language, it has borrowed much vocabulary from Sanskrit and Pali, and religious texts in those languages have been both transliterated and translated into Khmer. The Khmer script is also used to render a number of regional minority languages, such as Tampuan, Krung, and Cham.

The Khmer script, called *aksaa khmae* ("Khmer letters"), is also the official script of Cambodia. It is descended from the Brahmi script of South India, as are Thai, Lao, Myanmar, Old Mon, and others. The exact sources have not been determined, but there is a great similarity between the earliest inscriptions in the region and the Pallawa script of the Coromandel coast of India. Khmer has been a unique and independent script for more than 1,400 years. Modern Khmer has two basic styles of script: the *aksaa crieng* ("slanted script") and the *aksaa muul* ("round script"). There is no fundamental structural difference between the two. The slanted script (in its "standing" variant) is chosen as representative in *Chapter 17, Code Charts*.

Principles of the Khmer Script

Structurally, the Khmer script has many features in common with other Brahmi-derived scripts, such as Devanagari and Myanmar. Consonant characters bear an inherent vowel sound, with additional signs placed before, above, below, and/or after the consonants to indicate a vowel other than the inherent one. The overall writing direction is left to right.

In comparison with the Devanagari script, explained in detail in *Section 9.1, Devanagari*, the Khmer script has developed several distinctive features during its evolution.

Glottal Consonant. The Khmer script has a consonant character for a glottal stop (*qa*) that bears an inherent vowel sound and can have an optional vowel sign. While Khmer also has independent vowel characters like Devanagari, as shown in *Table 11-4*, in principle many of its sounds can be represented by using *qa* and a vowel sign. This does not mean these representations are always interchangeable in real words. Some words are written with one variant to the exclusion of others.

Subscript Consonants. Subscript consonant signs differ from independent consonant characters and are called *coeng* (literally, "foot, leg") after their subscript position. While a consonant character can constitute an orthographic syllable by itself, a subscript consonant sign cannot. Note that U+17A1 ឡ KHMER LETTER LA does not have a corresponding subscript consonant sign in standard Khmer, but does have a subscript in the Khmer script used in Thailand.

Table 11-4. Independent Khmer Vowel Characters

Name	Independent Vowel	Qa with Vowel Sign
i	ឥ	អិ, អុិ, អី
ii	ឦ	អី, អុី
u	ឧ	អុ, អុិ
uk	ឨ	អុក
uu	ឩ	អូ, អូិ
uuv	ឪ	អូវ
ry	ឫ	រឹ
ryy	ឬ	រឺ
ly	ឭ	លឹ
lyy	ឮ	លឺ
e	ឯ	អេ, អែ
ai	ឰ	អៃ
oo	ឱ, ឲ	អោ
au	ឳ	អៅ

Subscript consonant signs are used to represent any consonant following the first consonant in an orthographic syllable. They also have an inherent vowel sound, which may be suppressed if the syllable bears a vowel sign or another subscript consonant.

The subscript consonant signs are often used to represent a consonant cluster. Two consecutive consonant characters cannot represent a consonant cluster because the inherent vowel sound in between is retained. To suppress the vowel, a subscript consonant sign (or rarely a subscript independent vowel) replaces the second consonant character. Theoretically, any consonant cluster composed of any number of consonant sounds without inherent vowel sounds in between can be represented systematically by a consonant character and as many subscript consonant signs as necessary.

Examples of subscript consonant signs for a consonant cluster follow:

> ល្ង *lo + coeng + ngo* [lŋɔ̀:] "sesame" (compare លង *lo + ngo* [lɔ̀:ŋ] "to haunt")
>
> លក្ស្មី *lo + ka + coeng + sa + coeng + mo + ii* [lèəksmei] "beauty, luck"
>
> កាហ្វេ *ka + aa + ha + coeng + vo + e* [ka:fe:] "coffee"

The subscript consonant signs in the Khmer script can be used to denote a final consonant, although this practice is uncommon.

Examples of subscript consonant signs for a closing consonant follow:

> ទាំ្ង *to* + *aa* + *nikahit* + *coeng* + *ngo* [tèəŋ] "both" (= ទាំង) (≠ *ទ្ងាំ [tŋɔ̀əm])
>
> ហើ្យ *ha* + *oe* + *coeng* + *yo* [haəi] "already" (= ហើយ) (≠ *ហ្យើ [hyaə])

While these subscript consonant signs are usually attached to a consonant character, they can also be attached to an independent vowel character. Although this practice is relatively rare, it is used in one very common word, meaning "to give."

Examples of subscript consonant signs attached to an independent vowel character follow:

> ឱ្យ *qoo-1* + *coeng* + *yo* [ʔaoi] "to give" (= ឱយ and also ឲ្យ)
>
> ឱ្ម *qoo-1* + *coeng* + *mo* [ʔaom] "exclamation of solemn affirmation" (= ឱម)

Subscript Independent Vowel Signs. Some independent vowel characters also have corresponding subscript independent vowel signs, although these are rarely used today.

Examples of subscript independent vowel signs follow:

> ផ្ឯម *pha* + *coeng* + *qe* + *mo* [p^{h}ʔaem] "sweet" (= ផ្អែម *pha* + *coeng* + *qa* + *ae* + *mo*)
>
> ហ្ឫទ័យ *ha* + *coeng* + *ry* + *to* + *samyok sannya* + *yo* [harɯtey] "heart" (*royal*) (= ហឫទ័យ *ha* + *ry* + *to* + *samyok sannya* + *yo*)

Consonant Registers. The Khmer language has a richer set of vowels than the languages for which the ancestral script was used, although it has a smaller set of consonant sounds. The Khmer script takes advantage of this situation by assigning different characters to represent the same consonant using different inherent vowels. Khmer consonant characters and signs are organized into two series or registers, whose inherent vowels are nominally *-a* in the first register and *-o* in the second register, as shown in *Table 11-5*. The register of a consonant character is generally reflected on the last letter of its transliterated name. Some consonant characters and signs have a counterpart whose consonant sound is the same but whose register is different, as *ka* and *ko* in the first row of the table. For the other consonant characters and signs, two "shifter" signs are available. U+17C9 KHMER SIGN MUUSIKATOAN converts a consonant character and sign from the second to the first register, while U+17CA KHMER SIGN TRIISAP converts a consonant from the first register to the second (rows 2–4). To represent *pa*, however, *muusikatoan* is attached not to *po* but to *ba*, in an exceptional use (row 5). The phonetic value of a dependent vowel sign may also change depending on the context of the consonant(s) to which it is attached (row 6).

Encoding Principles. Like other related scripts, the Khmer encoding represents only the basic underlying characters; multiple glyphs and rendering transformations are required to assemble the final visual form for each orthographic syllable. Individual characters, such as U+1789 KHMER LETTER NYO, may assume variant forms depending on the other characters with which they combine.

Table 11-5. Two Registers of Khmer Consonants

Row	First Register	Second Register
1	ក *ka* [kɔː] "neck"	គ *ko* [kɔ̀ː] "mute"
2	រ៉ *ro + muusikatoan* [rɔː] "small saw"	រ *ro* [rɔ̀ː] "fence (in the water)"
3	សក *sa + ka* [sɔːk] "to peel, to shed one's skin"	ស៊ក *sa + triisap + ka* [sɔ̀ːk] "to insert"
4	បក *ba + ka* [bɔːk] "to return"	*ប៊ក *ba + triisap + ka* [bɔ̀ːk]
5	ប៉ម *ba + muusikatoan + mo* [pɔːm] "blockhouse"	ពម *po + mo* [pɔ̀ːm] "to put into the mouth"
6	កូរ *ka + u + ro* [koː] "to stir"	គូរ *ko + u + ro* [kuː] "to sketch"

Subscript Consonant Signs. In the way that many Cambodians analyze Khmer today, subscript consonant signs are considered to be different entities from consonant characters. The Unicode Standard does not assign independent code points for the subscript consonant signs. Instead, each of these signs is represented by the sequence of two characters: a special control character (U+17D2 KHMER SIGN COENG) and a corresponding consonant character. This is analogous to the virama model employed for representing conjuncts in other related scripts. Subscripted independent vowels are encoded in the same manner. Because the *coeng sign* character does not exist as a letter or sign in the Khmer script, the Unicode model departs from the ordinary way that Khmer is conceived of and taught to native Khmer speakers. Consequently, the encoding may not be intuitive to a native user of the Khmer writing system, although it is able to represent Khmer correctly.

U+17D2 ◌្ KHMER SIGN COENG is not actually a *coeng* but a *coeng* generator, because *coeng* in Khmer refers to the subscript consonant sign. The glyph for U+17D2 ◌្ KHMER SIGN COENG shown in the code charts is arbitrary and is not actually rendered directly; the dotted box around the glyph indicates that special rendering is required. To aid Khmer script users, a listing of typical Khmer subscript consonant letters has been provided in *Table 11-6* together with their descriptive names following preferred Khmer practice. While the Unicode encoding represents both the subscripts and the combined vowel letters with a pair of code points, they should be treated as a unit for most processing purposes. In other words, the sequence functions as if it had been encoded as a single character. A number of independent vowels also have subscript forms, as shown in *Table 11-8*.

Table 11-6. Khmer Subscript Consonant Signs

Glyph	Code	Name
◌្ក	17D2 1780	*khmer consonant sign coeng ka*
◌្ខ	17D2 1781	*khmer consonant sign coeng kha*
◌្គ	17D2 1782	*khmer consonant sign coeng ko*

Table 11-6. Khmer Subscript Consonant Signs (Continued)

Glyph	Code	Name
◌្ឃ	17D2 1783	*khmer consonant sign coeng kho*
◌្ង	17D2 1784	*khmer consonant sign coeng ngo*
◌្ច	17D2 1785	*khmer consonant sign coeng ca*
◌្ឆ	17D2 1786	*khmer consonant sign coeng cha*
◌្ជ	17D2 1787	*khmer consonant sign coeng co*
◌្ឈ	17D2 1788	*khmer consonant sign coeng cho*
◌្ញ	17D2 1789	*khmer consonant sign coeng nyo*
◌្ដ	17D2 178A	*khmer consonant sign coeng da*
◌្ឋ	17D2 178B	*khmer consonant sign coeng ttha*
◌្ឌ	17D2 178C	*khmer consonant sign coeng do*
◌្ឍ	17D2 178D	*khmer consonant sign coeng ttho*
◌្ណ	17D2 178E	*khmer consonant sign coeng na*
◌្ត	17D2 178F	*khmer consonant sign coeng ta*
◌្ថ	17D2 1790	*khmer consonant sign coeng tha*
◌្ទ	17D2 1791	*khmer consonant sign coeng to*
◌្ធ	17D2 1792	*khmer consonant sign coeng tho*
◌្ន	17D2 1793	*khmer consonant sign coeng no*
◌្ប	17D2 1794	*khmer consonant sign coeng ba*
◌្ផ	17D2 1795	*khmer consonant sign coeng pha*
◌្ព	17D2 1796	*khmer consonant sign coeng po*
◌្ភ	17D2 1797	*khmer consonant sign coeng pho*
◌្ម	17D2 1798	*khmer consonant sign coeng mo*
◌្យ	17D2 1799	*khmer consonant sign coeng yo*
◌្រ	17D2 179A	*khmer consonant sign coeng ro*
◌្ល	17D2 179B	*khmer consonant sign coeng lo*
◌្វ	17D2 179C	*khmer consonant sign coeng vo*
◌្ឝ	17D2 179D	*khmer consonant sign coeng sha*
◌្ឞ	17D2 179E	*khmer consonant sign coeng ssa*

Table 11-6. Khmer Subscript Consonant Signs (Continued)

Glyph	Code	Name
◌្ស	17D2 179F	*khmer consonant sign coeng sa*
◌្ហ	17D2 17A0	*khmer consonant sign coeng ha*
◌្ឡ	17D2 17A1	*khmer consonant sign coeng la*
◌្អ	17D2 17A2	*khmer vowel sign coeng qa*

As noted earlier, <U+17D2, U+17A1> represents a subscript form of *la* that is not used in Cambodia, although it is employed in Thailand.

Dependent Vowel Signs. Most of the Khmer dependent vowel signs are represented with a single character that is applied after the base consonant character and optional subscript consonant signs. Three of these Khmer vowel signs are not encoded as single characters in in the Unicode Standard. The vowel sign *am* is encoded as a nasalization sign, U+17C6 KHMER SIGN NIKAHIT. Two vowel signs, *om* and *aam*, have not been assigned independent code points. They are represented by the sequence of a vowel (U+17BB KHMER VOWEL SIGN U and U+17B6 KHMER VOWEL SIGN AA, respectively) and U+17C6 KHMER SIGN NIKAHIT.

The *nikahit* is superficially similar to *anusvara*, the nasalization sign in the Devanagari script, although in Khmer it is usually regarded as a vowel sign *am*. *Anusvara* not only represents a special nasal sound, but also can be used in place of one of the five nasal consonants homorganic to the subsequent consonant (velar, palatal, retroflex, dental, or labial, respectively). *Anusvara* can be used concurrently with any vowel sign in the same orthographic syllable. *Nikahit*, in contrast, functions differently. Its final sound is [m], irrespective of the type of the subsequent consonant. It is not used concurrently with the vowels *ii*, *e*, *ua*, *oe*, *oo*, and so on, although it is used with the vowel signs *aa* and *u*. In these cases the combination is sometimes regarded as a unit—*aam* and *om*, respectively. The sound that *aam* represents is [ɔ̀əm], not [a:m]. The sequences used for these combinations are shown in *Table 11-7*.

Table 11-7. Khmer Composite Dependent Vowel Signs with Nikahit

Glyph	Code	Name
◌ុំ	17BB 17C6	*khmer vowel sign om*
◌ាំ	17B6 17C6	*khmer vowel sign aam*

Examples of dependent vowel signs ending with [m] follow:

> ដំ *da* + *nikahit* [dɔm] "to pound" (compare ដម *da* + *mo* [dɔ:m] "nectar")
>
> ពាំ *po* + *aa* + *nikahit* [pɔ̀əm] "to carry in the beak" (compare ពាម *po* + *aa* + *mo* [pèəm] "mouth of a river")

Independent Vowel Characters. In Khmer, as in other Brahmic scripts, some independent vowels have their own letterforms, although the sounds they represent may more often be represented with the consonant character for the glottal stop (U+17A2 KHMER LETTER QA) modified by vowel signs (and optionally a consonant character). These independent vowels are encoded as separate characters in the Unicode Standard.

Subscript Independent Vowel Signs. Some independent vowels have corresponding subscript independent vowel signs, although these are rarely used. Each is represented by the sequence of U+17D2 KHMER SIGN COENG and an independent vowel, as shown in *Table 11-8.*

Table 11-8. Khmer Subscript Independent Vowel Signs

Glyph	Code	Name
◌្ឧ	17D2 17A7	*khmer independent vowel sign coeng qu*
◌្ឫ	17D2 17AB	*khmer independent vowel sign coeng ry*
◌្ឬ	17D2 17AC	*khmer independent vowel sign coeng ryy*
◌្ឯ	17D2 17AF	*khmer independent vowel sign coeng qe*

Other Signs as Syllabic Components. The Khmer sign *robat* historically corresponds to the Devanagari *repha*, a representation of syllable-initial *r-*. However, the Khmer script can treat the initial *r-* in the same way as the other initial consonants—namely, a consonant character *ro* and as many subscript consonant signs as necessary. Some old loan words from Sanskrit and Pali include *robat*, but in some of them the *robat* is not pronounced and is preserved in a fossilized spelling. Because *robat* is a distinct sign from the consonant character *ro*, the Unicode Standard encodes U+17CC KHMER SIGN ROBAT, but it treats the Devanagari *repha* as a part of a ligature without encoding it. The authoritative Chuon Nath dictionary sorts *robat* as if it were a base consonant character, just as the *repha* is sorted in scripts that use it. The consonant over which *robat* resides is then sorted as if it were a subscript.

Examples of consonant clusters beginning with *ro* and *robat* follow:

> រាជរ្សី *ro* + *aa* + *co* + *ro* + *coeng* + *sa* + *ii* [rèəcrsei] "king hermit"
>
> អាយ៌ *qa* + *aa* + *yo* + *robat* [ʔa:rya] "civilized" (= អារ្យ *qa* + *aa* + *ro* + *coeng* + *yo*)
>
> ពត៌មាន *po* + *ta* + *robat* + *mo* + *aa* + *no* [pɔ̀:dɔmèən] "news" (compare Sanskrit वर्तमान *vartamāna* "the present time")

U+17DD KHMER SIGN ATTHACAN is a rarely used sign that denotes that the base consonant character keeps its inherent vowel sound. In this respect it is similar to U+17D1 KHMER SIGN VIRIAM. U+17CB KHMER SIGN BANTOC shortens the vowel sound of the previous orthographic syllable. U+17C7 KHMER SIGN REAHMUK, U+17C8 KHMER SIGN YUUKALEAPINTU, U+17CD KHMER SIGN TOANDAKHIAT, U+17CE KHMER SIGN KAKABAT, U+17CF KHMER SIGN AHSDA, and U+17D0 KHMER SIGN SAMYOK SANNYA are also explicitly encoded signs used to compose an orthographic syllable.

Ligatures. Some vowel signs form ligatures with consonant characters and signs. These ligatures are not encoded separately, but should be presented graphically by the rendering software. Some common ligatures are shown in *Figure 11-1*.

Figure 11-1. Common Ligatures in Khmer

ក *ka* + ◌ា *aa* + រ *ro* = ការ [ka:] "job"

ប *ba* + ◌ា *aa* = បា [ba:] "father, male of an animal"; used to prevent confusion with ហ *ha*

ប *ba* + ◌ៅ *au* = បៅ [baw] "to suck"

ម *mo* + ◌្ស *coeng sa* + ◌ៅ *au* = ម្សៅ [msaw] "powder"

ស *sa* + ង *ngo* + ◌្ខ *coeng kha* + ◌្យ *coeng yo* + ◌ា *aa* = សង្ខ្យា [sɔŋk^{h}ya:] "counting"

Multiple Glyphs. A single character may assume different forms according to context. For example, a part of the glyph for *nyo* is omitted when a subscript consonant sign is attached. The implementation must render the correct glyph according to context. *Coeng nyo* also changes its shape when it is attached to *nyo*. The correct glyph for the sequence <U+17D2 KHMER SIGN COENG, U+1789 KHMER LETTER NYO> is rendered according to context, as shown in *Figure 11-2*. This kind of glyph alternation is very common in Khmer. Some spacing subscript consonant signs change their height depending on the orthographic context. Similarly, the vertical position of many signs varies according to context. Their presentation is left to the rendering software.

U+17B2 ឲ KHMER INDEPENDENT VOWEL QOO TYPE TWO is thought to be a variant of U+17B1 ឱ KHMER INDEPENDENT VOWEL QOO TYPE ONE, but it is explicitly encoded in the Unicode Standard. The variant is used in very few words, but these include the very common word *aoi* "to give," as noted in *Figure 11-2*.

Figure 11-2. Common Multiple Forms in Khmer

ញញឹម *nyo* + *nyo* + *y* + *mo* [ɲɔ̀ɲɯm] "to smile"

ចិញ្ចើម *ca* + *i* + *nyo* + *coeng* + *ca* + *oe* + *mo* [ceɲcaəm] "eyebrow"

ស្ញប់ *sa* + *coeng nyo* + *ba* + *bantoc* [sɲɔp] "to respect"

កញ្ញា *ka* + *nyo* + *coeng* + *nyo* + *aa* [kaɲɲa:] "girl, Miss, September"

ឲ្យ *qoo-2* + *coeng* + *yo* (= ឱ្យ *qoo-1* + *coeng* + *yo*) [ʔaoi] "to give"

Characters Whose Use Is Discouraged. Some of the Khmer characters encoded in the Unicode Standard are not recommended for use for various reasons.

The use of U+17A3 KHMER INDEPENDENT VOWEL QAQ and U+17A4 KHMER INDEPENDENT VOWEL QAA is discouraged. One feature of the Khmer script is the introduction of the consonant character for a glottal stop (U+17A2 KHMER LETTER QA). This made it unnecessary for each initial vowel sound to have its own independent vowel character, although some independent vowels exist. Neither U+17A3 nor U+17A4 actually exists in the Khmer script. Other related scripts, including the Devanagari script, have independent vowel characters corresponding to them (*a* and *aa*), but they can be transliterated by *khmer letter qa* and *khmer letter qa + khmer vowel aa,* respectively, without ambiguity because these scripts have no consonant character corresponding to the *khmer qa.*

The use of U+17B4 KHMER VOWEL INHERENT AQ and U+17B5 KHMER VOWEL INHERENT AA is discouraged. These newly invented characters do not exist in the Khmer script. They were intended to be used to represent a phonetic difference not expressed by the spelling, so as to assist in phonetic sorting. However, they are insufficient for that purpose and should be considered errors in the encoding.

The use of U+17D8 KHMER SIGN BEYYAL is discouraged. It was supposed to represent "et cetera" in Khmer. However, it is a word rather than a symbol. Moreover, it has several different spellings. It should be spelled out fully using normal letters. *Beyyal* can be written as follows:

> ។បេ។ *khan + ba + e + khan*
>
> –បេ– *en dash + ba + e + en dash*
>
> ។ល។ *khan + lo + khan*
>
> –ល– *en dash + lo + en dash*

Ordering of Syllable Components. The standard order of components in an orthographic syllable as expressed in BNF is

$$B\{R \mid C\}\ \{S\ \{R\}\}^*\ \{\{Z\}\ V\}\ \{O\}\ \{S\}$$

where

> B is a base character (consonant character, independent vowel character, and so on)
>
> R is a *robat*
>
> C is a consonant shifter
>
> S is a subscript consonant or independent vowel sign
>
> V is a dependent vowel sign
>
> Z is a zero width non-joiner or a zero width joiner
>
> O is any other sign

For example, the common word ខ្ញុំ khnyom "I" is composed of the following three elements: (1) consonant character *kha* as B; (2) subscript consonant sign *coeng nyo* as S; and

(3) dependent vowel sign *om* as *V*. In the Unicode Standard, *coeng nyo* and *om* are further decomposed, and the whole word is represented by five coded characters.

ខ្ញុំ *kha* + *coeng* + *nyo* + *u* + *nikahit* [kʰɲom] "I"

The order of coded characters does not always match the visual order. For example, some of the dependent vowel signs and their fragments may seem to precede a consonant character, but they are always put after it in the sequence of coded characters. This is also the case with *coeng ro*. Examples of visual reordering and other aspects of syllabic order are shown in *Figure 11-3*.

Figure 11-3. Examples of Syllabic Order in Khmer

ទេ *to* + *e* [tèː] "much"

ច្រើន *ca* + *coeng* + *ro* + *oe* + *no* [craən] "much"

សង្គ្រាម *sa* + *ngo* + *coeng* + *ko* + *coeng* + *ro* + *aa* + *mo* [sɔŋkrèəm] "war"

ហើ្យ *ha* + *oe* + *coeng* + *yo* [haəi] "already"

សញ្ញា *sa* + *nyo* + *coeng* + *nyo* + *aa* [saɲɲaː] "sign"

ស៊ី *sa* + *triisap* + *ii* [siː] "eat"

ប៉ី *ba* + *muusikatoan* + *ii* [pei] "a kind of flute"

Consonant Shifters. U+17C9 KHMER SIGN MUUSIKATOAN and U+17CA KHMER SIGN TRIISAP are consonant shifters, also known as register shifters. In the presence of other superscript glyphs, both of these signs are usually rendered with the same glyph shape as that of U+17BB KHMER VOWEL SIGN U, as shown in the last two examples of *Figure 11-3*.

Although the consonant shifter in handwriting may be written after the subscript, the consonant shifter should always be encoded immediately following the base consonant, except when it is preceded by U+200C ZERO WIDTH NON-JOINER. This provides Khmer with a fixed order of character placement, making it easier to search for words in a document.

ម៉្ងៃ *mo* + *muusikatoan* + *coeng* + *ngo* + *ai* [mŋai] "one day"

ម៊្ហែតៗ *mo* + *triisap* + *coeng* + *ha* + *ae* + *ta* + *lek too* [mhɛ̀ːtmhɛ̀ːt] "bland"

If either *muusikatoan* or *triisap* needs to keep its superscript shape (as an exception to the general rule that states other superscripts typically force the alternative subscript glyph for either character), U+200C ZERO WIDTH NON-JOINER should be inserted before the consonant shifter to show the normal glyph for a consonant shifter when the general rule requires the alternative glyph. In such cases, U+200C ZERO WIDTH NON-JOINER is inserted before the vowel sign, as shown in the following examples:

ប‌៊ីយែរ *ba* + [ZWNJ] + *triisap* + *ii* + *yo* + *ae* + *ro* [biyɛ̀ː] "beer"

ប្រតឹងអ‌៊ឹះ *ba* + *coeng* + *ro* + *ta* + *yy* + *ngo* + *qa* + [ZWNJ] + *triisap* + *y* + *reahmuk* [prɔtəːŋʔɯh] "urgent, too busy"

ប្រតឹងអ៊ឹះ *ba* + *coeng* + *ro* + *ta* + *yy* + *ngo* + *qa* + *triisap* + *y* + *reahmuk*

Ligature Control. In the *askaa muul* font style, some vowel signs ligate with the consonant characters to which they are applied. The font tables should determine whether they form a ligature; ligature use in *muul* fonts does not affect the meaning. However, U+200C ZERO WIDTH NON-JOINER may be inserted before the vowel sign to explicitly suppress such a ligature, as shown in *Figure 11-4* for the word "savant," pronounced [vituː].

Figure 11-4. Ligation in *Muul* Style in Khmer

វិទូ	*vo* + *i* + *to* + *uu*	(*aksaa crieng* font)
វិទូ, វិទូ	*vo* + *i* + *to* + *uu*	(ligature dependent on the *muul* font)
វ‌ិទូ	*vo* + [ZWNJ] + *i* + *to* + *uu*	([ZWNJ] to prevent the ligature in a *muul* font)
វ‍ិទូ	*vo* + [ZWJ] + *i* + *to* + *uu*	([ZWJ] to request the ligature in a *muul* font)

Spacing. Khmer does not use whitespace between words, although it does use whitespace between clauses and between parts of a name. If word boundary indications are desired—for example, as part of automatic line layout algorithms—the character U+200B ZERO WIDTH SPACE should be used to place invisible marks for such breaks. The ZERO WIDTH SPACE can grow to have a visible width when justified. See *Figure 16-2*.

Khmer Symbols: U+19E0–U+19FF

Symbols. Many symbols for punctuation, digits, and numerals for divination lore are encoded as independent entities. Symbols for the lunar calendar are encoded as single characters that cannot be decomposed even if their appearance might seem to be decomposable. U+19E0 KHMER SYMBOL PATHAMASAT and U+19F0 KHMER SYMBOL TUTEYASAT represent the first and second of August, respectively, in a leap year. The 15 characters from U+19E1 KHMER SYMBOL MUOY KOET to U+19EF KHMER SYMBOL DAP-PRAM KOET represent the first through the fifteenth lunar waxing days, respectively. The 15 characters from U+19F1 KHMER SYMBOL MUOY ROC through U+19FF KHMER SYMBOL DAP-PRAM ROC represent the first through the fifteenth waning days, respectively. The typographical form of these lunar dates is a top and bottom section of the same size text. The dividing line between the upper and lower halves of the symbol is the vertical center of the line height.

11.5 Tai Le

Tai Le: U+1950–U+197F

The Tai Le script has a history of 700–800 years, during which time several orthographic conventions were used. The modern form of the script was developed in the years following 1954; it rationalized the older system and added a systematic representation of tones with the use of combining diacritics. The new system was revised again in 1988, when spacing tone marks were introduced to replace the combining diacritics. The Unicode encoding of Tai Le handles both the modern form of the script and its more recent revision.

The Tai Le language is also known as Tai Nüa, Dehong Dai, Tai Mau, Tai Kong, and Chinese Shan. *Tai Le* is a transliteration of the indigenous designation, ᥖᥭᥰ ᥘᥫᥴ [tai² lə⁶] (in older orthography ᥖᥭ̈ ᥘᥫ́). The modern Tai Le orthographies are straightforward: initial consonants precede vowels, vowels precede final consonants, and tone marks, if any, follow the entire syllable. There is a one-to-one correspondence between the tone mark letters now used and existing nonspacing marks in the Unicode Standard. The tone mark is the last character in a syllable string in both orthographies. When one of the combining diacritics follows a tall letter ᥣ, ᥤ, ᥥ, ᥦ, ᥫ or ᥬ, it is displayed to the right of the letter, as shown in *Table 11-9.*

Table 11-9. Tai Le Tone Marks

Syllable	New Orthography	Old Orthography
ta	ᥖ	ᥖ
ta²	ᥖᥰ	ᥖ̈
ta³	ᥖᥱ	ᥖ̌
ta⁴	ᥖᥲ	ᥖ̀
ta⁵	ᥖᥳ	ᥖ̇
ta⁶	ᥖᥴ	ᥖ́
ti	ᥖᥤ	ᥖᥤ
ti²	ᥖᥤᥰ	ᥖᥤ̈
ti³	ᥖᥤᥱ	ᥖᥤ̌
ti⁴	ᥖᥤᥲ	ᥖᥤ̀
ti⁵	ᥖᥤᥳ	ᥖᥤ̇
ti⁶	ᥖᥤᥴ	ᥖᥤ́

Digits. In China, European digits (U+0030..U+0039) are mainly used, although Myanmar digits (U+1040..U+1049) are also used with slight glyph variants, as shown in *Table 11-10.*

Table 11-10. Myanmar Digits

Myanmar-Style Glyphs	Tai Le-Style Glyphs
၀ ၁ ၂ ၃ ၄ ၅ ၆ ၇ ၈ ၉	၀ ၁ ၂ ၃ ၄ ၅ ၆ ၇ ၈ ၉
0 1 2 3 4 5 6 7 8 9	0 1 2 3 4 5 6 7 8 9

Punctuation. Both CJK punctuation and Western punctuation are used. Typographically, European digits are about the same height and depth as the tall characters ᥖ and ᥗ. In some fonts, the baseline for punctuation is the depth of those characters.

11.6 New Tai Lue

New Tai Lue: U+1980–U+19DF

The New Tai Lue script, also known as Xishuang Banna Dai, is used mainly in southern China. The script was developed in the twentieth century as an orthographic simplification of the historic Lanna script used to write the Tai Lue language. "Lanna" refers to a region in present-day northern Thailand as well as to a Tai principality that existed in that region from approximately the late thirteenth century to the early twenieth century. The Lanna script grew out of the Mon script and was adapted in various forms in the Lanna kingdom and by Tai-speaking communities in surrounding areas that had close contact with the kingdom, including southern China. The Lanna script is still used to write various languages of the Tai family today, including Tai Lue. The approved orthography for this language uses the New Tai Lue script; however, usage of the older orthography based on a variant of Lanna script can still be found.

New Tai Lue differs from Lanna in that it regularizes the consonant repertoire, simplifies the writing of consonant clusters and syllable-final consonants, and uses only spacing vowel signs, which appear before or after the consonants they modify. By contrast, Lanna uses both spacing vowel signs and nonspacing vowel signs, which appear above or below the consonants they modify.

Syllabic Structure. All vowel signs in New Tai Lue are considered combining characters and follow their base consonants in the text stream. Where a syllable is composed of a vowel sign to the left and a vowel or tone mark on the right of the consonant, a sequence of characters is used, in the order *consonant + vowel + tone mark*, as shown in *Table 11-11.*

Final Consonants. A virama or killer character is not used to create conjunct consonants in New Tai Lue, because clusters of consonants do not regularly occur. New Tai Lue has a limited set of final consonants, which are modified with a hook showing that the inherent vowel is killed.

Table 11-11. New Tai Lue Vowel Placement

ᦂ	ka	+	ᦵ◌	e	+	◌ᧈ	t1					→	ᦵᦂᧈ	[ke:^{2}]
ᦂ	ka	+	ᦵ◌	e	+	◌ᦲ	i					→	ᦵᦂᦲ	[kə:^{1}]
ᦂ	ka	+	ᦵ◌	e	+	◌ᧀ	iy					→	ᦵᦂᧀ	[kəi^1]
ᦂ	ka	+	ᦵ◌	e	+	◌ᧀ	iy	+	◌ᧈ	t1		→	ᦵᦂᧀᧈ	[kəi^2]
ᦂ	ka	+	ᦵ◌	e	+	◌ᧀ	iy	+	◌ᧉ	t2		→	ᦵᦂᧀᧉ	[kəi^3]

Tones. Similar to the Thai and Lao scripts, New Tai Lue consonant letters come in pairs that denote two tonal registers. The tone of a syllable is indicated by the combination of the tonal register of the consonant letter plus a tone mark written at the end of the syllable, as shown in *Table 11-12*.

Table 11-12. New Tai Lue Registers and Tones

Display	Sequence	Register	Tone Mark	Tone	Transcription
ᦂ	ka^h	high		1	[ka^1]
ᦂᧈ	ka^h + t1	high	t1	2	[ka^2]
ᦂᧉ	ka^h + t2	high	t2	3	[ka^3]
ᦅ	ka^l	low		4	[ka^4]
ᦅᧈ	ka^l + t1	low	t1	5	[ka^5]
ᦅᧉ	ka^l + t2	low	t2	6	[ka^6]

11.7 Philippine Scripts

Tagalog: U+1700–U+171F
Hanunóo: U+1720–U+173F
Buhid: U+1740–U+175F
Tagbanwa: U+1760–U+177F

The first of these four scripts—Tagalog—is no longer used, whereas the other three—Hanunóo, Buhid, and Tagbanwa—are living scripts of the Philippines. South Indian scripts of the Pallava dynasty made their way to the Philippines, although the exact route is uncertain. They may have been transported by way of the Kavi scripts of Western Java between the tenth and fourteenth centuries CE.

Written accounts of the Tagalog script by Spanish missionaries and documents in Tagalog date from the mid-1500s. The first book in this script was printed in Manila in 1593. While the Tagalog script was used to write Tagalog, Bisaya, Ilocano, and other languages, it fell out of normal use by the mid-1700s. The modern Tagalog language—also known as Filipino—is now written in the Latin script.

The three living scripts—Hanunóo, Buhid, and Tagbanwa—are related to Tagalog but may not be directly descended from it. The Hanunóo and the Buhid peoples live in Mindoro, while the Tagbanwa live in Palawan. Hanunóo enjoys the most use; it is widely used to write love poetry, a popular pastime among the Hanunóo. Tagbanwa is used less often.

Principles of the Philippine Scripts

The Philippine scripts share features with the other Brahmi-derived scripts to which they are related.

Consonant Letters. Philippine scripts have consonants containing an inherent *-a* vowel, which may be modified by the addition of vowel signs or canceled (killed) by the use of a virama-type mark.

Independent Vowel Letters. Philippine scripts have null consonants, which are used to write syllables that start with a vowel.

Dependent Vowel Signs. The vowel *-i* is written with a mark above the associated consonant, and the vowel *-u* with an identical mark below. The mark is known as *kudlit* "diacritic," *tuldik* "accent," or *tuldok* "dot" in Tagalog, and as *ulitan* "diacritic" in Tagbanwa. The Philippine scripts employ only the two vowel signs *i* and *u*, which are also used to stand for the vowels *e* and *o*, respectively.

Virama. Although all languages normally written with the Philippine scripts have syllables ending in consonants, not all of the scripts have a mechanism for expressing the canceled *-a*. As a result, in those orthographies, the final consonants are unexpressed. Francisco Lopez introduced a cross-shaped *virama* in his 1620 catechism in the Ilocano language, but this innovation did not seem to find favor with native users, who seem to have considered the script adequate without it (they preferred ᜃᜃᜉᜒ *kakapi* to ᜃᜃᜋ᜔ᜉᜒ *kakampi*). A similar reform for the Hanunóo script seems to have been better received. The Hanunóo *pamudpod* was devised by Antoon Postma, who went to the Philippines from the Netherlands in the mid-1950s. In traditional orthography, ᜰᜲ ᜠᜩᜳ ᜪ ᜢᜩᜧ *si apu ba upada* is, with the *pamudpod*, rendered more accurately as ᜰᜲ ᜠᜬ᜴ᜩᜳᜧ᜴ ᜪᜬ᜴ ᜢᜩᜧᜨ᜴ *si aypud bay upadan*; the Hanunóo pronunciation is *si aypod bay upadan*. The Tagalog *virama* and Hanunóo *pamudpod* cancel only the inherent *-a*. No conjunct consonants are employed in the Philippine scripts.

Directionality. The Philippine scripts are read from left to right in horizontal lines running from top to bottom. They may be written or carved either in that manner or in vertical lines running from bottom to top, moving from left to right. In the latter case, the letters are written sideways so they may be read horizontally. This method of writing is probably due to the medium and writing implements used. Text is often scratched with a sharp instrument onto beaten strips of bamboo, which are held pointing away from the body and worked from the proximal to distal ends, in columns from left to right.

Rendering. In Tagalog and Tagbanwa, the vowel signs simply rest over or under the consonants. In Hanunóo and Buhid, ligatures are often formed, as shown in *Table 11-13.*

Table 11-13. Hanunóo and Buhid Vowel Sign Combinations

Hanunóo		
x	*x* + ◌ᜲ	*x* + ◌ᜳ
ᜣ	ᜣᜲ	ᜣᜳ
ᜤ	ᜤᜲ	ᜤᜳ
ᜥ	ᜥᜲ	ᜥᜳ
ᜦ	ᜦᜲ	ᜦᜳ
ᜧ	ᜧᜲ	ᜧᜳ
ᜨ	ᜨᜲ	ᜨᜳ
ᜩ	ᜩᜲ	ᜩᜳ
ᜪ	ᜪᜲ	ᜪᜳ
ᜫ	ᜫᜲ	ᜫᜳ
ᜬ	ᜬᜲ	ᜬᜳ
ᜭ	ᜭᜲ	ᜭᜳ
ᜮ	ᜮᜲ	ᜮᜳ
ᜯ	ᜯᜲ	ᜯᜳ
ᜰ	ᜰᜲ	ᜰᜳ
ᜱ	ᜱᜲ	ᜱᜳ

Buhid		
x	*x* + ◌ᝒ	*x* + ◌ᝓ
ᝃ	ᝃᝒ	ᝃᝓ
ᝄ	ᝄᝒ	ᝄᝓ
ᝅ	ᝅᝒ	ᝅᝓ
ᝆ	ᝆᝒ	ᝆᝓ
ᝇ	ᝇᝒ	ᝇᝓ
ᝈ	ᝈᝒ	ᝈᝓ
ᝉ	ᝉᝒ	ᝉᝓ
ᝊ	ᝊᝒ	ᝊᝓ
ᝋ	ᝋᝒ	ᝋᝓ
ᝌ	ᝌᝒ	ᝌᝓ
ᝍ	ᝍᝒ	ᝍᝓ
ᝎ	ᝎᝒ	ᝎᝓ
ᝏ	ᝏᝒ	ᝏᝓ
ᝐ	ᝐᝒ	ᝐᝓ
ᝑ	ᝑᝒ	ᝑᝓ

Punctuation. Punctuation has been unified for the Philippine scripts. In the Hanunóo block, U+1735 PHILIPPINE SINGLE PUNCTUATION and U+1736 PHILIPPINE DOUBLE PUNCTUATION are encoded. Tagalog makes use of only the latter; Hanunóo, Buhid, and Tagbanwa make use of both marks.

11.8 Buginese

Buginese: U+1A00–U+1A1F

The Buginese script is used on the island of Sulawesi, mainly in the southwest. A variety of traditional literature has been printed in it. As of 1971, as many as 2.3 million speakers of Buginese were reported in the southern part of Sulawesi. The Buginese script is one of the easternmost of the Brahmi scripts and is perhaps related to Javanese. It is attested as early as the fourteenth century CE. Buginese bears some affinity to Tagalog and, like Tagalog, does not traditionally record final consonants. The Buginese language, an Austronesian language with a rich traditional literature, is one of the foremost languages of Indonesia. The script was previously also used to write the Makassar, Bimanese, and Madurese languages.

Structure. Buginese vowel signs are used in a manner similar to that seen in other Brahmi-derived scripts. Consonants have an inherent /a/ vowel sound. Consonant conjuncts are not formed. Traditionally, a virama does not exist, but is included for modern usage in transcribing many non-Buginese words. This innovation is paralleled by a similar innovation in Hanunóo and Tagalog. The virama is always a visible sign. Because conjuncts are not formed in Buginese, U+200C ZERO WIDTH NON-JOINER is not necessary to force the display of the virama.

Ligature. One ligature is found in the Buginese script. It is formed by the ligation of <*a*, *-i*> + *ya* to represent *îya*, as shown in the first line of *Figure 11-5*. The ligature takes the shape of the Buginese letter *ya*, but with a dot applied at the far left side. Contrast that with the normal representation of the syllable *yi*, in which the dot indicating the vowel sign occurs in a centered position, as shown in the second line of *Figure 11-5*. The ligature for *îya* is not obligatory; it would be requested by inserting a *zero width joiner.*

Figure 11-5. Buginese Ligature

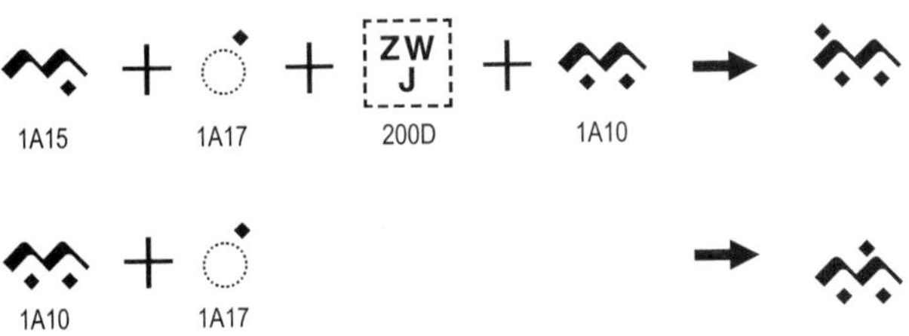

Order. Several orderings are possible for Buginese. The Unicode Standard encodes the Buginese characters in the Matthes order.

Punctuation. Buginese uses spaces between certain units. One punctuation symbol, U+1A1E BUGINESE PALLAWA, is functionally similar to the full stop and comma of the Latin script. There is also another separation mark, U+1A1F BUGINESE END OF SECTION.

U+0662 ARABIC-INDIC DIGIT TWO or a doubling of the vowel sign (especially U+1A19 BUGINESE VOWEL SIGN E and U+1A1A BUGINESE VOWEL SIGN O) is used sometimes to denote word reduplication.

Numerals. There are no known digits specific to the Buginese script.

11.9 Balinese

Balinese: U+1B00–U+1B7F

The Balinese script, or *aksara Bali,* is used for writing the Balinese language, the native language of the people of Bali, known locally as *basa Bali.* It is a descendant of the ancient Brahmi script of India, and therefore it has many similarities with modern scripts of South Asia and Southeast Asia, which are also members of that family. The Balinese script is used to write Kawi, or Old Javanese, which strongly influenced the Balinese language in the eleventh century CE. A slightly modified version of the script is used to write the Sasak language, which is spoken on the island of Lombok to the east of Bali. Some Balinese words have been borrowed from Sanskrit, which may also be written in the Balinese script.

Structure. Balinese consonants have an inherent *-a* vowel sound. Consonants combine with following consonants in the usual Brahmic fashion: the inherent vowel is "killed" by U+1B44 BALINESE ADEG ADEG (*virama*), and the following consonant is subjoined or postfixed, often with a change in shape. *Table 11-14* shows the base consonants and their conjunct forms.

Table 11-14. Balinese Base Consonants and Conjunct Forms

Consonant	Base Form	Conjunct Form
ka	ᬓ	◌᭄ᬓ
kha	ᬔ	◌᭄ᬔ
ga	ᬕ	◌᭄ᬕ
gha	ᬖ	◌᭄ᬖ
nga	ᬗ	◌᭄ᬗ
ca	ᬘ	◌᭄ᬘ
cha	ᬙ	◌᭄ᬙ
ja	ᬚ	◌᭄ᬚ
jha	ᬛ	◌᭄ᬛ
nya	ᬜ	◌᭄ᬜ
tta	ᬝ	◌᭄ᬝ
ttha	ᬞ	◌᭄ᬞ
dda	ᬟ	◌᭄ᬟ
ddha	ᬠ	◌᭄ᬠ

Table 11-14. Balinese Base Consonants and Conjunct Forms (Continued)

Consonant	Base Form	Conjunct Form
nna	ᬡ	◌᭄ᬡ
ta	ᬢ	◌᭄ᬢ
tha	ᬣ	◌᭄ᬣ
da	ᬤ	◌᭄ᬤ
dha	ᬥ	◌᭄ᬥ
na	ᬦ	◌᭄ᬦ
pa	ᬧ	◌᭄ᬧ
pha	ᬨ	◌᭄ᬨ
ba	ᬩ	◌᭄ᬩ
bha	ᬪ	◌᭄ᬪ
ma	ᬫ	◌᭄ᬫ
ya	ᬬ	◌᭄ᬬ
ra	ᬭ	◌᭄ᬭ
la	ᬮ	◌᭄ᬮ
wa	ᬯ	◌᭄ᬯ
ssa	ᬱ	◌᭄ᬱ
sha	ᬰ	◌᭄ᬰ
sa	ᬲ	◌᭄ᬲ
ha	ᬳ	◌᭄ᬳ
r	ᬋ	◌᭄ᬋ

The seven letters U+1B45 BALINESE LETTER KAF SASAK through U+1B4B BALINESE LETTER ASYURA SASAK are base consonant extensions for the Sasak language. Their base forms and conjunct forms are shown in *Table 11-15*.

Balinese dependent vowel signs are used in a manner similar to that employed by other Brahmic scripts.

Independent vowels are used in a manner similar to that seen in other Brahmic scripts, with a few differences. For example, U+1B05 BALINESE LETTER AKARA and U+1B0B BALINESE LETTER RA REPA can be treated as consonants; that is, they can be followed by

Table 11-15. Sasak Extensions for Balinese

Consonant	Base Form	Conjunct Form
kaf	ᭅ	◌᭄ᭅ
khot	ᭆ	◌᭄ᭆ
tzir	ᭇ	◌᭄ᭇ
ef	ᭈ	◌᭄ᭈ
ve	ᭉ	◌᭄ᭉ
zal	ᭊ	◌᭄ᭊ
asyura	ᭋ	◌᭄ᭋ

adeg adeg. In Sasak, the vowel letter *akara* can be followed by an explicit *adeg adeg* ᬅ᭄ in word- or syllable-final position, where it indicates the glottal stop; other consonants can also be subjoined to it.

***Behavior of* ra.** The behavior of the U+1B2D BALINESE LETTER RA is unique to Balinese. The inherited Kawi form of the script used a *repha* glyph in the same way as many Brahmic scripts do—it represented *ra* as the first element of a syllable. This is seen in the first example in *Figure 11-6*, where the sequence <*ra*, *virama*, *ma*> is rendered with the *repha* glyph. However, because many syllables end in *-r* in the Balinese language, this written form was reanalyzed and would be pronounced *damar.* Furthermore, *damar* would be represented using U+1B03 BALINESE SIGN SURANG for the *-r*, as shown in example 3. The character sequence used in Kawi for spelling *dharma* would in Balinese render as shown in example 2, where the base letter *ra* with a subjoined *ma* is not well formed for the writing system. The correct representation of *dharma* in Balinese is shown in example 4, where the reanalyzed *repha* is represented by the *surang* and is rendered above the first syllable instead of the second.

Because of its relationship to *ra*, *surang* should be treated as equivalent to *ra* for searching and sorting purposes. Two other combining signs are also equivalent to base letters for searching and sorting: U+1B02 BALINESE SIGN CECEK (*anusvara*) is equivalent to *nga*, and U+1B04 BALINESE SIGN BISAH (*visarga*) is equivalent to *ha*.

***Behavior of* ra repa.** The unique behavior of BALINESE LETTER RA REPA (*vocalic ṛ*) results from a reanalysis of the independent vowel letter as a consonant. In a compound word in which the first element ends in a consonant and the second element begins with an original *ra* + *pepet*, such as *Pak Rërëh* ᬧᬓ᭄ᬋᬋᬄ "Mr Rërëh", the postfixed form of ᬋ *ra repa* is used; this particular sequence is encoded *ka* + *adeg adeg* + *ra repa*. However, in other contexts where the *ra repa* represents the original Sanskrit vowel, U+1B3A BALINESE VOWEL SIGN RA REPA is used, as in *Krësna* ᬓᬺᬱ᭄ᬡ.

Figure 11-6. Writing *dharma* in Balinese

①	ᬥ	+	ᬭ	+	◌᭄	+	ᬫ	→	ᬥᬃᬫ (Kawi)
	dha 1B25		ra 1B2D		adeg adeg 1B44		ma 1B2B		dha-rma
②	ᬥ	+	ᬭ	+	◌᭄	+	ᬫ	→	*ᬥᬭ᭄ᬫ (Balinese)
	dha 1B25		ra 1B2D		adeg adeg 1B44		ma 1B2B		dha-rma
③	ᬥ	+	ᬫ	+	◌ᬃ			→	ᬥᬫᬃ
	dha 1B25		ma 1B2B		surang 1B03				dha-mar
④	ᬥ	+	◌ᬃ	+	ᬫ			→	ᬥᬃᬫ
	dha 1B25		surang 1B03		ma 1B2B				dhar-ma

Rendering. The vowel signs /u/ and /u:/ take different forms when combined with subscripted consonant clusters, as shown in *Table 11-16*. The upper limit of consonant clusters is three, the last of which can be *-ya*, *-wa*, or *-ra*.

Table 11-16. Balinese Consonant Clusters with u and u:

Syllable	**Glyph**
kyu	ᬓ᭄ᬬᬸ
kyú	ᬓ᭄ᬬᬹ
kwu	ᬓ᭄ᬯᬸ
kwú	ᬓ᭄ᬯᬹ
kru	ᬓ᭄ᬭᬸ
krú	ᬓ᭄ᬭᬹ

Table 11-16. Balinese Consonant Clusters with u and u: (Continued)

Syllable	Glyph
kyu	ᬓ᭄ᬬᬸ
kryu	ᬓ᭄ᬭ᭄ᬬᬸ
kryú	ᬓ᭄ᬭ᭄ᬬᬹ
skru	ᬲ᭄ᬓ᭄ᬭᬸ
skrú	ᬲ᭄ᬓ᭄ᬭᬹ

Nukta. The combining mark U+1B34 BALINESE SIGN REREKAN (*nukta*) and a similar sign in Javanese are used to extend the character repertoire for foreign sounds. In recent times, Sasak users have abandoned the Javanese-influenced *rerekan* in favor of the series of modified letters shown in *Table 11-15*, also making use of some unused Kawi letters for these Arabic sounds.

Ordering. The traditional order *ha na ca ra ka* | *da ta sa wa la* | *ma ga ba nga* | *pa ja ya nya* is taught in schools, although van der Tuuk followed the Javanese order *pa ja ya nya* | *ma ga ba nga* for the second half. The arrangement of characters in the code charts follows the Brahmic ordering.

Punctuation. Both U+1B5A BALINESE PANTI and U+1B5B BALINESE PAMADA are used to begin a section in text. U+1B5D BALINESE CARIK PAMUNGKAH is used as a colon. U+1B5E BALINESE CARIK SIKI and U+1B5F BALINESE CARIK PAREREN are used as comma and full stop, respectively. At the end of a section, ᭟᭜᭟ *pasalinan* and ᭛᭜᭛ *carik agung* may be used (depending on which sign began the section). They are encoded using the punctuation ring U+1B5C BALINESE WINDU together with *carik pareren* and *pamada*.

Hyphenation. Traditional Balinese texts are written on palm leaves; books of these bound leaves together are called *lontar*. U+1B60 BALINESE PAMENENG is inserted in lontar texts where a word must be broken at the end of a line (always after a full syllable). This sign is not used as a word-joining hyphen—it is used only in line breaking.

Musical Symbols. Bali is well known for its rich musical heritage. A number of related notation systems are used to write music. To represent degrees of a scale, the syllables *ding dong dang deng dung* are used (encoded at U+1B61..U+1B64, U+1B66), in the same way that *do re mi fa so la ti* is used in Western tradition. The symbols representing these syllables are based on the vowel matras, together with some other symbols. However, unlike the regular vowel matras, these stand-alone spacing characters take diacritical marks. They also have different positions and sizes relative to the baseline. These matra-like symbols are encoded in the range U+1B61..U+1B6A, along with a modified *aikara*. Some notation systems use other spacing letters, such as U+1B09 BALINESE LETTER UKARA and U+1B27 BALINESE LETTER PA, which are not separately encoded for musical use. The U+1B01 BALINESE SIGN ULU CANDRA (*candrabindu*) can also be used with U+1B62 BALINESE MUSI-

CAL SYMBOL DENG and U+1B68 BALINESE MUSICAL SYMBOL DEUNG, and possibly others. BALINESE SIGN ULU CANDRA can be used to indicate modre symbols as well.

A range of diacritical marks is used with these musical notation base characters to indicate metrical information. Some additional combining marks indicate the instruments used; this set is encoded at U+1B6B..U+1B73. A set of symbols describing certain features of performance are encoded at U+1B74..U+1B7C. These symbols describe the use of the right or left hand, the open or closed hand position, the "male" or "female" drum (of the pair) which is struck, and the quality of the striking.

Modre Symbols. The Balinese script also includes a range of "holy letters" called modre symbols. Most of these letters can be composed from the constituent parts currently encoded, including U+1B01 BALINESE SIGN ULU CANDRA. Additional characters, known to be used inline in text (as opposed to decoratively on drawings), are expected to be proposed as Balinese extensions in due course.

CHAPTER

12

Chapter 12

East Asian Scripts

This chapter presents the following scripts:

Han	*Hiragana*	*Hangul*
Bopomofo	*Katakana*	*Yi*

The characters that are now called East Asian ideographs, and known as Han ideographs in the Unicode Standard, were developed in China in the second millennium BCE. The basic system of writing Chinese using ideographs has not changed since that time, although the set of ideographs used, their specific shapes, and the technologies involved have developed over the centuries. The encoding of Chinese ideographs in the Unicode Standard is described in *Section 12.1, Han.*

As civilizations developed surrounding China, they frequently adapted China's ideographs for writing their own languages. Japan, Korea, and Vietnam all borrowed and modified Chinese ideographs for their own languages. Chinese is an isolating language, monosyllabic and noninflecting, and ideographic writing suits it well. As Han ideographs were adopted for unrelated languages, however, extensive modifications were required.

Chinese ideographs were originally used to write Japanese, for which they are, in fact, ill suited. As an adaptation, the Japanese developed two syllabaries, *hiragana* and *katakana*, whose shapes are simplified or stylized versions of certain ideographs. (See *Section 12.4, Hiragana and Katakana.*) Chinese ideographs are called *kanji* in Japanese and are still used, in combination with *hiragana* and *katakana*, in modern Japanese.

In Korea, Chinese ideographs were originally used to write Korean, for which they are also ill suited. The Koreans developed an alphabetic system, *Hangul*, discussed in *Section 12.6, Hangul.* The shapes of Hangul syllables or the letter-like *jamos* from which they are composed are not directly influenced by Chinese ideographs. However, the individual jamos are grouped into syllabic blocks that resemble ideographs both visually and in the relationship they have to the spoken language (one syllable per block). Chinese ideographs are called *hanja* in Korean and are still used together with Hangul in South Korea for modern Korean. The Unicode Standard includes a complete set of Korean Hangul syllables as well as the individual jamos, which can also be used to write Korean. *Section 3.12, Conjoining Jamo Behavior*, describes how to use the conjoining jamos and how to convert between the two methods for representing Korean.

In Vietnam, a set of native ideographs was created for Vietnamese based on the same principles used to create new ideographs for Chinese. These Vietnamese ideographs were used through the beginning of the twentieth century and are occasionally used in more recent signage and other limited contexts.

Yi was originally written using a set of ideographs invented in imitation of the Chinese. Modern Yi as encoded in the Unicode Standard is a syllabary derived from these ideographs and is discussed in *Section 12.7, Yi.*

Bopomofo, discussed in *Section 12.3, Bopomofo*, is another recently invented syllabic system, used to represent Chinese phonetics.

In all these East Asian scripts, the characters (Chinese ideographs, Japanese *kana*, Korean Hangul syllables, and Yi syllables) are written within uniformly sized rectangles, usually squares. Traditionally, the basic writing direction followed the conventions of Chinese handwriting, in top-down vertical lines arranged from right to left across the page. Under the influence of Western printing technologies, a horizontal, left-to-right directionality has become common, and proportional fonts are seeing increased use, particularly in Japan. Horizontal, right-to-left text is also found on occasion, usually for shorter texts such as inscriptions or store signs. Diacritical marks are rarely used, although phonetic annotations are not uncommon. Older editions of the Chinese classics sometimes use the ideographic tone marks (U+302A..U+302D) to indicate unusual pronunciations of characters.

Many older character sets include characters intended to simplify the implementation of East Asian scripts, such as variant punctuation forms for text written vertically, halfwidth forms (which occupy only half a rectangle), and fullwidth forms (which allow Latin letters to occupy a full rectangle). These characters are included in the Unicode Standard for compatibility with older standards.

Appendix E, Han Unification History, describes how the diverse typographic traditions of mainland China, Taiwan, Japan, Korea, and Vietnam have been reconciled to provide a common set of ideographs in the Unicode Standard for all these languages and regions.

12.1 Han

CJK Unified Ideographs

The Unicode Standard contains a set of unified Han ideographic characters used in the written Chinese, Japanese, and Korean languages.[1] The term *Han*, derived from the Chinese Han Dynasty, refers generally to Chinese traditional culture. The Han ideographic

1. Although the term "CJK"—Chinese, Japanese, and Korean—is used throughout this text to describe the languages that currently use Han ideographic characters, it should be noted that earlier Vietnamese writing systems were based on Han ideographs. Consequently, the term "CJKV" would be more accurate in a historical sense. Han ideographs are still used for historical, religious, and pedagogical purposes in Vietnam.

characters make up a coherent script, which was traditionally written vertically, with the vertical lines ordered from right to left. In modern usage, especially in technical works and in computer-rendered text, the Han script is written horizontally from left to right and is freely mixed with Latin or other scripts. When used in writing Japanese or Korean, the Han characters are interspersed with other scripts unique to those languages (Hiragana and Katakana for Japanese; Hangul syllables for Korean).

The term "Han ideographic characters" is used within the Unicode Standard as a common term traditionally used in Western texts, although "sinogram" is preferred by professional linguists. Taken literally, the word "ideograph" applies only to some of the ancient original character forms, which indeed arose as ideographic depictions. The vast majority of Han characters were developed later via composition, borrowing, and other non-ideographic principles, but the term "Han ideographs" remains in English usage as a conventional cover term for the script as a whole.

The Han ideographic characters constitute a very large set, numbering in the tens of thousands. They have a long history of use in East Asia. Enormous compendia of Han ideographic characters exist because of a continuous, millennia-long scholarly tradition of collecting all Han character citations, including variant, mistaken, and nonce forms, into annotated character dictionaries.

Because of the large size of the Han ideographic character repertoire, and because of the particular problems that the characters pose for standardizing their encoding, this character block description is more extended than that for other scripts and is divided into subsections. The first two subsections, "CJK Standards" and "Blocks Containing Han Ideographs," describe the character set standards used as sources and the way in which the Unicode Standard divides Han ideographs into blocks. These subsections are followed by an extended discussion of the characteristics of Han characters, with particular attention being paid to the problem of unification of encoding for characters used for different languages. There is a formal statement of the principles behind the Unified Han character encoding adopted in the Unicode Standard and the order of its arrangement. For a detailed account of the background and history of development of the Unified Han character encoding, see *Appendix E, Han Unification History*.

CJK Standards

The Unicode Standard draws its unified Han character repertoire of 70,229 characters from a number of character set standards. These standards are grouped into seven initial sources, as indicated in *Table 12-1*. The primary work of unifying and ordering the characters from these sources was done by the Ideographic Rapporteur Group (IRG), a subgroup of ISO/IEC JTC1/SC2/WG2.

The G, T, J, K, KP, and V sources represent the characters submitted to the IRG by its member bodies. The G source consists of submissions from mainland China, the Hong Kong SAR, and Singapore. The other five sources are the submissions from Taiwan, Japan, South and North Korea, and Vietnam, respectively. The U source represents character set stan-

Table 12-1. Initial Sources for Unified Han

G source:	G0	GB 2312-80
	G1	GB 12345-90 with 58 Hong Kong and 92 Korean "Idu" characters
	G3	GB 7589-87 unsimplified forms
	G5	GB 7590-87 unsimplified forms
	G7	General Purpose Hanzi List for Modern Chinese Language, and General List of Simplified Hanzi
	GS	Singapore Characters
	G8	GB 8565-88
	GE	GB 16500-95
T source:	T1	CNS 11643-1992 1st plane
	T2	CNS 11643-1992 2nd plane
	T3	CNS 11643-1992 3rd plane with some additional characters
	T4	CNS 11643-1992 4th plane
	T5	CNS 11643-1992 5th plane
	T6	CNS 11643-1992 6th plane
	T7	CNS 11643-1992 7th plane
	TF	CNS 11643-1992 15th plane
J source:	J0	JIS X 0208-1990
	J1	JIS X 0212-1990
	JA	Unified Japanese IT Vendors Contemporary Ideographs, 1993
K source:	K0	KS C 5601-1987 (unique ideographs)
	K1	KS C 5657-1991
	K2	PKS C 5700-1 1994
	K3	PKS C 5700-2 1994
KP source:	KP0	KPS 9566-97
	KP1	KPS 10721-2000
V source:	V0	TCVN 5773:1993
	V1	TCVN 6056:1995
U source:		KS C 5601-1987 (duplicate ideographs)
		ANSI Z39.64-1989 (EACC)
		Big-5 (Taiwan)
		CCCII, level 1
		GB 12052-89 (Korean)
		JEF (Fujitsu)
		PRC Telegraph Code
		Taiwan Telegraph Code (CCDC)
		Xerox Chinese
		Han Character Shapes Permitted for Personal Names (Japan)
		IBM Selected Japanese and Korean Ideographs

dards that were not submitted to the IRG by any member body but that were used by the Unicode Consortium.

For each of the IRG sources, the table contains an abbreviated source name in the second column and a descriptive source name in the third column. The abbreviated names are used in various data files published by the Unicode Consortium and ISO/IEC to identify the specific IRG sources.

In some cases, the entire ideographic repertoire of the original character set standards was *not* included in the corresponding source. Three reasons explain this decision:

1. Where the repertoires of two of the character set standards within a single source have considerable overlap, the characters in the overlap might be included only once in the source. This approach is used, for example, with GB 2312-80 and GB 12345-90, which have many ideographs in common. Characters in GB 12345-90 that are duplicates of characters in GB 2312-80 are not included in the G source.

2. Where a character set standard is based on unification rules that differ substantially from those used by the IRG, many variant characters found in the character set standard will not be included in the source. This situation is the case with CNS 11643-1992, EACC, and CCCII. It is the only case where full round-trip compatibility with the Han ideograph repertoire of the relevant character set standards is not guaranteed.

3. KS C 5601-1987 contains numerous duplicate ideographs included because they have multiple pronunciations in Korean. These multiply encoded ideographs are not included in the K source but are included in the U source. They are encoded in the CJK Compatibility Ideographs block to provide full round-trip compatibility with KS C 5601-1987 (now known as KS X 1001:1998).

Blocks Containing Han Ideographs

Han ideographic characters are found in five main blocks of the Unicode Standard, as shown in *Table 12-2*.

Table 12-2. Blocks Containing Han Ideographs

Block	**Range**	**Comment**
CJK Unified Ideographs	4E00-9FFF	Common
CJK Unified Ideographs Extension A	3400-4DFF	Rare
CJK Unified Ideographs Extension B	20000-2A6DF	Rare, historic
CJK Compatibility Ideographs	F900-FAFF	Duplicates, unifiable variants, corporate characters
CJK Compatibility Ideographs Supplement	2F800-2FA1F	Unifiable variants

Characters in the three unified ideographs blocks are defined by the IRG, based on Han unification principles explained later in this section.

The two compatibility ideographs blocks contain various duplicate or unifiable variant characters encoded for round-trip compatibility with various legacy standards.

The initial repertoire of the CJK Unified Ideographs block contains characters submitted to the IRG prior to 1992, consisting of commonly used characters. That initial repertoire was derived entirely from the G, T, J, and K sources. It has subsequently been extended with small sets of unified ideographs or ideographic components needed for interoperability with the HKSCS standard (U+9FA6..U+9FB3) and with the GB 18030 standard (U+9FB4..U+9FBB).

Characters in the CJK Unified Ideographs Extension A block are rare and are not unifiable with characters in the CJK Unified Ideographs block. They were submitted to the IRG during 1992–1998 and are derived entirely from the G, T, J, K, and V sources.

The CJK Unified Ideographs Extension B block contains rare and historic characters that are also not unifiable with characters in the CJK Unified Ideographs block. They were submitted to the IRG during 1998–2002 and are derived from a long list of additional sources, including major dictionaries, as documented in *Table 12-8*.

The only principled difference in the unification work done by the IRG on the three unified ideograph blocks is that the Source Separation Rule (rule R1) was applied only to the original CJK Unified Ideographs block and not to the two extension blocks. The Source Separation Rule states that ideographs that are distinctly encoded in a source must not be unified. (For further discussion, see "Principles of Han Unification" later in this section.)

The three unified ideograph blocks are not closed repertoires. Each contains a small range of reserved code points at the end of the block. Additional unified ideographs may eventually be encoded in those ranges—as has already occurred in the CJK Unified Ideographs block itself. There is no guarantee that any such Han ideographic additions would be of the same types or from the same sources as preexisting characters in the block, and implementations should be careful not to make hard-coded assumptions regarding the range of assignments within the Han ideographic blocks in general.

Unifiable Han characters unique to the U source are found in the CJK Compatibility Ideographs block. There are 12 of these characters: U+FA0E, U+FA0F, U+FA11, U+FA13, U+FA14, U+FA1F, U+FA21, U+FA23, U+FA24, U+FA27, U+FA28, and U+FA29. The remaining characters in the CJK Compatibility Ideographs block and the CJK Compatibility Ideographs Supplement block are either duplicates or unifiable variants of a character in one of the blocks of unified ideographs.

IICore. IICore (International Ideograph Core) is an important set of Han ideographs, incorporating characters from all the defined blocks. This set of nearly 10,000 characters has been developed by the IRG and represents the set of characters in everyday use throughout East Asia. By covering the characters in IICore, developers guarantee that they can handle all the needs of almost all of their customers. This coverage is of particular use on devices such as cell phones or PDAs, which have relatively stringent resource limitations. Characters in IICore are explicitly tagged as such in the Unihan Database (see "Unihan Database" in *Section 4.1, Unicode Character Database*).

General Characteristics of Han Ideographs

The authoritative Japanese dictionary *Koujien* defines Han characters to be

> characters that originated among the Chinese to write the Chinese language. They are now used in China, Japan, and Korea. They are logographic (each character represents a word, not just a sound) characters that developed from pictographic and ideographic principles. They are also used phonetically. In Japan they are generally called *kanji* (Han, that is, Chinese, characters) including the "national characters" (*kokuji*) such as *touge* (mountain pass), which have been created using the same principles. They are also called *mana* (true names, as opposed to *kana*, false or borrowed names).[2]

For many centuries, written Chinese was the accepted written standard throughout East Asia. The influence of the Chinese language and its written form on the modern East Asian languages is similar to the influence of Latin on the vocabulary and written forms of languages in the West. This influence is immediately visible in the mixture of Han characters and native phonetic scripts (*kana* in Japan, *hangul* in Korea) as now used in the orthographies of Japan and Korea (see *Table 12-3*).

Table 12-3. Common Han Characters

Han Character	*Chinese*	*Japanese*	*Korean*	*English Translation*
天	tiān	ten, ame	chen	heaven, sky
地	dì	chi, tsuchi	ci	earth, ground
人	rén	jin, hito	in	man, person
山	shān	san, yama	san	mountain
水	shuǐ	sui, mizu	swu	water
上	shàng	jou, ue	sang	above
下	xià	ka, shita	ha	below

The evolution of character shapes and semantic drift over the centuries has resulted in changes to the original forms and meanings. For example, the Chinese character 湯 *tāng* (Japanese *tou* or *yu*, Korean *thang*), which originally meant "hot water," has come to mean "soup" in Chinese. "Hot water" remains the primary meaning in Japanese and Korean, whereas "soup" appears in more recent borrowings from Chinese, such as "soup noodles"

2. Lee Collins' translation from the Japanese, *Koujien*, Izuru, Shinmura, ed. (Tokyo: Iwanami Shoten, 1983).

(Japanese *tanmen*; Korean *thangmyen*). Still, the identical appearance and similarities in meaning are dramatic and more than justify the concept of a unified Han script that transcends language.

The "nationality" of the Han characters became an issue only when each country began to create coded character sets (for example, China's GB 2312-80, Japan's JIS X 0208-1978, and Korea's KS C 5601-87) based on purely local needs. This problem appears to have arisen more from the priority placed on local requirements and lack of coordination with other countries, rather than out of conscious design. Nevertheless, the identity of the Han characters is fundamentally independent of language, as shown by dictionary definitions, vocabulary lists, and encoding standards.

Terminology. Several standard romanizations of the term used to refer to East Asian ideographic characters are commonly used. They include *hànzì* (Chinese), *kanzi* (Japanese), *kanji* (colloquial Japanese), *hanja* (Korean), and *Chữ hán* (Vietnamese). The standard English translations for these terms are interchangeable: Han character, Han ideographic character, East Asian ideographic character, or CJK ideographic character. For the purpose of clarity, the Unicode Standard uses some subset of the English terms when referring to these characters. The term *Kanzi* is used in reference to a specific Japanese government publication. The unrelated term *KangXi* (which is a Chinese reign name, rather than another romanization of "Han character") is used only when referring to the primary dictionary used for determining Han character arrangement in the Unicode Standard. (See *Table 12-7*.)

Distinguishing Han Character Usage Between Languages. There is some concern that unifying the Han characters may lead to confusion because they are sometimes used differently by the various East Asian languages. Computationally, Han character unification presents no more difficulty than employing a single Latin character set that is used to write languages as different as English and French. Programmers do not expect the characters "c", "h", "a", and "t" alone to tell us whether *chat* is a French word for cat or an English word meaning "informal talk." Likewise, we depend on context to identify the American hood (of a car) with the British bonnet. Few computer users are confused by the fact that ASCII can also be used to represent such words as the Welsh word *ynghyd*, which are strange looking to English eyes. Although it would be convenient to identify words by language for programs such as spell-checkers, it is neither practical nor productive to encode a separate Latin character set for every language that uses it.

Similarly, the Han characters are often combined to "spell" words whose meaning may not be evident from the constituent characters. For example, the two characters "to cut" and "hand" mean "postage stamp" in Japanese, but the compound may appear to be nonsense to a speaker of Chinese or Korean (see *Figure 12-1*).

Figure 12-1. Han Spelling

切	+	手	=	1. Japanese "stamp"
to cut		hand		2. Chinese "cut hand"

Even within one language, a computer requires context to distinguish the meanings of words represented by coded characters. The word *chuugoku* in Japanese, for example, may refer to China or to a district in central west Honshuu (see *Figure 12-2*).

Figure 12-2. Semantic Context for Han Characters

中	+	国	=	1. China
middle		country		2. Chuugoku district of Honshuu

Coding these two characters as four so as to capture this distinction would probably cause more confusion and still not provide a general solution. The Unicode Standard leaves the issues of language tagging and word recognition up to a higher level of software and does not attempt to encode the language of the Han characters.

Simplified and Traditional Chinese. There are currently two main varieties of written Chinese: "simplified Chinese" (*jiǎntǐzì*), used in most parts of the People's Republic of China (PRC) and Singapore, and "traditional Chinese" (*fántǐzì*), used predominantly in the Hong Kong and Macao SARs, Taiwan, and overseas Chinese communities. The process of interconverting between the two is a complex one. This complexity arises largely because a single simplified form may correspond to multiple traditional forms, such as U+53F0 台, which is a traditional character in its own right and the simplified form for U+6AAF 檯, U+81FA 臺, and U+98B1 颱. Moreover, vocabulary differences have arisen between Mandarin as spoken in Taiwan and Mandarin as spoken in the PRC, the most notable of which is the usual name of the language itself: *guóyǔ* (the National Language) in Taiwan and *pǔtōnghuà* (the Common Speech) in the PRC. Merely converting the character content of a text from simplified Chinese to the appropriate traditional counterpart is insufficient to change a simplified Chinese document to traditional Chinese, or vice versa. (The vast majority of Chinese characters are the same in both simplified and traditional Chinese.)

There are two PRC national standards, GB 2312-80 and GB 12345-90, which are intended to represent simplified and traditional Chinese, respectively. The character repertoires of the two are the same, but the simplified forms occur in GB 2312-80 and the traditional ones in GB 12345-90. These are both part of the IRG G source, with traditional forms and simplified forms separated where they differ. As a result, the Unicode Standard contains a number of distinct simplifications for characters, such as U+8AAC 說 and U+8BF4 说.

While there are lists of official simplifications published by the PRC, most of these are obtained by applying a few general principles to specific areas. In particular, there is a set of radicals (such as U+2F94 ⾔ KANGXI RADICAL SPEECH, U+2F99 ⾙ KANGXI RADICAL SHELL, U+2FA8 ⾨ KANGXI RADICAL GATE, and U+2FC3 ⿃ KANGXI RADICAL BIRD) for which simplifications exist (U+2EC8 ⻈ CJK RADICAL C-SIMPLIFIED SPEECH, U+2EC9 ⻉ CJK RADICAL C-SIMPLIFIED SHELL, U+2ED4 ⻔ CJK RADICAL C-SIMPLIFIED GATE, and U+2EE6 ⻦ CJK RADICAL C-SIMPLIFIED BIRD). The basic technique for simplifying a character containing one of these radicals is to substitute the simplified radical, as in the previous example.

The Unicode Standard does not explicitly encode all simplified forms for traditional Chinese characters. Where the simplified and traditional forms exist as different encoded characters, each should be used as appropriate. The Unicode Standard does not specify how to represent a new simplified form (or, more rarely, a new traditional form) that can be derived algorithmically from an encoded traditional form (simplified form).

Dialects of Chinese. Chinese is not a single language, but a complex of spoken forms that share a single written form. Although these spoken forms are referred to as dialects, they are actually mutually unintelligible and distinct languages. Virtually all modern written Chinese is Mandarin, the dominant language in both the PRC and Taiwan. Speakers of other Chinese languages learn to read and write Mandarin, although they pronounce it using the rules of their own language. (This would be like having Spanish children read and write only French, but pronouncing it as if it were Spanish.) The major non-Mandarin Chinese languages are Cantonese (spoken in the Hong Kong and Macao SARs, in many overseas Chinese communities, and in much of Guangzhou province), Wu, Min, Hakka, Gan, and Xiang.

Prior to the twentieth century, the standard form of written Chinese was literary Chinese, a form derived from the classical Chinese written, but probably not spoken by Confucius in the sixth century BCE.

The ideographic repertoire of the Unicode Standard is sufficient for all but the most specialized texts of modern Chinese, literary Chinese, and classical Chinese. Preclassical Chinese, written using *seal forms* or *oracle bone forms*, has not been systematically incorporated into the Unicode Standard. Of Chinese languages, Cantonese is occasionally found in printed materials; the others are almost never seen in printed form. There is less standardization for the ideographic repertoires of these languages, and no fully systematic effort has been undertaken to catalog the nonstandard ideographs they use. Because of efforts on the part of the government of the Hong Kong SAR, however, the current ideographic repertoire of the Unicode Standard should be adequate for many—but not all—written Cantonese texts.

Sorting Han Ideographs. The Unicode Standard does not define a method by which ideographic characters are sorted; the requirements for sorting differ by locale and application. Possible collating sequences include phonetic, radical-stroke (*KangXi*, *Xinhua Zidian*, and so on), four-corner, and total stroke count. Raw character codes alone are seldom sufficient to achieve a usable ordering in any of these schemes; ancillary data are usually required. (See *Table 12-7*.)

Character Glyphs. In form, Han characters are monospaced. Every character takes the same vertical and horizontal space, regardless of how simple or complex its particular form is. This practice follows from the long history of printing and typographical practice in China, which traditionally placed each character in a square cell. When written vertically, there are also a number of named cursive styles for Han characters, but the cursive forms of the characters tend to be quite idiosyncratic and are not implemented in general-purpose Han character fonts for computers.

There may be a wide variation in the glyphs used in different countries and for different applications. The most commonly used typefaces in one country may not be used in others.

The types of glyphs used to depict characters in the Han ideographic repertoire of the Unicode Standard have been constrained by available fonts. Users are advised to consult authoritative sources for the appropriate glyphs for individual markets and applications. It is assumed that most Unicode implementations will provide users with the ability to select the font (or mixture of fonts) that is most appropriate for a given locale.

Principles of Han Unification

Three-Dimensional Conceptual Model. To develop the explicit rules for unification, a conceptual framework was developed to model the nature of Han ideographic characters. This model expresses written elements in terms of three primary attributes: semantic (meaning, function), abstract shape (general form), and actual shape (instantiated, typeface form). These attributes are graphically represented in three dimensions according to the *X*, *Y*, and *Z* axes (see *Figure 12-3*).

Figure 12-3. Three-Dimensional Conceptual Model

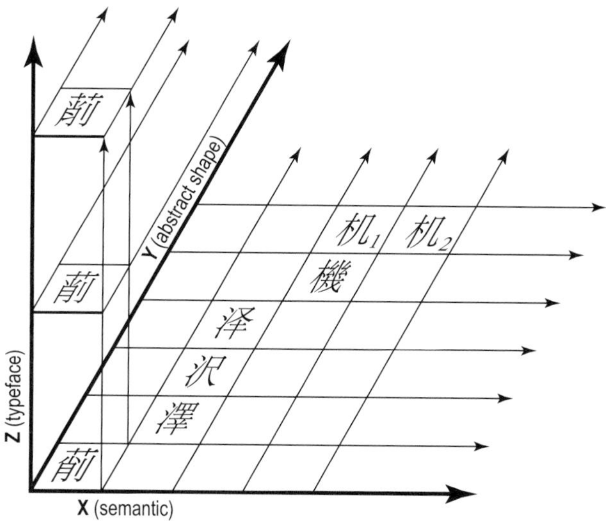

The semantic attribute (represented along the *X* axis) distinguishes characters by meaning and usage. Distinctions are made between entirely unrelated characters such as 澤 (marsh) and 機 (machine) as well as extensions or borrowings beyond the original semantic cluster such as $机_1$ (a phonetic borrowing used as a simplified form of 機) and $机_2$ (table, the original meaning).

The abstract shape attribute (the *Y* axis) distinguishes the variant forms of a single character with a single semantic attribute (that is, a character with a single position on the *X* axis).

The actual shape (typeface) attribute (the *Z* axis) is for differences of type design (the actual shape used in imaging) of each variant form.

Only characters that have the same abstract shape (that is, occupy a single point on the *X* and *Y* axes) are potential candidates for unification. *Z*-axis typeface and stylistic differences are generally ignored.

Unification Rules

The following rules were applied during the process of merging Han characters from the different source character sets.

R1 Source Separation Rule. If two ideographs are distinct in a primary source standard, then they are not unified.

- This rule is sometimes called the *round-trip rule* because its goal is to facilitate a round-trip conversion of character data between an IRG source standard and the Unicode Standard without loss of information.
- This rule was applied only for the work on the original CJK Unified Ideographs block [also known as the Unified Repertoire and Ordering (URO)]. The IRG dropped this rule in 1992 and will not use it in future work.

Figure 12-4 illustrates six variants of the CJK ideograph meaning "sword."

Figure 12-4. CJK Source Separation

剣 劍 剱 劔 劒 釼

"sword"

Each of the six variants in *Figure 12-4* is separately encoded in one of the primary source standards—in this case, J0 (JIS X 0208-1990), as shown in *Table 12-4*.

Table 12-4. Source Encoding for Sword Variants

Unicode	JIS
U+5263	J0-3775
U+528D	J0-5178
U+5271	J0-517B
U+5294	J0-5179
U+5292	J0-517A
U+91FC	J0-6E5F

Because the six sword characters are historically related, they are not subject to disunification by the Noncognate Rule (R2) and thus would ordinarily have been considered for possible abstract shape-based unification by R3. Under that rule, the fourth and fifth variants would probably have been unified for encoding. However, the Source Separation Rule required that all six variants be separately encoded, precluding them from any consideration of shape-based unification. Further variants of the "sword" ideograph, U+5251 and U+528E, are also separately encoded because of application of the Source Separation Rule—in that case applied to one or more Chinese primary source standards, rather than to the J0 Japanese primary source standard.

R2 ***Noncognate Rule. In general, if two ideographs are unrelated in historical derivation (noncognate characters), then they are not unified.***

For example, the ideographs in *Figure 12-5*, although visually quite similar, are nevertheless not unified because they are historically unrelated and have distinct meanings.

Figure 12-5. Not Cognates, Not Unified

土 ≠ 士

earth warrior, scholar

R3 ***By means of a two-level classification (described next), the abstract shape of each ideograph is determined. Any two ideographs that possess the same abstract shape are then unified provided that their unification is not disallowed by either the Source Separation Rule or the Noncognate Rule.***

Abstract Shape

Two-Level Classification. Using the three-dimensional model, characters are analyzed in a two-level classification. The two-level classification distinguishes characters by abstract shape (*Y* axis) and actual shape of a particular typeface (*Z* axis). Variant forms are identified based on the difference of abstract shapes.

To determine differences in abstract shape and actual shape, the structure and features of each component of an ideograph are analyzed as follows.

Ideographic Component Structure. The component structure of each ideograph is examined. A component is a geometrical combination of primitive elements. Various ideographs can be configured with these components used in conjunction with other components. Some components can be combined to make a component more complicated in its structure. Therefore, an ideograph can be defined as a component tree with the entire ideograph as the root node and with the bottom nodes consisting of primitive elements (see *Figure 12-6* and *Figure 12-7*).

Ideograph Features. The following features of each ideograph to be compared are examined:

Figure 12-6. Ideographic Component Structure

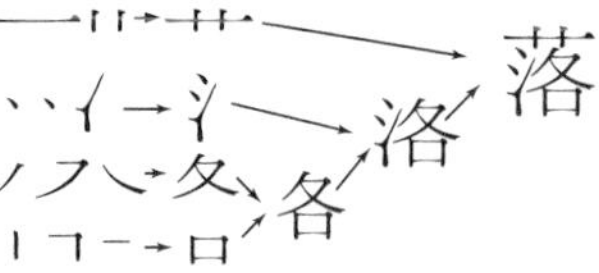

Figure 12-7. The Most Superior Node of an Ideographic Component

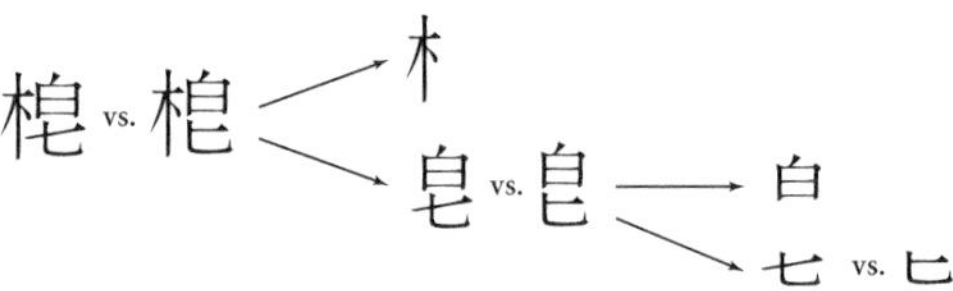

- Number of components
- Relative positions of components in each complete ideograph
- Structure of a corresponding component
- Treatment in a source character set
- Radical contained in a component

Uniqueness or Unification. If one or more of these features are different between the ideographs compared, the ideographs are considered to have different abstract shapes and, therefore, are considered unique characters and are not unified. If all of these features are identical between the ideographs, the ideographs are considered to have the same abstract shape and are unified.

Spatial Positioning. Ideographs may exist as a unit or may be a component of more complex ideographs. A source standard may describe a requirement for a component with a specific spatial positioning that would be otherwise unified on the principle of having the same abstract shape as an existing full ideograph. Examples of spatial positioning for ideographic components are left half, top half, and so on.

Examples. *Table 12-5* gives examples of some typical differences in abstract character shape, resulting in decisions not to unify characters. Also included in the table are all three instances of disunification based on distinctions in spatial positioning.

Differences in the actual shapes of ideographs that *have* been unified are illustrated in *Table 12-6*.

Han Ideograph Arrangement

The arrangement of the Unicode Han characters is based on the positions of characters as they are listed in four major dictionaries. The *KangXi Zidian* was chosen as primary

Table 12-5. Ideographs Not Unified

Characters	Reason
崖 ≠ 厓	Different number of components
峰 ≠ 峯	Same number of components placed in different relative positions
拡 ≠ 擴	Same number and same relative position of components, corresponding components structured differently
区 ≠ 區	Characters treated differently in a source character set
祕 ≠ 秘	Characters with different radical in a component
爲 ≠ 為	Same abstract shape, different actual shape
鿻 ≠ 䜌	Same abstract shape, different position (U+9FBB versus U+470C)
鿹 ≠ 𠔉	Same abstract shape, different position (U+9FB9 versus U+20509)
鿺 ≠ 𠦝	Same abstract shape, different position (U+9FBA versus U+2099D)

Table 12-6. Ideographs Unified

Characters	Reason
周 ≈ 周	Different writing sequence
雪 ≈ 雪	Differences in overshoot at the stroke termination
酉 ≈ 酉	Differences in contact of strokes
鉅 ≈ 鉅	Differences in protrusion at the folded corner of strokes
垔 ≈ 垔	Differences in bent strokes
朱 ≈ 朱	Differences in stroke termination
父 ≈ 父	Differences in accent at the stroke initiation
八 ≈ 八	Difference in rooftop modification
說 ≈ 説	Difference in rotated strokes/dots[a]

a. These ideographs (having the same abstract shape) would have been unified except for the Source Separation Rule.

because it contains most of the source characters and because the dictionary itself and the principles of character ordering it employs are commonly used throughout East Asia.

The Han ideograph arrangement follows the index (page and position) of the dictionaries listed in *Table 12-7* with their priorities.

When a character is found in the *KangXi Zidian*, it follows the *KangXi Zidian* order. When it is not found in the *KangXi Zidian* and it is found in *Dai Kan-Wa Jiten*, it is given a position extrapolated from the *KangXi* position of the preceding character in *Dai Kan-Wa Jiten*.

Table 12-7. Han Ideograph Arrangement

Priority	Dictionary	City	Publisher	Version
1	*KangXi Zidian*	Beijing	Zhonghua Bookstore, 1989	Seventh edition
2	*Dai Kan-Wa Jiten*	Tokyo	Taishuukan Shoten, 1986	Revised edition
3	*Hanyu Da Zidian*	Chengdu	Sichuan Cishu Publishing, 1986	First edition
4	*Dae Jaweon*	Seoul	Samseong Publishing Co. Ltd, 1988	First edition

When it is not found in either *KangXi* or *Dai Kan-Wa*, then the *Hanyu Da Zidian* and *Dae Jaweon* dictionaries are consulted in a similar manner.

Ideographs with simplified *KangXi* radicals are placed in a group following the traditional *KangXi* radical from which the simplified radical is derived. For example, characters with the simplified radical 讠 corresponding to *KangXi* radical 言 follow the last nonsimplified character having 言 as a radical. The arrangement for these simplified characters is that of the *Hanyu Da Zidian*.

The few characters that are not found in any of the four dictionaries are placed following characters with the same *KangXi* radical and stroke count.

Radical-Stroke Order. The radical-stroke order that results is a culturally neutral order. It does not exactly match the order found in common dictionaries. Information for sorting all CJK ideographs by the radical-stroke method is found in the Unihan Database (see "Unihan Database" in *Section 4.1, Unicode Character Database*). It should be used if characters from the various blocks containing ideographs (see *Table 12-2*) are to be properly interleaved. Note, however, that there is no standard way of ordering characters with the same radical-stroke count; for most purposes, Unicode code point order would be as acceptable as any other way.

A radical-stroke index to the IICore subset of the CJK unified ideographs is provided in *Chapter 18, Han Radical-Stroke Index*, to help locate the most useful and common Han characters in the standard. A full radical-stroke index of all CJK unified ideographs, together with a complete chart listing, can be found on the Unicode Web site. Details regarding the form of the online charts for the CJK unified ideographs are discussed in *Section 17.2, CJK Unified Ideographs.*

Mappings for Han Ideographs

The mappings defined by the IRG between the ideographs in the Unicode Standard and the IRG sources are specified in the Unihan Database. These mappings are considered to be normative parts of ISO/IEC 10646 and of the Unicode Standard; that is, the characters are *defined* to be the targets for conversion of these characters in these character set standards.

These mappings have been derived from editions of the source standards provided directly to the IRG by its member bodies, and they may not match mappings derived from the published editions of these standards. For this reason, developers may choose to use alternative mappings more directly correlated with published editions.

Specialized conversion systems may also choose more sophisticated mapping mechanisms—for example, semantic conversion, variant normalization, or conversion between simplified and traditional Chinese.

The Unicode Consortium also provides mapping information that extends beyond the normative mappings defined by the IRG. These additional mappings include mappings to character set standards included in the U source, including duplicate characters from KS C 5601-1987, mappings to portions of character set standards omitted from IRG sources, references to standard dictionaries, and suggested character/stroke counts.

CJK Unified Ideographs Extension B: U+20000–U+2A6D6

The ideographs in the CJK Unified Ideographs Extension B block represent an additional set of 42,711 ideographs beyond the 27,496 included in *The Unicode Standard, Version 3.0*. The same principles underlying the selection, organization, and unification of Han ideographs apply to these ideographs.

The ideographs in this block are derived from the six IRG sources: G source, H source, T source, J source, K source, and V source. There is no U source for ideographs in the CJK Unified Ideographs Extension B block. The H source represents a new IRG source beyond the ones used for earlier blocks of Han ideographs and is used for characters derived from standards published by the Hong Kong SAR. The standards and other references associated with these six IRG sources are listed in *Table 12-8*.

Table 12-8. Sources Added for Extension B

G source:	G_KX	KangXi dictionary ideographs (including the addendum) not already encoded in the BMP
	G_HZ	Hanyu Da Zidian ideographs not already encoded in the BMP
	G_CY	Ci Yuan
	G_CH	Ci Hai
	G_HC	Hanyu Da Cidian
	G_BK	Chinese Encyclopedia
	G_FZ	Founder Press System
	G_4K	Siku Quanshu
H source:	H	Hong Kong Supplementary Character Set
T source:	T4	CNS 11643-1992, 4th plane
	T5	CNS 11643-1992, 5th plane
	T6	CNS 11643-1992, 6th plane
	T7	CNS 11643-1992, 7th plane
	TF	CNS 11643-1992, 15th plane
J source:	J3	JIS X 0213:2000, level 3
	J3A	JIS X 0213:2004, level 3
	J4	JIS X 0213:2000, level 4
K source:	K4	PKS 5700-3:1998
V source:	V0	TCVN 5773:1993
	V2	VHN 01:1998
	V3	VHN 02:1998

For each of the six IRG sources, the second column of *Table 12-8* contains an abbreviated name of the source; the third column gives a descriptive name. The abbreviated names are used in various data files published by the Unicode Consortium and ISO/IEC to identify the specific IRG sources. For a more detailed explanation of the format of *Table 12-8*, refer to *Table 12-1*.

As with other Han ideograph blocks, the ideographs in the CJK Unified Ideographs Extension B block are derived from versions of national standards submitted to the IRG by its members. They may in some instances differ slightly from published versions of these standards.

As with other CJK unified ideographs, the names for these characters are algorithmically assigned. Thus CJK UNIFIED IDEOGRAPH-20000 is the name for the ideograph at U+20000.

These ideographs may be used in Ideographic Description Sequences, which are described in *Section 12.2, Ideographic Description Characters.*

CJK Compatibility Ideographs: U+F900–U+FAFF

The Korean national standard KS C 5601-1987 (now known as KS X 1001:1998), which served as one of the primary source sets for the Unified CJK Ideograph Repertoire and Ordering, Version 2.0, contains 268 duplicate encodings of identical ideograph forms to denote alternative pronunciations. That is, in certain cases, the standard encodes a single character multiple times to denote different linguistic uses. This approach is like encoding the letter "a" five times to denote the different pronunciations it has in the words *hat, able, art, father*, and *adrift*. Because they are in all ways identical in shape to their nominal counterparts, they were excluded by the IRG from its sources. For round-trip conversion with KS C 5601-1987, they are encoded separately from the primary CJK Unified Ideographs block.

Another 34 ideographs from various regional and industry standards were encoded in this block, primarily to achieve round-trip conversion compatibility. Twelve of these ideographs (U+FA0E, U+FA0F, U+FA11, U+FA13, U+FA14, U+FA1F, U+FA21, U+FA23, U+FA24, U+FA27, U+FA28, and U+FA29) are not encoded in the CJK Unified Ideographs Areas. These 12 characters are not duplicates and should be treated as a small extension to the set of unified ideographs.

Except for the 12 unified ideographs just enumerated, CJK compatibility ideographs from this block are not used in Ideographic Description Sequences.

An additional 59 compatibility ideographs are found from U+FA30..U+FA6A. They are included in the Unicode Standard to provide full round-trip compatibility with the ideographic repertoire of JIS X 0213:2000 and should not be used for any other purpose.

An additional 106 compatibility ideographs are encoded at the range U+FA70 to U+FAD9. They are included in the Unicode Standard to provide full round-trip compatibility with the ideographic repertoire of PKS 5700 parts 1, 2, and 3. They should not be used for any other purpose.

The names for the compatibility ideographs are also algorithmically derived. Thus the name for the compatibility ideograph U+F900 is CJK COMPATIBILITY IDEOGRAPH-F900.

CJK Compatibility Supplement: U+2F800–U+2FA1D

The CJK Compatibility Ideographs Supplement block consists of additional compatibility ideographs required for round-trip compatibility with CNS 11643-1992, planes 3, 4, 5, 6, 7, and 15. They should not be used for any other purpose and, in particular, may not be used in Ideographic Description Sequences.

Kanbun: U+3190–U+319F

This block contains a set of Kanbun marks used in Japanese texts to indicate the Japanese reading order of classical Chinese texts. These marks are not encoded in any current character encoding standards but are widely used in literature. They are typically written in an annotation style to the left of each line of vertically rendered Chinese text. For more details, see JIS X 4501.

Symbols Derived from Han Ideographs

A number of symbols derived from Han ideographs can be found in other blocks. See "Enclosed CJK Letters and Months: U+3200..U+32FF" and "CJK Compatibility: U+3300..U+33FF" in *Section 15.9, Enclosed and Square.*

CJK and KangXi Radicals: U+2E80–U+2FD5

East Asian ideographic *radicals* are ideographs or fragments of ideographs used to index dictionaries and word lists, and as the basis for creating new ideographs. The term *radical* comes from the Latin *radix*, meaning "root," and refers to the part of the character under which the character is classified in dictionaries. *Chapter 18, Han Radical-Stroke Index*, provides information on how to use radical-stroke lookup to locate ideographs encoded in the Unicode Standard.

There is no single radical set in general use throughout East Asia. However, the set of 214 radicals used in the eighteenth-century *KangXi* dictionary is universally recognized.

The visual appearance of radicals is often very different when they are used as radicals than their appearance when they are stand-alone ideographs. Indeed, many radicals have multiple graphic forms when used as parts of characters. A standard example is the water radical, which is written 水 when an ideograph and generally 氵 when part of an ideograph.

The Unicode Standard includes two blocks of encoded radicals: the KangXi Radicals block (U+2F00..U+2FD5), which contains the base forms for the 214 radicals, and the CJK Radicals Supplement block (U+2E80..U+2EF3), which contains a set of variant shapes taken by the radicals either when they occur as parts of characters or when they are used for simplified Chinese. These variant shapes are commonly found as independent and distinct characters in dictionary indices—such as for the radical-stroke charts in the Unicode Standard.

As such, they have not been subject to the usual unification rules used for other characters in the standard.

Most of the characters in the CJK and KangXi Radicals blocks are equivalents of characters in the CJK Unified Ideographs block of the Unicode Standard. Radicals that have one graphic form as an ideograph and another as part of an ideograph are generally encoded in both forms in the CJK Unified Ideographs block (such as U+6C34 and U+6C35 for the water radical).

Standards. CNS 11643-1992 includes a block of radicals separate from its ideograph block. This block includes 212 of the 214 KangXi radicals. These characters are included in the KangXi Radicals block.

Those radicals that are ideographs in their own right have a definite meaning and are usually referred to by that meaning. Accordingly, most of the characters in the KangXi Radicals block have been assigned names reflecting their meaning. The other radicals have been given names based on their shape.

Semantics. Characters in the CJK and KangXi Radicals blocks should never be used as ideographs. They have different properties and meanings. U+2F00 KANGXI RADICAL ONE is not equivalent to U+4E00 CJK UNIFIED IDEOGRAPH-4E00, for example. The former is to be treated as a symbol, the latter as a word or part of a word.

The characters in the CJK and KangXi Radicals blocks are compatibility characters. Except in cases where it is necessary to make a semantic distinction between a Chinese character in its role as a radical and the same Chinese character in its role as an ideograph, the characters from the Unified Ideographs blocks should be used instead of the compatibility radicals. To emphasize this difference, radicals may be given a distinct font style from their ideographic counterparts.

CJK Additions from HKSCS and GB 18030

Several characters have been encoded because of developments in HKSCS-2001 (the Hong Kong Supplementary Character Set) and GB 18030-2000 (the PRC National Standard). Both of these encoding standards were published with mappings to Unicode Private Use Area code points. PUA ideographic characters that could not be remapped to non-PUA CJK ideographs were added to the existing block of CJK Unified Ideographs. Fourteen new ideographs (U+9FA6..U+9FB3) were added from HKSCS, and eight multistroke ideographic components (U+9FB4..U+9FBB) were added from GB 18030.

To complete the mapping to these two Chinese standards, a number of non-ideographic characters were encoded elsewhere in the standard. In particular, two symbol characters from HKSCS were added to the existing Miscellaneous Technical block: U+23DA EARTH GROUND and U+23DB FUSE. A new block, CJK Strokes (U+31C0..U+31EF), was created and populated with a number of stroke symbols from HKSCS. Another block, Vertical Forms (U+FE10..U+FE1F), was created for vertical punctuation compatibility characters from GB 18030.

CJK Strokes: U+31C0–U+31EF

Characters in the CJK Strokes block are single-stroke components of CJK ideographs. The first characters assigned to this block were 16 HKSCS-2001 PUA characters that had been excluded from CJK Unified Ideograph Extension B on the grounds that they were not true ideographs. CJK strokes are used with highly specific semantics (primarily to index ideographs), but they lack the monosyllabic pronunciations and logographic functions typically associated with independent ideographs. The encoded characters in this block are single strokes of well-defined types; these constitute the basic elements of all CJK ideographs. Any traditionally defined stroke type attested in the representative forms appearing in the Unicode CJK ideograph code charts or attested in pre-unification source glyphs is a candidate for future inclusion in this block.

12.2 Ideographic Description Characters

Ideographic Description: U+2FF0–U+2FFB

Although the Unicode Standard includes more than 70,000 ideographs, many thousands of extremely rare ideographs were nevertheless left unencoded. Research into cataloging additional ideographs for encoding continues, but it is anticipated that at no point will the entire set of potential, encodable ideographs be completely exhausted. In particular, ideographs continue to be coined and such new coinages will invariably be unencoded.

The 12 characters in the Ideographic Description block provide a mechanism for the standard interchange of text that must reference unencoded ideographs. Unencoded ideographs can be described using these characters and encoded ideographs; the reader can then create a mental picture of the ideographs from the description.

This process is different from a formal *encoding* of an ideograph. There is no canonical description of unencoded ideographs; there is no semantic assigned to described ideographs; there is no equivalence defined for described ideographs. Conceptually, ideograph descriptions are more akin to the English phrase "an 'e' with an acute accent on it" than to the character sequence <U+006E, U+0301>.

In particular, support for the characters in the Ideographic Description block does *not* require the rendering engine to recreate the graphic appearance of the described character.

Note also that many of the ideographs that users might represent using the Ideographic Description characters will be formally encoded in future versions of the Unicode Standard.

The Ideographic Description Algorithm depends on the fact that virtually all CJK ideographs can be broken down into smaller pieces that are themselves ideographs. The broad coverage of the ideographs already encoded in the Unicode Standard implies that the vast majority of unencoded ideographs can be represented using the Ideographic Description characters.

Although Ideographic Description Sequences are intended primarily to represent unencoded ideographs and should not be used in data interchange to represent encoded ideographs, they also have pedagogical and analytic uses. A researcher, for example, may choose to represent the character U+86D9 蛙 as "⿰虫圭" in a database to provide a link between it and other characters sharing its phonetic, such as U+5A03 娃. The IRG is using Ideographic Description Sequences in this fashion to help provide a first-approximation, machine-generated set of unifications for its current work.

Ideographic Description Sequences. Ideographic Description Sequences are defined by the following grammar. The list of characters associated with the *Unified_CJK_Ideograph* and *CJK_Radical* properties can be found in the Unicode Character Database. See *Appendix A, Notational Conventions*, for the notational conventions used here.

IDS := *Unified_CJK_Ideograph* | *CJK_Radical* | *IDS_BinaryOperator IDS IDS*
| *IDS_TrinaryOperator IDS IDS IDS*

IDS_BinaryOperator := U+2FF0 | U+2FF1 | U+2FF4 | U+2FF5 | U+2FF6 | U+2FF7 |
U+2FF8 | U+2FF9 | U+2FFA | U+2FFB

IDS_TrinaryOperator:= U+2FF2 | U+2FF3

In addition to the above grammar, Ideographic Description Sequences have two other length constraints:

- No sequence can be longer than 16 Unicode code points in length.
- No sequence can contain more than six *Unified_CJK_Ideographs* or *CJK_Radicals* in a row without an intervening Ideographic Description character.

A sequence of characters that includes Ideographic Description characters but does not conform to the grammar and length constraints described here is not an Ideographic Description Sequence.

The operators indicate the relative graphic positions of the operands running from left to right and from top to bottom.

Non-unique compatibility ideographs (U+F900..U+FA6B and U+2F800..U+2FA1D, but not U+FA0E, U+FA0F, U+FA11, U+FA13, U+FA14, U+FA1F, U+FA21, U+FA23, U+FA24, U+FA27, U+FA28, or U+FA29) are not counted as unified ideographs for the purposes of this grammar, although they do have the ideographic property (see *Section 4.10, Letters, Alphabetic, and Ideographic*). These ideographs are excluded from Ideographic Description Sequences to incrementally reduce the ambiguity of such sequences. Non-unique compatibility ideographs have canonical equivalences and are excluded on that basis. Some *CJK_Radical* characters have compatibility equivalences to unified ideographs, but compatibility equivalence is not considered a basis for exclusion from Ideographic Description Sequences, because the shape differences involved may be relevant to description of the forms of unencoded ideographs.

Figure 12-8 illustrates the use of this grammar to provide descriptions of unencoded ideographs.

Figure 12-8. Using the Ideographic Description Characters

① → ⿱ 井 蛙
2FF1 4E95 86D9

② → ⿱ 井 ⿰ 虫 圭
2FF1 4E95 2FF0 866B 572D

③ → ⿱ 井 ⿰ 虫 ⿱ 土 土
2FF1 4E95 2FF0 866B 2FF1 571F 571F

④ → ⿸ 厂 ⿱ 今 止
2FF8 5382 2FF1 4ECA 6B62

⑤ → ⿰ 水 ⿱ 口 巛
2FF0 6C34 2FF1 53E3 5DDB

⑥ → ⿰ 氵 ⿱ 口 巛
2FF0 6C35 2FF1 53E3 5DDB

⑦ → ⿰ ⽔ ⿱ 口 巛
2FF0 2F54 2FF1 53E3 5DDB

⑧ → ⿰ ⺡ ⿱ 口 巛
2FF0 2EA1 2FF1 53E3 5DDB

⑨ → ⿱ ⿰ 鳥 龜 火
2FF1 2FF0 9CE5 9F9C 706B

⑩ → ⿳ ⿲ 丂 彡 丂 彐 皿
2FF3 2FF2 4E02 5F61 4E02 5F50 76BF

⑪ → ⿰ ⿳ ⿻ ⿰ 日 日 工 网 丂 乞
2FF0 2FF3 2FFB 2FF0 65E5 65E5 5DE5 7F51 4E02 4E5E

⑫ → ⿴ 囗 ⿰ ⿱ 鹵 凼 邑
2FF4 56D7 2FF0 2FF1 9E75 51FC 9091

⑬ → ⿰ 氵 ⿱ ⿰ 保 厽 土
2FF0 6C35 2FF1 2FF0 4FDD 53BD 571F

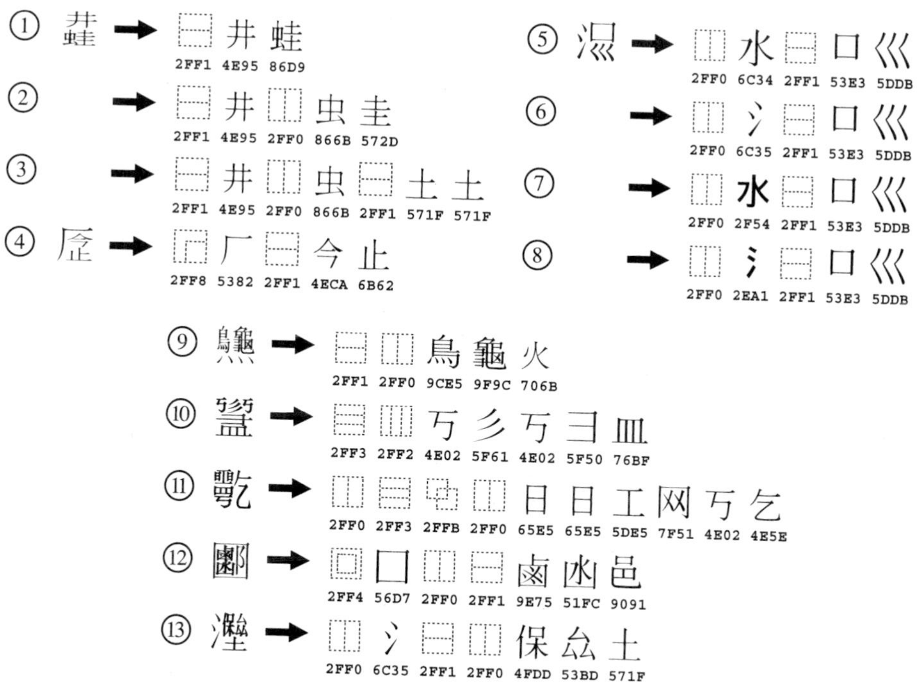

A user wishing to represent an unencoded ideograph will need to analyze its structure to determine how to describe it using an Ideographic Description Sequence. As a rule, it is best to use the natural radical-phonetic division for an ideograph if it has one and to use as short a description sequence as possible; however, there is no requirement that these rules be followed. Beyond that, the shortest possible Ideographic Description Sequence is preferred.

The length constraints allow random access into a string of ideographs to have well-defined limits. Only a small number of characters need to be scanned backward to determine whether those characters are part of an Ideographic Description Sequence.

The fact that Ideographic Description Sequences can contain other Ideographic Description Sequences means that implementations may need to be aware of the *recursion depth* of a sequence and its *back-scan length*. The recursion depth of an Ideographic Description Sequence is the maximum number of pending operations encountered in the process of parsing an Ideographic Description Sequence. In *Figure 12-8*, the maximum recursion depth is shown in the eleventh example, where four operations are still pending at the end of the Ideographic Description Sequence.

The back-scan length is the maximum number of ideographs unbroken by Ideographic Description characters in the sequence. None of the examples in *Figure 12-8* has more than six ideographs in a row; for many, the back-scan length is two.

The Unicode Standard places no formal limits on the recursion depth of Ideographic Description Sequences. It does, however, limit the back-scan length for valid Ideographic Description Sequences to be six or less.

Examples 9–13 illustrate more complex Ideographic Description Sequences showing the use of some of the less common operators.

Equivalence. Many unencoded ideographs can be described in more than one way using this algorithm, either because the pieces of a description can themselves be broken down further (examples 1–3 in *Figure 12-8*) or because duplications appear within the Unicode Standard (examples 5 and 6 in *Figure 12-8*).

The Unicode Standard does not define equivalence for two Ideographic Description Sequences that are not identical. *Figure 12-8* contains numerous examples illustrating how different Ideographic Description Sequences might be used to describe the same ideograph.

In particular, Ideographic Description Sequences should not be used to provide alternative graphic representations of encoded ideographs in data interchange. Searching, collation, and other content-based text operations would then fail.

Interaction with the Ideographic Variation Mark. As with ideographs proper, the Ideographic Variation Mark (U+303E) may be placed before an Ideographic Description Sequence to indicate that the description is merely an approximation of the original ideograph desired. A sequence of characters that includes an Ideographic Variation Mark is not an Ideographic Description Sequence.

Rendering. Ideographic Description characters are visible characters and are not to be treated as control characters. Thus the sequence U+2FF1 U+4E95 U+86D9 must have a distinct appearance from U+4E95 U+86D9.

An implementation may render a valid Ideographic Description Sequence either by rendering the individual characters separately or by parsing the Ideographic Description Sequence and drawing the ideograph so described. In the latter case, the Ideographic Description Sequence should be treated as a ligature of the individual characters for purposes of hit testing, cursor movement, and other user interface operations. (See *Section 5.11, Editing and Selection*.)

Character Boundaries. Ideographic Description characters are not combining characters, and there is no requirement that they affect character or word boundaries. Thus U+2FF1 U+4E95 U+86D9 may be treated as a sequence of three characters or even three words.

Implementations of the Unicode Standard may choose to parse Ideographic Description Sequences when calculating word and character boundaries. Note that such a decision will make the algorithms involved significantly more complicated and slower.

Standards. The Ideographic Description characters are found in GBK—an extension to GB 2312-80 that adds all Unicode ideographs not already in GB 2312-80. GBK is defined as a normative annex of GB 13000.1-93.

12.3 Bopomofo

Bopomofo: U+3100–U+312F

Bopomofo constitute a set of characters used to annotate or teach the phonetics of Chinese, primarily the standard Mandarin language. These characters are used in dictionaries and teaching materials, but not in the actual writing of Chinese text. The formal Chinese names for this alphabet are *Zhuyin-Zimu* ("phonetic alphabet") and *Zhuyin-Fuhao* ("phonetic symbols"), but the informal term "Bopomofo" (analogous to "ABCs") provides a more serviceable English name and is also used in China. The Bopomofo were developed as part of a populist literacy campaign following the 1911 revolution; thus they are acceptable to all branches of modern Chinese culture, although in the People's Republic of China their function has been largely taken over by the Pinyin romanization system.

Bopomofo is a hybrid writing system—part alphabet and part syllabary. The letters of Bopomofo are used to represent either the initial parts or the final parts of a Chinese syllable. The initials are just consonants, as for an alphabet. The finals constitute either simple vowels, vocalic diphthongs, or vowels plus nasal consonant combinations. Because a number of Chinese syllables have no initial consonant, the Bopomofo letters for finals may constitute an entire syllable by themselves. More typically, a Chinese syllable is represented by one initial consonant letter, followed by one final letter. In some instances, a third letter is used to indicate a complex vowel nucleus for the syllable. For example, the syllable that would be written *luan* in Pinyin is segmented l-u-an in Bopomofo—that is, <U+310C, U+3128, U+3122>.

Standards. The standard Mandarin set of Bopomofo is included in the People's Republic of China standards GB 2312 and GB 18030, and in the Republic of China (Taiwan) standard CNS 11643.

Mandarin Tone Marks. Small modifier letters used to indicate the five Mandarin tones are part of the Bopomofo system. In the Unicode Standard they have been unified into the Modifier Letter range, as shown in *Table 12-9.*

Table 12-9. Mandarin Tone Marks

first tone	U+02C9 MODIFIER LETTER MACRON
second tone	U+02CA MODIFIER LETTER ACUTE ACCENT
third tone	U+02C7 CARON
fourth tone	U+02CB MODIFIER LETTER GRAVE ACCENT
light tone	U+02D9 DOT ABOVE

Standard Mandarin Bopomofo. The order of the Mandarin Bopomofo letters U+3105..U+3129 is standard worldwide. The code offset of the first letter U+3105 BOPOMOFO LETTER B from a multiple of 16 is included to match the offset in the ISO-registered standard GB 2312. The character U+3127 BOPOMOFO LETTER I may be rendered as either a horizontal stroke or a vertical stroke. Often the glyph is chosen to stand perpendicular to the text baseline (for example, a horizontal stroke in vertically set text), but other usage is also common. In the Unicode Standard, the form shown in the charts is a vertical stroke; the horizontal stroke form is considered to be a rendering variant. The variant glyph is not assigned a separate character code.

Extended Bopomofo. To represent the sounds of Chinese dialects other than Mandarin, the basic Bopomofo set U+3105..U+3129 has been augmented by additional phonetic characters. These extensions are much less broadly recognized than the basic Mandarin set. The three extended Bopomofo characters U+312A..U+312C are cited in some standard reference works, such as the encyclopedia *Xin Ci Hai.* Another set of 24 extended Bopomofo, encoded at U+31A0..U+31B7, was designed in 1948 to cover additional sounds of the Minnan and Hakka dialects. The extensions are used together with the main set of Bopomofo characters to provide a complete phonetic orthography for those dialects. There are no standard Bopomofo letters for the phonetics of Cantonese or several other Southern Chinese dialects.

The small characters encoded at U+31B4..U+31B7 represent syllable-final consonants not present in standard Mandarin or in Mandarin dialects. They have the same shapes as Bopomofo "b", "d", "k", and "h", respectively, but are rendered in a smaller form than the initial consonants; they are also generally shown close to the syllable medial vowel character. These final letters are encoded separately so that the Minnan and Hakka dialects can be represented unambiguously in plain text without having to resort to subscripting or other fancy text mechanisms to represent the final consonants.

Extended Bopomofo Tone Marks. In addition to the Mandarin tone marks enumerated in *Table 12-9*, other tone marks appropriate for use with the extended Bopomofo transcriptions of Minnan and Hakka can be found in the Modifier Letter range, as shown in *Table 12-10.* The "departing tone" refers to the *qusheng* in traditional Chinese tonal analysis, with the *yin* variant historically derived from voiceless initials and the *yang* variant from voiced initials. Southern Chinese dialects in general maintain more tonal distinctions than Mandarin does.

Table 12-10. Minnan and Hakka Tone Marks

yin departing tone	U+02EA MODIFIER LETTER YIN DEPARTING TONE MARK
yang departing tone	U+02EB MODIFIER LETTER YANG DEPARTING TONE MARK

Rendering of Bopomofo. Bopomofo is rendered from left to right in horizontal text, but also commonly appears in vertical text. It may be used by itself in either orientation, but typically appears in interlinear annotation of Chinese (Han character) text. Children's books are often completely annotated with Bopomofo pronunciations for every character. This interlinear annotation is structurally quite similar to the system of Japanese *ruby* annotation, but it has additional complications that result from the explicit usage of tone marks with the Bopomofo letters.

In horizontal interlineation, the Bopomofo is generally placed above the corresponding Han character(s); tone marks, if present, appear at the end of each syllabic group of Bopomofo letters. In vertical interlineation, the Bopomofo is generally placed on the right side of the corresponding Han character(s); tone marks, if present, appear in a separate interlinear row to the right side of the vowel letter. When using extended Bopomofo for Minnan and Hakka, the tone marks may also be mixed with Latin digits 0–9 to express changes in actual tonetic values resulting from juxtaposition of basic tones.

12.4 Hiragana and Katakana

Hiragana: U+3040–U+309F

Hiragana is the cursive syllabary used to write Japanese words phonetically and to write sentence particles and inflectional endings. It is also commonly used to indicate the pronunciation of Japanese words. Hiragana syllables are phonetically equivalent to the corresponding Katakana syllables.

Standards. The Hiragana block is based on the JIS X 0208-1990 standard, extended by the nonstandard syllable U+3094 HIRAGANA LETTER VU, which is included in some Japanese corporate standards. Some additions are based on the JIS X 0213:2000 standard.

Combining Marks. Hiragana and the related script Katakana use U+3099 COMBINING KATAKANA-HIRAGANA VOICED SOUND MARK and U+309A COMBINING KATAKANA-HIRAGANA SEMI-VOICED SOUND MARK to generate voiced and semivoiced syllables from the base syllables, respectively. All common precomposed combinations of base syllable forms using these marks are already encoded as characters, and use of these precomposed forms is the predominant JIS usage. These combining marks must follow the base character to which they apply. Because most implementations and JIS standards treat these marks as spacing characters, the Unicode Standard contains two corresponding noncombining (spacing) marks at U+309B and U+309C.

Iteration Marks. The two characters U+309D HIRAGANA ITERATION MARK and U+309E HIRAGANA VOICED ITERATION MARK are punctuation-like characters that denote the iteration (repetition) of a previous syllable according to whether the repeated syllable has an unvoiced or voiced consonant, respectively.

Vertical Text Digraph. U+309F HIRAGANA DIGRAPH YORI is a digraph form used only when Hiragana is displayed vertically.

Katakana: U+30A0–U+30FF

Katakana is the noncursive syllabary used to write non-Japanese (usually Western) words phonetically in Japanese. It is also used to write Japanese words with visual emphasis. Katakana syllables are phonetically equivalent to corresponding Hiragana syllables. Katakana contains two characters, U+30F5 KATAKANA LETTER SMALL KA and U+30F6 KATAKANA

LETTER SMALL KE, that are used in special Japanese spelling conventions (for example, the spelling of place names that include archaic Japanese connective particles).

Standards. The Katakana block is based on the JIS X 0208-1990 standard. Some additions are based on the JIS X 0213:2000 standard.

Punctuation-like Characters. U+30FB KATAKANA MIDDLE DOT is used to separate words when writing non-Japanese phrases. U+30A0 KATAKANA-HIRAGANA DOUBLE HYPHEN is a delimiter occasionally used in analyzed Katakana or Hiragana textual material.

U+30FC KATAKANA-HIRAGANA PROLONGED SOUND MARK is used predominantly with Katakana and occasionally with Hiragana to denote a lengthened vowel of the previously written syllable. The two iteration marks, U+30FD KATAKANA ITERATION MARK and U+30FE KATAKANA VOICED ITERATION MARK, serve the same function in Katakana writing that the two Hiragana iteration marks serve in Hiragana writing.

Vertical Text Digraph. U+30FF KATAKANA DIGRAPH KOTO is a digraph form used only when Katakana is displayed vertically.

Katakana Phonetic Extensions: U+31F0–U+31FF

These extensions to the Katakana syllabary are all "small" variants. They are used in Japan for phonetic transcription of Ainu and other languages. They may be used in combination with U+3099 COMBINING KATAKANA-HIRAGANA VOICED SOUND MARK and U+309A COMBINING KATAKANA-HIRAGANA SEMI-VOICED SOUND MARK to indicate modification of the sounds represented.

Standards. The Katakana Phonetic Extensions block is based on the JIS X 0213:2000 standard.

12.5 Halfwidth and Fullwidth Forms

Halfwidth and Fullwidth Forms: U+FF00–U+FFEF

In the context of East Asian coding systems, a double-byte character set (DBCS), such as JIS X 0208-1990 or KS X 1001:1998, is generally used together with a single-byte character set (SBCS), such as ASCII or a variant of ASCII. Text that is encoded with both a DBCS and SBCS is typically displayed such that the glyphs representing DBCS characters occupy two display cells—where a display cell is defined in terms of the glyphs used to display the SBCS (ASCII) characters. In these systems, the two-display-cell width is known as the *fullwidth* or *zenkaku* form, and the one-display-cell width is known as the *halfwidth* or *hankaku* form. While *zenkaku* and *hankaku* are Japanese terms, the display-width concepts apply equally to Korean and Chinese implementations.

Because of this mixture of display widths, certain characters often appear twice—once in fullwidth form in the DBCS repertoire and once in halfwidth form in the SBCS repertoire.

To achieve round-trip conversion compatibility with such mixed-width encoding systems, it is necessary to encode both fullwidth and halfwidth forms of certain characters. This block consists of the additional forms needed to support conversion for existing texts that employ both forms.

In the context of conversion to and from such mixed-width encodings, all characters in the General Scripts Area should be construed as halfwidth (*hankaku*) characters if they have a fullwidth equivalent elsewhere in the standard or if they do not occur in the mixed-width encoding; otherwise, they should be construed as fullwidth (*zenkaku*). Specifically, most characters in the CJK Miscellaneous Area and the CJKV Ideograph Area, along with the characters in the CJK Compatibility Ideographs, CJK Compatibility Forms, and Small Form Variants blocks, should be construed as fullwidth (*zenkaku*) characters. For a complete description of the East Asian Width property, see Unicode Standard Annex #11, "East Asian Width."

The characters in this block consist of fullwidth forms of the ASCII block (except SPACE), certain characters of the Latin-1 Supplement, and some currency symbols. In addition, this block contains halfwidth forms of the Katakana and Hangul Compatibility Jamo characters. Finally, a number of symbol characters are replicated here (U+FFE8..U+FFEE) with explicit halfwidth semantics.

Unifications. The fullwidth form of U+0020 SPACE is unified with U+3000 IDEOGRAPHIC SPACE.

12.6 Hangul

Hangul Jamo: U+1100–U+11FF

Korean Hangul may be considered a featural syllabic script. As opposed to many other syllabic scripts, the syllables are formed from a set of alphabetic components in a regular fashion. These alphabetic components are called *jamo.*

The name *Hangul* itself is just one of several terms that may be used to refer to the script. In some contexts, the preferred term is simply the generic *Korean characters. Hangul* is used more frequently in South Korea, whereas a basically synonymous term *Choseongul* is preferred in North Korea. A politically neutral term, *Jeongum*, may also be used.

The Unicode Standard contains both the complete set of precomposed modern Hangul syllable blocks and the set of conjoining Hangul jamo. This set of conjoining Hangul jamo can be used to encode all modern and ancient syllable blocks. For a description of conjoining jamo behavior and precomposed Hangul syllables, see *Section 3.12, Conjoining Jamo Behavior,* and the description of the Hangul Syllables block (U+AC00..U+D7A3), which follows in this section.

The Hangul jamo are divided into three classes: *choseong* (leading consonants, or syllable-initial characters), *jungseong* (vowels, or syllable-peak characters), and *jongseong* (trailing consonants, or syllable-final characters). In the following discussion, these classes are abbreviated as *L* (leading consonant), *V* (vowel), and *T* (trailing consonant).

For use in composition, two invisible filler characters act as placeholders for *choseong* or *jungseong*: U+115F HANGUL CHOSEONG FILLER and U+1160 HANGUL JUNGSEONG FILLER.

Collation. The unit of collation in Korean text is normally the Hangul syllable block. Because of the arrangement of the conjoining jamo, their sequences may be collated with a binary comparison. For example, in comparing (a) *LVTLV* with (b) *LVLV*, the first syllable block of (a) *LVT* should be compared with the first syllable block of (b) *LV*. Supposing the first two characters are identical, the *T* would compare as greater than the second *L* in (b) because all trailing consonants have binary values greater than all leading consonants. This result produces the correct ordering between the strings. The positions of the fillers in the code charts were also chosen with this condition in mind.

As with any coded characters, collation cannot depend simply on a binary comparison. Odd sequences such as superfluous fillers will produce an incorrect sort, as will cases where a non-jamo character follows a sequence (such as comparing *LVT* with *LVX*, where *X* is a Unicode character above U+11FF, such as U+3000 IDEOGRAPHIC SPACE).

If mixtures of precomposed syllable blocks and jamo are collated, the easiest approach is to decompose the precomposed syllable blocks into conjoining jamo before comparing. See Unicode Technical Report #10, "Unicode Collation Algorithm," for more discussion about the collation of Korean.

Hangul Compatibility Jamo: U+3130–U+318F

This block consists of spacing, nonconjoining Hangul consonant and vowel (jamo) elements. These characters are provided solely for compatibility with the KS X 1001:1998 standard. Unlike the characters found in the Hangul Jamo block (U+1100..U+11FF), the jamo characters in this block have no conjoining semantics.

The characters of this block are considered to be fullwidth forms in contrast with the halfwidth Hangul compatibility jamo found at U+FFA0..U+FFDF.

Standards. The Unicode Standard follows KS X 1001:1998 for Hangul Jamo elements.

Normalization. When Hangul compatibility jamo are transformed with a compatibility normalization form, NFKD or NFKC, the characters are converted to the corresponding conjoining jamo characters. Where the characters are intended to remain in separate syllables after such transformation, they may require separation from adjacent characters. This separation can be achieved by inserting any non-Korean character.

- U+200B ZERO WIDTH SPACE is recommended where the characters are to allow a line break.
- U+2060 WORD JOINER can be used where the characters are not to break across lines.

Table 12-11 illustrates how two Hangul compatibility jamo can be separated in display, even after transforming them with NFKD or NFKC.

Table 12-11. Separating Jamo Characters

Original	NFKD	NFKC	Display
ㄱ ㅏ 3131 314F	ᄀ ᅡ 1100 1161	가 AC00	가
ㄱ ZW SP ㅏ 3131 200B 314F	ᄀ ZW SP ᅡ 1100 200B 1161	ᄀ ZW SP ᅡ 1100 200B 1161	가

Hangul Syllables: U+AC00–U+D7A3

The Hangul script used in the Korean writing system consists of individual consonant and vowel letters (jamo) that are visually combined into square display cells to form entire syllable blocks. Hangul syllables may be encoded directly as precomposed combinations of individual jamo or as decomposed sequences of conjoining jamo. The latter encoding is supported by the Hangul Jamo block (U+1100..U+11FF). The syllabic encoding method is described here.

Modern Hangul syllable blocks can be expressed with either two or three jamo, either in the form *consonant* + *vowel* or in the form *consonant* + *vowel* + *consonant*. There are 19 possible leading (initial) consonants (*choseong*), 21 vowels (*jungseong*), and 27 trailing (final) consonants (*jongseong*). Thus there are 399 possible two-jamo syllable blocks and 10,773 possible three-jamo syllable blocks, giving a total of 11,172 modern Hangul syllable blocks. This collection of 11,172 modern Hangul syllables encoded in this block is known as the *Johab* set.

Standards. The Hangul syllables are taken from KS C 5601-1992, representing the full Johab set. This group represents a superset of the Hangul syllables encoded in earlier versions of Korean standards (KS C 5601-1987 and KS C 5657-1991).

Equivalence. Each of the Hangul syllables encoded in this block may be encoded by an equivalent sequence of conjoining jamo. The converse is not true because thousands of archaic Hangul syllables may be encoded only as a sequence of conjoining jamo. Implementations that use a conjoining jamo encoding are able to represent these archaic Hangul syllables.

Hangul Syllable Composition. The Hangul syllables can be derived from conjoining jamo by a regular process of composition. The algorithm that maps a sequence of conjoining jamo to the encoding point for a Hangul syllable in the Johab set is detailed in *Section 3.12, Conjoining Jamo Behavior*.

Hangul Syllable Decomposition. Any Hangul syllable from the Johab set can be decomposed into a sequence of conjoining jamo characters. The algorithm that details the formula for decomposition is also provided in *Section 3.12, Conjoining Jamo Behavior*.

Hangul Syllable Name. The character names for Hangul syllables are derived algorithmically from the decomposition. (For full details, see *Section 3.12, Conjoining Jamo Behavior.*)

Hangul Syllable Representative Glyph. The representative glyph for a Hangul syllable can be formed from its decomposition based on the categorization of vowels shown in *Table 12-12*.

Table 12-12. Line-Based Placement of Jungseong

Vertical		Horizontal		Both	
1161	A	1169	O	116A	WA
1162	AE	116D	YO	116B	WAE
1163	YA	116E	U	116C	OE
1164	YAE	1172	YU	116F	WEO
1165	EO	1173	EU	1170	WE
1166	E			1171	WI
1167	YEO			1174	YI
1168	YE				
1175	I				

If the vowel of the syllable is based on a vertical line, place the preceding consonant to its left. If the vowel is based on a horizontal line, place the preceding consonant above it. If the vowel is based on a combination of vertical and horizontal lines, place the preceding consonant above the horizontal line and to the left of the vertical line. In either case, place a following consonant, if any, below the middle of the resulting group.

In any particular font, the exact placement, shape, and size of the components will vary according to the shapes of the other characters and the overall design of the font.

For other blocks containing characters related to Hangul, see "Enclosed CJK Letters and Months: U+3200–U+32FF" and "CJK Compatibility: U+3300–U+33FF" in *Section 15.9, Enclosed and Square*, as well as *Section 12.5, Halfwidth and Fullwidth Forms.*

12.7 Yi

Yi: U+A000–U+A4CF

The Yi syllabary encoded in Unicode is used to write the Liangshan dialect of the Yi language, a member of the Sino-Tibetan language family.

Yi is the Chinese name for one of the largest ethnic minorities in the People's Republic of China. The Yi, also known historically and in English as the Lolo, do not have a single ethnonym, but refer to themselves variously as Nuosu, Sani, Axi or Misapo. According to the 1990 census, more than 6.5 million Yi live in southwestern China in the provinces of Sichuan, Guizhou, Yunnan, and Guangxi. Smaller populations of Yi are also to be found in

Myanmar, Laos, and Vietnam. Yi is one of the official languages of the PRC, with between 4 and 5 million speakers.

The Yi language is divided into six major dialects. The Northern dialect, which is also known as the Liangshan dialect because it is spoken throughout the region of the Greater and Lesser Liangshan Mountains, is the largest and linguistically most coherent of these dialects. In 1991, there were about 1.6 million speakers of the Liangshan Yi dialect. The ethnonym of speakers of the Liangshan dialect is Nuosu.

Traditional Yi Script. The traditional Yi script, historically known as Cuan or Wei, is an ideographic script. Unlike in other Sinoform scripts, however, its ideographs appear not to be derived from Han ideographs. One of the more widespread traditions relates that the script, comprising about 1,840 ideographs, was devised by someone named Aki during the Tang dynasty (618–907 CE). The earliest surviving examples of the Yi script are monumental inscriptions dating from about 500 years ago; the earliest example is an inscription on a bronze bell dated 1485.

There is no single unified Yi script, but rather many local script traditions that vary considerably with regard to the repertoire, shapes, and orientations of individual glyphs and the overall writing direction. The profusion of local script variants occurred largely because until modern times the Yi script was mainly used for writing religious, magical, medical, or genealogical texts that were handed down from generation to generation by the priests of individual villages, and not as a means of communication between different communities or for the general dissemination of knowledge. Although a vast number of manuscripts written in the traditional Yi script have survived to the present day, the Yi script was not widely used in printing before the twentieth century.

Because the traditional Yi script is not standardized, a considerable number of glyphs are used in the various script traditions. According to one authority, there are more than 14,200 glyphs used in Yunnan, more than 8,000 in Sichuan, more than 7,000 in Guizhou, and more than 600 in Guangxi. However, these figures are misleading—most of the glyphs are simple variants of the same abstract character. For example, a 1989 dictionary of the Guizhou Yi script contains about 8,000 individual glyphs, but excluding glyph variants reduces this count to about 1,700 basic characters, which is quite close to the figure of 1,840 characters that Aki is reputed to have devised.

Standardized Yi Script. There has never been a high level of literacy in the traditional Yi script. Usage of the traditional script has remained limited even in modern times because the traditional script does not accurately reflect the phonetic characteristics of the modern Yi language, and because it has numerous variant glyphs and differences from locality to locality.

To improve literacy in Yi, a scheme for representing the Liangshan dialect using the Latin alphabet was introduced in 1956. A standardized form of the traditional script used for writing the Liangshan Yi dialect was devised in 1974 and officially promulgated in 1980. The standardized Liangshan Yi script encoded in Unicode is suitable for writing only the Liangshan Yi dialect; it is not intended as a unified script for writing all Yi dialects. Standardized versions of other local variants of traditional Yi scripts do not yet exist.

The standardized Yi syllabary comprises 1,164 signs representing each of the allowable syllables in the Liangshan Yi dialect. There are 819 unique signs representing syllables pronounced in the high level, low falling, and midlevel tones, and 345 composite signs representing syllables pronounced in the secondary high tone. The signs for syllables in the secondary high tone consist of the sign for the corresponding syllable in the midlevel tone (or in three cases the low falling tone), plus a diacritic mark shaped like an inverted breve. For example, U+A001 YI SYLLABLE IX is the same as U+A002 YI SYLLABLE I plus a diacritic mark. In addition to the 1,164 signs representing specific syllables, a syllable iteration mark is used to indicate reduplication of the preceding syllable, which is frequently used in interrogative constructs.

Standards. In 1991, a national standard for Yi was adopted by China as GB 13134-91. This encoding includes all 1,164 Yi syllables as well as the syllable iteration mark, and is the basis for the encoding in the Unicode Standard. The syllables in the secondary high tone, which are differentiated from the corresponding syllable in the midlevel tone or the low falling tone by a diacritic mark, are not decomposable.

Naming Conventions and Order. The Yi syllables are named on the basis of the spelling of the syllable in the standard Liangshan Yi romanization introduced in 1956. The tone of the syllable is indicated by the final letter: "t" indicates the high level tone, "p" indicates the low falling tone, "x" indicates the secondary high tone, and an absence of final "t", "p", or "x" indicates the midlevel tone.

With the exception of U+A015, the Yi syllables are ordered according to their phonetic order in the Liangshan Yi romanization—that is, by initial consonant, then by vowel, and finally by tone (t, x, unmarked, and p). This is the order used in dictionaries of Liangshan Yi that are ordered phonetically.

Yi Syllable Iteration Mark. U+A015 YI SYLLABLE WU does not represent a specific syllable in the Yi language, but rather is used as a syllable iteration mark. Its character properties therefore differ from those for the rest of the Yi syllable characters. The misnomer of U+A015 as YI SYLLABLE WU derives from the fact that it is represented by the letter *w* in the romanized Yi alphabet, and from some confusion about the meaning of the gap in traditional Yi syllable charts for the hypothetical syllable "wu".

The Yi syllable iteration mark is used to replace the second occurrence of a reduplicated syllable under all circumstances. It is very common in both formal and informal Yi texts.

Punctuation. The standardized Yi script does not have any special punctuation marks, but relies on the same set of punctuation marks used for writing modern Chinese in the PRC, including U+3001 IDEOGRAPHIC COMMA and U+3002 IDEOGRAPHIC FULL STOP.

Rendering. The traditional Yi script used a variety of writing directions—for example, right to left in the Liangshan region of Sichuan, and top to bottom in columns running from left to right in Guizhou and Yunnan. The standardized Yi script follows the writing rules for Han ideographs, so characters are generally written from left to right or occasionally from top to bottom. There is no typographic interaction between individual characters of the Yi script.

Yi Radicals. To facilitate the lookup of Yi characters in dictionaries, sets of radicals modeled on Han radicals have been devised for the various Yi scripts. (For information on Han radicals, see "CJK and KangXi Radicals" in *Section 12.1, Han*). The traditional Guizhou Yi script has 119 radicals; the traditional Liangshan Yi script has 170 radicals; and the traditional Yunnan Sani Yi script has 25 radicals. The standardized Liangshan Yi script encoded in Unicode has a set of 55 radical characters, which are encoded in the Yi Radicals block (U+A490..U+A4C5). Each radical represents a distinctive stroke element that is common to a subset of the characters encoded in the Yi Syllables block. The name used for each radical character is that of the corresponding Yi syllable closest to it in shape.

CHAPTER

13

Chapter 13

Additional Modern Scripts

This chapter contains a collection of additional scripts in modern use that do not fit well into the script categories featured in other chapters:

Ethiopic	*Tifinagh*	*Canadian Aboriginal Syllabics*
Mongolian	*N'Ko*	*Deseret*
Osmanya	*Cherokee*	*Shavian*

Ethiopic, Mongolian, and Tifinagh are scripts with long histories. Although their roots can be traced back to the original Semitic and North African writing systems, they would not be classified as Middle Eastern scripts today.

The remaining scripts in this chapter have been developed relatively recently. Some of them show roots in Latin and other letterforms, including shorthand. They are all original creative contributions intended specifically to serve the linguistic communities that use them.

13.1 Ethiopic

Ethiopic: U+1200–U+137F

The Ethiopic syllabary originally evolved for writing the Semitic language Ge'ez. Indeed, the English noun "Ethiopic" simply means "the Ge'ez language." Ge'ez itself is now limited to liturgical usage, but its script has been adopted for modern use in writing several languages of central east Africa, including Amharic, Tigre, and Oromo.

Basic and Extended Ethiopic. The Ethiopic characters encoded here are the basic set that has become established in common usage for writing major languages. As with other productive scripts, the basic Ethiopic forms are sometimes modified to produce an extended range of characters for writing additional languages.

Encoding Principles. The syllables of the Ethiopic script are traditionally presented as a two-dimensional matrix of consonant-vowel combinations. The encoding follows this structure; in particular, the codespace range U+1200..U+1357 is interpreted as a matrix of 43 consonants crossed with 8 vowels, making 344 conceptual syllables. Most of these consonant-vowel syllables are represented by characters in the script, but some of them happen to be unused, accounting for the blank cells in the matrix.

Variant Glyph Forms. A given Ethiopic syllable may be represented by different glyph forms, analogous to the glyph variants of Latin lowercase "a" or "g", which do not coexist in the same font. Thus the particular glyph shown in the code chart for each position in the matrix is merely one representation of that conceptual syllable, and the glyph itself is not the object that is encoded.

Labialized Subseries. A few Ethiopic consonants have labialized ("W") forms that are traditionally allotted their own consonant series in the syllable matrix, although only a subset of the possible vowel forms are realized. Each of these derivative series is encoded immediately after the corresponding main consonant series. Because the standard vowel series includes both "AA" and "WAA", two different cells of the syllable matrix might represent the "consonant + W + AA" syllable. For example:

U+1257 = QH + WAA: potential but unused version of QHWAA

U+125B = QHW + AA: ETHIOPIC SYLLABLE QHWAA

In these cases, where the two conceptual syllables are equivalent, the entry in the labialized subseries is encoded and not the "consonant + WAA" entry in the main syllable series. The six specific cases are enumerated in *Table 13-1*. In three of these cases, the -WAA position in the syllable matrix has been reanalyzed and used for encoding a syllable in -OA for extended Ethiopic.

Table 13-1. Labialized Forms in Ethiopic -WAA

-WAA Form	Encoded as	Not Used	Contrast
QWAA	U+124B ቋ	1247	U+1247 ቇ QOA
QHWAA	U+125B ቛ	1257	
XWAA	U+128B ኋ	1287	U+1287 ኇ XOA
KWAA	U+12B3 ኳ	12AF	U+12AF ኯ KOA
KXWAA	U+12C3 ዃ	12BF	
GWAA	U+1313 ጓ	130F	

Also, *within* the labialized subseries, the sixth vowel ("-E") forms are sometimes considered to be second vowel ("-U") forms. For example:

U+1249 = QW + U: unused version of QWE

U+124D = QW + E: ETHIOPIC SYLLABLE QWE

In these cases, where the two syllables are nearly equivalent, the "-E" entry is encoded and not the "-U" entry. The six specific cases are enumerated in *Table 13-2*.

Keyboard Input. Because the Ethiopic script includes more than 300 characters, the units of keyboard input must constitute some smaller set of entities, typically 43+8 codes interpreted as the coordinates of the syllable matrix. Because these keyboard input codes are expected to be transient entities that are resolved into syllabic characters before they enter stored text, keyboard input codes are not specified in this standard.

Table 13-2. Labialized Forms in Ethiopic -WE

"-WE" Form	Encoded as	Not Used
QWE	U+124D ቍ	1249
QHWE	U+125D ቝ	1259
XWE	U+128D ኍ	1289
KWE	U+12B5 ኵ	12B1
KXWE	U+12C5 ዅ	12C1
GWE	U+1315 ጕ	1311

Syllable Names. The Ethiopic script often has multiple syllables corresponding to the same Latin letter, making it difficult to assign unique Latin names. Therefore the names list makes use of certain devices (such as doubling a Latin letter in the name) merely to create uniqueness; this device has no relation to the phonetics of these syllables in any particular language.

Encoding Order and Sorting. The order of the consonants in the encoding is based on the traditional alphabetical order. It may differ from the sort order used for one or another language, if only because in many languages various pairs or triplets of syllables are treated as equivalent in the first sorting pass. For example, an Amharic dictionary may start out with a section headed by *three* H-like syllables:

U+1200 ETHIOPIC SYLLABLE HA

U+1210 ETHIOPIC SYLLABLE HHA

U+1280 ETHIOPIC SYLLABLE XA

Thus the encoding order cannot and does not implement a collation procedure for any particular language using this script.

Word Separators. The traditional word separator is U+1361 ETHIOPIC WORDSPACE (:). In modern usage, a plain white wordspace (U+0020 SPACE) is becoming common.

Section Mark. One or more *section marks* are typically used on a separate line to mark the separation of sections. Commonly, an odd number is used and they are separated by spaces.

Diacritical Marks. The Ethiopic script generally makes no use of diacritical marks, but they are sometimes employed for scholarly or didactic purposes. In particular, U+135F ETHIOPIC COMBINING GEMINATION MARK and U+030E COMBINING DOUBLE VERTICAL LINE ABOVE are sometimes used to indicate emphasis or gemination (consonant doubling).

Numbers. Ethiopic digit glyphs are derived from the Greek alphabet, possibly borrowed from Coptic letterforms. In modern use, European digits are often used. The Ethiopic number system does not use a zero, nor is it based on digital-positional notation. A number is denoted as a sequence of powers of 100, each preceded by a coefficient (2 through 99). In each term of the series, the power 100^n is indicated by n HUNDRED characters (merged to a digraph when n = 2). The coefficient is indicated by a *tens* digit and a *ones* digit, either of which is absent if its value is zero.

For example, the number 2345 is represented by

2345 = (20 + 3)*100^1 + (40 + 5)*100^0

= 20 3 100 40 5

= TWENTY THREE HUNDRED FORTY FIVE

= 1373 136B 137B 1375 136D ፳፫፻፵፭

A language using the Ethiopic script may have a *word* for "thousand," such as Amharic "SHI" (U+123A), and a quantity such as 2,345 may also be written as it is spoken in that language, which in the case of Amharic happens to parallel English:

2,345 = TWO thousand THREE HUNDRED FORTY FIVE

= 136A 123A 136B 137B 1375 136D ፪ሺ፫፻፵፭

Ethiopic Extensions: U+1380–U+139F, U+2D80–U+2DDF

The Ethiopic script is used for a large number of languages and dialects in Ethiopia and in some instances has been extended significantly beyond the set of characters used for major languages such as Amharic and Tigre. There are two blocks of extensions to the Ethiopic script: Ethiopic Supplement U+1380..U+139F and Ethiopic Extended U+2D80..U+2DDF. Those extensions cover such languages as Me'en, Blin, and Sebatbeit, which use many additional characters. Several other characters for Ethiopic script extensions can be found in the main Ethiopic script block in the range U+1200..U+137F.

The Ethiopic Supplement block also contains a set of tonal marks. They are used in multiline scored layout. Like other musical (an)notational systems of this type, these tonal marks require a higher-level protocol to enable proper rendering.

13.2 Mongolian

Mongolian: U+1800–U+18AF

The Mongolians are key representatives of a cultural-linguistic group known as Altaic, after the Altai mountains of central Asia. In the past, these peoples have dominated the vast expanses of Asia and beyond, from the Baltic to the Sea of Japan. Echoes of Altaic languages remain from Finland, Hungary, and Turkey, across central Asia, to Korea and Japan. Today the Mongolians are represented politically in Mongolia proper (formally the Mongolian People's Republic, also known as Outer Mongolia) and Inner Mongolia (formally the Inner Mongolia Autonomous Region, China), with Mongolian populations also living in other areas of China.

The Mongolian block unifies Mongolian and the three derivative scripts Todo, Manchu, and Sibe. Each of the three derivative scripts shares some common letters with Mongolian, and these letters are encoded only once. Each derivative script also has a number of modified letter forms or new letters, which are encoded separately.

Mongolian, Todo, and Manchu also have a number special "Ali Gali" letters that are used for transcribing Tibetan and Sanskrit in Buddhist texts.

History. The Mongolian script was derived from the Uighur script around the beginning of the thirteenth century, during the reign of Genghis Khan. The Uighur script, which was in use from about the eighth to the fifteenth centuries, was derived from Sogdian Aramaic, a Semitic script written horizontally from right to left. Probably under the influence of the Chinese script, the Uighur script became rotated 90 degrees counterclockwise so that the lines of text read vertically in columns running from left to right. The Mongolian script inherited this directionality from the Uighur script.

The Mongolian script has remained in continuous use for writing Mongolian within the Inner Mongolia Autonomous Region of the People's Republic of China and elsewhere in China. However, in the Mongolian People's Republic (Outer Mongolia), the traditional script was replaced by a Cyrillic orthography in the early 1940s. The traditional script has been revived to an extent since the early 1990s, so that now both the Cyrillic and the Mongolian scripts are used. The spelling used with the traditional Mongolian script represents the literary language of the seventeenth and early eighteenth centuries, whereas the Cyrillic script is used to represent the modern, colloquial pronunciation of words. As a consequence, there is no one-to-one relationship between the traditional Mongolian orthography and Cyrillic orthography. Approximate correspondence mappings are indicated in the code charts, but are not necessarily unique in either direction. All of the Cyrillic characters needed to write Mongolian are included in the Cyrillic block of the Unicode Standard.

In addition to the traditional Mongolian script of Mongolia, several historical modifications and adaptations of the Mongolian script have emerged elsewhere. These adaptations are often referred to as scripts in their own right, although for the purposes of character encoding in the Unicode Standard they are treated as styles of the Mongolian script and share encoding of their basic letters.

The Todo script is a modified and improved version of the Mongolian script, devised in 1648 by Zaya Pandita for use by the Kalmyk Mongolians, who had migrated to Russia in the sixteenth century, and who now inhabit the Republic of Kalmykia in the Russian Federation. The name *Todo* means "clear" in Mongolian; it refers to the fact that the new script eliminates the ambiguities inherent in the original Mongolian script. The orthography of the Todo script also reflects the Oirat-Kalmyk dialects of Mongolian rather than literary Mongolian. In Kalmykia, the Todo script was replaced by a succession of Cyrillic and Latin orthographies from the mid-1920s and is no longer in active use. Until very recently the Todo script was still used by speakers of the Oirat and Kalmyk dialects within Xinjiang and Qinghai in China.

The Manchu script is an adaptation of the Mongolian script used to write Manchu, a Tungusic language that is not closely related to Mongolian. The Mongolian script was first adapted for writing Manchu in 1599 under the orders of the Manchu leader Nurhachi, but few examples of this early form of the Manchu script survive. In 1632, the Manchu scholar

Dahai reformed the script by adding circles and dots to certain letters in an effort to distinguish their different sounds and by devising new letters to represent the sounds of the Chinese language. When the Manchu people conquered China to rule as the Qing dynasty (1644–1911), Manchu become the language of state. The ensuing systematic program of translation from Chinese created a large and important corpus of books written in Manchu. Over time the Manchu people became completely sinified, and as a spoken language Manchu is now almost extinct.

The Sibe (also spelled Sibo, Xibe, or Xibo) people are closely related to the Manchus, and their language is often classified as a dialect of Manchu. The Sibe people are widely dispersed across northwest and northeast China due to deliberate programs of ethnic dispersal during the Qing dynasty. The majority have become assimilated into the local population and no longer speak the Sibe language. However, there is a substantial Sibe population in the Sibe Autonomous County in the Ili River valley in Western Xinjiang, the descendants of border guards posted to Xinjiang in 1764, who still speak and write the Sibe language. The Sibe script is based on the Manchu script, with a few modified letters.

Directionality. The Mongolian script is written vertically from top to bottom in columns running from left to right. In modern contexts, words or phrases may be embedded in horizontal scripts. In such a case, the Mongolian text will be rotated 90 degrees counterclockwise so that it reads from left to right.

When rendering Mongolian text in a system that does not support vertical layout, the text should be laid out in horizontal lines running left to right, with the glyphs rotated 90 degrees counterclockwise with respect to their orientation in the code charts. If such text is viewed sideways, the usual Mongolian column order appears reversed, but this orientation can be workable for short stretches of text. There are no bidirectional effects in such a layout because all text is horizontal left to right.

Encoding Principles. The encoding model for Mongolian is somewhat different from that for any other script within Unicode, and in many respects it is the most complicated. For this reason, only the essential features of Mongolian shaping behavior are presented here; the precise details are to be presented in a separate technical report.

The Semitic alphabet from which the Mongolian script was ultimately derived is fundamentally inadequate for representing the sounds of the Mongolian language. As a result, many of the Mongolian letters are used to represent two different sounds, and the correct pronunciation of a letter may be known only from the context. In this respect, Mongolian orthography is similar to English spelling, in which the pronunciation of a letter such as *c* may be known only from the context.

Unlike in the Latin script, in which *c* /k/ and *c* /s/ are treated as the same letter and encoded as a single character, in the Mongolian script different phonetic values of the same glyph may be encoded as distinct characters. Modern Mongolian grammars consider the phonetic value of a letter to be its distinguishing feature, rather than its glyph shape. For example, the four Mongolian vowels *o*, *u*, *ö*, and *ü* are considered four distinct letters and are encoded as four characters (U+1823, U+1824, U+1825, and U+1826, respectively), even though *o* is written identically to *u* in all positional forms, *ö* is written identically to *ü* in all positional forms, *o* and *u* are normally distinguished from *ö* and *ü* only in the first syllable of a word. Likewise, the letters *t* (U+1832) and *d* (U+1833) are often indistinguishable. For example, pairs of Mongolian words such as *urtu* "long" and *ordu* "palace, camp, horde" or *ende* "here" and *ada* "devil" are written identically, but are represented using different sequences of Unicode characters, as shown in *Figure 13-1*. There are many such examples in Mongolian, but not in Todo, Manchu, or Sibe, which have largely eliminated ambiguous letters.

Figure 13-1. Mongolian Glyph Convergence

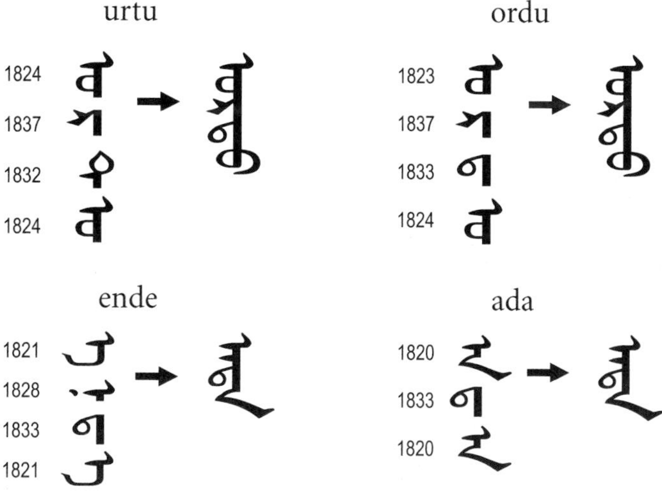

Cursive Joining. The Mongolian script is cursive, and the letters constituting a word are normally joined together. In most cases the letters join together naturally along a vertical stem, but in the case of certain "bowed" consonants (for example, U+182A MONGOLIAN LETTER BA and the feminine form of U+182C MONGOLIAN LETTER QA), which lack a trailing vertical stem, they may form ligatures with a following vowel. This is illustrated in *Figure 13-2*, where the letter *ba* combines with the letter *u* to form a ligature in the Mongolian word *abu* "father."

Figure 13-2. Mongolian Consonant Ligation

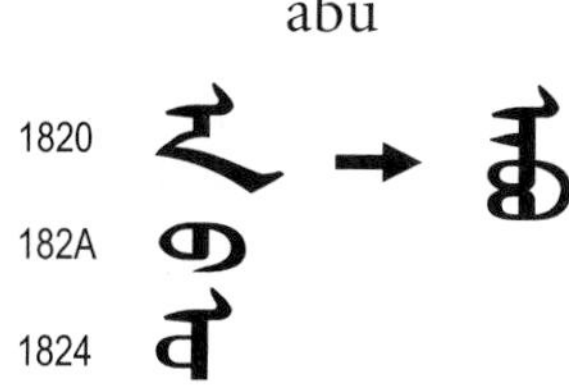

Many letters also have distinct glyph forms depending on their position within a word. These positional forms are classified as initial, medial, final, or isolate. The medial form is often the same as the initial form, but the final form is always distinct from the initial or medial form. *Figure 13-3* shows the Mongolian letters U+1823 *o* and U+1821 *e*, rendered with distinct positional forms initially and finally in the Mongolian words *odo* "now" and *ene* "this."

Figure 13-3. Mongolian Positional Forms

U+200C ZERO WIDTH NON-JOINER (ZWNJ) and U+200D ZERO WIDTH JOINER (ZWJ) may be used to select a particular positional form of a letter in isolation or to override the expected positional form within a word. Basically, they evoke the same contextual selection effects in neighboring letters as do non-joining or joining regular letters, but are themselves invisible (see *Chapter 16, Special Areas and Format Characters*). For example, the various positional forms of U+1820 MONGOLIAN LETTER A may be selected by means of the following character sequences:

<1820> selects the isolate form.

<1820 200D> selects the initial form.

<200D 1820> selects the final form.

<200D 1820 200D> selects the medial form.

Some letters have additional variant forms that do not depend on their position within a word, but instead reflect differences between modern versus traditional orthographic practice or lexical considerations—for example, special forms used for writing foreign words. On occasion, other contextual rules may condition a variant form selection. For example, a certain variant of a letter may be required when it occurs in the first syllable of a word or when it occurs immediately after a particular letter.

The various positional and variant glyph forms of a letter are considered presentation forms and are not encoded separately. It is the responsibility of the rendering system to select the correct glyph form for a letter according to its context.

Free Variation Selectors. When a glyph form that cannot be predicted algorithmically is required (for example, when writing a foreign word), the user needs to append an appropriate variation selector to the letter to indicate to the rendering system which glyph form is required. The following free variation selectors are provided for use specifically with the Mongolian block:

U+180B MONGOLIAN FREE VARIATION SELECTOR ONE (FVS1)

U+180C MONGOLIAN FREE VARIATION SELECTOR TWO (FVS2)

U+180D MONGOLIAN FREE VARIATION SELECTOR THREE (FVS3)

These format characters normally have no visual appearance. When required, a free variation selector immediately follows the base character it modifies. This combination of base character and variation selector is known as a standardized variant. The table of standardized variants, StandardizedVariants.txt, in the Unicode Character Database exhaustively lists all currently defined standardized variants. All combinations not listed in the table are unspecified and are reserved for future standardization; no conformant process may interpret them as standardized variants. Therefore, any free variation selector not immediately preceded by one of their defined base characters will be ignored.

Figure 13-4 gives an example of how a free variation selector may be used to select a particular glyph variant. In modern orthography, the initial letter *ga* in the Mongolian word *gal* "fire" is written with two dots; in traditional orthography, the letter *ga* is written without any dots. By default, the dotted form of the letter *ga* is selected, but this behavior may be overridden by means of FVS1, so that *ga* plus FVS1 selects the undotted form of the letter *ga*.

Figure 13-4. Mongolian Free Variation Selector

It is important to appreciate that even though a particular standardized variant may be defined for a letter, the user needs to apply the appropriate free variation selector only if the correct glyph form cannot be predicted automatically by the rendering system. In most cases, in running text, there will be few occasions when a free variation selector is required to disambiguate the glyph form.

Older documentation, external to the Unicode Standard, listed the action of the free variation selectors by using ZWJ to explicitly indicate the shaping environment affected by the variation selector. The relative order of the ZWJ and the free variation selector in these documents was different from the one required by *Section 16.4, Variation Selectors*. Older implementations of Mongolian free variation selectors may therefore interpret a sequence such as a base character followed by first by ZWJ and then by FVS1 as if it were a base character followed first by FVS1 and then by ZWJ.

Representative Glyphs. The representative glyph in the code charts is generally the isolate form for the vowels and the initial form for the consonants. Letters that share the same glyph forms are distinguished by using different positional forms for the representative glyph. For example, the representative glyph for U+1823 MONGOLIAN LETTER O is the isolate form, whereas the representative glyph for U+1824 MONGOLIAN LETTER U is the initial form. However, this distinction is only nominal, as the glyphs for the two characters are identical for the same positional form. Likewise, the representative glyphs for U+1863 MONGOLIAN LETTER SIBE KA and U+1874 MONGOLIAN LETTER MANCHU KA both take the final form, as their initial forms are identical to the representative glyph for U+182C MONGOLIAN LETTER QA (the initial form).

Vowel Harmony. Mongolian has a system of vowel harmony, whereby the vowels in a word are either all "masculine" and "neuter" vowels (that is, back vowels plus /i/) or all "feminine" and "neuter" vowels (that is, front vowels plus /i/). Words that are written with masculine/neuter vowels are considered to be masculine, and words that are written with feminine/neuter vowels are considered to be feminine. Words with only neuter vowels behave as feminine words (for example, take feminine suffixes). Manchu and Sibe have a similar system of vowel harmony, although it is not so strict. Some words in these two scripts may include both masculine and feminine vowels, and separated suffixes with masculine or feminine vowels may be applied to a stem irrespective of its gender.

Vowel harmony is an important element of the encoding model, as the gender of a word determines the glyph form of the velar series of consonant letters for Mongolian, Todo, Sibe, and Manchu. In each script, the velar letters have both masculine and feminine forms. For Mongolian and Todo, the masculine and feminine forms of these letters have different pronunciations.

When one of the velar consonants precedes a vowel, it takes the masculine form before masculine vowels, and the feminine form before feminine or neuter vowels. In the latter case, a ligature of the consonant and vowel is required.

When one of these consonants precedes another consonant or is the final letter in a word, it may take either a masculine or feminine glyph form, depending on its context. The rendering system should automatically select the correct gender form for these letters based on the gender of the word (in Mongolian and Todo) or the gender of the preceding vowel (in Manchu and Sibe). This is illustrated by *Figure 13-5*, where U+182D MONGOLIAN LETTER GA takes a masculine glyph form when it occurs finally in the masculine word *jarlig* "order," but takes a feminine glyph form when it occurs finally in the feminine word *chirig* "soldier." In this example, the gender form of the final letter *ga* depends on whether the first vowel in the word is a back (masculine) vowel or a front (feminine or neuter) vowel. Where the gender is ambiguous or a form not derivable from the context is required, the user needs to specify which form is required by means of the appropriate free variation selector.

Narrow No-Break Space. In Mongolian, Todo, Manchu, and Sibe, certain grammatical suffixes are separated from the stem of a word or from other suffixes by a narrow gap. There are many such suffixes in Mongolian, usually occurring in masculine and feminine pairs (for example, the dative suffixes *-dur* and *-dür*), and a stem may take multiple suffixes. In

Figure 13-5. Mongolian Gender Forms

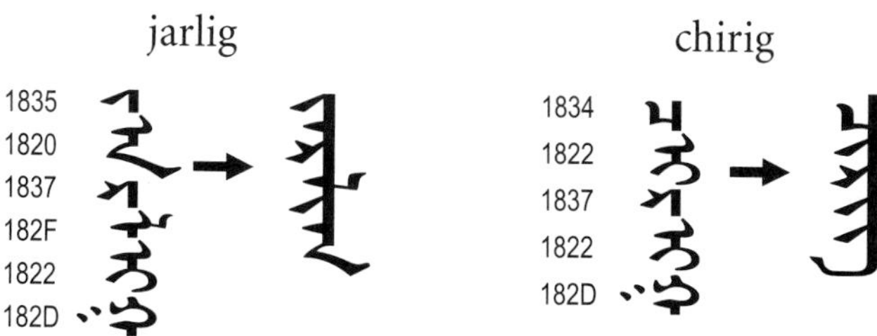

contrast, there are only six separated suffixes for Manchu and Sibe, and stems do not take more than one suffix at a time.

As any suffixes are considered to be an integral part of the word as a whole, a line break opportunity does not occur before a suffix, and the whitespace is represented using U+202F NARROW NO-BREAK SPACE (NNBSP). For a Mongolian font it is recommended that the width of NNBSP should be one-third the width of an ordinary space (U+0020 SPACE).

NNBSP affects the form of the preceding and following letters. The final letter of the stem or suffix preceding the NNBSP takes the final positional form, whereas the first letter of the suffix following NNBSP may take the normal initial form, a variant initial form, a medial form, or a final form, depending on the particular suffix.

Mongolian Vowel Separator. In Mongolian, the letters *a* (U+1820) and *e* (U+1821) in a word-final position may take a "forward tail" form or a "backward tail" form depending on the preceding consonant that they are attached to. In some words, a final letter *a* or *e* is separated from the preceding consonant by a narrow gap, in which case the vowel always takes the "forward tail" form. U+180E MONGOLIAN VOWEL SEPARATOR (MVS) is used to represent the whitespace that separates a final letter *a* or *e* from the rest of the word. MVS is very similar in function to NNBSP, as it divides a word with a narrow non-breaking whitespace. Whereas NNBSP marks off a grammatical suffix, however, the *a* or *e* following MVS is not a suffix but an integral part of the word stem. Whether a final letter *a* or *e* is joined or separated is purely lexical and is not a question of varying orthography. For example, the word *qana* <182C, 1820, 1828, 1820> without a gap before the final letter *a* means "the outer casing of a vein," whereas the word *qana* <182C, 1820, 1828, 180E, 1820> with a gap before the final letter *a* means "the wall of a tent," as shown in *Figure 13-6*.

Figure 13-6. Mongolian Vowel Separator

Qana with Connected Final

Qana with Separated Final

The MVS has a twofold effect on shaping. On the one hand, it always selects the forward tail form of a following letter *a* or *e*. On the other hand, it may affect the form of the preceding letter. The particular form that is taken by a letter preceding an MVS depends on the particular letter and in some cases on whether traditional or modern orthography is being used. The MVS is not needed for writing Todo, Manchu, or Sibe.

Numbers. The Mongolian and Todo scripts use a set of ten digits derived from the Tibetan digits. In vertical text, numbers are traditionally written from left to right across the width of the column. In modern contexts, they are frequently rotated so that they follow the vertical flow of the text.

The Manchu and Sibe scripts do not use any special digits, although Chinese number ideographs may be employed—for example, for page numbering in traditional books.

Punctuation. Traditional punctuation marks used for Mongolian and Todo include the U+1800 MONGOLIAN BIRGA (marks the start of a passage or the recto side of a folio), U+1802 MONGOLIAN COMMA, U+1803 MONGOLIAN FULL STOP, and U+1805 MONGOLIAN FOUR DOTS (marks the end of a passage). The *birga* occurs in several different glyph forms.

In writing Todo, U+1806 MONGOLIAN TODO SOFT HYPHEN is used at the beginning of the second line to indicate resumption of a broken word. It functions like U+2010 HYPHEN, except that U+1806 appears at the beginning of a line rather than at the end.

The Manchu script normally uses only two punctuation marks: U+1808 MONGOLIAN MANCHU COMMA and U+1809 MONGOLIAN MANCHU FULL STOP.

In modern contexts, Mongolian, Todo, and Sibe may use a variety of Western punctuation marks, such as parentheses, quotation marks, question marks, and exclamation marks. U+2048 QUESTION EXCLAMATION MARK and U+2049 EXCLAMATION QUESTION MARK are used for side-by-side display of a question mark and an exclamation mark together in vertical text. Todo and Sibe may additionally use punctuation marks borrowed from Chinese, such as U+3001 IDEOGRAPHIC COMMA, U+3002 IDEOGRAPHIC FULL STOP, U+300A LEFT DOUBLE ANGLE BRACKET, and U+300B RIGHT DOUBLE ANGLE BRACKET.

Nirugu. U+180A MONGOLIAN NIRUGU acts as a stem extender. In traditional Mongolian typography, it is used to physically extend the stem joining letters, so as to increase the separation between all letters in a word. This stretching behavior should preferably be carried out in the font rather than by the user manually inserting U+180A.

The *nirugu* may also be used to separate two parts of a compound word. For example, *altan-agula* "The Golden Mountains" may be written with the words *altan*, "golden," and *agula*, "mountains," joined together using the *nirugu*. In this usage the *nirugu* is similar to the use of hyphen in Latin scripts, but it is nonbreaking.

Syllable Boundary Marker. U+1807 MONGOLIAN SIBE SYLLABLE BOUNDARY MARKER, which is derived from the medial form of the letter *a* (U+1820), is used to disambiguate syllable boundaries within a word. It is mainly used for writing Sibe, but may also occur in Manchu texts. In native Manchu or Sibe words, syllable boundaries are never ambiguous; when transcribing Chinese proper names in the Manchu or Sibe script, however, the syllable boundary may be ambiguous. In such cases, U+1807 may be inserted into the character sequence at the syllable boundary.

13.3 Osmanya

Osmanya: U+10480–U+104AF

The Osmanya script, which in Somali is called 𐒍𐒖𐒇 𐒈𐒝𐒑𐒛𐒐𐒘 *far Soomaali* "Somali writing" or 𐒋𐒘𐒈𐒑𐒛𐒒𐒕𐒖 *Cismaanya*, was devised in 1920–1922 by 𐒋𐒘𐒈𐒑𐒛𐒒 𐒕𐒚𐒓𐒈𐒚𐒍 𐒏𐒜𐒒𐒖𐒆𐒘𐒕𐒆 (Cismaan Yuusuf Keenadiid) to represent the Somali language. It replaced an attempt by Sheikh Uweys of the Confraternity Qadiriyyah (died 1909) to devise an Arabic-based orthography for Somali. It has, in turn, been replaced by the Latin orthography of Muuse Xaaji Ismaaciil Galaal (1914–1980). In 1961, both the Latin and the Osmanya scripts were adopted for use in Somalia, but in 1969 there was a coup, with one of its stated aims being the resolution of the debate over the country's writing system. A Latin orthography was finally adopted in 1973. Gregersen (1977) states that some 20,000 or more people use Osmanya in private correspondence and bookkeeping, and that several books and a biweekly journal *Horseed* ("*Vanguard*") were published in cyclostyled format.

Structure. Osmanya is an alphabetic script, read from left to right in horizontal lines running from top to bottom. It has 22 consonants and 8 vowels. Unique long vowels are written for U+1049B 𐒛 OSMANYA LETTER AA, U+1049C 𐒜 OSMANYA LETTER EE, and U+1049D 𐒝 OSMANYA LETTER OO; long *uu* and *ii* are written with the consonants U+10493 𐒓 OSMANYA LETTER WAW and U+10495 𐒕 OSMANYA LETTER YA, respectively.

Ordering. Alphabetical ordering is based on the order of the Arabic alphabet, as specified by Osman Abdihalim Yuusuf Osman Keenadiid. This ordering is similar to the ordering given in Diringer (1996).

Names and Glyphs. The character names used in the Unicode Standard are as given by Osman. The glyphs shown in the code charts are taken from *Afkeenna iyo fartysa* ("Our language and its handwriting") 1971.

13.4 Tifinagh

Tifinagh: U+2D30–U+2D7F

The Tifinagh script is used by approximately 20 million people who speak varieties of languages commonly called Berber or Amazigh. The three main varieties in Morocco are known as Tarifite, Tamazighe, and Tachelhite. In Morocco, more than 40% of the population speaks Berber. In accordance with recent governmental decisions, the teaching of the Berber language, written in the Tifinagh script, will be generalized and compulsory in Morocco in all public schools by 2008.

Tifinagh is an alphabetic writing system. It uses spaces to separate words and makes use of Western punctuation.

History. The earliest variety of the Berber alphabet is Libyan. Two forms exist: a Western form and an Eastern form. The Western variety was used along the Mediterranean coast from Kabylia to Morocco and most probably to the Canary Islands. The Eastern variety, Old Tifinagh, is also called Libyan-Berber or Old Tuareg. It contains signs not found in the Libyan variety and was used to transcribe Old Tuareg. The word *tifinagh* is a feminine plural noun whose singular would be *tafniqt*; it means "the Phoenician (letters)."

Neo-Tifinagh refers to the writing systems that were developed to represent the Maghreb Berber dialects. A number of variants of Neo-Tifinagh exist, the first of which was proposed in the 1960s by the Académie Berbère. That variant has spread in Morocco and in Algeria, especially in Kabylia. Other Neo-Tifinagh systems are nearly identical to the Académie Berbère system. The encoding in the Tifinagh block is based on the Neo-Tifinagh systems.

Source Standards. The encoding consists of four Tifinagh character subsets: the basic set of the Institut Royal de la Culture Amazighe (IRCAM), the extended IRCAM set, other Neo-Tifinagh letters in use, and modern Tuareg letters. The first subset represents the set of characters chosen by IRCAM to unify the orthography of the different Moroccan modern-day Berber dialects while using the historical Tifinagh script.

Ordering. The letters are arranged according to the order specified by IRCAM. Other Neo-Tifinagh and Tuareg letters are interspersed according to their pronunciation. The modifier letter U+2D6F TIFINAGH MODIFIER LETTER LABIALIZATION is found at the end of the block.

Directionality. Historically, Berber texts did not have a fixed direction. Early inscriptions were written horizontally from left to right, from right to left, vertically (bottom to top, top to bottom); boustrophedon directionality was also known. Modern-day Berber script is most frequently written in horizontal lines from left to right; therefore the bidirectional class for Tifinagh letters is specified as strong left to right. Displaying Berber texts in other directions can be accomplished by the use of directional overrides or by the use of higher-level protocols.

13.5 N'Ko

N'Ko: U+07C0–U+07FF

N'Ko is a literary dialect used by the Manden (or Manding) people, who live primarily in West Africa. The script was devised by Solomana Kante in 1949 as a writing system for the Manden languages. The Manden language group is known as *Mandenkan*, where the suffix *-kan* means "language of." In addition to the substantial number of Mandens, some non-Mandens speak *Mandenkan* as a second language. There are an estimated 20 million Mandenkan speakers.

The major dialects of the Manden language are Bamanan, Jula, Maninka, and Mandinka. There are a number of other related dialects. When Mandens from different subgroups talk to each other, it is common practice for them to switch—consciously or subconsciously—from their own dialect to the conventional, literary dialect commonly known as *Kangbe*, "the clear language," also known as N'Ko. This dialect switching can occur in conversations between the Bamanan of Mali, the Maninka of Guinea, the Jula of the Ivory Coast, and the Mandinka of Gambia or Senegal, for example. Although there are great similarities between their dialects, speakers sometimes find it necessary to switch to *Kangbe* (N'Ko) by using a common word or phrase, similar to the accommodations Danes, Swedes, and Norwegians sometimes make when speaking to one another. For example, the word for "name" in Bamanan is *togo*, while it is *tooh* in Maninka. Speakers of both dialects will write it as ߕߐ߮ , although each may pronounce it differently.

Structure. The N'Ko script is written from right to left. It is phonetic in nature (one symbol, one sound). N'Ko has seven vowels, each of which can bear one of seven diacritical marks that modify the tone of the vowel as well as an optional diacritical mark that indicates nasalization. N'Ko has 19 consonants and two "abstract" consonants, U+07E0 NKO LETTER NA WOLOSO and U+07E7 NKO LETTER NYA WOLOSO, which indicate original consonants mutated by a preceding nasal, either word-internally or across word boundaries. Some consonants can bear one of three diacritical marks to transcribe foreign sounds or to transliterate foreign letters.

U+07D2 NKO LETTER N is considered neither a vowel nor a consonant; it indicates a syllabic alveolar or velar nasal. It can bear a diacritical mark, but cannot bear the nasal diacritic. The letter U+07D1 NKO LETTER DAGBASINNA has a special function in N'Ko orthography. The standard spelling rule is that when two successive syllables have the same vowel, the vowel is written only after the second of the two syllables. For example, ߓߟߏ <ba, la, oo> is pronounced [bolo], but in a foreign syllable to be pronounced [blo], the *dagbasinna* is inserted for ߓߑߟߏ <ba, dagbasinna, la, oo> to show that a consonant cluster is intended.

Digits. N'Ko uses decimal digits specific to the script. These digits have strong right-to-left directionality. Numbers are stored in text in logical order with most significant digit first; when displayed, numerals are then laid out in right-to-left order, with the most significant digit at the rightmost side, as illustrated for the numeral 144 in *Figure 13-7*. This situation differs from how numerals are handled in Hebrew and Arabic, where numerals are laid out in left-to-right order, even though the overall text direction is right to left.

Diacritical Marks. N'Ko diacritical marks are script-specific, despite superficial resemblances to other diacritical marks encoded for more general use. Some N'Ko diacritics have a wider range of glyph representation than the generic marks do, and are typically drawn rather higher and bolder than the generic marks.

Table 13-3 shows the use of the tone diacritics when applied to vowels.

When applied to a vowel, U+07F2 NKO COMBINING NASALIZATION MARK indicates the nasalization of that vowel. In the text stream, this mark is applied before any of the tone marks because combining marks below precede combining marks above in canonical order.

Table 13-3. N'Ko Tone Diacritics on Vowels

Character		Tone	Applied To
U+07EB	NKO COMBINING SHORT HIGH TONE	high	short vowel
U+07EC	NKO COMBINING SHORT LOW TONE	low	short vowel
U+07ED	NKO COMBINING SHORT RISING TONE	rising-falling	short vowel
U+07EE	NKO COMBINING LONG DESCENDING TONE	descending	long vowel
U+07EF	NKO COMBINING LONG HIGH TONE	high	long vowel
U+07F0	NKO COMBINING LONG LOW TONE	long low	long vowel
U+07F1	NKO COMBINING LONG RISING TONE	rising	long vowel

Two of the tone diacritics, when applied to consonants, indicate specific sounds from other languages—in particular, Arabic or French language sounds. U+07F3 NKO COMBINING DOUBLE DOT ABOVE is also used as a diacritic to represent sounds from other languages. The combinations used are as shown in *Table 13-4*.

Table 13-4. Other N'Ko Diacritic Usage

Character	Applied To	Represents
U+07EB NKO COMBINING SHORT HIGH TONE	SA	[s] or Arabic ص SAD
	GBA	[ɣ] or Arabic غ GHAIN
	KA	[q] or Arabic ق QAF
U+07ED NKO COMBINING SHORT RISING TONE	BA	[bʰ]
	TA	[ŧ] or Arabic ط TAH
	JA	[z] or Arabic ز ZAIN
	CA	[ð] or Arabic ذ THAL and also French [ʒ]
	DA	[đ] or Arabic ض ZAD
	RA	French [ʀ]
	SA	[ʃ] or Arabic ش SHEEN
	GBA	[g]
	FA	[v]
	KA	[ḫ] or Arabic خ KHAH
	LA	[lʰ]
	MA	[mʰ]
	NYA	[nʰ]
	HA	[ḥ] or Arabic ح HAH
	YA	[yʰ]
U+07F3 NKO COMBINING DOUBLE DOT ABOVE	A	[ʕa] or Arabic ع AIN + A
	EE	French [ə]
	U	French [y]
	JA	[ẓ] or Arabic ظ ZAH
	DA	[dʰ]
	SA	[θ] or Arabic ث THEH
	GBA	[kp]

Ordinal Numbers. Diacritical marks are also used to mark ordinal numbers. The first ordinal is indicated by applying U+07ED NKO COMBINING SHORT RISING TONE (a dot above) to

U+07C1 NKO DIGIT ONE. All other ordinal numbers are indicated by applying U+07F2 NKO COMBINING NASALIZATION MARK (an oval dot below) to the last digit in any sequence of digits composing the number. Thus the nasalization mark under the digit two would indicate the ordinal value 2nd, while the nasalization mark under the final digit four in the numeral 144 would indicate the ordinal value 144th, as shown in *Figure 13-7*.

Figure 13-7. Examples of N'Ko Ordinals

߁߭	1st
߂߲	2nd
߃߲	3rd
߁߄߄߲	144th

Punctuation. N'Ko uses a number of punctuation marks in common with other scripts. U+061F ARABIC QUESTION MARK, U+060C ARABIC COMMA, U+061B ARABIC SEMICOLON, and the paired U+FD3E ORNATE LEFT PARENTHESIS and U+FD3F ORNATE RIGHT PARENTHESIS are used, often with different shapes than are used in Arabic. A script-specific U+07F8 NKO COMMA and U+07F9 NKO EXCLAMATION MARK are encoded. The NKO COMMA differs in shape from the ARABIC COMMA, and the two are sometimes used distinctively in the same N'Ko text.

The character U+07F6 NKO SYMBOL OO DENNEN is used as an addition to phrases to indicate remote future placement of the topic under discussion. The decorative U+07F7 ߷ NKO SYMBOL GBAKURUNEN represents the three stones that hold a cooking pot over the fire and is used to end major sections of text.

The two tonal apostrophes, U+07F4 NKO HIGH TONE APOSTROPHE and U+07F5 NKO LOW TONE APOSTROPHE, are used to show the elision of a vowel while preserving the tonal information of the syllable. Their glyph representations can vary in height relative to the baseline. N'Ko also uses a set of paired punctuation, U+2E1C LEFT LOW PARAPHRASE BRACKET and U+2E1D RIGHT LOW PARAPHRASE BRACKET, to indicate indirect quotations.

Character Names and Block Name. Although the traditional name of the N'Ko language and script includes an apostrophe, apostrophes are disallowed in Unicode character and block names. Because of this, the formal block name is "NKo" and the script portion of the Unicode character names is "NKO".

Ordering. The order of N'Ko characters in the code charts reflects the traditional ordering of N'Ko. However, in collation, the three archaic letters U+07E8 NKO LETTER JONA JA, U+07E9 NKO LETTER JONA CHA, and U+07EA NKO LETTER JONA RA should be weighted as variants of U+07D6 NKO LETTER JA, U+07D7 NKO LETTER CHA, and U+07D9 NKO LETTER RA, respectively.

Rendering. N'Ko letters have shaping behavior similar to that of Arabic. Each letter can take one of four possible forms, as shown in *Table 13-5*.

Table 13-5. N'Ko Letter Shaping

Character	X_n	X_r	X_m	X_l
A	ߊ	‍ߊ	‍ߊ‍	ߊ‍
EE	ߋ	‍ߋ	‍ߋ‍	ߋ‍
I	ߌ	‍ߌ	‍ߌ‍	ߌ‍
E	ߍ	‍ߍ	‍ߍ‍	ߍ‍
U	ߎ	‍ߎ	‍ߎ‍	ߎ‍
OO	ߏ	‍ߏ	‍ߏ‍	ߏ‍
O	ߐ	‍ߐ	‍ߐ‍	ߐ‍
DAGBASINNA	ߑ	‍ߑ	‍ߑ‍	ߑ‍
N	ߒ	‍ߒ	‍ߒ‍	ߒ‍
BA	ߓ	‍ߓ	‍ߓ‍	ߓ‍
PA	ߔ	‍ߔ	‍ߔ‍	ߔ‍
TA	ߕ	‍ߕ	‍ߕ‍	ߕ‍
JA	ߖ	‍ߖ	‍ߖ‍	ߖ‍
CHA	ߗ	‍ߗ	‍ߗ‍	ߗ‍
DA	ߘ	‍ߘ	‍ߘ‍	ߘ‍
RA	ߙ	‍ߙ	‍ߙ‍	ߙ‍
RRA	ߚ	‍ߚ	‍ߚ‍	ߚ‍
SA	ߛ	‍ߛ	‍ߛ‍	ߛ‍
GBA	ߜ	‍ߜ	‍ߜ‍	ߜ‍
FA	ߝ	‍ߝ	‍ߝ‍	ߝ‍
KA	ߞ	‍ߞ	‍ߞ‍	ߞ‍
LA	ߟ	‍ߟ	‍ߟ‍	ߟ‍
NA WOLOSO	ߠ	‍ߠ	‍ߠ‍	ߠ‍
MA	ߡ	‍ߡ	‍ߡ‍	ߡ‍
NYA	ߢ	‍ߢ	‍ߢ‍	ߢ‍

Table 13-5. N'Ko Letter Shaping (Continued)

Character	X_n	X_r	X_m	X_l
NA	ߠ	ߠ	ߠ	ߠ
HA	ߤ	ߤ	ߤ	ߤ
WA	ߥ	ߥ	ߥ	ߥ
YA	ߦ	ߦ	ߦ	ߦ
NYA WOLOSO	ߧ	ߧ	ߧ	ߧ
JONA JA	ߨ	ߨ	ߨ	ߨ
JONA CHA	ߩ	ߩ	ߩ	ߩ
JONA RA	ߪ	ߪ	ߪ	ߪ

A noncursive style of N'Ko writing exists where no joining line is used between the letters in a word. This is a font convention, not a dynamic style like bold or italic, both of which are also valid dynamic styles for N'Ko. Noncursive fonts are mostly used as display fonts for the titles of books and articles. U+07FA NKO LAJANYALAN is sometimes used like U+0640 ARABIC TATWEEL to justify lines, although Latin-style justification where space is increased tends to be more common.

13.6 Cherokee

Cherokee: U+13A0–U+13FF

The Cherokee script is used to write the Cherokee language. Cherokee is a member of the Iroquioan language family. It is related to Cayuga, Seneca, Onondaga, Wyandot-Huron, Tuscarora, Oneida, and Mohawk. The relationship is not close because roughly 3,000 years ago the Cherokees migrated southeastward from the Great Lakes region of North America to what is now North Carolina, Tennessee, and Georgia. Cherokee is the native tongue of approximately 20,000 people, although most speakers today use it as a second language. The Cherokee word for both the language and the people is ᏣᎳᎩ *Tsalagi.*

The Cherokee syllabary, as invented by Sequoyah between 1815 and 1821, contained 6 vowels and 17 consonants. Sequoyah avoided copying from other alphabets, but his original letters were modified to make them easier to print. The first font for Cherokee was designed by Dr. Samuel A. Worcester. Using fonts available to him, he assigned a number of Latin letters to the Cherokee syllables. At this time the Cherokee letter "HV" was dropped, and the Cherokee syllabary reached its current size of 85 letters. Dr. Worcester's press printed 13,980,000 pages of Native American-language text, most of it in Cherokee.

Tones. Each Cherokee syllable can be spoken on one of four pitch or tone levels, or can slide from one pitch to one or two others within the same syllable. However, only in certain words does the tone of a syllable change the meaning. Tones are unmarked.

Case and Spelling. The Cherokee script is caseless, although for purposes of emphasis occasionally one letter will be made larger than the others. Cherokee spelling is not standardized: each person spells as the word sounds to him or her.

Numbers. Although Sequoyah invented a Cherokee number system, it was not adopted and is not encoded here. The Cherokee Nation uses European numbers. Cherokee speakers pay careful attention to the use of ordinal and cardinal numbers. When speaking of a numbered series, they will use ordinals. For example, when numbering chapters in a book, Cherokee headings would use First Chapter, Second Chapter, and so on, instead of Chapter One, Chapter Two, and so on.

Rendering and Input. Cherokee is a left-to-right script, which requires no combining characters. Several keyboarding conventions exist for inputting Cherokee. Some involve dead-key input based on Latin transliterations; some are based on sound-mnemonics related to Latin letters on keyboards; and some are ergonomic systems based on frequency of the syllables in the Cherokee language.

Punctuation. Cherokee uses standard Latin punctuation.

Standards. There are no other encoding standards for Cherokee.

13.7 Canadian Aboriginal Syllabics

Canadian Aboriginal Syllabics: U+1400–U+167F

The characters in this block are a unification of various local syllabaries of Canada into a single repertoire based on character appearance. The syllabics were invented in the late 1830s by James Evans for Algonquian languages. As other communities and linguistic groups adopted the script, the main structural principles described in this section were adopted. The primary user community for this script consists of several aboriginal groups throughout Canada, including Algonquian, Inuktitut, and Athapascan language families. The script is also used by governmental agencies and in business, education, and media.

Organization. The repertoire is organized primarily on structural principles found in the CASEC [1994] report, and is essentially a glyphic encoding. The canonical structure of each character series consists of a consonant shape with five variants. Typically the shape points down when the consonant is combined with the vowel /e/, up when combined with the vowel /i/, right when combined with the vowel /o/, and left when combined with the vowel /a/. It is reduced and superscripted when in syllable-final position, not followed by a vowel. For example:

ᐯ	ᐱ	ᐳ	ᐸ	ᑉ
PE	PI	PO	PA	P

Some variations in vowels also occur. For example, in Inuktitut usage, the syllable U+1450 ᑐ CANADIAN SYLLABICS TO is transcribed into Latin letters as "TU" rather than "TO", but the structure of the syllabary is generally the same regardless of language.

Arrangement. The arrangement of signs follows the Algonquian ordering (down-pointing, up-pointing, right-pointing, left-pointing), as in the previous example.

Sorted within each series are the variant forms for that series. Algonquian variants appear first, then Inuktitut variants, then Athapascan variants. This arrangement is convenient and consistent with the historical diffusion of Syllabics writing; it does not imply any hierarchy.

Some glyphs do not show the same down/up/right/left directions in the typical fashion—for example, beginning with U+146B ᑫ CANADIAN SYLLABICS KE. These glyphs are variations of the rule because of the shape of the basic glyph; they do not affect the convention.

Vowel length and labialization modify the character series through the addition of various marks (for example, U+143E ᐾ CANADIAN SYLLABICS PWII). Such modified characters are considered unique syllables. They are not decomposed into base characters and one or more diacritics. Some language families have different conventions for placement of the modifying mark. For the sake of consistency and simplicity, and to support multiple North American languages in the same document, each of these variants is assigned a unique code point.

13.8 Deseret

Deseret: U+10400–U+1044F

Deseret is a phonemic alphabet devised to write the English language. It was originally developed in the 1850s by the regents of the University of Deseret, now the University of Utah. It was promoted by The Church of Jesus Christ of Latter-day Saints, also known as the "Mormon" or LDS Church, under Church President Brigham Young (1801–1877). The name *Deseret* is taken from a word in the Book of Mormon defined to mean "honeybee" and reflects the LDS use of the beehive as a symbol of cooperative industry. Most literature about the script treats the term *Deseret Alphabet* as a proper noun and capitalizes it as such.

Among the designers of the Deseret Alphabet was George D. Watt, who had been trained in shorthand and served as Brigham Young's secretary. It is possible that, under Watt's influence, Sir Isaac Pitman's 1847 English Phonotypic Alphabet was used as the model for the Deseret Alphabet.

The Deseret Alphabet was a work in progress through most of the 1850s, with the set of letters and their shapes changing from time to time. The final version was used for the printed material of the late 1860s, but earlier versions are found in handwritten manuscripts.

The Church commissioned two typefaces and published four books using the Deseret Alphabet. The Church-owned *Deseret News* also published passages of scripture using the alphabet on occasion. In addition, some historical records, diaries, and other materials were handwritten using this script, and it had limited use on coins and signs. There is also one tombstone in Cedar City, Utah, written in the Deseret Alphabet. However, the script failed to gain wide acceptance and was not actively promoted after 1869. Today, the Deseret Alphabet remains of interest primarily to historians and hobbyists.

Letter Names and Shapes. Pedagogical materials produced by the LDS Church gave names to all of the non-vowel letters and indicated the vowel sounds with English examples. In the Unicode Standard, the spelling of the non-vowel letter names has been modified to clarify their pronunciations, and the vowels have been given names that emphasize the parallel structure of the two vowel runs.

The glyphs used in the Unicode Standard are derived from the second typeface commissioned by the LDS Church and represent the shapes most commonly encountered. Alternate glyphs are found in the first typeface and in some instructional material.

Structure. The final version of the script consists of 38 letters, LONG I through ENG. Two additional letters, OI and EW, found only in handwritten materials, are encoded after the first 38. The alphabet is bicameral; capital and small letters differ only in size and not in shape. The order of the letters is phonetic: letters for similar classes of sound are grouped together. In particular, most consonants come in unvoiced/voiced pairs. Forty-letter versions of the alphabet inserted OI after AY and EW after OW.

Sorting. The order of the letters in the Unicode Standard is the one used in all but one of the nineteenth-century descriptions of the alphabet. The exception is one in which the letters WU and YEE are inverted. The order YEE-WU follows the order of the "coalescents" in Pitman's work; the order WU-YEE appears in a greater number of Deseret materials, however, and has been followed here.

Alphabetized material followed the standard order of the Deseret Alphabet in the code charts, except that the short and long vowel pairs are grouped together, in the order long vowel first, and then short vowel.

Typographic Conventions. The Deseret Alphabet is written from left to right. Punctuation, capitalization, and digits are the same as in English. All words are written phonemically with the exception of short words that have pronunciations equivalent to letter names, as shown in *Figure 13-8*.

Figure 13-8. Short Words Equivalent to Deseret Letter Names

𐐌 AY is written for *eye* or *I*

𐐏 YEE is written for *ye*

𐐒 BEE is written for *be* or *bee*

𐐘 GAY is written for *gay*

𐐜 THEE is written for *the* or *thee*

Phonetics. An approximate IPA transcription of the sounds represented by the Deseret Alphabet is shown in *Table 13-6*.

Table 13-6. IPA Transcription of Deseret

𐐀𐐨	LONG I	ɪː	𐐒𐐺	BEE	b
𐐁𐐩	LONG E	eɪ	𐐓𐐻	TEE	t
𐐂𐐪	LONG A	ɑː	𐐔𐐼	DEE	d
𐐃𐐫	LONG AH	ɔː	𐐕𐐽	CHEE	tʃ
𐐄𐐬	LONG O	oː	𐐖𐐾	JEE	dʒ
𐐅𐐭	LONG OO	uː	𐐗𐐿	KAY	k
𐐆𐐮	SHORT I	ɪ	𐐘𐑀	GAY	ɡ
𐐇𐐯	SHORT E	ɛ	𐐙𐑁	EF	f
𐐈𐐰	SHORT A	æ	𐐚𐑂	VEE	v
𐐉𐐱	SHORT AH	ɔ	𐐛𐑃	ETH	θ
𐐊𐐲	SHORT O	ʌ	𐐜𐑄	THEE	ð
𐐋𐐳	SHORT OO	ʊ	𐐝𐑅	ES	s
𐐌𐐴	AY	ɑɪ	𐐞𐑆	ZEE	z
𐐦𐑎	OI	ɔɪ	𐐟𐑇	ESH	ʃ
𐐍𐐵	OW	ɑʊ	𐐠𐑈	ZHEE	ʒ
𐐧𐑏	EW	ju	𐐡𐑉	ER	r
𐐎𐐶	WU	w	𐐢𐑊	EL	l
𐐏𐐷	YEE	j	𐐣𐑋	EM	m
𐐐𐐸	H	h	𐐤𐑌	EN	n
𐐑𐐹	PEE	p	𐐥𐑍	ENG	ŋ

13.9 Shavian

Shavian: U+10450–U+1047F

The playwright George Bernard Shaw (1856–1950) was an outspoken critic of the idiosyncrasies of English orthography. In his will, he directed that Britain's Public Trustee seek out and publish an alphabet of no fewer than 40 letters to provide for the phonetic spelling of English. The alphabet finally selected was designed by Kingsley Read and is variously known as Shavian, Shaw's alphabet, and the Proposed British Alphabet. Also in accordance with Shaw's will, an edition of his play, *Androcles and the Lion*, was published and distributed to libraries, containing the text both in the standard Latin alphabet and in Shavian.

As with other attempts at spelling reform in English, the alphabet has met with little success. Nonetheless, it has its advocates and users. The normative version of Shavian is taken to be the version in *Androcles and the Lion*.

Structure. The alphabet consists of 48 letters and 1 punctuation mark. The letters have no case. The digits and other punctuation marks are the same as for the Latin script. The one additional punctuation mark is a "name mark," used to indicate proper nouns. U+00B7 MIDDLE DOT should be used to represent the "name mark." The letter names are intended to be indicative of their sounds; thus the sound /p/ is represented by U+10450 𐑐 SHAVIAN LETTER PEEP.

The first 40 letters are divided into four groups of 10. The first 10 and second 10 are 180-degree rotations of one another; the letters of the third and fourth groups often show a similar relationship of shape.

The first 10 letters are tall letters, which ascend above the x-height and generally represent unvoiced consonants. The next 10 letters are "deep" letters, which descend below the baseline and generally represent voiced consonants. The next 20 are the vowels and liquids. Again, each of these letters usually has a close phonetic relationship to the letter in its matching set of 10.

The remaining 8 letters are technically ligatures, the first 6 involving vowels plus /r/. Because ligation is not optional, these 8 letters are included in the encoding.

Collation. The problem of collation is not addressed by the alphabet's designers.

1

Chapter 14

Archaic Scripts

The following historic scripts are encoded in Version 5.0 of the Unicode Standard:

Ogham	*Linear B*	*Ugaritic*
Old Italic	*Cypriot*	*Old Persian*
Runic	*Phoenician*	*Sumero-Akkadian*
Gothic		

Unicode encodes a number of historic scripts. Although they are no longer used to write living languages, documents and inscriptions using these scripts exist, both for extinct and precursors of modern languages. The primary user communities for these scripts are scholars interested in studying the scripts and the languages written in them. Some of the historical scripts are related to each other and to modern alphabets.

The Ogham script is indigenous to Ireland. While its originators may have been aware of the Latin or Greek scripts, it seems clear that the sound values of Ogham letters were suited to the phonology of a form of Primitive Irish.

Old Italic was derived from Greek and was used to write Etruscan and other languages in Italy. It was borrowed by the Romans and is the immediate ancestor of the Latin script now used worldwide. Old Italic had other descendants, too: The Alpine alphabets seem to have been influential in devising the Runic script, which has a distinct angular appearance owing to its use in carving inscriptions in stone and wood. Gothic, like Cyrillic, was developed on the basis of Greek at a much later date than Old Italic.

The two historic scripts of northwestern Europe, Runic and Ogham, have a distinct appearance owing to their primary use in carving inscriptions in stone and wood. They are conventionally rendered from left to right in scholarly literature, but on the original stone carvings often proceeded in an arch tracing the outline of the stone.

Both Linear B and Cypriot are syllabaries that were used to write Greek. Linear B is the older of the two scripts, and there are some similarities between a few of the characters that may not be accidental. Cypriot may descend from Cypro-Minoan, which in turn may descend from Linear B.

The Phoenician alphabet was used in various forms around the Mediterranean. It is ancestral to Latin, Greek, Hebrew, and many other scripts both modern and historical.

Three ancient cuneiform scripts are described in this chapter: Ugaritic, Old Persian, and Sumero-Akkadian. The largest and oldest of these is Sumero-Akkadian. The other two scripts are not derived directly from the Sumero-Akkadian tradition but had common writing technology, consisting of wedges indented into clay tablets with reed styluses. Ugaritic texts are about as old as the earliest extant Biblical texts. Old Persian texts are newer, dating from the fifth century BCE.

14.1 Ogham

Ogham: U+1680–U+169F

Ogham is an alphabetic script devised to write a very early form of Irish. Monumental Ogham inscriptions are found in Ireland, Wales, Scotland, England, and on the Isle of Man. Many of the Scottish inscriptions are undeciphered and may be in Pictish. It is probable that Ogham (Old Irish "Ogam") was widely written in wood in early times. The main flowering of "classical" Ogham, rendered in monumental stone, was in the fifth and sixth centuries CE. Such inscriptions were mainly employed as territorial markers and memorials; the more ancient examples are standing stones.

The script was originally written along the edges of stone where two faces meet; when written on paper, the central "stemlines" of the script can be said to represent the edge of the stone. Inscriptions written on stemlines cut into the face of the stone, instead of along its edge, are known as "scholastic" and are of a later date (post-seventh century). Notes were also commonly written in Ogham in manuscripts as recently as the sixteenth century.

Structure. The Ogham alphabet consists of 26 distinct characters (*feda*), the first 20 of which are considered to be primary and the last 6 (*forfeda*) supplementary. The four primary series are called *aicmí* (plural of *aicme*, meaning "family"). Each *aicme* was named after its first character, (*Aicme Beithe*, *Aicme Uatha*, meaning "the B Family," "the H Family," and so forth). The character names used in this standard reflect the spelling of the names in modern Irish Gaelic, except that the acute accent is stripped from *Úr*, *Éabhadh*, *Ór*, and *Ifín*, and the mutation of *nGéadal* is not reflected.

Rendering. Ogham text is read beginning from the bottom left side of a stone, continuing upward, across the top, and down the right side (in the case of long inscriptions). Monumental Ogham was incised chiefly in a bottom-to-top direction, though there are examples of left-to-right bilingual inscriptions in Irish and Latin. Manuscript Ogham accommodated the horizontal left-to-right direction of the Latin script, and the vowels were written as vertical strokes as opposed to the incised notches of the inscriptions. Ogham should therefore be rendered on computers from left to right or from bottom to top (never starting from top to bottom).

Forfeda (Supplementary Characters). In printed and in manuscript Ogham, the fonts are conventionally designed with a central stemline, but this convention is not necessary. In implementations without the stemline, the character U+1680 OGHAM SPACE MARK should be given its conventional width and simply left blank like U+0020 SPACE. U+169B OGHAM FEATHER MARK and U+169C OGHAM REVERSED FEATHER MARK are used at the beginning and the end of Ogham text, particularly in manuscript Ogham. In some cases, only the *Ogham feather mark* is used, which can indicate the direction of the text.

The word *latheirt* ᚛ᚂᚐᚈᚆᚓᚔᚏᚈ᚜ shows the use of the feather marks. This word was written in the margin of a ninth-century Latin grammar and means "massive hangover," which may be the scribe's apology for any errors in his text.

14.2 Old Italic

Old Italic: U+10300–U+1032F

The Old Italic script unifies a number of related historical alphabets located on the Italian peninsula. Some of these were used for non-Indo-European languages (Etruscan and probably North Picene), and some for various Indo-European languages belonging to the Italic branch (Faliscan and members of the Sabellian group, including Oscan, Umbrian, and South Picene). The ultimate source for the alphabets in ancient Italy is Euboean Greek used at Ischia and Cumae in the bay of Naples in the eighth century BCE. Unfortunately, no Greek abecedaries from southern Italy have survived. Faliscan, Oscan, Umbrian, North Picene, and South Picene all derive from an Etruscan form of the alphabet.

There are some 10,000 inscriptions in Etruscan. By the time of the earliest Etruscan inscriptions, circa 700 BCE, local distinctions are already found in the use of the alphabet. Three major stylistic divisions are identified: the Northern, Southern, and Caere/Veii. Use of Etruscan can be divided into two stages, owing largely to the phonological changes that occurred: the "archaic Etruscan alphabet," used from the seventh to the fifth centuries BCE, and the "neo-Etruscan alphabet," used from the fourth to the first centuries BCE. Glyphs for eight of the letters differ between the two periods; additionally, neo-Etruscan abandoned the letters KA, KU, and EKS.

The unification of these alphabets into a single Old Italic script requires language-specific fonts because the glyphs most commonly used may differ somewhat depending on the language being represented.

Most of the languages have added characters to the common repertoire: Etruscan and Faliscan add LETTER EF; Oscan adds LETTER EF, LETTER II, and LETTER UU; Umbrian adds LETTER EF, LETTER ERS, and LETTER CHE; North Picene adds LETTER UU; and Adriatic adds LETTER II and LETTER UU.

The Latin script itself derives from a south Etruscan model, probably from Caere or Veii, around the mid-seventh century BCE or a bit earlier. However, because there are significant differences between Latin and Faliscan of the seventh and sixth centuries BCE in terms of formal differences (glyph shapes, directionality) and differences in the repertoire of letters used, this warrants a distinctive character block. Fonts for early Latin should use the *uppercase* code positions U+0041..U+005A. The unified Alpine script, which includes the

Venetic, Rhaetic, Lepontic, and Gallic alphabets, has not yet been proposed for addition to the Unicode Standard but is considered to differ enough from both Old Italic and Latin to warrant independent encoding. The Alpine script is thought to be the source for Runic, which is encoded at U+16A0..U+16FF. (See *Section 14.3, Runic.*)

Character names assigned to the Old Italic block are unattested but have been reconstructed according to the analysis made by Sampson (1985). While the Greek character names (ALPHA, BETA, GAMMA, and so on) were borrowed directly from the Phoenician names (modified to Greek phonology), the Etruscans are thought to have abandoned the Greek names in favor of a phonetically based nomenclature, where stops were pronounced with a following -e sound, and liquids and sibilants (which can be pronounced more or less on their own) were pronounced with a leading e- sound (so [k], [d] became [ke:], [de:] became [l:], [m:] became [el], [em]). It is these names, according to Sampson, which were borrowed by the Romans when they took their script from the Etruscans.

Directionality. Most early Etruscan texts have right-to-left directionality. From the third century BCE, left-to-right texts appear, showing the influence of Latin. Oscan, Umbrian, and Faliscan also generally have right-to-left directionality. Boustrophedon appears rarely, and not especially early (for instance, the Forum inscription dates to 550–500 BCE). Despite this, for reasons of implementation simplicity, many scholars prefer left-to-right presentation of texts, as this is also their practice when transcribing the texts into Latin script. Accordingly, the Old Italic script has a default directionality of strong left-to-right in this standard. If the default directionality of the script is overridden to produce a right-to-left presentation, the glyphs in Old Italic fonts should also be mirrored from the representative glyphs shown in the code charts. This kind of behavior is not uncommon in archaic scripts; for example, archaic Greek letters may be mirrored when written from right to left in boustrophedon.

Punctuation. The earliest inscriptions are written with no space between words in what is called *scriptio continua*. There are numerous Etruscan inscriptions with dots separating word forms, attested as early as the second quarter of the seventh century BCE. This punctuation is sometimes, but only rarely, used to separate syllables rather than words. From the sixth century BCE, words were often separated by one, two, or three dots spaced vertically above each other.

Numerals. Etruscan numerals are not well attested in the available materials, but are employed in the same fashion as Roman numerals. Several additional numerals are attested, but as their use is at present uncertain, they are not yet encoded in the Unicode Standard.

Glyphs. The default glyphs in the code charts are based on the most common shapes found for each letter. Most of these are similar to the Marsiliana abecedary (mid-seventh century BCE). Note that the phonetic values for U+10317 OLD ITALIC LETTER EKS [ks] and U+10319 OLD ITALIC LETTER KHE [kh] show the influence of western, Euboean Greek; eastern Greek has U+03A7 GREEK CAPITAL LETTER CHI [x] and U+03A8 GREEK CAPITAL LETTER PSI [ps] instead.

The geographic distribution of the Old Italic script is shown in *Figure 14-1.* In the figure, the approximate distribution of the ancient languages that used Old Italic alphabets is shown in white. Areas for the ancient languages that used other scripts are shown in gray, and the labels for those languages are shown in oblique type. In particular, note that the ancient Greek colonies of the southern Italian and Sicilian coasts used the Greek script proper. Also, languages such as Ligurian, Venetic, and so on, of the far north of Italy made use of alphabets of the Alpine script. Rome, of course, is shown in gray, because Latin was written with the Latin alphabet, now encoded in the Latin script.

Figure 14-1. Distribution of Old Italic

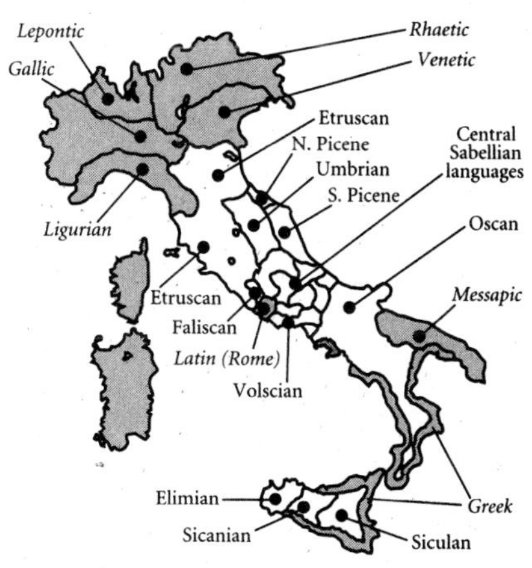

14.3 Runic

Runic: U+16A0–U+16F0

The Runic script was historically used to write the languages of the early and medieval societies in the German, Scandinavian, and Anglo-Saxon areas. Use of the Runic script in various forms covers a period from the first century to the nineteenth century. Some 6,000 Runic inscriptions are known. They form an indispensable source of information about the development of the Germanic languages.

Historical Script. The Runic script is an historical script, whose most important use today is in scholarly and popular works about the old Runic inscriptions and their interpretation. The Runic script illustrates many technical problems that are typical for this kind of script. Unlike many other scripts in the Unicode Standard, which predominantly serve the needs of the modern user community—with occasional extensions for historic forms—the encoding of the Runic script attempts to suit the needs of texts from different periods of time and from distinct societies that had little contact with one another.

Direction. Like other early writing systems, runes could be written either from left to right or from right to left, or moving first in one direction and then the other (*boustrophedon*), or following the outlines of the inscribed object. At times, characters appear in mirror image, or upside down, or both. In modern scholarly literature, Runic is written from left to right. Therefore, the letters of the Runic script have a default directionality of strong left-to-right in this standard.

The Runic Alphabet. Present-day knowledge about runes is incomplete. The set of graphemically distinct units shows greater variation in its graphical shapes than most modern scripts. The Runic alphabet changed several times during its history, both in the number and the shapes of the letters contained in it. The shapes of most runes can be related to some Latin capital letter, but not necessarily to a letter representing the same sound. The most conspicuous difference between the Latin and the Runic alphabets is the order of the letters.

The Runic alphabet is known as the *futhark* from the name of its first six letters. The original *old futhark* contained 24 runes:

ᚠ ᚢ ᚦ ᚨ ᚱ ᚲ ᚷ ᚹ ᚺ ᚾ ᛁ ᛃ ᛇ ᛈ ᛉ ᛊ ᛏ ᛒ ᛖ ᛗ ᛚ ᛜ ᛞ ᛟ

They are usually transliterated in this way:

f u þ a r k g w h n i j ï p z s t b e m l ŋ d o

In England and Friesland, seven more runes were added from the fifth to the ninth century.

In the Scandinavian countries, the *futhark* changed in a different way; in the eighth century, the simplified younger *futhark* appeared. It consists of only 16 runes, some of which are used in two different forms. The long-branch form is shown here:

ᚠ ᚢ ᚦ ᚬ ᚱ ᚴ ᚼ ᚾ ᛁ ᛅ ᛋ ᛏ ᛒ ᛘ ᛚ ᛦ

f u þ o r k h n i a s t b m l ʀ

The use of runes continued in Scandinavia during the Middle Ages. During that time, the *futhark* was influenced by the Latin alphabet and new runes were invented so that there was full correspondence with the Latin letters.

Representative Glyphs. The known inscriptions can include considerable variations of shape for a given rune, sometimes to the point where the nonspecialist will mistake the shape for a different rune. There is no dominant main form for some runes, particularly for many runes added in the Anglo-Friesian and medieval Nordic systems. When transcribing a Runic inscription into its Unicode-encoded form, one cannot rely on the idealized *representative glyph* shape in the character charts alone. One must take into account to which of the four Runic systems an inscription belongs and be knowledgeable about the permitted form variations within each system. The representative glyphs were chosen to provide an image that distinguishes each rune visually from all other runes in the same system. For actual use, it might be advisable to use a separate font for each Runic system. Of particular note is the fact that the glyph for U+16C4 ᛄ RUNIC LETTER GER is actually a rare form, as the more common form is already used for U+16E1 ᛡ RUNIC LETTER IOR.

Unifications. When a rune in an earlier writing system evolved into several different runes in a later system, the unification of the earlier rune with one of the later runes was based on similarity in graphic form rather than similarity in sound value. In cases where a substantial change in the typical graphical form has occurred, though the historical continuity is undisputed, unification has not been attempted. When runes from different writing systems have the same graphic form but different origins and denote different sounds, they have been coded as separate characters.

Long-Branch and Short-Twig. Two sharply different graphic forms, the *long-branch* and the *short-twig* form, were used for 9 of the 16 Viking Age Nordic runes. Although only one form is used in a given inscription, there are runologically important exceptions. In some cases, the two forms were used to convey different meanings in later use in the medieval system. Therefore the two forms have been separated in the Unicode Standard.

Staveless Runes. Staveless runes are a third form of the Viking Age Nordic runes, a kind of Runic shorthand. The number of known inscriptions is small and the graphic forms of many of the runes show great variability between inscriptions. For this reason, staveless runes have been unified with the corresponding Viking Age Nordic runes. The corresponding Viking Age Nordic runes must be used to encode these characters—specifically the short-twig characters, where both short-twig and long-branch characters exist.

Punctuation Marks. The wide variety of Runic punctuation marks has been reduced to three distinct characters based on simple aspects of their graphical form, as very little is known about any difference in intended meaning between marks that look different. Any other punctuation marks have been unified with shared punctuation marks elsewhere in the Unicode Standard.

Golden Numbers. Runes were used as symbols for Sunday letters and golden numbers on calendar staves used in Scandinavia during the Middle Ages. To complete the number series 1–19, three more calendar runes were added. They are included after the punctuation marks.

Encoding. A total of 81 characters of the Runic script are included in the Unicode Standard. Of these, 75 are Runic letters, 3 are punctuation marks, and 3 are Runic symbols. The order of the Runic characters follows the traditional *futhark* order, with variants and derived runes being inserted directly after the corresponding ancestor.

Runic character names are based as much as possible on the sometimes several traditional names for each rune, often with the Latin transliteration at the end of the name.

14.4 Gothic

Gothic: U+10330–U+1034F

The Gothic script was devised in the fourth century by the Gothic bishop, Wulfila (311–383 CE), to provide his people with a written language and a means of reading his translation of the Bible. Written Gothic materials are largely restricted to fragments of Wulfila's translation of the Bible; these fragments are of considerable importance in New Testament textual studies. The chief manuscript, kept at Uppsala, is the Codex Argenteus or "the Silver Book," which is partly written in gold on purple parchment. Gothic is an East Germanic language; this branch of Germanic has died out and thus the Gothic texts are of great importance in historical and comparative linguistics. Wulfila appears to have used the Greek script as a source for the Gothic, as can be seen from the basic alphabetical order. Some of the character shapes suggest Runic or Latin influence, but this is apparently coincidental.

Diacritics. The tenth letter U+10339 GOTHIC LETTER EIS is used with U+0308 COMBINING DIAERESIS when word-initial, when syllable-initial after a vowel, and in compounds with a verb as second member as shown below:

𐍃𐍅𐌴 𐌲𐌰𐌼𐌴𐌻𐌹𐌸 𐌹̈𐍃𐍄 𐌹̈𐌽 𐌴𐍃𐌰𐌹̈𐌹̈𐌽 𐍀𐍂𐌰𐌿𐍆𐌴𐍄𐌰𐌿
swe gameliþ ïst ïn esaïïn praufetau
"as is written in Isaiah the prophet"

To indicate contractions or omitted letters, U+0305 COMBINING OVERLINE is used.

Numerals. Gothic letters, like those of other early Western alphabets, can be used as numbers; two of the characters have only a numeric value and are not used alphabetically. To indicate numeric use of a letter, it is either flanked on one side by U+00B7 MIDDLE DOT or followed by both U+0304 COMBINING MACRON and U+0331 COMBINING MACRON BELOW, as shown in the following example:

·𐌴· or 𐌴̱̄ means "5"

Punctuation. Gothic manuscripts are written with no space between words in what is called *scriptio continua*. Sentences and major phrases are often separated by U+0020 SPACE, U+00B7 MIDDLE DOT, or U+003A COLON.

14.5 Linear B

Linear B Syllabary: U+10000–U+1007F

The Linear B script is a syllabic writing system that was used on the island of Crete and parts of the nearby mainland to write the oldest recorded variety of the Greek language. Linear B clay tablets predate Homeric Greek by some 700 years; the latest tablets date from the mid- to late thirteenth century BCE. Major archaeological sites include Knossos, first uncovered about 1900 by Sir Arthur Evans, and a major site near Pylos. The majority of currently known inscriptions are inventories of commodities and accounting records.

Early attempts to decipher the script failed until Michael Ventris, an architect and amateur decipherer, came to the realization that the language might be Greek and not, as previously thought, a completely unknown language. Ventris worked together with John Chadwick, and decipherment proceeded quickly. The two published a joint paper in 1953.

Linear B was written from left to right with no nonspacing marks. The script mainly consists of phonetic signs representing the combination of a consonant and a vowel. There are about 60 known phonetic signs, in addition to a few signs that seem to be mainly free variants (also known as Chadwick's optional signs), a few unidentified signs, numerals, and a number of ideographic signs, which were used mainly as counters for commodities. Some ligatures formed from combinations of syllables were apparently used as well. Chadwick gives several examples of these ligatures, the most common of which are included in the Unicode Standard. Other ligatures are the responsibility of the rendering system.

Standards. The catalog numbers used in the Unicode character names for Linear B syllables are based on the Wingspread Convention, as documented in Bennett (1964). The letter "B" is prepended arbitrarily, so that name parts will not start with a digit, thus conforming to ISO/IEC 10646 naming rules. The same naming conventions, using catalog numbers based on the Wingspread Convention, are used for Linear B ideograms.

Linear B Ideograms: U+10080–U+108FF

The Linear B Ideograms block contains the list of Linear B signs known to constitute ideograms (logographs), rather than syllables. When generally agreed upon, the names include the meaning associated with them—for example, U+10080 𐂀 LINEAR B IDEOGRAM B100 MAN. In other instances, the names of the ideograms simply carry their catalog number.

Aegean Numbers: U+10100–U+1013F

The signs used to denote Aegean whole numbers (U+10107..U+10133) derive from the non-Greek Linear A script. The signs are used in Linear B. The Cypriot syllabary appears to use the same system, as evidenced by the fact that the lower digits appear in extant texts. For measurements of agricultural and industrial products, Linear B uses three series of signs: liquid measures, dry measures, and weights. No set of signs for linear measurement has been found yet. Liquid and dry measures share the same symbols for the two smaller subunits; the system of weights retains its own unique subunits. Though several of the signs originate in Linear A, the measuring system of Linear B differs from that of Linear A. Linear B relies on units and subunits, much like the imperial "quart," "pint," and "cup," whereas Linear A uses whole numbers and fractions. The absolute values of the measurements have not yet been completely agreed upon.

14.6 Cypriot Syllabary

Cypriot Syllabary: U+10800–U+1083F

The Cypriot syllabary was used to write the Cypriot dialect of Greek from about 800 to 200 BCE. It is related to both Linear B and Cypro-Minoan, a script used for a language that has not yet been identified. Interpretation has been aided by the fact that, as use of the Cypriot syllabary died out, inscriptions were carved using both the Greek alphabet and the Cypriot syllabary. Unlike Linear B and Cypro-Minoan, the Cypriot syllabary was usually written from right to left, and accordingly the characters in this script have strong right-to-left directionality.

Word breaks can be indicated by spaces or by separating punctuation, although separating punctuation is also used between larger word groups.

Although both Linear B and the Cypriot syllabary were used to write Greek dialects, Linear B has a more highly abbreviated spelling. Structurally, the Cypriot syllabary consists of combinations of up to 12 initial consonants and 5 different vowels. Long and short vowels are not distinguished. The Cypriot syllabary distinguishes among a different set of initial consonants than Linear B; for example, unlike Linear B, Cypriot maintained a distinction between [l] and [r], though not between [d] and [t], as shown in *Table 14-1*. Not all of the 60 possible consonant-vowel combinations are represented. As is the case for Linear B, the Cypriot syllabary is well understood and documented.

Table 14-1. Similar Characters in Linear B and Cypriot

Linear B		Cypriot	
da	𐀅	*ta*	𐠭
na	𐀙	*na*	𐠙
pa	𐀞	*pa*	𐠞
ro	𐀫	*lo*	𐠒
se	𐀮	*se*	𐠩
ti	𐀴	*ti*	𐠯
to	𐀵	*to*	𐠰

For Aegean numbers, see the subsection “Aegean Numbers: U+10100–U+1013F” in *Section 14.5, Linear B.*

14.7 Phoenician

Phoenician: U+10900–U+1091F

The Phoenician alphabet and its successors were widely used over a broad area surrounding the Mediterranean Sea. Phoenician evolved over the period from about the twelfth century BCE until the second century BCE, with the last neo-Punic inscriptions dating from about the third century CE. Phoenician came into its own from the ninth century BCE. An older form of the Phoenician alphabet is a forerunner of the Greek, Old Italic (Etruscan),

Latin, Hebrew, Arabic, and Syriac scripts among others, many of which are still in modern use. It has also been suggested that Phoenician is the ultimate source of Kharoshthi and of the Indic scripts descending from Brahmi.

Phoenician is an historic script, and as for many other historic scripts, which often saw continuous change in use over periods of hundreds or thousands of years, its delineation as a script is somewhat problematic. This issue is particularly acute for historic Semitic scripts, which share basically identical repertoires of letters, which are historically related to each other, and which were used to write closely related Semitic languages.

In the Unicode Standard, the Phoenician script is intended for the representation of text in Palaeo-Hebrew, Archaic Phoenician, Phoenician, Early Aramaic, Late Phoenician cursive, Phoenician papyri, Siloam Hebrew, Hebrew seals, Ammonite, Moabite, and Punic. The line from Phoenician to Punic is taken to constitute a single continuous branch of script evolution, distinct from that of other related but separately encoded Semitic scripts.

The earliest Hebrew language texts were written in the Palaeo-Hebrew alphabet, one of the forms of writing considered to be encompassed within the Phoenician script as encoded in the Unicode Standard. The Samaritans who did not go into exile continued to use Palaeo-Hebrew forms, eventually developing them into the distinct Samaritan script, which is not yet encoded in the Unicode Standard. The Jews in exile gave up the Palaeo-Hebrew alphabet and instead adopted Imperial Aramaic writing, which was a descendant of the Early Aramaic form of the Phoenician script. Later, they transformed Imperial Aramaic into the "Jewish Aramaic" script now called (Square) Hebrew, separately encoded in the Hebrew block in the Unicode Standard.

Some scholars conceive of the language written in the Palaeo-Hebrew form of the Phoenician script as being quintessentially Hebrew and consistently transliterate it into Square Hebrew. In such contexts, Palaeo-Hebrew texts are often considered to simply *be* Hebrew, and because the relationship between the Palaeo-Hebrew letters and Square Hebrew letters is one-to-one and quite regular, the transliteration is conceived of as simply a font change. Other scholars of Phoenician transliterate texts into Latin. The encoding of the Phoenician script in the Unicode Standard does not invalidate such scholarly practice; it is simply intended to make it possible to represent Phoenician, Punic, and similar textual materials directly in the historic script, rather than as specialized font displays of transliterations in modern Square Hebrew.

Directionality. Phoenician is written horizontally from right to left. The characters of the Phoenician script are all given strong right-to-left directionality.

Punctuation. Inscriptions and other texts in the various forms of the Phoenician script generally have no space between words. Dots are sometimes found between words in later exemplars—for example, in Moabite inscriptions—and U+1091F PHOENICIAN WORD SEPARATOR should be used to represent this punctuation.

Stylistic Variation. The letters for Phoenician proper and especially for Punic have very exaggerated descenders. These descenders help distinguish the main line of Phoenician script evolution toward Punic, as contrasted with the Hebrew forms, where the descenders instead grew shorter over time.

Numerals. Phoenician numerals are built up from four elements in combination. Like the letters, Phoenician numbers are written from right to left: 𐤙𐤘𐤘𐤖𐤖𐤖 means 143 (100 + 20 + 20 + 1 + 1 + 1). This practice differs from modern Semitic scripts like Hebrew and Arabic, which use decimal numbers written from left to right.

Names. The names used for the characters here are those reconstructed by Theodor Nöldeke in 1904, as given in Powell (1996).

14.8 Ugaritic

Ugaritic: U+10380–U+1039F

The city state of Ugarit was an important seaport on the Phoenician coast (directly east of Cyprus, north of the modern town of Minet el-Beida) from about 1400 BCE until it was completely destroyed in the twelfth century BCE. The site of Ugarit, now called Ras Shamra (south of Latakia on the Syrian coast), was apparently continuously occupied from Neolithic times (circa 5000 BCE). It was first uncovered by a local inhabitant while plowing a field in 1928 and subsequently excavated by Claude Schaeffer and Georges Chenet beginning in 1929, in which year the first of many tablets written in the Ugaritic script were discovered. They later proved to contain extensive portions of an important Canaanite mythological and religious literature that had long been sought and that revolutionized Biblical studies. The script was first deciphered in a remarkably short time jointly by Hans Bauer, Edouard Dhorme, and Charles Virolleaud.

The Ugaritic language is Semitic, variously regarded by scholars as being a distinct language related to Akkadian and Canaanite, or a Canaanite dialect. Ugaritic is generally written from left to right horizontally, sometimes using U+1039F 𐎟 UGARITIC WORD DIVIDER. In the city of Ugarit, this script was also used to write the Hurrian language. The letters U+1039B 𐎛 UGARITIC LETTER I, U+1039C 𐎜 UGARITIC LETTER U, and U+1039D 𐎝 UGARITIC LETTER SSU are used for Hurrian.

Variant Glyphs. There is substantial variation in glyph representation for Ugaritic. Glyphs for U+10398 𐎘 UGARITIC LETTER THANNA, U+10399 𐎙 UGARITIC LETTER GHAIN, and U+1038F 𐎏 UGARITIC LETTER DHAL differ somewhat between modern reference sources, as do some transliterations. U+10398 𐎘 UGARITIC LETTER THANNA is most often displayed with a glyph that looks like an occurrence of U+10393 𐎓 UGARITIC LETTER AIN overlaid with U+10382 𐎂 UGARITIC LETTER GAMLA.

Ordering. The ancient Ugaritic alphabetical order, which differs somewhat from the modern Hebrew order for similar characters, has been used to encode Ugaritic in the Unicode Standard.

Character Names. Some of the Ugaritic character names have been reconstructed; others appear in an early fragmentary document.

14.9 Old Persian

Old Persian: U+103A0–U+103DF

The Old Persian script is found in a number of inscriptions in the Old Persian language dating from the Achaemenid Empire. Scholars today agree that the character inventory of Old Persian was invented for use in monumental inscriptions of the Achaemenid king, Darius I, by about 525 BCE. Old Persian is an alphabetic writing system with some syllabic aspects. While the shapes of some Old Persian letters look similar to signs in Sumero-Akkadian Cuneiform, it is clear that only one of them, U+103BE 𐎾 OLD PERSIAN SIGN LA, was actually borrowed. It was derived from the New Assyrian historic variant of Sumero-Akkadian U+121B7 𒆷 CUNEIFORM SIGN LA, because *la* is a foreign sound not used in the Old Persian language.

Directionality. Old Persian is written from left to right.

Repertoire. The repertoire contains 36 signs. These represent consonants, vowels, or consonant plus vowel syllables. There are also five numbers, one word divider, and eight ideograms. It is considered unlikely that any additional characters will be discovered.

Numerals. The attested numbers are built up by stringing the base numbers (1, 2, 10, 20, and 100) in sequences.

Variants. The signs U+103C8 OLD PERSIAN SIGN AURAMAZDAA and U+103C9 OLD PERSIAN SIGN AURAMAZDAA-2, and the signs U+103CC OLD PERSIAN SIGN DAHYAAUSH and U+103CD OLD PERSIAN SIGN DAHYAAUSH-2, have been encoded separately because their conventional attestation in the corpus of Old Persian texts is quite limited and scholars consider it advantageous to distinguish the forms in plain text representation.

14.10 Sumero-Akkadian

Cuneiform: U+12000–U+123FF

Sumero-Akkadian Cuneiform is a logographic writing system with a strong syllabic component. It was written from left to right on clay tablets.

Early History of Cuneiform. The earliest stage of Mesopotamian Cuneiform as a complete system of writing is first attested in Uruk during the so-called Uruk IV period (circa 3500–3200 BCE) with an initial repertoire of about 700 characters or "signs" as Cuneiform scholars customarily call them.

Late fourth millennium ideographic tablets were also found at Susa and several other sites in western Iran, in Assyria at Nineveh (northern Iraq), at Tell Brak (northwestern Syria), and at Habuba Kabira in Syria. The writing system developed in Sumer (southeastern Iraq) was repeatedly exported to peripheral regions in the third, second, and first millennia BCE. Local variations in usage are attested, but the core of the system is the Sumero-Akkadian writing system.

Writing emerged in Sumer simultaneously with a sudden growth in urbanization and an attendant increase in the scope and scale of administrative needs. A large proportion of the elements of the early writing system repertoire was devised to represent quantities and commodities for bureaucratic purposes.

At this earliest stage, signs were mainly pictographic, in that a relatively faithful facsimile of the thing signified was traced, although some items were strictly ideographic and represented by completely arbitrary abstractions, such as the symbol for sheep ⊕. Some scholars believe that the abstract symbols were derived from an earlier "token" system of accounting, but there is no general agreement on this point. Where the pictographs are concerned, interpretation was relatively straightforward. The head of a bull was used to denote "cattle"; an ear of barley was used to denote "barley." In some cases, pictographs were also interpreted logographically, so that meaning was derived from the symbol by close conceptual association. For example, the representation of a bowl might mean "bowl," but it could indicate concepts associated with bowls, such as "food." Renditions of a leg might variously suggest "leg," "stand," or "walk."

By the next chronological period of south Mesopotamian history (the Uruk III period, 3200–2900 BCE), logographic usage seems to have become much more widespread. In addition, individual signs were combined into more complex designs to express other concepts. For example, a head with a bowl next to it was used to denote "eat" or "drink." This is the point during script development at which one can truly speak of the first Sumerian texts. In due course, the early graphs underwent change, conditioned by factors such as the most widely available writing medium and writing tools, and the need to record information more quickly and efficiently from the standpoint of the bureaucracy that spawned the system.

Clay was the obvious writing medium in Sumer because it was widely available and easily molded into cushion- or pillow-shaped tablets. Writing utensils were easily made for it by sharpening pieces of reed. Because it was awkward and slow to inscribe curvilinear lines in a piece of clay with a sharpened reed (called a *stylus*), scribes tended to approximate the pictographs by means of short, wedge-shaped impressions made with the edge of the stylus. These short, mainly straight shapes gave rise to the modern word "cuneiform" from the Latin *cuneus*, meaning "wedge." Cuneiform proper was common from about 2700 BCE, although experts use the term "cuneiform" to include the earlier forms as well.

Geographic Range. The Sumerians did not live in complete isolation, and there is very early evidence of another significant linguistic group in the area immediately north of Sumer known as Agade or Akkad. Those peoples spoke a Semitic language whose dialects are subsumed by scholars under the heading "Akkadian." In the long run, the Akkadian speakers became the primary users and promulgators of Cuneiform script. Because of their trade involvement with their neighbors, Cuneiform spread through Babylonia (the umbrella term for Sumer and Akkad) to Elam, Assyria, eastern Syria, southern Anatolia, and even Egypt. Ultimately, many languages came to be written in Cuneiform script, the most notable being Sumerian, Akkadian (including Babylonian, Assyrian, Eblaite), Elamite, Hittite, and Hurrian.

Periods of script usage are defined according to geography and primary linguistic representation, as shown in *Table 14-2.*

Table 14-2. Cuneiform Script Usage

<table>
<tr><td colspan="3">Archaic Period
(to 2901 BCE)</td></tr>
<tr><td colspan="3">Early Dynastic
(2900–2335 BCE)</td></tr>
<tr><td colspan="3">Old Akkadian
(2334–2154 BCE)</td></tr>
<tr><td colspan="2">Ur III (NeoSumerian)
(2112–2095 BCE)</td><td rowspan="6">Elamite
(2100–360 BCE)</td></tr>
<tr><td>Old Assyrian
(1900–1750 BCE)</td><td>Old Babylonian
(2004–1595 BCE)</td></tr>
<tr><td>Middle Assyrian
(1500-1000 BCE)</td><td rowspan="2">Middle Babylonian
(1595–627 BCE)</td></tr>
<tr><td>Neo-Assyrian
(1000-609 BCE)</td></tr>
<tr><td></td><td>Neo-Babylonian
(626–539 BCE)</td></tr>
<tr><td colspan="2">Hittite
(1570-1220 BCE)</td></tr>
</table>

Sources and Coverage. The base character repertoire for the Cuneiform block was distilled from the list of Ur III signs compiled by the Cuneiform Digital Library Initiative (UCLA) in union with the list constructed independently by Miguel Civil. This repertoire is comprehensive from the Ur III period onward. Old Akkadian, Early Dynastic, and Archiac Cuneiform are not covered by this repertoire.

Simple Signs. Most Cuneiform signs are simple units; each sign of this type is represented by a single character in the standard.

Complex and Compound Signs. Some Cuneiform signs are categorized as either complex or compound signs. Complex signs are made up of a primary sign with one of more secondary signs written within it or conjoined to it, such that the whole is generally treated by scholars as a unit; this includes linear sequences of two or more signs or wedge-clusters where one or more of those clusters have not been clearly identified as characters in their own right. Complex signs, which present a relative visual unity, are assigned single individual code points irrespective of their components.

Compound signs are linear sequences of two or more signs or wedge-clusters generally treated by scholars as a single unit, when each and every such wedge-cluster exists as a clearly identified character in its own right. Compound signs are encoded as sequences of their component characters. Signs that shift from compound to complex, or vice versa, generally have been treated according to their Ur III manifestation.

Mergers and Splits. Over the long history of Cuneiform, an number of signs have simplified and merged; in other cases, a single sign has diverged and developed into more than one distinct sign. The choice of signs for encoding as characters was made at the point of maximum differentiation in the case of either mergers or splits to enable the most comprehensive set for the representation of text in any period.

Fonts for the representation of Cuneiform text may need to be designed distinctly for optimal use for different historic periods. Fonts for some periods will contain duplicate glyphs depending on the status of merged or split signs at that point of the development of the writing system.

Glyph Variants Acquiring Independent Semantic Status. Glyph variants such as U+122EC 𒋬 CUNEIFORM SIGN TA ASTERISK, a Middle Assyrian form of the sign U+122EB 𒋫 CUNEIFORM SIGN TA, which in Neo-Assyrian usage has its own logographic interpretation, have been assigned separate code positions. They are to be used only when the new interpretation applies.

Formatting. Cuneiform was often written between incised lines or in blocks surrounded by drawn boxes known as *case rules*. These boxes and lines are considered formatting and are not part of the script. Case ruling and the like are not to be treated as punctuation.

Ordering. The characters are encoded in the Unicode Standard in Latin alphabetical order by primary sign name. Complex signs based on the primary sign are organized according to graphic principles; in some cases, these correspond to the native analyses.

Other Standards. There is no standard legacy encoding of Cuneiform primarily because it was not possible to encode the huge number of characters in the pre-Unicode world of 8-bit fonts.

Cuneiform Numbers and Punctuation: U+12400–U+1247F

Cuneiform Punctuation. A small number of signs are occasionally used in Cuneiform to indicate word division, repetition, or phrase separation.

Cuneiform Numerals. In general, numerals have been encoded separately from signs that are visually identical but semantically different (for example, U+1244F 𒑏 CUNEIFORM NUMERIC SIGN ONE BAN2, U+12450 𒑐 CUNEIFORM NUMERIC SIGN TWO BAN2, and so on, versus U+12226 𒈦 CUNEIFORM SIGN MASH, U+1227A 𒉺 CUNEIFORM SIGN PA, and so on).

CHAPTER 15

Chapter 15

Symbols

The universe of symbols is rich and open-ended. The collection of encoded symbols in the Unicode Standard encompasses the following:

- *Currency symbols*
- *Letterlike symbols*
- *Mathematical alphabets*
- *Number forms*
- *Mathematical symbols*
- *Invisible mathematical operators*
- *Technical symbols*
- *Geometrical symbols*
- *Miscellaneous symbols and dingbats*
- *Enclosed and square symbols*
- *Braille patterns*
- *Western and Byzantine musical symbols*
- *Ancient Greek musical notation*

There are other notational systems not covered by the Unicode Standard. Some symbols mark the transition between pictorial items and text elements; because they do not have a well-defined place in plain text, they are not encoded here.

Combining marks may be used with symbols, particularly the set encoded at U+20D0..U+20FF (see *Section 7.9, Combining Marks*).

Letterlike and currency symbols, as well as number forms including superscripts and subscripts, are typically subject to the same font and style changes as the surrounding text. Where square and enclosed symbols occur in East Asian contexts, they generally follow the prevailing type styles.

Other symbols have an appearance that is independent of type style, or a more limited or altogether different range of type style variation than the regular text surrounding them. For example, mathematical alphanumeric symbols are typically used for mathematical variables; those letterlike symbols that are part of this set carry semantic information in their type style. This fact restricts—but does not completely eliminate—possible style variations. However, symbols such as mathematical operators can be used with any script or independent of any script.

Special invisible operator characters can be used to explicitly encode some mathematical operations, such as multiplication, which are normally implied by juxtaposition. This aids in automatic interpretation of mathematical notation.

In a bidirectional context (see Unicode Standard Annex #9, "The Bidirectional Algorithm"), symbol characters have no inherent directionality but resolve according to the Unicode Bidirectional Algorithm. Where the image of a symbol is not bilaterally symmetric, the mirror image is used when the character is part of the right-to-left text stream (see *Section 4.7, Bidi Mirrored—Normative*).

Dingbats and optical character recognition characters are different from all other characters in the standard, in that they are encoded based on their precise appearance.

Braille patterns are a special case, because they can be used to write text. They are included as symbols, as the Unicode Standard encodes only their shapes; the association of letters to patterns is left to other standards. When a character stream is intended primarily to convey text information, it should be coded using one of the scripts. Only when it is intended to convey a particular binding of text to Braille pattern sequence should it be coded using the Braille patterns.

Musical notation—particularly Western musical notation—is different from ordinary text in the way it is laid out, especially the representation of pitch and duration in Western musical notation. However, ordinary text commonly refers to the basic graphical elements that are used in musical notation, and it is primarily those symbols that are encoded in the Unicode Standard. Additional sets of symbols are encoded to support historical systems of musical notation.

Many symbols encoded in the Unicode Standard are intended to support legacy implementations and obsolescent practices, such as terminal emulation or other character mode user interfaces. Examples include box drawing components and control pictures.

Many of the symbols encoded in Unicode can be used as operators or given some other syntactical function in a formal language syntax. For more information, see Unicode Standard Annex #31, "Identifier and Pattern Syntax."

15.1 Currency Symbols

Currency symbols are intended to encode the customary symbolic signs used to indicate certain currencies in general text. These signs vary in shape and are often used for more than one currency. Not all currencies are represented by a special currency symbol; some use multiple-letter strings instead, such as "Sfr" for Swiss franc. Moreover, the abbreviations for currencies can vary by language. The Common Locale Data Registry (CLDR) provides further information; see *Section B.6, Other Unicode Online Resources*. Therefore, implementations that are concerned with the *exact* identity of a currency should not depend on an encoded currency sign character. Instead, they should follow standards such as the ISO 4217 three-letter currency codes, which are *specific* to currencies—for example, USD for U.S. dollar, CAD for Canadian dollar.

Unification. The Unicode Standard does not duplicate encodings where more than one currency is expressed with the same symbol. Many currency symbols are overstruck letters.

There are therefore many minor variants, such as the U+0024 DOLLAR SIGN $, with one or two vertical bars, or other graphical variation, as shown in *Figure 15-1*.

Figure 15-1. Alternative Glyphs for Dollar Sign

$ $

Claims that glyph variants of a certain currency symbol are used consistently to indicate a particular currency could not be substantiated upon further research. Therefore, the Unicode Standard considers these variants to be typographical and provides a single encoding for them. See ISO/IEC 10367, Annex B (informative), for an example of multiple renderings for U+00A3 POUND SIGN.

Fonts. Currency symbols are commonly designed to display at the same width as a digit (most often a European digit, U+0030..U+0039) to assist in alignment of monetary values in tabular displays. Like letters, they tend to follow the stylistic design features of particular fonts because they are used often and need to harmonize with body text. In particular, even though there may be more or less normative designs for the currency sign per se, as for the euro sign, type designers freely adapt such designs to make them fit the logic of the rest of their fonts. This partly explains why currency signs show more glyph variation than other types of symbols.

Currency Symbols: U+20A0–U+20CF

This block contains currency symbols that are not encoded in other blocks. Common currency symbols encoded in other blocks are listed in *Table 15-1*.

Table 15-1. Currency Symbols Encoded in Other Blocks

Currency	Unicode Code Point	
Dollar, milreis, escudo, peso	U+0024	DOLLAR SIGN
Cent	U+00A2	CENT SIGN
Pound and lira	U+00A3	POUND SIGN
General currency	U+00A4	CURRENCY SIGN
Yen or yuan	U+00A5	YEN SIGN
Dutch florin	U+0192	LATIN SMALL LETTER F WITH HOOK
Afghani	U+060B	AFGHANI SIGN
Rupee	U+09F2	BENGALI RUPEE MARK
Rupee	U+09F3	BENGALI RUPEE SIGN
Rupee	U+0AF1	GUJARATI RUPEE SIGN
Rupee	U+0BF9	TAMIL RUPEE SIGN
Baht	U+0E3F	THAI CURRENCY SYMBOL BAHT
Riel	U+17DB	KHMER CURRENCY SYMBOL RIEL
German mark (historic)	U+2133	SCRIPT CAPITAL M
Yuan, yen, won, HKD	U+5143	CJK UNIFIED IDEOGRAPH-5143
Yen	U+5186	CJK UNIFIED IDEOGRAPH-5186
Yuan	U+5706	CJK UNIFIED IDEOGRAPH-5706

Table 15-1. Currency Symbols Encoded in Other Blocks (Continued)

Yuan, yen, won, HKD, NTD	U+5713	CJK UNIFIED IDEOGRAPH-5713
Rial	U+FDFC	RIAL SIGN

Lira Sign. A separate currency sign U+20A4 LIRA SIGN is encoded for compatibility with the HP Roman-8 character set, which is still widely implemented in printers. In general, U+00A3 POUND SIGN should be used for both the various currencies known as pound (or punt) and the various currencies known as lira—for example, the former currency of Italy and the lira still in use in Turkey. Widespread implementation practice in Italian and Turkish systems has long made use of U+00A3 as the currency sign for the lira. As in the case of the dollar sign, the glyphic distinction between single- and double-bar versions of the sign is not indicative of a systematic difference in the currency.

Yen and Yuan. Like the dollar sign and the pound sign, U+00A5 YEN SIGN has been used as the currency sign for more than one currency. While there may be some preferences to use a double-bar glyph for the yen currency of Japan (JPY) and a single-bar glyph for the yuan (renminbi) currency of China (CNY), this distinction is not systematic in all font designs, and there is considerable overlap in usage. As listed in *Table 15-1*, there are also a number of CJK ideographs to represent the words *yen* (or *en*) and *yuan*, as well as the Korean word *won*, and these also tend to overlap in use as currency symbols. In the Unicode Standard, U+00A5 YEN SIGN is intended to be the character for the currency sign for both the yen and the yuan, with details of glyphic presentation left to font choice and local preferences.

Euro Sign. The single currency for member countries of the European Economic and Monetary Union is the euro (EUR). The euro character is encoded in the Unicode Standard as U+20AC EURO SIGN.

For additional forms of currency symbols, see Fullwidth Forms (U+FFE0..U+FFE6).

15.2 Letterlike Symbols

Letterlike Symbols: U+2100–U+214F

Letterlike symbols are symbols derived in some way from ordinary letters of an alphabetic script. This block includes symbols based on Latin, Greek, and Hebrew letters. Stylistic variations of single letters are used for semantics in mathematical notation. See "Mathematical Alphanumeric Symbols" in this section for the use of letterlike symbols in mathematical formulas. Some letterforms have given rise to specialized symbols, such as U+211E PRESCRIPTION TAKE.

Numero Sign. U+2116 NUMERO SIGN is provided both for Cyrillic use, where it looks like №, and for compatibility with Asian standards, where it looks like №. *Figure 15-2* illustrates a number of alternative glyphs for this sign. Instead of using a special symbol, French practice is to use an "N" or an "n", according to context, followed by a superscript small letter "o" (N^o or n^o; plural N^{os} or n^{os}). Legacy data encoded in ISO/IEC 8859-1 (Latin-1) or other 8-bit character sets may also have represented the *numero sign* by a sequence of "N" followed by the *degree sign* (U+00B0 DEGREE SIGN). Implementations interworking with legacy data should be aware of such alternative representations for the *numero sign* when converting data.

Figure 15-2. Alternative Glyphs for Numero Sign

№ № No. №

Unit Symbols. Several letterlike symbols are used to indicate units. In most cases, however, such as for SI units (Système International), the use of regular letters or other symbols is preferred. U+2113 SCRIPT SMALL L is commonly used as a non-SI symbol for the *liter*. Official SI usage prefers the regular *lowercase letter l*.

Three letterlike symbols have been given canonical equivalence to regular letters: U+2126 OHM SIGN, U+212A KELVIN SIGN, and U+212B ANGSTROM SIGN. In all three instances, the regular letter should be used. If text is normalized according to Unicode Standard Annex #15, "Unicode Normalization Forms," these three characters will be replaced by their regular equivalents.

In normal use, it is better to represent degrees Celsius "°C" with a sequence of U+00B0 DEGREE SIGN + U+0043 LATIN CAPITAL LETTER C, rather than U+2103 DEGREE CELSIUS. For searching, treat these two sequences as identical. Similarly, the sequence U+00B0 DEGREE SIGN + U+0046 LATIN CAPITAL LETTER F is preferred over U+2109 DEGREE FAHRENHEIT, and those two sequences should be treated as identical for searching.

Compatibility. Some symbols are composites of several letters. Many of these composite symbols are encoded for compatibility with Asian and other legacy encodings. (See also "CJK Compatibility Ideographs" in *Section 12.1, Han.*) The use of these composite symbols is discouraged where their presence is not required by compatibility. For example, in normal use, the symbols U+2121 TEL TELEPHONE SIGN and U+213B FAX FACSIMILE SIGN are simply spelled out.

In the context of East Asian typography, many letterlike symbols, and in particular composites, form part of a collection of compatibility symbols, the larger part of which is located in the CJK Compatibility block (see *Section 15.9, Enclosed and Square*). When used in this way, these symbols are rendered as "wide" characters occupying a full cell. They remain upright in vertical layout, contrary to the rotated rendering of their regular letter equivalents. See Unicode Standard Annex #11, "East Asian Width," for more information.

Where the letterlike symbols have alphabetic equivalents, they collate in alphabetic sequence; otherwise, they should be treated as neutral symbols. The letterlike symbols may have different directional properties than normal letters. For example, the four transfinite cardinal symbols (U+2135..U+2138) are used in ordinary mathematical text and do not share the strong right-to-left directionality of the Hebrew letters from which they are derived.

Styles. The letterlike symbols include some of the few instances in which the Unicode Standard encodes stylistic variants of letters as distinct characters. For example, there are instances of blackletter (*Fraktur*), double-struck, italic, and script styles for certain Latin letters used as mathematical symbols. The choice of these stylistic variants for encoding reflects their common use as distinct symbols. They form part of the larger set of mathematical alphanumeric symbols. For the complete set and more information on its use, see "Mathematical Alphanumeric Symbols" in this section. These symbols should not be used in ordinary, nonscientific texts.

Despite its name, U+2118 SCRIPT CAPITAL P is neither script nor capital—it is uniquely the Weierstrass elliptic function symbol derived from a calligraphic *lowercase* p. U+2113 SCRIPT SMALL L is derived from a special *italic* form of the *lowercase letter l* and, when it occurs in mathematical notation, is known as the symbol *ell*. Use U+1D4C1 MATHEMATICAL SCRIPT SMALL L as the *lowercase script l* for mathematical notation.

Standards. The Unicode Standard encodes letterlike symbols from many different national standards and corporate collections.

Mathematical Alphanumeric Symbols: U+1D400–U+1D7FF

The Mathematical Alphanumeric Symbols block contains a large extension of letterlike symbols used in mathematical notation, typically for variables. The characters in this block are intended for use only in mathematical or technical notation; they are not intended for use in nontechnical text. When used with markup languages—for example, with Mathematical Markup Language (MathML)—the characters are expected to be used directly, instead of indirectly via entity references or by composing them from base letters and style markup.

Words Used as Variables. In some specialties, whole words are used as variables, not just single letters. For these cases, style markup is preferred because in ordinary mathematical notation the juxtaposition of variables generally implies multiplication, not word formation as in ordinary text. Markup not only provides the necessary scoping in these cases, but also allows the use of a more extended alphabet.

Mathematical Alphabets

Basic Set of Alphanumeric Characters. Mathematical notation uses a basic set of mathematical alphanumeric characters, which consists of the following:

- The set of basic Latin digits (0–9) (U+0030..U+0039)
- The set of basic uppercase and lowercase Latin letters (a– z, A–Z)
- The uppercase Greek letters Α–Ω (U+0391..U+03A9), plus the nabla ∇ (U+2207) and the variant of theta ϴ given by U+03F4
- The lowercase Greek letters α–ω (U+03B1..U+03C9), plus the partial differential sign ∂ (U+2202), and the six glyph variants ϵ, ϑ, ϰ, ϕ, ϱ, and ϖ, given by U+03F5, U+03D1, U+03F0, U+03D5, U+03F1, and U+03D6, respectively

Only unaccented forms of the letters are used for mathematical notation, because general accents such as the acute accent would interfere with common mathematical diacritics. Examples of common mathematical diacritics that can interfere with general accents are the circumflex, macron, or the single or double dot above, the latter two of which are used in physics to denote derivatives with respect to the time variable. Mathematical symbols with diacritics are always represented by combining character sequences.

For some characters in the basic set of Greek characters, two variants of the same character are included. This is because they can appear in the same mathematical document with different meanings, even though they would have the same meaning in Greek text. (See "Variant Letterforms" in *Section 7.2, Greek.*)

Additional Characters. In addition to this basic set, mathematical notation uses the uppercase and lowercase digamma, in regular (U+03DC and U+03DD) and bold (U+1D7CA and U+1D7CB), and the four Hebrew-derived characters (U+2135..U+2138). Occasional uses of other alphabetic and numeric characters are known. Examples include U+0428 CYRILLIC CAPITAL LETTER SHA, U+306E HIRAGANA LETTER NO, and Eastern Arabic-Indic digits (U+06F0..U+06F9). However, these characters are used only in their basic forms, rather than in multiple mathematical styles.

Dotless Characters. In the Unicode Standard, the characters "i" and "j", including their variations in the mathematical alphabets, have the Soft_Dotted property. Any conformant renderer will remove the dot when the character is followed by a nonspacing combining mark above. Therefore, using an individual mathematical italic *i* or *j* with math accents would result in the intended display. However, in mathematical equations an entire subexpression can be placed underneath a math accent—for example, when a "wide hat" is placed on top of *i+j*, as shown in *Figure 15-3.*

Figure 15-3. Wide Mathematical Accents

$$\widehat{\imath+\jmath} = \hat{\imath} + \hat{\jmath}$$

In such a situation, a renderer can no longer rely simply on the presence of an adjacent combining character to substitute for the un-dotted glyph, and whether the dots should be removed in such a situation is no longer predictable. Authors differ in whether they expect the dotted or dotless forms in that case.

In some documents *mathematical italic dotless* i or *j* is used explicitly without any combining marks, or even in contrast to the dotted versions. Therefore, the Unicode Standard provides the explicitly dotless characters U+1D6A4 MATHEMATICAL ITALIC SMALL DOTLESS I and U+1D6A5 MATHEMATICAL ITALIC SMALL DOTLESS J. These two characters map to the ISOAMSO entities *imath* and *jmath* or the TEX macros *\imath* and *\jmath*. These entities are, by default, always italic. The appearance of these two characters in the code charts is similar to the shapes of the entities documented in the ISO 9573-13 entity sets and used by TEX. The mathematical dotless characters do not have case mappings.

Semantic Distinctions. Mathematical notation requires a number of Latin and Greek alphabets that initially appear to be mere font variations of one another. The letter H can appear as plain or upright (H), bold (**H**), italic (*H*), as well as script, Fraktur, and other styles. However, in any given document, these characters have distinct, and usually unrelated, mathematical semantics. For example, a normal H represents a different variable from a bold **H**, and so on. If these attributes are dropped in plain text, the distinctions are lost and the meaning of the text is altered. Without the distinctions, the well-known Hamiltonian formula turns into the *integral* equation in the variable H as shown in *Figure 15-4*.

Figure 15-4. Style Variants and Semantic Distinctions in Mathematics

Hamiltonian formula: $\mathcal{H} = \int d\tau(\epsilon E^2 + \mu H^2)$

Integral equation: $\mathrm{H} = \int \mathrm{d}\tau(\varepsilon \mathrm{E}^2 + \mu \mathrm{H}^2)$

Mathematicians will object that a properly formatted integral equation requires all the letters in this example (except for the "d") to be in italics. However, because the distinction between $\mathcal{H}$ and *H* has been lost, they would recognize it as a fallback representation of an integral equation, and not as a fallback representation of the Hamiltonian. By encoding a separate set of alphabets, it is possible to preserve such distinctions in plain text.

Mathematical Alphabets. The alphanumeric symbols encountered in mathematics and encoded in the Unicode Standard are given in *Table 15-2*.

Table 15-2. Mathematical Alphanumeric Symbols

Math Style	Characters from Basic Set	Location
plain (upright, serifed)	Latin, Greek, and digits	BMP
bold	Latin, Greek, and digits	Plane 1
italic	Latin and Greek	Plane 1
bold italic	Latin and Greek	Plane 1
script (calligraphic)	Latin	Plane 1
bold script (calligraphic)	Latin	Plane 1
Fraktur	Latin	Plane 1
bold Fraktur	Latin	Plane 1
double-struck	Latin and digits	Plane 1
sans-serif	Latin and digits	Plane 1
sans-serif bold	Latin, Greek, and digits	Plane 1
sans-serif italic	Latin	Plane 1
sans-serif bold italic	Latin and Greek	Plane 1
monospace	Latin and digits	Plane 1

The plain letters have been unified with the existing characters in the Basic Latin and Greek blocks. There are 24 double-struck, italic, Fraktur, and script characters that already exist in the Letterlike Symbols block (U+2100..U+214F). These are explicitly unified with the characters in this block, and corresponding holes have been left in the mathematical alphabets.

The alphabets in this block encode only semantic distinction, but not which specific font will be used to supply the actual plain, script, Fraktur, double-struck, sans-serif, or monospace glyphs. Especially the script and double-struck styles can show considerable variation across fonts. Characters from the Mathematical Alphanumeric Symbols block are not to be used for nonmathematical styled text.

Compatibility Decompositions. All mathematical alphanumeric symbols have compatibility decompositions to the base Latin and Greek letters. This does not imply that the use of these characters is discouraged for mathematical use. Folding away such distinctions by applying the compatibility mappings is usually not desirable, however, as it loses the semantic distinctions for which these characters were encoded. See Unicode Standard Annex #15, "Unicode Normalization Forms."

Fonts Used for Mathematical Alphabets

Mathematicians place strict requirements on the *specific* fonts used to represent mathematical variables. Readers of a mathematical text need to be able to distinguish single-letter variables from each other, even when they do not appear in close proximity. They must be able to recognize the letter itself, whether it is part of the text or is a mathematical variable, and lastly which mathematical alphabet it is from.

Fraktur. The blackletter style is often referred to as *Fraktur* or *Gothic* in various sources. Technically, Fraktur and Gothic typefaces are distinct designs from blackletter, but any of several font styles similar in appearance to the forms shown in the charts can be used. Note that in East Asian typography, the term *Gothic* is commonly used to indicate a sans-serif type style.

Math Italics. Mathematical variables are most commonly set in a form of italics, but not all italic fonts can be used successfully. For example, a math italic font should avoid a "tail" on the lowercase *italic letter z* because it clashes with subscripts. In common text fonts, the *italic letter v* and *Greek letter nu* are not very distinct. A rounded *italic letter v* is therefore preferred in a mathematical font. There are other characters that sometimes have similar shapes and require special attention to avoid ambiguity. Examples are shown in *Figure 15-5.*

Hard-to-Distinguish Letters. Not all sans-serif fonts allow an easy distinction between *lowercase l* and *uppercase I*, and not all monospaced (monowidth) fonts allow a distinction between the *letter l* and the *digit one.* Such fonts are not usable for mathematics. In Fraktur, the letters ℑ and 𝔍, in particular, must be made distinguishable. Overburdened blackletter forms are inappropriate for mathematical notation. Similarly, the *digit zero* must be distinct from the *uppercase letter O* for all mathematical alphanumeric sets. Some characters are so similar that even mathematical fonts do not attempt to provide distinct glyphs for

Figure 15-5. Easily Confused Shapes for Mathematical Glyphs

italic a	a	α	alpha
italic v (pointed)	v	ν	nu
italic v (rounded)	υ	υ	upsilon
script X	$\mathcal{X}$	χ	chi
plain Y	Y	Υ	Upsilon

them. Their use is normally avoided in mathematical notation unless no confusion is possible in a given context—for example, *uppercase A* and *uppercase Alpha.*

Font Support for Combining Diacritics. Mathematical equations require that characters be combined with diacritics (dots, tilde, circumflex, or arrows above are common), as well as followed or preceded by superscripted or subscripted letters or numbers. This requirement leads to designs for *italic* styles that are less inclined and *script* styles that have smaller overhangs and less slant than equivalent styles commonly used for text such as wedding invitations.

Type Style for Script Characters. In some instances, a deliberate unification with a non-mathematical symbol has been undertaken; for example, U+2133 is unified with the pre-1949 symbol for the German currency unit *Mark*. This unification restricts the range of glyphs that can be used for this character in the charts. Therefore the font used for the representative glyphs in the code charts is based on a simplified "English Script" style, as per recommendation by the American Mathematical Society. For consistency, other script characters in the Letterlike Symbols block are now shown in the same type style.

Double-Struck Characters. The double-struck glyphs shown in earlier editions of the standard attempted to match the design used for all the other Latin characters in the standard, which is based on Times. The current set of fonts was prepared in consultation with the American Mathematical Society and leading mathematical publishers; it shows much simpler forms that are derived from the forms written on a blackboard. However, both serifed and non-serifed forms can be used in mathematical texts, and inline fonts are found in works published by certain publishers.

15.3 Number Forms

Number Forms: U+2150–U+218F

Many number form characters are composite or duplicate forms encoded solely for compatibility with existing standards. The use of these composite symbols is discouraged where their presence is not required by compatibility.

Fractions. The Number Forms block contains a series of vulgar fraction characters, encoded for compatibility with legacy character encoding standards. These characters are intended to represent both of the common forms of vulgar fractions: forms with a right-slanted division slash, such as ¼, as shown in the code charts, and forms with a horizontal division line, such as $\frac{1}{4}$, which are considered to be alternative glyphs for the same fractions, as shown in *Figure 15-6.* A few other vulgar fraction characters are located in the Latin-1 block in the range U+00BC..U+00BE.

Figure 15-6. Alternate Forms of Vulgar Fractions

¼ $\frac{1}{4}$

The vulgar fraction characters are given compatibility decompositions using U+2044 "⁄" FRACTION SLASH. Use of the *fraction slash* is the more generic way to represent fractions in text; it can be used to construct fractional number forms that are not included in the collections of vulgar fraction characters. For more information on the *fraction slash*, see "Other Punctuation" in *Section 6.2, General Punctuation.*

Roman Numerals. For most purposes, it is preferable to compose the Roman numerals from sequences of the appropriate Latin letters. However, the uppercase and lowercase variants of the Roman numerals through 12, plus L, C, D, and M, have been encoded for compatibility with East Asian standards. Unlike sequences of Latin letters, these symbols remain upright in vertical layout. Additionally, in certain locales, compact date formats use Roman numerals for the month, but may expect the use of a single character.

In identifiers, the use of Roman numeral symbols—particularly those based on a single letter of the Latin alphabet—can lead to spoofing. For more information, see Unicode Technical Report #36, "Unicode Security Considerations."

U+2180 ROMAN NUMERAL ONE THOUSAND C D and U+216F ROMAN NUMERAL ONE THOUSAND can be considered to be glyphic variants of the same Roman numeral, but are distinguished because they are not generally interchangeable and because U+2180 cannot be considered to be a compatibility equivalent to the Latin letter M. U+2181 ROMAN NUMERAL FIVE THOUSAND and U+2182 ROMAN NUMERAL TEN THOUSAND are distinct characters used in Roman numerals; they do not have compatibility decompositions in the Unicode Standard. U+2183 ROMAN NUMERAL REVERSED ONE HUNDRED is a form used in combinations with C and/or I to form large numbers—some of which vary with single character number forms such as D, M, U+2181, or others. U+2183 is also used for the Claudian letter *antisigma.*

CJK Number Forms

Chinese Counting-Rod Numerals. Counting-rod numerals were used in pre-modern East Asian mathematical texts in conjunction with counting rods used to represent and manipulate numbers. The counting rods were a set of small sticks, several centimeters long that were arranged in patterns on a gridded counting board. Counting rods and the counting board provided a flexible system for mathematicians to manipulate numbers, allowing for considerable sophistication in mathematics.

The specifics of the patterns used to represent various numbers using counting rods varied, but there are two main constants: Two sets of numbers were used for alternate columns; one set was used for the ones, hundreds, and ten-thousands columns in the grid, while the other set was used for the tens and thousands. The shapes used for the counting-rod numerals in the Unicode Standard follow conventions from the Song dynasty in China, when traditional Chinese mathematics had reached its peak. Fragmentary material from many early Han dynasty texts shows different orientation conventions for the numerals, with horizontal and vertical marks swapped for the digits and tens places.

Zero was indicated by a blank square on the counting board and was either avoided in written texts or was represented with U+3007 IDEOGRAPHIC NUMBER ZERO. (Historically, U+3007 IDEOGRAPHIC NUMBER ZERO originated as a dot; as time passed, it increased in size until it became the same size as an ideograph. The actual size of U+3007 IDEOGRAPHIC NUMBER ZERO in mathematical texts varies, but this variation should be considered a font difference.) Written texts could also take advantage of the alternating shapes for the numerals to avoid having to explicitly represent zero. Thus 6,708 can be distinguished from 678, because the former would be 𝍮𝍦𝍧, whereas the latter would be 𝍥𝍯𝍧.

Negative numbers were originally indicated on the counting board by using rods of a different color. In written texts, a diagonal slash from lower right to upper left is overlaid upon the rightmost digit. On occasion, the slash might not be actually overlaid. U+20E5 COMBINING REVERSE SOLIDUS OVERLAY should be used for this negative sign.

The predominant use of counting-rod numerals in texts was as part of diagrams of counting boards. They are, however, occasionally used in other contexts, and they may even occur within the body of modern texts.

Suzhou-Style Numerals. The Suzhou-style numerals (Mandarin *su1zhou1ma3zi*) are CJK ideographic number forms encoded in the CJK Symbols and Punctuation block in the ranges U+3021..U+3029 and U+3038..U+303A.

The Suzhou-style numerals are modified forms of CJK ideographic numerals that are used by shopkeepers in China to mark prices. They are also known as "commercial forms," "shop units," or "grass numbers." They are encoded for compatibility with the CNS 11643-1992 and Big Five standards. The forms for ten, twenty, and thirty, encoded at U+3038..U+303A, are also encoded as CJK unified ideographs: U+5341, U+5344, and U+5345, respectively. (For twenty, see also U+5EFE and U+5EFF.)

These commercial forms of Chinese numerals should be distinguished from the use of other CJK unified ideographs as accounting numbers to deter fraud. See *Table 4-9* in *Section 4.6, Numeric Value—Normative*, for a list of ideographs used as accounting numbers.

Why are the Suzhou numbers called Hangzhou numerals in the Unicode names? No one has been able to trace this back. Hangzhou is a district in China that is near the Suzhou district, but the name "Hangzhou" does not occur in other sources that discuss these number forms.

Superscripts and Subscripts: U+2070–U+209F

In general, the Unicode Standard does not attempt to describe the positioning of a character above or below the baseline in typographical layout. Therefore, the preferred means to encode superscripted letters or digits, such as "1st" or "$DC00_{16}$", is by style or markup in rich text. However, in some instances superscript or subscript letters are used as part of the plain text content of specialized phonetic alphabets, such as the Uralic Phonetic Alphabet. These superscript and subscript letters are mostly from the Latin or Greek scripts. These characters are encoded in other character blocks, along with other modifier letters or phonetic letters. In addition, superscript digits are used to indicate tone in transliteration of many languages. The use of *superscript two* and *superscript three* is common legacy practice when referring to units of area and volume in general texts.

A certain number of additional superscript and subscript characters are needed for round-trip conversions to other standards and legacy code pages. Most such characters are encoded in this block and are considered compatibility characters.

Parsing of Superscript and Subscript Digits. In the Unicode Character Database, superscript and subscript digits have not been given the General_Category property value Decimal_Number (gc=Nd), so as to prevent expressions like 2^3 from being interpreted like 23 by simplistic parsers. This should not be construed as preventing more sophisticated numeric parsers, such as general mathematical expression parsers, from correctly identifying these compatibility superscript and subscript characters as digits and interpreting them appropriately.

Standards. Many of the characters in the Superscripts and Subscripts block are from character sets registered in the ISO International Register of Coded Character Sets to be Used With Escape Sequences, under the registration standard ISO/IEC 2375, for use with ISO/IEC 2022. Two MARC 21 character sets used by libraries include the digits, plus signs, minus signs, and parentheses.

Superscripts and Subscripts in Other Blocks. The superscript digits one, two, and three are coded in the Latin-1 Supplement block to provide code point compatibility with ISO/IEC 8859-1. For a discussion of U+00AA FEMININE ORDINAL INDICATOR and U+00BA MASCULINE ORDINAL INDICATOR, see "Letters of the Latin-1 Supplement" in *Section 7.1, Latin*. U+2120 SERVICE MARK and U+2122 TRADE MARK SIGN are commonly used symbols that are encoded in the Letterlike Symbols block (U+2100..U+214F); they consist of sequences of two superscripted letters each.

For phonetic usage, there are a small number of superscript letters located in the Spacing Modifier Letters block (U+02B0..U+02FF) and a large number of superscript and subscript letters in the Phonetic Extensions block (U+1D00..U+1D7F) and in the Phonetic Extensions Supplement block (U+1D80..U+1DBF). The superscripted letters do not contain the word "superscript" in their character names, but are simply called modifier letters. Finally, a small set of superscripted CJK ideographs, used for the Japanese system of syntactic markup of Classical Chinese text for reading, is located in the Kanbun block (U+3190..U+319F).

15.4 Mathematical Symbols

The Unicode Standard provides a large set of standard mathematical characters to support publications of scientific, technical, and mathematical texts on and off the Web. In addition to the mathematical symbols and arrows contained in the blocks described in this section, mathematical operators are found in the Basic Latin (ASCII) and Latin-1 Supplement blocks. A few of the symbols from the Miscellaneous Technical, Miscellaneous Symbols, and Dingbats blocks, as well as characters from General Punctuation, are also used in mathematical notation. For Latin and Greek letters in special font styles that are used as mathematical variables, such as U+210B ℋ SCRIPT CAPITAL H, as well as the Hebrew letter *alef* used as the first transfinite cardinal symbol encoded by U+2135 ℵ ALEF SYMBOL, see "Letterlike Symbols" and "Mathematical Alphanumeric Symbols" in *Section 15.2, Letterlike Symbols.*

The repertoire of mathematical symbols in Unicode enables the display of virtually all standard mathematical symbols. Nevertheless, no collection of mathematical symbols can ever be considered complete; mathematicians and other scientists are continually inventing new mathematical symbols. More symbols will be added as they become widely accepted in the scientific communities.

Semantics. The same mathematical symbol may have different meanings in different subdisciplines or different contexts. The Unicode Standard encodes only a single character for a single symbolic form. For example, the "+" symbol normally denotes addition in a mathematical context, but it might refer to concatenation in a computer science context dealing with strings, indicate incrementation, or have any number of other functions in given contexts. It is up to the application to distinguish such meanings according to the appropriate context. Where information is available about the usage (or usages) of particular symbols, it has been indicated in the character annotations in *Chapter 17, Code Charts.*

Mathematical Property. The mathematical (*math*) property is an informative property of characters that are used as operators in mathematical formulas. The mathematical property may be useful in identifying characters commonly used in mathematical text and formulas. However, a number of these characters have multiple usages and may occur with nonmathematical semantics. For example, U+002D HYPHEN-MINUS may also be used as a hyphen—and not as a mathematical minus sign. Other characters, including some alphabetic, numeric, punctuation, spaces, arrows, and geometric shapes, are used in mathematical expressions as well, but are even more dependent on the context for their identification. A list of characters with the mathematical property is provided in the Unicode Character Database.

For a classification of mathematical characters by typographical behavior and mapping to ISO 9573-13 entity sets, see Unicode Technical Report #25, "Unicode Support for Mathematics."

Mathematical Operators: U+2200–U+22FF

The Mathematical Operators block includes character encodings for operators, relations, geometric symbols, and a few other symbols with special usages confined largely to mathematical contexts.

Standards. Many national standards' mathematical operators are covered by the characters encoded in this block. These standards include such special collections as ANSI Y10.20, ISO 6862, ISO 8879, and portions of the collection of the American Mathematical Society, as well as the original repertoire of TEX.

Encoding Principles. Mathematical operators often have more than one meaning. Therefore the encoding of this block is intentionally rather shape-based, with numerous instances in which several semantic values can be attributed to the same Unicode code point. For example, U+2218 ∘ RING OPERATOR may be the equivalent of *white small circle* or *composite function* or *apl jot*. The Unicode Standard does not attempt to distinguish all possible semantic values that may be applied to mathematical operators or relation symbols.

The Unicode Standard does include many characters that appear to be quite similar to one another, but that may well convey different meanings in a given context. Conversely, mathematical operators, and especially relation symbols, may appear in various standards, handbooks, and fonts with a large number of purely graphical variants. Where variants were recognizable as such from the sources, they were not encoded separately. For relation symbols, the choice of a vertical or forward-slanting stroke typically seems to be an aesthetic one, but both slants might appear in a given context. However, a back-slanted stroke almost always has a distinct meaning compared to the forward-slanted stroke. See *Section 16.4, Variation Selectors*, for more information on some particular variants.

Unifications. Mathematical operators such as *implies* ⇒ and *if and only if* ↔ have been unified with the corresponding arrows (U+21D2 RIGHTWARDS DOUBLE ARROW and U+2194 LEFT RIGHT ARROW, respectively) in the Arrows block.

The operator U+2208 ELEMENT OF is occasionally rendered with a taller shape than shown in the code charts. Mathematical handbooks and standards consulted treat these characters as variants of the same glyph. U+220A SMALL ELEMENT OF is a distinctively small version of the *element of* that originates in mathematical pi fonts.

The operators U+226B MUCH GREATER-THAN and U+226A MUCH LESS-THAN are sometimes rendered in a nested shape. The nested shapes are encoded separately as U+2AA2 DOUBLE NESTED GREATER-THAN and U+2AA1 DOUBLE NESTED LESS-THAN.

A large class of unifications applies to variants of relation symbols involving negation. Variants involving vertical or slanted *negation slashes* and *negation slashes* of different lengths are not separately encoded. For example, U+2288 NEITHER A SUBSET OF NOR EQUAL TO is the archetype for several different glyph variants noted in various collections.

In two instances in this block, essentially stylistic variants are separately encoded: U+2265 GREATER-THAN OR EQUAL TO is distinguished from U+2267 GREATER-THAN OVER EQUAL TO; the same distinction applies to U+2264 LESS-THAN OR EQUAL TO and U+2266 LESS-

THAN OVER EQUAL TO. Further instances of the encoding of such stylistic variants can be found in the supplemental blocks of mathematical operators. The primary reason for such duplication is for compatibility with existing standards.

Greek-Derived Symbols. Several mathematical operators derived from Greek characters have been given separate encodings because they are used differently from the corresponding letters. These operators may occasionally occur in context with Greek-letter variables. They include U+2206 ∆ INCREMENT, U+220F ∏ N-ARY PRODUCT, and U+2211 ∑ N-ARY SUMMATION. The latter two are large operators that take limits.

Other duplicated Greek characters are those for U+00B5 µ MICRO SIGN in the Latin-1 Supplement block, U+2126 Ω OHM SIGN in Letterlike Symbols, and several characters among the APL functional symbols in the Miscellaneous Technical block. Most other Greek characters with special mathematical semantics are found in the Greek block because duplicates were not required for compatibility. Additional sets of mathematical-style Greek alphabets are found in the Mathematical Alphanumeric Symbols block.

N-ary Operators. N-ary operators are distinguished from binary operators by their larger size and by the fact that in mathematical layout, they take limit expressions.

Invisible Operators. In mathematics, some operators or punctuation are often implied but not displayed. For a set of invisible operators that can be used to mark these implied operators in the text, see *Section 15.5, Invisible Mathematical Operators.*

Minus Sign. U+2212 "−" MINUS SIGN is a mathematical operator, to be distinguished from the ASCII-derived U+002D "-" HYPHEN-MINUS, which may look the same as a minus sign or be shorter in length. (For a complete list of dashes in the Unicode Standard, see *Table* 6-3.) U+22EE..U+22F1 are a set of ellipses used in matrix notation. U+2052 "⁒" COMMERCIAL MINUS SIGN is a specialized form of the minus sign. Its use is described in *Section 6.2, General Punctuation.*

Delimiters. Many mathematical delimiters are unified with punctuation characters. See *Section 6.2, General Punctuation*, for more information. Some of the set of ornamental Brackets in the range U+2768..U+2775 are also used as mathematical delimiters. See *Section 15.8, Miscellaneous Symbols and Dingbats.* See also *Section 15.6, Technical Symbols*, for specialized characters used for large vertical or horizontal delimiters.

Bidirectional Layout. In a bidirectional context, with the exception of arrows, the glyphs for mathematical operators and delimiters are adjusted as described in Unicode Standard Annex #9, "The Bidirectional Algorithm." See *Section 4.7, Bidi Mirrored—Normative*, and "Semantics of Paired Punctuation" in *Section 6.2, General Punctuation.*

Other Elements of Mathematical Notation. In addition to the symbols in these blocks, mathematical and scientific notation makes frequent use of arrows, punctuation characters, letterlike symbols, geometrical shapes, and miscellaneous and technical symbols.

For an extensive discussion of mathematical alphanumeric symbols, see *Section 15.2, Letterlike Symbols.* For additional information on all the mathematical operators and other symbols, see Unicode Technical Report #25, "Unicode Support for Mathematics."

Supplements to Mathematical Symbols and Arrows

The Unicode Standard defines a number of additional blocks to supplement the repertoire of mathematical operators and arrows. These additions are intended to extend the Unicode repertoire sufficiently to cover the needs of such applications as MathML, modern mathematical formula editing and presentation software, and symbolic algebra systems.

Standards. MathML, an XML application, is intended to support the full legacy collection of the ISO mathematical entity sets. Accordingly, the repertoire of mathematical symbols for the Unicode Standard has been supplemented by the full list of mathematical entity sets in ISO TR 9573-13, *Public entity sets for mathematics and science*. An additional repertoire was provided from the amalgamated collection of the STIX Project (Scientific and Technical Information Exchange). That collection includes, but is not limited to, symbols gleaned from mathematical publications by experts of the American Mathematical Society and symbol sets provided by Elsevier Publishing and by the American Physical Society.

Supplemental Mathematical Operators: U+2A00–U+2AFF

The Supplemental Mathematical Operators block contains many additional symbols to supplement the collection of mathematical operators. In addition, the Miscellaneous Symbols and Arrows block (U+2B00..U+2BFF) has been set aside to encode additional mathematical symbols, arrows, and geometric shapes.

Miscellaneous Mathematical Symbols-A: U+27C0–U+27EF

The Miscellaneous Mathematical Symbols-A block contains symbols that are used mostly as operators or delimiters in mathematical notation.

Mathematical Brackets. The mathematical white square brackets, angle brackets, and double angle brackets encoded at U+27E6..U+27EB are intended for ordinary mathematical use of these particular bracket types. They are unambiguously narrow, for use in mathematical and scientific notation, and should be distinguished from the corresponding wide forms of white square brackets, angle brackets, and double angle brackets used in CJK typography. (See the discussion of the CJK Symbols and Punctuation block in *Section 6.2, General Punctuation*.) Note especially that the "bra" and "ket" angle brackets (U+2329 LEFT-POINTING ANGLE BRACKET and U+232A RIGHT-POINTING ANGLE BRACKET, respectively) are now deprecated for use with mathematics because of their canonical equivalence to CJK angle brackets, which is likely to result in unintended spacing problems if used in mathematical formulae.

Miscellaneous Mathematical Symbols-B: U+2980–U+29FF

The Miscellaneous Mathematical Symbols-B block contains miscellaneous symbols used for mathematical notation, including fences and other delimiters. Some of the symbols in this block may also be used as operators in some contexts.

Wiggly Fence. U+29D8 LEFT WIGGLY FENCE has a superficial similarity to U+FE34 PRESENTATION FORM FOR VERTICAL WAVY LOW LINE. The latter is a wiggly sidebar character, intended for legacy support as a style of underlining character in a vertical text layout context; it has a compatibility mapping to U+005F LOW LINE. This represents a very different usage from the standard use of fence characters in mathematical notation.

Arrows: U+2190–U+21FF

Arrows are used for a variety of purposes: to imply directional relation, to show logical derivation or implication, and to represent the cursor control keys.

Accordingly, the Unicode Standard includes a fairly extensive set of generic arrow shapes, especially those for which there are established usages with well-defined semantics. It does not attempt to encode every possible stylistic variant of arrows separately, especially where their use is mainly decorative. For most arrow variants, the Unicode Standard provides encodings in the two horizontal directions, often in the four cardinal directions. For the single and double arrows, the Unicode Standard provides encodings in eight directions.

Bidirectional Layout. In bidirectional layout, arrows are not automatically mirrored, because the direction of the arrow could be relative to the text direction or relative to an absolute direction. Therefore, if text is copied from a left-to-right to a right-to-left context, or vice versa, the character code for the desired arrow direction in the new context must be used. For example, it might be necessary to change U+21D2 RIGHTWARDS DOUBLE ARROW to U+21D0 LEFTWARDS DOUBLE ARROW to maintain the semantics of "implies" in a right-to-left context. For more information on bidirectional layout, see Unicode Standard Annex #9, "The Bidirectional Algorithm."

Standards. The Unicode Standard encodes arrows from many different international and national standards as well as corporate collections.

Unifications. Arrows expressing mathematical relations have been encoded in the Arrows block as well as in the supplemental arrows blocks. An example is U+21D2 ⇒ RIGHTWARDS DOUBLE ARROW, which may be used to denote *implies*. Where available, such usage information is indicated in the annotations to individual characters in *Chapter 17, Code Charts*. However, because the arrows have such a wide variety of applications, there may be several semantic values for the same Unicode character value.

Supplemental Arrows

The Supplemental Arrows-A (U+27F0..U+27FF), Supplemental Arrows-B (U+2900..U+297F), and Miscellaneous Symbols and Arrows (U+2B00..U+2BFF) blocks contain a large repertoire of arrows to supplement the main set in the Arrows block.

Long Arrows. The long arrows encoded in the range U+27F5..U+27FF map to standard SGML entity sets supported by MathML. Long arrows represent distinct semantics from their short counterparts, rather than mere stylistic glyph differences. For example, the shorter forms of arrows are often used in connection with limits, whereas the longer ones are associated with mappings. The use of the long arrows is so common that they were assigned entity names in the ISOAMSA entity set, one of the suite of mathematical symbol entity sets covered by the Unicode Standard.

Standardized Variants of Mathematical Symbols

These mathematical variants are all produced with the addition of U+FE00 VARIATION SELECTOR-1 (VS1) to mathematical operator base characters. The valid combinations are listed in the file StandardizedVariants.txt in the Unicode Character Database. All combinations not listed there are unspecified and are reserved for future standardization; no conformant process may interpret them as standardized variants.

Change in Representative Glyphs for U+2278 and U+2279. In Version 3.2 of the Unicode Standard, the representative glyphs for U+2278 NEITHER LESS-THAN NOR GREATER-THAN and U+2279 NEITHER GREATER-THAN NOR LESS-THAN were changed from using a vertical cancellation to using a slanted cancellation. This change was made to match the longstanding canonical decompositions for these characters, which use U+0338 COMBINING LONG SOLIDUS OVERLAY. The symmetric forms using the vertical stroke continue to be acceptable glyph variants. Using U+2278 or U+2279 with VS1 will request these variants explicitly, as will using U+2276 LESS-THAN OR GREATER-THAN or U+2277 GREATER-THAN OR LESS-THAN with U+20D2 COMBINING LONG VERTICAL LINE OVERLAY. Unless fonts are created with the intention to add support for both forms (via VS1 for the upright forms), there is no need to revise the glyphs in existing fonts; the glyphic range implied by using the base character code alone encompasses both shapes. For more information, see *Section 16.4, Variation Selectors.*

15.5 Invisible Mathematical Operators

In mathematics, some operators and punctuation are often implied but not displayed. The General Punctuation block contains several special format control characters known as *invisible operators*, which can be used to make such operators explicit for use in machine interpretation of mathematical expressions. Use of invisible operators is optional and is intended for interchange with math-aware programs.

A more complete discussion of mathematical notation can be found in Unicode Technical Report #25, "Unicode Support for Mathematics."

Invisible Separator. U+2063 INVISIBLE SEPARATOR (also known as *invisible comma*) is intended for use in index expressions and other mathematical notation where two adjacent variables form a list and are not implicitly multiplied. In mathematical notation, commas are not always explicitly present, but they need to be indicated for symbolic calculation software to help it disambiguate a sequence from a multiplication. For example, the double $_{ij}$ subscript in the variable a_{ij} means $a_{i,\,j}$—that is, the *i* and *j* are separate indices and not a single variable with the name *ij* or even the product of *i* and *j*. To represent the implied list separation in the subscript $_{ij}$, one can insert a nondisplaying *invisible separator* between the *i* and the *j*. In addition, use of the invisible comma would hint to a math layout program that it should typeset a small space between the variables.

Invisible Multiplication. Similarly, an expression like mc^2 implies that the mass m multiplies the square of the speed c. To represent the implied multiplication in mc^2, one inserts a nondisplaying U+2062 INVISIBLE TIMES between the m and the c. Another example can be seen in the expression $f^{ij}(\cos(ab))$, which has the same meaning as $f^{ij}(\cos(a \times b))$, where $\times$ represents *multiplication*, not the *cross product*. Note that the spacing between characters may also depend on whether the adjacent variables are part of a list or are to be concatenated (that is, multiplied).

Invisible Function Application. U+2061 FUNCTION APPLICATION is used for an implied function dependence, as in $f(x + y)$. To indicate that this is the function f of the quantity $x + y$ and not the expression $fx + fy$, one can insert the nondisplaying *function application symbol* between the f and the left parenthesis.

15.6 Technical Symbols

Control Pictures: U+2400–U+243F

The need to show the presence of the C0 control codes unequivocally when data are displayed has led to conventional representations for these nongraphic characters.

Code Points for Pictures for Control Codes. By definition, control codes themselves are manifested only by their action. However, it is sometimes necessary to show the position of a control code within a data stream. Conventional illustrations for the ASCII C0 control codes have been developed—but the characters U+2400..U+241F and U+2424 are intended for use as unspecified graphics for the corresponding control codes. This choice allows a particular application to use *any* desired pictorial representation of the given control code. It assumes that the particular pictures used to represent control codes are often specific to different systems and are rarely the subject of text interchange between systems.

Pictures for ASCII Space. By definition, the SPACE is a blank graphic. Conventions have also been established for the visible representation of the space. Three specific characters are provided that may be used to visually represent the ASCII space character, U+2420 SYMBOL FOR SPACE, U+2422 BLANK SYMBOL, and U+2423 OPEN BOX.

Standards. The CNS 11643 standard encodes characters for pictures of control codes. Standard representations for control characters have been defined—for example, in ANSI X3.32 and ISO 2047. If desired, the characters U+2400..U+241F may be used for these representations.

Miscellaneous Technical: U+2300–U+23FF

This block encodes technical symbols, including keytop labels such as U+232B ERASE TO THE LEFT. Excluded from consideration were symbols that are not normally used in one-dimensional text but are intended for two-dimensional diagrammatic use, such as most symbols for electronic circuits.

Keytop Labels. Where possible, keytop labels have been unified with other symbols of like appearance—for example, U+21E7 UPWARDS WHITE ARROW to indicate the Shift key. While symbols such as U+2318 PLACE OF INTEREST SIGN and U+2388 HELM SYMBOL are generic symbols that have been adapted to use on keytops, other symbols specifically follow ISO/IEC 9995-7.

Corner Brackets. Applications that need corner brackets may use the floor and ceiling symbols encoded at U+2308..U+230B. These symbols should not be confused with the CJK corner brackets at U+300C and U+300D, which are used as quotation marks. Specific types of editorial punctuation, including corner bracket forms, can also be found in the Supplemental Punctuation block (U+2E00..U+2E7F).

Crops and Quine Corners. Crops and quine corners are most properly used in two-dimensional layout but may be referred to in plain text. This usage of crops and quine corners is as indicated in *Figure 15-7*. The quine corners are also used in pairs (upper and lower) in mathematical notation.

Figure 15-7. Usage of Crops and Quine Corners

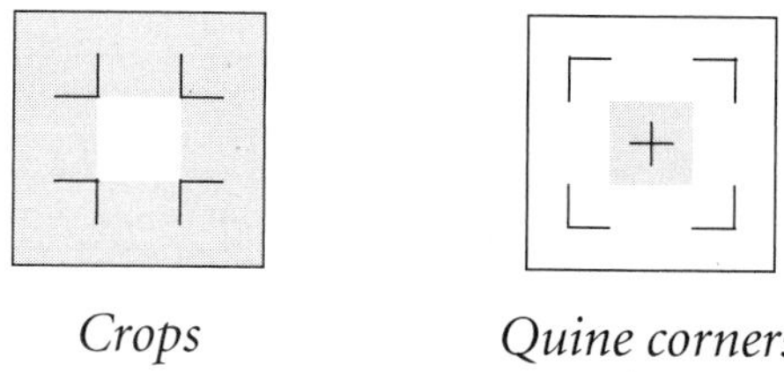

Angle Brackets. U+2329 LEFT-POINTING ANGLE BRACKET and U+232A RIGHT-POINTING ANGLE BRACKET have long been canonically equivalent to the CJK punctuation characters U+3008 LEFT ANGLE BRACKET and U+3009 RIGHT ANGLE BRACKET, respectively. This canonical equivalence implies that the use of the latter (CJK) code points is preferred and that U+2329 and U+232A are also "wide" characters. (See Unicode Standard Annex #11, "East Asian Width," for the definition of the East Asian wide property.) For this reason, the use of U+2329 and U+232A is deprecated for mathematics and for technical publication, where the wide property of the characters has the potential to interfere with the proper formatting of mathematical formulae. The angle brackets specifically provided for mathematics, U+27E8 MATHEMATICAL LEFT ANGLE BRACKET and U+27E9 MATHEMATICAL RIGHT ANGLE BRACKET, should be used instead. See *Section 15.4, Mathematical Symbols*.

APL Functional Symbols. APL (A Programming Language) makes extensive use of functional symbols constructed by composition with other, more primitive functional symbols. It used backspace and overstrike mechanisms in early computer implementations. In principle, functional composition is productive in APL; in practice, a relatively small number of composed functional symbols have become standard operators in APL. This relatively small set is encoded in its entirety in this block. All other APL extensions can be encoded by composition of other Unicode characters. For example, the APL symbol *a underbar* can be represented by U+0061 LATIN SMALL LETTER A + U+0332 COMBINING LOW LINE.

Symbol Pieces. The characters in the range U+239B..U+23B3, plus U+23B7, constitute a set of bracket and other symbol fragments for use in mathematical typesetting. These pieces originated in older font standards but have been used in past mathematical processing as characters in their own right to make up extra-tall glyphs for enclosing multiline mathematical formulae. Mathematical fences are ordinarily sized to the content that they enclose. However, in creating a large fence, the glyph is not scaled proportionally; in particular, the displayed stem weights must remain compatible with the accompanying smaller characters. Thus simple scaling of font outlines cannot be used to create tall brackets. Instead, a common technique is to build up the symbol from pieces. In particular, the characters U+239B LEFT PARENTHESIS UPPER HOOK through U+23B3 SUMMATION BOTTOM represent a set of glyph pieces for building up large versions of the fences (,), [,], {, and }, and of the large operators ∑ and ∫. These brace and operator pieces are compatibility characters. They should not be used in stored mathematical text, although they are often used in the data stream created by display and print drivers.

Table 15-3 shows which pieces are intended to be used together to create specific symbols.

Table 15-3. Use of Mathematical Symbol Pieces

	Two-Row	Three-Row	Five-Row
Summation	23B2, 23B3		
Integral	2320, 2321	2320, 23AE, 2321	2320, 3×23AE, 2321
Left parenthesis	239B, 239D	239B, 239C, 239D	239B, 3×239C, 239D
Right parenthesis	239E, 23A0	239E, 239F, 23A0	239E, 3×239F, 23A0
Left bracket	23A1, 23A3	23A1, 23A2, 23A3	23A1, 3×23A2, 23A3
Right bracket	23A4, 23A6	23A4, 23A5, 23A6	23A4, 3×23A5, 23A6
Left brace	23B0, 23B1	23A7, 23A8, 23A9	23A7, 23AA, 23A8, 23AA, 23A9
Right brace	23B1, 23B0	23AB, 23AC, 23AD	23AB, 23AA, 23AC, 23AA, 23AD

For example, an instance of U+239B can be positioned relative to instances of U+239C and U+239D to form an extra-tall (three or more line) left parenthesis. The center sections encoded here are meant to be used only with the top and bottom pieces encoded adjacent to them because the segments are usually graphically constructed within the fonts so that they match perfectly when positioned at the same *x* coordinates.

Horizontal Brackets. In mathematical equations, delimiters are often used horizontally, where they expand to the width of the expression they encompass. The six bracket characters in the range U+23DC..U+23E1 can be used for this purpose. In the context of mathematical layout, U+23B4 TOP SQUARE BRACKET and U+23B5 BOTTOM SQUARE BRACKET are also used that way. For more information, see Unicode Technical Report #25, "Unicode Support for Mathematics."

The set of horizontal square brackets, U+23B4 TOP SQUARE BRACKET and U+23B5 BOTTOM SQUARE BRACKET, together with U+23B6 BOTTOM SQUARE BRACKET OVER TOP SQUARE BRACKET, are used by certain legacy applications to delimit vertical runs of text in non-CJK terminal emulation. U+23B6 BOTTOM SQUARE BRACKET OVER TOP SQUARE BRACKET is used where a single character cell is both the end of one such run and the start of another. The use of these characters in terminal emulation should not be confused with the use of rotated forms of brackets for vertically rendered CJK text. See the further discussion of this issue in *Section 6.2, General Punctuation*.

Terminal Graphics Characters. In addition to the box drawing characters in the Box Drawing block, a small number of vertical or horizontal line characters are encoded in the Miscellaneous Technical symbols block to complete the set of compatibility characters needed for applications that need to emulate various old terminals. The horizontal scan line characters, U+23BA HORIZONTAL SCAN LINE-1 through U+23BD HORIZONTAL SCAN LINE-9, in particular, represent characters that were encoded in character ROM for use with nine-line character graphic cells. Horizontal scan line characters are encoded for scan lines 1, 3, 7, and 9. The horizontal scan line character for scan line 5 is unified with U+2500 BOX DRAWINGS LIGHT HORIZONTAL.

Dental Symbols. The set of symbols from U+23BE to U+23CC form a set of symbols from JIS X 0213 for use in dental notation.

Metrical Symbols. The symbols in the range U+23D1..U+23D9 are a set of spacing symbols used in the metrical analysis of poetry and lyrics.

Electrotechnical Symbols. The Miscellaneous Technical block also contains a smattering of electrotechnical symbols. These characters are not intended to constitute a complete encoding of all symbols used in electrical diagrams, but rather are compatibility characters encoded primarily for mapping to other standards. The symbols in the range U+238D..U+2394 are from the character set with the International Registry number 181. U+23DA EARTH GROUND and U+23DB FUSE are from HKSCS-2001.

Standards. This block contains a large number of symbols from ISO/IEC 9995-7:1994, *Information technology—Keyboard layouts for text and office systems—Part 7: Symbols used to represent functions.*

ISO/IEC 9995-7 contains many symbols that have been unified with existing and closely related symbols in Unicode. These symbols are shown with their ordinary shapes in the code charts, not with the particular glyph variation required by conformance to ISO/IEC 9995-7. Implementations wishing to be conformant to ISO/IEC 9995-7 in the depiction of these symbols should make use of a suitable font.

Optical Character Recognition: U+2440–U+245F

This block includes those symbolic characters of the OCR-A character set that do not correspond to ASCII characters as well as magnetic ink character recognition (MICR) symbols used in check processing.

Standards. Both sets of symbols are specified in ISO 2033.

15.7 Geometrical Symbols

Geometrical symbols are a collection of geometric shapes and their derivatives plus block elements and characters used for box drawing in legacy environments. In addition to the blocks described in this section, the Miscellaneous Technical (U+2300..U+23FF), Miscellaneous Symbols (U+2600..U+26FF), and Miscellaneous Symbols and Arrows (U+2B00.. U+2BFF) blocks contain geometrical symbols that complete the set of shapes in the Geometric Shapes block.

Box Drawing and Box Elements

Box drawing and block element characters are graphic compatibility characters in the Unicode Standard. A number of existing national and vendor standards, including IBM PC Code Page 437, contain sets of characters intended to enable a simple kind of display cell graphics, assuming terminal-type screen displays of fixed-pitch character cells. The Unicode Standard does not encourage this kind of character-cell-based graphics model, but does include sets of such characters for backward compatibility with the existing standards.

Box Drawing. The Box Drawing block (U+2500..U+257F) contains a collection of graphic compatibility characters that originate in legacy standards and that are intended for drawing boxes of various shapes and line widths for user interface components in character-cell-based graphic systems.

The "light," "heavy," and "double" attributes for some of these characters reflect the fact that the original sets often had a two-way distinction, between a light versus heavy line or a single versus double line, and included sufficient pieces to enable construction of graphic boxes with distinct styles that abutted each other in display.

The lines in the box drawing characters typically extend to the middle of the top, bottom, left, and/or right of the bounding box for the character cell. They are designed to connect together into continuous lines, with no gaps between them. When emulating terminal applications, fonts that implement the box drawing characters should do likewise.

Block Elements. The Block Elements block (U+2580..U+259F) contains another collection of graphic compatibility characters. Unlike the box drawing characters, the legacy block elements are designed to fill some defined fraction of each display cell or to fill each display cell with some defined degree of shading. These elements were used to create crude graphic displays in terminals or in terminal modes on displays where bit-mapped graphics were unavailable.

Half-block fill characters are included for each half of a display cell, plus a graduated series of vertical and horizontal fractional fills based on one-eighth parts. The fractional fills do not form a logically complete set but are intended only for backward compatibility. There is also a set of quadrant fill characters, U+2596..U+259F, which are designed to complement the half-block fill characters and U+2588 FULL BLOCK. When emulating terminal applications, fonts that implement the block element characters should be designed so that adjacent glyphs for characters such as U+2588 FULL BLOCK create solid patterns with no gaps between them.

Standards. The box drawing and block element characters were derived from GB 2312, KS X 1001, a variety of industry standards, and several terminal graphics sets. The Videotex Mosaic characters, which have similar appearances and functions, are unified against these sets.

Geometric Shapes: U+25A0–U+25FF

The Geometric Shapes are a collection of characters intended to encode prototypes for various commonly used geometrical shapes—mostly squares, triangles, and circles. The collection is somewhat arbitrary in scope; it is a compendium of shapes from various character and glyph standards. The typical distinctions more systematically encoded include black versus white, large versus small, basic shape (square versus triangle versus circle), orientation, and top versus bottom or left versus right part.

Hatched Squares. The hatched and cross-hatched squares at U+25A4..U+25A9 are derived from the Korean national standard (KS X 1001), in which they were probably intended as representations of fill patterns. Because the semantics of those characters are insufficiently defined in that standard, the Unicode character encoding simply carries the glyphs themselves as geometric shapes to provide a mapping for the Korean standard.

Lozenge. U+25CA ◊ LOZENGE is a typographical symbol seen in PostScript and in the Macintosh character set. It should be distinguished from both the generic U+25C7 WHITE DIAMOND and the U+2662 WHITE DIAMOND SUIT, as well as from another character sometimes called a lozenge, U+2311 SQUARE LOZENGE.

Use in Mathematics. Many geometric shapes are used in mathematics. When used for this purpose, the center points of the glyphs representing geometrical shapes should line up at the center line of the mathematical font. This differs from the alignment used for some of the representative glyphs in the code charts.

For several simple geometrical shapes—circle, square, triangle, diamond, and lozenge—differences in size carry semantic distinctions in mathematical notation, such as the difference between use of the symbol as a variable or as one of a variety of operator types. In some cases, other blocks, such as General Punctuation, Mathematical Operators, Block Elements, and Miscellaneous Symbols, contain these other sizes of geometrical symbols.

For more details on the use of geometrical shapes in mathematics, see Unicode Technical Report #25, "Unicode Support for Mathematics."

Standards. The Geometric Shapes are derived from a large range of national and vendor character standards. The squares and triangles at U+25E7..U+25EE are derived from the Linotype font collection. U+25EF LARGE CIRCLE is included for compatibility with the JIS X 0208-1990 Japanese standard.

15.8 Miscellaneous Symbols and Dingbats

Miscellaneous Symbols: U+2600–U+26FF

The Miscellaneous Symbols block consists of a very heterogeneous collection of symbols that do not fit in any other Unicode character block and that tend to be rather pictographic in nature. These symbols are typically used for text decorations, but they may also be treated as normal text characters in applications such as typesetting chess books, card game manuals, and horoscopes.

Characters in the Miscellaneous Symbols block may be rendered in more than one way, unlike characters in the Dingbats block, in which characters generally correspond to an explicit glyph. For example, both U+2641 EARTH and U+2645 URANUS have common alternative glyphs. EARTH can be rendered as ♁ or ⊕, and URANUS can be rendered as ♅ or ⛢.

The order of the Miscellaneous Symbols is completely arbitrary, but an attempt has been made to keep like symbols together and to group subsets of them into meaningful orders. Some of these subsets include weather and astronomical symbols, pointing hands, religious and ideological symbols, the Yijing (I Ching) trigrams, planet and zodiacal symbols, chess pieces, card suits, musical dingbats, and recycling symbols. (For other moon phases, see the circle-based shapes in the Geometric Shapes block.)

Corporate logos and collections of pictures of animals, vehicles, foods, and so on are not included because they tend either to be very specific in usage (logos, political party symbols) or nonconventional in appearance and semantic interpretation (pictures of cows or of cats; fizzing champagne bottles), and hence are inappropriate for encoding as characters. The Unicode Standard recommends that such items be incorporated in text via higher protocols that allow intermixing of graphic images with text, rather than by indefinite extension of the number of miscellaneous symbols encoded as characters.

Plastic Bottle Material Code System. The seven numbered logos encoded from U+2673 to U+2679, ♳♴♵♶♷♸♹, are from "The Plastic Bottle Material Code System," which was introduced in 1988 by the Society of the Plastics Industry (SPI). This set consistently uses thin, two-dimensional curved arrows suitable for use in plastics molding. In actual use, the symbols often are combined with an abbreviation of the material class below the triangle. Such abbreviations are not universal; therefore, they are not present in the representative glyphs in *Chapter 17, Code Charts*.

Recycling Symbol for Generic Materials. An unnumbered plastic resin code symbol U+267A ♺ RECYCLING SYMBOL FOR GENERIC MATERIALS is not formally part of the SPI system but is found in many fonts. Occasional use of this symbol as a generic materials code symbol can be found in the field, usually with a text legend below, but sometimes also surrounding or overlaid by other text or symbols. Sometimes the UNIVERSAL RECYCLING SYMBOL is substituted for the generic symbol in this context.

Universal Recycling Symbol. Unicode encodes two common glyph variants of this symbol: U+2672 ♲ UNIVERSAL RECYCLING SYMBOL and U+267B ♻ BLACK UNIVERSAL RECYCLING SYMBOL. Both are used to indicate that the material is recyclable. The white form is the traditional version of the symbol, but the black form is sometimes substituted, presumably because the thin outlines of the white form do not always reproduce well.

Paper Recycling Symbols. The two paper recycling symbols, U+267C ♼ RECYCLED PAPER SYMBOL and U+267D ♽ PARTIALLY-RECYCLED PAPER SYMBOL, can be used to distinguish between fully and partially recycled fiber content in paper products or packaging. They are usually accompanied by additional text.

Gender Symbols. The characters in the range U+26A2..U+26A9 are gender symbols. These are part of a set with U+2640 FEMALE SIGN, U+2642 MALE SIGN, U+26AA MEDIUM WHITE CIRCLE, and U+26B2 NEUTER. They are used in sexual studies and biology, for example. Some of these symbols have other uses as well, as astrological or alchemical symbols.

Genealogical Symbols. The characters in the range U+26AD..U+26B1 are sometimes seen in genealogical tables, where they indicate marriage and burial status. They may be augmented by other symbols, including the small circle indicating betrothal.

Standards. The Miscellaneous Symbols are derived from a large range of national and vendor character standards.

Dingbats: U+2700–U+27BF

The Dingbats are derived from a well-established set of glyphs, the ITC Zapf Dingbats series 100, which constitutes the industry standard "Zapf Dingbat" font currently available in most laser printers. Other series of dingbat glyphs also exist, but are not encoded in the Unicode Standard because they are not widely implemented in existing hardware and software as character-encoded fonts. The order of the Dingbats block basically follows the PostScript encoding.

Unifications. Where a dingbat from the ITC Zapf Dingbats series 100 could be unified with a generic symbol widely used in other contexts, only the generic symbol was encoded. This accounts for the encoding gaps in the Dingbats block. Examples of such unifications include card suits, BLACK STAR, BLACK TELEPHONE, and BLACK RIGHT-POINTING INDEX (see the Miscellaneous Symbols block); BLACK CIRCLE and BLACK SQUARE (see the Geometric Shapes block); white encircled numbers 1 to 10 (see the Enclosed Alphanumerics block); and several generic arrows (see the Arrows block). Those four entries appear elsewhere in this chapter.

In other instances, other glyphs from the ITC Zapf Dingbats series 100 glyphs have come to be recognized as having applicability as generic symbols, despite having originally been encoded in the Dingbats block. For example, the series of negative (black) circled numbers 1 to 10 are now treated as generic symbols for this sequence, the continuation of which can be found in the Enclosed Alphanumerics block. Other examples include U+2708 AIRPLANE and U+2709 ENVELOPE, which have definite semantics independent of the specific glyph shape, and which therefore should be considered generic symbols rather than symbols representing only the Zapf Dingbats glyph shapes.

For many of the remaining characters in the Dingbats block, their semantic value is primarily their shape; unlike characters that represent letters from a script, there is no well-established range of typeface variations for a dingbat that will retain its identity and therefore its semantics. It would be incorrect to arbitrarily replace U+279D TRIANGLE-HEADED RIGHTWARDS ARROW with any other right arrow dingbat or with any of the generic arrows from the Arrows block (U+2190..U+21FF). However, exact shape retention for the glyphs is not always required to maintain the relevant distinctions. For example, ornamental characters such as U+2741 EIGHT PETALLED OUTLINED BLACK FLORETTE have been successfully implemented in font faces other than Zapf Dingbats with glyph shapes that are similar, but not identical to the ITC Zapf Dingbats series 100.

The following guidelines are provided for font developers wishing to support this block of characters. Characters showing large sets of contrastive glyph shapes in the Dingbats block, and in particular the various arrow shapes at U+2794..U+27BE, should have glyphs that are closely modeled on the ITC Zapf Dingbats series 100, which are shown as representative glyphs in the code charts. The same applies to the various stars, asterisks, snowflakes, dropshadowed squares, check marks, and x's, many of which are ornamental and have elaborate names describing their glyphs.

Where the preceding guidelines do not apply, or where dingbats have more generic applicability as symbols, their glyphs do not need to match the representative glyphs in the code charts in every detail.

Ornamental Brackets. The 14 ornamental brackets encoded at U+2768..U+2775 are part of the set of Zapf Dingbats. Although they have always been included in Zapf Dingbats fonts, they were unencoded in PostScript versions of the fonts on some platforms. The Unicode Standard treats these brackets as punctuation characters.

Yijing Hexagram Symbols: U+4DC0–U+4DFF

Usage of the Yijing Hexagram Symbols in China begins with a text called《周易》*Zhou Yi*, ("the Zhou Dynasty classic of change"), said to have originated circa 1000 BCE. This text is now popularly known as the *Yijing*, *I Ching*, or *Book of Changes*. These symbols represent a primary level of notation in this ancient philosophical text, which is traditionally considered the first and most important of the Chinese classics. Today, these symbols appear in many print and electronic publications, produced in Asia and all over the world. The important Chinese character lexicon *Hanyu Da Zidian*, for example, makes use of these symbols in running text. These symbols are semantically distinct written signs associated with specific words. Each of the 64 hexagrams has a unique one- or two-syllable name. Each hexagram name is intimately connected with interpretation of the six lines. Related characters are Monogram and Digram Symbols (U+268A..U+268F), Yijing Trigram Symbols (U+2630..U+2637), and Tai Xuan Jing Symbols (U+1D300..U+1D356).

Tai Xuan Jing Symbols: U+1D300–U+1D356

Usage of these symbols in China begins with a text called《太玄經》*Tai Xuan Jing* (literally, "the exceedingly arcane classic"). Composed by a man named 楊雄 Yang Xiong (53 BCE–18 CE), the first draft of this work was completed in 2 BCE, in the decade before the fall of the Western Han Dynasty. This text is popularly known in the West under several titles, including *The Alternative I Ching* and *The Elemental Changes*. A number of annotated editions of *Tai Xuan Jing* have been published and reprinted in the 2,000 years since the original work appeared.

These symbols represent a primary level of notation in the original ancient text, following and expanding upon the traditions of the Chinese classic *Yijing*. The tetragram signs are less well known and less widely used than the hexagram signs. For this reason they were encoded on Plane 1 rather than the BMP.

Monograms. U+1D300 MONOGRAM FOR EARTH is an extension of the traditional Yijing monogram symbols, U+268A MONOGRAM FOR YANG and U+268B MONOGRAM FOR YIN. Because *yang* is typically associated with heaven (Chinese *tian*) and *yin* is typically associated with earth (Chinese *di*), the character U+1D300 has an unfortunate name. Tai Xuan Jing studies typically associate it with human (Chinese *ren*), as midway between heaven and earth.

Digrams. The range of characters U+1D301..U+1D302 constitutes an extension of the Yijing digram symbols encoded in the range U+268C..U+268F. They consist of the combinations of the human (*ren*) monogram with either the *yang* or the *yin* monogram. Because of the naming problem for U+1D300, these digrams also have infelicitous character names. Users are advised to identify the digram symbols by their representative glyphs or by the Chinese aliases provided for them in *Chapter 17, Code Charts*.

Tetragrams. The bulk of the symbols in the Tai Xuan Jing Symbols block are the tetragram signs. These tetragram symbols are semantically distinct written signs associated with specific words. Each of the 81 tetragrams has a unique monosyllabic name, and each tetragram name is intimately connected with interpretation of the four lines.

The 81 tetragram symbols (U+1D306..U+1D356) encoded on Plane 1 constitute a complete set. Within this set of 81 signs, a subset of 16 signs known as the Yijing tetragrams is of importance to Yijing scholarship. These are used in the study of the "nuclear trigrams." Related characters are the Yijing Trigram symbols (U+2630..U+2637) and the Yijing Hexagram symbols (U+4DC0..U+4DFF).

15.9 Enclosed and Square

Enclosed Alphanumerics: U+2460–U+24FF

The enclosed numbers and Latin letters of this block come from several sources—chiefly East Asian standards—and are provided for compatibility with them.

Standards. Enclosed letters and numbers occur in the Korean national standard, KS X 1001:1998, and in the Chinese national standard, GB 2312, as well as in various East Asian industry standards.

The Zapf Dingbats character set in widespread industry use contains four sets of encircled numbers (including encircled zero). The black-on-white set that has numbers with serifs is encoded here (U+2460..U+2468 and U+24EA). The other three sets are encoded in the range U+2776..U+2793 in the Dingbats block.

Decompositions. The parenthesized letters or numbers have compatibility decompositions to a sequence of opening parenthesis, letter or digit(s), closing parenthesis. The numbers with a period may be decomposed to digit(s), followed by a period. The encircled letters and single-digit numbers may be decomposed to a letter or digit followed by U+20DD ◌⃝ COMBINING ENCLOSING CIRCLE. Decompositions for the encircled numbers 10 through 20 are not supported in Unicode plain text.

Enclosed CJK Letters and Months: U+3200–U+32FF

Standards. This block provides mapping for all the enclosed Hangul elements from Korean standard KS X 1001:1998 as well as parenthesized ideographic characters from the JIS X 0208-1990 standard, CNS 11643, and several corporate registries.

CJK Compatibility: U+3300–U+33FF

CJK squared Katakana words are Katakana-spelled words that fill a single display cell (em-square) when intermixed with CJK ideographs. Likewise, squared Latin abbreviation symbols are designed to fill a single character position when mixed with CJK ideographs.

These characters are provided solely for compatibility with existing character encoding standards. Modern software can supply an infinite repertoire of Kana-spelled words or squared abbreviations on the fly.

Standards. CJK Compatibility characters are derived from the KS X 1001:1998 and CNS 11643 national standards, and from various company registries.

Japanese Era Names. The Japanese era names refer to the dates given in *Table 15-4*.

Table 15-4. Japanese Era Names

Code Point	Name	Dates
U+337B	SQUARE ERA NAME HEISEI	1989-01-07 to present day
U+337C	SQUARE ERA NAME SYOUWA	1926-12-24 to 1989-01-06
U+337D	SQUARE ERA NAME TAISYOU	1912-07-29 to 1926-12-23
U+337E	SQUARE ERA NAME MEIZI	1867 to 1912-07-28

15.10 Braille

Braille Patterns: U+2800–U+28FF

Braille is a writing system used by blind people worldwide. It uses a system of six or eight raised dots, arranged in two vertical rows of three or four dots, respectively. Eight-dot systems build on six-dot systems by adding two extra dots above or below the core matrix. Six-dot Braille allows 64 possible combinations, and eight-dot Braille allows 256 possible patterns of dot combinations. There is no fixed correspondence between a dot pattern and a character or symbol of any given script. Dot pattern assignments are dependent on context and user community. A single pattern can represent an abbreviation or a frequently occurring short word. For a number of contexts and user communities, the series of ISO technical reports starting with ISO/TR 11548-1 provide standardized correspondence tables as well as invocation sequences to indicate a context switch.

The Unicode Standard encodes a single complete set of 256 eight-dot patterns. This set includes the 64 dot patterns needed for six-dot Braille.

The character names for Braille patterns are based on the assignments of the dots of the Braille pattern to digits 1 to 8 as follows:

1	●●	4
2	●●	5
3	●●	6
7	●●	8

The designation of dots 1 to 6 corresponds to that of six-dot Braille. The additional dots 7 and 8 are added beneath. The character name for a Braille pattern consists of BRAILLE PATTERN DOTS-12345678, where only those digits corresponding to dots in the pattern are included. The name for the empty pattern is BRAILLE PATTERN BLANK.

The 256 Braille patterns are arranged in the same sequence as in ISO/TR 11548-1, which is based on an octal number generated from the pattern arrangement. Octal numbers are associated with each dot of a Braille pattern in the following way:

1	●●	10
2	●●	20
4	●●	40
100	●●	200

The octal number is obtained by adding the values corresponding to the dots present in the pattern. Octal numbers smaller than 100 are expanded to three digits by inserting leading zeroes. For example, the dots of BRAILLE PATTERN DOTS-1247 are assigned to the octal values of 1_8, 2_8, 10_8, and 100_8. The octal number representing the sum of these values is 113_8.

The assignment of meanings to Braille patterns is outside the scope of this standard.

Example. According to ISO/TR 11548-2, the character LATIN CAPITAL LETTER F can be represented in eight-dot Braille by the combination of the dots 1, 2, 4, and 7 (BRAILLE PATTERN DOTS-1247). A full circle corresponds to a tangible (set) dot, and empty circles serve as position indicators for dots not set within the dot matrix:

1	●	●	4
2	●	○	5
3	○	○	6
7	●	○	8

Usage Model. The eight-dot Braille patterns in the Unicode Standard are intended to be used with either style of eight-dot Braille system, whether the additional two dots are considered to be in the top row or in the bottom row. These two systems are never intermixed in the same context, so their distinction is a matter of convention. The intent of encoding the 256 Braille patterns in the Unicode Standard is to allow input and output devices to be implemented that can interchange Braille data without having to go through a context-dependent conversion from semantic values to patterns, or vice versa. In this manner, final-form documents can be exchanged and faithfully rendered. At the same time, processing of textual data that require semantic support is intended to take place using the regular character assignments in the Unicode Standard.

Imaging. When output on a Braille device, dots shown as black are intended to be rendered as tangible. Dots shown in the standard as open circles are blank (not rendered as tangible). The Unicode Standard does not specify any physical dimension of Braille characters.

In the absence of a higher-level protocol, Braille patterns are output from left to right. When used to render final form (tangible) documents, Braille patterns are normally not intermixed with any other Unicode characters except control codes.

15.11 Western Musical Symbols

Musical Symbols: U+1D100–U+1D1FF

The musical symbols encoded in the Musical Symbols block are intended to cover basic Western musical notation and its antecedents: mensural notation and plainsong (or Gregorian) notation. The most comprehensive coded language in regular use for representing sound is the common musical notation (CMN) of the Western world. Western musical notation is a system of symbols that is relatively, but not completely, self-consistent and relatively stable but still, like music itself, evolving. This open-ended system has survived over time partly because of its flexibility and extensibility. In the Unicode Standard, musical symbols have been drawn primarily from CMN. Commonly recognized additions to the CMN repertoire, such as quarter-tone accidentals, cluster noteheads, and shape-note noteheads, have also been included.

Graphical score elements are not included in the Musical Symbols block. These pictographs are usually created for a specific repertoire or sometimes even a single piece. Characters that have some specialized meaning in music but that are found in other character blocks are not included. They include numbers for time signatures and figured basses, letters for section labels and Roman numeral harmonic analysis, and so on.

Musical symbols are used worldwide in a more or less standard manner by a very large group of users. The symbols frequently occur in running text and may be treated as simple spacing characters with no special properties, with a few exceptions. Musical symbols are used in contexts such as theoretical works, pedagogical texts, terminological dictionaries, bibliographic databases, thematic catalogs, and databases of musical data. The musical symbol characters are also intended to be used within higher-level protocols, such as music description languages and file formats for the representation of musical data and musical scores.

Because of the complexities of layout and of pitch representation in general, the encoding of musical pitch is intentionally outside the scope of the Unicode Standard. The Musical Symbols block provides a common set of elements for interchange and processing. Encoding of pitch, and layout of the resulting musical structure, involves specifications not only for the vertical relationship between multiple notes simultaneously, but also in multiple staves, between instrumental parts, and so forth. These musical features are expected to be handled entirely in higher-level protocols making use of the graphical elements provided. Lack of pitch encoding is not a shortcoming, but rather is a necessary feature of the encoding.

Glyphs. The glyphs for musical symbols shown in *Chapter 17, Code Charts*, are representative of typical cases; however, note in particular that the stem direction is not specified by the Unicode Standard and can be determined only in context. For a font that is intended to provide musical symbols in running text, either stem direction is acceptable. In some contexts—particularly for applications in early music—note heads, stems, flags, and other associated symbols may need to be rendered in different colors—for example, red.

Symbols in Other Blocks. U+266D MUSIC FLAT SIGN, U+266E MUSIC NATURAL SIGN, and U+266F MUSIC SHARP SIGN—three characters that occur frequently in musical notation—are encoded in the Miscellaneous Symbols block (U+2600..U+267F). However, four characters also encoded in that block are to be interpreted merely as dingbats or miscellaneous symbols, not as representing actual musical notes:

U+2669 QUARTER NOTE

U+266A EIGHTH NOTE

U+266B BEAMED EIGHTH NOTES

U+266C BEAMED SIXTEENTH NOTES

Gregorian. The *punctum*, or Gregorian *brevis*, a square shape, is unified with U+1D147 MUSICAL SYMBOL SQUARE NOTEHEAD BLACK. The Gregorian *semibrevis*, a diamond or lozenge shape, is unified with U+1D1BA MUSICAL SYMBOL SEMIBREVIS BLACK. Thus Gregorian notation, medieval notation, and modern notation either require separate fonts in practice or need font features to make subtle differentiations between shapes where required.

Processing. Most musical symbols can be thought of as simple spacing characters when used inline within texts and examples, even though they behave in a more complex manner in full musical layout. Some characters are meant only to be combined with others to produce combined character sequences, representing musical notes and their particular articulations. Musical symbols can be input, processed, and displayed in a manner similar to mathematical symbols. When embedded in text, most of the symbols are simple spacing characters with no special properties. A few characters have format control functions, as described later in this section.

Input Methods. Musical symbols can be entered via standard alphanumeric keyboard, via piano keyboard or other device, or by a graphical method. Keyboard input of the musical symbols may make use of techniques similar to those used for Chinese, Japanese, and Korean. In addition, input methods utilizing pointing devices or piano keyboards could be developed similar to those in existing musical layout systems. For example, within a graphical user interface, the user could choose symbols from a palette-style menu.

Directionality. When combined with right-to-left texts—in Hebrew or Arabic, for example—the musical notation is usually written from left to right in the normal manner. The words are divided into syllables and placed under or above the notes in the same fashion as for Latin and other left-to-right scripts. The individual words or syllables corresponding to each note, however, are written in the dominant direction of the script.

The opposite approach is also known: in some traditions, the musical notation is actually written from right to left. In that case, some of the symbols, such as clef signs, are mirrored; other symbols, such as notes, flags, and accidentals, are *not* mirrored. All responsibility for such details of bidirectional layout lies with higher-level protocols and is not reflected in any character properties. *Figure 15-8* exemplifies this principle with two musical passages. The first example shows Turkish lyrics in Arabic script with ordinary left-to-right musical notation; the second shows right-to-left musical notation. Note the partial mirroring.

Figure 15-8. Examples of Specialized Music Layout

Format Characters. Extensive ligature-like beams are used frequently in musical notation between groups of notes having short values. The practice is widespread and very predictable, so it is therefore amenable to algorithmic handling. The format characters U+1D173 MUSICAL SYMBOL BEGIN BEAM and U+1D174 MUSICAL SYMBOL END BEAM can be used to indicate the extents of beam groupings. In some exceptional cases, beams are left unclosed on one end. This status can be indicated with a U+1D159 MUSICAL SYMBOL NULL NOTEHEAD character if no stem is to appear at the end of the beam.

Similarly, format characters have been provided for other connecting structures. The characters U+1D175 MUSICAL SYMBOL BEGIN TIE, U+1D176 MUSICAL SYMBOL END TIE, U+1D177 MUSICAL SYMBOL BEGIN SLUR, U+1D178 MUSICAL SYMBOL END SLUR, U+1D179 MUSICAL SYMBOL BEGIN PHRASE, and U+1D17A MUSICAL SYMBOL END PHRASE indicate the extent of these features. Like beaming, these features are easily handled in an algorithmic fashion.

These pairs of characters modify the layout and grouping of notes and phrases in full musical notation. When musical examples are written or rendered in plain text without special software, the start/end format characters may be rendered as brackets or left uninterpreted. To the extent possible, more sophisticated software that renders musical examples inline with natural-language text might interpret them in their actual format control capacity, rendering slurs, beams, and so forth, as appropriate.

Precomposed Note Characters. For maximum flexibility, the character set includes both precomposed note values and primitives from which complete notes may be constructed. The precomposed versions are provided mainly for convenience. However, if any normalization form is applied, including NFC, the characters will be decomposed. For further information, see Unicode Standard Annex #15, "Unicode Normalization Forms." The canonical equivalents for these characters are given in the Unicode Character Database and are illustrated in *Figure 15-9.*

Figure 15-9. Precomposed Note Characters

1D15E = 1D157 + 1D165
1D15F = 1D158 + 1D165
1D160 = 1D158 + 1D165 + 1D16E
1D161 = 1D158 + 1D165 + 1D16F
1D162 = 1D158 + 1D165 + 1D170
1D163 = 1D158 + 1D165 + 1D171
1D164 = 1D158 + 1D165 + 1D172

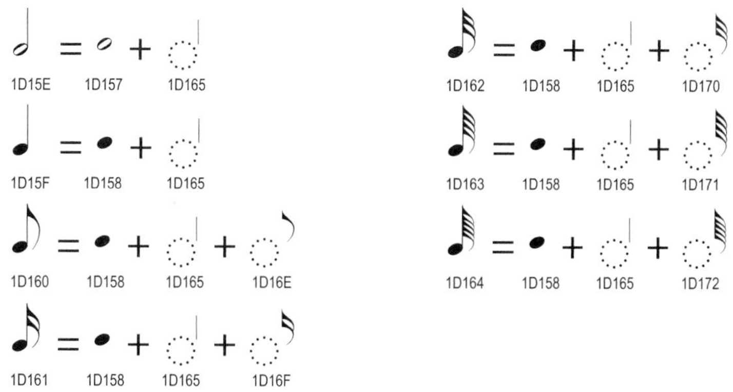

Alternative Noteheads. More complex notes built up from alternative noteheads, stems, flags, and articulation symbols are necessary for complete implementations and complex scores. Examples of their use include American shape-note and modern percussion notations, as shown in *Figure 15-10.*

Figure 15-10. Alternative Noteheads

1D147 1D165

1D143 1D165

Augmentation Dots and Articulation Symbols. Augmentation dots and articulation symbols may be appended to either the precomposed or built-up notes. In addition, augmentation dots and articulation symbols may be repeated as necessary to build a complete note symbol. Examples of the use of augmentation dots are shown in *Figure 15-11.*

Figure 15-11. Augmentation Dots and Articulation Symbols

1D158 1D165 1D16E 1D16D

1D158 1D165 1D17C

1D158 1D165 1D16E 1D17B 1D16D 1D16D

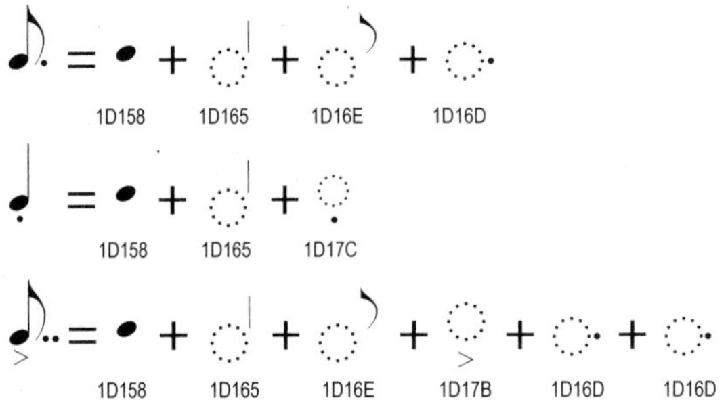

Ornamentation. *Table 15-5* lists common eighteenth-century ornaments and the sequences of characters from which they can be generated.

Table 15-5. Examples of Ornamentation

	1D19C STROKE-2 + 1D19D STROKE-3
	1D19C STROKE-2 + 1D1A0 STROKE-6 + 1D19D STROKE-3
	1D1A0 STROKE-6 + 1D19C STROKE-2 + 1D19C STROKE-2 + 1D19D STROKE-3
	1D19C STROKE-2 + 1D19C STROKE-2 + 1D1A0 STROKE-6 + 1D19D STROKE-3
	1D19C STROKE-2 + 1D19C STROKE-2 + 1D1A3 STROKE-9
	1D1A1 STROKE-7 + 1D19C STROKE-2 + 1D19C STROKE-2 + 1D19D STROKE-3

Table 15-5. Examples of Ornamentation (Continued)

	1D1A2 STROKE-8 + 1D19C STROKE-2 + 1D19C STROKE-2 + 1D19D STROKE-3
	1D19C STROKE-2 + 1D19C STROKE-2 + 1D19D STROKE-3 + 1D19F STROKE-5
	1D1A1 STROKE-7 + 1D19C STROKE-2 + 1D19C STROKE-2 + 1D1A0 STROKE-6 + 1D19D STROKE-3
	1D1A1 STROKE-7 + 1D19C STROKE-2 + 1D19C STROKE-2 + 1D19D STROKE-3 + 1D19F STROKE-5
	1D1A2 STROKE-8 + 1D19C STROKE-2 + 1D19C STROKE-2 + 1D1A0 STROKE-6 + 1D19D STROKE-3
	1D19B STROKE-1 + 1D19C STROKE-2 + 1D19C STROKE-2 + 1D19D STROKE-3
	1D19B STROKE-1 + 1D19C STROKE-2 + 1D19C STROKE-2 + 1D19D STROKE-3 + 1D19E STROKE-4
	1D19C STROKE-2 + 1D19D STROKE-3 + 1D19E STROKE-4

15.12 Byzantine Musical Symbols

Byzantine Musical Symbols: U+1D000–U+1D0FF

Byzantine musical notation first appeared in the seventh or eighth century CE, developing more fully by the tenth century. These musical symbols are chiefly used to write the religious music and hymns of the Christian Orthodox Church, although folk music manuscripts are also known. In 1881, the Orthodox Patriarchy Musical Committee redefined some of the signs and established the New Analytical Byzantine Musical Notation System, which is in use today. About 95 percent of the more than 7,000 musical manuscripts using this system are in Greek. Other manuscripts are in Russian, Bulgarian, Romanian, and Arabic.

Processing. Computer representation of Byzantine musical symbols is quite recent, although typographic publication of religious music books began in 1820. Two kinds of applications have been developed: applications to enable musicians to write the books they use, and applications that compare or convert this musical notation system to the standard Western system. (See *Section 15.11, Western Musical Symbols.*)

Byzantine musical symbols are divided into 15 classes according to function. Characters interact with one another in the horizontal and vertical dimension. There are three horizontal "stripes" in which various classes generally appear and rules as to how other characters interact within them. These rules, which are still being specified, are the responsibilities of higher-level protocols.

15.13 Ancient Greek Musical Notation

Ancient Greek Musical Notation: U+1D200–U+1D24F

Ancient Greeks developed their own distinct system of musical notation, which is found in a large number of ancient texts ranging from a fragment of Euripides' *Orestes* to Christian hymns. It is also used in the modern publication of these texts as well as in modern studies of ancient music.

The system covers about three octaves, and symbols can be grouped by threes: one symbol corresponds to a "natural" note on a diatonic scale, and the two others to successive sharpenings of that first note. There is no distinction between enharmonic and chromatic scales. The system uses two series of symbols: one for vocal melody and one for instrumental melody.

The symbols are based on Greek letters, comparable to the modern usage of the Latin letters A through G to refer to notes of the Western musical scale. However, rather than using a sharp and flat notation to indicate semitones, or casing and other diacritics to indicate distinct octaves, the Ancient Greek system extended the basic Greek alphabet by rotating and flipping letterforms in various ways and by adding a few more symbols not directly based on letters.

Unification. In the Unicode Standard, the vocal and instrumental systems are unified with each other and with the basic Greek alphabet, based on shape. *Table 15-6* gives the correspondence between modern notes, the numbering used by modern scholars, and the Unicode characters or sequences of characters to use to represent them.

Table 15-6. Representation of Ancient Greek Vocal and Instrumental Notation

Modern Note	Modern Number	Vocal Notation	Instrumental Notation
g"	70	2127, 0374	1D23C, 0374
	69	0391, 0374	1D23B, 0374
	68	0392, 0374	1D23A, 0374
f"	67	0393, 0374	039D, 0374
	66	0394, 0374	1D239, 0374
	65	0395, 0374	1D208, 0374
e"	64	0396, 0374	1D238, 0374
	63	0397, 0374	1D237, 0374
	62	0398, 0374	1D20D, 0374
d"	61	0399, 0374	1D236, 0374
	60	039A, 0374	1D235, 0374
	59	039B, 0374	1D234, 0374
c"	58	039C, 0374	1D233, 0374
	57	039D, 0374	1D232, 0374
	56	039E, 0374	1D20E, 0374

Table 15-6. Representation of Ancient Greek Vocal and Instrumental Notation (Continued)

Modern Note	Modern Number	Vocal Notation	Instrumental Notation
b’	55	039F, 0374	039A, 0374
	54	1D21C	1D241
	53	1D21B	1D240
a’	52	1D21A	1D23F
	51	1D219	1D23E
	50	1D218	1D23D
g’	49	2127	1D23C
	48	0391	1D23B
	47	0392	1D23A
f’	46	0393	039D
	45	0394	1D239
	44	0395	1D208
e’	43	0396	1D238
	42	0397	1D237
	41	0398	1D20D
d’	40	0399	1D236
	39	039A	1D235
	38	039B	1D234
c’	37	039C	1D233
	36	039D	1D232
	35	039E	1D20E
b	34	039F	039A
	33	03A0	03FD
	32	03A1	1D231
a	31	03F9	03F9
	30	03A4	1D230
	29	03A5	1D22F
g	28	03A6	1D213
	27	03A7	1D22E
	26	03A8	1D22D
f	25	03A9	1D22C
	24	1D217	1D22B
	23	1D216	1D22A
e	22	1D215	0393
	21	1D214	1D205
	20	1D213	1D21C
d	19	1D212	1D229
	18	1D211	1D228
	17	1D210	1D227
c	16	1D20F	0395
	15	1D20E	1D211
	14	1D20D	1D226

Table 15-6. Representation of Ancient Greek Vocal and Instrumental Notation (Continued)

Modern Note	Modern Number	Vocal Notation	Instrumental Notation
B	13	1D20C	1D225
	12	1D20B	1D224
	11	1D20A	1D223
A	10	1D209	0397
	9	1D208	1D206
	8	1D207	1D222
G	7	1D206	1D221
	6	1D205	03A4
	5	1D204	1D220
F	4	1D203	1D21F
	3	1D202	1D202
	2	1D201	1D21E
E	1	1D200	1D21D

Naming Conventions. The character names are based on the standard names widely used by modern scholars. There is no standardized ancient system for naming these characters. Apparent gaps in the numbering sequence are due to the unification with standard letters and between vocal and instrumental notations.

If a symbol is used in both the vocal notation system and the instrumental notation system, its Unicode character name is based on the vocal notation system catalog number. Thus U+1D20D GREEK VOCAL NOTATION SYMBOL-14 has a glyph based on an inverted capital lambda. In the vocal notation system, it represents the first sharp of B; in the instrumental notation system, it represents the first sharp of d'. Because it is used in both systems, its name is based on its sequence in the vocal notation system, rather than its sequence in the instrumental notation system. The character names list in the Unicode Character Database is fully annotated with the functions of the symbols for each system.

Font. Scholars usually typeset musical characters in sans-serif fonts to distinguish them from standard letters, which are usually represented with a serifed font. However, this is not required. The code charts use a font without serifs for reasons of clarity.

Combining Marks. The combining marks encoded in the range U+1D242..U+1D244 are placed over the vocal or instrumental notation symbols. They are used to indicate metrical qualities.

Chapter 16

Special Areas and Format Characters

This chapter describes several kinds of characters that have special properties as well as areas of the codespace that are set aside for special purposes:

Control codes	*Surrogates area*	*Noncharacters*
Layout controls	*Variation selectors*	*Specials*
Deprecated format characters	*Private-use characters*	*Tag characters*

In addition to regular characters, the Unicode Standard contains a number of format characters. These characters are not normally rendered directly, but rather influence the layout of text or otherwise affect the operation of text processes.

The Unicode Standard contains code positions for the 64 control characters and the DEL character found in ISO standards and many vendor character sets. The choice of control function associated with a given character code is outside the scope of the Unicode Standard, with the exception of those control characters specified in this chapter.

Layout controls are not themselves rendered visibly, but influence the behavior of algorithms for line breaking, word breaking, glyph selection, and bidirectional ordering.

Surrogate code points are reserved and are to be used in pairs—called surrogate pairs—to access 1,048,544 supplementary characters.

Variation selectors allow the specification of standardized variants of characters. This ability is particularly useful where the majority of implementations would treat the two variants as two forms of the same character, but where some implementations need to differentiate between the two. By using a variation selector, such differentiation can be made explicit.

Private-use characters are reserved for private use. Their meaning is defined by private agreement.

Noncharacters are code points that are permanently reserved and will never have characters assigned to them.

The Specials block contains characters that are neither graphic characters nor traditional controls.

Tag characters support a general scheme for the internal tagging of text streams in the absence of other mechanisms, such as markup languages. They are reserved for use with specific plain text-based protocols that specify their usage. Their use in ordinary text is strongly discouraged.

16.1 Control Codes

There are 65 code points set aside in the Unicode Standard for compatibility with the C0 and C1 control codes defined in the ISO/IEC 2022 framework. The ranges of these code points are U+0000..U+001F, U+007F, and U+0080..U+009F, which correspond to the 8-bit controls 00_{16} to $1F_{16}$ (C0 controls), $7F_{16}$ (*delete*), and 80_{16} to $9F_{16}$ (C1 controls), respectively. For example, the 8-bit legacy control code *character tabulation* (or *tab*) is the byte value 09_{16}; the Unicode Standard encodes the corresponding control code at U+0009.

The Unicode Standard provides for the intact interchange of these code points, neither adding to nor subtracting from their semantics. The semantics of the control codes are generally determined by the application with which they are used. However, in the absence of specific application uses, they may be interpreted according to the control function semantics specified in ISO/IEC 6429:1992.

In general, the use of control codes constitutes a higher-level protocol and is beyond the scope of the Unicode Standard. For example, the use of ISO/IEC 6429 control sequences for controlling bidirectional formatting would be a legitimate higher-level protocol layered on top of the plain text of the Unicode Standard. Higher-level protocols are not specified by the Unicode Standard; their existence cannot be assumed without a separate agreement between the parties interchanging such data.

Representing Control Sequences

There is a simple, one-to-one mapping between 7-bit (and 8-bit) control codes and the Unicode control codes: every 7-bit (or 8-bit) control code is numerically equal to its corresponding Unicode code point. For example, if the ASCII *line feed* control code ($0A_{16}$) is to be used for line break control, then the text "WX<LF>YZ" would be transmitted in Unicode plain text as the following coded character sequence: <0057, 0058, 000A, 0059, 005A>.

Control sequences that are part of Unicode text must be represented in terms of the Unicode encoding forms. For example, suppose that an application allows embedded font information to be transmitted by means of markup using plain text and control codes. A font tag specified as "^ATimes^B", where ^A refers to the C0 control code 01_{16} and ^B refers to the C0 control code 02_{16}, would then be expressed by the following coded character sequence: <0001, 0054, 0069, 006D, 0065, 0073, 0002>. The representation of the control codes in the three Unicode encoding forms simply follows the rules for any other code points in the standard:

UTF-8: <01 54 69 6D 65 73 02>

UTF-16: <0001 0054 0069 006D 0065 0073 0002>

UTF-32: <00000001 00000054 00000069 0000006D 00000065 00000073 00000002>

Escape Sequences. Escape sequences are a particular type of protocol that consists of the use of some set of ASCII characters introduced by the *escape* control code, $1B_{16}$, to convey extra-textual information. When converting escape sequences into and out of Unicode text, they should be converted on a character-by-character basis. For instance, "ESC-A" <1B 41> would be converted into the Unicode coded character sequence <001B, 0041>. Interpretation of U+0041 as part of the escape sequence, rather than as *latin capital letter a*, is the responsibility of the higher-level protocol that makes use of such escape sequences. This approach allows for low-level conversion processes to conformantly convert escape sequences into and out of the Unicode Standard without needing to actually recognize the escape sequences as such.

If a process uses escape sequences or other configurations of control code sequences to embed additional information about text (such as formatting attributes or structure), then such sequences constitute a higher-level protocol that is outside the scope of the Unicode Standard.

Specification of Control Code Semantics

Several control codes are commonly used in plain text, particularly those involved in line and paragraph formatting. The use of these control codes is widespread and important to interoperability. Therefore, the Unicode Standard specifies semantics for their use with the rest of the encoded characters in the standard. *Table 16-1* lists those control codes.

Table 16-1. Control Codes Specified in the Unicode Standard

Code Point	Abbreviation	ISO/IEC 6429 Name
U+0009	HT	character tabulation (tab)
U+000A	LF	line feed
U+000B	VT	line tabulation (vertical tab)
U+000C	FF	form feed
U+000D	CR	carriage return
U+001C	FS	information separator four
U+001D	GS	information separator three
U+001E	RS	information separator two
U+001F	US	information separator one
U+0085	NEL	next line

Most of the control codes in *Table 16-1* have the White_Space property. They have the directional property values of S, B, or WS, rather than the default of ON used for other control codes. (See Unicode Standard Annex #9, "The Bidirectional Algorithm.") In addition, the separator semantics of the control codes U+001C..U+001F are recognized in the Bidirectional Algorithm. U+0009..U+000D and U+0085 also have line breaking property values that differ from the default CM value for other control codes. (See Unicode Standard Annex #14, "Line Breaking Properties.")

U+0000 *null* may be used as a Unicode string terminator, as in the C language. Such usage is outside the scope of the Unicode Standard, which does not require any particular formal language representation of a string or any particular usage of null.

Newline Function. In particular, one or more of the control codes U+000A *line feed*, U+000D *carriage return*, and the Unicode equivalent of the EBCDIC *next line* can encode a *newline function*. A newline function can act like a *line separator* or a *paragraph separator*, depending on the application. See *Section 16.2, Layout Controls*, for information on how to interpret a line or paragraph separator. The exact encoding of a newline function depends on the application domain. For information on how to identify a newline function, see *Section 5.8, Newline Guidelines*.

16.2 Layout Controls

The effect of layout controls is specific to particular text processes. As much as possible, layout controls are transparent to those text processes for which they were not intended. In other words, their effects are mutually orthogonal.

Line and Word Breaking

The following gives a brief summary of the intended behavior of certain layout controls. For a full description of line and word breaking layout controls, see Unicode Standard Annex #14, "Line Breaking Properties."

No-Break Space. U+00A0 NO-BREAK SPACE has the same width as U+0020 SPACE, but the NO-BREAK SPACE indicates that, under normal circumstances, no line breaks are permitted between it and surrounding characters, unless the preceding or following character is a line or paragraph separator or space or zero width space. For a complete list of space characters in the Unicode Standard, see *Table 6-2*.

Word Joiner. U+2060 WORD JOINER behaves like U+00A0 NO-BREAK SPACE in that it indicates the absence of word boundaries; however, the *word joiner* has no width. The function of the character is to indicate that line breaks are not allowed between the adjoining characters, except next to hard line breaks. For example, the *word joiner* can be inserted after the fourth character in the text "base+delta" to indicate that there should be no line break between the "e" and the "+". The *word joiner* can be used to prevent line breaking with other characters that do not have nonbreaking variants, such as U+2009 THIN SPACE or U+2015 HORIZONTAL BAR, by bracketing the character.

The word joiner must not be confused with the *zero width joiner* or the *combining grapheme joiner*, which have very different functions. In particular, inserting a word joiner between two characters has no effect on their ligating and cursive joining behavior. The word joiner should be ignored in contexts other than word or line breaking.

Zero Width No-Break Space. In addition to its primary meaning of *byte order mark* (see "Byte Order Mark" in *Section 16.8, Specials*), the code point U+FEFF possesses the semantics of ZERO WIDTH NO-BREAK SPACE, which matches that of *word joiner*. Until Unicode 3.2, U+FEFF was the only code point with word joining semantics, but because it is more commonly used as *byte order mark*, the use of U+2060 WORD JOINER to indicate word joining is strongly preferred for any new text. Implementations should continue to support the word joining semantics of U+FEFF for backward compatibility.

Zero Width Space. The U+200B ZERO WIDTH SPACE indicates a word boundary, except that it has no width. Zero-width space characters are intended to be used in languages that have no visible word spacing to represent word breaks, such as Thai, Khmer, and Japanese. When text is justified, ZWSP has no effect on letter spacing—for example, in English or Japanese usage.

There may be circumstances with other scripts, such as Thai, where extra space is applied around ZWSP as a result of justification, as shown in *Table 16-2*. This approach is unlike the use of fixed-width space characters, such as U+2002 EN SPACE, that have specified width and should not be automatically expanded during justification (see *Section 6.2, General Punctuation*).

Table 16-2. Letter Spacing

Type	Justification Examples	Explanation
Memory	the ISP®[ZWSP]Charts	The [ZWSP] is inserted to allow line break after ®
Display 1	the ISP®Charts	Without letter spacing
Display 2	the ISP®Charts	Increased letter spacing
Display 3	the ISP®Charts	"Thai-style" letter spacing
Display 4	the ISP ®Charts	[ZWSP] incorrectly inhibiting letter spacing (after ®)

In some languages such as German and Russian, increased letter spacing is used to indicate emphasis. Implementers should be aware of this issue.

Zero-Width Spaces and Joiner Characters. The zero-width spaces are not to be confused with the zero-width joiner characters. U+200C ZERO WIDTH NON-JOINER and U+200D ZERO WIDTH JOINER have no effect on word boundaries, and ZERO WIDTH NO-BREAK SPACE and ZERO WIDTH SPACE have no effect on joining or linking behavior. In other words, the zero-width joiner characters should be ignored when determining word boundaries; ZERO

WIDTH SPACE should be ignored when determining cursive joining behavior. See "Cursive Connection" later in this section.

Hyphenation. U+00AD SOFT HYPHEN (SHY) indicates an intraword break point, where a line break is preferred if a word must be hyphenated or otherwise broken across lines. Such break points are generally determined by an automatic hyphenator. SHY can be used with any script, but its use is generally limited to situations where users need to override the behavior of such a hyphenator. The visible rendering of a line break at an intraword break point, whether automatically determined or indicated by a SHY, depends on the surrounding characters, the rules governing the script and language used, and, at times, the meaning of the word. The precise rules are outside the scope of this standard, but see Unicode Standard Annex #14, "Line Breaking Properties," for additional information. A common default rendering is to insert a hyphen before the line break, but this is insufficient or even incorrect in many situations.

Contrast this usage with U+2027 HYPHENATION POINT, which is used for a visible indication of the place of hyphenation in dictionaries. For a complete list of dash characters in the Unicode Standard, including all the hyphens, see *Table 6-3*.

The Unicode Standard includes two nonbreaking hyphen characters: U+2011 NON-BREAKING HYPHEN and U+0F0C TIBETAN MARK DELIMITER TSHEG BSTAR. See *Section 10.2, Tibetan*, for more discussion of the Tibetan-specific line breaking behavior.

Line and Paragraph Separator. The Unicode Standard provides two unambiguous characters, U+2028 LINE SEPARATOR and U+2029 PARAGRAPH SEPARATOR, to separate lines and paragraphs. They are considered the default form of denoting line and paragraph boundaries in Unicode plain text. A new line is begun after each LINE SEPARATOR. A new paragraph is begun after each PARAGRAPH SEPARATOR. As these characters are separator codes, it is not necessary either to start the first line or paragraph or to end the last line or paragraph with them. Doing so would indicate that there was an empty paragraph or line following. The PARAGRAPH SEPARATOR can be inserted between paragraphs of text. Its use allows the creation of plain text files, which can be laid out on a different line width at the receiving end. The LINE SEPARATOR can be used to indicate an unconditional end of line.

A paragraph separator indicates where a new paragraph should start. Any interparagraph formatting would be applied. This formatting could cause, for example, the line to be broken, any interparagraph line spacing to be applied, and the first line to be indented. A *line separator* indicates that a line break should occur at this point; although the text continues on the next line, it does not start a new paragraph—no interparagraph line spacing or paragraphic indentation is applied. For more information on line separators, see *Section 5.8, Newline Guidelines*.

Cursive Connection and Ligatures

In some fonts for some scripts, consecutive characters in a text stream may be rendered via adjacent glyphs that cursively join to each other, so as to emulate connected handwriting.

For example, cursive joining is implemented in nearly all fonts for the Arabic scripts and in a few handwriting-like fonts for the Latin script.

Cursive rendering is implemented by joining glyphs in the font and by using a process that selects the particular joining glyph to represent each individual character occurrence, based on the joining nature of its neighboring characters. This glyph selection is implemented in the rendering engine, typically using information in the font.

In many cases there is an even closer binding, where a sequence of characters is represented by a single glyph, called a ligature. Ligatures can occur in both cursive and noncursive fonts. Where ligatures are available, it is the task of the rendering system to select a ligature to create the most appropriate line layout. However, the rendering system cannot define the locations where ligatures are possible because there are many languages in which ligature formation requires more information. For example, in some languages, ligatures are never formed across syllable boundaries.

On occasion, an author may wish to override the normal automatic selection of connecting glyphs or ligatures. Typically, this choice is made to achieve one of the following effects:

- Cause nondefault joining appearance (for example, as is sometimes required in writing Persian using the Arabic script)
- Exhibit the joining-variant glyphs themselves in isolation
- Request a ligature to be formed where it normally would not be
- Request a ligature not to be formed where it normally would be

The Unicode Standard provides two characters that influence joining and ligature glyph selection: U+200C ZERO WIDTH NON-JOINER and U+200D ZERO WIDTH JOINER. The zero width joiner and non-joiner request a rendering system to have more or less of a connection between characters than they would otherwise have. Such a connection may be a simple cursive link, or it may include control of ligatures.

The zero width joiner and non-joiner characters are designed for use in plain text; they should not be used where higher-level ligation and cursive control is available. (See Unicode Technical Report #20, "Unicode in XML and Other Markup Languages," for more information.) Moreover, they are essentially requests for the rendering system to take into account when laying out the text; while a rendering system should consider them, it is perfectly acceptable for the system to disregard these requests.

The ZWJ and ZWNJ are designed for marking the unusual cases where ligatures or cursive connections are required or prohibited. These characters are not to be used in all cases where ligatures or cursive connections are desired; instead, they are meant only for overriding the normal behavior of the text.

Joiner. U+200D ZERO WIDTH JOINER is intended to produce a more connected rendering of adjacent characters than would otherwise be the case, if possible. In particular:

- If the two characters could form a ligature but do not normally, ZWJ requests that the ligature be used.

- Otherwise, if either of the characters could cursively connect but do not normally, ZWJ requests that each of the characters take a cursive-connection form where possible.

In a sequence like <X, ZWJ, Y>, where a cursive form exists for X but not for Y, the presence of ZWJ requests a cursive form for X. Otherwise, where neither a ligature nor a cursive connection is available, the ZWJ has no effect. In other words, given the three broad categories below, ZWJ requests that glyphs in the highest available category (for the given font) be used:

1. Ligated
2. Cursively connected
3. Unconnected

Non-joiner. U+200C ZERO WIDTH NON-JOINER is intended to break both cursive connections and ligatures in rendering.

ZWNJ requests that glyphs in the lowest available category (for the given font) be used.

For those unusual circumstances where someone wants to forbid ligatures in a sequence XY but promote cursive connection, the sequence <X, ZWJ, ZWNJ, ZWJ, Y> can be used. The ZWNJ breaks ligatures, while the two adjacent joiners cause the X and Y to take adjacent cursive forms (where they exist). Similarly, if someone wanted to have X take a cursive form but Y be isolated, then the sequence <X, ZWJ, ZWNJ, Y> could be used (as in previous versions of the Unicode Standard). Examples are shown in *Figure 16-3*.

Cursive Connection. For cursive connection, the joiner and non-joiner characters typically do not modify the contextual selection process itself, but instead change the context of a particular character occurrence. By providing a non-joining adjacent character where the adjacent character otherwise would be joining, or vice versa, they indicate that the rendering process should select a different joining glyph. This process can be used in two ways: to prevent a cursive joining or to exhibit joining glyphs in isolation.

In *Figure 16-1*, the insertion of the ZWNJ overrides the normal cursive joining of *sad* and *lam*.

Figure 16-1. Prevention of Joining

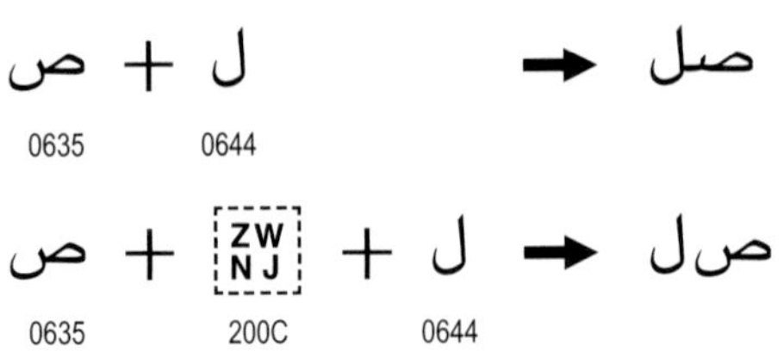

ص + ل → صل
0635 0644

ص + ZWNJ + ل → ص‌ل
0635 200C 0644

In *Figure 16-2*, the normal display of *ghain* without ZWJ before or after it uses the nominal (isolated) glyph form. When preceded and followed by ZWJ characters, however, the *ghain* is rendered with its medial form glyph in isolation.

Figure 16-2. Exhibition of Joining Glyphs in Isolation

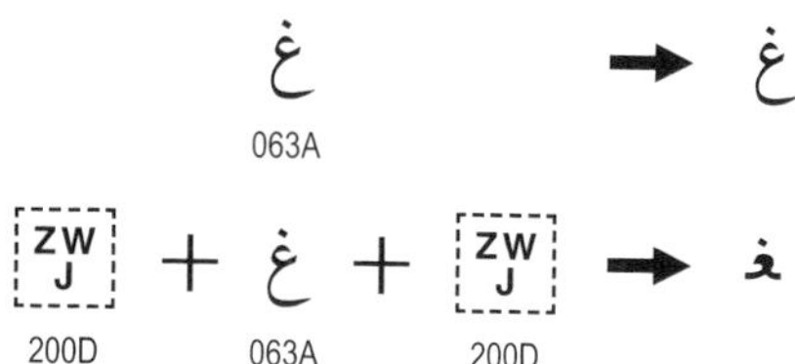

The examples in *Figure 16-1* and *Figure 16-2* are adapted from the Iranian national coded character set standard, ISIRI 3342, which defines ZWNJ and ZWJ as "pseudo space" and "pseudo connection," respectively.

Examples. *Figure 16-3* provides samples of desired renderings when the joiner or non-joiner is inserted between two characters. The examples presume that all of the glyphs are available in the font. If, for example, the ligatures are not available, the display would fall back to the unligated forms. Each of the entries in the first column of *Figure 16-3* shows two characters in visual display order. The column headings show characters to be inserted between those two characters. The cells below show the respective display when the joiners in the heading row are inserted between the original two characters.

Figure 16-3. Effect of Intervening Joiners

Character Sequences	As Is	ZWNJ	ZWJ ZWNJ ZWJ	ZWJ
f i 0066 0069	f i *or* ﬁ	f i	f i	ﬁ
ا ل 0627 0644	لا	ل‌ا	ل‍‌‍ا	ل‍ا
ج م 062C 0645	مج *or* مج	م‌ج	مج	مج
ج و 062C 0648	وج	وج	وج	وج

For backward compatibility, between Arabic characters a ZWJ acts just like the sequence <ZWJ, ZWNJ, ZWJ>, preventing a ligature from forming instead of requesting the use of a ligature that would not normally be used. As a result, there is no plain text mechanism for requesting the use of a ligature in Arabic text.

Transparency. The property value of Joining_Type=Transparent applies to characters that should not interfere with cursive connection, even when they occur in sequence between two characters that are connected cursively. These include all nonspacing marks and most format control characters, except for ZWJ and ZWNJ themselves. Note, in particular, that enclosing combining marks are also transparent as regards cursive connection. For example, using U+20DD COMBINING ENCLOSING CIRCLE to circle an Arabic letter in a sequence should not cause that Arabic letter to change its cursive connections to neighboring letters. See *Section 8.2, Arabic*, for more on joining classes and the details regarding Arabic cursive joining.

Joiner and Non-joiner in Indic Scripts. In Indic text, the ZWJ and ZWNJ are used to request particular display forms. A ZWJ after a sequence of consonant plus virama requests what is called a "half-form" of that consonant. A ZWNJ after a sequence of consonant plus virama requests that conjunct formation be interrupted, usually resulting in an explicit virama on that consonant. There are a few more specialized uses as well. For more information, see the discussions in *Chapter 9, South Asian Scripts-I.*

Implementation Notes. For modern font technologies, such as OpenType or AAT, font vendors should add ZWJ to their ligature mapping tables as appropriate. Thus, where a font had a mapping from "f" + "i" to ﬁ, the font designer should add the mapping from "f" + ZWJ + "i" to ﬁ. In contrast, ZWNJ will normally have the desired effect naturally for most fonts without any change, as it simply obstructs the normal ligature/cursive connection behavior. As with all other alternate format characters, fonts should use an invisible zero-width glyph for representation of both ZWJ and ZWNJ.

Filtering Joiner and Non-joiner. ZERO WIDTH JOINER and ZERO WIDTH NON-JOINER are format control characters. As such, and in common with other format control characters, they are ordinarily ignored by processes that analyze text content. For example, a spell-checker or a search operation should filter them out when checking for matches. There are exceptions, however. In particular scripts—most notably the Indic scripts—ZWJ and ZWNJ have specialized usages that may be of orthographic significance. In those contexts, blind filtering of all instances of ZWJ or ZWNJ may result in ignoring distinctions relevant to the user's notion of text content. Implementers should be aware of these exceptional circumstances, so that searching and matching operations behave as expected for those scripts.

Combining Grapheme Joiner

U+034F COMBINING GRAPHEME JOINER (CGJ) is used to affect the collation of adjacent characters for purposes of language-sensitive collation and searching. It is also used to distinguish sequences that would otherwise be canonically equivalent.

Formally, the combining grapheme joiner is not a format control character, but rather a combining mark. It has the General_Category value gc=Mn and the canonical combining class value ccc=0.

As a result of these properties, the presence of a combining grapheme joiner in the midst of a combining character sequence does not interrupt the combining character sequence; any process that is accumulating and processing all the characters of a combining character sequence would include a combining grapheme joiner as part of that sequence. This differs from the behavior of most format control characters, whose presence would interrupt a combining character sequence.

In addition, because the combining grapheme joiner has the canonical combining class of 0, canonical reordering will not reorder any adjacent combining marks around a combining grapheme joiner. (See the definition of canonical reordering in *Section 3.11, Canonical Ordering Behavior*.) In turn, this means that insertion of a combining grapheme joiner between two combining marks will prevent normalization from switching the positions of those two combining marks, regardless of their own combining classes.

Blocking Reordering. The CGJ has no visible glyph and no other format effect on neighboring characters but simply blocks reordering of combining marks. It can therefore be used as a tool to distinguish two alternative orderings of a sequence of combining marks for some exceptional processing or rendering purpose, whenever normalization would otherwise eliminate the distinction between the two sequences.

For example, using CGJ to block reordering is one way to maintain distinction between differently ordered sequences of certain Hebrew accents and marks. These distinctions are necessary for analytic and text representational purposes. However, these characters were assigned fixed-position combining classes despite the fact that they interact typographically. As a result, normalization treats differently ordered sequences as equivalent. In particular, the sequence

<lamed, patah, hiriq, finalmem>

is canonically equivalent to

<lamed, hiriq, patah, finalmem>

because the canonical combining classes of U+05B4 HEBREW POINT HIRIQ and U+05B7 HEBREW POINT PATAH are distinct. However, the sequence

<lamed, patah, CGJ, hiriq, finalmem>

is not canonically equivalent to the other two. The presence of the combining grapheme joiner, which has ccc=0, blocks the reordering of *hiriq* before *patah* by canonical reordering and thus allows a *patah* following a *hiriq* and a *patah* preceding a *hiriq* to be reliably distinguished, whether for display or for other processing.

The use of CGJ with double diacritics is discussed in *Section 7.9, Combining Marks*; see *Figure 7-10*.

CGJ and Collation. The Unicode Collation Algorithm normalizes Unicode text strings before applying collation weighting. The combining grapheme joiner is ordinarily ignored in collation key weighting in the UCA. However, whenever it blocks the reordering of combining marks in a string, it affects the order of secondary key weights associated with those combining marks, giving the two strings distinct keys. That makes it possible to treat them distinctly in searching and sorting without having to tailor the weights for either the combining grapheme joiner or the combining marks.

The CGJ can also be used to prevent the formation of contractions in the Unicode Collation Algorithm. For example, while "ch" is sorted as a single unit in a tailored Slovak collation, the sequence <c, CGJ, h> will sort as a "c" followed by an "h". The CGJ can also be used in German, for example, to distinguish in sorting between "ü" in the meaning of u-umlaut, which is the more common case and often sorted like <u,e>, and "ü" in the meaning u-diaeresis, which is comparatively rare and sorted like "u" with a secondary key weight. This also requires no tailoring of either the combining grapheme joiner or the sequence. Because CGJ is invisible and has the default_ignorable property, data that are marked up with a CGJ should not cause problems for other processes.

It is possible to give sequences of characters that include the combining grapheme joiner special tailored weights. Thus the sequence <c, CGJ, h> could be weighted completely differently from the contraction "ch" or from the way "c" and "h" would have sorted without the contraction. However, such an application of CGJ is not recommended. For more information on the use of CGJ with sorting, matching, and searching, see Unicode Technical Report #10, "Unicode Collation Algorithm."

Rendering. For rendering, the combining grapheme joiner is invisible. However, some older implementations may treat a sequence of grapheme clusters linked by combining grapheme joiners as a single unit for the application of enclosing combining marks. For more information on grapheme clusters, see Unicode Technical Report #29, "Text Boundaries." For more information on enclosing combining marks, see *Section 3.11, Canonical Ordering Behavior.*

CGJ and Joiner Characters. The combining grapheme joiner must not be confused with the *zero width joiner* or the *word joiner*, which have very different functions. In particular, inserting a combining grapheme joiner between two characters should have no effect on their ligation or cursive joining behavior. Where the prevention of line breaking is the desired effect, the word joiner should be used. For more information on the behavior of these characters in line breaking, see Unicode Standard Annex #14, "Line Breaking Properties."

Bidirectional Ordering Controls

Bidirectional ordering controls are used in the Bidirectional Algorithm, described in Unicode Standard Annex #9, "The Bidirectional Algorithm." Systems that handle right-to-left scripts such as Arabic, Syriac, and Hebrew, for example, should interpret these format control characters. The bidirectional ordering controls are shown in *Table 16-3.*

As with other format control characters, bidirectional ordering controls affect the layout of the text in which they are contained but should be ignored for other text processes, such as sorting or searching. However, text processes that modify text content must maintain these characters correctly, because matching pairs of bidirectional ordering controls must be

Table 16-3. Bidirectional Ordering Controls

Code	Name	Abbreviation
U+200E	LEFT-TO-RIGHT MARK	LRM
U+200F	RIGHT-TO-LEFT MARK	RLM
U+202A	LEFT-TO-RIGHT EMBEDDING	LRE
U+202B	RIGHT-TO-LEFT EMBEDDING	RLE
U+202C	POP DIRECTIONAL FORMATTING	PDF
U+202D	LEFT-TO-RIGHT OVERRIDE	LRO
U+202E	RIGHT-TO-LEFT OVERRIDE	RLO

coordinated, so as not to disrupt the layout and interpretation of bidirectional text. Each instance of a LRE, RLE, LRO, or RLO is normally paired with a corresponding PDF.

U+200E LEFT-TO-RIGHT MARK and U+200F RIGHT-TO-LEFT MARK have the semantics of an invisible character of zero width, except that these characters have strong directionality. They are intended to be used to resolve cases of ambiguous directionality in the context of bidirectional texts; they are not paired. Unlike U+200B ZERO WIDTH SPACE, these characters carry no word breaking semantics. (See Unicode Standard Annex #9, "The Bidirectional Algorithm," for more information.)

16.3 Deprecated Format Characters

Deprecated Format Characters: U+206A–U+206F

Three pairs of deprecated format characters are encoded in this block:

- Symmetric swapping format characters used to control the glyphs that depict characters such as "(" (The default state is *activated.*)
- Character shaping selectors used to control the shaping behavior of the Arabic compatibility characters (The default state is *inhibited.*)
- Numeric shape selectors used to override the normal shapes of the Western digits (The default state is *nominal.*)

The use of these character shaping selectors and codes for digit shapes is *strongly* discouraged in the Unicode Standard. Instead, the appropriate character codes should be used with the default state. For example, if contextual forms for Arabic characters are desired, then the nominal characters should be used, not the presentation forms with the shaping selectors. Similarly, if the Arabic digit forms are desired, then the explicit characters should be used, such as U+0660 ARABIC-INDIC DIGIT ZERO.

Symmetric Swapping. The symmetric swapping format characters are used in conjunction with the class of left- and right-handed pairs of characters (symmetric characters), such as parentheses. The characters thus affected are listed in *Section 4.7, Bidi Mirrored—Norma-*

tive. They indicate whether the interpretation of the term LEFT or RIGHT in the character names should be interpreted as meaning *opening* or *closing*, respectively. They do not nest. The default state of symmetric swapping may be set by a higher-level protocol or standard, such as ISO 6429. In the absence of such a protocol, the default state is *activated*.

From the point of encountering U+206A INHIBIT SYMMETRIC SWAPPING format character up to a subsequent U+206B ACTIVATE SYMMETRIC SWAPPING (if any), the symmetric characters will be interpreted and rendered as left and right.

From the point of encountering U+206B ACTIVATE SYMMETRIC SWAPPING format character up to a subsequent U+206A INHIBIT SYMMETRIC SWAPPING (if any), the symmetric characters will be interpreted and rendered as opening and closing. This state (*activated*) is the default state in the absence of any symmetric swapping code or a higher-level protocol.

Character Shaping Selectors. The character shaping selector format characters are used in conjunction with Arabic presentation forms. During the presentation process, certain letterforms may be joined together in cursive connection or ligatures. The shaping selector codes indicate that the character shape determination (glyph selection) process used to achieve this presentation effect is to be either activated or inhibited. The shaping selector codes do not nest.

From the point of encountering a U+206C INHIBIT ARABIC FORM SHAPING format character up to a subsequent U+206D ACTIVATE ARABIC FORM SHAPING (if any), the character shaping determination process should be inhibited. If the backing store contains Arabic presentation forms (for example, U+FE80..U+FEFC), then these forms should be presented without shape modification. This state (*inhibited*) is the default state in the absence of any character shaping selector or a higher-level protocol.

From the point of encountering a U+206D ACTIVATE ARABIC FORM SHAPING format character up to a subsequent U+206C INHIBIT ARABIC FORM SHAPING (if any), any Arabic presentation forms that appear in the backing store should be presented with shape modification by means of the character shaping (glyph selection) process.

The shaping selectors have no effect on nominal Arabic characters (U+0660..U+06FF), which are always subject to character shaping (glyph selection).

Numeric Shape Selectors. The numeric shape selector format characters allow the selection of the shapes in which the digits U+0030..U+0039 are to be rendered. These format characters do not nest.

From the point of encountering a U+206E NATIONAL DIGIT SHAPES format character up to a subsequent U+206F NOMINAL DIGIT SHAPES (if any), the European digits (U+0030..U+0039) should be depicted using the appropriate national digit shapes as specified by means of appropriate agreements. For example, they could be displayed with shapes such as the ARABIC-INDIC DIGITS (U+0660..U+0669). The actual character shapes (glyphs) used to display national digit shapes are not specified by the Unicode Standard.

From the point of encountering a U+206F NOMINAL DIGIT SHAPES format character up to a subsequent U+206E NATIONAL DIGIT SHAPES (if any), the European digits (U+0030..

U+0039) should be depicted using glyphs that represent the nominal digit shapes shown in the code tables for these digits. This state (*nominal*) is the default state in the absence of any numeric shape selector or a higher-level protocol.

16.4 Variation Selectors

Characters in the Unicode Standard can be represented by a wide variety of glyphs, as discussed in *Chapter 2, General Structure*. Occasionally the need arises in text processing to restrict or change the set of glyphs that are to be used to represent a character. Normally such changes are indicated by choice of font or style in rich text documents. In special circumstances, such a variation from the normal range of appearance needs to be expressed side-by-side in the same document in plain text contexts, where it is impossible or inconvenient to exchange formatted text. For example, in languages employing the Mongolian script, sometimes a specific variant range of glyphs is needed for a specific textual purpose for which the range of "generic" glyphs is considered inappropriate.

Variation selectors provide a mechanism for specifying a restriction on the set of glyphs that are used to represent a particular character. They also provide a mechanism for specifying variants, such as for CJK ideographs and Mongolian letters, that have essentially the same semantics but substantially different ranges of glyphs.

Variation Sequence. A variation sequence, which always consists of a base character followed by the variation selector, may be specified as part of the Unicode Standard. That sequence is referred to as a *variant* of the base character. The variation selector affects *only* the appearance of the base character, and only in the variation sequences defined in this Standard. The variation selector is *not* used as a general code extension mechanism.

> *Only the variation sequences specifically defined in the file StandardizedVariants.txt in the Unicode Character Database are sanctioned for standard use. In all other cases, the variation selector cannot change the visual appearance of the preceding base character from what it would have had in the absence of the variation selector.*

The base character in a variation sequence is never a combining character or a decomposable character. The variation selectors themselves are combining marks of combining class 0 and are default ignorable characters. Thus, if the variation sequence is not supported, the variation selector should be invisible and ignored. As with all default ignorable characters, this does not preclude modes or environments where the variation selectors should be given visible appearance. For example, a "Show Hidden" mode could reveal the presence of such characters with specialized glyphs, or a particular environment could use or require a visual indication of a base character (such as a wavy underline) to show that it is part of a standardized variation sequence that cannot be supported by the current font.

The standardization or support of a particular variation sequence does *not* limit the set of glyphs that can be used to represent the base character alone. If a user *requires* a visual distinction between a character and a particular variant of that character, then fonts must be used to make that distinction. The existence of a variation sequence does not preclude the later encoding of a new character with distinct semantics and a similar or overlapping range of glyphs.

Mongolian. For the behavior of older implementations of Mongolian using variation selectors, see the discussion of Mongolian free variation selectors in *Section 13.2, Mongolian.*

16.5 Private-Use Characters

Private-use characters are assigned Unicode code points whose interpretation is not specified by this standard and whose use may be determined by private agreement among cooperating users. These characters are designated for private use and do not have defined, interpretable semantics except by private agreement.

Private-use characters are often used to implement end-user defined characters (EUDC), which are common in East Asian computing environments.

No charts are provided for private-use characters, as any such characters are, by their very nature, defined only outside the context of this standard.

Three distinct blocks of private-use characters are provided in the Unicode Standard: the primary Private Use Area (PUA) in the BMP and two supplementary Private Use Areas in the supplemental planes.

All code points in the blocks of private-use characters in the Unicode Standard are permanently designated for private use. No assignment to a particular standard set of characters will ever be endorsed or documented by the Unicode Consortium for any of these code points.

Any prior use of a character as a private-use character has no direct bearing on any eventual encoding decisions regarding whether and how to encode that character. Standardization of characters must always follow the normal process for encoding of new characters or scripts.

Properties. The Unicode Character Database provides default character properties, which implementations can use for the processing of private-use characters. In addition, users of private-use characters may exchange external data that allow them also to exchange private-use characters in a semantically consistent way between implementations. The Unicode Standard provides no predefined format for such an exchange.

Normalization. The canonical and compatibility decompositions of any private-use character (for example, U+E000) are equal to the character itself. This is normatively defined by the Unicode Standard and cannot be changed by private agreement. The treatment of all private-use characters for normalization forms NFC, NFD, NFKD, and NFKC is also normatively defined by the Unicode Standard on the basis of these decompositions. (See Unicode Standard Annex #15, "Unicode Normalization Forms.") No private agreement may change these forms—for example, by changing the standard canonical or compatibility decompositions for private-use characters.

This does not preclude private agreements on other transformations. Thus one could define a transformation "MyCompanyComposition" that was identical to NFC except that it mapped U+E000 to "a". The forms NFC, NFD, NFKD, and NFKC themselves, however, cannot be changed by such agreements.

Private Use Area: U+E000–U+F8FF

The primary Private Use Area consists of code points in the range U+E000 to U+F8FF, for a total of 6,400 private-use characters.

Encoding Structure. By convention, the primary Private Use Area is divided into a corporate use subarea for platform writers, starting at U+F8FF and extending downward in values, and an end-user subarea, starting at U+E000 and extending upward.

By following this convention, the likelihood of collision between private-use characters defined by platform writers with private-use characters defined by end users can be reduced. However, it should be noted that this is only a convention, not a normative specification. In principle, any user can define any interpretation of any private-use character.

Corporate Use Subarea. Systems vendors and/or software developers may need to reserve some private-use characters for internal use by their software. The corporate use subarea is the preferred area for such reservations. Assignments of character semantics in this subarea may be completely internal, hidden from end users, and used only for vendor-specific application support, or they may be published as vendor-specific character assignments available to applications and end users. An example of the former case would be the assignment of a character code to a system support operation such as <MOVE> or <COPY>; an example of the latter case would be the assignment of a character code to a vendor-specific logo character such as Apple's *apple* character.

Note, however, that systems vendors may need to support full end-user definability for all private-use characters, for such purposes as *gaiji* support or for transient cross-mapping tables. The use of noncharacters (see *Section 16.7, Noncharacters*, and definition D14 in *Section 3.4, Characters and Encoding*) is the preferred way to make use of *non-interchangeable* internal system sentinels of various sorts.

End-User Subarea. The end-user subarea is intended for private-use character definitions by end users or for scratch allocations of character space by end-user applications.

Allocation of Subareas. Vendors may choose to reserve ranges of private-use characters in the corporate use subarea and make some defined portion of the end-user subarea available for completely free end-user definition. The convention of separating the two subareas is merely a suggestion for the convenience of system vendors and software developers. No firm dividing line between the two subareas is defined in this standard, as different users may have different requirements. No provision is made in the Unicode Standard for avoiding a "stack-heap collision" between the two subareas; in other words, there is no guarantee that end users will not define a private-use character at a code point that overlaps and conflicts with a particular corporate private-use definition at the same code point. Avoiding such overlaps in definition is up to implementations and users.

Supplementary Private Use Areas

Encoding Structure. The entire Plane 15, with the exception of the noncharacters U+FFFFE and U+FFFFF, is defined to be the Supplementary Private Use Area-A. The entire Plane 16, with the exception of the noncharacters U+10FFFE and U+10FFFF, is defined to be the Supplementary Private Use Area-B. Together these areas make an additional 131,068 code points available for private use.

The supplementary PUAs provide additional undifferentiated space for private-use characters for implementations for which the 6,400 private-use characters in the primary PUA prove to be insufficient.

16.6 Surrogates Area

Surrogates Area: U+D800–U+DFFF

When using UTF-16 to represent supplementary characters, pairs of 16-bit code units are used for each character. These units are called *surrogates*. To distinguish them from ordinary characters, they are allocated in a separate area. The Surrogates Area consists of 1,024 low-half surrogate code points and 1,024 high-half surrogate code points. For the formal definition of a *surrogate pair* and the role of surrogate pairs in the Unicode Conformance Clause, see *Section 3.8, Surrogates,* and *Section 5.4, Handling Surrogate Pairs in UTF-16.*

The use of surrogate pairs in the Unicode Standard is formally equivalent to the Universal Transformation Format-16 (UTF-16) defined in ISO 10646. For more information, see *Appendix C, Relationship to ISO/IEC 10646.* For a complete statement of UTF-16, see *Section 3.9, Unicode Encoding Forms.*

High-Surrogate. The high-surrogate code points are assigned to the range U+D800..U+DBFF. The high-surrogate code point is always the first element of a surrogate pair.

Low-Surrogate. The low-surrogate code points are assigned to the range U+DC00..U+DFFF. The low-surrogate code point is always the second element of a surrogate pair.

Private-Use High-Surrogates. The high-surrogate code points from U+DB80..U+DBFF are private-use high-surrogate code points (a total of 128 code points). Characters represented by means of a surrogate pair, where the high-surrogate code point is a private-use high-surrogate, are private-use characters from the supplementary private use areas. For more information on private-use characters, see *Section 16.5, Private-Use Characters.*

The code tables do not have charts or name list entries for the range D800..DFFF because individual, unpaired surrogates merely have code points.

16.7 Noncharacters

Noncharacters: U+FFFE, U+FFFF, and Others

Noncharacters are code points that are permanently reserved in the Unicode Standard for internal use. They are forbidden for use in open interchange of Unicode text data. See *Section 3.4, Characters and Encoding*, for the formal definition of noncharacters and conformance requirements related to their use.

The Unicode Standard sets aside 66 noncharacter code points. The last two code points of each plane are noncharacters: U+FFFE and U+FFFF on the BMP, U+1FFFE and U+1FFFF on Plane 1, and so on, up to U+10FFFE and U+10FFFF on Plane 16, for a total of 34 code points. In addition, there is a contiguous range of another 32 noncharacter code points in the BMP: U+FDD0..U+FDEF. For historical reasons, the range U+FDD0..U+FDEF is contained within the Arabic Presentation Forms-A block, but those noncharacters are not "Arabic noncharacters" or "right-to-left noncharacters," and are not distinguished in any other way from the other noncharacters, except in their code point values.

Applications are free to use any of these noncharacter code points internally but should *never* attempt to exchange them. If a noncharacter is received in open interchange, an application is not required to interpret it in any way. It is good practice, however, to recognize it as a noncharacter and to take appropriate action, such as removing it from the text. Note that Unicode conformance freely allows the removal of these characters. (See conformance clause C7 in *Section 3.2, Conformance Requirements.*)

In effect, noncharacters can be thought of as application-internal private-use code points. Unlike the private-use characters discussed in *Section 16.5, Private-Use Characters*, which *are* assigned characters and which *are* intended for use in open interchange, subject to interpretation by private agreement, noncharacters are permanently reserved (unassigned) and have no interpretation whatsoever outside of their possible application-internal private uses.

U+FFFF and U+10FFFF. These two noncharacter code points have the attribute of being associated with the largest code unit values for particular Unicode encoding forms. In UTF-16, U+FFFF is associated with the largest 16-bit code unit value, $FFFF_{16}$. U+10FFFF is associated with the largest legal UTF-32 32-bit code unit value, $10FFFF_{16}$. This attribute renders these two noncharacter code points useful for internal purposes as sentinels. For example, they might be used to indicate the end of a list, to represent a value in an index guaranteed to be higher than any valid character value, and so on.

U+FFFE. This noncharacter has the intended peculiarity that, when represented in UTF-16 and then serialized, it has the opposite byte sequence of U+FEFF, the *byte order mark*. This means that applications should reserve U+FFFE as an internal signal that a UTF-16 text stream is in a reversed byte format. Detection of U+FFFE at the start of an input stream should be taken as a strong indication that the input stream should be byte-swapped before interpretation. For more on the use of the *byte order mark* and its interaction with the noncharacter U+FFFE, see *Section 16.8, Specials*.

16.8 Specials

The Specials block contains code points that are interpreted as neither control nor graphic characters but that are provided to facilitate current software practices.

For information about the noncharacter code points U+FFFE and U+FFFF, see *Section 16.7, Noncharacters*.

Byte Order Mark (BOM): U+FEFF

For historical reasons, the character U+FEFF used for the *byte order mark* is named ZERO WIDTH NO-BREAK SPACE. Except for compatibility with versions of Unicode prior to Version 3.2, U+FEFF is not used with the semantics of *zero width no-break space* (see *Section 16.2, Layout Controls*). Instead, its most common and most important usage is in the following two circumstances:

1. Unmarked Byte Order. Some machine architectures use the so-called big-endian byte order, while others use the little-endian byte order. When Unicode text is serialized into bytes, the bytes can go in either order, depending on the architecture. Sometimes this byte order is not externally marked, which causes problems in interchange between different systems.
2. Unmarked Character Set. In some circumstances, the character set information for a stream of coded characters (such as a file) is not available. The only information available is that the stream contains text, but the precise character set is not known.

In these two cases, the character U+FEFF is used as a signature to indicate the byte order and the character set by using the byte serializations described in *Section 3.10, Unicode Encoding Schemes*. Because the byte-swapped version U+FFFE is a noncharacter, when an interpreting process finds U+FFFE as the first character, it signals either that the process has encountered text that is of the incorrect byte order or that the file is not valid Unicode text.

In the UTF-16 encoding scheme, U+FEFF at the very beginning of a file or stream explicitly signals the byte order.

The byte sequences <FE_{16} FF_{16}> or <FF_{16} FE_{16}> may also serve as a signature to identify a file as containing UTF-16 text. Either sequence is exceedingly rare at the outset of text files using other character encodings, whether single- or multiple-byte, and therefore not likely to be confused with real text data. For example, in systems that employ ISO Latin-1 (ISO/IEC 8859-1) or the Microsoft Windows ANSI Code Page 1252, the byte sequence <FE_{16} FF_{16}> constitutes the string <*thorn, y diaeresis*> "þÿ"; in systems that employ the Apple Macintosh Roman character set or the Adobe Standard Encoding, this sequence represents the sequence <*ogonek, hacek*> "˛ ˇ"; in systems that employ other common IBM PC code pages (for example, CP 437, 850), this sequence represents <*black square, no-break space*> "■ ".

In UTF-8, the BOM corresponds to the byte sequence <EF_{16} BB_{16} BF_{16}>. Although there are never any questions of byte order with UTF-8 text, this sequence can serve as signature for UTF-8 encoded text where the character set is unmarked. As with a BOM in UTF-16, this sequence of bytes will be extremely rare at the beginning of text files in other character encodings. For example, in systems that employ Microsoft Windows ANSI Code Page 1252, <EF_{16} BB_{16} BF_{16}> corresponds to the sequence <*i diaeresis, guillemet, inverted question mark*> "ï » ¿".

For compatibility with versions of the Unicode Standard prior to Version 3.2, the code point U+FEFF has the word-joining semantics of *zero width no-break space* when it is not used as a BOM. In new text, these semantics should be encoded by U+2060 WORD JOINER. See "Line and Word Breaking" in *Section 16.2, Layout Controls*, for more information.

Where the byte order is explicitly specified, such as in UTF-16BE or UTF-16LE, then all U+FEFF characters—even at the very beginning of the text—are to be interpreted as *zero width no-break spaces*. Similarly, where Unicode text has known byte order, initial U+FEFF characters are not required, but for backward compatibility are to be interpreted as *zero width no-break spaces*. For example, for strings in an API, the memory architecture of the processor provides the explicit byte order. For databases and similar structures, it is much more efficient and robust to use a uniform byte order for the same field (if not the entire database), thereby avoiding use of the *byte order mark*.

Systems that use the *byte order mark* must recognize when an initial U+FEFF signals the byte order. In those cases, it is not part of the textual content and should be removed before processing, because otherwise it may be mistaken for a legitimate *zero width no-break space*. To represent an initial U+FEFF ZERO WIDTH NO-BREAK SPACE in a UTF-16 file, use U+FEFF twice in a row. The first one is a *byte order mark*; the second one is the initial *zero width no-break space*. See *Table 16-4* for a summary of encoding scheme signatures.

Table 16-4. Unicode Encoding Scheme Signatures

Encoding Scheme	Signature
UTF-8	EF BB BF
UTF-16 Big-endian	FE FF
UTF-16 Little-endian	FF FE
UTF-32 Big-endian	00 00 FE FF
UTF-32 Little-endian	FF FE 00 00

If U+FEFF had only the semantics of a signature code point, it could be freely deleted from text without affecting the interpretation of the rest of the text. Carelessly appending files together, for example, can result in a signature code point in the middle of text. Unfortunately, U+FEFF also has significance as a character. As a *zero width no-break space*, it indicates that line breaks are not allowed between the adjoining characters. Thus U+FEFF affects the interpretation of text and cannot be freely deleted. The overloading of semantics for this code point has caused problems for programs and protocols. The new character U+2060 WORD JOINER has the same semantics in all cases as U+FEFF, except that it *cannot* be used as a signature. Implementers are strongly encouraged to use *word joiner* in those circumstances whenever word joining semantics are intended.

An initial U+FEFF also takes a characteristic form in other charsets designed for Unicode text. (The term "charset" refers to a wide range of text encodings, including encoding schemes as well as compression schemes and text-specific transformation formats.) The characteristic sequences of bytes associated with an initial U+FEFF can serve as signatures in those cases, as shown in *Table 16-5*.

Table 16-5. U+FEFF Signature in Other Charsets

Charset	Signature
SCSU	0E FE FF
BOCU-1	FB EE 28
UTF-7	2B 2F 76 38 or 2B 2F 76 39 or 2B 2F 76 2B or 2B 2F 76 2F
UTF-EBCDIC	DD 73 66 73

Most signatures can be deleted either before or after conversion of an input stream into a Unicode encoding form. However, in the case of BOCU-1 and UTF-7, the input byte sequence must be converted before the initial U+FEFF can be deleted, because stripping the signature byte sequence without conversion destroys context necessary for the correct interpretation of subsequent bytes in the input sequence.

Specials: U+FFF0–U+FFF8

The nine unassigned Unicode code points in the range U+FFF0..U+FFF8 are reserved for special character definitions.

Annotation Characters: U+FFF9–U+FFFB

An *interlinear annotation* consists of *annotating text* that is related to a sequence of *annotated* characters. For all regular editing and text-processing algorithms, the annotated characters are treated as part of the text stream. The annotating text is also part of the content, but for all or some text processing, it does not form part of the main text stream. However, within the annotating text, characters are accessible to the same kind of layout, text-processing, and editing algorithms as the base text. The *annotation characters* delimit the annotating and the annotated text, and identify them as part of an annotation. See *Figure 16-4*.

The annotation characters are used in internal processing when out-of-band information is associated with a character stream, very similarly to the usage of U+FFFC OBJECT REPLACE-

Figure 16-4. Annotation Characters

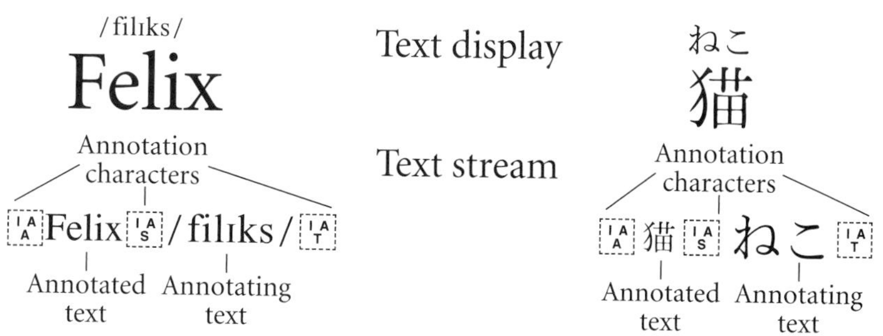

MENT CHARACTER. However, unlike the opaque objects hidden by the latter character, the annotation itself is textual.

Conformance. A conformant implementation that supports annotation characters interprets the base text as if it were part of an unannotated text stream. Within the annotating text, it interprets the annotating characters with their regular Unicode semantics.

U+FFF9 INTERLINEAR ANNOTATION ANCHOR is an anchor character, preceding the interlinear annotation. The exact nature and formatting of the annotation depend on additional information that is not part of the plain text stream. This situation is analogous to that for U+FFFC OBJECT REPLACEMENT CHARACTER.

U+FFFA INTERLINEAR ANNOTATION SEPARATOR separates the base characters in the text stream from the annotation characters that follow. The exact interpretation of this character depends on the nature of the annotation. More than one separator may be present. Additional separators delimit parts of a multipart annotating text.

U+FFFB INTERLINEAR ANNOTATION TERMINATOR terminates the annotation object (and returns to the regular text stream).

Use in Plain Text. Usage of the annotation characters in plain text interchange is strongly discouraged without prior agreement between the sender and the receiver, because the content may be misinterpreted otherwise. Simply filtering out the annotation characters on input will produce an unreadable result or, even worse, an opposite meaning. On input, a plain text receiver should either preserve all characters or remove the interlinear annotation characters as well as the annotating text included between the INTERLINEAR ANNOTATION SEPARATOR and the INTERLINEAR ANNOTATION TERMINATOR.

When an output for plain text usage is desired but the receiver is unknown to the sender, these interlinear annotation characters should be removed as well as the annotating text included between the INTERLINEAR ANNOTATION SEPARATOR and the INTERLINEAR ANNOTATION TERMINATOR.

This restriction does not preclude the use of annotation characters in plain text interchange, but it requires a prior agreement between the sender and the receiver for correct interpretation of the annotations.

Lexical Restrictions. If an implementation encounters a paragraph break between an *anchor* and its corresponding *terminator,* it shall terminate any open annotations at this point. Anchor characters must precede their corresponding terminator characters. Unpaired anchors or terminators shall be ignored. A *separator* occurring outside a pair of delimiters, shall be ignored. Annotations may be nested.

Formatting. All formatting information for an annotation is provided by higher-level protocols. The details of the layout of the annotation are implementation-defined. Correct formatting may require additional information that is not present in the character stream, but rather is maintained out-of-band. Therefore, annotation markers serve as placeholders for an implementation that has access to that information from another source. The formatting of annotations and other special line layout features of Japanese is discussed in JIS X 4501.

Input. Annotation characters are not normally input or edited directly by end users. Their insertion and management in text are typically handled by an application, which will present a user interface for selecting and annotating text.

Collation. With the exception of the special case where the annotation is intended to be used as a sort key, annotations are typically ignored for collation or optionally preprocessed to act as tie breakers only. Importantly, annotation base characters are not ignored, but rather are treated like regular text.

Replacement Characters: U+FFFC–U+FFFD

U+FFFC. The U+FFFC OBJECT REPLACEMENT CHARACTER is used as an insertion point for objects located within a stream of text. All other information about the object is kept outside the character data stream. Internally it is a dummy character that acts as an anchor point for the object's formatting information. In addition to assuring correct placement of an object in a data stream, the object replacement character allows the use of general stream-based algorithms for any textual aspects of embedded objects.

U+FFFD. The U+FFFD REPLACEMENT CHARACTER is the general substitute character in the Unicode Standard. It can be substituted for any "unknown" character in another encoding that cannot be mapped in terms of known Unicode characters (see *Section 5.3, Unknown and Missing Characters*).

16.9 Tag Characters

Tag Characters: U+E0000–U+E007F

The characters in this block provide a mechanism for language tagging in Unicode plain text. *The use of these characters is strongly discouraged.* The characters in this block are reserved for use with special protocols. They are *not* to be used in the absence of such protocols or with *any* protocols that provide alternate means for language tagging, such as

HTML or XML. See Unicode Technical Report #20, "Unicode in XML and Other Markup Languages." The requirement for language information embedded in plain text data is often overstated. See *Section 5.10, Language Information in Plain Text.*

This block encodes a set of 95 special-use tag characters to enable the spelling out of ASCII-based string tags using characters that can be strictly separated from ordinary text content characters in Unicode. These tag characters can be embedded by protocols into plain text. They can be identified and/or ignored by implementations with trivial algorithms because there is no overloading of usage for these tag characters—they can express only tag values and never textual content itself.

In addition to these 95 characters, one language tag identification character and one cancel tag character are encoded. The language tag identification character identifies a tag string as a language tag; the language tag itself makes use of RFC 4646 (or its successors) language tag strings spelled out using the tag characters from this block.

Syntax for Embedding Tags

To embed any ASCII-derived tag in Unicode plain text, the tag is spelled out with corresponding tag characters, prefixed with the relevant tag identification character. The resultant string is embedded directly in the text.

Tag Identification. The tag identification character is used as a mechanism for identifying tags of different types. In the future, this could enable multiple types of tags embedded in plain text to coexist.

Tag Termination. No termination character is required for the tag itself, because all characters that make up the tag are numerically distinct from any non-tag character. A tag terminates either at the first non-tag character (that is, any other normal Unicode character) or at next tag identification character. A detailed BNF syntax for tags is listed in "Formal Tag Syntax" later in this section.

Language Tags. A string of tag characters prefixed by U+E0001 LANGUAGE TAG is specified to constitute a language tag. Furthermore, the tag values for the language tag are to be spelled out as specified in RFC 4646, making use only of registered tag values or of user-defined language tags starting with the characters "x-".

For example, consider the task of embedding a language tag for Japanese. The Japanese tag from RFC 4646 is "ja" (composed of ISO 639 language id) or, alternatively, "ja-JP" (composed of ISO 639 language id plus ISO 3166 country id). Because RFC 4646 specifies that language tags are not case significant, it is recommended that for language tags, the entire tag be lowercased before conversion to tag characters.

Thus the entire language tag "ja-JP" would be converted to the tag characters as follows:

<U+E0001, U+E006A, U+E0061, U+E002D, U+E006A, U+E0070>

The language tag, in its shorter, "ja" form, would be expressed as follows:

<U+E0001, U+E006A, U+E0061>

Tag Scope and Nesting. The value of an established tag continues from the point at which the tag is embedded in text until either

> A. The text itself goes out of scope, as defined by the application, for example, for line-oriented protocols, when reaching the end-of-line or end-of-string; for text streams, when reaching the end-of-stream; and so on),

or

> B. The tag is explicitly canceled by the U+E007F CANCEL TAG character.

Tags of the *same* type cannot be nested in any way. For example, if a new embedded language tag occurs following text that was already language tagged, the tagged value for subsequent text simply changes to that specified in the new tag.

Tags of different types can have interdigitating scope, but not hierarchical scope. In effect, tags of different types completely ignore each other, so that the use of language tags can be completely asynchronous with the use of future tag types. These relationships are illustrated in *Figure 16-5.*

Figure 16-5. Tag Characters

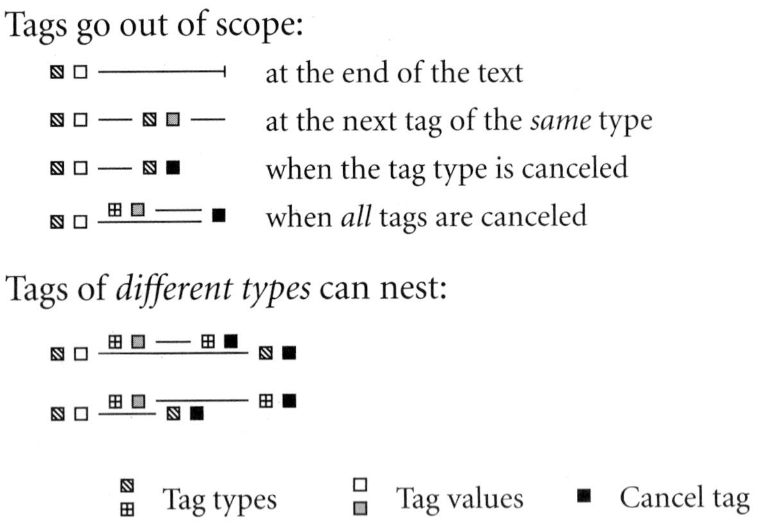

Tags go out of scope:

at the end of the text

at the next tag of the *same* type

when the tag type is canceled

when *all* tags are canceled

Tags of *different types* can nest:

Tag types Tag values Cancel tag

Canceling Tag Values. The main function of CANCEL TAG is to make possible operations such as blind concatenation of strings in a tagged context without the propagation of inappropriate tag values across the string boundaries. There are two uses of CANCEL TAG. To cancel a tag value of a particular type, prefix the CANCEL TAG character with the tag identification character of the appropriate type. For example, the complete string to cancel a language tag is <U+E0001, U+E007F>. The value of the relevant tag type returns to the default state for that tag type—namely, no tag value specified, the same as untagged text. To cancel any tag values of any type that may be in effect, use CANCEL TAG without a prefixed tag identification character.

Currently there is no observable difference in the two uses of CANCEL TAG, because only one tag identification character (and therefore one tag type) is defined. Inserting a bare CANCEL TAG in places where only the language tag needs to be canceled could lead to unanticipated side effects if this text were to be inserted in the future into a text that supports more than one tag type.

Working with Language Tags

Avoiding Language Tags. Because of the extra implementation burden, language tags should be avoided in plain text unless language information is required and the receivers of the text are certain to properly recognize and maintain the tags. However, where language tags must be used, implementers should consider the following implementation issues involved in supporting language information with tags and decide how to handle tags where they are not fully supported. This discussion applies to any mechanism for providing language tags in a plain text environment.

Higher-Level Protocols. Language tags should be avoided wherever higher-level protocols, such as a rich text format, HTML, or MIME, provide language attributes. This practice prevents cases where the higher-level protocol and the language tags disagree. See Unicode Technical Report #20, "Unicode in XML and Other Markup Languages."

Effect of Tags on Interpretation of Text. Implementations that support language tags may need to take them into account for special processing, such as hyphenation or choice of font. However, the tag characters themselves have no display and do not affect line breaking, character shaping or joining, or any other format or layout properties. Processes interpreting the tag may choose to impose such behavior based on the tag value that it represents.

Display. Characters in the tag character block have no visible rendering in normal text and the language tags themselves are not displayed. This choice may not require modification of the displaying program, if the fonts on that platform have the language tag characters mapped to zero-width, invisible glyphs. For debugging or other operations that must render the tags themselves visible, it is advisable that the tag characters be rendered using the corresponding ASCII character glyphs (perhaps modified systematically to differentiate them from normal ASCII characters). The tag character values have been chosen, however, so that the tag characters will be interpretable in most debuggers even without display support.

Processing. Sequential access to the text is generally straightforward. If language codes are not relevant to the particular processing operation, then they should be ignored. Random access to stateful tags is more problematic. Because the current state of the text depends on tags that appeared previous to it, the text must be searched backward, sometimes all the way to the start. With these exceptions, tags pose no particular difficulties as long as no modifications are made to the text.

Range Checking for Tag Characters. Tag characters are encoded in Plane 14 to support easy range checking. The following C/C++ source code snippets show efficient implementations of range checks for characters E0000..E007F expressed in each of the three significant Unicode encoding forms. Range checks allow implementations that do not want to support these tag characters to efficiently filter for them.

Range check expressed in UTF-32:

```
if ( ((unsigned)  *s)  - 0xE0000  <= 0x7F  )
```

Range check expressed in UTF-16:

```
if ( ( *s == 0xDB40 ) && ( ((unsigned)*(s+1)) - 0xDC00  <= 0x7F ) )
```

Range check expressed in UTF-8:

```
if ( ( *s == 0xF3 ) && ( *(s+1) == 0xA0 ) &&
         ( ( *(s+2) & 0xFE ) == 0x80 ) )
```

Alternatively, the range checks for UTF-32 and UTF-16 can be coded with bit masks. Both versions should be equally efficient.

Range check expressed in UTF-32:

```
if ( ((*s) & 0xFFFFFF80)  == 0xE0000 )
```

Range check expressed in UTF-16:

```
if ( ( *s == 0xDB40 ) && ( *(s+1) & 0xDC80) == 0xDC00 )
```

Editing and Modification. Inline tags present particular problems for text changes, because they are stateful. Any modifications of the text are more complicated, as those modifications need to be aware of the current language status and the <start>...<end> tags must be properly maintained. If an editing program is unaware that certain tags are stateful and cannot process them correctly, then it is very easy for the user to modify text in ways that corrupt it. For example, a user might delete part of a tag or paste text including a tag into the wrong context.

Dangers of Incomplete Support. Even programs that do not interpret the tags should not allow editing operations to break initial tags or leave tags unpaired. Unpaired tags should be discarded upon a save or send operation.

Nonetheless, malformed text may be produced and transmitted by a tag-unaware editor. Therefore, implementations that do not ignore language tags must be prepared to receive malformed tags. On reception of a malformed or unpaired tag, language tag-aware implementations should reset the language to NONE and then ignore the tag.

Unicode Conformance Issues

The rules for Unicode conformance for the tag characters are exactly the same as those for any other Unicode characters. A conformant process is not required to interpret the tag characters. If it does interpret them, it should interpret them according to the standard—that is, as spelled-out tags. However, there is no requirement to provide a particular interpretation of the text because it is tagged with a given language. If an application does not interpret tag characters, it should leave their values undisturbed and do whatever it does with any other uninterpreted characters.

The presence of a well-formed tag is no guarantee that the data are correctly tagged. For example, an application could erroneously label French data with a Spanish tag.

Implementations of Unicode that already make use of out-of-band mechanisms for language tagging or "heavy-weight" in-band mechanisms such as XML or HTML will continue to do exactly what they are doing and will ignore the tag characters completely. They may even prohibit their use to prevent conflicts with the equivalent markup.

Formal Tag Syntax

An extended BNF description of the tags specified in this section is given here.

```
tag := language-tag | cancel-all-tag

language-tag := language-tag-introducer (language-tag-arg
                  | tag-cancel)

language-tag-arg := tag-argument
```

> In this rule, `tag-argument` is constrained to be a valid language identifier according to RFC 4646, with the assumption that the appropriate conversions from tag character values to ASCII are performed before checking for syntactic correctness against RFC 4646. For example, U+E0041 TAG LATIN CAPITAL LETTER A is mapped to U+0041 LATIN CAPITAL LETTER A, and so on.

```
cancel-all-tag := tag-cancel

tag-argument := tag-character+

tag-character := [U+E0020 - U+E007E]

language-tag-introducer := U+E0001

tag-cancel := U+E007F
```

Chapter 17

Code Charts

> ***Disclaimer***
>
> Character images shown in the code charts are not prescriptive. In actual fonts, considerable variations are to be expected.

The code charts that follow present the characters of the Unicode Standard. Characters are organized into related groups called *blocks*. Many scripts are fully contained within a single character block, but other scripts, including some of the most widely used scripts, have characters divided across several blocks. Separate blocks contain common punctuation characters and different types of symbols.

A character names list follows each character chart. The character names list itemizes every character in the block and provides supplementary information in many cases.

Charts for CJK Unified Ideographs and for Hangul syllables are not printed in this chapter, but are available online, as discussed in *Section 17.2, CJK Unified Ideographs*, and *Section 17.3, Hangul Syllables*.

An index to distinctive character names is found at the back of this book; a full set of character names appears in the Unicode Character Database.

17.1 Character Names List

The following illustration identifies the components of typical entries in the character names list.

code	*image*	*entry*	
00AE	®	REGISTERED SIGN	
		= registered trade mark sign (1.0)	*(Version 1.0 name)*
00AF	¯	MACRON	*(Unicode name)*
		= overline, APL overbar	*(alternative names)*
		• this is a spacing character	*(informative note)*
		→ 02C9 ˉ modifier letter macron	*(cross reference)*

→ 0304 ̄ combining macron
→ 0305 ̅ combining overline
≈ 0020 [SP] 0304 ̄ *(compatibility decomposition)*

00E5 å LATIN SMALL LETTER A WITH RING ABOVE
• Danish, Norwegian, Swedish, Walloon *(sample of language use)*
≡ 0061 a 030A ̊ *(canonical decomposition)*

Images in the Code Charts and Character Lists

Each character in these code charts is shown with a representative glyph. A representative glyph is not a prescriptive form of the character, but rather one that enables recognition of the intended character to a knowledgeable user and facilitates lookup of the character in the code charts. In many cases, there are more or less well-established alternative glyphic representations for the same character.

Designers of high-quality fonts will do their own research into the preferred glyphic appearance of Unicode characters. In addition, many scripts require context-dependent glyph shaping, glyph positioning, or ligatures, none of which is shown in the code charts.

The representative glyphs for the Latin, Greek, and Cyrillic scripts in the code charts are based on a serifed, Times-like font. Some characters have alternative forms. For example, even the ASCII character U+0061 LATIN SMALL LETTER A has two common alternative forms: the "a" used in Times and the "ɑ" that occurs in many other font styles. In a Times-like font, the character U+03A5 GREEK CAPITAL LETTER UPSILON looks like "Y"; the form ϒ is common in other font styles.

The fonts used for other scripts are similar to Times in that each represents a common, widely used design, with variable stroke width and serifs or similar devices, where applicable, to show each character as distinctly as possible. Sans-serif fonts with uniform stroke width tend to have less visibly distinct characters. In the code charts, sans-serif fonts are used for archaic scripts that predate the invention of serifs, for example.

A different case is U+010F LATIN SMALL LETTER D WITH CARON, which is commonly typeset as ď instead of ď. In such cases, the code charts show the more common variant in preference to a more didactic archetypical shape.

Many characters have been unified and have different appearances in different language contexts. The shape shown for U+2116 № NUMERO SIGN is a fullwidth shape as it would be used in East Asian fonts. In Cyrillic usage, № is the universally recognized glyph. See *Figure 15-2.*

In certain cases, characters need to be represented by more or less condensed, shifted, or distorted glyphs to make them fit the format of the code charts. For example, U+0D10 ഐ MALAYALAM LETTER AI is shown in a reduced size to fit the character cell.

Sometimes characters need to be given artificial shapes to make them recognizable in the code charts. Examples are the space characters and such characters as U+00AD [SHY] SOFT HYPHEN and U+2011 [NB] NON-BREAKING HYPHEN, where the special behavior of the hyphen is indicated by the dashed box and the letters. This use of a dashed box is not correlated with the General Category value of the character.

When characters are used in context, the surrounding text gives important clues as to identity, size, and positioning. In the code charts, these clues are absent. For example, U+2075 ⁵ SUPERSCRIPT FIVE is shown much smaller than it would be in a Times-like text font.

Combining characters are shown with a dotted circle—for example, U+0940 ◌ी DEVANAGARI VOWEL SIGN II. The relative position of the dotted circle gives an approximate indication of the location of the base character in relation to the combining mark. During rendering, additional adjustments are necessary. Accents such as U+0302 COMBINING CIRCUMFLEX ACCENT are adjusted vertically and horizontally based on the height and width of the base character, as in " î " versus "Ŵ".

For non-European scripts, typical typefaces were selected that allow as much distinction as possible among the different characters.

The Unicode Standard contains many characters that are used in writing minority languages or that are historical characters, often used primarily in manuscripts or inscriptions. Where there is no strong tradition of printed materials, the typography of a character may not be settled.

Character Names

The character names in the code charts precisely match the normative character names in the Unicode Character Database. Character names are unique and stable. By convention, they are in uppercase. Because character names are stable, mistaken names will not be revised, but may be annotated. For example:

2118 ℘ SCRIPT CAPITAL P
= Weierstrass elliptic function
• actually this has the form of a lowercase calligraphic p, despite its name

For more information on character names, see *Section 4.8, Name—Normative.*

Informative Aliases

An informative alias (preceded by =) is an alternate name for a character. Characters may have several aliases, and aliases for different characters are not guaranteed to be unique. Aliases are informative and may be updated. By convention, aliases are in lowercase, except where they contain proper names. Where an alias matches the name of a character in *The Unicode Standard, Version 1.0*, it is listed first, followed by "1.0" in parentheses. Because the formal character names may differ in unexpected ways from commonly used names (for example, PILCROW SIGN = paragraph sign), some aliases may be useful alternate choices for indicating characters in user interfaces. In the Hangul Jamo block, U+1100..U+11FF, the normative short jamo names are given as aliases.

Normative Aliases

A normative character name alias (one preceded by ※) is a formal, unique, and stable alternate name for a character. Characters are given normative character name aliases in certain cases where there is a defect in the character name. They do not replace the character name, but rather allow users to formally refer to the character without requiring the use of a defective name. For more information, see *Section 4.8, Name—Normative*. By convention, normative character aliases are written in uppercase letters.

FE18 ︘ PRESENTATION FORM FOR VERTICAL RIGHT WHITE LENTICULAR BRAKCET

※ PRESENTATION FORM FOR VERTICAL RIGHT WHITE LENTICULAR BRACKET
• misspelling of "BRACKET" in character name is a known defect
≈ <vertical> 3017

Cross References

Cross references (preceded by →) are used to indicate a related character of interest, but without indicating the nature of the relation. Possibilities are a different character of similar appearance or name, the other member of a case pair, or some other linguistic relationship.

Explicit Inequality. The two characters are not identical, although the glyphs that depict them are identical or very close.

003A : COLON
→ 0589 : armenian full stop
→ 2236 : ratio

Other Linguistic Relationships. These relationships include transliterations (such as between Serbian and Croatian), typographically unrelated characters used to represent the same sound, and so on.

01C9 lj LATIN SMALL LETTER LJ
→ 0459 љ cyrillic small letter lje
≈ 006C l 006A j

Cross references are neither exhaustive nor symmetric. Typically a general character would have cross references to more specialized characters, but not the other way around.

Information About Languages

An informative note may include a list of one or more of the languages using that character where this information is considered useful. For case pairs, the annotation is given only for the lowercase form to avoid needless repetition. An ellipsis "..." indicates that the listed languages cited are merely the principal ones among many.

Case Mappings

When a case mapping corresponds *solely* to a difference based on SMALL versus CAPITAL in the names of the characters, the case mapping is not given in the names list but only in the Unicode Character Database.

0041	A	LATIN CAPITAL LETTER A
01F2	Dz	LATIN CAPITAL LETTER D WITH SMALL LETTER Z ≈ 0044 D 007A z

When the case mapping cannot be predicted from the name, the casing information is sometimes given in a note.

00DF	ß	LATIN SMALL LETTER SHARP S = Eszett • German • uppercase is "SS" • in origin a ligature of 017F ſ and 0073 s → 03B2 β greek small letter beta

For more information about case and case mappings, see *Section 4.2, Case—Normative.*

Decompositions

The decomposition sequence (one or more letters) given for a character is either its canonical mapping or its compatibility mapping. The canonical mapping is marked with an *identical to* symbol ≡.

00E5	å	LATIN SMALL LETTER A WITH RING ABOVE • Danish, Norwegian, Swedish, Walloon ≡ 0061 a 030A ◌̊
212B	Å	ANGSTROM SIGN ≡ 00C5 Å latin capital letter a with ring above

Compatibility mappings are marked with an *almost equal to* symbol ≈. Formatting information may be indicated with a formatting tag, shown inside angle brackets.

01F2	Dz	LATIN CAPITAL LETTER D WITH SMALL LETTER Z ≈ 0044 D 007A z
FF21	Ａ	FULLWIDTH LATIN CAPITAL LETTER A ≈ <wide> 0041 A

The following compatibility formatting tags are used in the Unicode Character Database:

<font>	A font variant (for example, a blackletter form)
<noBreak>	A no-break version of a space, hyphen, or other punctuation
<initial>	An initial presentation form (Arabic)
<medial>	A medial presentation form (Arabic)
<final>	A final presentation form (Arabic)
<isolated>	An isolated presentation form (Arabic)

<circle>	An encircled form
<super>	A superscript form
<sub>	A subscript form
<vertical>	A vertical layout presentation form
<wide>	A fullwidth (or zenkaku) compatibility character
<narrow>	A halfwidth (or hankaku) compatibility character
<small>	A small variant form (CNS compatibility)
<square>	A CJK squared font variant
<fraction>	A vulgar fraction form
<compat>	Otherwise unspecified compatibility character

In the character names list accompanying the code charts, the "<compat>" label is suppressed, but all other compatibility formatting tags are explicitly listed in the compatibility mapping.

Decompositions are not necessarily full decompositions. For example, the decomposition for U+212B Å ANGSTROM SIGN can be further decomposed using the canonical mapping for U+00C5 Å LATIN CAPITAL LETTER A WITH RING ABOVE. (For more information on decomposition, see *Section 3.7, Decomposition.*)

Compatibility decompositions do not attempt to retain or emulate the formatting of the original character. For example, compatibility decompositions with the <noBreak> formatting tag do not use U+2060 WORD JOINER to emulate nonbreaking behavior; compatibility decompositions with the <circle> formatting tag do not use U+20DD COMBINING ENCLOSING CIRCLE; and compatibility decompositions with formatting tags <initial>, <medial>, <final>, or <isolate> for explicit positional forms do not use ZWJ or ZWNJ. The one exception is the use of U+2044 FRACTION SLASH to express the <fraction> semantics of compatibility decompositions for vulgar fractions.

Reserved Characters

Character codes that are marked "<reserved>" are unassigned and reserved for future encoding. Reserved codes are indicated by a ▧ glyph. To ensure readability, many instances of reserved characters have been suppressed from the names list. Reserved codes may also have cross references to assigned characters located elsewhere.

2073 ▧ <reserved>
→ 00B3 ^{3} superscript three

Noncharacters

Character codes that are marked "<not a character>" refer to noncharacters. They are designated code points that will never be assigned to a character. These codes are indicated by a ■ glyph. Noncharacters are shown in the code charts only where they occur together with other characters in the same block. For a complete list of noncharacters, see *Section 16.7, Noncharacters.*

FFFF ■ <not a character>
• the value FFFF ■ is guaranteed not to be a Unicode character at all

Subheads

The character names list contains a number of informative subheads that help divide up the list into smaller sublists of similar characters. For example, in the Miscellaneous Symbols block, U+2600..U+26FF, there are subheads for "Astrological symbols," "Chess symbols," and so on. Such subheads are editorial and informative; they should not be taken as providing any definitive, normative status information about characters in the sublists they mark or about any constraints on what characters could be encoded in the future at reserved code points within their ranges. The subheads are subject to change.

17.2 CJK Unified Ideographs

Because of their bulk, the charts for CJK Unified Ideographs are included in this book only as a printable file on the CD-ROM. They are available online at the Unicode Web site. (See "Charts" in *Section B.6, Other Unicode Online Resources.*)

Character names are not provided for any of the online charts of CJK Unified Ideograph character blocks, because the name of a unified ideograph simply consists of its Unicode code point preceded by CJK UNIFIED IDEOGRAPH-.

As is the case for the other character charts, each CJK Unified Ideograph character in the online charts is shown with its Unicode code point and a single representative glyph. Note that varying typographic practices throughout East Asia may require glyphs other than the representative one to be used so that the display is correct for a particular country or language.

Mappings between the CJK ideographs included in the Unicode Standard and those in other character set standards are included in the Unihan Database (see "Unihan Database" in *Section 4.1, Unicode Character Database*).

A radical-stroke index to the IICore subset of CJK ideographs is provided in *Chapter 18, Han Radical-Stroke Index.* A printable version of the complete radical-stroke index is included on the CD-ROM and available as part of the online character charts on the Unicode Web site.

17.3 Hangul Syllables

Because of their bulk, charts for the Hangul Syllables are included in this book only as a printable file on the CD-ROM. They are available online at the Unicode Web site. (See "Charts" in *Section B.6, Other Unicode Online Resources*.)

As in the case of CJK Unified Ideographs, a character names list is not provided for the online chart of characters in the Hangul Syllables block, U+AC00..U+D7AF, because the name of a Hangul syllable can be determined by algorithm as described in *Section 3.12, Conjoining Jamo Behavior*. The short names used in that algorithm are listed in the code charts as aliases in the Hangul Jamo block, U+1100..U+11FF, as well as in Jamo.txt in the Unicode Character Database.

	000	001	002	003	004	005	006	007
0	NUL 0000	DLE 0010	SP 0020	0 0030	@ 0040	P 0050	` 0060	p 0070
1	SOH 0001	DC1 0011	! 0021	1 0031	A 0041	Q 0051	a 0061	q 0071
2	STX 0002	DC2 0012	" 0022	2 0032	B 0042	R 0052	b 0062	r 0072
3	ETX 0003	DC3 0013	# 0023	3 0033	C 0043	S 0053	c 0063	s 0073
4	EOT 0004	DC4 0014	$ 0024	4 0034	D 0044	T 0054	d 0064	t 0074
5	ENQ 0005	NAK 0015	% 0025	5 0035	E 0045	U 0055	e 0065	u 0075
6	ACK 0006	SYN 0016	& 0026	6 0036	F 0046	V 0056	f 0066	v 0076
7	BEL 0007	ETB 0017	' 0027	7 0037	G 0047	W 0057	g 0067	w 0077
8	BS 0008	CAN 0018	(0028	8 0038	H 0048	X 0058	h 0068	x 0078
9	HT 0009	EM 0019	) 0029	9 0039	I 0049	Y 0059	i 0069	y 0079
A	LF 000A	SUB 001A	* 002A	: 003A	J 004A	Z 005A	j 006A	z 007A
B	VT 000B	ESC 001B	+ 002B	; 003B	K 004B	[005B	k 006B	{ 007B
C	FF 000C	FS 001C	, 002C	< 003C	L 004C	\ 005C	l 006C	| 007C
D	CR 000D	GS 001D	- 002D	= 003D	M 004D	] 005D	m 006D	} 007D
E	SO 000E	RS 001E	. 002E	> 003E	N 004E	^ 005E	n 006E	~ 007E
F	SI 000F	US 001F	/ 002F	? 003F	O 004F	_ 005F	o 006F	DEL 007F

C0 controls

Alias names are those for ISO/IEC 6429:1992. Commonly used alternative aliases are also shown.

0000 NUL <control>
= NULL

0001 SOH <control>
= START OF HEADING

0002 STX <control>
= START OF TEXT

0003 ETX <control>
= END OF TEXT

0004 EOT <control>
= END OF TRANSMISSION

0005 ENQ <control>
= ENQUIRY

0006 ACK <control>
= ACKNOWLEDGE

0007 BEL <control>
= BELL

0008 BS <control>
= BACKSPACE

0009 HT <control>
= CHARACTER TABULATION
= horizontal tabulation (HT), tab

000A LF <control>
= LINE FEED (LF)
= new line (NL), end of line (EOL)

000B VT <control>
= LINE TABULATION
= vertical tabulation (VT)

000C FF <control>
= FORM FEED (FF)

000D CR <control>
= CARRIAGE RETURN (CR)

000E SO <control>
= SHIFT OUT

000F SI <control>
= SHIFT IN

0010 DLE <control>
= DATA LINK ESCAPE

0011 DC1 <control>
= DEVICE CONTROL ONE

0012 DC2 <control>
= DEVICE CONTROL TWO

0013 DC3 <control>
= DEVICE CONTROL THREE

0014 DC4 <control>
= DEVICE CONTROL FOUR

0015 NAK <control>
= NEGATIVE ACKNOWLEDGE

0016 SYN <control>
= SYNCHRONOUS IDLE

0017 ETB <control>
= END OF TRANSMISSION BLOCK

0018 CAN <control>
= CANCEL

0019 EM <control>
= END OF MEDIUM

001A SUB <control>
= SUBSTITUTE
→ FFFD � replacement character

001B ESC <control>
= ESCAPE

001C FS <control>
= INFORMATION SEPARATOR FOUR
= file separator (FS)

001D GS <control>
= INFORMATION SEPARATOR THREE
= group separator (GS)

001E RS <control>
= INFORMATION SEPARATOR TWO
= record separator (RS)

001F US <control>
= INFORMATION SEPARATOR ONE
= unit separator (US)

ASCII punctuation and symbols

Based on ISO/IEC 646.

0020 SP SPACE
• sometimes considered a control code
• other space characters: 2000 NQSP –200A HSP
→ 00A0 NBSP no-break space
→ 200B ZWSP zero width space
→ 2060 WJ word joiner
→ 3000 IDSP ideographic space
→ FEFF ZWNBSP zero width no-break space

0021 ! EXCLAMATION MARK
= factorial
= bang
→ 00A1 ¡ inverted exclamation mark
→ 01C3 ǃ latin letter retroflex click
→ 203C ‼ double exclamation mark
→ 203D ‽ interrobang
→ 2762 ❢ heavy exclamation mark ornament

0022 " QUOTATION MARK
• neutral (vertical), used as opening or closing quotation mark
• preferred characters in English for paired quotation marks are 201C " & 201D "
→ 02BA ʺ modifier letter double prime
→ 030B ◌̋ combining double acute accent
→ 030E ◌̎ combining double vertical line above
→ 2033 ″ double prime
→ 3003 〃 ditto mark

0023 # NUMBER SIGN
= pound sign, hash, crosshatch, octothorpe
→ 2114 ℔ l b bar symbol
→ 266F ♯ music sharp sign

0024 $ DOLLAR SIGN
= milreis, escudo
• glyph may have one or two vertical bars
• other currency symbol characters: 20A0 ₠ –20B5 ₵
→ 00A4 ¤ currency sign

0025 % PERCENT SIGN
→ 066A ٪ arabic percent sign
→ 2030 ‰ per mille sign
→ 2031 ‱ per ten thousand sign
→ 2052 ⁒ commercial minus sign

0026 & AMPERSAND
→ 204A ⁊ tironian sign et
→ 214B ⅋ turned ampersand

0027 ' APOSTROPHE
= apostrophe-quote (1.0)
= APL quote
• neutral (vertical) glyph with mixed usage
• 2019 ’ is preferred for apostrophe
• preferred characters in English for paired quotation marks are 2018 ‘ & 2019 ’
→ 02B9 ʹ modifier letter prime
→ 02BC ʼ modifier letter apostrophe
→ 02C8 ˈ modifier letter vertical line
→ 0301 ◌́ combining acute accent
→ 2032 ′ prime

0028 (LEFT PARENTHESIS
= opening parenthesis (1.0)

0029) RIGHT PARENTHESIS
= closing parenthesis (1.0)
• see discussion on semantics of paired bracketing characters

002A * ASTERISK
= star (on phone keypads)
→ 066D ٭ arabic five pointed star
→ 204E ⁎ low asterisk
→ 2217 ∗ asterisk operator
→ 2731 ✱ heavy asterisk

002B + PLUS SIGN

002C , COMMA
= decimal separator
→ 060C ، arabic comma
→ 201A ‚ single low-9 quotation mark
→ 3001 、 ideographic comma

002D - HYPHEN-MINUS
= hyphen or minus sign
• used for either hyphen or minus sign
→ 2010 ‐ hyphen
→ 2011 ‑ non-breaking hyphen
→ 2012 ‒ figure dash
→ 2013 – en dash
→ 2212 − minus sign

002E . FULL STOP
= period, dot, decimal point
• may be rendered as a raised decimal point in old style numbers
→ 06D4 ۔ arabic full stop
→ 3002 。 ideographic full stop

002F / SOLIDUS
= slash, virgule
→ 01C0 ǀ latin letter dental click
→ 0338 ◌̸ combining long solidus overlay
→ 2044 ⁄ fraction slash
→ 2215 ∕ division slash

ASCII digits

0030 0 DIGIT ZERO
0031 1 DIGIT ONE
0032 2 DIGIT TWO
0033 3 DIGIT THREE
0034 4 DIGIT FOUR
0035 5 DIGIT FIVE
0036 6 DIGIT SIX
0037 7 DIGIT SEVEN
0038 8 DIGIT EIGHT
0039 9 DIGIT NINE

ASCII punctuation and symbols

003A : COLON
→ 0589 ։ armenian full stop
→ 05C3 ׃ hebrew punctuation sof pasuq
→ 2236 ∶ ratio

003B ; SEMICOLON
• this, and not 037E ;, is the preferred character for 'Greek question mark'
→ 037E ; greek question mark
→ 061B ؛ arabic semicolon
→ 204F ⁏ reversed semicolon

003C < LESS-THAN SIGN
→ 2039 ‹ single left-pointing angle quotation mark
→ 2329 〈 left-pointing angle bracket
→ 27E8 ⟨ mathematical left angle bracket
→ 3008 〈 left angle bracket

003D = EQUALS SIGN
• other related characters: 2241 ≁–2263 ≣
→ 2260 ≠ not equal to
→ 2261 ≡ identical to

003E > GREATER-THAN SIGN
→ 203A › single right-pointing angle quotation mark
→ 232A 〉 right-pointing angle bracket
→ 27E9 ⟩ mathematical right angle bracket
→ 3009 〉 right angle bracket

003F ? QUESTION MARK
→ 00BF ¿ inverted question mark
→ 037E ; greek question mark
→ 061F ؟ arabic question mark
→ 203D ‽ interrobang
→ 2048 ⁈ question exclamation mark
→ 2049 ⁉ exclamation question mark

0040 @ COMMERCIAL AT
= at sign

Uppercase Latin alphabet

0041 A LATIN CAPITAL LETTER A
0042 B LATIN CAPITAL LETTER B
→ 212C ℬ script capital b
0043 C LATIN CAPITAL LETTER C
→ 2102 ℂ double-struck capital c
→ 212D ℭ black-letter capital c
0044 D LATIN CAPITAL LETTER D
0045 E LATIN CAPITAL LETTER E
→ 2107 ℇ euler constant
→ 2130 ℰ script capital e
0046 F LATIN CAPITAL LETTER F
→ 2131 ℱ script capital f
→ 2132 Ⅎ turned capital f
0047 G LATIN CAPITAL LETTER G
0048 H LATIN CAPITAL LETTER H
→ 210B ℋ script capital h
→ 210C ℌ black-letter capital h
→ 210D ℍ double-struck capital h

0049 I LATIN CAPITAL LETTER I
- Turkish and Azerbaijani use 0131 ı for lowercase
- → 0130 İ latin capital letter i with dot above
- → 0406 І cyrillic capital letter byelorussian-ukrainian i
- → 04C0 Ӏ cyrillic letter palochka
- → 2110 ℐ script capital i
- → 2111 ℑ black-letter capital i
- → 2160 Ⅰ roman numeral one

004A J LATIN CAPITAL LETTER J

004B K LATIN CAPITAL LETTER K
- → 212A K kelvin sign

004C L LATIN CAPITAL LETTER L
- → 2112 ℒ script capital l

004D M LATIN CAPITAL LETTER M
- → 2133 ℳ script capital m

004E N LATIN CAPITAL LETTER N
- → 2115 ℕ double-struck capital n

004F O LATIN CAPITAL LETTER O

0050 P LATIN CAPITAL LETTER P
- → 2119 ℙ double-struck capital p

0051 Q LATIN CAPITAL LETTER Q
- → 211A ℚ double-struck capital q

0052 R LATIN CAPITAL LETTER R
- → 211B ℛ script capital r
- → 211C ℜ black-letter capital r
- → 211D ℝ double-struck capital r

0053 S LATIN CAPITAL LETTER S

0054 T LATIN CAPITAL LETTER T

0055 U LATIN CAPITAL LETTER U

0056 V LATIN CAPITAL LETTER V

0057 W LATIN CAPITAL LETTER W

0058 X LATIN CAPITAL LETTER X

0059 Y LATIN CAPITAL LETTER Y

005A Z LATIN CAPITAL LETTER Z
- → 2124 ℤ double-struck capital z
- → 2128 ℨ black-letter capital z

ASCII punctuation and symbols

005B [LEFT SQUARE BRACKET
- = opening square bracket (1.0)
- other bracket characters: 27E6 ⟦ –27EB ⟫ , 2983 ⦃ –2998 ⦘ , 3008 〈 –301B 〛

005C \ REVERSE SOLIDUS
- = backslash
- → 20E5 ⃥ combining reverse solidus overlay
- → 2216 ∖ set minus

005D] RIGHT SQUARE BRACKET
- = closing square bracket (1.0)

005E ^ CIRCUMFLEX ACCENT
- this is a spacing character
- → 02C4 ˄ modifier letter up arrowhead
- → 02C6 ˆ modifier letter circumflex accent
- → 0302 ̂ combining circumflex accent
- → 2038 ‸ caret
- → 2303 ⌃ up arrowhead

005F _ LOW LINE
- = spacing underscore (1.0)
- this is a spacing character
- → 02CD ˍ modifier letter low macron
- → 0331 ̱ combining macron below
- → 0332 ̲ combining low line
- → 2017 ‗ double low line

0060 ` GRAVE ACCENT
- this is a spacing character
- → 02CB ˋ modifier letter grave accent
- → 0300 ̀ combining grave accent
- → 2035 ‵ reversed prime

Lowercase Latin alphabet

0061 a LATIN SMALL LETTER A

0062 b LATIN SMALL LETTER B

0063 c LATIN SMALL LETTER C

0064 d LATIN SMALL LETTER D

0065 e LATIN SMALL LETTER E
- → 212E ℮ estimated symbol
- → 212F ℯ script small e

0066 f LATIN SMALL LETTER F

0067 g LATIN SMALL LETTER G
- → 0261 ɡ latin small letter script g
- → 210A ℊ script small g

0068 h LATIN SMALL LETTER H
- → 04BB һ cyrillic small letter shha
- → 210E ℎ planck constant

0069 i LATIN SMALL LETTER I
- Turkish and Azerbaijani use 0130 İ for uppercase
- → 0131 ı latin small letter dotless i
- → 1D6A4 𝚤 mathematical italic small dotless i

006A j LATIN SMALL LETTER J
- → 0237 ȷ latin small letter dotless j
- → 1D6A5 𝚥 mathematical italic small dotless j

006B k LATIN SMALL LETTER K

006C l LATIN SMALL LETTER L
- → 2113 ℓ script small l
- → 1D4C1 𝓁 mathematical script small l

006D m LATIN SMALL LETTER M

006E n LATIN SMALL LETTER N
- → 207F ⁿ superscript latin small letter n

006F o LATIN SMALL LETTER O
- → 2134 ℴ script small o

0070 p LATIN SMALL LETTER P

0071 q LATIN SMALL LETTER Q

0072 r LATIN SMALL LETTER R

0073 s LATIN SMALL LETTER S

0074 t LATIN SMALL LETTER T

0075 u LATIN SMALL LETTER U

0076 v LATIN SMALL LETTER V

0077 w LATIN SMALL LETTER W

0078 x LATIN SMALL LETTER X

0079 y LATIN SMALL LETTER Y

007A z LATIN SMALL LETTER Z
- → 01B6 ƶ latin small letter z with stroke

ASCII punctuation and symbols

007B { LEFT CURLY BRACKET
- = opening curly bracket (1.0)
- = left brace

007C | VERTICAL LINE
- = vertical bar
- used in pairs to indicate absolute value
- → 01C0 ǀ latin letter dental click
- → 05C0 ׀ hebrew punctuation paseq
- → 2223 ∣ divides
- → 2758 ❘ light vertical bar

007D } RIGHT CURLY BRACKET
- = closing curly bracket (1.0)
- = right brace

007E ~ TILDE
- this is a spacing character
→ 02DC ˜ small tilde
→ 0303 ◌̃ combining tilde
→ 2053 ⁓ swung dash
→ 223C ∼ tilde operator
→ FF5E ～ fullwidth tilde

Control character

007F DEL <control>
= DELETE

	008	009	00A	00B	00C	00D	00E	00F
0	XXX 0080	DCS 0090	NB SP 00A0	° 00B0	À 00C0	Ð 00D0	à 00E0	ð 00F0
1	XXX 0081	PU1 0091	¡ 00A1	± 00B1	Á 00C1	Ñ 00D1	á 00E1	ñ 00F1
2	BPH 0082	PU2 0092	¢ 00A2	^{2} 00B2	Â 00C2	Ò 00D2	â 00E2	ò 00F2
3	NBH 0083	STS 0093	£ 00A3	^{3} 00B3	Ã 00C3	Ó 00D3	ã 00E3	ó 00F3
4	IND 0084	CCH 0094	¤ 00A4	´ 00B4	Ä 00C4	Ô 00D4	ä 00E4	ô 00F4
5	NEL 0085	MW 0095	¥ 00A5	µ 00B5	Å 00C5	Õ 00D5	å 00E5	õ 00F5
6	SSA 0086	SPA 0096	¦ 00A6	¶ 00B6	Æ 00C6	Ö 00D6	æ 00E6	ö 00F6
7	ESA 0087	EPA 0097	§ 00A7	· 00B7	Ç 00C7	× 00D7	ç 00E7	÷ 00F7
8	HTS 0088	SOS 0098	¨ 00A8	¸ 00B8	È 00C8	Ø 00D8	è 00E8	ø 00F8
9	HTJ 0089	XXX 0099	© 00A9	^{1} 00B9	É 00C9	Ù 00D9	é 00E9	ù 00F9
A	VTS 008A	SCI 009A	ª 00AA	º 00BA	Ê 00CA	Ú 00DA	ê 00EA	ú 00FA
B	PLD 008B	CSI 009B	« 00AB	» 00BB	Ë 00CB	Û 00DB	ë 00EB	û 00FB
C	PLU 008C	ST 009C	¬ 00AC	¼ 00BC	Ì 00CC	Ü 00DC	ì 00EC	ü 00FC
D	RI 008D	OSC 009D	SHY 00AD	½ 00BD	Í 00CD	Ý 00DD	í 00ED	ý 00FD
E	SS2 008E	PM 009E	® 00AE	¾ 00BE	Î 00CE	Þ 00DE	î 00EE	þ 00FE
F	SS3 008F	APC 009F	¯ 00AF	¿ 00BF	Ï 00CF	ß 00DF	ï 00EF	ÿ 00FF

C1 controls

Alias names are those for ISO/IEC 6429:1992.

0080 XXX <control>

0081 XXX <control>

0082 BPH <control>
= BREAK PERMITTED HERE
→ 200B ZWSP zero width space

0083 NBH <control>
= NO BREAK HERE
→ 2060 WJ word joiner

0084 IND <control>
• formerly known as INDEX

0085 NEL <control>
= NEXT LINE (NEL)

0086 SSA <control>
= START OF SELECTED AREA

0087 ESA <control>
= END OF SELECTED AREA

0088 HTS <control>
= CHARACTER TABULATION SET

0089 HTJ <control>
= CHARACTER TABULATION WITH JUSTIFICATION

008A VTS <control>
= LINE TABULATION SET

008B PLD <control>
= PARTIAL LINE FORWARD

008C PLU <control>
= PARTIAL LINE BACKWARD

008D RI <control>
= REVERSE LINE FEED

008E SS2 <control>
= SINGLE SHIFT TWO

008F SS3 <control>
= SINGLE SHIFT THREE

0090 DCS <control>
= DEVICE CONTROL STRING

0091 PU1 <control>
= PRIVATE USE ONE

0092 PU2 <control>
= PRIVATE USE TWO

0093 STS <control>
= SET TRANSMIT STATE

0094 CCH <control>
= CANCEL CHARACTER

0095 MW <control>
= MESSAGE WAITING

0096 SPA <control>
= START OF GUARDED AREA

0097 EPA <control>
= END OF GUARDED AREA

0098 SOS <control>
= START OF STRING

0099 XXX <control>

009A SCI <control>
= SINGLE CHARACTER INTRODUCER

009B CSI <control>
= CONTROL SEQUENCE INTRODUCER

009C ST <control>
= STRING TERMINATOR

009D OSC <control>
= OPERATING SYSTEM COMMAND

009E PM <control>
= PRIVACY MESSAGE

009F APC <control>
= APPLICATION PROGRAM COMMAND

Latin-1 punctuation and symbols

Based on ISO/IEC 8859-1 (aka Latin-1) from here.

00A0 NBSP NO-BREAK SPACE
• commonly abbreviated as NBSP
→ 0020 SP space
→ 2007 FSP figure space
→ 202F NNBSP narrow no-break space
→ 2060 WJ word joiner
→ FEFF ZWNBSP zero width no-break space
≈ <noBreak> 0020 SP

00A1 ¡ INVERTED EXCLAMATION MARK
• Spanish, Asturian, Galician
→ 0021 ! exclamation mark

00A2 ¢ CENT SIGN

00A3 £ POUND SIGN
= pound sterling, Irish punt, Italian lira, Turkish lira, etc.
→ 20A4 ₤ lira sign

00A4 ¤ CURRENCY SIGN
• other currency symbol characters: 20A0 ₠ –20B5 ₵
→ 0024 $ dollar sign

00A5 ¥ YEN SIGN
= yuan sign
• glyph may have one or two crossbars

00A6 ¦ BROKEN BAR
= broken vertical bar (1.0)
= parted rule (in typography)

00A7 § SECTION SIGN
• paragraph sign in some European usage

00A8 ¨ DIAERESIS
• this is a spacing character
→ 0308 ◌̈ combining diaeresis
≈ 0020 SP 0308 ◌̈

00A9 © COPYRIGHT SIGN
→ 2117 ℗ sound recording copyright
→ 24B8 Ⓒ circled latin capital letter c

00AA ª FEMININE ORDINAL INDICATOR
• Spanish
≈ <super> 0061 a

00AB « LEFT-POINTING DOUBLE ANGLE QUOTATION MARK
= left guillemet
= chevrons (in typography)
• usually opening, sometimes closing
→ 226A ≪ much less-than
→ 300A 《 left double angle bracket

00AC ¬ NOT SIGN
= angled dash (in typography)
→ 2310 ⌐ reversed not sign

00AD SHY SOFT HYPHEN
= discretionary hyphen
• commonly abbreviated as SHY

00AE ® REGISTERED SIGN
= registered trade mark sign (1.0)
→ 24C7 Ⓡ circled latin capital letter r

00AF ¯ MACRON
= overline, APL overbar
• this is a spacing character
→ 02C9 ˉ modifier letter macron
→ 0304 ◌̄ combining macron
→ 0305 ◌̅ combining overline
≈ 0020 SP 0304 ◌̄

00B0 ° DEGREE SIGN
• this is a spacing character
→ 02DA ˚ ring above
→ 030A ̊ combining ring above
→ 2070 ⁰ superscript zero
→ 2218 ∘ ring operator

00B1 ± PLUS-MINUS SIGN
→ 2213 ∓ minus-or-plus sign

00B2 ² SUPERSCRIPT TWO
= squared
• other superscript digit characters: 2070 ⁰–2079 ⁹
→ 00B9 ¹ superscript one
≈ <super> 0032 2

00B3 ³ SUPERSCRIPT THREE
= cubed
→ 00B9 ¹ superscript one
≈ <super> 0033 3

00B4 ´ ACUTE ACCENT
• this is a spacing character
→ 02B9 ʹ modifier letter prime
→ 02CA ˊ modifier letter acute accent
→ 0301 ́ combining acute accent
→ 2032 ′ prime
≈ 0020 [SP] 0301 ́

00B5 µ MICRO SIGN
≈ 03BC μ greek small letter mu

00B6 ¶ PILCROW SIGN
= paragraph sign
• section sign in some European usage
→ 204B ⁋ reversed pilcrow sign
→ 2761 ❡ curved stem paragraph sign ornament

00B7 · MIDDLE DOT
= midpoint (in typography)
= Georgian comma
= Greek middle dot (ano teleia)
→ 0387 · greek ano teleia
→ 2022 • bullet
→ 2024 ․ one dot leader
→ 2027 ‧ hyphenation point
→ 2219 ∙ bullet operator
→ 22C5 ⋅ dot operator
→ 30FB ・ katakana middle dot

00B8 ¸ CEDILLA
• this is a spacing character
• other spacing accent characters: 02D8 ˘–02DB ˛
→ 0327 ̧ combining cedilla
≈ 0020 [SP] 0327 ̧

00B9 ¹ SUPERSCRIPT ONE
→ 00B2 ² superscript two
→ 00B3 ³ superscript three
≈ <super> 0031 1

00BA º MASCULINE ORDINAL INDICATOR
• Spanish
≈ <super> 006F o

00BB » RIGHT-POINTING DOUBLE ANGLE QUOTATION MARK
= right guillemet
• usually closing, sometimes opening
→ 226B ≫ much greater-than
→ 300B 》 right double angle bracket

00BC ¼ VULGAR FRACTION ONE QUARTER
• bar may be horizontal or slanted
• other fraction characters: 2153 ⅓–215E ⅞
≈ <fraction> 0031 1 2044 ⁄ 0034 4

00BD ½ VULGAR FRACTION ONE HALF
• bar may be horizontal or slanted
≈ <fraction> 0031 1 2044 ⁄ 0032 2

00BE ¾ VULGAR FRACTION THREE QUARTERS
• bar may be horizontal or slanted
≈ <fraction> 0033 3 2044 ⁄ 0034 4

00BF ¿ INVERTED QUESTION MARK
= turned question mark
• Spanish
→ 003F ? question mark

Letters

00C0 À LATIN CAPITAL LETTER A WITH GRAVE
≡ 0041 A 0300 ̀

00C1 Á LATIN CAPITAL LETTER A WITH ACUTE
≡ 0041 A 0301 ́

00C2 Â LATIN CAPITAL LETTER A WITH CIRCUMFLEX
≡ 0041 A 0302 ̂

00C3 Ã LATIN CAPITAL LETTER A WITH TILDE
≡ 0041 A 0303 ̃

00C4 Ä LATIN CAPITAL LETTER A WITH DIAERESIS
≡ 0041 A 0308 ̈

00C5 Å LATIN CAPITAL LETTER A WITH RING ABOVE
→ 212B Å angstrom sign
≡ 0041 A 030A ̊

00C6 Æ LATIN CAPITAL LETTER AE
= latin capital ligature ae (1.0)

00C7 Ç LATIN CAPITAL LETTER C WITH CEDILLA
≡ 0043 C 0327 ̧

00C8 È LATIN CAPITAL LETTER E WITH GRAVE
≡ 0045 E 0300 ̀

00C9 É LATIN CAPITAL LETTER E WITH ACUTE
≡ 0045 E 0301 ́

00CA Ê LATIN CAPITAL LETTER E WITH CIRCUMFLEX
≡ 0045 E 0302 ̂

00CB Ë LATIN CAPITAL LETTER E WITH DIAERESIS
≡ 0045 E 0308 ̈

00CC Ì LATIN CAPITAL LETTER I WITH GRAVE
≡ 0049 I 0300 ̀

00CD Í LATIN CAPITAL LETTER I WITH ACUTE
≡ 0049 I 0301 ́

00CE Î LATIN CAPITAL LETTER I WITH CIRCUMFLEX
≡ 0049 I 0302 ̂

00CF Ï LATIN CAPITAL LETTER I WITH DIAERESIS
≡ 0049 I 0308 ̈

00D0 Ð LATIN CAPITAL LETTER ETH
→ 00F0 ð latin small letter eth
→ 0110 Đ latin capital letter d with stroke
→ 0189 Ɖ latin capital letter african d

00D1 Ñ LATIN CAPITAL LETTER N WITH TILDE
≡ 004E N 0303 ̃

00D2 Ò LATIN CAPITAL LETTER O WITH GRAVE
≡ 004F O 0300 ̀

00D3 Ó LATIN CAPITAL LETTER O WITH ACUTE
≡ 004F O 0301 ́

00D4 Ô LATIN CAPITAL LETTER O WITH CIRCUMFLEX
≡ 004F O 0302 ̂

00D5 Õ LATIN CAPITAL LETTER O WITH TILDE
≡ 004F O 0303 ̃

00D6 Ö LATIN CAPITAL LETTER O WITH DIAERESIS
≡ 004F O 0308 ̈

Mathematical operator

00D7 × MULTIPLICATION SIGN
= z notation Cartesian product

Letters

00D8 Ø LATIN CAPITAL LETTER O WITH STROKE
= o slash
→ 2205 ∅ empty set

00D9 Ù LATIN CAPITAL LETTER U WITH GRAVE
≡ 0055 U 0300 ̀

00DA Ú LATIN CAPITAL LETTER U WITH ACUTE
≡ 0055 U 0301 ́

00DB Û LATIN CAPITAL LETTER U WITH CIRCUMFLEX
≡ 0055 U 0302 ̂

00DC Ü LATIN CAPITAL LETTER U WITH DIAERESIS
≡ 0055 U 0308 ̈

00DD Ý LATIN CAPITAL LETTER Y WITH ACUTE
≡ 0059 Y 0301 ́

00DE Þ LATIN CAPITAL LETTER THORN

00DF ß LATIN SMALL LETTER SHARP S
= Eszett
• German
• uppercase is "SS"
• in origin a ligature of 017F ſ and 0073 s
→ 03B2 β greek small letter beta

00E0 à LATIN SMALL LETTER A WITH GRAVE
≡ 0061 a 0300 ̀

00E1 á LATIN SMALL LETTER A WITH ACUTE
≡ 0061 a 0301 ́

00E2 â LATIN SMALL LETTER A WITH CIRCUMFLEX
≡ 0061 a 0302 ̂

00E3 ã LATIN SMALL LETTER A WITH TILDE
• Portuguese
≡ 0061 a 0303 ̃

00E4 ä LATIN SMALL LETTER A WITH DIAERESIS
≡ 0061 a 0308 ̈

00E5 å LATIN SMALL LETTER A WITH RING ABOVE
• Danish, Norwegian, Swedish, Walloon
≡ 0061 a 030A ̊

00E6 æ LATIN SMALL LETTER AE
= latin small ligature ae (1.0)
= ash (from Old English æsc)
• Danish, Norwegian, Icelandic, Faroese, Old English, French, IPA
→ 0153 œ latin small ligature oe
→ 04D5 ӕ cyrillic small ligature a ie

00E7 ç LATIN SMALL LETTER C WITH CEDILLA
≡ 0063 c 0327 ̧

00E8 è LATIN SMALL LETTER E WITH GRAVE
≡ 0065 e 0300 ̀

00E9 é LATIN SMALL LETTER E WITH ACUTE
≡ 0065 e 0301 ́

00EA ê LATIN SMALL LETTER E WITH CIRCUMFLEX
≡ 0065 e 0302 ̂

00EB ë LATIN SMALL LETTER E WITH DIAERESIS
≡ 0065 e 0308 ̈

00EC ì LATIN SMALL LETTER I WITH GRAVE
• Italian, Malagasy
≡ 0069 i 0300 ̀

00ED í LATIN SMALL LETTER I WITH ACUTE
≡ 0069 i 0301 ́

00EE î LATIN SMALL LETTER I WITH CIRCUMFLEX
≡ 0069 i 0302 ̂

00EF ï LATIN SMALL LETTER I WITH DIAERESIS
≡ 0069 i 0308 ̈

00F0 ð LATIN SMALL LETTER ETH
• Icelandic, Faroese, Old English, IPA
→ 00D0 Đ latin capital letter eth
→ 03B4 δ greek small letter delta
→ 2202 ∂ partial differential

00F1 ñ LATIN SMALL LETTER N WITH TILDE
≡ 006E n 0303 ̃

00F2 ò LATIN SMALL LETTER O WITH GRAVE
≡ 006F o 0300 ̀

00F3 ó LATIN SMALL LETTER O WITH ACUTE
≡ 006F o 0301 ́

00F4 ô LATIN SMALL LETTER O WITH CIRCUMFLEX
≡ 006F o 0302 ̂

00F5 õ LATIN SMALL LETTER O WITH TILDE
• Portuguese, Estonian
≡ 006F o 0303 ̃

00F6 ö LATIN SMALL LETTER O WITH DIAERESIS
≡ 006F o 0308 ̈

Mathematical operator

00F7 ÷ DIVISION SIGN
→ 2215 ∕ division slash
→ 2223 ∣ divides

Letters

00F8 ø LATIN SMALL LETTER O WITH STROKE
= o slash
• Danish, Norwegian, Faroese, IPA

00F9 ù LATIN SMALL LETTER U WITH GRAVE
• French, Italian
≡ 0075 u 0300 ̀

00FA ú LATIN SMALL LETTER U WITH ACUTE
≡ 0075 u 0301 ́

00FB û LATIN SMALL LETTER U WITH CIRCUMFLEX
≡ 0075 u 0302 ̂

00FC ü LATIN SMALL LETTER U WITH DIAERESIS
≡ 0075 u 0308 ̈

00FD ý LATIN SMALL LETTER Y WITH ACUTE
• Czech, Slovak, Icelandic, Faroese, Welsh, Malagasy
≡ 0079 y 0301 ́

00FE þ LATIN SMALL LETTER THORN
• Icelandic, Old English, phonetics
• Runic letter borrowed into Latin script
→ 16A6 ᚦ runic letter thurisaz thurs thorn

00FF ÿ LATIN SMALL LETTER Y WITH DIAERESIS
• French
→ 0178 Ÿ latin capital letter y with diaeresis
≡ 0079 y 0308 ̈

	010	011	012	013	014	015	016	017
0	Ā 0100	Đ 0110	Ġ 0120	İ 0130	ŀ 0140	Ő 0150	Š 0160	Ű 0170
1	ā 0101	đ 0111	ġ 0121	ı 0131	Ł 0141	ő 0151	š 0161	ű 0171
2	Ă 0102	Ē 0112	Ģ 0122	Ĳ 0132	ł 0142	Œ 0152	Ţ 0162	Ų 0172
3	ă 0103	ē 0113	ģ 0123	ĳ 0133	Ń 0143	œ 0153	ţ 0163	ų 0173
4	Ą 0104	Ĕ 0114	Ĥ 0124	Ĵ 0134	ń 0144	Ŕ 0154	Ť 0164	Ŵ 0174
5	ą 0105	ĕ 0115	ĥ 0125	ĵ 0135	Ņ 0145	ŕ 0155	ť 0165	ŵ 0175
6	Ć 0106	Ė 0116	Ħ 0126	Ķ 0136	ņ 0146	Ŗ 0156	Ŧ 0166	Ŷ 0176
7	ć 0107	ė 0117	ħ 0127	ķ 0137	Ň 0147	ŗ 0157	ŧ 0167	ŷ 0177
8	Ĉ 0108	Ę 0118	Ĩ 0128	ĸ 0138	ň 0148	Ř 0158	Ũ 0168	Ÿ 0178
9	ĉ 0109	ę 0119	ĩ 0129	Ĺ 0139	ŉ 0149	ř 0159	ũ 0169	Ź 0179
A	Ċ 010A	Ě 011A	Ī 012A	ĺ 013A	Ŋ 014A	Ś 015A	Ū 016A	ź 017A
B	ċ 010B	ě 011B	ī 012B	Ļ 013B	ŋ 014B	ś 015B	ū 016B	Ż 017B
C	Č 010C	Ĝ 011C	Ĭ 012C	ļ 013C	Ō 014C	Ŝ 015C	Ŭ 016C	ż 017C
D	č 010D	ĝ 011D	ĭ 012D	Ľ 013D	ō 014D	ŝ 015D	ŭ 016D	Ž 017D
E	Ď 010E	Ğ 011E	Į 012E	ľ 013E	Ŏ 014E	Ş 015E	Ů 016E	ž 017E
F	ď 010F	ğ 011F	į 012F	Ŀ 013F	ŏ 014F	ş 015F	ů 016F	ſ 017F

European Latin

0100 Ā LATIN CAPITAL LETTER A WITH MACRON
≡ 0041 A 0304 ◌̄

0101 ā LATIN SMALL LETTER A WITH MACRON
• Latvian, Latin, ...
≡ 0061 a 0304 ◌̄

0102 Ă LATIN CAPITAL LETTER A WITH BREVE
≡ 0041 A 0306 ◌̆

0103 ă LATIN SMALL LETTER A WITH BREVE
• Romanian, Vietnamese, Latin, ...
≡ 0061 a 0306 ◌̆

0104 Ą LATIN CAPITAL LETTER A WITH OGONEK
≡ 0041 A 0328 ◌̨

0105 ą LATIN SMALL LETTER A WITH OGONEK
• Polish, Lithuanian, ...
≡ 0061 a 0328 ◌̨

0106 Ć LATIN CAPITAL LETTER C WITH ACUTE
≡ 0043 C 0301 ◌́

0107 ć LATIN SMALL LETTER C WITH ACUTE
• Polish, Croatian, ...
→ 045B ћ cyrillic small letter tshe
≡ 0063 c 0301 ◌́

0108 Ĉ LATIN CAPITAL LETTER C WITH CIRCUMFLEX
≡ 0043 C 0302 ◌̂

0109 ĉ LATIN SMALL LETTER C WITH CIRCUMFLEX
• Esperanto
≡ 0063 c 0302 ◌̂

010A Ċ LATIN CAPITAL LETTER C WITH DOT ABOVE
≡ 0043 C 0307 ◌̇

010B ċ LATIN SMALL LETTER C WITH DOT ABOVE
• Maltese, Irish Gaelic (old orthography)
≡ 0063 c 0307 ◌̇

010C Č LATIN CAPITAL LETTER C WITH CARON
≡ 0043 C 030C ◌̌

010D č LATIN SMALL LETTER C WITH CARON
• Czech, Slovak, Slovenian, and many other languages
≡ 0063 c 030C ◌̌

010E Ď LATIN CAPITAL LETTER D WITH CARON
• the form using caron/hacek is preferred in all contexts
≡ 0044 D 030C ◌̌

010F ď LATIN SMALL LETTER D WITH CARON
• Czech, Slovak
• the form using apostrophe is preferred in typesetting
≡ 0064 d 030C ◌̌

0110 Đ LATIN CAPITAL LETTER D WITH STROKE
→ 00D0 Ð latin capital letter eth
→ 0111 đ latin small letter d with stroke
→ 0189 Ɖ latin capital letter african d

0111 đ LATIN SMALL LETTER D WITH STROKE
• Croatian, Vietnamese, Sami
• an alternate glyph with the stroke through the bowl is used in Americanist orthographies
→ 0110 Đ latin capital letter d with stroke
→ 0452 ђ cyrillic small letter dje

0112 Ē LATIN CAPITAL LETTER E WITH MACRON
≡ 0045 E 0304 ◌̄

0113 ē LATIN SMALL LETTER E WITH MACRON
• Latvian, Latin, ...
≡ 0065 e 0304 ◌̄

0114 Ĕ LATIN CAPITAL LETTER E WITH BREVE
≡ 0045 E 0306 ◌̆

0115 ĕ LATIN SMALL LETTER E WITH BREVE
• Malay, Latin, ...
≡ 0065 e 0306 ◌̆

0116 Ė LATIN CAPITAL LETTER E WITH DOT ABOVE
≡ 0045 E 0307 ◌̇

0117 ė LATIN SMALL LETTER E WITH DOT ABOVE
• Lithuanian
≡ 0065 e 0307 ◌̇

0118 Ę LATIN CAPITAL LETTER E WITH OGONEK
≡ 0045 E 0328 ◌̨

0119 ę LATIN SMALL LETTER E WITH OGONEK
• Polish, Lithuanian, ...
≡ 0065 e 0328 ◌̨

011A Ě LATIN CAPITAL LETTER E WITH CARON
≡ 0045 E 030C ◌̌

011B ě LATIN SMALL LETTER E WITH CARON
• Czech, ...
≡ 0065 e 030C ◌̌

011C Ĝ LATIN CAPITAL LETTER G WITH CIRCUMFLEX
≡ 0047 G 0302 ◌̂

011D ĝ LATIN SMALL LETTER G WITH CIRCUMFLEX
• Esperanto
≡ 0067 g 0302 ◌̂

011E Ğ LATIN CAPITAL LETTER G WITH BREVE
≡ 0047 G 0306 ◌̆

011F ğ LATIN SMALL LETTER G WITH BREVE
• Turkish, Azerbaijani
→ 01E7 ǧ latin small letter g with caron
≡ 0067 g 0306 ◌̆

0120 Ġ LATIN CAPITAL LETTER G WITH DOT ABOVE
≡ 0047 G 0307 ◌̇

0121 ġ LATIN SMALL LETTER G WITH DOT ABOVE
• Maltese, Irish Gaelic (old orthography)
≡ 0067 g 0307 ◌̇

0122 Ģ LATIN CAPITAL LETTER G WITH CEDILLA
≡ 0047 G 0327 ◌̧

0123 ģ LATIN SMALL LETTER G WITH CEDILLA
• Latvian
• there are three major glyph variants
≡ 0067 g 0327 ◌̧

0124 Ĥ LATIN CAPITAL LETTER H WITH CIRCUMFLEX
≡ 0048 H 0302 ◌̂

0125 ĥ LATIN SMALL LETTER H WITH CIRCUMFLEX
• Esperanto
≡ 0068 h 0302 ◌̂

0126 Ħ LATIN CAPITAL LETTER H WITH STROKE

0127 ħ LATIN SMALL LETTER H WITH STROKE
• Maltese, IPA, ...
→ 045B ћ cyrillic small letter tshe
→ 210F ℏ planck constant over two pi

0128 Ĩ LATIN CAPITAL LETTER I WITH TILDE
≡ 0049 I 0303 ◌̃

0129 ĩ LATIN SMALL LETTER I WITH TILDE
• Greenlandic (old orthography)
≡ 0069 i 0303 ◌̃

012A Ī LATIN CAPITAL LETTER I WITH MACRON
≡ 0049 I 0304 ◌̄

012B ī LATIN SMALL LETTER I WITH MACRON
• Latvian, Latin, ...
≡ 0069 i 0304 ◌̄

012C Ĭ LATIN CAPITAL LETTER I WITH BREVE
≡ 0049 I 0306 ◌̆

012D ĭ LATIN SMALL LETTER I WITH BREVE
• Latin, ...
≡ 0069 i 0306 ̆

012E Į LATIN CAPITAL LETTER I WITH OGONEK
≡ 0049 I 0328 ̨

012F į LATIN SMALL LETTER I WITH OGONEK
• Lithuanian, ...
≡ 0069 i 0328 ̨

0130 İ LATIN CAPITAL LETTER I WITH DOT ABOVE
= i dot
• Turkish, Azerbaijani
• lowercase is 0069 i
→ 0049 I latin capital letter i
≡ 0049 I 0307 ̇

0131 ı LATIN SMALL LETTER DOTLESS I
• Turkish, Azerbaijani
• uppercase is 0049 I
→ 0069 i latin small letter i

0132 Ĳ LATIN CAPITAL LIGATURE IJ
≈ 0049 I 004A J

0133 ĳ LATIN SMALL LIGATURE IJ
• Dutch
≈ 0069 i 006A j

0134 Ĵ LATIN CAPITAL LETTER J WITH CIRCUMFLEX
≡ 004A J 0302 ̂

0135 ĵ LATIN SMALL LETTER J WITH CIRCUMFLEX
• Esperanto
≡ 006A j 0302 ̂

0136 Ķ LATIN CAPITAL LETTER K WITH CEDILLA
≡ 004B K 0327 ̧

0137 ķ LATIN SMALL LETTER K WITH CEDILLA
• Latvian
≡ 006B k 0327 ̧

0138 ĸ LATIN SMALL LETTER KRA
• Greenlandic (old orthography)

0139 Ĺ LATIN CAPITAL LETTER L WITH ACUTE
≡ 004C L 0301 ́

013A ĺ LATIN SMALL LETTER L WITH ACUTE
• Slovak
≡ 006C l 0301 ́

013B Ļ LATIN CAPITAL LETTER L WITH CEDILLA
≡ 004C L 0327 ̧

013C ļ LATIN SMALL LETTER L WITH CEDILLA
• Latvian
≡ 006C l 0327 ̧

013D Ľ LATIN CAPITAL LETTER L WITH CARON
• the form using apostrophe is preferred in typesetting
≡ 004C L 030C ̌

013E ľ LATIN SMALL LETTER L WITH CARON
• Slovak
• the form using apostrophe is preferred in typesetting
≡ 006C l 030C ̌

013F Ŀ LATIN CAPITAL LETTER L WITH MIDDLE DOT
• some fonts show the middle dot inside the L, but the preferred form has the dot following the L
≈ 004C L 00B7 ·

0140 ŀ LATIN SMALL LETTER L WITH MIDDLE DOT
• Catalan legacy compatibility character for ISO 6937
• preferred representation for Catalan: 006C l 00B7 ·
≈ 006C l 00B7 ·

0141 Ł LATIN CAPITAL LETTER L WITH STROKE
→ 023D Ƚ latin capital letter l with bar

0142 ł LATIN SMALL LETTER L WITH STROKE
• Polish, ...
→ 019A ƚ latin small letter l with bar

0143 Ń LATIN CAPITAL LETTER N WITH ACUTE
≡ 004E N 0301 ́

0144 ń LATIN SMALL LETTER N WITH ACUTE
• Polish, ...
≡ 006E n 0301 ́

0145 Ņ LATIN CAPITAL LETTER N WITH CEDILLA
≡ 004E N 0327 ̧

0146 ņ LATIN SMALL LETTER N WITH CEDILLA
• Latvian
≡ 006E n 0327 ̧

0147 Ň LATIN CAPITAL LETTER N WITH CARON
≡ 004E N 030C ̌

0148 ň LATIN SMALL LETTER N WITH CARON
• Czech, Slovak
≡ 006E n 030C ̌

0149 ŉ LATIN SMALL LETTER N PRECEDED BY APOSTROPHE
= latin small letter apostrophe n (1.0)
• Afrikaans
• legacy compatibility character for ISO/IEC 6937
• uppercase is 02BC ʼ 004E N
≈ 02BC ʼ 006E n

014A Ŋ LATIN CAPITAL LETTER ENG
• glyph may also have appearance of large form of the small letter

014B ŋ LATIN SMALL LETTER ENG
• Sami, Mende, IPA, ...

014C Ō LATIN CAPITAL LETTER O WITH MACRON
≡ 004F O 0304 ̄

014D ō LATIN SMALL LETTER O WITH MACRON
• Latvian, Latin, ...
≡ 006F o 0304 ̄

014E Ŏ LATIN CAPITAL LETTER O WITH BREVE
≡ 004F O 0306 ̆

014F ŏ LATIN SMALL LETTER O WITH BREVE
• Latin
≡ 006F o 0306 ̆

0150 Ő LATIN CAPITAL LETTER O WITH DOUBLE ACUTE
≡ 004F O 030B ̋

0151 ő LATIN SMALL LETTER O WITH DOUBLE ACUTE
• Hungarian
≡ 006F o 030B ̋

0152 Œ LATIN CAPITAL LIGATURE OE

0153 œ LATIN SMALL LIGATURE OE
= ethel (from Old English eðel)
• French, IPA, Old Icelandic, Old English, ...
→ 00E6 æ latin small letter ae
→ 0276 ɶ latin letter small capital oe

0154 Ŕ LATIN CAPITAL LETTER R WITH ACUTE
≡ 0052 R 0301 ́

0155 ŕ LATIN SMALL LETTER R WITH ACUTE
• Slovak, ...
≡ 0072 r 0301 ́

0156 Ŗ LATIN CAPITAL LETTER R WITH CEDILLA
≡ 0052 R 0327 ̧
0157 ŗ LATIN SMALL LETTER R WITH CEDILLA
• Livonian
≡ 0072 r 0327 ̧
0158 Ř LATIN CAPITAL LETTER R WITH CARON
≡ 0052 R 030C ̌
0159 ř LATIN SMALL LETTER R WITH CARON
• Czech, ...
≡ 0072 r 030C ̌
015A Ś LATIN CAPITAL LETTER S WITH ACUTE
≡ 0053 S 0301 ́
015B ś LATIN SMALL LETTER S WITH ACUTE
• Polish, Indic transliteration, ...
≡ 0073 s 0301 ́
015C Ŝ LATIN CAPITAL LETTER S WITH CIRCUMFLEX
≡ 0053 S 0302 ̂
015D ŝ LATIN SMALL LETTER S WITH CIRCUMFLEX
• Esperanto
≡ 0073 s 0302 ̂
015E Ş LATIN CAPITAL LETTER S WITH CEDILLA
≡ 0053 S 0327 ̧
015F ş LATIN SMALL LETTER S WITH CEDILLA
• Turkish, Azerbaijani, Romanian, ...
• this character is used in both Turkish and Romanian data
• a glyph variant with comma below is preferred for Romanian
→ 0219 ș latin small letter s with comma below
≡ 0073 s 0327 ̧
0160 Š LATIN CAPITAL LETTER S WITH CARON
≡ 0053 S 030C ̌
0161 š LATIN SMALL LETTER S WITH CARON
• Czech, Estonian, Finnish, Slovak, and many other languages
≡ 0073 s 030C ̌
0162 Ţ LATIN CAPITAL LETTER T WITH CEDILLA
≡ 0054 T 0327 ̧
0163 ţ LATIN SMALL LETTER T WITH CEDILLA
• Romanian, Semitic transliteration, ...
• this character is used in Romanian data
• a glyph variant with comma below is preferred for Romanian
→ 021B ț latin small letter t with comma below
≡ 0074 t 0327 ̧
0164 Ť LATIN CAPITAL LETTER T WITH CARON
• the form using caron/hacek is preferred in all contexts
≡ 0054 T 030C ̌
0165 ť LATIN SMALL LETTER T WITH CARON
• Czech, Slovak
• the form using apostrophe is preferred in typesetting
≡ 0074 t 030C ̌
0166 Ŧ LATIN CAPITAL LETTER T WITH STROKE
0167 ŧ LATIN SMALL LETTER T WITH STROKE
• Sami
0168 Ũ LATIN CAPITAL LETTER U WITH TILDE
≡ 0055 U 0303 ̃
0169 ũ LATIN SMALL LETTER U WITH TILDE
• Greenlandic (old orthography)
≡ 0075 u 0303 ̃
016A Ū LATIN CAPITAL LETTER U WITH MACRON
≡ 0055 U 0304 ̄
016B ū LATIN SMALL LETTER U WITH MACRON
• Latvian, Lithuanian, Latin, ...
≡ 0075 u 0304 ̄
016C Ŭ LATIN CAPITAL LETTER U WITH BREVE
≡ 0055 U 0306 ̆
016D ŭ LATIN SMALL LETTER U WITH BREVE
• Latin, Esperanto, ...
≡ 0075 u 0306 ̆
016E Ů LATIN CAPITAL LETTER U WITH RING ABOVE
≡ 0055 U 030A ̊
016F ů LATIN SMALL LETTER U WITH RING ABOVE
• Czech, ...
≡ 0075 u 030A ̊
0170 Ű LATIN CAPITAL LETTER U WITH DOUBLE ACUTE
≡ 0055 U 030B ̋
0171 ű LATIN SMALL LETTER U WITH DOUBLE ACUTE
• Hungarian
≡ 0075 u 030B ̋
0172 Ų LATIN CAPITAL LETTER U WITH OGONEK
≡ 0055 U 0328 ̨
0173 ų LATIN SMALL LETTER U WITH OGONEK
• Lithuanian
≡ 0075 u 0328 ̨
0174 Ŵ LATIN CAPITAL LETTER W WITH CIRCUMFLEX
≡ 0057 W 0302 ̂
0175 ŵ LATIN SMALL LETTER W WITH CIRCUMFLEX
• Welsh
≡ 0077 w 0302 ̂
0176 Ŷ LATIN CAPITAL LETTER Y WITH CIRCUMFLEX
≡ 0059 Y 0302 ̂
0177 ŷ LATIN SMALL LETTER Y WITH CIRCUMFLEX
• Welsh
≡ 0079 y 0302 ̂
0178 Ÿ LATIN CAPITAL LETTER Y WITH DIAERESIS
• French, Igbo
→ 00FF ÿ latin small letter y with diaeresis
≡ 0059 Y 0308 ̈
0179 Ź LATIN CAPITAL LETTER Z WITH ACUTE
≡ 005A Z 0301 ́
017A ź LATIN SMALL LETTER Z WITH ACUTE
• Polish, ...
≡ 007A z 0301 ́
017B Ż LATIN CAPITAL LETTER Z WITH DOT ABOVE
≡ 005A Z 0307 ̇
017C ż LATIN SMALL LETTER Z WITH DOT ABOVE
• Polish, ...
≡ 007A z 0307 ̇
017D Ž LATIN CAPITAL LETTER Z WITH CARON
≡ 005A Z 030C ̌
017E ž LATIN SMALL LETTER Z WITH CARON
• Czech, Estonian, Finnish, Slovak, Slovenian, and many other languages
≡ 007A z 030C ̌
017F ſ LATIN SMALL LETTER LONG S
• in common use in Roman types until the 18th century
• in current use in Fraktur and Gaelic types
≈ 0073 s latin small letter s

	018	019	01A	01B	01C	01D	01E	01F	020	021	022	023	024
0	ƀ 0180	Ɛ 0190	Ơ 01A0	ư 01B0	ǀ 01C0	ǐ 01D0	Ǡ 01E0	ǰ 01F0	Ȁ 0200	Ȑ 0210	Ƞ 0220	Ȱ 0230	ɀ 0240
1	Ɓ 0181	Ƒ 0191	ơ 01A1	Ʊ 01B1	ǁ 01C1	Ǒ 01D1	ǡ 01E1	Ǳ 01F1	ȁ 0201	ȑ 0211	ȡ 0221	ȱ 0231	Ɂ 0241
2	Ƃ 0182	ƒ 0192	Ƣ 01A2	Ʋ 01B2	ǂ 01C2	ǒ 01D2	Ǣ 01E2	ǲ 01F2	Ȃ 0202	Ȓ 0212	Ȣ 0222	Ȳ 0232	ɂ 0242
3	ƃ 0183	Ɠ 0193	ƣ 01A3	Ƴ 01B3	ǃ 01C3	Ǔ 01D3	ǣ 01E3	ǳ 01F3	ȃ 0203	ȓ 0213	ȣ 0223	ȳ 0233	Ƀ 0243
4	Ƅ 0184	Ɣ 0194	Ƥ 01A4	ƴ 01B4	Ǆ 01C4	ǔ 01D4	Ǥ 01E4	Ǵ 01F4	Ȅ 0204	Ȕ 0214	Ȥ 0224	ȴ 0234	Ʉ 0244
5	ƅ 0185	ƕ 0195	ƥ 01A5	Ƶ 01B5	ǅ 01C5	Ǖ 01D5	ǥ 01E5	ǵ 01F5	ȅ 0205	ȕ 0215	ȥ 0225	ȵ 0235	Ʌ 0245
6	Ɔ 0186	Ɩ 0196	Ʀ 01A6	ƶ 01B6	ǆ 01C6	ǖ 01D6	Ǧ 01E6	Ƕ 01F6	Ȇ 0206	Ȗ 0216	Ȧ 0226	ȶ 0236	Ɇ 0246
7	Ƈ 0187	Ɨ 0197	Ƨ 01A7	Ʒ 01B7	Ǉ 01C7	Ǘ 01D7	ǧ 01E7	Ƿ 01F7	ȇ 0207	ȗ 0217	ȧ 0227	ȷ 0237	ɇ 0247
8	ƈ 0188	Ƙ 0198	ƨ 01A8	Ƹ 01B8	ǈ 01C8	ǘ 01D8	Ǩ 01E8	Ǹ 01F8	Ȉ 0208	Ș 0218	Ȩ 0228	ȸ 0238	Ɉ 0248
9	Ɖ 0189	ƙ 0199	Ʃ 01A9	ƹ 01B9	ǉ 01C9	Ǚ 01D9	ǩ 01E9	ǹ 01F9	ȉ 0209	ș 0219	ȩ 0229	ȹ 0239	ɉ 0249
A	Ɗ 018A	ƚ 019A	ƪ 01AA	ƺ 01BA	Ǌ 01CA	ǚ 01DA	Ǫ 01EA	Ǻ 01FA	Ȋ 020A	Ț 021A	Ȫ 022A	Ⱥ 023A	Ɋ 024A
B	Ƌ 018B	ƛ 019B	ƫ 01AB	ƻ 01BB	ǋ 01CB	Ǜ 01DB	ǫ 01EB	ǻ 01FB	ȋ 020B	ț 021B	ȫ 022B	Ȼ 023B	ɋ 024B
C	ƌ 018C	Ɯ 019C	Ƭ 01AC	Ƽ 01BC	ǌ 01CC	ǜ 01DC	Ǭ 01EC	Ǽ 01FC	Ȍ 020C	Ȝ 021C	Ȭ 022C	ȼ 023C	Ɍ 024C
D	ƍ 018D	Ɲ 019D	ƭ 01AD	ƽ 01BD	Ǎ 01CD	ǝ 01DD	ǭ 01ED	ǽ 01FD	ȍ 020D	ȝ 021D	ȭ 022D	Ƚ 023D	ɍ 024D
E	Ǝ 018E	ƞ 019E	Ʈ 01AE	ƾ 01BE	ǎ 01CE	Ǟ 01DE	Ǯ 01EE	Ǿ 01FE	Ȏ 020E	Ȟ 021E	Ȯ 022E	Ⱦ 023E	Ɏ 024E
F	Ə 018F	Ɵ 019F	Ư 01AF	ƿ 01BF	Ǐ 01CF	ǟ 01DF	ǯ 01EF	ǿ 01FF	ȏ 020F	ȟ 021F	ȯ 022F	ȿ 023F	ɏ 024F

Non-European and historic Latin

0180 ƀ LATIN SMALL LETTER B WITH STROKE
- Americanist and Indo-Europeanist usage for phonetic beta
- Americanist orthographies use an alternate glyph with the stroke through the bowl
- Old Saxon
- uppercase is 0243 Ƀ

→ 03B2 β greek small letter beta
→ 2422 ␢ blank symbol

0181 Ɓ LATIN CAPITAL LETTER B WITH HOOK
- Zulu, Pan-Nigerian alphabet

→ 0253 ɓ latin small letter b with hook

0182 Ƃ LATIN CAPITAL LETTER B WITH TOPBAR

0183 ƃ LATIN SMALL LETTER B WITH TOPBAR
- Zhuang (old orthography)
- former Soviet minority language scripts

→ 0411 Б cyrillic capital letter be

0184 Ƅ LATIN CAPITAL LETTER TONE SIX

0185 ƅ LATIN SMALL LETTER TONE SIX
- Zhuang (old orthography)
- Zhuang tone three is Cyrillic ze
- Zhuang tone four is Cyrillic che

→ 01A8 ƨ latin small letter tone two
→ 01BD ƽ latin small letter tone five
→ 0437 з cyrillic small letter ze
→ 0447 ч cyrillic small letter che
→ 044C ь cyrillic small letter soft sign

0186 Ɔ LATIN CAPITAL LETTER OPEN O
- typographically a turned C
- African

→ 0254 ɔ latin small letter open o

0187 Ƈ LATIN CAPITAL LETTER C WITH HOOK

0188 ƈ LATIN SMALL LETTER C WITH HOOK
- African

0189 Ɖ LATIN CAPITAL LETTER AFRICAN D
- Ewe

→ 00D0 Ð latin capital letter eth
→ 0110 Đ latin capital letter d with stroke
→ 0256 ɖ latin small letter d with tail

018A Ɗ LATIN CAPITAL LETTER D WITH HOOK
- Pan-Nigerian alphabet

→ 0257 ɗ latin small letter d with hook

018B Ƌ LATIN CAPITAL LETTER D WITH TOPBAR

018C ƌ LATIN SMALL LETTER D WITH TOPBAR
- former-Soviet minority language scripts
- Zhuang (old orthography)

018D ƍ LATIN SMALL LETTER TURNED DELTA

= reversed Polish-hook o
- archaic phonetic for labialized alveolar fricative
- recommended spellings 007A z 02B7 ʷ or 007A z 032B ◌̫

018E Ǝ LATIN CAPITAL LETTER REVERSED E

= turned e
- Pan-Nigerian alphabet
- lowercase is 01DD ǝ

018F Ə LATIN CAPITAL LETTER SCHWA
- Azerbaijani, ...

→ 0259 ə latin small letter schwa
→ 04D8 Ә cyrillic capital letter schwa

0190 Ɛ LATIN CAPITAL LETTER OPEN E

= epsilon
- African

→ 025B ɛ latin small letter open e
→ 2107 ℇ euler constant

0191 Ƒ LATIN CAPITAL LETTER F WITH HOOK
- African

0192 ƒ LATIN SMALL LETTER F WITH HOOK

= script f
= Florin currency symbol (Netherlands)
= function symbol
- used as abbreviation convention for folder

0193 Ɠ LATIN CAPITAL LETTER G WITH HOOK
- African

→ 0260 ɠ latin small letter g with hook

0194 Ɣ LATIN CAPITAL LETTER GAMMA
- African

→ 0263 ɣ latin small letter gamma

0195 ƕ LATIN SMALL LETTER HV
- Gothic transliteration
- uppercase is 01F6 Ƕ

0196 Ɩ LATIN CAPITAL LETTER IOTA
- African

→ 0269 ɩ latin small letter iota

0197 Ɨ LATIN CAPITAL LETTER I WITH STROKE

= barred i, i bar
- African
- ISO 6438 gives lowercase as 026A ɪ, not 0268 ɨ

→ 026A ɪ latin letter small capital i

0198 Ƙ LATIN CAPITAL LETTER K WITH HOOK

0199 ƙ LATIN SMALL LETTER K WITH HOOK
- Hausa, Pan-Nigerian alphabet

019A ƚ LATIN SMALL LETTER L WITH BAR

= barred l
- Americanist phonetic usage for 026C ɬ

→ 0142 ł latin small letter l with stroke
→ 023D Ƚ latin capital letter l with bar

019B ƛ LATIN SMALL LETTER LAMBDA WITH STROKE

= barred lambda, lambda bar
- Americanist phonetic usage

019C Ɯ LATIN CAPITAL LETTER TURNED M
- Zhuang (old orthography)

→ 026F ɯ latin small letter turned m

019D Ɲ LATIN CAPITAL LETTER N WITH LEFT HOOK
- African

→ 0272 ɲ latin small letter n with left hook

019E ƞ LATIN SMALL LETTER N WITH LONG RIGHT LEG
- archaic phonetic for Japanese 3093 ん
- recommended spelling for syllabic n is 006E n 0329 ◌̩
- Lakota (indicates nasalization of vowel)

→ 0220 Ƞ latin capital letter n with long right leg

019F Ɵ LATIN CAPITAL LETTER O WITH MIDDLE TILDE

= barred o, o bar
- lowercase is 0275 ɵ
- African

→ 04E8 Ө cyrillic capital letter barred o

01A0 Ơ LATIN CAPITAL LETTER O WITH HORN

≡ 004F O 031B ◌̛

01A1 ơ LATIN SMALL LETTER O WITH HORN
- Vietnamese

≡ 006F o 031B ◌̛

01A2 Ƣ LATIN CAPITAL LETTER OI

※ LATIN CAPITAL LETTER GHA

01A3 ƣ LATIN SMALL LETTER OI
※ LATIN SMALL LETTER GHA
• Pan-Turkic Latin alphabets
01A4 Ƥ LATIN CAPITAL LETTER P WITH HOOK
01A5 ƥ LATIN SMALL LETTER P WITH HOOK
• African
01A6 Ʀ LATIN LETTER YR
• Old Norse
• from German Standard DIN 31624 and ISO 5246-2
• lowercase is 0280 ʀ
01A7 Ƨ LATIN CAPITAL LETTER TONE TWO
01A8 ƨ LATIN SMALL LETTER TONE TWO
• Zhuang (old orthography)
• typographically a reversed S
→ 0185 ƅ latin small letter tone six
01A9 Ʃ LATIN CAPITAL LETTER ESH
• African
→ 0283 ʃ latin small letter esh
→ 03A3 Σ greek capital letter sigma
01AA ƪ LATIN LETTER REVERSED ESH LOOP
• archaic phonetic for labialized palatoalveolar or palatal fricative
• Twi
• recommended spellings 0283 ʃ 02B7 ʷ, 00E7 ç 02B7 ʷ, 0068 h 0265 ɥ, etc.
01AB ƫ LATIN SMALL LETTER T WITH PALATAL HOOK
• archaic phonetic for palatalized alveolar or dental stop
• recommended spelling 0074 t 02B2 ʲ
01AC Ƭ LATIN CAPITAL LETTER T WITH HOOK
• a glyph variant with hook at the right also occurs
01AD ƭ LATIN SMALL LETTER T WITH HOOK
• African
01AE Ʈ LATIN CAPITAL LETTER T WITH RETROFLEX HOOK
• African
→ 0288 ʈ latin small letter t with retroflex hook
01AF Ư LATIN CAPITAL LETTER U WITH HORN
≡ 0055 U 031B ◌̛
01B0 ư LATIN SMALL LETTER U WITH HORN
• Vietnamese
≡ 0075 u 031B ◌̛
01B1 Ʊ LATIN CAPITAL LETTER UPSILON
• African
• typographically based on turned capital Greek omega
→ 028A ʊ latin small letter upsilon
→ 2127 ℧ inverted ohm sign
01B2 Ʋ LATIN CAPITAL LETTER V WITH HOOK
= script v
• African
→ 028B ʋ latin small letter v with hook
01B3 Ƴ LATIN CAPITAL LETTER Y WITH HOOK
• a glyph variant with hook at the left also occurs
01B4 ƴ LATIN SMALL LETTER Y WITH HOOK
• Bini, Esoko, and other Edo languages in West Africa
01B5 Ƶ LATIN CAPITAL LETTER Z WITH STROKE
01B6 ƶ LATIN SMALL LETTER Z WITH STROKE
= barred z, z bar
• Pan-Turkic Latin orthography
• handwritten variant of Latin "z"
→ 007A z latin small letter z
01B7 Ʒ LATIN CAPITAL LETTER EZH
• African, Skolt Sami
• lowercase is 0292 ʒ
→ 021C Ȝ latin capital letter yogh
→ 04E0 Ӡ cyrillic capital letter abkhasian dze
01B8 Ƹ LATIN CAPITAL LETTER EZH REVERSED
01B9 ƹ LATIN SMALL LETTER EZH REVERSED
• archaic phonetic for voiced pharyngeal fricative
• sometimes typographically rendered with a turned digit 3
• recommended spelling 0295 ʕ
→ 0295 ʕ latin letter pharyngeal voiced fricative
→ 0639 ع arabic letter ain
01BA ƺ LATIN SMALL LETTER EZH WITH TAIL
• archaic phonetic for labialized voiced palatoalveolar or palatal fricative
• Twi
• recommended spellings 0292 ʒ 02B7 ʷ or 006A j 02B7 ʷ
01BB ƻ LATIN LETTER TWO WITH STROKE
• archaic phonetic for [dz] affricate
• recommended spellings 0292 ʒ or 0064 d 007A z
01BC Ƽ LATIN CAPITAL LETTER TONE FIVE
01BD ƽ LATIN SMALL LETTER TONE FIVE
• Zhuang (old orthography)
→ 0185 ƅ latin small letter tone six
01BE ƾ LATIN LETTER INVERTED GLOTTAL STOP WITH STROKE
• archaic phonetic for [ts] affricate
• recommended spelling 0074 t 0073 s
• letter form is actually derived from ligation of ts, rather than inverted glottal stop
01BF ƿ LATIN LETTER WYNN
= wen
• Runic letter borrowed into Latin script
• replaced by "w" in modern transcriptions of Old English
• uppercase is 01F7 Ƿ
→ 16B9 ᚹ runic letter wunjo wynn w

African letters for clicks

01C0 ǀ LATIN LETTER DENTAL CLICK
= pipe
• Khoisan tradition
• "c" in Zulu orthography
→ 002F / solidus
→ 007C | vertical line
→ 0287 ʇ latin small letter turned t
→ 2223 ∣ divides
01C1 ǁ LATIN LETTER LATERAL CLICK
= double pipe
• Khoisan tradition
• "x" in Zulu orthography
→ 0296 ʖ latin letter inverted glottal stop
→ 2225 ∥ parallel to
01C2 ǂ LATIN LETTER ALVEOLAR CLICK
= double-barred pipe
• Khoisan tradition
→ 2260 ≠ not equal to

01C3 ! LATIN LETTER RETROFLEX CLICK
= latin letter exclamation mark (1.0)
• Khoisan tradition
• "q" in Zulu orthography
→ 0021 ! exclamation mark
→ 0297 ʗ latin letter stretched c

Croatian digraphs matching Serbian Cyrillic letters

01C4 Ǆ LATIN CAPITAL LETTER DZ WITH CARON
≈ 0044 D 017D Ž

01C5 ǅ LATIN CAPITAL LETTER D WITH SMALL LETTER Z WITH CARON
≈ 0044 D 017E ž

01C6 ǆ LATIN SMALL LETTER DZ WITH CARON
→ 045F џ cyrillic small letter dzhe
≈ 0064 d 017E ž

01C7 Ǉ LATIN CAPITAL LETTER LJ
≈ 004C L 004A J

01C8 ǈ LATIN CAPITAL LETTER L WITH SMALL LETTER J
≈ 004C L 006A j

01C9 ǉ LATIN SMALL LETTER LJ
→ 0459 љ cyrillic small letter lje
≈ 006C l 006A j

01CA Ǌ LATIN CAPITAL LETTER NJ
≈ 004E N 004A J

01CB ǋ LATIN CAPITAL LETTER N WITH SMALL LETTER J
≈ 004E N 006A j

01CC ǌ LATIN SMALL LETTER NJ
→ 045A њ cyrillic small letter nje
≈ 006E n 006A j

Pinyin diacritic-vowel combinations

01CD Ǎ LATIN CAPITAL LETTER A WITH CARON
≡ 0041 A 030C ̌

01CE ǎ LATIN SMALL LETTER A WITH CARON
• Pinyin third tone
≡ 0061 a 030C ̌

01CF Ǐ LATIN CAPITAL LETTER I WITH CARON
≡ 0049 I 030C ̌

01D0 ǐ LATIN SMALL LETTER I WITH CARON
• Pinyin third tone
≡ 0069 i 030C ̌

01D1 Ǒ LATIN CAPITAL LETTER O WITH CARON
≡ 004F O 030C ̌

01D2 ǒ LATIN SMALL LETTER O WITH CARON
• Pinyin third tone
≡ 006F o 030C ̌

01D3 Ǔ LATIN CAPITAL LETTER U WITH CARON
≡ 0055 U 030C ̌

01D4 ǔ LATIN SMALL LETTER U WITH CARON
• Pinyin third tone
≡ 0075 u 030C ̌

01D5 Ǖ LATIN CAPITAL LETTER U WITH DIAERESIS AND MACRON
≡ 00DC Ü 0304 ̄

01D6 ǖ LATIN SMALL LETTER U WITH DIAERESIS AND MACRON
• Pinyin first tone
≡ 00FC ü 0304 ̄

01D7 Ǘ LATIN CAPITAL LETTER U WITH DIAERESIS AND ACUTE
≡ 00DC Ü 0301 ́

01D8 ǘ LATIN SMALL LETTER U WITH DIAERESIS AND ACUTE
• Pinyin second tone
≡ 00FC ü 0301 ́

01D9 Ǚ LATIN CAPITAL LETTER U WITH DIAERESIS AND CARON
≡ 00DC Ü 030C ̌

01DA ǚ LATIN SMALL LETTER U WITH DIAERESIS AND CARON
• Pinyin third tone
≡ 00FC ü 030C ̌

01DB Ǜ LATIN CAPITAL LETTER U WITH DIAERESIS AND GRAVE
≡ 00DC Ü 0300 ̀

01DC ǜ LATIN SMALL LETTER U WITH DIAERESIS AND GRAVE
• Pinyin fourth tone
≡ 00FC ü 0300 ̀

Phonetic and historic letters

01DD ǝ LATIN SMALL LETTER TURNED E
• Pan-Nigerian alphabet
• all other usages of schwa are 0259 ə
• uppercase is 018E Ǝ
→ 0259 ə latin small letter schwa

01DE Ǟ LATIN CAPITAL LETTER A WITH DIAERESIS AND MACRON
≡ 00C4 Ä 0304 ̄

01DF ǟ LATIN SMALL LETTER A WITH DIAERESIS AND MACRON
• Livonian, Uralicist usage
≡ 00E4 ä 0304 ̄

01E0 Ǡ LATIN CAPITAL LETTER A WITH DOT ABOVE AND MACRON
≡ 0226 Ȧ 0304 ̄

01E1 ǡ LATIN SMALL LETTER A WITH DOT ABOVE AND MACRON
• Uralicist usage
≡ 0227 ȧ 0304 ̄

01E2 Ǣ LATIN CAPITAL LETTER AE WITH MACRON
≡ 00C6 Æ 0304 ̄

01E3 ǣ LATIN SMALL LETTER AE WITH MACRON
• Old Norse, Old English
≡ 00E6 æ 0304 ̄

01E4 Ǥ LATIN CAPITAL LETTER G WITH STROKE

01E5 ǥ LATIN SMALL LETTER G WITH STROKE
• Skolt Sami

01E6 Ǧ LATIN CAPITAL LETTER G WITH CARON
≡ 0047 G 030C ̌

01E7 ǧ LATIN SMALL LETTER G WITH CARON
• Skolt Sami
→ 011F ğ latin small letter g with breve
≡ 0067 g 030C ̌

01E8 Ǩ LATIN CAPITAL LETTER K WITH CARON
≡ 004B K 030C ̌

01E9 ǩ LATIN SMALL LETTER K WITH CARON
• Skolt Sami
≡ 006B k 030C ̌

01EA Ǫ LATIN CAPITAL LETTER O WITH OGONEK
≡ 004F O 0328 ̨

01EB ǫ LATIN SMALL LETTER O WITH OGONEK
• Sami, Iroquoian, Old Icelandic
≡ 006F o 0328 ̨

01EC Ǭ LATIN CAPITAL LETTER O WITH OGONEK AND MACRON
≡ 01EA Ǫ 0304 ◌̄

01ED ǭ LATIN SMALL LETTER O WITH OGONEK AND MACRON
• Old Icelandic
≡ 01EB ǫ 0304 ◌̄

01EE Ǯ LATIN CAPITAL LETTER EZH WITH CARON
≡ 01B7 Ʒ 030C ◌̌

01EF ǯ LATIN SMALL LETTER EZH WITH CARON
• Skolt Sami
≡ 0292 ʒ 030C ◌̌

01F0 ǰ LATIN SMALL LETTER J WITH CARON
• IPA and many languages
≡ 006A j 030C ◌̌

01F1 Ǳ LATIN CAPITAL LETTER DZ
≈ 0044 D 005A Z

01F2 ǲ LATIN CAPITAL LETTER D WITH SMALL LETTER Z
≈ 0044 D 007A z

01F3 ǳ LATIN SMALL LETTER DZ
≈ 0064 d 007A z

01F4 Ǵ LATIN CAPITAL LETTER G WITH ACUTE
≡ 0047 G 0301 ◌́

01F5 ǵ LATIN SMALL LETTER G WITH ACUTE
• Macedonian and Serbian transliteration
≡ 0067 g 0301 ◌́

01F6 Ƕ LATIN CAPITAL LETTER HWAIR
• lowercase is 0195 ƕ

01F7 Ƿ LATIN CAPITAL LETTER WYNN
= wen
• lowercase is 01BF ƿ

01F8 Ǹ LATIN CAPITAL LETTER N WITH GRAVE
≡ 004E N 0300 ◌̀

01F9 ǹ LATIN SMALL LETTER N WITH GRAVE
• Pinyin
≡ 006E n 0300 ◌̀

01FA Ǻ LATIN CAPITAL LETTER A WITH RING ABOVE AND ACUTE
≡ 00C5 Å 0301 ◌́

01FB ǻ LATIN SMALL LETTER A WITH RING ABOVE AND ACUTE
≡ 00E5 å 0301 ◌́

01FC Ǽ LATIN CAPITAL LETTER AE WITH ACUTE
≡ 00C6 Æ 0301 ◌́

01FD ǽ LATIN SMALL LETTER AE WITH ACUTE
≡ 00E6 æ 0301 ◌́

01FE Ǿ LATIN CAPITAL LETTER O WITH STROKE AND ACUTE
≡ 00D8 Ø 0301 ◌́

01FF ǿ LATIN SMALL LETTER O WITH STROKE AND ACUTE
≡ 00F8 ø 0301 ◌́

Additions for Slovenian and Croatian

0200 Ȁ LATIN CAPITAL LETTER A WITH DOUBLE GRAVE
≡ 0041 A 030F ◌̏

0201 ȁ LATIN SMALL LETTER A WITH DOUBLE GRAVE
≡ 0061 a 030F ◌̏

0202 Ȃ LATIN CAPITAL LETTER A WITH INVERTED BREVE
≡ 0041 A 0311 ◌̑

0203 ȃ LATIN SMALL LETTER A WITH INVERTED BREVE
≡ 0061 a 0311 ◌̑

0204 Ȅ LATIN CAPITAL LETTER E WITH DOUBLE GRAVE
≡ 0045 E 030F ◌̏

0205 ȅ LATIN SMALL LETTER E WITH DOUBLE GRAVE
≡ 0065 e 030F ◌̏

0206 Ȇ LATIN CAPITAL LETTER E WITH INVERTED BREVE
≡ 0045 E 0311 ◌̑

0207 ȇ LATIN SMALL LETTER E WITH INVERTED BREVE
≡ 0065 e 0311 ◌̑

0208 Ȉ LATIN CAPITAL LETTER I WITH DOUBLE GRAVE
≡ 0049 I 030F ◌̏

0209 ȉ LATIN SMALL LETTER I WITH DOUBLE GRAVE
≡ 0069 i 030F ◌̏

020A Ȋ LATIN CAPITAL LETTER I WITH INVERTED BREVE
≡ 0049 I 0311 ◌̑

020B ȋ LATIN SMALL LETTER I WITH INVERTED BREVE
≡ 0069 i 0311 ◌̑

020C Ȍ LATIN CAPITAL LETTER O WITH DOUBLE GRAVE
≡ 004F O 030F ◌̏

020D ȍ LATIN SMALL LETTER O WITH DOUBLE GRAVE
≡ 006F o 030F ◌̏

020E Ȏ LATIN CAPITAL LETTER O WITH INVERTED BREVE
≡ 004F O 0311 ◌̑

020F ȏ LATIN SMALL LETTER O WITH INVERTED BREVE
≡ 006F o 0311 ◌̑

0210 Ȑ LATIN CAPITAL LETTER R WITH DOUBLE GRAVE
≡ 0052 R 030F ◌̏

0211 ȑ LATIN SMALL LETTER R WITH DOUBLE GRAVE
≡ 0072 r 030F ◌̏

0212 Ȓ LATIN CAPITAL LETTER R WITH INVERTED BREVE
≡ 0052 R 0311 ◌̑

0213 ȓ LATIN SMALL LETTER R WITH INVERTED BREVE
≡ 0072 r 0311 ◌̑

0214 Ȕ LATIN CAPITAL LETTER U WITH DOUBLE GRAVE
≡ 0055 U 030F ◌̏

0215 ȕ LATIN SMALL LETTER U WITH DOUBLE GRAVE
≡ 0075 u 030F ◌̏

0216 Ȗ LATIN CAPITAL LETTER U WITH INVERTED BREVE
≡ 0055 U 0311 ◌̑

0217 ȗ LATIN SMALL LETTER U WITH INVERTED BREVE
≡ 0075 u 0311 ◌̑

Additions for Romanian

0218 Ș LATIN CAPITAL LETTER S WITH COMMA BELOW
≡ 0053 S 0326 ◌̦

0219 ș LATIN SMALL LETTER S WITH COMMA BELOW
• Romanian, when distinct comma below form is required
→ 015F ş latin small letter s with cedilla
≡ 0073 s 0326 ◌̦

021A Ț LATIN CAPITAL LETTER T WITH COMMA BELOW
≡ 0054 T 0326 ◌̦

021B ț LATIN SMALL LETTER T WITH COMMA BELOW
• Romanian, when distinct comma below form is required
→ 0163 ţ latin small letter t with cedilla
≡ 0074 t 0326 ◌̦

Miscellaneous additions

021C Ȝ LATIN CAPITAL LETTER YOGH
→ 01B7 Ʒ latin capital letter ezh

021D ȝ LATIN SMALL LETTER YOGH
- Middle English, Scots
→ 0292 ʒ latin small letter ezh
→ 1D79 ᵹ latin small letter insular g
→ 2125 ℥ ounce sign

021E Ȟ LATIN CAPITAL LETTER H WITH CARON
≡ 0048 H 030C ̌

021F ȟ LATIN SMALL LETTER H WITH CARON
- Finnish Romany
≡ 0068 h 030C ̌

0220 Ƞ LATIN CAPITAL LETTER N WITH LONG RIGHT LEG
- Lakota
→ 019E ƞ latin small letter n with long right leg

0221 ȡ LATIN SMALL LETTER D WITH CURL
- phonetic use in Sinology

0222 Ȣ LATIN CAPITAL LETTER OU

0223 ȣ LATIN SMALL LETTER OU
- Algonquin, Huron
→ 0038 8 digit eight

0224 Ȥ LATIN CAPITAL LETTER Z WITH HOOK

0225 ȥ LATIN SMALL LETTER Z WITH HOOK
- Middle High German

0226 Ȧ LATIN CAPITAL LETTER A WITH DOT ABOVE
≡ 0041 A 0307 ̇

0227 ȧ LATIN SMALL LETTER A WITH DOT ABOVE
- Uralicist usage
≡ 0061 a 0307 ̇

0228 Ȩ LATIN CAPITAL LETTER E WITH CEDILLA
≡ 0045 E 0327 ̧

0229 ȩ LATIN SMALL LETTER E WITH CEDILLA
≡ 0065 e 0327 ̧

Additions for Livonian

022A Ȫ LATIN CAPITAL LETTER O WITH DIAERESIS AND MACRON
≡ 00D6 Ö 0304 ̄

022B ȫ LATIN SMALL LETTER O WITH DIAERESIS AND MACRON
≡ 00F6 ö 0304 ̄

022C Ȭ LATIN CAPITAL LETTER O WITH TILDE AND MACRON
≡ 00D5 Õ 0304 ̄

022D ȭ LATIN SMALL LETTER O WITH TILDE AND MACRON
≡ 00F5 õ 0304 ̄

022E Ȯ LATIN CAPITAL LETTER O WITH DOT ABOVE
≡ 004F O 0307 ̇

022F ȯ LATIN SMALL LETTER O WITH DOT ABOVE
≡ 006F o 0307 ̇

0230 Ȱ LATIN CAPITAL LETTER O WITH DOT ABOVE AND MACRON
≡ 022E Ȯ 0304 ̄

0231 ȱ LATIN SMALL LETTER O WITH DOT ABOVE AND MACRON
≡ 022F ȯ 0304 ̄

0232 Ȳ LATIN CAPITAL LETTER Y WITH MACRON
≡ 0059 Y 0304 ̄

0233 ȳ LATIN SMALL LETTER Y WITH MACRON
- also Cornish
≡ 0079 y 0304 ̄

Additions for Sinology

0234 ȴ LATIN SMALL LETTER L WITH CURL

0235 ȵ LATIN SMALL LETTER N WITH CURL

0236 ȶ LATIN SMALL LETTER T WITH CURL

Miscellaneous additions

0237 ȷ LATIN SMALL LETTER DOTLESS J
→ 1D6A5 𝚥 mathematical italic small dotless j

0238 ȸ LATIN SMALL LETTER DB DIGRAPH
- used in Africanist linguistics

0239 ȹ LATIN SMALL LETTER QP DIGRAPH
- used in Africanist linguistics

023A Ⱥ LATIN CAPITAL LETTER A WITH STROKE
- Sencoten
- lowercase is 2C65 ⱥ

023B Ȼ LATIN CAPITAL LETTER C WITH STROKE
- Sencoten

023C ȼ LATIN SMALL LETTER C WITH STROKE
- used in Americanist linguistics

023D Ƚ LATIN CAPITAL LETTER L WITH BAR
- Sencoten
- lowercase is 019A ƚ

023E Ⱦ LATIN CAPITAL LETTER T WITH DIAGONAL STROKE
- Sencoten
- lowercase is 2C66 ⱦ

023F ȿ LATIN SMALL LETTER S WITH SWASH TAIL

0240 ɀ LATIN SMALL LETTER Z WITH SWASH TAIL

0241 Ɂ LATIN CAPITAL LETTER GLOTTAL STOP

0242 ɂ LATIN SMALL LETTER GLOTTAL STOP
- casing use in Chipewyan, Dogrib, Slavey (Canadian aboriginal orthographies)
→ 0294 ʔ latin letter glottal stop
→ 02C0 ˀ modifier letter glottal stop

0243 Ƀ LATIN CAPITAL LETTER B WITH STROKE
- lowercase is 0180 ƀ

0244 Ʉ LATIN CAPITAL LETTER U BAR
- lowercase is 0289 ʉ

0245 Ʌ LATIN CAPITAL LETTER TURNED V
- lowercase is 028C ʌ

0246 Ɇ LATIN CAPITAL LETTER E WITH STROKE

0247 ɇ LATIN SMALL LETTER E WITH STROKE

0248 Ɉ LATIN CAPITAL LETTER J WITH STROKE

0249 ɉ LATIN SMALL LETTER J WITH STROKE

024A Ɋ LATIN CAPITAL LETTER SMALL Q WITH HOOK TAIL

024B ɋ LATIN SMALL LETTER Q WITH HOOK TAIL

024C Ɍ LATIN CAPITAL LETTER R WITH STROKE

024D ɍ LATIN SMALL LETTER R WITH STROKE

024E Ɏ LATIN CAPITAL LETTER Y WITH STROKE

024F ɏ LATIN SMALL LETTER Y WITH STROKE

	025	026	027	028	029	02A
0	ɐ 0250	ɠ 0260	ɰ 0270	ʀ 0280	ʐ 0290	ʠ 02A0
1	ɑ 0251	ɡ 0261	ɱ 0271	ʁ 0281	ʑ 0291	ʡ 02A1
2	ɒ 0252	ɢ 0262	ɲ 0272	ʂ 0282	ʒ 0292	ʢ 02A2
3	ɓ 0253	ɣ 0263	ɳ 0273	ʃ 0283	ʓ 0293	ʣ 02A3
4	ɔ 0254	ɤ 0264	ɴ 0274	ʄ 0284	ʔ 0294	ʤ 02A4
5	ɕ 0255	ɥ 0265	ɵ 0275	ʅ 0285	ʕ 0295	ʥ 02A5
6	ɖ 0256	ɦ 0266	ɶ 0276	ʆ 0286	ʖ 0296	ʦ 02A6
7	ɗ 0257	ɧ 0267	ɷ 0277	ʇ 0287	ʗ 0297	ʧ 02A7
8	ɘ 0258	ɨ 0268	ɸ 0278	ʈ 0288	ʘ 0298	ʨ 02A8
9	ə 0259	ɩ 0269	ɹ 0279	ʉ 0289	ʙ 0299	ʩ 02A9
A	ɚ 025A	ɪ 026A	ɺ 027A	ʊ 028A	ʚ 029A	ʪ 02AA
B	ɛ 025B	ɫ 026B	ɻ 027B	ʋ 028B	ʛ 029B	ʫ 02AB
C	ɜ 025C	ɬ 026C	ɼ 027C	ʌ 028C	ʜ 029C	ʬ 02AC
D	ɝ 025D	ɭ 026D	ɽ 027D	ʍ 028D	ʝ 029D	ʭ 02AD
E	ɞ 025E	ɮ 026E	ɾ 027E	ʎ 028E	ʞ 029E	ʮ 02AE
F	ɟ 025F	ɯ 026F	ɿ 027F	ʏ 028F	ʟ 029F	ʯ 02AF

IPA extensions

IPA includes basic Latin letters and a number of Latin or Greek letters from other blocks.

→ 00E6 æ latin small letter ae
→ 00E7 ç latin small letter c with cedilla
→ 00F0 ð latin small letter eth
→ 00F8 ø latin small letter o with stroke
→ 0127 ħ latin small letter h with stroke
→ 014B ŋ latin small letter eng
→ 0153 œ latin small ligature oe
→ 03B2 β greek small letter beta
→ 03B8 θ greek small letter theta
→ 03BB λ greek small letter lamda
→ 03C7 χ greek small letter chi

0250 ɐ LATIN SMALL LETTER TURNED A
• low central unrounded vowel

0251 ɑ LATIN SMALL LETTER ALPHA
= latin small letter script a (1.0)
• low back unrounded vowel
→ 03B1 α greek small letter alpha

0252 ɒ LATIN SMALL LETTER TURNED ALPHA
• low back rounded vowel

0253 ɓ LATIN SMALL LETTER B WITH HOOK
• implosive bilabial stop
• Pan-Nigerian alphabet
→ 0181 Ɓ latin capital letter b with hook

0254 ɔ LATIN SMALL LETTER OPEN O
• typographically a turned c
• lower-mid back rounded vowel
→ 0186 Ɔ latin capital letter open o

0255 ɕ LATIN SMALL LETTER C WITH CURL
• voiceless alveolo-palatal laminal fricative
• used in transcription of Mandarin Chinese
• sound spelled with 015B ś in Polish

0256 ɖ LATIN SMALL LETTER D WITH TAIL
= d retroflex hook
• voiced retroflex stop
→ 0189 Đ latin capital letter african d

0257 ɗ LATIN SMALL LETTER D WITH HOOK
• implosive dental or alveolar stop
• Ewe, Pan-Nigerian alphabet
→ 018A Ɗ latin capital letter d with hook

0258 ɘ LATIN SMALL LETTER REVERSED E
• upper-mid central unrounded vowel

0259 ə LATIN SMALL LETTER SCHWA
• mid-central unrounded vowel
• variant uppercase form 018E Ǝ is associated with 01DD ǝ
→ 018F Ə latin capital letter schwa
→ 01DD ǝ latin small letter turned e
→ 04D9 ә cyrillic small letter schwa

025A ɚ LATIN SMALL LETTER SCHWA WITH HOOK
• rhotacized schwa

025B ɛ LATIN SMALL LETTER OPEN E
= epsilon
• lower-mid front unrounded vowel
→ 0190 Ɛ latin capital letter open e
→ 03B5 ε greek small letter epsilon

025C ɜ LATIN SMALL LETTER REVERSED OPEN E
• lower-mid central unrounded vowel

025D ɝ LATIN SMALL LETTER REVERSED OPEN E WITH HOOK
• rhotacized lower-mid central vowel

025E ɞ LATIN SMALL LETTER CLOSED REVERSED OPEN E
= closed reversed epsilon
• lower-mid central rounded vowel

025F ɟ LATIN SMALL LETTER DOTLESS J WITH STROKE
• voiced palatal stop
• typographically a turned f, but better thought of as a form of j
• "gy" in Hungarian orthography
• also archaic phonetic for palatoalveolar affricate 02A4 ʤ

0260 ɠ LATIN SMALL LETTER G WITH HOOK
• implosive velar stop
→ 0193 Ɠ latin capital letter g with hook

0261 ɡ LATIN SMALL LETTER SCRIPT G
• voiced velar stop
→ 0067 g latin small letter g

0262 ɢ LATIN LETTER SMALL CAPITAL G
• voiced uvular stop

0263 ɣ LATIN SMALL LETTER GAMMA
• voiced velar fricative
→ 0194 Ɣ latin capital letter gamma
→ 03B3 γ greek small letter gamma

0264 ɤ LATIN SMALL LETTER RAMS HORN
= latin small letter baby gamma (1.0)
• upper-mid back unrounded vowel

0265 ɥ LATIN SMALL LETTER TURNED H
• voiced rounded palatal approximant

0266 ɦ LATIN SMALL LETTER H WITH HOOK
• breathy-voiced glottal fricative
→ 02B1 ʱ modifier letter small h with hook

0267 ɧ LATIN SMALL LETTER HENG WITH HOOK
• voiceless coarticulated velar and palatoalveolar fricative
• "tj" or "kj" or "sj" in some Swedish dialects

0268 ɨ LATIN SMALL LETTER I WITH STROKE
= barred i, i bar
• high central unrounded vowel
• ISO 6438 gives lowercase of 0197 Ɨ as 026A ɪ, not 0268 ɨ

0269 ɩ LATIN SMALL LETTER IOTA
• semi-high front unrounded vowel
• obsoleted by IPA in 1989
• preferred use is 026A ɪ latin letter small capital i
→ 0196 Ɩ latin capital letter iota
→ 03B9 ι greek small letter iota

026A ɪ LATIN LETTER SMALL CAPITAL I
• semi-high front unrounded vowel
• preferred IPA alternate for 0269 ɩ
→ 0197 Ɨ latin capital letter i with stroke

026B ɫ LATIN SMALL LETTER L WITH MIDDLE TILDE
• velarized voiced alveolar lateral approximant
• uppercase is 2C62 Ɫ

026C ɬ LATIN SMALL LETTER L WITH BELT
• voiceless alveolar lateral fricative

026D ɭ LATIN SMALL LETTER L WITH RETROFLEX HOOK
• voiced retroflex lateral

026E ɮ LATIN SMALL LETTER LEZH
• voiced lateral fricative
• "dhl" in Zulu orthography

026F ɯ LATIN SMALL LETTER TURNED M
• high back unrounded vowel
→ 019C Ɯ latin capital letter turned m

0270 ɰ LATIN SMALL LETTER TURNED M WITH LONG LEG
• voiced velar approximant

0271 ɱ LATIN SMALL LETTER M WITH HOOK
• voiced labiodental nasal

0272 ɲ LATIN SMALL LETTER N WITH LEFT HOOK
• voiced palatal nasal
→ 019D Ɲ latin capital letter n with left hook

0273 ɳ LATIN SMALL LETTER N WITH RETROFLEX HOOK
• voiced retroflex nasal

0274 ɴ LATIN LETTER SMALL CAPITAL N
• voiced uvular nasal

0275 ɵ LATIN SMALL LETTER BARRED O
= o bar
• rounded mid-central vowel, i.e. rounded schwa
• uppercase is 019F Ɵ
→ 03B8 θ greek small letter theta
→ 0473 ѳ cyrillic small letter fita
→ 04E9 ө cyrillic small letter barred o

0276 ɶ LATIN LETTER SMALL CAPITAL OE
• low front rounded vowel
→ 0153 œ latin small ligature oe

0277 ɷ LATIN SMALL LETTER CLOSED OMEGA
• semi-high back rounded vowel
• obsoleted by IPA in 1989
• preferred use is 028A ʊ latin small letter upsilon

0278 ɸ LATIN SMALL LETTER PHI
• voiceless bilabial fricative
→ 03C6 φ greek small letter phi

0279 ɹ LATIN SMALL LETTER TURNED R
• voiced alveolar approximant
→ 02B4 ʴ modifier letter small turned r

027A ɺ LATIN SMALL LETTER TURNED R WITH LONG LEG
• voiced lateral flap

027B ɻ LATIN SMALL LETTER TURNED R WITH HOOK
• voiced retroflex approximant
→ 02B5 ʵ modifier letter small turned r with hook

027C ɼ LATIN SMALL LETTER R WITH LONG LEG
• voiced strident apico-alveolar trill
• obsoleted by IPA in 1989
• sound spelled with 0159 ř in Czech
• preferred phonetic representation for Czech is 0072 r 031D ◌̝
• in current use in Gaelic types (as glyph variant of 0072 r)

027D ɽ LATIN SMALL LETTER R WITH TAIL
• voiced retroflex flap
• uppercase is 2C64 Ɽ

027E ɾ LATIN SMALL LETTER R WITH FISHHOOK
• voiced alveolar flap or tap

027F ɿ LATIN SMALL LETTER REVERSED R WITH FISHHOOK
= long leg turned iota (a misnomer)
• apical dental vowel
• used by linguists working on Chinese and other Sino-Tibetan languages
• IPA spelling - 007A z 0329 ◌̩

0280 ʀ LATIN LETTER SMALL CAPITAL R
• voiced uvular trill
• Germanic, Old Norse
• uppercase is 01A6 Ʀ

0281 ʁ LATIN LETTER SMALL CAPITAL INVERTED R
• voiced uvular fricative or approximant
→ 02B6 ʶ modifier letter small capital inverted r

0282 ʂ LATIN SMALL LETTER S WITH HOOK
• voiceless retroflex fricative

0283 ʃ LATIN SMALL LETTER ESH
• voiceless postalveolar fricative
→ 01A9 Ʃ latin capital letter esh
→ 222B ∫ integral

0284 ʄ LATIN SMALL LETTER DOTLESS J WITH STROKE AND HOOK
• implosive palatal stop
• typographically based on 025F ɟ, not on 0283 ʃ

0285 ʅ LATIN SMALL LETTER SQUAT REVERSED ESH
• apical retroflex vowel
• used by linguists working on Chinese and other Sino-Tibetan languages
• IPA spelling - 0290 ʐ 0329 ◌̩
• in origin 027F ɿ plus the retroflex hook 0322 ◌̢, despite its name

0286 ʆ LATIN SMALL LETTER ESH WITH CURL
• palatalized voiceless postalveolar fricative
• suggested spelling - 0283 ʃ 02B2 ʲ

0287 ʇ LATIN SMALL LETTER TURNED T
• dental click (sound of "tsk tsk")
→ 01C0 ǀ latin letter dental click

0288 ʈ LATIN SMALL LETTER T WITH RETROFLEX HOOK
• voiceless retroflex stop
→ 01AE Ʈ latin capital letter t with retroflex hook

0289 ʉ LATIN SMALL LETTER U BAR
• high central rounded vowel
• uppercase is 0244 Ʉ

028A ʊ LATIN SMALL LETTER UPSILON
• semi-high back rounded vowel
• preferred IPA alternate to 0277 ɷ
→ 01B1 Ʊ latin capital letter upsilon
→ 03C5 υ greek small letter upsilon

028B ʋ LATIN SMALL LETTER V WITH HOOK
= latin small letter script v (1.0)
• voiced labiodental approximant
→ 01B2 Ʋ latin capital letter v with hook
→ 03C5 υ greek small letter upsilon

028C ʌ LATIN SMALL LETTER TURNED V
= caret, wedge
• lower-mid back unrounded vowel
• uppercase is 0245 Ʌ
→ 039B Λ greek capital letter lamda
→ 2038 ‸ caret
→ 2227 ∧ logical and

028D ʍ LATIN SMALL LETTER TURNED W
• voiceless rounded labiovelar approximant

028E ʎ LATIN SMALL LETTER TURNED Y
• voiced lateral approximant

028F ʏ LATIN LETTER SMALL CAPITAL Y
• semi-high front rounded vowel

0290 ʐ LATIN SMALL LETTER Z WITH RETROFLEX HOOK
• voiced retroflex fricative

0291 ʑ LATIN SMALL LETTER Z WITH CURL
• voiced alveolo-palatal laminal fricative
• sound spelled with 017A ź in Polish

0292 ʒ LATIN SMALL LETTER EZH
= dram
• voiced postalveolar fricative
• mistakenly named yogh in Unicode 1.0
• uppercase is 01B7 Ʒ
• Skolt Sami
→ 021D ȝ latin small letter yogh
→ 04E1 ӡ cyrillic small letter abkhasian dze
→ 2125 ℥ ounce sign

0293 ʓ LATIN SMALL LETTER EZH WITH CURL
• palatalized voiced postalveolar fricative

0294 ʔ LATIN LETTER GLOTTAL STOP
• this is a caseless letter
• used in IPA, other phonetic notations, and those orthographies which use a caseless glottal stop
→ 0241 Ɂ latin capital letter glottal stop
→ 02C0 ˀ modifier letter glottal stop

0295 ʕ LATIN LETTER PHARYNGEAL VOICED FRICATIVE
= reversed glottal stop
• voiced pharyngeal fricative
• ain
→ 01B9 ƹ latin small letter ezh reversed
→ 02C1 ˁ modifier letter reversed glottal stop

0296 ʖ LATIN LETTER INVERTED GLOTTAL STOP
• lateral click
→ 01C1 ǁ latin letter lateral click

0297 ʗ LATIN LETTER STRETCHED C
• palatal (or alveolar) click
→ 01C3 ǃ latin letter retroflex click
→ 2201 ∁ complement

0298 ʘ LATIN LETTER BILABIAL CLICK
= bullseye
→ 2299 ⊙ circled dot operator

0299 ʙ LATIN LETTER SMALL CAPITAL B
• bilabial trill

029A ʚ LATIN SMALL LETTER CLOSED OPEN E
= closed epsilon
• lower-mid front rounded vowel
• non-IPA alternate for the preferred 0153 œ

029B ʛ LATIN LETTER SMALL CAPITAL G WITH HOOK
• voiced uvular implosive

029C ʜ LATIN LETTER SMALL CAPITAL H
• voiceless epiglottal fricative

029D ʝ LATIN SMALL LETTER J WITH CROSSED-TAIL
• voiced palatal fricative

029E ʞ LATIN SMALL LETTER TURNED K
• proposed for velar click
• withdrawn by IPA in 1970

029F ʟ LATIN LETTER SMALL CAPITAL L
• velar lateral approximant

02A0 ʠ LATIN SMALL LETTER Q WITH HOOK
• voiceless uvular implosive

02A1 ʡ LATIN LETTER GLOTTAL STOP WITH STROKE
• voiced epiglottal stop

02A2 ʢ LATIN LETTER REVERSED GLOTTAL STOP WITH STROKE
• voiced epiglottal fricative

02A3 ʣ LATIN SMALL LETTER DZ DIGRAPH
• voiced dental affricate

02A4 ʤ LATIN SMALL LETTER DEZH DIGRAPH
• voiced postalveolar affricate

02A5 ʥ LATIN SMALL LETTER DZ DIGRAPH WITH CURL
• voiced alveolo-palatal affricate

02A6 ʦ LATIN SMALL LETTER TS DIGRAPH
• voiceless dental affricate

02A7 ʧ LATIN SMALL LETTER TESH DIGRAPH
• voiceless postalveolar affricate

02A8 ʨ LATIN SMALL LETTER TC DIGRAPH WITH CURL
• voiceless alveolo-palatal affricate

IPA characters for disordered speech

02A9 ʩ LATIN SMALL LETTER FENG DIGRAPH
• velopharyngeal fricative

02AA ʪ LATIN SMALL LETTER LS DIGRAPH
• lateral alveolar fricative (lisp)

02AB ʫ LATIN SMALL LETTER LZ DIGRAPH
• voiced lateral alveolar fricative

02AC ʬ LATIN LETTER BILABIAL PERCUSSIVE
• audible lip smack

02AD ʭ LATIN LETTER BIDENTAL PERCUSSIVE
• audible teeth gnashing

Additions for Sinology

02AE ʮ LATIN SMALL LETTER TURNED H WITH FISHHOOK

02AF ʯ LATIN SMALL LETTER TURNED H WITH FISHHOOK AND TAIL

	02B	02C	02D	02E	02F
0	ʰ 02B0	ˀ 02C0	ː 02D0	ˠ 02E0	˰ 02F0
1	ʱ 02B1	ˁ 02C1	ˑ 02D1	ˡ 02E1	˱ 02F1
2	ʲ 02B2	˂ 02C2	˒ 02D2	ˢ 02E2	˲ 02F2
3	ʳ 02B3	˃ 02C3	˓ 02D3	ˣ 02E3	˳ 02F3
4	ʴ 02B4	˄ 02C4	˔ 02D4	ˤ 02E4	˴ 02F4
5	ʵ 02B5	˅ 02C5	˕ 02D5	˥ 02E5	˵ 02F5
6	ʶ 02B6	ˆ 02C6	˖ 02D6	˦ 02E6	˶ 02F6
7	ʷ 02B7	ˇ 02C7	˗ 02D7	˧ 02E7	˷ 02F7
8	ʸ 02B8	ˈ 02C8	˘ 02D8	˨ 02E8	˸ 02F8
9	ʹ 02B9	ˉ 02C9	˙ 02D9	˩ 02E9	˹ 02F9
A	ʺ 02BA	ˊ 02CA	˚ 02DA	˪ 02EA	˺ 02FA
B	ʻ 02BB	ˋ 02CB	˛ 02DB	˫ 02EB	˻ 02FB
C	ʼ 02BC	ˌ 02CC	˜ 02DC	ˬ 02EC	˼ 02FC
D	ʽ 02BD	ˍ 02CD	˝ 02DD	˭ 02ED	˽ 02FD
E	ʾ 02BE	ˎ 02CE	˞ 02DE	ˮ 02EE	˾ 02FE
F	ʿ 02BF	ˏ 02CF	˟ 02DF	˯ 02EF	˿ 02FF

Latin superscript modifier letters

02B0 ʰ MODIFIER LETTER SMALL H
- aspiration
≈ <super> 0068 h

02B1 ʱ MODIFIER LETTER SMALL H WITH HOOK
- breathy voiced, murmured
→ 0266 ɦ latin small letter h with hook
→ 0324 ◌̤ combining diaeresis below
≈ <super> 0266 ɦ

02B2 ʲ MODIFIER LETTER SMALL J
- palatalization
→ 0321 ◌̡ combining palatalized hook below
≈ <super> 006A j

02B3 ʳ MODIFIER LETTER SMALL R
≈ <super> 0072 r

02B4 ʴ MODIFIER LETTER SMALL TURNED R
→ 0279 ɹ latin small letter turned r
≈ <super> 0279 ɹ

02B5 ʵ MODIFIER LETTER SMALL TURNED R WITH HOOK
→ 027B ɻ latin small letter turned r with hook
≈ <super> 027B ɻ

02B6 ʶ MODIFIER LETTER SMALL CAPITAL INVERTED R
- preceding four used for r-coloring or r-offglides
→ 0281 ʁ latin letter small capital inverted r
≈ <super> 0281 ʁ

02B7 ʷ MODIFIER LETTER SMALL W
- labialization
→ 032B ◌̫ combining inverted double arch below
≈ <super> 0077 w

02B8 ʸ MODIFIER LETTER SMALL Y
- palatalization
- common Americanist usage for 02B2 ʲ
≈ <super> 0079 y

Miscellaneous phonetic modifiers

02B9 ʹ MODIFIER LETTER PRIME
- primary stress, emphasis
- transliteration of mjagkij znak (Cyrillic soft sign: palatalization)
→ 0027 ' apostrophe
→ 00B4 ´ acute accent
→ 02CA ˊ modifier letter acute accent
→ 0301 ◌́ combining acute accent
→ 0374 ʹ greek numeral sign
→ 2032 ′ prime

02BA ʺ MODIFIER LETTER DOUBLE PRIME
- exaggerated stress, contrastive stress
- transliteration of tverdyj znak (Cyrillic hard sign: no palatalization)
→ 0022 " quotation mark
→ 030B ◌̋ combining double acute accent
→ 2033 ″ double prime

02BB ʻ MODIFIER LETTER TURNED COMMA
- typographical alternate for 02BD ʽ or 02BF ʿ
- used in Hawai`ian orthography as `okina (glottal stop)
→ 0312 ◌̒ combining turned comma above
→ 07F5 ߵ nko low tone apostrophe
→ 2018 ‘ left single quotation mark

02BC ʼ MODIFIER LETTER APOSTROPHE
= apostrophe
- glottal stop, glottalization, ejective
- spacing clone of Greek smooth breathing mark
- many languages use this as a letter of their alphabets
- 2019 ’ is the preferred character for a punctuation apostrophe
→ 0027 ' apostrophe
→ 0313 ◌̓ combining comma above
→ 0315 ◌̕ combining comma above right
→ 055A ՚ armenian apostrophe
→ 07F4 ߴ nko high tone apostrophe
→ 2019 ’ right single quotation mark

02BD ʽ MODIFIER LETTER REVERSED COMMA
- weak aspiration
- spacing clone of Greek rough breathing mark
→ 0314 ◌̔ combining reversed comma above
→ 0559 ՙ armenian modifier letter left half ring
→ 201B ‛ single high-reversed-9 quotation mark

02BE ʾ MODIFIER LETTER RIGHT HALF RING
- transliteration of Arabic hamza (glottal stop)
→ 055A ՚ armenian apostrophe
→ 0621 ء arabic letter hamza

02BF ʿ MODIFIER LETTER LEFT HALF RING
- transliteration of Arabic ain (voiced pharyngeal fricative)
→ 0559 ՙ armenian modifier letter left half ring
→ 0639 ع arabic letter ain

02C0 ˀ MODIFIER LETTER GLOTTAL STOP
- ejective or glottalized
- typographical alternate for 02BC ʼ or 02BE ʾ
→ 0294 ʔ latin letter glottal stop
→ 0309 ◌̉ combining hook above

02C1 ˁ MODIFIER LETTER REVERSED GLOTTAL STOP
- typographical alternate for 02BF ʿ
→ 0295 ʕ latin letter pharyngeal voiced fricative

02C2 ˂ MODIFIER LETTER LEFT ARROWHEAD
- fronted articulation

02C3 ˃ MODIFIER LETTER RIGHT ARROWHEAD
- backed articulation

02C4 ˄ MODIFIER LETTER UP ARROWHEAD
- raised articulation
→ 005E ^ circumflex accent
→ 2303 ⌃ up arrowhead

02C5 ˅ MODIFIER LETTER DOWN ARROWHEAD
- lowered articulation

02C6 ˆ MODIFIER LETTER CIRCUMFLEX ACCENT
- rising-falling tone, falling tone, secondary stress, etc.
→ 005E ^ circumflex accent
→ 0302 ◌̂ combining circumflex accent

02C7 ˇ CARON
= hacek
- falling-rising tone
- Mandarin Chinese third tone
→ 030C ◌̌ combining caron

02C8 ˈ MODIFIER LETTER VERTICAL LINE
- primary stress, downstep
- precedes letter or syllable modified
→ 0027 ' apostrophe
→ 030D ◌̍ combining vertical line above

02C9 ˉ MODIFIER LETTER MACRON
- high level tone
- precedes or follows letter or syllable modified
- Mandarin Chinese first tone
→ 00AF ¯ macron
→ 0304 ◌̄ combining macron

02CA ˊ MODIFIER LETTER ACUTE ACCENT
- high-rising tone (IPA), high tone, primary stress
- Mandarin Chinese second tone
→ 00B4 ´ acute accent
→ 02B9 ʹ modifier letter prime
→ 0301 ◌́ combining acute accent
→ 0374 ʹ greek numeral sign
→ 055B ՛ armenian emphasis mark

02CB ˋ MODIFIER LETTER GRAVE ACCENT
- high-falling tone (IPA), low tone, secondary or tertiary stress
- Mandarin Chinese fourth tone
→ 0060 ` grave accent
→ 0300 ◌̀ combining grave accent
→ 055D ՝ armenian comma

02CC ˌ MODIFIER LETTER LOW VERTICAL LINE
- secondary stress
- precedes letter or syllable modified
→ 0329 ◌̩ combining vertical line below

02CD ˍ MODIFIER LETTER LOW MACRON
- low level tone
→ 005F _ low line
→ 0331 ◌̱ combining macron below

02CE ˎ MODIFIER LETTER LOW GRAVE ACCENT
- low-falling tone

02CF ˏ MODIFIER LETTER LOW ACUTE ACCENT
- low-rising tone
→ 0375 ͵ greek lower numeral sign

02D0 ː MODIFIER LETTER TRIANGULAR COLON
- length mark
→ 003A : colon

02D1 ˑ MODIFIER LETTER HALF TRIANGULAR COLON
- half-length mark
→ 00B7 · middle dot

02D2 ˒ MODIFIER LETTER CENTRED RIGHT HALF RING
- more rounded articulation

02D3 ˓ MODIFIER LETTER CENTRED LEFT HALF RING
- less rounded articulation

02D4 ˔ MODIFIER LETTER UP TACK
- vowel raising or closing
→ 031D ◌̝ combining up tack below
→ 0323 ◌̣ combining dot below

02D5 ˕ MODIFIER LETTER DOWN TACK
- vowel lowering or opening
→ 031C ◌̜ combining left half ring below
→ 031E ◌̞ combining down tack below

02D6 ˖ MODIFIER LETTER PLUS SIGN
- advanced or fronted articulation
→ 031F ◌̟ combining plus sign below

02D7 ˗ MODIFIER LETTER MINUS SIGN
- retracted or backed articulation
- glyph may have small end-serifs
→ 0320 ◌̠ combining minus sign below
→ 2212 − minus sign

Spacing clones of diacritics

02D8 ˘ BREVE
→ 0306 ◌̆ combining breve
≈ 0020 SP 0306 ◌̆

02D9 ˙ DOT ABOVE
- Mandarin Chinese fifth tone (light or neutral)
→ 0307 ◌̇ combining dot above
≈ 0020 SP 0307 ◌̇

02DA ˚ RING ABOVE
→ 00B0 ° degree sign
→ 030A ◌̊ combining ring above
≈ 0020 SP 030A ◌̊

02DB ˛ OGONEK
→ 0328 ◌̨ combining ogonek
≈ 0020 SP 0328 ◌̨

02DC ˜ SMALL TILDE
→ 007E ~ tilde
→ 0303 ◌̃ combining tilde
→ 223C ∼ tilde operator
≈ 0020 SP 0303 ◌̃

02DD ˝ DOUBLE ACUTE ACCENT
→ 030B ◌̋ combining double acute accent
≈ 0020 SP 030B ◌̋

Additions based on 1989 IPA

02DE ˞ MODIFIER LETTER RHOTIC HOOK
- rhotacization in vowel
- often ligated: 025A ɚ = 0259 ə + 02DE ˞; 025D ɝ = 025C ɜ + 02DE ˞

02DF ˟ MODIFIER LETTER CROSS ACCENT
- Swedish grave accent

02E0 ˠ MODIFIER LETTER SMALL GAMMA
- these modifier letters are occasionally used in transcription of affricates
≈ <super> 0263 ɣ

02E1 ˡ MODIFIER LETTER SMALL L
≈ <super> 006C l

02E2 ˢ MODIFIER LETTER SMALL S
≈ <super> 0073 s

02E3 ˣ MODIFIER LETTER SMALL X
≈ <super> 0078 x

02E4 ˤ MODIFIER LETTER SMALL REVERSED GLOTTAL STOP
≈ <super> 0295 ʕ

Tone letters

02E5 ˥ MODIFIER LETTER EXTRA-HIGH TONE BAR
02E6 ˦ MODIFIER LETTER HIGH TONE BAR
02E7 ˧ MODIFIER LETTER MID TONE BAR
02E8 ˨ MODIFIER LETTER LOW TONE BAR
02E9 ˩ MODIFIER LETTER EXTRA-LOW TONE BAR

Extended Bopomofo tone marks

02EA ˪ MODIFIER LETTER YIN DEPARTING TONE MARK
02EB ˫ MODIFIER LETTER YANG DEPARTING TONE MARK

IPA modifiers

02EC ˬ MODIFIER LETTER VOICING
02ED ˭ MODIFIER LETTER UNASPIRATED

Other modifier letter

02EE ˮ MODIFIER LETTER DOUBLE APOSTROPHE
- Nenets

UPA modifiers

02EF ˯ MODIFIER LETTER LOW DOWN ARROWHEAD

Code	Glyph	Name
02F0	˰	MODIFIER LETTER LOW UP ARROWHEAD
02F1	˱	MODIFIER LETTER LOW LEFT ARROWHEAD
02F2	˲	MODIFIER LETTER LOW RIGHT ARROWHEAD
02F3	˳	MODIFIER LETTER LOW RING
02F4	˴	MODIFIER LETTER MIDDLE GRAVE ACCENT
02F5	˵	MODIFIER LETTER MIDDLE DOUBLE GRAVE ACCENT
02F6	˶	MODIFIER LETTER MIDDLE DOUBLE ACUTE ACCENT
02F7	˷	MODIFIER LETTER LOW TILDE
02F8	˸	MODIFIER LETTER RAISED COLON
02F9	˹	MODIFIER LETTER BEGIN HIGH TONE
02FA	˺	MODIFIER LETTER END HIGH TONE
02FB	˻	MODIFIER LETTER BEGIN LOW TONE
02FC	˼	MODIFIER LETTER END LOW TONE
02FD	˽	MODIFIER LETTER SHELF
02FE	˾	MODIFIER LETTER OPEN SHELF
02FF	˿	MODIFIER LETTER LOW LEFT ARROW

	030	031	032	033	034	035	036
0	0300	0310	0320	0330	0340	0350	0360
1	0301	0311	0321	0331	0341	0351	0361
2	0302	0312	0322	0332	0342	0352	0362
3	0303	0313	0323	0333	0343	0353	a 0363
4	0304	0314	0324	0334	0344	0354	e 0364
5	0305	0315	0325	0335	0345	0355	i 0365
6	0306	0316	0326	0336	0346	0356	o 0366
7	0307	0317	0327	0337	0347	0357	u 0367
8	0308	0318	0328	0338	0348	0358	c 0368
9	0309	0319	0329	0339	0349	0359	d 0369
A	030A	031A	032A	033A	034A	035A	h 036A
B	030B	031B	032B	033B	034B	035B	m 036B
C	030C	031C	032C	033C	034C	035C	r 036C
D	030D	031D	032D	033D	034D	035D	t 036D
E	030E	031E	032E	033E	034E	035E	v 036E
F	030F	031F	032F	033F	CGJ 034F	035F	x 036F

Ordinary diacritics

0300 ◌̀ COMBINING GRAVE ACCENT
= Greek varia
→ 0060 ` grave accent
→ 02CB ˋ modifier letter grave accent

0301 ◌́ COMBINING ACUTE ACCENT
= stress mark
= Greek oxia, tonos
→ 0027 ' apostrophe
→ 00B4 ´ acute accent
→ 02B9 ʹ modifier letter prime
→ 02CA ˊ modifier letter acute accent
→ 0384 ΄ greek tonos

0302 ◌̂ COMBINING CIRCUMFLEX ACCENT
= hat
→ 005E ^ circumflex accent
→ 02C6 ˆ modifier letter circumflex accent

0303 ◌̃ COMBINING TILDE
• IPA: nasalization
• Vietnamese tone mark
→ 007E ~ tilde
→ 02DC ˜ small tilde

0304 ◌̄ COMBINING MACRON
= long
• distinguish from the following
→ 00AF ¯ macron
→ 02C9 ˉ modifier letter macron

0305 ◌̅ COMBINING OVERLINE
= overscore, vinculum
• connects on left and right
→ 00AF ¯ macron

0306 ◌̆ COMBINING BREVE
= short
= Greek vrachy
→ 02D8 ˘ breve

0307 ◌̇ COMBINING DOT ABOVE
= derivative (Newtonian notation)
• IPA (withdrawn in 1976): palatalization
→ 02D9 ˙ dot above

0308 ◌̈ COMBINING DIAERESIS
= double dot above, umlaut
= Greek dialytika
= double derivative
→ 00A8 ¨ diaeresis

0309 ◌̉ COMBINING HOOK ABOVE
= hoi
• kerns left or right of circumflex over vowels
• Vietnamese tone mark
→ 02C0 ˀ modifier letter glottal stop

030A ◌̊ COMBINING RING ABOVE
→ 00B0 ° degree sign
→ 02DA ˚ ring above

030B ◌̋ COMBINING DOUBLE ACUTE ACCENT
• Hungarian, Chuvash
→ 0022 " quotation mark
→ 02BA ʺ modifier letter double prime
→ 02DD ˝ double acute accent

030C ◌̌ COMBINING CARON
= hacek, V above
→ 02C7 ˇ caron

030D ◌̍ COMBINING VERTICAL LINE ABOVE
• this is not the Greek tonos
• Marshallese
→ 02C8 ˈ modifier letter vertical line

030E ◌̎ COMBINING DOUBLE VERTICAL LINE ABOVE
• Marshallese
→ 0022 " quotation mark

030F ◌̏ COMBINING DOUBLE GRAVE ACCENT
• Serbian and Croatian poetics

0310 ◌̐ COMBINING CANDRABINDU
→ 0901 ◌ँ devanagari sign candrabindu

0311 ◌̑ COMBINING INVERTED BREVE

0312 ◌̒ COMBINING TURNED COMMA ABOVE
= cedilla above
• Latvian (but not used in decomposition)
→ 02BB ʻ modifier letter turned comma

0313 ◌̓ COMBINING COMMA ABOVE
= Greek psili, smooth breathing mark
• Americanist: ejective or glottalization
→ 02BC ʼ modifier letter apostrophe
→ 0486 ◌҆ combining cyrillic psili pneumata
→ 055A ՚ armenian apostrophe

0314 ◌̔ COMBINING REVERSED COMMA ABOVE
= Greek dasia, rough breathing mark
→ 02BD ʽ modifier letter reversed comma
→ 0485 ◌҅ combining cyrillic dasia pneumata
→ 0559 ՙ armenian modifier letter left half ring

0315 ◌̕ COMBINING COMMA ABOVE RIGHT
→ 02BC ʼ modifier letter apostrophe

0316 ◌̖ COMBINING GRAVE ACCENT BELOW

0317 ◌̗ COMBINING ACUTE ACCENT BELOW

0318 ◌̘ COMBINING LEFT TACK BELOW

0319 ◌̙ COMBINING RIGHT TACK BELOW

031A ◌̚ COMBINING LEFT ANGLE ABOVE
• IPA: unreleased stop

031B ◌̛ COMBINING HORN
• Vietnamese

031C ◌̜ COMBINING LEFT HALF RING BELOW
• IPA: open variety of vowel
→ 02D5 ˕ modifier letter down tack

031D ◌̝ COMBINING UP TACK BELOW
• IPA: vowel raising or closing
→ 02D4 ˔ modifier letter up tack

031E ◌̞ COMBINING DOWN TACK BELOW
• IPA: vowel lowering or opening
→ 02D5 ˕ modifier letter down tack

031F ◌̟ COMBINING PLUS SIGN BELOW
• IPA: advanced or fronted articulation
→ 02D6 ˖ modifier letter plus sign

0320 ◌̠ COMBINING MINUS SIGN BELOW
• IPA: retracted or backed articulation
• glyph may have small end-serifs
→ 02D7 ˗ modifier letter minus sign

0321 ◌̡ COMBINING PALATALIZED HOOK BELOW
• IPA: palatalization
→ 02B2 ʲ modifier letter small j

0322 ◌̢ COMBINING RETROFLEX HOOK BELOW
• IPA: retroflexion

0323 ◌̣ COMBINING DOT BELOW
= nang
• IPA: closer variety of vowel
• Americanist and Indo-Europeanist: retraction or retroflexion
• Semiticist: velarization or pharyngealization
• Vietnamese tone mark
→ 02D4 ˔ modifier letter up tack

0324 ◌̤ COMBINING DIAERESIS BELOW
• IPA: breathy-voice or murmur
→ 02B1 ʱ modifier letter small h with hook

0325 ◌̥ COMBINING RING BELOW
• IPA: voiceless
• vocalic (in Latin transliteration of Indic sonorants)
• Madurese

0326 ◌̦ COMBINING COMMA BELOW
• Romanian, Latvian, Livonian

0327 ◌̧ COMBINING CEDILLA
• French, Turkish, Azerbaijani
→ 00B8 ¸ cedilla

0328 ◌̨ COMBINING OGONEK
= nasal hook
• Americanist: nasalization
• Polish, Lithuanian
→ 02DB ˛ ogonek

0329 ◌̩ COMBINING VERTICAL LINE BELOW
• IPA: syllabic
• Yoruba
→ 02CC ˌ modifier letter low vertical line

032A ◌̪ COMBINING BRIDGE BELOW
• IPA: dental

032B ◌̫ COMBINING INVERTED DOUBLE ARCH BELOW
• IPA: labialization
→ 02B7 ʷ modifier letter small w

032C ◌̬ COMBINING CARON BELOW
• IPA: voiced

032D ◌̭ COMBINING CIRCUMFLEX ACCENT BELOW
• Americanist: fronted articulation

032E ◌̮ COMBINING BREVE BELOW
• Hittite transcription

032F ◌̯ COMBINING INVERTED BREVE BELOW
• Americanist: fronted articulation (variant of 032D ◌̭)
• Indo-Europeanist: semivowel

0330 ◌̰ COMBINING TILDE BELOW
• IPA: creaky voice

0331 ◌̱ COMBINING MACRON BELOW
→ 005F _ low line
→ 02CD ˍ modifier letter low macron

0332 ◌̲ COMBINING LOW LINE
= underline, underscore
• connects on left and right
→ 005F _ low line

0333 ◌̳ COMBINING DOUBLE LOW LINE
= double underline, double underscore
• connects on left and right
→ 0347 ◌͇ combining equals sign below
→ 2017 ‗ double low line

Overstruck diacritics

0334 ◌̴ COMBINING TILDE OVERLAY
• IPA: velarization or pharyngealization

0335 ◌̵ COMBINING SHORT STROKE OVERLAY

0336 ◌̶ COMBINING LONG STROKE OVERLAY

0337 ◌̷ COMBINING SHORT SOLIDUS OVERLAY
= short slash overlay

0338 ◌̸ COMBINING LONG SOLIDUS OVERLAY
= long slash overlay

Additions

0339 ◌̹ COMBINING RIGHT HALF RING BELOW

033A ◌̺ COMBINING INVERTED BRIDGE BELOW

033B ◌̻ COMBINING SQUARE BELOW

033C ◌̼ COMBINING SEAGULL BELOW

033D ◌̽ COMBINING X ABOVE

033E ◌̾ COMBINING VERTICAL TILDE
• Cyrillic palatalization
→ 0484 ◌҄ combining cyrillic palatalization

033F ◌̿ COMBINING DOUBLE OVERLINE

Vietnamese tone marks (deprecated)

Vietnamese-specific accent placement should be handled by specialized rendering of 0300 and 0301.

0340 ◌̀ COMBINING GRAVE TONE MARK
≡ 0300 ◌̀ combining grave accent

0341 ◌́ COMBINING ACUTE TONE MARK
≡ 0301 ◌́ combining acute accent

Additions for Greek

0342 ◌͂ COMBINING GREEK PERISPOMENI

0343 ◌̓ COMBINING GREEK KORONIS
≡ 0313 ◌̓ combining comma above

0344 ◌̈́ COMBINING GREEK DIALYTIKA TONOS
• use of this character is discouraged
≡ 0308 ◌̈ 0301 ◌́

0345 ◌ͅ COMBINING GREEK YPOGEGRAMMENI
= greek non-spacing iota below (1.0)
= iota subscript
• note special casing issues
→ 037A ͺ greek ypogegrammeni
→ 0399 Ι greek capital letter iota

Additions for IPA

0346 ◌͆ COMBINING BRIDGE ABOVE
• IPA: dentolabial
→ 20E9 ◌⃩ combining wide bridge above

0347 ◌͇ COMBINING EQUALS SIGN BELOW
• IPA: alveolar

0348 ◌͈ COMBINING DOUBLE VERTICAL LINE BELOW
• IPA: strong articulation

0349 ◌͉ COMBINING LEFT ANGLE BELOW
• IPA: weak articulation

034A ◌͊ COMBINING NOT TILDE ABOVE
• IPA: denasal

IPA diacritics for disordered speech

034B ◌͋ COMBINING HOMOTHETIC ABOVE
• IPA: nasal escape

034C ◌͌ COMBINING ALMOST EQUAL TO ABOVE
• IPA: velopharyngeal friction

034D ◌͍ COMBINING LEFT RIGHT ARROW BELOW
• IPA: labial spreading

034E ◌͎ COMBINING UPWARDS ARROW BELOW
• IPA: whistled articulation

Grapheme joiner

034F CGJ COMBINING GRAPHEME JOINER
• commonly abbreviated as CGJ
• has no visible glyph
• the name of this character is misleading; it does not actually join graphemes

Additions for the Uralic Phonetic Alphabet

0350 ◌͐ COMBINING RIGHT ARROWHEAD ABOVE

0351 ◌͑ COMBINING LEFT HALF RING ABOVE

0352 ◌͒ COMBINING FERMATA

0353 ◌͓ COMBINING X BELOW

0354 ◌͔ COMBINING LEFT ARROWHEAD BELOW

0355 ◌͕ COMBINING RIGHT ARROWHEAD BELOW

0356 ◌͖ COMBINING RIGHT ARROWHEAD AND UP ARROWHEAD BELOW
0357 ◌͗ COMBINING RIGHT HALF RING ABOVE

Miscellaneous additions

0358 ◌͘ COMBINING DOT ABOVE RIGHT
- Latin transliterations of the Southern Min dialects of Chinese

0359 ◌͙ COMBINING ASTERISK BELOW
→ 204E ⁎ low asterisk

035A ◌͚ COMBINING DOUBLE RING BELOW
- Kharoshthi transliteration

035B ◌͛ COMBINING ZIGZAG ABOVE
- Latin abbreviation, Lithuanian phonetics and mediaevalist transcriptions

Double diacritics

035C ◌͜ COMBINING DOUBLE BREVE BELOW
= ligature tie below, papyrological hyphen
- a common glyph alternate connects the horizontal midpoints of the characters

→ 035D ◌͝ combining double breve
→ 0361 ◌͡ combining double inverted breve

035D ◌͝ COMBINING DOUBLE BREVE
035E ◌͞ COMBINING DOUBLE MACRON
035F ◌͟ COMBINING DOUBLE MACRON BELOW
0360 ◌͠ COMBINING DOUBLE TILDE
0361 ◌͡ COMBINING DOUBLE INVERTED BREVE
= ligature tie

0362 ◌͢ COMBINING DOUBLE RIGHTWARDS ARROW BELOW
- IPA: sliding articulation

Medieval superscript letter diacritics

These are letter diacritics written directly above other letters. They appear primarily in medieval Germanic manuscripts, but saw some usage as late as the 19th century in some languages.

0363 ◌ͣ COMBINING LATIN SMALL LETTER A
0364 ◌ͤ COMBINING LATIN SMALL LETTER E
0365 ◌ͥ COMBINING LATIN SMALL LETTER I
0366 ◌ͦ COMBINING LATIN SMALL LETTER O
0367 ◌ͧ COMBINING LATIN SMALL LETTER U
0368 ◌ͨ COMBINING LATIN SMALL LETTER C
0369 ◌ͩ COMBINING LATIN SMALL LETTER D
036A ◌ͪ COMBINING LATIN SMALL LETTER H
036B ◌ͫ COMBINING LATIN SMALL LETTER M
036C ◌ͬ COMBINING LATIN SMALL LETTER R
036D ◌ͭ COMBINING LATIN SMALL LETTER T
036E ◌ͮ COMBINING LATIN SMALL LETTER V
036F ◌ͯ COMBINING LATIN SMALL LETTER X

	037	038	039	03A	03B	03C	03D	03E	03F
0			ΐ 0390	Π 03A0	ΰ 03B0	π 03C0	ϐ 03D0	Ϡ 03E0	ϰ 03F0
1			Α 0391	Ρ 03A1	α 03B1	ρ 03C1	ϑ 03D1	ϡ 03E1	ϱ 03F1
2			Β 0392		β 03B2	ς 03C2	ϒ 03D2	Ϣ 03E2	ϲ 03F2
3			Γ 0393	Σ 03A3	γ 03B3	σ 03C3	ϓ 03D3	ϣ 03E3	ϳ 03F3
4	ʹ 0374	΄ 0384	Δ 0394	Τ 03A4	δ 03B4	τ 03C4	ϔ 03D4	Ϥ 03E4	ϴ 03F4
5	͵ 0375	΅ 0385	Ε 0395	Υ 03A5	ε 03B5	υ 03C5	ϕ 03D5	ϥ 03E5	ϵ 03F5
6		Ά 0386	Ζ 0396	Φ 03A6	ζ 03B6	φ 03C6	ϖ 03D6	Ϧ 03E6	϶ 03F6
7		· 0387	Η 0397	Χ 03A7	η 03B7	χ 03C7	ϗ 03D7	ϧ 03E7	Ϸ 03F7
8		Έ 0388	Θ 0398	Ψ 03A8	θ 03B8	ψ 03C8	Ϙ 03D8	Ϩ 03E8	ϸ 03F8
9		Ή 0389	Ι 0399	Ω 03A9	ι 03B9	ω 03C9	ϙ 03D9	ϩ 03E9	Ϲ 03F9
A	ͺ 037A	Ί 038A	Κ 039A	Ϊ 03AA	κ 03BA	ϊ 03CA	Ϛ 03DA	Ϫ 03EA	Ϻ 03FA
B	ͻ 037B		Λ 039B	Ϋ 03AB	λ 03BB	ϋ 03CB	ϛ 03DB	ϫ 03EB	ϻ 03FB
C	ͼ 037C	Ό 038C	Μ 039C	ά 03AC	μ 03BC	ό 03CC	Ϝ 03DC	Ϭ 03EC	ϼ 03FC
D	ͽ 037D		Ν 039D	έ 03AD	ν 03BD	ύ 03CD	ϝ 03DD	ϭ 03ED	Ͻ 03FD
E	; 037E	Ύ 038E	Ξ 039E	ή 03AE	ξ 03BE	ώ 03CE	Ϟ 03DE	Ϯ 03EE	Ͼ 03FE
F		Ώ 038F	Ο 039F	ί 03AF	ο 03BF		ϟ 03DF	ϯ 03EF	Ͽ 03FF

Numeral signs

0374 ʹ GREEK NUMERAL SIGN
- = dexia keraia
- • indicates numeric use of letters
- → 02CA ˊ modifier letter acute accent
- ≡ 02B9 ʹ modifier letter prime

0375 ͵ GREEK LOWER NUMERAL SIGN
- = aristeri keraia
- • indicates numeric use of letters
- → 02CF ˏ modifier letter low acute accent

Iota subscript

037A ͺ GREEK YPOGEGRAMMENI
- = iota subscript
- → 0345 ͅ combining greek ypogegrammeni
- ≈ 0020 SP 0345 ͅ

Lowercase of editorial symbols

037B ͻ GREEK SMALL REVERSED LUNATE SIGMA SYMBOL

037C ͼ GREEK SMALL DOTTED LUNATE SIGMA SYMBOL

037D ͽ GREEK SMALL REVERSED DOTTED LUNATE SIGMA SYMBOL

Punctuation

037E ; GREEK QUESTION MARK
- = erotimatiko
- • sentence-final punctuation
- • 003B ; is the preferred character
- → 003F ? question mark
- ≡ 003B ; semicolon

Spacing accent marks

0384 ΄ GREEK TONOS
- → 00B4 ´ acute accent
- → 030D ̍ combining vertical line above
- ≈ 0020 SP 0301 ́

0385 ΅ GREEK DIALYTIKA TONOS
- ≡ 00A8 ¨ 0301 ́

Letter

0386 Ά GREEK CAPITAL LETTER ALPHA WITH TONOS
- ≡ 0391 Α 0301 ́

Punctuation

0387 · GREEK ANO TELEIA
- • functions in Greek like a semicolon
- • 00B7 · is the preferred character
- ≡ 00B7 · middle dot

Letters

0388 Έ GREEK CAPITAL LETTER EPSILON WITH TONOS
- ≡ 0395 Ε 0301 ́

0389 Ή GREEK CAPITAL LETTER ETA WITH TONOS
- ≡ 0397 Η 0301 ́

038A Ί GREEK CAPITAL LETTER IOTA WITH TONOS
- ≡ 0399 Ι 0301 ́

038B <reserved>

038C Ό GREEK CAPITAL LETTER OMICRON WITH TONOS
- ≡ 039F Ο 0301 ́

038D <reserved>

038E Ύ GREEK CAPITAL LETTER UPSILON WITH TONOS
- ≡ 03A5 Υ 0301 ́

038F Ώ GREEK CAPITAL LETTER OMEGA WITH TONOS
- ≡ 03A9 Ω 0301 ́

0390 ΐ GREEK SMALL LETTER IOTA WITH DIALYTIKA AND TONOS
- ≡ 03CA ϊ 0301 ́

0391 Α GREEK CAPITAL LETTER ALPHA

0392 Β GREEK CAPITAL LETTER BETA

0393 Γ GREEK CAPITAL LETTER GAMMA
- = gamma function
- → 213E ℾ double-struck capital gamma

0394 Δ GREEK CAPITAL LETTER DELTA
- → 2206 ∆ increment

0395 Ε GREEK CAPITAL LETTER EPSILON

0396 Ζ GREEK CAPITAL LETTER ZETA

0397 Η GREEK CAPITAL LETTER ETA

0398 Θ GREEK CAPITAL LETTER THETA

0399 Ι GREEK CAPITAL LETTER IOTA
- = iota adscript

039A Κ GREEK CAPITAL LETTER KAPPA

039B Λ GREEK CAPITAL LETTER LAMDA

039C Μ GREEK CAPITAL LETTER MU

039D Ν GREEK CAPITAL LETTER NU

039E Ξ GREEK CAPITAL LETTER XI

039F Ο GREEK CAPITAL LETTER OMICRON

03A0 Π GREEK CAPITAL LETTER PI
- → 213F ℿ double-struck capital pi
- → 220F ∏ n-ary product

03A1 Ρ GREEK CAPITAL LETTER RHO

03A2 <reserved>

03A3 Σ GREEK CAPITAL LETTER SIGMA
- → 01A9 Ʃ latin capital letter esh
- → 2211 ∑ n-ary summation

03A4 Τ GREEK CAPITAL LETTER TAU

03A5 Υ GREEK CAPITAL LETTER UPSILON

03A6 Φ GREEK CAPITAL LETTER PHI

03A7 Χ GREEK CAPITAL LETTER CHI

03A8 Ψ GREEK CAPITAL LETTER PSI

03A9 Ω GREEK CAPITAL LETTER OMEGA
- → 2126 Ω ohm sign
- → 2127 ℧ inverted ohm sign

03AA Ϊ GREEK CAPITAL LETTER IOTA WITH DIALYTIKA
- ≡ 0399 Ι 0308 ̈

03AB Ϋ GREEK CAPITAL LETTER UPSILON WITH DIALYTIKA
- ≡ 03A5 Υ 0308 ̈

03AC ά GREEK SMALL LETTER ALPHA WITH TONOS
- ≡ 03B1 α 0301 ́

03AD έ GREEK SMALL LETTER EPSILON WITH TONOS
- ≡ 03B5 ε 0301 ́

03AE ή GREEK SMALL LETTER ETA WITH TONOS
- ≡ 03B7 η 0301 ́

03AF ί GREEK SMALL LETTER IOTA WITH TONOS
- ≡ 03B9 ι 0301 ́

03B0 ΰ GREEK SMALL LETTER UPSILON WITH DIALYTIKA AND TONOS
- ≡ 03CB ϋ 0301 ́

03B1 α GREEK SMALL LETTER ALPHA
- → 0251 ɑ latin small letter alpha
- → 221D ∝ proportional to

03B2 β GREEK SMALL LETTER BETA
- → 00DF ß latin small letter sharp s
- → 0180 ƀ latin small letter b with stroke

03B3 γ GREEK SMALL LETTER GAMMA
- → 0263 ɣ latin small letter gamma
- → 213D ℽ double-struck small gamma

03B4 δ GREEK SMALL LETTER DELTA

03B5 ε GREEK SMALL LETTER EPSILON
→ 025B ɛ latin small letter open e
03B6 ζ GREEK SMALL LETTER ZETA
03B7 η GREEK SMALL LETTER ETA
03B8 θ GREEK SMALL LETTER THETA
→ 0275 ɵ latin small letter barred o
→ 0473 ѳ cyrillic small letter fita
03B9 ι GREEK SMALL LETTER IOTA
→ 0269 ɩ latin small letter iota
→ 2129 ℩ turned greek small letter iota
03BA κ GREEK SMALL LETTER KAPPA
03BB λ GREEK SMALL LETTER LAMDA
= lambda
03BC μ GREEK SMALL LETTER MU
→ 00B5 µ micro sign
03BD ν GREEK SMALL LETTER NU
03BE ξ GREEK SMALL LETTER XI
03BF ο GREEK SMALL LETTER OMICRON
03C0 π GREEK SMALL LETTER PI
• math constant 3.141592...
03C1 ρ GREEK SMALL LETTER RHO
03C2 ς GREEK SMALL LETTER FINAL SIGMA
= stigma (the Modern Greek name for this letterform)
• not to be confused with the actual stigma letter
→ 03DB ϛ greek small letter stigma
03C3 σ GREEK SMALL LETTER SIGMA
• used symbolically with a numeric value 200
03C4 τ GREEK SMALL LETTER TAU
03C5 υ GREEK SMALL LETTER UPSILON
→ 028A ʊ latin small letter upsilon
→ 028B ʋ latin small letter v with hook
03C6 φ GREEK SMALL LETTER PHI
→ 0278 ɸ latin small letter phi
→ 03D5 ϕ greek phi symbol
• the ordinary Greek letter, showing considerable glyph variation
• in mathematical contexts, the loopy glyph is preferred, to contrast with 03D5 ϕ
03C7 χ GREEK SMALL LETTER CHI
03C8 ψ GREEK SMALL LETTER PSI
03C9 ω GREEK SMALL LETTER OMEGA
03CA ϊ GREEK SMALL LETTER IOTA WITH DIALYTIKA
≡ 03B9 ι 0308 ̈
03CB ϋ GREEK SMALL LETTER UPSILON WITH DIALYTIKA
≡ 03C5 υ 0308 ̈
03CC ό GREEK SMALL LETTER OMICRON WITH TONOS
≡ 03BF ο 0301 ́
03CD ύ GREEK SMALL LETTER UPSILON WITH TONOS
≡ 03C5 υ 0301 ́
03CE ώ GREEK SMALL LETTER OMEGA WITH TONOS
≡ 03C9 ω 0301 ́

Variant letterforms

03D0 ϐ GREEK BETA SYMBOL
= curled beta
≈ 03B2 β greek small letter beta
03D1 ϑ GREEK THETA SYMBOL
= script theta
• used as a technical symbol
≈ 03B8 θ greek small letter theta
03D2 ϒ GREEK UPSILON WITH HOOK SYMBOL
≈ 03A5 Υ greek capital letter upsilon
03D3 ϓ GREEK UPSILON WITH ACUTE AND HOOK SYMBOL
≡ 03D2 ϒ 0301 ́
03D4 ϔ GREEK UPSILON WITH DIAERESIS AND HOOK SYMBOL
≡ 03D2 ϒ 0308 ̈
03D5 ϕ GREEK PHI SYMBOL
• used as a technical symbol, with a stroked glyph
• maps to "phi1" symbol entities
≈ 03C6 φ greek small letter phi
03D6 ϖ GREEK PI SYMBOL
= omega pi
• used as a technical symbol
• a variant of pi, looking like omega
≈ 03C0 π greek small letter pi
03D7 ϗ GREEK KAI SYMBOL
• used as an ampersand
→ 2CE4 ⳤ coptic symbol kai

Archaic letters

03D8 Ϙ GREEK LETTER ARCHAIC KOPPA
03D9 ϙ GREEK SMALL LETTER ARCHAIC KOPPA
• the Q-shaped archaic koppas are the ordinary alphabetic letters and can also be used as symbols with a numeric value of 90 in classical and pre-classical texts
03DA Ϛ GREEK LETTER STIGMA
• apparently in origin a cursive form of digamma
• the name "stigma" originally applied to a medieval sigma-tau ligature, whose shape was confusably similar to the cursive digamma
• used as a symbol with a numeric value of 6
03DB ϛ GREEK SMALL LETTER STIGMA
→ 03C2 ς greek small letter final sigma
03DC Ϝ GREEK LETTER DIGAMMA
03DD ϝ GREEK SMALL LETTER DIGAMMA
• used as a symbol with a numeric value of 6
03DE Ϟ GREEK LETTER KOPPA
03DF ϟ GREEK SMALL LETTER KOPPA
• used in modern Greek as a symbol with a numeric value of 90, as in the dating of legal documentation
03E0 Ϡ GREEK LETTER SAMPI
03E1 ϡ GREEK SMALL LETTER SAMPI
• used as a symbol with a numeric value of 900

Coptic letters derived from Demotic

For other Coptic letters see the Coptic Block.

03E2 Ϣ COPTIC CAPITAL LETTER SHEI
03E3 ϣ COPTIC SMALL LETTER SHEI
03E4 Ϥ COPTIC CAPITAL LETTER FEI
03E5 ϥ COPTIC SMALL LETTER FEI
03E6 Ϧ COPTIC CAPITAL LETTER KHEI
03E7 ϧ COPTIC SMALL LETTER KHEI
03E8 Ϩ COPTIC CAPITAL LETTER HORI
03E9 ϩ COPTIC SMALL LETTER HORI
03EA Ϫ COPTIC CAPITAL LETTER GANGIA
03EB ϫ COPTIC SMALL LETTER GANGIA
03EC Ϭ COPTIC CAPITAL LETTER SHIMA
03ED ϭ COPTIC SMALL LETTER SHIMA
03EE Ϯ COPTIC CAPITAL LETTER DEI
03EF ϯ COPTIC SMALL LETTER DEI

Variant letterforms

03F0 ϰ GREEK KAPPA SYMBOL
= script kappa
• used as technical symbol
≈ 03BA κ greek small letter kappa

03F1 ϱ GREEK RHO SYMBOL
= tailed rho
• used as technical symbol
≈ 03C1 ρ greek small letter rho

03F2 ϲ GREEK LUNATE SIGMA SYMBOL
= greek small letter lunate sigma (1.0)
≈ 03C2 ς greek small letter final sigma

Additional letter

03F3 ϳ GREEK LETTER YOT

Variant letterforms and symbols

03F4 ϴ GREEK CAPITAL THETA SYMBOL
→ 0472 Ѳ cyrillic capital letter fita
≈ 0398 Θ greek capital letter theta

03F5 ϵ GREEK LUNATE EPSILON SYMBOL
= straight epsilon
→ 220A ∊ small element of
≈ 03B5 ε greek small letter epsilon

03F6 ϶ GREEK REVERSED LUNATE EPSILON SYMBOL
= reversed straight epsilon
→ 220D ∍ small contains as member

Additional archaic letters for Bactrian

03F7 Ϸ GREEK CAPITAL LETTER SHO

03F8 ϸ GREEK SMALL LETTER SHO

Variant letterform

03F9 Ϲ GREEK CAPITAL LUNATE SIGMA SYMBOL
≈ 03A3 Σ greek capital letter sigma

Archaic letters

03FA Ϻ GREEK CAPITAL LETTER SAN

03FB ϻ GREEK SMALL LETTER SAN

Symbol

03FC ϼ GREEK RHO WITH STROKE SYMBOL
• used with abbreviations containing 03C1 ρ

Editorial symbols

03FD Ͻ GREEK CAPITAL REVERSED LUNATE SIGMA SYMBOL
= antisigma

03FE Ͼ GREEK CAPITAL DOTTED LUNATE SIGMA SYMBOL
= sigma periestigmenon

03FF Ͽ GREEK CAPITAL REVERSED DOTTED LUNATE SIGMA SYMBOL
= antisigma periestigmenon

	040	041	042	043	044	045	046	047	048	049	04A	04B	04C	04D	04E	04F
0	Ѐ 0400	А 0410	Р 0420	а 0430	р 0440	ѐ 0450	Ѡ 0460	Ѱ 0470	Ҁ 0480	Ґ 0490	Ҡ 04A0	Ұ 04B0	Ӏ 04C0	Ӑ 04D0	Ӡ 04E0	Ӱ 04F0
1	Ё 0401	Б 0411	С 0421	б 0431	с 0441	ё 0451	ѡ 0461	ѱ 0471	ҁ 0481	ґ 0491	ҡ 04A1	ұ 04B1	Ӂ 04C1	ӑ 04D1	ӡ 04E1	ӱ 04F1
2	Ђ 0402	В 0412	Т 0422	в 0432	т 0442	ђ 0452	Ѣ 0462	Ѳ 0472	҂ 0482	Ғ 0492	Ң 04A2	Ҳ 04B2	ӂ 04C2	Ӓ 04D2	Ӣ 04E2	Ӳ 04F2
3	Ѓ 0403	Г 0413	У 0423	г 0433	у 0443	ѓ 0453	ѣ 0463	ѳ 0473	◌҃ 0483	ғ 0493	ң 04A3	ҳ 04B3	Ӄ 04C3	ӓ 04D3	ӣ 04E3	ӳ 04F3
4	Є 0404	Д 0414	Ф 0424	д 0434	ф 0444	є 0454	Ѥ 0464	Ѵ 0474	◌҄ 0484	Ҕ 0494	Ҥ 04A4	Ҵ 04B4	ӄ 04C4	Ӕ 04D4	Ӥ 04E4	Ӵ 04F4
5	Ѕ 0405	Е 0415	Х 0425	е 0435	х 0445	ѕ 0455	ѥ 0465	ѵ 0475	◌҅ 0485	ҕ 0495	ҥ 04A5	ҵ 04B5	Ӆ 04C5	ӕ 04D5	ӥ 04E5	ӵ 04F5
6	І 0406	Ж 0416	Ц 0426	ж 0436	ц 0446	і 0456	Ѧ 0466	Ѷ 0476	◌҆ 0486	Җ 0496	Ҧ 04A6	Ҷ 04B6	ӆ 04C6	Ӗ 04D6	Ӧ 04E6	Ӷ 04F6
7	Ї 0407	З 0417	Ч 0427	з 0437	ч 0447	ї 0457	ѧ 0467	ѷ 0477		җ 0497	ҧ 04A7	ҷ 04B7	Ӈ 04C7	ӗ 04D7	ӧ 04E7	ӷ 04F7
8	Ј 0408	И 0418	Ш 0428	и 0438	ш 0448	ј 0458	Ѩ 0468	Ѹ 0478	◌҈ 0488	Ҙ 0498	Ҩ 04A8	Ҹ 04B8	ӈ 04C8	Ә 04D8	Ө 04E8	Ӹ 04F8
9	Љ 0409	Й 0419	Щ 0429	й 0439	щ 0449	љ 0459	ѩ 0469	ѹ 0479	◌҉ 0489	ҙ 0499	ҩ 04A9	ҹ 04B9	Ӊ 04C9	ә 04D9	ө 04E9	ӹ 04F9
A	Њ 040A	К 041A	Ъ 042A	к 043A	ъ 044A	њ 045A	Ѫ 046A	Ѻ 047A	Ҋ 048A	Қ 049A	Ҫ 04AA	Һ 04BA	ӊ 04CA	Ӛ 04DA	Ӫ 04EA	Ӻ 04FA
B	Ћ 040B	Л 041B	Ы 042B	л 043B	ы 044B	ћ 045B	ѫ 046B	ѻ 047B	ҋ 048B	қ 049B	ҫ 04AB	һ 04BB	Ӌ 04CB	ӛ 04DB	ӫ 04EB	ӻ 04FB
C	Ќ 040C	М 041C	Ь 042C	м 043C	ь 044C	ќ 045C	Ѭ 046C	Ѽ 047C	Ҍ 048C	Ҝ 049C	Ҭ 04AC	Ҽ 04BC	ӌ 04CC	Ӝ 04DC	Ӭ 04EC	Ӽ 04FC
D	Ѝ 040D	Н 041D	Э 042D	н 043D	э 044D	ѝ 045D	ѭ 046D	ѽ 047D	ҍ 048D	ҝ 049D	ҭ 04AD	ҽ 04BD	Ӎ 04CD	ӝ 04DD	ӭ 04ED	ӽ 04FD
E	Ў 040E	О 041E	Ю 042E	о 043E	ю 044E	ў 045E	Ѯ 046E	Ѿ 047E	Ҏ 048E	Ҟ 049E	Ү 04AE	Ҿ 04BE	ӎ 04CE	Ӟ 04DE	Ӯ 04EE	Ӿ 04FE
F	Џ 040F	П 041F	Я 042F	п 043F	я 044F	џ 045F	ѯ 046F	ѿ 047F	ҏ 048F	ҟ 049F	ү 04AF	ҿ 04BF	ӏ 04CF	ӟ 04DF	ӯ 04EF	ӿ 04FF

Cyrillic extensions

0400 Ѐ CYRILLIC CAPITAL LETTER IE WITH GRAVE
≡ 0415 Е 0300 ̀

0401 Ё CYRILLIC CAPITAL LETTER IO
≡ 0415 Е 0308 ̈

0402 Ђ CYRILLIC CAPITAL LETTER DJE

0403 Ѓ CYRILLIC CAPITAL LETTER GJE
≡ 0413 Г 0301 ́

0404 Є CYRILLIC CAPITAL LETTER UKRAINIAN IE

0405 Ѕ CYRILLIC CAPITAL LETTER DZE

0406 І CYRILLIC CAPITAL LETTER BYELORUSSIAN-UKRAINIAN I
→ 0049 I latin capital letter i
→ 0456 і cyrillic small letter byelorussian-ukrainian i
→ 04C0 Ӏ cyrillic letter palochka

0407 Ї CYRILLIC CAPITAL LETTER YI
≡ 0406 І 0308 ̈

0408 Ј CYRILLIC CAPITAL LETTER JE

0409 Љ CYRILLIC CAPITAL LETTER LJE

040A Њ CYRILLIC CAPITAL LETTER NJE

040B Ћ CYRILLIC CAPITAL LETTER TSHE

040C Ќ CYRILLIC CAPITAL LETTER KJE
≡ 041A К 0301 ́

040D Ѝ CYRILLIC CAPITAL LETTER I WITH GRAVE
≡ 0418 И 0300 ̀

040E Ў CYRILLIC CAPITAL LETTER SHORT U
≡ 0423 У 0306 ̆

040F Џ CYRILLIC CAPITAL LETTER DZHE

Basic Russian alphabet

0410 А CYRILLIC CAPITAL LETTER A

0411 Б CYRILLIC CAPITAL LETTER BE
→ 0183 ƃ latin small letter b with topbar

0412 В CYRILLIC CAPITAL LETTER VE

0413 Г CYRILLIC CAPITAL LETTER GHE

0414 Д CYRILLIC CAPITAL LETTER DE

0415 Е CYRILLIC CAPITAL LETTER IE

0416 Ж CYRILLIC CAPITAL LETTER ZHE

0417 З CYRILLIC CAPITAL LETTER ZE

0418 И CYRILLIC CAPITAL LETTER I

0419 Й CYRILLIC CAPITAL LETTER SHORT I
≡ 0418 И 0306 ̆

041A К CYRILLIC CAPITAL LETTER KA

041B Л CYRILLIC CAPITAL LETTER EL

041C М CYRILLIC CAPITAL LETTER EM

041D Н CYRILLIC CAPITAL LETTER EN

041E О CYRILLIC CAPITAL LETTER O

041F П CYRILLIC CAPITAL LETTER PE

0420 Р CYRILLIC CAPITAL LETTER ER

0421 С CYRILLIC CAPITAL LETTER ES

0422 Т CYRILLIC CAPITAL LETTER TE

0423 У CYRILLIC CAPITAL LETTER U
→ 0478 Ѹ cyrillic capital letter uk
→ 04AF ү cyrillic small letter straight u

0424 Ф CYRILLIC CAPITAL LETTER EF

0425 Х CYRILLIC CAPITAL LETTER HA

0426 Ц CYRILLIC CAPITAL LETTER TSE

0427 Ч CYRILLIC CAPITAL LETTER CHE

0428 Ш CYRILLIC CAPITAL LETTER SHA

0429 Щ CYRILLIC CAPITAL LETTER SHCHA

042A Ъ CYRILLIC CAPITAL LETTER HARD SIGN

042B Ы CYRILLIC CAPITAL LETTER YERU

042C Ь CYRILLIC CAPITAL LETTER SOFT SIGN

042D Э CYRILLIC CAPITAL LETTER E

042E Ю CYRILLIC CAPITAL LETTER YU

042F Я CYRILLIC CAPITAL LETTER YA

0430 а CYRILLIC SMALL LETTER A

0431 б CYRILLIC SMALL LETTER BE

0432 в CYRILLIC SMALL LETTER VE

0433 г CYRILLIC SMALL LETTER GHE

0434 д CYRILLIC SMALL LETTER DE

0435 е CYRILLIC SMALL LETTER IE

0436 ж CYRILLIC SMALL LETTER ZHE

0437 з CYRILLIC SMALL LETTER ZE

0438 и CYRILLIC SMALL LETTER I

0439 й CYRILLIC SMALL LETTER SHORT I
≡ 0438 и 0306 ̆

043A к CYRILLIC SMALL LETTER KA

043B л CYRILLIC SMALL LETTER EL

043C м CYRILLIC SMALL LETTER EM

043D н CYRILLIC SMALL LETTER EN

043E о CYRILLIC SMALL LETTER O

043F п CYRILLIC SMALL LETTER PE

0440 р CYRILLIC SMALL LETTER ER

0441 с CYRILLIC SMALL LETTER ES

0442 т CYRILLIC SMALL LETTER TE

0443 у CYRILLIC SMALL LETTER U

0444 ф CYRILLIC SMALL LETTER EF

0445 х CYRILLIC SMALL LETTER HA

0446 ц CYRILLIC SMALL LETTER TSE

0447 ч CYRILLIC SMALL LETTER CHE

0448 ш CYRILLIC SMALL LETTER SHA

0449 щ CYRILLIC SMALL LETTER SHCHA

044A ъ CYRILLIC SMALL LETTER HARD SIGN

044B ы CYRILLIC SMALL LETTER YERU

044C ь CYRILLIC SMALL LETTER SOFT SIGN
→ 0185 ƅ latin small letter tone six

044D э CYRILLIC SMALL LETTER E

044E ю CYRILLIC SMALL LETTER YU

044F я CYRILLIC SMALL LETTER YA

Cyrillic extensions

0450 ѐ CYRILLIC SMALL LETTER IE WITH GRAVE
• Macedonian
≡ 0435 е 0300 ̀

0451 ё CYRILLIC SMALL LETTER IO
• Russian, ...
≡ 0435 е 0308 ̈

0452 ђ CYRILLIC SMALL LETTER DJE
• Serbian
→ 0111 đ latin small letter d with stroke

0453 ѓ CYRILLIC SMALL LETTER GJE
• Macedonian
≡ 0433 г 0301 ́

0454 є CYRILLIC SMALL LETTER UKRAINIAN IE
= Old Cyrillic yest

0455 ѕ CYRILLIC SMALL LETTER DZE
= Old Cyrillic zelo
• Macedonian

0456 і CYRILLIC SMALL LETTER BYELORUSSIAN-UKRAINIAN I
= Old Cyrillic i

0457 ї CYRILLIC SMALL LETTER YI
• Ukrainian
≡ 0456 і 0308 ̈

0458 ј CYRILLIC SMALL LETTER JE
• Serbian, Azerbaijani, Altay

0459 љ CYRILLIC SMALL LETTER LJE
• Serbian, Macedonian
→ 01C9 ǉ latin small letter lj

045A њ CYRILLIC SMALL LETTER NJE
• Serbian, Macedonian
→ 01CC ǌ latin small letter nj

045B ћ CYRILLIC SMALL LETTER TSHE
= Old Cyrillic derv
• Serbian
→ 0107 ć latin small letter c with acute
→ 0127 ħ latin small letter h with stroke
→ 040B Ћ cyrillic capital letter tshe
→ 210F ℏ planck constant over two pi

045C ќ CYRILLIC SMALL LETTER KJE
• Macedonian
≡ 043A к 0301 ◌́

045D ѝ CYRILLIC SMALL LETTER I WITH GRAVE
• Macedonian, Bulgarian
≡ 0438 и 0300 ◌̀

045E ў CYRILLIC SMALL LETTER SHORT U
• Byelorussian, Uzbek
≡ 0443 у 0306 ◌̆

045F џ CYRILLIC SMALL LETTER DZHE
• Serbian, Macedonian, Abkhasian
→ 01C6 ǆ latin small letter dz with caron

Historic letters

0460 Ѡ CYRILLIC CAPITAL LETTER OMEGA
0461 ѡ CYRILLIC SMALL LETTER OMEGA
0462 Ѣ CYRILLIC CAPITAL LETTER YAT
0463 ѣ CYRILLIC SMALL LETTER YAT
0464 Ѥ CYRILLIC CAPITAL LETTER IOTIFIED E
0465 ѥ CYRILLIC SMALL LETTER IOTIFIED E
0466 Ѧ CYRILLIC CAPITAL LETTER LITTLE YUS
0467 ѧ CYRILLIC SMALL LETTER LITTLE YUS
0468 Ѩ CYRILLIC CAPITAL LETTER IOTIFIED LITTLE YUS
0469 ѩ CYRILLIC SMALL LETTER IOTIFIED LITTLE YUS
046A Ѫ CYRILLIC CAPITAL LETTER BIG YUS
046B ѫ CYRILLIC SMALL LETTER BIG YUS
046C Ѭ CYRILLIC CAPITAL LETTER IOTIFIED BIG YUS
046D ѭ CYRILLIC SMALL LETTER IOTIFIED BIG YUS
046E Ѯ CYRILLIC CAPITAL LETTER KSI
046F ѯ CYRILLIC SMALL LETTER KSI
0470 Ѱ CYRILLIC CAPITAL LETTER PSI
0471 ѱ CYRILLIC SMALL LETTER PSI
0472 Ѳ CYRILLIC CAPITAL LETTER FITA
0473 ѳ CYRILLIC SMALL LETTER FITA
→ 0275 ɵ latin small letter barred o
→ 03B8 θ greek small letter theta

0474 Ѵ CYRILLIC CAPITAL LETTER IZHITSA
0475 ѵ CYRILLIC SMALL LETTER IZHITSA
0476 Ѷ CYRILLIC CAPITAL LETTER IZHITSA WITH DOUBLE GRAVE ACCENT
≡ 0474 Ѵ 030F ◌̏

0477 ѷ CYRILLIC SMALL LETTER IZHITSA WITH DOUBLE GRAVE ACCENT
≡ 0475 ѵ 030F ◌̏

0478 Ѹ CYRILLIC CAPITAL LETTER UK
• basic Old Cyrillic uk is unified with cyrillic letter u
→ 0423 У cyrillic capital letter u

0479 ѹ CYRILLIC SMALL LETTER UK
047A Ѻ CYRILLIC CAPITAL LETTER ROUND OMEGA
047B ѻ CYRILLIC SMALL LETTER ROUND OMEGA
047C Ѽ CYRILLIC CAPITAL LETTER OMEGA WITH TITLO
047D ѽ CYRILLIC SMALL LETTER OMEGA WITH TITLO
• the exact identity of these broad omegas is unclear and may require revision of glyphs

047E Ѿ CYRILLIC CAPITAL LETTER OT
047F ѿ CYRILLIC SMALL LETTER OT
0480 Ҁ CYRILLIC CAPITAL LETTER KOPPA
0481 ҁ CYRILLIC SMALL LETTER KOPPA

Historic miscellaneous

0482 ҂ CYRILLIC THOUSANDS SIGN
0483 ◌҃ COMBINING CYRILLIC TITLO
0484 ◌҄ COMBINING CYRILLIC PALATALIZATION
→ 033E ◌̾ combining vertical tilde

0485 ◌҅ COMBINING CYRILLIC DASIA PNEUMATA
→ 0314 ◌̔ combining reversed comma above

0486 ◌҆ COMBINING CYRILLIC PSILI PNEUMATA
→ 0313 ◌̓ combining comma above

0487 <reserved>
0488 ◌҈ COMBINING CYRILLIC HUNDRED THOUSANDS SIGN
• use 20DD ⃝ for ten thousands sign

0489 ◌҉ COMBINING CYRILLIC MILLIONS SIGN

Extended Cyrillic

048A Ҋ CYRILLIC CAPITAL LETTER SHORT I WITH TAIL
048B ҋ CYRILLIC SMALL LETTER SHORT I WITH TAIL
• Kildin Sami

048C Ҍ CYRILLIC CAPITAL LETTER SEMISOFT SIGN
048D ҍ CYRILLIC SMALL LETTER SEMISOFT SIGN
• Kildin Sami

048E Ҏ CYRILLIC CAPITAL LETTER ER WITH TICK
048F ҏ CYRILLIC SMALL LETTER ER WITH TICK
• Kildin Sami

0490 Ґ CYRILLIC CAPITAL LETTER GHE WITH UPTURN
0491 ґ CYRILLIC SMALL LETTER GHE WITH UPTURN
• Ukrainian

0492 Ғ CYRILLIC CAPITAL LETTER GHE WITH STROKE
0493 ғ CYRILLIC SMALL LETTER GHE WITH STROKE
• Azerbaijani, Bashkir, ...
• full bar form preferred over half-barred "F"-type

0494 Ҕ CYRILLIC CAPITAL LETTER GHE WITH MIDDLE HOOK
0495 ҕ CYRILLIC SMALL LETTER GHE WITH MIDDLE HOOK
• Abkhasian, Yakut

0496 Җ CYRILLIC CAPITAL LETTER ZHE WITH DESCENDER
0497 җ CYRILLIC SMALL LETTER ZHE WITH DESCENDER
• Tatar, ...

0498 Ҙ CYRILLIC CAPITAL LETTER ZE WITH DESCENDER
0499 ҙ CYRILLIC SMALL LETTER ZE WITH DESCENDER
• Bashkir
• letterforms with right hooks are preferred, although occasional variants with left hooks occur

049A Қ CYRILLIC CAPITAL LETTER KA WITH DESCENDER
049B қ CYRILLIC SMALL LETTER KA WITH DESCENDER
• Abkhasian, Tajik, ...

049C Ҝ CYRILLIC CAPITAL LETTER KA WITH VERTICAL STROKE

049D ҝ CYRILLIC SMALL LETTER KA WITH VERTICAL STROKE
- Azerbaijani

049E Ҟ CYRILLIC CAPITAL LETTER KA WITH STROKE

049F ҟ CYRILLIC SMALL LETTER KA WITH STROKE
- Abkhasian

04A0 Ҡ CYRILLIC CAPITAL LETTER BASHKIR KA

04A1 ҡ CYRILLIC SMALL LETTER BASHKIR KA

04A2 Ң CYRILLIC CAPITAL LETTER EN WITH DESCENDER

04A3 ң CYRILLIC SMALL LETTER EN WITH DESCENDER
- Bashkir, ...

04A4 Ҥ CYRILLIC CAPITAL LIGATURE EN GHE

04A5 ҥ CYRILLIC SMALL LIGATURE EN GHE
- Altay, Mari, Yakut
- this is not a decomposable ligature

04A6 Ҧ CYRILLIC CAPITAL LETTER PE WITH MIDDLE HOOK

04A7 ҧ CYRILLIC SMALL LETTER PE WITH MIDDLE HOOK
- Abkhasian

04A8 Ҩ CYRILLIC CAPITAL LETTER ABKHASIAN HA

04A9 ҩ CYRILLIC SMALL LETTER ABKHASIAN HA

04AA Ҫ CYRILLIC CAPITAL LETTER ES WITH DESCENDER

04AB ҫ CYRILLIC SMALL LETTER ES WITH DESCENDER
- Bashkir, Chuvash
- letterforms with right hooks are preferred, although occasional variants with left hooks occur
- in Chuvashia, letterforms identical to or similar in form to 00E7 ç regularly occur

04AC Ҭ CYRILLIC CAPITAL LETTER TE WITH DESCENDER

04AD ҭ CYRILLIC SMALL LETTER TE WITH DESCENDER
- Abkhasian

04AE Ү CYRILLIC CAPITAL LETTER STRAIGHT U

04AF ү CYRILLIC SMALL LETTER STRAIGHT U
- stem is straight, unlike LETTER U
- Azerbaijani, Bashkir, ...
- → 0423 У cyrillic capital letter u

04B0 Ұ CYRILLIC CAPITAL LETTER STRAIGHT U WITH STROKE

04B1 ұ CYRILLIC SMALL LETTER STRAIGHT U WITH STROKE
- Kazakh

04B2 Ҳ CYRILLIC CAPITAL LETTER HA WITH DESCENDER

04B3 ҳ CYRILLIC SMALL LETTER HA WITH DESCENDER
- Abkhasian, Tajik, Uzbek

04B4 Ҵ CYRILLIC CAPITAL LIGATURE TE TSE

04B5 ҵ CYRILLIC SMALL LIGATURE TE TSE
- Abkhasian
- this is not a decomposable ligature

04B6 Ҷ CYRILLIC CAPITAL LETTER CHE WITH DESCENDER

04B7 ҷ CYRILLIC SMALL LETTER CHE WITH DESCENDER
- Abkhasian, Tajik

04B8 Ҹ CYRILLIC CAPITAL LETTER CHE WITH VERTICAL STROKE

04B9 ҹ CYRILLIC SMALL LETTER CHE WITH VERTICAL STROKE
- Azerbaijani

04BA Һ CYRILLIC CAPITAL LETTER SHHA

04BB һ CYRILLIC SMALL LETTER SHHA
- originally derived from Latin "h", but uppercase form 04BA Һ is closer to an inverted che (0427 Ч)
- Azerbaijani, Bashkir, ...
- → 0068 h latin small letter h

04BC Ҽ CYRILLIC CAPITAL LETTER ABKHASIAN CHE

04BD ҽ CYRILLIC SMALL LETTER ABKHASIAN CHE

04BE Ҿ CYRILLIC CAPITAL LETTER ABKHASIAN CHE WITH DESCENDER

04BF ҿ CYRILLIC SMALL LETTER ABKHASIAN CHE WITH DESCENDER
- ogonek form preferred

04C0 Ӏ CYRILLIC LETTER PALOCHKA
- aspiration sign in many Caucasian languages
- is usually not cased, but the formal lowercase is 04CF ӏ
- → 0049 I latin capital letter i
- → 0406 І cyrillic capital letter byelorussian-ukrainian i

04C1 Ӂ CYRILLIC CAPITAL LETTER ZHE WITH BREVE
- ≡ 0416 Ж 0306 ̆

04C2 ӂ CYRILLIC SMALL LETTER ZHE WITH BREVE
- Moldavian
- ≡ 0436 ж 0306 ̆

04C3 Ӄ CYRILLIC CAPITAL LETTER KA WITH HOOK

04C4 ӄ CYRILLIC SMALL LETTER KA WITH HOOK
- Khanty, Chukchi

04C5 Ӆ CYRILLIC CAPITAL LETTER EL WITH TAIL

04C6 ӆ CYRILLIC SMALL LETTER EL WITH TAIL
- Kildin Sami

04C7 Ӈ CYRILLIC CAPITAL LETTER EN WITH HOOK

04C8 ӈ CYRILLIC SMALL LETTER EN WITH HOOK
- Khanty, Chukchi, Nenets

04C9 Ӊ CYRILLIC CAPITAL LETTER EN WITH TAIL

04CA ӊ CYRILLIC SMALL LETTER EN WITH TAIL
- Kildin Sami

04CB Ӌ CYRILLIC CAPITAL LETTER KHAKASSIAN CHE

04CC ӌ CYRILLIC SMALL LETTER KHAKASSIAN CHE

04CD Ӎ CYRILLIC CAPITAL LETTER EM WITH TAIL

04CE ӎ CYRILLIC SMALL LETTER EM WITH TAIL
- Kildin Sami

04CF ӏ CYRILLIC SMALL LETTER PALOCHKA

04D0 Ӑ CYRILLIC CAPITAL LETTER A WITH BREVE
- ≡ 0410 А 0306 ̆

04D1 ӑ CYRILLIC SMALL LETTER A WITH BREVE
- ≡ 0430 а 0306 ̆

04D2 Ӓ CYRILLIC CAPITAL LETTER A WITH DIAERESIS
- ≡ 0410 А 0308 ̈

04D3 ӓ CYRILLIC SMALL LETTER A WITH DIAERESIS
- ≡ 0430 а 0308 ̈

04D4 Ӕ CYRILLIC CAPITAL LIGATURE A IE

04D5 ӕ CYRILLIC SMALL LIGATURE A IE
- this is not a decomposable ligature
- → 00E6 æ latin small letter ae

04D6 Ӗ CYRILLIC CAPITAL LETTER IE WITH BREVE
- ≡ 0415 Е 0306 ̆

04D7 ӗ CYRILLIC SMALL LETTER IE WITH BREVE
- ≡ 0435 е 0306 ̆

04D8 Ә CYRILLIC CAPITAL LETTER SCHWA

04D9 ә CYRILLIC SMALL LETTER SCHWA
- → 0259 ə latin small letter schwa

04DA Ӛ CYRILLIC CAPITAL LETTER SCHWA WITH DIAERESIS
≡ 04D8 Ә 0308 ö
04DB ӛ CYRILLIC SMALL LETTER SCHWA WITH DIAERESIS
≡ 04D9 ә 0308 ö
04DC Ӝ CYRILLIC CAPITAL LETTER ZHE WITH DIAERESIS
≡ 0416 Ж 0308 ö
04DD ӝ CYRILLIC SMALL LETTER ZHE WITH DIAERESIS
≡ 0436 ж 0308 ö
04DE Ӟ CYRILLIC CAPITAL LETTER ZE WITH DIAERESIS
≡ 0417 З 0308 ö
04DF ӟ CYRILLIC SMALL LETTER ZE WITH DIAERESIS
≡ 0437 з 0308 ö
04E0 Ӡ CYRILLIC CAPITAL LETTER ABKHASIAN DZE
04E1 ӡ CYRILLIC SMALL LETTER ABKHASIAN DZE
→ 0292 ʒ latin small letter ezh
04E2 Ӣ CYRILLIC CAPITAL LETTER I WITH MACRON
≡ 0418 И 0304 ō
04E3 ӣ CYRILLIC SMALL LETTER I WITH MACRON
≡ 0438 и 0304 ō
04E4 Ӥ CYRILLIC CAPITAL LETTER I WITH DIAERESIS
≡ 0418 И 0308 ö
04E5 ӥ CYRILLIC SMALL LETTER I WITH DIAERESIS
≡ 0438 и 0308 ö
04E6 Ӧ CYRILLIC CAPITAL LETTER O WITH DIAERESIS
≡ 041E О 0308 ö
04E7 ӧ CYRILLIC SMALL LETTER O WITH DIAERESIS
≡ 043E о 0308 ö
04E8 Ө CYRILLIC CAPITAL LETTER BARRED O
04E9 ө CYRILLIC SMALL LETTER BARRED O
→ 0275 ɵ latin small letter barred o
04EA Ӫ CYRILLIC CAPITAL LETTER BARRED O WITH DIAERESIS
≡ 04E8 Ө 0308 ö
04EB ӫ CYRILLIC SMALL LETTER BARRED O WITH DIAERESIS
≡ 04E9 ө 0308 ö
04EC Ӭ CYRILLIC CAPITAL LETTER E WITH DIAERESIS
≡ 042D Э 0308 ö
04ED ӭ CYRILLIC SMALL LETTER E WITH DIAERESIS
• Kildin Sami
≡ 044D э 0308 ö
04EE Ӯ CYRILLIC CAPITAL LETTER U WITH MACRON
≡ 0423 У 0304 ō
04EF ӯ CYRILLIC SMALL LETTER U WITH MACRON
≡ 0443 у 0304 ō
04F0 Ӱ CYRILLIC CAPITAL LETTER U WITH DIAERESIS
≡ 0423 У 0308 ö
04F1 ӱ CYRILLIC SMALL LETTER U WITH DIAERESIS
≡ 0443 у 0308 ö
04F2 Ӳ CYRILLIC CAPITAL LETTER U WITH DOUBLE ACUTE
≡ 0423 У 030B ő
04F3 ӳ CYRILLIC SMALL LETTER U WITH DOUBLE ACUTE
≡ 0443 у 030B ő
04F4 Ӵ CYRILLIC CAPITAL LETTER CHE WITH DIAERESIS
≡ 0427 Ч 0308 ö
04F5 ӵ CYRILLIC SMALL LETTER CHE WITH DIAERESIS
≡ 0447 ч 0308 ö
04F6 Ӷ CYRILLIC CAPITAL LETTER GHE WITH DESCENDER
04F7 ӷ CYRILLIC SMALL LETTER GHE WITH DESCENDER
• Yupik
04F8 Ӹ CYRILLIC CAPITAL LETTER YERU WITH DIAERESIS
≡ 042B Ы 0308 ö
04F9 ӹ CYRILLIC SMALL LETTER YERU WITH DIAERESIS
≡ 044B ы 0308 ö

Additions for Nivkh

04FA Ӻ CYRILLIC CAPITAL LETTER GHE WITH STROKE AND HOOK
04FB ӻ CYRILLIC SMALL LETTER GHE WITH STROKE AND HOOK
04FC Ӽ CYRILLIC CAPITAL LETTER HA WITH HOOK
04FD ӽ CYRILLIC SMALL LETTER HA WITH HOOK
04FE Ӿ CYRILLIC CAPITAL LETTER HA WITH STROKE
04FF ӿ CYRILLIC SMALL LETTER HA WITH STROKE

	050	051	052
0	Ԁ 0500	Ԑ 0510	
1	ԁ 0501	ԑ 0511	
2	Ԃ 0502	Ԓ 0512	
3	ԃ 0503	ԓ 0513	
4	Ԅ 0504		
5	ԅ 0505		
6	Ԇ 0506		
7	ԇ 0507		
8	Ԉ 0508		
9	ԉ 0509		
A	Ԋ 050A		
B	ԋ 050B		
C	Ԍ 050C		
D	ԍ 050D		
E	Ԏ 050E		
F	ԏ 050F		

Komi letters

0500 Ԁ CYRILLIC CAPITAL LETTER KOMI DE
0501 ԁ CYRILLIC SMALL LETTER KOMI DE
0502 Ԃ CYRILLIC CAPITAL LETTER KOMI DJE
0503 ԃ CYRILLIC SMALL LETTER KOMI DJE
0504 Ԅ CYRILLIC CAPITAL LETTER KOMI ZJE
0505 ԅ CYRILLIC SMALL LETTER KOMI ZJE
0506 Ԇ CYRILLIC CAPITAL LETTER KOMI DZJE
0507 ԇ CYRILLIC SMALL LETTER KOMI DZJE
0508 Ԉ CYRILLIC CAPITAL LETTER KOMI LJE
0509 ԉ CYRILLIC SMALL LETTER KOMI LJE
050A Ԋ CYRILLIC CAPITAL LETTER KOMI NJE
050B ԋ CYRILLIC SMALL LETTER KOMI NJE
050C Ԍ CYRILLIC CAPITAL LETTER KOMI SJE
050D ԍ CYRILLIC SMALL LETTER KOMI SJE
050E Ԏ CYRILLIC CAPITAL LETTER KOMI TJE
050F ԏ CYRILLIC SMALL LETTER KOMI TJE

Cyrillic extensions

0510 Ԑ CYRILLIC CAPITAL LETTER REVERSED ZE
0511 ԑ CYRILLIC SMALL LETTER REVERSED ZE
• Enets, Khanty
0512 Ԓ CYRILLIC CAPITAL LETTER EL WITH HOOK
0513 ԓ CYRILLIC SMALL LETTER EL WITH HOOK
• Chukchi, Itelmen, Khanty

	053	054	055	056	057	058
0		Հ 0540	Ր 0550		հ 0570	ր 0580
1	Ա 0531	Ձ 0541	Ց 0551	ա 0561	ձ 0571	ց 0581
2	Բ 0532	Ղ 0542	Ւ 0552	բ 0562	ղ 0572	ւ 0582
3	Գ 0533	Ճ 0543	Փ 0553	գ 0563	ճ 0573	փ 0583
4	Դ 0534	Մ 0544	Ք 0554	դ 0564	մ 0574	ք 0584
5	Ե 0535	Յ 0545	Օ 0555	ե 0565	յ 0575	օ 0585
6	Զ 0536	Ն 0546	Ֆ 0556	զ 0566	ն 0576	ֆ 0586
7	Է 0537	Շ 0547		է 0567	շ 0577	և 0587
8	Ը 0538	Ո 0548		ը 0568	ո 0578	
9	Թ 0539	Չ 0549	ՙ 0559	թ 0569	չ 0579	։ 0589
A	Ժ 053A	Պ 054A	՚ 055A	ժ 056A	պ 057A	֊ 058A
B	Ի 053B	Ջ 054B	՛ 055B	ի 056B	ջ 057B	
C	Լ 053C	Ռ 054C	՜ 055C	լ 056C	ռ 057C	
D	Խ 053D	Ս 054D	՝ 055D	խ 056D	ս 057D	
E	Ծ 053E	Վ 054E	՞ 055E	ծ 056E	վ 057E	
F	Կ 053F	Տ 054F	՟ 055F	կ 056F	տ 057F	

Uppercase letters

0531 Ա ARMENIAN CAPITAL LETTER AYB
0532 Բ ARMENIAN CAPITAL LETTER BEN
0533 Գ ARMENIAN CAPITAL LETTER GIM
0534 Դ ARMENIAN CAPITAL LETTER DA
0535 Ե ARMENIAN CAPITAL LETTER ECH
0536 Զ ARMENIAN CAPITAL LETTER ZA
0537 Է ARMENIAN CAPITAL LETTER EH
0538 Ը ARMENIAN CAPITAL LETTER ET
0539 Թ ARMENIAN CAPITAL LETTER TO
053A Ժ ARMENIAN CAPITAL LETTER ZHE
053B Ի ARMENIAN CAPITAL LETTER INI
053C Լ ARMENIAN CAPITAL LETTER LIWN
053D Խ ARMENIAN CAPITAL LETTER XEH
053E Ծ ARMENIAN CAPITAL LETTER CA
053F Կ ARMENIAN CAPITAL LETTER KEN
0540 Հ ARMENIAN CAPITAL LETTER HO
0541 Ձ ARMENIAN CAPITAL LETTER JA
0542 Ղ ARMENIAN CAPITAL LETTER GHAD
0543 Ճ ARMENIAN CAPITAL LETTER CHEH
0544 Մ ARMENIAN CAPITAL LETTER MEN
0545 Յ ARMENIAN CAPITAL LETTER YI
0546 Ն ARMENIAN CAPITAL LETTER NOW
0547 Շ ARMENIAN CAPITAL LETTER SHA
0548 Ո ARMENIAN CAPITAL LETTER VO
0549 Չ ARMENIAN CAPITAL LETTER CHA
054A Պ ARMENIAN CAPITAL LETTER PEH
054B Ջ ARMENIAN CAPITAL LETTER JHEH
054C Ռ ARMENIAN CAPITAL LETTER RA
054D Ս ARMENIAN CAPITAL LETTER SEH
054E Վ ARMENIAN CAPITAL LETTER VEW
054F Տ ARMENIAN CAPITAL LETTER TIWN
0550 Ր ARMENIAN CAPITAL LETTER REH
0551 Ց ARMENIAN CAPITAL LETTER CO
0552 Ւ ARMENIAN CAPITAL LETTER YIWN
0553 Փ ARMENIAN CAPITAL LETTER PIWR
0554 Ք ARMENIAN CAPITAL LETTER KEH
0555 Օ ARMENIAN CAPITAL LETTER OH
0556 Ֆ ARMENIAN CAPITAL LETTER FEH

Modifier letters

0559 ՙ ARMENIAN MODIFIER LETTER LEFT HALF RING
→ 02BD ʽ modifier letter reversed comma
→ 02BF ʿ modifier letter left half ring
→ 0314 ◌̔ combining reversed comma above
055A ՚ ARMENIAN APOSTROPHE
= armenian modifier letter right half ring (1.0)
→ 02BC ʼ modifier letter apostrophe
→ 02BE ʾ modifier letter right half ring
→ 0313 ◌̓ combining comma above
055B ՛ ARMENIAN EMPHASIS MARK
= shesht
→ 02CA ˊ modifier letter acute accent
055C ՜ ARMENIAN EXCLAMATION MARK
= batsaganchakan nshan
055D ՝ ARMENIAN COMMA
= bowt
→ 02CB ˋ modifier letter grave accent
055E ՞ ARMENIAN QUESTION MARK
= hartsakan nshan
055F ՟ ARMENIAN ABBREVIATION MARK
= patiw

Lowercase letters

0561 ա ARMENIAN SMALL LETTER AYB
0562 բ ARMENIAN SMALL LETTER BEN
0563 գ ARMENIAN SMALL LETTER GIM
0564 դ ARMENIAN SMALL LETTER DA
0565 ե ARMENIAN SMALL LETTER ECH
0566 զ ARMENIAN SMALL LETTER ZA
0567 է ARMENIAN SMALL LETTER EH
0568 ը ARMENIAN SMALL LETTER ET
0569 թ ARMENIAN SMALL LETTER TO
056A ժ ARMENIAN SMALL LETTER ZHE
056B ի ARMENIAN SMALL LETTER INI
056C լ ARMENIAN SMALL LETTER LIWN
056D խ ARMENIAN SMALL LETTER XEH
056E ծ ARMENIAN SMALL LETTER CA
056F կ ARMENIAN SMALL LETTER KEN
0570 հ ARMENIAN SMALL LETTER HO
0571 ձ ARMENIAN SMALL LETTER JA
0572 ղ ARMENIAN SMALL LETTER GHAD
0573 ճ ARMENIAN SMALL LETTER CHEH
0574 մ ARMENIAN SMALL LETTER MEN
0575 յ ARMENIAN SMALL LETTER YI
0576 ն ARMENIAN SMALL LETTER NOW
0577 շ ARMENIAN SMALL LETTER SHA
0578 ո ARMENIAN SMALL LETTER VO
0579 չ ARMENIAN SMALL LETTER CHA
057A պ ARMENIAN SMALL LETTER PEH
057B ջ ARMENIAN SMALL LETTER JHEH
057C ռ ARMENIAN SMALL LETTER RA
057D ս ARMENIAN SMALL LETTER SEH
057E վ ARMENIAN SMALL LETTER VEW
057F տ ARMENIAN SMALL LETTER TIWN
0580 ր ARMENIAN SMALL LETTER REH
0581 ց ARMENIAN SMALL LETTER CO
0582 ւ ARMENIAN SMALL LETTER YIWN
0583 փ ARMENIAN SMALL LETTER PIWR
0584 ք ARMENIAN SMALL LETTER KEH
0585 օ ARMENIAN SMALL LETTER OH
0586 ֆ ARMENIAN SMALL LETTER FEH
0587 և ARMENIAN SMALL LIGATURE ECH YIWN
≈ 0565 ե 0582 ւ

Punctuation

0589 ։ ARMENIAN FULL STOP
= vertsaket
• may also be used for Georgian
→ 003A : colon
058A ֊ ARMENIAN HYPHEN
= yentamna

	059	05A	05B	05C	05D	05E	05F
0		◌֠ 05A0	◌ְ 05B0	׀ 05C0	א 05D0	נ 05E0	װ 05F0
1	◌֑ 0591	◌֡ 05A1	◌ֱ 05B1	◌ׁ 05C1	ב 05D1	ס 05E1	ױ 05F1
2	◌֒ 0592	◌֢ 05A2	◌ֲ 05B2	◌ׂ 05C2	ג 05D2	ע 05E2	ײ 05F2
3	◌֓ 0593	◌֣ 05A3	◌ֳ 05B3	׃ 05C3	ד 05D3	ף 05E3	׳ 05F3
4	◌֔ 0594	◌֤ 05A4	◌ִ 05B4	◌ׄ 05C4	ה 05D4	פ 05E4	״ 05F4
5	◌֕ 0595	◌֥ 05A5	◌ֵ 05B5	◌ׅ 05C5	ו 05D5	ץ 05E5	
6	◌֖ 0596	◌֦ 05A6	◌ֶ 05B6	׆ 05C6	ז 05D6	צ 05E6	
7	◌֗ 0597	◌֧ 05A7	◌ַ 05B7	◌ׇ 05C7	ח 05D7	ק 05E7	
8	◌֘ 0598	◌֨ 05A8	◌ָ 05B8		ט 05D8	ר 05E8	
9	◌֙ 0599	◌֩ 05A9	◌ֹ 05B9		י 05D9	ש 05E9	
A	◌֚ 059A	◌֪ 05AA	◌ֺ 05BA		ך 05DA	ת 05EA	
B	◌֛ 059B	◌֫ 05AB	◌ֻ 05BB		כ 05DB		
C	◌֜ 059C	◌֬ 05AC	◌ּ 05BC		ל 05DC		
D	◌֝ 059D	◌֭ 05AD	◌ֽ 05BD		ם 05DD		
E	◌֞ 059E	◌֮ 05AE	־ 05BE		מ 05DE		
F	◌֟ 059F	◌֯ 05AF	◌ֿ 05BF		ן 05DF		

Cantillation marks

0591 ◌֑ HEBREW ACCENT ETNAHTA
= atnah

0592 ◌֒ HEBREW ACCENT SEGOL
= segolta

0593 ◌֓ HEBREW ACCENT SHALSHELET

0594 ◌֔ HEBREW ACCENT ZAQEF QATAN

0595 ◌֕ HEBREW ACCENT ZAQEF GADOL

0596 ◌֖ HEBREW ACCENT TIPEHA
= tarha, me'ayla ~ mayla

0597 ◌֗ HEBREW ACCENT REVIA

0598 ◌֘ HEBREW ACCENT ZARQA
= tsinorit, zinorit; tsinor, zinor
• This character is to be used when Zarqa or Tsinor are placed above, and also for Tsinorit.
→ 05AE ◌֮ hebrew accent zinor

0599 ◌֙ HEBREW ACCENT PASHTA

059A ◌֚ HEBREW ACCENT YETIV

059B ◌֛ HEBREW ACCENT TEVIR

059C ◌֜ HEBREW ACCENT GERESH
= teres

059D ◌֝ HEBREW ACCENT GERESH MUQDAM

059E ◌֞ HEBREW ACCENT GERSHAYIM

059F ◌֟ HEBREW ACCENT QARNEY PARA
= pazer gadol

05A0 ◌֠ HEBREW ACCENT TELISHA GEDOLA

05A1 ◌֡ HEBREW ACCENT PAZER
= pazer qatan

05A2 ◌֢ HEBREW ACCENT ATNAH HAFUKH
→ 05AA ◌֪ hebrew accent yerah ben yomo

05A3 ◌֣ HEBREW ACCENT MUNAH

05A4 ◌֤ HEBREW ACCENT MAHAPAKH

05A5 ◌֥ HEBREW ACCENT MERKHA
= yored

05A6 ◌֦ HEBREW ACCENT MERKHA KEFULA

05A7 ◌֧ HEBREW ACCENT DARGA

05A8 ◌֨ HEBREW ACCENT QADMA
= azla

05A9 ◌֩ HEBREW ACCENT TELISHA QETANA

05AA ◌֪ HEBREW ACCENT YERAH BEN YOMO
= galgal
→ 05A2 ◌֢ hebrew accent atnah hafukh

05AB ◌֫ HEBREW ACCENT OLE

05AC ◌֬ HEBREW ACCENT ILUY

05AD ◌֭ HEBREW ACCENT DEHI

05AE ◌֮ HEBREW ACCENT ZINOR
= tsinor; zarqa
• This character is to be used when Zarqa or Tsinor are placed above left.
→ 0598 ◌֘ hebrew accent zarqa

05AF ◌֯ HEBREW MARK MASORA CIRCLE

Points and punctuation

05B0 ◌ְ HEBREW POINT SHEVA

05B1 ◌ֱ HEBREW POINT HATAF SEGOL

05B2 ◌ֲ HEBREW POINT HATAF PATAH

05B3 ◌ֳ HEBREW POINT HATAF QAMATS

05B4 ◌ִ HEBREW POINT HIRIQ

05B5 ◌ֵ HEBREW POINT TSERE

05B6 ◌ֶ HEBREW POINT SEGOL

05B7 ◌ַ HEBREW POINT PATAH
• furtive patah is not a distinct character

05B8 ◌ָ HEBREW POINT QAMATS
→ 05C7 ◌ׇ hebrew point qamats qatan

05B9 ◌ֹ HEBREW POINT HOLAM

05BA ◌ֺ HEBREW POINT HOLAM HASER FOR VAV

05BB ◌ֻ HEBREW POINT QUBUTS

05BC ◌ּ HEBREW POINT DAGESH OR MAPIQ
= shuruq
• falls within the base letter

05BD ◌ֽ HEBREW POINT METEG
= siluq
• may be used as a Hebrew accent sof pasuq

05BE ־ HEBREW PUNCTUATION MAQAF

05BF ◌ֿ HEBREW POINT RAFE
→ FB1E ◌ﬞ hebrew point judeo-spanish varika

05C0 ׀ HEBREW PUNCTUATION PASEQ
= legarmeh
• may be treated as spacing punctuation, not as a point
→ 007C | vertical line

05C1 ◌ׁ HEBREW POINT SHIN DOT

05C2 ◌ׂ HEBREW POINT SIN DOT

05C3 ׃ HEBREW PUNCTUATION SOF PASUQ
• may be used as a Hebrew punctuation colon
→ 003A : colon

Puncta extraordinaria

05C4 ◌ׄ HEBREW MARK UPPER DOT

05C5 ◌ׅ HEBREW MARK LOWER DOT
• punctum extraordinarium (Psalms 27:13)
→ 05B4 ◌ִ hebrew point hiriq

Points and punctuation

05C6 ׆ HEBREW PUNCTUATION NUN HAFUKHA
• does not historically derive from the letter nun
→ 05E0 נ hebrew letter nun

05C7 ◌ׇ HEBREW POINT QAMATS QATAN
→ 05B8 ◌ָ hebrew point qamats

Based on ISO 8859-8

05D0 א HEBREW LETTER ALEF
= aleph
→ 2135 ℵ alef symbol

05D1 ב HEBREW LETTER BET
→ 2136 ℶ bet symbol

05D2 ג HEBREW LETTER GIMEL
→ 2137 ℷ gimel symbol

05D3 ד HEBREW LETTER DALET
→ 2138 ℸ dalet symbol

05D4 ה HEBREW LETTER HE

05D5 ו HEBREW LETTER VAV

05D6 ז HEBREW LETTER ZAYIN

05D7 ח HEBREW LETTER HET

05D8 ט HEBREW LETTER TET

05D9 י HEBREW LETTER YOD

05DA ך HEBREW LETTER FINAL KAF

05DB כ HEBREW LETTER KAF

05DC ל HEBREW LETTER LAMED

05DD ם HEBREW LETTER FINAL MEM

05DE מ HEBREW LETTER MEM

05DF ן HEBREW LETTER FINAL NUN

05E0 נ HEBREW LETTER NUN

05E1 ס HEBREW LETTER SAMEKH

05E2 ע HEBREW LETTER AYIN

05E3 ף HEBREW LETTER FINAL PE

05E4 פ HEBREW LETTER PE

05E5 ץ HEBREW LETTER FINAL TSADI

05E6 צ HEBREW LETTER TSADI
= zade

05E7 ק HEBREW LETTER QOF

05E8 ר HEBREW LETTER RESH
05E9 ש HEBREW LETTER SHIN
05EA ת HEBREW LETTER TAV

Yiddish digraphs

05F0 װ HEBREW LIGATURE YIDDISH DOUBLE VAV
= tsvey vovn
05F1 ױ HEBREW LIGATURE YIDDISH VAV YOD
05F2 ײ HEBREW LIGATURE YIDDISH DOUBLE YOD
= tsvey yudn

Additional punctuation

05F3 ׳ HEBREW PUNCTUATION GERESH
05F4 ״ HEBREW PUNCTUATION GERSHAYIM

	060	061	062	063	064	065	066	067	068	069	06A	06B	06C	06D	06E	06F
0	؀ 0600	◌ؐ 0610		ذ 0630	ـ 0640	◌ِ 0650	٠ 0660	◌ٰ 0670	ڀ 0680	ڐ 0690	ڠ 06A0	ڰ 06B0	ۀ 06C0	ې 06D0	◌۠ 06E0	۰ 06F0
1	؁ 0601	◌ؑ 0611	ء 0621	ر 0631	ف 0641	◌ّ 0651	١ 0661	ٱ 0671	ځ 0681	ڑ 0691	ڡ 06A1	ڱ 06B1	ہ 06C1	ۑ 06D1	◌ۡ 06E1	۱ 06F1
2	؂ 0602	◌ؒ 0612	آ 0622	ز 0632	ق 0642	◌ْ 0652	٢ 0662	ٲ 0672	ڂ 0682	ڒ 0692	ڢ 06A2	ڲ 06B2	ۂ 06C2	ے 06D2	◌ۢ 06E2	۲ 06F2
3	؃ 0603	◌ؓ 0613	أ 0623	س 0633	ك 0643	◌ٓ 0653	٣ 0663	ٳ 0673	ڃ 0683	ړ 0693	ڣ 06A3	ڳ 06B3	ۃ 06C3	ۓ 06D3	◌ۣ 06E3	۳ 06F3
4		◌ؔ 0614	ؤ 0624	ش 0634	ل 0644	◌ٔ 0654	٤ 0664	ٴ 0674	ڄ 0684	ڔ 0694	ڤ 06A4	ڴ 06B4	ۄ 06C4	۔ 06D4	◌ۤ 06E4	۴ 06F4
5		◌ؕ 0615	إ 0625	ص 0635	م 0645	◌ٕ 0655	٥ 0665	ٵ 0675	څ 0685	ڕ 0695	ڥ 06A5	ڵ 06B5	ۅ 06C5	ە 06D5	ۥ 06E5	۵ 06F5
6			ئ 0626	ض 0636	ن 0646	◌ٖ 0656	٦ 0666	ٶ 0676	چ 0686	ږ 0696	ڦ 06A6	ڶ 06B6	ۆ 06C6	◌ۖ 06D6	ۦ 06E6	۶ 06F6
7			ا 0627	ط 0637	ه 0647	◌ٗ 0657	٧ 0667	ٷ 0677	ڇ 0687	ڗ 0697	ڧ 06A7	ڷ 06B7	ۇ 06C7	◌ۗ 06D7	◌ۧ 06E7	۷ 06F7
8			ب 0628	ظ 0638	و 0648	◌٘ 0658	٨ 0668	ٸ 0678	ڈ 0688	ژ 0698	ڨ 06A8	ڸ 06B8	ۈ 06C8	◌ۘ 06D8	◌ۨ 06E8	۸ 06F8
9			ة 0629	ع 0639	ى 0649	◌ٙ 0659	٩ 0669	ٹ 0679	ډ 0689	ڙ 0699	ک 06A9	ڹ 06B9	ۉ 06C9	◌ۙ 06D9	۩ 06E9	۹ 06F9
A			ت 062A	غ 063A	ي 064A	◌ٚ 065A	٪ 066A	ٺ 067A	ڊ 068A	ښ 069A	ڪ 06AA	ں 06BA	ۊ 06CA	◌ۚ 06DA	◌۪ 06EA	ۺ 06FA
B	؋ 060B	؛ 061B	ث 062B		◌ً 064B	◌ٛ 065B	٫ 066B	ٻ 067B	ڋ 068B	ڛ 069B	ګ 06AB	ڻ 06BB	ۋ 06CB	◌ۛ 06DB	◌۫ 06EB	ۻ 06FB
C	، 060C		ج 062C		◌ٌ 064C	◌ٜ 065C	٬ 066C	ټ 067C	ڌ 068C	ڜ 069C	ڬ 06AC	ڼ 06BC	ی 06CC	◌ۜ 06DC	◌۬ 06EC	ۼ 06FC
D	؍ 060D		ح 062D		◌ٍ 064D	◌ٝ 065D	٭ 066D	ٽ 067D	ڍ 068D	ڝ 069D	ڭ 06AD	ڽ 06BD	ۍ 06CD	۝ 06DD	◌ۭ 06ED	۽ 06FD
E	؎ 060E	؞ 061E	خ 062E		◌َ 064E	◌ٞ 065E	ٮ 066E	پ 067E	ڎ 068E	ڞ 069E	ڮ 06AE	ھ 06BE	ێ 06CE	۞ 06DE	ۮ 06EE	۾ 06FE
F	؏ 060F	؟ 061F	د 062F		◌ُ 064F		ٯ 066F	ٿ 067F	ڏ 068F	ڟ 069F	گ 06AF	ڿ 06BF	ۏ 06CF	◌۟ 06DF	ۯ 06EF	ۿ 06FF

Subtending marks

0600 ؀ ARABIC NUMBER SIGN
0601 ؁ ARABIC SIGN SANAH
0602 ؂ ARABIC FOOTNOTE MARKER
0603 ؃ ARABIC SIGN SAFHA

Currency sign

060B ؋ AFGHANI SIGN

Punctuation

060C ، ARABIC COMMA
- also used with Thaana and Syriac in modern text

→ 002C , comma

060D ؍ ARABIC DATE SEPARATOR

Poetic marks

060E ؎ ARABIC POETIC VERSE SIGN
060F ؏ ARABIC SIGN MISRA

Honorifics

0610 ◌ؐ ARABIC SIGN SALLALLAHOU ALAYHE WASSALLAM
- represents sallallahu alayhe wasallam "may God's peace and blessings be upon him"

0611 ◌ؑ ARABIC SIGN ALAYHE ASSALLAM
- represents alayhe assalam "upon him be peace"

0612 ◌ؒ ARABIC SIGN RAHMATULLAH ALAYHE
- represents rahmatullah alayhe "may God have mercy upon him"

0613 ◌ؓ ARABIC SIGN RADI ALLAHOU ANHU
- represents radi allahu 'anhu "may God be pleased with him"

0614 ◌ؔ ARABIC SIGN TAKHALLUS
- sign placed over the name or nom-de-plume of a poet, or in some writings used to mark all proper names

Koranic annotation sign

0615 ◌ؕ ARABIC SMALL HIGH TAH
- marks a recommended pause position in some Korans published in Iran and Pakistan
- should not be confused with the small TAH sign used as a diacritic for some letters such as 0679 ٹ

Punctuation

061B ؛ ARABIC SEMICOLON
- also used with Thaana and Syriac in modern text

→ 003B ; semicolon

061C <reserved>
061D <reserved>
061E ؞ ARABIC TRIPLE DOT PUNCTUATION MARK
061F ؟ ARABIC QUESTION MARK
- also used with Thaana and Syriac in modern text

→ 003F ? question mark

Based on ISO 8859-6

0621 ء ARABIC LETTER HAMZA

→ 02BE ʾ modifier letter right half ring

0622 آ ARABIC LETTER ALEF WITH MADDA ABOVE

≡ 0627 ا 0653 ◌ٓ

0623 أ ARABIC LETTER ALEF WITH HAMZA ABOVE

≡ 0627 ا 0654 ◌ٔ

0624 ؤ ARABIC LETTER WAW WITH HAMZA ABOVE

≡ 0648 و 0654 ◌ٔ

0625 إ ARABIC LETTER ALEF WITH HAMZA BELOW

≡ 0627 ا 0655 ◌ٕ

0626 ئ ARABIC LETTER YEH WITH HAMZA ABOVE

≡ 064A ي 0654 ◌ٔ

0627 ا ARABIC LETTER ALEF
0628 ب ARABIC LETTER BEH
0629 ة ARABIC LETTER TEH MARBUTA
062A ت ARABIC LETTER TEH
062B ث ARABIC LETTER THEH
062C ج ARABIC LETTER JEEM
062D ح ARABIC LETTER HAH
062E خ ARABIC LETTER KHAH
062F د ARABIC LETTER DAL
0630 ذ ARABIC LETTER THAL
0631 ر ARABIC LETTER REH
0632 ز ARABIC LETTER ZAIN
0633 س ARABIC LETTER SEEN
0634 ش ARABIC LETTER SHEEN
0635 ص ARABIC LETTER SAD
0636 ض ARABIC LETTER DAD
0637 ط ARABIC LETTER TAH
0638 ظ ARABIC LETTER ZAH
0639 ع ARABIC LETTER AIN

→ 01B9 ƹ latin small letter ezh reversed
→ 02BF ʿ modifier letter left half ring

063A غ ARABIC LETTER GHAIN
063B <reserved>
063C <reserved>
063D <reserved>
063E <reserved>
063F <reserved>
0640 ـ ARABIC TATWEEL

= kashida
- inserted to stretch characters
- also used with Syriac

0641 ف ARABIC LETTER FEH
0642 ق ARABIC LETTER QAF
0643 ك ARABIC LETTER KAF
0644 ل ARABIC LETTER LAM
0645 م ARABIC LETTER MEEM
0646 ن ARABIC LETTER NOON
0647 ه ARABIC LETTER HEH
0648 و ARABIC LETTER WAW
0649 ى ARABIC LETTER ALEF MAKSURA
- represents YEH-shaped letter with no dots in any positional form

064A ي ARABIC LETTER YEH

Points from ISO 8859-6

064B ◌ً ARABIC FATHATAN
064C ◌ٌ ARABIC DAMMATAN
064D ◌ٍ ARABIC KASRATAN
064E ◌َ ARABIC FATHA
064F ◌ُ ARABIC DAMMA
0650 ◌ِ ARABIC KASRA
0651 ◌ّ ARABIC SHADDA
0652 ◌ْ ARABIC SUKUN
- marks absence of a vowel after the base consonant
- used in some Korans to mark a long vowel as ignored
- can have a variety of shapes, including a circular one and a shape that looks like '◌ۡ'

→ 06E1 ◌ۡ arabic small high dotless head of khah

Combining maddah and hamza

0653 ◌ٓ ARABIC MADDAH ABOVE
0654 ◌ٔ ARABIC HAMZA ABOVE
0655 ◌ٕ ARABIC HAMZA BELOW

Other combining marks

0656 ◌ٖ ARABIC SUBSCRIPT ALEF
0657 ◌ٗ ARABIC INVERTED DAMMA
0658 ◌٘ ARABIC MARK NOON GHUNNA
• Kashmiri and Baluchi
• indicates nasalization in Urdu
0659 ◌ٙ ARABIC ZWARAKAY
• Pashto
065A ◌ٚ ARABIC VOWEL SIGN SMALL V ABOVE
• African languages
065B ◌ٛ ARABIC VOWEL SIGN INVERTED SMALL V ABOVE
• African languages
065C ◌ٜ ARABIC VOWEL SIGN DOT BELOW
• African languages
065D ◌ٝ ARABIC REVERSED DAMMA
• Ormuri, African languages
065E ◌ٞ ARABIC FATHA WITH TWO DOTS
• Kalami

Arabic-Indic digits

These digits are used with Arabic proper; for languages of Iran, Pakistan, and India, see the Eastern Arabic-Indic digits at 06F0..06F9.

0660 ٠ ARABIC-INDIC DIGIT ZERO
0661 ١ ARABIC-INDIC DIGIT ONE
0662 ٢ ARABIC-INDIC DIGIT TWO
0663 ٣ ARABIC-INDIC DIGIT THREE
0664 ٤ ARABIC-INDIC DIGIT FOUR
0665 ٥ ARABIC-INDIC DIGIT FIVE
0666 ٦ ARABIC-INDIC DIGIT SIX
0667 ٧ ARABIC-INDIC DIGIT SEVEN
0668 ٨ ARABIC-INDIC DIGIT EIGHT
0669 ٩ ARABIC-INDIC DIGIT NINE

Punctuation

066A ٪ ARABIC PERCENT SIGN
→ 0025 % percent sign
066B ٫ ARABIC DECIMAL SEPARATOR
066C ٬ ARABIC THOUSANDS SEPARATOR
→ 0027 ' apostrophe
→ 2019 ’ right single quotation mark
066D ٭ ARABIC FIVE POINTED STAR
→ 002A * asterisk

Archaic letters

066E ٮ ARABIC LETTER DOTLESS BEH
066F ٯ ARABIC LETTER DOTLESS QAF

Point

0670 ◌ٰ ARABIC LETTER SUPERSCRIPT ALEF
• actually a vowel sign, despite the name

Extended Arabic letters

0671 ٱ ARABIC LETTER ALEF WASLA
• Koranic Arabic
0672 ٲ ARABIC LETTER ALEF WITH WAVY HAMZA ABOVE
• Baluchi, Kashmiri
0673 ٳ ARABIC LETTER ALEF WITH WAVY HAMZA BELOW
• Baluchi, Kashmiri
0674 ٴ ARABIC LETTER HIGH HAMZA
• Kazakh
• forms digraphs
0675 ٵ ARABIC LETTER HIGH HAMZA ALEF
• Kazakh
≈ 0627 ا 0674 ٴ
0676 ٶ ARABIC LETTER HIGH HAMZA WAW
• Kazakh
≈ 0648 و 0674 ٴ
0677 ٷ ARABIC LETTER U WITH HAMZA ABOVE
• Kazakh
≈ 06C7 ۇ 0674 ٴ
0678 ٸ ARABIC LETTER HIGH HAMZA YEH
• Kazakh
≈ 064A ي 0674 ٴ
0679 ٹ ARABIC LETTER TTEH
• Urdu
067A ٺ ARABIC LETTER TTEHEH
• Sindhi
067B ٻ ARABIC LETTER BEEH
• Sindhi
067C ټ ARABIC LETTER TEH WITH RING
• Pashto
067D ٽ ARABIC LETTER TEH WITH THREE DOTS ABOVE DOWNWARDS
• Sindhi
067E پ ARABIC LETTER PEH
• Persian, Urdu, ...
067F ٿ ARABIC LETTER TEHEH
• Sindhi
0680 ڀ ARABIC LETTER BEHEH
• Sindhi
0681 ځ ARABIC LETTER HAH WITH HAMZA ABOVE
• Pashto letter “dze”
0682 ڂ ARABIC LETTER HAH WITH TWO DOTS VERTICAL ABOVE
• not used in modern Pashto
0683 ڃ ARABIC LETTER NYEH
• Sindhi
0684 ڄ ARABIC LETTER DYEH
• Sindhi
0685 څ ARABIC LETTER HAH WITH THREE DOTS ABOVE
• Pashto
0686 چ ARABIC LETTER TCHEH
• Persian, Urdu, ...
0687 ڇ ARABIC LETTER TCHEHEH
• Sindhi
0688 ڈ ARABIC LETTER DDAL
• Urdu
0689 ډ ARABIC LETTER DAL WITH RING
• Pashto
068A ڊ ARABIC LETTER DAL WITH DOT BELOW
• Sindhi
068B ڋ ARABIC LETTER DAL WITH DOT BELOW AND SMALL TAH
• Lahnda
068C ڌ ARABIC LETTER DAHAL
• Sindhi
068D ڍ ARABIC LETTER DDAHAL
• Sindhi
068E ڎ ARABIC LETTER DUL
• older shape for DUL, now obsolete in Sindhi
• Burushaski

068F ڏ ARABIC LETTER DAL WITH THREE DOTS ABOVE DOWNWARDS
• Sindhi
• current shape used for DUL

0690 ڐ ARABIC LETTER DAL WITH FOUR DOTS ABOVE
• old Urdu, not in current use

0691 ڑ ARABIC LETTER RREH
• Urdu

0692 ڒ ARABIC LETTER REH WITH SMALL V
• Kurdish

0693 ړ ARABIC LETTER REH WITH RING
• Pashto

0694 ڔ ARABIC LETTER REH WITH DOT BELOW
• Kurdish

0695 ڕ ARABIC LETTER REH WITH SMALL V BELOW
• Kurdish

0696 ږ ARABIC LETTER REH WITH DOT BELOW AND DOT ABOVE
• Pashto

0697 ڗ ARABIC LETTER REH WITH TWO DOTS ABOVE
• Dargwa

0698 ژ ARABIC LETTER JEH
• Persian, Urdu, ...

0699 ڙ ARABIC LETTER REH WITH FOUR DOTS ABOVE
• Sindhi

069A ښ ARABIC LETTER SEEN WITH DOT BELOW AND DOT ABOVE
• Pashto

069B ڛ ARABIC LETTER SEEN WITH THREE DOTS BELOW

069C ڜ ARABIC LETTER SEEN WITH THREE DOTS BELOW AND THREE DOTS ABOVE
• Moroccan Arabic

069D ڝ ARABIC LETTER SAD WITH TWO DOTS BELOW
• Turkic

069E ڞ ARABIC LETTER SAD WITH THREE DOTS ABOVE
• Berber, Burushaski

069F ڟ ARABIC LETTER TAH WITH THREE DOTS ABOVE
• old Hausa

06A0 ڠ ARABIC LETTER AIN WITH THREE DOTS ABOVE
• old Malay

06A1 ڡ ARABIC LETTER DOTLESS FEH
• Adighe

06A2 ڢ ARABIC LETTER FEH WITH DOT MOVED BELOW
• Maghrib Arabic

06A3 ڣ ARABIC LETTER FEH WITH DOT BELOW
• Ingush

06A4 ڤ ARABIC LETTER VEH
• Middle Eastern Arabic for foreign words
• Kurdish

06A5 ڥ ARABIC LETTER FEH WITH THREE DOTS BELOW
• North African Arabic for foreign words

06A6 ڦ ARABIC LETTER PEHEH
• Sindhi

06A7 ڧ ARABIC LETTER QAF WITH DOT ABOVE
• Maghrib Arabic

06A8 ڨ ARABIC LETTER QAF WITH THREE DOTS ABOVE
• Tunisian Arabic

06A9 ک ARABIC LETTER KEHEH
• Persian, Urdu, ...

06AA ڪ ARABIC LETTER SWASH KAF

06AB ګ ARABIC LETTER KAF WITH RING
• Pashto
• may appear like an Arabic KAF (0643 ك) with a ring below the base

06AC ڬ ARABIC LETTER KAF WITH DOT ABOVE
• old Malay

06AD ڭ ARABIC LETTER NG
• Uighur, Kazakh, old Malay, ...

06AE ڮ ARABIC LETTER KAF WITH THREE DOTS BELOW
• Berber

06AF گ ARABIC LETTER GAF
• Persian, Urdu, ...

06B0 ڰ ARABIC LETTER GAF WITH RING
• Lahnda

06B1 ڱ ARABIC LETTER NGOEH
• Sindhi

06B2 ڲ ARABIC LETTER GAF WITH TWO DOTS BELOW
• not used in Sindhi

06B3 ڳ ARABIC LETTER GUEH
• Sindhi

06B4 ڴ ARABIC LETTER GAF WITH THREE DOTS ABOVE
• not used in Sindhi

06B5 ڵ ARABIC LETTER LAM WITH SMALL V
• Kurdish

06B6 ڶ ARABIC LETTER LAM WITH DOT ABOVE
• Kurdish

06B7 ڷ ARABIC LETTER LAM WITH THREE DOTS ABOVE
• Kurdish

06B8 ڸ ARABIC LETTER LAM WITH THREE DOTS BELOW

06B9 ڹ ARABIC LETTER NOON WITH DOT BELOW

06BA ں ARABIC LETTER NOON GHUNNA
• Urdu

06BB ڻ ARABIC LETTER RNOON
• Sindhi

06BC ڼ ARABIC LETTER NOON WITH RING
• Pashto

06BD ڽ ARABIC LETTER NOON WITH THREE DOTS ABOVE
• old Malay

06BE ھ ARABIC LETTER HEH DOACHASHMEE
• Urdu
• forms aspirate digraphs

06BF ڿ ARABIC LETTER TCHEH WITH DOT ABOVE

06C0 ۀ ARABIC LETTER HEH WITH YEH ABOVE
= arabic letter hamzah on ha (1.0)
= izafet
• Urdu
• actually a ligature, not an independent letter
≡ 06D5 ە 0654 ◌ٔ

06C1 ہ ARABIC LETTER HEH GOAL
• Urdu

06C2 ۂ ARABIC LETTER HEH GOAL WITH HAMZA ABOVE
• Urdu
• actually a ligature, not an independent letter
≡ 06C1 ہ 0654 ◌ٔ

06C3 ۃ ARABIC LETTER TEH MARBUTA GOAL
• Urdu

06C4 ۄ ARABIC LETTER WAW WITH RING
• Kashmiri

06C5 ۅ ARABIC LETTER KIRGHIZ OE
• Kirghiz

06C6 ۆ ARABIC LETTER OE
• Uighur, Kurdish, Kazakh

06C7 ۇ ARABIC LETTER U
- Kirghiz

06C8 ۈ ARABIC LETTER YU
- Uighur

06C9 ۉ ARABIC LETTER KIRGHIZ YU
- Kazakh, Kirghiz

06CA ۊ ARABIC LETTER WAW WITH TWO DOTS ABOVE
- Kurdish

06CB ۋ ARABIC LETTER VE
- Uighur, Kazakh

06CC ی ARABIC LETTER FARSI YEH
- Arabic, Persian, Urdu, ...
- initial and medial forms of this letter have dots

→ 0649 ى arabic letter alef maksura
→ 064A ي arabic letter yeh

06CD ۍ ARABIC LETTER YEH WITH TAIL
- Pashto, Sindhi

06CE ێ ARABIC LETTER YEH WITH SMALL V
- Kurdish

06CF ۏ ARABIC LETTER WAW WITH DOT ABOVE

06D0 ې ARABIC LETTER E
- Pashto, Uighur
- used as the letter bbeh in Sindhi

06D1 ۑ ARABIC LETTER YEH WITH THREE DOTS BELOW
- old Malay

06D2 ے ARABIC LETTER YEH BARREE
- Urdu

06D3 ۓ ARABIC LETTER YEH BARREE WITH HAMZA ABOVE
- Urdu
- actually a ligature, not an independent letter

≡ 06D2 ے 0654 ◌ٔ

Punctuation

06D4 ۔ ARABIC FULL STOP
- Urdu

Extended Arabic letter

06D5 ە ARABIC LETTER AE
- Uighur, Kazakh, Kirghiz

Koranic annotation signs

06D6 ◌ۖ ARABIC SMALL HIGH LIGATURE SAD WITH LAM WITH ALEF MAKSURA

06D7 ◌ۗ ARABIC SMALL HIGH LIGATURE QAF WITH LAM WITH ALEF MAKSURA

06D8 ◌ۘ ARABIC SMALL HIGH MEEM INITIAL FORM

06D9 ◌ۙ ARABIC SMALL HIGH LAM ALEF

06DA ◌ۚ ARABIC SMALL HIGH JEEM

06DB ◌ۛ ARABIC SMALL HIGH THREE DOTS

06DC ◌ۜ ARABIC SMALL HIGH SEEN

06DD ۝ ARABIC END OF AYAH

06DE ۞ ARABIC START OF RUB EL HIZB

06DF ◌۟ ARABIC SMALL HIGH ROUNDED ZERO
- smaller than the typical circular shape used for 0652 ◌ْ

06E0 ◌۠ ARABIC SMALL HIGH UPRIGHT RECTANGULAR ZERO

06E1 ◌ۡ ARABIC SMALL HIGH DOTLESS HEAD OF KHAH

= Arabic jazm
- presentation form of 0652 ◌ْ, using font technology to select the variant is preferred
- used in some Korans to mark absence of a vowel

→ 0652 ◌ْ arabic sukun

06E2 ◌ۢ ARABIC SMALL HIGH MEEM ISOLATED FORM

06E3 ◌ۣ ARABIC SMALL LOW SEEN

06E4 ◌ۤ ARABIC SMALL HIGH MADDA

06E5 ۥ ARABIC SMALL WAW

06E6 ۦ ARABIC SMALL YEH

06E7 ◌ۧ ARABIC SMALL HIGH YEH

06E8 ◌ۨ ARABIC SMALL HIGH NOON

06E9 ۩ ARABIC PLACE OF SAJDAH
- there is a range of acceptable glyphs for this character

06EA ◌۪ ARABIC EMPTY CENTRE LOW STOP

06EB ◌۫ ARABIC EMPTY CENTRE HIGH STOP

06EC ◌۬ ARABIC ROUNDED HIGH STOP WITH FILLED CENTRE

06ED ◌ۭ ARABIC SMALL LOW MEEM

Extended Arabic letters for Parkari

06EE ۮ ARABIC LETTER DAL WITH INVERTED V

06EF ۯ ARABIC LETTER REH WITH INVERTED V

Eastern Arabic-Indic digits

These digits are used with Arabic-script languages of Iran, Pakistan, and India (Persian, Sindhi, Urdu, etc.). For details of variations in preferred glyphs, see the block description for the Arabic script.

06F0 ۰ EXTENDED ARABIC-INDIC DIGIT ZERO

06F1 ۱ EXTENDED ARABIC-INDIC DIGIT ONE

06F2 ۲ EXTENDED ARABIC-INDIC DIGIT TWO

06F3 ۳ EXTENDED ARABIC-INDIC DIGIT THREE

06F4 ۴ EXTENDED ARABIC-INDIC DIGIT FOUR
- Persian has a different glyph than Sindhi and Urdu

06F5 ۵ EXTENDED ARABIC-INDIC DIGIT FIVE
- Persian, Sindhi, and Urdu share glyph different from Arabic

06F6 ۶ EXTENDED ARABIC-INDIC DIGIT SIX
- Persian, Sindhi, and Urdu have glyphs different from Arabic

06F7 ۷ EXTENDED ARABIC-INDIC DIGIT SEVEN
- Urdu and Sindhi have glyphs different from Arabic

06F8 ۸ EXTENDED ARABIC-INDIC DIGIT EIGHT

06F9 ۹ EXTENDED ARABIC-INDIC DIGIT NINE

Extended Arabic letters

06FA ۺ ARABIC LETTER SHEEN WITH DOT BELOW

06FB ۻ ARABIC LETTER DAD WITH DOT BELOW

06FC ۼ ARABIC LETTER GHAIN WITH DOT BELOW

Signs for Sindhi

06FD ۽ ARABIC SIGN SINDHI AMPERSAND

06FE ۾ ARABIC SIGN SINDHI POSTPOSITION MEN

Extended Arabic letter for Parkari

06FF ۿ ARABIC LETTER HEH WITH INVERTED V

	070	071	072	073	074
0	0700	0710	0720	0730	0740
1	0701	0711	0721	0731	0741
2	0702	0712	0722	0732	0742
3	0703	0713	0723	0733	0743
4	0704	0714	0724	0734	0744
5	0705	0715	0725	0735	0745
6	0706	0716	0726	0736	0746
7	0707	0717	0727	0737	0747
8	0708	0718	0728	0738	0748
9	0709	0719	0729	0739	0749
A	070A	071A	072A	073A	074A
B	070B	071B	072B	073B	
C	070C	071C	072C	073C	
D	070D	071D	072D	073D	074D
E		071E	072E	073E	074E
F	SAM 070F	071F	072F	073F	074F

Syriac punctuation and signs

0700 ܀ SYRIAC END OF PARAGRAPH
- marks the end of a paragraph

0701 ܁ SYRIAC SUPRALINEAR FULL STOP
- marks interrogations, imperatives, and pauses, especially in Biblical texts

0702 ܂ SYRIAC SUBLINEAR FULL STOP
- marks subordinate clauses and minor pauses, especially in Biblical texts

0703 ܃ SYRIAC SUPRALINEAR COLON
- marks expressions of wonder and has a distinct pausal value in Biblical texts

0704 ܄ SYRIAC SUBLINEAR COLON
- used at the end of verses of supplications

0705 ܅ SYRIAC HORIZONTAL COLON
- joins two words closely together in a context to which a rising tone is suitable

0706 ܆ SYRIAC COLON SKEWED LEFT
- marks a dependent clause

0707 ܇ SYRIAC COLON SKEWED RIGHT
- marks the end of a subdivision of the apodosis, or latter part of a Biblical verse

0708 ܈ SYRIAC SUPRALINEAR COLON SKEWED LEFT
- marks a minor phrase division

0709 ܉ SYRIAC SUBLINEAR COLON SKEWED RIGHT
- marks the end of a real or rhetorical question

070A ܊ SYRIAC CONTRACTION
- a contraction mark, mostly used in East Syriac
- placed at the end of an incomplete word

070B ܋ SYRIAC HARKLEAN OBELUS
- marks the beginning of a phrase, word, or morpheme that has a marginal note

070C ܌ SYRIAC HARKLEAN METOBELUS
- marks the end of a section with a marginal note

070D ܍ SYRIAC HARKLEAN ASTERISCUS
- marks the beginning of a phrase, word, or morpheme that has a marginal note

Syriac format control character

070F [SAM] SYRIAC ABBREVIATION MARK
= SAM
- marks the beginning of a Syriac abbreviation

Syriac letters

0710 ܐ SYRIAC LETTER ALAPH
0711 ܑ SYRIAC LETTER SUPERSCRIPT ALAPH
- used in East Syriac texts to indicate an etymological Alaph

0712 ܒ SYRIAC LETTER BETH
0713 ܓ SYRIAC LETTER GAMAL
0714 ܔ SYRIAC LETTER GAMAL GARSHUNI
- used in Garshuni documents

0715 ܕ SYRIAC LETTER DALATH
0716 ܖ SYRIAC LETTER DOTLESS DALATH RISH
- ambiguous form for undifferentiated early dalath/rish

0717 ܗ SYRIAC LETTER HE
0718 ܘ SYRIAC LETTER WAW
0719 ܙ SYRIAC LETTER ZAIN
071A ܚ SYRIAC LETTER HETH
071B ܛ SYRIAC LETTER TETH
071C ܜ SYRIAC LETTER TETH GARSHUNI
- used in Garshuni documents

071D ܝ SYRIAC LETTER YUDH
071E ܞ SYRIAC LETTER YUDH HE
- mostly used in East Syriac texts

071F ܟ SYRIAC LETTER KAPH
0720 ܠ SYRIAC LETTER LAMADH
0721 ܡ SYRIAC LETTER MIM
0722 ܢ SYRIAC LETTER NUN
0723 ܣ SYRIAC LETTER SEMKATH
0724 ܤ SYRIAC LETTER FINAL SEMKATH
0725 ܥ SYRIAC LETTER E
0726 ܦ SYRIAC LETTER PE
0727 ܧ SYRIAC LETTER REVERSED PE
- used in Christian Palestinian Aramaic

0728 ܨ SYRIAC LETTER SADHE
0729 ܩ SYRIAC LETTER QAPH
072A ܪ SYRIAC LETTER RISH
072B ܫ SYRIAC LETTER SHIN
072C ܬ SYRIAC LETTER TAW

Persian letters

072D ܭ SYRIAC LETTER PERSIAN BHETH
072E ܮ SYRIAC LETTER PERSIAN GHAMAL
072F ܯ SYRIAC LETTER PERSIAN DHALATH

Syriac points (vowels)

0730 ◌ܰ SYRIAC PTHAHA ABOVE
0731 ◌ܱ SYRIAC PTHAHA BELOW
0732 ◌ܲ SYRIAC PTHAHA DOTTED
0733 ◌ܳ SYRIAC ZQAPHA ABOVE
0734 ◌ܴ SYRIAC ZQAPHA BELOW
0735 ◌ܵ SYRIAC ZQAPHA DOTTED
0736 ◌ܶ SYRIAC RBASA ABOVE
0737 ◌ܷ SYRIAC RBASA BELOW
0738 ◌ܸ SYRIAC DOTTED ZLAMA HORIZONTAL
0739 ◌ܹ SYRIAC DOTTED ZLAMA ANGULAR
073A ◌ܺ SYRIAC HBASA ABOVE
073B ◌ܻ SYRIAC HBASA BELOW
073C ◌ܼ SYRIAC HBASA-ESASA DOTTED
073D ◌ܽ SYRIAC ESASA ABOVE
073E ◌ܾ SYRIAC ESASA BELOW
073F ◌ܿ SYRIAC RWAHA

Syriac marks

0740 ◌݀ SYRIAC FEMININE DOT
- feminine marker used with the Taw feminine suffix

0741 ◌݁ SYRIAC QUSHSHAYA
- indicates a plosive pronunciation

0742 ◌݂ SYRIAC RUKKAKHA
- indicates an aspirated (spirantized) pronunciation

0743 ◌݃ SYRIAC TWO VERTICAL DOTS ABOVE
- accent mark used in ancient manuscripts

0744 ◌݄ SYRIAC TWO VERTICAL DOTS BELOW
- accent mark used in ancient manuscripts

0745 ◌݅ SYRIAC THREE DOTS ABOVE
- diacritic used in Turoyo for letters not found in Syriac

0746 ◌݆ SYRIAC THREE DOTS BELOW
- diacritic used in Turoyo for letters not found in Syriac

0747 ◌݇ SYRIAC OBLIQUE LINE ABOVE
- indication of a silent letter

0748 ◌݈ SYRIAC OBLIQUE LINE BELOW
- indication of a silent letter
- also used to indicate numbers multiplied by a certain constant

0749 ◌݉ SYRIAC MUSIC
- a music mark
- also used in the Syrian Orthodox Anaphora book to mark the breaking of the Eucharist bread

074A ◌݊ SYRIAC BARREKH
- a diacritic cross used in liturgical texts

Sogdian letters

074D ݍ SYRIAC LETTER SOGDIAN ZHAIN
074E ݎ SYRIAC LETTER SOGDIAN KHAPH
074F ݏ SYRIAC LETTER SOGDIAN FE

	075	076	077
0	ݐ 0750	ݠ 0760	
1	ݑ 0751	ݡ 0761	
2	ݒ 0752	ݢ 0762	
3	ݓ 0753	ݣ 0763	
4	ݔ 0754	ݤ 0764	
5	ݕ 0755	ݥ 0765	
6	ݖ 0756	ݦ 0766	
7	ݗ 0757	ݧ 0767	
8	ݘ 0758	ݨ 0768	
9	ݙ 0759	ݩ 0769	
A	ݚ 075A	ݪ 076A	
B	ݛ 075B	ݫ 076B	
C	ݜ 075C	ݬ 076C	
D	ݝ 075D	ݭ 076D	
E	ݞ 075E		
F	ݟ 075F		

Extended Arabic letters

These are primarily used in Arabic-script orthographies of African languages.

0750 ݐ ARABIC LETTER BEH WITH THREE DOTS HORIZONTALLY BELOW

0751 ݑ ARABIC LETTER BEH WITH DOT BELOW AND THREE DOTS ABOVE

0752 ݒ ARABIC LETTER BEH WITH THREE DOTS POINTING UPWARDS BELOW

0753 ݓ ARABIC LETTER BEH WITH THREE DOTS POINTING UPWARDS BELOW AND TWO DOTS ABOVE

0754 ݔ ARABIC LETTER BEH WITH TWO DOTS BELOW AND DOT ABOVE

0755 ݕ ARABIC LETTER BEH WITH INVERTED SMALL V BELOW

0756 ݖ ARABIC LETTER BEH WITH SMALL V

0757 ݗ ARABIC LETTER HAH WITH TWO DOTS ABOVE

0758 ݘ ARABIC LETTER HAH WITH THREE DOTS POINTING UPWARDS BELOW

0759 ݙ ARABIC LETTER DAL WITH TWO DOTS VERTICALLY BELOW AND SMALL TAH
- Saraiki

075A ݚ ARABIC LETTER DAL WITH INVERTED SMALL V BELOW

075B ݛ ARABIC LETTER REH WITH STROKE

075C ݜ ARABIC LETTER SEEN WITH FOUR DOTS ABOVE
- Shina

075D ݝ ARABIC LETTER AIN WITH TWO DOTS ABOVE

075E ݞ ARABIC LETTER AIN WITH THREE DOTS POINTING DOWNWARDS ABOVE

075F ݟ ARABIC LETTER AIN WITH TWO DOTS VERTICALLY ABOVE

0760 ݠ ARABIC LETTER FEH WITH TWO DOTS BELOW

0761 ݡ ARABIC LETTER FEH WITH THREE DOTS POINTING UPWARDS BELOW

0762 ݢ ARABIC LETTER KEHEH WITH DOT ABOVE
- old Malay, preferred to 06AC ڬ
- → 06AC ڬ arabic letter kaf with dot above

0763 ݣ ARABIC LETTER KEHEH WITH THREE DOTS ABOVE
- Moroccan Arabic, Amazigh, Burushaski
- → 06AD ڭ arabic letter ng

0764 ݤ ARABIC LETTER KEHEH WITH THREE DOTS POINTING UPWARDS BELOW

0765 ݥ ARABIC LETTER MEEM WITH DOT ABOVE

0766 ݦ ARABIC LETTER MEEM WITH DOT BELOW
- Maba

0767 ݧ ARABIC LETTER NOON WITH TWO DOTS BELOW

0768 ݨ ARABIC LETTER NOON WITH SMALL TAH
- Saraiki, Pathwari

0769 ݩ ARABIC LETTER NOON WITH SMALL V
- Gojri

076A ݪ ARABIC LETTER LAM WITH BAR

076B ݫ ARABIC LETTER REH WITH TWO DOTS VERTICALLY ABOVE
- Torwali, Ormuri

076C ݬ ARABIC LETTER REH WITH HAMZA ABOVE
- Ormuri

076D ݭ ARABIC LETTER SEEN WITH TWO DOTS VERTICALLY ABOVE
- Kalami, Ormuri

	078	079	07A	07B
0	ހ 0780	ސ 0790	ޠ 07A0	◌ް 07B0
1	ށ 0781	ޑ 0791	ޡ 07A1	ޱ 07B1
2	ނ 0782	ޒ 0792	ޢ 07A2	
3	ރ 0783	ޓ 0793	ޣ 07A3	
4	ބ 0784	ޔ 0794	ޤ 07A4	
5	ޅ 0785	ޕ 0795	ޥ 07A5	
6	ކ 0786	ޖ 0796	◌ަ 07A6	
7	އ 0787	ޗ 0797	◌ާ 07A7	
8	ވ 0788	ޘ 0798	◌ި 07A8	
9	މ 0789	ޙ 0799	◌ީ 07A9	
A	ފ 078A	ޚ 079A	◌ު 07AA	
B	ދ 078B	ޛ 079B	◌ޫ 07AB	
C	ތ 078C	ޜ 079C	◌ެ 07AC	
D	ލ 078D	ޝ 079D	◌ޭ 07AD	
E	ގ 078E	ޞ 079E	◌ޮ 07AE	
F	ޏ 078F	ޟ 079F	◌ޯ 07AF	

Basic consonants

0780 ހ THAANA LETTER HAA
0781 ށ THAANA LETTER SHAVIYANI
0782 ނ THAANA LETTER NOONU
0783 ރ THAANA LETTER RAA
0784 ބ THAANA LETTER BAA
0785 ޅ THAANA LETTER LHAVIYANI
0786 ކ THAANA LETTER KAAFU
0787 އ THAANA LETTER ALIFU
0788 ވ THAANA LETTER VAAVU
0789 މ THAANA LETTER MEEMU
078A ފ THAANA LETTER FAAFU
078B ދ THAANA LETTER DHAALU
078C ތ THAANA LETTER THAA
078D ލ THAANA LETTER LAAMU
078E ގ THAANA LETTER GAAFU
078F ޏ THAANA LETTER GNAVIYANI
0790 ސ THAANA LETTER SEENU
0791 ޑ THAANA LETTER DAVIYANI
0792 ޒ THAANA LETTER ZAVIYANI
0793 ޓ THAANA LETTER TAVIYANI
0794 ޔ THAANA LETTER YAA
0795 ޕ THAANA LETTER PAVIYANI
0796 ޖ THAANA LETTER JAVIYANI
0797 ޗ THAANA LETTER CHAVIYANI

Extensions for Arabic

0798 ޘ THAANA LETTER TTAA
0799 ޙ THAANA LETTER HHAA
079A ޚ THAANA LETTER KHAA
079B ޛ THAANA LETTER THAALU
079C ޜ THAANA LETTER ZAA
079D ޝ THAANA LETTER SHEENU
079E ޞ THAANA LETTER SAADHU
079F ޟ THAANA LETTER DAADHU
07A0 ޠ THAANA LETTER TO
07A1 ޡ THAANA LETTER ZO
07A2 ޢ THAANA LETTER AINU
07A3 ޣ THAANA LETTER GHAINU
07A4 ޤ THAANA LETTER QAAFU
07A5 ޥ THAANA LETTER WAAVU

Vowels

07A6 ◌ަ THAANA ABAFILI
07A7 ◌ާ THAANA AABAAFILI
07A8 ◌ި THAANA IBIFILI
07A9 ◌ީ THAANA EEBEEFILI
07AA ◌ު THAANA UBUFILI
07AB ◌ޫ THAANA OOBOOFILI
07AC ◌ެ THAANA EBEFILI
07AD ◌ޭ THAANA EYBEYFILI
07AE ◌ޮ THAANA OBOFILI
07AF ◌ޯ THAANA OABOAFILI
07B0 ◌ް THAANA SUKUN

Consonant for Addu dialect

07B1 ޱ THAANA LETTER NAA

	07C	07D	07E	07F
0	߀ 07C0	ߐ 07D0	ߠ 07E0	◌߰ 07F0
1	߁ 07C1	ߑ 07D1	ߡ 07E1	◌߱ 07F1
2	߂ 07C2	ߒ 07D2	ߢ 07E2	◌߲ 07F2
3	߃ 07C3	ߓ 07D3	ߣ 07E3	◌߳ 07F3
4	߄ 07C4	ߔ 07D4	ߤ 07E4	ߴ 07F4
5	߅ 07C5	ߕ 07D5	ߥ 07E5	ߵ 07F5
6	߆ 07C6	ߖ 07D6	ߦ 07E6	߶ 07F6
7	߇ 07C7	ߗ 07D7	ߧ 07E7	߷ 07F7
8	߈ 07C8	ߘ 07D8	ߨ 07E8	߸ 07F8
9	߉ 07C9	ߙ 07D9	ߩ 07E9	߹ 07F9
A	ߊ 07CA	ߚ 07DA	ߪ 07EA	ߺ 07FA
B	ߋ 07CB	ߛ 07DB	◌߫ 07EB	
C	ߌ 07CC	ߜ 07DC	◌߬ 07EC	
D	ߍ 07CD	ߝ 07DD	◌߭ 07ED	
E	ߎ 07CE	ߞ 07DE	◌߮ 07EE	
F	ߏ 07CF	ߟ 07DF	◌߯ 07EF	

Digits

07C0 ߀ NKO DIGIT ZERO
07C1 ߁ NKO DIGIT ONE
07C2 ߂ NKO DIGIT TWO
07C3 ߃ NKO DIGIT THREE
07C4 ߄ NKO DIGIT FOUR
07C5 ߅ NKO DIGIT FIVE
07C6 ߆ NKO DIGIT SIX
07C7 ߇ NKO DIGIT SEVEN
07C8 ߈ NKO DIGIT EIGHT
07C9 ߉ NKO DIGIT NINE

Letters

07CA ߊ NKO LETTER A
07CB ߋ NKO LETTER EE
07CC ߌ NKO LETTER I
07CD ߍ NKO LETTER E
07CE ߎ NKO LETTER U
07CF ߏ NKO LETTER OO
07D0 ߐ NKO LETTER O
07D1 ߑ NKO LETTER DAGBASINNA
07D2 ߒ NKO LETTER N
07D3 ߓ NKO LETTER BA
07D4 ߔ NKO LETTER PA
07D5 ߕ NKO LETTER TA
07D6 ߖ NKO LETTER JA
07D7 ߗ NKO LETTER CHA
07D8 ߘ NKO LETTER DA
07D9 ߙ NKO LETTER RA
07DA ߚ NKO LETTER RRA
07DB ߛ NKO LETTER SA
07DC ߜ NKO LETTER GBA
07DD ߝ NKO LETTER FA
07DE ߞ NKO LETTER KA
07DF ߟ NKO LETTER LA
07E0 ߠ NKO LETTER NA WOLOSO
07E1 ߡ NKO LETTER MA
07E2 ߢ NKO LETTER NYA
07E3 ߣ NKO LETTER NA
07E4 ߤ NKO LETTER HA
07E5 ߥ NKO LETTER WA
07E6 ߦ NKO LETTER YA
07E7 ߧ NKO LETTER NYA WOLOSO

Archaic letters

07E8 ߨ NKO LETTER JONA JA
07E9 ߩ NKO LETTER JONA CHA
07EA ߪ NKO LETTER JONA RA
→ 07D9 ߙ nko letter ra

Tone marks

07EB ◌߫ NKO COMBINING SHORT HIGH TONE
→ 0304 ◌̄ combining macron
07EC ◌߬ NKO COMBINING SHORT LOW TONE
→ 0303 ◌̃ combining tilde
07ED ◌߭ NKO COMBINING SHORT RISING TONE
→ 0307 ◌̇ combining dot above
07EE ◌߮ NKO COMBINING LONG DESCENDING TONE
→ 0302 ◌̂ combining circumflex accent
07EF ◌߯ NKO COMBINING LONG HIGH TONE
07F0 ◌߰ NKO COMBINING LONG LOW TONE
07F1 ◌߱ NKO COMBINING LONG RISING TONE
07F2 ◌߲ NKO COMBINING NASALIZATION MARK
→ 0323 ◌̣ combining dot below
07F3 ◌߳ NKO COMBINING DOUBLE DOT ABOVE
→ 0308 ◌̈ combining diaeresis
07F4 ߴ NKO HIGH TONE APOSTROPHE
→ 02BC ʼ modifier letter apostrophe
07F5 ߵ NKO LOW TONE APOSTROPHE
→ 02BB ʻ modifier letter turned comma

Symbol

07F6 ߶ NKO SYMBOL OO DENNEN

Punctuation

07F7 ߷ NKO SYMBOL GBAKURUNEN
07F8 ߸ NKO COMMA
07F9 ߹ NKO EXCLAMATION MARK

Letter extender

07FA ߺ NKO LAJANYALAN
→ 005F _ low line
→ 0640 ـ arabic tatweel

	090	091	092	093	094	095	096	097
0		ऐ 0910	ठ 0920	र 0930	◌ी 0940	ॐ 0950	ॠ 0960	॰ 0970
1	◌ँ 0901	ऑ 0911	ड 0921	ऱ 0931	◌ु 0941	◌॑ 0951	ॡ 0961	
2	◌ं 0902	ऒ 0912	ढ 0922	ल 0932	◌ू 0942	◌॒ 0952	◌ॢ 0962	
3	◌ः 0903	ओ 0913	ण 0923	ळ 0933	◌ृ 0943	◌॓ 0953	◌ॣ 0963	
4	ऄ 0904	औ 0914	त 0924	ऴ 0934	◌ॄ 0944	◌॔ 0954	। 0964	
5	अ 0905	क 0915	थ 0925	व 0935	◌ॅ 0945		॥ 0965	
6	आ 0906	ख 0916	द 0926	श 0936	◌ॆ 0946		० 0966	
7	इ 0907	ग 0917	ध 0927	ष 0937	◌े 0947		१ 0967	
8	ई 0908	घ 0918	न 0928	स 0938	◌ै 0948	क़ 0958	२ 0968	
9	उ 0909	ङ 0919	ऩ 0929	ह 0939	◌ॉ 0949	ख़ 0959	३ 0969	
A	ऊ 090A	च 091A	प 092A		◌ॊ 094A	ग़ 095A	४ 096A	
B	ऋ 090B	छ 091B	फ 092B		◌ो 094B	ज़ 095B	५ 096B	ॻ 097B
C	ऌ 090C	ज 091C	ब 092C	◌़ 093C	◌ौ 094C	ड़ 095C	६ 096C	ॼ 097C
D	ऍ 090D	झ 091D	भ 092D	ऽ 093D	◌् 094D	ढ़ 095D	७ 096D	ॽ 097D
E	ऎ 090E	ञ 091E	म 092E	◌ा 093E		फ़ 095E	८ 096E	ॾ 097E
F	ए 090F	ट 091F	य 092F	◌ि 093F		य़ 095F	९ 096F	ॿ 097F

Based on ISCII 1988

Various signs

0901 ◌ँ DEVANAGARI SIGN CANDRABINDU
 = anunasika
 → 0310 ◌̐ combining candrabindu
0902 ◌ं DEVANAGARI SIGN ANUSVARA
 = bindu
0903 ◌ः DEVANAGARI SIGN VISARGA

Independent vowels

0904 ऄ DEVANAGARI LETTER SHORT A
0905 अ DEVANAGARI LETTER A
0906 आ DEVANAGARI LETTER AA
0907 इ DEVANAGARI LETTER I
0908 ई DEVANAGARI LETTER II
0909 उ DEVANAGARI LETTER U
090A ऊ DEVANAGARI LETTER UU
090B ऋ DEVANAGARI LETTER VOCALIC R
090C ऌ DEVANAGARI LETTER VOCALIC L
090D ऍ DEVANAGARI LETTER CANDRA E
090E ऎ DEVANAGARI LETTER SHORT E
 • for transcribing Dravidian short e
090F ए DEVANAGARI LETTER E
0910 ऐ DEVANAGARI LETTER AI
0911 ऑ DEVANAGARI LETTER CANDRA O
0912 ऒ DEVANAGARI LETTER SHORT O
 • for transcribing Dravidian short o
0913 ओ DEVANAGARI LETTER O
0914 औ DEVANAGARI LETTER AU

Consonants

0915 क DEVANAGARI LETTER KA
0916 ख DEVANAGARI LETTER KHA
0917 ग DEVANAGARI LETTER GA
0918 घ DEVANAGARI LETTER GHA
0919 ङ DEVANAGARI LETTER NGA
091A च DEVANAGARI LETTER CA
091B छ DEVANAGARI LETTER CHA
091C ज DEVANAGARI LETTER JA
091D झ DEVANAGARI LETTER JHA
091E ञ DEVANAGARI LETTER NYA
091F ट DEVANAGARI LETTER TTA
0920 ठ DEVANAGARI LETTER TTHA
0921 ड DEVANAGARI LETTER DDA
0922 ढ DEVANAGARI LETTER DDHA
0923 ण DEVANAGARI LETTER NNA
0924 त DEVANAGARI LETTER TA
0925 थ DEVANAGARI LETTER THA
0926 द DEVANAGARI LETTER DA
0927 ध DEVANAGARI LETTER DHA
0928 न DEVANAGARI LETTER NA
0929 ऩ DEVANAGARI LETTER NNNA
 • for transcribing Dravidian alveolar n
 ≡ 0928 न 093C ◌़
092A प DEVANAGARI LETTER PA
092B फ DEVANAGARI LETTER PHA
092C ब DEVANAGARI LETTER BA
092D भ DEVANAGARI LETTER BHA
092E म DEVANAGARI LETTER MA
092F य DEVANAGARI LETTER YA
0930 र DEVANAGARI LETTER RA
0931 ऱ DEVANAGARI LETTER RRA
 • for transcribing Dravidian alveolar r
 • half form is represented as "Eyelash RA"
 ≡ 0930 र 093C ◌़
0932 ल DEVANAGARI LETTER LA
0933 ळ DEVANAGARI LETTER LLA
0934 ऴ DEVANAGARI LETTER LLLA
 • for transcribing Dravidian l
 ≡ 0933 ळ 093C ◌़
0935 व DEVANAGARI LETTER VA
0936 श DEVANAGARI LETTER SHA
0937 ष DEVANAGARI LETTER SSA
0938 स DEVANAGARI LETTER SA
0939 ह DEVANAGARI LETTER HA

Various signs

093C ◌़ DEVANAGARI SIGN NUKTA
 • for extending the alphabet to new letters
093D ऽ DEVANAGARI SIGN AVAGRAHA

Dependent vowel signs

093E ◌ा DEVANAGARI VOWEL SIGN AA
093F ◌ि DEVANAGARI VOWEL SIGN I
 • stands to the left of the consonant
0940 ◌ी DEVANAGARI VOWEL SIGN II
0941 ◌ु DEVANAGARI VOWEL SIGN U
0942 ◌ू DEVANAGARI VOWEL SIGN UU
0943 ◌ृ DEVANAGARI VOWEL SIGN VOCALIC R
0944 ◌ॄ DEVANAGARI VOWEL SIGN VOCALIC RR
0945 ◌ॅ DEVANAGARI VOWEL SIGN CANDRA E
 = candra
0946 ◌ॆ DEVANAGARI VOWEL SIGN SHORT E
 • for transcribing Dravidian vowels
0947 ◌े DEVANAGARI VOWEL SIGN E
0948 ◌ै DEVANAGARI VOWEL SIGN AI
0949 ◌ॉ DEVANAGARI VOWEL SIGN CANDRA O
094A ◌ॊ DEVANAGARI VOWEL SIGN SHORT O
 • for transcribing Dravidian vowels
094B ◌ो DEVANAGARI VOWEL SIGN O
094C ◌ौ DEVANAGARI VOWEL SIGN AU

Various signs

094D ◌् DEVANAGARI SIGN VIRAMA
 = halant (the preferred Hindi name)
 • suppresses inherent vowel
094E <reserved>
094F <reserved>
0950 ॐ DEVANAGARI OM
0951 ◌॑ DEVANAGARI STRESS SIGN UDATTA
 • mostly used for Rigvedic svarita, with rare use for Yajurvedic udatta
0952 ◌॒ DEVANAGARI STRESS SIGN ANUDATTA
0953 ◌॓ DEVANAGARI GRAVE ACCENT
0954 ◌॔ DEVANAGARI ACUTE ACCENT

Additional consonants

0958 क़ DEVANAGARI LETTER QA
 ≡ 0915 क 093C ◌़
0959 ख़ DEVANAGARI LETTER KHHA
 ≡ 0916 ख 093C ◌़
095A ग़ DEVANAGARI LETTER GHHA
 ≡ 0917 ग 093C ◌़
095B ज़ DEVANAGARI LETTER ZA
 ≡ 091C ज 093C ◌़
095C ड़ DEVANAGARI LETTER DDDHA
 ≡ 0921 ड 093C ◌़

095D ढ़ DEVANAGARI LETTER RHA
≡ 0922 ढ 093C ़
095E फ़ DEVANAGARI LETTER FA
≡ 092B फ 093C ़
095F य़ DEVANAGARI LETTER YYA
≡ 092F य 093C ़

Additional vowels for Sanskrit

0960 ॠ DEVANAGARI LETTER VOCALIC RR
0961 ॡ DEVANAGARI LETTER VOCALIC LL
0962 ॢ DEVANAGARI VOWEL SIGN VOCALIC L
0963 ॣ DEVANAGARI VOWEL SIGN VOCALIC LL

Generic punctuation for scripts of India

Note that despite the fact that these characters have "DEVANAGARI" in their names, these punctuation marks are intended for common use for the scripts of India.

0964 । DEVANAGARI DANDA
= purna viram
• phrase separator
0965 ॥ DEVANAGARI DOUBLE DANDA
= deergh viram

Digits

0966 ० DEVANAGARI DIGIT ZERO
0967 १ DEVANAGARI DIGIT ONE
0968 २ DEVANAGARI DIGIT TWO
0969 ३ DEVANAGARI DIGIT THREE
096A ४ DEVANAGARI DIGIT FOUR
096B ५ DEVANAGARI DIGIT FIVE
096C ६ DEVANAGARI DIGIT SIX
096D ७ DEVANAGARI DIGIT SEVEN
096E ८ DEVANAGARI DIGIT EIGHT
096F ९ DEVANAGARI DIGIT NINE

Devanagari-specific additions

0970 ॰ DEVANAGARI ABBREVIATION SIGN

Sindhi implosives

These are added from Amendment 3 to 10646:2003.

097B ॻ DEVANAGARI LETTER GGA
097C ॼ DEVANAGARI LETTER JJA

Glottal stop

097D ॽ DEVANAGARI LETTER GLOTTAL STOP
• used for writing Limbu in Devanagari
• a glyph variant has the connecting top bar

Sindhi implosives

These are added from Amendment 3 to 10646:2003.

097E ॾ DEVANAGARI LETTER DDDA
097F ॿ DEVANAGARI LETTER BBA

	098	099	09A	09B	09C	09D	09E	09F
0		ঐ 0990	ঠ 09A0	র 09B0	◌ী 09C0		ৠ 09E0	ৰ 09F0
1	◌ঁ 0981		ড 09A1		◌ু 09C1		ৡ 09E1	ৱ 09F1
2	◌ং 0982		ঢ 09A2	ল 09B2	◌ূ 09C2		◌ৢ 09E2	৲ 09F2
3	◌ঃ 0983	ও 0993	ণ 09A3		◌ৃ 09C3		◌ৣ 09E3	৳ 09F3
4		ঔ 0994	ত 09A4		◌ৄ 09C4			৴ 09F4
5	অ 0985	ক 0995	থ 09A5					৵ 09F5
6	আ 0986	খ 0996	দ 09A6	শ 09B6			০ 09E6	৶ 09F6
7	ই 0987	গ 0997	ধ 09A7	ষ 09B7	◌ে 09C7	◌ৗ 09D7	১ 09E7	৷ 09F7
8	ঈ 0988	ঘ 0998	ন 09A8	স 09B8	◌ৈ 09C8		২ 09E8	৸ 09F8
9	উ 0989	ঙ 0999		হ 09B9			৩ 09E9	৹ 09F9
A	ঊ 098A	চ 099A	প 09AA				৪ 09EA	৺ 09FA
B	ঋ 098B	ছ 099B	ফ 09AB		◌ো 09CB		৫ 09EB	
C	ঌ 098C	জ 099C	ব 09AC	◌় 09BC	◌ৌ 09CC	ড় 09DC	৬ 09EC	
D		ঝ 099D	ভ 09AD	ঽ 09BD	◌্ 09CD	ঢ় 09DD	৭ 09ED	
E		ঞ 099E	ম 09AE	◌া 09BE	ৎ 09CE		৮ 09EE	
F	এ 098F	ট 099F	য 09AF	◌ি 09BF		য় 09DF	৯ 09EF	

Based on ISCII 1988

Various signs

0981 ◌ঁ BENGALI SIGN CANDRABINDU
0982 ◌ং BENGALI SIGN ANUSVARA
0983 ◌ঃ BENGALI SIGN VISARGA

Independent vowels

0985 অ BENGALI LETTER A
0986 আ BENGALI LETTER AA
0987 ই BENGALI LETTER I
0988 ঈ BENGALI LETTER II
0989 উ BENGALI LETTER U
098A ঊ BENGALI LETTER UU
098B ঋ BENGALI LETTER VOCALIC R
098C ঌ BENGALI LETTER VOCALIC L
098D <reserved>
098E <reserved>
098F এ BENGALI LETTER E
0990 ঐ BENGALI LETTER AI
0991 <reserved>
0992 <reserved>
0993 ও BENGALI LETTER O
0994 ঔ BENGALI LETTER AU

Consonants

0995 ক BENGALI LETTER KA
0996 খ BENGALI LETTER KHA
0997 গ BENGALI LETTER GA
0998 ঘ BENGALI LETTER GHA
0999 ঙ BENGALI LETTER NGA
099A চ BENGALI LETTER CA
099B ছ BENGALI LETTER CHA
099C জ BENGALI LETTER JA
099D ঝ BENGALI LETTER JHA
099E ঞ BENGALI LETTER NYA
099F ট BENGALI LETTER TTA
09A0 ঠ BENGALI LETTER TTHA
09A1 ড BENGALI LETTER DDA
09A2 ঢ BENGALI LETTER DDHA
09A3 ণ BENGALI LETTER NNA
09A4 ত BENGALI LETTER TA
09A5 থ BENGALI LETTER THA
09A6 দ BENGALI LETTER DA
09A7 ধ BENGALI LETTER DHA
09A8 ন BENGALI LETTER NA
09A9 <reserved>
09AA প BENGALI LETTER PA
09AB ফ BENGALI LETTER PHA
09AC ব BENGALI LETTER BA
= Bengali va, wa
09AD ভ BENGALI LETTER BHA
09AE ম BENGALI LETTER MA
09AF য BENGALI LETTER YA
09B0 র BENGALI LETTER RA
09B1 <reserved>
09B2 ল BENGALI LETTER LA
09B3 <reserved>
09B4 <reserved>
09B5 <reserved>
09B6 শ BENGALI LETTER SHA
09B7 ষ BENGALI LETTER SSA
09B8 স BENGALI LETTER SA
09B9 হ BENGALI LETTER HA

Various signs

09BC ◌় BENGALI SIGN NUKTA
• for extending the alphabet to new letters
09BD ঽ BENGALI SIGN AVAGRAHA

Dependent vowel signs

09BE ◌া BENGALI VOWEL SIGN AA
09BF ◌ি BENGALI VOWEL SIGN I
• stands to the left of the consonant
09C0 ◌ী BENGALI VOWEL SIGN II
09C1 ◌ু BENGALI VOWEL SIGN U
09C2 ◌ূ BENGALI VOWEL SIGN UU
09C3 ◌ৃ BENGALI VOWEL SIGN VOCALIC R
09C4 ◌ৄ BENGALI VOWEL SIGN VOCALIC RR
09C5 <reserved>
09C6 <reserved>
09C7 ◌ে BENGALI VOWEL SIGN E
• stands to the left of the consonant
09C8 ◌ৈ BENGALI VOWEL SIGN AI
• stands to the left of the consonant

Two-part dependent vowel signs

These two-part dependent vowel signs have glyph pieces which stand on both sides of the consonant. These vowel signs follow the consonant in logical order, and should be handled as a unit for most processing.

09CB ◌ো BENGALI VOWEL SIGN O
≡ 09C7 ◌ে 09BE ◌া
09CC ◌ৌ BENGALI VOWEL SIGN AU
≡ 09C7 ◌ে 09D7 ◌ৗ

Sign

09CD ◌্ BENGALI SIGN VIRAMA
= hasant (Bengali term for halant)

Additional consonant

09CE ৎ BENGALI LETTER KHANDA TA

Sign

09D7 ◌ৗ BENGALI AU LENGTH MARK

Additional consonants

09DC ড় BENGALI LETTER RRA
≡ 09A1 ড 09BC ◌়
09DD ঢ় BENGALI LETTER RHA
≡ 09A2 ঢ 09BC ◌়
09DE <reserved>
09DF য় BENGALI LETTER YYA
≡ 09AF য 09BC ◌়

Additional vowels for Sanskrit

09E0 ৠ BENGALI LETTER VOCALIC RR
09E1 ৡ BENGALI LETTER VOCALIC LL
09E2 ◌ৢ BENGALI VOWEL SIGN VOCALIC L
09E3 ◌ৣ BENGALI VOWEL SIGN VOCALIC LL

Reserved

For viram punctuation, use the generic Indic 0964 and 0965.

09E4 <reserved>
→ 0964 । devanagari danda
09E5 <reserved>
→ 0965 ॥ devanagari double danda

Digits

09E6 ০ BENGALI DIGIT ZERO
09E7 ১ BENGALI DIGIT ONE
09E8 ২ BENGALI DIGIT TWO
09E9 ৩ BENGALI DIGIT THREE

09EA ৪ BENGALI DIGIT FOUR
09EB ৫ BENGALI DIGIT FIVE
09EC ৬ BENGALI DIGIT SIX
09ED ৭ BENGALI DIGIT SEVEN
09EE ৮ BENGALI DIGIT EIGHT
09EF ৯ BENGALI DIGIT NINE

Bengali-specific additions

09F0 ৰ BENGALI LETTER RA WITH MIDDLE DIAGONAL
• Assamese
09F1 ৱ BENGALI LETTER RA WITH LOWER DIAGONAL
= bengali letter va with lower diagonal (1.0)
• Assamese
09F2 ৲ BENGALI RUPEE MARK
09F3 ৳ BENGALI RUPEE SIGN
09F4 ৴ BENGALI CURRENCY NUMERATOR ONE
• not in current usage
09F5 ৵ BENGALI CURRENCY NUMERATOR TWO
• not in current usage
09F6 ৶ BENGALI CURRENCY NUMERATOR THREE
• not in current usage
09F7 ৷ BENGALI CURRENCY NUMERATOR FOUR
09F8 ৸ BENGALI CURRENCY NUMERATOR ONE LESS THAN THE DENOMINATOR
09F9 ৹ BENGALI CURRENCY DENOMINATOR SIXTEEN
09FA ৺ BENGALI ISSHAR

	0A0	0A1	0A2	0A3	0A4	0A5	0A6	0A7
0		ਐ 0A10	ਠ 0A20	ਰ 0A30	◌ੀ 0A40			◌ੰ 0A70
1	◌ਁ 0A01		ਡ 0A21		◌ੁ 0A41			◌ੱ 0A71
2	◌ਂ 0A02		ਢ 0A22	ਲ 0A32	◌ੂ 0A42			ੲ 0A72
3	◌ਃ 0A03	ਓ 0A13	ਣ 0A23	ਲ਼ 0A33				ੳ 0A73
4		ਔ 0A14	ਤ 0A24					ੴ 0A74
5	ਅ 0A05	ਕ 0A15	ਥ 0A25	ਵ 0A35				
6	ਆ 0A06	ਖ 0A16	ਦ 0A26	ਸ਼ 0A36			੦ 0A66	
7	ਇ 0A07	ਗ 0A17	ਧ 0A27		◌ੇ 0A47		੧ 0A67	
8	ਈ 0A08	ਘ 0A18	ਨ 0A28	ਸ 0A38	◌ੈ 0A48		੨ 0A68	
9	ਉ 0A09	ਙ 0A19		ਹ 0A39		ਖ਼ 0A59	੩ 0A69	
A	ਊ 0A0A	ਚ 0A1A	ਪ 0A2A			ਗ਼ 0A5A	੪ 0A6A	
B		ਛ 0A1B	ਫ 0A2B		◌ੋ 0A4B	ਜ਼ 0A5B	੫ 0A6B	
C		ਜ 0A1C	ਬ 0A2C	◌਼ 0A3C	◌ੌ 0A4C	ੜ 0A5C	੬ 0A6C	
D		ਝ 0A1D	ਭ 0A2D		◌੍ 0A4D		੭ 0A6D	
E		ਞ 0A1E	ਮ 0A2E	◌ਾ 0A3E		ਫ਼ 0A5E	੮ 0A6E	
F	ਏ 0A0F	ਟ 0A1F	ਯ 0A2F	◌ਿ 0A3F			੯ 0A6F	

Based on ISCII 1988

Various signs

0A01 ◌ਁ GURMUKHI SIGN ADAK BINDI
0A02 ◌ਂ GURMUKHI SIGN BINDI
0A03 ◌ਃ GURMUKHI SIGN VISARGA

Independent vowels

0A05 ਅ GURMUKHI LETTER A
= aira
0A06 ਆ GURMUKHI LETTER AA
0A07 ਇ GURMUKHI LETTER I
0A08 ਈ GURMUKHI LETTER II
0A09 ਉ GURMUKHI LETTER U
0A0A ਊ GURMUKHI LETTER UU
0A0B <reserved>
0A0C <reserved>
0A0D <reserved>
0A0E <reserved>
0A0F ਏ GURMUKHI LETTER EE
0A10 ਐ GURMUKHI LETTER AI
0A11 <reserved>
0A12 <reserved>
0A13 ਓ GURMUKHI LETTER OO
0A14 ਔ GURMUKHI LETTER AU

Consonants

0A15 ਕ GURMUKHI LETTER KA
0A16 ਖ GURMUKHI LETTER KHA
0A17 ਗ GURMUKHI LETTER GA
0A18 ਘ GURMUKHI LETTER GHA
0A19 ਙ GURMUKHI LETTER NGA
0A1A ਚ GURMUKHI LETTER CA
0A1B ਛ GURMUKHI LETTER CHA
0A1C ਜ GURMUKHI LETTER JA
0A1D ਝ GURMUKHI LETTER JHA
0A1E ਞ GURMUKHI LETTER NYA
0A1F ਟ GURMUKHI LETTER TTA
0A20 ਠ GURMUKHI LETTER TTHA
0A21 ਡ GURMUKHI LETTER DDA
0A22 ਢ GURMUKHI LETTER DDHA
0A23 ਣ GURMUKHI LETTER NNA
0A24 ਤ GURMUKHI LETTER TA
0A25 ਥ GURMUKHI LETTER THA
0A26 ਦ GURMUKHI LETTER DA
0A27 ਧ GURMUKHI LETTER DHA
0A28 ਨ GURMUKHI LETTER NA
0A29 <reserved>
0A2A ਪ GURMUKHI LETTER PA
0A2B ਫ GURMUKHI LETTER PHA
0A2C ਬ GURMUKHI LETTER BA
0A2D ਭ GURMUKHI LETTER BHA
0A2E ਮ GURMUKHI LETTER MA
0A2F ਯ GURMUKHI LETTER YA
0A30 ਰ GURMUKHI LETTER RA
0A31 <reserved>
0A32 ਲ GURMUKHI LETTER LA
0A33 ਲ਼ GURMUKHI LETTER LLA
≡ 0A32 ਲ 0A3C ◌਼
0A34 <reserved>
0A35 ਵ GURMUKHI LETTER VA
0A36 ਸ਼ GURMUKHI LETTER SHA
≡ 0A38 ਸ 0A3C ◌਼
0A37 <reserved>
0A38 ਸ GURMUKHI LETTER SA
0A39 ਹ GURMUKHI LETTER HA

Various signs

0A3C ◌਼ GURMUKHI SIGN NUKTA
= pairin bindi
• for extending the alphabet to new letters

Dependent vowel signs

0A3E ◌ਾ GURMUKHI VOWEL SIGN AA
= kanna
0A3F ਿ◌ GURMUKHI VOWEL SIGN I
= sihari
• stands to the left of the consonant
0A40 ◌ੀ GURMUKHI VOWEL SIGN II
= bihari
0A41 ◌ੁ GURMUKHI VOWEL SIGN U
= aunkar
0A42 ◌ੂ GURMUKHI VOWEL SIGN UU
= dulainkar
0A43 <reserved>
0A44 <reserved>
0A45 <reserved>
0A46 <reserved>
0A47 ◌ੇ GURMUKHI VOWEL SIGN EE
= lanvan
0A48 ◌ੈ GURMUKHI VOWEL SIGN AI
= dulanvan
0A49 <reserved>
0A4A <reserved>
0A4B ◌ੋ GURMUKHI VOWEL SIGN OO
= hora
0A4C ◌ੌ GURMUKHI VOWEL SIGN AU
= kanaura

Various signs

0A4D ◌੍ GURMUKHI SIGN VIRAMA

Additional consonants

0A59 ਖ਼ GURMUKHI LETTER KHHA
≡ 0A16 ਖ 0A3C ◌਼
0A5A ਗ਼ GURMUKHI LETTER GHHA
≡ 0A17 ਗ 0A3C ◌਼
0A5B ਜ਼ GURMUKHI LETTER ZA
≡ 0A1C ਜ 0A3C ◌਼
0A5C ੜ GURMUKHI LETTER RRA
0A5D <reserved>
0A5E ਫ਼ GURMUKHI LETTER FA
≡ 0A2B ਫ 0A3C ◌਼

Reserved

For viram punctuation, use the generic Indic 0964 and 0965.

0A64 <reserved>
→ 0964 । devanagari danda
0A65 <reserved>
→ 0965 ॥ devanagari double danda

Digits

0A66 ੦ GURMUKHI DIGIT ZERO
0A67 ੧ GURMUKHI DIGIT ONE
0A68 ੨ GURMUKHI DIGIT TWO
0A69 ੩ GURMUKHI DIGIT THREE
0A6A ੪ GURMUKHI DIGIT FOUR
0A6B ੫ GURMUKHI DIGIT FIVE
0A6C ੬ GURMUKHI DIGIT SIX
0A6D ੭ GURMUKHI DIGIT SEVEN
0A6E ੮ GURMUKHI DIGIT EIGHT
0A6F ੯ GURMUKHI DIGIT NINE

Gurmukhi-specific additions

0A70 ੰ GURMUKHI TIPPI
• nasalization

0A71 ੱ GURMUKHI ADDAK
• doubles following consonant

0A72 ੲ GURMUKHI IRI
• base for vowels

0A73 ੳ GURMUKHI URA
• base for vowels

0A74 ੴ GURMUKHI EK ONKAR
• God is One

	0A8	0A9	0AA	0AB	0AC	0AD	0AE	0AF
0		ઐ 0A90	ઠ 0AA0	ર 0AB0	◌ી 0AC0	ૐ 0AD0	ૠ 0AE0	
1	◌ઁ 0A81	ઑ 0A91	ડ 0AA1		◌ુ 0AC1		ૡ 0AE1	૱ 0AF1
2	◌ં 0A82		ઢ 0AA2	લ 0AB2	◌ૂ 0AC2		◌ૢ 0AE2	
3	◌ઃ 0A83	ઓ 0A93	ણ 0AA3	ળ 0AB3	◌ૃ 0AC3		◌ૣ 0AE3	
4		ઔ 0A94	ત 0AA4		◌ૄ 0AC4			
5	અ 0A85	ક 0A95	થ 0AA5	વ 0AB5	◌ૅ 0AC5			
6	આ 0A86	ખ 0A96	દ 0AA6	શ 0AB6			૦ 0AE6	
7	ઇ 0A87	ગ 0A97	ધ 0AA7	ષ 0AB7	◌ે 0AC7		૧ 0AE7	
8	ઈ 0A88	ઘ 0A98	ન 0AA8	સ 0AB8	◌ૈ 0AC8		૨ 0AE8	
9	ઉ 0A89	ઙ 0A99		હ 0AB9	◌ૉ 0AC9		૩ 0AE9	
A	ઊ 0A8A	ચ 0A9A	પ 0AAA				૪ 0AEA	
B	ઋ 0A8B	છ 0A9B	ફ 0AAB		◌ો 0ACB		૫ 0AEB	
C	ઌ 0A8C	જ 0A9C	બ 0AAC	◌઼ 0ABC	◌ૌ 0ACC		૬ 0AEC	
D	ઍ 0A8D	ઝ 0A9D	ભ 0AAD	ઽ 0ABD	◌્ 0ACD		૭ 0AED	
E		ઞ 0A9E	મ 0AAE	◌ા 0ABE			૮ 0AEE	
F	એ 0A8F	ટ 0A9F	ય 0AAF	◌િ 0ABF			૯ 0AEF	

Based on ISCII 1988

Various signs

0A81 ઁ GUJARATI SIGN CANDRABINDU
0A82 ં GUJARATI SIGN ANUSVARA
0A83 ઃ GUJARATI SIGN VISARGA

Independent vowels

0A85 અ GUJARATI LETTER A
0A86 આ GUJARATI LETTER AA
0A87 ઇ GUJARATI LETTER I
0A88 ઈ GUJARATI LETTER II
0A89 ઉ GUJARATI LETTER U
0A8A ઊ GUJARATI LETTER UU
0A8B ઋ GUJARATI LETTER VOCALIC R
0A8C ઌ GUJARATI LETTER VOCALIC L
- used with Sanskrit text

0A8D ઍ GUJARATI VOWEL CANDRA E
0A8E <reserved>
0A8F એ GUJARATI LETTER E
0A90 ઐ GUJARATI LETTER AI
0A91 ઑ GUJARATI VOWEL CANDRA O
0A92 <reserved>
0A93 ઓ GUJARATI LETTER O
0A94 ઔ GUJARATI LETTER AU

Consonants

0A95 ક GUJARATI LETTER KA
0A96 ખ GUJARATI LETTER KHA
0A97 ગ GUJARATI LETTER GA
0A98 ઘ GUJARATI LETTER GHA
0A99 ઙ GUJARATI LETTER NGA
0A9A ચ GUJARATI LETTER CA
0A9B છ GUJARATI LETTER CHA
0A9C જ GUJARATI LETTER JA
0A9D ઝ GUJARATI LETTER JHA
0A9E ઞ GUJARATI LETTER NYA
0A9F ટ GUJARATI LETTER TTA
0AA0 ઠ GUJARATI LETTER TTHA
0AA1 ડ GUJARATI LETTER DDA
0AA2 ઢ GUJARATI LETTER DDHA
0AA3 ણ GUJARATI LETTER NNA
0AA4 ત GUJARATI LETTER TA
0AA5 થ GUJARATI LETTER THA
0AA6 દ GUJARATI LETTER DA
0AA7 ધ GUJARATI LETTER DHA
0AA8 ન GUJARATI LETTER NA
0AA9 <reserved>
0AAA પ GUJARATI LETTER PA
0AAB ફ GUJARATI LETTER PHA
0AAC બ GUJARATI LETTER BA
0AAD ભ GUJARATI LETTER BHA
0AAE મ GUJARATI LETTER MA
0AAF ય GUJARATI LETTER YA
0AB0 ર GUJARATI LETTER RA
0AB1 <reserved>
0AB2 લ GUJARATI LETTER LA
0AB3 ળ GUJARATI LETTER LLA
0AB4 <reserved>
0AB5 વ GUJARATI LETTER VA
0AB6 શ GUJARATI LETTER SHA
0AB7 ષ GUJARATI LETTER SSA
0AB8 સ GUJARATI LETTER SA
0AB9 હ GUJARATI LETTER HA

Various signs

0ABC ઼ GUJARATI SIGN NUKTA
- for extending the alphabet to new letters

0ABD ઽ GUJARATI SIGN AVAGRAHA

Dependent vowel signs

0ABE ા GUJARATI VOWEL SIGN AA
0ABF િ GUJARATI VOWEL SIGN I
- stands to the left of the consonant

0AC0 ી GUJARATI VOWEL SIGN II
0AC1 ુ GUJARATI VOWEL SIGN U
0AC2 ૂ GUJARATI VOWEL SIGN UU
0AC3 ૃ GUJARATI VOWEL SIGN VOCALIC R
0AC4 ૄ GUJARATI VOWEL SIGN VOCALIC RR
0AC5 ૅ GUJARATI VOWEL SIGN CANDRA E
0AC6 <reserved>
0AC7 ે GUJARATI VOWEL SIGN E
0AC8 ૈ GUJARATI VOWEL SIGN AI
0AC9 ૉ GUJARATI VOWEL SIGN CANDRA O
0ACA <reserved>
0ACB ો GUJARATI VOWEL SIGN O
0ACC ૌ GUJARATI VOWEL SIGN AU

Various signs

0ACD ્ GUJARATI SIGN VIRAMA
0ACE <reserved>
0ACF <reserved>
0AD0 ૐ GUJARATI OM

Additional vowels for Sanskrit

0AE0 ૠ GUJARATI LETTER VOCALIC RR
0AE1 ૡ GUJARATI LETTER VOCALIC LL
0AE2 ૢ GUJARATI VOWEL SIGN VOCALIC L
0AE3 ૣ GUJARATI VOWEL SIGN VOCALIC LL

Reserved

For viram punctuation, use the generic Indic 0964 and 0965.

0AE4 <reserved>
→ 0964 । devanagari danda

0AE5 <reserved>
→ 0965 ॥ devanagari double danda

Digits

0AE6 ૦ GUJARATI DIGIT ZERO
0AE7 ૧ GUJARATI DIGIT ONE
0AE8 ૨ GUJARATI DIGIT TWO
0AE9 ૩ GUJARATI DIGIT THREE
0AEA ૪ GUJARATI DIGIT FOUR
0AEB ૫ GUJARATI DIGIT FIVE
0AEC ૬ GUJARATI DIGIT SIX
0AED ૭ GUJARATI DIGIT SEVEN
0AEE ૮ GUJARATI DIGIT EIGHT
0AEF ૯ GUJARATI DIGIT NINE

Currency sign

0AF1 ૱ GUJARATI RUPEE SIGN

	0B0	0B1	0B2	0B3	0B4	0B5	0B6	0B7
0		ଐ 0B10	ଠ 0B20	ର 0B30	◌ୀ 0B40		ୠ 0B60	୰ 0B70
1	◌ଁ 0B01		ଡ 0B21		◌ୁ 0B41		ୡ 0B61	ୱ 0B71
2	◌ଂ 0B02		ଢ 0B22	ଲ 0B32	◌ୂ 0B42			
3	◌ଃ 0B03	ଓ 0B13	ଣ 0B23	ଳ 0B33	◌ୃ 0B43			
4		ଔ 0B14	ତ 0B24					
5	ଅ 0B05	କ 0B15	ଥ 0B25	ଵ 0B35				
6	ଆ 0B06	ଖ 0B16	ଦ 0B26	ଶ 0B36		◌ୖ 0B56	୦ 0B66	
7	ଇ 0B07	ଗ 0B17	ଧ 0B27	ଷ 0B37	◌େ 0B47	◌ୗ 0B57	୧ 0B67	
8	ଈ 0B08	ଘ 0B18	ନ 0B28	ସ 0B38	◌ୈ 0B48		୨ 0B68	
9	ଉ 0B09	ଙ 0B19		ହ 0B39			୩ 0B69	
A	ଊ 0B0A	ଚ 0B1A	ପ 0B2A				୪ 0B6A	
B	ଋ 0B0B	ଛ 0B1B	ଫ 0B2B		◌ୋ 0B4B		୫ 0B6B	
C	ଌ 0B0C	ଜ 0B1C	ବ 0B2C	◌଼ 0B3C	◌ୌ 0B4C	ଡ଼ 0B5C	୬ 0B6C	
D		ଝ 0B1D	ଭ 0B2D	ଽ 0B3D	◌୍ 0B4D	ଢ଼ 0B5D	୭ 0B6D	
E		ଞ 0B1E	ମ 0B2E	◌ା 0B3E			୮ 0B6E	
F	ଏ 0B0F	ଟ 0B1F	ଯ 0B2F	◌ି 0B3F		ୟ 0B5F	୯ 0B6F	

Based on ISCII 1988

Various signs

0B01 ◌ଁ ORIYA SIGN CANDRABINDU
0B02 ◌ଂ ORIYA SIGN ANUSVARA
0B03 ◌ଃ ORIYA SIGN VISARGA

Independent vowels

0B05 ଅ ORIYA LETTER A
0B06 ଆ ORIYA LETTER AA
0B07 ଇ ORIYA LETTER I
0B08 ଈ ORIYA LETTER II
0B09 ଉ ORIYA LETTER U
0B0A ଊ ORIYA LETTER UU
0B0B ଋ ORIYA LETTER VOCALIC R
0B0C ଌ ORIYA LETTER VOCALIC L
0B0D <reserved>
0B0E <reserved>
0B0F ଏ ORIYA LETTER E
0B10 ଐ ORIYA LETTER AI
0B11 <reserved>
0B12 <reserved>
0B13 ଓ ORIYA LETTER O
0B14 ଔ ORIYA LETTER AU

Consonants

0B15 କ ORIYA LETTER KA
0B16 ଖ ORIYA LETTER KHA
0B17 ଗ ORIYA LETTER GA
0B18 ଘ ORIYA LETTER GHA
0B19 ଙ ORIYA LETTER NGA
0B1A ଚ ORIYA LETTER CA
0B1B ଛ ORIYA LETTER CHA
0B1C ଜ ORIYA LETTER JA
0B1D ଝ ORIYA LETTER JHA
0B1E ଞ ORIYA LETTER NYA
0B1F ଟ ORIYA LETTER TTA
0B20 ଠ ORIYA LETTER TTHA
0B21 ଡ ORIYA LETTER DDA
0B22 ଢ ORIYA LETTER DDHA
0B23 ଣ ORIYA LETTER NNA
0B24 ତ ORIYA LETTER TA
0B25 ଥ ORIYA LETTER THA
0B26 ଦ ORIYA LETTER DA
0B27 ଧ ORIYA LETTER DHA
0B28 ନ ORIYA LETTER NA
0B29 <reserved>
0B2A ପ ORIYA LETTER PA
0B2B ଫ ORIYA LETTER PHA
0B2C ବ ORIYA LETTER BA
→ 0B35 ଵ oriya letter va
0B2D ଭ ORIYA LETTER BHA
0B2E ମ ORIYA LETTER MA
0B2F ଯ ORIYA LETTER YA
= ja
0B30 ର ORIYA LETTER RA
0B31 <reserved>
0B32 ଲ ORIYA LETTER LA
0B33 ଳ ORIYA LETTER LLA
0B34 <reserved>
0B35 ଵ ORIYA LETTER VA
→ 0B2C ବ oriya letter ba
0B36 ଶ ORIYA LETTER SHA
0B37 ଷ ORIYA LETTER SSA
0B38 ସ ORIYA LETTER SA
0B39 ହ ORIYA LETTER HA

Various signs

0B3C ◌଼ ORIYA SIGN NUKTA
• for extending the alphabet to new letters
0B3D ଽ ORIYA SIGN AVAGRAHA

Dependent vowel signs

0B3E ◌ା ORIYA VOWEL SIGN AA
0B3F ◌ି ORIYA VOWEL SIGN I
0B40 ◌ୀ ORIYA VOWEL SIGN II
0B41 ◌ୁ ORIYA VOWEL SIGN U
0B42 ◌ୂ ORIYA VOWEL SIGN UU
0B43 ◌ୃ ORIYA VOWEL SIGN VOCALIC R
0B44 <reserved>
0B45 <reserved>
0B46 <reserved>
0B47 ◌େ ORIYA VOWEL SIGN E
• stands to the left of the consonant
0B48 ◌ୈ ORIYA VOWEL SIGN AI
• pieces left of and above the consonant
≡ 0B47 ◌େ 0B56 ◌ୖ

Two-part dependent vowel signs

These two-part dependent vowel signs have glyph pieces which stand on both sides of the consonant. These vowel signs follow the consonant in logical order, and should be handled as a unit for most processing.

0B4B ◌ୋ ORIYA VOWEL SIGN O
≡ 0B47 ◌େ 0B3E ◌ା
0B4C ◌ୌ ORIYA VOWEL SIGN AU
≡ 0B47 ◌େ 0B57 ◌ୗ

Various signs

0B4D ◌୍ ORIYA SIGN VIRAMA
0B4E <reserved>
0B4F <reserved>
0B50 <reserved>
0B51 <reserved>
0B52 <reserved>
0B53 <reserved>
0B54 <reserved>
0B55 <reserved>
0B56 ◌ୖ ORIYA AI LENGTH MARK
0B57 ◌ୗ ORIYA AU LENGTH MARK

Additional consonants

0B5C ଡ଼ ORIYA LETTER RRA
= dda
≡ 0B21 ଡ 0B3C ◌଼
0B5D ଢ଼ ORIYA LETTER RHA
= ddha
≡ 0B22 ଢ 0B3C ◌଼
0B5E <reserved>
0B5F ୟ ORIYA LETTER YYA
= ya

Additional vowels for Sanskrit

0B60 ୠ ORIYA LETTER VOCALIC RR
0B61 ୡ ORIYA LETTER VOCALIC LL

Reserved

For viram punctuation, use the generic Indic 0964 and 0965.

0B64 <reserved>
→ 0964 । devanagari danda
0B65 <reserved>
→ 0965 ॥ devanagari double danda

Digits

0B66 ୦ ORIYA DIGIT ZERO
0B67 ୧ ORIYA DIGIT ONE
0B68 ୨ ORIYA DIGIT TWO
0B69 ୩ ORIYA DIGIT THREE
0B6A ୪ ORIYA DIGIT FOUR
0B6B ୫ ORIYA DIGIT FIVE
0B6C ୬ ORIYA DIGIT SIX
0B6D ୭ ORIYA DIGIT SEVEN
0B6E ୮ ORIYA DIGIT EIGHT
0B6F ୯ ORIYA DIGIT NINE

Oriya-specific additions

0B70 ୰ ORIYA ISSHAR
0B71 ୱ ORIYA LETTER WA
→ 0B13 ଓ oriya letter o
→ 0B35 ଵ oriya letter va

	0B8	0B9	0BA	0BB	0BC	0BD	0BE	0BF
0		ஐ 0B90		ர 0BB0	◌ீ 0BC0			௰ 0BF0
1				ற 0BB1	◌ு 0BC1			௱ 0BF1
2	◌ஂ 0B82	ஒ 0B92		ல 0BB2	◌ூ 0BC2			௲ 0BF2
3	ஃ 0B83	ஓ 0B93	ண 0BA3	ள 0BB3				௳ 0BF3
4		ஔ 0B94	த 0BA4	ழ 0BB4				௴ 0BF4
5	அ 0B85	க 0B95		வ 0BB5				௵ 0BF5
6	ஆ 0B86			ஶ 0BB6	◌ெ 0BC6		௦ 0BE6	௶ 0BF6
7	இ 0B87			ஷ 0BB7	◌ே 0BC7	◌ௗ 0BD7	௧ 0BE7	௷ 0BF7
8	ஈ 0B88		ந 0BA8	ஸ 0BB8	◌ை 0BC8		௨ 0BE8	௸ 0BF8
9	உ 0B89	ங 0B99	ன 0BA9	ஹ 0BB9			௩ 0BE9	௹ 0BF9
A	ஊ 0B8A	ச 0B9A	ப 0BAA		◌ொ 0BCA		௪ 0BEA	௺ 0BFA
B					◌ோ 0BCB		௫ 0BEB	
C		ஜ 0B9C			◌ௌ 0BCC		௬ 0BEC	
D					◌் 0BCD		௭ 0BED	
E	எ 0B8E	ஞ 0B9E	ம 0BAE	◌ா 0BBE			௮ 0BEE	
F	ஏ 0B8F	ட 0B9F	ய 0BAF	◌ி 0BBF			௯ 0BEF	

Based on ISCII 1988

Various signs

0B82 ◌ஂ TAMIL SIGN ANUSVARA
• not used in Tamil
0B83 ஃ TAMIL SIGN VISARGA
= aytham

Independent vowels

0B85 அ TAMIL LETTER A
0B86 ஆ TAMIL LETTER AA
0B87 இ TAMIL LETTER I
0B88 ஈ TAMIL LETTER II
0B89 உ TAMIL LETTER U
0B8A ஊ TAMIL LETTER UU
0B8B <reserved>
0B8C <reserved>
0B8D <reserved>
0B8E எ TAMIL LETTER E
0B8F ஏ TAMIL LETTER EE
0B90 ஐ TAMIL LETTER AI
0B91 <reserved>
0B92 ஒ TAMIL LETTER O
0B93 ஓ TAMIL LETTER OO
0B94 ஔ TAMIL LETTER AU
≡ 0B92 ஒ 0BD7 ◌ௗ

Consonants

0B95 க TAMIL LETTER KA
0B96 <reserved>
0B97 <reserved>
0B98 <reserved>
0B99 ங TAMIL LETTER NGA
0B9A ச TAMIL LETTER CA
0B9B <reserved>
0B9C ஜ TAMIL LETTER JA
0B9D <reserved>
0B9E ஞ TAMIL LETTER NYA
0B9F ட TAMIL LETTER TTA
0BA0 <reserved>
0BA1 <reserved>
0BA2 <reserved>
0BA3 ண TAMIL LETTER NNA
0BA4 த TAMIL LETTER TA
0BA5 <reserved>
0BA6 <reserved>
0BA7 <reserved>
0BA8 ந TAMIL LETTER NA
0BA9 ன TAMIL LETTER NNNA
0BAA ப TAMIL LETTER PA
0BAB <reserved>
0BAC <reserved>
0BAD <reserved>
0BAE ம TAMIL LETTER MA
0BAF ய TAMIL LETTER YA
0BB0 ர TAMIL LETTER RA
0BB1 ற TAMIL LETTER RRA
0BB2 ல TAMIL LETTER LA
0BB3 ள TAMIL LETTER LLA
0BB4 ழ TAMIL LETTER LLLA
0BB5 வ TAMIL LETTER VA
0BB6 ஶ TAMIL LETTER SHA
0BB7 ஷ TAMIL LETTER SSA
0BB8 ஸ TAMIL LETTER SA
0BB9 ஹ TAMIL LETTER HA

Dependent vowel signs

0BBE ◌ா TAMIL VOWEL SIGN AA
0BBF ◌ி TAMIL VOWEL SIGN I
0BC0 ◌ீ TAMIL VOWEL SIGN II
0BC1 ◌ு TAMIL VOWEL SIGN U
0BC2 ◌ூ TAMIL VOWEL SIGN UU
0BC3 <reserved>
0BC4 <reserved>
0BC5 <reserved>
0BC6 ◌ெ TAMIL VOWEL SIGN E
• stands to the left of the consonant
0BC7 ◌ே TAMIL VOWEL SIGN EE
• stands to the left of the consonant
0BC8 ◌ை TAMIL VOWEL SIGN AI
• stands to the left of the consonant

Two-part dependent vowel signs

These two-part dependent vowel signs have glyph pieces which stand on both sides of the consonant. These vowel signs follow the consonant in logical order, and should be handled as a unit for most processing.

0BCA ◌ொ TAMIL VOWEL SIGN O
≡ 0BC6 ◌ெ 0BBE ◌ா
0BCB ◌ோ TAMIL VOWEL SIGN OO
≡ 0BC7 ◌ே 0BBE ◌ா
0BCC ◌ௌ TAMIL VOWEL SIGN AU
≡ 0BC6 ◌ெ 0BD7 ◌ௗ

Various signs

0BCD ◌் TAMIL SIGN VIRAMA
0BCE <reserved>
0BCF <reserved>
0BD0 <reserved>
0BD1 <reserved>
0BD2 <reserved>
0BD3 <reserved>
0BD4 <reserved>
0BD5 <reserved>
0BD6 <reserved>
0BD7 ◌ௗ TAMIL AU LENGTH MARK

Reserved

For viram punctuation, use the generic Indic 0964 and 0965.

0BE4 <reserved>
→ 0964 । devanagari danda
0BE5 <reserved>
→ 0965 ॥ devanagari double danda

Digits

0BE6 ௦ TAMIL DIGIT ZERO
0BE7 ௧ TAMIL DIGIT ONE
0BE8 ௨ TAMIL DIGIT TWO
0BE9 ௩ TAMIL DIGIT THREE
0BEA ௪ TAMIL DIGIT FOUR
0BEB ௫ TAMIL DIGIT FIVE
0BEC ௬ TAMIL DIGIT SIX
0BED ௭ TAMIL DIGIT SEVEN
0BEE ௮ TAMIL DIGIT EIGHT
0BEF ௯ TAMIL DIGIT NINE

Tamil numerics

0BF0 ௰ TAMIL NUMBER TEN
0BF1 ௱ TAMIL NUMBER ONE HUNDRED
0BF2 ௲ TAMIL NUMBER ONE THOUSAND

Tamil symbols

0BF3 ௳ TAMIL DAY SIGN
0BF4 ௴ TAMIL MONTH SIGN
0BF5 ௵ TAMIL YEAR SIGN
0BF6 ௶ TAMIL DEBIT SIGN
0BF7 ௷ TAMIL CREDIT SIGN
0BF8 ௸ TAMIL AS ABOVE SIGN

Currency symbol

0BF9 ௹ TAMIL RUPEE SIGN

Tamil symbol

0BFA ௺ TAMIL NUMBER SIGN

	0C0	0C1	0C2	0C3	0C4	0C5	0C6	0C7
0		ఐ 0C10	ఠ 0C20	ర 0C30	◌ీ 0C40		ౠ 0C60	
1	◌ఁ 0C01		డ 0C21	ఱ 0C31	◌ు 0C41		ౡ 0C61	
2	◌ం 0C02	ఒ 0C12	ఢ 0C22	ల 0C32	◌ూ 0C42			
3	◌ః 0C03	ఓ 0C13	ణ 0C23	ళ 0C33	◌ృ 0C43			
4		ఔ 0C14	త 0C24		◌ౄ 0C44			
5	అ 0C05	క 0C15	థ 0C25	వ 0C35		◌ౕ 0C55		
6	ఆ 0C06	ఖ 0C16	ద 0C26	శ 0C36	◌ె 0C46	◌ౖ 0C56	౦ 0C66	
7	ఇ 0C07	గ 0C17	ధ 0C27	ష 0C37	◌ే 0C47		౧ 0C67	
8	ఈ 0C08	ఘ 0C18	న 0C28	స 0C38	◌ై 0C48		౨ 0C68	
9	ఉ 0C09	ఙ 0C19		హ 0C39			౩ 0C69	
A	ఊ 0C0A	చ 0C1A	ప 0C2A		◌ొ 0C4A		౪ 0C6A	
B	ఋ 0C0B	ఛ 0C1B	ఫ 0C2B		◌ో 0C4B		౫ 0C6B	
C	ఌ 0C0C	జ 0C1C	బ 0C2C		◌ౌ 0C4C		౬ 0C6C	
D		ఝ 0C1D	భ 0C2D		◌్ 0C4D		౭ 0C6D	
E	ఎ 0C0E	ఞ 0C1E	మ 0C2E	◌ా 0C3E			౮ 0C6E	
F	ఏ 0C0F	ట 0C1F	య 0C2F	◌ి 0C3F			౯ 0C6F	

Based on ISCII 1988

Various signs

0C01 ఁ TELUGU SIGN CANDRABINDU
0C02 ం TELUGU SIGN ANUSVARA
= sunna
0C03 ః TELUGU SIGN VISARGA

Independent vowels

0C05 అ TELUGU LETTER A
0C06 ఆ TELUGU LETTER AA
0C07 ఇ TELUGU LETTER I
0C08 ఈ TELUGU LETTER II
0C09 ఉ TELUGU LETTER U
0C0A ఊ TELUGU LETTER UU
0C0B ఋ TELUGU LETTER VOCALIC R
0C0C ఌ TELUGU LETTER VOCALIC L
0C0D <reserved>
0C0E ఎ TELUGU LETTER E
0C0F ఏ TELUGU LETTER EE
0C10 ఐ TELUGU LETTER AI
0C11 <reserved>
0C12 ఒ TELUGU LETTER O
0C13 ఓ TELUGU LETTER OO
0C14 ఔ TELUGU LETTER AU

Consonants

0C15 క TELUGU LETTER KA
0C16 ఖ TELUGU LETTER KHA
0C17 గ TELUGU LETTER GA
0C18 ఘ TELUGU LETTER GHA
0C19 ఙ TELUGU LETTER NGA
0C1A చ TELUGU LETTER CA
0C1B ఛ TELUGU LETTER CHA
0C1C జ TELUGU LETTER JA
0C1D ఝ TELUGU LETTER JHA
0C1E ఞ TELUGU LETTER NYA
0C1F ట TELUGU LETTER TTA
0C20 ఠ TELUGU LETTER TTHA
0C21 డ TELUGU LETTER DDA
0C22 ఢ TELUGU LETTER DDHA
0C23 ణ TELUGU LETTER NNA
0C24 త TELUGU LETTER TA
0C25 థ TELUGU LETTER THA
0C26 ద TELUGU LETTER DA
0C27 ధ TELUGU LETTER DHA
0C28 న TELUGU LETTER NA
0C29 <reserved>
0C2A ప TELUGU LETTER PA
0C2B ఫ TELUGU LETTER PHA
0C2C బ TELUGU LETTER BA
0C2D భ TELUGU LETTER BHA
0C2E మ TELUGU LETTER MA
0C2F య TELUGU LETTER YA
0C30 ర TELUGU LETTER RA
0C31 ఱ TELUGU LETTER RRA
0C32 ల TELUGU LETTER LA
0C33 ళ TELUGU LETTER LLA
0C34 <reserved>
0C35 వ TELUGU LETTER VA
0C36 శ TELUGU LETTER SHA
0C37 ష TELUGU LETTER SSA
0C38 స TELUGU LETTER SA
0C39 హ TELUGU LETTER HA

Dependent vowel signs

0C3E ా TELUGU VOWEL SIGN AA
0C3F ి TELUGU VOWEL SIGN I
0C40 ీ TELUGU VOWEL SIGN II
0C41 ు TELUGU VOWEL SIGN U
0C42 ూ TELUGU VOWEL SIGN UU
0C43 ృ TELUGU VOWEL SIGN VOCALIC R
0C44 ౄ TELUGU VOWEL SIGN VOCALIC RR
0C45 <reserved>
0C46 ె TELUGU VOWEL SIGN E
0C47 ే TELUGU VOWEL SIGN EE
0C48 ై TELUGU VOWEL SIGN AI
≡ 0C46 ె 0C56 ౖ
0C49 <reserved>
0C4A ొ TELUGU VOWEL SIGN O
0C4B ో TELUGU VOWEL SIGN OO
0C4C ౌ TELUGU VOWEL SIGN AU

Various signs

0C4D ్ TELUGU SIGN VIRAMA
= halant (the preferred name)
0C4E <reserved>
0C4F <reserved>
0C50 <reserved>
0C51 <reserved>
0C52 <reserved>
0C53 <reserved>
0C54 <reserved>
0C55 ౕ TELUGU LENGTH MARK
0C56 ౖ TELUGU AI LENGTH MARK

Additional vowels for Sanskrit

0C60 ౠ TELUGU LETTER VOCALIC RR
0C61 ౡ TELUGU LETTER VOCALIC LL

Reserved

For viram punctuation, use the generic Indic 0964 and 0965.

0C64 <reserved>
→ 0964 । devanagari danda
0C65 <reserved>
→ 0965 ॥ devanagari double danda

Digits

0C66 ౦ TELUGU DIGIT ZERO
0C67 ౧ TELUGU DIGIT ONE
0C68 ౨ TELUGU DIGIT TWO
0C69 ౩ TELUGU DIGIT THREE
0C6A ౪ TELUGU DIGIT FOUR
0C6B ౫ TELUGU DIGIT FIVE
0C6C ౬ TELUGU DIGIT SIX
0C6D ౭ TELUGU DIGIT SEVEN
0C6E ౮ TELUGU DIGIT EIGHT
0C6F ౯ TELUGU DIGIT NINE

	0C8	0C9	0CA	0CB	0CC	0CD	0CE	0CF
0		ಐ 0C90	ಠ 0CA0	ರ 0CB0	◌ೀ 0CC0		ೠ 0CE0	
1			ಡ 0CA1	ಱ 0CB1	◌ು 0CC1		ೡ 0CE1	ೱ 0CF1
2	◌ಂ 0C82	ಒ 0C92	ಢ 0CA2	ಲ 0CB2	◌ೂ 0CC2		◌ೢ 0CE2	ೲ 0CF2
3	◌ಃ 0C83	ಓ 0C93	ಣ 0CA3	ಳ 0CB3	◌ೃ 0CC3		◌ೣ 0CE3	
4		ಔ 0C94	ತ 0CA4		◌ೄ 0CC4			
5	ಅ 0C85	ಕ 0C95	ಥ 0CA5	ವ 0CB5		◌ೕ 0CD5		
6	ಆ 0C86	ಖ 0C96	ದ 0CA6	ಶ 0CB6	◌ೆ 0CC6	◌ೖ 0CD6	೦ 0CE6	
7	ಇ 0C87	ಗ 0C97	ಧ 0CA7	ಷ 0CB7	◌ೇ 0CC7		೧ 0CE7	
8	ಈ 0C88	ಘ 0C98	ನ 0CA8	ಸ 0CB8	◌ೈ 0CC8		೨ 0CE8	
9	ಉ 0C89	ಙ 0C99		ಹ 0CB9			೩ 0CE9	
A	ಊ 0C8A	ಚ 0C9A	ಪ 0CAA		◌ೊ 0CCA		೪ 0CEA	
B	ಋ 0C8B	ಛ 0C9B	ಫ 0CAB		◌ೋ 0CCB		೫ 0CEB	
C	ಌ 0C8C	ಜ 0C9C	ಬ 0CAC	◌಼ 0CBC	◌ೌ 0CCC		೬ 0CEC	
D		ಝ 0C9D	ಭ 0CAD	ಽ 0CBD	◌್ 0CCD		೭ 0CED	
E	ಎ 0C8E	ಞ 0C9E	ಮ 0CAE	◌ಾ 0CBE		ೞ 0CDE	೮ 0CEE	
F	ಏ 0C8F	ಟ 0C9F	ಯ 0CAF	◌ಿ 0CBF			೯ 0CEF	

Based on ISCII 1988

Various signs

0C82 ◌ಂ KANNADA SIGN ANUSVARA
0C83 ◌ಃ KANNADA SIGN VISARGA

Independent vowels

0C85 ಅ KANNADA LETTER A
0C86 ಆ KANNADA LETTER AA
0C87 ಇ KANNADA LETTER I
0C88 ಈ KANNADA LETTER II
0C89 ಉ KANNADA LETTER U
0C8A ಊ KANNADA LETTER UU
0C8B ಋ KANNADA LETTER VOCALIC R
0C8C ಌ KANNADA LETTER VOCALIC L
0C8D <reserved>
0C8E ಎ KANNADA LETTER E
0C8F ಏ KANNADA LETTER EE
0C90 ಐ KANNADA LETTER AI
0C91 <reserved>
0C92 ಒ KANNADA LETTER O
0C93 ಓ KANNADA LETTER OO
0C94 ಔ KANNADA LETTER AU

Consonants

0C95 ಕ KANNADA LETTER KA
0C96 ಖ KANNADA LETTER KHA
0C97 ಗ KANNADA LETTER GA
0C98 ಘ KANNADA LETTER GHA
0C99 ಙ KANNADA LETTER NGA
0C9A ಚ KANNADA LETTER CA
0C9B ಛ KANNADA LETTER CHA
0C9C ಜ KANNADA LETTER JA
0C9D ಝ KANNADA LETTER JHA
0C9E ಞ KANNADA LETTER NYA
0C9F ಟ KANNADA LETTER TTA
0CA0 ಠ KANNADA LETTER TTHA
0CA1 ಡ KANNADA LETTER DDA
0CA2 ಢ KANNADA LETTER DDHA
0CA3 ಣ KANNADA LETTER NNA
0CA4 ತ KANNADA LETTER TA
0CA5 ಥ KANNADA LETTER THA
0CA6 ದ KANNADA LETTER DA
0CA7 ಧ KANNADA LETTER DHA
0CA8 ನ KANNADA LETTER NA
0CA9 <reserved>
0CAA ಪ KANNADA LETTER PA
0CAB ಫ KANNADA LETTER PHA
0CAC ಬ KANNADA LETTER BA
0CAD ಭ KANNADA LETTER BHA
0CAE ಮ KANNADA LETTER MA
0CAF ಯ KANNADA LETTER YA
0CB0 ರ KANNADA LETTER RA
0CB1 ಱ KANNADA LETTER RRA
0CB2 ಲ KANNADA LETTER LA
0CB3 ಳ KANNADA LETTER LLA
0CB4 <reserved>
0CB5 ವ KANNADA LETTER VA
0CB6 ಶ KANNADA LETTER SHA
0CB7 ಷ KANNADA LETTER SSA
0CB8 ಸ KANNADA LETTER SA
0CB9 ಹ KANNADA LETTER HA

Various signs

0CBC ◌಼ KANNADA SIGN NUKTA
0CBD ಽ KANNADA SIGN AVAGRAHA

Dependent vowel signs

0CBE ◌ಾ KANNADA VOWEL SIGN AA
0CBF ◌ಿ KANNADA VOWEL SIGN I
0CC0 ◌ೀ KANNADA VOWEL SIGN II
≡ 0CBF ◌ಿ 0CD5 ◌ೕ
0CC1 ◌ು KANNADA VOWEL SIGN U
0CC2 ◌ೂ KANNADA VOWEL SIGN UU
0CC3 ◌ೃ KANNADA VOWEL SIGN VOCALIC R
0CC4 ◌ೄ KANNADA VOWEL SIGN VOCALIC RR
0CC5 <reserved>
0CC6 ◌ೆ KANNADA VOWEL SIGN E
0CC7 ◌ೇ KANNADA VOWEL SIGN EE
≡ 0CC6 ◌ೆ 0CD5 ◌ೕ
0CC8 ◌ೈ KANNADA VOWEL SIGN AI
≡ 0CC6 ◌ೆ 0CD6 ◌ೖ
0CC9 <reserved>
0CCA ◌ೊ KANNADA VOWEL SIGN O
≡ 0CC6 ◌ೆ 0CC2 ◌ೂ
0CCB ◌ೋ KANNADA VOWEL SIGN OO
≡ 0CCA ◌ೊ 0CD5 ◌ೕ
0CCC ◌ೌ KANNADA VOWEL SIGN AU

Sign

0CCD ◌್ KANNADA SIGN VIRAMA
• preferred name is halant

Various signs

0CD5 ◌ೕ KANNADA LENGTH MARK
0CD6 ◌ೖ KANNADA AI LENGTH MARK

Additional consonants

0CDE ೞ KANNADA LETTER FA
※ KANNADA LETTER LLLA
• obsolete historic letter
• name is a mistake for LLLA

Additional vowels for Sanskrit

0CE0 ೠ KANNADA LETTER VOCALIC RR
0CE1 ೡ KANNADA LETTER VOCALIC LL
0CE2 ◌ೢ KANNADA VOWEL SIGN VOCALIC L
0CE3 ◌ೣ KANNADA VOWEL SIGN VOCALIC LL

Reserved

For viram punctuation, use the generic Indic 0964 and 0965.

0CE4 <reserved>
→ 0964 । devanagari danda
0CE5 <reserved>
→ 0965 ॥ devanagari double danda

Digits

0CE6 ೦ KANNADA DIGIT ZERO
0CE7 ೧ KANNADA DIGIT ONE
0CE8 ೨ KANNADA DIGIT TWO
0CE9 ೩ KANNADA DIGIT THREE
0CEA ೪ KANNADA DIGIT FOUR
0CEB ೫ KANNADA DIGIT FIVE
0CEC ೬ KANNADA DIGIT SIX
0CED ೭ KANNADA DIGIT SEVEN
0CEE ೮ KANNADA DIGIT EIGHT
0CEF ೯ KANNADA DIGIT NINE

Various signs

0CF1 ೱ KANNADA SIGN JIHVAMULIYA
0CF2 ೲ KANNADA SIGN UPADHMANIYA

	0D0	0D1	0D2	0D3	0D4	0D5	0D6	0D7
0		ഐ 0D10	ഠ 0D20	ര 0D30	◌ീ 0D40		ൠ 0D60	
1			ഡ 0D21	റ 0D31	◌ു 0D41		ൡ 0D61	
2	◌ം 0D02	ഒ 0D12	ഢ 0D22	ല 0D32	◌ൂ 0D42			
3	◌ഃ 0D03	ഓ 0D13	ണ 0D23	ള 0D33	◌ൃ 0D43			
4		ഔ 0D14	ത 0D24	ഴ 0D34				
5	അ 0D05	ക 0D15	ഥ 0D25	വ 0D35				
6	ആ 0D06	ഖ 0D16	ദ 0D26	ശ 0D36	െ◌ 0D46		൦ 0D66	
7	ഇ 0D07	ഗ 0D17	ധ 0D27	ഷ 0D37	േ◌ 0D47	◌ൗ 0D57	൧ 0D67	
8	ഈ 0D08	ഘ 0D18	ന 0D28	സ 0D38	ൈ◌ 0D48		൨ 0D68	
9	ഉ 0D09	ങ 0D19		ഹ 0D39			൩ 0D69	
A	ഊ 0D0A	ച 0D1A	പ 0D2A		◌ൊ 0D4A		൪ 0D6A	
B	ഋ 0D0B	ഛ 0D1B	ഫ 0D2B		◌ോ 0D4B		൫ 0D6B	
C	ഌ 0D0C	ജ 0D1C	ബ 0D2C		◌ൌ 0D4C		൬ 0D6C	
D		ഝ 0D1D	ഭ 0D2D		◌് 0D4D		൭ 0D6D	
E	എ 0D0E	ഞ 0D1E	മ 0D2E	◌ാ 0D3E			൮ 0D6E	
F	ഏ 0D0F	ട 0D1F	യ 0D2F	◌ി 0D3F			൯ 0D6F	

Based on ISCII 1988

Various signs

0D02 ◌ം MALAYALAM SIGN ANUSVARA
0D03 ◌ഃ MALAYALAM SIGN VISARGA

Independent vowels

0D05 അ MALAYALAM LETTER A
0D06 ആ MALAYALAM LETTER AA
0D07 ഇ MALAYALAM LETTER I
0D08 ഈ MALAYALAM LETTER II
0D09 ഉ MALAYALAM LETTER U
0D0A ഊ MALAYALAM LETTER UU
0D0B ഋ MALAYALAM LETTER VOCALIC R
0D0C ഌ MALAYALAM LETTER VOCALIC L
0D0D <reserved>
0D0E എ MALAYALAM LETTER E
0D0F ഏ MALAYALAM LETTER EE
0D10 ഐ MALAYALAM LETTER AI
0D11 <reserved>
0D12 ഒ MALAYALAM LETTER O
0D13 ഓ MALAYALAM LETTER OO
0D14 ഔ MALAYALAM LETTER AU

Consonants

Alternate romanizations are shown as aliases for some letters to clarify their identity.

0D15 ക MALAYALAM LETTER KA
0D16 ഖ MALAYALAM LETTER KHA
0D17 ഗ MALAYALAM LETTER GA
0D18 ഘ MALAYALAM LETTER GHA
0D19 ങ MALAYALAM LETTER NGA
0D1A ച MALAYALAM LETTER CA
= cha
0D1B ഛ MALAYALAM LETTER CHA
= chha
0D1C ജ MALAYALAM LETTER JA
0D1D ഝ MALAYALAM LETTER JHA
0D1E ഞ MALAYALAM LETTER NYA
= nha
0D1F ട MALAYALAM LETTER TTA
= ta
0D20 ഠ MALAYALAM LETTER TTHA
= tta
0D21 ഡ MALAYALAM LETTER DDA
= hard da
0D22 ഢ MALAYALAM LETTER DDHA
= hard dda
0D23 ണ MALAYALAM LETTER NNA
= hard na
0D24 ത MALAYALAM LETTER TA
= tha
0D25 ഥ MALAYALAM LETTER THA
= ttha
0D26 ദ MALAYALAM LETTER DA
= soft da
0D27 ധ MALAYALAM LETTER DHA
= soft dda
0D28 ന MALAYALAM LETTER NA
0D29 <reserved>
0D2A പ MALAYALAM LETTER PA
0D2B ഫ MALAYALAM LETTER PHA
0D2C ബ MALAYALAM LETTER BA
0D2D ഭ MALAYALAM LETTER BHA
0D2E മ MALAYALAM LETTER MA
0D2F യ MALAYALAM LETTER YA
0D30 ര MALAYALAM LETTER RA
0D31 റ MALAYALAM LETTER RRA
0D32 ല MALAYALAM LETTER LA
0D33 ള MALAYALAM LETTER LLA
0D34 ഴ MALAYALAM LETTER LLLA
= zha
0D35 വ MALAYALAM LETTER VA
0D36 ശ MALAYALAM LETTER SHA
= soft sha
0D37 ഷ MALAYALAM LETTER SSA
= sha
0D38 സ MALAYALAM LETTER SA
0D39 ഹ MALAYALAM LETTER HA

Dependent vowel signs

0D3E ◌ാ MALAYALAM VOWEL SIGN AA
0D3F ◌ി MALAYALAM VOWEL SIGN I
0D40 ◌ീ MALAYALAM VOWEL SIGN II
0D41 ◌ു MALAYALAM VOWEL SIGN U
0D42 ◌ൂ MALAYALAM VOWEL SIGN UU
0D43 ◌ൃ MALAYALAM VOWEL SIGN VOCALIC R
0D44 <reserved>
0D45 <reserved>
0D46 ◌െ MALAYALAM VOWEL SIGN E
• stands to the left of the consonant
0D47 ◌േ MALAYALAM VOWEL SIGN EE
• stands to the left of the consonant
0D48 ◌ൈ MALAYALAM VOWEL SIGN AI
• stands to the left of the consonant

Two-part dependent vowel signs

These two-part dependent vowel signs have glyph pieces which stand on both sides of the consonant. These vowel signs follow the consonant in logical order, and should be handled as a unit for most processing.

0D4A ◌ൊ MALAYALAM VOWEL SIGN O
≡ 0D46 ◌െ 0D3E ◌ാ
0D4B ◌ോ MALAYALAM VOWEL SIGN OO
≡ 0D47 ◌േ 0D3E ◌ാ
0D4C ◌ൌ MALAYALAM VOWEL SIGN AU
• archaic form of the /au/ dependent vowel
→ 0D57 ◌ൗ malayalam au length mark
≡ 0D46 ◌െ 0D57 ◌ൗ

Various signs

0D4D ◌് MALAYALAM SIGN VIRAMA
= chandrakkala (the preferred name)
= vowel half-u
0D4E <reserved>
0D4F <reserved>
0D50 <reserved>
0D51 <reserved>
0D52 <reserved>
0D53 <reserved>
0D54 <reserved>
0D55 <reserved>
0D56 <reserved>
0D57 ◌ൗ MALAYALAM AU LENGTH MARK
• used alone to write the /au/ dependent vowel in modern texts
→ 0D4C ◌ൌ malayalam vowel sign au

Additional vowels for Sanskrit

0D60 ൠ MALAYALAM LETTER VOCALIC RR
0D61 ൡ MALAYALAM LETTER VOCALIC LL

Reserved

For viram punctuation, use the generic Indic 0964 and 0965.

0D64 <reserved>
→ 0964 । devanagari danda

0D65 <reserved>
→ 0965 ॥ devanagari double danda

Digits

0D66 ൦ MALAYALAM DIGIT ZERO
0D67 ൧ MALAYALAM DIGIT ONE
0D68 ൨ MALAYALAM DIGIT TWO
0D69 ൩ MALAYALAM DIGIT THREE
0D6A ൪ MALAYALAM DIGIT FOUR
0D6B ൫ MALAYALAM DIGIT FIVE
0D6C ൬ MALAYALAM DIGIT SIX
0D6D ൭ MALAYALAM DIGIT SEVEN
0D6E ൮ MALAYALAM DIGIT EIGHT
0D6F ൯ MALAYALAM DIGIT NINE

	0D8	0D9	0DA	0DB	0DC	0DD	0DE	0DF
0		ඐ 0D90	ච 0DA0	ධ 0DB0	ව 0DC0	◌ැ 0DD0		
1		එ 0D91	ඡ 0DA1	න 0DB1	ශ 0DC1	◌ෑ 0DD1		
2	◌ං 0D82	ඒ 0D92	ජ 0DA2		ෂ 0DC2	◌ි 0DD2		◌ෲ 0DF2
3	◌ඃ 0D83	ඓ 0D93	ඣ 0DA3	ඳ 0DB3	ස 0DC3	◌ී 0DD3		◌ෳ 0DF3
4		ඔ 0D94	ඤ 0DA4	ප 0DB4	හ 0DC4	◌ු 0DD4		෴ 0DF4
5	අ 0D85	ඕ 0D95	ඥ 0DA5	ඵ 0DB5	ළ 0DC5			
6	ආ 0D86	ඖ 0D96	ඦ 0DA6	බ 0DB6	ෆ 0DC6	◌ූ 0DD6		
7	ඇ 0D87		ට 0DA7	භ 0DB7				
8	ඈ 0D88		ඨ 0DA8	ම 0DB8		◌ෘ 0DD8		
9	ඉ 0D89		ඩ 0DA9	ඹ 0DB9		◌ෙ 0DD9		
A	ඊ 0D8A	ක 0D9A	ඪ 0DAA	ය 0DBA	◌් 0DCA	◌ේ 0DDA		
B	උ 0D8B	ඛ 0D9B	ණ 0DAB	ර 0DBB		◌ෛ 0DDB		
C	ඌ 0D8C	ග 0D9C	ඬ 0DAC			◌ො 0DDC		
D	ඍ 0D8D	ඝ 0D9D	ත 0DAD	ල 0DBD		◌ෝ 0DDD		
E	ඎ 0D8E	ඞ 0D9E	ථ 0DAE			◌ෞ 0DDE		
F	ඏ 0D8F	ඟ 0D9F	ද 0DAF		◌ා 0DCF	◌ෟ 0DDF		

Various signs

0D82 ◌ං SINHALA SIGN ANUSVARAYA
= anusvara

0D83 ◌ඃ SINHALA SIGN VISARGAYA
= visarga

Independent vowels

0D85 අ SINHALA LETTER AYANNA
= sinhala letter a

0D86 ආ SINHALA LETTER AAYANNA
= sinhala letter aa

0D87 ඇ SINHALA LETTER AEYANNA
= sinhala letter ae

0D88 ඈ SINHALA LETTER AEEYANNA
= sinhala letter aae

0D89 ඉ SINHALA LETTER IYANNA
= sinhala letter i

0D8A ඊ SINHALA LETTER IIYANNA
= sinhala letter ii

0D8B උ SINHALA LETTER UYANNA
= sinhala letter u

0D8C ඌ SINHALA LETTER UUYANNA
= sinhala letter uu

0D8D ඍ SINHALA LETTER IRUYANNA
= sinhala letter vocalic r

0D8E ඎ SINHALA LETTER IRUUYANNA
= sinhala letter vocalic rr

0D8F ඏ SINHALA LETTER ILUYANNA
= sinhala letter vocalic l

0D90 ඐ SINHALA LETTER ILUUYANNA
= sinhala letter vocalic ll

0D91 එ SINHALA LETTER EYANNA
= sinhala letter e

0D92 ඒ SINHALA LETTER EEYANNA
= sinhala letter ee

0D93 ඓ SINHALA LETTER AIYANNA
= sinhala letter ai

0D94 ඔ SINHALA LETTER OYANNA
= sinhala letter o

0D95 ඕ SINHALA LETTER OOYANNA
= sinhala letter oo

0D96 ඖ SINHALA LETTER AUYANNA
= sinhala letter au

Consonants

0D9A ක SINHALA LETTER ALPAPRAANA KAYANNA
= sinhala letter ka

0D9B ඛ SINHALA LETTER MAHAAPRAANA KAYANNA
= sinhala letter kha

0D9C ග SINHALA LETTER ALPAPRAANA GAYANNA
= sinhala letter ga

0D9D ඝ SINHALA LETTER MAHAAPRAANA GAYANNA
= sinhala letter gha

0D9E ඞ SINHALA LETTER KANTAJA NAASIKYAYA
= sinhala letter nga

0D9F ඟ SINHALA LETTER SANYAKA GAYANNA
= sinhala letter nnga

0DA0 ච SINHALA LETTER ALPAPRAANA CAYANNA
= sinhala letter ca

0DA1 ඡ SINHALA LETTER MAHAAPRAANA CAYANNA
= sinhala letter cha

0DA2 ජ SINHALA LETTER ALPAPRAANA JAYANNA
= sinhala letter ja

0DA3 ඣ SINHALA LETTER MAHAAPRAANA JAYANNA
= sinhala letter jha

0DA4 ඤ SINHALA LETTER TAALUJA NAASIKYAYA
= sinhala letter nya

0DA5 ඥ SINHALA LETTER TAALUJA SANYOOGA NAAKSIKYAYA
= sinhala letter jnya

0DA6 ඦ SINHALA LETTER SANYAKA JAYANNA
= sinhala letter nyja

0DA7 ට SINHALA LETTER ALPAPRAANA TTAYANNA
= sinhala letter tta

0DA8 ඨ SINHALA LETTER MAHAAPRAANA TTAYANNA
= sinhala letter ttha

0DA9 ඩ SINHALA LETTER ALPAPRAANA DDAYANNA
= sinhala letter dda

0DAA ඪ SINHALA LETTER MAHAAPRAANA DDAYANNA
= sinhala letter ddha

0DAB ණ SINHALA LETTER MUURDHAJA NAYANNA
= sinhala letter nna

0DAC ඬ SINHALA LETTER SANYAKA DDAYANNA
= sinhala letter nndda

0DAD ත SINHALA LETTER ALPAPRAANA TAYANNA
= sinhala letter ta

0DAE ථ SINHALA LETTER MAHAAPRAANA TAYANNA
= sinhala letter tha

0DAF ද SINHALA LETTER ALPAPRAANA DAYANNA
= sinhala letter da

0DB0 ධ SINHALA LETTER MAHAAPRAANA DAYANNA
= sinhala letter dha

0DB1 න SINHALA LETTER DANTAJA NAYANNA
= sinhala letter na

0DB2 <reserved>

0DB3 ඳ SINHALA LETTER SANYAKA DAYANNA
= sinhala letter nda

0DB4 ප SINHALA LETTER ALPAPRAANA PAYANNA
= sinhala letter pa

0DB5 ඵ SINHALA LETTER MAHAAPRAANA PAYANNA
= sinhala letter pha

0DB6 බ SINHALA LETTER ALPAPRAANA BAYANNA
= sinhala letter ba

0DB7 භ SINHALA LETTER MAHAAPRAANA BAYANNA
= sinhala letter bha

0DB8 ම SINHALA LETTER MAYANNA
= sinhala letter ma

0DB9 ඹ SINHALA LETTER AMBA BAYANNA
= sinhala letter mba

0DBA ය SINHALA LETTER YAYANNA
= sinhala letter ya

0DBB ර SINHALA LETTER RAYANNA
= sinhala letter ra

0DBC <reserved>

0DBD ල SINHALA LETTER DANTAJA LAYANNA
= sinhala letter la
• dental

0DBE <reserved>

0DBF <reserved>

0DC0 ව SINHALA LETTER VAYANNA
= sinhala letter va

0DC1 ශ SINHALA LETTER TAALUJA SAYANNA
= sinhala letter sha

0DC2 ෂ SINHALA LETTER MUURDHAJA SAYANNA
= sinhala letter ssa
• retroflex

0DC3 ස SINHALA LETTER DANTAJA SAYANNA
= sinhala letter sa
• dental

0DC4 හ SINHALA LETTER HAYANNA
= sinhala letter ha

0DC5 ළ SINHALA LETTER MUURDHAJA LAYANNA
= sinhala letter lla
• retroflex

0DC6 ෆ SINHALA LETTER FAYANNA
= sinhala letter fa

Sign

0DCA ◌් SINHALA SIGN AL-LAKUNA
= virama

Dependent vowel signs

0DCF ◌ා SINHALA VOWEL SIGN AELA-PILLA
= sinhala vowel sign aa

0DD0 ◌ැ SINHALA VOWEL SIGN KETTI AEDA-PILLA
= sinhala vowel sign ae

0DD1 ◌ෑ SINHALA VOWEL SIGN DIGA AEDA-PILLA
= sinhala vowel sign aae

0DD2 ◌ි SINHALA VOWEL SIGN KETTI IS-PILLA
= sinhala vowel sign i

0DD3 ◌ී SINHALA VOWEL SIGN DIGA IS-PILLA
= sinhala vowel sign ii

0DD4 ◌ු SINHALA VOWEL SIGN KETTI PAA-PILLA
= sinhala vowel sign u

0DD5 <reserved>

0DD6 ◌ූ SINHALA VOWEL SIGN DIGA PAA-PILLA
= sinhala vowel sign uu

0DD7 <reserved>

0DD8 ◌ෘ SINHALA VOWEL SIGN GAETTA-PILLA
= sinhala vowel sign vocalic r

0DD9 ◌ෙ SINHALA VOWEL SIGN KOMBUVA
= sinhala vowel sign e

0DDA ◌ේ SINHALA VOWEL SIGN DIGA KOMBUVA
= sinhala vowel sign ee
≡ 0DD9 ◌ෙ 0DCA ◌්

0DDB ◌ෛ SINHALA VOWEL SIGN KOMBU DEKA
= sinhala vowel sign ai

Two-part dependent vowel signs

These two-part dependent vowel signs have glyph pieces which stand on both sides of the consonant. These vowel signs follow the consonant in logical order, and should be handled as a unit for most processing.

0DDC ◌ො SINHALA VOWEL SIGN KOMBUVA HAA AELA-PILLA
= sinhala vowel sign o
≡ 0DD9 ◌ෙ 0DCF ◌ා

0DDD ◌ෝ SINHALA VOWEL SIGN KOMBUVA HAA DIGA AELA-PILLA
= sinhala vowel sign oo
≡ 0DDC ◌ො 0DCA ◌්

0DDE ◌ෞ SINHALA VOWEL SIGN KOMBUVA HAA GAYANUKITTA
= sinhala vowel sign au
≡ 0DD9 ◌ෙ 0DDF ◌ෟ

Dependent vowel sign

0DDF ◌ෟ SINHALA VOWEL SIGN GAYANUKITTA
= sinhala vowel sign vocalic l

Additional dependent vowel signs

0DF2 ◌ෲ SINHALA VOWEL SIGN DIGA GAETTA-PILLA
= sinhala vowel sign vocalic rr

0DF3 ◌ෳ SINHALA VOWEL SIGN DIGA GAYANUKITTA
= sinhala vowel sign vocalic ll

Punctuation

0DF4 ෴ SINHALA PUNCTUATION KUNDDALIYA

	0E0	0E1	0E2	0E3	0E4	0E5	0E6	0E7
0		ฐ 0E10	ภ 0E20	ะ 0E30	เ 0E40	๐ 0E50		
1	ก 0E01	ฑ 0E11	ม 0E21	◌ั 0E31	แ 0E41	๑ 0E51		
2	ข 0E02	ฒ 0E12	ย 0E22	า 0E32	โ 0E42	๒ 0E52		
3	ฃ 0E03	ณ 0E13	ร 0E23	ำ 0E33	ใ 0E43	๓ 0E53		
4	ค 0E04	ด 0E14	ฤ 0E24	◌ิ 0E34	ไ 0E44	๔ 0E54		
5	ฅ 0E05	ต 0E15	ล 0E25	◌ี 0E35	ๅ 0E45	๕ 0E55		
6	ฆ 0E06	ถ 0E16	ฦ 0E26	◌ึ 0E36	ๆ 0E46	๖ 0E56		
7	ง 0E07	ท 0E17	ว 0E27	◌ื 0E37	◌็ 0E47	๗ 0E57		
8	จ 0E08	ธ 0E18	ศ 0E28	◌ุ 0E38	◌่ 0E48	๘ 0E58		
9	ฉ 0E09	น 0E19	ษ 0E29	◌ู 0E39	◌้ 0E49	๙ 0E59		
A	ช 0E0A	บ 0E1A	ส 0E2A	◌ฺ 0E3A	◌๊ 0E4A	๚ 0E5A		
B	ซ 0E0B	ป 0E1B	ห 0E2B		◌๋ 0E4B	๛ 0E5B		
C	ฌ 0E0C	ผ 0E1C	ฬ 0E2C		◌์ 0E4C			
D	ญ 0E0D	ฝ 0E1D	อ 0E2D		◌ํ 0E4D			
E	ฎ 0E0E	พ 0E1E	ฮ 0E2E		◌๎ 0E4E			
F	ฏ 0E0F	ฟ 0E1F	ฯ 0E2F	฿ 0E3F	๏ 0E4F			

Based on TIS 620-2533

Consonants

0E01 ก THAI CHARACTER KO KAI
0E02 ข THAI CHARACTER KHO KHAI
0E03 ฃ THAI CHARACTER KHO KHUAT
0E04 ค THAI CHARACTER KHO KHWAI
0E05 ฅ THAI CHARACTER KHO KHON
0E06 ฆ THAI CHARACTER KHO RAKHANG
0E07 ง THAI CHARACTER NGO NGU
0E08 จ THAI CHARACTER CHO CHAN
0E09 ฉ THAI CHARACTER CHO CHING
0E0A ช THAI CHARACTER CHO CHANG
0E0B ซ THAI CHARACTER SO SO
0E0C ฌ THAI CHARACTER CHO CHOE
0E0D ญ THAI CHARACTER YO YING
0E0E ฎ THAI CHARACTER DO CHADA
0E0F ฏ THAI CHARACTER TO PATAK
0E10 ฐ THAI CHARACTER THO THAN
0E11 ฑ THAI CHARACTER THO NANGMONTHO
0E12 ฒ THAI CHARACTER THO PHUTHAO
0E13 ณ THAI CHARACTER NO NEN
0E14 ด THAI CHARACTER DO DEK
0E15 ต THAI CHARACTER TO TAO
0E16 ถ THAI CHARACTER THO THUNG
0E17 ท THAI CHARACTER THO THAHAN
0E18 ธ THAI CHARACTER THO THONG
0E19 น THAI CHARACTER NO NU
0E1A บ THAI CHARACTER BO BAIMAI
0E1B ป THAI CHARACTER PO PLA
0E1C ผ THAI CHARACTER PHO PHUNG
0E1D ฝ THAI CHARACTER FO FA
0E1E พ THAI CHARACTER PHO PHAN
0E1F ฟ THAI CHARACTER FO FAN
0E20 ภ THAI CHARACTER PHO SAMPHAO
0E21 ม THAI CHARACTER MO MA
0E22 ย THAI CHARACTER YO YAK
0E23 ร THAI CHARACTER RO RUA
0E24 ฤ THAI CHARACTER RU
• independent vowel letter used to write Sanskrit
0E25 ล THAI CHARACTER LO LING
0E26 ฦ THAI CHARACTER LU
• independent vowel letter used to write Sanskrit
0E27 ว THAI CHARACTER WO WAEN
0E28 ศ THAI CHARACTER SO SALA
0E29 ษ THAI CHARACTER SO RUSI
0E2A ส THAI CHARACTER SO SUA
0E2B ห THAI CHARACTER HO HIP
0E2C ฬ THAI CHARACTER LO CHULA
0E2D อ THAI CHARACTER O ANG
0E2E ฮ THAI CHARACTER HO NOKHUK
= ho nok huk

Sign

0E2F ฯ THAI CHARACTER PAIYANNOI
= paiyan noi
• ellipsis, abbreviation

Vowels

0E30 ะ THAI CHARACTER SARA A
0E31 ◌ั THAI CHARACTER MAI HAN-AKAT
0E32 า THAI CHARACTER SARA AA
→ 0E45 ๅ thai character lakkhangyao
0E33 ำ THAI CHARACTER SARA AM
≈ 0E4D ◌ํ 0E32 า
0E34 ◌ิ THAI CHARACTER SARA I
0E35 ◌ี THAI CHARACTER SARA II
0E36 ◌ึ THAI CHARACTER SARA UE
0E37 ◌ื THAI CHARACTER SARA UEE
= sara uue
0E38 ◌ุ THAI CHARACTER SARA U
0E39 ◌ู THAI CHARACTER SARA UU
0E3A ◌ฺ THAI CHARACTER PHINTHU
• Pali virama

Currency symbol

0E3F ฿ THAI CURRENCY SYMBOL BAHT

Vowels

0E40 เ THAI CHARACTER SARA E
0E41 แ THAI CHARACTER SARA AE
0E42 โ THAI CHARACTER SARA O
0E43 ใ THAI CHARACTER SARA AI MAIMUAN
= sara ai mai muan
0E44 ไ THAI CHARACTER SARA AI MAIMALAI
= sara ai mai malai
0E45 ๅ THAI CHARACTER LAKKHANGYAO
= lakkhang yao
• special vowel length indication used with 0E24 ฤ or 0E26 ฦ
→ 0E32 า thai character sara aa

Sign

0E46 ๆ THAI CHARACTER MAIYAMOK
= mai yamok
• repetition

Vowel

0E47 ◌็ THAI CHARACTER MAITAIKHU
= mai taikhu

Tone marks

0E48 ◌่ THAI CHARACTER MAI EK
0E49 ◌้ THAI CHARACTER MAI THO
0E4A ◌๊ THAI CHARACTER MAI TRI
0E4B ◌๋ THAI CHARACTER MAI CHATTAWA

Signs

0E4C ◌์ THAI CHARACTER THANTHAKHAT
• cancellation mark
0E4D ◌ํ THAI CHARACTER NIKHAHIT
= nikkhahit
• final nasal
0E4E ◌๎ THAI CHARACTER YAMAKKAN
0E4F ๏ THAI CHARACTER FONGMAN
• used as a bullet
→ 17D9 ៙ khmer sign phnaek muan

Digits

0E50 ๐ THAI DIGIT ZERO
0E51 ๑ THAI DIGIT ONE
0E52 ๒ THAI DIGIT TWO
0E53 ๓ THAI DIGIT THREE
0E54 ๔ THAI DIGIT FOUR
0E55 ๕ THAI DIGIT FIVE
0E56 ๖ THAI DIGIT SIX
0E57 ๗ THAI DIGIT SEVEN
0E58 ๘ THAI DIGIT EIGHT
0E59 ๙ THAI DIGIT NINE

Signs

0E5A ๚ THAI CHARACTER ANGKHANKHU
- used to mark end of long sections
- used in combination with 0E30 ะ to mark end of a verse

0E5B ๛ THAI CHARACTER KHOMUT
- used to mark end of chapter or document

→ 17DA ៚ khmer sign koomuut

	0E8	0E9	0EA	0EB	0EC	0ED	0EE	0EF
0				ະ 0EB0	ເ 0EC0	໐ 0ED0		
1	ກ 0E81		ມ 0EA1	◌ັ 0EB1	ແ 0EC1	໑ 0ED1		
2	ຂ 0E82		ຢ 0EA2	າ 0EB2	ໂ 0EC2	໒ 0ED2		
3			ຣ 0EA3	ຳ 0EB3	ໃ 0EC3	໓ 0ED3		
4	ຄ 0E84	ດ 0E94		◌ິ 0EB4	ໄ 0EC4	໔ 0ED4		
5		ຕ 0E95	ລ 0EA5	◌ີ 0EB5		໕ 0ED5		
6		ຖ 0E96		◌ຶ 0EB6	ໆ 0EC6	໖ 0ED6		
7	ງ 0E87	ທ 0E97	ວ 0EA7	◌ື 0EB7		໗ 0ED7		
8	ຈ 0E88			◌ຸ 0EB8	◌່ 0EC8	໘ 0ED8		
9		ນ 0E99		◌ູ 0EB9	◌້ 0EC9	໙ 0ED9		
A	ຊ 0E8A	ບ 0E9A	ສ 0EAA		◌໊ 0ECA			
B		ປ 0E9B	ຫ 0EAB	◌ົ 0EBB	◌໋ 0ECB			
C		ຜ 0E9C		◌ຼ 0EBC	◌໌ 0ECC	ໜ 0EDC		
D	ຍ 0E8D	ຝ 0E9D	ອ 0EAD	ຽ 0EBD	◌ໍ 0ECD	ໝ 0EDD		
E		ພ 0E9E	ຮ 0EAE					
F		ຟ 0E9F	ຯ 0EAF					

Consonants

0E81 ກ LAO LETTER KO
  = ko kay

0E82 ຂ LAO LETTER KHO SUNG
  = kho khay

0E83 <reserved>

0E84 ຄ LAO LETTER KHO TAM
  = kho khuay

0E85 <reserved>

0E86 <reserved>

0E87 ງ LAO LETTER NGO
  = ngo ngu, ngo ngua

0E88 ຈ LAO LETTER CO
  = co cok, co cua

0E89 <reserved>

0E8A ຊ LAO LETTER SO TAM
  = so sang

0E8B <reserved>

0E8C <reserved>

0E8D ຍ LAO LETTER NYO
  = nyo nyung

0E8E <reserved>

0E8F <reserved>

0E90 <reserved>

0E91 <reserved>

0E92 <reserved>

0E93 <reserved>

0E94 ດ LAO LETTER DO
  = do dek

0E95 ຕ LAO LETTER TO
  = to ta

0E96 ຖ LAO LETTER THO SUNG
  = tho thong

0E97 ທ LAO LETTER THO TAM
  = tho thung

0E98 <reserved>

0E99 ນ LAO LETTER NO
  = no nok

0E9A ບ LAO LETTER BO
  = bo be, bo bet

0E9B ປ LAO LETTER PO
  = po pa

0E9C ຜ LAO LETTER PHO SUNG
  = pho pheng

0E9D ຝ LAO LETTER FO TAM
  ※ LAO LETTER FO FON
  = fo fa
  • name is a mistake for fo sung

0E9E ພ LAO LETTER PHO TAM
  = pho phu

0E9F ຟ LAO LETTER FO SUNG
  ※ LAO LETTER FO FAY
  • name is a mistake for fo tam

0EA0 <reserved>

0EA1 ມ LAO LETTER MO
  = mo mew, mo ma

0EA2 ຢ LAO LETTER YO
  = yo ya

0EA3 ຣ LAO LETTER LO LING
  ※ LAO LETTER RO
  = ro rot
  • name is a mistake, lo ling is the mnemonic for 0EA5 ລ

0EA4 <reserved>

0EA5 ລ LAO LETTER LO LOOT
  ※ LAO LETTER LO
  = lo ling
  • name is a mistake, lo loot is the mnemonic for 0EA3 ຣ

0EA6 <reserved>

0EA7 ວ LAO LETTER WO
  = wo wi

0EA8 <reserved>

0EA9 <reserved>

0EAA ສ LAO LETTER SO SUNG
  = so sya

0EAB ຫ LAO LETTER HO SUNG
  = ho hay, ho han

0EAC <reserved>

0EAD ອ LAO LETTER O
  = o o

0EAE ຮ LAO LETTER HO TAM
  = ho hya, ho hyan

Sign

0EAF ຯ LAO ELLIPSIS

Vowels

0EB0 ະ LAO VOWEL SIGN A

0EB1 ◌ັ LAO VOWEL SIGN MAI KAN
  • vowel shortener

0EB2 າ LAO VOWEL SIGN AA

0EB3 ຳ LAO VOWEL SIGN AM
  ≈ 0ECD ◌ໍ 0EB2 າ

0EB4 ◌ິ LAO VOWEL SIGN I

0EB5 ◌ີ LAO VOWEL SIGN II

0EB6 ◌ຶ LAO VOWEL SIGN Y

0EB7 ◌ື LAO VOWEL SIGN YY

0EB8 ◌ຸ LAO VOWEL SIGN U

0EB9 ◌ູ LAO VOWEL SIGN UU

0EBA <reserved>

0EBB ◌ົ LAO VOWEL SIGN MAI KON
  = mai kong

Signs

0EBC ◌ຼ LAO SEMIVOWEL SIGN LO

0EBD ຽ LAO SEMIVOWEL SIGN NYO
  = nyo fyang

Vowels

0EC0 ເ LAO VOWEL SIGN E

0EC1 ແ LAO VOWEL SIGN EI

0EC2 ໂ LAO VOWEL SIGN O

0EC3 ໃ LAO VOWEL SIGN AY
  = mai muan

0EC4 ໄ LAO VOWEL SIGN AI
  = mai may

Sign

0EC6 ໆ LAO KO LA
  • repetition

Tone marks

0EC8 ◌່ LAO TONE MAI EK

0EC9 ◌້ LAO TONE MAI THO

0ECA ◌໊ LAO TONE MAI TI

0ECB ◌໋ LAO TONE MAI CATAWA

Signs

0ECC ◌໌ LAO CANCELLATION MARK

0ECD ◌ໍ LAO NIGGAHITA
  • final nasal or long o vowel

Digits

0ED0 ໐ LAO DIGIT ZERO
0ED1 ໑ LAO DIGIT ONE
0ED2 ໒ LAO DIGIT TWO
0ED3 ໓ LAO DIGIT THREE
0ED4 ໔ LAO DIGIT FOUR
0ED5 ໕ LAO DIGIT FIVE
0ED6 ໖ LAO DIGIT SIX
0ED7 ໗ LAO DIGIT SEVEN
0ED8 ໘ LAO DIGIT EIGHT
0ED9 ໙ LAO DIGIT NINE

Digraphs

0EDC ໜ LAO HO NO
≈ 0EAB ຫ 0E99 ນ
0EDD ໝ LAO HO MO
≈ 0EAB ຫ 0EA1 ມ

	0F0	0F1	0F2	0F3	0F4	0F5	0F6	0F7	0F8	0F9	0FA	0FB	0FC	0FD	0FE	0FF
0	ༀ 0F00	༐ 0F10	༠ 0F20	༰ 0F30	ཀ 0F40	ཐ 0F50	འ 0F60		◌ྀ 0F80	◌ྐ 0F90	◌ྠ 0FA0	◌ྰ 0FB0	࿀ 0FC0	࿐ 0FD0		
1	༁ 0F01	༑ 0F11	༡ 0F21	༱ 0F31	ཁ 0F41	ད 0F51	ཡ 0F61	◌ཱ 0F71	◌ཱྀ 0F81	◌ྑ 0F91	◌ྡ 0FA1	◌ྱ 0FB1	࿁ 0FC1	࿑ 0FD1		
2	༂ 0F02	༒ 0F12	༢ 0F22	༲ 0F32	ག 0F42	དྷ 0F52	ར 0F62	◌ི 0F72	◌ྂ 0F82	◌ྒ 0F92	◌ྡྷ 0FA2	◌ྲ 0FB2	࿂ 0FC2			
3	༃ 0F03	༓ 0F13	༣ 0F23	༳ 0F33	གྷ 0F43	ན 0F53	ལ 0F63	◌ཱི 0F73	◌ྃ 0F83	◌ྒྷ 0F93	◌ྣ 0FA3	◌ླ 0FB3	࿃ 0FC3			
4	༄ 0F04	༔ 0F14	༤ 0F24	༴ 0F34	ང 0F44	པ 0F54	ཤ 0F64	◌ུ 0F74	◌྄ 0F84	◌ྔ 0F94	◌ྤ 0FA4	◌ྴ 0FB4	࿄ 0FC4			
5	༅ 0F05	༕ 0F15	༥ 0F25	◌༵ 0F35	ཅ 0F45	ཕ 0F55	ཥ 0F65	◌ཱུ 0F75	྅ 0F85	◌ྕ 0F95	◌ྥ 0FA5	◌ྵ 0FB5	࿅ 0FC5			
6	༆ 0F06	༖ 0F16	༦ 0F26	༶ 0F36	ཆ 0F46	བ 0F56	ས 0F66	◌ྲྀ 0F76	◌྆ 0F86	◌ྖ 0F96	◌ྦ 0FA6	◌ྶ 0FB6	◌࿆ 0FC6			
7	༇ 0F07	༗ 0F17	༧ 0F27	◌༷ 0F37	ཇ 0F47	བྷ 0F57	ཧ 0F67	◌ཷ 0F77	◌྇ 0F87	◌ྗ 0F97	◌ྦྷ 0FA7	◌ྷ 0FB7	࿇ 0FC7			
8	༈ 0F08	◌༘ 0F18	༨ 0F28	༸ 0F38		མ 0F58	ཨ 0F68	◌ླྀ 0F78	ྈ 0F88		◌ྨ 0FA8	◌ྸ 0FB8	࿈ 0FC8			
9	༉ 0F09	◌༙ 0F19	༩ 0F29	◌༹ 0F39	ཉ 0F49	ཙ 0F59	ཀྵ 0F69	◌ཹ 0F79	ྉ 0F89	◌ྙ 0F99	◌ྩ 0FA9	◌ྐྵ 0FB9	࿉ 0FC9			
A	༊ 0F0A	༚ 0F1A	༪ 0F2A	༺ 0F3A	ཊ 0F4A	ཚ 0F5A	ཪ 0F6A	◌ེ 0F7A	ྊ 0F8A	◌ྚ 0F9A	◌ྪ 0FAA	◌ྺ 0FBA	࿊ 0FCA			
B	་ 0F0B	༛ 0F1B	༫ 0F2B	༻ 0F3B	ཋ 0F4B	ཛ 0F5B		◌ཻ 0F7B	ྋ 0F8B	◌ྛ 0F9B	◌ྫ 0FAB	◌ྻ 0FBB	࿋ 0FCB			
C	༌ 0F0C	༜ 0F1C	༬ 0F2C	༼ 0F3C	ཌ 0F4C	ཛྷ 0F5C		◌ོ 0F7C		◌ྜ 0F9C	◌ྫྷ 0FAC	◌ྼ 0FBC	࿌ 0FCC			
D	། 0F0D	༝ 0F1D	༭ 0F2D	༽ 0F3D	ཌྷ 0F4D	ཝ 0F5D		◌ཽ 0F7D		◌ྜྷ 0F9D	◌ྭ 0FAD					
E	༎ 0F0E	༞ 0F1E	༮ 0F2E	༾ 0F3E	ཎ 0F4E	ཞ 0F5E		◌ཾ 0F7E		◌ྞ 0F9E	◌ྮ 0FAE	྾ 0FBE				
F	༏ 0F0F	༟ 0F1F	༯ 0F2F	༿ 0F3F	ཏ 0F4F	ཟ 0F5F		◌ཿ 0F7F		◌ྟ 0F9F	◌ྯ 0FAF	྿ 0FBF	࿏ 0FCF			

Syllable

0F00 ༀ TIBETAN SYLLABLE OM

Head marks

0F01 ༁ TIBETAN MARK GTER YIG MGO TRUNCATED A
0F02 ༂ TIBETAN MARK GTER YIG MGO -UM RNAM BCAD MA
0F03 ༃ TIBETAN MARK GTER YIG MGO -UM GTER TSHEG MA
0F04 ༄ TIBETAN MARK INITIAL YIG MGO MDUN MA
- honorific; marks beginning of text or start of new folio
→ 1800 ᠀ mongolian birga

0F05 ༅ TIBETAN MARK CLOSING YIG MGO SGAB MA
- follows and ligates with initial yig-mgo

0F06 ༆ TIBETAN MARK CARET YIG MGO PHUR SHAD MA
0F07 ༇ TIBETAN MARK YIG MGO TSHEG SHAD MA

Marks and signs

0F08 ༈ TIBETAN MARK SBRUL SHAD
- separates sections of meaning equivalent to topics and sub-topics

0F09 ༉ TIBETAN MARK BSKUR YIG MGO
- list enumerator, used in Bhutan

0F0A ༊ TIBETAN MARK BKA- SHOG YIG MGO
- petition honorific, used in Bhutan

0F0B ་ TIBETAN MARK INTERSYLLABIC TSHEG
- morpheme delimiter (approximate meaning)
- the normal tsheg; provides a break opportunity
- character name is a misnomer

0F0C ༌ TIBETAN MARK DELIMITER TSHEG BSTAR
- a non-breaking tsheg; inhibits line breaking
- character name is a misnomer
≈ <noBreak> 0F0B ་

0F0D ། TIBETAN MARK SHAD
- marks end of a section of text (tshig-grub)
→ 0964 । devanagari danda

0F0E ༎ TIBETAN MARK NYIS SHAD
- marks end of a whole topic (don-tshan)
→ 0965 ॥ devanagari double danda

0F0F ༏ TIBETAN MARK TSHEG SHAD
0F10 ༐ TIBETAN MARK NYIS TSHEG SHAD
0F11 ༑ TIBETAN MARK RIN CHEN SPUNGS SHAD
- shad which follows a tsheg-bar that starts a new line

0F12 ༒ TIBETAN MARK RGYA GRAM SHAD
0F13 ༓ TIBETAN MARK CARET -DZUD RTAGS ME LONG CAN
0F14 ༔ TIBETAN MARK GTER TSHEG
- used as a comma-like text delimiter
→ 17D6 ៖ khmer sign camnuc pii kuuh

Astrological signs

0F15 ༕ TIBETAN LOGOTYPE SIGN CHAD RTAGS
0F16 ༖ TIBETAN LOGOTYPE SIGN LHAG RTAGS
0F17 ༗ TIBETAN ASTROLOGICAL SIGN SGRA GCAN -CHAR RTAGS
0F18 ༘ TIBETAN ASTROLOGICAL SIGN -KHYUD PA
- combines with digits

0F19 ༙ TIBETAN ASTROLOGICAL SIGN SDONG TSHUGS
- combines with digits

0F1A ༚ TIBETAN SIGN RDEL DKAR GCIG
0F1B ༛ TIBETAN SIGN RDEL DKAR GNYIS
0F1C ༜ TIBETAN SIGN RDEL DKAR GSUM
0F1D ༝ TIBETAN SIGN RDEL NAG GCIG
0F1E ༞ TIBETAN SIGN RDEL NAG GNYIS
0F1F ༟ TIBETAN SIGN RDEL DKAR RDEL NAG

Digits

0F20 ༠ TIBETAN DIGIT ZERO
0F21 ༡ TIBETAN DIGIT ONE
0F22 ༢ TIBETAN DIGIT TWO
0F23 ༣ TIBETAN DIGIT THREE
0F24 ༤ TIBETAN DIGIT FOUR
0F25 ༥ TIBETAN DIGIT FIVE
0F26 ༦ TIBETAN DIGIT SIX
0F27 ༧ TIBETAN DIGIT SEVEN
0F28 ༨ TIBETAN DIGIT EIGHT
0F29 ༩ TIBETAN DIGIT NINE

Digits minus half

0F2A ༪ TIBETAN DIGIT HALF ONE
0F2B ༫ TIBETAN DIGIT HALF TWO
0F2C ༬ TIBETAN DIGIT HALF THREE
0F2D ༭ TIBETAN DIGIT HALF FOUR
0F2E ༮ TIBETAN DIGIT HALF FIVE
0F2F ༯ TIBETAN DIGIT HALF SIX
0F30 ༰ TIBETAN DIGIT HALF SEVEN
0F31 ༱ TIBETAN DIGIT HALF EIGHT
0F32 ༲ TIBETAN DIGIT HALF NINE
0F33 ༳ TIBETAN DIGIT HALF ZERO

Marks and signs

0F34 ༴ TIBETAN MARK BSDUS RTAGS
- repetition

0F35 ༵ TIBETAN MARK NGAS BZUNG NYI ZLA
- honorific, emphasis; used like underlining

0F36 ༶ TIBETAN MARK CARET -DZUD RTAGS BZHI MIG CAN
- marks point of text insertion or annotation

0F37 ༷ TIBETAN MARK NGAS BZUNG SGOR RTAGS
- emphasis; used like underlining

0F38 ༸ TIBETAN MARK CHE MGO
0F39 ༹ TIBETAN MARK TSA -PHRU
- a lenition mark

Paired punctuation

0F3A ༺ TIBETAN MARK GUG RTAGS GYON
0F3B ༻ TIBETAN MARK GUG RTAGS GYAS
- brackets

0F3C ༼ TIBETAN MARK ANG KHANG GYON
0F3D ༽ TIBETAN MARK ANG KHANG GYAS
- used for bracketing with a roof over

Astrological signs

0F3E ༾ TIBETAN SIGN YAR TSHES
0F3F ༿ TIBETAN SIGN MAR TSHES
- marks which combine with digits

Consonants

0F40 ཀ TIBETAN LETTER KA
0F41 ཁ TIBETAN LETTER KHA
0F42 ག TIBETAN LETTER GA
0F43 གྷ TIBETAN LETTER GHA
≡ 0F42 ག 0FB7 ྷ

0F44 ང TIBETAN LETTER NGA
0F45 ཅ TIBETAN LETTER CA
0F46 ཆ TIBETAN LETTER CHA
0F47 ཇ TIBETAN LETTER JA
0F48 <reserved>
0F49 ཉ TIBETAN LETTER NYA
0F4A ཊ TIBETAN LETTER TTA

0F4B ཋ TIBETAN LETTER TTHA
0F4C ཌ TIBETAN LETTER DDA
0F4D ཌྷ TIBETAN LETTER DDHA
  ≡ 0F4C ཌ 0FB7 ◌ྷ
0F4E ཎ TIBETAN LETTER NNA
0F4F ཏ TIBETAN LETTER TA
0F50 ཐ TIBETAN LETTER THA
0F51 ད TIBETAN LETTER DA
0F52 དྷ TIBETAN LETTER DHA
  ≡ 0F51 ད 0FB7 ◌ྷ
0F53 ན TIBETAN LETTER NA
0F54 པ TIBETAN LETTER PA
0F55 ཕ TIBETAN LETTER PHA
0F56 བ TIBETAN LETTER BA
0F57 བྷ TIBETAN LETTER BHA
  ≡ 0F56 བ 0FB7 ◌ྷ
0F58 མ TIBETAN LETTER MA
0F59 ཙ TIBETAN LETTER TSA
0F5A ཚ TIBETAN LETTER TSHA
0F5B ཛ TIBETAN LETTER DZA
0F5C ཛྷ TIBETAN LETTER DZHA
  ≡ 0F5B ཛ 0FB7 ◌ྷ
0F5D ཝ TIBETAN LETTER WA
0F5E ཞ TIBETAN LETTER ZHA
0F5F ཟ TIBETAN LETTER ZA
0F60 འ TIBETAN LETTER -A
0F61 ཡ TIBETAN LETTER YA
0F62 ར TIBETAN LETTER RA
  • when followed by a subjoined letter = ra mgo
0F63 ལ TIBETAN LETTER LA
0F64 ཤ TIBETAN LETTER SHA
0F65 ཥ TIBETAN LETTER SSA
  = reversed sha
0F66 ས TIBETAN LETTER SA
0F67 ཧ TIBETAN LETTER HA
0F68 ཨ TIBETAN LETTER A
  • base for dependent vowels
0F69 ཀྵ TIBETAN LETTER KSSA
  ≡ 0F40 ཀ 0FB5 ◌ྵ
0F6A ཪ TIBETAN LETTER FIXED-FORM RA
  • used only in transliteration and transcription

Dependent vowel signs

0F71 ◌ཱ TIBETAN VOWEL SIGN AA
  = a-chung
  • common, vowel-lengthening mark
0F72 ◌ི TIBETAN VOWEL SIGN I
0F73 ◌ཱི TIBETAN VOWEL SIGN II
  • use of this character is discouraged
  ≡ 0F71 ◌ཱ 0F72 ◌ི
0F74 ◌ུ TIBETAN VOWEL SIGN U
0F75 ◌ཱུ TIBETAN VOWEL SIGN UU
  • use of this character is discouraged
  ≡ 0F71 ◌ཱ 0F74 ◌ུ
0F76 ◌ྲྀ TIBETAN VOWEL SIGN VOCALIC R
  ≡ 0FB2 ◌ྲ 0F80 ◌ྀ
0F77 ◌ཷ TIBETAN VOWEL SIGN VOCALIC RR
  • use of this character is strongly discouraged
  ≈ 0FB2 ◌ྲ 0F81 ◌ཱྀ
0F78 ◌ླྀ TIBETAN VOWEL SIGN VOCALIC L
  ≡ 0FB3 ◌ླ 0F80 ◌ྀ
0F79 ◌ཹ TIBETAN VOWEL SIGN VOCALIC LL
  • use of this character is strongly discouraged
  ≈ 0FB3 ◌ླ 0F81 ◌ཱྀ
0F7A ◌ེ TIBETAN VOWEL SIGN E
0F7B ◌ཻ TIBETAN VOWEL SIGN EE
0F7C ◌ོ TIBETAN VOWEL SIGN O
0F7D ◌ཽ TIBETAN VOWEL SIGN OO

Vocalic modification

0F7E ◌ཾ TIBETAN SIGN RJES SU NGA RO
  = anusvara
0F7F ◌ཿ TIBETAN SIGN RNAM BCAD
  = visarga

Dependent vowel signs

0F80 ◌ྀ TIBETAN VOWEL SIGN REVERSED I
0F81 ◌ཱྀ TIBETAN VOWEL SIGN REVERSED II
  • use of this character is discouraged
  ≡ 0F71 ◌ཱ 0F80 ◌ྀ

Marks and signs

0F82 ◌ྂ TIBETAN SIGN NYI ZLA NAA DA
0F83 ◌ྃ TIBETAN SIGN SNA LDAN
  → 0901 ◌ँ devanagari sign candrabindu
0F84 ◌྄ TIBETAN MARK HALANTA
  = srog med
  → 094D ◌् devanagari sign virama
0F85 ྅ TIBETAN MARK PALUTA
  • transliteration of Sanskrit avagraha
  → 093D ऽ devanagari sign avagraha
0F86 ◌྆ TIBETAN SIGN LCI RTAGS
0F87 ◌྇ TIBETAN SIGN YANG RTAGS

Transliteration head letters

0F88 ྈ TIBETAN SIGN LCE TSA CAN
0F89 ྉ TIBETAN SIGN MCHU CAN
0F8A ྊ TIBETAN SIGN GRU CAN RGYINGS
  • always followed by 0F82 ◌ྂ
0F8B ྋ TIBETAN SIGN GRU MED RGYINGS

Subjoined consonants

0F90 ◌ྐ TIBETAN SUBJOINED LETTER KA
0F91 ◌ྑ TIBETAN SUBJOINED LETTER KHA
0F92 ◌ྒ TIBETAN SUBJOINED LETTER GA
0F93 ◌ྒྷ TIBETAN SUBJOINED LETTER GHA
  ≡ 0F92 ◌ྒ 0FB7 ◌ྷ
0F94 ◌ྔ TIBETAN SUBJOINED LETTER NGA
0F95 ◌ྕ TIBETAN SUBJOINED LETTER CA
0F96 ◌ྖ TIBETAN SUBJOINED LETTER CHA
0F97 ◌ྗ TIBETAN SUBJOINED LETTER JA
0F98 <reserved>
0F99 ◌ྙ TIBETAN SUBJOINED LETTER NYA
0F9A ◌ྚ TIBETAN SUBJOINED LETTER TTA
0F9B ◌ྛ TIBETAN SUBJOINED LETTER TTHA
0F9C ◌ྜ TIBETAN SUBJOINED LETTER DDA
0F9D ◌ྜྷ TIBETAN SUBJOINED LETTER DDHA
  ≡ 0F9C ◌ྜ 0FB7 ◌ྷ
0F9E ◌ྞ TIBETAN SUBJOINED LETTER NNA
0F9F ◌ྟ TIBETAN SUBJOINED LETTER TA
0FA0 ◌ྠ TIBETAN SUBJOINED LETTER THA
0FA1 ◌ྡ TIBETAN SUBJOINED LETTER DA
0FA2 ◌ྡྷ TIBETAN SUBJOINED LETTER DHA
  ≡ 0FA1 ◌ྡ 0FB7 ◌ྷ
0FA3 ◌ྣ TIBETAN SUBJOINED LETTER NA
0FA4 ◌ྤ TIBETAN SUBJOINED LETTER PA
0FA5 ◌ྥ TIBETAN SUBJOINED LETTER PHA
0FA6 ◌ྦ TIBETAN SUBJOINED LETTER BA
0FA7 ◌ྦྷ TIBETAN SUBJOINED LETTER BHA
  ≡ 0FA6 ◌ྦ 0FB7 ◌ྷ

0FA8 ྨ TIBETAN SUBJOINED LETTER MA
0FA9 ྩ TIBETAN SUBJOINED LETTER TSA
0FAA ྪ TIBETAN SUBJOINED LETTER TSHA
0FAB ྫ TIBETAN SUBJOINED LETTER DZA
0FAC ྫྷ TIBETAN SUBJOINED LETTER DZHA
≡ 0FAB ྫ 0FB7 ྷ
0FAD ྭ TIBETAN SUBJOINED LETTER WA
= wa-zur, wa-btags
0FAE ྮ TIBETAN SUBJOINED LETTER ZHA
0FAF ྯ TIBETAN SUBJOINED LETTER ZA
0FB0 ྰ TIBETAN SUBJOINED LETTER -A
= a-chung
• rare, only used for full-sized subjoined letter
→ 0F71 ཱ tibetan vowel sign aa
0FB1 ྱ TIBETAN SUBJOINED LETTER YA
= ya-btags
0FB2 ྲ TIBETAN SUBJOINED LETTER RA
= ra-btags
0FB3 ླ TIBETAN SUBJOINED LETTER LA
0FB4 ྴ TIBETAN SUBJOINED LETTER SHA
0FB5 ྵ TIBETAN SUBJOINED LETTER SSA
= reversed subjoined sha
0FB6 ྶ TIBETAN SUBJOINED LETTER SA
0FB7 ྷ TIBETAN SUBJOINED LETTER HA
0FB8 ྸ TIBETAN SUBJOINED LETTER A
0FB9 ྐྵ TIBETAN SUBJOINED LETTER KSSA
≡ 0F90 ྐ 0FB5 ྵ

Fixed-form subjoined consonants

These characters are used only for transliteration and transcription.

0FBA ྺ TIBETAN SUBJOINED LETTER FIXED-FORM WA
0FBB ྻ TIBETAN SUBJOINED LETTER FIXED-FORM YA
0FBC ྼ TIBETAN SUBJOINED LETTER FIXED-FORM RA

Signs

0FBE ྾ TIBETAN KU RU KHA
• often repeated three times; indicates a refrain
0FBF ྿ TIBETAN KU RU KHA BZHI MIG CAN
• marks point of text insertion or annotation
→ 203B ※ reference mark

Cantillation signs

0FC0 ࿀ TIBETAN CANTILLATION SIGN HEAVY BEAT
• marks a heavy drum beat
0FC1 ࿁ TIBETAN CANTILLATION SIGN LIGHT BEAT
• marks a light drum beat
0FC2 ࿂ TIBETAN CANTILLATION SIGN CANG TE-U
• symbol of a small Tibetan hand drum
0FC3 ࿃ TIBETAN CANTILLATION SIGN SBUB -CHAL
• symbol of a Tibetan cymbal

Symbols

0FC4 ࿄ TIBETAN SYMBOL DRIL BU
• symbol of a Tibetan hand bell
0FC5 ࿅ TIBETAN SYMBOL RDO RJE
0FC6 ࿆ TIBETAN SYMBOL PADMA GDAN
0FC7 ࿇ TIBETAN SYMBOL RDO RJE RGYA GRAM
0FC8 ࿈ TIBETAN SYMBOL PHUR PA
0FC9 ࿉ TIBETAN SYMBOL NOR BU
0FCA ࿊ TIBETAN SYMBOL NOR BU NYIS -KHYIL
• the double body symbol
→ 262F ☯ yin yang
0FCB ࿋ TIBETAN SYMBOL NOR BU GSUM -KHYIL
• the tri-kaya or triple body symbol
0FCC ࿌ TIBETAN SYMBOL NOR BU BZHI -KHYIL
• the quadruple body symbol, a form of the swastika
→ 534D 卍 cjk unified ideograph-534D

Astrological sign

0FCF ࿏ TIBETAN SIGN RDEL NAG GSUM

Marks

0FD0 ࿐ TIBETAN MARK BSKA- SHOG GI MGO RGYAN
※ TIBETAN MARK BKA- SHOG GI MGO RGYAN
• used in Bhutan
0FD1 ࿑ TIBETAN MARK MNYAM YIG GI MGO RGYAN
• used in Bhutan

	100	101	102	103	104	105	106	107	108	109
0	က 1000	တ 1010	ဠ 1020	◌ူ 1030	၀ 1040	ၐ 1050				
1	ခ 1001	ထ 1011	အ 1021	◌ေ 1031	၁ 1041	ၑ 1051				
2	ဂ 1002	ဒ 1012		◌ဲ 1032	၂ 1042	ၒ 1052				
3	ဃ 1003	ဓ 1013	ဣ 1023		၃ 1043	ၓ 1053				
4	င 1004	န 1014	ဤ 1024		၄ 1044	ၔ 1054				
5	စ 1005	ပ 1015	ဥ 1025		၅ 1045	ၕ 1055				
6	ဆ 1006	ဖ 1016	ဦ 1026	◌ံ 1036	၆ 1046	◌ၖ 1056				
7	ဇ 1007	ဗ 1017	ဧ 1027	◌့ 1037	၇ 1047	◌ၗ 1057				
8	ဈ 1008	ဘ 1018		◌း 1038	၈ 1048	◌ၘ 1058				
9	ဉ 1009	မ 1019	ဩ 1029	◌္ 1039	၉ 1049	◌ၙ 1059				
A	ည 100A	ယ 101A	ဪ 102A		၊ 104A					
B	ဋ 100B	ရ 101B			။ 104B					
C	ဌ 100C	လ 101C	◌ာ 102C		၌ 104C					
D	ဍ 100D	ဝ 101D	◌ိ 102D		၍ 104D					
E	ဎ 100E	သ 101E	◌ီ 102E		၎ 104E					
F	ဏ 100F	ဟ 101F	◌ု 102F		၏ 104F					

Consonants

1000 က MYANMAR LETTER KA

1001 ခ MYANMAR LETTER KHA

1002 ဂ MYANMAR LETTER GA

1003 ဃ MYANMAR LETTER GHA

1004 င MYANMAR LETTER NGA

1005 စ MYANMAR LETTER CA

1006 ဆ MYANMAR LETTER CHA

1007 ဇ MYANMAR LETTER JA

1008 ဈ MYANMAR LETTER JHA

1009 ဉ MYANMAR LETTER NYA

100A ည MYANMAR LETTER NNYA

100B ဋ MYANMAR LETTER TTA

100C ဌ MYANMAR LETTER TTHA

100D ဍ MYANMAR LETTER DDA

100E ဎ MYANMAR LETTER DDHA

100F ဏ MYANMAR LETTER NNA

1010 တ MYANMAR LETTER TA

1011 ထ MYANMAR LETTER THA

1012 ဒ MYANMAR LETTER DA

1013 ဓ MYANMAR LETTER DHA

1014 န MYANMAR LETTER NA

1015 ပ MYANMAR LETTER PA

1016 ဖ MYANMAR LETTER PHA

1017 ဗ MYANMAR LETTER BA

1018 ဘ MYANMAR LETTER BHA

1019 မ MYANMAR LETTER MA

101A ယ MYANMAR LETTER YA

101B ရ MYANMAR LETTER RA

101C လ MYANMAR LETTER LA

101D ဝ MYANMAR LETTER WA

101E သ MYANMAR LETTER SA

101F ဟ MYANMAR LETTER HA

1020 ဠ MYANMAR LETTER LLA

Independent vowels

1021 အ MYANMAR LETTER A
- also represents the glottal stop as a consonant

1022 <reserved>

1023 ဣ MYANMAR LETTER I

1024 ဤ MYANMAR LETTER II

1025 ဥ MYANMAR LETTER U

1026 ဦ MYANMAR LETTER UU
≡ 1025 ဥ 102E ◌ီ

1027 ဧ MYANMAR LETTER E

1028 <reserved>

1029 ဩ MYANMAR LETTER O

102A ဪ MYANMAR LETTER AU

Dependent vowel signs

102C ◌ာ MYANMAR VOWEL SIGN AA

102D ◌ိ MYANMAR VOWEL SIGN I

102E ◌ီ MYANMAR VOWEL SIGN II

102F ◌ု MYANMAR VOWEL SIGN U

1030 ◌ူ MYANMAR VOWEL SIGN UU

1031 ◌ေ MYANMAR VOWEL SIGN E
- stands to the left of the consonant

1032 ◌ဲ MYANMAR VOWEL SIGN AI

Various signs

1036 ◌ံ MYANMAR SIGN ANUSVARA

1037 ◌့ MYANMAR SIGN DOT BELOW
= aukmyit
- a tone mark

1038 ◌း MYANMAR SIGN VISARGA

1039 ◌္ MYANMAR SIGN VIRAMA
= killer (when rendered visibly)

Digits

1040 ၀ MYANMAR DIGIT ZERO

1041 ၁ MYANMAR DIGIT ONE

1042 ၂ MYANMAR DIGIT TWO

1043 ၃ MYANMAR DIGIT THREE

1044 ၄ MYANMAR DIGIT FOUR

1045 ၅ MYANMAR DIGIT FIVE

1046 ၆ MYANMAR DIGIT SIX

1047 ၇ MYANMAR DIGIT SEVEN

1048 ၈ MYANMAR DIGIT EIGHT

1049 ၉ MYANMAR DIGIT NINE

Punctuation

104A ၊ MYANMAR SIGN LITTLE SECTION
→ 0964 । devanagari danda

104B ။ MYANMAR SIGN SECTION
→ 0965 ॥ devanagari double danda

Various signs

104C ၌ MYANMAR SYMBOL LOCATIVE

104D ၍ MYANMAR SYMBOL COMPLETED

104E ၎ MYANMAR SYMBOL AFOREMENTIONED

104F ၏ MYANMAR SYMBOL GENITIVE

Pali and Sanskrit extensions

1050 ၐ MYANMAR LETTER SHA

1051 ၑ MYANMAR LETTER SSA

1052 ၒ MYANMAR LETTER VOCALIC R

1053 ၓ MYANMAR LETTER VOCALIC RR

1054 ၔ MYANMAR LETTER VOCALIC L

1055 ၕ MYANMAR LETTER VOCALIC LL

1056 ◌ၖ MYANMAR VOWEL SIGN VOCALIC R

1057 ◌ၗ MYANMAR VOWEL SIGN VOCALIC RR

1058 ◌ၘ MYANMAR VOWEL SIGN VOCALIC L

1059 ◌ၙ MYANMAR VOWEL SIGN VOCALIC LL

	10A	10B	10C	10D	10E	10F
0	Ⴀ 10A0	Ⴐ 10B0	Ⴠ 10C0	ა 10D0	რ 10E0	ჰ 10F0
1	Ⴁ 10A1	Ⴑ 10B1	Ⴡ 10C1	ბ 10D1	ს 10E1	ჱ 10F1
2	Ⴂ 10A2	Ⴒ 10B2	Ⴢ 10C2	გ 10D2	ტ 10E2	ჲ 10F2
3	Ⴃ 10A3	Ⴓ 10B3	Ⴣ 10C3	დ 10D3	უ 10E3	ჳ 10F3
4	Ⴄ 10A4	Ⴔ 10B4	Ⴤ 10C4	ე 10D4	ფ 10E4	ჴ 10F4
5	Ⴅ 10A5	Ⴕ 10B5	Ⴥ 10C5	ვ 10D5	ქ 10E5	ჵ 10F5
6	Ⴆ 10A6	Ⴖ 10B6		ზ 10D6	ღ 10E6	ჶ 10F6
7	Ⴇ 10A7	Ⴗ 10B7		თ 10D7	ყ 10E7	ჷ 10F7
8	Ⴈ 10A8	Ⴘ 10B8		ი 10D8	შ 10E8	ჸ 10F8
9	Ⴉ 10A9	Ⴙ 10B9		კ 10D9	ჩ 10E9	ჹ 10F9
A	Ⴊ 10AA	Ⴚ 10BA		ლ 10DA	ც 10EA	ჺ 10FA
B	Ⴋ 10AB	Ⴛ 10BB		მ 10DB	ძ 10EB	჻ 10FB
C	Ⴌ 10AC	Ⴜ 10BC		ნ 10DC	წ 10EC	ჼ 10FC
D	Ⴍ 10AD	Ⴝ 10BD		ო 10DD	ჭ 10ED	
E	Ⴎ 10AE	Ⴞ 10BE		პ 10DE	ხ 10EE	
F	Ⴏ 10AF	Ⴟ 10BF		ჟ 10DF	ჯ 10EF	

Capital letters (Khutsuri)

This is the uppercase of the old ecclesiastical alphabet. The style shown in the code charts is known as Asomtavruli. See the Georgian Supplement block for lowercase Nuskhuri.

10A0 Ⴀ GEORGIAN CAPITAL LETTER AN
10A1 Ⴁ GEORGIAN CAPITAL LETTER BAN
10A2 Ⴂ GEORGIAN CAPITAL LETTER GAN
10A3 Ⴃ GEORGIAN CAPITAL LETTER DON
10A4 Ⴄ GEORGIAN CAPITAL LETTER EN
10A5 Ⴅ GEORGIAN CAPITAL LETTER VIN
10A6 Ⴆ GEORGIAN CAPITAL LETTER ZEN
10A7 Ⴇ GEORGIAN CAPITAL LETTER TAN
10A8 Ⴈ GEORGIAN CAPITAL LETTER IN
10A9 Ⴉ GEORGIAN CAPITAL LETTER KAN
10AA Ⴊ GEORGIAN CAPITAL LETTER LAS
10AB Ⴋ GEORGIAN CAPITAL LETTER MAN
10AC Ⴌ GEORGIAN CAPITAL LETTER NAR
10AD Ⴍ GEORGIAN CAPITAL LETTER ON
10AE Ⴎ GEORGIAN CAPITAL LETTER PAR
10AF Ⴏ GEORGIAN CAPITAL LETTER ZHAR
10B0 Ⴐ GEORGIAN CAPITAL LETTER RAE
10B1 Ⴑ GEORGIAN CAPITAL LETTER SAN
10B2 Ⴒ GEORGIAN CAPITAL LETTER TAR
10B3 Ⴓ GEORGIAN CAPITAL LETTER UN
10B4 Ⴔ GEORGIAN CAPITAL LETTER PHAR
10B5 Ⴕ GEORGIAN CAPITAL LETTER KHAR
10B6 Ⴖ GEORGIAN CAPITAL LETTER GHAN
10B7 Ⴗ GEORGIAN CAPITAL LETTER QAR
10B8 Ⴘ GEORGIAN CAPITAL LETTER SHIN
10B9 Ⴙ GEORGIAN CAPITAL LETTER CHIN
10BA Ⴚ GEORGIAN CAPITAL LETTER CAN
10BB Ⴛ GEORGIAN CAPITAL LETTER JIL
10BC Ⴜ GEORGIAN CAPITAL LETTER CIL
10BD Ⴝ GEORGIAN CAPITAL LETTER CHAR
10BE Ⴞ GEORGIAN CAPITAL LETTER XAN
10BF Ⴟ GEORGIAN CAPITAL LETTER JHAN
10C0 Ⴠ GEORGIAN CAPITAL LETTER HAE
10C1 Ⴡ GEORGIAN CAPITAL LETTER HE
10C2 Ⴢ GEORGIAN CAPITAL LETTER HIE
10C3 Ⴣ GEORGIAN CAPITAL LETTER WE
10C4 Ⴤ GEORGIAN CAPITAL LETTER HAR
10C5 Ⴥ GEORGIAN CAPITAL LETTER HOE

Mkhedruli

This is the modern secular alphabet, which is caseless.

10D0 ა GEORGIAN LETTER AN
10D1 ბ GEORGIAN LETTER BAN
10D2 გ GEORGIAN LETTER GAN
10D3 დ GEORGIAN LETTER DON
10D4 ე GEORGIAN LETTER EN
10D5 ვ GEORGIAN LETTER VIN
10D6 ზ GEORGIAN LETTER ZEN
10D7 თ GEORGIAN LETTER TAN
10D8 ი GEORGIAN LETTER IN
10D9 კ GEORGIAN LETTER KAN
10DA ლ GEORGIAN LETTER LAS
10DB მ GEORGIAN LETTER MAN
10DC ნ GEORGIAN LETTER NAR
10DD ო GEORGIAN LETTER ON
10DE პ GEORGIAN LETTER PAR
10DF ჟ GEORGIAN LETTER ZHAR
10E0 რ GEORGIAN LETTER RAE
10E1 ს GEORGIAN LETTER SAN
10E2 ტ GEORGIAN LETTER TAR
10E3 უ GEORGIAN LETTER UN
10E4 ფ GEORGIAN LETTER PHAR
10E5 ქ GEORGIAN LETTER KHAR
10E6 ღ GEORGIAN LETTER GHAN
10E7 ყ GEORGIAN LETTER QAR
10E8 შ GEORGIAN LETTER SHIN
10E9 ჩ GEORGIAN LETTER CHIN
10EA ც GEORGIAN LETTER CAN
10EB ძ GEORGIAN LETTER JIL
10EC წ GEORGIAN LETTER CIL
10ED ჭ GEORGIAN LETTER CHAR
10EE ხ GEORGIAN LETTER XAN
10EF ჯ GEORGIAN LETTER JHAN
10F0 ჰ GEORGIAN LETTER HAE

Archaic letters

10F1 ჱ GEORGIAN LETTER HE
10F2 ჲ GEORGIAN LETTER HIE
10F3 ჳ GEORGIAN LETTER WE
10F4 ჴ GEORGIAN LETTER HAR
10F5 ჵ GEORGIAN LETTER HOE
10F6 ჶ GEORGIAN LETTER FI

Additional letters for Mingrelian and Svan

10F7 ჷ GEORGIAN LETTER YN
10F8 ჸ GEORGIAN LETTER ELIFI

Additional letters

10F9 ჹ GEORGIAN LETTER TURNED GAN
10FA ჺ GEORGIAN LETTER AIN

Punctuation

10FB ჻ GEORGIAN PARAGRAPH SEPARATOR

Modifier letter

10FC ჼ MODIFIER LETTER GEORGIAN NAR
≈ <super> 10DC ნ

	110	111	112	113	114	115	116	117	118	119	11A	11B	11C	11D	11E	11F
0	ᄀ 1100	ᄐ 1110	ᄠ 1120	ᄰ 1130	ᅀ 1140	ᅐ 1150	HJF 1160	ᅰ 1170	ᆀ 1180	ᆐ 1190	ᆠ 11A0	ᆰ 11B0	ᇀ 11C0	ᇐ 11D0	ᇠ 11E0	ᇰ 11F0
1	ᄁ 1101	ᄑ 1111	ᄡ 1121	ᄱ 1131	ᅁ 1141	ᅑ 1151	ᅡ 1161	ᅱ 1171	ᆁ 1181	ᆑ 1191	ᆡ 11A1	ᆱ 11B1	ᇁ 11C1	ᇑ 11D1	ᇡ 11E1	ᇱ 11F1
2	ᄂ 1102	ᄒ 1112	ᄢ 1122	ᄲ 1132	ᅂ 1142	ᅒ 1152	ᅢ 1162	ᅲ 1172	ᆂ 1182	ᆒ 1192	ᆢ 11A2	ᆲ 11B2	ᇂ 11C2	ᇒ 11D2	ᇢ 11E2	ᇲ 11F2
3	ᄃ 1103	ᄓ 1113	ᄣ 1123	ᄳ 1133	ᅃ 1143	ᅓ 1153	ᅣ 1163	ᅳ 1173	ᆃ 1183	ᆓ 1193		ᆳ 11B3	ᇃ 11C3	ᇓ 11D3	ᇣ 11E3	ᇳ 11F3
4	ᄄ 1104	ᄔ 1114	ᄤ 1124	ᄴ 1134	ᅄ 1144	ᅔ 1154	ᅤ 1164	ᅴ 1174	ᆄ 1184	ᆔ 1194		ᆴ 11B4	ᇄ 11C4	ᇔ 11D4	ᇤ 11E4	ᇴ 11F4
5	ᄅ 1105	ᄕ 1115	ᄥ 1125	ᄵ 1135	ᅅ 1145	ᅕ 1155	ᅥ 1165	ᅵ 1175	ᆅ 1185	ᆕ 1195		ᆵ 11B5	ᇅ 11C5	ᇕ 11D5	ᇥ 11E5	ᇵ 11F5
6	ᄆ 1106	ᄖ 1116	ᄦ 1126	ᄶ 1136	ᅆ 1146	ᅖ 1156	ᅦ 1166	ᅶ 1176	ᆆ 1186	ᆖ 1196		ᆶ 11B6	ᇆ 11C6	ᇖ 11D6	ᇦ 11E6	ᇶ 11F6
7	ᄇ 1107	ᄗ 1117	ᄧ 1127	ᄷ 1137	ᅇ 1147	ᅗ 1157	ᅧ 1167	ᅷ 1177	ᆇ 1187	ᆗ 1197		ᆷ 11B7	ᇇ 11C7	ᇗ 11D7	ᇧ 11E7	ᇷ 11F7
8	ᄈ 1108	ᄘ 1118	ᄨ 1128	ᄸ 1138	ᅈ 1148	ᅘ 1158	ᅨ 1168	ᅸ 1178	ᆈ 1188	ᆘ 1198	ᆨ 11A8	ᆸ 11B8	ᇈ 11C8	ᇘ 11D8	ᇨ 11E8	ᇸ 11F8
9	ᄉ 1109	ᄙ 1119	ᄩ 1129	ᄹ 1139	ᅉ 1149	ᅙ 1159	ᅩ 1169	ᅹ 1179	ᆉ 1189	ᆙ 1199	ᆩ 11A9	ᆹ 11B9	ᇉ 11C9	ᇙ 11D9	ᇩ 11E9	ᇹ 11F9
A	ᄊ 110A	ᄚ 111A	ᄪ 112A	ᄺ 113A	ᅊ 114A		ᅪ 116A	ᅺ 117A	ᆊ 118A	ᆚ 119A	ᆪ 11AA	ᆺ 11BA	ᇊ 11CA	ᇚ 11DA	ᇪ 11EA	
B	ᄋ 110B	ᄛ 111B	ᄫ 112B	ᄻ 113B	ᅋ 114B		ᅫ 116B	ᅻ 117B	ᆋ 118B	ᆛ 119B	ᆫ 11AB	ᆻ 11BB	ᇋ 11CB	ᇛ 11DB	ᇫ 11EB	
C	ᄌ 110C	ᄜ 111C	ᄬ 112C	ᄼ 113C	ᅌ 114C		ᅬ 116C	ᅼ 117C	ᆌ 118C	ᆜ 119C	ᆬ 11AC	ᆼ 11BC	ᇌ 11CC	ᇜ 11DC	ᇬ 11EC	
D	ᄍ 110D	ᄝ 111D	ᄭ 112D	ᄽ 113D	ᅍ 114D		ᅭ 116D	ᅽ 117D	ᆍ 118D	ᆝ 119D	ᆭ 11AD	ᆽ 11BD	ᇍ 11CD	ᇝ 11DD	ᇭ 11ED	
E	ᄎ 110E	ᄞ 111E	ᄮ 112E	ᄾ 113E	ᅎ 114E		ᅮ 116E	ᅾ 117E	ᆎ 118E	ᆞ 119E	ᆮ 11AE	ᆾ 11BE	ᇎ 11CE	ᇞ 11DE	ᇮ 11EE	
F	ᄏ 110F	ᄟ 111F	ᄯ 112F	ᄿ 113F	ᅏ 114F	HCF 115F	ᅯ 116F	ᅿ 117F	ᆏ 118F	ᆟ 119F	ᆯ 11AF	ᆿ 11BF	ᇏ 11CF	ᇟ 11DF	ᇯ 11EF	

The aliases in this block represent the Jamo short names.

Korean combining alphabet

Initial consonants

1100 ᄀ HANGUL CHOSEONG KIYEOK
= G
1101 ᄁ HANGUL CHOSEONG SSANGKIYEOK
= GG
1102 ᄂ HANGUL CHOSEONG NIEUN
= N
1103 ᄃ HANGUL CHOSEONG TIKEUT
= D
1104 ᄄ HANGUL CHOSEONG SSANGTIKEUT
= DD
1105 ᄅ HANGUL CHOSEONG RIEUL
= R
1106 ᄆ HANGUL CHOSEONG MIEUM
= M
1107 ᄇ HANGUL CHOSEONG PIEUP
= B
1108 ᄈ HANGUL CHOSEONG SSANGPIEUP
= BB
1109 ᄉ HANGUL CHOSEONG SIOS
= S
110A ᄊ HANGUL CHOSEONG SSANGSIOS
= SS
110B ᄋ HANGUL CHOSEONG IEUNG
110C ᄌ HANGUL CHOSEONG CIEUC
= J
110D ᄍ HANGUL CHOSEONG SSANGCIEUC
= JJ
110E ᄎ HANGUL CHOSEONG CHIEUCH
= C
110F ᄏ HANGUL CHOSEONG KHIEUKH
= K
1110 ᄐ HANGUL CHOSEONG THIEUTH
= T
1111 ᄑ HANGUL CHOSEONG PHIEUPH
= P
1112 ᄒ HANGUL CHOSEONG HIEUH
= H
1113 ᄓ HANGUL CHOSEONG NIEUN-KIYEOK
1114 ᄔ HANGUL CHOSEONG SSANGNIEUN
1115 ᄕ HANGUL CHOSEONG NIEUN-TIKEUT
1116 ᄖ HANGUL CHOSEONG NIEUN-PIEUP
1117 ᄗ HANGUL CHOSEONG TIKEUT-KIYEOK
1118 ᄘ HANGUL CHOSEONG RIEUL-NIEUN
1119 ᄙ HANGUL CHOSEONG SSANGRIEUL
111A ᄚ HANGUL CHOSEONG RIEUL-HIEUH
111B ᄛ HANGUL CHOSEONG KAPYEOUNRIEUL
111C ᄜ HANGUL CHOSEONG MIEUM-PIEUP
111D ᄝ HANGUL CHOSEONG KAPYEOUNMIEUM
111E ᄞ HANGUL CHOSEONG PIEUP-KIYEOK
111F ᄟ HANGUL CHOSEONG PIEUP-NIEUN
1120 ᄠ HANGUL CHOSEONG PIEUP-TIKEUT
1121 ᄡ HANGUL CHOSEONG PIEUP-SIOS
1122 ᄢ HANGUL CHOSEONG PIEUP-SIOS-KIYEOK
1123 ᄣ HANGUL CHOSEONG PIEUP-SIOS-TIKEUT
1124 ᄤ HANGUL CHOSEONG PIEUP-SIOS-PIEUP
1125 ᄥ HANGUL CHOSEONG PIEUP-SSANGSIOS
1126 ᄦ HANGUL CHOSEONG PIEUP-SIOS-CIEUC
1127 ᄧ HANGUL CHOSEONG PIEUP-CIEUC
1128 ᄨ HANGUL CHOSEONG PIEUP-CHIEUCH
1129 ᄩ HANGUL CHOSEONG PIEUP-THIEUTH
112A ᄪ HANGUL CHOSEONG PIEUP-PHIEUPH
112B ᄫ HANGUL CHOSEONG KAPYEOUNPIEUP
112C ᄬ HANGUL CHOSEONG KAPYEOUNSSANGPIEUP
112D ᄭ HANGUL CHOSEONG SIOS-KIYEOK
112E ᄮ HANGUL CHOSEONG SIOS-NIEUN
112F ᄯ HANGUL CHOSEONG SIOS-TIKEUT
1130 ᄰ HANGUL CHOSEONG SIOS-RIEUL
1131 ᄱ HANGUL CHOSEONG SIOS-MIEUM
1132 ᄲ HANGUL CHOSEONG SIOS-PIEUP
1133 ᄳ HANGUL CHOSEONG SIOS-PIEUP-KIYEOK
1134 ᄴ HANGUL CHOSEONG SIOS-SSANGSIOS
1135 ᄵ HANGUL CHOSEONG SIOS-IEUNG
1136 ᄶ HANGUL CHOSEONG SIOS-CIEUC
1137 ᄷ HANGUL CHOSEONG SIOS-CHIEUCH
1138 ᄸ HANGUL CHOSEONG SIOS-KHIEUKH
1139 ᄹ HANGUL CHOSEONG SIOS-THIEUTH
113A ᄺ HANGUL CHOSEONG SIOS-PHIEUPH
113B ᄻ HANGUL CHOSEONG SIOS-HIEUH
113C ᄼ HANGUL CHOSEONG CHITUEUMSIOS
113D ᄽ HANGUL CHOSEONG CHITUEUMSSANGSIOS
113E ᄾ HANGUL CHOSEONG CEONGCHIEUMSIOS
113F ᄿ HANGUL CHOSEONG CEONGCHIEUMSSANGSIOS
1140 ᅀ HANGUL CHOSEONG PANSIOS
1141 ᅁ HANGUL CHOSEONG IEUNG-KIYEOK
1142 ᅂ HANGUL CHOSEONG IEUNG-TIKEUT
1143 ᅃ HANGUL CHOSEONG IEUNG-MIEUM
1144 ᅄ HANGUL CHOSEONG IEUNG-PIEUP
1145 ᅅ HANGUL CHOSEONG IEUNG-SIOS
1146 ᅆ HANGUL CHOSEONG IEUNG-PANSIOS
1147 ᅇ HANGUL CHOSEONG SSANGIEUNG
1148 ᅈ HANGUL CHOSEONG IEUNG-CIEUC
1149 ᅉ HANGUL CHOSEONG IEUNG-CHIEUCH
114A ᅊ HANGUL CHOSEONG IEUNG-THIEUTH
114B ᅋ HANGUL CHOSEONG IEUNG-PHIEUPH
114C ᅌ HANGUL CHOSEONG YESIEUNG
114D ᅍ HANGUL CHOSEONG CIEUC-IEUNG
114E ᅎ HANGUL CHOSEONG CHITUEUMCIEUC
114F ᅏ HANGUL CHOSEONG CHITUEUMSSANGCIEUC
1150 ᅐ HANGUL CHOSEONG CEONGCHIEUMCIEUC
1151 ᅑ HANGUL CHOSEONG CEONGCHIEUMSSANGCIEUC
1152 ᅒ HANGUL CHOSEONG CHIEUCH-KHIEUKH
1153 ᅓ HANGUL CHOSEONG CHIEUCH-HIEUH
1154 ᅔ HANGUL CHOSEONG CHITUEUMCHIEUCH
1155 ᅕ HANGUL CHOSEONG CEONGCHIEUMCHIEUCH
1156 ᅖ HANGUL CHOSEONG PHIEUPH-PIEUP
1157 ᅗ HANGUL CHOSEONG KAPYEOUNPHIEUPH
1158 ᅘ HANGUL CHOSEONG SSANGHIEUH
1159 ᅙ HANGUL CHOSEONG YEORINHIEUH
115A <reserved>
115B <reserved>
115C <reserved>
115D <reserved>
115E <reserved>
115F HC F HANGUL CHOSEONG FILLER

Medial vowels

1160 HJ F HANGUL JUNGSEONG FILLER
1161 ᅡ HANGUL JUNGSEONG A
= A
1162 ᅢ HANGUL JUNGSEONG AE
= AE
1163 ᅣ HANGUL JUNGSEONG YA
= YA

1164 ᅤ HANGUL JUNGSEONG YAE
= YAE

1165 ᅥ HANGUL JUNGSEONG EO
= EO

1166 ᅦ HANGUL JUNGSEONG E
= E

1167 ᅧ HANGUL JUNGSEONG YEO
= YEO

1168 ᅨ HANGUL JUNGSEONG YE
= YE

1169 ᅩ HANGUL JUNGSEONG O
= O

116A ᅪ HANGUL JUNGSEONG WA
= WA

116B ᅫ HANGUL JUNGSEONG WAE
= WAE

116C ᅬ HANGUL JUNGSEONG OE
= OE

116D ᅭ HANGUL JUNGSEONG YO
= YO

116E ᅮ HANGUL JUNGSEONG U
= U

116F ᅯ HANGUL JUNGSEONG WEO
= WEO

1170 ᅰ HANGUL JUNGSEONG WE
= WE

1171 ᅱ HANGUL JUNGSEONG WI
= WI

1172 ᅲ HANGUL JUNGSEONG YU
= YU

1173 ᅳ HANGUL JUNGSEONG EU
= EU

1174 ᅴ HANGUL JUNGSEONG YI
= YI

1175 ᅵ HANGUL JUNGSEONG I
= I

1176 ᅶ HANGUL JUNGSEONG A-O

1177 ᅷ HANGUL JUNGSEONG A-U

1178 ᅸ HANGUL JUNGSEONG YA-O

1179 ᅹ HANGUL JUNGSEONG YA-YO

117A ᅺ HANGUL JUNGSEONG EO-O

117B ᅻ HANGUL JUNGSEONG EO-U

117C ᅼ HANGUL JUNGSEONG EO-EU

117D ᅽ HANGUL JUNGSEONG YEO-O

117E ᅾ HANGUL JUNGSEONG YEO-U

117F ᅿ HANGUL JUNGSEONG O-EO

1180 ᆀ HANGUL JUNGSEONG O-E

1181 ᆁ HANGUL JUNGSEONG O-YE

1182 ᆂ HANGUL JUNGSEONG O-O

1183 ᆃ HANGUL JUNGSEONG O-U

1184 ᆄ HANGUL JUNGSEONG YO-YA

1185 ᆅ HANGUL JUNGSEONG YO-YAE

1186 ᆆ HANGUL JUNGSEONG YO-YEO

1187 ᆇ HANGUL JUNGSEONG YO-O

1188 ᆈ HANGUL JUNGSEONG YO-I

1189 ᆉ HANGUL JUNGSEONG U-A

118A ᆊ HANGUL JUNGSEONG U-AE

118B ᆋ HANGUL JUNGSEONG U-EO-EU

118C ᆌ HANGUL JUNGSEONG U-YE

118D ᆍ HANGUL JUNGSEONG U-U

118E ᆎ HANGUL JUNGSEONG YU-A

118F ᆏ HANGUL JUNGSEONG YU-EO

1190 ᆐ HANGUL JUNGSEONG YU-E

1191 ᆑ HANGUL JUNGSEONG YU-YEO

1192 ᆒ HANGUL JUNGSEONG YU-YE

1193 ᆓ HANGUL JUNGSEONG YU-U

1194 ᆔ HANGUL JUNGSEONG YU-I

1195 ᆕ HANGUL JUNGSEONG EU-U

1196 ᆖ HANGUL JUNGSEONG EU-EU

1197 ᆗ HANGUL JUNGSEONG YI-U

1198 ᆘ HANGUL JUNGSEONG I-A

1199 ᆙ HANGUL JUNGSEONG I-YA

119A ᆚ HANGUL JUNGSEONG I-O

119B ᆛ HANGUL JUNGSEONG I-U

119C ᆜ HANGUL JUNGSEONG I-EU

119D ᆝ HANGUL JUNGSEONG I-ARAEA

119E ᆞ HANGUL JUNGSEONG ARAEA

119F ᆟ HANGUL JUNGSEONG ARAEA-EO

11A0 ᆠ HANGUL JUNGSEONG ARAEA-U

11A1 ᆡ HANGUL JUNGSEONG ARAEA-I

11A2 ᆢ HANGUL JUNGSEONG SSANGARAEA

Final consonants

11A8 ᆨ HANGUL JONGSEONG KIYEOK
= G

11A9 ᆩ HANGUL JONGSEONG SSANGKIYEOK
= GG

11AA ᆪ HANGUL JONGSEONG KIYEOK-SIOS
= GS

11AB ᆫ HANGUL JONGSEONG NIEUN
= N

11AC ᆬ HANGUL JONGSEONG NIEUN-CIEUC
= NJ

11AD ᆭ HANGUL JONGSEONG NIEUN-HIEUH
= NH

11AE ᆮ HANGUL JONGSEONG TIKEUT
= D

11AF ᆯ HANGUL JONGSEONG RIEUL
= L

11B0 ᆰ HANGUL JONGSEONG RIEUL-KIYEOK
= LG

11B1 ᆱ HANGUL JONGSEONG RIEUL-MIEUM
= LM

11B2 ᆲ HANGUL JONGSEONG RIEUL-PIEUP
= LB

11B3 ᆳ HANGUL JONGSEONG RIEUL-SIOS
= LS

11B4 ᆴ HANGUL JONGSEONG RIEUL-THIEUTH
= LT

11B5 ᆵ HANGUL JONGSEONG RIEUL-PHIEUPH
= LP

11B6 ᆶ HANGUL JONGSEONG RIEUL-HIEUH
= LH

11B7 ᆷ HANGUL JONGSEONG MIEUM
= M

11B8 ᆸ HANGUL JONGSEONG PIEUP
= B

11B9 ᆹ HANGUL JONGSEONG PIEUP-SIOS
= BS

11BA ᆺ HANGUL JONGSEONG SIOS
= S

11BB ᆻ HANGUL JONGSEONG SSANGSIOS
= SS

11BC ᆼ HANGUL JONGSEONG IEUNG
= NG

11BD ᆽ HANGUL JONGSEONG CIEUC
= J

11BE ᆾ HANGUL JONGSEONG CHIEUCH
= C

11BF ᆿ HANGUL JONGSEONG KHIEUKH
= K

11C0 ᇀ HANGUL JONGSEONG THIEUTH
= T

11C1 ᇁ HANGUL JONGSEONG PHIEUPH
= P

11C2 ᇂ HANGUL JONGSEONG HIEUH
= H

11C3 ᇃ HANGUL JONGSEONG KIYEOK-RIEUL

11C4 ᇄ HANGUL JONGSEONG KIYEOK-SIOS-KIYEOK

11C5 ᇅ HANGUL JONGSEONG NIEUN-KIYEOK

11C6 ᇆ HANGUL JONGSEONG NIEUN-TIKEUT

11C7 ᇇ HANGUL JONGSEONG NIEUN-SIOS

11C8 ᇈ HANGUL JONGSEONG NIEUN-PANSIOS

11C9 ᇉ HANGUL JONGSEONG NIEUN-THIEUTH

11CA ᇊ HANGUL JONGSEONG TIKEUT-KIYEOK

11CB ᇋ HANGUL JONGSEONG TIKEUT-RIEUL

11CC ᇌ HANGUL JONGSEONG RIEUL-KIYEOK-SIOS

11CD ᇍ HANGUL JONGSEONG RIEUL-NIEUN

11CE ᇎ HANGUL JONGSEONG RIEUL-TIKEUT

11CF ᇏ HANGUL JONGSEONG RIEUL-TIKEUT-HIEUH

11D0 ᇐ HANGUL JONGSEONG SSANGRIEUL

11D1 ᇑ HANGUL JONGSEONG RIEUL-MIEUM-KIYEOK

11D2 ᇒ HANGUL JONGSEONG RIEUL-MIEUM-SIOS

11D3 ᇓ HANGUL JONGSEONG RIEUL-PIEUP-SIOS

11D4 ᇔ HANGUL JONGSEONG RIEUL-PIEUP-HIEUH

11D5 ᇕ HANGUL JONGSEONG RIEUL-KAPYEOUNPIEUP

11D6 ᇖ HANGUL JONGSEONG RIEUL-SSANGSIOS

11D7 ᇗ HANGUL JONGSEONG RIEUL-PANSIOS

11D8 ᇘ HANGUL JONGSEONG RIEUL-KHIEUKH

11D9 ᇙ HANGUL JONGSEONG RIEUL-YEORINHIEUH

11DA ᇚ HANGUL JONGSEONG MIEUM-KIYEOK

11DB ᇛ HANGUL JONGSEONG MIEUM-RIEUL

11DC ᇜ HANGUL JONGSEONG MIEUM-PIEUP

11DD ᇝ HANGUL JONGSEONG MIEUM-SIOS

11DE ᇞ HANGUL JONGSEONG MIEUM-SSANGSIOS

11DF ᇟ HANGUL JONGSEONG MIEUM-PANSIOS

11E0 ᇠ HANGUL JONGSEONG MIEUM-CHIEUCH

11E1 ᇡ HANGUL JONGSEONG MIEUM-HIEUH

11E2 ᇢ HANGUL JONGSEONG KAPYEOUNMIEUM

11E3 ᇣ HANGUL JONGSEONG PIEUP-RIEUL

11E4 ᇤ HANGUL JONGSEONG PIEUP-PHIEUPH

11E5 ᇥ HANGUL JONGSEONG PIEUP-HIEUH

11E6 ᇦ HANGUL JONGSEONG KAPYEOUNPIEUP

11E7 ᇧ HANGUL JONGSEONG SIOS-KIYEOK

11E8 ᇨ HANGUL JONGSEONG SIOS-TIKEUT

11E9 ᇩ HANGUL JONGSEONG SIOS-RIEUL

11EA ᇪ HANGUL JONGSEONG SIOS-PIEUP

11EB ᇫ HANGUL JONGSEONG PANSIOS

11EC ᇬ HANGUL JONGSEONG IEUNG-KIYEOK

11ED ᇭ HANGUL JONGSEONG IEUNG-SSANGKIYEOK

11EE ᇮ HANGUL JONGSEONG SSANGIEUNG

11EF ᇯ HANGUL JONGSEONG IEUNG-KHIEUKH

11F0 ᇰ HANGUL JONGSEONG YESIEUNG

11F1 ᇱ HANGUL JONGSEONG YESIEUNG-SIOS

11F2 ᇲ HANGUL JONGSEONG YESIEUNG-PANSIOS

11F3 ᇳ HANGUL JONGSEONG PHIEUPH-PIEUP

11F4 ᇴ HANGUL JONGSEONG KAPYEOUNPHIEUPH

11F5 ᇵ HANGUL JONGSEONG HIEUH-NIEUN

11F6 ᇶ HANGUL JONGSEONG HIEUH-RIEUL

11F7 ᇷ HANGUL JONGSEONG HIEUH-MIEUM

11F8 ᇸ HANGUL JONGSEONG HIEUH-PIEUP

11F9 ᇹ HANGUL JONGSEONG YEORINHIEUH

	120	121	122	123	124	125	126	127	128	129	12A	12B
0	ሀ 1200	ሐ 1210	ሠ 1220	ሰ 1230	ቀ 1240	ቐ 1250	በ 1260	ተ 1270	ኀ 1280	ነ 1290	አ 12A0	ኰ 12B0
1	ሁ 1201	ሑ 1211	ሡ 1221	ሱ 1231	ቁ 1241	ቑ 1251	ቡ 1261	ቱ 1271	ኁ 1281	ኑ 1291	ኡ 12A1	
2	ሂ 1202	ሒ 1212	ሢ 1222	ሲ 1232	ቂ 1242	ቒ 1252	ቢ 1262	ቲ 1272	ኂ 1282	ኒ 1292	ኢ 12A2	ኲ 12B2
3	ሃ 1203	ሓ 1213	ሣ 1223	ሳ 1233	ቃ 1243	ቓ 1253	ባ 1263	ታ 1273	ኃ 1283	ና 1293	ኣ 12A3	ኳ 12B3
4	ሄ 1204	ሔ 1214	ሤ 1224	ሴ 1234	ቄ 1244	ቔ 1254	ቤ 1264	ቴ 1274	ኄ 1284	ኔ 1294	ኤ 12A4	ኴ 12B4
5	ህ 1205	ሕ 1215	ሥ 1225	ስ 1235	ቅ 1245	ቕ 1255	ብ 1265	ት 1275	ኅ 1285	ን 1295	እ 12A5	ኵ 12B5
6	ሆ 1206	ሖ 1216	ሦ 1226	ሶ 1236	ቆ 1246	ቖ 1256	ቦ 1266	ቶ 1276	ኆ 1286	ኖ 1296	ኦ 12A6	
7	ሇ 1207	ሗ 1217	ሧ 1227	ሷ 1237	ቇ 1247		ቧ 1267	ቷ 1277	ኇ 1287	ኗ 1297	ኧ 12A7	
8	ለ 1208	መ 1218	ረ 1228	ሸ 1238	ቈ 1248	ቘ 1258	ቨ 1268	ቸ 1278	ኈ 1288	ኘ 1298	ከ 12A8	ኸ 12B8
9	ሉ 1209	ሙ 1219	ሩ 1229	ሹ 1239			ቩ 1269	ቹ 1279		ኙ 1299	ኩ 12A9	ኹ 12B9
A	ሊ 120A	ሚ 121A	ሪ 122A	ሺ 123A	ቊ 124A	ቚ 125A	ቪ 126A	ቺ 127A	ኊ 128A	ኚ 129A	ኪ 12AA	ኺ 12BA
B	ላ 120B	ማ 121B	ራ 122B	ሻ 123B	ቋ 124B	ቛ 125B	ቫ 126B	ቻ 127B	ኋ 128B	ኛ 129B	ካ 12AB	ኻ 12BB
C	ሌ 120C	ሜ 121C	ሬ 122C	ሼ 123C	ቌ 124C	ቜ 125C	ቬ 126C	ቼ 127C	ኌ 128C	ኜ 129C	ኬ 12AC	ኼ 12BC
D	ል 120D	ም 121D	ር 122D	ሽ 123D	ቍ 124D	ቝ 125D	ቭ 126D	ች 127D	ኍ 128D	ኝ 129D	ክ 12AD	ኽ 12BD
E	ሎ 120E	ሞ 121E	ሮ 122E	ሾ 123E			ቮ 126E	ቾ 127E		ኞ 129E	ኮ 12AE	ኾ 12BE
F	ሏ 120F	ሟ 121F	ሯ 122F	ሿ 123F			ቯ 126F	ቿ 127F		ኟ 129F	ኯ 12AF	

	12C	12D	12E	12F	130	131	132	133	134	135	136	137
0	ኰ 12C0	ዐ 12D0	ዠ 12E0	ደ 12F0	ጀ 1300	ጐ 1310	ጠ 1320	ጰ 1330	ፀ 1340	ፐ 1350	፠ 1360	፰ 1370
1		ዑ 12D1	ዡ 12E1	ዱ 12F1	ጁ 1301		ጡ 1321	ጱ 1331	ፁ 1341	ፑ 1351	፡ 1361	፱ 1371
2	ኲ 12C2	ዒ 12D2	ዢ 12E2	ዲ 12F2	ጂ 1302	ጒ 1312	ጢ 1322	ጲ 1332	ፂ 1342	ፒ 1352	። 1362	፲ 1372
3	ኳ 12C3	ዓ 12D3	ዣ 12E3	ዳ 12F3	ጃ 1303	ጓ 1313	ጣ 1323	ጳ 1333	ፃ 1343	ፓ 1353	፣ 1363	፳ 1373
4	ኴ 12C4	ዔ 12D4	ዤ 12E4	ዴ 12F4	ጄ 1304	ጔ 1314	ጤ 1324	ጴ 1334	ፄ 1344	ፔ 1354	፤ 1364	፴ 1374
5	ኵ 12C5	ዕ 12D5	ዥ 12E5	ድ 12F5	ጅ 1305	ጕ 1315	ጥ 1325	ጵ 1335	ፅ 1345	ፕ 1355	፥ 1365	፵ 1375
6		ዖ 12D6	ዦ 12E6	ዶ 12F6	ጆ 1306		ጦ 1326	ጶ 1336	ፆ 1346	ፖ 1356	፦ 1366	፶ 1376
7			ዧ 12E7	ዷ 12F7	ጇ 1307		ጧ 1327	ጷ 1337	ፇ 1347	ፗ 1357	፧ 1367	፷ 1377
8	ወ 12C8	ዘ 12D8	የ 12E8	ዸ 12F8	ገ 1308	ጘ 1318	ጨ 1328	ጸ 1338	ፈ 1348	ፘ 1358	፨ 1368	፸ 1378
9	ዉ 12C9	ዙ 12D9	ዩ 12E9	ዹ 12F9	ጉ 1309	ጙ 1319	ጩ 1329	ጹ 1339	ፉ 1349	ፙ 1359	፩ 1369	፹ 1379
A	ዊ 12CA	ዚ 12DA	ዪ 12EA	ዺ 12FA	ጊ 130A	ጚ 131A	ጪ 132A	ጺ 133A	ፊ 134A	ፚ 135A	፪ 136A	፺ 137A
B	ዋ 12CB	ዛ 12DB	ያ 12EB	ዻ 12FB	ጋ 130B	ጛ 131B	ጫ 132B	ጻ 133B	ፋ 134B		፫ 136B	፻ 137B
C	ዌ 12CC	ዜ 12DC	ዬ 12EC	ዼ 12FC	ጌ 130C	ጜ 131C	ጬ 132C	ጼ 133C	ፌ 134C		፬ 136C	፼ 137C
D	ው 12CD	ዝ 12DD	ይ 12ED	ዽ 12FD	ግ 130D	ጝ 131D	ጭ 132D	ጽ 133D	ፍ 134D		፭ 136D	
E	ዎ 12CE	ዞ 12DE	ዮ 12EE	ዾ 12FE	ጎ 130E	ጞ 131E	ጮ 132E	ጾ 133E	ፎ 134E		፮ 136E	
F	ዏ 12CF	ዟ 12DF	ዯ 12EF	ዿ 12FF	ጏ 130F	ጟ 131F	ጯ 132F	ጿ 133F	ፏ 134F	◌፟ 135F	፯ 136F	

Syllables

Code	Glyph	Name
1200	ሀ	ETHIOPIC SYLLABLE HA
1201	ሁ	ETHIOPIC SYLLABLE HU
1202	ሂ	ETHIOPIC SYLLABLE HI
1203	ሃ	ETHIOPIC SYLLABLE HAA
1204	ሄ	ETHIOPIC SYLLABLE HEE
1205	ህ	ETHIOPIC SYLLABLE HE
1206	ሆ	ETHIOPIC SYLLABLE HO
1207	ሇ	ETHIOPIC SYLLABLE HOA
1208	ለ	ETHIOPIC SYLLABLE LA
1209	ሉ	ETHIOPIC SYLLABLE LU
120A	ሊ	ETHIOPIC SYLLABLE LI
120B	ላ	ETHIOPIC SYLLABLE LAA
120C	ሌ	ETHIOPIC SYLLABLE LEE
120D	ል	ETHIOPIC SYLLABLE LE
120E	ሎ	ETHIOPIC SYLLABLE LO
120F	ሏ	ETHIOPIC SYLLABLE LWA
1210	ሐ	ETHIOPIC SYLLABLE HHA
1211	ሑ	ETHIOPIC SYLLABLE HHU
1212	ሒ	ETHIOPIC SYLLABLE HHI
1213	ሓ	ETHIOPIC SYLLABLE HHAA
1214	ሔ	ETHIOPIC SYLLABLE HHEE
1215	ሕ	ETHIOPIC SYLLABLE HHE
1216	ሖ	ETHIOPIC SYLLABLE HHO
1217	ሗ	ETHIOPIC SYLLABLE HHWA
1218	መ	ETHIOPIC SYLLABLE MA
1219	ሙ	ETHIOPIC SYLLABLE MU
121A	ሚ	ETHIOPIC SYLLABLE MI
121B	ማ	ETHIOPIC SYLLABLE MAA
121C	ሜ	ETHIOPIC SYLLABLE MEE
121D	ም	ETHIOPIC SYLLABLE ME
121E	ሞ	ETHIOPIC SYLLABLE MO
121F	ሟ	ETHIOPIC SYLLABLE MWA
1220	ሠ	ETHIOPIC SYLLABLE SZA
1221	ሡ	ETHIOPIC SYLLABLE SZU
1222	ሢ	ETHIOPIC SYLLABLE SZI
1223	ሣ	ETHIOPIC SYLLABLE SZAA
1224	ሤ	ETHIOPIC SYLLABLE SZEE
1225	ሥ	ETHIOPIC SYLLABLE SZE
1226	ሦ	ETHIOPIC SYLLABLE SZO
1227	ሧ	ETHIOPIC SYLLABLE SZWA
1228	ረ	ETHIOPIC SYLLABLE RA
1229	ሩ	ETHIOPIC SYLLABLE RU
122A	ሪ	ETHIOPIC SYLLABLE RI
122B	ራ	ETHIOPIC SYLLABLE RAA
122C	ሬ	ETHIOPIC SYLLABLE REE
122D	ር	ETHIOPIC SYLLABLE RE
122E	ሮ	ETHIOPIC SYLLABLE RO
122F	ሯ	ETHIOPIC SYLLABLE RWA
1230	ሰ	ETHIOPIC SYLLABLE SA
1231	ሱ	ETHIOPIC SYLLABLE SU
1232	ሲ	ETHIOPIC SYLLABLE SI
1233	ሳ	ETHIOPIC SYLLABLE SAA
1234	ሴ	ETHIOPIC SYLLABLE SEE
1235	ስ	ETHIOPIC SYLLABLE SE
1236	ሶ	ETHIOPIC SYLLABLE SO
1237	ሷ	ETHIOPIC SYLLABLE SWA
1238	ሸ	ETHIOPIC SYLLABLE SHA
1239	ሹ	ETHIOPIC SYLLABLE SHU
123A	ሺ	ETHIOPIC SYLLABLE SHI
123B	ሻ	ETHIOPIC SYLLABLE SHAA
123C	ሼ	ETHIOPIC SYLLABLE SHEE
123D	ሽ	ETHIOPIC SYLLABLE SHE
123E	ሾ	ETHIOPIC SYLLABLE SHO
123F	ሿ	ETHIOPIC SYLLABLE SHWA
1240	ቀ	ETHIOPIC SYLLABLE QA
1241	ቁ	ETHIOPIC SYLLABLE QU
1242	ቂ	ETHIOPIC SYLLABLE QI
1243	ቃ	ETHIOPIC SYLLABLE QAA
1244	ቄ	ETHIOPIC SYLLABLE QEE
1245	ቅ	ETHIOPIC SYLLABLE QE
1246	ቆ	ETHIOPIC SYLLABLE QO
1247	ቇ	ETHIOPIC SYLLABLE QOA
1248	ቈ	ETHIOPIC SYLLABLE QWA
1249		<reserved>
124A	ቊ	ETHIOPIC SYLLABLE QWI
124B	ቋ	ETHIOPIC SYLLABLE QWAA
124C	ቌ	ETHIOPIC SYLLABLE QWEE
124D	ቍ	ETHIOPIC SYLLABLE QWE
124E		<reserved>
124F		<reserved>
1250	ቐ	ETHIOPIC SYLLABLE QHA
1251	ቑ	ETHIOPIC SYLLABLE QHU
1252	ቒ	ETHIOPIC SYLLABLE QHI
1253	ቓ	ETHIOPIC SYLLABLE QHAA
1254	ቔ	ETHIOPIC SYLLABLE QHEE
1255	ቕ	ETHIOPIC SYLLABLE QHE
1256	ቖ	ETHIOPIC SYLLABLE QHO
1257		<reserved>
1258	ቘ	ETHIOPIC SYLLABLE QHWA
1259		<reserved>
125A	ቚ	ETHIOPIC SYLLABLE QHWI
125B	ቛ	ETHIOPIC SYLLABLE QHWAA
125C	ቜ	ETHIOPIC SYLLABLE QHWEE
125D	ቝ	ETHIOPIC SYLLABLE QHWE
125E		<reserved>
125F		<reserved>
1260	በ	ETHIOPIC SYLLABLE BA
1261	ቡ	ETHIOPIC SYLLABLE BU
1262	ቢ	ETHIOPIC SYLLABLE BI
1263	ባ	ETHIOPIC SYLLABLE BAA
1264	ቤ	ETHIOPIC SYLLABLE BEE
1265	ብ	ETHIOPIC SYLLABLE BE
1266	ቦ	ETHIOPIC SYLLABLE BO
1267	ቧ	ETHIOPIC SYLLABLE BWA
1268	ቨ	ETHIOPIC SYLLABLE VA
1269	ቩ	ETHIOPIC SYLLABLE VU
126A	ቪ	ETHIOPIC SYLLABLE VI
126B	ቫ	ETHIOPIC SYLLABLE VAA
126C	ቬ	ETHIOPIC SYLLABLE VEE
126D	ቭ	ETHIOPIC SYLLABLE VE
126E	ቮ	ETHIOPIC SYLLABLE VO
126F	ቯ	ETHIOPIC SYLLABLE VWA
1270	ተ	ETHIOPIC SYLLABLE TA
1271	ቱ	ETHIOPIC SYLLABLE TU
1272	ቲ	ETHIOPIC SYLLABLE TI
1273	ታ	ETHIOPIC SYLLABLE TAA
1274	ቴ	ETHIOPIC SYLLABLE TEE
1275	ት	ETHIOPIC SYLLABLE TE
1276	ቶ	ETHIOPIC SYLLABLE TO
1277	ቷ	ETHIOPIC SYLLABLE TWA
1278	ቸ	ETHIOPIC SYLLABLE CA
1279	ቹ	ETHIOPIC SYLLABLE CU
127A	ቺ	ETHIOPIC SYLLABLE CI
127B	ቻ	ETHIOPIC SYLLABLE CAA
127C	ቼ	ETHIOPIC SYLLABLE CEE

127D ች ETHIOPIC SYLLABLE CE
127E ቾ ETHIOPIC SYLLABLE CO
127F ቿ ETHIOPIC SYLLABLE CWA
1280 ኀ ETHIOPIC SYLLABLE XA
1281 ኁ ETHIOPIC SYLLABLE XU
1282 ኂ ETHIOPIC SYLLABLE XI
1283 ኃ ETHIOPIC SYLLABLE XAA
1284 ኄ ETHIOPIC SYLLABLE XEE
1285 ኅ ETHIOPIC SYLLABLE XE
1286 ኆ ETHIOPIC SYLLABLE XO
1287 ኇ ETHIOPIC SYLLABLE XOA
1288 ኈ ETHIOPIC SYLLABLE XWA
1289 <reserved>
128A ኊ ETHIOPIC SYLLABLE XWI
128B ኋ ETHIOPIC SYLLABLE XWAA
128C ኌ ETHIOPIC SYLLABLE XWEE
128D ኍ ETHIOPIC SYLLABLE XWE
128E <reserved>
128F <reserved>
1290 ነ ETHIOPIC SYLLABLE NA
1291 ኑ ETHIOPIC SYLLABLE NU
1292 ኒ ETHIOPIC SYLLABLE NI
1293 ና ETHIOPIC SYLLABLE NAA
1294 ኔ ETHIOPIC SYLLABLE NEE
1295 ን ETHIOPIC SYLLABLE NE
1296 ኖ ETHIOPIC SYLLABLE NO
1297 ኗ ETHIOPIC SYLLABLE NWA
1298 ኘ ETHIOPIC SYLLABLE NYA
1299 ኙ ETHIOPIC SYLLABLE NYU
129A ኚ ETHIOPIC SYLLABLE NYI
129B ኛ ETHIOPIC SYLLABLE NYAA
129C ኜ ETHIOPIC SYLLABLE NYEE
129D ኝ ETHIOPIC SYLLABLE NYE
129E ኞ ETHIOPIC SYLLABLE NYO
129F ኟ ETHIOPIC SYLLABLE NYWA
12A0 አ ETHIOPIC SYLLABLE GLOTTAL A
12A1 ኡ ETHIOPIC SYLLABLE GLOTTAL U
12A2 ኢ ETHIOPIC SYLLABLE GLOTTAL I
12A3 ኣ ETHIOPIC SYLLABLE GLOTTAL AA
12A4 ኤ ETHIOPIC SYLLABLE GLOTTAL EE
12A5 እ ETHIOPIC SYLLABLE GLOTTAL E
12A6 ኦ ETHIOPIC SYLLABLE GLOTTAL O
12A7 ኧ ETHIOPIC SYLLABLE GLOTTAL WA
12A8 ከ ETHIOPIC SYLLABLE KA
12A9 ኩ ETHIOPIC SYLLABLE KU
12AA ኪ ETHIOPIC SYLLABLE KI
12AB ካ ETHIOPIC SYLLABLE KAA
12AC ኬ ETHIOPIC SYLLABLE KEE
12AD ክ ETHIOPIC SYLLABLE KE
12AE ኮ ETHIOPIC SYLLABLE KO
12AF ኯ ETHIOPIC SYLLABLE KOA
12B0 ኰ ETHIOPIC SYLLABLE KWA
12B1 <reserved>
12B2 ኲ ETHIOPIC SYLLABLE KWI
12B3 ኳ ETHIOPIC SYLLABLE KWAA
12B4 ኴ ETHIOPIC SYLLABLE KWEE
12B5 ኵ ETHIOPIC SYLLABLE KWE
12B6 <reserved>
12B7 <reserved>
12B8 ኸ ETHIOPIC SYLLABLE KXA
12B9 ኹ ETHIOPIC SYLLABLE KXU
12BA ኺ ETHIOPIC SYLLABLE KXI
12BB ኻ ETHIOPIC SYLLABLE KXAA
12BC ኼ ETHIOPIC SYLLABLE KXEE
12BD ኽ ETHIOPIC SYLLABLE KXE
12BE ኾ ETHIOPIC SYLLABLE KXO
12BF <reserved>
12C0 ዀ ETHIOPIC SYLLABLE KXWA
12C1 <reserved>
12C2 ዂ ETHIOPIC SYLLABLE KXWI
12C3 ዃ ETHIOPIC SYLLABLE KXWAA
12C4 ዄ ETHIOPIC SYLLABLE KXWEE
12C5 ዅ ETHIOPIC SYLLABLE KXWE
12C6 <reserved>
12C7 <reserved>
12C8 ወ ETHIOPIC SYLLABLE WA
12C9 ዉ ETHIOPIC SYLLABLE WU
12CA ዊ ETHIOPIC SYLLABLE WI
12CB ዋ ETHIOPIC SYLLABLE WAA
12CC ዌ ETHIOPIC SYLLABLE WEE
12CD ው ETHIOPIC SYLLABLE WE
12CE ዎ ETHIOPIC SYLLABLE WO
12CF ዏ ETHIOPIC SYLLABLE WOA
12D0 ዐ ETHIOPIC SYLLABLE PHARYNGEAL A
12D1 ዑ ETHIOPIC SYLLABLE PHARYNGEAL U
12D2 ዒ ETHIOPIC SYLLABLE PHARYNGEAL I
12D3 ዓ ETHIOPIC SYLLABLE PHARYNGEAL AA
12D4 ዔ ETHIOPIC SYLLABLE PHARYNGEAL EE
12D5 ዕ ETHIOPIC SYLLABLE PHARYNGEAL E
12D6 ዖ ETHIOPIC SYLLABLE PHARYNGEAL O
12D7 <reserved>
12D8 ዘ ETHIOPIC SYLLABLE ZA
12D9 ዙ ETHIOPIC SYLLABLE ZU
12DA ዚ ETHIOPIC SYLLABLE ZI
12DB ዛ ETHIOPIC SYLLABLE ZAA
12DC ዜ ETHIOPIC SYLLABLE ZEE
12DD ዝ ETHIOPIC SYLLABLE ZE
12DE ዞ ETHIOPIC SYLLABLE ZO
12DF ዟ ETHIOPIC SYLLABLE ZWA
12E0 ዠ ETHIOPIC SYLLABLE ZHA
12E1 ዡ ETHIOPIC SYLLABLE ZHU
12E2 ዢ ETHIOPIC SYLLABLE ZHI
12E3 ዣ ETHIOPIC SYLLABLE ZHAA
12E4 ዤ ETHIOPIC SYLLABLE ZHEE
12E5 ዥ ETHIOPIC SYLLABLE ZHE
12E6 ዦ ETHIOPIC SYLLABLE ZHO
12E7 ዧ ETHIOPIC SYLLABLE ZHWA
12E8 የ ETHIOPIC SYLLABLE YA
12E9 ዩ ETHIOPIC SYLLABLE YU
12EA ዪ ETHIOPIC SYLLABLE YI
12EB ያ ETHIOPIC SYLLABLE YAA
12EC ዬ ETHIOPIC SYLLABLE YEE
12ED ይ ETHIOPIC SYLLABLE YE
12EE ዮ ETHIOPIC SYLLABLE YO
12EF ዯ ETHIOPIC SYLLABLE YOA
12F0 ደ ETHIOPIC SYLLABLE DA
12F1 ዱ ETHIOPIC SYLLABLE DU
12F2 ዲ ETHIOPIC SYLLABLE DI
12F3 ዳ ETHIOPIC SYLLABLE DAA
12F4 ዴ ETHIOPIC SYLLABLE DEE
12F5 ድ ETHIOPIC SYLLABLE DE
12F6 ዶ ETHIOPIC SYLLABLE DO
12F7 ዷ ETHIOPIC SYLLABLE DWA
12F8 ዸ ETHIOPIC SYLLABLE DDA
12F9 ዹ ETHIOPIC SYLLABLE DDU
12FA ዺ ETHIOPIC SYLLABLE DDI

12FB ዻ ETHIOPIC SYLLABLE DDAA
12FC ዼ ETHIOPIC SYLLABLE DDEE
12FD ዽ ETHIOPIC SYLLABLE DDE
12FE ዾ ETHIOPIC SYLLABLE DDO
12FF ዿ ETHIOPIC SYLLABLE DDWA
1300 ጀ ETHIOPIC SYLLABLE JA
1301 ጁ ETHIOPIC SYLLABLE JU
1302 ጂ ETHIOPIC SYLLABLE JI
1303 ጃ ETHIOPIC SYLLABLE JAA
1304 ጄ ETHIOPIC SYLLABLE JEE
1305 ጅ ETHIOPIC SYLLABLE JE
1306 ጆ ETHIOPIC SYLLABLE JO
1307 ጇ ETHIOPIC SYLLABLE JWA
1308 ገ ETHIOPIC SYLLABLE GA
1309 ጉ ETHIOPIC SYLLABLE GU
130A ጊ ETHIOPIC SYLLABLE GI
130B ጋ ETHIOPIC SYLLABLE GAA
130C ጌ ETHIOPIC SYLLABLE GEE
130D ግ ETHIOPIC SYLLABLE GE
130E ጎ ETHIOPIC SYLLABLE GO
130F ጏ ETHIOPIC SYLLABLE GOA
1310 ጐ ETHIOPIC SYLLABLE GWA
1311 <reserved>
1312 ጒ ETHIOPIC SYLLABLE GWI
1313 ጓ ETHIOPIC SYLLABLE GWAA
1314 ጔ ETHIOPIC SYLLABLE GWEE
1315 ጕ ETHIOPIC SYLLABLE GWE
1316 <reserved>
1317 <reserved>
1318 ጘ ETHIOPIC SYLLABLE GGA
1319 ጙ ETHIOPIC SYLLABLE GGU
131A ጚ ETHIOPIC SYLLABLE GGI
131B ጛ ETHIOPIC SYLLABLE GGAA
131C ጜ ETHIOPIC SYLLABLE GGEE
131D ጝ ETHIOPIC SYLLABLE GGE
131E ጞ ETHIOPIC SYLLABLE GGO
131F ጟ ETHIOPIC SYLLABLE GGWAA
1320 ጠ ETHIOPIC SYLLABLE THA
1321 ጡ ETHIOPIC SYLLABLE THU
1322 ጢ ETHIOPIC SYLLABLE THI
1323 ጣ ETHIOPIC SYLLABLE THAA
1324 ጤ ETHIOPIC SYLLABLE THEE
1325 ጥ ETHIOPIC SYLLABLE THE
1326 ጦ ETHIOPIC SYLLABLE THO
1327 ጧ ETHIOPIC SYLLABLE THWA
1328 ጨ ETHIOPIC SYLLABLE CHA
1329 ጩ ETHIOPIC SYLLABLE CHU
132A ጪ ETHIOPIC SYLLABLE CHI
132B ጫ ETHIOPIC SYLLABLE CHAA
132C ጬ ETHIOPIC SYLLABLE CHEE
132D ጭ ETHIOPIC SYLLABLE CHE
132E ጮ ETHIOPIC SYLLABLE CHO
132F ጯ ETHIOPIC SYLLABLE CHWA
1330 ጰ ETHIOPIC SYLLABLE PHA
1331 ጱ ETHIOPIC SYLLABLE PHU
1332 ጲ ETHIOPIC SYLLABLE PHI
1333 ጳ ETHIOPIC SYLLABLE PHAA
1334 ጴ ETHIOPIC SYLLABLE PHEE
1335 ጵ ETHIOPIC SYLLABLE PHE
1336 ጶ ETHIOPIC SYLLABLE PHO
1337 ጷ ETHIOPIC SYLLABLE PHWA
1338 ጸ ETHIOPIC SYLLABLE TSA
1339 ጹ ETHIOPIC SYLLABLE TSU
133A ጺ ETHIOPIC SYLLABLE TSI
133B ጻ ETHIOPIC SYLLABLE TSAA
133C ጼ ETHIOPIC SYLLABLE TSEE
133D ጽ ETHIOPIC SYLLABLE TSE
133E ጾ ETHIOPIC SYLLABLE TSO
133F ጿ ETHIOPIC SYLLABLE TSWA
1340 ፀ ETHIOPIC SYLLABLE TZA
1341 ፁ ETHIOPIC SYLLABLE TZU
1342 ፂ ETHIOPIC SYLLABLE TZI
1343 ፃ ETHIOPIC SYLLABLE TZAA
1344 ፄ ETHIOPIC SYLLABLE TZEE
1345 ፅ ETHIOPIC SYLLABLE TZE
1346 ፆ ETHIOPIC SYLLABLE TZO
1347 ፇ ETHIOPIC SYLLABLE TZOA
1348 ፈ ETHIOPIC SYLLABLE FA
1349 ፉ ETHIOPIC SYLLABLE FU
134A ፊ ETHIOPIC SYLLABLE FI
134B ፋ ETHIOPIC SYLLABLE FAA
134C ፌ ETHIOPIC SYLLABLE FEE
134D ፍ ETHIOPIC SYLLABLE FE
134E ፎ ETHIOPIC SYLLABLE FO
134F ፏ ETHIOPIC SYLLABLE FWA
1350 ፐ ETHIOPIC SYLLABLE PA
1351 ፑ ETHIOPIC SYLLABLE PU
1352 ፒ ETHIOPIC SYLLABLE PI
1353 ፓ ETHIOPIC SYLLABLE PAA
1354 ፔ ETHIOPIC SYLLABLE PEE
1355 ፕ ETHIOPIC SYLLABLE PE
1356 ፖ ETHIOPIC SYLLABLE PO
1357 ፗ ETHIOPIC SYLLABLE PWA
1358 ፘ ETHIOPIC SYLLABLE RYA
1359 ፙ ETHIOPIC SYLLABLE MYA
135A ፚ ETHIOPIC SYLLABLE FYA

Combining mark

135F ◌፟ ETHIOPIC COMBINING GEMINATION MARK

Punctuation

1360 ፠ ETHIOPIC SECTION MARK
1361 ፡ ETHIOPIC WORDSPACE
1362 ። ETHIOPIC FULL STOP
1363 ፣ ETHIOPIC COMMA
1364 ፤ ETHIOPIC SEMICOLON
1365 ፥ ETHIOPIC COLON
1366 ፦ ETHIOPIC PREFACE COLON
1367 ፧ ETHIOPIC QUESTION MARK
1368 ፨ ETHIOPIC PARAGRAPH SEPARATOR

Digits

1369 ፩ ETHIOPIC DIGIT ONE
136A ፪ ETHIOPIC DIGIT TWO
136B ፫ ETHIOPIC DIGIT THREE
136C ፬ ETHIOPIC DIGIT FOUR
136D ፭ ETHIOPIC DIGIT FIVE
136E ፮ ETHIOPIC DIGIT SIX
136F ፯ ETHIOPIC DIGIT SEVEN
1370 ፰ ETHIOPIC DIGIT EIGHT
1371 ፱ ETHIOPIC DIGIT NINE

Numbers

1372 ፲ ETHIOPIC NUMBER TEN
1373 ፳ ETHIOPIC NUMBER TWENTY
1374 ፴ ETHIOPIC NUMBER THIRTY
1375 ፵ ETHIOPIC NUMBER FORTY
1376 ፶ ETHIOPIC NUMBER FIFTY
1377 ፷ ETHIOPIC NUMBER SIXTY

1378 ፸ ETHIOPIC NUMBER SEVENTY
1379 ፹ ETHIOPIC NUMBER EIGHTY
137A ፺ ETHIOPIC NUMBER NINETY
137B ፻ ETHIOPIC NUMBER HUNDRED
137C ፼ ETHIOPIC NUMBER TEN THOUSAND

	138	139
0	ᎀ 1380	᎐ 1390
1	ᎁ 1381	᎑ 1391
2	ᎂ 1382	᎒ 1392
3	ᎃ 1383	᎓ 1393
4	ᎄ 1384	᎔ 1394
5	ᎅ 1385	᎕ 1395
6	ᎆ 1386	᎖ 1396
7	ᎇ 1387	᎗ 1397
8	ᎈ 1388	᎘ 1398
9	ᎉ 1389	᎙ 1399
A	ᎊ 138A	
B	ᎋ 138B	
C	ᎌ 138C	
D	ᎍ 138D	
E	ᎎ 138E	
F	ᎏ 138F	

Syllables for Sebatbeit

1380 ᎀ ETHIOPIC SYLLABLE SEBATBEIT MWA
1381 ᎁ ETHIOPIC SYLLABLE MWI
1382 ᎂ ETHIOPIC SYLLABLE MWEE
1383 ᎃ ETHIOPIC SYLLABLE MWE
1384 ᎄ ETHIOPIC SYLLABLE SEBATBEIT BWA
1385 ᎅ ETHIOPIC SYLLABLE BWI
1386 ᎆ ETHIOPIC SYLLABLE BWEE
1387 ᎇ ETHIOPIC SYLLABLE BWE
1388 ᎈ ETHIOPIC SYLLABLE SEBATBEIT FWA
1389 ᎉ ETHIOPIC SYLLABLE FWI
138A ᎊ ETHIOPIC SYLLABLE FWEE
138B ᎋ ETHIOPIC SYLLABLE FWE
138C ᎌ ETHIOPIC SYLLABLE SEBATBEIT PWA
138D ᎍ ETHIOPIC SYLLABLE PWI
138E ᎎ ETHIOPIC SYLLABLE PWEE
138F ᎏ ETHIOPIC SYLLABLE PWE

Tonal marks

Intended for use with a multiline scored layout

1390 ᎐ ETHIOPIC TONAL MARK YIZET
1391 ᎑ ETHIOPIC TONAL MARK DERET
1392 ᎒ ETHIOPIC TONAL MARK RIKRIK
1393 ᎓ ETHIOPIC TONAL MARK SHORT RIKRIK
1394 ᎔ ETHIOPIC TONAL MARK DIFAT
1395 ᎕ ETHIOPIC TONAL MARK KENAT
1396 ᎖ ETHIOPIC TONAL MARK CHIRET
1397 ᎗ ETHIOPIC TONAL MARK HIDET
1398 ᎘ ETHIOPIC TONAL MARK DERET-HIDET
1399 ᎙ ETHIOPIC TONAL MARK KURT

	13A	13B	13C	13D	13E	13F
0	Ꭰ 13A0	Ꮀ 13B0	Ꮐ 13C0	Ꮠ 13D0	Ꮰ 13E0	Ᏸ 13F0
1	Ꭱ 13A1	Ꮁ 13B1	Ꮑ 13C1	Ꮡ 13D1	Ꮱ 13E1	Ᏹ 13F1
2	Ꭲ 13A2	Ꮂ 13B2	Ꮒ 13C2	Ꮢ 13D2	Ꮲ 13E2	Ᏺ 13F2
3	Ꭳ 13A3	Ꮃ 13B3	Ꮓ 13C3	Ꮣ 13D3	Ꮳ 13E3	Ᏻ 13F3
4	Ꭴ 13A4	Ꮄ 13B4	Ꮔ 13C4	Ꮤ 13D4	Ꮴ 13E4	Ᏼ 13F4
5	Ꭵ 13A5	Ꮅ 13B5	Ꮕ 13C5	Ꮥ 13D5	Ꮵ 13E5	
6	Ꭶ 13A6	Ꮆ 13B6	Ꮖ 13C6	Ꮦ 13D6	Ꮶ 13E6	
7	Ꭷ 13A7	Ꮇ 13B7	Ꮗ 13C7	Ꮧ 13D7	Ꮷ 13E7	
8	Ꭸ 13A8	Ꮈ 13B8	Ꮘ 13C8	Ꮨ 13D8	Ꮸ 13E8	
9	Ꭹ 13A9	Ꮉ 13B9	Ꮙ 13C9	Ꮩ 13D9	Ꮹ 13E9	
A	Ꭺ 13AA	Ꮊ 13BA	Ꮚ 13CA	Ꮪ 13DA	Ꮺ 13EA	
B	Ꭻ 13AB	Ꮋ 13BB	Ꮛ 13CB	Ꮫ 13DB	Ꮻ 13EB	
C	Ꭼ 13AC	Ꮌ 13BC	Ꮜ 13CC	Ꮬ 13DC	Ꮼ 13EC	
D	Ꭽ 13AD	Ꮍ 13BD	Ꮝ 13CD	Ꮭ 13DD	Ꮽ 13ED	
E	Ꭾ 13AE	Ꮎ 13BE	Ꮞ 13CE	Ꮮ 13DE	Ꮾ 13EE	
F	Ꭿ 13AF	Ꮏ 13BF	Ꮟ 13CF	Ꮯ 13DF	Ꮿ 13EF	

Syllables

13A0 Ꭰ CHEROKEE LETTER A
13A1 Ꭱ CHEROKEE LETTER E
13A2 Ꭲ CHEROKEE LETTER I
13A3 Ꭳ CHEROKEE LETTER O
13A4 Ꭴ CHEROKEE LETTER U
13A5 Ꭵ CHEROKEE LETTER V
13A6 Ꭶ CHEROKEE LETTER GA
13A7 Ꭷ CHEROKEE LETTER KA
13A8 Ꭸ CHEROKEE LETTER GE
13A9 Ꭹ CHEROKEE LETTER GI
13AA Ꭺ CHEROKEE LETTER GO
13AB Ꭻ CHEROKEE LETTER GU
13AC Ꭼ CHEROKEE LETTER GV
13AD Ꭽ CHEROKEE LETTER HA
13AE Ꭾ CHEROKEE LETTER HE
13AF Ꭿ CHEROKEE LETTER HI
13B0 Ꮀ CHEROKEE LETTER HO
13B1 Ꮁ CHEROKEE LETTER HU
13B2 Ꮂ CHEROKEE LETTER HV
13B3 Ꮃ CHEROKEE LETTER LA
13B4 Ꮄ CHEROKEE LETTER LE
13B5 Ꮅ CHEROKEE LETTER LI
13B6 Ꮆ CHEROKEE LETTER LO
13B7 Ꮇ CHEROKEE LETTER LU
13B8 Ꮈ CHEROKEE LETTER LV
13B9 Ꮉ CHEROKEE LETTER MA
13BA Ꮊ CHEROKEE LETTER ME
13BB Ꮋ CHEROKEE LETTER MI
13BC Ꮌ CHEROKEE LETTER MO
13BD Ꮍ CHEROKEE LETTER MU
13BE Ꮎ CHEROKEE LETTER NA
13BF Ꮏ CHEROKEE LETTER HNA
13C0 Ꮐ CHEROKEE LETTER NAH
13C1 Ꮑ CHEROKEE LETTER NE
13C2 Ꮒ CHEROKEE LETTER NI
13C3 Ꮓ CHEROKEE LETTER NO
13C4 Ꮔ CHEROKEE LETTER NU
13C5 Ꮕ CHEROKEE LETTER NV
13C6 Ꮖ CHEROKEE LETTER QUA
13C7 Ꮗ CHEROKEE LETTER QUE
13C8 Ꮘ CHEROKEE LETTER QUI
13C9 Ꮙ CHEROKEE LETTER QUO
13CA Ꮚ CHEROKEE LETTER QUU
13CB Ꮛ CHEROKEE LETTER QUV
13CC Ꮜ CHEROKEE LETTER SA
13CD Ꮝ CHEROKEE LETTER S
13CE Ꮞ CHEROKEE LETTER SE
13CF Ꮟ CHEROKEE LETTER SI
13D0 Ꮠ CHEROKEE LETTER SO
13D1 Ꮡ CHEROKEE LETTER SU
13D2 Ꮢ CHEROKEE LETTER SV
13D3 Ꮣ CHEROKEE LETTER DA
13D4 Ꮤ CHEROKEE LETTER TA
13D5 Ꮥ CHEROKEE LETTER DE
13D6 Ꮦ CHEROKEE LETTER TE
13D7 Ꮧ CHEROKEE LETTER DI
13D8 Ꮨ CHEROKEE LETTER TI
13D9 Ꮩ CHEROKEE LETTER DO
13DA Ꮪ CHEROKEE LETTER DU
13DB Ꮫ CHEROKEE LETTER DV
13DC Ꮬ CHEROKEE LETTER DLA
13DD Ꮭ CHEROKEE LETTER TLA
13DE Ꮮ CHEROKEE LETTER TLE
13DF Ꮯ CHEROKEE LETTER TLI
13E0 Ꮰ CHEROKEE LETTER TLO
13E1 Ꮱ CHEROKEE LETTER TLU
13E2 Ꮲ CHEROKEE LETTER TLV
13E3 Ꮳ CHEROKEE LETTER TSA
13E4 Ꮴ CHEROKEE LETTER TSE
13E5 Ꮵ CHEROKEE LETTER TSI
13E6 Ꮶ CHEROKEE LETTER TSO
13E7 Ꮷ CHEROKEE LETTER TSU
13E8 Ꮸ CHEROKEE LETTER TSV
13E9 Ꮹ CHEROKEE LETTER WA
13EA Ꮺ CHEROKEE LETTER WE
13EB Ꮻ CHEROKEE LETTER WI
13EC Ꮼ CHEROKEE LETTER WO
13ED Ꮽ CHEROKEE LETTER WU
13EE Ꮾ CHEROKEE LETTER WV
13EF Ꮿ CHEROKEE LETTER YA
13F0 Ᏸ CHEROKEE LETTER YE
13F1 Ᏹ CHEROKEE LETTER YI
13F2 Ᏺ CHEROKEE LETTER YO
13F3 Ᏻ CHEROKEE LETTER YU
13F4 Ᏼ CHEROKEE LETTER YV

	140	141	142	143	144	145	146	147	148	149	14A	14B	14C	14D
0		ᐐ 1410	ᐠ 1420	ᐰ 1430	ᑀ 1440	ᑐ 1450	ᑠ 1460	ᑰ 1470	ᒀ 1480	ᒐ 1490	ᒠ 14A0	ᒰ 14B0	ᓀ 14C0	ᓐ 14D0
1	ᐁ 1401	ᐑ 1411	ᐡ 1421	ᐱ 1431	ᑁ 1441	ᑑ 1451	ᑡ 1461	ᑱ 1471	ᒁ 1481	ᒑ 1491	ᒡ 14A1	ᒱ 14B1	ᓁ 14C1	ᓑ 14D1
2	ᐂ 1402	ᐒ 1412	ᐢ 1422	ᐲ 1432	ᑂ 1442	ᑒ 1452	ᑢ 1462	ᑲ 1472	ᒂ 1482	ᒒ 1492	ᒢ 14A2	ᒲ 14B2	ᓂ 14C2	ᓒ 14D2
3	ᐃ 1403	ᐓ 1413	ᐣ 1423	ᐳ 1433	ᑃ 1443	ᑓ 1453	ᑣ 1463	ᑳ 1473	ᒃ 1483	ᒓ 1493	ᒣ 14A3	ᒳ 14B3	ᓃ 14C3	ᓓ 14D3
4	ᐄ 1404	ᐔ 1414	1424	ᐴ 1434	ᑄ 1444	ᑔ 1454	ᑤ 1464	ᑴ 1474	ᒄ 1484	ᒔ 1494	ᒤ 14A4	ᒴ 14B4	ᓄ 14C4	ᓔ 14D4
5	ᐅ 1405	ᐕ 1415	ᐥ 1425	ᐵ 1435	ᑅ 1445	ᑕ 1455	ᑥ 1465	ᑵ 1475	ᒅ 1485	ᒕ 1495	ᒥ 14A5	ᒵ 14B5	ᓅ 14C5	ᓕ 14D5
6	ᐆ 1406	ᐖ 1416	1426	ᐶ 1436	ᑆ 1446	ᑖ 1456	ᑦ 1466	ᑶ 1476	ᒆ 1486	ᒖ 1496	ᒦ 14A6	ᒶ 14B6	ᓆ 14C6	ᓖ 14D6
7	ᐇ 1407	ᐗ 1417	ᐧ 1427	ᐷ 1437	ᑇ 1447	ᑗ 1457	ᑧ 1467	ᑷ 1477	1487	ᒗ 1497	ᒧ 14A7	ᒷ 14B7	ᓇ 14C7	ᓗ 14D7
8	ᐈ 1408	ᐘ 1418	ᐨ 1428	ᐸ 1438	ᑈ 1448	ᑘ 1458	ᑨ 1468	ᑸ 1478	ᒈ 1488	ᒘ 1498	ᒨ 14A8	ᒸ 14B8	ᓈ 14C8	ᓘ 14D8
9	ᐉ 1409	ᐙ 1419	ᐩ 1429	ᐹ 1439	ᑉ 1449	ᑙ 1459	ᑩ 1469	ᑹ 1479	ᒉ 1489	ᒙ 1499	ᒩ 14A9	ᒹ 14B9	ᓉ 14C9	ᓙ 14D9
A	ᐊ 140A	ᐚ 141A	ᐪ 142A	ᐺ 143A	ᑊ 144A	ᑚ 145A	ᑪ 146A	ᑺ 147A	ᒊ 148A	ᒚ 149A	ᒪ 14AA	ᒺ 14BA	ᓊ 14CA	ᓚ 14DA
B	ᐋ 140B	ᐛ 141B	ᐫ 142B	ᐻ 143B	ᑋ 144B	ᑛ 145B	ᑫ 146B	ᑻ 147B	ᒋ 148B	ᒛ 149B	ᒫ 14AB	ᒻ 14BB	ᓋ 14CB	ᓛ 14DB
C	ᐌ 140C	ᐜ 141C	ᐬ 142C	ᐼ 143C	ᑌ 144C	ᑜ 145C	ᑬ 146C	ᑼ 147C	ᒌ 148C	ᒜ 149C	ᒬ 14AC	ᒼ 14BC	ᓌ 14CC	ᓜ 14DC
D	ᐍ 140D	ᐝ 141D	ᐭ 142D	ᐽ 143D	ᑍ 144D	ᑝ 145D	ᑭ 146D	ᑽ 147D	ᒍ 148D	ᒝ 149D	ᒭ 14AD	ᒽ 14BD	ᓍ 14CD	ᓝ 14DD
E	ᐎ 140E	ᐞ 141E	ᐮ 142E	ᐾ 143E	ᑎ 144E	ᑞ 145E	ᑮ 146E	ᑾ 147E	ᒎ 148E	ᒞ 149E	ᒮ 14AE	ᒾ 14BE	ᓎ 14CE	ᓞ 14DE
F	ᐏ 140F	ᐟ 141F	ᐯ 142F	ᐿ 143F	ᑏ 144F	ᑟ 145F	ᑯ 146F	ᑿ 147F	ᒏ 148F	ᒟ 149F	ᒯ 14AF	ᒿ 14BF	ᓏ 14CF	ᓟ 14DF

	14E	14F	150	151	152	153	154	155	156	157	158	159	15A
0	14E0	14F0	1500	1510	1520	1530	1540	1550	1560	1570	1580	1590	15A0
1	14E1	14F1	1501	1511	1521	1531	1541	1551	1561	1571	1581	1591	15A1
2	14E2	14F2	1502	1512	1522	1532	1542	1552	1562	1572	1582	1592	15A2
3	14E3	14F3	1503	1513	1523	1533	1543	1553	1563	1573	1583	1593	15A3
4	14E4	14F4	1504	1514	1524	1534	1544	1554	1564	1574	1584	1594	15A4
5	14E5	14F5	1505	1515	1525	1535	1545	1555	1565	1575	1585	1595	15A5
6	14E6	14F6	1506	1516	1526	1536	1546	1556	1566	1576	1586	1596	15A6
7	14E7	14F7	1507	1517	1527	1537	1547	1557	1567	1577	1587	1597	15A7
8	14E8	14F8	1508	1518	1528	1538	1548	1558	1568	1578	1588	1598	15A8
9	14E9	14F9	1509	1519	1529	1539	1549	1559	1569	1579	1589	1599	15A9
A	14EA	14FA	150A	151A	152A	153A	154A	155A	156A	157A	158A	159A	15AA
B	14EB	14FB	150B	151B	152B	153B	154B	155B	156B	157B	158B	159B	15AB
C	14EC	14FC	150C	151C	152C	153C	154C	155C	156C	157C	158C	159C	15AC
D	14ED	14FD	150D	151D	152D	153D	154D	155D	156D	157D	158D	159D	15AD
E	14EE	14FE	150E	151E	152E	153E	154E	155E	156E	157E	158E	159E	15AE
F	14EF	14FF	150F	151F	152F	153F	154F	155F	156F	157F	158F	159F	15AF

	15B	15C	15D	15E	15F	160	161	162	163	164	165	166	167
0	15B0	15C0	15D0	15E0	15F0	1600	1610	1620	1630	1640	1650	1660	1670
1	15B1	15C1	15D1	15E1	15F1	1601	1611	1621	1631	1641	1651	1661	1671
2	15B2	15C2	15D2	15E2	15F2	1602	1612	1622	1632	1642	1652	1662	1672
3	15B3	15C3	15D3	15E3	15F3	1603	1613	1623	1633	1643	1653	1663	1673
4	15B4	15C4	15D4	15E4	15F4	1604	1614	1624	1634	1644	1654	1664	1674
5	15B5	15C5	15D5	15E5	15F5	1605	1615	1625	1635	1645	1655	1665	1675
6	15B6	15C6	15D6	15E6	15F6	1606	1616	1626	1636	1646	1656	1666	1676
7	15B7	15C7	15D7	15E7	15F7	1607	1617	1627	1637	1647	1657	1667	
8	15B8	15C8	15D8	15E8	15F8	1608	1618	1628	1638	1648	1658	1668	
9	15B9	15C9	15D9	15E9	15F9	1609	1619	1629	1639	1649	1659	1669	
A	15BA	15CA	15DA	15EA	15FA	160A	161A	162A	163A	164A	165A	166A	
B	15BB	15CB	15DB	15EB	15FB	160B	161B	162B	163B	164B	165B	166B	
C	15BC	15CC	15DC	15EC	15FC	160C	161C	162C	163C	164C	165C	166C	
D	15BD	15CD	15DD	15ED	15FD	160D	161D	162D	163D	164D	165D	166D	
E	15BE	15CE	15DE	15EE	15FE	160E	161E	162E	163E	164E	165E	166E	
F	15BF	15CF	15DF	15EF	15FF	160F	161F	162F	163F	164F	165F	166F	

Syllables

1401 ᐁ CANADIAN SYLLABICS E
• Inuktitut (AI), Carrier (U)

1402 ᐂ CANADIAN SYLLABICS AAI
• Inuktitut

1403 ᐃ CANADIAN SYLLABICS I
• Carrier (O)

1404 ᐄ CANADIAN SYLLABICS II

1405 ᐅ CANADIAN SYLLABICS O
• Inuktitut (U), Carrier (E)

1406 ᐆ CANADIAN SYLLABICS OO
• Inuktitut (UU)

1407 ᐇ CANADIAN SYLLABICS Y-CREE OO

1408 ᐈ CANADIAN SYLLABICS CARRIER EE

1409 ᐉ CANADIAN SYLLABICS CARRIER I

140A ᐊ CANADIAN SYLLABICS A

140B ᐋ CANADIAN SYLLABICS AA

140C ᐌ CANADIAN SYLLABICS WE

140D ᐍ CANADIAN SYLLABICS WEST-CREE WE

140E ᐎ CANADIAN SYLLABICS WI

140F ᐏ CANADIAN SYLLABICS WEST-CREE WI

1410 ᐐ CANADIAN SYLLABICS WII

1411 ᐑ CANADIAN SYLLABICS WEST-CREE WII

1412 ᐒ CANADIAN SYLLABICS WO

1413 ᐓ CANADIAN SYLLABICS WEST-CREE WO

1414 ᐔ CANADIAN SYLLABICS WOO

1415 ᐕ CANADIAN SYLLABICS WEST-CREE WOO

1416 ᐖ CANADIAN SYLLABICS NASKAPI WOO

1417 ᐗ CANADIAN SYLLABICS WA

1418 ᐘ CANADIAN SYLLABICS WEST-CREE WA

1419 ᐙ CANADIAN SYLLABICS WAA

141A ᐚ CANADIAN SYLLABICS WEST-CREE WAA

141B ᐛ CANADIAN SYLLABICS NASKAPI WAA

141C ᐜ CANADIAN SYLLABICS AI
• East Cree

141D ᐝ CANADIAN SYLLABICS Y-CREE W

141E ᐞ CANADIAN SYLLABICS GLOTTAL STOP
• Moose Cree (Y), Algonquian (GLOTTAL STOP)

141F ᐟ CANADIAN SYLLABICS FINAL ACUTE
• West Cree (T), East Cree (Y), Inuktitut (GLOTTAL STOP)
• Athapascan (B/P), Sayisi (I), Carrier (G)

1420 ᐠ CANADIAN SYLLABICS FINAL GRAVE
• West Cree (K), Athapascan (K), Carrier (KH)

1421 ᐡ CANADIAN SYLLABICS FINAL BOTTOM HALF RING
• N Cree (SH), Sayisi (R), Carrier (NG)

1422 ᐢ CANADIAN SYLLABICS FINAL TOP HALF RING
• Algonquian (S), Chipewyan (R), Sayisi (S)

1423 ᐣ CANADIAN SYLLABICS FINAL RIGHT HALF RING
• West Cree (N), Athapascan (D/T), Sayisi (N), Carrier (N)

1424 ᐤ CANADIAN SYLLABICS FINAL RING
• West Cree (W), Sayisi (O)

1425 ᐥ CANADIAN SYLLABICS FINAL DOUBLE ACUTE
• Chipewyan (TT), South Slavey (GH)

1426 ᐦ CANADIAN SYLLABICS FINAL DOUBLE SHORT VERTICAL STROKES
• Algonquian (H), Carrier (R)

1427 ᐧ CANADIAN SYLLABICS FINAL MIDDLE DOT
• Moose Cree (W), Athapascan (Y), Sayisi (YU)

1428 ᐨ CANADIAN SYLLABICS FINAL SHORT HORIZONTAL STROKE
• West Cree (C), Sayisi (D)

1429 ᐩ CANADIAN SYLLABICS FINAL PLUS
• Athapascan (N), Sayisi (AI)

142A ᐪ CANADIAN SYLLABICS FINAL DOWN TACK
• N Cree (L), Carrier (D)
→ 22A4 ⊤ down tack

142B ᐫ CANADIAN SYLLABICS EN

142C ᐬ CANADIAN SYLLABICS IN

142D ᐭ CANADIAN SYLLABICS ON

142E ᐮ CANADIAN SYLLABICS AN

142F ᐯ CANADIAN SYLLABICS PE
• Inuktitut (PAI), Athapascan (BE), Carrier (HU)

1430 ᐰ CANADIAN SYLLABICS PAAI
• Inuktitut

1431 ᐱ CANADIAN SYLLABICS PI

1432 ᐲ CANADIAN SYLLABICS PII

1433 ᐳ CANADIAN SYLLABICS PO
• Inuktitut (PU), Athapascan (BO), Carrier (HE)

1434 ᐴ CANADIAN SYLLABICS POO
• Inuktitut (PUU)

1435 ᐵ CANADIAN SYLLABICS Y-CREE POO

1436 ᐶ CANADIAN SYLLABICS CARRIER HEE

1437 ᐷ CANADIAN SYLLABICS CARRIER HI

1438 ᐸ CANADIAN SYLLABICS PA
• Athapascan (BA), Carrier (HA)

1439 ᐹ CANADIAN SYLLABICS PAA

143A ᐺ CANADIAN SYLLABICS PWE

143B ᐻ CANADIAN SYLLABICS WEST-CREE PWE

143C ᐼ CANADIAN SYLLABICS PWI

143D ᐽ CANADIAN SYLLABICS WEST-CREE PWI

143E ᐾ CANADIAN SYLLABICS PWII

143F ᐿ CANADIAN SYLLABICS WEST-CREE PWII

1440 ᑀ CANADIAN SYLLABICS PWO

1441 ᑁ CANADIAN SYLLABICS WEST-CREE PWO

1442 ᑂ CANADIAN SYLLABICS PWOO

1443 ᑃ CANADIAN SYLLABICS WEST-CREE PWOO

1444 ᑄ CANADIAN SYLLABICS PWA

1445 ᑅ CANADIAN SYLLABICS WEST-CREE PWA

1446 ᑆ CANADIAN SYLLABICS PWAA

1447 ᑇ CANADIAN SYLLABICS WEST-CREE PWAA

1448 ᑈ CANADIAN SYLLABICS Y-CREE PWAA

1449 ᑉ CANADIAN SYLLABICS P

144A ᑊ CANADIAN SYLLABICS WEST-CREE P
• Sayisi (G)

144B ᑋ CANADIAN SYLLABICS CARRIER H

144C ᑌ CANADIAN SYLLABICS TE
• Inuktitut (TAI), Athapascan (DI), Carrier (DU)

144D ᑍ CANADIAN SYLLABICS TAAI
• Inuktitut

144E ᑎ CANADIAN SYLLABICS TI
• Athapascan (DE), Carrier (DO)

144F ᑏ CANADIAN SYLLABICS TII

1450 ᑐ CANADIAN SYLLABICS TO
• Inuktitut (TU), Athapascan (DO), Carrier (DE), Sayisi (DU)

1451 ᑑ CANADIAN SYLLABICS TOO
• Inuktitut (TUU)

1452 ᑒ CANADIAN SYLLABICS Y-CREE TOO

1453 ᑓ CANADIAN SYLLABICS CARRIER DEE

1454 ᑔ CANADIAN SYLLABICS CARRIER DI

1455 ᑕ CANADIAN SYLLABICS TA
• Athapascan (DA)

1456 ᑖ CANADIAN SYLLABICS TAA

1457 ᑗ CANADIAN SYLLABICS TWE

1458 ᑘ CANADIAN SYLLABICS WEST-CREE TWE

1459 ᑙ CANADIAN SYLLABICS TWI
145A ᑚ CANADIAN SYLLABICS WEST-CREE TWI
145B ᑛ CANADIAN SYLLABICS TWII
145C ᑜ CANADIAN SYLLABICS WEST-CREE TWII
145D ᑝ CANADIAN SYLLABICS TWO
145E ᑞ CANADIAN SYLLABICS WEST-CREE TWO
145F ᑟ CANADIAN SYLLABICS TWOO
1460 ᑠ CANADIAN SYLLABICS WEST-CREE TWOO
1461 ᑡ CANADIAN SYLLABICS TWA
1462 ᑢ CANADIAN SYLLABICS WEST-CREE TWA
1463 ᑣ CANADIAN SYLLABICS TWAA
1464 ᑤ CANADIAN SYLLABICS WEST-CREE TWAA
1465 ᑥ CANADIAN SYLLABICS NASKAPI TWAA
1466 ᑦ CANADIAN SYLLABICS T
1467 ᑧ CANADIAN SYLLABICS TTE
• South Slavey (DEH)
1468 ᑨ CANADIAN SYLLABICS TTI
• South Slavey (DIH)
1469 ᑩ CANADIAN SYLLABICS TTO
• South Slavey (DOH)
146A ᑪ CANADIAN SYLLABICS TTA
• South Slavey (DAH)
146B ᑫ CANADIAN SYLLABICS KE
• Inuktitut (KAI)
146C ᑬ CANADIAN SYLLABICS KAAI
• Inuktitut
146D ᑭ CANADIAN SYLLABICS KI
146E ᑮ CANADIAN SYLLABICS KII
146F ᑯ CANADIAN SYLLABICS KO
• Inuktitut (KU), Sayisi (KU)
1470 ᑰ CANADIAN SYLLABICS KOO
• Inuktitut (KUU)
1471 ᑱ CANADIAN SYLLABICS Y-CREE KOO
1472 ᑲ CANADIAN SYLLABICS KA
1473 ᑳ CANADIAN SYLLABICS KAA
1474 ᑴ CANADIAN SYLLABICS KWE
1475 ᑵ CANADIAN SYLLABICS WEST-CREE KWE
1476 ᑶ CANADIAN SYLLABICS KWI
1477 ᑷ CANADIAN SYLLABICS WEST-CREE KWI
1478 ᑸ CANADIAN SYLLABICS KWII
1479 ᑹ CANADIAN SYLLABICS WEST-CREE KWII
147A ᑺ CANADIAN SYLLABICS KWO
147B ᑻ CANADIAN SYLLABICS WEST-CREE KWO
147C ᑼ CANADIAN SYLLABICS KWOO
147D ᑽ CANADIAN SYLLABICS WEST-CREE KWOO
147E ᑾ CANADIAN SYLLABICS KWA
147F ᑿ CANADIAN SYLLABICS WEST-CREE KWA
1480 ᒀ CANADIAN SYLLABICS KWAA
1481 ᒁ CANADIAN SYLLABICS WEST-CREE KWAA
1482 ᒂ CANADIAN SYLLABICS NASKAPI KWAA
1483 ᒃ CANADIAN SYLLABICS K
1484 ᒄ CANADIAN SYLLABICS KW
• East Cree
1485 ᒅ CANADIAN SYLLABICS SOUTH-SLAVEY KEH
1486 ᒆ CANADIAN SYLLABICS SOUTH-SLAVEY KIH
1487 CANADIAN SYLLABICS SOUTH-SLAVEY KOH
1488 ᒈ CANADIAN SYLLABICS SOUTH-SLAVEY KAH
1489 ᒉ CANADIAN SYLLABICS CE
• Inuktitut (GAI), Athapascan (DHE), Sayisi (THE)
148A ᒊ CANADIAN SYLLABICS CAAI
• Inuktitut (GAAI)
148B ᒋ CANADIAN SYLLABICS CI
• Inuktitut (GI), Athapascan (DHI), Sayisi (THI)
148C ᒌ CANADIAN SYLLABICS CII
• Inuktitut (GII)
148D ᒍ CANADIAN SYLLABICS CO
• Inuktitut (GU), Athapascan (DHO), Sayisi (THO)
148E ᒎ CANADIAN SYLLABICS COO
• Inuktitut (GUU)
148F ᒏ CANADIAN SYLLABICS Y-CREE COO
1490 ᒐ CANADIAN SYLLABICS CA
• Inuktitut (GA), Athapascan (DHA), Sayisi (THA)
1491 ᒑ CANADIAN SYLLABICS CAA
• Inuktitut (GAA)
1492 ᒒ CANADIAN SYLLABICS CWE
1493 ᒓ CANADIAN SYLLABICS WEST-CREE CWE
1494 ᒔ CANADIAN SYLLABICS CWI
1495 ᒕ CANADIAN SYLLABICS WEST-CREE CWI
1496 ᒖ CANADIAN SYLLABICS CWII
1497 ᒗ CANADIAN SYLLABICS WEST-CREE CWII
1498 ᒘ CANADIAN SYLLABICS CWO
1499 ᒙ CANADIAN SYLLABICS WEST-CREE CWO
149A ᒚ CANADIAN SYLLABICS CWOO
149B ᒛ CANADIAN SYLLABICS WEST-CREE CWOO
149C ᒜ CANADIAN SYLLABICS CWA
149D ᒝ CANADIAN SYLLABICS WEST-CREE CWA
149E ᒞ CANADIAN SYLLABICS CWAA
149F ᒟ CANADIAN SYLLABICS WEST-CREE CWAA
14A0 ᒠ CANADIAN SYLLABICS NASKAPI CWAA
14A1 ᒡ CANADIAN SYLLABICS C
• Inuktitut (G), Sayisi (T)
14A2 ᒢ CANADIAN SYLLABICS SAYISI TH
• Athapascan (DH)
14A3 ᒣ CANADIAN SYLLABICS ME
• Inuktitut (MAI)
14A4 ᒤ CANADIAN SYLLABICS MAAI
• Inuktitut
14A5 ᒥ CANADIAN SYLLABICS MI
14A6 ᒦ CANADIAN SYLLABICS MII
14A7 ᒧ CANADIAN SYLLABICS MO
• Inuktitut (MU), Sayisi (MU)
14A8 ᒨ CANADIAN SYLLABICS MOO
• Inuktitut (MUU)
14A9 ᒩ CANADIAN SYLLABICS Y-CREE MOO
14AA ᒪ CANADIAN SYLLABICS MA
14AB ᒫ CANADIAN SYLLABICS MAA
14AC ᒬ CANADIAN SYLLABICS MWE
14AD ᒭ CANADIAN SYLLABICS WEST-CREE MWE
14AE ᒮ CANADIAN SYLLABICS MWI
14AF ᒯ CANADIAN SYLLABICS WEST-CREE MWI
14B0 ᒰ CANADIAN SYLLABICS MWII
14B1 ᒱ CANADIAN SYLLABICS WEST-CREE MWII
14B2 ᒲ CANADIAN SYLLABICS MWO
14B3 ᒳ CANADIAN SYLLABICS WEST-CREE MWO
14B4 ᒴ CANADIAN SYLLABICS MWOO
14B5 ᒵ CANADIAN SYLLABICS WEST-CREE MWOO
14B6 ᒶ CANADIAN SYLLABICS MWA
14B7 ᒷ CANADIAN SYLLABICS WEST-CREE MWA
14B8 ᒸ CANADIAN SYLLABICS MWAA
14B9 ᒹ CANADIAN SYLLABICS WEST-CREE MWAA
14BA ᒺ CANADIAN SYLLABICS NASKAPI MWAA
14BB ᒻ CANADIAN SYLLABICS M
14BC ᒼ CANADIAN SYLLABICS WEST-CREE M
• Carrier (M)
14BD ᒽ CANADIAN SYLLABICS MH
14BE ᒾ CANADIAN SYLLABICS ATHAPASCAN M

14BF ᒿ CANADIAN SYLLABICS SAYISI M
14C0 ᓀ CANADIAN SYLLABICS NE
• Inuktitut (NAI)
14C1 ᓁ CANADIAN SYLLABICS NAAI
• Inuktitut
14C2 ᓂ CANADIAN SYLLABICS NI
14C3 ᓃ CANADIAN SYLLABICS NII
14C4 ᓄ CANADIAN SYLLABICS NO
• Inuktitut (NU), Sayisi (NU)
14C5 ᓅ CANADIAN SYLLABICS NOO
• Inuktitut (NUU)
14C6 ᓆ CANADIAN SYLLABICS Y-CREE NOO
14C7 ᓇ CANADIAN SYLLABICS NA
14C8 ᓈ CANADIAN SYLLABICS NAA
14C9 ᓉ CANADIAN SYLLABICS NWE
14CA ᓊ CANADIAN SYLLABICS WEST-CREE NWE
14CB ᓋ CANADIAN SYLLABICS NWA
14CC ᓌ CANADIAN SYLLABICS WEST-CREE NWA
14CD ᓍ CANADIAN SYLLABICS NWAA
14CE ᓎ CANADIAN SYLLABICS WEST-CREE NWAA
14CF ᓏ CANADIAN SYLLABICS NASKAPI NWAA
14D0 ᓐ CANADIAN SYLLABICS N
14D1 ᓑ CANADIAN SYLLABICS CARRIER NG
14D2 ᓒ CANADIAN SYLLABICS NH
14D3 ᓓ CANADIAN SYLLABICS LE
• Inuktitut (LAI)
14D4 ᓔ CANADIAN SYLLABICS LAAI
• Inuktitut
14D5 ᓕ CANADIAN SYLLABICS LI
14D6 ᓖ CANADIAN SYLLABICS LII
14D7 ᓗ CANADIAN SYLLABICS LO
• Inuktitut (LU)
14D8 ᓘ CANADIAN SYLLABICS LOO
• Inuktitut (LUU)
14D9 ᓙ CANADIAN SYLLABICS Y-CREE LOO
14DA ᓚ CANADIAN SYLLABICS LA
14DB ᓛ CANADIAN SYLLABICS LAA
14DC ᓜ CANADIAN SYLLABICS LWE
14DD ᓝ CANADIAN SYLLABICS WEST-CREE LWE
14DE ᓞ CANADIAN SYLLABICS LWI
14DF ᓟ CANADIAN SYLLABICS WEST-CREE LWI
14E0 ᓠ CANADIAN SYLLABICS LWII
14E1 ᓡ CANADIAN SYLLABICS WEST-CREE LWII
14E2 ᓢ CANADIAN SYLLABICS LWO
14E3 ᓣ CANADIAN SYLLABICS WEST-CREE LWO
14E4 ᓤ CANADIAN SYLLABICS LWOO
14E5 ᓥ CANADIAN SYLLABICS WEST-CREE LWOO
14E6 ᓦ CANADIAN SYLLABICS LWA
14E7 ᓧ CANADIAN SYLLABICS WEST-CREE LWA
14E8 ᓨ CANADIAN SYLLABICS LWAA
14E9 ᓩ CANADIAN SYLLABICS WEST-CREE LWAA
14EA ᓪ CANADIAN SYLLABICS L
14EB ᓫ CANADIAN SYLLABICS WEST-CREE L
14EC ᓬ CANADIAN SYLLABICS MEDIAL L
14ED ᓭ CANADIAN SYLLABICS SE
• Inuktitut (SAI)
14EE ᓮ CANADIAN SYLLABICS SAAI
• Inuktitut
14EF ᓯ CANADIAN SYLLABICS SI
14F0 ᓰ CANADIAN SYLLABICS SII
14F1 ᓱ CANADIAN SYLLABICS SO
• Inuktitut (SU), Sayisi (SU)
14F2 ᓲ CANADIAN SYLLABICS SOO
• Inuktitut (SUU)
14F3 ᓳ CANADIAN SYLLABICS Y-CREE SOO
14F4 ᓴ CANADIAN SYLLABICS SA
14F5 ᓵ CANADIAN SYLLABICS SAA
14F6 ᓶ CANADIAN SYLLABICS SWE
14F7 ᓷ CANADIAN SYLLABICS WEST-CREE SWE
14F8 ᓸ CANADIAN SYLLABICS SWI
14F9 ᓹ CANADIAN SYLLABICS WEST-CREE SWI
14FA ᓺ CANADIAN SYLLABICS SWII
14FB ᓻ CANADIAN SYLLABICS WEST-CREE SWII
14FC ᓼ CANADIAN SYLLABICS SWO
14FD ᓽ CANADIAN SYLLABICS WEST-CREE SWO
14FE ᓾ CANADIAN SYLLABICS SWOO
14FF ᓿ CANADIAN SYLLABICS WEST-CREE SWOO
1500 ᔀ CANADIAN SYLLABICS SWA
1501 ᔁ CANADIAN SYLLABICS WEST-CREE SWA
1502 ᔂ CANADIAN SYLLABICS SWAA
1503 ᔃ CANADIAN SYLLABICS WEST-CREE SWAA
1504 ᔄ CANADIAN SYLLABICS NASKAPI SWAA
1505 ᔅ CANADIAN SYLLABICS S
1506 ᔆ CANADIAN SYLLABICS ATHAPASCAN S
1507 ᔇ CANADIAN SYLLABICS SW
1508 ᔈ CANADIAN SYLLABICS BLACKFOOT S
1509 ᔉ CANADIAN SYLLABICS MOOSE-CREE SK
150A ᔊ CANADIAN SYLLABICS NASKAPI SKW
150B ᔋ CANADIAN SYLLABICS NASKAPI S-W
150C ᔌ CANADIAN SYLLABICS NASKAPI SPWA
150D ᔍ CANADIAN SYLLABICS NASKAPI STWA
150E ᔎ CANADIAN SYLLABICS NASKAPI SKWA
150F ᔏ CANADIAN SYLLABICS NASKAPI SCWA
1510 ᔐ CANADIAN SYLLABICS SHE
1511 ᔑ CANADIAN SYLLABICS SHI
1512 ᔒ CANADIAN SYLLABICS SHII
1513 ᔓ CANADIAN SYLLABICS SHO
1514 ᔔ CANADIAN SYLLABICS SHOO
1515 ᔕ CANADIAN SYLLABICS SHA
1516 ᔖ CANADIAN SYLLABICS SHAA
1517 ᔗ CANADIAN SYLLABICS SHWE
1518 ᔘ CANADIAN SYLLABICS WEST-CREE SHWE
1519 ᔙ CANADIAN SYLLABICS SHWI
151A ᔚ CANADIAN SYLLABICS WEST-CREE SHWI
151B ᔛ CANADIAN SYLLABICS SHWII
151C ᔜ CANADIAN SYLLABICS WEST-CREE SHWII
151D ᔝ CANADIAN SYLLABICS SHWO
151E ᔞ CANADIAN SYLLABICS WEST-CREE SHWO
151F ᔟ CANADIAN SYLLABICS SHWOO
1520 ᔠ CANADIAN SYLLABICS WEST-CREE SHWOO
1521 ᔡ CANADIAN SYLLABICS SHWA
1522 ᔢ CANADIAN SYLLABICS WEST-CREE SHWA
1523 ᔣ CANADIAN SYLLABICS SHWAA
1524 ᔤ CANADIAN SYLLABICS WEST-CREE SHWAA
1525 ᔥ CANADIAN SYLLABICS SH
1526 ᔦ CANADIAN SYLLABICS YE
• Inuktitut (YAI)
1527 ᔧ CANADIAN SYLLABICS YAAI
• Inuktitut
1528 ᔨ CANADIAN SYLLABICS YI
1529 ᔩ CANADIAN SYLLABICS YII
152A ᔪ CANADIAN SYLLABICS YO
• Inuktitut (YU)
152B ᔫ CANADIAN SYLLABICS YOO
• Inuktitut (YUU)

152C ᔬ CANADIAN SYLLABICS Y-CREE YOO
152D ᔭ CANADIAN SYLLABICS YA
152E ᔮ CANADIAN SYLLABICS YAA
152F ᔯ CANADIAN SYLLABICS YWE
1530 ᔰ CANADIAN SYLLABICS WEST-CREE YWE
1531 ᔱ CANADIAN SYLLABICS YWI
1532 ᔲ CANADIAN SYLLABICS WEST-CREE YWI
1533 ᔳ CANADIAN SYLLABICS YWII
1534 ᔴ CANADIAN SYLLABICS WEST-CREE YWII
1535 ᔵ CANADIAN SYLLABICS YWO
1536 ᔶ CANADIAN SYLLABICS WEST-CREE YWO
1537 ᔷ CANADIAN SYLLABICS YWOO
1538 ᔸ CANADIAN SYLLABICS WEST-CREE YWOO
1539 ᔹ CANADIAN SYLLABICS YWA
153A ᔺ CANADIAN SYLLABICS WEST-CREE YWA
153B ᔻ CANADIAN SYLLABICS YWAA
153C ᔼ CANADIAN SYLLABICS WEST-CREE YWAA
153D ᔽ CANADIAN SYLLABICS NASKAPI YWAA
153E ᔾ CANADIAN SYLLABICS Y
153F ᔿ CANADIAN SYLLABICS BIBLE-CREE Y
1540 ᕀ CANADIAN SYLLABICS WEST-CREE Y
1541 ᕁ CANADIAN SYLLABICS SAYISI YI
1542 ᕂ CANADIAN SYLLABICS RE
• Inuktitut (RAI)
1543 ᕃ CANADIAN SYLLABICS R-CREE RE
• Athapascan (LE)
1544 ᕄ CANADIAN SYLLABICS WEST-CREE LE
• Athapascan (LI)
1545 ᕅ CANADIAN SYLLABICS RAAI
• Inuktitut
1546 ᕆ CANADIAN SYLLABICS RI
1547 ᕇ CANADIAN SYLLABICS RII
1548 ᕈ CANADIAN SYLLABICS RO
• Inuktitut (RU)
1549 ᕉ CANADIAN SYLLABICS ROO
• Inuktitut (RUU)
154A ᕊ CANADIAN SYLLABICS WEST-CREE LO
• Sayisi (LU)
154B ᕋ CANADIAN SYLLABICS RA
154C ᕌ CANADIAN SYLLABICS RAA
154D ᕍ CANADIAN SYLLABICS WEST-CREE LA
154E ᕎ CANADIAN SYLLABICS RWAA
154F ᕏ CANADIAN SYLLABICS WEST-CREE RWAA
1550 ᕐ CANADIAN SYLLABICS R
1551 ᕑ CANADIAN SYLLABICS WEST-CREE R
1552 ᕒ CANADIAN SYLLABICS MEDIAL R
1553 ᕓ CANADIAN SYLLABICS FE
• Inuktitut (FAI)
1554 ᕔ CANADIAN SYLLABICS FAAI
• Inuktitut
1555 ᕕ CANADIAN SYLLABICS FI
1556 ᕖ CANADIAN SYLLABICS FII
1557 ᕗ CANADIAN SYLLABICS FO
1558 ᕘ CANADIAN SYLLABICS FOO
1559 ᕙ CANADIAN SYLLABICS FA
155A ᕚ CANADIAN SYLLABICS FAA
155B ᕛ CANADIAN SYLLABICS FWAA
155C ᕜ CANADIAN SYLLABICS WEST-CREE FWAA
155D ᕝ CANADIAN SYLLABICS F
155E ᕞ CANADIAN SYLLABICS THE
• Sayisi (TE)
155F ᕟ CANADIAN SYLLABICS N-CREE THE
1560 ᕠ CANADIAN SYLLABICS THI
• Sayisi (TI)
1561 ᕡ CANADIAN SYLLABICS N-CREE THI
1562 ᕢ CANADIAN SYLLABICS THII
1563 ᕣ CANADIAN SYLLABICS N-CREE THII
1564 ᕤ CANADIAN SYLLABICS THO
• Sayisi (TU)
1565 ᕥ CANADIAN SYLLABICS THOO
1566 ᕦ CANADIAN SYLLABICS THA
• Sayisi (TA)
1567 ᕧ CANADIAN SYLLABICS THAA
1568 ᕨ CANADIAN SYLLABICS THWAA
1569 ᕩ CANADIAN SYLLABICS WEST-CREE THWAA
156A ᕪ CANADIAN SYLLABICS TH
156B ᕫ CANADIAN SYLLABICS TTHE
156C ᕬ CANADIAN SYLLABICS TTHI
156D ᕭ CANADIAN SYLLABICS TTHO
• Sayisi (TTHU)
156E ᕮ CANADIAN SYLLABICS TTHA
156F ᕯ CANADIAN SYLLABICS TTH
• probably a mistaken interpretation of an asterisk used to mark a proper noun
→ 002A * asterisk
1570 ᕰ CANADIAN SYLLABICS TYE
1571 ᕱ CANADIAN SYLLABICS TYI
1572 ᕲ CANADIAN SYLLABICS TYO
1573 ᕳ CANADIAN SYLLABICS TYA
1574 ᕴ CANADIAN SYLLABICS NUNAVIK HE
1575 ᕵ CANADIAN SYLLABICS NUNAVIK HI
1576 ᕶ CANADIAN SYLLABICS NUNAVIK HII
1577 ᕷ CANADIAN SYLLABICS NUNAVIK HO
1578 ᕸ CANADIAN SYLLABICS NUNAVIK HOO
1579 ᕹ CANADIAN SYLLABICS NUNAVIK HA
157A ᕺ CANADIAN SYLLABICS NUNAVIK HAA
157B ᕻ CANADIAN SYLLABICS NUNAVIK H
157C ᕼ CANADIAN SYLLABICS NUNAVUT H
157D ᕽ CANADIAN SYLLABICS HK
• Algonquian
157E ᕾ CANADIAN SYLLABICS QAAI
• Inuktitut
157F ᕿ CANADIAN SYLLABICS QI
1580 ᖀ CANADIAN SYLLABICS QII
1581 ᖁ CANADIAN SYLLABICS QO
• Inuktitut (QU)
1582 ᖂ CANADIAN SYLLABICS QOO
• Inuktitut (QUU)
1583 ᖃ CANADIAN SYLLABICS QA
1584 ᖄ CANADIAN SYLLABICS QAA
1585 ᖅ CANADIAN SYLLABICS Q
1586 ᖆ CANADIAN SYLLABICS TLHE
• Sayisi (KLE)
1587 ᖇ CANADIAN SYLLABICS TLHI
• Sayisi (KLI)
1588 ᖈ CANADIAN SYLLABICS TLHO
• Sayisi (KLU)
1589 ᖉ CANADIAN SYLLABICS TLHA
• Sayisi (KLA)
158A ᖊ CANADIAN SYLLABICS WEST-CREE RE
158B ᖋ CANADIAN SYLLABICS WEST-CREE RI
158C ᖌ CANADIAN SYLLABICS WEST-CREE RO
158D ᖍ CANADIAN SYLLABICS WEST-CREE RA
158E ᖎ CANADIAN SYLLABICS NGAAI
• Inuktitut
158F ᖏ CANADIAN SYLLABICS NGI

1590 ᖐ CANADIAN SYLLABICS NGII
1591 ᖑ CANADIAN SYLLABICS NGO
• Inuktitut (NGU)
1592 ᖒ CANADIAN SYLLABICS NGOO
• Inuktitut (NGUU)
1593 ᖓ CANADIAN SYLLABICS NGA
1594 ᖔ CANADIAN SYLLABICS NGAA
1595 ᖕ CANADIAN SYLLABICS NG
1596 ᖖ CANADIAN SYLLABICS NNG
1597 ᖗ CANADIAN SYLLABICS SAYISI SHE
1598 ᖘ CANADIAN SYLLABICS SAYISI SHI
1599 ᖙ CANADIAN SYLLABICS SAYISI SHO
• Sayisi (SHU)
159A ᖚ CANADIAN SYLLABICS SAYISI SHA
159B ᖛ CANADIAN SYLLABICS WOODS-CREE THE
159C ᖜ CANADIAN SYLLABICS WOODS-CREE THI
159D ᖝ CANADIAN SYLLABICS WOODS-CREE THO
159E ᖞ CANADIAN SYLLABICS WOODS-CREE THA
159F ᖟ CANADIAN SYLLABICS WOODS-CREE TH
15A0 ᖠ CANADIAN SYLLABICS LHI
15A1 ᖡ CANADIAN SYLLABICS LHII
15A2 ᖢ CANADIAN SYLLABICS LHO
• Inuktitut (LHU)
15A3 ᖣ CANADIAN SYLLABICS LHOO
• Inuktitut (LHUU)
15A4 ᖤ CANADIAN SYLLABICS LHA
15A5 ᖥ CANADIAN SYLLABICS LHAA
15A6 ᖦ CANADIAN SYLLABICS LH
15A7 ᖧ CANADIAN SYLLABICS TH-CREE THE
15A8 ᖨ CANADIAN SYLLABICS TH-CREE THI
15A9 ᖩ CANADIAN SYLLABICS TH-CREE THII
15AA ᖪ CANADIAN SYLLABICS TH-CREE THO
15AB ᖫ CANADIAN SYLLABICS TH-CREE THOO
15AC ᖬ CANADIAN SYLLABICS TH-CREE THA
15AD ᖭ CANADIAN SYLLABICS TH-CREE THAA
15AE ᖮ CANADIAN SYLLABICS TH-CREE TH
15AF ᖯ CANADIAN SYLLABICS AIVILIK B
15B0 ᖰ CANADIAN SYLLABICS BLACKFOOT E
15B1 ᖱ CANADIAN SYLLABICS BLACKFOOT I
15B2 ᖲ CANADIAN SYLLABICS BLACKFOOT O
15B3 ᖳ CANADIAN SYLLABICS BLACKFOOT A
15B4 ᖴ CANADIAN SYLLABICS BLACKFOOT WE
15B5 ᖵ CANADIAN SYLLABICS BLACKFOOT WI
15B6 ᖶ CANADIAN SYLLABICS BLACKFOOT WO
15B7 ᖷ CANADIAN SYLLABICS BLACKFOOT WA
15B8 ᖸ CANADIAN SYLLABICS BLACKFOOT NE
15B9 ᖹ CANADIAN SYLLABICS BLACKFOOT NI
15BA ᖺ CANADIAN SYLLABICS BLACKFOOT NO
15BB ᖻ CANADIAN SYLLABICS BLACKFOOT NA
15BC ᖼ CANADIAN SYLLABICS BLACKFOOT KE
15BD ᖽ CANADIAN SYLLABICS BLACKFOOT KI
15BE ᖾ CANADIAN SYLLABICS BLACKFOOT KO
15BF ᖿ CANADIAN SYLLABICS BLACKFOOT KA
15C0 ᗀ CANADIAN SYLLABICS SAYISI HE
15C1 ᗁ CANADIAN SYLLABICS SAYISI HI
15C2 ᗂ CANADIAN SYLLABICS SAYISI HO
• Sayisi (HU)
15C3 ᗃ CANADIAN SYLLABICS SAYISI HA
15C4 ᗄ CANADIAN SYLLABICS CARRIER GHU
15C5 ᗅ CANADIAN SYLLABICS CARRIER GHO
15C6 ᗆ CANADIAN SYLLABICS CARRIER GHE
15C7 ᗇ CANADIAN SYLLABICS CARRIER GHEE
15C8 ᗈ CANADIAN SYLLABICS CARRIER GHI
15C9 ᗉ CANADIAN SYLLABICS CARRIER GHA
15CA ᗊ CANADIAN SYLLABICS CARRIER RU
15CB ᗋ CANADIAN SYLLABICS CARRIER RO
15CC ᗌ CANADIAN SYLLABICS CARRIER RE
15CD ᗍ CANADIAN SYLLABICS CARRIER REE
15CE ᗎ CANADIAN SYLLABICS CARRIER RI
15CF ᗏ CANADIAN SYLLABICS CARRIER RA
15D0 ᗐ CANADIAN SYLLABICS CARRIER WU
15D1 ᗑ CANADIAN SYLLABICS CARRIER WO
15D2 ᗒ CANADIAN SYLLABICS CARRIER WE
15D3 ᗓ CANADIAN SYLLABICS CARRIER WEE
15D4 ᗔ CANADIAN SYLLABICS CARRIER WI
15D5 ᗕ CANADIAN SYLLABICS CARRIER WA
15D6 ᗖ CANADIAN SYLLABICS CARRIER HWU
15D7 ᗗ CANADIAN SYLLABICS CARRIER HWO
15D8 ᗘ CANADIAN SYLLABICS CARRIER HWE
15D9 ᗙ CANADIAN SYLLABICS CARRIER HWEE
15DA ᗚ CANADIAN SYLLABICS CARRIER HWI
15DB ᗛ CANADIAN SYLLABICS CARRIER HWA
15DC ᗜ CANADIAN SYLLABICS CARRIER THU
15DD ᗝ CANADIAN SYLLABICS CARRIER THO
15DE ᗞ CANADIAN SYLLABICS CARRIER THE
15DF ᗟ CANADIAN SYLLABICS CARRIER THEE
15E0 ᗠ CANADIAN SYLLABICS CARRIER THI
15E1 ᗡ CANADIAN SYLLABICS CARRIER THA
15E2 ᗢ CANADIAN SYLLABICS CARRIER TTU
15E3 ᗣ CANADIAN SYLLABICS CARRIER TTO
15E4 ᗤ CANADIAN SYLLABICS CARRIER TTE
15E5 ᗥ CANADIAN SYLLABICS CARRIER TTEE
15E6 ᗦ CANADIAN SYLLABICS CARRIER TTI
15E7 ᗧ CANADIAN SYLLABICS CARRIER TTA
15E8 ᗨ CANADIAN SYLLABICS CARRIER PU
15E9 ᗩ CANADIAN SYLLABICS CARRIER PO
15EA ᗪ CANADIAN SYLLABICS CARRIER PE
15EB ᗫ CANADIAN SYLLABICS CARRIER PEE
15EC ᗬ CANADIAN SYLLABICS CARRIER PI
15ED ᗭ CANADIAN SYLLABICS CARRIER PA
15EE ᗮ CANADIAN SYLLABICS CARRIER P
15EF ᗯ CANADIAN SYLLABICS CARRIER GU
15F0 ᗰ CANADIAN SYLLABICS CARRIER GO
15F1 ᗱ CANADIAN SYLLABICS CARRIER GE
15F2 ᗲ CANADIAN SYLLABICS CARRIER GEE
15F3 ᗳ CANADIAN SYLLABICS CARRIER GI
15F4 ᗴ CANADIAN SYLLABICS CARRIER GA
15F5 ᗵ CANADIAN SYLLABICS CARRIER KHU
15F6 ᗶ CANADIAN SYLLABICS CARRIER KHO
15F7 ᗷ CANADIAN SYLLABICS CARRIER KHE
15F8 ᗸ CANADIAN SYLLABICS CARRIER KHEE
15F9 ᗹ CANADIAN SYLLABICS CARRIER KHI
15FA ᗺ CANADIAN SYLLABICS CARRIER KHA
15FB ᗻ CANADIAN SYLLABICS CARRIER KKU
15FC ᗼ CANADIAN SYLLABICS CARRIER KKO
15FD ᗽ CANADIAN SYLLABICS CARRIER KKE
15FE ᗾ CANADIAN SYLLABICS CARRIER KKEE
15FF ᗿ CANADIAN SYLLABICS CARRIER KKI
1600 ᘀ CANADIAN SYLLABICS CARRIER KKA
1601 ᘁ CANADIAN SYLLABICS CARRIER KK
1602 ᘂ CANADIAN SYLLABICS CARRIER NU
1603 ᘃ CANADIAN SYLLABICS CARRIER NO
1604 ᘄ CANADIAN SYLLABICS CARRIER NE
1605 ᘅ CANADIAN SYLLABICS CARRIER NEE
1606 ᘆ CANADIAN SYLLABICS CARRIER NI
1607 ᘇ CANADIAN SYLLABICS CARRIER NA

1608 ᘈ CANADIAN SYLLABICS CARRIER MU
1609 ᘉ CANADIAN SYLLABICS CARRIER MO
160A ᘊ CANADIAN SYLLABICS CARRIER ME
160B ᘋ CANADIAN SYLLABICS CARRIER MEE
160C ᘌ CANADIAN SYLLABICS CARRIER MI
160D ᘍ CANADIAN SYLLABICS CARRIER MA
160E ᘎ CANADIAN SYLLABICS CARRIER YU
160F ᘏ CANADIAN SYLLABICS CARRIER YO
1610 ᘐ CANADIAN SYLLABICS CARRIER YE
1611 ᘑ CANADIAN SYLLABICS CARRIER YEE
1612 ᘒ CANADIAN SYLLABICS CARRIER YI
1613 ᘓ CANADIAN SYLLABICS CARRIER YA
1614 ᘔ CANADIAN SYLLABICS CARRIER JU
- Athapascan (ZA), Sayisi (TZO), South Slavey (DHA)

1615 ᘕ CANADIAN SYLLABICS SAYISI JU
- Athapascan (ZO), Sayisi (TZU), South Slavey (DHO)

1616 ᘖ CANADIAN SYLLABICS CARRIER JO
1617 ᘗ CANADIAN SYLLABICS CARRIER JE
1618 ᘘ CANADIAN SYLLABICS CARRIER JEE
1619 ᘙ CANADIAN SYLLABICS CARRIER JI
161A ᘚ CANADIAN SYLLABICS SAYISI JI
- Athapascan (ZE), Sayisi (TZE), South Slavey (DHE)

161B ᘛ CANADIAN SYLLABICS CARRIER JA
- Athapascan (ZI), Sayisi (TZI), South Slavey (DHI)

161C ᘜ CANADIAN SYLLABICS CARRIER JJU
161D ᘝ CANADIAN SYLLABICS CARRIER JJO
161E ᘞ CANADIAN SYLLABICS CARRIER JJE
161F ᘟ CANADIAN SYLLABICS CARRIER JJEE
1620 ᘠ CANADIAN SYLLABICS CARRIER JJI
1621 ᘡ CANADIAN SYLLABICS CARRIER JJA
1622 ᘢ CANADIAN SYLLABICS CARRIER LU
1623 ᘣ CANADIAN SYLLABICS CARRIER LO
1624 ᘤ CANADIAN SYLLABICS CARRIER LE
1625 ᘥ CANADIAN SYLLABICS CARRIER LEE
1626 ᘦ CANADIAN SYLLABICS CARRIER LI
1627 ᘧ CANADIAN SYLLABICS CARRIER LA
1628 ᘨ CANADIAN SYLLABICS CARRIER DLU
1629 ᘩ CANADIAN SYLLABICS CARRIER DLO
162A ᘪ CANADIAN SYLLABICS CARRIER DLE
162B ᘫ CANADIAN SYLLABICS CARRIER DLEE
162C ᘬ CANADIAN SYLLABICS CARRIER DLI
162D ᘭ CANADIAN SYLLABICS CARRIER DLA
162E ᘮ CANADIAN SYLLABICS CARRIER LHU
162F ᘯ CANADIAN SYLLABICS CARRIER LHO
1630 ᘰ CANADIAN SYLLABICS CARRIER LHE
1631 ᘱ CANADIAN SYLLABICS CARRIER LHEE
1632 ᘲ CANADIAN SYLLABICS CARRIER LHI
1633 ᘳ CANADIAN SYLLABICS CARRIER LHA
1634 ᘴ CANADIAN SYLLABICS CARRIER TLHU
1635 ᘵ CANADIAN SYLLABICS CARRIER TLHO
1636 ᘶ CANADIAN SYLLABICS CARRIER TLHE
1637 ᘷ CANADIAN SYLLABICS CARRIER TLHEE
1638 ᘸ CANADIAN SYLLABICS CARRIER TLHI
1639 ᘹ CANADIAN SYLLABICS CARRIER TLHA
163A ᘺ CANADIAN SYLLABICS CARRIER TLU
163B ᘻ CANADIAN SYLLABICS CARRIER TLO
163C ᘼ CANADIAN SYLLABICS CARRIER TLE
163D ᘽ CANADIAN SYLLABICS CARRIER TLEE
163E ᘾ CANADIAN SYLLABICS CARRIER TLI
163F ᘿ CANADIAN SYLLABICS CARRIER TLA
1640 ᙀ CANADIAN SYLLABICS CARRIER ZU
1641 ᙁ CANADIAN SYLLABICS CARRIER ZO
1642 ᙂ CANADIAN SYLLABICS CARRIER ZE
1643 ᙃ CANADIAN SYLLABICS CARRIER ZEE
1644 ᙄ CANADIAN SYLLABICS CARRIER ZI
1645 ᙅ CANADIAN SYLLABICS CARRIER ZA
1646 ᙆ CANADIAN SYLLABICS CARRIER Z
1647 ᙇ CANADIAN SYLLABICS CARRIER INITIAL Z
1648 ᙈ CANADIAN SYLLABICS CARRIER DZU
1649 ᙉ CANADIAN SYLLABICS CARRIER DZO
164A ᙊ CANADIAN SYLLABICS CARRIER DZE
164B ᙋ CANADIAN SYLLABICS CARRIER DZEE
164C ᙌ CANADIAN SYLLABICS CARRIER DZI
164D ᙍ CANADIAN SYLLABICS CARRIER DZA
164E ᙎ CANADIAN SYLLABICS CARRIER SU
164F ᙏ CANADIAN SYLLABICS CARRIER SO
1650 ᙐ CANADIAN SYLLABICS CARRIER SE
1651 ᙑ CANADIAN SYLLABICS CARRIER SEE
1652 ᙒ CANADIAN SYLLABICS CARRIER SI
1653 ᙓ CANADIAN SYLLABICS CARRIER SA
1654 ᙔ CANADIAN SYLLABICS CARRIER SHU
1655 ᙕ CANADIAN SYLLABICS CARRIER SHO
1656 ᙖ CANADIAN SYLLABICS CARRIER SHE
1657 ᙗ CANADIAN SYLLABICS CARRIER SHEE
1658 ᙘ CANADIAN SYLLABICS CARRIER SHI
1659 ᙙ CANADIAN SYLLABICS CARRIER SHA
165A ᙚ CANADIAN SYLLABICS CARRIER SH
165B ᙛ CANADIAN SYLLABICS CARRIER TSU
165C ᙜ CANADIAN SYLLABICS CARRIER TSO
165D ᙝ CANADIAN SYLLABICS CARRIER TSE
165E ᙞ CANADIAN SYLLABICS CARRIER TSEE
165F ᙟ CANADIAN SYLLABICS CARRIER TSI
1660 ᙠ CANADIAN SYLLABICS CARRIER TSA
1661 ᙡ CANADIAN SYLLABICS CARRIER CHU
1662 ᙢ CANADIAN SYLLABICS CARRIER CHO
1663 ᙣ CANADIAN SYLLABICS CARRIER CHE
1664 ᙤ CANADIAN SYLLABICS CARRIER CHEE
1665 ᙥ CANADIAN SYLLABICS CARRIER CHI
1666 ᙦ CANADIAN SYLLABICS CARRIER CHA
1667 ᙧ CANADIAN SYLLABICS CARRIER TTSU
1668 ᙨ CANADIAN SYLLABICS CARRIER TTSO
1669 ᙩ CANADIAN SYLLABICS CARRIER TTSE
166A ᙪ CANADIAN SYLLABICS CARRIER TTSEE
166B ᙫ CANADIAN SYLLABICS CARRIER TTSI
166C ᙬ CANADIAN SYLLABICS CARRIER TTSA

Symbol

166D ᙭ CANADIAN SYLLABICS CHI SIGN
- Algonquian
- used as a symbol to denote Christ

→ 2627 ☧ chi rho

Punctuation

166E ᙮ CANADIAN SYLLABICS FULL STOP

Syllables

166F ᙯ CANADIAN SYLLABICS QAI
1670 ᙰ CANADIAN SYLLABICS NGAI
1671 ᙱ CANADIAN SYLLABICS NNGI
1672 ᙲ CANADIAN SYLLABICS NNGII
1673 ᙳ CANADIAN SYLLABICS NNGO
- Inuktitut (NNGU)

1674 ᙴ CANADIAN SYLLABICS NNGOO
- Inuktitut (NNGUU)

1675 ᙵ CANADIAN SYLLABICS NNGA
1676 ᙶ CANADIAN SYLLABICS NNGAA

	168	169
0	1680	ᚐ 1690
1	ᚁ 1681	ᚑ 1691
2	ᚂ 1682	ᚒ 1692
3	ᚃ 1683	ᚓ 1693
4	ᚄ 1684	ᚔ 1694
5	ᚅ 1685	ᚕ 1695
6	ᚆ 1686	ᚖ 1696
7	ᚇ 1687	ᚗ 1697
8	ᚈ 1688	ᚘ 1698
9	ᚉ 1689	ᚙ 1699
A	ᚊ 168A	ᚚ 169A
B	ᚋ 168B	᚛ 169B
C	ᚌ 168C	᚜ 169C
D	ᚍ 168D	
E	ᚎ 168E	
F	ᚏ 168F	

Punctuation

1680   OGHAM SPACE MARK
- glyph is blank in “stemless” style fonts

Traditional letters

1681 ᚁ OGHAM LETTER BEITH
1682 ᚂ OGHAM LETTER LUIS
1683 ᚃ OGHAM LETTER FEARN
1684 ᚄ OGHAM LETTER SAIL
1685 ᚅ OGHAM LETTER NION
1686 ᚆ OGHAM LETTER UATH
1687 ᚇ OGHAM LETTER DAIR
1688 ᚈ OGHAM LETTER TINNE
1689 ᚉ OGHAM LETTER COLL
168A ᚊ OGHAM LETTER CEIRT
168B ᚋ OGHAM LETTER MUIN
168C ᚌ OGHAM LETTER GORT
168D ᚍ OGHAM LETTER NGEADAL
168E ᚎ OGHAM LETTER STRAIF
168F ᚏ OGHAM LETTER RUIS
1690 ᚐ OGHAM LETTER AILM
1691 ᚑ OGHAM LETTER ONN
1692 ᚒ OGHAM LETTER UR
1693 ᚓ OGHAM LETTER EADHADH
1694 ᚔ OGHAM LETTER IODHADH

Forfeda (supplementary letters)

1695 ᚕ OGHAM LETTER EABHADH
1696 ᚖ OGHAM LETTER OR
1697 ᚗ OGHAM LETTER UILLEANN
1698 ᚘ OGHAM LETTER IFIN
1699 ᚙ OGHAM LETTER EAMHANCHOLL
169A ᚚ OGHAM LETTER PEITH

Punctuation

169B ᚛ OGHAM FEATHER MARK
- marks beginning of Ogham text

169C ᚜ OGHAM REVERSED FEATHER MARK
- marks end of Ogham text

	16A	16B	16C	16D	16E	16F
0	ᚠ 16A0	ᚰ 16B0	ᛀ 16C0	ᛐ 16D0	ᛠ 16E0	ᛰ 16F0
1	ᚡ 16A1	ᚱ 16B1	ᛁ 16C1	ᛑ 16D1	ᛡ 16E1	
2	ᚢ 16A2	ᚲ 16B2	ᛂ 16C2	ᛒ 16D2	ᛢ 16E2	
3	ᚣ 16A3	ᚳ 16B3	ᛃ 16C3	ᛓ 16D3	ᛣ 16E3	
4	ᚤ 16A4	ᚴ 16B4	ᛄ 16C4	ᛔ 16D4	ᛤ 16E4	
5	ᚥ 16A5	ᚵ 16B5	ᛅ 16C5	ᛕ 16D5	ᛥ 16E5	
6	ᚦ 16A6	ᚶ 16B6	ᛆ 16C6	ᛖ 16D6	ᛦ 16E6	
7	ᚧ 16A7	ᚷ 16B7	ᛇ 16C7	ᛗ 16D7	ᛧ 16E7	
8	ᚨ 16A8	ᚸ 16B8	ᛈ 16C8	ᛘ 16D8	ᛨ 16E8	
9	ᚩ 16A9	ᚹ 16B9	ᛉ 16C9	ᛙ 16D9	ᛩ 16E9	
A	ᚪ 16AA	ᚺ 16BA	ᛊ 16CA	ᛚ 16DA	ᛪ 16EA	
B	ᚫ 16AB	ᚻ 16BB	ᛋ 16CB	ᛛ 16DB	᛫ 16EB	
C	ᚬ 16AC	ᚼ 16BC	ᛌ 16CC	ᛜ 16DC	᛬ 16EC	
D	ᚭ 16AD	ᚽ 16BD	ᛍ 16CD	ᛝ 16DD	᛭ 16ED	
E	ᚮ 16AE	ᚾ 16BE	ᛎ 16CE	ᛞ 16DE	ᛮ 16EE	
F	ᚯ 16AF	ᚿ 16BF	ᛏ 16CF	ᛟ 16DF	ᛯ 16EF	

Letters

16A0 ᚠ RUNIC LETTER FEHU FEOH FE F
16A1 ᚡ RUNIC LETTER V
16A2 ᚢ RUNIC LETTER URUZ UR U
16A3 ᚣ RUNIC LETTER YR
16A4 ᚤ RUNIC LETTER Y
16A5 ᚥ RUNIC LETTER W
16A6 ᚦ RUNIC LETTER THURISAZ THURS THORN
→ 00FE þ latin small letter thorn
16A7 ᚧ RUNIC LETTER ETH
16A8 ᚨ RUNIC LETTER ANSUZ A
16A9 ᚩ RUNIC LETTER OS O
16AA ᚪ RUNIC LETTER AC A
16AB ᚫ RUNIC LETTER AESC
16AC ᚬ RUNIC LETTER LONG-BRANCH-OSS O
16AD ᚭ RUNIC LETTER SHORT-TWIG-OSS O
16AE ᚮ RUNIC LETTER O
16AF ᚯ RUNIC LETTER OE
16B0 ᚰ RUNIC LETTER ON
16B1 ᚱ RUNIC LETTER RAIDO RAD REID R
16B2 ᚲ RUNIC LETTER KAUNA
16B3 ᚳ RUNIC LETTER CEN
16B4 ᚴ RUNIC LETTER KAUN K
16B5 ᚵ RUNIC LETTER G
16B6 ᚶ RUNIC LETTER ENG
16B7 ᚷ RUNIC LETTER GEBO GYFU G
16B8 ᚸ RUNIC LETTER GAR
16B9 ᚹ RUNIC LETTER WUNJO WYNN W
→ 01BF ƿ latin letter wynn
16BA ᚺ RUNIC LETTER HAGLAZ H
16BB ᚻ RUNIC LETTER HAEGL H
16BC ᚼ RUNIC LETTER LONG-BRANCH-HAGALL H
16BD ᚽ RUNIC LETTER SHORT-TWIG-HAGALL H
16BE ᚾ RUNIC LETTER NAUDIZ NYD NAUD N
16BF ᚿ RUNIC LETTER SHORT-TWIG-NAUD N
16C0 ᛀ RUNIC LETTER DOTTED-N
16C1 ᛁ RUNIC LETTER ISAZ IS ISS I
16C2 ᛂ RUNIC LETTER E
16C3 ᛃ RUNIC LETTER JERAN J
16C4 ᛄ RUNIC LETTER GER
16C5 ᛅ RUNIC LETTER LONG-BRANCH-AR AE
16C6 ᛆ RUNIC LETTER SHORT-TWIG-AR A
16C7 ᛇ RUNIC LETTER IWAZ EOH
16C8 ᛈ RUNIC LETTER PERTHO PEORTH P
16C9 ᛉ RUNIC LETTER ALGIZ EOLHX
16CA ᛊ RUNIC LETTER SOWILO S
16CB ᛋ RUNIC LETTER SIGEL LONG-BRANCH-SOL S
16CC ᛌ RUNIC LETTER SHORT-TWIG-SOL S
16CD ᛍ RUNIC LETTER C
16CE ᛎ RUNIC LETTER Z
16CF ᛏ RUNIC LETTER TIWAZ TIR TYR T
16D0 ᛐ RUNIC LETTER SHORT-TWIG-TYR T
16D1 ᛑ RUNIC LETTER D
16D2 ᛒ RUNIC LETTER BERKANAN BEORC BJARKAN B
16D3 ᛓ RUNIC LETTER SHORT-TWIG-BJARKAN B
16D4 ᛔ RUNIC LETTER DOTTED-P
16D5 ᛕ RUNIC LETTER OPEN-P
16D6 ᛖ RUNIC LETTER EHWAZ EH E
16D7 ᛗ RUNIC LETTER MANNAZ MAN M
16D8 ᛘ RUNIC LETTER LONG-BRANCH-MADR M
16D9 ᛙ RUNIC LETTER SHORT-TWIG-MADR M
16DA ᛚ RUNIC LETTER LAUKAZ LAGU LOGR L
16DB ᛛ RUNIC LETTER DOTTED-L
16DC ᛜ RUNIC LETTER INGWAZ
16DD ᛝ RUNIC LETTER ING
16DE ᛞ RUNIC LETTER DAGAZ DAEG D
16DF ᛟ RUNIC LETTER OTHALAN ETHEL O
16E0 ᛠ RUNIC LETTER EAR
16E1 ᛡ RUNIC LETTER IOR
16E2 ᛢ RUNIC LETTER CWEORTH
16E3 ᛣ RUNIC LETTER CALC
16E4 ᛤ RUNIC LETTER CEALC
16E5 ᛥ RUNIC LETTER STAN
16E6 ᛦ RUNIC LETTER LONG-BRANCH-YR
16E7 ᛧ RUNIC LETTER SHORT-TWIG-YR
16E8 ᛨ RUNIC LETTER ICELANDIC-YR
16E9 ᛩ RUNIC LETTER Q
16EA ᛪ RUNIC LETTER X

Punctuation

16EB ᛫ RUNIC SINGLE PUNCTUATION
16EC ᛬ RUNIC MULTIPLE PUNCTUATION
16ED ᛭ RUNIC CROSS PUNCTUATION

Golden number runes

16EE ᛮ RUNIC ARLAUG SYMBOL
• golden number 17
16EF ᛯ RUNIC TVIMADUR SYMBOL
• golden number 18
16F0 ᛰ RUNIC BELGTHOR SYMBOL
• golden number 19

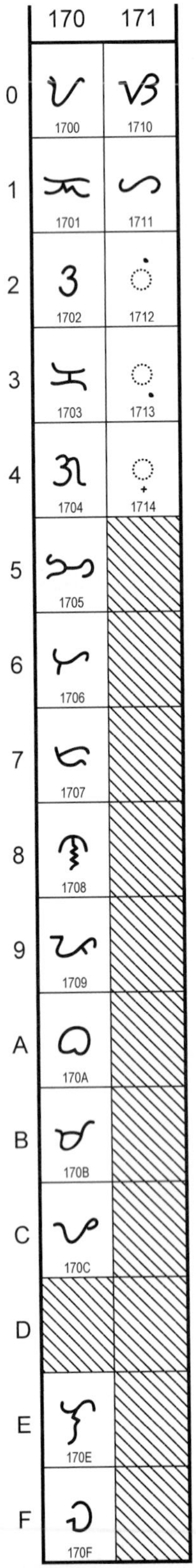

	170	171
0	ᜀ 1700	ᜐ 1710
1	ᜁ 1701	ᜑ 1711
2	ᜂ 1702	◌ᜒ 1712
3	ᜃ 1703	◌ᜓ 1713
4	ᜄ 1704	◌᜔ 1714
5	ᜅ 1705	
6	ᜆ 1706	
7	ᜇ 1707	
8	ᜈ 1708	
9	ᜉ 1709	
A	ᜊ 170A	
B	ᜋ 170B	
C	ᜌ 170C	
D		
E	ᜎ 170E	
F	ᜏ 170F	

Independent vowels

1700 ᜀ TAGALOG LETTER A
1701 ᜁ TAGALOG LETTER I
1702 ᜂ TAGALOG LETTER U

Consonants

1703 ᜃ TAGALOG LETTER KA
1704 ᜄ TAGALOG LETTER GA
1705 ᜅ TAGALOG LETTER NGA
1706 ᜆ TAGALOG LETTER TA
1707 ᜇ TAGALOG LETTER DA
1708 ᜈ TAGALOG LETTER NA
1709 ᜉ TAGALOG LETTER PA
170A ᜊ TAGALOG LETTER BA
170B ᜋ TAGALOG LETTER MA
170C ᜌ TAGALOG LETTER YA
170D <reserved>
170E ᜎ TAGALOG LETTER LA
170F ᜏ TAGALOG LETTER WA
1710 ᜐ TAGALOG LETTER SA
1711 ᜑ TAGALOG LETTER HA

Dependent vowel signs

1712 ◌ᜒ TAGALOG VOWEL SIGN I
1713 ◌ᜓ TAGALOG VOWEL SIGN U

Virama

1714 ◌᜔ TAGALOG SIGN VIRAMA

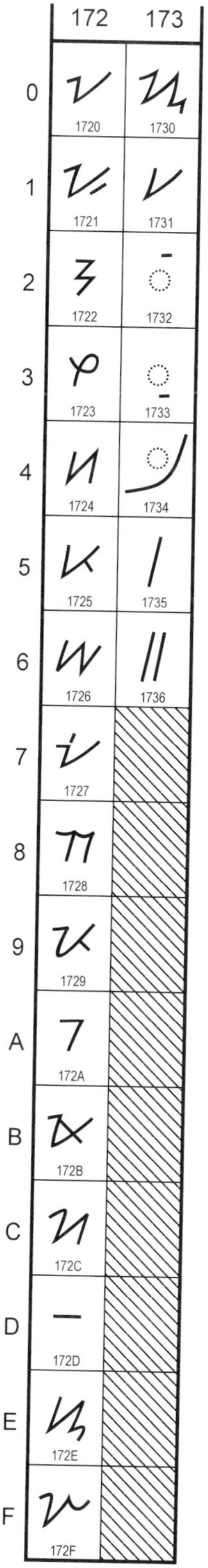

	172	173
0	ᜠ 1720	ᜰ 1730
1	ᜡ 1721	ᜱ 1731
2	ᜢ 1722	◌ᜲ 1732
3	ᜣ 1723	◌ᜳ 1733
4	ᜤ 1724	◌᜴ 1734
5	ᜥ 1725	᜵ 1735
6	ᜦ 1726	᜶ 1736
7	ᜧ 1727	
8	ᜨ 1728	
9	ᜩ 1729	
A	ᜪ 172A	
B	ᜫ 172B	
C	ᜬ 172C	
D	ᜭ 172D	
E	ᜮ 172E	
F	ᜯ 172F	

Independent vowels

1720 ᜠ HANUNOO LETTER A
1721 ᜡ HANUNOO LETTER I
1722 ᜢ HANUNOO LETTER U

Consonants

1723 ᜣ HANUNOO LETTER KA
1724 ᜤ HANUNOO LETTER GA
1725 ᜥ HANUNOO LETTER NGA
1726 ᜦ HANUNOO LETTER TA
1727 ᜧ HANUNOO LETTER DA
1728 ᜨ HANUNOO LETTER NA
1729 ᜩ HANUNOO LETTER PA
172A ᜪ HANUNOO LETTER BA
172B ᜫ HANUNOO LETTER MA
172C ᜬ HANUNOO LETTER YA
172D ᜭ HANUNOO LETTER RA
172E ᜮ HANUNOO LETTER LA
172F ᜯ HANUNOO LETTER WA
1730 ᜰ HANUNOO LETTER SA
1731 ᜱ HANUNOO LETTER HA

Dependent vowel signs

1732 ◌ᜲ HANUNOO VOWEL SIGN I
1733 ◌ᜳ HANUNOO VOWEL SIGN U

Virama

1734 ◌᜴ HANUNOO SIGN PAMUDPOD

Generic punctuation for Philippine scripts

1735 ᜵ PHILIPPINE SINGLE PUNCTUATION
→ 0964 । devanagari danda
1736 ᜶ PHILIPPINE DOUBLE PUNCTUATION
→ 0965 ॥ devanagari double danda

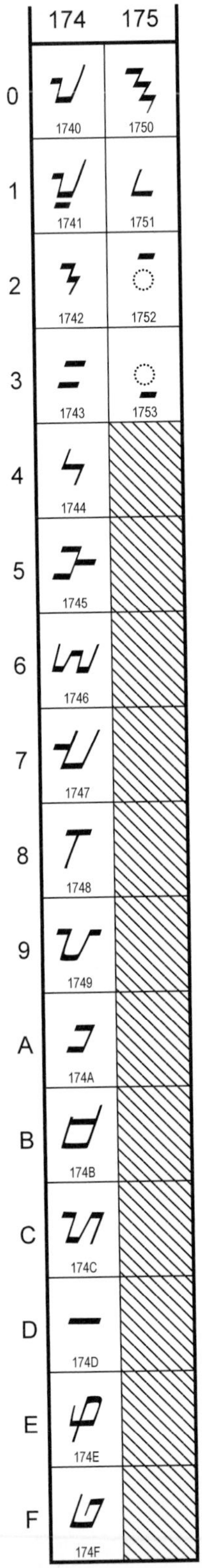

	174	175
0	ᝀ 1740	ᝐ 1750
1	ᝁ 1741	ᝑ 1751
2	ᝂ 1742	◌ᝒ 1752
3	ᝃ 1743	◌ᝓ 1753
4	ᝄ 1744	
5	ᝅ 1745	
6	ᝆ 1746	
7	ᝇ 1747	
8	ᝈ 1748	
9	ᝉ 1749	
A	ᝊ 174A	
B	ᝋ 174B	
C	ᝌ 174C	
D	ᝍ 174D	
E	ᝎ 174E	
F	ᝏ 174F	

Independent vowels

1740 ᝀ BUHID LETTER A
1741 ᝁ BUHID LETTER I
1742 ᝂ BUHID LETTER U

Consonants

1743 ᝃ BUHID LETTER KA
1744 ᝄ BUHID LETTER GA
1745 ᝅ BUHID LETTER NGA
1746 ᝆ BUHID LETTER TA
1747 ᝇ BUHID LETTER DA
1748 ᝈ BUHID LETTER NA
1749 ᝉ BUHID LETTER PA
174A ᝊ BUHID LETTER BA
174B ᝋ BUHID LETTER MA
174C ᝌ BUHID LETTER YA
174D ᝍ BUHID LETTER RA
174E ᝎ BUHID LETTER LA
174F ᝏ BUHID LETTER WA
1750 ᝐ BUHID LETTER SA
1751 ᝑ BUHID LETTER HA

Dependent vowel signs

1752 ◌ᝒ BUHID VOWEL SIGN I
1753 ◌ᝓ BUHID VOWEL SIGN U

	176	177
0	ᝠ 1760	ᝰ 1770
1	ᝡ 1761	
2	ᝢ 1762	◌ᝲ 1772
3	ᝣ 1763	◌ᝳ 1773
4	ᝤ 1764	
5	ᝥ 1765	
6	ᝦ 1766	
7	ᝧ 1767	
8	ᝨ 1768	
9	ᝩ 1769	
A	ᝪ 176A	
B	ᝫ 176B	
C	ᝬ 176C	
D		
E	ᝮ 176E	
F	ᝯ 176F	

Independent vowels

1760 ᝠ TAGBANWA LETTER A
1761 ᝡ TAGBANWA LETTER I
1762 ᝢ TAGBANWA LETTER U

Consonants

1763 ᝣ TAGBANWA LETTER KA
1764 ᝤ TAGBANWA LETTER GA
1765 ᝥ TAGBANWA LETTER NGA
1766 ᝦ TAGBANWA LETTER TA
1767 ᝧ TAGBANWA LETTER DA
1768 ᝨ TAGBANWA LETTER NA
1769 ᝩ TAGBANWA LETTER PA
176A ᝪ TAGBANWA LETTER BA
176B ᝫ TAGBANWA LETTER MA
176C ᝬ TAGBANWA LETTER YA
176D <reserved>
176E ᝮ TAGBANWA LETTER LA
176F ᝯ TAGBANWA LETTER WA
1770 ᝰ TAGBANWA LETTER SA

Dependent vowel signs

1772 ◌ᝲ TAGBANWA VOWEL SIGN I
1773 ◌ᝳ TAGBANWA VOWEL SIGN U

	178	179	17A	17B	17C	17D	17E	17F
0	ក 1780	ថ 1790	ហ 17A0	ឰ 17B0	◌ៀ 17C0	◌័ 17D0	០ 17E0	៰ 17F0
1	ខ 1781	ទ 1791	ឡ 17A1	ឱ 17B1	◌េ 17C1	◌៑ 17D1	១ 17E1	៱ 17F1
2	គ 1782	ធ 1792	អ 17A2	ឲ 17B2	◌ែ 17C2	◌្ 17D2	២ 17E2	៲ 17F2
3	ឃ 1783	ន 1793	ឣ 17A3	ឳ 17B3	◌ៃ 17C3	◌៓ 17D3	៣ 17E3	៳ 17F3
4	ង 1784	ប 1794	ឤ 17A4	KIV AQ 17B4	◌ោ 17C4	។ 17D4	៤ 17E4	៴ 17F4
5	ច 1785	ផ 1795	ឥ 17A5	KIV AA 17B5	◌ៅ 17C5	៕ 17D5	៥ 17E5	៵ 17F5
6	ឆ 1786	ព 1796	ឦ 17A6	◌ា 17B6	◌ំ 17C6	៖ 17D6	៦ 17E6	៶ 17F6
7	ជ 1787	ភ 1797	ឧ 17A7	◌ិ 17B7	◌ះ 17C7	ៗ 17D7	៧ 17E7	៷ 17F7
8	ឈ 1788	ម 1798	ឨ 17A8	◌ី 17B8	◌ៈ 17C8	៘ 17D8	៨ 17E8	៸ 17F8
9	ញ 1789	យ 1799	ឩ 17A9	◌ឹ 17B9	◌៉ 17C9	៙ 17D9	៩ 17E9	៹ 17F9
A	ដ 178A	រ 179A	ឪ 17AA	◌ឺ 17BA	◌៊ 17CA	៚ 17DA		
B	ឋ 178B	ល 179B	ឫ 17AB	◌ុ 17BB	◌់ 17CB	៛ 17DB		
C	ឌ 178C	វ 179C	ឬ 17AC	◌ូ 17BC	◌៌ 17CC	ៜ 17DC		
D	ឍ 178D	ឝ 179D	ឭ 17AD	◌ួ 17BD	◌៍ 17CD	◌៝ 17DD		
E	ណ 178E	ឞ 179E	ឮ 17AE	◌ើ 17BE	◌៎ 17CE			
F	ត 178F	ស 179F	ឯ 17AF	◌ឿ 17BF	◌៏ 17CF			

Consonants

1780 ក KHMER LETTER KA
1781 ខ KHMER LETTER KHA
1782 គ KHMER LETTER KO
1783 ឃ KHMER LETTER KHO
1784 ង KHMER LETTER NGO
1785 ច KHMER LETTER CA
1786 ឆ KHMER LETTER CHA
1787 ជ KHMER LETTER CO
1788 ឈ KHMER LETTER CHO
1789 ញ KHMER LETTER NYO
178A ដ KHMER LETTER DA
178B ឋ KHMER LETTER TTHA
178C ឌ KHMER LETTER DO
178D ឍ KHMER LETTER TTHO
178E ណ KHMER LETTER NNO
- as this character belongs to the first register, its correct transliteration is nna, not nno

178F ត KHMER LETTER TA
1790 ថ KHMER LETTER THA
1791 ទ KHMER LETTER TO
1792 ធ KHMER LETTER THO
1793 ន KHMER LETTER NO
1794 ប KHMER LETTER BA
1795 ផ KHMER LETTER PHA
1796 ព KHMER LETTER PO
1797 ភ KHMER LETTER PHO
1798 ម KHMER LETTER MO
1799 យ KHMER LETTER YO
179A រ KHMER LETTER RO
179B ល KHMER LETTER LO
179C វ KHMER LETTER VO
179D ឝ KHMER LETTER SHA
- used only for Pali/Sanskrit transliteration

179E ឞ KHMER LETTER SSO
- used only for Pali/Sanskrit transliteration
- as this character belongs to the first register, its correct transliteration is ssa, not sso

179F ស KHMER LETTER SA
17A0 ហ KHMER LETTER HA
17A1 ឡ KHMER LETTER LA
17A2 អ KHMER LETTER QA
- glottal stop

Independent vowel (deprecated)

17A3 ឣ KHMER INDEPENDENT VOWEL QAQ
- originally intended only for Pali/Sanskrit transliteration
- use of this character is strongly discouraged; 17A2 អ should be used instead

Independent vowels

17A4 ឤ KHMER INDEPENDENT VOWEL QAA
- used only for Pali/Sanskrit transliteration
- use of this character is discouraged; the sequence 17A2 អ 17B6 ◌ា should be used instead

17A5 ឥ KHMER INDEPENDENT VOWEL QI
17A6 ឦ KHMER INDEPENDENT VOWEL QII
17A7 ឧ KHMER INDEPENDENT VOWEL QU
17A8 ឨ KHMER INDEPENDENT VOWEL QUK
- obsolete ligature for the sequence 17A7 ឧ 1780 ក
- use of the sequence is now preferred

17A9 ឩ KHMER INDEPENDENT VOWEL QUU
17AA ឪ KHMER INDEPENDENT VOWEL QUUV
17AB ឫ KHMER INDEPENDENT VOWEL RY
17AC ឬ KHMER INDEPENDENT VOWEL RYY
17AD ឭ KHMER INDEPENDENT VOWEL LY
17AE ឮ KHMER INDEPENDENT VOWEL LYY
17AF ឯ KHMER INDEPENDENT VOWEL QE
17B0 ឰ KHMER INDEPENDENT VOWEL QAI
17B1 ឱ KHMER INDEPENDENT VOWEL QOO TYPE ONE
17B2 ឲ KHMER INDEPENDENT VOWEL QOO TYPE TWO
- this is a variant for 17B1 ឱ, used in only two words
- 17B1 ឱ is the normal variant of this vowel

17B3 ឳ KHMER INDEPENDENT VOWEL QAU

Inherent vowels

These are for phonetic transcription to distinguish Indic language inherent vowels from Khmer inherent vowels. These characters are included solely for compatibility with particular applications; their use in other contexts is discouraged.

17B4 KIV AQ KHMER VOWEL INHERENT AQ
17B5 KIV AA KHMER VOWEL INHERENT AA

Dependent vowel signs

17B6 ◌ា KHMER VOWEL SIGN AA
17B7 ◌ិ KHMER VOWEL SIGN I
17B8 ◌ី KHMER VOWEL SIGN II
17B9 ◌ឹ KHMER VOWEL SIGN Y
17BA ◌ឺ KHMER VOWEL SIGN YY
17BB ◌ុ KHMER VOWEL SIGN U
17BC ◌ូ KHMER VOWEL SIGN UU
17BD ◌ួ KHMER VOWEL SIGN UA

Two-part dependent vowel signs

These two-part dependent vowel signs have glyph pieces which stand on both sides of the consonant. These vowel signs follow the consonant in logical order, and should be handled as a unit for processing.

17BE ◌ើ KHMER VOWEL SIGN OE
17BF ◌ឿ KHMER VOWEL SIGN YA
17C0 ◌ៀ KHMER VOWEL SIGN IE

Dependent vowel signs

17C1 ◌េ KHMER VOWEL SIGN E
17C2 ◌ែ KHMER VOWEL SIGN AE
17C3 ◌ៃ KHMER VOWEL SIGN AI

Two-part dependent vowel signs

These two-part dependent vowel signs have glyph pieces which stand on both sides of the consonant. These vowel signs follow the consonant in logical order, and should be handled as a unit for processing.

17C4 ◌ោ KHMER VOWEL SIGN OO
17C5 ◌ៅ KHMER VOWEL SIGN AU

Various signs

17C6 ◌ំ KHMER SIGN NIKAHIT
= srak am
= anusvara
- final nasalization
- this character is usually regarded as a vowel sign am, along with om and aam

→ 0E4D ◌ํ thai character nikhahit
→ 1036 ◌ံ myanmar sign anusvara

17C7 ◌ះ KHMER SIGN REAHMUK
= srak ah
= visarga
→ 1038 ◌း myanmar sign visarga

17C8 ◌ៈ KHMER SIGN YUUKALEAPINTU
• inserts a short inherent vowel with abrupt glottal stop
• the preferred transliteration is yukaleakpintu

Consonant shifters

These signs shift the base consonant between registers.

17C9 ◌៉ KHMER SIGN MUUSIKATOAN
• changes the second register to the first
• the preferred transliteration is muusekatoan

17CA ◌៊ KHMER SIGN TRIISAP
• changes the first register to the second
• the preferred transliteration is treisap

Various signs

17CB ◌់ KHMER SIGN BANTOC
• shortens the vowel sound in the previous orthographic syllable
• the preferred transliteration is bantak

17CC ◌៌ KHMER SIGN ROBAT
• a diacritic historically corresponding to the repha form of ra in Devanagari

17CD ◌៍ KHMER SIGN TOANDAKHIAT
• indicates that the base character is not pronounced

17CE ◌៎ KHMER SIGN KAKABAT
• sign used with some exclamations

17CF ◌៏ KHMER SIGN AHSDA
• denotes stressed intonation in some single-consonant words

17D0 ◌័ KHMER SIGN SAMYOK SANNYA
• denotes deviation from the general rules of pronunciation, mostly used in loan words from Pali/Sanskrit, French, and so on

17D1 ◌៑ KHMER SIGN VIRIAM
• mostly obsolete, a "killer"
• indicates that the base character is the final consonant of a word without its inherent vowel sound

17D2 ◌្ KHMER SIGN COENG
• functions to indicate that the following Khmer letter is to be rendered subscripted
• shape shown is arbitrary and is not visibly rendered

Lunar date sign (deprecated)

17D3 ◌៓ KHMER SIGN BATHAMASAT
• originally intended as part of lunar date symbols
• use of this character is strongly discouraged in favor of the complete set of lunar date symbols
→ 19E0 ᧠ khmer symbol pathamasat

Various signs

17D4 ។ KHMER SIGN KHAN
• functions as a full stop, period
→ 0E2F ฯ thai character paiyannoi
→ 104A ၊ myanmar sign little section

17D5 ៕ KHMER SIGN BARIYOOSAN
• indicates the end of a section or a text
→ 0E5A ๚ thai character angkhankhu
→ 104B ။ myanmar sign section

17D6 ៖ KHMER SIGN CAMNUC PII KUUH
• functions as colon
• the preferred transliteration is camnoc pii kuuh
→ 00F7 ÷ division sign
→ 0F14 ༔ tibetan mark gter tsheg

17D7 ៗ KHMER SIGN LEK TOO
• repetition sign
→ 0E46 ๆ thai character maiyamok

17D8 ៘ KHMER SIGN BEYYAL
• et cetera
• use of this character is discouraged; other abbreviations for et cetera also exist
• preferred spelling: 17D4 ។ 179B ល 17D4 ។

17D9 ៙ KHMER SIGN PHNAEK MUAN
• indicates the beginning of a book or a treatise
• the preferred transliteration is phnek moan
→ 0E4F ๏ thai character fongman

17DA ៚ KHMER SIGN KOOMUUT
• indicates the end of a book or treatise
• this forms a pair with 17D9 ៙
• the preferred transliteration is koomoot
→ 0E5B ๛ thai character khomut

Currency symbol

17DB ៛ KHMER CURRENCY SYMBOL RIEL

Various signs

17DC ៜ KHMER SIGN AVAKRAHASANYA
• rare, shows an omitted Sanskrit vowel, like an apostrophe
• the preferred transliteration is avakraha sannya
→ 093D ऽ devanagari sign avagraha

17DD ◌៝ KHMER SIGN ATTHACAN
• mostly obsolete
• indicates that the base character is the final consonant of a word with its inherent vowel sound
→ 17D1 ◌៑ khmer sign viriam

Digits

17E0 ០ KHMER DIGIT ZERO
17E1 ១ KHMER DIGIT ONE
17E2 ២ KHMER DIGIT TWO
17E3 ៣ KHMER DIGIT THREE
17E4 ៤ KHMER DIGIT FOUR
17E5 ៥ KHMER DIGIT FIVE
17E6 ៦ KHMER DIGIT SIX
17E7 ៧ KHMER DIGIT SEVEN
17E8 ៨ KHMER DIGIT EIGHT
17E9 ៩ KHMER DIGIT NINE

Numeric symbols for divination lore

These characters have numeric values 0-9, respectively, but are not used for calculation.

17F0 ៰ KHMER SYMBOL LEK ATTAK SON
17F1 ៱ KHMER SYMBOL LEK ATTAK MUOY
17F2 ៲ KHMER SYMBOL LEK ATTAK PII
17F3 ៳ KHMER SYMBOL LEK ATTAK BEI
17F4 ៴ KHMER SYMBOL LEK ATTAK BUON
17F5 ៵ KHMER SYMBOL LEK ATTAK PRAM
17F6 ៶ KHMER SYMBOL LEK ATTAK PRAM-MUOY
17F7 ៷ KHMER SYMBOL LEK ATTAK PRAM-PII
17F8 ៸ KHMER SYMBOL LEK ATTAK PRAM-BEI
17F9 ៹ KHMER SYMBOL LEK ATTAK PRAM-BUON

	180	181	182	183	184	185	186	187	188	189	18A
0	1800	1810	1820	1830	1840	1850	1860	1870	1880	1890	18A0
1	1801	1811	1821	1831	1841	1851	1861	1871	1881	1891	18A1
2	1802	1812	1822	1832	1842	1852	1862	1872	1882	1892	18A2
3	1803	1813	1823	1833	1843	1853	1863	1873	1883	1893	18A3
4	1804	1814	1824	1834	1844	1854	1864	1874	1884	1894	18A4
5	1805	1815	1825	1835	1845	1855	1865	1875	1885	1895	18A5
6	1806	1816	1826	1836	1846	1856	1866	1876	1886	1896	18A6
7	1807	1817	1827	1837	1847	1857	1867	1877	1887	1897	18A7
8	1808	1818	1828	1838	1848	1858	1868		1888	1898	18A8
9	1809	1819	1829	1839	1849	1859	1869		1889	1899	18A9
A	180A		182A	183A	184A	185A	186A		188A	189A	
B	FVS1 180B		182B	183B	184B	185B	186B		188B	189B	
C	FVS2 180C		182C	183C	184C	185C	186C		188C	189C	
D	FVS3 180D		182D	183D	184D	185D	186D		188D	189D	
E	MVS 180E		182E	183E	184E	185E	186E		188E	189E	
F			182F	183F	184F	185F	186F		188F	189F	

Punctuation

1800 MONGOLIAN BIRGA
→ 0F04 ༄ tibetan mark initial yig mgo mdun ma
1801 MONGOLIAN ELLIPSIS
1802 MONGOLIAN COMMA
1803 MONGOLIAN FULL STOP
1804 MONGOLIAN COLON
1805 MONGOLIAN FOUR DOTS
• marks the end of a chapter
1806 MONGOLIAN TODO SOFT HYPHEN
• not a format control character, but simply a hyphen for Todo
→ 00AD soft hyphen
1807 MONGOLIAN SIBE SYLLABLE BOUNDARY MARKER
1808 MONGOLIAN MANCHU COMMA
1809 MONGOLIAN MANCHU FULL STOP
180A MONGOLIAN NIRUGU

Format controls

180B MONGOLIAN FREE VARIATION SELECTOR ONE
• abbreviated FVS1
180C MONGOLIAN FREE VARIATION SELECTOR TWO
• abbreviated FVS2
180D MONGOLIAN FREE VARIATION SELECTOR THREE
• abbreviated FVS3
180E MONGOLIAN VOWEL SEPARATOR
• abbreviated MVS

Digits

1810 MONGOLIAN DIGIT ZERO
1811 MONGOLIAN DIGIT ONE
1812 MONGOLIAN DIGIT TWO
1813 MONGOLIAN DIGIT THREE
1814 MONGOLIAN DIGIT FOUR
1815 MONGOLIAN DIGIT FIVE
1816 MONGOLIAN DIGIT SIX
1817 MONGOLIAN DIGIT SEVEN
1818 MONGOLIAN DIGIT EIGHT
1819 MONGOLIAN DIGIT NINE

Basic letters

1820 MONGOLIAN LETTER A
→ 0430 а cyrillic small letter a
1821 MONGOLIAN LETTER E
→ 044D э cyrillic small letter e
1822 MONGOLIAN LETTER I
→ 0438 и cyrillic small letter i
1823 MONGOLIAN LETTER O
→ 043E о cyrillic small letter o
1824 MONGOLIAN LETTER U
→ 0443 у cyrillic small letter u
1825 MONGOLIAN LETTER OE
→ 04E9 ө cyrillic small letter barred o
1826 MONGOLIAN LETTER UE
→ 04AF ү cyrillic small letter straight u
1827 MONGOLIAN LETTER EE
1828 MONGOLIAN LETTER NA
→ 043D н cyrillic small letter en
1829 MONGOLIAN LETTER ANG
182A MONGOLIAN LETTER BA
→ 0431 б cyrillic small letter be
182B MONGOLIAN LETTER PA
→ 043F п cyrillic small letter pe
182C MONGOLIAN LETTER QA
→ 0445 х cyrillic small letter ha
182D MONGOLIAN LETTER GA
→ 0433 г cyrillic small letter ghe
182E MONGOLIAN LETTER MA
→ 043C м cyrillic small letter em
182F MONGOLIAN LETTER LA
→ 043B л cyrillic small letter el
1830 MONGOLIAN LETTER SA
→ 0441 с cyrillic small letter es
1831 MONGOLIAN LETTER SHA
→ 0448 ш cyrillic small letter sha
1832 MONGOLIAN LETTER TA
→ 0442 т cyrillic small letter te
1833 MONGOLIAN LETTER DA
→ 0434 д cyrillic small letter de
1834 MONGOLIAN LETTER CHA
→ 0447 ч cyrillic small letter che
1835 MONGOLIAN LETTER JA
→ 0436 ж cyrillic small letter zhe
1836 MONGOLIAN LETTER YA
→ 0439 й cyrillic small letter short i
1837 MONGOLIAN LETTER RA
→ 0440 р cyrillic small letter er
1838 MONGOLIAN LETTER WA
→ 0432 в cyrillic small letter ve
1839 MONGOLIAN LETTER FA
→ 0444 ф cyrillic small letter ef
183A MONGOLIAN LETTER KA
→ 0445 х cyrillic small letter ha
183B MONGOLIAN LETTER KHA
→ 043A к cyrillic small letter ka
183C MONGOLIAN LETTER TSA
→ 0446 ц cyrillic small letter tse
183D MONGOLIAN LETTER ZA
→ 0437 з cyrillic small letter ze
183E MONGOLIAN LETTER HAA
→ 0445 х cyrillic small letter ha
183F MONGOLIAN LETTER ZRA
→ 0436 ж cyrillic small letter zhe
1840 MONGOLIAN LETTER LHA
1841 MONGOLIAN LETTER ZHI
1842 MONGOLIAN LETTER CHI

Todo letters

1843 MONGOLIAN LETTER TODO LONG VOWEL SIGN
1844 MONGOLIAN LETTER TODO E
1845 MONGOLIAN LETTER TODO I
1846 MONGOLIAN LETTER TODO O
1847 MONGOLIAN LETTER TODO U
1848 MONGOLIAN LETTER TODO OE
1849 MONGOLIAN LETTER TODO UE
184A MONGOLIAN LETTER TODO ANG
184B MONGOLIAN LETTER TODO BA
184C MONGOLIAN LETTER TODO PA
184D MONGOLIAN LETTER TODO QA
184E MONGOLIAN LETTER TODO GA
184F MONGOLIAN LETTER TODO MA
1850 MONGOLIAN LETTER TODO TA
1851 MONGOLIAN LETTER TODO DA
1852 MONGOLIAN LETTER TODO CHA
1853 MONGOLIAN LETTER TODO JA
1854 MONGOLIAN LETTER TODO TSA

1855 ᡕ MONGOLIAN LETTER TODO YA

1856 ᡖ MONGOLIAN LETTER TODO WA

1857 ᡗ MONGOLIAN LETTER TODO KA

1858 ᡘ MONGOLIAN LETTER TODO GAA

1859 ᡙ MONGOLIAN LETTER TODO HAA

185A ᡚ MONGOLIAN LETTER TODO JIA

185B ᡛ MONGOLIAN LETTER TODO NIA

185C ᡜ MONGOLIAN LETTER TODO DZA

Sibe letters

185D ᡝ MONGOLIAN LETTER SIBE E

185E ᡞ MONGOLIAN LETTER SIBE I

185F ᡟ MONGOLIAN LETTER SIBE IY

1860 ᡠ MONGOLIAN LETTER SIBE UE

1861 ᡡ MONGOLIAN LETTER SIBE U

1862 ᡢ MONGOLIAN LETTER SIBE ANG

1863 ᡣ MONGOLIAN LETTER SIBE KA

1864 ᡤ MONGOLIAN LETTER SIBE GA

1865 ᡥ MONGOLIAN LETTER SIBE HA

1866 ᡦ MONGOLIAN LETTER SIBE PA

1867 ᡧ MONGOLIAN LETTER SIBE SHA

1868 ᡨ MONGOLIAN LETTER SIBE TA

1869 ᡩ MONGOLIAN LETTER SIBE DA

186A ᡪ MONGOLIAN LETTER SIBE JA

186B ᡫ MONGOLIAN LETTER SIBE FA

186C ᡬ MONGOLIAN LETTER SIBE GAA

186D ᡭ MONGOLIAN LETTER SIBE HAA

186E ᡮ MONGOLIAN LETTER SIBE TSA

186F ᡯ MONGOLIAN LETTER SIBE ZA

1870 ᡰ MONGOLIAN LETTER SIBE RAA

1871 ᡱ MONGOLIAN LETTER SIBE CHA

1872 ᡲ MONGOLIAN LETTER SIBE ZHA

Manchu letters

1873 ᡳ MONGOLIAN LETTER MANCHU I

1874 ᡴ MONGOLIAN LETTER MANCHU KA

1875 ᡵ MONGOLIAN LETTER MANCHU RA

1876 ᡶ MONGOLIAN LETTER MANCHU FA

1877 ᡷ MONGOLIAN LETTER MANCHU ZHA

Extensions for Sanskrit and Tibetan

1880 ᢀ MONGOLIAN LETTER ALI GALI ANUSVARA ONE
→ 0F83 ྃ tibetan sign sna ldan

1881 ᢁ MONGOLIAN LETTER ALI GALI VISARGA ONE
→ 0F7F ཿ tibetan sign rnam bcad

1882 ᢂ MONGOLIAN LETTER ALI GALI DAMARU
→ 0F88 ྈ tibetan sign lce tsa can

1883 ᢃ MONGOLIAN LETTER ALI GALI UBADAMA

1884 ᢄ MONGOLIAN LETTER ALI GALI INVERTED UBADAMA

1885 ᢅ MONGOLIAN LETTER ALI GALI BALUDA
→ 0F85 ྅ tibetan mark paluta

1886 ᢆ MONGOLIAN LETTER ALI GALI THREE BALUDA

1887 ᢇ MONGOLIAN LETTER ALI GALI A

1888 ᢈ MONGOLIAN LETTER ALI GALI I

1889 ᢉ MONGOLIAN LETTER ALI GALI KA

188A ᢊ MONGOLIAN LETTER ALI GALI NGA

188B ᢋ MONGOLIAN LETTER ALI GALI CA

188C ᢌ MONGOLIAN LETTER ALI GALI TTA

188D ᢍ MONGOLIAN LETTER ALI GALI TTHA

188E ᢎ MONGOLIAN LETTER ALI GALI DDA

188F ᢏ MONGOLIAN LETTER ALI GALI NNA

1890 ᢐ MONGOLIAN LETTER ALI GALI TA

1891 ᢑ MONGOLIAN LETTER ALI GALI DA

1892 ᢒ MONGOLIAN LETTER ALI GALI PA

1893 ᢓ MONGOLIAN LETTER ALI GALI PHA

1894 ᢔ MONGOLIAN LETTER ALI GALI SSA

1895 ᢕ MONGOLIAN LETTER ALI GALI ZHA

1896 ᢖ MONGOLIAN LETTER ALI GALI ZA

1897 ᢗ MONGOLIAN LETTER ALI GALI AH

1898 ᢘ MONGOLIAN LETTER TODO ALI GALI TA

1899 ᢙ MONGOLIAN LETTER TODO ALI GALI ZHA

189A ᢚ MONGOLIAN LETTER MANCHU ALI GALI GHA

189B ᢛ MONGOLIAN LETTER MANCHU ALI GALI NGA

189C ᢜ MONGOLIAN LETTER MANCHU ALI GALI CA

189D ᢝ MONGOLIAN LETTER MANCHU ALI GALI JHA

189E ᢞ MONGOLIAN LETTER MANCHU ALI GALI TTA

189F ᢟ MONGOLIAN LETTER MANCHU ALI GALI DDHA

18A0 ᢠ MONGOLIAN LETTER MANCHU ALI GALI TA

18A1 ᢡ MONGOLIAN LETTER MANCHU ALI GALI DHA

18A2 ᢢ MONGOLIAN LETTER MANCHU ALI GALI SSA

18A3 ᢣ MONGOLIAN LETTER MANCHU ALI GALI CYA

18A4 ᢤ MONGOLIAN LETTER MANCHU ALI GALI ZHA

18A5 ᢥ MONGOLIAN LETTER MANCHU ALI GALI ZA

18A6 ᢦ MONGOLIAN LETTER ALI GALI HALF U

18A7 ᢧ MONGOLIAN LETTER ALI GALI HALF YA

18A8 ᢨ MONGOLIAN LETTER MANCHU ALI GALI BHA

18A9 ◌ᢩ MONGOLIAN LETTER ALI GALI DAGALGA

	190	191	192	193	194
0	ᤀ 1900	ᤐ 1910	◌ᤠ 1920	◌ᤰ 1930	᥀ 1940
1	ᤁ 1901	ᤑ 1911	◌ᤡ 1921	◌ᤱ 1931	
2	ᤂ 1902	ᤒ 1912	◌ᤢ 1922	◌ᤲ 1932	
3	ᤃ 1903	ᤓ 1913	◌ᤣ 1923	◌ᤳ 1933	
4	ᤄ 1904	ᤔ 1914	◌ᤤ 1924	◌ᤴ 1934	᥄ 1944
5	ᤅ 1905	ᤕ 1915	◌ᤥ 1925	◌ᤵ 1935	᥅ 1945
6	ᤆ 1906	ᤖ 1916	◌ᤦ 1926	◌ᤶ 1936	᥆ 1946
7	ᤇ 1907	ᤗ 1917	◌ᤧ 1927	◌ᤷ 1937	᥇ 1947
8	ᤈ 1908	ᤘ 1918	◌ᤨ 1928	◌ᤸ 1938	᥈ 1948
9	ᤉ 1909	ᤙ 1919	◌ᤩ 1929	◌᤹ 1939	᥉ 1949
A	ᤊ 190A	ᤚ 191A	◌ᤪ 192A	◌᤺ 193A	᥊ 194A
B	ᤋ 190B	ᤛ 191B	◌ᤫ 192B	◌᤻ 193B	᥋ 194B
C	ᤌ 190C	ᤜ 191C			᥌ 194C
D	ᤍ 190D				᥍ 194D
E	ᤎ 190E				᥎ 194E
F	ᤏ 190F				᥏ 194F

Consonants

1900 ᤀ LIMBU VOWEL-CARRIER LETTER
1901 ᤁ LIMBU LETTER KA
1902 ᤂ LIMBU LETTER KHA
1903 ᤃ LIMBU LETTER GA
1904 ᤄ LIMBU LETTER GHA
1905 ᤅ LIMBU LETTER NGA
1906 ᤆ LIMBU LETTER CA
1907 ᤇ LIMBU LETTER CHA
1908 ᤈ LIMBU LETTER JA
1909 ᤉ LIMBU LETTER JHA
190A ᤊ LIMBU LETTER YAN
190B ᤋ LIMBU LETTER TA
190C ᤌ LIMBU LETTER THA
190D ᤍ LIMBU LETTER DA
190E ᤎ LIMBU LETTER DHA
190F ᤏ LIMBU LETTER NA
1910 ᤐ LIMBU LETTER PA
1911 ᤑ LIMBU LETTER PHA
1912 ᤒ LIMBU LETTER BA
1913 ᤓ LIMBU LETTER BHA
1914 ᤔ LIMBU LETTER MA
1915 ᤕ LIMBU LETTER YA
1916 ᤖ LIMBU LETTER RA
1917 ᤗ LIMBU LETTER LA
1918 ᤘ LIMBU LETTER WA
1919 ᤙ LIMBU LETTER SHA
191A ᤚ LIMBU LETTER SSA
191B ᤛ LIMBU LETTER SA
191C ᤜ LIMBU LETTER HA

Dependent vowel signs

1920 ◌ᤠ LIMBU VOWEL SIGN A
1921 ◌ᤡ LIMBU VOWEL SIGN I
1922 ◌ᤢ LIMBU VOWEL SIGN U
1923 ◌ᤣ LIMBU VOWEL SIGN EE
1924 ◌ᤤ LIMBU VOWEL SIGN AI
1925 ◌ᤥ LIMBU VOWEL SIGN OO
1926 ◌ᤦ LIMBU VOWEL SIGN AU
1927 ◌ᤧ LIMBU VOWEL SIGN E
1928 ◌ᤨ LIMBU VOWEL SIGN O

Subjoined consonants

1929 ◌ᤩ LIMBU SUBJOINED LETTER YA
192A ◌ᤪ LIMBU SUBJOINED LETTER RA
192B ◌ᤫ LIMBU SUBJOINED LETTER WA

Final consonants

1930 ◌ᤰ LIMBU SMALL LETTER KA
1931 ◌ᤱ LIMBU SMALL LETTER NGA
1932 ◌ᤲ LIMBU SMALL LETTER ANUSVARA
1933 ◌ᤳ LIMBU SMALL LETTER TA
1934 ◌ᤴ LIMBU SMALL LETTER NA
1935 ◌ᤵ LIMBU SMALL LETTER PA
1936 ◌ᤶ LIMBU SMALL LETTER MA
1937 ◌ᤷ LIMBU SMALL LETTER RA
1938 ◌ᤸ LIMBU SMALL LETTER LA

Various signs

1939 ◌᤹ LIMBU SIGN MUKPHRENG
193A ◌᤺ LIMBU SIGN KEMPHRENG
193B ◌᤻ LIMBU SIGN SA-I
193C <reserved>
193D <reserved>
193E <reserved>
193F <reserved>
1940 ᥀ LIMBU SIGN LOO
1941 <reserved>
1942 <reserved>
1943 <reserved>
1944 ᥄ LIMBU EXCLAMATION MARK
1945 ᥅ LIMBU QUESTION MARK

Digits

1946 ᥆ LIMBU DIGIT ZERO
1947 ᥇ LIMBU DIGIT ONE
1948 ᥈ LIMBU DIGIT TWO
1949 ᥉ LIMBU DIGIT THREE
194A ᥊ LIMBU DIGIT FOUR
194B ᥋ LIMBU DIGIT FIVE
194C ᥌ LIMBU DIGIT SIX
194D ᥍ LIMBU DIGIT SEVEN
194E ᥎ LIMBU DIGIT EIGHT
194F ᥏ LIMBU DIGIT NINE

	195	196	197
0	ᥐ 1950	ᥠ 1960	ᥰ 1970
1	ᥑ 1951	ᥡ 1961	ᥱ 1971
2	ᥒ 1952	ᥢ 1962	ᥲ 1972
3	ᥓ 1953	ᥣ 1963	ᥳ 1973
4	ᥔ 1954	ᥤ 1964	ᥴ 1974
5	ᥕ 1955	ᥥ 1965	
6	ᥖ 1956	ᥦ 1966	
7	ᥗ 1957	ᥧ 1967	
8	ᥘ 1958	ᥨ 1968	
9	ᥙ 1959	ᥩ 1969	
A	ᥚ 195A	ᥪ 196A	
B	ᥛ 195B	ᥫ 196B	
C	ᥜ 195C	ᥬ 196C	
D	ᥝ 195D	ᥭ 196D	
E	ᥞ 195E		
F	ᥟ 195F		

Note the similarly named but distinct New Tai Lue script encoded at U+1980..U+19DF.

Consonants

1950 ᥐ TAI LE LETTER KA
1951 ᥑ TAI LE LETTER XA
1952 ᥒ TAI LE LETTER NGA
1953 ᥓ TAI LE LETTER TSA
1954 ᥔ TAI LE LETTER SA
1955 ᥕ TAI LE LETTER YA
1956 ᥖ TAI LE LETTER TA
1957 ᥗ TAI LE LETTER THA
1958 ᥘ TAI LE LETTER LA
1959 ᥙ TAI LE LETTER PA
195A ᥚ TAI LE LETTER PHA
195B ᥛ TAI LE LETTER MA
195C ᥜ TAI LE LETTER FA
195D ᥝ TAI LE LETTER VA
195E ᥞ TAI LE LETTER HA
195F ᥟ TAI LE LETTER QA
1960 ᥠ TAI LE LETTER KHA
1961 ᥡ TAI LE LETTER TSHA
1962 ᥢ TAI LE LETTER NA

Vowels

1963 ᥣ TAI LE LETTER A
1964 ᥤ TAI LE LETTER I
1965 ᥥ TAI LE LETTER EE
1966 ᥦ TAI LE LETTER EH
1967 ᥧ TAI LE LETTER U
1968 ᥨ TAI LE LETTER OO
1969 ᥩ TAI LE LETTER O
196A ᥪ TAI LE LETTER UE
196B ᥫ TAI LE LETTER E
196C ᥬ TAI LE LETTER AUE
196D ᥭ TAI LE LETTER AI

Tone letters

1970 ᥰ TAI LE LETTER TONE-2
1971 ᥱ TAI LE LETTER TONE-3
1972 ᥲ TAI LE LETTER TONE-4
1973 ᥳ TAI LE LETTER TONE-5
1974 ᥴ TAI LE LETTER TONE-6

	198	199	19A	19B	19C	19D
0	ᦀ 1980	ᦐ 1990	ᦠ 19A0	◌ᦰ 19B0	◌ᧀ 19C0	᧐ 19D0
1	ᦁ 1981	ᦑ 1991	ᦡ 19A1	◌ᦱ 19B1	ᧁ 19C1	᧑ 19D1
2	ᦂ 1982	ᦒ 1992	ᦢ 19A2	◌ᦲ 19B2	ᧂ 19C2	᧒ 19D2
3	ᦃ 1983	ᦓ 1993	ᦣ 19A3	◌ᦳ 19B3	ᧃ 19C3	᧓ 19D3
4	ᦄ 1984	ᦔ 1994	ᦤ 19A4	◌ᦴ 19B4	ᧄ 19C4	᧔ 19D4
5	ᦅ 1985	ᦕ 1995	ᦥ 19A5	ᦵ◌ 19B5	ᧅ 19C5	᧕ 19D5
6	ᦆ 1986	ᦖ 1996	ᦦ 19A6	ᦶ◌ 19B6	ᧆ 19C6	᧖ 19D6
7	ᦇ 1987	ᦗ 1997	ᦧ 19A7	ᦷ◌ 19B7	ᧇ 19C7	᧗ 19D7
8	ᦈ 1988	ᦘ 1998	ᦨ 19A8	◌ᦸ 19B8	◌ᧈ 19C8	᧘ 19D8
9	ᦉ 1989	ᦙ 1999	ᦩ 19A9	◌ᦹ 19B9	◌ᧉ 19C9	᧙ 19D9
A	ᦊ 198A	ᦚ 199A		ᦺ◌ 19BA		
B	ᦋ 198B	ᦛ 199B		◌ᦻ 19BB		
C	ᦌ 198C	ᦜ 199C		◌ᦼ 19BC		
D	ᦍ 198D	ᦝ 199D		◌ᦽ 19BD		
E	ᦎ 198E	ᦞ 199E		◌ᦾ 19BE		᧞ 19DE
F	ᦏ 198F	ᦟ 199F		◌ᦿ 19BF		᧟ 19DF

Note the similarly named but distinct Tai Le script encoded at U+1950..U+197F. The New Tai Lue script is also known as Xishuang Banna Dai.

Consonants

1980 ᦀ NEW TAI LUE LETTER HIGH QA
1981 ᦁ NEW TAI LUE LETTER LOW QA
1982 ᦂ NEW TAI LUE LETTER HIGH KA
1983 ᦃ NEW TAI LUE LETTER HIGH XA
1984 ᦄ NEW TAI LUE LETTER HIGH NGA
1985 ᦅ NEW TAI LUE LETTER LOW KA
1986 ᦆ NEW TAI LUE LETTER LOW XA
1987 ᦇ NEW TAI LUE LETTER LOW NGA
1988 ᦈ NEW TAI LUE LETTER HIGH TSA
1989 ᦉ NEW TAI LUE LETTER HIGH SA
198A ᦊ NEW TAI LUE LETTER HIGH YA
198B ᦋ NEW TAI LUE LETTER LOW TSA
198C ᦌ NEW TAI LUE LETTER LOW SA
198D ᦍ NEW TAI LUE LETTER LOW YA
198E ᦎ NEW TAI LUE LETTER HIGH TA
198F ᦏ NEW TAI LUE LETTER HIGH THA
1990 ᦐ NEW TAI LUE LETTER HIGH NA
1991 ᦑ NEW TAI LUE LETTER LOW TA
1992 ᦒ NEW TAI LUE LETTER LOW THA
1993 ᦓ NEW TAI LUE LETTER LOW NA
1994 ᦔ NEW TAI LUE LETTER HIGH PA
1995 ᦕ NEW TAI LUE LETTER HIGH PHA
1996 ᦖ NEW TAI LUE LETTER HIGH MA
1997 ᦗ NEW TAI LUE LETTER LOW PA
1998 ᦘ NEW TAI LUE LETTER LOW PHA
1999 ᦙ NEW TAI LUE LETTER LOW MA
199A ᦚ NEW TAI LUE LETTER HIGH FA
199B ᦛ NEW TAI LUE LETTER HIGH VA
199C ᦜ NEW TAI LUE LETTER HIGH LA
199D ᦝ NEW TAI LUE LETTER LOW FA
199E ᦞ NEW TAI LUE LETTER LOW VA
199F ᦟ NEW TAI LUE LETTER LOW LA
19A0 ᦠ NEW TAI LUE LETTER HIGH HA
19A1 ᦡ NEW TAI LUE LETTER HIGH DA
19A2 ᦢ NEW TAI LUE LETTER HIGH BA
19A3 ᦣ NEW TAI LUE LETTER LOW HA
19A4 ᦤ NEW TAI LUE LETTER LOW DA
19A5 ᦥ NEW TAI LUE LETTER LOW BA
19A6 ᦦ NEW TAI LUE LETTER HIGH KVA
19A7 ᦧ NEW TAI LUE LETTER HIGH XVA
19A8 ᦨ NEW TAI LUE LETTER LOW KVA
19A9 ᦩ NEW TAI LUE LETTER LOW XVA

Vowel signs

19B0 ◌ᦰ NEW TAI LUE VOWEL SIGN VOWEL SHORTENER
19B1 ◌ᦱ NEW TAI LUE VOWEL SIGN AA
19B2 ◌ᦲ NEW TAI LUE VOWEL SIGN II
19B3 ◌ᦳ NEW TAI LUE VOWEL SIGN U
19B4 ◌ᦴ NEW TAI LUE VOWEL SIGN UU
19B5 ᦵ◌ NEW TAI LUE VOWEL SIGN E
19B6 ᦶ◌ NEW TAI LUE VOWEL SIGN AE
19B7 ᦷ◌ NEW TAI LUE VOWEL SIGN O
19B8 ◌ᦸ NEW TAI LUE VOWEL SIGN OA
19B9 ◌ᦹ NEW TAI LUE VOWEL SIGN UE
19BA ᦺ◌ NEW TAI LUE VOWEL SIGN AY
19BB ◌ᦻ NEW TAI LUE VOWEL SIGN AAY
19BC ◌ᦼ NEW TAI LUE VOWEL SIGN UY
19BD ◌ᦽ NEW TAI LUE VOWEL SIGN OY
19BE ◌ᦾ NEW TAI LUE VOWEL SIGN OAY
19BF ◌ᦿ NEW TAI LUE VOWEL SIGN UEY
19C0 ◌ᧀ NEW TAI LUE VOWEL SIGN IY

Final consonants

19C1 ᧁ NEW TAI LUE LETTER FINAL V
19C2 ᧂ NEW TAI LUE LETTER FINAL NG
19C3 ᧃ NEW TAI LUE LETTER FINAL N
19C4 ᧄ NEW TAI LUE LETTER FINAL M
19C5 ᧅ NEW TAI LUE LETTER FINAL K
19C6 ᧆ NEW TAI LUE LETTER FINAL D
19C7 ᧇ NEW TAI LUE LETTER FINAL B

Tone marks

19C8 ◌ᧈ NEW TAI LUE TONE MARK-1
19C9 ◌ᧉ NEW TAI LUE TONE MARK-2

Digits

19D0 ᧐ NEW TAI LUE DIGIT ZERO
19D1 ᧑ NEW TAI LUE DIGIT ONE
19D2 ᧒ NEW TAI LUE DIGIT TWO
19D3 ᧓ NEW TAI LUE DIGIT THREE
19D4 ᧔ NEW TAI LUE DIGIT FOUR
19D5 ᧕ NEW TAI LUE DIGIT FIVE
19D6 ᧖ NEW TAI LUE DIGIT SIX
19D7 ᧗ NEW TAI LUE DIGIT SEVEN
19D8 ᧘ NEW TAI LUE DIGIT EIGHT
19D9 ᧙ NEW TAI LUE DIGIT NINE

Various signs

19DE ᧞ NEW TAI LUE SIGN LAE
• conjunction: and
19DF ᧟ NEW TAI LUE SIGN LAEV
• perfective

	19E	19F
0	᧠ 19E0	᧰ 19F0
1	᧡ 19E1	᧱ 19F1
2	᧢ 19E2	᧲ 19F2
3	᧣ 19E3	᧳ 19F3
4	᧤ 19E4	᧴ 19F4
5	᧥ 19E5	᧵ 19F5
6	᧦ 19E6	᧶ 19F6
7	᧧ 19E7	᧷ 19F7
8	᧨ 19E8	᧸ 19F8
9	᧩ 19E9	᧹ 19F9
A	᧪ 19EA	᧺ 19FA
B	᧫ 19EB	᧻ 19FB
C	᧬ 19EC	᧼ 19FC
D	᧭ 19ED	᧽ 19FD
E	᧮ 19EE	᧾ 19FE
F	᧯ 19EF	᧿ 19FF

Lunar date symbols

19E0 ᧠ KHMER SYMBOL PATHAMASAT
- represents the first August in a leap year

The following fifteen characters represent the first through the fifteenth waxing days, respectively.

19E1 ᧡ KHMER SYMBOL MUOY KOET
19E2 ᧢ KHMER SYMBOL PII KOET
19E3 ᧣ KHMER SYMBOL BEI KOET
19E4 ᧤ KHMER SYMBOL BUON KOET
19E5 ᧥ KHMER SYMBOL PRAM KOET
19E6 ᧦ KHMER SYMBOL PRAM-MUOY KOET
19E7 ᧧ KHMER SYMBOL PRAM-PII KOET
19E8 ᧨ KHMER SYMBOL PRAM-BEI KOET
19E9 ᧩ KHMER SYMBOL PRAM-BUON KOET
19EA ᧪ KHMER SYMBOL DAP KOET
19EB ᧫ KHMER SYMBOL DAP-MUOY KOET
19EC ᧬ KHMER SYMBOL DAP-PII KOET
19ED ᧭ KHMER SYMBOL DAP-BEI KOET
19EE ᧮ KHMER SYMBOL DAP-BUON KOET
19EF ᧯ KHMER SYMBOL DAP-PRAM KOET
19F0 ᧰ KHMER SYMBOL TUTEYASAT
- represents the second August in a leap year

The following fifteen characters represent the first through the fifteenth waning days, respectively.

19F1 ᧱ KHMER SYMBOL MUOY ROC
19F2 ᧲ KHMER SYMBOL PII ROC
19F3 ᧳ KHMER SYMBOL BEI ROC
19F4 ᧴ KHMER SYMBOL BUON ROC
19F5 ᧵ KHMER SYMBOL PRAM ROC
19F6 ᧶ KHMER SYMBOL PRAM-MUOY ROC
19F7 ᧷ KHMER SYMBOL PRAM-PII ROC
19F8 ᧸ KHMER SYMBOL PRAM-BEI ROC
19F9 ᧹ KHMER SYMBOL PRAM-BUON ROC
19FA ᧺ KHMER SYMBOL DAP ROC
19FB ᧻ KHMER SYMBOL DAP-MUOY ROC
19FC ᧼ KHMER SYMBOL DAP-PII ROC
19FD ᧽ KHMER SYMBOL DAP-BEI ROC
19FE ᧾ KHMER SYMBOL DAP-BUON ROC
19FF ᧿ KHMER SYMBOL DAP-PRAM ROC

	1A0	1A1
0	ᨀ 1A00	ᨐ 1A10
1	ᨁ 1A01	ᨑ 1A11
2	ᨂ 1A02	ᨒ 1A12
3	ᨃ 1A03	ᨓ 1A13
4	ᨄ 1A04	ᨔ 1A14
5	ᨅ 1A05	ᨕ 1A15
6	ᨆ 1A06	ᨖ 1A16
7	ᨇ 1A07	◌ᨗ 1A17
8	ᨈ 1A08	◌ᨘ 1A18
9	ᨉ 1A09	◌ᨙ 1A19
A	ᨊ 1A0A	◌ᨚ 1A1A
B	ᨋ 1A0B	◌ᨛ 1A1B
C	ᨌ 1A0C	
D	ᨍ 1A0D	
E	ᨎ 1A0E	᨞ 1A1E
F	ᨏ 1A0F	᨟ 1A1F

This script is also known as Lontara.

Consonants

1A00 ᨀ BUGINESE LETTER KA
1A01 ᨁ BUGINESE LETTER GA
1A02 ᨂ BUGINESE LETTER NGA
1A03 ᨃ BUGINESE LETTER NGKA
1A04 ᨄ BUGINESE LETTER PA
1A05 ᨅ BUGINESE LETTER BA
1A06 ᨆ BUGINESE LETTER MA
1A07 ᨇ BUGINESE LETTER MPA
1A08 ᨈ BUGINESE LETTER TA
1A09 ᨉ BUGINESE LETTER DA
1A0A ᨊ BUGINESE LETTER NA
1A0B ᨋ BUGINESE LETTER NRA
1A0C ᨌ BUGINESE LETTER CA
1A0D ᨍ BUGINESE LETTER JA
1A0E ᨎ BUGINESE LETTER NYA
1A0F ᨏ BUGINESE LETTER NYCA
1A10 ᨐ BUGINESE LETTER YA
1A11 ᨑ BUGINESE LETTER RA
1A12 ᨒ BUGINESE LETTER LA
1A13 ᨓ BUGINESE LETTER VA
1A14 ᨔ BUGINESE LETTER SA
1A15 ᨕ BUGINESE LETTER A
1A16 ᨖ BUGINESE LETTER HA

Vowels

1A17 ◌ᨗ BUGINESE VOWEL SIGN I
1A18 ◌ᨘ BUGINESE VOWEL SIGN U
1A19 ◌ᨙ BUGINESE VOWEL SIGN E
1A1A ◌ᨚ BUGINESE VOWEL SIGN O
1A1B ◌ᨛ BUGINESE VOWEL SIGN AE

Various signs

1A1E ᨞ BUGINESE PALLAWA
1A1F ᨟ BUGINESE END OF SECTION

	1B0	1B1	1B2	1B3	1B4	1B5	1B6	1B7
0	1B00	1B10	1B20	1B30	1B40	1B50	1B60	1B70
1	1B01	1B11	1B21	1B31	1B41	1B51	1B61	1B71
2	1B02	1B12	1B22	1B32	1B42	1B52	1B62	1B72
3	1B03	1B13	1B23	1B33	1B43	1B53	1B63	1B73
4	1B04	1B14	1B24	1B34	1B44	1B54	1B64	1B74
5	1B05	1B15	1B25	1B35	1B45	1B55	1B65	1B75
6	1B06	1B16	1B26	1B36	1B46	1B56	1B66	1B76
7	1B07	1B17	1B27	1B37	1B47	1B57	1B67	1B77
8	1B08	1B18	1B28	1B38	1B48	1B58	1B68	1B78
9	1B09	1B19	1B29	1B39	1B49	1B59	1B69	1B79
A	1B0A	1B1A	1B2A	1B3A	1B4A	1B5A	1B6A	1B7A
B	1B0B	1B1B	1B2B	1B3B	1B4B	1B5B	1B6B	1B7B
C	1B0C	1B1C	1B2C	1B3C		1B5C	1B6C	1B7C
D	1B0D	1B1D	1B2D	1B3D		1B5D	1B6D	
E	1B0E	1B1E	1B2E	1B3E		1B5E	1B6E	
F	1B0F	1B1F	1B2F	1B3F		1B5F	1B6F	

Various signs

1B00 ◌ᬀ BALINESE SIGN ULU RICEM
= ardhacandra

1B01 ◌ᬁ BALINESE SIGN ULU CANDRA
= candrabindu

1B02 ◌ᬂ BALINESE SIGN CECEK
= anusvara

1B03 ◌ᬃ BALINESE SIGN SURANG
= repha

1B04 ◌ᬄ BALINESE SIGN BISAH
= visarga

Independent vowels

1B05 ᬅ BALINESE LETTER AKARA
= a

1B06 ᬆ BALINESE LETTER AKARA TEDUNG
= aa
≡ 1B05 ᬅ 1B35 ◌ᬵ

1B07 ᬇ BALINESE LETTER IKARA
= i

1B08 ᬈ BALINESE LETTER IKARA TEDUNG
= ii
≡ 1B07 ᬇ 1B35 ◌ᬵ

1B09 ᬉ BALINESE LETTER UKARA
= u

1B0A ᬊ BALINESE LETTER UKARA TEDUNG
= uu
≡ 1B09 ᬉ 1B35 ◌ᬵ

1B0B ᬋ BALINESE LETTER RA REPA
= vocalic r

1B0C ᬌ BALINESE LETTER RA REPA TEDUNG
= vocalic rr
≡ 1B0B ᬋ 1B35 ◌ᬵ

1B0D ᬍ BALINESE LETTER LA LENGA
= vocalic l

1B0E ᬎ BALINESE LETTER LA LENGA TEDUNG
= vocalic ll
≡ 1B0D ᬍ 1B35 ◌ᬵ

1B0F ᬏ BALINESE LETTER EKARA
= e

1B10 ᬐ BALINESE LETTER AIKARA
= ai

1B11 ᬑ BALINESE LETTER OKARA
= o

1B12 ᬒ BALINESE LETTER OKARA TEDUNG
= au
≡ 1B11 ᬑ 1B35 ◌ᬵ

Consonants

1B13 ᬓ BALINESE LETTER KA

1B14 ᬔ BALINESE LETTER KA MAHAPRANA
= kha

1B15 ᬕ BALINESE LETTER GA

1B16 ᬖ BALINESE LETTER GA GORA
= gha

1B17 ᬗ BALINESE LETTER NGA

1B18 ᬘ BALINESE LETTER CA

1B19 ᬙ BALINESE LETTER CA LACA
= cha

1B1A ᬚ BALINESE LETTER JA

1B1B ᬛ BALINESE LETTER JA JERA
= jha

1B1C ᬜ BALINESE LETTER NYA

1B1D ᬝ BALINESE LETTER TA LATIK
= tta

1B1E ᬞ BALINESE LETTER TA MURDA MAHAPRANA
= ttha

1B1F ᬟ BALINESE LETTER DA MURDA ALPAPRANA
= dda

1B20 ᬠ BALINESE LETTER DA MURDA MAHAPRANA
= ddha

1B21 ᬡ BALINESE LETTER NA RAMBAT
= nna

1B22 ᬢ BALINESE LETTER TA

1B23 ᬣ BALINESE LETTER TA TAWA
= tha

1B24 ᬤ BALINESE LETTER DA

1B25 ᬥ BALINESE LETTER DA MADU
= dha

1B26 ᬦ BALINESE LETTER NA

1B27 ᬧ BALINESE LETTER PA

1B28 ᬨ BALINESE LETTER PA KAPAL
= pha

1B29 ᬩ BALINESE LETTER BA

1B2A ᬪ BALINESE LETTER BA KEMBANG
= bha

1B2B ᬫ BALINESE LETTER MA

1B2C ᬬ BALINESE LETTER YA

1B2D ᬭ BALINESE LETTER RA

1B2E ᬮ BALINESE LETTER LA

1B2F ᬯ BALINESE LETTER WA

1B30 ᬰ BALINESE LETTER SA SAGA
= sha

1B31 ᬱ BALINESE LETTER SA SAPA
= ssa

1B32 ᬲ BALINESE LETTER SA

1B33 ᬳ BALINESE LETTER HA

Sign

1B34 ◌᬴ BALINESE SIGN REREKAN
= nukta

Dependent vowel signs

1B35 ◌ᬵ BALINESE VOWEL SIGN TEDUNG
= aa

1B36 ◌ᬶ BALINESE VOWEL SIGN ULU
= i

1B37 ◌ᬷ BALINESE VOWEL SIGN ULU SARI
= ii

1B38 ◌ᬸ BALINESE VOWEL SIGN SUKU
= u

1B39 ◌ᬹ BALINESE VOWEL SIGN SUKU ILUT
= uu

1B3A ◌ᬺ BALINESE VOWEL SIGN RA REPA
= vocalic r

1B3B ◌ᬻ BALINESE VOWEL SIGN RA REPA TEDUNG
= vocalic rr
≡ 1B3A ◌ᬺ 1B35 ◌ᬵ

1B3C ◌ᬼ BALINESE VOWEL SIGN LA LENGA
= vocalic l

1B3D ◌ᬽ BALINESE VOWEL SIGN LA LENGA TEDUNG
= vocalic ll
≡ 1B3C ◌ᬼ 1B35 ◌ᬵ

1B3E ◌ᬾ BALINESE VOWEL SIGN TALING
= e

1B3F ◌ᬿ BALINESE VOWEL SIGN TALING REPA
= ai

1B40 ◌ᭀ BALINESE VOWEL SIGN TALING TEDUNG
= o
≡ 1B3E ◌ᬾ 1B35 ◌ᬵ

1B41 ◌ᭁ BALINESE VOWEL SIGN TALING REPA TEDUNG
= au
≡ 1B3F ◌ᬿ 1B35 ◌ᬵ

1B42 ◌ᭂ BALINESE VOWEL SIGN PEPET
= ae

1B43 ◌ᭃ BALINESE VOWEL SIGN PEPET TEDUNG
= oe
≡ 1B42 ◌ᭂ 1B35 ◌ᬵ

Sign

1B44 ◌᭄ BALINESE ADEG ADEG
= virama

Additional consonants

1B45 ᭅ BALINESE LETTER KAF SASAK
1B46 ᭆ BALINESE LETTER KHOT SASAK
1B47 ᭇ BALINESE LETTER TZIR SASAK
1B48 ᭈ BALINESE LETTER EF SASAK
1B49 ᭉ BALINESE LETTER VE SASAK
1B4A ᭊ BALINESE LETTER ZAL SASAK
1B4B ᭋ BALINESE LETTER ASYURA SASAK

Digits

1B50 ᭐ BALINESE DIGIT ZERO
1B51 ᭑ BALINESE DIGIT ONE
1B52 ᭒ BALINESE DIGIT TWO
1B53 ᭓ BALINESE DIGIT THREE
1B54 ᭔ BALINESE DIGIT FOUR
1B55 ᭕ BALINESE DIGIT FIVE
1B56 ᭖ BALINESE DIGIT SIX
1B57 ᭗ BALINESE DIGIT SEVEN
1B58 ᭘ BALINESE DIGIT EIGHT
1B59 ᭙ BALINESE DIGIT NINE

Punctuation

1B5A ᭚ BALINESE PANTI
= section

1B5B ᭛ BALINESE PAMADA
= honorific section

1B5C ᭜ BALINESE WINDU
= punctuation ring

1B5D ᭝ BALINESE CARIK PAMUNGKAH
= colon

1B5E ᭞ BALINESE CARIK SIKI
= danda
→ 0964 । devanagari danda

1B5F ᭟ BALINESE CARIK PAREREN
= double danda
→ 0965 ॥ devanagari double danda

1B60 ᭠ BALINESE PAMENENG
= line-breaking hyphen

Musical symbols for notes

1B61 ᭡ BALINESE MUSICAL SYMBOL DONG
1B62 ᭢ BALINESE MUSICAL SYMBOL DENG
1B63 ᭣ BALINESE MUSICAL SYMBOL DUNG
1B64 ᭤ BALINESE MUSICAL SYMBOL DANG
1B65 ᭥ BALINESE MUSICAL SYMBOL DANG SURANG
1B66 ᭦ BALINESE MUSICAL SYMBOL DING
1B67 ᭧ BALINESE MUSICAL SYMBOL DAENG
1B68 ᭨ BALINESE MUSICAL SYMBOL DEUNG
1B69 ᭩ BALINESE MUSICAL SYMBOL DAING
1B6A ᭪ BALINESE MUSICAL SYMBOL DANG GEDE

Diacritical marks for musical symbols

1B6B ◌᭫ BALINESE MUSICAL SYMBOL COMBINING TEGEH
1B6C ◌᭬ BALINESE MUSICAL SYMBOL COMBINING ENDEP
1B6D ◌᭭ BALINESE MUSICAL SYMBOL COMBINING KEMPUL
1B6E ◌᭮ BALINESE MUSICAL SYMBOL COMBINING KEMPLI
1B6F ◌᭯ BALINESE MUSICAL SYMBOL COMBINING JEGOGAN
1B70 ◌᭰ BALINESE MUSICAL SYMBOL COMBINING KEMPUL WITH JEGOGAN
1B71 ◌᭱ BALINESE MUSICAL SYMBOL COMBINING KEMPLI WITH JEGOGAN
1B72 ◌᭲ BALINESE MUSICAL SYMBOL COMBINING BENDE
1B73 ◌᭳ BALINESE MUSICAL SYMBOL COMBINING GONG

Musical symbols

1B74 ᭴ BALINESE MUSICAL SYMBOL RIGHT-HAND OPEN DUG
1B75 ᭵ BALINESE MUSICAL SYMBOL RIGHT-HAND OPEN DAG
1B76 ᭶ BALINESE MUSICAL SYMBOL RIGHT-HAND CLOSED TUK
1B77 ᭷ BALINESE MUSICAL SYMBOL RIGHT-HAND CLOSED TAK
1B78 ᭸ BALINESE MUSICAL SYMBOL LEFT-HAND OPEN PANG
1B79 ᭹ BALINESE MUSICAL SYMBOL LEFT-HAND OPEN PUNG
1B7A ᭺ BALINESE MUSICAL SYMBOL LEFT-HAND CLOSED PLAK
1B7B ᭻ BALINESE MUSICAL SYMBOL LEFT-HAND CLOSED PLUK
1B7C ᭼ BALINESE MUSICAL SYMBOL LEFT-HAND OPEN PING

	1D0	1D1	1D2	1D3	1D4	1D5	1D6	1D7
0	ᴀ 1D00	ᴐ 1D10	ᴠ 1D20	ᴰ 1D30	ᵀ 1D40	ᵐ 1D50	ᵠ 1D60	ᵰ 1D70
1	ᴁ 1D01	ᴑ 1D11	ᴡ 1D21	ᴱ 1D31	ᵁ 1D41	ᵑ 1D51	ᵡ 1D61	ᵱ 1D71
2	ᴂ 1D02	ᴒ 1D12	ᴢ 1D22	ᴲ 1D32	ᵂ 1D42	ᵒ 1D52	ᵢ 1D62	ᵲ 1D72
3	ᴃ 1D03	ᴓ 1D13	ᴣ 1D23	ᴳ 1D33	ᵃ 1D43	ᵓ 1D53	ᵣ 1D63	ᵳ 1D73
4	ᴄ 1D04	ᴔ 1D14	ᴤ 1D24	ᴴ 1D34	ᵄ 1D44	ᵔ 1D54	ᵤ 1D64	ᵴ 1D74
5	ᴅ 1D05	ᴕ 1D15	ᴥ 1D25	ᴵ 1D35	ᵅ 1D45	ᵕ 1D55	ᵥ 1D65	ᵵ 1D75
6	ᴆ 1D06	ᴖ 1D16	ᴦ 1D26	ᴶ 1D36	ᵆ 1D46	ᵖ 1D56	ᵦ 1D66	ᵶ 1D76
7	ᴇ 1D07	ᴗ 1D17	ᴧ 1D27	ᴷ 1D37	ᵇ 1D47	ᵗ 1D57	ᵧ 1D67	ᵷ 1D77
8	ᴈ 1D08	ᴘ 1D18	ᴨ 1D28	ᴸ 1D38	ᵈ 1D48	ᵘ 1D58	ᵨ 1D68	ᵸ 1D78
9	ᴉ 1D09	ᴙ 1D19	ᴩ 1D29	ᴹ 1D39	ᵉ 1D49	ᵙ 1D59	ᵩ 1D69	ᵹ 1D79
A	ᴊ 1D0A	ᴚ 1D1A	ᴪ 1D2A	ᴺ 1D3A	ᵊ 1D4A	ᵚ 1D5A	ᵪ 1D6A	ᵺ 1D7A
B	ᴋ 1D0B	ᴛ 1D1B	ᴫ 1D2B	ᴻ 1D3B	ᵋ 1D4B	ᵛ 1D5B	ᵫ 1D6B	ᵻ 1D7B
C	ᴌ 1D0C	ᴜ 1D1C	ᴬ 1D2C	ᴼ 1D3C	ᵌ 1D4C	ᵜ 1D5C	ᵬ 1D6C	ᵼ 1D7C
D	ᴍ 1D0D	ᴝ 1D1D	ᴭ 1D2D	ᴽ 1D3D	ᵍ 1D4D	ᵝ 1D5D	ᵭ 1D6D	ᵽ 1D7D
E	ᴎ 1D0E	ᴞ 1D1E	ᴮ 1D2E	ᴾ 1D3E	ᵎ 1D4E	ᵞ 1D5E	ᵮ 1D6E	ᵾ 1D7E
F	ᴏ 1D0F	ᴟ 1D1F	ᴯ 1D2F	ᴿ 1D3F	ᵏ 1D4F	ᵟ 1D5F	ᵯ 1D6F	ᵿ 1D7F

These are non-IPA phonetic extensions, mostly for the Uralic Phonetic Alphabet (UPA).

The small capitals, superscript, and subscript forms are for phonetic representations where style variations are semantically important.

For general text, use regular Latin, Greek or Cyrillic letters with markup instead.

Latin letters

1D00 ᴀ LATIN LETTER SMALL CAPITAL A
1D01 ᴁ LATIN LETTER SMALL CAPITAL AE
1D02 ᴂ LATIN SMALL LETTER TURNED AE
• glyph can also have sideways orientation
1D03 ᴃ LATIN LETTER SMALL CAPITAL BARRED B
1D04 ᴄ LATIN LETTER SMALL CAPITAL C
1D05 ᴅ LATIN LETTER SMALL CAPITAL D
1D06 ᴆ LATIN LETTER SMALL CAPITAL ETH
1D07 ᴇ LATIN LETTER SMALL CAPITAL E
1D08 ᴈ LATIN SMALL LETTER TURNED OPEN E
1D09 ᴉ LATIN SMALL LETTER TURNED I
1D0A ᴊ LATIN LETTER SMALL CAPITAL J
1D0B ᴋ LATIN LETTER SMALL CAPITAL K
1D0C ᴌ LATIN LETTER SMALL CAPITAL L WITH STROKE
1D0D ᴍ LATIN LETTER SMALL CAPITAL M
1D0E ᴎ LATIN LETTER SMALL CAPITAL REVERSED N
1D0F ᴏ LATIN LETTER SMALL CAPITAL O
1D10 ᴐ LATIN LETTER SMALL CAPITAL OPEN O
1D11 ᴑ LATIN SMALL LETTER SIDEWAYS O
1D12 ᴒ LATIN SMALL LETTER SIDEWAYS OPEN O
1D13 ᴓ LATIN SMALL LETTER SIDEWAYS O WITH STROKE
1D14 ᴔ LATIN SMALL LETTER TURNED OE
• glyph can also have sideways orientation
1D15 ᴕ LATIN LETTER SMALL CAPITAL OU
1D16 ᴖ LATIN SMALL LETTER TOP HALF O
1D17 ᴗ LATIN SMALL LETTER BOTTOM HALF O
1D18 ᴘ LATIN LETTER SMALL CAPITAL P
• represents a semi-voiced [p]
1D19 ᴙ LATIN LETTER SMALL CAPITAL REVERSED R
1D1A ᴚ LATIN LETTER SMALL CAPITAL TURNED R
1D1B ᴛ LATIN LETTER SMALL CAPITAL T
1D1C ᴜ LATIN LETTER SMALL CAPITAL U
1D1D ᴝ LATIN SMALL LETTER SIDEWAYS U
1D1E ᴞ LATIN SMALL LETTER SIDEWAYS DIAERESIZED U
• glyph can also have turned orientation
1D1F ᴟ LATIN SMALL LETTER SIDEWAYS TURNED M
1D20 ᴠ LATIN LETTER SMALL CAPITAL V
1D21 ᴡ LATIN LETTER SMALL CAPITAL W
1D22 ᴢ LATIN LETTER SMALL CAPITAL Z
1D23 ᴣ LATIN LETTER SMALL CAPITAL EZH
1D24 ᴤ LATIN LETTER VOICED LARYNGEAL SPIRANT
1D25 ᴥ LATIN LETTER AIN

Greek letters

1D26 ᴦ GREEK LETTER SMALL CAPITAL GAMMA
1D27 ᴧ GREEK LETTER SMALL CAPITAL LAMDA
1D28 ᴨ GREEK LETTER SMALL CAPITAL PI
1D29 ᴩ GREEK LETTER SMALL CAPITAL RHO
• represents a voiceless uvular trill
1D2A ᴪ GREEK LETTER SMALL CAPITAL PSI

Cyrillic letter

1D2B ᴫ CYRILLIC LETTER SMALL CAPITAL EL
• in italic style, the glyph is obliqued, not italicized
→ 043B л cyrillic small letter el

Latin superscript modifier letters

1D2C ᴬ MODIFIER LETTER CAPITAL A
≈ <super> 0041 A
1D2D ᴭ MODIFIER LETTER CAPITAL AE
≈ <super> 00C6 Æ
1D2E ᴮ MODIFIER LETTER CAPITAL B
≈ <super> 0042 B
1D2F ᴯ MODIFIER LETTER CAPITAL BARRED B
1D30 ᴰ MODIFIER LETTER CAPITAL D
≈ <super> 0044 D
1D31 ᴱ MODIFIER LETTER CAPITAL E
≈ <super> 0045 E
1D32 ᴲ MODIFIER LETTER CAPITAL REVERSED E
≈ <super> 018E Ǝ
1D33 ᴳ MODIFIER LETTER CAPITAL G
≈ <super> 0047 G
1D34 ᴴ MODIFIER LETTER CAPITAL H
≈ <super> 0048 H
1D35 ᴵ MODIFIER LETTER CAPITAL I
≈ <super> 0049 I
1D36 ᴶ MODIFIER LETTER CAPITAL J
≈ <super> 004A J
1D37 ᴷ MODIFIER LETTER CAPITAL K
≈ <super> 004B K
1D38 ᴸ MODIFIER LETTER CAPITAL L
≈ <super> 004C L
1D39 ᴹ MODIFIER LETTER CAPITAL M
≈ <super> 004D M
1D3A ᴺ MODIFIER LETTER CAPITAL N
≈ <super> 004E N
1D3B ᴻ MODIFIER LETTER CAPITAL REVERSED N
1D3C ᴼ MODIFIER LETTER CAPITAL O
≈ <super> 004F O
1D3D ᴽ MODIFIER LETTER CAPITAL OU
≈ <super> 0222 Ȣ
1D3E ᴾ MODIFIER LETTER CAPITAL P
≈ <super> 0050 P
1D3F ᴿ MODIFIER LETTER CAPITAL R
≈ <super> 0052 R
1D40 ᵀ MODIFIER LETTER CAPITAL T
≈ <super> 0054 T
1D41 ᵁ MODIFIER LETTER CAPITAL U
≈ <super> 0055 U
1D42 ᵂ MODIFIER LETTER CAPITAL W
≈ <super> 0057 W
1D43 ᵃ MODIFIER LETTER SMALL A
≈ <super> 0061 a
1D44 ᵄ MODIFIER LETTER SMALL TURNED A
≈ <super> 0250 ɐ
1D45 ᵅ MODIFIER LETTER SMALL ALPHA
≈ <super> 0251 ɑ
1D46 ᵆ MODIFIER LETTER SMALL TURNED AE
≈ <super> 1D02 ᴂ
1D47 ᵇ MODIFIER LETTER SMALL B
≈ <super> 0062 b
1D48 ᵈ MODIFIER LETTER SMALL D
≈ <super> 0064 d

1D49 ᵉ MODIFIER LETTER SMALL E
≈ <super> 0065 e
1D4A ᵊ MODIFIER LETTER SMALL SCHWA
≈ <super> 0259 ə
1D4B ᵋ MODIFIER LETTER SMALL OPEN E
≈ <super> 025B ɛ
1D4C ᵌ MODIFIER LETTER SMALL TURNED OPEN E
• more appropriate equivalence would be to 1D08 ᴈ
≈ <super> 025C ɜ
1D4D ᵍ MODIFIER LETTER SMALL G
≈ <super> 0067 g
1D4E ᵎ MODIFIER LETTER SMALL TURNED I
1D4F ᵏ MODIFIER LETTER SMALL K
≈ <super> 006B k
1D50 ᵐ MODIFIER LETTER SMALL M
≈ <super> 006D m
1D51 ᵑ MODIFIER LETTER SMALL ENG
≈ <super> 014B ŋ
1D52 ᵒ MODIFIER LETTER SMALL O
≈ <super> 006F o
1D53 ᵓ MODIFIER LETTER SMALL OPEN O
≈ <super> 0254 ɔ
1D54 ᵔ MODIFIER LETTER SMALL TOP HALF O
≈ <super> 1D16 ᴖ
1D55 ᵕ MODIFIER LETTER SMALL BOTTOM HALF O
≈ <super> 1D17 ᴗ
1D56 ᵖ MODIFIER LETTER SMALL P
≈ <super> 0070 p
1D57 ᵗ MODIFIER LETTER SMALL T
≈ <super> 0074 t
1D58 ᵘ MODIFIER LETTER SMALL U
≈ <super> 0075 u
1D59 ᵙ MODIFIER LETTER SMALL SIDEWAYS U
≈ <super> 1D1D ᴝ
1D5A ᵚ MODIFIER LETTER SMALL TURNED M
≈ <super> 026F ɯ
1D5B ᵛ MODIFIER LETTER SMALL V
≈ <super> 0076 v
1D5C ᵜ MODIFIER LETTER SMALL AIN
≈ <super> 1D25 ᴥ

Greek superscript modifier letters

1D5D ᵝ MODIFIER LETTER SMALL BETA
≈ <super> 03B2 β
1D5E ᵞ MODIFIER LETTER SMALL GREEK GAMMA
≈ <super> 03B3 γ
1D5F ᵟ MODIFIER LETTER SMALL DELTA
≈ <super> 03B4 δ
1D60 ᵠ MODIFIER LETTER SMALL GREEK PHI
≈ <super> 03C6 φ
1D61 ᵡ MODIFIER LETTER SMALL CHI
≈ <super> 03C7 χ

Latin subscript modifier letters

1D62 ᵢ LATIN SUBSCRIPT SMALL LETTER I
≈ <sub> 0069 i
1D63 ᵣ LATIN SUBSCRIPT SMALL LETTER R
≈ <sub> 0072 r
1D64 ᵤ LATIN SUBSCRIPT SMALL LETTER U
≈ <sub> 0075 u
1D65 ᵥ LATIN SUBSCRIPT SMALL LETTER V
≈ <sub> 0076 v

Greek subscript modifier letters

1D66 ᵦ GREEK SUBSCRIPT SMALL LETTER BETA
≈ <sub> 03B2 β
1D67 ᵧ GREEK SUBSCRIPT SMALL LETTER GAMMA
≈ <sub> 03B3 γ
1D68 ᵨ GREEK SUBSCRIPT SMALL LETTER RHO
≈ <sub> 03C1 ρ
1D69 ᵩ GREEK SUBSCRIPT SMALL LETTER PHI
≈ <sub> 03C6 φ
1D6A ᵪ GREEK SUBSCRIPT SMALL LETTER CHI
≈ <sub> 03C7 χ

Latin letter

1D6B ᵫ LATIN SMALL LETTER UE

Latin letters with middle tilde

An additional letter with middle tilde is found in another block.

→ 026B ɫ latin small letter l with middle tilde
1D6C ᵬ LATIN SMALL LETTER B WITH MIDDLE TILDE
1D6D ᵭ LATIN SMALL LETTER D WITH MIDDLE TILDE
1D6E ᵮ LATIN SMALL LETTER F WITH MIDDLE TILDE
1D6F ᵯ LATIN SMALL LETTER M WITH MIDDLE TILDE
1D70 ᵰ LATIN SMALL LETTER N WITH MIDDLE TILDE
1D71 ᵱ LATIN SMALL LETTER P WITH MIDDLE TILDE
1D72 ᵲ LATIN SMALL LETTER R WITH MIDDLE TILDE
1D73 ᵳ LATIN SMALL LETTER R WITH FISHHOOK AND MIDDLE TILDE
1D74 ᵴ LATIN SMALL LETTER S WITH MIDDLE TILDE
1D75 ᵵ LATIN SMALL LETTER T WITH MIDDLE TILDE
1D76 ᵶ LATIN SMALL LETTER Z WITH MIDDLE TILDE

Caucasian linguistics

1D77 ᵷ LATIN SMALL LETTER TURNED G
• Georgian transcription
→ 10F9 ჹ georgian letter turned gan
1D78 ᵸ MODIFIER LETTER CYRILLIC EN
≈ <super> 043D н

Other phonetic symbols

1D79 ᵹ LATIN SMALL LETTER INSULAR G
• older Irish phonetic notation
→ 0067 g latin small letter g
→ 021D ȝ latin small letter yogh
→ 0261 ɡ latin small letter script g
→ 0263 ɣ latin small letter gamma
1D7A ᵺ LATIN SMALL LETTER TH WITH STRIKETHROUGH
• American dictionary usage
→ 03B8 θ greek small letter theta
1D7B ᵻ LATIN SMALL CAPITAL LETTER I WITH STROKE
• used with different meanings by Americanists and Oxford dictionaries
1D7C ᵼ LATIN SMALL LETTER IOTA WITH STROKE
• used by Russianists
1D7D ᵽ LATIN SMALL LETTER P WITH STROKE
• used by Americanists
• uppercase is 2C63 Ᵽ
1D7E ᵾ LATIN SMALL CAPITAL LETTER U WITH STROKE
• used by Americanists
1D7F ᵿ LATIN SMALL LETTER UPSILON WITH STROKE
• used by Americanists and Oxford dictionaries

	1D8	1D9	1DA	1DB
0	ᶀ 1D80	ᶐ 1D90	ᶠ 1DA0	ᶰ 1DB0
1	ᶁ 1D81	ᶑ 1D91	ᶡ 1DA1	ᶱ 1DB1
2	ᶂ 1D82	ᶒ 1D92	ᶢ 1DA2	ᶲ 1DB2
3	ᶃ 1D83	ᶓ 1D93	ᶣ 1DA3	ᶳ 1DB3
4	ᶄ 1D84	ᶔ 1D94	ᶤ 1DA4	ᶴ 1DB4
5	ᶅ 1D85	ᶕ 1D95	ᶥ 1DA5	ᶵ 1DB5
6	ᶆ 1D86	ᶖ 1D96	ᶦ 1DA6	ᶶ 1DB6
7	ᶇ 1D87	ᶗ 1D97	ᶧ 1DA7	ᶷ 1DB7
8	ᶈ 1D88	ᶘ 1D98	ᶨ 1DA8	ᶸ 1DB8
9	ᶉ 1D89	ᶙ 1D99	ᶩ 1DA9	ᶹ 1DB9
A	ᶊ 1D8A	ᶚ 1D9A	ᶪ 1DAA	ᶺ 1DBA
B	ᶋ 1D8B	ᶛ 1D9B	ᶫ 1DAB	ᶻ 1DBB
C	ᶌ 1D8C	ᶜ 1D9C	ᶬ 1DAC	ᶼ 1DBC
D	ᶍ 1D8D	ᶝ 1D9D	ᶭ 1DAD	ᶽ 1DBD
E	ᶎ 1D8E	ᶞ 1D9E	ᶮ 1DAE	ᶾ 1DBE
F	ᶏ 1D8F	ᶟ 1D9F	ᶯ 1DAF	ᶿ 1DBF

Latin letters with palatal hook

An additional letter with palatal hook is found in another block.

→ 01AB ƫ latin small letter t with palatal hook

1D80 ᶀ LATIN SMALL LETTER B WITH PALATAL HOOK
1D81 ᶁ LATIN SMALL LETTER D WITH PALATAL HOOK
1D82 ᶂ LATIN SMALL LETTER F WITH PALATAL HOOK
1D83 ᶃ LATIN SMALL LETTER G WITH PALATAL HOOK
1D84 ᶄ LATIN SMALL LETTER K WITH PALATAL HOOK
1D85 ᶅ LATIN SMALL LETTER L WITH PALATAL HOOK
1D86 ᶆ LATIN SMALL LETTER M WITH PALATAL HOOK
1D87 ᶇ LATIN SMALL LETTER N WITH PALATAL HOOK
1D88 ᶈ LATIN SMALL LETTER P WITH PALATAL HOOK
1D89 ᶉ LATIN SMALL LETTER R WITH PALATAL HOOK
1D8A ᶊ LATIN SMALL LETTER S WITH PALATAL HOOK
1D8B ᶋ LATIN SMALL LETTER ESH WITH PALATAL HOOK
1D8C ᶌ LATIN SMALL LETTER V WITH PALATAL HOOK
1D8D ᶍ LATIN SMALL LETTER X WITH PALATAL HOOK
1D8E ᶎ LATIN SMALL LETTER Z WITH PALATAL HOOK

Latin letters with retroflex hook

IPA recommends transcribing vowels with r-coloring (rhoticity) with the rhotic hook instead.

→ 02DE ˞ modifier letter rhotic hook

Additional letters with retroflex hook are found in other blocks.

→ 01AE Ʈ latin capital letter t with retroflex hook
→ 0256 ɖ latin small letter d with tail
→ 026D ɭ latin small letter l with retroflex hook
→ 0273 ɳ latin small letter n with retroflex hook
→ 027B ɻ latin small letter turned r with hook
→ 027D ɽ latin small letter r with tail
→ 0282 ʂ latin small letter s with hook
→ 0285 ʅ latin small letter squat reversed esh
→ 0288 ʈ latin small letter t with retroflex hook
→ 0290 ʐ latin small letter z with retroflex hook
→ 02AF ʯ latin small letter turned h with fishhook and tail

1D8F ᶏ LATIN SMALL LETTER A WITH RETROFLEX HOOK
1D90 ᶐ LATIN SMALL LETTER ALPHA WITH RETROFLEX HOOK
1D91 ᶑ LATIN SMALL LETTER D WITH HOOK AND TAIL
1D92 ᶒ LATIN SMALL LETTER E WITH RETROFLEX HOOK
1D93 ᶓ LATIN SMALL LETTER OPEN E WITH RETROFLEX HOOK
1D94 ᶔ LATIN SMALL LETTER REVERSED OPEN E WITH RETROFLEX HOOK
→ 025D ɝ latin small letter reversed open e with hook
1D95 ᶕ LATIN SMALL LETTER SCHWA WITH RETROFLEX HOOK
→ 025A ɚ latin small letter schwa with hook
1D96 ᶖ LATIN SMALL LETTER I WITH RETROFLEX HOOK
1D97 ᶗ LATIN SMALL LETTER OPEN O WITH RETROFLEX HOOK
1D98 ᶘ LATIN SMALL LETTER ESH WITH RETROFLEX HOOK
1D99 ᶙ LATIN SMALL LETTER U WITH RETROFLEX HOOK
1D9A ᶚ LATIN SMALL LETTER EZH WITH RETROFLEX HOOK

Modifier letters

Other modifier letters can be found in the Spacing Modifier Letters, Phonetic Extensions, as well as Superscripts and Subscripts blocks.

1D9B ᶛ MODIFIER LETTER SMALL TURNED ALPHA
≈ <super> 0252 ɒ
1D9C ᶜ MODIFIER LETTER SMALL C
≈ <super> 0063 c
1D9D ᶝ MODIFIER LETTER SMALL C WITH CURL
≈ <super> 0255 ɕ
1D9E ᶞ MODIFIER LETTER SMALL ETH
≈ <super> 00F0 ð
1D9F ᶟ MODIFIER LETTER SMALL REVERSED OPEN E
≈ <super> 025C ɜ
1DA0 ᶠ MODIFIER LETTER SMALL F
≈ <super> 0066 f
1DA1 ᶡ MODIFIER LETTER SMALL DOTLESS J WITH STROKE
≈ <super> 025F ɟ
1DA2 ᶢ MODIFIER LETTER SMALL SCRIPT G
≈ <super> 0261 ɡ
1DA3 ᶣ MODIFIER LETTER SMALL TURNED H
≈ <super> 0265 ɥ
1DA4 ᶤ MODIFIER LETTER SMALL I WITH STROKE
≈ <super> 0268 ɨ
1DA5 ᶥ MODIFIER LETTER SMALL IOTA
≈ <super> 0269 ɩ
1DA6 ᶦ MODIFIER LETTER SMALL CAPITAL I
≈ <super> 026A ɪ
1DA7 ᶧ MODIFIER LETTER SMALL CAPITAL I WITH STROKE
≈ <super> 1D7B ᵻ
1DA8 ᶨ MODIFIER LETTER SMALL J WITH CROSSED-TAIL
≈ <super> 029D ʝ
1DA9 ᶩ MODIFIER LETTER SMALL L WITH RETROFLEX HOOK
≈ <super> 026D ɭ
1DAA ᶪ MODIFIER LETTER SMALL L WITH PALATAL HOOK
≈ <super> 1D85 ᶅ
1DAB ᶫ MODIFIER LETTER SMALL CAPITAL L
≈ <super> 029F ʟ
1DAC ᶬ MODIFIER LETTER SMALL M WITH HOOK
≈ <super> 0271 ɱ
1DAD ᶭ MODIFIER LETTER SMALL TURNED M WITH LONG LEG
≈ <super> 0270 ɰ
1DAE ᶮ MODIFIER LETTER SMALL N WITH LEFT HOOK
≈ <super> 0272 ɲ
1DAF ᶯ MODIFIER LETTER SMALL N WITH RETROFLEX HOOK
≈ <super> 0273 ɳ
1DB0 ᶰ MODIFIER LETTER SMALL CAPITAL N
≈ <super> 0274 ɴ
1DB1 ᶱ MODIFIER LETTER SMALL BARRED O
≈ <super> 0275 ɵ
1DB2 ᶲ MODIFIER LETTER SMALL PHI
≈ <super> 0278 ɸ
1DB3 ᶳ MODIFIER LETTER SMALL S WITH HOOK
≈ <super> 0282 ʂ
1DB4 ᶴ MODIFIER LETTER SMALL ESH
≈ <super> 0283 ʃ

1DB5 ᶵ MODIFIER LETTER SMALL T WITH PALATAL HOOK
≈ <super> 01AB ƫ
1DB6 ᶶ MODIFIER LETTER SMALL U BAR
≈ <super> 0289 ʉ
1DB7 ᶷ MODIFIER LETTER SMALL UPSILON
≈ <super> 028A ʊ
1DB8 ᶸ MODIFIER LETTER SMALL CAPITAL U
≈ <super> 1D1C ᴜ
1DB9 ᶹ MODIFIER LETTER SMALL V WITH HOOK
≈ <super> 028B ʋ
1DBA ᶺ MODIFIER LETTER SMALL TURNED V
≈ <super> 028C ʌ
1DBB ᶻ MODIFIER LETTER SMALL Z
≈ <super> 007A z
1DBC ᶼ MODIFIER LETTER SMALL Z WITH RETROFLEX HOOK
≈ <super> 0290 ʐ
1DBD ᶽ MODIFIER LETTER SMALL Z WITH CURL
≈ <super> 0291 ʑ
1DBE ᶾ MODIFIER LETTER SMALL EZH
≈ <super> 0292 ʒ
1DBF ᶿ MODIFIER LETTER SMALL THETA
≈ <super> 03B8 θ

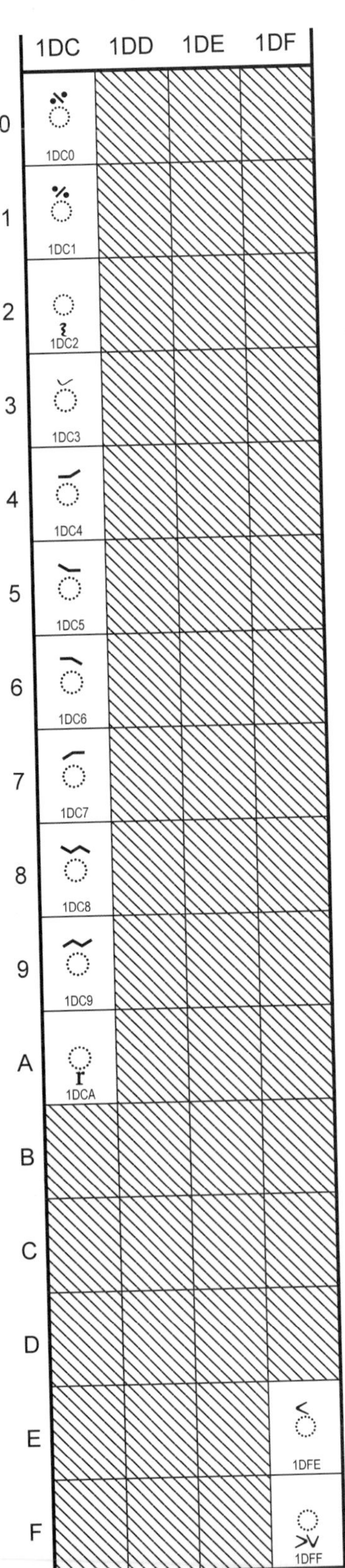

Used for Ancient Greek

These are used as editorial signs for Ancient Greek to indicate scribal deletion of erroneous accent marks.

1DC0 ◌᷀ COMBINING DOTTED GRAVE ACCENT
→ 1FED ῭ greek dialytika and varia

1DC1 ◌᷁ COMBINING DOTTED ACUTE ACCENT
→ 0344 ◌̈́ combining greek dialytika tonos
→ 1FEE ΅ greek dialytika and oxia

Miscellaneous marks

1DC2 ◌᷂ COMBINING SNAKE BELOW

1DC3 ◌᷃ COMBINING SUSPENSION MARK
• Glagolitic
→ 0306 ◌̆ combining breve

Contour tone marks

1DC4 ◌᷄ COMBINING MACRON-ACUTE

1DC5 ◌᷅ COMBINING GRAVE-MACRON

1DC6 ◌᷆ COMBINING MACRON-GRAVE

1DC7 ◌᷇ COMBINING ACUTE-MACRON

1DC8 ◌᷈ COMBINING GRAVE-ACUTE-GRAVE

1DC9 ◌᷉ COMBINING ACUTE-GRAVE-ACUTE

Miscellaneous mark

1DCA ◌᷊ COMBINING LATIN SMALL LETTER R BELOW

Additional marks for UPA

1DFE ◌᷾ COMBINING LEFT ARROWHEAD ABOVE

1DFF ◌᷿ COMBINING RIGHT ARROWHEAD AND DOWN ARROWHEAD BELOW

	1E0	1E1	1E2	1E3	1E4	1E5	1E6	1E7	1E8	1E9	1EA	1EB	1EC	1ED	1EE	1EF
0	Ḁ 1E00	Ḑ 1E10	Ḡ 1E20	Ḱ 1E30	Ṁ 1E40	Ṑ 1E50	Ṡ 1E60	Ṱ 1E70	Ẁ 1E80	Ẑ 1E90	Ạ 1EA0	Ằ 1EB0	Ề 1EC0	Ố 1ED0	Ỡ 1EE0	Ự 1EF0
1	ḁ 1E01	ḑ 1E11	ḡ 1E21	ḱ 1E31	ṁ 1E41	ṑ 1E51	ṡ 1E61	ṱ 1E71	ẁ 1E81	ẑ 1E91	ạ 1EA1	ằ 1EB1	ề 1EC1	ố 1ED1	ỡ 1EE1	ự 1EF1
2	Ḃ 1E02	Ḓ 1E12	Ḣ 1E22	Ḳ 1E32	Ṃ 1E42	Ṓ 1E52	Ṣ 1E62	Ṳ 1E72	Ẃ 1E82	Ẓ 1E92	Ả 1EA2	Ẳ 1EB2	Ể 1EC2	Ồ 1ED2	Ợ 1EE2	Ỳ 1EF2
3	ḃ 1E03	ḓ 1E13	ḣ 1E23	ḳ 1E33	ṃ 1E43	ṓ 1E53	ṣ 1E63	ṳ 1E73	ẃ 1E83	ẓ 1E93	ả 1EA3	ẳ 1EB3	ể 1EC3	ồ 1ED3	ợ 1EE3	ỳ 1EF3
4	Ḅ 1E04	Ḕ 1E14	Ḥ 1E24	Ḵ 1E34	Ṅ 1E44	Ṕ 1E54	Ṥ 1E64	Ṵ 1E74	Ẅ 1E84	Ẕ 1E94	Ấ 1EA4	Ẵ 1EB4	Ễ 1EC4	Ổ 1ED4	Ụ 1EE4	Ỵ 1EF4
5	ḅ 1E05	ḕ 1E15	ḥ 1E25	ḵ 1E35	ṅ 1E45	ṕ 1E55	ṥ 1E65	ṵ 1E75	ẅ 1E85	ẕ 1E95	ấ 1EA5	ẵ 1EB5	ễ 1EC5	ổ 1ED5	ụ 1EE5	ỵ 1EF5
6	Ḇ 1E06	Ḗ 1E16	Ḧ 1E26	Ḷ 1E36	Ṇ 1E46	Ṗ 1E56	Ṧ 1E66	Ṷ 1E76	Ẇ 1E86	ẖ 1E96	Ầ 1EA6	Ặ 1EB6	Ệ 1EC6	Ỗ 1ED6	Ủ 1EE6	Ỷ 1EF6
7	ḇ 1E07	ḗ 1E17	ḧ 1E27	ḷ 1E37	ṇ 1E47	ṗ 1E57	ṧ 1E67	ṷ 1E77	ẇ 1E87	ẗ 1E97	ầ 1EA7	ặ 1EB7	ệ 1EC7	ỗ 1ED7	ủ 1EE7	ỷ 1EF7
8	Ḉ 1E08	Ḙ 1E18	Ḩ 1E28	Ḹ 1E38	Ṉ 1E48	Ṙ 1E58	Ṩ 1E68	Ṹ 1E78	Ẉ 1E88	ẘ 1E98	Ẩ 1EA8	Ẹ 1EB8	Ỉ 1EC8	Ộ 1ED8	Ứ 1EE8	Ỹ 1EF8
9	ḉ 1E09	ḙ 1E19	ḩ 1E29	ḹ 1E39	ṉ 1E49	ṙ 1E59	ṩ 1E69	ṹ 1E79	ẉ 1E89	ẙ 1E99	ẩ 1EA9	ẹ 1EB9	ỉ 1EC9	ộ 1ED9	ứ 1EE9	ỹ 1EF9
A	Ḋ 1E0A	Ḛ 1E1A	Ḫ 1E2A	Ḻ 1E3A	Ṋ 1E4A	Ṛ 1E5A	Ṫ 1E6A	Ṻ 1E7A	Ẋ 1E8A	ẚ 1E9A	Ẫ 1EAA	Ẻ 1EBA	Ị 1ECA	Ớ 1EDA	Ừ 1EEA	
B	ḋ 1E0B	ḛ 1E1B	ḫ 1E2B	ḻ 1E3B	ṋ 1E4B	ṛ 1E5B	ṫ 1E6B	ṻ 1E7B	ẋ 1E8B	ẛ 1E9B	ẫ 1EAB	ẻ 1EBB	ị 1ECB	ớ 1EDB	ừ 1EEB	
C	Ḍ 1E0C	Ḝ 1E1C	Ḭ 1E2C	Ḽ 1E3C	Ṍ 1E4C	Ṝ 1E5C	Ṭ 1E6C	Ṽ 1E7C	Ẍ 1E8C		Ậ 1EAC	Ẽ 1EBC	Ọ 1ECC	Ờ 1EDC	Ử 1EEC	
D	ḍ 1E0D	ḝ 1E1D	ḭ 1E2D	ḽ 1E3D	ṍ 1E4D	ṝ 1E5D	ṭ 1E6D	ṽ 1E7D	ẍ 1E8D		ậ 1EAD	ẽ 1EBD	ọ 1ECD	ờ 1EDD	ử 1EED	
E	Ḏ 1E0E	Ḟ 1E1E	Ḯ 1E2E	Ḿ 1E3E	Ṏ 1E4E	Ṟ 1E5E	Ṯ 1E6E	Ṿ 1E7E	Ẏ 1E8E		Ắ 1EAE	Ế 1EBE	Ỏ 1ECE	Ở 1EDE	Ữ 1EEE	
F	ḏ 1E0F	ḟ 1E1F	ḯ 1E2F	ḿ 1E3F	ṏ 1E4F	ṟ 1E5F	ṯ 1E6F	ṿ 1E7F	ẏ 1E8F		ắ 1EAF	ế 1EBF	ỏ 1ECF	ở 1EDF	ữ 1EEF	

In this block the names "WITH LINE BELOW" refer to a macron below the letter.

Latin general use extensions

1E00 Ḁ LATIN CAPITAL LETTER A WITH RING BELOW
≡ 0041 A 0325 ◌̥

1E01 ḁ LATIN SMALL LETTER A WITH RING BELOW
≡ 0061 a 0325 ◌̥

1E02 Ḃ LATIN CAPITAL LETTER B WITH DOT ABOVE
≡ 0042 B 0307 ◌̇

1E03 ḃ LATIN SMALL LETTER B WITH DOT ABOVE
• Irish Gaelic (old orthography)
≡ 0062 b 0307 ◌̇

1E04 Ḅ LATIN CAPITAL LETTER B WITH DOT BELOW
≡ 0042 B 0323 ◌̣

1E05 ḅ LATIN SMALL LETTER B WITH DOT BELOW
≡ 0062 b 0323 ◌̣

1E06 Ḇ LATIN CAPITAL LETTER B WITH LINE BELOW
≡ 0042 B 0331 ◌̱

1E07 ḇ LATIN SMALL LETTER B WITH LINE BELOW
≡ 0062 b 0331 ◌̱

1E08 Ḉ LATIN CAPITAL LETTER C WITH CEDILLA AND ACUTE
≡ 00C7 Ç 0301 ◌́

1E09 ḉ LATIN SMALL LETTER C WITH CEDILLA AND ACUTE
≡ 00E7 ç 0301 ◌́

1E0A Ḋ LATIN CAPITAL LETTER D WITH DOT ABOVE
≡ 0044 D 0307 ◌̇

1E0B ḋ LATIN SMALL LETTER D WITH DOT ABOVE
• Irish Gaelic (old orthography)
≡ 0064 d 0307 ◌̇

1E0C Ḍ LATIN CAPITAL LETTER D WITH DOT BELOW
≡ 0044 D 0323 ◌̣

1E0D ḍ LATIN SMALL LETTER D WITH DOT BELOW
• Indic transliteration
≡ 0064 d 0323 ◌̣

1E0E Ḏ LATIN CAPITAL LETTER D WITH LINE BELOW
≡ 0044 D 0331 ◌̱

1E0F ḏ LATIN SMALL LETTER D WITH LINE BELOW
≡ 0064 d 0331 ◌̱

1E10 Ḑ LATIN CAPITAL LETTER D WITH CEDILLA
≡ 0044 D 0327 ◌̧

1E11 ḑ LATIN SMALL LETTER D WITH CEDILLA
• Livonian
≡ 0064 d 0327 ◌̧

1E12 Ḓ LATIN CAPITAL LETTER D WITH CIRCUMFLEX BELOW
≡ 0044 D 032D ◌̭

1E13 ḓ LATIN SMALL LETTER D WITH CIRCUMFLEX BELOW
≡ 0064 d 032D ◌̭

1E14 Ḕ LATIN CAPITAL LETTER E WITH MACRON AND GRAVE
≡ 0112 Ē 0300 ◌̀

1E15 ḕ LATIN SMALL LETTER E WITH MACRON AND GRAVE
≡ 0113 ē 0300 ◌̀

1E16 Ḗ LATIN CAPITAL LETTER E WITH MACRON AND ACUTE
≡ 0112 Ē 0301 ◌́

1E17 ḗ LATIN SMALL LETTER E WITH MACRON AND ACUTE
≡ 0113 ē 0301 ◌́

1E18 Ḙ LATIN CAPITAL LETTER E WITH CIRCUMFLEX BELOW
≡ 0045 E 032D ◌̭

1E19 ḙ LATIN SMALL LETTER E WITH CIRCUMFLEX BELOW
≡ 0065 e 032D ◌̭

1E1A Ḛ LATIN CAPITAL LETTER E WITH TILDE BELOW
≡ 0045 E 0330 ◌̰

1E1B ḛ LATIN SMALL LETTER E WITH TILDE BELOW
≡ 0065 e 0330 ◌̰

1E1C Ḝ LATIN CAPITAL LETTER E WITH CEDILLA AND BREVE
≡ 0228 Ȩ 0306 ◌̆

1E1D ḝ LATIN SMALL LETTER E WITH CEDILLA AND BREVE
≡ 0229 ȩ 0306 ◌̆

1E1E Ḟ LATIN CAPITAL LETTER F WITH DOT ABOVE
≡ 0046 F 0307 ◌̇

1E1F ḟ LATIN SMALL LETTER F WITH DOT ABOVE
• Irish Gaelic (old orthography)
≡ 0066 f 0307 ◌̇

1E20 Ḡ LATIN CAPITAL LETTER G WITH MACRON
≡ 0047 G 0304 ◌̄

1E21 ḡ LATIN SMALL LETTER G WITH MACRON
≡ 0067 g 0304 ◌̄

1E22 Ḣ LATIN CAPITAL LETTER H WITH DOT ABOVE
≡ 0048 H 0307 ◌̇

1E23 ḣ LATIN SMALL LETTER H WITH DOT ABOVE
≡ 0068 h 0307 ◌̇

1E24 Ḥ LATIN CAPITAL LETTER H WITH DOT BELOW
≡ 0048 H 0323 ◌̣

1E25 ḥ LATIN SMALL LETTER H WITH DOT BELOW
• Indic transliteration
≡ 0068 h 0323 ◌̣

1E26 Ḧ LATIN CAPITAL LETTER H WITH DIAERESIS
≡ 0048 H 0308 ◌̈

1E27 ḧ LATIN SMALL LETTER H WITH DIAERESIS
≡ 0068 h 0308 ◌̈

1E28 Ḩ LATIN CAPITAL LETTER H WITH CEDILLA
≡ 0048 H 0327 ◌̧

1E29 ḩ LATIN SMALL LETTER H WITH CEDILLA
≡ 0068 h 0327 ◌̧

1E2A Ḫ LATIN CAPITAL LETTER H WITH BREVE BELOW
≡ 0048 H 032E ◌̮

1E2B ḫ LATIN SMALL LETTER H WITH BREVE BELOW
• Semitic transliteration
≡ 0068 h 032E ◌̮

1E2C Ḭ LATIN CAPITAL LETTER I WITH TILDE BELOW
≡ 0049 I 0330 ◌̰

1E2D ḭ LATIN SMALL LETTER I WITH TILDE BELOW
≡ 0069 i 0330 ◌̰

1E2E Ḯ LATIN CAPITAL LETTER I WITH DIAERESIS AND ACUTE
≡ 00CF Ï 0301 ◌́

1E2F ḯ LATIN SMALL LETTER I WITH DIAERESIS AND ACUTE
≡ 00EF ï 0301 ◌́

1E30 Ḱ LATIN CAPITAL LETTER K WITH ACUTE
≡ 004B K 0301 ◌́

1E31 ḱ LATIN SMALL LETTER K WITH ACUTE
• Macedonian transliteration
≡ 006B k 0301 ◌́

1E32 Ḳ LATIN CAPITAL LETTER K WITH DOT BELOW
≡ 004B K 0323 ◌̣

1E33 ḳ LATIN SMALL LETTER K WITH DOT BELOW
≡ 006B k 0323 ◌̣

1E34 Ḵ LATIN CAPITAL LETTER K WITH LINE BELOW
≡ 004B K 0331 ◌̱

1E35 ḵ LATIN SMALL LETTER K WITH LINE BELOW
≡ 006B k 0331 ◌̱

1E36 Ḷ LATIN CAPITAL LETTER L WITH DOT BELOW
≡ 004C L 0323 ◌̣

1E37 ḷ LATIN SMALL LETTER L WITH DOT BELOW
- Indic transliteration
- see ISO 15919 on the use of dot below versus ring below in Indic transliteration

→ 0325 ◌̥ combining ring below
≡ 006C l 0323 ◌̣

1E38 Ḹ LATIN CAPITAL LETTER L WITH DOT BELOW AND MACRON
≡ 1E36 Ḷ 0304 ◌̄

1E39 ḹ LATIN SMALL LETTER L WITH DOT BELOW AND MACRON
- Indic transliteration

≡ 1E37 ḷ 0304 ◌̄

1E3A Ḻ LATIN CAPITAL LETTER L WITH LINE BELOW
≡ 004C L 0331 ◌̱

1E3B ḻ LATIN SMALL LETTER L WITH LINE BELOW
- Indic transliteration

≡ 006C l 0331 ◌̱

1E3C Ḽ LATIN CAPITAL LETTER L WITH CIRCUMFLEX BELOW
≡ 004C L 032D ◌̭

1E3D ḽ LATIN SMALL LETTER L WITH CIRCUMFLEX BELOW
≡ 006C l 032D ◌̭

1E3E Ḿ LATIN CAPITAL LETTER M WITH ACUTE
≡ 004D M 0301 ◌́

1E3F ḿ LATIN SMALL LETTER M WITH ACUTE
≡ 006D m 0301 ◌́

1E40 Ṁ LATIN CAPITAL LETTER M WITH DOT ABOVE
≡ 004D M 0307 ◌̇

1E41 ṁ LATIN SMALL LETTER M WITH DOT ABOVE
- Irish Gaelic (old orthography)

≡ 006D m 0307 ◌̇

1E42 Ṃ LATIN CAPITAL LETTER M WITH DOT BELOW
≡ 004D M 0323 ◌̣

1E43 ṃ LATIN SMALL LETTER M WITH DOT BELOW
- Indic transliteration

≡ 006D m 0323 ◌̣

1E44 Ṅ LATIN CAPITAL LETTER N WITH DOT ABOVE
≡ 004E N 0307 ◌̇

1E45 ṅ LATIN SMALL LETTER N WITH DOT ABOVE
- Indic transliteration

≡ 006E n 0307 ◌̇

1E46 Ṇ LATIN CAPITAL LETTER N WITH DOT BELOW
≡ 004E N 0323 ◌̣

1E47 ṇ LATIN SMALL LETTER N WITH DOT BELOW
- Indic transliteration

≡ 006E n 0323 ◌̣

1E48 Ṉ LATIN CAPITAL LETTER N WITH LINE BELOW
≡ 004E N 0331 ◌̱

1E49 ṉ LATIN SMALL LETTER N WITH LINE BELOW
- Indic transliteration

≡ 006E n 0331 ◌̱

1E4A Ṋ LATIN CAPITAL LETTER N WITH CIRCUMFLEX BELOW
≡ 004E N 032D ◌̭

1E4B ṋ LATIN SMALL LETTER N WITH CIRCUMFLEX BELOW
≡ 006E n 032D ◌̭

1E4C Ṍ LATIN CAPITAL LETTER O WITH TILDE AND ACUTE
≡ 00D5 Õ 0301 ◌́

1E4D ṍ LATIN SMALL LETTER O WITH TILDE AND ACUTE
≡ 00F5 õ 0301 ◌́

1E4E Ṏ LATIN CAPITAL LETTER O WITH TILDE AND DIAERESIS
≡ 00D5 Õ 0308 ◌̈

1E4F ṏ LATIN SMALL LETTER O WITH TILDE AND DIAERESIS
≡ 00F5 õ 0308 ◌̈

1E50 Ṑ LATIN CAPITAL LETTER O WITH MACRON AND GRAVE
≡ 014C Ō 0300 ◌̀

1E51 ṑ LATIN SMALL LETTER O WITH MACRON AND GRAVE
≡ 014D ō 0300 ◌̀

1E52 Ṓ LATIN CAPITAL LETTER O WITH MACRON AND ACUTE
≡ 014C Ō 0301 ◌́

1E53 ṓ LATIN SMALL LETTER O WITH MACRON AND ACUTE
≡ 014D ō 0301 ◌́

1E54 Ṕ LATIN CAPITAL LETTER P WITH ACUTE
≡ 0050 P 0301 ◌́

1E55 ṕ LATIN SMALL LETTER P WITH ACUTE
≡ 0070 p 0301 ◌́

1E56 Ṗ LATIN CAPITAL LETTER P WITH DOT ABOVE
≡ 0050 P 0307 ◌̇

1E57 ṗ LATIN SMALL LETTER P WITH DOT ABOVE
- Irish Gaelic (old orthography)

≡ 0070 p 0307 ◌̇

1E58 Ṙ LATIN CAPITAL LETTER R WITH DOT ABOVE
≡ 0052 R 0307 ◌̇

1E59 ṙ LATIN SMALL LETTER R WITH DOT ABOVE
≡ 0072 r 0307 ◌̇

1E5A Ṛ LATIN CAPITAL LETTER R WITH DOT BELOW
≡ 0052 R 0323 ◌̣

1E5B ṛ LATIN SMALL LETTER R WITH DOT BELOW
- Indic transliteration
- see ISO 15919 on the use of dot below versus ring below in Indic transliteration

→ 0325 ◌̥ combining ring below
≡ 0072 r 0323 ◌̣

1E5C Ṝ LATIN CAPITAL LETTER R WITH DOT BELOW AND MACRON
≡ 1E5A Ṛ 0304 ◌̄

1E5D ṝ LATIN SMALL LETTER R WITH DOT BELOW AND MACRON
- Indic transliteration

≡ 1E5B ṛ 0304 ◌̄

1E5E Ṟ LATIN CAPITAL LETTER R WITH LINE BELOW
≡ 0052 R 0331 ◌̱

1E5F ṟ LATIN SMALL LETTER R WITH LINE BELOW
- Indic transliteration

≡ 0072 r 0331 ◌̱

1E60 Ṡ LATIN CAPITAL LETTER S WITH DOT ABOVE
≡ 0053 S 0307 ◌̇

1E61 ṡ LATIN SMALL LETTER S WITH DOT ABOVE
- Irish Gaelic (old orthography)

≡ 0073 s 0307 ◌̇

1E62 Ṣ LATIN CAPITAL LETTER S WITH DOT BELOW
≡ 0053 S 0323 ◌̣

1E63 ṣ LATIN SMALL LETTER S WITH DOT BELOW
• Indic transliteration
≡ 0073 s 0323 ◌̣

1E64 Ṥ LATIN CAPITAL LETTER S WITH ACUTE AND DOT ABOVE
≡ 015A Ś 0307 ◌̇

1E65 ṥ LATIN SMALL LETTER S WITH ACUTE AND DOT ABOVE
≡ 015B ś 0307 ◌̇

1E66 Ṧ LATIN CAPITAL LETTER S WITH CARON AND DOT ABOVE
≡ 0160 Š 0307 ◌̇

1E67 ṧ LATIN SMALL LETTER S WITH CARON AND DOT ABOVE
≡ 0161 š 0307 ◌̇

1E68 Ṩ LATIN CAPITAL LETTER S WITH DOT BELOW AND DOT ABOVE
≡ 1E62 Ṣ 0307 ◌̇

1E69 ṩ LATIN SMALL LETTER S WITH DOT BELOW AND DOT ABOVE
≡ 1E63 ṣ 0307 ◌̇

1E6A Ṫ LATIN CAPITAL LETTER T WITH DOT ABOVE
≡ 0054 T 0307 ◌̇

1E6B ṫ LATIN SMALL LETTER T WITH DOT ABOVE
• Irish Gaelic (old orthography)
≡ 0074 t 0307 ◌̇

1E6C Ṭ LATIN CAPITAL LETTER T WITH DOT BELOW
≡ 0054 T 0323 ◌̣

1E6D ṭ LATIN SMALL LETTER T WITH DOT BELOW
• Indic transliteration
≡ 0074 t 0323 ◌̣

1E6E Ṯ LATIN CAPITAL LETTER T WITH LINE BELOW
≡ 0054 T 0331 ◌̱

1E6F ṯ LATIN SMALL LETTER T WITH LINE BELOW
• Semitic transliteration
≡ 0074 t 0331 ◌̱

1E70 Ṱ LATIN CAPITAL LETTER T WITH CIRCUMFLEX BELOW
≡ 0054 T 032D ◌̭

1E71 ṱ LATIN SMALL LETTER T WITH CIRCUMFLEX BELOW
≡ 0074 t 032D ◌̭

1E72 Ṳ LATIN CAPITAL LETTER U WITH DIAERESIS BELOW
≡ 0055 U 0324 ◌̤

1E73 ṳ LATIN SMALL LETTER U WITH DIAERESIS BELOW
≡ 0075 u 0324 ◌̤

1E74 Ṵ LATIN CAPITAL LETTER U WITH TILDE BELOW
≡ 0055 U 0330 ◌̰

1E75 ṵ LATIN SMALL LETTER U WITH TILDE BELOW
≡ 0075 u 0330 ◌̰

1E76 Ṷ LATIN CAPITAL LETTER U WITH CIRCUMFLEX BELOW
≡ 0055 U 032D ◌̭

1E77 ṷ LATIN SMALL LETTER U WITH CIRCUMFLEX BELOW
≡ 0075 u 032D ◌̭

1E78 Ṹ LATIN CAPITAL LETTER U WITH TILDE AND ACUTE
≡ 0168 Ũ 0301 ◌́

1E79 ṹ LATIN SMALL LETTER U WITH TILDE AND ACUTE
≡ 0169 ũ 0301 ◌́

1E7A Ṻ LATIN CAPITAL LETTER U WITH MACRON AND DIAERESIS
≡ 016A Ū 0308 ◌̈

1E7B ṻ LATIN SMALL LETTER U WITH MACRON AND DIAERESIS
≡ 016B ū 0308 ◌̈

1E7C Ṽ LATIN CAPITAL LETTER V WITH TILDE
≡ 0056 V 0303 ◌̃

1E7D ṽ LATIN SMALL LETTER V WITH TILDE
≡ 0076 v 0303 ◌̃

1E7E Ṿ LATIN CAPITAL LETTER V WITH DOT BELOW
≡ 0056 V 0323 ◌̣

1E7F ṿ LATIN SMALL LETTER V WITH DOT BELOW
≡ 0076 v 0323 ◌̣

1E80 Ẁ LATIN CAPITAL LETTER W WITH GRAVE
≡ 0057 W 0300 ◌̀

1E81 ẁ LATIN SMALL LETTER W WITH GRAVE
• Welsh
≡ 0077 w 0300 ◌̀

1E82 Ẃ LATIN CAPITAL LETTER W WITH ACUTE
≡ 0057 W 0301 ◌́

1E83 ẃ LATIN SMALL LETTER W WITH ACUTE
• Welsh
≡ 0077 w 0301 ◌́

1E84 Ẅ LATIN CAPITAL LETTER W WITH DIAERESIS
≡ 0057 W 0308 ◌̈

1E85 ẅ LATIN SMALL LETTER W WITH DIAERESIS
• Welsh
≡ 0077 w 0308 ◌̈

1E86 Ẇ LATIN CAPITAL LETTER W WITH DOT ABOVE
≡ 0057 W 0307 ◌̇

1E87 ẇ LATIN SMALL LETTER W WITH DOT ABOVE
≡ 0077 w 0307 ◌̇

1E88 Ẉ LATIN CAPITAL LETTER W WITH DOT BELOW
≡ 0057 W 0323 ◌̣

1E89 ẉ LATIN SMALL LETTER W WITH DOT BELOW
≡ 0077 w 0323 ◌̣

1E8A Ẋ LATIN CAPITAL LETTER X WITH DOT ABOVE
≡ 0058 X 0307 ◌̇

1E8B ẋ LATIN SMALL LETTER X WITH DOT ABOVE
≡ 0078 x 0307 ◌̇

1E8C Ẍ LATIN CAPITAL LETTER X WITH DIAERESIS
≡ 0058 X 0308 ◌̈

1E8D ẍ LATIN SMALL LETTER X WITH DIAERESIS
≡ 0078 x 0308 ◌̈

1E8E Ẏ LATIN CAPITAL LETTER Y WITH DOT ABOVE
≡ 0059 Y 0307 ◌̇

1E8F ẏ LATIN SMALL LETTER Y WITH DOT ABOVE
≡ 0079 y 0307 ◌̇

1E90 Ẑ LATIN CAPITAL LETTER Z WITH CIRCUMFLEX
≡ 005A Z 0302 ◌̂

1E91 ẑ LATIN SMALL LETTER Z WITH CIRCUMFLEX
≡ 007A z 0302 ◌̂

1E92 Ẓ LATIN CAPITAL LETTER Z WITH DOT BELOW
≡ 005A Z 0323 ◌̣

1E93 ẓ LATIN SMALL LETTER Z WITH DOT BELOW
• Indic transliteration
≡ 007A z 0323 ◌̣

1E94 Ẕ LATIN CAPITAL LETTER Z WITH LINE BELOW
≡ 005A Z 0331 ◌̱

1E95 ẕ LATIN SMALL LETTER Z WITH LINE BELOW
• Semitic transliteration
≡ 007A z 0331 ̱

1E96 ẖ LATIN SMALL LETTER H WITH LINE BELOW
• Semitic transliteration
≡ 0068 h 0331 ̱

1E97 ẗ LATIN SMALL LETTER T WITH DIAERESIS
≡ 0074 t 0308 ̈

1E98 ẘ LATIN SMALL LETTER W WITH RING ABOVE
≡ 0077 w 030A ̊

1E99 ẙ LATIN SMALL LETTER Y WITH RING ABOVE
≡ 0079 y 030A ̊

1E9A ẚ LATIN SMALL LETTER A WITH RIGHT HALF RING
≈ 0061 a 02BE ʾ

1E9B ẛ LATIN SMALL LETTER LONG S WITH DOT ABOVE
• in current use in Gaelic types (as glyph variant of 1E61 ṡ)
≡ 017F ſ 0307 ̇

Latin extensions for Vietnamese

1EA0 Ạ LATIN CAPITAL LETTER A WITH DOT BELOW
≡ 0041 A 0323 ̣

1EA1 ạ LATIN SMALL LETTER A WITH DOT BELOW
≡ 0061 a 0323 ̣

1EA2 Ả LATIN CAPITAL LETTER A WITH HOOK ABOVE
≡ 0041 A 0309 ̉

1EA3 ả LATIN SMALL LETTER A WITH HOOK ABOVE
≡ 0061 a 0309 ̉

1EA4 Ấ LATIN CAPITAL LETTER A WITH CIRCUMFLEX AND ACUTE
≡ 00C2 Â 0301 ́

1EA5 ấ LATIN SMALL LETTER A WITH CIRCUMFLEX AND ACUTE
≡ 00E2 â 0301 ́

1EA6 Ầ LATIN CAPITAL LETTER A WITH CIRCUMFLEX AND GRAVE
≡ 00C2 Â 0300 ̀

1EA7 ầ LATIN SMALL LETTER A WITH CIRCUMFLEX AND GRAVE
≡ 00E2 â 0300 ̀

1EA8 Ẩ LATIN CAPITAL LETTER A WITH CIRCUMFLEX AND HOOK ABOVE
≡ 00C2 Â 0309 ̉

1EA9 ẩ LATIN SMALL LETTER A WITH CIRCUMFLEX AND HOOK ABOVE
≡ 00E2 â 0309 ̉

1EAA Ẫ LATIN CAPITAL LETTER A WITH CIRCUMFLEX AND TILDE
≡ 00C2 Â 0303 ̃

1EAB ẫ LATIN SMALL LETTER A WITH CIRCUMFLEX AND TILDE
≡ 00E2 â 0303 ̃

1EAC Ậ LATIN CAPITAL LETTER A WITH CIRCUMFLEX AND DOT BELOW
≡ 1EA0 Ạ 0302 ̂

1EAD ậ LATIN SMALL LETTER A WITH CIRCUMFLEX AND DOT BELOW
≡ 1EA1 ạ 0302 ̂

1EAE Ắ LATIN CAPITAL LETTER A WITH BREVE AND ACUTE
≡ 0102 Ă 0301 ́

1EAF ắ LATIN SMALL LETTER A WITH BREVE AND ACUTE
≡ 0103 ă 0301 ́

1EB0 Ằ LATIN CAPITAL LETTER A WITH BREVE AND GRAVE
≡ 0102 Ă 0300 ̀

1EB1 ằ LATIN SMALL LETTER A WITH BREVE AND GRAVE
≡ 0103 ă 0300 ̀

1EB2 Ẳ LATIN CAPITAL LETTER A WITH BREVE AND HOOK ABOVE
≡ 0102 Ă 0309 ̉

1EB3 ẳ LATIN SMALL LETTER A WITH BREVE AND HOOK ABOVE
≡ 0103 ă 0309 ̉

1EB4 Ẵ LATIN CAPITAL LETTER A WITH BREVE AND TILDE
≡ 0102 Ă 0303 ̃

1EB5 ẵ LATIN SMALL LETTER A WITH BREVE AND TILDE
≡ 0103 ă 0303 ̃

1EB6 Ặ LATIN CAPITAL LETTER A WITH BREVE AND DOT BELOW
≡ 1EA0 Ạ 0306 ̆

1EB7 ặ LATIN SMALL LETTER A WITH BREVE AND DOT BELOW
≡ 1EA1 ạ 0306 ̆

1EB8 Ẹ LATIN CAPITAL LETTER E WITH DOT BELOW
≡ 0045 E 0323 ̣

1EB9 ẹ LATIN SMALL LETTER E WITH DOT BELOW
≡ 0065 e 0323 ̣

1EBA Ẻ LATIN CAPITAL LETTER E WITH HOOK ABOVE
≡ 0045 E 0309 ̉

1EBB ẻ LATIN SMALL LETTER E WITH HOOK ABOVE
≡ 0065 e 0309 ̉

1EBC Ẽ LATIN CAPITAL LETTER E WITH TILDE
≡ 0045 E 0303 ̃

1EBD ẽ LATIN SMALL LETTER E WITH TILDE
≡ 0065 e 0303 ̃

1EBE Ế LATIN CAPITAL LETTER E WITH CIRCUMFLEX AND ACUTE
≡ 00CA Ê 0301 ́

1EBF ế LATIN SMALL LETTER E WITH CIRCUMFLEX AND ACUTE
≡ 00EA ê 0301 ́

1EC0 Ề LATIN CAPITAL LETTER E WITH CIRCUMFLEX AND GRAVE
≡ 00CA Ê 0300 ̀

1EC1 ề LATIN SMALL LETTER E WITH CIRCUMFLEX AND GRAVE
≡ 00EA ê 0300 ̀

1EC2 Ể LATIN CAPITAL LETTER E WITH CIRCUMFLEX AND HOOK ABOVE
≡ 00CA Ê 0309 ̉

1EC3 ể LATIN SMALL LETTER E WITH CIRCUMFLEX AND HOOK ABOVE
≡ 00EA ê 0309 ̉

1EC4 Ễ LATIN CAPITAL LETTER E WITH CIRCUMFLEX AND TILDE
≡ 00CA Ê 0303 ̃

1EC5 ễ LATIN SMALL LETTER E WITH CIRCUMFLEX AND TILDE
≡ 00EA ê 0303 ̃

1EC6 Ệ LATIN CAPITAL LETTER E WITH CIRCUMFLEX AND DOT BELOW
≡ 1EB8 Ẹ 0302 ̂

1EC7 ệ LATIN SMALL LETTER E WITH CIRCUMFLEX AND DOT BELOW
≡ 1EB9 ẹ 0302 ̂

1EC8 Ỉ LATIN CAPITAL LETTER I WITH HOOK ABOVE
≡ 0049 I 0309 ◌̉

1EC9 ỉ LATIN SMALL LETTER I WITH HOOK ABOVE
≡ 0069 i 0309 ◌̉

1ECA Ị LATIN CAPITAL LETTER I WITH DOT BELOW
≡ 0049 I 0323 ◌̣

1ECB ị LATIN SMALL LETTER I WITH DOT BELOW
≡ 0069 i 0323 ◌̣

1ECC Ọ LATIN CAPITAL LETTER O WITH DOT BELOW
≡ 004F O 0323 ◌̣

1ECD ọ LATIN SMALL LETTER O WITH DOT BELOW
≡ 006F o 0323 ◌̣

1ECE Ỏ LATIN CAPITAL LETTER O WITH HOOK ABOVE
≡ 004F O 0309 ◌̉

1ECF ỏ LATIN SMALL LETTER O WITH HOOK ABOVE
≡ 006F o 0309 ◌̉

1ED0 Ố LATIN CAPITAL LETTER O WITH CIRCUMFLEX AND ACUTE
≡ 00D4 Ô 0301 ◌́

1ED1 ố LATIN SMALL LETTER O WITH CIRCUMFLEX AND ACUTE
≡ 00F4 ô 0301 ◌́

1ED2 Ồ LATIN CAPITAL LETTER O WITH CIRCUMFLEX AND GRAVE
≡ 00D4 Ô 0300 ◌̀

1ED3 ồ LATIN SMALL LETTER O WITH CIRCUMFLEX AND GRAVE
≡ 00F4 ô 0300 ◌̀

1ED4 Ổ LATIN CAPITAL LETTER O WITH CIRCUMFLEX AND HOOK ABOVE
≡ 00D4 Ô 0309 ◌̉

1ED5 ổ LATIN SMALL LETTER O WITH CIRCUMFLEX AND HOOK ABOVE
≡ 00F4 ô 0309 ◌̉

1ED6 Ỗ LATIN CAPITAL LETTER O WITH CIRCUMFLEX AND TILDE
≡ 00D4 Ô 0303 ◌̃

1ED7 ỗ LATIN SMALL LETTER O WITH CIRCUMFLEX AND TILDE
00F4 ô 0303 ◌̃

1ED8 Ộ LATIN CAPITAL LETTER O WITH CIRCUMFLEX AND DOT BELOW
≡ 1ECC Ọ 0302 ◌̂

1ED9 ộ LATIN SMALL LETTER O WITH CIRCUMFLEX AND DOT BELOW
≡ 1ECD ọ 0302 ◌̂

1EDA Ớ LATIN CAPITAL LETTER O WITH HORN AND ACUTE
≡ 01A0 Ơ 0301 ◌́

1EDB ớ LATIN SMALL LETTER O WITH HORN AND ACUTE
≡ 01A1 ơ 0301 ◌́

1EDC Ờ LATIN CAPITAL LETTER O WITH HORN AND GRAVE
≡ 01A0 Ơ 0300 ◌̀

1EDD ờ LATIN SMALL LETTER O WITH HORN AND GRAVE
≡ 01A1 ơ 0300 ◌̀

1EDE Ở LATIN CAPITAL LETTER O WITH HORN AND HOOK ABOVE
≡ 01A0 Ơ 0309 ◌̉

1EDF ở LATIN SMALL LETTER O WITH HORN AND HOOK ABOVE
≡ 01A1 ơ 0309 ◌̉

1EE0 Ỡ LATIN CAPITAL LETTER O WITH HORN AND TILDE
≡ 01A0 Ơ 0303 ◌̃

1EE1 ỡ LATIN SMALL LETTER O WITH HORN AND TILDE
≡ 01A1 ơ 0303 ◌̃

1EE2 Ợ LATIN CAPITAL LETTER O WITH HORN AND DOT BELOW
≡ 01A0 Ơ 0323 ◌̣

1EE3 ợ LATIN SMALL LETTER O WITH HORN AND DOT BELOW
≡ 01A1 ơ 0323 ◌̣

1EE4 Ụ LATIN CAPITAL LETTER U WITH DOT BELOW
≡ 0055 U 0323 ◌̣

1EE5 ụ LATIN SMALL LETTER U WITH DOT BELOW
≡ 0075 u 0323 ◌̣

1EE6 Ủ LATIN CAPITAL LETTER U WITH HOOK ABOVE
≡ 0055 U 0309 ◌̉

1EE7 ủ LATIN SMALL LETTER U WITH HOOK ABOVE
≡ 0075 u 0309 ◌̉

1EE8 Ứ LATIN CAPITAL LETTER U WITH HORN AND ACUTE
≡ 01AF Ư 0301 ◌́

1EE9 ứ LATIN SMALL LETTER U WITH HORN AND ACUTE
≡ 01B0 ư 0301 ◌́

1EEA Ừ LATIN CAPITAL LETTER U WITH HORN AND GRAVE
≡ 01AF Ư 0300 ◌̀

1EEB ừ LATIN SMALL LETTER U WITH HORN AND GRAVE
≡ 01B0 ư 0300 ◌̀

1EEC Ử LATIN CAPITAL LETTER U WITH HORN AND HOOK ABOVE
≡ 01AF Ư 0309 ◌̉

1EED ử LATIN SMALL LETTER U WITH HORN AND HOOK ABOVE
≡ 01B0 ư 0309 ◌̉

1EEE Ữ LATIN CAPITAL LETTER U WITH HORN AND TILDE
≡ 01AF Ư 0303 ◌̃

1EEF ữ LATIN SMALL LETTER U WITH HORN AND TILDE
≡ 01B0 ư 0303 ◌̃

1EF0 Ự LATIN CAPITAL LETTER U WITH HORN AND DOT BELOW
≡ 01AF Ư 0323 ◌̣

1EF1 ự LATIN SMALL LETTER U WITH HORN AND DOT BELOW
≡ 01B0 ư 0323 ◌̣

1EF2 Ỳ LATIN CAPITAL LETTER Y WITH GRAVE
≡ 0059 Y 0300 ◌̀

1EF3 ỳ LATIN SMALL LETTER Y WITH GRAVE
• Welsh
≡ 0079 y 0300 ◌̀

1EF4 Ỵ LATIN CAPITAL LETTER Y WITH DOT BELOW
≡ 0059 Y 0323 ◌̣

1EF5 ỵ LATIN SMALL LETTER Y WITH DOT BELOW
≡ 0079 y 0323 ◌̣

1EF6 Ỷ LATIN CAPITAL LETTER Y WITH HOOK ABOVE
≡ 0059 Y 0309 ◌̉

1EF7 ỷ LATIN SMALL LETTER Y WITH HOOK ABOVE
≡ 0079 y 0309 ◌̉

1EF8 Ỹ LATIN CAPITAL LETTER Y WITH TILDE
≡ 0059 Y 0303 ◌̃

1EF9 ỹ LATIN SMALL LETTER Y WITH TILDE
≡ 0079 y 0303 ◌̃

	1F0	1F1	1F2	1F3	1F4	1F5	1F6	1F7	1F8	1F9	1FA	1FB	1FC	1FD	1FE	1FF
0	ἀ 1F00	ἐ 1F10	ἠ 1F20	ἰ 1F30	ὀ 1F40	ὐ 1F50	ὠ 1F60	ὰ 1F70	ᾀ 1F80	ᾐ 1F90	ᾠ 1FA0	ᾰ 1FB0	῀ 1FC0	ῐ 1FD0	ῠ 1FE0	
1	ἁ 1F01	ἑ 1F11	ἡ 1F21	ἱ 1F31	ὁ 1F41	ὑ 1F51	ὡ 1F61	ά 1F71	ᾁ 1F81	ᾑ 1F91	ᾡ 1FA1	ᾱ 1FB1	῁ 1FC1	ῑ 1FD1	ῡ 1FE1	
2	ἂ 1F02	ἒ 1F12	ἢ 1F22	ἲ 1F32	ὂ 1F42	ὒ 1F52	ὢ 1F62	ὲ 1F72	ᾂ 1F82	ᾒ 1F92	ᾢ 1FA2	ᾲ 1FB2	ῂ 1FC2	ῒ 1FD2	ῢ 1FE2	ῲ 1FF2
3	ἃ 1F03	ἓ 1F13	ἣ 1F23	ἳ 1F33	ὃ 1F43	ὓ 1F53	ὣ 1F63	έ 1F73	ᾃ 1F83	ᾓ 1F93	ᾣ 1FA3	ᾳ 1FB3	ῃ 1FC3	ΐ 1FD3	ΰ 1FE3	ῳ 1FF3
4	ἄ 1F04	ἔ 1F14	ἤ 1F24	ἴ 1F34	ὄ 1F44	ὔ 1F54	ὤ 1F64	ὴ 1F74	ᾄ 1F84	ᾔ 1F94	ᾤ 1FA4	ᾴ 1FB4	ῄ 1FC4		ῤ 1FE4	ῴ 1FF4
5	ἅ 1F05	ἕ 1F15	ἥ 1F25	ἵ 1F35	ὅ 1F45	ὕ 1F55	ὥ 1F65	ή 1F75	ᾅ 1F85	ᾕ 1F95	ᾥ 1FA5				ῥ 1FE5	
6	ἆ 1F06		ἦ 1F26	ἶ 1F36		ὖ 1F56	ὦ 1F66	ὶ 1F76	ᾆ 1F86	ᾖ 1F96	ᾦ 1FA6	ᾶ 1FB6	ῆ 1FC6	ῖ 1FD6	ῦ 1FE6	ῶ 1FF6
7	ἇ 1F07		ἧ 1F27	ἷ 1F37		ὗ 1F57	ὧ 1F67	ί 1F77	ᾇ 1F87	ᾗ 1F97	ᾧ 1FA7	ᾷ 1FB7	ῇ 1FC7	ῗ 1FD7	ῧ 1FE7	ῷ 1FF7
8	Ἀ 1F08	Ἐ 1F18	Ἠ 1F28	Ἰ 1F38	Ὀ 1F48		Ὠ 1F68	ὸ 1F78	ᾈ 1F88	ᾘ 1F98	ᾨ 1FA8	Ᾰ 1FB8	Ὲ 1FC8	Ῐ 1FD8	Ῠ 1FE8	Ὸ 1FF8
9	Ἁ 1F09	Ἑ 1F19	Ἡ 1F29	Ἱ 1F39	Ὁ 1F49	Ὑ 1F59	Ὡ 1F69	ό 1F79	ᾉ 1F89	ᾙ 1F99	ᾩ 1FA9	Ᾱ 1FB9	Έ 1FC9	Ῑ 1FD9	Ῡ 1FE9	Ό 1FF9
A	Ἂ 1F0A	Ἒ 1F1A	Ἢ 1F2A	Ἲ 1F3A	Ὂ 1F4A		Ὢ 1F6A	ὺ 1F7A	ᾊ 1F8A	ᾚ 1F9A	ᾪ 1FAA	Ὰ 1FBA	Ὴ 1FCA	Ὶ 1FDA	Ὺ 1FEA	Ὼ 1FFA
B	Ἃ 1F0B	Ἓ 1F1B	Ἣ 1F2B	Ἳ 1F3B	Ὃ 1F4B	Ὓ 1F5B	Ὣ 1F6B	ύ 1F7B	ᾋ 1F8B	ᾛ 1F9B	ᾫ 1FAB	Ά 1FBB	Ή 1FCB	Ί 1FDB	Ύ 1FEB	Ώ 1FFB
C	Ἄ 1F0C	Ἔ 1F1C	Ἤ 1F2C	Ἴ 1F3C	Ὄ 1F4C		Ὤ 1F6C	ὼ 1F7C	ᾌ 1F8C	ᾜ 1F9C	ᾬ 1FAC	ᾼ 1FBC	ῌ 1FCC		Ῥ 1FEC	ῼ 1FFC
D	Ἅ 1F0D	Ἕ 1F1D	Ἥ 1F2D	Ἵ 1F3D	Ὅ 1F4D	Ὕ 1F5D	Ὥ 1F6D	ώ 1F7D	ᾍ 1F8D	ᾝ 1F9D	ᾭ 1FAD	᾽ 1FBD	῍ 1FCD	῝ 1FDD	῭ 1FED	´ 1FFD
E	Ἆ 1F0E		Ἦ 1F2E	Ἶ 1F3E			Ὦ 1F6E		ᾎ 1F8E	ᾞ 1F9E	ᾮ 1FAE	ι 1FBE	῎ 1FCE	῞ 1FDE	΅ 1FEE	῾ 1FFE
F	Ἇ 1F0F		Ἧ 1F2F	Ἷ 1F3F		Ὗ 1F5F	Ὧ 1F6F		ᾏ 1F8F	ᾟ 1F9F	ᾯ 1FAF	᾿ 1FBF	῏ 1FCF	῟ 1FDF	` 1FEF	

Precomposed polytonic Greek

1F00 ἀ GREEK SMALL LETTER ALPHA WITH PSILI
 ≡ 03B1 α 0313 ◌̓

1F01 ἁ GREEK SMALL LETTER ALPHA WITH DASIA
 ≡ 03B1 α 0314 ◌̔

1F02 ἂ GREEK SMALL LETTER ALPHA WITH PSILI AND VARIA
 ≡ 1F00 ἀ 0300 ◌̀

1F03 ἃ GREEK SMALL LETTER ALPHA WITH DASIA AND VARIA
 ≡ 1F01 ἁ 0300 ◌̀

1F04 ἄ GREEK SMALL LETTER ALPHA WITH PSILI AND OXIA
 ≡ 1F00 ἀ 0301 ◌́

1F05 ἅ GREEK SMALL LETTER ALPHA WITH DASIA AND OXIA
 ≡ 1F01 ἁ 0301 ◌́

1F06 ἆ GREEK SMALL LETTER ALPHA WITH PSILI AND PERISPOMENI
 ≡ 1F00 ἀ 0342 ◌͂

1F07 ἇ GREEK SMALL LETTER ALPHA WITH DASIA AND PERISPOMENI
 ≡ 1F01 ἁ 0342 ◌͂

1F08 Ἀ GREEK CAPITAL LETTER ALPHA WITH PSILI
 ≡ 0391 Α 0313 ◌̓

1F09 Ἁ GREEK CAPITAL LETTER ALPHA WITH DASIA
 ≡ 0391 Α 0314 ◌̔

1F0A Ἂ GREEK CAPITAL LETTER ALPHA WITH PSILI AND VARIA
 ≡ 1F08 Ἀ 0300 ◌̀

1F0B Ἃ GREEK CAPITAL LETTER ALPHA WITH DASIA AND VARIA
 ≡ 1F09 Ἁ 0300 ◌̀

1F0C Ἄ GREEK CAPITAL LETTER ALPHA WITH PSILI AND OXIA
 ≡ 1F08 Ἀ 0301 ◌́

1F0D Ἅ GREEK CAPITAL LETTER ALPHA WITH DASIA AND OXIA
 ≡ 1F09 Ἁ 0301 ◌́

1F0E Ἆ GREEK CAPITAL LETTER ALPHA WITH PSILI AND PERISPOMENI
 ≡ 1F08 Ἀ 0342 ◌͂

1F0F Ἇ GREEK CAPITAL LETTER ALPHA WITH DASIA AND PERISPOMENI
 ≡ 1F09 Ἁ 0342 ◌͂

1F10 ἐ GREEK SMALL LETTER EPSILON WITH PSILI
 ≡ 03B5 ε 0313 ◌̓

1F11 ἑ GREEK SMALL LETTER EPSILON WITH DASIA
 ≡ 03B5 ε 0314 ◌̔

1F12 ἒ GREEK SMALL LETTER EPSILON WITH PSILI AND VARIA
 ≡ 1F10 ἐ 0300 ◌̀

1F13 ἓ GREEK SMALL LETTER EPSILON WITH DASIA AND VARIA
 ≡ 1F11 ἑ 0300 ◌̀

1F14 ἔ GREEK SMALL LETTER EPSILON WITH PSILI AND OXIA
 ≡ 1F10 ἐ 0301 ◌́

1F15 ἕ GREEK SMALL LETTER EPSILON WITH DASIA AND OXIA
 ≡ 1F11 ἑ 0301 ◌́

1F16 <reserved>

1F17 <reserved>

1F18 Ἐ GREEK CAPITAL LETTER EPSILON WITH PSILI
 ≡ 0395 Ε 0313 ◌̓

1F19 Ἑ GREEK CAPITAL LETTER EPSILON WITH DASIA
 ≡ 0395 Ε 0314 ◌̔

1F1A Ἒ GREEK CAPITAL LETTER EPSILON WITH PSILI AND VARIA
 ≡ 1F18 Ἐ 0300 ◌̀

1F1B Ἓ GREEK CAPITAL LETTER EPSILON WITH DASIA AND VARIA
 ≡ 1F19 Ἑ 0300 ◌̀

1F1C Ἔ GREEK CAPITAL LETTER EPSILON WITH PSILI AND OXIA
 ≡ 1F18 Ἐ 0301 ◌́

1F1D Ἕ GREEK CAPITAL LETTER EPSILON WITH DASIA AND OXIA
 ≡ 1F19 Ἑ 0301 ◌́

1F1E <reserved>

1F1F <reserved>

1F20 ἠ GREEK SMALL LETTER ETA WITH PSILI
 ≡ 03B7 η 0313 ◌̓

1F21 ἡ GREEK SMALL LETTER ETA WITH DASIA
 ≡ 03B7 η 0314 ◌̔

1F22 ἢ GREEK SMALL LETTER ETA WITH PSILI AND VARIA
 ≡ 1F20 ἠ 0300 ◌̀

1F23 ἣ GREEK SMALL LETTER ETA WITH DASIA AND VARIA
 ≡ 1F21 ἡ 0300 ◌̀

1F24 ἤ GREEK SMALL LETTER ETA WITH PSILI AND OXIA
 ≡ 1F20 ἠ 0301 ◌́

1F25 ἥ GREEK SMALL LETTER ETA WITH DASIA AND OXIA
 ≡ 1F21 ἡ 0301 ◌́

1F26 ἦ GREEK SMALL LETTER ETA WITH PSILI AND PERISPOMENI
 ≡ 1F20 ἠ 0342 ◌͂

1F27 ἧ GREEK SMALL LETTER ETA WITH DASIA AND PERISPOMENI
 ≡ 1F21 ἡ 0342 ◌͂

1F28 Ἠ GREEK CAPITAL LETTER ETA WITH PSILI
 ≡ 0397 Η 0313 ◌̓

1F29 Ἡ GREEK CAPITAL LETTER ETA WITH DASIA
 ≡ 0397 Η 0314 ◌̔

1F2A Ἢ GREEK CAPITAL LETTER ETA WITH PSILI AND VARIA
 ≡ 1F28 Ἠ 0300 ◌̀

1F2B Ἣ GREEK CAPITAL LETTER ETA WITH DASIA AND VARIA
 ≡ 1F29 Ἡ 0300 ◌̀

1F2C Ἤ GREEK CAPITAL LETTER ETA WITH PSILI AND OXIA
 ≡ 1F28 Ἠ 0301 ◌́

1F2D Ἥ GREEK CAPITAL LETTER ETA WITH DASIA AND OXIA
 ≡ 1F29 Ἡ 0301 ◌́

1F2E Ἦ GREEK CAPITAL LETTER ETA WITH PSILI AND PERISPOMENI
 ≡ 1F28 Ἠ 0342 ◌͂

1F2F Ἧ GREEK CAPITAL LETTER ETA WITH DASIA AND PERISPOMENI
 ≡ 1F29 Ἡ 0342 ◌͂

1F30 ἰ GREEK SMALL LETTER IOTA WITH PSILI
 ≡ 03B9 ι 0313 ◌̓

1F31 ἱ GREEK SMALL LETTER IOTA WITH DASIA
 ≡ 03B9 ι 0314 ◌̔

1F32 ἲ GREEK SMALL LETTER IOTA WITH PSILI AND VARIA
≡ 1F30 ἰ 0300 ◌̀
1F33 ἳ GREEK SMALL LETTER IOTA WITH DASIA AND VARIA
≡ 1F31 ἱ 0300 ◌̀
1F34 ἴ GREEK SMALL LETTER IOTA WITH PSILI AND OXIA
≡ 1F30 ἰ 0301 ◌́
1F35 ἵ GREEK SMALL LETTER IOTA WITH DASIA AND OXIA
≡ 1F31 ἱ 0301 ◌́
1F36 ἶ GREEK SMALL LETTER IOTA WITH PSILI AND PERISPOMENI
≡ 1F30 ἰ 0342 ◌͂
1F37 ἷ GREEK SMALL LETTER IOTA WITH DASIA AND PERISPOMENI
≡ 1F31 ἱ 0342 ◌͂
1F38 Ἰ GREEK CAPITAL LETTER IOTA WITH PSILI
≡ 0399 Ι 0313 ◌̓
1F39 Ἱ GREEK CAPITAL LETTER IOTA WITH DASIA
≡ 0399 Ι 0314 ◌̔
1F3A Ἲ GREEK CAPITAL LETTER IOTA WITH PSILI AND VARIA
≡ 1F38 Ἰ 0300 ◌̀
1F3B Ἳ GREEK CAPITAL LETTER IOTA WITH DASIA AND VARIA
≡ 1F39 Ἱ 0300 ◌̀
1F3C Ἴ GREEK CAPITAL LETTER IOTA WITH PSILI AND OXIA
≡ 1F38 Ἰ 0301 ◌́
1F3D Ἵ GREEK CAPITAL LETTER IOTA WITH DASIA AND OXIA
≡ 1F39 Ἱ 0301 ◌́
1F3E Ἶ GREEK CAPITAL LETTER IOTA WITH PSILI AND PERISPOMENI
≡ 1F38 Ἰ 0342 ◌͂
1F3F Ἷ GREEK CAPITAL LETTER IOTA WITH DASIA AND PERISPOMENI
≡ 1F39 Ἱ 0342 ◌͂
1F40 ὀ GREEK SMALL LETTER OMICRON WITH PSILI
≡ 03BF ο 0313 ◌̓
1F41 ὁ GREEK SMALL LETTER OMICRON WITH DASIA
≡ 03BF ο 0314 ◌̔
1F42 ὂ GREEK SMALL LETTER OMICRON WITH PSILI AND VARIA
≡ 1F40 ὀ 0300 ◌̀
1F43 ὃ GREEK SMALL LETTER OMICRON WITH DASIA AND VARIA
≡ 1F41 ὁ 0300 ◌̀
1F44 ὄ GREEK SMALL LETTER OMICRON WITH PSILI AND OXIA
≡ 1F40 ὀ 0301 ◌́
1F45 ὅ GREEK SMALL LETTER OMICRON WITH DASIA AND OXIA
≡ 1F41 ὁ 0301 ◌́
1F46 <reserved>
1F47 <reserved>
1F48 Ὀ GREEK CAPITAL LETTER OMICRON WITH PSILI
≡ 039F Ο 0313 ◌̓
1F49 Ὁ GREEK CAPITAL LETTER OMICRON WITH DASIA
≡ 039F Ο 0314 ◌̔
1F4A Ὂ GREEK CAPITAL LETTER OMICRON WITH PSILI AND VARIA
≡ 1F48 Ὀ 0300 ◌̀
1F4B Ὃ GREEK CAPITAL LETTER OMICRON WITH DASIA AND VARIA
≡ 1F49 Ὁ 0300 ◌̀
1F4C Ὄ GREEK CAPITAL LETTER OMICRON WITH PSILI AND OXIA
≡ 1F48 Ὀ 0301 ◌́
1F4D Ὅ GREEK CAPITAL LETTER OMICRON WITH DASIA AND OXIA
≡ 1F49 Ὁ 0301 ◌́
1F4E <reserved>
1F4F <reserved>
1F50 ὐ GREEK SMALL LETTER UPSILON WITH PSILI
≡ 03C5 υ 0313 ◌̓
1F51 ὑ GREEK SMALL LETTER UPSILON WITH DASIA
≡ 03C5 υ 0314 ◌̔
1F52 ὒ GREEK SMALL LETTER UPSILON WITH PSILI AND VARIA
≡ 1F50 ὐ 0300 ◌̀
1F53 ὓ GREEK SMALL LETTER UPSILON WITH DASIA AND VARIA
≡ 1F51 ὑ 0300 ◌̀
1F54 ὔ GREEK SMALL LETTER UPSILON WITH PSILI AND OXIA
≡ 1F50 ὐ 0301 ◌́
1F55 ὕ GREEK SMALL LETTER UPSILON WITH DASIA AND OXIA
≡ 1F51 ὑ 0301 ◌́
1F56 ὖ GREEK SMALL LETTER UPSILON WITH PSILI AND PERISPOMENI
≡ 1F50 ὐ 0342 ◌͂
1F57 ὗ GREEK SMALL LETTER UPSILON WITH DASIA AND PERISPOMENI
≡ 1F51 ὑ 0342 ◌͂
1F58 <reserved>
1F59 Ὑ GREEK CAPITAL LETTER UPSILON WITH DASIA
≡ 03A5 Υ 0314 ◌̔
1F5A <reserved>
1F5B Ὓ GREEK CAPITAL LETTER UPSILON WITH DASIA AND VARIA
≡ 1F59 Ὑ 0300 ◌̀
1F5C <reserved>
1F5D Ὕ GREEK CAPITAL LETTER UPSILON WITH DASIA AND OXIA
≡ 1F59 Ὑ 0301 ◌́
1F5E <reserved>
1F5F Ὗ GREEK CAPITAL LETTER UPSILON WITH DASIA AND PERISPOMENI
≡ 1F59 Ὑ 0342 ◌͂
1F60 ὠ GREEK SMALL LETTER OMEGA WITH PSILI
≡ 03C9 ω 0313 ◌̓
1F61 ὡ GREEK SMALL LETTER OMEGA WITH DASIA
≡ 03C9 ω 0314 ◌̔
1F62 ὢ GREEK SMALL LETTER OMEGA WITH PSILI AND VARIA
≡ 1F60 ὠ 0300 ◌̀
1F63 ὣ GREEK SMALL LETTER OMEGA WITH DASIA AND VARIA
≡ 1F61 ὡ 0300 ◌̀
1F64 ὤ GREEK SMALL LETTER OMEGA WITH PSILI AND OXIA
≡ 1F60 ὠ 0301 ◌́
1F65 ὥ GREEK SMALL LETTER OMEGA WITH DASIA AND OXIA
≡ 1F61 ὡ 0301 ◌́

1F66 ὦ GREEK SMALL LETTER OMEGA WITH PSILI AND PERISPOMENI
≡ 1F60 ὠ 0342 ◌͂

1F67 ὧ GREEK SMALL LETTER OMEGA WITH DASIA AND PERISPOMENI
≡ 1F61 ὡ 0342 ◌͂

1F68 Ὠ GREEK CAPITAL LETTER OMEGA WITH PSILI
≡ 03A9 Ω 0313 ◌̓

1F69 Ὡ GREEK CAPITAL LETTER OMEGA WITH DASIA
≡ 03A9 Ω 0314 ◌̔

1F6A Ὢ GREEK CAPITAL LETTER OMEGA WITH PSILI AND VARIA
≡ 1F68 Ὠ 0300 ◌̀

1F6B Ὣ GREEK CAPITAL LETTER OMEGA WITH DASIA AND VARIA
≡ 1F69 Ὡ 0300 ◌̀

1F6C Ὤ GREEK CAPITAL LETTER OMEGA WITH PSILI AND OXIA
≡ 1F68 Ὠ 0301 ◌́

1F6D Ὥ GREEK CAPITAL LETTER OMEGA WITH DASIA AND OXIA
≡ 1F69 Ὡ 0301 ◌́

1F6E Ὦ GREEK CAPITAL LETTER OMEGA WITH PSILI AND PERISPOMENI
≡ 1F68 Ὠ 0342 ◌͂

1F6F Ὧ GREEK CAPITAL LETTER OMEGA WITH DASIA AND PERISPOMENI
≡ 1F69 Ὡ 0342 ◌͂

1F70 ὰ GREEK SMALL LETTER ALPHA WITH VARIA
≡ 03B1 α 0300 ◌̀

1F71 ά GREEK SMALL LETTER ALPHA WITH OXIA
≡ 03AC ά greek small letter alpha with tonos

1F72 ὲ GREEK SMALL LETTER EPSILON WITH VARIA
≡ 03B5 ε 0300 ◌̀

1F73 έ GREEK SMALL LETTER EPSILON WITH OXIA
≡ 03AD έ greek small letter epsilon with tonos

1F74 ὴ GREEK SMALL LETTER ETA WITH VARIA
≡ 03B7 η 0300 ◌̀

1F75 ή GREEK SMALL LETTER ETA WITH OXIA
≡ 03AE ή greek small letter eta with tonos

1F76 ὶ GREEK SMALL LETTER IOTA WITH VARIA
≡ 03B9 ι 0300 ◌̀

1F77 ί GREEK SMALL LETTER IOTA WITH OXIA
≡ 03AF ί greek small letter iota with tonos

1F78 ὸ GREEK SMALL LETTER OMICRON WITH VARIA
≡ 03BF ο 0300 ◌̀

1F79 ό GREEK SMALL LETTER OMICRON WITH OXIA
≡ 03CC ό greek small letter omicron with tonos

1F7A ὺ GREEK SMALL LETTER UPSILON WITH VARIA
≡ 03C5 υ 0300 ◌̀

1F7B ύ GREEK SMALL LETTER UPSILON WITH OXIA
≡ 03CD ύ greek small letter upsilon with tonos

1F7C ὼ GREEK SMALL LETTER OMEGA WITH VARIA
≡ 03C9 ω 0300 ◌̀

1F7D ώ GREEK SMALL LETTER OMEGA WITH OXIA
≡ 03CE ώ greek small letter omega with tonos

1F7E <reserved>

1F7F <reserved>

1F80 ᾀ GREEK SMALL LETTER ALPHA WITH PSILI AND YPOGEGRAMMENI
≡ 1F00 ἀ 0345 ◌ͅ

1F81 ᾁ GREEK SMALL LETTER ALPHA WITH DASIA AND YPOGEGRAMMENI
≡ 1F01 ἁ 0345 ◌ͅ

1F82 ᾂ GREEK SMALL LETTER ALPHA WITH PSILI AND VARIA AND YPOGEGRAMMENI
≡ 1F02 ἂ 0345 ◌ͅ

1F83 ᾃ GREEK SMALL LETTER ALPHA WITH DASIA AND VARIA AND YPOGEGRAMMENI
≡ 1F03 ἃ 0345 ◌ͅ

1F84 ᾄ GREEK SMALL LETTER ALPHA WITH PSILI AND OXIA AND YPOGEGRAMMENI
≡ 1F04 ἄ 0345 ◌ͅ

1F85 ᾅ GREEK SMALL LETTER ALPHA WITH DASIA AND OXIA AND YPOGEGRAMMENI
≡ 1F05 ἅ 0345 ◌ͅ

1F86 ᾆ GREEK SMALL LETTER ALPHA WITH PSILI AND PERISPOMENI AND YPOGEGRAMMENI
≡ 1F06 ἆ 0345 ◌ͅ

1F87 ᾇ GREEK SMALL LETTER ALPHA WITH DASIA AND PERISPOMENI AND YPOGEGRAMMENI
≡ 1F07 ἇ 0345 ◌ͅ

1F88 ᾈ GREEK CAPITAL LETTER ALPHA WITH PSILI AND PROSGEGRAMMENI
≡ 1F08 Ἀ 0345 ◌ͅ

1F89 ᾉ GREEK CAPITAL LETTER ALPHA WITH DASIA AND PROSGEGRAMMENI
≡ 1F09 Ἁ 0345 ◌ͅ

1F8A ᾊ GREEK CAPITAL LETTER ALPHA WITH PSILI AND VARIA AND PROSGEGRAMMENI
≡ 1F0A Ἂ 0345 ◌ͅ

1F8B ᾋ GREEK CAPITAL LETTER ALPHA WITH DASIA AND VARIA AND PROSGEGRAMMENI
≡ 1F0B Ἃ 0345 ◌ͅ

1F8C ᾌ GREEK CAPITAL LETTER ALPHA WITH PSILI AND OXIA AND PROSGEGRAMMENI
≡ 1F0C Ἄ 0345 ◌ͅ

1F8D ᾍ GREEK CAPITAL LETTER ALPHA WITH DASIA AND OXIA AND PROSGEGRAMMENI
≡ 1F0D Ἅ 0345 ◌ͅ

1F8E ᾎ GREEK CAPITAL LETTER ALPHA WITH PSILI AND PERISPOMENI AND PROSGEGRAMMENI
≡ 1F0E Ἆ 0345 ◌ͅ

1F8F ᾏ GREEK CAPITAL LETTER ALPHA WITH DASIA AND PERISPOMENI AND PROSGEGRAMMENI
≡ 1F0F Ἇ 0345 ◌ͅ

1F90 ᾐ GREEK SMALL LETTER ETA WITH PSILI AND YPOGEGRAMMENI
≡ 1F20 ἠ 0345 ◌ͅ

1F91 ᾑ GREEK SMALL LETTER ETA WITH DASIA AND YPOGEGRAMMENI
≡ 1F21 ἡ 0345 ◌ͅ

1F92 ᾒ GREEK SMALL LETTER ETA WITH PSILI AND VARIA AND YPOGEGRAMMENI
≡ 1F22 ἢ 0345 ◌ͅ

1F93 ᾓ GREEK SMALL LETTER ETA WITH DASIA AND VARIA AND YPOGEGRAMMENI
≡ 1F23 ἣ 0345 ◌ͅ

1F94 ᾔ GREEK SMALL LETTER ETA WITH PSILI AND OXIA AND YPOGEGRAMMENI
≡ 1F24 ἤ 0345 ◌ͅ

1F95 ᾕ GREEK SMALL LETTER ETA WITH DASIA AND OXIA AND YPOGEGRAMMENI
≡ 1F25 ἥ 0345 ◌ͅ

1F96 ᾖ GREEK SMALL LETTER ETA WITH PSILI AND PERISPOMENI AND YPOGEGRAMMENI
≡ 1F26 ἦ 0345 ◌ͅ

1F97 ᾗ GREEK SMALL LETTER ETA WITH DASIA AND PERISPOMENI AND YPOGEGRAMMENI
≡ 1F27 ἧ 0345 ◌ͅ

1F98 ᾘ GREEK CAPITAL LETTER ETA WITH PSILI AND PROSGEGRAMMENI
≡ 1F28 Ἠ 0345 ◌ͅ

1F99 ᾙ GREEK CAPITAL LETTER ETA WITH DASIA AND PROSGEGRAMMENI
≡ 1F29 Ἡ 0345 ◌ͅ

1F9A ᾚ GREEK CAPITAL LETTER ETA WITH PSILI AND VARIA AND PROSGEGRAMMENI
≡ 1F2A Ἢ 0345 ◌ͅ

1F9B ᾛ GREEK CAPITAL LETTER ETA WITH DASIA AND VARIA AND PROSGEGRAMMENI
≡ 1F2B Ἣ 0345 ◌ͅ

1F9C ᾜ GREEK CAPITAL LETTER ETA WITH PSILI AND OXIA AND PROSGEGRAMMENI
≡ 1F2C Ἤ 0345 ◌ͅ

1F9D ᾝ GREEK CAPITAL LETTER ETA WITH DASIA AND OXIA AND PROSGEGRAMMENI
≡ 1F2D Ἥ 0345 ◌ͅ

1F9E ᾞ GREEK CAPITAL LETTER ETA WITH PSILI AND PERISPOMENI AND PROSGEGRAMMENI
≡ 1F2E Ἦ 0345 ◌ͅ

1F9F ᾟ GREEK CAPITAL LETTER ETA WITH DASIA AND PERISPOMENI AND PROSGEGRAMMENI
≡ 1F2F Ἧ 0345 ◌ͅ

1FA0 ᾠ GREEK SMALL LETTER OMEGA WITH PSILI AND YPOGEGRAMMENI
≡ 1F60 ὠ 0345 ◌ͅ

1FA1 ᾡ GREEK SMALL LETTER OMEGA WITH DASIA AND YPOGEGRAMMENI
≡ 1F61 ὡ 0345 ◌ͅ

1FA2 ᾢ GREEK SMALL LETTER OMEGA WITH PSILI AND VARIA AND YPOGEGRAMMENI
≡ 1F62 ὢ 0345 ◌ͅ

1FA3 ᾣ GREEK SMALL LETTER OMEGA WITH DASIA AND VARIA AND YPOGEGRAMMENI
≡ 1F63 ὣ 0345 ◌ͅ

1FA4 ᾤ GREEK SMALL LETTER OMEGA WITH PSILI AND OXIA AND YPOGEGRAMMENI
≡ 1F64 ὤ 0345 ◌ͅ

1FA5 ᾥ GREEK SMALL LETTER OMEGA WITH DASIA AND OXIA AND YPOGEGRAMMENI
≡ 1F65 ὥ 0345 ◌ͅ

1FA6 ᾦ GREEK SMALL LETTER OMEGA WITH PSILI AND PERISPOMENI AND YPOGEGRAMMENI
≡ 1F66 ὦ 0345 ◌ͅ

1FA7 ᾧ GREEK SMALL LETTER OMEGA WITH DASIA AND PERISPOMENI AND YPOGEGRAMMENI
≡ 1F67 ὧ 0345 ◌ͅ

1FA8 ᾨ GREEK CAPITAL LETTER OMEGA WITH PSILI AND PROSGEGRAMMENI
≡ 1F68 Ὠ 0345 ◌ͅ

1FA9 ᾩ GREEK CAPITAL LETTER OMEGA WITH DASIA AND PROSGEGRAMMENI
≡ 1F69 Ὡ 0345 ◌ͅ

1FAA ᾪ GREEK CAPITAL LETTER OMEGA WITH PSILI AND VARIA AND PROSGEGRAMMENI
≡ 1F6A Ὢ 0345 ◌ͅ

1FAB ᾫ GREEK CAPITAL LETTER OMEGA WITH DASIA AND VARIA AND PROSGEGRAMMENI
≡ 1F6B Ὣ 0345 ◌ͅ

1FAC ᾬ GREEK CAPITAL LETTER OMEGA WITH PSILI AND OXIA AND PROSGEGRAMMENI
≡ 1F6C Ὤ 0345 ◌ͅ

1FAD ᾭ GREEK CAPITAL LETTER OMEGA WITH DASIA AND OXIA AND PROSGEGRAMMENI
≡ 1F6D Ὥ 0345 ◌ͅ

1FAE ᾮ GREEK CAPITAL LETTER OMEGA WITH PSILI AND PERISPOMENI AND PROSGEGRAMMENI
≡ 1F6E Ὦ 0345 ◌ͅ

1FAF ᾯ GREEK CAPITAL LETTER OMEGA WITH DASIA AND PERISPOMENI AND PROSGEGRAMMENI
≡ 1F6F Ὧ 0345 ◌ͅ

1FB0 ᾰ GREEK SMALL LETTER ALPHA WITH VRACHY
≡ 03B1 α 0306 ◌̆

1FB1 ᾱ GREEK SMALL LETTER ALPHA WITH MACRON
≡ 03B1 α 0304 ◌̄

1FB2 ᾲ GREEK SMALL LETTER ALPHA WITH VARIA AND YPOGEGRAMMENI
≡ 1F70 ὰ 0345 ◌ͅ

1FB3 ᾳ GREEK SMALL LETTER ALPHA WITH YPOGEGRAMMENI
≡ 03B1 α 0345 ◌ͅ

1FB4 ᾴ GREEK SMALL LETTER ALPHA WITH OXIA AND YPOGEGRAMMENI
≡ 03AC ά 0345 ◌ͅ

1FB5 <reserved>

1FB6 ᾶ GREEK SMALL LETTER ALPHA WITH PERISPOMENI
≡ 03B1 α 0342 ◌͂

1FB7 ᾷ GREEK SMALL LETTER ALPHA WITH PERISPOMENI AND YPOGEGRAMMENI
≡ 1FB6 ᾶ 0345 ◌ͅ

1FB8 Ᾰ GREEK CAPITAL LETTER ALPHA WITH VRACHY
≡ 0391 Α 0306 ◌̆

1FB9 Ᾱ GREEK CAPITAL LETTER ALPHA WITH MACRON
≡ 0391 Α 0304 ◌̄

1FBA Ὰ GREEK CAPITAL LETTER ALPHA WITH VARIA
≡ 0391 Α 0300 ◌̀

1FBB Ά GREEK CAPITAL LETTER ALPHA WITH OXIA
≡ 0386 Ά greek capital letter alpha with tonos

1FBC ᾼ GREEK CAPITAL LETTER ALPHA WITH PROSGEGRAMMENI
≡ 0391 Α 0345 ◌ͅ

1FBD ᾽ GREEK KORONIS
≈ 0020 SP 0313 ◌̓

1FBE ι GREEK PROSGEGRAMMENI
≡ 03B9 ι greek small letter iota

1FBF ᾿ GREEK PSILI
≈ 0020 SP 0313 ◌̓

1FC0 ῀ GREEK PERISPOMENI
≈ 0020 SP 0342 ◌͂

1FC1 ῁ GREEK DIALYTIKA AND PERISPOMENI
≡ 00A8 ¨ 0342 ◌͂

1FC2 ῂ GREEK SMALL LETTER ETA WITH VARIA AND YPOGEGRAMMENI
≡ 1F74 ὴ 0345 ◌ͅ

1FC3 ῃ GREEK SMALL LETTER ETA WITH YPOGEGRAMMENI
≡ 03B7 η 0345 ◌ͅ

1FC4 ῄ GREEK SMALL LETTER ETA WITH OXIA AND YPOGEGRAMMENI
≡ 03AE ή 0345 ◌ͅ

1FC5 <reserved>

1FC6 ῆ GREEK SMALL LETTER ETA WITH PERISPOMENI
≡ 03B7 η 0342 ◌͂

1FC7 ῇ GREEK SMALL LETTER ETA WITH PERISPOMENI AND YPOGEGRAMMENI
≡ 1FC6 ῆ 0345 ◌ͅ

1FC8 Ὲ GREEK CAPITAL LETTER EPSILON WITH VARIA
≡ 0395 Ε 0300 ◌̀

1FC9 Έ GREEK CAPITAL LETTER EPSILON WITH OXIA
≡ 0388 Έ greek capital letter epsilon with tonos

1FCA Ὴ GREEK CAPITAL LETTER ETA WITH VARIA
≡ 0397 Η 0300 ◌̀

1FCB Ή GREEK CAPITAL LETTER ETA WITH OXIA
≡ 0389 Ή greek capital letter eta with tonos

1FCC ῌ GREEK CAPITAL LETTER ETA WITH PROSGEGRAMMENI
≡ 0397 Η 0345 ◌ͅ

1FCD ῍ GREEK PSILI AND VARIA
≡ 1FBF ᾿ 0300 ◌̀

1FCE ῎ GREEK PSILI AND OXIA
≡ 1FBF ᾿ 0301 ◌́

1FCF ῏ GREEK PSILI AND PERISPOMENI
≡ 1FBF ᾿ 0342 ◌͂

1FD0 ῐ GREEK SMALL LETTER IOTA WITH VRACHY
≡ 03B9 ι 0306 ◌̆

1FD1 ῑ GREEK SMALL LETTER IOTA WITH MACRON
≡ 03B9 ι 0304 ◌̄

1FD2 ῒ GREEK SMALL LETTER IOTA WITH DIALYTIKA AND VARIA
≡ 03CA ϊ 0300 ◌̀

1FD3 ΐ GREEK SMALL LETTER IOTA WITH DIALYTIKA AND OXIA
≡ 0390 ΐ greek small letter iota with dialytika and tonos

1FD4 <reserved>

1FD5 <reserved>

1FD6 ῖ GREEK SMALL LETTER IOTA WITH PERISPOMENI
≡ 03B9 ι 0342 ◌͂

1FD7 ῗ GREEK SMALL LETTER IOTA WITH DIALYTIKA AND PERISPOMENI
≡ 03CA ϊ 0342 ◌͂

1FD8 Ῐ GREEK CAPITAL LETTER IOTA WITH VRACHY
≡ 0399 Ι 0306 ◌̆

1FD9 Ῑ GREEK CAPITAL LETTER IOTA WITH MACRON
≡ 0399 Ι 0304 ◌̄

1FDA Ὶ GREEK CAPITAL LETTER IOTA WITH VARIA
≡ 0399 Ι 0300 ◌̀

1FDB Ί GREEK CAPITAL LETTER IOTA WITH OXIA
≡ 038A Ί greek capital letter iota with tonos

1FDC <reserved>

1FDD ῝ GREEK DASIA AND VARIA
≡ 1FFE ῾ 0300 ◌̀

1FDE ῞ GREEK DASIA AND OXIA
≡ 1FFE ῾ 0301 ◌́

1FDF ῟ GREEK DASIA AND PERISPOMENI
≡ 1FFE ῾ 0342 ◌͂

1FE0 ῠ GREEK SMALL LETTER UPSILON WITH VRACHY
≡ 03C5 υ 0306 ◌̆

1FE1 ῡ GREEK SMALL LETTER UPSILON WITH MACRON
≡ 03C5 υ 0304 ◌̄

1FE2 ῢ GREEK SMALL LETTER UPSILON WITH DIALYTIKA AND VARIA
≡ 03CB ϋ 0300 ◌̀

1FE3 ΰ GREEK SMALL LETTER UPSILON WITH DIALYTIKA AND OXIA
≡ 03B0 ΰ greek small letter upsilon with dialytika and tonos

1FE4 ῤ GREEK SMALL LETTER RHO WITH PSILI
≡ 03C1 ρ 0313 ◌̓

1FE5 ῥ GREEK SMALL LETTER RHO WITH DASIA
≡ 03C1 ρ 0314 ◌̔

1FE6 ῦ GREEK SMALL LETTER UPSILON WITH PERISPOMENI
≡ 03C5 υ 0342 ◌͂

1FE7 ῧ GREEK SMALL LETTER UPSILON WITH DIALYTIKA AND PERISPOMENI
≡ 03CB ϋ 0342 ◌͂

1FE8 Ῠ GREEK CAPITAL LETTER UPSILON WITH VRACHY
≡ 03A5 Υ 0306 ◌̆

1FE9 Ῡ GREEK CAPITAL LETTER UPSILON WITH MACRON
≡ 03A5 Υ 0304 ◌̄

1FEA Ὺ GREEK CAPITAL LETTER UPSILON WITH VARIA
≡ 03A5 Υ 0300 ◌̀

1FEB Ύ GREEK CAPITAL LETTER UPSILON WITH OXIA
≡ 038E Ύ greek capital letter upsilon with tonos

1FEC Ῥ GREEK CAPITAL LETTER RHO WITH DASIA
≡ 03A1 Ρ 0314 ◌̔

1FED ῭ GREEK DIALYTIKA AND VARIA
≡ 00A8 ¨ 0300 ◌̀

1FEE ΅ GREEK DIALYTIKA AND OXIA
≡ 0385 ΅ greek dialytika tonos

1FEF ` GREEK VARIA
≡ 0060 ` grave accent

1FF0 <reserved>

1FF1 <reserved>

1FF2 ῲ GREEK SMALL LETTER OMEGA WITH VARIA AND YPOGEGRAMMENI
≡ 1F7C ὼ 0345 ◌ͅ

1FF3 ῳ GREEK SMALL LETTER OMEGA WITH YPOGEGRAMMENI
≡ 03C9 ω 0345 ◌ͅ

1FF4 ῴ GREEK SMALL LETTER OMEGA WITH OXIA AND YPOGEGRAMMENI
≡ 03CE ώ 0345 ◌ͅ

1FF5 <reserved>

1FF6 ῶ GREEK SMALL LETTER OMEGA WITH PERISPOMENI
≡ 03C9 ω 0342 ◌͂

1FF7 ῷ GREEK SMALL LETTER OMEGA WITH PERISPOMENI AND YPOGEGRAMMENI
≡ 1FF6 ῶ 0345 ◌ͅ

1FF8 Ὸ GREEK CAPITAL LETTER OMICRON WITH VARIA
≡ 039F Ο 0300 ◌̀

1FF9 Ό GREEK CAPITAL LETTER OMICRON WITH OXIA
≡ 038C Ό greek capital letter omicron with tonos

1FFA Ὼ GREEK CAPITAL LETTER OMEGA WITH VARIA
≡ 03A9 Ω 0300 ◌̀

1FFB Ώ GREEK CAPITAL LETTER OMEGA WITH OXIA
≡ 038F Ώ greek capital letter omega with tonos

1FFC ῼ GREEK CAPITAL LETTER OMEGA WITH PROSGEGRAMMENI
≡ 03A9 Ω 0345 ◌ͅ

1FFD ´ GREEK OXIA
≡ 00B4 ´ acute accent

1FFE ῾ GREEK DASIA
≈ 0020 SP 0314 ◌̔

	200	201	202	203	204	205	206
0	NQ SP 2000	‐ 2010	† 2020	‰ 2030	⁀ 2040	⁐ 2050	WJ 2060
1	MQ SP 2001	NB ‑ 2011	‡ 2021	‱ 2031	⁁ 2041	⁑ 2051	f() 2061
2	EN SP 2002	‒ 2012	• 2022	′ 2032	⁂ 2042	⁒ 2052	× 2062
3	EM SP 2003	– 2013	‣ 2023	″ 2033	⁃ 2043	⁓ 2053	, 2063
4	3/M SP 2004	— 2014	․ 2024	‴ 2034	⁄ 2044	⁔ 2054	
5	4/M SP 2005	― 2015	‥ 2025	‵ 2035	⁅ 2045	⁕ 2055	
6	6/M SP 2006	‖ 2016	… 2026	‶ 2036	⁆ 2046	⁖ 2056	
7	F SP 2007	‗ 2017	‧ 2027	‷ 2037	⁇ 2047	⁗ 2057	
8	P SP 2008	‘ 2018	L SEP 2028	‸ 2038	⁈ 2048	⁘ 2058	
9	TH SP 2009	’ 2019	P SEP 2029	‹ 2039	⁉ 2049	⁙ 2059	
A	H SP 200A	‚ 201A	LRE 202A	› 203A	⁊ 204A	⁚ 205A	I SS 206A
B	ZW SP 200B	‛ 201B	RLE 202B	※ 203B	⁋ 204B	⁛ 205B	A SS 206B
C	ZW NJ 200C	“ 201C	PDF 202C	‼ 203C	⁌ 204C	⁜ 205C	I AFS 206C
D	ZW J 200D	” 201D	LRO 202D	‽ 203D	⁍ 204D	⁝ 205D	A AFS 206D
E	LRM 200E	„ 201E	RLO 202E	‾ 203E	⁎ 204E	⁞ 205E	NA DS 206E
F	RLM 200F	‟ 201F	NNB SP 202F	‿ 203F	⁏ 204F	MM SP 205F	NO DS 206F

For additional general punctuation characters see also Basic Latin, Latin-1, Supplemental Punctuation and CJK Symbols and Punctuation.

Spaces

2000 NQSP EN QUAD
- ≡ 2002 ENSP en space

2001 MQSP EM QUAD
- = mutton quad
- ≡ 2003 EMSP em space

2002 ENSP EN SPACE
- = nut
- • half an em
- ≈ 0020 SP space

2003 EMSP EM SPACE
- = mutton
- • nominally, a space equal to the type size in points
- • may scale by the condensation factor of a font
- ≈ 0020 SP space

2004 3/MSP THREE-PER-EM SPACE
- = thick space
- ≈ 0020 SP space

2005 4/MSP FOUR-PER-EM SPACE
- = mid space
- ≈ 0020 SP space

2006 6/MSP SIX-PER-EM SPACE
- • in computer typography sometimes equated to thin space
- ≈ 0020 SP space

2007 FSP FIGURE SPACE
- • space equal to tabular width of a font
- • this is equivalent to the digit width of fonts with fixed-width digits
- ≈ <noBreak> 0020 SP

2008 PSP PUNCTUATION SPACE
- • space equal to narrow punctuation of a font
- ≈ 0020 SP space

2009 THSP THIN SPACE
- • a fifth of an em (or sometimes a sixth)
- ≈ 0020 SP space

200A HSP HAIR SPACE
- • thinner than a thin space
- • in traditional typography, the thinnest space available
- ≈ 0020 SP space

200B ZWSP ZERO WIDTH SPACE
- • commonly abbreviated ZWSP
- • this character is intended for line break control; it has no width, but its presence between two characters does not prevent increased letter spacing in justification

Format characters

200C ZWNJ ZERO WIDTH NON-JOINER
- • commonly abbreviated ZWNJ

200D ZWJ ZERO WIDTH JOINER
- • commonly abbreviated ZWJ

200E LRM LEFT-TO-RIGHT MARK
- • commonly abbreviated LRM

200F RLM RIGHT-TO-LEFT MARK
- • commonly abbreviated RLM

Dashes

2010 ‐ HYPHEN
- → 002D - hyphen-minus
- → 00AD SHY soft hyphen

2011 NB NON-BREAKING HYPHEN
- → 002D - hyphen-minus
- → 00AD SHY soft hyphen
- ≈ <noBreak> 2010 ‐

2012 ‒ FIGURE DASH

2013 – EN DASH

2014 — EM DASH
- • may be used in pairs to offset parenthetical text
- → 30FC ー katakana-hiragana prolonged sound mark

2015 ― HORIZONTAL BAR
- = quotation dash
- • long dash introducing quoted text

General punctuation

2016 ‖ DOUBLE VERTICAL LINE
- • used in pairs to indicate norm of a matrix
- → 20E6 ⃦ combining double vertical stroke overlay
- → 2225 ∥ parallel to

2017 ‗ DOUBLE LOW LINE
- • this is a spacing character
- → 005F _ low line
- → 0333 ̳ combining double low line
- ≈ 0020 SP 0333 ̳

2018 ‘ LEFT SINGLE QUOTATION MARK
- = single turned comma quotation mark
- • this is the preferred character (as opposed to 201B ‛)
- → 0027 ' apostrophe
- → 02BB ʻ modifier letter turned comma
- → 275B ❛ heavy single turned comma quotation mark ornament

2019 ’ RIGHT SINGLE QUOTATION MARK
- = single comma quotation mark
- • this is the preferred character to use for apostrophe
- → 0027 ' apostrophe
- → 02BC ʼ modifier letter apostrophe
- → 275C ❜ heavy single comma quotation mark ornament

201A ‚ SINGLE LOW-9 QUOTATION MARK
- = low single comma quotation mark
- • used as opening single quotation mark in some languages

201B ‛ SINGLE HIGH-REVERSED-9 QUOTATION MARK
- = single reversed comma quotation mark
- • has same semantic as 2018 ‘, but differs in appearance
- → 02BD ʽ modifier letter reversed comma

201C “ LEFT DOUBLE QUOTATION MARK
- = double turned comma quotation mark
- • this is the preferred character (as opposed to 201F ‟)
- → 0022 " quotation mark
- → 275D ❝ heavy double turned comma quotation mark ornament
- → 301D 〝 reversed double prime quotation mark

201D ” RIGHT DOUBLE QUOTATION MARK
= double comma quotation mark
→ 0022 " quotation mark
→ 2033 ″ double prime
→ 275E ❞ heavy double comma quotation mark ornament
→ 301E 〞 double prime quotation mark

201E „ DOUBLE LOW-9 QUOTATION MARK
= low double comma quotation mark
• used as opening double quotation mark in some languages
→ 301F 〟 low double prime quotation mark

201F ‟ DOUBLE HIGH-REVERSED-9 QUOTATION MARK
= double reversed comma quotation mark
• has same semantic as 201C “ , but differs in appearance

2020 † DAGGER
= obelisk, obelus, long cross

2021 ‡ DOUBLE DAGGER
= diesis, double obelisk

2022 • BULLET
= black small circle
→ 00B7 · middle dot
→ 2024 . one dot leader
→ 2219 ∙ bullet operator
→ 25D8 ◘ inverse bullet
→ 25E6 ◦ white bullet

2023 ‣ TRIANGULAR BULLET
→ 220E ∎ end of proof
→ 25B8 ▸ black right-pointing small triangle

2024 . ONE DOT LEADER
• also used as an Armenian semicolon (mijaket)
→ 00B7 · middle dot
→ 2022 • bullet
→ 2219 ∙ bullet operator
≈ 002E . full stop

2025 ‥ TWO DOT LEADER
≈ 002E . 002E .

2026 … HORIZONTAL ELLIPSIS
= three dot leader
→ 22EE ⋮ vertical ellipsis
→ FE19 ︙ presentation form for vertical horizontal ellipsis
≈ 002E . 002E . 002E .

2027 ‧ HYPHENATION POINT

Format characters

2028 [LSEP] LINE SEPARATOR
• may be used to represent this semantic unambiguously

2029 [PSEP] PARAGRAPH SEPARATOR
• may be used to represent this semantic unambiguously

202A [LRE] LEFT-TO-RIGHT EMBEDDING
• commonly abbreviated LRE

202B [RLE] RIGHT-TO-LEFT EMBEDDING
• commonly abbreviated RLE

202C [PDF] POP DIRECTIONAL FORMATTING
• commonly abbreviated PDF

202D [LRO] LEFT-TO-RIGHT OVERRIDE
• commonly abbreviated LRO

202E [RLO] RIGHT-TO-LEFT OVERRIDE
• commonly abbreviated RLO

202F [NNBSP] NARROW NO-BREAK SPACE
• commonly abbreviated NNBSP
→ 00A0 [NBSP] no-break space
≈ <noBreak> 0020 [SP]

General punctuation

2030 ‰ PER MILLE SIGN
= permille, per thousand
• used, for example, in measures of blood alcohol content, salinity, etc.
→ 0025 % percent sign

2031 ‱ PER TEN THOUSAND SIGN
= permyriad
• percent of a percent, rarely used
→ 0025 % percent sign

2032 ′ PRIME
= minutes, feet
→ 0027 ' apostrophe
→ 00B4 ´ acute accent
→ 02B9 ʹ modifier letter prime

2033 ″ DOUBLE PRIME
= seconds, inches
→ 0022 " quotation mark
→ 02BA ʺ modifier letter double prime
→ 201D ” right double quotation mark
→ 3003 〃 ditto mark
→ 301E 〞 double prime quotation mark
≈ 2032 ′ 2032 ′

2034 ‴ TRIPLE PRIME
= lines (old measure, 1/12 of an inch)
≈ 2032 ′ 2032 ′ 2032 ′

2035 ‵ REVERSED PRIME
→ 0060 ` grave accent

2036 ‶ REVERSED DOUBLE PRIME
→ 301D 〝 reversed double prime quotation mark
≈ 2035 ‵ 2035 ‵

2037 ‷ REVERSED TRIPLE PRIME
≈ 2035 ‵ 2035 ‵ 2035 ‵

2038 ‸ CARET
→ 2303 ⌃ up arrowhead

2039 ‹ SINGLE LEFT-POINTING ANGLE QUOTATION MARK
= left pointing single guillemet
• usually opening, sometimes closing
→ 003C < less-than sign
→ 2329 〈 left-pointing angle bracket
→ 3008 〈 left angle bracket

203A › SINGLE RIGHT-POINTING ANGLE QUOTATION MARK
= right pointing single guillemet
• usually closing, sometimes opening
→ 003E > greater-than sign
→ 232A 〉 right-pointing angle bracket
→ 3009 〉 right angle bracket

203B ※ REFERENCE MARK
= Japanese kome
= Urdu paragraph separator
→ 0FBF ྿ tibetan ku ru kha bzhi mig can
→ 200AD 𠂭 cjk unified ideograph-200AD

Double punctuation for vertical text

203C ‼ DOUBLE EXCLAMATION MARK
→ 0021 ! exclamation mark
≈ 0021 ! 0021 !

General punctuation

203D ‽ INTERROBANG
→ 0021 ! exclamation mark
→ 003F ? question mark

203E ‾ OVERLINE
= spacing overscore
≈ 0020 SP 0305 ◌̅

203F ‿ UNDERTIE
= Greek enotikon
→ 2323 ⌣ smile

2040 ⁀ CHARACTER TIE
= z notation sequence concatenation
→ 2322 ⌢ frown

2041 ⁁ CARET INSERTION POINT
• proofreader's mark: insert here
→ 22CC ⋌ right semidirect product

2042 ⁂ ASTERISM

2043 ⁃ HYPHEN BULLET

2044 ⁄ FRACTION SLASH
= solidus (in typography)
• for composing arbitrary fractions
→ 002F / solidus
→ 2215 ∕ division slash

2045 ⁅ LEFT SQUARE BRACKET WITH QUILL

2046 ⁆ RIGHT SQUARE BRACKET WITH QUILL

Double punctuation for vertical text

2047 ⁇ DOUBLE QUESTION MARK
≈ 003F ? 003F ?

2048 ⁈ QUESTION EXCLAMATION MARK
≈ 003F ? 0021 !

2049 ⁉ EXCLAMATION QUESTION MARK
≈ 0021 ! 003F ?

General punctuation

204A ⁊ TIRONIAN SIGN ET
• Irish Gaelic, Old English, ...
→ 0026 & ampersand

204B ⁋ REVERSED PILCROW SIGN
→ 00B6 ¶ pilcrow sign

204C ⁌ BLACK LEFTWARDS BULLET

204D ⁍ BLACK RIGHTWARDS BULLET

204E ⁎ LOW ASTERISK
→ 002A * asterisk
→ 0359 ◌͙ combining asterisk below

204F ⁏ REVERSED SEMICOLON
→ 003B ; semicolon

2050 ⁐ CLOSE UP
• editing mark

2051 ⁑ TWO ASTERISKS ALIGNED VERTICALLY

2052 ⁒ COMMERCIAL MINUS SIGN
= abzüglich (German), med avdrag av (Swedish), piska (Swedish, "whip")
• a common glyph variant and fallback representation looks like ./.
• may also be used as a dingbat to indicate correctness
• used in Finno-Ugric Phonetic Alphabet to indicate a related borrowed form with different sound
→ 0025 % percent sign
→ 066A ٪ arabic percent sign

2053 ⁓ SWUNG DASH
→ 007E ~ tilde

2054 ⁔ INVERTED UNDERTIE

2055 ⁕ FLOWER PUNCTUATION MARK
= phul, puspika
• used as a punctuation mark with Syloti Nagri, Bengali and other Indic scripts
→ 274B ❋ heavy eight teardrop-spoked propeller asterisk

Archaic punctuation

2056 ⁖ THREE DOT PUNCTUATION

General punctuation

2057 ⁗ QUADRUPLE PRIME
≈ 2032 ′ 2032 ′ 2032 ′ 2032 ′

Archaic punctuation

2058 ⁘ FOUR DOT PUNCTUATION

2059 ⁙ FIVE DOT PUNCTUATION
= Greek pentonkion
= quincunx
→ 2684 ⚄ die face-5

205A ⁚ TWO DOT PUNCTUATION
• historically used to indicate the end of a sentence or change of speaker
• extends from baseline to cap height
→ FE30 ︰ presentation form for vertical two dot leader
→ 1015B 𐅛 greek acrophonic epidaurean two

205B ⁛ FOUR DOT MARK
• used by scribes in the margin as highlighter mark
• this is centered on the line, but extends beyond top and bottom of the line

205C ⁜ DOTTED CROSS
• used by scribes in the margin as highlighter mark

205D ⁝ TRICOLON
= Epidaurean acrophonic symbol three
→ 22EE ⋮ vertical ellipsis
→ 2AF6 ⫶ triple colon operator
→ FE19 ︙ presentation form for vertical horizontal ellipsis

205E ⁞ VERTICAL FOUR DOTS
• used in dictionaries to indicate legal but undesirable word break
• glyph extends the whole height of the line

Space

205F MMSP MEDIUM MATHEMATICAL SPACE
• abbreviated MMSP
• four-eighteenths of an em
≈ 0020 SP space

Format character

2060 WJ WORD JOINER
• commonly abbreviated WJ
• a zero width non-breaking space (only)
• intended for disambiguation of functions for byte order mark
→ FEFF ZWNBSP zero width no-break space

Invisible operators

2061 f() FUNCTION APPLICATION
• contiguity operator indicating application of a function

2062 × INVISIBLE TIMES
• contiguity operator indicating multiplication

2063 ⁣ INVISIBLE SEPARATOR
= invisible comma
• contiguity operator indicating that adjacent mathematical symbols form a list, e.g. when no visible comma is used between multiple indices

Deprecated

206A INHIBIT SYMMETRIC SWAPPING
206B ACTIVATE SYMMETRIC SWAPPING
206C INHIBIT ARABIC FORM SHAPING
206D ACTIVATE ARABIC FORM SHAPING
206E NATIONAL DIGIT SHAPES
206F NOMINAL DIGIT SHAPES

	207	208	209
0	^{0} 2070	$_{0}$ 2080	$_{a}$ 2090
1	^{i} 2071	$_{1}$ 2081	$_{e}$ 2091
2		$_{2}$ 2082	$_{o}$ 2092
3		$_{3}$ 2083	$_{x}$ 2093
4	^{4} 2074	$_{4}$ 2084	$_{ə}$ 2094
5	^{5} 2075	$_{5}$ 2085	
6	^{6} 2076	$_{6}$ 2086	
7	^{7} 2077	$_{7}$ 2087	
8	^{8} 2078	$_{8}$ 2088	
9	^{9} 2079	$_{9}$ 2089	
A	$^{+}$ 207A	$_{+}$ 208A	
B	$^{-}$ 207B	$_{-}$ 208B	
C	$^{=}$ 207C	$_{=}$ 208C	
D	$^{(}$ 207D	$_{(}$ 208D	
E	$^{)}$ 207E	$_{)}$ 208E	
F	^{n} 207F		

Superscripts

2070 ^{0} SUPERSCRIPT ZERO
≈ <super> 0030 0

2071 ^{i} SUPERSCRIPT LATIN SMALL LETTER I
≈ <super> 0069 i

2072 <reserved>
→ 00B2 ^{2} superscript two

2073 <reserved>
→ 00B3 ^{3} superscript three

2074 ^{4} SUPERSCRIPT FOUR
≈ <super> 0034 4

2075 ^{5} SUPERSCRIPT FIVE
≈ <super> 0035 5

2076 ^{6} SUPERSCRIPT SIX
≈ <super> 0036 6

2077 ^{7} SUPERSCRIPT SEVEN
≈ <super> 0037 7

2078 ^{8} SUPERSCRIPT EIGHT
≈ <super> 0038 8

2079 ^{9} SUPERSCRIPT NINE
≈ <super> 0039 9

207A $^{+}$ SUPERSCRIPT PLUS SIGN
≈ <super> 002B +

207B $^{-}$ SUPERSCRIPT MINUS
≈ <super> 2212 −

207C $^{=}$ SUPERSCRIPT EQUALS SIGN
≈ <super> 003D =

207D $^{(}$ SUPERSCRIPT LEFT PARENTHESIS
≈ <super> 0028 (

207E $^{)}$ SUPERSCRIPT RIGHT PARENTHESIS
≈ <super> 0029)

207F ^{n} SUPERSCRIPT LATIN SMALL LETTER N
≈ <super> 006E n

Subscripts

2080 $_{0}$ SUBSCRIPT ZERO
≈ <sub> 0030 0

2081 $_{1}$ SUBSCRIPT ONE
≈ <sub> 0031 1

2082 $_{2}$ SUBSCRIPT TWO
≈ <sub> 0032 2

2083 $_{3}$ SUBSCRIPT THREE
≈ <sub> 0033 3

2084 $_{4}$ SUBSCRIPT FOUR
≈ <sub> 0034 4

2085 $_{5}$ SUBSCRIPT FIVE
≈ <sub> 0035 5

2086 $_{6}$ SUBSCRIPT SIX
≈ <sub> 0036 6

2087 $_{7}$ SUBSCRIPT SEVEN
≈ <sub> 0037 7

2088 $_{8}$ SUBSCRIPT EIGHT
≈ <sub> 0038 8

2089 $_{9}$ SUBSCRIPT NINE
≈ <sub> 0039 9

208A $_{+}$ SUBSCRIPT PLUS SIGN
≈ <sub> 002B +

208B $_{-}$ SUBSCRIPT MINUS
≈ <sub> 2212 −

208C $_{=}$ SUBSCRIPT EQUALS SIGN
≈ <sub> 003D =

208D $_{(}$ SUBSCRIPT LEFT PARENTHESIS
≈ <sub> 0028 (

208E $_{)}$ SUBSCRIPT RIGHT PARENTHESIS
≈ <sub> 0029)

208F <reserved>

2090 $_{a}$ LATIN SUBSCRIPT SMALL LETTER A
≈ <sub> 0061 a

2091 $_{e}$ LATIN SUBSCRIPT SMALL LETTER E
≈ <sub> 0065 e

2092 $_{o}$ LATIN SUBSCRIPT SMALL LETTER O
≈ <sub> 006F o

2093 $_{x}$ LATIN SUBSCRIPT SMALL LETTER X
≈ <sub> 0078 x

2094 $_{ə}$ LATIN SUBSCRIPT SMALL LETTER SCHWA
≈ <sub> 0259 ə

	20A	20B	20C
0	₠ 20A0	₰ 20B0	
1	₡ 20A1	₱ 20B1	
2	₢ 20A2	₲ 20B2	
3	₣ 20A3	₳ 20B3	
4	₤ 20A4	₴ 20B4	
5	₥ 20A5	₵ 20B5	
6	₦ 20A6		
7	₧ 20A7		
8	₨ 20A8		
9	₩ 20A9		
A	₪ 20AA		
B	₫ 20AB		
C	€ 20AC		
D	₭ 20AD		
E	₮ 20AE		
F	₯ 20AF		

Currency symbols

A number of currency symbols are found in other blocks. Fullwidth versions of some currency symbols are found in the Halfwidth and Fullwidth Forms block.

→ 0024 $ dollar sign
→ 00A2 ¢ cent sign
→ 00A3 £ pound sign
→ 00A4 ¤ currency sign
→ 00A5 ¥ yen sign
→ 0192 ƒ latin small letter f with hook
→ 060B ؋ afghani sign
→ 09F2 ৲ bengali rupee mark
→ 09F3 ৳ bengali rupee sign
→ 0AF1 ૱ gujarati rupee sign
→ 0BF9 ௹ tamil rupee sign
→ 0E3F ฿ thai currency symbol baht
→ 17DB ៛ khmer currency symbol riel
→ 2133 ℳ script capital m
→ 5143 元 cjk unified ideograph-5143
→ 5186 円 cjk unified ideograph-5186
→ 5706 圆 cjk unified ideograph-5706
→ 5713 圓 cjk unified ideograph-5713
→ FDFC ﷼ rial sign

20A0 ₠ EURO-CURRENCY SIGN
- intended for ECU, but not widely used
- historical character; this is NOT the euro!

→ 20AC € euro sign

20A1 ₡ COLON SIGN
- Costa Rica, El Salvador

20A2 ₢ CRUZEIRO SIGN
- Brazil

20A3 ₣ FRENCH FRANC SIGN
- France

20A4 ₤ LIRA SIGN
- intended for lira, but not widely used
- preferred character for lira is 00A3 £

→ 00A3 £ pound sign

20A5 ₥ MILL SIGN
- USA (1/10 cent)

20A6 ₦ NAIRA SIGN
- Nigeria

20A7 ₧ PESETA SIGN
- Spain

→ 20B1 ₱ peso sign

20A8 ₨ RUPEE SIGN
- India

≈ 0052 R 0073 s

20A9 ₩ WON SIGN
- Korea

20AA ₪ NEW SHEQEL SIGN
- Israel

20AB ₫ DONG SIGN
- Vietnam

20AC € EURO SIGN
- currency sign for the European Monetary Union
- euro, not ecu

→ 20A0 ₠ euro-currency sign

20AD ₭ KIP SIGN
- Laos

20AE ₮ TUGRIK SIGN
- Mongolia
- also transliterated as tugrug, tugric, tugrog, togrog, tögrög

20AF ₯ DRACHMA SIGN
- Greece

20B0 ₰ GERMAN PENNY SIGN

20B1 ₱ PESO SIGN
- Philippines
- the Mexican peso is indicated with the dollar sign

→ 20A7 ₧ peseta sign

20B2 ₲ GUARANI SIGN
- Paraguay
- Often represented by G. or Gs.

20B3 ₳ AUSTRAL SIGN
- former Argentinian currency

20B4 ₴ HRYVNIA SIGN
- Ukraine

20B5 ₵ CEDI SIGN
- Ghana
- glyph may look like 'Ȼ' or like C with a short vertical stroke through the upper arm

→ 00A2 ¢ cent sign
→ 023B Ȼ latin capital letter c with stroke

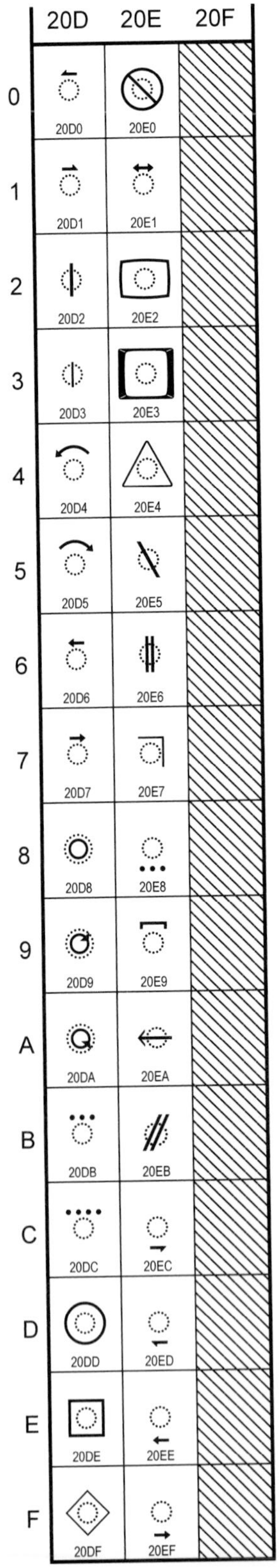

	20D	20E	20F
0	20D0	20E0	
1	20D1	20E1	
2	20D2	20E2	
3	20D3	20E3	
4	20D4	20E4	
5	20D5	20E5	
6	20D6	20E6	
7	20D7	20E7	
8	20D8	20E8	
9	20D9	20E9	
A	20DA	20EA	
B	20DB	20EB	
C	20DC	20EC	
D	20DD	20ED	
E	20DE	20EE	
F	20DF	20EF	

Combining diacritical marks for symbols

20D0 ⃐ COMBINING LEFT HARPOON ABOVE
20D1 ⃑ COMBINING RIGHT HARPOON ABOVE
• vector
20D2 ⃒ COMBINING LONG VERTICAL LINE OVERLAY
• negation
20D3 ⃓ COMBINING SHORT VERTICAL LINE OVERLAY
• occasional variant for negation
20D4 ⃔ COMBINING ANTICLOCKWISE ARROW ABOVE
20D5 ⃕ COMBINING CLOCKWISE ARROW ABOVE
• rotation
20D6 ⃖ COMBINING LEFT ARROW ABOVE
20D7 ⃗ COMBINING RIGHT ARROW ABOVE
• vector
20D8 ⃘ COMBINING RING OVERLAY
20D9 ⃙ COMBINING CLOCKWISE RING OVERLAY
20DA ⃚ COMBINING ANTICLOCKWISE RING OVERLAY
20DB ⃛ COMBINING THREE DOTS ABOVE
= third derivative
20DC ⃜ COMBINING FOUR DOTS ABOVE
= fourth derivative

Enclosing diacritics

20DD ⃝ COMBINING ENCLOSING CIRCLE
= JIS composition circle
= Cyrillic combining ten thousands sign
→ 25CB ○ white circle
→ 25EF ◯ large circle
→ 3007 〇 ideographic number zero
20DE ⃞ COMBINING ENCLOSING SQUARE
→ 25A1 □ white square
20DF ⃟ COMBINING ENCLOSING DIAMOND
→ 25C7 ◇ white diamond
20E0 ⃠ COMBINING ENCLOSING CIRCLE BACKSLASH
• prohibition

Additional diacritical mark for symbols

20E1 ⃡ COMBINING LEFT RIGHT ARROW ABOVE
• tensor

Additional enclosing diacritics

20E2 ⃢ COMBINING ENCLOSING SCREEN
→ 239A ⎚ clear screen symbol
20E3 ⃣ COMBINING ENCLOSING KEYCAP
20E4 ⃤ COMBINING ENCLOSING UPWARD POINTING TRIANGLE
→ 25B3 △ white up-pointing triangle

Additional diacritical marks for symbols

20E5 ⃥ COMBINING REVERSE SOLIDUS OVERLAY
→ 005C \ reverse solidus
20E6 ⃦ COMBINING DOUBLE VERTICAL STROKE OVERLAY
= z notation finite function diacritic
→ 2016 ‖ double vertical line
20E7 ⃧ COMBINING ANNUITY SYMBOL
= actuarial bend
→ 2309 ⌉ right ceiling
20E8 ⃨ COMBINING TRIPLE UNDERDOT
20E9 ⃩ COMBINING WIDE BRIDGE ABOVE
= contraction operator
• extends the full width of the base character
→ 0346 ͆ combining bridge above
20EA ⃪ COMBINING LEFTWARDS ARROW OVERLAY
→ 2190 ← leftwards arrow
20EB ⃫ COMBINING LONG DOUBLE SOLIDUS OVERLAY
= long double slash overlay
20EC ⃬ COMBINING RIGHTWARDS HARPOON WITH BARB DOWNWARDS
20ED ⃭ COMBINING LEFTWARDS HARPOON WITH BARB DOWNWARDS
20EE ⃮ COMBINING LEFT ARROW BELOW
20EF ⃯ COMBINING RIGHT ARROW BELOW

	210	211	212	213	214
0	℀ 2100	ℐ 2110	℠ 2120	ℰ 2130	⅀ 2140
1	℁ 2101	ℑ 2111	℡ 2121	ℱ 2131	⅁ 2141
2	ℂ 2102	ℒ 2112	™ 2122	Ⅎ 2132	⅂ 2142
3	℃ 2103	ℓ 2113	℣ 2123	ℳ 2133	⅃ 2143
4	℄ 2104	℔ 2114	ℤ 2124	ℴ 2134	⅄ 2144
5	℅ 2105	ℕ 2115	℥ 2125	ℵ 2135	ⅅ 2145
6	℆ 2106	№ 2116	Ω 2126	ℶ 2136	ⅆ 2146
7	ℇ 2107	℗ 2117	℧ 2127	ℷ 2137	ⅇ 2147
8	℈ 2108	℘ 2118	ℨ 2128	ℸ 2138	ⅈ 2148
9	℉ 2109	ℙ 2119	℩ 2129	ℹ 2139	ⅉ 2149
A	ℊ 210A	ℚ 211A	K 212A	℺ 213A	⅊ 214A
B	ℋ 210B	ℛ 211B	Å 212B	℻ 213B	⅋ 214B
C	ℌ 210C	ℜ 211C	ℬ 212C	ℼ 213C	⅌ 214C
D	ℍ 210D	ℝ 211D	ℭ 212D	ℽ 213D	⅍ 214D
E	ℎ 210E	℞ 211E	℮ 212E	ℾ 213E	ⅎ 214E
F	ℏ 210F	℟ 211F	ℯ 212F	ℿ 213F	

Letterlike symbols

Some of the letterlike symbols are intended to complete the set of mathematical alphanumeric symbols starting at U+1D400.

2100 ℀ ACCOUNT OF
≈ 0061 a 002F / 0063 c

2101 ℁ ADDRESSED TO THE SUBJECT
→ 214D ⅍ aktieselskab
≈ 0061 a 002F / 0073 s

2102 ℂ DOUBLE-STRUCK CAPITAL C
= the set of complex numbers
≈ <font> 0043 C latin capital letter c

2103 ℃ DEGREE CELSIUS
= degrees Centigrade
≈ 00B0 ° 0043 C

2104 ℄ CENTRE LINE SYMBOL
= clone

2105 ℅ CARE OF
≈ 0063 c 002F / 006F o

2106 ℆ CADA UNA
≈ 0063 c 002F / 0075 u

2107 ℇ EULER CONSTANT
→ 0045 E latin capital letter e
≈ 0190 Ɛ latin capital letter open e

2108 ℈ SCRUPLE

2109 ℉ DEGREE FAHRENHEIT
≈ 00B0 ° 0046 F

210A ℊ SCRIPT SMALL G
= real number symbol
≈ <font> 0067 g latin small letter g

210B ℋ SCRIPT CAPITAL H
= Hamiltonian operator
≈ <font> 0048 H latin capital letter h

210C ℌ BLACK-LETTER CAPITAL H
= Hilbert space
≈ <font> 0048 H latin capital letter h

210D ℍ DOUBLE-STRUCK CAPITAL H
≈ <font> 0048 H latin capital letter h

210E ℎ PLANCK CONSTANT
= height, specific enthalpy, ...
• simply a mathematical italic h; this character's name results from legacy usage
≈ <font> 0068 h latin small letter h

210F ℏ PLANCK CONSTANT OVER TWO PI
→ 045B ћ cyrillic small letter tshe
≈ <font> 0127 ħ latin small letter h with stroke

2110 ℐ SCRIPT CAPITAL I
≈ <font> 0049 I latin capital letter i

2111 ℑ BLACK-LETTER CAPITAL I
= imaginary part
≈ <font> 0049 I latin capital letter i

2112 ℒ SCRIPT CAPITAL L
= Laplace transform
≈ <font> 004C L latin capital letter l

2113 ℓ SCRIPT SMALL L
= mathematical symbol 'ell'
= liter (traditional symbol)
• despite its character name, this symbol is derived from a special italicized version of the small letter l
• the SI recommended symbol for liter is 006C l
→ 1D4C1 𝓁 mathematical script small l
≈ <font> 006C l latin small letter l

2114 ℔ L B BAR SYMBOL
= pounds
→ 0023 # number sign

2115 ℕ DOUBLE-STRUCK CAPITAL N
= natural number
≈ <font> 004E N latin capital letter n

2116 № NUMERO SIGN
≈ 004E N 006F o

2117 ℗ SOUND RECORDING COPYRIGHT
= published
= phonorecord sign
→ 00A9 © copyright sign
→ 24C5 Ⓟ circled latin capital letter p

2118 ℘ SCRIPT CAPITAL P
= Weierstrass elliptic function
• actually this has the form of a lowercase calligraphic p, despite its name

2119 ℙ DOUBLE-STRUCK CAPITAL P
≈ <font> 0050 P latin capital letter p

211A ℚ DOUBLE-STRUCK CAPITAL Q
= the set of rational numbers
≈ <font> 0051 Q latin capital letter q

211B ℛ SCRIPT CAPITAL R
= Riemann Integral
≈ <font> 0052 R latin capital letter r

211C ℜ BLACK-LETTER CAPITAL R
= real part
≈ <font> 0052 R latin capital letter r

211D ℝ DOUBLE-STRUCK CAPITAL R
= the set of real numbers
≈ <font> 0052 R latin capital letter r

211E ℞ PRESCRIPTION TAKE
= recipe
= cross ratio

211F ℟ RESPONSE

2120 ℠ SERVICE MARK
≈ <super> 0053 S 004D M

2121 ℡ TELEPHONE SIGN
• typical forms for this symbol may use lower case, small caps or superscripted letter shapes
→ 260E ☎ black telephone
→ 2706 ✆ telephone location sign
≈ 0054 T 0045 E 004C L

2122 ™ TRADE MARK SIGN
≈ <super> 0054 T 004D M

2123 ℣ VERSICLE

2124 ℤ DOUBLE-STRUCK CAPITAL Z
= the set of integers
≈ <font> 005A Z latin capital letter z

2125 ℥ OUNCE SIGN
→ 021D ȝ latin small letter yogh

2126 Ω OHM SIGN
• SI unit of resistance, named after G. S. Ohm, German physicist
• preferred representation is 03A9 Ω
≡ 03A9 Ω greek capital letter omega

2127 ℧ INVERTED OHM SIGN
= mho
• archaic unit of conductance (= the SI unit siemens)
• typographically a turned greek capital letter omega
→ 01B1 Ʊ latin capital letter upsilon
→ 03A9 Ω greek capital letter omega

2128 ℨ BLACK-LETTER CAPITAL Z
≈ <font> 005A Z latin capital letter z

2129 ℩ TURNED GREEK SMALL LETTER IOTA
- unique element fulfilling a description (logic)
- → 03B9 ι greek small letter iota

212A K KELVIN SIGN
- ≡ 004B K latin capital letter k

212B Å ANGSTROM SIGN
- non SI length unit (=0.1 nm) named after A. J. Ångström, Swedish physicist
- preferred representation is 00C5 Å
- ≡ 00C5 Å latin capital letter a with ring above

212C ℬ SCRIPT CAPITAL B
- = Bernoulli function
- ≈ <font> 0042 B latin capital letter b

212D ℭ BLACK-LETTER CAPITAL C
- ≈ <font> 0043 C latin capital letter c

212E ℮ ESTIMATED SYMBOL
- used in European packaging
- → 0065 e latin small letter e

212F ℯ SCRIPT SMALL E
- = error
- = natural exponent
- ≈ <font> 0065 e latin small letter e

2130 ℰ SCRIPT CAPITAL E
- = emf (electromotive force)
- ≈ <font> 0045 E latin capital letter e

2131 ℱ SCRIPT CAPITAL F
- = Fourier transform
- ≈ <font> 0046 F latin capital letter f

2132 Ⅎ TURNED CAPITAL F
- = Claudian digamma inversum
- lowercase is 214E ⅎ
- → 0046 F latin capital letter f
- → 03DC Ϝ greek letter digamma

2133 ℳ SCRIPT CAPITAL M
- = M-matrix (physics)
- = German Mark currency symbol, before WWII
- ≈ <font> 004D M latin capital letter m

2134 ℴ SCRIPT SMALL O
- = order, of inferior order to
- ≈ <font> 006F o latin small letter o

Hebrew letterlike math symbols

These are left-to-right characters.

2135 ℵ ALEF SYMBOL
- = first transfinite cardinal (countable)
- ≈ 05D0 א hebrew letter alef

2136 ℶ BET SYMBOL
- = second transfinite cardinal (the continuum)
- ≈ 05D1 ב hebrew letter bet

2137 ℷ GIMEL SYMBOL
- = third transfinite cardinal (functions of a real variable)
- ≈ 05D2 ג hebrew letter gimel

2138 ℸ DALET SYMBOL
- = fourth transfinite cardinal
- ≈ 05D3 ד hebrew letter dalet

Additional letterlike symbols

2139 ℹ INFORMATION SOURCE
- intended for use with 20DD⃝
- ≈ <font> 0069 i latin small letter i

213A ℺ ROTATED CAPITAL Q
- a binding signature mark

213B ℻ FACSIMILE SIGN
- typical forms for this symbol may use lower case, small caps or superscripted letter shapes
- → 2121 ℡ telephone sign
- ≈ 0046 F 0041 A 0058 X

213C ℼ DOUBLE-STRUCK SMALL PI
- ≈ <font> 03C0 π greek small letter pi

213D ℽ DOUBLE-STRUCK SMALL GAMMA
- ≈ <font> 03B3 γ greek small letter gamma

213E ℾ DOUBLE-STRUCK CAPITAL GAMMA
- ≈ <font> 0393 Γ greek capital letter gamma

213F ℿ DOUBLE-STRUCK CAPITAL PI
- ≈ <font> 03A0 Π greek capital letter pi

Double-struck large operator

2140 ⅀ DOUBLE-STRUCK N-ARY SUMMATION
- ≈ <font> 2211 ∑ n-ary summation

Additional letterlike symbols

2141 ⅁ TURNED SANS-SERIF CAPITAL G
- = game

2142 ⅂ TURNED SANS-SERIF CAPITAL L

2143 ⅃ REVERSED SANS-SERIF CAPITAL L

2144 ⅄ TURNED SANS-SERIF CAPITAL Y

Double-struck italic math symbols

These stylized mathematical symbols are used in some documents to distinguish special mathematical usages from ordinary variables.

2145 ⅅ DOUBLE-STRUCK ITALIC CAPITAL D
- sometimes used for the differential
- ≈ <font> 0044 D latin capital letter d

2146 ⅆ DOUBLE-STRUCK ITALIC SMALL D
- sometimes used for the differential
- ≈ <font> 0064 d latin small letter d

2147 ⅇ DOUBLE-STRUCK ITALIC SMALL E
- sometimes used for the natural exponent
- ≈ <font> 0065 e latin small letter e

2148 ⅈ DOUBLE-STRUCK ITALIC SMALL I
- sometimes used for the imaginary unit
- ≈ <font> 0069 i latin small letter i

2149 ⅉ DOUBLE-STRUCK ITALIC SMALL J
- sometimes used for the imaginary unit
- ≈ <font> 006A j latin small letter j

Additional letterlike symbols

214A ⅊ PROPERTY LINE

214B ⅋ TURNED AMPERSAND
- used in linear logic
- → 0026 & ampersand

214C ⅌ PER SIGN
- abbreviates the word 'per'

214D ⅍ AKTIESELSKAB
- → 2101 ℁ addressed to the subject

Lowercase Claudian letter

Claudian letters in inscriptions are uppercase, but may be transcribed by scholars in lowercase.

214E ⅎ TURNED SMALL F
- uppercase is 2132 Ⅎ
- → 03DD ϝ greek small letter digamma

	215	216	217	218
0		Ⅰ 2160	ⅰ 2170	ↀ 2180
1		Ⅱ 2161	ⅱ 2171	ↁ 2181
2		Ⅲ 2162	ⅲ 2172	ↂ 2182
3	⅓ 2153	Ⅳ 2163	ⅳ 2173	Ↄ 2183
4	⅔ 2154	Ⅴ 2164	ⅴ 2174	ↄ 2184
5	⅕ 2155	Ⅵ 2165	ⅵ 2175	
6	⅖ 2156	Ⅶ 2166	ⅶ 2176	
7	⅗ 2157	Ⅷ 2167	ⅷ 2177	
8	⅘ 2158	Ⅸ 2168	ⅸ 2178	
9	⅙ 2159	Ⅹ 2169	ⅹ 2179	
A	⅚ 215A	Ⅺ 216A	ⅺ 217A	
B	⅛ 215B	Ⅻ 216B	ⅻ 217B	
C	⅜ 215C	Ⅼ 216C	ⅼ 217C	
D	⅝ 215D	Ⅽ 216D	ⅽ 217D	
E	⅞ 215E	Ⅾ 216E	ⅾ 217E	
F	⅟ 215F	Ⅿ 216F	ⅿ 217F	

Fractions

Other fraction number forms are found in the Latin-1 Supplement block.

→ 00BC ¼ vulgar fraction one quarter
→ 00BD ½ vulgar fraction one half
→ 00BE ¾ vulgar fraction three quarters

2153 ⅓ VULGAR FRACTION ONE THIRD
≈ <fraction> 0031 1 2044 ⁄ 0033 3

2154 ⅔ VULGAR FRACTION TWO THIRDS
≈ <fraction> 0032 2 2044 ⁄ 0033 3

2155 ⅕ VULGAR FRACTION ONE FIFTH
≈ <fraction> 0031 1 2044 ⁄ 0035 5

2156 ⅖ VULGAR FRACTION TWO FIFTHS
≈ <fraction> 0032 2 2044 ⁄ 0035 5

2157 ⅗ VULGAR FRACTION THREE FIFTHS
≈ <fraction> 0033 3 2044 ⁄ 0035 5

2158 ⅘ VULGAR FRACTION FOUR FIFTHS
≈ <fraction> 0034 4 2044 ⁄ 0035 5

2159 ⅙ VULGAR FRACTION ONE SIXTH
≈ <fraction> 0031 1 2044 ⁄ 0036 6

215A ⅚ VULGAR FRACTION FIVE SIXTHS
≈ <fraction> 0035 5 2044 ⁄ 0036 6

215B ⅛ VULGAR FRACTION ONE EIGHTH
≈ <fraction> 0031 1 2044 ⁄ 0038 8

215C ⅜ VULGAR FRACTION THREE EIGHTHS
≈ <fraction> 0033 3 2044 ⁄ 0038 8

215D ⅝ VULGAR FRACTION FIVE EIGHTHS
≈ <fraction> 0035 5 2044 ⁄ 0038 8

215E ⅞ VULGAR FRACTION SEVEN EIGHTHS
≈ <fraction> 0037 7 2044 ⁄ 0038 8

215F ⅟ FRACTION NUMERATOR ONE
≈ <fraction> 0031 1 2044 ⁄

Roman numerals

2160 Ⅰ ROMAN NUMERAL ONE
≈ 0049 I latin capital letter i

2161 Ⅱ ROMAN NUMERAL TWO
≈ 0049 I 0049 I

2162 Ⅲ ROMAN NUMERAL THREE
≈ 0049 I 0049 I 0049 I

2163 Ⅳ ROMAN NUMERAL FOUR
≈ 0049 I 0056 V

2164 Ⅴ ROMAN NUMERAL FIVE
≈ 0056 V latin capital letter v

2165 Ⅵ ROMAN NUMERAL SIX
≈ 0056 V 0049 I

2166 Ⅶ ROMAN NUMERAL SEVEN
≈ 0056 V 0049 I 0049 I

2167 Ⅷ ROMAN NUMERAL EIGHT
≈ 0056 V 0049 I 0049 I 0049 I

2168 Ⅸ ROMAN NUMERAL NINE
≈ 0049 I 0058 X

2169 Ⅹ ROMAN NUMERAL TEN
≈ 0058 X latin capital letter x

216A Ⅺ ROMAN NUMERAL ELEVEN
≈ 0058 X 0049 I

216B Ⅻ ROMAN NUMERAL TWELVE
≈ 0058 X 0049 I 0049 I

216C Ⅼ ROMAN NUMERAL FIFTY
≈ 004C L latin capital letter l

216D Ⅽ ROMAN NUMERAL ONE HUNDRED
≈ 0043 C latin capital letter c

216E Ⅾ ROMAN NUMERAL FIVE HUNDRED
≈ 0044 D latin capital letter d

216F Ⅿ ROMAN NUMERAL ONE THOUSAND
≈ 004D M latin capital letter m

2170 ⅰ SMALL ROMAN NUMERAL ONE
≈ 0069 i latin small letter i

2171 ⅱ SMALL ROMAN NUMERAL TWO
≈ 0069 i 0069 i

2172 ⅲ SMALL ROMAN NUMERAL THREE
≈ 0069 i 0069 i 0069 i

2173 ⅳ SMALL ROMAN NUMERAL FOUR
≈ 0069 i 0076 v

2174 ⅴ SMALL ROMAN NUMERAL FIVE
≈ 0076 v latin small letter v

2175 ⅵ SMALL ROMAN NUMERAL SIX
≈ 0076 v 0069 i

2176 ⅶ SMALL ROMAN NUMERAL SEVEN
≈ 0076 v 0069 i 0069 i

2177 ⅷ SMALL ROMAN NUMERAL EIGHT
≈ 0076 v 0069 i 0069 i 0069 i

2178 ⅸ SMALL ROMAN NUMERAL NINE
≈ 0069 i 0078 x

2179 ⅹ SMALL ROMAN NUMERAL TEN
≈ 0078 x latin small letter x

217A ⅺ SMALL ROMAN NUMERAL ELEVEN
≈ 0078 x 0069 i

217B ⅻ SMALL ROMAN NUMERAL TWELVE
≈ 0078 x 0069 i 0069 i

217C ⅼ SMALL ROMAN NUMERAL FIFTY
≈ 006C l latin small letter l

217D ⅽ SMALL ROMAN NUMERAL ONE HUNDRED
≈ 0063 c latin small letter c

217E ⅾ SMALL ROMAN NUMERAL FIVE HUNDRED
≈ 0064 d latin small letter d

217F ⅿ SMALL ROMAN NUMERAL ONE THOUSAND
≈ 006D m latin small letter m

2180 ↀ ROMAN NUMERAL ONE THOUSAND C D

2181 ↁ ROMAN NUMERAL FIVE THOUSAND

2182 ↂ ROMAN NUMERAL TEN THOUSAND

2183 Ↄ ROMAN NUMERAL REVERSED ONE HUNDRED
= apostrophic C
= Claudian antisigma
• used in combination with C and I to form large numbers
• lowercase is 2184 ↄ
→ 03FD Ͻ greek capital reversed lunate sigma symbol

Lowercase Claudian letter

Claudian letters in inscriptions are uppercase, but may be transcribed by scholars in lowercase.

2184 ↄ LATIN SMALL LETTER REVERSED C
→ 037B ͻ greek small reversed lunate sigma symbol

	219	21A	21B	21C	21D	21E	21F
0	← 2190	↠ 21A0	↰ 21B0	⇀ 21C0	⇐ 21D0	⇠ 21E0	⇰ 21F0
1	↑ 2191	↡ 21A1	↱ 21B1	⇁ 21C1	⇑ 21D1	⇡ 21E1	⇱ 21F1
2	→ 2192	↢ 21A2	↲ 21B2	⇂ 21C2	⇒ 21D2	⇢ 21E2	⇲ 21F2
3	↓ 2193	↣ 21A3	↳ 21B3	⇃ 21C3	⇓ 21D3	⇣ 21E3	⇳ 21F3
4	↔ 2194	↤ 21A4	↴ 21B4	⇄ 21C4	⇔ 21D4	⇤ 21E4	⇴ 21F4
5	↕ 2195	↥ 21A5	↵ 21B5	⇅ 21C5	⇕ 21D5	⇥ 21E5	⇵ 21F5
6	↖ 2196	↦ 21A6	↶ 21B6	⇆ 21C6	⇖ 21D6	⇦ 21E6	⇶ 21F6
7	↗ 2197	↧ 21A7	↷ 21B7	⇇ 21C7	⇗ 21D7	⇧ 21E7	⇷ 21F7
8	↘ 2198	↨ 21A8	↸ 21B8	⇈ 21C8	⇘ 21D8	⇨ 21E8	⇸ 21F8
9	↙ 2199	↩ 21A9	↹ 21B9	⇉ 21C9	⇙ 21D9	⇩ 21E9	⇹ 21F9
A	↚ 219A	↪ 21AA	↺ 21BA	⇊ 21CA	⇚ 21DA	⇪ 21EA	⇺ 21FA
B	↛ 219B	↫ 21AB	↻ 21BB	⇋ 21CB	⇛ 21DB	⇫ 21EB	⇻ 21FB
C	↜ 219C	↬ 21AC	↼ 21BC	⇌ 21CC	⇜ 21DC	⇬ 21EC	⇼ 21FC
D	↝ 219D	↭ 21AD	↽ 21BD	⇍ 21CD	⇝ 21DD	⇭ 21ED	⇽ 21FD
E	↞ 219E	↮ 21AE	↾ 21BE	⇎ 21CE	⇞ 21DE	⇮ 21EE	⇾ 21FE
F	↟ 219F	↯ 21AF	↿ 21BF	⇏ 21CF	⇟ 21DF	⇯ 21EF	⇿ 21FF

Simple arrows

2190 ← LEFTWARDS ARROW
→ 20EA ⃪ combining leftwards arrow overlay
2191 ↑ UPWARDS ARROW
• IPA: egressive airflow
2192 → RIGHTWARDS ARROW
= z notation total function
2193 ↓ DOWNWARDS ARROW
• IPA: ingressive airflow
2194 ↔ LEFT RIGHT ARROW
= z notation relation
2195 ↕ UP DOWN ARROW
2196 ↖ NORTH WEST ARROW
2197 ↗ NORTH EAST ARROW
2198 ↘ SOUTH EAST ARROW
2199 ↙ SOUTH WEST ARROW

Arrows with modifications

219A ↚ LEFTWARDS ARROW WITH STROKE
• negation of 2190 ←
≡ 2190 ← 0338 ̸
219B ↛ RIGHTWARDS ARROW WITH STROKE
• negation of 2192 →
≡ 2192 → 0338 ̸
219C ↜ LEFTWARDS WAVE ARROW
219D ↝ RIGHTWARDS WAVE ARROW
219E ↞ LEFTWARDS TWO HEADED ARROW
= fast cursor left
219F ↟ UPWARDS TWO HEADED ARROW
= fast cursor up
21A0 ↠ RIGHTWARDS TWO HEADED ARROW
= z notation total surjection
= fast cursor right
21A1 ↡ DOWNWARDS TWO HEADED ARROW
= form feed
= fast cursor down
21A2 ↢ LEFTWARDS ARROW WITH TAIL
21A3 ↣ RIGHTWARDS ARROW WITH TAIL
= z notation total injection
21A4 ↤ LEFTWARDS ARROW FROM BAR
21A5 ↥ UPWARDS ARROW FROM BAR
21A6 ↦ RIGHTWARDS ARROW FROM BAR
= z notation maplet
21A7 ↧ DOWNWARDS ARROW FROM BAR
= depth symbol
21A8 ↨ UP DOWN ARROW WITH BASE
21A9 ↩ LEFTWARDS ARROW WITH HOOK
21AA ↪ RIGHTWARDS ARROW WITH HOOK
21AB ↫ LEFTWARDS ARROW WITH LOOP
21AC ↬ RIGHTWARDS ARROW WITH LOOP
21AD ↭ LEFT RIGHT WAVE ARROW
21AE ↮ LEFT RIGHT ARROW WITH STROKE
• negation of 2194 ↔
≡ 2194 ↔ 0338 ̸
21AF ↯ DOWNWARDS ZIGZAG ARROW
= electrolysis

Arrows with bent tips

Other arrows with bent tips to complete this set can be found in the Miscellaneous Symbols and Arrows block.

21B0 ↰ UPWARDS ARROW WITH TIP LEFTWARDS
21B1 ↱ UPWARDS ARROW WITH TIP RIGHTWARDS
21B2 ↲ DOWNWARDS ARROW WITH TIP LEFTWARDS
21B3 ↳ DOWNWARDS ARROW WITH TIP RIGHTWARDS

Keyboard symbols and circle arrows

21B4 ↴ RIGHTWARDS ARROW WITH CORNER DOWNWARDS
= line feed
21B5 ↵ DOWNWARDS ARROW WITH CORNER LEFTWARDS
• may indicate a carriage return or new line
→ 23CE ⏎ return symbol
21B6 ↶ ANTICLOCKWISE TOP SEMICIRCLE ARROW
21B7 ↷ CLOCKWISE TOP SEMICIRCLE ARROW
21B8 ↸ NORTH WEST ARROW TO LONG BAR
= home
21B9 ↹ LEFTWARDS ARROW TO BAR OVER RIGHTWARDS ARROW TO BAR
= tab with shift tab
21BA ↺ ANTICLOCKWISE OPEN CIRCLE ARROW
21BB ↻ CLOCKWISE OPEN CIRCLE ARROW

Harpoons

21BC ↼ LEFTWARDS HARPOON WITH BARB UPWARDS
21BD ↽ LEFTWARDS HARPOON WITH BARB DOWNWARDS
21BE ↾ UPWARDS HARPOON WITH BARB RIGHTWARDS
21BF ↿ UPWARDS HARPOON WITH BARB LEFTWARDS
21C0 ⇀ RIGHTWARDS HARPOON WITH BARB UPWARDS
21C1 ⇁ RIGHTWARDS HARPOON WITH BARB DOWNWARDS
21C2 ⇂ DOWNWARDS HARPOON WITH BARB RIGHTWARDS
21C3 ⇃ DOWNWARDS HARPOON WITH BARB LEFTWARDS

Paired arrows and harpoons

21C4 ⇄ RIGHTWARDS ARROW OVER LEFTWARDS ARROW
21C5 ⇅ UPWARDS ARROW LEFTWARDS OF DOWNWARDS ARROW
21C6 ⇆ LEFTWARDS ARROW OVER RIGHTWARDS ARROW
21C7 ⇇ LEFTWARDS PAIRED ARROWS
21C8 ⇈ UPWARDS PAIRED ARROWS
21C9 ⇉ RIGHTWARDS PAIRED ARROWS
21CA ⇊ DOWNWARDS PAIRED ARROWS
21CB ⇋ LEFTWARDS HARPOON OVER RIGHTWARDS HARPOON
21CC ⇌ RIGHTWARDS HARPOON OVER LEFTWARDS HARPOON

Double arrows

21CD ⇍ LEFTWARDS DOUBLE ARROW WITH STROKE
• negation of 21D0 ⇐
≡ 21D0 ⇐ 0338 ̸
21CE ⇎ LEFT RIGHT DOUBLE ARROW WITH STROKE
• negation of 21D4 ⇔
≡ 21D4 ⇔ 0338 ̸
21CF ⇏ RIGHTWARDS DOUBLE ARROW WITH STROKE
• negation of 21D2 ⇒
≡ 21D2 ⇒ 0338 ̸
21D0 ⇐ LEFTWARDS DOUBLE ARROW
21D1 ⇑ UPWARDS DOUBLE ARROW
21D2 ⇒ RIGHTWARDS DOUBLE ARROW
21D3 ⇓ DOWNWARDS DOUBLE ARROW
21D4 ⇔ LEFT RIGHT DOUBLE ARROW
21D5 ⇕ UP DOWN DOUBLE ARROW
21D6 ⇖ NORTH WEST DOUBLE ARROW

21D7 ⇗ NORTH EAST DOUBLE ARROW
21D8 ⇘ SOUTH EAST DOUBLE ARROW
21D9 ⇙ SOUTH WEST DOUBLE ARROW

Miscellaneous arrows and keyboard symbols

21DA ⇚ LEFTWARDS TRIPLE ARROW
21DB ⇛ RIGHTWARDS TRIPLE ARROW
21DC ⇜ LEFTWARDS SQUIGGLE ARROW
21DD ⇝ RIGHTWARDS SQUIGGLE ARROW
21DE ⇞ UPWARDS ARROW WITH DOUBLE STROKE
= page up
21DF ⇟ DOWNWARDS ARROW WITH DOUBLE STROKE
= page down
21E0 ⇠ LEFTWARDS DASHED ARROW
21E1 ⇡ UPWARDS DASHED ARROW
21E2 ⇢ RIGHTWARDS DASHED ARROW
21E3 ⇣ DOWNWARDS DASHED ARROW
21E4 ⇤ LEFTWARDS ARROW TO BAR
= leftward tab
21E5 ⇥ RIGHTWARDS ARROW TO BAR
= rightward tab

White arrows and keyboard symbols

21E6 ⇦ LEFTWARDS WHITE ARROW
21E7 ⇧ UPWARDS WHITE ARROW
= shift
21E8 ⇨ RIGHTWARDS WHITE ARROW
21E9 ⇩ DOWNWARDS WHITE ARROW
21EA ⇪ UPWARDS WHITE ARROW FROM BAR
= caps lock
21EB ⇫ UPWARDS WHITE ARROW ON PEDESTAL
= level 2 lock
21EC ⇬ UPWARDS WHITE ARROW ON PEDESTAL WITH HORIZONTAL BAR
= caps lock
21ED ⇭ UPWARDS WHITE ARROW ON PEDESTAL WITH VERTICAL BAR
= numerics lock
21EE ⇮ UPWARDS WHITE DOUBLE ARROW
= level 3 select
21EF ⇯ UPWARDS WHITE DOUBLE ARROW ON PEDESTAL
= level 3 lock
21F0 ⇰ RIGHTWARDS WHITE ARROW FROM WALL
= group lock
21F1 ⇱ NORTH WEST ARROW TO CORNER
= home
21F2 ⇲ SOUTH EAST ARROW TO CORNER
= end
21F3 ⇳ UP DOWN WHITE ARROW
= scrolling

Miscellaneous arrows

21F4 ⇴ RIGHT ARROW WITH SMALL CIRCLE
21F5 ⇵ DOWNWARDS ARROW LEFTWARDS OF UPWARDS ARROW
21F6 ⇶ THREE RIGHTWARDS ARROWS
21F7 ⇷ LEFTWARDS ARROW WITH VERTICAL STROKE
21F8 ⇸ RIGHTWARDS ARROW WITH VERTICAL STROKE
= z notation partial function
21F9 ⇹ LEFT RIGHT ARROW WITH VERTICAL STROKE
= z notation partial relation
21FA ⇺ LEFTWARDS ARROW WITH DOUBLE VERTICAL STROKE
21FB ⇻ RIGHTWARDS ARROW WITH DOUBLE VERTICAL STROKE
= z notation finite function
21FC ⇼ LEFT RIGHT ARROW WITH DOUBLE VERTICAL STROKE
= z notation finite relation
21FD ⇽ LEFTWARDS OPEN-HEADED ARROW
21FE ⇾ RIGHTWARDS OPEN-HEADED ARROW
21FF ⇿ LEFT RIGHT OPEN-HEADED ARROW

	220	221	222	223	224	225	226	227	228	229	22A	22B	22C	22D	22E	22F
0	∀ 2200	∐ 2210	∠ 2220	∰ 2230	≀ 2240	≐ 2250	≠ 2260	≰ 2270	⊀ 2280	⊐ 2290	⊠ 22A0	⊰ 22B0	⋀ 22C0	⋐ 22D0	⋠ 22E0	⋰ 22F0
1	∁ 2201	∑ 2211	∡ 2221	∱ 2231	≁ 2241	≑ 2251	≡ 2261	≱ 2271	⊁ 2281	⊑ 2291	⊡ 22A1	⊱ 22B1	⋁ 22C1	⋑ 22D1	⋡ 22E1	⋱ 22F1
2	∂ 2202	− 2212	∢ 2222	∲ 2232	≂ 2242	≒ 2252	≢ 2262	≲ 2272	⊂ 2282	⊒ 2292	⊢ 22A2	⊲ 22B2	⋂ 22C2	⋒ 22D2	⋢ 22E2	⋲ 22F2
3	∃ 2203	∓ 2213	∣ 2223	∳ 2233	≃ 2243	≓ 2253	≣ 2263	≳ 2273	⊃ 2283	⊓ 2293	⊣ 22A3	⊳ 22B3	⋃ 22C3	⋓ 22D3	⋣ 22E3	⋳ 22F3
4	∄ 2204	∔ 2214	∤ 2224	∴ 2234	≄ 2244	≔ 2254	≤ 2264	≴ 2274	⊄ 2284	⊔ 2294	⊤ 22A4	⊴ 22B4	⋄ 22C4	⋔ 22D4	⋤ 22E4	⋴ 22F4
5	∅ 2205	∕ 2215	∥ 2225	∵ 2235	≅ 2245	≕ 2255	≥ 2265	≵ 2275	⊅ 2285	⊕ 2295	⊥ 22A5	⊵ 22B5	⋅ 22C5	⋕ 22D5	⋥ 22E5	⋵ 22F5
6	∆ 2206	∖ 2216	∦ 2226	∶ 2236	≆ 2246	≖ 2256	≦ 2266	≶ 2276	⊆ 2286	⊖ 2296	⊦ 22A6	⊶ 22B6	⋆ 22C6	⋖ 22D6	⋦ 22E6	⋶ 22F6
7	∇ 2207	∗ 2217	∧ 2227	∷ 2237	≇ 2247	≗ 2257	≧ 2267	≷ 2277	⊇ 2287	⊗ 2297	⊧ 22A7	⊷ 22B7	⋇ 22C7	⋗ 22D7	⋧ 22E7	⋷ 22F7
8	∈ 2208	∘ 2218	∨ 2228	∸ 2238	≈ 2248	≘ 2258	≨ 2268	≸ 2278	⊈ 2288	⊘ 2298	⊨ 22A8	⊸ 22B8	⋈ 22C8	⋘ 22D8	⋨ 22E8	⋸ 22F8
9	∉ 2209	∙ 2219	∩ 2229	∹ 2239	≉ 2249	≙ 2259	≩ 2269	≹ 2279	⊉ 2289	⊙ 2299	⊩ 22A9	⊹ 22B9	⋉ 22C9	⋙ 22D9	⋩ 22E9	⋹ 22F9
A	∊ 220A	√ 221A	∪ 222A	∺ 223A	≊ 224A	≚ 225A	≪ 226A	≺ 227A	⊊ 228A	⊚ 229A	⊪ 22AA	⊺ 22BA	⋊ 22CA	⋚ 22DA	⋪ 22EA	⋺ 22FA
B	∋ 220B	∛ 221B	∫ 222B	∻ 223B	≋ 224B	≛ 225B	≫ 226B	≻ 227B	⊋ 228B	⊛ 229B	⊫ 22AB	⊻ 22BB	⋋ 22CB	⋛ 22DB	⋫ 22EB	⋻ 22FB
C	∌ 220C	∜ 221C	∬ 222C	∼ 223C	≌ 224C	≜ 225C	≬ 226C	≼ 227C	⊌ 228C	⊜ 229C	⊬ 22AC	⊼ 22BC	⋌ 22CC	⋜ 22DC	⋬ 22EC	⋼ 22FC
D	∍ 220D	∝ 221D	∭ 222D	∽ 223D	≍ 224D	≝ 225D	≭ 226D	≽ 227D	⊍ 228D	⊝ 229D	⊭ 22AD	⊽ 22BD	⋍ 22CD	⋝ 22DD	⋭ 22ED	⋽ 22FD
E	∎ 220E	∞ 221E	∮ 222E	∾ 223E	≎ 224E	≞ 225E	≮ 226E	≾ 227E	⊎ 228E	⊞ 229E	⊮ 22AE	⊾ 22BE	⋎ 22CE	⋞ 22DE	⋮ 22EE	⋾ 22FE
F	∏ 220F	∟ 221F	∯ 222F	∿ 223F	≏ 224F	≟ 225F	≯ 226F	≿ 227F	⊏ 228F	⊟ 229F	⊯ 22AF	⊿ 22BF	⋏ 22CF	⋟ 22DF	⋯ 22EF	⋿ 22FF

Miscellaneous mathematical symbols

2200 ∀ FOR ALL
= universal quantifier

2201 ∁ COMPLEMENT
→ 0297 ʗ latin letter stretched c

2202 ∂ PARTIAL DIFFERENTIAL

2203 ∃ THERE EXISTS
= existential quantifier

2204 ∄ THERE DOES NOT EXIST
≡ 2203 ∃ 0338 ̸

2205 ∅ EMPTY SET
= null set
• used in linguistics to indicate a null morpheme or phonological "zero"
→ 00D8 Ø latin capital letter o with stroke
→ 2300 ⌀ diameter sign

2206 ∆ INCREMENT
= Laplace operator
= forward difference
= symmetric difference of sets
→ 0394 Δ greek capital letter delta
→ 25B3 △ white up-pointing triangle

2207 ∇ NABLA
= backward difference
= gradient, del
• used for Laplacian operator (written with superscript 2)
→ 25BD ▽ white down-pointing triangle

Set membership

2208 ∈ ELEMENT OF

2209 ∉ NOT AN ELEMENT OF
≡ 2208 ∈ 0338 ̸

220A ∊ SMALL ELEMENT OF
• originates in math pi fonts; not the straight epsilon
→ 03F5 ϵ greek lunate epsilon symbol

220B ∋ CONTAINS AS MEMBER
= such that

220C ∌ DOES NOT CONTAIN AS MEMBER
≡ 220B ∋ 0338 ̸

220D ∍ SMALL CONTAINS AS MEMBER
→ 03F6 ϶ greek reversed lunate epsilon symbol

Miscellaneous mathematical symbol

220E ∎ END OF PROOF
= q.e.d.
→ 2023 ‣ triangular bullet
→ 25AE ▮ black vertical rectangle

N-ary operators

220F ∏ N-ARY PRODUCT
= product sign
→ 03A0 Π greek capital letter pi

2210 ∐ N-ARY COPRODUCT
= coproduct sign

2211 ∑ N-ARY SUMMATION
= summation sign
→ 03A3 Σ greek capital letter sigma
→ 2140 ⅀ double-struck n-ary summation

Operators

2212 − MINUS SIGN
→ 002D - hyphen-minus

2213 ∓ MINUS-OR-PLUS SIGN
→ 00B1 ± plus-minus sign

2214 ∔ DOT PLUS

2215 ∕ DIVISION SLASH
• generic division operator
→ 002F / solidus
→ 2044 ⁄ fraction slash

2216 ∖ SET MINUS
→ 005C \ reverse solidus

2217 ∗ ASTERISK OPERATOR
→ 002A * asterisk

2218 ∘ RING OPERATOR
= composite function
= APL jot
→ 00B0 ° degree sign
→ 25E6 ◦ white bullet

2219 ∙ BULLET OPERATOR
→ 00B7 · middle dot
→ 2022 • bullet
→ 2024 ․ one dot leader

221A √ SQUARE ROOT
= radical sign
→ 2713 ✓ check mark

221B ∛ CUBE ROOT

221C ∜ FOURTH ROOT

221D ∝ PROPORTIONAL TO
→ 03B1 α greek small letter alpha

Miscellaneous mathematical symbols

221E ∞ INFINITY

221F ∟ RIGHT ANGLE

2220 ∠ ANGLE

2221 ∡ MEASURED ANGLE

2222 ∢ SPHERICAL ANGLE
= angle arc

Operators

2223 ∣ DIVIDES
= such that
= APL stile
→ 007C | vertical line
→ 01C0 ǀ latin letter dental click

2224 ∤ DOES NOT DIVIDE
≡ 2223 ∣ 0338 ̸

2225 ∥ PARALLEL TO
→ 01C1 ǁ latin letter lateral click
→ 2016 ‖ double vertical line

2226 ∦ NOT PARALLEL TO
≡ 2225 ∥ 0338 ̸

Logical and set operators

2227 ∧ LOGICAL AND
= wedge, conjunction
→ 22C0 ⋀ n-ary logical and
→ 2303 ⌃ up arrowhead

2228 ∨ LOGICAL OR
= vee, disjunction
→ 22C1 ⋁ n-ary logical or
→ 2304 ⌄ down arrowhead

2229 ∩ INTERSECTION
= cap, hat
→ 22C2 ⋂ n-ary intersection

222A ∪ UNION
= cup
→ 22C3 ⋃ n-ary union

Integrals

222B ∫ INTEGRAL
→ 0283 ʃ latin small letter esh

222C ∬ DOUBLE INTEGRAL
≈ 222B ∫ 222B ∫

222D ∭ TRIPLE INTEGRAL
→ 2A0C ⨌ quadruple integral operator
≈ 222B ∫ 222B ∫ 222B ∫

222E ∮ CONTOUR INTEGRAL
→ 2A15 ⨕ integral around a point operator

222F ∯ SURFACE INTEGRAL
≈ 222E ∮ 222E ∮

2230 ∰ VOLUME INTEGRAL
≈ 222E ∮ 222E ∮ 222E ∮

2231 ∱ CLOCKWISE INTEGRAL

2232 ∲ CLOCKWISE CONTOUR INTEGRAL

2233 ∳ ANTICLOCKWISE CONTOUR INTEGRAL
• clockwise or anticlockwise arrows do not reverse during layout mirroring

Miscellaneous mathematical symbols

2234 ∴ THEREFORE

2235 ∵ BECAUSE

Relations

2236 ∶ RATIO
→ 003A : colon

2237 ∷ PROPORTION

Operator

2238 ∸ DOT MINUS
= saturating subtraction

Relation

2239 ∹ EXCESS

Operator

223A ∺ GEOMETRIC PROPORTION

Relations

223B ∻ HOMOTHETIC
→ 2A6B ⩫ tilde operator with rising dots

223C ∼ TILDE OPERATOR
= varies with (proportional to)
= difference between
= similar to
= not
= cycle
= APL tilde
→ 007E ~ tilde
→ 00AC ¬ not sign
→ 02DC ˜ small tilde

223D ∽ REVERSED TILDE
= lazy S
• reversed tilde and lazy S are glyph variants

223E ∾ INVERTED LAZY S
= most positive

Miscellaneous mathematical symbol

223F ∿ SINE WAVE
= alternating current

Operator

2240 ≀ WREATH PRODUCT

Relations

2241 ≁ NOT TILDE
≡ 223C ∼ 0338 ̸

2242 ≂ MINUS TILDE

2243 ≃ ASYMPTOTICALLY EQUAL TO

2244 ≄ NOT ASYMPTOTICALLY EQUAL TO
≡ 2243 ≃ 0338 ̸

2245 ≅ APPROXIMATELY EQUAL TO

2246 ≆ APPROXIMATELY BUT NOT ACTUALLY EQUAL TO

2247 ≇ NEITHER APPROXIMATELY NOR ACTUALLY EQUAL TO
≡ 2245 ≅ 0338 ̸

2248 ≈ ALMOST EQUAL TO
= asymptotic to

2249 ≉ NOT ALMOST EQUAL TO
≡ 2248 ≈ 0338 ̸

224A ≊ ALMOST EQUAL OR EQUAL TO

224B ≋ TRIPLE TILDE

224C ≌ ALL EQUAL TO
• reversed tilde and lazy S are glyph variants

224D ≍ EQUIVALENT TO

224E ≎ GEOMETRICALLY EQUIVALENT TO

224F ≏ DIFFERENCE BETWEEN

2250 ≐ APPROACHES THE LIMIT

2251 ≑ GEOMETRICALLY EQUAL TO

2252 ≒ APPROXIMATELY EQUAL TO OR THE IMAGE OF
= nearly equals

2253 ≓ IMAGE OF OR APPROXIMATELY EQUAL TO

2254 ≔ COLON EQUALS

2255 ≕ EQUALS COLON

2256 ≖ RING IN EQUAL TO

2257 ≗ RING EQUAL TO
= approximately equal to

2258 ≘ CORRESPONDS TO

2259 ≙ ESTIMATES
= corresponds to

225A ≚ EQUIANGULAR TO

225B ≛ STAR EQUALS

225C ≜ DELTA EQUAL TO
= equiangular
= equal to by definition

225D ≝ EQUAL TO BY DEFINITION

225E ≞ MEASURED BY

225F ≟ QUESTIONED EQUAL TO

2260 ≠ NOT EQUAL TO
→ 003D = equals sign
→ 01C2 ǂ latin letter alveolar click
≡ 003D = 0338 ̸

2261 ≡ IDENTICAL TO

2262 ≢ NOT IDENTICAL TO
≡ 2261 ≡ 0338 ̸

2263 ≣ STRICTLY EQUIVALENT TO

2264 ≤ LESS-THAN OR EQUAL TO

2265 ≥ GREATER-THAN OR EQUAL TO

2266 ≦ LESS-THAN OVER EQUAL TO

2267 ≧ GREATER-THAN OVER EQUAL TO

2268 ≨ LESS-THAN BUT NOT EQUAL TO

2269 ≩ GREATER-THAN BUT NOT EQUAL TO

226A ≪ MUCH LESS-THAN
→ 00AB « left-pointing double angle quotation mark

226B ≫ MUCH GREATER-THAN
→ 00BB » right-pointing double angle quotation mark

226C ≬ BETWEEN
= plaintiff, quantic

226D ≭ NOT EQUIVALENT TO
≡ 224D ≍ 0338 ̸

226E ≮ NOT LESS-THAN
≡ 003C < 0338 ̸

226F ≯ NOT GREATER-THAN
≡ 003E > 0338 ̸

2270 ≰ NEITHER LESS-THAN NOR EQUAL TO
≡ 2264 ≤ 0338 ◌̸
2271 ≱ NEITHER GREATER-THAN NOR EQUAL TO
≡ 2265 ≥ 0338 ◌̸
2272 ≲ LESS-THAN OR EQUIVALENT TO
2273 ≳ GREATER-THAN OR EQUIVALENT TO
2274 ≴ NEITHER LESS-THAN NOR EQUIVALENT TO
≡ 2272 ≲ 0338 ◌̸
2275 ≵ NEITHER GREATER-THAN NOR EQUIVALENT TO
≡ 2273 ≳ 0338 ◌̸
2276 ≶ LESS-THAN OR GREATER-THAN
2277 ≷ GREATER-THAN OR LESS-THAN
2278 ≸ NEITHER LESS-THAN NOR GREATER-THAN
≡ 2276 ≶ 0338 ◌̸
2279 ≹ NEITHER GREATER-THAN NOR LESS-THAN
≡ 2277 ≷ 0338 ◌̸
227A ≺ PRECEDES
= lower rank than
→ 22B0 ⊰ precedes under relation
227B ≻ SUCCEEDS
= higher rank than
→ 22B1 ⊱ succeeds under relation
227C ≼ PRECEDES OR EQUAL TO
227D ≽ SUCCEEDS OR EQUAL TO
227E ≾ PRECEDES OR EQUIVALENT TO
227F ≿ SUCCEEDS OR EQUIVALENT TO
2280 ⊀ DOES NOT PRECEDE
≡ 227A ≺ 0338 ◌̸
2281 ⊁ DOES NOT SUCCEED
≡ 227B ≻ 0338 ◌̸
2282 ⊂ SUBSET OF
= included in set
2283 ⊃ SUPERSET OF
= includes in set
2284 ⊄ NOT A SUBSET OF
≡ 2282 ⊂ 0338 ◌̸
2285 ⊅ NOT A SUPERSET OF
≡ 2283 ⊃ 0338 ◌̸
2286 ⊆ SUBSET OF OR EQUAL TO
2287 ⊇ SUPERSET OF OR EQUAL TO
2288 ⊈ NEITHER A SUBSET OF NOR EQUAL TO
≡ 2286 ⊆ 0338 ◌̸
2289 ⊉ NEITHER A SUPERSET OF NOR EQUAL TO
≡ 2287 ⊇ 0338 ◌̸
228A ⊊ SUBSET OF WITH NOT EQUAL TO
228B ⊋ SUPERSET OF WITH NOT EQUAL TO

Operators

228C ⊌ MULTISET
228D ⊍ MULTISET MULTIPLICATION
→ 2A03 ⨃ n-ary union operator with dot
→ 2A40 ⩀ intersection with dot
228E ⊎ MULTISET UNION
= z notation bag addition
→ 2A04 ⨄ n-ary union operator with plus

Relations

228F ⊏ SQUARE IMAGE OF
2290 ⊐ SQUARE ORIGINAL OF
2291 ⊑ SQUARE IMAGE OF OR EQUAL TO
2292 ⊒ SQUARE ORIGINAL OF OR EQUAL TO

Operators

2293 ⊓ SQUARE CAP
→ 2A05 ⨅ n-ary square intersection operator
2294 ⊔ SQUARE CUP
2295 ⊕ CIRCLED PLUS
= direct sum
= vector pointing into page
→ 2641 ♁ earth
→ 2A01 ⨁ n-ary circled plus operator
2296 ⊖ CIRCLED MINUS
= symmetric difference
→ 29B5 ⦵ circle with horizontal bar
2297 ⊗ CIRCLED TIMES
= tensor product
= vector pointing into page
→ 2A02 ⨂ n-ary circled times operator
2298 ⊘ CIRCLED DIVISION SLASH
2299 ⊙ CIRCLED DOT OPERATOR
= direct product
= vector pointing out of page
→ 0298 ʘ latin letter bilabial click
→ 2609 ☉ sun
→ 2A00 ⨀ n-ary circled dot operator
229A ⊚ CIRCLED RING OPERATOR
→ 233E ⌾ apl functional symbol circle jot
→ 25CE ◎ bullseye
229B ⊛ CIRCLED ASTERISK OPERATOR
→ 235F ⍟ apl functional symbol circle star
229C ⊜ CIRCLED EQUALS
229D ⊝ CIRCLED DASH
229E ⊞ SQUARED PLUS
229F ⊟ SQUARED MINUS
22A0 ⊠ SQUARED TIMES
→ 2612 ☒ ballot box with x
22A1 ⊡ SQUARED DOT OPERATOR
22A2 ⊢ RIGHT TACK
= turnstile
= proves, implies, yields
= reducible
22A3 ⊣ LEFT TACK
= reverse turnstile
= non-theorem, does not yield

Miscellaneous mathematical symbols

22A4 ⊤ DOWN TACK
= top
→ 2E06 ⸆ raised interpolation marker
22A5 ⊥ UP TACK
= base, bottom
→ 27C2 ⟂ perpendicular

Relations

22A6 ⊦ ASSERTION
= reduces to
22A7 ⊧ MODELS
22A8 ⊨ TRUE
= statement is true, valid
= is a tautology
= satisfies
= results in
22A9 ⊩ FORCES
22AA ⊪ TRIPLE VERTICAL BAR RIGHT TURNSTILE
22AB ⊫ DOUBLE VERTICAL BAR DOUBLE RIGHT TURNSTILE
22AC ⊬ DOES NOT PROVE
≡ 22A2 ⊢ 0338 ◌̸
22AD ⊭ NOT TRUE
≡ 22A8 ⊨ 0338 ◌̸

22AE ⊮ DOES NOT FORCE
≡ 22A9 ⊩ 0338 ◌̸
22AF ⊯ NEGATED DOUBLE VERTICAL BAR DOUBLE RIGHT TURNSTILE
≡ 22AB ⊫ 0338 ◌̸
22B0 ⊰ PRECEDES UNDER RELATION
→ 227A ≺ precedes
22B1 ⊱ SUCCEEDS UNDER RELATION
→ 227B ≻ succeeds
22B2 ⊲ NORMAL SUBGROUP OF
→ 25C5 ◅ white left-pointing pointer
22B3 ⊳ CONTAINS AS NORMAL SUBGROUP
→ 25BB ▻ white right-pointing pointer
22B4 ⊴ NORMAL SUBGROUP OF OR EQUAL TO
22B5 ⊵ CONTAINS AS NORMAL SUBGROUP OR EQUAL TO
22B6 ⊶ ORIGINAL OF
22B7 ⊷ IMAGE OF
22B8 ⊸ MULTIMAP
22B9 ⊹ HERMITIAN CONJUGATE MATRIX

Operators

22BA ⊺ INTERCALATE
22BB ⊻ XOR
22BC ⊼ NAND
→ 2305 ⌅ projective
22BD ⊽ NOR

Miscellaneous mathematical symbols

22BE ⊾ RIGHT ANGLE WITH ARC
22BF ⊿ RIGHT TRIANGLE

N-ary operators

22C0 ⋀ N-ARY LOGICAL AND
• also used to denote the universal quantifier
→ 2227 ∧ logical and
22C1 ⋁ N-ARY LOGICAL OR
• also used to denote the existential quantifier
→ 2228 ∨ logical or
22C2 ⋂ N-ARY INTERSECTION
= z notation generalised intersection
→ 2229 ∩ intersection
22C3 ⋃ N-ARY UNION
= z notation generalised union
→ 222A ∪ union

Operators

22C4 ⋄ DIAMOND OPERATOR
→ 25C7 ◇ white diamond
22C5 ⋅ DOT OPERATOR
→ 00B7 · middle dot
22C6 ⋆ STAR OPERATOR
• APL
→ 066D ٭ arabic five pointed star
→ 2605 ★ black star
22C7 ⋇ DIVISION TIMES

Relation

22C8 ⋈ BOWTIE
→ 2445 ⑅ ocr bow tie

Operators

22C9 ⋉ LEFT NORMAL FACTOR SEMIDIRECT PRODUCT
22CA ⋊ RIGHT NORMAL FACTOR SEMIDIRECT PRODUCT
22CB ⋋ LEFT SEMIDIRECT PRODUCT
22CC ⋌ RIGHT SEMIDIRECT PRODUCT
→ 2041 ⁁ caret insertion point

Relation

22CD ⋍ REVERSED TILDE EQUALS

Logical operators

22CE ⋎ CURLY LOGICAL OR
22CF ⋏ CURLY LOGICAL AND

Relations

22D0 ⋐ DOUBLE SUBSET
22D1 ⋑ DOUBLE SUPERSET

Operators

22D2 ⋒ DOUBLE INTERSECTION
22D3 ⋓ DOUBLE UNION

Relations

22D4 ⋔ PITCHFORK
= proper intersection
22D5 ⋕ EQUAL AND PARALLEL TO
→ 2317 ⌗ viewdata square
22D6 ⋖ LESS-THAN WITH DOT
22D7 ⋗ GREATER-THAN WITH DOT
22D8 ⋘ VERY MUCH LESS-THAN
22D9 ⋙ VERY MUCH GREATER-THAN
22DA ⋚ LESS-THAN EQUAL TO OR GREATER-THAN
22DB ⋛ GREATER-THAN EQUAL TO OR LESS-THAN
22DC ⋜ EQUAL TO OR LESS-THAN
22DD ⋝ EQUAL TO OR GREATER-THAN
22DE ⋞ EQUAL TO OR PRECEDES
22DF ⋟ EQUAL TO OR SUCCEEDS
22E0 ⋠ DOES NOT PRECEDE OR EQUAL
≡ 227C ≼ 0338 ◌̸
22E1 ⋡ DOES NOT SUCCEED OR EQUAL
≡ 227D ≽ 0338 ◌̸
22E2 ⋢ NOT SQUARE IMAGE OF OR EQUAL TO
≡ 2291 ⊑ 0338 ◌̸
22E3 ⋣ NOT SQUARE ORIGINAL OF OR EQUAL TO
≡ 2292 ⊒ 0338 ◌̸
22E4 ⋤ SQUARE IMAGE OF OR NOT EQUAL TO
22E5 ⋥ SQUARE ORIGINAL OF OR NOT EQUAL TO
22E6 ⋦ LESS-THAN BUT NOT EQUIVALENT TO
22E7 ⋧ GREATER-THAN BUT NOT EQUIVALENT TO
22E8 ⋨ PRECEDES BUT NOT EQUIVALENT TO
22E9 ⋩ SUCCEEDS BUT NOT EQUIVALENT TO
22EA ⋪ NOT NORMAL SUBGROUP OF
≡ 22B2 ⊲ 0338 ◌̸
22EB ⋫ DOES NOT CONTAIN AS NORMAL SUBGROUP
≡ 22B3 ⊳ 0338 ◌̸
22EC ⋬ NOT NORMAL SUBGROUP OF OR EQUAL TO
≡ 22B4 ⊴ 0338 ◌̸
22ED ⋭ DOES NOT CONTAIN AS NORMAL SUBGROUP OR EQUAL
≡ 22B5 ⊵ 0338 ◌̸
22EE ⋮ VERTICAL ELLIPSIS
• these four ellipses are used for matrix row/column elision
→ 205D ⁝ tricolon
→ 2026 … horizontal ellipsis
→ FE19 ︙ presentation form for vertical horizontal ellipsis
22EF ⋯ MIDLINE HORIZONTAL ELLIPSIS
22F0 ⋰ UP RIGHT DIAGONAL ELLIPSIS
22F1 ⋱ DOWN RIGHT DIAGONAL ELLIPSIS

22F2	⋲	ELEMENT OF WITH LONG HORIZONTAL STROKE
22F3	⋳	ELEMENT OF WITH VERTICAL BAR AT END OF HORIZONTAL STROKE
22F4	⋴	SMALL ELEMENT OF WITH VERTICAL BAR AT END OF HORIZONTAL STROKE
22F5	⋵	ELEMENT OF WITH DOT ABOVE
22F6	⋶	ELEMENT OF WITH OVERBAR
22F7	⋷	SMALL ELEMENT OF WITH OVERBAR
22F8	⋸	ELEMENT OF WITH UNDERBAR
22F9	⋹	ELEMENT OF WITH TWO HORIZONTAL STROKES
22FA	⋺	CONTAINS WITH LONG HORIZONTAL STROKE
22FB	⋻	CONTAINS WITH VERTICAL BAR AT END OF HORIZONTAL STROKE
22FC	⋼	SMALL CONTAINS WITH VERTICAL BAR AT END OF HORIZONTAL STROKE
22FD	⋽	CONTAINS WITH OVERBAR
22FE	⋾	SMALL CONTAINS WITH OVERBAR
22FF	⋿	Z NOTATION BAG MEMBERSHIP

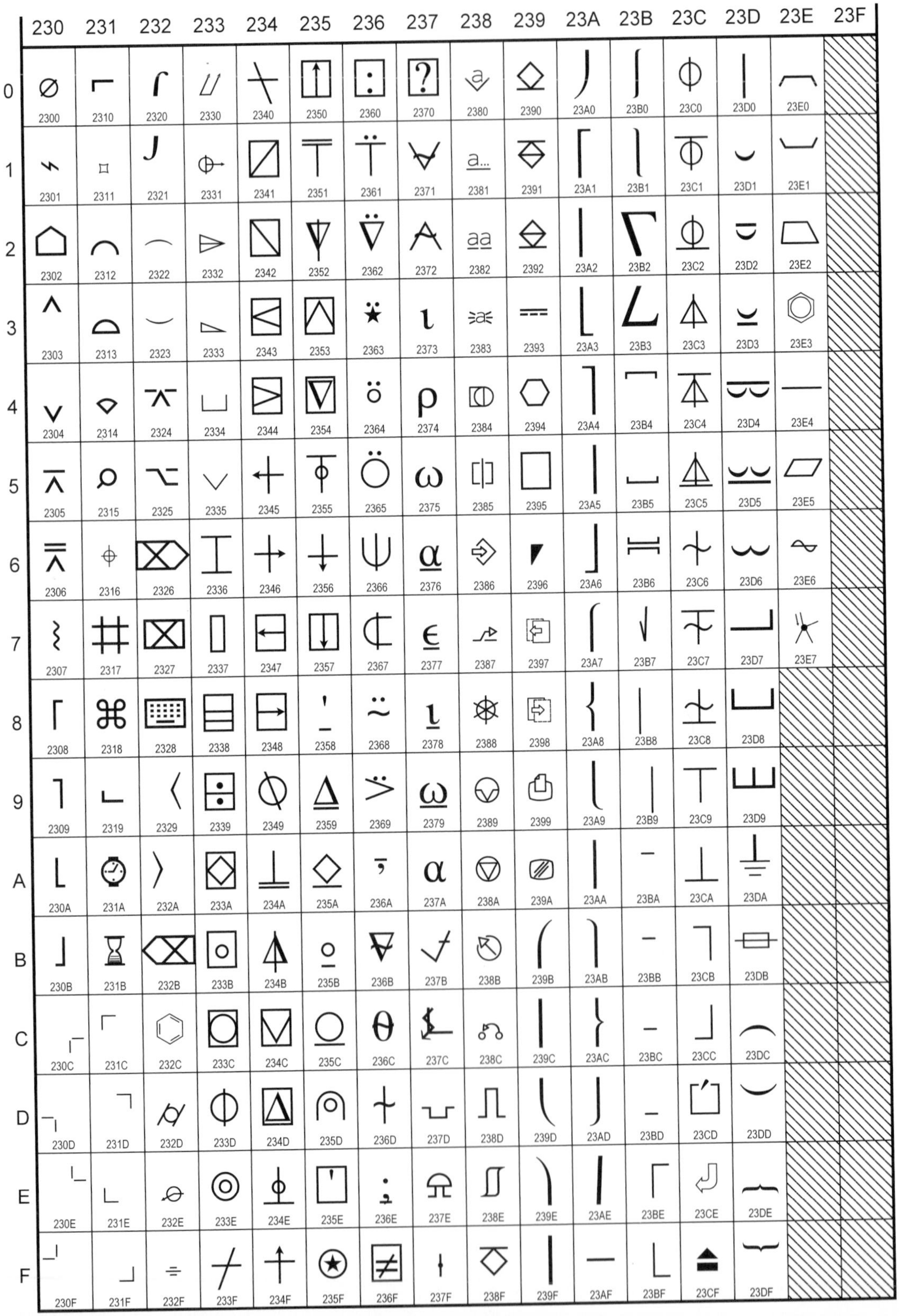

	230	231	232	233	234	235	236	237	238	239	23A	23B	23C	23D	23E	23F
0	2300	2310	2320	2330	2340	2350	2360	2370	2380	2390	23A0	23B0	23C0	23D0	23E0	
1	2301	2311	2321	2331	2341	2351	2361	2371	2381	2391	23A1	23B1	23C1	23D1	23E1	
2	2302	2312	2322	2332	2342	2352	2362	2372	2382	2392	23A2	23B2	23C2	23D2	23E2	
3	2303	2313	2323	2333	2343	2353	2363	2373	2383	2393	23A3	23B3	23C3	23D3	23E3	
4	2304	2314	2324	2334	2344	2354	2364	2374	2384	2394	23A4	23B4	23C4	23D4	23E4	
5	2305	2315	2325	2335	2345	2355	2365	2375	2385	2395	23A5	23B5	23C5	23D5	23E5	
6	2306	2316	2326	2336	2346	2356	2366	2376	2386	2396	23A6	23B6	23C6	23D6	23E6	
7	2307	2317	2327	2337	2347	2357	2367	2377	2387	2397	23A7	23B7	23C7	23D7	23E7	
8	2308	2318	2328	2338	2348	2358	2368	2378	2388	2398	23A8	23B8	23C8	23D8		
9	2309	2319	2329	2339	2349	2359	2369	2379	2389	2399	23A9	23B9	23C9	23D9		
A	230A	231A	232A	233A	234A	235A	236A	237A	238A	239A	23AA	23BA	23CA	23DA		
B	230B	231B	232B	233B	234B	235B	236B	237B	238B	239B	23AB	23BB	23CB	23DB		
C	230C	231C	232C	233C	234C	235C	236C	237C	238C	239C	23AC	23BC	23CC	23DC		
D	230D	231D	232D	233D	234D	235D	236D	237D	238D	239D	23AD	23BD	23CD	23DD		
E	230E	231E	232E	233E	234E	235E	236E	237E	238E	239E	23AE	23BE	23CE	23DE		
F	230F	231F	232F	233F	234F	235F	236F	237F	238F	239F	23AF	23BF	23CF	23DF		

Miscellaneous technical

2300 ⌀ DIAMETER SIGN
→ 2205 ∅ empty set

2301 ⌁ ELECTRIC ARROW
• from ISO 2047
• symbol for End of Transmission

2302 ⌂ HOUSE

2303 ⌃ UP ARROWHEAD
→ 005E ^ circumflex accent
→ 02C4 ˄ modifier letter up arrowhead
→ 2038 ‸ caret
→ 2227 ∧ logical and

2304 ⌄ DOWN ARROWHEAD
→ 02C5 ˅ modifier letter down arrowhead
→ 2228 ∨ logical or
→ 2335 ⌵ countersink

2305 ⌅ PROJECTIVE
→ 22BC ⊼ nand

2306 ⌆ PERSPECTIVE

2307 ⌇ WAVY LINE
→ 3030 〰 wavy dash

Corner brackets

The ceiling and floor characters are recommended for general-purpose corner brackets, rather than the CJK corner brackets, which are wide quotation marks.

2308 ⌈ LEFT CEILING
= APL upstile
→ 300C 「 left corner bracket

2309 ⌉ RIGHT CEILING
→ 20E7 ⃧ combining annuity symbol

230A ⌊ LEFT FLOOR
= APL downstile

230B ⌋ RIGHT FLOOR
→ 300D 」 right corner bracket

Crops

230C ⌌ BOTTOM RIGHT CROP
• set of four "crop" corners, arranged facing outward

230D ⌍ BOTTOM LEFT CROP

230E ⌎ TOP RIGHT CROP

230F ⌏ TOP LEFT CROP

Miscellaneous technical

2310 ⌐ REVERSED NOT SIGN
= beginning of line
→ 00AC ¬ not sign

2311 ⌑ SQUARE LOZENGE
= Kissen (pillow)
• used as a command delimiter in some very old computers

2312 ⌒ ARC
→ 25E0 ◠ upper half circle

2313 ⌓ SEGMENT

2314 ⌔ SECTOR

2315 ⌕ TELEPHONE RECORDER

2316 ⌖ POSITION INDICATOR

2317 ⌗ VIEWDATA SQUARE
→ 22D5 ⋕ equal and parallel to

2318 ⌘ PLACE OF INTEREST SIGN
= command key (1.0)

2319 ⌙ TURNED NOT SIGN
= line marker

GUI icons

231A ⌚ WATCH

231B ⌛ HOURGLASS

Quine corners

231C ⌜ TOP LEFT CORNER
• set of four "quine" corners, for quincuncial arrangement
• these are also used in mathematics in upper and lower pairs
→ 2E00 ⸀ right angle substitution marker

231D ⌝ TOP RIGHT CORNER

231E ⌞ BOTTOM LEFT CORNER

231F ⌟ BOTTOM RIGHT CORNER

Integral pieces

2320 ⌠ TOP HALF INTEGRAL
→ 23AE ⎮ integral extension

2321 ⌡ BOTTOM HALF INTEGRAL

Frown and smile

2322 ⌢ FROWN
→ 2040 ⁀ character tie

2323 ⌣ SMILE
→ 203F ‿ undertie

Keyboard symbols

2324 ⌤ UP ARROWHEAD BETWEEN TWO HORIZONTAL BARS
= enter key

2325 ⌥ OPTION KEY

2326 ⌦ ERASE TO THE RIGHT
= delete to the right key

2327 ⌧ X IN A RECTANGLE BOX
= clear key

2328 ⌨ KEYBOARD

Angle brackets

These are discouraged for mathematical use because of their canonical equivalence to CJK punctuation.

2329 〈 LEFT-POINTING ANGLE BRACKET
→ 003C < less-than sign
→ 2039 ‹ single left-pointing angle quotation mark
→ 27E8 ⟨ mathematical left angle bracket
≡ 3008 〈 left angle bracket

232A 〉 RIGHT-POINTING ANGLE BRACKET
→ 003E > greater-than sign
→ 203A › single right-pointing angle quotation mark
→ 27E9 ⟩ mathematical right angle bracket
≡ 3009 〉 right angle bracket

Keyboard symbol

232B ⌫ ERASE TO THE LEFT
= delete to the left key

Chemistry symbol

232C ⌬ BENZENE RING

Drafting symbols

232D ⌭ CYLINDRICITY

232E ⌮ ALL AROUND-PROFILE

232F ⌯ SYMMETRY

2330 ⌰ TOTAL RUNOUT

2331 ⌱ DIMENSION ORIGIN

2332 ⌲ CONICAL TAPER

2333 ⌳ SLOPE
→ 25FA ◺ lower left triangle

2334 ⌴ COUNTERBORE
→ 2423 ␣ open box
2335 ⌵ COUNTERSINK
→ 2304 ⌄ down arrowhead

APL

2336 ⌶ APL FUNCTIONAL SYMBOL I-BEAM
2337 ⌷ APL FUNCTIONAL SYMBOL SQUISH QUAD
→ 2395 ⎕ apl functional symbol quad
→ 25AF ▯ white vertical rectangle
→ 2AFF ⫿ n-ary white vertical bar
2338 ⌸ APL FUNCTIONAL SYMBOL QUAD EQUAL
2339 ⌹ APL FUNCTIONAL SYMBOL QUAD DIVIDE
233A ⌺ APL FUNCTIONAL SYMBOL QUAD DIAMOND
233B ⌻ APL FUNCTIONAL SYMBOL QUAD JOT
→ 29C7 ⧇ squared small circle
233C ⌼ APL FUNCTIONAL SYMBOL QUAD CIRCLE
233D ⌽ APL FUNCTIONAL SYMBOL CIRCLE STILE
233E ⌾ APL FUNCTIONAL SYMBOL CIRCLE JOT
→ 229A ⊚ circled ring operator
→ 29BE ⦾ circled white bullet
233F ⌿ APL FUNCTIONAL SYMBOL SLASH BAR
2340 ⍀ APL FUNCTIONAL SYMBOL BACKSLASH BAR
2341 ⍁ APL FUNCTIONAL SYMBOL QUAD SLASH
→ 29C4 ⧄ squared rising diagonal slash
2342 ⍂ APL FUNCTIONAL SYMBOL QUAD BACKSLASH
→ 29C5 ⧅ squared falling diagonal slash
2343 ⍃ APL FUNCTIONAL SYMBOL QUAD LESS-THAN
2344 ⍄ APL FUNCTIONAL SYMBOL QUAD GREATER-THAN
2345 ⍅ APL FUNCTIONAL SYMBOL LEFTWARDS VANE
2346 ⍆ APL FUNCTIONAL SYMBOL RIGHTWARDS VANE
2347 ⍇ APL FUNCTIONAL SYMBOL QUAD LEFTWARDS ARROW
2348 ⍈ APL FUNCTIONAL SYMBOL QUAD RIGHTWARDS ARROW
2349 ⍉ APL FUNCTIONAL SYMBOL CIRCLE BACKSLASH
→ 29B0 ⦰ reversed empty set
234A ⍊ APL FUNCTIONAL SYMBOL DOWN TACK UNDERBAR
= up tack underbar
• preferred naming for APL tack symbols now follows the London Convention in ISO/IEC 13751:2000 (APL Extended)
→ 22A5 ⊥ up tack
234B ⍋ APL FUNCTIONAL SYMBOL DELTA STILE
234C ⍌ APL FUNCTIONAL SYMBOL QUAD DOWN CARET
234D ⍍ APL FUNCTIONAL SYMBOL QUAD DELTA
234E ⍎ APL FUNCTIONAL SYMBOL DOWN TACK JOT
= up tack jot
→ 22A5 ⊥ up tack
234F ⍏ APL FUNCTIONAL SYMBOL UPWARDS VANE
2350 ⍐ APL FUNCTIONAL SYMBOL QUAD UPWARDS ARROW
2351 ⍑ APL FUNCTIONAL SYMBOL UP TACK OVERBAR
= down tack overbar
→ 22A4 ⊤ down tack
→ 3012 〒 postal mark
2352 ⍒ APL FUNCTIONAL SYMBOL DEL STILE
2353 ⍓ APL FUNCTIONAL SYMBOL QUAD UP CARET
2354 ⍔ APL FUNCTIONAL SYMBOL QUAD DEL
2355 ⍕ APL FUNCTIONAL SYMBOL UP TACK JOT
= down tack jot
→ 22A4 ⊤ down tack
2356 ⍖ APL FUNCTIONAL SYMBOL DOWNWARDS VANE
2357 ⍗ APL FUNCTIONAL SYMBOL QUAD DOWNWARDS ARROW
2358 ⍘ APL FUNCTIONAL SYMBOL QUOTE UNDERBAR
2359 ⍙ APL FUNCTIONAL SYMBOL DELTA UNDERBAR
235A ⍚ APL FUNCTIONAL SYMBOL DIAMOND UNDERBAR
235B ⍛ APL FUNCTIONAL SYMBOL JOT UNDERBAR
235C ⍜ APL FUNCTIONAL SYMBOL CIRCLE UNDERBAR
235D ⍝ APL FUNCTIONAL SYMBOL UP SHOE JOT
→ 2A40 ⩀ intersection with dot
235E ⍞ APL FUNCTIONAL SYMBOL QUOTE QUAD
235F ⍟ APL FUNCTIONAL SYMBOL CIRCLE STAR
→ 229B ⊛ circled asterisk operator
2360 ⍠ APL FUNCTIONAL SYMBOL QUAD COLON
2361 ⍡ APL FUNCTIONAL SYMBOL UP TACK DIAERESIS
= down tack diaeresis
→ 22A4 ⊤ down tack
2362 ⍢ APL FUNCTIONAL SYMBOL DEL DIAERESIS
2363 ⍣ APL FUNCTIONAL SYMBOL STAR DIAERESIS
2364 ⍤ APL FUNCTIONAL SYMBOL JOT DIAERESIS
= hoot
2365 ⍥ APL FUNCTIONAL SYMBOL CIRCLE DIAERESIS
= holler
2366 ⍦ APL FUNCTIONAL SYMBOL DOWN SHOE STILE
2367 ⍧ APL FUNCTIONAL SYMBOL LEFT SHOE STILE
2368 ⍨ APL FUNCTIONAL SYMBOL TILDE DIAERESIS
= smirk
2369 ⍩ APL FUNCTIONAL SYMBOL GREATER-THAN DIAERESIS
236A ⍪ APL FUNCTIONAL SYMBOL COMMA BAR
236B ⍫ APL FUNCTIONAL SYMBOL DEL TILDE
236C ⍬ APL FUNCTIONAL SYMBOL ZILDE
236D ⍭ APL FUNCTIONAL SYMBOL STILE TILDE
236E ⍮ APL FUNCTIONAL SYMBOL SEMICOLON UNDERBAR
236F ⍯ APL FUNCTIONAL SYMBOL QUAD NOT EQUAL
2370 ⍰ APL FUNCTIONAL SYMBOL QUAD QUESTION
2371 ⍱ APL FUNCTIONAL SYMBOL DOWN CARET TILDE
2372 ⍲ APL FUNCTIONAL SYMBOL UP CARET TILDE
2373 ⍳ APL FUNCTIONAL SYMBOL IOTA
2374 ⍴ APL FUNCTIONAL SYMBOL RHO
2375 ⍵ APL FUNCTIONAL SYMBOL OMEGA
2376 ⍶ APL FUNCTIONAL SYMBOL ALPHA UNDERBAR
2377 ⍷ APL FUNCTIONAL SYMBOL EPSILON UNDERBAR
2378 ⍸ APL FUNCTIONAL SYMBOL IOTA UNDERBAR
2379 ⍹ APL FUNCTIONAL SYMBOL OMEGA UNDERBAR
237A ⍺ APL FUNCTIONAL SYMBOL ALPHA

Graphics for control codes

237B ⍻ NOT CHECK MARK
• from ISO 2047
• symbol for Negative Acknowledge

Miscellaneous technical

237C ⍼ RIGHT ANGLE WITH DOWNWARDS ZIGZAG ARROW

Graphics for control codes

237D ⍽ SHOULDERED OPEN BOX
• from ISO 9995-7
• keyboard symbol for No Break Space
→ 2423 ␣ open box

237E ⍾ BELL SYMBOL
• from ISO 2047
237F ⍿ VERTICAL LINE WITH MIDDLE DOT
• from ISO 2047
• symbol for End of Medium

Keyboard symbols from ISO 9995-7

2380 ⎀ INSERTION SYMBOL
2381 ⎁ CONTINUOUS UNDERLINE SYMBOL
2382 ⎂ DISCONTINUOUS UNDERLINE SYMBOL
2383 ⎃ EMPHASIS SYMBOL
2384 ⎄ COMPOSITION SYMBOL
2385 ⎅ WHITE SQUARE WITH CENTRE VERTICAL LINE
= center
2386 ⎆ ENTER SYMBOL
2387 ⎇ ALTERNATIVE KEY SYMBOL
2388 ⎈ HELM SYMBOL
= control
→ 2638 ☸ wheel of dharma
2389 ⎉ CIRCLED HORIZONTAL BAR WITH NOTCH
= pause
238A ⎊ CIRCLED TRIANGLE DOWN
= interrupt
238B ⎋ BROKEN CIRCLE WITH NORTHWEST ARROW
= escape
238C ⎌ UNDO SYMBOL

Electrotechnical symbols from IR 181

238D ⎍ MONOSTABLE SYMBOL
238E ⎎ HYSTERESIS SYMBOL
238F ⎏ OPEN-CIRCUIT-OUTPUT H-TYPE SYMBOL
2390 ⎐ OPEN-CIRCUIT-OUTPUT L-TYPE SYMBOL
2391 ⎑ PASSIVE-PULL-DOWN-OUTPUT SYMBOL
2392 ⎒ PASSIVE-PULL-UP-OUTPUT SYMBOL
2393 ⎓ DIRECT CURRENT SYMBOL FORM TWO
2394 ⎔ SOFTWARE-FUNCTION SYMBOL

APL

2395 ⎕ APL FUNCTIONAL SYMBOL QUAD
→ 2337 ⌷ apl functional symbol squish quad
→ 25AF ▯ white vertical rectangle

Keyboard symbols from ISO 9995-7

2396 ⎖ DECIMAL SEPARATOR KEY SYMBOL
2397 ⎗ PREVIOUS PAGE
2398 ⎘ NEXT PAGE
2399 ⎙ PRINT SCREEN SYMBOL
239A ⎚ CLEAR SCREEN SYMBOL
→ 20E2 ⃢ combining enclosing screen

Bracket pieces

239B ⎛ LEFT PARENTHESIS UPPER HOOK
239C ⎜ LEFT PARENTHESIS EXTENSION
239D ⎝ LEFT PARENTHESIS LOWER HOOK
239E ⎞ RIGHT PARENTHESIS UPPER HOOK
239F ⎟ RIGHT PARENTHESIS EXTENSION
23A0 ⎠ RIGHT PARENTHESIS LOWER HOOK
23A1 ⎡ LEFT SQUARE BRACKET UPPER CORNER
23A2 ⎢ LEFT SQUARE BRACKET EXTENSION
23A3 ⎣ LEFT SQUARE BRACKET LOWER CORNER
23A4 ⎤ RIGHT SQUARE BRACKET UPPER CORNER
23A5 ⎥ RIGHT SQUARE BRACKET EXTENSION
23A6 ⎦ RIGHT SQUARE BRACKET LOWER CORNER
23A7 ⎧ LEFT CURLY BRACKET UPPER HOOK
23A8 ⎨ LEFT CURLY BRACKET MIDDLE PIECE
23A9 ⎩ LEFT CURLY BRACKET LOWER HOOK
23AA ⎪ CURLY BRACKET EXTENSION
23AB ⎫ RIGHT CURLY BRACKET UPPER HOOK
23AC ⎬ RIGHT CURLY BRACKET MIDDLE PIECE
23AD ⎭ RIGHT CURLY BRACKET LOWER HOOK

Special character extensions

23AE ⎮ INTEGRAL EXTENSION
→ 2320 ⌠ top half integral
→ 2321 ⌡ bottom half integral
23AF ⎯ HORIZONTAL LINE EXTENSION
• used for extension of arrows
→ 23D0 ⏐ vertical line extension

Bracket pieces

23B0 ⎰ UPPER LEFT OR LOWER RIGHT CURLY BRACKET SECTION
= left moustache
23B1 ⎱ UPPER RIGHT OR LOWER LEFT CURLY BRACKET SECTION
= right moustache

Summation sign parts

23B2 ⎲ SUMMATION TOP
23B3 ⎳ SUMMATION BOTTOM

Horizontal brackets

These characters are also used as delimiters of vertical text in non-CJK terminal emulation.

23B4 ⎴ TOP SQUARE BRACKET
→ FE47 ﹇ presentation form for vertical left square bracket
23B5 ⎵ BOTTOM SQUARE BRACKET
→ FE48 ﹈ presentation form for vertical right square bracket
23B6 ⎶ BOTTOM SQUARE BRACKET OVER TOP SQUARE BRACKET
• only used for terminal emulation

Terminal graphic characters

23B7 ⎷ RADICAL SYMBOL BOTTOM
23B8 ⎸ LEFT VERTICAL BOX LINE
23B9 ⎹ RIGHT VERTICAL BOX LINE

Scan lines for terminal graphics

The scan line numbers here refer to old, low-resolution technology for terminals, with only 9 scan lines per fixed-size character glyph. Even-numbered scan lines are unified with box-drawing graphics.

23BA ⎺ HORIZONTAL SCAN LINE-1
23BB ⎻ HORIZONTAL SCAN LINE-3
23BC ⎼ HORIZONTAL SCAN LINE-7
23BD ⎽ HORIZONTAL SCAN LINE-9

Dentistry notation symbols

23BE ⎾ DENTISTRY SYMBOL LIGHT VERTICAL AND TOP RIGHT
→ 2308 ⌈ left ceiling
23BF ⎿ DENTISTRY SYMBOL LIGHT VERTICAL AND BOTTOM RIGHT
→ 230A ⌊ left floor
23C0 ⏀ DENTISTRY SYMBOL LIGHT VERTICAL WITH CIRCLE
23C1 ⏁ DENTISTRY SYMBOL LIGHT DOWN AND HORIZONTAL WITH CIRCLE
23C2 ⏂ DENTISTRY SYMBOL LIGHT UP AND HORIZONTAL WITH CIRCLE
23C3 ⏃ DENTISTRY SYMBOL LIGHT VERTICAL WITH TRIANGLE
23C4 ⏄ DENTISTRY SYMBOL LIGHT DOWN AND HORIZONTAL WITH TRIANGLE

23C5 ⏅ DENTISTRY SYMBOL LIGHT UP AND HORIZONTAL WITH TRIANGLE
23C6 ⏆ DENTISTRY SYMBOL LIGHT VERTICAL AND WAVE
23C7 ⏇ DENTISTRY SYMBOL LIGHT DOWN AND HORIZONTAL WITH WAVE
23C8 ⏈ DENTISTRY SYMBOL LIGHT UP AND HORIZONTAL WITH WAVE
23C9 ⏉ DENTISTRY SYMBOL LIGHT DOWN AND HORIZONTAL
→ 22A4 ⊤ down tack
→ 252C ┬ box drawings light down and horizontal
23CA ⏊ DENTISTRY SYMBOL LIGHT UP AND HORIZONTAL
→ 22A5 ⊥ up tack
→ 2534 ┴ box drawings light up and horizontal
23CB ⏋ DENTISTRY SYMBOL LIGHT VERTICAL AND TOP LEFT
→ 2309 ⌉ right ceiling
23CC ⏌ DENTISTRY SYMBOL LIGHT VERTICAL AND BOTTOM LEFT
→ 230B ⌋ right floor

Miscellaneous technical

23CD ⏍ SQUARE FOOT

Keyboard and UI symbols

23CE ⏎ RETURN SYMBOL
• may be shown with either hollow or filled glyph
→ 21B5 ↵ downwards arrow with corner leftwards
23CF ⏏ EJECT SYMBOL
• UI symbol to eject media

Special character extension

23D0 ⏐ VERTICAL LINE EXTENSION
• used for extension of arrows
→ 23AF ⎯ horizontal line extension

Metrical symbols

23D1 ⏑ METRICAL BREVE
23D2 ⏒ METRICAL LONG OVER SHORT
23D3 ⏓ METRICAL SHORT OVER LONG
23D4 ⏔ METRICAL LONG OVER TWO SHORTS
23D5 ⏕ METRICAL TWO SHORTS OVER LONG
23D6 ⏖ METRICAL TWO SHORTS JOINED
23D7 ⏗ METRICAL TRISEME
→ 1D242 ◌𝉂 combining greek musical triseme
23D8 ⏘ METRICAL TETRASEME
→ 1D243 ◌𝉃 combining greek musical tetraseme
23D9 ⏙ METRICAL PENTASEME
→ 1D244 ◌𝉄 combining greek musical pentaseme

Electrotechnical symbols

23DA ⏚ EARTH GROUND
23DB ⏛ FUSE

Horizontal brackets

These are intended for bracketing terms of mathematical expressions where their glyph extends to accommodate the width of the bracketed expression

23DC ⏜ TOP PARENTHESIS
→ FE35 ︵ presentation form for vertical left parenthesis
23DD ⏝ BOTTOM PARENTHESIS
→ FE36 ︶ presentation form for vertical right parenthesis
23DE ⏞ TOP CURLY BRACKET
→ FE37 ︷ presentation form for vertical left curly bracket
23DF ⏟ BOTTOM CURLY BRACKET
→ FE38 ︸ presentation form for vertical right curly bracket
23E0 ⏠ TOP TORTOISE SHELL BRACKET
→ FE39 ︹ presentation form for vertical left tortoise shell bracket
23E1 ⏡ BOTTOM TORTOISE SHELL BRACKET
→ FE3A ︺ presentation form for vertical right tortoise shell bracket

Miscellaneous technical

23E2 ⏢ WHITE TRAPEZIUM

Chemistry symbol

23E3 ⏣ BENZENE RING WITH CIRCLE

Miscellaneous technical

23E4 ⏤ STRAIGHTNESS
23E5 ⏥ FLATNESS
23E6 ⏦ AC CURRENT
23E7 ⏧ ELECTRICAL INTERSECTION

	240	241	242	243
0	␀ 2400	␐ 2410	␠ 2420	
1	␁ 2401	␑ 2411	␡ 2421	
2	␂ 2402	␒ 2412	␢ 2422	
3	␃ 2403	␓ 2413	␣ 2423	
4	␄ 2404	␔ 2414	␤ 2424	
5	␅ 2405	␕ 2415	␥ 2425	
6	␆ 2406	␖ 2416	␦ 2426	
7	␇ 2407	␗ 2417		
8	␈ 2408	␘ 2418		
9	␉ 2409	␙ 2419		
A	␊ 240A	␚ 241A		
B	␋ 240B	␛ 241B		
C	␌ 240C	␜ 241C		
D	␍ 240D	␝ 241D		
E	␎ 240E	␞ 241E		
F	␏ 240F	␟ 241F		

The diagonal lettering glyphs are only exemplary; alternate representations may be, and often are used in the visible display of control codes.

Graphic pictures for control codes

2400 ␀ SYMBOL FOR NULL
2401 ␁ SYMBOL FOR START OF HEADING
2402 ␂ SYMBOL FOR START OF TEXT
2403 ␃ SYMBOL FOR END OF TEXT
2404 ␄ SYMBOL FOR END OF TRANSMISSION
2405 ␅ SYMBOL FOR ENQUIRY
2406 ␆ SYMBOL FOR ACKNOWLEDGE
2407 ␇ SYMBOL FOR BELL
2408 ␈ SYMBOL FOR BACKSPACE
2409 ␉ SYMBOL FOR HORIZONTAL TABULATION
240A ␊ SYMBOL FOR LINE FEED
240B ␋ SYMBOL FOR VERTICAL TABULATION
240C ␌ SYMBOL FOR FORM FEED
240D ␍ SYMBOL FOR CARRIAGE RETURN
240E ␎ SYMBOL FOR SHIFT OUT
240F ␏ SYMBOL FOR SHIFT IN
2410 ␐ SYMBOL FOR DATA LINK ESCAPE
2411 ␑ SYMBOL FOR DEVICE CONTROL ONE
2412 ␒ SYMBOL FOR DEVICE CONTROL TWO
2413 ␓ SYMBOL FOR DEVICE CONTROL THREE
2414 ␔ SYMBOL FOR DEVICE CONTROL FOUR
2415 ␕ SYMBOL FOR NEGATIVE ACKNOWLEDGE
2416 ␖ SYMBOL FOR SYNCHRONOUS IDLE
2417 ␗ SYMBOL FOR END OF TRANSMISSION BLOCK
2418 ␘ SYMBOL FOR CANCEL
2419 ␙ SYMBOL FOR END OF MEDIUM
241A ␚ SYMBOL FOR SUBSTITUTE
241B ␛ SYMBOL FOR ESCAPE
241C ␜ SYMBOL FOR FILE SEPARATOR
241D ␝ SYMBOL FOR GROUP SEPARATOR
241E ␞ SYMBOL FOR RECORD SEPARATOR
241F ␟ SYMBOL FOR UNIT SEPARATOR
2420 ␠ SYMBOL FOR SPACE
2421 ␡ SYMBOL FOR DELETE

Specific symbols for space

2422 ␢ BLANK SYMBOL
- graphic for space
- → 0180 ƀ latin small letter b with stroke

2423 ␣ OPEN BOX
- graphic for space
- → 2334 ⌴ counterbore

Graphic picture for control code

2424 ␤ SYMBOL FOR NEWLINE

Keyboard symbol

2425 ␥ SYMBOL FOR DELETE FORM TWO
- from ISO 9995-7
- keyboard symbol for undoable delete

Specific symbol for control code

2426 ␦ SYMBOL FOR SUBSTITUTE FORM TWO
- from ISO 2047
- → 061F ؟ arabic question mark

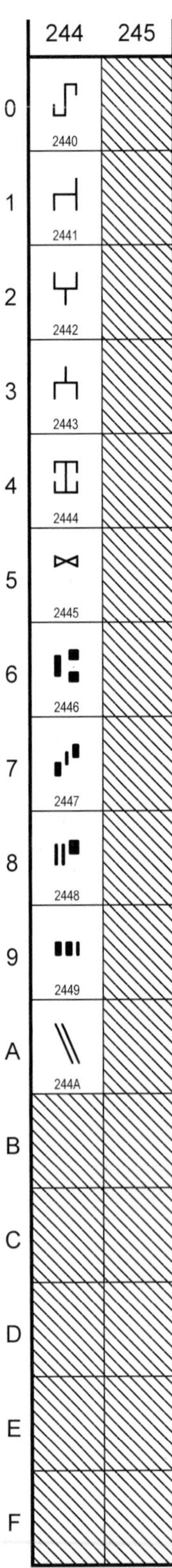

OCR

2440 ⑀ OCR HOOK
2441 ⑁ OCR CHAIR
2442 ⑂ OCR FORK
2443 ⑃ OCR INVERTED FORK
2444 ⑄ OCR BELT BUCKLE
2445 ⑅ OCR BOW TIE
→ 22C8 ⋈ bowtie
2446 ⑆ OCR BRANCH BANK IDENTIFICATION
= transit
2447 ⑇ OCR AMOUNT OF CHECK
2448 ⑈ OCR DASH
= on us
2449 ⑉ OCR CUSTOMER ACCOUNT NUMBER
= dash
244A ⑊ OCR DOUBLE BACKSLASH

	246	247	248	249	24A	24B	24C	24D	24E	24F
0	① 2460	⑰ 2470	⒀ 2480	⒐ 2490	⒠ 24A0	⒰ 24B0	Ⓚ 24C0	ⓐ 24D0	ⓠ 24E0	⓰ 24F0
1	② 2461	⑱ 2471	⒁ 2481	⒑ 2491	⒡ 24A1	⒱ 24B1	Ⓛ 24C1	ⓑ 24D1	ⓡ 24E1	⓱ 24F1
2	③ 2462	⑲ 2472	⒂ 2482	⒒ 2492	⒢ 24A2	⒲ 24B2	Ⓜ 24C2	ⓒ 24D2	ⓢ 24E2	⓲ 24F2
3	④ 2463	⑳ 2473	⒃ 2483	⒓ 2493	⒣ 24A3	⒳ 24B3	Ⓝ 24C3	ⓓ 24D3	ⓣ 24E3	⓳ 24F3
4	⑤ 2464	⑴ 2474	⒄ 2484	⒔ 2494	⒤ 24A4	⒴ 24B4	Ⓞ 24C4	ⓔ 24D4	ⓤ 24E4	⓴ 24F4
5	⑥ 2465	⑵ 2475	⒅ 2485	⒕ 2495	⒥ 24A5	⒵ 24B5	Ⓟ 24C5	ⓕ 24D5	ⓥ 24E5	⓵ 24F5
6	⑦ 2466	⑶ 2476	⒆ 2486	⒖ 2496	⒦ 24A6	Ⓐ 24B6	Ⓠ 24C6	ⓖ 24D6	ⓦ 24E6	⓶ 24F6
7	⑧ 2467	⑷ 2477	⒇ 2487	⒗ 2497	⒧ 24A7	Ⓑ 24B7	Ⓡ 24C7	ⓗ 24D7	ⓧ 24E7	⓷ 24F7
8	⑨ 2468	⑸ 2478	⒈ 2488	⒘ 2498	⒨ 24A8	Ⓒ 24B8	Ⓢ 24C8	ⓘ 24D8	ⓨ 24E8	⓸ 24F8
9	⑩ 2469	⑹ 2479	⒉ 2489	⒙ 2499	⒩ 24A9	Ⓓ 24B9	Ⓣ 24C9	ⓙ 24D9	ⓩ 24E9	⓹ 24F9
A	⑪ 246A	⑺ 247A	⒊ 248A	⒚ 249A	⒪ 24AA	Ⓔ 24BA	Ⓤ 24CA	ⓚ 24DA	⓪ 24EA	⓺ 24FA
B	⑫ 246B	⑻ 247B	⒋ 248B	⒛ 249B	⒫ 24AB	Ⓕ 24BB	Ⓥ 24CB	ⓛ 24DB	⓫ 24EB	⓻ 24FB
C	⑬ 246C	⑼ 247C	⒌ 248C	⒜ 249C	⒬ 24AC	Ⓖ 24BC	Ⓦ 24CC	ⓜ 24DC	⓬ 24EC	⓼ 24FC
D	⑭ 246D	⑽ 247D	⒍ 248D	⒝ 249D	⒭ 24AD	Ⓗ 24BD	Ⓧ 24CD	ⓝ 24DD	⓭ 24ED	⓽ 24FD
E	⑮ 246E	⑾ 247E	⒎ 248E	⒞ 249E	⒮ 24AE	Ⓘ 24BE	Ⓨ 24CE	ⓞ 24DE	⓮ 24EE	⓾ 24FE
F	⑯ 246F	⑿ 247F	⒏ 248F	⒟ 249F	⒯ 24AF	Ⓙ 24BF	Ⓩ 24CF	ⓟ 24DF	⓯ 24EF	⓿ 24FF

Circled numbers

2460 ① CIRCLED DIGIT ONE
≈ <circle> 0031 1
2461 ② CIRCLED DIGIT TWO
≈ <circle> 0032 2
2462 ③ CIRCLED DIGIT THREE
≈ <circle> 0033 3
2463 ④ CIRCLED DIGIT FOUR
≈ <circle> 0034 4
2464 ⑤ CIRCLED DIGIT FIVE
≈ <circle> 0035 5
2465 ⑥ CIRCLED DIGIT SIX
≈ <circle> 0036 6
2466 ⑦ CIRCLED DIGIT SEVEN
≈ <circle> 0037 7
2467 ⑧ CIRCLED DIGIT EIGHT
≈ <circle> 0038 8
2468 ⑨ CIRCLED DIGIT NINE
≈ <circle> 0039 9
2469 ⑩ CIRCLED NUMBER TEN
≈ <circle> 0031 1 0030 0
246A ⑪ CIRCLED NUMBER ELEVEN
≈ <circle> 0031 1 0031 1
246B ⑫ CIRCLED NUMBER TWELVE
≈ <circle> 0031 1 0032 2
246C ⑬ CIRCLED NUMBER THIRTEEN
≈ <circle> 0031 1 0033 3
246D ⑭ CIRCLED NUMBER FOURTEEN
≈ <circle> 0031 1 0034 4
246E ⑮ CIRCLED NUMBER FIFTEEN
≈ <circle> 0031 1 0035 5
246F ⑯ CIRCLED NUMBER SIXTEEN
≈ <circle> 0031 1 0036 6
2470 ⑰ CIRCLED NUMBER SEVENTEEN
≈ <circle> 0031 1 0037 7
2471 ⑱ CIRCLED NUMBER EIGHTEEN
≈ <circle> 0031 1 0038 8
2472 ⑲ CIRCLED NUMBER NINETEEN
≈ <circle> 0031 1 0039 9
2473 ⑳ CIRCLED NUMBER TWENTY
≈ <circle> 0032 2 0030 0

Parenthesized numbers

2474 ⑴ PARENTHESIZED DIGIT ONE
≈ 0028 (0031 1 0029)
2475 ⑵ PARENTHESIZED DIGIT TWO
≈ 0028 (0032 2 0029)
2476 ⑶ PARENTHESIZED DIGIT THREE
≈ 0028 (0033 3 0029)
2477 ⑷ PARENTHESIZED DIGIT FOUR
≈ 0028 (0034 4 0029)
2478 ⑸ PARENTHESIZED DIGIT FIVE
≈ 0028 (0035 5 0029)
2479 ⑹ PARENTHESIZED DIGIT SIX
≈ 0028 (0036 6 0029)
247A ⑺ PARENTHESIZED DIGIT SEVEN
≈ 0028 (0037 7 0029)
247B ⑻ PARENTHESIZED DIGIT EIGHT
≈ 0028 (0038 8 0029)
247C ⑼ PARENTHESIZED DIGIT NINE
≈ 0028 (0039 9 0029)
247D ⑽ PARENTHESIZED NUMBER TEN
≈ 0028 (0031 1 0030 0 0029)
247E ⑾ PARENTHESIZED NUMBER ELEVEN
≈ 0028 (0031 1 0031 1 0029)
247F ⑿ PARENTHESIZED NUMBER TWELVE
≈ 0028 (0031 1 0032 2 0029)
2480 ⒀ PARENTHESIZED NUMBER THIRTEEN
≈ 0028 (0031 1 0033 3 0029)
2481 ⒁ PARENTHESIZED NUMBER FOURTEEN
≈ 0028 (0031 1 0034 4 0029)
2482 ⒂ PARENTHESIZED NUMBER FIFTEEN
≈ 0028 (0031 1 0035 5 0029)
2483 ⒃ PARENTHESIZED NUMBER SIXTEEN
≈ 0028 (0031 1 0036 6 0029)
2484 ⒄ PARENTHESIZED NUMBER SEVENTEEN
≈ 0028 (0031 1 0037 7 0029)
2485 ⒅ PARENTHESIZED NUMBER EIGHTEEN
≈ 0028 (0031 1 0038 8 0029)
2486 ⒆ PARENTHESIZED NUMBER NINETEEN
≈ 0028 (0031 1 0039 9 0029)
2487 ⒇ PARENTHESIZED NUMBER TWENTY
≈ 0028 (0032 2 0030 0 0029)

Numbers period

2488 ⒈ DIGIT ONE FULL STOP
≈ 0031 1 002E .
2489 ⒉ DIGIT TWO FULL STOP
≈ 0032 2 002E .
248A ⒊ DIGIT THREE FULL STOP
≈ 0033 3 002E .
248B ⒋ DIGIT FOUR FULL STOP
≈ 0034 4 002E .
248C ⒌ DIGIT FIVE FULL STOP
≈ 0035 5 002E .
248D ⒍ DIGIT SIX FULL STOP
≈ 0036 6 002E .
248E ⒎ DIGIT SEVEN FULL STOP
≈ 0037 7 002E .
248F ⒏ DIGIT EIGHT FULL STOP
≈ 0038 8 002E .
2490 ⒐ DIGIT NINE FULL STOP
≈ 0039 9 002E .
2491 ⒑ NUMBER TEN FULL STOP
≈ 0031 1 0030 0 002E .
2492 ⒒ NUMBER ELEVEN FULL STOP
≈ 0031 1 0031 1 002E .
2493 ⒓ NUMBER TWELVE FULL STOP
≈ 0031 1 0032 2 002E .
2494 ⒔ NUMBER THIRTEEN FULL STOP
≈ 0031 1 0033 3 002E .
2495 ⒕ NUMBER FOURTEEN FULL STOP
≈ 0031 1 0034 4 002E .
2496 ⒖ NUMBER FIFTEEN FULL STOP
≈ 0031 1 0035 5 002E .
2497 ⒗ NUMBER SIXTEEN FULL STOP
≈ 0031 1 0036 6 002E .
2498 ⒘ NUMBER SEVENTEEN FULL STOP
≈ 0031 1 0037 7 002E .
2499 ⒙ NUMBER EIGHTEEN FULL STOP
≈ 0031 1 0038 8 002E .
249A ⒚ NUMBER NINETEEN FULL STOP
≈ 0031 1 0039 9 002E .
249B ⒛ NUMBER TWENTY FULL STOP
≈ 0032 2 0030 0 002E .

Parenthesized Latin letters

249C ⒜ PARENTHESIZED LATIN SMALL LETTER A
≈ 0028 (0061 a 0029)
249D ⒝ PARENTHESIZED LATIN SMALL LETTER B
≈ 0028 (0062 b 0029)
249E ⒞ PARENTHESIZED LATIN SMALL LETTER C
≈ 0028 (0063 c 0029)
249F ⒟ PARENTHESIZED LATIN SMALL LETTER D
≈ 0028 (0064 d 0029)
24A0 ⒠ PARENTHESIZED LATIN SMALL LETTER E
≈ 0028 (0065 e 0029)
24A1 ⒡ PARENTHESIZED LATIN SMALL LETTER F
≈ 0028 (0066 f 0029)
24A2 ⒢ PARENTHESIZED LATIN SMALL LETTER G
≈ 0028 (0067 g 0029)
24A3 ⒣ PARENTHESIZED LATIN SMALL LETTER H
≈ 0028 (0068 h 0029)
24A4 ⒤ PARENTHESIZED LATIN SMALL LETTER I
≈ 0028 (0069 i 0029)
24A5 ⒥ PARENTHESIZED LATIN SMALL LETTER J
≈ 0028 (006A j 0029)
24A6 ⒦ PARENTHESIZED LATIN SMALL LETTER K
≈ 0028 (006B k 0029)
24A7 ⒧ PARENTHESIZED LATIN SMALL LETTER L
≈ 0028 (006C l 0029)
24A8 ⒨ PARENTHESIZED LATIN SMALL LETTER M
≈ 0028 (006D m 0029)
24A9 ⒩ PARENTHESIZED LATIN SMALL LETTER N
≈ 0028 (006E n 0029)
24AA ⒪ PARENTHESIZED LATIN SMALL LETTER O
≈ 0028 (006F o 0029)
24AB ⒫ PARENTHESIZED LATIN SMALL LETTER P
≈ 0028 (0070 p 0029)
24AC ⒬ PARENTHESIZED LATIN SMALL LETTER Q
≈ 0028 (0071 q 0029)
24AD ⒭ PARENTHESIZED LATIN SMALL LETTER R
≈ 0028 (0072 r 0029)
24AE ⒮ PARENTHESIZED LATIN SMALL LETTER S
≈ 0028 (0073 s 0029)
24AF ⒯ PARENTHESIZED LATIN SMALL LETTER T
≈ 0028 (0074 t 0029)
24B0 ⒰ PARENTHESIZED LATIN SMALL LETTER U
≈ 0028 (0075 u 0029)
24B1 ⒱ PARENTHESIZED LATIN SMALL LETTER V
≈ 0028 (0076 v 0029)
24B2 ⒲ PARENTHESIZED LATIN SMALL LETTER W
≈ 0028 (0077 w 0029)
24B3 ⒳ PARENTHESIZED LATIN SMALL LETTER X
≈ 0028 (0078 x 0029)
24B4 ⒴ PARENTHESIZED LATIN SMALL LETTER Y
≈ 0028 (0079 y 0029)
24B5 ⒵ PARENTHESIZED LATIN SMALL LETTER Z
≈ 0028 (007A z 0029)

Circled Latin letters

24B6 Ⓐ CIRCLED LATIN CAPITAL LETTER A
≈ <circle> 0041 A
24B7 Ⓑ CIRCLED LATIN CAPITAL LETTER B
≈ <circle> 0042 B
24B8 Ⓒ CIRCLED LATIN CAPITAL LETTER C
→ 00A9 © copyright sign
≈ <circle> 0043 C
24B9 Ⓓ CIRCLED LATIN CAPITAL LETTER D
≈ <circle> 0044 D
24BA Ⓔ CIRCLED LATIN CAPITAL LETTER E
≈ <circle> 0045 E
24BB Ⓕ CIRCLED LATIN CAPITAL LETTER F
≈ <circle> 0046 F
24BC Ⓖ CIRCLED LATIN CAPITAL LETTER G
≈ <circle> 0047 G
24BD Ⓗ CIRCLED LATIN CAPITAL LETTER H
≈ <circle> 0048 H
24BE Ⓘ CIRCLED LATIN CAPITAL LETTER I
≈ <circle> 0049 I
24BF Ⓙ CIRCLED LATIN CAPITAL LETTER J
≈ <circle> 004A J
24C0 Ⓚ CIRCLED LATIN CAPITAL LETTER K
≈ <circle> 004B K
24C1 Ⓛ CIRCLED LATIN CAPITAL LETTER L
≈ <circle> 004C L
24C2 Ⓜ CIRCLED LATIN CAPITAL LETTER M
≈ <circle> 004D M
24C3 Ⓝ CIRCLED LATIN CAPITAL LETTER N
≈ <circle> 004E N
24C4 Ⓞ CIRCLED LATIN CAPITAL LETTER O
≈ <circle> 004F O
24C5 Ⓟ CIRCLED LATIN CAPITAL LETTER P
→ 2117 ℗ sound recording copyright
≈ <circle> 0050 P
24C6 Ⓠ CIRCLED LATIN CAPITAL LETTER Q
≈ <circle> 0051 Q
24C7 Ⓡ CIRCLED LATIN CAPITAL LETTER R
→ 00AE ® registered sign
≈ <circle> 0052 R
24C8 Ⓢ CIRCLED LATIN CAPITAL LETTER S
≈ <circle> 0053 S
24C9 Ⓣ CIRCLED LATIN CAPITAL LETTER T
≈ <circle> 0054 T
24CA Ⓤ CIRCLED LATIN CAPITAL LETTER U
≈ <circle> 0055 U
24CB Ⓥ CIRCLED LATIN CAPITAL LETTER V
≈ <circle> 0056 V
24CC Ⓦ CIRCLED LATIN CAPITAL LETTER W
≈ <circle> 0057 W
24CD Ⓧ CIRCLED LATIN CAPITAL LETTER X
≈ <circle> 0058 X
24CE Ⓨ CIRCLED LATIN CAPITAL LETTER Y
≈ <circle> 0059 Y
24CF Ⓩ CIRCLED LATIN CAPITAL LETTER Z
≈ <circle> 005A Z
24D0 ⓐ CIRCLED LATIN SMALL LETTER A
≈ <circle> 0061 a
24D1 ⓑ CIRCLED LATIN SMALL LETTER B
≈ <circle> 0062 b
24D2 ⓒ CIRCLED LATIN SMALL LETTER C
≈ <circle> 0063 c
24D3 ⓓ CIRCLED LATIN SMALL LETTER D
≈ <circle> 0064 d
24D4 ⓔ CIRCLED LATIN SMALL LETTER E
≈ <circle> 0065 e
24D5 ⓕ CIRCLED LATIN SMALL LETTER F
≈ <circle> 0066 f
24D6 ⓖ CIRCLED LATIN SMALL LETTER G
≈ <circle> 0067 g
24D7 ⓗ CIRCLED LATIN SMALL LETTER H
≈ <circle> 0068 h

24D8 ⓘ CIRCLED LATIN SMALL LETTER I
≈ <circle> 0069 i
24D9 ⓙ CIRCLED LATIN SMALL LETTER J
≈ <circle> 006A j
24DA ⓚ CIRCLED LATIN SMALL LETTER K
≈ <circle> 006B k
24DB ⓛ CIRCLED LATIN SMALL LETTER L
≈ <circle> 006C l
24DC ⓜ CIRCLED LATIN SMALL LETTER M
≈ <circle> 006D m
24DD ⓝ CIRCLED LATIN SMALL LETTER N
≈ <circle> 006E n
24DE ⓞ CIRCLED LATIN SMALL LETTER O
≈ <circle> 006F o
24DF ⓟ CIRCLED LATIN SMALL LETTER P
≈ <circle> 0070 p
24E0 ⓠ CIRCLED LATIN SMALL LETTER Q
≈ <circle> 0071 q
24E1 ⓡ CIRCLED LATIN SMALL LETTER R
≈ <circle> 0072 r
24E2 ⓢ CIRCLED LATIN SMALL LETTER S
≈ <circle> 0073 s
24E3 ⓣ CIRCLED LATIN SMALL LETTER T
≈ <circle> 0074 t
24E4 ⓤ CIRCLED LATIN SMALL LETTER U
≈ <circle> 0075 u
24E5 ⓥ CIRCLED LATIN SMALL LETTER V
≈ <circle> 0076 v
24E6 ⓦ CIRCLED LATIN SMALL LETTER W
≈ <circle> 0077 w
24E7 ⓧ CIRCLED LATIN SMALL LETTER X
≈ <circle> 0078 x
24E8 ⓨ CIRCLED LATIN SMALL LETTER Y
≈ <circle> 0079 y
24E9 ⓩ CIRCLED LATIN SMALL LETTER Z
≈ <circle> 007A z

Additional circled number

24EA ⓪ CIRCLED DIGIT ZERO
≈ <circle> 0030 0

White on black circled numbers

24EB ⓫ NEGATIVE CIRCLED NUMBER ELEVEN
24EC ⓬ NEGATIVE CIRCLED NUMBER TWELVE
24ED ⓭ NEGATIVE CIRCLED NUMBER THIRTEEN
24EE ⓮ NEGATIVE CIRCLED NUMBER FOURTEEN
24EF ⓯ NEGATIVE CIRCLED NUMBER FIFTEEN
24F0 ⓰ NEGATIVE CIRCLED NUMBER SIXTEEN
24F1 ⓱ NEGATIVE CIRCLED NUMBER SEVENTEEN
24F2 ⓲ NEGATIVE CIRCLED NUMBER EIGHTEEN
24F3 ⓳ NEGATIVE CIRCLED NUMBER NINETEEN
24F4 ⓴ NEGATIVE CIRCLED NUMBER TWENTY

Double circled numbers

24F5 ⓵ DOUBLE CIRCLED DIGIT ONE
24F6 ⓶ DOUBLE CIRCLED DIGIT TWO
24F7 ⓷ DOUBLE CIRCLED DIGIT THREE
24F8 ⓸ DOUBLE CIRCLED DIGIT FOUR
24F9 ⓹ DOUBLE CIRCLED DIGIT FIVE
24FA ⓺ DOUBLE CIRCLED DIGIT SIX
24FB ⓻ DOUBLE CIRCLED DIGIT SEVEN
24FC ⓼ DOUBLE CIRCLED DIGIT EIGHT
24FD ⓽ DOUBLE CIRCLED DIGIT NINE
24FE ⓾ DOUBLE CIRCLED NUMBER TEN

Additional white on black circled number

24FF ⓿ NEGATIVE CIRCLED DIGIT ZERO
→ 2776 ❶ dingbat negative circled digit one

	250	251	252	253	254	255	256	257
0	─ 2500	┐ 2510	┠ 2520	┰ 2530	╀ 2540	═ 2550	╠ 2560	╰ 2570
1	━ 2501	┑ 2511	┡ 2521	┱ 2531	╁ 2541	║ 2551	╡ 2561	╱ 2571
2	│ 2502	┒ 2512	┢ 2522	┲ 2532	╂ 2542	╒ 2552	╢ 2562	╲ 2572
3	┃ 2503	┓ 2513	┣ 2523	┳ 2533	╃ 2543	╓ 2553	╣ 2563	╳ 2573
4	┄ 2504	└ 2514	┤ 2524	┴ 2534	╄ 2544	╔ 2554	╤ 2564	╴ 2574
5	┅ 2505	┕ 2515	┥ 2525	┵ 2535	╅ 2545	╕ 2555	╥ 2565	╵ 2575
6	┆ 2506	┖ 2516	┦ 2526	┶ 2536	╆ 2546	╖ 2556	╦ 2566	╶ 2576
7	┇ 2507	┗ 2517	┧ 2527	┷ 2537	╇ 2547	╗ 2557	╧ 2567	╷ 2577
8	┈ 2508	┘ 2518	┨ 2528	┸ 2538	╈ 2548	╘ 2558	╨ 2568	╸ 2578
9	┉ 2509	┙ 2519	┩ 2529	┹ 2539	╉ 2549	╙ 2559	╩ 2569	╹ 2579
A	┊ 250A	┚ 251A	┪ 252A	┺ 253A	╊ 254A	╚ 255A	╪ 256A	╺ 257A
B	┋ 250B	┛ 251B	┫ 252B	┻ 253B	╋ 254B	╛ 255B	╫ 256B	╻ 257B
C	┌ 250C	├ 251C	┬ 252C	┼ 253C	╌ 254C	╜ 255C	╬ 256C	╼ 257C
D	┍ 250D	┝ 251D	┭ 252D	┽ 253D	╍ 254D	╝ 255D	╭ 256D	╽ 257D
E	┎ 250E	┞ 251E	┮ 252E	┾ 253E	╎ 254E	╞ 255E	╮ 256E	╾ 257E
F	┏ 250F	┟ 251F	┯ 252F	┿ 253F	╏ 254F	╟ 255F	╯ 256F	╿ 257F

Form and chart components

2500 ─ BOX DRAWINGS LIGHT HORIZONTAL
= Videotex Mosaic DG 15

2501 ━ BOX DRAWINGS HEAVY HORIZONTAL

2502 │ BOX DRAWINGS LIGHT VERTICAL
= Videotex Mosaic DG 14

2503 ┃ BOX DRAWINGS HEAVY VERTICAL

2504 ┄ BOX DRAWINGS LIGHT TRIPLE DASH HORIZONTAL

2505 ┅ BOX DRAWINGS HEAVY TRIPLE DASH HORIZONTAL

2506 ┆ BOX DRAWINGS LIGHT TRIPLE DASH VERTICAL

2507 ┇ BOX DRAWINGS HEAVY TRIPLE DASH VERTICAL

2508 ┈ BOX DRAWINGS LIGHT QUADRUPLE DASH HORIZONTAL

2509 ┉ BOX DRAWINGS HEAVY QUADRUPLE DASH HORIZONTAL

250A ┊ BOX DRAWINGS LIGHT QUADRUPLE DASH VERTICAL

250B ┋ BOX DRAWINGS HEAVY QUADRUPLE DASH VERTICAL

250C ┌ BOX DRAWINGS LIGHT DOWN AND RIGHT
= Videotex Mosaic DG 16

250D ┍ BOX DRAWINGS DOWN LIGHT AND RIGHT HEAVY

250E ┎ BOX DRAWINGS DOWN HEAVY AND RIGHT LIGHT

250F ┏ BOX DRAWINGS HEAVY DOWN AND RIGHT

2510 ┐ BOX DRAWINGS LIGHT DOWN AND LEFT
= Videotex Mosaic DG 17

2511 ┑ BOX DRAWINGS DOWN LIGHT AND LEFT HEAVY

2512 ┒ BOX DRAWINGS DOWN HEAVY AND LEFT LIGHT

2513 ┓ BOX DRAWINGS HEAVY DOWN AND LEFT

2514 └ BOX DRAWINGS LIGHT UP AND RIGHT
= Videotex Mosaic DG 18

2515 ┕ BOX DRAWINGS UP LIGHT AND RIGHT HEAVY

2516 ┖ BOX DRAWINGS UP HEAVY AND RIGHT LIGHT

2517 ┗ BOX DRAWINGS HEAVY UP AND RIGHT

2518 ┘ BOX DRAWINGS LIGHT UP AND LEFT
= Videotex Mosaic DG 19

2519 ┙ BOX DRAWINGS UP LIGHT AND LEFT HEAVY

251A ┚ BOX DRAWINGS UP HEAVY AND LEFT LIGHT

251B ┛ BOX DRAWINGS HEAVY UP AND LEFT

251C ├ BOX DRAWINGS LIGHT VERTICAL AND RIGHT
= Videotex Mosaic DG 20

251D ┝ BOX DRAWINGS VERTICAL LIGHT AND RIGHT HEAVY
= Videotex Mosaic DG 03

251E ┞ BOX DRAWINGS UP HEAVY AND RIGHT DOWN LIGHT

251F ┟ BOX DRAWINGS DOWN HEAVY AND RIGHT UP LIGHT

2520 ┠ BOX DRAWINGS VERTICAL HEAVY AND RIGHT LIGHT

2521 ┡ BOX DRAWINGS DOWN LIGHT AND RIGHT UP HEAVY

2522 ┢ BOX DRAWINGS UP LIGHT AND RIGHT DOWN HEAVY

2523 ┣ BOX DRAWINGS HEAVY VERTICAL AND RIGHT

2524 ┤ BOX DRAWINGS LIGHT VERTICAL AND LEFT
= Videotex Mosaic DG 21

2525 ┥ BOX DRAWINGS VERTICAL LIGHT AND LEFT HEAVY
= Videotex Mosaic DG 04

2526 ┦ BOX DRAWINGS UP HEAVY AND LEFT DOWN LIGHT

2527 ┧ BOX DRAWINGS DOWN HEAVY AND LEFT UP LIGHT

2528 ┨ BOX DRAWINGS VERTICAL HEAVY AND LEFT LIGHT

2529 ┩ BOX DRAWINGS DOWN LIGHT AND LEFT UP HEAVY

252A ┪ BOX DRAWINGS UP LIGHT AND LEFT DOWN HEAVY

252B ┫ BOX DRAWINGS HEAVY VERTICAL AND LEFT

252C ┬ BOX DRAWINGS LIGHT DOWN AND HORIZONTAL
= Videotex Mosaic DG 22

252D ┭ BOX DRAWINGS LEFT HEAVY AND RIGHT DOWN LIGHT

252E ┮ BOX DRAWINGS RIGHT HEAVY AND LEFT DOWN LIGHT

252F ┯ BOX DRAWINGS DOWN LIGHT AND HORIZONTAL HEAVY
= Videotex Mosaic DG 02

2530 ┰ BOX DRAWINGS DOWN HEAVY AND HORIZONTAL LIGHT

2531 ┱ BOX DRAWINGS RIGHT LIGHT AND LEFT DOWN HEAVY

2532 ┲ BOX DRAWINGS LEFT LIGHT AND RIGHT DOWN HEAVY

2533 ┳ BOX DRAWINGS HEAVY DOWN AND HORIZONTAL

2534 ┴ BOX DRAWINGS LIGHT UP AND HORIZONTAL
= Videotex Mosaic DG 23

2535 ┵ BOX DRAWINGS LEFT HEAVY AND RIGHT UP LIGHT

2536 ┶ BOX DRAWINGS RIGHT HEAVY AND LEFT UP LIGHT

2537 ┷ BOX DRAWINGS UP LIGHT AND HORIZONTAL HEAVY
= Videotex Mosaic DG 01

2538 ┸ BOX DRAWINGS UP HEAVY AND HORIZONTAL LIGHT

2539 ┹ BOX DRAWINGS RIGHT LIGHT AND LEFT UP HEAVY

253A ┺ BOX DRAWINGS LEFT LIGHT AND RIGHT UP HEAVY

253B ┻ BOX DRAWINGS HEAVY UP AND HORIZONTAL

253C ┼ BOX DRAWINGS LIGHT VERTICAL AND HORIZONTAL
= Videotex Mosaic DG 24

253D ┽ BOX DRAWINGS LEFT HEAVY AND RIGHT VERTICAL LIGHT

253E ┾ BOX DRAWINGS RIGHT HEAVY AND LEFT VERTICAL LIGHT

253F ┿ BOX DRAWINGS VERTICAL LIGHT AND HORIZONTAL HEAVY
= Videotex Mosaic DG 13

2540 ╀ BOX DRAWINGS UP HEAVY AND DOWN HORIZONTAL LIGHT

2541 ╁ BOX DRAWINGS DOWN HEAVY AND UP HORIZONTAL LIGHT

2542 ╂ BOX DRAWINGS VERTICAL HEAVY AND HORIZONTAL LIGHT

2543 ╃ BOX DRAWINGS LEFT UP HEAVY AND RIGHT DOWN LIGHT

2544 ╄ BOX DRAWINGS RIGHT UP HEAVY AND LEFT DOWN LIGHT

2545 ╅ BOX DRAWINGS LEFT DOWN HEAVY AND RIGHT UP LIGHT

2546 ┮ BOX DRAWINGS RIGHT DOWN HEAVY AND LEFT UP LIGHT
2547 ┯ BOX DRAWINGS DOWN LIGHT AND UP HORIZONTAL HEAVY
2548 ╈ BOX DRAWINGS UP LIGHT AND DOWN HORIZONTAL HEAVY
2549 ╉ BOX DRAWINGS RIGHT LIGHT AND LEFT VERTICAL HEAVY
254A ╊ BOX DRAWINGS LEFT LIGHT AND RIGHT VERTICAL HEAVY
254B ╋ BOX DRAWINGS HEAVY VERTICAL AND HORIZONTAL
254C ╌ BOX DRAWINGS LIGHT DOUBLE DASH HORIZONTAL
254D ╍ BOX DRAWINGS HEAVY DOUBLE DASH HORIZONTAL
254E ╎ BOX DRAWINGS LIGHT DOUBLE DASH VERTICAL
254F ╏ BOX DRAWINGS HEAVY DOUBLE DASH VERTICAL
2550 ═ BOX DRAWINGS DOUBLE HORIZONTAL
2551 ║ BOX DRAWINGS DOUBLE VERTICAL
2552 ╒ BOX DRAWINGS DOWN SINGLE AND RIGHT DOUBLE
2553 ╓ BOX DRAWINGS DOWN DOUBLE AND RIGHT SINGLE
2554 ╔ BOX DRAWINGS DOUBLE DOWN AND RIGHT
2555 ╕ BOX DRAWINGS DOWN SINGLE AND LEFT DOUBLE
2556 ╖ BOX DRAWINGS DOWN DOUBLE AND LEFT SINGLE
2557 ╗ BOX DRAWINGS DOUBLE DOWN AND LEFT
2558 ╘ BOX DRAWINGS UP SINGLE AND RIGHT DOUBLE
2559 ╙ BOX DRAWINGS UP DOUBLE AND RIGHT SINGLE
255A ╚ BOX DRAWINGS DOUBLE UP AND RIGHT
255B ╛ BOX DRAWINGS UP SINGLE AND LEFT DOUBLE
255C ╜ BOX DRAWINGS UP DOUBLE AND LEFT SINGLE
255D ╝ BOX DRAWINGS DOUBLE UP AND LEFT
255E ╞ BOX DRAWINGS VERTICAL SINGLE AND RIGHT DOUBLE
255F ╟ BOX DRAWINGS VERTICAL DOUBLE AND RIGHT SINGLE
2560 ╠ BOX DRAWINGS DOUBLE VERTICAL AND RIGHT
2561 ╡ BOX DRAWINGS VERTICAL SINGLE AND LEFT DOUBLE
2562 ╢ BOX DRAWINGS VERTICAL DOUBLE AND LEFT SINGLE
2563 ╣ BOX DRAWINGS DOUBLE VERTICAL AND LEFT
2564 ╤ BOX DRAWINGS DOWN SINGLE AND HORIZONTAL DOUBLE
2565 ╥ BOX DRAWINGS DOWN DOUBLE AND HORIZONTAL SINGLE
2566 ╦ BOX DRAWINGS DOUBLE DOWN AND HORIZONTAL
2567 ╧ BOX DRAWINGS UP SINGLE AND HORIZONTAL DOUBLE
2568 ╨ BOX DRAWINGS UP DOUBLE AND HORIZONTAL SINGLE
2569 ╩ BOX DRAWINGS DOUBLE UP AND HORIZONTAL
256A ╪ BOX DRAWINGS VERTICAL SINGLE AND HORIZONTAL DOUBLE
256B ╫ BOX DRAWINGS VERTICAL DOUBLE AND HORIZONTAL SINGLE
256C ╬ BOX DRAWINGS DOUBLE VERTICAL AND HORIZONTAL
256D ╭ BOX DRAWINGS LIGHT ARC DOWN AND RIGHT
256E ╮ BOX DRAWINGS LIGHT ARC DOWN AND LEFT
256F ╯ BOX DRAWINGS LIGHT ARC UP AND LEFT
2570 ╰ BOX DRAWINGS LIGHT ARC UP AND RIGHT
2571 ╱ BOX DRAWINGS LIGHT DIAGONAL UPPER RIGHT TO LOWER LEFT
2572 ╲ BOX DRAWINGS LIGHT DIAGONAL UPPER LEFT TO LOWER RIGHT
2573 ╳ BOX DRAWINGS LIGHT DIAGONAL CROSS
2574 ╴ BOX DRAWINGS LIGHT LEFT
2575 ╵ BOX DRAWINGS LIGHT UP
2576 ╶ BOX DRAWINGS LIGHT RIGHT
2577 ╷ BOX DRAWINGS LIGHT DOWN
2578 ╸ BOX DRAWINGS HEAVY LEFT
2579 ╹ BOX DRAWINGS HEAVY UP
257A ╺ BOX DRAWINGS HEAVY RIGHT
257B ╻ BOX DRAWINGS HEAVY DOWN
257C ╼ BOX DRAWINGS LIGHT LEFT AND HEAVY RIGHT
257D ╽ BOX DRAWINGS LIGHT UP AND HEAVY DOWN
257E ╾ BOX DRAWINGS HEAVY LEFT AND LIGHT RIGHT
257F ╿ BOX DRAWINGS HEAVY UP AND LIGHT DOWN

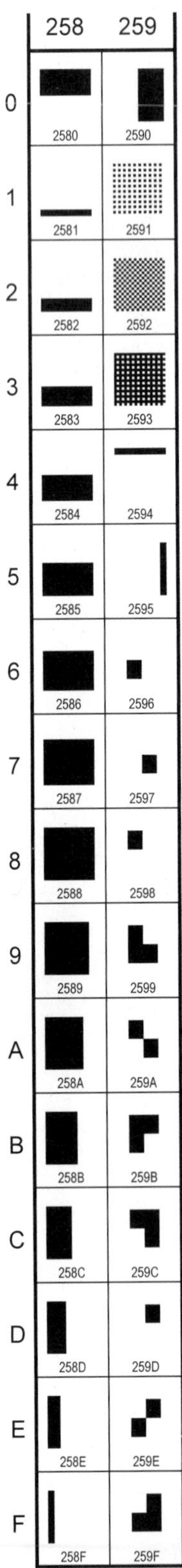

Block elements

2580 ▀ UPPER HALF BLOCK
2581 ▁ LOWER ONE EIGHTH BLOCK
2582 ▂ LOWER ONE QUARTER BLOCK
2583 ▃ LOWER THREE EIGHTHS BLOCK
2584 ▄ LOWER HALF BLOCK
2585 ▅ LOWER FIVE EIGHTHS BLOCK
2586 ▆ LOWER THREE QUARTERS BLOCK
2587 ▇ LOWER SEVEN EIGHTHS BLOCK
2588 █ FULL BLOCK
= solid
→ 25A0 ■ black square
2589 ▉ LEFT SEVEN EIGHTHS BLOCK
258A ▊ LEFT THREE QUARTERS BLOCK
258B ▋ LEFT FIVE EIGHTHS BLOCK
258C ▌ LEFT HALF BLOCK
258D ▍ LEFT THREE EIGHTHS BLOCK
258E ▎ LEFT ONE QUARTER BLOCK
258F ▏ LEFT ONE EIGHTH BLOCK
2590 ▐ RIGHT HALF BLOCK

Shade characters

2591 ░ LIGHT SHADE
• 25%
2592 ▒ MEDIUM SHADE
• 50%
2593 ▓ DARK SHADE
• 75%

Block elements

2594 ▔ UPPER ONE EIGHTH BLOCK
2595 ▕ RIGHT ONE EIGHTH BLOCK

Terminal graphic characters

2596 ▖ QUADRANT LOWER LEFT
2597 ▗ QUADRANT LOWER RIGHT
2598 ▘ QUADRANT UPPER LEFT
2599 ▙ QUADRANT UPPER LEFT AND LOWER LEFT AND LOWER RIGHT
259A ▚ QUADRANT UPPER LEFT AND LOWER RIGHT
259B ▛ QUADRANT UPPER LEFT AND UPPER RIGHT AND LOWER LEFT
259C ▜ QUADRANT UPPER LEFT AND UPPER RIGHT AND LOWER RIGHT
259D ▝ QUADRANT UPPER RIGHT
259E ▞ QUADRANT UPPER RIGHT AND LOWER LEFT
259F ▟ QUADRANT UPPER RIGHT AND LOWER LEFT AND LOWER RIGHT

	25A	25B	25C	25D	25E	25F
0	25A0	25B0	25C0	25D0	25E0	25F0
1	25A1	25B1	25C1	25D1	25E1	25F1
2	25A2	25B2	25C2	25D2	25E2	25F2
3	25A3	25B3	25C3	25D3	25E3	25F3
4	25A4	25B4	25C4	25D4	25E4	25F4
5	25A5	25B5	25C5	25D5	25E5	25F5
6	25A6	25B6	25C6	25D6	25E6	25F6
7	25A7	25B7	25C7	25D7	25E7	25F7
8	25A8	25B8	25C8	25D8	25E8	25F8
9	25A9	25B9	25C9	25D9	25E9	25F9
A	25AA	25BA	25CA	25DA	25EA	25FA
B	25AB	25BB	25CB	25DB	25EB	25FB
C	25AC	25BC	25CC	25DC	25EC	25FC
D	25AD	25BD	25CD	25DD	25ED	25FD
E	25AE	25BE	25CE	25DE	25EE	25FE
F	25AF	25BF	25CF	25DF	25EF	25FF

Geometric shapes

Other geometric shapes complementing this set are found in the Miscellaneous Symbols and Arrows block.

25A0 ■ BLACK SQUARE
= moding mark (in ideographic text)
→ 2588 █ full block

25A1 □ WHITE SQUARE
= quadrature
• may be used to represent a missing ideograph
→ 20DE ⃞ combining enclosing square
→ 2610 ☐ ballot box
→ 3013 〓 geta mark

25A2 ▢ WHITE SQUARE WITH ROUNDED CORNERS
25A3 ▣ WHITE SQUARE CONTAINING BLACK SMALL SQUARE
25A4 ▤ SQUARE WITH HORIZONTAL FILL
25A5 ▥ SQUARE WITH VERTICAL FILL
25A6 ▦ SQUARE WITH ORTHOGONAL CROSSHATCH FILL
25A7 ▧ SQUARE WITH UPPER LEFT TO LOWER RIGHT FILL
25A8 ▨ SQUARE WITH UPPER RIGHT TO LOWER LEFT FILL
25A9 ▩ SQUARE WITH DIAGONAL CROSSHATCH FILL
25AA ▪ BLACK SMALL SQUARE
25AB ▫ WHITE SMALL SQUARE
25AC ▬ BLACK RECTANGLE
25AD ▭ WHITE RECTANGLE

25AE ▮ BLACK VERTICAL RECTANGLE
= histogram marker
→ 220E ∎ end of proof

25AF ▯ WHITE VERTICAL RECTANGLE
→ 2337 ⌷ apl functional symbol squish quad
→ 2395 ⎕ apl functional symbol quad

25B0 ▰ BLACK PARALLELOGRAM
25B1 ▱ WHITE PARALLELOGRAM
25B2 ▲ BLACK UP-POINTING TRIANGLE

25B3 △ WHITE UP-POINTING TRIANGLE
= trine
→ 20E4 ⃤ combining enclosing upward pointing triangle
→ 2206 ∆ increment

25B4 ▴ BLACK UP-POINTING SMALL TRIANGLE
25B5 ▵ WHITE UP-POINTING SMALL TRIANGLE
25B6 ▶ BLACK RIGHT-POINTING TRIANGLE

25B7 ▷ WHITE RIGHT-POINTING TRIANGLE
= z notation range restriction

25B8 ▸ BLACK RIGHT-POINTING SMALL TRIANGLE
→ 2023 ‣ triangular bullet

25B9 ▹ WHITE RIGHT-POINTING SMALL TRIANGLE
25BA ► BLACK RIGHT-POINTING POINTER

25BB ▻ WHITE RIGHT-POINTING POINTER
= forward arrow indicator
→ 22B3 ⊳ contains as normal subgroup

25BC ▼ BLACK DOWN-POINTING TRIANGLE

25BD ▽ WHITE DOWN-POINTING TRIANGLE
= Hamilton operator
→ 2207 ∇ nabla

25BE ▾ BLACK DOWN-POINTING SMALL TRIANGLE
25BF ▿ WHITE DOWN-POINTING SMALL TRIANGLE
25C0 ◀ BLACK LEFT-POINTING TRIANGLE

25C1 ◁ WHITE LEFT-POINTING TRIANGLE
= z notation domain restriction

25C2 ◂ BLACK LEFT-POINTING SMALL TRIANGLE
25C3 ◃ WHITE LEFT-POINTING SMALL TRIANGLE
25C4 ◄ BLACK LEFT-POINTING POINTER

25C5 ◅ WHITE LEFT-POINTING POINTER
= backward arrow indicator
→ 22B2 ⊲ normal subgroup of

25C6 ◆ BLACK DIAMOND
→ 2666 ♦ black diamond suit

25C7 ◇ WHITE DIAMOND
→ 20DF ⃟ combining enclosing diamond
→ 22C4 ⋄ diamond operator
→ 2662 ♢ white diamond suit

25C8 ◈ WHITE DIAMOND CONTAINING BLACK SMALL DIAMOND

25C9 ◉ FISHEYE
= tainome (Japanese, a kind of bullet)

25CA ◊ LOZENGE
→ 2662 ♢ white diamond suit

25CB ○ WHITE CIRCLE
→ 20DD ⃝ combining enclosing circle
→ 25EF ◯ large circle
→ 3007 〇 ideographic number zero

25CC ◌ DOTTED CIRCLE
• note that the reference glyph for this character is intentionally larger than the dotted circle glyph used to indicate combining characters in this standard; see, for example, 0300 ◌̀

25CD ◍ CIRCLE WITH VERTICAL FILL

25CE ◎ BULLSEYE
→ 229A ⊚ circled ring operator

25CF ● BLACK CIRCLE
25D0 ◐ CIRCLE WITH LEFT HALF BLACK
25D1 ◑ CIRCLE WITH RIGHT HALF BLACK
25D2 ◒ CIRCLE WITH LOWER HALF BLACK
25D3 ◓ CIRCLE WITH UPPER HALF BLACK
25D4 ◔ CIRCLE WITH UPPER RIGHT QUADRANT BLACK
25D5 ◕ CIRCLE WITH ALL BUT UPPER LEFT QUADRANT BLACK
25D6 ◖ LEFT HALF BLACK CIRCLE
25D7 ◗ RIGHT HALF BLACK CIRCLE

25D8 ◘ INVERSE BULLET
→ 2022 • bullet
→ 25E6 ◦ white bullet

25D9 ◙ INVERSE WHITE CIRCLE
25DA ◚ UPPER HALF INVERSE WHITE CIRCLE
25DB ◛ LOWER HALF INVERSE WHITE CIRCLE
25DC ◜ UPPER LEFT QUADRANT CIRCULAR ARC
25DD ◝ UPPER RIGHT QUADRANT CIRCULAR ARC
25DE ◞ LOWER RIGHT QUADRANT CIRCULAR ARC
25DF ◟ LOWER LEFT QUADRANT CIRCULAR ARC

25E0 ◠ UPPER HALF CIRCLE
→ 2312 ⌒ arc

25E1 ◡ LOWER HALF CIRCLE
25E2 ◢ BLACK LOWER RIGHT TRIANGLE
25E3 ◣ BLACK LOWER LEFT TRIANGLE
25E4 ◤ BLACK UPPER LEFT TRIANGLE
25E5 ◥ BLACK UPPER RIGHT TRIANGLE

25E6 ◦ WHITE BULLET
→ 2022 • bullet
→ 2218 ∘ ring operator
→ 25D8 ◘ inverse bullet

25E7 ◧ SQUARE WITH LEFT HALF BLACK
→ 2B12 ⬒ square with top half black

25E8 ◨ SQUARE WITH RIGHT HALF BLACK

25E9 ◩ SQUARE WITH UPPER LEFT DIAGONAL HALF BLACK
25EA ◪ SQUARE WITH LOWER RIGHT DIAGONAL HALF BLACK
25EB ◫ WHITE SQUARE WITH VERTICAL BISECTING LINE
25EC ◬ WHITE UP-POINTING TRIANGLE WITH DOT
25ED ◭ UP-POINTING TRIANGLE WITH LEFT HALF BLACK
25EE ◮ UP-POINTING TRIANGLE WITH RIGHT HALF BLACK
25EF ◯ LARGE CIRCLE
→ 20DD ⃝ combining enclosing circle
→ 25CB ○ white circle
→ 3007 〇 ideographic number zero

Control code graphics

25F0 ◰ WHITE SQUARE WITH UPPER LEFT QUADRANT
25F1 ◱ WHITE SQUARE WITH LOWER LEFT QUADRANT
25F2 ◲ WHITE SQUARE WITH LOWER RIGHT QUADRANT
25F3 ◳ WHITE SQUARE WITH UPPER RIGHT QUADRANT
25F4 ◴ WHITE CIRCLE WITH UPPER LEFT QUADRANT
25F5 ◵ WHITE CIRCLE WITH LOWER LEFT QUADRANT
25F6 ◶ WHITE CIRCLE WITH LOWER RIGHT QUADRANT
25F7 ◷ WHITE CIRCLE WITH UPPER RIGHT QUADRANT

Geometric shapes

25F8 ◸ UPPER LEFT TRIANGLE
25F9 ◹ UPPER RIGHT TRIANGLE
25FA ◺ LOWER LEFT TRIANGLE
→ 22BF ⊿ right triangle
25FB ◻ WHITE MEDIUM SQUARE
= always (modal operator)
→ 25A1 □ white square
25FC ◼ BLACK MEDIUM SQUARE
→ 25A0 ■ black square
25FD ◽ WHITE MEDIUM SMALL SQUARE
→ 25AB ▫ white small square
25FE ◾ BLACK MEDIUM SMALL SQUARE
→ 25AA ▪ black small square
25FF ◿ LOWER RIGHT TRIANGLE
→ 22BF ⊿ right triangle

	260	261	262	263	264	265	266	267	268	269	26A	26B	26C	26D	26E	26F
0	☀ 2600	☐ 2610	☠ 2620	☰ 2630	♀ 2640	♐ 2650	♠ 2660	♰ 2670	⚀ 2680	⚐ 2690	⚠ 26A0	⚰ 26B0				
1	☁ 2601	☑ 2611	☡ 2621	☱ 2631	♁ 2641	♑ 2651	♡ 2661	♱ 2671	⚁ 2681	⚑ 2691	⚡ 26A1	⚱ 26B1				
2	☂ 2602	☒ 2612	☢ 2622	☲ 2632	♂ 2642	♒ 2652	♢ 2662	♲ 2672	⚂ 2682	⚒ 2692	⚢ 26A2	⚲ 26B2				
3	☃ 2603	☓ 2613	☣ 2623	☳ 2633	♃ 2643	♓ 2653	♣ 2663	♳ 2673	⚃ 2683	⚓ 2693	⚣ 26A3					
4	☄ 2604	☔ 2614	☤ 2624	☴ 2634	♄ 2644	♔ 2654	♤ 2664	♴ 2674	⚄ 2684	⚔ 2694	⚤ 26A4					
5	★ 2605	☕ 2615	☥ 2625	☵ 2635	♅ 2645	♕ 2655	♥ 2665	♵ 2675	⚅ 2685	⚕ 2695	⚥ 26A5					
6	☆ 2606	☖ 2616	☦ 2626	☶ 2636	♆ 2646	♖ 2656	♦ 2666	♶ 2676	⚆ 2686	⚖ 2696	⚦ 26A6					
7	☇ 2607	☗ 2617	☧ 2627	☷ 2637	♇ 2647	♗ 2657	♧ 2667	♷ 2677	⚇ 2687	⚗ 2697	⚧ 26A7					
8	☈ 2608	☘ 2618	☨ 2628	☸ 2638	♈ 2648	♘ 2658	♨ 2668	♸ 2678	⚈ 2688	⚘ 2698	⚨ 26A8					
9	☉ 2609	☙ 2619	☩ 2629	☹ 2639	♉ 2649	♙ 2659	♩ 2669	♹ 2679	⚉ 2689	⚙ 2699	⚩ 26A9					
A	☊ 260A	☚ 261A	☪ 262A	☺ 263A	♊ 264A	♚ 265A	♪ 266A	♺ 267A	⚊ 268A	⚚ 269A	⚪ 26AA					
B	☋ 260B	☛ 261B	☫ 262B	☻ 263B	♋ 264B	♛ 265B	♫ 266B	♻ 267B	⚋ 268B	⚛ 269B	⚫ 26AB					
C	☌ 260C	☜ 261C	☬ 262C	☼ 263C	♌ 264C	♜ 265C	♬ 266C	♼ 267C	⚌ 268C	⚜ 269C	⚬ 26AC					
D	☍ 260D	☝ 261D	☭ 262D	☽ 263D	♍ 264D	♝ 265D	♭ 266D	♽ 267D	⚍ 268D		⚭ 26AD					
E	☎ 260E	☞ 261E	☮ 262E	☾ 263E	♎ 264E	♞ 265E	♮ 266E	♾ 267E	⚎ 268E		⚮ 26AE					
F	☏ 260F	☟ 261F	☯ 262F	☿ 263F	♏ 264F	♟ 265F	♯ 266F	♿ 267F	⚏ 268F		⚯ 26AF					

Weather and astrological symbols

2600 ☀ BLACK SUN WITH RAYS
= clear weather
→ 2609 ☉ sun

2601 ☁ CLOUD
= cloudy weather

2602 ☂ UMBRELLA
= rainy weather

2603 ☃ SNOWMAN
= snowy weather

2604 ☄ COMET

2605 ★ BLACK STAR
→ 22C6 ⋆ star operator

2606 ☆ WHITE STAR
→ 2729 ✩ stress outlined white star

2607 ☇ LIGHTNING

2608 ☈ THUNDERSTORM

2609 ☉ SUN
→ 2299 ⊙ circled dot operator
→ 2600 ☀ black sun with rays
→ 263C ☼ white sun with rays

260A ☊ ASCENDING NODE

260B ☋ DESCENDING NODE

260C ☌ CONJUNCTION

260D ☍ OPPOSITION

Miscellaneous symbols

260E ☎ BLACK TELEPHONE
→ 2121 ℡ telephone sign
→ 2706 ✆ telephone location sign

260F ☏ WHITE TELEPHONE

2610 ☐ BALLOT BOX
→ 25A1 □ white square

2611 ☑ BALLOT BOX WITH CHECK

2612 ☒ BALLOT BOX WITH X
→ 22A0 ⊠ squared times

2613 ☓ SALTIRE
= St. Andrew's Cross
→ 2717 ✗ ballot x

Weather symbol

2614 ☔ UMBRELLA WITH RAIN DROPS
= showery weather

Miscellaneous symbol

2615 ☕ HOT BEVERAGE
= tea or coffee, depending on locale
• can be used to indicate a wait
→ 231A ⌚ watch
→ 231B ⌛ hourglass

Japanese chess symbols

2616 ☖ WHITE SHOGI PIECE

2617 ☗ BLACK SHOGI PIECE

Miscellaneous symbols

2618 ☘ SHAMROCK

2619 ☙ REVERSED ROTATED FLORAL HEART BULLET
• a binding signature mark
→ 2767 ❧ rotated floral heart bullet

Pointing hand symbols

261A ☚ BLACK LEFT POINTING INDEX

261B ☛ BLACK RIGHT POINTING INDEX

261C ☜ WHITE LEFT POINTING INDEX

261D ☝ WHITE UP POINTING INDEX

261E ☞ WHITE RIGHT POINTING INDEX
= fist (typographic term)

261F ☟ WHITE DOWN POINTING INDEX

Warning signs

2620 ☠ SKULL AND CROSSBONES
= poison

2621 ☡ CAUTION SIGN

2622 ☢ RADIOACTIVE SIGN

2623 ☣ BIOHAZARD SIGN

Medical and healing symbols

2624 ☤ CADUCEUS
→ 2695 ⚕ staff of aesculapius

2625 ☥ ANKH

Religious and political symbols

2626 ☦ ORTHODOX CROSS

2627 ☧ CHI RHO
= Constantine's cross, Christogram
→ 2CE9 ⳩ coptic symbol khi ro

2628 ☨ CROSS OF LORRAINE

2629 ☩ CROSS OF JERUSALEM

262A ☪ STAR AND CRESCENT

262B ☫ FARSI SYMBOL
= symbol of iran (1.0)

262C ☬ ADI SHAKTI
= Gurmukhi khanda

262D ☭ HAMMER AND SICKLE

262E ☮ PEACE SYMBOL

262F ☯ YIN YANG
→ 0FCA ࿊ tibetan symbol nor bu nyis -khyil

Yijing trigram symbols

2630 ☰ TRIGRAM FOR HEAVEN
= qian2

2631 ☱ TRIGRAM FOR LAKE
= dui4

2632 ☲ TRIGRAM FOR FIRE
= li2

2633 ☳ TRIGRAM FOR THUNDER
= zhen4

2634 ☴ TRIGRAM FOR WIND
= xun4

2635 ☵ TRIGRAM FOR WATER
= kan3

2636 ☶ TRIGRAM FOR MOUNTAIN
= gen4

2637 ☷ TRIGRAM FOR EARTH
= kun1

Miscellaneous symbols

2638 ☸ WHEEL OF DHARMA
→ 2388 ⎈ helm symbol

2639 ☹ WHITE FROWNING FACE

263A ☺ WHITE SMILING FACE
= have a nice day!

263B ☻ BLACK SMILING FACE

263C ☼ WHITE SUN WITH RAYS
= compass
→ 2609 ☉ sun

Astrological symbols

263D ☽ FIRST QUARTER MOON

263E ☾ LAST QUARTER MOON

263F ☿ MERCURY

2640 ♀ FEMALE SIGN
= Venus

2641 ♁ EARTH
→ 2295 ⊕ circled plus
2642 ♂ MALE SIGN
= Mars
2643 ♃ JUPITER
2644 ♄ SATURN
2645 ♅ URANUS
2646 ♆ NEPTUNE
2647 ♇ PLUTO

Zodiacal symbols

2648 ♈ ARIES
2649 ♉ TAURUS
264A ♊ GEMINI
264B ♋ CANCER
264C ♌ LEO
264D ♍ VIRGO
= minim (alternate glyph)
264E ♎ LIBRA
264F ♏ SCORPIUS
= minim, drop
2650 ♐ SAGITTARIUS
2651 ♑ CAPRICORN
2652 ♒ AQUARIUS
2653 ♓ PISCES

Chess symbols

2654 ♔ WHITE CHESS KING
2655 ♕ WHITE CHESS QUEEN
2656 ♖ WHITE CHESS ROOK
2657 ♗ WHITE CHESS BISHOP
2658 ♘ WHITE CHESS KNIGHT
2659 ♙ WHITE CHESS PAWN
265A ♚ BLACK CHESS KING
265B ♛ BLACK CHESS QUEEN
265C ♜ BLACK CHESS ROOK
265D ♝ BLACK CHESS BISHOP
265E ♞ BLACK CHESS KNIGHT
265F ♟ BLACK CHESS PAWN

Playing card symbols

2660 ♠ BLACK SPADE SUIT
2661 ♡ WHITE HEART SUIT
2662 ♢ WHITE DIAMOND SUIT
→ 25C7 ◇ white diamond
→ 25CA ◊ lozenge
2663 ♣ BLACK CLUB SUIT
→ 2618 ☘ shamrock
2664 ♤ WHITE SPADE SUIT
2665 ♥ BLACK HEART SUIT
= valentine
→ 2764 ❤ heavy black heart
2666 ♦ BLACK DIAMOND SUIT
→ 25C6 ◆ black diamond
2667 ♧ WHITE CLUB SUIT

Miscellaneous symbol

2668 ♨ HOT SPRINGS

Musical symbols

2669 ♩ QUARTER NOTE
266A ♪ EIGHTH NOTE
266B ♫ BEAMED EIGHTH NOTES
266C ♬ BEAMED SIXTEENTH NOTES
266D ♭ MUSIC FLAT SIGN
266E ♮ MUSIC NATURAL SIGN
266F ♯ MUSIC SHARP SIGN
= z notation infix bag count
→ 0023 # number sign

Syriac cross symbols

These symbols are used in liturgical texts of Syriac-speaking churches.

2670 ♰ WEST SYRIAC CROSS
2671 ♱ EAST SYRIAC CROSS

Recycling symbols

2672 ♲ UNIVERSAL RECYCLING SYMBOL
• used as generic symbol for recycling or to indicate that material is recyclable
2673 ♳ RECYCLING SYMBOL FOR TYPE-1 PLASTICS
• polyethylene terephthalate
2674 ♴ RECYCLING SYMBOL FOR TYPE-2 PLASTICS
• high density polyethylene
2675 ♵ RECYCLING SYMBOL FOR TYPE-3 PLASTICS
• vinyl, polyvinyl chloride
2676 ♶ RECYCLING SYMBOL FOR TYPE-4 PLASTICS
• low density polyethylene
2677 ♷ RECYCLING SYMBOL FOR TYPE-5 PLASTICS
• polypropylene
2678 ♸ RECYCLING SYMBOL FOR TYPE-6 PLASTICS
• polystyrene
2679 ♹ RECYCLING SYMBOL FOR TYPE-7 PLASTICS
• other plastics
267A ♺ RECYCLING SYMBOL FOR GENERIC MATERIALS
• used together with other text and labels to indicate the type of material to be recycled
267B ♻ BLACK UNIVERSAL RECYCLING SYMBOL
267C ♼ RECYCLED PAPER SYMBOL
• used to indicate 100% recycled paper content
267D ♽ PARTIALLY-RECYCLED PAPER SYMBOL
• percentage of recycled paper content indicated in overlay or next to this symbol

Miscellaneous symbols

267E ♾ PERMANENT PAPER SIGN
267F ♿ WHEELCHAIR SYMBOL

Dice

2680 ⚀ DIE FACE-1
2681 ⚁ DIE FACE-2
2682 ⚂ DIE FACE-3
2683 ⚃ DIE FACE-4
2684 ⚄ DIE FACE-5
2685 ⚅ DIE FACE-6

Go markers

2686 ⚆ WHITE CIRCLE WITH DOT RIGHT
2687 ⚇ WHITE CIRCLE WITH TWO DOTS
2688 ⚈ BLACK CIRCLE WITH WHITE DOT RIGHT
2689 ⚉ BLACK CIRCLE WITH TWO WHITE DOTS

Yijing monogram and digram symbols

These form a subset of the larger collection found in the Tai Xuan Jing Symbols block.

268A ⚊ MONOGRAM FOR YANG
268B ⚋ MONOGRAM FOR YIN
268C ⚌ DIGRAM FOR GREATER YANG
268D ⚍ DIGRAM FOR LESSER YIN
268E ⚎ DIGRAM FOR LESSER YANG
268F ⚏ DIGRAM FOR GREATER YIN

Dictionary and map symbols

2690 ⚐ WHITE FLAG
2691 ⚑ BLACK FLAG
2692 ⚒ HAMMER AND PICK
= mining, working day (in timetables)
2693 ⚓ ANCHOR
= nautical term, harbor (on maps)
2694 ⚔ CROSSED SWORDS
= military term, battleground (on maps), killed in action
2695 ⚕ STAFF OF AESCULAPIUS
= medical term
• both inclined or upright renderings of this symbol are common
→ 2624 ☤ caduceus
2696 ⚖ SCALES
= legal term, jurisprudence
2697 ⚗ ALEMBIC
= chemical term, chemistry
2698 ⚘ FLOWER
= botanical term
→ 2055 ⁕ flower punctuation mark
→ 2618 ☘ shamrock
→ 2740 ❀ white florette
2699 ⚙ GEAR
= technology, tools
269A ⚚ STAFF OF HERMES
• signifies a commercial term or commerce
• glyph shows a heraldic staff with a winged wheel
269B ⚛ ATOM SYMBOL
= nuclear installation (on maps)

Miscellaneous symbols

269C ⚜ FLEUR-DE-LIS
269D <reserved>
269E <reserved>
269F <reserved>
26A0 ⚠ WARNING SIGN
26A1 ⚡ HIGH VOLTAGE SIGN

Gender symbols

26A2 ⚢ DOUBLED FEMALE SIGN
= lesbianism
26A3 ⚣ DOUBLED MALE SIGN
• a glyph variant has the two circles on the same line
= male homosexuality
26A4 ⚤ INTERLOCKED FEMALE AND MALE SIGN
• a glyph variant has the two circles on the same line
= bisexuality
26A5 ⚥ MALE AND FEMALE SIGN
= transgendered sexuality
= hermaphrodite (in entomology)
26A6 ⚦ MALE WITH STROKE SIGN
= transgendered sexuality
26A7 ⚧ MALE WITH STROKE AND MALE AND FEMALE SIGN
= transgendered sexuality
26A8 ⚨ VERTICAL MALE WITH STROKE SIGN
= ferrous iron sulphate (alchemy and older chemistry)
26A9 ⚩ HORIZONTAL MALE WITH STROKE SIGN
= magnesium (alchemy and older chemistry)

Circles

26AA ⚪ MEDIUM WHITE CIRCLE
= asexuality, sexless, genderless
= engaged, betrothed
• base for male or female sign
26AB ⚫ MEDIUM BLACK CIRCLE
• UI symbol for record function
26AC ⚬ MEDIUM SMALL WHITE CIRCLE
= engaged, betrothed (genealogy)
• can represent wedding ring

Genealogical symbols

26AD ⚭ MARRIAGE SYMBOL
→ 221E ∞ infinity
26AE ⚮ DIVORCE SYMBOL
→ 29DE ⧞ infinity negated with vertical bar
26AF ⚯ UNMARRIED PARTNERSHIP SYMBOL
→ 29DF ⧟ double-ended multimap
26B0 ⚰ COFFIN
= buried (genealogy)
→ 25AD ▭ white rectangle
26B1 ⚱ FUNERAL URN
= cremated (genealogy)

Gender symbol

26B2 ⚲ NEUTER

	270	271	272	273	274	275	276	277	278	279	27A	27B
0		2710	2720	2730	2740	2750		2770	2780	2790	27A0	
1	2701	2711	2721	2731	2741	2751	2761	2771	2781	2791	27A1	27B1
2	2702	2712	2722	2732	2742	2752	2762	2772	2782	2792	27A2	27B2
3	2703	2713	2723	2733	2743		2763	2773	2783	2793	27A3	27B3
4	2704	2714	2724	2734	2744		2764	2774	2784	2794	27A4	27B4
5		2715	2725	2735	2745		2765	2775	2785		27A5	27B5
6	2706	2716	2726	2736	2746	2756	2766	2776	2786		27A6	27B6
7	2707	2717	2727	2737	2747		2767	2777	2787		27A7	27B7
8	2708	2718		2738	2748	2758	2768	2778	2788	2798	27A8	27B8
9	2709	2719	2729	2739	2749	2759	2769	2779	2789	2799	27A9	27B9
A		271A	272A	273A	274A	275A	276A	277A	278A	279A	27AA	27BA
B		271B	272B	273B	274B	275B	276B	277B	278B	279B	27AB	27BB
C	270C	271C	272C	273C		275C	276C	277C	278C	279C	27AC	27BC
D	270D	271D	272D	273D	274D	275D	276D	277D	278D	279D	27AD	27BD
E	270E	271E	272E	273E		275E	276E	277E	278E	279E	27AE	27BE
F	270F	271F	272F	273F	274F		276F	277F	278F	279F	27AF	

ITC Zapf dingbats series 100

Miscellaneous

- 2701 ✁ UPPER BLADE SCISSORS
- 2702 ✂ BLACK SCISSORS
- 2703 ✃ LOWER BLADE SCISSORS
- 2704 ✄ WHITE SCISSORS
- 2705 <reserved>
  - → 260E ☎ black telephone
- 2706 ✆ TELEPHONE LOCATION SIGN
  - → 2121 ℡ telephone sign
- 2707 ✇ TAPE DRIVE
- 2708 ✈ AIRPLANE
- 2709 ✉ ENVELOPE
- 270A <reserved>
  - → 261B ☛ black right pointing index
- 270B <reserved>
  - → 261E ☞ white right pointing index
- 270C ✌ VICTORY HAND
- 270D ✍ WRITING HAND
- 270E ✎ LOWER RIGHT PENCIL
- 270F ✏ PENCIL
- 2710 ✐ UPPER RIGHT PENCIL
- 2711 ✑ WHITE NIB
- 2712 ✒ BLACK NIB
- 2713 ✓ CHECK MARK
  - → 221A √ square root
- 2714 ✔ HEAVY CHECK MARK
- 2715 ✕ MULTIPLICATION X
  - → 00D7 × multiplication sign
  - → 2573 ╳ box drawings light diagonal cross
- 2716 ✖ HEAVY MULTIPLICATION X
- 2717 ✗ BALLOT X
  - → 2613 ☓ saltire
- 2718 ✘ HEAVY BALLOT X

Crosses

- 2719 ✙ OUTLINED GREEK CROSS
- 271A ✚ HEAVY GREEK CROSS
- 271B ✛ OPEN CENTRE CROSS
- 271C ✜ HEAVY OPEN CENTRE CROSS
- 271D ✝ LATIN CROSS
- 271E ✞ SHADOWED WHITE LATIN CROSS
- 271F ✟ OUTLINED LATIN CROSS
- 2720 ✠ MALTESE CROSS
  - • Historically, the Maltese cross took many forms; the shape shown in the Zapf Dingbats is similar to one known as the Cross Formée.

Stars, asterisks and snowflakes

- 2721 ✡ STAR OF DAVID
- 2722 ✢ FOUR TEARDROP-SPOKED ASTERISK
- 2723 ✣ FOUR BALLOON-SPOKED ASTERISK
- 2724 ✤ HEAVY FOUR BALLOON-SPOKED ASTERISK
- 2725 ✥ FOUR CLUB-SPOKED ASTERISK
- 2726 ✦ BLACK FOUR POINTED STAR
- 2727 ✧ WHITE FOUR POINTED STAR
- 2728 <reserved>
  - → 2605 ★ black star
- 2729 ✩ STRESS OUTLINED WHITE STAR
  - → 2606 ☆ white star
- 272A ✪ CIRCLED WHITE STAR
- 272B ✫ OPEN CENTRE BLACK STAR
- 272C ✬ BLACK CENTRE WHITE STAR
- 272D ✭ OUTLINED BLACK STAR
- 272E ✮ HEAVY OUTLINED BLACK STAR
- 272F ✯ PINWHEEL STAR
- 2730 ✰ SHADOWED WHITE STAR
- 2731 ✱ HEAVY ASTERISK
  - → 002A * asterisk
- 2732 ✲ OPEN CENTRE ASTERISK
- 2733 ✳ EIGHT SPOKED ASTERISK
- 2734 ✴ EIGHT POINTED BLACK STAR
- 2735 ✵ EIGHT POINTED PINWHEEL STAR
- 2736 ✶ SIX POINTED BLACK STAR
  - = sextile
- 2737 ✷ EIGHT POINTED RECTILINEAR BLACK STAR
- 2738 ✸ HEAVY EIGHT POINTED RECTILINEAR BLACK STAR
- 2739 ✹ TWELVE POINTED BLACK STAR
- 273A ✺ SIXTEEN POINTED ASTERISK
  - = starburst
- 273B ✻ TEARDROP-SPOKED ASTERISK
- 273C ✼ OPEN CENTRE TEARDROP-SPOKED ASTERISK
- 273D ✽ HEAVY TEARDROP-SPOKED ASTERISK
- 273E ✾ SIX PETALLED BLACK AND WHITE FLORETTE
- 273F ✿ BLACK FLORETTE
- 2740 ❀ WHITE FLORETTE
- 2741 ❁ EIGHT PETALLED OUTLINED BLACK FLORETTE
- 2742 ❂ CIRCLED OPEN CENTRE EIGHT POINTED STAR
- 2743 ❃ HEAVY TEARDROP-SPOKED PINWHEEL ASTERISK
- 2744 ❄ SNOWFLAKE
- 2745 ❅ TIGHT TRIFOLIATE SNOWFLAKE
- 2746 ❆ HEAVY CHEVRON SNOWFLAKE
- 2747 ❇ SPARKLE
- 2748 ❈ HEAVY SPARKLE
- 2749 ❉ BALLOON-SPOKED ASTERISK
  - = jack
- 274A ❊ EIGHT TEARDROP-SPOKED PROPELLER ASTERISK
- 274B ❋ HEAVY EIGHT TEARDROP-SPOKED PROPELLER ASTERISK
  - = turbofan

Miscellaneous

- 274C <reserved>
  - → 25CF ● black circle
- 274D ❍ SHADOWED WHITE CIRCLE
- 274E <reserved>
  - → 25A0 ■ black square
- 274F ❏ LOWER RIGHT DROP-SHADOWED WHITE SQUARE
- 2750 ❐ UPPER RIGHT DROP-SHADOWED WHITE SQUARE
- 2751 ❑ LOWER RIGHT SHADOWED WHITE SQUARE
- 2752 ❒ UPPER RIGHT SHADOWED WHITE SQUARE
- 2753 <reserved>
  - → 25B2 ▲ black up-pointing triangle
- 2754 <reserved>
  - → 25BC ▼ black down-pointing triangle
- 2755 <reserved>
  - → 25C6 ◆ black diamond
- 2756 ❖ BLACK DIAMOND MINUS WHITE X
- 2757 <reserved>
  - → 25D7 ◗ right half black circle
- 2758 ❘ LIGHT VERTICAL BAR
  - → 007C | vertical line
- 2759 ❙ MEDIUM VERTICAL BAR
- 275A ❚ HEAVY VERTICAL BAR

Punctuation ornaments

275B ❛ HEAVY SINGLE TURNED COMMA QUOTATION MARK ORNAMENT
→ 2018 ‘ left single quotation mark

275C ❜ HEAVY SINGLE COMMA QUOTATION MARK ORNAMENT
→ 2019 ’ right single quotation mark

275D ❝ HEAVY DOUBLE TURNED COMMA QUOTATION MARK ORNAMENT
→ 201C “ left double quotation mark

275E ❞ HEAVY DOUBLE COMMA QUOTATION MARK ORNAMENT
→ 201D ” right double quotation mark

275F <reserved>

2760 <reserved>

2761 ❡ CURVED STEM PARAGRAPH SIGN ORNAMENT
→ 00B6 ¶ pilcrow sign

2762 ❢ HEAVY EXCLAMATION MARK ORNAMENT
→ 0021 ! exclamation mark

2763 ❣ HEAVY HEART EXCLAMATION MARK ORNAMENT

2764 ❤ HEAVY BLACK HEART
→ 2665 ♥ black heart suit

2765 ❥ ROTATED HEAVY BLACK HEART BULLET

2766 ❦ FLORAL HEART
= Aldus leaf

2767 ❧ ROTATED FLORAL HEART BULLET
= hedera, ivy leaf
→ 2619 ☙ reversed rotated floral heart bullet

Ornamental brackets

2768 ❨ MEDIUM LEFT PARENTHESIS ORNAMENT
→ 0028 (left parenthesis

2769 ❩ MEDIUM RIGHT PARENTHESIS ORNAMENT
→ 0029) right parenthesis

276A ❪ MEDIUM FLATTENED LEFT PARENTHESIS ORNAMENT

276B ❫ MEDIUM FLATTENED RIGHT PARENTHESIS ORNAMENT

276C ❬ MEDIUM LEFT-POINTING ANGLE BRACKET ORNAMENT
→ 2329 〈 left-pointing angle bracket

276D ❭ MEDIUM RIGHT-POINTING ANGLE BRACKET ORNAMENT
→ 232A 〉 right-pointing angle bracket

276E ❮ HEAVY LEFT-POINTING ANGLE QUOTATION MARK ORNAMENT
→ 2039 ‹ single left-pointing angle quotation mark

276F ❯ HEAVY RIGHT-POINTING ANGLE QUOTATION MARK ORNAMENT
→ 203A › single right-pointing angle quotation mark

2770 ❰ HEAVY LEFT-POINTING ANGLE BRACKET ORNAMENT

2771 ❱ HEAVY RIGHT-POINTING ANGLE BRACKET ORNAMENT

2772 ❲ LIGHT LEFT TORTOISE SHELL BRACKET ORNAMENT
→ 3014 〔 left tortoise shell bracket

2773 ❳ LIGHT RIGHT TORTOISE SHELL BRACKET ORNAMENT
→ 3015 〕 right tortoise shell bracket

2774 ❴ MEDIUM LEFT CURLY BRACKET ORNAMENT
→ 007B { left curly bracket

2775 ❵ MEDIUM RIGHT CURLY BRACKET ORNAMENT
→ 007D } right curly bracket

Dingbat circled digits

2776 ❶ DINGBAT NEGATIVE CIRCLED DIGIT ONE

2777 ❷ DINGBAT NEGATIVE CIRCLED DIGIT TWO

2778 ❸ DINGBAT NEGATIVE CIRCLED DIGIT THREE

2779 ❹ DINGBAT NEGATIVE CIRCLED DIGIT FOUR

277A ❺ DINGBAT NEGATIVE CIRCLED DIGIT FIVE

277B ❻ DINGBAT NEGATIVE CIRCLED DIGIT SIX

277C ❼ DINGBAT NEGATIVE CIRCLED DIGIT SEVEN

277D ❽ DINGBAT NEGATIVE CIRCLED DIGIT EIGHT

277E ❾ DINGBAT NEGATIVE CIRCLED DIGIT NINE

277F ❿ DINGBAT NEGATIVE CIRCLED NUMBER TEN

2780 ➀ DINGBAT CIRCLED SANS-SERIF DIGIT ONE

2781 ➁ DINGBAT CIRCLED SANS-SERIF DIGIT TWO

2782 ➂ DINGBAT CIRCLED SANS-SERIF DIGIT THREE

2783 ➃ DINGBAT CIRCLED SANS-SERIF DIGIT FOUR

2784 ➄ DINGBAT CIRCLED SANS-SERIF DIGIT FIVE

2785 ➅ DINGBAT CIRCLED SANS-SERIF DIGIT SIX

2786 ➆ DINGBAT CIRCLED SANS-SERIF DIGIT SEVEN

2787 ➇ DINGBAT CIRCLED SANS-SERIF DIGIT EIGHT

2788 ➈ DINGBAT CIRCLED SANS-SERIF DIGIT NINE

2789 ➉ DINGBAT CIRCLED SANS-SERIF NUMBER TEN

278A ➊ DINGBAT NEGATIVE CIRCLED SANS-SERIF DIGIT ONE

278B ➋ DINGBAT NEGATIVE CIRCLED SANS-SERIF DIGIT TWO

278C ➌ DINGBAT NEGATIVE CIRCLED SANS-SERIF DIGIT THREE

278D ➍ DINGBAT NEGATIVE CIRCLED SANS-SERIF DIGIT FOUR

278E ➎ DINGBAT NEGATIVE CIRCLED SANS-SERIF DIGIT FIVE

278F ➏ DINGBAT NEGATIVE CIRCLED SANS-SERIF DIGIT SIX

2790 ➐ DINGBAT NEGATIVE CIRCLED SANS-SERIF DIGIT SEVEN

2791 ➑ DINGBAT NEGATIVE CIRCLED SANS-SERIF DIGIT EIGHT

2792 ➒ DINGBAT NEGATIVE CIRCLED SANS-SERIF DIGIT NINE

2793 ➓ DINGBAT NEGATIVE CIRCLED SANS-SERIF NUMBER TEN

Dingbat arrows

2794 ➔ HEAVY WIDE-HEADED RIGHTWARDS ARROW

2795 <reserved>
→ 2192 → rightwards arrow

2796 <reserved>
→ 2194 ↔ left right arrow

2797 <reserved>
→ 2195 ↕ up down arrow

2798 ➘ HEAVY SOUTH EAST ARROW

2799 ➙ HEAVY RIGHTWARDS ARROW

279A ➚ HEAVY NORTH EAST ARROW

279B ➛ DRAFTING POINT RIGHTWARDS ARROW

279C ➜ HEAVY ROUND-TIPPED RIGHTWARDS ARROW

279D ➝ TRIANGLE-HEADED RIGHTWARDS ARROW

279E ➞ HEAVY TRIANGLE-HEADED RIGHTWARDS ARROW

279F ➟ DASHED TRIANGLE-HEADED RIGHTWARDS ARROW

27A0 ➠ HEAVY DASHED TRIANGLE-HEADED RIGHTWARDS ARROW

27A1 ➡ BLACK RIGHTWARDS ARROW

27A2 ➢ THREE-D TOP-LIGHTED RIGHTWARDS ARROWHEAD
27A3 ➣ THREE-D BOTTOM-LIGHTED RIGHTWARDS ARROWHEAD
27A4 ➤ BLACK RIGHTWARDS ARROWHEAD
27A5 ➥ HEAVY BLACK CURVED DOWNWARDS AND RIGHTWARDS ARROW
27A6 ➦ HEAVY BLACK CURVED UPWARDS AND RIGHTWARDS ARROW
27A7 ➧ SQUAT BLACK RIGHTWARDS ARROW
27A8 ➨ HEAVY CONCAVE-POINTED BLACK RIGHTWARDS ARROW
27A9 ➩ RIGHT-SHADED WHITE RIGHTWARDS ARROW
27AA ➪ LEFT-SHADED WHITE RIGHTWARDS ARROW
27AB ➫ BACK-TILTED SHADOWED WHITE RIGHTWARDS ARROW
27AC ➬ FRONT-TILTED SHADOWED WHITE RIGHTWARDS ARROW
27AD ➭ HEAVY LOWER RIGHT-SHADOWED WHITE RIGHTWARDS ARROW
27AE ➮ HEAVY UPPER RIGHT-SHADOWED WHITE RIGHTWARDS ARROW
27AF ➯ NOTCHED LOWER RIGHT-SHADOWED WHITE RIGHTWARDS ARROW
27B0 <reserved>
27B1 ➱ NOTCHED UPPER RIGHT-SHADOWED WHITE RIGHTWARDS ARROW
27B2 ➲ CIRCLED HEAVY WHITE RIGHTWARDS ARROW
27B3 ➳ WHITE-FEATHERED RIGHTWARDS ARROW
27B4 ➴ BLACK-FEATHERED SOUTH EAST ARROW
27B5 ➵ BLACK-FEATHERED RIGHTWARDS ARROW
27B6 ➶ BLACK-FEATHERED NORTH EAST ARROW
27B7 ➷ HEAVY BLACK-FEATHERED SOUTH EAST ARROW
27B8 ➸ HEAVY BLACK-FEATHERED RIGHTWARDS ARROW
27B9 ➹ HEAVY BLACK-FEATHERED NORTH EAST ARROW
27BA ➺ TEARDROP-BARBED RIGHTWARDS ARROW
27BB ➻ HEAVY TEARDROP-SHANKED RIGHTWARDS ARROW
27BC ➼ WEDGE-TAILED RIGHTWARDS ARROW
27BD ➽ HEAVY WEDGE-TAILED RIGHTWARDS ARROW
27BE ➾ OPEN-OUTLINED RIGHTWARDS ARROW

	27C	27D	27E
0	⟀ 27C0	⟐ 27D0	⟠ 27E0
1	⟁ 27C1	⟑ 27D1	⟡ 27E1
2	⟂ 27C2	⟒ 27D2	⟢ 27E2
3	⟃ 27C3	⟓ 27D3	⟣ 27E3
4	⟄ 27C4	⟔ 27D4	⟤ 27E4
5	⟅ 27C5	⟕ 27D5	⟥ 27E5
6	⟆ 27C6	⟖ 27D6	⟦ 27E6
7	⟇ 27C7	⟗ 27D7	⟧ 27E7
8	⟈ 27C8	⟘ 27D8	⟨ 27E8
9	⟉ 27C9	⟙ 27D9	⟩ 27E9
A	⟊ 27CA	⟚ 27DA	⟪ 27EA
B		⟛ 27DB	⟫ 27EB
C		⟜ 27DC	
D		⟝ 27DD	
E		⟞ 27DE	
F		⟟ 27DF	

Miscellaneous symbols

27C0 ⟀ THREE DIMENSIONAL ANGLE
• used by Euclid

27C1 ⟁ WHITE TRIANGLE CONTAINING SMALL WHITE TRIANGLE
• used by Euclid

27C2 ⟂ PERPENDICULAR
= orthogonal to
• relation, typeset with additional spacing
→ 22A5 ⊥ up tack

27C3 ⟃ OPEN SUBSET

27C4 ⟄ OPEN SUPERSET

27C5 ⟅ LEFT S-SHAPED BAG DELIMITER

27C6 ⟆ RIGHT S-SHAPED BAG DELIMITER

27C7 ⟇ OR WITH DOT INSIDE

27C8 ⟈ REVERSE SOLIDUS PRECEDING SUBSET

27C9 ⟉ SUPERSET PRECEDING SOLIDUS

Vertical line operator

27CA ⟊ VERTICAL BAR WITH HORIZONTAL STROKE
→ 2AF2 ⫲ parallel with horizontal stroke
→ 2AF5 ⫵ triple vertical bar with horizontal stroke

Miscellaneous symbol

27D0 ⟐ WHITE DIAMOND WITH CENTRED DOT

Operators

27D1 ⟑ AND WITH DOT
→ 2227 ∧ logical and
→ 2A40 ⩀ intersection with dot

27D2 ⟒ ELEMENT OF OPENING UPWARDS
→ 2AD9 ⫙ element of opening downwards

27D3 ⟓ LOWER RIGHT CORNER WITH DOT
= pullback
→ 230B ⌋ right floor

27D4 ⟔ UPPER LEFT CORNER WITH DOT
= pushout
→ 2308 ⌈ left ceiling

Database theory operators

27D5 ⟕ LEFT OUTER JOIN

27D6 ⟖ RIGHT OUTER JOIN

27D7 ⟗ FULL OUTER JOIN
→ 2A1D ⨝ join

Tacks and turnstiles

27D8 ⟘ LARGE UP TACK
→ 22A5 ⊥ up tack

27D9 ⟙ LARGE DOWN TACK
→ 22A4 ⊤ down tack

27DA ⟚ LEFT AND RIGHT DOUBLE TURNSTILE
→ 22A8 ⊨ true
→ 2AE4 ⫤ vertical bar double left turnstile

27DB ⟛ LEFT AND RIGHT TACK
→ 22A2 ⊢ right tack

27DC ⟜ LEFT MULTIMAP
→ 22B8 ⊸ multimap

27DD ⟝ LONG RIGHT TACK
→ 22A2 ⊢ right tack

27DE ⟞ LONG LEFT TACK
→ 22A3 ⊣ left tack

27DF ⟟ UP TACK WITH CIRCLE ABOVE
= radial component
→ 2AF1 ⫱ down tack with circle below

Modal logic operators

27E0 ⟠ LOZENGE DIVIDED BY HORIZONTAL RULE
• used as form of possibility in modal logic
→ 25CA ◊ lozenge

27E1 ⟡ WHITE CONCAVE-SIDED DIAMOND
= never (modal operator)

27E2 ⟢ WHITE CONCAVE-SIDED DIAMOND WITH LEFTWARDS TICK
= was never (modal operator)

27E3 ⟣ WHITE CONCAVE-SIDED DIAMOND WITH RIGHTWARDS TICK
= will never be (modal operator)

27E4 ⟤ WHITE SQUARE WITH LEFTWARDS TICK
= was always (modal operator)
→ 25A1 □ white square

27E5 ⟥ WHITE SQUARE WITH RIGHTWARDS TICK
= will always be (modal operator)

Mathematical brackets

27E6 ⟦ MATHEMATICAL LEFT WHITE SQUARE BRACKET
= z notation left bag bracket
→ 301A 〚 left white square bracket

27E7 ⟧ MATHEMATICAL RIGHT WHITE SQUARE BRACKET
= z notation right bag bracket
→ 301B 〛 right white square bracket

27E8 ⟨ MATHEMATICAL LEFT ANGLE BRACKET
= bra
= z notation left sequence bracket
→ 2329 〈 left-pointing angle bracket
→ 3008 〈 left angle bracket

27E9 ⟩ MATHEMATICAL RIGHT ANGLE BRACKET
= ket
= z notation right sequence bracket
→ 232A 〉 right-pointing angle bracket
→ 3009 〉 right angle bracket

27EA ⟪ MATHEMATICAL LEFT DOUBLE ANGLE BRACKET
= z notation left chevron bracket
→ 300A 《 left double angle bracket

27EB ⟫ MATHEMATICAL RIGHT DOUBLE ANGLE BRACKET
= z notation right chevron bracket
→ 300B 》 right double angle bracket

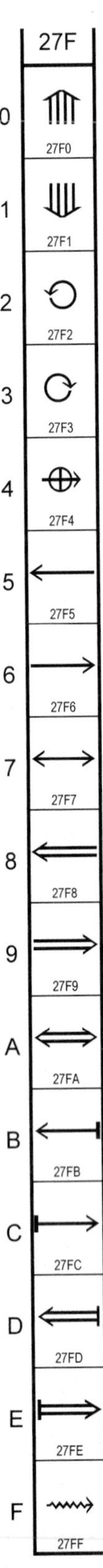

Arrows

27F0 ⟰ UPWARDS QUADRUPLE ARROW
→ 290A ⤊ upwards triple arrow

27F1 ⟱ DOWNWARDS QUADRUPLE ARROW
→ 290B ⤋ downwards triple arrow

27F2 ⟲ ANTICLOCKWISE GAPPED CIRCLE ARROW
→ 21BA ↺ anticlockwise open circle arrow
→ 2940 ⥀ anticlockwise closed circle arrow

27F3 ⟳ CLOCKWISE GAPPED CIRCLE ARROW
→ 21BB ↻ clockwise open circle arrow
→ 2941 ⥁ clockwise closed circle arrow

27F4 ⟴ RIGHT ARROW WITH CIRCLED PLUS

Long arrows

The long arrows are used for mapping whereas the short forms would be used in limits. They are also needed for MathML to complete mapping to the AMSA sets.

27F5 ⟵ LONG LEFTWARDS ARROW
→ 2190 ← leftwards arrow

27F6 ⟶ LONG RIGHTWARDS ARROW
→ 2192 → rightwards arrow

27F7 ⟷ LONG LEFT RIGHT ARROW
→ 2194 ↔ left right arrow

27F8 ⟸ LONG LEFTWARDS DOUBLE ARROW
→ 21D0 ⇐ leftwards double arrow

27F9 ⟹ LONG RIGHTWARDS DOUBLE ARROW
→ 21D2 ⇒ rightwards double arrow

27FA ⟺ LONG LEFT RIGHT DOUBLE ARROW
→ 21D4 ⇔ left right double arrow

27FB ⟻ LONG LEFTWARDS ARROW FROM BAR
= maps from
→ 21A4 ↤ leftwards arrow from bar

27FC ⟼ LONG RIGHTWARDS ARROW FROM BAR
= maps to
→ 21A6 ↦ rightwards arrow from bar

27FD ⟽ LONG LEFTWARDS DOUBLE ARROW FROM BAR
→ 2906 ⤆ leftwards double arrow from bar

27FE ⟾ LONG RIGHTWARDS DOUBLE ARROW FROM BAR
→ 2907 ⤇ rightwards double arrow from bar

27FF ⟿ LONG RIGHTWARDS SQUIGGLE ARROW
→ 21DD ⇝ rightwards squiggle arrow

	280	281	282	283	284	285	286	287	288	289	28A	28B	28C	28D	28E	28F
0	2800	2810	2820	2830	2840	2850	2860	2870	2880	2890	28A0	28B0	28C0	28D0	28E0	28F0
1	2801	2811	2821	2831	2841	2851	2861	2871	2881	2891	28A1	28B1	28C1	28D1	28E1	28F1
2	2802	2812	2822	2832	2842	2852	2862	2872	2882	2892	28A2	28B2	28C2	28D2	28E2	28F2
3	2803	2813	2823	2833	2843	2853	2863	2873	2883	2893	28A3	28B3	28C3	28D3	28E3	28F3
4	2804	2814	2824	2834	2844	2854	2864	2874	2884	2894	28A4	28B4	28C4	28D4	28E4	28F4
5	2805	2815	2825	2835	2845	2855	2865	2875	2885	2895	28A5	28B5	28C5	28D5	28E5	28F5
6	2806	2816	2826	2836	2846	2856	2866	2876	2886	2896	28A6	28B6	28C6	28D6	28E6	28F6
7	2807	2817	2827	2837	2847	2857	2867	2877	2887	2897	28A7	28B7	28C7	28D7	28E7	28F7
8	2808	2818	2828	2838	2848	2858	2868	2878	2888	2898	28A8	28B8	28C8	28D8	28E8	28F8
9	2809	2819	2829	2839	2849	2859	2869	2879	2889	2899	28A9	28B9	28C9	28D9	28E9	28F9
A	280A	281A	282A	283A	284A	285A	286A	287A	288A	289A	28AA	28BA	28CA	28DA	28EA	28FA
B	280B	281B	282B	283B	284B	285B	286B	287B	288B	289B	28AB	28BB	28CB	28DB	28EB	28FB
C	280C	281C	282C	283C	284C	285C	286C	287C	288C	289C	28AC	28BC	28CC	28DC	28EC	28FC
D	280D	281D	282D	283D	284D	285D	286D	287D	288D	289D	28AD	28BD	28CD	28DD	28ED	28FD
E	280E	281E	282E	283E	284E	285E	286E	287E	288E	289E	28AE	28BE	28CE	28DE	28EE	28FE
F	280F	281F	282F	283F	284F	285F	286F	287F	288F	289F	28AF	28BF	28CF	28DF	28EF	28FF

When braille patterns are punched, the filled circles shown here correspond to punch impression.

Braille patterns

2800 ⠀ BRAILLE PATTERN BLANK
- while this character is imaged as a fixed-width blank in many fonts, it does not act as a space

2801 ⠁ BRAILLE PATTERN DOTS-1
2802 ⠂ BRAILLE PATTERN DOTS-2
2803 ⠃ BRAILLE PATTERN DOTS-12
2804 ⠄ BRAILLE PATTERN DOTS-3
2805 ⠅ BRAILLE PATTERN DOTS-13
2806 ⠆ BRAILLE PATTERN DOTS-23
2807 ⠇ BRAILLE PATTERN DOTS-123
2808 ⠈ BRAILLE PATTERN DOTS-4
2809 ⠉ BRAILLE PATTERN DOTS-14
280A ⠊ BRAILLE PATTERN DOTS-24
280B ⠋ BRAILLE PATTERN DOTS-124
280C ⠌ BRAILLE PATTERN DOTS-34
280D ⠍ BRAILLE PATTERN DOTS-134
280E ⠎ BRAILLE PATTERN DOTS-234
280F ⠏ BRAILLE PATTERN DOTS-1234
2810 ⠐ BRAILLE PATTERN DOTS-5
2811 ⠑ BRAILLE PATTERN DOTS-15
2812 ⠒ BRAILLE PATTERN DOTS-25
2813 ⠓ BRAILLE PATTERN DOTS-125
2814 ⠔ BRAILLE PATTERN DOTS-35
2815 ⠕ BRAILLE PATTERN DOTS-135
2816 ⠖ BRAILLE PATTERN DOTS-235
2817 ⠗ BRAILLE PATTERN DOTS-1235
2818 ⠘ BRAILLE PATTERN DOTS-45
2819 ⠙ BRAILLE PATTERN DOTS-145
281A ⠚ BRAILLE PATTERN DOTS-245
281B ⠛ BRAILLE PATTERN DOTS-1245
281C ⠜ BRAILLE PATTERN DOTS-345
281D ⠝ BRAILLE PATTERN DOTS-1345
281E ⠞ BRAILLE PATTERN DOTS-2345
281F ⠟ BRAILLE PATTERN DOTS-12345
2820 ⠠ BRAILLE PATTERN DOTS-6
2821 ⠡ BRAILLE PATTERN DOTS-16
2822 ⠢ BRAILLE PATTERN DOTS-26
2823 ⠣ BRAILLE PATTERN DOTS-126
2824 ⠤ BRAILLE PATTERN DOTS-36
2825 ⠥ BRAILLE PATTERN DOTS-136
2826 ⠦ BRAILLE PATTERN DOTS-236
2827 ⠧ BRAILLE PATTERN DOTS-1236
2828 ⠨ BRAILLE PATTERN DOTS-46
2829 ⠩ BRAILLE PATTERN DOTS-146
282A ⠪ BRAILLE PATTERN DOTS-246
282B ⠫ BRAILLE PATTERN DOTS-1246
282C ⠬ BRAILLE PATTERN DOTS-346
282D ⠭ BRAILLE PATTERN DOTS-1346
282E ⠮ BRAILLE PATTERN DOTS-2346
282F ⠯ BRAILLE PATTERN DOTS-12346
2830 ⠰ BRAILLE PATTERN DOTS-56
2831 ⠱ BRAILLE PATTERN DOTS-156
2832 ⠲ BRAILLE PATTERN DOTS-256
2833 ⠳ BRAILLE PATTERN DOTS-1256
2834 ⠴ BRAILLE PATTERN DOTS-356
2835 ⠵ BRAILLE PATTERN DOTS-1356
2836 ⠶ BRAILLE PATTERN DOTS-2356
2837 ⠷ BRAILLE PATTERN DOTS-12356
2838 ⠸ BRAILLE PATTERN DOTS-456
2839 ⠹ BRAILLE PATTERN DOTS-1456
283A ⠺ BRAILLE PATTERN DOTS-2456
283B ⠻ BRAILLE PATTERN DOTS-12456
283C ⠼ BRAILLE PATTERN DOTS-3456
283D ⠽ BRAILLE PATTERN DOTS-13456
283E ⠾ BRAILLE PATTERN DOTS-23456
283F ⠿ BRAILLE PATTERN DOTS-123456
2840 ⡀ BRAILLE PATTERN DOTS-7
2841 ⡁ BRAILLE PATTERN DOTS-17
2842 ⡂ BRAILLE PATTERN DOTS-27
2843 ⡃ BRAILLE PATTERN DOTS-127
2844 ⡄ BRAILLE PATTERN DOTS-37
2845 ⡅ BRAILLE PATTERN DOTS-137
2846 ⡆ BRAILLE PATTERN DOTS-237
2847 ⡇ BRAILLE PATTERN DOTS-1237
2848 ⡈ BRAILLE PATTERN DOTS-47
2849 ⡉ BRAILLE PATTERN DOTS-147
284A ⡊ BRAILLE PATTERN DOTS-247
284B ⡋ BRAILLE PATTERN DOTS-1247
284C ⡌ BRAILLE PATTERN DOTS-347
284D ⡍ BRAILLE PATTERN DOTS-1347
284E ⡎ BRAILLE PATTERN DOTS-2347
284F ⡏ BRAILLE PATTERN DOTS-12347
2850 ⡐ BRAILLE PATTERN DOTS-57
2851 ⡑ BRAILLE PATTERN DOTS-157
2852 ⡒ BRAILLE PATTERN DOTS-257
2853 ⡓ BRAILLE PATTERN DOTS-1257
2854 ⡔ BRAILLE PATTERN DOTS-357
2855 ⡕ BRAILLE PATTERN DOTS-1357
2856 ⡖ BRAILLE PATTERN DOTS-2357
2857 ⡗ BRAILLE PATTERN DOTS-12357
2858 ⡘ BRAILLE PATTERN DOTS-457
2859 ⡙ BRAILLE PATTERN DOTS-1457
285A ⡚ BRAILLE PATTERN DOTS-2457
285B ⡛ BRAILLE PATTERN DOTS-12457
285C ⡜ BRAILLE PATTERN DOTS-3457
285D ⡝ BRAILLE PATTERN DOTS-13457
285E ⡞ BRAILLE PATTERN DOTS-23457
285F ⡟ BRAILLE PATTERN DOTS-123457
2860 ⡠ BRAILLE PATTERN DOTS-67
2861 ⡡ BRAILLE PATTERN DOTS-167
2862 ⡢ BRAILLE PATTERN DOTS-267
2863 ⡣ BRAILLE PATTERN DOTS-1267
2864 ⡤ BRAILLE PATTERN DOTS-367
2865 ⡥ BRAILLE PATTERN DOTS-1367
2866 ⡦ BRAILLE PATTERN DOTS-2367
2867 ⡧ BRAILLE PATTERN DOTS-12367
2868 ⡨ BRAILLE PATTERN DOTS-467
2869 ⡩ BRAILLE PATTERN DOTS-1467
286A ⡪ BRAILLE PATTERN DOTS-2467
286B ⡫ BRAILLE PATTERN DOTS-12467
286C ⡬ BRAILLE PATTERN DOTS-3467
286D ⡭ BRAILLE PATTERN DOTS-13467
286E ⡮ BRAILLE PATTERN DOTS-23467
286F ⡯ BRAILLE PATTERN DOTS-123467
2870 ⡰ BRAILLE PATTERN DOTS-567
2871 ⡱ BRAILLE PATTERN DOTS-1567
2872 ⡲ BRAILLE PATTERN DOTS-2567
2873 ⡳ BRAILLE PATTERN DOTS-12567
2874 ⡴ BRAILLE PATTERN DOTS-3567
2875 ⡵ BRAILLE PATTERN DOTS-13567
2876 ⡶ BRAILLE PATTERN DOTS-23567
2877 ⡷ BRAILLE PATTERN DOTS-123567
2878 ⡸ BRAILLE PATTERN DOTS-4567

2879 ⡹ BRAILLE PATTERN DOTS-14567
287A ⡺ BRAILLE PATTERN DOTS-24567
287B ⡻ BRAILLE PATTERN DOTS-124567
287C ⡼ BRAILLE PATTERN DOTS-34567
287D ⡽ BRAILLE PATTERN DOTS-134567
287E ⡾ BRAILLE PATTERN DOTS-234567
287F ⡿ BRAILLE PATTERN DOTS-1234567
2880 ⢀ BRAILLE PATTERN DOTS-8
2881 ⢁ BRAILLE PATTERN DOTS-18
2882 ⢂ BRAILLE PATTERN DOTS-28
2883 ⢃ BRAILLE PATTERN DOTS-128
2884 ⢄ BRAILLE PATTERN DOTS-38
2885 ⢅ BRAILLE PATTERN DOTS-138
2886 ⢆ BRAILLE PATTERN DOTS-238
2887 ⢇ BRAILLE PATTERN DOTS-1238
2888 ⢈ BRAILLE PATTERN DOTS-48
2889 ⢉ BRAILLE PATTERN DOTS-148
288A ⢊ BRAILLE PATTERN DOTS-248
288B ⢋ BRAILLE PATTERN DOTS-1248
288C ⢌ BRAILLE PATTERN DOTS-348
288D ⢍ BRAILLE PATTERN DOTS-1348
288E ⢎ BRAILLE PATTERN DOTS-2348
288F ⢏ BRAILLE PATTERN DOTS-12348
2890 ⢐ BRAILLE PATTERN DOTS-58
2891 ⢑ BRAILLE PATTERN DOTS-158
2892 ⢒ BRAILLE PATTERN DOTS-258
2893 ⢓ BRAILLE PATTERN DOTS-1258
2894 ⢔ BRAILLE PATTERN DOTS-358
2895 ⢕ BRAILLE PATTERN DOTS-1358
2896 ⢖ BRAILLE PATTERN DOTS-2358
2897 ⢗ BRAILLE PATTERN DOTS-12358
2898 ⢘ BRAILLE PATTERN DOTS-458
2899 ⢙ BRAILLE PATTERN DOTS-1458
289A ⢚ BRAILLE PATTERN DOTS-2458
289B ⢛ BRAILLE PATTERN DOTS-12458
289C ⢜ BRAILLE PATTERN DOTS-3458
289D ⢝ BRAILLE PATTERN DOTS-13458
289E ⢞ BRAILLE PATTERN DOTS-23458
289F ⢟ BRAILLE PATTERN DOTS-123458
28A0 ⢠ BRAILLE PATTERN DOTS-68
28A1 ⢡ BRAILLE PATTERN DOTS-168
28A2 ⢢ BRAILLE PATTERN DOTS-268
28A3 ⢣ BRAILLE PATTERN DOTS-1268
28A4 ⢤ BRAILLE PATTERN DOTS-368
28A5 ⢥ BRAILLE PATTERN DOTS-1368
28A6 ⢦ BRAILLE PATTERN DOTS-2368
28A7 ⢧ BRAILLE PATTERN DOTS-12368
28A8 ⢨ BRAILLE PATTERN DOTS-468
28A9 ⢩ BRAILLE PATTERN DOTS-1468
28AA ⢪ BRAILLE PATTERN DOTS-2468
28AB ⢫ BRAILLE PATTERN DOTS-12468
28AC ⢬ BRAILLE PATTERN DOTS-3468
28AD ⢭ BRAILLE PATTERN DOTS-13468
28AE ⢮ BRAILLE PATTERN DOTS-23468
28AF ⢯ BRAILLE PATTERN DOTS-123468
28B0 ⢰ BRAILLE PATTERN DOTS-568
28B1 ⢱ BRAILLE PATTERN DOTS-1568
28B2 ⢲ BRAILLE PATTERN DOTS-2568
28B3 ⢳ BRAILLE PATTERN DOTS-12568
28B4 ⢴ BRAILLE PATTERN DOTS-3568
28B5 ⢵ BRAILLE PATTERN DOTS-13568
28B6 ⢶ BRAILLE PATTERN DOTS-23568
28B7 ⢷ BRAILLE PATTERN DOTS-123568
28B8 ⢸ BRAILLE PATTERN DOTS-4568
28B9 ⢹ BRAILLE PATTERN DOTS-14568
28BA ⢺ BRAILLE PATTERN DOTS-24568
28BB ⢻ BRAILLE PATTERN DOTS-124568
28BC ⢼ BRAILLE PATTERN DOTS-34568
28BD ⢽ BRAILLE PATTERN DOTS-134568
28BE ⢾ BRAILLE PATTERN DOTS-234568
28BF ⢿ BRAILLE PATTERN DOTS-1234568
28C0 ⣀ BRAILLE PATTERN DOTS-78
28C1 ⣁ BRAILLE PATTERN DOTS-178
28C2 ⣂ BRAILLE PATTERN DOTS-278
28C3 ⣃ BRAILLE PATTERN DOTS-1278
28C4 ⣄ BRAILLE PATTERN DOTS-378
28C5 ⣅ BRAILLE PATTERN DOTS-1378
28C6 ⣆ BRAILLE PATTERN DOTS-2378
28C7 ⣇ BRAILLE PATTERN DOTS-12378
28C8 ⣈ BRAILLE PATTERN DOTS-478
28C9 ⣉ BRAILLE PATTERN DOTS-1478
28CA ⣊ BRAILLE PATTERN DOTS-2478
28CB ⣋ BRAILLE PATTERN DOTS-12478
28CC ⣌ BRAILLE PATTERN DOTS-3478
28CD ⣍ BRAILLE PATTERN DOTS-13478
28CE ⣎ BRAILLE PATTERN DOTS-23478
28CF ⣏ BRAILLE PATTERN DOTS-123478
28D0 ⣐ BRAILLE PATTERN DOTS-578
28D1 ⣑ BRAILLE PATTERN DOTS-1578
28D2 ⣒ BRAILLE PATTERN DOTS-2578
28D3 ⣓ BRAILLE PATTERN DOTS-12578
28D4 ⣔ BRAILLE PATTERN DOTS-3578
28D5 ⣕ BRAILLE PATTERN DOTS-13578
28D6 ⣖ BRAILLE PATTERN DOTS-23578
28D7 ⣗ BRAILLE PATTERN DOTS-123578
28D8 ⣘ BRAILLE PATTERN DOTS-4578
28D9 ⣙ BRAILLE PATTERN DOTS-14578
28DA ⣚ BRAILLE PATTERN DOTS-24578
28DB ⣛ BRAILLE PATTERN DOTS-124578
28DC ⣜ BRAILLE PATTERN DOTS-34578
28DD ⣝ BRAILLE PATTERN DOTS-134578
28DE ⣞ BRAILLE PATTERN DOTS-234578
28DF ⣟ BRAILLE PATTERN DOTS-1234578
28E0 ⣠ BRAILLE PATTERN DOTS-678
28E1 ⣡ BRAILLE PATTERN DOTS-1678
28E2 ⣢ BRAILLE PATTERN DOTS-2678
28E3 ⣣ BRAILLE PATTERN DOTS-12678
28E4 ⣤ BRAILLE PATTERN DOTS-3678
28E5 ⣥ BRAILLE PATTERN DOTS-13678
28E6 ⣦ BRAILLE PATTERN DOTS-23678
28E7 ⣧ BRAILLE PATTERN DOTS-123678
28E8 ⣨ BRAILLE PATTERN DOTS-4678
28E9 ⣩ BRAILLE PATTERN DOTS-14678
28EA ⣪ BRAILLE PATTERN DOTS-24678
28EB ⣫ BRAILLE PATTERN DOTS-124678
28EC ⣬ BRAILLE PATTERN DOTS-34678
28ED ⣭ BRAILLE PATTERN DOTS-134678
28EE ⣮ BRAILLE PATTERN DOTS-234678
28EF ⣯ BRAILLE PATTERN DOTS-1234678
28F0 ⣰ BRAILLE PATTERN DOTS-5678
28F1 ⣱ BRAILLE PATTERN DOTS-15678
28F2 ⣲ BRAILLE PATTERN DOTS-25678
28F3 ⣳ BRAILLE PATTERN DOTS-125678
28F4 ⣴ BRAILLE PATTERN DOTS-35678
28F5 ⣵ BRAILLE PATTERN DOTS-135678
28F6 ⣶ BRAILLE PATTERN DOTS-235678

28F7 ⣷ BRAILLE PATTERN DOTS-1235678
28F8 ⣸ BRAILLE PATTERN DOTS-45678
28F9 ⣹ BRAILLE PATTERN DOTS-145678
28FA ⣺ BRAILLE PATTERN DOTS-245678
28FB ⣻ BRAILLE PATTERN DOTS-1245678
28FC ⣼ BRAILLE PATTERN DOTS-345678
28FD ⣽ BRAILLE PATTERN DOTS-1345678
28FE ⣾ BRAILLE PATTERN DOTS-2345678
28FF ⣿ BRAILLE PATTERN DOTS-12345678

	290	291	292	293	294	295	296	297
0	⤀ 2900	⤐ 2910	⤠ 2920	⤰ 2930	⥀ 2940	⥐ 2950	⥠ 2960	⥰ 2970
1	⤁ 2901	⤑ 2911	⤡ 2921	⤱ 2931	⥁ 2941	⥑ 2951	⥡ 2961	⥱ 2971
2	⤂ 2902	⤒ 2912	⤢ 2922	⤲ 2932	⥂ 2942	⥒ 2952	⥢ 2962	⥲ 2972
3	⤃ 2903	⤓ 2913	⤣ 2923	⤳ 2933	⥃ 2943	⥓ 2953	⥣ 2963	⥳ 2973
4	⤄ 2904	⤔ 2914	⤤ 2924	⤴ 2934	⥄ 2944	⥔ 2954	⥤ 2964	⥴ 2974
5	⤅ 2905	⤕ 2915	⤥ 2925	⤵ 2935	⥅ 2945	⥕ 2955	⥥ 2965	⥵ 2975
6	⤆ 2906	⤖ 2916	⤦ 2926	⤶ 2936	⥆ 2946	⥖ 2956	⥦ 2966	⥶ 2976
7	⤇ 2907	⤗ 2917	⤧ 2927	⤷ 2937	⥇ 2947	⥗ 2957	⥧ 2967	⥷ 2977
8	⤈ 2908	⤘ 2918	⤨ 2928	⤸ 2938	⥈ 2948	⥘ 2958	⥨ 2968	⥸ 2978
9	⤉ 2909	⤙ 2919	⤩ 2929	⤹ 2939	⥉ 2949	⥙ 2959	⥩ 2969	⥹ 2979
A	⤊ 290A	⤚ 291A	⤪ 292A	⤺ 293A	⥊ 294A	⥚ 295A	⥪ 296A	⥺ 297A
B	⤋ 290B	⤛ 291B	⤫ 292B	⤻ 293B	⥋ 294B	⥛ 295B	⥫ 296B	⥻ 297B
C	⤌ 290C	⤜ 291C	⤬ 292C	⤼ 293C	⥌ 294C	⥜ 295C	⥬ 296C	⥼ 297C
D	⤍ 290D	⤝ 291D	⤭ 292D	⤽ 293D	⥍ 294D	⥝ 295D	⥭ 296D	⥽ 297D
E	⤎ 290E	⤞ 291E	⤮ 292E	⤾ 293E	⥎ 294E	⥞ 295E	⥮ 296E	⥾ 297E
F	⤏ 290F	⤟ 291F	⤯ 292F	⤿ 293F	⥏ 294F	⥟ 295F	⥯ 296F	⥿ 297F

Miscellaneous arrows

2900 ⤀ RIGHTWARDS TWO-HEADED ARROW WITH VERTICAL STROKE
= z notation partial surjection

2901 ⤁ RIGHTWARDS TWO-HEADED ARROW WITH DOUBLE VERTICAL STROKE
= z notation finite surjection

2902 ⤂ LEFTWARDS DOUBLE ARROW WITH VERTICAL STROKE

2903 ⤃ RIGHTWARDS DOUBLE ARROW WITH VERTICAL STROKE

2904 ⤄ LEFT RIGHT DOUBLE ARROW WITH VERTICAL STROKE

2905 ⤅ RIGHTWARDS TWO-HEADED ARROW FROM BAR
= maps to

2906 ⤆ LEFTWARDS DOUBLE ARROW FROM BAR
= maps from
→ 27FB ⟻ long leftwards arrow from bar

2907 ⤇ RIGHTWARDS DOUBLE ARROW FROM BAR
= maps to
→ 27FC ⟼ long rightwards arrow from bar

2908 ⤈ DOWNWARDS ARROW WITH HORIZONTAL STROKE

2909 ⤉ UPWARDS ARROW WITH HORIZONTAL STROKE

290A ⤊ UPWARDS TRIPLE ARROW
→ 21D1 ⇑ upwards double arrow
→ 27F0 ⟰ upwards quadruple arrow

290B ⤋ DOWNWARDS TRIPLE ARROW
→ 21D3 ⇓ downwards double arrow
→ 27F1 ⟱ downwards quadruple arrow

290C ⤌ LEFTWARDS DOUBLE DASH ARROW

290D ⤍ RIGHTWARDS DOUBLE DASH ARROW

290E ⤎ LEFTWARDS TRIPLE DASH ARROW

290F ⤏ RIGHTWARDS TRIPLE DASH ARROW

2910 ⤐ RIGHTWARDS TWO-HEADED TRIPLE DASH ARROW

2911 ⤑ RIGHTWARDS ARROW WITH DOTTED STEM

2912 ⤒ UPWARDS ARROW TO BAR

2913 ⤓ DOWNWARDS ARROW TO BAR

2914 ⤔ RIGHTWARDS ARROW WITH TAIL WITH VERTICAL STROKE
= z notation partial injection

2915 ⤕ RIGHTWARDS ARROW WITH TAIL WITH DOUBLE VERTICAL STROKE
= z notation finite injection

2916 ⤖ RIGHTWARDS TWO-HEADED ARROW WITH TAIL
= bijective mapping
= z notation bijection

2917 ⤗ RIGHTWARDS TWO-HEADED ARROW WITH TAIL WITH VERTICAL STROKE
= z notation surjective injection

2918 ⤘ RIGHTWARDS TWO-HEADED ARROW WITH TAIL WITH DOUBLE VERTICAL STROKE
= z notation finite surjective injection

Arrow tails

2919 ⤙ LEFTWARDS ARROW-TAIL

291A ⤚ RIGHTWARDS ARROW-TAIL

291B ⤛ LEFTWARDS DOUBLE ARROW-TAIL

291C ⤜ RIGHTWARDS DOUBLE ARROW-TAIL

Miscellaneous arrows

291D ⤝ LEFTWARDS ARROW TO BLACK DIAMOND

291E ⤞ RIGHTWARDS ARROW TO BLACK DIAMOND

291F ⤟ LEFTWARDS ARROW FROM BAR TO BLACK DIAMOND

2920 ⤠ RIGHTWARDS ARROW FROM BAR TO BLACK DIAMOND

2921 ⤡ NORTH WEST AND SOUTH EAST ARROW

2922 ⤢ NORTH EAST AND SOUTH WEST ARROW

2923 ⤣ NORTH WEST ARROW WITH HOOK

2924 ⤤ NORTH EAST ARROW WITH HOOK

2925 ⤥ SOUTH EAST ARROW WITH HOOK

2926 ⤦ SOUTH WEST ARROW WITH HOOK

Crossing arrows for knot theory

2927 ⤧ NORTH WEST ARROW AND NORTH EAST ARROW

2928 ⤨ NORTH EAST ARROW AND SOUTH EAST ARROW

2929 ⤩ SOUTH EAST ARROW AND SOUTH WEST ARROW

292A ⤪ SOUTH WEST ARROW AND NORTH WEST ARROW

292B ⤫ RISING DIAGONAL CROSSING FALLING DIAGONAL

292C ⤬ FALLING DIAGONAL CROSSING RISING DIAGONAL

292D ⤭ SOUTH EAST ARROW CROSSING NORTH EAST ARROW

292E ⤮ NORTH EAST ARROW CROSSING SOUTH EAST ARROW

292F ⤯ FALLING DIAGONAL CROSSING NORTH EAST ARROW

2930 ⤰ RISING DIAGONAL CROSSING SOUTH EAST ARROW

2931 ⤱ NORTH EAST ARROW CROSSING NORTH WEST ARROW

2932 ⤲ NORTH WEST ARROW CROSSING NORTH EAST ARROW

Miscellaneous curved arrows

2933 ⤳ WAVE ARROW POINTING DIRECTLY RIGHT
→ 219D ↝ rightwards wave arrow

2934 ⤴ ARROW POINTING RIGHTWARDS THEN CURVING UPWARDS

2935 ⤵ ARROW POINTING RIGHTWARDS THEN CURVING DOWNWARDS

2936 ⤶ ARROW POINTING DOWNWARDS THEN CURVING LEFTWARDS

2937 ⤷ ARROW POINTING DOWNWARDS THEN CURVING RIGHTWARDS

2938 ⤸ RIGHT-SIDE ARC CLOCKWISE ARROW

2939 ⤹ LEFT-SIDE ARC ANTICLOCKWISE ARROW

293A ⤺ TOP ARC ANTICLOCKWISE ARROW

293B ⤻ BOTTOM ARC ANTICLOCKWISE ARROW

293C ⤼ TOP ARC CLOCKWISE ARROW WITH MINUS

293D ⤽ TOP ARC ANTICLOCKWISE ARROW WITH PLUS

293E ⤾ LOWER RIGHT SEMICIRCULAR CLOCKWISE ARROW

293F ⤿ LOWER LEFT SEMICIRCULAR ANTICLOCKWISE ARROW

2940 ⥀ ANTICLOCKWISE CLOSED CIRCLE ARROW
→ 20DA ◌⃚ combining anticlockwise ring overlay

2941 ⥁ CLOCKWISE CLOSED CIRCLE ARROW
→ 20D9 ◌⃙ combining clockwise ring overlay

Arrows combined with operators

2942 ⥂ RIGHTWARDS ARROW ABOVE SHORT LEFTWARDS ARROW

2943 ⥃ LEFTWARDS ARROW ABOVE SHORT RIGHTWARDS ARROW

2944 ⥄ SHORT RIGHTWARDS ARROW ABOVE LEFTWARDS ARROW
2945 ⥅ RIGHTWARDS ARROW WITH PLUS BELOW
2946 ⥆ LEFTWARDS ARROW WITH PLUS BELOW
2947 ⥇ RIGHTWARDS ARROW THROUGH X
2948 ⥈ LEFT RIGHT ARROW THROUGH SMALL CIRCLE
2949 ⥉ UPWARDS TWO-HEADED ARROW FROM SMALL CIRCLE

Double-barbed harpoons

294A ⥊ LEFT BARB UP RIGHT BARB DOWN HARPOON
294B ⥋ LEFT BARB DOWN RIGHT BARB UP HARPOON
294C ⥌ UP BARB RIGHT DOWN BARB LEFT HARPOON
294D ⥍ UP BARB LEFT DOWN BARB RIGHT HARPOON
294E ⥎ LEFT BARB UP RIGHT BARB UP HARPOON
294F ⥏ UP BARB RIGHT DOWN BARB RIGHT HARPOON
2950 ⥐ LEFT BARB DOWN RIGHT BARB DOWN HARPOON
2951 ⥑ UP BARB LEFT DOWN BARB LEFT HARPOON

Modified harpoons

2952 ⥒ LEFTWARDS HARPOON WITH BARB UP TO BAR
2953 ⥓ RIGHTWARDS HARPOON WITH BARB UP TO BAR
2954 ⥔ UPWARDS HARPOON WITH BARB RIGHT TO BAR
2955 ⥕ DOWNWARDS HARPOON WITH BARB RIGHT TO BAR
2956 ⥖ LEFTWARDS HARPOON WITH BARB DOWN TO BAR
2957 ⥗ RIGHTWARDS HARPOON WITH BARB DOWN TO BAR
2958 ⥘ UPWARDS HARPOON WITH BARB LEFT TO BAR
2959 ⥙ DOWNWARDS HARPOON WITH BARB LEFT TO BAR
295A ⥚ LEFTWARDS HARPOON WITH BARB UP FROM BAR
295B ⥛ RIGHTWARDS HARPOON WITH BARB UP FROM BAR
295C ⥜ UPWARDS HARPOON WITH BARB RIGHT FROM BAR
295D ⥝ DOWNWARDS HARPOON WITH BARB RIGHT FROM BAR
295E ⥞ LEFTWARDS HARPOON WITH BARB DOWN FROM BAR
295F ⥟ RIGHTWARDS HARPOON WITH BARB DOWN FROM BAR
2960 ⥠ UPWARDS HARPOON WITH BARB LEFT FROM BAR
2961 ⥡ DOWNWARDS HARPOON WITH BARB LEFT FROM BAR

Paired harpoons

2962 ⥢ LEFTWARDS HARPOON WITH BARB UP ABOVE LEFTWARDS HARPOON WITH BARB DOWN
2963 ⥣ UPWARDS HARPOON WITH BARB LEFT BESIDE UPWARDS HARPOON WITH BARB RIGHT
2964 ⥤ RIGHTWARDS HARPOON WITH BARB UP ABOVE RIGHTWARDS HARPOON WITH BARB DOWN
2965 ⥥ DOWNWARDS HARPOON WITH BARB LEFT BESIDE DOWNWARDS HARPOON WITH BARB RIGHT
2966 ⥦ LEFTWARDS HARPOON WITH BARB UP ABOVE RIGHTWARDS HARPOON WITH BARB UP
2967 ⥧ LEFTWARDS HARPOON WITH BARB DOWN ABOVE RIGHTWARDS HARPOON WITH BARB DOWN
2968 ⥨ RIGHTWARDS HARPOON WITH BARB UP ABOVE LEFTWARDS HARPOON WITH BARB UP
2969 ⥩ RIGHTWARDS HARPOON WITH BARB DOWN ABOVE LEFTWARDS HARPOON WITH BARB DOWN
296A ⥪ LEFTWARDS HARPOON WITH BARB UP ABOVE LONG DASH
296B ⥫ LEFTWARDS HARPOON WITH BARB DOWN BELOW LONG DASH
296C ⥬ RIGHTWARDS HARPOON WITH BARB UP ABOVE LONG DASH
296D ⥭ RIGHTWARDS HARPOON WITH BARB DOWN BELOW LONG DASH
296E ⥮ UPWARDS HARPOON WITH BARB LEFT BESIDE DOWNWARDS HARPOON WITH BARB RIGHT
296F ⥯ DOWNWARDS HARPOON WITH BARB LEFT BESIDE UPWARDS HARPOON WITH BARB RIGHT

Miscellaneous arrow

2970 ⥰ RIGHT DOUBLE ARROW WITH ROUNDED HEAD
→ 2283 ⊃ superset of

Arrows combined with relations

2971 ⥱ EQUALS SIGN ABOVE RIGHTWARDS ARROW
2972 ⥲ TILDE OPERATOR ABOVE RIGHTWARDS ARROW
2973 ⥳ LEFTWARDS ARROW ABOVE TILDE OPERATOR
2974 ⥴ RIGHTWARDS ARROW ABOVE TILDE OPERATOR
2975 ⥵ RIGHTWARDS ARROW ABOVE ALMOST EQUAL TO
2976 ⥶ LESS-THAN ABOVE LEFTWARDS ARROW
2977 ⥷ LEFTWARDS ARROW THROUGH LESS-THAN
2978 ⥸ GREATER-THAN ABOVE RIGHTWARDS ARROW
2979 ⥹ SUBSET ABOVE RIGHTWARDS ARROW
297A ⥺ LEFTWARDS ARROW THROUGH SUBSET
297B ⥻ SUPERSET ABOVE LEFTWARDS ARROW

Fish tails

297C ⥼ LEFT FISH TAIL
297D ⥽ RIGHT FISH TAIL
297E ⥾ UP FISH TAIL
297F ⥿ DOWN FISH TAIL

	298	299	29A	29B	29C	29D	29E	29F
0	⦀ 2980	⦐ 2990	⦠ 29A0	⦰ 29B0	⧀ 29C0	⧐ 29D0	⧠ 29E0	⧰ 29F0
1	⦁ 2981	⦑ 2991	⦡ 29A1	⦱ 29B1	⧁ 29C1	⧑ 29D1	⧡ 29E1	⧱ 29F1
2	⦂ 2982	⦒ 2992	⦢ 29A2	⦲ 29B2	⧂ 29C2	⧒ 29D2	⧢ 29E2	⧲ 29F2
3	⦃ 2983	⦓ 2993	⦣ 29A3	⦳ 29B3	⧃ 29C3	⧓ 29D3	⧣ 29E3	⧳ 29F3
4	⦄ 2984	⦔ 2994	⦤ 29A4	⦴ 29B4	⧄ 29C4	⧔ 29D4	⧤ 29E4	⧴ 29F4
5	⦅ 2985	⦕ 2995	⦥ 29A5	⦵ 29B5	⧅ 29C5	⧕ 29D5	⧥ 29E5	⧵ 29F5
6	⦆ 2986	⦖ 2996	⦦ 29A6	⦶ 29B6	⧆ 29C6	⧖ 29D6	⧦ 29E6	⧶ 29F6
7	⦇ 2987	⦗ 2997	⦧ 29A7	⦷ 29B7	⧇ 29C7	⧗ 29D7	⧧ 29E7	⧷ 29F7
8	⦈ 2988	⦘ 2998	⦨ 29A8	⦸ 29B8	⧈ 29C8	⧘ 29D8	⧨ 29E8	⧸ 29F8
9	⦉ 2989	⦙ 2999	⦩ 29A9	⦹ 29B9	⧉ 29C9	⧙ 29D9	⧩ 29E9	⧹ 29F9
A	⦊ 298A	⦚ 299A	⦪ 29AA	⦺ 29BA	⧊ 29CA	⧚ 29DA	⧪ 29EA	⧺ 29FA
B	⦋ 298B	⦛ 299B	⦫ 29AB	⦻ 29BB	⧋ 29CB	⧛ 29DB	⧫ 29EB	⧻ 29FB
C	⦌ 298C	⦜ 299C	⦬ 29AC	⦼ 29BC	⧌ 29CC	⧜ 29DC	⧬ 29EC	⧼ 29FC
D	⦍ 298D	⦝ 299D	⦭ 29AD	⦽ 29BD	⧍ 29CD	⧝ 29DD	⧭ 29ED	⧽ 29FD
E	⦎ 298E	⦞ 299E	⦮ 29AE	⦾ 29BE	⧎ 29CE	⧞ 29DE	⧮ 29EE	⧾ 29FE
F	⦏ 298F	⦟ 299F	⦯ 29AF	⦿ 29BF	⧏ 29CF	⧟ 29DF	⧯ 29EF	⧿ 29FF

Miscellaneous mathematical symbols

2980 ⦀ TRIPLE VERTICAL BAR DELIMITER
→ 2AF4 ⫴ triple vertical bar binary relation
→ 2AFC ⫼ large triple vertical bar operator
2981 ⦁ Z NOTATION SPOT
• medium-small-sized black circle
→ 2219 ∙ bullet operator
→ 25CF ● black circle
2982 ⦂ Z NOTATION TYPE COLON
→ 0F7F ཿ tibetan sign rnam bcad

Brackets

2983 ⦃ LEFT WHITE CURLY BRACKET
2984 ⦄ RIGHT WHITE CURLY BRACKET
2985 ⦅ LEFT WHITE PARENTHESIS
→ FF5F ｟ fullwidth left white parenthesis
2986 ⦆ RIGHT WHITE PARENTHESIS
• used for Bourbakist intervals
→ FF60 ｠ fullwidth right white parenthesis
2987 ⦇ Z NOTATION LEFT IMAGE BRACKET
2988 ⦈ Z NOTATION RIGHT IMAGE BRACKET
2989 ⦉ Z NOTATION LEFT BINDING BRACKET
298A ⦊ Z NOTATION RIGHT BINDING BRACKET
298B ⦋ LEFT SQUARE BRACKET WITH UNDERBAR
298C ⦌ RIGHT SQUARE BRACKET WITH UNDERBAR
298D ⦍ LEFT SQUARE BRACKET WITH TICK IN TOP CORNER
298E ⦎ RIGHT SQUARE BRACKET WITH TICK IN BOTTOM CORNER
298F ⦏ LEFT SQUARE BRACKET WITH TICK IN BOTTOM CORNER
2990 ⦐ RIGHT SQUARE BRACKET WITH TICK IN TOP CORNER
2991 ⦑ LEFT ANGLE BRACKET WITH DOT
2992 ⦒ RIGHT ANGLE BRACKET WITH DOT
2993 ⦓ LEFT ARC LESS-THAN BRACKET
2994 ⦔ RIGHT ARC GREATER-THAN BRACKET
2995 ⦕ DOUBLE LEFT ARC GREATER-THAN BRACKET
2996 ⦖ DOUBLE RIGHT ARC LESS-THAN BRACKET
2997 ⦗ LEFT BLACK TORTOISE SHELL BRACKET
→ 3014 〔 left tortoise shell bracket
→ 3018 〘 left white tortoise shell bracket
2998 ⦘ RIGHT BLACK TORTOISE SHELL BRACKET

Fences

2999 ⦙ DOTTED FENCE
• four close dots vertical
299A ⦚ VERTICAL ZIGZAG LINE
→ 2307 ⌇ wavy line

Angles

299B ⦛ MEASURED ANGLE OPENING LEFT
→ 2221 ∡ measured angle
299C ⦜ RIGHT ANGLE VARIANT WITH SQUARE
→ 221F ∟ right angle
299D ⦝ MEASURED RIGHT ANGLE WITH DOT
299E ⦞ ANGLE WITH S INSIDE
299F ⦟ ACUTE ANGLE
29A0 ⦠ SPHERICAL ANGLE OPENING LEFT
→ 2222 ∢ spherical angle
29A1 ⦡ SPHERICAL ANGLE OPENING UP
29A2 ⦢ TURNED ANGLE
→ 2220 ∠ angle
29A3 ⦣ REVERSED ANGLE
29A4 ⦤ ANGLE WITH UNDERBAR
29A5 ⦥ REVERSED ANGLE WITH UNDERBAR
29A6 ⦦ OBLIQUE ANGLE OPENING UP
29A7 ⦧ OBLIQUE ANGLE OPENING DOWN
29A8 ⦨ MEASURED ANGLE WITH OPEN ARM ENDING IN ARROW POINTING UP AND RIGHT
29A9 ⦩ MEASURED ANGLE WITH OPEN ARM ENDING IN ARROW POINTING UP AND LEFT
29AA ⦪ MEASURED ANGLE WITH OPEN ARM ENDING IN ARROW POINTING DOWN AND RIGHT
29AB ⦫ MEASURED ANGLE WITH OPEN ARM ENDING IN ARROW POINTING DOWN AND LEFT
29AC ⦬ MEASURED ANGLE WITH OPEN ARM ENDING IN ARROW POINTING RIGHT AND UP
29AD ⦭ MEASURED ANGLE WITH OPEN ARM ENDING IN ARROW POINTING LEFT AND UP
29AE ⦮ MEASURED ANGLE WITH OPEN ARM ENDING IN ARROW POINTING RIGHT AND DOWN
29AF ⦯ MEASURED ANGLE WITH OPEN ARM ENDING IN ARROW POINTING LEFT AND DOWN

Empty sets

29B0 ⦰ REVERSED EMPTY SET
→ 2205 ∅ empty set
→ 2349 ⍉ apl functional symbol circle backslash
29B1 ⦱ EMPTY SET WITH OVERBAR
29B2 ⦲ EMPTY SET WITH SMALL CIRCLE ABOVE
29B3 ⦳ EMPTY SET WITH RIGHT ARROW ABOVE
29B4 ⦴ EMPTY SET WITH LEFT ARROW ABOVE

Circle symbols

29B5 ⦵ CIRCLE WITH HORIZONTAL BAR
→ 2296 ⊖ circled minus
29B6 ⦶ CIRCLED VERTICAL BAR
29B7 ⦷ CIRCLED PARALLEL
29B8 ⦸ CIRCLED REVERSE SOLIDUS
29B9 ⦹ CIRCLED PERPENDICULAR
29BA ⦺ CIRCLE DIVIDED BY HORIZONTAL BAR AND TOP HALF DIVIDED BY VERTICAL BAR
29BB ⦻ CIRCLE WITH SUPERIMPOSED X
→ 2297 ⊗ circled times
29BC ⦼ CIRCLED ANTICLOCKWISE-ROTATED DIVISION SIGN
29BD ⦽ UP ARROW THROUGH CIRCLE
29BE ⦾ CIRCLED WHITE BULLET
→ 229A ⊚ circled ring operator
→ 233E ⌾ apl functional symbol circle jot
→ 25CE ◎ bullseye
29BF ⦿ CIRCLED BULLET
• forms part of a graduated set of circles with enclosed black circle of different sizes
→ 2299 ⊙ circled dot operator
→ 25C9 ◉ fisheye
→ 2A00 ⨀ n-ary circled dot operator
29C0 ⧀ CIRCLED LESS-THAN
29C1 ⧁ CIRCLED GREATER-THAN
29C2 ⧂ CIRCLE WITH SMALL CIRCLE TO THE RIGHT
29C3 ⧃ CIRCLE WITH TWO HORIZONTAL STROKES TO THE RIGHT

Square symbols

29C4 ⧄ SQUARED RISING DIAGONAL SLASH
→ 2341 ⍁ apl functional symbol quad slash
→ 303C 〼 masu mark
29C5 ⧅ SQUARED FALLING DIAGONAL SLASH
→ 2342 ⍂ apl functional symbol quad backslash
29C6 ⧆ SQUARED ASTERISK

29C7 ⧇ SQUARED SMALL CIRCLE
→ 233B ⌻ apl functional symbol quad jot
29C8 ⧈ SQUARED SQUARE
29C9 ⧉ TWO JOINED SQUARES

Triangle symbols

29CA ⧊ TRIANGLE WITH DOT ABOVE
29CB ⧋ TRIANGLE WITH UNDERBAR
29CC ⧌ S IN TRIANGLE
29CD ⧍ TRIANGLE WITH SERIFS AT BOTTOM
→ 25B3 △ white up-pointing triangle
29CE ⧎ RIGHT TRIANGLE ABOVE LEFT TRIANGLE
29CF ⧏ LEFT TRIANGLE BESIDE VERTICAL BAR
29D0 ⧐ VERTICAL BAR BESIDE RIGHT TRIANGLE

Bowtie symbols

29D1 ⧑ BOWTIE WITH LEFT HALF BLACK
→ 22C8 ⋈ bowtie
29D2 ⧒ BOWTIE WITH RIGHT HALF BLACK
29D3 ⧓ BLACK BOWTIE
29D4 ⧔ TIMES WITH LEFT HALF BLACK
→ 22C9 ⋉ left normal factor semidirect product
29D5 ⧕ TIMES WITH RIGHT HALF BLACK
→ 22CA ⋊ right normal factor semidirect product
29D6 ⧖ WHITE HOURGLASS
= vertical bowtie
= white framus
→ 231B ⌛ hourglass
29D7 ⧗ BLACK HOURGLASS

Fences

29D8 ⧘ LEFT WIGGLY FENCE
→ FE34 ︴ presentation form for vertical wavy low line
29D9 ⧙ RIGHT WIGGLY FENCE
29DA ⧚ LEFT DOUBLE WIGGLY FENCE
29DB ⧛ RIGHT DOUBLE WIGGLY FENCE

Miscellaneous mathematical symbols

29DC ⧜ INCOMPLETE INFINITY
= ISOtech entity ⧜
→ 221E ∞ infinity
29DD ⧝ TIE OVER INFINITY
29DE ⧞ INFINITY NEGATED WITH VERTICAL BAR
29DF ⧟ DOUBLE-ENDED MULTIMAP
→ 22B8 ⊸ multimap
29E0 ⧠ SQUARE WITH CONTOURED OUTLINE
= D'Alembertian
→ 274F ❏ lower right drop-shadowed white square
29E1 ⧡ INCREASES AS
→ 22B4 ⊴ normal subgroup of or equal to
29E2 ⧢ SHUFFLE PRODUCT
→ 22FF ⋿ z notation bag membership

Relations

29E3 ⧣ EQUALS SIGN AND SLANTED PARALLEL
→ 0023 # number sign
→ 22D5 ⋕ equal and parallel to
29E4 ⧤ EQUALS SIGN AND SLANTED PARALLEL WITH TILDE ABOVE
29E5 ⧥ IDENTICAL TO AND SLANTED PARALLEL
→ 2A68 ⩨ triple horizontal bar with double vertical stroke
29E6 ⧦ GLEICH STARK
= tautological equivalent

Miscellaneous mathematical symbols

29E7 ⧧ THERMODYNAMIC
• vertical bar crossed by two horizontals
→ 2260 ≠ not equal to
29E8 ⧨ DOWN-POINTING TRIANGLE WITH LEFT HALF BLACK
→ 25ED ◭ up-pointing triangle with left half black
29E9 ⧩ DOWN-POINTING TRIANGLE WITH RIGHT HALF BLACK
→ 25EE ◮ up-pointing triangle with right half black
29EA ⧪ BLACK DIAMOND WITH DOWN ARROW
29EB ⧫ BLACK LOZENGE
→ 25CA ◊ lozenge
29EC ⧬ WHITE CIRCLE WITH DOWN ARROW
29ED ⧭ BLACK CIRCLE WITH DOWN ARROW

Error bar symbols

29EE ⧮ ERROR-BARRED WHITE SQUARE
29EF ⧯ ERROR-BARRED BLACK SQUARE
29F0 ⧰ ERROR-BARRED WHITE DIAMOND
29F1 ⧱ ERROR-BARRED BLACK DIAMOND
29F2 ⧲ ERROR-BARRED WHITE CIRCLE
29F3 ⧳ ERROR-BARRED BLACK CIRCLE

Miscellaneous mathematical symbols

29F4 ⧴ RULE-DELAYED
= colon right arrow
29F5 ⧵ REVERSE SOLIDUS OPERATOR
→ 005C \ reverse solidus
→ 2216 ∖ set minus
29F6 ⧶ SOLIDUS WITH OVERBAR
29F7 ⧷ REVERSE SOLIDUS WITH HORIZONTAL STROKE

Large operators

29F8 ⧸ BIG SOLIDUS
→ 2215 ∕ division slash
29F9 ⧹ BIG REVERSE SOLIDUS
= z notation schema hiding
→ 2216 ∖ set minus

Specialized plus sign operators

29FA ⧺ DOUBLE PLUS
29FB ⧻ TRIPLE PLUS

Brackets

29FC ⧼ LEFT-POINTING CURVED ANGLE BRACKET
→ 227A ≺ precedes
→ 2329 〈 left-pointing angle bracket
29FD ⧽ RIGHT-POINTING CURVED ANGLE BRACKET
→ 227B ≻ succeeds
→ 232A 〉 right-pointing angle bracket

Miscellaneous mathematical symbols

29FE ⧾ TINY
→ 002B + plus sign
29FF ⧿ MINY
→ 2212 − minus sign

	2A0	2A1	2A2	2A3	2A4	2A5	2A6	2A7	2A8	2A9	2AA	2AB	2AC	2AD	2AE	2AF
0	⨀ 2A00	⨐ 2A10	⨠ 2A20	⨰ 2A30	⩀ 2A40	⩐ 2A50	⩠ 2A60	⩰ 2A70	⪀ 2A80	⪐ 2A90	⪠ 2AA0	⪰ 2AB0	⫀ 2AC0	⫐ 2AD0	⫠ 2AE0	⫰ 2AF0
1	⨁ 2A01	⨑ 2A11	⨡ 2A21	⨱ 2A31	⩁ 2A41	⩑ 2A51	⩡ 2A61	⩱ 2A71	⪁ 2A81	⪑ 2A91	⪡ 2AA1	⪱ 2AB1	⫁ 2AC1	⫑ 2AD1	⫡ 2AE1	⫱ 2AF1
2	⨂ 2A02	⨒ 2A12	⨢ 2A22	⨲ 2A32	⩂ 2A42	⩒ 2A52	⩢ 2A62	⩲ 2A72	⪂ 2A82	⪒ 2A92	⪢ 2AA2	⪲ 2AB2	⫂ 2AC2	⫒ 2AD2	⫢ 2AE2	⫲ 2AF2
3	⨃ 2A03	⨓ 2A13	⨣ 2A23	⨳ 2A33	⩃ 2A43	⩓ 2A53	⩣ 2A63	⩳ 2A73	⪃ 2A83	⪓ 2A93	⪣ 2AA3	⪳ 2AB3	⫃ 2AC3	⫓ 2AD3	⫣ 2AE3	⫳ 2AF3
4	⨄ 2A04	⨔ 2A14	⨤ 2A24	⨴ 2A34	⩄ 2A44	⩔ 2A54	⩤ 2A64	⩴ 2A74	⪄ 2A84	⪔ 2A94	⪤ 2AA4	⪴ 2AB4	⫄ 2AC4	⫔ 2AD4	⫤ 2AE4	⫴ 2AF4
5	⨅ 2A05	⨕ 2A15	⨥ 2A25	⨵ 2A35	⩅ 2A45	⩕ 2A55	⩥ 2A65	⩵ 2A75	⪅ 2A85	⪕ 2A95	⪥ 2AA5	⪵ 2AB5	⫅ 2AC5	⫕ 2AD5	⫥ 2AE5	⫵ 2AF5
6	⨆ 2A06	⨖ 2A16	⨦ 2A26	⨶ 2A36	⩆ 2A46	⩖ 2A56	⩦ 2A66	⩶ 2A76	⪆ 2A86	⪖ 2A96	⪦ 2AA6	⪶ 2AB6	⫆ 2AC6	⫖ 2AD6	⫦ 2AE6	⫶ 2AF6
7	⨇ 2A07	⨗ 2A17	⨧ 2A27	⨷ 2A37	⩇ 2A47	⩗ 2A57	⩧ 2A67	⩷ 2A77	⪇ 2A87	⪗ 2A97	⪧ 2AA7	⪷ 2AB7	⫇ 2AC7	⫗ 2AD7	⫧ 2AE7	⫷ 2AF7
8	⨈ 2A08	⨘ 2A18	⨨ 2A28	⨸ 2A38	⩈ 2A48	⩘ 2A58	⩨ 2A68	⩸ 2A78	⪈ 2A88	⪘ 2A98	⪨ 2AA8	⪸ 2AB8	⫈ 2AC8	⫘ 2AD8	⫨ 2AE8	⫸ 2AF8
9	⨉ 2A09	⨙ 2A19	⨩ 2A29	⨹ 2A39	⩉ 2A49	⩙ 2A59	⩩ 2A69	⩹ 2A79	⪉ 2A89	⪙ 2A99	⪩ 2AA9	⪹ 2AB9	⫉ 2AC9	⫙ 2AD9	⫩ 2AE9	⫹ 2AF9
A	⨊ 2A0A	⨚ 2A1A	⨪ 2A2A	⨺ 2A3A	⩊ 2A4A	⩚ 2A5A	⩪ 2A6A	⩺ 2A7A	⪊ 2A8A	⪚ 2A9A	⪪ 2AAA	⪺ 2ABA	⫊ 2ACA	⫚ 2ADA	⫪ 2AEA	⫺ 2AFA
B	⨋ 2A0B	⨛ 2A1B	⨫ 2A2B	⨻ 2A3B	⩋ 2A4B	⩛ 2A5B	⩫ 2A6B	⩻ 2A7B	⪋ 2A8B	⪛ 2A9B	⪫ 2AAB	⪻ 2ABB	⫋ 2ACB	⫛ 2ADB	⫫ 2AEB	⫻ 2AFB
C	⨌ 2A0C	⨜ 2A1C	⨬ 2A2C	⨼ 2A3C	⩌ 2A4C	⩜ 2A5C	⩬ 2A6C	⩼ 2A7C	⪌ 2A8C	⪜ 2A9C	⪬ 2AAC	⪼ 2ABC	⫌ 2ACC	⫝̸ 2ADC	⫬ 2AEC	⫼ 2AFC
D	⨍ 2A0D	⨝ 2A1D	⨭ 2A2D	⨽ 2A3D	⩍ 2A4D	⩝ 2A5D	⩭ 2A6D	⩽ 2A7D	⪍ 2A8D	⪝ 2A9D	⪭ 2AAD	⪽ 2ABD	⫍ 2ACD	⫝ 2ADD	⫭ 2AED	⫽ 2AFD
E	⨎ 2A0E	⨞ 2A1E	⨮ 2A2E	⨾ 2A3E	⩎ 2A4E	⩞ 2A5E	⩮ 2A6E	⩾ 2A7E	⪎ 2A8E	⪞ 2A9E	⪮ 2AAE	⪾ 2ABE	⫎ 2ACE	⫞ 2ADE	⫮ 2AEE	⫾ 2AFE
F	⨏ 2A0F	⨟ 2A1F	⨯ 2A2F	⨿ 2A3F	⩏ 2A4F	⩟ 2A5F	⩯ 2A6F	⩿ 2A7F	⪏ 2A8F	⪟ 2A9F	⪯ 2AAF	⪿ 2ABF	⫏ 2ACF	⫟ 2ADF	⫯ 2AEF	⫿ 2AFF

N-ary operators

2A00 ⨀ N-ARY CIRCLED DOT OPERATOR
→ 2299 ⊙ circled dot operator
→ 25C9 ◉ fisheye

2A01 ⨁ N-ARY CIRCLED PLUS OPERATOR
→ 2295 ⊕ circled plus

2A02 ⨂ N-ARY CIRCLED TIMES OPERATOR
→ 2297 ⊗ circled times

2A03 ⨃ N-ARY UNION OPERATOR WITH DOT

2A04 ⨄ N-ARY UNION OPERATOR WITH PLUS
→ 228E ⊎ multiset union

2A05 ⨅ N-ARY SQUARE INTERSECTION OPERATOR
→ 2293 ⊓ square cap

2A06 ⨆ N-ARY SQUARE UNION OPERATOR
→ 2294 ⊔ square cup

2A07 ⨇ TWO LOGICAL AND OPERATOR
= merge
→ 2A55 ⩕ two intersecting logical and

2A08 ⨈ TWO LOGICAL OR OPERATOR
→ 2A56 ⩖ two intersecting logical or

2A09 ⨉ N-ARY TIMES OPERATOR
→ 00D7 × multiplication sign

Summations and integrals

2A0A ⨊ MODULO TWO SUM
→ 2211 ∑ n-ary summation

2A0B ⨋ SUMMATION WITH INTEGRAL

2A0C ⨌ QUADRUPLE INTEGRAL OPERATOR
→ 222D ∭ triple integral
≈ 222B ∫ 222B ∫ 222B ∫ 222B ∫

2A0D ⨍ FINITE PART INTEGRAL

2A0E ⨎ INTEGRAL WITH DOUBLE STROKE

2A0F ⨏ INTEGRAL AVERAGE WITH SLASH

2A10 ⨐ CIRCULATION FUNCTION

2A11 ⨑ ANTICLOCKWISE INTEGRATION

2A12 ⨒ LINE INTEGRATION WITH RECTANGULAR PATH AROUND POLE

2A13 ⨓ LINE INTEGRATION WITH SEMICIRCULAR PATH AROUND POLE

2A14 ⨔ LINE INTEGRATION NOT INCLUDING THE POLE

2A15 ⨕ INTEGRAL AROUND A POINT OPERATOR
→ 222E ∮ contour integral

2A16 ⨖ QUATERNION INTEGRAL OPERATOR

2A17 ⨗ INTEGRAL WITH LEFTWARDS ARROW WITH HOOK

2A18 ⨘ INTEGRAL WITH TIMES SIGN

2A19 ⨙ INTEGRAL WITH INTERSECTION

2A1A ⨚ INTEGRAL WITH UNION

2A1B ⨛ INTEGRAL WITH OVERBAR
= upper integral

2A1C ⨜ INTEGRAL WITH UNDERBAR
= lower integral

Miscellaneous large operators

2A1D ⨝ JOIN
= large bowtie
• relational database theory
→ 22C8 ⋈ bowtie
→ 27D7 ⟗ full outer join

2A1E ⨞ LARGE LEFT TRIANGLE OPERATOR
• relational database theory
→ 25C1 ◁ white left-pointing triangle

2A1F ⨟ Z NOTATION SCHEMA COMPOSITION
→ 2A3E ⨾ z notation relational composition

2A20 ⨠ Z NOTATION SCHEMA PIPING
→ 226B ≫ much greater-than

2A21 ⨡ Z NOTATION SCHEMA PROJECTION
→ 21BE ↾ upwards harpoon with barb rightwards

Plus and minus sign operators

2A22 ⨢ PLUS SIGN WITH SMALL CIRCLE ABOVE

2A23 ⨣ PLUS SIGN WITH CIRCUMFLEX ACCENT ABOVE

2A24 ⨤ PLUS SIGN WITH TILDE ABOVE
= positive difference or sum

2A25 ⨥ PLUS SIGN WITH DOT BELOW
→ 2214 ∔ dot plus

2A26 ⨦ PLUS SIGN WITH TILDE BELOW
= sum or positive difference

2A27 ⨧ PLUS SIGN WITH SUBSCRIPT TWO
= nim-addition

2A28 ⨨ PLUS SIGN WITH BLACK TRIANGLE

2A29 ⨩ MINUS SIGN WITH COMMA ABOVE

2A2A ⨪ MINUS SIGN WITH DOT BELOW
→ 2238 ∸ dot minus

2A2B ⨫ MINUS SIGN WITH FALLING DOTS

2A2C ⨬ MINUS SIGN WITH RISING DOTS

2A2D ⨭ PLUS SIGN IN LEFT HALF CIRCLE

2A2E ⨮ PLUS SIGN IN RIGHT HALF CIRCLE

Multiplication and division sign operators

2A2F ⨯ VECTOR OR CROSS PRODUCT
→ 00D7 × multiplication sign

2A30 ⨰ MULTIPLICATION SIGN WITH DOT ABOVE

2A31 ⨱ MULTIPLICATION SIGN WITH UNDERBAR

2A32 ⨲ SEMIDIRECT PRODUCT WITH BOTTOM CLOSED

2A33 ⨳ SMASH PRODUCT

2A34 ⨴ MULTIPLICATION SIGN IN LEFT HALF CIRCLE

2A35 ⨵ MULTIPLICATION SIGN IN RIGHT HALF CIRCLE

2A36 ⨶ CIRCLED MULTIPLICATION SIGN WITH CIRCUMFLEX ACCENT

2A37 ⨷ MULTIPLICATION SIGN IN DOUBLE CIRCLE

2A38 ⨸ CIRCLED DIVISION SIGN

Miscellaneous mathematical operators

2A39 ⨹ PLUS SIGN IN TRIANGLE

2A3A ⨺ MINUS SIGN IN TRIANGLE

2A3B ⨻ MULTIPLICATION SIGN IN TRIANGLE

2A3C ⨼ INTERIOR PRODUCT
→ 230B ⌋ right floor

2A3D ⨽ RIGHTHAND INTERIOR PRODUCT
→ 230A ⌊ left floor
→ 2319 ⌙ turned not sign

2A3E ⨾ Z NOTATION RELATIONAL COMPOSITION
→ 2A1F ⨟ z notation schema composition

2A3F ⨿ AMALGAMATION OR COPRODUCT
→ 2210 ∐ n-ary coproduct

Intersections and unions

2A40 ⩀ INTERSECTION WITH DOT
→ 2227 ∧ logical and
→ 27D1 ⟑ and with dot

2A41 ⩁ UNION WITH MINUS SIGN
= z notation bag subtraction
→ 228E ⊎ multiset union

2A42 ⩂ UNION WITH OVERBAR

2A43 ⩃ INTERSECTION WITH OVERBAR

2A44 ⩄ INTERSECTION WITH LOGICAL AND

2A45 ⩅ UNION WITH LOGICAL OR

2A46 ⩆ UNION ABOVE INTERSECTION

2A47 ⩇ INTERSECTION ABOVE UNION

2A48 ⩈ UNION ABOVE BAR ABOVE INTERSECTION
2A49 ⩉ INTERSECTION ABOVE BAR ABOVE UNION
2A4A ⩊ UNION BESIDE AND JOINED WITH UNION
2A4B ⩋ INTERSECTION BESIDE AND JOINED WITH INTERSECTION
2A4C ⩌ CLOSED UNION WITH SERIFS
→ 222A ∪ union
2A4D ⩍ CLOSED INTERSECTION WITH SERIFS
→ 2229 ∩ intersection
2A4E ⩎ DOUBLE SQUARE INTERSECTION
2A4F ⩏ DOUBLE SQUARE UNION
2A50 ⩐ CLOSED UNION WITH SERIFS AND SMASH PRODUCT

Logical ands and ors

2A51 ⩑ LOGICAL AND WITH DOT ABOVE
2A52 ⩒ LOGICAL OR WITH DOT ABOVE
2A53 ⩓ DOUBLE LOGICAL AND
2A54 ⩔ DOUBLE LOGICAL OR
2A55 ⩕ TWO INTERSECTING LOGICAL AND
→ 2A07 ⨇ two logical and operator
2A56 ⩖ TWO INTERSECTING LOGICAL OR
→ 2A08 ⨈ two logical or operator
2A57 ⩗ SLOPING LARGE OR
2A58 ⩘ SLOPING LARGE AND
2A59 ⩙ LOGICAL OR OVERLAPPING LOGICAL AND
2A5A ⩚ LOGICAL AND WITH MIDDLE STEM
2A5B ⩛ LOGICAL OR WITH MIDDLE STEM
2A5C ⩜ LOGICAL AND WITH HORIZONTAL DASH
2A5D ⩝ LOGICAL OR WITH HORIZONTAL DASH
2A5E ⩞ LOGICAL AND WITH DOUBLE OVERBAR
→ 2306 ⌆ perspective
2A5F ⩟ LOGICAL AND WITH UNDERBAR
2A60 ⩠ LOGICAL AND WITH DOUBLE UNDERBAR
→ 2259 ≙ estimates
2A61 ⩡ SMALL VEE WITH UNDERBAR
→ 225A ≚ equiangular to
2A62 ⩢ LOGICAL OR WITH DOUBLE OVERBAR
2A63 ⩣ LOGICAL OR WITH DOUBLE UNDERBAR
→ 225A ≚ equiangular to

Miscellaneous mathematical operators

2A64 ⩤ Z NOTATION DOMAIN ANTIRESTRICTION
2A65 ⩥ Z NOTATION RANGE ANTIRESTRICTION
→ 2332 ⌲ conical taper

Relational operators

2A66 ⩦ EQUALS SIGN WITH DOT BELOW
→ 2250 ≐ approaches the limit
2A67 ⩧ IDENTICAL WITH DOT ABOVE
2A68 ⩨ TRIPLE HORIZONTAL BAR WITH DOUBLE VERTICAL STROKE
= identical and parallel to
→ 22D5 ⋕ equal and parallel to
→ 29E5 ⧥ identical to and slanted parallel
2A69 ⩩ TRIPLE HORIZONTAL BAR WITH TRIPLE VERTICAL STROKE
2A6A ⩪ TILDE OPERATOR WITH DOT ABOVE
2A6B ⩫ TILDE OPERATOR WITH RISING DOTS
→ 223B ∻ homothetic
2A6C ⩬ SIMILAR MINUS SIMILAR
2A6D ⩭ CONGRUENT WITH DOT ABOVE
→ 2245 ≅ approximately equal to
2A6E ⩮ EQUALS WITH ASTERISK
→ 225B ≛ star equals
2A6F ⩯ ALMOST EQUAL TO WITH CIRCUMFLEX ACCENT
2A70 ⩰ APPROXIMATELY EQUAL OR EQUAL TO
2A71 ⩱ EQUALS SIGN ABOVE PLUS SIGN
• black stands slightly better (chess notation)
2A72 ⩲ PLUS SIGN ABOVE EQUALS SIGN
• white stands slightly better (chess notation)
2A73 ⩳ EQUALS SIGN ABOVE TILDE OPERATOR
2A74 ⩴ DOUBLE COLON EQUAL
≈ 003A : 003A : 003D =
2A75 ⩵ TWO CONSECUTIVE EQUALS SIGNS
≈ 003D = 003D =
2A76 ⩶ THREE CONSECUTIVE EQUALS SIGNS
≈ 003D = 003D = 003D =
2A77 ⩷ EQUALS SIGN WITH TWO DOTS ABOVE AND TWO DOTS BELOW
2A78 ⩸ EQUIVALENT WITH FOUR DOTS ABOVE
2A79 ⩹ LESS-THAN WITH CIRCLE INSIDE
2A7A ⩺ GREATER-THAN WITH CIRCLE INSIDE
2A7B ⩻ LESS-THAN WITH QUESTION MARK ABOVE
2A7C ⩼ GREATER-THAN WITH QUESTION MARK ABOVE
2A7D ⩽ LESS-THAN OR SLANTED EQUAL TO
→ 2264 ≤ less-than or equal to
2A7E ⩾ GREATER-THAN OR SLANTED EQUAL TO
→ 2265 ≥ greater-than or equal to
2A7F ⩿ LESS-THAN OR SLANTED EQUAL TO WITH DOT INSIDE
2A80 ⪀ GREATER-THAN OR SLANTED EQUAL TO WITH DOT INSIDE
2A81 ⪁ LESS-THAN OR SLANTED EQUAL TO WITH DOT ABOVE
2A82 ⪂ GREATER-THAN OR SLANTED EQUAL TO WITH DOT ABOVE
2A83 ⪃ LESS-THAN OR SLANTED EQUAL TO WITH DOT ABOVE RIGHT
2A84 ⪄ GREATER-THAN OR SLANTED EQUAL TO WITH DOT ABOVE LEFT
2A85 ⪅ LESS-THAN OR APPROXIMATE
2A86 ⪆ GREATER-THAN OR APPROXIMATE
2A87 ⪇ LESS-THAN AND SINGLE-LINE NOT EQUAL TO
→ 2268 ≨ less-than but not equal to
2A88 ⪈ GREATER-THAN AND SINGLE-LINE NOT EQUAL TO
→ 2269 ≩ greater-than but not equal to
2A89 ⪉ LESS-THAN AND NOT APPROXIMATE
2A8A ⪊ GREATER-THAN AND NOT APPROXIMATE
2A8B ⪋ LESS-THAN ABOVE DOUBLE-LINE EQUAL ABOVE GREATER-THAN
→ 22DA ⋚ less-than equal to or greater-than
2A8C ⪌ GREATER-THAN ABOVE DOUBLE-LINE EQUAL ABOVE LESS-THAN
→ 22DB ⋛ greater-than equal to or less-than
2A8D ⪍ LESS-THAN ABOVE SIMILAR OR EQUAL
2A8E ⪎ GREATER-THAN ABOVE SIMILAR OR EQUAL
2A8F ⪏ LESS-THAN ABOVE SIMILAR ABOVE GREATER-THAN
2A90 ⪐ GREATER-THAN ABOVE SIMILAR ABOVE LESS-THAN
2A91 ⪑ LESS-THAN ABOVE GREATER-THAN ABOVE DOUBLE-LINE EQUAL
2A92 ⪒ GREATER-THAN ABOVE LESS-THAN ABOVE DOUBLE-LINE EQUAL
2A93 ⪓ LESS-THAN ABOVE SLANTED EQUAL ABOVE GREATER-THAN ABOVE SLANTED EQUAL
2A94 ⪔ GREATER-THAN ABOVE SLANTED EQUAL ABOVE LESS-THAN ABOVE SLANTED EQUAL

2A95 ⪕ SLANTED EQUAL TO OR LESS-THAN
→ 22DC ⋜ equal to or less-than
2A96 ⪖ SLANTED EQUAL TO OR GREATER-THAN
→ 22DD ⋝ equal to or greater-than
2A97 ⪗ SLANTED EQUAL TO OR LESS-THAN WITH DOT INSIDE
2A98 ⪘ SLANTED EQUAL TO OR GREATER-THAN WITH DOT INSIDE
2A99 ⪙ DOUBLE-LINE EQUAL TO OR LESS-THAN
→ 22DC ⋜ equal to or less-than
2A9A ⪚ DOUBLE-LINE EQUAL TO OR GREATER-THAN
→ 22DD ⋝ equal to or greater-than
2A9B ⪛ DOUBLE-LINE SLANTED EQUAL TO OR LESS-THAN
2A9C ⪜ DOUBLE-LINE SLANTED EQUAL TO OR GREATER-THAN
2A9D ⪝ SIMILAR OR LESS-THAN
2A9E ⪞ SIMILAR OR GREATER-THAN
2A9F ⪟ SIMILAR ABOVE LESS-THAN ABOVE EQUALS SIGN
2AA0 ⪠ SIMILAR ABOVE GREATER-THAN ABOVE EQUALS SIGN
2AA1 ⪡ DOUBLE NESTED LESS-THAN
= absolute continuity
→ 226A ≪ much less-than
2AA2 ⪢ DOUBLE NESTED GREATER-THAN
→ 226B ≫ much greater-than
2AA3 ⪣ DOUBLE NESTED LESS-THAN WITH UNDERBAR
2AA4 ⪤ GREATER-THAN OVERLAPPING LESS-THAN
2AA5 ⪥ GREATER-THAN BESIDE LESS-THAN
2AA6 ⪦ LESS-THAN CLOSED BY CURVE
2AA7 ⪧ GREATER-THAN CLOSED BY CURVE
2AA8 ⪨ LESS-THAN CLOSED BY CURVE ABOVE SLANTED EQUAL
2AA9 ⪩ GREATER-THAN CLOSED BY CURVE ABOVE SLANTED EQUAL
2AAA ⪪ SMALLER THAN
2AAB ⪫ LARGER THAN
2AAC ⪬ SMALLER THAN OR EQUAL TO
2AAD ⪭ LARGER THAN OR EQUAL TO
2AAE ⪮ EQUALS SIGN WITH BUMPY ABOVE
→ 224F ≏ difference between
2AAF ⪯ PRECEDES ABOVE SINGLE-LINE EQUALS SIGN
→ 227C ≼ precedes or equal to
2AB0 ⪰ SUCCEEDS ABOVE SINGLE-LINE EQUALS SIGN
→ 227D ≽ succeeds or equal to
2AB1 ⪱ PRECEDES ABOVE SINGLE-LINE NOT EQUAL TO
2AB2 ⪲ SUCCEEDS ABOVE SINGLE-LINE NOT EQUAL TO
2AB3 ⪳ PRECEDES ABOVE EQUALS SIGN
2AB4 ⪴ SUCCEEDS ABOVE EQUALS SIGN
2AB5 ⪵ PRECEDES ABOVE NOT EQUAL TO
2AB6 ⪶ SUCCEEDS ABOVE NOT EQUAL TO
2AB7 ⪷ PRECEDES ABOVE ALMOST EQUAL TO
2AB8 ⪸ SUCCEEDS ABOVE ALMOST EQUAL TO
2AB9 ⪹ PRECEDES ABOVE NOT ALMOST EQUAL TO
2ABA ⪺ SUCCEEDS ABOVE NOT ALMOST EQUAL TO
2ABB ⪻ DOUBLE PRECEDES
2ABC ⪼ DOUBLE SUCCEEDS

Subset and superset relations

2ABD ⪽ SUBSET WITH DOT
2ABE ⪾ SUPERSET WITH DOT
2ABF ⪿ SUBSET WITH PLUS SIGN BELOW
2AC0 ⫀ SUPERSET WITH PLUS SIGN BELOW
2AC1 ⫁ SUBSET WITH MULTIPLICATION SIGN BELOW
2AC2 ⫂ SUPERSET WITH MULTIPLICATION SIGN BELOW
2AC3 ⫃ SUBSET OF OR EQUAL TO WITH DOT ABOVE
2AC4 ⫄ SUPERSET OF OR EQUAL TO WITH DOT ABOVE
2AC5 ⫅ SUBSET OF ABOVE EQUALS SIGN
2AC6 ⫆ SUPERSET OF ABOVE EQUALS SIGN
2AC7 ⫇ SUBSET OF ABOVE TILDE OPERATOR
2AC8 ⫈ SUPERSET OF ABOVE TILDE OPERATOR
2AC9 ⫉ SUBSET OF ABOVE ALMOST EQUAL TO
2ACA ⫊ SUPERSET OF ABOVE ALMOST EQUAL TO
2ACB ⫋ SUBSET OF ABOVE NOT EQUAL TO
2ACC ⫌ SUPERSET OF ABOVE NOT EQUAL TO
2ACD ⫍ SQUARE LEFT OPEN BOX OPERATOR
2ACE ⫎ SQUARE RIGHT OPEN BOX OPERATOR
2ACF ⫏ CLOSED SUBSET
→ 2282 ⊂ subset of
2AD0 ⫐ CLOSED SUPERSET
→ 2283 ⊃ superset of
2AD1 ⫑ CLOSED SUBSET OR EQUAL TO
2AD2 ⫒ CLOSED SUPERSET OR EQUAL TO
2AD3 ⫓ SUBSET ABOVE SUPERSET
2AD4 ⫔ SUPERSET ABOVE SUBSET
2AD5 ⫕ SUBSET ABOVE SUBSET
2AD6 ⫖ SUPERSET ABOVE SUPERSET
2AD7 ⫗ SUPERSET BESIDE SUBSET
2AD8 ⫘ SUPERSET BESIDE AND JOINED BY DASH WITH SUBSET

Forks

2AD9 ⫙ ELEMENT OF OPENING DOWNWARDS
→ 2208 ∈ element of
→ 27D2 ⟒ element of opening upwards
2ADA ⫚ PITCHFORK WITH TEE TOP
→ 22D4 ⋔ pitchfork
2ADB ⫛ TRANSVERSAL INTERSECTION
→ 22D4 ⋔ pitchfork
2ADC ⫝̸ FORKING
= not independent
• an equational logic symbol, not a computing science symbol
• non-independence (original concept) is related to forking
≡ 2ADD ⫝ 0338 ̸
2ADD ⫝ NONFORKING
= independent
• an equational logic symbol, not a computing science symbol
• independence (original concept) is related to non-forking

Tacks and turnstiles

2ADE ⫞ SHORT LEFT TACK
→ 22A3 ⊣ left tack
2ADF ⫟ SHORT DOWN TACK
→ 22A4 ⊤ down tack
2AE0 ⫠ SHORT UP TACK
→ 22A5 ⊥ up tack
2AE1 ⫡ PERPENDICULAR WITH S
2AE2 ⫢ VERTICAL BAR TRIPLE RIGHT TURNSTILE
= ordinarily satisfies
2AE3 ⫣ DOUBLE VERTICAL BAR LEFT TURNSTILE
→ 22A9 ⊩ forces
2AE4 ⫤ VERTICAL BAR DOUBLE LEFT TURNSTILE
→ 22A8 ⊨ true
2AE5 ⫥ DOUBLE VERTICAL BAR DOUBLE LEFT TURNSTILE

2AE6 ⫦ LONG DASH FROM LEFT MEMBER OF DOUBLE VERTICAL
→ 22A9 ⊩ forces
2AE7 ⫧ SHORT DOWN TACK WITH OVERBAR
→ 22A4 ⊤ down tack
→ 2351 ⍑ apl functional symbol up tack overbar
2AE8 ⫨ SHORT UP TACK WITH UNDERBAR
→ 22A5 ⊥ up tack
→ 234A ⍊ apl functional symbol down tack underbar
2AE9 ⫩ SHORT UP TACK ABOVE SHORT DOWN TACK
2AEA ⫪ DOUBLE DOWN TACK
2AEB ⫫ DOUBLE UP TACK
= independence
• probability theory
2AEC ⫬ DOUBLE STROKE NOT SIGN
→ 00AC ¬ not sign
2AED ⫭ REVERSED DOUBLE STROKE NOT SIGN
→ 2310 ⌐ reversed not sign

Vertical line operators

2AEE ⫮ DOES NOT DIVIDE WITH REVERSED NEGATION SLASH
→ 2224 ∤ does not divide
2AEF ⫯ VERTICAL LINE WITH CIRCLE ABOVE
2AF0 ⫰ VERTICAL LINE WITH CIRCLE BELOW
2AF1 ⫱ DOWN TACK WITH CIRCLE BELOW
= necessarily satisfies
→ 27DF ⟟ up tack with circle above
2AF2 ⫲ PARALLEL WITH HORIZONTAL STROKE
→ 2226 ∦ not parallel to
→ 27CA ⟊ vertical bar with horizontal stroke
2AF3 ⫳ PARALLEL WITH TILDE OPERATOR
2AF4 ⫴ TRIPLE VERTICAL BAR BINARY RELATION
= interleave
→ 2980 ⦀ triple vertical bar delimiter
2AF5 ⫵ TRIPLE VERTICAL BAR WITH HORIZONTAL STROKE
→ 27CA ⟊ vertical bar with horizontal stroke

Miscellaneous mathematical operator

2AF6 ⫶ TRIPLE COLON OPERATOR
• logic
→ 205D ⁝ tricolon
→ 22EE ⋮ vertical ellipsis

Relations

2AF7 ⫷ TRIPLE NESTED LESS-THAN
→ 22D8 ⋘ very much less-than
2AF8 ⫸ TRIPLE NESTED GREATER-THAN
→ 22D9 ⋙ very much greater-than
2AF9 ⫹ DOUBLE-LINE SLANTED LESS-THAN OR EQUAL TO
→ 2266 ≦ less-than over equal to
2AFA ⫺ DOUBLE-LINE SLANTED GREATER-THAN OR EQUAL TO
→ 2267 ≧ greater-than over equal to
2AFB ⫻ TRIPLE SOLIDUS BINARY RELATION
→ 2AF4 ⫴ triple vertical bar binary relation

Operators

2AFC ⫼ LARGE TRIPLE VERTICAL BAR OPERATOR
• often n-ary
→ 2AF4 ⫴ triple vertical bar binary relation
→ 2980 ⦀ triple vertical bar delimiter
2AFD ⫽ DOUBLE SOLIDUS OPERATOR
→ 2225 ∥ parallel to
2AFE ⫾ WHITE VERTICAL BAR
= Dijkstra choice
2AFF ⫿ N-ARY WHITE VERTICAL BAR
= n-ary Dijkstra choice

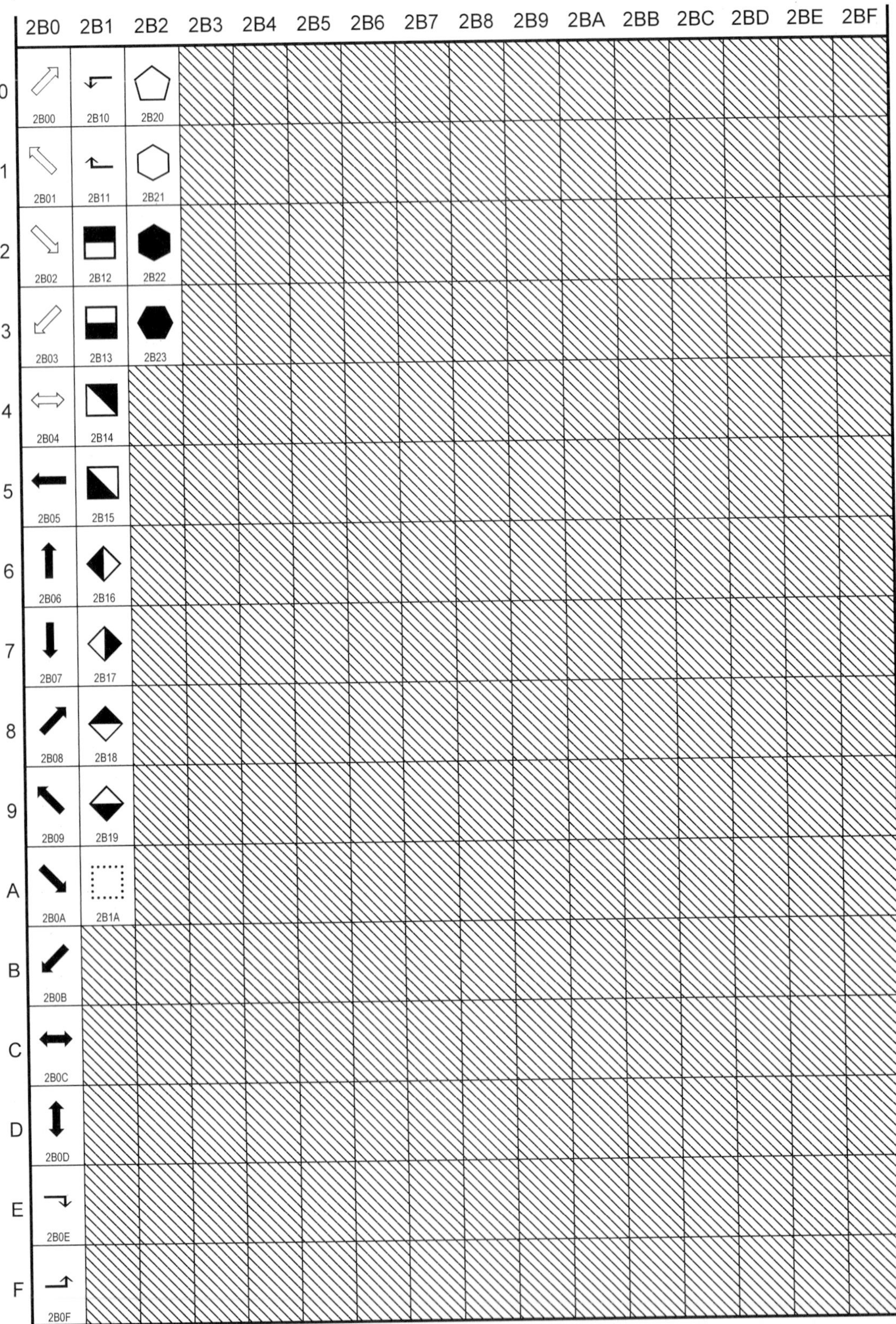
2B0
2B1
2B2
2B3
2B4
2B5
2B6
2B7
2B8
2B9
2BA
2BB
2BC
2BD
2BE
2BF
0
1
2
3
4
5
6
7
8
9
A
B
C
D
E
F
2B00
2B01
2B02
2B03
2B04
2B05
2B06
2B07
2B08
2B09
2B0A
2B0B
2B0C
2B0D
2B0E
2B0F
2B10
2B11
2B12
2B13
2B14
2B15
2B16
2B17
2B18
2B19
2B1A
2B20
2B21
2B22
2B23

White and black arrows

Other white and black arrows to complete this set can be found in the Arrows and Dingbats blocks.

2B00 ⬀ NORTH EAST WHITE ARROW
2B01 ⬁ NORTH WEST WHITE ARROW
2B02 ⬂ SOUTH EAST WHITE ARROW
2B03 ⬃ SOUTH WEST WHITE ARROW
2B04 ⬄ LEFT RIGHT WHITE ARROW
2B05 ⬅ LEFTWARDS BLACK ARROW
2B06 ⬆ UPWARDS BLACK ARROW
2B07 ⬇ DOWNWARDS BLACK ARROW
2B08 ⬈ NORTH EAST BLACK ARROW
2B09 ⬉ NORTH WEST BLACK ARROW
2B0A ⬊ SOUTH EAST BLACK ARROW
2B0B ⬋ SOUTH WEST BLACK ARROW
2B0C ⬌ LEFT RIGHT BLACK ARROW
2B0D ⬍ UP DOWN BLACK ARROW

Arrows with bent tips

Other arrows with bent tips to complete this set can be found in the Arrows block.

2B0E ⬎ RIGHTWARDS ARROW WITH TIP DOWNWARDS
2B0F ⬏ RIGHTWARDS ARROW WITH TIP UPWARDS
2B10 ⬐ LEFTWARDS ARROW WITH TIP DOWNWARDS
2B11 ⬑ LEFTWARDS ARROW WITH TIP UPWARDS

Squares

2B12 ⬒ SQUARE WITH TOP HALF BLACK
→ 25E7 ◧ square with left half black
2B13 ⬓ SQUARE WITH BOTTOM HALF BLACK
2B14 ⬔ SQUARE WITH UPPER RIGHT DIAGONAL HALF BLACK
2B15 ⬕ SQUARE WITH LOWER LEFT DIAGONAL HALF BLACK

Diamonds

2B16 ⬖ DIAMOND WITH LEFT HALF BLACK
2B17 ⬗ DIAMOND WITH RIGHT HALF BLACK
2B18 ⬘ DIAMOND WITH TOP HALF BLACK
2B19 ⬙ DIAMOND WITH BOTTOM HALF BLACK

Square

2B1A ⬚ DOTTED SQUARE

Pentagon

2B20 ⬠ WHITE PENTAGON

Hexagons

2B21 ⬡ WHITE HEXAGON
2B22 ⬢ BLACK HEXAGON
2B23 ⬣ HORIZONTAL BLACK HEXAGON

	2C0	2C1	2C2	2C3	2C4	2C5
0	Ⰰ 2C00	Ⱀ 2C10	Ⱐ 2C20	ⰰ 2C30	ⱀ 2C40	ⱐ 2C50
1	Ⰱ 2C01	Ⱁ 2C11	Ⱑ 2C21	ⰱ 2C31	ⱁ 2C41	ⱑ 2C51
2	Ⰲ 2C02	Ⱂ 2C12	Ⱒ 2C22	ⰲ 2C32	ⱂ 2C42	ⱒ 2C52
3	Ⰳ 2C03	Ⱃ 2C13	Ⱓ 2C23	ⰳ 2C33	ⱃ 2C43	ⱓ 2C53
4	Ⰴ 2C04	Ⱄ 2C14	Ⱔ 2C24	ⰴ 2C34	ⱄ 2C44	ⱔ 2C54
5	Ⰵ 2C05	Ⱅ 2C15	Ⱕ 2C25	ⰵ 2C35	ⱅ 2C45	ⱕ 2C55
6	Ⰶ 2C06	Ⱆ 2C16	Ⱖ 2C26	ⰶ 2C36	ⱆ 2C46	ⱖ 2C56
7	Ⰷ 2C07	Ⱇ 2C17	Ⱗ 2C27	ⰷ 2C37	ⱇ 2C47	ⱗ 2C57
8	Ⰸ 2C08	Ⱈ 2C18	Ⱘ 2C28	ⰸ 2C38	ⱈ 2C48	ⱘ 2C58
9	Ⰹ 2C09	Ⱉ 2C19	Ⱙ 2C29	ⰹ 2C39	ⱉ 2C49	ⱙ 2C59
A	Ⰺ 2C0A	Ⱊ 2C1A	Ⱚ 2C2A	ⰺ 2C3A	ⱊ 2C4A	ⱚ 2C5A
B	Ⰻ 2C0B	Ⱋ 2C1B	Ⱛ 2C2B	ⰻ 2C3B	ⱋ 2C4B	ⱛ 2C5B
C	Ⰼ 2C0C	Ⱌ 2C1C	Ⱜ 2C2C	ⰼ 2C3C	ⱌ 2C4C	ⱜ 2C5C
D	Ⰽ 2C0D	Ⱍ 2C1D	Ⱝ 2C2D	ⰽ 2C3D	ⱍ 2C4D	ⱝ 2C5D
E	Ⰾ 2C0E	Ⱎ 2C1E	Ⱞ 2C2E	ⰾ 2C3E	ⱎ 2C4E	ⱞ 2C5E
F	Ⰿ 2C0F	Ⱏ 2C1F		ⰿ 2C3F	ⱏ 2C4F	

Capital letters

2C00 Ⰰ GLAGOLITIC CAPITAL LETTER AZU
2C01 Ⰱ GLAGOLITIC CAPITAL LETTER BUKY
2C02 Ⰲ GLAGOLITIC CAPITAL LETTER VEDE
2C03 Ⰳ GLAGOLITIC CAPITAL LETTER GLAGOLI
2C04 Ⰴ GLAGOLITIC CAPITAL LETTER DOBRO
2C05 Ⰵ GLAGOLITIC CAPITAL LETTER YESTU
2C06 Ⰶ GLAGOLITIC CAPITAL LETTER ZHIVETE
2C07 Ⰷ GLAGOLITIC CAPITAL LETTER DZELO
2C08 Ⰸ GLAGOLITIC CAPITAL LETTER ZEMLJA
2C09 Ⰹ GLAGOLITIC CAPITAL LETTER IZHE
2C0A Ⰺ GLAGOLITIC CAPITAL LETTER INITIAL IZHE
2C0B Ⰻ GLAGOLITIC CAPITAL LETTER I
2C0C Ⰼ GLAGOLITIC CAPITAL LETTER DJERVI
2C0D Ⰽ GLAGOLITIC CAPITAL LETTER KAKO
2C0E Ⰾ GLAGOLITIC CAPITAL LETTER LJUDIJE
2C0F Ⰿ GLAGOLITIC CAPITAL LETTER MYSLITE
2C10 Ⱀ GLAGOLITIC CAPITAL LETTER NASHI
2C11 Ⱁ GLAGOLITIC CAPITAL LETTER ONU
2C12 Ⱂ GLAGOLITIC CAPITAL LETTER POKOJI
2C13 Ⱃ GLAGOLITIC CAPITAL LETTER RITSI
2C14 Ⱄ GLAGOLITIC CAPITAL LETTER SLOVO
2C15 Ⱅ GLAGOLITIC CAPITAL LETTER TVRIDO
2C16 Ⱆ GLAGOLITIC CAPITAL LETTER UKU
2C17 Ⱇ GLAGOLITIC CAPITAL LETTER FRITU
2C18 Ⱈ GLAGOLITIC CAPITAL LETTER HERU
2C19 Ⱉ GLAGOLITIC CAPITAL LETTER OTU
2C1A Ⱊ GLAGOLITIC CAPITAL LETTER PE
2C1B Ⱋ GLAGOLITIC CAPITAL LETTER SHTA
2C1C Ⱌ GLAGOLITIC CAPITAL LETTER TSI
2C1D Ⱍ GLAGOLITIC CAPITAL LETTER CHRIVI
2C1E Ⱎ GLAGOLITIC CAPITAL LETTER SHA
2C1F Ⱏ GLAGOLITIC CAPITAL LETTER YERU
2C20 Ⱐ GLAGOLITIC CAPITAL LETTER YERI
2C21 Ⱑ GLAGOLITIC CAPITAL LETTER YATI
2C22 Ⱒ GLAGOLITIC CAPITAL LETTER SPIDERY HA
2C23 Ⱓ GLAGOLITIC CAPITAL LETTER YU
2C24 Ⱔ GLAGOLITIC CAPITAL LETTER SMALL YUS
2C25 Ⱕ GLAGOLITIC CAPITAL LETTER SMALL YUS WITH TAIL
2C26 Ⱖ GLAGOLITIC CAPITAL LETTER YO
2C27 Ⱗ GLAGOLITIC CAPITAL LETTER IOTATED SMALL YUS
2C28 Ⱘ GLAGOLITIC CAPITAL LETTER BIG YUS
2C29 Ⱙ GLAGOLITIC CAPITAL LETTER IOTATED BIG YUS
2C2A Ⱚ GLAGOLITIC CAPITAL LETTER FITA
2C2B Ⱛ GLAGOLITIC CAPITAL LETTER IZHITSA
2C2C Ⱜ GLAGOLITIC CAPITAL LETTER SHTAPIC
2C2D Ⱝ GLAGOLITIC CAPITAL LETTER TROKUTASTI A
2C2E Ⱞ GLAGOLITIC CAPITAL LETTER LATINATE MYSLITE

Small letters

2C30 ⰰ GLAGOLITIC SMALL LETTER AZU
2C31 ⰱ GLAGOLITIC SMALL LETTER BUKY
2C32 ⰲ GLAGOLITIC SMALL LETTER VEDE
2C33 ⰳ GLAGOLITIC SMALL LETTER GLAGOLI
2C34 ⰴ GLAGOLITIC SMALL LETTER DOBRO
2C35 ⰵ GLAGOLITIC SMALL LETTER YESTU
2C36 ⰶ GLAGOLITIC SMALL LETTER ZHIVETE
2C37 ⰷ GLAGOLITIC SMALL LETTER DZELO
2C38 ⰸ GLAGOLITIC SMALL LETTER ZEMLJA
2C39 ⰹ GLAGOLITIC SMALL LETTER IZHE
2C3A ⰺ GLAGOLITIC SMALL LETTER INITIAL IZHE
2C3B ⰻ GLAGOLITIC SMALL LETTER I
2C3C ⰼ GLAGOLITIC SMALL LETTER DJERVI
2C3D ⰽ GLAGOLITIC SMALL LETTER KAKO
2C3E ⰾ GLAGOLITIC SMALL LETTER LJUDIJE
2C3F ⰿ GLAGOLITIC SMALL LETTER MYSLITE
2C40 ⱀ GLAGOLITIC SMALL LETTER NASHI
2C41 ⱁ GLAGOLITIC SMALL LETTER ONU
2C42 ⱂ GLAGOLITIC SMALL LETTER POKOJI
2C43 ⱃ GLAGOLITIC SMALL LETTER RITSI
2C44 ⱄ GLAGOLITIC SMALL LETTER SLOVO
2C45 ⱅ GLAGOLITIC SMALL LETTER TVRIDO
2C46 ⱆ GLAGOLITIC SMALL LETTER UKU
2C47 ⱇ GLAGOLITIC SMALL LETTER FRITU
2C48 ⱈ GLAGOLITIC SMALL LETTER HERU
2C49 ⱉ GLAGOLITIC SMALL LETTER OTU
2C4A ⱊ GLAGOLITIC SMALL LETTER PE
2C4B ⱋ GLAGOLITIC SMALL LETTER SHTA
2C4C ⱌ GLAGOLITIC SMALL LETTER TSI
2C4D ⱍ GLAGOLITIC SMALL LETTER CHRIVI
2C4E ⱎ GLAGOLITIC SMALL LETTER SHA
2C4F ⱏ GLAGOLITIC SMALL LETTER YERU
2C50 ⱐ GLAGOLITIC SMALL LETTER YERI
2C51 ⱑ GLAGOLITIC SMALL LETTER YATI
2C52 ⱒ GLAGOLITIC SMALL LETTER SPIDERY HA
2C53 ⱓ GLAGOLITIC SMALL LETTER YU
2C54 ⱔ GLAGOLITIC SMALL LETTER SMALL YUS
2C55 ⱕ GLAGOLITIC SMALL LETTER SMALL YUS WITH TAIL
2C56 ⱖ GLAGOLITIC SMALL LETTER YO
2C57 ⱗ GLAGOLITIC SMALL LETTER IOTATED SMALL YUS
2C58 ⱘ GLAGOLITIC SMALL LETTER BIG YUS
2C59 ⱙ GLAGOLITIC SMALL LETTER IOTATED BIG YUS
2C5A ⱚ GLAGOLITIC SMALL LETTER FITA
2C5B ⱛ GLAGOLITIC SMALL LETTER IZHITSA
2C5C ⱜ GLAGOLITIC SMALL LETTER SHTAPIC
2C5D ⱝ GLAGOLITIC SMALL LETTER TROKUTASTI A
2C5E ⱞ GLAGOLITIC SMALL LETTER LATINATE MYSLITE

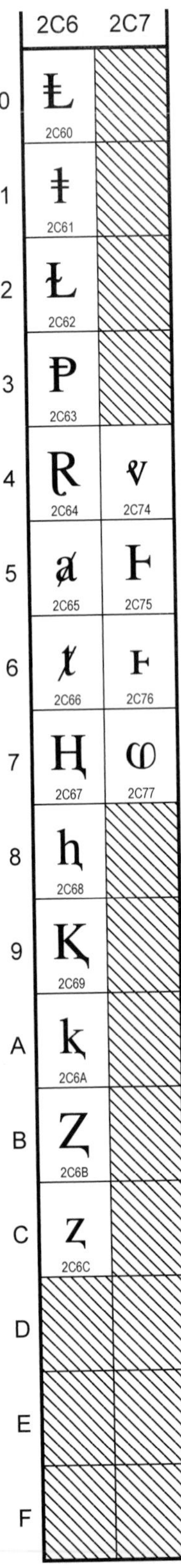

Orthographic Latin additions

2C60 Ⱡ LATIN CAPITAL LETTER L WITH DOUBLE BAR
2C61 ⱡ LATIN SMALL LETTER L WITH DOUBLE BAR
2C62 Ɫ LATIN CAPITAL LETTER L WITH MIDDLE TILDE
• lowercase is 026B ɫ
2C63 Ᵽ LATIN CAPITAL LETTER P WITH STROKE
• lowercase is 1D7D ᵽ
2C64 Ɽ LATIN CAPITAL LETTER R WITH TAIL
• lowercase is 027D ɽ
2C65 ⱥ LATIN SMALL LETTER A WITH STROKE
• uppercase is 023A Ⱥ
2C66 ⱦ LATIN SMALL LETTER T WITH DIAGONAL STROKE
• uppercase is 023E Ⱦ

Additions for Uighur

2C67 Ⱨ LATIN CAPITAL LETTER H WITH DESCENDER
2C68 ⱨ LATIN SMALL LETTER H WITH DESCENDER
2C69 Ⱪ LATIN CAPITAL LETTER K WITH DESCENDER
2C6A ⱪ LATIN SMALL LETTER K WITH DESCENDER
2C6B Ⱬ LATIN CAPITAL LETTER Z WITH DESCENDER
2C6C ⱬ LATIN SMALL LETTER Z WITH DESCENDER

Miscellaneous addition

2C74 ⱴ LATIN SMALL LETTER V WITH CURL

Claudian letters

Claudian letters in inscriptions are uppercase, but may be transcribed by scholars in lowercase.

2C75 Ⱶ LATIN CAPITAL LETTER HALF H
→ 2132 Ⅎ turned capital f
→ 2183 Ↄ roman numeral reversed one hundred
2C76 ⱶ LATIN SMALL LETTER HALF H

Addition for UPA

2C77 ⱷ LATIN SMALL LETTER TAILLESS PHI
• medium rounded o

	2C8	2C9	2CA	2CB	2CC	2CD	2CE	2CF
0	Ⲁ 2C80	Ⲑ 2C90	Ⲡ 2CA0	Ⲱ 2CB0	Ⳁ 2CC0	Ⳑ 2CD0	Ⳡ 2CE0	
1	ⲁ 2C81	ⲑ 2C91	ⲡ 2CA1	ⲱ 2CB1	ⳁ 2CC1	ⳑ 2CD1	ⳡ 2CE1	
2	Ⲃ 2C82	Ⲓ 2C92	Ⲣ 2CA2	Ⲳ 2CB2	Ⳃ 2CC2	Ⳓ 2CD2	Ⳣ 2CE2	
3	ⲃ 2C83	ⲓ 2C93	ⲣ 2CA3	ⲳ 2CB3	ⳃ 2CC3	ⳓ 2CD3	ⳣ 2CE3	
4	Ⲅ 2C84	Ⲕ 2C94	Ⲥ 2CA4	Ⲵ 2CB4	Ⳅ 2CC4	Ⳕ 2CD4	ⳤ 2CE4	
5	ⲅ 2C85	ⲕ 2C95	ⲥ 2CA5	ⲵ 2CB5	ⳅ 2CC5	ⳕ 2CD5	⳥ 2CE5	
6	Ⲇ 2C86	Ⲗ 2C96	Ⲧ 2CA6	Ⲷ 2CB6	Ⳇ 2CC6	Ⳗ 2CD6	⳦ 2CE6	
7	ⲇ 2C87	ⲗ 2C97	ⲧ 2CA7	ⲷ 2CB7	ⳇ 2CC7	ⳗ 2CD7	⳧ 2CE7	
8	Ⲉ 2C88	Ⲙ 2C98	Ⲩ 2CA8	Ⲹ 2CB8	Ⳉ 2CC8	Ⳙ 2CD8	⳨ 2CE8	
9	ⲉ 2C89	ⲙ 2C99	ⲩ 2CA9	ⲹ 2CB9	ⳉ 2CC9	ⳙ 2CD9	⳩ 2CE9	⳹ 2CF9
A	Ⲋ 2C8A	Ⲛ 2C9A	Ⲫ 2CAA	Ⲻ 2CBA	Ⳋ 2CCA	Ⳛ 2CDA	⳪ 2CEA	⳺ 2CFA
B	ⲋ 2C8B	ⲛ 2C9B	ⲫ 2CAB	ⲻ 2CBB	ⳋ 2CCB	ⳛ 2CDB		⳻ 2CFB
C	Ⲍ 2C8C	Ⲝ 2C9C	Ⲭ 2CAC	Ⲽ 2CBC	Ⳍ 2CCC	Ⳝ 2CDC		⳼ 2CFC
D	ⲍ 2C8D	ⲝ 2C9D	ⲭ 2CAD	ⲽ 2CBD	ⳍ 2CCD	ⳝ 2CDD		⳽ 2CFD
E	Ⲏ 2C8E	Ⲟ 2C9E	Ⲯ 2CAE	Ⲿ 2CBE	Ⳏ 2CCE	Ⳟ 2CDE		⳾ 2CFE
F	ⲏ 2C8F	ⲟ 2C9F	ⲯ 2CAF	ⲿ 2CBF	ⳏ 2CCF	ⳟ 2CDF		⳿ 2CFF

Other Coptic letters derived from Demotic are encoded in the Greek and Coptic block.

Bohairic Coptic letters

2C80 Ⲁ COPTIC CAPITAL LETTER ALFA
2C81 ⲁ COPTIC SMALL LETTER ALFA
2C82 Ⲃ COPTIC CAPITAL LETTER VIDA
2C83 ⲃ COPTIC SMALL LETTER VIDA
2C84 Ⲅ COPTIC CAPITAL LETTER GAMMA
2C85 ⲅ COPTIC SMALL LETTER GAMMA
2C86 Ⲇ COPTIC CAPITAL LETTER DALDA
2C87 ⲇ COPTIC SMALL LETTER DALDA
2C88 Ⲉ COPTIC CAPITAL LETTER EIE
2C89 ⲉ COPTIC SMALL LETTER EIE
2C8A Ⲋ COPTIC CAPITAL LETTER SOU
2C8B ⲋ COPTIC SMALL LETTER SOU
2C8C Ⲍ COPTIC CAPITAL LETTER ZATA
2C8D ⲍ COPTIC SMALL LETTER ZATA
2C8E Ⲏ COPTIC CAPITAL LETTER HATE
2C8F ⲏ COPTIC SMALL LETTER HATE
2C90 Ⲑ COPTIC CAPITAL LETTER THETHE
2C91 ⲑ COPTIC SMALL LETTER THETHE
2C92 Ⲓ COPTIC CAPITAL LETTER IAUDA
2C93 ⲓ COPTIC SMALL LETTER IAUDA
2C94 Ⲕ COPTIC CAPITAL LETTER KAPA
2C95 ⲕ COPTIC SMALL LETTER KAPA
2C96 Ⲗ COPTIC CAPITAL LETTER LAULA
2C97 ⲗ COPTIC SMALL LETTER LAULA
2C98 Ⲙ COPTIC CAPITAL LETTER MI
2C99 ⲙ COPTIC SMALL LETTER MI
2C9A Ⲛ COPTIC CAPITAL LETTER NI
2C9B ⲛ COPTIC SMALL LETTER NI
2C9C Ⲝ COPTIC CAPITAL LETTER KSI
2C9D ⲝ COPTIC SMALL LETTER KSI
2C9E Ⲟ COPTIC CAPITAL LETTER O
2C9F ⲟ COPTIC SMALL LETTER O
2CA0 Ⲡ COPTIC CAPITAL LETTER PI
2CA1 ⲡ COPTIC SMALL LETTER PI
2CA2 Ⲣ COPTIC CAPITAL LETTER RO
2CA3 ⲣ COPTIC SMALL LETTER RO
2CA4 Ⲥ COPTIC CAPITAL LETTER SIMA
2CA5 ⲥ COPTIC SMALL LETTER SIMA
2CA6 Ⲧ COPTIC CAPITAL LETTER TAU
2CA7 ⲧ COPTIC SMALL LETTER TAU
2CA8 Ⲩ COPTIC CAPITAL LETTER UA
2CA9 ⲩ COPTIC SMALL LETTER UA
2CAA Ⲫ COPTIC CAPITAL LETTER FI
2CAB ⲫ COPTIC SMALL LETTER FI
2CAC Ⲭ COPTIC CAPITAL LETTER KHI
2CAD ⲭ COPTIC SMALL LETTER KHI
2CAE Ⲯ COPTIC CAPITAL LETTER PSI
2CAF ⲯ COPTIC SMALL LETTER PSI
2CB0 Ⲱ COPTIC CAPITAL LETTER OOU
2CB1 ⲱ COPTIC SMALL LETTER OOU

Old Coptic and dialect letters

2CB2 Ⲳ COPTIC CAPITAL LETTER DIALECT-P ALEF
2CB3 ⲳ COPTIC SMALL LETTER DIALECT-P ALEF
2CB4 Ⲵ COPTIC CAPITAL LETTER OLD COPTIC AIN
2CB5 ⲵ COPTIC SMALL LETTER OLD COPTIC AIN
2CB6 Ⲷ COPTIC CAPITAL LETTER CRYPTOGRAMMIC EIE
2CB7 ⲷ COPTIC SMALL LETTER CRYPTOGRAMMIC EIE
2CB8 Ⲹ COPTIC CAPITAL LETTER DIALECT-P KAPA
2CB9 ⲹ COPTIC SMALL LETTER DIALECT-P KAPA
2CBA Ⲻ COPTIC CAPITAL LETTER DIALECT-P NI
2CBB ⲻ COPTIC SMALL LETTER DIALECT-P NI
2CBC Ⲽ COPTIC CAPITAL LETTER CRYPTOGRAMMIC NI
2CBD ⲽ COPTIC SMALL LETTER CRYPTOGRAMMIC NI
2CBE Ⲿ COPTIC CAPITAL LETTER OLD COPTIC OOU
2CBF ⲿ COPTIC SMALL LETTER OLD COPTIC OOU
2CC0 Ⳁ COPTIC CAPITAL LETTER SAMPI
2CC1 ⳁ COPTIC SMALL LETTER SAMPI
2CC2 Ⳃ COPTIC CAPITAL LETTER CROSSED SHEI
2CC3 ⳃ COPTIC SMALL LETTER CROSSED SHEI
2CC4 Ⳅ COPTIC CAPITAL LETTER OLD COPTIC SHEI
2CC5 ⳅ COPTIC SMALL LETTER OLD COPTIC SHEI
2CC6 Ⳇ COPTIC CAPITAL LETTER OLD COPTIC ESH
2CC7 ⳇ COPTIC SMALL LETTER OLD COPTIC ESH
2CC8 Ⳉ COPTIC CAPITAL LETTER AKHMIMIC KHEI
2CC9 ⳉ COPTIC SMALL LETTER AKHMIMIC KHEI
2CCA Ⳋ COPTIC CAPITAL LETTER DIALECT-P HORI
2CCB ⳋ COPTIC SMALL LETTER DIALECT-P HORI
2CCC Ⳍ COPTIC CAPITAL LETTER OLD COPTIC HORI
2CCD ⳍ COPTIC SMALL LETTER OLD COPTIC HORI
2CCE Ⳏ COPTIC CAPITAL LETTER OLD COPTIC HA
2CCF ⳏ COPTIC SMALL LETTER OLD COPTIC HA
2CD0 Ⳑ COPTIC CAPITAL LETTER L-SHAPED HA
2CD1 ⳑ COPTIC SMALL LETTER L-SHAPED HA
2CD2 Ⳓ COPTIC CAPITAL LETTER OLD COPTIC HEI
2CD3 ⳓ COPTIC SMALL LETTER OLD COPTIC HEI
2CD4 Ⳕ COPTIC CAPITAL LETTER OLD COPTIC HAT
2CD5 ⳕ COPTIC SMALL LETTER OLD COPTIC HAT
2CD6 Ⳗ COPTIC CAPITAL LETTER OLD COPTIC GANGIA
2CD7 ⳗ COPTIC SMALL LETTER OLD COPTIC GANGIA
2CD8 Ⳙ COPTIC CAPITAL LETTER OLD COPTIC DJA
2CD9 ⳙ COPTIC SMALL LETTER OLD COPTIC DJA
2CDA Ⳛ COPTIC CAPITAL LETTER OLD COPTIC SHIMA
2CDB ⳛ COPTIC SMALL LETTER OLD COPTIC SHIMA

Old Nubian letters

2CDC Ⳝ COPTIC CAPITAL LETTER OLD NUBIAN SHIMA
2CDD ⳝ COPTIC SMALL LETTER OLD NUBIAN SHIMA
2CDE Ⳟ COPTIC CAPITAL LETTER OLD NUBIAN NGI
2CDF ⳟ COPTIC SMALL LETTER OLD NUBIAN NGI
2CE0 Ⳡ COPTIC CAPITAL LETTER OLD NUBIAN NYI
2CE1 ⳡ COPTIC SMALL LETTER OLD NUBIAN NYI
2CE2 Ⳣ COPTIC CAPITAL LETTER OLD NUBIAN WAU
2CE3 ⳣ COPTIC SMALL LETTER OLD NUBIAN WAU

Symbols

2CE4 ⳤ COPTIC SYMBOL KAI
→ 03D7 ϗ greek kai symbol
2CE5 ⳥ COPTIC SYMBOL MI RO
2CE6 ⳦ COPTIC SYMBOL PI RO
2CE7 ⳧ COPTIC SYMBOL STAUROS
2CE8 ⳨ COPTIC SYMBOL TAU RO
2CE9 ⳩ COPTIC SYMBOL KHI RO
→ 2627 ☧ chi rho
2CEA ⳪ COPTIC SYMBOL SHIMA SIMA

Old Nubian punctuation

2CF9 ⳹ COPTIC OLD NUBIAN FULL STOP
2CFA ⳺ COPTIC OLD NUBIAN DIRECT QUESTION MARK
2CFB ⳻ COPTIC OLD NUBIAN INDIRECT QUESTION MARK
2CFC ⳼ COPTIC OLD NUBIAN VERSE DIVIDER

Numeric character

2CFD ⳽ COPTIC FRACTION ONE HALF

Punctuation

2CFE ⳾ COPTIC FULL STOP
2CFF ⳿ COPTIC MORPHOLOGICAL DIVIDER

	2D0	2D1	2D2
0	ⴀ 2D00	ⴐ 2D10	ⴠ 2D20
1	ⴁ 2D01	ⴑ 2D11	ⴡ 2D21
2	ⴂ 2D02	ⴒ 2D12	ⴢ 2D22
3	ⴃ 2D03	ⴓ 2D13	ⴣ 2D23
4	ⴄ 2D04	ⴔ 2D14	ⴤ 2D24
5	ⴅ 2D05	ⴕ 2D15	ⴥ 2D25
6	ⴆ 2D06	ⴖ 2D16	
7	ⴇ 2D07	ⴗ 2D17	
8	ⴈ 2D08	ⴘ 2D18	
9	ⴉ 2D09	ⴙ 2D19	
A	ⴊ 2D0A	ⴚ 2D1A	
B	ⴋ 2D0B	ⴛ 2D1B	
C	ⴌ 2D0C	ⴜ 2D1C	
D	ⴍ 2D0D	ⴝ 2D1D	
E	ⴎ 2D0E	ⴞ 2D1E	
F	ⴏ 2D0F	ⴟ 2D1F	

Small letters (Khutsuri)

This is the lowercase of the old ecclesiastical alphabet. See the Georgian block for uppercase Asomtavruli.

2D00 ⴀ GEORGIAN SMALL LETTER AN
2D01 ⴁ GEORGIAN SMALL LETTER BAN
2D02 ⴂ GEORGIAN SMALL LETTER GAN
2D03 ⴃ GEORGIAN SMALL LETTER DON
2D04 ⴄ GEORGIAN SMALL LETTER EN
2D05 ⴅ GEORGIAN SMALL LETTER VIN
2D06 ⴆ GEORGIAN SMALL LETTER ZEN
2D07 ⴇ GEORGIAN SMALL LETTER TAN
2D08 ⴈ GEORGIAN SMALL LETTER IN
2D09 ⴉ GEORGIAN SMALL LETTER KAN
2D0A ⴊ GEORGIAN SMALL LETTER LAS
2D0B ⴋ GEORGIAN SMALL LETTER MAN
2D0C ⴌ GEORGIAN SMALL LETTER NAR
2D0D ⴍ GEORGIAN SMALL LETTER ON
2D0E ⴎ GEORGIAN SMALL LETTER PAR
2D0F ⴏ GEORGIAN SMALL LETTER ZHAR
2D10 ⴐ GEORGIAN SMALL LETTER RAE
2D11 ⴑ GEORGIAN SMALL LETTER SAN
2D12 ⴒ GEORGIAN SMALL LETTER TAR
2D13 ⴓ GEORGIAN SMALL LETTER UN
2D14 ⴔ GEORGIAN SMALL LETTER PHAR
2D15 ⴕ GEORGIAN SMALL LETTER KHAR
2D16 ⴖ GEORGIAN SMALL LETTER GHAN
2D17 ⴗ GEORGIAN SMALL LETTER QAR
2D18 ⴘ GEORGIAN SMALL LETTER SHIN
2D19 ⴙ GEORGIAN SMALL LETTER CHIN
2D1A ⴚ GEORGIAN SMALL LETTER CAN
2D1B ⴛ GEORGIAN SMALL LETTER JIL
2D1C ⴜ GEORGIAN SMALL LETTER CIL
2D1D ⴝ GEORGIAN SMALL LETTER CHAR
2D1E ⴞ GEORGIAN SMALL LETTER XAN
2D1F ⴟ GEORGIAN SMALL LETTER JHAN
2D20 ⴠ GEORGIAN SMALL LETTER HAE
2D21 ⴡ GEORGIAN SMALL LETTER HE
2D22 ⴢ GEORGIAN SMALL LETTER HIE
2D23 ⴣ GEORGIAN SMALL LETTER WE
2D24 ⴤ GEORGIAN SMALL LETTER HAR
2D25 ⴥ GEORGIAN SMALL LETTER HOE

	2D3	2D4	2D5	2D6	2D7
0	ⴰ 2D30	ⵀ 2D40	ⵐ 2D50	ⵠ 2D60	
1	ⴱ 2D31	ⵁ 2D41	ⵑ 2D51	ⵡ 2D61	
2	ⴲ 2D32	ⵂ 2D42	ⵒ 2D52	ⵢ 2D62	
3	ⴳ 2D33	ⵃ 2D43	ⵓ 2D53	ⵣ 2D63	
4	ⴴ 2D34	ⵄ 2D44	ⵔ 2D54	ⵤ 2D64	
5	ⴵ 2D35	ⵅ 2D45	ⵕ 2D55	ⵥ 2D65	
6	ⴶ 2D36	ⵆ 2D46	ⵖ 2D56		
7	ⴷ 2D37	ⵇ 2D47	ⵗ 2D57		
8	ⴸ 2D38	ⵈ 2D48	ⵘ 2D58		
9	ⴹ 2D39	ⵉ 2D49	ⵙ 2D59		
A	ⴺ 2D3A	ⵊ 2D4A	ⵚ 2D5A		
B	ⴻ 2D3B	ⵋ 2D4B	ⵛ 2D5B		
C	ⴼ 2D3C	ⵌ 2D4C	ⵜ 2D5C		
D	ⴽ 2D3D	ⵍ 2D4D	ⵝ 2D5D		
E	ⴾ 2D3E	ⵎ 2D4E	ⵞ 2D5E		
F	ⴿ 2D3F	ⵏ 2D4F	ⵟ 2D5F	ⵯ 2D6F	

Letters

2D30 ⴰ TIFINAGH LETTER YA
2D31 ⴱ TIFINAGH LETTER YAB
2D32 ⴲ TIFINAGH LETTER YABH
2D33 ⴳ TIFINAGH LETTER YAG
2D34 ⴴ TIFINAGH LETTER YAGHH
2D35 ⴵ TIFINAGH LETTER BERBER ACADEMY YAJ
2D36 ⴶ TIFINAGH LETTER YAJ
2D37 ⴷ TIFINAGH LETTER YAD
2D38 ⴸ TIFINAGH LETTER YADH
2D39 ⴹ TIFINAGH LETTER YADD
2D3A ⴺ TIFINAGH LETTER YADDH
2D3B ⴻ TIFINAGH LETTER YEY
2D3C ⴼ TIFINAGH LETTER YAF
2D3D ⴽ TIFINAGH LETTER YAK
2D3E ⴾ TIFINAGH LETTER TUAREG YAK
2D3F ⴿ TIFINAGH LETTER YAKHH
2D40 ⵀ TIFINAGH LETTER YAH
= Tuareg yab
2D41 ⵁ TIFINAGH LETTER BERBER ACADEMY YAH
2D42 ⵂ TIFINAGH LETTER TUAREG YAH
2D43 ⵃ TIFINAGH LETTER YAHH
2D44 ⵄ TIFINAGH LETTER YAA
2D45 ⵅ TIFINAGH LETTER YAKH
2D46 ⵆ TIFINAGH LETTER TUAREG YAKH
2D47 ⵇ TIFINAGH LETTER YAQ
2D48 ⵈ TIFINAGH LETTER TUAREG YAQ
2D49 ⵉ TIFINAGH LETTER YI
2D4A ⵊ TIFINAGH LETTER YAZH
2D4B ⵋ TIFINAGH LETTER AHAGGAR YAZH
2D4C ⵌ TIFINAGH LETTER TUAREG YAZH
2D4D ⵍ TIFINAGH LETTER YAL
2D4E ⵎ TIFINAGH LETTER YAM
2D4F ⵏ TIFINAGH LETTER YAN
2D50 ⵐ TIFINAGH LETTER TUAREG YAGN
2D51 ⵑ TIFINAGH LETTER TUAREG YANG
2D52 ⵒ TIFINAGH LETTER YAP
2D53 ⵓ TIFINAGH LETTER YU
= Tuareg yaw
2D54 ⵔ TIFINAGH LETTER YAR
2D55 ⵕ TIFINAGH LETTER YARR
2D56 ⵖ TIFINAGH LETTER YAGH
2D57 ⵗ TIFINAGH LETTER TUAREG YAGH
2D58 ⵘ TIFINAGH LETTER AYER YAGH
= Adrar yaj
2D59 ⵙ TIFINAGH LETTER YAS
2D5A ⵚ TIFINAGH LETTER YASS
2D5B ⵛ TIFINAGH LETTER YASH
2D5C ⵜ TIFINAGH LETTER YAT
2D5D ⵝ TIFINAGH LETTER YATH
2D5E ⵞ TIFINAGH LETTER YACH
2D5F ⵟ TIFINAGH LETTER YATT
2D60 ⵠ TIFINAGH LETTER YAV
2D61 ⵡ TIFINAGH LETTER YAW
2D62 ⵢ TIFINAGH LETTER YAY
2D63 ⵣ TIFINAGH LETTER YAZ
2D64 ⵤ TIFINAGH LETTER TAWELLEMET YAZ
= harpoon yaz
2D65 ⵥ TIFINAGH LETTER YAZZ

Modifier letter

2D6F ⵯ TIFINAGH MODIFIER LETTER LABIALIZATION MARK
= tamatart
≈ <super> 2D61 ⵡ

	2D8	2D9	2DA	2DB	2DC	2DD
0	ⶀ 2D80	ⶐ 2D90	ⶠ 2DA0	ⶰ 2DB0	ⷀ 2DC0	ⷐ 2DD0
1	ⶁ 2D81	ⶑ 2D91	ⶡ 2DA1	ⶱ 2DB1	ⷁ 2DC1	ⷑ 2DD1
2	ⶂ 2D82	ⶒ 2D92	ⶢ 2DA2	ⶲ 2DB2	ⷂ 2DC2	ⷒ 2DD2
3	ⶃ 2D83	ⶓ 2D93	ⶣ 2DA3	ⶳ 2DB3	ⷃ 2DC3	ⷓ 2DD3
4	ⶄ 2D84	ⶔ 2D94	ⶤ 2DA4	ⶴ 2DB4	ⷄ 2DC4	ⷔ 2DD4
5	ⶅ 2D85	ⶕ 2D95	ⶥ 2DA5	ⶵ 2DB5	ⷅ 2DC5	ⷕ 2DD5
6	ⶆ 2D86	ⶖ 2D96	ⶦ 2DA6	ⶶ 2DB6	ⷆ 2DC6	ⷖ 2DD6
7	ⶇ 2D87					
8	ⶈ 2D88		ⶨ 2DA8	ⶸ 2DB8	ⷈ 2DC8	ⷘ 2DD8
9	ⶉ 2D89		ⶩ 2DA9	ⶹ 2DB9	ⷉ 2DC9	ⷙ 2DD9
A	ⶊ 2D8A		ⶪ 2DAA	ⶺ 2DBA	ⷊ 2DCA	ⷚ 2DDA
B	ⶋ 2D8B		ⶫ 2DAB	ⶻ 2DBB	ⷋ 2DCB	ⷛ 2DDB
C	ⶌ 2D8C		ⶬ 2DAC	ⶼ 2DBC	ⷌ 2DCC	ⷜ 2DDC
D	ⶍ 2D8D		ⶭ 2DAD	ⶽ 2DBD	ⷍ 2DCD	ⷝ 2DDD
E	ⶎ 2D8E		ⶮ 2DAE	ⶾ 2DBE	ⷎ 2DCE	ⷞ 2DDE
F	ⶏ 2D8F					

Syllables for Me'en

Code	Glyph	Name
2D80	ⶀ	ETHIOPIC SYLLABLE LOA
2D81	ⶁ	ETHIOPIC SYLLABLE MOA
2D82	ⶂ	ETHIOPIC SYLLABLE ROA
2D83	ⶃ	ETHIOPIC SYLLABLE SOA
2D84	ⶄ	ETHIOPIC SYLLABLE SHOA
2D85	ⶅ	ETHIOPIC SYLLABLE BOA
2D86	ⶆ	ETHIOPIC SYLLABLE TOA
2D87	ⶇ	ETHIOPIC SYLLABLE COA
2D88	ⶈ	ETHIOPIC SYLLABLE NOA
2D89	ⶉ	ETHIOPIC SYLLABLE NYOA
2D8A	ⶊ	ETHIOPIC SYLLABLE GLOTTAL OA
2D8B	ⶋ	ETHIOPIC SYLLABLE ZOA
2D8C	ⶌ	ETHIOPIC SYLLABLE DOA
2D8D	ⶍ	ETHIOPIC SYLLABLE DDOA
2D8E	ⶎ	ETHIOPIC SYLLABLE JOA
2D8F	ⶏ	ETHIOPIC SYLLABLE THOA
2D90	ⶐ	ETHIOPIC SYLLABLE CHOA
2D91	ⶑ	ETHIOPIC SYLLABLE PHOA
2D92	ⶒ	ETHIOPIC SYLLABLE POA

Syllables for Blin

Code	Glyph	Name
2D93	ⶓ	ETHIOPIC SYLLABLE GGWA
2D94	ⶔ	ETHIOPIC SYLLABLE GGWI
2D95	ⶕ	ETHIOPIC SYLLABLE GGWEE
2D96	ⶖ	ETHIOPIC SYLLABLE GGWE

Syllables for Sebatbeit

Code	Glyph	Name
2DA0	ⶠ	ETHIOPIC SYLLABLE SSA
2DA1	ⶡ	ETHIOPIC SYLLABLE SSU
2DA2	ⶢ	ETHIOPIC SYLLABLE SSI
2DA3	ⶣ	ETHIOPIC SYLLABLE SSAA
2DA4	ⶤ	ETHIOPIC SYLLABLE SSEE
2DA5	ⶥ	ETHIOPIC SYLLABLE SSE
2DA6	ⶦ	ETHIOPIC SYLLABLE SSO
2DA7		<reserved>
2DA8	ⶨ	ETHIOPIC SYLLABLE CCA
2DA9	ⶩ	ETHIOPIC SYLLABLE CCU
2DAA	ⶪ	ETHIOPIC SYLLABLE CCI
2DAB	ⶫ	ETHIOPIC SYLLABLE CCAA
2DAC	ⶬ	ETHIOPIC SYLLABLE CCEE
2DAD	ⶭ	ETHIOPIC SYLLABLE CCE
2DAE	ⶮ	ETHIOPIC SYLLABLE CCO
2DAF		<reserved>
2DB0	ⶰ	ETHIOPIC SYLLABLE ZZA
2DB1	ⶱ	ETHIOPIC SYLLABLE ZZU
2DB2	ⶲ	ETHIOPIC SYLLABLE ZZI
2DB3	ⶳ	ETHIOPIC SYLLABLE ZZAA
2DB4	ⶴ	ETHIOPIC SYLLABLE ZZEE
2DB5	ⶵ	ETHIOPIC SYLLABLE ZZE
2DB6	ⶶ	ETHIOPIC SYLLABLE ZZO
2DB7		<reserved>
2DB8	ⶸ	ETHIOPIC SYLLABLE CCHA
2DB9	ⶹ	ETHIOPIC SYLLABLE CCHU
2DBA	ⶺ	ETHIOPIC SYLLABLE CCHI
2DBB	ⶻ	ETHIOPIC SYLLABLE CCHAA
2DBC	ⶼ	ETHIOPIC SYLLABLE CCHEE
2DBD	ⶽ	ETHIOPIC SYLLABLE CCHE
2DBE	ⶾ	ETHIOPIC SYLLABLE CCHO
2DBF		<reserved>
2DC0	ⷀ	ETHIOPIC SYLLABLE QYA
2DC1	ⷁ	ETHIOPIC SYLLABLE QYU
2DC2	ⷂ	ETHIOPIC SYLLABLE QYI
2DC3	ⷃ	ETHIOPIC SYLLABLE QYAA
2DC4	ⷄ	ETHIOPIC SYLLABLE QYEE
2DC5	ⷅ	ETHIOPIC SYLLABLE QYE
2DC6	ⷆ	ETHIOPIC SYLLABLE QYO
2DC7		<reserved>
2DC8	ⷈ	ETHIOPIC SYLLABLE KYA
2DC9	ⷉ	ETHIOPIC SYLLABLE KYU
2DCA	ⷊ	ETHIOPIC SYLLABLE KYI
2DCB	ⷋ	ETHIOPIC SYLLABLE KYAA
2DCC	ⷌ	ETHIOPIC SYLLABLE KYEE
2DCD	ⷍ	ETHIOPIC SYLLABLE KYE
2DCE	ⷎ	ETHIOPIC SYLLABLE KYO
2DCF		<reserved>
2DD0	ⷐ	ETHIOPIC SYLLABLE XYA
2DD1	ⷑ	ETHIOPIC SYLLABLE XYU
2DD2	ⷒ	ETHIOPIC SYLLABLE XYI
2DD3	ⷓ	ETHIOPIC SYLLABLE XYAA
2DD4	ⷔ	ETHIOPIC SYLLABLE XYEE
2DD5	ⷕ	ETHIOPIC SYLLABLE XYE
2DD6	ⷖ	ETHIOPIC SYLLABLE XYO
2DD7		<reserved>
2DD8	ⷘ	ETHIOPIC SYLLABLE GYA
2DD9	ⷙ	ETHIOPIC SYLLABLE GYU
2DDA	ⷚ	ETHIOPIC SYLLABLE GYI
2DDB	ⷛ	ETHIOPIC SYLLABLE GYAA
2DDC	ⷜ	ETHIOPIC SYLLABLE GYEE
2DDD	ⷝ	ETHIOPIC SYLLABLE GYE
2DDE	ⷞ	ETHIOPIC SYLLABLE GYO

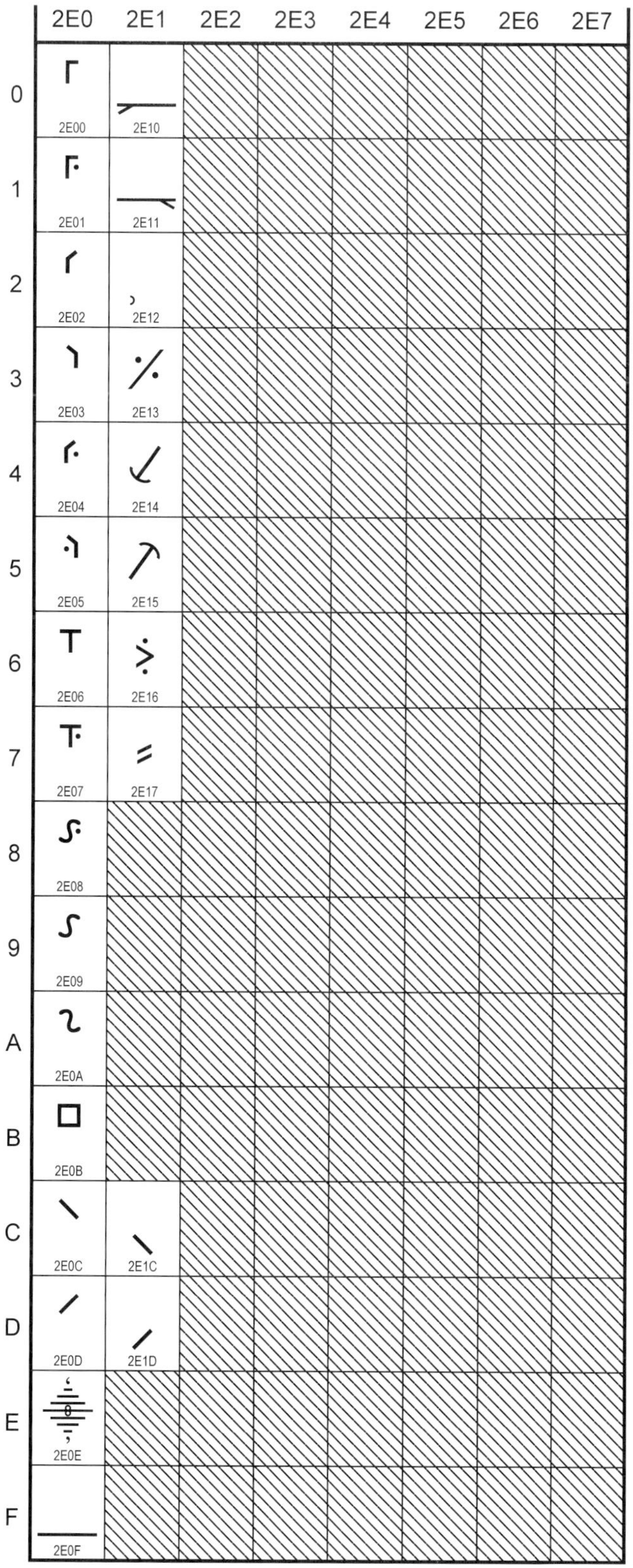

	2E0	2E1	2E2	2E3	2E4	2E5	2E6	2E7
0	2E00	2E10						
1	2E01	2E11						
2	2E02	2E12						
3	2E03	2E13						
4	2E04	2E14						
5	2E05	2E15						
6	2E06	2E16						
7	2E07	2E17						
8	2E08							
9	2E09							
A	2E0A							
B	2E0B							
C	2E0C	2E1C						
D	2E0D	2E1D						
E	2E0E							
F	2E0F							

New Testament editorial symbols

2E00 ⸀ RIGHT ANGLE SUBSTITUTION MARKER
→ 231C ⌜ top left corner
2E01 ⸁ RIGHT ANGLE DOTTED SUBSTITUTION MARKER
2E02 ⸂ LEFT SUBSTITUTION BRACKET
2E03 ⸃ RIGHT SUBSTITUTION BRACKET
2E04 ⸄ LEFT DOTTED SUBSTITUTION BRACKET
2E05 ⸅ RIGHT DOTTED SUBSTITUTION BRACKET
2E06 ⸆ RAISED INTERPOLATION MARKER
→ 22A4 ⊤ down tack
2E07 ⸇ RAISED DOTTED INTERPOLATION MARKER
2E08 ⸈ DOTTED TRANSPOSITION MARKER
2E09 ⸉ LEFT TRANSPOSITION BRACKET
2E0A ⸊ RIGHT TRANSPOSITION BRACKET
2E0B ⸋ RAISED SQUARE
• used as an opening raised omission bracket
2E0C ⸌ LEFT RAISED OMISSION BRACKET
• used as an opening or closing raised omission bracket
2E0D ⸍ RIGHT RAISED OMISSION BRACKET
• used as a closing or opening raised omission bracket

Ancient Greek textual symbols

2E0E ⸎ EDITORIAL CORONIS
→ 1FBD ᾽ greek koronis
2E0F ⸏ PARAGRAPHOS
2E10 ⸐ FORKED PARAGRAPHOS
2E11 ⸑ REVERSED FORKED PARAGRAPHOS
2E12 ⸒ HYPODIASTOLE
2E13 ⸓ DOTTED OBELOS
• glyph variants may look like '÷' or '∸'
→ 2052 ⁒ commercial minus sign
2E14 ⸔ DOWNWARDS ANCORA
• contrary to its formal name this symbol points upwards
2E15 ⸕ UPWARDS ANCORA
• contrary to its formal name this symbol points downwards
2E16 ⸖ DOTTED RIGHT-POINTING ANGLE
= diple periestigmene

Ancient Near-Eastern linguistic symbol

2E17 ⸗ DOUBLE OBLIQUE HYPHEN
• used in ancient Near-Eastern linguistics
• hyphen in Fraktur text uses 002D - or 2010 ‐, but with a '⸗' glyph in Fraktur fonts
→ 002D - hyphen-minus
→ 003D = equals sign
→ 2010 ‐ hyphen

Brackets

2E1C ⸜ LEFT LOW PARAPHRASE BRACKET
2E1D ⸝ RIGHT LOW PARAPHRASE BRACKET
• used in N'Ko

	2E8	2E9	2EA	2EB	2EC	2ED	2EE	2EF
0	⺀ 2E80	⺐ 2E90	⺠ 2EA0	⺰ 2EB0	⻀ 2EC0	⻐ 2ED0	⻠ 2EE0	⻰ 2EF0
1	⺁ 2E81	⺑ 2E91	⺡ 2EA1	⺱ 2EB1	⻁ 2EC1	⻑ 2ED1	⻡ 2EE1	⻱ 2EF1
2	⺂ 2E82	⺒ 2E92	⺢ 2EA2	⺲ 2EB2	⻂ 2EC2	⻒ 2ED2	⻢ 2EE2	⻲ 2EF2
3	⺃ 2E83	⺓ 2E93	⺣ 2EA3	⺳ 2EB3	⻃ 2EC3	⻓ 2ED3	⻣ 2EE3	⻳ 2EF3
4	⺄ 2E84	⺔ 2E94	⺤ 2EA4	⺴ 2EB4	⻄ 2EC4	⻔ 2ED4	⻤ 2EE4	
5	⺅ 2E85	⺕ 2E95	⺥ 2EA5	⺵ 2EB5	⻅ 2EC5	⻕ 2ED5	⻥ 2EE5	
6	⺆ 2E86	⺖ 2E96	⺦ 2EA6	⺶ 2EB6	⻆ 2EC6	⻖ 2ED6	⻦ 2EE6	
7	⺇ 2E87	⺗ 2E97	⺧ 2EA7	⺷ 2EB7	⻇ 2EC7	⻗ 2ED7	⻧ 2EE7	
8	⺈ 2E88	⺘ 2E98	⺨ 2EA8	⺸ 2EB8	⻈ 2EC8	⻘ 2ED8	⻨ 2EE8	
9	⺉ 2E89	⺙ 2E99	⺩ 2EA9	⺹ 2EB9	⻉ 2EC9	⻙ 2ED9	⻩ 2EE9	
A	⺊ 2E8A		⺪ 2EAA	⺺ 2EBA	⻊ 2ECA	⻚ 2EDA	⻪ 2EEA	
B	⺋ 2E8B	⺛ 2E9B	⺫ 2EAB	⺻ 2EBB	⻋ 2ECB	⻛ 2EDB	⻫ 2EEB	
C	⺌ 2E8C	⺜ 2E9C	⺬ 2EAC	⺼ 2EBC	⻌ 2ECC	⻜ 2EDC	⻬ 2EEC	
D	⺍ 2E8D	⺝ 2E9D	⺭ 2EAD	⺽ 2EBD	⻍ 2ECD	⻝ 2EDD	⻭ 2EED	
E	⺎ 2E8E	⺞ 2E9E	⺮ 2EAE	⺾ 2EBE	⻎ 2ECE	⻞ 2EDE	⻮ 2EEE	
F	⺏ 2E8F	⺟ 2E9F	⺯ 2EAF	⺿ 2EBF	⻏ 2ECF	⻟ 2EDF	⻯ 2EEF	

CJK radicals supplement

2E80 ⺀ CJK RADICAL REPEAT
2E81 ⺁ CJK RADICAL CLIFF
- → 5382 厂

2E82 ⺂ CJK RADICAL SECOND ONE
- → 4E5B 乛

2E83 ⺃ CJK RADICAL SECOND TWO
- → 4E5A 乚

2E84 ⺄ CJK RADICAL SECOND THREE
- → 4E59 乙

2E85 ⺅ CJK RADICAL PERSON
- • form used on left side
- → 4EBB 亻

2E86 ⺆ CJK RADICAL BOX
- → 5182 冂

2E87 ⺇ CJK RADICAL TABLE
- → 51E0 几

2E88 ⺈ CJK RADICAL KNIFE ONE
- • form used at top
- → 5200 刀

2E89 ⺉ CJK RADICAL KNIFE TWO
- • form used on right side
- → 5202 刂

2E8A ⺊ CJK RADICAL DIVINATION
- • form used at top
- → 535C 卜

2E8B ⺋ CJK RADICAL SEAL
- • form used at bottom
- → 353E 㔾

2E8C ⺌ CJK RADICAL SMALL ONE
- • form used at top
- → 5C0F 小

2E8D ⺍ CJK RADICAL SMALL TWO
- • form used at top
- → 5C0F 小

2E8E ⺎ CJK RADICAL LAME ONE
- → 5C22 尢

2E8F ⺏ CJK RADICAL LAME TWO
- → 5C23 尣

2E90 ⺐ CJK RADICAL LAME THREE
- → 5C22 尢

2E91 ⺑ CJK RADICAL LAME FOUR
- → 5C23 尣

2E92 ⺒ CJK RADICAL SNAKE
- → 5DF3 巳

2E93 ⺓ CJK RADICAL THREAD
- → 5E7A 幺

2E94 ⺔ CJK RADICAL SNOUT ONE
- → 5F51 彑

2E95 ⺕ CJK RADICAL SNOUT TWO
- → 5F50 彐

2E96 ⺖ CJK RADICAL HEART ONE
- • form used on left side
- → 5FC4 忄

2E97 ⺗ CJK RADICAL HEART TWO
- • form used at bottom
- → 5FC3 心

2E98 ⺘ CJK RADICAL HAND
- • form used on left side
- → 624C 扌

2E99 ⺙ CJK RADICAL RAP
- • form used on right side
- → 6535 攵

2E9A <reserved>
2E9B ⺛ CJK RADICAL CHOKE
- → 65E1 旡

2E9C ⺜ CJK RADICAL SUN
- → 65E5 日

2E9D ⺝ CJK RADICAL MOON
- → 6708 月

2E9E ⺞ CJK RADICAL DEATH
- → 6B7A 歺

2E9F ⺟ CJK RADICAL MOTHER
- ≈ 6BCD 母

2EA0 ⺠ CJK RADICAL CIVILIAN
- → 6C11 民

2EA1 ⺡ CJK RADICAL WATER ONE
- • form used on left side
- → 6C35 氵

2EA2 ⺢ CJK RADICAL WATER TWO
- • form used (rarely) at bottom
- → 6C3A 氺

2EA3 ⺣ CJK RADICAL FIRE
- • form used at bottom
- → 706C 灬

2EA4 ⺤ CJK RADICAL PAW ONE
- • form used at top
- → 722B 爫

2EA5 ⺥ CJK RADICAL PAW TWO
- • form used at top
- → 722B 爫

2EA6 ⺦ CJK RADICAL SIMPLIFIED HALF TREE TRUNK
- → 4E2C 丬

2EA7 ⺧ CJK RADICAL COW
- → 725B 牛

2EA8 ⺨ CJK RADICAL DOG
- • form used on left side
- → 72AD 犭

2EA9 ⺩ CJK RADICAL JADE
- • form used on left side
- → 738B 王

2EAA ⺪ CJK RADICAL BOLT OF CLOTH
- • form used on left side
- → 758B 疋

2EAB ⺫ CJK RADICAL EYE
- • form used at top
- → 2EB2 ⺲ cjk radical net two
- → 76EE 目

2EAC ⺬ CJK RADICAL SPIRIT ONE
- → 793A 示

2EAD ⺭ CJK RADICAL SPIRIT TWO
- → 793B 礻

2EAE ⺮ CJK RADICAL BAMBOO
- → 7AF9 竹

2EAF ⺯ CJK RADICAL SILK
- • form used on left side
- → 7CF9 糹

2EB0 ⺰ CJK RADICAL C-SIMPLIFIED SILK
- • form used on left side
- → 7E9F 纟

2EB1 ⺱ CJK RADICAL NET ONE
- → 7F53 罓

2EB2 ⺲ CJK RADICAL NET TWO
- → 2EAB ⺫ cjk radical eye
- → 7F52 罒

2EB3 ⺳ CJK RADICAL NET THREE
→ 7F51 网
2EB4 ⺴ CJK RADICAL NET FOUR
→ 7F51 网
2EB5 ⺵ CJK RADICAL MESH
→ 2626B 𦉫
2EB6 ⺶ CJK RADICAL SHEEP
• form used on left side
→ 7F8A 羊
2EB7 ⺷ CJK RADICAL RAM
• form used at top
→ 7F8A 羊
2EB8 ⺸ CJK RADICAL EWE
→ 7F8B 羋
2EB9 ⺹ CJK RADICAL OLD
→ 8002 耂
2EBA ⺺ CJK RADICAL BRUSH ONE
→ 8080 肀
2EBB ⺻ CJK RADICAL BRUSH TWO
→ 807F 聿
2EBC ⺼ CJK RADICAL MEAT
→ 8089 肉
2EBD ⺽ CJK RADICAL MORTAR
→ 81FC 臼
2EBE ⺾ CJK RADICAL GRASS ONE
→ 8279 艹
2EBF ⺿ CJK RADICAL GRASS TWO
→ 8279 艹
2EC0 ⻀ CJK RADICAL GRASS THREE
→ 8279 艹
2EC1 ⻁ CJK RADICAL TIGER
→ 864E 虎
2EC2 ⻂ CJK RADICAL CLOTHES
• form used on left side
→ 8864 衤
2EC3 ⻃ CJK RADICAL WEST ONE
• form used at top
→ 8980 覀
2EC4 ⻄ CJK RADICAL WEST TWO
• form used on left side
→ 897F 西
2EC5 ⻅ CJK RADICAL C-SIMPLIFIED SEE
→ 89C1 见
2EC6 ⻆ CJK RADICAL SIMPLIFIED HORN
→ 89D2 角
2EC7 ⻇ CJK RADICAL HORN
→ 278B2 𧢲
2EC8 ⻈ CJK RADICAL C-SIMPLIFIED SPEECH
→ 8BA0 讠
2EC9 ⻉ CJK RADICAL C-SIMPLIFIED SHELL
→ 8D1D 贝
2ECA ⻊ CJK RADICAL FOOT
• form used on left side
→ 8DB3 足
2ECB ⻋ CJK RADICAL C-SIMPLIFIED CART
→ 8F66 车
2ECC ⻌ CJK RADICAL SIMPLIFIED WALK
→ 8FB6 辶
2ECD ⻍ CJK RADICAL WALK ONE
→ 8FB6 辶
2ECE ⻎ CJK RADICAL WALK TWO
→ 8FB6 辶
2ECF ⻏ CJK RADICAL CITY
• form used on right side
→ 9091 邑
2ED0 ⻐ CJK RADICAL C-SIMPLIFIED GOLD
→ 9485 钅
2ED1 ⻑ CJK RADICAL LONG ONE
→ 9577 長
2ED2 ⻒ CJK RADICAL LONG TWO
• form used on left side
→ 9578 镸
2ED3 ⻓ CJK RADICAL C-SIMPLIFIED LONG
→ 957F 长
2ED4 ⻔ CJK RADICAL C-SIMPLIFIED GATE
→ 95E8 门
2ED5 ⻕ CJK RADICAL MOUND ONE
→ 961C 阜
→ 28E0F 𨸏
2ED6 ⻖ CJK RADICAL MOUND TWO
• form used on left side
→ 961D 阝
2ED7 ⻗ CJK RADICAL RAIN
→ 96E8 雨
2ED8 ⻘ CJK RADICAL BLUE
→ 9752 青
2ED9 ⻙ CJK RADICAL C-SIMPLIFIED TANNED LEATHER
→ 97E6 韦
2EDA ⻚ CJK RADICAL C-SIMPLIFIED LEAF
→ 9875 页
2EDB ⻛ CJK RADICAL C-SIMPLIFIED WIND
→ 98CE 风
2EDC ⻜ CJK RADICAL C-SIMPLIFIED FLY
→ 98DE 飞
2EDD ⻝ CJK RADICAL EAT ONE
• form used at bottom
→ 98DF 食
2EDE ⻞ CJK RADICAL EAT TWO
• form used on left side
→ 2967F 𩙿
2EDF ⻟ CJK RADICAL EAT THREE
• form used on left side
→ 98E0 飠
2EE0 ⻠ CJK RADICAL C-SIMPLIFIED EAT
• form used on left side
→ 9963 饣
2EE1 ⻡ CJK RADICAL HEAD
→ 29810 𩠐
2EE2 ⻢ CJK RADICAL C-SIMPLIFIED HORSE
→ 9A6C 马
2EE3 ⻣ CJK RADICAL BONE
→ 9AA8 骨
2EE4 ⻤ CJK RADICAL GHOST
→ 9B3C 鬼
2EE5 ⻥ CJK RADICAL C-SIMPLIFIED FISH
→ 9C7C 鱼
2EE6 ⻦ CJK RADICAL C-SIMPLIFIED BIRD
→ 9E1F 鸟
2EE7 ⻧ CJK RADICAL C-SIMPLIFIED SALT
→ 9E75 卤
2EE8 ⻨ CJK RADICAL SIMPLIFIED WHEAT
→ 9EA6 麦
2EE9 ⻩ CJK RADICAL SIMPLIFIED YELLOW
→ 9EC4 黄

2EEA 黾 CJK RADICAL C-SIMPLIFIED FROG
→ 9EFE 黾
2EEB 斉 CJK RADICAL J-SIMPLIFIED EVEN
→ 6589 斉
2EEC 齐 CJK RADICAL C-SIMPLIFIED EVEN
→ 9F50 齐
2EED 歯 CJK RADICAL J-SIMPLIFIED TOOTH
→ 6B6F 歯
2EEE 齿 CJK RADICAL C-SIMPLIFIED TOOTH
→ 9F7F 齿
2EEF 竜 CJK RADICAL J-SIMPLIFIED DRAGON
→ 9F8D 龍
2EF0 龙 CJK RADICAL C-SIMPLIFIED DRAGON
→ 9F99 龙
2EF1 龜 CJK RADICAL TURTLE
→ 9F9C 龜
2EF2 亀 CJK RADICAL J-SIMPLIFIED TURTLE
→ 4E80 亀
2EF3 龟 CJK RADICAL C-SIMPLIFIED TURTLE
≈ 9F9F 龟

	2F0	2F1	2F2	2F3	2F4	2F5	2F6	2F7	2F8	2F9	2FA	2FB	2FC	2FD
0	⼀ 2F00	⼐ 2F10	⼠ 2F20	⼰ 2F30	⽀ 2F40	⽐ 2F50	⽠ 2F60	⽰ 2F70	⾀ 2F80	⾐ 2F90	⾠ 2FA0	⾰ 2FB0	⿀ 2FC0	⿐ 2FD0
1	⼁ 2F01	⼑ 2F11	⼡ 2F21	⼱ 2F31	⽁ 2F41	⽑ 2F51	⽡ 2F61	⽱ 2F71	⾁ 2F81	⾑ 2F91	⾡ 2FA1	⾱ 2FB1	⿁ 2FC1	⿑ 2FD1
2	⼂ 2F02	⼒ 2F12	⼢ 2F22	⼲ 2F32	⽂ 2F42	⽒ 2F52	⽢ 2F62	⽲ 2F72	⾂ 2F82	⾒ 2F92	⾢ 2FA2	⾲ 2FB2	⿂ 2FC2	⿒ 2FD2
3	⼃ 2F03	⼓ 2F13	⼣ 2F23	⼳ 2F33	⽃ 2F43	⽓ 2F53	⽣ 2F63	⽳ 2F73	⾃ 2F83	⾓ 2F93	⾣ 2FA3	⾳ 2FB3	⿃ 2FC3	⿓ 2FD3
4	⼄ 2F04	⼔ 2F14	⼤ 2F24	⼴ 2F34	⽄ 2F44	⽔ 2F54	⽤ 2F64	⽴ 2F74	⾄ 2F84	⾔ 2F94	⾤ 2FA4	⾴ 2FB4	⿄ 2FC4	⿔ 2FD4
5	⼅ 2F05	⼕ 2F15	⼥ 2F25	⼵ 2F35	⽅ 2F45	⽕ 2F55	⽥ 2F65	⽵ 2F75	⾅ 2F85	⾕ 2F95	⾥ 2FA5	⾵ 2FB5	⿅ 2FC5	⿕ 2FD5
6	⼆ 2F06	⼖ 2F16	⼦ 2F26	⼶ 2F36	⽆ 2F46	⽖ 2F56	⽦ 2F66	⽶ 2F76	⾆ 2F86	⾖ 2F96	⾦ 2FA6	⾶ 2FB6	⿆ 2FC6	
7	⼇ 2F07	⼗ 2F17	⼧ 2F27	⼷ 2F37	⽇ 2F47	⽗ 2F57	⽧ 2F67	⽷ 2F77	⾇ 2F87	⾗ 2F97	⾧ 2FA7	⾷ 2FB7	⿇ 2FC7	
8	⼈ 2F08	⼘ 2F18	⼨ 2F28	⼸ 2F38	⽈ 2F48	⽘ 2F58	⽨ 2F68	⽸ 2F78	⾈ 2F88	⾘ 2F98	⾨ 2FA8	⾸ 2FB8	⿈ 2FC8	
9	⼉ 2F09	⼙ 2F19	⼩ 2F29	⼹ 2F39	⽉ 2F49	⽙ 2F59	⽩ 2F69	⽹ 2F79	⾉ 2F89	⾙ 2F99	⾩ 2FA9	⾹ 2FB9	⿉ 2FC9	
A	⼊ 2F0A	⼚ 2F1A	⼪ 2F2A	⼺ 2F3A	⽊ 2F4A	⽚ 2F5A	⽪ 2F6A	⽺ 2F7A	⾊ 2F8A	⾚ 2F9A	⾪ 2FAA	⾺ 2FBA	⿊ 2FCA	
B	⼋ 2F0B	⼛ 2F1B	⼫ 2F2B	⼻ 2F3B	⽋ 2F4B	⽛ 2F5B	⽫ 2F6B	⽻ 2F7B	⾋ 2F8B	⾛ 2F9B	⾫ 2FAB	⾻ 2FBB	⿋ 2FCB	
C	⼌ 2F0C	⼜ 2F1C	⼬ 2F2C	⼼ 2F3C	⽌ 2F4C	⽜ 2F5C	⽬ 2F6C	⽼ 2F7C	⾌ 2F8C	⾜ 2F9C	⾬ 2FAC	⾼ 2FBC	⿌ 2FCC	
D	⼍ 2F0D	⼝ 2F1D	⼭ 2F2D	⼽ 2F3D	⽍ 2F4D	⽝ 2F5D	⽭ 2F6D	⽽ 2F7D	⾍ 2F8D	⾝ 2F9D	⾭ 2FAD	⾽ 2FBD	⿍ 2FCD	
E	⼎ 2F0E	⼞ 2F1E	⼮ 2F2E	⼾ 2F3E	⽎ 2F4E	⽞ 2F5E	⽮ 2F6E	⽾ 2F7E	⾎ 2F8E	⾞ 2F9E	⾮ 2FAE	⾾ 2FBE	⿎ 2FCE	
F	⼏ 2F0F	⼟ 2F1F	⼯ 2F2F	⼿ 2F3F	⽏ 2F4F	⽟ 2F5F	⽯ 2F6F	⽿ 2F7F	⾏ 2F8F	⾟ 2F9F	⾯ 2FAF	⾿ 2FBF	⿏ 2FCF	

Kangxi radicals

2F00 ⼀ KANGXI RADICAL ONE
≈ 4E00 一
2F01 ⼁ KANGXI RADICAL LINE
≈ 4E28 丨
2F02 ⼂ KANGXI RADICAL DOT
≈ 4E36 丶
2F03 ⼃ KANGXI RADICAL SLASH
≈ 4E3F 丿
2F04 ⼄ KANGXI RADICAL SECOND
≈ 4E59 乙
2F05 ⼅ KANGXI RADICAL HOOK
≈ 4E85 亅
2F06 ⼆ KANGXI RADICAL TWO
≈ 4E8C 二
2F07 ⼇ KANGXI RADICAL LID
≈ 4EA0 亠
2F08 ⼈ KANGXI RADICAL MAN
≈ 4EBA 人
2F09 ⼉ KANGXI RADICAL LEGS
≈ 513F 儿
2F0A ⼊ KANGXI RADICAL ENTER
≈ 5165 入
2F0B ⼋ KANGXI RADICAL EIGHT
≈ 516B 八
2F0C ⼌ KANGXI RADICAL DOWN BOX
≈ 5182 冂
2F0D ⼍ KANGXI RADICAL COVER
≈ 5196 冖
2F0E ⼎ KANGXI RADICAL ICE
≈ 51AB 冫
2F0F ⼏ KANGXI RADICAL TABLE
≈ 51E0 几
2F10 ⼐ KANGXI RADICAL OPEN BOX
≈ 51F5 凵
2F11 ⼑ KANGXI RADICAL KNIFE
≈ 5200 刀
2F12 ⼒ KANGXI RADICAL POWER
≈ 529B 力
2F13 ⼓ KANGXI RADICAL WRAP
≈ 52F9 勹
2F14 ⼔ KANGXI RADICAL SPOON
≈ 5315 匕
2F15 ⼕ KANGXI RADICAL RIGHT OPEN BOX
≈ 531A 匚
2F16 ⼖ KANGXI RADICAL HIDING ENCLOSURE
≈ 5338 匸
2F17 ⼗ KANGXI RADICAL TEN
≈ 5341 十
2F18 ⼘ KANGXI RADICAL DIVINATION
≈ 535C 卜
2F19 ⼙ KANGXI RADICAL SEAL
≈ 5369 卩
2F1A ⼚ KANGXI RADICAL CLIFF
≈ 5382 厂
2F1B ⼛ KANGXI RADICAL PRIVATE
≈ 53B6 厶
2F1C ⼜ KANGXI RADICAL AGAIN
≈ 53C8 又
2F1D ⼝ KANGXI RADICAL MOUTH
≈ 53E3 口
2F1E ⼞ KANGXI RADICAL ENCLOSURE
≈ 56D7 囗
2F1F ⼟ KANGXI RADICAL EARTH
≈ 571F 土
2F20 ⼠ KANGXI RADICAL SCHOLAR
≈ 58EB 士
2F21 ⼡ KANGXI RADICAL GO
≈ 5902 夂
2F22 ⼢ KANGXI RADICAL GO SLOWLY
≈ 590A 夊
2F23 ⼣ KANGXI RADICAL EVENING
≈ 5915 夕
2F24 ⼤ KANGXI RADICAL BIG
≈ 5927 大
2F25 ⼥ KANGXI RADICAL WOMAN
≈ 5973 女
2F26 ⼦ KANGXI RADICAL CHILD
≈ 5B50 子
2F27 ⼧ KANGXI RADICAL ROOF
≈ 5B80 宀
2F28 ⼨ KANGXI RADICAL INCH
≈ 5BF8 寸
2F29 ⼩ KANGXI RADICAL SMALL
≈ 5C0F 小
2F2A ⼪ KANGXI RADICAL LAME
≈ 5C22 尢
2F2B ⼫ KANGXI RADICAL CORPSE
≈ 5C38 尸
2F2C ⼬ KANGXI RADICAL SPROUT
≈ 5C6E 屮
2F2D ⼭ KANGXI RADICAL MOUNTAIN
≈ 5C71 山
2F2E ⼮ KANGXI RADICAL RIVER
≈ 5DDB 巛
2F2F ⼯ KANGXI RADICAL WORK
≈ 5DE5 工
2F30 ⼰ KANGXI RADICAL ONESELF
≈ 5DF1 己
2F31 ⼱ KANGXI RADICAL TURBAN
≈ 5DFE 巾
2F32 ⼲ KANGXI RADICAL DRY
≈ 5E72 干
2F33 ⼳ KANGXI RADICAL SHORT THREAD
≈ 5E7A 幺
2F34 ⼴ KANGXI RADICAL DOTTED CLIFF
≈ 5E7F 广
2F35 ⼵ KANGXI RADICAL LONG STRIDE
≈ 5EF4 廴
2F36 ⼶ KANGXI RADICAL TWO HANDS
≈ 5EFE 廾
2F37 ⼷ KANGXI RADICAL SHOOT
≈ 5F0B 弋
2F38 ⼸ KANGXI RADICAL BOW
≈ 5F13 弓
2F39 ⼹ KANGXI RADICAL SNOUT
≈ 5F50 彐
2F3A ⼺ KANGXI RADICAL BRISTLE
≈ 5F61 彡
2F3B ⼻ KANGXI RADICAL STEP
≈ 5F73 彳
2F3C ⼼ KANGXI RADICAL HEART
≈ 5FC3 心

2F3D 戈 KANGXI RADICAL HALBERD
≈ 6208 戈
2F3E 戶 KANGXI RADICAL DOOR
≈ 6236 戶
2F3F 手 KANGXI RADICAL HAND
≈ 624B 手
2F40 支 KANGXI RADICAL BRANCH
≈ 652F 支
2F41 攴 KANGXI RADICAL RAP
≈ 6534 攴
2F42 文 KANGXI RADICAL SCRIPT
≈ 6587 文
2F43 斗 KANGXI RADICAL DIPPER
≈ 6597 斗
2F44 斤 KANGXI RADICAL AXE
≈ 65A4 斤
2F45 方 KANGXI RADICAL SQUARE
≈ 65B9 方
2F46 无 KANGXI RADICAL NOT
≈ 65E0 无
2F47 日 KANGXI RADICAL SUN
≈ 65E5 日
2F48 曰 KANGXI RADICAL SAY
≈ 66F0 曰
2F49 月 KANGXI RADICAL MOON
≈ 6708 月
2F4A 木 KANGXI RADICAL TREE
≈ 6728 木
2F4B 欠 KANGXI RADICAL LACK
≈ 6B20 欠
2F4C 止 KANGXI RADICAL STOP
≈ 6B62 止
2F4D 歹 KANGXI RADICAL DEATH
≈ 6B79 歹
2F4E 殳 KANGXI RADICAL WEAPON
≈ 6BB3 殳
2F4F 毋 KANGXI RADICAL DO NOT
≈ 6BCB 毋
2F50 比 KANGXI RADICAL COMPARE
≈ 6BD4 比
2F51 毛 KANGXI RADICAL FUR
≈ 6BDB 毛
2F52 氏 KANGXI RADICAL CLAN
≈ 6C0F 氏
2F53 气 KANGXI RADICAL STEAM
≈ 6C14 气
2F54 水 KANGXI RADICAL WATER
≈ 6C34 水
2F55 火 KANGXI RADICAL FIRE
≈ 706B 火
2F56 爪 KANGXI RADICAL CLAW
≈ 722A 爪
2F57 父 KANGXI RADICAL FATHER
≈ 7236 父
2F58 爻 KANGXI RADICAL DOUBLE X
≈ 723B 爻
2F59 爿 KANGXI RADICAL HALF TREE TRUNK
≈ 723F 爿
2F5A 片 KANGXI RADICAL SLICE
≈ 7247 片
2F5B 牙 KANGXI RADICAL FANG
≈ 7259 牙

2F5C 牛 KANGXI RADICAL COW
≈ 725B 牛
2F5D 犬 KANGXI RADICAL DOG
≈ 72AC 犬
2F5E 玄 KANGXI RADICAL PROFOUND
≈ 7384 玄
2F5F 玉 KANGXI RADICAL JADE
≈ 7389 玉
2F60 瓜 KANGXI RADICAL MELON
≈ 74DC 瓜
2F61 瓦 KANGXI RADICAL TILE
≈ 74E6 瓦
2F62 甘 KANGXI RADICAL SWEET
≈ 7518 甘
2F63 生 KANGXI RADICAL LIFE
≈ 751F 生
2F64 用 KANGXI RADICAL USE
≈ 7528 用
2F65 田 KANGXI RADICAL FIELD
≈ 7530 田
2F66 疋 KANGXI RADICAL BOLT OF CLOTH
≈ 758B 疋
2F67 疒 KANGXI RADICAL SICKNESS
≈ 7592 疒
2F68 癶 KANGXI RADICAL DOTTED TENT
≈ 7676 癶
2F69 白 KANGXI RADICAL WHITE
≈ 767D 白
2F6A 皮 KANGXI RADICAL SKIN
≈ 76AE 皮
2F6B 皿 KANGXI RADICAL DISH
≈ 76BF 皿
2F6C 目 KANGXI RADICAL EYE
≈ 76EE 目
2F6D 矛 KANGXI RADICAL SPEAR
≈ 77DB 矛
2F6E 矢 KANGXI RADICAL ARROW
≈ 77E2 矢
2F6F 石 KANGXI RADICAL STONE
≈ 77F3 石
2F70 示 KANGXI RADICAL SPIRIT
≈ 793A 示
2F71 禸 KANGXI RADICAL TRACK
≈ 79B8 禸
2F72 禾 KANGXI RADICAL GRAIN
≈ 79BE 禾
2F73 穴 KANGXI RADICAL CAVE
≈ 7A74 穴
2F74 立 KANGXI RADICAL STAND
≈ 7ACB 立
2F75 竹 KANGXI RADICAL BAMBOO
≈ 7AF9 竹
2F76 米 KANGXI RADICAL RICE
≈ 7C73 米
2F77 糸 KANGXI RADICAL SILK
≈ 7CF8 糸
2F78 缶 KANGXI RADICAL JAR
≈ 7F36 缶
2F79 网 KANGXI RADICAL NET
≈ 7F51 网
2F7A 羊 KANGXI RADICAL SHEEP
≈ 7F8A 羊

2F7B 羽 KANGXI RADICAL FEATHER
≈ 7FBD 羽
2F7C 老 KANGXI RADICAL OLD
≈ 8001 老
2F7D 而 KANGXI RADICAL AND
≈ 800C 而
2F7E 耒 KANGXI RADICAL PLOW
≈ 8012 耒
2F7F 耳 KANGXI RADICAL EAR
≈ 8033 耳
2F80 聿 KANGXI RADICAL BRUSH
≈ 807F 聿
2F81 肉 KANGXI RADICAL MEAT
≈ 8089 肉
2F82 臣 KANGXI RADICAL MINISTER
≈ 81E3 臣
2F83 自 KANGXI RADICAL SELF
≈ 81EA 自
2F84 至 KANGXI RADICAL ARRIVE
≈ 81F3 至
2F85 臼 KANGXI RADICAL MORTAR
≈ 81FC 臼
2F86 舌 KANGXI RADICAL TONGUE
≈ 820C 舌
2F87 舛 KANGXI RADICAL OPPOSE
≈ 821B 舛
2F88 舟 KANGXI RADICAL BOAT
≈ 821F 舟
2F89 艮 KANGXI RADICAL STOPPING
≈ 826E 艮
2F8A 色 KANGXI RADICAL COLOR
≈ 8272 色
2F8B 艸 KANGXI RADICAL GRASS
≈ 8278 艸
2F8C 虍 KANGXI RADICAL TIGER
≈ 864D 虍
2F8D 虫 KANGXI RADICAL INSECT
≈ 866B 虫
2F8E 血 KANGXI RADICAL BLOOD
≈ 8840 血
2F8F 行 KANGXI RADICAL WALK ENCLOSURE
≈ 884C 行
2F90 衣 KANGXI RADICAL CLOTHES
≈ 8863 衣
2F91 襾 KANGXI RADICAL WEST
≈ 897E 襾
2F92 見 KANGXI RADICAL SEE
≈ 898B 見
2F93 角 KANGXI RADICAL HORN
≈ 89D2 角
2F94 言 KANGXI RADICAL SPEECH
≈ 8A00 言
2F95 谷 KANGXI RADICAL VALLEY
≈ 8C37 谷
2F96 豆 KANGXI RADICAL BEAN
≈ 8C46 豆
2F97 豕 KANGXI RADICAL PIG
≈ 8C55 豕
2F98 豸 KANGXI RADICAL BADGER
≈ 8C78 豸
2F99 貝 KANGXI RADICAL SHELL
≈ 8C9D 貝
2F9A 赤 KANGXI RADICAL RED
≈ 8D64 赤
2F9B 走 KANGXI RADICAL RUN
≈ 8D70 走
2F9C 足 KANGXI RADICAL FOOT
≈ 8DB3 足
2F9D 身 KANGXI RADICAL BODY
≈ 8EAB 身
2F9E 車 KANGXI RADICAL CART
≈ 8ECA 車
2F9F 辛 KANGXI RADICAL BITTER
≈ 8F9B 辛
2FA0 辰 KANGXI RADICAL MORNING
≈ 8FB0 辰
2FA1 辵 KANGXI RADICAL WALK
≈ 8FB5 辵
2FA2 邑 KANGXI RADICAL CITY
≈ 9091 邑
2FA3 酉 KANGXI RADICAL WINE
≈ 9149 酉
2FA4 釆 KANGXI RADICAL DISTINGUISH
≈ 91C6 釆
2FA5 里 KANGXI RADICAL VILLAGE
≈ 91CC 里
2FA6 金 KANGXI RADICAL GOLD
≈ 91D1 金
2FA7 長 KANGXI RADICAL LONG
≈ 9577 長
2FA8 門 KANGXI RADICAL GATE
≈ 9580 門
2FA9 阜 KANGXI RADICAL MOUND
≈ 961C 阜
2FAA 隶 KANGXI RADICAL SLAVE
≈ 96B6 隶
2FAB 隹 KANGXI RADICAL SHORT TAILED BIRD
≈ 96B9 隹
2FAC 雨 KANGXI RADICAL RAIN
≈ 96E8 雨
2FAD 靑 KANGXI RADICAL BLUE
≈ 9751 靑
2FAE 非 KANGXI RADICAL WRONG
≈ 975E 非
2FAF 面 KANGXI RADICAL FACE
≈ 9762 面
2FB0 革 KANGXI RADICAL LEATHER
≈ 9769 革
2FB1 韋 KANGXI RADICAL TANNED LEATHER
≈ 97CB 韋
2FB2 韭 KANGXI RADICAL LEEK
≈ 97ED 韭
2FB3 音 KANGXI RADICAL SOUND
≈ 97F3 音
2FB4 頁 KANGXI RADICAL LEAF
≈ 9801 頁
2FB5 風 KANGXI RADICAL WIND
≈ 98A8 風
2FB6 飛 KANGXI RADICAL FLY
≈ 98DB 飛
2FB7 食 KANGXI RADICAL EAT
≈ 98DF 食
2FB8 首 KANGXI RADICAL HEAD
≈ 9996 首

2FB9 香 KANGXI RADICAL FRAGRANT
≈ 9999 香
2FBA 馬 KANGXI RADICAL HORSE
≈ 99AC 馬
2FBB 骨 KANGXI RADICAL BONE
≈ 9AA8 骨
2FBC 高 KANGXI RADICAL TALL
≈ 9AD8 高
2FBD 髟 KANGXI RADICAL HAIR
≈ 9ADF 髟
2FBE 鬥 KANGXI RADICAL FIGHT
≈ 9B25 鬥
2FBF 鬯 KANGXI RADICAL SACRIFICIAL WINE
≈ 9B2F 鬯
2FC0 鬲 KANGXI RADICAL CAULDRON
≈ 9B32 鬲
2FC1 鬼 KANGXI RADICAL GHOST
≈ 9B3C 鬼
2FC2 魚 KANGXI RADICAL FISH
≈ 9B5A 魚
2FC3 鳥 KANGXI RADICAL BIRD
≈ 9CE5 鳥
2FC4 鹵 KANGXI RADICAL SALT
≈ 9E75 鹵
2FC5 鹿 KANGXI RADICAL DEER
≈ 9E7F 鹿
2FC6 麥 KANGXI RADICAL WHEAT
≈ 9EA5 麥
2FC7 麻 KANGXI RADICAL HEMP
≈ 9EBB 麻
2FC8 黃 KANGXI RADICAL YELLOW
≈ 9EC3 黃
2FC9 黍 KANGXI RADICAL MILLET
≈ 9ECD 黍
2FCA 黑 KANGXI RADICAL BLACK
≈ 9ED1 黑
2FCB 黹 KANGXI RADICAL EMBROIDERY
≈ 9EF9 黹
2FCC 黽 KANGXI RADICAL FROG
≈ 9EFD 黽
2FCD 鼎 KANGXI RADICAL TRIPOD
≈ 9F0E 鼎
2FCE 鼓 KANGXI RADICAL DRUM
≈ 9F13 鼓
2FCF 鼠 KANGXI RADICAL RAT
≈ 9F20 鼠
2FD0 鼻 KANGXI RADICAL NOSE
≈ 9F3B 鼻
2FD1 齊 KANGXI RADICAL EVEN
≈ 9F4A 齊
2FD2 齒 KANGXI RADICAL TOOTH
≈ 9F52 齒
2FD3 龍 KANGXI RADICAL DRAGON
≈ 9F8D 龍
2FD4 龜 KANGXI RADICAL TURTLE
≈ 9F9C 龜
2FD5 龠 KANGXI RADICAL FLUTE
≈ 9FA0 龠

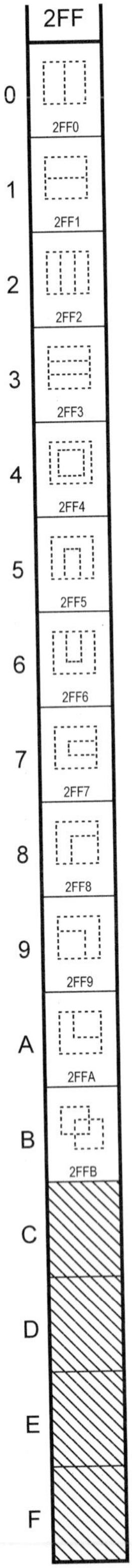

	2FF
0	2FF0
1	2FF1
2	2FF2
3	2FF3
4	2FF4
5	2FF5
6	2FF6
7	2FF7
8	2FF8
9	2FF9
A	2FFA
B	2FFB
C	
D	
E	
F	

Ideographic description characters

These are visibly displayed graphic characters, not invisible composition controls.

2FF0 ⿰ IDEOGRAPHIC DESCRIPTION CHARACTER LEFT TO RIGHT
2FF1 ⿱ IDEOGRAPHIC DESCRIPTION CHARACTER ABOVE TO BELOW
2FF2 ⿲ IDEOGRAPHIC DESCRIPTION CHARACTER LEFT TO MIDDLE AND RIGHT
2FF3 ⿳ IDEOGRAPHIC DESCRIPTION CHARACTER ABOVE TO MIDDLE AND BELOW
2FF4 ⿴ IDEOGRAPHIC DESCRIPTION CHARACTER FULL SURROUND
2FF5 ⿵ IDEOGRAPHIC DESCRIPTION CHARACTER SURROUND FROM ABOVE
2FF6 ⿶ IDEOGRAPHIC DESCRIPTION CHARACTER SURROUND FROM BELOW
2FF7 ⿷ IDEOGRAPHIC DESCRIPTION CHARACTER SURROUND FROM LEFT
2FF8 ⿸ IDEOGRAPHIC DESCRIPTION CHARACTER SURROUND FROM UPPER LEFT
2FF9 ⿹ IDEOGRAPHIC DESCRIPTION CHARACTER SURROUND FROM UPPER RIGHT
2FFA ⿺ IDEOGRAPHIC DESCRIPTION CHARACTER SURROUND FROM LOWER LEFT
2FFB ⿻ IDEOGRAPHIC DESCRIPTION CHARACTER OVERLAID

	300	301	302	303
0	ID SP 3000	【 3010	〠 3020	〰 3030
1	、 3001	】 3011	〡 3021	〱 3031
2	。 3002	〒 3012	〢 3022	〲 3032
3	〃 3003	〓 3013	〣 3023	〳 3033
4	〄 3004	〔 3014	〤 3024	〴 3034
5	々 3005	〕 3015	〥 3025	〵 3035
6	〆 3006	〖 3016	〦 3026	〶 3036
7	〇 3007	〗 3017	〧 3027	〷 3037
8	〈 3008	〘 3018	〨 3028	〸 3038
9	〉 3009	〙 3019	〩 3029	〹 3039
A	《 300A	〚 301A	◌〪 302A	〺 303A
B	》 300B	〛 301B	◌〫 302B	〻 303B
C	「 300C	〜 301C	◌〬 302C	〼 303C
D	」 300D	〝 301D	◌〭 302D	〽 303D
E	『 300E	〞 301E	◌〮 302E	〾 303E
F	』 300F	〟 301F	◌〯 302F	〿 303F

CJK symbols and punctuation

3000 IDEOGRAPHIC SPACE
→ 0020 space
≈ <wide> 0020

3001 、 IDEOGRAPHIC COMMA
→ 002C , comma

3002 。 IDEOGRAPHIC FULL STOP
→ 002E . full stop

3003 〃 DITTO MARK
→ 2033 ″ double prime

3004 〄 JAPANESE INDUSTRIAL STANDARD SYMBOL

3005 々 IDEOGRAPHIC ITERATION MARK

3006 〆 IDEOGRAPHIC CLOSING MARK

3007 〇 IDEOGRAPHIC NUMBER ZERO
→ 20DD ⃝ combining enclosing circle
→ 25CB ○ white circle
→ 25EF ◯ large circle

CJK angle brackets

3008 〈 LEFT ANGLE BRACKET
→ 003C < less-than sign
→ 2039 ‹ single left-pointing angle quotation mark
→ 2329 〈 left-pointing angle bracket
→ 27E8 ⟨ mathematical left angle bracket

3009 〉 RIGHT ANGLE BRACKET
→ 003E > greater-than sign
→ 203A › single right-pointing angle quotation mark
→ 232A 〉 right-pointing angle bracket
→ 27E9 ⟩ mathematical right angle bracket

300A 《 LEFT DOUBLE ANGLE BRACKET
→ 00AB « left-pointing double angle quotation mark
→ 27EA ⟪ mathematical left double angle bracket

300B 》 RIGHT DOUBLE ANGLE BRACKET
→ 00BB » right-pointing double angle quotation mark
→ 27EB ⟫ mathematical right double angle bracket

CJK corner brackets

The CJK corner brackets, which function as quotation marks, are not recommended for general-purpose corner brackets. See the ceiling and floor characters, instead.

300C 「 LEFT CORNER BRACKET
→ 2308 ⌈ left ceiling

300D 」 RIGHT CORNER BRACKET
• used as quotation marks
→ 230B ⌋ right floor

300E 『 LEFT WHITE CORNER BRACKET

300F 』 RIGHT WHITE CORNER BRACKET
• used as quotation marks

CJK brackets

3010 【 LEFT BLACK LENTICULAR BRACKET

3011 】 RIGHT BLACK LENTICULAR BRACKET

CJK symbols

3012 〒 POSTAL MARK

3013 〓 GETA MARK
• substitute for ideograph not in font

CJK brackets

3014 〔 LEFT TORTOISE SHELL BRACKET

3015 〕 RIGHT TORTOISE SHELL BRACKET

3016 〖 LEFT WHITE LENTICULAR BRACKET

3017 〗 RIGHT WHITE LENTICULAR BRACKET

3018 〘 LEFT WHITE TORTOISE SHELL BRACKET

3019 〙 RIGHT WHITE TORTOISE SHELL BRACKET

301A 〚 LEFT WHITE SQUARE BRACKET
= left abstract syntax bracket
→ 27E6 ⟦ mathematical left white square bracket

301B 〛 RIGHT WHITE SQUARE BRACKET
= right abstract syntax bracket
→ 27E7 ⟧ mathematical right white square bracket

CJK symbols and punctuation

301C 〜 WAVE DASH
• This character was encoded to match JIS C 6226-1978 1-33 "wave dash". The JIS standards and some industry practice disagree in mapping.
→ 3030 〰 wavy dash
→ FF5E ～ fullwidth tilde

301D 〝 REVERSED DOUBLE PRIME QUOTATION MARK
• sometimes depicted as double prime quotation mark
→ 201C " left double quotation mark
→ 2036 ‶ reversed double prime

301E 〞 DOUBLE PRIME QUOTATION MARK
• this is a mistaken analogue to 201D ";
301F 〟 is preferred
→ 201D " right double quotation mark
→ 2033 ″ double prime

301F 〟 LOW DOUBLE PRIME QUOTATION MARK
• may be depicted as low inverse double prime quotation mark

3020 〠 POSTAL MARK FACE

Suzhou numerals

The Suzhou numerals (Chinese su1zhou1ma3zi) are special numeric forms used by traders to display the prices of goods. The use of "HANGZHOU" in the names is a misnomer.

3021 〡 HANGZHOU NUMERAL ONE

3022 〢 HANGZHOU NUMERAL TWO

3023 〣 HANGZHOU NUMERAL THREE

3024 〤 HANGZHOU NUMERAL FOUR

3025 〥 HANGZHOU NUMERAL FIVE

3026 〦 HANGZHOU NUMERAL SIX

3027 〧 HANGZHOU NUMERAL SEVEN

3028 〨 HANGZHOU NUMERAL EIGHT

3029 〩 HANGZHOU NUMERAL NINE

Diacritics

302A ◌〪 IDEOGRAPHIC LEVEL TONE MARK

302B ◌〫 IDEOGRAPHIC RISING TONE MARK

302C ◌〬 IDEOGRAPHIC DEPARTING TONE MARK

302D ◌〭 IDEOGRAPHIC ENTERING TONE MARK

302E ◌〮 HANGUL SINGLE DOT TONE MARK
= single dot Bangjeom

302F ◌〯 HANGUL DOUBLE DOT TONE MARK
= double dot Bangjeom

Other CJK symbols

3030 〰 WAVY DASH
→ 2307 ⌇ wavy line
→ 301C 〜 wave dash

3031 〱 VERTICAL KANA REPEAT MARK

3032 〲 VERTICAL KANA REPEAT WITH VOICED SOUND MARK
- the preceding two semantic characters are preferred to the following three glyphic forms

3033 〳 VERTICAL KANA REPEAT MARK UPPER HALF
3034 〴 VERTICAL KANA REPEAT WITH VOICED SOUND MARK UPPER HALF
- the preceding two are glyphs used in conjunction with the following glyph

3035 〵 VERTICAL KANA REPEAT MARK LOWER HALF
3036 〶 CIRCLED POSTAL MARK
≈ 3012 〒 postal mark
3037 〷 IDEOGRAPHIC TELEGRAPH LINE FEED SEPARATOR SYMBOL

Additional Suzhou numerals

3038 〸 HANGZHOU NUMERAL TEN
≈ 5341 十
3039 〹 HANGZHOU NUMERAL TWENTY
≈ 5344 卄
303A 〺 HANGZHOU NUMERAL THIRTY
≈ 5345 卅

Other CJK punctuation

303B 〻 VERTICAL IDEOGRAPHIC ITERATION MARK
303C 〼 MASU MARK
- informal abbreviation for Japanese -masu ending

→ 29C4 ⧄ squared rising diagonal slash
303D 〽 PART ALTERNATION MARK
- marks the start of a song part in Japanese

Special CJK indicators

These are visibly displayed graphic characters, not invisible format control characters.

303E 〾 IDEOGRAPHIC VARIATION INDICATOR
- visual indicator that the following ideograph is to be taken as a variant of the intended character

303F 〿 IDEOGRAPHIC HALF FILL SPACE
- visual indicator of a screen space for half of an ideograph

	304	305	306	307	308	309
0	(hatched)	ぐ 3050	だ 3060	ば 3070	む 3080	ゐ 3090
1	ぁ 3041	け 3051	ち 3061	ぱ 3071	め 3081	ゑ 3091
2	あ 3042	げ 3052	ぢ 3062	ひ 3072	も 3082	を 3092
3	ぃ 3043	こ 3053	っ 3063	び 3073	ゃ 3083	ん 3093
4	い 3044	ご 3054	つ 3064	ぴ 3074	や 3084	ゔ 3094
5	ぅ 3045	さ 3055	づ 3065	ふ 3075	ゅ 3085	ゕ 3095
6	う 3046	ざ 3056	て 3066	ぶ 3076	ゆ 3086	ゖ 3096
7	ぇ 3047	し 3057	で 3067	ぷ 3077	ょ 3087	(hatched)
8	え 3048	じ 3058	と 3068	へ 3078	よ 3088	(hatched)
9	ぉ 3049	す 3059	ど 3069	べ 3079	ら 3089	◌゙ 3099
A	お 304A	ず 305A	な 306A	ぺ 307A	り 308A	◌゚ 309A
B	か 304B	せ 305B	に 306B	ほ 307B	る 308B	゛ 309B
C	が 304C	ぜ 305C	ぬ 306C	ぼ 307C	れ 308C	゜ 309C
D	き 304D	そ 305D	ね 306D	ぽ 307D	ろ 308D	ゝ 309D
E	ぎ 304E	ぞ 305E	の 306E	ま 307E	ゎ 308E	ゞ 309E
F	く 304F	た 305F	は 306F	み 307F	わ 308F	ゟ 309F

Based on JIS X 0208

3041 ぁ HIRAGANA LETTER SMALL A
3042 あ HIRAGANA LETTER A
3043 ぃ HIRAGANA LETTER SMALL I
3044 い HIRAGANA LETTER I
3045 ぅ HIRAGANA LETTER SMALL U
3046 う HIRAGANA LETTER U
3047 ぇ HIRAGANA LETTER SMALL E
3048 え HIRAGANA LETTER E
3049 ぉ HIRAGANA LETTER SMALL O
304A お HIRAGANA LETTER O
304B か HIRAGANA LETTER KA
304C が HIRAGANA LETTER GA
≡ 304B か 3099 ◌゙
304D き HIRAGANA LETTER KI
304E ぎ HIRAGANA LETTER GI
≡ 304D き 3099 ◌゙
304F く HIRAGANA LETTER KU
3050 ぐ HIRAGANA LETTER GU
≡ 304F く 3099 ◌゙
3051 け HIRAGANA LETTER KE
3052 げ HIRAGANA LETTER GE
≡ 3051 け 3099 ◌゙
3053 こ HIRAGANA LETTER KO
3054 ご HIRAGANA LETTER GO
≡ 3053 こ 3099 ◌゙
3055 さ HIRAGANA LETTER SA
3056 ざ HIRAGANA LETTER ZA
≡ 3055 さ 3099 ◌゙
3057 し HIRAGANA LETTER SI
= SHI
3058 じ HIRAGANA LETTER ZI
= JI (not unique)
≡ 3057 し 3099 ◌゙
3059 す HIRAGANA LETTER SU
305A ず HIRAGANA LETTER ZU
≡ 3059 す 3099 ◌゙
305B せ HIRAGANA LETTER SE
305C ぜ HIRAGANA LETTER ZE
≡ 305B せ 3099 ◌゙
305D そ HIRAGANA LETTER SO
305E ぞ HIRAGANA LETTER ZO
≡ 305D そ 3099 ◌゙
305F た HIRAGANA LETTER TA
3060 だ HIRAGANA LETTER DA
≡ 305F た 3099 ◌゙
3061 ち HIRAGANA LETTER TI
= CHI
3062 ぢ HIRAGANA LETTER DI
= JI (not unique)
≡ 3061 ち 3099 ◌゙
3063 っ HIRAGANA LETTER SMALL TU
= SMALL TSU
3064 つ HIRAGANA LETTER TU
= TSU
3065 づ HIRAGANA LETTER DU
= ZU (not unique)
≡ 3064 つ 3099 ◌゙
3066 て HIRAGANA LETTER TE
3067 で HIRAGANA LETTER DE
≡ 3066 て 3099 ◌゙
3068 と HIRAGANA LETTER TO
3069 ど HIRAGANA LETTER DO
≡ 3068 と 3099 ◌゙
306A な HIRAGANA LETTER NA
306B に HIRAGANA LETTER NI
306C ぬ HIRAGANA LETTER NU
306D ね HIRAGANA LETTER NE
306E の HIRAGANA LETTER NO
306F は HIRAGANA LETTER HA
3070 ば HIRAGANA LETTER BA
≡ 306F は 3099 ◌゙
3071 ぱ HIRAGANA LETTER PA
≡ 306F は 309A ◌゚
3072 ひ HIRAGANA LETTER HI
3073 び HIRAGANA LETTER BI
≡ 3072 ひ 3099 ◌゙
3074 ぴ HIRAGANA LETTER PI
≡ 3072 ひ 309A ◌゚
3075 ふ HIRAGANA LETTER HU
= FU
3076 ぶ HIRAGANA LETTER BU
≡ 3075 ふ 3099 ◌゙
3077 ぷ HIRAGANA LETTER PU
≡ 3075 ふ 309A ◌゚
3078 へ HIRAGANA LETTER HE
3079 べ HIRAGANA LETTER BE
≡ 3078 へ 3099 ◌゙
307A ぺ HIRAGANA LETTER PE
≡ 3078 へ 309A ◌゚
307B ほ HIRAGANA LETTER HO
307C ぼ HIRAGANA LETTER BO
≡ 307B ほ 3099 ◌゙
307D ぽ HIRAGANA LETTER PO
≡ 307B ほ 309A ◌゚
307E ま HIRAGANA LETTER MA
307F み HIRAGANA LETTER MI
3080 む HIRAGANA LETTER MU
3081 め HIRAGANA LETTER ME
3082 も HIRAGANA LETTER MO
3083 ゃ HIRAGANA LETTER SMALL YA
3084 や HIRAGANA LETTER YA
3085 ゅ HIRAGANA LETTER SMALL YU
3086 ゆ HIRAGANA LETTER YU
3087 ょ HIRAGANA LETTER SMALL YO
3088 よ HIRAGANA LETTER YO
3089 ら HIRAGANA LETTER RA
308A り HIRAGANA LETTER RI
308B る HIRAGANA LETTER RU
308C れ HIRAGANA LETTER RE
308D ろ HIRAGANA LETTER RO
308E ゎ HIRAGANA LETTER SMALL WA
308F わ HIRAGANA LETTER WA
3090 ゐ HIRAGANA LETTER WI
3091 ゑ HIRAGANA LETTER WE
3092 を HIRAGANA LETTER WO
3093 ん HIRAGANA LETTER N
3094 ゔ HIRAGANA LETTER VU
≡ 3046 う 3099 ◌゙

Small letters

3095 ゕ HIRAGANA LETTER SMALL KA
3096 ゖ HIRAGANA LETTER SMALL KE

Voicing marks

3099 ◌゙ COMBINING KATAKANA-HIRAGANA VOICED SOUND MARK
309A ◌゚ COMBINING KATAKANA-HIRAGANA SEMI-VOICED SOUND MARK

309B ゛ KATAKANA-HIRAGANA VOICED SOUND MARK
≈ 0020 SP 3099 ゙

309C ゜ KATAKANA-HIRAGANA SEMI-VOICED SOUND MARK
≈ 0020 SP 309A ゚

Iteration marks

309D ゝ HIRAGANA ITERATION MARK

309E ゞ HIRAGANA VOICED ITERATION MARK
≡ 309D ゝ 3099 ゙

Vertical form digraph

309F ゟ HIRAGANA DIGRAPH YORI
≈ <vertical> 3088 よ 308A り

	30A	30B	30C	30D	30E	30F
0	゠ 30A0	グ 30B0	ダ 30C0	バ 30D0	ム 30E0	ヰ 30F0
1	ァ 30A1	ケ 30B1	チ 30C1	パ 30D1	メ 30E1	ヱ 30F1
2	ア 30A2	ゲ 30B2	ヂ 30C2	ヒ 30D2	モ 30E2	ヲ 30F2
3	ィ 30A3	コ 30B3	ッ 30C3	ビ 30D3	ャ 30E3	ン 30F3
4	イ 30A4	ゴ 30B4	ツ 30C4	ピ 30D4	ヤ 30E4	ヴ 30F4
5	ゥ 30A5	サ 30B5	ヅ 30C5	フ 30D5	ュ 30E5	ヵ 30F5
6	ウ 30A6	ザ 30B6	テ 30C6	ブ 30D6	ユ 30E6	ヶ 30F6
7	ェ 30A7	シ 30B7	デ 30C7	プ 30D7	ョ 30E7	ヷ 30F7
8	エ 30A8	ジ 30B8	ト 30C8	ヘ 30D8	ヨ 30E8	ヸ 30F8
9	ォ 30A9	ス 30B9	ド 30C9	ベ 30D9	ラ 30E9	ヹ 30F9
A	オ 30AA	ズ 30BA	ナ 30CA	ペ 30DA	リ 30EA	ヺ 30FA
B	カ 30AB	セ 30BB	ニ 30CB	ホ 30DB	ル 30EB	・ 30FB
C	ガ 30AC	ゼ 30BC	ヌ 30CC	ボ 30DC	レ 30EC	ー 30FC
D	キ 30AD	ソ 30BD	ネ 30CD	ポ 30DD	ロ 30ED	ヽ 30FD
E	ギ 30AE	ゾ 30BE	ノ 30CE	マ 30DE	ヮ 30EE	ヾ 30FE
F	ク 30AF	タ 30BF	ハ 30CF	ミ 30DF	ワ 30EF	ヿ 30FF

Katakana punctuation

30A0 = KATAKANA-HIRAGANA DOUBLE HYPHEN
→ 003D = equals sign

Based on JIS X 0208

30A1 ァ KATAKANA LETTER SMALL A
30A2 ア KATAKANA LETTER A
30A3 ィ KATAKANA LETTER SMALL I
30A4 イ KATAKANA LETTER I
30A5 ゥ KATAKANA LETTER SMALL U
30A6 ウ KATAKANA LETTER U
30A7 ェ KATAKANA LETTER SMALL E
30A8 エ KATAKANA LETTER E
30A9 ォ KATAKANA LETTER SMALL O
30AA オ KATAKANA LETTER O
30AB カ KATAKANA LETTER KA
30AC ガ KATAKANA LETTER GA
≡ 30AB カ 3099 ◌゙
30AD キ KATAKANA LETTER KI
30AE ギ KATAKANA LETTER GI
≡ 30AD キ 3099 ◌゙
30AF ク KATAKANA LETTER KU
30B0 グ KATAKANA LETTER GU
≡ 30AF ク 3099 ◌゙
30B1 ケ KATAKANA LETTER KE
30B2 ゲ KATAKANA LETTER GE
≡ 30B1 ケ 3099 ◌゙
30B3 コ KATAKANA LETTER KO
30B4 ゴ KATAKANA LETTER GO
≡ 30B3 コ 3099 ◌゙
30B5 サ KATAKANA LETTER SA
30B6 ザ KATAKANA LETTER ZA
≡ 30B5 サ 3099 ◌゙
30B7 シ KATAKANA LETTER SI
= SHI
30B8 ジ KATAKANA LETTER ZI
= JI (not unique)
≡ 30B7 シ 3099 ◌゙
30B9 ス KATAKANA LETTER SU
30BA ズ KATAKANA LETTER ZU
≡ 30B9 ス 3099 ◌゙
30BB セ KATAKANA LETTER SE
30BC ゼ KATAKANA LETTER ZE
≡ 30BB セ 3099 ◌゙
30BD ソ KATAKANA LETTER SO
30BE ゾ KATAKANA LETTER ZO
≡ 30BD ソ 3099 ◌゙
30BF タ KATAKANA LETTER TA
30C0 ダ KATAKANA LETTER DA
≡ 30BF タ 3099 ◌゙
30C1 チ KATAKANA LETTER TI
= CHI
30C2 ヂ KATAKANA LETTER DI
= JI (not unique)
≡ 30C1 チ 3099 ◌゙
30C3 ッ KATAKANA LETTER SMALL TU
= SMALL TSU
30C4 ツ KATAKANA LETTER TU
= TSU
30C5 ヅ KATAKANA LETTER DU
= ZU (not unique)
≡ 30C4 ツ 3099 ◌゙
30C6 テ KATAKANA LETTER TE
30C7 デ KATAKANA LETTER DE
≡ 30C6 テ 3099 ◌゙
30C8 ト KATAKANA LETTER TO
30C9 ド KATAKANA LETTER DO
≡ 30C8 ト 3099 ◌゙
30CA ナ KATAKANA LETTER NA
30CB ニ KATAKANA LETTER NI
30CC ヌ KATAKANA LETTER NU
30CD ネ KATAKANA LETTER NE
30CE ノ KATAKANA LETTER NO
30CF ハ KATAKANA LETTER HA
30D0 バ KATAKANA LETTER BA
≡ 30CF ハ 3099 ◌゙
30D1 パ KATAKANA LETTER PA
≡ 30CF ハ 309A ◌゚
30D2 ヒ KATAKANA LETTER HI
30D3 ビ KATAKANA LETTER BI
≡ 30D2 ヒ 3099 ◌゙
30D4 ピ KATAKANA LETTER PI
≡ 30D2 ヒ 309A ◌゚
30D5 フ KATAKANA LETTER HU
= FU
30D6 ブ KATAKANA LETTER BU
≡ 30D5 フ 3099 ◌゙
30D7 プ KATAKANA LETTER PU
≡ 30D5 フ 309A ◌゚
30D8 ヘ KATAKANA LETTER HE
30D9 ベ KATAKANA LETTER BE
≡ 30D8 ヘ 3099 ◌゙
30DA ペ KATAKANA LETTER PE
≡ 30D8 ヘ 309A ◌゚
30DB ホ KATAKANA LETTER HO
30DC ボ KATAKANA LETTER BO
≡ 30DB ホ 3099 ◌゙
30DD ポ KATAKANA LETTER PO
≡ 30DB ホ 309A ◌゚
30DE マ KATAKANA LETTER MA
30DF ミ KATAKANA LETTER MI
30E0 ム KATAKANA LETTER MU
30E1 メ KATAKANA LETTER ME
30E2 モ KATAKANA LETTER MO
30E3 ャ KATAKANA LETTER SMALL YA
30E4 ヤ KATAKANA LETTER YA
30E5 ュ KATAKANA LETTER SMALL YU
30E6 ユ KATAKANA LETTER YU
30E7 ョ KATAKANA LETTER SMALL YO
30E8 ヨ KATAKANA LETTER YO
30E9 ラ KATAKANA LETTER RA
30EA リ KATAKANA LETTER RI
30EB ル KATAKANA LETTER RU
30EC レ KATAKANA LETTER RE
30ED ロ KATAKANA LETTER RO
30EE ヮ KATAKANA LETTER SMALL WA
30EF ワ KATAKANA LETTER WA
30F0 ヰ KATAKANA LETTER WI
30F1 ヱ KATAKANA LETTER WE
30F2 ヲ KATAKANA LETTER WO
30F3 ン KATAKANA LETTER N
30F4 ヴ KATAKANA LETTER VU
≡ 30A6 ウ 3099 ◌゙
30F5 ヵ KATAKANA LETTER SMALL KA
30F6 ヶ KATAKANA LETTER SMALL KE

30F7 ヷ KATAKANA LETTER VA
≡ 30EF ワ 3099 ◌゙
30F8 ヸ KATAKANA LETTER VI
≡ 30F0 ヰ 3099 ◌゙
30F9 ヹ KATAKANA LETTER VE
≡ 30F1 ヱ 3099 ◌゙
30FA ヺ KATAKANA LETTER VO
≡ 30F2 ヲ 3099 ◌゙

Conjunction and length marks

30FB ・ KATAKANA MIDDLE DOT
→ 00B7 · middle dot
30FC ー KATAKANA-HIRAGANA PROLONGED SOUND MARK
→ 2014 — em dash

Iteration marks

30FD ヽ KATAKANA ITERATION MARK
30FE ヾ KATAKANA VOICED ITERATION MARK
≡ 30FD ヽ 3099 ◌゙

Vertical form digraph

30FF ヿ KATAKANA DIGRAPH KOTO
≈ <vertical> 30B3 コ 30C8 ト

	310	311	312
0		ㄐ 3110	ㄠ 3120
1		ㄑ 3111	ㄡ 3121
2		ㄒ 3112	ㄢ 3122
3		ㄓ 3113	ㄣ 3123
4		ㄔ 3114	ㄤ 3124
5	ㄅ 3105	ㄕ 3115	ㄥ 3125
6	ㄆ 3106	ㄖ 3116	ㄦ 3126
7	ㄇ 3107	ㄗ 3117	ㄧ 3127
8	ㄈ 3108	ㄘ 3118	ㄨ 3128
9	ㄉ 3109	ㄙ 3119	ㄩ 3129
A	ㄊ 310A	ㄚ 311A	ㄪ 312A
B	ㄋ 310B	ㄛ 311B	ㄫ 312B
C	ㄌ 310C	ㄜ 311C	ㄬ 312C
D	ㄍ 310D	ㄝ 311D	
E	ㄎ 310E	ㄞ 311E	
F	ㄏ 310F	ㄟ 311F	

See also the Bopomofo Extended block

Based on GB 2312

3105 ㄅ BOPOMOFO LETTER B
3106 ㄆ BOPOMOFO LETTER P
3107 ㄇ BOPOMOFO LETTER M
3108 ㄈ BOPOMOFO LETTER F
3109 ㄉ BOPOMOFO LETTER D
310A ㄊ BOPOMOFO LETTER T
310B ㄋ BOPOMOFO LETTER N
310C ㄌ BOPOMOFO LETTER L
310D ㄍ BOPOMOFO LETTER G
310E ㄎ BOPOMOFO LETTER K
310F ㄏ BOPOMOFO LETTER H
3110 ㄐ BOPOMOFO LETTER J
3111 ㄑ BOPOMOFO LETTER Q
3112 ㄒ BOPOMOFO LETTER X
3113 ㄓ BOPOMOFO LETTER ZH
3114 ㄔ BOPOMOFO LETTER CH
3115 ㄕ BOPOMOFO LETTER SH
3116 ㄖ BOPOMOFO LETTER R
3117 ㄗ BOPOMOFO LETTER Z
3118 ㄘ BOPOMOFO LETTER C
3119 ㄙ BOPOMOFO LETTER S
311A ㄚ BOPOMOFO LETTER A
311B ㄛ BOPOMOFO LETTER O
311C ㄜ BOPOMOFO LETTER E
311D ㄝ BOPOMOFO LETTER EH
311E ㄞ BOPOMOFO LETTER AI
311F ㄟ BOPOMOFO LETTER EI
3120 ㄠ BOPOMOFO LETTER AU
3121 ㄡ BOPOMOFO LETTER OU
3122 ㄢ BOPOMOFO LETTER AN
3123 ㄣ BOPOMOFO LETTER EN
3124 ㄤ BOPOMOFO LETTER ANG
3125 ㄥ BOPOMOFO LETTER ENG
3126 ㄦ BOPOMOFO LETTER ER
3127 ㄧ BOPOMOFO LETTER I
3128 ㄨ BOPOMOFO LETTER U
3129 ㄩ BOPOMOFO LETTER IU

Dialect (non-Mandarin) letters

312A ㄪ BOPOMOFO LETTER V
312B ㄫ BOPOMOFO LETTER NG
312C ㄬ BOPOMOFO LETTER GN

	313	314	315	316	317	318
0		ㅀ 3140	ㅐ 3150	ㅠ 3160	ㅰ 3170	ㆀ 3180
1	ㄱ 3131	ㅁ 3141	ㅑ 3151	ㅡ 3161	ㅱ 3171	ㆁ 3181
2	ㄲ 3132	ㅂ 3142	ㅒ 3152	ㅢ 3162	ㅲ 3172	ㆂ 3182
3	ㄳ 3133	ㅃ 3143	ㅓ 3153	ㅣ 3163	ㅳ 3173	ㆃ 3183
4	ㄴ 3134	ㅄ 3144	ㅔ 3154	HF 3164	ㅴ 3174	ㆄ 3184
5	ㄵ 3135	ㅅ 3145	ㅕ 3155	ㅥ 3165	ㅵ 3175	ㆅ 3185
6	ㄶ 3136	ㅆ 3146	ㅖ 3156	ㅦ 3166	ㅶ 3176	ㆆ 3186
7	ㄷ 3137	ㅇ 3147	ㅗ 3157	ㅧ 3167	ㅷ 3177	ㆇ 3187
8	ㄸ 3138	ㅈ 3148	ㅘ 3158	ㅨ 3168	ㅸ 3178	ㆈ 3188
9	ㄹ 3139	ㅉ 3149	ㅙ 3159	ㅩ 3169	ㅹ 3179	ㆉ 3189
A	ㄺ 313A	ㅊ 314A	ㅚ 315A	ㅪ 316A	ㅺ 317A	ㆊ 318A
B	ㄻ 313B	ㅋ 314B	ㅛ 315B	ㅫ 316B	ㅻ 317B	ㆋ 318B
C	ㄼ 313C	ㅌ 314C	ㅜ 315C	ㅬ 316C	ㅼ 317C	ㆌ 318C
D	ㄽ 313D	ㅍ 314D	ㅝ 315D	ㅭ 316D	ㅽ 317D	ㆍ 318D
E	ㄾ 313E	ㅎ 314E	ㅞ 315E	ㅮ 316E	ㅾ 317E	ㆎ 318E
F	ㄿ 313F	ㅏ 314F	ㅟ 315F	ㅯ 316F	ㅿ 317F	

Modern letters

3131 ㄱ HANGUL LETTER KIYEOK
≈ 1100 ᄀ hangul choseong kiyeok
3132 ㄲ HANGUL LETTER SSANGKIYEOK
≈ 1101 ᄁ hangul choseong ssangkiyeok
3133 ㄳ HANGUL LETTER KIYEOK-SIOS
≈ 11AA ᆪ hangul jongseong kiyeok-sios
3134 ㄴ HANGUL LETTER NIEUN
≈ 1102 ᄂ hangul choseong nieun
3135 ㄵ HANGUL LETTER NIEUN-CIEUC
≈ 11AC ᆬ hangul jongseong nieun-cieuc
3136 ㄶ HANGUL LETTER NIEUN-HIEUH
≈ 11AD ᆭ hangul jongseong nieun-hieuh
3137 ㄷ HANGUL LETTER TIKEUT
≈ 1103 ᄃ hangul choseong tikeut
3138 ㄸ HANGUL LETTER SSANGTIKEUT
≈ 1104 ᄄ hangul choseong ssangtikeut
3139 ㄹ HANGUL LETTER RIEUL
≈ 1105 ᄅ hangul choseong rieul
313A ㄺ HANGUL LETTER RIEUL-KIYEOK
≈ 11B0 ᆰ hangul jongseong rieul-kiyeok
313B ㄻ HANGUL LETTER RIEUL-MIEUM
≈ 11B1 ᆱ hangul jongseong rieul-mieum
313C ㄼ HANGUL LETTER RIEUL-PIEUP
≈ 11B2 ᆲ hangul jongseong rieul-pieup
313D ㄽ HANGUL LETTER RIEUL-SIOS
≈ 11B3 ᆳ hangul jongseong rieul-sios
313E ㄾ HANGUL LETTER RIEUL-THIEUTH
≈ 11B4 ᆴ hangul jongseong rieul-thieuth
313F ㄿ HANGUL LETTER RIEUL-PHIEUPH
≈ 11B5 ᆵ hangul jongseong rieul-phieuph
3140 ㅀ HANGUL LETTER RIEUL-HIEUH
≈ 111A ᄚ hangul choseong rieul-hieuh
3141 ㅁ HANGUL LETTER MIEUM
≈ 1106 ᄆ hangul choseong mieum
3142 ㅂ HANGUL LETTER PIEUP
≈ 1107 ᄇ hangul choseong pieup
3143 ㅃ HANGUL LETTER SSANGPIEUP
≈ 1108 ᄈ hangul choseong ssangpieup
3144 ㅄ HANGUL LETTER PIEUP-SIOS
≈ 1121 ᄡ hangul choseong pieup-sios
3145 ㅅ HANGUL LETTER SIOS
≈ 1109 ᄉ hangul choseong sios
3146 ㅆ HANGUL LETTER SSANGSIOS
≈ 110A ᄊ hangul choseong ssangsios
3147 ㅇ HANGUL LETTER IEUNG
≈ 110B ᄋ hangul choseong ieung
3148 ㅈ HANGUL LETTER CIEUC
≈ 110C ᄌ hangul choseong cieuc
3149 ㅉ HANGUL LETTER SSANGCIEUC
≈ 110D ᄍ hangul choseong ssangcieuc
314A ㅊ HANGUL LETTER CHIEUCH
≈ 110E ᄎ hangul choseong chieuch
314B ㅋ HANGUL LETTER KHIEUKH
≈ 110F ᄏ hangul choseong khieukh
314C ㅌ HANGUL LETTER THIEUTH
≈ 1110 ᄐ hangul choseong thieuth
314D ㅍ HANGUL LETTER PHIEUPH
≈ 1111 ᄑ hangul choseong phieuph
314E ㅎ HANGUL LETTER HIEUH
≈ 1112 ᄒ hangul choseong hieuh
314F ㅏ HANGUL LETTER A
≈ 1161 ᅡ hangul jungseong a
3150 ㅐ HANGUL LETTER AE
≈ 1162 ᅢ hangul jungseong ae
3151 ㅑ HANGUL LETTER YA
≈ 1163 ᅣ hangul jungseong ya
3152 ㅒ HANGUL LETTER YAE
≈ 1164 ᅤ hangul jungseong yae
3153 ㅓ HANGUL LETTER EO
≈ 1165 ᅥ hangul jungseong eo
3154 ㅔ HANGUL LETTER E
≈ 1166 ᅦ hangul jungseong e
3155 ㅕ HANGUL LETTER YEO
≈ 1167 ᅧ hangul jungseong yeo
3156 ㅖ HANGUL LETTER YE
≈ 1168 ᅨ hangul jungseong ye
3157 ㅗ HANGUL LETTER O
≈ 1169 ᅩ hangul jungseong o
3158 ㅘ HANGUL LETTER WA
≈ 116A ᅪ hangul jungseong wa
3159 ㅙ HANGUL LETTER WAE
≈ 116B ᅫ hangul jungseong wae
315A ㅚ HANGUL LETTER OE
≈ 116C ᅬ hangul jungseong oe
315B ㅛ HANGUL LETTER YO
≈ 116D ᅭ hangul jungseong yo
315C ㅜ HANGUL LETTER U
≈ 116E ᅮ hangul jungseong u
315D ㅝ HANGUL LETTER WEO
≈ 116F ᅯ hangul jungseong weo
315E ㅞ HANGUL LETTER WE
≈ 1170 ᅰ hangul jungseong we
315F ㅟ HANGUL LETTER WI
≈ 1171 ᅱ hangul jungseong wi
3160 ㅠ HANGUL LETTER YU
≈ 1172 ᅲ hangul jungseong yu
3161 ㅡ HANGUL LETTER EU
≈ 1173 ᅳ hangul jungseong eu
3162 ㅢ HANGUL LETTER YI
≈ 1174 ᅴ hangul jungseong yi
3163 ㅣ HANGUL LETTER I
≈ 1175 ᅵ hangul jungseong i

Special character

3164 [HF] HANGUL FILLER
= cae om
≈ 1160 [HJF] hangul jungseong filler

Archaic letters

3165 ㅥ HANGUL LETTER SSANGNIEUN
≈ 1114 ᄔ hangul choseong ssangnieun
3166 ㅦ HANGUL LETTER NIEUN-TIKEUT
≈ 1115 ᄕ hangul choseong nieun-tikeut
3167 ㅧ HANGUL LETTER NIEUN-SIOS
≈ 11C7 ᇇ hangul jongseong nieun-sios
3168 ㅨ HANGUL LETTER NIEUN-PANSIOS
≈ 11C8 ᇈ hangul jongseong nieun-pansios
3169 ㅩ HANGUL LETTER RIEUL-KIYEOK-SIOS
≈ 11CC ᇌ hangul jongseong rieul-kiyeok-sios
316A ㅪ HANGUL LETTER RIEUL-TIKEUT
≈ 11CE ᇎ hangul jongseong rieul-tikeut
316B ㅫ HANGUL LETTER RIEUL-PIEUP-SIOS
≈ 11D3 ᇓ hangul jongseong rieul-pieup-sios

316C ㅬ HANGUL LETTER RIEUL-PANSIOS
≈ 11D7 ᇗ hangul jongseong rieul-pansios
316D ㅭ HANGUL LETTER RIEUL-YEORINHIEUH
≈ 11D9 ᇙ hangul jongseong rieul-yeorinhieuh
316E ㅮ HANGUL LETTER MIEUM-PIEUP
≈ 111C ᄜ hangul choseong mieum-pieup
316F ㅯ HANGUL LETTER MIEUM-SIOS
≈ 11DD ᇝ hangul jongseong mieum-sios
3170 ㅰ HANGUL LETTER MIEUM-PANSIOS
≈ 11DF ᇟ hangul jongseong mieum-pansios
3171 ㅱ HANGUL LETTER KAPYEOUNMIEUM
≈ 111D ᄝ hangul choseong kapyeounmieum
3172 ㅲ HANGUL LETTER PIEUP-KIYEOK
≈ 111E ᄞ hangul choseong pieup-kiyeok
3173 ㅳ HANGUL LETTER PIEUP-TIKEUT
≈ 1120 ᄠ hangul choseong pieup-tikeut
3174 ㅴ HANGUL LETTER PIEUP-SIOS-KIYEOK
≈ 1122 ᄢ hangul choseong pieup-sios-kiyeok
3175 ㅵ HANGUL LETTER PIEUP-SIOS-TIKEUT
≈ 1123 ᄣ hangul choseong pieup-sios-tikeut
3176 ㅶ HANGUL LETTER PIEUP-CIEUC
≈ 1127 ᄧ hangul choseong pieup-cieuc
3177 ㅷ HANGUL LETTER PIEUP-THIEUTH
≈ 1129 ᄩ hangul choseong pieup-thieuth
3178 ㅸ HANGUL LETTER KAPYEOUNPIEUP
≈ 112B ᄫ hangul choseong kapyeounpieup
3179 ㅹ HANGUL LETTER KAPYEOUNSSANGPIEUP
≈ 112C ᄬ hangul choseong kapyeounssangpieup
317A ㅺ HANGUL LETTER SIOS-KIYEOK
≈ 112D ᄭ hangul choseong sios-kiyeok
317B ㅻ HANGUL LETTER SIOS-NIEUN
≈ 112E ᄮ hangul choseong sios-nieun
317C ㅼ HANGUL LETTER SIOS-TIKEUT
≈ 112F ᄯ hangul choseong sios-tikeut
317D ㅽ HANGUL LETTER SIOS-PIEUP
≈ 1132 ᄲ hangul choseong sios-pieup
317E ㅾ HANGUL LETTER SIOS-CIEUC
≈ 1136 ᄶ hangul choseong sios-cieuc
317F ㅿ HANGUL LETTER PANSIOS
≈ 1140 ᅀ hangul choseong pansios
3180 ㆀ HANGUL LETTER SSANGIEUNG
≈ 1147 ᅇ hangul choseong ssangieung
3181 ㆁ HANGUL LETTER YESIEUNG
• archaic velar nasal
≈ 114C ᅌ hangul choseong yesieung
3182 ㆂ HANGUL LETTER YESIEUNG-SIOS
≈ 11F1 ᇱ hangul jongseong yesieung-sios
3183 ㆃ HANGUL LETTER YESIEUNG-PANSIOS
≈ 11F2 ᇲ hangul jongseong yesieung-pansios
3184 ㆄ HANGUL LETTER KAPYEOUNPHIEUPH
≈ 1157 ᅗ hangul choseong kapyeounphieuph
3185 ㆅ HANGUL LETTER SSANGHIEUH
≈ 1158 ᅘ hangul choseong ssanghieuh
3186 ㆆ HANGUL LETTER YEORINHIEUH
• archaic glottal stop
≈ 1159 ᅙ hangul choseong yeorinhieuh
3187 ㆇ HANGUL LETTER YO-YA
≈ 1184 ᆄ hangul jungseong yo-ya
3188 ㆈ HANGUL LETTER YO-YAE
≈ 1185 ᆅ hangul jungseong yo-yae
3189 ㆉ HANGUL LETTER YO-I
≈ 1188 ᆈ hangul jungseong yo-i
318A ㆊ HANGUL LETTER YU-YEO
≈ 1191 ᆑ hangul jungseong yu-yeo
318B ㆋ HANGUL LETTER YU-YE
≈ 1192 ᆒ hangul jungseong yu-ye
318C ㆌ HANGUL LETTER YU-I
≈ 1194 ᆔ hangul jungseong yu-i
318D ㆍ HANGUL LETTER ARAEA
≈ 119E ᆞ hangul jungseong araea
318E ㆎ HANGUL LETTER ARAEAE
≈ 11A1 ᆡ hangul jungseong araea-i

	319
0	㆐ 3190
1	㆑ 3191
2	㆒ 3192
3	㆓ 3193
4	㆔ 3194
5	㆕ 3195
6	㆖ 3196
7	㆗ 3197
8	㆘ 3198
9	㆙ 3199
A	㆚ 319A
B	㆛ 319B
C	㆜ 319C
D	㆝ 319D
E	㆞ 319E
F	㆟ 319F

Kanbun

3190 ㆐ IDEOGRAPHIC ANNOTATION LINKING MARK
= tateten
3191 ㆑ IDEOGRAPHIC ANNOTATION REVERSE MARK
= kaeriten re
3192 ㆒ IDEOGRAPHIC ANNOTATION ONE MARK
≈ <super> 4E00 一
3193 ㆓ IDEOGRAPHIC ANNOTATION TWO MARK
≈ <super> 4E8C 二
3194 ㆔ IDEOGRAPHIC ANNOTATION THREE MARK
≈ <super> 4E09 三
3195 ㆕ IDEOGRAPHIC ANNOTATION FOUR MARK
≈ <super> 56DB 四
3196 ㆖ IDEOGRAPHIC ANNOTATION TOP MARK
≈ <super> 4E0A 上
3197 ㆗ IDEOGRAPHIC ANNOTATION MIDDLE MARK
≈ <super> 4E2D 中
3198 ㆘ IDEOGRAPHIC ANNOTATION BOTTOM MARK
≈ <super> 4E0B 下
3199 ㆙ IDEOGRAPHIC ANNOTATION FIRST MARK
≈ <super> 7532 甲
319A ㆚ IDEOGRAPHIC ANNOTATION SECOND MARK
≈ <super> 4E59 乙
319B ㆛ IDEOGRAPHIC ANNOTATION THIRD MARK
≈ <super> 4E19 丙
319C ㆜ IDEOGRAPHIC ANNOTATION FOURTH MARK
≈ <super> 4E01 丁
319D ㆝ IDEOGRAPHIC ANNOTATION HEAVEN MARK
≈ <super> 5929 天
319E ㆞ IDEOGRAPHIC ANNOTATION EARTH MARK
≈ <super> 5730 地
319F ㆟ IDEOGRAPHIC ANNOTATION MAN MARK
≈ <super> 4EBA 人

	31A	31B
0	ㆠ 31A0	ㆰ 31B0
1	ㆡ 31A1	ㆱ 31B1
2	ㆢ 31A2	ㆲ 31B2
3	ㆣ 31A3	ㆳ 31B3
4	ㆤ 31A4	ㆴ 31B4
5	ㆥ 31A5	ㆵ 31B5
6	ㆦ 31A6	ㆶ 31B6
7	ㆧ 31A7	ㆷ 31B7
8	ㆨ 31A8	
9	ㆩ 31A9	
A	ㆪ 31AA	
B	ㆫ 31AB	
C	ㆬ 31AC	
D	ㆭ 31AD	
E	ㆮ 31AE	
F	ㆯ 31AF	

See also the Bopomofo block

Extended Bopomofo for Minnan and Hakka

31A0 ㆠ BOPOMOFO LETTER BU
31A1 ㆡ BOPOMOFO LETTER ZI
31A2 ㆢ BOPOMOFO LETTER JI
31A3 ㆣ BOPOMOFO LETTER GU
31A4 ㆤ BOPOMOFO LETTER EE
31A5 ㆥ BOPOMOFO LETTER ENN
31A6 ㆦ BOPOMOFO LETTER OO
31A7 ㆧ BOPOMOFO LETTER ONN
31A8 ㆨ BOPOMOFO LETTER IR
31A9 ㆩ BOPOMOFO LETTER ANN
31AA ㆪ BOPOMOFO LETTER INN
31AB ㆫ BOPOMOFO LETTER UNN
31AC ㆬ BOPOMOFO LETTER IM
31AD ㆭ BOPOMOFO LETTER NGG
31AE ㆮ BOPOMOFO LETTER AINN
31AF ㆯ BOPOMOFO LETTER AUNN
31B0 ㆰ BOPOMOFO LETTER AM
31B1 ㆱ BOPOMOFO LETTER OM
31B2 ㆲ BOPOMOFO LETTER ONG
31B3 ㆳ BOPOMOFO LETTER INNN
31B4 ㆴ BOPOMOFO FINAL LETTER P
31B5 ㆵ BOPOMOFO FINAL LETTER T
31B6 ㆶ BOPOMOFO FINAL LETTER K
31B7 ㆷ BOPOMOFO FINAL LETTER H

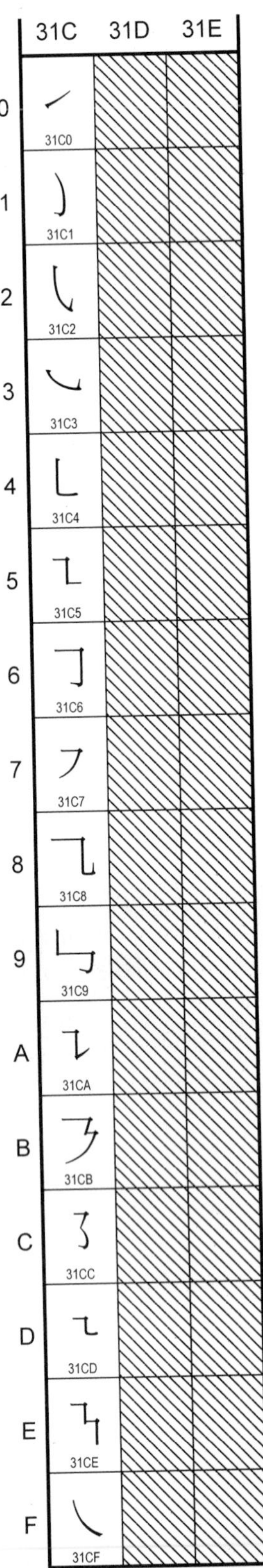

CJK strokes

31C0	㇀	CJK STROKE T
31C1	㇁	CJK STROKE WG
31C2	㇂	CJK STROKE XG
31C3	㇃	CJK STROKE BXG
31C4	㇄	CJK STROKE SW
31C5	㇅	CJK STROKE HZZ
31C6	㇆	CJK STROKE HZG
31C7	㇇	CJK STROKE HP
31C8	㇈	CJK STROKE HZWG
31C9	㇉	CJK STROKE SZWG
31CA	㇊	CJK STROKE HZT
31CB	㇋	CJK STROKE HZZP
31CC	㇌	CJK STROKE HPWG
31CD	㇍	CJK STROKE HZW
31CE	㇎	CJK STROKE HZZZ
31CF	㇏	CJK STROKE N

	31F
0	ㇰ 31F0
1	ㇱ 31F1
2	ㇲ 31F2
3	ㇳ 31F3
4	ㇴ 31F4
5	ㇵ 31F5
6	ㇶ 31F6
7	ㇷ 31F7
8	ㇸ 31F8
9	ㇹ 31F9
A	ㇺ 31FA
B	ㇻ 31FB
C	ㇼ 31FC
D	ㇽ 31FD
E	ㇾ 31FE
F	ㇿ 31FF

Phonetic extensions for Ainu

31F0 ㇰ KATAKANA LETTER SMALL KU
31F1 ㇱ KATAKANA LETTER SMALL SI
31F2 ㇲ KATAKANA LETTER SMALL SU
31F3 ㇳ KATAKANA LETTER SMALL TO
31F4 ㇴ KATAKANA LETTER SMALL NU
31F5 ㇵ KATAKANA LETTER SMALL HA
31F6 ㇶ KATAKANA LETTER SMALL HI
31F7 ㇷ KATAKANA LETTER SMALL HU
31F8 ㇸ KATAKANA LETTER SMALL HE
31F9 ㇹ KATAKANA LETTER SMALL HO
31FA ㇺ KATAKANA LETTER SMALL MU
31FB ㇻ KATAKANA LETTER SMALL RA
31FC ㇼ KATAKANA LETTER SMALL RI
31FD ㇽ KATAKANA LETTER SMALL RU
31FE ㇾ KATAKANA LETTER SMALL RE
31FF ㇿ KATAKANA LETTER SMALL RO

	320	321	322	323	324	325	326	327	328	329	32A	32B	32C	32D	32E	32F
0	㈀ 3200	㈐ 3210	㈠ 3220	㈰ 3230	㉀ 3240	㉐ 3250	㉠ 3260	㉰ 3270	㊀ 3280	㊐ 3290	㊠ 32A0	㊰ 32B0	㋀ 32C0	㋐ 32D0	㋠ 32E0	㋰ 32F0
1	㈁ 3201	㈑ 3211	㈡ 3221	㈱ 3231	㉁ 3241	㉑ 3251	㉡ 3261	㉱ 3271	㊁ 3281	㊑ 3291	㊡ 32A1	㊱ 32B1	㋁ 32C1	㋑ 32D1	㋡ 32E1	㋱ 32F1
2	㈂ 3202	㈒ 3212	㈢ 3222	㈲ 3232	㉂ 3242	㉒ 3252	㉢ 3262	㉲ 3272	㊂ 3282	㊒ 3292	㊢ 32A2	㊲ 32B2	㋂ 32C2	㋒ 32D2	㋢ 32E2	㋲ 32F2
3	㈃ 3203	㈓ 3213	㈣ 3223	㈳ 3233	㉃ 3243	㉓ 3253	㉣ 3263	㉳ 3273	㊃ 3283	㊓ 3293	㊣ 32A3	㊳ 32B3	㋃ 32C3	㋓ 32D3	㋣ 32E3	㋳ 32F3
4	㈄ 3204	㈔ 3214	㈤ 3224	㈴ 3234		㉔ 3254	㉤ 3264	㉴ 3274	㊄ 3284	㊔ 3294	㊤ 32A4	㊴ 32B4	㋄ 32C4	㋔ 32D4	㋤ 32E4	㋴ 32F4
5	㈅ 3205	㈕ 3215	㈥ 3225	㈵ 3235		㉕ 3255	㉥ 3265	㉵ 3275	㊅ 3285	㊕ 3295	㊥ 32A5	㊵ 32B5	㋅ 32C5	㋕ 32D5	㋥ 32E5	㋵ 32F5
6	㈆ 3206	㈖ 3216	㈦ 3226	㈶ 3236		㉖ 3256	㉦ 3266	㉶ 3276	㊆ 3286	㊖ 3296	㊦ 32A6	㊶ 32B6	㋆ 32C6	㋖ 32D6	㋦ 32E6	㋶ 32F6
7	㈇ 3207	㈗ 3217	㈧ 3227	㈷ 3237		㉗ 3257	㉧ 3267	㉷ 3277	㊇ 3287	㊗ 3297	㊧ 32A7	㊷ 32B7	㋇ 32C7	㋗ 32D7	㋧ 32E7	㋷ 32F7
8	㈈ 3208	㈘ 3218	㈨ 3228	㈸ 3238		㉘ 3258	㉨ 3268	㉸ 3278	㊈ 3288	㊘ 3298	㊨ 32A8	㊸ 32B8	㋈ 32C8	㋘ 32D8	㋨ 32E8	㋸ 32F8
9	㈉ 3209	㈙ 3219	㈩ 3229	㈹ 3239		㉙ 3259	㉩ 3269	㉹ 3279	㊉ 3289	㊙ 3299	㊩ 32A9	㊹ 32B9	㋉ 32C9	㋙ 32D9	㋩ 32E9	㋹ 32F9
A	㈊ 320A	㈚ 321A	㈪ 322A	㈺ 323A		㉚ 325A	㉪ 326A	㉺ 327A	㊊ 328A	㊚ 329A	㊪ 32AA	㊺ 32BA	㋊ 32CA	㋚ 32DA	㋪ 32EA	㋺ 32FA
B	㈋ 320B	㈛ 321B	㈫ 322B	㈻ 323B		㉛ 325B	㉫ 326B	㉻ 327B	㊋ 328B	㊛ 329B	㊫ 32AB	㊻ 32BB	㋋ 32CB	㋛ 32DB	㋫ 32EB	㋻ 32FB
C	㈌ 320C	㈜ 321C	㈬ 322C	㈼ 323C		㉜ 325C	㉬ 326C	㉼ 327C	㊌ 328C	㊜ 329C	㊬ 32AC	㊼ 32BC	㋌ 32CC	㋜ 32DC	㋬ 32EC	㋼ 32FC
D	㈍ 320D	㈝ 321D	㈭ 322D	㈽ 323D		㉝ 325D	㉭ 326D	㉽ 327D	㊍ 328D	㊝ 329D	㊭ 32AD	㊽ 32BD	㋍ 32CD	㋝ 32DD	㋭ 32ED	㋽ 32FD
E	㈎ 320E	㈞ 321E	㈮ 322E	㈾ 323E		㉞ 325E	㉮ 326E	㉾ 327E	㊎ 328E	㊞ 329E	㊮ 32AE	㊾ 32BE	㋎ 32CE	㋞ 32DE	㋮ 32EE	㋾ 32FE
F	㈏ 320F		㈯ 322F	㈿ 323F		㉟ 325F	㉯ 326F	㉿ 327F	㊏ 328F	㊟ 329F	㊯ 32AF	㊿ 32BF	㋏ 32CF	㋟ 32DF	㋯ 32EF	

Parenthesized Hangul elements

3200 ㈀ PARENTHESIZED HANGUL KIYEOK
≈ 0028 (1100 ᄀ 0029)
3201 ㈁ PARENTHESIZED HANGUL NIEUN
≈ 0028 (1102 ᄂ 0029)
3202 ㈂ PARENTHESIZED HANGUL TIKEUT
≈ 0028 (1103 ᄃ 0029)
3203 ㈃ PARENTHESIZED HANGUL RIEUL
≈ 0028 (1105 ᄅ 0029)
3204 ㈄ PARENTHESIZED HANGUL MIEUM
≈ 0028 (1106 ᄆ 0029)
3205 ㈅ PARENTHESIZED HANGUL PIEUP
≈ 0028 (1107 ᄇ 0029)
3206 ㈆ PARENTHESIZED HANGUL SIOS
≈ 0028 (1109 ᄉ 0029)
3207 ㈇ PARENTHESIZED HANGUL IEUNG
≈ 0028 (110B ᄋ 0029)
3208 ㈈ PARENTHESIZED HANGUL CIEUC
≈ 0028 (110C ᄌ 0029)
3209 ㈉ PARENTHESIZED HANGUL CHIEUCH
≈ 0028 (110E ᄎ 0029)
320A ㈊ PARENTHESIZED HANGUL KHIEUKH
≈ 0028 (110F ᄏ 0029)
320B ㈋ PARENTHESIZED HANGUL THIEUTH
≈ 0028 (1110 ᄐ 0029)
320C ㈌ PARENTHESIZED HANGUL PHIEUPH
≈ 0028 (1111 ᄑ 0029)
320D ㈍ PARENTHESIZED HANGUL HIEUH
≈ 0028 (1112 ᄒ 0029)

Parenthesized Hangul syllables

320E ㈎ PARENTHESIZED HANGUL KIYEOK A
≈ 0028 (1100 ᄀ 1161 ᅡ 0029)
320F ㈏ PARENTHESIZED HANGUL NIEUN A
≈ 0028 (1102 ᄂ 1161 ᅡ 0029)
3210 ㈐ PARENTHESIZED HANGUL TIKEUT A
≈ 0028 (1103 ᄃ 1161 ᅡ 0029)
3211 ㈑ PARENTHESIZED HANGUL RIEUL A
≈ 0028 (1105 ᄅ 1161 ᅡ 0029)
3212 ㈒ PARENTHESIZED HANGUL MIEUM A
≈ 0028 (1106 ᄆ 1161 ᅡ 0029)
3213 ㈓ PARENTHESIZED HANGUL PIEUP A
≈ 0028 (1107 ᄇ 1161 ᅡ 0029)
3214 ㈔ PARENTHESIZED HANGUL SIOS A
≈ 0028 (1109 ᄉ 1161 ᅡ 0029)
3215 ㈕ PARENTHESIZED HANGUL IEUNG A
≈ 0028 (110B ᄋ 1161 ᅡ 0029)
3216 ㈖ PARENTHESIZED HANGUL CIEUC A
≈ 0028 (110C ᄌ 1161 ᅡ 0029)
3217 ㈗ PARENTHESIZED HANGUL CHIEUCH A
≈ 0028 (110E ᄎ 1161 ᅡ 0029)
3218 ㈘ PARENTHESIZED HANGUL KHIEUKH A
≈ 0028 (110F ᄏ 1161 ᅡ 0029)
3219 ㈙ PARENTHESIZED HANGUL THIEUTH A
≈ 0028 (1110 ᄐ 1161 ᅡ 0029)
321A ㈚ PARENTHESIZED HANGUL PHIEUPH A
≈ 0028 (1111 ᄑ 1161 ᅡ 0029)
321B ㈛ PARENTHESIZED HANGUL HIEUH A
≈ 0028 (1112 ᄒ 1161 ᅡ 0029)
321C ㈜ PARENTHESIZED HANGUL CIEUC U
≈ 0028 (110C ᄌ 116E ᅮ 0029)

Parenthesized Korean words

321D ㈝ PARENTHESIZED KOREAN CHARACTER OJEON
≈ 0028 (110B ᄋ 1169 ᅩ 110C ᄌ 1165 ᅥ 11AB ᆫ 0029)
321E ㈞ PARENTHESIZED KOREAN CHARACTER O HU
≈ 0028 (110B ᄋ 1169 ᅩ 1112 ᄒ 116E ᅮ 0029)

Parenthesized ideographs

3220 ㈠ PARENTHESIZED IDEOGRAPH ONE
≈ 0028 (4E00 一 0029)
3221 ㈡ PARENTHESIZED IDEOGRAPH TWO
≈ 0028 (4E8C 二 0029)
3222 ㈢ PARENTHESIZED IDEOGRAPH THREE
≈ 0028 (4E09 三 0029)
3223 ㈣ PARENTHESIZED IDEOGRAPH FOUR
≈ 0028 (56DB 四 0029)
3224 ㈤ PARENTHESIZED IDEOGRAPH FIVE
≈ 0028 (4E94 五 0029)
3225 ㈥ PARENTHESIZED IDEOGRAPH SIX
≈ 0028 (516D 六 0029)
3226 ㈦ PARENTHESIZED IDEOGRAPH SEVEN
≈ 0028 (4E03 七 0029)
3227 ㈧ PARENTHESIZED IDEOGRAPH EIGHT
≈ 0028 (516B 八 0029)
3228 ㈨ PARENTHESIZED IDEOGRAPH NINE
≈ 0028 (4E5D 九 0029)
3229 ㈩ PARENTHESIZED IDEOGRAPH TEN
≈ 0028 (5341 十 0029)
322A ㈪ PARENTHESIZED IDEOGRAPH MOON
• Monday
≈ 0028 (6708 月 0029)
322B ㈫ PARENTHESIZED IDEOGRAPH FIRE
• Tuesday
≈ 0028 (706B 火 0029)
322C ㈬ PARENTHESIZED IDEOGRAPH WATER
• Wednesday
≈ 0028 (6C34 水 0029)
322D ㈭ PARENTHESIZED IDEOGRAPH WOOD
• Thursday
≈ 0028 (6728 木 0029)
322E ㈮ PARENTHESIZED IDEOGRAPH METAL
• Friday
≈ 0028 (91D1 金 0029)
322F ㈯ PARENTHESIZED IDEOGRAPH EARTH
• Saturday
≈ 0028 (571F 土 0029)
3230 ㈰ PARENTHESIZED IDEOGRAPH SUN
• Sunday
≈ 0028 (65E5 日 0029)
3231 ㈱ PARENTHESIZED IDEOGRAPH STOCK
• incorporated
≈ 0028 (682A 株 0029)
3232 ㈲ PARENTHESIZED IDEOGRAPH HAVE
• limited
≈ 0028 (6709 有 0029)
3233 ㈳ PARENTHESIZED IDEOGRAPH SOCIETY
• company
≈ 0028 (793E 社 0029)
3234 ㈴ PARENTHESIZED IDEOGRAPH NAME
≈ 0028 (540D 名 0029)
3235 ㈵ PARENTHESIZED IDEOGRAPH SPECIAL
≈ 0028 (7279 特 0029)

3236 ㈶ PARENTHESIZED IDEOGRAPH FINANCIAL
≈ 0028 (8CA1 財 0029)

3237 ㈷ PARENTHESIZED IDEOGRAPH CONGRATULATION
≈ 0028 (795D 祝 0029)

3238 ㈸ PARENTHESIZED IDEOGRAPH LABOR
≈ 0028 (52B4 労 0029)

3239 ㈹ PARENTHESIZED IDEOGRAPH REPRESENT
≈ 0028 (4EE3 代 0029)

323A ㈺ PARENTHESIZED IDEOGRAPH CALL
≈ 0028 (547C 呼 0029)

323B ㈻ PARENTHESIZED IDEOGRAPH STUDY
≈ 0028 (5B66 学 0029)

323C ㈼ PARENTHESIZED IDEOGRAPH SUPERVISE
≈ 0028 (76E3 監 0029)

323D ㈽ PARENTHESIZED IDEOGRAPH ENTERPRISE
≈ 0028 (4F01 企 0029)

323E ㈾ PARENTHESIZED IDEOGRAPH RESOURCE
≈ 0028 (8CC7 資 0029)

323F ㈿ PARENTHESIZED IDEOGRAPH ALLIANCE
≈ 0028 (5354 協 0029)

3240 ㉀ PARENTHESIZED IDEOGRAPH FESTIVAL
≈ 0028 (796D 祭 0029)

3241 ㉁ PARENTHESIZED IDEOGRAPH REST
≈ 0028 (4F11 休 0029)

3242 ㉂ PARENTHESIZED IDEOGRAPH SELF
• from
≈ 0028 (81EA 自 0029)

3243 ㉃ PARENTHESIZED IDEOGRAPH REACH
• to
≈ 0028 (81F3 至 0029)

Squared Latin abbreviation

3250 ㉐ PARTNERSHIP SIGN
≈ <square> 0050 P 0054 T 0045 E

Circled numbers

3251 ㉑ CIRCLED NUMBER TWENTY ONE
≈ <circle> 0032 2 0031 1

3252 ㉒ CIRCLED NUMBER TWENTY TWO
≈ <circle> 0032 2 0032 2

3253 ㉓ CIRCLED NUMBER TWENTY THREE
≈ <circle> 0032 2 0033 3

3254 ㉔ CIRCLED NUMBER TWENTY FOUR
≈ <circle> 0032 2 0034 4

3255 ㉕ CIRCLED NUMBER TWENTY FIVE
≈ <circle> 0032 2 0035 5

3256 ㉖ CIRCLED NUMBER TWENTY SIX
≈ <circle> 0032 2 0036 6

3257 ㉗ CIRCLED NUMBER TWENTY SEVEN
≈ <circle> 0032 2 0037 7

3258 ㉘ CIRCLED NUMBER TWENTY EIGHT
≈ <circle> 0032 2 0038 8

3259 ㉙ CIRCLED NUMBER TWENTY NINE
≈ <circle> 0032 2 0039 9

325A ㉚ CIRCLED NUMBER THIRTY
≈ <circle> 0033 3 0030 0

325B ㉛ CIRCLED NUMBER THIRTY ONE
≈ <circle> 0033 3 0031 1

325C ㉜ CIRCLED NUMBER THIRTY TWO
≈ <circle> 0033 3 0032 2

325D ㉝ CIRCLED NUMBER THIRTY THREE
≈ <circle> 0033 3 0033 3

325E ㉞ CIRCLED NUMBER THIRTY FOUR
≈ <circle> 0033 3 0034 4

325F ㉟ CIRCLED NUMBER THIRTY FIVE
≈ <circle> 0033 3 0035 5

Circled Hangul elements

3260 ㉠ CIRCLED HANGUL KIYEOK
≈ <circle> 1100 ᄀ

3261 ㉡ CIRCLED HANGUL NIEUN
≈ <circle> 1102 ᄂ

3262 ㉢ CIRCLED HANGUL TIKEUT
≈ <circle> 1103 ᄃ

3263 ㉣ CIRCLED HANGUL RIEUL
≈ <circle> 1105 ᄅ

3264 ㉤ CIRCLED HANGUL MIEUM
≈ <circle> 1106 ᄆ

3265 ㉥ CIRCLED HANGUL PIEUP
≈ <circle> 1107 ᄇ

3266 ㉦ CIRCLED HANGUL SIOS
≈ <circle> 1109 ᄉ

3267 ㉧ CIRCLED HANGUL IEUNG
≈ <circle> 110B ᄋ

3268 ㉨ CIRCLED HANGUL CIEUC
≈ <circle> 110C ᄌ

3269 ㉩ CIRCLED HANGUL CHIEUCH
≈ <circle> 110E ᄎ

326A ㉪ CIRCLED HANGUL KHIEUKH
≈ <circle> 110F ᄏ

326B ㉫ CIRCLED HANGUL THIEUTH
≈ <circle> 1110 ᄐ

326C ㉬ CIRCLED HANGUL PHIEUPH
≈ <circle> 1111 ᄑ

326D ㉭ CIRCLED HANGUL HIEUH
≈ <circle> 1112 ᄒ

Circled Hangul syllables

326E ㉮ CIRCLED HANGUL KIYEOK A
≈ <circle> 1100 ᄀ 1161 ᅡ

326F ㉯ CIRCLED HANGUL NIEUN A
≈ <circle> 1102 ᄂ 1161 ᅡ

3270 ㉰ CIRCLED HANGUL TIKEUT A
≈ <circle> 1103 ᄃ 1161 ᅡ

3271 ㉱ CIRCLED HANGUL RIEUL A
≈ <circle> 1105 ᄅ 1161 ᅡ

3272 ㉲ CIRCLED HANGUL MIEUM A
≈ <circle> 1106 ᄆ 1161 ᅡ

3273 ㉳ CIRCLED HANGUL PIEUP A
≈ <circle> 1107 ᄇ 1161 ᅡ

3274 ㉴ CIRCLED HANGUL SIOS A
≈ <circle> 1109 ᄉ 1161 ᅡ

3275 ㉵ CIRCLED HANGUL IEUNG A
≈ <circle> 110B ᄋ 1161 ᅡ

3276 ㉶ CIRCLED HANGUL CIEUC A
≈ <circle> 110C ᄌ 1161 ᅡ

3277 ㉷ CIRCLED HANGUL CHIEUCH A
≈ <circle> 110E ᄎ 1161 ᅡ

3278 ㉸ CIRCLED HANGUL KHIEUKH A
≈ <circle> 110F ᄏ 1161 ᅡ

3279 ㉹ CIRCLED HANGUL THIEUTH A
≈ <circle> 1110 ᄐ 1161 ᅡ

327A ㉺ CIRCLED HANGUL PHIEUPH A
≈ <circle> 1111 ᄑ 1161 ᅡ

327B ㉻ CIRCLED HANGUL HIEUH A
≈ <circle> 1112 ᄒ 1161 ᅡ

Circled Korean words

327C ㉼ CIRCLED KOREAN CHARACTER CHAMKO
≈ <circle> 110E ᄎ 1161 ᅡ 11B7 ᆷ 1100 ᄀ 1169 ᅩ

327D ㉽ CIRCLED KOREAN CHARACTER JUEUI
≈ <circle> 110C ᄌ 116E ᅮ 110B ᄋ 1174 ᅴ

Circled Hangul syllable

327E ㉾ CIRCLED HANGUL IEUNG U
• postal code mark
≈ <circle> 110B ᄋ 116E ᅮ

Symbol

327F ㉿ KOREAN STANDARD SYMBOL

Circled ideographs

3280 ㊀ CIRCLED IDEOGRAPH ONE
= maru-iti, symbol of unification
≈ <circle> 4E00 一

3281 ㊁ CIRCLED IDEOGRAPH TWO
≈ <circle> 4E8C 二

3282 ㊂ CIRCLED IDEOGRAPH THREE
≈ <circle> 4E09 三

3283 ㊃ CIRCLED IDEOGRAPH FOUR
≈ <circle> 56DB 四

3284 ㊄ CIRCLED IDEOGRAPH FIVE
≈ <circle> 4E94 五

3285 ㊅ CIRCLED IDEOGRAPH SIX
≈ <circle> 516D 六

3286 ㊆ CIRCLED IDEOGRAPH SEVEN
≈ <circle> 4E03 七

3287 ㊇ CIRCLED IDEOGRAPH EIGHT
≈ <circle> 516B 八

3288 ㊈ CIRCLED IDEOGRAPH NINE
≈ <circle> 4E5D 九

3289 ㊉ CIRCLED IDEOGRAPH TEN
≈ <circle> 5341 十

328A ㊊ CIRCLED IDEOGRAPH MOON
• Monday
≈ <circle> 6708 月

328B ㊋ CIRCLED IDEOGRAPH FIRE
• Tuesday
≈ <circle> 706B 火

328C ㊌ CIRCLED IDEOGRAPH WATER
• Wednesday
≈ <circle> 6C34 水

328D ㊍ CIRCLED IDEOGRAPH WOOD
• Thursday
≈ <circle> 6728 木

328E ㊎ CIRCLED IDEOGRAPH METAL
• Friday
≈ <circle> 91D1 金

328F ㊏ CIRCLED IDEOGRAPH EARTH
• Saturday
≈ <circle> 571F 土

3290 ㊐ CIRCLED IDEOGRAPH SUN
• Sunday
≈ <circle> 65E5 日

3291 ㊑ CIRCLED IDEOGRAPH STOCK
• incorporated
≈ <circle> 682A 株

3292 ㊒ CIRCLED IDEOGRAPH HAVE
• limited
≈ <circle> 6709 有

3293 ㊓ CIRCLED IDEOGRAPH SOCIETY
• company
≈ <circle> 793E 社

3294 ㊔ CIRCLED IDEOGRAPH NAME
≈ <circle> 540D 名

3295 ㊕ CIRCLED IDEOGRAPH SPECIAL
≈ <circle> 7279 特

3296 ㊖ CIRCLED IDEOGRAPH FINANCIAL
≈ <circle> 8CA1 財

3297 ㊗ CIRCLED IDEOGRAPH CONGRATULATION
≈ <circle> 795D 祝

3298 ㊘ CIRCLED IDEOGRAPH LABOR
≈ <circle> 52B4 労

3299 ㊙ CIRCLED IDEOGRAPH SECRET
≈ <circle> 79D8 秘

329A ㊚ CIRCLED IDEOGRAPH MALE
≈ <circle> 7537 男

329B ㊛ CIRCLED IDEOGRAPH FEMALE
≈ <circle> 5973 女

329C ㊜ CIRCLED IDEOGRAPH SUITABLE
≈ <circle> 9069 適

329D ㊝ CIRCLED IDEOGRAPH EXCELLENT
≈ <circle> 512A 優

329E ㊞ CIRCLED IDEOGRAPH PRINT
• name seal
≈ <circle> 5370 印

329F ㊟ CIRCLED IDEOGRAPH ATTENTION
≈ <circle> 6CE8 注

32A0 ㊠ CIRCLED IDEOGRAPH ITEM
≈ <circle> 9805 項

32A1 ㊡ CIRCLED IDEOGRAPH REST
• holiday
≈ <circle> 4F11 休

32A2 ㊢ CIRCLED IDEOGRAPH COPY
≈ <circle> 5199 写

32A3 ㊣ CIRCLED IDEOGRAPH CORRECT
≈ <circle> 6B63 正

32A4 ㊤ CIRCLED IDEOGRAPH HIGH
≈ <circle> 4E0A 上

32A5 ㊥ CIRCLED IDEOGRAPH CENTRE
≈ <circle> 4E2D 中

32A6 ㊦ CIRCLED IDEOGRAPH LOW
≈ <circle> 4E0B 下

32A7 ㊧ CIRCLED IDEOGRAPH LEFT
≈ <circle> 5DE6 左

32A8 ㊨ CIRCLED IDEOGRAPH RIGHT
≈ <circle> 53F3 右

32A9 ㊩ CIRCLED IDEOGRAPH MEDICINE
≈ <circle> 533B 医

32AA ㊪ CIRCLED IDEOGRAPH RELIGION
≈ <circle> 5B97 宗

32AB ㊫ CIRCLED IDEOGRAPH STUDY
≈ <circle> 5B66 学

32AC ㊬ CIRCLED IDEOGRAPH SUPERVISE
≈ <circle> 76E3 監

32AD ㊭ CIRCLED IDEOGRAPH ENTERPRISE
≈ <circle> 4F01 企

32AE ㊮ CIRCLED IDEOGRAPH RESOURCE
≈ <circle> 8CC7 資

32AF ㊯ CIRCLED IDEOGRAPH ALLIANCE
≈ <circle> 5354 協

32B0 ㊰ CIRCLED IDEOGRAPH NIGHT
≈ <circle> 591C 夜

Circled numbers

32B1 ㊱ CIRCLED NUMBER THIRTY SIX
≈ <circle> 0033 3 0036 6
32B2 ㊲ CIRCLED NUMBER THIRTY SEVEN
≈ <circle> 0033 3 0037 7
32B3 ㊳ CIRCLED NUMBER THIRTY EIGHT
≈ <circle> 0033 3 0038 8
32B4 ㊴ CIRCLED NUMBER THIRTY NINE
≈ <circle> 0033 3 0039 9
32B5 ㊵ CIRCLED NUMBER FORTY
≈ <circle> 0034 4 0030 0
32B6 ㊶ CIRCLED NUMBER FORTY ONE
≈ <circle> 0034 4 0031 1
32B7 ㊷ CIRCLED NUMBER FORTY TWO
≈ <circle> 0034 4 0032 2
32B8 ㊸ CIRCLED NUMBER FORTY THREE
≈ <circle> 0034 4 0033 3
32B9 ㊹ CIRCLED NUMBER FORTY FOUR
≈ <circle> 0034 4 0034 4
32BA ㊺ CIRCLED NUMBER FORTY FIVE
≈ <circle> 0034 4 0035 5
32BB ㊻ CIRCLED NUMBER FORTY SIX
≈ <circle> 0034 4 0036 6
32BC ㊼ CIRCLED NUMBER FORTY SEVEN
≈ <circle> 0034 4 0037 7
32BD ㊽ CIRCLED NUMBER FORTY EIGHT
≈ <circle> 0034 4 0038 8
32BE ㊾ CIRCLED NUMBER FORTY NINE
≈ <circle> 0034 4 0039 9
32BF ㊿ CIRCLED NUMBER FIFTY
≈ <circle> 0035 5 0030 0

Telegraph symbols for months

32C0 ㋀ IDEOGRAPHIC TELEGRAPH SYMBOL FOR JANUARY
≈ 0031 1 6708 月
32C1 ㋁ IDEOGRAPHIC TELEGRAPH SYMBOL FOR FEBRUARY
≈ 0032 2 6708 月
32C2 ㋂ IDEOGRAPHIC TELEGRAPH SYMBOL FOR MARCH
≈ 0033 3 6708 月
32C3 ㋃ IDEOGRAPHIC TELEGRAPH SYMBOL FOR APRIL
≈ 0034 4 6708 月
32C4 ㋄ IDEOGRAPHIC TELEGRAPH SYMBOL FOR MAY
≈ 0035 5 6708 月
32C5 ㋅ IDEOGRAPHIC TELEGRAPH SYMBOL FOR JUNE
≈ 0036 6 6708 月
32C6 ㋆ IDEOGRAPHIC TELEGRAPH SYMBOL FOR JULY
≈ 0037 7 6708 月
32C7 ㋇ IDEOGRAPHIC TELEGRAPH SYMBOL FOR AUGUST
≈ 0038 8 6708 月
32C8 ㋈ IDEOGRAPHIC TELEGRAPH SYMBOL FOR SEPTEMBER
≈ 0039 9 6708 月
32C9 ㋉ IDEOGRAPHIC TELEGRAPH SYMBOL FOR OCTOBER
≈ 0031 1 0030 0 6708 月
32CA ㋊ IDEOGRAPHIC TELEGRAPH SYMBOL FOR NOVEMBER
≈ 0031 1 0031 1 6708 月
32CB ㋋ IDEOGRAPHIC TELEGRAPH SYMBOL FOR DECEMBER
≈ 0031 1 0032 2 6708 月

Squared Latin abbreviations

32CC ㋌ SQUARE HG
≈ <square> 0048 H 0067 g
32CD ㋍ SQUARE ERG
≈ <square> 0065 e 0072 r 0067 g
32CE ㋎ SQUARE EV
≈ <square> 0065 e 0056 V
32CF ㋏ LIMITED LIABILITY SIGN
≈ <square> 004C L 0054 T 0044 D

Circled Katakana

32D0 ㋐ CIRCLED KATAKANA A
≈ <circle> 30A2 ア
32D1 ㋑ CIRCLED KATAKANA I
≈ <circle> 30A4 イ
32D2 ㋒ CIRCLED KATAKANA U
≈ <circle> 30A6 ウ
32D3 ㋓ CIRCLED KATAKANA E
≈ <circle> 30A8 エ
32D4 ㋔ CIRCLED KATAKANA O
≈ <circle> 30AA オ
32D5 ㋕ CIRCLED KATAKANA KA
≈ <circle> 30AB カ
32D6 ㋖ CIRCLED KATAKANA KI
≈ <circle> 30AD キ
32D7 ㋗ CIRCLED KATAKANA KU
≈ <circle> 30AF ク
32D8 ㋘ CIRCLED KATAKANA KE
≈ <circle> 30B1 ケ
32D9 ㋙ CIRCLED KATAKANA KO
≈ <circle> 30B3 コ
32DA ㋚ CIRCLED KATAKANA SA
≈ <circle> 30B5 サ
32DB ㋛ CIRCLED KATAKANA SI
≈ <circle> 30B7 シ
32DC ㋜ CIRCLED KATAKANA SU
≈ <circle> 30B9 ス
32DD ㋝ CIRCLED KATAKANA SE
≈ <circle> 30BB セ
32DE ㋞ CIRCLED KATAKANA SO
≈ <circle> 30BD ソ
32DF ㋟ CIRCLED KATAKANA TA
≈ <circle> 30BF タ
32E0 ㋠ CIRCLED KATAKANA TI
≈ <circle> 30C1 チ
32E1 ㋡ CIRCLED KATAKANA TU
≈ <circle> 30C4 ツ
32E2 ㋢ CIRCLED KATAKANA TE
≈ <circle> 30C6 テ
32E3 ㋣ CIRCLED KATAKANA TO
≈ <circle> 30C8 ト
32E4 ㋤ CIRCLED KATAKANA NA
≈ <circle> 30CA ナ
32E5 ㋥ CIRCLED KATAKANA NI
≈ <circle> 30CB ニ
32E6 ㋦ CIRCLED KATAKANA NU
≈ <circle> 30CC ヌ
32E7 ㋧ CIRCLED KATAKANA NE
≈ <circle> 30CD ネ
32E8 ㋨ CIRCLED KATAKANA NO
≈ <circle> 30CE ノ
32E9 ㋩ CIRCLED KATAKANA HA
≈ <circle> 30CF ハ

32EA ㋪ CIRCLED KATAKANA HI
≈ <circle> 30D2 ヒ
32EB ㋫ CIRCLED KATAKANA HU
≈ <circle> 30D5 フ
32EC ㋬ CIRCLED KATAKANA HE
≈ <circle> 30D8 ヘ
32ED ㋭ CIRCLED KATAKANA HO
≈ <circle> 30DB ホ
32EE ㋮ CIRCLED KATAKANA MA
≈ <circle> 30DE マ
32EF ㋯ CIRCLED KATAKANA MI
≈ <circle> 30DF ミ
32F0 ㋰ CIRCLED KATAKANA MU
≈ <circle> 30E0 ム
32F1 ㋱ CIRCLED KATAKANA ME
≈ <circle> 30E1 メ
32F2 ㋲ CIRCLED KATAKANA MO
≈ <circle> 30E2 モ
32F3 ㋳ CIRCLED KATAKANA YA
≈ <circle> 30E4 ヤ
32F4 ㋴ CIRCLED KATAKANA YU
≈ <circle> 30E6 ユ
32F5 ㋵ CIRCLED KATAKANA YO
≈ <circle> 30E8 ヨ
32F6 ㋶ CIRCLED KATAKANA RA
≈ <circle> 30E9 ラ
32F7 ㋷ CIRCLED KATAKANA RI
≈ <circle> 30EA リ
32F8 ㋸ CIRCLED KATAKANA RU
≈ <circle> 30EB ル
32F9 ㋹ CIRCLED KATAKANA RE
≈ <circle> 30EC レ
32FA ㋺ CIRCLED KATAKANA RO
≈ <circle> 30ED ロ
32FB ㋻ CIRCLED KATAKANA WA
≈ <circle> 30EF ワ
32FC ㋼ CIRCLED KATAKANA WI
≈ <circle> 30F0 ヰ
32FD ㋽ CIRCLED KATAKANA WE
≈ <circle> 30F1 ヱ
32FE ㋾ CIRCLED KATAKANA WO
≈ <circle> 30F2 ヲ

	330	331	332	333	334	335	336	337	338	339	33A	33B	33C	33D	33E	33F
0	アパート 3300	ギガ 3310	サンチーム 3320	ピコ 3330	ポンド 3340	ユアン 3350	8点 3360	24点 3370	pA 3380	Hz 3390	cm^2 33A0	ps 33B0	kΩ 33C0	lm 33D0	1日 33E0	17日 33F0
1	アルファ 3301	ギニー 3311	シリング 3321	ビル 3331	ホール 3341	リットル 3351	9点 3361	hPa 3371	nA 3381	kHz 3391	m^2 33A1	ns 33B1	MΩ 33C1	ln 33D1	2日 33E1	18日 33F1
2	アンペア 3302	キュリー 3312	センチ 3322	ファラッド 3332	ホーン 3342	リラ 3352	10点 3362	da 3372	μA 3382	MHz 3392	km^2 33A2	μs 33B2	a.m. 33C2	log 33D2	3日 33E2	19日 33F2
3	アール 3303	ギルダー 3313	セント 3323	フィート 3333	マイクロ 3343	ルピー 3353	11点 3363	AU 3373	mA 3383	GHz 3393	mm^3 33A3	ms 33B3	Bq 33C3	lx 33D3	4日 33E3	20日 33F3
4	イニング 3304	キロ 3314	ダース 3324	ブッシェル 3334	マイル 3344	ルーブル 3354	12点 3364	bar 3374	kA 3384	THz 3394	cm^3 33A4	pV 33B4	cc 33C4	mb 33D4	5日 33E4	21日 33F4
5	インチ 3305	キログラム 3315	デシ 3325	フラン 3335	マッハ 3345	レム 3355	13点 3365	oV 3375	KB 3385	μℓ 3395	m^3 33A5	nV 33B5	cd 33C5	mil 33D5	6日 33E5	22日 33F5
6	ウオン 3306	キロメートル 3316	ドル 3326	ヘクタール 3336	マルク 3346	レントゲン 3356	14点 3366	pc 3376	MB 3386	mℓ 3396	km^3 33A6	μV 33B6	C/kg 33C6	mol 33D6	7日 33E6	23日 33F6
7	エスクード 3307	キロワット 3317	トン 3327	ペソ 3337	マンション 3347	ワット 3357	15点 3367	dm 3377	GB 3387	dℓ 3397	m/s 33A7	mV 33B7	Co. 33C7	pH 33D7	8日 33E7	24日 33F7
8	エーカー 3308	グラム 3318	ナノ 3328	ペニヒ 3338	ミクロン 3348	0点 3358	16点 3368	dm^2 3378	cal 3388	kℓ 3398	m/s^2 33A8	kV 33B8	dB 33C8	p.m. 33D8	9日 33E8	25日 33F8
9	オンス 3309	グラムトン 3319	ノット 3329	ヘルツ 3339	ミリ 3349	1点 3359	17点 3369	dm^3 3379	kcal 3389	fm 3399	Pa 33A9	MV 33B9	Gy 33C9	PPM 33D9	10日 33E9	26日 33F9
A	オーム 330A	クルゼイロ 331A	ハイツ 332A	ペンス 333A	ミリバール 334A	2点 335A	18点 336A	IU 337A	pF 338A	nm 339A	kPa 33AA	pW 33BA	ha 33CA	PR 33DA	11日 33EA	27日 33FA
B	カイリ 330B	クローネ 331B	パーセント 332B	ページ 333B	メガ 334B	3点 335B	19点 336B	平成 337B	nF 338B	μm 339B	MPa 33AB	nW 33BB	HP 33CB	sr 33DB	12日 33EB	28日 33FB
C	カラット 330C	ケース 331C	パーツ 332C	ベータ 333C	メガトン 334C	4点 335C	20点 336C	昭和 337C	μF 338C	mm 339C	GPa 33AC	μW 33BC	in 33CC	Sv 33DC	13日 33EC	29日 33FC
D	カロリー 330D	コルナ 331D	バーレル 332D	ポイント 333D	メートル 334D	5点 335D	21点 336D	大正 337D	μg 338D	cm 339D	rad 33AD	mW 33BD	K.K. 33CD	Wb 33DD	14日 33ED	30日 33FD
E	ガロン 330E	コーポ 331E	ピアストル 332E	ボルト 333E	ヤード 334E	6点 335E	22点 336E	明治 337E	mg 338E	km 339E	rad/s 33AE	kW 33BE	KM 33CE	V/m 33DE	15日 33EE	31日 33FE
F	ガンマ 330F	サイクル 331F	ピクル 332F	ホン 333F	ヤール 334F	7点 335F	23点 336F	株式会社 337F	kg 338F	mm^2 339F	rad/s^2 33AF	MW 33BF	kt 33CF	A/m 33DF	16日 33EF	gal 33FF

Squared Katakana words

3300 ㌀ SQUARE APAATO
• apartment
≈ <square> 30A2 ア 30D1 パ 30FC ー 30C8 ト

3301 ㌁ SQUARE ARUHUA
• alpha
≈ <square> 30A2 ア 30EB ル 30D5 フ 30A1 ァ

3302 ㌂ SQUARE ANPEA
• ampere
≈ <square> 30A2 ア 30F3 ン 30DA ペ 30A2 ア

3303 ㌃ SQUARE AARU
• are (unit of area)
≈ <square> 30A2 ア 30FC ー 30EB ル

3304 ㌄ SQUARE ININGU
• inning
≈ <square> 30A4 イ 30CB ニ 30F3 ン 30B0 グ

3305 ㌅ SQUARE INTI
• inch
≈ <square> 30A4 イ 30F3 ン 30C1 チ

3306 ㌆ SQUARE UON
• won (Korean currency)
≈ <square> 30A6 ウ 30A9 ォ 30F3 ン

3307 ㌇ SQUARE ESUKUUDO
• escudo (Portuguese currency)
≈ <square> 30A8 エ 30B9 ス 30AF ク 30FC ー 30C9 ド

3308 ㌈ SQUARE EEKAA
• acre
≈ <square> 30A8 エ 30FC ー 30AB カ 30FC ー

3309 ㌉ SQUARE ONSU
• ounce
≈ <square> 30AA オ 30F3 ン 30B9 ス

330A ㌊ SQUARE OOMU
• ohm
≈ <square> 30AA オ 30FC ー 30E0 ム

330B ㌋ SQUARE KAIRI
• kai-ri: nautical mile
≈ <square> 30AB カ 30A4 イ 30EA リ

330C ㌌ SQUARE KARATTO
• carat
≈ <square> 30AB カ 30E9 ラ 30C3 ッ 30C8 ト

330D ㌍ SQUARE KARORII
• calorie
≈ <square> 30AB カ 30ED ロ 30EA リ 30FC ー

330E ㌎ SQUARE GARON
• gallon
≈ <square> 30AC ガ 30ED ロ 30F3 ン

330F ㌏ SQUARE GANMA
• gamma
≈ <square> 30AC ガ 30F3 ン 30DE マ

3310 ㌐ SQUARE GIGA
• giga-
≈ <square> 30AE ギ 30AC ガ

3311 ㌑ SQUARE GINII
• guinea
≈ <square> 30AE ギ 30CB ニ 30FC ー

3312 ㌒ SQUARE KYURII
• curie
≈ <square> 30AD キ 30E5 ュ 30EA リ 30FC ー

3313 ㌓ SQUARE GIRUDAA
• guilder
≈ <square> 30AE ギ 30EB ル 30C0 ダ 30FC ー

3314 ㌔ SQUARE KIRO
• kilo-
≈ <square> 30AD キ 30ED ロ

3315 ㌕ SQUARE KIROGURAMU
• kilogram
≈ <square> 30AD キ 30ED ロ 30B0 グ 30E9 ラ 30E0 ム

3316 ㌖ SQUARE KIROMEETORU
• kilometer
≈ <square> 30AD キ 30ED ロ 30E1 メ 30FC ー 30C8 ト 30EB ル

3317 ㌗ SQUARE KIROWATTO
• kilowatt
≈ <square> 30AD キ 30ED ロ 30EF ワ 30C3 ッ 30C8 ト

3318 ㌘ SQUARE GURAMU
• gram
≈ <square> 30B0 グ 30E9 ラ 30E0 ム

3319 ㌙ SQUARE GURAMUTON
• gram ton
≈ <square> 30B0 グ 30E9 ラ 30E0 ム 30C8 ト 30F3 ン

331A ㌚ SQUARE KURUZEIRO
• cruzeiro (Brazilian currency)
≈ <square> 30AF ク 30EB ル 30BC ゼ 30A4 イ 30ED ロ

331B ㌛ SQUARE KUROONE
• krone
≈ <square> 30AF ク 30ED ロ 30FC ー 30CD ネ

331C ㌜ SQUARE KEESU
• case
≈ <square> 30B1 ケ 30FC ー 30B9 ス

331D ㌝ SQUARE KORUNA
• koruna (Czech currency)
≈ <square> 30B3 コ 30EB ル 30CA ナ

331E ㌞ SQUARE KOOPO
• co-op
≈ <square> 30B3 コ 30FC ー 30DD ポ

331F ㌟ SQUARE SAIKURU
• cycle
≈ <square> 30B5 サ 30A4 イ 30AF ク 30EB ル

3320 ㌠ SQUARE SANTIIMU
• centime
≈ <square> 30B5 サ 30F3 ン 30C1 チ 30FC ー 30E0 ム

3321 ㌡ SQUARE SIRINGU
• shilling
≈ <square> 30B7 シ 30EA リ 30F3 ン 30B0 グ

3322 ㌢ SQUARE SENTI
• centi-
≈ <square> 30BB セ 30F3 ン 30C1 チ

3323 ㌣ **SQUARE SENTO**
• cent
≈ <square> 30BB セ 30F3 ン 30C8 ト

3324 ㌤ **SQUARE DAASU**
• dozen
≈ <square> 30C0 ダ 30FC ー 30B9 ス

3325 ㌥ **SQUARE DESI**
• deci-
≈ <square> 30C7 デ 30B7 シ

3326 ㌦ **SQUARE DORU**
• dollar
≈ <square> 30C9 ド 30EB ル

3327 ㌧ **SQUARE TON**
• ton
≈ <square> 30C8 ト 30F3 ン

3328 ㌨ **SQUARE NANO**
• nano-
≈ <square> 30CA ナ 30CE ノ

3329 ㌩ **SQUARE NOTTO**
• knot, nautical mile
≈ <square> 30CE ノ 30C3 ッ 30C8 ト

332A ㌪ **SQUARE HAITU**
• heights
≈ <square> 30CF ハ 30A4 イ 30C4 ツ

332B ㌫ **SQUARE PAASENTO**
• percent
≈ <square> 30D1 パ 30FC ー 30BB セ 30F3 ン 30C8 ト

332C ㌬ **SQUARE PAATU**
• parts
≈ <square> 30D1 パ 30FC ー 30C4 ツ

332D ㌭ **SQUARE BAARERU**
• barrel
≈ <square> 30D0 バ 30FC ー 30EC レ 30EB ル

332E ㌮ **SQUARE PIASUTORU**
• piaster
≈ <square> 30D4 ピ 30A2 ア 30B9 ス 30C8 ト 30EB ル

332F ㌯ **SQUARE PIKURU**
• picul (unit of weight)
≈ <square> 30D4 ピ 30AF ク 30EB ル

3330 ㌰ **SQUARE PIKO**
• pico-
≈ <square> 30D4 ピ 30B3 コ

3331 ㌱ **SQUARE BIRU**
• building
≈ <square> 30D3 ビ 30EB ル

3332 ㌲ **SQUARE HUARADDO**
• farad
≈ <square> 30D5 フ 30A1 ァ 30E9 ラ 30C3 ッ 30C9 ド

3333 ㌳ **SQUARE HUIITO**
• feet
≈ <square> 30D5 フ 30A3 ィ 30FC ー 30C8 ト

3334 ㌴ **SQUARE BUSSYERU**
• bushel
≈ <square> 30D6 ブ 30C3 ッ 30B7 シ 30A7 ェ 30EB ル

3335 ㌵ **SQUARE HURAN**
• franc
≈ <square> 30D5 フ 30E9 ラ 30F3 ン

3336 ㌶ **SQUARE HEKUTAARU**
• hectare
≈ <square> 30D8 ヘ 30AF ク 30BF タ 30FC ー 30EB ル

3337 ㌷ **SQUARE PESO**
• peso
≈ <square> 30DA ペ 30BD ソ

3338 ㌸ **SQUARE PENIHI**
• pfennig
≈ <square> 30DA ペ 30CB ニ 30D2 ヒ

3339 ㌹ **SQUARE HERUTU**
• hertz
≈ <square> 30D8 ヘ 30EB ル 30C4 ツ

333A ㌺ **SQUARE PENSU**
• pence
≈ <square> 30DA ペ 30F3 ン 30B9 ス

333B ㌻ **SQUARE PEEZI**
• page
≈ <square> 30DA ペ 30FC ー 30B8 ジ

333C ㌼ **SQUARE BEETA**
• beta
≈ <square> 30D9 ベ 30FC ー 30BF タ

333D ㌽ **SQUARE POINTO**
• point
≈ <square> 30DD ポ 30A4 イ 30F3 ン 30C8 ト

333E ㌾ **SQUARE BORUTO**
• volt, bolt
≈ <square> 30DC ボ 30EB ル 30C8 ト

333F ㌿ **SQUARE HON**
• hon: volume
≈ <square> 30DB ホ 30F3 ン

3340 ㍀ **SQUARE PONDO**
• pound
≈ <square> 30DD ポ 30F3 ン 30C9 ド

3341 ㍁ **SQUARE HOORU**
• hall
≈ <square> 30DB ホ 30FC ー 30EB ル

3342 ㍂ **SQUARE HOON**
• horn
≈ <square> 30DB ホ 30FC ー 30F3 ン

3343 ㍃ **SQUARE MAIKURO**
• micro-
≈ <square> 30DE マ 30A4 イ 30AF ク 30ED ロ

3344 ㍄ **SQUARE MAIRU**
• mile
≈ <square> 30DE マ 30A4 イ 30EB ル

3345 ㍅ **SQUARE MAHHA**
• mach
≈ <square> 30DE マ 30C3 ッ 30CF ハ

3346 ㍆ **SQUARE MARUKU**
• mark
≈ <square> 30DE マ 30EB ル 30AF ク

3347 ㍇ **SQUARE MANSYON**
• mansion (i.e. better quality apartment)
≈ <square> 30DE マ 30F3 ン 30B7 シ 30E7 ョ 30F3 ン

3348 ㍈ **SQUARE MIKURON**
• micron
≈ <square> 30DF ミ 30AF ク 30ED ロ 30F3 ン

3349 ㍉ SQUARE MIRI
• milli-
≈ <square> 30DF ミ 30EA リ

334A ㍊ SQUARE MIRIBAARU
• millibar
≈ <square> 30DF ミ 30EA リ 30D0 バ 30FC ー 30EB ル

334B ㍋ SQUARE MEGA
• mega-
≈ <square> 30E1 メ 30AC ガ

334C ㍌ SQUARE MEGATON
• megaton
≈ <square> 30E1 メ 30AC ガ 30C8 ト 30F3 ン

334D ㍍ SQUARE MEETORU
• meter
≈ <square> 30E1 メ 30FC ー 30C8 ト 30EB ル

334E ㍎ SQUARE YAADO
• yard
≈ <square> 30E4 ヤ 30FC ー 30C9 ド

334F ㍏ SQUARE YAARU
• yard
≈ <square> 30E4 ヤ 30FC ー 30EB ル

3350 ㍐ SQUARE YUAN
• yuan (Chinese currency)
≈ <square> 30E6 ユ 30A2 ア 30F3 ン

3351 ㍑ SQUARE RITTORU
• liter
≈ <square> 30EA リ 30C3 ッ 30C8 ト 30EB ル

3352 ㍒ SQUARE RIRA
• lira
≈ <square> 30EA リ 30E9 ラ

3353 ㍓ SQUARE RUPII
• rupee
≈ <square> 30EB ル 30D4 ピ 30FC ー

3354 ㍔ SQUARE RUUBURU
• ruble
≈ <square> 30EB ル 30FC ー 30D6 ブ 30EB ル

3355 ㍕ SQUARE REMU
• rem (unit of radiation)
≈ <square> 30EC レ 30E0 ム

3356 ㍖ SQUARE RENTOGEN
• roentgen
≈ <square> 30EC レ 30F3 ン 30C8 ト 30B2 ゲ 30F3 ン

3357 ㍗ SQUARE WATTO
• watt
≈ <square> 30EF ワ 30C3 ッ 30C8 ト

Telegraph symbols for hours

3358 ㍘ IDEOGRAPHIC TELEGRAPH SYMBOL FOR HOUR ZERO
≈ 0030 0 70B9 点

3359 ㍙ IDEOGRAPHIC TELEGRAPH SYMBOL FOR HOUR ONE
≈ 0031 1 70B9 点

335A ㍚ IDEOGRAPHIC TELEGRAPH SYMBOL FOR HOUR TWO
≈ 0032 2 70B9 点

335B ㍛ IDEOGRAPHIC TELEGRAPH SYMBOL FOR HOUR THREE
≈ 0033 3 70B9 点

335C ㍜ IDEOGRAPHIC TELEGRAPH SYMBOL FOR HOUR FOUR
≈ 0034 4 70B9 点

335D ㍝ IDEOGRAPHIC TELEGRAPH SYMBOL FOR HOUR FIVE
≈ 0035 5 70B9 点

335E ㍞ IDEOGRAPHIC TELEGRAPH SYMBOL FOR HOUR SIX
≈ 0036 6 70B9 点

335F ㍟ IDEOGRAPHIC TELEGRAPH SYMBOL FOR HOUR SEVEN
≈ 0037 7 70B9 点

3360 ㍠ IDEOGRAPHIC TELEGRAPH SYMBOL FOR HOUR EIGHT
≈ 0038 8 70B9 点

3361 ㍡ IDEOGRAPHIC TELEGRAPH SYMBOL FOR HOUR NINE
≈ 0039 9 70B9 点

3362 ㍢ IDEOGRAPHIC TELEGRAPH SYMBOL FOR HOUR TEN
≈ 0031 1 0030 0 70B9 点

3363 ㍣ IDEOGRAPHIC TELEGRAPH SYMBOL FOR HOUR ELEVEN
≈ 0031 1 0031 1 70B9 点

3364 ㍤ IDEOGRAPHIC TELEGRAPH SYMBOL FOR HOUR TWELVE
≈ 0031 1 0032 2 70B9 点

3365 ㍥ IDEOGRAPHIC TELEGRAPH SYMBOL FOR HOUR THIRTEEN
≈ 0031 1 0033 3 70B9 点

3366 ㍦ IDEOGRAPHIC TELEGRAPH SYMBOL FOR HOUR FOURTEEN
≈ 0031 1 0034 4 70B9 点

3367 ㍧ IDEOGRAPHIC TELEGRAPH SYMBOL FOR HOUR FIFTEEN
≈ 0031 1 0035 5 70B9 点

3368 ㍨ IDEOGRAPHIC TELEGRAPH SYMBOL FOR HOUR SIXTEEN
≈ 0031 1 0036 6 70B9 点

3369 ㍩ IDEOGRAPHIC TELEGRAPH SYMBOL FOR HOUR SEVENTEEN
≈ 0031 1 0037 7 70B9 点

336A ㍪ IDEOGRAPHIC TELEGRAPH SYMBOL FOR HOUR EIGHTEEN
≈ 0031 1 0038 8 70B9 点

336B ㍫ IDEOGRAPHIC TELEGRAPH SYMBOL FOR HOUR NINETEEN
≈ 0031 1 0039 9 70B9 点

336C ㍬ IDEOGRAPHIC TELEGRAPH SYMBOL FOR HOUR TWENTY
≈ 0032 2 0030 0 70B9 点

336D ㍭ IDEOGRAPHIC TELEGRAPH SYMBOL FOR HOUR TWENTY-ONE
≈ 0032 2 0031 1 70B9 点

336E ㍮ IDEOGRAPHIC TELEGRAPH SYMBOL FOR HOUR TWENTY-TWO
≈ 0032 2 0032 2 70B9 点

336F ㍯ IDEOGRAPHIC TELEGRAPH SYMBOL FOR HOUR TWENTY-THREE
≈ 0032 2 0033 3 70B9 点

3370 ㍰ IDEOGRAPHIC TELEGRAPH SYMBOL FOR HOUR TWENTY-FOUR
≈ 0032 2 0034 4 70B9 点

Squared Latin abbreviations

3371 ㍱ SQUARE HPA
≈ <square> 0068 h 0050 P 0061 a

3372 ㍲ SQUARE DA
≈ <square> 0064 d 0061 a

3373 ㍳ SQUARE AU
≈ <square> 0041 A 0055 U

3374 ㍴ SQUARE BAR
≈ <square> 0062 b 0061 a 0072 r

3375 ㍵ SQUARE OV
≈ <square> 006F o 0056 V

3376 ㍶ SQUARE PC
≈ <square> 0070 p 0063 c

3377 ㍷ SQUARE DM
≈ <square> 0064 d 006D m

3378 ㍸ SQUARE DM SQUARED
≈ <square> 0064 d 006D m 00B2 ²

3379 ㍹ SQUARE DM CUBED
≈ <square> 0064 d 006D m 00B3 ³

337A ㍺ SQUARE IU
≈ <square> 0049 I 0055 U

Japanese era names

337B ㍻ SQUARE ERA NAME HEISEI
≈ <square> 5E73 平 6210 成

337C ㍼ SQUARE ERA NAME SYOUWA
≈ <square> 662D 昭 548C 和

337D ㍽ SQUARE ERA NAME TAISYOU
≈ <square> 5927 大 6B63 正

337E ㍾ SQUARE ERA NAME MEIZI
≈ <square> 660E 明 6CBB 治

Japanese corporation

337F ㍿ SQUARE CORPORATION
= kabusiki-gaisya
• incorporated
≈ <square> 682A 株 5F0F 式 4F1A 会 793E 社

Squared Latin abbreviations

3380 ㎀ SQUARE PA AMPS
≈ <square> 0070 p 0041 A

3381 ㎁ SQUARE NA
≈ <square> 006E n 0041 A

3382 ㎂ SQUARE MU A
≈ <square> 03BC μ 0041 A

3383 ㎃ SQUARE MA
≈ <square> 006D m 0041 A

3384 ㎄ SQUARE KA
≈ <square> 006B k 0041 A

3385 ㎅ SQUARE KB
≈ <square> 004B K 0042 B

3386 ㎆ SQUARE MB
≈ <square> 004D M 0042 B

3387 ㎇ SQUARE GB
≈ <square> 0047 G 0042 B

3388 ㎈ SQUARE CAL
≈ <square> 0063 c 0061 a 006C l

3389 ㎉ SQUARE KCAL
≈ <square> 006B k 0063 c 0061 a 006C l

338A ㎊ SQUARE PF
≈ <square> 0070 p 0046 F

338B ㎋ SQUARE NF
≈ <square> 006E n 0046 F

338C ㎌ SQUARE MU F
≈ <square> 03BC μ 0046 F

338D ㎍ SQUARE MU G
≈ <square> 03BC μ 0067 g

338E ㎎ SQUARE MG
≈ <square> 006D m 0067 g

338F ㎏ SQUARE KG
≈ <square> 006B k 0067 g

3390 ㎐ SQUARE HZ
≈ <square> 0048 H 007A z

3391 ㎑ SQUARE KHZ
≈ <square> 006B k 0048 H 007A z

3392 ㎒ SQUARE MHZ
≈ <square> 004D M 0048 H 007A z

3393 ㎓ SQUARE GHZ
≈ <square> 0047 G 0048 H 007A z

3394 ㎔ SQUARE THZ
≈ <square> 0054 T 0048 H 007A z

3395 ㎕ SQUARE MU L
≈ <square> 03BC μ 2113 ℓ

3396 ㎖ SQUARE ML
≈ <square> 006D m 2113 ℓ

3397 ㎗ SQUARE DL
≈ <square> 0064 d 2113 ℓ

3398 ㎘ SQUARE KL
≈ <square> 006B k 2113 ℓ

3399 ㎙ SQUARE FM
≈ <square> 0066 f 006D m

339A ㎚ SQUARE NM
≈ <square> 006E n 006D m

339B ㎛ SQUARE MU M
≈ <square> 03BC μ 006D m

339C ㎜ SQUARE MM
≈ <square> 006D m 006D m

339D ㎝ SQUARE CM
≈ <square> 0063 c 006D m

339E ㎞ SQUARE KM
≈ <square> 006B k 006D m

339F ㎟ SQUARE MM SQUARED
≈ <square> 006D m 006D m 00B2 ²

33A0 ㎠ SQUARE CM SQUARED
≈ <square> 0063 c 006D m 00B2 ²

33A1 ㎡ SQUARE M SQUARED
≈ <square> 006D m 00B2 ²

33A2 ㎢ SQUARE KM SQUARED
≈ <square> 006B k 006D m 00B2 ²

33A3 ㎣ SQUARE MM CUBED
≈ <square> 006D m 006D m 00B3 ³

33A4 ㎤ SQUARE CM CUBED
≈ <square> 0063 c 006D m 00B3 ³

33A5 ㎥ SQUARE M CUBED
≈ <square> 006D m 00B3 ³

33A6 ㎦ SQUARE KM CUBED
≈ <square> 006B k 006D m 00B3 ³

33A7 ㎧ SQUARE M OVER S
≈ <square> 006D m 2215 ∕ 0073 s

33A8 ㎨ SQUARE M OVER S SQUARED
≈ <square> 006D m 2215 ∕ 0073 s 00B2 ²

33A9 ㎩ SQUARE PA
≈ <square> 0050 P 0061 a

33AA ㎪ SQUARE KPA
≈ <square> 006B k 0050 P 0061 a

33AB ㎫ SQUARE MPA
≈ <square> 004D M 0050 P 0061 a

33AC ㎬ SQUARE GPA
≈ <square> 0047 G 0050 P 0061 a

33AD rad SQUARE RAD
≈ <square> 0072 r 0061 a 0064 d
33AE rad/s SQUARE RAD OVER S
≈ <square> 0072 r 0061 a 0064 d 2215 / 0073 s
33AF rad/s² SQUARE RAD OVER S SQUARED
≈ <square> 0072 r 0061 a 0064 d 2215 / 0073 s 00B2 ²
33B0 ps SQUARE PS
≈ <square> 0070 p 0073 s
33B1 ns SQUARE NS
≈ <square> 006E n 0073 s
33B2 μs SQUARE MU S
≈ <square> 03BC μ 0073 s
33B3 ms SQUARE MS
≈ <square> 006D m 0073 s
33B4 pV SQUARE PV
≈ <square> 0070 p 0056 V
33B5 nV SQUARE NV
≈ <square> 006E n 0056 V
33B6 μV SQUARE MU V
≈ <square> 03BC μ 0056 V
33B7 mV SQUARE MV
≈ <square> 006D m 0056 V
33B8 kV SQUARE KV
≈ <square> 006B k 0056 V
33B9 MV SQUARE MV MEGA
≈ <square> 004D M 0056 V
33BA pW SQUARE PW
≈ <square> 0070 p 0057 W
33BB nW SQUARE NW
≈ <square> 006E n 0057 W
33BC μW SQUARE MU W
≈ <square> 03BC μ 0057 W
33BD mW SQUARE MW
≈ <square> 006D m 0057 W
33BE kW SQUARE KW
≈ <square> 006B k 0057 W
33BF MW SQUARE MW MEGA
≈ <square> 004D M 0057 W
33C0 kΩ SQUARE K OHM
≈ <square> 006B k 03A9 Ω
33C1 MΩ SQUARE M OHM
≈ <square> 004D M 03A9 Ω
33C2 a.m. SQUARE AM
≈ <square> 0061 a 002E . 006D m 002E .
33C3 Bq SQUARE BQ
≈ <square> 0042 B 0071 q
33C4 cc SQUARE CC
≈ <square> 0063 c 0063 c
33C5 cd SQUARE CD
≈ <square> 0063 c 0064 d
33C6 C/kg SQUARE C OVER KG
≈ <square> 0043 C 2215 / 006B k 0067 g
33C7 Co. SQUARE CO
≈ <square> 0043 C 006F o 002E .
33C8 dB SQUARE DB
≈ <square> 0064 d 0042 B
33C9 Gy SQUARE GY
≈ <square> 0047 G 0079 y
33CA ha SQUARE HA
≈ <square> 0068 h 0061 a
33CB HP SQUARE HP
≈ <square> 0048 H 0050 P
33CC in SQUARE IN
≈ <square> 0069 i 006E n
33CD K.K. SQUARE KK
≈ <square> 004B K 004B K
33CE KM SQUARE KM CAPITAL
≈ <square> 004B K 004D M
33CF kt SQUARE KT
≈ <square> 006B k 0074 t
33D0 lm SQUARE LM
≈ <square> 006C l 006D m
33D1 ln SQUARE LN
≈ <square> 006C l 006E n
33D2 log SQUARE LOG
≈ <square> 006C l 006F o 0067 g
33D3 lx SQUARE LX
≈ <square> 006C l 0078 x
33D4 mb SQUARE MB SMALL
≈ <square> 006D m 0062 b
33D5 mil SQUARE MIL
≈ <square> 006D m 0069 i 006C l
33D6 mol SQUARE MOL
≈ <square> 006D m 006F o 006C l
33D7 pH SQUARE PH
≈ <square> 0050 P 0048 H
33D8 p.m. SQUARE PM
≈ <square> 0070 p 002E . 006D m 002E .
33D9 PPM SQUARE PPM
≈ <square> 0050 P 0050 P 004D M
33DA PR SQUARE PR
≈ <square> 0050 P 0052 R
33DB sr SQUARE SR
≈ <square> 0073 s 0072 r
33DC Sv SQUARE SV
≈ <square> 0053 S 0076 v
33DD Wb SQUARE WB
≈ <square> 0057 W 0062 b
33DE V/m SQUARE V OVER M
≈ <square> 0056 V 2215 / 006D m
33DF A/m SQUARE A OVER M
≈ <square> 0041 A 2215 / 006D m

Telegraph symbols for days

33E0 1日 IDEOGRAPHIC TELEGRAPH SYMBOL FOR DAY ONE
≈ 0031 1 65E5 日
33E1 2日 IDEOGRAPHIC TELEGRAPH SYMBOL FOR DAY TWO
≈ 0032 2 65E5 日
33E2 3日 IDEOGRAPHIC TELEGRAPH SYMBOL FOR DAY THREE
≈ 0033 3 65E5 日
33E3 4日 IDEOGRAPHIC TELEGRAPH SYMBOL FOR DAY FOUR
≈ 0034 4 65E5 日
33E4 5日 IDEOGRAPHIC TELEGRAPH SYMBOL FOR DAY FIVE
≈ 0035 5 65E5 日
33E5 6日 IDEOGRAPHIC TELEGRAPH SYMBOL FOR DAY SIX
≈ 0036 6 65E5 日
33E6 7日 IDEOGRAPHIC TELEGRAPH SYMBOL FOR DAY SEVEN
≈ 0037 7 65E5 日

33E7 8日 IDEOGRAPHIC TELEGRAPH SYMBOL FOR DAY EIGHT
≈ 0038 8 65E5 日

33E8 9日 IDEOGRAPHIC TELEGRAPH SYMBOL FOR DAY NINE
≈ 0039 9 65E5 日

33E9 10日 IDEOGRAPHIC TELEGRAPH SYMBOL FOR DAY TEN
≈ 0031 1 0030 0 65E5 日

33EA 11日 IDEOGRAPHIC TELEGRAPH SYMBOL FOR DAY ELEVEN
≈ 0031 1 0031 1 65E5 日

33EB 12日 IDEOGRAPHIC TELEGRAPH SYMBOL FOR DAY TWELVE
≈ 0031 1 0032 2 65E5 日

33EC 13日 IDEOGRAPHIC TELEGRAPH SYMBOL FOR DAY THIRTEEN
≈ 0031 1 0033 3 65E5 日

33ED 14日 IDEOGRAPHIC TELEGRAPH SYMBOL FOR DAY FOURTEEN
≈ 0031 1 0034 4 65E5 日

33EE 15日 IDEOGRAPHIC TELEGRAPH SYMBOL FOR DAY FIFTEEN
≈ 0031 1 0035 5 65E5 日

33EF 16日 IDEOGRAPHIC TELEGRAPH SYMBOL FOR DAY SIXTEEN
≈ 0031 1 0036 6 65E5 日

33F0 17日 IDEOGRAPHIC TELEGRAPH SYMBOL FOR DAY SEVENTEEN
≈ 0031 1 0037 7 65E5 日

33F1 18日 IDEOGRAPHIC TELEGRAPH SYMBOL FOR DAY EIGHTEEN
≈ 0031 1 0038 8 65E5 日

33F2 19日 IDEOGRAPHIC TELEGRAPH SYMBOL FOR DAY NINETEEN
≈ 0031 1 0039 9 65E5 日

33F3 20日 IDEOGRAPHIC TELEGRAPH SYMBOL FOR DAY TWENTY
≈ 0032 2 0030 0 65E5 日

33F4 21日 IDEOGRAPHIC TELEGRAPH SYMBOL FOR DAY TWENTY-ONE
≈ 0032 2 0031 1 65E5 日

33F5 22日 IDEOGRAPHIC TELEGRAPH SYMBOL FOR DAY TWENTY-TWO
≈ 0032 2 0032 2 65E5 日

33F6 23日 IDEOGRAPHIC TELEGRAPH SYMBOL FOR DAY TWENTY-THREE
≈ 0032 2 0033 3 65E5 日

33F7 24日 IDEOGRAPHIC TELEGRAPH SYMBOL FOR DAY TWENTY-FOUR
≈ 0032 2 0034 4 65E5 日

33F8 25日 IDEOGRAPHIC TELEGRAPH SYMBOL FOR DAY TWENTY-FIVE
≈ 0032 2 0035 5 65E5 日

33F9 26日 IDEOGRAPHIC TELEGRAPH SYMBOL FOR DAY TWENTY-SIX
≈ 0032 2 0036 6 65E5 日

33FA 27日 IDEOGRAPHIC TELEGRAPH SYMBOL FOR DAY TWENTY-SEVEN
≈ 0032 2 0037 7 65E5 日

33FB 28日 IDEOGRAPHIC TELEGRAPH SYMBOL FOR DAY TWENTY-EIGHT
≈ 0032 2 0038 8 65E5 日

33FC 29日 IDEOGRAPHIC TELEGRAPH SYMBOL FOR DAY TWENTY-NINE
≈ 0032 2 0039 9 65E5 日

33FD 30日 IDEOGRAPHIC TELEGRAPH SYMBOL FOR DAY THIRTY
≈ 0033 3 0030 0 65E5 日

33FE 31日 IDEOGRAPHIC TELEGRAPH SYMBOL FOR DAY THIRTY-ONE
≈ 0033 3 0031 1 65E5 日

Squared Latin abbreviation

33FF gal SQUARE GAL
≈ <square> 0067 g 0061 a 006C l

	4DC	4DD	4DE	4DF
0	䷀ 4DC0	䷐ 4DD0	䷠ 4DE0	䷰ 4DF0
1	䷁ 4DC1	䷑ 4DD1	䷡ 4DE1	䷱ 4DF1
2	䷂ 4DC2	䷒ 4DD2	䷢ 4DE2	䷲ 4DF2
3	䷃ 4DC3	䷓ 4DD3	䷣ 4DE3	䷳ 4DF3
4	䷄ 4DC4	䷔ 4DD4	䷤ 4DE4	䷴ 4DF4
5	䷅ 4DC5	䷕ 4DD5	䷥ 4DE5	䷵ 4DF5
6	䷆ 4DC6	䷖ 4DD6	䷦ 4DE6	䷶ 4DF6
7	䷇ 4DC7	䷗ 4DD7	䷧ 4DE7	䷷ 4DF7
8	䷈ 4DC8	䷘ 4DD8	䷨ 4DE8	䷸ 4DF8
9	䷉ 4DC9	䷙ 4DD9	䷩ 4DE9	䷹ 4DF9
A	䷊ 4DCA	䷚ 4DDA	䷪ 4DEA	䷺ 4DFA
B	䷋ 4DCB	䷛ 4DDB	䷫ 4DEB	䷻ 4DFB
C	䷌ 4DCC	䷜ 4DDC	䷬ 4DEC	䷼ 4DFC
D	䷍ 4DCD	䷝ 4DDD	䷭ 4DED	䷽ 4DFD
E	䷎ 4DCE	䷞ 4DDE	䷮ 4DEE	䷾ 4DFE
F	䷏ 4DCF	䷟ 4DDF	䷯ 4DEF	䷿ 4DFF

Yijing hexagram symbols

4DC0 ䷀ HEXAGRAM FOR THE CREATIVE HEAVEN
4DC1 ䷁ HEXAGRAM FOR THE RECEPTIVE EARTH
4DC2 ䷂ HEXAGRAM FOR DIFFICULTY AT THE BEGINNING
4DC3 ䷃ HEXAGRAM FOR YOUTHFUL FOLLY
4DC4 ䷄ HEXAGRAM FOR WAITING
4DC5 ䷅ HEXAGRAM FOR CONFLICT
4DC6 ䷆ HEXAGRAM FOR THE ARMY
4DC7 ䷇ HEXAGRAM FOR HOLDING TOGETHER
4DC8 ䷈ HEXAGRAM FOR SMALL TAMING
4DC9 ䷉ HEXAGRAM FOR TREADING
4DCA ䷊ HEXAGRAM FOR PEACE
4DCB ䷋ HEXAGRAM FOR STANDSTILL
4DCC ䷌ HEXAGRAM FOR FELLOWSHIP
4DCD ䷍ HEXAGRAM FOR GREAT POSSESSION
4DCE ䷎ HEXAGRAM FOR MODESTY
4DCF ䷏ HEXAGRAM FOR ENTHUSIASM
4DD0 ䷐ HEXAGRAM FOR FOLLOWING
4DD1 ䷑ HEXAGRAM FOR WORK ON THE DECAYED
4DD2 ䷒ HEXAGRAM FOR APPROACH
4DD3 ䷓ HEXAGRAM FOR CONTEMPLATION
4DD4 ䷔ HEXAGRAM FOR BITING THROUGH
4DD5 ䷕ HEXAGRAM FOR GRACE
4DD6 ䷖ HEXAGRAM FOR SPLITTING APART
4DD7 ䷗ HEXAGRAM FOR RETURN
4DD8 ䷘ HEXAGRAM FOR INNOCENCE
4DD9 ䷙ HEXAGRAM FOR GREAT TAMING
4DDA ䷚ HEXAGRAM FOR MOUTH CORNERS
4DDB ䷛ HEXAGRAM FOR GREAT PREPONDERANCE
4DDC ䷜ HEXAGRAM FOR THE ABYSMAL WATER
4DDD ䷝ HEXAGRAM FOR THE CLINGING FIRE
4DDE ䷞ HEXAGRAM FOR INFLUENCE
4DDF ䷟ HEXAGRAM FOR DURATION
4DE0 ䷠ HEXAGRAM FOR RETREAT
4DE1 ䷡ HEXAGRAM FOR GREAT POWER
4DE2 ䷢ HEXAGRAM FOR PROGRESS
4DE3 ䷣ HEXAGRAM FOR DARKENING OF THE LIGHT
4DE4 ䷤ HEXAGRAM FOR THE FAMILY
4DE5 ䷥ HEXAGRAM FOR OPPOSITION
4DE6 ䷦ HEXAGRAM FOR OBSTRUCTION
4DE7 ䷧ HEXAGRAM FOR DELIVERANCE
4DE8 ䷨ HEXAGRAM FOR DECREASE
4DE9 ䷩ HEXAGRAM FOR INCREASE
4DEA ䷪ HEXAGRAM FOR BREAKTHROUGH
4DEB ䷫ HEXAGRAM FOR COMING TO MEET
4DEC ䷬ HEXAGRAM FOR GATHERING TOGETHER
4DED ䷭ HEXAGRAM FOR PUSHING UPWARD
4DEE ䷮ HEXAGRAM FOR OPPRESSION
4DEF ䷯ HEXAGRAM FOR THE WELL
4DF0 ䷰ HEXAGRAM FOR REVOLUTION
4DF1 ䷱ HEXAGRAM FOR THE CAULDRON
4DF2 ䷲ HEXAGRAM FOR THE AROUSING THUNDER
4DF3 ䷳ HEXAGRAM FOR THE KEEPING STILL MOUNTAIN
4DF4 ䷴ HEXAGRAM FOR DEVELOPMENT
4DF5 ䷵ HEXAGRAM FOR THE MARRYING MAIDEN
4DF6 ䷶ HEXAGRAM FOR ABUNDANCE
4DF7 ䷷ HEXAGRAM FOR THE WANDERER
4DF8 ䷸ HEXAGRAM FOR THE GENTLE WIND
4DF9 ䷹ HEXAGRAM FOR THE JOYOUS LAKE
4DFA ䷺ HEXAGRAM FOR DISPERSION
4DFB ䷻ HEXAGRAM FOR LIMITATION
4DFC ䷼ HEXAGRAM FOR INNER TRUTH
4DFD ䷽ HEXAGRAM FOR SMALL PREPONDERANCE
4DFE ䷾ HEXAGRAM FOR AFTER COMPLETION
4DFF ䷿ HEXAGRAM FOR BEFORE COMPLETION

	A00	A01	A02	A03	A04	A05	A06	A07	A08	A09	A0A	A0B	A0C	A0D	A0E
0	A000	A010	A020	A030	A040	A050	A060	A070	A080	A090	A0A0	A0B0	A0C0	A0D0	A0E0
1	A001	A011	A021	A031	A041	A051	A061	A071	A081	A091	A0A1	A0B1	A0C1	A0D1	A0E1
2	A002	A012	A022	A032	A042	A052	A062	A072	A082	A092	A0A2	A0B2	A0C2	A0D2	A0E2
3	A003	A013	A023	A033	A043	A053	A063	A073	A083	A093	A0A3	A0B3	A0C3	A0D3	A0E3
4	A004	A014	A024	A034	A044	A054	A064	A074	A084	A094	A0A4	A0B4	A0C4	A0D4	A0E4
5	A005	A015	A025	A035	A045	A055	A065	A075	A085	A095	A0A5	A0B5	A0C5	A0D5	A0E5
6	A006	A016	A026	A036	A046	A056	A066	A076	A086	A096	A0A6	A0B6	A0C6	A0D6	A0E6
7	A007	A017	A027	A037	A047	A057	A067	A077	A087	A097	A0A7	A0B7	A0C7	A0D7	A0E7
8	A008	A018	A028	A038	A048	A058	A068	A078	A088	A098	A0A8	A0B8	A0C8	A0D8	A0E8
9	A009	A019	A029	A039	A049	A059	A069	A079	A089	A099	A0A9	A0B9	A0C9	A0D9	A0E9
A	A00A	A01A	A02A	A03A	A04A	A05A	A06A	A07A	A08A	A09A	A0AA	A0BA	A0CA	A0DA	A0EA
B	A00B	A01B	A02B	A03B	A04B	A05B	A06B	A07B	A08B	A09B	A0AB	A0BB	A0CB	A0DB	A0EB
C	A00C	A01C	A02C	A03C	A04C	A05C	A06C	A07C	A08C	A09C	A0AC	A0BC	A0CC	A0DC	A0EC
D	A00D	A01D	A02D	A03D	A04D	A05D	A06D	A07D	A08D	A09D	A0AD	A0BD	A0CD	A0DD	A0ED
E	A00E	A01E	A02E	A03E	A04E	A05E	A06E	A07E	A08E	A09E	A0AE	A0BE	A0CE	A0DE	A0EE
F	A00F	A01F	A02F	A03F	A04F	A05F	A06F	A07F	A08F	A09F	A0AF	A0BF	A0CF	A0DF	A0EF

	A0F	A10	A11	A12	A13	A14	A15	A16	A17	A18	A19	A1A	A1B	A1C	A1D
0	ꃰ A0F0	ꄀ A100	ꄐ A110	ꄠ A120	ꄰ A130	ꅀ A140	ꅐ A150	ꅠ A160	ꅰ A170	ꆀ A180	ꆐ A190	ꆠ A1A0	ꆰ A1B0	ꇀ A1C0	ꇐ A1D0
1	ꃱ A0F1	ꄁ A101	ꄑ A111	ꄡ A121	ꄱ A131	ꅁ A141	ꅑ A151	ꅡ A161	ꅱ A171	ꆁ A181	ꆑ A191	ꆡ A1A1	ꆱ A1B1	ꇁ A1C1	ꇑ A1D1
2	ꃲ A0F2	ꄂ A102	ꄒ A112	ꄢ A122	ꄲ A132	ꅂ A142	ꅒ A152	ꅢ A162	ꅲ A172	ꆂ A182	ꆒ A192	ꆢ A1A2	ꆲ A1B2	ꇂ A1C2	ꇒ A1D2
3	ꃳ A0F3	ꄃ A103	ꄓ A113	ꄣ A123	ꄳ A133	ꅃ A143	ꅓ A153	ꅣ A163	ꅳ A173	ꆃ A183	ꆓ A193	ꆣ A1A3	ꆳ A1B3	ꇃ A1C3	ꇓ A1D3
4	ꃴ A0F4	ꄄ A104	ꄔ A114	ꄤ A124	ꄴ A134	ꅄ A144	ꅔ A154	ꅤ A164	ꅴ A174	ꆄ A184	ꆔ A194	ꆤ A1A4	ꆴ A1B4	ꇄ A1C4	ꇔ A1D4
5	ꃵ A0F5	ꄅ A105	ꄕ A115	ꄥ A125	ꄵ A135	ꅅ A145	ꅕ A155	ꅥ A165	ꅵ A175	ꆅ A185	ꆕ A195	ꆥ A1A5	ꆵ A1B5	ꇅ A1C5	ꇕ A1D5
6	ꃶ A0F6	ꄆ A106	ꄖ A116	ꄦ A126	ꄶ A136	ꅆ A146	ꅖ A156	ꅦ A166	ꅶ A176	ꆆ A186	ꆖ A196	ꆦ A1A6	ꆶ A1B6	ꇆ A1C6	ꇖ A1D6
7	ꃷ A0F7	ꄇ A107	ꄗ A117	ꄧ A127	ꄷ A137	ꅇ A147	ꅗ A157	ꅧ A167	ꅷ A177	ꆇ A187	ꆗ A197	ꆧ A1A7	ꆷ A1B7	ꇇ A1C7	ꇗ A1D7
8	ꃸ A0F8	ꄈ A108	ꄘ A118	ꄨ A128	ꄸ A138	ꅈ A148	ꅘ A158	ꅨ A168	ꅸ A178	ꆈ A188	ꆘ A198	ꆨ A1A8	ꆸ A1B8	ꇈ A1C8	ꇘ A1D8
9	ꃹ A0F9	ꄉ A109	ꄙ A119	ꄩ A129	ꄹ A139	ꅉ A149	ꅙ A159	ꅩ A169	ꅹ A179	ꆉ A189	ꆙ A199	ꆩ A1A9	ꆹ A1B9	ꇉ A1C9	ꇙ A1D9
A	ꃺ A0FA	ꄊ A10A	ꄚ A11A	ꄪ A12A	ꄺ A13A	ꅊ A14A	ꅚ A15A	ꅪ A16A	ꅺ A17A	ꆊ A18A	ꆚ A19A	ꆪ A1AA	ꆺ A1BA	ꇊ A1CA	ꇚ A1DA
B	ꃻ A0FB	ꄋ A10B	ꄛ A11B	ꄫ A12B	ꄻ A13B	ꅋ A14B	ꅛ A15B	ꅫ A16B	ꅻ A17B	ꆋ A18B	ꆛ A19B	ꆫ A1AB	ꆻ A1BB	ꇋ A1CB	ꇛ A1DB
C	ꃼ A0FC	ꄌ A10C	ꄜ A11C	ꄬ A12C	ꄼ A13C	ꅌ A14C	ꅜ A15C	ꅬ A16C	ꅼ A17C	ꆌ A18C	ꆜ A19C	ꆬ A1AC	ꆼ A1BC	ꇌ A1CC	ꇜ A1DC
D	ꃽ A0FD	ꄍ A10D	ꄝ A11D	ꄭ A12D	ꄽ A13D	ꅍ A14D	ꅝ A15D	ꅭ A16D	ꅽ A17D	ꆍ A18D	ꆝ A19D	ꆭ A1AD	ꆽ A1BD	ꇍ A1CD	ꇝ A1DD
E	ꃾ A0FE	ꄎ A10E	ꄞ A11E	ꄮ A12E	ꄾ A13E	ꅎ A14E	ꅞ A15E	ꅮ A16E	ꅾ A17E	ꆎ A18E	ꆞ A19E	ꆮ A1AE	ꆾ A1BE	ꇎ A1CE	ꇞ A1DE
F	ꃿ A0FF	ꄏ A10F	ꄟ A11F	ꄯ A12F	ꄿ A13F	ꅏ A14F	ꅟ A15F	ꅯ A16F	ꅿ A17F	ꆏ A18F	ꆟ A19F	ꆯ A1AF	ꆿ A1BF	ꇏ A1CF	ꇟ A1DF

	A1E	A1F	A20	A21	A22	A23	A24	A25	A26	A27	A28	A29	A2A	A2B	A2C
0	A1E0	A1F0	A200	A210	A220	A230	A240	A250	A260	A270	A280	A290	A2A0	A2B0	A2C0
1	A1E1	A1F1	A201	A211	A221	A231	A241	A251	A261	A271	A281	A291	A2A1	A2B1	A2C1
2	A1E2	A1F2	A202	A212	A222	A232	A242	A252	A262	A272	A282	A292	A2A2	A2B2	A2C2
3	A1E3	A1F3	A203	A213	A223	A233	A243	A253	A263	A273	A283	A293	A2A3	A2B3	A2C3
4	A1E4	A1F4	A204	A214	A224	A234	A244	A254	A264	A274	A284	A294	A2A4	A2B4	A2C4
5	A1E5	A1F5	A205	A215	A225	A235	A245	A255	A265	A275	A285	A295	A2A5	A2B5	A2C5
6	A1E6	A1F6	A206	A216	A226	A236	A246	A256	A266	A276	A286	A296	A2A6	A2B6	A2C6
7	A1E7	A1F7	A207	A217	A227	A237	A247	A257	A267	A277	A287	A297	A2A7	A2B7	A2C7
8	A1E8	A1F8	A208	A218	A228	A238	A248	A258	A268	A278	A288	A298	A2A8	A2B8	A2C8
9	A1E9	A1F9	A209	A219	A229	A239	A249	A259	A269	A279	A289	A299	A2A9	A2B9	A2C9
A	A1EA	A1FA	A20A	A21A	A22A	A23A	A24A	A25A	A26A	A27A	A28A	A29A	A2AA	A2BA	A2CA
B	A1EB	A1FB	A20B	A21B	A22B	A23B	A24B	A25B	A26B	A27B	A28B	A29B	A2AB	A2BB	A2CB
C	A1EC	A1FC	A20C	A21C	A22C	A23C	A24C	A25C	A26C	A27C	A28C	A29C	A2AC	A2BC	A2CC
D	A1ED	A1FD	A20D	A21D	A22D	A23D	A24D	A25D	A26D	A27D	A28D	A29D	A2AD	A2BD	A2CD
E	A1EE	A1FE	A20E	A21E	A22E	A23E	A24E	A25E	A26E	A27E	A28E	A29E	A2AE	A2BE	A2CE
F	A1EF	A1FF	A20F	A21F	A22F	A23F	A24F	A25F	A26F	A27F	A28F	A29F	A2AF	A2BF	A2CF

	A2D	A2E	A2F	A30	A31	A32	A33	A34	A35	A36	A37	A38	A39	A3A
0	ꋐ A2D0	ꋠ A2E0	ꋰ A2F0	ꌀ A300	ꌐ A310	ꌠ A320	ꌰ A330	ꍀ A340	ꍐ A350	ꍠ A360	ꍰ A370	ꎀ A380	ꎐ A390	ꎠ A3A0
1	ꋑ A2D1	ꋡ A2E1	ꋱ A2F1	ꌁ A301	ꌑ A311	ꌡ A321	ꌱ A331	ꍁ A341	ꍑ A351	ꍡ A361	ꍱ A371	ꎁ A381	ꎑ A391	ꎡ A3A1
2	ꋒ A2D2	ꋢ A2E2	ꋲ A2F2	ꌂ A302	ꌒ A312	ꌢ A322	ꌲ A332	ꍂ A342	ꍒ A352	ꍢ A362	ꍲ A372	ꎂ A382	ꎒ A392	ꎢ A3A2
3	ꋓ A2D3	ꋣ A2E3	ꋳ A2F3	ꌃ A303	ꌓ A313	ꌣ A323	ꌳ A333	ꍃ A343	ꍓ A353	ꍣ A363	ꍳ A373	ꎃ A383	ꎓ A393	ꎣ A3A3
4	ꋔ A2D4	ꋤ A2E4	ꋴ A2F4	ꌄ A304	ꌔ A314	ꌤ A324	ꌴ A334	ꍄ A344	ꍔ A354	ꍤ A364	ꍴ A374	ꎄ A384	ꎔ A394	ꎤ A3A4
5	ꋕ A2D5	ꋥ A2E5	ꋵ A2F5	ꌅ A305	ꌕ A315	ꌥ A325	ꌵ A335	ꍅ A345	ꍕ A355	ꍥ A365	ꍵ A375	ꎅ A385	ꎕ A395	ꎥ A3A5
6	ꋖ A2D6	ꋦ A2E6	ꋶ A2F6	ꌆ A306	ꌖ A316	ꌦ A326	ꌶ A336	ꍆ A346	ꍖ A356	ꍦ A366	ꍶ A376	ꎆ A386	ꎖ A396	ꎦ A3A6
7	ꋗ A2D7	ꋧ A2E7	ꋷ A2F7	ꌇ A307	ꌗ A317	ꌧ A327	ꌷ A337	ꍇ A347	ꍗ A357	ꍧ A367	ꍷ A377	ꎇ A387	ꎗ A397	ꎧ A3A7
8	ꋘ A2D8	ꋨ A2E8	ꋸ A2F8	ꌈ A308	ꌘ A318	ꌨ A328	ꌸ A338	ꍈ A348	ꍘ A358	ꍨ A368	ꍸ A378	ꎈ A388	ꎘ A398	ꎨ A3A8
9	ꋙ A2D9	ꋩ A2E9	ꋹ A2F9	ꌉ A309	ꌙ A319	ꌩ A329	ꌹ A339	ꍉ A349	ꍙ A359	ꍩ A369	ꍹ A379	ꎉ A389	ꎙ A399	ꎩ A3A9
A	ꋚ A2DA	ꋪ A2EA	ꋺ A2FA	ꌊ A30A	ꌚ A31A	ꌪ A32A	ꌺ A33A	ꍊ A34A	ꍚ A35A	ꍪ A36A	ꍺ A37A	ꎊ A38A	ꎚ A39A	ꎪ A3AA
B	ꋛ A2DB	ꋫ A2EB	ꋻ A2FB	ꌋ A30B	ꌛ A31B	ꌫ A32B	ꌻ A33B	ꍋ A34B	ꍛ A35B	ꍫ A36B	ꍻ A37B	ꎋ A38B	ꎛ A39B	ꎫ A3AB
C	ꋜ A2DC	ꋬ A2EC	ꋼ A2FC	ꌌ A30C	ꌜ A31C	ꌬ A32C	ꌼ A33C	ꍌ A34C	ꍜ A35C	ꍬ A36C	ꍼ A37C	ꎌ A38C	ꎜ A39C	ꎬ A3AC
D	ꋝ A2DD	ꋭ A2ED	ꋽ A2FD	ꌍ A30D	ꌝ A31D	ꌭ A32D	ꌽ A33D	ꍍ A34D	ꍝ A35D	ꍭ A36D	ꍽ A37D	ꎍ A38D	ꎝ A39D	ꎭ A3AD
E	ꋞ A2DE	ꋮ A2EE	ꋾ A2FE	ꌎ A30E	ꌞ A31E	ꌮ A32E	ꌾ A33E	ꍎ A34E	ꍞ A35E	ꍮ A36E	ꍾ A37E	ꎎ A38E	ꎞ A39E	ꎮ A3AE
F	ꋟ A2DF	ꋯ A2EF	ꋿ A2FF	ꌏ A30F	ꌟ A31F	ꌯ A32F	ꌿ A33F	ꍏ A34F	ꍟ A35F	ꍯ A36F	ꍿ A37F	ꎏ A38F	ꎟ A39F	ꎯ A3AF

	A3B	A3C	A3D	A3E	A3F	A40	A41	A42	A43	A44	A45	A46	A47	A48
0	ꎰ A3B0	ꏀ A3C0	ꏐ A3D0	ꏠ A3E0	ꏰ A3F0	ꐀ A400	ꐐ A410	ꐠ A420	ꐰ A430	ꑀ A440	ꑐ A450	ꑠ A460	ꑰ A470	ꒀ A480
1	ꎱ A3B1	ꏁ A3C1	ꏑ A3D1	ꏡ A3E1	ꏱ A3F1	ꐁ A401	ꐑ A411	ꐡ A421	ꐱ A431	ꑁ A441	ꑑ A451	ꑡ A461	ꑱ A471	ꒁ A481
2	ꎲ A3B2	ꏂ A3C2	ꏒ A3D2	ꏢ A3E2	ꏲ A3F2	ꐂ A402	ꐒ A412	ꐢ A422	ꐲ A432	ꑂ A442	ꑒ A452	ꑢ A462	ꑲ A472	ꒂ A482
3	ꎳ A3B3	ꏃ A3C3	ꏓ A3D3	ꏣ A3E3	ꏳ A3F3	ꐃ A403	ꐓ A413	ꐣ A423	ꐳ A433	ꑃ A443	ꑓ A453	ꑣ A463	ꑳ A473	ꒃ A483
4	ꎴ A3B4	ꏄ A3C4	ꏔ A3D4	ꏤ A3E4	ꏴ A3F4	ꐄ A404	ꐔ A414	ꐤ A424	ꐴ A434	ꑄ A444	ꑔ A454	ꑤ A464	ꑴ A474	ꒄ A484
5	ꎵ A3B5	ꏅ A3C5	ꏕ A3D5	ꏥ A3E5	ꏵ A3F5	ꐅ A405	ꐕ A415	ꐥ A425	ꐵ A435	ꑅ A445	ꑕ A455	ꑥ A465	ꑵ A475	ꒅ A485
6	ꎶ A3B6	ꏆ A3C6	ꏖ A3D6	ꏦ A3E6	ꏶ A3F6	ꐆ A406	ꐖ A416	ꐦ A426	ꐶ A436	ꑆ A446	ꑖ A456	ꑦ A466	ꑶ A476	ꒆ A486
7	ꎷ A3B7	ꏇ A3C7	ꏗ A3D7	ꏧ A3E7	ꏷ A3F7	ꐇ A407	ꐗ A417	ꐧ A427	ꐷ A437	ꑇ A447	ꑗ A457	ꑧ A467	ꑷ A477	ꒇ A487
8	ꎸ A3B8	ꏈ A3C8	ꏘ A3D8	ꏨ A3E8	ꏸ A3F8	ꐈ A408	ꐘ A418	ꐨ A428	ꐸ A438	ꑈ A448	ꑘ A458	ꑨ A468	ꑸ A478	ꒈ A488
9	ꎹ A3B9	ꏉ A3C9	ꏙ A3D9	ꏩ A3E9	ꏹ A3F9	ꐉ A409	ꐙ A419	ꐩ A429	ꐹ A439	ꑉ A449	ꑙ A459	ꑩ A469	ꑹ A479	ꒉ A489
A	ꎺ A3BA	ꏊ A3CA	ꏚ A3DA	ꏪ A3EA	ꏺ A3FA	ꐊ A40A	ꐚ A41A	ꐪ A42A	ꐺ A43A	ꑊ A44A	ꑚ A45A	ꑪ A46A	ꑺ A47A	ꒊ A48A
B	ꎻ A3BB	ꏋ A3CB	ꏛ A3DB	ꏫ A3EB	ꏻ A3FB	ꐋ A40B	ꐛ A41B	ꐫ A42B	ꐻ A43B	ꑋ A44B	ꑛ A45B	ꑫ A46B	ꑻ A47B	ꒋ A48B
C	ꎼ A3BC	ꏌ A3CC	ꏜ A3DC	ꏬ A3EC	ꏼ A3FC	ꐌ A40C	ꐜ A41C	ꐬ A42C	ꐼ A43C	ꑌ A44C	ꑜ A45C	ꑬ A46C	ꑼ A47C	ꒌ A48C
D	ꎽ A3BD	ꏍ A3CD	ꏝ A3DD	ꏭ A3ED	ꏽ A3FD	ꐍ A40D	ꐝ A41D	ꐭ A42D	ꐽ A43D	ꑍ A44D	ꑝ A45D	ꑭ A46D	ꑽ A47D	
E	ꎾ A3BE	ꏎ A3CE	ꏞ A3DE	ꏮ A3EE	ꏾ A3FE	ꐎ A40E	ꐞ A41E	ꐮ A42E	ꐾ A43E	ꑎ A44E	ꑞ A45E	ꑮ A46E	ꑾ A47E	
F	ꎿ A3BF	ꏏ A3CF	ꏟ A3DF	ꏯ A3EF	ꏿ A3FF	ꐏ A40F	ꐟ A41F	ꐯ A42F	ꐿ A43F	ꑏ A44F	ꑟ A45F	ꑯ A46F	ꑿ A47F	

Syllables

A000 ꀀ YI SYLLABLE IT
A001 ꀁ YI SYLLABLE IX
A002 ꀂ YI SYLLABLE I
A003 ꀃ YI SYLLABLE IP
A004 ꀄ YI SYLLABLE IET
A005 ꀅ YI SYLLABLE IEX
A006 ꀆ YI SYLLABLE IE
A007 ꀇ YI SYLLABLE IEP
A008 ꀈ YI SYLLABLE AT
A009 ꀉ YI SYLLABLE AX
A00A ꀊ YI SYLLABLE A
A00B ꀋ YI SYLLABLE AP
A00C ꀌ YI SYLLABLE UOX
A00D ꀍ YI SYLLABLE UO
A00E ꀎ YI SYLLABLE UOP
A00F ꀏ YI SYLLABLE OT
A010 ꀐ YI SYLLABLE OX
A011 ꀑ YI SYLLABLE O
A012 ꀒ YI SYLLABLE OP
A013 ꀓ YI SYLLABLE EX
A014 ꀔ YI SYLLABLE E

Syllable iteration mark

A015 ꀕ YI SYLLABLE WU
※ YI SYLLABLE ITERATION MARK
• name is a misnomer

Syllables

A016 ꀖ YI SYLLABLE BIT
A017 ꀗ YI SYLLABLE BIX
A018 ꀘ YI SYLLABLE BI
A019 ꀙ YI SYLLABLE BIP
A01A ꀚ YI SYLLABLE BIET
A01B ꀛ YI SYLLABLE BIEX
A01C ꀜ YI SYLLABLE BIE
A01D ꀝ YI SYLLABLE BIEP
A01E ꀞ YI SYLLABLE BAT
A01F ꀟ YI SYLLABLE BAX
A020 ꀠ YI SYLLABLE BA
A021 ꀡ YI SYLLABLE BAP
A022 ꀢ YI SYLLABLE BUOX
A023 ꀣ YI SYLLABLE BUO
A024 ꀤ YI SYLLABLE BUOP
A025 ꀥ YI SYLLABLE BOT
A026 ꀦ YI SYLLABLE BOX
A027 ꀧ YI SYLLABLE BO
A028 ꀨ YI SYLLABLE BOP
A029 ꀩ YI SYLLABLE BEX
A02A ꀪ YI SYLLABLE BE
A02B ꀫ YI SYLLABLE BEP
A02C ꀬ YI SYLLABLE BUT
A02D ꀭ YI SYLLABLE BUX
A02E ꀮ YI SYLLABLE BU
A02F ꀯ YI SYLLABLE BUP
A030 ꀰ YI SYLLABLE BURX
A031 ꀱ YI SYLLABLE BUR
A032 ꀲ YI SYLLABLE BYT
A033 ꀳ YI SYLLABLE BYX
A034 ꀴ YI SYLLABLE BY
A035 ꀵ YI SYLLABLE BYP
A036 ꀶ YI SYLLABLE BYRX
A037 ꀷ YI SYLLABLE BYR
A038 ꀸ YI SYLLABLE PIT
A039 ꀹ YI SYLLABLE PIX
A03A ꀺ YI SYLLABLE PI
A03B ꀻ YI SYLLABLE PIP
A03C ꀼ YI SYLLABLE PIEX
A03D ꀽ YI SYLLABLE PIE
A03E ꀾ YI SYLLABLE PIEP
A03F ꀿ YI SYLLABLE PAT
A040 ꁀ YI SYLLABLE PAX
A041 ꁁ YI SYLLABLE PA
A042 ꁂ YI SYLLABLE PAP
A043 ꁃ YI SYLLABLE PUOX
A044 ꁄ YI SYLLABLE PUO
A045 ꁅ YI SYLLABLE PUOP
A046 ꁆ YI SYLLABLE POT
A047 ꁇ YI SYLLABLE POX
A048 ꁈ YI SYLLABLE PO
A049 ꁉ YI SYLLABLE POP
A04A ꁊ YI SYLLABLE PUT
A04B ꁋ YI SYLLABLE PUX
A04C ꁌ YI SYLLABLE PU
A04D ꁍ YI SYLLABLE PUP
A04E ꁎ YI SYLLABLE PURX
A04F ꁏ YI SYLLABLE PUR
A050 ꁐ YI SYLLABLE PYT
A051 ꁑ YI SYLLABLE PYX
A052 ꁒ YI SYLLABLE PY
A053 ꁓ YI SYLLABLE PYP
A054 ꁔ YI SYLLABLE PYRX
A055 ꁕ YI SYLLABLE PYR
A056 ꁖ YI SYLLABLE BBIT
A057 ꁗ YI SYLLABLE BBIX
A058 ꁘ YI SYLLABLE BBI
A059 ꁙ YI SYLLABLE BBIP
A05A ꁚ YI SYLLABLE BBIET
A05B ꁛ YI SYLLABLE BBIEX
A05C ꁜ YI SYLLABLE BBIE
A05D ꁝ YI SYLLABLE BBIEP
A05E ꁞ YI SYLLABLE BBAT
A05F ꁟ YI SYLLABLE BBAX
A060 ꁠ YI SYLLABLE BBA
A061 ꁡ YI SYLLABLE BBAP
A062 ꁢ YI SYLLABLE BBUOX
A063 ꁣ YI SYLLABLE BBUO
A064 ꁤ YI SYLLABLE BBUOP
A065 ꁥ YI SYLLABLE BBOT
A066 ꁦ YI SYLLABLE BBOX
A067 ꁧ YI SYLLABLE BBO
A068 ꁨ YI SYLLABLE BBOP
A069 ꁩ YI SYLLABLE BBEX
A06A ꁪ YI SYLLABLE BBE
A06B ꁫ YI SYLLABLE BBEP
A06C ꁬ YI SYLLABLE BBUT
A06D ꁭ YI SYLLABLE BBUX
A06E ꁮ YI SYLLABLE BBU
A06F ꁯ YI SYLLABLE BBUP
A070 ꁰ YI SYLLABLE BBURX
A071 ꁱ YI SYLLABLE BBUR
A072 ꁲ YI SYLLABLE BBYT
A073 ꁳ YI SYLLABLE BBYX
A074 ꁴ YI SYLLABLE BBY
A075 ꁵ YI SYLLABLE BBYP
A076 ꁶ YI SYLLABLE NBIT
A077 ꁷ YI SYLLABLE NBIX

A078 ꁸ YI SYLLABLE NBI
A079 ꁹ YI SYLLABLE NBIP
A07A ꁺ YI SYLLABLE NBIEX
A07B ꁻ YI SYLLABLE NBIE
A07C ꁼ YI SYLLABLE NBIEP
A07D ꁽ YI SYLLABLE NBAT
A07E ꁾ YI SYLLABLE NBAX
A07F ꁿ YI SYLLABLE NBA
A080 ꂀ YI SYLLABLE NBAP
A081 ꂁ YI SYLLABLE NBOT
A082 ꂂ YI SYLLABLE NBOX
A083 ꂃ YI SYLLABLE NBO
A084 ꂄ YI SYLLABLE NBOP
A085 ꂅ YI SYLLABLE NBUT
A086 ꂆ YI SYLLABLE NBUX
A087 ꂇ YI SYLLABLE NBU
A088 ꂈ YI SYLLABLE NBUP
A089 ꂉ YI SYLLABLE NBURX
A08A ꂊ YI SYLLABLE NBUR
A08B ꂋ YI SYLLABLE NBYT
A08C ꂌ YI SYLLABLE NBYX
A08D ꂍ YI SYLLABLE NBY
A08E ꂎ YI SYLLABLE NBYP
A08F ꂏ YI SYLLABLE NBYRX
A090 ꂐ YI SYLLABLE NBYR
A091 ꂑ YI SYLLABLE HMIT
A092 ꂒ YI SYLLABLE HMIX
A093 ꂓ YI SYLLABLE HMI
A094 ꂔ YI SYLLABLE HMIP
A095 ꂕ YI SYLLABLE HMIEX
A096 ꂖ YI SYLLABLE HMIE
A097 ꂗ YI SYLLABLE HMIEP
A098 ꂘ YI SYLLABLE HMAT
A099 ꂙ YI SYLLABLE HMAX
A09A ꂚ YI SYLLABLE HMA
A09B ꂛ YI SYLLABLE HMAP
A09C ꂜ YI SYLLABLE HMUOX
A09D ꂝ YI SYLLABLE HMUO
A09E ꂞ YI SYLLABLE HMUOP
A09F ꂟ YI SYLLABLE HMOT
A0A0 ꂠ YI SYLLABLE HMOX
A0A1 ꂡ YI SYLLABLE HMO
A0A2 ꂢ YI SYLLABLE HMOP
A0A3 ꂣ YI SYLLABLE HMUT
A0A4 ꂤ YI SYLLABLE HMUX
A0A5 ꂥ YI SYLLABLE HMU
A0A6 ꂦ YI SYLLABLE HMUP
A0A7 ꂧ YI SYLLABLE HMURX
A0A8 ꂨ YI SYLLABLE HMUR
A0A9 ꂩ YI SYLLABLE HMYX
A0AA ꂪ YI SYLLABLE HMY
A0AB ꂫ YI SYLLABLE HMYP
A0AC ꂬ YI SYLLABLE HMYRX
A0AD ꂭ YI SYLLABLE HMYR
A0AE ꂮ YI SYLLABLE MIT
A0AF ꂯ YI SYLLABLE MIX
A0B0 ꂰ YI SYLLABLE MI
A0B1 ꂱ YI SYLLABLE MIP
A0B2 ꂲ YI SYLLABLE MIEX
A0B3 ꂳ YI SYLLABLE MIE
A0B4 ꂴ YI SYLLABLE MIEP
A0B5 ꂵ YI SYLLABLE MAT
A0B6 ꂶ YI SYLLABLE MAX
A0B7 ꂷ YI SYLLABLE MA
A0B8 ꂸ YI SYLLABLE MAP
A0B9 ꂹ YI SYLLABLE MUOT
A0BA ꂺ YI SYLLABLE MUOX
A0BB ꂻ YI SYLLABLE MUO
A0BC ꂼ YI SYLLABLE MUOP
A0BD ꂽ YI SYLLABLE MOT
A0BE ꂾ YI SYLLABLE MOX
A0BF ꂿ YI SYLLABLE MO
A0C0 ꃀ YI SYLLABLE MOP
A0C1 ꃁ YI SYLLABLE MEX
A0C2 ꃂ YI SYLLABLE ME
A0C3 ꃃ YI SYLLABLE MUT
A0C4 ꃄ YI SYLLABLE MUX
A0C5 ꃅ YI SYLLABLE MU
A0C6 ꃆ YI SYLLABLE MUP
A0C7 ꃇ YI SYLLABLE MURX
A0C8 ꃈ YI SYLLABLE MUR
A0C9 ꃉ YI SYLLABLE MYT
A0CA ꃊ YI SYLLABLE MYX
A0CB ꃋ YI SYLLABLE MY
A0CC ꃌ YI SYLLABLE MYP
A0CD ꃍ YI SYLLABLE FIT
A0CE ꃎ YI SYLLABLE FIX
A0CF ꃏ YI SYLLABLE FI
A0D0 ꃐ YI SYLLABLE FIP
A0D1 ꃑ YI SYLLABLE FAT
A0D2 ꃒ YI SYLLABLE FAX
A0D3 ꃓ YI SYLLABLE FA
A0D4 ꃔ YI SYLLABLE FAP
A0D5 ꃕ YI SYLLABLE FOX
A0D6 ꃖ YI SYLLABLE FO
A0D7 ꃗ YI SYLLABLE FOP
A0D8 ꃘ YI SYLLABLE FUT
A0D9 ꃙ YI SYLLABLE FUX
A0DA ꃚ YI SYLLABLE FU
A0DB ꃛ YI SYLLABLE FUP
A0DC ꃜ YI SYLLABLE FURX
A0DD ꃝ YI SYLLABLE FUR
A0DE ꃞ YI SYLLABLE FYT
A0DF ꃟ YI SYLLABLE FYX
A0E0 ꃠ YI SYLLABLE FY
A0E1 ꃡ YI SYLLABLE FYP
A0E2 ꃢ YI SYLLABLE VIT
A0E3 ꃣ YI SYLLABLE VIX
A0E4 ꃤ YI SYLLABLE VI
A0E5 ꃥ YI SYLLABLE VIP
A0E6 ꃦ YI SYLLABLE VIET
A0E7 ꃧ YI SYLLABLE VIEX
A0E8 ꃨ YI SYLLABLE VIE
A0E9 ꃩ YI SYLLABLE VIEP
A0EA ꃪ YI SYLLABLE VAT
A0EB ꃫ YI SYLLABLE VAX
A0EC ꃬ YI SYLLABLE VA
A0ED ꃭ YI SYLLABLE VAP
A0EE ꃮ YI SYLLABLE VOT
A0EF ꃯ YI SYLLABLE VOX
A0F0 ꃰ YI SYLLABLE VO
A0F1 ꃱ YI SYLLABLE VOP
A0F2 ꃲ YI SYLLABLE VEX
A0F3 ꃳ YI SYLLABLE VEP
A0F4 ꃴ YI SYLLABLE VUT
A0F5 ꃵ YI SYLLABLE VUX

A0F6 ꃶ YI SYLLABLE VU
A0F7 ꃷ YI SYLLABLE VUP
A0F8 ꃸ YI SYLLABLE VURX
A0F9 ꃹ YI SYLLABLE VUR
A0FA ꃺ YI SYLLABLE VYT
A0FB ꃻ YI SYLLABLE VYX
A0FC ꃼ YI SYLLABLE VY
A0FD ꃽ YI SYLLABLE VYP
A0FE ꃾ YI SYLLABLE VYRX
A0FF ꃿ YI SYLLABLE VYR
A100 ꄀ YI SYLLABLE DIT
A101 ꄁ YI SYLLABLE DIX
A102 ꄂ YI SYLLABLE DI
A103 ꄃ YI SYLLABLE DIP
A104 ꄄ YI SYLLABLE DIEX
A105 ꄅ YI SYLLABLE DIE
A106 ꄆ YI SYLLABLE DIEP
A107 ꄇ YI SYLLABLE DAT
A108 ꄈ YI SYLLABLE DAX
A109 ꄉ YI SYLLABLE DA
A10A ꄊ YI SYLLABLE DAP
A10B ꄋ YI SYLLABLE DUOX
A10C ꄌ YI SYLLABLE DUO
A10D ꄍ YI SYLLABLE DOT
A10E ꄎ YI SYLLABLE DOX
A10F ꄏ YI SYLLABLE DO
A110 ꄐ YI SYLLABLE DOP
A111 ꄑ YI SYLLABLE DEX
A112 ꄒ YI SYLLABLE DE
A113 ꄓ YI SYLLABLE DEP
A114 ꄔ YI SYLLABLE DUT
A115 ꄕ YI SYLLABLE DUX
A116 ꄖ YI SYLLABLE DU
A117 ꄗ YI SYLLABLE DUP
A118 ꄘ YI SYLLABLE DURX
A119 ꄙ YI SYLLABLE DUR
A11A ꄚ YI SYLLABLE TIT
A11B ꄛ YI SYLLABLE TIX
A11C ꄜ YI SYLLABLE TI
A11D ꄝ YI SYLLABLE TIP
A11E ꄞ YI SYLLABLE TIEX
A11F ꄟ YI SYLLABLE TIE
A120 ꄠ YI SYLLABLE TIEP
A121 ꄡ YI SYLLABLE TAT
A122 ꄢ YI SYLLABLE TAX
A123 ꄣ YI SYLLABLE TA
A124 ꄤ YI SYLLABLE TAP
A125 ꄥ YI SYLLABLE TUOT
A126 ꄦ YI SYLLABLE TUOX
A127 ꄧ YI SYLLABLE TUO
A128 ꄨ YI SYLLABLE TUOP
A129 ꄩ YI SYLLABLE TOT
A12A ꄪ YI SYLLABLE TOX
A12B ꄫ YI SYLLABLE TO
A12C ꄬ YI SYLLABLE TOP
A12D ꄭ YI SYLLABLE TEX
A12E ꄮ YI SYLLABLE TE
A12F ꄯ YI SYLLABLE TEP
A130 ꄰ YI SYLLABLE TUT
A131 ꄱ YI SYLLABLE TUX
A132 ꄲ YI SYLLABLE TU
A133 ꄳ YI SYLLABLE TUP
A134 ꄴ YI SYLLABLE TURX
A135 ꄵ YI SYLLABLE TUR
A136 ꄶ YI SYLLABLE DDIT
A137 ꄷ YI SYLLABLE DDIX
A138 ꄸ YI SYLLABLE DDI
A139 ꄹ YI SYLLABLE DDIP
A13A ꄺ YI SYLLABLE DDIEX
A13B ꄻ YI SYLLABLE DDIE
A13C ꄼ YI SYLLABLE DDIEP
A13D ꄽ YI SYLLABLE DDAT
A13E ꄾ YI SYLLABLE DDAX
A13F ꄿ YI SYLLABLE DDA
A140 ꅀ YI SYLLABLE DDAP
A141 ꅁ YI SYLLABLE DDUOX
A142 ꅂ YI SYLLABLE DDUO
A143 ꅃ YI SYLLABLE DDUOP
A144 ꅄ YI SYLLABLE DDOT
A145 ꅅ YI SYLLABLE DDOX
A146 ꅆ YI SYLLABLE DDO
A147 ꅇ YI SYLLABLE DDOP
A148 ꅈ YI SYLLABLE DDEX
A149 ꅉ YI SYLLABLE DDE
A14A ꅊ YI SYLLABLE DDEP
A14B ꅋ YI SYLLABLE DDUT
A14C ꅌ YI SYLLABLE DDUX
A14D ꅍ YI SYLLABLE DDU
A14E ꅎ YI SYLLABLE DDUP
A14F ꅏ YI SYLLABLE DDURX
A150 ꅐ YI SYLLABLE DDUR
A151 ꅑ YI SYLLABLE NDIT
A152 ꅒ YI SYLLABLE NDIX
A153 ꅓ YI SYLLABLE NDI
A154 ꅔ YI SYLLABLE NDIP
A155 ꅕ YI SYLLABLE NDIEX
A156 ꅖ YI SYLLABLE NDIE
A157 ꅗ YI SYLLABLE NDAT
A158 ꅘ YI SYLLABLE NDAX
A159 ꅙ YI SYLLABLE NDA
A15A ꅚ YI SYLLABLE NDAP
A15B ꅛ YI SYLLABLE NDOT
A15C ꅜ YI SYLLABLE NDOX
A15D ꅝ YI SYLLABLE NDO
A15E ꅞ YI SYLLABLE NDOP
A15F ꅟ YI SYLLABLE NDEX
A160 ꅠ YI SYLLABLE NDE
A161 ꅡ YI SYLLABLE NDEP
A162 ꅢ YI SYLLABLE NDUT
A163 ꅣ YI SYLLABLE NDUX
A164 ꅤ YI SYLLABLE NDU
A165 ꅥ YI SYLLABLE NDUP
A166 ꅦ YI SYLLABLE NDURX
A167 ꅧ YI SYLLABLE NDUR
A168 ꅨ YI SYLLABLE HNIT
A169 ꅩ YI SYLLABLE HNIX
A16A ꅪ YI SYLLABLE HNI
A16B ꅫ YI SYLLABLE HNIP
A16C ꅬ YI SYLLABLE HNIET
A16D ꅭ YI SYLLABLE HNIEX
A16E ꅮ YI SYLLABLE HNIE
A16F ꅯ YI SYLLABLE HNIEP
A170 ꅰ YI SYLLABLE HNAT
A171 ꅱ YI SYLLABLE HNAX
A172 ꅲ YI SYLLABLE HNA
A173 ꅳ YI SYLLABLE HNAP

A174 YI SYLLABLE HNUOX
A175 YI SYLLABLE HNUO
A176 YI SYLLABLE HNOT
A177 YI SYLLABLE HNOX
A178 YI SYLLABLE HNOP
A179 YI SYLLABLE HNEX
A17A YI SYLLABLE HNE
A17B YI SYLLABLE HNEP
A17C YI SYLLABLE HNUT
A17D YI SYLLABLE NIT
A17E YI SYLLABLE NIX
A17F YI SYLLABLE NI
A180 YI SYLLABLE NIP
A181 YI SYLLABLE NIEX
A182 YI SYLLABLE NIE
A183 YI SYLLABLE NIEP
A184 YI SYLLABLE NAX
A185 YI SYLLABLE NA
A186 YI SYLLABLE NAP
A187 YI SYLLABLE NUOX
A188 YI SYLLABLE NUO
A189 YI SYLLABLE NUOP
A18A YI SYLLABLE NOT
A18B YI SYLLABLE NOX
A18C YI SYLLABLE NO
A18D YI SYLLABLE NOP
A18E YI SYLLABLE NEX
A18F YI SYLLABLE NE
A190 YI SYLLABLE NEP
A191 YI SYLLABLE NUT
A192 YI SYLLABLE NUX
A193 YI SYLLABLE NU
A194 YI SYLLABLE NUP
A195 YI SYLLABLE NURX
A196 YI SYLLABLE NUR
A197 YI SYLLABLE HLIT
A198 YI SYLLABLE HLIX
A199 YI SYLLABLE HLI
A19A YI SYLLABLE HLIP
A19B YI SYLLABLE HLIEX
A19C YI SYLLABLE HLIE
A19D YI SYLLABLE HLIEP
A19E YI SYLLABLE HLAT
A19F YI SYLLABLE HLAX
A1A0 YI SYLLABLE HLA
A1A1 YI SYLLABLE HLAP
A1A2 YI SYLLABLE HLUOX
A1A3 YI SYLLABLE HLUO
A1A4 YI SYLLABLE HLUOP
A1A5 YI SYLLABLE HLOX
A1A6 YI SYLLABLE HLO
A1A7 YI SYLLABLE HLOP
A1A8 YI SYLLABLE HLEX
A1A9 YI SYLLABLE HLE
A1AA YI SYLLABLE HLEP
A1AB YI SYLLABLE HLUT
A1AC YI SYLLABLE HLUX
A1AD YI SYLLABLE HLU
A1AE YI SYLLABLE HLUP
A1AF YI SYLLABLE HLURX
A1B0 YI SYLLABLE HLUR
A1B1 YI SYLLABLE HLYT
A1B2 YI SYLLABLE HLYX
A1B3 YI SYLLABLE HLY
A1B4 YI SYLLABLE HLYP
A1B5 YI SYLLABLE HLYRX
A1B6 YI SYLLABLE HLYR
A1B7 YI SYLLABLE LIT
A1B8 YI SYLLABLE LIX
A1B9 YI SYLLABLE LI
A1BA YI SYLLABLE LIP
A1BB YI SYLLABLE LIET
A1BC YI SYLLABLE LIEX
A1BD YI SYLLABLE LIE
A1BE YI SYLLABLE LIEP
A1BF YI SYLLABLE LAT
A1C0 YI SYLLABLE LAX
A1C1 YI SYLLABLE LA
A1C2 YI SYLLABLE LAP
A1C3 YI SYLLABLE LUOT
A1C4 YI SYLLABLE LUOX
A1C5 YI SYLLABLE LUO
A1C6 YI SYLLABLE LUOP
A1C7 YI SYLLABLE LOT
A1C8 YI SYLLABLE LOX
A1C9 YI SYLLABLE LO
A1CA YI SYLLABLE LOP
A1CB YI SYLLABLE LEX
A1CC YI SYLLABLE LE
A1CD YI SYLLABLE LEP
A1CE YI SYLLABLE LUT
A1CF YI SYLLABLE LUX
A1D0 YI SYLLABLE LU
A1D1 YI SYLLABLE LUP
A1D2 YI SYLLABLE LURX
A1D3 YI SYLLABLE LUR
A1D4 YI SYLLABLE LYT
A1D5 YI SYLLABLE LYX
A1D6 YI SYLLABLE LY
A1D7 YI SYLLABLE LYP
A1D8 YI SYLLABLE LYRX
A1D9 YI SYLLABLE LYR
A1DA YI SYLLABLE GIT
A1DB YI SYLLABLE GIX
A1DC YI SYLLABLE GI
A1DD YI SYLLABLE GIP
A1DE YI SYLLABLE GIET
A1DF YI SYLLABLE GIEX
A1E0 YI SYLLABLE GIE
A1E1 YI SYLLABLE GIEP
A1E2 YI SYLLABLE GAT
A1E3 YI SYLLABLE GAX
A1E4 YI SYLLABLE GA
A1E5 YI SYLLABLE GAP
A1E6 YI SYLLABLE GUOT
A1E7 YI SYLLABLE GUOX
A1E8 YI SYLLABLE GUO
A1E9 YI SYLLABLE GUOP
A1EA YI SYLLABLE GOT
A1EB YI SYLLABLE GOX
A1EC YI SYLLABLE GO
A1ED YI SYLLABLE GOP
A1EE YI SYLLABLE GET
A1EF YI SYLLABLE GEX
A1F0 YI SYLLABLE GE
A1F1 YI SYLLABLE GEP

A1F2 ꇲ YI SYLLABLE GUT
A1F3 ꇳ YI SYLLABLE GUX
A1F4 ꇴ YI SYLLABLE GU
A1F5 ꇵ YI SYLLABLE GUP
A1F6 ꇶ YI SYLLABLE GURX
A1F7 ꇷ YI SYLLABLE GUR
A1F8 ꇸ YI SYLLABLE KIT
A1F9 ꇹ YI SYLLABLE KIX
A1FA ꇺ YI SYLLABLE KI
A1FB ꇻ YI SYLLABLE KIP
A1FC ꇼ YI SYLLABLE KIEX
A1FD ꇽ YI SYLLABLE KIE
A1FE ꇾ YI SYLLABLE KIEP
A1FF ꇿ YI SYLLABLE KAT
A200 ꈀ YI SYLLABLE KAX
A201 ꈁ YI SYLLABLE KA
A202 ꈂ YI SYLLABLE KAP
A203 ꈃ YI SYLLABLE KUOX
A204 ꈄ YI SYLLABLE KUO
A205 ꈅ YI SYLLABLE KUOP
A206 ꈆ YI SYLLABLE KOT
A207 ꈇ YI SYLLABLE KOX
A208 ꈈ YI SYLLABLE KO
A209 ꈉ YI SYLLABLE KOP
A20A ꈊ YI SYLLABLE KET
A20B ꈋ YI SYLLABLE KEX
A20C ꈌ YI SYLLABLE KE
A20D ꈍ YI SYLLABLE KEP
A20E ꈎ YI SYLLABLE KUT
A20F ꈏ YI SYLLABLE KUX
A210 ꈐ YI SYLLABLE KU
A211 ꈑ YI SYLLABLE KUP
A212 ꈒ YI SYLLABLE KURX
A213 ꈓ YI SYLLABLE KUR
A214 ꈔ YI SYLLABLE GGIT
A215 ꈕ YI SYLLABLE GGIX
A216 ꈖ YI SYLLABLE GGI
A217 ꈗ YI SYLLABLE GGIEX
A218 ꈘ YI SYLLABLE GGIE
A219 ꈙ YI SYLLABLE GGIEP
A21A ꈚ YI SYLLABLE GGAT
A21B ꈛ YI SYLLABLE GGAX
A21C ꈜ YI SYLLABLE GGA
A21D ꈝ YI SYLLABLE GGAP
A21E ꈞ YI SYLLABLE GGUOT
A21F ꈟ YI SYLLABLE GGUOX
A220 ꈠ YI SYLLABLE GGUO
A221 ꈡ YI SYLLABLE GGUOP
A222 ꈢ YI SYLLABLE GGOT
A223 ꈣ YI SYLLABLE GGOX
A224 ꈤ YI SYLLABLE GGO
A225 ꈥ YI SYLLABLE GGOP
A226 ꈦ YI SYLLABLE GGET
A227 ꈧ YI SYLLABLE GGEX
A228 ꈨ YI SYLLABLE GGE
A229 ꈩ YI SYLLABLE GGEP
A22A ꈪ YI SYLLABLE GGUT
A22B ꈫ YI SYLLABLE GGUX
A22C ꈬ YI SYLLABLE GGU
A22D ꈭ YI SYLLABLE GGUP
A22E ꈮ YI SYLLABLE GGURX
A22F ꈯ YI SYLLABLE GGUR
A230 ꈰ YI SYLLABLE MGIEX
A231 ꈱ YI SYLLABLE MGIE
A232 ꈲ YI SYLLABLE MGAT
A233 ꈳ YI SYLLABLE MGAX
A234 ꈴ YI SYLLABLE MGA
A235 ꈵ YI SYLLABLE MGAP
A236 ꈶ YI SYLLABLE MGUOX
A237 ꈷ YI SYLLABLE MGUO
A238 ꈸ YI SYLLABLE MGUOP
A239 ꈹ YI SYLLABLE MGOT
A23A ꈺ YI SYLLABLE MGOX
A23B ꈻ YI SYLLABLE MGO
A23C ꈼ YI SYLLABLE MGOP
A23D ꈽ YI SYLLABLE MGEX
A23E ꈾ YI SYLLABLE MGE
A23F ꈿ YI SYLLABLE MGEP
A240 ꉀ YI SYLLABLE MGUT
A241 ꉁ YI SYLLABLE MGUX
A242 ꉂ YI SYLLABLE MGU
A243 ꉃ YI SYLLABLE MGUP
A244 ꉄ YI SYLLABLE MGURX
A245 ꉅ YI SYLLABLE MGUR
A246 ꉆ YI SYLLABLE HXIT
A247 ꉇ YI SYLLABLE HXIX
A248 ꉈ YI SYLLABLE HXI
A249 ꉉ YI SYLLABLE HXIP
A24A ꉊ YI SYLLABLE HXIET
A24B ꉋ YI SYLLABLE HXIEX
A24C ꉌ YI SYLLABLE HXIE
A24D ꉍ YI SYLLABLE HXIEP
A24E ꉎ YI SYLLABLE HXAT
A24F ꉏ YI SYLLABLE HXAX
A250 ꉐ YI SYLLABLE HXA
A251 ꉑ YI SYLLABLE HXAP
A252 ꉒ YI SYLLABLE HXUOT
A253 ꉓ YI SYLLABLE HXUOX
A254 ꉔ YI SYLLABLE HXUO
A255 ꉕ YI SYLLABLE HXUOP
A256 ꉖ YI SYLLABLE HXOT
A257 ꉗ YI SYLLABLE HXOX
A258 ꉘ YI SYLLABLE HXO
A259 ꉙ YI SYLLABLE HXOP
A25A ꉚ YI SYLLABLE HXEX
A25B ꉛ YI SYLLABLE HXE
A25C ꉜ YI SYLLABLE HXEP
A25D ꉝ YI SYLLABLE NGIEX
A25E ꉞ YI SYLLABLE NGIE
A25F ꉟ YI SYLLABLE NGIEP
A260 ꉠ YI SYLLABLE NGAT
A261 ꉡ YI SYLLABLE NGAX
A262 ꉢ YI SYLLABLE NGA
A263 ꉣ YI SYLLABLE NGAP
A264 ꉤ YI SYLLABLE NGUOT
A265 ꉥ YI SYLLABLE NGUOX
A266 ꉦ YI SYLLABLE NGUO
A267 ꉧ YI SYLLABLE NGOT
A268 ꉨ YI SYLLABLE NGOX
A269 ꉩ YI SYLLABLE NGO
A26A ꉪ YI SYLLABLE NGOP
A26B ꉫ YI SYLLABLE NGEX
A26C ꉬ YI SYLLABLE NGE
A26D ꉭ YI SYLLABLE NGEP
A26E ꉮ YI SYLLABLE HIT
A26F ꉯ YI SYLLABLE HIEX

A270 ꉰ YI SYLLABLE HIE
A271 ꉱ YI SYLLABLE HAT
A272 ꉲ YI SYLLABLE HAX
A273 ꉳ YI SYLLABLE HA
A274 ꉴ YI SYLLABLE HAP
A275 ꉵ YI SYLLABLE HUOT
A276 ꉶ YI SYLLABLE HUOX
A277 ꉷ YI SYLLABLE HUO
A278 ꉸ YI SYLLABLE HUOP
A279 ꉹ YI SYLLABLE HOT
A27A ꉺ YI SYLLABLE HOX
A27B ꉻ YI SYLLABLE HO
A27C ꉼ YI SYLLABLE HOP
A27D ꉽ YI SYLLABLE HEX
A27E ꉾ YI SYLLABLE HE
A27F ꉿ YI SYLLABLE HEP
A280 ꊀ YI SYLLABLE WAT
A281 ꊁ YI SYLLABLE WAX
A282 ꊂ YI SYLLABLE WA
A283 ꊃ YI SYLLABLE WAP
A284 ꊄ YI SYLLABLE WUOX
A285 ꊅ YI SYLLABLE WUO
A286 ꊆ YI SYLLABLE WUOP
A287 ꊇ YI SYLLABLE WOX
A288 ꊈ YI SYLLABLE WO
A289 ꊉ YI SYLLABLE WOP
A28A ꊊ YI SYLLABLE WEX
A28B ꊋ YI SYLLABLE WE
A28C ꊌ YI SYLLABLE WEP
A28D ꊍ YI SYLLABLE ZIT
A28E ꊎ YI SYLLABLE ZIX
A28F ꊏ YI SYLLABLE ZI
A290 ꊐ YI SYLLABLE ZIP
A291 ꊑ YI SYLLABLE ZIEX
A292 ꊒ YI SYLLABLE ZIE
A293 ꊓ YI SYLLABLE ZIEP
A294 ꊔ YI SYLLABLE ZAT
A295 ꊕ YI SYLLABLE ZAX
A296 ꊖ YI SYLLABLE ZA
A297 ꊗ YI SYLLABLE ZAP
A298 ꊘ YI SYLLABLE ZUOX
A299 ꊙ YI SYLLABLE ZUO
A29A ꊚ YI SYLLABLE ZUOP
A29B ꊛ YI SYLLABLE ZOT
A29C ꊜ YI SYLLABLE ZOX
A29D ꊝ YI SYLLABLE ZO
A29E ꊞ YI SYLLABLE ZOP
A29F ꊟ YI SYLLABLE ZEX
A2A0 ꊠ YI SYLLABLE ZE
A2A1 ꊡ YI SYLLABLE ZEP
A2A2 ꊢ YI SYLLABLE ZUT
A2A3 ꊣ YI SYLLABLE ZUX
A2A4 ꊤ YI SYLLABLE ZU
A2A5 ꊥ YI SYLLABLE ZUP
A2A6 ꊦ YI SYLLABLE ZURX
A2A7 ꊧ YI SYLLABLE ZUR
A2A8 ꊨ YI SYLLABLE ZYT
A2A9 ꊩ YI SYLLABLE ZYX
A2AA ꊪ YI SYLLABLE ZY
A2AB ꊫ YI SYLLABLE ZYP
A2AC ꊬ YI SYLLABLE ZYRX
A2AD ꊭ YI SYLLABLE ZYR
A2AE ꊮ YI SYLLABLE CIT
A2AF ꊯ YI SYLLABLE CIX
A2B0 ꊰ YI SYLLABLE CI
A2B1 ꊱ YI SYLLABLE CIP
A2B2 ꊲ YI SYLLABLE CIET
A2B3 ꊳ YI SYLLABLE CIEX
A2B4 ꊴ YI SYLLABLE CIE
A2B5 ꊵ YI SYLLABLE CIEP
A2B6 ꊶ YI SYLLABLE CAT
A2B7 ꊷ YI SYLLABLE CAX
A2B8 ꊸ YI SYLLABLE CA
A2B9 ꊹ YI SYLLABLE CAP
A2BA ꊺ YI SYLLABLE CUOX
A2BB ꊻ YI SYLLABLE CUO
A2BC ꊼ YI SYLLABLE CUOP
A2BD ꊽ YI SYLLABLE COT
A2BE ꊾ YI SYLLABLE COX
A2BF ꊿ YI SYLLABLE CO
A2C0 ꋀ YI SYLLABLE COP
A2C1 ꋁ YI SYLLABLE CEX
A2C2 ꋂ YI SYLLABLE CE
A2C3 ꋃ YI SYLLABLE CEP
A2C4 ꋄ YI SYLLABLE CUT
A2C5 ꋅ YI SYLLABLE CUX
A2C6 ꋆ YI SYLLABLE CU
A2C7 ꋇ YI SYLLABLE CUP
A2C8 ꋈ YI SYLLABLE CURX
A2C9 ꋉ YI SYLLABLE CUR
A2CA ꋊ YI SYLLABLE CYT
A2CB ꋋ YI SYLLABLE CYX
A2CC ꋌ YI SYLLABLE CY
A2CD ꋍ YI SYLLABLE CYP
A2CE ꋎ YI SYLLABLE CYRX
A2CF ꋏ YI SYLLABLE CYR
A2D0 ꋐ YI SYLLABLE ZZIT
A2D1 ꋑ YI SYLLABLE ZZIX
A2D2 ꋒ YI SYLLABLE ZZI
A2D3 ꋓ YI SYLLABLE ZZIP
A2D4 ꋔ YI SYLLABLE ZZIET
A2D5 ꋕ YI SYLLABLE ZZIEX
A2D6 ꋖ YI SYLLABLE ZZIE
A2D7 ꋗ YI SYLLABLE ZZIEP
A2D8 ꋘ YI SYLLABLE ZZAT
A2D9 ꋙ YI SYLLABLE ZZAX
A2DA ꋚ YI SYLLABLE ZZA
A2DB ꋛ YI SYLLABLE ZZAP
A2DC ꋜ YI SYLLABLE ZZOX
A2DD ꋝ YI SYLLABLE ZZO
A2DE ꋞ YI SYLLABLE ZZOP
A2DF ꋟ YI SYLLABLE ZZEX
A2E0 ꋠ YI SYLLABLE ZZE
A2E1 ꋡ YI SYLLABLE ZZEP
A2E2 ꋢ YI SYLLABLE ZZUX
A2E3 ꋣ YI SYLLABLE ZZU
A2E4 ꋤ YI SYLLABLE ZZUP
A2E5 ꋥ YI SYLLABLE ZZURX
A2E6 ꋦ YI SYLLABLE ZZUR
A2E7 ꋧ YI SYLLABLE ZZYT
A2E8 ꋨ YI SYLLABLE ZZYX
A2E9 ꋩ YI SYLLABLE ZZY
A2EA ꋪ YI SYLLABLE ZZYP
A2EB ꋫ YI SYLLABLE ZZYRX
A2EC ꋬ YI SYLLABLE ZZYR
A2ED ꋭ YI SYLLABLE NZIT

A2EE YI SYLLABLE NZIX
A2EF YI SYLLABLE NZI
A2F0 YI SYLLABLE NZIP
A2F1 YI SYLLABLE NZIEX
A2F2 YI SYLLABLE NZIE
A2F3 YI SYLLABLE NZIEP
A2F4 YI SYLLABLE NZAT
A2F5 YI SYLLABLE NZAX
A2F6 YI SYLLABLE NZA
A2F7 YI SYLLABLE NZAP
A2F8 YI SYLLABLE NZUOX
A2F9 YI SYLLABLE NZUO
A2FA YI SYLLABLE NZOX
A2FB YI SYLLABLE NZOP
A2FC YI SYLLABLE NZEX
A2FD YI SYLLABLE NZE
A2FE YI SYLLABLE NZUX
A2FF YI SYLLABLE NZU
A300 YI SYLLABLE NZUP
A301 YI SYLLABLE NZURX
A302 YI SYLLABLE NZUR
A303 YI SYLLABLE NZYT
A304 YI SYLLABLE NZYX
A305 YI SYLLABLE NZY
A306 YI SYLLABLE NZYP
A307 YI SYLLABLE NZYRX
A308 YI SYLLABLE NZYR
A309 YI SYLLABLE SIT
A30A YI SYLLABLE SIX
A30B YI SYLLABLE SI
A30C YI SYLLABLE SIP
A30D YI SYLLABLE SIEX
A30E YI SYLLABLE SIE
A30F YI SYLLABLE SIEP
A310 YI SYLLABLE SAT
A311 YI SYLLABLE SAX
A312 YI SYLLABLE SA
A313 YI SYLLABLE SAP
A314 YI SYLLABLE SUOX
A315 YI SYLLABLE SUO
A316 YI SYLLABLE SUOP
A317 YI SYLLABLE SOT
A318 YI SYLLABLE SOX
A319 YI SYLLABLE SO
A31A YI SYLLABLE SOP
A31B YI SYLLABLE SEX
A31C YI SYLLABLE SE
A31D YI SYLLABLE SEP
A31E YI SYLLABLE SUT
A31F YI SYLLABLE SUX
A320 YI SYLLABLE SU
A321 YI SYLLABLE SUP
A322 YI SYLLABLE SURX
A323 YI SYLLABLE SUR
A324 YI SYLLABLE SYT
A325 YI SYLLABLE SYX
A326 YI SYLLABLE SY
A327 YI SYLLABLE SYP
A328 YI SYLLABLE SYRX
A329 YI SYLLABLE SYR
A32A YI SYLLABLE SSIT
A32B YI SYLLABLE SSIX
A32C YI SYLLABLE SSI
A32D YI SYLLABLE SSIP
A32E YI SYLLABLE SSIEX
A32F YI SYLLABLE SSIE
A330 YI SYLLABLE SSIEP
A331 YI SYLLABLE SSAT
A332 YI SYLLABLE SSAX
A333 YI SYLLABLE SSA
A334 YI SYLLABLE SSAP
A335 YI SYLLABLE SSOT
A336 YI SYLLABLE SSOX
A337 YI SYLLABLE SSO
A338 YI SYLLABLE SSOP
A339 YI SYLLABLE SSEX
A33A YI SYLLABLE SSE
A33B YI SYLLABLE SSEP
A33C YI SYLLABLE SSUT
A33D YI SYLLABLE SSUX
A33E YI SYLLABLE SSU
A33F YI SYLLABLE SSUP
A340 YI SYLLABLE SSYT
A341 YI SYLLABLE SSYX
A342 YI SYLLABLE SSY
A343 YI SYLLABLE SSYP
A344 YI SYLLABLE SSYRX
A345 YI SYLLABLE SSYR
A346 YI SYLLABLE ZHAT
A347 YI SYLLABLE ZHAX
A348 YI SYLLABLE ZHA
A349 YI SYLLABLE ZHAP
A34A YI SYLLABLE ZHUOX
A34B YI SYLLABLE ZHUO
A34C YI SYLLABLE ZHUOP
A34D YI SYLLABLE ZHOT
A34E YI SYLLABLE ZHOX
A34F YI SYLLABLE ZHO
A350 YI SYLLABLE ZHOP
A351 YI SYLLABLE ZHET
A352 YI SYLLABLE ZHEX
A353 YI SYLLABLE ZHE
A354 YI SYLLABLE ZHEP
A355 YI SYLLABLE ZHUT
A356 YI SYLLABLE ZHUX
A357 YI SYLLABLE ZHU
A358 YI SYLLABLE ZHUP
A359 YI SYLLABLE ZHURX
A35A YI SYLLABLE ZHUR
A35B YI SYLLABLE ZHYT
A35C YI SYLLABLE ZHYX
A35D YI SYLLABLE ZHY
A35E YI SYLLABLE ZHYP
A35F YI SYLLABLE ZHYRX
A360 YI SYLLABLE ZHYR
A361 YI SYLLABLE CHAT
A362 YI SYLLABLE CHAX
A363 YI SYLLABLE CHA
A364 YI SYLLABLE CHAP
A365 YI SYLLABLE CHUOT
A366 YI SYLLABLE CHUOX
A367 YI SYLLABLE CHUO
A368 YI SYLLABLE CHUOP
A369 YI SYLLABLE CHOT
A36A YI SYLLABLE CHOX
A36B YI SYLLABLE CHO

A36C	ꍬ	YI SYLLABLE CHOP
A36D	ꍭ	YI SYLLABLE CHET
A36E	ꍮ	YI SYLLABLE CHEX
A36F	ꍯ	YI SYLLABLE CHE
A370	ꍰ	YI SYLLABLE CHEP
A371	ꍱ	YI SYLLABLE CHUX
A372	ꍲ	YI SYLLABLE CHU
A373	ꍳ	YI SYLLABLE CHUP
A374	ꍴ	YI SYLLABLE CHURX
A375	ꍵ	YI SYLLABLE CHUR
A376	ꍶ	YI SYLLABLE CHYT
A377	ꍷ	YI SYLLABLE CHYX
A378	ꍸ	YI SYLLABLE CHY
A379	ꍹ	YI SYLLABLE CHYP
A37A	ꍺ	YI SYLLABLE CHYRX
A37B	ꍻ	YI SYLLABLE CHYR
A37C	ꍼ	YI SYLLABLE RRAX
A37D	ꍽ	YI SYLLABLE RRA
A37E	ꍾ	YI SYLLABLE RRUOX
A37F	ꍿ	YI SYLLABLE RRUO
A380	ꎀ	YI SYLLABLE RROT
A381	ꎁ	YI SYLLABLE RROX
A382	ꎂ	YI SYLLABLE RRO
A383	ꎃ	YI SYLLABLE RROP
A384	ꎄ	YI SYLLABLE RRET
A385	ꎅ	YI SYLLABLE RREX
A386	ꎆ	YI SYLLABLE RRE
A387	ꎇ	YI SYLLABLE RREP
A388	ꎈ	YI SYLLABLE RRUT
A389	ꎉ	YI SYLLABLE RRUX
A38A	ꎊ	YI SYLLABLE RRU
A38B	ꎋ	YI SYLLABLE RRUP
A38C	ꎌ	YI SYLLABLE RRURX
A38D	ꎍ	YI SYLLABLE RRUR
A38E	ꎎ	YI SYLLABLE RRYT
A38F	ꎏ	YI SYLLABLE RRYX
A390	ꎐ	YI SYLLABLE RRY
A391	ꎑ	YI SYLLABLE RRYP
A392	ꎒ	YI SYLLABLE RRYRX
A393	ꎓ	YI SYLLABLE RRYR
A394	ꎔ	YI SYLLABLE NRAT
A395	ꎕ	YI SYLLABLE NRAX
A396	ꎖ	YI SYLLABLE NRA
A397	ꎗ	YI SYLLABLE NRAP
A398	ꎘ	YI SYLLABLE NROX
A399	ꎙ	YI SYLLABLE NRO
A39A	ꎚ	YI SYLLABLE NROP
A39B	ꎛ	YI SYLLABLE NRET
A39C	ꎜ	YI SYLLABLE NREX
A39D	ꎝ	YI SYLLABLE NRE
A39E	ꎞ	YI SYLLABLE NREP
A39F	ꎟ	YI SYLLABLE NRUT
A3A0	ꎠ	YI SYLLABLE NRUX
A3A1	ꎡ	YI SYLLABLE NRU
A3A2	ꎢ	YI SYLLABLE NRUP
A3A3	ꎣ	YI SYLLABLE NRURX
A3A4	ꎤ	YI SYLLABLE NRUR
A3A5	ꎥ	YI SYLLABLE NRYT
A3A6	ꎦ	YI SYLLABLE NRYX
A3A7	ꎧ	YI SYLLABLE NRY
A3A8	ꎨ	YI SYLLABLE NRYP
A3A9	ꎩ	YI SYLLABLE NRYRX
A3AA	ꎪ	YI SYLLABLE NRYR
A3AB	ꎫ	YI SYLLABLE SHAT
A3AC	ꎬ	YI SYLLABLE SHAX
A3AD	ꎭ	YI SYLLABLE SHA
A3AE	ꎮ	YI SYLLABLE SHAP
A3AF	ꎯ	YI SYLLABLE SHUOX
A3B0	ꎰ	YI SYLLABLE SHUO
A3B1	ꎱ	YI SYLLABLE SHUOP
A3B2	ꎲ	YI SYLLABLE SHOT
A3B3	ꎳ	YI SYLLABLE SHOX
A3B4	ꎴ	YI SYLLABLE SHO
A3B5	ꎵ	YI SYLLABLE SHOP
A3B6	ꎶ	YI SYLLABLE SHET
A3B7	ꎷ	YI SYLLABLE SHEX
A3B8	ꎸ	YI SYLLABLE SHE
A3B9	ꎹ	YI SYLLABLE SHEP
A3BA	ꎺ	YI SYLLABLE SHUT
A3BB	ꎻ	YI SYLLABLE SHUX
A3BC	ꎼ	YI SYLLABLE SHU
A3BD	ꎽ	YI SYLLABLE SHUP
A3BE	ꎾ	YI SYLLABLE SHURX
A3BF	ꎿ	YI SYLLABLE SHUR
A3C0	ꏀ	YI SYLLABLE SHYT
A3C1	ꏁ	YI SYLLABLE SHYX
A3C2	ꏂ	YI SYLLABLE SHY
A3C3	ꏃ	YI SYLLABLE SHYP
A3C4	ꏄ	YI SYLLABLE SHYRX
A3C5	ꏅ	YI SYLLABLE SHYR
A3C6	ꏆ	YI SYLLABLE RAT
A3C7	ꏇ	YI SYLLABLE RAX
A3C8	ꏈ	YI SYLLABLE RA
A3C9	ꏉ	YI SYLLABLE RAP
A3CA	ꏊ	YI SYLLABLE RUOX
A3CB	ꏋ	YI SYLLABLE RUO
A3CC	ꏌ	YI SYLLABLE RUOP
A3CD	ꏍ	YI SYLLABLE ROT
A3CE	ꏎ	YI SYLLABLE ROX
A3CF	ꏏ	YI SYLLABLE RO
A3D0	ꏐ	YI SYLLABLE ROP
A3D1	ꏑ	YI SYLLABLE REX
A3D2	ꏒ	YI SYLLABLE RE
A3D3	ꏓ	YI SYLLABLE REP
A3D4	ꏔ	YI SYLLABLE RUT
A3D5	ꏕ	YI SYLLABLE RUX
A3D6	ꏖ	YI SYLLABLE RU
A3D7	ꏗ	YI SYLLABLE RUP
A3D8	ꏘ	YI SYLLABLE RURX
A3D9	ꏙ	YI SYLLABLE RUR
A3DA	ꏚ	YI SYLLABLE RYT
A3DB	ꏛ	YI SYLLABLE RYX
A3DC	ꏜ	YI SYLLABLE RY
A3DD	ꏝ	YI SYLLABLE RYP
A3DE	ꏞ	YI SYLLABLE RYRX
A3DF	ꏟ	YI SYLLABLE RYR
A3E0	ꏠ	YI SYLLABLE JIT
A3E1	ꏡ	YI SYLLABLE JIX
A3E2	ꏢ	YI SYLLABLE JI
A3E3	ꏣ	YI SYLLABLE JIP
A3E4	ꏤ	YI SYLLABLE JIET
A3E5	ꏥ	YI SYLLABLE JIEX
A3E6	ꏦ	YI SYLLABLE JIE
A3E7	ꏧ	YI SYLLABLE JIEP
A3E8	ꏨ	YI SYLLABLE JUOT
A3E9	ꏩ	YI SYLLABLE JUOX

A3EA ꏪ YI SYLLABLE JUO
A3EB ꏫ YI SYLLABLE JUOP
A3EC ꏬ YI SYLLABLE JOT
A3ED ꏭ YI SYLLABLE JOX
A3EE ꏮ YI SYLLABLE JO
A3EF ꏯ YI SYLLABLE JOP
A3F0 ꏰ YI SYLLABLE JUT
A3F1 ꏱ YI SYLLABLE JUX
A3F2 ꏲ YI SYLLABLE JU
A3F3 ꏳ YI SYLLABLE JUP
A3F4 ꏴ YI SYLLABLE JURX
A3F5 ꏵ YI SYLLABLE JUR
A3F6 ꏶ YI SYLLABLE JYT
A3F7 ꏷ YI SYLLABLE JYX
A3F8 ꏸ YI SYLLABLE JY
A3F9 ꏹ YI SYLLABLE JYP
A3FA ꏺ YI SYLLABLE JYRX
A3FB ꏻ YI SYLLABLE JYR
A3FC ꏼ YI SYLLABLE QIT
A3FD ꏽ YI SYLLABLE QIX
A3FE ꏾ YI SYLLABLE QI
A3FF ꏿ YI SYLLABLE QIP
A400 ꐀ YI SYLLABLE QIET
A401 ꐁ YI SYLLABLE QIEX
A402 ꐂ YI SYLLABLE QIE
A403 ꐃ YI SYLLABLE QIEP
A404 ꐄ YI SYLLABLE QUOT
A405 ꐅ YI SYLLABLE QUOX
A406 ꐆ YI SYLLABLE QUO
A407 ꐇ YI SYLLABLE QUOP
A408 ꐈ YI SYLLABLE QOT
A409 ꐉ YI SYLLABLE QOX
A40A ꐊ YI SYLLABLE QO
A40B ꐋ YI SYLLABLE QOP
A40C ꐌ YI SYLLABLE QUT
A40D ꐍ YI SYLLABLE QUX
A40E ꐎ YI SYLLABLE QU
A40F ꐏ YI SYLLABLE QUP
A410 ꐐ YI SYLLABLE QURX
A411 ꐑ YI SYLLABLE QUR
A412 ꐒ YI SYLLABLE QYT
A413 ꐓ YI SYLLABLE QYX
A414 ꐔ YI SYLLABLE QY
A415 ꐕ YI SYLLABLE QYP
A416 ꐖ YI SYLLABLE QYRX
A417 ꐗ YI SYLLABLE QYR
A418 ꐘ YI SYLLABLE JJIT
A419 ꐙ YI SYLLABLE JJIX
A41A ꐚ YI SYLLABLE JJI
A41B ꐛ YI SYLLABLE JJIP
A41C ꐜ YI SYLLABLE JJIET
A41D ꐝ YI SYLLABLE JJIEX
A41E ꐞ YI SYLLABLE JJIE
A41F ꐟ YI SYLLABLE JJIEP
A420 ꐠ YI SYLLABLE JJUOX
A421 ꐡ YI SYLLABLE JJUO
A422 ꐢ YI SYLLABLE JJUOP
A423 ꐣ YI SYLLABLE JJOT
A424 ꐤ YI SYLLABLE JJOX
A425 ꐥ YI SYLLABLE JJO
A426 ꐦ YI SYLLABLE JJOP
A427 ꐧ YI SYLLABLE JJUT
A428 ꐨ YI SYLLABLE JJUX
A429 ꐩ YI SYLLABLE JJU
A42A ꐪ YI SYLLABLE JJUP
A42B ꐫ YI SYLLABLE JJURX
A42C ꐬ YI SYLLABLE JJUR
A42D ꐭ YI SYLLABLE JJYT
A42E ꐮ YI SYLLABLE JJYX
A42F ꐯ YI SYLLABLE JJY
A430 ꐰ YI SYLLABLE JJYP
A431 ꐱ YI SYLLABLE NJIT
A432 ꐲ YI SYLLABLE NJIX
A433 ꐳ YI SYLLABLE NJI
A434 ꐴ YI SYLLABLE NJIP
A435 ꐵ YI SYLLABLE NJIET
A436 ꐶ YI SYLLABLE NJIEX
A437 ꐷ YI SYLLABLE NJIE
A438 ꐸ YI SYLLABLE NJIEP
A439 ꐹ YI SYLLABLE NJUOX
A43A ꐺ YI SYLLABLE NJUO
A43B ꐻ YI SYLLABLE NJOT
A43C ꐼ YI SYLLABLE NJOX
A43D ꐽ YI SYLLABLE NJO
A43E ꐾ YI SYLLABLE NJOP
A43F ꐿ YI SYLLABLE NJUX
A440 ꑀ YI SYLLABLE NJU
A441 ꑁ YI SYLLABLE NJUP
A442 ꑂ YI SYLLABLE NJURX
A443 ꑃ YI SYLLABLE NJUR
A444 ꑄ YI SYLLABLE NJYT
A445 ꑅ YI SYLLABLE NJYX
A446 ꑆ YI SYLLABLE NJY
A447 ꑇ YI SYLLABLE NJYP
A448 ꑈ YI SYLLABLE NJYRX
A449 ꑉ YI SYLLABLE NJYR
A44A ꑊ YI SYLLABLE NYIT
A44B ꑋ YI SYLLABLE NYIX
A44C ꑌ YI SYLLABLE NYI
A44D ꑍ YI SYLLABLE NYIP
A44E ꑎ YI SYLLABLE NYIET
A44F ꑏ YI SYLLABLE NYIEX
A450 ꑐ YI SYLLABLE NYIE
A451 ꑑ YI SYLLABLE NYIEP
A452 ꑒ YI SYLLABLE NYUOX
A453 ꑓ YI SYLLABLE NYUO
A454 ꑔ YI SYLLABLE NYUOP
A455 ꑕ YI SYLLABLE NYOT
A456 ꑖ YI SYLLABLE NYOX
A457 ꑗ YI SYLLABLE NYO
A458 ꑘ YI SYLLABLE NYOP
A459 ꑙ YI SYLLABLE NYUT
A45A ꑚ YI SYLLABLE NYUX
A45B ꑛ YI SYLLABLE NYU
A45C ꑜ YI SYLLABLE NYUP
A45D ꑝ YI SYLLABLE XIT
A45E ꑞ YI SYLLABLE XIX
A45F ꑟ YI SYLLABLE XI
A460 ꑠ YI SYLLABLE XIP
A461 ꑡ YI SYLLABLE XIET
A462 ꑢ YI SYLLABLE XIEX
A463 ꑣ YI SYLLABLE XIE
A464 ꑤ YI SYLLABLE XIEP
A465 ꑥ YI SYLLABLE XUOX
A466 ꑦ YI SYLLABLE XUO
A467 ꑧ YI SYLLABLE XOT

A468 ꑨ YI SYLLABLE XOX
A469 ꑩ YI SYLLABLE XO
A46A ꑪ YI SYLLABLE XOP
A46B ꑫ YI SYLLABLE XYT
A46C ꑬ YI SYLLABLE XYX
A46D ꑭ YI SYLLABLE XY
A46E ꑮ YI SYLLABLE XYP
A46F ꑯ YI SYLLABLE XYRX
A470 ꑰ YI SYLLABLE XYR
A471 ꑱ YI SYLLABLE YIT
A472 ꑲ YI SYLLABLE YIX
A473 ꑳ YI SYLLABLE YI
A474 ꑴ YI SYLLABLE YIP
A475 ꑵ YI SYLLABLE YIET
A476 ꑶ YI SYLLABLE YIEX
A477 ꑷ YI SYLLABLE YIE
A478 ꑸ YI SYLLABLE YIEP
A479 ꑹ YI SYLLABLE YUOT
A47A ꑺ YI SYLLABLE YUOX
A47B ꑻ YI SYLLABLE YUO
A47C ꑼ YI SYLLABLE YUOP
A47D ꑽ YI SYLLABLE YOT
A47E ꑾ YI SYLLABLE YOX
A47F ꑿ YI SYLLABLE YO
A480 ꒀ YI SYLLABLE YOP
A481 ꒁ YI SYLLABLE YUT
A482 ꒂ YI SYLLABLE YUX
A483 ꒃ YI SYLLABLE YU
A484 ꒄ YI SYLLABLE YUP
A485 ꒅ YI SYLLABLE YURX
A486 ꒆ YI SYLLABLE YUR
A487 ꒇ YI SYLLABLE YYT
A488 ꒈ YI SYLLABLE YYX
A489 ꒉ YI SYLLABLE YY
A48A ꒊ YI SYLLABLE YYP
A48B ꒋ YI SYLLABLE YYRX
A48C ꒌ YI SYLLABLE YYR

	A49	A4A	A4B	A4C
0	꒐ A490	꒠ A4A0	꒰ A4B0	꓀ A4C0
1	꒑ A491	꒡ A4A1	꒱ A4B1	꓁ A4C1
2	꒒ A492	꒢ A4A2	꒲ A4B2	꓂ A4C2
3	꒓ A493	꒣ A4A3	꒳ A4B3	꓃ A4C3
4	꒔ A494	꒤ A4A4	꒴ A4B4	꓄ A4C4
5	꒕ A495	꒥ A4A5	꒵ A4B5	꓅ A4C5
6	꒖ A496	꒦ A4A6	꒶ A4B6	꓆ A4C6
7	꒗ A497	꒧ A4A7	꒷ A4B7	
8	꒘ A498	꒨ A4A8	꒸ A4B8	
9	꒙ A499	꒩ A4A9	꒹ A4B9	
A	꒚ A49A	꒪ A4AA	꒺ A4BA	
B	꒛ A49B	꒫ A4AB	꒻ A4BB	
C	꒜ A49C	꒬ A4AC	꒼ A4BC	
D	꒝ A49D	꒭ A4AD	꒽ A4BD	
E	꒞ A49E	꒮ A4AE	꒾ A4BE	
F	꒟ A49F	꒯ A4AF	꒿ A4BF	

Yi radicals

Yi radicals are named based on the Yi syllable their shape is abstracted from. This is illustrated with crossreferences for the first two radicals.

A490 ꒐ YI RADICAL QOT
→ A408 ꐈ yi syllable qot
A491 ꒑ YI RADICAL LI
→ A1B9 ꆹ yi syllable li
A492 ꒒ YI RADICAL KIT
A493 ꒓ YI RADICAL NYIP
A494 ꒔ YI RADICAL CYP
A495 ꒕ YI RADICAL SSI
A496 ꒖ YI RADICAL GGOP
A497 ꒗ YI RADICAL GEP
A498 ꒘ YI RADICAL MI
A499 ꒙ YI RADICAL HXIT
A49A ꒚ YI RADICAL LYR
A49B ꒛ YI RADICAL BBUT
A49C ꒜ YI RADICAL MOP
A49D ꒝ YI RADICAL YO
A49E ꒞ YI RADICAL PUT
A49F ꒟ YI RADICAL HXUO
A4A0 ꒠ YI RADICAL TAT
A4A1 ꒡ YI RADICAL GA
A4A2 ꒢ YI RADICAL ZUP
A4A3 ꒣ YI RADICAL CYT
A4A4 ꒤ YI RADICAL DDUR
A4A5 ꒥ YI RADICAL BUR
A4A6 ꒦ YI RADICAL GGUO
A4A7 ꒧ YI RADICAL NYOP
A4A8 ꒨ YI RADICAL TU
A4A9 ꒩ YI RADICAL OP
A4AA ꒪ YI RADICAL JJUT
A4AB ꒫ YI RADICAL ZOT
A4AC ꒬ YI RADICAL PYT
A4AD ꒭ YI RADICAL HMO
A4AE ꒮ YI RADICAL YIT
A4AF ꒯ YI RADICAL VUR
A4B0 ꒰ YI RADICAL SHY
A4B1 ꒱ YI RADICAL VEP
A4B2 ꒲ YI RADICAL ZA
A4B3 ꒳ YI RADICAL JO
A4B4 ꒴ YI RADICAL NZUP
A4B5 ꒵ YI RADICAL JJY
A4B6 ꒶ YI RADICAL GOT
A4B7 ꒷ YI RADICAL JJIE
A4B8 ꒸ YI RADICAL WO
A4B9 ꒹ YI RADICAL DU
A4BA ꒺ YI RADICAL SHUR
A4BB ꒻ YI RADICAL LIE
A4BC ꒼ YI RADICAL CY
A4BD ꒽ YI RADICAL CUOP
A4BE ꒾ YI RADICAL CIP
A4BF ꒿ YI RADICAL HXOP
A4C0 ꓀ YI RADICAL SHAT
A4C1 ꓁ YI RADICAL ZUR
A4C2 ꓂ YI RADICAL SHOP
A4C3 ꓃ YI RADICAL CHE
A4C4 ꓄ YI RADICAL ZZIET
A4C5 ꓅ YI RADICAL NBIE
A4C6 ꓆ YI RADICAL KE

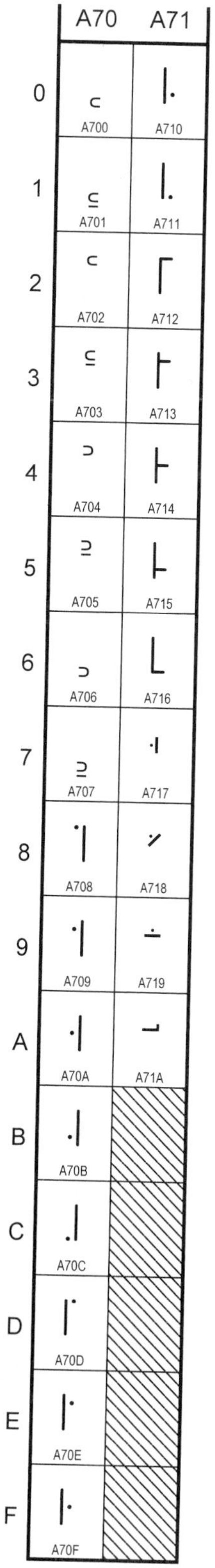

	A70	A71
0	꜀ A700	꜐ A710
1	꜁ A701	꜑ A711
2	꜂ A702	꜒ A712
3	꜃ A703	꜓ A713
4	꜄ A704	꜔ A714
5	꜅ A705	꜕ A715
6	꜆ A706	꜖ A716
7	꜇ A707	ꜗ A717
8	꜈ A708	ꜘ A718
9	꜉ A709	ꜙ A719
A	꜊ A70A	ꜚ A71A
B	꜋ A70B	
C	꜌ A70C	
D	꜍ A70D	
E	꜎ A70E	
F	꜏ A70F	

Corner tone marks for Chinese

A700 ꜀ MODIFIER LETTER CHINESE TONE YIN PING
A701 ꜁ MODIFIER LETTER CHINESE TONE YANG PING
A702 ꜂ MODIFIER LETTER CHINESE TONE YIN SHANG
A703 ꜃ MODIFIER LETTER CHINESE TONE YANG SHANG
A704 ꜄ MODIFIER LETTER CHINESE TONE YIN QU
A705 ꜅ MODIFIER LETTER CHINESE TONE YANG QU
A706 ꜆ MODIFIER LETTER CHINESE TONE YIN RU
A707 ꜇ MODIFIER LETTER CHINESE TONE YANG RU

Dotted tone letters

A708 ꜈ MODIFIER LETTER EXTRA-HIGH DOTTED TONE BAR
A709 ꜉ MODIFIER LETTER HIGH DOTTED TONE BAR
A70A ꜊ MODIFIER LETTER MID DOTTED TONE BAR
A70B ꜋ MODIFIER LETTER LOW DOTTED TONE BAR
A70C ꜌ MODIFIER LETTER EXTRA-LOW DOTTED TONE BAR
A70D ꜍ MODIFIER LETTER EXTRA-HIGH DOTTED LEFT-STEM TONE BAR
A70E ꜎ MODIFIER LETTER HIGH DOTTED LEFT-STEM TONE BAR
A70F ꜏ MODIFIER LETTER MID DOTTED LEFT-STEM TONE BAR
A710 ꜐ MODIFIER LETTER LOW DOTTED LEFT-STEM TONE BAR
A711 ꜑ MODIFIER LETTER EXTRA-LOW DOTTED LEFT-STEM TONE BAR

Left-stem tone letters

A712 ꜒ MODIFIER LETTER EXTRA-HIGH LEFT-STEM TONE BAR
A713 ꜓ MODIFIER LETTER HIGH LEFT-STEM TONE BAR
A714 ꜔ MODIFIER LETTER MID LEFT-STEM TONE BAR
A715 ꜕ MODIFIER LETTER LOW LEFT-STEM TONE BAR
A716 ꜖ MODIFIER LETTER EXTRA-LOW LEFT-STEM TONE BAR

Chinantec tone marks

A717 ꜗ MODIFIER LETTER DOT VERTICAL BAR
A718 ꜘ MODIFIER LETTER DOT SLASH
A719 ꜙ MODIFIER LETTER DOT HORIZONTAL BAR
A71A ꜚ MODIFIER LETTER LOWER RIGHT CORNER ANGLE

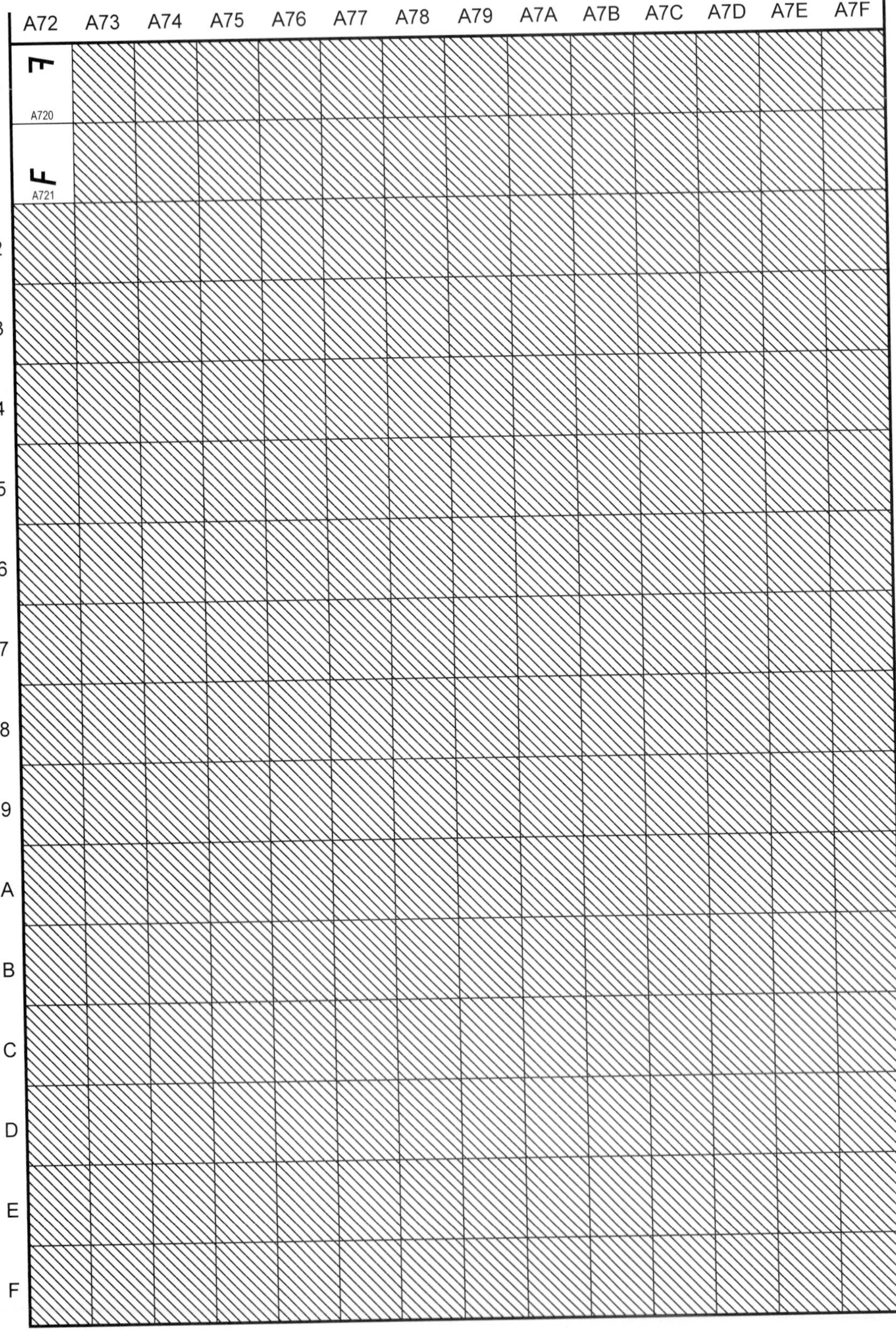
A72
A73
A74
A75
A76
A77
A78
A79
A7A
A7B
A7C
A7D
A7E
A7F
0
1
2
3
4
5
6
7
8
9
A
B
C
D
E
F
A720
A721

Additions for UPA

A720 ꜠ MODIFIER LETTER STRESS AND HIGH TONE
A721 ꜡ MODIFIER LETTER STRESS AND LOW TONE

	A80	A81	A82
0	ꠀ A800	ꠐ A810	ꠠ A820
1	ꠁ A801	ꠑ A811	ꠡ A821
2	◌ꠂ A802	ꠒ A812	ꠢ A822
3	ꠃ A803	ꠓ A813	◌ꠣ A823
4	ꠄ A804	ꠔ A814	◌ꠤ A824
5	ꠅ A805	ꠕ A815	◌ꠥ A825
6	◌꠆ A806	ꠖ A816	◌ꠦ A826
7	ꠇ A807	ꠗ A817	◌ꠧ A827
8	ꠈ A808	ꠘ A818	꠨ A828
9	ꠉ A809	ꠙ A819	꠩ A829
A	ꠊ A80A	ꠚ A81A	꠪ A82A
B	◌ꠋ A80B	ꠛ A81B	꠫ A82B
C	ꠌ A80C	ꠜ A81C	
D	ꠍ A80D	ꠝ A81D	
E	ꠎ A80E	ꠞ A81E	
F	ꠏ A80F	ꠟ A81F	

Independent vowels and dvisvara

A800 ꠀ SYLOTI NAGRI LETTER A
A801 ꠁ SYLOTI NAGRI LETTER I
A802 ◌ꠂ SYLOTI NAGRI SIGN DVISVARA
A803 ꠃ SYLOTI NAGRI LETTER U
A804 ꠄ SYLOTI NAGRI LETTER E
A805 ꠅ SYLOTI NAGRI LETTER O

Sign

A806 ◌꠆ SYLOTI NAGRI SIGN HASANTA
= halant, virama

Consonants and consonant signs

A807 ꠇ SYLOTI NAGRI LETTER KO
A808 ꠈ SYLOTI NAGRI LETTER KHO
A809 ꠉ SYLOTI NAGRI LETTER GO
A80A ꠊ SYLOTI NAGRI LETTER GHO
A80B ◌ꠋ SYLOTI NAGRI SIGN ANUSVARA
A80C ꠌ SYLOTI NAGRI LETTER CO
A80D ꠍ SYLOTI NAGRI LETTER CHO
A80E ꠎ SYLOTI NAGRI LETTER JO
A80F ꠏ SYLOTI NAGRI LETTER JHO
A810 ꠐ SYLOTI NAGRI LETTER TTO
A811 ꠑ SYLOTI NAGRI LETTER TTHO
A812 ꠒ SYLOTI NAGRI LETTER DDO
A813 ꠓ SYLOTI NAGRI LETTER DDHO
A814 ꠔ SYLOTI NAGRI LETTER TO
A815 ꠕ SYLOTI NAGRI LETTER THO
A816 ꠖ SYLOTI NAGRI LETTER DO
A817 ꠗ SYLOTI NAGRI LETTER DHO
A818 ꠘ SYLOTI NAGRI LETTER NO
A819 ꠙ SYLOTI NAGRI LETTER PO
A81A ꠚ SYLOTI NAGRI LETTER PHO
A81B ꠛ SYLOTI NAGRI LETTER BO
A81C ꠜ SYLOTI NAGRI LETTER BHO
A81D ꠝ SYLOTI NAGRI LETTER MO
A81E ꠞ SYLOTI NAGRI LETTER RO
A81F ꠟ SYLOTI NAGRI LETTER LO
A820 ꠠ SYLOTI NAGRI LETTER RRO
A821 ꠡ SYLOTI NAGRI LETTER SO
A822 ꠢ SYLOTI NAGRI LETTER HO

Dependent vowel signs

A823 ◌ꠣ SYLOTI NAGRI VOWEL SIGN A
A824 ◌ꠤ SYLOTI NAGRI VOWEL SIGN I
A825 ◌ꠥ SYLOTI NAGRI VOWEL SIGN U
A826 ◌ꠦ SYLOTI NAGRI VOWEL SIGN E
A827 ◌ꠧ SYLOTI NAGRI VOWEL SIGN OO

Poetry marks

A828 ꠨ SYLOTI NAGRI POETRY MARK-1
A829 ꠩ SYLOTI NAGRI POETRY MARK-2
A82A ꠪ SYLOTI NAGRI POETRY MARK-3
A82B ꠫ SYLOTI NAGRI POETRY MARK-4

	A84	A85	A86	A87
0	ꡀ A840	ꡐ A850	ꡠ A860	ꡰ A870
1	ꡁ A841	ꡑ A851	ꡡ A861	ꡱ A871
2	ꡂ A842	ꡒ A852	ꡢ A862	ꡲ A872
3	ꡃ A843	ꡓ A853	ꡣ A863	ꡳ A873
4	ꡄ A844	ꡔ A854	ꡤ A864	꡴ A874
5	ꡅ A845	ꡕ A855	ꡥ A865	꡵ A875
6	ꡆ A846	ꡖ A856	ꡦ A866	꡶ A876
7	ꡇ A847	ꡗ A857	ꡧ A867	꡷ A877
8	ꡈ A848	ꡘ A858	ꡨ A868	
9	ꡉ A849	ꡙ A859	ꡩ A869	
A	ꡊ A84A	ꡚ A85A	ꡪ A86A	
B	ꡋ A84B	ꡛ A85B	ꡫ A86B	
C	ꡌ A84C	ꡜ A85C	ꡬ A86C	
D	ꡍ A84D	ꡝ A85D	ꡭ A86D	
E	ꡎ A84E	ꡞ A85E	ꡮ A86E	
F	ꡏ A84F	ꡟ A85F	ꡯ A86F	

Phags-pa letters are used for Mongolian, Chinese, Uighur, Tibetan, and Sanskrit unless annotated with a more restricted list of languages.

Consonants

A840 ꡀ PHAGS-PA LETTER KA
• Mongolian, Chinese, Tibetan, Sanskrit
→ 0F40 ཀ tibetan letter ka
A841 ꡁ PHAGS-PA LETTER KHA
→ 0F41 ཁ tibetan letter kha
A842 ꡂ PHAGS-PA LETTER GA
→ 0F42 ག tibetan letter ga
A843 ꡃ PHAGS-PA LETTER NGA
• Mongolian, Chinese, Tibetan, Sanskrit
→ 0F44 ང tibetan letter nga
A844 ꡄ PHAGS-PA LETTER CA
• Chinese, Tibetan
→ 0F45 ཅ tibetan letter ca
A845 ꡅ PHAGS-PA LETTER CHA
• Mongolian, Chinese, Uighur, Tibetan
→ 0F46 ཆ tibetan letter cha
A846 ꡆ PHAGS-PA LETTER JA
• Mongolian, Chinese, Uighur, Tibetan
→ 0F47 ཇ tibetan letter ja
A847 ꡇ PHAGS-PA LETTER NYA
• Chinese, Tibetan, Sanskrit
→ 0F49 ཉ tibetan letter nya
A848 ꡈ PHAGS-PA LETTER TA
• Mongolian, Chinese, Tibetan, Sanskrit
→ 0F4F ཏ tibetan letter ta
A849 ꡉ PHAGS-PA LETTER THA
→ 0F50 ཐ tibetan letter tha
A84A ꡊ PHAGS-PA LETTER DA
→ 0F51 ད tibetan letter da
A84B ꡋ PHAGS-PA LETTER NA
→ 0F53 ན tibetan letter na
A84C ꡌ PHAGS-PA LETTER PA
• Mongolian, Chinese, Tibetan, Sanskrit
→ 0F54 པ tibetan letter pa
A84D ꡍ PHAGS-PA LETTER PHA
• Chinese, Tibetan, Sanskrit
→ 0F55 ཕ tibetan letter pha
A84E ꡎ PHAGS-PA LETTER BA
→ 0F56 བ tibetan letter ba
A84F ꡏ PHAGS-PA LETTER MA
→ 0F58 མ tibetan letter ma
A850 ꡐ PHAGS-PA LETTER TSA
• Chinese, Tibetan, Sanskrit
→ 0F59 ཙ tibetan letter tsa
A851 ꡑ PHAGS-PA LETTER TSHA
• Mongolian, Chinese, Tibetan, Sanskrit
→ 0F5A ཚ tibetan letter tsha
A852 ꡒ PHAGS-PA LETTER DZA
• Chinese, Tibetan, Sanskrit
→ 0F5B ཛ tibetan letter dza
A853 ꡓ PHAGS-PA LETTER WA
→ 0F5D ཝ tibetan letter wa
A854 ꡔ PHAGS-PA LETTER ZHA
• Chinese, Tibetan
→ 0F5E ཞ tibetan letter zha
A855 ꡕ PHAGS-PA LETTER ZA
• Mongolian, Chinese, Tibetan
→ 0F5F ཟ tibetan letter za
A856 ꡖ PHAGS-PA LETTER SMALL A
→ 0F60 འ tibetan letter -a
A857 ꡗ PHAGS-PA LETTER YA
→ 0F61 ཡ tibetan letter ya
A858 ꡘ PHAGS-PA LETTER RA
• Mongolian, Uighur, Tibetan, Sanskrit
→ 0F62 ར tibetan letter ra
A859 ꡙ PHAGS-PA LETTER LA
→ 0F63 ལ tibetan letter la
A85A ꡚ PHAGS-PA LETTER SHA
→ 0F64 ཤ tibetan letter sha
A85B ꡛ PHAGS-PA LETTER SA
→ 0F66 ས tibetan letter sa
A85C ꡜ PHAGS-PA LETTER HA
→ 0F67 ཧ tibetan letter ha

Letter A

A85D ꡝ PHAGS-PA LETTER A
→ 0F68 ཨ tibetan letter a

Vowels

A85E ꡞ PHAGS-PA LETTER I
→ 0F72 ི tibetan vowel sign i
A85F ꡟ PHAGS-PA LETTER U
→ 0F74 ུ tibetan vowel sign u
A860 ꡠ PHAGS-PA LETTER E
→ 0F7A ེ tibetan vowel sign e
A861 ꡡ PHAGS-PA LETTER O
→ 0F7C ོ tibetan vowel sign o

Consonants

A862 ꡢ PHAGS-PA LETTER QA
• Mongolian, Uighur
A863 ꡣ PHAGS-PA LETTER XA
• Mongolian, Chinese
A864 ꡤ PHAGS-PA LETTER FA
• Chinese, Uighur
→ A85C ꡜ phags-pa letter ha
A865 ꡥ PHAGS-PA LETTER GGA
• language usage unknown
• created by reversal of A862 ꡢ

Vowel

A866 ꡦ PHAGS-PA LETTER EE
• Mongolian, Chinese, Uighur

Subjoined Consonants

A867 ꡧ PHAGS-PA SUBJOINED LETTER WA
• Chinese, Tibetan, Sanskrit
→ 0FAD ྭ tibetan subjoined letter wa
A868 ꡨ PHAGS-PA SUBJOINED LETTER YA
• Chinese, Tibetan, Sanskrit
→ 0FB1 ྱ tibetan subjoined letter ya

Consonant additions for Sanskrit

A869 ꡩ PHAGS-PA LETTER TTA
• Sanskrit
→ 0F4A ཊ tibetan letter tta
A86A ꡪ PHAGS-PA LETTER TTHA
• Sanskrit
→ 0F4B ཋ tibetan letter ttha
A86B ꡫ PHAGS-PA LETTER DDA
• Sanskrit
→ 0F4C ཌ tibetan letter dda

A86C PHAGS-PA LETTER NNA
• Sanskrit
→ 0F4E tibetan letter nna

Alternate consonant forms for Chinese

A86D PHAGS-PA LETTER ALTERNATE YA
• Chinese
→ A857 phags-pa letter ya

A86E PHAGS-PA LETTER VOICELESS SHA
• Chinese
→ A85A phags-pa letter sha

A86F PHAGS-PA LETTER VOICED HA
• Chinese
→ A85C phags-pa letter ha

A870 PHAGS-PA LETTER ASPIRATED FA
• Chinese
→ A864 phags-pa letter fa

Subjoined consonant

A871 PHAGS-PA SUBJOINED LETTER RA
• Tibetan, Sanskrit
→ 0FB2 tibetan subjoined letter ra

Consonant addition for Tibetan

A872 PHAGS-PA SUPERFIXED LETTER RA
• Tibetan
→ 0F62 tibetan letter ra

Candrabindu

A873 PHAGS-PA LETTER CANDRABINDU
• Sanskrit
→ 0F83 tibetan sign sna ldan
→ 0F7E tibetan sign rjes su nga ro
→ 1880 mongolian letter ali gali anusvara one

Head marks for Tibetan

A874 PHAGS-PA SINGLE HEAD MARK
• Tibetan
• marks beginning of text
→ 0F04 tibetan mark initial yig mgo mdun ma
→ 1800 mongolian birga

A875 PHAGS-PA DOUBLE HEAD MARK
• Tibetan
• marks beginning of text

Punctuation for Tibetan

A876 PHAGS-PA MARK SHAD
• Tibetan
→ 0F0D tibetan mark shad

A877 PHAGS-PA MARK DOUBLE SHAD
• Tibetan
→ 0F0E tibetan mark nyis shad

	F90	F91	F92	F93	F94	F95	F96	F97	F98	F99	F9A	F9B	F9C	F9D	F9E	F9F
0	豈 F900	蘿 F910	鸞 F920	擄 F930	鹿 F940	縷 F950	怒 F960	殺 F970	呂 F980	戀 F990	裂 F9A0	聆 F9B0	燎 F9C0	類 F9D0	易 F9E0	藺 F9F0
1	更 F901	螺 F911	嵐 F921	櫓 F931	論 F941	陋 F951	率 F961	辰 F971	女 F981	撚 F991	說 F9A1	鈴 F9B1	療 F9C1	六 F9D1	李 F9E1	隣 F9F1
2	車 F902	裸 F912	濫 F922	爐 F932	壟 F942	勒 F952	異 F962	沈 F972	廬 F982	漣 F992	廉 F9A2	零 F9B2	蓼 F9C2	戮 F9D2	梨 F9E2	鱗 F9F2
3	賈 F903	邏 F913	藍 F923	盧 F933	弄 F943	肋 F953	北 F963	拾 F973	旅 F983	煉 F993	念 F9A3	靈 F9B3	遼 F9C3	陸 F9D3	泥 F9E3	麟 F9F3
4	滑 F904	樂 F914	襤 F924	老 F934	籠 F944	凜 F954	磻 F964	若 F974	濾 F984	璉 F994	捻 F9A4	領 F9B4	龍 F9C4	倫 F9D4	理 F9E4	林 F9F4
5	串 F905	洛 F915	拉 F925	蘆 F935	聾 F945	凌 F955	便 F965	掠 F975	礪 F985	秊 F995	殮 F9A5	例 F9B5	暈 F9C5	崙 F9D5	痢 F9E5	淋 F9F5
6	句 F906	烙 F916	臘 F926	虜 F936	牢 F946	稜 F956	復 F966	略 F976	閭 F986	練 F996	簾 F9A6	禮 F9B6	阮 F9C6	淪 F9D6	罹 F9E6	臨 F9F6
7	龜 F907	珞 F917	蠟 F927	路 F937	磊 F947	綾 F957	不 F967	亮 F977	驪 F987	聯 F997	獵 F9A7	醴 F9B7	劉 F9C7	輪 F9D7	裏 F9E7	立 F9F7
8	龜 F908	落 F918	廊 F928	露 F938	賂 F948	菱 F958	泌 F968	兩 F978	麗 F988	輦 F998	令 F9A8	隸 F9B8	杻 F9C8	律 F9D8	裡 F9E8	笠 F9F8
9	契 F909	酪 F919	朗 F929	魯 F939	雷 F949	陵 F959	數 F969	凉 F979	黎 F989	蓮 F999	囹 F9A9	惡 F9B9	柳 F9C9	慄 F9D9	里 F9E9	粒 F9F9
A	金 F90A	駱 F91A	浪 F92A	鷺 F93A	壘 F94A	讀 F95A	索 F96A	梁 F97A	力 F98A	連 F99A	寧 F9AA	了 F9BA	流 F9CA	栗 F9DA	離 F9EA	狀 F9FA
B	喇 F90B	亂 F91B	狼 F92B	碌 F93B	屢 F94B	拏 F95B	參 F96B	糧 F97B	曆 F98B	鍊 F99B	嶺 F9AB	僚 F9BB	溜 F9CB	率 F9DB	匿 F9EB	炙 F9FB
C	奈 F90C	卵 F91C	郎 F92C	祿 F93C	樓 F94C	樂 F95C	塞 F96C	良 F97C	歷 F98C	列 F99C	怜 F9AC	寮 F9BC	琉 F9CC	隆 F9DC	溺 F9EC	識 F9FC
D	懶 F90D	欄 F91D	來 F92D	綠 F93D	淚 F94D	諾 F95D	省 F96D	諒 F97D	轢 F98D	劣 F99D	玲 F9AD	尿 F9BD	留 F9CD	利 F9DD	吝 F9ED	什 F9FD
E	癩 F90E	爛 F91E	冷 F92E	菉 F93E	漏 F94E	丹 F95E	葉 F96E	量 F97E	年 F98E	咽 F99E	瑩 F9AE	料 F9BE	硫 F9CE	吏 F9DE	燐 F9EE	茶 F9FE
F	羅 F90F	蘭 F91F	勞 F92F	錄 F93F	累 F94F	寧 F95F	說 F96F	勵 F97F	憐 F98F	烈 F99F	羚 F9AF	樂 F9BF	紐 F9CF	履 F9DF	璘 F9EF	刺 F9FF

	FA0	FA1	FA2	FA3	FA4	FA5	FA6	FA7	FA8	FA9	FAA	FAB	FAC	FAD	FAE	FAF
0	切 FA00	塚 FA10	蘒 FA20	侮 FA30	懲 FA40	祖 FA50	褐 FA60	並 FA70	婢 FA80	敖 FA90	猪 FAA0	練 FAB0	變 FAC0	𢡄 FAD0		
1	度 FA01	﨑 FA11	﨡 FA21	僧 FA31	敏 FA41	祝 FA51	視 FA61	况 FA71	嬨 FA81	晴 FA91	瑱 FAA1	缾 FAB1	贈 FAC1	𣏕 FAD1		
2	拓 FA02	晴 FA12	諸 FA22	免 FA32	既 FA42	禍 FA52	謁 FA62	全 FA72	廒 FA82	朗 FA92	甆 FAA2	者 FAB2	輸 FAC2	㮝 FAD2		
3	糖 FA03	﨓 FA13	﨣 FA23	勉 FA33	暑 FA43	禎 FA53	謹 FA63	侀 FA73	廙 FA83	望 FA93	画 FAA3	荒 FAB3	遲 FAC3	䀘 FAD3		
4	宅 FA04	﨔 FA14	﨤 FA24	勤 FA34	梅 FA44	穀 FA54	賓 FA64	充 FA74	彩 FA84	杖 FA94	瘝 FAA4	華 FAB4	醙 FAC4	䀹 FAD4		
5	洞 FA05	凞 FA15	逸 FA25	卑 FA35	海 FA45	突 FA55	贈 FA65	冀 FA75	徭 FA85	歹 FA95	瘟 FAA5	蝹 FAB5	鉶 FAC5	𥉉 FAD5		
6	暴 FA06	猪 FA16	都 FA26	喝 FA36	渚 FA46	節 FA56	辶 FA66	勇 FA76	惘 FA86	殺 FA96	益 FAA6	襁 FAB6	陼 FAC6	𥳐 FAD6		
7	輻 FA07	益 FA17	﨧 FA27	嘆 FA37	漢 FA47	練 FA57	逸 FA67	勺 FA77	慎 FA87	流 FA97	盛 FAA7	覆 FAB7	難 FAC7	𧻓 FAD7		
8	行 FA08	礼 FA18	﨨 FA28	器 FA38	煮 FA48	縉 FA58	難 FA68	喝 FA78	愈 FA88	滛 FA98	直 FAA8	視 FAB8	靖 FAC8	齃 FAD8		
9	降 FA09	神 FA19	﨩 FA29	塀 FA39	爫 FA49	繁 FA59	響 FA69	啕 FA79	憎 FA89	滋 FA99	睊 FAA9	調 FAB9	韛 FAC9	龎 FAD9		
A	見 FA0A	祥 FA1A	飯 FA2A	墨 FA3A	琢 FA4A	署 FA5A	頻 FA6A	喙 FA7A	慠 FA8A	漢 FA9A	着 FAAA	諸 FABA	響 FACA			
B	廓 FA0B	福 FA1B	飼 FA2B	層 FA3B	碑 FA4B	者 FA5B		嗢 FA7B	懲 FA8B	瀞 FA9B	磌 FAAB	請 FABB	頋 FACB			
C	兀 FA0C	靖 FA1C	館 FA2C	屮 FA3C	社 FA4C	臭 FA5C		塚 FA7C	戴 FA8C	煮 FA9C	窱 FAAC	謁 FABC	頻 FACC			
D	嗀 FA0D	精 FA1D	鶴 FA2D	悔 FA3D	祉 FA4D	艹 FA5D		墳 FA7D	揄 FA8D	瞧 FA9D	節 FAAD	諾 FABD	鬒 FACD			
E	﨎 FA0E	羽 FA1E		慨 FA3E	祈 FA4E	艹 FA5E		奄 FA7E	搜 FA8E	爵 FA9E	类 FAAE	諭 FABE	龜 FACE			
F	﨏 FA0F	﨟 FA1F		憎 FA3F	祐 FA4F	著 FA5F		奔 FA7F	摒 FA8F	犯 FA9F	絛 FAAF	謹 FABF	𢡊 FACF			

Pronunciation variants from KS X 1001:1998

F900 豈 CJK COMPATIBILITY IDEOGRAPH-F900
≡ 8C48 豈
F901 更 CJK COMPATIBILITY IDEOGRAPH-F901
≡ 66F4 更
F902 車 CJK COMPATIBILITY IDEOGRAPH-F902
≡ 8ECA 車
F903 賈 CJK COMPATIBILITY IDEOGRAPH-F903
≡ 8CC8 賈
F904 滑 CJK COMPATIBILITY IDEOGRAPH-F904
≡ 6ED1 滑
F905 串 CJK COMPATIBILITY IDEOGRAPH-F905
≡ 4E32 串
F906 句 CJK COMPATIBILITY IDEOGRAPH-F906
≡ 53E5 句
F907 龜 CJK COMPATIBILITY IDEOGRAPH-F907
≡ 9F9C 龜
F908 龜 CJK COMPATIBILITY IDEOGRAPH-F908
≡ 9F9C 龜
F909 契 CJK COMPATIBILITY IDEOGRAPH-F909
≡ 5951 契
F90A 金 CJK COMPATIBILITY IDEOGRAPH-F90A
≡ 91D1 金
F90B 喇 CJK COMPATIBILITY IDEOGRAPH-F90B
≡ 5587 喇
F90C 奈 CJK COMPATIBILITY IDEOGRAPH-F90C
≡ 5948 奈
F90D 懶 CJK COMPATIBILITY IDEOGRAPH-F90D
≡ 61F6 懶
F90E 癩 CJK COMPATIBILITY IDEOGRAPH-F90E
≡ 7669 癩
F90F 羅 CJK COMPATIBILITY IDEOGRAPH-F90F
≡ 7F85 羅
F910 蘿 CJK COMPATIBILITY IDEOGRAPH-F910
≡ 863F 蘿
F911 螺 CJK COMPATIBILITY IDEOGRAPH-F911
≡ 87BA 螺
F912 裸 CJK COMPATIBILITY IDEOGRAPH-F912
≡ 88F8 裸
F913 邏 CJK COMPATIBILITY IDEOGRAPH-F913
≡ 908F 邏
F914 樂 CJK COMPATIBILITY IDEOGRAPH-F914
≡ 6A02 樂
F915 洛 CJK COMPATIBILITY IDEOGRAPH-F915
≡ 6D1B 洛
F916 烙 CJK COMPATIBILITY IDEOGRAPH-F916
≡ 70D9 烙
F917 珞 CJK COMPATIBILITY IDEOGRAPH-F917
≡ 73DE 珞
F918 落 CJK COMPATIBILITY IDEOGRAPH-F918
≡ 843D 落
F919 酪 CJK COMPATIBILITY IDEOGRAPH-F919
≡ 916A 酪
F91A 駱 CJK COMPATIBILITY IDEOGRAPH-F91A
≡ 99F1 駱
F91B 亂 CJK COMPATIBILITY IDEOGRAPH-F91B
≡ 4E82 亂
F91C 卵 CJK COMPATIBILITY IDEOGRAPH-F91C
≡ 5375 卵
F91D 欄 CJK COMPATIBILITY IDEOGRAPH-F91D
≡ 6B04 欄
F91E 爛 CJK COMPATIBILITY IDEOGRAPH-F91E
≡ 721B 爛
F91F 蘭 CJK COMPATIBILITY IDEOGRAPH-F91F
≡ 862D 蘭
F920 鸞 CJK COMPATIBILITY IDEOGRAPH-F920
≡ 9E1E 鸞
F921 嵐 CJK COMPATIBILITY IDEOGRAPH-F921
≡ 5D50 嵐
F922 濫 CJK COMPATIBILITY IDEOGRAPH-F922
≡ 6FEB 濫
F923 藍 CJK COMPATIBILITY IDEOGRAPH-F923
≡ 85CD 藍
F924 襤 CJK COMPATIBILITY IDEOGRAPH-F924
≡ 8964 襤
F925 拉 CJK COMPATIBILITY IDEOGRAPH-F925
≡ 62C9 拉
F926 臘 CJK COMPATIBILITY IDEOGRAPH-F926
≡ 81D8 臘
F927 蠟 CJK COMPATIBILITY IDEOGRAPH-F927
≡ 881F 蠟
F928 廊 CJK COMPATIBILITY IDEOGRAPH-F928
≡ 5ECA 廊
F929 朗 CJK COMPATIBILITY IDEOGRAPH-F929
≡ 6717 朗
F92A 浪 CJK COMPATIBILITY IDEOGRAPH-F92A
≡ 6D6A 浪
F92B 狼 CJK COMPATIBILITY IDEOGRAPH-F92B
≡ 72FC 狼
F92C 郎 CJK COMPATIBILITY IDEOGRAPH-F92C
≡ 90CE 郎
F92D 來 CJK COMPATIBILITY IDEOGRAPH-F92D
≡ 4F86 來
F92E 冷 CJK COMPATIBILITY IDEOGRAPH-F92E
≡ 51B7 冷
F92F 勞 CJK COMPATIBILITY IDEOGRAPH-F92F
≡ 52DE 勞
F930 擄 CJK COMPATIBILITY IDEOGRAPH-F930
≡ 64C4 擄
F931 櫓 CJK COMPATIBILITY IDEOGRAPH-F931
≡ 6AD3 櫓
F932 爐 CJK COMPATIBILITY IDEOGRAPH-F932
≡ 7210 爐
F933 盧 CJK COMPATIBILITY IDEOGRAPH-F933
≡ 76E7 盧
F934 老 CJK COMPATIBILITY IDEOGRAPH-F934
≡ 8001 老
F935 蘆 CJK COMPATIBILITY IDEOGRAPH-F935
≡ 8606 蘆
F936 虜 CJK COMPATIBILITY IDEOGRAPH-F936
≡ 865C 虜
F937 路 CJK COMPATIBILITY IDEOGRAPH-F937
≡ 8DEF 路
F938 露 CJK COMPATIBILITY IDEOGRAPH-F938
≡ 9732 露
F939 魯 CJK COMPATIBILITY IDEOGRAPH-F939
≡ 9B6F 魯
F93A 鷺 CJK COMPATIBILITY IDEOGRAPH-F93A
≡ 9DFA 鷺
F93B 碌 CJK COMPATIBILITY IDEOGRAPH-F93B
≡ 788C 碌
F93C 祿 CJK COMPATIBILITY IDEOGRAPH-F93C
≡ 797F 祿

F93D 綠 CJK COMPATIBILITY IDEOGRAPH-F93D
≡ 7DA0 綠
F93E 菉 CJK COMPATIBILITY IDEOGRAPH-F93E
≡ 83C9 菉
F93F 錄 CJK COMPATIBILITY IDEOGRAPH-F93F
≡ 9304 錄
F940 鹿 CJK COMPATIBILITY IDEOGRAPH-F940
≡ 9E7F 鹿
F941 論 CJK COMPATIBILITY IDEOGRAPH-F941
≡ 8AD6 論
F942 壟 CJK COMPATIBILITY IDEOGRAPH-F942
≡ 58DF 壟
F943 弄 CJK COMPATIBILITY IDEOGRAPH-F943
≡ 5F04 弄
F944 籠 CJK COMPATIBILITY IDEOGRAPH-F944
≡ 7C60 籠
F945 聾 CJK COMPATIBILITY IDEOGRAPH-F945
≡ 807E 聾
F946 牢 CJK COMPATIBILITY IDEOGRAPH-F946
≡ 7262 牢
F947 磊 CJK COMPATIBILITY IDEOGRAPH-F947
≡ 78CA 磊
F948 賂 CJK COMPATIBILITY IDEOGRAPH-F948
≡ 8CC2 賂
F949 雷 CJK COMPATIBILITY IDEOGRAPH-F949
≡ 96F7 雷
F94A 壘 CJK COMPATIBILITY IDEOGRAPH-F94A
≡ 58D8 壘
F94B 屢 CJK COMPATIBILITY IDEOGRAPH-F94B
≡ 5C62 屢
F94C 樓 CJK COMPATIBILITY IDEOGRAPH-F94C
≡ 6A13 樓
F94D 淚 CJK COMPATIBILITY IDEOGRAPH-F94D
≡ 6DDA 淚
F94E 漏 CJK COMPATIBILITY IDEOGRAPH-F94E
≡ 6F0F 漏
F94F 累 CJK COMPATIBILITY IDEOGRAPH-F94F
≡ 7D2F 累
F950 縷 CJK COMPATIBILITY IDEOGRAPH-F950
≡ 7E37 縷
F951 陋 CJK COMPATIBILITY IDEOGRAPH-F951
≡ 964B 陋
F952 勒 CJK COMPATIBILITY IDEOGRAPH-F952
≡ 52D2 勒
F953 肋 CJK COMPATIBILITY IDEOGRAPH-F953
≡ 808B 肋
F954 凜 CJK COMPATIBILITY IDEOGRAPH-F954
≡ 51DC 凜
F955 凌 CJK COMPATIBILITY IDEOGRAPH-F955
≡ 51CC 凌
F956 稜 CJK COMPATIBILITY IDEOGRAPH-F956
≡ 7A1C 稜
F957 綾 CJK COMPATIBILITY IDEOGRAPH-F957
≡ 7DBE 綾
F958 菱 CJK COMPATIBILITY IDEOGRAPH-F958
≡ 83F1 菱
F959 陵 CJK COMPATIBILITY IDEOGRAPH-F959
≡ 9675 陵
F95A 讀 CJK COMPATIBILITY IDEOGRAPH-F95A
≡ 8B80 讀
F95B 拏 CJK COMPATIBILITY IDEOGRAPH-F95B
≡ 62CF 拏
F95C 樂 CJK COMPATIBILITY IDEOGRAPH-F95C
≡ 6A02 樂
F95D 諾 CJK COMPATIBILITY IDEOGRAPH-F95D
≡ 8AFE 諾
F95E 丹 CJK COMPATIBILITY IDEOGRAPH-F95E
≡ 4E39 丹
F95F 寧 CJK COMPATIBILITY IDEOGRAPH-F95F
≡ 5BE7 寧
F960 怒 CJK COMPATIBILITY IDEOGRAPH-F960
≡ 6012 怒
F961 率 CJK COMPATIBILITY IDEOGRAPH-F961
≡ 7387 率
F962 異 CJK COMPATIBILITY IDEOGRAPH-F962
≡ 7570 異
F963 北 CJK COMPATIBILITY IDEOGRAPH-F963
≡ 5317 北
F964 磻 CJK COMPATIBILITY IDEOGRAPH-F964
≡ 78FB 磻
F965 便 CJK COMPATIBILITY IDEOGRAPH-F965
≡ 4FBF 便
F966 復 CJK COMPATIBILITY IDEOGRAPH-F966
≡ 5FA9 復
F967 不 CJK COMPATIBILITY IDEOGRAPH-F967
≡ 4E0D 不
F968 泌 CJK COMPATIBILITY IDEOGRAPH-F968
≡ 6CCC 泌
F969 數 CJK COMPATIBILITY IDEOGRAPH-F969
≡ 6578 數
F96A 索 CJK COMPATIBILITY IDEOGRAPH-F96A
≡ 7D22 索
F96B 參 CJK COMPATIBILITY IDEOGRAPH-F96B
≡ 53C3 參
F96C 塞 CJK COMPATIBILITY IDEOGRAPH-F96C
≡ 585E 塞
F96D 省 CJK COMPATIBILITY IDEOGRAPH-F96D
≡ 7701 省
F96E 葉 CJK COMPATIBILITY IDEOGRAPH-F96E
≡ 8449 葉
F96F 說 CJK COMPATIBILITY IDEOGRAPH-F96F
≡ 8AAA 說
F970 殺 CJK COMPATIBILITY IDEOGRAPH-F970
≡ 6BBA 殺
F971 辰 CJK COMPATIBILITY IDEOGRAPH-F971
≡ 8FB0 辰
F972 沈 CJK COMPATIBILITY IDEOGRAPH-F972
≡ 6C88 沈
F973 拾 CJK COMPATIBILITY IDEOGRAPH-F973
≡ 62FE 拾
F974 若 CJK COMPATIBILITY IDEOGRAPH-F974
≡ 82E5 若
F975 掠 CJK COMPATIBILITY IDEOGRAPH-F975
≡ 63A0 掠
F976 略 CJK COMPATIBILITY IDEOGRAPH-F976
≡ 7565 略
F977 亮 CJK COMPATIBILITY IDEOGRAPH-F977
≡ 4EAE 亮
F978 兩 CJK COMPATIBILITY IDEOGRAPH-F978
≡ 5169 兩
F979 凉 CJK COMPATIBILITY IDEOGRAPH-F979
≡ 51C9 凉
F97A 梁 CJK COMPATIBILITY IDEOGRAPH-F97A
≡ 6881 梁

F97B 糧 CJK COMPATIBILITY IDEOGRAPH-F97B
≡ 7CE7 糧
F97C 良 CJK COMPATIBILITY IDEOGRAPH-F97C
≡ 826F 良
F97D 諒 CJK COMPATIBILITY IDEOGRAPH-F97D
≡ 8AD2 諒
F97E 量 CJK COMPATIBILITY IDEOGRAPH-F97E
≡ 91CF 量
F97F 勵 CJK COMPATIBILITY IDEOGRAPH-F97F
≡ 52F5 勵
F980 呂 CJK COMPATIBILITY IDEOGRAPH-F980
≡ 5442 呂
F981 女 CJK COMPATIBILITY IDEOGRAPH-F981
≡ 5973 女
F982 廬 CJK COMPATIBILITY IDEOGRAPH-F982
≡ 5EEC 廬
F983 旅 CJK COMPATIBILITY IDEOGRAPH-F983
≡ 65C5 旅
F984 濾 CJK COMPATIBILITY IDEOGRAPH-F984
≡ 6FFE 濾
F985 礪 CJK COMPATIBILITY IDEOGRAPH-F985
≡ 792A 礪
F986 閭 CJK COMPATIBILITY IDEOGRAPH-F986
≡ 95AD 閭
F987 驪 CJK COMPATIBILITY IDEOGRAPH-F987
≡ 9A6A 驪
F988 麗 CJK COMPATIBILITY IDEOGRAPH-F988
≡ 9E97 麗
F989 黎 CJK COMPATIBILITY IDEOGRAPH-F989
≡ 9ECE 黎
F98A 力 CJK COMPATIBILITY IDEOGRAPH-F98A
≡ 529B 力
F98B 曆 CJK COMPATIBILITY IDEOGRAPH-F98B
≡ 66C6 曆
F98C 歷 CJK COMPATIBILITY IDEOGRAPH-F98C
≡ 6B77 歷
F98D 轢 CJK COMPATIBILITY IDEOGRAPH-F98D
≡ 8F62 轢
F98E 年 CJK COMPATIBILITY IDEOGRAPH-F98E
≡ 5E74 年
F98F 憐 CJK COMPATIBILITY IDEOGRAPH-F98F
≡ 6190 憐
F990 戀 CJK COMPATIBILITY IDEOGRAPH-F990
≡ 6200 戀
F991 撚 CJK COMPATIBILITY IDEOGRAPH-F991
≡ 649A 撚
F992 漣 CJK COMPATIBILITY IDEOGRAPH-F992
≡ 6F23 漣
F993 煉 CJK COMPATIBILITY IDEOGRAPH-F993
≡ 7149 煉
F994 璉 CJK COMPATIBILITY IDEOGRAPH-F994
≡ 7489 璉
F995 秊 CJK COMPATIBILITY IDEOGRAPH-F995
≡ 79CA 秊
F996 練 CJK COMPATIBILITY IDEOGRAPH-F996
≡ 7DF4 練
F997 聯 CJK COMPATIBILITY IDEOGRAPH-F997
≡ 806F 聯
F998 輦 CJK COMPATIBILITY IDEOGRAPH-F998
≡ 8F26 輦
F999 蓮 CJK COMPATIBILITY IDEOGRAPH-F999
≡ 84EE 蓮
F99A 連 CJK COMPATIBILITY IDEOGRAPH-F99A
≡ 9023 連
F99B 鍊 CJK COMPATIBILITY IDEOGRAPH-F99B
≡ 934A 鍊
F99C 列 CJK COMPATIBILITY IDEOGRAPH-F99C
≡ 5217 列
F99D 劣 CJK COMPATIBILITY IDEOGRAPH-F99D
≡ 52A3 劣
F99E 咽 CJK COMPATIBILITY IDEOGRAPH-F99E
≡ 54BD 咽
F99F 烈 CJK COMPATIBILITY IDEOGRAPH-F99F
≡ 70C8 烈
F9A0 裂 CJK COMPATIBILITY IDEOGRAPH-F9A0
≡ 88C2 裂
F9A1 說 CJK COMPATIBILITY IDEOGRAPH-F9A1
≡ 8AAA 說
F9A2 廉 CJK COMPATIBILITY IDEOGRAPH-F9A2
≡ 5EC9 廉
F9A3 念 CJK COMPATIBILITY IDEOGRAPH-F9A3
≡ 5FF5 念
F9A4 捻 CJK COMPATIBILITY IDEOGRAPH-F9A4
≡ 637B 捻
F9A5 殮 CJK COMPATIBILITY IDEOGRAPH-F9A5
≡ 6BAE 殮
F9A6 簾 CJK COMPATIBILITY IDEOGRAPH-F9A6
≡ 7C3E 簾
F9A7 獵 CJK COMPATIBILITY IDEOGRAPH-F9A7
≡ 7375 獵
F9A8 令 CJK COMPATIBILITY IDEOGRAPH-F9A8
≡ 4EE4 令
F9A9 囹 CJK COMPATIBILITY IDEOGRAPH-F9A9
≡ 56F9 囹
F9AA 寧 CJK COMPATIBILITY IDEOGRAPH-F9AA
≡ 5BE7 寧
F9AB 嶺 CJK COMPATIBILITY IDEOGRAPH-F9AB
≡ 5DBA 嶺
F9AC 怜 CJK COMPATIBILITY IDEOGRAPH-F9AC
≡ 601C 怜
F9AD 玲 CJK COMPATIBILITY IDEOGRAPH-F9AD
≡ 73B2 玲
F9AE 瑩 CJK COMPATIBILITY IDEOGRAPH-F9AE
≡ 7469 瑩
F9AF 羚 CJK COMPATIBILITY IDEOGRAPH-F9AF
≡ 7F9A 羚
F9B0 聆 CJK COMPATIBILITY IDEOGRAPH-F9B0
≡ 8046 聆
F9B1 鈴 CJK COMPATIBILITY IDEOGRAPH-F9B1
≡ 9234 鈴
F9B2 零 CJK COMPATIBILITY IDEOGRAPH-F9B2
≡ 96F6 零
F9B3 靈 CJK COMPATIBILITY IDEOGRAPH-F9B3
≡ 9748 靈
F9B4 領 CJK COMPATIBILITY IDEOGRAPH-F9B4
≡ 9818 領
F9B5 例 CJK COMPATIBILITY IDEOGRAPH-F9B5
≡ 4F8B 例
F9B6 禮 CJK COMPATIBILITY IDEOGRAPH-F9B6
≡ 79AE 禮
F9B7 醴 CJK COMPATIBILITY IDEOGRAPH-F9B7
≡ 91B4 醴
F9B8 隸 CJK COMPATIBILITY IDEOGRAPH-F9B8
→ 96B7 隷 cjk unified ideograph-96B7
≡ 96B8 隸

F9B9 惡 CJK COMPATIBILITY IDEOGRAPH-F9B9
≡ 60E1 惡
F9BA 了 CJK COMPATIBILITY IDEOGRAPH-F9BA
≡ 4E86 了
F9BB 僚 CJK COMPATIBILITY IDEOGRAPH-F9BB
≡ 50DA 僚
F9BC 寮 CJK COMPATIBILITY IDEOGRAPH-F9BC
≡ 5BEE 寮
F9BD 尿 CJK COMPATIBILITY IDEOGRAPH-F9BD
≡ 5C3F 尿
F9BE 料 CJK COMPATIBILITY IDEOGRAPH-F9BE
≡ 6599 料
F9BF 樂 CJK COMPATIBILITY IDEOGRAPH-F9BF
≡ 6A02 樂
F9C0 燎 CJK COMPATIBILITY IDEOGRAPH-F9C0
≡ 71CE 燎
F9C1 療 CJK COMPATIBILITY IDEOGRAPH-F9C1
≡ 7642 療
F9C2 蓼 CJK COMPATIBILITY IDEOGRAPH-F9C2
≡ 84FC 蓼
F9C3 遼 CJK COMPATIBILITY IDEOGRAPH-F9C3
≡ 907C 遼
F9C4 龍 CJK COMPATIBILITY IDEOGRAPH-F9C4
≡ 9F8D 龍
F9C5 暈 CJK COMPATIBILITY IDEOGRAPH-F9C5
≡ 6688 暈
F9C6 阮 CJK COMPATIBILITY IDEOGRAPH-F9C6
≡ 962E 阮
F9C7 劉 CJK COMPATIBILITY IDEOGRAPH-F9C7
≡ 5289 劉
F9C8 杻 CJK COMPATIBILITY IDEOGRAPH-F9C8
≡ 677B 杻
F9C9 柳 CJK COMPATIBILITY IDEOGRAPH-F9C9
≡ 67F3 柳
F9CA 流 CJK COMPATIBILITY IDEOGRAPH-F9CA
≡ 6D41 流
F9CB 溜 CJK COMPATIBILITY IDEOGRAPH-F9CB
≡ 6E9C 溜
F9CC 琉 CJK COMPATIBILITY IDEOGRAPH-F9CC
≡ 7409 琉
F9CD 留 CJK COMPATIBILITY IDEOGRAPH-F9CD
≡ 7559 留
F9CE 硫 CJK COMPATIBILITY IDEOGRAPH-F9CE
≡ 786B 硫
F9CF 紐 CJK COMPATIBILITY IDEOGRAPH-F9CF
≡ 7D10 紐
F9D0 類 CJK COMPATIBILITY IDEOGRAPH-F9D0
≡ 985E 類
F9D1 六 CJK COMPATIBILITY IDEOGRAPH-F9D1
≡ 516D 六
F9D2 戮 CJK COMPATIBILITY IDEOGRAPH-F9D2
≡ 622E 戮
F9D3 陸 CJK COMPATIBILITY IDEOGRAPH-F9D3
≡ 9678 陸
F9D4 倫 CJK COMPATIBILITY IDEOGRAPH-F9D4
≡ 502B 倫
F9D5 崙 CJK COMPATIBILITY IDEOGRAPH-F9D5
≡ 5D19 崙
F9D6 淪 CJK COMPATIBILITY IDEOGRAPH-F9D6
≡ 6DEA 淪
F9D7 輪 CJK COMPATIBILITY IDEOGRAPH-F9D7
≡ 8F2A 輪
F9D8 律 CJK COMPATIBILITY IDEOGRAPH-F9D8
≡ 5F8B 律
F9D9 慄 CJK COMPATIBILITY IDEOGRAPH-F9D9
≡ 6144 慄
F9DA 栗 CJK COMPATIBILITY IDEOGRAPH-F9DA
≡ 6817 栗
F9DB 率 CJK COMPATIBILITY IDEOGRAPH-F9DB
≡ 7387 率
F9DC 隆 CJK COMPATIBILITY IDEOGRAPH-F9DC
≡ 9686 隆
F9DD 利 CJK COMPATIBILITY IDEOGRAPH-F9DD
≡ 5229 利
F9DE 吏 CJK COMPATIBILITY IDEOGRAPH-F9DE
≡ 540F 吏
F9DF 履 CJK COMPATIBILITY IDEOGRAPH-F9DF
≡ 5C65 履
F9E0 易 CJK COMPATIBILITY IDEOGRAPH-F9E0
≡ 6613 易
F9E1 李 CJK COMPATIBILITY IDEOGRAPH-F9E1
≡ 674E 李
F9E2 梨 CJK COMPATIBILITY IDEOGRAPH-F9E2
≡ 68A8 梨
F9E3 泥 CJK COMPATIBILITY IDEOGRAPH-F9E3
≡ 6CE5 泥
F9E4 理 CJK COMPATIBILITY IDEOGRAPH-F9E4
≡ 7406 理
F9E5 痢 CJK COMPATIBILITY IDEOGRAPH-F9E5
≡ 75E2 痢
F9E6 罹 CJK COMPATIBILITY IDEOGRAPH-F9E6
≡ 7F79 罹
F9E7 裏 CJK COMPATIBILITY IDEOGRAPH-F9E7
≡ 88CF 裏
F9E8 裡 CJK COMPATIBILITY IDEOGRAPH-F9E8
≡ 88E1 裡
F9E9 里 CJK COMPATIBILITY IDEOGRAPH-F9E9
≡ 91CC 里
F9EA 離 CJK COMPATIBILITY IDEOGRAPH-F9EA
≡ 96E2 離
F9EB 匿 CJK COMPATIBILITY IDEOGRAPH-F9EB
≡ 533F 匿
F9EC 溺 CJK COMPATIBILITY IDEOGRAPH-F9EC
≡ 6EBA 溺
F9ED 吝 CJK COMPATIBILITY IDEOGRAPH-F9ED
≡ 541D 吝
F9EE 燐 CJK COMPATIBILITY IDEOGRAPH-F9EE
≡ 71D0 燐
F9EF 璘 CJK COMPATIBILITY IDEOGRAPH-F9EF
≡ 7498 璘
F9F0 藺 CJK COMPATIBILITY IDEOGRAPH-F9F0
≡ 85FA 藺
F9F1 隣 CJK COMPATIBILITY IDEOGRAPH-F9F1
≡ 96A3 隣
F9F2 鱗 CJK COMPATIBILITY IDEOGRAPH-F9F2
≡ 9C57 鱗
F9F3 麟 CJK COMPATIBILITY IDEOGRAPH-F9F3
≡ 9E9F 麟
F9F4 林 CJK COMPATIBILITY IDEOGRAPH-F9F4
≡ 6797 林
F9F5 淋 CJK COMPATIBILITY IDEOGRAPH-F9F5
≡ 6DCB 淋
F9F6 臨 CJK COMPATIBILITY IDEOGRAPH-F9F6
≡ 81E8 臨

F9F7 立 CJK COMPATIBILITY IDEOGRAPH-F9F7
≡ 7ACB 立
F9F8 笠 CJK COMPATIBILITY IDEOGRAPH-F9F8
≡ 7B20 笠
F9F9 粒 CJK COMPATIBILITY IDEOGRAPH-F9F9
≡ 7C92 粒
F9FA 狀 CJK COMPATIBILITY IDEOGRAPH-F9FA
≡ 72C0 狀
F9FB 炙 CJK COMPATIBILITY IDEOGRAPH-F9FB
≡ 7099 炙
F9FC 識 CJK COMPATIBILITY IDEOGRAPH-F9FC
≡ 8B58 識
F9FD 什 CJK COMPATIBILITY IDEOGRAPH-F9FD
≡ 4EC0 什
F9FE 茶 CJK COMPATIBILITY IDEOGRAPH-F9FE
≡ 8336 茶
F9FF 刺 CJK COMPATIBILITY IDEOGRAPH-F9FF
≡ 523A 刺
FA00 切 CJK COMPATIBILITY IDEOGRAPH-FA00
≡ 5207 切
FA01 度 CJK COMPATIBILITY IDEOGRAPH-FA01
≡ 5EA6 度
FA02 拓 CJK COMPATIBILITY IDEOGRAPH-FA02
≡ 62D3 拓
FA03 糖 CJK COMPATIBILITY IDEOGRAPH-FA03
≡ 7CD6 糖
FA04 宅 CJK COMPATIBILITY IDEOGRAPH-FA04
≡ 5B85 宅
FA05 洞 CJK COMPATIBILITY IDEOGRAPH-FA05
≡ 6D1E 洞
FA06 暴 CJK COMPATIBILITY IDEOGRAPH-FA06
≡ 66B4 暴
FA07 輻 CJK COMPATIBILITY IDEOGRAPH-FA07
≡ 8F3B 輻
FA08 行 CJK COMPATIBILITY IDEOGRAPH-FA08
≡ 884C 行
FA09 降 CJK COMPATIBILITY IDEOGRAPH-FA09
≡ 964D 降
FA0A 見 CJK COMPATIBILITY IDEOGRAPH-FA0A
≡ 898B 見
FA0B 廓 CJK COMPATIBILITY IDEOGRAPH-FA0B
≡ 5ED3 廓

Duplicate characters from Big 5

FA0C 兀 CJK COMPATIBILITY IDEOGRAPH-FA0C
≡ 5140 兀
FA0D 嗀 CJK COMPATIBILITY IDEOGRAPH-FA0D
≡ 55C0 嗀

The IBM 32 compatibility ideographs

FA0E 﨎 CJK COMPATIBILITY IDEOGRAPH-FA0E
• a unified CJK ideograph, not a compatibility ideograph, despite its name
FA0F 﨏 CJK COMPATIBILITY IDEOGRAPH-FA0F
• a unified CJK ideograph, not a compatibility ideograph, despite its name
FA10 塚 CJK COMPATIBILITY IDEOGRAPH-FA10
≡ 585A 塚
FA11 﨑 CJK COMPATIBILITY IDEOGRAPH-FA11
• a unified CJK ideograph, not a compatibility ideograph, despite its name
FA12 晴 CJK COMPATIBILITY IDEOGRAPH-FA12
≡ 6674 晴
FA13 﨓 CJK COMPATIBILITY IDEOGRAPH-FA13
• a unified CJK ideograph, not a compatibility ideograph, despite its name
FA14 﨔 CJK COMPATIBILITY IDEOGRAPH-FA14
• a unified CJK ideograph, not a compatibility ideograph, despite its name
FA15 凞 CJK COMPATIBILITY IDEOGRAPH-FA15
≡ 51DE 凞
FA16 猪 CJK COMPATIBILITY IDEOGRAPH-FA16
≡ 732A 猪
FA17 益 CJK COMPATIBILITY IDEOGRAPH-FA17
≡ 76CA 益
FA18 礼 CJK COMPATIBILITY IDEOGRAPH-FA18
≡ 793C 礼
FA19 神 CJK COMPATIBILITY IDEOGRAPH-FA19
≡ 795E 神
FA1A 祥 CJK COMPATIBILITY IDEOGRAPH-FA1A
≡ 7965 祥
FA1B 福 CJK COMPATIBILITY IDEOGRAPH-FA1B
≡ 798F 福
FA1C 靖 CJK COMPATIBILITY IDEOGRAPH-FA1C
≡ 9756 靖
FA1D 精 CJK COMPATIBILITY IDEOGRAPH-FA1D
≡ 7CBE 精
FA1E 羽 CJK COMPATIBILITY IDEOGRAPH-FA1E
≡ 7FBD 羽
FA1F 﨟 CJK COMPATIBILITY IDEOGRAPH-FA1F
• a unified CJK ideograph, not a compatibility ideograph, despite its name
FA20 蘒 CJK COMPATIBILITY IDEOGRAPH-FA20
≡ 8612 蘒
FA21 﨡 CJK COMPATIBILITY IDEOGRAPH-FA21
• a unified CJK ideograph, not a compatibility ideograph, despite its name
FA22 諸 CJK COMPATIBILITY IDEOGRAPH-FA22
≡ 8AF8 諸
FA23 﨣 CJK COMPATIBILITY IDEOGRAPH-FA23
• a unified CJK ideograph, not a compatibility ideograph, despite its name
FA24 﨤 CJK COMPATIBILITY IDEOGRAPH-FA24
• a unified CJK ideograph, not a compatibility ideograph, despite its name
FA25 逸 CJK COMPATIBILITY IDEOGRAPH-FA25
≡ 9038 逸
FA26 都 CJK COMPATIBILITY IDEOGRAPH-FA26
≡ 90FD 都
FA27 﨧 CJK COMPATIBILITY IDEOGRAPH-FA27
• a unified CJK ideograph, not a compatibility ideograph, despite its name
FA28 﨨 CJK COMPATIBILITY IDEOGRAPH-FA28
• a unified CJK ideograph, not a compatibility ideograph, despite its name
FA29 﨩 CJK COMPATIBILITY IDEOGRAPH-FA29
• a unified CJK ideograph, not a compatibility ideograph, despite its name
FA2A 飯 CJK COMPATIBILITY IDEOGRAPH-FA2A
≡ 98EF 飯
FA2B 飼 CJK COMPATIBILITY IDEOGRAPH-FA2B
≡ 98FC 飼
FA2C 館 CJK COMPATIBILITY IDEOGRAPH-FA2C
≡ 9928 館
FA2D 鶴 CJK COMPATIBILITY IDEOGRAPH-FA2D
≡ 9DB4 鶴

JIS X 0213 compatibility ideographs

FA30 侮 CJK COMPATIBILITY IDEOGRAPH-FA30
≡ 4FAE 侮
FA31 僧 CJK COMPATIBILITY IDEOGRAPH-FA31
≡ 50E7 僧
FA32 免 CJK COMPATIBILITY IDEOGRAPH-FA32
≡ 514D 免
FA33 勉 CJK COMPATIBILITY IDEOGRAPH-FA33
≡ 52C9 勉
FA34 勤 CJK COMPATIBILITY IDEOGRAPH-FA34
≡ 52E4 勤
FA35 卑 CJK COMPATIBILITY IDEOGRAPH-FA35
≡ 5351 卑
FA36 喝 CJK COMPATIBILITY IDEOGRAPH-FA36
≡ 559D 喝
FA37 嘆 CJK COMPATIBILITY IDEOGRAPH-FA37
≡ 5606 嘆
FA38 器 CJK COMPATIBILITY IDEOGRAPH-FA38
≡ 5668 器
FA39 塀 CJK COMPATIBILITY IDEOGRAPH-FA39
≡ 5840 塀
FA3A 墨 CJK COMPATIBILITY IDEOGRAPH-FA3A
≡ 58A8 墨
FA3B 層 CJK COMPATIBILITY IDEOGRAPH-FA3B
≡ 5C64 層
FA3C 屮 CJK COMPATIBILITY IDEOGRAPH-FA3C
≡ 5C6E 屮
FA3D 悔 CJK COMPATIBILITY IDEOGRAPH-FA3D
≡ 6094 悔
FA3E 慨 CJK COMPATIBILITY IDEOGRAPH-FA3E
≡ 6168 慨
FA3F 憎 CJK COMPATIBILITY IDEOGRAPH-FA3F
≡ 618E 憎
FA40 懲 CJK COMPATIBILITY IDEOGRAPH-FA40
≡ 61F2 懲
FA41 敏 CJK COMPATIBILITY IDEOGRAPH-FA41
≡ 654F 敏
FA42 既 CJK COMPATIBILITY IDEOGRAPH-FA42
≡ 65E2 既
FA43 暑 CJK COMPATIBILITY IDEOGRAPH-FA43
≡ 6691 暑
FA44 梅 CJK COMPATIBILITY IDEOGRAPH-FA44
≡ 6885 梅
FA45 海 CJK COMPATIBILITY IDEOGRAPH-FA45
≡ 6D77 海
FA46 渚 CJK COMPATIBILITY IDEOGRAPH-FA46
≡ 6E1A 渚
FA47 漢 CJK COMPATIBILITY IDEOGRAPH-FA47
≡ 6F22 漢
FA48 煮 CJK COMPATIBILITY IDEOGRAPH-FA48
≡ 716E 煮
FA49 爫 CJK COMPATIBILITY IDEOGRAPH-FA49
≡ 722B 爫
FA4A 琢 CJK COMPATIBILITY IDEOGRAPH-FA4A
≡ 7422 琢
FA4B 碑 CJK COMPATIBILITY IDEOGRAPH-FA4B
≡ 7891 碑
FA4C 社 CJK COMPATIBILITY IDEOGRAPH-FA4C
≡ 793E 社
FA4D 祉 CJK COMPATIBILITY IDEOGRAPH-FA4D
≡ 7949 祉
FA4E 祈 CJK COMPATIBILITY IDEOGRAPH-FA4E
≡ 7948 祈
FA4F 祐 CJK COMPATIBILITY IDEOGRAPH-FA4F
≡ 7950 祐
FA50 祖 CJK COMPATIBILITY IDEOGRAPH-FA50
≡ 7956 祖
FA51 祝 CJK COMPATIBILITY IDEOGRAPH-FA51
≡ 795D 祝
FA52 禍 CJK COMPATIBILITY IDEOGRAPH-FA52
≡ 798D 禍
FA53 禎 CJK COMPATIBILITY IDEOGRAPH-FA53
≡ 798E 禎
FA54 穀 CJK COMPATIBILITY IDEOGRAPH-FA54
≡ 7A40 穀
FA55 突 CJK COMPATIBILITY IDEOGRAPH-FA55
≡ 7A81 突
FA56 節 CJK COMPATIBILITY IDEOGRAPH-FA56
≡ 7BC0 節
FA57 練 CJK COMPATIBILITY IDEOGRAPH-FA57
≡ 7DF4 練
FA58 縉 CJK COMPATIBILITY IDEOGRAPH-FA58
≡ 7E09 縉
FA59 繁 CJK COMPATIBILITY IDEOGRAPH-FA59
≡ 7E41 繁
FA5A 署 CJK COMPATIBILITY IDEOGRAPH-FA5A
≡ 7F72 署
FA5B 者 CJK COMPATIBILITY IDEOGRAPH-FA5B
≡ 8005 者
FA5C 臭 CJK COMPATIBILITY IDEOGRAPH-FA5C
≡ 81ED 臭
FA5D 艹 CJK COMPATIBILITY IDEOGRAPH-FA5D
≡ 8279 艹
FA5E 艹 CJK COMPATIBILITY IDEOGRAPH-FA5E
≡ 8279 艹
FA5F 著 CJK COMPATIBILITY IDEOGRAPH-FA5F
≡ 8457 著
FA60 褐 CJK COMPATIBILITY IDEOGRAPH-FA60
≡ 8910 褐
FA61 視 CJK COMPATIBILITY IDEOGRAPH-FA61
≡ 8996 視
FA62 謁 CJK COMPATIBILITY IDEOGRAPH-FA62
≡ 8B01 謁
FA63 謹 CJK COMPATIBILITY IDEOGRAPH-FA63
≡ 8B39 謹
FA64 賓 CJK COMPATIBILITY IDEOGRAPH-FA64
≡ 8CD3 賓
FA65 贈 CJK COMPATIBILITY IDEOGRAPH-FA65
≡ 8D08 贈
FA66 辶 CJK COMPATIBILITY IDEOGRAPH-FA66
≡ 8FB6 辶
FA67 逸 CJK COMPATIBILITY IDEOGRAPH-FA67
≡ 9038 逸
FA68 難 CJK COMPATIBILITY IDEOGRAPH-FA68
≡ 96E3 難
FA69 響 CJK COMPATIBILITY IDEOGRAPH-FA69
≡ 97FF 響
FA6A 頻 CJK COMPATIBILITY IDEOGRAPH-FA6A
≡ 983B 頻

DPRK compatibility ideographs

FA70 並 CJK COMPATIBILITY IDEOGRAPH-FA70
≡ 4E26 並

FA71 况 CJK COMPATIBILITY IDEOGRAPH-FA71
≡ 51B5 况
FA72 全 CJK COMPATIBILITY IDEOGRAPH-FA72
≡ 5168 全
FA73 侀 CJK COMPATIBILITY IDEOGRAPH-FA73
≡ 4F80 侀
FA74 充 CJK COMPATIBILITY IDEOGRAPH-FA74
≡ 5145 充
FA75 冀 CJK COMPATIBILITY IDEOGRAPH-FA75
≡ 5180 冀
FA76 勇 CJK COMPATIBILITY IDEOGRAPH-FA76
≡ 52C7 勇
FA77 勺 CJK COMPATIBILITY IDEOGRAPH-FA77
≡ 52FA 勺
FA78 喝 CJK COMPATIBILITY IDEOGRAPH-FA78
≡ 559D 喝
FA79 啕 CJK COMPATIBILITY IDEOGRAPH-FA79
≡ 5555 啕
FA7A 喙 CJK COMPATIBILITY IDEOGRAPH-FA7A
≡ 5599 喙
FA7B 嗢 CJK COMPATIBILITY IDEOGRAPH-FA7B
≡ 55E2 嗢
FA7C 塚 CJK COMPATIBILITY IDEOGRAPH-FA7C
≡ 585A 塚
FA7D 墳 CJK COMPATIBILITY IDEOGRAPH-FA7D
≡ 58B3 墳
FA7E 奄 CJK COMPATIBILITY IDEOGRAPH-FA7E
≡ 5944 奄
FA7F 奔 CJK COMPATIBILITY IDEOGRAPH-FA7F
≡ 5954 奔
FA80 婢 CJK COMPATIBILITY IDEOGRAPH-FA80
≡ 5A62 婢
FA81 嬨 CJK COMPATIBILITY IDEOGRAPH-FA81
≡ 5B28 嬨
FA82 廒 CJK COMPATIBILITY IDEOGRAPH-FA82
≡ 5ED2 廒
FA83 廙 CJK COMPATIBILITY IDEOGRAPH-FA83
≡ 5ED9 廙
FA84 彩 CJK COMPATIBILITY IDEOGRAPH-FA84
≡ 5F69 彩
FA85 徭 CJK COMPATIBILITY IDEOGRAPH-FA85
≡ 5FAD 徭
FA86 惘 CJK COMPATIBILITY IDEOGRAPH-FA86
≡ 60D8 惘
FA87 慎 CJK COMPATIBILITY IDEOGRAPH-FA87
≡ 614E 慎
FA88 愈 CJK COMPATIBILITY IDEOGRAPH-FA88
≡ 6108 愈
FA89 憎 CJK COMPATIBILITY IDEOGRAPH-FA89
≡ 618E 憎
FA8A 慠 CJK COMPATIBILITY IDEOGRAPH-FA8A
≡ 6160 慠
FA8B 懲 CJK COMPATIBILITY IDEOGRAPH-FA8B
≡ 61F2 懲
FA8C 戴 CJK COMPATIBILITY IDEOGRAPH-FA8C
≡ 6234 戴
FA8D 揄 CJK COMPATIBILITY IDEOGRAPH-FA8D
≡ 63C4 揄
FA8E 搜 CJK COMPATIBILITY IDEOGRAPH-FA8E
≡ 641C 搜
FA8F 摒 CJK COMPATIBILITY IDEOGRAPH-FA8F
≡ 6452 摒
FA90 敖 CJK COMPATIBILITY IDEOGRAPH-FA90
≡ 6556 敖
FA91 晴 CJK COMPATIBILITY IDEOGRAPH-FA91
≡ 6674 晴
FA92 朗 CJK COMPATIBILITY IDEOGRAPH-FA92
≡ 6717 朗
FA93 望 CJK COMPATIBILITY IDEOGRAPH-FA93
≡ 671B 望
FA94 杖 CJK COMPATIBILITY IDEOGRAPH-FA94
≡ 6756 杖
FA95 歹 CJK COMPATIBILITY IDEOGRAPH-FA95
≡ 6B79 歹
FA96 殺 CJK COMPATIBILITY IDEOGRAPH-FA96
≡ 6BBA 殺
FA97 流 CJK COMPATIBILITY IDEOGRAPH-FA97
≡ 6D41 流
FA98 滛 CJK COMPATIBILITY IDEOGRAPH-FA98
≡ 6EDB 滛
FA99 滋 CJK COMPATIBILITY IDEOGRAPH-FA99
≡ 6ECB 滋
FA9A 漢 CJK COMPATIBILITY IDEOGRAPH-FA9A
≡ 6F22 漢
FA9B 瀞 CJK COMPATIBILITY IDEOGRAPH-FA9B
≡ 701E 瀞
FA9C 煮 CJK COMPATIBILITY IDEOGRAPH-FA9C
≡ 716E 煮
FA9D 瞧 CJK COMPATIBILITY IDEOGRAPH-FA9D
≡ 77A7 瞧
FA9E 爵 CJK COMPATIBILITY IDEOGRAPH-FA9E
≡ 7235 爵
FA9F 犯 CJK COMPATIBILITY IDEOGRAPH-FA9F
≡ 72AF 犯
FAA0 猪 CJK COMPATIBILITY IDEOGRAPH-FAA0
≡ 732A 猪
FAA1 瑱 CJK COMPATIBILITY IDEOGRAPH-FAA1
≡ 7471 瑱
FAA2 甆 CJK COMPATIBILITY IDEOGRAPH-FAA2
≡ 7506 甆
FAA3 画 CJK COMPATIBILITY IDEOGRAPH-FAA3
≡ 753B 画
FAA4 瘝 CJK COMPATIBILITY IDEOGRAPH-FAA4
≡ 761D 瘝
FAA5 瘟 CJK COMPATIBILITY IDEOGRAPH-FAA5
≡ 761F 瘟
FAA6 益 CJK COMPATIBILITY IDEOGRAPH-FAA6
≡ 76CA 益
FAA7 盛 CJK COMPATIBILITY IDEOGRAPH-FAA7
≡ 76DB 盛
FAA8 直 CJK COMPATIBILITY IDEOGRAPH-FAA8
≡ 76F4 直
FAA9 睊 CJK COMPATIBILITY IDEOGRAPH-FAA9
≡ 774A 睊
FAAA 着 CJK COMPATIBILITY IDEOGRAPH-FAAA
≡ 7740 着
FAAB 磌 CJK COMPATIBILITY IDEOGRAPH-FAAB
≡ 78CC 磌
FAAC 窱 CJK COMPATIBILITY IDEOGRAPH-FAAC
≡ 7AB1 窱
FAAD 節 CJK COMPATIBILITY IDEOGRAPH-FAAD
≡ 7BC0 節
FAAE 类 CJK COMPATIBILITY IDEOGRAPH-FAAE
≡ 7C7B 类

FAAF 條 CJK COMPATIBILITY IDEOGRAPH-FAAF
≡ 7D5B 絛
FAB0 練 CJK COMPATIBILITY IDEOGRAPH-FAB0
≡ 7DF4 練
FAB1 缾 CJK COMPATIBILITY IDEOGRAPH-FAB1
≡ 7F3E 缾
FAB2 者 CJK COMPATIBILITY IDEOGRAPH-FAB2
≡ 8005 者
FAB3 荒 CJK COMPATIBILITY IDEOGRAPH-FAB3
≡ 8352 荒
FAB4 華 CJK COMPATIBILITY IDEOGRAPH-FAB4
≡ 83EF 華
FAB5 蝹 CJK COMPATIBILITY IDEOGRAPH-FAB5
≡ 8779 蝹
FAB6 襁 CJK COMPATIBILITY IDEOGRAPH-FAB6
≡ 8941 襁
FAB7 覆 CJK COMPATIBILITY IDEOGRAPH-FAB7
≡ 8986 覆
FAB8 視 CJK COMPATIBILITY IDEOGRAPH-FAB8
≡ 8996 視
FAB9 調 CJK COMPATIBILITY IDEOGRAPH-FAB9
≡ 8ABF 調
FABA 諸 CJK COMPATIBILITY IDEOGRAPH-FABA
≡ 8AF8 諸
FABB 請 CJK COMPATIBILITY IDEOGRAPH-FABB
≡ 8ACB 請
FABC 謁 CJK COMPATIBILITY IDEOGRAPH-FABC
≡ 8B01 謁
FABD 諾 CJK COMPATIBILITY IDEOGRAPH-FABD
≡ 8AFE 諾
FABE 諭 CJK COMPATIBILITY IDEOGRAPH-FABE
≡ 8AED 諭
FABF 謹 CJK COMPATIBILITY IDEOGRAPH-FABF
≡ 8B39 謹
FAC0 變 CJK COMPATIBILITY IDEOGRAPH-FAC0
≡ 8B8A 變
FAC1 贈 CJK COMPATIBILITY IDEOGRAPH-FAC1
≡ 8D08 贈
FAC2 輸 CJK COMPATIBILITY IDEOGRAPH-FAC2
≡ 8F38 輸
FAC3 遲 CJK COMPATIBILITY IDEOGRAPH-FAC3
≡ 9072 遲
FAC4 醙 CJK COMPATIBILITY IDEOGRAPH-FAC4
≡ 9199 醙
FAC5 鉶 CJK COMPATIBILITY IDEOGRAPH-FAC5
≡ 9276 鉶
FAC6 陼 CJK COMPATIBILITY IDEOGRAPH-FAC6
≡ 967C 陼
FAC7 難 CJK COMPATIBILITY IDEOGRAPH-FAC7
≡ 96E3 難
FAC8 靖 CJK COMPATIBILITY IDEOGRAPH-FAC8
≡ 9756 靖
FAC9 韛 CJK COMPATIBILITY IDEOGRAPH-FAC9
≡ 97DB 韛
FACA 響 CJK COMPATIBILITY IDEOGRAPH-FACA
≡ 97FF 響
FACB 頋 CJK COMPATIBILITY IDEOGRAPH-FACB
≡ 980B 頋
FACC 頻 CJK COMPATIBILITY IDEOGRAPH-FACC
≡ 983B 頻
FACD 鬒 CJK COMPATIBILITY IDEOGRAPH-FACD
≡ 9B12 鬒
FACE 龜 CJK COMPATIBILITY IDEOGRAPH-FACE
≡ 9F9C 龜
FACF 𢡊 CJK COMPATIBILITY IDEOGRAPH-FACF
≡ 2284A 𢡊
FAD0 𢡄 CJK COMPATIBILITY IDEOGRAPH-FAD0
≡ 22844 𢡄
FAD1 𣏕 CJK COMPATIBILITY IDEOGRAPH-FAD1
≡ 233D5 𣏕
FAD2 㮝 CJK COMPATIBILITY IDEOGRAPH-FAD2
≡ 3B9D 㮝
FAD3 䀘 CJK COMPATIBILITY IDEOGRAPH-FAD3
≡ 4018 䀘
FAD4 䀹 CJK COMPATIBILITY IDEOGRAPH-FAD4
≡ 4039 䀹
FAD5 𥉉 CJK COMPATIBILITY IDEOGRAPH-FAD5
≡ 25249 𥉉
FAD6 𥳐 CJK COMPATIBILITY IDEOGRAPH-FAD6
≡ 25CD0 𥳐
FAD7 𧻓 CJK COMPATIBILITY IDEOGRAPH-FAD7
≡ 27ED3 𧻓
FAD8 齃 CJK COMPATIBILITY IDEOGRAPH-FAD8
≡ 9F43 齃
FAD9 龎 CJK COMPATIBILITY IDEOGRAPH-FAD9
≡ 9F8E 龎

	FB0	FB1	FB2	FB3	FB4
0	ﬀ FB00		ﬠ FB20	אַ FB30	נּ FB40
1	ﬁ FB01		ﬡ FB21	בּ FB31	סּ FB41
2	ﬂ FB02		ﬢ FB22	גּ FB32	
3	ﬃ FB03	ﬓ FB13	ﬣ FB23	דּ FB33	ףּ FB43
4	ﬄ FB04	ﬔ FB14	ﬤ FB24	הּ FB34	פּ FB44
5	ﬅ FB05	ﬕ FB15	ﬥ FB25	וּ FB35	
6	ﬆ FB06	ﬖ FB16	ﬦ FB26	זּ FB36	צּ FB46
7		ﬗ FB17	ﬧ FB27		קּ FB47
8			ﬨ FB28	טּ FB38	רּ FB48
9			﬩ FB29	יּ FB39	שּ FB49
A			שׁ FB2A	ךּ FB3A	תּ FB4A
B			שׂ FB2B	כּ FB3B	וֹ FB4B
C			שּׁ FB2C	לּ FB3C	בֿ FB4C
D		יִ FB1D	שּׂ FB2D		כֿ FB4D
E		◌ﬞ FB1E	אַ FB2E	מּ FB3E	פֿ FB4E
F		ײַ FB1F	אָ FB2F		ﭏ FB4F

Latin ligatures

See the Basic Latin block starting at 0020

FB00 ﬀ LATIN SMALL LIGATURE FF
≈ 0066 f 0066 f

FB01 ﬁ LATIN SMALL LIGATURE FI
≈ 0066 f 0069 i

FB02 ﬂ LATIN SMALL LIGATURE FL
≈ 0066 f 006C l

FB03 ﬃ LATIN SMALL LIGATURE FFI
≈ 0066 f 0066 f 0069 i

FB04 ﬄ LATIN SMALL LIGATURE FFL
≈ 0066 f 0066 f 006C l

FB05 ﬅ LATIN SMALL LIGATURE LONG S T
≈ 017F ſ 0074 t

FB06 ﬆ LATIN SMALL LIGATURE ST
≈ 0073 s 0074 t

Armenian ligatures

See the Armenian block starting at 0530

FB13 ﬓ ARMENIAN SMALL LIGATURE MEN NOW
≈ 0574 մ 0576 ն

FB14 ﬔ ARMENIAN SMALL LIGATURE MEN ECH
≈ 0574 մ 0565 ե

FB15 ﬕ ARMENIAN SMALL LIGATURE MEN INI
≈ 0574 մ 056B ի

FB16 ﬖ ARMENIAN SMALL LIGATURE VEW NOW
≈ 057E վ 0576 ն

FB17 ﬗ ARMENIAN SMALL LIGATURE MEN XEH
≈ 0574 մ 056D խ

Hebrew presentation forms

See the Hebrew block starting at 0590

FB1D יִ HEBREW LETTER YOD WITH HIRIQ
≡ 05D9 י 05B4 ◌ִ

FB1E ◌ﬞ HEBREW POINT JUDEO-SPANISH VARIKA
• a glyph variant of 05BF ◌ֿ

FB1F ײַ HEBREW LIGATURE YIDDISH YOD YOD PATAH
≡ 05F2 ײ 05B7 ◌ַ

FB20 ﬠ HEBREW LETTER ALTERNATIVE AYIN
• this form of AYIN has no descender, for use with marks placed below the letter
≈ <font> 05E2 ע hebrew letter ayin

FB21 ﬡ HEBREW LETTER WIDE ALEF
≈ <font> 05D0 א hebrew letter alef

FB22 ﬢ HEBREW LETTER WIDE DALET
≈ <font> 05D3 ד hebrew letter dalet

FB23 ﬣ HEBREW LETTER WIDE HE
≈ <font> 05D4 ה hebrew letter he

FB24 ﬤ HEBREW LETTER WIDE KAF
≈ <font> 05DB כ hebrew letter kaf

FB25 ﬥ HEBREW LETTER WIDE LAMED
≈ <font> 05DC ל hebrew letter lamed

FB26 ﬦ HEBREW LETTER WIDE FINAL MEM
≈ <font> 05DD ם hebrew letter final mem

FB27 ﬧ HEBREW LETTER WIDE RESH
≈ <font> 05E8 ר hebrew letter resh

FB28 ﬨ HEBREW LETTER WIDE TAV
≈ <font> 05EA ת hebrew letter tav

FB29 ﬩ HEBREW LETTER ALTERNATIVE PLUS SIGN
≈ <font> 002B + plus sign

FB2A שׁ HEBREW LETTER SHIN WITH SHIN DOT
≡ 05E9 ש 05C1 ◌ׁ

FB2B שׂ HEBREW LETTER SHIN WITH SIN DOT
≡ 05E9 ש 05C2 ◌ׂ

FB2C שּׁ HEBREW LETTER SHIN WITH DAGESH AND SHIN DOT
≡ FB49 שּ 05C1 ◌ׁ

FB2D שּׂ HEBREW LETTER SHIN WITH DAGESH AND SIN DOT
≡ FB49 שּ 05C2 ◌ׂ

FB2E אַ HEBREW LETTER ALEF WITH PATAH
≡ 05D0 א 05B7 ◌ַ

FB2F אָ HEBREW LETTER ALEF WITH QAMATS
≡ 05D0 א 05B8 ◌ָ

FB30 אּ HEBREW LETTER ALEF WITH MAPIQ
≡ 05D0 א 05BC ◌ּ

FB31 בּ HEBREW LETTER BET WITH DAGESH
≡ 05D1 ב 05BC ◌ּ

FB32 גּ HEBREW LETTER GIMEL WITH DAGESH
≡ 05D2 ג 05BC ◌ּ

FB33 דּ HEBREW LETTER DALET WITH DAGESH
≡ 05D3 ד 05BC ◌ּ

FB34 הּ HEBREW LETTER HE WITH MAPIQ
≡ 05D4 ה 05BC ◌ּ

FB35 וּ HEBREW LETTER VAV WITH DAGESH
≡ 05D5 ו 05BC ◌ּ

FB36 זּ HEBREW LETTER ZAYIN WITH DAGESH
≡ 05D6 ז 05BC ◌ּ

FB37 <reserved>

FB38 טּ HEBREW LETTER TET WITH DAGESH
≡ 05D8 ט 05BC ◌ּ

FB39 יּ HEBREW LETTER YOD WITH DAGESH
≡ 05D9 י 05BC ◌ּ

FB3A ךּ HEBREW LETTER FINAL KAF WITH DAGESH
≡ 05DA ך 05BC ◌ּ

FB3B כּ HEBREW LETTER KAF WITH DAGESH
≡ 05DB כ 05BC ◌ּ

FB3C לּ HEBREW LETTER LAMED WITH DAGESH
≡ 05DC ל 05BC ◌ּ

FB3D <reserved>

FB3E מּ HEBREW LETTER MEM WITH DAGESH
≡ 05DE מ 05BC ◌ּ

FB3F <reserved>

FB40 נּ HEBREW LETTER NUN WITH DAGESH
≡ 05E0 נ 05BC ◌ּ

FB41 סּ HEBREW LETTER SAMEKH WITH DAGESH
≡ 05E1 ס 05BC ◌ּ

FB42 <reserved>

FB43 ףּ HEBREW LETTER FINAL PE WITH DAGESH
≡ 05E3 ף 05BC ◌ּ

FB44 פּ HEBREW LETTER PE WITH DAGESH
≡ 05E4 פ 05BC ◌ּ

FB45 <reserved>

FB46 צּ HEBREW LETTER TSADI WITH DAGESH
≡ 05E6 צ 05BC ◌ּ

FB47 קּ HEBREW LETTER QOF WITH DAGESH
≡ 05E7 ק 05BC ◌ּ

FB48 רּ HEBREW LETTER RESH WITH DAGESH
≡ 05E8 ר 05BC ◌ּ

FB49 שּ HEBREW LETTER SHIN WITH DAGESH
≡ 05E9 ש 05BC ◌ּ

FB4A תּ HEBREW LETTER TAV WITH DAGESH
≡ 05EA ת 05BC ◌ּ

FB4B וֹ HEBREW LETTER VAV WITH HOLAM
≡ 05D5 ו 05B9 ◌ֹ

FB4C בֿ HEBREW LETTER BET WITH RAFE
≡ 05D1 ב 05BF ◌ֿ
FB4D כֿ HEBREW LETTER KAF WITH RAFE
≡ 05DB כ 05BF ◌ֿ
FB4E פֿ HEBREW LETTER PE WITH RAFE
≡ 05E4 פ 05BF ◌ֿ
FB4F ﭏ HEBREW LIGATURE ALEF LAMED
≈ 05D0 א 05DC ל

	FB5	FB6	FB7	FB8	FB9	FBA	FBB	FBC	FBD	FBE	FBF	FC0	FC1	FC2	FC3
0	FB50	FB60	FB70	FB80	FB90	FBA0	FBB0			FBE0	FBF0	FC00	FC10	FC20	FC30
1	FB51	FB61	FB71	FB81	FB91	FBA1	FBB1			FBE1	FBF1	FC01	FC11	FC21	FC31
2	FB52	FB62	FB72	FB82	FB92	FBA2				FBE2	FBF2	FC02	FC12	FC22	FC32
3	FB53	FB63	FB73	FB83	FB93	FBA3			FBD3	FBE3	FBF3	FC03	FC13	FC23	FC33
4	FB54	FB64	FB74	FB84	FB94	FBA4			FBD4	FBE4	FBF4	FC04	FC14	FC24	FC34
5	FB55	FB65	FB75	FB85	FB95	FBA5			FBD5	FBE5	FBF5	FC05	FC15	FC25	FC35
6	FB56	FB66	FB76	FB86	FB96	FBA6			FBD6	FBE6	FBF6	FC06	FC16	FC26	FC36
7	FB57	FB67	FB77	FB87	FB97	FBA7			FBD7	FBE7	FBF7	FC07	FC17	FC27	FC37
8	FB58	FB68	FB78	FB88	FB98	FBA8			FBD8	FBE8	FBF8	FC08	FC18	FC28	FC38
9	FB59	FB69	FB79	FB89	FB99	FBA9			FBD9	FBE9	FBF9	FC09	FC19	FC29	FC39
A	FB5A	FB6A	FB7A	FB8A	FB9A	FBAA			FBDA	FBEA	FBFA	FC0A	FC1A	FC2A	FC3A
B	FB5B	FB6B	FB7B	FB8B	FB9B	FBAB			FBDB	FBEB	FBFB	FC0B	FC1B	FC2B	FC3B
C	FB5C	FB6C	FB7C	FB8C	FB9C	FBAC			FBDC	FBEC	FBFC	FC0C	FC1C	FC2C	FC3C
D	FB5D	FB6D	FB7D	FB8D	FB9D	FBAD			FBDD	FBED	FBFD	FC0D	FC1D	FC2D	FC3D
E	FB5E	FB6E	FB7E	FB8E	FB9E	FBAE			FBDE	FBEE	FBFE	FC0E	FC1E	FC2E	FC3E
F	FB5F	FB6F	FB7F	FB8F	FB9F	FBAF			FBDF	FBEF	FBFF	FC0F	FC1F	FC2F	FC3F

	FC4	FC5	FC6	FC7	FC8	FC9	FCA	FCB	FCC	FCD	FCE	FCF	FD0	FD1
0	ﱀ FC40	ﱐ FC50	ﱠ FC60	ﱰ FC70	ﲀ FC80	ﲐ FC90	ﲠ FCA0	ﲰ FCB0	ﳀ FCC0	ﳐ FCD0	ﳠ FCE0	ﳰ FCF0	ﴀ FD00	ﴐ FD10
1	ﱁ FC41	ﱑ FC51	ﱡ FC61	ﱱ FC71	ﲁ FC81	ﲑ FC91	ﲡ FCA1	ﲱ FCB1	ﳁ FCC1	ﳑ FCD1	ﳡ FCE1	ﳱ FCF1	ﴁ FD01	ﴑ FD11
2	ﱂ FC42	ﱒ FC52	ﱢ FC62	ﱲ FC72	ﲂ FC82	ﲒ FC92	ﲢ FCA2	ﲲ FCB2	ﳂ FCC2	ﳒ FCD2	ﳢ FCE2	ﳲ FCF2	ﴂ FD02	ﴒ FD12
3	ﱃ FC43	ﱓ FC53	ﱣ FC63	ﱳ FC73	ﲃ FC83	ﲓ FC93	ﲣ FCA3	ﲳ FCB3	ﳃ FCC3	ﳓ FCD3	ﳣ FCE3	ﳳ FCF3	ﴃ FD03	ﴓ FD13
4	ﱄ FC44	ﱔ FC54	ﱤ FC64	ﱴ FC74	ﲄ FC84	ﲔ FC94	ﲤ FCA4	ﲴ FCB4	ﳄ FCC4	ﳔ FCD4	ﳤ FCE4	ﳴ FCF4	ﴄ FD04	ﴔ FD14
5	ﱅ FC45	ﱕ FC55	ﱥ FC65	ﱵ FC75	ﲅ FC85	ﲕ FC95	ﲥ FCA5	ﲵ FCB5	ﳅ FCC5	ﳕ FCD5	ﳥ FCE5	ﳵ FCF5	ﴅ FD05	ﴕ FD15
6	ﱆ FC46	ﱖ FC56	ﱦ FC66	ﱶ FC76	ﲆ FC86	ﲖ FC96	ﲦ FCA6	ﲶ FCB6	ﳆ FCC6	ﳖ FCD6	ﳦ FCE6	ﳶ FCF6	ﴆ FD06	ﴖ FD16
7	ﱇ FC47	ﱗ FC57	ﱧ FC67	ﱷ FC77	ﲇ FC87	ﲗ FC97	ﲧ FCA7	ﲷ FCB7	ﳇ FCC7	ﳗ FCD7	ﳧ FCE7	ﳷ FCF7	ﴇ FD07	ﴗ FD17
8	ﱈ FC48	ﱘ FC58	ﱨ FC68	ﱸ FC78	ﲈ FC88	ﲘ FC98	ﲨ FCA8	ﲸ FCB8	ﳈ FCC8	ﳘ FCD8	ﳨ FCE8	ﳸ FCF8	ﴈ FD08	ﴘ FD18
9	ﱉ FC49	ﱙ FC59	ﱩ FC69	ﱹ FC79	ﲉ FC89	ﲙ FC99	ﲩ FCA9	ﲹ FCB9	ﳉ FCC9	ﳙ FCD9	ﳩ FCE9	ﳹ FCF9	ﴉ FD09	ﴙ FD19
A	ﱊ FC4A	ﱚ FC5A	ﱪ FC6A	ﱺ FC7A	ﲊ FC8A	ﲚ FC9A	ﲪ FCAA	ﲺ FCBA	ﳊ FCCA	ﳚ FCDA	ﳪ FCEA	ﳺ FCFA	ﴊ FD0A	ﴚ FD1A
B	ﱋ FC4B	ﱛ FC5B	ﱫ FC6B	ﱻ FC7B	ﲋ FC8B	ﲛ FC9B	ﲫ FCAB	ﲻ FCBB	ﳋ FCCB	ﳛ FCDB	ﳫ FCEB	ﳻ FCFB	ﴋ FD0B	ﴛ FD1B
C	ﱌ FC4C	ﱜ FC5C	ﱬ FC6C	ﱼ FC7C	ﲌ FC8C	ﲜ FC9C	ﲬ FCAC	ﲼ FCBC	ﳌ FCCC	ﳜ FCDC	ﳬ FCEC	ﳼ FCFC	ﴌ FD0C	ﴜ FD1C
D	ﱍ FC4D	ﱝ FC5D	ﱭ FC6D	ﱽ FC7D	ﲍ FC8D	ﲝ FC9D	ﲭ FCAD	ﲽ FCBD	ﳍ FCCD	ﳝ FCDD	ﳭ FCED	ﳽ FCFD	ﴍ FD0D	ﴝ FD1D
E	ﱎ FC4E	ﱞ FC5E	ﱮ FC6E	ﱾ FC7E	ﲎ FC8E	ﲞ FC9E	ﲮ FCAE	ﲾ FCBE	ﳎ FCCE	ﳞ FCDE	ﳮ FCEE	ﳾ FCFE	ﴎ FD0E	ﴞ FD1E
F	ﱏ FC4F	ﱟ FC5F	ﱯ FC6F	ﱿ FC7F	ﲏ FC8F	ﲟ FC9F	ﲯ FCAF	ﲿ FCBF	ﳏ FCCF	ﳟ FCDF	ﳯ FCEF	ﳿ FCFF	ﴏ FD0F	ﴟ FD1F

	FD2	FD3	FD4	FD5	FD6	FD7	FD8	FD9	FDA	FDB	FDC	FDD	FDE	FDF
0	ﴠ FD20	ﴰ FD30		ﵐ FD50	ﵠ FD60	ﵰ FD70	ﶀ FD80		ﶠ FDA0	ﶰ FDB0	ﷀ FDC0	FDD0	FDE0	ﷰ FDF0
1	ﴡ FD21	ﴱ FD31		ﵑ FD51	ﵡ FD61	ﵱ FD71	ﶁ FD81		ﶡ FDA1	ﶱ FDB1	ﷁ FDC1	FDD1	FDE1	ﷱ FDF1
2	ﴢ FD22	ﴲ FD32		ﵒ FD52	ﵢ FD62	ﵲ FD72	ﶂ FD82	ﶒ FD92	ﶢ FDA2	ﶲ FDB2	ﷂ FDC2	FDD2	FDE2	ﷲ FDF2
3	ﴣ FD23	ﴳ FD33		ﵓ FD53	ﵣ FD63	ﵳ FD73	ﶃ FD83	ﶓ FD93	ﶣ FDA3	ﶳ FDB3	ﷃ FDC3	FDD3	FDE3	ﷳ FDF3
4	ﴤ FD24	ﴴ FD34		ﵔ FD54	ﵤ FD64	ﵴ FD74	ﶄ FD84	ﶔ FD94	ﶤ FDA4	ﶴ FDB4	ﷄ FDC4	FDD4	FDE4	ﷴ FDF4
5	ﴥ FD25	ﴵ FD35		ﵕ FD55	ﵥ FD65	ﵵ FD75	ﶅ FD85	ﶕ FD95	ﶥ FDA5	ﶵ FDB5	ﷅ FDC5	FDD5	FDE5	ﷵ FDF5
6	ﴦ FD26	ﴶ FD36		ﵖ FD56	ﵦ FD66	ﵶ FD76	ﶆ FD86	ﶖ FD96	ﶦ FDA6	ﶶ FDB6	ﷆ FDC6	FDD6	FDE6	ﷶ FDF6
7	ﴧ FD27	ﴷ FD37		ﵗ FD57	ﵧ FD67	ﵷ FD77	ﶇ FD87	ﶗ FD97	ﶧ FDA7	ﶷ FDB7	ﷇ FDC7	FDD7	FDE7	ﷷ FDF7
8	ﴨ FD28	ﴸ FD38		ﵘ FD58	ﵨ FD68	ﵸ FD78	ﶈ FD88	ﶘ FD98	ﶨ FDA8	ﶸ FDB8		FDD8	FDE8	ﷸ FDF8
9	ﴩ FD29	ﴹ FD39		ﵙ FD59	ﵩ FD69	ﵹ FD79	ﶉ FD89	ﶙ FD99	ﶩ FDA9	ﶹ FDB9		FDD9	FDE9	ﷹ FDF9
A	ﴪ FD2A	ﴺ FD3A		ﵚ FD5A	ﵪ FD6A	ﵺ FD7A	ﶊ FD8A	ﶚ FD9A	ﶪ FDAA	ﶺ FDBA		FDDA	FDEA	ﷺ FDFA
B	ﴫ FD2B	ﴻ FD3B		ﵛ FD5B	ﵫ FD6B	ﵻ FD7B	ﶋ FD8B	ﶛ FD9B	ﶫ FDAB	ﶻ FDBB		FDDB	FDEB	ﷻ FDFB
C	ﴬ FD2C	ﴼ FD3C		ﵜ FD5C	ﵬ FD6C	ﵼ FD7C	ﶌ FD8C	ﶜ FD9C	ﶬ FDAC	ﶼ FDBC		FDDC	FDEC	﷼ FDFC
D	ﴭ FD2D	ﴽ FD3D		ﵝ FD5D	ﵭ FD6D	ﵽ FD7D	ﶍ FD8D	ﶝ FD9D	ﶭ FDAD	ﶽ FDBD		FDDD	FDED	﷽ FDFD
E	ﴮ FD2E	﴾ FD3E		ﵞ FD5E	ﵮ FD6E	ﵾ FD7E	ﶎ FD8E	ﶞ FD9E	ﶮ FDAE	ﶾ FDBE		FDDE	FDEE	
F	ﴯ FD2F	﴿ FD3F		ﵟ FD5F	ﵯ FD6F	ﵿ FD7F	ﶏ FD8F	ﶟ FD9F	ﶯ FDAF	ﶿ FDBF		FDDF	FDEF	

Preferred characters are found in the Arabic block 0600 - 06FF. This block also contains 32 noncharacters in the range FDD0 - FDDF.

Glyphs for contextual forms of letters for Persian, Urdu, Sindhi, etc.

FB50 ﭐ ARABIC LETTER ALEF WASLA ISOLATED FORM
≈ <isolated> 0671 ٱ

FB51 ﭑ ARABIC LETTER ALEF WASLA FINAL FORM
≈ <final> 0671 ٱ

FB52 ﭒ ARABIC LETTER BEEH ISOLATED FORM
≈ <isolated> 067B ٻ

FB53 ﭓ ARABIC LETTER BEEH FINAL FORM
≈ <final> 067B ٻ

FB54 ﭔ ARABIC LETTER BEEH INITIAL FORM
≈ <initial> 067B ٻ

FB55 ﭕ ARABIC LETTER BEEH MEDIAL FORM
≈ <medial> 067B ٻ

FB56 ﭖ ARABIC LETTER PEH ISOLATED FORM
≈ <isolated> 067E پ

FB57 ﭗ ARABIC LETTER PEH FINAL FORM
≈ <final> 067E پ

FB58 ﭘ ARABIC LETTER PEH INITIAL FORM
≈ <initial> 067E پ

FB59 ﭙ ARABIC LETTER PEH MEDIAL FORM
≈ <medial> 067E پ

FB5A ﭚ ARABIC LETTER BEHEH ISOLATED FORM
≈ <isolated> 0680 ڀ

FB5B ﭛ ARABIC LETTER BEHEH FINAL FORM
≈ <final> 0680 ڀ

FB5C ﭜ ARABIC LETTER BEHEH INITIAL FORM
≈ <initial> 0680 ڀ

FB5D ﭝ ARABIC LETTER BEHEH MEDIAL FORM
≈ <medial> 0680 ڀ

FB5E ﭞ ARABIC LETTER TTEHEH ISOLATED FORM
≈ <isolated> 067A ٺ

FB5F ﭟ ARABIC LETTER TTEHEH FINAL FORM
≈ <final> 067A ٺ

FB60 ﭠ ARABIC LETTER TTEHEH INITIAL FORM
≈ <initial> 067A ٺ

FB61 ﭡ ARABIC LETTER TTEHEH MEDIAL FORM
≈ <medial> 067A ٺ

FB62 ﭢ ARABIC LETTER TEHEH ISOLATED FORM
≈ <isolated> 067F ٿ

FB63 ﭣ ARABIC LETTER TEHEH FINAL FORM
≈ <final> 067F ٿ

FB64 ﭤ ARABIC LETTER TEHEH INITIAL FORM
≈ <initial> 067F ٿ

FB65 ﭥ ARABIC LETTER TEHEH MEDIAL FORM
≈ <medial> 067F ٿ

FB66 ﭦ ARABIC LETTER TTEH ISOLATED FORM
≈ <isolated> 0679 ٹ

FB67 ﭧ ARABIC LETTER TTEH FINAL FORM
≈ <final> 0679 ٹ

FB68 ﭨ ARABIC LETTER TTEH INITIAL FORM
≈ <initial> 0679 ٹ

FB69 ﭩ ARABIC LETTER TTEH MEDIAL FORM
≈ <medial> 0679 ٹ

FB6A ﭪ ARABIC LETTER VEH ISOLATED FORM
≈ <isolated> 06A4 ڤ

FB6B ﭫ ARABIC LETTER VEH FINAL FORM
≈ <final> 06A4 ڤ

FB6C ﭬ ARABIC LETTER VEH INITIAL FORM
≈ <initial> 06A4 ڤ

FB6D ﭭ ARABIC LETTER VEH MEDIAL FORM
≈ <medial> 06A4 ڤ

FB6E ﭮ ARABIC LETTER PEHEH ISOLATED FORM
≈ <isolated> 06A6 ڦ

FB6F ﭯ ARABIC LETTER PEHEH FINAL FORM
≈ <final> 06A6 ڦ

FB70 ﭰ ARABIC LETTER PEHEH INITIAL FORM
≈ <initial> 06A6 ڦ

FB71 ﭱ ARABIC LETTER PEHEH MEDIAL FORM
≈ <medial> 06A6 ڦ

FB72 ﭲ ARABIC LETTER DYEH ISOLATED FORM
≈ <isolated> 0684 ڄ

FB73 ﭳ ARABIC LETTER DYEH FINAL FORM
≈ <final> 0684 ڄ

FB74 ﭴ ARABIC LETTER DYEH INITIAL FORM
≈ <initial> 0684 ڄ

FB75 ﭵ ARABIC LETTER DYEH MEDIAL FORM
≈ <medial> 0684 ڄ

FB76 ﭶ ARABIC LETTER NYEH ISOLATED FORM
≈ <isolated> 0683 ڃ

FB77 ﭷ ARABIC LETTER NYEH FINAL FORM
≈ <final> 0683 ڃ

FB78 ﭸ ARABIC LETTER NYEH INITIAL FORM
≈ <initial> 0683 ڃ

FB79 ﭹ ARABIC LETTER NYEH MEDIAL FORM
≈ <medial> 0683 ڃ

FB7A ﭺ ARABIC LETTER TCHEH ISOLATED FORM
≈ <isolated> 0686 چ

FB7B ﭻ ARABIC LETTER TCHEH FINAL FORM
≈ <final> 0686 چ

FB7C ﭼ ARABIC LETTER TCHEH INITIAL FORM
≈ <initial> 0686 چ

FB7D ﭽ ARABIC LETTER TCHEH MEDIAL FORM
≈ <medial> 0686 چ

FB7E ﭾ ARABIC LETTER TCHEHEH ISOLATED FORM
≈ <isolated> 0687 ڇ

FB7F ﭿ ARABIC LETTER TCHEHEH FINAL FORM
≈ <final> 0687 ڇ

FB80 ﮀ ARABIC LETTER TCHEHEH INITIAL FORM
≈ <initial> 0687 ڇ

FB81 ﮁ ARABIC LETTER TCHEHEH MEDIAL FORM
≈ <medial> 0687 ڇ

FB82 ﮂ ARABIC LETTER DDAHAL ISOLATED FORM
≈ <isolated> 068D ڍ

FB83 ﮃ ARABIC LETTER DDAHAL FINAL FORM
≈ <final> 068D ڍ

FB84 ﮄ ARABIC LETTER DAHAL ISOLATED FORM
≈ <isolated> 068C ڌ

FB85 ﮅ ARABIC LETTER DAHAL FINAL FORM
≈ <final> 068C ڌ

FB86 ﮆ ARABIC LETTER DUL ISOLATED FORM
≈ <isolated> 068E ڎ

FB87 ﮇ ARABIC LETTER DUL FINAL FORM
≈ <final> 068E ڎ

FB88 ﮈ ARABIC LETTER DDAL ISOLATED FORM
≈ <isolated> 0688 ڈ

FB89 ﮉ ARABIC LETTER DDAL FINAL FORM
≈ <final> 0688 ڈ

FB8A ﮊ ARABIC LETTER JEH ISOLATED FORM
≈ <isolated> 0698 ژ

FB8B ﮋ ARABIC LETTER JEH FINAL FORM
≈ <final> 0698 ژ

FB8C ﮌ ARABIC LETTER RREH ISOLATED FORM
≈ <isolated> 0691 ڑ

FB8D ﮍ ARABIC LETTER RREH FINAL FORM
≈ <final> 0691 ڑ

FB8E ﮎ ARABIC LETTER KEHEH ISOLATED FORM
≈ <isolated> 06A9 ک

FB8F ﮏ ARABIC LETTER KEHEH FINAL FORM
≈ <final> 06A9 ک

FB90 ﮐ ARABIC LETTER KEHEH INITIAL FORM
≈ <initial> 06A9 ک

FB91 ﮑ ARABIC LETTER KEHEH MEDIAL FORM
≈ <medial> 06A9 ک

FB92 ﮒ ARABIC LETTER GAF ISOLATED FORM
≈ <isolated> 06AF گ

FB93 ﮓ ARABIC LETTER GAF FINAL FORM
≈ <final> 06AF گ

FB94 ﮔ ARABIC LETTER GAF INITIAL FORM
≈ <initial> 06AF گ

FB95 ﮕ ARABIC LETTER GAF MEDIAL FORM
≈ <medial> 06AF گ

FB96 ﮖ ARABIC LETTER GUEH ISOLATED FORM
≈ <isolated> 06B3 ڳ

FB97 ﮗ ARABIC LETTER GUEH FINAL FORM
≈ <final> 06B3 ڳ

FB98 ﮘ ARABIC LETTER GUEH INITIAL FORM
≈ <initial> 06B3 ڳ

FB99 ﮙ ARABIC LETTER GUEH MEDIAL FORM
≈ <medial> 06B3 ڳ

FB9A ﮚ ARABIC LETTER NGOEH ISOLATED FORM
≈ <isolated> 06B1 ڱ

FB9B ﮛ ARABIC LETTER NGOEH FINAL FORM
≈ <final> 06B1 ڱ

FB9C ﮜ ARABIC LETTER NGOEH INITIAL FORM
≈ <initial> 06B1 ڱ

FB9D ﮝ ARABIC LETTER NGOEH MEDIAL FORM
≈ <medial> 06B1 ڱ

FB9E ﮞ ARABIC LETTER NOON GHUNNA ISOLATED FORM
≈ <isolated> 06BA ں

FB9F ﮟ ARABIC LETTER NOON GHUNNA FINAL FORM
≈ <final> 06BA ں

FBA0 ﮠ ARABIC LETTER RNOON ISOLATED FORM
≈ <isolated> 06BB ڻ

FBA1 ﮡ ARABIC LETTER RNOON FINAL FORM
≈ <final> 06BB ڻ

FBA2 ﮢ ARABIC LETTER RNOON INITIAL FORM
≈ <initial> 06BB ڻ

FBA3 ﮣ ARABIC LETTER RNOON MEDIAL FORM
≈ <medial> 06BB ڻ

FBA4 ﮤ ARABIC LETTER HEH WITH YEH ABOVE ISOLATED FORM
≈ <isolated> 06C0 ۀ

FBA5 ﮥ ARABIC LETTER HEH WITH YEH ABOVE FINAL FORM
≈ <final> 06C0 ۀ

FBA6 ﮦ ARABIC LETTER HEH GOAL ISOLATED FORM
≈ <isolated> 06C1 ہ

FBA7 ﮧ ARABIC LETTER HEH GOAL FINAL FORM
≈ <final> 06C1 ہ

FBA8 ﮨ ARABIC LETTER HEH GOAL INITIAL FORM
≈ <initial> 06C1 ہ

FBA9 ﮩ ARABIC LETTER HEH GOAL MEDIAL FORM
≈ <medial> 06C1 ہ

FBAA ﮪ ARABIC LETTER HEH DOACHASHMEE ISOLATED FORM
≈ <isolated> 06BE ھ

FBAB ﮫ ARABIC LETTER HEH DOACHASHMEE FINAL FORM
≈ <final> 06BE ھ

FBAC ﮬ ARABIC LETTER HEH DOACHASHMEE INITIAL FORM
≈ <initial> 06BE ھ

FBAD ﮭ ARABIC LETTER HEH DOACHASHMEE MEDIAL FORM
≈ <medial> 06BE ھ

FBAE ﮮ ARABIC LETTER YEH BARREE ISOLATED FORM
≈ <isolated> 06D2 ے

FBAF ﮯ ARABIC LETTER YEH BARREE FINAL FORM
≈ <final> 06D2 ے

FBB0 ﮰ ARABIC LETTER YEH BARREE WITH HAMZA ABOVE ISOLATED FORM
≈ <isolated> 06D3 ۓ

FBB1 ﮱ ARABIC LETTER YEH BARREE WITH HAMZA ABOVE FINAL FORM
≈ <final> 06D3 ۓ

Glyphs for contextual forms of letters for Central Asian languages

FBD3 ﯓ ARABIC LETTER NG ISOLATED FORM
≈ <isolated> 06AD ڭ

FBD4 ﯔ ARABIC LETTER NG FINAL FORM
≈ <final> 06AD ڭ

FBD5 ﯕ ARABIC LETTER NG INITIAL FORM
≈ <initial> 06AD ڭ

FBD6 ﯖ ARABIC LETTER NG MEDIAL FORM
≈ <medial> 06AD ڭ

FBD7 ﯗ ARABIC LETTER U ISOLATED FORM
≈ <isolated> 06C7 ۇ

FBD8 ﯘ ARABIC LETTER U FINAL FORM
≈ <final> 06C7 ۇ

FBD9 ﯙ ARABIC LETTER OE ISOLATED FORM
≈ <isolated> 06C6 ۆ

FBDA ﯚ ARABIC LETTER OE FINAL FORM
≈ <final> 06C6 ۆ

FBDB ﯛ ARABIC LETTER YU ISOLATED FORM
≈ <isolated> 06C8 ۈ

FBDC ﯜ ARABIC LETTER YU FINAL FORM
≈ <final> 06C8 ۈ

FBDD ﯝ ARABIC LETTER U WITH HAMZA ABOVE ISOLATED FORM
≈ <isolated> 0677 ٷ

FBDE ﯞ ARABIC LETTER VE ISOLATED FORM
≈ <isolated> 06CB ۋ

FBDF ﯟ ARABIC LETTER VE FINAL FORM
≈ <final> 06CB ۋ

FBE0 ﯠ ARABIC LETTER KIRGHIZ OE ISOLATED FORM
≈ <isolated> 06C5 ۅ

FBE1 ﯡ ARABIC LETTER KIRGHIZ OE FINAL FORM
≈ <final> 06C5 ۅ

FBE2 ﯢ ARABIC LETTER KIRGHIZ YU ISOLATED FORM
≈ <isolated> 06C9 ۉ

FBE3 ﯣ ARABIC LETTER KIRGHIZ YU FINAL FORM
≈ <final> 06C9 ۉ

FBE4 ﯤ ARABIC LETTER E ISOLATED FORM
≈ <isolated> 06D0 ې

FBE5 ﯥ ARABIC LETTER E FINAL FORM
≈ <final> 06D0 ې

FBE6 ﯦ ARABIC LETTER E INITIAL FORM
≈ <initial> 06D0 ې

FBE7 ﯧ ARABIC LETTER E MEDIAL FORM
≈ <medial> 06D0 ې

FBE8 ﯨ ARABIC LETTER UIGHUR KAZAKH KIRGHIZ ALEF MAKSURA INITIAL FORM
≈ <initial> 0649 ى

FBE9 ﯩ ARABIC LETTER UIGHUR KAZAKH KIRGHIZ ALEF MAKSURA MEDIAL FORM
≈ <medial> 0649 ى

Ligatures (two elements)

FBEA ﯪ ARABIC LIGATURE YEH WITH HAMZA ABOVE WITH ALEF ISOLATED FORM
≈ <isolated> 0626 ئ 0627 ا

FBEB ﯫ ARABIC LIGATURE YEH WITH HAMZA ABOVE WITH ALEF FINAL FORM
≈ <final> 0626 ئ 0627 ا

FBEC ﯬ ARABIC LIGATURE YEH WITH HAMZA ABOVE WITH AE ISOLATED FORM
≈ <isolated> 0626 ئ 06D5 ە

FBED ﯭ ARABIC LIGATURE YEH WITH HAMZA ABOVE WITH AE FINAL FORM
≈ <final> 0626 ئ 06D5 ە

FBEE ﯮ ARABIC LIGATURE YEH WITH HAMZA ABOVE WITH WAW ISOLATED FORM
≈ <isolated> 0626 ئ 0648 و

FBEF ﯯ ARABIC LIGATURE YEH WITH HAMZA ABOVE WITH WAW FINAL FORM
≈ <final> 0626 ئ 0648 و

FBF0 ﯰ ARABIC LIGATURE YEH WITH HAMZA ABOVE WITH U ISOLATED FORM
≈ <isolated> 0626 ئ 06C7 ۇ

FBF1 ﯱ ARABIC LIGATURE YEH WITH HAMZA ABOVE WITH U FINAL FORM
≈ <final> 0626 ئ 06C7 ۇ

FBF2 ﯲ ARABIC LIGATURE YEH WITH HAMZA ABOVE WITH OE ISOLATED FORM
≈ <isolated> 0626 ئ 06C6 ۆ

FBF3 ﯳ ARABIC LIGATURE YEH WITH HAMZA ABOVE WITH OE FINAL FORM
≈ <final> 0626 ئ 06C6 ۆ

FBF4 ﯴ ARABIC LIGATURE YEH WITH HAMZA ABOVE WITH YU ISOLATED FORM
≈ <isolated> 0626 ئ 06C8 ۈ

FBF5 ﯵ ARABIC LIGATURE YEH WITH HAMZA ABOVE WITH YU FINAL FORM
≈ <final> 0626 ئ 06C8 ۈ

FBF6 ﯶ ARABIC LIGATURE YEH WITH HAMZA ABOVE WITH E ISOLATED FORM
≈ <isolated> 0626 ئ 06D0 ې

FBF7 ﯷ ARABIC LIGATURE YEH WITH HAMZA ABOVE WITH E FINAL FORM
≈ <final> 0626 ئ 06D0 ې

FBF8 ﯸ ARABIC LIGATURE YEH WITH HAMZA ABOVE WITH E INITIAL FORM
≈ <initial> 0626 ئ 06D0 ې

FBF9 ﯹ ARABIC LIGATURE UIGHUR KIRGHIZ YEH WITH HAMZA ABOVE WITH ALEF MAKSURA ISOLATED FORM
≈ <isolated> 0626 ئ 0649 ى

FBFA ﯺ ARABIC LIGATURE UIGHUR KIRGHIZ YEH WITH HAMZA ABOVE WITH ALEF MAKSURA FINAL FORM
≈ <final> 0626 ئ 0649 ى

FBFB ﯻ ARABIC LIGATURE UIGHUR KIRGHIZ YEH WITH HAMZA ABOVE WITH ALEF MAKSURA INITIAL FORM
≈ <initial> 0626 ئ 0649 ى

FBFC ﯼ ARABIC LETTER FARSI YEH ISOLATED FORM
≈ <isolated> 06CC ی

FBFD ﯽ ARABIC LETTER FARSI YEH FINAL FORM
≈ <final> 06CC ی

FBFE ﯾ ARABIC LETTER FARSI YEH INITIAL FORM
≈ <initial> 06CC ی

FBFF ﯿ ARABIC LETTER FARSI YEH MEDIAL FORM
≈ <medial> 06CC ی

FC00 ﰀ ARABIC LIGATURE YEH WITH HAMZA ABOVE WITH JEEM ISOLATED FORM
≈ <isolated> 0626 ئ 062C ج

FC01 ﰁ ARABIC LIGATURE YEH WITH HAMZA ABOVE WITH HAH ISOLATED FORM
≈ <isolated> 0626 ئ 062D ح

FC02 ﰂ ARABIC LIGATURE YEH WITH HAMZA ABOVE WITH MEEM ISOLATED FORM
≈ <isolated> 0626 ئ 0645 م

FC03 ﰃ ARABIC LIGATURE YEH WITH HAMZA ABOVE WITH ALEF MAKSURA ISOLATED FORM
≈ <isolated> 0626 ئ 0649 ى

FC04 ﰄ ARABIC LIGATURE YEH WITH HAMZA ABOVE WITH YEH ISOLATED FORM
≈ <isolated> 0626 ئ 064A ي

FC05 ﰅ ARABIC LIGATURE BEH WITH JEEM ISOLATED FORM
≈ <isolated> 0628 ب 062C ج

FC06 ﰆ ARABIC LIGATURE BEH WITH HAH ISOLATED FORM
≈ <isolated> 0628 ب 062D ح

FC07 ﰇ ARABIC LIGATURE BEH WITH KHAH ISOLATED FORM
≈ <isolated> 0628 ب 062E خ

FC08 ﰈ ARABIC LIGATURE BEH WITH MEEM ISOLATED FORM
≈ <isolated> 0628 ب 0645 م

FC09 ﰉ ARABIC LIGATURE BEH WITH ALEF MAKSURA ISOLATED FORM
≈ <isolated> 0628 ب 0649 ى

FC0A ﰊ ARABIC LIGATURE BEH WITH YEH ISOLATED FORM
≈ <isolated> 0628 ب 064A ي

FC0B ﰋ ARABIC LIGATURE TEH WITH JEEM ISOLATED FORM
≈ <isolated> 062A ت 062C ج

FC0C ﰌ ARABIC LIGATURE TEH WITH HAH ISOLATED FORM
≈ <isolated> 062A ت 062D ح

FC0D ﰍ ARABIC LIGATURE TEH WITH KHAH ISOLATED FORM
≈ <isolated> 062A ت 062E خ

FC0E ﰎ ARABIC LIGATURE TEH WITH MEEM ISOLATED FORM
≈ <isolated> 062A ت 0645 م

FC0F ﰏ ARABIC LIGATURE TEH WITH ALEF MAKSURA ISOLATED FORM
≈ <isolated> 062A ت 0649 ى

FC10 ﰐ ARABIC LIGATURE TEH WITH YEH ISOLATED FORM
≈ <isolated> 062A ت 064A ي

FC11 ﰑ ARABIC LIGATURE THEH WITH JEEM ISOLATED FORM
≈ <isolated> 062B ث 062C ج

FC12 ﰒ ARABIC LIGATURE THEH WITH MEEM ISOLATED FORM
≈ <isolated> 062B ث 0645 م

FC13 ﰓ ARABIC LIGATURE THEH WITH ALEF MAKSURA ISOLATED FORM
≈ <isolated> 062B ث 0649 ى

FC14 ﰔ ARABIC LIGATURE THEH WITH YEH ISOLATED FORM
≈ <isolated> 062B ث 064A ي

FC15 ﰕ ARABIC LIGATURE JEEM WITH HAH ISOLATED FORM
≈ <isolated> 062C ج 062D ح

FC16 ﰖ ARABIC LIGATURE JEEM WITH MEEM ISOLATED FORM
≈ <isolated> 062C ج 0645 م

FC17 ﰗ ARABIC LIGATURE HAH WITH JEEM ISOLATED FORM
≈ <isolated> 062D ح 062C ج

FC18 ﰘ ARABIC LIGATURE HAH WITH MEEM ISOLATED FORM
≈ <isolated> 062D ح 0645 م

FC19 ﰙ ARABIC LIGATURE KHAH WITH JEEM ISOLATED FORM
≈ <isolated> 062E خ 062C ج

FC1A ﰚ ARABIC LIGATURE KHAH WITH HAH ISOLATED FORM
≈ <isolated> 062E خ 062D ح

FC1B ﰛ ARABIC LIGATURE KHAH WITH MEEM ISOLATED FORM
≈ <isolated> 062E خ 0645 م

FC1C ﰜ ARABIC LIGATURE SEEN WITH JEEM ISOLATED FORM
≈ <isolated> 0633 س 062C ج

FC1D ﰝ ARABIC LIGATURE SEEN WITH HAH ISOLATED FORM
≈ <isolated> 0633 س 062D ح

FC1E ﰞ ARABIC LIGATURE SEEN WITH KHAH ISOLATED FORM
≈ <isolated> 0633 س 062E خ

FC1F ﰟ ARABIC LIGATURE SEEN WITH MEEM ISOLATED FORM
≈ <isolated> 0633 س 0645 م

FC20 ﰠ ARABIC LIGATURE SAD WITH HAH ISOLATED FORM
≈ <isolated> 0635 ص 062D ح

FC21 ﰡ ARABIC LIGATURE SAD WITH MEEM ISOLATED FORM
≈ <isolated> 0635 ص 0645 م

FC22 ﰢ ARABIC LIGATURE DAD WITH JEEM ISOLATED FORM
≈ <isolated> 0636 ض 062C ج

FC23 ﰣ ARABIC LIGATURE DAD WITH HAH ISOLATED FORM
≈ <isolated> 0636 ض 062D ح

FC24 ﰤ ARABIC LIGATURE DAD WITH KHAH ISOLATED FORM
≈ <isolated> 0636 ض 062E خ

FC25 ﰥ ARABIC LIGATURE DAD WITH MEEM ISOLATED FORM
≈ <isolated> 0636 ض 0645 م

FC26 ﰦ ARABIC LIGATURE TAH WITH HAH ISOLATED FORM
≈ <isolated> 0637 ط 062D ح

FC27 ﰧ ARABIC LIGATURE TAH WITH MEEM ISOLATED FORM
≈ <isolated> 0637 ط 0645 م

FC28 ﰨ ARABIC LIGATURE ZAH WITH MEEM ISOLATED FORM
≈ <isolated> 0638 ظ 0645 م

FC29 ﰩ ARABIC LIGATURE AIN WITH JEEM ISOLATED FORM
≈ <isolated> 0639 ع 062C ج

FC2A ﰪ ARABIC LIGATURE AIN WITH MEEM ISOLATED FORM
≈ <isolated> 0639 ع 0645 م

FC2B ﰫ ARABIC LIGATURE GHAIN WITH JEEM ISOLATED FORM
≈ <isolated> 063A غ 062C ج

FC2C ﰬ ARABIC LIGATURE GHAIN WITH MEEM ISOLATED FORM
≈ <isolated> 063A غ 0645 م

FC2D ﰭ ARABIC LIGATURE FEH WITH JEEM ISOLATED FORM
≈ <isolated> 0641 ف 062C ج

FC2E ﰮ ARABIC LIGATURE FEH WITH HAH ISOLATED FORM
≈ <isolated> 0641 ف 062D ح

FC2F ﰯ ARABIC LIGATURE FEH WITH KHAH ISOLATED FORM
≈ <isolated> 0641 ف 062E خ

FC30 ﰰ ARABIC LIGATURE FEH WITH MEEM ISOLATED FORM
≈ <isolated> 0641 ف 0645 م

FC31 ﰱ ARABIC LIGATURE FEH WITH ALEF MAKSURA ISOLATED FORM
≈ <isolated> 0641 ف 0649 ى

FC32 ﰲ ARABIC LIGATURE FEH WITH YEH ISOLATED FORM
≈ <isolated> 0641 ف 064A ي

FC33 ﰳ ARABIC LIGATURE QAF WITH HAH ISOLATED FORM
≈ <isolated> 0642 ق 062D ح

FC34 ﰴ ARABIC LIGATURE QAF WITH MEEM ISOLATED FORM
≈ <isolated> 0642 ق 0645 م

FC35 ﰵ ARABIC LIGATURE QAF WITH ALEF MAKSURA ISOLATED FORM
≈ <isolated> 0642 ق 0649 ى

FC36 ﰶ ARABIC LIGATURE QAF WITH YEH ISOLATED FORM
≈ <isolated> 0642 ق 064A ي

FC37 ﰷ ARABIC LIGATURE KAF WITH ALEF ISOLATED FORM
≈ <isolated> 0643 ك 0627 ا

FC38 ﰸ ARABIC LIGATURE KAF WITH JEEM ISOLATED FORM
≈ <isolated> 0643 ك 062C ج

FC39 ﰹ ARABIC LIGATURE KAF WITH HAH ISOLATED FORM
≈ <isolated> 0643 ك 062D ح

FC3A ﰺ ARABIC LIGATURE KAF WITH KHAH ISOLATED FORM
≈ <isolated> 0643 ك 062E خ

FC3B ﰻ ARABIC LIGATURE KAF WITH LAM ISOLATED FORM
≈ <isolated> 0643 ك 0644 ل

FC3C ﰼ ARABIC LIGATURE KAF WITH MEEM ISOLATED FORM
≈ <isolated> 0643 ك 0645 م

FC3D ﰽ ARABIC LIGATURE KAF WITH ALEF MAKSURA ISOLATED FORM
≈ <isolated> 0643 ك 0649 ى

FC3E ﰾ ARABIC LIGATURE KAF WITH YEH ISOLATED FORM
≈ <isolated> 0643 ك 064A ي

FC3F ﰿ ARABIC LIGATURE LAM WITH JEEM ISOLATED FORM
≈ <isolated> 0644 ل 062C ج

FC40 ﱀ ARABIC LIGATURE LAM WITH HAH ISOLATED FORM
≈ <isolated> 0644 ل 062D ح

FC41 ﱁ ARABIC LIGATURE LAM WITH KHAH ISOLATED FORM
≈ <isolated> 0644 ل 062E خ

FC42 ﱂ ARABIC LIGATURE LAM WITH MEEM ISOLATED FORM
≈ <isolated> 0644 ل 0645 م

FC43 ﱃ ARABIC LIGATURE LAM WITH ALEF MAKSURA ISOLATED FORM
≈ <isolated> 0644 ل 0649 ى

FC44 ﱄ ARABIC LIGATURE LAM WITH YEH ISOLATED FORM
≈ <isolated> 0644 ل 064A ي

FC45 ﱅ ARABIC LIGATURE MEEM WITH JEEM ISOLATED FORM
≈ <isolated> 0645 م 062C ج

FC46 ﱆ ARABIC LIGATURE MEEM WITH HAH ISOLATED FORM
≈ <isolated> 0645 م 062D ح

FC47 ﱇ ARABIC LIGATURE MEEM WITH KHAH ISOLATED FORM
≈ <isolated> 0645 م 062E خ

FC48 ﱈ ARABIC LIGATURE MEEM WITH MEEM ISOLATED FORM
≈ <isolated> 0645 م 0645 م

FC49 ﱉ ARABIC LIGATURE MEEM WITH ALEF MAKSURA ISOLATED FORM
≈ <isolated> 0645 م 0649 ى

FC4A ﱊ ARABIC LIGATURE MEEM WITH YEH ISOLATED FORM
≈ <isolated> 0645 م 064A ي

FC4B ﱋ ARABIC LIGATURE NOON WITH JEEM ISOLATED FORM
≈ <isolated> 0646 ن 062C ج

FC4C ﱌ ARABIC LIGATURE NOON WITH HAH ISOLATED FORM
≈ <isolated> 0646 ن 062D ح

FC4D ﱍ ARABIC LIGATURE NOON WITH KHAH ISOLATED FORM
≈ <isolated> 0646 ن 062E خ

FC4E ﱎ ARABIC LIGATURE NOON WITH MEEM ISOLATED FORM
≈ <isolated> 0646 ن 0645 م

FC4F ﱏ ARABIC LIGATURE NOON WITH ALEF MAKSURA ISOLATED FORM
≈ <isolated> 0646 ن 0649 ى

FC50 ﱐ ARABIC LIGATURE NOON WITH YEH ISOLATED FORM
≈ <isolated> 0646 ن 064A ي

FC51 ﱑ ARABIC LIGATURE HEH WITH JEEM ISOLATED FORM
≈ <isolated> 0647 ه 062C ج

FC52 ﱒ ARABIC LIGATURE HEH WITH MEEM ISOLATED FORM
≈ <isolated> 0647 ه 0645 م

FC53 ﱓ ARABIC LIGATURE HEH WITH ALEF MAKSURA ISOLATED FORM
≈ <isolated> 0647 ه 0649 ى

FC54 ﱔ ARABIC LIGATURE HEH WITH YEH ISOLATED FORM
≈ <isolated> 0647 ه 064A ي

FC55 ﱕ ARABIC LIGATURE YEH WITH JEEM ISOLATED FORM
≈ <isolated> 064A ي 062C ج

FC56 ﱖ ARABIC LIGATURE YEH WITH HAH ISOLATED FORM
≈ <isolated> 064A ي 062D ح

FC57 ﱗ ARABIC LIGATURE YEH WITH KHAH ISOLATED FORM
≈ <isolated> 064A ي 062E خ

FC58 ﱘ ARABIC LIGATURE YEH WITH MEEM ISOLATED FORM
≈ <isolated> 064A ي 0645 م

FC59 ﱙ ARABIC LIGATURE YEH WITH ALEF MAKSURA ISOLATED FORM
≈ <isolated> 064A ي 0649 ى

FC5A ﱚ ARABIC LIGATURE YEH WITH YEH ISOLATED FORM
≈ <isolated> 064A ي 064A ي

FC5B ﱛ ARABIC LIGATURE THAL WITH SUPERSCRIPT ALEF ISOLATED FORM
≈ <isolated> 0630 ذ 0670 ◌ٰ

FC5C ﱜ ARABIC LIGATURE REH WITH SUPERSCRIPT ALEF ISOLATED FORM
≈ <isolated> 0631 ر 0670 ◌ٰ

FC5D ﱝ ARABIC LIGATURE ALEF MAKSURA WITH SUPERSCRIPT ALEF ISOLATED FORM
≈ <isolated> 0649 ى 0670 ◌ٰ

FC5E ﱞ ARABIC LIGATURE SHADDA WITH DAMMATAN ISOLATED FORM
≈ <isolated> 0020 SP 064C ◌ٌ 0651 ◌ّ

FC5F ﱟ ARABIC LIGATURE SHADDA WITH KASRATAN ISOLATED FORM
≈ <isolated> 0020 SP 064D ◌ٍ 0651 ◌ّ

FC60 ﱠ ARABIC LIGATURE SHADDA WITH FATHA ISOLATED FORM
≈ <isolated> 0020 SP 064E ◌َ 0651 ◌ّ

FC61 ﱡ ARABIC LIGATURE SHADDA WITH DAMMA ISOLATED FORM
≈ <isolated> 0020 SP 064F ◌ُ 0651 ◌ّ

FC62 ﱢ ARABIC LIGATURE SHADDA WITH KASRA ISOLATED FORM
≈ <isolated> 0020 SP 0650 ◌ِ 0651 ◌ّ

FC63 ﱣ ARABIC LIGATURE SHADDA WITH SUPERSCRIPT ALEF ISOLATED FORM
≈ <isolated> 0020 SP 0651 ◌ّ 0670 ◌ٰ

FC64 ﱤ ARABIC LIGATURE YEH WITH HAMZA ABOVE WITH REH FINAL FORM
≈ <final> 0626 ئ 0631 ر

FC65 ﱥ ARABIC LIGATURE YEH WITH HAMZA ABOVE WITH ZAIN FINAL FORM
≈ <final> 0626 ئ 0632 ز

FC66 ﱦ ARABIC LIGATURE YEH WITH HAMZA ABOVE WITH MEEM FINAL FORM
≈ <final> 0626 ئ 0645 م

FC67 ﱧ ARABIC LIGATURE YEH WITH HAMZA ABOVE WITH NOON FINAL FORM
≈ <final> 0626 ئ 0646 ن

FC68 ﱨ ARABIC LIGATURE YEH WITH HAMZA ABOVE WITH ALEF MAKSURA FINAL FORM
≈ <final> 0626 ئ 0649 ى

FC69 ﱩ ARABIC LIGATURE YEH WITH HAMZA ABOVE WITH YEH FINAL FORM
≈ <final> 0626 ئ 064A ي

FC6A ﱪ ARABIC LIGATURE BEH WITH REH FINAL FORM
≈ <final> 0628 ب 0631 ر

FC6B ﱫ ARABIC LIGATURE BEH WITH ZAIN FINAL FORM
≈ <final> 0628 ب 0632 ز

FC6C ﱬ ARABIC LIGATURE BEH WITH MEEM FINAL FORM
≈ <final> 0628 ب 0645 م

FC6D ﱭ ARABIC LIGATURE BEH WITH NOON FINAL FORM
≈ <final> 0628 ب 0646 ن

FC6E ﱮ ARABIC LIGATURE BEH WITH ALEF MAKSURA FINAL FORM
≈ <final> 0628 ب 0649 ى

FC6F ﱯ ARABIC LIGATURE BEH WITH YEH FINAL FORM
≈ <final> 0628 ب 064A ي

FC70 ﱰ ARABIC LIGATURE TEH WITH REH FINAL FORM
≈ <final> 062A ت 0631 ر

FC71 ﱱ ARABIC LIGATURE TEH WITH ZAIN FINAL FORM
≈ <final> 062A ت 0632 ز

FC72 ﱲ ARABIC LIGATURE TEH WITH MEEM FINAL FORM
≈ <final> 062A ت 0645 م

FC73 ﱳ ARABIC LIGATURE TEH WITH NOON FINAL FORM
≈ <final> 062A ت 0646 ن

FC74 ﱴ ARABIC LIGATURE TEH WITH ALEF MAKSURA FINAL FORM
≈ <final> 062A ت 0649 ى

FC75 ﱵ ARABIC LIGATURE TEH WITH YEH FINAL FORM
≈ <final> 062A ت 064A ي

FC76 ﱶ ARABIC LIGATURE THEH WITH REH FINAL FORM
≈ <final> 062B ث 0631 ر

FC77 ﱷ ARABIC LIGATURE THEH WITH ZAIN FINAL FORM
≈ <final> 062B ث 0632 ز

FC78 ﱸ ARABIC LIGATURE THEH WITH MEEM FINAL FORM
≈ <final> 062B ث 0645 م

FC79 ﱹ ARABIC LIGATURE THEH WITH NOON FINAL FORM
≈ <final> 062B ث 0646 ن

FC7A ﱺ ARABIC LIGATURE THEH WITH ALEF MAKSURA FINAL FORM
≈ <final> 062B ث 0649 ى

FC7B ﱻ ARABIC LIGATURE THEH WITH YEH FINAL FORM
≈ <final> 062B ث 064A ي

FC7C ﱼ ARABIC LIGATURE FEH WITH ALEF MAKSURA FINAL FORM
≈ <final> 0641 ف 0649 ى

FC7D ﱽ ARABIC LIGATURE FEH WITH YEH FINAL FORM
≈ <final> 0641 ف 064A ي

FC7E ﱾ ARABIC LIGATURE QAF WITH ALEF MAKSURA FINAL FORM
≈ <final> 0642 ق 0649 ى

FC7F ﱿ ARABIC LIGATURE QAF WITH YEH FINAL FORM
≈ <final> 0642 ق 064A ي

FC80 ﲀ ARABIC LIGATURE KAF WITH ALEF FINAL FORM
≈ <final> 0643 ك 0627 ا

FC81 ﲁ ARABIC LIGATURE KAF WITH LAM FINAL FORM
≈ <final> 0643 ك 0644 ل

FC82 ﲂ ARABIC LIGATURE KAF WITH MEEM FINAL FORM
≈ <final> 0643 ك 0645 م

FC83 ﲃ ARABIC LIGATURE KAF WITH ALEF MAKSURA FINAL FORM
≈ <final> 0643 ك 0649 ى

FC84 ﲄ ARABIC LIGATURE KAF WITH YEH FINAL FORM
≈ <final> 0643 ك 064A ي

FC85 ﲅ ARABIC LIGATURE LAM WITH MEEM FINAL FORM
≈ <final> 0644 ل 0645 م

FC86 ﲆ ARABIC LIGATURE LAM WITH ALEF MAKSURA FINAL FORM
≈ <final> 0644 ل 0649 ى

FC87 ﲇ ARABIC LIGATURE LAM WITH YEH FINAL FORM
≈ <final> 0644 ل 064A ي

FC88 ﲈ ARABIC LIGATURE MEEM WITH ALEF FINAL FORM
≈ <final> 0645 م 0627 ا

FC89 ﲉ ARABIC LIGATURE MEEM WITH MEEM FINAL FORM
≈ <final> 0645 م 0645 م

FC8A ﲊ ARABIC LIGATURE NOON WITH REH FINAL FORM
≈ <final> 0646 ن 0631 ر

FC8B ﲋ ARABIC LIGATURE NOON WITH ZAIN FINAL FORM
≈ <final> 0646 ن 0632 ز

FC8C ﲌ ARABIC LIGATURE NOON WITH MEEM FINAL FORM
≈ <final> 0646 ن 0645 م

FC8D ﲍ ARABIC LIGATURE NOON WITH NOON FINAL FORM
≈ <final> 0646 ن 0646 ن

FC8E ﲎ ARABIC LIGATURE NOON WITH ALEF MAKSURA FINAL FORM
≈ <final> 0646 ن 0649 ى

FC8F ﲏ ARABIC LIGATURE NOON WITH YEH FINAL FORM
≈ <final> 0646 ن 064A ي

FC90 ﲐ ARABIC LIGATURE ALEF MAKSURA WITH SUPERSCRIPT ALEF FINAL FORM
≈ <final> 0649 ى 0670 ٰ

FC91 ﲑ ARABIC LIGATURE YEH WITH REH FINAL FORM
≈ <final> 064A ي 0631 ر

FC92 ﲒ ARABIC LIGATURE YEH WITH ZAIN FINAL FORM
≈ <final> 064A ي 0632 ز

FC93 ﲓ ARABIC LIGATURE YEH WITH MEEM FINAL FORM
≈ <final> 064A ي 0645 م

FC94 ﲔ ARABIC LIGATURE YEH WITH NOON FINAL FORM
≈ <final> 064A ي 0646 ن

FC95 ﲕ ARABIC LIGATURE YEH WITH ALEF MAKSURA FINAL FORM
≈ <final> 064A ي 0649 ى

FC96 ﲖ ARABIC LIGATURE YEH WITH YEH FINAL FORM
≈ <final> 064A ي 064A ي

FC97 ﲗ ARABIC LIGATURE YEH WITH HAMZA ABOVE WITH JEEM INITIAL FORM
≈ <initial> 0626 ئ 062C ج

FC98 ﲘ ARABIC LIGATURE YEH WITH HAMZA ABOVE WITH HAH INITIAL FORM
≈ <initial> 0626 ئ 062D ح

FC99 ﲙ ARABIC LIGATURE YEH WITH HAMZA ABOVE WITH KHAH INITIAL FORM
≈ <initial> 0626 ئ 062E خ

FC9A ﲚ ARABIC LIGATURE YEH WITH HAMZA ABOVE WITH MEEM INITIAL FORM
≈ <initial> 0626 ئ 0645 م

FC9B ﲛ ARABIC LIGATURE YEH WITH HAMZA ABOVE WITH HEH INITIAL FORM
≈ <initial> 0626 ئ 0647 ه

FC9C ﲜ ARABIC LIGATURE BEH WITH JEEM INITIAL FORM
≈ <initial> 0628 ب 062C ج

FC9D ﲝ ARABIC LIGATURE BEH WITH HAH INITIAL FORM
≈ <initial> 0628 ب 062D ح

FC9E ﲞ ARABIC LIGATURE BEH WITH KHAH INITIAL FORM
≈ <initial> 0628 ب 062E خ

FC9F ﲟ ARABIC LIGATURE BEH WITH MEEM INITIAL FORM
≈ <initial> 0628 ب 0645 م

FCA0 ﲠ ARABIC LIGATURE BEH WITH HEH INITIAL FORM
≈ <initial> 0628 ب 0647 ه

FCA1 ﲡ ARABIC LIGATURE TEH WITH JEEM INITIAL FORM
≈ <initial> 062A ت 062C ج

FCA2 ﲢ ARABIC LIGATURE TEH WITH HAH INITIAL FORM
≈ <initial> 062A ت 062D ح

FCA3 ﲣ ARABIC LIGATURE TEH WITH KHAH INITIAL FORM
≈ <initial> 062A ت 062E خ

FCA4 ﲤ ARABIC LIGATURE TEH WITH MEEM INITIAL FORM
≈ <initial> 062A ت 0645 م

FCA5 ﲥ ARABIC LIGATURE TEH WITH HEH INITIAL FORM
≈ <initial> 062A ت 0647 ه

FCA6 ﲦ ARABIC LIGATURE THEH WITH MEEM INITIAL FORM
≈ <initial> 062B ث 0645 م

FCA7 ﲧ ARABIC LIGATURE JEEM WITH HAH INITIAL FORM
≈ <initial> 062C ج 062D ح

FCA8 ﲨ ARABIC LIGATURE JEEM WITH MEEM INITIAL FORM
≈ <initial> 062C ج 0645 م

FCA9 ﲩ ARABIC LIGATURE HAH WITH JEEM INITIAL FORM
≈ <initial> 062D ح 062C ج

FCAA ﲪ ARABIC LIGATURE HAH WITH MEEM INITIAL FORM
≈ <initial> 062D ح 0645 م

FCAB ﲫ ARABIC LIGATURE KHAH WITH JEEM INITIAL FORM
≈ <initial> 062E خ 062C ج

FCAC ﲬ ARABIC LIGATURE KHAH WITH MEEM INITIAL FORM
≈ <initial> 062E خ 0645 م

FCAD ﲭ ARABIC LIGATURE SEEN WITH JEEM INITIAL FORM
≈ <initial> 0633 س 062C ج

FCAE ﲮ ARABIC LIGATURE SEEN WITH HAH INITIAL FORM
≈ <initial> 0633 س 062D ح

FCAF ﲯ ARABIC LIGATURE SEEN WITH KHAH INITIAL FORM
≈ <initial> 0633 س 062E خ

FCB0 ﲰ ARABIC LIGATURE SEEN WITH MEEM INITIAL FORM
≈ <initial> 0633 س 0645 م

FCB1 ﲱ ARABIC LIGATURE SAD WITH HAH INITIAL FORM
≈ <initial> 0635 ص 062D ح

FCB2 ﲲ ARABIC LIGATURE SAD WITH KHAH INITIAL FORM
≈ <initial> 0635 ص 062E خ

FCB3 ﲳ ARABIC LIGATURE SAD WITH MEEM INITIAL FORM
≈ <initial> 0635 ص 0645 م

FCB4 ﲴ ARABIC LIGATURE DAD WITH JEEM INITIAL FORM
≈ <initial> 0636 ض 062C ج

FCB5 ﲵ ARABIC LIGATURE DAD WITH HAH INITIAL FORM
≈ <initial> 0636 ض 062D ح

FCB6 ﲶ ARABIC LIGATURE DAD WITH KHAH INITIAL FORM
≈ <initial> 0636 ض 062E خ

FCB7 ﲷ ARABIC LIGATURE DAD WITH MEEM INITIAL FORM
≈ <initial> 0636 ض 0645 م

FCB8 ﲸ ARABIC LIGATURE TAH WITH HAH INITIAL FORM
≈ <initial> 0637 ط 062D ح

FCB9 ﲹ ARABIC LIGATURE ZAH WITH MEEM INITIAL FORM
≈ <initial> 0638 ظ 0645 م

FCBA ﲺ ARABIC LIGATURE AIN WITH JEEM INITIAL FORM
≈ <initial> 0639 ع 062C ج

FCBB ﲻ ARABIC LIGATURE AIN WITH MEEM INITIAL FORM
≈ <initial> 0639 ع 0645 م

FCBC ﲼ ARABIC LIGATURE GHAIN WITH JEEM INITIAL FORM
≈ <initial> 063A غ 062C ج

FCBD ﲽ ARABIC LIGATURE GHAIN WITH MEEM INITIAL FORM
≈ <initial> 063A غ 0645 م

FCBE ﲾ ARABIC LIGATURE FEH WITH JEEM INITIAL FORM
≈ <initial> 0641 ف 062C ج

FCBF ﲿ ARABIC LIGATURE FEH WITH HAH INITIAL FORM
≈ <initial> 0641 ف 062D ح

FCC0 ﳀ ARABIC LIGATURE FEH WITH KHAH INITIAL FORM
≈ <initial> 0641 ف 062E خ

FCC1 ﳁ ARABIC LIGATURE FEH WITH MEEM INITIAL FORM
≈ <initial> 0641 ف 0645 م

FCC2 ﳂ ARABIC LIGATURE QAF WITH HAH INITIAL FORM
≈ <initial> 0642 ق 062D ح

FCC3 ﳃ ARABIC LIGATURE QAF WITH MEEM INITIAL FORM
≈ <initial> 0642 ق 0645 م

FCC4 ﳄ ARABIC LIGATURE KAF WITH JEEM INITIAL FORM
≈ <initial> 0643 ك 062C ج

FCC5 ﳅ ARABIC LIGATURE KAF WITH HAH INITIAL FORM
≈ <initial> 0643 ك 062D ح

FCC6 ﳆ ARABIC LIGATURE KAF WITH KHAH INITIAL FORM
≈ <initial> 0643 ك 062E خ

FCC7 ﳇ ARABIC LIGATURE KAF WITH LAM INITIAL FORM
≈ <initial> 0643 ك 0644 ل

FCC8 ﳈ ARABIC LIGATURE KAF WITH MEEM INITIAL FORM
≈ <initial> 0643 ك 0645 م

FCC9 ﳉ ARABIC LIGATURE LAM WITH JEEM INITIAL FORM
≈ <initial> 0644 ل 062C ج

FCCA ﳊ ARABIC LIGATURE LAM WITH HAH INITIAL FORM
≈ <initial> 0644 ل 062D ح

FCCB ﳋ ARABIC LIGATURE LAM WITH KHAH INITIAL FORM
≈ <initial> 0644 ل 062E خ

FCCC ﳌ ARABIC LIGATURE LAM WITH MEEM INITIAL FORM
≈ <initial> 0644 ل 0645 م

FCCD ﳍ ARABIC LIGATURE LAM WITH HEH INITIAL FORM
≈ <initial> 0644 ل 0647 ه

FCCE ﳎ ARABIC LIGATURE MEEM WITH JEEM INITIAL FORM
≈ <initial> 0645 م 062C ج

FCCF ﳏ ARABIC LIGATURE MEEM WITH HAH INITIAL FORM
≈ <initial> 0645 م 062D ح

FCD0 ﳐ ARABIC LIGATURE MEEM WITH KHAH INITIAL FORM
≈ <initial> 0645 م 062E خ

FCD1 ﳑ ARABIC LIGATURE MEEM WITH MEEM INITIAL FORM
≈ <initial> 0645 م 0645 م

FCD2 ﳒ ARABIC LIGATURE NOON WITH JEEM INITIAL FORM
≈ <initial> 0646 ن 062C ج

FCD3 ﳓ ARABIC LIGATURE NOON WITH HAH INITIAL FORM
≈ <initial> 0646 ن 062D ح

FCD4 ﳔ ARABIC LIGATURE NOON WITH KHAH INITIAL FORM
≈ <initial> 0646 ن 062E خ

FCD5 ﳕ ARABIC LIGATURE NOON WITH MEEM INITIAL FORM
≈ <initial> 0646 ن 0645 م

FCD6 ﳖ ARABIC LIGATURE NOON WITH HEH INITIAL FORM
≈ <initial> 0646 ن 0647 ه

FCD7 ﳗ ARABIC LIGATURE HEH WITH JEEM INITIAL FORM
≈ <initial> 0647 ه 062C ج

FCD8 ﳘ ARABIC LIGATURE HEH WITH MEEM INITIAL FORM
≈ <initial> 0647 ه 0645 م

FCD9 ﳙ ARABIC LIGATURE HEH WITH SUPERSCRIPT ALEF INITIAL FORM
≈ <initial> 0647 ه 0670 ٰ

FCDA ﳚ ARABIC LIGATURE YEH WITH JEEM INITIAL FORM
≈ <initial> 064A ي 062C ج

FCDB ﳛ ARABIC LIGATURE YEH WITH HAH INITIAL FORM
≈ <initial> 064A ي 062D ح

FCDC ﳜ ARABIC LIGATURE YEH WITH KHAH INITIAL FORM
≈ <initial> 064A ي 062E خ

FCDD ﳝ ARABIC LIGATURE YEH WITH MEEM INITIAL FORM
≈ <initial> 064A ي 0645 م

FCDE ﳞ ARABIC LIGATURE YEH WITH HEH INITIAL FORM
≈ <initial> 064A ي 0647 ه

FCDF ﳟ ARABIC LIGATURE YEH WITH HAMZA ABOVE WITH MEEM MEDIAL FORM
≈ <medial> 0626 ئ 0645 م

FCE0 ﳠ ARABIC LIGATURE YEH WITH HAMZA ABOVE WITH HEH MEDIAL FORM
≈ <medial> 0626 ئ 0647 ه

FCE1 ﳡ ARABIC LIGATURE BEH WITH MEEM MEDIAL FORM
≈ <medial> 0628 ب 0645 م

FCE2 ﳢ ARABIC LIGATURE BEH WITH HEH MEDIAL FORM
≈ <medial> 0628 ب 0647 ه

FCE3 ﳣ ARABIC LIGATURE TEH WITH MEEM MEDIAL FORM
≈ <medial> 062A ت 0645 م

FCE4 ﳤ ARABIC LIGATURE TEH WITH HEH MEDIAL FORM
≈ <medial> 062A ت 0647 ه

FCE5 ﳥ ARABIC LIGATURE THEH WITH MEEM MEDIAL FORM
≈ <medial> 062B ث 0645 م

FCE6 ﳦ ARABIC LIGATURE THEH WITH HEH MEDIAL FORM
≈ <medial> 062B ث 0647 ه

FCE7 ﳧ ARABIC LIGATURE SEEN WITH MEEM MEDIAL FORM
≈ <medial> 0633 س 0645 م

FCE8 ﳨ ARABIC LIGATURE SEEN WITH HEH MEDIAL FORM
≈ <medial> 0633 س 0647 ه

FCE9 ﳩ ARABIC LIGATURE SHEEN WITH MEEM MEDIAL FORM
≈ <medial> 0634 ش 0645 م

FCEA ﳪ ARABIC LIGATURE SHEEN WITH HEH MEDIAL FORM
≈ <medial> 0634 ش 0647 ه

FCEB ﳫ ARABIC LIGATURE KAF WITH LAM MEDIAL FORM
≈ <medial> 0643 ك 0644 ل

FCEC ﳬ ARABIC LIGATURE KAF WITH MEEM MEDIAL FORM
≈ <medial> 0643 ك 0645 م

FCED ﳭ ARABIC LIGATURE LAM WITH MEEM MEDIAL FORM
≈ <medial> 0644 ل 0645 م

FCEE ﳮ ARABIC LIGATURE NOON WITH MEEM MEDIAL FORM
≈ <medial> 0646 ن 0645 م

FCEF ﳯ ARABIC LIGATURE NOON WITH HEH MEDIAL FORM
≈ <medial> 0646 ن 0647 ه

FCF0 ﳰ ARABIC LIGATURE YEH WITH MEEM MEDIAL FORM
≈ <medial> 064A ي 0645 م

FCF1 ﳱ ARABIC LIGATURE YEH WITH HEH MEDIAL FORM
≈ <medial> 064A ي 0647 ه

FCF2 ﳲ ARABIC LIGATURE SHADDA WITH FATHA MEDIAL FORM
≈ <medial> 0640 - 064E ◌َ 0651 ◌ّ

FCF3 ﳳ ARABIC LIGATURE SHADDA WITH DAMMA MEDIAL FORM
≈ <medial> 0640 - 064F ◌ُ 0651 ◌ّ

FCF4 ﳴ ARABIC LIGATURE SHADDA WITH KASRA MEDIAL FORM
≈ <medial> 0640 - 0650 ◌ِ 0651 ◌ّ

FCF5 ﳵ ARABIC LIGATURE TAH WITH ALEF MAKSURA ISOLATED FORM
≈ <isolated> 0637 ط 0649 ى

FCF6 ﳶ ARABIC LIGATURE TAH WITH YEH ISOLATED FORM
≈ <isolated> 0637 ط 064A ي

FCF7 ﳷ ARABIC LIGATURE AIN WITH ALEF MAKSURA ISOLATED FORM
≈ <isolated> 0639 ع 0649 ى

FCF8 ﳸ ARABIC LIGATURE AIN WITH YEH ISOLATED FORM
≈ <isolated> 0639 ع 064A ي

FCF9 ﳹ ARABIC LIGATURE GHAIN WITH ALEF MAKSURA ISOLATED FORM
≈ <isolated> 063A غ 0649 ى

FCFA ﳺ ARABIC LIGATURE GHAIN WITH YEH ISOLATED FORM
≈ <isolated> 063A غ 064A ي

FCFB ﳻ ARABIC LIGATURE SEEN WITH ALEF MAKSURA ISOLATED FORM
≈ <isolated> 0633 س 0649 ى

FCFC ﳼ ARABIC LIGATURE SEEN WITH YEH ISOLATED FORM
≈ <isolated> 0633 س 064A ي

FCFD ﳽ ARABIC LIGATURE SHEEN WITH ALEF MAKSURA ISOLATED FORM
≈ <isolated> 0634 ش 0649 ى

FCFE ﳾ ARABIC LIGATURE SHEEN WITH YEH ISOLATED FORM
≈ <isolated> 0634 ش 064A ي

FCFF ﳿ ARABIC LIGATURE HAH WITH ALEF MAKSURA ISOLATED FORM
≈ <isolated> 062D ح 0649 ى

FD00 ﴀ ARABIC LIGATURE HAH WITH YEH ISOLATED FORM
≈ <isolated> 062D ح 064A ي

FD01 ﴁ ARABIC LIGATURE JEEM WITH ALEF MAKSURA ISOLATED FORM
≈ <isolated> 062C ج 0649 ى

FD02 ﴂ ARABIC LIGATURE JEEM WITH YEH ISOLATED FORM
≈ <isolated> 062C ج 064A ي

FD03 ﴃ ARABIC LIGATURE KHAH WITH ALEF MAKSURA ISOLATED FORM
≈ <isolated> 062E خ 0649 ى

FD04 ﴄ ARABIC LIGATURE KHAH WITH YEH ISOLATED FORM
≈ <isolated> 062E خ 064A ي

FD05 ﴅ ARABIC LIGATURE SAD WITH ALEF MAKSURA ISOLATED FORM
≈ <isolated> 0635 ص 0649 ى

FD06 ﴆ ARABIC LIGATURE SAD WITH YEH ISOLATED FORM
≈ <isolated> 0635 ص 064A ي

FD07 ﴇ ARABIC LIGATURE DAD WITH ALEF MAKSURA ISOLATED FORM
≈ <isolated> 0636 ض 0649 ى

FD08 ﴈ ARABIC LIGATURE DAD WITH YEH ISOLATED FORM
≈ <isolated> 0636 ض 064A ي

FD09 ﴉ ARABIC LIGATURE SHEEN WITH JEEM ISOLATED FORM
≈ <isolated> 0634 ش 062C ج

FD0A ﴊ ARABIC LIGATURE SHEEN WITH HAH ISOLATED FORM
≈ <isolated> 0634 ش 062D ح

FD0B ﴋ ARABIC LIGATURE SHEEN WITH KHAH ISOLATED FORM
≈ <isolated> 0634 ش 062E خ

FD0C ﴌ ARABIC LIGATURE SHEEN WITH MEEM ISOLATED FORM
≈ <isolated> 0634 ش 0645 م

FD0D ﴍ ARABIC LIGATURE SHEEN WITH REH ISOLATED FORM
≈ <isolated> 0634 ش 0631 ر

FD0E ﴎ ARABIC LIGATURE SEEN WITH REH ISOLATED FORM
≈ <isolated> 0633 س 0631 ر

FD0F ﴏ ARABIC LIGATURE SAD WITH REH ISOLATED FORM
≈ <isolated> 0635 ص 0631 ر

FD10 ﴐ ARABIC LIGATURE DAD WITH REH ISOLATED FORM
≈ <isolated> 0636 ض 0631 ر

FD11 ﴑ ARABIC LIGATURE TAH WITH ALEF MAKSURA FINAL FORM
≈ <final> 0637 ط 0649 ى

FD12 ﴒ ARABIC LIGATURE TAH WITH YEH FINAL FORM
≈ <final> 0637 ط 064A ي

FD13 ﴓ ARABIC LIGATURE AIN WITH ALEF MAKSURA FINAL FORM
≈ <final> 0639 ع 0649 ى

FD14 ﴔ ARABIC LIGATURE AIN WITH YEH FINAL FORM
≈ <final> 0639 ع 064A ي

FD15 ﴕ ARABIC LIGATURE GHAIN WITH ALEF MAKSURA FINAL FORM
≈ <final> 063A غ 0649 ى

FD16 ﴖ ARABIC LIGATURE GHAIN WITH YEH FINAL FORM
≈ <final> 063A غ 064A ي

FD17 ﴗ ARABIC LIGATURE SEEN WITH ALEF MAKSURA FINAL FORM
≈ <final> 0633 س 0649 ى

FD18 ﴘ ARABIC LIGATURE SEEN WITH YEH FINAL FORM
≈ <final> 0633 س 064A ي

FD19 ﴙ ARABIC LIGATURE SHEEN WITH ALEF MAKSURA FINAL FORM
≈ <final> 0634 ش 0649 ى

FD1A ﴚ ARABIC LIGATURE SHEEN WITH YEH FINAL FORM
≈ <final> 0634 ش 064A ي

FD1B ﴛ ARABIC LIGATURE HAH WITH ALEF MAKSURA FINAL FORM
≈ <final> 062D ح 0649 ى

FD1C ﴜ ARABIC LIGATURE HAH WITH YEH FINAL FORM
≈ <final> 062D ح 064A ي

FD1D ﴝ ARABIC LIGATURE JEEM WITH ALEF MAKSURA FINAL FORM
≈ <final> 062C ج 0649 ى
FD1E ﴞ ARABIC LIGATURE JEEM WITH YEH FINAL FORM
≈ <final> 062C ج 064A ي
FD1F ﴟ ARABIC LIGATURE KHAH WITH ALEF MAKSURA FINAL FORM
≈ <final> 062E خ 0649 ى
FD20 ﴠ ARABIC LIGATURE KHAH WITH YEH FINAL FORM
≈ <final> 062E خ 064A ي
FD21 ﴡ ARABIC LIGATURE SAD WITH ALEF MAKSURA FINAL FORM
≈ <final> 0635 ص 0649 ى
FD22 ﴢ ARABIC LIGATURE SAD WITH YEH FINAL FORM
≈ <final> 0635 ص 064A ي
FD23 ﴣ ARABIC LIGATURE DAD WITH ALEF MAKSURA FINAL FORM
≈ <final> 0636 ض 0649 ى
FD24 ﴤ ARABIC LIGATURE DAD WITH YEH FINAL FORM
≈ <final> 0636 ض 064A ي
FD25 ﴥ ARABIC LIGATURE SHEEN WITH JEEM FINAL FORM
≈ <final> 0634 ش 062C ج
FD26 ﴦ ARABIC LIGATURE SHEEN WITH HAH FINAL FORM
≈ <final> 0634 ش 062D ح
FD27 ﴧ ARABIC LIGATURE SHEEN WITH KHAH FINAL FORM
≈ <final> 0634 ش 062E خ
FD28 ﴨ ARABIC LIGATURE SHEEN WITH MEEM FINAL FORM
≈ <final> 0634 ش 0645 م
FD29 ﴩ ARABIC LIGATURE SHEEN WITH REH FINAL FORM
≈ <final> 0634 ش 0631 ر
FD2A ﴪ ARABIC LIGATURE SEEN WITH REH FINAL FORM
≈ <final> 0633 س 0631 ر
FD2B ﴫ ARABIC LIGATURE SAD WITH REH FINAL FORM
≈ <final> 0635 ص 0631 ر
FD2C ﴬ ARABIC LIGATURE DAD WITH REH FINAL FORM
≈ <final> 0636 ض 0631 ر
FD2D ﴭ ARABIC LIGATURE SHEEN WITH JEEM INITIAL FORM
≈ <initial> 0634 ش 062C ج
FD2E ﴮ ARABIC LIGATURE SHEEN WITH HAH INITIAL FORM
≈ <initial> 0634 ش 062D ح
FD2F ﴯ ARABIC LIGATURE SHEEN WITH KHAH INITIAL FORM
≈ <initial> 0634 ش 062E خ
FD30 ﴰ ARABIC LIGATURE SHEEN WITH MEEM INITIAL FORM
≈ <initial> 0634 ش 0645 م
FD31 ﴱ ARABIC LIGATURE SEEN WITH HEH INITIAL FORM
≈ <initial> 0633 س 0647 ه
FD32 ﴲ ARABIC LIGATURE SHEEN WITH HEH INITIAL FORM
≈ <initial> 0634 ش 0647 ه
FD33 ﴳ ARABIC LIGATURE TAH WITH MEEM INITIAL FORM
≈ <initial> 0637 ط 0645 م
FD34 ﴴ ARABIC LIGATURE SEEN WITH JEEM MEDIAL FORM
≈ <medial> 0633 س 062C ج
FD35 ﴵ ARABIC LIGATURE SEEN WITH HAH MEDIAL FORM
≈ <medial> 0633 س 062D ح
FD36 ﴶ ARABIC LIGATURE SEEN WITH KHAH MEDIAL FORM
≈ <medial> 0633 س 062E خ
FD37 ﴷ ARABIC LIGATURE SHEEN WITH JEEM MEDIAL FORM
≈ <medial> 0634 ش 062C ج
FD38 ﴸ ARABIC LIGATURE SHEEN WITH HAH MEDIAL FORM
≈ <medial> 0634 ش 062D ح
FD39 ﴹ ARABIC LIGATURE SHEEN WITH KHAH MEDIAL FORM
≈ <medial> 0634 ش 062E خ
FD3A ﴺ ARABIC LIGATURE TAH WITH MEEM MEDIAL FORM
≈ <medial> 0637 ط 0645 م
FD3B ﴻ ARABIC LIGATURE ZAH WITH MEEM MEDIAL FORM
≈ <medial> 0638 ظ 0645 م
FD3C ﴼ ARABIC LIGATURE ALEF WITH FATHATAN FINAL FORM
≈ <final> 0627 ا 064B ◌ً
FD3D ﴽ ARABIC LIGATURE ALEF WITH FATHATAN ISOLATED FORM
≈ <isolated> 0627 ا 064B ◌ً

Punctuation

FD3E ﴾ ORNATE LEFT PARENTHESIS
FD3F ﴿ ORNATE RIGHT PARENTHESIS

Ligatures (three elements)

FD50 ﵐ ARABIC LIGATURE TEH WITH JEEM WITH MEEM INITIAL FORM
≈ <initial> 062A ت 062C ج 0645 م
FD51 ﵑ ARABIC LIGATURE TEH WITH HAH WITH JEEM FINAL FORM
≈ <final> 062A ت 062D ح 062C ج
FD52 ﵒ ARABIC LIGATURE TEH WITH HAH WITH JEEM INITIAL FORM
≈ <initial> 062A ت 062D ح 062C ج
FD53 ﵓ ARABIC LIGATURE TEH WITH HAH WITH MEEM INITIAL FORM
≈ <initial> 062A ت 062D ح 0645 م
FD54 ﵔ ARABIC LIGATURE TEH WITH KHAH WITH MEEM INITIAL FORM
≈ <initial> 062A ت 062E خ 0645 م
FD55 ﵕ ARABIC LIGATURE TEH WITH MEEM WITH JEEM INITIAL FORM
≈ <initial> 062A ت 0645 م 062C ج
FD56 ﵖ ARABIC LIGATURE TEH WITH MEEM WITH HAH INITIAL FORM
≈ <initial> 062A ت 0645 م 062D ح
FD57 ﵗ ARABIC LIGATURE TEH WITH MEEM WITH KHAH INITIAL FORM
≈ <initial> 062A ت 0645 م 062E خ
FD58 ﵘ ARABIC LIGATURE JEEM WITH MEEM WITH HAH FINAL FORM
≈ <final> 062C ج 0645 م 062D ح
FD59 ﵙ ARABIC LIGATURE JEEM WITH MEEM WITH HAH INITIAL FORM
≈ <initial> 062C ج 0645 م 062D ح

FD5A ﵚ ARABIC LIGATURE HAH WITH MEEM WITH YEH FINAL FORM
≈ <final> 062D ح 0645 م 064A ي

FD5B ﵛ ARABIC LIGATURE HAH WITH MEEM WITH ALEF MAKSURA FINAL FORM
≈ <final> 062D ح 0645 م 0649 ى

FD5C ﵜ ARABIC LIGATURE SEEN WITH HAH WITH JEEM INITIAL FORM
≈ <initial> 0633 س 062D ح 062C ج

FD5D ﵝ ARABIC LIGATURE SEEN WITH JEEM WITH HAH INITIAL FORM
≈ <initial> 0633 س 062C ج 062D ح

FD5E ﵞ ARABIC LIGATURE SEEN WITH JEEM WITH ALEF MAKSURA FINAL FORM
≈ <final> 0633 س 062C ج 0649 ى

FD5F ﵟ ARABIC LIGATURE SEEN WITH MEEM WITH HAH FINAL FORM
≈ <final> 0633 س 0645 م 062D ح

FD60 ﵠ ARABIC LIGATURE SEEN WITH MEEM WITH HAH INITIAL FORM
≈ <initial> 0633 س 0645 م 062D ح

FD61 ﵡ ARABIC LIGATURE SEEN WITH MEEM WITH JEEM INITIAL FORM
≈ <initial> 0633 س 0645 م 062C ج

FD62 ﵢ ARABIC LIGATURE SEEN WITH MEEM WITH MEEM FINAL FORM
≈ <final> 0633 س 0645 م 0645 م

FD63 ﵣ ARABIC LIGATURE SEEN WITH MEEM WITH MEEM INITIAL FORM
≈ <initial> 0633 س 0645 م 0645 م

FD64 ﵤ ARABIC LIGATURE SAD WITH HAH WITH HAH FINAL FORM
≈ <final> 0635 ص 062D ح 062D ح

FD65 ﵥ ARABIC LIGATURE SAD WITH HAH WITH HAH INITIAL FORM
≈ <initial> 0635 ص 062D ح 062D ح

FD66 ﵦ ARABIC LIGATURE SAD WITH MEEM WITH MEEM FINAL FORM
≈ <final> 0635 ص 0645 م 0645 م

FD67 ﵧ ARABIC LIGATURE SHEEN WITH HAH WITH MEEM FINAL FORM
≈ <final> 0634 ش 062D ح 0645 م

FD68 ﵨ ARABIC LIGATURE SHEEN WITH HAH WITH MEEM INITIAL FORM
≈ <initial> 0634 ش 062D ح 0645 م

FD69 ﵩ ARABIC LIGATURE SHEEN WITH JEEM WITH YEH FINAL FORM
≈ <final> 0634 ش 062C ج 064A ي

FD6A ﵪ ARABIC LIGATURE SHEEN WITH MEEM WITH KHAH FINAL FORM
≈ <final> 0634 ش 0645 م 062E خ

FD6B ﵫ ARABIC LIGATURE SHEEN WITH MEEM WITH KHAH INITIAL FORM
≈ <initial> 0634 ش 0645 م 062E خ

FD6C ﵬ ARABIC LIGATURE SHEEN WITH MEEM WITH MEEM FINAL FORM
≈ <final> 0634 ش 0645 م 0645 م

FD6D ﵭ ARABIC LIGATURE SHEEN WITH MEEM WITH MEEM INITIAL FORM
≈ <initial> 0634 ش 0645 م 0645 م

FD6E ﵮ ARABIC LIGATURE DAD WITH HAH WITH ALEF MAKSURA FINAL FORM
≈ <final> 0636 ض 062D ح 0649 ى

FD6F ﵯ ARABIC LIGATURE DAD WITH KHAH WITH MEEM FINAL FORM
≈ <final> 0636 ض 062E خ 0645 م

FD70 ﵰ ARABIC LIGATURE DAD WITH KHAH WITH MEEM INITIAL FORM
≈ <initial> 0636 ض 062E خ 0645 م

FD71 ﵱ ARABIC LIGATURE TAH WITH MEEM WITH HAH FINAL FORM
≈ <final> 0637 ط 0645 م 062D ح

FD72 ﵲ ARABIC LIGATURE TAH WITH MEEM WITH HAH INITIAL FORM
≈ <initial> 0637 ط 0645 م 062D ح

FD73 ﵳ ARABIC LIGATURE TAH WITH MEEM WITH MEEM INITIAL FORM
≈ <initial> 0637 ط 0645 م 0645 م

FD74 ﵴ ARABIC LIGATURE TAH WITH MEEM WITH YEH FINAL FORM
≈ <final> 0637 ط 0645 م 064A ي

FD75 ﵵ ARABIC LIGATURE AIN WITH JEEM WITH MEEM FINAL FORM
≈ <final> 0639 ع 062C ج 0645 م

FD76 ﵶ ARABIC LIGATURE AIN WITH MEEM WITH MEEM FINAL FORM
≈ <final> 0639 ع 0645 م 0645 م

FD77 ﵷ ARABIC LIGATURE AIN WITH MEEM WITH MEEM INITIAL FORM
≈ <initial> 0639 ع 0645 م 0645 م

FD78 ﵸ ARABIC LIGATURE AIN WITH MEEM WITH ALEF MAKSURA FINAL FORM
≈ <final> 0639 ع 0645 م 0649 ى

FD79 ﵹ ARABIC LIGATURE GHAIN WITH MEEM WITH MEEM FINAL FORM
≈ <final> 063A غ 0645 م 0645 م

FD7A ﵺ ARABIC LIGATURE GHAIN WITH MEEM WITH YEH FINAL FORM
≈ <final> 063A غ 0645 م 064A ي

FD7B ﵻ ARABIC LIGATURE GHAIN WITH MEEM WITH ALEF MAKSURA FINAL FORM
≈ <final> 063A غ 0645 م 0649 ى

FD7C ﵼ ARABIC LIGATURE FEH WITH KHAH WITH MEEM FINAL FORM
≈ <final> 0641 ف 062E خ 0645 م

FD7D ﵽ ARABIC LIGATURE FEH WITH KHAH WITH MEEM INITIAL FORM
≈ <initial> 0641 ف 062E خ 0645 م

FD7E ﵾ ARABIC LIGATURE QAF WITH MEEM WITH HAH FINAL FORM
≈ <final> 0642 ق 0645 م 062D ح

FD7F ﵿ ARABIC LIGATURE QAF WITH MEEM WITH MEEM FINAL FORM
≈ <final> 0642 ق 0645 م 0645 م

FD80 ﶀ ARABIC LIGATURE LAM WITH HAH WITH MEEM FINAL FORM
≈ <final> 0644 ل 062D ح 0645 م

FD81 ﶁ ARABIC LIGATURE LAM WITH HAH WITH YEH FINAL FORM
≈ <final> 0644 ل 062D ح 064A ي

FD82 ﶂ ARABIC LIGATURE LAM WITH HAH WITH ALEF MAKSURA FINAL FORM
≈ <final> 0644 ل 062D ح 0649 ى

FD83 ﶃ ARABIC LIGATURE LAM WITH JEEM WITH JEEM INITIAL FORM
≈ <initial> 0644 ل 062C ج 062C ج

FD84 ﶄ ARABIC LIGATURE LAM WITH JEEM WITH JEEM FINAL FORM
≈ <final> 0644 ل 062C ج 062C ج

FD85 ﶅ ARABIC LIGATURE LAM WITH KHAH WITH MEEM FINAL FORM
≈ <final> 0644 ل 062E خ 0645 م

FD86 ﶆ ARABIC LIGATURE LAM WITH KHAH WITH MEEM INITIAL FORM
≈ <initial> 0644 ل 062E خ 0645 م

FD87 ﶇ ARABIC LIGATURE LAM WITH MEEM WITH HAH FINAL FORM
≈ <final> 0644 ل 0645 م 062D ح

FD88 ﶈ ARABIC LIGATURE LAM WITH MEEM WITH HAH INITIAL FORM
≈ <initial> 0644 ل 0645 م 062D ح

FD89 ﶉ ARABIC LIGATURE MEEM WITH HAH WITH JEEM INITIAL FORM
≈ <initial> 0645 م 062D ح 062C ج

FD8A ﶊ ARABIC LIGATURE MEEM WITH HAH WITH MEEM INITIAL FORM
≈ <initial> 0645 م 062D ح 0645 م

FD8B ﶋ ARABIC LIGATURE MEEM WITH HAH WITH YEH FINAL FORM
≈ <final> 0645 م 062D ح 064A ي

FD8C ﶌ ARABIC LIGATURE MEEM WITH JEEM WITH HAH INITIAL FORM
≈ <initial> 0645 م 062C ج 062D ح

FD8D ﶍ ARABIC LIGATURE MEEM WITH JEEM WITH MEEM INITIAL FORM
≈ <initial> 0645 م 062C ج 0645 م

FD8E ﶎ ARABIC LIGATURE MEEM WITH KHAH WITH JEEM INITIAL FORM
≈ <initial> 0645 م 062E خ 062C ج

FD8F ﶏ ARABIC LIGATURE MEEM WITH KHAH WITH MEEM INITIAL FORM
≈ <initial> 0645 م 062E خ 0645 م

FD90 <reserved>

FD91 <reserved>

FD92 ﶒ ARABIC LIGATURE MEEM WITH JEEM WITH KHAH INITIAL FORM
≈ <initial> 0645 م 062C ج 062E خ

FD93 ﶓ ARABIC LIGATURE HEH WITH MEEM WITH JEEM INITIAL FORM
≈ <initial> 0647 ه 0645 م 062C ج

FD94 ﶔ ARABIC LIGATURE HEH WITH MEEM WITH MEEM INITIAL FORM
≈ <initial> 0647 ه 0645 م 0645 م

FD95 ﶕ ARABIC LIGATURE NOON WITH HAH WITH MEEM INITIAL FORM
≈ <initial> 0646 ن 062D ح 0645 م

FD96 ﶖ ARABIC LIGATURE NOON WITH HAH WITH ALEF MAKSURA FINAL FORM
≈ <final> 0646 ن 062D ح 0649 ى

FD97 ﶗ ARABIC LIGATURE NOON WITH JEEM WITH MEEM FINAL FORM
≈ <final> 0646 ن 062C ج 0645 م

FD98 ﶘ ARABIC LIGATURE NOON WITH JEEM WITH MEEM INITIAL FORM
≈ <initial> 0646 ن 062C ج 0645 م

FD99 ﶙ ARABIC LIGATURE NOON WITH JEEM WITH ALEF MAKSURA FINAL FORM
≈ <final> 0646 ن 062C ج 0649 ى

FD9A ﶚ ARABIC LIGATURE NOON WITH MEEM WITH YEH FINAL FORM
≈ <final> 0646 ن 0645 م 064A ي

FD9B ﶛ ARABIC LIGATURE NOON WITH MEEM WITH ALEF MAKSURA FINAL FORM
≈ <final> 0646 ن 0645 م 0649 ى

FD9C ﶜ ARABIC LIGATURE YEH WITH MEEM WITH MEEM FINAL FORM
≈ <final> 064A ي 0645 م 0645 م

FD9D ﶝ ARABIC LIGATURE YEH WITH MEEM WITH MEEM INITIAL FORM
≈ <initial> 064A ي 0645 م 0645 م

FD9E ﶞ ARABIC LIGATURE BEH WITH KHAH WITH YEH FINAL FORM
≈ <final> 0628 ب 062E خ 064A ي

FD9F ﶟ ARABIC LIGATURE TEH WITH JEEM WITH YEH FINAL FORM
≈ <final> 062A ت 062C ج 064A ي

FDA0 ﶠ ARABIC LIGATURE TEH WITH JEEM WITH ALEF MAKSURA FINAL FORM
≈ <final> 062A ت 062C ج 0649 ى

FDA1 ﶡ ARABIC LIGATURE TEH WITH KHAH WITH YEH FINAL FORM
≈ <final> 062A ت 062E خ 064A ي

FDA2 ﶢ ARABIC LIGATURE TEH WITH KHAH WITH ALEF MAKSURA FINAL FORM
≈ <final> 062A ت 062E خ 0649 ى

FDA3 ﶣ ARABIC LIGATURE TEH WITH MEEM WITH YEH FINAL FORM
≈ <final> 062A ت 0645 م 064A ي

FDA4 ﶤ ARABIC LIGATURE TEH WITH MEEM WITH ALEF MAKSURA FINAL FORM
≈ <final> 062A ت 0645 م 0649 ى

FDA5 ﶥ ARABIC LIGATURE JEEM WITH MEEM WITH YEH FINAL FORM
≈ <final> 062C ج 0645 م 064A ي

FDA6 ﶦ ARABIC LIGATURE JEEM WITH HAH WITH ALEF MAKSURA FINAL FORM
≈ <final> 062C ج 062D ح 0649 ى

FDA7 ﶧ ARABIC LIGATURE JEEM WITH MEEM WITH ALEF MAKSURA FINAL FORM
≈ <final> 062C ج 0645 م 0649 ى

FDA8 ﶨ ARABIC LIGATURE SEEN WITH KHAH WITH ALEF MAKSURA FINAL FORM
≈ <final> 0633 س 062E خ 0649 ى

FDA9 ﶩ ARABIC LIGATURE SAD WITH HAH WITH YEH FINAL FORM
≈ <final> 0635 ص 062D ح 064A ي

FDAA ﶪ ARABIC LIGATURE SHEEN WITH HAH WITH YEH FINAL FORM
≈ <final> 0634 ش 062D ح 064A ي

FDAB ﶫ ARABIC LIGATURE DAD WITH HAH WITH YEH FINAL FORM
≈ <final> 0636 ض 062D ح 064A ي

FDAC ﶬ ARABIC LIGATURE LAM WITH JEEM WITH YEH FINAL FORM
≈ <final> 0644 ل 062C ج 064A ي

FDAD ﶭ ARABIC LIGATURE LAM WITH MEEM WITH YEH FINAL FORM
≈ <final> 0644 ل 0645 م 064A ي

FDAE ﶮ ARABIC LIGATURE YEH WITH HAH WITH YEH FINAL FORM
≈ <final> 064A ي 062D ح 064A ي

FDAF ﶯ ARABIC LIGATURE YEH WITH JEEM WITH YEH FINAL FORM
≈ <final> 064A ي 062C ج 064A ي

FDB0 ﶰ ARABIC LIGATURE YEH WITH MEEM WITH YEH FINAL FORM
≈ <final> 064A ي 0645 م 064A ي

FDB1 ﶱ ARABIC LIGATURE MEEM WITH MEEM WITH YEH FINAL FORM
≈ <final> 0645 م 0645 م 064A ي

FDB2 ﶲ ARABIC LIGATURE QAF WITH MEEM WITH YEH FINAL FORM
≈ <final> 0642 ق 0645 م 064A ي

FDB3 ﶳ ARABIC LIGATURE NOON WITH HAH WITH YEH FINAL FORM
≈ <final> 0646 ن 062D ح 064A ي

FDB4 ﶴ ARABIC LIGATURE QAF WITH MEEM WITH HAH INITIAL FORM
≈ <initial> 0642 ق 0645 م 062D ح

FDB5 ﶵ ARABIC LIGATURE LAM WITH HAH WITH MEEM INITIAL FORM
≈ <initial> 0644 ل 062D ح 0645 م

FDB6 ﶶ ARABIC LIGATURE AIN WITH MEEM WITH YEH FINAL FORM
≈ <final> 0639 ع 0645 م 064A ي

FDB7 ﶷ ARABIC LIGATURE KAF WITH MEEM WITH YEH FINAL FORM
≈ <final> 0643 ك 0645 م 064A ي

FDB8 ﶸ ARABIC LIGATURE NOON WITH JEEM WITH HAH INITIAL FORM
≈ <initial> 0646 ن 062C ج 062D ح

FDB9 ﶹ ARABIC LIGATURE MEEM WITH KHAH WITH YEH FINAL FORM
≈ <final> 0645 م 062E خ 064A ي

FDBA ﶺ ARABIC LIGATURE LAM WITH JEEM WITH MEEM INITIAL FORM
≈ <initial> 0644 ل 062C ج 0645 م

FDBB ﶻ ARABIC LIGATURE KAF WITH MEEM WITH MEEM FINAL FORM
≈ <final> 0643 ك 0645 م 0645 م

FDBC ﶼ ARABIC LIGATURE LAM WITH JEEM WITH MEEM FINAL FORM
≈ <final> 0644 ل 062C ج 0645 م

FDBD ﶽ ARABIC LIGATURE NOON WITH JEEM WITH HAH FINAL FORM
≈ <final> 0646 ن 062C ج 062D ح

FDBE ﶾ ARABIC LIGATURE JEEM WITH HAH WITH YEH FINAL FORM
≈ <final> 062C ج 062D ح 064A ي

FDBF ﶿ ARABIC LIGATURE HAH WITH JEEM WITH YEH FINAL FORM
≈ <final> 062D ح 062C ج 064A ي

FDC0 ﷀ ARABIC LIGATURE MEEM WITH JEEM WITH YEH FINAL FORM
≈ <final> 0645 م 062C ج 064A ي

FDC1 ﷁ ARABIC LIGATURE FEH WITH MEEM WITH YEH FINAL FORM
≈ <final> 0641 ف 0645 م 064A ي

FDC2 ﷂ ARABIC LIGATURE BEH WITH HAH WITH YEH FINAL FORM
≈ <final> 0628 ب 062D ح 064A ي

FDC3 ﷃ ARABIC LIGATURE KAF WITH MEEM WITH MEEM INITIAL FORM
≈ <initial> 0643 ك 0645 م 0645 م

FDC4 ﷄ ARABIC LIGATURE AIN WITH JEEM WITH MEEM INITIAL FORM
≈ <initial> 0639 ع 062C ج 0645 م

FDC5 ﷅ ARABIC LIGATURE SAD WITH MEEM WITH MEEM INITIAL FORM
≈ <initial> 0635 ص 0645 م 0645 م

FDC6 ﷆ ARABIC LIGATURE SEEN WITH KHAH WITH YEH FINAL FORM
≈ <final> 0633 س 062E خ 064A ي

FDC7 ﷇ ARABIC LIGATURE NOON WITH JEEM WITH YEH FINAL FORM
≈ <final> 0646 ن 062C ج 064A ي

Noncharacters

These codes are intended for process-internal uses, but are not permitted for interchange.

FDD0 <not a character>
FDD1 <not a character>
FDD2 <not a character>
FDD3 <not a character>
FDD4 <not a character>
FDD5 <not a character>
FDD6 <not a character>
FDD7 <not a character>
FDD8 <not a character>
FDD9 <not a character>
FDDA <not a character>
FDDB <not a character>
FDDC <not a character>
FDDD <not a character>
FDDE <not a character>
FDDF <not a character>
FDE0 <not a character>
FDE1 <not a character>
FDE2 <not a character>
FDE3 <not a character>
FDE4 <not a character>
FDE5 <not a character>
FDE6 <not a character>
FDE7 <not a character>
FDE8 <not a character>
FDE9 <not a character>
FDEA <not a character>
FDEB <not a character>
FDEC <not a character>
FDED <not a character>
FDEE <not a character>
FDEF <not a character>

Word ligatures

FDF0 ﷰ ARABIC LIGATURE SALLA USED AS KORANIC STOP SIGN ISOLATED FORM
≈ <isolated> 0635 ص 0644 ل 06D2 ے

FDF1 ﷱ ARABIC LIGATURE QALA USED AS KORANIC STOP SIGN ISOLATED FORM
≈ <isolated> 0642 ق 0644 ل 06D2 ے

FDF2 ﷲ ARABIC LIGATURE ALLAH ISOLATED FORM
≈ <isolated> 0627 ا 0644 ل 0644 ل 0647 ه

FDF3 ﷳ ARABIC LIGATURE AKBAR ISOLATED FORM
≈ <isolated> 0627 ا 0643 ك 0628 ب 0631 ر

FDF4 ﷴ ARABIC LIGATURE MOHAMMAD ISOLATED FORM
≈ <isolated> 0645 م 062D ح 0645 م 062F د

FDF5 ﷵ ARABIC LIGATURE SALAM ISOLATED FORM
≈ <isolated> 0635 ص 0644 ل 0639 ع 0645 م

FDF6 ﷶ ARABIC LIGATURE RASOUL ISOLATED FORM
≈ <isolated> 0631 ر 0633 س 0648 و 0644 ل

FDF7 ﷷ ARABIC LIGATURE ALAYHE ISOLATED FORM
≈ <isolated> 0639 ع 0644 ل 064A ي 0647 ه

FDF8 ﷸ ARABIC LIGATURE WASALLAM ISOLATED FORM
≈ <isolated> 0648 و 0633 س 0644 ل 0645 م

FDF9 ﷹ ARABIC LIGATURE SALLA ISOLATED FORM
≈ <isolated> 0635 ص 0644 ل 0649 ى

FDFA ﷺ ARABIC LIGATURE SALLALLAHOU ALAYHE WASALLAM
≈ <isolated> 0635 ص 0644 ل 0649 ى 0020 SP 0627 ا 0644 ل 0644 ل 0647 ه 0020 SP 0639 ع 0644 ل 064A ي 0647 ه 0020 SP 0648 و 0633 س 0644 ل 0645 م

FDFB ﷻ ARABIC LIGATURE JALLAJALALOUHOU
≈ <isolated> 062C ج 0644 ل 0020 SP 062C ج 0644 ل 0627 ا 0644 ل 0647 ه

Currency sign

FDFC ﷼ RIAL SIGN
≈ <isolated> 0631 ر 06CC ی 0627 ا 0644 ل

Symbol

FDFD ﷽ ARABIC LIGATURE BISMILLAH AR-RAHMAN AR-RAHEEM

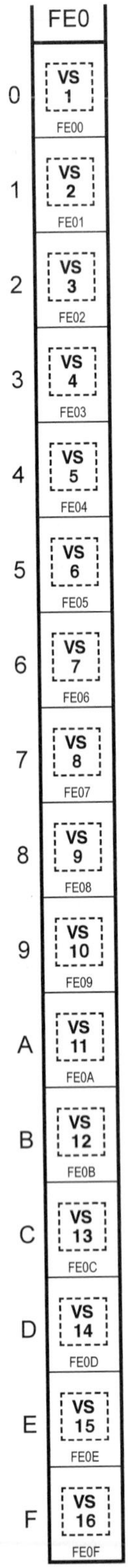

	FE0
0	VS 1 FE00
1	VS 2 FE01
2	VS 3 FE02
3	VS 4 FE03
4	VS 5 FE04
5	VS 6 FE05
6	VS 7 FE06
7	VS 8 FE07
8	VS 9 FE08
9	VS 10 FE09
A	VS 11 FE0A
B	VS 12 FE0B
C	VS 13 FE0C
D	VS 14 FE0D
E	VS 15 FE0E
F	VS 16 FE0F

Variation selectors

Combining characters; in conjunction with the preceding character these indicate a predetermined choice of variant glyph

FE00 VS1 VARIATION SELECTOR-1
• these are abbreviated VS1, and so on
FE01 VS2 VARIATION SELECTOR-2
FE02 VS3 VARIATION SELECTOR-3
FE03 VS4 VARIATION SELECTOR-4
FE04 VS5 VARIATION SELECTOR-5
FE05 VS6 VARIATION SELECTOR-6
FE06 VS7 VARIATION SELECTOR-7
FE07 VS8 VARIATION SELECTOR-8
FE08 VS9 VARIATION SELECTOR-9
FE09 VS10 VARIATION SELECTOR-10
FE0A VS11 VARIATION SELECTOR-11
FE0B VS12 VARIATION SELECTOR-12
FE0C VS13 VARIATION SELECTOR-13
FE0D VS14 VARIATION SELECTOR-14
FE0E VS15 VARIATION SELECTOR-15
FE0F VS16 VARIATION SELECTOR-16

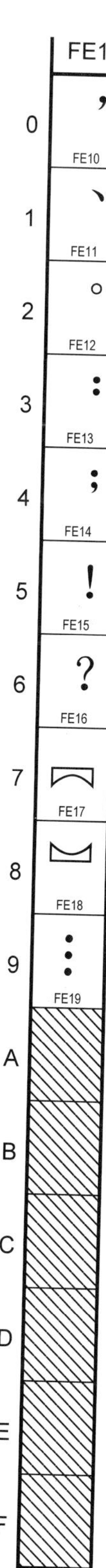

These characters are compatibility characters needed to map to GB 18030.

Glyphs for vertical variants

FE10 ︐ PRESENTATION FORM FOR VERTICAL COMMA
→ FE50 ﹐ small comma
≈ <vertical> 002C ,

FE11 ︑ PRESENTATION FORM FOR VERTICAL IDEOGRAPHIC COMMA
→ FE45 ﹅ sesame dot
→ FE51 ﹑ small ideographic comma
≈ <vertical> 3001 、

FE12 ︒ PRESENTATION FORM FOR VERTICAL IDEOGRAPHIC FULL STOP
≈ <vertical> 3002 。

FE13 ︓ PRESENTATION FORM FOR VERTICAL COLON
→ FE55 ﹕ small colon
≈ <vertical> 003A :

FE14 ︔ PRESENTATION FORM FOR VERTICAL SEMICOLON
→ FE54 ﹔ small semicolon
≈ <vertical> 003B ;

FE15 ︕ PRESENTATION FORM FOR VERTICAL EXCLAMATION MARK
→ FE57 ﹗ small exclamation mark
≈ <vertical> 0021 !

FE16 ︖ PRESENTATION FORM FOR VERTICAL QUESTION MARK
→ FE56 ﹖ small question mark
≈ <vertical> 003F ?

FE17 ︗ PRESENTATION FORM FOR VERTICAL LEFT WHITE LENTICULAR BRACKET
≈ <vertical> 3016 〖

FE18 ︘ PRESENTATION FORM FOR VERTICAL RIGHT WHITE LENTICULAR BRAKCET
※ PRESENTATION FORM FOR VERTICAL RIGHT WHITE LENTICULAR BRACKET
• misspelling of "BRACKET" in character name is a known defect
≈ <vertical> 3017 〗

FE19 ︙ PRESENTATION FORM FOR VERTICAL HORIZONTAL ELLIPSIS
→ 22EE ⋮ vertical ellipsis
≈ <vertical> 2026 …

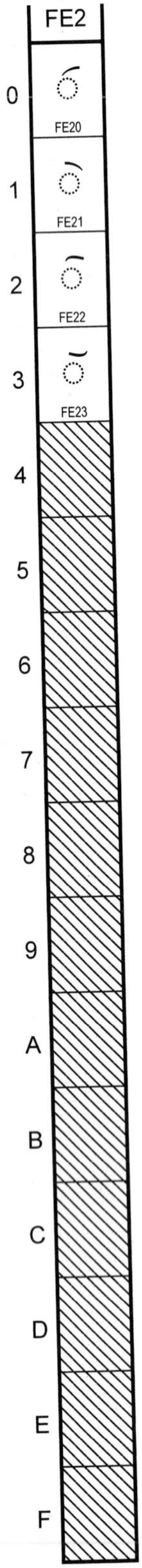

	FE2
0	◌︠ FE20
1	◌︡ FE21
2	◌︢ FE22
3	◌︣ FE23
4	
5	
6	
7	
8	
9	
A	
B	
C	
D	
E	
F	

Combining half marks

FE20 ◌︠ COMBINING LIGATURE LEFT HALF
FE21 ◌︡ COMBINING LIGATURE RIGHT HALF
FE22 ◌︢ COMBINING DOUBLE TILDE LEFT HALF
FE23 ◌︣ COMBINING DOUBLE TILDE RIGHT HALF

	FE3	FE4
0	︰ FE30	﹀ FE40
1	︱ FE31	﹁ FE41
2	︲ FE32	﹂ FE42
3	︳ FE33	﹃ FE43
4	︴ FE34	﹄ FE44
5	︵ FE35	﹅ FE45
6	︶ FE36	﹆ FE46
7	︷ FE37	﹇ FE47
8	︸ FE38	﹈ FE48
9	︹ FE39	﹉ FE49
A	︺ FE3A	﹊ FE4A
B	︻ FE3B	﹋ FE4B
C	︼ FE3C	﹌ FE4C
D	︽ FE3D	﹍ FE4D
E	︾ FE3E	﹎ FE4E
F	︿ FE3F	﹏ FE4F

Glyphs for vertical variants

FE30 ︰ PRESENTATION FORM FOR VERTICAL TWO DOT LEADER
≈ <vertical> 2025 ‥

FE31 ︱ PRESENTATION FORM FOR VERTICAL EM DASH
≈ <vertical> 2014 —

FE32 ︲ PRESENTATION FORM FOR VERTICAL EN DASH
≈ <vertical> 2013 –

FE33 ︳ PRESENTATION FORM FOR VERTICAL LOW LINE
≈ <vertical> 005F _

FE34 ︴ PRESENTATION FORM FOR VERTICAL WAVY LOW LINE
≈ <vertical> 005F _

FE35 ︵ PRESENTATION FORM FOR VERTICAL LEFT PARENTHESIS
→ 23DC ⏜ top parenthesis
≈ <vertical> 0028 (

FE36 ︶ PRESENTATION FORM FOR VERTICAL RIGHT PARENTHESIS
→ 23DD ⏝ bottom parenthesis
≈ <vertical> 0029)

FE37 ︷ PRESENTATION FORM FOR VERTICAL LEFT CURLY BRACKET
→ 23DE ⏞ top curly bracket
≈ <vertical> 007B {

FE38 ︸ PRESENTATION FORM FOR VERTICAL RIGHT CURLY BRACKET
→ 23DF ⏟ bottom curly bracket
≈ <vertical> 007D }

FE39 ︹ PRESENTATION FORM FOR VERTICAL LEFT TORTOISE SHELL BRACKET
→ 23E0 ⏠ top tortoise shell bracket
≈ <vertical> 3014 〔

FE3A ︺ PRESENTATION FORM FOR VERTICAL RIGHT TORTOISE SHELL BRACKET
→ 23E1 ⏡ bottom tortoise shell bracket
≈ <vertical> 3015 〕

FE3B ︻ PRESENTATION FORM FOR VERTICAL LEFT BLACK LENTICULAR BRACKET
≈ <vertical> 3010 【

FE3C ︼ PRESENTATION FORM FOR VERTICAL RIGHT BLACK LENTICULAR BRACKET
≈ <vertical> 3011 】

FE3D ︽ PRESENTATION FORM FOR VERTICAL LEFT DOUBLE ANGLE BRACKET
≈ <vertical> 300A 《

FE3E ︾ PRESENTATION FORM FOR VERTICAL RIGHT DOUBLE ANGLE BRACKET
≈ <vertical> 300B 》

FE3F ︿ PRESENTATION FORM FOR VERTICAL LEFT ANGLE BRACKET
≈ <vertical> 3008 〈

FE40 ﹀ PRESENTATION FORM FOR VERTICAL RIGHT ANGLE BRACKET
≈ <vertical> 3009 〉

FE41 ﹁ PRESENTATION FORM FOR VERTICAL LEFT CORNER BRACKET
≈ <vertical> 300C 「

FE42 ﹂ PRESENTATION FORM FOR VERTICAL RIGHT CORNER BRACKET
≈ <vertical> 300D 」

FE43 ﹃ PRESENTATION FORM FOR VERTICAL LEFT WHITE CORNER BRACKET
≈ <vertical> 300E 『

FE44 ﹄ PRESENTATION FORM FOR VERTICAL RIGHT WHITE CORNER BRACKET
≈ <vertical> 300F 』

Sidelining emphasis marks

FE45 ﹅ SESAME DOT
→ FE51 ﹑ small ideographic comma

FE46 ﹆ WHITE SESAME DOT
• sesame dots are used beside vertical text for emphasis

Glyphs for vertical variants

FE47 ﹇ PRESENTATION FORM FOR VERTICAL LEFT SQUARE BRACKET
→ 23B4 ⎴ top square bracket
≈ <vertical> 005B [

FE48 ﹈ PRESENTATION FORM FOR VERTICAL RIGHT SQUARE BRACKET
→ 23B5 ⎵ bottom square bracket
≈ <vertical> 005D]

Overscores and underscores

FE49 ﹉ DASHED OVERLINE
≈ 203E ‾ overline

FE4A ﹊ CENTRELINE OVERLINE
≈ 203E ‾ overline

FE4B ﹋ WAVY OVERLINE
≈ 203E ‾ overline

FE4C ﹌ DOUBLE WAVY OVERLINE
≈ 203E ‾ overline

FE4D ﹍ DASHED LOW LINE
≈ 005F _ low line

FE4E ﹎ CENTRELINE LOW LINE
≈ 005F _ low line

FE4F ﹏ WAVY LOW LINE
≈ 005F _ low line

	FE5	FE6
0	﹐ FE50	﹠ FE60
1	﹑ FE51	﹡ FE61
2	﹒ FE52	﹢ FE62
3	(reserved)	﹣ FE63
4	﹔ FE54	﹤ FE64
5	﹕ FE55	﹥ FE65
6	﹖ FE56	﹦ FE66
7	﹗ FE57	(reserved)
8	﹘ FE58	﹨ FE68
9	﹙ FE59	﹩ FE69
A	﹚ FE5A	﹪ FE6A
B	﹛ FE5B	﹫ FE6B
C	﹜ FE5C	(reserved)
D	﹝ FE5D	(reserved)
E	﹞ FE5E	(reserved)
F	﹟ FE5F	(reserved)

Compatibility variants for CNS 11643.

Small form variants

FE50 ﹐ SMALL COMMA
→ FE10 ︐ presentation form for vertical comma
≈ <small> 002C ,

FE51 ﹑ SMALL IDEOGRAPHIC COMMA
→ FE11 ︑ presentation form for vertical ideographic comma
→ FE45 ﹅ sesame dot
≈ <small> 3001 、

FE52 ﹒ SMALL FULL STOP
≈ <small> 002E .

FE53 <reserved>

FE54 ﹔ SMALL SEMICOLON
→ FE14 ︔ presentation form for vertical semicolon
≈ <small> 003B ;

FE55 ﹕ SMALL COLON
→ FE13 ︓ presentation form for vertical colon
≈ <small> 003A :

FE56 ﹖ SMALL QUESTION MARK
≈ <small> 003F ?

FE57 ﹗ SMALL EXCLAMATION MARK
≈ <small> 0021 !

FE58 ﹘ SMALL EM DASH
≈ <small> 2014 —

FE59 ﹙ SMALL LEFT PARENTHESIS
≈ <small> 0028 (

FE5A ﹚ SMALL RIGHT PARENTHESIS
≈ <small> 0029)

FE5B ﹛ SMALL LEFT CURLY BRACKET
≈ <small> 007B {

FE5C ﹜ SMALL RIGHT CURLY BRACKET
≈ <small> 007D }

FE5D ﹝ SMALL LEFT TORTOISE SHELL BRACKET
≈ <small> 3014 〔

FE5E ﹞ SMALL RIGHT TORTOISE SHELL BRACKET
≈ <small> 3015 〕

FE5F ﹟ SMALL NUMBER SIGN
≈ <small> 0023 #

FE60 ﹠ SMALL AMPERSAND
≈ <small> 0026 &

FE61 ﹡ SMALL ASTERISK
≈ <small> 002A *

FE62 ﹢ SMALL PLUS SIGN
≈ <small> 002B +

FE63 ﹣ SMALL HYPHEN-MINUS
≈ <small> 002D -

FE64 ﹤ SMALL LESS-THAN SIGN
≈ <small> 003C <

FE65 ﹥ SMALL GREATER-THAN SIGN
≈ <small> 003E >

FE66 ﹦ SMALL EQUALS SIGN
≈ <small> 003D =

FE67 <reserved>

FE68 ﹨ SMALL REVERSE SOLIDUS
≈ <small> 005C \

FE69 ﹩ SMALL DOLLAR SIGN
≈ <small> 0024 $

FE6A ﹪ SMALL PERCENT SIGN
≈ <small> 0025 %

FE6B ﹫ SMALL COMMERCIAL AT
≈ <small> 0040 @

	FE7	FE8	FE9	FEA	FEB	FEC	FED	FEE	FEF
0	ﹰ FE70	ﺀ FE80	ﺐ FE90	ﺠ FEA0	ﺰ FEB0	ﻀ FEC0	ﻐ FED0	ﻠ FEE0	ﻰ FEF0
1	ﹱ FE71	ﺁ FE81	ﺑ FE91	ﺡ FEA1	ﺱ FEB1	ﻁ FEC1	ﻑ FED1	ﻡ FEE1	ﻱ FEF1
2	ﹲ FE72	ﺂ FE82	ﺒ FE92	ﺢ FEA2	ﺲ FEB2	ﻂ FEC2	ﻒ FED2	ﻢ FEE2	ﻲ FEF2
3	ﹳ FE73	ﺃ FE83	ﺓ FE93	ﺣ FEA3	ﺳ FEB3	ﻃ FEC3	ﻓ FED3	ﻣ FEE3	ﻳ FEF3
4	ﹴ FE74	ﺄ FE84	ﺔ FE94	ﺤ FEA4	ﺴ FEB4	ﻄ FEC4	ﻔ FED4	ﻤ FEE4	ﻴ FEF4
5		ﺅ FE85	ﺕ FE95	ﺥ FEA5	ﺵ FEB5	ﻅ FEC5	ﻕ FED5	ﻥ FEE5	ﻵ FEF5
6	ﹶ FE76	ﺆ FE86	ﺖ FE96	ﺦ FEA6	ﺶ FEB6	ﻆ FEC6	ﻖ FED6	ﻦ FEE6	ﻶ FEF6
7	ﹷ FE77	ﺇ FE87	ﺗ FE97	ﺧ FEA7	ﺷ FEB7	ﻇ FEC7	ﻗ FED7	ﻧ FEE7	ﻷ FEF7
8	ﹸ FE78	ﺈ FE88	ﺘ FE98	ﺨ FEA8	ﺸ FEB8	ﻈ FEC8	ﻘ FED8	ﻨ FEE8	ﻸ FEF8
9	ﹹ FE79	ﺉ FE89	ﺙ FE99	ﺩ FEA9	ﺹ FEB9	ﻉ FEC9	ﻙ FED9	ﻩ FEE9	ﻹ FEF9
A	ﹺ FE7A	ﺊ FE8A	ﺚ FE9A	ﺪ FEAA	ﺺ FEBA	ﻊ FECA	ﻚ FEDA	ﻪ FEEA	ﻺ FEFA
B	ﹻ FE7B	ﺋ FE8B	ﺛ FE9B	ﺫ FEAB	ﺻ FEBB	ﻋ FECB	ﻛ FEDB	ﻫ FEEB	ﻻ FEFB
C	ﹼ FE7C	ﺌ FE8C	ﺜ FE9C	ﺬ FEAC	ﺼ FEBC	ﻌ FECC	ﻜ FEDC	ﻬ FEEC	ﻼ FEFC
D	ﹽ FE7D	ﺍ FE8D	ﺝ FE9D	ﺭ FEAD	ﺽ FEBD	ﻍ FECD	ﻝ FEDD	ﻭ FEED	
E	ﹾ FE7E	ﺎ FE8E	ﺞ FE9E	ﺮ FEAE	ﺾ FEBE	ﻎ FECE	ﻞ FEDE	ﻮ FEEE	
F	ﹿ FE7F	ﺏ FE8F	ﺟ FE9F	ﺯ FEAF	ﺿ FEBF	ﻏ FECF	ﻟ FEDF	ﻯ FEEF	ZWN BSP FEFF

Preferred characters are found in the Arabic block 0600 - 06FF. Some of these characters are used for Arabic mathematics where contextual shape variations are important semantically.

Glyphs for spacing forms of Arabic points

FE70 ﹰ ARABIC FATHATAN ISOLATED FORM
≈ <isolated> 0020 [SP] 064B ◌ً

FE71 ﹱ ARABIC TATWEEL WITH FATHATAN ABOVE
≈ <medial> 0640 ـ 064B ◌ً

FE72 ﹲ ARABIC DAMMATAN ISOLATED FORM
≈ <isolated> 0020 [SP] 064C ◌ٌ

Glyph part

FE73 ﹳ ARABIC TAIL FRAGMENT
• for compatibility with certain legacy character sets

Glyphs for spacing forms of Arabic points

FE74 ﹴ ARABIC KASRATAN ISOLATED FORM
≈ <isolated> 0020 [SP] 064D ◌ٍ

FE75 <reserved>

FE76 ﹶ ARABIC FATHA ISOLATED FORM
≈ <isolated> 0020 [SP] 064E ◌َ

FE77 ﹷ ARABIC FATHA MEDIAL FORM
≈ <medial> 0640 ـ 064E ◌َ

FE78 ﹸ ARABIC DAMMA ISOLATED FORM
≈ <isolated> 0020 [SP] 064F ◌ُ

FE79 ﹹ ARABIC DAMMA MEDIAL FORM
≈ <medial> 0640 ـ 064F ◌ُ

FE7A ﹺ ARABIC KASRA ISOLATED FORM
≈ <isolated> 0020 [SP] 0650 ◌ِ

FE7B ﹻ ARABIC KASRA MEDIAL FORM
≈ <medial> 0640 ـ 0650 ◌ِ

FE7C ﹼ ARABIC SHADDA ISOLATED FORM
≈ <isolated> 0020 [SP] 0651 ◌ّ

FE7D ﹽ ARABIC SHADDA MEDIAL FORM
≈ <medial> 0640 ـ 0651 ◌ّ

FE7E ﹾ ARABIC SUKUN ISOLATED FORM
≈ <isolated> 0020 [SP] 0652 ◌ْ

FE7F ﹿ ARABIC SUKUN MEDIAL FORM
≈ <medial> 0640 ـ 0652 ◌ْ

Basic glyphs for Arabic language contextual forms

FE80 ﺀ ARABIC LETTER HAMZA ISOLATED FORM
≈ <isolated> 0621 ء

FE81 ﺁ ARABIC LETTER ALEF WITH MADDA ABOVE ISOLATED FORM
≈ <isolated> 0622 آ

FE82 ﺂ ARABIC LETTER ALEF WITH MADDA ABOVE FINAL FORM
≈ <final> 0622 آ

FE83 ﺃ ARABIC LETTER ALEF WITH HAMZA ABOVE ISOLATED FORM
≈ <isolated> 0623 أ

FE84 ﺄ ARABIC LETTER ALEF WITH HAMZA ABOVE FINAL FORM
≈ <final> 0623 أ

FE85 ﺅ ARABIC LETTER WAW WITH HAMZA ABOVE ISOLATED FORM
≈ <isolated> 0624 ؤ

FE86 ﺆ ARABIC LETTER WAW WITH HAMZA ABOVE FINAL FORM
≈ <final> 0624 ؤ

FE87 ﺇ ARABIC LETTER ALEF WITH HAMZA BELOW ISOLATED FORM
≈ <isolated> 0625 إ

FE88 ﺈ ARABIC LETTER ALEF WITH HAMZA BELOW FINAL FORM
≈ <final> 0625 إ

FE89 ﺉ ARABIC LETTER YEH WITH HAMZA ABOVE ISOLATED FORM
≈ <isolated> 0626 ئ

FE8A ﺊ ARABIC LETTER YEH WITH HAMZA ABOVE FINAL FORM
≈ <final> 0626 ئ

FE8B ﺋ ARABIC LETTER YEH WITH HAMZA ABOVE INITIAL FORM
≈ <initial> 0626 ئ

FE8C ﺌ ARABIC LETTER YEH WITH HAMZA ABOVE MEDIAL FORM
≈ <medial> 0626 ئ

FE8D ﺍ ARABIC LETTER ALEF ISOLATED FORM
≈ <isolated> 0627 ا

FE8E ﺎ ARABIC LETTER ALEF FINAL FORM
≈ <final> 0627 ا

FE8F ﺏ ARABIC LETTER BEH ISOLATED FORM
≈ <isolated> 0628 ب

FE90 ﺐ ARABIC LETTER BEH FINAL FORM
≈ <final> 0628 ب

FE91 ﺑ ARABIC LETTER BEH INITIAL FORM
≈ <initial> 0628 ب

FE92 ﺒ ARABIC LETTER BEH MEDIAL FORM
≈ <medial> 0628 ب

FE93 ﺓ ARABIC LETTER TEH MARBUTA ISOLATED FORM
≈ <isolated> 0629 ة

FE94 ﺔ ARABIC LETTER TEH MARBUTA FINAL FORM
≈ <final> 0629 ة

FE95 ﺕ ARABIC LETTER TEH ISOLATED FORM
≈ <isolated> 062A ت

FE96 ﺖ ARABIC LETTER TEH FINAL FORM
≈ <final> 062A ت

FE97 ﺗ ARABIC LETTER TEH INITIAL FORM
≈ <initial> 062A ت

FE98 ﺘ ARABIC LETTER TEH MEDIAL FORM
≈ <medial> 062A ت

FE99 ﺙ ARABIC LETTER THEH ISOLATED FORM
≈ <isolated> 062B ث

FE9A ﺚ ARABIC LETTER THEH FINAL FORM
≈ <final> 062B ث

FE9B ﺛ ARABIC LETTER THEH INITIAL FORM
≈ <initial> 062B ث

FE9C ﺜ ARABIC LETTER THEH MEDIAL FORM
≈ <medial> 062B ث

FE9D ﺝ ARABIC LETTER JEEM ISOLATED FORM
≈ <isolated> 062C ج

FE9E ﺞ ARABIC LETTER JEEM FINAL FORM
≈ <final> 062C ج

FE9F ﺟ ARABIC LETTER JEEM INITIAL FORM
≈ <initial> 062C ج

FEA0 ﺠ ARABIC LETTER JEEM MEDIAL FORM
≈ <medial> 062C ج

FEA1 ﺡ ARABIC LETTER HAH ISOLATED FORM
≈ <isolated> 062D ح

FEA2 ﺢ ARABIC LETTER HAH FINAL FORM
≈ <final> 062D ح

FEA3 ﺣ ARABIC LETTER HAH INITIAL FORM
≈ <initial> 062D ح

FEA4 ﺤ ARABIC LETTER HAH MEDIAL FORM
≈ <medial> 062D ح

FEA5 ﺥ ARABIC LETTER KHAH ISOLATED FORM
≈ <isolated> 062E خ

FEA6 ﺦ ARABIC LETTER KHAH FINAL FORM
≈ <final> 062E خ

FEA7 ﺧ ARABIC LETTER KHAH INITIAL FORM
≈ <initial> 062E خ

FEA8 ﺨ ARABIC LETTER KHAH MEDIAL FORM
≈ <medial> 062E خ

FEA9 ﺩ ARABIC LETTER DAL ISOLATED FORM
≈ <isolated> 062F د

FEAA ﺪ ARABIC LETTER DAL FINAL FORM
≈ <final> 062F د

FEAB ﺫ ARABIC LETTER THAL ISOLATED FORM
≈ <isolated> 0630 ذ

FEAC ﺬ ARABIC LETTER THAL FINAL FORM
≈ <final> 0630 ذ

FEAD ﺭ ARABIC LETTER REH ISOLATED FORM
≈ <isolated> 0631 ر

FEAE ﺮ ARABIC LETTER REH FINAL FORM
≈ <final> 0631 ر

FEAF ﺯ ARABIC LETTER ZAIN ISOLATED FORM
≈ <isolated> 0632 ز

FEB0 ﺰ ARABIC LETTER ZAIN FINAL FORM
≈ <final> 0632 ز

FEB1 ﺱ ARABIC LETTER SEEN ISOLATED FORM
≈ <isolated> 0633 س

FEB2 ﺲ ARABIC LETTER SEEN FINAL FORM
≈ <final> 0633 س

FEB3 ﺳ ARABIC LETTER SEEN INITIAL FORM
≈ <initial> 0633 س

FEB4 ﺴ ARABIC LETTER SEEN MEDIAL FORM
≈ <medial> 0633 س

FEB5 ﺵ ARABIC LETTER SHEEN ISOLATED FORM
≈ <isolated> 0634 ش

FEB6 ﺶ ARABIC LETTER SHEEN FINAL FORM
≈ <final> 0634 ش

FEB7 ﺷ ARABIC LETTER SHEEN INITIAL FORM
≈ <initial> 0634 ش

FEB8 ﺸ ARABIC LETTER SHEEN MEDIAL FORM
≈ <medial> 0634 ش

FEB9 ﺹ ARABIC LETTER SAD ISOLATED FORM
≈ <isolated> 0635 ص

FEBA ﺺ ARABIC LETTER SAD FINAL FORM
≈ <final> 0635 ص

FEBB ﺻ ARABIC LETTER SAD INITIAL FORM
≈ <initial> 0635 ص

FEBC ﺼ ARABIC LETTER SAD MEDIAL FORM
≈ <medial> 0635 ص

FEBD ﺽ ARABIC LETTER DAD ISOLATED FORM
≈ <isolated> 0636 ض

FEBE ﺾ ARABIC LETTER DAD FINAL FORM
≈ <final> 0636 ض

FEBF ﺿ ARABIC LETTER DAD INITIAL FORM
≈ <initial> 0636 ض

FEC0 ﻀ ARABIC LETTER DAD MEDIAL FORM
≈ <medial> 0636 ض

FEC1 ﻁ ARABIC LETTER TAH ISOLATED FORM
≈ <isolated> 0637 ط

FEC2 ﻂ ARABIC LETTER TAH FINAL FORM
≈ <final> 0637 ط

FEC3 ﻃ ARABIC LETTER TAH INITIAL FORM
≈ <initial> 0637 ط

FEC4 ﻄ ARABIC LETTER TAH MEDIAL FORM
≈ <medial> 0637 ط

FEC5 ﻅ ARABIC LETTER ZAH ISOLATED FORM
≈ <isolated> 0638 ظ

FEC6 ﻆ ARABIC LETTER ZAH FINAL FORM
≈ <final> 0638 ظ

FEC7 ﻇ ARABIC LETTER ZAH INITIAL FORM
≈ <initial> 0638 ظ

FEC8 ﻈ ARABIC LETTER ZAH MEDIAL FORM
≈ <medial> 0638 ظ

FEC9 ﻉ ARABIC LETTER AIN ISOLATED FORM
≈ <isolated> 0639 ع

FECA ﻊ ARABIC LETTER AIN FINAL FORM
≈ <final> 0639 ع

FECB ﻋ ARABIC LETTER AIN INITIAL FORM
≈ <initial> 0639 ع

FECC ﻌ ARABIC LETTER AIN MEDIAL FORM
≈ <medial> 0639 ع

FECD ﻍ ARABIC LETTER GHAIN ISOLATED FORM
≈ <isolated> 063A غ

FECE ﻎ ARABIC LETTER GHAIN FINAL FORM
≈ <final> 063A غ

FECF ﻏ ARABIC LETTER GHAIN INITIAL FORM
≈ <initial> 063A غ

FED0 ﻐ ARABIC LETTER GHAIN MEDIAL FORM
≈ <medial> 063A غ

FED1 ﻑ ARABIC LETTER FEH ISOLATED FORM
≈ <isolated> 0641 ف

FED2 ﻒ ARABIC LETTER FEH FINAL FORM
≈ <final> 0641 ف

FED3 ﻓ ARABIC LETTER FEH INITIAL FORM
≈ <initial> 0641 ف

FED4 ﻔ ARABIC LETTER FEH MEDIAL FORM
≈ <medial> 0641 ف

FED5 ﻕ ARABIC LETTER QAF ISOLATED FORM
≈ <isolated> 0642 ق

FED6 ﻖ ARABIC LETTER QAF FINAL FORM
≈ <final> 0642 ق

FED7 ﻗ ARABIC LETTER QAF INITIAL FORM
≈ <initial> 0642 ق

FED8 ﻘ ARABIC LETTER QAF MEDIAL FORM
≈ <medial> 0642 ق

FED9 ﻙ ARABIC LETTER KAF ISOLATED FORM
≈ <isolated> 0643 ك

FEDA ﻚ ARABIC LETTER KAF FINAL FORM
≈ <final> 0643 ك

FEDB ﻛ ARABIC LETTER KAF INITIAL FORM
≈ <initial> 0643 ك

FEDC ﻜ ARABIC LETTER KAF MEDIAL FORM
≈ <medial> 0643 ك

FEDD ﻝ ARABIC LETTER LAM ISOLATED FORM
≈ <isolated> 0644 ل

FEDE ﻞ ARABIC LETTER LAM FINAL FORM
≈ <final> 0644 ل

FEDF ﻟ ARABIC LETTER LAM INITIAL FORM
≈ <initial> 0644 ل

FEE0 ﻠ ARABIC LETTER LAM MEDIAL FORM
≈ <medial> 0644 ل

FEE1 ﻡ ARABIC LETTER MEEM ISOLATED FORM
≈ <isolated> 0645 م
FEE2 ﻢ ARABIC LETTER MEEM FINAL FORM
≈ <final> 0645 م
FEE3 ﻣ ARABIC LETTER MEEM INITIAL FORM
≈ <initial> 0645 م
FEE4 ﻤ ARABIC LETTER MEEM MEDIAL FORM
≈ <medial> 0645 م
FEE5 ﻥ ARABIC LETTER NOON ISOLATED FORM
≈ <isolated> 0646 ن
FEE6 ﻦ ARABIC LETTER NOON FINAL FORM
≈ <final> 0646 ن
FEE7 ﻧ ARABIC LETTER NOON INITIAL FORM
≈ <initial> 0646 ن
FEE8 ﻨ ARABIC LETTER NOON MEDIAL FORM
≈ <medial> 0646 ن
FEE9 ﻩ ARABIC LETTER HEH ISOLATED FORM
≈ <isolated> 0647 ه
FEEA ﻪ ARABIC LETTER HEH FINAL FORM
≈ <final> 0647 ه
FEEB ﻫ ARABIC LETTER HEH INITIAL FORM
≈ <initial> 0647 ه
FEEC ﻬ ARABIC LETTER HEH MEDIAL FORM
≈ <medial> 0647 ه
FEED ﻭ ARABIC LETTER WAW ISOLATED FORM
≈ <isolated> 0648 و
FEEE ﻮ ARABIC LETTER WAW FINAL FORM
≈ <final> 0648 و
FEEF ﻯ ARABIC LETTER ALEF MAKSURA ISOLATED FORM
≈ <isolated> 0649 ى
FEF0 ﻰ ARABIC LETTER ALEF MAKSURA FINAL FORM
≈ <final> 0649 ى
FEF1 ﻱ ARABIC LETTER YEH ISOLATED FORM
≈ <isolated> 064A ي
FEF2 ﻲ ARABIC LETTER YEH FINAL FORM
≈ <final> 064A ي
FEF3 ﻳ ARABIC LETTER YEH INITIAL FORM
≈ <initial> 064A ي
FEF4 ﻴ ARABIC LETTER YEH MEDIAL FORM
≈ <medial> 064A ي
FEF5 ﻵ ARABIC LIGATURE LAM WITH ALEF WITH MADDA ABOVE ISOLATED FORM
≈ <isolated> 0644 ل 0622 آ
FEF6 ﻶ ARABIC LIGATURE LAM WITH ALEF WITH MADDA ABOVE FINAL FORM
≈ <final> 0644 ل 0622 آ
FEF7 ﻷ ARABIC LIGATURE LAM WITH ALEF WITH HAMZA ABOVE ISOLATED FORM
≈ <isolated> 0644 ل 0623 أ
FEF8 ﻸ ARABIC LIGATURE LAM WITH ALEF WITH HAMZA ABOVE FINAL FORM
≈ <final> 0644 ل 0623 أ
FEF9 ﻹ ARABIC LIGATURE LAM WITH ALEF WITH HAMZA BELOW ISOLATED FORM
≈ <isolated> 0644 ل 0625 إ
FEFA ﻺ ARABIC LIGATURE LAM WITH ALEF WITH HAMZA BELOW FINAL FORM
≈ <final> 0644 ل 0625 إ
FEFB ﻻ ARABIC LIGATURE LAM WITH ALEF ISOLATED FORM
≈ <isolated> 0644 ل 0627 ا
FEFC ﻼ ARABIC LIGATURE LAM WITH ALEF FINAL FORM
≈ <final> 0644 ل 0627 ا

Special

FEFF [ZWNBSP] ZERO WIDTH NO-BREAK SPACE
= BYTE ORDER MARK (BOM), ZWNBSP
• may be used to detect byte order by contrast with the noncharacter code point FFFE
• use as an indication of non-breaking is deprecated; see 2060 [WJ] instead
→ 200B [ZWSP] zero width space
→ 2060 [WJ] word joiner
→ FFFE <not a character>

	FF0	FF1	FF2	FF3	FF4	FF5	FF6	FF7	FF8	FF9	FFA	FFB	FFC	FFD	FFE
0		０ FF10	＠ FF20	Ｐ FF30	｀ FF40	ｐ FF50	｠ FF60	ｰ FF70	ﾀ FF80	ﾐ FF90	HW HF FFA0	ﾰ FFB0			￠ FFE0
1	！ FF01	１ FF11	Ａ FF21	Ｑ FF31	ａ FF41	ｑ FF51	｡ FF61	ｱ FF71	ﾁ FF81	ﾑ FF91	ﾡ FFA1	ﾱ FFB1			￡ FFE1
2	＂ FF02	２ FF12	Ｂ FF22	Ｒ FF32	ｂ FF42	ｒ FF52	｢ FF62	ｲ FF72	ﾂ FF82	ﾒ FF92	ﾢ FFA2	ﾲ FFB2	ￂ FFC2	ￒ FFD2	￢ FFE2
3	＃ FF03	３ FF13	Ｃ FF23	Ｓ FF33	ｃ FF43	ｓ FF53	｣ FF63	ｳ FF73	ﾃ FF83	ﾓ FF93	ﾣ FFA3	ﾳ FFB3	ￃ FFC3	ￓ FFD3	￣ FFE3
4	＄ FF04	４ FF14	Ｄ FF24	Ｔ FF34	ｄ FF44	ｔ FF54	､ FF64	ｴ FF74	ﾄ FF84	ﾔ FF94	ﾤ FFA4	ﾴ FFB4	ￄ FFC4	ￔ FFD4	￤ FFE4
5	％ FF05	５ FF15	Ｅ FF25	Ｕ FF35	ｅ FF45	ｕ FF55	･ FF65	ｵ FF75	ﾅ FF85	ﾕ FF95	ﾥ FFA5	ﾵ FFB5	ￅ FFC5	ￕ FFD5	￥ FFE5
6	＆ FF06	６ FF16	Ｆ FF26	Ｖ FF36	ｆ FF46	ｖ FF56	ｦ FF66	ｶ FF76	ﾆ FF86	ﾖ FF96	ﾦ FFA6	ﾶ FFB6	ￆ FFC6	ￖ FFD6	￦ FFE6
7	＇ FF07	７ FF17	Ｇ FF27	Ｗ FF37	ｇ FF47	ｗ FF57	ｧ FF67	ｷ FF77	ﾇ FF87	ﾗ FF97	ﾧ FFA7	ﾷ FFB7	ￇ FFC7	ￗ FFD7	
8	（ FF08	８ FF18	Ｈ FF28	Ｘ FF38	ｈ FF48	ｘ FF58	ｨ FF68	ｸ FF78	ﾈ FF88	ﾘ FF98	ﾨ FFA8	ﾸ FFB8			￨ FFE8
9	） FF09	９ FF19	Ｉ FF29	Ｙ FF39	ｉ FF49	ｙ FF59	ｩ FF69	ｹ FF79	ﾉ FF89	ﾙ FF99	ﾩ FFA9	ﾹ FFB9			￩ FFE9
A	＊ FF0A	： FF1A	Ｊ FF2A	Ｚ FF3A	ｊ FF4A	ｚ FF5A	ｪ FF6A	ｺ FF7A	ﾊ FF8A	ﾚ FF9A	ﾪ FFAA	ﾺ FFBA	ￊ FFCA	ￚ FFDA	￪ FFEA
B	＋ FF0B	； FF1B	Ｋ FF2B	［ FF3B	ｋ FF4B	｛ FF5B	ｫ FF6B	ｻ FF7B	ﾋ FF8B	ﾛ FF9B	ﾫ FFAB	ﾻ FFBB	ￋ FFCB	ￛ FFDB	￫ FFEB
C	， FF0C	＜ FF1C	Ｌ FF2C	＼ FF3C	ｌ FF4C	｜ FF5C	ｬ FF6C	ｼ FF7C	ﾌ FF8C	ﾜ FF9C	ﾬ FFAC	ﾼ FFBC	ￌ FFCC	ￜ FFDC	￬ FFEC
D	－ FF0D	＝ FF1D	Ｍ FF2D	］ FF3D	ｍ FF4D	｝ FF5D	ｭ FF6D	ｽ FF7D	ﾍ FF8D	ﾝ FF9D	ﾭ FFAD	ﾽ FFBD	ￍ FFCD		￭ FFED
E	． FF0E	＞ FF1E	Ｎ FF2E	＾ FF3E	ｎ FF4E	～ FF5E	ｮ FF6E	ｾ FF7E	ﾎ FF8E	ﾞ FF9E	ﾮ FFAE	ﾾ FFBE	ￎ FFCE		￮ FFEE
F	／ FF0F	？ FF1F	Ｏ FF2F	＿ FF3F	ｏ FF4F	｟ FF5F	ｯ FF6F	ｿ FF7F	ﾏ FF8F	ﾟ FF9F	ﾯ FFAF		ￏ FFCF		

Fullwidth ASCII variants

See ASCII 0020 - 007E

FF01 ！ FULLWIDTH EXCLAMATION MARK
≈ <wide> 0021 !

FF02 ＂ FULLWIDTH QUOTATION MARK
≈ <wide> 0022 "

FF03 ＃ FULLWIDTH NUMBER SIGN
≈ <wide> 0023 #

FF04 ＄ FULLWIDTH DOLLAR SIGN
≈ <wide> 0024 $

FF05 ％ FULLWIDTH PERCENT SIGN
≈ <wide> 0025 %

FF06 ＆ FULLWIDTH AMPERSAND
≈ <wide> 0026 &

FF07 ＇ FULLWIDTH APOSTROPHE
≈ <wide> 0027 '

FF08 （ FULLWIDTH LEFT PARENTHESIS
≈ <wide> 0028 (

FF09 ） FULLWIDTH RIGHT PARENTHESIS
≈ <wide> 0029)

FF0A ＊ FULLWIDTH ASTERISK
≈ <wide> 002A *

FF0B ＋ FULLWIDTH PLUS SIGN
≈ <wide> 002B +

FF0C ， FULLWIDTH COMMA
≈ <wide> 002C ,

FF0D － FULLWIDTH HYPHEN-MINUS
≈ <wide> 002D -

FF0E ． FULLWIDTH FULL STOP
≈ <wide> 002E .

FF0F ／ FULLWIDTH SOLIDUS
≈ <wide> 002F /

FF10 ０ FULLWIDTH DIGIT ZERO
≈ <wide> 0030 0

FF11 １ FULLWIDTH DIGIT ONE
≈ <wide> 0031 1

FF12 ２ FULLWIDTH DIGIT TWO
≈ <wide> 0032 2

FF13 ３ FULLWIDTH DIGIT THREE
≈ <wide> 0033 3

FF14 ４ FULLWIDTH DIGIT FOUR
≈ <wide> 0034 4

FF15 ５ FULLWIDTH DIGIT FIVE
≈ <wide> 0035 5

FF16 ６ FULLWIDTH DIGIT SIX
≈ <wide> 0036 6

FF17 ７ FULLWIDTH DIGIT SEVEN
≈ <wide> 0037 7

FF18 ８ FULLWIDTH DIGIT EIGHT
≈ <wide> 0038 8

FF19 ９ FULLWIDTH DIGIT NINE
≈ <wide> 0039 9

FF1A ： FULLWIDTH COLON
≈ <wide> 003A :

FF1B ； FULLWIDTH SEMICOLON
≈ <wide> 003B ;

FF1C ＜ FULLWIDTH LESS-THAN SIGN
≈ <wide> 003C <

FF1D ＝ FULLWIDTH EQUALS SIGN
≈ <wide> 003D =

FF1E ＞ FULLWIDTH GREATER-THAN SIGN
≈ <wide> 003E >

FF1F ？ FULLWIDTH QUESTION MARK
≈ <wide> 003F ?

FF20 ＠ FULLWIDTH COMMERCIAL AT
≈ <wide> 0040 @

FF21 Ａ FULLWIDTH LATIN CAPITAL LETTER A
≈ <wide> 0041 A

FF22 Ｂ FULLWIDTH LATIN CAPITAL LETTER B
≈ <wide> 0042 B

FF23 Ｃ FULLWIDTH LATIN CAPITAL LETTER C
≈ <wide> 0043 C

FF24 Ｄ FULLWIDTH LATIN CAPITAL LETTER D
≈ <wide> 0044 D

FF25 Ｅ FULLWIDTH LATIN CAPITAL LETTER E
≈ <wide> 0045 E

FF26 Ｆ FULLWIDTH LATIN CAPITAL LETTER F
≈ <wide> 0046 F

FF27 Ｇ FULLWIDTH LATIN CAPITAL LETTER G
≈ <wide> 0047 G

FF28 Ｈ FULLWIDTH LATIN CAPITAL LETTER H
≈ <wide> 0048 H

FF29 Ｉ FULLWIDTH LATIN CAPITAL LETTER I
≈ <wide> 0049 I

FF2A Ｊ FULLWIDTH LATIN CAPITAL LETTER J
≈ <wide> 004A J

FF2B Ｋ FULLWIDTH LATIN CAPITAL LETTER K
≈ <wide> 004B K

FF2C Ｌ FULLWIDTH LATIN CAPITAL LETTER L
≈ <wide> 004C L

FF2D Ｍ FULLWIDTH LATIN CAPITAL LETTER M
≈ <wide> 004D M

FF2E Ｎ FULLWIDTH LATIN CAPITAL LETTER N
≈ <wide> 004E N

FF2F Ｏ FULLWIDTH LATIN CAPITAL LETTER O
≈ <wide> 004F O

FF30 Ｐ FULLWIDTH LATIN CAPITAL LETTER P
≈ <wide> 0050 P

FF31 Ｑ FULLWIDTH LATIN CAPITAL LETTER Q
≈ <wide> 0051 Q

FF32 Ｒ FULLWIDTH LATIN CAPITAL LETTER R
≈ <wide> 0052 R

FF33 Ｓ FULLWIDTH LATIN CAPITAL LETTER S
≈ <wide> 0053 S

FF34 Ｔ FULLWIDTH LATIN CAPITAL LETTER T
≈ <wide> 0054 T

FF35 Ｕ FULLWIDTH LATIN CAPITAL LETTER U
≈ <wide> 0055 U

FF36 Ｖ FULLWIDTH LATIN CAPITAL LETTER V
≈ <wide> 0056 V

FF37 Ｗ FULLWIDTH LATIN CAPITAL LETTER W
≈ <wide> 0057 W

FF38 Ｘ FULLWIDTH LATIN CAPITAL LETTER X
≈ <wide> 0058 X

FF39 Ｙ FULLWIDTH LATIN CAPITAL LETTER Y
≈ <wide> 0059 Y

FF3A Ｚ FULLWIDTH LATIN CAPITAL LETTER Z
≈ <wide> 005A Z

FF3B ［ FULLWIDTH LEFT SQUARE BRACKET
≈ <wide> 005B [

FF3C ＼ FULLWIDTH REVERSE SOLIDUS
≈ <wide> 005C \

FF3D ］ FULLWIDTH RIGHT SQUARE BRACKET
≈ <wide> 005D]

FF3E ＾ FULLWIDTH CIRCUMFLEX ACCENT
≈ <wide> 005E ^
FF3F ＿ FULLWIDTH LOW LINE
≈ <wide> 005F _
FF40 ｀ FULLWIDTH GRAVE ACCENT
≈ <wide> 0060 `
FF41 ａ FULLWIDTH LATIN SMALL LETTER A
≈ <wide> 0061 a
FF42 ｂ FULLWIDTH LATIN SMALL LETTER B
≈ <wide> 0062 b
FF43 ｃ FULLWIDTH LATIN SMALL LETTER C
≈ <wide> 0063 c
FF44 ｄ FULLWIDTH LATIN SMALL LETTER D
≈ <wide> 0064 d
FF45 ｅ FULLWIDTH LATIN SMALL LETTER E
≈ <wide> 0065 e
FF46 ｆ FULLWIDTH LATIN SMALL LETTER F
≈ <wide> 0066 f
FF47 ｇ FULLWIDTH LATIN SMALL LETTER G
≈ <wide> 0067 g
FF48 ｈ FULLWIDTH LATIN SMALL LETTER H
≈ <wide> 0068 h
FF49 ｉ FULLWIDTH LATIN SMALL LETTER I
≈ <wide> 0069 i
FF4A ｊ FULLWIDTH LATIN SMALL LETTER J
≈ <wide> 006A j
FF4B ｋ FULLWIDTH LATIN SMALL LETTER K
≈ <wide> 006B k
FF4C ｌ FULLWIDTH LATIN SMALL LETTER L
≈ <wide> 006C l
FF4D ｍ FULLWIDTH LATIN SMALL LETTER M
≈ <wide> 006D m
FF4E ｎ FULLWIDTH LATIN SMALL LETTER N
≈ <wide> 006E n
FF4F ｏ FULLWIDTH LATIN SMALL LETTER O
≈ <wide> 006F o
FF50 ｐ FULLWIDTH LATIN SMALL LETTER P
≈ <wide> 0070 p
FF51 ｑ FULLWIDTH LATIN SMALL LETTER Q
≈ <wide> 0071 q
FF52 ｒ FULLWIDTH LATIN SMALL LETTER R
≈ <wide> 0072 r
FF53 ｓ FULLWIDTH LATIN SMALL LETTER S
≈ <wide> 0073 s
FF54 ｔ FULLWIDTH LATIN SMALL LETTER T
≈ <wide> 0074 t
FF55 ｕ FULLWIDTH LATIN SMALL LETTER U
≈ <wide> 0075 u
FF56 ｖ FULLWIDTH LATIN SMALL LETTER V
≈ <wide> 0076 v
FF57 ｗ FULLWIDTH LATIN SMALL LETTER W
≈ <wide> 0077 w
FF58 ｘ FULLWIDTH LATIN SMALL LETTER X
≈ <wide> 0078 x
FF59 ｙ FULLWIDTH LATIN SMALL LETTER Y
≈ <wide> 0079 y
FF5A ｚ FULLWIDTH LATIN SMALL LETTER Z
≈ <wide> 007A z
FF5B ｛ FULLWIDTH LEFT CURLY BRACKET
≈ <wide> 007B {
FF5C ｜ FULLWIDTH VERTICAL LINE
≈ <wide> 007C |
FF5D ｝ FULLWIDTH RIGHT CURLY BRACKET
≈ <wide> 007D }
FF5E ～ FULLWIDTH TILDE
≈ <wide> 007E ~

Fullwidth brackets

FF5F ｟ FULLWIDTH LEFT WHITE PARENTHESIS
≈ <wide> 2985 ⦅
FF60 ｠ FULLWIDTH RIGHT WHITE PARENTHESIS
• the most commonly occurring glyph variant looks like doubled parentheses
≈ <wide> 2986 ⦆

Halfwidth CJK punctuation

See CJK punctuation 3000 - 303F

FF61 ｡ HALFWIDTH IDEOGRAPHIC FULL STOP
≈ <narrow> 3002 。
FF62 ｢ HALFWIDTH LEFT CORNER BRACKET
≈ <narrow> 300C 「
FF63 ｣ HALFWIDTH RIGHT CORNER BRACKET
≈ <narrow> 300D 」
FF64 ､ HALFWIDTH IDEOGRAPHIC COMMA
≈ <narrow> 3001 、

Halfwidth Katakana variants

See Katakana 30A0 - 30FF

FF65 ･ HALFWIDTH KATAKANA MIDDLE DOT
≈ <narrow> 30FB ・
FF66 ｦ HALFWIDTH KATAKANA LETTER WO
≈ <narrow> 30F2 ヲ
FF67 ｧ HALFWIDTH KATAKANA LETTER SMALL A
≈ <narrow> 30A1 ァ
FF68 ｨ HALFWIDTH KATAKANA LETTER SMALL I
≈ <narrow> 30A3 ィ
FF69 ｩ HALFWIDTH KATAKANA LETTER SMALL U
≈ <narrow> 30A5 ゥ
FF6A ｪ HALFWIDTH KATAKANA LETTER SMALL E
≈ <narrow> 30A7 ェ
FF6B ｫ HALFWIDTH KATAKANA LETTER SMALL O
≈ <narrow> 30A9 ォ
FF6C ｬ HALFWIDTH KATAKANA LETTER SMALL YA
≈ <narrow> 30E3 ャ
FF6D ｭ HALFWIDTH KATAKANA LETTER SMALL YU
≈ <narrow> 30E5 ュ
FF6E ｮ HALFWIDTH KATAKANA LETTER SMALL YO
≈ <narrow> 30E7 ョ
FF6F ｯ HALFWIDTH KATAKANA LETTER SMALL TU
≈ <narrow> 30C3 ッ
FF70 ｰ HALFWIDTH KATAKANA-HIRAGANA PROLONGED SOUND MARK
≈ <narrow> 30FC ー
FF71 ｱ HALFWIDTH KATAKANA LETTER A
≈ <narrow> 30A2 ア
FF72 ｲ HALFWIDTH KATAKANA LETTER I
≈ <narrow> 30A4 イ
FF73 ｳ HALFWIDTH KATAKANA LETTER U
≈ <narrow> 30A6 ウ
FF74 ｴ HALFWIDTH KATAKANA LETTER E
≈ <narrow> 30A8 エ
FF75 ｵ HALFWIDTH KATAKANA LETTER O
≈ <narrow> 30AA オ
FF76 ｶ HALFWIDTH KATAKANA LETTER KA
≈ <narrow> 30AB カ
FF77 ｷ HALFWIDTH KATAKANA LETTER KI
≈ <narrow> 30AD キ

FF78 ｸ HALFWIDTH KATAKANA LETTER KU
≈ <narrow> 30AF ク
FF79 ｹ HALFWIDTH KATAKANA LETTER KE
≈ <narrow> 30B1 ケ
FF7A ｺ HALFWIDTH KATAKANA LETTER KO
≈ <narrow> 30B3 コ
FF7B ｻ HALFWIDTH KATAKANA LETTER SA
≈ <narrow> 30B5 サ
FF7C ｼ HALFWIDTH KATAKANA LETTER SI
≈ <narrow> 30B7 シ
FF7D ｽ HALFWIDTH KATAKANA LETTER SU
≈ <narrow> 30B9 ス
FF7E ｾ HALFWIDTH KATAKANA LETTER SE
≈ <narrow> 30BB セ
FF7F ｿ HALFWIDTH KATAKANA LETTER SO
≈ <narrow> 30BD ソ
FF80 ﾀ HALFWIDTH KATAKANA LETTER TA
≈ <narrow> 30BF タ
FF81 ﾁ HALFWIDTH KATAKANA LETTER TI
≈ <narrow> 30C1 チ
FF82 ﾂ HALFWIDTH KATAKANA LETTER TU
≈ <narrow> 30C4 ツ
FF83 ﾃ HALFWIDTH KATAKANA LETTER TE
≈ <narrow> 30C6 テ
FF84 ﾄ HALFWIDTH KATAKANA LETTER TO
≈ <narrow> 30C8 ト
FF85 ﾅ HALFWIDTH KATAKANA LETTER NA
≈ <narrow> 30CA ナ
FF86 ﾆ HALFWIDTH KATAKANA LETTER NI
≈ <narrow> 30CB ニ
FF87 ﾇ HALFWIDTH KATAKANA LETTER NU
≈ <narrow> 30CC ヌ
FF88 ﾈ HALFWIDTH KATAKANA LETTER NE
≈ <narrow> 30CD ネ
FF89 ﾉ HALFWIDTH KATAKANA LETTER NO
≈ <narrow> 30CE ノ
FF8A ﾊ HALFWIDTH KATAKANA LETTER HA
≈ <narrow> 30CF ハ
FF8B ﾋ HALFWIDTH KATAKANA LETTER HI
≈ <narrow> 30D2 ヒ
FF8C ﾌ HALFWIDTH KATAKANA LETTER HU
≈ <narrow> 30D5 フ
FF8D ﾍ HALFWIDTH KATAKANA LETTER HE
≈ <narrow> 30D8 ヘ
FF8E ﾎ HALFWIDTH KATAKANA LETTER HO
≈ <narrow> 30DB ホ
FF8F ﾏ HALFWIDTH KATAKANA LETTER MA
≈ <narrow> 30DE マ
FF90 ﾐ HALFWIDTH KATAKANA LETTER MI
≈ <narrow> 30DF ミ
FF91 ﾑ HALFWIDTH KATAKANA LETTER MU
≈ <narrow> 30E0 ム
FF92 ﾒ HALFWIDTH KATAKANA LETTER ME
≈ <narrow> 30E1 メ
FF93 ﾓ HALFWIDTH KATAKANA LETTER MO
≈ <narrow> 30E2 モ
FF94 ﾔ HALFWIDTH KATAKANA LETTER YA
≈ <narrow> 30E4 ヤ
FF95 ﾕ HALFWIDTH KATAKANA LETTER YU
≈ <narrow> 30E6 ユ
FF96 ﾖ HALFWIDTH KATAKANA LETTER YO
≈ <narrow> 30E8 ヨ
FF97 ﾗ HALFWIDTH KATAKANA LETTER RA
≈ <narrow> 30E9 ラ
FF98 ﾘ HALFWIDTH KATAKANA LETTER RI
≈ <narrow> 30EA リ
FF99 ﾙ HALFWIDTH KATAKANA LETTER RU
≈ <narrow> 30EB ル
FF9A ﾚ HALFWIDTH KATAKANA LETTER RE
≈ <narrow> 30EC レ
FF9B ﾛ HALFWIDTH KATAKANA LETTER RO
≈ <narrow> 30ED ロ
FF9C ﾜ HALFWIDTH KATAKANA LETTER WA
≈ <narrow> 30EF ワ
FF9D ﾝ HALFWIDTH KATAKANA LETTER N
≈ <narrow> 30F3 ン
FF9E ﾞ HALFWIDTH KATAKANA VOICED SOUND MARK
≈ <narrow> 3099 ◌゙
FF9F ﾟ HALFWIDTH KATAKANA SEMI-VOICED SOUND MARK
≈ <narrow> 309A ◌゚

Halfwidth Hangul variants

See Hangul Compatibility Jamo 3130 - 318F

FFA0 ﾠ HALFWIDTH HANGUL FILLER
≈ <narrow> 3164 ㅤ
FFA1 ﾡ HALFWIDTH HANGUL LETTER KIYEOK
≈ <narrow> 3131 ㄱ
FFA2 ﾢ HALFWIDTH HANGUL LETTER SSANGKIYEOK
≈ <narrow> 3132 ㄲ
FFA3 ﾣ HALFWIDTH HANGUL LETTER KIYEOK-SIOS
≈ <narrow> 3133 ㄳ
FFA4 ﾤ HALFWIDTH HANGUL LETTER NIEUN
≈ <narrow> 3134 ㄴ
FFA5 ﾥ HALFWIDTH HANGUL LETTER NIEUN-CIEUC
≈ <narrow> 3135 ㄵ
FFA6 ﾦ HALFWIDTH HANGUL LETTER NIEUN-HIEUH
≈ <narrow> 3136 ㄶ
FFA7 ﾧ HALFWIDTH HANGUL LETTER TIKEUT
≈ <narrow> 3137 ㄷ
FFA8 ﾨ HALFWIDTH HANGUL LETTER SSANGTIKEUT
≈ <narrow> 3138 ㄸ
FFA9 ﾩ HALFWIDTH HANGUL LETTER RIEUL
≈ <narrow> 3139 ㄹ
FFAA ﾪ HALFWIDTH HANGUL LETTER RIEUL-KIYEOK
≈ <narrow> 313A ㄺ
FFAB ﾫ HALFWIDTH HANGUL LETTER RIEUL-MIEUM
≈ <narrow> 313B ㄻ
FFAC ﾬ HALFWIDTH HANGUL LETTER RIEUL-PIEUP
≈ <narrow> 313C ㄼ
FFAD ﾭ HALFWIDTH HANGUL LETTER RIEUL-SIOS
≈ <narrow> 313D ㄽ
FFAE ﾮ HALFWIDTH HANGUL LETTER RIEUL-THIEUTH
≈ <narrow> 313E ㄾ
FFAF ﾯ HALFWIDTH HANGUL LETTER RIEUL-PHIEUPH
≈ <narrow> 313F ㄿ
FFB0 ﾰ HALFWIDTH HANGUL LETTER RIEUL-HIEUH
≈ <narrow> 3140 ㅀ
FFB1 ﾱ HALFWIDTH HANGUL LETTER MIEUM
≈ <narrow> 3141 ㅁ
FFB2 ﾲ HALFWIDTH HANGUL LETTER PIEUP
≈ <narrow> 3142 ㅂ
FFB3 ﾳ HALFWIDTH HANGUL LETTER SSANGPIEUP
≈ <narrow> 3143 ㅃ

FFB4 ﾴ HALFWIDTH HANGUL LETTER PIEUP-SIOS
≈ <narrow> 3144 ㅄ

FFB5 ﾵ HALFWIDTH HANGUL LETTER SIOS
≈ <narrow> 3145 ㅅ

FFB6 ﾶ HALFWIDTH HANGUL LETTER SSANGSIOS
≈ <narrow> 3146 ㅆ

FFB7 ﾷ HALFWIDTH HANGUL LETTER IEUNG
≈ <narrow> 3147 ㅇ

FFB8 ﾸ HALFWIDTH HANGUL LETTER CIEUC
≈ <narrow> 3148 ㅈ

FFB9 ﾹ HALFWIDTH HANGUL LETTER SSANGCIEUC
≈ <narrow> 3149 ㅉ

FFBA ﾺ HALFWIDTH HANGUL LETTER CHIEUCH
≈ <narrow> 314A ㅊ

FFBB ﾻ HALFWIDTH HANGUL LETTER KHIEUKH
≈ <narrow> 314B ㅋ

FFBC ﾼ HALFWIDTH HANGUL LETTER THIEUTH
≈ <narrow> 314C ㅌ

FFBD ﾽ HALFWIDTH HANGUL LETTER PHIEUPH
≈ <narrow> 314D ㅍ

FFBE ﾾ HALFWIDTH HANGUL LETTER HIEUH
≈ <narrow> 314E ㅎ

FFBF <reserved>

FFC0 <reserved>

FFC1 <reserved>

FFC2 ￂ HALFWIDTH HANGUL LETTER A
≈ <narrow> 314F ㅏ

FFC3 ￃ HALFWIDTH HANGUL LETTER AE
≈ <narrow> 3150 ㅐ

FFC4 ￄ HALFWIDTH HANGUL LETTER YA
≈ <narrow> 3151 ㅑ

FFC5 ￅ HALFWIDTH HANGUL LETTER YAE
≈ <narrow> 3152 ㅒ

FFC6 ￆ HALFWIDTH HANGUL LETTER EO
≈ <narrow> 3153 ㅓ

FFC7 ￇ HALFWIDTH HANGUL LETTER E
≈ <narrow> 3154 ㅔ

FFC8 <reserved>

FFC9 <reserved>

FFCA ￊ HALFWIDTH HANGUL LETTER YEO
≈ <narrow> 3155 ㅕ

FFCB ￋ HALFWIDTH HANGUL LETTER YE
≈ <narrow> 3156 ㅖ

FFCC ￌ HALFWIDTH HANGUL LETTER O
≈ <narrow> 3157 ㅗ

FFCD ￍ HALFWIDTH HANGUL LETTER WA
≈ <narrow> 3158 ㅘ

FFCE ￎ HALFWIDTH HANGUL LETTER WAE
≈ <narrow> 3159 ㅙ

FFCF ￏ HALFWIDTH HANGUL LETTER OE
≈ <narrow> 315A ㅚ

FFD0 <reserved>

FFD1 <reserved>

FFD2 ￒ HALFWIDTH HANGUL LETTER YO
≈ <narrow> 315B ㅛ

FFD3 ￓ HALFWIDTH HANGUL LETTER U
≈ <narrow> 315C ㅜ

FFD4 ￔ HALFWIDTH HANGUL LETTER WEO
≈ <narrow> 315D ㅝ

FFD5 ￕ HALFWIDTH HANGUL LETTER WE
≈ <narrow> 315E ㅞ

FFD6 ￖ HALFWIDTH HANGUL LETTER WI
≈ <narrow> 315F ㅟ

FFD7 ￗ HALFWIDTH HANGUL LETTER YU
≈ <narrow> 3160 ㅠ

FFD8 <reserved>

FFD9 <reserved>

FFDA ￚ HALFWIDTH HANGUL LETTER EU
≈ <narrow> 3161 ㅡ

FFDB ￛ HALFWIDTH HANGUL LETTER YI
≈ <narrow> 3162 ㅢ

FFDC ￜ HALFWIDTH HANGUL LETTER I
≈ <narrow> 3163 ㅣ

Fullwidth symbol variants

See Latin-1 00A0 - 00FF

FFE0 ￠ FULLWIDTH CENT SIGN
≈ <wide> 00A2 ¢

FFE1 ￡ FULLWIDTH POUND SIGN
≈ <wide> 00A3 £

FFE2 ￢ FULLWIDTH NOT SIGN
≈ <wide> 00AC ¬

FFE3 ￣ FULLWIDTH MACRON
• sometimes treated as fullwidth overline
→ 203E ‾ overline
≈ <wide> 00AF ¯

FFE4 ￤ FULLWIDTH BROKEN BAR
≈ <wide> 00A6 ¦

FFE5 ￥ FULLWIDTH YEN SIGN
≈ <wide> 00A5 ¥

FFE6 ￦ FULLWIDTH WON SIGN
≈ <wide> 20A9 ₩

Halfwidth symbol variants

FFE8 ￨ HALFWIDTH FORMS LIGHT VERTICAL
≈ <narrow> 2502 │

FFE9 ￩ HALFWIDTH LEFTWARDS ARROW
≈ <narrow> 2190 ←

FFEA ￪ HALFWIDTH UPWARDS ARROW
≈ <narrow> 2191 ↑

FFEB ￫ HALFWIDTH RIGHTWARDS ARROW
≈ <narrow> 2192 →

FFEC ￬ HALFWIDTH DOWNWARDS ARROW
≈ <narrow> 2193 ↓

FFED ￭ HALFWIDTH BLACK SQUARE
≈ <narrow> 25A0 ■

FFEE ￮ HALFWIDTH WHITE CIRCLE
≈ <narrow> 25CB ○

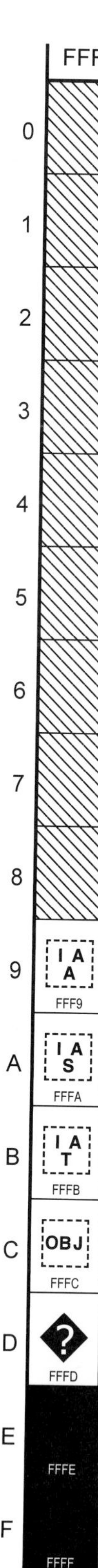

Interlinear annotation

Used internally for Japanese Ruby (furigana), etc.

FFF9 INTERLINEAR ANNOTATION ANCHOR
- marks start of annotated text

FFFA INTERLINEAR ANNOTATION SEPARATOR
- marks start of annotating character(s)

FFFB INTERLINEAR ANNOTATION TERMINATOR
- marks end of annotation block

Replacement characters

FFFC OBJECT REPLACEMENT CHARACTER
- used as placeholder in text for an otherwise unspecified object

FFFD � REPLACEMENT CHARACTER
- used to replace an incoming character whose value is unknown or unrepresentable in Unicode
- compare the use of 001A as a control character to indicate the substitute function

Noncharacters

These codes are intended for process-internal uses, but are not permitted for interchange.

FFFE <not a character>
- the value FFFE is guaranteed not to be a Unicode character at all
- may be used to detect byte order by contrast with FEFF which is a character

→ FEFF zero width no-break space

FFFF <not a character>
- the value FFFF is guaranteed not to be a Unicode character at all

	1000	1001	1002	1003	1004	1005	1006	1007
0	10000	10010	10020	10030	10040	10050		
1	10001	10011	10021	10031	10041	10051		
2	10002	10012	10022	10032	10042	10052		
3	10003	10013	10023	10033	10043	10053		
4	10004	10014	10024	10034	10044	10054		
5	10005	10015	10025	10035	10045	10055		
6	10006	10016	10026	10036	10046	10056		
7	10007	10017		10037	10047	10057		
8	10008	10018	10028	10038	10048	10058		
9	10009	10019	10029	10039	10049	10059		
A	1000A	1001A	1002A	1003A	1004A	1005A		
B	1000B	1001B	1002B		1004B	1005B		
C		1001C	1002C	1003C	1004C	1005C		
D	1000D	1001D	1002D	1003D	1004D	1005D		
E	1000E	1001E	1002E					
F	1000F	1001F	1002F	1003F				

Basic syllables

10000 𐀀 LINEAR B SYLLABLE B008 A
10001 𐀁 LINEAR B SYLLABLE B038 E
10002 𐀂 LINEAR B SYLLABLE B028 I
10003 𐀃 LINEAR B SYLLABLE B061 O
10004 𐀄 LINEAR B SYLLABLE B010 U
10005 𐀅 LINEAR B SYLLABLE B001 DA
10006 𐀆 LINEAR B SYLLABLE B045 DE
10007 𐀇 LINEAR B SYLLABLE B007 DI
10008 𐀈 LINEAR B SYLLABLE B014 DO
10009 𐀉 LINEAR B SYLLABLE B051 DU
1000A 𐀊 LINEAR B SYLLABLE B057 JA
1000B 𐀋 LINEAR B SYLLABLE B046 JE
1000C <reserved>
1000D 𐀍 LINEAR B SYLLABLE B036 JO
1000E 𐀎 LINEAR B SYLLABLE B065 JU
= ideogram B129 flour
1000F 𐀏 LINEAR B SYLLABLE B077 KA
10010 𐀐 LINEAR B SYLLABLE B044 KE
10011 𐀑 LINEAR B SYLLABLE B067 KI
10012 𐀒 LINEAR B SYLLABLE B070 KO
10013 𐀓 LINEAR B SYLLABLE B081 KU
10014 𐀔 LINEAR B SYLLABLE B080 MA
10015 𐀕 LINEAR B SYLLABLE B013 ME
10016 𐀖 LINEAR B SYLLABLE B073 MI
10017 𐀗 LINEAR B SYLLABLE B015 MO
10018 𐀘 LINEAR B SYLLABLE B023 MU
= ideogram B109 ox
10019 𐀙 LINEAR B SYLLABLE B006 NA
1001A 𐀚 LINEAR B SYLLABLE B024 NE
1001B 𐀛 LINEAR B SYLLABLE B030 NI
= ideogram B030 figs
1001C 𐀜 LINEAR B SYLLABLE B052 NO
1001D 𐀝 LINEAR B SYLLABLE B055 NU
1001E 𐀞 LINEAR B SYLLABLE B003 PA
1001F 𐀟 LINEAR B SYLLABLE B072 PE
10020 𐀠 LINEAR B SYLLABLE B039 PI
10021 𐀡 LINEAR B SYLLABLE B011 PO
10022 𐀢 LINEAR B SYLLABLE B050 PU
10023 𐀣 LINEAR B SYLLABLE B016 QA
10024 𐀤 LINEAR B SYLLABLE B078 QE
10025 𐀥 LINEAR B SYLLABLE B021 QI
= ideogram B106 sheep
10026 𐀦 LINEAR B SYLLABLE B032 QO
10027 <reserved>
10028 𐀨 LINEAR B SYLLABLE B060 RA
10029 𐀩 LINEAR B SYLLABLE B027 RE
1002A 𐀪 LINEAR B SYLLABLE B053 RI
1002B 𐀫 LINEAR B SYLLABLE B002 RO
1002C 𐀬 LINEAR B SYLLABLE B026 RU
1002D 𐀭 LINEAR B SYLLABLE B031 SA
= ideogram B031 flax
1002E 𐀮 LINEAR B SYLLABLE B009 SE
1002F 𐀯 LINEAR B SYLLABLE B041 SI
10030 𐀰 LINEAR B SYLLABLE B012 SO
10031 𐀱 LINEAR B SYLLABLE B058 SU
10032 𐀲 LINEAR B SYLLABLE B059 TA
10033 𐀳 LINEAR B SYLLABLE B004 TE
10034 𐀴 LINEAR B SYLLABLE B037 TI
10035 𐀵 LINEAR B SYLLABLE B005 TO
10036 𐀶 LINEAR B SYLLABLE B069 TU
10037 𐀷 LINEAR B SYLLABLE B054 WA
10038 𐀸 LINEAR B SYLLABLE B075 WE
10039 𐀹 LINEAR B SYLLABLE B040 WI
1003A 𐀺 LINEAR B SYLLABLE B042 WO
1003B <reserved>
1003C 𐀼 LINEAR B SYLLABLE B017 ZA
1003D 𐀽 LINEAR B SYLLABLE B074 ZE
1003E <reserved>
1003F 𐀿 LINEAR B SYLLABLE B020 ZO

Supplementary signs

10040 𐁀 LINEAR B SYLLABLE B025 A2
10041 𐁁 LINEAR B SYLLABLE B043 A3
10042 𐁂 LINEAR B SYLLABLE B085 AU
= ideogram B108 pig
10043 𐁃 LINEAR B SYLLABLE B071 DWE
10044 𐁄 LINEAR B SYLLABLE B090 DWO
10045 𐁅 LINEAR B SYLLABLE B048 NWA
10046 𐁆 LINEAR B SYLLABLE B029 PU2
10047 𐁇 LINEAR B SYLLABLE B062 PTE
10048 𐁈 LINEAR B SYLLABLE B076 RA2
10049 𐁉 LINEAR B SYLLABLE B033 RA3
= ideogram B144 saffron
1004A 𐁊 LINEAR B SYLLABLE B068 RO2
1004B 𐁋 LINEAR B SYLLABLE B066 TA2
1004C 𐁌 LINEAR B SYLLABLE B087 TWE
1004D 𐁍 LINEAR B SYLLABLE B091 TWO

Symbols

10050 𐁐 LINEAR B SYMBOL B018
10051 𐁑 LINEAR B SYMBOL B019
10052 𐁒 LINEAR B SYMBOL B022
= ideogram B107 goat
10053 𐁓 LINEAR B SYMBOL B034
10054 𐁔 LINEAR B SYMBOL B047
10055 𐁕 LINEAR B SYMBOL B049
10056 𐁖 LINEAR B SYMBOL B056
10057 𐁗 LINEAR B SYMBOL B063
10058 𐁘 LINEAR B SYMBOL B064
10059 𐁙 LINEAR B SYMBOL B079
1005A 𐁚 LINEAR B SYMBOL B082
1005B 𐁛 LINEAR B SYMBOL B083
1005C 𐁜 LINEAR B SYMBOL B086
1005D 𐁝 LINEAR B SYMBOL B089

	1008	1009	100A	100B	100C	100D	100E	100F
0	𐂀 10080	𐂐 10090	𐂠 100A0	𐂰 100B0	𐃀 100C0	𐃐 100D0	𐃠 100E0	𐃰 100F0
1	𐂁 10081	𐂑 10091	𐂡 100A1	𐂱 100B1	𐃁 100C1	𐃑 100D1	𐃡 100E1	𐃱 100F1
2	𐂂 10082	𐂒 10092	𐂢 100A2	𐂲 100B2	𐃂 100C2	𐃒 100D2	𐃢 100E2	𐃲 100F2
3	𐂃 10083	𐂓 10093	𐂣 100A3	𐂳 100B3	𐃃 100C3	𐃓 100D3	𐃣 100E3	𐃳 100F3
4	𐂄 10084	𐂔 10094	𐂤 100A4	𐂴 100B4	𐃄 100C4	𐃔 100D4	𐃤 100E4	𐃴 100F4
5	𐂅 10085	𐂕 10095	𐂥 100A5	𐂵 100B5	𐃅 100C5	𐃕 100D5	𐃥 100E5	𐃵 100F5
6	𐂆 10086	𐂖 10096	𐂦 100A6	𐂶 100B6	𐃆 100C6	𐃖 100D6	𐃦 100E6	𐃶 100F6
7	𐂇 10087	𐂗 10097	𐂧 100A7	𐂷 100B7	𐃇 100C7	𐃗 100D7	𐃧 100E7	𐃷 100F7
8	𐂈 10088	𐂘 10098	𐂨 100A8	𐂸 100B8	𐃈 100C8	𐃘 100D8	𐃨 100E8	𐃸 100F8
9	𐂉 10089	𐂙 10099	𐂩 100A9	𐂹 100B9	𐃉 100C9	𐃙 100D9	𐃩 100E9	𐃹 100F9
A	𐂊 1008A	𐂚 1009A	𐂪 100AA	𐂺 100BA	𐃊 100CA	𐃚 100DA	𐃪 100EA	𐃺 100FA
B	𐂋 1008B	𐂛 1009B	𐂫 100AB	𐂻 100BB	𐃋 100CB	𐃛 100DB	𐃫 100EB	
C	𐂌 1008C	𐂜 1009C	𐂬 100AC	𐂼 100BC	𐃌 100CC	𐃜 100DC	𐃬 100EC	
D	𐂍 1008D	𐂝 1009D	𐂭 100AD	𐂽 100BD	𐃍 100CD	𐃝 100DD	𐃭 100ED	
E	𐂎 1008E	𐂞 1009E	𐂮 100AE	𐂾 100BE	𐃎 100CE	𐃞 100DE	𐃮 100EE	
F	𐂏 1008F	𐂟 1009F	𐂯 100AF	𐂿 100BF	𐃏 100CF	𐃟 100DF	𐃯 100EF	

Some Linear B syllables are also used as Linear B ideograms.

→ 10025 𐀥 linear b syllable b021 qi
→ 10052 𐁒 linear b symbol b022
→ 10018 𐀘 linear b syllable b023 mu
→ 1001B 𐀛 linear b syllable b030 ni
→ 1002D 𐀭 linear b syllable b031 sa
→ 10049 𐁉 linear b syllable b033 ra3
→ 1000E 𐀎 linear b syllable b065 ju
→ 10042 𐁂 linear b syllable b085 au

People and animals

10080 𐂀 LINEAR B IDEOGRAM B100 MAN
10081 𐂁 LINEAR B IDEOGRAM B102 WOMAN
10082 𐂂 LINEAR B IDEOGRAM B104 DEER
10083 𐂃 LINEAR B IDEOGRAM B105 EQUID
10084 𐂄 LINEAR B IDEOGRAM B105F MARE
10085 𐂅 LINEAR B IDEOGRAM B105M STALLION
10086 𐂆 LINEAR B IDEOGRAM B106F EWE
10087 𐂇 LINEAR B IDEOGRAM B106M RAM
10088 𐂈 LINEAR B IDEOGRAM B107F SHE-GOAT
10089 𐂉 LINEAR B IDEOGRAM B107M HE-GOAT
1008A 𐂊 LINEAR B IDEOGRAM B108F SOW
1008B 𐂋 LINEAR B IDEOGRAM B108M BOAR
1008C 𐂌 LINEAR B IDEOGRAM B109F COW
1008D 𐂍 LINEAR B IDEOGRAM B109M BULL

Cereals and plants

1008E 𐂎 LINEAR B IDEOGRAM B120 WHEAT
1008F 𐂏 LINEAR B IDEOGRAM B121 BARLEY
10090 𐂐 LINEAR B IDEOGRAM B122 OLIVE
10091 𐂑 LINEAR B IDEOGRAM B123 SPICE
10092 𐂒 LINEAR B IDEOGRAM B125 CYPERUS
10093 𐂓 LINEAR B MONOGRAM B127 KAPO
= fruit
10094 𐂔 LINEAR B MONOGRAM B128 KANAKO
= saffron

Extracts

10095 𐂕 LINEAR B IDEOGRAM B130 OIL
10096 𐂖 LINEAR B IDEOGRAM B131 WINE
10097 𐂗 LINEAR B IDEOGRAM B132
10098 𐂘 LINEAR B MONOGRAM B133 AREPA
= ointment
10099 𐂙 LINEAR B MONOGRAM B135 MERI
= honey

Metals

1009A 𐂚 LINEAR B IDEOGRAM B140 BRONZE
1009B 𐂛 LINEAR B IDEOGRAM B141 GOLD
1009C 𐂜 LINEAR B IDEOGRAM B142

Other materials

1009D 𐂝 LINEAR B IDEOGRAM B145 WOOL
1009E 𐂞 LINEAR B IDEOGRAM B146
1009F 𐂟 LINEAR B IDEOGRAM B150
100A0 𐂠 LINEAR B IDEOGRAM B151 HORN
100A1 𐂡 LINEAR B IDEOGRAM B152
100A2 𐂢 LINEAR B IDEOGRAM B153
100A3 𐂣 LINEAR B IDEOGRAM B154
100A4 𐂤 LINEAR B MONOGRAM B156 TURO2
= cheese
100A5 𐂥 LINEAR B IDEOGRAM B157
100A6 𐂦 LINEAR B IDEOGRAM B158
100A7 𐂧 LINEAR B IDEOGRAM B159 CLOTH
100A8 𐂨 LINEAR B IDEOGRAM B160
100A9 𐂩 LINEAR B IDEOGRAM B161
100AA 𐂪 LINEAR B IDEOGRAM B162 GARMENT
100AB 𐂫 LINEAR B IDEOGRAM B163 ARMOUR
100AC 𐂬 LINEAR B IDEOGRAM B164
100AD 𐂭 LINEAR B IDEOGRAM B165
100AE 𐂮 LINEAR B IDEOGRAM B166
100AF 𐂯 LINEAR B IDEOGRAM B167
100B0 𐂰 LINEAR B IDEOGRAM B168
100B1 𐂱 LINEAR B IDEOGRAM B169
100B2 𐂲 LINEAR B IDEOGRAM B170
100B3 𐂳 LINEAR B IDEOGRAM B171
100B4 𐂴 LINEAR B IDEOGRAM B172
100B5 𐂵 LINEAR B IDEOGRAM B173 MONTH
100B6 𐂶 LINEAR B IDEOGRAM B174
100B7 𐂷 LINEAR B IDEOGRAM B176 TREE
100B8 𐂸 LINEAR B IDEOGRAM B177
100B9 𐂹 LINEAR B IDEOGRAM B178
100BA 𐂺 LINEAR B IDEOGRAM B179
100BB 𐂻 LINEAR B IDEOGRAM B180
100BC 𐂼 LINEAR B IDEOGRAM B181
100BD 𐂽 LINEAR B IDEOGRAM B182
100BE 𐂾 LINEAR B IDEOGRAM B183
100BF 𐂿 LINEAR B IDEOGRAM B184
• the shape of this ideogram is only partially known
100C0 𐃀 LINEAR B IDEOGRAM B185
100C1 𐃁 LINEAR B IDEOGRAM B189
100C2 𐃂 LINEAR B IDEOGRAM B190
100C3 𐃃 LINEAR B IDEOGRAM B191 HELMET
100C4 𐃄 LINEAR B IDEOGRAM B220 FOOTSTOOL
100C5 𐃅 LINEAR B IDEOGRAM B225 BATHTUB
100C6 𐃆 LINEAR B IDEOGRAM B230 SPEAR
100C7 𐃇 LINEAR B IDEOGRAM B231 ARROW
100C8 𐃈 LINEAR B IDEOGRAM B232
100C9 𐃉 LINEAR B IDEOGRAM B233 SWORD
= pugio
100CA 𐃊 LINEAR B IDEOGRAM B234
100CB 𐃋 LINEAR B IDEOGRAM B236
= "gupio", inverted sword
100CC 𐃌 LINEAR B IDEOGRAM B240 WHEELED CHARIOT
100CD 𐃍 LINEAR B IDEOGRAM B241 CHARIOT
100CE 𐃎 LINEAR B IDEOGRAM B242 CHARIOT FRAME
100CF 𐃏 LINEAR B IDEOGRAM B243 WHEEL
100D0 𐃐 LINEAR B IDEOGRAM B245
100D1 𐃑 LINEAR B IDEOGRAM B246
100D2 𐃒 LINEAR B MONOGRAM B247 DIPTE
100D3 𐃓 LINEAR B IDEOGRAM B248
100D4 𐃔 LINEAR B IDEOGRAM B249
100D5 𐃕 LINEAR B IDEOGRAM B251
• the shape of this ideogram is only partially known
100D6 𐃖 LINEAR B IDEOGRAM B252
• the shape of this ideogram is only partially known
100D7 𐃗 LINEAR B IDEOGRAM B253
100D8 𐃘 LINEAR B IDEOGRAM B254 DART
100D9 𐃙 LINEAR B IDEOGRAM B255
100DA 𐃚 LINEAR B IDEOGRAM B256
100DB 𐃛 LINEAR B IDEOGRAM B257
100DC 𐃜 LINEAR B IDEOGRAM B258
100DD 𐃝 LINEAR B IDEOGRAM B259

Vessels

100DE 𐃞 LINEAR B IDEOGRAM VESSEL B155
100DF 𐃟 LINEAR B IDEOGRAM VESSEL B200
100E0 𐃠 LINEAR B IDEOGRAM VESSEL B201

100E1 𐃡 LINEAR B IDEOGRAM VESSEL B202
100E2 𐃢 LINEAR B IDEOGRAM VESSEL B203
100E3 𐃣 LINEAR B IDEOGRAM VESSEL B204
100E4 𐃤 LINEAR B IDEOGRAM VESSEL B205
100E5 𐃥 LINEAR B IDEOGRAM VESSEL B206
100E6 𐃦 LINEAR B IDEOGRAM VESSEL B207
100E7 𐃧 LINEAR B IDEOGRAM VESSEL B208
100E8 𐃨 LINEAR B IDEOGRAM VESSEL B209
100E9 𐃩 LINEAR B IDEOGRAM VESSEL B210
100EA 𐃪 LINEAR B IDEOGRAM VESSEL B211
100EB 𐃫 LINEAR B IDEOGRAM VESSEL B212
100EC 𐃬 LINEAR B IDEOGRAM VESSEL B213
100ED 𐃭 LINEAR B IDEOGRAM VESSEL B214
100EE 𐃮 LINEAR B IDEOGRAM VESSEL B215
100EF 𐃯 LINEAR B IDEOGRAM VESSEL B216
100F0 𐃰 LINEAR B IDEOGRAM VESSEL B217
100F1 𐃱 LINEAR B IDEOGRAM VESSEL B218
100F2 𐃲 LINEAR B IDEOGRAM VESSEL B219
100F3 𐃳 LINEAR B IDEOGRAM VESSEL B221
100F4 𐃴 LINEAR B IDEOGRAM VESSEL B222
100F5 𐃵 LINEAR B IDEOGRAM VESSEL B226
100F6 𐃶 LINEAR B IDEOGRAM VESSEL B227
100F7 𐃷 LINEAR B IDEOGRAM VESSEL B228
100F8 𐃸 LINEAR B IDEOGRAM VESSEL B229
100F9 𐃹 LINEAR B IDEOGRAM VESSEL B250
100FA 𐃺 LINEAR B IDEOGRAM VESSEL B305
- the shape of this ideogram is only partially known

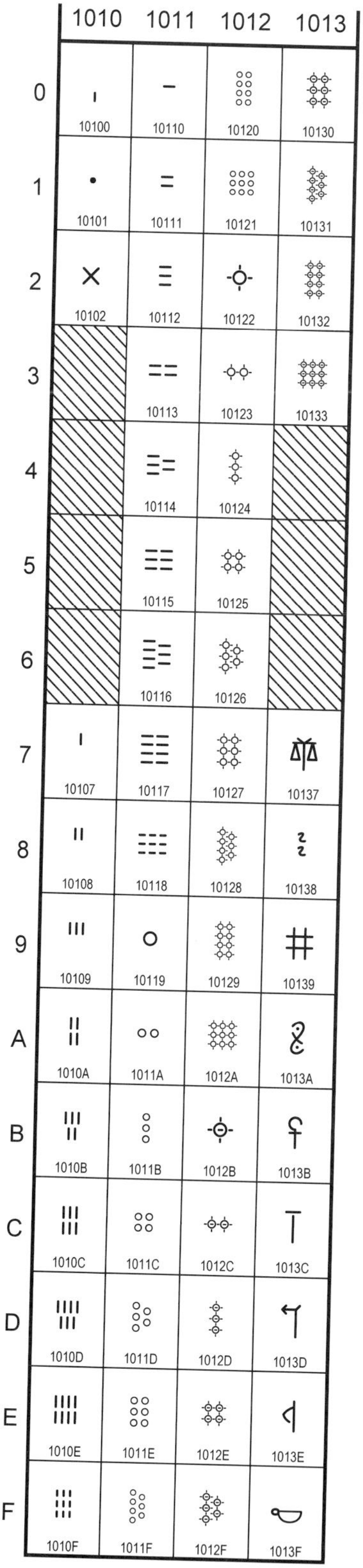

	1010	1011	1012	1013
0	10100	10110	10120	10130
1	10101	10111	10121	10131
2	10102	10112	10122	10132
3		10113	10123	10133
4		10114	10124	
5		10115	10125	
6		10116	10126	
7	10107	10117	10127	10137
8	10108	10118	10128	10138
9	10109	10119	10129	10139
A	1010A	1011A	1012A	1013A
B	1010B	1011B	1012B	1013B
C	1010C	1011C	1012C	1013C
D	1010D	1011D	1012D	1013D
E	1010E	1011E	1012E	1013E
F	1010F	1011F	1012F	1013F

Punctuation

10100 AEGEAN WORD SEPARATOR LINE
10101 AEGEAN WORD SEPARATOR DOT
10102 AEGEAN CHECK MARK

Numbers

10107 AEGEAN NUMBER ONE
10108 AEGEAN NUMBER TWO
10109 AEGEAN NUMBER THREE
1010A AEGEAN NUMBER FOUR
1010B AEGEAN NUMBER FIVE
1010C AEGEAN NUMBER SIX
1010D AEGEAN NUMBER SEVEN
1010E AEGEAN NUMBER EIGHT
1010F AEGEAN NUMBER NINE
10110 AEGEAN NUMBER TEN
10111 AEGEAN NUMBER TWENTY
10112 AEGEAN NUMBER THIRTY
10113 AEGEAN NUMBER FORTY
10114 AEGEAN NUMBER FIFTY
10115 AEGEAN NUMBER SIXTY
10116 AEGEAN NUMBER SEVENTY
10117 AEGEAN NUMBER EIGHTY
10118 AEGEAN NUMBER NINETY
10119 AEGEAN NUMBER ONE HUNDRED
1011A AEGEAN NUMBER TWO HUNDRED
1011B AEGEAN NUMBER THREE HUNDRED
1011C AEGEAN NUMBER FOUR HUNDRED
1011D AEGEAN NUMBER FIVE HUNDRED
1011E AEGEAN NUMBER SIX HUNDRED
1011F AEGEAN NUMBER SEVEN HUNDRED
10120 AEGEAN NUMBER EIGHT HUNDRED
10121 AEGEAN NUMBER NINE HUNDRED
10122 AEGEAN NUMBER ONE THOUSAND
10123 AEGEAN NUMBER TWO THOUSAND
10124 AEGEAN NUMBER THREE THOUSAND
10125 AEGEAN NUMBER FOUR THOUSAND
10126 AEGEAN NUMBER FIVE THOUSAND
10127 AEGEAN NUMBER SIX THOUSAND
10128 AEGEAN NUMBER SEVEN THOUSAND
10129 AEGEAN NUMBER EIGHT THOUSAND
1012A AEGEAN NUMBER NINE THOUSAND
1012B AEGEAN NUMBER TEN THOUSAND
1012C AEGEAN NUMBER TWENTY THOUSAND
1012D AEGEAN NUMBER THIRTY THOUSAND
1012E AEGEAN NUMBER FORTY THOUSAND
1012F AEGEAN NUMBER FIFTY THOUSAND
10130 AEGEAN NUMBER SIXTY THOUSAND
10131 AEGEAN NUMBER SEVENTY THOUSAND
10132 AEGEAN NUMBER EIGHTY THOUSAND
10133 AEGEAN NUMBER NINETY THOUSAND

Measures

10137 AEGEAN WEIGHT BASE UNIT
10138 AEGEAN WEIGHT FIRST SUBUNIT
10139 AEGEAN WEIGHT SECOND SUBUNIT
1013A AEGEAN WEIGHT THIRD SUBUNIT
1013B AEGEAN WEIGHT FOURTH SUBUNIT
1013C AEGEAN DRY MEASURE FIRST SUBUNIT
1013D AEGEAN LIQUID MEASURE FIRST SUBUNIT
1013E AEGEAN MEASURE SECOND SUBUNIT
1013F AEGEAN MEASURE THIRD SUBUNIT

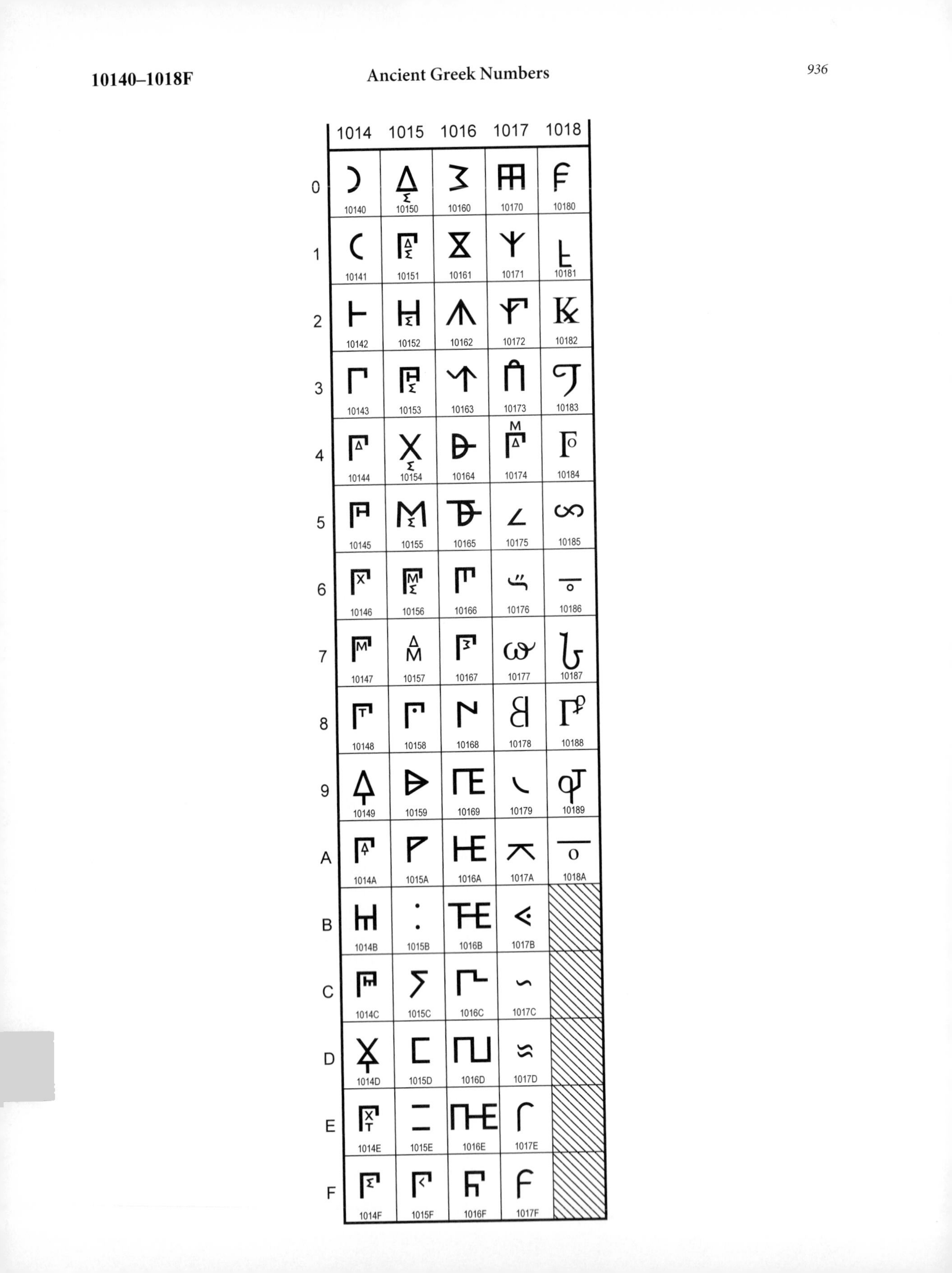

	1014	1015	1016	1017	1018
0	10140	10150	10160	10170	10180
1	10141	10151	10161	10171	10181
2	10142	10152	10162	10172	10182
3	10143	10153	10163	10173	10183
4	10144	10154	10164	10174	10184
5	10145	10155	10165	10175	10185
6	10146	10156	10166	10176	10186
7	10147	10157	10167	10177	10187
8	10148	10158	10168	10178	10188
9	10149	10159	10169	10179	10189
A	1014A	1015A	1016A	1017A	1018A
B	1014B	1015B	1016B	1017B	
C	1014C	1015C	1016C	1017C	
D	1014D	1015D	1016D	1017D	
E	1014E	1015E	1016E	1017E	
F	1014F	1015F	1016F	1017F	

Ancient Greek acrophonic numerals

These are shown as sans-serif forms because that corresponds more closely to their appearance in ancient texts.

10140 𐅀 GREEK ACROPHONIC ATTIC ONE QUARTER
10141 𐅁 GREEK ACROPHONIC ATTIC ONE HALF
10142 𐅂 GREEK ACROPHONIC ATTIC ONE DRACHMA
10143 𐅃 GREEK ACROPHONIC ATTIC FIVE
10144 𐅄 GREEK ACROPHONIC ATTIC FIFTY
10145 𐅅 GREEK ACROPHONIC ATTIC FIVE HUNDRED
10146 𐅆 GREEK ACROPHONIC ATTIC FIVE THOUSAND
10147 𐅇 GREEK ACROPHONIC ATTIC FIFTY THOUSAND
10148 𐅈 GREEK ACROPHONIC ATTIC FIVE TALENTS
10149 𐅉 GREEK ACROPHONIC ATTIC TEN TALENTS
1014A 𐅊 GREEK ACROPHONIC ATTIC FIFTY TALENTS
1014B 𐅋 GREEK ACROPHONIC ATTIC ONE HUNDRED TALENTS
1014C 𐅌 GREEK ACROPHONIC ATTIC FIVE HUNDRED TALENTS
1014D 𐅍 GREEK ACROPHONIC ATTIC ONE THOUSAND TALENTS
1014E 𐅎 GREEK ACROPHONIC ATTIC FIVE THOUSAND TALENTS
1014F 𐅏 GREEK ACROPHONIC ATTIC FIVE STATERS
10150 𐅐 GREEK ACROPHONIC ATTIC TEN STATERS
10151 𐅑 GREEK ACROPHONIC ATTIC FIFTY STATERS
10152 𐅒 GREEK ACROPHONIC ATTIC ONE HUNDRED STATERS
10153 𐅓 GREEK ACROPHONIC ATTIC FIVE HUNDRED STATERS
10154 𐅔 GREEK ACROPHONIC ATTIC ONE THOUSAND STATERS
10155 𐅕 GREEK ACROPHONIC ATTIC TEN THOUSAND STATERS
10156 𐅖 GREEK ACROPHONIC ATTIC FIFTY THOUSAND STATERS
10157 𐅗 GREEK ACROPHONIC ATTIC TEN MNAS
10158 𐅘 GREEK ACROPHONIC HERAEUM ONE PLETHRON
10159 𐅙 GREEK ACROPHONIC THESPIAN ONE
1015A 𐅚 GREEK ACROPHONIC HERMIONIAN ONE
1015B 𐅛 GREEK ACROPHONIC EPIDAUREAN TWO
→ 205A ⁚ two dot punctuation
1015C 𐅜 GREEK ACROPHONIC THESPIAN TWO
1015D 𐅝 GREEK ACROPHONIC CYRENAIC TWO DRACHMAS
1015E 𐅞 GREEK ACROPHONIC EPIDAUREAN TWO DRACHMAS
• top line is at cap height, unlike 10111 𐄑
→ 10111 𐄑 aegean number twenty
1015F 𐅟 GREEK ACROPHONIC TROEZENIAN FIVE
10160 𐅠 GREEK ACROPHONIC TROEZENIAN TEN
10161 𐅡 GREEK ACROPHONIC TROEZENIAN TEN ALTERNATE FORM
10162 𐅢 GREEK ACROPHONIC HERMIONIAN TEN
10163 𐅣 GREEK ACROPHONIC MESSENIAN TEN
10164 𐅤 GREEK ACROPHONIC THESPIAN TEN
10165 𐅥 GREEK ACROPHONIC THESPIAN THIRTY
10166 𐅦 GREEK ACROPHONIC TROEZENIAN FIFTY
10167 𐅧 GREEK ACROPHONIC TROEZENIAN FIFTY ALTERNATE FORM
10168 𐅨 GREEK ACROPHONIC HERMIONIAN FIFTY
10169 𐅩 GREEK ACROPHONIC THESPIAN FIFTY
1016A 𐅪 GREEK ACROPHONIC THESPIAN ONE HUNDRED
1016B 𐅫 GREEK ACROPHONIC THESPIAN THREE HUNDRED
1016C 𐅬 GREEK ACROPHONIC EPIDAUREAN FIVE HUNDRED
1016D 𐅭 GREEK ACROPHONIC TROEZENIAN FIVE HUNDRED
1016E 𐅮 GREEK ACROPHONIC THESPIAN FIVE HUNDRED
1016F 𐅯 GREEK ACROPHONIC CARYSTIAN FIVE HUNDRED
10170 𐅰 GREEK ACROPHONIC NAXIAN FIVE HUNDRED
10171 𐅱 GREEK ACROPHONIC THESPIAN ONE THOUSAND
10172 𐅲 GREEK ACROPHONIC THESPIAN FIVE THOUSAND
10173 𐅳 GREEK ACROPHONIC DELPHIC FIVE MNAS
10174 𐅴 GREEK ACROPHONIC STRATIAN FIFTY MNAS

Ancient Greek papyrological numbers

10175 𐅵 GREEK ONE HALF SIGN
10176 𐅶 GREEK ONE HALF SIGN ALTERNATE FORM
10177 𐅷 GREEK TWO THIRDS SIGN
10178 𐅸 GREEK THREE QUARTERS SIGN
10179 𐅹 GREEK YEAR SIGN
1017A 𐅺 GREEK TALENT SIGN
1017B 𐅻 GREEK DRACHMA SIGN
1017C 𐅼 GREEK OBOL SIGN
1017D 𐅽 GREEK TWO OBOLS SIGN
1017E 𐅾 GREEK THREE OBOLS SIGN
1017F 𐅿 GREEK FOUR OBOLS SIGN
10180 𐆀 GREEK FIVE OBOLS SIGN
10181 𐆁 GREEK METRETES SIGN
10182 𐆂 GREEK KYATHOS BASE SIGN
10183 𐆃 GREEK LITRA SIGN
10184 𐆄 GREEK OUNKIA SIGN
10185 𐆅 GREEK XESTES SIGN
10186 𐆆 GREEK ARTABE SIGN
10187 𐆇 GREEK AROURA SIGN
10188 𐆈 GREEK GRAMMA SIGN
10189 𐆉 GREEK TRYBLION BASE SIGN
1018A 𐆊 GREEK ZERO SIGN

	1030	1031	1032
0	𐌀 10300	𐌐 10310	𐌠 10320
1	𐌁 10301	𐌑 10311	𐌡 10321
2	𐌂 10302	𐌒 10312	𐌢 10322
3	𐌃 10303	𐌓 10313	𐌣 10323
4	𐌄 10304	𐌔 10314	
5	𐌅 10305	𐌕 10315	
6	𐌆 10306	𐌖 10316	
7	𐌇 10307	𐌗 10317	
8	𐌈 10308	𐌘 10318	
9	𐌉 10309	𐌙 10319	
A	𐌊 1030A	𐌚 1031A	
B	𐌋 1030B	𐌛 1031B	
C	𐌌 1030C	𐌜 1031C	
D	𐌍 1030D	𐌝 1031D	
E	𐌎 1030E	𐌞 1031E	
F	𐌏 1030F		

Letters

10300 𐌀 OLD ITALIC LETTER A
10301 𐌁 OLD ITALIC LETTER BE
10302 𐌂 OLD ITALIC LETTER KE
10303 𐌃 OLD ITALIC LETTER DE
10304 𐌄 OLD ITALIC LETTER E
10305 𐌅 OLD ITALIC LETTER VE
10306 𐌆 OLD ITALIC LETTER ZE
10307 𐌇 OLD ITALIC LETTER HE
10308 𐌈 OLD ITALIC LETTER THE
10309 𐌉 OLD ITALIC LETTER I
1030A 𐌊 OLD ITALIC LETTER KA
1030B 𐌋 OLD ITALIC LETTER EL
1030C 𐌌 OLD ITALIC LETTER EM
1030D 𐌍 OLD ITALIC LETTER EN
1030E 𐌎 OLD ITALIC LETTER ESH
1030F 𐌏 OLD ITALIC LETTER O
10310 𐌐 OLD ITALIC LETTER PE
10311 𐌑 OLD ITALIC LETTER SHE
10312 𐌒 OLD ITALIC LETTER KU
10313 𐌓 OLD ITALIC LETTER ER
10314 𐌔 OLD ITALIC LETTER ES
10315 𐌕 OLD ITALIC LETTER TE
10316 𐌖 OLD ITALIC LETTER U
10317 𐌗 OLD ITALIC LETTER EKS
10318 𐌘 OLD ITALIC LETTER PHE
10319 𐌙 OLD ITALIC LETTER KHE
1031A 𐌚 OLD ITALIC LETTER EF
1031B 𐌛 OLD ITALIC LETTER ERS
1031C 𐌜 OLD ITALIC LETTER CHE
1031D 𐌝 OLD ITALIC LETTER II
1031E 𐌞 OLD ITALIC LETTER UU

Numerals

10320 𐌠 OLD ITALIC NUMERAL ONE
10321 𐌡 OLD ITALIC NUMERAL FIVE
10322 𐌢 OLD ITALIC NUMERAL TEN
10323 𐌣 OLD ITALIC NUMERAL FIFTY

	1033	1034
0	𐌰 10330	𐍀 10340
1	𐌱 10331	𐍁 10341
2	𐌲 10332	𐍂 10342
3	𐌳 10333	𐍃 10343
4	𐌴 10334	𐍄 10344
5	𐌵 10335	𐍅 10345
6	𐌶 10336	𐍆 10346
7	𐌷 10337	𐍇 10347
8	𐌸 10338	𐍈 10348
9	𐌹 10339	𐍉 10349
A	𐌺 1033A	𐍊 1034A
B	𐌻 1033B	
C	𐌼 1033C	
D	𐌽 1033D	
E	𐌾 1033E	
F	𐌿 1033F	

Letters

10330 𐌰 GOTHIC LETTER AHSA
10331 𐌱 GOTHIC LETTER BAIRKAN
10332 𐌲 GOTHIC LETTER GIBA
10333 𐌳 GOTHIC LETTER DAGS
10334 𐌴 GOTHIC LETTER AIHVUS
10335 𐌵 GOTHIC LETTER QAIRTHRA
10336 𐌶 GOTHIC LETTER IUJA
10337 𐌷 GOTHIC LETTER HAGL
10338 𐌸 GOTHIC LETTER THIUTH
10339 𐌹 GOTHIC LETTER EIS
1033A 𐌺 GOTHIC LETTER KUSMA
1033B 𐌻 GOTHIC LETTER LAGUS
1033C 𐌼 GOTHIC LETTER MANNA
1033D 𐌽 GOTHIC LETTER NAUTHS
1033E 𐌾 GOTHIC LETTER JER
1033F 𐌿 GOTHIC LETTER URUS
10340 𐍀 GOTHIC LETTER PAIRTHRA
10341 𐍁 GOTHIC LETTER NINETY
10342 𐍂 GOTHIC LETTER RAIDA
10343 𐍃 GOTHIC LETTER SAUIL
10344 𐍄 GOTHIC LETTER TEIWS
10345 𐍅 GOTHIC LETTER WINJA
10346 𐍆 GOTHIC LETTER FAIHU
10347 𐍇 GOTHIC LETTER IGGWS
10348 𐍈 GOTHIC LETTER HWAIR
10349 𐍉 GOTHIC LETTER OTHAL
1034A 𐍊 GOTHIC LETTER NINE HUNDRED

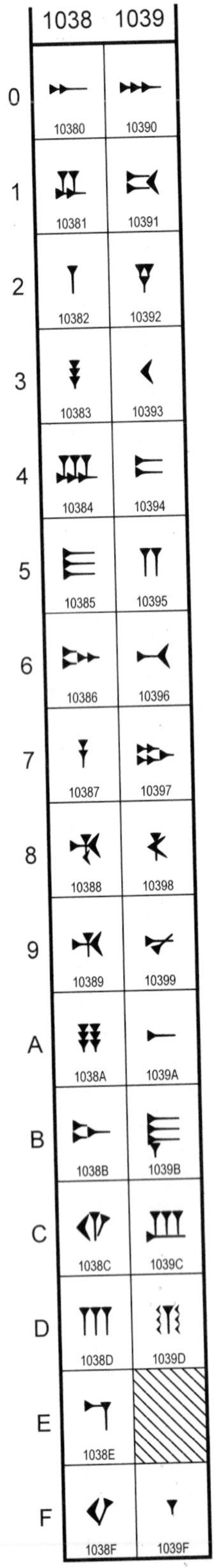

	1038	1039
0	𐎀 10380	𐎐 10390
1	𐎁 10381	𐎑 10391
2	𐎂 10382	𐎒 10392
3	𐎃 10383	𐎓 10393
4	𐎄 10384	𐎔 10394
5	𐎅 10385	𐎕 10395
6	𐎆 10386	𐎖 10396
7	𐎇 10387	𐎗 10397
8	𐎈 10388	𐎘 10398
9	𐎉 10389	𐎙 10399
A	𐎊 1038A	𐎚 1039A
B	𐎋 1038B	𐎛 1039B
C	𐎌 1038C	𐎜 1039C
D	𐎍 1038D	𐎝 1039D
E	𐎎 1038E	
F	𐎏 1038F	𐎟 1039F

Letters

10380 𐎀 UGARITIC LETTER ALPA
10381 𐎁 UGARITIC LETTER BETA
10382 𐎂 UGARITIC LETTER GAMLA
10383 𐎃 UGARITIC LETTER KHA
10384 𐎄 UGARITIC LETTER DELTA
10385 𐎅 UGARITIC LETTER HO
10386 𐎆 UGARITIC LETTER WO
10387 𐎇 UGARITIC LETTER ZETA
10388 𐎈 UGARITIC LETTER HOTA
10389 𐎉 UGARITIC LETTER TET
1038A 𐎊 UGARITIC LETTER YOD
1038B 𐎋 UGARITIC LETTER KAF
1038C 𐎌 UGARITIC LETTER SHIN
1038D 𐎍 UGARITIC LETTER LAMDA
1038E 𐎎 UGARITIC LETTER MEM
1038F 𐎏 UGARITIC LETTER DHAL
10390 𐎐 UGARITIC LETTER NUN
10391 𐎑 UGARITIC LETTER ZU
10392 𐎒 UGARITIC LETTER SAMKA
10393 𐎓 UGARITIC LETTER AIN
10394 𐎔 UGARITIC LETTER PU
10395 𐎕 UGARITIC LETTER SADE
10396 𐎖 UGARITIC LETTER QOPA
10397 𐎗 UGARITIC LETTER RASHA
10398 𐎘 UGARITIC LETTER THANNA
10399 𐎙 UGARITIC LETTER GHAIN
1039A 𐎚 UGARITIC LETTER TO
1039B 𐎛 UGARITIC LETTER I
1039C 𐎜 UGARITIC LETTER U
1039D 𐎝 UGARITIC LETTER SSU

Punctuation

1039F 𐎟 UGARITIC WORD DIVIDER

	103A	103B	103C	103D
0	𐎠 103A0	𐎰 103B0	𐏀 103C0	𐏐 103D0
1	𐎡 103A1	𐎱 103B1	𐏁 103C1	𐏑 103D1
2	𐎢 103A2	𐎲 103B2	𐏂 103C2	𐏒 103D2
3	𐎣 103A3	𐎳 103B3	𐏃 103C3	𐏓 103D3
4	𐎤 103A4	𐎴 103B4		𐏔 103D4
5	𐎥 103A5	𐎵 103B5		𐏕 103D5
6	𐎦 103A6	𐎶 103B6		
7	𐎧 103A7	𐎷 103B7		
8	𐎨 103A8	𐎸 103B8	𐏈 103C8	
9	𐎩 103A9	𐎹 103B9	𐏉 103C9	
A	𐎪 103AA	𐎺 103BA	𐏊 103CA	
B	𐎫 103AB	𐎻 103BB	𐏋 103CB	
C	𐎬 103AC	𐎼 103BC	𐏌 103CC	
D	𐎭 103AD	𐎽 103BD	𐏍 103CD	
E	𐎮 103AE	𐎾 103BE	𐏎 103CE	
F	𐎯 103AF	𐎿 103BF	𐏏 103CF	

Independent vowels

103A0 𐎠 OLD PERSIAN SIGN A
103A1 𐎡 OLD PERSIAN SIGN I
103A2 𐎢 OLD PERSIAN SIGN U

Consonants

103A3 𐎣 OLD PERSIAN SIGN KA
103A4 𐎤 OLD PERSIAN SIGN KU
103A5 𐎥 OLD PERSIAN SIGN GA
103A6 𐎦 OLD PERSIAN SIGN GU
103A7 𐎧 OLD PERSIAN SIGN XA
103A8 𐎨 OLD PERSIAN SIGN CA
103A9 𐎩 OLD PERSIAN SIGN JA
103AA 𐎪 OLD PERSIAN SIGN JI
103AB 𐎫 OLD PERSIAN SIGN TA
103AC 𐎬 OLD PERSIAN SIGN TU
103AD 𐎭 OLD PERSIAN SIGN DA
103AE 𐎮 OLD PERSIAN SIGN DI
103AF 𐎯 OLD PERSIAN SIGN DU
103B0 𐎰 OLD PERSIAN SIGN THA
103B1 𐎱 OLD PERSIAN SIGN PA
103B2 𐎲 OLD PERSIAN SIGN BA
103B3 𐎳 OLD PERSIAN SIGN FA
103B4 𐎴 OLD PERSIAN SIGN NA
103B5 𐎵 OLD PERSIAN SIGN NU
103B6 𐎶 OLD PERSIAN SIGN MA
103B7 𐎷 OLD PERSIAN SIGN MI
103B8 𐎸 OLD PERSIAN SIGN MU
103B9 𐎹 OLD PERSIAN SIGN YA
103BA 𐎺 OLD PERSIAN SIGN VA
103BB 𐎻 OLD PERSIAN SIGN VI
103BC 𐎼 OLD PERSIAN SIGN RA
103BD 𐎽 OLD PERSIAN SIGN RU
103BE 𐎾 OLD PERSIAN SIGN LA
103BF 𐎿 OLD PERSIAN SIGN SA
103C0 𐏀 OLD PERSIAN SIGN ZA
103C1 𐏁 OLD PERSIAN SIGN SHA
103C2 𐏂 OLD PERSIAN SIGN SSA
103C3 𐏃 OLD PERSIAN SIGN HA

Various signs

103C8 𐏈 OLD PERSIAN SIGN AURAMAZDAA
103C9 𐏉 OLD PERSIAN SIGN AURAMAZDAA-2
103CA 𐏊 OLD PERSIAN SIGN AURAMAZDAAHA
103CB 𐏋 OLD PERSIAN SIGN XSHAAYATHIYA
103CC 𐏌 OLD PERSIAN SIGN DAHYAAUSH
103CD 𐏍 OLD PERSIAN SIGN DAHYAAUSH-2
103CE 𐏎 OLD PERSIAN SIGN BAGA
103CF 𐏏 OLD PERSIAN SIGN BUUMISH

Punctuation

103D0 𐏐 OLD PERSIAN WORD DIVIDER

Numbers

103D1 𐏑 OLD PERSIAN NUMBER ONE
103D2 𐏒 OLD PERSIAN NUMBER TWO
103D3 𐏓 OLD PERSIAN NUMBER TEN
103D4 𐏔 OLD PERSIAN NUMBER TWENTY
103D5 𐏕 OLD PERSIAN NUMBER HUNDRED

	1040	1041	1042	1043	1044
0	𐐀 10400	𐐐 10410	𐐠 10420	𐐰 10430	𐑀 10440
1	𐐁 10401	𐐑 10411	𐐡 10421	𐐱 10431	𐑁 10441
2	𐐂 10402	𐐒 10412	𐐢 10422	𐐲 10432	𐑂 10442
3	𐐃 10403	𐐓 10413	𐐣 10423	𐐳 10433	𐑃 10443
4	𐐄 10404	𐐔 10414	𐐤 10424	𐐴 10434	𐑄 10444
5	𐐅 10405	𐐕 10415	𐐥 10425	𐐵 10435	𐑅 10445
6	𐐆 10406	𐐖 10416	𐐦 10426	𐐶 10436	𐑆 10446
7	𐐇 10407	𐐗 10417	𐐧 10427	𐐷 10437	𐑇 10447
8	𐐈 10408	𐐘 10418	𐐨 10428	𐐸 10438	𐑈 10448
9	𐐉 10409	𐐙 10419	𐐩 10429	𐐹 10439	𐑉 10449
A	𐐊 1040A	𐐚 1041A	𐐪 1042A	𐐺 1043A	𐑊 1044A
B	𐐋 1040B	𐐛 1041B	𐐫 1042B	𐐻 1043B	𐑋 1044B
C	𐐌 1040C	𐐜 1041C	𐐬 1042C	𐐼 1043C	𐑌 1044C
D	𐐍 1040D	𐐝 1041D	𐐭 1042D	𐐽 1043D	𐑍 1044D
E	𐐎 1040E	𐐞 1041E	𐐮 1042E	𐐾 1043E	𐑎 1044E
F	𐐏 1040F	𐐟 1041F	𐐯 1042F	𐐿 1043F	𐑏 1044F

Uppercase letters

10400 𐐀 DESERET CAPITAL LETTER LONG I
10401 𐐁 DESERET CAPITAL LETTER LONG E
10402 𐐂 DESERET CAPITAL LETTER LONG A
10403 𐐃 DESERET CAPITAL LETTER LONG AH
10404 𐐄 DESERET CAPITAL LETTER LONG O
10405 𐐅 DESERET CAPITAL LETTER LONG OO
10406 𐐆 DESERET CAPITAL LETTER SHORT I
10407 𐐇 DESERET CAPITAL LETTER SHORT E
10408 𐐈 DESERET CAPITAL LETTER SHORT A
10409 𐐉 DESERET CAPITAL LETTER SHORT AH
1040A 𐐊 DESERET CAPITAL LETTER SHORT O
1040B 𐐋 DESERET CAPITAL LETTER SHORT OO
1040C 𐐌 DESERET CAPITAL LETTER AY
1040D 𐐍 DESERET CAPITAL LETTER OW
1040E 𐐎 DESERET CAPITAL LETTER WU
1040F 𐐏 DESERET CAPITAL LETTER YEE
10410 𐐐 DESERET CAPITAL LETTER H
10411 𐐑 DESERET CAPITAL LETTER PEE
10412 𐐒 DESERET CAPITAL LETTER BEE
10413 𐐓 DESERET CAPITAL LETTER TEE
10414 𐐔 DESERET CAPITAL LETTER DEE
10415 𐐕 DESERET CAPITAL LETTER CHEE
10416 𐐖 DESERET CAPITAL LETTER JEE
10417 𐐗 DESERET CAPITAL LETTER KAY
10418 𐐘 DESERET CAPITAL LETTER GAY
10419 𐐙 DESERET CAPITAL LETTER EF
1041A 𐐚 DESERET CAPITAL LETTER VEE
1041B 𐐛 DESERET CAPITAL LETTER ETH
1041C 𐐜 DESERET CAPITAL LETTER THEE
1041D 𐐝 DESERET CAPITAL LETTER ES
1041E 𐐞 DESERET CAPITAL LETTER ZEE
1041F 𐐟 DESERET CAPITAL LETTER ESH
10420 𐐠 DESERET CAPITAL LETTER ZHEE
10421 𐐡 DESERET CAPITAL LETTER ER
10422 𐐢 DESERET CAPITAL LETTER EL
10423 𐐣 DESERET CAPITAL LETTER EM
10424 𐐤 DESERET CAPITAL LETTER EN
10425 𐐥 DESERET CAPITAL LETTER ENG
10426 𐐦 DESERET CAPITAL LETTER OI
10427 𐐧 DESERET CAPITAL LETTER EW

Lowercase letters

10428 𐐨 DESERET SMALL LETTER LONG I
10429 𐐩 DESERET SMALL LETTER LONG E
1042A 𐐪 DESERET SMALL LETTER LONG A
1042B 𐐫 DESERET SMALL LETTER LONG AH
1042C 𐐬 DESERET SMALL LETTER LONG O
1042D 𐐭 DESERET SMALL LETTER LONG OO
1042E 𐐮 DESERET SMALL LETTER SHORT I
1042F 𐐯 DESERET SMALL LETTER SHORT E
10430 𐐰 DESERET SMALL LETTER SHORT A
10431 𐐱 DESERET SMALL LETTER SHORT AH
10432 𐐲 DESERET SMALL LETTER SHORT O
10433 𐐳 DESERET SMALL LETTER SHORT OO
10434 𐐴 DESERET SMALL LETTER AY
10435 𐐵 DESERET SMALL LETTER OW
10436 𐐶 DESERET SMALL LETTER WU
10437 𐐷 DESERET SMALL LETTER YEE
10438 𐐸 DESERET SMALL LETTER H
10439 𐐹 DESERET SMALL LETTER PEE
1043A 𐐺 DESERET SMALL LETTER BEE
1043B 𐐻 DESERET SMALL LETTER TEE
1043C 𐐼 DESERET SMALL LETTER DEE
1043D 𐐽 DESERET SMALL LETTER CHEE
1043E 𐐾 DESERET SMALL LETTER JEE
1043F 𐐿 DESERET SMALL LETTER KAY
10440 𐑀 DESERET SMALL LETTER GAY
10441 𐑁 DESERET SMALL LETTER EF
10442 𐑂 DESERET SMALL LETTER VEE
10443 𐑃 DESERET SMALL LETTER ETH
10444 𐑄 DESERET SMALL LETTER THEE
10445 𐑅 DESERET SMALL LETTER ES
10446 𐑆 DESERET SMALL LETTER ZEE
10447 𐑇 DESERET SMALL LETTER ESH
10448 𐑈 DESERET SMALL LETTER ZHEE
10449 𐑉 DESERET SMALL LETTER ER
1044A 𐑊 DESERET SMALL LETTER EL
1044B 𐑋 DESERET SMALL LETTER EM
1044C 𐑌 DESERET SMALL LETTER EN
1044D 𐑍 DESERET SMALL LETTER ENG
1044E 𐑎 DESERET SMALL LETTER OI
1044F 𐑏 DESERET SMALL LETTER EW

	1045	1046	1047
0	𐑐 10450	𐑠 10460	𐑰 10470
1	𐑑 10451	𐑡 10461	𐑱 10471
2	𐑒 10452	𐑢 10462	𐑲 10472
3	𐑓 10453	𐑣 10463	𐑳 10473
4	𐑔 10454	𐑤 10464	𐑴 10474
5	𐑕 10455	𐑥 10465	𐑵 10475
6	𐑖 10456	𐑦 10466	𐑶 10476
7	𐑗 10457	𐑧 10467	𐑷 10477
8	𐑘 10458	𐑨 10468	𐑸 10478
9	𐑙 10459	𐑩 10469	𐑹 10479
A	𐑚 1045A	𐑪 1046A	𐑺 1047A
B	𐑛 1045B	𐑫 1046B	𐑻 1047B
C	𐑜 1045C	𐑬 1046C	𐑼 1047C
D	𐑝 1045D	𐑭 1046D	𐑽 1047D
E	𐑞 1045E	𐑮 1046E	𐑾 1047E
F	𐑟 1045F	𐑯 1046F	𐑿 1047F

Consonants

10450 𐑐 SHAVIAN LETTER PEEP
10451 𐑑 SHAVIAN LETTER TOT
10452 𐑒 SHAVIAN LETTER KICK
10453 𐑓 SHAVIAN LETTER FEE
10454 𐑔 SHAVIAN LETTER THIGH
10455 𐑕 SHAVIAN LETTER SO
10456 𐑖 SHAVIAN LETTER SURE
10457 𐑗 SHAVIAN LETTER CHURCH
10458 𐑘 SHAVIAN LETTER YEA
10459 𐑙 SHAVIAN LETTER HUNG
1045A 𐑚 SHAVIAN LETTER BIB
1045B 𐑛 SHAVIAN LETTER DEAD
1045C 𐑜 SHAVIAN LETTER GAG
1045D 𐑝 SHAVIAN LETTER VOW
1045E 𐑞 SHAVIAN LETTER THEY
1045F 𐑟 SHAVIAN LETTER ZOO
10460 𐑠 SHAVIAN LETTER MEASURE
10461 𐑡 SHAVIAN LETTER JUDGE
10462 𐑢 SHAVIAN LETTER WOE
10463 𐑣 SHAVIAN LETTER HA-HA
10464 𐑤 SHAVIAN LETTER LOLL
10465 𐑥 SHAVIAN LETTER MIME

Vowels

10466 𐑦 SHAVIAN LETTER IF
10467 𐑧 SHAVIAN LETTER EGG
10468 𐑨 SHAVIAN LETTER ASH
10469 𐑩 SHAVIAN LETTER ADO
1046A 𐑪 SHAVIAN LETTER ON
1046B 𐑫 SHAVIAN LETTER WOOL
1046C 𐑬 SHAVIAN LETTER OUT
1046D 𐑭 SHAVIAN LETTER AH
1046E 𐑮 SHAVIAN LETTER ROAR
1046F 𐑯 SHAVIAN LETTER NUN
10470 𐑰 SHAVIAN LETTER EAT
10471 𐑱 SHAVIAN LETTER AGE
10472 𐑲 SHAVIAN LETTER ICE
10473 𐑳 SHAVIAN LETTER UP
10474 𐑴 SHAVIAN LETTER OAK
10475 𐑵 SHAVIAN LETTER OOZE
10476 𐑶 SHAVIAN LETTER OIL
10477 𐑷 SHAVIAN LETTER AWE
10478 𐑸 SHAVIAN LETTER ARE
10479 𐑹 SHAVIAN LETTER OR
1047A 𐑺 SHAVIAN LETTER AIR
1047B 𐑻 SHAVIAN LETTER ERR
1047C 𐑼 SHAVIAN LETTER ARRAY
1047D 𐑽 SHAVIAN LETTER EAR
1047E 𐑾 SHAVIAN LETTER IAN
1047F 𐑿 SHAVIAN LETTER YEW

	1048	1049	104A
0	𐒀 10480	𐒐 10490	𐒠 104A0
1	𐒁 10481	𐒑 10491	𐒡 104A1
2	𐒂 10482	𐒒 10492	𐒢 104A2
3	𐒃 10483	𐒓 10493	𐒣 104A3
4	𐒄 10484	𐒔 10494	𐒤 104A4
5	𐒅 10485	𐒕 10495	𐒥 104A5
6	𐒆 10486	𐒖 10496	𐒦 104A6
7	𐒇 10487	𐒗 10497	𐒧 104A7
8	𐒈 10488	𐒘 10498	𐒨 104A8
9	𐒉 10489	𐒙 10499	𐒩 104A9
A	𐒊 1048A	𐒚 1049A	
B	𐒋 1048B	𐒛 1049B	
C	𐒌 1048C	𐒜 1049C	
D	𐒍 1048D	𐒝 1049D	
E	𐒎 1048E		
F	𐒏 1048F		

Letters

10480 𐒀 OSMANYA LETTER ALEF
10481 𐒁 OSMANYA LETTER BA
10482 𐒂 OSMANYA LETTER TA
10483 𐒃 OSMANYA LETTER JA
10484 𐒄 OSMANYA LETTER XA
10485 𐒅 OSMANYA LETTER KHA
10486 𐒆 OSMANYA LETTER DEEL
10487 𐒇 OSMANYA LETTER RA
10488 𐒈 OSMANYA LETTER SA
10489 𐒉 OSMANYA LETTER SHIIN
1048A 𐒊 OSMANYA LETTER DHA
1048B 𐒋 OSMANYA LETTER CAYN
1048C 𐒌 OSMANYA LETTER GA
1048D 𐒍 OSMANYA LETTER FA
1048E 𐒎 OSMANYA LETTER QAAF
1048F 𐒏 OSMANYA LETTER KAAF
10490 𐒐 OSMANYA LETTER LAAN
10491 𐒑 OSMANYA LETTER MIIN
10492 𐒒 OSMANYA LETTER NUUN
10493 𐒓 OSMANYA LETTER WAW
10494 𐒔 OSMANYA LETTER HA
10495 𐒕 OSMANYA LETTER YA
10496 𐒖 OSMANYA LETTER A
10497 𐒗 OSMANYA LETTER E
10498 𐒘 OSMANYA LETTER I
10499 𐒙 OSMANYA LETTER O
1049A 𐒚 OSMANYA LETTER U
1049B 𐒛 OSMANYA LETTER AA
1049C 𐒜 OSMANYA LETTER EE
1049D 𐒝 OSMANYA LETTER OO

Digits

104A0 𐒠 OSMANYA DIGIT ZERO
104A1 𐒡 OSMANYA DIGIT ONE
104A2 𐒢 OSMANYA DIGIT TWO
104A3 𐒣 OSMANYA DIGIT THREE
104A4 𐒤 OSMANYA DIGIT FOUR
104A5 𐒥 OSMANYA DIGIT FIVE
104A6 𐒦 OSMANYA DIGIT SIX
104A7 𐒧 OSMANYA DIGIT SEVEN
104A8 𐒨 OSMANYA DIGIT EIGHT
104A9 𐒩 OSMANYA DIGIT NINE

	1080	1081	1082	1083
0	10800	10810	10820	10830
1	10801	10811	10821	10831
2	10802	10812	10822	10832
3	10803	10813	10823	10833
4	10804	10814	10824	10834
5	10805	10815	10825	10835
6		10816	10826	
7		10817	10827	10837
8	10808	10818	10828	10838
9		10819	10829	
A	1080A	1081A	1082A	
B	1080B	1081B	1082B	
C	1080C	1081C	1082C	1083C
D	1080D	1081D	1082D	
E	1080E	1081E	1082E	
F	1080F	1081F	1082F	1083F

Syllables

Code	Glyph	Name
10800	𐠀	CYPRIOT SYLLABLE A
10801	𐠁	CYPRIOT SYLLABLE E
10802	𐠂	CYPRIOT SYLLABLE I
10803	𐠃	CYPRIOT SYLLABLE O
10804	𐠄	CYPRIOT SYLLABLE U
10805	𐠅	CYPRIOT SYLLABLE JA
10806		<reserved>
10807		<reserved>
10808	𐠈	CYPRIOT SYLLABLE JO
10809		<reserved>
1080A	𐠊	CYPRIOT SYLLABLE KA
1080B	𐠋	CYPRIOT SYLLABLE KE
1080C	𐠌	CYPRIOT SYLLABLE KI
1080D	𐠍	CYPRIOT SYLLABLE KO
1080E	𐠎	CYPRIOT SYLLABLE KU
1080F	𐠏	CYPRIOT SYLLABLE LA
10810	𐠐	CYPRIOT SYLLABLE LE
10811	𐠑	CYPRIOT SYLLABLE LI
10812	𐠒	CYPRIOT SYLLABLE LO
10813	𐠓	CYPRIOT SYLLABLE LU
10814	𐠔	CYPRIOT SYLLABLE MA
10815	𐠕	CYPRIOT SYLLABLE ME
10816	𐠖	CYPRIOT SYLLABLE MI
10817	𐠗	CYPRIOT SYLLABLE MO
10818	𐠘	CYPRIOT SYLLABLE MU
10819	𐠙	CYPRIOT SYLLABLE NA
1081A	𐠚	CYPRIOT SYLLABLE NE
1081B	𐠛	CYPRIOT SYLLABLE NI
1081C	𐠜	CYPRIOT SYLLABLE NO
1081D	𐠝	CYPRIOT SYLLABLE NU
1081E	𐠞	CYPRIOT SYLLABLE PA
1081F	𐠟	CYPRIOT SYLLABLE PE
10820	𐠠	CYPRIOT SYLLABLE PI
10821	𐠡	CYPRIOT SYLLABLE PO
10822	𐠢	CYPRIOT SYLLABLE PU
10823	𐠣	CYPRIOT SYLLABLE RA
10824	𐠤	CYPRIOT SYLLABLE RE
10825	𐠥	CYPRIOT SYLLABLE RI
10826	𐠦	CYPRIOT SYLLABLE RO
10827	𐠧	CYPRIOT SYLLABLE RU
10828	𐠨	CYPRIOT SYLLABLE SA
10829	𐠩	CYPRIOT SYLLABLE SE
1082A	𐠪	CYPRIOT SYLLABLE SI
1082B	𐠫	CYPRIOT SYLLABLE SO
1082C	𐠬	CYPRIOT SYLLABLE SU
1082D	𐠭	CYPRIOT SYLLABLE TA
1082E	𐠮	CYPRIOT SYLLABLE TE
1082F	𐠯	CYPRIOT SYLLABLE TI
10830	𐠰	CYPRIOT SYLLABLE TO
10831	𐠱	CYPRIOT SYLLABLE TU
10832	𐠲	CYPRIOT SYLLABLE WA
10833	𐠳	CYPRIOT SYLLABLE WE
10834	𐠴	CYPRIOT SYLLABLE WI
10835	𐠵	CYPRIOT SYLLABLE WO
10836		<reserved>
10837	𐠷	CYPRIOT SYLLABLE XA
10838	𐠸	CYPRIOT SYLLABLE XE
10839		<reserved>
1083A		<reserved>
1083B		<reserved>
1083C	𐠼	CYPRIOT SYLLABLE ZA
1083D		<reserved>
1083E		<reserved>
1083F	𐠿	CYPRIOT SYLLABLE ZO

	1090	1091
0	𐤀 10900	𐤐 10910
1	𐤁 10901	𐤑 10911
2	𐤂 10902	𐤒 10912
3	𐤃 10903	𐤓 10913
4	𐤄 10904	𐤔 10914
5	𐤅 10905	𐤕 10915
6	𐤆 10906	𐤖 10916
7	𐤇 10907	𐤗 10917
8	𐤈 10908	𐤘 10918
9	𐤉 10909	𐤙 10919
A	𐤊 1090A	
B	𐤋 1090B	
C	𐤌 1090C	
D	𐤍 1090D	
E	𐤎 1090E	
F	𐤏 1090F	𐤟 1091F

Letters

10900 𐤀 PHOENICIAN LETTER ALF
→ 05D0 א hebrew letter alef

10901 𐤁 PHOENICIAN LETTER BET
→ 05D1 ב hebrew letter bet

10902 𐤂 PHOENICIAN LETTER GAML
→ 05D2 ג hebrew letter gimel

10903 𐤃 PHOENICIAN LETTER DELT
→ 05D3 ד hebrew letter dalet

10904 𐤄 PHOENICIAN LETTER HE
→ 05D4 ה hebrew letter he

10905 𐤅 PHOENICIAN LETTER WAU
→ 05D5 ו hebrew letter vav

10906 𐤆 PHOENICIAN LETTER ZAI
→ 05D6 ז hebrew letter zayin

10907 𐤇 PHOENICIAN LETTER HET
→ 05D7 ח hebrew letter het

10908 𐤈 PHOENICIAN LETTER TET
→ 05D8 ט hebrew letter tet

10909 𐤉 PHOENICIAN LETTER YOD
→ 05D9 י hebrew letter yod

1090A 𐤊 PHOENICIAN LETTER KAF
→ 05DB כ hebrew letter kaf

1090B 𐤋 PHOENICIAN LETTER LAMD
→ 05DC ל hebrew letter lamed

1090C 𐤌 PHOENICIAN LETTER MEM
→ 05DE מ hebrew letter mem

1090D 𐤍 PHOENICIAN LETTER NUN
→ 05E0 נ hebrew letter nun

1090E 𐤎 PHOENICIAN LETTER SEMK
→ 05E1 ס hebrew letter samekh

1090F 𐤏 PHOENICIAN LETTER AIN
→ 05E2 ע hebrew letter ayin

10910 𐤐 PHOENICIAN LETTER PE
→ 05E4 פ hebrew letter pe

10911 𐤑 PHOENICIAN LETTER SADE
→ 05E6 צ hebrew letter tsadi

10912 𐤒 PHOENICIAN LETTER QOF
→ 05E7 ק hebrew letter qof

10913 𐤓 PHOENICIAN LETTER ROSH
→ 05E8 ר hebrew letter resh

10914 𐤔 PHOENICIAN LETTER SHIN
→ 05E9 ש hebrew letter shin

10915 𐤕 PHOENICIAN LETTER TAU
→ 05EA ת hebrew letter tav

Numbers

10916 𐤖 PHOENICIAN NUMBER ONE
10917 𐤗 PHOENICIAN NUMBER TEN
10918 𐤘 PHOENICIAN NUMBER TWENTY
10919 𐤙 PHOENICIAN NUMBER ONE HUNDRED

Punctuation

1091F 𐤟 PHOENICIAN WORD SEPARATOR
→ 00B7 · middle dot

	10A0	10A1	10A2	10A3	10A4	10A5
0	10A00	10A10	10A20	10A30	10A40	10A50
1	10A01	10A11	10A21	10A31	10A41	10A51
2	10A02	10A12	10A22	10A32	10A42	10A52
3	10A03	10A13	10A23	10A33	10A43	10A53
4			10A24		10A44	10A54
5	10A05	10A15	10A25		10A45	10A55
6	10A06	10A16	10A26		10A46	10A56
7		10A17	10A27		10A47	10A57
8			10A28	10A38		10A58
9		10A19	10A29	10A39		
A		10A1A	10A2A	10A3A		
B		10A1B	10A2B			
C	10A0C	10A1C	10A2C			
D	10A0D	10A1D	10A2D			
E	10A0E	10A1E	10A2E			
F	10A0F	10A1F	10A2F	10A3F		

Vowels

10A00 𐨀 KHAROSHTHI LETTER A
10A01 ◌𐨁 KHAROSHTHI VOWEL SIGN I
10A02 ◌𐨂 KHAROSHTHI VOWEL SIGN U
10A03 ◌𐨃 KHAROSHTHI VOWEL SIGN VOCALIC R
10A04 <reserved>
10A05 ◌𐨅 KHAROSHTHI VOWEL SIGN E
10A06 ◌𐨆 KHAROSHTHI VOWEL SIGN O

Length mark

10A0C ◌𐨌 KHAROSHTHI VOWEL LENGTH MARK

Various signs

10A0D ◌𐨍 KHAROSHTHI SIGN DOUBLE RING BELOW
10A0E ◌𐨎 KHAROSHTHI SIGN ANUSVARA
10A0F ◌𐨏 KHAROSHTHI SIGN VISARGA

Consonants

10A10 𐨐 KHAROSHTHI LETTER KA
10A11 𐨑 KHAROSHTHI LETTER KHA
10A12 𐨒 KHAROSHTHI LETTER GA
10A13 𐨓 KHAROSHTHI LETTER GHA
10A14 <reserved>
10A15 𐨕 KHAROSHTHI LETTER CA
10A16 𐨖 KHAROSHTHI LETTER CHA
10A17 𐨗 KHAROSHTHI LETTER JA
10A18 <reserved>
10A19 𐨙 KHAROSHTHI LETTER NYA
10A1A 𐨚 KHAROSHTHI LETTER TTA
10A1B 𐨛 KHAROSHTHI LETTER TTHA
10A1C 𐨜 KHAROSHTHI LETTER DDA
10A1D 𐨝 KHAROSHTHI LETTER DDHA
10A1E 𐨞 KHAROSHTHI LETTER NNA
10A1F 𐨟 KHAROSHTHI LETTER TA
10A20 𐨠 KHAROSHTHI LETTER THA
10A21 𐨡 KHAROSHTHI LETTER DA
10A22 𐨢 KHAROSHTHI LETTER DHA
10A23 𐨣 KHAROSHTHI LETTER NA
10A24 𐨤 KHAROSHTHI LETTER PA
10A25 𐨥 KHAROSHTHI LETTER PHA
10A26 𐨦 KHAROSHTHI LETTER BA
10A27 𐨧 KHAROSHTHI LETTER BHA
10A28 𐨨 KHAROSHTHI LETTER MA
10A29 𐨩 KHAROSHTHI LETTER YA
10A2A 𐨪 KHAROSHTHI LETTER RA
10A2B 𐨫 KHAROSHTHI LETTER LA
10A2C 𐨬 KHAROSHTHI LETTER VA
10A2D 𐨭 KHAROSHTHI LETTER SHA
10A2E 𐨮 KHAROSHTHI LETTER SSA
10A2F 𐨯 KHAROSHTHI LETTER SA
10A30 𐨰 KHAROSHTHI LETTER ZA
10A31 𐨱 KHAROSHTHI LETTER HA
10A32 𐨲 KHAROSHTHI LETTER KKA
10A33 𐨳 KHAROSHTHI LETTER TTTHA

Various signs

10A38 ◌𐨸 KHAROSHTHI SIGN BAR ABOVE
10A39 ◌𐨹 KHAROSHTHI SIGN CAUDA
10A3A ◌𐨺 KHAROSHTHI SIGN DOT BELOW

Virama

10A3F ◌𐨿 KHAROSHTHI VIRAMA
= halant
• suppresses inherent vowel
• shape shown is arbitrary and is not visibly rendered

Digits

10A40 𐩀 KHAROSHTHI DIGIT ONE
10A41 𐩁 KHAROSHTHI DIGIT TWO
10A42 𐩂 KHAROSHTHI DIGIT THREE
10A43 𐩃 KHAROSHTHI DIGIT FOUR

Numbers

10A44 𐩄 KHAROSHTHI NUMBER TEN
10A45 𐩅 KHAROSHTHI NUMBER TWENTY
10A46 𐩆 KHAROSHTHI NUMBER ONE HUNDRED
10A47 𐩇 KHAROSHTHI NUMBER ONE THOUSAND

Punctuation

10A50 𐩐 KHAROSHTHI PUNCTUATION DOT
10A51 𐩑 KHAROSHTHI PUNCTUATION SMALL CIRCLE
10A52 𐩒 KHAROSHTHI PUNCTUATION CIRCLE
10A53 𐩓 KHAROSHTHI PUNCTUATION CRESCENT BAR
10A54 𐩔 KHAROSHTHI PUNCTUATION MANGALAM
10A55 𐩕 KHAROSHTHI PUNCTUATION LOTUS
10A56 𐩖 KHAROSHTHI PUNCTUATION DANDA
10A57 𐩗 KHAROSHTHI PUNCTUATION DOUBLE DANDA
10A58 𐩘 KHAROSHTHI PUNCTUATION LINES

	1200	1201	1202	1203	1204	1205	1206	1207	1208	1209	120A	120B	120C	120D	120E	120F
0	12000	12010	12020	12030	12040	12050	12060	12070	12080	12090	120A0	120B0	120C0	120D0	120E0	120F0
1	12001	12011	12021	12031	12041	12051	12061	12071	12081	12091	120A1	120B1	120C1	120D1	120E1	120F1
2	12002	12012	12022	12032	12042	12052	12062	12072	12082	12092	120A2	120B2	120C2	120D2	120E2	120F2
3	12003	12013	12023	12033	12043	12053	12063	12073	12083	12093	120A3	120B3	120C3	120D3	120E3	120F3
4	12004	12014	12024	12034	12044	12054	12064	12074	12084	12094	120A4	120B4	120C4	120D4	120E4	120F4
5	12005	12015	12025	12035	12045	12055	12065	12075	12085	12095	120A5	120B5	120C5	120D5	120E5	120F5
6	12006	12016	12026	12036	12046	12056	12066	12076	12086	12096	120A6	120B6	120C6	120D6	120E6	120F6
7	12007	12017	12027	12037	12047	12057	12067	12077	12087	12097	120A7	120B7	120C7	120D7	120E7	120F7
8	12008	12018	12028	12038	12048	12058	12068	12078	12088	12098	120A8	120B8	120C8	120D8	120E8	120F8
9	12009	12019	12029	12039	12049	12059	12069	12079	12089	12099	120A9	120B9	120C9	120D9	120E9	120F9
A	1200A	1201A	1202A	1203A	1204A	1205A	1206A	1207A	1208A	1209A	120AA	120BA	120CA	120DA	120EA	120FA
B	1200B	1201B	1202B	1203B	1204B	1205B	1206B	1207B	1208B	1209B	120AB	120BB	120CB	120DB	120EB	120FB
C	1200C	1201C	1202C	1203C	1204C	1205C	1206C	1207C	1208C	1209C	120AC	120BC	120CC	120DC	120EC	120FC
D	1200D	1201D	1202D	1203D	1204D	1205D	1206D	1207D	1208D	1209D	120AD	120BD	120CD	120DD	120ED	120FD
E	1200E	1201E	1202E	1203E	1204E	1205E	1206E	1207E	1208E	1209E	120AE	120BE	120CE	120DE	120EE	120FE
F	1200F	1201F	1202F	1203F	1204F	1205F	1206F	1207F	1208F	1209F	120AF	120BF	120CF	120DF	120EF	120FF

	1210	1211	1212	1213	1214	1215	1216	1217	1218	1219	121A	121B	121C	121D	121E	121F
0	12100	12110	12120	12130	12140	12150	12160	12170	12180	12190	121A0	121B0	121C0	121D0	121E0	121F0
1	12101	12111	12121	12131	12141	12151	12161	12171	12181	12191	121A1	121B1	121C1	121D1	121E1	121F1
2	12102	12112	12122	12132	12142	12152	12162	12172	12182	12192	121A2	121B2	121C2	121D2	121E2	121F2
3	12103	12113	12123	12133	12143	12153	12163	12173	12183	12193	121A3	121B3	121C3	121D3	121E3	121F3
4	12104	12114	12124	12134	12144	12154	12164	12174	12184	12194	121A4	121B4	121C4	121D4	121E4	121F4
5	12105	12115	12125	12135	12145	12155	12165	12175	12185	12195	121A5	121B5	121C5	121D5	121E5	121F5
6	12106	12116	12126	12136	12146	12156	12166	12176	12186	12196	121A6	121B6	121C6	121D6	121E6	121F6
7	12107	12117	12127	12137	12147	12157	12167	12177	12187	12197	121A7	121B7	121C7	121D7	121E7	121F7
8	12108	12118	12128	12138	12148	12158	12168	12178	12188	12198	121A8	121B8	121C8	121D8	121E8	121F8
9	12109	12119	12129	12139	12149	12159	12169	12179	12189	12199	121A9	121B9	121C9	121D9	121E9	121F9
A	1210A	1211A	1212A	1213A	1214A	1215A	1216A	1217A	1218A	1219A	121AA	121BA	121CA	121DA	121EA	121FA
B	1210B	1211B	1212B	1213B	1214B	1215B	1216B	1217B	1218B	1219B	121AB	121BB	121CB	121DB	121EB	121FB
C	1210C	1211C	1212C	1213C	1214C	1215C	1216C	1217C	1218C	1219C	121AC	121BC	121CC	121DC	121EC	121FC
D	1210D	1211D	1212D	1213D	1214D	1215D	1216D	1217D	1218D	1219D	121AD	121BD	121CD	121DD	121ED	121FD
E	1210E	1211E	1212E	1213E	1214E	1215E	1216E	1217E	1218E	1219E	121AE	121BE	121CE	121DE	121EE	121FE
F	1210F	1211F	1212F	1213F	1214F	1215F	1216F	1217F	1218F	1219F	121AF	121BF	121CF	121DF	121EF	121FF

	1220	1221	1222	1223	1224	1225	1226	1227	1228	1229	122A	122B	122C	122D	122E	122F
0	12200	12210	12220	12230	12240	12250	12260	12270	12280	12290	122A0	122B0	122C0	122D0	122E0	122F0
1	12201	12211	12221	12231	12241	12251	12261	12271	12281	12291	122A1	122B1	122C1	122D1	122E1	122F1
2	12202	12212	12222	12232	12242	12252	12262	12272	12282	12292	122A2	122B2	122C2	122D2	122E2	122F2
3	12203	12213	12223	12233	12243	12253	12263	12273	12283	12293	122A3	122B3	122C3	122D3	122E3	122F3
4	12204	12214	12224	12234	12244	12254	12264	12274	12284	12294	122A4	122B4	122C4	122D4	122E4	122F4
5	12205	12215	12225	12235	12245	12255	12265	12275	12285	12295	122A5	122B5	122C5	122D5	122E5	122F5
6	12206	12216	12226	12236	12246	12256	12266	12276	12286	12296	122A6	122B6	122C6	122D6	122E6	122F6
7	12207	12217	12227	12237	12247	12257	12267	12277	12287	12297	122A7	122B7	122C7	122D7	122E7	122F7
8	12208	12218	12228	12238	12248	12258	12268	12278	12288	12298	122A8	122B8	122C8	122D8	122E8	122F8
9	12209	12219	12229	12239	12249	12259	12269	12279	12289	12299	122A9	122B9	122C9	122D9	122E9	122F9
A	1220A	1221A	1222A	1223A	1224A	1225A	1226A	1227A	1228A	1229A	122AA	122BA	122CA	122DA	122EA	122FA
B	1220B	1221B	1222B	1223B	1224B	1225B	1226B	1227B	1228B	1229B	122AB	122BB	122CB	122DB	122EB	122FB
C	1220C	1221C	1222C	1223C	1224C	1225C	1226C	1227C	1228C	1229C	122AC	122BC	122CC	122DC	122EC	122FC
D	1220D	1221D	1222D	1223D	1224D	1225D	1226D	1227D	1228D	1229D	122AD	122BD	122CD	122DD	122ED	122FD
E	1220E	1221E	1222E	1223E	1224E	1225E	1226E	1227E	1228E	1229E	122AE	122BE	122CE	122DE	122EE	122FE
F	1220F	1221F	1222F	1223F	1224F	1225F	1226F	1227F	1228F	1229F	122AF	122BF	122CF	122DF	122EF	122FF

	1230	1231	1232	1233	1234	1235	1236	1237	1238	1239	123A	123B	123C	123D	123E	123F
0	12300	12310	12320	12330	12340	12350	12360									
1	12301	12311	12321	12331	12341	12351	12361									
2	12302	12312	12322	12332	12342	12352	12362									
3	12303	12313	12323	12333	12343	12353	12363									
4	12304	12314	12324	12334	12344	12354	12364									
5	12305	12315	12325	12335	12345	12355	12365									
6	12306	12316	12326	12336	12346	12356	12366									
7	12307	12317	12327	12337	12347	12357	12367									
8	12308	12318	12328	12338	12348	12358	12368									
9	12309	12319	12329	12339	12349	12359	12369									
A	1230A	1231A	1232A	1233A	1234A	1235A	1236A									
B	1230B	1231B	1232B	1233B	1234B	1235B	1236B									
C	1230C	1231C	1232C	1233C	1234C	1235C	1236C									
D	1230D	1231D	1232D	1233D	1234D	1235D	1236D									
E	1230E	1231E	1232E	1233E	1234E	1235E	1236E									
F	1230F	1231F	1232F	1233F	1234F	1235F										

Signs

12000 CUNEIFORM SIGN A
12001 CUNEIFORM SIGN A TIMES A
12002 CUNEIFORM SIGN A TIMES BAD
12003 CUNEIFORM SIGN A TIMES GAN2 TENU
12004 CUNEIFORM SIGN A TIMES HA
12005 CUNEIFORM SIGN A TIMES IGI
12006 CUNEIFORM SIGN A TIMES LAGAR GUNU
12007 CUNEIFORM SIGN A TIMES MUSH
12008 CUNEIFORM SIGN A TIMES SAG
12009 CUNEIFORM SIGN A2
1200A CUNEIFORM SIGN AB
1200B CUNEIFORM SIGN AB TIMES ASH2
1200C CUNEIFORM SIGN AB TIMES DUN3 GUNU
1200D CUNEIFORM SIGN AB TIMES GAL
1200E CUNEIFORM SIGN AB TIMES GAN2 TENU
1200F CUNEIFORM SIGN AB TIMES HA
12010 CUNEIFORM SIGN AB TIMES IGI GUNU
12011 CUNEIFORM SIGN AB TIMES IMIN
12012 CUNEIFORM SIGN AB TIMES LAGAB
12013 CUNEIFORM SIGN AB TIMES SHESH
12014 CUNEIFORM SIGN AB TIMES U PLUS U PLUS U
12015 CUNEIFORM SIGN AB GUNU
12016 CUNEIFORM SIGN AB2
12017 CUNEIFORM SIGN AB2 TIMES BALAG
12018 CUNEIFORM SIGN AB2 TIMES GAN2 TENU
12019 CUNEIFORM SIGN AB2 TIMES ME PLUS EN
1201A CUNEIFORM SIGN AB2 TIMES SHA3
1201B CUNEIFORM SIGN AB2 TIMES TAK4
1201C CUNEIFORM SIGN AD
1201D CUNEIFORM SIGN AK
1201E CUNEIFORM SIGN AK TIMES ERIN2
1201F CUNEIFORM SIGN AK TIMES SHITA PLUS GISH
12020 CUNEIFORM SIGN AL
12021 CUNEIFORM SIGN AL TIMES AL
12022 CUNEIFORM SIGN AL TIMES DIM2
12023 CUNEIFORM SIGN AL TIMES GISH
12024 CUNEIFORM SIGN AL TIMES HA
12025 CUNEIFORM SIGN AL TIMES KAD3
12026 CUNEIFORM SIGN AL TIMES KI
12027 CUNEIFORM SIGN AL TIMES SHE
12028 CUNEIFORM SIGN AL TIMES USH
12029 CUNEIFORM SIGN ALAN
1202A CUNEIFORM SIGN ALEPH
1202B CUNEIFORM SIGN AMAR
1202C CUNEIFORM SIGN AMAR TIMES SHE
1202D CUNEIFORM SIGN AN
1202E CUNEIFORM SIGN AN OVER AN
1202F CUNEIFORM SIGN AN THREE TIMES
12030 CUNEIFORM SIGN AN PLUS NAGA OPPOSING AN PLUS NAGA
12031 CUNEIFORM SIGN AN PLUS NAGA SQUARED
12032 CUNEIFORM SIGN ANSHE
12033 CUNEIFORM SIGN APIN
12034 CUNEIFORM SIGN ARAD
12035 CUNEIFORM SIGN ARAD TIMES KUR
12036 CUNEIFORM SIGN ARKAB
12037 CUNEIFORM SIGN ASAL2
12038 CUNEIFORM SIGN ASH
12039 CUNEIFORM SIGN ASH ZIDA TENU
1203A CUNEIFORM SIGN ASH KABA TENU
1203B CUNEIFORM SIGN ASH OVER ASH TUG2 OVER TUG2 TUG2 OVER TUG2 PAP
1203C CUNEIFORM SIGN ASH OVER ASH OVER ASH
1203D CUNEIFORM SIGN ASH OVER ASH OVER ASH CROSSING ASH OVER ASH OVER ASH
1203E CUNEIFORM SIGN ASH2
1203F CUNEIFORM SIGN ASHGAB
12040 CUNEIFORM SIGN BA
12041 CUNEIFORM SIGN BAD
12042 CUNEIFORM SIGN BAG3
12043 CUNEIFORM SIGN BAHAR2
12044 CUNEIFORM SIGN BAL
12045 CUNEIFORM SIGN BAL OVER BAL
12046 CUNEIFORM SIGN BALAG
12047 CUNEIFORM SIGN BAR
12048 CUNEIFORM SIGN BARA2
12049 CUNEIFORM SIGN BI
1204A CUNEIFORM SIGN BI TIMES A
1204B CUNEIFORM SIGN BI TIMES GAR
1204C CUNEIFORM SIGN BI TIMES IGI GUNU
1204D CUNEIFORM SIGN BU
1204E CUNEIFORM SIGN BU OVER BU AB
1204F CUNEIFORM SIGN BU OVER BU UN
12050 CUNEIFORM SIGN BU CROSSING BU
12051 CUNEIFORM SIGN BULUG
12052 CUNEIFORM SIGN BULUG OVER BULUG
12053 CUNEIFORM SIGN BUR
12054 CUNEIFORM SIGN BUR2
12055 CUNEIFORM SIGN DA
12056 CUNEIFORM SIGN DAG
12057 CUNEIFORM SIGN DAG KISIM5 TIMES A PLUS MASH
12058 CUNEIFORM SIGN DAG KISIM5 TIMES AMAR
12059 CUNEIFORM SIGN DAG KISIM5 TIMES BALAG
1205A CUNEIFORM SIGN DAG KISIM5 TIMES BI
1205B CUNEIFORM SIGN DAG KISIM5 TIMES GA
1205C CUNEIFORM SIGN DAG KISIM5 TIMES GA PLUS MASH
1205D CUNEIFORM SIGN DAG KISIM5 TIMES GI
1205E CUNEIFORM SIGN DAG KISIM5 TIMES GIR2
1205F CUNEIFORM SIGN DAG KISIM5 TIMES GUD
12060 CUNEIFORM SIGN DAG KISIM5 TIMES HA
12061 CUNEIFORM SIGN DAG KISIM5 TIMES IR
12062 CUNEIFORM SIGN DAG KISIM5 TIMES IR PLUS LU
12063 CUNEIFORM SIGN DAG KISIM5 TIMES KAK
12064 CUNEIFORM SIGN DAG KISIM5 TIMES LA
12065 CUNEIFORM SIGN DAG KISIM5 TIMES LU
12066 CUNEIFORM SIGN DAG KISIM5 TIMES LU PLUS MASH2
12067 CUNEIFORM SIGN DAG KISIM5 TIMES LUM
12068 CUNEIFORM SIGN DAG KISIM5 TIMES NE
12069 CUNEIFORM SIGN DAG KISIM5 TIMES PAP PLUS PAP
1206A CUNEIFORM SIGN DAG KISIM5 TIMES SI
1206B CUNEIFORM SIGN DAG KISIM5 TIMES TAK4
1206C CUNEIFORM SIGN DAG KISIM5 TIMES U2 PLUS GIR2
1206D CUNEIFORM SIGN DAG KISIM5 TIMES USH
1206E CUNEIFORM SIGN DAM
1206F CUNEIFORM SIGN DAR
12070 CUNEIFORM SIGN DARA3
12071 CUNEIFORM SIGN DARA4
12072 CUNEIFORM SIGN DI
12073 CUNEIFORM SIGN DIB
12074 CUNEIFORM SIGN DIM
12075 CUNEIFORM SIGN DIM TIMES SHE
12076 CUNEIFORM SIGN DIM2

12077 CUNEIFORM SIGN DIN
12078 CUNEIFORM SIGN DIN KASKAL U GUNU DISH
12079 CUNEIFORM SIGN DISH
1207A CUNEIFORM SIGN DU
1207B CUNEIFORM SIGN DU OVER DU
1207C CUNEIFORM SIGN DU GUNU
1207D CUNEIFORM SIGN DU SHESHIG
1207E CUNEIFORM SIGN DUB
1207F CUNEIFORM SIGN DUB TIMES ESH2
12080 CUNEIFORM SIGN DUB2
12081 CUNEIFORM SIGN DUG
12082 CUNEIFORM SIGN DUGUD
12083 CUNEIFORM SIGN DUH
12084 CUNEIFORM SIGN DUN
12085 CUNEIFORM SIGN DUN3
12086 CUNEIFORM SIGN DUN3 GUNU
12087 CUNEIFORM SIGN DUN3 GUNU GUNU
12088 CUNEIFORM SIGN DUN4
12089 CUNEIFORM SIGN DUR2
1208A CUNEIFORM SIGN E
1208B CUNEIFORM SIGN E TIMES PAP
1208C CUNEIFORM SIGN E OVER E NUN OVER NUN
1208D CUNEIFORM SIGN E2
1208E CUNEIFORM SIGN E2 TIMES A PLUS HA PLUS DA
1208F CUNEIFORM SIGN E2 TIMES GAR
12090 CUNEIFORM SIGN E2 TIMES MI
12091 CUNEIFORM SIGN E2 TIMES SAL
12092 CUNEIFORM SIGN E2 TIMES SHE
12093 CUNEIFORM SIGN E2 TIMES U
12094 CUNEIFORM SIGN EDIN
12095 CUNEIFORM SIGN EGIR
12096 CUNEIFORM SIGN EL
12097 CUNEIFORM SIGN EN
12098 CUNEIFORM SIGN EN TIMES GAN2
12099 CUNEIFORM SIGN EN TIMES GAN2 TENU
1209A CUNEIFORM SIGN EN TIMES ME
1209B CUNEIFORM SIGN EN CROSSING EN
1209C CUNEIFORM SIGN EN OPPOSING EN
1209D CUNEIFORM SIGN EN SQUARED
1209E CUNEIFORM SIGN EREN
1209F CUNEIFORM SIGN ERIN2
120A0 CUNEIFORM SIGN ESH2
120A1 CUNEIFORM SIGN EZEN
120A2 CUNEIFORM SIGN EZEN TIMES A
120A3 CUNEIFORM SIGN EZEN TIMES A PLUS LAL
120A4 CUNEIFORM SIGN EZEN TIMES A PLUS LAL TIMES LAL
120A5 CUNEIFORM SIGN EZEN TIMES AN
120A6 CUNEIFORM SIGN EZEN TIMES BAD
120A7 CUNEIFORM SIGN EZEN TIMES DUN3 GUNU
120A8 CUNEIFORM SIGN EZEN TIMES DUN3 GUNU GUNU
120A9 CUNEIFORM SIGN EZEN TIMES HA
120AA CUNEIFORM SIGN EZEN TIMES HA GUNU
120AB CUNEIFORM SIGN EZEN TIMES IGI GUNU
120AC CUNEIFORM SIGN EZEN TIMES KASKAL
120AD CUNEIFORM SIGN EZEN TIMES KASKAL SQUARED
120AE CUNEIFORM SIGN EZEN TIMES KU3
120AF CUNEIFORM SIGN EZEN TIMES LA
120B0 CUNEIFORM SIGN EZEN TIMES LAL TIMES LAL
120B1 CUNEIFORM SIGN EZEN TIMES LI
120B2 CUNEIFORM SIGN EZEN TIMES LU
120B3 CUNEIFORM SIGN EZEN TIMES U2
120B4 CUNEIFORM SIGN EZEN TIMES UD
120B5 CUNEIFORM SIGN GA
120B6 CUNEIFORM SIGN GA GUNU
120B7 CUNEIFORM SIGN GA2
120B8 CUNEIFORM SIGN GA2 TIMES A PLUS DA PLUS HA
120B9 CUNEIFORM SIGN GA2 TIMES A PLUS HA
120BA CUNEIFORM SIGN GA2 TIMES A PLUS IGI
120BB CUNEIFORM SIGN GA2 TIMES AB2 TENU PLUS TAB
120BC CUNEIFORM SIGN GA2 TIMES AN
120BD CUNEIFORM SIGN GA2 TIMES ASH
120BE CUNEIFORM SIGN GA2 TIMES ASH2 PLUS GAL
120BF CUNEIFORM SIGN GA2 TIMES BAD
120C0 CUNEIFORM SIGN GA2 TIMES BAR PLUS RA
120C1 CUNEIFORM SIGN GA2 TIMES BUR
120C2 CUNEIFORM SIGN GA2 TIMES BUR PLUS RA
120C3 CUNEIFORM SIGN GA2 TIMES DA
120C4 CUNEIFORM SIGN GA2 TIMES DI
120C5 CUNEIFORM SIGN GA2 TIMES DIM TIMES SHE
120C6 CUNEIFORM SIGN GA2 TIMES DUB
120C7 CUNEIFORM SIGN GA2 TIMES EL
120C8 CUNEIFORM SIGN GA2 TIMES EL PLUS LA
120C9 CUNEIFORM SIGN GA2 TIMES EN
120CA CUNEIFORM SIGN GA2 TIMES EN TIMES GAN2 TENU
120CB CUNEIFORM SIGN GA2 TIMES GAN2 TENU
120CC CUNEIFORM SIGN GA2 TIMES GAR
120CD CUNEIFORM SIGN GA2 TIMES GI
120CE CUNEIFORM SIGN GA2 TIMES GI4
120CF CUNEIFORM SIGN GA2 TIMES GI4 PLUS A
120D0 CUNEIFORM SIGN GA2 TIMES GIR2 PLUS SU
120D1 CUNEIFORM SIGN GA2 TIMES HA PLUS LU PLUS ESH2
120D2 CUNEIFORM SIGN GA2 TIMES HAL
120D3 CUNEIFORM SIGN GA2 TIMES HAL PLUS LA
120D4 CUNEIFORM SIGN GA2 TIMES HI PLUS LI
120D5 CUNEIFORM SIGN GA2 TIMES HUB2
120D6 CUNEIFORM SIGN GA2 TIMES IGI GUNU
120D7 CUNEIFORM SIGN GA2 TIMES ISH PLUS HU PLUS ASH
120D8 CUNEIFORM SIGN GA2 TIMES KAK
120D9 CUNEIFORM SIGN GA2 TIMES KASKAL
120DA CUNEIFORM SIGN GA2 TIMES KID
120DB CUNEIFORM SIGN GA2 TIMES KID PLUS LAL
120DC CUNEIFORM SIGN GA2 TIMES KU3 PLUS AN
120DD CUNEIFORM SIGN GA2 TIMES LA
120DE CUNEIFORM SIGN GA2 TIMES ME PLUS EN
120DF CUNEIFORM SIGN GA2 TIMES MI
120E0 CUNEIFORM SIGN GA2 TIMES NUN
120E1 CUNEIFORM SIGN GA2 TIMES NUN OVER NUN
120E2 CUNEIFORM SIGN GA2 TIMES PA
120E3 CUNEIFORM SIGN GA2 TIMES SAL
120E4 CUNEIFORM SIGN GA2 TIMES SAR
120E5 CUNEIFORM SIGN GA2 TIMES SHE
120E6 CUNEIFORM SIGN GA2 TIMES SHE PLUS TUR
120E7 CUNEIFORM SIGN GA2 TIMES SHID
120E8 CUNEIFORM SIGN GA2 TIMES SUM
120E9 CUNEIFORM SIGN GA2 TIMES TAK4
120EA CUNEIFORM SIGN GA2 TIMES U
120EB CUNEIFORM SIGN GA2 TIMES UD
120EC CUNEIFORM SIGN GA2 TIMES UD PLUS DU
120ED CUNEIFORM SIGN GA2 OVER GA2

120EE CUNEIFORM SIGN GABA
120EF CUNEIFORM SIGN GABA CROSSING GABA
120F0 CUNEIFORM SIGN GAD
120F1 CUNEIFORM SIGN GAD OVER GAD GAR OVER GAR
120F2 CUNEIFORM SIGN GAL
120F3 CUNEIFORM SIGN GAL GAD OVER GAD GAR OVER GAR
120F4 CUNEIFORM SIGN GALAM
120F5 CUNEIFORM SIGN GAM
120F6 CUNEIFORM SIGN GAN
120F7 CUNEIFORM SIGN GAN2
120F8 CUNEIFORM SIGN GAN2 TENU
120F9 CUNEIFORM SIGN GAN2 OVER GAN2
120FA CUNEIFORM SIGN GAN2 CROSSING GAN2
120FB CUNEIFORM SIGN GAR
120FC CUNEIFORM SIGN GAR3
120FD CUNEIFORM SIGN GASHAN
120FE CUNEIFORM SIGN GESHTIN
120FF CUNEIFORM SIGN GESHTIN TIMES KUR
12100 CUNEIFORM SIGN GI
12101 CUNEIFORM SIGN GI TIMES E
12102 CUNEIFORM SIGN GI TIMES U
12103 CUNEIFORM SIGN GI CROSSING GI
12104 CUNEIFORM SIGN GI4
12105 CUNEIFORM SIGN GI4 OVER GI4
12106 CUNEIFORM SIGN GI4 CROSSING GI4
12107 CUNEIFORM SIGN GIDIM
12108 CUNEIFORM SIGN GIR2
12109 CUNEIFORM SIGN GIR2 GUNU
1210A CUNEIFORM SIGN GIR3
1210B CUNEIFORM SIGN GIR3 TIMES A PLUS IGI
1210C CUNEIFORM SIGN GIR3 TIMES GAN2 TENU
1210D CUNEIFORM SIGN GIR3 TIMES IGI
1210E CUNEIFORM SIGN GIR3 TIMES LU PLUS IGI
1210F CUNEIFORM SIGN GIR3 TIMES PA
12110 CUNEIFORM SIGN GISAL
12111 CUNEIFORM SIGN GISH
12112 CUNEIFORM SIGN GISH CROSSING GISH
12113 CUNEIFORM SIGN GISH TIMES BAD
12114 CUNEIFORM SIGN GISH TIMES TAK4
12115 CUNEIFORM SIGN GISH TENU
12116 CUNEIFORM SIGN GU
12117 CUNEIFORM SIGN GU CROSSING GU
12118 CUNEIFORM SIGN GU2
12119 CUNEIFORM SIGN GU2 TIMES KAK
1211A CUNEIFORM SIGN GU2 TIMES KAK TIMES IGI GUNU
1211B CUNEIFORM SIGN GU2 TIMES NUN
1211C CUNEIFORM SIGN GU2 TIMES SAL PLUS TUG2
1211D CUNEIFORM SIGN GU2 GUNU
1211E CUNEIFORM SIGN GUD
1211F CUNEIFORM SIGN GUD TIMES A PLUS KUR
12120 CUNEIFORM SIGN GUD TIMES KUR
12121 CUNEIFORM SIGN GUD OVER GUD LUGAL
12122 CUNEIFORM SIGN GUL
12123 CUNEIFORM SIGN GUM
12124 CUNEIFORM SIGN GUM TIMES SHE
12125 CUNEIFORM SIGN GUR
12126 CUNEIFORM SIGN GUR7
12127 CUNEIFORM SIGN GURUN
12128 CUNEIFORM SIGN GURUSH
12129 CUNEIFORM SIGN HA
1212A CUNEIFORM SIGN HA TENU
1212B CUNEIFORM SIGN HA GUNU
1212C CUNEIFORM SIGN HAL
1212D CUNEIFORM SIGN HI
1212E CUNEIFORM SIGN HI TIMES ASH
1212F CUNEIFORM SIGN HI TIMES ASH2
12130 CUNEIFORM SIGN HI TIMES BAD
12131 CUNEIFORM SIGN HI TIMES DISH
12132 CUNEIFORM SIGN HI TIMES GAD
12133 CUNEIFORM SIGN HI TIMES KIN
12134 CUNEIFORM SIGN HI TIMES NUN
12135 CUNEIFORM SIGN HI TIMES SHE
12136 CUNEIFORM SIGN HI TIMES U
12137 CUNEIFORM SIGN HU
12138 CUNEIFORM SIGN HUB2
12139 CUNEIFORM SIGN HUB2 TIMES AN
1213A CUNEIFORM SIGN HUB2 TIMES HAL
1213B CUNEIFORM SIGN HUB2 TIMES KASKAL
1213C CUNEIFORM SIGN HUB2 TIMES LISH
1213D CUNEIFORM SIGN HUB2 TIMES UD
1213E CUNEIFORM SIGN HUL2
1213F CUNEIFORM SIGN I
12140 CUNEIFORM SIGN I A
12141 CUNEIFORM SIGN IB
12142 CUNEIFORM SIGN IDIM
12143 CUNEIFORM SIGN IDIM OVER IDIM BUR
12144 CUNEIFORM SIGN IDIM OVER IDIM SQUARED
12145 CUNEIFORM SIGN IG
12146 CUNEIFORM SIGN IGI
12147 CUNEIFORM SIGN IGI DIB
12148 CUNEIFORM SIGN IGI RI
12149 CUNEIFORM SIGN IGI OVER IGI SHIR OVER SHIR UD OVER UD
1214A CUNEIFORM SIGN IGI GUNU
1214B CUNEIFORM SIGN IL
1214C CUNEIFORM SIGN IL TIMES GAN2 TENU
1214D CUNEIFORM SIGN IL2
1214E CUNEIFORM SIGN IM
1214F CUNEIFORM SIGN IM TIMES TAK4
12150 CUNEIFORM SIGN IM CROSSING IM
12151 CUNEIFORM SIGN IM OPPOSING IM
12152 CUNEIFORM SIGN IM SQUARED
12153 CUNEIFORM SIGN IMIN
12154 CUNEIFORM SIGN IN
12155 CUNEIFORM SIGN IR
12156 CUNEIFORM SIGN ISH
12157 CUNEIFORM SIGN KA
12158 CUNEIFORM SIGN KA TIMES A
12159 CUNEIFORM SIGN KA TIMES AD
1215A CUNEIFORM SIGN KA TIMES AD PLUS KU3
1215B CUNEIFORM SIGN KA TIMES ASH2
1215C CUNEIFORM SIGN KA TIMES BAD
1215D CUNEIFORM SIGN KA TIMES BALAG
1215E CUNEIFORM SIGN KA TIMES BAR
1215F CUNEIFORM SIGN KA TIMES BI
12160 CUNEIFORM SIGN KA TIMES ERIN2
12161 CUNEIFORM SIGN KA TIMES ESH2
12162 CUNEIFORM SIGN KA TIMES GA
12163 CUNEIFORM SIGN KA TIMES GAL
12164 CUNEIFORM SIGN KA TIMES GAN2 TENU
12165 CUNEIFORM SIGN KA TIMES GAR
12166 CUNEIFORM SIGN KA TIMES GAR PLUS SHA3 PLUS A
12167 CUNEIFORM SIGN KA TIMES GI
12168 CUNEIFORM SIGN KA TIMES GIR2

12169 CUNEIFORM SIGN KA TIMES GISH PLUS SAR
1216A CUNEIFORM SIGN KA TIMES GISH CROSSING GISH
1216B CUNEIFORM SIGN KA TIMES GU
1216C CUNEIFORM SIGN KA TIMES GUR7
1216D CUNEIFORM SIGN KA TIMES IGI
1216E CUNEIFORM SIGN KA TIMES IM
1216F CUNEIFORM SIGN KA TIMES KAK
12170 CUNEIFORM SIGN KA TIMES KI
12171 CUNEIFORM SIGN KA TIMES KID
12172 CUNEIFORM SIGN KA TIMES LI
12173 CUNEIFORM SIGN KA TIMES LU
12174 CUNEIFORM SIGN KA TIMES ME
12175 CUNEIFORM SIGN KA TIMES ME PLUS DU
12176 CUNEIFORM SIGN KA TIMES ME PLUS GI
12177 CUNEIFORM SIGN KA TIMES ME PLUS TE
12178 CUNEIFORM SIGN KA TIMES MI
12179 CUNEIFORM SIGN KA TIMES MI PLUS NUNUZ
1217A CUNEIFORM SIGN KA TIMES NE
1217B CUNEIFORM SIGN KA TIMES NUN
1217C CUNEIFORM SIGN KA TIMES PI
1217D CUNEIFORM SIGN KA TIMES RU
1217E CUNEIFORM SIGN KA TIMES SA
1217F CUNEIFORM SIGN KA TIMES SAR
12180 CUNEIFORM SIGN KA TIMES SHA
12181 CUNEIFORM SIGN KA TIMES SHE
12182 CUNEIFORM SIGN KA TIMES SHID
12183 CUNEIFORM SIGN KA TIMES SHU
12184 CUNEIFORM SIGN KA TIMES SIG
12185 CUNEIFORM SIGN KA TIMES SUHUR
12186 CUNEIFORM SIGN KA TIMES TAR
12187 CUNEIFORM SIGN KA TIMES U
12188 CUNEIFORM SIGN KA TIMES U2
12189 CUNEIFORM SIGN KA TIMES UD
1218A CUNEIFORM SIGN KA TIMES UMUM TIMES PA
1218B CUNEIFORM SIGN KA TIMES USH
1218C CUNEIFORM SIGN KA TIMES ZI
1218D CUNEIFORM SIGN KA2
1218E CUNEIFORM SIGN KA2 CROSSING KA2
1218F CUNEIFORM SIGN KAB
12190 CUNEIFORM SIGN KAD2
12191 CUNEIFORM SIGN KAD3
12192 CUNEIFORM SIGN KAD4
12193 CUNEIFORM SIGN KAD5
12194 CUNEIFORM SIGN KAD5 OVER KAD5
12195 CUNEIFORM SIGN KAK
12196 CUNEIFORM SIGN KAK TIMES IGI GUNU
12197 CUNEIFORM SIGN KAL
12198 CUNEIFORM SIGN KAL TIMES BAD
12199 CUNEIFORM SIGN KAL CROSSING KAL
1219A CUNEIFORM SIGN KAM2
1219B CUNEIFORM SIGN KAM4
1219C CUNEIFORM SIGN KASKAL
1219D CUNEIFORM SIGN KASKAL LAGAB TIMES U OVER LAGAB TIMES U
1219E CUNEIFORM SIGN KASKAL OVER KASKAL LAGAB TIMES U OVER LAGAB TIMES U
1219F CUNEIFORM SIGN KESH2
121A0 CUNEIFORM SIGN KI
121A1 CUNEIFORM SIGN KI TIMES BAD
121A2 CUNEIFORM SIGN KI TIMES U
121A3 CUNEIFORM SIGN KI TIMES UD
121A4 CUNEIFORM SIGN KID
121A5 CUNEIFORM SIGN KIN
121A6 CUNEIFORM SIGN KISAL
121A7 CUNEIFORM SIGN KISH
121A8 CUNEIFORM SIGN KISIM5
121A9 CUNEIFORM SIGN KISIM5 OVER KISIM5
121AA CUNEIFORM SIGN KU
121AB CUNEIFORM SIGN KU OVER HI TIMES ASH2 KU OVER HI TIMES ASH2
121AC CUNEIFORM SIGN KU3
121AD CUNEIFORM SIGN KU4
121AE CUNEIFORM SIGN KU4 VARIANT FORM
121AF CUNEIFORM SIGN KU7
121B0 CUNEIFORM SIGN KUL
121B1 CUNEIFORM SIGN KUL GUNU
121B2 CUNEIFORM SIGN KUN
121B3 CUNEIFORM SIGN KUR
121B4 CUNEIFORM SIGN KUR OPPOSING KUR
121B5 CUNEIFORM SIGN KUSHU2
121B6 CUNEIFORM SIGN KWU318
121B7 CUNEIFORM SIGN LA
121B8 CUNEIFORM SIGN LAGAB
121B9 CUNEIFORM SIGN LAGAB TIMES A
121BA CUNEIFORM SIGN LAGAB TIMES A PLUS DA PLUS HA
121BB CUNEIFORM SIGN LAGAB TIMES A PLUS GAR
121BC CUNEIFORM SIGN LAGAB TIMES A PLUS LAL
121BD CUNEIFORM SIGN LAGAB TIMES AL
121BE CUNEIFORM SIGN LAGAB TIMES AN
121BF CUNEIFORM SIGN LAGAB TIMES ASH ZIDA TENU
121C0 CUNEIFORM SIGN LAGAB TIMES BAD
121C1 CUNEIFORM SIGN LAGAB TIMES BI
121C2 CUNEIFORM SIGN LAGAB TIMES DAR
121C3 CUNEIFORM SIGN LAGAB TIMES EN
121C4 CUNEIFORM SIGN LAGAB TIMES GA
121C5 CUNEIFORM SIGN LAGAB TIMES GAR
121C6 CUNEIFORM SIGN LAGAB TIMES GUD
121C7 CUNEIFORM SIGN LAGAB TIMES GUD PLUS GUD
121C8 CUNEIFORM SIGN LAGAB TIMES HA
121C9 CUNEIFORM SIGN LAGAB TIMES HAL
121CA CUNEIFORM SIGN LAGAB TIMES HI TIMES NUN
121CB CUNEIFORM SIGN LAGAB TIMES IGI GUNU
121CC CUNEIFORM SIGN LAGAB TIMES IM
121CD CUNEIFORM SIGN LAGAB TIMES IM PLUS HA
121CE CUNEIFORM SIGN LAGAB TIMES IM PLUS LU
121CF CUNEIFORM SIGN LAGAB TIMES KI
121D0 CUNEIFORM SIGN LAGAB TIMES KIN
121D1 CUNEIFORM SIGN LAGAB TIMES KU3
121D2 CUNEIFORM SIGN LAGAB TIMES KUL
121D3 CUNEIFORM SIGN LAGAB TIMES KUL PLUS HI PLUS A
121D4 CUNEIFORM SIGN LAGAB TIMES LAGAB
121D5 CUNEIFORM SIGN LAGAB TIMES LISH
121D6 CUNEIFORM SIGN LAGAB TIMES LU
121D7 CUNEIFORM SIGN LAGAB TIMES LUL
121D8 CUNEIFORM SIGN LAGAB TIMES ME
121D9 CUNEIFORM SIGN LAGAB TIMES ME PLUS EN
121DA CUNEIFORM SIGN LAGAB TIMES MUSH
121DB CUNEIFORM SIGN LAGAB TIMES NE
121DC CUNEIFORM SIGN LAGAB TIMES SHE PLUS SUM
121DD CUNEIFORM SIGN LAGAB TIMES SHITA PLUS GISH PLUS ERIN2
121DE CUNEIFORM SIGN LAGAB TIMES SHITA PLUS GISH TENU
121DF CUNEIFORM SIGN LAGAB TIMES SHU2

121E0 CUNEIFORM SIGN LAGAB TIMES SHU2 PLUS SHU2
121E1 CUNEIFORM SIGN LAGAB TIMES SUM
121E2 CUNEIFORM SIGN LAGAB TIMES TAG
121E3 CUNEIFORM SIGN LAGAB TIMES TAK4
121E4 CUNEIFORM SIGN LAGAB TIMES TE PLUS A PLUS SU PLUS NA
121E5 CUNEIFORM SIGN LAGAB TIMES U
121E6 CUNEIFORM SIGN LAGAB TIMES U PLUS A
121E7 CUNEIFORM SIGN LAGAB TIMES U PLUS U PLUS U
121E8 CUNEIFORM SIGN LAGAB TIMES U2 PLUS ASH
121E9 CUNEIFORM SIGN LAGAB TIMES UD
121EA CUNEIFORM SIGN LAGAB TIMES USH
121EB CUNEIFORM SIGN LAGAB SQUARED
121EC CUNEIFORM SIGN LAGAR
121ED CUNEIFORM SIGN LAGAR TIMES SHE
121EE CUNEIFORM SIGN LAGAR TIMES SHE PLUS SUM
121EF CUNEIFORM SIGN LAGAR GUNU
121F0 CUNEIFORM SIGN LAGAR GUNU OVER LAGAR GUNU SHE
121F1 CUNEIFORM SIGN LAHSHU
121F2 CUNEIFORM SIGN LAL
121F3 CUNEIFORM SIGN LAL TIMES LAL
121F4 CUNEIFORM SIGN LAM
121F5 CUNEIFORM SIGN LAM TIMES KUR
121F6 CUNEIFORM SIGN LAM TIMES KUR PLUS RU
121F7 CUNEIFORM SIGN LI
121F8 CUNEIFORM SIGN LIL
121F9 CUNEIFORM SIGN LIMMU2
121FA CUNEIFORM SIGN LISH
121FB CUNEIFORM SIGN LU
121FC CUNEIFORM SIGN LU TIMES BAD
121FD CUNEIFORM SIGN LU2
121FE CUNEIFORM SIGN LU2 TIMES AL
121FF CUNEIFORM SIGN LU2 TIMES BAD
12200 CUNEIFORM SIGN LU2 TIMES ESH2
12201 CUNEIFORM SIGN LU2 TIMES ESH2 TENU
12202 CUNEIFORM SIGN LU2 TIMES GAN2 TENU
12203 CUNEIFORM SIGN LU2 TIMES HI TIMES BAD
12204 CUNEIFORM SIGN LU2 TIMES IM
12205 CUNEIFORM SIGN LU2 TIMES KAD2
12206 CUNEIFORM SIGN LU2 TIMES KAD3
12207 CUNEIFORM SIGN LU2 TIMES KAD3 PLUS ASH
12208 CUNEIFORM SIGN LU2 TIMES KI
12209 CUNEIFORM SIGN LU2 TIMES LA PLUS ASH
1220A CUNEIFORM SIGN LU2 TIMES LAGAB
1220B CUNEIFORM SIGN LU2 TIMES ME PLUS EN
1220C CUNEIFORM SIGN LU2 TIMES NE
1220D CUNEIFORM SIGN LU2 TIMES NU
1220E CUNEIFORM SIGN LU2 TIMES SI PLUS ASH
1220F CUNEIFORM SIGN LU2 TIMES SIK2 PLUS BU
12210 CUNEIFORM SIGN LU2 TIMES TUG2
12211 CUNEIFORM SIGN LU2 TENU
12212 CUNEIFORM SIGN LU2 CROSSING LU2
12213 CUNEIFORM SIGN LU2 OPPOSING LU2
12214 CUNEIFORM SIGN LU2 SQUARED
12215 CUNEIFORM SIGN LU2 SHESHIG
12216 CUNEIFORM SIGN LU3
12217 CUNEIFORM SIGN LUGAL
12218 CUNEIFORM SIGN LUGAL OVER LUGAL
12219 CUNEIFORM SIGN LUGAL OPPOSING LUGAL
1221A CUNEIFORM SIGN LUGAL SHESHIG
1221B CUNEIFORM SIGN LUH
1221C CUNEIFORM SIGN LUL
1221D CUNEIFORM SIGN LUM
1221E CUNEIFORM SIGN LUM OVER LUM
1221F CUNEIFORM SIGN LUM OVER LUM GAR OVER GAR
12220 CUNEIFORM SIGN MA
12221 CUNEIFORM SIGN MA TIMES TAK4
12222 CUNEIFORM SIGN MA GUNU
12223 CUNEIFORM SIGN MA2
12224 CUNEIFORM SIGN MAH
12225 CUNEIFORM SIGN MAR
12226 CUNEIFORM SIGN MASH
12227 CUNEIFORM SIGN MASH2
12228 CUNEIFORM SIGN ME
12229 CUNEIFORM SIGN MES
1222A CUNEIFORM SIGN MI
1222B CUNEIFORM SIGN MIN
1222C CUNEIFORM SIGN MU
1222D CUNEIFORM SIGN MU OVER MU
1222E CUNEIFORM SIGN MUG
1222F CUNEIFORM SIGN MUG GUNU
12230 CUNEIFORM SIGN MUNSUB
12231 CUNEIFORM SIGN MURGU2
12232 CUNEIFORM SIGN MUSH
12233 CUNEIFORM SIGN MUSH TIMES A
12234 CUNEIFORM SIGN MUSH TIMES KUR
12235 CUNEIFORM SIGN MUSH TIMES ZA
12236 CUNEIFORM SIGN MUSH OVER MUSH
12237 CUNEIFORM SIGN MUSH OVER MUSH TIMES A PLUS NA
12238 CUNEIFORM SIGN MUSH CROSSING MUSH
12239 CUNEIFORM SIGN MUSH3
1223A CUNEIFORM SIGN MUSH3 TIMES A
1223B CUNEIFORM SIGN MUSH3 TIMES A PLUS DI
1223C CUNEIFORM SIGN MUSH3 TIMES DI
1223D CUNEIFORM SIGN MUSH3 GUNU
1223E CUNEIFORM SIGN NA
1223F CUNEIFORM SIGN NA2
12240 CUNEIFORM SIGN NAGA
12241 CUNEIFORM SIGN NAGA INVERTED
12242 CUNEIFORM SIGN NAGA TIMES SHU TENU
12243 CUNEIFORM SIGN NAGA OPPOSING NAGA
12244 CUNEIFORM SIGN NAGAR
12245 CUNEIFORM SIGN NAM NUTILLU
12246 CUNEIFORM SIGN NAM
12247 CUNEIFORM SIGN NAM2
12248 CUNEIFORM SIGN NE
12249 CUNEIFORM SIGN NE TIMES A
1224A CUNEIFORM SIGN NE TIMES UD
1224B CUNEIFORM SIGN NE SHESHIG
1224C CUNEIFORM SIGN NI
1224D CUNEIFORM SIGN NI TIMES E
1224E CUNEIFORM SIGN NI2
1224F CUNEIFORM SIGN NIM
12250 CUNEIFORM SIGN NIM TIMES GAN2 TENU
12251 CUNEIFORM SIGN NIM TIMES GAR PLUS GAN2 TENU
12252 CUNEIFORM SIGN NINDA2
12253 CUNEIFORM SIGN NINDA2 TIMES AN
12254 CUNEIFORM SIGN NINDA2 TIMES ASH
12255 CUNEIFORM SIGN NINDA2 TIMES ASH PLUS ASH
12256 CUNEIFORM SIGN NINDA2 TIMES GUD

12257 CUNEIFORM SIGN NINDA2 TIMES ME PLUS GAN2 TENU
12258 CUNEIFORM SIGN NINDA2 TIMES NE
12259 CUNEIFORM SIGN NINDA2 TIMES NUN
1225A CUNEIFORM SIGN NINDA2 TIMES SHE
1225B CUNEIFORM SIGN NINDA2 TIMES SHE PLUS A AN
1225C CUNEIFORM SIGN NINDA2 TIMES SHE PLUS ASH
1225D CUNEIFORM SIGN NINDA2 TIMES SHE PLUS ASH PLUS ASH
1225E CUNEIFORM SIGN NINDA2 TIMES U2 PLUS ASH
1225F CUNEIFORM SIGN NINDA2 TIMES USH
12260 CUNEIFORM SIGN NISAG
12261 CUNEIFORM SIGN NU
12262 CUNEIFORM SIGN NU11
12263 CUNEIFORM SIGN NUN
12264 CUNEIFORM SIGN NUN LAGAR TIMES GAR
12265 CUNEIFORM SIGN NUN LAGAR TIMES MASH
12266 CUNEIFORM SIGN NUN LAGAR TIMES SAL
12267 CUNEIFORM SIGN NUN LAGAR TIMES SAL OVER NUN LAGAR TIMES SAL
12268 CUNEIFORM SIGN NUN LAGAR TIMES USH
12269 CUNEIFORM SIGN NUN TENU
1226A CUNEIFORM SIGN NUN OVER NUN
1226B CUNEIFORM SIGN NUN CROSSING NUN
1226C CUNEIFORM SIGN NUN CROSSING NUN LAGAR OVER LAGAR
1226D CUNEIFORM SIGN NUNUZ
1226E CUNEIFORM SIGN NUNUZ AB2 TIMES ASHGAB
1226F CUNEIFORM SIGN NUNUZ AB2 TIMES BI
12270 CUNEIFORM SIGN NUNUZ AB2 TIMES DUG
12271 CUNEIFORM SIGN NUNUZ AB2 TIMES GUD
12272 CUNEIFORM SIGN NUNUZ AB2 TIMES IGI GUNU
12273 CUNEIFORM SIGN NUNUZ AB2 TIMES KAD3
12274 CUNEIFORM SIGN NUNUZ AB2 TIMES LA
12275 CUNEIFORM SIGN NUNUZ AB2 TIMES NE
12276 CUNEIFORM SIGN NUNUZ AB2 TIMES SILA3
12277 CUNEIFORM SIGN NUNUZ AB2 TIMES U2
12278 CUNEIFORM SIGN NUNUZ KISIM5 TIMES BI
12279 CUNEIFORM SIGN NUNUZ KISIM5 TIMES BI U
1227A CUNEIFORM SIGN PA
1227B CUNEIFORM SIGN PAD
1227C CUNEIFORM SIGN PAN
1227D CUNEIFORM SIGN PAP
1227E CUNEIFORM SIGN PESH2
1227F CUNEIFORM SIGN PI
12280 CUNEIFORM SIGN PI TIMES A
12281 CUNEIFORM SIGN PI TIMES AB
12282 CUNEIFORM SIGN PI TIMES BI
12283 CUNEIFORM SIGN PI TIMES BU
12284 CUNEIFORM SIGN PI TIMES E
12285 CUNEIFORM SIGN PI TIMES I
12286 CUNEIFORM SIGN PI TIMES IB
12287 CUNEIFORM SIGN PI TIMES U
12288 CUNEIFORM SIGN PI TIMES U2
12289 CUNEIFORM SIGN PI CROSSING PI
1228A CUNEIFORM SIGN PIRIG
1228B CUNEIFORM SIGN PIRIG TIMES KAL
1228C CUNEIFORM SIGN PIRIG TIMES UD
1228D CUNEIFORM SIGN PIRIG TIMES ZA
1228E CUNEIFORM SIGN PIRIG OPPOSING PIRIG
1228F CUNEIFORM SIGN RA
12290 CUNEIFORM SIGN RAB
12291 CUNEIFORM SIGN RI
12292 CUNEIFORM SIGN RU
12293 CUNEIFORM SIGN SA
12294 CUNEIFORM SIGN SAG NUTILLU
12295 CUNEIFORM SIGN SAG
12296 CUNEIFORM SIGN SAG TIMES A
12297 CUNEIFORM SIGN SAG TIMES DU
12298 CUNEIFORM SIGN SAG TIMES DUB
12299 CUNEIFORM SIGN SAG TIMES HA
1229A CUNEIFORM SIGN SAG TIMES KAK
1229B CUNEIFORM SIGN SAG TIMES KUR
1229C CUNEIFORM SIGN SAG TIMES LUM
1229D CUNEIFORM SIGN SAG TIMES MI
1229E CUNEIFORM SIGN SAG TIMES NUN
1229F CUNEIFORM SIGN SAG TIMES SAL
122A0 CUNEIFORM SIGN SAG TIMES SHID
122A1 CUNEIFORM SIGN SAG TIMES TAB
122A2 CUNEIFORM SIGN SAG TIMES U2
122A3 CUNEIFORM SIGN SAG TIMES UB
122A4 CUNEIFORM SIGN SAG TIMES UM
122A5 CUNEIFORM SIGN SAG TIMES UR
122A6 CUNEIFORM SIGN SAG TIMES USH
122A7 CUNEIFORM SIGN SAG OVER SAG
122A8 CUNEIFORM SIGN SAG GUNU
122A9 CUNEIFORM SIGN SAL
122AA CUNEIFORM SIGN SAL LAGAB TIMES ASH2
122AB CUNEIFORM SIGN SANGA2
122AC CUNEIFORM SIGN SAR
122AD CUNEIFORM SIGN SHA
122AE CUNEIFORM SIGN SHA3
122AF CUNEIFORM SIGN SHA3 TIMES A
122B0 CUNEIFORM SIGN SHA3 TIMES BAD
122B1 CUNEIFORM SIGN SHA3 TIMES GISH
122B2 CUNEIFORM SIGN SHA3 TIMES NE
122B3 CUNEIFORM SIGN SHA3 TIMES SHU2
122B4 CUNEIFORM SIGN SHA3 TIMES TUR
122B5 CUNEIFORM SIGN SHA3 TIMES U
122B6 CUNEIFORM SIGN SHA3 TIMES U PLUS A
122B7 CUNEIFORM SIGN SHA6
122B8 CUNEIFORM SIGN SHAB6
122B9 ● CUNEIFORM SIGN SHAR2
• formed by making a circular indentation with the end of the stylus
122BA CUNEIFORM SIGN SHE
122BB CUNEIFORM SIGN SHE HU
122BC CUNEIFORM SIGN SHE OVER SHE GAD OVER GAD GAR OVER GAR
122BD CUNEIFORM SIGN SHE OVER SHE TAB OVER TAB GAR OVER GAR
122BE CUNEIFORM SIGN SHEG9
122BF CUNEIFORM SIGN SHEN
122C0 CUNEIFORM SIGN SHESH
122C1 CUNEIFORM SIGN SHESH2
122C2 CUNEIFORM SIGN SHESHLAM
122C3 CUNEIFORM SIGN SHID
122C4 CUNEIFORM SIGN SHID TIMES A
122C5 CUNEIFORM SIGN SHID TIMES IM
122C6 CUNEIFORM SIGN SHIM
122C7 CUNEIFORM SIGN SHIM TIMES A
122C8 CUNEIFORM SIGN SHIM TIMES BAL
122C9 CUNEIFORM SIGN SHIM TIMES BULUG
122CA CUNEIFORM SIGN SHIM TIMES DIN
122CB CUNEIFORM SIGN SHIM TIMES GAR
122CC CUNEIFORM SIGN SHIM TIMES IGI

122CD CUNEIFORM SIGN SHIM TIMES IGI GUNU
122CE CUNEIFORM SIGN SHIM TIMES KUSHU2
122CF CUNEIFORM SIGN SHIM TIMES LUL
122D0 CUNEIFORM SIGN SHIM TIMES MUG
122D1 CUNEIFORM SIGN SHIM TIMES SAL
122D2 CUNEIFORM SIGN SHINIG
122D3 CUNEIFORM SIGN SHIR
122D4 CUNEIFORM SIGN SHIR TENU
122D5 CUNEIFORM SIGN SHIR OVER SHIR BUR OVER BUR
122D6 CUNEIFORM SIGN SHITA
122D7 CUNEIFORM SIGN SHU
122D8 CUNEIFORM SIGN SHU OVER INVERTED SHU
122D9 CUNEIFORM SIGN SHU2
122DA CUNEIFORM SIGN SHUBUR
122DB CUNEIFORM SIGN SI
122DC CUNEIFORM SIGN SI GUNU
122DD CUNEIFORM SIGN SIG
122DE CUNEIFORM SIGN SIG4
122DF CUNEIFORM SIGN SIG4 OVER SIG4 SHU2
122E0 CUNEIFORM SIGN SIK2
122E1 CUNEIFORM SIGN SILA3
122E2 CUNEIFORM SIGN SU
122E3 CUNEIFORM SIGN SU OVER SU
122E4 CUNEIFORM SIGN SUD
122E5 CUNEIFORM SIGN SUD2
122E6 CUNEIFORM SIGN SUHUR
122E7 CUNEIFORM SIGN SUM
122E8 CUNEIFORM SIGN SUMASH
122E9 CUNEIFORM SIGN SUR
122EA CUNEIFORM SIGN SUR9
122EB CUNEIFORM SIGN TA
122EC CUNEIFORM SIGN TA ASTERISK
122ED CUNEIFORM SIGN TA TIMES HI
122EE CUNEIFORM SIGN TA TIMES MI
122EF CUNEIFORM SIGN TA GUNU
122F0 CUNEIFORM SIGN TAB
122F1 CUNEIFORM SIGN TAB OVER TAB NI OVER NI DISH OVER DISH
122F2 CUNEIFORM SIGN TAB SQUARED
122F3 CUNEIFORM SIGN TAG
122F4 CUNEIFORM SIGN TAG TIMES BI
122F5 CUNEIFORM SIGN TAG TIMES GUD
122F6 CUNEIFORM SIGN TAG TIMES SHE
122F7 CUNEIFORM SIGN TAG TIMES SHU
122F8 CUNEIFORM SIGN TAG TIMES TUG2
122F9 CUNEIFORM SIGN TAG TIMES UD
122FA CUNEIFORM SIGN TAK4
122FB CUNEIFORM SIGN TAR
122FC CUNEIFORM SIGN TE
122FD CUNEIFORM SIGN TE GUNU
122FE CUNEIFORM SIGN TI
122FF CUNEIFORM SIGN TI TENU
12300 CUNEIFORM SIGN TIL
12301 CUNEIFORM SIGN TIR
12302 CUNEIFORM SIGN TIR TIMES TAK4
12303 CUNEIFORM SIGN TIR OVER TIR
12304 CUNEIFORM SIGN TIR OVER TIR GAD OVER GAD GAR OVER GAR
12305 CUNEIFORM SIGN TU
12306 CUNEIFORM SIGN TUG2
12307 CUNEIFORM SIGN TUK
12308 CUNEIFORM SIGN TUM
12309 CUNEIFORM SIGN TUR
1230A CUNEIFORM SIGN TUR OVER TUR ZA OVER ZA
1230B CUNEIFORM SIGN U
1230C CUNEIFORM SIGN U GUD
1230D CUNEIFORM SIGN U U U
1230E CUNEIFORM SIGN U OVER U PA OVER PA GAR OVER GAR
1230F CUNEIFORM SIGN U OVER U SUR OVER SUR
12310 CUNEIFORM SIGN U OVER U U REVERSED OVER U REVERSED
12311 CUNEIFORM SIGN U2
12312 CUNEIFORM SIGN UB
12313 CUNEIFORM SIGN UD
12314 CUNEIFORM SIGN UD KUSHU2
12315 CUNEIFORM SIGN UD TIMES BAD
12316 CUNEIFORM SIGN UD TIMES MI
12317 CUNEIFORM SIGN UD TIMES U PLUS U PLUS U
12318 CUNEIFORM SIGN UD TIMES U PLUS U PLUS U GUNU
12319 CUNEIFORM SIGN UD GUNU
1231A CUNEIFORM SIGN UD SHESHIG
1231B CUNEIFORM SIGN UD SHESHIG TIMES BAD
1231C CUNEIFORM SIGN UDUG
1231D CUNEIFORM SIGN UM
1231E CUNEIFORM SIGN UM TIMES LAGAB
1231F CUNEIFORM SIGN UM TIMES ME PLUS DA
12320 CUNEIFORM SIGN UM TIMES SHA3
12321 CUNEIFORM SIGN UM TIMES U
12322 CUNEIFORM SIGN UMBIN
12323 CUNEIFORM SIGN UMUM
12324 CUNEIFORM SIGN UMUM TIMES KASKAL
12325 CUNEIFORM SIGN UMUM TIMES PA
12326 CUNEIFORM SIGN UN
12327 CUNEIFORM SIGN UN GUNU
12328 CUNEIFORM SIGN UR
12329 CUNEIFORM SIGN UR CROSSING UR
1232A CUNEIFORM SIGN UR SHESHIG
1232B CUNEIFORM SIGN UR2
1232C CUNEIFORM SIGN UR2 TIMES A PLUS HA
1232D CUNEIFORM SIGN UR2 TIMES A PLUS NA
1232E CUNEIFORM SIGN UR2 TIMES AL
1232F CUNEIFORM SIGN UR2 TIMES HA
12330 CUNEIFORM SIGN UR2 TIMES NUN
12331 CUNEIFORM SIGN UR2 TIMES U2
12332 CUNEIFORM SIGN UR2 TIMES U2 PLUS ASH
12333 CUNEIFORM SIGN UR2 TIMES U2 PLUS BI
12334 CUNEIFORM SIGN UR4
12335 CUNEIFORM SIGN URI
12336 CUNEIFORM SIGN URI3
12337 CUNEIFORM SIGN URU
12338 CUNEIFORM SIGN URU TIMES A
12339 CUNEIFORM SIGN URU TIMES ASHGAB
1233A CUNEIFORM SIGN URU TIMES BAR
1233B CUNEIFORM SIGN URU TIMES DUN
1233C CUNEIFORM SIGN URU TIMES GA
1233D CUNEIFORM SIGN URU TIMES GAL
1233E CUNEIFORM SIGN URU TIMES GAN2 TENU
1233F CUNEIFORM SIGN URU TIMES GAR
12340 CUNEIFORM SIGN URU TIMES GU
12341 CUNEIFORM SIGN URU TIMES HA
12342 CUNEIFORM SIGN URU TIMES IGI
12343 CUNEIFORM SIGN URU TIMES IM
12344 CUNEIFORM SIGN URU TIMES ISH
12345 CUNEIFORM SIGN URU TIMES KI
12346 CUNEIFORM SIGN URU TIMES LUM

12347 CUNEIFORM SIGN URU TIMES MIN
12348 CUNEIFORM SIGN URU TIMES PA
12349 CUNEIFORM SIGN URU TIMES SHE
1234A CUNEIFORM SIGN URU TIMES SIG4
1234B CUNEIFORM SIGN URU TIMES TU
1234C CUNEIFORM SIGN URU TIMES U PLUS GUD
1234D CUNEIFORM SIGN URU TIMES UD
1234E CUNEIFORM SIGN URU TIMES URUDA
1234F CUNEIFORM SIGN URUDA
12350 CUNEIFORM SIGN URUDA TIMES U
12351 CUNEIFORM SIGN USH
12352 CUNEIFORM SIGN USH TIMES A
12353 CUNEIFORM SIGN USH TIMES KU
12354 CUNEIFORM SIGN USH TIMES KUR
12355 CUNEIFORM SIGN USH TIMES TAK4
12356 CUNEIFORM SIGN USHX
12357 CUNEIFORM SIGN USH2
12358 CUNEIFORM SIGN USHUMX
12359 CUNEIFORM SIGN UTUKI
1235A CUNEIFORM SIGN UZ3
1235B CUNEIFORM SIGN UZ3 TIMES KASKAL
1235C CUNEIFORM SIGN UZU
1235D CUNEIFORM SIGN ZA
1235E CUNEIFORM SIGN ZA TENU
1235F CUNEIFORM SIGN ZA SQUARED TIMES KUR
12360 CUNEIFORM SIGN ZAG
12361 CUNEIFORM SIGN ZAMX
12362 CUNEIFORM SIGN ZE2
12363 CUNEIFORM SIGN ZI
12364 CUNEIFORM SIGN ZI OVER ZI
12365 CUNEIFORM SIGN ZI3
12366 CUNEIFORM SIGN ZIB
12367 CUNEIFORM SIGN ZIB KABA TENU
12368 CUNEIFORM SIGN ZIG
12369 CUNEIFORM SIGN ZIZ2
1236A CUNEIFORM SIGN ZU
1236B CUNEIFORM SIGN ZU5
1236C CUNEIFORM SIGN ZU5 TIMES A
1236D CUNEIFORM SIGN ZUBUR
1236E CUNEIFORM SIGN ZUM

	1240	1241	1242	1243	1244	1245	1246	1247
0	12400	12410	12420	12430	12440	12450	12460	12470
1	12401	12411	12421	12431	12441	12451	12461	12471
2	12402	12412	12422	12432	12442	12452	12462	12472
3	12403	12413	12423	12433	12443	12453		12473
4	12404	12414	12424	12434	12444	12454		
5	12405	12415	12425	12435	12445	12455		
6	12406	12416	12426	12436	12446	12456		
7	12407	12417	12427	12437	12447	12457		
8	12408	12418	12428	12438	12448	12458		
9	12409	12419	12429	12439	12449	12459		
A	1240A	1241A	1242A	1243A	1244A	1245A		
B	1240B	1241B	1242B	1243B	1244B	1245B		
C	1240C	1241C	1242C	1243C	1244C	1245C		
D	1240D	1241D	1242D	1243D	1244D	1245D		
E	1240E	1241E	1242E	1243E	1244E	1245E		
F	1240F	1241F	1242F	1243F	1244F	1245F		

Numeric signs

12400 CUNEIFORM NUMERIC SIGN TWO ASH
12401 CUNEIFORM NUMERIC SIGN THREE ASH
12402 CUNEIFORM NUMERIC SIGN FOUR ASH
12403 CUNEIFORM NUMERIC SIGN FIVE ASH
12404 CUNEIFORM NUMERIC SIGN SIX ASH
12405 CUNEIFORM NUMERIC SIGN SEVEN ASH
12406 CUNEIFORM NUMERIC SIGN EIGHT ASH
12407 CUNEIFORM NUMERIC SIGN NINE ASH
12408 CUNEIFORM NUMERIC SIGN THREE DISH
12409 CUNEIFORM NUMERIC SIGN FOUR DISH
1240A CUNEIFORM NUMERIC SIGN FIVE DISH
1240B CUNEIFORM NUMERIC SIGN SIX DISH
1240C CUNEIFORM NUMERIC SIGN SEVEN DISH
1240D CUNEIFORM NUMERIC SIGN EIGHT DISH
1240E CUNEIFORM NUMERIC SIGN NINE DISH
1240F CUNEIFORM NUMERIC SIGN FOUR U
12410 CUNEIFORM NUMERIC SIGN FIVE U
12411 CUNEIFORM NUMERIC SIGN SIX U
12412 CUNEIFORM NUMERIC SIGN SEVEN U
12413 CUNEIFORM NUMERIC SIGN EIGHT U
12414 CUNEIFORM NUMERIC SIGN NINE U
12415 CUNEIFORM NUMERIC SIGN ONE GESH2
12416 CUNEIFORM NUMERIC SIGN TWO GESH2
12417 CUNEIFORM NUMERIC SIGN THREE GESH2
12418 CUNEIFORM NUMERIC SIGN FOUR GESH2
12419 CUNEIFORM NUMERIC SIGN FIVE GESH2
1241A CUNEIFORM NUMERIC SIGN SIX GESH2
1241B CUNEIFORM NUMERIC SIGN SEVEN GESH2
1241C CUNEIFORM NUMERIC SIGN EIGHT GESH2
1241D CUNEIFORM NUMERIC SIGN NINE GESH2
1241E CUNEIFORM NUMERIC SIGN ONE GESHU
1241F CUNEIFORM NUMERIC SIGN TWO GESHU
12420 CUNEIFORM NUMERIC SIGN THREE GESHU
12421 CUNEIFORM NUMERIC SIGN FOUR GESHU
12422 CUNEIFORM NUMERIC SIGN FIVE GESHU
12423 CUNEIFORM NUMERIC SIGN TWO SHAR2
12424 CUNEIFORM NUMERIC SIGN THREE SHAR2
12425 CUNEIFORM NUMERIC SIGN THREE SHAR2 VARIANT FORM
12426 CUNEIFORM NUMERIC SIGN FOUR SHAR2
12427 CUNEIFORM NUMERIC SIGN FIVE SHAR2
12428 CUNEIFORM NUMERIC SIGN SIX SHAR2
12429 CUNEIFORM NUMERIC SIGN SEVEN SHAR2
1242A CUNEIFORM NUMERIC SIGN EIGHT SHAR2
1242B CUNEIFORM NUMERIC SIGN NINE SHAR2
1242C CUNEIFORM NUMERIC SIGN ONE SHARU
1242D CUNEIFORM NUMERIC SIGN TWO SHARU
1242E CUNEIFORM NUMERIC SIGN THREE SHARU
1242F CUNEIFORM NUMERIC SIGN THREE SHARU VARIANT FORM
12430 CUNEIFORM NUMERIC SIGN FOUR SHARU
12431 CUNEIFORM NUMERIC SIGN FIVE SHARU
12432 CUNEIFORM NUMERIC SIGN SHAR2 TIMES GAL PLUS DISH
12433 CUNEIFORM NUMERIC SIGN SHAR2 TIMES GAL PLUS MIN
12434 CUNEIFORM NUMERIC SIGN ONE BURU
12435 CUNEIFORM NUMERIC SIGN TWO BURU
12436 CUNEIFORM NUMERIC SIGN THREE BURU
12437 CUNEIFORM NUMERIC SIGN THREE BURU VARIANT FORM
12438 CUNEIFORM NUMERIC SIGN FOUR BURU
12439 CUNEIFORM NUMERIC SIGN FIVE BURU
1243A CUNEIFORM NUMERIC SIGN THREE VARIANT FORM ESH16
1243B CUNEIFORM NUMERIC SIGN THREE VARIANT FORM ESH21
1243C CUNEIFORM NUMERIC SIGN FOUR VARIANT FORM LIMMU
1243D CUNEIFORM NUMERIC SIGN FOUR VARIANT FORM LIMMU4
1243E CUNEIFORM NUMERIC SIGN FOUR VARIANT FORM LIMMU A
1243F CUNEIFORM NUMERIC SIGN FOUR VARIANT FORM LIMMU B
12440 CUNEIFORM NUMERIC SIGN SIX VARIANT FORM ASH9
12441 CUNEIFORM NUMERIC SIGN SEVEN VARIANT FORM IMIN3
12442 CUNEIFORM NUMERIC SIGN SEVEN VARIANT FORM IMIN A
12443 CUNEIFORM NUMERIC SIGN SEVEN VARIANT FORM IMIN B
12444 CUNEIFORM NUMERIC SIGN EIGHT VARIANT FORM USSU
12445 CUNEIFORM NUMERIC SIGN EIGHT VARIANT FORM USSU3
12446 CUNEIFORM NUMERIC SIGN NINE VARIANT FORM ILIMMU
12447 CUNEIFORM NUMERIC SIGN NINE VARIANT FORM ILIMMU3
12448 CUNEIFORM NUMERIC SIGN NINE VARIANT FORM ILIMMU4
12449 CUNEIFORM NUMERIC SIGN NINE VARIANT FORM ILIMMU A
1244A CUNEIFORM NUMERIC SIGN TWO ASH TENU
1244B CUNEIFORM NUMERIC SIGN THREE ASH TENU
1244C CUNEIFORM NUMERIC SIGN FOUR ASH TENU
1244D CUNEIFORM NUMERIC SIGN FIVE ASH TENU
1244E CUNEIFORM NUMERIC SIGN SIX ASH TENU
1244F CUNEIFORM NUMERIC SIGN ONE BAN2
12450 CUNEIFORM NUMERIC SIGN TWO BAN2
12451 CUNEIFORM NUMERIC SIGN THREE BAN2
12452 CUNEIFORM NUMERIC SIGN FOUR BAN2
12453 CUNEIFORM NUMERIC SIGN FOUR BAN2 VARIANT FORM
12454 CUNEIFORM NUMERIC SIGN FIVE BAN2
12455 CUNEIFORM NUMERIC SIGN FIVE BAN2 VARIANT FORM
12456 CUNEIFORM NUMERIC SIGN NIGIDAMIN
12457 CUNEIFORM NUMERIC SIGN NIGIDAESH
12458 CUNEIFORM NUMERIC SIGN ONE ESHE3
12459 CUNEIFORM NUMERIC SIGN TWO ESHE3

Fractions

1245A CUNEIFORM NUMERIC SIGN ONE THIRD DISH
1245B CUNEIFORM NUMERIC SIGN TWO THIRDS DISH
1245C CUNEIFORM NUMERIC SIGN FIVE SIXTHS DISH
1245D CUNEIFORM NUMERIC SIGN ONE THIRD VARIANT FORM A
1245E CUNEIFORM NUMERIC SIGN TWO THIRDS VARIANT FORM A
1245F CUNEIFORM NUMERIC SIGN ONE EIGHTH ASH
12460 CUNEIFORM NUMERIC SIGN ONE QUARTER ASH
12461 CUNEIFORM NUMERIC SIGN OLD ASSYRIAN ONE SIXTH
12462 CUNEIFORM NUMERIC SIGN OLD ASSYRIAN ONE QUARTER

Punctuation

12470 𒑰 CUNEIFORM PUNCTUATION SIGN OLD ASSYRIAN WORD DIVIDER
→ 1039F 𐎟 ugaritic word divider
→ 103D0 𐏐 old persian word divider

12471 𒑱 CUNEIFORM PUNCTUATION SIGN VERTICAL COLON

12472 𒑲 CUNEIFORM PUNCTUATION SIGN DIAGONAL COLON

12473 𒑳 CUNEIFORM PUNCTUATION SIGN DIAGONAL TRICOLON

	1D00	1D01	1D02	1D03	1D04	1D05	1D06	1D07	1D08	1D09	1D0A	1D0B	1D0C	1D0D	1D0E	1D0F
0	1D000	1D010	1D020	1D030	1D040	1D050	1D060	1D070	1D080	1D090	1D0A0	1D0B0	1D0C0	1D0D0	1D0E0	1D0F0
1	1D001	1D011	1D021	1D031	1D041	1D051	1D061	1D071	1D081	1D091	1D0A1	1D0B1	1D0C1	1D0D1	1D0E1	1D0F1
2	1D002	1D012	1D022	1D032	1D042	1D052	1D062	1D072	1D082	1D092	1D0A2	1D0B2	1D0C2	1D0D2	1D0E2	1D0F2
3	1D003	1D013	1D023	1D033	1D043	1D053	1D063	1D073	1D083	1D093	1D0A3	1D0B3	1D0C3	1D0D3	1D0E3	1D0F3
4	1D004	1D014	1D024	1D034	1D044	1D054	1D064	1D074	1D084	1D094	1D0A4	1D0B4	1D0C4	1D0D4	1D0E4	1D0F4
5	1D005	1D015	1D025	1D035	1D045	1D055	1D065	1D075	1D085	1D095	1D0A5	1D0B5	1D0C5	1D0D5	1D0E5	1D0F5
6	1D006	1D016	1D026	1D036	1D046	1D056	1D066	1D076	1D086	1D096	1D0A6	1D0B6	1D0C6	1D0D6	1D0E6	
7	1D007	1D017	1D027	1D037	1D047	1D057	1D067	1D077	1D087	1D097	1D0A7	1D0B7	1D0C7	1D0D7	1D0E7	
8	1D008	1D018	1D028	1D038	1D048	1D058	1D068	1D078	1D088	1D098	1D0A8	1D0B8	1D0C8	1D0D8	1D0E8	
9	1D009	1D019	1D029	1D039	1D049	1D059	1D069	1D079	1D089	1D099	1D0A9	1D0B9	1D0C9	1D0D9	1D0E9	
A	1D00A	1D01A	1D02A	1D03A	1D04A	1D05A	1D06A	1D07A	1D08A	1D09A	1D0AA	1D0BA	1D0CA	1D0DA	1D0EA	
B	1D00B	1D01B	1D02B	1D03B	1D04B	1D05B	1D06B	1D07B	1D08B	1D09B	1D0AB	1D0BB	1D0CB	1D0DB	1D0EB	
C	1D00C	1D01C	1D02C	1D03C	1D04C	1D05C	1D06C	1D07C	1D08C	1D09C	1D0AC	1D0BC	1D0CC	1D0DC	1D0EC	
D	1D00D	1D01D	1D02D	1D03D	1D04D	1D05D	1D06D	1D07D	1D08D	1D09D	1D0AD	1D0BD	1D0CD	1D0DD	1D0ED	
E	1D00E	1D01E	1D02E	1D03E	1D04E	1D05E	1D06E	1D07E	1D08E	1D09E	1D0AE	1D0BE	1D0CE	1D0DE	1D0EE	
F	1D00F	1D01F	1D02F	1D03F	1D04F	1D05F	1D06F	1D07F	1D08F	1D09F	1D0AF	1D0BF	1D0CF	1D0DF	1D0EF	

Prosodies (Prosodics)

These three characters are not actually attested in musical contexts.

1D000 BYZANTINE MUSICAL SYMBOL PSILI
1D001 BYZANTINE MUSICAL SYMBOL DASEIA
1D002 BYZANTINE MUSICAL SYMBOL PERISPOMENI

Ekfonetika

1D003 BYZANTINE MUSICAL SYMBOL OXEIA EKFONITIKON
1D004 BYZANTINE MUSICAL SYMBOL OXEIA DIPLI
1D005 BYZANTINE MUSICAL SYMBOL VAREIA EKFONITIKON
1D006 BYZANTINE MUSICAL SYMBOL VAREIA DIPLI
1D007 BYZANTINE MUSICAL SYMBOL KATHISTI
1D008 BYZANTINE MUSICAL SYMBOL SYRMATIKI
1D009 BYZANTINE MUSICAL SYMBOL PARAKLITIKI
1D00A BYZANTINE MUSICAL SYMBOL YPOKRISIS
1D00B BYZANTINE MUSICAL SYMBOL YPOKRISIS DIPLI
1D00C BYZANTINE MUSICAL SYMBOL KREMASTI
1D00D BYZANTINE MUSICAL SYMBOL APESO EKFONITIKON
1D00E BYZANTINE MUSICAL SYMBOL EXO EKFONITIKON
1D00F BYZANTINE MUSICAL SYMBOL TELEIA
1D010 BYZANTINE MUSICAL SYMBOL KENTIMATA
1D011 BYZANTINE MUSICAL SYMBOL APOSTROFOS
1D012 BYZANTINE MUSICAL SYMBOL APOSTROFOS DIPLI
1D013 BYZANTINE MUSICAL SYMBOL SYNEVMA
1D014 BYZANTINE MUSICAL SYMBOL THITA

Melodimata (Melodics)

1D015 BYZANTINE MUSICAL SYMBOL OLIGON ARCHAION
1D016 BYZANTINE MUSICAL SYMBOL GORGON ARCHAION
1D017 BYZANTINE MUSICAL SYMBOL PSILON
1D018 BYZANTINE MUSICAL SYMBOL CHAMILON
1D019 BYZANTINE MUSICAL SYMBOL VATHY
1D01A BYZANTINE MUSICAL SYMBOL ISON ARCHAION
1D01B BYZANTINE MUSICAL SYMBOL KENTIMA ARCHAION
1D01C BYZANTINE MUSICAL SYMBOL KENTIMATA ARCHAION
1D01D BYZANTINE MUSICAL SYMBOL SAXIMATA
1D01E BYZANTINE MUSICAL SYMBOL PARICHON
1D01F BYZANTINE MUSICAL SYMBOL STAVROS APODEXIA
1D020 BYZANTINE MUSICAL SYMBOL OXEIAI ARCHAION
1D021 BYZANTINE MUSICAL SYMBOL VAREIAI ARCHAION
1D022 BYZANTINE MUSICAL SYMBOL APODERMA ARCHAION
1D023 BYZANTINE MUSICAL SYMBOL APOTHEMA
1D024 BYZANTINE MUSICAL SYMBOL KLASMA
1D025 BYZANTINE MUSICAL SYMBOL REVMA
1D026 BYZANTINE MUSICAL SYMBOL PIASMA ARCHAION
1D027 BYZANTINE MUSICAL SYMBOL TINAGMA
1D028 BYZANTINE MUSICAL SYMBOL ANATRICHISMA
1D029 BYZANTINE MUSICAL SYMBOL SEISMA
1D02A BYZANTINE MUSICAL SYMBOL SYNAGMA ARCHAION
1D02B BYZANTINE MUSICAL SYMBOL SYNAGMA META STAVROU
1D02C BYZANTINE MUSICAL SYMBOL OYRANISMA ARCHAION
1D02D BYZANTINE MUSICAL SYMBOL THEMA
1D02E BYZANTINE MUSICAL SYMBOL LEMOI
1D02F BYZANTINE MUSICAL SYMBOL DYO
1D030 BYZANTINE MUSICAL SYMBOL TRIA
1D031 BYZANTINE MUSICAL SYMBOL TESSERA
1D032 BYZANTINE MUSICAL SYMBOL KRATIMATA
1D033 BYZANTINE MUSICAL SYMBOL APESO EXO NEO
1D034 BYZANTINE MUSICAL SYMBOL FTHORA ARCHAION
1D035 BYZANTINE MUSICAL SYMBOL IMIFTHORA
1D036 BYZANTINE MUSICAL SYMBOL TROMIKON ARCHAION
1D037 BYZANTINE MUSICAL SYMBOL KATAVA TROMIKON
1D038 BYZANTINE MUSICAL SYMBOL PELASTON
1D039 BYZANTINE MUSICAL SYMBOL PSIFISTON
1D03A BYZANTINE MUSICAL SYMBOL KONTEVMA
1D03B BYZANTINE MUSICAL SYMBOL CHOREVMA ARCHAION
1D03C BYZANTINE MUSICAL SYMBOL RAPISMA
1D03D BYZANTINE MUSICAL SYMBOL PARAKALESMA ARCHAION
1D03E BYZANTINE MUSICAL SYMBOL PARAKLITIKI ARCHAION
1D03F BYZANTINE MUSICAL SYMBOL ICHADIN
1D040 BYZANTINE MUSICAL SYMBOL NANA
1D041 BYZANTINE MUSICAL SYMBOL PETASMA
1D042 BYZANTINE MUSICAL SYMBOL KONTEVMA ALLO
1D043 BYZANTINE MUSICAL SYMBOL TROMIKON ALLO
1D044 BYZANTINE MUSICAL SYMBOL STRAGGISMATA
1D045 BYZANTINE MUSICAL SYMBOL GRONTHISMATA

Fonitika (Vocals)

1D046 BYZANTINE MUSICAL SYMBOL ISON NEO
1D047 BYZANTINE MUSICAL SYMBOL OLIGON NEO
1D048 BYZANTINE MUSICAL SYMBOL OXEIA NEO
1D049 BYZANTINE MUSICAL SYMBOL PETASTI
1D04A BYZANTINE MUSICAL SYMBOL KOUFISMA
1D04B BYZANTINE MUSICAL SYMBOL PETASTOKOUFISMA
1D04C BYZANTINE MUSICAL SYMBOL KRATIMOKOUFISMA
1D04D BYZANTINE MUSICAL SYMBOL PELASTON NEO
1D04E BYZANTINE MUSICAL SYMBOL KENTIMATA NEO ANO
1D04F BYZANTINE MUSICAL SYMBOL KENTIMA NEO ANO
1D050 BYZANTINE MUSICAL SYMBOL YPSILI
1D051 BYZANTINE MUSICAL SYMBOL APOSTROFOS NEO
1D052 BYZANTINE MUSICAL SYMBOL APOSTROFOI SYNDESMOS NEO
1D053 BYZANTINE MUSICAL SYMBOL YPORROI
1D054 BYZANTINE MUSICAL SYMBOL KRATIMOYPORROON
1D055 BYZANTINE MUSICAL SYMBOL ELAFRON
1D056 BYZANTINE MUSICAL SYMBOL CHAMILI

Afona or Ypostaseis (Mutes or Hypostases)

1D057 BYZANTINE MUSICAL SYMBOL MIKRON ISON
1D058 BYZANTINE MUSICAL SYMBOL VAREIA NEO
1D059 BYZANTINE MUSICAL SYMBOL PIASMA NEO
1D05A BYZANTINE MUSICAL SYMBOL PSIFISTON NEO
1D05B BYZANTINE MUSICAL SYMBOL OMALON
1D05C BYZANTINE MUSICAL SYMBOL ANTIKENOMA
1D05D BYZANTINE MUSICAL SYMBOL LYGISMA
1D05E BYZANTINE MUSICAL SYMBOL PARAKLITIKI NEO
1D05F BYZANTINE MUSICAL SYMBOL PARAKALESMA NEO
1D060 BYZANTINE MUSICAL SYMBOL ETERON PARAKALESMA
1D061 BYZANTINE MUSICAL SYMBOL KYLISMA
1D062 BYZANTINE MUSICAL SYMBOL ANTIKENOKYLISMA
1D063 BYZANTINE MUSICAL SYMBOL TROMIKON NEO
1D064 BYZANTINE MUSICAL SYMBOL EKSTREPTON
1D065 BYZANTINE MUSICAL SYMBOL SYNAGMA NEO
1D066 BYZANTINE MUSICAL SYMBOL SYRMA
1D067 BYZANTINE MUSICAL SYMBOL CHOREVMA NEO
1D068 BYZANTINE MUSICAL SYMBOL EPEGERMA
1D069 BYZANTINE MUSICAL SYMBOL SEISMA NEO
1D06A BYZANTINE MUSICAL SYMBOL XIRON KLASMA
1D06B BYZANTINE MUSICAL SYMBOL TROMIKOPSIFISTON
1D06C BYZANTINE MUSICAL SYMBOL PSIFISTOLYGISMA
1D06D BYZANTINE MUSICAL SYMBOL TROMIKOLYGISMA
1D06E BYZANTINE MUSICAL SYMBOL TROMIKOPARAKALESMA
1D06F BYZANTINE MUSICAL SYMBOL PSIFISTOPARAKALESMA
1D070 BYZANTINE MUSICAL SYMBOL TROMIKOSYNAGMA
1D071 BYZANTINE MUSICAL SYMBOL PSIFISTOSYNAGMA
1D072 BYZANTINE MUSICAL SYMBOL GORGOSYNTHETON
1D073 BYZANTINE MUSICAL SYMBOL ARGOSYNTHETON
1D074 BYZANTINE MUSICAL SYMBOL ETERON ARGOSYNTHETON
1D075 BYZANTINE MUSICAL SYMBOL OYRANISMA NEO
1D076 BYZANTINE MUSICAL SYMBOL THEMATISMOS ESO
1D077 BYZANTINE MUSICAL SYMBOL THEMATISMOS EXO
1D078 BYZANTINE MUSICAL SYMBOL THEMA APLOUN
1D079 BYZANTINE MUSICAL SYMBOL THES KAI APOTHES
1D07A BYZANTINE MUSICAL SYMBOL KATAVASMA
1D07B BYZANTINE MUSICAL SYMBOL ENDOFONON
1D07C BYZANTINE MUSICAL SYMBOL YFEN KATO
1D07D BYZANTINE MUSICAL SYMBOL YFEN ANO
1D07E BYZANTINE MUSICAL SYMBOL STAVROS

Argies (Retards)

1D07F BYZANTINE MUSICAL SYMBOL KLASMA ANO
1D080 BYZANTINE MUSICAL SYMBOL DIPLI ARCHAION
1D081 BYZANTINE MUSICAL SYMBOL KRATIMA ARCHAION
1D082 BYZANTINE MUSICAL SYMBOL KRATIMA ALLO
1D083 BYZANTINE MUSICAL SYMBOL KRATIMA NEO
1D084 BYZANTINE MUSICAL SYMBOL APODERMA NEO
1D085 BYZANTINE MUSICAL SYMBOL APLI
1D086 BYZANTINE MUSICAL SYMBOL DIPLI
1D087 BYZANTINE MUSICAL SYMBOL TRIPLI
1D088 BYZANTINE MUSICAL SYMBOL TETRAPLI
1D089 BYZANTINE MUSICAL SYMBOL KORONIS

Leimmata or Siopes (Leimmas or Silencers)

1D08A BYZANTINE MUSICAL SYMBOL LEIMMA ENOS CHRONOU
1D08B BYZANTINE MUSICAL SYMBOL LEIMMA DYO CHRONON
1D08C BYZANTINE MUSICAL SYMBOL LEIMMA TRION CHRONON
1D08D BYZANTINE MUSICAL SYMBOL LEIMMA TESSARON CHRONON
1D08E BYZANTINE MUSICAL SYMBOL LEIMMA IMISEOS CHRONOU

Synagmata or Gorgotites (Synagmas or Quickeners)

1D08F BYZANTINE MUSICAL SYMBOL GORGON NEO ANO
1D090 BYZANTINE MUSICAL SYMBOL GORGON PARESTIGMENON ARISTERA
1D091 BYZANTINE MUSICAL SYMBOL GORGON PARESTIGMENON DEXIA
1D092 BYZANTINE MUSICAL SYMBOL DIGORGON
1D093 BYZANTINE MUSICAL SYMBOL DIGORGON PARESTIGMENON ARISTERA KATO
1D094 BYZANTINE MUSICAL SYMBOL DIGORGON PARESTIGMENON ARISTERA ANO
1D095 BYZANTINE MUSICAL SYMBOL DIGORGON PARESTIGMENON DEXIA
1D096 BYZANTINE MUSICAL SYMBOL TRIGORGON
1D097 BYZANTINE MUSICAL SYMBOL ARGON
1D098 BYZANTINE MUSICAL SYMBOL IMIDIARGON
- called diargon by some authorities

1D099 BYZANTINE MUSICAL SYMBOL DIARGON
- called triargon by some authorities

Agogika (Conduits)

Glyphs shown for conduits reflect Greek practice, with chi as the base letter; different national traditions use glyphs with different base letters.

1D09A BYZANTINE MUSICAL SYMBOL AGOGI POLI ARGI
1D09B BYZANTINE MUSICAL SYMBOL AGOGI ARGOTERI
1D09C BYZANTINE MUSICAL SYMBOL AGOGI ARGI
1D09D BYZANTINE MUSICAL SYMBOL AGOGI METRIA
1D09E BYZANTINE MUSICAL SYMBOL AGOGI MESI
1D09F BYZANTINE MUSICAL SYMBOL AGOGI GORGI
1D0A0 BYZANTINE MUSICAL SYMBOL AGOGI GORGOTERI
1D0A1 BYZANTINE MUSICAL SYMBOL AGOGI POLI GORGI

Ichimata and Martyrika (Ichimas and Evidentials)

1D0A2 BYZANTINE MUSICAL SYMBOL MARTYRIA PROTOS ICHOS
1D0A3 BYZANTINE MUSICAL SYMBOL MARTYRIA ALLI PROTOS ICHOS

1D0A4 BYZANTINE MUSICAL SYMBOL MARTYRIA DEYTEROS ICHOS
1D0A5 BYZANTINE MUSICAL SYMBOL MARTYRIA ALLI DEYTEROS ICHOS
1D0A6 BYZANTINE MUSICAL SYMBOL MARTYRIA TRITOS ICHOS
1D0A7 BYZANTINE MUSICAL SYMBOL MARTYRIA TRIFONIAS
1D0A8 BYZANTINE MUSICAL SYMBOL MARTYRIA TETARTOS ICHOS
1D0A9 BYZANTINE MUSICAL SYMBOL MARTYRIA TETARTOS LEGETOS ICHOS
1D0AA BYZANTINE MUSICAL SYMBOL MARTYRIA LEGETOS ICHOS
1D0AB BYZANTINE MUSICAL SYMBOL MARTYRIA PLAGIOS ICHOS
1D0AC BYZANTINE MUSICAL SYMBOL ISAKIA TELOUS ICHIMATOS
1D0AD BYZANTINE MUSICAL SYMBOL APOSTROFOI TELOUS ICHIMATOS
1D0AE BYZANTINE MUSICAL SYMBOL FANEROSIS TETRAFONIAS
1D0AF BYZANTINE MUSICAL SYMBOL FANEROSIS MONOFONIAS
1D0B0 BYZANTINE MUSICAL SYMBOL FANEROSIS DIFONIAS
1D0B1 BYZANTINE MUSICAL SYMBOL MARTYRIA VARYS ICHOS
1D0B2 BYZANTINE MUSICAL SYMBOL MARTYRIA PROTOVARYS ICHOS
1D0B3 BYZANTINE MUSICAL SYMBOL MARTYRIA PLAGIOS TETARTOS ICHOS
1D0B4 BYZANTINE MUSICAL SYMBOL GORTHMIKON N APLOUN
- used in intonation formulas instead of nu, before phonemes a, i, o, u

→ 03BD ν greek small letter nu

1D0B5 BYZANTINE MUSICAL SYMBOL GORTHMIKON N DIPLOUN
- used in intonation formulas instead of nu, before phoneme e

→ 03BD ν greek small letter nu

Fthores (Destroyers)

1D0B6 BYZANTINE MUSICAL SYMBOL ENARXIS KAI FTHORA VOU
1D0B7 BYZANTINE MUSICAL SYMBOL IMIFONON
1D0B8 BYZANTINE MUSICAL SYMBOL IMIFTHORON
1D0B9 BYZANTINE MUSICAL SYMBOL FTHORA ARCHAION DEYTEROU ICHOU
1D0BA BYZANTINE MUSICAL SYMBOL FTHORA DIATONIKI PA
1D0BB BYZANTINE MUSICAL SYMBOL FTHORA DIATONIKI NANA
1D0BC BYZANTINE MUSICAL SYMBOL FTHORA NAOS ICHOS
1D0BD BYZANTINE MUSICAL SYMBOL FTHORA DIATONIKI DI
1D0BE BYZANTINE MUSICAL SYMBOL FTHORA SKLIRON DIATONON DI
1D0BF BYZANTINE MUSICAL SYMBOL FTHORA DIATONIKI KE
1D0C0 BYZANTINE MUSICAL SYMBOL FTHORA DIATONIKI ZO
1D0C1 BYZANTINE MUSICAL SYMBOL FTHORA DIATONIKI NI KATO
1D0C2 BYZANTINE MUSICAL SYMBOL FTHORA DIATONIKI NI ANO
1D0C3 BYZANTINE MUSICAL SYMBOL FTHORA MALAKON CHROMA DIFONIAS
1D0C4 BYZANTINE MUSICAL SYMBOL FTHORA MALAKON CHROMA MONOFONIAS
1D0C5 BYZANTINE MUSICAL SYMBOL FHTORA SKLIRON CHROMA VASIS

※ BYZANTINE MUSICAL SYMBOL FTHORA SKLIRON CHROMA VASIS
- misspelling of "FTHORA" in character name is a known defect

1D0C6 BYZANTINE MUSICAL SYMBOL FTHORA SKLIRON CHROMA SYNAFI
1D0C7 BYZANTINE MUSICAL SYMBOL FTHORA NENANO
1D0C8 BYZANTINE MUSICAL SYMBOL CHROA ZYGOS
1D0C9 BYZANTINE MUSICAL SYMBOL CHROA KLITON
1D0CA BYZANTINE MUSICAL SYMBOL CHROA SPATHI

Alloioseis (Differentiators)

1D0CB BYZANTINE MUSICAL SYMBOL FTHORA I YFESIS TETARTIMORION
1D0CC BYZANTINE MUSICAL SYMBOL FTHORA ENARMONIOS ANTIFONIA
1D0CD BYZANTINE MUSICAL SYMBOL YFESIS TRITIMORION
1D0CE BYZANTINE MUSICAL SYMBOL DIESIS TRITIMORION
1D0CF BYZANTINE MUSICAL SYMBOL DIESIS TETARTIMORION
1D0D0 BYZANTINE MUSICAL SYMBOL DIESIS APLI DYO DODEKATA
1D0D1 BYZANTINE MUSICAL SYMBOL DIESIS MONOGRAMMOS TESSERA DODEKATA
1D0D2 BYZANTINE MUSICAL SYMBOL DIESIS DIGRAMMOS EX DODEKATA
1D0D3 BYZANTINE MUSICAL SYMBOL DIESIS TRIGRAMMOS OKTO DODEKATA
1D0D4 BYZANTINE MUSICAL SYMBOL YFESIS APLI DYO DODEKATA
1D0D5 BYZANTINE MUSICAL SYMBOL YFESIS MONOGRAMMOS TESSERA DODEKATA
1D0D6 BYZANTINE MUSICAL SYMBOL YFESIS DIGRAMMOS EX DODEKATA
1D0D7 BYZANTINE MUSICAL SYMBOL YFESIS TRIGRAMMOS OKTO DODEKATA
1D0D8 BYZANTINE MUSICAL SYMBOL GENIKI DIESIS
1D0D9 BYZANTINE MUSICAL SYMBOL GENIKI YFESIS

Rythmika (Rhythmics)

1D0DA BYZANTINE MUSICAL SYMBOL DIASTOLI APLI MIKRI

→ 1D105 | musical symbol short barline

1D0DB BYZANTINE MUSICAL SYMBOL DIASTOLI APLI MEGALI

→ 1D100 | musical symbol single barline

1D0DC BYZANTINE MUSICAL SYMBOL DIASTOLI DIPLI
1D0DD BYZANTINE MUSICAL SYMBOL DIASTOLI THESEOS
1D0DE BYZANTINE MUSICAL SYMBOL SIMANSIS THESEOS
1D0DF BYZANTINE MUSICAL SYMBOL SIMANSIS THESEOS DISIMOU
1D0E0 BYZANTINE MUSICAL SYMBOL SIMANSIS THESEOS TRISIMOU
1D0E1 BYZANTINE MUSICAL SYMBOL SIMANSIS THESEOS TETRASIMOU
1D0E2 BYZANTINE MUSICAL SYMBOL SIMANSIS ARSEOS

1D0E3 BYZANTINE MUSICAL SYMBOL SIMANSIS ARSEOS DISIMOU
1D0E4 BYZANTINE MUSICAL SYMBOL SIMANSIS ARSEOS TRISIMOU
1D0E5 BYZANTINE MUSICAL SYMBOL SIMANSIS ARSEOS TETRASIMOU

Grammata (Letters)

The first three characters are not actually attested in musical contexts.

1D0E6 BYZANTINE MUSICAL SYMBOL DIGRAMMA GG
1D0E7 BYZANTINE MUSICAL SYMBOL DIFTOGGOS OU
→ 0223 ȣ latin small letter ou
1D0E8 BYZANTINE MUSICAL SYMBOL STIGMA
→ 03DB ϛ greek small letter stigma
1D0E9 BYZANTINE MUSICAL SYMBOL ARKTIKO PA
1D0EA BYZANTINE MUSICAL SYMBOL ARKTIKO VOU
1D0EB BYZANTINE MUSICAL SYMBOL ARKTIKO GA
1D0EC BYZANTINE MUSICAL SYMBOL ARKTIKO DI
1D0ED BYZANTINE MUSICAL SYMBOL ARKTIKO KE
1D0EE BYZANTINE MUSICAL SYMBOL ARKTIKO ZO
1D0EF BYZANTINE MUSICAL SYMBOL ARKTIKO NI

Specials

1D0F0 BYZANTINE MUSICAL SYMBOL KENTIMATA NEO MESO
1D0F1 BYZANTINE MUSICAL SYMBOL KENTIMA NEO MESO
1D0F2 BYZANTINE MUSICAL SYMBOL KENTIMATA NEO KATO
1D0F3 BYZANTINE MUSICAL SYMBOL KENTIMA NEO KATO
1D0F4 BYZANTINE MUSICAL SYMBOL KLASMA KATO
1D0F5 BYZANTINE MUSICAL SYMBOL GORGON NEO KATO

	1D10	1D11	1D12	1D13	1D14	1D15	1D16	1D17	1D18	1D19	1D1A	1D1B	1D1C	1D1D	1D1E	1D1F
0	1D100	1D110	1D120	1D130	1D140	1D150	1D160	1D170	1D180	m 1D190	1D1A0	1D1B0	1D1C0	1D1D0		
1	1D101	1D111	1D121	1D131	1D141	1D151	1D161	1D171	1D181	f 1D191	1D1A1	1D1B1	1D1C1	1D1D1		
2	1D102	1D112	1D122	1D132	1D142	1D152	1D162	1D172	1D182	1D192	1D1A2	1D1B2	1D1C2	1D1D2		
3	1D103	1D113	1D123	1D133	1D143	1D153	1D163	BEGIN BEAM 1D173	1D183	1D193	1D1A3	1D1B3	1D1C3	1D1D3		
4	1D104	1D114	1D124	1D134	1D144	1D154	1D164	END BEAM 1D174	1D184	1D194	1D1A4	1D1B4	1D1C4	1D1D4		
5	1D105	1D115	1D125	1D135	1D145	1D155	1D165	BEGIN TIE 1D175	1D185	1D195	1D1A5	1D1B5	1D1C5	1D1D5		
6	1D106	1D116	1D126	8va 1D136	1D146	1D156	1D166	END TIE 1D176	1D186	tr 1D196	1D1A6	1D1B6	1D1C6	1D1D6		
7	1D107	1D117		8vb 1D137	1D147	1D157	1D167	BEGIN SLUR 1D177	1D187	1D197	1D1A7	1D1B7	1D1C7	1D1D7		
8	1D108	1D118		15ma 1D138	1D148	1D158	1D168	END SLUR 1D178	1D188	1D198	1D1A8	1D1B8	1D1C8	1D1D8		
9	D.S. 1D109	1D119		15mb 1D139	1D149	NULL NOTE HEAD 1D159	1D169	BEGIN PHR. 1D179	1D189	1D199	1D1A9	1D1B9	1D1C9	1D1D9		
A	D.C. 1D10A	1D11A	1D12A	1D13A	1D14A	1D15A	1D16A	END PHR. 1D17A	1D18A	1D19A	1D1AA	1D1BA	1D1CA	1D1DA		
B	1D10B	1D11B	1D12B	1D13B	1D14B	1D15B	1D16B	1D17B	1D18B	1D19B	1D1AB	1D1BB	1D1CB	1D1DB		
C	1D10C	1D11C	1D12C	1D13C	1D14C	1D15C	1D16C	1D17C	r 1D18C	1D19C	1D1AC	1D1BC	1D1CC	1D1DC		
D	1D10D	1D11D	1D12D	1D13D	1D14D	1D15D	1D16D	1D17D	s 1D18D	1D19D	1D1AD	1D1BD	1D1CD	1D1DD		
E	1D10E	1D11E	1D12E	1D13E	1D14E	1D15E	1D16E	1D17E	z 1D18E	1D19E	Ped. 1D1AE	1D1BE	1D1CE			
F	1D10F	1D11F	1D12F	1D13F	1D14F	1D15F	1D16F	1D17F	p 1D18F	1D19F	1D1AF	1D1BF	1D1CF			

Bars
1D100 MUSICAL SYMBOL SINGLE BARLINE
1D101 MUSICAL SYMBOL DOUBLE BARLINE
1D102 MUSICAL SYMBOL FINAL BARLINE
1D103 MUSICAL SYMBOL REVERSE FINAL BARLINE
1D104 MUSICAL SYMBOL DASHED BARLINE
1D105 MUSICAL SYMBOL SHORT BARLINE

Codas
1D106 MUSICAL SYMBOL LEFT REPEAT SIGN
1D107 MUSICAL SYMBOL RIGHT REPEAT SIGN
1D108 MUSICAL SYMBOL REPEAT DOTS
1D109 D.S. MUSICAL SYMBOL DAL SEGNO
1D10A D.C. MUSICAL SYMBOL DA CAPO
1D10B MUSICAL SYMBOL SEGNO
1D10C MUSICAL SYMBOL CODA

Figure repetitions
1D10D MUSICAL SYMBOL REPEATED FIGURE-1
1D10E MUSICAL SYMBOL REPEATED FIGURE-2
1D10F MUSICAL SYMBOL REPEATED FIGURE-3

Holds and pauses
1D110 MUSICAL SYMBOL FERMATA
1D111 MUSICAL SYMBOL FERMATA BELOW
1D112 MUSICAL SYMBOL BREATH MARK
1D113 MUSICAL SYMBOL CAESURA

Staff brackets
1D114 MUSICAL SYMBOL BRACE
1D115 MUSICAL SYMBOL BRACKET

Staves
1D116 MUSICAL SYMBOL ONE-LINE STAFF
1D117 MUSICAL SYMBOL TWO-LINE STAFF
1D118 MUSICAL SYMBOL THREE-LINE STAFF
1D119 MUSICAL SYMBOL FOUR-LINE STAFF
1D11A MUSICAL SYMBOL FIVE-LINE STAFF
1D11B MUSICAL SYMBOL SIX-LINE STAFF

Tablature
1D11C MUSICAL SYMBOL SIX-STRING FRETBOARD
1D11D MUSICAL SYMBOL FOUR-STRING FRETBOARD

Clefs
1D11E MUSICAL SYMBOL G CLEF
1D11F MUSICAL SYMBOL G CLEF OTTAVA ALTA
1D120 MUSICAL SYMBOL G CLEF OTTAVA BASSA
1D121 MUSICAL SYMBOL C CLEF
1D122 MUSICAL SYMBOL F CLEF
1D123 MUSICAL SYMBOL F CLEF OTTAVA ALTA
1D124 MUSICAL SYMBOL F CLEF OTTAVA BASSA
1D125 MUSICAL SYMBOL DRUM CLEF-1
1D126 MUSICAL SYMBOL DRUM CLEF-2

Accidentals
1D127 <reserved>
→ 266D ♭ music flat sign
1D128 <reserved>
→ 266E ♮ music natural sign
1D129 <reserved>
→ 266F ♯ music sharp sign
1D12A MUSICAL SYMBOL DOUBLE SHARP
1D12B MUSICAL SYMBOL DOUBLE FLAT
1D12C MUSICAL SYMBOL FLAT UP
1D12D MUSICAL SYMBOL FLAT DOWN
1D12E MUSICAL SYMBOL NATURAL UP
1D12F MUSICAL SYMBOL NATURAL DOWN
1D130 MUSICAL SYMBOL SHARP UP
1D131 MUSICAL SYMBOL SHARP DOWN
1D132 MUSICAL SYMBOL QUARTER TONE SHARP
1D133 MUSICAL SYMBOL QUARTER TONE FLAT

Time signatures
1D134 MUSICAL SYMBOL COMMON TIME
1D135 MUSICAL SYMBOL CUT TIME

Octaves
1D136 MUSICAL SYMBOL OTTAVA ALTA
1D137 MUSICAL SYMBOL OTTAVA BASSA
1D138 MUSICAL SYMBOL QUINDICESIMA ALTA
1D139 MUSICAL SYMBOL QUINDICESIMA BASSA

Rests
1D13A MUSICAL SYMBOL MULTI REST
= double whole-rest, breve rest
1D13B MUSICAL SYMBOL WHOLE REST
= semibreve rest
1D13C MUSICAL SYMBOL HALF REST
= minim rest
1D13D MUSICAL SYMBOL QUARTER REST
= crochet rest
1D13E MUSICAL SYMBOL EIGHTH REST
1D13F MUSICAL SYMBOL SIXTEENTH REST
1D140 MUSICAL SYMBOL THIRTY-SECOND REST
1D141 MUSICAL SYMBOL SIXTY-FOURTH REST
1D142 MUSICAL SYMBOL ONE HUNDRED TWENTY-EIGHTH REST

Noteheads
1D143 MUSICAL SYMBOL X NOTEHEAD
1D144 MUSICAL SYMBOL PLUS NOTEHEAD
1D145 MUSICAL SYMBOL CIRCLE X NOTEHEAD
1D146 MUSICAL SYMBOL SQUARE NOTEHEAD WHITE
1D147 MUSICAL SYMBOL SQUARE NOTEHEAD BLACK
1D148 MUSICAL SYMBOL TRIANGLE NOTEHEAD UP WHITE
1D149 MUSICAL SYMBOL TRIANGLE NOTEHEAD UP BLACK
1D14A MUSICAL SYMBOL TRIANGLE NOTEHEAD LEFT WHITE
1D14B MUSICAL SYMBOL TRIANGLE NOTEHEAD LEFT BLACK
1D14C MUSICAL SYMBOL TRIANGLE NOTEHEAD RIGHT WHITE
1D14D MUSICAL SYMBOL TRIANGLE NOTEHEAD RIGHT BLACK
1D14E MUSICAL SYMBOL TRIANGLE NOTEHEAD DOWN WHITE
1D14F MUSICAL SYMBOL TRIANGLE NOTEHEAD DOWN BLACK
1D150 MUSICAL SYMBOL TRIANGLE NOTEHEAD UP RIGHT WHITE
1D151 MUSICAL SYMBOL TRIANGLE NOTEHEAD UP RIGHT BLACK
1D152 MUSICAL SYMBOL MOON NOTEHEAD WHITE
1D153 MUSICAL SYMBOL MOON NOTEHEAD BLACK
1D154 MUSICAL SYMBOL TRIANGLE-ROUND NOTEHEAD DOWN WHITE
1D155 MUSICAL SYMBOL TRIANGLE-ROUND NOTEHEAD DOWN BLACK
1D156 MUSICAL SYMBOL PARENTHESIS NOTEHEAD
1D157 MUSICAL SYMBOL VOID NOTEHEAD
1D158 MUSICAL SYMBOL NOTEHEAD BLACK
1D159 MUSICAL SYMBOL NULL NOTEHEAD
1D15A MUSICAL SYMBOL CLUSTER NOTEHEAD WHITE

1D15B MUSICAL SYMBOL CLUSTER NOTEHEAD BLACK

Notes

1D15C MUSICAL SYMBOL BREVE
1D15D MUSICAL SYMBOL WHOLE NOTE
1D15E MUSICAL SYMBOL HALF NOTE
≡ 1D157 1D165
1D15F MUSICAL SYMBOL QUARTER NOTE
≡ 1D158 1D165
1D160 MUSICAL SYMBOL EIGHTH NOTE
≡ 1D15F 1D16E
1D161 MUSICAL SYMBOL SIXTEENTH NOTE
≡ 1D15F 1D16F
1D162 MUSICAL SYMBOL THIRTY-SECOND NOTE
≡ 1D15F 1D170
1D163 MUSICAL SYMBOL SIXTY-FOURTH NOTE
≡ 1D15F 1D171
1D164 MUSICAL SYMBOL ONE HUNDRED TWENTY-EIGHTH NOTE
≡ 1D15F 1D172

Stems

1D165 MUSICAL SYMBOL COMBINING STEM
1D166 MUSICAL SYMBOL COMBINING SPRECHGESANG STEM

Tremolos

1D167 MUSICAL SYMBOL COMBINING TREMOLO-1
1D168 MUSICAL SYMBOL COMBINING TREMOLO-2
1D169 MUSICAL SYMBOL COMBINING TREMOLO-3
1D16A MUSICAL SYMBOL FINGERED TREMOLO-1
1D16B MUSICAL SYMBOL FINGERED TREMOLO-2
1D16C MUSICAL SYMBOL FINGERED TREMOLO-3

Augmentation dot

1D16D MUSICAL SYMBOL COMBINING AUGMENTATION DOT

Flags

1D16E MUSICAL SYMBOL COMBINING FLAG-1
1D16F MUSICAL SYMBOL COMBINING FLAG-2
1D170 MUSICAL SYMBOL COMBINING FLAG-3
1D171 MUSICAL SYMBOL COMBINING FLAG-4
1D172 MUSICAL SYMBOL COMBINING FLAG-5

Beams and slurs

1D173 BEGIN BEAM MUSICAL SYMBOL BEGIN BEAM
1D174 END BEAM MUSICAL SYMBOL END BEAM
1D175 BEGIN TIE MUSICAL SYMBOL BEGIN TIE
1D176 END TIE MUSICAL SYMBOL END TIE
1D177 BEGIN SLUR MUSICAL SYMBOL BEGIN SLUR
1D178 END SLUR MUSICAL SYMBOL END SLUR
1D179 BEGIN PHR MUSICAL SYMBOL BEGIN PHRASE
1D17A END PHR MUSICAL SYMBOL END PHRASE

Articulation

1D17B MUSICAL SYMBOL COMBINING ACCENT
1D17C MUSICAL SYMBOL COMBINING STACCATO
1D17D MUSICAL SYMBOL COMBINING TENUTO
1D17E MUSICAL SYMBOL COMBINING STACCATISSIMO
1D17F MUSICAL SYMBOL COMBINING MARCATO
1D180 MUSICAL SYMBOL COMBINING MARCATO-STACCATO
1D181 MUSICAL SYMBOL COMBINING ACCENT-STACCATO
1D182 MUSICAL SYMBOL COMBINING LOURE
1D183 MUSICAL SYMBOL ARPEGGIATO UP
1D184 MUSICAL SYMBOL ARPEGGIATO DOWN
1D185 MUSICAL SYMBOL COMBINING DOIT
1D186 MUSICAL SYMBOL COMBINING RIP
1D187 MUSICAL SYMBOL COMBINING FLIP
1D188 MUSICAL SYMBOL COMBINING SMEAR
1D189 MUSICAL SYMBOL COMBINING BEND
1D18A MUSICAL SYMBOL COMBINING DOUBLE TONGUE
1D18B MUSICAL SYMBOL COMBINING TRIPLE TONGUE
1D18C MUSICAL SYMBOL RINFORZANDO
1D18D MUSICAL SYMBOL SUBITO
1D18E MUSICAL SYMBOL Z

Dynamics

1D18F MUSICAL SYMBOL PIANO
1D190 MUSICAL SYMBOL MEZZO
1D191 MUSICAL SYMBOL FORTE
1D192 MUSICAL SYMBOL CRESCENDO
1D193 MUSICAL SYMBOL DECRESCENDO

Ornaments

1D194 MUSICAL SYMBOL GRACE NOTE SLASH
1D195 MUSICAL SYMBOL GRACE NOTE NO SLASH
1D196 MUSICAL SYMBOL TR
1D197 MUSICAL SYMBOL TURN
1D198 MUSICAL SYMBOL INVERTED TURN
1D199 MUSICAL SYMBOL TURN SLASH
1D19A MUSICAL SYMBOL TURN UP
1D19B MUSICAL SYMBOL ORNAMENT STROKE-1
1D19C MUSICAL SYMBOL ORNAMENT STROKE-2
1D19D MUSICAL SYMBOL ORNAMENT STROKE-3
1D19E MUSICAL SYMBOL ORNAMENT STROKE-4
1D19F MUSICAL SYMBOL ORNAMENT STROKE-5
1D1A0 MUSICAL SYMBOL ORNAMENT STROKE-6
1D1A1 MUSICAL SYMBOL ORNAMENT STROKE-7
1D1A2 MUSICAL SYMBOL ORNAMENT STROKE-8
1D1A3 MUSICAL SYMBOL ORNAMENT STROKE-9
1D1A4 MUSICAL SYMBOL ORNAMENT STROKE-10
1D1A5 MUSICAL SYMBOL ORNAMENT STROKE-11

Analytics

1D1A6 MUSICAL SYMBOL HAUPTSTIMME
1D1A7 MUSICAL SYMBOL NEBENSTIMME
1D1A8 MUSICAL SYMBOL END OF STIMME
1D1A9 MUSICAL SYMBOL DEGREE SLASH

Instrumentation

1D1AA MUSICAL SYMBOL COMBINING DOWN BOW
1D1AB MUSICAL SYMBOL COMBINING UP BOW
1D1AC MUSICAL SYMBOL COMBINING HARMONIC
1D1AD MUSICAL SYMBOL COMBINING SNAP PIZZICATO

Pedals

1D1AE MUSICAL SYMBOL PEDAL MARK
1D1AF MUSICAL SYMBOL PEDAL UP MARK
1D1B0 MUSICAL SYMBOL HALF PEDAL MARK

Miscellaneous symbols

1D1B1 MUSICAL SYMBOL GLISSANDO UP
1D1B2 MUSICAL SYMBOL GLISSANDO DOWN
1D1B3 MUSICAL SYMBOL WITH FINGERNAILS
1D1B4 MUSICAL SYMBOL DAMP
1D1B5 MUSICAL SYMBOL DAMP ALL

Mensural notation

1D1B6 MUSICAL SYMBOL MAXIMA

1D1B7 𝆷 MUSICAL SYMBOL LONGA
1D1B8 𝆸 MUSICAL SYMBOL BREVIS
1D1B9 𝆹 MUSICAL SYMBOL SEMIBREVIS WHITE
1D1BA 𝆺 MUSICAL SYMBOL SEMIBREVIS BLACK
1D1BB 𝆹𝅥 MUSICAL SYMBOL MINIMA
≡ 1D1B9 𝆹 1D165 𝅥
1D1BC 𝆺𝅥 MUSICAL SYMBOL MINIMA BLACK
≡ 1D1BA 𝆺 1D165 𝅥
1D1BD 𝆹𝅥𝅮 MUSICAL SYMBOL SEMIMINIMA WHITE
≡ 1D1BB 𝆹𝅥 1D16E 𝅮
1D1BE 𝆺𝅥𝅮 MUSICAL SYMBOL SEMIMINIMA BLACK
≡ 1D1BC 𝆺𝅥 1D16E 𝅮
1D1BF 𝆹𝅥𝅯 MUSICAL SYMBOL FUSA WHITE
≡ 1D1BB 𝆹𝅥 1D16F 𝅯
1D1C0 𝆺𝅥𝅯 MUSICAL SYMBOL FUSA BLACK
≡ 1D1BC 𝆺𝅥 1D16F 𝅯

Mensural rests

1D1C1 𝇁 MUSICAL SYMBOL LONGA PERFECTA REST
1D1C2 𝇂 MUSICAL SYMBOL LONGA IMPERFECTA REST
1D1C3 𝇃 MUSICAL SYMBOL BREVIS REST
1D1C4 𝇄 MUSICAL SYMBOL SEMIBREVIS REST
1D1C5 𝇅 MUSICAL SYMBOL MINIMA REST
1D1C6 𝇆 MUSICAL SYMBOL SEMIMINIMA REST

Mensural prolations

1D1C7 𝇇 MUSICAL SYMBOL TEMPUS PERFECTUM CUM PROLATIONE PERFECTA
1D1C8 𝇈 MUSICAL SYMBOL TEMPUS PERFECTUM CUM PROLATIONE IMPERFECTA
1D1C9 𝇉 MUSICAL SYMBOL TEMPUS PERFECTUM CUM PROLATIONE PERFECTA DIMINUTION-1
1D1CA 𝇊 MUSICAL SYMBOL TEMPUS IMPERFECTUM CUM PROLATIONE PERFECTA
1D1CB 𝇋 MUSICAL SYMBOL TEMPUS IMPERFECTUM CUM PROLATIONE IMPERFECTA
1D1CC 𝇌 MUSICAL SYMBOL TEMPUS IMPERFECTUM CUM PROLATIONE IMPERFECTA DIMINUTION-1
1D1CD 𝇍 MUSICAL SYMBOL TEMPUS IMPERFECTUM CUM PROLATIONE IMPERFECTA DIMINUTION-2
1D1CE 𝇎 MUSICAL SYMBOL TEMPUS IMPERFECTUM CUM PROLATIONE IMPERFECTA DIMINUTION-3

Miscellaneous symbol

1D1CF 𝇏 MUSICAL SYMBOL CROIX

Gregorian notation

1D1D0 𝇐 MUSICAL SYMBOL GREGORIAN C CLEF
1D1D1 𝇑 MUSICAL SYMBOL GREGORIAN F CLEF
1D1D2 𝇒 MUSICAL SYMBOL SQUARE B
1D1D3 𝇓 MUSICAL SYMBOL VIRGA
1D1D4 𝇔 MUSICAL SYMBOL PODATUS
1D1D5 𝇕 MUSICAL SYMBOL CLIVIS
1D1D6 𝇖 MUSICAL SYMBOL SCANDICUS
1D1D7 𝇗 MUSICAL SYMBOL CLIMACUS
1D1D8 𝇘 MUSICAL SYMBOL TORCULUS
1D1D9 𝇙 MUSICAL SYMBOL PORRECTUS
1D1DA 𝇚 MUSICAL SYMBOL PORRECTUS FLEXUS
1D1DB 𝇛 MUSICAL SYMBOL SCANDICUS FLEXUS
1D1DC 𝇜 MUSICAL SYMBOL TORCULUS RESUPINUS
1D1DD 𝇝 MUSICAL SYMBOL PES SUBPUNCTIS

	1D20	1D21	1D22	1D23	1D24
0	1D200	1D210	1D220	1D230	1D240
1	1D201	1D211	1D221	1D231	1D241
2	1D202	1D212	1D222	1D232	1D242
3	1D203	1D213	1D223	1D233	1D243
4	1D204	1D214	1D224	1D234	1D244
5	1D205	1D215	1D225	1D235	1D245
6	1D206	1D216	1D226	1D236	
7	1D207	1D217	1D227	1D237	
8	1D208	1D218	1D228	1D238	
9	1D209	1D219	1D229	1D239	
A	1D20A	1D21A	1D22A	1D23A	
B	1D20B	1D21B	1D22B	1D23B	
C	1D20C	1D21C	1D22C	1D23C	
D	1D20D	1D21D	1D22D	1D23D	
E	1D20E	1D21E	1D22E	1D23E	
F	1D20F	1D21F	1D22F	1D23F	

Ancient Greek vocalic notation

In a few instances vocalic and instrumental symbols have been unified with each other. In other instances they have been unified with regular Greek letters.

1D200 𝈀 GREEK VOCAL NOTATION SYMBOL-1
- vocal E

1D201 𝈁 GREEK VOCAL NOTATION SYMBOL-2
- vocal first sharp of E

1D202 𝈂 GREEK VOCAL NOTATION SYMBOL-3
= Greek instrumental notation symbol-3
- vocal or instrumental second sharp of E

1D203 𝈃 GREEK VOCAL NOTATION SYMBOL-4
- vocal F

1D204 𝈄 GREEK VOCAL NOTATION SYMBOL-5
- vocal first sharp of F

1D205 𝈅 GREEK VOCAL NOTATION SYMBOL-6
= Greek instrumental notation symbol-21
- vocal second sharp of F
- instrumental second sharp of d

1D206 𝈆 GREEK VOCAL NOTATION SYMBOL-7
= Greek instrumental notation symbol-9
- vocal G
- instrumental second sharp of G

1D207 𝈇 GREEK VOCAL NOTATION SYMBOL-8
- vocal first sharp of G

1D208 𝈈 GREEK VOCAL NOTATION SYMBOL-9
= Greek instrumental notation symbol-44
- vocal second sharp of G
- instrumental first sharp of e′

1D209 𝈉 GREEK VOCAL NOTATION SYMBOL-10
- vocal A
- this is a modification of 039F Ο and is therefore not the same as 03D8 Ϙ

1D20A 𝈊 GREEK VOCAL NOTATION SYMBOL-11
- vocal first sharp of A

1D20B 𝈋 GREEK VOCAL NOTATION SYMBOL-12
- vocal second sharp of A

1D20C 𝈌 GREEK VOCAL NOTATION SYMBOL-13
- vocal B

1D20D 𝈍 GREEK VOCAL NOTATION SYMBOL-14
= Greek instrumental notation symbol-41
- vocal first sharp of B
- instrumental first sharp of d′

→ 0056 V latin capital letter v

1D20E 𝈎 GREEK VOCAL NOTATION SYMBOL-15
= Greek instrumental notation symbol-35
- vocal second sharp of B
- instrumental first sharp of b

1D20F 𝈏 GREEK VOCAL NOTATION SYMBOL-16
- vocal c
- unlike 1D23B 𝈻 this character has a glyph variant that looks like a horizontal line

1D210 𝈐 GREEK VOCAL NOTATION SYMBOL-17
- vocal first sharp of c

1D211 𝈑 GREEK VOCAL NOTATION SYMBOL-18
= Greek instrumental notation symbol-15
- vocal second sharp of c
- instrumental second sharp of B

1D212 𝈒 GREEK VOCAL NOTATION SYMBOL-19
- vocal d

1D213 𝈓 GREEK VOCAL NOTATION SYMBOL-20
= Greek instrumental notation symbol-28
- vocal first sharp of d
- instrumental g
- this is a modification of 0395 Ε and is therefore not the same as 0046 F

1D214 𝈔 GREEK VOCAL NOTATION SYMBOL-21
- vocal second sharp of d

1D215 𝈕 GREEK VOCAL NOTATION SYMBOL-22
- vocal e

1D216 𝈖 GREEK VOCAL NOTATION SYMBOL-23
- vocal first sharp of e
- this is a modification of 0392 Β and is therefore not the same as 0052 R

1D217 𝈗 GREEK VOCAL NOTATION SYMBOL-24
- vocal second sharp of e

1D218 𝈘 GREEK VOCAL NOTATION SYMBOL-50
- vocal first sharp of g′

1D219 𝈙 GREEK VOCAL NOTATION SYMBOL-51
- vocal second sharp of g′

1D21A 𝈚 GREEK VOCAL NOTATION SYMBOL-52
- vocal a′

1D21B 𝈛 GREEK VOCAL NOTATION SYMBOL-53
- vocal first sharp of a′

1D21C 𝈜 GREEK VOCAL NOTATION SYMBOL-54
= Greek instrumental notation symbol-20
- vocal second sharp of a′
- instrumental first sharp of d

Ancient Greek instrumental notation

1D21D 𝈝 GREEK INSTRUMENTAL NOTATION SYMBOL-1
- instrumental E

1D21E 𝈞 GREEK INSTRUMENTAL NOTATION SYMBOL-2
- instrumental first sharp of E

1D21F 𝈟 GREEK INSTRUMENTAL NOTATION SYMBOL-4
- instrumental F

1D220 𝈠 GREEK INSTRUMENTAL NOTATION SYMBOL-5
- instrumental first sharp of F

1D221 𝈡 GREEK INSTRUMENTAL NOTATION SYMBOL-7
- instrumental G

1D222 𝈢 GREEK INSTRUMENTAL NOTATION SYMBOL-8
- instrumental first sharp of G

1D223 𝈣 GREEK INSTRUMENTAL NOTATION SYMBOL-11
- instrumental first sharp of A

1D224 𝈤 GREEK INSTRUMENTAL NOTATION SYMBOL-12
- instrumental second sharp of A

1D225 𝈥 GREEK INSTRUMENTAL NOTATION SYMBOL-13
- instrumental B

1D226 𝈦 GREEK INSTRUMENTAL NOTATION SYMBOL-14
- instrumental first sharp of B

1D227 𝈧 GREEK INSTRUMENTAL NOTATION SYMBOL-17
- instrumental first sharp of c

1D228 𝈨 GREEK INSTRUMENTAL NOTATION SYMBOL-18
- instrumental second sharp of c

1D229 𝈩 GREEK INSTRUMENTAL NOTATION SYMBOL-19
- instrumental d

1D22A 𝈪 GREEK INSTRUMENTAL NOTATION SYMBOL-23
- instrumental first sharp of e

1D22B 𝈫 GREEK INSTRUMENTAL NOTATION SYMBOL-24
- instrumental second sharp of e

1D22C 𝈬 GREEK INSTRUMENTAL NOTATION SYMBOL-25
- instrumental f

1D22D 𝈭 GREEK INSTRUMENTAL NOTATION SYMBOL-26
- instrumental first sharp of f

1D22E 𝈮 GREEK INSTRUMENTAL NOTATION SYMBOL-27
- instrumental second sharp of f

1D22F 𝈯 GREEK INSTRUMENTAL NOTATION SYMBOL-29
- instrumental first sharp of g

1D230 𝈰 GREEK INSTRUMENTAL NOTATION SYMBOL-30
- instrumental second sharp of g

1D231 𝈱 GREEK INSTRUMENTAL NOTATION SYMBOL-32
- instrumental first sharp of a

1D232 𝈲 GREEK INSTRUMENTAL NOTATION SYMBOL-36
- instrumental second sharp of b

1D233 𝈳 GREEK INSTRUMENTAL NOTATION SYMBOL-37
- instrumental c′

1D234 𝈴 GREEK INSTRUMENTAL NOTATION SYMBOL-38
- instrumental first sharp of c′

1D235 𝈵 GREEK INSTRUMENTAL NOTATION SYMBOL-39
- instrumental second sharp of c′

1D236 𝈶 GREEK INSTRUMENTAL NOTATION SYMBOL-40
- instrumental d′

1D237 𝈷 GREEK INSTRUMENTAL NOTATION SYMBOL-42
- instrumental second sharp of d′

1D238 𝈸 GREEK INSTRUMENTAL NOTATION SYMBOL-43
- instrumental e′

1D239 𝈹 GREEK INSTRUMENTAL NOTATION SYMBOL-45
- instrumental second sharp of e′

1D23A 𝈺 GREEK INSTRUMENTAL NOTATION SYMBOL-47
- instrumental first sharp of f′
- similar but not identical to 002F /

1D23B 𝈻 GREEK INSTRUMENTAL NOTATION SYMBOL-48
- instrumental second sharp of f′
- similar but not identical to 005C \

1D23C 𝈼 GREEK INSTRUMENTAL NOTATION SYMBOL-49
- instrumental g′

1D23D 𝈽 GREEK INSTRUMENTAL NOTATION SYMBOL-50
- instrumental first sharp of g′

1D23E 𝈾 GREEK INSTRUMENTAL NOTATION SYMBOL-51
- instrumental second sharp of g′

1D23F 𝈿 GREEK INSTRUMENTAL NOTATION SYMBOL-52
- instrumental a′

1D240 𝉀 GREEK INSTRUMENTAL NOTATION SYMBOL-53
- instrumental first sharp of a′

1D241 𝉁 GREEK INSTRUMENTAL NOTATION SYMBOL-54
- instrumental second sharp of a′

Further Greek musical notation symbols

1D242 ◌𝉂 COMBINING GREEK MUSICAL TRISEME
→ 23D7 ⏗ metrical triseme

1D243 ◌𝉃 COMBINING GREEK MUSICAL TETRASEME
→ 23D8 ⏘ metrical tetraseme

1D244 ◌𝉄 COMBINING GREEK MUSICAL PENTASEME
→ 23D9 ⏙ metrical pentaseme

1D245 𝉅 GREEK MUSICAL LEIMMA

	1D30	1D31	1D32	1D33	1D34	1D35
0	1D300	1D310	1D320	1D330	1D340	1D350
1	1D301	1D311	1D321	1D331	1D341	1D351
2	1D302	1D312	1D322	1D332	1D342	1D352
3	1D303	1D313	1D323	1D333	1D343	1D353
4	1D304	1D314	1D324	1D334	1D344	1D354
5	1D305	1D315	1D325	1D335	1D345	1D355
6	1D306	1D316	1D326	1D336	1D346	1D356
7	1D307	1D317	1D327	1D337	1D347	
8	1D308	1D318	1D328	1D338	1D348	
9	1D309	1D319	1D329	1D339	1D349	
A	1D30A	1D31A	1D32A	1D33A	1D34A	
B	1D30B	1D31B	1D32B	1D33B	1D34B	
C	1D30C	1D31C	1D32C	1D33C	1D34C	
D	1D30D	1D31D	1D32D	1D33D	1D34D	
E	1D30E	1D31E	1D32E	1D33E	1D34E	
F	1D30F	1D31F	1D32F	1D33F	1D34F	

These symbols are an extension of the better-known Yijing symbols found in the Miscellaneous Symbols block. The names for the monogram and digram symbols here are not correct translations of the usual Chinese terminology.

Monogram

1D300 𝌀 MONOGRAM FOR EARTH
= ren
• usually associated with human (Chinese ren), rather than earth
→ 268A ⚊ monogram for yang
→ 268B ⚋ monogram for yin

Digrams

The digrams extend the set of Yijing digrams; note that the Chinese aliases more correctly represent their interpretation.

1D301 𝌁 DIGRAM FOR HEAVENLY EARTH
= tian ren

1D302 𝌂 DIGRAM FOR HUMAN EARTH
= di ren

1D303 𝌃 DIGRAM FOR EARTHLY HEAVEN
= ren tian

1D304 𝌄 DIGRAM FOR EARTHLY HUMAN
= ren di

1D305 𝌅 DIGRAM FOR EARTH
= ren ren

Tetragrams

1D306 𝌆 TETRAGRAM FOR CENTRE
1D307 𝌇 TETRAGRAM FOR FULL CIRCLE
1D308 𝌈 TETRAGRAM FOR MIRED
1D309 𝌉 TETRAGRAM FOR BARRIER
1D30A 𝌊 TETRAGRAM FOR KEEPING SMALL
1D30B 𝌋 TETRAGRAM FOR CONTRARIETY
1D30C 𝌌 TETRAGRAM FOR ASCENT
1D30D 𝌍 TETRAGRAM FOR OPPOSITION
1D30E 𝌎 TETRAGRAM FOR BRANCHING OUT
1D30F 𝌏 TETRAGRAM FOR DEFECTIVENESS OR DISTORTION
1D310 𝌐 TETRAGRAM FOR DIVERGENCE
1D311 𝌑 TETRAGRAM FOR YOUTHFULNESS
1D312 𝌒 TETRAGRAM FOR INCREASE
1D313 𝌓 TETRAGRAM FOR PENETRATION
1D314 𝌔 TETRAGRAM FOR REACH
1D315 𝌕 TETRAGRAM FOR CONTACT
1D316 𝌖 TETRAGRAM FOR HOLDING BACK
1D317 𝌗 TETRAGRAM FOR WAITING
1D318 𝌘 TETRAGRAM FOR FOLLOWING
1D319 𝌙 TETRAGRAM FOR ADVANCE
1D31A 𝌚 TETRAGRAM FOR RELEASE
1D31B 𝌛 TETRAGRAM FOR RESISTANCE
1D31C 𝌜 TETRAGRAM FOR EASE
1D31D 𝌝 TETRAGRAM FOR JOY
1D31E 𝌞 TETRAGRAM FOR CONTENTION
1D31F 𝌟 TETRAGRAM FOR ENDEAVOUR
1D320 𝌠 TETRAGRAM FOR DUTIES
1D321 𝌡 TETRAGRAM FOR CHANGE
1D322 𝌢 TETRAGRAM FOR DECISIVENESS
1D323 𝌣 TETRAGRAM FOR BOLD RESOLUTION
1D324 𝌤 TETRAGRAM FOR PACKING
1D325 𝌥 TETRAGRAM FOR LEGION
1D326 𝌦 TETRAGRAM FOR CLOSENESS
1D327 𝌧 TETRAGRAM FOR KINSHIP
1D328 𝌨 TETRAGRAM FOR GATHERING
1D329 𝌩 TETRAGRAM FOR STRENGTH
1D32A 𝌪 TETRAGRAM FOR PURITY
1D32B 𝌫 TETRAGRAM FOR FULLNESS
1D32C 𝌬 TETRAGRAM FOR RESIDENCE
1D32D 𝌭 TETRAGRAM FOR LAW OR MODEL
1D32E 𝌮 TETRAGRAM FOR RESPONSE
1D32F 𝌯 TETRAGRAM FOR GOING TO MEET
1D330 𝌰 TETRAGRAM FOR ENCOUNTERS
1D331 𝌱 TETRAGRAM FOR STOVE
1D332 𝌲 TETRAGRAM FOR GREATNESS
1D333 𝌳 TETRAGRAM FOR ENLARGEMENT
1D334 𝌴 TETRAGRAM FOR PATTERN
1D335 𝌵 TETRAGRAM FOR RITUAL
1D336 𝌶 TETRAGRAM FOR FLIGHT
1D337 𝌷 TETRAGRAM FOR VASTNESS OR WASTING
1D338 𝌸 TETRAGRAM FOR CONSTANCY
1D339 𝌹 TETRAGRAM FOR MEASURE
1D33A 𝌺 TETRAGRAM FOR ETERNITY
1D33B 𝌻 TETRAGRAM FOR UNITY
1D33C 𝌼 TETRAGRAM FOR DIMINISHMENT
1D33D 𝌽 TETRAGRAM FOR CLOSED MOUTH
1D33E 𝌾 TETRAGRAM FOR GUARDEDNESS
1D33F 𝌿 TETRAGRAM FOR GATHERING IN
1D340 𝍀 TETRAGRAM FOR MASSING
1D341 𝍁 TETRAGRAM FOR ACCUMULATION
1D342 𝍂 TETRAGRAM FOR EMBELLISHMENT
1D343 𝍃 TETRAGRAM FOR DOUBT
1D344 𝍄 TETRAGRAM FOR WATCH
1D345 𝍅 TETRAGRAM FOR SINKING
1D346 𝍆 TETRAGRAM FOR INNER
1D347 𝍇 TETRAGRAM FOR DEPARTURE
1D348 𝍈 TETRAGRAM FOR DARKENING
1D349 𝍉 TETRAGRAM FOR DIMMING
1D34A 𝍊 TETRAGRAM FOR EXHAUSTION
1D34B 𝍋 TETRAGRAM FOR SEVERANCE
1D34C 𝍌 TETRAGRAM FOR STOPPAGE
1D34D 𝍍 TETRAGRAM FOR HARDNESS
1D34E 𝍎 TETRAGRAM FOR COMPLETION
1D34F 𝍏 TETRAGRAM FOR CLOSURE
1D350 𝍐 TETRAGRAM FOR FAILURE
1D351 𝍑 TETRAGRAM FOR AGGRAVATION
1D352 𝍒 TETRAGRAM FOR COMPLIANCE
1D353 𝍓 TETRAGRAM FOR ON THE VERGE
1D354 𝍔 TETRAGRAM FOR DIFFICULTIES
1D355 𝍕 TETRAGRAM FOR LABOURING
1D356 𝍖 TETRAGRAM FOR FOSTERING

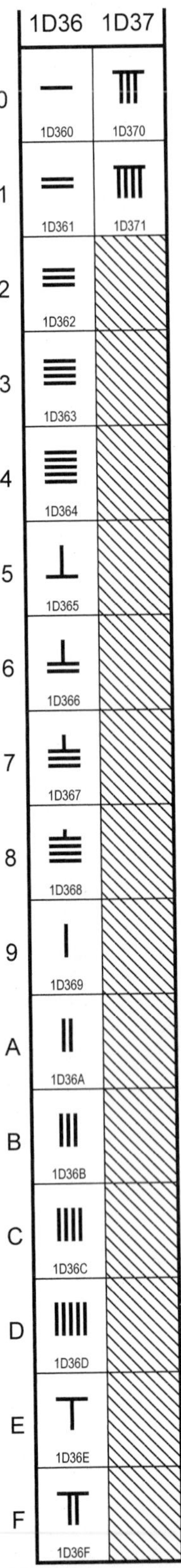

Counting rod units

1D360 𝍠 COUNTING ROD UNIT DIGIT ONE
1D361 𝍡 COUNTING ROD UNIT DIGIT TWO
1D362 𝍢 COUNTING ROD UNIT DIGIT THREE
1D363 𝍣 COUNTING ROD UNIT DIGIT FOUR
1D364 𝍤 COUNTING ROD UNIT DIGIT FIVE
1D365 𝍥 COUNTING ROD UNIT DIGIT SIX
1D366 𝍦 COUNTING ROD UNIT DIGIT SEVEN
1D367 𝍧 COUNTING ROD UNIT DIGIT EIGHT
1D368 𝍨 COUNTING ROD UNIT DIGIT NINE
1D369 𝍩 COUNTING ROD TENS DIGIT ONE
1D36A 𝍪 COUNTING ROD TENS DIGIT TWO
1D36B 𝍫 COUNTING ROD TENS DIGIT THREE
1D36C 𝍬 COUNTING ROD TENS DIGIT FOUR
1D36D 𝍭 COUNTING ROD TENS DIGIT FIVE
1D36E 𝍮 COUNTING ROD TENS DIGIT SIX
1D36F 𝍯 COUNTING ROD TENS DIGIT SEVEN
1D370 𝍰 COUNTING ROD TENS DIGIT EIGHT
1D371 𝍱 COUNTING ROD TENS DIGIT NINE

	1D40	1D41	1D42	1D43	1D44	1D45	1D46	1D47	1D48	1D49	1D4A	1D4B	1D4C	1D4D	1D4E	1D4F
0	**A** 1D400	**Q** 1D410	**g** 1D420	**w** 1D430	*M* 1D440	*c* 1D450	*s* 1D460	***I*** 1D470	***Y*** 1D480	***o*** 1D490		U 1D4B0	k 1D4C0	**A** 1D4D0	**Q** 1D4E0	**g** 1D4F0
1	**B** 1D401	**R** 1D411	**h** 1D421	**x** 1D431	*N* 1D441	*d* 1D451	*t* 1D461	***J*** 1D471	***Z*** 1D481	***p*** 1D491		V 1D4B1	l 1D4C1	**B** 1D4D1	**R** 1D4E1	**h** 1D4F1
2	**C** 1D402	**S** 1D412	**i** 1D422	**y** 1D432	*O* 1D442	*e* 1D452	*u* 1D462	***K*** 1D472	***a*** 1D482	***q*** 1D492	G 1D4A2	W 1D4B2	m 1D4C2	**C** 1D4D2	**S** 1D4E2	**i** 1D4F2
3	**D** 1D403	**T** 1D413	**j** 1D423	**z** 1D433	*P* 1D443	*f* 1D453	*v* 1D463	***L*** 1D473	***b*** 1D483	***r*** 1D493		X 1D4B3	n 1D4C3	**D** 1D4D3	**T** 1D4E3	**j** 1D4F3
4	**E** 1D404	**U** 1D414	**k** 1D424	*A* 1D434	*Q* 1D444	*g* 1D454	*w* 1D464	***M*** 1D474	***c*** 1D484	***s*** 1D494		Y 1D4B4		**E** 1D4D4	**U** 1D4E4	**k** 1D4F4
5	**F** 1D405	**V** 1D415	**l** 1D425	*B* 1D435	*R* 1D445		*x* 1D465	***N*** 1D475	***d*** 1D485	***t*** 1D495	J 1D4A5	Z 1D4B5	p 1D4C5	**F** 1D4D5	**V** 1D4E5	**l** 1D4F5
6	**G** 1D406	**W** 1D416	**m** 1D426	*C* 1D436	*S* 1D446	*i* 1D456	*y* 1D466	***O*** 1D476	***e*** 1D486	***u*** 1D496	K 1D4A6	a 1D4B6	q 1D4C6	**G** 1D4D6	**W** 1D4E6	**m** 1D4F6
7	**H** 1D407	**X** 1D417	**n** 1D427	*D* 1D437	*T* 1D447	*j* 1D457	*z* 1D467	***P*** 1D477	***f*** 1D487	***v*** 1D497		b 1D4B7	r 1D4C7	**H** 1D4D7	**X** 1D4E7	**n** 1D4F7
8	**I** 1D408	**Y** 1D418	**o** 1D428	*E* 1D438	*U* 1D448	*k* 1D458	***A*** 1D468	***Q*** 1D478	***g*** 1D488	***w*** 1D498		c 1D4B8	s 1D4C8	**I** 1D4D8	**Y** 1D4E8	**o** 1D4F8
9	**J** 1D409	**Z** 1D419	**p** 1D429	*F* 1D439	*V* 1D449	*l* 1D459	***B*** 1D469	***R*** 1D479	***h*** 1D489	***x*** 1D499	N 1D4A9	d 1D4B9	t 1D4C9	**J** 1D4D9	**Z** 1D4E9	**p** 1D4F9
A	**K** 1D40A	**a** 1D41A	**q** 1D42A	*G* 1D43A	*W* 1D44A	*m* 1D45A	***C*** 1D46A	***S*** 1D47A	***i*** 1D48A	***y*** 1D49A	O 1D4AA		u 1D4CA	**K** 1D4DA	**a** 1D4EA	**q** 1D4FA
B	**L** 1D40B	**b** 1D41B	**r** 1D42B	*H* 1D43B	*X* 1D44B	*n* 1D45B	***D*** 1D46B	***T*** 1D47B	***j*** 1D48B	***z*** 1D49B	P 1D4AB	f 1D4BB	v 1D4CB	**L** 1D4DB	**b** 1D4EB	**r** 1D4FB
C	**M** 1D40C	**c** 1D41C	**s** 1D42C	*I* 1D43C	*Y* 1D44C	*o* 1D45C	***E*** 1D46C	***U*** 1D47C	***k*** 1D48C	A 1D49C	Q 1D4AC		w 1D4CC	**M** 1D4DC	**c** 1D4EC	**s** 1D4FC
D	**N** 1D40D	**d** 1D41D	**t** 1D42D	*J* 1D43D	*Z* 1D44D	*p* 1D45D	***F*** 1D46D	***V*** 1D47D	***l*** 1D48D			h 1D4BD	x 1D4CD	**N** 1D4DD	**d** 1D4ED	**t** 1D4FD
E	**O** 1D40E	**e** 1D41E	**u** 1D42E	*K* 1D43E	*a* 1D44E	*q* 1D45E	***G*** 1D46E	***W*** 1D47E	***m*** 1D48E	C 1D49E	S 1D4AE	i 1D4BE	y 1D4CE	**O** 1D4DE	**e** 1D4EE	**u** 1D4FE
F	**P** 1D40F	**f** 1D41F	**v** 1D42F	*L* 1D43F	*b* 1D44F	*r* 1D45F	***H*** 1D46F	***X*** 1D47F	***n*** 1D48F	D 1D49F	T 1D4AF	j 1D4BF	z 1D4CF	**P** 1D4DF	**f** 1D4EF	**v** 1D4FF

	1D50	1D51	1D52	1D53	1D54	1D55	1D56	1D57	1D58	1D59	1D5A	1D5B	1D5C	1D5D	1D5E	1D5F
0	𝔀 1D500	𝔐 1D510	𝔠 1D520	𝔰 1D530	𝕀 1D540	𝕐 1D550	𝕠 1D560	𝕰 1D570	𝖀 1D580	𝖐 1D590	𝖠 1D5A0	𝖰 1D5B0	𝗀 1D5C0	𝗐 1D5D0	𝗠 1D5E0	𝗰 1D5F0
1	𝔁 1D501	𝔑 1D511	𝔡 1D521	𝔱 1D531	𝕁 1D541		𝕡 1D561	𝕱 1D571	𝖁 1D581	𝖑 1D591	𝖡 1D5A1	𝖱 1D5B1	𝗁 1D5C1	𝗑 1D5D1	𝗡 1D5E1	𝗱 1D5F1
2	𝔂 1D502	𝔒 1D512	𝔢 1D522	𝔲 1D532	𝕂 1D542	𝕒 1D552	𝕢 1D562	𝕲 1D572	𝖂 1D582	𝖒 1D592	𝖢 1D5A2	𝖲 1D5B2	𝗂 1D5C2	𝗒 1D5D2	𝗢 1D5E2	𝗲 1D5F2
3	𝔃 1D503	𝔓 1D513	𝔣 1D523	𝔳 1D533	𝕃 1D543	𝕓 1D553	𝕣 1D563	𝕳 1D573	𝖃 1D583	𝖓 1D593	𝖣 1D5A3	𝖳 1D5B3	𝗃 1D5C3	𝗓 1D5D3	𝗣 1D5E3	𝗳 1D5F3
4	𝔄 1D504	𝔔 1D514	𝔤 1D524	𝔴 1D534	𝕄 1D544	𝕔 1D554	𝕤 1D564	𝕴 1D574	𝖄 1D584	𝖔 1D594	𝖤 1D5A4	𝖴 1D5B4	𝗄 1D5C4	𝗔 1D5D4	𝗤 1D5E4	𝗴 1D5F4
5	𝔅 1D505		𝔥 1D525	𝔵 1D535		𝕕 1D555	𝕥 1D565	𝕵 1D575	𝖅 1D585	𝖕 1D595	𝖥 1D5A5	𝖵 1D5B5	𝗅 1D5C5	𝗕 1D5D5	𝗥 1D5E5	𝗵 1D5F5
6		𝔖 1D516	𝔦 1D526	𝔶 1D536	𝕆 1D546	𝕖 1D556	𝕦 1D566	𝕶 1D576	𝖆 1D586	𝖖 1D596	𝖦 1D5A6	𝖶 1D5B6	𝗆 1D5C6	𝗖 1D5D6	𝗦 1D5E6	𝗶 1D5F6
7	𝔇 1D507	𝔗 1D517	𝔧 1D527	𝔷 1D537		𝕗 1D557	𝕧 1D567	𝕷 1D577	𝖇 1D587	𝖗 1D597	𝖧 1D5A7	𝖷 1D5B7	𝗇 1D5C7	𝗗 1D5D7	𝗧 1D5E7	𝗷 1D5F7
8	𝔈 1D508	𝔘 1D518	𝔨 1D528	𝔸 1D538		𝕘 1D558	𝕨 1D568	𝕸 1D578	𝖈 1D588	𝖘 1D598	𝖨 1D5A8	𝖸 1D5B8	𝗈 1D5C8	𝗘 1D5D8	𝗨 1D5E8	𝗸 1D5F8
9	𝔉 1D509	𝔙 1D519	𝔩 1D529	𝔹 1D539		𝕙 1D559	𝕩 1D569	𝕹 1D579	𝖉 1D589	𝖙 1D599	𝖩 1D5A9	𝖹 1D5B9	𝗉 1D5C9	𝗙 1D5D9	𝗩 1D5E9	𝗹 1D5F9
A	𝔊 1D50A	𝔚 1D51A	𝔪 1D52A		𝕊 1D54A	𝕚 1D55A	𝕪 1D56A	𝕺 1D57A	𝖊 1D58A	𝖚 1D59A	𝖪 1D5AA	𝖺 1D5BA	𝗊 1D5CA	𝗚 1D5DA	𝗪 1D5EA	𝗺 1D5FA
B		𝔛 1D51B	𝔫 1D52B	𝔻 1D53B	𝕋 1D54B	𝕛 1D55B	𝕫 1D56B	𝕻 1D57B	𝖋 1D58B	𝖛 1D59B	𝖫 1D5AB	𝖻 1D5BB	𝗋 1D5CB	𝗛 1D5DB	𝗫 1D5EB	𝗻 1D5FB
C		𝔜 1D51C	𝔬 1D52C	𝔼 1D53C	𝕌 1D54C	𝕜 1D55C	𝕬 1D56C	𝕼 1D57C	𝖌 1D58C	𝖜 1D59C	𝖬 1D5AC	𝖼 1D5BC	𝗌 1D5CC	𝗜 1D5DC	𝗬 1D5EC	𝗼 1D5FC
D	𝔍 1D50D		𝔭 1D52D	𝔽 1D53D	𝕍 1D54D	𝕝 1D55D	𝕭 1D56D	𝕽 1D57D	𝖍 1D58D	𝖝 1D59D	𝖭 1D5AD	𝖽 1D5BD	𝗍 1D5CD	𝗝 1D5DD	𝗭 1D5ED	𝗽 1D5FD
E	𝔎 1D50E	𝔞 1D51E	𝔮 1D52E	𝔾 1D53E	𝕎 1D54E	𝕞 1D55E	𝕮 1D56E	𝕾 1D57E	𝖎 1D58E	𝖞 1D59E	𝖮 1D5AE	𝖾 1D5BE	𝗎 1D5CE	𝗞 1D5DE	𝗮 1D5EE	𝗾 1D5FE
F	𝔏 1D50F	𝔟 1D51F	𝔯 1D52F		𝕏 1D54F	𝕟 1D55F	𝕯 1D56F	𝕿 1D57F	𝖏 1D58F	𝖟 1D59F	𝖯 1D5AF	𝖿 1D5BF	𝗏 1D5CF	𝗟 1D5DF	𝗯 1D5EF	𝗿 1D5FF

	1D60	1D61	1D62	1D63	1D64	1D65	1D66	1D67	1D68	1D69	1D6A	1D6B	1D6C	1D6D	1D6E	1D6F
0	𝘀 1D600	𝘐 1D610	𝘠 1D620	𝘰 1D630	𝙀 1D640	𝙐 1D650	𝙠 1D660	𝙰 1D670	𝚀 1D680	𝚐 1D690	𝚠 1D6A0	𝚰 1D6B0	𝛀 1D6C0	𝛐 1D6D0	𝛠 1D6E0	𝛰 1D6F0
1	𝘁 1D601	𝘑 1D611	𝘡 1D621	𝘱 1D631	𝙁 1D641	𝙑 1D651	𝙡 1D661	𝙱 1D671	𝚁 1D681	𝚑 1D691	𝚡 1D6A1	𝚱 1D6B1	𝛁 1D6C1	𝛑 1D6D1	𝛡 1D6E1	𝛱 1D6F1
2	𝘂 1D602	𝘒 1D612	𝘢 1D622	𝘲 1D632	𝙂 1D642	𝙒 1D652	𝙢 1D662	𝙲 1D672	𝚂 1D682	𝚒 1D692	𝚢 1D6A2	𝚲 1D6B2	𝛂 1D6C2	𝛒 1D6D2	𝛢 1D6E2	𝛲 1D6F2
3	𝘃 1D603	𝘓 1D613	𝘣 1D623	𝘳 1D633	𝙃 1D643	𝙓 1D653	𝙣 1D663	𝙳 1D673	𝚃 1D683	𝚓 1D693	𝚣 1D6A3	𝚳 1D6B3	𝛃 1D6C3	𝛓 1D6D3	𝛣 1D6E3	𝛳 1D6F3
4	𝘄 1D604	𝘔 1D614	𝘤 1D624	𝘴 1D634	𝙄 1D644	𝙔 1D654	𝙤 1D664	𝙴 1D674	𝚄 1D684	𝚔 1D694	𝚤 1D6A4	𝚴 1D6B4	𝛄 1D6C4	𝛔 1D6D4	𝛤 1D6E4	𝛴 1D6F4
5	𝘅 1D605	𝘕 1D615	𝘥 1D625	𝘵 1D635	𝙅 1D645	𝙕 1D655	𝙥 1D665	𝙵 1D675	𝚅 1D685	𝚕 1D695	𝚥 1D6A5	𝚵 1D6B5	𝛅 1D6C5	𝛕 1D6D5	𝛥 1D6E5	𝛵 1D6F5
6	𝘆 1D606	𝘖 1D616	𝘦 1D626	𝘶 1D636	𝙆 1D646	𝙖 1D656	𝙦 1D666	𝙶 1D676	𝚆 1D686	𝚖 1D696		𝚶 1D6B6	𝛆 1D6C6	𝛖 1D6D6	𝛦 1D6E6	𝛶 1D6F6
7	𝘇 1D607	𝘗 1D617	𝘧 1D627	𝘷 1D637	𝙇 1D647	𝙗 1D657	𝙧 1D667	𝙷 1D677	𝚇 1D687	𝚗 1D697		𝚷 1D6B7	𝛇 1D6C7	𝛗 1D6D7	𝛧 1D6E7	𝛷 1D6F7
8	𝘈 1D608	𝘘 1D618	𝘨 1D628	𝘸 1D638	𝙈 1D648	𝙘 1D658	𝙨 1D668	𝙸 1D678	𝚈 1D688	𝚘 1D698	𝚨 1D6A8	𝚸 1D6B8	𝛈 1D6C8	𝛘 1D6D8	𝛨 1D6E8	𝛸 1D6F8
9	𝘉 1D609	𝘙 1D619	𝘩 1D629	𝘹 1D639	𝙉 1D649	𝙙 1D659	𝙩 1D669	𝙹 1D679	𝚉 1D689	𝚙 1D699	𝚩 1D6A9	𝚹 1D6B9	𝛉 1D6C9	𝛙 1D6D9	𝛩 1D6E9	𝛹 1D6F9
A	𝘊 1D60A	𝘚 1D61A	𝘪 1D62A	𝘺 1D63A	𝙊 1D64A	𝙚 1D65A	𝙪 1D66A	𝙺 1D67A	𝚊 1D68A	𝚚 1D69A	𝚪 1D6AA	𝚺 1D6BA	𝛊 1D6CA	𝛚 1D6DA	𝛪 1D6EA	𝛺 1D6FA
B	𝘋 1D60B	𝘛 1D61B	𝘫 1D62B	𝘻 1D63B	𝙋 1D64B	𝙛 1D65B	𝙫 1D66B	𝙻 1D67B	𝚋 1D68B	𝚛 1D69B	𝚫 1D6AB	𝚻 1D6BB	𝛋 1D6CB	𝛛 1D6DB	𝛫 1D6EB	𝛻 1D6FB
C	𝘌 1D60C	𝘜 1D61C	𝘬 1D62C	𝘼 1D63C	𝙌 1D64C	𝙜 1D65C	𝙬 1D66C	𝙼 1D67C	𝚌 1D68C	𝚜 1D69C	𝚬 1D6AC	𝚼 1D6BC	𝛌 1D6CC	𝛜 1D6DC	𝛬 1D6EC	𝛼 1D6FC
D	𝘍 1D60D	𝘝 1D61D	𝘭 1D62D	𝘽 1D63D	𝙍 1D64D	𝙝 1D65D	𝙭 1D66D	𝙽 1D67D	𝚍 1D68D	𝚝 1D69D	𝚭 1D6AD	𝚽 1D6BD	𝛍 1D6CD	𝛝 1D6DD	𝛭 1D6ED	𝛽 1D6FD
E	𝘎 1D60E	𝘞 1D61E	𝘮 1D62E	𝘾 1D63E	𝙎 1D64E	𝙞 1D65E	𝙮 1D66E	𝙾 1D67E	𝚎 1D68E	𝚞 1D69E	𝚮 1D6AE	𝚾 1D6BE	𝛎 1D6CE	𝛞 1D6DE	𝛮 1D6EE	𝛾 1D6FE
F	𝘏 1D60F	𝘟 1D61F	𝘯 1D62F	𝘿 1D63F	𝙏 1D64F	𝙟 1D65F	𝙯 1D66F	𝙿 1D67F	𝚏 1D68F	𝚟 1D69F	𝚯 1D6AF	𝚿 1D6BF	𝛏 1D6CF	𝛟 1D6DF	𝛯 1D6EF	𝛿 1D6FF

	1D70	1D71	1D72	1D73	1D74	1D75	1D76	1D77	1D78	1D79	1D7A	1D7B	1D7C	1D7D	1D7E	1D7F
0	ε 1D700	υ 1D710	Ε 1D720	Υ 1D730	λ 1D740	ϵ 1D750	Λ 1D760	α 1D770	ρ 1D780	Α 1D790	Ρ 1D7A0	η 1D7B0	χ 1D7C0	2 1D7D0	8 1D7E0	4 1D7F0
1	ζ 1D701	φ 1D711	Ζ 1D721	Φ 1D731	μ 1D741	ϑ 1D751	Μ 1D761	β 1D771	ς 1D781	Β 1D791	ϴ 1D7A1	θ 1D7B1	ψ 1D7C1	3 1D7D1	9 1D7E1	5 1D7F1
2	η 1D702	χ 1D712	Η 1D722	Χ 1D732	ν 1D742	ϰ 1D752	Ν 1D762	γ 1D772	σ 1D782	Γ 1D792	Σ 1D7A2	ι 1D7B2	ω 1D7C2	4 1D7D2	0 1D7E2	6 1D7F2
3	θ 1D703	ψ 1D713	Θ 1D723	Ψ 1D733	ξ 1D743	ϕ 1D753	Ξ 1D763	δ 1D773	τ 1D783	Δ 1D793	Τ 1D7A3	κ 1D7B3	∂ 1D7C3	5 1D7D3	1 1D7E3	7 1D7F3
4	ι 1D704	ω 1D714	Ι 1D724	Ω 1D734	ο 1D744	ϱ 1D754	Ο 1D764	ε 1D774	υ 1D784	Ε 1D794	Υ 1D7A4	λ 1D7B4	ϵ 1D7C4	6 1D7D4	2 1D7E4	8 1D7F4
5	κ 1D705	∂ 1D715	Κ 1D725	∇ 1D735	π 1D745	ϖ 1D755	Π 1D765	ζ 1D775	φ 1D785	Ζ 1D795	Φ 1D7A5	μ 1D7B5	ϑ 1D7C5	7 1D7D5	3 1D7E5	9 1D7F5
6	λ 1D706	ϵ 1D716	Λ 1D726	α 1D736	ρ 1D746	Α 1D756	Ρ 1D766	η 1D776	χ 1D786	Η 1D796	Χ 1D7A6	ν 1D7B6	ϰ 1D7C6	8 1D7D6	4 1D7E6	0 1D7F6
7	μ 1D707	ϑ 1D717	Μ 1D727	β 1D737	ς 1D747	Β 1D757	ϴ 1D767	θ 1D777	ψ 1D787	Θ 1D797	Ψ 1D7A7	ξ 1D7B7	ϕ 1D7C7	9 1D7D7	5 1D7E7	1 1D7F7
8	ν 1D708	ϰ 1D718	Ν 1D728	γ 1D738	σ 1D748	Γ 1D758	Σ 1D768	ι 1D778	ω 1D788	Ι 1D798	Ω 1D7A8	ο 1D7B8	ϱ 1D7C8	0 1D7D8	6 1D7E8	2 1D7F8
9	ξ 1D709	ϕ 1D719	Ξ 1D729	δ 1D739	τ 1D749	Δ 1D759	Τ 1D769	κ 1D779	∂ 1D789	Κ 1D799	∇ 1D7A9	π 1D7B9	ϖ 1D7C9	1 1D7D9	7 1D7E9	3 1D7F9
A	ο 1D70A	ϱ 1D71A	Ο 1D72A	ε 1D73A	υ 1D74A	Ε 1D75A	Υ 1D76A	λ 1D77A	ϵ 1D78A	Λ 1D79A	α 1D7AA	ρ 1D7BA	Ϝ 1D7CA	2 1D7DA	8 1D7EA	4 1D7FA
B	π 1D70B	ϖ 1D71B	Π 1D72B	ζ 1D73B	φ 1D74B	Ζ 1D75B	Φ 1D76B	μ 1D77B	ϑ 1D78B	Μ 1D79B	β 1D7AB	ς 1D7BB	ϝ 1D7CB	3 1D7DB	9 1D7EB	5 1D7FB
C	ρ 1D70C	Α 1D71C	Ρ 1D72C	η 1D73C	χ 1D74C	Η 1D75C	Χ 1D76C	ν 1D77C	ϰ 1D78C	Ν 1D79C	γ 1D7AC	σ 1D7BC		4 1D7DC	0 1D7EC	6 1D7FC
D	ς 1D70D	Β 1D71D	ϴ 1D72D	θ 1D73D	ψ 1D74D	Θ 1D75D	Ψ 1D76D	ξ 1D77D	ϕ 1D78D	Ξ 1D79D	δ 1D7AD	τ 1D7BD		5 1D7DD	1 1D7ED	7 1D7FD
E	σ 1D70E	Γ 1D71E	Σ 1D72E	ι 1D73E	ω 1D74E	Ι 1D75E	Ω 1D76E	ο 1D77E	ϱ 1D78E	Ο 1D79E	ε 1D7AE	υ 1D7BE	0 1D7CE	6 1D7DE	2 1D7EE	8 1D7FE
F	τ 1D70F	Δ 1D71F	Τ 1D72F	κ 1D73F	∂ 1D74F	Κ 1D75F	∇ 1D76F	π 1D77F	ϖ 1D78F	Π 1D79F	ζ 1D7AF	φ 1D7BF	1 1D7CF	7 1D7DF	3 1D7EF	9 1D7FF

To be used for mathematical variables where style variations are important semantically. For general text, use standard Latin and Greek letters with markup.

Bold symbols

1D400 **A** MATHEMATICAL BOLD CAPITAL A
≈ <font> 0041 A latin capital letter a

1D401 **B** MATHEMATICAL BOLD CAPITAL B
≈ <font> 0042 B latin capital letter b

1D402 **C** MATHEMATICAL BOLD CAPITAL C
≈ <font> 0043 C latin capital letter c

1D403 **D** MATHEMATICAL BOLD CAPITAL D
≈ <font> 0044 D latin capital letter d

1D404 **E** MATHEMATICAL BOLD CAPITAL E
≈ <font> 0045 E latin capital letter e

1D405 **F** MATHEMATICAL BOLD CAPITAL F
≈ <font> 0046 F latin capital letter f

1D406 **G** MATHEMATICAL BOLD CAPITAL G
≈ <font> 0047 G latin capital letter g

1D407 **H** MATHEMATICAL BOLD CAPITAL H
≈ <font> 0048 H latin capital letter h

1D408 **I** MATHEMATICAL BOLD CAPITAL I
≈ <font> 0049 I latin capital letter i

1D409 **J** MATHEMATICAL BOLD CAPITAL J
≈ <font> 004A J latin capital letter j

1D40A **K** MATHEMATICAL BOLD CAPITAL K
≈ <font> 004B K latin capital letter k

1D40B **L** MATHEMATICAL BOLD CAPITAL L
≈ <font> 004C L latin capital letter l

1D40C **M** MATHEMATICAL BOLD CAPITAL M
≈ <font> 004D M latin capital letter m

1D40D **N** MATHEMATICAL BOLD CAPITAL N
≈ <font> 004E N latin capital letter n

1D40E **O** MATHEMATICAL BOLD CAPITAL O
≈ <font> 004F O latin capital letter o

1D40F **P** MATHEMATICAL BOLD CAPITAL P
≈ <font> 0050 P latin capital letter p

1D410 **Q** MATHEMATICAL BOLD CAPITAL Q
≈ <font> 0051 Q latin capital letter q

1D411 **R** MATHEMATICAL BOLD CAPITAL R
≈ <font> 0052 R latin capital letter r

1D412 **S** MATHEMATICAL BOLD CAPITAL S
≈ <font> 0053 S latin capital letter s

1D413 **T** MATHEMATICAL BOLD CAPITAL T
≈ <font> 0054 T latin capital letter t

1D414 **U** MATHEMATICAL BOLD CAPITAL U
≈ <font> 0055 U latin capital letter u

1D415 **V** MATHEMATICAL BOLD CAPITAL V
≈ <font> 0056 V latin capital letter v

1D416 **W** MATHEMATICAL BOLD CAPITAL W
≈ <font> 0057 W latin capital letter w

1D417 **X** MATHEMATICAL BOLD CAPITAL X
≈ <font> 0058 X latin capital letter x

1D418 **Y** MATHEMATICAL BOLD CAPITAL Y
≈ <font> 0059 Y latin capital letter y

1D419 **Z** MATHEMATICAL BOLD CAPITAL Z
≈ <font> 005A Z latin capital letter z

1D41A **a** MATHEMATICAL BOLD SMALL A
≈ <font> 0061 a latin small letter a

1D41B **b** MATHEMATICAL BOLD SMALL B
≈ <font> 0062 b latin small letter b

1D41C **c** MATHEMATICAL BOLD SMALL C
≈ <font> 0063 c latin small letter c

1D41D **d** MATHEMATICAL BOLD SMALL D
≈ <font> 0064 d latin small letter d

1D41E **e** MATHEMATICAL BOLD SMALL E
≈ <font> 0065 e latin small letter e

1D41F **f** MATHEMATICAL BOLD SMALL F
≈ <font> 0066 f latin small letter f

1D420 **g** MATHEMATICAL BOLD SMALL G
≈ <font> 0067 g latin small letter g

1D421 **h** MATHEMATICAL BOLD SMALL H
≈ <font> 0068 h latin small letter h

1D422 **i** MATHEMATICAL BOLD SMALL I
≈ <font> 0069 i latin small letter i

1D423 **j** MATHEMATICAL BOLD SMALL J
≈ <font> 006A j latin small letter j

1D424 **k** MATHEMATICAL BOLD SMALL K
≈ <font> 006B k latin small letter k

1D425 **l** MATHEMATICAL BOLD SMALL L
≈ <font> 006C l latin small letter l

1D426 **m** MATHEMATICAL BOLD SMALL M
≈ <font> 006D m latin small letter m

1D427 **n** MATHEMATICAL BOLD SMALL N
≈ <font> 006E n latin small letter n

1D428 **o** MATHEMATICAL BOLD SMALL O
≈ <font> 006F o latin small letter o

1D429 **p** MATHEMATICAL BOLD SMALL P
≈ <font> 0070 p latin small letter p

1D42A **q** MATHEMATICAL BOLD SMALL Q
≈ <font> 0071 q latin small letter q

1D42B **r** MATHEMATICAL BOLD SMALL R
≈ <font> 0072 r latin small letter r

1D42C **s** MATHEMATICAL BOLD SMALL S
≈ <font> 0073 s latin small letter s

1D42D **t** MATHEMATICAL BOLD SMALL T
≈ <font> 0074 t latin small letter t

1D42E **u** MATHEMATICAL BOLD SMALL U
≈ <font> 0075 u latin small letter u

1D42F **v** MATHEMATICAL BOLD SMALL V
≈ <font> 0076 v latin small letter v

1D430 **w** MATHEMATICAL BOLD SMALL W
≈ <font> 0077 w latin small letter w

1D431 **x** MATHEMATICAL BOLD SMALL X
≈ <font> 0078 x latin small letter x

1D432 **y** MATHEMATICAL BOLD SMALL Y
≈ <font> 0079 y latin small letter y

1D433 **z** MATHEMATICAL BOLD SMALL Z
≈ <font> 007A z latin small letter z

Italic symbols

Several italic symbols have been previously coded in the Letterlike Symbols block and are retained there to ensure unambiguous representation.

1D434 *A* MATHEMATICAL ITALIC CAPITAL A
≈ <font> 0041 A latin capital letter a

1D435 *B* MATHEMATICAL ITALIC CAPITAL B
≈ <font> 0042 B latin capital letter b

1D436 *C* MATHEMATICAL ITALIC CAPITAL C
≈ <font> 0043 C latin capital letter c

1D437 *D* MATHEMATICAL ITALIC CAPITAL D
≈ <font> 0044 D latin capital letter d

1D438 *E* MATHEMATICAL ITALIC CAPITAL E
≈ <font> 0045 E latin capital letter e

1D439 *F* MATHEMATICAL ITALIC CAPITAL F
≈ <font> 0046 F latin capital letter f

1D43A *G* MATHEMATICAL ITALIC CAPITAL G
≈ <font> 0047 G latin capital letter g
1D43B *H* MATHEMATICAL ITALIC CAPITAL H
≈ <font> 0048 H latin capital letter h
1D43C *I* MATHEMATICAL ITALIC CAPITAL I
≈ <font> 0049 I latin capital letter i
1D43D *J* MATHEMATICAL ITALIC CAPITAL J
≈ <font> 004A J latin capital letter j
1D43E *K* MATHEMATICAL ITALIC CAPITAL K
≈ <font> 004B K latin capital letter k
1D43F *L* MATHEMATICAL ITALIC CAPITAL L
≈ <font> 004C L latin capital letter l
1D440 *M* MATHEMATICAL ITALIC CAPITAL M
≈ <font> 004D M latin capital letter m
1D441 *N* MATHEMATICAL ITALIC CAPITAL N
≈ <font> 004E N latin capital letter n
1D442 *O* MATHEMATICAL ITALIC CAPITAL O
≈ <font> 004F O latin capital letter o
1D443 *P* MATHEMATICAL ITALIC CAPITAL P
≈ <font> 0050 P latin capital letter p
1D444 *Q* MATHEMATICAL ITALIC CAPITAL Q
≈ <font> 0051 Q latin capital letter q
1D445 *R* MATHEMATICAL ITALIC CAPITAL R
≈ <font> 0052 R latin capital letter r
1D446 *S* MATHEMATICAL ITALIC CAPITAL S
≈ <font> 0053 S latin capital letter s
1D447 *T* MATHEMATICAL ITALIC CAPITAL T
≈ <font> 0054 T latin capital letter t
1D448 *U* MATHEMATICAL ITALIC CAPITAL U
≈ <font> 0055 U latin capital letter u
1D449 *V* MATHEMATICAL ITALIC CAPITAL V
≈ <font> 0056 V latin capital letter v
1D44A *W* MATHEMATICAL ITALIC CAPITAL W
≈ <font> 0057 W latin capital letter w
1D44B *X* MATHEMATICAL ITALIC CAPITAL X
≈ <font> 0058 X latin capital letter x
1D44C *Y* MATHEMATICAL ITALIC CAPITAL Y
≈ <font> 0059 Y latin capital letter y
1D44D *Z* MATHEMATICAL ITALIC CAPITAL Z
≈ <font> 005A Z latin capital letter z
1D44E *a* MATHEMATICAL ITALIC SMALL A
≈ <font> 0061 a latin small letter a
1D44F *b* MATHEMATICAL ITALIC SMALL B
≈ <font> 0062 b latin small letter b
1D450 *c* MATHEMATICAL ITALIC SMALL C
≈ <font> 0063 c latin small letter c
1D451 *d* MATHEMATICAL ITALIC SMALL D
≈ <font> 0064 d latin small letter d
1D452 *e* MATHEMATICAL ITALIC SMALL E
≈ <font> 0065 e latin small letter e
1D453 *f* MATHEMATICAL ITALIC SMALL F
≈ <font> 0066 f latin small letter f
1D454 *g* MATHEMATICAL ITALIC SMALL G
≈ <font> 0067 g latin small letter g
1D455 <reserved>
→ 210E *h* planck constant
1D456 *i* MATHEMATICAL ITALIC SMALL I
≈ <font> 0069 i latin small letter i
1D457 *j* MATHEMATICAL ITALIC SMALL J
≈ <font> 006A j latin small letter j
1D458 *k* MATHEMATICAL ITALIC SMALL K
≈ <font> 006B k latin small letter k
1D459 *l* MATHEMATICAL ITALIC SMALL L
≈ <font> 006C l latin small letter l
1D45A *m* MATHEMATICAL ITALIC SMALL M
≈ <font> 006D m latin small letter m
1D45B *n* MATHEMATICAL ITALIC SMALL N
≈ <font> 006E n latin small letter n
1D45C *o* MATHEMATICAL ITALIC SMALL O
≈ <font> 006F o latin small letter o
1D45D *p* MATHEMATICAL ITALIC SMALL P
≈ <font> 0070 p latin small letter p
1D45E *q* MATHEMATICAL ITALIC SMALL Q
≈ <font> 0071 q latin small letter q
1D45F *r* MATHEMATICAL ITALIC SMALL R
≈ <font> 0072 r latin small letter r
1D460 *s* MATHEMATICAL ITALIC SMALL S
≈ <font> 0073 s latin small letter s
1D461 *t* MATHEMATICAL ITALIC SMALL T
≈ <font> 0074 t latin small letter t
1D462 *u* MATHEMATICAL ITALIC SMALL U
≈ <font> 0075 u latin small letter u
1D463 *v* MATHEMATICAL ITALIC SMALL V
≈ <font> 0076 v latin small letter v
1D464 *w* MATHEMATICAL ITALIC SMALL W
≈ <font> 0077 w latin small letter w
1D465 *x* MATHEMATICAL ITALIC SMALL X
≈ <font> 0078 x latin small letter x
1D466 *y* MATHEMATICAL ITALIC SMALL Y
≈ <font> 0079 y latin small letter y
1D467 *z* MATHEMATICAL ITALIC SMALL Z
≈ <font> 007A z latin small letter z

Bold italic symbols

1D468 ***A*** MATHEMATICAL BOLD ITALIC CAPITAL A
≈ <font> 0041 A latin capital letter a
1D469 ***B*** MATHEMATICAL BOLD ITALIC CAPITAL B
≈ <font> 0042 B latin capital letter b
1D46A ***C*** MATHEMATICAL BOLD ITALIC CAPITAL C
≈ <font> 0043 C latin capital letter c
1D46B ***D*** MATHEMATICAL BOLD ITALIC CAPITAL D
≈ <font> 0044 D latin capital letter d
1D46C ***E*** MATHEMATICAL BOLD ITALIC CAPITAL E
≈ <font> 0045 E latin capital letter e
1D46D ***F*** MATHEMATICAL BOLD ITALIC CAPITAL F
≈ <font> 0046 F latin capital letter f
1D46E ***G*** MATHEMATICAL BOLD ITALIC CAPITAL G
≈ <font> 0047 G latin capital letter g
1D46F ***H*** MATHEMATICAL BOLD ITALIC CAPITAL H
≈ <font> 0048 H latin capital letter h
1D470 ***I*** MATHEMATICAL BOLD ITALIC CAPITAL I
≈ <font> 0049 I latin capital letter i
1D471 ***J*** MATHEMATICAL BOLD ITALIC CAPITAL J
≈ <font> 004A J latin capital letter j
1D472 ***K*** MATHEMATICAL BOLD ITALIC CAPITAL K
≈ <font> 004B K latin capital letter k
1D473 ***L*** MATHEMATICAL BOLD ITALIC CAPITAL L
≈ <font> 004C L latin capital letter l
1D474 ***M*** MATHEMATICAL BOLD ITALIC CAPITAL M
≈ <font> 004D M latin capital letter m
1D475 ***N*** MATHEMATICAL BOLD ITALIC CAPITAL N
≈ <font> 004E N latin capital letter n
1D476 ***O*** MATHEMATICAL BOLD ITALIC CAPITAL O
≈ <font> 004F O latin capital letter o
1D477 ***P*** MATHEMATICAL BOLD ITALIC CAPITAL P
≈ <font> 0050 P latin capital letter p

1D478 *Q* MATHEMATICAL BOLD ITALIC CAPITAL Q
≈ <font> 0051 Q latin capital letter q
1D479 *R* MATHEMATICAL BOLD ITALIC CAPITAL R
≈ <font> 0052 R latin capital letter r
1D47A *S* MATHEMATICAL BOLD ITALIC CAPITAL S
≈ <font> 0053 S latin capital letter s
1D47B *T* MATHEMATICAL BOLD ITALIC CAPITAL T
≈ <font> 0054 T latin capital letter t
1D47C *U* MATHEMATICAL BOLD ITALIC CAPITAL U
≈ <font> 0055 U latin capital letter u
1D47D *V* MATHEMATICAL BOLD ITALIC CAPITAL V
≈ <font> 0056 V latin capital letter v
1D47E *W* MATHEMATICAL BOLD ITALIC CAPITAL W
≈ <font> 0057 W latin capital letter w
1D47F *X* MATHEMATICAL BOLD ITALIC CAPITAL X
≈ <font> 0058 X latin capital letter x
1D480 *Y* MATHEMATICAL BOLD ITALIC CAPITAL Y
≈ <font> 0059 Y latin capital letter y
1D481 *Z* MATHEMATICAL BOLD ITALIC CAPITAL Z
≈ <font> 005A Z latin capital letter z
1D482 *a* MATHEMATICAL BOLD ITALIC SMALL A
≈ <font> 0061 a latin small letter a
1D483 *b* MATHEMATICAL BOLD ITALIC SMALL B
≈ <font> 0062 b latin small letter b
1D484 *c* MATHEMATICAL BOLD ITALIC SMALL C
≈ <font> 0063 c latin small letter c
1D485 *d* MATHEMATICAL BOLD ITALIC SMALL D
≈ <font> 0064 d latin small letter d
1D486 *e* MATHEMATICAL BOLD ITALIC SMALL E
≈ <font> 0065 e latin small letter e
1D487 *f* MATHEMATICAL BOLD ITALIC SMALL F
≈ <font> 0066 f latin small letter f
1D488 *g* MATHEMATICAL BOLD ITALIC SMALL G
≈ <font> 0067 g latin small letter g
1D489 *h* MATHEMATICAL BOLD ITALIC SMALL H
≈ <font> 0068 h latin small letter h
1D48A *i* MATHEMATICAL BOLD ITALIC SMALL I
≈ <font> 0069 i latin small letter i
1D48B *j* MATHEMATICAL BOLD ITALIC SMALL J
≈ <font> 006A j latin small letter j
1D48C *k* MATHEMATICAL BOLD ITALIC SMALL K
≈ <font> 006B k latin small letter k
1D48D *l* MATHEMATICAL BOLD ITALIC SMALL L
≈ <font> 006C l latin small letter l
1D48E *m* MATHEMATICAL BOLD ITALIC SMALL M
≈ <font> 006D m latin small letter m
1D48F *n* MATHEMATICAL BOLD ITALIC SMALL N
≈ <font> 006E n latin small letter n
1D490 *o* MATHEMATICAL BOLD ITALIC SMALL O
≈ <font> 006F o latin small letter o
1D491 *p* MATHEMATICAL BOLD ITALIC SMALL P
≈ <font> 0070 p latin small letter p
1D492 *q* MATHEMATICAL BOLD ITALIC SMALL Q
≈ <font> 0071 q latin small letter q
1D493 *r* MATHEMATICAL BOLD ITALIC SMALL R
≈ <font> 0072 r latin small letter r
1D494 *s* MATHEMATICAL BOLD ITALIC SMALL S
≈ <font> 0073 s latin small letter s
1D495 *t* MATHEMATICAL BOLD ITALIC SMALL T
≈ <font> 0074 t latin small letter t
1D496 *u* MATHEMATICAL BOLD ITALIC SMALL U
≈ <font> 0075 u latin small letter u
1D497 *v* MATHEMATICAL BOLD ITALIC SMALL V
≈ <font> 0076 v latin small letter v
1D498 *w* MATHEMATICAL BOLD ITALIC SMALL W
≈ <font> 0077 w latin small letter w
1D499 *x* MATHEMATICAL BOLD ITALIC SMALL X
≈ <font> 0078 x latin small letter x
1D49A *y* MATHEMATICAL BOLD ITALIC SMALL Y
≈ <font> 0079 y latin small letter y
1D49B *z* MATHEMATICAL BOLD ITALIC SMALL Z
≈ <font> 007A z latin small letter z

Script symbols

Several script symbols have been previously coded in the Letterlike Symbols block and are retained there to ensure unambiguous representation.

1D49C 𝒜 MATHEMATICAL SCRIPT CAPITAL A
≈ <font> 0041 A latin capital letter a
1D49D ▧ <reserved>
→ 212C ℬ script capital b
1D49E 𝒞 MATHEMATICAL SCRIPT CAPITAL C
≈ <font> 0043 C latin capital letter c
1D49F 𝒟 MATHEMATICAL SCRIPT CAPITAL D
≈ <font> 0044 D latin capital letter d
1D4A0 ▧ <reserved>
→ 2130 ℰ script capital e
1D4A1 ▧ <reserved>
→ 2131 ℱ script capital f
1D4A2 𝒢 MATHEMATICAL SCRIPT CAPITAL G
≈ <font> 0047 G latin capital letter g
1D4A3 ▧ <reserved>
→ 210B ℋ script capital h
1D4A4 ▧ <reserved>
→ 2110 ℐ script capital i
1D4A5 𝒥 MATHEMATICAL SCRIPT CAPITAL J
≈ <font> 004A J latin capital letter j
1D4A6 𝒦 MATHEMATICAL SCRIPT CAPITAL K
≈ <font> 004B K latin capital letter k
1D4A7 ▧ <reserved>
→ 2112 ℒ script capital l
1D4A8 ▧ <reserved>
→ 2133 ℳ script capital m
1D4A9 𝒩 MATHEMATICAL SCRIPT CAPITAL N
≈ <font> 004E N latin capital letter n
1D4AA 𝒪 MATHEMATICAL SCRIPT CAPITAL O
≈ <font> 004F O latin capital letter o
1D4AB 𝒫 MATHEMATICAL SCRIPT CAPITAL P
= power set
≈ <font> 0050 P latin capital letter p
1D4AC 𝒬 MATHEMATICAL SCRIPT CAPITAL Q
≈ <font> 0051 Q latin capital letter q
1D4AD ▧ <reserved>
→ 211B ℛ script capital r
1D4AE 𝒮 MATHEMATICAL SCRIPT CAPITAL S
≈ <font> 0053 S latin capital letter s
1D4AF 𝒯 MATHEMATICAL SCRIPT CAPITAL T
≈ <font> 0054 T latin capital letter t
1D4B0 𝒰 MATHEMATICAL SCRIPT CAPITAL U
≈ <font> 0055 U latin capital letter u
1D4B1 𝒱 MATHEMATICAL SCRIPT CAPITAL V
≈ <font> 0056 V latin capital letter v
1D4B2 𝒲 MATHEMATICAL SCRIPT CAPITAL W
≈ <font> 0057 W latin capital letter w

1D4B3 𝒳 MATHEMATICAL SCRIPT CAPITAL X
≈ <font> 0058 X latin capital letter x
1D4B4 𝒴 MATHEMATICAL SCRIPT CAPITAL Y
≈ <font> 0059 Y latin capital letter y
1D4B5 𝒵 MATHEMATICAL SCRIPT CAPITAL Z
≈ <font> 005A Z latin capital letter z
1D4B6 𝒶 MATHEMATICAL SCRIPT SMALL A
≈ <font> 0061 a latin small letter a
1D4B7 𝒷 MATHEMATICAL SCRIPT SMALL B
≈ <font> 0062 b latin small letter b
1D4B8 𝒸 MATHEMATICAL SCRIPT SMALL C
≈ <font> 0063 c latin small letter c
1D4B9 𝒹 MATHEMATICAL SCRIPT SMALL D
≈ <font> 0064 d latin small letter d
1D4BA <reserved>
→ 212F ℯ script small e
1D4BB 𝒻 MATHEMATICAL SCRIPT SMALL F
≈ <font> 0066 f latin small letter f
1D4BC <reserved>
→ 210A ℊ script small g
1D4BD 𝒽 MATHEMATICAL SCRIPT SMALL H
≈ <font> 0068 h latin small letter h
1D4BE 𝒾 MATHEMATICAL SCRIPT SMALL I
≈ <font> 0069 i latin small letter i
1D4BF 𝒿 MATHEMATICAL SCRIPT SMALL J
≈ <font> 006A j latin small letter j
1D4C0 𝓀 MATHEMATICAL SCRIPT SMALL K
≈ <font> 006B k latin small letter k
1D4C1 𝓁 MATHEMATICAL SCRIPT SMALL L
→ 2113 ℓ script small l
≈ <font> 006C l latin small letter l
1D4C2 𝓂 MATHEMATICAL SCRIPT SMALL M
≈ <font> 006D m latin small letter m
1D4C3 𝓃 MATHEMATICAL SCRIPT SMALL N
≈ <font> 006E n latin small letter n
1D4C4 <reserved>
→ 2134 ℴ script small o
1D4C5 𝓅 MATHEMATICAL SCRIPT SMALL P
≈ <font> 0070 p latin small letter p
1D4C6 𝓆 MATHEMATICAL SCRIPT SMALL Q
≈ <font> 0071 q latin small letter q
1D4C7 𝓇 MATHEMATICAL SCRIPT SMALL R
≈ <font> 0072 r latin small letter r
1D4C8 𝓈 MATHEMATICAL SCRIPT SMALL S
≈ <font> 0073 s latin small letter s
1D4C9 𝓉 MATHEMATICAL SCRIPT SMALL T
≈ <font> 0074 t latin small letter t
1D4CA 𝓊 MATHEMATICAL SCRIPT SMALL U
≈ <font> 0075 u latin small letter u
1D4CB 𝓋 MATHEMATICAL SCRIPT SMALL V
≈ <font> 0076 v latin small letter v
1D4CC 𝓌 MATHEMATICAL SCRIPT SMALL W
≈ <font> 0077 w latin small letter w
1D4CD 𝓍 MATHEMATICAL SCRIPT SMALL X
≈ <font> 0078 x latin small letter x
1D4CE 𝓎 MATHEMATICAL SCRIPT SMALL Y
≈ <font> 0079 y latin small letter y
1D4CF 𝓏 MATHEMATICAL SCRIPT SMALL Z
≈ <font> 007A z latin small letter z

Bold script symbols

1D4D0 𝓐 MATHEMATICAL BOLD SCRIPT CAPITAL A
≈ <font> 0041 A latin capital letter a
1D4D1 𝓑 MATHEMATICAL BOLD SCRIPT CAPITAL B
≈ <font> 0042 B latin capital letter b
1D4D2 𝓒 MATHEMATICAL BOLD SCRIPT CAPITAL C
≈ <font> 0043 C latin capital letter c
1D4D3 𝓓 MATHEMATICAL BOLD SCRIPT CAPITAL D
≈ <font> 0044 D latin capital letter d
1D4D4 𝓔 MATHEMATICAL BOLD SCRIPT CAPITAL E
≈ <font> 0045 E latin capital letter e
1D4D5 𝓕 MATHEMATICAL BOLD SCRIPT CAPITAL F
≈ <font> 0046 F latin capital letter f
1D4D6 𝓖 MATHEMATICAL BOLD SCRIPT CAPITAL G
≈ <font> 0047 G latin capital letter g
1D4D7 𝓗 MATHEMATICAL BOLD SCRIPT CAPITAL H
≈ <font> 0048 H latin capital letter h
1D4D8 𝓘 MATHEMATICAL BOLD SCRIPT CAPITAL I
≈ <font> 0049 I latin capital letter i
1D4D9 𝓙 MATHEMATICAL BOLD SCRIPT CAPITAL J
≈ <font> 004A J latin capital letter j
1D4DA 𝓚 MATHEMATICAL BOLD SCRIPT CAPITAL K
≈ <font> 004B K latin capital letter k
1D4DB 𝓛 MATHEMATICAL BOLD SCRIPT CAPITAL L
≈ <font> 004C L latin capital letter l
1D4DC 𝓜 MATHEMATICAL BOLD SCRIPT CAPITAL M
≈ <font> 004D M latin capital letter m
1D4DD 𝓝 MATHEMATICAL BOLD SCRIPT CAPITAL N
≈ <font> 004E N latin capital letter n
1D4DE 𝓞 MATHEMATICAL BOLD SCRIPT CAPITAL O
≈ <font> 004F O latin capital letter o
1D4DF 𝓟 MATHEMATICAL BOLD SCRIPT CAPITAL P
≈ <font> 0050 P latin capital letter p
1D4E0 𝓠 MATHEMATICAL BOLD SCRIPT CAPITAL Q
≈ <font> 0051 Q latin capital letter q
1D4E1 𝓡 MATHEMATICAL BOLD SCRIPT CAPITAL R
≈ <font> 0052 R latin capital letter r
1D4E2 𝓢 MATHEMATICAL BOLD SCRIPT CAPITAL S
≈ <font> 0053 S latin capital letter s
1D4E3 𝓣 MATHEMATICAL BOLD SCRIPT CAPITAL T
≈ <font> 0054 T latin capital letter t
1D4E4 𝓤 MATHEMATICAL BOLD SCRIPT CAPITAL U
≈ <font> 0055 U latin capital letter u
1D4E5 𝓥 MATHEMATICAL BOLD SCRIPT CAPITAL V
≈ <font> 0056 V latin capital letter v
1D4E6 𝓦 MATHEMATICAL BOLD SCRIPT CAPITAL W
≈ <font> 0057 W latin capital letter w
1D4E7 𝓧 MATHEMATICAL BOLD SCRIPT CAPITAL X
≈ <font> 0058 X latin capital letter x
1D4E8 𝓨 MATHEMATICAL BOLD SCRIPT CAPITAL Y
≈ <font> 0059 Y latin capital letter y
1D4E9 𝓩 MATHEMATICAL BOLD SCRIPT CAPITAL Z
≈ <font> 005A Z latin capital letter z
1D4EA 𝓪 MATHEMATICAL BOLD SCRIPT SMALL A
≈ <font> 0061 a latin small letter a
1D4EB 𝓫 MATHEMATICAL BOLD SCRIPT SMALL B
≈ <font> 0062 b latin small letter b
1D4EC 𝓬 MATHEMATICAL BOLD SCRIPT SMALL C
≈ <font> 0063 c latin small letter c
1D4ED 𝓭 MATHEMATICAL BOLD SCRIPT SMALL D
≈ <font> 0064 d latin small letter d
1D4EE 𝓮 MATHEMATICAL BOLD SCRIPT SMALL E
≈ <font> 0065 e latin small letter e
1D4EF 𝓯 MATHEMATICAL BOLD SCRIPT SMALL F
≈ <font> 0066 f latin small letter f

1D4F0 𝓰 MATHEMATICAL BOLD SCRIPT SMALL G
≈ <font> 0067 g latin small letter g
1D4F1 𝓱 MATHEMATICAL BOLD SCRIPT SMALL H
≈ <font> 0068 h latin small letter h
1D4F2 𝓲 MATHEMATICAL BOLD SCRIPT SMALL I
≈ <font> 0069 i latin small letter i
1D4F3 𝓳 MATHEMATICAL BOLD SCRIPT SMALL J
≈ <font> 006A j latin small letter j
1D4F4 𝓴 MATHEMATICAL BOLD SCRIPT SMALL K
≈ <font> 006B k latin small letter k
1D4F5 𝓵 MATHEMATICAL BOLD SCRIPT SMALL L
≈ <font> 006C l latin small letter l
1D4F6 𝓶 MATHEMATICAL BOLD SCRIPT SMALL M
≈ <font> 006D m latin small letter m
1D4F7 𝓷 MATHEMATICAL BOLD SCRIPT SMALL N
≈ <font> 006E n latin small letter n
1D4F8 𝓸 MATHEMATICAL BOLD SCRIPT SMALL O
≈ <font> 006F o latin small letter o
1D4F9 𝓹 MATHEMATICAL BOLD SCRIPT SMALL P
≈ <font> 0070 p latin small letter p
1D4FA 𝓺 MATHEMATICAL BOLD SCRIPT SMALL Q
≈ <font> 0071 q latin small letter q
1D4FB 𝓻 MATHEMATICAL BOLD SCRIPT SMALL R
≈ <font> 0072 r latin small letter r
1D4FC 𝓼 MATHEMATICAL BOLD SCRIPT SMALL S
≈ <font> 0073 s latin small letter s
1D4FD 𝓽 MATHEMATICAL BOLD SCRIPT SMALL T
≈ <font> 0074 t latin small letter t
1D4FE 𝓾 MATHEMATICAL BOLD SCRIPT SMALL U
≈ <font> 0075 u latin small letter u
1D4FF 𝓿 MATHEMATICAL BOLD SCRIPT SMALL V
≈ <font> 0076 v latin small letter v
1D500 𝔀 MATHEMATICAL BOLD SCRIPT SMALL W
≈ <font> 0077 w latin small letter w
1D501 𝔁 MATHEMATICAL BOLD SCRIPT SMALL X
≈ <font> 0078 x latin small letter x
1D502 𝔂 MATHEMATICAL BOLD SCRIPT SMALL Y
≈ <font> 0079 y latin small letter y
1D503 𝔃 MATHEMATICAL BOLD SCRIPT SMALL Z
≈ <font> 007A z latin small letter z

Fraktur symbols

This style is sometimes known as black-letter. Several black-letter symbols have been previously coded in the Letterlike Symbols block and are retained there to ensure unambiguous representation.

1D504 𝔄 MATHEMATICAL FRAKTUR CAPITAL A
≈ <font> 0041 A latin capital letter a
1D505 𝔅 MATHEMATICAL FRAKTUR CAPITAL B
≈ <font> 0042 B latin capital letter b
1D506 ▧ <reserved>
→ 212D ℭ black-letter capital c
1D507 𝔇 MATHEMATICAL FRAKTUR CAPITAL D
≈ <font> 0044 D latin capital letter d
1D508 𝔈 MATHEMATICAL FRAKTUR CAPITAL E
≈ <font> 0045 E latin capital letter e
1D509 𝔉 MATHEMATICAL FRAKTUR CAPITAL F
≈ <font> 0046 F latin capital letter f
1D50A 𝔊 MATHEMATICAL FRAKTUR CAPITAL G
≈ <font> 0047 G latin capital letter g
1D50B ▧ <reserved>
→ 210C ℌ black-letter capital h
1D50C ▧ <reserved>
→ 2111 ℑ black-letter capital i
1D50D 𝔍 MATHEMATICAL FRAKTUR CAPITAL J
≈ <font> 004A J latin capital letter j
1D50E 𝔎 MATHEMATICAL FRAKTUR CAPITAL K
≈ <font> 004B K latin capital letter k
1D50F 𝔏 MATHEMATICAL FRAKTUR CAPITAL L
≈ <font> 004C L latin capital letter l
1D510 𝔐 MATHEMATICAL FRAKTUR CAPITAL M
= New Testament majority text
≈ <font> 004D M latin capital letter m
1D511 𝔑 MATHEMATICAL FRAKTUR CAPITAL N
≈ <font> 004E N latin capital letter n
1D512 𝔒 MATHEMATICAL FRAKTUR CAPITAL O
≈ <font> 004F O latin capital letter o
1D513 𝔓 MATHEMATICAL FRAKTUR CAPITAL P
≈ <font> 0050 P latin capital letter p
1D514 𝔔 MATHEMATICAL FRAKTUR CAPITAL Q
≈ <font> 0051 Q latin capital letter q
1D515 ▧ <reserved>
→ 211C ℜ black-letter capital r
1D516 𝔖 MATHEMATICAL FRAKTUR CAPITAL S
= Septuagint, Greek Old Testament
≈ <font> 0053 S latin capital letter s
1D517 𝔗 MATHEMATICAL FRAKTUR CAPITAL T
≈ <font> 0054 T latin capital letter t
1D518 𝔘 MATHEMATICAL FRAKTUR CAPITAL U
≈ <font> 0055 U latin capital letter u
1D519 𝔙 MATHEMATICAL FRAKTUR CAPITAL V
≈ <font> 0056 V latin capital letter v
1D51A 𝔚 MATHEMATICAL FRAKTUR CAPITAL W
≈ <font> 0057 W latin capital letter w
1D51B 𝔛 MATHEMATICAL FRAKTUR CAPITAL X
≈ <font> 0058 X latin capital letter x
1D51C 𝔜 MATHEMATICAL FRAKTUR CAPITAL Y
≈ <font> 0059 Y latin capital letter y
1D51D ▧ <reserved>
→ 2128 ℨ black-letter capital z
1D51E 𝔞 MATHEMATICAL FRAKTUR SMALL A
≈ <font> 0061 a latin small letter a
1D51F 𝔟 MATHEMATICAL FRAKTUR SMALL B
≈ <font> 0062 b latin small letter b
1D520 𝔠 MATHEMATICAL FRAKTUR SMALL C
≈ <font> 0063 c latin small letter c
1D521 𝔡 MATHEMATICAL FRAKTUR SMALL D
≈ <font> 0064 d latin small letter d
1D522 𝔢 MATHEMATICAL FRAKTUR SMALL E
≈ <font> 0065 e latin small letter e
1D523 𝔣 MATHEMATICAL FRAKTUR SMALL F
≈ <font> 0066 f latin small letter f
1D524 𝔤 MATHEMATICAL FRAKTUR SMALL G
≈ <font> 0067 g latin small letter g
1D525 𝔥 MATHEMATICAL FRAKTUR SMALL H
≈ <font> 0068 h latin small letter h
1D526 𝔦 MATHEMATICAL FRAKTUR SMALL I
≈ <font> 0069 i latin small letter i
1D527 𝔧 MATHEMATICAL FRAKTUR SMALL J
≈ <font> 006A j latin small letter j
1D528 𝔨 MATHEMATICAL FRAKTUR SMALL K
≈ <font> 006B k latin small letter k
1D529 𝔩 MATHEMATICAL FRAKTUR SMALL L
≈ <font> 006C l latin small letter l

1D52A 𝔪 MATHEMATICAL FRAKTUR SMALL M
≈ <font> 006D m latin small letter m
1D52B 𝔫 MATHEMATICAL FRAKTUR SMALL N
≈ <font> 006E n latin small letter n
1D52C 𝔬 MATHEMATICAL FRAKTUR SMALL O
≈ <font> 006F o latin small letter o
1D52D 𝔭 MATHEMATICAL FRAKTUR SMALL P
≈ <font> 0070 p latin small letter p
1D52E 𝔮 MATHEMATICAL FRAKTUR SMALL Q
≈ <font> 0071 q latin small letter q
1D52F 𝔯 MATHEMATICAL FRAKTUR SMALL R
≈ <font> 0072 r latin small letter r
1D530 𝔰 MATHEMATICAL FRAKTUR SMALL S
≈ <font> 0073 s latin small letter s
1D531 𝔱 MATHEMATICAL FRAKTUR SMALL T
≈ <font> 0074 t latin small letter t
1D532 𝔲 MATHEMATICAL FRAKTUR SMALL U
≈ <font> 0075 u latin small letter u
1D533 𝔳 MATHEMATICAL FRAKTUR SMALL V
≈ <font> 0076 v latin small letter v
1D534 𝔴 MATHEMATICAL FRAKTUR SMALL W
≈ <font> 0077 w latin small letter w
1D535 𝔵 MATHEMATICAL FRAKTUR SMALL X
≈ <font> 0078 x latin small letter x
1D536 𝔶 MATHEMATICAL FRAKTUR SMALL Y
≈ <font> 0079 y latin small letter y
1D537 𝔷 MATHEMATICAL FRAKTUR SMALL Z
≈ <font> 007A z latin small letter z

Double-struck symbols

This style is sometimes known as open-face or blackboard-bold. Several double-struck symbols have been previously coded in the Letterlike Symbols block and are retained there to ensure unambiguous representation.

1D538 𝔸 MATHEMATICAL DOUBLE-STRUCK CAPITAL A
≈ <font> 0041 A latin capital letter a
1D539 𝔹 MATHEMATICAL DOUBLE-STRUCK CAPITAL B
≈ <font> 0042 B latin capital letter b
1D53A <reserved>
→ 2102 ℂ double-struck capital c
1D53B 𝔻 MATHEMATICAL DOUBLE-STRUCK CAPITAL D
≈ <font> 0044 D latin capital letter d
1D53C 𝔼 MATHEMATICAL DOUBLE-STRUCK CAPITAL E
≈ <font> 0045 E latin capital letter e
1D53D 𝔽 MATHEMATICAL DOUBLE-STRUCK CAPITAL F
≈ <font> 0046 F latin capital letter f
1D53E 𝔾 MATHEMATICAL DOUBLE-STRUCK CAPITAL G
≈ <font> 0047 G latin capital letter g
1D53F <reserved>
→ 210D ℍ double-struck capital h
1D540 𝕀 MATHEMATICAL DOUBLE-STRUCK CAPITAL I
≈ <font> 0049 I latin capital letter i
1D541 𝕁 MATHEMATICAL DOUBLE-STRUCK CAPITAL J
≈ <font> 004A J latin capital letter j
1D542 𝕂 MATHEMATICAL DOUBLE-STRUCK CAPITAL K
≈ <font> 004B K latin capital letter k
1D543 𝕃 MATHEMATICAL DOUBLE-STRUCK CAPITAL L
≈ <font> 004C L latin capital letter l
1D544 𝕄 MATHEMATICAL DOUBLE-STRUCK CAPITAL M
≈ <font> 004D M latin capital letter m
1D545 <reserved>
→ 2115 ℕ double-struck capital n
1D546 𝕆 MATHEMATICAL DOUBLE-STRUCK CAPITAL O
≈ <font> 004F O latin capital letter o
1D547 <reserved>
→ 2119 ℙ double-struck capital p
1D548 <reserved>
→ 211A ℚ double-struck capital q
1D549 <reserved>
→ 211D ℝ double-struck capital r
1D54A 𝕊 MATHEMATICAL DOUBLE-STRUCK CAPITAL S
≈ <font> 0053 S latin capital letter s
1D54B 𝕋 MATHEMATICAL DOUBLE-STRUCK CAPITAL T
≈ <font> 0054 T latin capital letter t
1D54C 𝕌 MATHEMATICAL DOUBLE-STRUCK CAPITAL U
≈ <font> 0055 U latin capital letter u
1D54D 𝕍 MATHEMATICAL DOUBLE-STRUCK CAPITAL V
≈ <font> 0056 V latin capital letter v
1D54E 𝕎 MATHEMATICAL DOUBLE-STRUCK CAPITAL W
≈ <font> 0057 W latin capital letter w
1D54F 𝕏 MATHEMATICAL DOUBLE-STRUCK CAPITAL X
≈ <font> 0058 X latin capital letter x
1D550 𝕐 MATHEMATICAL DOUBLE-STRUCK CAPITAL Y
≈ <font> 0059 Y latin capital letter y
1D551 <reserved>
→ 2124 ℤ double-struck capital z
1D552 𝕒 MATHEMATICAL DOUBLE-STRUCK SMALL A
≈ <font> 0061 a latin small letter a
1D553 𝕓 MATHEMATICAL DOUBLE-STRUCK SMALL B
≈ <font> 0062 b latin small letter b
1D554 𝕔 MATHEMATICAL DOUBLE-STRUCK SMALL C
≈ <font> 0063 c latin small letter c
1D555 𝕕 MATHEMATICAL DOUBLE-STRUCK SMALL D
≈ <font> 0064 d latin small letter d
1D556 𝕖 MATHEMATICAL DOUBLE-STRUCK SMALL E
≈ <font> 0065 e latin small letter e
1D557 𝕗 MATHEMATICAL DOUBLE-STRUCK SMALL F
≈ <font> 0066 f latin small letter f
1D558 𝕘 MATHEMATICAL DOUBLE-STRUCK SMALL G
≈ <font> 0067 g latin small letter g
1D559 𝕙 MATHEMATICAL DOUBLE-STRUCK SMALL H
≈ <font> 0068 h latin small letter h
1D55A 𝕚 MATHEMATICAL DOUBLE-STRUCK SMALL I
≈ <font> 0069 i latin small letter i
1D55B 𝕛 MATHEMATICAL DOUBLE-STRUCK SMALL J
≈ <font> 006A j latin small letter j
1D55C 𝕜 MATHEMATICAL DOUBLE-STRUCK SMALL K
≈ <font> 006B k latin small letter k
1D55D 𝕝 MATHEMATICAL DOUBLE-STRUCK SMALL L
≈ <font> 006C l latin small letter l
1D55E 𝕞 MATHEMATICAL DOUBLE-STRUCK SMALL M
≈ <font> 006D m latin small letter m
1D55F 𝕟 MATHEMATICAL DOUBLE-STRUCK SMALL N
≈ <font> 006E n latin small letter n
1D560 𝕠 MATHEMATICAL DOUBLE-STRUCK SMALL O
≈ <font> 006F o latin small letter o
1D561 𝕡 MATHEMATICAL DOUBLE-STRUCK SMALL P
≈ <font> 0070 p latin small letter p
1D562 𝕢 MATHEMATICAL DOUBLE-STRUCK SMALL Q
≈ <font> 0071 q latin small letter q
1D563 𝕣 MATHEMATICAL DOUBLE-STRUCK SMALL R
≈ <font> 0072 r latin small letter r
1D564 𝕤 MATHEMATICAL DOUBLE-STRUCK SMALL S
≈ <font> 0073 s latin small letter s

1D565 𝕥 MATHEMATICAL DOUBLE-STRUCK SMALL T
≈ <font> 0074 t latin small letter t

1D566 𝕦 MATHEMATICAL DOUBLE-STRUCK SMALL U
≈ <font> 0075 u latin small letter u

1D567 𝕧 MATHEMATICAL DOUBLE-STRUCK SMALL V
≈ <font> 0076 v latin small letter v

1D568 𝕨 MATHEMATICAL DOUBLE-STRUCK SMALL W
≈ <font> 0077 w latin small letter w

1D569 𝕩 MATHEMATICAL DOUBLE-STRUCK SMALL X
≈ <font> 0078 x latin small letter x

1D56A 𝕪 MATHEMATICAL DOUBLE-STRUCK SMALL Y
≈ <font> 0079 y latin small letter y

1D56B 𝕫 MATHEMATICAL DOUBLE-STRUCK SMALL Z
≈ <font> 007A z latin small letter z

Bold Fraktur symbols

1D56C 𝕬 MATHEMATICAL BOLD FRAKTUR CAPITAL A
≈ <font> 0041 A latin capital letter a

1D56D 𝕭 MATHEMATICAL BOLD FRAKTUR CAPITAL B
≈ <font> 0042 B latin capital letter b

1D56E 𝕮 MATHEMATICAL BOLD FRAKTUR CAPITAL C
≈ <font> 0043 C latin capital letter c

1D56F 𝕯 MATHEMATICAL BOLD FRAKTUR CAPITAL D
≈ <font> 0044 D latin capital letter d

1D570 𝕰 MATHEMATICAL BOLD FRAKTUR CAPITAL E
≈ <font> 0045 E latin capital letter e

1D571 𝕱 MATHEMATICAL BOLD FRAKTUR CAPITAL F
≈ <font> 0046 F latin capital letter f

1D572 𝕲 MATHEMATICAL BOLD FRAKTUR CAPITAL G
≈ <font> 0047 G latin capital letter g

1D573 𝕳 MATHEMATICAL BOLD FRAKTUR CAPITAL H
≈ <font> 0048 H latin capital letter h

1D574 𝕴 MATHEMATICAL BOLD FRAKTUR CAPITAL I
≈ <font> 0049 I latin capital letter i

1D575 𝕵 MATHEMATICAL BOLD FRAKTUR CAPITAL J
≈ <font> 004A J latin capital letter j

1D576 𝕶 MATHEMATICAL BOLD FRAKTUR CAPITAL K
≈ <font> 004B K latin capital letter k

1D577 𝕷 MATHEMATICAL BOLD FRAKTUR CAPITAL L
≈ <font> 004C L latin capital letter l

1D578 𝕸 MATHEMATICAL BOLD FRAKTUR CAPITAL M
≈ <font> 004D M latin capital letter m

1D579 𝕹 MATHEMATICAL BOLD FRAKTUR CAPITAL N
≈ <font> 004E N latin capital letter n

1D57A 𝕺 MATHEMATICAL BOLD FRAKTUR CAPITAL O
≈ <font> 004F O latin capital letter o

1D57B 𝕻 MATHEMATICAL BOLD FRAKTUR CAPITAL P
≈ <font> 0050 P latin capital letter p

1D57C 𝕼 MATHEMATICAL BOLD FRAKTUR CAPITAL Q
≈ <font> 0051 Q latin capital letter q

1D57D 𝕽 MATHEMATICAL BOLD FRAKTUR CAPITAL R
≈ <font> 0052 R latin capital letter r

1D57E 𝕾 MATHEMATICAL BOLD FRAKTUR CAPITAL S
≈ <font> 0053 S latin capital letter s

1D57F 𝕿 MATHEMATICAL BOLD FRAKTUR CAPITAL T
≈ <font> 0054 T latin capital letter t

1D580 𝖀 MATHEMATICAL BOLD FRAKTUR CAPITAL U
≈ <font> 0055 U latin capital letter u

1D581 𝖁 MATHEMATICAL BOLD FRAKTUR CAPITAL V
≈ <font> 0056 V latin capital letter v

1D582 𝖂 MATHEMATICAL BOLD FRAKTUR CAPITAL W
≈ <font> 0057 W latin capital letter w

1D583 𝖃 MATHEMATICAL BOLD FRAKTUR CAPITAL X
≈ <font> 0058 X latin capital letter x

1D584 𝖄 MATHEMATICAL BOLD FRAKTUR CAPITAL Y
≈ <font> 0059 Y latin capital letter y

1D585 𝖅 MATHEMATICAL BOLD FRAKTUR CAPITAL Z
≈ <font> 005A Z latin capital letter z

1D586 𝖆 MATHEMATICAL BOLD FRAKTUR SMALL A
≈ <font> 0061 a latin small letter a

1D587 𝖇 MATHEMATICAL BOLD FRAKTUR SMALL B
≈ <font> 0062 b latin small letter b

1D588 𝖈 MATHEMATICAL BOLD FRAKTUR SMALL C
≈ <font> 0063 c latin small letter c

1D589 𝖉 MATHEMATICAL BOLD FRAKTUR SMALL D
≈ <font> 0064 d latin small letter d

1D58A 𝖊 MATHEMATICAL BOLD FRAKTUR SMALL E
≈ <font> 0065 e latin small letter e

1D58B 𝖋 MATHEMATICAL BOLD FRAKTUR SMALL F
≈ <font> 0066 f latin small letter f

1D58C 𝖌 MATHEMATICAL BOLD FRAKTUR SMALL G
≈ <font> 0067 g latin small letter g

1D58D 𝖍 MATHEMATICAL BOLD FRAKTUR SMALL H
≈ <font> 0068 h latin small letter h

1D58E 𝖎 MATHEMATICAL BOLD FRAKTUR SMALL I
≈ <font> 0069 i latin small letter i

1D58F 𝖏 MATHEMATICAL BOLD FRAKTUR SMALL J
≈ <font> 006A j latin small letter j

1D590 𝖐 MATHEMATICAL BOLD FRAKTUR SMALL K
≈ <font> 006B k latin small letter k

1D591 𝖑 MATHEMATICAL BOLD FRAKTUR SMALL L
≈ <font> 006C l latin small letter l

1D592 𝖒 MATHEMATICAL BOLD FRAKTUR SMALL M
≈ <font> 006D m latin small letter m

1D593 𝖓 MATHEMATICAL BOLD FRAKTUR SMALL N
≈ <font> 006E n latin small letter n

1D594 𝖔 MATHEMATICAL BOLD FRAKTUR SMALL O
≈ <font> 006F o latin small letter o

1D595 𝖕 MATHEMATICAL BOLD FRAKTUR SMALL P
≈ <font> 0070 p latin small letter p

1D596 𝖖 MATHEMATICAL BOLD FRAKTUR SMALL Q
≈ <font> 0071 q latin small letter q

1D597 𝖗 MATHEMATICAL BOLD FRAKTUR SMALL R
≈ <font> 0072 r latin small letter r

1D598 𝖘 MATHEMATICAL BOLD FRAKTUR SMALL S
≈ <font> 0073 s latin small letter s

1D599 𝖙 MATHEMATICAL BOLD FRAKTUR SMALL T
≈ <font> 0074 t latin small letter t

1D59A 𝖚 MATHEMATICAL BOLD FRAKTUR SMALL U
≈ <font> 0075 u latin small letter u

1D59B 𝖛 MATHEMATICAL BOLD FRAKTUR SMALL V
≈ <font> 0076 v latin small letter v

1D59C 𝖜 MATHEMATICAL BOLD FRAKTUR SMALL W
≈ <font> 0077 w latin small letter w

1D59D 𝖝 MATHEMATICAL BOLD FRAKTUR SMALL X
≈ <font> 0078 x latin small letter x

1D59E 𝖞 MATHEMATICAL BOLD FRAKTUR SMALL Y
≈ <font> 0079 y latin small letter y

1D59F 𝖟 MATHEMATICAL BOLD FRAKTUR SMALL Z
≈ <font> 007A z latin small letter z

Sans-serif symbols

1D5A0 𝖠 MATHEMATICAL SANS-SERIF CAPITAL A
≈ <font> 0041 A latin capital letter a

1D5A1 𝖡 MATHEMATICAL SANS-SERIF CAPITAL B
≈ <font> 0042 B latin capital letter b

1D5A2 𝖢 MATHEMATICAL SANS-SERIF CAPITAL C
≈ <font> 0043 C latin capital letter c

1D5A3 D MATHEMATICAL SANS-SERIF CAPITAL D
≈ <font> 0044 D latin capital letter d

1D5A4 E MATHEMATICAL SANS-SERIF CAPITAL E
≈ <font> 0045 E latin capital letter e

1D5A5 F MATHEMATICAL SANS-SERIF CAPITAL F
≈ <font> 0046 F latin capital letter f

1D5A6 G MATHEMATICAL SANS-SERIF CAPITAL G
≈ <font> 0047 G latin capital letter g

1D5A7 H MATHEMATICAL SANS-SERIF CAPITAL H
≈ <font> 0048 H latin capital letter h

1D5A8 I MATHEMATICAL SANS-SERIF CAPITAL I
≈ <font> 0049 I latin capital letter i

1D5A9 J MATHEMATICAL SANS-SERIF CAPITAL J
≈ <font> 004A J latin capital letter j

1D5AA K MATHEMATICAL SANS-SERIF CAPITAL K
≈ <font> 004B K latin capital letter k

1D5AB L MATHEMATICAL SANS-SERIF CAPITAL L
≈ <font> 004C L latin capital letter l

1D5AC M MATHEMATICAL SANS-SERIF CAPITAL M
≈ <font> 004D M latin capital letter m

1D5AD N MATHEMATICAL SANS-SERIF CAPITAL N
≈ <font> 004E N latin capital letter n

1D5AE O MATHEMATICAL SANS-SERIF CAPITAL O
≈ <font> 004F O latin capital letter o

1D5AF P MATHEMATICAL SANS-SERIF CAPITAL P
≈ <font> 0050 P latin capital letter p

1D5B0 Q MATHEMATICAL SANS-SERIF CAPITAL Q
≈ <font> 0051 Q latin capital letter q

1D5B1 R MATHEMATICAL SANS-SERIF CAPITAL R
≈ <font> 0052 R latin capital letter r

1D5B2 S MATHEMATICAL SANS-SERIF CAPITAL S
≈ <font> 0053 S latin capital letter s

1D5B3 T MATHEMATICAL SANS-SERIF CAPITAL T
≈ <font> 0054 T latin capital letter t

1D5B4 U MATHEMATICAL SANS-SERIF CAPITAL U
≈ <font> 0055 U latin capital letter u

1D5B5 V MATHEMATICAL SANS-SERIF CAPITAL V
≈ <font> 0056 V latin capital letter v

1D5B6 W MATHEMATICAL SANS-SERIF CAPITAL W
≈ <font> 0057 W latin capital letter w

1D5B7 X MATHEMATICAL SANS-SERIF CAPITAL X
≈ <font> 0058 X latin capital letter x

1D5B8 Y MATHEMATICAL SANS-SERIF CAPITAL Y
≈ <font> 0059 Y latin capital letter y

1D5B9 Z MATHEMATICAL SANS-SERIF CAPITAL Z
≈ <font> 005A Z latin capital letter z

1D5BA a MATHEMATICAL SANS-SERIF SMALL A
≈ <font> 0061 a latin small letter a

1D5BB b MATHEMATICAL SANS-SERIF SMALL B
≈ <font> 0062 b latin small letter b

1D5BC c MATHEMATICAL SANS-SERIF SMALL C
≈ <font> 0063 c latin small letter c

1D5BD d MATHEMATICAL SANS-SERIF SMALL D
≈ <font> 0064 d latin small letter d

1D5BE e MATHEMATICAL SANS-SERIF SMALL E
≈ <font> 0065 e latin small letter e

1D5BF f MATHEMATICAL SANS-SERIF SMALL F
≈ <font> 0066 f latin small letter f

1D5C0 g MATHEMATICAL SANS-SERIF SMALL G
≈ <font> 0067 g latin small letter g

1D5C1 h MATHEMATICAL SANS-SERIF SMALL H
≈ <font> 0068 h latin small letter h

1D5C2 i MATHEMATICAL SANS-SERIF SMALL I
≈ <font> 0069 i latin small letter i

1D5C3 j MATHEMATICAL SANS-SERIF SMALL J
≈ <font> 006A j latin small letter j

1D5C4 k MATHEMATICAL SANS-SERIF SMALL K
≈ <font> 006B k latin small letter k

1D5C5 l MATHEMATICAL SANS-SERIF SMALL L
≈ <font> 006C l latin small letter l

1D5C6 m MATHEMATICAL SANS-SERIF SMALL M
≈ <font> 006D m latin small letter m

1D5C7 n MATHEMATICAL SANS-SERIF SMALL N
≈ <font> 006E n latin small letter n

1D5C8 o MATHEMATICAL SANS-SERIF SMALL O
≈ <font> 006F o latin small letter o

1D5C9 p MATHEMATICAL SANS-SERIF SMALL P
≈ <font> 0070 p latin small letter p

1D5CA q MATHEMATICAL SANS-SERIF SMALL Q
≈ <font> 0071 q latin small letter q

1D5CB r MATHEMATICAL SANS-SERIF SMALL R
≈ <font> 0072 r latin small letter r

1D5CC s MATHEMATICAL SANS-SERIF SMALL S
≈ <font> 0073 s latin small letter s

1D5CD t MATHEMATICAL SANS-SERIF SMALL T
≈ <font> 0074 t latin small letter t

1D5CE u MATHEMATICAL SANS-SERIF SMALL U
≈ <font> 0075 u latin small letter u

1D5CF v MATHEMATICAL SANS-SERIF SMALL V
≈ <font> 0076 v latin small letter v

1D5D0 w MATHEMATICAL SANS-SERIF SMALL W
≈ <font> 0077 w latin small letter w

1D5D1 x MATHEMATICAL SANS-SERIF SMALL X
≈ <font> 0078 x latin small letter x

1D5D2 y MATHEMATICAL SANS-SERIF SMALL Y
≈ <font> 0079 y latin small letter y

1D5D3 z MATHEMATICAL SANS-SERIF SMALL Z
≈ <font> 007A z latin small letter z

Sans-serif bold symbols

1D5D4 **A** MATHEMATICAL SANS-SERIF BOLD CAPITAL A
≈ <font> 0041 A latin capital letter a

1D5D5 **B** MATHEMATICAL SANS-SERIF BOLD CAPITAL B
≈ <font> 0042 B latin capital letter b

1D5D6 **C** MATHEMATICAL SANS-SERIF BOLD CAPITAL C
≈ <font> 0043 C latin capital letter c

1D5D7 **D** MATHEMATICAL SANS-SERIF BOLD CAPITAL D
≈ <font> 0044 D latin capital letter d

1D5D8 **E** MATHEMATICAL SANS-SERIF BOLD CAPITAL E
≈ <font> 0045 E latin capital letter e

1D5D9 **F** MATHEMATICAL SANS-SERIF BOLD CAPITAL F
≈ <font> 0046 F latin capital letter f

1D5DA **G** MATHEMATICAL SANS-SERIF BOLD CAPITAL G
≈ <font> 0047 G latin capital letter g

1D5DB **H** MATHEMATICAL SANS-SERIF BOLD CAPITAL H
≈ <font> 0048 H latin capital letter h

1D5DC **I** MATHEMATICAL SANS-SERIF BOLD CAPITAL I
≈ <font> 0049 I latin capital letter i

1D5DD **J** MATHEMATICAL SANS-SERIF BOLD CAPITAL J
≈ <font> 004A J latin capital letter j

1D5DE **K** MATHEMATICAL SANS-SERIF BOLD CAPITAL K
≈ <font> 004B K latin capital letter k

1D5DF **L** MATHEMATICAL SANS-SERIF BOLD CAPITAL L
≈ <font> 004C L latin capital letter l

1D5E0 **M** MATHEMATICAL SANS-SERIF BOLD CAPITAL M
≈ <font> 004D M latin capital letter m

1D5E1 **N** MATHEMATICAL SANS-SERIF BOLD CAPITAL N
≈ <font> 004E N latin capital letter n

1D5E2 **O** MATHEMATICAL SANS-SERIF BOLD CAPITAL O
≈ <font> 004F O latin capital letter o

1D5E3 **P** MATHEMATICAL SANS-SERIF BOLD CAPITAL P
≈ <font> 0050 P latin capital letter p

1D5E4 **Q** MATHEMATICAL SANS-SERIF BOLD CAPITAL Q
≈ <font> 0051 Q latin capital letter q

1D5E5 **R** MATHEMATICAL SANS-SERIF BOLD CAPITAL R
≈ <font> 0052 R latin capital letter r

1D5E6 **S** MATHEMATICAL SANS-SERIF BOLD CAPITAL S
≈ <font> 0053 S latin capital letter s

1D5E7 **T** MATHEMATICAL SANS-SERIF BOLD CAPITAL T
≈ <font> 0054 T latin capital letter t

1D5E8 **U** MATHEMATICAL SANS-SERIF BOLD CAPITAL U
≈ <font> 0055 U latin capital letter u

1D5E9 **V** MATHEMATICAL SANS-SERIF BOLD CAPITAL V
≈ <font> 0056 V latin capital letter v

1D5EA **W** MATHEMATICAL SANS-SERIF BOLD CAPITAL W
≈ <font> 0057 W latin capital letter w

1D5EB **X** MATHEMATICAL SANS-SERIF BOLD CAPITAL X
≈ <font> 0058 X latin capital letter x

1D5EC **Y** MATHEMATICAL SANS-SERIF BOLD CAPITAL Y
≈ <font> 0059 Y latin capital letter y

1D5ED **Z** MATHEMATICAL SANS-SERIF BOLD CAPITAL Z
≈ <font> 005A Z latin capital letter z

1D5EE **a** MATHEMATICAL SANS-SERIF BOLD SMALL A
≈ <font> 0061 a latin small letter a

1D5EF **b** MATHEMATICAL SANS-SERIF BOLD SMALL B
≈ <font> 0062 b latin small letter b

1D5F0 **c** MATHEMATICAL SANS-SERIF BOLD SMALL C
≈ <font> 0063 c latin small letter c

1D5F1 **d** MATHEMATICAL SANS-SERIF BOLD SMALL D
≈ <font> 0064 d latin small letter d

1D5F2 **e** MATHEMATICAL SANS-SERIF BOLD SMALL E
≈ <font> 0065 e latin small letter e

1D5F3 **f** MATHEMATICAL SANS-SERIF BOLD SMALL F
≈ <font> 0066 f latin small letter f

1D5F4 **g** MATHEMATICAL SANS-SERIF BOLD SMALL G
≈ <font> 0067 g latin small letter g

1D5F5 **h** MATHEMATICAL SANS-SERIF BOLD SMALL H
≈ <font> 0068 h latin small letter h

1D5F6 **i** MATHEMATICAL SANS-SERIF BOLD SMALL I
≈ <font> 0069 i latin small letter i

1D5F7 **j** MATHEMATICAL SANS-SERIF BOLD SMALL J
≈ <font> 006A j latin small letter j

1D5F8 **k** MATHEMATICAL SANS-SERIF BOLD SMALL K
≈ <font> 006B k latin small letter k

1D5F9 **l** MATHEMATICAL SANS-SERIF BOLD SMALL L
≈ <font> 006C l latin small letter l

1D5FA **m** MATHEMATICAL SANS-SERIF BOLD SMALL M
≈ <font> 006D m latin small letter m

1D5FB **n** MATHEMATICAL SANS-SERIF BOLD SMALL N
≈ <font> 006E n latin small letter n

1D5FC **o** MATHEMATICAL SANS-SERIF BOLD SMALL O
≈ <font> 006F o latin small letter o

1D5FD **p** MATHEMATICAL SANS-SERIF BOLD SMALL P
≈ <font> 0070 p latin small letter p

1D5FE **q** MATHEMATICAL SANS-SERIF BOLD SMALL Q
≈ <font> 0071 q latin small letter q

1D5FF **r** MATHEMATICAL SANS-SERIF BOLD SMALL R
≈ <font> 0072 r latin small letter r

1D600 **s** MATHEMATICAL SANS-SERIF BOLD SMALL S
≈ <font> 0073 s latin small letter s

1D601 **t** MATHEMATICAL SANS-SERIF BOLD SMALL T
≈ <font> 0074 t latin small letter t

1D602 **u** MATHEMATICAL SANS-SERIF BOLD SMALL U
≈ <font> 0075 u latin small letter u

1D603 **v** MATHEMATICAL SANS-SERIF BOLD SMALL V
≈ <font> 0076 v latin small letter v

1D604 **w** MATHEMATICAL SANS-SERIF BOLD SMALL W
≈ <font> 0077 w latin small letter w

1D605 **x** MATHEMATICAL SANS-SERIF BOLD SMALL X
≈ <font> 0078 x latin small letter x

1D606 **y** MATHEMATICAL SANS-SERIF BOLD SMALL Y
≈ <font> 0079 y latin small letter y

1D607 **z** MATHEMATICAL SANS-SERIF BOLD SMALL Z
≈ <font> 007A z latin small letter z

Sans-serif italic symbols

1D608 *A* MATHEMATICAL SANS-SERIF ITALIC CAPITAL A
≈ <font> 0041 A latin capital letter a

1D609 *B* MATHEMATICAL SANS-SERIF ITALIC CAPITAL B
≈ <font> 0042 B latin capital letter b

1D60A *C* MATHEMATICAL SANS-SERIF ITALIC CAPITAL C
≈ <font> 0043 C latin capital letter c

1D60B *D* MATHEMATICAL SANS-SERIF ITALIC CAPITAL D
≈ <font> 0044 D latin capital letter d

1D60C *E* MATHEMATICAL SANS-SERIF ITALIC CAPITAL E
≈ <font> 0045 E latin capital letter e

1D60D *F* MATHEMATICAL SANS-SERIF ITALIC CAPITAL F
≈ <font> 0046 F latin capital letter f

1D60E *G* MATHEMATICAL SANS-SERIF ITALIC CAPITAL G
≈ <font> 0047 G latin capital letter g

1D60F *H* MATHEMATICAL SANS-SERIF ITALIC CAPITAL H
≈ <font> 0048 H latin capital letter h

1D610 *I* MATHEMATICAL SANS-SERIF ITALIC CAPITAL I
≈ <font> 0049 I latin capital letter i

1D611 *J* MATHEMATICAL SANS-SERIF ITALIC CAPITAL J
≈ <font> 004A J latin capital letter j

1D612 *K* MATHEMATICAL SANS-SERIF ITALIC CAPITAL K
≈ <font> 004B K latin capital letter k

1D613 *L* MATHEMATICAL SANS-SERIF ITALIC CAPITAL L
≈ <font> 004C L latin capital letter l

1D614 *M* MATHEMATICAL SANS-SERIF ITALIC CAPITAL M
≈ <font> 004D M latin capital letter m

1D615 *N* MATHEMATICAL SANS-SERIF ITALIC CAPITAL N
≈ <font> 004E N latin capital letter n

1D616 *O* MATHEMATICAL SANS-SERIF ITALIC CAPITAL O
≈ <font> 004F O latin capital letter o

1D617 *P* MATHEMATICAL SANS-SERIF ITALIC CAPITAL P
≈ <font> 0050 P latin capital letter p

1D618 *Q* MATHEMATICAL SANS-SERIF ITALIC CAPITAL Q
≈ <font> 0051 Q latin capital letter q

1D619 *R* MATHEMATICAL SANS-SERIF ITALIC CAPITAL R
≈ <font> 0052 R latin capital letter r

1D61A *S* MATHEMATICAL SANS-SERIF ITALIC CAPITAL S
≈ <font> 0053 S latin capital letter s

1D61B *T* MATHEMATICAL SANS-SERIF ITALIC CAPITAL T
≈ <font> 0054 T latin capital letter t

1D61C *U* MATHEMATICAL SANS-SERIF ITALIC CAPITAL U
≈ <font> 0055 U latin capital letter u

1D61D *V* MATHEMATICAL SANS-SERIF ITALIC CAPITAL V
≈ <font> 0056 V latin capital letter v

1D61E *W* MATHEMATICAL SANS-SERIF ITALIC CAPITAL W
≈ <font> 0057 W latin capital letter w

1D61F *X* MATHEMATICAL SANS-SERIF ITALIC CAPITAL X
≈ <font> 0058 X latin capital letter x

1D620 *Y* MATHEMATICAL SANS-SERIF ITALIC CAPITAL Y
≈ <font> 0059 Y latin capital letter y

1D621 *Z* MATHEMATICAL SANS-SERIF ITALIC CAPITAL Z
≈ <font> 005A Z latin capital letter z

1D622 *a* MATHEMATICAL SANS-SERIF ITALIC SMALL A
≈ <font> 0061 a latin small letter a

1D623 *b* MATHEMATICAL SANS-SERIF ITALIC SMALL B
≈ <font> 0062 b latin small letter b

1D624 *c* MATHEMATICAL SANS-SERIF ITALIC SMALL C
≈ <font> 0063 c latin small letter c

1D625 *d* MATHEMATICAL SANS-SERIF ITALIC SMALL D
≈ <font> 0064 d latin small letter d

1D626 *e* MATHEMATICAL SANS-SERIF ITALIC SMALL E
≈ <font> 0065 e latin small letter e

1D627 *f* MATHEMATICAL SANS-SERIF ITALIC SMALL F
≈ <font> 0066 f latin small letter f

1D628 *g* MATHEMATICAL SANS-SERIF ITALIC SMALL G
≈ <font> 0067 g latin small letter g

1D629 *h* MATHEMATICAL SANS-SERIF ITALIC SMALL H
≈ <font> 0068 h latin small letter h

1D62A *i* MATHEMATICAL SANS-SERIF ITALIC SMALL I
≈ <font> 0069 i latin small letter i

1D62B *j* MATHEMATICAL SANS-SERIF ITALIC SMALL J
≈ <font> 006A j latin small letter j

1D62C *k* MATHEMATICAL SANS-SERIF ITALIC SMALL K
≈ <font> 006B k latin small letter k

1D62D *l* MATHEMATICAL SANS-SERIF ITALIC SMALL L
≈ <font> 006C l latin small letter l

1D62E *m* MATHEMATICAL SANS-SERIF ITALIC SMALL M
≈ <font> 006D m latin small letter m

1D62F *n* MATHEMATICAL SANS-SERIF ITALIC SMALL N
≈ <font> 006E n latin small letter n

1D630 *o* MATHEMATICAL SANS-SERIF ITALIC SMALL O
≈ <font> 006F o latin small letter o

1D631 *p* MATHEMATICAL SANS-SERIF ITALIC SMALL P
≈ <font> 0070 p latin small letter p

1D632 *q* MATHEMATICAL SANS-SERIF ITALIC SMALL Q
≈ <font> 0071 q latin small letter q

1D633 *r* MATHEMATICAL SANS-SERIF ITALIC SMALL R
≈ <font> 0072 r latin small letter r

1D634 *s* MATHEMATICAL SANS-SERIF ITALIC SMALL S
≈ <font> 0073 s latin small letter s

1D635 *t* MATHEMATICAL SANS-SERIF ITALIC SMALL T
≈ <font> 0074 t latin small letter t

1D636 *u* MATHEMATICAL SANS-SERIF ITALIC SMALL U
≈ <font> 0075 u latin small letter u

1D637 *v* MATHEMATICAL SANS-SERIF ITALIC SMALL V
≈ <font> 0076 v latin small letter v

1D638 *w* MATHEMATICAL SANS-SERIF ITALIC SMALL W
≈ <font> 0077 w latin small letter w

1D639 *x* MATHEMATICAL SANS-SERIF ITALIC SMALL X
≈ <font> 0078 x latin small letter x

1D63A *y* MATHEMATICAL SANS-SERIF ITALIC SMALL Y
≈ <font> 0079 y latin small letter y

1D63B *z* MATHEMATICAL SANS-SERIF ITALIC SMALL Z
≈ <font> 007A z latin small letter z

Sans-serif bold italic symbols

1D63C ***A*** MATHEMATICAL SANS-SERIF BOLD ITALIC CAPITAL A
≈ <font> 0041 A latin capital letter a

1D63D ***B*** MATHEMATICAL SANS-SERIF BOLD ITALIC CAPITAL B
≈ <font> 0042 B latin capital letter b

1D63E ***C*** MATHEMATICAL SANS-SERIF BOLD ITALIC CAPITAL C
≈ <font> 0043 C latin capital letter c

1D63F ***D*** MATHEMATICAL SANS-SERIF BOLD ITALIC CAPITAL D
≈ <font> 0044 D latin capital letter d

1D640 ***E*** MATHEMATICAL SANS-SERIF BOLD ITALIC CAPITAL E
≈ <font> 0045 E latin capital letter e

1D641 ***F*** MATHEMATICAL SANS-SERIF BOLD ITALIC CAPITAL F
≈ <font> 0046 F latin capital letter f

1D642 ***G*** MATHEMATICAL SANS-SERIF BOLD ITALIC CAPITAL G
≈ <font> 0047 G latin capital letter g

1D643 ***H*** MATHEMATICAL SANS-SERIF BOLD ITALIC CAPITAL H
≈ <font> 0048 H latin capital letter h

1D644 ***I*** MATHEMATICAL SANS-SERIF BOLD ITALIC CAPITAL I
≈ <font> 0049 I latin capital letter i

1D645 ***J*** MATHEMATICAL SANS-SERIF BOLD ITALIC CAPITAL J
≈ <font> 004A J latin capital letter j

1D646 ***K*** MATHEMATICAL SANS-SERIF BOLD ITALIC CAPITAL K
≈ <font> 004B K latin capital letter k

1D647 ***L*** MATHEMATICAL SANS-SERIF BOLD ITALIC CAPITAL L
≈ <font> 004C L latin capital letter l

1D648 ***M*** MATHEMATICAL SANS-SERIF BOLD ITALIC CAPITAL M
≈ <font> 004D M latin capital letter m

1D649 ***N*** MATHEMATICAL SANS-SERIF BOLD ITALIC CAPITAL N
≈ <font> 004E N latin capital letter n

1D64A ***O*** MATHEMATICAL SANS-SERIF BOLD ITALIC CAPITAL O
≈ <font> 004F O latin capital letter o

1D64B ***P*** MATHEMATICAL SANS-SERIF BOLD ITALIC CAPITAL P
≈ <font> 0050 P latin capital letter p

1D64C ***Q*** MATHEMATICAL SANS-SERIF BOLD ITALIC CAPITAL Q
≈ <font> 0051 Q latin capital letter q

1D64D ***R*** MATHEMATICAL SANS-SERIF BOLD ITALIC CAPITAL R
≈ <font> 0052 R latin capital letter r

1D64E ***S*** MATHEMATICAL SANS-SERIF BOLD ITALIC CAPITAL S
≈ <font> 0053 S latin capital letter s

1D64F ***T*** MATHEMATICAL SANS-SERIF BOLD ITALIC CAPITAL T
≈ <font> 0054 T latin capital letter t

1D650 ***U*** MATHEMATICAL SANS-SERIF BOLD ITALIC CAPITAL U
≈ <font> 0055 U latin capital letter u

1D651 ***V*** MATHEMATICAL SANS-SERIF BOLD ITALIC CAPITAL V
≈ <font> 0056 V latin capital letter v

1D652 ***W*** MATHEMATICAL SANS-SERIF BOLD ITALIC CAPITAL W
≈ <font> 0057 W latin capital letter w

1D653 ***X*** MATHEMATICAL SANS-SERIF BOLD ITALIC CAPITAL X
≈ <font> 0058 X latin capital letter x

1D654 ***Y*** MATHEMATICAL SANS-SERIF BOLD ITALIC CAPITAL Y
≈ <font> 0059 Y latin capital letter y

1D655 ***Z*** MATHEMATICAL SANS-SERIF BOLD ITALIC CAPITAL Z
≈ <font> 005A Z latin capital letter z

1D656 ***a*** MATHEMATICAL SANS-SERIF BOLD ITALIC SMALL A
≈ <font> 0061 a latin small letter a

1D657 ***b*** MATHEMATICAL SANS-SERIF BOLD ITALIC SMALL B
≈ <font> 0062 b latin small letter b

1D658 ***c*** MATHEMATICAL SANS-SERIF BOLD ITALIC SMALL C
≈ <font> 0063 c latin small letter c

1D659 ***d*** MATHEMATICAL SANS-SERIF BOLD ITALIC SMALL D
≈ <font> 0064 d latin small letter d

1D65A ***e*** MATHEMATICAL SANS-SERIF BOLD ITALIC SMALL E
≈ <font> 0065 e latin small letter e

1D65B ***f*** MATHEMATICAL SANS-SERIF BOLD ITALIC SMALL F
≈ <font> 0066 f latin small letter f

1D65C ***g*** MATHEMATICAL SANS-SERIF BOLD ITALIC SMALL G
≈ <font> 0067 g latin small letter g

1D65D ***h*** MATHEMATICAL SANS-SERIF BOLD ITALIC SMALL H
≈ <font> 0068 h latin small letter h

1D65E ***i*** MATHEMATICAL SANS-SERIF BOLD ITALIC SMALL I
≈ <font> 0069 i latin small letter i

1D65F ***j*** MATHEMATICAL SANS-SERIF BOLD ITALIC SMALL J
≈ <font> 006A j latin small letter j

1D660 ***k*** MATHEMATICAL SANS-SERIF BOLD ITALIC SMALL K
≈ <font> 006B k latin small letter k

1D661 ***l*** MATHEMATICAL SANS-SERIF BOLD ITALIC SMALL L
≈ <font> 006C l latin small letter l

1D662 ***m*** MATHEMATICAL SANS-SERIF BOLD ITALIC SMALL M
≈ <font> 006D m latin small letter m

1D663 ***n*** MATHEMATICAL SANS-SERIF BOLD ITALIC SMALL N
≈ <font> 006E n latin small letter n

1D664 ***o*** MATHEMATICAL SANS-SERIF BOLD ITALIC SMALL O
≈ <font> 006F o latin small letter o

1D665 ***p*** MATHEMATICAL SANS-SERIF BOLD ITALIC SMALL P
≈ <font> 0070 p latin small letter p

1D666 ***q*** MATHEMATICAL SANS-SERIF BOLD ITALIC SMALL Q
≈ <font> 0071 q latin small letter q

1D667 ***r*** MATHEMATICAL SANS-SERIF BOLD ITALIC SMALL R
≈ <font> 0072 r latin small letter r

1D668 ***s*** MATHEMATICAL SANS-SERIF BOLD ITALIC SMALL S
≈ <font> 0073 s latin small letter s

1D669 ***t*** MATHEMATICAL SANS-SERIF BOLD ITALIC SMALL T
≈ <font> 0074 t latin small letter t

1D66A ***u*** MATHEMATICAL SANS-SERIF BOLD ITALIC SMALL U
≈ <font> 0075 u latin small letter u

1D66B ***v*** MATHEMATICAL SANS-SERIF BOLD ITALIC SMALL V
≈ <font> 0076 v latin small letter v

1D66C ***w*** MATHEMATICAL SANS-SERIF BOLD ITALIC SMALL W
≈ <font> 0077 w latin small letter w

1D66D ***x*** MATHEMATICAL SANS-SERIF BOLD ITALIC SMALL X
≈ <font> 0078 x latin small letter x

1D66E ***y*** MATHEMATICAL SANS-SERIF BOLD ITALIC SMALL Y
≈ <font> 0079 y latin small letter y

1D66F ***z*** MATHEMATICAL SANS-SERIF BOLD ITALIC SMALL Z
≈ <font> 007A z latin small letter z

Monospace symbols

1D670 `A` MATHEMATICAL MONOSPACE CAPITAL A
≈ <font> 0041 A latin capital letter a

1D671 `B` MATHEMATICAL MONOSPACE CAPITAL B
≈ <font> 0042 B latin capital letter b

1D672 `C` MATHEMATICAL MONOSPACE CAPITAL C
≈ <font> 0043 C latin capital letter c

1D673 `D` MATHEMATICAL MONOSPACE CAPITAL D
≈ <font> 0044 D latin capital letter d

1D674 `E` MATHEMATICAL MONOSPACE CAPITAL E
≈ <font> 0045 E latin capital letter e

1D675 `F` MATHEMATICAL MONOSPACE CAPITAL F
≈ <font> 0046 F latin capital letter f

1D676 `G` MATHEMATICAL MONOSPACE CAPITAL G
≈ <font> 0047 G latin capital letter g

1D677 `H` MATHEMATICAL MONOSPACE CAPITAL H
≈ <font> 0048 H latin capital letter h

1D678 `I` MATHEMATICAL MONOSPACE CAPITAL I
≈ <font> 0049 I latin capital letter i

1D679 `J` MATHEMATICAL MONOSPACE CAPITAL J
≈ <font> 004A J latin capital letter j

1D67A `K` MATHEMATICAL MONOSPACE CAPITAL K
≈ <font> 004B K latin capital letter k

1D67B `L` MATHEMATICAL MONOSPACE CAPITAL L
≈ <font> 004C L latin capital letter l

1D67C `M` MATHEMATICAL MONOSPACE CAPITAL M
≈ <font> 004D M latin capital letter m

1D67D `N` MATHEMATICAL MONOSPACE CAPITAL N
≈ <font> 004E N latin capital letter n

1D67E `O` MATHEMATICAL MONOSPACE CAPITAL O
≈ <font> 004F O latin capital letter o

1D67F `P` MATHEMATICAL MONOSPACE CAPITAL P
≈ <font> 0050 P latin capital letter p

1D680 `Q` MATHEMATICAL MONOSPACE CAPITAL Q
≈ <font> 0051 Q latin capital letter q

1D681 `R` MATHEMATICAL MONOSPACE CAPITAL R
≈ <font> 0052 R latin capital letter r

1D682 `S` MATHEMATICAL MONOSPACE CAPITAL S
≈ <font> 0053 S latin capital letter s

1D683 `T` MATHEMATICAL MONOSPACE CAPITAL T
≈ <font> 0054 T latin capital letter t

1D684 `U` MATHEMATICAL MONOSPACE CAPITAL U
≈ <font> 0055 U latin capital letter u

1D685 V MATHEMATICAL MONOSPACE CAPITAL V
≈ <font> 0056 V latin capital letter v
1D686 W MATHEMATICAL MONOSPACE CAPITAL W
≈ <font> 0057 W latin capital letter w
1D687 X MATHEMATICAL MONOSPACE CAPITAL X
≈ <font> 0058 X latin capital letter x
1D688 Y MATHEMATICAL MONOSPACE CAPITAL Y
≈ <font> 0059 Y latin capital letter y
1D689 Z MATHEMATICAL MONOSPACE CAPITAL Z
≈ <font> 005A Z latin capital letter z
1D68A a MATHEMATICAL MONOSPACE SMALL A
≈ <font> 0061 a latin small letter a
1D68B b MATHEMATICAL MONOSPACE SMALL B
≈ <font> 0062 b latin small letter b
1D68C c MATHEMATICAL MONOSPACE SMALL C
≈ <font> 0063 c latin small letter c
1D68D d MATHEMATICAL MONOSPACE SMALL D
≈ <font> 0064 d latin small letter d
1D68E e MATHEMATICAL MONOSPACE SMALL E
≈ <font> 0065 e latin small letter e
1D68F f MATHEMATICAL MONOSPACE SMALL F
≈ <font> 0066 f latin small letter f
1D690 g MATHEMATICAL MONOSPACE SMALL G
≈ <font> 0067 g latin small letter g
1D691 h MATHEMATICAL MONOSPACE SMALL H
≈ <font> 0068 h latin small letter h
1D692 i MATHEMATICAL MONOSPACE SMALL I
≈ <font> 0069 i latin small letter i
1D693 j MATHEMATICAL MONOSPACE SMALL J
≈ <font> 006A j latin small letter j
1D694 k MATHEMATICAL MONOSPACE SMALL K
≈ <font> 006B k latin small letter k
1D695 l MATHEMATICAL MONOSPACE SMALL L
≈ <font> 006C l latin small letter l
1D696 m MATHEMATICAL MONOSPACE SMALL M
≈ <font> 006D m latin small letter m
1D697 n MATHEMATICAL MONOSPACE SMALL N
≈ <font> 006E n latin small letter n
1D698 o MATHEMATICAL MONOSPACE SMALL O
≈ <font> 006F o latin small letter o
1D699 p MATHEMATICAL MONOSPACE SMALL P
≈ <font> 0070 p latin small letter p
1D69A q MATHEMATICAL MONOSPACE SMALL Q
≈ <font> 0071 q latin small letter q
1D69B r MATHEMATICAL MONOSPACE SMALL R
≈ <font> 0072 r latin small letter r
1D69C s MATHEMATICAL MONOSPACE SMALL S
≈ <font> 0073 s latin small letter s
1D69D t MATHEMATICAL MONOSPACE SMALL T
≈ <font> 0074 t latin small letter t
1D69E u MATHEMATICAL MONOSPACE SMALL U
≈ <font> 0075 u latin small letter u
1D69F v MATHEMATICAL MONOSPACE SMALL V
≈ <font> 0076 v latin small letter v
1D6A0 w MATHEMATICAL MONOSPACE SMALL W
≈ <font> 0077 w latin small letter w
1D6A1 x MATHEMATICAL MONOSPACE SMALL X
≈ <font> 0078 x latin small letter x
1D6A2 y MATHEMATICAL MONOSPACE SMALL Y
≈ <font> 0079 y latin small letter y
1D6A3 z MATHEMATICAL MONOSPACE SMALL Z
≈ <font> 007A z latin small letter z

Dotless symbols

For use as independent symbols. These are not required as base characters for accents since regular i and j are soft-dotted in Unicode.

1D6A4 ı MATHEMATICAL ITALIC SMALL DOTLESS I
= \imath
→ 0131 ı latin small letter dotless i
→ 1D456 *i* mathematical italic small i
≈ <font> 0131 ı latin small letter dotless i
1D6A5 ȷ MATHEMATICAL ITALIC SMALL DOTLESS J
= \jmath
→ 0237 ȷ latin small letter dotless j
→ 1D457 *j* mathematical italic small j
≈ <font> 0237 ȷ latin small letter dotless j

Bold Greek symbols

1D6A8 **Α** MATHEMATICAL BOLD CAPITAL ALPHA
≈ <font> 0391 Α greek capital letter alpha
1D6A9 **Β** MATHEMATICAL BOLD CAPITAL BETA
≈ <font> 0392 Β greek capital letter beta
1D6AA **Γ** MATHEMATICAL BOLD CAPITAL GAMMA
≈ <font> 0393 Γ greek capital letter gamma
1D6AB **Δ** MATHEMATICAL BOLD CAPITAL DELTA
≈ <font> 0394 Δ greek capital letter delta
1D6AC **Ε** MATHEMATICAL BOLD CAPITAL EPSILON
≈ <font> 0395 Ε greek capital letter epsilon
1D6AD **Ζ** MATHEMATICAL BOLD CAPITAL ZETA
≈ <font> 0396 Ζ greek capital letter zeta
1D6AE **Η** MATHEMATICAL BOLD CAPITAL ETA
≈ <font> 0397 Η greek capital letter eta
1D6AF **Θ** MATHEMATICAL BOLD CAPITAL THETA
≈ <font> 0398 Θ greek capital letter theta
1D6B0 **Ι** MATHEMATICAL BOLD CAPITAL IOTA
≈ <font> 0399 Ι greek capital letter iota
1D6B1 **Κ** MATHEMATICAL BOLD CAPITAL KAPPA
≈ <font> 039A Κ greek capital letter kappa
1D6B2 **Λ** MATHEMATICAL BOLD CAPITAL LAMDA
≈ <font> 039B Λ greek capital letter lamda
1D6B3 **Μ** MATHEMATICAL BOLD CAPITAL MU
≈ <font> 039C Μ greek capital letter mu
1D6B4 **Ν** MATHEMATICAL BOLD CAPITAL NU
≈ <font> 039D Ν greek capital letter nu
1D6B5 **Ξ** MATHEMATICAL BOLD CAPITAL XI
≈ <font> 039E Ξ greek capital letter xi
1D6B6 **Ο** MATHEMATICAL BOLD CAPITAL OMICRON
≈ <font> 039F Ο greek capital letter omicron
1D6B7 **Π** MATHEMATICAL BOLD CAPITAL PI
≈ <font> 03A0 Π greek capital letter pi
1D6B8 **Ρ** MATHEMATICAL BOLD CAPITAL RHO
≈ <font> 03A1 Ρ greek capital letter rho
1D6B9 **ϴ** MATHEMATICAL BOLD CAPITAL THETA SYMBOL
≈ <font> 03F4 ϴ greek capital theta symbol
1D6BA **Σ** MATHEMATICAL BOLD CAPITAL SIGMA
≈ <font> 03A3 Σ greek capital letter sigma
1D6BB **Τ** MATHEMATICAL BOLD CAPITAL TAU
≈ <font> 03A4 Τ greek capital letter tau
1D6BC **Υ** MATHEMATICAL BOLD CAPITAL UPSILON
≈ <font> 03A5 Υ greek capital letter upsilon
1D6BD **Φ** MATHEMATICAL BOLD CAPITAL PHI
≈ <font> 03A6 Φ greek capital letter phi
1D6BE **Χ** MATHEMATICAL BOLD CAPITAL CHI
≈ <font> 03A7 Χ greek capital letter chi

1D6BF Ψ MATHEMATICAL BOLD CAPITAL PSI
≈ <font> 03A8 Ψ greek capital letter psi

1D6C0 Ω MATHEMATICAL BOLD CAPITAL OMEGA
≈ <font> 03A9 Ω greek capital letter omega

1D6C1 ∇ MATHEMATICAL BOLD NABLA
≈ <font> 2207 ∇ nabla

1D6C2 α MATHEMATICAL BOLD SMALL ALPHA
≈ <font> 03B1 α greek small letter alpha

1D6C3 β MATHEMATICAL BOLD SMALL BETA
≈ <font> 03B2 β greek small letter beta

1D6C4 γ MATHEMATICAL BOLD SMALL GAMMA
≈ <font> 03B3 γ greek small letter gamma

1D6C5 δ MATHEMATICAL BOLD SMALL DELTA
≈ <font> 03B4 δ greek small letter delta

1D6C6 ε MATHEMATICAL BOLD SMALL EPSILON
≈ <font> 03B5 ε greek small letter epsilon

1D6C7 ζ MATHEMATICAL BOLD SMALL ZETA
≈ <font> 03B6 ζ greek small letter zeta

1D6C8 η MATHEMATICAL BOLD SMALL ETA
≈ <font> 03B7 η greek small letter eta

1D6C9 θ MATHEMATICAL BOLD SMALL THETA
≈ <font> 03B8 θ greek small letter theta

1D6CA ι MATHEMATICAL BOLD SMALL IOTA
≈ <font> 03B9 ι greek small letter iota

1D6CB κ MATHEMATICAL BOLD SMALL KAPPA
≈ <font> 03BA κ greek small letter kappa

1D6CC λ MATHEMATICAL BOLD SMALL LAMDA
≈ <font> 03BB λ greek small letter lamda

1D6CD μ MATHEMATICAL BOLD SMALL MU
≈ <font> 03BC μ greek small letter mu

1D6CE ν MATHEMATICAL BOLD SMALL NU
≈ <font> 03BD ν greek small letter nu

1D6CF ξ MATHEMATICAL BOLD SMALL XI
≈ <font> 03BE ξ greek small letter xi

1D6D0 ο MATHEMATICAL BOLD SMALL OMICRON
≈ <font> 03BF ο greek small letter omicron

1D6D1 π MATHEMATICAL BOLD SMALL PI
≈ <font> 03C0 π greek small letter pi

1D6D2 ρ MATHEMATICAL BOLD SMALL RHO
≈ <font> 03C1 ρ greek small letter rho

1D6D3 ς MATHEMATICAL BOLD SMALL FINAL SIGMA
≈ <font> 03C2 ς greek small letter final sigma

1D6D4 σ MATHEMATICAL BOLD SMALL SIGMA
≈ <font> 03C3 σ greek small letter sigma

1D6D5 τ MATHEMATICAL BOLD SMALL TAU
≈ <font> 03C4 τ greek small letter tau

1D6D6 υ MATHEMATICAL BOLD SMALL UPSILON
≈ <font> 03C5 υ greek small letter upsilon

1D6D7 φ MATHEMATICAL BOLD SMALL PHI
≈ <font> 03C6 φ greek small letter phi

1D6D8 χ MATHEMATICAL BOLD SMALL CHI
≈ <font> 03C7 χ greek small letter chi

1D6D9 ψ MATHEMATICAL BOLD SMALL PSI
≈ <font> 03C8 ψ greek small letter psi

1D6DA ω MATHEMATICAL BOLD SMALL OMEGA
≈ <font> 03C9 ω greek small letter omega

Additional bold Greek symbols

1D6DB ∂ MATHEMATICAL BOLD PARTIAL DIFFERENTIAL
≈ <font> 2202 ∂ partial differential

1D6DC ϵ MATHEMATICAL BOLD EPSILON SYMBOL
≈ <font> 03F5 ϵ greek lunate epsilon symbol

1D6DD ϑ MATHEMATICAL BOLD THETA SYMBOL
≈ <font> 03D1 ϑ greek theta symbol

1D6DE ϰ MATHEMATICAL BOLD KAPPA SYMBOL
≈ <font> 03F0 ϰ greek kappa symbol

1D6DF ϕ MATHEMATICAL BOLD PHI SYMBOL
≈ <font> 03D5 ϕ greek phi symbol

1D6E0 ϱ MATHEMATICAL BOLD RHO SYMBOL
≈ <font> 03F1 ϱ greek rho symbol

1D6E1 ϖ MATHEMATICAL BOLD PI SYMBOL
≈ <font> 03D6 ϖ greek pi symbol

Italic Greek symbols

1D6E2 Α MATHEMATICAL ITALIC CAPITAL ALPHA
≈ <font> 0391 Α greek capital letter alpha

1D6E3 Β MATHEMATICAL ITALIC CAPITAL BETA
≈ <font> 0392 Β greek capital letter beta

1D6E4 Γ MATHEMATICAL ITALIC CAPITAL GAMMA
≈ <font> 0393 Γ greek capital letter gamma

1D6E5 Δ MATHEMATICAL ITALIC CAPITAL DELTA
≈ <font> 0394 Δ greek capital letter delta

1D6E6 Ε MATHEMATICAL ITALIC CAPITAL EPSILON
≈ <font> 0395 Ε greek capital letter epsilon

1D6E7 Ζ MATHEMATICAL ITALIC CAPITAL ZETA
≈ <font> 0396 Ζ greek capital letter zeta

1D6E8 Η MATHEMATICAL ITALIC CAPITAL ETA
≈ <font> 0397 Η greek capital letter eta

1D6E9 Θ MATHEMATICAL ITALIC CAPITAL THETA
≈ <font> 0398 Θ greek capital letter theta

1D6EA Ι MATHEMATICAL ITALIC CAPITAL IOTA
≈ <font> 0399 Ι greek capital letter iota

1D6EB Κ MATHEMATICAL ITALIC CAPITAL KAPPA
≈ <font> 039A Κ greek capital letter kappa

1D6EC Λ MATHEMATICAL ITALIC CAPITAL LAMDA
≈ <font> 039B Λ greek capital letter lamda

1D6ED Μ MATHEMATICAL ITALIC CAPITAL MU
≈ <font> 039C Μ greek capital letter mu

1D6EE Ν MATHEMATICAL ITALIC CAPITAL NU
≈ <font> 039D Ν greek capital letter nu

1D6EF Ξ MATHEMATICAL ITALIC CAPITAL XI
≈ <font> 039E Ξ greek capital letter xi

1D6F0 Ο MATHEMATICAL ITALIC CAPITAL OMICRON
≈ <font> 039F Ο greek capital letter omicron

1D6F1 Π MATHEMATICAL ITALIC CAPITAL PI
≈ <font> 03A0 Π greek capital letter pi

1D6F2 Ρ MATHEMATICAL ITALIC CAPITAL RHO
≈ <font> 03A1 Ρ greek capital letter rho

1D6F3 ϴ MATHEMATICAL ITALIC CAPITAL THETA SYMBOL
≈ <font> 03F4 ϴ greek capital theta symbol

1D6F4 Σ MATHEMATICAL ITALIC CAPITAL SIGMA
≈ <font> 03A3 Σ greek capital letter sigma

1D6F5 Τ MATHEMATICAL ITALIC CAPITAL TAU
≈ <font> 03A4 Τ greek capital letter tau

1D6F6 Υ MATHEMATICAL ITALIC CAPITAL UPSILON
≈ <font> 03A5 Υ greek capital letter upsilon

1D6F7 Φ MATHEMATICAL ITALIC CAPITAL PHI
≈ <font> 03A6 Φ greek capital letter phi

1D6F8 Χ MATHEMATICAL ITALIC CAPITAL CHI
≈ <font> 03A7 Χ greek capital letter chi

1D6F9 Ψ MATHEMATICAL ITALIC CAPITAL PSI
≈ <font> 03A8 Ψ greek capital letter psi

1D6FA Ω MATHEMATICAL ITALIC CAPITAL OMEGA
≈ <font> 03A9 Ω greek capital letter omega

1D6FB 𝛻 MATHEMATICAL ITALIC NABLA
≈ <font> 2207 ∇ nabla

1D6FC 𝛼 MATHEMATICAL ITALIC SMALL ALPHA
≈ <font> 03B1 α greek small letter alpha

1D6FD 𝛽 MATHEMATICAL ITALIC SMALL BETA
≈ <font> 03B2 β greek small letter beta

1D6FE 𝛾 MATHEMATICAL ITALIC SMALL GAMMA
≈ <font> 03B3 γ greek small letter gamma

1D6FF 𝛿 MATHEMATICAL ITALIC SMALL DELTA
≈ <font> 03B4 δ greek small letter delta

1D700 𝜀 MATHEMATICAL ITALIC SMALL EPSILON
≈ <font> 03B5 ε greek small letter epsilon

1D701 𝜁 MATHEMATICAL ITALIC SMALL ZETA
≈ <font> 03B6 ζ greek small letter zeta

1D702 𝜂 MATHEMATICAL ITALIC SMALL ETA
≈ <font> 03B7 η greek small letter eta

1D703 𝜃 MATHEMATICAL ITALIC SMALL THETA
≈ <font> 03B8 θ greek small letter theta

1D704 𝜄 MATHEMATICAL ITALIC SMALL IOTA
≈ <font> 03B9 ι greek small letter iota

1D705 𝜅 MATHEMATICAL ITALIC SMALL KAPPA
≈ <font> 03BA κ greek small letter kappa

1D706 𝜆 MATHEMATICAL ITALIC SMALL LAMDA
≈ <font> 03BB λ greek small letter lamda

1D707 𝜇 MATHEMATICAL ITALIC SMALL MU
≈ <font> 03BC μ greek small letter mu

1D708 𝜈 MATHEMATICAL ITALIC SMALL NU
≈ <font> 03BD ν greek small letter nu

1D709 𝜉 MATHEMATICAL ITALIC SMALL XI
≈ <font> 03BE ξ greek small letter xi

1D70A 𝜊 MATHEMATICAL ITALIC SMALL OMICRON
≈ <font> 03BF ο greek small letter omicron

1D70B 𝜋 MATHEMATICAL ITALIC SMALL PI
≈ <font> 03C0 π greek small letter pi

1D70C 𝜌 MATHEMATICAL ITALIC SMALL RHO
≈ <font> 03C1 ρ greek small letter rho

1D70D 𝜍 MATHEMATICAL ITALIC SMALL FINAL SIGMA
≈ <font> 03C2 ς greek small letter final sigma

1D70E 𝜎 MATHEMATICAL ITALIC SMALL SIGMA
≈ <font> 03C3 σ greek small letter sigma

1D70F 𝜏 MATHEMATICAL ITALIC SMALL TAU
≈ <font> 03C4 τ greek small letter tau

1D710 𝜐 MATHEMATICAL ITALIC SMALL UPSILON
≈ <font> 03C5 υ greek small letter upsilon

1D711 𝜑 MATHEMATICAL ITALIC SMALL PHI
≈ <font> 03C6 φ greek small letter phi

1D712 𝜒 MATHEMATICAL ITALIC SMALL CHI
≈ <font> 03C7 χ greek small letter chi

1D713 𝜓 MATHEMATICAL ITALIC SMALL PSI
≈ <font> 03C8 ψ greek small letter psi

1D714 𝜔 MATHEMATICAL ITALIC SMALL OMEGA
≈ <font> 03C9 ω greek small letter omega

Additional italic Greek symbols

1D715 𝜕 MATHEMATICAL ITALIC PARTIAL DIFFERENTIAL
≈ <font> 2202 ∂ partial differential

1D716 𝜖 MATHEMATICAL ITALIC EPSILON SYMBOL
≈ <font> 03F5 ϵ greek lunate epsilon symbol

1D717 𝜗 MATHEMATICAL ITALIC THETA SYMBOL
≈ <font> 03D1 ϑ greek theta symbol

1D718 𝜘 MATHEMATICAL ITALIC KAPPA SYMBOL
≈ <font> 03F0 ϰ greek kappa symbol

1D719 𝜙 MATHEMATICAL ITALIC PHI SYMBOL
≈ <font> 03D5 ϕ greek phi symbol

1D71A 𝜚 MATHEMATICAL ITALIC RHO SYMBOL
≈ <font> 03F1 ϱ greek rho symbol

1D71B 𝜛 MATHEMATICAL ITALIC PI SYMBOL
≈ <font> 03D6 ϖ greek pi symbol

Bold italic Greek symbols

1D71C 𝜜 MATHEMATICAL BOLD ITALIC CAPITAL ALPHA
≈ <font> 0391 Α greek capital letter alpha

1D71D 𝜝 MATHEMATICAL BOLD ITALIC CAPITAL BETA
≈ <font> 0392 Β greek capital letter beta

1D71E 𝜞 MATHEMATICAL BOLD ITALIC CAPITAL GAMMA
≈ <font> 0393 Γ greek capital letter gamma

1D71F 𝜟 MATHEMATICAL BOLD ITALIC CAPITAL DELTA
≈ <font> 0394 Δ greek capital letter delta

1D720 𝜠 MATHEMATICAL BOLD ITALIC CAPITAL EPSILON
≈ <font> 0395 Ε greek capital letter epsilon

1D721 𝜡 MATHEMATICAL BOLD ITALIC CAPITAL ZETA
≈ <font> 0396 Ζ greek capital letter zeta

1D722 𝜢 MATHEMATICAL BOLD ITALIC CAPITAL ETA
≈ <font> 0397 Η greek capital letter eta

1D723 𝜣 MATHEMATICAL BOLD ITALIC CAPITAL THETA
≈ <font> 0398 Θ greek capital letter theta

1D724 𝜤 MATHEMATICAL BOLD ITALIC CAPITAL IOTA
≈ <font> 0399 Ι greek capital letter iota

1D725 𝜥 MATHEMATICAL BOLD ITALIC CAPITAL KAPPA
≈ <font> 039A Κ greek capital letter kappa

1D726 𝜦 MATHEMATICAL BOLD ITALIC CAPITAL LAMDA
≈ <font> 039B Λ greek capital letter lamda

1D727 𝜧 MATHEMATICAL BOLD ITALIC CAPITAL MU
≈ <font> 039C Μ greek capital letter mu

1D728 𝜨 MATHEMATICAL BOLD ITALIC CAPITAL NU
≈ <font> 039D Ν greek capital letter nu

1D729 𝜩 MATHEMATICAL BOLD ITALIC CAPITAL XI
≈ <font> 039E Ξ greek capital letter xi

1D72A 𝜪 MATHEMATICAL BOLD ITALIC CAPITAL OMICRON
≈ <font> 039F Ο greek capital letter omicron

1D72B 𝜫 MATHEMATICAL BOLD ITALIC CAPITAL PI
≈ <font> 03A0 Π greek capital letter pi

1D72C 𝜬 MATHEMATICAL BOLD ITALIC CAPITAL RHO
≈ <font> 03A1 Ρ greek capital letter rho

1D72D 𝜭 MATHEMATICAL BOLD ITALIC CAPITAL THETA SYMBOL
≈ <font> 03F4 ϴ greek capital theta symbol

1D72E 𝜮 MATHEMATICAL BOLD ITALIC CAPITAL SIGMA
≈ <font> 03A3 Σ greek capital letter sigma

1D72F 𝜯 MATHEMATICAL BOLD ITALIC CAPITAL TAU
≈ <font> 03A4 Τ greek capital letter tau

1D730 𝜰 MATHEMATICAL BOLD ITALIC CAPITAL UPSILON
≈ <font> 03A5 Υ greek capital letter upsilon

1D731 𝜱 MATHEMATICAL BOLD ITALIC CAPITAL PHI
≈ <font> 03A6 Φ greek capital letter phi

1D732 𝜲 MATHEMATICAL BOLD ITALIC CAPITAL CHI
≈ <font> 03A7 Χ greek capital letter chi

1D733 𝜳 MATHEMATICAL BOLD ITALIC CAPITAL PSI
≈ <font> 03A8 Ψ greek capital letter psi

1D734 𝜴 MATHEMATICAL BOLD ITALIC CAPITAL OMEGA
≈ <font> 03A9 Ω greek capital letter omega

1D735 𝜵 MATHEMATICAL BOLD ITALIC NABLA
≈ <font> 2207 ∇ nabla
1D736 𝜶 MATHEMATICAL BOLD ITALIC SMALL ALPHA
≈ <font> 03B1 α greek small letter alpha
1D737 𝜷 MATHEMATICAL BOLD ITALIC SMALL BETA
≈ <font> 03B2 β greek small letter beta
1D738 𝜸 MATHEMATICAL BOLD ITALIC SMALL GAMMA
≈ <font> 03B3 γ greek small letter gamma
1D739 𝜹 MATHEMATICAL BOLD ITALIC SMALL DELTA
≈ <font> 03B4 δ greek small letter delta
1D73A 𝜺 MATHEMATICAL BOLD ITALIC SMALL EPSILON
≈ <font> 03B5 ε greek small letter epsilon
1D73B 𝜻 MATHEMATICAL BOLD ITALIC SMALL ZETA
≈ <font> 03B6 ζ greek small letter zeta
1D73C 𝜼 MATHEMATICAL BOLD ITALIC SMALL ETA
≈ <font> 03B7 η greek small letter eta
1D73D 𝜽 MATHEMATICAL BOLD ITALIC SMALL THETA
≈ <font> 03B8 θ greek small letter theta
1D73E 𝜾 MATHEMATICAL BOLD ITALIC SMALL IOTA
≈ <font> 03B9 ι greek small letter iota
1D73F 𝜿 MATHEMATICAL BOLD ITALIC SMALL KAPPA
≈ <font> 03BA κ greek small letter kappa
1D740 𝝀 MATHEMATICAL BOLD ITALIC SMALL LAMDA
≈ <font> 03BB λ greek small letter lamda
1D741 𝝁 MATHEMATICAL BOLD ITALIC SMALL MU
≈ <font> 03BC μ greek small letter mu
1D742 𝝂 MATHEMATICAL BOLD ITALIC SMALL NU
≈ <font> 03BD ν greek small letter nu
1D743 𝝃 MATHEMATICAL BOLD ITALIC SMALL XI
≈ <font> 03BE ξ greek small letter xi
1D744 𝝄 MATHEMATICAL BOLD ITALIC SMALL OMICRON
≈ <font> 03BF ο greek small letter omicron
1D745 𝝅 MATHEMATICAL BOLD ITALIC SMALL PI
≈ <font> 03C0 π greek small letter pi
1D746 𝝆 MATHEMATICAL BOLD ITALIC SMALL RHO
≈ <font> 03C1 ρ greek small letter rho
1D747 𝝇 MATHEMATICAL BOLD ITALIC SMALL FINAL SIGMA
≈ <font> 03C2 ς greek small letter final sigma
1D748 𝝈 MATHEMATICAL BOLD ITALIC SMALL SIGMA
≈ <font> 03C3 σ greek small letter sigma
1D749 𝝉 MATHEMATICAL BOLD ITALIC SMALL TAU
≈ <font> 03C4 τ greek small letter tau
1D74A 𝝊 MATHEMATICAL BOLD ITALIC SMALL UPSILON
≈ <font> 03C5 υ greek small letter upsilon
1D74B 𝝋 MATHEMATICAL BOLD ITALIC SMALL PHI
≈ <font> 03C6 φ greek small letter phi
1D74C 𝝌 MATHEMATICAL BOLD ITALIC SMALL CHI
≈ <font> 03C7 χ greek small letter chi
1D74D 𝝍 MATHEMATICAL BOLD ITALIC SMALL PSI
≈ <font> 03C8 ψ greek small letter psi
1D74E 𝝎 MATHEMATICAL BOLD ITALIC SMALL OMEGA
≈ <font> 03C9 ω greek small letter omega

Additional bold italic Greek symbols

1D74F 𝝏 MATHEMATICAL BOLD ITALIC PARTIAL DIFFERENTIAL
≈ <font> 2202 ∂ partial differential
1D750 𝝐 MATHEMATICAL BOLD ITALIC EPSILON SYMBOL
≈ <font> 03F5 ϵ greek lunate epsilon symbol
1D751 𝝑 MATHEMATICAL BOLD ITALIC THETA SYMBOL
≈ <font> 03D1 ϑ greek theta symbol
1D752 𝝒 MATHEMATICAL BOLD ITALIC KAPPA SYMBOL
≈ <font> 03F0 ϰ greek kappa symbol
1D753 𝝓 MATHEMATICAL BOLD ITALIC PHI SYMBOL
≈ <font> 03D5 ϕ greek phi symbol
1D754 𝝔 MATHEMATICAL BOLD ITALIC RHO SYMBOL
≈ <font> 03F1 ϱ greek rho symbol
1D755 𝝕 MATHEMATICAL BOLD ITALIC PI SYMBOL
≈ <font> 03D6 ϖ greek pi symbol

Sans-serif bold Greek symbols

1D756 𝝖 MATHEMATICAL SANS-SERIF BOLD CAPITAL ALPHA
≈ <font> 0391 Α greek capital letter alpha
1D757 𝝗 MATHEMATICAL SANS-SERIF BOLD CAPITAL BETA
≈ <font> 0392 Β greek capital letter beta
1D758 𝝘 MATHEMATICAL SANS-SERIF BOLD CAPITAL GAMMA
≈ <font> 0393 Γ greek capital letter gamma
1D759 𝝙 MATHEMATICAL SANS-SERIF BOLD CAPITAL DELTA
≈ <font> 0394 Δ greek capital letter delta
1D75A 𝝚 MATHEMATICAL SANS-SERIF BOLD CAPITAL EPSILON
≈ <font> 0395 Ε greek capital letter epsilon
1D75B 𝝛 MATHEMATICAL SANS-SERIF BOLD CAPITAL ZETA
≈ <font> 0396 Ζ greek capital letter zeta
1D75C 𝝜 MATHEMATICAL SANS-SERIF BOLD CAPITAL ETA
≈ <font> 0397 Η greek capital letter eta
1D75D 𝝝 MATHEMATICAL SANS-SERIF BOLD CAPITAL THETA
≈ <font> 0398 Θ greek capital letter theta
1D75E 𝝞 MATHEMATICAL SANS-SERIF BOLD CAPITAL IOTA
≈ <font> 0399 Ι greek capital letter iota
1D75F 𝝟 MATHEMATICAL SANS-SERIF BOLD CAPITAL KAPPA
≈ <font> 039A Κ greek capital letter kappa
1D760 𝝠 MATHEMATICAL SANS-SERIF BOLD CAPITAL LAMDA
≈ <font> 039B Λ greek capital letter lamda
1D761 𝝡 MATHEMATICAL SANS-SERIF BOLD CAPITAL MU
≈ <font> 039C Μ greek capital letter mu
1D762 𝝢 MATHEMATICAL SANS-SERIF BOLD CAPITAL NU
≈ <font> 039D Ν greek capital letter nu
1D763 𝝣 MATHEMATICAL SANS-SERIF BOLD CAPITAL XI
≈ <font> 039E Ξ greek capital letter xi
1D764 𝝤 MATHEMATICAL SANS-SERIF BOLD CAPITAL OMICRON
≈ <font> 039F Ο greek capital letter omicron
1D765 𝝥 MATHEMATICAL SANS-SERIF BOLD CAPITAL PI
≈ <font> 03A0 Π greek capital letter pi
1D766 𝝦 MATHEMATICAL SANS-SERIF BOLD CAPITAL RHO
≈ <font> 03A1 Ρ greek capital letter rho
1D767 𝝧 MATHEMATICAL SANS-SERIF BOLD CAPITAL THETA SYMBOL
≈ <font> 03F4 ϴ greek capital theta symbol
1D768 𝝨 MATHEMATICAL SANS-SERIF BOLD CAPITAL SIGMA
≈ <font> 03A3 Σ greek capital letter sigma

1D769 Τ MATHEMATICAL SANS-SERIF BOLD CAPITAL TAU
≈ <font> 03A4 Τ greek capital letter tau

1D76A Υ MATHEMATICAL SANS-SERIF BOLD CAPITAL UPSILON
≈ <font> 03A5 Υ greek capital letter upsilon

1D76B Φ MATHEMATICAL SANS-SERIF BOLD CAPITAL PHI
≈ <font> 03A6 Φ greek capital letter phi

1D76C Χ MATHEMATICAL SANS-SERIF BOLD CAPITAL CHI
≈ <font> 03A7 Χ greek capital letter chi

1D76D Ψ MATHEMATICAL SANS-SERIF BOLD CAPITAL PSI
≈ <font> 03A8 Ψ greek capital letter psi

1D76E Ω MATHEMATICAL SANS-SERIF BOLD CAPITAL OMEGA
≈ <font> 03A9 Ω greek capital letter omega

1D76F ∇ MATHEMATICAL SANS-SERIF BOLD NABLA
≈ <font> 2207 ∇ nabla

1D770 α MATHEMATICAL SANS-SERIF BOLD SMALL ALPHA
≈ <font> 03B1 α greek small letter alpha

1D771 β MATHEMATICAL SANS-SERIF BOLD SMALL BETA
≈ <font> 03B2 β greek small letter beta

1D772 γ MATHEMATICAL SANS-SERIF BOLD SMALL GAMMA
≈ <font> 03B3 γ greek small letter gamma

1D773 δ MATHEMATICAL SANS-SERIF BOLD SMALL DELTA
≈ <font> 03B4 δ greek small letter delta

1D774 ε MATHEMATICAL SANS-SERIF BOLD SMALL EPSILON
≈ <font> 03B5 ε greek small letter epsilon

1D775 ζ MATHEMATICAL SANS-SERIF BOLD SMALL ZETA
≈ <font> 03B6 ζ greek small letter zeta

1D776 η MATHEMATICAL SANS-SERIF BOLD SMALL ETA
≈ <font> 03B7 η greek small letter eta

1D777 θ MATHEMATICAL SANS-SERIF BOLD SMALL THETA
≈ <font> 03B8 θ greek small letter theta

1D778 ι MATHEMATICAL SANS-SERIF BOLD SMALL IOTA
≈ <font> 03B9 ι greek small letter iota

1D779 κ MATHEMATICAL SANS-SERIF BOLD SMALL KAPPA
≈ <font> 03BA κ greek small letter kappa

1D77A λ MATHEMATICAL SANS-SERIF BOLD SMALL LAMDA
≈ <font> 03BB λ greek small letter lamda

1D77B μ MATHEMATICAL SANS-SERIF BOLD SMALL MU
≈ <font> 03BC μ greek small letter mu

1D77C ν MATHEMATICAL SANS-SERIF BOLD SMALL NU
≈ <font> 03BD ν greek small letter nu

1D77D ξ MATHEMATICAL SANS-SERIF BOLD SMALL XI
≈ <font> 03BE ξ greek small letter xi

1D77E ο MATHEMATICAL SANS-SERIF BOLD SMALL OMICRON
≈ <font> 03BF ο greek small letter omicron

1D77F π MATHEMATICAL SANS-SERIF BOLD SMALL PI
≈ <font> 03C0 π greek small letter pi

1D780 ρ MATHEMATICAL SANS-SERIF BOLD SMALL RHO
≈ <font> 03C1 ρ greek small letter rho

1D781 ς MATHEMATICAL SANS-SERIF BOLD SMALL FINAL SIGMA
≈ <font> 03C2 ς greek small letter final sigma

1D782 σ MATHEMATICAL SANS-SERIF BOLD SMALL SIGMA
≈ <font> 03C3 σ greek small letter sigma

1D783 τ MATHEMATICAL SANS-SERIF BOLD SMALL TAU
≈ <font> 03C4 τ greek small letter tau

1D784 υ MATHEMATICAL SANS-SERIF BOLD SMALL UPSILON
≈ <font> 03C5 υ greek small letter upsilon

1D785 φ MATHEMATICAL SANS-SERIF BOLD SMALL PHI
≈ <font> 03C6 φ greek small letter phi

1D786 χ MATHEMATICAL SANS-SERIF BOLD SMALL CHI
≈ <font> 03C7 χ greek small letter chi

1D787 ψ MATHEMATICAL SANS-SERIF BOLD SMALL PSI
≈ <font> 03C8 ψ greek small letter psi

1D788 ω MATHEMATICAL SANS-SERIF BOLD SMALL OMEGA
≈ <font> 03C9 ω greek small letter omega

Additional sans-serif bold Greek symbols

1D789 ∂ MATHEMATICAL SANS-SERIF BOLD PARTIAL DIFFERENTIAL
≈ <font> 2202 ∂ partial differential

1D78A ϵ MATHEMATICAL SANS-SERIF BOLD EPSILON SYMBOL
≈ <font> 03F5 ϵ greek lunate epsilon symbol

1D78B ϑ MATHEMATICAL SANS-SERIF BOLD THETA SYMBOL
≈ <font> 03D1 ϑ greek theta symbol

1D78C ϰ MATHEMATICAL SANS-SERIF BOLD KAPPA SYMBOL
≈ <font> 03F0 ϰ greek kappa symbol

1D78D ϕ MATHEMATICAL SANS-SERIF BOLD PHI SYMBOL
≈ <font> 03D5 ϕ greek phi symbol

1D78E ϱ MATHEMATICAL SANS-SERIF BOLD RHO SYMBOL
≈ <font> 03F1 ϱ greek rho symbol

1D78F ϖ MATHEMATICAL SANS-SERIF BOLD PI SYMBOL
≈ <font> 03D6 ϖ greek pi symbol

Sans-serif bold italic Greek symbols

1D790 *Α* MATHEMATICAL SANS-SERIF BOLD ITALIC CAPITAL ALPHA
≈ <font> 0391 Α greek capital letter alpha

1D791 *Β* MATHEMATICAL SANS-SERIF BOLD ITALIC CAPITAL BETA
≈ <font> 0392 Β greek capital letter beta

1D792 *Γ* MATHEMATICAL SANS-SERIF BOLD ITALIC CAPITAL GAMMA
≈ <font> 0393 Γ greek capital letter gamma

1D793 *Δ* MATHEMATICAL SANS-SERIF BOLD ITALIC CAPITAL DELTA
≈ <font> 0394 Δ greek capital letter delta

1D794 *Ε* MATHEMATICAL SANS-SERIF BOLD ITALIC CAPITAL EPSILON
≈ <font> 0395 Ε greek capital letter epsilon

1D795 *Ζ* MATHEMATICAL SANS-SERIF BOLD ITALIC CAPITAL ZETA
≈ <font> 0396 Ζ greek capital letter zeta

1D796 *Η* MATHEMATICAL SANS-SERIF BOLD ITALIC CAPITAL ETA
≈ <font> 0397 Η greek capital letter eta

1D797 *Θ* MATHEMATICAL SANS-SERIF BOLD ITALIC CAPITAL THETA
≈ <font> 0398 Θ greek capital letter theta

1D798 *Ι* MATHEMATICAL SANS-SERIF BOLD ITALIC CAPITAL IOTA
≈ <font> 0399 Ι greek capital letter iota

1D799 *Κ* MATHEMATICAL SANS-SERIF BOLD ITALIC CAPITAL KAPPA
≈ <font> 039A Κ greek capital letter kappa

1D79A *Λ* MATHEMATICAL SANS-SERIF BOLD ITALIC CAPITAL LAMDA
≈ <font> 039B Λ greek capital letter lamda

1D79B *Μ* MATHEMATICAL SANS-SERIF BOLD ITALIC CAPITAL MU
≈ <font> 039C Μ greek capital letter mu

1D79C *Ν* MATHEMATICAL SANS-SERIF BOLD ITALIC CAPITAL NU
≈ <font> 039D Ν greek capital letter nu

1D79D *Ξ* MATHEMATICAL SANS-SERIF BOLD ITALIC CAPITAL XI
≈ <font> 039E Ξ greek capital letter xi

1D79E *Ο* MATHEMATICAL SANS-SERIF BOLD ITALIC CAPITAL OMICRON
≈ <font> 039F Ο greek capital letter omicron

1D79F *Π* MATHEMATICAL SANS-SERIF BOLD ITALIC CAPITAL PI
≈ <font> 03A0 Π greek capital letter pi

1D7A0 *Ρ* MATHEMATICAL SANS-SERIF BOLD ITALIC CAPITAL RHO
≈ <font> 03A1 Ρ greek capital letter rho

1D7A1 *ϴ* MATHEMATICAL SANS-SERIF BOLD ITALIC CAPITAL THETA SYMBOL
≈ <font> 03F4 ϴ greek capital theta symbol

1D7A2 *Σ* MATHEMATICAL SANS-SERIF BOLD ITALIC CAPITAL SIGMA
≈ <font> 03A3 Σ greek capital letter sigma

1D7A3 *Τ* MATHEMATICAL SANS-SERIF BOLD ITALIC CAPITAL TAU
≈ <font> 03A4 Τ greek capital letter tau

1D7A4 *Υ* MATHEMATICAL SANS-SERIF BOLD ITALIC CAPITAL UPSILON
≈ <font> 03A5 Υ greek capital letter upsilon

1D7A5 *Φ* MATHEMATICAL SANS-SERIF BOLD ITALIC CAPITAL PHI
≈ <font> 03A6 Φ greek capital letter phi

1D7A6 *Χ* MATHEMATICAL SANS-SERIF BOLD ITALIC CAPITAL CHI
≈ <font> 03A7 Χ greek capital letter chi

1D7A7 *Ψ* MATHEMATICAL SANS-SERIF BOLD ITALIC CAPITAL PSI
≈ <font> 03A8 Ψ greek capital letter psi

1D7A8 *Ω* MATHEMATICAL SANS-SERIF BOLD ITALIC CAPITAL OMEGA
≈ <font> 03A9 Ω greek capital letter omega

1D7A9 *∇* MATHEMATICAL SANS-SERIF BOLD ITALIC NABLA
≈ <font> 2207 ∇ nabla

1D7AA *α* MATHEMATICAL SANS-SERIF BOLD ITALIC SMALL ALPHA
≈ <font> 03B1 α greek small letter alpha

1D7AB *β* MATHEMATICAL SANS-SERIF BOLD ITALIC SMALL BETA
≈ <font> 03B2 β greek small letter beta

1D7AC *γ* MATHEMATICAL SANS-SERIF BOLD ITALIC SMALL GAMMA
≈ <font> 03B3 γ greek small letter gamma

1D7AD *δ* MATHEMATICAL SANS-SERIF BOLD ITALIC SMALL DELTA
≈ <font> 03B4 δ greek small letter delta

1D7AE *ε* MATHEMATICAL SANS-SERIF BOLD ITALIC SMALL EPSILON
≈ <font> 03B5 ε greek small letter epsilon

1D7AF *ζ* MATHEMATICAL SANS-SERIF BOLD ITALIC SMALL ZETA
≈ <font> 03B6 ζ greek small letter zeta

1D7B0 *η* MATHEMATICAL SANS-SERIF BOLD ITALIC SMALL ETA
≈ <font> 03B7 η greek small letter eta

1D7B1 *θ* MATHEMATICAL SANS-SERIF BOLD ITALIC SMALL THETA
≈ <font> 03B8 θ greek small letter theta

1D7B2 *ι* MATHEMATICAL SANS-SERIF BOLD ITALIC SMALL IOTA
≈ <font> 03B9 ι greek small letter iota

1D7B3 *κ* MATHEMATICAL SANS-SERIF BOLD ITALIC SMALL KAPPA
≈ <font> 03BA κ greek small letter kappa

1D7B4 *λ* MATHEMATICAL SANS-SERIF BOLD ITALIC SMALL LAMDA
≈ <font> 03BB λ greek small letter lamda

1D7B5 *μ* MATHEMATICAL SANS-SERIF BOLD ITALIC SMALL MU
≈ <font> 03BC μ greek small letter mu

1D7B6 *ν* MATHEMATICAL SANS-SERIF BOLD ITALIC SMALL NU
≈ <font> 03BD ν greek small letter nu

1D7B7 *ξ* MATHEMATICAL SANS-SERIF BOLD ITALIC SMALL XI
≈ <font> 03BE ξ greek small letter xi

1D7B8 *ο* MATHEMATICAL SANS-SERIF BOLD ITALIC SMALL OMICRON
≈ <font> 03BF ο greek small letter omicron

1D7B9 *π* MATHEMATICAL SANS-SERIF BOLD ITALIC SMALL PI
≈ <font> 03C0 π greek small letter pi

1D7BA *ρ* MATHEMATICAL SANS-SERIF BOLD ITALIC SMALL RHO
≈ <font> 03C1 ρ greek small letter rho

1D7BB *ς* MATHEMATICAL SANS-SERIF BOLD ITALIC SMALL FINAL SIGMA
≈ <font> 03C2 ς greek small letter final sigma

1D7BC *σ* MATHEMATICAL SANS-SERIF BOLD ITALIC SMALL SIGMA
≈ <font> 03C3 σ greek small letter sigma

1D7BD *τ* MATHEMATICAL SANS-SERIF BOLD ITALIC SMALL TAU
≈ <font> 03C4 τ greek small letter tau

1D7BE *υ* MATHEMATICAL SANS-SERIF BOLD ITALIC SMALL UPSILON
≈ <font> 03C5 υ greek small letter upsilon

1D7BF *φ* MATHEMATICAL SANS-SERIF BOLD ITALIC SMALL PHI
≈ <font> 03C6 φ greek small letter phi

1D7C0 *χ* MATHEMATICAL SANS-SERIF BOLD ITALIC SMALL CHI
≈ <font> 03C7 χ greek small letter chi

1D7C1 *ψ* MATHEMATICAL SANS-SERIF BOLD ITALIC SMALL PSI
≈ <font> 03C8 ψ greek small letter psi

1D7C2 𝟂 MATHEMATICAL SANS-SERIF BOLD ITALIC SMALL OMEGA
≈ <font> 03C9 ω greek small letter omega

Additional sans-serif bold italic Greek symbols

1D7C3 𝟃 MATHEMATICAL SANS-SERIF BOLD ITALIC PARTIAL DIFFERENTIAL
≈ <font> 2202 ∂ partial differential

1D7C4 𝟄 MATHEMATICAL SANS-SERIF BOLD ITALIC EPSILON SYMBOL
≈ <font> 03F5 ϵ greek lunate epsilon symbol

1D7C5 𝟅 MATHEMATICAL SANS-SERIF BOLD ITALIC THETA SYMBOL
≈ <font> 03D1 ϑ greek theta symbol

1D7C6 𝟆 MATHEMATICAL SANS-SERIF BOLD ITALIC KAPPA SYMBOL
≈ <font> 03F0 ϰ greek kappa symbol

1D7C7 𝟇 MATHEMATICAL SANS-SERIF BOLD ITALIC PHI SYMBOL
≈ <font> 03D5 ϕ greek phi symbol

1D7C8 𝟈 MATHEMATICAL SANS-SERIF BOLD ITALIC RHO SYMBOL
≈ <font> 03F1 ϱ greek rho symbol

1D7C9 𝟉 MATHEMATICAL SANS-SERIF BOLD ITALIC PI SYMBOL
≈ <font> 03D6 ϖ greek pi symbol

Additional bold Greek symbols

1D7CA 𝟊 MATHEMATICAL BOLD CAPITAL DIGAMMA
≈ <font> 03DC Ϝ greek letter digamma

1D7CB 𝟋 MATHEMATICAL BOLD SMALL DIGAMMA
≈ <font> 03DD ϝ greek small letter digamma

Bold digits

1D7CE 𝟎 MATHEMATICAL BOLD DIGIT ZERO
≈ <font> 0030 0 digit zero

1D7CF 𝟏 MATHEMATICAL BOLD DIGIT ONE
≈ <font> 0031 1 digit one

1D7D0 𝟐 MATHEMATICAL BOLD DIGIT TWO
≈ <font> 0032 2 digit two

1D7D1 𝟑 MATHEMATICAL BOLD DIGIT THREE
≈ <font> 0033 3 digit three

1D7D2 𝟒 MATHEMATICAL BOLD DIGIT FOUR
≈ <font> 0034 4 digit four

1D7D3 𝟓 MATHEMATICAL BOLD DIGIT FIVE
≈ <font> 0035 5 digit five

1D7D4 𝟔 MATHEMATICAL BOLD DIGIT SIX
≈ <font> 0036 6 digit six

1D7D5 𝟕 MATHEMATICAL BOLD DIGIT SEVEN
≈ <font> 0037 7 digit seven

1D7D6 𝟖 MATHEMATICAL BOLD DIGIT EIGHT
≈ <font> 0038 8 digit eight

1D7D7 𝟗 MATHEMATICAL BOLD DIGIT NINE
≈ <font> 0039 9 digit nine

Double-struck digits

1D7D8 𝟘 MATHEMATICAL DOUBLE-STRUCK DIGIT ZERO
≈ <font> 0030 0 digit zero

1D7D9 𝟙 MATHEMATICAL DOUBLE-STRUCK DIGIT ONE
≈ <font> 0031 1 digit one

1D7DA 𝟚 MATHEMATICAL DOUBLE-STRUCK DIGIT TWO
≈ <font> 0032 2 digit two

1D7DB 𝟛 MATHEMATICAL DOUBLE-STRUCK DIGIT THREE
≈ <font> 0033 3 digit three

1D7DC 𝟜 MATHEMATICAL DOUBLE-STRUCK DIGIT FOUR
≈ <font> 0034 4 digit four

1D7DD 𝟝 MATHEMATICAL DOUBLE-STRUCK DIGIT FIVE
≈ <font> 0035 5 digit five

1D7DE 𝟞 MATHEMATICAL DOUBLE-STRUCK DIGIT SIX
≈ <font> 0036 6 digit six

1D7DF 𝟟 MATHEMATICAL DOUBLE-STRUCK DIGIT SEVEN
≈ <font> 0037 7 digit seven

1D7E0 𝟠 MATHEMATICAL DOUBLE-STRUCK DIGIT EIGHT
≈ <font> 0038 8 digit eight

1D7E1 𝟡 MATHEMATICAL DOUBLE-STRUCK DIGIT NINE
≈ <font> 0039 9 digit nine

Sans-serif digits

1D7E2 𝟢 MATHEMATICAL SANS-SERIF DIGIT ZERO
≈ <font> 0030 0 digit zero

1D7E3 𝟣 MATHEMATICAL SANS-SERIF DIGIT ONE
≈ <font> 0031 1 digit one

1D7E4 𝟤 MATHEMATICAL SANS-SERIF DIGIT TWO
≈ <font> 0032 2 digit two

1D7E5 𝟥 MATHEMATICAL SANS-SERIF DIGIT THREE
≈ <font> 0033 3 digit three

1D7E6 𝟦 MATHEMATICAL SANS-SERIF DIGIT FOUR
≈ <font> 0034 4 digit four

1D7E7 𝟧 MATHEMATICAL SANS-SERIF DIGIT FIVE
≈ <font> 0035 5 digit five

1D7E8 𝟨 MATHEMATICAL SANS-SERIF DIGIT SIX
≈ <font> 0036 6 digit six

1D7E9 𝟩 MATHEMATICAL SANS-SERIF DIGIT SEVEN
≈ <font> 0037 7 digit seven

1D7EA 𝟪 MATHEMATICAL SANS-SERIF DIGIT EIGHT
≈ <font> 0038 8 digit eight

1D7EB 𝟫 MATHEMATICAL SANS-SERIF DIGIT NINE
≈ <font> 0039 9 digit nine

Sans-serif bold digits

1D7EC 𝟬 MATHEMATICAL SANS-SERIF BOLD DIGIT ZERO
≈ <font> 0030 0 digit zero

1D7ED 𝟭 MATHEMATICAL SANS-SERIF BOLD DIGIT ONE
≈ <font> 0031 1 digit one

1D7EE 𝟮 MATHEMATICAL SANS-SERIF BOLD DIGIT TWO
≈ <font> 0032 2 digit two

1D7EF 𝟯 MATHEMATICAL SANS-SERIF BOLD DIGIT THREE
≈ <font> 0033 3 digit three

1D7F0 𝟰 MATHEMATICAL SANS-SERIF BOLD DIGIT FOUR
≈ <font> 0034 4 digit four

1D7F1 𝟱 MATHEMATICAL SANS-SERIF BOLD DIGIT FIVE
≈ <font> 0035 5 digit five

1D7F2 𝟲 MATHEMATICAL SANS-SERIF BOLD DIGIT SIX
≈ <font> 0036 6 digit six

1D7F3 𝟳 MATHEMATICAL SANS-SERIF BOLD DIGIT SEVEN
≈ <font> 0037 7 digit seven

1D7F4 𝟴 MATHEMATICAL SANS-SERIF BOLD DIGIT EIGHT
≈ <font> 0038 8 digit eight

1D7F5 𝟵 MATHEMATICAL SANS-SERIF BOLD DIGIT NINE
≈ <font> 0039 9 digit nine

Monospace digits

1D7F6 𝟶 MATHEMATICAL MONOSPACE DIGIT ZERO
≈ <font> 0030 0 digit zero

1D7F7 𝟷 MATHEMATICAL MONOSPACE DIGIT ONE
≈ <font> 0031 1 digit one

1D7F8 𝟸 MATHEMATICAL MONOSPACE DIGIT TWO
≈ <font> 0032 2 digit two

1D7F9 3 MATHEMATICAL MONOSPACE DIGIT THREE
≈ <font> 0033 3 digit three
1D7FA 4 MATHEMATICAL MONOSPACE DIGIT FOUR
≈ <font> 0034 4 digit four
1D7FB 5 MATHEMATICAL MONOSPACE DIGIT FIVE
≈ <font> 0035 5 digit five
1D7FC 6 MATHEMATICAL MONOSPACE DIGIT SIX
≈ <font> 0036 6 digit six
1D7FD 7 MATHEMATICAL MONOSPACE DIGIT SEVEN
≈ <font> 0037 7 digit seven
1D7FE 8 MATHEMATICAL MONOSPACE DIGIT EIGHT
≈ <font> 0038 8 digit eight
1D7FF 9 MATHEMATICAL MONOSPACE DIGIT NINE
≈ <font> 0039 9 digit nine

	2F80	2F81	2F82	2F83	2F84	2F85	2F86	2F87	2F88	2F89	2F8A	2F8B
0	丽 2F800	兤 2F810	刻 2F820	卽 2F830	咢 2F840	切 2F850	𡚨 2F860	寳 2F870	嵼 2F880	廾 2F890	悁 2F8A0	懲 2F8B0
1	丸 2F801	具 2F811	剆 2F821	卿 2F831	哶 2F841	壮 2F851	𡛪 2F861	𡬘 2F871	巡 2F881	𢌱 2F891	㤺 2F8A1	懶 2F8B1
2	乁 2F802	𠔜 2F812	割 2F822	卿 2F832	唐 2F842	城 2F852	姬 2F862	寿 2F872	巢 2F882	𢌱 2F892	㤜 2F8A2	成 2F8B2
3	𠄢 2F803	㒹 2F813	剷 2F823	卿 2F833	啓 2F843	埴 2F853	娛 2F863	将 2F873	㠯 2F883	舁 2F893	悔 2F8A3	戛 2F8B3
4	你 2F804	內 2F814	㔕 2F824	𠨬 2F834	啣 2F844	堍 2F854	娧 2F864	当 2F874	巽 2F884	弢 2F894	𢛔 2F8A4	扝 2F8B4
5	侮 2F805	再 2F815	勇 2F825	灰 2F835	善 2F845	型 2F855	姘 2F865	尢 2F875	帨 2F885	弢 2F895	惇 2F8A5	抱 2F8B5
6	侻 2F806	𠕋 2F816	勉 2F826	及 2F836	善 2F846	堲 2F856	婦 2F866	㞁 2F876	帽 2F886	㣇 2F896	慈 2F8A6	拔 2F8B6
7	倂 2F807	冗 2F817	勤 2F827	叟 2F837	喙 2F847	報 2F857	㛮 2F867	屠 2F877	幩 2F887	𣊸 2F897	慌 2F8A7	捐 2F8B7
8	偺 2F808	冤 2F818	勺 2F828	𠭣 2F838	喫 2F848	墬 2F858	㛼 2F868	屮 2F878	㡢 2F888	𦇚 2F898	慎 2F8A8	𢬌 2F8B8
9	備 2F809	仌 2F819	包 2F829	叫 2F839	喳 2F849	𡓤 2F859	嬈 2F869	峀 2F879	𢆃 2F889	形 2F899	慌 2F8A9	挽 2F8B9
A	僧 2F80A	冬 2F81A	匆 2F82A	叱 2F83A	嗂 2F84A	売 2F85A	嬾 2F86A	岍 2F87A	㡼 2F88A	彫 2F89A	慺 2F8AA	拼 2F8BA
B	像 2F80B	况 2F81B	北 2F82B	吆 2F83B	圖 2F84B	壷 2F85B	嬾 2F86B	𡷤 2F87B	庰 2F88B	㣣 2F89B	憎 2F8AB	捨 2F8BB
C	㒞 2F80C	𩇟 2F81C	卉 2F82C	咞 2F83C	嘆 2F84C	夆 2F85C	𡧈 2F86C	嵃 2F87C	庳 2F88C	徚 2F89C	憲 2F8AC	掃 2F8BC
D	𠘺 2F80D	凵 2F81D	卑 2F82D	吸 2F83D	圗 2F84D	多 2F85D	寃 2F86D	𡷦 2F87D	庶 2F88D	忍 2F89D	憤 2F8AD	揤 2F8BD
E	免 2F80E	刃 2F81E	博 2F82E	呈 2F83E	噑 2F84E	夢 2F85E	寘 2F86E	嵮 2F87E	廊 2F88E	志 2F89E	憯 2F8AE	𢯱 2F8BE
F	兔 2F80F	㓟 2F81F	即 2F82F	周 2F83F	噴 2F84F	奢 2F85F	寧 2F86F	嵫 2F87F	𪎒 2F88F	忹 2F89F	懞 2F8AF	搢 2F8BF

	2F8C	2F8D	2F8E	2F8F	2F90	2F91	2F92	2F93	2F94	2F95	2F96
0	揅 2F8C0	㬈 2F8D0	枅 2F8E0	𣢧 2F8F0	派 2F900	𣽞 2F910	爨 2F920	瑱 2F930	直 2F940	磌 2F950	䈂 2F960
1	掩 2F8C1	㫤 2F8D1	桒 2F8E1	歔 2F8F1	海 2F901	𣾎 2F911	爵 2F921	璅 2F931	𥃳 2F941	䃣 2F951	𥮫 2F961
2	㨮 2F8C2	冒 2F8D2	梅 2F8E2	㱎 2F8F2	流 2F902	濆 2F912	牐 2F922	瓊 2F932	𥃲 2F942	𥘦 2F952	篆 2F962
3	摩 2F8C3	冕 2F8D3	𣑭 2F8E3	歲 2F8F3	浩 2F903	瀹 2F913	𤘈 2F923	㼛 2F933	𥄙 2F943	祖 2F953	築 2F963
4	摾 2F8C4	最 2F8D4	梎 2F8E4	殟 2F8F4	浸 2F904	瀞 2F914	犀 2F924	甤 2F934	𥄳 2F944	𥚚 2F954	䈧 2F964
5	撝 2F8C5	暜 2F8D5	栟 2F8E5	殺 2F8F5	涅 2F905	瀛 2F915	犕 2F925	𤰶 2F935	眞 2F945	𥛅 2F955	𥲀 2F965
6	摷 2F8C6	肭 2F8D6	椔 2F8E6	殻 2F8F6	𣴞 2F906	㶖 2F916	𤜵 2F926	甾 2F936	真 2F946	福 2F956	糒 2F966
7	㩬 2F8C7	䏙 2F8D7	㮝 2F8E7	𣪍 2F8F7	洴 2F907	灊 2F917	𤠔 2F927	𤲒 2F937	真 2F947	秫 2F957	䊠 2F967
8	敏 2F8C8	朗 2F8D8	楂 2F8E8	𡴋 2F8F8	港 2F908	災 2F918	獺 2F928	異 2F938	睊 2F948	䄯 2F958	糨 2F968
9	敬 2F8C9	望 2F8D9	榣 2F8E9	𣫺 2F8F9	湮 2F909	灷 2F919	王 2F929	𢆟 2F939	䀹 2F949	穀 2F959	糣 2F969
A	𣀊 2F8CA	朡 2F8DA	槪 2F8EA	汎 2F8FA	㴳 2F90A	炭 2F91A	㺬 2F92A	瘐 2F93A	瞋 2F94A	穊 2F95A	紀 2F96A
B	旣 2F8CB	杞 2F8DB	檨 2F8EB	𣲼 2F8FB	滋 2F90B	𠔥 2F91B	玥 2F92B	𤾡 2F93B	䁆 2F94B	穏 2F95B	𥾆 2F96B
C	書 2F8CC	杓 2F8DC	𣚣 2F8EC	沿 2F8FC	滇 2F90C	煅 2F91C	㺸 2F92C	𤾸 2F93C	䂖 2F94C	𥥼 2F95C	絣 2F96C
D	晉 2F8CD	𣏃 2F8DD	櫛 2F8ED	泍 2F8FD	𣻑 2F90D	𤉣 2F91D	㺸 2F92D	𥁄 2F93D	𥐝 2F94D	𥪧 2F95D	䌁 2F96D
E	㬙 2F8CE	㭉 2F8DE	㰘 2F8EE	汧 2F8FE	淹 2F90E	熜 2F91E	瑇 2F92E	㿼 2F93E	硎 2F94E	𥪧 2F95E	緇 2F96E
F	暑 2F8CF	柺 2F8DF	次 2F8EF	洖 2F8FF	潮 2F90F	𤎫 2F91F	瑜 2F92F	䀈 2F93F	碌 2F94F	竮 2F95F	縂 2F96F

	2F97	2F98	2F99	2F9A	2F9B	2F9C	2F9D	2F9E	2F9F	2FA0	2FA1
0	繅 2F970	𣍟 2F980	芋 2F990	荓 2F9A0	𦾱 2F9B0	蟡 2F9C0	諭 2F9D0	𨗒 2F9E0	閷 2F9F0	頩 2FA00	𪃎 2FA10
1	䌴 2F971	䏕 2F981	芝 2F991	菊 2F9A1	𧃒 2F9B1	蠁 2F9C1	變 2F9D1	𨗭 2F9E1	𨵷 2F9F1	𩖶 2FA01	䳸 2FA11
2	𦈨 2F972	育 2F982	劳 2F992	菌 2F9A2	䕫 2F9B2	䗹 2F9C2	豕 2F9D2	邔 2F9E2	䧦 2F9F2	飢 2FA02	𪄅 2FA12
3	𦉇 2F973	脃 2F983	花 2F993	菜 2F9A3	虐 2F9B3	衠 2F9C3	𧲨 2F9D3	郱 2F9E3	雃 2F9F3	䬳 2FA03	𪈎 2FA13
4	䍙 2F974	䐋 2F984	芳 2F994	𦰶 2F9A4	虜 2F9B4	衣 2F9C4	貫 2F9D4	鄑 2F9E4	嶲 2F9F4	餩 2FA04	𪊑 2FA14
5	𦋙 2F975	脾 2F985	芽 2F995	𦵫 2F9A5	虧 2F9B5	𧙧 2F9C5	賁 2F9D5	𨜮 2F9E5	霣 2F9F5	馧 2FA05	麻 2FA15
6	罺 2F976	媵 2F986	苦 2F996	𦳕 2F9A6	虩 2F9B6	裗 2F9C6	贛 2F9D6	鄛 2F9E6	𩅅 2F9F6	駂 2FA06	䵖 2FA16
7	𦌾 2F977	𦞧 2F987	𦬼 2F997	䔫 2F9A7	蚩 2F9B7	裞 2F9C7	起 2F9D7	鈸 2F9E7	𩈚 2F9F7	駾 2FA07	黹 2FA17
8	羕 2F978	𦞵 2F988	若 2F998	蓱 2F9A8	蚈 2F9B8	䘵 2F9C8	𧼯 2F9D8	鋗 2F9E8	䩮 2F9F8	䯎 2FA08	黾 2FA18
9	翺 2F979	𣎓 2F989	茝 2F999	蓳 2F9A9	蜎 2F9B9	裺 2F9C9	𠠄 2F9D9	鋘 2F9E9	䩶 2F9F9	𩬰 2FA09	鼅 2FA19
A	者 2F97A	𣎜 2F98A	荣 2F99A	蔖 2F9AA	蛢 2F9BA	㒻 2F9CA	跋 2F9DA	鉼 2F9EA	韠 2F9FA	鬒 2FA0A	鼏 2FA1A
B	𦓚 2F97B	舁 2F98B	莭 2F99B	𧏊 2F9AB	蝹 2F9BB	𧢮 2F9CB	趼 2F9DB	鏹 2F9EB	𩐊 2F9FB	鱀 2FA0B	鼖 2FA1B
C	𦔣 2F97C	舄 2F98C	茣 2F99C	蕤 2F9AC	蜨 2F9BC	𧥦 2F9CC	跰 2F9DC	鐕 2F9EC	䪲 2F9FC	鳽 2FA0C	鼻 2FA1C
D	聠 2F97D	辞 2F98D	莽 2F99D	𦼬 2F9AD	蝫 2F9BD	䚾 2F9CD	𠣞 2F9DD	𨯺 2F9ED	𩒖 2F9FD	䳎 2FA0D	𪘀 2FA1D
E	𦖨 2F97E	䑫 2F98E	菧 2F99E	䕝 2F9AE	螆 2F9BE	䛇 2F9CE	軔 2F9DE	開 2F9EE	頋 2F9FE	䳭 2FA0E	
F	聰 2F97F	芑 2F98F	著 2F99F	䕡 2F9AF	䗗 2F9BF	誠 2F9CF	輸 2F9DF	䦕 2F9EF	頋 2F9FF	鵧 2FA0F	

Duplicate characters from CNS 11643-1992

2F800 丽 CJK COMPATIBILITY IDEOGRAPH-2F800
≡ 4E3D 丽
2F801 丸 CJK COMPATIBILITY IDEOGRAPH-2F801
≡ 4E38 丸
2F802 乁 CJK COMPATIBILITY IDEOGRAPH-2F802
≡ 4E41 乁
2F803 𠄢 CJK COMPATIBILITY IDEOGRAPH-2F803
≡ 20122 𠄢
2F804 你 CJK COMPATIBILITY IDEOGRAPH-2F804
≡ 4F60 你
2F805 侮 CJK COMPATIBILITY IDEOGRAPH-2F805
≡ 4FAE 侮
2F806 侻 CJK COMPATIBILITY IDEOGRAPH-2F806
≡ 4FBB 侻
2F807 倂 CJK COMPATIBILITY IDEOGRAPH-2F807
≡ 5002 倂
2F808 偺 CJK COMPATIBILITY IDEOGRAPH-2F808
≡ 507A 偺
2F809 備 CJK COMPATIBILITY IDEOGRAPH-2F809
≡ 5099 備
2F80A 僧 CJK COMPATIBILITY IDEOGRAPH-2F80A
≡ 50E7 僧
2F80B 像 CJK COMPATIBILITY IDEOGRAPH-2F80B
≡ 50CF 像
2F80C 㒞 CJK COMPATIBILITY IDEOGRAPH-2F80C
≡ 349E 㒞
2F80D 𠘺 CJK COMPATIBILITY IDEOGRAPH-2F80D
→ 5145 充
≡ 2063A 𠘺
2F80E 免 CJK COMPATIBILITY IDEOGRAPH-2F80E
≡ 514D 免
2F80F 兔 CJK COMPATIBILITY IDEOGRAPH-2F80F
≡ 5154 兔
2F810 兤 CJK COMPATIBILITY IDEOGRAPH-2F810
≡ 5164 兤
2F811 具 CJK COMPATIBILITY IDEOGRAPH-2F811
≡ 5177 具
2F812 𠔜 CJK COMPATIBILITY IDEOGRAPH-2F812
≡ 2051C 𠔜
2F813 㒹 CJK COMPATIBILITY IDEOGRAPH-2F813
≡ 34B9 㒹
2F814 內 CJK COMPATIBILITY IDEOGRAPH-2F814
→ 5185 内
≡ 5167 內
2F815 再 CJK COMPATIBILITY IDEOGRAPH-2F815
≡ 518D 再
2F816 𠕋 CJK COMPATIBILITY IDEOGRAPH-2F816
≡ 2054B 𠕋
2F817 冗 CJK COMPATIBILITY IDEOGRAPH-2F817
≡ 5197 冗
2F818 冤 CJK COMPATIBILITY IDEOGRAPH-2F818
≡ 51A4 冤
2F819 仌 CJK COMPATIBILITY IDEOGRAPH-2F819
≡ 4ECC 仌
2F81A 冬 CJK COMPATIBILITY IDEOGRAPH-2F81A
≡ 51AC 冬
2F81B 况 CJK COMPATIBILITY IDEOGRAPH-2F81B
≡ 51B5 况
2F81C 𩇟 CJK COMPATIBILITY IDEOGRAPH-2F81C
≡ 291DF 𩇟
2F81D 凵 CJK COMPATIBILITY IDEOGRAPH-2F81D
≡ 51F5 凵
2F81E 刃 CJK COMPATIBILITY IDEOGRAPH-2F81E
≡ 5203 刃
2F81F 㓟 CJK COMPATIBILITY IDEOGRAPH-2F81F
≡ 34DF 㓟
2F820 刻 CJK COMPATIBILITY IDEOGRAPH-2F820
≡ 523B 刻
2F821 剆 CJK COMPATIBILITY IDEOGRAPH-2F821
≡ 5246 剆
2F822 割 CJK COMPATIBILITY IDEOGRAPH-2F822
≡ 5272 割
2F823 剷 CJK COMPATIBILITY IDEOGRAPH-2F823
≡ 5277 剷
2F824 㔕 CJK COMPATIBILITY IDEOGRAPH-2F824
≡ 3515 㔕
2F825 勇 CJK COMPATIBILITY IDEOGRAPH-2F825
≡ 52C7 勇
2F826 勉 CJK COMPATIBILITY IDEOGRAPH-2F826
≡ 52C9 勉
2F827 勤 CJK COMPATIBILITY IDEOGRAPH-2F827
≡ 52E4 勤
2F828 勺 CJK COMPATIBILITY IDEOGRAPH-2F828
≡ 52FA 勺
2F829 包 CJK COMPATIBILITY IDEOGRAPH-2F829
≡ 5305 包
2F82A 匆 CJK COMPATIBILITY IDEOGRAPH-2F82A
≡ 5306 匆
2F82B 北 CJK COMPATIBILITY IDEOGRAPH-2F82B
≡ 5317 北
2F82C 卉 CJK COMPATIBILITY IDEOGRAPH-2F82C
≡ 5349 卉
2F82D 卑 CJK COMPATIBILITY IDEOGRAPH-2F82D
≡ 5351 卑
2F82E 博 CJK COMPATIBILITY IDEOGRAPH-2F82E
≡ 535A 博
2F82F 即 CJK COMPATIBILITY IDEOGRAPH-2F82F
≡ 5373 即
2F830 卽 CJK COMPATIBILITY IDEOGRAPH-2F830
≡ 537D 卽
2F831 卿 CJK COMPATIBILITY IDEOGRAPH-2F831
≡ 537F 卿
2F832 卿 CJK COMPATIBILITY IDEOGRAPH-2F832
≡ 537F 卿
2F833 卿 CJK COMPATIBILITY IDEOGRAPH-2F833
≡ 537F 卿
2F834 𠨬 CJK COMPATIBILITY IDEOGRAPH-2F834
≡ 20A2C 𠨬
2F835 灰 CJK COMPATIBILITY IDEOGRAPH-2F835
≡ 7070 灰
2F836 及 CJK COMPATIBILITY IDEOGRAPH-2F836
≡ 53CA 及
2F837 叟 CJK COMPATIBILITY IDEOGRAPH-2F837
≡ 53DF 叟
2F838 𠭣 CJK COMPATIBILITY IDEOGRAPH-2F838
≡ 20B63 𠭣
2F839 叫 CJK COMPATIBILITY IDEOGRAPH-2F839
≡ 53EB 叫
2F83A 叱 CJK COMPATIBILITY IDEOGRAPH-2F83A
≡ 53F1 叱
2F83B 吆 CJK COMPATIBILITY IDEOGRAPH-2F83B
≡ 5406 吆
2F83C 咞 CJK COMPATIBILITY IDEOGRAPH-2F83C
≡ 549E 咞

2F83D 吸 CJK COMPATIBILITY IDEOGRAPH-2F83D
≡ 5438 吸
2F83E 呈 CJK COMPATIBILITY IDEOGRAPH-2F83E
≡ 5448 呈
2F83F 周 CJK COMPATIBILITY IDEOGRAPH-2F83F
≡ 5468 周
2F840 咢 CJK COMPATIBILITY IDEOGRAPH-2F840
≡ 54A2 咢
2F841 哶 CJK COMPATIBILITY IDEOGRAPH-2F841
≡ 54F6 哶
2F842 唐 CJK COMPATIBILITY IDEOGRAPH-2F842
≡ 5510 唐
2F843 啓 CJK COMPATIBILITY IDEOGRAPH-2F843
≡ 5553 啓
2F844 啣 CJK COMPATIBILITY IDEOGRAPH-2F844
≡ 5563 啣
2F845 善 CJK COMPATIBILITY IDEOGRAPH-2F845
≡ 5584 善
2F846 善 CJK COMPATIBILITY IDEOGRAPH-2F846
≡ 5584 善
2F847 喙 CJK COMPATIBILITY IDEOGRAPH-2F847
≡ 5599 喙
2F848 喫 CJK COMPATIBILITY IDEOGRAPH-2F848
≡ 55AB 喫
2F849 喳 CJK COMPATIBILITY IDEOGRAPH-2F849
≡ 55B3 喳
2F84A 嗂 CJK COMPATIBILITY IDEOGRAPH-2F84A
≡ 55C2 嗂
2F84B 圖 CJK COMPATIBILITY IDEOGRAPH-2F84B
≡ 5716 圖
2F84C 嘆 CJK COMPATIBILITY IDEOGRAPH-2F84C
≡ 5606 嘆
2F84D 圗 CJK COMPATIBILITY IDEOGRAPH-2F84D
≡ 5717 圗
2F84E 噑 CJK COMPATIBILITY IDEOGRAPH-2F84E
≡ 5651 噑
2F84F 噴 CJK COMPATIBILITY IDEOGRAPH-2F84F
≡ 5674 噴
2F850 切 CJK COMPATIBILITY IDEOGRAPH-2F850
≡ 5207 切
2F851 壮 CJK COMPATIBILITY IDEOGRAPH-2F851
≡ 58EE 壮
2F852 城 CJK COMPATIBILITY IDEOGRAPH-2F852
≡ 57CE 城
2F853 埴 CJK COMPATIBILITY IDEOGRAPH-2F853
≡ 57F4 埴
2F854 堍 CJK COMPATIBILITY IDEOGRAPH-2F854
≡ 580D 堍
2F855 型 CJK COMPATIBILITY IDEOGRAPH-2F855
≡ 578B 型
2F856 堲 CJK COMPATIBILITY IDEOGRAPH-2F856
≡ 5832 堲
2F857 報 CJK COMPATIBILITY IDEOGRAPH-2F857
≡ 5831 報
2F858 墬 CJK COMPATIBILITY IDEOGRAPH-2F858
≡ 58AC 墬
2F859 𡓤 CJK COMPATIBILITY IDEOGRAPH-2F859
≡ 214E4 𡓤
2F85A 売 CJK COMPATIBILITY IDEOGRAPH-2F85A
→ 58F3 壳
≡ 58F2 売
2F85B 壷 CJK COMPATIBILITY IDEOGRAPH-2F85B
→ 21533 𡔳
≡ 58F7 壷
2F85C 夆 CJK COMPATIBILITY IDEOGRAPH-2F85C
≡ 5906 夆
2F85D 多 CJK COMPATIBILITY IDEOGRAPH-2F85D
≡ 591A 多
2F85E 夢 CJK COMPATIBILITY IDEOGRAPH-2F85E
≡ 5922 夢
2F85F 奢 CJK COMPATIBILITY IDEOGRAPH-2F85F
≡ 5962 奢
2F860 𡚨 CJK COMPATIBILITY IDEOGRAPH-2F860
≡ 216A8 𡚨
2F861 𡛪 CJK COMPATIBILITY IDEOGRAPH-2F861
≡ 216EA 𡛪
2F862 姬 CJK COMPATIBILITY IDEOGRAPH-2F862
≡ 59EC 姬
2F863 娛 CJK COMPATIBILITY IDEOGRAPH-2F863
≡ 5A1B 娛
2F864 娧 CJK COMPATIBILITY IDEOGRAPH-2F864
≡ 5A27 娧
2F865 姘 CJK COMPATIBILITY IDEOGRAPH-2F865
≡ 59D8 姘
2F866 婦 CJK COMPATIBILITY IDEOGRAPH-2F866
≡ 5A66 婦
2F867 㛮 CJK COMPATIBILITY IDEOGRAPH-2F867
≡ 36EE 㛮
2F868 㛼 CJK COMPATIBILITY IDEOGRAPH-2F868
≡ 36FC 㛼
2F869 嬈 CJK COMPATIBILITY IDEOGRAPH-2F869
≡ 5B08 嬈
2F86A 嬾 CJK COMPATIBILITY IDEOGRAPH-2F86A
≡ 5B3E 嬾
2F86B 嬾 CJK COMPATIBILITY IDEOGRAPH-2F86B
≡ 5B3E 嬾
2F86C 𡧈 CJK COMPATIBILITY IDEOGRAPH-2F86C
≡ 219C8 𡧈
2F86D 寃 CJK COMPATIBILITY IDEOGRAPH-2F86D
≡ 5BC3 寃
2F86E 寘 CJK COMPATIBILITY IDEOGRAPH-2F86E
≡ 5BD8 寘
2F86F 寧 CJK COMPATIBILITY IDEOGRAPH-2F86F
≡ 5BE7 寧
2F870 寳 CJK COMPATIBILITY IDEOGRAPH-2F870
≡ 5BF3 寳
2F871 𡬘 CJK COMPATIBILITY IDEOGRAPH-2F871
≡ 21B18 𡬘
2F872 寿 CJK COMPATIBILITY IDEOGRAPH-2F872
≡ 5BFF 寿
2F873 将 CJK COMPATIBILITY IDEOGRAPH-2F873
≡ 5C06 将
2F874 当 CJK COMPATIBILITY IDEOGRAPH-2F874
≡ 5F53 当
2F875 尢 CJK COMPATIBILITY IDEOGRAPH-2F875
≡ 5C22 尢
2F876 㞁 CJK COMPATIBILITY IDEOGRAPH-2F876
≡ 3781 㞁
2F877 屠 CJK COMPATIBILITY IDEOGRAPH-2F877
≡ 5C60 屠
2F878 屮 CJK COMPATIBILITY IDEOGRAPH-2F878
≡ 5C6E 屮
2F879 峀 CJK COMPATIBILITY IDEOGRAPH-2F879
≡ 5CC0 峀

2F87A 岍 CJK COMPATIBILITY IDEOGRAPH-2F87A
≡ 5C8D 岍
2F87B 峀 CJK COMPATIBILITY IDEOGRAPH-2F87B
≡ 21DE4 峀
2F87C 峰 CJK COMPATIBILITY IDEOGRAPH-2F87C
≡ 5D43 峰
2F87D 𡷦 CJK COMPATIBILITY IDEOGRAPH-2F87D
≡ 21DE6 𡷦
2F87E 嵃 CJK COMPATIBILITY IDEOGRAPH-2F87E
≡ 5D6E 嵮
2F87F 嵫 CJK COMPATIBILITY IDEOGRAPH-2F87F
≡ 5D6B 嵫
2F880 嵼 CJK COMPATIBILITY IDEOGRAPH-2F880
≡ 5D7C 嵼
2F881 巡 CJK COMPATIBILITY IDEOGRAPH-2F881
≡ 5DE1 巡
2F882 巢 CJK COMPATIBILITY IDEOGRAPH-2F882
≡ 5DE2 巢
2F883 㠯 CJK COMPATIBILITY IDEOGRAPH-2F883
≡ 382F 㠯
2F884 巽 CJK COMPATIBILITY IDEOGRAPH-2F884
≡ 5DFD 巽
2F885 帨 CJK COMPATIBILITY IDEOGRAPH-2F885
≡ 5E28 帨
2F886 帽 CJK COMPATIBILITY IDEOGRAPH-2F886
≡ 5E3D 帽
2F887 幩 CJK COMPATIBILITY IDEOGRAPH-2F887
≡ 5E69 幩
2F888 㡢 CJK COMPATIBILITY IDEOGRAPH-2F888
≡ 3862 㡢
2F889 𢆃 CJK COMPATIBILITY IDEOGRAPH-2F889
≡ 22183 𢆃
2F88A 㡼 CJK COMPATIBILITY IDEOGRAPH-2F88A
≡ 387C 㡼
2F88B 庰 CJK COMPATIBILITY IDEOGRAPH-2F88B
≡ 5EB0 庰
2F88C 庳 CJK COMPATIBILITY IDEOGRAPH-2F88C
≡ 5EB3 庳
2F88D 庶 CJK COMPATIBILITY IDEOGRAPH-2F88D
≡ 5EB6 庶
2F88E 廊 CJK COMPATIBILITY IDEOGRAPH-2F88E
≡ 5ECA 廊
2F88F 𪎒 CJK COMPATIBILITY IDEOGRAPH-2F88F
≡ 2A392 𪎒
2F890 廾 CJK COMPATIBILITY IDEOGRAPH-2F890
≡ 5EFE 廾
2F891 𢌱 CJK COMPATIBILITY IDEOGRAPH-2F891
≡ 22331 𢌱
2F892 𢌱 CJK COMPATIBILITY IDEOGRAPH-2F892
≡ 22331 𢌱
2F893 舁 CJK COMPATIBILITY IDEOGRAPH-2F893
≡ 8201 舁
2F894 弢 CJK COMPATIBILITY IDEOGRAPH-2F894
≡ 5F22 弢
2F895 弢 CJK COMPATIBILITY IDEOGRAPH-2F895
≡ 5F22 弢
2F896 㣇 CJK COMPATIBILITY IDEOGRAPH-2F896
≡ 38C7 㣇
2F897 𣊸 CJK COMPATIBILITY IDEOGRAPH-2F897
≡ 232B8 𣊸
2F898 𦇚 CJK COMPATIBILITY IDEOGRAPH-2F898
≡ 261DA 𦇚
2F899 形 CJK COMPATIBILITY IDEOGRAPH-2F899
≡ 5F62 形
2F89A 彫 CJK COMPATIBILITY IDEOGRAPH-2F89A
≡ 5F6B 彫
2F89B 㣣 CJK COMPATIBILITY IDEOGRAPH-2F89B
≡ 38E3 㣣
2F89C 徚 CJK COMPATIBILITY IDEOGRAPH-2F89C
→ 22505 𢔅
≡ 5F9A 徚
2F89D 忍 CJK COMPATIBILITY IDEOGRAPH-2F89D
≡ 5FCD 忍
2F89E 志 CJK COMPATIBILITY IDEOGRAPH-2F89E
≡ 5FD7 志
2F89F 忹 CJK COMPATIBILITY IDEOGRAPH-2F89F
≡ 5FF9 忹
2F8A0 悁 CJK COMPATIBILITY IDEOGRAPH-2F8A0
≡ 6081 悁
2F8A1 㤺 CJK COMPATIBILITY IDEOGRAPH-2F8A1
≡ 393A 㤺
2F8A2 㤜 CJK COMPATIBILITY IDEOGRAPH-2F8A2
≡ 391C 㤜
2F8A3 悔 CJK COMPATIBILITY IDEOGRAPH-2F8A3
≡ 6094 悔
2F8A4 𢛔 CJK COMPATIBILITY IDEOGRAPH-2F8A4
≡ 226D4 𢛔
2F8A5 惇 CJK COMPATIBILITY IDEOGRAPH-2F8A5
≡ 60C7 惇
2F8A6 慈 CJK COMPATIBILITY IDEOGRAPH-2F8A6
≡ 6148 慈
2F8A7 慌 CJK COMPATIBILITY IDEOGRAPH-2F8A7
≡ 614C 慌
2F8A8 慎 CJK COMPATIBILITY IDEOGRAPH-2F8A8
≡ 614E 慎
2F8A9 慌 CJK COMPATIBILITY IDEOGRAPH-2F8A9
≡ 614C 慌
2F8AA 慺 CJK COMPATIBILITY IDEOGRAPH-2F8AA
≡ 617A 慺
2F8AB 憎 CJK COMPATIBILITY IDEOGRAPH-2F8AB
≡ 618E 憎
2F8AC 憲 CJK COMPATIBILITY IDEOGRAPH-2F8AC
≡ 61B2 憲
2F8AD 憤 CJK COMPATIBILITY IDEOGRAPH-2F8AD
≡ 61A4 憤
2F8AE 憯 CJK COMPATIBILITY IDEOGRAPH-2F8AE
≡ 61AF 憯
2F8AF 懞 CJK COMPATIBILITY IDEOGRAPH-2F8AF
≡ 61DE 懞
2F8B0 懲 CJK COMPATIBILITY IDEOGRAPH-2F8B0
≡ 61F2 懲
2F8B1 懶 CJK COMPATIBILITY IDEOGRAPH-2F8B1
≡ 61F6 懶
2F8B2 成 CJK COMPATIBILITY IDEOGRAPH-2F8B2
≡ 6210 成
2F8B3 戛 CJK COMPATIBILITY IDEOGRAPH-2F8B3
≡ 621B 戛
2F8B4 扝 CJK COMPATIBILITY IDEOGRAPH-2F8B4
≡ 625D 扝
2F8B5 抱 CJK COMPATIBILITY IDEOGRAPH-2F8B5
≡ 62B1 抱
2F8B6 拔 CJK COMPATIBILITY IDEOGRAPH-2F8B6
≡ 62D4 拔
2F8B7 捐 CJK COMPATIBILITY IDEOGRAPH-2F8B7
≡ 6350 捐

2F8B8 抜 CJK COMPATIBILITY IDEOGRAPH-2F8B8
≡ 22B0C 抜
2F8B9 挽 CJK COMPATIBILITY IDEOGRAPH-2F8B9
≡ 633D 挽
2F8BA 拼 CJK COMPATIBILITY IDEOGRAPH-2F8BA
≡ 62FC 拼
2F8BB 捨 CJK COMPATIBILITY IDEOGRAPH-2F8BB
≡ 6368 捨
2F8BC 掃 CJK COMPATIBILITY IDEOGRAPH-2F8BC
≡ 6383 掃
2F8BD 揤 CJK COMPATIBILITY IDEOGRAPH-2F8BD
≡ 63E4 揤
2F8BE 搜 CJK COMPATIBILITY IDEOGRAPH-2F8BE
≡ 22BF1 搜
2F8BF 揅 CJK COMPATIBILITY IDEOGRAPH-2F8BF
≡ 6422 揅
2F8C0 掔 CJK COMPATIBILITY IDEOGRAPH-2F8C0
≡ 63C5 掔
2F8C1 掩 CJK COMPATIBILITY IDEOGRAPH-2F8C1
≡ 63A9 掩
2F8C2 㨮 CJK COMPATIBILITY IDEOGRAPH-2F8C2
≡ 3A2E 㨮
2F8C3 摩 CJK COMPATIBILITY IDEOGRAPH-2F8C3
≡ 6469 摩
2F8C4 摾 CJK COMPATIBILITY IDEOGRAPH-2F8C4
≡ 647E 摾
2F8C5 撝 CJK COMPATIBILITY IDEOGRAPH-2F8C5
≡ 649D 撝
2F8C6 摷 CJK COMPATIBILITY IDEOGRAPH-2F8C6
≡ 6477 摷
2F8C7 㩬 CJK COMPATIBILITY IDEOGRAPH-2F8C7
≡ 3A6C 㩬
2F8C8 敏 CJK COMPATIBILITY IDEOGRAPH-2F8C8
≡ 654F 敏
2F8C9 敬 CJK COMPATIBILITY IDEOGRAPH-2F8C9
≡ 656C 敬
2F8CA 𣀊 CJK COMPATIBILITY IDEOGRAPH-2F8CA
≡ 2300A 𣀊
2F8CB 旣 CJK COMPATIBILITY IDEOGRAPH-2F8CB
≡ 65E3 旣
2F8CC 書 CJK COMPATIBILITY IDEOGRAPH-2F8CC
≡ 66F8 書
2F8CD 晉 CJK COMPATIBILITY IDEOGRAPH-2F8CD
≡ 6649 晉
2F8CE 㬙 CJK COMPATIBILITY IDEOGRAPH-2F8CE
≡ 3B19 㬙
2F8CF 暑 CJK COMPATIBILITY IDEOGRAPH-2F8CF
≡ 6691 暑
2F8D0 㬈 CJK COMPATIBILITY IDEOGRAPH-2F8D0
≡ 3B08 㬈
2F8D1 㫤 CJK COMPATIBILITY IDEOGRAPH-2F8D1
≡ 3AE4 㫤
2F8D2 冒 CJK COMPATIBILITY IDEOGRAPH-2F8D2
≡ 5192 冒
2F8D3 冕 CJK COMPATIBILITY IDEOGRAPH-2F8D3
≡ 5195 冕
2F8D4 最 CJK COMPATIBILITY IDEOGRAPH-2F8D4
≡ 6700 最
2F8D5 暜 CJK COMPATIBILITY IDEOGRAPH-2F8D5
≡ 669C 暜
2F8D6 肭 CJK COMPATIBILITY IDEOGRAPH-2F8D6
≡ 80AD 肭
2F8D7 䏙 CJK COMPATIBILITY IDEOGRAPH-2F8D7
≡ 43D9 䏙
2F8D8 朗 CJK COMPATIBILITY IDEOGRAPH-2F8D8
≡ 6717 朗
2F8D9 望 CJK COMPATIBILITY IDEOGRAPH-2F8D9
≡ 671B 望
2F8DA 朡 CJK COMPATIBILITY IDEOGRAPH-2F8DA
≡ 6721 朡
2F8DB 杞 CJK COMPATIBILITY IDEOGRAPH-2F8DB
≡ 675E 杞
2F8DC 杓 CJK COMPATIBILITY IDEOGRAPH-2F8DC
≡ 6753 杓
2F8DD 𣏃 CJK COMPATIBILITY IDEOGRAPH-2F8DD
≡ 233C3 𣏃
2F8DE 㭉 CJK COMPATIBILITY IDEOGRAPH-2F8DE
≡ 3B49 㭉
2F8DF 柺 CJK COMPATIBILITY IDEOGRAPH-2F8DF
≡ 67FA 柺
2F8E0 枅 CJK COMPATIBILITY IDEOGRAPH-2F8E0
≡ 6785 枅
2F8E1 桒 CJK COMPATIBILITY IDEOGRAPH-2F8E1
≡ 6852 桒
2F8E2 梅 CJK COMPATIBILITY IDEOGRAPH-2F8E2
≡ 6885 梅
2F8E3 𣑭 CJK COMPATIBILITY IDEOGRAPH-2F8E3
≡ 2346D 𣑭
2F8E4 梎 CJK COMPATIBILITY IDEOGRAPH-2F8E4
≡ 688E 梎
2F8E5 栟 CJK COMPATIBILITY IDEOGRAPH-2F8E5
≡ 681F 栟
2F8E6 椔 CJK COMPATIBILITY IDEOGRAPH-2F8E6
≡ 6914 椔
2F8E7 㮝 CJK COMPATIBILITY IDEOGRAPH-2F8E7
≡ 3B9D 㮝
2F8E8 楂 CJK COMPATIBILITY IDEOGRAPH-2F8E8
≡ 6942 楂
2F8E9 榣 CJK COMPATIBILITY IDEOGRAPH-2F8E9
≡ 69A3 榣
2F8EA 槪 CJK COMPATIBILITY IDEOGRAPH-2F8EA
≡ 69EA 槪
2F8EB 檨 CJK COMPATIBILITY IDEOGRAPH-2F8EB
≡ 6AA8 檨
2F8EC 𣚣 CJK COMPATIBILITY IDEOGRAPH-2F8EC
≡ 236A3 𣚣
2F8ED 櫛 CJK COMPATIBILITY IDEOGRAPH-2F8ED
≡ 6ADB 櫛
2F8EE 㰘 CJK COMPATIBILITY IDEOGRAPH-2F8EE
≡ 3C18 㰘
2F8EF 次 CJK COMPATIBILITY IDEOGRAPH-2F8EF
≡ 6B21 次
2F8F0 𣢧 CJK COMPATIBILITY IDEOGRAPH-2F8F0
≡ 238A7 𣢧
2F8F1 歔 CJK COMPATIBILITY IDEOGRAPH-2F8F1
≡ 6B54 歔
2F8F2 㱎 CJK COMPATIBILITY IDEOGRAPH-2F8F2
≡ 3C4E 㱎
2F8F3 歲 CJK COMPATIBILITY IDEOGRAPH-2F8F3
≡ 6B72 歲
2F8F4 殟 CJK COMPATIBILITY IDEOGRAPH-2F8F4
≡ 6B9F 殟
2F8F5 殺 CJK COMPATIBILITY IDEOGRAPH-2F8F5
≡ 6BBA 殺

2F8F6 殻 CJK COMPATIBILITY IDEOGRAPH-2F8F6
≡ 6BBB 殻
2F8F7 𣪍 CJK COMPATIBILITY IDEOGRAPH-2F8F7
≡ 23A8D 𣪍
2F8F8 𡴋 CJK COMPATIBILITY IDEOGRAPH-2F8F8
≡ 21D0B 𡴋
2F8F9 𣫺 CJK COMPATIBILITY IDEOGRAPH-2F8F9
≡ 23AFA 𣫺
2F8FA 汎 CJK COMPATIBILITY IDEOGRAPH-2F8FA
≡ 6C4E 汎
2F8FB 𣲼 CJK COMPATIBILITY IDEOGRAPH-2F8FB
≡ 23CBC 𣲼
2F8FC 沿 CJK COMPATIBILITY IDEOGRAPH-2F8FC
≡ 6CBF 沿
2F8FD 泍 CJK COMPATIBILITY IDEOGRAPH-2F8FD
≡ 6CCD 泍
2F8FE 汧 CJK COMPATIBILITY IDEOGRAPH-2F8FE
≡ 6C67 汧
2F8FF 洖 CJK COMPATIBILITY IDEOGRAPH-2F8FF
≡ 6D16 洖
2F900 派 CJK COMPATIBILITY IDEOGRAPH-2F900
≡ 6D3E 派
2F901 海 CJK COMPATIBILITY IDEOGRAPH-2F901
≡ 6D77 海
2F902 流 CJK COMPATIBILITY IDEOGRAPH-2F902
≡ 6D41 流
2F903 浩 CJK COMPATIBILITY IDEOGRAPH-2F903
≡ 6D69 浩
2F904 浸 CJK COMPATIBILITY IDEOGRAPH-2F904
≡ 6D78 浸
2F905 涅 CJK COMPATIBILITY IDEOGRAPH-2F905
≡ 6D85 涅
2F906 𣴞 CJK COMPATIBILITY IDEOGRAPH-2F906
≡ 23D1E 𣴞
2F907 洴 CJK COMPATIBILITY IDEOGRAPH-2F907
≡ 6D34 洴
2F908 港 CJK COMPATIBILITY IDEOGRAPH-2F908
≡ 6E2F 港
2F909 湮 CJK COMPATIBILITY IDEOGRAPH-2F909
≡ 6E6E 湮
2F90A 㴳 CJK COMPATIBILITY IDEOGRAPH-2F90A
≡ 3D33 㴳
2F90B 滋 CJK COMPATIBILITY IDEOGRAPH-2F90B
≡ 6ECB 滋
2F90C 滇 CJK COMPATIBILITY IDEOGRAPH-2F90C
≡ 6EC7 滇
2F90D 𣻑 CJK COMPATIBILITY IDEOGRAPH-2F90D
≡ 23ED1 𣻑
2F90E 淹 CJK COMPATIBILITY IDEOGRAPH-2F90E
≡ 6DF9 淹
2F90F 潮 CJK COMPATIBILITY IDEOGRAPH-2F90F
≡ 6F6E 潮
2F910 𣽞 CJK COMPATIBILITY IDEOGRAPH-2F910
≡ 23F5E 𣽞
2F911 𣾎 CJK COMPATIBILITY IDEOGRAPH-2F911
≡ 23F8E 𣾎
2F912 濆 CJK COMPATIBILITY IDEOGRAPH-2F912
≡ 6FC6 濆
2F913 瀹 CJK COMPATIBILITY IDEOGRAPH-2F913
≡ 7039 瀹
2F914 瀞 CJK COMPATIBILITY IDEOGRAPH-2F914
≡ 701E 瀞
2F915 瀛 CJK COMPATIBILITY IDEOGRAPH-2F915
≡ 701B 瀛
2F916 㶖 CJK COMPATIBILITY IDEOGRAPH-2F916
≡ 3D96 㶖
2F917 灊 CJK COMPATIBILITY IDEOGRAPH-2F917
≡ 704A 灊
2F918 災 CJK COMPATIBILITY IDEOGRAPH-2F918
≡ 707D 災
2F919 灷 CJK COMPATIBILITY IDEOGRAPH-2F919
≡ 7077 灷
2F91A 炭 CJK COMPATIBILITY IDEOGRAPH-2F91A
≡ 70AD 炭
2F91B 𠔥 CJK COMPATIBILITY IDEOGRAPH-2F91B
≡ 20525 𠔥
2F91C 煅 CJK COMPATIBILITY IDEOGRAPH-2F91C
≡ 7145 煅
2F91D 𤉣 CJK COMPATIBILITY IDEOGRAPH-2F91D
≡ 24263 𤉣
2F91E 熜 CJK COMPATIBILITY IDEOGRAPH-2F91E
≡ 719C 熜
2F91F 𤎫 CJK COMPATIBILITY IDEOGRAPH-2F91F
≡ 243AB 𤎫
2F920 爨 CJK COMPATIBILITY IDEOGRAPH-2F920
≡ 7228 爨
2F921 爵 CJK COMPATIBILITY IDEOGRAPH-2F921
≡ 7235 爵
2F922 牐 CJK COMPATIBILITY IDEOGRAPH-2F922
≡ 7250 牐
2F923 𤘈 CJK COMPATIBILITY IDEOGRAPH-2F923
≡ 24608 𤘈
2F924 犀 CJK COMPATIBILITY IDEOGRAPH-2F924
≡ 7280 犀
2F925 犕 CJK COMPATIBILITY IDEOGRAPH-2F925
≡ 7295 犕
2F926 𤜵 CJK COMPATIBILITY IDEOGRAPH-2F926
≡ 24735 𤜵
2F927 𤠔 CJK COMPATIBILITY IDEOGRAPH-2F927
≡ 24814 𤠔
2F928 獺 CJK COMPATIBILITY IDEOGRAPH-2F928
≡ 737A 獺
2F929 王 CJK COMPATIBILITY IDEOGRAPH-2F929
≡ 738B 王
2F92A 㺬 CJK COMPATIBILITY IDEOGRAPH-2F92A
≡ 3EAC 㺬
2F92B 玥 CJK COMPATIBILITY IDEOGRAPH-2F92B
≡ 73A5 玥
2F92C 㺸 CJK COMPATIBILITY IDEOGRAPH-2F92C
≡ 3EB8 㺸
2F92D 㺸 CJK COMPATIBILITY IDEOGRAPH-2F92D
≡ 3EB8 㺸
2F92E 瑇 CJK COMPATIBILITY IDEOGRAPH-2F92E
≡ 7447 瑇
2F92F 瑜 CJK COMPATIBILITY IDEOGRAPH-2F92F
≡ 745C 瑜
2F930 瑱 CJK COMPATIBILITY IDEOGRAPH-2F930
≡ 7471 瑱
2F931 璅 CJK COMPATIBILITY IDEOGRAPH-2F931
≡ 7485 璅
2F932 瓊 CJK COMPATIBILITY IDEOGRAPH-2F932
≡ 74CA 瓊
2F933 㼛 CJK COMPATIBILITY IDEOGRAPH-2F933
≡ 3F1B 㼛

2F934 猪 CJK COMPATIBILITY IDEOGRAPH-2F934
≡ 7524 猪
2F935 𤰶 CJK COMPATIBILITY IDEOGRAPH-2F935
≡ 24C36 𤰶
2F936 甾 CJK COMPATIBILITY IDEOGRAPH-2F936
≡ 753E 甾
2F937 𤲒 CJK COMPATIBILITY IDEOGRAPH-2F937
≡ 24C92 𤲒
2F938 異 CJK COMPATIBILITY IDEOGRAPH-2F938
≡ 7570 異
2F939 𢆟 CJK COMPATIBILITY IDEOGRAPH-2F939
≡ 2219F 𢆟
2F93A 瘐 CJK COMPATIBILITY IDEOGRAPH-2F93A
≡ 7610 瘐
2F93B 𤾡 CJK COMPATIBILITY IDEOGRAPH-2F93B
≡ 24FA1 𤾡
2F93C 𤾸 CJK COMPATIBILITY IDEOGRAPH-2F93C
≡ 24FB8 𤾸
2F93D 𥁄 CJK COMPATIBILITY IDEOGRAPH-2F93D
≡ 25044 𥁄
2F93E 㿼 CJK COMPATIBILITY IDEOGRAPH-2F93E
≡ 3FFC 㿼
2F93F 䀈 CJK COMPATIBILITY IDEOGRAPH-2F93F
≡ 4008 䀈
2F940 直 CJK COMPATIBILITY IDEOGRAPH-2F940
≡ 76F4 直
2F941 𥃳 CJK COMPATIBILITY IDEOGRAPH-2F941
≡ 250F3 𥃳
2F942 𥃲 CJK COMPATIBILITY IDEOGRAPH-2F942
≡ 250F2 𥃲
2F943 𥄙 CJK COMPATIBILITY IDEOGRAPH-2F943
≡ 25119 𥄙
2F944 𥄳 CJK COMPATIBILITY IDEOGRAPH-2F944
≡ 25133 𥄳
2F945 眞 CJK COMPATIBILITY IDEOGRAPH-2F945
≡ 771E 眞
2F946 真 CJK COMPATIBILITY IDEOGRAPH-2F946
≡ 771F 真
2F947 真 CJK COMPATIBILITY IDEOGRAPH-2F947
≡ 771F 真
2F948 睊 CJK COMPATIBILITY IDEOGRAPH-2F948
≡ 774A 睊
2F949 䀹 CJK COMPATIBILITY IDEOGRAPH-2F949
≡ 4039 䀹
2F94A 瞋 CJK COMPATIBILITY IDEOGRAPH-2F94A
≡ 778B 瞋
2F94B 䁆 CJK COMPATIBILITY IDEOGRAPH-2F94B
≡ 4046 䁆
2F94C 䂖 CJK COMPATIBILITY IDEOGRAPH-2F94C
≡ 4096 䂖
2F94D 𥐝 CJK COMPATIBILITY IDEOGRAPH-2F94D
≡ 2541D 𥐝
2F94E 硎 CJK COMPATIBILITY IDEOGRAPH-2F94E
≡ 784E 硎
2F94F 碌 CJK COMPATIBILITY IDEOGRAPH-2F94F
≡ 788C 碌
2F950 磌 CJK COMPATIBILITY IDEOGRAPH-2F950
≡ 78CC 磌
2F951 䃣 CJK COMPATIBILITY IDEOGRAPH-2F951
≡ 40E3 䃣
2F952 𥘦 CJK COMPATIBILITY IDEOGRAPH-2F952
≡ 25626 𥘦
2F953 祖 CJK COMPATIBILITY IDEOGRAPH-2F953
≡ 7956 祖
2F954 𥚚 CJK COMPATIBILITY IDEOGRAPH-2F954
≡ 2569A 𥚚
2F955 𥛅 CJK COMPATIBILITY IDEOGRAPH-2F955
≡ 256C5 𥛅
2F956 福 CJK COMPATIBILITY IDEOGRAPH-2F956
≡ 798F 福
2F957 秫 CJK COMPATIBILITY IDEOGRAPH-2F957
≡ 79EB 秫
2F958 䄯 CJK COMPATIBILITY IDEOGRAPH-2F958
≡ 412F 䄯
2F959 穀 CJK COMPATIBILITY IDEOGRAPH-2F959
≡ 7A40 穀
2F95A 穊 CJK COMPATIBILITY IDEOGRAPH-2F95A
≡ 7A4A 穊
2F95B 穏 CJK COMPATIBILITY IDEOGRAPH-2F95B
≡ 7A4F 穏
2F95C 𥥼 CJK COMPATIBILITY IDEOGRAPH-2F95C
≡ 2597C 𥥼
2F95D 𥪧 CJK COMPATIBILITY IDEOGRAPH-2F95D
≡ 25AA7 𥪧
2F95E 𥪧 CJK COMPATIBILITY IDEOGRAPH-2F95E
≡ 25AA7 𥪧
2F95F 竮 CJK COMPATIBILITY IDEOGRAPH-2F95F
≡ 7AEE 竮
2F960 䈂 CJK COMPATIBILITY IDEOGRAPH-2F960
≡ 4202 䈂
2F961 𥮫 CJK COMPATIBILITY IDEOGRAPH-2F961
≡ 25BAB 𥮫
2F962 篆 CJK COMPATIBILITY IDEOGRAPH-2F962
≡ 7BC6 篆
2F963 築 CJK COMPATIBILITY IDEOGRAPH-2F963
≡ 7BC9 築
2F964 䈧 CJK COMPATIBILITY IDEOGRAPH-2F964
≡ 4227 䈧
2F965 𥲀 CJK COMPATIBILITY IDEOGRAPH-2F965
≡ 25C80 𥲀
2F966 糒 CJK COMPATIBILITY IDEOGRAPH-2F966
≡ 7CD2 糒
2F967 䊠 CJK COMPATIBILITY IDEOGRAPH-2F967
≡ 42A0 䊠
2F968 糨 CJK COMPATIBILITY IDEOGRAPH-2F968
≡ 7CE8 糨
2F969 糣 CJK COMPATIBILITY IDEOGRAPH-2F969
≡ 7CE3 糣
2F96A 紀 CJK COMPATIBILITY IDEOGRAPH-2F96A
≡ 7D00 紀
2F96B 𥾆 CJK COMPATIBILITY IDEOGRAPH-2F96B
≡ 25F86 𥾆
2F96C 絣 CJK COMPATIBILITY IDEOGRAPH-2F96C
≡ 7D63 絣
2F96D 䌁 CJK COMPATIBILITY IDEOGRAPH-2F96D
≡ 4301 䌁
2F96E 緇 CJK COMPATIBILITY IDEOGRAPH-2F96E
≡ 7DC7 緇
2F96F 縂 CJK COMPATIBILITY IDEOGRAPH-2F96F
≡ 7E02 縂
2F970 繅 CJK COMPATIBILITY IDEOGRAPH-2F970
≡ 7E45 繅
2F971 䌴 CJK COMPATIBILITY IDEOGRAPH-2F971
≡ 4334 䌴

2F972 𦈨 CJK COMPATIBILITY IDEOGRAPH-2F972
≡ 26228 𦈨
2F973 𦉇 CJK COMPATIBILITY IDEOGRAPH-2F973
≡ 26247 𦉇
2F974 䍙 CJK COMPATIBILITY IDEOGRAPH-2F974
≡ 4359 䍙
2F975 𦋙 CJK COMPATIBILITY IDEOGRAPH-2F975
≡ 262D9 𦋙
2F976 罺 CJK COMPATIBILITY IDEOGRAPH-2F976
≡ 7F7A 罺
2F977 𦌾 CJK COMPATIBILITY IDEOGRAPH-2F977
≡ 2633E 𦌾
2F978 羕 CJK COMPATIBILITY IDEOGRAPH-2F978
≡ 7F95 羕
2F979 翺 CJK COMPATIBILITY IDEOGRAPH-2F979
≡ 7FFA 翺
2F97A 者 CJK COMPATIBILITY IDEOGRAPH-2F97A
≡ 8005 者
2F97B 𦓚 CJK COMPATIBILITY IDEOGRAPH-2F97B
≡ 264DA 𦓚
2F97C 𦔣 CJK COMPATIBILITY IDEOGRAPH-2F97C
≡ 26523 𦔣
2F97D 聠 CJK COMPATIBILITY IDEOGRAPH-2F97D
≡ 8060 聠
2F97E 𦖨 CJK COMPATIBILITY IDEOGRAPH-2F97E
≡ 265A8 𦖨
2F97F 聰 CJK COMPATIBILITY IDEOGRAPH-2F97F
≡ 8070 聰
2F980 𣍟 CJK COMPATIBILITY IDEOGRAPH-2F980
≡ 2335F 𣍟
2F981 䏕 CJK COMPATIBILITY IDEOGRAPH-2F981
≡ 43D5 䏕
2F982 育 CJK COMPATIBILITY IDEOGRAPH-2F982
≡ 80B2 育
2F983 脃 CJK COMPATIBILITY IDEOGRAPH-2F983
≡ 8103 脃
2F984 䐋 CJK COMPATIBILITY IDEOGRAPH-2F984
≡ 440B 䐋
2F985 脾 CJK COMPATIBILITY IDEOGRAPH-2F985
≡ 813E 脾
2F986 媵 CJK COMPATIBILITY IDEOGRAPH-2F986
≡ 5AB5 媵
2F987 𦞧 CJK COMPATIBILITY IDEOGRAPH-2F987
≡ 267A7 𦞧
2F988 𦞵 CJK COMPATIBILITY IDEOGRAPH-2F988
≡ 267B5 𦞵
2F989 𣎓 CJK COMPATIBILITY IDEOGRAPH-2F989
≡ 23393 𣎓
2F98A 𣎜 CJK COMPATIBILITY IDEOGRAPH-2F98A
≡ 2339C 𣎜
2F98B 舁 CJK COMPATIBILITY IDEOGRAPH-2F98B
≡ 8201 舁
2F98C 舄 CJK COMPATIBILITY IDEOGRAPH-2F98C
≡ 8204 舄
2F98D 辞 CJK COMPATIBILITY IDEOGRAPH-2F98D
≡ 8F9E 辞
2F98E 䑫 CJK COMPATIBILITY IDEOGRAPH-2F98E
≡ 446B 䑫
2F98F 芑 CJK COMPATIBILITY IDEOGRAPH-2F98F
≡ 8291 芑
2F990 芋 CJK COMPATIBILITY IDEOGRAPH-2F990
≡ 828B 芋
2F991 芝 CJK COMPATIBILITY IDEOGRAPH-2F991
≡ 829D 芝
2F992 劳 CJK COMPATIBILITY IDEOGRAPH-2F992
≡ 52B3 劳
2F993 花 CJK COMPATIBILITY IDEOGRAPH-2F993
≡ 82B1 花
2F994 芳 CJK COMPATIBILITY IDEOGRAPH-2F994
≡ 82B3 芳
2F995 芽 CJK COMPATIBILITY IDEOGRAPH-2F995
≡ 82BD 芽
2F996 苦 CJK COMPATIBILITY IDEOGRAPH-2F996
≡ 82E6 苦
2F997 𦬼 CJK COMPATIBILITY IDEOGRAPH-2F997
≡ 26B3C 𦬼
2F998 若 CJK COMPATIBILITY IDEOGRAPH-2F998
≡ 82E5 若
2F999 茝 CJK COMPATIBILITY IDEOGRAPH-2F999
≡ 831D 茝
2F99A 荣 CJK COMPATIBILITY IDEOGRAPH-2F99A
≡ 8363 荣
2F99B 莭 CJK COMPATIBILITY IDEOGRAPH-2F99B
≡ 83AD 莭
2F99C 茣 CJK COMPATIBILITY IDEOGRAPH-2F99C
≡ 8323 茣
2F99D 莽 CJK COMPATIBILITY IDEOGRAPH-2F99D
≡ 83BD 莽
2F99E 菧 CJK COMPATIBILITY IDEOGRAPH-2F99E
≡ 83E7 菧
2F99F 著 CJK COMPATIBILITY IDEOGRAPH-2F99F
≡ 8457 著
2F9A0 荓 CJK COMPATIBILITY IDEOGRAPH-2F9A0
≡ 8353 荓
2F9A1 菊 CJK COMPATIBILITY IDEOGRAPH-2F9A1
≡ 83CA 菊
2F9A2 菌 CJK COMPATIBILITY IDEOGRAPH-2F9A2
≡ 83CC 菌
2F9A3 菜 CJK COMPATIBILITY IDEOGRAPH-2F9A3
≡ 83DC 菜
2F9A4 𦰶 CJK COMPATIBILITY IDEOGRAPH-2F9A4
≡ 26C36 𦰶
2F9A5 𦵫 CJK COMPATIBILITY IDEOGRAPH-2F9A5
≡ 26D6B 𦵫
2F9A6 𦳕 CJK COMPATIBILITY IDEOGRAPH-2F9A6
≡ 26CD5 𦳕
2F9A7 䔫 CJK COMPATIBILITY IDEOGRAPH-2F9A7
≡ 452B 䔫
2F9A8 蓱 CJK COMPATIBILITY IDEOGRAPH-2F9A8
≡ 84F1 蓱
2F9A9 蓳 CJK COMPATIBILITY IDEOGRAPH-2F9A9
≡ 84F3 蓳
2F9AA 蔖 CJK COMPATIBILITY IDEOGRAPH-2F9AA
≡ 8516 蔖
2F9AB 𧏊 CJK COMPATIBILITY IDEOGRAPH-2F9AB
≡ 273CA 𧏊
2F9AC 蕤 CJK COMPATIBILITY IDEOGRAPH-2F9AC
≡ 8564 蕤
2F9AD 𦼬 CJK COMPATIBILITY IDEOGRAPH-2F9AD
≡ 26F2C 𦼬
2F9AE 䕝 CJK COMPATIBILITY IDEOGRAPH-2F9AE
≡ 455D 䕝
2F9AF 䕡 CJK COMPATIBILITY IDEOGRAPH-2F9AF
≡ 4561 䕡

2F9B0 䕫 CJK COMPATIBILITY IDEOGRAPH-2F9B0
≡ 26FB1 䕫
2F9B1 𧃒 CJK COMPATIBILITY IDEOGRAPH-2F9B1
≡ 270D2 𧃒
2F9B2 䕫 CJK COMPATIBILITY IDEOGRAPH-2F9B2
→ 5914 夔
→ 270CD 𧃍
→ 270F0 𧃰
≡ 456B 䕫
2F9B3 虐 CJK COMPATIBILITY IDEOGRAPH-2F9B3
≡ 8650 虐
2F9B4 虜 CJK COMPATIBILITY IDEOGRAPH-2F9B4
≡ 865C 虜
2F9B5 虧 CJK COMPATIBILITY IDEOGRAPH-2F9B5
≡ 8667 虧
2F9B6 虩 CJK COMPATIBILITY IDEOGRAPH-2F9B6
→ 27205 𧈅
≡ 8669 虩
2F9B7 蚩 CJK COMPATIBILITY IDEOGRAPH-2F9B7
≡ 86A9 蚩
2F9B8 蚈 CJK COMPATIBILITY IDEOGRAPH-2F9B8
≡ 8688 蚈
2F9B9 蜎 CJK COMPATIBILITY IDEOGRAPH-2F9B9
≡ 870E 蜎
2F9BA 蛢 CJK COMPATIBILITY IDEOGRAPH-2F9BA
≡ 86E2 蛢
2F9BB 蝹 CJK COMPATIBILITY IDEOGRAPH-2F9BB
≡ 8779 蝹
2F9BC 蜨 CJK COMPATIBILITY IDEOGRAPH-2F9BC
≡ 8728 蜨
2F9BD 蝫 CJK COMPATIBILITY IDEOGRAPH-2F9BD
≡ 876B 蝫
2F9BE 螆 CJK COMPATIBILITY IDEOGRAPH-2F9BE
≡ 8786 螆
2F9BF 䗗 CJK COMPATIBILITY IDEOGRAPH-2F9BF
≡ 45D7 䗗
2F9C0 蟡 CJK COMPATIBILITY IDEOGRAPH-2F9C0
≡ 87E1 蟡
2F9C1 蠁 CJK COMPATIBILITY IDEOGRAPH-2F9C1
≡ 8801 蠁
2F9C2 䗹 CJK COMPATIBILITY IDEOGRAPH-2F9C2
≡ 45F9 䗹
2F9C3 衠 CJK COMPATIBILITY IDEOGRAPH-2F9C3
≡ 8860 衠
2F9C4 衣 CJK COMPATIBILITY IDEOGRAPH-2F9C4
≡ 8863 衣
2F9C5 𧙧 CJK COMPATIBILITY IDEOGRAPH-2F9C5
≡ 27667 𧙧
2F9C6 裗 CJK COMPATIBILITY IDEOGRAPH-2F9C6
≡ 88D7 裗
2F9C7 裞 CJK COMPATIBILITY IDEOGRAPH-2F9C7
≡ 88DE 裞
2F9C8 䘵 CJK COMPATIBILITY IDEOGRAPH-2F9C8
≡ 4635 䘵
2F9C9 裺 CJK COMPATIBILITY IDEOGRAPH-2F9C9
≡ 88FA 裺
2F9CA 㒻 CJK COMPATIBILITY IDEOGRAPH-2F9CA
≡ 34BB 㒻
2F9CB 𧢮 CJK COMPATIBILITY IDEOGRAPH-2F9CB
→ 4695 䚕
≡ 278AE 𧢮
2F9CC 𧥦 CJK COMPATIBILITY IDEOGRAPH-2F9CC
≡ 27966 𧥦
2F9CD 䚾 CJK COMPATIBILITY IDEOGRAPH-2F9CD
≡ 46BE 䚾
2F9CE 䛇 CJK COMPATIBILITY IDEOGRAPH-2F9CE
≡ 46C7 䛇
2F9CF 誠 CJK COMPATIBILITY IDEOGRAPH-2F9CF
≡ 8AA0 誠
2F9D0 諭 CJK COMPATIBILITY IDEOGRAPH-2F9D0
≡ 8AED 諭
2F9D1 變 CJK COMPATIBILITY IDEOGRAPH-2F9D1
≡ 8B8A 變
2F9D2 豕 CJK COMPATIBILITY IDEOGRAPH-2F9D2
≡ 8C55 豕
2F9D3 𧲨 CJK COMPATIBILITY IDEOGRAPH-2F9D3
≡ 27CA8 𧲨
2F9D4 貫 CJK COMPATIBILITY IDEOGRAPH-2F9D4
≡ 8CAB 貫
2F9D5 賁 CJK COMPATIBILITY IDEOGRAPH-2F9D5
≡ 8CC1 賁
2F9D6 贛 CJK COMPATIBILITY IDEOGRAPH-2F9D6
→ 25AD4 𥫔
≡ 8D1B 贛
2F9D7 起 CJK COMPATIBILITY IDEOGRAPH-2F9D7
≡ 8D77 起
2F9D8 𧼯 CJK COMPATIBILITY IDEOGRAPH-2F9D8
≡ 27F2F 𧼯
2F9D9 𠠄 CJK COMPATIBILITY IDEOGRAPH-2F9D9
≡ 20804 𠠄
2F9DA 跋 CJK COMPATIBILITY IDEOGRAPH-2F9DA
≡ 8DCB 跋
2F9DB 趼 CJK COMPATIBILITY IDEOGRAPH-2F9DB
≡ 8DBC 趼
2F9DC 跰 CJK COMPATIBILITY IDEOGRAPH-2F9DC
≡ 8DF0 跰
2F9DD 𠣞 CJK COMPATIBILITY IDEOGRAPH-2F9DD
≡ 208DE 𠣞
2F9DE 軔 CJK COMPATIBILITY IDEOGRAPH-2F9DE
≡ 8ED4 軔
2F9DF 輸 CJK COMPATIBILITY IDEOGRAPH-2F9DF
≡ 8F38 輸
2F9E0 𨗒 CJK COMPATIBILITY IDEOGRAPH-2F9E0
≡ 285D2 𨗒
2F9E1 𨗭 CJK COMPATIBILITY IDEOGRAPH-2F9E1
≡ 285ED 𨗭
2F9E2 邔 CJK COMPATIBILITY IDEOGRAPH-2F9E2
≡ 9094 邔
2F9E3 郱 CJK COMPATIBILITY IDEOGRAPH-2F9E3
≡ 90F1 郱
2F9E4 鄑 CJK COMPATIBILITY IDEOGRAPH-2F9E4
≡ 9111 鄑
2F9E5 𨜮 CJK COMPATIBILITY IDEOGRAPH-2F9E5
≡ 2872E 𨜮
2F9E6 鄛 CJK COMPATIBILITY IDEOGRAPH-2F9E6
≡ 911B 鄛
2F9E7 鈸 CJK COMPATIBILITY IDEOGRAPH-2F9E7
≡ 9238 鈸
2F9E8 鋗 CJK COMPATIBILITY IDEOGRAPH-2F9E8
≡ 92D7 鋗
2F9E9 鋘 CJK COMPATIBILITY IDEOGRAPH-2F9E9
≡ 92D8 鋘
2F9EA 鉼 CJK COMPATIBILITY IDEOGRAPH-2F9EA
≡ 927C 鉼
2F9EB 鏹 CJK COMPATIBILITY IDEOGRAPH-2F9EB
≡ 93F9 鏹

2F9EC 鐯 CJK COMPATIBILITY IDEOGRAPH-2F9EC
≡ 9415 鐕
2F9ED 𨯺 CJK COMPATIBILITY IDEOGRAPH-2F9ED
≡ 28BFA 𨯺
2F9EE 開 CJK COMPATIBILITY IDEOGRAPH-2F9EE
≡ 958B 開
2F9EF 䦕 CJK COMPATIBILITY IDEOGRAPH-2F9EF
≡ 4995 䦕
2F9F0 閷 CJK COMPATIBILITY IDEOGRAPH-2F9F0
≡ 95B7 閷
2F9F1 𨵷 CJK COMPATIBILITY IDEOGRAPH-2F9F1
≡ 28D77 𨵷
2F9F2 䧦 CJK COMPATIBILITY IDEOGRAPH-2F9F2
≡ 49E6 䧦
2F9F3 雃 CJK COMPATIBILITY IDEOGRAPH-2F9F3
≡ 96C3 雃
2F9F4 嶲 CJK COMPATIBILITY IDEOGRAPH-2F9F4
≡ 5DB2 嶲
2F9F5 霣 CJK COMPATIBILITY IDEOGRAPH-2F9F5
≡ 9723 霣
2F9F6 𩅅 CJK COMPATIBILITY IDEOGRAPH-2F9F6
≡ 29145 𩅅
2F9F7 𩈚 CJK COMPATIBILITY IDEOGRAPH-2F9F7
≡ 2921A 𩈚
2F9F8 䩮 CJK COMPATIBILITY IDEOGRAPH-2F9F8
≡ 4A6E 䩮
2F9F9 䩶 CJK COMPATIBILITY IDEOGRAPH-2F9F9
≡ 4A76 䩶
2F9FA 韠 CJK COMPATIBILITY IDEOGRAPH-2F9FA
≡ 97E0 韠
2F9FB 𩐊 CJK COMPATIBILITY IDEOGRAPH-2F9FB
≡ 2940A 𩐊
2F9FC 䪲 CJK COMPATIBILITY IDEOGRAPH-2F9FC
≡ 4AB2 䪲
2F9FD 𩒖 CJK COMPATIBILITY IDEOGRAPH-2F9FD
≡ 29496 𩒖
2F9FE 頋 CJK COMPATIBILITY IDEOGRAPH-2F9FE
≡ 980B 頋
2F9FF 頋 CJK COMPATIBILITY IDEOGRAPH-2F9FF
≡ 980B 頋
2FA00 頩 CJK COMPATIBILITY IDEOGRAPH-2FA00
≡ 9829 頩
2FA01 𩖶 CJK COMPATIBILITY IDEOGRAPH-2FA01
≡ 295B6 𩖶
2FA02 飢 CJK COMPATIBILITY IDEOGRAPH-2FA02
≡ 98E2 飢
2FA03 䬳 CJK COMPATIBILITY IDEOGRAPH-2FA03
≡ 4B33 䬳
2FA04 餩 CJK COMPATIBILITY IDEOGRAPH-2FA04
≡ 9929 餩
2FA05 馧 CJK COMPATIBILITY IDEOGRAPH-2FA05
≡ 99A7 馧
2FA06 駂 CJK COMPATIBILITY IDEOGRAPH-2FA06
≡ 99C2 駂
2FA07 駾 CJK COMPATIBILITY IDEOGRAPH-2FA07
≡ 99FE 駾
2FA08 䯎 CJK COMPATIBILITY IDEOGRAPH-2FA08
≡ 4BCE 䯎
2FA09 𩬰 CJK COMPATIBILITY IDEOGRAPH-2FA09
≡ 29B30 𩬰
2FA0A 鬒 CJK COMPATIBILITY IDEOGRAPH-2FA0A
≡ 9B12 鬒
2FA0B 鱀 CJK COMPATIBILITY IDEOGRAPH-2FA0B
≡ 9C40 鱀
2FA0C 鳽 CJK COMPATIBILITY IDEOGRAPH-2FA0C
≡ 9CFD 鳽
2FA0D 䳎 CJK COMPATIBILITY IDEOGRAPH-2FA0D
≡ 4CCE 䳎
2FA0E 䳭 CJK COMPATIBILITY IDEOGRAPH-2FA0E
≡ 4CED 䳭
2FA0F 鵧 CJK COMPATIBILITY IDEOGRAPH-2FA0F
≡ 9D67 鵧
2FA10 𪃎 CJK COMPATIBILITY IDEOGRAPH-2FA10
≡ 2A0CE 𪃎
2FA11 䳸 CJK COMPATIBILITY IDEOGRAPH-2FA11
≡ 4CF8 䳸
2FA12 𪄅 CJK COMPATIBILITY IDEOGRAPH-2FA12
≡ 2A105 𪄅
2FA13 𪈎 CJK COMPATIBILITY IDEOGRAPH-2FA13
≡ 2A20E 𪈎
2FA14 𪊑 CJK COMPATIBILITY IDEOGRAPH-2FA14
≡ 2A291 𪊑
2FA15 麻 CJK COMPATIBILITY IDEOGRAPH-2FA15
≡ 9EBB 麻
2FA16 䵖 CJK COMPATIBILITY IDEOGRAPH-2FA16
≡ 4D56 䵖
2FA17 黹 CJK COMPATIBILITY IDEOGRAPH-2FA17
≡ 9EF9 黹
2FA18 黾 CJK COMPATIBILITY IDEOGRAPH-2FA18
≡ 9EFE 黾
2FA19 鼅 CJK COMPATIBILITY IDEOGRAPH-2FA19
≡ 9F05 鼅
2FA1A 鼏 CJK COMPATIBILITY IDEOGRAPH-2FA1A
≡ 9F0F 鼏
2FA1B 鼖 CJK COMPATIBILITY IDEOGRAPH-2FA1B
≡ 9F16 鼖
2FA1C 鼻 CJK COMPATIBILITY IDEOGRAPH-2FA1C
≡ 9F3B 鼻
2FA1D 𪘀 CJK COMPATIBILITY IDEOGRAPH-2FA1D
≡ 2A600 𪘀

	E000	E001	E002	E003	E004	E005	E006	E007
0			SP E0020	0 E0030	@ E0040	P E0050	` E0060	p E0070
1	E0001		! E0021	1 E0031	A E0041	Q E0051	a E0061	q E0071
2			" E0022	2 E0032	B E0042	R E0052	b E0062	r E0072
3			# E0023	3 E0033	C E0043	S E0053	c E0063	s E0073
4			$ E0024	4 E0034	D E0044	T E0054	d E0064	t E0074
5			% E0025	5 E0035	E E0045	U E0055	e E0065	u E0075
6			& E0026	6 E0036	F E0046	V E0056	f E0066	v E0076
7			' E0027	7 E0037	G E0047	W E0057	g E0067	w E0077
8			(E0028	8 E0038	H E0048	X E0058	h E0068	x E0078
9			) E0029	9 E0039	I E0049	Y E0059	i E0069	y E0079
A			* E002A	: E003A	J E004A	Z E005A	j E006A	z E007A
B			+ E002B	; E003B	K E004B	[E005B	k E006B	{ E007B
C			, E002C	< E003C	L E004C	\ E005C	l E006C	| E007C
D			- E002D	= E003D	M E004D	] E005D	m E006D	} E007D
E			. E002E	> E003E	N E004E	^ E005E	n E006E	~ E007E
F			/ E002F	? E003F	O E004F	_ E005F	o E006F	E007F

Tag identifiers

E0001 LANGUAGE TAG

Tag components

E0020 TAG SPACE
E0021 TAG EXCLAMATION MARK
E0022 TAG QUOTATION MARK
E0023 TAG NUMBER SIGN
E0024 TAG DOLLAR SIGN
E0025 TAG PERCENT SIGN
E0026 TAG AMPERSAND
E0027 TAG APOSTROPHE
E0028 TAG LEFT PARENTHESIS
E0029 TAG RIGHT PARENTHESIS
E002A TAG ASTERISK
E002B TAG PLUS SIGN
E002C TAG COMMA
E002D TAG HYPHEN-MINUS
E002E TAG FULL STOP
E002F TAG SOLIDUS
E0030 TAG DIGIT ZERO
E0031 TAG DIGIT ONE
E0032 TAG DIGIT TWO
E0033 TAG DIGIT THREE
E0034 TAG DIGIT FOUR
E0035 TAG DIGIT FIVE
E0036 TAG DIGIT SIX
E0037 TAG DIGIT SEVEN
E0038 TAG DIGIT EIGHT
E0039 TAG DIGIT NINE
E003A TAG COLON
E003B TAG SEMICOLON
E003C TAG LESS-THAN SIGN
E003D TAG EQUALS SIGN
E003E TAG GREATER-THAN SIGN
E003F TAG QUESTION MARK
E0040 TAG COMMERCIAL AT
E0041 TAG LATIN CAPITAL LETTER A
E0042 TAG LATIN CAPITAL LETTER B
E0043 TAG LATIN CAPITAL LETTER C
E0044 TAG LATIN CAPITAL LETTER D
E0045 TAG LATIN CAPITAL LETTER E
E0046 TAG LATIN CAPITAL LETTER F
E0047 TAG LATIN CAPITAL LETTER G
E0048 TAG LATIN CAPITAL LETTER H
E0049 TAG LATIN CAPITAL LETTER I
E004A TAG LATIN CAPITAL LETTER J
E004B TAG LATIN CAPITAL LETTER K
E004C TAG LATIN CAPITAL LETTER L
E004D TAG LATIN CAPITAL LETTER M
E004E TAG LATIN CAPITAL LETTER N
E004F TAG LATIN CAPITAL LETTER O
E0050 TAG LATIN CAPITAL LETTER P
E0051 TAG LATIN CAPITAL LETTER Q
E0052 TAG LATIN CAPITAL LETTER R
E0053 TAG LATIN CAPITAL LETTER S
E0054 TAG LATIN CAPITAL LETTER T
E0055 TAG LATIN CAPITAL LETTER U
E0056 TAG LATIN CAPITAL LETTER V
E0057 TAG LATIN CAPITAL LETTER W
E0058 TAG LATIN CAPITAL LETTER X
E0059 TAG LATIN CAPITAL LETTER Y
E005A TAG LATIN CAPITAL LETTER Z
E005B TAG LEFT SQUARE BRACKET
E005C TAG REVERSE SOLIDUS
E005D TAG RIGHT SQUARE BRACKET
E005E TAG CIRCUMFLEX ACCENT
E005F TAG LOW LINE
E0060 TAG GRAVE ACCENT
E0061 TAG LATIN SMALL LETTER A
E0062 TAG LATIN SMALL LETTER B
E0063 TAG LATIN SMALL LETTER C
E0064 TAG LATIN SMALL LETTER D
E0065 TAG LATIN SMALL LETTER E
E0066 TAG LATIN SMALL LETTER F
E0067 TAG LATIN SMALL LETTER G
E0068 TAG LATIN SMALL LETTER H
E0069 TAG LATIN SMALL LETTER I
E006A TAG LATIN SMALL LETTER J
E006B TAG LATIN SMALL LETTER K
E006C TAG LATIN SMALL LETTER L
E006D TAG LATIN SMALL LETTER M
E006E TAG LATIN SMALL LETTER N
E006F TAG LATIN SMALL LETTER O
E0070 TAG LATIN SMALL LETTER P
E0071 TAG LATIN SMALL LETTER Q
E0072 TAG LATIN SMALL LETTER R
E0073 TAG LATIN SMALL LETTER S
E0074 TAG LATIN SMALL LETTER T
E0075 TAG LATIN SMALL LETTER U
E0076 TAG LATIN SMALL LETTER V
E0077 TAG LATIN SMALL LETTER W
E0078 TAG LATIN SMALL LETTER X
E0079 TAG LATIN SMALL LETTER Y
E007A TAG LATIN SMALL LETTER Z
E007B TAG LEFT CURLY BRACKET
E007C TAG VERTICAL LINE
E007D TAG RIGHT CURLY BRACKET
E007E TAG TILDE
E007F CANCEL TAG

	E010	E011	E012	E013	E014	E015	E016	E017	E018	E019	E01A	E01B	E01C	E01D	E01E
0	VS 17 E0100	VS 33 E0110	VS 49 E0120	VS 65 E0130	VS 81 E0140	VS 97 E0150	VS 113 E0160	VS 129 E0170	VS 145 E0180	VS 161 E0190	VS 177 E01A0	VS 193 E01B0	VS 209 E01C0	VS 225 E01D0	VS 241 E01E0
1	VS 18 E0101	VS 34 E0111	VS 50 E0121	VS 66 E0131	VS 82 E0141	VS 98 E0151	VS 114 E0161	VS 130 E0171	VS 146 E0181	VS 162 E0191	VS 178 E01A1	VS 194 E01B1	VS 210 E01C1	VS 226 E01D1	VS 242 E01E1
2	VS 19 E0102	VS 35 E0112	VS 51 E0122	VS 67 E0132	VS 83 E0142	VS 99 E0152	VS 115 E0162	VS 131 E0172	VS 147 E0182	VS 163 E0192	VS 179 E01A2	VS 195 E01B2	VS 211 E01C2	VS 227 E01D2	VS 243 E01E2
3	VS 20 E0103	VS 36 E0113	VS 52 E0123	VS 68 E0133	VS 84 E0143	VS 100 E0153	VS 116 E0163	VS 132 E0173	VS 148 E0183	VS 164 E0193	VS 180 E01A3	VS 196 E01B3	VS 212 E01C3	VS 228 E01D3	VS 244 E01E3
4	VS 21 E0104	VS 37 E0114	VS 53 E0124	VS 69 E0134	VS 85 E0144	VS 101 E0154	VS 117 E0164	VS 133 E0174	VS 149 E0184	VS 165 E0194	VS 181 E01A4	VS 197 E01B4	VS 213 E01C4	VS 229 E01D4	VS 245 E01E4
5	VS 22 E0105	VS 38 E0115	VS 54 E0125	VS 70 E0135	VS 86 E0145	VS 102 E0155	VS 118 E0165	VS 134 E0175	VS 150 E0185	VS 166 E0195	VS 182 E01A5	VS 198 E01B5	VS 214 E01C5	VS 230 E01D5	VS 246 E01E5
6	VS 23 E0106	VS 39 E0116	VS 55 E0126	VS 71 E0136	VS 87 E0146	VS 103 E0156	VS 119 E0166	VS 135 E0176	VS 151 E0186	VS 167 E0196	VS 183 E01A6	VS 199 E01B6	VS 215 E01C6	VS 231 E01D6	VS 247 E01E6
7	VS 24 E0107	VS 40 E0117	VS 56 E0127	VS 72 E0137	VS 88 E0147	VS 104 E0157	VS 120 E0167	VS 136 E0177	VS 152 E0187	VS 168 E0197	VS 184 E01A7	VS 200 E01B7	VS 216 E01C7	VS 232 E01D7	VS 248 E01E7
8	VS 25 E0108	VS 41 E0118	VS 57 E0128	VS 73 E0138	VS 89 E0148	VS 105 E0158	VS 121 E0168	VS 137 E0178	VS 153 E0188	VS 169 E0198	VS 185 E01A8	VS 201 E01B8	VS 217 E01C8	VS 233 E01D8	VS 249 E01E8
9	VS 26 E0109	VS 42 E0119	VS 58 E0129	VS 74 E0139	VS 90 E0149	VS 106 E0159	VS 122 E0169	VS 138 E0179	VS 154 E0189	VS 170 E0199	VS 186 E01A9	VS 202 E01B9	VS 218 E01C9	VS 234 E01D9	VS 250 E01E9
A	VS 27 E010A	VS 43 E011A	VS 59 E012A	VS 75 E013A	VS 91 E014A	VS 107 E015A	VS 123 E016A	VS 139 E017A	VS 155 E018A	VS 171 E019A	VS 187 E01AA	VS 203 E01BA	VS 219 E01CA	VS 235 E01DA	VS 251 E01EA
B	VS 28 E010B	VS 44 E011B	VS 60 E012B	VS 76 E013B	VS 92 E014B	VS 108 E015B	VS 124 E016B	VS 140 E017B	VS 156 E018B	VS 172 E019B	VS 188 E01AB	VS 204 E01BB	VS 220 E01CB	VS 236 E01DB	VS 252 E01EB
C	VS 29 E010C	VS 45 E011C	VS 61 E012C	VS 77 E013C	VS 93 E014C	VS 109 E015C	VS 125 E016C	VS 141 E017C	VS 157 E018C	VS 173 E019C	VS 189 E01AC	VS 205 E01BC	VS 221 E01CC	VS 237 E01DC	VS 253 E01EC
D	VS 30 E010D	VS 46 E011D	VS 62 E012D	VS 78 E013D	VS 94 E014D	VS 110 E015D	VS 126 E016D	VS 142 E017D	VS 158 E018D	VS 174 E019D	VS 190 E01AD	VS 206 E01BD	VS 222 E01CD	VS 238 E01DD	VS 254 E01ED
E	VS 31 E010E	VS 47 E011E	VS 63 E012E	VS 79 E013E	VS 95 E014E	VS 111 E015E	VS 127 E016E	VS 143 E017E	VS 159 E018E	VS 175 E019E	VS 191 E01AE	VS 207 E01BE	VS 223 E01CE	VS 239 E01DE	VS 255 E01EE
F	VS 32 E010F	VS 48 E011F	VS 64 E012F	VS 80 E013F	VS 96 E014F	VS 112 E015F	VS 128 E016F	VS 144 E017F	VS 160 E018F	VS 176 E019F	VS 192 E01AF	VS 208 E01BF	VS 224 E01CF	VS 240 E01DF	VS 256 E01EF

These complete the set started at FE00 to FE0F

Variation selectors

E0100 VS17 VARIATION SELECTOR-17
• these are abbreviated VS17, and so on
E0101 VS18 VARIATION SELECTOR-18
E0102 VS19 VARIATION SELECTOR-19
E0103 VS20 VARIATION SELECTOR-20
E0104 VS21 VARIATION SELECTOR-21
E0105 VS22 VARIATION SELECTOR-22
E0106 VS23 VARIATION SELECTOR-23
E0107 VS24 VARIATION SELECTOR-24
E0108 VS25 VARIATION SELECTOR-25
E0109 VS26 VARIATION SELECTOR-26
E010A VS27 VARIATION SELECTOR-27
E010B VS28 VARIATION SELECTOR-28
E010C VS29 VARIATION SELECTOR-29
E010D VS30 VARIATION SELECTOR-30
E010E VS31 VARIATION SELECTOR-31
E010F VS32 VARIATION SELECTOR-32
E0110 VS33 VARIATION SELECTOR-33
E0111 VS34 VARIATION SELECTOR-34
E0112 VS35 VARIATION SELECTOR-35
E0113 VS36 VARIATION SELECTOR-36
E0114 VS37 VARIATION SELECTOR-37
E0115 VS38 VARIATION SELECTOR-38
E0116 VS39 VARIATION SELECTOR-39
E0117 VS40 VARIATION SELECTOR-40
E0118 VS41 VARIATION SELECTOR-41
E0119 VS42 VARIATION SELECTOR-42
E011A VS43 VARIATION SELECTOR-43
E011B VS44 VARIATION SELECTOR-44
E011C VS45 VARIATION SELECTOR-45
E011D VS46 VARIATION SELECTOR-46
E011E VS47 VARIATION SELECTOR-47
E011F VS48 VARIATION SELECTOR-48
E0120 VS49 VARIATION SELECTOR-49
E0121 VS50 VARIATION SELECTOR-50
E0122 VS51 VARIATION SELECTOR-51
E0123 VS52 VARIATION SELECTOR-52
E0124 VS53 VARIATION SELECTOR-53
E0125 VS54 VARIATION SELECTOR-54
E0126 VS55 VARIATION SELECTOR-55
E0127 VS56 VARIATION SELECTOR-56
E0128 VS57 VARIATION SELECTOR-57
E0129 VS58 VARIATION SELECTOR-58
E012A VS59 VARIATION SELECTOR-59
E012B VS60 VARIATION SELECTOR-60
E012C VS61 VARIATION SELECTOR-61
E012D VS62 VARIATION SELECTOR-62
E012E VS63 VARIATION SELECTOR-63
E012F VS64 VARIATION SELECTOR-64
E0130 VS65 VARIATION SELECTOR-65
E0131 VS66 VARIATION SELECTOR-66
E0132 VS67 VARIATION SELECTOR-67
E0133 VS68 VARIATION SELECTOR-68
E0134 VS69 VARIATION SELECTOR-69
E0135 VS70 VARIATION SELECTOR-70
E0136 VS71 VARIATION SELECTOR-71
E0137 VS72 VARIATION SELECTOR-72
E0138 VS73 VARIATION SELECTOR-73
E0139 VS74 VARIATION SELECTOR-74
E013A VS75 VARIATION SELECTOR-75
E013B VS76 VARIATION SELECTOR-76
E013C VS77 VARIATION SELECTOR-77
E013D VS78 VARIATION SELECTOR-78
E013E VS79 VARIATION SELECTOR-79
E013F VS80 VARIATION SELECTOR-80
E0140 VS81 VARIATION SELECTOR-81
E0141 VS82 VARIATION SELECTOR-82
E0142 VS83 VARIATION SELECTOR-83
E0143 VS84 VARIATION SELECTOR-84
E0144 VS85 VARIATION SELECTOR-85
E0145 VS86 VARIATION SELECTOR-86
E0146 VS87 VARIATION SELECTOR-87
E0147 VS88 VARIATION SELECTOR-88
E0148 VS89 VARIATION SELECTOR-89
E0149 VS90 VARIATION SELECTOR-90
E014A VS91 VARIATION SELECTOR-91
E014B VS92 VARIATION SELECTOR-92
E014C VS93 VARIATION SELECTOR-93
E014D VS94 VARIATION SELECTOR-94
E014E VS95 VARIATION SELECTOR-95
E014F VS96 VARIATION SELECTOR-96
E0150 VS97 VARIATION SELECTOR-97
E0151 VS98 VARIATION SELECTOR-98
E0152 VS99 VARIATION SELECTOR-99
E0153 VS100 VARIATION SELECTOR-100
E0154 VS101 VARIATION SELECTOR-101
E0155 VS102 VARIATION SELECTOR-102
E0156 VS103 VARIATION SELECTOR-103
E0157 VS104 VARIATION SELECTOR-104
E0158 VS105 VARIATION SELECTOR-105
E0159 VS106 VARIATION SELECTOR-106
E015A VS107 VARIATION SELECTOR-107
E015B VS108 VARIATION SELECTOR-108
E015C VS109 VARIATION SELECTOR-109
E015D VS110 VARIATION SELECTOR-110
E015E VS111 VARIATION SELECTOR-111
E015F VS112 VARIATION SELECTOR-112
E0160 VS113 VARIATION SELECTOR-113
E0161 VS114 VARIATION SELECTOR-114
E0162 VS115 VARIATION SELECTOR-115
E0163 VS116 VARIATION SELECTOR-116
E0164 VS117 VARIATION SELECTOR-117
E0165 VS118 VARIATION SELECTOR-118
E0166 VS119 VARIATION SELECTOR-119
E0167 VS120 VARIATION SELECTOR-120
E0168 VS121 VARIATION SELECTOR-121
E0169 VS122 VARIATION SELECTOR-122
E016A VS123 VARIATION SELECTOR-123
E016B VS124 VARIATION SELECTOR-124
E016C VS125 VARIATION SELECTOR-125
E016D VS126 VARIATION SELECTOR-126
E016E VS127 VARIATION SELECTOR-127
E016F VS128 VARIATION SELECTOR-128
E0170 VS129 VARIATION SELECTOR-129
E0171 VS130 VARIATION SELECTOR-130
E0172 VS131 VARIATION SELECTOR-131
E0173 VS132 VARIATION SELECTOR-132
E0174 VS133 VARIATION SELECTOR-133
E0175 VS134 VARIATION SELECTOR-134
E0176 VS135 VARIATION SELECTOR-135
E0177 VS136 VARIATION SELECTOR-136
E0178 VS137 VARIATION SELECTOR-137
E0179 VS138 VARIATION SELECTOR-138
E017A VS139 VARIATION SELECTOR-139

E017B VS 140 VARIATION SELECTOR-140
E017C VS 141 VARIATION SELECTOR-141
E017D VS 142 VARIATION SELECTOR-142
E017E VS 143 VARIATION SELECTOR-143
E017F VS 144 VARIATION SELECTOR-144
E0180 VS 145 VARIATION SELECTOR-145
E0181 VS 146 VARIATION SELECTOR-146
E0182 VS 147 VARIATION SELECTOR-147
E0183 VS 148 VARIATION SELECTOR-148
E0184 VS 149 VARIATION SELECTOR-149
E0185 VS 150 VARIATION SELECTOR-150
E0186 VS 151 VARIATION SELECTOR-151
E0187 VS 152 VARIATION SELECTOR-152
E0188 VS 153 VARIATION SELECTOR-153
E0189 VS 154 VARIATION SELECTOR-154
E018A VS 155 VARIATION SELECTOR-155
E018B VS 156 VARIATION SELECTOR-156
E018C VS 157 VARIATION SELECTOR-157
E018D VS 158 VARIATION SELECTOR-158
E018E VS 159 VARIATION SELECTOR-159
E018F VS 160 VARIATION SELECTOR-160
E0190 VS 161 VARIATION SELECTOR-161
E0191 VS 162 VARIATION SELECTOR-162
E0192 VS 163 VARIATION SELECTOR-163
E0193 VS 164 VARIATION SELECTOR-164
E0194 VS 165 VARIATION SELECTOR-165
E0195 VS 166 VARIATION SELECTOR-166
E0196 VS 167 VARIATION SELECTOR-167
E0197 VS 168 VARIATION SELECTOR-168
E0198 VS 169 VARIATION SELECTOR-169
E0199 VS 170 VARIATION SELECTOR-170
E019A VS 171 VARIATION SELECTOR-171
E019B VS 172 VARIATION SELECTOR-172
E019C VS 173 VARIATION SELECTOR-173
E019D VS 174 VARIATION SELECTOR-174
E019E VS 175 VARIATION SELECTOR-175
E019F VS 176 VARIATION SELECTOR-176
E01A0 VS 177 VARIATION SELECTOR-177
E01A1 VS 178 VARIATION SELECTOR-178
E01A2 VS 179 VARIATION SELECTOR-179
E01A3 VS 180 VARIATION SELECTOR-180
E01A4 VS 181 VARIATION SELECTOR-181
E01A5 VS 182 VARIATION SELECTOR-182
E01A6 VS 183 VARIATION SELECTOR-183
E01A7 VS 184 VARIATION SELECTOR-184
E01A8 VS 185 VARIATION SELECTOR-185
E01A9 VS 186 VARIATION SELECTOR-186
E01AA VS 187 VARIATION SELECTOR-187
E01AB VS 188 VARIATION SELECTOR-188
E01AC VS 189 VARIATION SELECTOR-189
E01AD VS 190 VARIATION SELECTOR-190
E01AE VS 191 VARIATION SELECTOR-191
E01AF VS 192 VARIATION SELECTOR-192
E01B0 VS 193 VARIATION SELECTOR-193
E01B1 VS 194 VARIATION SELECTOR-194
E01B2 VS 195 VARIATION SELECTOR-195
E01B3 VS 196 VARIATION SELECTOR-196
E01B4 VS 197 VARIATION SELECTOR-197
E01B5 VS 198 VARIATION SELECTOR-198
E01B6 VS 199 VARIATION SELECTOR-199
E01B7 VS 200 VARIATION SELECTOR-200
E01B8 VS 201 VARIATION SELECTOR-201
E01B9 VS 202 VARIATION SELECTOR-202
E01BA VS 203 VARIATION SELECTOR-203
E01BB VS 204 VARIATION SELECTOR-204
E01BC VS 205 VARIATION SELECTOR-205
E01BD VS 206 VARIATION SELECTOR-206
E01BE VS 207 VARIATION SELECTOR-207
E01BF VS 208 VARIATION SELECTOR-208
E01C0 VS 209 VARIATION SELECTOR-209
E01C1 VS 210 VARIATION SELECTOR-210
E01C2 VS 211 VARIATION SELECTOR-211
E01C3 VS 212 VARIATION SELECTOR-212
E01C4 VS 213 VARIATION SELECTOR-213
E01C5 VS 214 VARIATION SELECTOR-214
E01C6 VS 215 VARIATION SELECTOR-215
E01C7 VS 216 VARIATION SELECTOR-216
E01C8 VS 217 VARIATION SELECTOR-217
E01C9 VS 218 VARIATION SELECTOR-218
E01CA VS 219 VARIATION SELECTOR-219
E01CB VS 220 VARIATION SELECTOR-220
E01CC VS 221 VARIATION SELECTOR-221
E01CD VS 222 VARIATION SELECTOR-222
E01CE VS 223 VARIATION SELECTOR-223
E01CF VS 224 VARIATION SELECTOR-224
E01D0 VS 225 VARIATION SELECTOR-225
E01D1 VS 226 VARIATION SELECTOR-226
E01D2 VS 227 VARIATION SELECTOR-227
E01D3 VS 228 VARIATION SELECTOR-228
E01D4 VS 229 VARIATION SELECTOR-229
E01D5 VS 230 VARIATION SELECTOR-230
E01D6 VS 231 VARIATION SELECTOR-231
E01D7 VS 232 VARIATION SELECTOR-232
E01D8 VS 233 VARIATION SELECTOR-233
E01D9 VS 234 VARIATION SELECTOR-234
E01DA VS 235 VARIATION SELECTOR-235
E01DB VS 236 VARIATION SELECTOR-236
E01DC VS 237 VARIATION SELECTOR-237
E01DD VS 238 VARIATION SELECTOR-238
E01DE VS 239 VARIATION SELECTOR-239
E01DF VS 240 VARIATION SELECTOR-240
E01E0 VS 241 VARIATION SELECTOR-241
E01E1 VS 242 VARIATION SELECTOR-242
E01E2 VS 243 VARIATION SELECTOR-243
E01E3 VS 244 VARIATION SELECTOR-244
E01E4 VS 245 VARIATION SELECTOR-245
E01E5 VS 246 VARIATION SELECTOR-246
E01E6 VS 247 VARIATION SELECTOR-247
E01E7 VS 248 VARIATION SELECTOR-248
E01E8 VS 249 VARIATION SELECTOR-249
E01E9 VS 250 VARIATION SELECTOR-250
E01EA VS 251 VARIATION SELECTOR-251
E01EB VS 252 VARIATION SELECTOR-252
E01EC VS 253 VARIATION SELECTOR-253
E01ED VS 254 VARIATION SELECTOR-254
E01EE VS 255 VARIATION SELECTOR-255
E01EF VS 256 VARIATION SELECTOR-256

CHAPTER
18

Chapter 18

Han Radical-Stroke Index

To expedite locating specific Han ideographic characters within the Unicode Han ideographic set, this chapter contains a radical-stroke index for the most important ideographs. Specifically, the radical-stroke index in this chapter covers the 9,810 characters within IICore (see *Section 12.1, Han*). A radical-stroke chart covering all of Unihan is available on the CD-ROM and the Unicode Web site.

Under the traditional radical-stroke system, each Han ideograph is considered to be written with one of a number of different character elements or radicals and a number of additional strokes. For example, the character 說 has the radical 言 and seven additional strokes. To find the character 說 within a dictionary, one would first locate the section for its radical, 言, and then find the subsection for characters with seven additional strokes.

This method is complicated by the fact that there are occasional ambiguities in the counting of strokes. Even worse, some characters are considered by different authorities to be written with different radicals; there is not, in fact, universal agreement about which set of radicals to use for certain characters, particularly with the increased use of simplified characters.

The most influential authority for radical-stroke information is the eighteenth-century *KangXi* dictionary, which contains 214 radicals. The main problem in using *KangXi* radicals today is that many simplified characters are difficult to classify under any of the 214 *KangXi* radicals. As a result, various modern radical sets have been introduced. None, however, is in general use, and the 214 *KangXi* radicals remain the best known. See "CJK and KangXi Radicals" in *Section 12.1, Han*.

The Unicode radical-stroke charts are based on the *KangXi* radicals. The Unicode Standard follows a number of different sources for radical-stroke classification. Where two sources are at odds as to radical or stroke count for a given character, the character is shown in *both* positions in the radical-stroke charts.

Simplified characters are, as a rule, considered to have the same radical as their traditional forms and are found under the appropriate radical. For example, the character 伣 is found under the same radical, 人, as its traditional form (俔).

1 stroke

2 strokes

3 strokes

4 strokes

一 1

一 4E00 **1** 丁 4E01 七 4E03 **2** 三 4E09 亐 4E90 上 4E0A 下 4E0B 丈 4E08 万 4E07 凡 51E1 兀 5140 卄 5344 **3** 与 4E0E
开 5F00 天 5929 专 4E13 丐 4E10 不 4E0D 冇 5187 丑 4E11 丹 4E39 弌 5F0C **4** 丕 4E15 世 4E16 业 4E1A 且 4E14 丙 4E19 丘 4E18
丛 4E1B 东 4E1C 丝 4E1D 冊 518A 册 518C 旦 65E6 氐 6C10 **5** 丟 4E1F 丢 4E22 亚 4E9A 両 4E21 百 767E 夹 5939 丞 4E1E 死 6B7B
6 严 4E25 两 4E24 丽 4E3D **7** 丧 4E27 並 4E26 **8** 閂 9582 **10** 晝 665D **12** 畺 757A

丨 2

2 个 4E2A 丫 4E2B **3** 丰 4E30 中 4E2D 书 4E66 引 5F15 **4** 旧 65E7 丱 4E31 **6** 串 4E32 **8** 临 4E34

丶 3

2 义 4E49 丸 4E38 凡 51E1 之 4E4B 勺 52FA **3** 丹 4E39 为 4E3A 太 592A **4** 主 4E3B 丼 4E3C **7** 丽 4E3D
8 举 4E3E

丿 4

1 乂 4E42 乃 4E43 **2** 义 4E49 久 4E45 么 4E48 及 53CA **3** 之 4E4B 乌 4E4C 尹 5C39 **4** 乏 4E4F 乍 4E4D 乎 4E4E
乐 4E50 **5** 乔 4E54 乒 4E52 乓 4E53 **6** 乕 4E55 **7** 垂 5782 乖 4E56 **8** 乗 4E57 **9** 乘 4E58

乙 5

乙 4E59 **1** 九 4E5D 乜 4E5C **2** 卫 536B 也 4E5F 乞 4E5E 飞 98DE 习 4E60 **3** 书 4E66 孔 5B54 扎 624E **4** 札 672D
礼 793C **5** 氹 6C39 乭 4E6D 乩 4E69 乪 4E6A 买 4E70 乫 4E6B **6** 乱 4E71 糺 7CFA 虬 866C **7** 乶 4E76 乸 4E78 乳 4E73
乷 4E77 軋 8ECB **10** 乾 4E7E 亀 4E80 **12** 亂 4E82

亅 6

1 了 4E86 **3** 予 4E88 **5** 争 4E89 **7** 事 4E8B

二 7

二 4E8C **1** 亐 4E90 于 4E8E 亏 4E8F **2** 互 4E92 五 4E94 亓 4E93 井 4E95 元 5143 云 4E91 仁 4EC1 匀 52FB **4** 亚 4E9A
亘 4E98 亙 4E99 **5** 亜 4E9C 些 4E9B **6** 亟 4E9F 亞 4E9E 竺 7AFA **9** 商 5546

亠 8

1 亡 4EA1 **2** 卞 535E 六 516D 亢 4EA2 **3** 主 4E3B 市 5E02 **4** 亦 4EA6 交 4EA4 产 4EA7 亥 4EA5 **5** 亩 4EA9
亨 4EA8 **6** 京 4EAC 享 4EAB 夜 591C 卒 5352 **7** 亭 4EAD 亮 4EAE 亲 4EB2 兗 5157 **8** 亳 4EB3 畝 755D **9** 毫 6BEB
商 5546 **10** 亵 4EB5 **11** 亶 4EB6 雍 96CD **15** 贏 8D62 **20** 饔 9954

人 9

人 4EBA **1** 亿 4EBF **2** 仁 4EC1 什 4EC0 仃 4EC3 仄 4EC4 仆 4EC6 介 4ECB 从 4ECE 仇 4EC7 仑 4ED1 化 5316 今 4ECA 仍 4ECD
仅 4EC5 仏 4ECF 仓 4ED3 内 5185 **3** 以 4EE5 仨 4EE8 仕 4ED5 仝 4EDD 付 4ED8 仗 4ED7 代 4EE3 仙 4ED9 仟 4EDF 仡 4EE1 仫 4EEB

人 人 9

们 4EEC 仪 4EEA 令 4EE4 仔 4ED4 他 4ED6 仞 4EDE 囚 56DA **4** 伋 4F0B 全 5168 伕 4F15 伟 4F1F 会 4F1A 伝 4F1D 传 4F20 休 4F11

伍 4F0D 伎 4F0E 伏 4F0F 优 4F18 伢 4F22 伐 4F10 仳 4EF3 佤 4F64 企 4F01 仲 4EF2 仵 4EF5 件 4EF6 任 4EFB 伤 4F24 伥 4F25 仮 4EEE

价 4EF7 众 4F17 伦 4F26 份 4EFD 伜 4F1C 仰 4EF0 伉 4F09 仿 4EFF 伞 4F1E 伙 4F19 伪 4F2A 伫 4F2B 伊 4F0A **5** 佢 4F62 似 4F3C

佘 4F58 余 4F59 佞 4F5E 估 4F30 体 4F53 何 4F55 佐 4F50 佑 4F51 佈 4F48 佔 4F54 但 4F46 伸 4F38 佃 4F43 佚 4F5A 作 4F5C 伯 4F2F

伶 4F36 佣 4F63 低 4F4E 你 4F60 佝 4F5D 佟 4F5F 住 4F4F 位 4F4D 伴 4F34 佇 4F47 佗 4F57 佖 4F56 伺 4F3A 佛 4F5B 伽 4F3D 坐 5750

巫 5DEB **6** 佳 4F73 侍 4F8D 佶 4F76 佬 4F6C 供 4F9B 侖 4F96 使 4F7F 命 547D 価 4FA1 佰 4F70 侑 4F91 來 4F86 例 4F8B 侠 4FA0

侥 4FA5 侄 4F84 侦 4FA6 侊 4F8A 侗 4F97 侣 4FA3 侃 4F83 侧 4FA7 侏 4F8F 侁 4F81 侨 4FA8 佺 4F7A 侩 4FA9 佻 4F7B 佾 4F7E 佩 4F69

侈 4F88 侪 4FAA 佼 4F7C 依 4F9D 佯 4F6F 併 4F75 侘 4F98 侬 4FAC 侭 4FAD 舍 820D 舎 820E **7** 臥 81E5 俦 4FE6 俨 4FE8 俥 4FE5

俞 4FDE 便 4FBF 俉 4FC9 俩 4FE9 俪 4FEA 俠 4FE0 俓 4FD3 俏 4FCF 俣 4FE3 俔 4FD4 俚 4FDA 保 4FDD 促 4FC3 侶 4FB6 俋 4FCB 俄 4FC4

俐 4FD0 俬 4FEC 侮 4FAE 俙 4FD9 俭 4FED 俎 4FCE 俗 4FD7 俘 4FD8 係 4FC2 信 4FE1 侵 4FB5 侯 4FAF 侷 4FB7 俑 4FD1 俟 4FDF 俊 4FCA

臾 81FE **8** 併 4F75 修 4FEE 俸 4FF8 倩 5029 债 503A 俵 4FF5 倀 5000 倖 5016 倻 503B 借 501F 值 503C 値 5024 倆 5006 倚 501A

俺 4FFA 倈 5008 倢 5022 倾 503E 倒 5012 俳 4FF3 俶 4FF6 倬 502C 倏 500F 倘 5018 俱 4FF1 倶 5036 們 5011 倡 5021 個 500B 候 5019

倭 502D 倪 502A 俾 4FFE 倂 5002 倫 502B 倹 5039 倜 501C 倞 501E 俯 4FEF 倅 5005 倍 500D 倣 5023 倦 5026 倧 5027 倥 5025 倌 500C

倉 5009 倨 5028 倔 5014 珡 73E1 閃 9583 **9** 偌 504C 健 5065 做 505A 偃 5043 偭 506D 偕 5055 偵 5075 偿 507F 側 5074 偶 5076

偈 5048 偎 504E 偲 5072 偷 5077 偸 5078 偺 507A 偯 506F 停 505C 偻 507B 偽 507D 偏 504F 假 5047 偉 5049 **10** 傀 5080 傣 50A3

備 5099 傅 5085 傈 5088 傥 50A5 傘 5098 傜 509C 傖 5096 傑 5091 傚 509A 傍 508D 傢 50A2 傧 50A7 储 50A8 傕 5095 傩 50A9

11 傲 50B2 債 50B5 僅 50C5 傳 50B3 僉 50C9 僊 50CA 傾 50BE 僂 50C2 催 50AC 傷 50B7 働 50CD 傻 50BB 傯 50AF 傭 50AD 僇 50C7

12 像 50CF 僣 50E3 僥 50E5 僨 50E8 僖 50D6 僳 50F3 僰 50F0 僚 50DA 僭 50ED 僕 50D5 僩 50E9 僑 50D1 僞 50DE 僮 50EE 僧 50E7

僱 50F1 僎 50CE **13** 儆 5106 儁 5101 僵 50F5 價 50F9 儅 5105 儂 5102 儉 5109 儈 5108 億 5104 儀 5100 僿 50FF 僻 50FB

14 僭 50ED 儚 511A 儔 5114 儒 5112 儕 5115 儐 5110 儘 5118 **15** 優 512A 償 511F 儡 5121 **16** 儲 5132 **17** 儳 5133

人 9
19 儷 5137 儺 513A 儸 5138 **20** 儼 513C 儻 513B

儿 10
儿 513F **1** 兀 5140 **2** 元 5143 允 5141 匹 5339 **3** 兄 5144 四 56DB **4** 兆 5146 尧 5C27 光 5149 先 5148 兇 5147
充 5145 **5** 克 514B 児 5150 兎 514E 兌 514C 免 514D 兑 5151 禿 79BF **6** 兕 5155 兒 5152 兔 5154 兖 5156 尭 5C2D 羌 7F8C
虎 864E **7** 兙 5159 兗 5157 **8** 兛 515B 党 515A **9** 兞 515E 兝 515D 兜 515C **11** 兡 5161 **12** 兢 5162
14 兣 5163

入 11
入 5165 **2** 內 5167 内 5185 **3** 込 8FBC **4** 全 5168 **6** 兩 5169 **7** 兪 516A **20** 糴 7CF4

八 12
八 516B **2** 六 516D 兮 516E 公 516C 分 5206 **3** 兰 5170 只 53EA 叭 53ED 扒 6252 **4** 关 5173 共 5171 兴 5174
5 兌 514C 兵 5175 **6** 其 5176 具 5177 单 5355 典 5178 **7** 养 517B 兹 5179 总 603B 酋 914B **8** 兼 517C
9 兽 517D **12** 舆 8206 **14** 冀 5180

冂 13
2 冇 5187 円 5186 内 5185 冈 5188 **3** 冊 518A 冉 5189 册 518C **4** 再 518D 同 540C **5** 冏 518F **6** 岡 5CA1
7 冒 5192 冑 5191 **9** 冕 5195 勗 52D7 晟 665F 曼 66FC **10** 最 6700

冖 14
2 冗 5197 **3** 写 5199 冚 519A **4** 军 519B 农 519C **7** 冠 51A0 軍 8ECD **8** 冧 51A7 冢 51A2 冥 51A5 冤 51A4
9 冨 51A8 **10** 幂 5E42 **14** 冪 51AA

冫 15
1 习 4E60 **2** 匀 5300 **3** 冬 51AC 冯 51AF **4** 冴 51B4 冲 51B2 冰 51B0 次 6B21 决 51B3 **5** 冻 51BB 况 51B5
冷 51B7 冶 51B6 **6** 冽 51BD 冼 51BC 冾 51BE 净 51C0 **7** 凃 51C3 **8** 凌 51CC 凍 51CD 凄 51C4 准 51C6 凈 51C8 凋 51CB
凉 51C9 **9** 凑 51D1 减 51CF 飡 98E1 **10** 馮 99AE 準 51D6 **13** 凛 51DB 凜 51DC **14** 凞 51DE 凝 51DD

几 16
几 51E0 **1** 凡 51E1 **2** 亢 4EA2 冗 5197 凤 51E4 **3** 凧 51E7 処 51E6 **4** 凩 51E9 凪 51EA 夙 5919 朵 6735 机 673A
肌 808C **6** 凯 51EF 凭 51ED 咒 5492 虎 864E **8** 飢 98E2 **9** 凰 51F0 **10** 凱 51F1 **11** 鳧 9CE7 麂 9E82
12 凳 51F3 鳳 9CF3

凵 17
凵 51F5 **2** 凶 51F6 **3** 击 51FB 凸 51F8 出 51FA 凹 51F9 **4** 凼 51FC **6** 函 51FD 画 753B **10** 凿 51FF

凵 17
15 豳 8C73

刀 18
刁 5201 刀 5200 **1** 刃 5203 **2** 切 5207 分 5206 刈 5208 **3** 刊 520A 刍 520D 叨 53E8 召 53EC 边 8FBA **4** 刑 5211
列 5217 划 5212 则 5219 刚 521A 创 521B 刖 5216 刎 520E 刘 5218 **5** 删 522A 别 5225 別 522B 利 5229 刪 5220 刨 5228 判 5224
初 521D **6** 㓤 34E4 刺 523A 刳 5233 到 5230 刿 523F 制 5236 𠜎 2070E 刮 522E 刽 523D 刹 5239 剁 5241 剂 5242 刻 523B 券 5238
刷 5237 **7** 剋 524B 剌 524C 剄 5244 削 524A 則 5247 剐 5250 剎 524E 剑 5251 剉 5249 前 524D 剃 5243 負 8CA0 **8** 荆 8346
剔 5254 剛 525B 𠜱 20731 剣 5263 剤 5264 剖 5256 剡 5261 剜 525C 剥 5265 剧 5267 剝 525D 釗 91D7 **9** 副 526F 𠝹 20779 剰 5270
剱 5271 剪 526A **10** 剴 5274 剩 5269 創 5275 割 5272 **11** 剽 527D 剷 5277 剿 527F 蒯 84AF **12** 劂 5282 劄 5284 劃 5283
敝 655D **13** 劇 5287 劏 528F 劍 528D 劊 528A 劉 5289 劈 5288 **14** 剿 527F 劓 5293 劒 5292 劑 5291

力 19
力 529B **2** 办 529E 劝 529D **3** 功 529F 劢 52A2 加 52A0 务 52A1 另 53E6 夯 592F 幼 5E7C **4** 动 52A8 攰 6530 劣 52A3
劤 52A4 劦 52A6 肋 808B **5** 劫 52AB 劳 52B3 励 52B1 助 52A9 男 7537 劬 52AC 労 52B4 努 52AA 劭 52AD 劲 52B2 **6** 劻 52BB
势 52BF 効 52B9 劾 52BE **7** 勃 52C3 勅 52C5 勁 52C1 勋 52CB 勉 52C9 勇 52C7 觔 89D4 **8** 勍 52CD 勐 52D0 **9** 務 52D9
勘 52D8 勒 52D2 勖 52D6 勗 52D7 動 52D5 **10** 勛 52DB 勝 52DD 勞 52DE **11** 募 52DF 勣 52E3 勢 52E2 勤 52E4 勧 52E7 勦 52E6
13 勲 52F2 勰 52F0 **14** 勳 52F3 辦 8FA6 **15** 勵 52F5 **17** 勷 52F7 **18** 勸 52F8

勹 20
1 勺 52FA **2** 勻 52FB 勿 52FF 匁 5301 匂 5302 匀 5300 勾 52FE **3** 句 53E5 匆 5306 包 5305 **4** 匈 5308 旬 65EC
5 甸 7538 **6** 匋 530B **7** 匍 530D **8** 芻 82BB **9** 匐 5310 匏 530F

匕 21
匕 5315 **2** 化 5316 匂 5302 **3** 北 5317 叱 53F1 它 5B83 尼 5C3C **4** 旨 65E8 此 6B64 牝 725D **5** 壱 58F1
9 匙 5319 頃 9803 **12** 疑 7591

匚 22
匚 531A **2** 区 533A 匹 5339 **3** 叵 53F5 匝 531D **4** 匡 5321 匠 5320 **5** 匣 5323 医 533B **8** 匪 532A 匿 533F
9 匭 532D 匮 532E 區 5340 **11** 匯 532F **12** 匱 5331 **13** 赜 8D5C

匸 23
2 区 533A 匹 5339 **5** 医 533B **9** 匿 533F 區 5340 匾 533E

十 24
十 5341 **1** 千 5343 卄 5344 **2** 廿 5EFF 卅 5345 午 5348 升 5347 什 4EC0 **3** 卉 5349 古 53E4 半 534A 叶 53F6 汁 6C41 辻 8FBB **4** 卍 534D 华 534E 协 534F 早 65E9 **5** 克 514B 孛 5B5B **6** 丧 4E27 卒 5352 单 5355 卓 5353 卑 5351 協 5354 卖 5356 **7** 南 5357 単 5358 計 8A08 **8** 真 771F 針 91DD 隼 96BC **9** 啬 556C **10** 傘 5098 凖 51D6 博 535A **11** 準 6E96 **19** 颦 98A6

卜 25
卜 535C **2** 卞 535E 仆 4EC6 **3** 卡 5361 卟 535F 占 5360 卢 5362 扑 6251 **4** 贞 8D1E 朴 6734 **5** 卤 5364 **6** 卓 5353 卦 5366 卧 5367 **7** 貞 8C9E 訃 8A03 赴 8D74 **8** 釙 91D9 **9** 卨 5368

卩 26
1 卫 536B **2** 厄 5384 **3** 卮 536E 卯 536F 叩 53E9 氾 6C3E 犯 72AF **4** 危 5371 印 5370 **5** 卵 5375 却 5374 即 5373 私 79C1 **6** 卹 5379 卷 5377 卸 5378 巻 5DFB **7** 卽 537D 卻 537B **9** 卿 537F

厂 27
厂 5382 **2** 仄 4EC4 厅 5385 历 5386 厄 5384 反 53CD **3** 厉 5389 圧 5727 **4** 质 8D28 压 538B 厌 538C 灰 7070 **5** 厎 538E **6** 厓 5393 厕 5395 **7** 厙 5399 厖 5396 厘 5398 厚 539A **8** 厝 539D 原 539F **9** 厢 53A2 厠 53A0 厩 53A9 **10** 厨 53A8 厦 53A6 雁 96C1 厥 53A5 **12** 厩 53A9 厮 53AE 厭 53AD 廐 5ED0 暦 66A6 歴 6B74 **13** 厲 53B2 靥 9765 鴈 9D08 **14** 赝 8D5D 曆 66C6 歷 6B77 **15** 厳 53B3 **17** 厴 53B4 贋 8D0B **22** 魘 9B58

厶 28
2 仏 4ECF 允 5141 公 516C 勾 52FE **3** 去 53BB 台 53F0 広 5E83 弁 5F01 弗 5F17 払 6255 **4** 牟 725F **5** 县 53BF 矣 77E3 **6** 叁 53C1 参 53C2 聀 8077 **9** 參 53C3 **12** 叆 53C6

又 29
又 53C8 **1** 叉 53C9 **2** 及 53CA 友 53CB 反 53CD 収 53CE 双 53CC **3** 发 53D1 圣 5723 奴 5974 **4** 权 6743 **6** 取 53D6 叔 53D4 受 53D7 变 53D8 艰 8270 **7** 叛 53DB 叙 53D9 叚 53DA **8** 叟 53DF 难 96BE 隻 96BB **10** 馭 99AD **11** 叠 53E0 **14** 叡 53E1 **15** 燮 71EE **16** 叢 53E2 雙 96D9

口 30
口 53E3 **2** 兄 5144 加 52A0 句 53E5 叵 53F5 古 53E4 卟 535F 占 5360 叮 53EE 可 53EF 叶 53F6 右 53F3 号 53F7 只 53EA 叭 53ED 史 53F2 叱 53F1 叽 53FD 司 53F8 叼 53FC 叩 53E9 叫 53EB 叾 53FE 另 53E6 叨 53E8 召 53EC 叻 53FB 台 53F0 叹 53F9 **3** 吏 540F 后 540E 同 540C 吁 5401 吉 5409 吐 5410 吋 540B 吓 5413 吕 5415 吊 540A 吃 5403 吒 5412 向 5411 合 5408 各 5404 名 540D 吖 5416

口

口 30

吔 5414 吗 5417 吆 5406 回 56DE 如 5982 扣 6263 舌 820C **4** 含 542B 吸 5438 呈 5448 吞 541E 吴 5434 呓 5453 呆 5446 吾 543E

吱 5431 否 5426 吠 5420 呔 5454 呕 5455 呃 5443 呀 5440 吨 5428 吡 5421 吵 5435 吶 5436 呐 5450 呗 5457 员 5458 吽 543D 告 544A

呑 5451 呂 5442 听 542C 吟 541F 吩 5429 呛 545B 吻 543B 吹 5439 呜 545C 吝 541D 吭 542D 启 542F 君 541B 吳 5433 呉 5449 呎 544E

吧 5427 吼 543C 吮 542E 杏 674F **5** 命 547D 周 5468 咓 5493 味 5473 咁 5481 咕 5495 呵 5475 咂 5482 咗 5497 呸 5478 咙 5499

呯 546F 咔 5494 咀 5480 呷 5477 呻 547B 呪 546A 咒 5492 咋 548B 和 548C 咐 5490 㕷 3577 呱 5471 呼 547C 呤 5464 咎 548E 咚 549A

鸣 9E23 咆 5486 呟 545F 咛 549B 咇 5487 咏 548F 呢 5462 咈 5488 咄 5484 呶 5476 咖 5496 呦 5466 咝 549D 呲 5472 知 77E5 舎 820E

6 哀 54C0 哎 54CE 哐 54D0 哇 54C7 咭 54AD 咾 54BE 哋 54CB 哉 54C9 哄 54C4 哑 54D1 𠱸 20C78 哂 54C2 咸 54B8 哒 54D2 咧 54A7

咦 54A6 哔 54D4 咣 54A3 咢 54A2 品 54C1 咽 54BD 骂 9A82 哖 54D6 咻 54BB 哗 54D7 咱 54B1 咿 54BF 响 54CD 哈 54C8 哚 54DA 𠱓 20C53

咯 54AF 哆 54C6 咬 54AC 咨 54A8 𠲖 20C96 咳 54B3 咩 54A9 咲 54B2 咪 54AA 咤 54A4 咹 54B9 哝 54DD 咫 54AB 哞 54DE 哟 54DF 虽 867D

7 哥 54E5 哿 54FF 哪 54EA 唜 551C 𠳏 20CCF 𠳕 20CD5 哧 54E7 哲 54F2 哮 54EE 唞 551E 唠 5520 唓 5513 哺 54FA 哽 54FD 唖 5516

唔 5514 唇 5507 哨 54E8 唢 5522 員 54E1 唄 5504 哩 54E9 哭 54ED 哦 54E6 唎 550E 唏 550F 唑 5511 唤 5524 唁 5501 哼 54FC 唥 5525

唐 5510 唧 5527 𠴕 20D15 唉 5509 唆 5506 **8** 商 5546 啬 556C 啊 554A 唪 552A 啧 5567 㖭 35AD 啩 5569 啪 556A 啦 5566 𠵿 20D7F

啞 555E 唭 552D 啉 5549 唵 5535 啄 5544 啭 556D 啡 5561 啃 5543 啮 556E 唬 552C 唱 5531 問 554F 啱 5571 啰 5570 唾 553E 啝 555D

售 552E 唯 552F 啤 5564 啲 5572 啟 555F 啥 5565 啋 554B 唸 5538 啁 5541 啕 5555 啗 5557 啍 554D 㖡 35A1 啐 5550 唷 5537 啖 5556

啵 5575 啶 5576 啷 5577 唳 5533 啓 5553 啸 5578 啹 5579 唰 5530 𠵼 20D7C 啜 555C 啣 5563 釦 91E6 **9** 啫 556B 㖿 35BF 喏 558F

喵 55B5 𠸏 20E0F 喎 558E 営 55B6 喫 55AB 喷 55B7 喆 5586 喜 559C 喋 558B 喪 55AA 喃 5583 喳 55B3 喇 5587 喊 558A 喱 55B1 喁 5581

喝 559D 喂 5582 喟 559F 單 55AE 喘 5598 啾 557E 喬 55AC 喺 55BA 喉 5589 喻 55BB 喩 55A9 喰 55B0 喚 559A 喼 55BC 喨 55A8 喑 5591

啻 557B 啼 557C 善 5584 喽 55BD 喧 55A7 喀 5580 喔 5594 𠸎 20E0E 㗎 35CE 喙 5599 喲 55B2 **10** 嗒 55D2 嗗 55D7 嗖 55D6 嗟 55DF

嗉 55C9 嗎 55CE 嗜 55DC 嗑 55D1 嗫 55EB 嘩 5629 嗬 55EC 嗔 55D4 嗇 55C7 𠺝 20E9D 嗦 55E6 嗝 55DD 嗄 55C4 嗩 55E9 嗣 55E3 嗯 55EF

嗰 55F0 嗅 55C5 嗥 55E5 嗚 55DA 嗱 55F1 嗲 55F2 嗳 55F3 嗆 55C6 嗡 55E1 嗌 55CC 嗨 55E8 嗐 55D0 𠺢 20EA2 嗤 55E4 𠹷 20E77 嗧 55E7

口 30

嗵 55F5 嗓 55D3 辔 8F94 **11** 嗷 55F7 𠻗 20ED7 嘖 5616 𠻺 20EFA 嘉 5609 嘆 5606 嘞 561E 嘈 5608 嗽 55FD 嘔 5614 嘌 560C 嘁 5601

嘎 560E 嘜 561C 𠽌 20F4C 嘘 5618 嘗 5617 嗶 55F6 嘢 5622 嘍 560D 嘓 5613 嘣 5623 嘤 5624 𠼭 20F2D 𠼮 20F2E 嘅 5605 鳴 9CF4 嘥 5625

嘛 561B 嘀 5600 嗾 55FE 𠻹 20EF9 嘧 5627 嘐 5610 噓 5653 囀 56C0 **12** 嘟 561F 嘩 5629 噴 5674 嘻 563B 嘭 562D 噎 564E 噁 5641

嘶 5636 嘲 5632 𠾴 20FB4 噘 5658 嘹 5639 噛 565B 噗 5657 嘿 563F 嘸 5638 㗳 35F3 噏 564F 噃 5643 噙 5659 噜 565C 噒 5652 噂 5642

噌 564C 嘮 562E 噚 565A 嘱 5631 噀 5640 噔 5654 𠾼 20FBC 噝 565D 嘰 5630 嘴 5634 嘯 562F 舖 8217 **13** 噠 5660 噶 5676 噢 5662

㗾 35FE 噩 5669 噤 5664 𠿪 20FEA 噸 5678 噱 5671 噹 5679 器 5668 噥 5665 噪 566A 噬 566C 噯 566F 噺 567A 噫 566B 噼 567C 舘 8218

14 𡁜 2105C 嚆 5686 𡁻 2107B 嚇 5687 𡁶 21076 嚏 568F 𡁵 21075 𡁯 2106F 嚅 5685 嚉 5689 嚐 5690 嚎 568E 嚓 5693 嚀 5680 嚮 56AE

囃 56C3 **15** 𡃁 210C1 嚡 56A1 嚢 56A2 嚙 5699 嚣 56A3 嚟 569F 嚕 5695 嚤 56A4 𡃉 210C9 **16** 嚮 56AE 嚭 56AD 嚥 56A5 嚦 56A6

嚬 56AC 嚨 56A8 **17** 嚴 56B4 嚱 56B1 嚶 56B6 嚹 56B9 嚷 56B7 **18** 嚿 56BF 嚼 56BC 囁 56C1 囀 56C0 囂 56C2 囃 56C3 囍 56CD

19 囊 56CA 囈 56C8 囉 56C9 轡 8F61 **20** 囌 56CC **21** 囓 56D3 囍 56CD 囑 56D1 **22** 囔 56D4 **25** 囖 56D6

囗 31

囗 56D7 **2** 囚 56DA 四 56DB **3** 囟 56DF 团 56E2 団 56E3 因 56E0 回 56DE 囝 56DD 囡 56E1 **4** 囪 56EA 囱 56F1 囲 56F2

园 56ED 围 56F4 困 56F0 囤 56E4 囮 56EE 囵 56F5 囫 56EB 図 56F3 **5** 国 56FD 固 56FA 囹 56F9 图 56FE **6** 囿 56FF 圀 5700

𡇙 211D9 **7** 圃 5703 圄 5704 圆 5706 **8** 圉 5709 國 570B 圇 5707 圈 5708 圏 570F **9** 圍 570D **10** 嗇 55C7 園 5712

圓 5713 **11** 團 5718 圖 5716 **13** 圜 571C

土 32

土 571F **2** 主 4E3B 去 53BB 圧 5727 圣 5723 **3** 吐 5410 圩 5729 圬 572C 圭 572D 在 5728 圳 5733 圮 572E 圯 572F 地 5730

场 573A 寺 5BFA 庄 5E84 **4** 圾 573E 坛 575B 坏 574F 坜 575C 址 5740 坚 575A 坔 5754 坝 575D 圻 573B 坂 5742 坐 5750 坌 574C

坎 574E 均 5747 坍 574D 坞 575E 坟 575F 坑 5751 坊 574A 块 5757 坠 5760 杜 675C 灶 7076 牡 7261 社 793E 肚 809A **5** 垂 5782

坩 5769 坷 5777 坯 576F 垄 5784 垅 5785 坪 576A 坦 5766 坤 5764 坰 5770 坵 5775 垈 5788 坼 577C 坻 577B 垃 5783 坨 5768 坭 576D

坡 5761 坮 576E 坳 5773 **6** 型 578B 垚 579A 垫 57AB 垩 57A9 垭 57AD 垣 57A3 垮 57AE 城 57CE 垰 57B0 垌 578C 垧 57A7 垕 5795

垢 57A2 垛 579B 垓 5793 垞 579E 垵 57B5 垠 57A0 垦 57A6 垒 5792 **7** 埔 57D4 埂 57C2 埗 57D7 埕 57D5 埋 57CB 埙 57D9 埚 57DA

土 32

埒 57D2 垺 57BA 埆 57C6 埓 57D3 垸 57B8 埇 57C7 埃 57C3 埈 57C8 **8** 埡 57E1 堊 580A 基 57FA 堇 5807 埴 57F4 埜 57DC 域 57DF

堅 5805 埼 57FC 堑 5811 堂 5802 埧 57E7 埸 57F8 堈 5808 堆 5806 埤 57E4 埰 57F0 埠 57E0 埻 57FB 培 57F9 堃 5803 堉 5809 執 57F7

埞 57DE 埭 57ED 堀 5800 堕 5815 **9** 堵 5835 堝 581D 堯 582F 堪 582A 堞 581E 堰 5830 堧 5827 堤 5824 場 5834 堣 5823 堺 583A

塁 5841 堡 5821 堭 582D 堠 5820 報 5831 堗 5817 塀 5840 **10** 塔 5854 塭 586D 塊 584A 塚 585A 填 586B 塒 5852 塌 584C 塤 5864

塏 584F 塩 5869 塢 5862 塡 5861 塯 586F 塙 5859 塘 5858 塑 5851 塋 584B 塗 5857 塞 585E 塱 5871 **11** 墓 5893 塳 5873 墊 588A

墐 5890 墘 5898 墙 5899 塹 5879 塼 587C 塽 587D 墅 5885 塾 587E 墉 5889 塵 5875 境 5883 墒 5892 增 5897 墀 5880 **12** 墟 589F

墮 58AE 墜 589C 墬 58AC 墳 58B3 墣 58A3 墨 58A8 墦 58A6 墩 58A9 墡 58A1 增 589E **13** 墺 58BA 壊 58CA 墻 58BB 壆 58C6 墾 58BE

壇 58C7 壌 58CC 壅 58C5 壂 58C2 壁 58C1 **14** 壓 58D3 壑 58D1 壎 58CE 壕 58D5 **15** 壙 58D9 壘 58D8 **16** 壢 58E2 壜 58DC

壞 58DE 壟 58DF **17** 壤 58E4 **21** 壩 58E9

士 33

士 58EB **1** 壬 58EC **2** 仕 4ED5 **3** 吉 5409 壮 58EE **4** 壱 58F1 売 58F2 壳 58F3 壯 58EF 声 58F0 志 5FD7

5 垂 5782 **7** 壶 58F6 **8** 壷 58F7 **9** 喆 5586 喜 559C 壻 58FB 壹 58F9 壺 58FA **10** 壼 58FC **11** 嘉 5609

壽 58FD 臺 81FA **12** 賣 8CE3 **19** 懿 61FF **21** 囍 56CD

夂 34

2 冬 51AC 処 51E6 务 52A1 处 5904 **3** 各 5404 **4** 夆 5906 条 6761 **5** 备 5907 **6** 变 5909 **9** 惫 60EB

10 愛 611B **12** 憂 6182

夊 35

5 夌 590C **6** 变 5909 复 590D **7** 夏 590F **19** 夔 5914

夕 36

夕 5915 **2** 外 5916 **3** 名 540D 夙 5919 多 591A 夛 591B 汐 6C50 **5** 夜 591C **8** 够 591F 夠 5920 悤 60A4

9 飧 98E7 **11** 夢 5922 夥 5925 夤 5924

大 37

大 5927 **1** 天 5929 夫 592B 夭 592D 太 592A 夬 592C **2** 头 5934 失 5931 央 592E 夯 592F **3** 夹 5939 乔 4E54 买 4E70

因 56E0 夸 5938 夺 593A 夷 5937 尖 5C16 **4** 奂 5942 夽 593D 奀 5940 奁 5941 夾 593E 戻 623B 旲 65F2 杕 6755 达 8FBE

5 奉 5949 奈 5948 奇 5947 奄 5944 奋 594B 突 7A81 **6** 奏 594F 奔 5954 契 5951 奎 594E 奐 5950 奖 5956 奕 5955 类 7C7B

大 37

牵 7275 美 7F8E 耷 8037 臭 81ED **7** 奘 5958 套 5957 奚 595A **8** 爽 723D **9** 奢 5962 奥 5965 奠 5960 **10** 奧 5967
奨 5968 馱 99B1 **11** 奩 5969 奪 596A 奬 596C 奫 596B **12** 器 5668 奭 596D 樊 6A0A **13** 奮 596E 養 990A

女 38

女 5973 **2** 奶 5976 奴 5974 **3** 囡 56E1 奸 5978 如 5982 奼 597C 妁 5981 妆 5986 妄 5984 妇 5987 妃 5983 好 597D 她 5979
妈 5988 安 5B89 汝 6C5D **4** 妍 598D 妩 59A9 妘 5998 妓 5993 妪 59AA 妣 59A3 妙 5999 妊 598A 妖 5996 妥 59A5 妗 5997 妏 598F
妨 59A8 妫 59AB 妒 5992 妞 599E 妝 599D 妤 59A4 **5** 姊 59CA 姒 59D2 妹 59B9 姃 59C3 姑 59D1 妸 59B8 妬 59AC 妻 59BB 妲 59B2
姐 59D0 妯 59AF 姍 59CD 姓 59D3 委 59D4 妳 59B3 姗 59D7 姉 59C9 妾 59BE 姅 59C5 妮 59AE 始 59CB 姆 59C6 **6** 妍 598D 姸 59F8
娃 5A03 姞 59DE 姥 59E5 娅 5A05 姮 59EE 姫 59EB 威 5A01 耍 800D 姨 59E8 娆 5A06 姪 59EA 姻 59FB 姝 59DD 娇 5A07 姙 59D9 姶 59F6
姚 59DA 姵 59F5 娈 5A08 姣 59E3 姿 59FF 姜 59DC 姘 59D8 娄 5A04 姹 59F9 姦 59E6 要 8981 **7** 娍 5A0D 娫 5A2B 娜 5A1C 姬 59EC
娠 5A20 娱 5A31 娌 5A0C 娉 5A09 娚 5A1A 娟 5A1F 娲 5A32 娛 5A1B 娯 5A2F 娥 5A25 娳 5A33 娩 5A29 娴 5A34 娣 5A23 娑 5A11 娘 5A18
娓 5A13 **8** 婀 5A40 婧 5A67 婊 5A4A 婭 5A6D 娶 5A36 婪 5A6A 婕 5A55 娼 5A3C 婁 5A41 婴 5A74 婢 5A62 婤 5A64 婚 5A5A 婵 5A75
婆 5A46 婶 5A76 婉 5A49 婠 5A60 婦 5A66 **9** 媧 5AA7 媒 5A92 媜 5A9C 媞 5A9E 媪 5AAA 媤 5AA4 媬 5AAC 媓 5A93 媛 5A9B 婷 5A77
媄 5A84 媗 5A97 媚 5A9A 婿 5A7F 婺 5A7A **10** 嫂 5AC2 媾 5ABE 媽 5ABD 媴 5AB4 嫄 5AC4 媺 5ABA 媼 5ABC 媳 5AB3 媲 5AB2 媱 5AB1
嫒 5AD2 嫉 5AC9 嫌 5ACC 嫈 5AC8 嫁 5AC1 嫔 5AD4 嫋 5ACB **11** 嫣 5AE3 嫤 5AE4 嫩 5AE9 嫗 5AD7 嫖 5AD6 嫦 5AE6 嫚 5ADA 嫘 5AD8
嫲 5AF2 嫡 5AE1 嫙 5AD9 嫪 5AEA **12** 嬅 5B05 嬈 5B08 嬉 5B09 嫻 5AFB 嫺 5AFA 嬋 5B0B 嫵 5AF5 嬌 5B0C 嬃 5B03 **13** 嬴 5B34
嬝 5B1D 嬡 5B21 嬗 5B17 嬢 5B22 嬖 5B16 **14** 嬬 5B2C 嬰 5B30 嬲 5B32 嬶 5B36 嬤 5B24 嬪 5B2A **15** 嬸 5B38 **16** 嬿 5B3F
17 孀 5B40 孃 5B43 **19** 孋 5B4B 孌 5B4C **20** 孍 5B4D

子 39

子 5B50 孑 5B51 孓 5B53 **1** 孔 5B54 **2** 仔 4ED4 孕 5B55 **3** 团 56DD 好 597D 存 5B58 孙 5B59 字 5B57 孖 5B56
4 孝 5B5D 孛 5B5B 孜 5B5C 孚 5B5A 李 674E **5** 享 4EAB 孟 5B5F 季 5B63 孤 5B64 孢 5B62 学 5B66 **6** 孪 5B6A 孩 5B69
籽 7C7D **7** 孬 5B6C 孭 5B6D 孫 5B6B 屘 5C58 **8** 孰 5B70 **9** 孱 5B71 **10** 孳 5B73 **11** 孵 5B75 **13** 學 5B78
14 孺 5B7A 孻 5B7B **16** 孼 5B7C **17** 孽 5B7D **19** 孿 5B7F

宀 40

2 宁 5B81 它 5B83 **3** 字 5B57 宇 5B87 守 5B88 宅 5B85 安 5B89 **4** 完 5B8C 宋 5B8B 宏 5B8F 牢 7262 宍 5B8D 灾 707E

5 実 5B9F 宝 5B9D 宗 5B97 定 5B9A 宕 5B95 宠 5BA0 宜 5B9C 审 5BA1 宙 5B99 宛 5B9B 实 5B9E 宓 5B93 官 5B98 宖 5B96

6 宣 5BA3 宦 5BA6 宥 5BA5 室 5BA4 宫 5BAB 宪 5BAA 客 5BA2 **7** 宬 5BAC 害 5BB3 宽 5BBD 宸 5BB8 家 5BB6 宵 5BB5 宴 5BB4

宮 5BAE 宾 5BBE 容 5BB9 宰 5BB0 案 6848 **8** 寇 5BC7 寅 5BC5 寄 5BC4 寂 5BC2 宿 5BBF 寀 5BC0 寃 5BC3 密 5BC6 **9** 寒 5BD2

富 5BCC 寔 5BD4 寓 5BD3 甯 752F 寍 5BCD 寐 5BD0 **10** 塞 585E 寛 5BDB 寝 5BDD 寗 5BD7 **11** 寞 5BDE 寨 5BE8 赛 8D5B 寡 5BE1

察 5BDF 寧 5BE7 寤 5BE4 寢 5BE2 寥 5BE5 實 5BE6 搴 6434 蜜 871C **12** 寬 5BEC 賓 8CD3 寮 5BEE 寫 5BEB 審 5BE9 **13** 寯 5BEF

寰 5BF0 憲 61B2 **14** 賽 8CFD 蹇 8E47 **16** 寳 5BF3 寵 5BF5 **17** 寶 5BF6 騫 9A2B

寸 41

寸 5BF8 **2** 付 4ED8 对 5BF9 **3** 吋 540B 団 56E3 守 5B88 寺 5BFA 寻 5BFB 导 5BFC 忖 5FD6 **4** 寿 5BFF 対 5BFE 村 6751

肘 8098 **6** 将 5C06 封 5C01 専 5C02 耐 8010 紂 7D02 **7** 射 5C04 討 8A0E 辱 8FB1 酎 914E **8** 將 5C07 專 5C08 尉 5C09

9 尊 5C0A 尋 5C0B **11** 對 5C0D **12** 導 5C0E

小 42

小 5C0F **1** 少 5C11 **2** 尔 5C14 尕 5C15 **3** 兴 5174 尘 5C18 尖 5C16 当 5F53 **4** 劳 52B4 肖 8096 **5** 学 5B66

尙 5C19 尚 5C1A **6** 単 5358 尝 5C1D 栄 6804 **7** 挙 6319 **8** 堂 5802 巣 5DE3 蛍 86CD 雀 96C0 **9** 営 55B6 辉 8F89

覚 899A **10** 誉 8A89 **13** 鴬 9D2C **14** 厳 53B3

尢 43

兀 5140 尢 5C22 **1** 尤 5C24 **3** 尧 5C27 **4** 尪 5C2A 尨 5C28 尬 5C2C **5** 尭 5C2D **6** 虺 867A **7** 軏 8ECF

9 就 5C31 堯 582F **10** 尴 5C34 **14** 尷 5C37

尸 44

尸 5C38 **1** 尹 5C39 尺 5C3A **2** 尻 5C3B 尼 5C3C **3** 尽 5C3D **4** 层 5C42 屁 5C41 尿 5C3F 尾 5C3E 局 5C40

5 届 5C46 屉 5C49 居 5C45 屆 5C4A 屈 5C48 **6** 昼 663C 咫 54AB 屍 5C4D 屋 5C4B 屌 5C4C 屏 5C4F 屎 5C4E **7** 屘 5C58

展 5C55 屑 5C51 屓 5C53 屐 5C50 **8** 屙 5C59 屝 5C5D 屛 5C5B 屜 5C5C **9** 孱 5B71 屠 5C60 属 5C5E 屡 5C61 犀 7280

11 屢 5C62 屣 5C63 **12** 履 5C65 層 5C64 **14** 屨 5C68 **18** 屬 5C6C **21** 屭 5C6D

屮 45

1 屯 5C6F **7** 芻 82BB

山 46

山 5C71 **2** 仙 4ED9 **3** 屿 5C7F 屹 5C79 岁 5C81 屺 5C7A 岂 5C82 汕 6C55 辿 8FBF **4** 岌 5C8C 岐 5C90 岖 5C96 岗 5C97

岘 5C98 岑 5C91 岔 5C94 岚 5C9A 岛 5C9B 岜 5C9C 杣 6763 氙 6C19 **5** 岡 5CA1 岠 5CA0 岵 5CB5 岸 5CB8 岩 5CA9 岾 5CBE 岿 5CBF

岨 5CA8 岬 5CAC 岫 5CAB 峀 5CC0 岳 5CB3 岱 5CB1 岭 5CAD 岺 5CBA 岣 5CA3 岷 5CB7 峄 5CC4 峅 5CC5 疝 759D 秈 79C8 **6** 峙 5CD9

峡 5CE1 峠 5CE0 峒 5CD2 峇 5CC7 峋 5CCB 峥 5CE5 峦 5CE6 幽 5E7D 炭 70AD 耑 8011 舢 8222 **7** 崁 5D01 崂 5D02 豈 8C48 峽 5CFD

崃 5D03 峭 5CED 峴 5CF4 峨 5CE8 島 5CF6 峪 5CEA 峯 5CEF 峰 5CF0 峻 5CFB 訕 8A15 **8** 崋 5D0B 崚 5D1A 崧 5D27 崠 5D20 崖 5D16

崎 5D0E 崍 5D0D 崭 5D2D 崑 5D11 崮 5D2E 崗 5D17 崔 5D14 崟 5D1F 崙 5D19 崤 5D24 崢 5D22 崩 5D29 崇 5D07 崆 5D06 崌 5D0C 崛 5D1B

9 嵌 5D4C 嵘 5D58 崴 5D34 嵎 5D4E 崽 5D3D 嵇 5D47 嵙 5D59 嵐 5D50 嵜 5D5C 嵄 5D44 嵝 5D5D 嵋 5D4B **10** 嵬 5D6C 嵯 5D6F

嵩 5D69 **11** 嶄 5D84 嶇 5D87 嶋 5D8B 嶌 5D8C 嶂 5D82 **12** 嶢 5DA2 嶠 5DA0 嶔 5D94 嶙 5D99 嶝 5D9D **13** 嶪 5DAA 嶮 5DAE

14 嶼 5DBC 嶺 5DBA 嶷 5DB7 嶽 5DBD 嶸 5DB8 豳 8C73 **16** 巅 5DC5 **17** 巌 5DCC 巉 5DC9 **18** 巍 5DCD **19** 巔 5DD4

巒 5DD2 **20** 巖 5DD6

巛 47

川 5DDD **1** 卅 5345 **3** 州 5DDE 圳 5733 **4** 巡 5DE1 災 707D 玔 7394 **5** 甽 753D 甾 753E **7** 訓 8A13 邕 9095

8 巢 5DE2 巣 5DE3 釧 91E7 **9** 順 9806 **10** 馴 99B4

工 48

工 5DE5 **2** 仝 4EDD 功 529F 巨 5DE8 左 5DE6 巧 5DE7 **3** 巩 5DE9 巪 5DEA 式 5F0F 扛 625B 江 6C5F 邛 909B **4** 巫 5DEB

攻 653B 杠 6760 杢 6762 汞 6C5E 肛 809B **5** 空 7A7A **6** 紅 7D05 缸 7F38 舡 8221 虹 8679 **7** 差 5DEE 訌 8A0C 貢 8CA2

8 釭 91ED **9** 項 9805

己 49

己 5DF1 已 5DF2 巳 5DF3 **1** 巴 5DF4 **2** 包 5305 **3** 圮 572E 圯 572F 妃 5983 屺 5C7A 异 5F02 汜 6C5C **4** 忌 5FCC

改 6539 杞 675E 玘 7398 **5** 祀 7940 **6** 巷 5DF7 巻 5DFB 紀 7D00 **7** 記 8A18 起 8D77 配 914D **9** 巽 5DFD

巾 50

巾 5DFE **1** 帀 5E01 巿 5DFF **2** 市 5E02 凧 51E7 匝 531D 布 5E03 帅 5E05 **3** 师 5E08 吊 540A 帆 5E06 **4** 乕 4E55

帏 5E0F 帐 5E10 希 5E0C **5** 帖 5E16 帜 5E1C 帙 5E19 帕 5E15 帛 5E1B 帘 5E18 帚 5E1A 帑 5E11 帔 5E14 **6** 帝 5E1D 带 5E26

帧 5E27 帥 5E25 帟 5E1F **7** 帮 5E2E 帯 5E2F 帱 5E31 帰 5E30 𢃇 220C7 師 5E2B 席 5E2D **8** 帳 5E33 帶 5E36 常 5E38 帼 5E3C

巾 50
帷 5E37 **9** 幂 5E42 幇 5E47 幅 5E45 幀 5E40 帽 5E3D 帿 5E3F 幄 5E44 幃 5E43 **10** 幌 5E4C **11** 幕 5E55 幔 5E54 幗 5E57
幛 5E5B **12** 幣 5E63 幡 5E61 幢 5E62 幟 5E5F **14** 幪 5E6A 幫 5E6B **15** 歸 6B78

干 51
干 5E72 **2** 平 5E73 刊 520A **3** 并 5E76 年 5E74 奸 5978 扞 625E 汗 6C57 舌 820C 邗 9097 **4** 罕 7F55 旱 65F1 杆 6746
玕 7395 肝 809D **5** 并 5E76 幸 5E78 幷 5E77 矸 77F8 **6** 竿 7AFF **7** 訐 8A10 赶 8D76 軒 8ED2 **9** 頇 9807
10 幹 5E79 **14** 鼾 9F3E

幺 52
么 4E48 乡 4E61 幺 5E7A **1** 幻 5E7B **2** 幼 5E7C **6** 幽 5E7D **9** 幾 5E7E **11** 麼 9EBC

广 53
广 5E7F **2** 庁 5E81 広 5E83 **3** 庄 5E84 庆 5E86 **4** 床 5E8A 库 5E93 庇 5E87 应 5E94 庐 5E90 序 5E8F 応 5FDC
5 庞 5E9E 店 5E97 庙 5E99 府 5E9C 底 5E95 庖 5E96 庚 5E9A 废 5E9F **6** 度 5EA6 庥 5EA5 庠 5EA0 **7** 唐 5510 席 5E2D
庭 5EAD 庫 5EAB 座 5EA7 **8** 庴 5EB4 庶 5EB6 庹 5EB9 庵 5EB5 康 5EB7 庸 5EB8 **9** 庾 5EBE 廊 5ECA 廂 5EC2 廁 5EC1 赓 8D53
廃 5EC3 **10** 廈 5EC8 廉 5EC9 **11** 廄 5EC4 廓 5ED3 廍 5ECD 廔 5ED4 廐 5ED0 廏 5ECF 廖 5ED6 腐 8150 **12** 廣 5EE3 慶 6176
廚 5EDA 廝 5EDD 廟 5EDF 廠 5EE0 廛 5EDB 廡 5EE1 賡 8CE1 廢 5EE2 **13** 廨 5EE8 **14** 應 61C9 膺 81BA **16** 廬 5EEC 龐 9F90
21 鷹 9DF9 **22** 廳 5EF3

廴 54
4 廷 5EF7 延 5EF6 **6** 廼 5EFC 廻 5EFB 建 5EFA

廾 55
廾 5EFE **1** 开 5F00 廿 5EFF **2** 卉 5349 弁 5F01 **3** 异 5F02 **4** 弃 5F03 弄 5F04 **5** 奔 5954 **6** 弇 5F07
弈 5F08 羿 7FBF **12** 弊 5F0A **13** 彛 5F5B **15** 彝 5F5D

弋 56
弋 5F0B **1** 弌 5F0C **2** 代 4EE3 **3** 弐 5F10 式 5F0F **4** 忒 5FD2 杙 6759 **5** 甙 7519 武 6B66 **6** 贰 8D30
9 貳 8CB3 弑 5F11 **10** 弒 5F12 **11** 鳶 9CF6

弓 57
弓 5F13 **1** 弔 5F14 引 5F15 **2** 弗 5F17 弘 5F18 **3** 夷 5937 弛 5F1B 芎 828E **4** 张 5F20 弟 5F1F **5** 弧 5F27
弥 5F25 弦 5F26 弩 5F29 穹 7A79 **6** 弭 5F2D 弯 5F2F **7** 弱 5F31 躬 8EAC **8** 張 5F35 弴 5F34 弹 5F39 強 5F37
9 弼 5F3C 强 5F3A 粥 7CA5 弾 5F3E **10** 彀 5F40 **11** 彅 5F45 **12** 彆 5F46 彈 5F48 **13** 彊 5F4A **14** 彌 5F4C

弓 57 **16** 疆 7586 **19** 彎 5F4E

彐 58 **1** 尹 5C39 **2** 刍 520D 归 5F52 **3** 夛 591B 寻 5BFB 当 5F53 **4** 灵 7075 **5** 秉 79C9 帚 5E1A 彔 5F54 录 5F55
6 彖 5F56 **7** 帰 5E30 **8** 彗 5F57 雪 96EA **9** 尋 5C0B 彘 5F58 **10** 彙 5F59 **13** 彛 5F5B **15** 彝 5F5D
歸 6B78

彡 59 **4** 尨 5C28 形 5F62 彤 5F64 彣 5F63 杉 6749 **5** 参 53C2 衫 886B **6** 须 987B 彥 5F65 彦 5F66 **7** 彧 5F67
8 參 53C3 彬 5F6C 彪 5F6A 彩 5F69 彫 5F6B **9** 彭 5F6D 須 9808 **11** 彰 5F70 **12** 影 5F71

彳 60 彳 5F73 **4** 彻 5F7B 役 5F79 彷 5F77 **5** 征 5F81 徂 5F82 往 5F80 彿 5F7F 彼 5F7C 径 5F84 **6** 待 5F85 徊 5F8A 徇 5F87
徉 5F89 律 5F8B 很 5F88 後 5F8C **7** 徒 5F92 徕 5F95 徑 5F91 徐 5F90 従 5F93 **8** 徠 5FA0 徘 5F98 徙 5F99 徜 5F9C 得 5F97
從 5F9E 御 5FA1 衔 8854 **9** 復 5FA9 徨 5FA8 循 5FAA 徧 5FA7 徫 5FAB **10** 微 5FAE 徭 5FAD 徬 5FAC **11** 徳 5FB3 徴 5FB4
12 德 5FB7 徵 5FB5 徹 5FB9 **14** 徽 5FBD **20** 黴 9EF4

心 61 心 5FC3 **1** 必 5FC5 忆 5FC6 **3** 志 5FD7 忑 5FD1 忖 5FD6 忒 5FD2 忐 5FD0 忏 5FCF 応 5FDC 忘 5FD8 忙 5FD9 忌 5FCC 忍 5FCD
沁 6C81 芯 82AF **4** 忝 5FDD 忮 5FEE 怀 6000 态 6001 忧 5FE7 忠 5FE0 忡 5FE1 忤 5FE4 忾 5FFE 怅 6005 忻 5FFB 怂 6002 念 5FF5
忿 5FFF 忪 5FEA 怆 6006 忰 5FF0 忽 5FFD 忞 5FDE 忟 5FDF 忱 5FF1 快 5FEB 忸 5FF8 **5** 总 603B 怔 6014 怯 602F 怙 6019 怵 6035
怖 6016 怦 6026 怛 601B 思 601D 怏 600F 性 6027 怎 600E 怕 6015 怜 601C 怱 6031 怨 6028 急 6025 怩 6029 怫 602B 怒 6012 怪 602A
怼 603C 怠 6020 怡 6021 **6** 恝 605D 恸 6078 恚 605A 恃 6043 恐 6050 恥 6065 恭 606D 恶 6076 恒 6052 恵 6075 恢 6062 恆 6046
虑 8651 恍 604D 恫 606B 恩 6069 恺 607A 恻 607B 恬 606C 恁 6041 息 606F 恤 6064 恰 6070 恂 6042 恪 606A 恋 604B 恼 607C 恣 6063
恙 6059 恽 607D 恨 6068 恳 6073 恕 6055 **7** 悖 6096 悪 60AA 悚 609A 悟 609F 悭 60AD 悄 6084 悍 608D 悬 60AC 患 60A3 悧 60A7
悔 6094 悠 60A0 您 60A8 悤 60A4 悅 6085 悉 6089 悋 608B 悯 60AF 悦 60A6 悌 608C 悩 60A9 恿 607F 悛 609B **8** 惫 60EB 情 60C5
惬 60EC 悵 60B5 悻 60BB 惡 60E1 惜 60DC 悳 60B3 惠 60E0 惑 60D1 悽 60BD 惭 60ED 悱 60B1 悲 60B2 悼 60BC 惧 60E7 悶 60B6 惕 60D5
惘 60D8 惣 60E3 悸 60B8 惟 60DF 惩 60E9 惆 60C6 惚 60DA 惊 60CA 惇 60C7 惦 60E6 悴 60B4 惮 60EE 悰 60B0 惋 60CB 惨 60E8 惯 60EF

心 61

鈊 920A **9** 惹 60F9 愜 611C 愤 6124 愖 6116 想 60F3 惰 60F0 感 611F 惻 60FB 愓 6113 愚 611A 愠 6120 惺 60FA 愒 6112 愕 6115
惴 60F4 愣 6123 愀 6100 愁 6101 愎 610E 惶 60F6 愆 6106 愈 6108 愉 6109 愛 611B 意 610F 愔 6114 愃 6103 惲 60F2 慨 6168 愍 610D
㥠 3960 惱 60F1 **10** 慌 614C 愧 6127 慈 6148 愫 612B 慑 6151 慎 614E 慄 6144 愿 613F 愰 6130 愷 6137 慍 614D 愾 613E 慇 6147
愴 6134 愼 613C 慊 614A 慂 6142 𢞵 227B5 態 614B **11** 慶 6176 慝 615D 慕 6155 慧 6167 慤 6164 慙 6159 慚 615A 慳 6173 慓 6153
慼 617C 慽 617D 憂 6182 慮 616E 慢 6162 慟 615F 慜 615C 憁 6181 慫 616B 慾 617E 慷 6177 慵 6175 慰 6170 慘 6158 慣 6163
12 慨 6168 憋 618B 憨 61A8 憤 61A4 憘 6198 憙 6199 憓 6193 憫 61AB 憬 61AC 憚 619A 憮 61AE 憩 61A9 憊 618A 憔 6194 憑 6191
憧 61A7 憐 6190 憎 618E 憲 61B2 **13** 懂 61C2 懊 61CA 懃 61C3 懋 61CB 懒 61D2 憾 61BE 懇 61C7 憺 61BA 懈 61C8 懐 61D0 懍 61CD
應 61C9 憶 61B6 懑 61D1 **14** 懞 61DE 懨 61E8 懦 61E6 懟 61DF 懣 61E3 **15** 懴 61F4 懲 61F2 **16** 懵 61F5 懸 61F8 懶 61F6
懷 61F7 **17** 懺 61FA **18** 懿 61FF 懾 61FE 懼 61FC **19** 戀 6200 **21** 戆 6206 **24** 戇 6207

戈 62

戈 6208 **1** 戊 620A **2** 伐 4F10 划 5212 戎 620E 戌 620C 戍 620D 成 6210 戏 620F **3** 我 6211 戒 6212 找 627E
4 戔 6214 或 6216 戕 6215 **5** 哉 54C9 咸 54B8 威 5A01 战 6218 **6** 载 8F7D 戙 6219 **7** 戛 621B 戚 621A
8 戟 621F 裁 88C1 戦 6226 **9** 戢 6222 戥 6225 載 8F09 戡 6221 **10** 截 622A 戩 6229 **11** 戯 622F 戮 622E 戱 6231
12 戰 6230 **13** 戴 6234 戲 6232 **14** 戳 6233

戶 63

戶 6236 户 6237 戸 6238 **3** 启 542F 妒 5992 戻 623B 沪 6CAA 芦 82A6 **4** 戾 623E 所 6240 房 623F 戽 623D 枦 67A6 炉 7089
肩 80A9 **5** 扁 6241 扃 6243 **6** 扇 6247 **7** 扈 6248 **8** 扉 6249 雇 96C7

手 64

才 624D 手 624B **1** 扎 624E **2** 打 6253 扑 6251 扒 6252 扔 6254 払 6255 **3** 扞 625E 扛 625B 扙 6259 扣 6263 扦 6266
托 6258 扥 6265 执 6267 扩 6269 扪 626A 扫 626B 扬 626C 扨 6268 扠 6260 **4** 承 627F 扱 6271 扶 6276 抚 629A 技 6280 抔 6294
抠 62A0 扰 6270 抜 629C 扼 627C 找 627E 批 6279 扯 626F 抄 6284 折 6298 抓 6293 扳 6273 抡 62A1 扮 626E 抢 62A2 扺 627A 抑 6291
抛 629B 投 6295 抆 6286 抗 6297 抖 6296 护 62A4 抉 6289 択 629E 扭 626D 把 628A 报 62A5 抒 6292 **5** 拜 62DC 拒 62D2 拟 62DF
抹 62B9 抦 62A6 拓 62D3 拢 62E2 拔 62D4 拋 62CB 抨 62A8 拣 62E3 拈 62C8 担 62C5 抻 62BB 押 62BC 抽 62BD 拐 62D0 拝 62DD 拃 62C3

手 64

拖 62D6 拊 62CA 拍 62CD 拆 62C6 抮 62AE 拎 62CE 拥 62E5 抵 62B5 拘 62D8 拠 62E0 抱 62B1 拄 62C4 拡 62E1 拉 62C9 拦 62E6 拌 62CC 手

㧟 39DF 拧 62E7 𢫕 22AD5 抿 62BF 拂 62C2 拙 62D9 拏 62CF 招 62DB 披 62AB 拨 62E8 择 62E9 拚 62DA 抬 62AC 拇 62C7 拗 62D7

6 挈 6308 拭 62ED 挂 6302 持 6301 拮 62EE 拷 62F7 挚 631A 拱 62F1 挝 631D 拵 62F5 挎 630E 挞 631E 挟 631F 挠 6320 挡 6321

拽 62FD 括 62EC 拴 62F4 拾 62FE 拿 62FF 挑 6311 指 6307 挣 6323 挛 631B 挤 6324 拼 62FC 拳 62F3 挙 6319 挖 6316 按 6309 挥 6325

拯 62EF 拶 62F6 **7** 挺 633A 挻 633B 挪 632A 挵 6335 挿 633F 捞 635E 捕 6355 捂 6342 𢭃 22B43 振 632F 挾 633E 捗 6357 捎 634E

捍 634D 捏 634F 捜 635C 捉 6349 捆 6346 捐 6350 损 635F 挹 6339 捌 634C 捡 6361 挫 632B 捋 634B 换 6362 挽 633D 捣 6363 㧸 39F8

挲 6332 捅 6345 挨 6328 **8** 捧 6367 掛 639B 措 63AA 捱 6371 捺 637A 掩 63A9 捷 6377 捿 637F 排 6392 掉 6389 掳 63B3 掌 638C

掴 63B4 捫 636B 掣 63A3 掰 63B0 捶 6376 推 63A8 捭 636D 𢯊 22BCA 掀 6380 捨 6368 掄 6384 採 63A1 授 6388 掙 6399 捻 637B 掏 638F

掐 6390 㧾 39FE 掬 63AC 掠 63A0 掂 6382 掖 6396 捽 637D 接 63A5 掷 63B7 捲 6372 掸 63B8 掟 639F 控 63A7 捩 6369 掮 63AE 探 63A2

掃 6383 据 636E 掘 6398 掹 63B9 掺 63BA 掻 63BB 掇 6387 **9** 揶 63F6 描 63CF 掲 63B2 揍 63CD 揷 63F7 揲 63F2 揸 63F8 揠 63E0

揦 63E6 揀 63C0 揼 63FC 𢱕 22C55 揩 63E9 揹 63F9 揽 63FD 㨘 3A18 提 63D0 揚 63DA 揖 63D6 揾 63FE 揭 63ED 揣 63E3 揿 63FF 插 63D2

揪 63EA 揄 63C4 揺 63FA 援 63F4 搀 6400 換 63DB 揞 63DE 搁 6401 搂 6402 揃 63C3 搅 6405 𢱑 22C51 揮 63EE 握 63E1 摒 6452 揆 63C6

揉 63C9 掾 63BE 撥 64A5 **10** 搽 643D 搭 642D 搜 641C 搥 6425 搓 6413 搔 6414 搆 6406 摃 6443 摂 6442 摄 6444 搢 6422 搏 640F

搣 6423 搨 6428 損 640D 摁 6441 摆 6446 搵 6435 携 643A 搗 6417 摀 6440 搬 642C 摇 6447 搶 6436 搇 6407 搖 6416 搞 641E 搪 642A

搐 6410 搴 6434 摈 6448 搾 643E 搧 6427 搦 6426 摊 644A 搡 6421 **11** 摩 6469 摒 6452 摸 6478 摹 6479 摰 6470 摯 646F 撃 6483

摶 6476 摳 6473 摵 6475 𢳂 22CC2 摟 645F 撂 6482 摞 645E 摑 6451 摧 6467 𢴈 22D08 摠 6460 摭 646D 摘 6458 摔 6454 撇 6487 摺 647A

摻 647B 摜 645C 摷 6477 **12** 𢵌 22D4C 撵 64B5 撓 6493 撷 64B7 撕 6495 撒 6492 撢 64A2 撅 6485 撩 64A9 撍 648D 撲 64B2 撐 6490

撑 6491 撮 64AE 𢵧 22D67 撫 64AB 撬 64AC 撳 64B3 播 64AD 撚 649A 撴 64B4 撞 649E 撤 64A4 撙 6499 撈 6488 撹 64B9 撰 64B0 撥 64A5

13 撾 64BE 撻 64BB 擎 64CE 擒 64D2 擀 64C0 㩒 3A52 擊 64CA 撼 64BC 擂 64C2 據 64DA 擄 64C4 擋 64CB 擝 64DD 操 64CD 擇 64C7

撿 64BF 擔 64D4 擅 64C5 擁 64C1 擞 64DE 擘 64D8 **14** 擭 64ED 擧 64E7 擡 64E1 擣 64E3 擱 64F1 擤 64E4 擬 64EC 擠 64E0 擦 64E6

手 64

擰 64F0 擢 64E2 **15** 擥 64E5 擴 64F4 擲 64F2 攆 6506 擷 64F7 攀 6500 擾 64FE 攄 6504 㩧 3A67 擻 64FB 擺 64FA **16** 攒 6512
攏 650F **17** 攖 6516 攔 6514 攙 6519 攘 6518 **18** 攝 651D 攜 651C **19** 攤 6524 攞 651E 攢 6522 攣 6523 **20** 攫 652B
攥 6525 攪 652A **21** 攬 652C **25** 𢺳 22EB3

支 65

支 652F **2** 伎 4F0E 攰 6530 **3** 吱 5431 妓 5993 岐 5C90 忮 5FEE 技 6280 芰 82B0 **4** 枝 679D 歧 6B67 肢 80A2
6 翅 7FC5 **7** 豉 8C49

攴 66

2 攷 6537 收 6536 **3** 孜 5B5C 攻 653B 攸 6538 改 6539 **4** 放 653E 政 653F 条 6761 枚 679A 牧 7267 玫 73AB
5 故 6545 敃 6543 畋 754B **6** 敌 654C 效 6548 敉 6549 致 81F4 **7** 敟 655F 敖 6556 教 6559 救 6551 敕 6555 敔 6554
敗 6557 敏 654F 敍 654D 敘 6558 敎 654E 敛 655B 赦 8D66 **8** 敝 655D 敢 6562 散 6563 敞 655E 敦 6566 敭 656D **9** 敬 656C
数 6570 **10** 敝 655D 敲 6572 **11** 敷 6577 數 6578 敵 6575 整 6574 **12** 敾 657E **13** 斂 6582 **14** 斃 6583
16 斅 6585 **19** 變 8B8A

文 67

文 6587 **2** 刘 5218 齐 9F50 **3** 吝 541D 坟 575F 对 5BFE 彣 5F63 汶 6C76 **4** 忞 5FDE 斉 6589 旻 65FB 旼 65FC 炆 7086
玟 739F **6** 斋 658B 紊 7D0A 紋 7D0B 虔 8654 蚊 868A **7** 斎 658E 斌 658C **8** 斑 6591 斐 6590 閔 9594 雯 96EF
12 斓 6593 **17** 斕 6595

斗 68

斗 6597 **3** 抖 6296 **4** 戽 623D 枓 6793 **5** 科 79D1 **6** 料 6599 蚪 86AA **7** 斜 659C 斛 659B **9** 斟 659F
10 斡 65A1 魁 9B41

斤 69

斤 65A4 **1** 斥 65A5 **2** 劤 52A4 匠 5320 **3** 听 542C 圻 573B 忻 5FFB 折 6298 沂 6C82 芹 82B9 近 8FD1 **4** 所 6240
斩 65A9 斧 65A7 欣 6B23 昕 6615 析 6790 炘 7098 祈 7948 **5** 斫 65AB **7** 斬 65AC 断 65AD 訢 8A22 **8** 斯 65AF
9 頎 980E 新 65B0 靳 9773 **10** 斲 65B2 **14** 斷 65B7

方 70

方 65B9 **2** 仿 4EFF **3** 坊 574A 妨 59A8 彷 5F77 芳 82B3 邡 90A1 防 9632 **4** 房 623F 放 653E 於 65BC 昉 6609 枋 678B
肪 80AA **5** 施 65BD **6** 旁 65C1 旂 65C2 旅 65C5 紡 7D21 舫 822B **7** 旌 65CC 族 65CF 旎 65CE 旋 65CB 訪 8A2A

方 70 — **8** 鈁 9201 **9** 旒 65D2 **10** 旗 65D7 旖 65D6 **11** 魴 9B74 **14** 旛 65DB

无 71 — 无 65E0 **5** 既 65E2 **7** 旣 65E3

日 72 — 日 65E5 **1** 旧 65E7 旦 65E6 **2** 早 65E9 旨 65E8 旬 65EC 旭 65ED 旮 65EE 旯 65EF 曳 66F3 **3** 旱 65F1 旴 65F4 时 65F6 旲 65F2 旷 65F7 旸 65F8 汩 6C68 阳 9633 **4** 畅 7545 旺 65FA 昊 660A 昙 6619 昔 6614 昃 6603 旽 65FD 昆 6606 昌 660C 旿 65FF 昇 6607 昕 6615 昑 6611 昐 6610 明 660E 昏 660F 易 6613 昀 6600 昂 6602 旻 65FB 旼 65FC 昉 6609 杲 6772 杳 6773 沓 6C93 炅 7085 者 8005 **5** 昼 663C 冒 5192 春 6625 昧 6627 昰 6630 是 662F 昻 663B 昞 661E 昺 663A 昜 661C 显 663E 映 6620 星 661F 昨 6628 昤 6624 昫 662B 昴 6634 昿 663F 昱 6631 昡 6621 昶 6636 昵 6635 昭 662D 曜 66DC 曷 66F7 **6** 時 6642 晋 664B 晅 6645 晒 6652 晓 6653 晉 6649 晃 6643 晄 6644 晔 6654 晌 664C 晁 6641 晏 664F 晕 6655 晖 6656 曺 66FA 書 66F8 耆 8006 **7** 晝 665D 勗 52D7 晟 665F 晢 6662 晤 6664 晨 6668 晛 665B 曼 66FC 晧 6667 晦 6666 晞 665E 晗 6657 晚 665A 晥 6665 晙 6659 晩 6669 曹 66F9 曽 66FD **8** 晴 6674 暁 6681 暑 6691 晰 6670 晳 6673 暂 6682 晫 666B 晶 6676 晹 6679 智 667A 晷 6677 景 666F 晾 667E 普 666E 晸 6678 替 66FF 最 6700 曾 66FE 量 91CF 間 9593 **9** 暎 668E 暘 6698 暍 668D 暖 6696 暗 6697 暄 6684 暈 6688 暉 6689 暇 6687 暋 668B 暐 6690 暌 668C 會 6703 **10** 嘗 5617 曄 66C4 暦 66A6 暢 66A2 暣 66A3 暧 66A7 暠 66A0 暝 669D 暨 66A8 馹 99B9 **11** 暱 66B1 暮 66AE 暳 66B3 暪 66AA 暴 66B4 暫 66AB 暲 66B2 魯 9B6F **12** 曄 66C4 暹 66B9 曉 66C9 曆 66C6 暸 66B8 曇 66C7 暻 66BB 曁 66C1 暾 66BE **13** 曖 66D6 **14** 曙 66D9 曜 66DC **15** 曠 66E0 曝 66DD **16** 曣 66E3 曦 66E6 **17** 曩 66E9 **19** 曬 66EC

曰 73 — 曰 66F0 **1** 电 7535 曱 66F1 **2** 曲 66F2 曳 66F3 **3** 更 66F4 **5** 曷 66F7 **6** 曺 66FA 書 66F8 **7** 勗 52D7 曼 66FC 曹 66F9 曽 66FD **8** 替 66FF 最 6700 曾 66FE **9** 會 6703

月 74 — 月 6708 **2** 刖 5216 有 6709 **3** 阴 9634 **4** 明 660E 朋 670B 服 670D 玥 73A5 **5** 朐 6710 **6** 朕 6715 朔 6714 **7** 朗 6717 望 671B **8** 勝 52DD 朞 671E 期 671F 朝 671D 渠 6E20 閒 9592 **11** 滕 6ED5 **12** 膶 81B6 螣 87A3 **13** 謄 8B04 賸 8CF8 **14** 朦 6726 **16** 朧 6727 騰 9A30

木 木 75

木 6728 **1** 未 672A 末 672B 本 672C 朮 672E 术 672F 札 672D **2** 朱 6731 休 4F11 凩 51E9 朽 673D 朴 6734 杀 6740 朵 6735

机 673A 杂 6742 朶 6736 权 6743 **3** 来 6765 呆 5446 困 56F0 宋 5B8B 床 5E8A 杆 6746 杜 675C 杠 6760 杢 6762 材 6750 村 6751

杕 6755 杖 6756 杙 6759 杏 674F 束 675F 杣 6763 杉 6749 杋 674B 杓 6753 条 6761 极 6781 杗 6757 杞 675E 李 674E 杨 6768 杈 6748

沐 6C90 **4** 來 4F86 枉 6789 林 6797 杮 676E 枝 679D 杯 676F 枢 67A2 枒 6792 枇 6787 杪 676A 東 6771 杲 6772 杳 6773 枏 678F

果 679C 㭎 3B4E 枘 6798 枣 67A3 杵 6775 枡 67A1 枚 679A 析 6790 板 677F 枞 679E 松 677E 枪 67AA 枠 67A0 枫 67AB 枭 67AD 构 6784

杭 676D 枋 678B 枓 6793 杰 6770 枦 67A6 枕 6795 杻 677B 杷 6777 杼 677C 采 91C7 牀 7240 **5** 柜 67DC 柰 67F0 标 6807 栈 6808

柾 67FE 枾 67BE 某 67D0 柑 67D1 枯 67AF 栉 6809 柯 67EF 柄 67C4 栃 6803 柘 67D8 柩 67E9 枰 67B0 栋 680B 栌 680C 查 67E5 査 67FB

相 76F8 柙 67D9 柚 67DA 柵 67F5 枳 67B3 枴 67B4 柺 67FA 柶 67F6 柬 67EC 柞 67DE 柏 67CF 柝 67DD 柢 67E2 栎 680E 枸 67B8 栅 6805

柳 67F3 柊 67CA 柱 67F1 柿 67FF 栏 680F 柒 67D2 染 67D3 栄 6804 柠 67E0 柁 67C1 架 67B6 枷 67B7 柖 67D6 树 6811 枱 67B1 柔 67D4

栂 6802 柴 67F4 **6** 唜 551C 栽 683D 框 6846 桟 685F 栻 683B 栞 681E 桂 6842 桔 6854 栳 6833 桠 6860 桓 6853 栗 6817 栖 6816

栢 6822 栯 682F 桎 684E 桌 684C 桢 6862 桄 6844 档 6863 桐 6850 株 682A 桥 6865 栴 6834 桕 6855 桦 6866 桁 6841 栓 6813 桧 6867

桃 6843 桅 6845 栒 6812 桀 6840 桝 685D 格 683C 栘 6818 栾 683E 桨 6868 桩 6869 校 6821 核 6838 样 6837 桜 685C 案 6848 桉 6849

根 6839 栩 6829 桑 6851 臬 81EC **7** 條 689D 梦 68A6 梆 6886 梠 68A0 梃 6883 梛 689B 梼 68BC 梇 6887 械 68B0 梵 68B5 梂 6882

梗 6897 梧 68A7 桭 686D 梢 68A2 桿 687F 桯 686F 梘 6898 梱 68B1 梏 688F 梨 68A8 梅 6885 梟 689F 梔 6894 检 68C0 梲 68B2 桴 6874

梓 6893 梳 68B3 梯 68AF 梁 6881 梡 68A1 桹 6879 棂 68C2 梶 68B6 桶 6876 梭 68AD **8** 椛 691B 棻 68FB 棒 68D2 棖 68D6 棱 68F1

椏 690F 棋 68CB 植 690D 森 68EE 棼 68FC 棟 68DF 椟 691F 椅 6905 棲 68F2 棧 68E7 椒 6912 棹 68F9 棠 68E0 棵 68F5 棍 68CD 椙 6919

椚 691A 棗 68D7 棘 68D8 棅 68C5 椎 690E 棉 68C9 検 691C 椧 6927 棚 68DA 椋 690B 椁 6901 椄 6904 棄 68C4 椪 692A 棪 68EA 棕 68D5

椀 6900 棺 68FA 棨 68E8 棣 68E3 椭 692D 渠 6E20 閑 9591 集 96C6 **9** 楮 696E 椰 6930 楛 695B 榔 6994 楗 6957 極 6975 楔 6954

椿 693F 楳 6973 椹 6939 楠 6960 楂 6942 楚 695A 楝 695D 楕 6955 楷 6977 楨 6968 榄 6984 業 696D 楊 694A 楫 696B 楬 696C 楞 695E

楸 6978 椴 6934 楽 697D 楯 696F 榆 6986 楡 6961 楓 6953 榈 6988 楼 697C 楢 6962 榉 6989 楦 6966 概 6982 楣 6963 楹 6979 楙 6959

木 75

椽 693D **10** 寨 5BE8 槐 69D0 槌 69CC 槎 69CE 榊 698A 榛 699B 構 69CB 榧 69A7 槓 69D3 榖 6996 樺 6A3A 槙 69D9 榦 69A6 榑 6991
榎 698E 槛 69DB 榥 69A5 榻 69BB 榫 69AB 榭 69AD 槃 69C3 榣 69A3 槍 69CD 槇 69C7 榴 69B4 槁 69C1 榜 699C 様 69D8 榮 69AE 槟 69DF
榨 69A8 榕 6995 榷 69B7 **11** 模 6A21 槤 69E4 槨 69E8 樋 6A0B 樁 6A01 槻 69FB 槿 69FF 横 6A2A 槽 69FD 樞 6A1E 樫 6A2B 標 6A19
槭 69ED 樗 6A17 樓 6A13 樱 6A31 権 6A29 槪 69EA 樂 6A02 樅 6A05 樊 6A0A 槲 69F2 樟 6A1F 樣 6A23 樑 6A11 樒 6A12 槳 69F3 樨 6A28
12 樺 6A3A 橡 6A61 橄 6A44 橢 6A62 橈 6A48 樾 6A3E 樹 6A39 橲 6A72 橫 6A6B 橱 6A71 橛 6A5B 橒 6A52 樸 6A38 橇 6A47 橋 6A4B
樵 6A35 橓 6A53 橹 6A79 橦 6A66 樽 6A3D 橙 6A59 橘 6A58 機 6A5F 橚 6A5A **13** 橽 6A7D 檠 6AA0 檎 6A8E 檨 6AA8 檉 6A89 檣 6AA3
橿 6A7F 檔 6A94 橾 6A7E 櫛 6ADB 檪 6AAA 檄 6A84 檢 6AA2 檜 6A9C 檐 6A90 檩 6AA9 檀 6A80 檍 6A8D 檗 6A97 **14** 檬 6AAC 櫆 6AC6
檯 6AAF 檮 6AAE 櫃 6AC3 檻 6ABB 檳 6AB3 檸 6AB8 櫂 6AC2 櫈 6AC8 **15** 櫛 6ADB 櫚 6ADA 櫝 6ADD 櫫 6AEB 櫟 6ADF 櫓 6AD3 櫥 6AE5
16 櫧 6AE7 櫪 6AEA 櫨 6AE8 櫬 6AEC 櫳 6AF3 櫶 6AF6 櫱 6AF1 **17** 櫸 6AF8 欌 6B0C 櫺 6AFA 櫻 6AFB 欄 6B04 欅 6B05
18 權 6B0A 欉 6B09 **19** 欐 6B10 欒 6B12 **21** 欗 6B17 欖 6B16 **22** 欝 6B1D **24** 欞 6B1E

欠 76

欠 6B20 **2** 次 6B21 欢 6B22 **3** 吹 5439 坎 574E 芡 82A1 **4** 欣 6B23 欧 6B27 炊 708A **5** 砍 780D **7** 欷 6B37
欲 6B32 欸 6B38 軟 8EDF **8** 款 6B3E 欺 6B3A 欽 6B3D 飲 98F2 **9** 歇 6B47 歃 6B43 歆 6B46 飮 98EE **10** 歌 6B4C 歉 6B49
11 歎 6B4E 歐 6B50 歓 6B53 **12** 歔 6B54 歙 6B59 **13** 歜 6B5C 歛 6B5B **14** 歟 6B5F **18** 歡 6B61

止 77

止 6B62 **1** 正 6B63 **2** 企 4F01 凪 51EA 此 6B64 **3** 址 5740 扯 626F 步 6B65 沚 6C9A 缶 7F36 芷 82B7 **4** 武 6B66
歧 6B67 歩 6B69 祉 7949 肯 80AF **5** 歪 6B6A **6** 耻 803B **7** 趾 8DBE **8** 歯 6B6F **9** 歲 6B72 歳 6B73
10 歴 6B74 **12** 歷 6B77 **14** 歸 6B78

歹 78

歹 6B79 **2** 列 5217 夙 5919 死 6B7B **3** 歼 6B7C **4** 歿 6B7F **5** 殂 6B82 殃 6B83 殇 6B87 殄 6B84 殆 6B86
6 残 6B8B 殊 6B8A 殉 6B89 **7** 殒 6B92 殓 6B93 **8** 殖 6B96 殘 6B98 殚 6B9A **9** 殛 6B9B **10** 殞 6B9E 殡 6BA1
11 殤 6BA4 **12** 殫 6BAB **13** 殭 6BAD 殮 6BAE **14** 殯 6BAF **17** 殲 6BB2

殳 79

殳 6BB3 **3** 役 5F79 投 6295 没 6CA1 芟 829F **4** 殴 6BB4 股 80A1 **5** 段 6BB5 疫 75AB **6** 殷 6BB7 般 822C

殳 79
7 殺 6BBA 殻 6BBB 設 8A2D **8** 殼 6BBC **9** 彀 5F40 毀 6BC0 毁 6BC1 殿 6BBF **10** 榖 6996 穀 7A40 骰 9AB0
11 毆 6BC6 毅 6BC5 **13** 轂 8F42

毋 80
毌 6BCC **1** 母 6BCD **2** 毎 6BCE **3** 乸 4E78 姆 59C6 拇 62C7 每 6BCF 毐 6BD0 苺 82FA **4** 毒 6BD2 **7** 貫 8CAB
9 毓 6BD3

比 81
比 6BD4 **2** 仳 4EF3 毕 6BD5 **3** 吡 5421 妣 59A3 屁 5C41 庇 5E87 批 6279 沘 6C98 **4** 昆 6606 枇 6787 玭 73AD
5 毗 6BD7 毘 6BD8 毖 6BD6 皆 7686 砒 7812 秕 79D5 **6** 毙 6BD9 粃 7C83 紕 7D15 **8** 琵 7435 **13** 毚 6BDA

毛 82
毛 6BDB **3** 尾 5C3E 芼 82BC **5** 毡 6BE1 **6** 笔 7B14 粍 7C8D 耄 8004 耗 8017 **7** 毫 6BEB 毬 6BEC **8** 毳 6BF3
毯 6BEF **9** 毽 6BFD **10** 髦 9AE6 **11** 麾 9EBE **12** 氅 6C05 **13** 氈 6C08

氏 83
氏 6C0F **1** 民 6C11 氐 6C10 **3** 抵 627A 芪 82AA **4** 氓 6C13 昏 660F 祇 7947 **5** 衹 8879 **6** 紙 7D19 舐 8210

气 84
气 6C14 **2** 気 6C17 氖 6C16 **3** 氙 6C19 汽 6C7D **4** 氛 6C1B **5** 氟 6C1F 氢 6C22 **6** 氩 6C29 氤 6C24 氦 6C26
氧 6C27 氣 6C23 氨 6C28 **7** 氪 6C2A 氫 6C2B **8** 氰 6C30 氬 6C2C 氮 6C2E 氯 6C2F **10** 氳 6C33

水 85
水 6C34 **1** 氹 6C39 氷 6C37 永 6C38 氶 6C36 **2** 求 6C42 冰 51B0 凼 51FC 汀 6C40 汁 6C41 汇 6C47 汆 6C46 汉 6C49 氾 6C3E
3 尿 5C3F 汗 6C57 汙 6C59 汚 6C5A 污 6C61 汞 6C5E 江 6C5F 汕 6C55 汍 6C4D 汎 6C4E 汐 6C50 汛 6C5B 汜 6C5C 池 6C60 汝 6C5D
汤 6C64 汊 6C4A **4** 沲 6C72 沣 6CA3 汪 6C6A 汫 6C6B 沅 6C85 沄 6C84 沐 6C90 沛 6C9B 沔 6C94 汰 6C70 沤 6CA4 沥 6CA5 沌 6C8C
沘 6C98 沍 6C8D 沏 6C8F 沚 6C9A 沙 6C99 汨 6C68 汩 6C69 沓 6C93 沖 6C96 汭 6C6D 汽 6C7D 沃 6C83 沂 6C82 沦 6CA6 汹 6C79 汾 6C7E
沧 6CA7 沕 6C95 沒 6C92 沟 6C9F 没 6CA1 汴 6C74 汶 6C76 沆 6C86 沩 6CA9 沪 6CAA 沈 6C88 沉 6C89 沁 6C81 決 6C7A 沢 6CA2 沇 6C87
5 泛 6CDB 泰 6CF0 沫 6CAB 沬 6CAC 法 6CD5 泄 6CC4 沽 6CBD 河 6CB3 泵 6CF5 泙 6CD9 沾 6CBE 泸 6CF8 沮 6CAE 泪 6CEA 油 6CB9
沺 6CBA 畓 7553 泱 6CF1 況 6CC1 泂 6CC2 泅 6CC5 泗 6CD7 𣲷 23CB7 泉 6CC9 泊 6CCA 泠 6CE0 泜 6CDC 沿 6CBF 泖 6CD6 泡 6CE1 注 6CE8
泣 6CE3 泫 6CEB 泮 6CEE 泞 6CDE 沱 6CB1 泻 6CFB 泌 6CCC 泳 6CF3 泥 6CE5 泯 6CEF 沸 6CB8 泓 6CD3 沼 6CBC 波 6CE2 泼 6CFC 泽 6CFD

水 85

泾 6CFE 治 6CBB **6** 浅 6D45 洼 6D3C 洁 6D01 洱 6D31 洪 6D2A 洹 6D39 洒 6D12 洧 6D27 洌 6D0C 浇 6D47 浈 6D48 洸 6D38 洩 6D29 水
浊 6D4A 洞 6D1E 洄 6D04 测 6D4B 洙 6D19 洗 6D17 活 6D3B 洑 6D11 洎 6D0E 洫 6D2B 洐 6D10 派 6D3E 浍 6D4D 洽 6D3D 洮 6D2E 洵 6D35
洶 6D36 洚 6D1A 洛 6D1B 洺 6D3A 浄 6D44 浆 6D46 浏 6D4F 济 6D4E 洨 6D28 洋 6D0B 洣 6D23 洲 6D32 浑 6D51 浒 6D52 浓 6D53 津 6D25
浔 6D54 流 6D41 衍 884D **7** 涏 6D8F 涎 6D8E 涛 6D9B 浙 6D59 涍 6D8D 涜 6D9C 涝 6D9D 浦 6D66 涑 6D91 浯 6D6F 酒 9152 浹 6D79
涞 6D9E 涟 6D9F 涇 6D87 涉 6D89 消 6D88 涅 6D85 浿 6D7F 浬 6D6C 浞 6D5E 涓 6D93 涡 6DA1 涢 6DA2 浥 6D65 涔 6D94 浩 6D69 海 6D77
浜 6D5C 涂 6D82 浴 6D74 浮 6D6E 涣 6DA3 涤 6DA4 润 6DA6 涧 6DA7 涕 6D95 浣 6D63 浤 6D64 浪 6D6A 浸 6D78 涨 6DA8 涩 6DA9 涊 6D8A
涌 6D8C 涘 6D98 浚 6D5A **8** 颍 988D 淼 6DFC 涙 6D99 清 6E05 淸 6DF8 渍 6E0D 添 6DFB 渚 6E1A 淩 6DE9 淇 6DC7 淋 6DCB 淅 6DC5
淞 6DDE 涷 6DB7 渎 6E0E 涯 6DAF 淹 6DF9 涿 6DBF 淒 6DD2 渐 6E10 淺 6DFA 淑 6DD1 渉 6E09 渋 6E0B 淖 6DD6 淌 6DCC 淏 6DCF 混 6DF7
渇 6E07 涸 6DB8 渑 6E11 淮 6DEE 淦 6DE6 淪 6DEA 淆 6DC6 渊 6E0A 渓 6E13 淫 6DEB 淨 6DE8 淍 6DCD 渔 6E14 淘 6DD8 涼 6DBC 淳 6DF3
液 6DB2 済 6E08 淬 6DEC 涪 6DAA 淤 6DE4 淯 6DEF 渕 6E15 淃 6DC3 淡 6DE1 淙 6DD9 淀 6DC0 淚 6DDA 深 6DF1 涮 6DAE 涵 6DB5 渗 6E17
淥 6DE5 淄 6DC4 淵 6DF5 **9** 渶 6E36 渠 6E20 渦 6E26 湊 6E4A 渽 6E3D 湛 6E5B 満 6E80 港 6E2F 渫 6E2B 滞 6EDE 湖 6E56 湳 6E73
渣 6E23 湘 6E58 渤 6E24 湮 6E6E 減 6E1B 湎 6E4E 湞 6E5E 湜 6E5C 渺 6E3A 測 6E2C 湯 6E6F 湿 6E7F 湡 6E61 温 6E29 渴 6E34 渭 6E2D
溃 6E83 湍 6E4D 溅 6E85 湃 6E43 湫 6E6B 湩 6E69 湺 6E7A 湟 6E5F 渝 6E1D 湲 6E72 渙 6E19 湾 6E7E 渟 6E1F 渡 6E21 游 6E38 渼 6E3C
溇 6E87 湔 6E54 滋 6ECB 渲 6E32 渾 6E3E 溉 6E89 渥 6E25 湣 6E63 湄 6E44 湧 6E67 溌 6E8C **10** 寨 5BE8 涢 6DA2 滑 6ED1 滁 6EC1
滟 6EDF 溱 6EB1 溝 6E9D 溘 6E98 满 6EE1 滢 6EE2 滇 6EC7 溥 6EA5 溧 6EA7 溽 6EBD 滅 6EC5 滙 6ED9 源 6E90 溼 6EBC 滤 6EE4 滥 6EE5
滉 6EC9 溫 6EAB 準 6E96 溴 6EB4 溵 6EB5 滔 6ED4 溪 6EAA 滄 6EC4 滕 6ED5 溜 6E9C 滦 6EE6 漓 6F13 溏 6E8F 滝 6EDD 滂 6EC2 溢 6EA2
溯 6EAF 滎 6ECE 滨 6EE8 溶 6EB6 滓 6ED3 溟 6E9F 滘 6ED8 溺 6EBA 滩 6EE9 **11** 潁 6F41 溇 6E87 漠 6F20 漣 6F23 滌 6ECC 滚 6EDA
漬 6F2C 漌 6F0C 漢 6F22 滿 6EFF 滯 6EEF 漧 6F27 潇 6F47 漆 6F06 漸 6F38 漕 6F15 漱 6F31 漚 6F1A 漂 6F02 滷 6EF7 漫 6F2B 漯 6F2F
潅 6F45 漑 6F11 潋 6F4B 漁 6F01 漪 6F2A 滸 6EF8 滾 6EFE 漉 6F09 漳 6F33 滴 6EF4 漩 6F29 漾 6F3E 演 6F14 漥 6F25 滬 6EEC 漏 6F0F
漲 6F32 漿 6F3F 滲 6EF2 潍 6F4D **12** 潢 6F62 潴 6F74 潔 6F54 潜 6F5C 澆 6F86 澍 6F8D 澎 6F8E 潮 6F6E 潸 6F78 潭 6F6D 潦 6F66

水 火

水 85

澐 6F90 潛 6F5B 澁 6F81 潤 6F64 澗 6F97 潣 6F63 潰 6F70 澂 6F82 潟 6F5F 潗 6F57 澔 6F94 潘 6F58 潼 6F7C 澈 6F88 澜 6F9C 潽 6F7D

潾 6F7E 澇 6F87 潯 6F6F 潺 6F7A 潠 6F60 澄 6F84 潑 6F51 潞 6F5E 潚 6F5A 澀 6F80 **13** 澾 6FBE 澳 6FB3 澣 6FA3 濑 6FD1 澪 6FAA

濊 6FCA 濒 6FD2 澯 6FAF 澠 6FA0 澧 6FA7 濃 6FC3 澡 6FA1 澤 6FA4 澴 6FB4 濁 6FC1 激 6FC0 澮 6FAE 澹 6FB9 澶 6FB6 濂 6FC2 澱 6FB1

澦 6FA6 **14** 潛 6F5B 濩 6FE9 濛 6FDB 濨 6FE8 鴻 9D3B 濤 6FE4 濫 6FEB 濡 6FE1 濬 6FEC 濶 6FF6 濕 6FD5 濮 6FEE 濠 6FE0 濟 6FDF

濚 6FDA 濱 6FF1 濘 6FD8 澀 6F80 濯 6FEF 濰 6FF0 瀞 701E **15** 瀆 7006 濾 6FFE 瀑 7011 濺 6FFA 瀏 700F 瀁 7001 瀅 7005 瀉 7009

瀋 700B **16** 瀦 7026 瀞 701E 瀚 701A 瀟 701F 瀬 702C 瀨 7028 瀜 701C 瀝 701D 瀕 7015 瀣 7023 瀘 7018 瀧 7027 瀛 701B

17 瀯 702F 瀾 703E 瀲 7032 瀰 7030 瀷 7037 **18** 灌 704C 灃 7043 灏 704F 灐 7050 **19** 灕 7055 灑 7051 灘 7058

21 灠 7060 灞 705E 灝 705D **22** 灣 7063 **23** 灥 7065 灤 7064 **28** 灩 7069

火 86

火 706B **1** 灭 706D **2** 伙 4F19 灯 706F 灰 7070 **3** 灵 7075 灶 7076 灿 707F 灸 7078 灼 707C 灾 707E 炀 7080 災 707D

狄 72C4 **4** 杰 6770 炜 709C 炖 7096 炒 7092 炅 7085 炚 709A 炘 7098 炊 708A 炙 7099 炆 7086 炕 7095 炎 708E 炉 7089 炔 7094

5 炬 70AC 炡 70A1 炳 70B3 炼 70BC 点 70B9 畑 7551 炽 70BD 炭 70AD 炯 70AF 炸 70B8 烁 70C1 炮 70AE 炷 70B7 炫 70AB 烂 70C2

為 70BA 炤 70A4 烃 70C3 疢 75A2 秋 79CB **6** 烓 70D3 烤 70E4 热 70ED 烘 70D8 烜 70DC 烦 70E6 烈 70C8 烧 70E7 烛 70DB 烔 70D4

烟 70DF 烋 70CB 烨 70E8 烏 70CF 烇 70C7 烩 70E9 烚 70DA 烙 70D9 烊 70CA 羔 7F94 烫 70EB 烬 70EC 烝 70DD 耿 803F **7** 焉 7109

焘 7118 烴 70F4 焊 710A 烱 70F1 烯 70EF 焕 7115 烽 70FD 烹 70F9 焖 7116 烷 70F7 烺 70FA 焄 7104 焗 7117 焌 710C **8** 焔 7114

煮 716E 焚 711A 焯 712F 焜 711C 無 7121 焦 7126 焰 7130 然 7136 焞 711E 焠 7120 焿 713F 焙 7119 焱 7131 焢 7122 煀 7140 焼 713C

9 煐 7150 煚 715A 煤 7164 煏 714F 煙 7159 煉 7149 煩 7169 煃 7143 煬 716C 煦 7166 煜 715C 照 7167 煨 7168 煅 7145 煲 7172

煌 714C 煖 7156 煥 7165 煞 715E 煎 714E 煊 714A 煇 7147 煸 7178 煆 7146 煒 7152 煕 7155 **10** 燁 71C1 熙 7199 㷧 3DE7 熀 7180

熉 7189 熈 7188 熏 718F 熄 7184 熗 7197 熒 7192 熔 7194 煽 717D 熊 718A 蒸 84B8 **11** 勲 52F2 熲 71B2 熬 71AC 熢 71A2 熥 71A5

熱 71B1 㷫 3DEB 熟 719F 熵 71B5 熨 71A8 熠 71A0 黙 9ED9 **12** 燊 71CA 燁 71C1 燒 71D2 熹 71B9 熺 71BA 燕 71D5 燎 71CE 燗 71D7

燜 71DC 燔 71D4 燄 71C4 燃 71C3 燉 71C9 熾 71BE 燐 71D0 燙 71D9 燈 71C8 **13** 凞 51DE 燵 71F5 燠 71E0 燧 71E7 營 71DF 燦 71E6

火 86
燶 71F6 燥 71E5 燭 71ED 燬 71EC 燴 71F4 燮 71EE **14** 爀 7200 燾 71FE 燹 71F9 燸 71F8 燻 71FB 燼 71FC 燿 71FF **15** 爌 720C
爆 7206 爍 720D **16** 爐 7210 爔 7214 **17** 爛 721B **19** 𤓓 244D3 **25** 爨 7228

爪 87
爪 722A **3** 妥 59A5 孚 5B5A 抓 6293 **4** 受 53D7 采 91C7 觅 89C5 争 722D 爬 722C **5** 爰 7230 **6** 奚 595A 爱 7231
笊 7B0A 舀 8200 **7** 覓 8993 **8** 爲 7232 **14** 爵 7235

父 88
父 7236 **2** 交 4EA4 爷 7237 **4** 斧 65A7 爸 7238 **6** 爹 7239 釜 91DC **9** 爺 723A

爻 89
爻 723B **5** 爼 723C **7** 爽 723D **10** 爾 723E 駁 99C1

爿 90
爿 723F **3** 壮 58EE 壯 58EF 妆 599D **4** 戕 6215 牀 7240 状 72B6 狀 72C0 **6** 将 5C06 **7** 將 5C07 **13** 牆 7246

片 91
片 7247 **4** 版 7248 **8** 牍 724D 牌 724C **9** 牒 7252 **11** 牖 7256 **15** 牘 7258

牙 92
牙 7259 **2** 冴 51B4 **3** 呀 5440 邪 90AA 芽 82BD **4** 枒 6792 迓 8FD3 **5** 穿 7A7F **6** 蚜 869C **7** 訝 8A1D
谺 8C3A **8** 雅 96C5 **11** 鴉 9D09

牛 93
牛 725B **2** 件 4EF6 牝 725D 牟 725F **3** 吽 543D 牢 7262 牡 7261 牤 7264 牠 7260 **4** 牦 7266 牧 7267 物 7269
5 牵 7275 牯 726F 牲 7272 牴 7274 **6** 特 7279 牺 727A **7** 牽 727D 牾 727E 犁 7281 **8** 犊 728A 犄 7284 犇 7287
犂 7282 犀 7280 **10** 犒 7292 犖 7296 **11** 犛 729B **12** 犟 729F **13** 犠 72A0 **15** 犡 72A1 犢 72A2 **16** 犧 72A7

犬 94
犬 72AC **2** 伏 4F0F 犰 72B0 犯 72AF **3** 吠 5420 状 72B6 犷 72B7 **4** 戻 623B 戾 623E 狀 72C0 狂 72C2 犹 72B9 狆 72C6
狈 72C8 狄 72C4 **5** 狙 72D9 狎 72CE 狛 72DB 狐 72D0 狗 72D7 狍 72CD 狞 72DE 狒 72D2 畎 754E **6** 哭 54ED 类 7C7B 狭 72ED
狮 72EE 独 72EC 狢 72E2 狰 72F0 狡 72E1 狩 72E9 狱 72F1 狠 72E0 狲 72F2 **7** 㹴 3E74 狹 72F9 狽 72FD 狸 72F8 狷 72F7 狼 72FC
8 猜 731C 猪 732A 猎 730E 猫 732B 猇 7307 猓 7313 猖 7316 猡 7321 猊 730A 猙 7319 猝 731D 猟 731F 猕 7315 猛 731B
9 猢 7322 献 732E 猩 7329 猥 7325 猬 732C 猴 7334 猶 7336 猷 7337 獁 7341 **10** 猾 733E 猿 733F 獃 7343 獅 7345 猻 733B

犬 94

11 獒 7352 獏 734F 獄 7344 獐 7350 獎 734E **12** 獗 7357 獠 7360 獢 7362 獤 7364 獣 7363 默 9ED8 **13** 獭 736D 獨 7368
獪 736A **14** 獲 7372 獴 7374 獰 7370 **15** 獷 7377 獸 7378 獵 7375 **16** 獺 737A 獻 737B **17** 獼 737C **18** 獾 737E
19 玀 7380

玄 95

玄 7384 **3** 呟 545F 弦 5F26 泫 6CEB **4** 昡 6621 炫 70AB 玹 73B9 **5** 玆 7386 畜 755C 眩 7729 **6** 率 7387 絃 7D43
舷 8237 衒 8852 **8** 鉉 9249

玉 96

玉 7389 王 738B **1** 主 4E3B **2** 匡 5321 玎 738E 玑 7391 **3** 呈 5448 国 56FD 宝 5B9D 尪 5C2A 弄 5F04 汪 6C6A 狂 72C2
玕 7395 玗 7397 玙 7399 玔 7394 玖 7396 玘 7398 玚 739A 玛 739B **4** 旺 65FA 曜 66DC 枉 6789 玨 73A8 玩 73A9 玮 73AE 环 73AF
玭 73AD 现 73B0 玫 73AB 玠 73A0 玢 73A2 玥 73A5 玟 739F 玦 73A6 玧 73A7 **5** 珏 73CF 珐 73D0 珂 73C2 珑 73D1 玷 73B7 珅 73C5
玳 73B3 珀 73C0 珍 73CD 玲 73B2 玺 73BA 珎 73CE 珊 73CA 玹 73B9 珌 73CC 珉 73C9 玿 73BF 珈 73C8 玻 73BB 皇 7687 **6** 珡 73E1
珪 73EA 珥 73E5 珙 73D9 顼 987C 珖 73D6 珰 73F0 珠 73E0 珤 73E4 珗 73D7 珦 73E6 珩 73E9 珮 73EE 珣 73E3 珞 73DE 珫 73EB 班 73ED
珲 73F2 珢 73E2 珝 73DD 琉 7409 **7** 望 671B 珹 73F9 琊 740A 珽 73FD 球 7403 珸 73F8 琏 740F 琐 7410 珵 73F5 現 73FE 理 7406
琄 7404 琍 740D 琇 7407 琁 7401 琓 7413 琅 7405 珺 73FA 㻐 3ED0 **8** 琤 7424 琫 742B 琵 7435 珷 73F7 琴 7434 琶 7436 琪 742A
琳 7433 琦 7426 琢 7422 琲 7432 琡 7421 琸 7438 琥 7425 琨 7428 琠 7420 琟 741F 琼 743C 琰 7430 琺 743A 琮 742E 琬 742C 琯 742F
琛 741B 琭 742D 琚 741A 鈺 923A 閏 958F **9** 瑛 745B 瑃 7443 瑟 745F 瑚 745A 頊 980A 瑌 744C 瑅 7445 瑁 7441 瑆 7446 瑞 745E
瑀 7440 瑜 745C 瑗 7457 瑄 7444 琿 743F 瑕 7455 瑋 744B 瑙 7459 聖 8056 **10** 瑯 746F 瑰 7470 瑳 7473 瑪 746A 瑱 7471 瑨 7468
瑣 7463 瑥 7465 瑶 7476 瑲 7472 瑤 7464 瑠 7460 瑭 746D 瑩 7469 瑢 7462 **11** 璉 7489 璃 7483 璂 7482 瑾 747E 璊 748A 璀 7480
璎 748E 璁 7481 瑽 747D 璋 748B 璇 7487 璆 7486 **12** 噩 5669 璜 749C 璡 74A1 璤 74A4 璞 749E 璟 749F 璠 74A0 璘 7498 璣 74A3
璐 7490 **13** 璥 74A5 璲 74B2 璱 74B1 璨 74A8 璩 74A9 璪 74AA 環 74B0 璦 74A6 璧 74A7 **14** 璵 74B5 璹 74B9 璽 74BD 璿 74BF
璸 74B8 **15** 瓊 74CA 瓈 74C8 瓆 74C6 **16** 瓒 74D2 瓏 74CF **17** 瓔 74D4 瓓 74D3 瓖 74D6 **18** 瓘 74D8 **19** 瓚 74DA

瓜 97
瓜 74DC **3** 呱 5471 孤 5B64 弧 5F27 狐 72D0 苽 82FD **5** 瓞 74DE **6** 瓠 74E0 **7** 觚 89DA **11** 瓢 74E2
14 瓣 74E3 **17** 瓤 74E4

瓦 98
瓦 74E6 **2** 佤 4F64 **3** 瓩 74E9 **4** 瓯 74EF 瓮 74EE **5** 瓴 74F4 **6** 瓷 74F7 瓶 74F6 **8** 甁 7501
9 甄 7504 **11** 甍 750D 甌 750C **12** 甑 7511 **13** 甕 7515

甘 99
甘 7518 **3** 咁 5481 坩 5769 甙 7519 苷 82F7 邯 90AF **4** 某 67D0 柑 67D1 甚 751A **5** 疳 75B3 **6** 甛 751B 甜 751C
紺 7D3A 蚶 86B6 **7** 酣 9163 **8** 鉗 9257

生 100
生 751F **3** 姓 59D3 性 6027 **4** 星 661F 牲 7272 **5** 甡 7521 **6** 產 7522 産 7523 笙 7B19 **7** 甥 7525 甦 7526

用 101
用 7528 甩 7529 **2** 佣 4F63 甫 752B 甬 752C **4** 甭 752D **7** 甯 752F

田 102
甲 7532 申 7533 由 7531 电 7535 曱 66F1 田 7530 甴 7534 **2** 佃 4F43 男 7537 町 753A 甸 7538 **3** 畅 7545 沺 6CBA 畀 7540
画 753B 甽 753D 甾 753E 苗 82D7 **4** 思 601D 毗 6BD7 毘 6BD8 畓 7553 畑 7551 畎 754E 畏 754F 畋 754B 畈 7548 界 754C 畇 7547
胃 80C3 **5** 畠 7560 畛 755B 留 7559 畝 755D 畜 755C 畔 7554 畚 755A **6** 畦 7566 畢 7562 異 7570 略 7565 累 7D2F 細 7D30
7 塁 5841 畴 7574 畬 756C 畲 7572 番 756A 畳 7573 畫 756B 畯 756F **8** 畺 757A 畸 7578 當 7576 畵 7575 畷 7577 鈿 923F
雷 96F7 **10** 畿 757F **11** 奮 596E 鴫 9D2B **14** 疇 7587 疆 7586 **17** 疊 758A

疋 103
疋 758B **4** 胥 80E5 **6** 蛋 86CB **7** 疎 758E 疏 758F **8** 楚 695A **9** 疑 7591

疒 104
2 疖 7596 疗 7597 **3** 疟 759F 疝 759D 疙 7599 疚 759A **4** 疡 75A1 疣 75A3 疪 75AA 疥 75A5 疮 75AE 疯 75AF 疫 75AB
疢 75A2 疤 75A4 **5** 症 75C7 疳 75B3 疴 75B4 病 75C5 疸 75B8 疽 75BD 疾 75BE 疹 75B9 痈 75C8 痀 75C0 疼 75BC 疱 75B1 痂 75C2
疲 75B2 痉 75C9 疵 75B5 痙 75D9 **6** 痔 75D4 痍 75CD 痊 75CA 痒 75D2 痕 75D5 **7** 𤶸 24DB8 痣 75E3 痨 75E8 痘 75D8 痞 75DE
痙 75D9 瘦 75E9 痢 75E2 痤 75E4 痪 75EA 痫 75EB 痧 75E7 痛 75DB 痠 75E0 **8** 痾 75FE 痲 75F2 痳 75F3 痱 75F1 痹 75F9 痼 75FC
痴 75F4 痿 75FF 痺 75FA 瘁 7601 瘀 7600 痰 75F0 𤷪 24DEA **9** 瘦 75E9 瘧 7627 瘍 760D 瘟 761F 瘉 7609 瘋 760B 瘓 7613 瘖 7616

疒 104

瘘 7618 **10** 瘩 7629 瘦 7626 瘙 7619 瘞 761E 瘪 762A 瘜 761C 瘢 7622 瘡 7621 瘤 7624 瘠 7620 瘫 762B **11** 瘼 763C 瘻 763B

瘴 7634 瘺 763A 瘾 763E 瘸 7638 **12** 癍 764D 療 7642 癎 764E 癇 7647 癌 764C 癆 7646 **13** 癘 7658 癞 765E 癤 7664 癒 7652

癖 7656 **14** 癟 765F 癣 7663 癡 7661 **15** 癤 7664 癦 7666 癥 7665 癢 7662 **16** 癫 766B 癩 7669 癪 766A **17** 癮 766E

癬 766C **18** 癰 7670 **19** 癱 7671 癲 7672

癶 105

4 癸 7678 発 767A **7** 登 767B 發 767C

白 106

白 767D **1** 百 767E **2** 伯 4F2F 皂 7682 **3** 帕 5E15 帛 5E1B 怕 6015 拍 62CD 泊 6CCA 狛 72DB 的 7684 迫 8FEB

4 柏 67CF 泉 6CC9 珀 73C0 皇 7687 皆 7686 皈 7688 **5** 畠 7560 皋 768B **6** 皐 7690 皑 7691 皎 768E 粕 7C95 習 7FD2

舶 8236 **7** 皓 7693 皖 7696 **8** 皙 7699 鉑 9251 **10** 皚 769A 皞 769E 魄 9B44 **12** 皤 76A4

皮 107

皮 76AE **3** 坡 5761 帔 5E14 彼 5F7C 披 62AB 波 6CE2 陂 9642 **4** 玻 73BB **5** 疲 75B2 皱 76B1 皰 76B0 破 7834 被 88AB

7 皴 76B4 詖 8A56 跛 8DDB **8** 鈹 9239 **9** 皸 76B8 頗 9817 **10** 皺 76BA

皿 108

皿 76BF **3** 孟 5B5F 盂 76C2 **4** 盃 76C3 盅 76C5 盆 76C6 盈 76C8 **5** 盏 76CF 盐 76D0 盍 76CD 监 76D1 盎 76CE 盌 76CC

益 76CA **6** 盔 76D4 盛 76DB 盘 76D8 盒 76D2 盗 76D7 盖 76D6 **7** 盜 76DC **8** 盞 76DE 盟 76DF **9** 監 76E3 盡 76E1

10 盤 76E4 **11** 盧 76E7 盥 76E5 **12** 盪 76EA **13** 盬 76EC **18** 蠱 8831 **20** 鹽 9E7D **23** 豔 8C54

目 109

目 76EE **2** 盯 76EF **3** 具 5177 直 76F4 泪 6CEA 盱 76F1 盲 76F2 苜 82DC **4** 冒 5192 相 76F8 𥄫 2512B 眄 7704 盹 76F9

省 7701 眇 7707 看 770B 盾 76FE 盼 76FC 盷 76F7 眈 7708 眉 7709 県 770C **5** 真 771F 眨 7728 眛 771B 眬 772C 眞 771E 眩 7729

眠 7720 眥 7725 **6** 眶 7736 眭 772D 眾 773E 眺 773A 睁 7741 眷 7737 眯 772F 眼 773C 眸 7738 **7** 着 7740 睐 7750 睍 774D

睏 774F 睑 7751 睇 7747 睆 7746 **8** 睛 775B 睦 7766 睪 776A 睚 775A 睞 775E 睫 776B 督 7763 睨 7768 睢 7762 睥 7765 睬 776C

睜 775C **9** 睾 777E 睹 7779 瞄 7784 睡 7761 睿 777F 瞅 7785 睽 777D **10** 瞍 778D 瞇 7787 瞌 778C 瞒 7792 瞋 778B 瞓 7793

瞎 778E 瞑 7791 **11** 䁥 4065 瞞 779E 䁪 406A 瞟 779F 瞠 77A0 **12** 瞥 77A5 瞰 77B0 瞭 77AD 瞧 77A7 瞬 77AC 瞳 77B3 瞩 77A9

瞪 77AA **13** 瞽 77BD 瞿 77BF 瞼 77BC 瞻 77BB **14** 矇 77C7 **15** 矋 77CB **16** 矓 77D3 **19** 矗 77D7 **21** 矚 77DA

矛 110 — 矛 77DB **3** 茅 8305 **4** 柔 67D4 矜 77DC **6** 袤 88A4 務 52D9

矢 111 — 矢 77E2 **2** 医 533B 矣 77E3 **3** 知 77E5 **4** 矧 77E7 **5** 疾 75BE 矩 77E9 **6** 矫 77EB **7** 短 77ED **8** 矮 77EE 雉 96C9 **9** 疑 7591 **12** 矯 77EF

石 112 — 石 77F3 **2** 矶 77F6 **3** 妬 59AC 宕 5B95 岩 5CA9 拓 62D3 矸 77F8 矻 77FB 矽 77FD 矾 77FE 矿 77FF 砀 7800 码 7801 **4** 斫 65AB 柘 67D8 泵 6CF5 研 7814 砖 7816 砒 7812 砌 780C 砂 7802 砚 781A 砕 7815 砍 780D 砇 7807 **5** 砭 782D 砝 781D 砵 7835 砸 7838 砺 783A 砻 783B 砰 7830 砧 7827 砠 7820 砷 7837 砟 781F 砱 7831 砥 7825 砾 783E 砲 7832 砿 783F 砬 782C 砣 7823 础 7840 破 7834 砦 7826 **6** 研 7814 硏 784F 硎 784E 硅 7845 硓 7853 硒 7852 硕 7855 硐 7850 硃 7843 硚 785A **7** 硦 7866 硬 786C 硤 7864 硝 785D 硯 786F 硷 7877 硲 7872 确 786E 硫 786B 跖 8DD6 **8** 碛 789B 䂻 40BB 碁 7881 碕 7895 碍 788D 碘 7898 碓 7893 碑 7891 碖 7896 硼 787C 碉 7889 碎 788E 碚 789A 碰 78B0 碇 7887 硿 787F 碗 7897 碌 788C 鉐 9250 **9** 碧 78A7 碟 789F 碴 78B4 碱 78B1 碩 78A9 碣 78A3 碳 78B3 磁 78C1 **10** 磋 78CB 碼 78BC 磕 78D5 磊 78CA 磐 78D0 磎 78CE 磔 78D4 碻 78BB 磅 78C5 確 78BA 碾 78BE **11** 磨 78E8 磧 78E7 磬 78EC 磡 78E1 磚 78DA **12** 硚 785A 磺 78FA 䃟 40DF 磵 78F5 礁 7901 磻 78FB 磷 78F7 磴 78F4 磯 78EF **13** 礎 790E 礑 7911 礖 7916 礒 7912 **14** 礡 7921 礙 7919 **15** 礪 792A 礦 7926 礬 792C 礫 792B **16** 礴 7934 礱 7931

示 113 — 示 793A **1** 礼 793C **2** 佘 4F58 礽 793D **3** 奈 5948 宗 5B97 祁 7941 社 793E 祀 7940 祂 7942 **4** 柰 67F0 祆 7946 祉 7949 视 89C6 祅 7945 祈 7948 祇 7947 **5** 祛 795B 祜 795C 祐 7950 祓 7953 祖 7956 神 795E 祝 795D 祚 795A 祗 7957 祢 7962 祕 7955 祠 7960 祟 795F **6** 票 7968 祯 796F 祭 796D 祥 7965 **7** 祷 7977 視 8996 祸 7978 禄 7984 **8** 禀 7980 祺 797A 禁 7981 祼 797C 禅 7985 祿 797F **9** 禍 798D 禊 798A 福 798F 禎 798E 禔 7994 禑 7991 禕 7995 **10** 禡 79A1 禛 799B 禚 799A **11** 禤 79A4 禦 79A6 **12** 禧 79A7 禪 79AA **13** 禮 79AE **14** 禱 79B1 禰 79B0 **17** 禳 79B3

禸 114 — **4** 禹 79B9 禺 79BA **6** 离 79BB **8** 禽 79BD 萬 842C

禾
穴
立
竹

禾 115

禾 (79BE) **2** 利 (5229) 禿 (79BF) 秃 (79C3) 秀 (79C0) 私 (79C1) **3** 秉 (79C9) 和 (548C) 委 (59D4) 季 (5B63) 秆 (79C6) 秈 (79C8) 秊 (79CA)
4 秕 (79D5) 秒 (79D2) 种 (79CD) 秋 (79CB) 科 (79D1) **5** 秭 (79ED) 秦 (79E6) 秣 (79E3) 秫 (79EB) 䄷 (4137) 秤 (79E4) 租 (79DF) 秞 (79DE) 秧 (79E7)
积 (79EF) 秩 (79E9) 称 (79F0) 秘 (79D8) **6** 秸 (79F8) 秽 (79FD) 移 (79FB) **7** 嵇 (5D47) 稍 (7A0D) 稈 (7A08) 程 (7A0B) 稀 (7A00) 税 (7A05) 稅 (7A0E)
酥 (9165) **8** 稜 (7A1C) 稙 (7A19) 稞 (7A1E) 稚 (7A1A) 稗 (7A17) 稔 (7A14) 稠 (7A20) 稣 (7A23) 稟 (7A1F) **9** 種 (7A2E) 稲 (7A32) 稱 (7A31) 稳 (7A33)
10 寨 (5BE8) 穀 (7A40) 穂 (7A42) 稶 (7A36) 稽 (7A3D) 稷 (7A37) 稻 (7A3B) 稿 (7A3F) 稼 (7A3C) **11** 穎 (7A4E) 積 (7A4D) 穑 (7A51) 穆 (7A46) 穏 (7A4F)
穐 (7A50) 穌 (7A4C) 穋 (7A4B) 麇 (9E87) **12** 穗 (7A57) 穉 (7A49) **13** 穡 (7A61) 穢 (7A62) 穠 (7A60) 穣 (7A63) **14** 穫 (7A6B) 穩 (7A69) 穨 (7A68)
穦 (7A66) **17** 穰 (7A70) 龢 (9FA2)

穴 116

穴 (7A74) **2** 究 (7A76) 穷 (7A77) **3** 帘 (5E18) 空 (7A7A) 穹 (7A79) **4** 穿 (7A7F) 突 (7A81) 穽 (7A7D) 窃 (7A83) **5** 窍 (7A8D) 窄 (7A84)
窈 (7A88) **6** 窒 (7A92) 窑 (7A91) 窕 (7A95) 窓 (7A93) **7** 窜 (7A9C) 窝 (7A9D) 窖 (7A96) 窗 (7A97) 窘 (7A98) **8** 窥 (7AA5) 窦 (7AA6) 窠 (7AA0)
窣 (7AA3) 窟 (7A9F) **9** 窩 (7AA9) 窪 (7AAA) **10** 窮 (7AAE) 窳 (7AB3) 窰 (7AB0) 窯 (7AAF) **11** 窺 (7ABA) 窸 (7AB8) **12** 窳 (7AB3) 窿 (7ABF)
竃 (7AC3) **13** 竄 (7AC4) 竅 (7AC5) **15** 竇 (7AC7) **16** 竈 (7AC8) **17** 竊 (7ACA)

立 117

立 (7ACB) **1** 产 (4EA7) **2** 位 (4F4D) **3** 垃 (5783) 妾 (59BE) 拉 (62C9) 泣 (6CE3) 苙 (82D9) **4** 亲 (4EB2) 昱 (6631) 竑 (7AD1) 竖 (7AD6)
竗 (7AD7) **5** 砬 (782C) 站 (7AD9) 竜 (7ADC) 竞 (7ADE) 竝 (7ADD) **6** 章 (7AE0) 竟 (7ADF) 翊 (7FCA) 笠 (7B20) 粒 (7C92) 翌 (7FCC) **7** 竦 (7AE6)
童 (7AE5) 竣 (7AE3) **8** 竪 (7AEA) 靖 (9756) **9** 竭 (7AED) 端 (7AEF) 颯 (98AF) **15** 競 (7AF6)

竹 118

竹 (7AF9) **2** 竺 (7AFA) **3** 竽 (7AFD) 竿 (7AFF) 笃 (7B03) **4** 笈 (7B08) 笄 (7B04) 笔 (7B14) 笑 (7B11) 笊 (7B0A) 笏 (7B0F) 笋 (7B0B) 笆 (7B06)
5 笫 (7B2B) 笺 (7B3A) 笹 (7B39) 笨 (7B28) 笼 (7B3C) 笘 (7B18) 笪 (7B2A) 笛 (7B1B) 笙 (7B19) 笮 (7B2E) 符 (7B26) 笭 (7B2D) 笠 (7B20) 笵 (7B35) 笥 (7B25)
第 (7B2C) 笤 (7B24) 笞 (7B1E) **6** 笄 (7B04) 筐 (7B50) 等 (7B49) 筑 (7B51) 策 (7B56) 筚 (7B5A) 筛 (7B5B) 筒 (7B52) 筅 (7B45) 筈 (7B48) 筏 (7B4F) 筌 (7B4C)
答 (7B54) 筋 (7B4B) 筍 (7B4D) 筝 (7B5D) 筊 (7B4A) 筆 (7B46) **7** 筬 (7B6C) 筥 (7B65) 筵 (7B75) 筹 (7B79) 筠 (7B60) 筮 (7B6E) 筲 (7B72) 筧 (7B67) 筯 (7B6F)
筽 (7B7D) 筱 (7B71) 筰 (7B70) 签 (7B7E) 简 (7B80) 筷 (7B77) 筦 (7B66) 節 (7BC0) 筩 (7B69) **8** 劄 (5284) 箝 (7B9D) 箍 (7B8D) 箕 (7B95) 箋 (7B8B) 箎 (7B8E)
算 (7B97) 箇 (7B87) 箩 (7BA9) 箆 (7B86) 箠 (7BA0) 箄 (7B84) 箚 (7B9A) 箏 (7B8F) 箙 (7B99) 箪 (7BAA) 箔 (7B94) 箜 (7B9C) 管 (7BA1) 箫 (7BAB) 箒 (7B92)

竹 118 **9** 節 7BC0 箸 7BB8 箬 7BAC 箱 7BB1 範 7BC4 箴 7BB4 篁 7BC1 篌 7BCC 篒 7BD2 篓 7BD3 箭 7BAD 篇 7BC7 篆 7BC6 簔 7C14

10 篝 7BDD 篤 7BE4 築 7BC9 篥 7BE5 篮 7BEE 篡 7BE1 篠 7BE0 篦 7BE6 篪 7BEA 篩 7BE9 簑 7C11 篙 7BD9 篭 7BED 篛 7BDB

11 篷 7BF7 篱 7BF1 簀 7C00 簌 7C0C 簒 7C12 篳 7BF3 簍 7C0D 篾 7BFE 簔 7C14 簇 7C07 簗 7C17 簋 7C0B **12** 簧 7C27 簪 7C2A

簡 7C21 簣 7C23 簞 7C1E 簰 7C30 簫 7C2B **13** 籀 7C40 簸 7C38 籁 7C41 簽 7C3D 簷 7C37 簾 7C3E 簿 7C3F **14** 簪 7C2A 籍 7C4D

籌 7C4C 籃 7C43 籏 7C4F 纂 7E82 **15** 籔 7C54 籐 7C50 籓 7C53 **16** 籜 7C5C 籟 7C5F 籗 7C57 籙 7C59 籠 7C60 **17** 籣 7C63

籥 7C65 籤 7C64 **19** 籬 7C6C 籮 7C6E **26** 籲 7C72

米 119 米 7C73 **2** 籴 7C74 **3** 咪 54AA 类 7C7B 娄 5A04 屎 5C4E 粁 7C81 粂 7C82 籸 7C78 籽 7C7D 籾 7C7E 迷 8FF7 **4** 敉 6549

料 6599 氣 6C23 粃 7C83 粍 7C8D 粄 7C84 粉 7C89 粋 7C8B 粑 7C91 **5** 眯 772F 粘 7C98 粗 7C97 粕 7C95 粒 7C92 粛 7C9B

6 粤 7CA4 粥 7CA5 粪 7CAA 粟 7C9F 粞 7C9E 粧 7CA7 **7** 粵 7CB5 糀 7CC0 粳 7CB3 粲 7CB2 粱 7CB1 粮 7CAE **8** 精 7CBE

粿 7CBF 粼 7CBC 粹 7CB9 粽 7CBD **9** 糊 7CCA 糎 7CCE 糍 7CCD 糅 7CC5 **10** 糗 7CD7 糖 7CD6 糕 7CD5 **11** 糜 7CDC 糢 7CE2

糙 7CD9 糟 7CDF 糞 7CDE 糠 7CE0 糝 7CDD 麋 9E8B **12** 糧 7CE7 **13** 糬 7CEC **14** 糯 7CEF 糰 7CF0 **16** 糴 7CF4

19 糶 7CF6

糸 120 糸 7CF8 **1** 系 7CFB 糺 7CFA **2** 糾 7CFE 纠 7EA0 **3** 紆 7D06 紅 7D05 红 7EA2 紂 7D02 纣 7EA3 纤 7EA4 紇 7D07 纥 7EA5

約 7D04 紈 7D08 约 7EA6 级 7EA7 纨 7EA8 紀 7D00 纪 7EAA 紉 7D09 纫 7EAB 纶 7EB6 **4** 級 7D1A 素 7D20 纬 7EAC 紜 7D1C 纭 7EAD

索 7D22 紘 7D18 純 7D14 纯 7EAF 紕 7D15 纰 7EB0 紧 7D27 紗 7D17 纱 7EB1 納 7D0D 纲 7EB2 纳 7EB3 纵 7EB5 紛 7D1B 纷 7EB7 紙 7D19

纸 7EB8 紊 7D0A 紋 7D0B 纹 7EB9 紡 7D21 纺 7EBA 紐 7D10 纽 7EBD 紓 7D13 **5** 线 7EBF 紺 7D3A 绀 7EC0 紲 7D32 紮 7D2E 紱 7D31

练 7EC3 組 7D44 组 7EC4 紳 7D33 绅 7EC5 紬 7D2C 累 7D2F 細 7D30 细 7EC6 织 7EC7 絅 7D45 終 7D42 终 7EC8 绉 7EC9 絋 7D4B 絃 7D43

絆 7D46 绊 7ECA 紵 7D35 紼 7D3C 絀 7D40 绌 7ECC 紹 7D39 绍 7ECD 绎 7ECE 経 7D4C 经 7ECF 紫 7D2B **6** 絜 7D5C 绑 7ED1 絨 7D68

绒 7ED2 絓 7D53 結 7D50 结 7ED3 絝 7D5D 绕 7ED5 絰 7D70 絖 7D56 絪 7D6A 絵 7D75 绘 7ED8 給 7D66 给 7ED9 絢 7D62 绚 7EDA 絳 7D73

绛 7EDB 絡 7D61 络 7EDC 絶 7D76 绝 7EDD 絞 7D5E 绞 7EDE 統 7D71 统 7EDF 絣 7D63 絮 7D6E 絕 7D55 絲 7D72 **7** 絛 7D5B 綁 7D81

糸 120

絽 7D7D 綎 7D8E 続 7D9A 絿 7D7F 經 7D93 綑 7D91 絹 7D79 绢 7EE2 綉 7D89 绣 7EE3 絺 7D7A 綏 7D8F 绥 7EE5 绦 7EE6 継 7D99 继 7EE7

綛 7D9B **8** 绩 7EE9 緒 7DD2 绪 7EEA 綾 7DBE 绫 7EEB 緊 7DCA 续 7EED 綺 7DBA 绮 7EEE 綫 7DAB 緋 7DCB 绯 7EEF 綽 7DBD 绰 7EF0

緄 7DC4 绳 7EF3 綱 7DB1 網 7DB2 綞 7D9E 維 7DAD 维 7EF4 綿 7DBF 绵 7EF5 綸 7DB8 綵 7DB5 綬 7DAC 绶 7EF6 総 7DCF 绷 7EF7 綢 7DA2

绸 7EF8 綯 7DAF 绺 7EFA 綣 7DA3 綜 7D9C 综 7EFC 綻 7DBB 绽 7EFD 綰 7DB0 绾 7EFE 緑 7DD1 绿 7EFF 綴 7DB4 缀 7F00 綠 7DA0 緇 7DC7

9 緖 7DD6 緙 7DD9 缂 7F02 練 7DF4 緘 7DD8 缄 7F04 縅 7E05 緬 7DEC 缅 7F05 缆 7F06 緹 7DF9 缇 7F07 緲 7DF2 缈 7F08 緝 7DDD

缉 7F09 縄 7E04 緞 7DDE 缎 7F0E 緜 7DDC 線 7DDA 緩 7DE9 缓 7F13 締 7DE0 缔 7F14 缕 7F15 編 7DE8 编 7F16 縁 7E01 緡 7DE1 緯 7DEF

緣 7DE3 缘 7F18 緻 7DFB **10** 縣 7E23 縋 7E0B 縒 7E12 缙 7F19 縝 7E1D 缜 7F1C 縛 7E1B 缚 7F1A 縟 7E1F 缛 7F1B 縉 7E09 縕 7E15

縧 7E27 縦 7E26 缝 7F1D 縐 7E10 縞 7E1E 缠 7F20 縊 7E0A 缢 7F22 縑 7E11 縈 7E08 缤 7F24 縡 7E21 **11** 縫 7E2B 縭 7E2D 績 7E3E

繊 7E4A 繋 7E4B 縳 7E33 縹 7E39 縥 7E25 縷 7E37 縵 7E35 缦 7F26 縲 7E32 繃 7E43 缨 7F28 繁 7E41 總 7E3D 縱 7E31 繇 7E47 縴 7E34

縯 7E2F 縮 7E2E 缩 7F29 繍 7E4D 繆 7E46 缪 7F2A 縿 7E3F 繅 7E45 缫 7F2B **12** 繈 7E48 繞 7E5E 繖 7E56 繚 7E5A 缭 7F2D 繙 7E59

織 7E54 繕 7E55 缮 7F2E 繒 7E52 繡 7E61 **13** 繋 7E4B 繭 7E6D 繫 7E6B 繮 7E6E 缰 7F30 繩 7E69 繰 7E70 缲 7F32 繹 7E79 繳 7E73

缴 7F34 繪 7E6A **14** 繾 7E7E 繻 7E7B 纂 7E82 辮 8FAE 繽 7E7D 繼 7E7C **15** 纈 7E88 續 7E8C 纍 7E8D 纏 7E8F 纐 7E90

16 纒 7E92 **17** 纓 7E93 纖 7E96 纔 7E94 **19** 纛 7E9B 纘 7E98 **21** 纜 7E9C

缶 121

缶 7F36 **2** 匋 530B **3** 缸 7F38 **4** 珤 73E4 缺 7F3A **5** 窑 7A91 缽 7F3D **8** 罂 7F42 **11** 罄 7F44 罅 7F45

罐 7F50 **12** 罈 7F48 𦉘 26258 **14** 罌 7F4C **15** 罍 7F4D **16** 罎 7F4E **18** 罐 7F50

网 122

网 7F51 **3** 罕 7F55 啰 5570 罗 7F57 罔 7F54 **4** 罚 7F5A **5** 罡 7F61 罢 7F62 罟 7F5F 罠 7F60 **6** 罣 7F63

7 詈 8A48 買 8CB7 **8** 罫 7F6B 署 7F72 置 7F6E 罪 7F6A 罩 7F69 **9** 罴 7F74 罰 7F70 **10** 罵 7F75 罷 7F77

11 罹 7F79 **12** 羁 7F81 **14** 羆 7F86 羅 7F85 **17** 羇 7F87 **19** 羈 7F88

羊 123

羊 7F8A **1** 羋 7F8B **2** 佯 4F6F 羌 7F8C **3** 咩 54A9 姜 59DC 庠 5EA0 徉 5F89 洋 6D0B 美 7F8E 羑 7F91 **4** 养 517B

恙 6059 氧 6C27 烊 70CA 羔 7F94 祥 7965 **5** 着 7740 痒 75D2 盖 76D6 羞 7F9E 羚 7F9A 羟 7F9F **6** 羡 7FA1 翔 7FD4

羊 123

7 羥 7FA5 義 7FA9 羨 7FA8 群 7FA4 羧 7FA7 詳 8A73 **9** 羯 7FAF 養 990A **10** 羱 7FB1 羲 7FB2 **11** 鮮 9BAE

13 羸 7FB8 羶 7FB6 羹 7FB9 **15** 羼 7FBC

羽 124

羽 7FBD **3** 羿 7FBF **4** 扇 6247 翅 7FC5 栩 6829 珝 73DD 翁 7FC1 **5** 翊 7FCA 習 7FD2 翎 7FCE 翌 7FCC **6** 翘 7FD8

翕 7FD5 翔 7FD4 翚 7FDA **7** 詡 8A61 **8** 翡 7FE1 翟 7FDF 翠 7FE0 **9** 翥 7FE5 翫 7FEB 翦 7FE6 翬 7FEC 翩 7FE9

10 翰 7FF0 翮 7FEE 翱 7FF1 **11** 翳 7FF3 翼 7FFC **12** 翹 7FF9 翻 7FFB **14** 耀 8000 **16** 糴 7CF4 **19** 糶 7CF6

老 125

老 8001 考 8003 **2** 佬 4F6C 考 8003 **3** 咾 54BE 姥 59E5 孝 5B5D 荖 8356 **4** 栳 6833 者 8005 耆 8006 耄 8004

5 耉 8009 耈 8008 **6** 耋 800B 蛯 86EF

而 126

而 800C **3** 耍 800D 耐 8010 耑 8011 **8** 需 9700

耒 127

耒 8012 **4** 耕 8015 耘 8018 耗 8017 耙 8019 **5** 耜 801C **8** 耥 8025 **9** 耦 8026 **10** 耨 8028 耪 802A

12 耭 802D

耳 128

耳 8033 **2** 取 53D6 職 8077 **3** 弭 5F2D 洱 6D31 耶 8036 耷 8037 茸 8338 **4** 恥 6065 珥 73E5 耻 803B 耸 8038 耿 803F

耽 803D 聂 8042 **5** 聋 804B 职 804C 聃 8043 聆 8046 聊 804A **6** 聒 8052 联 8054 **7** 聖 8056 聘 8058 **8** 聞 805E

聟 805F 聡 8061 聚 805A 餌 990C **9** 聩 8069 聪 806A **11** 聱 8071 聲 8072 聰 8070 聳 8073 聯 806F **12** 聴 8074 聶 8076

聵 8075 職 8077 **16** 聽 807D 聾 807E

聿 129

聿 807F **3** 建 5EFA 律 5F8B 津 6D25 **4** 肃 8083 **6** 筆 7B46 粛 7C9B **7** 肆 8086 肄 8084 肅 8085 **8** 肇 8087

肉 130

肉 8089 **2** 肏 808F 肌 808C 肋 808B **3** 肝 809D 肚 809A 肛 809B 肘 8098 肖 8096 肓 8093 肠 80A0 **4** 肤 80A4 肺 80BA

肢 80A2 肽 80BD 肱 80B1 肫 80AB 肯 80AF 肾 80BE 肿 80BF 胀 80C0 肴 80B4 股 80A1 肮 80AE 肪 80AA 育 80B2 肩 80A9 肥 80A5 胁 80C1

5 胤 80E4 胡 80E1 胚 80DA 胧 80E7 背 80CC 胆 80C6 胛 80DB 胃 80C3 胄 80C4 胜 80DC 胗 80D7 胝 80DD 胞 80DE 胖 80D6 脉 8109

肉 130

胥 80E5 胫 80EB 胎 80CE **6** 脔 8114 胯 80EF 胰 80F0 胱 80F1 胴 80F4 胭 80ED 脈 8108 脍 810D 脆 8106 脂 8102 胸 80F8 胳 80F3

脏 810F 脐 8110 胶 80F6 脊 810A 脑 8111 胼 80FC 胺 80FA 脓 8113 脅 8105 脇 8107 能 80FD **7** 脩 8129 脚 811A 脖 8116 脯 812F

脰 8130 脣 8123 脤 8124 豚 8C5A 脛 811B 脷 8137 脢 8122 脸 8138 脫 812B 脗 8117 脝 811D 脱 8131 脳 8133 脘 8118 脲 8132

8 㬹 3B39 腈 8148 脹 8139 腊 814A 腎 814E 腌 814C 腓 8153 腆 8146 脾 813E 腋 814B 腐 8150 腑 8151 腚 815A 腔 8154 腕 8155

9 腴 8174 腱 8171 腻 817B 腩 8169 腰 8170 腼 817C 腸 8178 腥 8165 腮 816E 腭 816D 腫 816B 腹 8179 腺 817A 腧 8167 腳 8173

腾 817E 腦 8166 **10** 膏 818F 腿 817F 膊 818A 膈 8188 膀 8180 膂 8182 膑 8191 𦟌 267CC **11** 膜 819C 膝 819D 膘 8198 膚 819A

膛 819B 膣 81A3 膙 8199 膠 81A0 **12** 膥 81A5 膵 81B5 膩 81A9 膨 81A8 膶 81B6 膳 81B3 **13** 臈 81C8 膿 81BF 臊 81CA 臉 81C9

膾 81BE 膽 81BD 膻 81BB 膺 81BA 臆 81C6 臃 81C3 臀 81C0 臂 81C2 **14** 臓 81D3 臍 81CD 臏 81CF **15** 臘 81D8 **16** 臚 81DA

臜 81DC **18** 臟 81DF **19** 臢 81E2 臠 81E0

臣 131

臣 81E3 **2** 臥 81E5 卧 5367 **3** 姫 59EB 宧 5BA6 **8** 臧 81E7 **9** 頤 9824 **11** 臨 81E8

自 132

自 81EA **3** 咱 54B1 洎 6D0E **4** 息 606F 臬 81EC 臭 81ED

至 133

至 81F3 **2** 侄 4F84 到 5230 **3** 姪 59EA 室 5BA4 屋 5C4B 致 81F4 郅 90C5 **4** 桎 684E **5** 窒 7A92 **6** 絰 7D70

耋 800B 蛭 86ED **7** 輊 8F0A **8** 臺 81FA **10** 臻 81FB **11** 鵄 9D44

臼 134

臼 81FC **2** 兒 5152 臾 81FE **4** 桕 6855 舀 8200 **5** 舂 8202 **6** 與 8207 裒 88D2 **7** 舅 8205 **8** 與 8207

9 興 8208 **10** 舆 8206 舉 8209 **12** 舊 820A **18** 釁 91C1

舌 135

舌 820C **1** 乱 4E71 **2** 刮 522E 舍 820D 舎 820E **3** 恬 606C 括 62EC 活 6D3B **4** 敌 654C 舐 8210 适 9002

5 甜 751C **6** 筈 7B48 聒 8052 舒 8212 蛞 86DE **7** 辞 8F9E 話 8A71 **8** 舔 8214 銛 929B **9** 舖 8216 舗 8217

10 舘 8218 **11** 𦧲 269F2 **16** 𦧺 269FA

廾 136

廾 821B **4** 桀 6840 桝 685D **6** 舜 821C **8** 舞 821E

舟 137

舟 821F **3** 舡 8221 舢 8222 **4** 舦 8226 舰 8230 舨 8228 舩 8229 舱 8231 般 822C 航 822A 舫 822B **5** 舸 8238 舺 823A

舟 137
舳 8233 舶 8236 船 8239 舷 8237 舵 8235 **7** 艇 8247 艅 8245 艀 8240 **8** 艋 824B **9** 艏 824F **10** 艘 8258 艙 8259
13 艤 8264 **14** 艦 8266 **15** 艪 826A

艮 138
艮 826E **1** 良 826F **2** 艰 8270 **3** 垦 57A0 很 5F88 恨 6068 狠 72E0 茛 831B 退 9000 限 9650 **4** 根 6839
5 痕 75D5 眼 773C **7** 跟 8DDF **8** 銀 9280 **11** 艱 8271 **15** 齦 9F66

色 139
色 8272 **4** 艳 8273 **6** 絶 7D76 **8** 銫 92AB **13** 艶 8276 **18** 艷 8277

艸 140
艸 8278 **1** 艺 827A **2** 艾 827E 节 8282 **3** 芋 828B 芊 828A 芃 8283 芍 828D 芒 8292 芎 828E **4** 芻 82BB 芈 7F8B
芝 829D 芙 8299 芜 829C 芫 82AB 苇 82C7 芸 82B8 芾 82BE 芰 82B0 芣 82A3 芽 82BD 芚 829A 芷 82B7 芮 82AE 苋 82CB 芼 82BC 苌 82CC
花 82B1 芹 82B9 苅 82C5 芥 82A5 芩 82A9 芬 82AC 苍 82CD 芪 82AA 芡 82A1 芟 829F 芳 82B3 苎 82CE 芦 82A6 芯 82AF 芵 82B5 芭 82AD
苏 82CF 芧 82A7 **5** 苣 82E3 苿 82BF 苡 82E1 茉 8309 苷 82F7 苦 82E6 苯 82EF 苛 82DB 若 82E5 茂 8302 茏 830F 苹 82F9 苫 82EB
苜 82DC 苖 82D6 苗 82D7 英 82F1 苒 82D2 茌 830C 苽 82FD 苓 82D3 苟 82DF 茍 830D 茆 8306 苳 82F3 苑 82D1 苞 82DE 苙 82D9 范 8303
苧 82E7 茔 8314 苾 82FE 茕 8315 茁 8301 苕 82D5 茄 8304 茎 830E 苔 82D4 茅 8305 苺 82FA **6** 兹 5179 荆 8346 荊 834A 荖 8356
茸 8338 茜 831C 茬 832C 荐 8350 荚 835A 荑 8351 荜 835C 草 8349 茧 8327 茼 833C 茵 8335 茴 8334 茱 8331 荞 835E 茯 832F 荏 834F
荇 8347 荃 8343 荟 835F 茶 8336 荀 8340 茗 8317 荘 8358 荠 8360 茭 832D 茨 8328 荒 8352 茫 832B 荡 8361 荣 8363 荤 8364 荥 8365
荦 8366 荧 8367 荨 8368 茛 831B 荩 8369 荪 836A 荫 836B 茹 8339 茘 8318 荔 8354 药 836F 茲 8332 **7** 莒 8392 莚 839A 荺 837A
莕 8395 荸 8378 莆 8386 荳 8373 莢 83A2 莽 83BD 莱 83B1 莲 83B2 莖 8396 莳 83B3 莫 83AB 莧 83A7 莴 83B4 莪 83AA 莉 8389 莠 83A0
莓 8393 荷 8377 莜 839C 莅 8385 莵 83B5 荼 837C 莩 83A9 荽 837D 莟 839F 获 83B7 荻 837B 莘 8398 莎 838E 莞 839E 莹 83B9 莨 83A8
莺 83BA 莙 8399 莊 838A 荵 8375 莼 83BC **8** 棻 68FB 華 83EF 菁 83C1 萇 8407 著 8457 菱 83F1 菈 83C8 萁 8401 菘 83D8 菫 83EB
莿 83BF 萘 8418 菴 83F4 萊 840A 萋 840B 菲 83F2 菽 83FD 菓 83D3 菖 83D6 萌 840C 䓪 44EA 萝 841D 菌 83CC 萎 840E 菜 83DC 萠 8420
菔 83D4 菟 83DF 萄 8404 萏 840F 菊 83CA 萃 8403 菩 83E9 菸 83F8 菏 83CF 萍 840D 菹 83F9 萢 8422 菠 83E0 萣 8423 萓 8413 菀 83C0
菅 83C5 萤 8424 营 8425 萦 8426 萧 8427 菉 83C9 菰 83F0 菡 83E1 萨 8428 菇 83C7 菑 83D1 **9** 募 52DF 孳 5B73 惹 60F9 萵 8435

艸 140

萸 8438 葚 845A 葉 8449 葫 846B 葙 8459 葳 8473 葬 846C 葺 847A 萬 842C 葛 845B 萼 843C 萩 8429 董 8463 葆 8446 葩 8469 葎 844E

葡 8461 葱 8471 蒋 848B 葶 8476 蒂 8482 蒌 848C 蒍 848D 落 843D 萱 8431 葷 8477 葭 846D 葦 8466 葵 8475 葯 846F 韮 97EE

10 夢 5922 蓚 84DA 蒐 8490 蓁 84C1 蒜 849C 蓍 84CD 蓋 84CB 蒝 849D 蓝 84DD 蒔 8494 蓦 84E6 蒨 84A8 蓓 84D3 蓖 84D6 蒼 84BC

蓊 84CA 蒯 84AF 蓟 84DF 蓑 84D1 蒿 84BF 蓆 84C6 蒺 84BA 蒟 849F 蒡 84A1 蓄 84C4 蒹 84B9 蒴 84B4 蒲 84B2 蒞 849E 蓉 84C9 蒙 8499

蓂 84C2 蒻 84BB 蓀 84C0 蒸 84B8 **11** 摹 6479 暮 66AE 蓮 84EE 蓬 84EC 蔀 8500 蔯 852F 蔭 852D 蓪 84EA 蔫 852B 蓳 84F3 蔷 8537

蓴 84F4 蔵 8535 蓽 84FD 蔞 851E 蔓 8513 蔑 8511 蔦 8526 蔥 8525 蓯 84EF 蔔 8514 蔡 8521 蔗 8517 蔴 8534 蔟 851F 蔺 853A 蔆 8506

蔻 853B 蓿 84FF 蔼 853C 蔚 851A 蔣 8523 蓼 84FC 蔘 8518 蔬 852C **12** 甍 750D 蔽 853D 蕙 8559 蕈 8548 蕨 8568 蕤 8564 蕓 8553

蕞 855E 蕪 856A 蕎 854E 蕉 8549 蕃 8543 蔿 853F 蕣 8563 蕲 8572 蕩 8569 蕊 854A 蕁 8541 蕴 8574 蕗 8557 蕭 856D **13** 薌 858C

薔 8594 薑 8591 蕾 857E 薗 8597 薨 85A8 薙 8599 薫 85AB 薬 85AC 薇 8587 薈 8588 薛 859B 薊 858A 薦 85A6 薪 85AA 薏 858F 蕹 8579

薮 85AE 薄 8584 薀 8580 薜 859C 薅 8585 蟇 87C7 **14** 舊 820A 蕴 8574 薯 85AF 薩 85A9 藉 85C9 薹 85B9 藍 85CD 薾 85BE 藏 85CF

薰 85B0 藐 85D0 藓 85D3 藁 85C1 薺 85BA 藎 85CE **15** 繭 7E6D 藕 85D5 藝 85DD 藪 85EA 藜 85DC 藠 85E0 藥 85E5 藤 85E4 藩 85E9

16 孽 5B7D 藷 85F7 藿 85FF 蘋 860B 蘆 8606 藺 85FA 蘄 8604 蘅 8605 蘇 8607 藹 85F9 蘑 8611 蘢 8622 藻 85FB 蘂 8602 蘊 860A

躉 8E89 **17** 蘦 8626 驀 9A40 蘭 862D 蘩 8629 蘞 861E 蘖 8616 蘚 861A 蘗 8617 **19** 囌 56CC 蘸 8638 蘿 863F

虍 141

2 虎 864E 虏 864F **3** 彪 5F6A 虐 8650 **4** 虑 8651 虔 8654 **5** 虚 865A 處 8655 **6** 虛 865B 虜 865C

7 號 865F 虞 865E **9** 慮 616E 虢 8662 膚 819A **10** 盧 76E7 **11** 虧 8667

虫 142

虫 866B **1** 虬 866C **2** 虯 866F 虱 8671 **3** 独 72EC 虹 8679 虾 867E 虺 867A 虽 867D 蚀 8680 虻 867B 蚁 8681 蚂 8682

4 蚤 86A4 蚌 868C 蚕 8695 蚜 869C 蚋 868B 蚣 86A3 蚊 868A 蚪 86AA 蚓 8693 蚩 86A9 **5** 蚶 86B6 蛄 86C4 蚵 86B5 蛎 86CE

蛆 86C6 蚺 86BA 蛊 86CA 蚱 86B1 蚯 86AF 蛉 86C9 蛀 86C0 蛍 86CD 蛇 86C7 蛋 86CB 蚴 86B4 **6** 蛙 86D9 蛯 86EF 蛰 86F0 蛲 86F2

蛭 86ED 蛐 86D0 蛔 86D4 蛛 86DB 蛞 86DE 蛤 86E4 蛮 86EE 蛟 86DF **7** 蜓 8713 蜒 8712 蜇 8707 蜃 8703 蛺 86FA 蛸 86F8 蜈 8708

蜆 8706 蜗 8717 蜀 8700 蛾 86FE 蜊 870A 蜍 870D 蛻 86FB 蜉 8709 蜂 8702 蜕 8715 蛹 86F9 触 89E6 **8** 蜣 8723 蜻 873B 蜞 871E

衣 145 襴 8974 **18** 襷 8977

襾 146 西 897F **3** 哂 54C2 廼 5EFC 洒 6D12 茜 831C 要 8981 **4** 晒 6652 栗 6817 栖 6816 迺 8FFA **5** 硒 7852 票 7968
6 粟 7C9F 粞 7C9E 覃 8983 **7** 賈 8CC8 **12** 覆 8986 **13** 覇 8987 覈 8988

見 147 見 898B 见 89C1 **2** 俔 4FD4 观 89C2 **3** 峴 5CF4 莧 83A7 **4** 晛 665B 梘 6898 觅 89C5 覓 8993 現 73FE 视 89C6 視 8996
規 898F 规 89C4 **5** 睍 774D 硯 786F 览 89C8 覚 899A 觉 89C9 覗 8997 **6** 寛 5BDB 筧 7B67 蜆 8706 觊 89CA 覜 899C
7 寬 5BEC 覡 89A1 觋 89CB **8** 覤 89A4 靚 975A **9** 覩 89A9 覧 89A7 覦 89A6 觎 89CE 親 89AA 靦 9766 **10** 覯 89AF
覬 89AC **11** 覲 89B2 觐 89D0 觑 89D1 観 89B3 **12** 覷 89B7 **13** 覺 89BA **14** 覽 89BD **15** 覿 89BF **18** 觀 89C0

角 148 角 89D2 **2** 觔 89D4 **3** 埆 57C6 **4** 斛 659B **5** 确 786E 觞 89DE 觚 89DA **6** 觜 89DC 觥 89E5 触 89E6 解 89E3
8 觭 89ED **11** 觴 89F4 **13** 觸 89F8 **15** 觼 89FC

言 149 言 8A00 **2** 信 4FE1 訂 8A02 計 8A08 计 8BA1 订 8BA2 訃 8A03 讣 8BA3 认 8BA4 訄 8A04 讥 8BA5 **3** 唁 5501 訏 8A0F 訐 8A10
訌 8A0C 讧 8BA7 討 8A0E 讨 8BA8 让 8BA9 訕 8A15 讪 8BAA 訖 8A16 託 8A17 讫 8BAB 訓 8A13 训 8BAD 议 8BAE 訊 8A0A 讯 8BAF 記 8A18
记 8BB0 訑 8A11 這 9019 **4** 讲 8BB2 讳 8BB3 讴 8BB4 訝 8A1D 讶 8BB6 訥 8A25 讷 8BB7 許 8A31 许 8BB8 訛 8A1B 讹 8BB9 䜣 4723
訢 8A22 论 8BBA 訟 8A1F 讼 8BBC 讽 8BBD 設 8A2D 设 8BBE 訪 8A2A 访 8BBF 訣 8A23 訳 8A33 诀 8BC0 **5** 詎 8A4E 証 8A3C 证 8BC1
詁 8A41 诂 8BC2 訶 8A36 诃 8BC3 評 8A55 评 8BC4 詛 8A5B 诅 8BC5 识 8BC6 詈 8A48 詐 8A50 诈 8BC8 訴 8A34 诉 8BC9 診 8A3A 诊 8BCA
詆 8A46 诋 8BCB 诌 8BCC 註 8A3B 詑 8A51 詠 8A60 詞 8A5E 词 8BCD 詔 8A54 诏 8BCF 詖 8A56 译 8BD1 詒 8A52 诒 8BD2 訾 8A3E
6 誆 8A86 诔 8BD4 試 8A66 试 8BD5 詩 8A69 诗 8BD7 詰 8A70 诘 8BD8 誇 8A87 詼 8A7C 诙 8BD9 誠 8AA0 诚 8BDA 誅 8A85 诛 8BDB
詵 8A75 話 8A71 话 8BDD 诞 8BDE 詬 8A6C 诟 8BDF 詮 8A6E 诠 8BE0 誂 8A82 詹 8A79 詭 8A6D 诡 8BE1 詢 8A62 詣 8A63 询 8BE2 诣 8BE3
詻 8A7B 诤 8BE4 詨 8A68 該 8A72 该 8BE5 詳 8A73 详 8BE6 誊 8A8A 誉 8A89 詫 8A6B 诧 8BE7 詡 8A61 诩 8BE9 **7** 誕 8A95 誡 8AA1
诫 8BEB 誓 8A93 読 8AAD 誌 8A8C 誣 8AA3 诬 8BEC 誧 8AA7 語 8A9E 语 8BED 誚 8A9A 诮 8BEE 誤 8AA4 误 8BEF 誥 8AA5 诰 8BF0 誘 8A98

言 149

诱 8BF1 誨 8AA8 诲 8BF2 說 8AAA 誑 8A91 诳 8BF3 説 8AAC 说 8BF4 認 8A8D 誦 8AA6 诵 8BF5 **8** 诞 8BDE 請 8ACB 请 8BF7 诸 8BF8

諏 8ACF 诺 8BFA 諌 8ACC 读 8BFB 誹 8AB9 诽 8BFD 課 8AB2 课 8BFE 誾 8ABE 諉 8AC9 诿 8BFF 谀 8C00 誰 8AB0 谁 8C01 論 8AD6 諍 8ACD

諗 8AD7 調 8ABF 调 8C03 諂 8AC2 谄 8C04 諒 8AD2 谅 8C05 諄 8AC4 谆 8C06 誶 8AB6 談 8AC7 谈 8C08 誼 8ABC 谊 8C0A 𧨾 27A3E

9 諸 8AF8 諾 8AFE 諛 8ADB 謀 8B00 谋 8C0B 諶 8AF6 谌 8C0C 諜 8ADC 谍 8C0D 谎 8C0E 諫 8AEB 谏 8C0F 諴 8AF4 諧 8AE7 谐 8C10

谑 8C11 謁 8B01 谒 8C12 謂 8B02 谓 8C13 諤 8AE4 谔 8C14 諭 8AED 谕 8C15 諡 8AE1 諼 8AFC 諷 8AF7 谗 8C17 諪 8AEA 諮 8AEE 諳 8AF3

谙 8C19 諺 8AFA 谚 8C1A 諦 8AE6 谛 8C1B 谜 8C1C 諢 8AE2 諱 8AF1 諝 8ADD **10** 謄 8B04 謊 8B0A 謔 8B14 謎 8B0E 講 8B1B 譁 8B41

谟 8C1F 谠 8C20 謖 8B16 谡 8C21 謢 8B22 謝 8B1D 谢 8C22 謡 8B21 谣 8C23 謠 8B20 謅 8B05 謗 8B17 谤 8C24 謚 8B1A 谥 8C25 謙 8B19

谦 8C26 謐 8B10 谧 8C27 **11** 謨 8B28 謮 8B2E 謦 8B26 謹 8B39 谨 8C28 謳 8B33 謾 8B3E 谩 8C29 謫 8B2B 謬 8B2C 谬 8C2C

12 譁 8B41 譊 8B4A 譆 8B46 譚 8B5A 谭 8C2D 譖 8B56 谮 8C2E 譙 8B59 谯 8C2F 識 8B58 谰 8C30 譜 8B5C 谱 8C31 證 8B49 譎 8B4E

谲 8C32 譏 8B4F **13** 譪 8B6A 警 8B66 谴 8C34 譟 8B5F 譯 8B6F 譭 8B6D 譫 8B6B 譠 8B60 譲 8B72 議 8B70 譬 8B6C **14** 譖 8B56

護 8B77 譴 8B74 譽 8B7D 辯 8FAF **15** 譿 8B7F 讃 8B83 讀 8B80 **16** 讌 8B8C 讎 8B8E 讐 8B90 變 8B8A **17** 讖 8B96 谶 8C36

讒 8B92 讓 8B93 **19** 讚 8B9A **20** 讞 8B9E 讜 8B9C

谷 150

谷 8C37 **2** 俗 4FD7 卻 537B **3** 容 5BB9 峪 5CEA 浴 6D74 郤 90E4 **4** 欲 6B32 谺 8C3A **5** 硲 7872 裕 88D5

10 谿 8C3F 豁 8C41

豆 151

豆 8C46 **3** 豈 8C48 荳 8373 逗 9017 **4** 脰 8130 豉 8C49 **5** 壹 58F9 痘 75D8 登 767B 短 77ED **6** 豊 8C4A

8 豎 8C4E 豌 8C4C **9** 頭 982D **11** 豐 8C50 **15** 懿 61FF **21** 豔 8C54

豕 152

豕 8C55 **3** 啄 5544 家 5BB6 逐 9010 **4** 琢 7422 豚 8C5A **5** 象 8C61 **6** 豢 8C62 **7** 豪 8C6A **9** 豫 8C6B

豬 8C6C 豭 8C6D **10** 豳 8C73

豸 153

豸 8C78 **3** 豺 8C7A 豹 8C79 **5** 貂 8C82 **6** 貊 8C8A 貉 8C89 **7** 貍 8C8D 貌 8C8C **9** 貓 8C93 **11** 貘 8C98

貝 154

貝 8C9D · 贝 8D1D · **2** 則 5247 · 贞 8D1E · 貞 8C9E · 負 8CA0 · 负 8D1F · **3** 員 54E1 · 唄 5504 · 屓 5C53 · 狽 72FD · 貢 8CA2 · 贡 8D21 · 財 8CA1

财 8D22 · **4** 质 8D28 · 败 8D25 · 敗 6557 · 責 8CAC · 责 8D23 · 贤 8D24 · 账 8D26 · 貨 8CA8 · 货 8D27 · 販 8CA9 · 贩 8D29 · 貪 8CAA · 贪 8D2A · 貧 8CA7

贫 8D2B · 贬 8D2C · 购 8D2D · 贮 8D2E · 貫 8CAB · 贯 8D2F · **5** 贰 8D30 · 貳 8CB3 · 貶 8CB6 · 贱 8D31 · 賁 8CC1 · 贲 8D32 · 貰 8CB0 · 貼 8CBC · 贴 8D34

貴 8CB4 · 贵 8D35 · 買 8CB7 · 貸 8CB8 · 贷 8D37 · 貿 8CBF · 贸 8D38 · 貯 8CAF · 費 8CBB · 费 8D39 · 賀 8CC0 · 贺 8D3A · 貽 8CBD · 贻 8D3B · 貲 8CB2

6 賎 8CCE · 賊 8CCA · 贼 8D3C · 贽 8D3D · 賈 8CC8 · 贾 8D3E · 賄 8CC4 · 贿 8D3F · 赀 8D40 · 賃 8CC3 · 赁 8D41 · 賂 8CC2 · 赂 8D42 · 赃 8D43 · 資 8CC7

资 8D44 · 賅 8CC5 · 赅 8D45 · **7** 賓 8CD3 · 實 5BE6 · 賑 8CD1 · 赈 8D48 · 赉 8D49 · 賒 8CD2 · 赊 8D4A · **8** 赓 8D53 · 賡 8CE1 · 賦 8CE6 · 赋 8D4B

賛 8CDB · 賬 8CEC · 賣 8CE3 · 赌 8D4C · 賢 8CE2 · 赎 8D4E · 賚 8CDA · 賤 8CE4 · 賞 8CDE · 赏 8D4F · 賜 8CDC · 赐 8D50 · 質 8CEA · 賠 8CE0 · 赔 8D54 · 鋇 92C7

9 賭 8CED · 賰 8CF0 · 賴 8CF4 · 赖 8D56 · 賱 8CF1 · **10** 赛 8D5B · 賽 8CFD · 赘 8D58 · 購 8CFC · 賻 8CFB · 賸 8CF8 · 賺 8CFA · 赚 8D5A

11 赜 8D5C · 贅 8D05 · 贄 8D04 · **12** 赝 8D5D · 寳 5BF3 · 贋 8D0B · 贊 8D0A · 赞 8D5E · 贇 8D07 · 赟 8D5F · 贈 8D08 · 赠 8D60 · **13** 赢 8D62

贏 8D0F · 寶 5BF6 · 贍 8D0D · 赡 8D61 · **14** 贓 8D13 · 贔 8D14 · 齎 9F4E · **15** 贗 8D17 · 贖 8D16 · **17** 贛 8D1B · 赣 8D63

赤 155

赤 8D64 · **3** 郝 90DD · **4** 赦 8D66 · 赧 8D67 · **7** 赫 8D6B · **9** 赭 8D6D

走 156

走 8D70 · **2** 赴 8D74 · 赵 8D75 · 赳 8D73 · **3** 徒 5F92 · 赶 8D76 · 起 8D77 · 陡 9661 · **5** 越 8D8A · 趄 8D84 · 趁 8D81 · 趋 8D8B · 超 8D85

6 趔 8D94 · **7** 趙 8D99 · 趕 8D95 · 趖 8D96 · **8** 趣 8DA3 · 趟 8D9F · **10** 趨 8DA8

足 157

足 8DB3 · **2** 促 4FC3 · 趴 8DB4 · **3** 捉 6349 · 浞 6D5E · 趸 8DB8 · 趵 8DB5 · **4** 趿 8DBF · 趺 8DBA · 趾 8DBE · 跃 8DC3 · 跄 8DC4

5 距 8DDD · 践 8DF5 · 跖 8DD6 · 跋 8DCB · 跌 8DCC · 跗 8DD7 · 跚 8DDA · 跑 8DD1 · 跎 8DCE · 跏 8DCF · 跛 8DDB · 跆 8DC6 · **6** 跬 8DEC · 跫 8DEB

跨 8DE8 · 跷 8DF7 · 跩 8DE9 · 跦 8DE6 · 跣 8DE3 · 跹 8DF9 · 跳 8DF3 · 跺 8DFA · 跪 8DEA · 路 8DEF · 跡 8DE1 · 跻 8DFB · 跤 8DE4 · 跟 8DDF · **7** 踌 8E0C

踅 8E05 · 䟴 47F4 · 踎 8E0E · 踉 8E09 · 跼 8DFC · 踊 8E0A · **8** 踜 8E1C · 踐 8E10 · 踝 8E1D · 踢 8E22 · 踏 8E0F · 踟 8E1F · 踩 8E29 · 踭 8E2D · 踮 8E2E

踯 8E2F · 踡 8E21 · 踪 8E2A · 踞 8E1E · 蹊 8E4A · **9** 踫 8E2B · 踼 8E3C · 踹 8E39 · 踵 8E35 · 踽 8E3D · 踰 8E30 · 踱 8E31 · 蹄 8E44 · 踴 8E34 · 蹂 8E42

10 蹉 8E49 · 蹑 8E51 · 蹒 8E52 · 蹋 8E4B · 蹈 8E48 · 蹊 8E4A · 蹌 8E4C · 蹓 8E53 · 蹇 8E47 · **11** 蹟 8E5F · 蹣 8E63 · 蹔 8E54 · 蹧 8E67 · 蹙 8E59

蹚 8E5A · 蹕 8E55 · 蹦 8E66 · 蹤 8E64 · 蹠 8E60 · 躀 8E80 · **12** 蹩 8E69 · 蹺 8E7A · 蹰 8E70 · 蹶 8E76 · 蹼 8E7C · 𨅝 2815D · 蹻 8E7B · 蹴 8E74 · 蹾 8E7E

足 157
蹲 8E72 蹭 8E6D 蹿 8E7F 蹬 8E6C **13** 躇 8E87 躂 8E82 躉 8E89 躁 8E81 躅 8E85 **14** 躊 8E8A 躏 8E8F 躋 8E8B 躍 8E8D
15 躑 8E91 躓 8E93 躕 8E95 齪 9F6A **16** 躙 8E99 **18** 躡 8EA1 躥 8EA5 **20** 躪 8EAA **21** 𨈇 28207

身 158
身 8EAB **3** 射 5C04 躬 8EAC **4** 躯 8EAF 躭 8EAD **5** 躰 8EB0 **6** 躲 8EB2 **8** 躺 8EBA **9** 躾 8EBE
11 軀 8EC0 **17** 軈 8EC8

車 159
車 8ECA 车 8F66 **1** 軋 8ECB 轧 8F67 **2** 俥 4FE5 军 519B 軍 8ECD 厙 5399 軌 8ECC 轨 8F68 **3** 庫 5EAB 軒 8ED2 轩 8F69
軏 8ECF 軔 8ED4 轫 8F6B 連 9023 陣 9663 **4** 斩 65A9 斬 65AC 転 8EE2 转 8F6C 軚 8EDA 軛 8EDB 轭 8F6D 轮 8F6E 軟 8EDF 软 8F6F
轰 8F70 **5** 軲 8EF2 轱 8F71 軻 8EFB 軸 8EF8 轴 8F74 軼 8EFC 轶 8F76 軫 8EEB 轸 8F78 軨 8EE8 轹 8F79 𨋢 282E2 軽 8EFD 轻 8F7B
6 载 8F7D 載 8F09 軾 8EFE 轼 8F7C 輌 8F0C 輊 8F0A 輋 8F0B 轿 8F7F 輅 8F05 較 8F03 较 8F83 **7** 輒 8F12 辄 8F84 輔 8F14
辅 8F85 辆 8F86 輕 8F15 輓 8F13 **8** 辉 8F89 輝 8F1D 輦 8F26 辇 8F87 輛 8F1B 輩 8F29 辈 8F88 輥 8F25 辊 8F8A 輞 8F1E 輧 8F27
輪 8F2A 輟 8F1F 辍 8F8D 輜 8F1C 辎 8F8E **9** 辔 8F94 輳 8F33 輻 8F3B 辐 8F90 輯 8F2F 辑 8F91 輹 8F39 輸 8F38 输 8F93
10 輿 8F3F 轂 8F42 轅 8F45 辕 8F95 轄 8F44 辖 8F96 輾 8F3E 辗 8F97 **11** 轉 8F49 轆 8F46 辘 8F98 **12** 轎 8F4E 轍 8F4D
辙 8F99 轔 8F54 **14** 轝 8F5D 轟 8F5F **15** 轡 8F61 轢 8F62 **16** 轤 8F64

辛 160
辛 8F9B **3** 宰 5BB0 莘 8398 **4** 梓 6893 **5** 辜 8F9C **6** 辞 8F9E 辟 8F9F **7** 辣 8FA3 **8** 鋅 92C5
9 辨 8FA8 辩 8FA9 辦 8FA6 **10** 辫 8FAB **12** 辭 8FAD **13** 瓣 74E3 辮 8FAE **14** 辯 8FAF

辰 161
辰 8FB0 **3** 唇 5507 娠 5A20 宸 5BB8 振 632F 辱 8FB1 **4** 晨 6668 脣 8123 脤 8124 **6** 蜃 8703 農 8FB2 **7** 賑 8CD1
8 震 9707

辵 162
2 辻 8FBB 込 8FBC 辽 8FBD 边 8FB9 辺 8FBA **3** 巡 5DE1 迂 8FC2 过 8FC7 达 8FBE 迈 8FC8 辿 8FBF 迁 8FC1 迄 8FC4 迅 8FC5
迆 8FC6 **4** 进 8FDB 远 8FDC 违 8FDD 运 8FD0 还 8FD8 连 8FDE 迓 8FD3 近 8FD1 返 8FD4 迎 8FCE 这 8FD9 迟 8FDF **5** 迲 8FF2
述 8FF0 迪 8FEA 迥 8FE5 迭 8FED 迤 8FE4 迫 8FEB 迩 8FE9 迢 8FE2 迦 8FE6 迳 8FF3 迨 8FE8 邇 9087 **6** 迺 8FFA 迴 8FF4 选 9009
适 9002 逈 9008 逅 9005 逃 9003 追 8FFD 迹 8FF9 迸 8FF8 送 9001 迷 8FF7 逆 9006 退 9000 逊 900A **7** 逝 901D 逑 9011 連 9023

辵 162

逋 900B 逑 901F 逗 9017 逐 9010 逕 9015 逍 900D 逞 901E 造 9020 透 900F 逓 9013 途 9014 逛 901B 逖 9016 逢 9022 這 9019 递 9012

通 901A 逡 9021 **8** 迸 8FF8 逵 9035 逹 9039 逻 903B 逶 9036 進 9032 週 9031 逸 9038 逮 902E 逯 902F **9** 過 904E 達 9054

逼 903C 遇 9047 遏 904F 遗 9057 遑 9051 遁 9041 逾 903E 遊 904A 遒 9052 道 9053 遂 9042 運 904B 遍 904D 遐 9050 遅 9045 違 9055

10 遘 9058 遠 9060 遢 9062 遣 9063 遝 905D 遞 905E 遥 9065 遙 9059 遛 905B 遡 9061 遜 905C **11** 遨 9068 遭 906D 遯 906F

遮 906E 適 9069 **12** 暹 66B9 遷 9077 遶 9076 遼 907C 遺 907A 遴 9074 遵 9075 遲 9072 選 9078 **13** 邁 9081 遽 907D 還 9084

邀 9080 邂 9082 避 907F 邉 9089 邃 9083 邊 908A **14** 邇 9087 邈 9088 **15** 邊 908A 邋 908B **19** 邐 9090 邏 908F

邑 163

邑 9091 **2** 俋 4FCB 邓 9093 **3** 挹 6339 浥 6D65 邗 9097 邛 909B 邝 909D 邙 9099 邕 9095 **4** 扈 6248 邪 90AA 祁 7941

邦 90A6 邢 90A2 䢵 48B5 邨 90A8 邬 90AC 邡 90A1 那 90A3 **5** 邯 90AF 邴 90B4 邳 90B3 邶 90B6 邺 90BA 邮 90AE 邱 90B1 邻 90BB

邸 90B8 邹 90B9 邵 90B5 邰 90B0 **6** 耶 8036 邽 90BD 䢼 48BC 郁 90C1 郏 90CF 郅 90C5 邾 90BE 郐 90D0 郃 90C3 郇 90C7 郊 90CA

郑 90D1 郎 90CE 郓 90D3 **7** 郝 90DD 郚 90DA 郦 90E6 䣅 48C5 郢 90E2 郧 90E7 郜 90DC 郗 90D7 郤 90E4 郞 90DE 郡 90E1

8 郴 90F4 郪 90EA 郵 90F5 郫 90EB 郭 90ED 部 90E8 郸 90F8 郯 90EF 郷 90F7 **9** 都 90FD 郾 90FE 鄂 9102 鄉 9109

10 郷 90F7 䣓 48D3 鄔 9114 鄒 9112 鄗 9117 鄌 910C 鄕 9115 **11** 鄢 9122 鄞 911E 鄙 9119 鄘 9118 **12** 鄲 9132 鄱 9131

鄯 912F 鄰 9130 鄭 912D 鄧 9127 **13** 鄴 9134 **14** 鄹 9139 **15** 鄺 913A **18** 酆 9146 **19** 酈 9148

酉 164

酉 9149 **2** 酊 914A 酋 914B **3** 酒 9152 酐 9150 酎 914E 酌 914C 配 914D **4** 酜 915C 酝 915D 酞 915E 酗 9157 酚 915A

酔 9154 **5** 酣 9163 酢 9162 酥 9165 **6** 酮 916E 酰 9170 酯 916F 酩 9169 酪 916A 酱 9171 酬 916C **7** 酵 9175 酽 917D

酷 9177 酶 9176 酴 9174 酿 917F 酸 9178 **8** 醋 918B 醃 9183 醇 9187 醉 9189 **9** 醐 9190 醍 918D 醒 9192 醗 9197

10 醛 919B 醜 919C 醚 919A 醞 919E 醤 91A4 醣 91A3 **11** 醫 91AB 醬 91AC 醪 91AA **12** 醮 91AE 醯 91AF 醱 91B1

13 醵 91B5 醴 91B4 醸 91B8 **14** 醺 91BA **17** 釀 91C0 **18** 釁 91C1 **20** 釅 91C5

釆 165

釆 91C6 **1** 采 91C7 **4** 悉 6089 釈 91C8 **5** 番 756A 釉 91C9 释 91CA **13** 釋 91CB

里 166

里 91CC **2** 重 91CD 俚 4FDA 厘 5398 **3** 哩 54E9 埋 57CB 娌 5A0C 浬 6D6C 狸 72F8 **4** 理 7406 野 91CE **5** 童 7AE5

里 166 — 裡 88E1 量 91CF **6** 裏 88CF **7** 貍 8C8D **8** 鋰 92F0 **11** 釐 91D0 鯉 9BC9 — 里

金 167 — 金 91D1 **2** 釘 91D8 針 91DD 针 9488 钉 9489 釗 91D7 钊 948A 釙 91D9 釜 91DC **3** 崟 5D1F 淦 6DE6 釪 91EA 釭 91ED 钍 948D — 金

釦 91E6 钎 948E 釧 91E7 钏 948F 釣 91E3 釩 91E9 钒 9492 钓 9493 釵 91F5 钗 9497 **4** 欽 6B3D 鈒 9212 鈇 9207 鈣 9223 钙 9499

鈈 9208 鈦 9226 钛 949B 鈜 921C 鈪 922A 鈍 920D 钝 949D 鈔 9214 钞 949E 钟 949F 鈉 9209 钠 94A0 钡 94A1 钢 94A2 鈑 9211 钣 94A3

鈐 9210 钥 94A5 钦 94A6 鈞 921E 钧 94A7 钨 94A8 鈎 920E 钩 94A9 鈁 9201 鈊 920A 鈕 9215 钮 94AE 鈀 9200 鈗 9217 **5** 鉅 9245

鈺 923A 钰 94B0 钱 94B1 鉦 9266 鉗 9257 钳 94B3 鈷 9237 钴 94B4 鉢 9262 钵 94B5 鉥 9265 鉐 9250 鈽 923D 鈸 9238 钹 94B9 鉞 925E

鉆 9246 钻 94BB 鉴 9274 鉬 926C 鉭 926D 钼 94BC 鉀 9240 钾 94BE 鈾 923E 鈿 923F 钿 94BF 铀 94C0 鉄 9244 铁 94C1 鉑 9251 铂 94C2

鈴 9234 铃 94C3 铄 94C4 鉛 925B 鉤 9264 铅 94C5 鉚 925A 铆 94C6 鉋 924B 鉱 9271 鉉 9249 铉 94C9 鉈 9248 铊 94CA 鉍 924D 鈮 922E

鈹 9239 铎 94CE **6** 銭 92AD 銬 92AC 铐 94D0 銎 928E 鉺 927A 鉷 9277 銊 928A 銕 9295 銧 92A7 铛 94DB 銅 9285 铜 94DC 铝 94DD

銦 92A6 铠 94E0 铡 94E1 銖 9296 铢 94E2 銑 9291 铣 94E3 铤 94E4 銛 929B 铧 94E7 銜 929C 銓 9293 铨 94E8 銚 929A 鉻 927B 銘 9298

铬 94EC 铭 94ED 铮 94EE 銫 92AB 铯 94EF 銮 92AE 鉸 9278 铰 94F0 銥 92A5 铱 94F1 铲 94F2 銃 9283 铳 94F3 鉼 927C 銨 92A8 铵 94F5

銀 9280 银 94F6 鉾 927E 鐺 943A **7** 鋁 92C1 鋌 92CC 鋳 92F3 铸 94F8 鋆 92C6 鋕 92D5 銶 92B6 鋪 92EA 铺 94FA 鋉 92C9 鋏 92CF

链 94FE 铿 94FF 銷 92B7 销 9500 锁 9501 銲 92B2 鋥 92E5 鋇 92C7 鋤 92E4 锄 9504 鋰 92F0 锂 9502 锅 9505 鋯 92EF 銹 92B9 锈 9508

鋲 92F2 銳 92B3 銼 92BC 锉 9509 鋒 92D2 锋 950B 鋅 92C5 锌 950C 锏 950F 鋭 92ED 锐 9510 銻 92BB 锑 9511 鋐 92D0 鋃 92C3 锒 9512

8 铮 94EE 鉼 927C 錺 933A 錆 9306 錶 9336 锗 9517 錂 9302 錏 930F 錤 9324 錯 932F 错 9519 锚 951A 鍈 9348 錬 932C 錛 931B

錡 9321 錸 9338 錾 933E 錢 9322 錕 9315 锟 951F 錩 9329 錫 932B 锡 9521 錮 932E 锢 9522 锣 9523 鋼 92FC 錘 9318 锤 9524 錐 9310

锥 9525 錦 9326 锦 9526 锨 9528 錚 931A 錞 931E 錟 931F 錠 9320 锭 952D 鋺 92FA 錧 9327 键 952E 録 9332 鋸 92F8 锯 952F 錳 9333

锰 9530 錣 9323 錄 9304 錙 9319 锱 9531 **9** 鍺 937A 錨 9328 鍋 934B 鍵 9375 鍥 9365 锲 9532 鍊 934A 鍼 937C 鍇 9347 锴 9534

鍘 9358 鍚 935A 鍶 9376 鍔 9354 锷 9537 鍤 9364 鍬 936C 锹 9539 鍾 937E 锺 953A 鍑 9351 鍛 935B 锻 953B 鍠 9360 鍮 936E 鍰 9370

锵 9535 鍍 934D 镀 9540 鎂 9382 镁 9541 镂 9542 鍙 9359 鍜 935C 鍪 936A **10** 鎯 93AF 鎚 939A 鎹 93B9 鎡 93A1 鎷 93B7 镊 954A

金 167

鏵 93F5 鎮 93AE 镇 9547 鎘 9398 镉 9549 鎖 9396 鎤 93A4 鎧 93A7 镌 954C 鎳 93B3 镍 954D 鎢 93A2 鎗 9397 鎭 93AD 鎬 93AC 镐 9550

鎊 938A 镑 9551 鎰 93B0 鎌 938C 鎣 93A3 鎏 938F 鎵 93B5 鎔 9394 镕 9555 **11** 鏈 93C8 鎩 93A9 鏋 93CB 鏨 93E8 鏄 93C4 鏗 93D7

鏢 93E2 镖 9556 鏜 93DC 镗 9557 鏤 93E4 鏝 93DD 镘 9558 鏍 93CD 鏞 93DE 镛 955B 鏖 93D6 鏡 93E1 镜 955C 鏟 93DF 鏑 93D1 鏃 93C3

鏘 93D8 鏹 93F9 **12** 鏵 93F5 鐄 9404 鐃 9403 鐡 9421 镢 9562 鐐 9410 镣 9563 鐧 9427 鏶 93F6 鐘 9418 鐥 9425 鐏 940F 鐙 9419

镫 956B 鏽 93FD **13** 鐫 942B 鐵 9435 鐳 9433 镭 956D 鐺 943A 鐸 9438 鐶 9436 鐲 9432 镯 956F 鐮 942E 镰 9570 鐿 943F

14 鑊 944A 鑓 9453 鑄 9444 鑑 9451 鑒 9452 鑂 9442 鑌 944C **15** 鑛 945B 鑚 945A 鑤 9464 鑠 9460 鑣 9463 镳 9573 鑞 945E

16 鑪 946A 鑫 946B **17** 鑰 9470 鑲 9472 镶 9576 **18** 鑵 9475 鑷 9477 **19** 鑼 947C 鑽 947D 鑾 947E 鑿 947F

長 168

长 957F 長 9577 **2** 倀 5000 **3** 套 5957 帳 5E33 張 5F35 悵 60B5 萇 8407 **4** 棖 68D6 脹 8139 **6** 肆 8086

7 賬 8CEC

門 169

門 9580 门 95E8 **1** 閂 9582 闩 95E9 **2** 們 5011 𨳍 28CCD 閃 9583 闪 95EA 𨳊 28CCA **3** 问 95EE 問 554F 捫 636B 闫 95EB

閉 9589 闭 95ED 𨳒 28CD2 闯 95EF **4** 悶 60B6 椚 691A 閏 958F 闰 95F0 開 958B 闱 95F1 閑 9591 闲 95F2 閎 958E 闳 95F3 間 9593

间 95F4 閒 9592 閔 9594 闵 95F5 闷 95F7 **5** 閘 9598 闸 95F8 闹 95F9 **6** 聞 805E 閨 95A8 闺 95FA 闻 95FB 閪 95AA 閩 95A9

闽 95FD 闾 95FE 閥 95A5 阀 9600 閤 95A4 閣 95A3 阁 9601 閡 95A1 阂 9602 関 95A2 **7** 誾 8ABE 閭 95AD 閫 95AB 閱 95B1 阄 9604

閲 95B2 阅 9605 閬 95AC 阆 9606 **8** 閾 95BE 阈 9608 閹 95B9 阉 9609 阋 960B 閻 95BB 阎 960E 閼 95BC 阐 9610 **9** 闌 95CC

阑 9611 闆 95C6 闇 95C7 闊 95CA 阔 9614 闈 95C8 闋 95CB 阕 9615 **10** 闖 95D6 闔 95D4 阖 9616 闐 95D0 阗 9617 闘 95D8 闕 95D5

阙 9619 **11** 阚 961A 關 95DC **12** 闡 95E1 **13** 闢 95E2

阜 170

阜 961C **2** 队 961F **3** 阡 9621 **4** 阱 9631 阮 962E 阨 9628 阵 9635 阳 9633 阪 962A 阶 9636 阴 9634 阬 962C 防 9632

阭 962D **5** 际 9645 陆 9646 阿 963F 陇 9647 陈 9648 阻 963B 附 9644 陀 9640 陂 9642 陉 9649 **6** 陋 964B 陌 964C 陕 9655

降 964D 陔 9654 限 9650 **7** 陡 9661 陣 9663 陜 965C 陝 965D 陛 965B 陘 9658 陟 965F 陨 9668 陞 965E 除 9664 险 9669 陥 9665

院 9662 **8** 陸 9678 陵 9675 陬 966C 陳 9673 陲 9672 陴 9674 険 967A 陰 9670 陶 9676 陷 9677 陪 966A 䧑 49D1 **9** 隋 968B

阜 170

随 968F 階 968E 隄 9684 陽 967D 隅 9685 隈 9688 隍 968D 隆 9686 隐 9690 隊 968A **10** 隗 9697 隔 9694 隙 9699 隕 9695 隘 9698

11 隠 96A0 際 969B 障 969C **12** 隣 96A3 **13** 隨 96A8 隧 96A7 險 96AA **14** 隲 96B2 隰 96B0 隱 96B1 **16** 隴 96B4

隶 171

隶 96B6 **3** 埭 57ED 康 5EB7 逮 902E **4** 棣 68E3 **8** 隷 96B7 **9** 隸 96B8

隹 172

隹 96B9 **2** 准 51C6 难 96BE 隼 96BC 隽 96BD 隻 96BB **3** 售 552E 唯 552F 堆 5806 崔 5D14 帷 5E37 惟 60DF 推 63A8 淮 6DEE

進 9032 雀 96C0 **4** 雁 96C1 椎 690E 焦 7126 雅 96C5 雃 96C3 集 96C6 雄 96C4 雇 96C7 **5** 雍 96CD 睢 7762 碓 7893 稚 7A1A

雋 96CB 雎 96CE 雉 96C9 雊 96CA 雏 96CF 雌 96CC **6** 維 7DAD 翟 7FDF 雑 96D1 雒 96D2 **7** 誰 8AB0 **8** 錐 9310 雕 96D5

霍 970D **9** 雖 96D6 **10** 瞿 77BF 雙 96D9 雞 96DE 雛 96DB 雜 96DC 騅 9A05 **11** 離 96E2 難 96E3

雨 173

雨 96E8 **3** 雩 96E9 雫 96EB 雪 96EA **4** 雲 96F2 雳 96F3 雰 96F0 雯 96EF **5** 電 96FB 雷 96F7 零 96F6 雾 96FE 雹 96F9

6 需 9700 霁 9701 䨒 4A12 **7** 霆 9706 霊 970A 震 9707 霄 9704 霉 9709 霂 9702 霈 9708 **8** 霖 9716 霏 970F 霓 9713

霍 970D 霎 970E 霑 9711 **9** 霙 9719 霜 971C 霞 971E **10** 霤 9724 **11** 霧 9727 霦 9726 霪 972A 霭 972D 霨 9728

12 霰 9730 露 9732 **13** 霸 9738 霹 9739 **14** 霾 973E 霽 973D **16** 靆 9746 靂 9742 靈 9748 靄 9744 **17** 靉 9749

19 靍 974D **21** 靏 974F

青 174

靑 9751 青 9752 **2** 倩 5029 **3** 婧 5A67 情 60C5 清 6E05 淸 6DF8 猜 731C 菁 83C1 **4** 晴 6674 靓 9753 **5** 睛 775B

靖 9756 **6** 精 7CBE 蜻 873B 静 9759 **7** 請 8ACB 靚 975A **8** 錆 9306 靜 975C 靛 975B **11** 鯖 9BD6 **13** 鼱 9F31

非 175

非 975E **2** 俳 4FF3 匪 532A **3** 啡 5561 徘 5F98 悱 60B1 排 6392 菲 83F2 **4** 悲 60B2 扉 6249 斐 6590 琲 7432 腓 8153

辈 8F88 **5** 痱 75F1 罪 7F6A **6** 緋 7DCB 翡 7FE1 蜚 871A 裴 88F4 裵 88F5 **7** 靠 9760 誹 8AB9 輩 8F29 **8** 霏 970F

11 靡 9761 鯡 9BE1

面 176

面 9762 **2** 偭 506D **3** 湎 6E4E **6** 靥 9765 緬 7DEC **7** 靦 9766 麺 9EBA **11** 麵 9EB5 **14** 靨 9768

革 韋 韭 音 頁 風

革 177

革 9769 **2** 勒 52D2 **3** 靭 976D 靱 9771 靫 976B **4** 靴 9774 靳 9773 靷 9777 靶 9776 **5** 靺 977A 鞆 9786 靼 977C
鞅 9785 鞄 9784 **6** 緙 7DD9 鞋 978B 鞏 978F 鞑 9791 鞍 978D **7** 鞘 9798 **8** 鞜 979C 鞠 97A0 **9** 鞨 97A8 鞦 97A6
鞭 97AD 鞫 97AB 鞣 97A3 **13** 韃 97C3 韁 97C1 **15** 韆 97C6 **17** 韉 97C9

韋 178

韋 97CB 韦 97E6 **2** 偉 5049 **3** 圍 570D 幃 5E43 徫 5FAB 葦 8466 違 9055 韌 97CC 韧 97E7 **4** 暐 6690 煒 7152 瑋 744B
5 禕 7995 褘 8918 **6** 緯 7DEF 衛 885B **7** 諱 8AF1 **8** 闈 95C8 韓 97D3 韩 97E9 **9** 韙 97D9 韪 97EA 韫 97EB
10 韞 97DE 韡 97E1 韜 97DC 韬 97EC **12** 韡 97E1

韭 179

韭 97ED **4** 韮 97EE **8** 韱 97F1

音 180

音 97F3 **2** 章 7AE0 竟 7ADF **3** 喑 5591 愔 6114 **4** 意 610F 暗 6697 歆 6B46 韵 97F5 **5** 瘖 7616 韶 97F6
7 諳 8AF3 **8** 闇 95C7 **9** 韹 97F9 **10** 韻 97FB **11** 韾 97FE 響 97FF **12** 黯 9EEF **13** 響 97FF
14 頀 9800

頁 181

頁 9801 页 9875 **2** 頂 9802 顶 9876 頃 9803 顷 9877 **3** 頇 9807 须 987B 須 9808 項 9805 项 9879 順 9806 顺 987A
4 頎 980E 煩 7169 顼 987C 頊 980A 頑 9811 顽 987D 顾 987E 頓 9813 顿 987F 頒 9812 颁 9881 頌 980C 颂 9882 預 9810 预 9884
5 颅 9885 領 9818 领 9886 䪸 4AB8 頗 9817 颇 9887 頚 981A 颈 9888 **6** 颍 988D 潁 6F41 熲 71B2 頡 9821 颉 9889 頬 982C
颊 988A 頜 981C 颌 988C 頫 982B 颏 988F **7** 穎 7A4E 頤 9824 颐 9890 頼 983C 頭 982D 頰 9830 頸 9838 頻 983B 频 9891 頹 9839
頽 983D 颓 9893 頷 9837 颔 9894 頴 9834 颖 9896 **8** 顆 9846 颗 9897 **9** 題 984C 题 9898 顕 9855 顎 984E 颚 989A 顓 9853
颛 989B 顏 984F 顔 9854 颜 989C 額 984D 额 989D **10** 颞 989E 顛 985B 颠 98A0 願 9858 顗 9857 顚 985A 類 985E 顙 9859
11 顢 9862 **12** 囂 56C2 顥 9865 颢 98A2 顧 9867 **13** 顫 986B 颤 98A4 **14** 顯 986F **15** 颦 98A6 顰 9870
16 顱 9871 **17** 颧 98A7 **18** 顴 9874 顳 9873

風 182

風 98A8 风 98CE **3** 嵐 5D50 **4** 楓 6953 **5** 瘋 760B 飒 98D2 颯 98AF 颱 98B1 **6** 颳 98B3 **7** 諷 8AF7
8 颶 98B6 飓 98D3 **9** 颺 98BA **10** 颼 98BC 飕 98D5 **11** 飄 98C4 飘 98D8 **12** 飆 98C6 飇 98C7 飙 98D9 飈 98C8

飛 183
飞 98DE 飛 98DB **12** 飜 98DC

食 184
食 98DF **2** 饤 9964 飢 98E2 饥 9965 飡 98E1 **3** 飧 98E7 飨 98E8 **4** 飩 98E9 饨 9968 飪 98EA 饪 996A 飭 98ED 饬 996C
飯 98EF 饭 996D 飮 98EE 飲 98F2 饮 996E **5** 饯 996F 飾 98FE 饰 9970 飽 98FD 饱 9971 飼 98FC 饲 9972 飴 98F4 饴 9974
6 餍 990D 蚀 8680 蝕 8755 餌 990C 饵 9975 饶 9976 餉 9909 饷 9977 饸 9978 饹 9979 餃 9903 饺 997A 養 990A 餅 9905 饼 997C
7 餑 9911 饽 997D 饾 997E 餐 9910 餓 9913 饿 997F 餘 9918 馀 9980 餒 9912 馁 9981 **8** 餅 9905 餞 991E 馃 9983 餛 991B
馄 9984 餠 9920 餚 991A 餡 9921 馅 9985 館 9928 馆 9986 **9** 餬 992C 餮 992E 餵 9935 馈 9988 馊 998A 馋 998B **10** 餿 993F
餽 993D 餸 9938 馍 998D 餾 993E 馏 998F 馐 9990 **11** 饈 9948 饉 9949 馑 9991 饅 9945 馒 9992 饗 9957 **12** 饒 9952 饋 994B
饍 994D 饌 994C 馔 9994 饑 9951 **13** 饗 9957 饕 9955 饔 9954 **14** 饜 995C **17** 饞 995E

首 185
首 9996 **2** 馗 9997

香 186
香 9999 **5** 馝 999D **9** 馥 99A5 **11** 馨 99A8

馬 187
馬 99AC 马 9A6C **2** 冯 51AF 馮 99AE 馭 99AD 驭 9A6D **3** 嗎 55CE 媽 5ABD 馱 99B1 驮 9A6E 馴 99B4 驯 9A6F 馳 99B3 驰 9A70
4 瑪 746A 駄 99C4 駆 99C6 驱 9A71 馹 99B9 駁 99C1 驳 9A73 驴 9A74 駅 99C5 **5** 碼 78BC 禡 79A1 罵 7F75 駛 99DB 驶 9A76
駟 99DF 驷 9A77 駈 99C8 駙 99D9 驸 9A78 駒 99D2 驹 9A79 駐 99D0 驻 9A7B 駝 99DD 驼 9A7C 駑 99D1 驽 9A7D 駕 99D5 驾 9A7E 驿 9A7F
駘 99D8 **6** 骂 9A82 篤 7BE4 螞 879E 骁 9A81 骄 9A84 骅 9A85 駱 99F1 骆 9A86 駭 99ED 骇 9A87 駢 99E2 骈 9A88 **7** 骊 9A8A
騁 9A01 骋 9A8B 验 9A8C 駸 99F8 駿 99FF 骏 9A8F **8** 闖 95D6 騏 9A0F 騎 9A0E 骑 9A91 騅 9A05 騈 9A08 験 9A13 騒 9A12
9 騨 9A28 騙 9A19 骗 9A97 骚 9A9A 騖 9A16 骛 9A9B **10** 騰 9A30 蓦 84E6 騷 9A37 驊 9A4A 騵 9A35 騮 9A2E 騶 9A36 騯 9A2F
騫 9A2B 骞 9A9E **11** 驀 9A40 驁 9A41 驅 9A45 驃 9A43 骠 9AA0 騾 9A3E 骡 9AA1 驄 9A44 **12** 驊 9A4A 驍 9A4D 驕 9A55 驌 9A4C
13 驚 9A5A 驛 9A5B 驗 9A57 **14** 驟 9A5F 骤 9AA4 **16** 骥 9AA5 驢 9A62 **17** 驥 9A65 驤 9A64 骧 9AA7 **18** 驩 9A69
19 驪 9A6A **20** 驫 9A6B

骨 188

骨 9AA8 **3** 嗗 55D7 滑 6ED1 猾 733E **4** 骰 9AB0 骯 9AAF **5** 骷 9AB7 骶 9AB6 **6** 骺 9ABA 骼 9ABC 骹 9AB9 骸 9AB8
7 骾 9ABE **8** 髁 9AC1 髀 9AC0 **9** 髄 9AC4 髅 9AC5 髂 9AC2 **10** 髋 9ACB **11** 髏 9ACF **13** 髒 9AD2 髓 9AD3
體 9AD4 髑 9AD1 **14** 髕 9AD5 **15** 髖 9AD6

高 189

高 9AD8 髙 9AD9 **3** 塙 5859 嵩 5D69 搞 641E 蒿 84BF 鄗 9117 **4** 敲 6572 暠 66A0 槁 69C1 犒 7292 **5** 碻 78BB 稿 7A3F
6 篙 7BD9 縞 7E1E **8** 鎬 93AC

髟 190

3 髡 9AE1 **4** 髪 9AEA 髥 9AE5 髦 9AE6 **5** 髮 9AEE 髯 9AEF 髭 9AED **6** 髻 9AFB 髷 9AF7 髹 9AF9 **8** 鬆 9B06
鬈 9B08 鬃 9B03 **9** 鬍 9B0D **10** 鬓 9B13 **11** 鬘 9B18 **12** 鬚 9B1A **13** 鬟 9B1F **14** 鬢 9B22 **15** 鬣 9B23

鬥 191

鬥 9B25 **5** 鬧 9B27 **6** 鬨 9B28 **8** 鬩 9B29 **10** 鬪 9B2A **17** 鬮 9B2E

鬯 192

鬯 9B2F **19** 鬱 9B31

鬲 193

鬲 9B32 **3** 嗝 55DD 隔 9694 **4** 膈 8188 **6** 翮 7FEE 融 878D **8** 鎘 9398

鬼 194

鬼 9B3C **2** 傀 5080 **3** 塊 584A 嵬 5D6C 愧 6127 蒐 8490 隗 9697 **4** 槐 69D0 瑰 7470 魂 9B42 魁 9B41 **5** 魅 9B45
魃 9B43 魆 9B46 魄 9B44 **6** 魇 9B47 **7** 醜 919C 魉 9B49 **8** 魎 9B4E 魍 9B4D 魏 9B4F **9** 餽 993D **11** 魔 9B54
魑 9B51 **14** 魘 9B58

魚 195

魚 9B5A 鱼 9C7C **3** 漁 6F01 魟 9B5F 魠 9B60 **4** 魷 9B77 鱿 9C7F 魨 9B68 魯 9B6F 鲁 9C81 魴 9B74 **5** 稣 7A23 穌 7A4C
魽 9B7D 鮎 9B8E 鲇 9C87 鲈 9C88 鮋 9B8B 鮓 9B93 鮒 9B92 鲋 9C8B 鮑 9B91 鲍 9C8D 𩶘 29D98 鮐 9B90 **6** 鮭 9BAD 鲑 9C91 鮪 9BAA
鮨 9BA8 鮫 9BAB 鮮 9BAE 鲜 9C9C 鮟 9B9F 鲟 9C9F 鰤 9C24 **7** 鯈 9BC8 鯁 9BC1 鲢 9CA2 鯉 9BC9 鲤 9CA4 鯓 9BD3 鮸 9BB8 鯀 9BC0
鲧 9CA7 鯊 9BCA 鲨 9CA8 鯇 9BC7 鯽 9BFD 鲫 9CAB 鯒 9BD2 **8** 鯗 9BD7 鯖 9BD6 鲭 9CAD 鯪 9BEA 鲮 9CAE 鯡 9BE1 鯱 9BF1 鯤 9BE4
鲲 9CB2 鯧 9BE7 鲳 9CB3 鯝 9BDD 鲵 9CB5 鯰 9BF0 鯛 9BDB 鯨 9BE8 鲸 9CB8 鯙 9BD9 鯭 9BED 鯵 9BF5 鯔 9BD4 **9** 鯽 9BFD 鰆 9C06
鰈 9C08 鰊 9C0A 鰄 9C04 鯷 9BF7 鰂 9C02 鰓 9C13 鳃 9CC3 鰐 9C10 鳄 9CC4 鰍 9C0D 鳅 9CC5 鰒 9C12 鰉 9C09 鰌 9C0C 鰕 9C15

黃 201 — **13** 黌 9ECC

黍 202 — 黍 9ECD **3** 黎 9ECE **5** 黏 9ECF **10** 黐 9ED0

黑 203 — 黑 9ED1 黒 9ED2 **3** 嘿 563F 墨 58A8 **4** 默 9ED8 黙 9ED9 黔 9ED4 **5** 點 9EDE 黛 9EDB 黜 9EDC 黝 9EDD **6** 黠 9EE0 黟 9EDF **8** 黩 9EE9 黨 9EE8 黥 9EE5 **9** 黯 9EEF **11** 黴 9EF4 **15** 黷 9EF7

黽 205 — 黽 9EFD **3** 澠 6FA0 **4** 黿 9EFF 鼋 9F0B **6** 蠅 8805 **10** 鼇 9F07 **12** 鼈 9F08

鼎 206 — 鼎 9F0E **2** 鼐 9F10

鼓 207 — 鼓 9F13 **5** 瞽 77BD 鼕 9F15 **8** 鼙 9F19

鼠 208 — 鼠 9F20 **5** 鼬 9F2C 鼩 9F29 **7** 鼯 9F2F **8** 鼱 9F31 **9** 鼴 9F34 **10** 鼹 9F39

鼻 209 — 鼻 9F3B **2** 劓 5293 **3** 嬶 5B36 擤 64E4 鼾 9F3E

齊 210 — 齐 9F50 斉 6589 齊 9F4A **2** 儕 5115 剤 5264 劑 5291 **3** 擠 64E0 斎 658E 済 6E08 濟 6FDF 薺 85BA 齋 9F4B **4** 臍 81CD **7** 躋 8E8B 齎 9F4E **8** 霽 973D **9** 齑 9F51

齒 211 — 歯 6B6F 齒 9F52 齿 9F7F **3** 噛 565B 嚙 5699 **5** 齟 9F5F 龃 9F83 齡 9F61 齢 9F62 龄 9F84 齣 9F63 齙 9F59 齜 9F5C **6** 齧 9F67 龇 9F87 齦 9F66 龈 9F88 **7** 齬 9F6C 龉 9F89 齪 9F6A 龊 9F8A **9** 齲 9F72 龋 9F8B 齷 9F77 龌 9F8C

龍 212 — 竜 7ADC 龍 9F8D 龙 9F99 **3** 嚨 56A8 垄 5784 壟 58DF 寵 5BF5 攏 650F 滝 6EDD 瀧 7027 蘢 8622 隴 96B4 龐 9F90 **4** 朧 6727 櫳 6AF3 瓏 74CF **5** 砻 783B 礱 7931 **6** 笼 7BED 籠 7C60 聾 807E 袭 88AD 襲 8972 龔 9F94 龚 9F9A 龕 9F95 龛 9F9B

龜 213 — 亀 4E80 龜 9F9C 龟 9F9F **4** 鼋 9F0B **5** 穐 7A50

龠 214 — **5** 龢 9FA2 **6** 籥 7C65 **8** 鑰 9470

APPENDICES
A

Appendix A

Notational Conventions

This appendix describes the typographic conventions used throughout this book.

Code Points

In running text, an individual Unicode code point is expressed as U+*n*, where *n* is four to six hexadecimal digits, using the digits 0–9 and uppercase letters A–F (for 10 through 15, respectively). Leading zeros are omitted, unless the code point would have fewer than four hexadecimal digits—for example, U+0001, U+0012, U+0123, U+1234, U+12345, U+102345.

- U+0416 is the Unicode code point for the character named CYRILLIC CAPITAL LETTER ZHE.

The *U+* may be omitted for brevity in tables or when denoting ranges.

A range of Unicode code points is expressed as *U+xxxx–U+yyyy* or *xxxx..yyyy*, where *xxxx* and *yyyy* are the first and last Unicode values in the range, and the long dash or two dots indicate a contiguous range inclusive of the endpoints. For ranges involving supplementary characters, the code points in the ranges are expressed with five or six hexadecimal digits.

- The range U+0900–U+097F contains 128 Unicode code points.
- The Plane 16 private-use characters are in the range 100000..10FFFD.

Character Names

In running text, a formal Unicode name is shown in small capitals (for example, GREEK SMALL LETTER MU), and alternative names (aliases) appear in italics (for example, *umlaut*). Italics are also used to refer to a text element that is not explicitly encoded (for example, *pasekh alef*) or to set off a non-English word (for example, the Welsh word *ynghyd*).

For more information on Unicode character names, see *Section 4.8, Name—Normative*.

For notational conventions used in the code charts, see *Section 17.1, Character Names List*.

Character Blocks

When referring to the normative names of character blocks in the text of the standard, the character block name is titlecased and is used with the term "block." For example:

the Latin Extended-B block

Optionally, an exact range for the character block may also be cited:

the Alphabetic Presentation Forms block (U+FB00..U+FB4F)

These references to normative character block names should not be confused with the headers used throughout the text of the standard, particularly in the block description chapters, to refer to particular ranges of characters. Such headers may be abbreviated in various ways and may refer to subranges within character blocks or ranges that cross character block boundaries. For example:

Latin Ligatures: U+FB00–U+FB06

The definitive list of normative character block names is Blocks.txt in the Unicode Character Database.

Sequences

A sequence of two or more code points may be represented by a comma-delimited list, set off by angle brackets. For this purpose, angle brackets consist of U+003C LESS-THAN SIGN and U+003E GREATER-THAN SIGN. Spaces are optional after the comma, and U+ notation for the code point is also optional—for example, "<U+0061, U+0300>".

When the usage is clear from the context, a sequence of characters may be represented with generic short names, as in "<a, grave>", or the angle brackets may be omitted.

In contrast to sequences of code points, a sequence of one or more code *units* may be represented by a list set off by angle brackets, but without comma delimitation or U+ notation. For example, the notation "<nn nn nn nn>" represents a sequence of bytes, as for the UTF-8 encoding form of a Unicode character. The notation "<nnnn nnnn>" represents a sequence of 16-bit code units, as for the UTF-16 encoding form of a Unicode character.

Rendering

A figure such as *Figure A-1* depicts how a sequence of characters is typically rendered.

Figure A-1. Example of Rendering

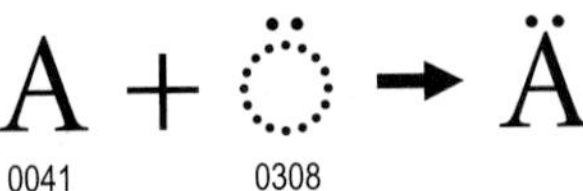

The sequence under discussion is depicted on the left of the arrow, using representative glyphs and code points below them. A possible rendering of that sequence is depicted on the right side of the arrow.

Properties and Property Values

The names of properties and property values appear in titlecase, with words connected by an underscore—for example, General_Category or Uppercase_Letter. In some instances, short names are used, such as gc=Lu, which is equivalent to General_Category = Uppercase_Letter. Long and short names for all properties and property values are defined in the Unicode Character Database; see also *Section 3.5, Properties.*

Occasionally, and especially when discussing character properties that have single words as names, such as *age* and *block,* the names appear in lowercase italics.

Miscellaneous

Phonemic transcriptions are shown between slashes, as in Khmer /khnyom/.

Phonetic transcriptions are shown between square brackets, using the International Phonetic Alphabet. (Full details on the IPA can be found on the International Phonetic Association's Web site, http://www2.arts.gla.ac.uk/IPA/ipa.html.)

A leading asterisk is used to represent an incorrect or nonoccurring linguistic form.

In the text of this book, the word "Unicode" when used alone as a noun refers to the Unicode Standard.

Unambiguous dates of the current common era, such as 1999, are unlabeled. In cases of ambiguity, CE is used. Dates before the common era are labeled with BCE.

The term *byte,* as used in this standard, always refers to a unit of eight bits. This corresponds to the use of the term *octet* in some other standards.

Extended BNF

The Unicode Standard and technical reports use an extended BNF format for describing syntax. As different conventions are used for BNF, *Table A-1* lists the notation used here.

Table A-1. Extended BNF

Symbols	Meaning
`x := ...`	production rule
`x y`	the sequence consisting of x then y
`x*`	zero or more occurrences of x
`x?`	zero or one occurrence of x
`x+`	one or more occurrences of x
`x | y`	either x or y
`( x )`	for grouping
`x || y`	equivalent to `(x | y | (x y))`
`{ x }`	equivalent to `(x)?`
`"abc"`	string literals ("_" is sometimes used to denote space for clarity)

Table A-1. Extended BNF (Continued)

Symbols	Meaning
'abc'	string literals (alternative form)
sot	start of text
eot	end of text
\u1234	Unicode code points within string literals or character classes
\U00101234	Unicode code points within string literals or character classes
U+HHHH	Unicode character literal: equivalent to '\uHHHH'
U-HHHHHHHH	Unicode character literal: equivalent to '\UHHHHHHHH'
[gc=Lu]	character class (syntax below)

In other environments, such as programming languages or markup, alternative notation for sequences of code points or code units may be used.

Character Classes. A *code point class* is a specification of an unordered set of code points. Whenever the code points are all assigned characters, it can also be referred to as a *character class*. The specification consists of any of the following:

- A literal code point
- A range of literal code points
- A set of code points having a given Unicode character property value, as defined in the Unicode Character Database (see PropertyAliases.txt and PropertyValueAliases.txt)
- Non-Boolean properties given as an expression <property> = <property_value> or <property> ≠ <property_value>, such as "General_Category=Titlecase_Letter"
- Boolean properties given as an expression <property> = true or <property> ≠ true, such as "Uppercase=true"
- Combinations of logical operations on classes

Further extensions to this specification of character classes are used in some Unicode Standard Annexes and Unicode Technical Reports. Such extensions are described in those documents, as appropriate.

A partial formal BNF syntax for character classes as used in this standard is given by the following:

```
char_class  := "[" char_class - char_class "]"          set difference
            := "[" item_list "]"
            := "[" property ("=" | "≠") property_value "]"
item_list   := item (","? item)?
item        := code_point                        either literal or escaped
            := code_point - code_point                   inclusive range
```

Whenever any character could be interpreted as a syntax character, it must be escaped. Where no ambiguity would result (with normal operator precedence), extra square brackets can be discarded. If a space character is used as a literal, it is escaped. Examples are found in *Table A-2*.

Table A-2. Character Class Examples

Syntax	Matches
`[a-z]`	English lowercase letters
`[a-z]-[c]`	English lowercase letters except for c
`[0-9]`	European decimal digits
`[\u0030-\u0039]`	(same as above, using Unicode escapes)
`[0-9 A-F a-f]`	hexadecimal digits
`[\p{gc=Letter} \p{gc=Nonspacing_Mark}]`	all letters and nonspacing marks
`[\p{gc=L} \p{gc=Mn}]`	(same as above, using abbreviated notation)
`[^\p{gc=Unassigned}]`	all assigned Unicode characters
`[\u0600-\u06FF - \p{gc=Unassigned}]`	all assigned Arabic characters
`[\p{Alphabetic}]`	all alphabetic characters
`[^\p{Line_Break=Infix_Numeric}]`	all code points that do not have the line break property of Infix_Numeric

For more information about character classes, see Unicode Technical Standard #18, "Unicode Regular Expression Guidelines."

Operators

Operators used in this standard are listed in *Table A-3*.

Table A-3. Operators

Symbol	Meaning
→	is transformed to, or behaves like
↛	is not transformed to
/	integer division (rounded down)
%	modulo operation; equivalent to the integer remainder for positive numbers
¬	logical not

Appendix B

Unicode Publications and Resources

This appendix provides information about the Unicode Consortium and its activities, particularly regarding publications other than the Unicode Standard. The Unicode Consortium publishes a number of technical standards and technical reports, and the current list of those, with abstracts of their content, is included here for convenient reference.

The Unicode Web site also has many useful online resources. *Section B.6, Other Unicode Online Resources*, provides a guide to the kinds of information available online.

B.1 The Unicode Consortium

The Unicode Consortium was incorporated in January 1991, under the name Unicode, Inc., to promote the Unicode Standard as an international encoding system for information interchange, to aid in its implementation, and to maintain quality control over future revisions.

To further these goals, the Unicode Consortium cooperates with the Joint Technical Committee 1 of the International Organization for Standardization and the International Electrotechnical Commission (ISO/IEC JTC1). It holds a Class C liaison membership with ISO/IEC JTC1/SC2; it participates in the work of both JTC1/SC2/WG2 (the technical working group for the subcommittee within JTC1 responsible for character set encoding) and the Ideographic Rapporteur Group (IRG) of WG2. The Consortium is a member company of the InterNational Committee for Information Technology Standards, Technical Committee L2 (INCITS/L2), an accredited U.S. standards organization. Many members of the Unicode Consortium have representatives in many countries who also work with other national standards bodies. In addition, a number of organizations are Liaison Members of the Consortium. For a list, see "Unicode Consortium Liaison Members" on page xlvii.

Membership in the Unicode Consortium is open to organizations and individuals anywhere in the world who support the Unicode Standard and who would like to assist in its extension and widespread implementation. Full, Institutional, Supporting, and Associate Members represent a broad spectrum of corporations and organizations in the computer and information processing industry. For a list, see "Unicode Consortium Members" on page xlv. The Consortium is supported financially solely through membership dues.

The Unicode Technical Committee

The Unicode Technical Committee (UTC) is the working group within the Consortium responsible for the creation, maintenance, and quality of the Unicode Standard. The UTC follows an open process in developing the Unicode Standard and its other technical publications. It coordinates and reviews all technical input to these documents and decides their contents. For more information on the UTC and the process by which the Unicode Standard and the other technical publications are developed, see:

http://www.unicode.org/consortium/utc.html

Other Activities

Going beyond developing technical standards, the Unicode Consortium acts as registration authority for the registration of script identifiers under ISO 15924, and it has a technical committee dedicated to the maintenance of the Common Locale Data Repository (CLDR). The repository contains a large and rapidly growing body of data used in the locale definition for software internationalization. For further information about these and other activities of the Unicode Consortium, visit:

http://www.unicode.org

B.2 Unicode Publications

In addition to the Unicode Standard, the Unicode Consortium publishes Unicode Technical Standards and Unicode Technical Reports. These materials are published as electronic documents only and, unlike Unicode Standard Annexes, do not form part of the Unicode Standard.

A *Unicode Standard Annex* (UAX) forms an integral part of the Unicode Standard. The Unicode Standard may require conformance to normative content in a Unicode Standard Annex, if so specified in the Conformance chapter of that version of the Unicode Standard. The version number of a UAX document corresponds to the version number of the Unicode Standard at the last point that the UAX document was updated. The Unicode Standard Annexes are printed in the back of this book, following the indices.

A *Unicode Technical Standard* (UTS) is a separate specification with its own conformance requirements. A UTS may include a requirement for an implementation of the UTS to also conform to a specific, base level of the Unicode Standard, but conformance to the Unicode Standard as such does not require conformance to any UTS.

A *Unicode Technical Report* (UTR) contains informative material. Unicode Technical Reports do not contain conformance requirements of their own, nor does conformance to the Unicode Standard require conformance to any specifications contained in any of the UTRs. Other specifications, however, are free to cite the material in UTRs and to make any level of conformance requirements within their own context.

In the past, some normative material was published as Unicode Technical Reports. Currently, however, such material is published either as a Unicode Technical Standard or a Unicode Standard Annex.

The Unicode Web site is the source for the most current version of all three categories of technical reports:

http://www.unicode.org/reports/

The following sections provide lists of abstracts for current Unicode Technical Standards and Unicode Technical Reports. They are listed numerically within each category. There are gaps in the numerical sequence become some of the reports have been superseded or have been incorporated into the text of the standard.

B.3 Unicode Technical Standards

UTS #6: A Standard Compression Scheme for Unicode

This report presents the specifications of a compression scheme for Unicode and sample implementation.

UTS #10: Unicode Collation Algorithm

This report provides the specification of the Unicode Collation Algorithm, which provides a specification for how to compare two Unicode strings while remaining conformant to the requirements of the Unicode Standard.

UTS #18: Unicode Regular Expression Guidelines

This document describes guidelines for how to adapt regular expression engines for use with the Unicode Standard.

UTS #22: Character Mapping Markup Language (CharMapML)

This document specifies an XML format for the interchange of mapping data for character encodings. It provides a complete description for such mappings in terms of a defined mapping to and from Unicode code points, and a description of alias tables for the interchange of mapping table names.

UTS #35: Locale Data Markup Language (LDML)

This document describes an XML format (*vocabulary*) for the exchange of structured locale data.

UTS #37: Ideographic Variation Database

This document describes the organization of the Ideographic Variation Database and the procedure to add sequences to that database.

UTS #39: Unicode Security Mechanisms

Because Unicode contains such a large number of characters and incorporates the varied writing systems of the world, incorrect usage can expose programs or systems to possible security attacks. This report specifies mechanisms that can be used in detecting possible security problems.

B.4 Unicode Technical Reports

UTR #16: UTF-EBCDIC

This document presents the specifications of UTF-EBCDIC: EBCDIC Friendly Unicode (or UCS) Transformation Format.

UTR #17: Character Encoding Model

This document clarifies a number of the terms used to describe character encodings and indicates where the different encoding forms of the Unicode Standard fit in. It elaborates the Internet Architecture Board's (IAB) three-layer "text stream" definitions into a five-layer structure.

UTR #20: Unicode in XML and Other Markup Languages

This document contains guidelines on the use of the Unicode Standard in conjunction with markup languages such as XML.

UTR #23: The Unicode Character Property Model

This document presents a conceptual model of character properties defined in the Unicode Standard.

UTR #25: Unicode Support for Mathematics

The Unicode Standard includes virtually all of the standard characters used in mathematics. This set supports a variety of math applications on computers, including document presentation languages like TEX, math markup languages like MathML and OpenMath, internal representations of mathematics in systems like Mathematica, Maple, and MathCAD, computer programs, and plain text. This document describes the Unicode mathematics character groups and gives some of their imputed default math properties.

UTR #26: Compatibility Encoding Scheme for UTF-16: 8-Bit (CESU-8)

This document specifies an 8-bit Compatibility Encoding Scheme for UTF-16 (CESU) that is intended for internal use within systems processing Unicode to provide an ASCII-compatible 8-bit encoding that is similar to UTF-8 but preserves UTF-16 binary collation. *It is not intended or recommended as an encoding used for open information exchange.* The Unicode Consortium does not encourage the use of CESU-8, but does recognize the existence of data in this encoding and supplies this technical report to clearly define the format and to distinguish it from UTF-8. This encoding does not replace or amend the definition of UTF-8.

UTR #30: Character Foldings

This report identifies a set of operations that map similar characters to a common target. Such operations, called character foldings, are used to ignore certain distinctions between similar characters. The report also provides an algorithm for applying these operations to searching, plus additional guidelines.

UTR #36: Unicode Security Considerations

Because Unicode contains such a large number of characters and incorporates the varied writing systems of the world, incorrect usage can expose programs or systems to possible security attacks. This document describes some of the security considerations that programmers, system analysts, standards developers, and users should take into account, and it provides specific recommendations to reduce the risk of problems.

B.5 Unicode Technical Notes

Unicode Technical Notes provide information on a variety of topics related to Unicode and internationalization technologies.

These technical notes are independent publications, not approved by any of the Unicode Technical Committees, nor are they part of the Unicode Standard or any other Unicode specification. Publication does not imply endorsement by the Unicode Consortium in any way. These documents are not subject to the Unicode Patent Policy. Unicode Technical Notes can be found on the Unicode Web site at:

http://www.unicode.org/notes/

The technical notes cover the following topics (among others):

- Algorithms
- Collation
- Compression and code set conversions
- Language identification

- Migration of software
- Modern and historical scripts
- Text layout and rendering
- Tutorials
- Social and cultural issues

B.6 Other Unicode Online Resources

The Unicode Consortium provides a number of online resources for obtaining information and data about the Unicode Standard as well as updates and corrigenda.

Unicode Online Resources

Unicode Web Site

http://www.unicode.org

Unicode Anonymous FTP Site

ftp://ftp.unicode.org

Charts. The charts section of the Web site provides online charts for all of the Unicode characters, plus specialized charts for normalization, collation, case mapping, script names, and Unified CJK Ideographs.

http://www.unicode.org/charts/

Common Locale Data Registry (CLDR). Machine-readable repository, in XML format, of locale information for use in application and system development.

http://www.unicode.org/cldr/

Conferences. The Internationalization and Unicode Conferences are of particular value to anyone implementing the Unicode Standard or working on internationalization. A variety of tutorials and conference sessions cover current topics related to the Unicode Standard, the World Wide Web, software, internationalization, and localization.

http://www.unicode.org/conference/

E-mail Discussion List. Subscription instructions for the public e-mail discussion list are posted on the Unicode Web site.

FAQ (Frequently Asked Questions). The FAQ pages provide an invaluable resource for understanding the Unicode Standard and its implications for users and implementers.

http://www.unicode.org/faq/

Online Unicode Character Database. This page supplies information about the online Unicode Character Database (UCD), including links to documentation files and the most up-to-date version of the data files, as well as instructions on how to access any particular version of the UCD.

http://www.unicode.org/ucd/

Online Unihan Database. The online Unihan Database provides interactive access to all of the property information associated with CJK ideographs in the Unicode Standard.

http://www.unicode.org/chart/unihan.html

Policies. These pages describe Unicode Consortium policies on stability, patents, and Unicode Web site privacy. The stability policies are particularly important for implementers, documenting invariants for the Unicode Standard that allow implementations to be compatible with future and past versions. Accordingly, the stability policies are also reprinted in this book in *Appendix F, Unicode Encoding Stability Policies*, for easy reference.

http://www.unicode.org/policies/

Updates and Errata. This page lists periodic updates with corrections of typographic errors and new clarifications of the text.

http://www.unicode.org/errata/

Versions. This page describes the version numbering used in the Unicode Standard, the nature of the Unicode character repertoire, and ways to cite and reference the Unicode Standard, the Unicode Character Database, and Unicode Technical Reports. It also specifies the exact contents of each and every version of the Unicode Standard, back to Unicode 1.0.0.

http://www.unicode.org/versions/

Where Is My Character? This page provides basic guidance to finding Unicode characters, especially those whose glyphs do not appear in the charts, or that are represented by sequences of Unicode characters.

http://www.unicode.org/standard/where/

How to Contact the Unicode Consortium

The best way to contact the Unicode Consortium to obtain membership information or order additional copies of this book is via the Web site:

http://www.unicode.org/contacts.html

The Web site also lists the current telephone, fax, and courier delivery address. The Consortium's postal address is:

P.O. Box 391476
Mountain View, CA 94039-1476
USA

Appendix C

Relationship to ISO/IEC 10646

The Unicode Consortium maintains a strong working relationship with ISO/IEC JTC1/SC2/WG2, the working group developing International Standard 10646. Today both organizations are firmly committed to maintaining the synchronization between the Unicode Standard and 10646. Each standard nevertheless uses its own form of reference and, to some degree, separate terminology. This appendix gives a brief history and explains how the standards are related.

C.1 History

Having recognized the benefits of developing a single universal character code standard, members of the Unicode Consortium worked with representatives from the International Organization for Standardization (ISO) during the summer and fall of 1991 to pursue this goal. Meetings between the two bodies resulted in mutually acceptable changes to both Unicode Version 1.0 and the first ISO/IEC Draft International Standard DIS 10646.1, which merged their combined repertoire into a single numerical character encoding. This work culminated in *The Unicode Standard, Version 1.1*.

ISO/IEC 10646-1:1993, *Information Technology—Universal Multiple-Octet*[1] *Coded Character Set (UCS)—Part 1: Architecture and Basic Multilingual Plane*, was published in May 1993 after final editorial changes were made to accommodate the comments of voting members. *The Unicode Standard, Version 1.1*, reflected the additional characters introduced from the DIS 10646.1 repertoire and incorporated minor editorial changes.

Merging *The Unicode Standard, Version 1.0*, and DIS 10646.1 consisted of aligning the numerical values of identical characters and then filling in some groups of characters that were present in DIS 10646.1, but not in the Unicode Standard. As a result, the encoded characters (code points and names) of ISO/IEC 10646-1:1993 and *The Unicode Standard, Version 1.1*, are precisely the same.

---

1. *Octet* is ISO/IEC terminology for *byte*—that is, an ordered sequence of 8 bits considered as a unit.

Versions 2.0, 2.1, and 3.0 of the Unicode Standard successively added more characters, matching a series of amendments to ISO/IEC 10646-1. *The Unicode Standard, Version 3.0,* is precisely aligned with the second edition of ISO/IEC 10646-1, known as ISO/IEC 10646-1:2000.

In 2001, Part 2 of ISO/IEC 10646 was published as ISO/IEC 10646-2:2001. Version 3.1 of the Unicode Standard was synchronized with that publication, which added supplementary characters for the first time. Subsequently, Versions 3.2 and 4.0 of the Unicode Standard added characters matching further amendments to both parts of ISO/IEC 10646. *The Unicode Standard, Version 4.0,* is precisely aligned with the third version of ISO/IEC 10646 (first edition), published as a single standard merging the former two parts: ISO/IEC 10646:2003.

Versions 4.1 and 5.0 of the Unicode Standard added characters matching Amendments 1 and 2 to ISO/IEC 10646:2003. Version 5.0 also adds four characters for Sindhi support from Amendment 3 to ISO/IEC 10646:2003.

Table C-1 gives the timeline for these efforts.

Table C-1. Timeline

Year	Version	Summary
1989	DP 10646	Draft proposal, independent of Unicode
1990	Unicode Prepublication	Prepublication review draft
1990	DIS-1 10646	First draft, independent of Unicode
1991	Unicode 1.0	Edition published by Addison-Wesley
1992	Unicode 1.0.1	Modified for merger compatibility
1992	DIS-2 10646	Second draft, merged with Unicode
1993	IS 10646-1:1993	Merged standard
1993	Unicode 1.1	Revised to match IS 10646-1:1993
1995	10646 amendments	Korean realigned, plus additions
1996	Unicode 2.0	Synchronized with 10646 amendments
1998	Unicode 2.1	Added euro sign and corrigenda
1999	10646 amendments	Additions
2000	Unicode 3.0	Synchronized with 10646 second edition
2000	IS 10646-1:2000	10646 part 1, second edition, publication with amendments to date
2001	IS 10646-2:2001	10646 part 2 (supplementary planes)
2001	Unicode 3.1	Synchronized with 10646 part 2
2002	Unicode 3.2	Synchronized with Amd 1 to 10646 part 1
2003	Unicode 4.0	Synchronized with 10646 third version
2003	IS 10646:2003	10646 third version (first edition), merging the two parts
2005	Unicode 4.1	Synchronized with Amd 1 to 10646:2003
2006	Unicode 5.0	Synchronized with Amd 2 to 10646:2003, plus Sindhi additions

Unicode 1.0

The combined repertoire presented in ISO/IEC 10646 is a superset of *The Unicode Standard, Version 1.0,* repertoire as amended by *The Unicode Standard, Version 1.0.1. The Unicode Standard, Version 1.0,* was amended by the *Unicode 1.0.1 Addendum* to make the Unicode Standard a proper subset of ISO/IEC 10646. This effort entailed both moving and eliminating a small number of characters.

Unicode 2.0

The Unicode Standard, Version 2.0, covered the repertoire of *The Unicode Standard, Version 1.1* (and IS 10646), plus the first seven amendments to IS 10646, as follows:

Amd. 1: UTF-16

Amd. 2: UTF-8

Amd. 3: Coding of C1 Controls

Amd. 4: Removal of Annex G: UTF-1

Amd. 5: Korean Hangul Character Collection

Amd. 6: Tibetan Character Collection

Amd. 7: 33 Additional Characters (Hebrew, Long S, Dong)

In addition, *The Unicode Standard, Version 2.0,* covered Technical Corrigendum No. 1 (on renaming of AE LIGATURE to LETTER) and such Editorial Corrigenda to ISO/IEC 10646 as were applicable to the Unicode Standard. The euro sign and the object replacement character were added in Version 2.1, per amendment 18 of ISO 10646-1.

Unicode 3.0

The Unicode Standard, Version 3.0, is synchronized with the second edition of ISO/IEC 10646-1. The latter contains all of the published amendments to 10646-1; the list includes the first seven amendments, plus the following:

Amd. 8: Addition of Annex T: Procedure for the Unification and Arrangement of CJK Ideographs

Amd. 9: Identifiers for Characters

Amd. 10: Ethiopic Character Collection

Amd. 11: Unified Canadian Aboriginal Syllabics Character Collection

Amd. 12: Cherokee Character Collection

Amd. 13: CJK Unified Ideographs with Supplementary Sources (Horizontal Extension)

Amd. 14: Yi Syllables and Yi Radicals Character Collection

Amd. 15: Kangxi Radicals, Hangzhou Numerals Character Collection

Amd. 16: Braille Patterns Character Collection

Amd. 17: CJK Unified Ideographs Extension A (Vertical Extension)

Amd. 18: Miscellaneous Letters and Symbols Character Collection (which includes the euro sign)

Amd. 19: Runic Character Collection

Amd. 20: Ogham Character Collection

Amd. 21: Sinhala Character Collection

Amd. 22: Keyboard Symbols Character Collection

Amd. 23: Bopomofo Extensions and Other Character Collection

Amd. 24: Thaana Character Collection

Amd. 25: Khmer Character Collection

Amd. 26: Myanmar Character Collection

Amd. 27: Syriac Character Collection

Amd. 28: Ideographic Description Characters

Amd. 29: Mongolian

Amd. 30: Additional Latin and Other Characters

Amd. 31: Tibetan Extension

The second edition of 10646-1 also contains the contents of Technical Corrigendum No. 2 and all the Editorial Corrigenda to the year 2000.

Unicode 4.0

The Unicode Standard, Version 4.0, is synchronized with the third version of ISO/IEC 10646. The third version of ISO/IEC 10646 is the result of the merger of the second edition of Part 1 (ISO/IEC 10646-1:2000) with the first edition of Part 2 (ISO/IEC 10646-2:2001) into a single publication. The third version incorporates the published amendments to 10646-1 and 10646-2:

Amd. 1 (to part 1): Mathematical symbols and other characters

Amd. 2 (to part 1): Limbu, Tai Le, Yijing, and other characters

Amd. 1 (to part 2): Aegean, Ugaritic, and other characters

The third version of 10646 also contains all the Editorial Corrigenda to date.

Unicode 5.0

The Unicode Standard, Version 5.0, is synchronized with ISO/IEC 10646:2003 plus its first two published amendments:

Amd. 1: Glagolitic, Coptic, Georgian and other characters

Amd. 2: N'Ko, Phags-Pa, Phoenician and Cuneiform

Four Devanagari characters for the support of the Sindhi language (U+097B, U+097C, U+097E, U+097F) were added in Version 5.0 per Amendment 3 of ISO 10646.

The synchronization of *The Unicode Standard, Version 5.0*, with the third version of ISO/IEC 10646 plus its amendments means that the repertoire, encoding, and names of all characters are identical between the two standards at those version levels, and that all other material from the amendments to 10646 that have a bearing on the text of the Unicode Standard have been taken into account in the revision of the Unicode Standard.

C.2 Encoding Forms in ISO/IEC 10646

ISO/IEC 10646 defines four alternative forms of encoding: UCS-4, UCS-2, UTF-8, and UTF-16. UTF-8 and UTF-16 are discussed in *Section C.3, UCS Transformation Formats.*

UCS-4. UCS-4 stands for "Universal Character Set coded in 4 octets" and is considered the canonical form for 10646. It is a four-octet (32-bit) encoding containing 2^{31} code positions. These code positions are conceptually divided into 128 *groups* of 256 *planes*, with each plane containing 256 *rows* of 256 *cells.*

ISO/IEC 10646 states that all future assignments of characters to 10646 will be allocated on the BMP or the first 14 supplementary planes. This is to ensure interoperability between the UCS transformation formats (see below). It also guarantees interoperability with implementations of the Unicode Standard, for which only code positions $0..10FFFF_{16}$ are meaningful. The former provision for private-use code positions in groups 60 to 7F and in planes E0 to FF in 10646 has been removed from 10646. As a consequence, UCS-4 can now be taken effectively as an alias for the Unicode encoding form UTF-32, except that UTF-32 has the extra requirement that additional Unicode semantics be observed for all characters.

UCS-2. UCS-2 stands for "Universal Character Set coded in 2 octets" and is also known as "the two-octet BMP form." It is the two-octet (16-bit) encoding consisting only of code positions for plane zero, the *Basic Multilingual Plane.*

Zero Extending

The character "A", U+0041 LATIN CAPITAL LETTER A, has the unchanging numerical value 41 hexadecimal. This value may be extended by any quantity of leading zeros to serve in the context of the following encoding standards and transformation formats (see *Table C-2*).

This design eliminates the problem of disparate values in all systems that use either of the standards and their transformation formats.

Table C-2. Zero Extending

Bits	Standard	Binary	Hex	Dec	Char
7	ASCII	1000001	41	65	A
8	8859-1	01000001	41	65	A
16	UTF-16, UCS-2	00000000 01000001	41	65	A
32	UTF-32, UCS-4	00000000 00000000 00000000 01000001	41	65	A

C.3 UCS Transformation Formats

UTF-8

The term *UTF-8* in ISO/IEC 10646 stands for "UCS Transformation Format, 8-bit form." UTF-8 is an alternative coded representation form for all of the characters of ISO/IEC 10646. The ISO/IEC definition is identical in format to UTF-8 as described under definition D92 in *Section 3.9, Unicode Encoding Forms.*

UTF-8 can be used to transmit text data through communications systems that assume that individual octets in the range of x00 to x7F have a definition according to ISO/IEC 4873, including a C0 set of control functions according to the 8-bit structure of ISO/IEC 2022. UTF-8 also avoids the use of octet values in this range that have special significance during the parsing of file name character strings in widely used file-handling systems.

The definition of UTF-8 in Annex D of ISO/IEC 10646:2003 also allows for the use of five- and six-byte sequences to encode characters that are outside the range of the Unicode character set; those five- and six-byte sequences are illegal for the use of UTF-8 as an encoding form of Unicode characters. ISO/IEC 10646 does not allow mapping of surrogate code positions, known as RC-elements in that standard; that restriction is identical to the restriction for the Unicode definition of UTF-8.

UTF-16

The term *UTF-16* in ISO/IEC 10646 stands for "UCS Transformation Format for 16 Planes of Group 00." It is defined in Annex C of ISO/IEC 10646:2003. In UTF-16, each BMP code position represents itself. Non-BMP code positions of ISO/IEC 10646 in planes 1 to 16 are represented using pairs of special codes. UTF-16 defines the transformation between the UCS-4 code positions in planes 1 to 16 of Group 00 and the pairs of special codes and is identical to the UTF-16 encoding form defined in the Unicode Standard under definition D91 in *Section 3.9, Unicode Encoding Forms.*

In ISO/IEC 10646, *high-surrogates* are called "RC-elements from the high-half zone" and *low-surrogates* are called "RC-elements from the low-half zone." Together, they constitute the S (Special) Zone of the BMP.

UTF-16 represents the BMP and the next 16 planes.

C.4 Synchronization of the Standards

Programmers and system users should treat the encoded character values from the Unicode Standard and ISO/IEC 10646 as identities, especially in the transmission of raw character data across system boundaries. The Unicode Consortium and ISO/IEC JTC1/SC2/WG2 are committed to maintaining the synchronization between the two standards.

However, the Unicode Standard and ISO/IEC 10646 differ in the precise terms of their conformance specifications. Any Unicode implementation will conform to ISO/IEC 10646, level 3, but because the Unicode Standard imposes additional constraints on character semantics and transmittability, not all implementations that are compliant with ISO/IEC 10646 will be compliant with the Unicode Standard.

C.5 Identification of Features for the Unicode Standard

ISO/IEC 10646 provides mechanisms for specifying a number of implementation parameters, generating what may be termed instantiations of the standard. ISO/IEC 10646 contains no means of explicitly declaring the Unicode Standard as such. As a whole, however, the Unicode Standard may be considered as encompassing the entire repertoire of ISO/IEC 10646 and having the following features (as well as additional semantics):

- Numbered subset 307 (UNICODE 5.0)
- UTF-8, UTF-16, or UCS-4 (= UTF-32)
- Implementation level 3 (allowing both combining marks and precomposed characters)
- Device type 1 (receiving device with full retransmission capability)

Few applications are expected to make use of all of the characters defined in ISO/IEC 10646. The conformance clauses of the two standards address this situation in very different ways. ISO/IEC 10646 provides a mechanism for specifying included subsets of the character repertoire, permitting implementations to ignore characters that are not included (see normative Annex A of ISO/IEC 10646). A Unicode implementation requires a minimal level of handling all character codes—namely, the ability to store and retransmit them undamaged. Thus the Unicode Standard encompasses the entire ISO/IEC 10646 repertoire without requiring that any particular subset be implemented.

The Unicode Standard does not provide formal mechanisms for identifying a stream of bytes as Unicode characters, although to some extent this function is served by use of the *byte order mark* (U+FEFF) to indicate byte ordering. ISO/IEC 10646 defines an ISO/IEC 2022 control sequence to introduce the use of 10646. ISO/IEC 10646 also allows the use of U+FEFF as a "signature" as described in ISO/IEC 10646. This optional "signature" convention for identification of UTF-8, UTF-16, and UCS-4 is described in the informative Annex

H of 10646. It is consistent with the description of the *byte order mark* in *Section 16.8, Specials.*

C.6 Character Names

Unicode character names follow the ISO/IEC character naming guidelines (summarized in informative Annex L of ISO/IEC 10646). In the first version of the Unicode Standard, the naming convention followed the ISO/IEC naming convention, but with some differences that were largely editorial. For example,

ISO/IEC 10646 name	029A	LATIN SMALL LETTER CLOSED OPEN E
Unicode 1.0 name	029A	LATIN SMALL LETTER CLOSED EPSILON

In the ISO/IEC framework, the unique character name is viewed as the major resource for both character semantics and cross-mapping among standards. In the framework of the Unicode Standard, character semantics are indicated via character properties, functional specifications, usage annotations, and name aliases; cross-mappings among standards are provided in the form of explicit tables available on the Unicode Web site. The disparities between the Unicode 1.0 names and ISO/IEC 10646 names have been remedied by adoption of ISO/IEC 10646 names in the Unicode Standard. The names adopted by the Unicode Standard are from the English-language version of ISO/IEC 10646, even when other language versions are published by ISO.

C.7 Character Functional Specifications

The core of a character code standard is a mapping of code points to characters, but in some cases the semantics or even the identity of the character may be unclear. Certainly a character is not simply the representative glyph used to depict it in the standard. For this reason, the Unicode Standard supplies the information necessary to specify the semantics of the characters it encodes.

Thus the Unicode Standard encompasses far more than a chart of code points. It also contains a set of extensive character functional specifications and data, as well as substantial background material designed to help implementers better understand how the characters interact. The Unicode Standard specifies properties and algorithms. Conformant implementations of the Unicode Standard will also be conformant with ISO/IEC 10646, level 3.

Compliant implementations of ISO/IEC 10646 can be conformant to the Unicode Standard—as long as the implementations conform to all additional specifications that apply to the characters of their adopted subsets, and as long as they support all Unicode characters outside their adopted subsets in the manner referred to in *Section C.5, Identification of Features for the Unicode Standard.*

Appendix D

Changes from Previous Versions

This appendix provides version history of the standard and summarizes updates that have been made to conformance specifications, character content, and data files in the Unicode Character Database since the publication of *The Unicode Standard, Version 3.0,* and *The Unicode Standard, Version 4.0.* For specific details on conformance requirements, always refer to *Chapter 3, Conformance.* Further information on all major, minor, and update versions of the Unicode Standard can be found on the Unicode Web site. Also see the subsection "Versions" in *Section B.6, Other Unicode Online Resources.*

D.1 Improvements to the Standard

Version 5.0 of the Unicode Standard incorporates into the text the knowledge gained from many years of worldwide industry implementation experience. It supersedes all previous versions and offers round-trip compatibility with the Chinese standards GB18030 and HKSCS, improved alignment of the Bidirectional Algorithm with norms of the industry, improved guidance on the segmentation of text and processing Unicode strings, and enhanced descriptions of rendering Indic scripts.

This latest version of the Unicode Standard is the basis for Unicode security mechanisms, the Unicode collation algorithm, the locale data provided by the Common Locale Data Repository, and support for Unicode in regular expressions. The significant improvements to the standard since Versions 3.0 and 4.0 include the further development of the Unicode encoding model, the introduction of the character property model, and the establishment of casing and identifier stability.

The text of the standard has been enhanced significantly:

- Two thirds of the definitions are new.
- One third of the conformance clauses are new.
- One half of the character repertoire is new.
- One fourth of the tables are new.
- Four fifths of the figures are new or updated.

- One half of the Unicode Standard Annexes are new.
- All Unicode Standard Annexes are included in the book for the first time.
- The form factor has been improved dramatically to make the book smaller and lighter.

D.2 Versions of the Unicode Standard

The Unicode Technical Committee updates the Unicode Standard to respond to the needs of implementers and users while maintaining consistency with ISO/IEC 10646. The relationship between these versions of Unicode and ISO/IEC 10646 is shown in *Table D-1*. For more detail on the relationship of Unicode and ISO/IEC 10646, see *Appendix C, Relationship to ISO/IEC 10646.*

Table D-1. Versions of Unicode and ISO/IEC 10646-1

Year	Version	Published	ISO/IEC 10646-1
1991	Unicode 1.0	Vol. 1, Addison-Wesley	Basis for Committee Draft 2 of 10646-1
1992	Unicode 1.0.1	Vol. 1, 2, Addison-Wesley	Interim merger version
1993	Unicode 1.1	Technical Report #4	Matches ISO 10646-1
1996	Unicode 2.0	Addison-Wesley	Matches ISO 10646-1 plus amendments
1998	Unicode 2.1	Technical Report #8	Matches ISO 10646-1 plus amendments
2000	Unicode 3.0	Addison-Wesley	Matches ISO 10646-1 second edition
2001	Unicode 3.1	Standard Annex #27	Matches ISO 10646-1 second edition plus two characters, 10646-2 first edition
2002	Unicode 3.2	Standard Annex #28	Matches ISO 10646-1 second edition plus amendment, 10646-2 first edition
2003	Unicode 4.0	Addison-Wesley	Matches ISO 10646:2003, third version
2005	Unicode 4.1	Web publication	Matches ISO 10646:2003, third version, plus Amd. 1
2006	Unicode 5.0	Addison-Wesley (2007)	Matches ISO 10646:2003, third version, plus Amd. 1, Amd. 2, and four characters from Amd. 3

The Unicode Standard has grown from having 28,294 assigned graphic and format characters in Version 1.0, to having 99,024 characters in Version 5.0. *Table D-2* documents the number of code points allocated in the different versions of the Unicode Standard. The row in *Table D-2* labeled "Graphic + Format" represents the traditional count of Unicode characters and is the typical answer to the question, "How many characters are in the Unicode Standard?"

Some of the values in *Table D-2* differ slightly from summary statistics published in earlier versions of the standard, primarily due to a refined accounting of the allocations in Unicode 1.0. Also note that the numbers for Han Compatibility include the 12 unified ideographs encoded in the CJK Compatibility Ideographs block.

Table D-2. Allocation of Code Points by Type

	V1.0.0	V1.0.1	V1.1	V2.0	V2.1	V3.0	V3.1	V3.2	V4.0	V4.1	V5.0
Alphabetics, Symbols	4,734	4,728	6,290	6,491	6,493	10,210	11,798	12,753	13,973	15,117	16,486
Han (URO)		20,902	20,902	20,902	20,902	20,902	20,902	20,902	20,902	20,902	20,902
Han (URO Extension)										22	22
Han Extension A						6,582	6,582	6,582	6,582	6,582	6,582
Han Extension B							42,711	42,711	42,711	42,711	42,711
Han Compatibility		302	302	302	302	302	844	903	903	1,009	1,009
Subtotal Han		21,204	21,204	21,204	21,204	27,786	71,039	71,098	71,098	71,226	71,226
Hangul Syllables	2,350	2,350	6,656	11,172	11,172	11,172	11,172	11,172	11,172	11,172	11,172
Graphic Characters	7,084	28,282	34,150	38,867	38,869	49,168	94,009	95,023	96,243	97,515	98,884
Format Characters	12	12	18	18	18	26	131	133	139	140	140
Graphic + Format	7,096	28,294	34,168	38,885	38,887	49,194	94,140	95,156	96,382	97,655	99,024
Controls	65	65	65	65	65	65	65	65	65	65	65
Private Use	5,632	6,144	6,400	137,468	137,468	137,468	137,468	137,468	137,468	137,468	137,468
Total Assigned	12,793	34,503	40,633	176,418	176,420	186,727	231,673	232,689	233,915	235,188	236,557
Surrogate Code Points				2,048	2,048	2,048	2,048	2,048	2,048	2,048	2,048
Noncharacters	2	2	2	34	34	34	66	66	66	66	66
Total Designated	12,795	34,505	40,635	178,500	178,502	188,809	233,787	234,803	236,029	237,302	238,671
Reserved Code Points	52,741	31,031	24,901	935,612	935,610	925,303	880,325	879,309	878,083	876,810	875,441

D.3 Clause and Definition Numbering Changes

In the time since the publication of *The Unicode Standard, Version 2.0*, there have been very substantial additions to the numbered conformance clauses and formal definitions in the standard. In prior versions, some effort was made to keep the numbering of clauses and definitions consistent between versions. However, with Version 5.0, it has proven necessary to renumber completely.

To assist in comparison of Version 5.0 to earlier versions of the standard, *Table D-3* provides a cross-mapping of clause and definitions numbers between Version 5.0 and other major versions.

Table D-3. Clause and Definition Numbering

V5.0	V4.0	V3.0	V2.0
n/a	C1–C3		
C1	C4	C4	C4
C2	C5	C5	C5
C3	C6	C6	C6
C4	C7	C7	C7
C5	C8	C8	C8
C6	C9	C9	C9
C7	C10	C10	C10
C8	C11	C1, C2, C11	C1, C2
C9	C12	C12	
C10	C12a	C12	
C11	C12b	C3	C3
C12	C13	C13	
C13	C14		
C14	C15		
C15	C16		
C16	C17		
C17	C18		
C18	C19		
C19	C19a		
C20	C20		
D1	D1	D1	D1
n/a	D2		
D2	D2a		
D3	D2b	D2	D2
D4–D6			
D7	D3	D3	D3
D8	D4	D4	D4
D9	D4a		

V5.0	V4.0	V3.0	V2.0
D10	D4b		
D11	D5		
D12	D6	D6	D6
n/a	D7		
D13	D7a	D7a	
D14	D7b		
D15	D7c		
D16	D8	D8	D8
D17	D8a		
D18–D32			
n/a	n/a	D9	D9
n/a	n/a	D10	D10
n/a	n/a	D10a	
n/a	n/a	D10b	
n/a	n/a	D11	D11
D33	D9		
D34			
D35	D9a		
D36	D9b		
D37–D44			
D45	D9c		
D46	D9d		
D47	D10		
D48	D10a		
n/a	D11		
D49	D12	D12	D12
n/a	D13	D13	D13
D50–D51			
D52	D14	D14	D14

Table D-3. Clause and Definition Numbering (Continued)

V5.0	V4.0	V3.0	V2.0
D53	D15	D15	D15
D54			
D55	D16	D16	D16
D56	D17	D17	D17
D57	D17a	D17a	
D58–D62			
D63	D18	D18	D18
D64	D19	D19	D19
D65	D20	D20	D20
D66	D21	D21	D21
D67	D22	D22	D22
D68	D23	D23	D23
D69	D23a		
D70	D24	D24	D24
D71	D25	D25	D25
D72	D25a		
D73	D26	D26	D26
D74	D26a		
D75	D27	D27	D27
D76	D28	D28	D28
D77	D28a	D5	D5
D78	D28b	D7	D7
D79	D29	D29	
D80	D29a		
D81	D29b		
D82	D29c		
D83	D29d		
D84	D30	D30	

V5.0	V4.0	V3.0	V2.0
D85	D30a		
D86	D30b		
D87	D30c		
D88	D30d		
D89	D30e		
n/a	n/a	D31	
D90	D31		
n/a	D32	D32	
n/a	D33–D34		
D91	D35		
D92	D36		
D93	D37		
D94	D38		
D95	D39	D36	
D96	D40	D33	
D97	D41	D34	
D98	D42	D35	
D99	D43		
D100	D44		
D101	D45		
D102–D103			
D104	D46	D37	D29
D105–D119			
D120	D47		
D121–D122			
D123	D48		
D124–D131			

An entry "n/a" in the Version 5.0 (V5.0) or Version 4.0 (V4.0) columns indicates a clause or definition that has become obsolete or has been superseded. In some cases, because of rewording of clauses or definitions over time, two or more entries from an earlier version might correspond to a single Unicode 5.0 entry, or vice versa.

D.4 Changes from Version 4.1 to Version 5.0

New Characters Added

In total, 1,369 new character assignments were made to the Unicode Standard, Version 5.0. These additions include new characters for Cyrillic, Greek, Hebrew, Kannada, Latin, math, phonetic extensions, symbols, and five new scripts: Balinese, N'Ko, Phags-pa, Phoenician, and Sumero-Akkadian Cuneiform.

The new character additions were to both the BMP and the SMP (Plane 1). For more information on these character allocations, see the file DerivedAge.txt in the Unicode Character Database (UCD).

Unicode Character Database Changes

The Unicode Character Database was extended to cover the character repertoire additions, and new block definitions and script values were added. A number of other updates were made, as listed here.

New Properties. Normative_Name_Alias was added to provide alternate identifiers for characters with problems in their names. The metaproperty termed "Deprecated" was added. The Jamo_Short_Name property was documented as a contributory property in PropertyAliases.txt and PropertyValueAliases.txt.

General Category. U+103D0 OLD PERSIAN WORD DIVIDER was changed to Po. The bracket characters U+23B4..U+23B6 were changed to So. U+0294 LATIN LETTER GLOTTAL STOP was changed to Lo. U+2132 TURNED CAPITAL F and U+2183 ROMAN NUMERAL REVERSED ONE HUNDRED were changed to Lu. U+10341 GOTHIC LETTER NINETY was changed to Nl.

Numeric Properties. The Numeric_Type of U+10341 GOTHIC LETTER NINETY was changed from None to Numeric, and it was given the Numeric_Value 90.

Bidirectional Behavior. The Bidi_Class property for Old Persian numerals U+103D1..U+103D5 and U+2132 TURNED CAPITAL F was changed to L. The list of characters with the Bidi_Mirrored property was made consistent for brackets and quotation marks.

Scripts. Unassigned code points were given a new Script property value of "Zzzz". Three Mongolian punctuation marks, U+1802, U+1803, and U+1805, were changed to Script=Common. U+1DBF MODIFIER LETTER SMALL THETA was changed to Script=Greek. U+2132 TURNED CAPITAL F was changed to Script=Latin.

Unihan. The kIICore field was made a normative property, and three new provisional properties were added: kCheungBauer, kCheungBauerIndex, and kFourCornerCoverage. There were numerous additions to the kCangjie property.

Text Breaking. Grapheme_Link was deprecated as a property and moved from PropList.txt to DerivedCoreProperties.txt.

Line Break. The Line_Break property of several punctuation characters (U+1735, U+1736, U+17D9, U+203D, U+2047..U+2049) and bracket characters (U+23B4..U+23B6) was changed to AL to better match their expected behavior. Numerous characters for Southeast Asian scripts, which require complex contextual line breaking, were changed to SA.

Case-Related Properties. The addition of the second member of a few case pairs (such as U+0243 LATIN CAPITAL LETTER B WITH STROKE) led to the revision of the uppercase, lowercase, and titlecase mappings for the already-encoded first member of the case pair.

For more information, see the file UCD.html in the Unicode Character Database.

Changes Affecting Conformance and Stability

Chapter 3, Conformance, was substantially improved by incorporating much of the Unicode Property Model, enhancing the treatment of combining characters, and further clarifying canonical ordering behavior through the addition of clearly defined principles. Additionally, conformance clauses and definitions were renumbered for overall readability and clarity of the text.

Significant clarifications or modifications to character behavior include those listed below.

Bidirectional Behavior. The Bidirectional Algorithm was modified to tighten up the conformance requirements for characters with the Bidi_Mirrored property.

Stability of Cased Letters. If uppercase characters are added in cased scripts, the corresponding lowercase characters will be added as well, so that case folding is stable.

Stability of Named Character Sequences. An initial provisional phase was incorporated into the process for defining Named Character Sequences, so that approved Named Character Sequences will be immutable.

Disunification of Diacritics. Criteria for disunifying diacritics were established.

Indic Scripts. Descriptions of Indic scripts were improved substantially. ZERO WIDTH JOINER and ZERO WIDTH NON-JOINER can now be used to encourage or discourage ligation in Bengali; the sequence for Gurmukhi double vowels was determined; and the shaping of *ra* in Tamil was updated.

Combining Marks. The use of the combining grapheme joiner with Latin script diacritics was clarified.

Unicode Standard Annexes

Changes to the Unicode Standard Annexes were made, as listed here.

> In UAX #9, "Bidirectional Algorithm," the definition of directional run was changed to be the same as level run, rule L4 and HL6 were updated in conjunction with the change in handling Bidi_Mirrored, and a caution was added on the use of higher-level protocols.

In UAX #14, "Line Breaking Properties," a number of rules were modified, the use of soft hyphen in cursive scripts was documented, the conformance clauses were restated and the algorithm was reorganized into tailorable and non-tailorable sections, and the normative status was made consistent with *Chapter 3, Conformance*. As a result of the restatement of conformance, the Line_Break property became normative.

In UAX #15, "Unicode Normalization Forms," the stability section was updated.

In UAX #29, "Text Boundaries," the definition of numeric was changed for both word and sentence breaks, the definition of ALetter was tied to the Line_Break property SA, text was added to explain why modifier letters are not parts of words, breaks within CRLF were forbidden, and rule 0 of section 4 was removed.

UAX #31, "Identifier and Pattern Syntax," introduced profiles and added notes on profiles of identifiers for natural languages and the use of spaces in identifiers.

Errata

An itemized list of errata incorporated since the publication of the Unicode Standard, Version 4.1, can be found online. See "Updates and Errata" in *Section B.6, Other Unicode Online Resources*.

D.5 Changes from Version 4.0 to Version 4.1

New Characters Added

In total, 1,273 new character assignments were made to the Unicode Standard, Version 4.1. These additions include characters to complete round-trip mapping of the HKSCS and GB 18030 standards; five new currency signs; new characters for Arabic, Ethiopic, Hebrew, Indic, and Korean; and eight new scripts: Buginese, Coptic, Glagolitic, Kharoshthi, New Tai Lue, Old Persian, Syloti Nagri, and Tifinagh. The addition of the Coptic script constituted a disunification of Coptic from Greek.

The Nuskhuri forms of Khutsuri Georgian were added. The new Nuskhuri forms are now to be taken as the lowercase pairs of the Asomtavruli Georgian and are a change from the previous documentation about Georgian.

The new character additions were to both the BMP and the SMP (Plane 1). For more information on the character allocations, see the file DerivedAge.txt in the Unicode Character Database.

Unicode Character Database Changes

The Unicode Character Database was extended to cover the character repertoire additions, and new block definitions and script values were added. A number of other updates were made, including those listed below.

New Properties. Grapheme_Cluster_Break, Sentence_Break, Word_Break, and STerm were added in support of text boundary determination. Other_ID_Continue was added to support identifier stability. Pattern_Syntax and Pattern_White_Space were added in support of pattern syntax matching. The property Variation_Selector was added as a convenience for referring to all variation selector characters.

Case Mapping. The case mapping contexts defined in SpecialCasing.txt were updated and supersede *Table 3-13*, "Context Specification for Casing," in *The Unicode Standard, Version 4.0*.

Alphabetic. The Alphabetic property was modified to be a superset of Lowercase and Uppercase for compatibility with POSIX-style character classes. The uppercase and lowercase circled letters A through Z, U+24B6..U+24E9, were added to Other_Alphabetic.

Bidirectional Behavior. The values of the Bidi_Class property were harmonized for a few compatibility equivalents of characters whose Bidi_Class values changed for Unicode 4.0.1. The Bidi_Class property for Braille symbols was changed to L. The properties for characters related to number and date formatting were changed.

General Category. U+30FB KATAKANA MIDDLE DOT and U+FF65 HALFWIDTH KATAKANA MIDDLE DOT were changed from Pc to Po. The Ethiopic digits (U+1369 and following) were changed from Nd to No. U+200B ZERO WIDTH SPACE was changed to Cf. U+A015 YI SYLLABLE WU was changed from Lo to Lm.

Numeric Properties. The Numeric_Type of U+1034A GOTHIC LETTER NINE HUNDRED was changed from None to Numeric, and it was given the Numeric_Value 900.

New Data Files. NamedSequences.txt was added. This data file defines specific names for some significant Unicode character sequences, giving their Unicode Sequence Identifier (USI) values.

Line Break. The Line_Break properties of Runic, certain Indic characters, Mongolian, Tibetan punctuation, Hangul, and spacing clones of European diacritical marks were revised to better match their expected behavior.

Unihan. Five provisional properties were added: kFennIndex, kGSR, kHDZRadBreak, kHanyuPinlu, and kRSAdobe_Japan1_6. kIICore was added as an informative property. kAlternateKangXi and kAlternateMorohashi were dropped.

Block Ranges. The end of the CJK Unified Ideographs range was changed from U+9FA5 to U+9FBB.

For more information, see the file UCD.html in the Unicode Character Database.

Changes Affecting Conformance and Stability

Several updates were made to *Chapter 3, Conformance. Section 3.13, Default Case Operations*, was updated to define case-ignorable characters and case-ignorable sequences. *Table 3-13*, "Context Specification for Casing," was replaced by a description of each context followed by the equivalent regular expression(s) describing the context before a character and the context after a character, or both. In *Section 3.7, Decomposition*, the phrase "according to the decomposition mappings found in the names list of *Section 16.1, Character Names List*," was changed to "according to the decomposition mappings found in the Unicode Character Database" in the relevant definitions.

Significant clarifications or modifications to character behavior include those listed below.

Space and No-Break Space. U+0020 SPACE is no longer recommended as a suitable base character for display of isolated nonspacing marks. Instead, U+00A0 NO-BREAK SPACE is the preferred base character for this function. Additionally, NO-BREAK SPACE is no longer considered equivalent to <U+FEFF ZERO WIDTH NO-BREAK SPACE, U+0020 SPACE, U+FEFF ZERO WIDTH NO-BREAK SPACE>.

Combining Grapheme Joiner. The function of U+034F COMBINING GRAPHEME JOINER was clarified.

Other Combining Characters. The control of the positioning of U+05BD HEBREW POINT METEG and the rendering of Thai combining marks were clarified.

Indic. U+09CE BENGALI LETTER KHANDA TA was added. This necessitates adjustment of Bengali script implementations.

Arabic. The joining type of U+06C2 ARABIC LETTER HEH GOAL WITH HAMZA ABOVE was changed to dual joining to align with U+06C1 ARABIC LETTER HEH GOAL.

Bidirectional Behavior. The Bidi_Class properties for +, -, and / were changed. This change affected number and date formatting. It was made to better align with industry practice.

Stability of Numeric Assignments. All characters with the property value Numeric_Type= Numeric are guaranteed to have a non-null Numeric_Value.

Unicode Standard Annexes

The following Unicode Standard Annexes were added:

- UAX #31: Identifier and Pattern Syntax
- UAX #34: Unicode Named Character Sequences

Changes to the Unicode Standard Annexes were made, as listed here.

> UAX #9, "Bidirectional Algorithm," added a note after N1 and clarified the example after N2. Overriding expected behavior by a higher-level protocol was constrained.

UAX #14, "Line Breaking Properties," was updated.

UAX #15, "Unicode Normalization Forms," corrected definition D2, which defines *blocked* characters.

In UAX #29, "Text Boundaries," the definition of numeric for both word and sentence breaks was changed to include all characters of the General Category Nd plus U+066B ARABIC DECIMAL SEPARATOR and U+066C ARABIC THOUSANDS SEPARATOR.

UAX #31, "Identifier and Pattern Syntax," was updated to contain information on identifiers formerly published in *Section 5.15* of *The Unicode Standard, Version 4.0*, as well as information formerly published in Annex 7 of UAX #15, "Unicode Normalization Forms."

Errata

An itemized list of errata incorporated since the publication of *The Unicode Standard, Version 4.0* can be found online. See "Updates and Errata" in *Section B.6, Other Unicode Online Resources*.

D.6 Changes from Unicode Version 3.2 to Version 4.0

New Characters Added

In total, 1,226 new character assignments were made to the Unicode Standard, Version 4.0. These additions include currency symbols, additional Latin and Cyrillic characters, the Limbu and Tai Le scripts, Yijing Hexagram symbols, Khmer symbols, Linear B syllables and ideograms, Cypriot, Ugaritic, and a new block of variation selectors. Double-diacritic characters were added for dictionary use. In total, 452 characters were added to the BMP; 774 were added to the supplementary planes.

These new characters extend the set of modern currency symbols and represent a greater coverage of minority and historical scripts. For more information on the allocations, see the file DerivedAge.txt in the Unicode Character Database.

In addition, substantial improvements were made to the script descriptions, particularly for Indic scripts.

Unicode Character Database Changes

The Unicode Character Database was extended to cover the character repertoire additions, and new block definitions and script values were added. A number of other updates were made, including those listed below.

Provisional and Fallback Properties. Unicode 4.0 introduced the concept of provisional properties, clarified the relationships between properties, and provided precisely defined fallback properties for characters not explicitly defined in the data files.

New Properties and Values. The Hangul_Syllable_Type and Other_ID_Start properties were added. For Unihan.txt, the Unicode_Radical_Stroke property was added and classified as informative; all other non-normative Unihan properties were classified as provisional. A number of numeric values were added for CJK ideographs.

General Category. U+00AD SOFT HYPHEN was changed to Cf, which also resulted in it gaining the Default_Ignorable_Code_Point property. Modifier letters U+02B9..U+02BA and U+02C6..U+02CF were changed to Lm. U+180E MONGOLIAN VOWEL SEPARATOR was changed to Zs.

Deprecated Characters. Two Khmer characters, U+17A3 KHMER INDEPENDENT VOWEL QAQ and U+17D3 KHMER SIGN BATHAMASAT, were deprecated.

Stabilized Properties. The Hyphen property was stabilized.

For more information, see the file UCD.html in the Unicode Character Database.

Changes Affecting Conformance and Stability

Chapter 3, Conformance, was substantially improved by incorporating the Unicode Character Encoding Model, resulting in fully specified definitions and conformance requirements of UTF-8, UTF-16, and UTF-32. Clearer terminology was introduced for code point assignments. In addition, the conformance section of UAXes, UTSes and UTRs was clarified. A section on default case operations was added, based on material incorporated from UAX #21, "Case Mappings."

Identifiers. A structure for ensuring backward-compatible programming language identifiers was introduced using the new property Other_ID_Start.

Bidirectional Behavior. The Bidirectional Algorithm was made to be invariant under canonical equivalence.

Significant clarifications or modifications to character behavior include those listed below.

Line Breaking and Boundaries. U+00AD SOFT HYPHEN was reclassified. Text boundaries were clarified.

Prefix Format Control. U+06DD ARABIC END OF AYAH and U+070F SYRIAC ABBREVIATION MARK were reclassified and have significantly different behavior as prefix format control characters. The new characters U+0600..U+0603 were given this behavior as well.

Unicode Standard Annexes

The following Unicode Standard Annex was added:

- UAX #29: Text Boundaries

UAX #29, "Text Boundaries," was updated to contain information on text boundary conditions formerly published in Chapter 5 of *The Unicode Standard, Version 3.0.*

The following Unicode Technical Report was upgraded in status to a Unicode Standard Annex:

- UAX #24: Script Names

The following Standard Annexes were superseded as a result of their incorporation into the text of the book:

- UAX #13: Unicode Newline Guidelines
- UAX #19: UTF-32
- UAX #21: Case Mappings
- UAX #27: Unicode 3.1
- UAX #28: Unicode 3.2

UAX #9, "The Bidirectional Algorithm," was updated to contain information on the Bidirectional Algorithm formerly published in Chapter 3 of *The Unicode Standard, Version 3.0.*

Errata

An itemized list of errata incorporated since the publication of the Unicode Standard, Version 3.2 can be found online. See "Updates and Errata" in *Section B.6, Other Unicode Online Resources.*

D.7 Changes from Unicode Version 3.1 to Version 3.2

New Characters Added

In total, 1,016 new character assignments were made to the Unicode Standard, Version 3.2. These additions included a large collection of mathematical symbols in support of MathML, other symbols such as recyling symbols, minority Philippine scripts, and a number of special characters, including U+034F COMBINING GRAPHEME JOINER and U+2060 WORD JOINER. The additional symbol sets benefit technical publishing needs.

All new character additions were to the BMP. For more information on these character allocations, see the file DerivedAge.txt in the Unicode Character Database.

Unicode Character Database Changes

The Unicode Character Database was extended to cover the character repertoire additions, and new block definitions and script values were added. A number of other updates were made, including those listed below.

Property Aliases. The new data files PropertyAliases.txt and PropertyValueAliases.txt were introduced, normatively specifying aliases for character properties and for the values of character properties.

Blocks. Normative blocks defined in Blocks.txt were adjusted slightly.

Variation Selectors. A specification of when variation selectors can be used was added.

New Properties. New properties were added, including properties for ideographic description categories, code points that are ignorable by default, deprecated characters, IDS operators, Han properties, grapheme properties, and the soft dotted property.

For more information, see the file UCD.html in the Unicode Character Database.

Changes Affecting Conformance

There was a significant update to the definition of UTF-8 to eliminate irregular sequences and bring the Unicode specification more in line with other specifications of UTF-8. Corrigendum #3 corrected the canonical decomposition mapping for U+F951 to map to U+964B.

Significant clarifications or modifications to character behavior include those listed below.

Word Joiner. U+2060 WORD JOINER was defined as the preferred character to express the word joining semantics previously implied by U+FEFF ZERO WIDTH NO-BREAK SPACE. This leaves ZERO WIDTH NO-BREAK SPACE to be used solely with the semantic of the byte order mark (BOM).

Special Properties. A number of characters with special properties, including boundary control, joining, and variation selection, were added.

Behavior of Hangul Syllables, Conjoining Jamo, and Combining Marks. Discussions of the application of combining marks to Hangul syllables and the behavior of syllable boundaries in a sequence of conjoining jamo were updated.

Unicode Standard Annexes

The following Technical Report was upgraded in status to a Unicode Standard Annex:

- UAX #21: Case Mappings

Errata

An itemized list of errata incorporated since the publication of the Unicode Standard, Version 3.1 can be found online. See "Updates and Errata" in *Section B.6, Other Unicode Online Resources.*

D.8 Changes from Unicode Version 3.0 to Version 3.1

New Characters Added

In total, 44,946 new character assignments were made to the Unicode Standard, Version 3.1, including a very large collection of additional CJK ideographs, historic scripts, and several sets of symbols. The CJK ideograph additions provide significant coverage for dictionary and historical usage. For the first time, graphic and format characters were added to the supplementary planes:

- Supplementary Multilingual Plane (SMP), U+10000..U+1FFFF
- Supplementary Ideographic Plane (SIP), U+20000..U+2FFFF
- Supplementary Special-purpose Plane (SSP), U+E0000..U+EFFFF

Several historic scripts, including Old Italic, Gothic, and Deseret, and sets of symbols covering mathematical alphanumeric and musical symbols, were added to the Supplementary Multilingual Plane, or Plane 1. The Supplementary Ideographic Plane, or Plane 2, saw the addition of a very large collection of unified Han ideographs as well as additional Han compatibility ideographs. A set of 97 tag characters was added to the Supplementary Special-purpose Plane, or Plane 14.

Additionally, two mathematical symbols were added to the BMP, and 32 more code points were allocated as noncharacters. For more information on these character allocations, see the file DerivedAge.txt in the Unicode Character Database.

Unicode Character Database Changes

The Unicode Character Database was extended to cover the character repertoire addition, and new block definitions and script values were added. A number of other updates were made, including those listed below.

PropList.txt. The supplementary property list file, PropList.txt, was significantly reorganized.

New Properties. A number of derived data files were added, and new properties were added for case folding and scripts.

Hex Notation. The convention of using five-digit hex notation for the representation of supplementary characters was introduced.

For more information, see the file UCD.html in the Unicode Character Database.

Changes Affecting Conformance and Stability

There were four major changes affecting conformance. The first was the addition of new noncharacters and a clarification regarding noncharacter status. The second was Corrigendum #1, which updated the definition of UTF-8 to address security issues, by excluding non-shortest forms. The third was the inclusion of UTF-32 as part of the standard. The fourth was Corrigendum #2, affecting normalization: U+FB1D was added to CompositionExclusions.txt in the Unicode Character Database.

Significant clarifications or modifications to character behavior include those listed below.

Ligature Formation. To allow for finer control over ligature formation, the semantics of U+200D ZERO WIDTH JOINER and U+200C ZERO WIDTH NON-JOINER were broadened to cover ligatures as well as cursive connection.

Stability Policy. The Unicode Character Encoding Stability policy was documented.

New Normative Properties. All of the General Category values and case mappings were made normative.

Unicode Standard Annexes

The following Technical Reports were upgraded in status to Unicode Standard Annexes:

- UAX #9: The Bidirectional Algorithm
- UAX #19: UTF-32

Errata

An itemized list of errata incorporated since the publication of the Unicode Standard, Version 3.0 can be found online. See "Updates and Errata" in *Section B.6, Other Unicode Online Resources.*

Appendix E

Han Unification History

Efforts to create a unified Han character encoding are at least as venerable as the existing national standards. The Chinese Character Code for Information Interchange (CCCII), first developed in Taiwan in 1980, contains characters for use in China, Taiwan, and Japan. In somewhat modified form, it has been adopted for use in the United States as ANSI Z39.64-1989, also known as the East Asian Character Code (EACC) for bibliographic use. In 1981, Takahashi Tokutaro of Japan's National Diet Library proposed standardization of a character set for common use among East Asian countries.

E.1 Development of the URO

The Unicode Han character set began with a project to create a Han character cross-reference database at Xerox in 1986. In 1988, a parallel effort began at Apple based on the RLG's CJK Thesaurus, which is used to maintain EACC. The merger of the Apple and Xerox databases in 1989 led to the first draft of the Unicode Han character set. At the September 1989 meeting of X3L2 (an accredited standards committee for codes and character sets operating under the procedures of the American National Standards Institute), the Unicode Working Group proposed this set for inclusion in ISO 10646.

The primary difference between the Unicode Han character repertoire and earlier efforts was that the Unicode Han character set extended the bibliographic sets to guarantee complete coverage of industry and newer national standards. The unification criteria employed in this original Unicode Han character repertoire were based on rules used by JIS and on a set of Han character identity principles (*rentong yuanze*) being developed in China by experts working with the Association for a Common Chinese Code (ACCC). An important principle was to preserve all character distinctions within existing and proposed national and industry standards.

The Unicode Han proposal stimulated interest in a unified Han set for inclusion in ISO 10646, which led to an ad hoc meeting to discuss the issue of unification. Held in Beijing in October 1989, this meeting was the beginning of informal cooperation between the Unicode Working Group and the ACCC to exchange information on each group's proposals for Han unification.

A second ad hoc meeting on Han unification was held in Seoul in February 1990. At this meeting, the Korean delegation proposed the establishment of a group composed of the East Asian countries and other interested organizations to study a unified Han encoding.

From this informal meeting emerged the Chinese/Japanese/Korean Joint Research Group (hereafter referred to as the CJK-JRG).

A second draft of the Unicode Han character repertoire was sent out for widespread review in December 1990 to coincide with the announcement of the formation of the Unicode Consortium. The December 1990 draft of the Unicode Han character set differed from the first draft in that it used the principle of *KangXi* radical-stroke ordering of the characters. To verify independently the soundness and accuracy of the unification, the Consortium arranged to have this draft reviewed in detail by East Asian scholars at the University of Toronto.

In the meantime, China announced that it was about to complete its own proposal for a Han Character Set, GB 13000. Concluding that the two drafts were similar in content and philosophy, the Unicode Consortium and the Center for Computer and Information Development Research, Ministry of Machinery and Electronic Industry (CCID, China's computer standards body), agreed to merge the two efforts into a single proposal. Each added missing characters from the other set and agreed upon a method for ordering the characters using the four-dictionary ordering scheme described in *Section 12.1, Han*. Both proposals benefited greatly from programmatic comparisons of the two databases.

As a result of the agreement to merge the Unicode Standard and ISO 10646, the Unicode Consortium agreed to adopt the unified Han character repertoire that was to be developed by the CJK-JRG.

The first CJK-JRG meeting was held in Tokyo in July 1991. The group recognized that there was a compelling requirement for unification of the existing CJK ideographic characters into one coherent coding standard. Two basic decisions were made: to use GB 13000 (previously merged with the Unicode Han repertoire) as the basis for what would be termed "The Unified Repertoire and Ordering," and to verify the unification results based on rules that had been developed by Professor Miyazawa Akira and other members of the Japanese delegation.

The formal review of GB 13000 began immediately. Subsequent meetings were held in Beijing and Hong Kong. On March 27, 1992, the CJK-JRG completed the *Unified Repertoire and Ordering* (URO), *Version 2.0*. This repertoire was subsequently published both by the Unicode Consortium in *The Unicode Standard, Version 1.0*, Volume 2, and by ISO in ISO/IEC 10646-1:1993.

E.2 Ideographic Rapporteur Group

In October 1993, the CJK-JRG became a formal subgroup of ISO/IEC JTC1/SC2/WG2 and was renamed the Ideographic Rapporteur Group (IRG). The IRG now has the formal responsibility of developing extensions to the URO 2.0 to expand the encoded repertoire of unified CJK ideographs. The Unicode Consortium participates in this group as a liaison member of ISO.

In its second meeting in Hanoi in February 1994, the IRG agreed to include Vietnamese Chữ Nôm ideographs in a future version of the URO and to add a fifth reference dictionary to the ordering scheme.

In 1998, the IRG completed work on the first ideographic supplement to the URO, CJK Unified Ideographs Extension A. This set of 6,582 characters was culled from national and industrial standards and historical literature and was first encoded in *The Unicode Standard, Version 3.0*. CJK Unified Ideographs Extension A represents the final set of CJK ideographs to be encoded on the BMP.

In 2000, the IRG completed work on the second ideographic supplement to the URO, a very large collection known as CJK Unified Ideographs Extension B. These 42,711 characters were derived from major classical dictionaries and literary sources, and from many additional national standards, as documented in *Table 12-8* in *Section 12.1, Han*. The Extension B collection was first encoded in *The Unicode Standard, Version 3.1*, and is the first collection of unified CJK ideographs to be encoded on Plane 2.

In 2005, the IRG identified a subset of the unified ideographs, called the Ideographic International Core (IICore). This subset is designed to serve as a relatively small collection of around 10,000 ideographs, mainly for use in devices with limited resources, such as mobile phones. The IICore subset is meant to cover the vast majority of modern texts in all locales where ideographs are used. The repertoire of the IICore subset is identified with the kIICore key in the *Unihan Database*.

Also in 2005, a small set of ideographs was encoded to support the complete repertoire of the of the GB 18030:2000 and HKSCS 2004 standards. In addition, an initial set of CJK strokes was encoded.

At the present time (summer 2006), the IRG is continuing work on the unification of additional CJKV ideographs, considering candidate repertoire submissions from China, Hong Kong, Taiwan, Macao, Japan, North Korea, South Korea, Vietnam, Singapore, and the United States.

Appendix F

Unicode Encoding Stability Policies

Unlike many other standards, the Unicode Standard is continually expanding—new characters are added to meet a variety of uses, ranging from technical symbols to letters for archaic languages. Character properties are also expanded or revised to meet implementation requirements.

In each new version of the Unicode Standard, the Unicode Consortium may add characters or make certain changes to characters that were encoded in a previous version of the standard. However, the Consortium imposes limitations on the types of changes that can be made in an effort to minimize the impact on existing implementations.

This appendix reproduces the text of the policies of the Unicode Consortium regarding character encoding stability in force at the time of publication. The most up-to-date version of these polices is found on the Unicode Web site. See the subsection "Policies" in *Section B.6, Other Unicode Online Resources*. For more information, see "Stability" in *Section 3.1, Versions of the Unicode Standard*.

While these policies guide the development of the standard, they are not formally part of the specification. Most fundamentally, these policies are intended to ensure that text encoded in one version of the standard remains valid and unchanged in later versions. In many cases, the constraints imposed by these stability policies allow implementers to simplify support for particular features of the standard, with the assurance that their implementations will not be invalidated by a later update to the standard.

In this appendix, the notation Unicode N.n+ means "The Unicode Standard, Version N.n and all subsequent versions." See also *Section 3.1, Versions of the Unicode Standard*.

F.1 Encoding Stability Policies for the Unicode Standard

Encoding Stability

Applicable Version: Unicode 2.0+

> ***Once a character is encoded, it will not be moved or removed.***

This policy ensures that implementers can always depend on each version of the Unicode Standard being a superset of the previous version. The Unicode Standard may deprecate the character (that is, formally discourage its use), but it will not reallocate, remove, or reassign the character.

- Ordering of characters is handled via collation, not by moving characters to different code points. For more information, see Unicode Technical Standard #10, "Unicode Collation Algorithm," and the Unicode FAQ on the Unicode Web site at http://www.unicode.org/faq/.

Name Stability

Applicable Version: Unicode 2.0+

Once a character is encoded, its character name will not be changed.

Together with the limitations in name syntax, this policy allows implementations to create unique identifiers from character names. The character names are used to distinguish between characters and do not always express the full meaning of each character. They are designed to be used programmatically and, therefore, must be stable.

In some cases the original name chosen to represent the character is inaccurate in one way or another. Any such inaccuracies are dealt with by adding annotations to the character name list (see *Chapter 17, Code Charts*) or by adding descriptive text to the standard.

- It is possible to produce translated names for the characters, to make the information conveyed by the name accessible to non-English speakers.
- In cases of outright errors in character names such as misspellings, a character may be given a formal name alias.

Formal Name Alias Stability

Applicable Version: Unicode 5.0+

Formal aliases, once assigned to a character, will not be changed or removed.

Formal aliases are defined in the file NameAliases.txt in the Unicode Character Database and listed in the character code charts.

Named Character Sequence Stability

Applicable Version: Unicode 5.0+

Named character sequences will not be changed or removed.

This stability guarantee applies both to the name of the named character sequence and to the sequence of characters so named.

Named character sequences are defined in the file NamedSequences.txt in the Unicode Character Database. For more information on named character sequences, see Unicode Standard Annex #34, "Unicode Named Character Sequences."

- There are also provisional named character sequences, which are included in the Unicode Character Database but are not covered by this stability policy.

Name Uniqueness

Applicable Version: Unicode 2.0+

> ***The names of characters, formal aliases, and named character sequences are unique within a shared namespace.***

The names of characters, named character sequences, and formal aliases for characters share a single namespace in which each name uniquely identifies either a single character or a single named character sequence. The definition of uniqueness is not just a simple comparison of the characters—instead, the loose matching rules from UCD.html in the Unicode Character Database are used.

Normalization Stability

Applicable Version: Unicode 3.1+

> ***If a string contains only characters from a given version of the Unicode, and it is put into a normalized form in accordance with that version of Unicode, then the result will also be in that normalized form according to any subsequent version of Unicode.***
>
> ***The result will also be in that normalized form according to any prior version of the standard that contains all of the characters in the string (back to the first applicable version, Unicode 3.1).***

In particular, once a character is encoded, its canonical combining class and decomposition mapping will not be changed in a way that will destabilize normalization. Thus the following constraints will be maintained under all circumstances.

> ***Decomposition Mapping: The decomposition mapping may not be changed except for the correction of exceptional errors which meet all of the following conditions (1–3):***
>
> ***1. There is a clear and evident error identified in the Unicode Character Database (such as a typographic mistake).***
>
> ***2. The error constitutes a clear violation of the identity stability policy.***
>
> ***3. The correction of such an error does not violate the following constraints (a–d):***
>
> ***a. No character will be given a decomposition mapping when it did not previously have one.***
>
> ***b. No decomposition mapping will be removed from a character.***
>
> ***c. No decomposition mapping will change in type (canonical to compatibility, or vice versa).***

d. The number of characters in a decomposition mapping will not change.

Canonical Combining Class: Once a character is assigned, the canonical combining class will not change.

If an implementation normalizes a string that contains characters that are not assigned in the version of Unicode that it supports, that string might not be in normalized form according to a future version of Unicode. For example, suppose that a Unicode 4.0 program normalizes a string that contains new Unicode 4.1 characters. That string might not be normalized according to Unicode 4.1.

In versions prior to Unicode 4.1, there were exceptional cases where the normalization algorithm had to be applied twice to put a string into normalized form. See Unicode Standard Annex #15, "Normalization Forms."

Identity Stability

Applicable Version: Unicode 1.1+

Once a character is encoded, its properties may still be changed, but not in such a way as to change the fundamental identity of the character.

The Consortium will endeavor to keep the values of the other properties as stable as possible, but some circumstances may arise that require changing them. Particularly in the situation where the Unicode Standard first encodes less well-documented characters and scripts, the exact character properties and behavior initially may not be well known.

As more experience is gathered in implementing the characters, adjustments in the properties may become necessary. Examples of such properties include, but are not limited to, the following:

- General_Category
- Case mappings
- Bidirectional properties
- Compatibility decomposition tags (such as <font> or <compat>)
- Representative glyphs

However, character properties will not be changed in a way that would affect character identity. For example, the representative glyph for U+0061 "A" cannot be changed to "B"; the General_Category for U+0061 "A" cannot be changed to Ll (lowercase letter); and the decomposition mapping for U+00C1 (Á) cannot be changed to <U+0042, U+0301> (B, ´).

Property Value Stability

Values of certain properties are limited by the constraints listed in *Table F-1*. The applicable version is given in the first column.

Table F-1. Constraints on Property Values

Applicable Versions	Constraints
Unicode 1.1.5+	Combining classes are limited to the values 0 to 255.
Unicode 1.1.5+	All characters other than those of General Category M* have the combining class 0.
Unicode 2.0+	Canonical and compatibility mappings are always in canonical order, and the resulting recursive decomposition will also be in canonical order.
Unicode 2.0+	Canonical mappings are always limited either to a single value or to a pair. The second character in the pair cannot itself have a canonical mapping.
Unicode 2.0+	Canonical mappings are always limited so that no string when normalized to NFC expands to more than 3× in length (measured in code units).
Unicode 2.1.3+	The General_Category values will not be further subdivided.
Unicode 3.0.0+	The Bidi_Category values will not be further subdivided.
Unicode 3.0.1+	Case folding mappings are limited so that no string when case folded expands to more than 3× in length (measured in code units).
Unicode 3.1+	The Noncharacter_Code_Point property is an immutable code point property, which means that its property values for all Unicode code points will never change.
Unicode 4.0+	The Bidirectional properties will be assigned so as to preserve canonical equivalence.
Unicode 4.1+	All characters with the Lowercase property and all characters with the Uppercase property have the Alphabetic property.
Unicode 4.1+	The Pattern_Syntax and Pattern_Whitespace properties are immutable code point properties, which means that their property values for all Unicode code points will never change.

These constraints ensure that implementers can simplify or optimize certain aspects of their support for character properties. For further description of these invariants, see the file UCD.html in the Unicode Character Database.

Identifier Stability

Applicable Version: Unicode 3.0+

> ***All strings that are valid default Unicode identifiers will continue to be valid default Unicode identifiers in all subsequent versions of Unicode. Furthermore, default identifiers never contain characters with the Pattern_Syntax or Pattern_Whitespace properties.***

If a string qualifies as an identifier under one version of Unicode, it will qualify as an identifier under all future versions. The reverse is not true—an identifier under Version 5.0 may not be an identifier under Version 4.0—it may contain a character that was unassigned under Unicode 4.0, or (very rarely) a Unicode 4.0 character that was not an identifier character in Unicode 4.0, but became one in Unicode 5.0.

For more information, see Unicode Standard Annex #31, "Identifier and Pattern Syntax."

Case Folding Stability

Applicable Version: Unicode 5.0+

> ***Caseless matching of Unicode strings used for identifiers is stable.***

Case folding stability ensures that identifiers created in different versions of Unicode can be reliably matched in a case-insensitive manner. For more information on identifiers, see Unicode Standard Annex #31, "Identifier and Pattern Syntax." Identifiers commonly exclude compatibility decomposable characters; therefore this policy formally applies only to strings normalized with NFKC. The toCaseFold() operation used for caseless matching is defined by rule R4 under "Default Case Conversion" in *Section 3.13, Default Case Algorithms.*

The formal statement of this policy is:

> ***For each string S containing characters only from a given Unicode version, toCasefold(NFKC(S)) under that version is identical to toCasefold(NFKC(S)) under any later version of Unicode.***

Glossary

Abjad. A writing system in which only consonants are indicated. The term "abjad" is derived from the first four letters of the traditional order of the Arabic script: *alef, beh, jeem, dal.* (See *Section 6.1, Writing Systems.*)

Abstract Character. A unit of information used for the organization, control, or representation of textual data. (See definition D7 in *Section 3.4, Characters and Encoding.*)

Abstract Character Sequence. An ordered sequence of one or more abstract characters. (See definition D8 in *Section 3.4, Characters and Encoding.*)

Abugida. A writing system in which consonants are indicated by the base letters that have an inherent vowel, and in which other vowels are indicated by additional distinguishing marks of some kind modifying the base letter. The term "abugida" is derived from the first four letters of the Ethiopic script in the Semitic order: *alf, bet, gaml, dant.* (See *Section 6.1, Writing Systems.*)

Accent Mark. A mark placed above, below, or to the side of a character to alter its phonetic value. (See also *diacritic.*)

Acrophonic. Denoting letters or numbers by the first letter of their name. For example, the Greek acrophonic numerals are variant forms of such initial letters.

Aksara. (1) In Sanskrit grammar, the term for "letter" in general, as opposed to consonant (*vyanjana*) or vowel (*svara*). Derived from the first and last letters of the traditional ordering of Sanskrit letters—"a" and "ksha". (2) More generally, in Indic writing systems, *aksara* refers to a "syllable," consisting of a consonant plus vowel sequence, where the vowel may or may not be the inherent vowel of the consonant letter. When multiple consonants are involved, the *aksara* represents the entire orthographic syllable, which can include two or more leading consonants that may be visually presented in conjunct forms; in such cases, the *aksara* may not be identical to the phonological syllable.

Algorithm. A term used in a broad sense in the Unicode Standard, to mean the logical description of a process used to achieve a specified result. This does not require the actual procedure described in the algorithm to be followed; any implementation is conformant as long as the results are the same.

Alphabet. A writing system in which both consonants and vowels are indicated. The term "alphabet" is derived from the first two letters of the Greek script: *alpha, beta.* (See *Section 6.1, Writing Systems.*)

Alphabetic Property. Informative property of the primary units of alphabets and/or syllabaries. (See *Section 4.10, Letters, Alphabetic, and Ideographic.*)

Alphabetic Sorting. (See *collation.*)

Annotation. The association of secondary textual content with a point or range of the primary text. (The value of a particular annotation *is* considered to be a part of the "content" of the text. Typical examples include glossing, citations, exemplification, Japanese yomi, and so on.)

ANSI. (1) The American National Standards Institute. (2) The Microsoft collective name for all Windows code pages. Sometimes used specifically for code page 1252, which is a superset of ISO/IEC 8859-1.

Apparatus Criticus. Collection of conventions used by editors to annotate and comment on text.

Arabic Digits. Forms of decimal digits used in most parts of the Arabic world (for instance, U+0660 ٠, U+0661 ١, U+0662 ٢, U+0663 ٣). Although *European digits* (1, 2, 3,…) derive historically from these forms, they are visually distinct and are coded separately. (Arabic digits are sometimes called Indic numerals; however, this nomenclature leads to confusion with the digits currently used with the scripts of India.) Arabic digits are referred to as *Arabic-Indic digits* in the Unicode Standard. Variant forms of Arabic digits used chiefly in Iran and Pakistan are referred to as *Eastern Arabic-Indic digits.* (See *Section 8.2, Arabic.*)

ASCII. (1) The American Standard Code for Information Interchange, a 7-bit coded character set for information interchange. It is the U.S. national variant of ISO/IEC 646 and is formally the U.S. standard ANSI X3.4. It was proposed by ANSI in 1963 and finalized in 1968. (2) The set of 128 Unicode characters from U+0000 to U+007F, including control codes as well as graphic characters. (3) ASCII has been incorrectly used to refer to various 8-bit character encodings that include ASCII characters in the first 128 positions.

Assigned Character. Synonym for assigned to an abstract character. This refers to graphic, format, control, and private-use characters that have been encoded in the Unicode Standard. (See *Section 2.4, Code Points and Characters.*)

Assigned Code Point. (See *designated code point.*)

Atomic Character. A character that is not decomposable. (See *decomposable character.*)

Base Character. Any graphic character except for those with the General Category of Combining Mark (M). (See definition D51 in *Section 3.6, Combination.*) In a combining character sequence, the base character is the initial character, which the combining marks are applied to.

Basic Multilingual Plane. Plane 0, abbreviated as BMP.

Bicameral. A script that distinguishes between two cases. (See *case.*) Most often used in the context of European alphabets.

BIDI. Abbreviation of bidirectional, in reference to mixed left-to-right and right-to-left text.

Bidirectional Display. The process or result of mixing left-to-right text and right-to-left text in a single line. (See Unicode Standard Annex #9, "The Bidirectional Algorithm.")

Big-endian. A computer architecture that stores multiple-byte numerical values with the most significant byte (MSB) values first.

Binary Files. Files containing nontextual information.

Block. A grouping of related characters within the Unicode encoding space. A block may contain unassigned positions, which are reserved.

BMP. Acronym for *Basic Multilingual Plane.*

BMP Character. A Unicode encoded character having a BMP code point. (See *supplementary character.*)

BMP Code Point. A Unicode code point between U+0000 and U+FFFF. (See *supplementary code point.*)

BNF. Acronym for *Backus-Naur Form*, a formal meta-syntax for describing context-free syntaxes. (For details, see *Appendix A, Notational Conventions.*)

BOCU-1. Acronym for Binary Ordered Compression for Unicode. A Unicode compression scheme that is MIME-compatible (directly usable for e-mail) and preserves binary order, which is useful for databases and sorted lists.

BOM. Acronym for *byte order mark.*

Bopomofo. An alphabetic script used primarily in the Republic of China (Taiwan) to write the sounds of Mandarin Chinese and some other dialects. Each symbol corresponds to either the syllable-initial or syllable-final sounds; it is therefore a subsyllabic script in its primary usage. The name is derived from the names of its first four elements. More properly known as *zhuyin zimu* or *zhuyin fuhao* in Mandarin Chinese.

Boustrophedon. A pattern of writing seen in some ancient manuscripts and inscriptions, where alternate lines of text are laid out in opposite directions, and where right-to-left lines generally use glyphs mirrored from their left-to-right forms. Literally, "as the ox turns," referring to the plowing of a field.

Braille. A writing system using a series of raised dots to be read with the fingers by people who are blind or whose eyesight is not sufficient for reading printed material. (See *Section 15.10, Braille.*)

Braille Pattern. One of the 64 (for six-dot Braille) or 256 (for eight-dot Braille) possible tangible dot combinations.

Byte. (1) The minimal unit of addressable storage for a particular computer architecture. (2) An octet. Note that many early computer architectures used bytes larger than 8 bits in size, but the industry has now standardized almost uniformly on 8-bit bytes. The Unicode Standard follows the current industry practice in equating the term *byte* with *octet* and using the more familiar term *byte* in all contexts. (See *octet.*)

Byte Order Mark. The Unicode character U+FEFF when used to indicate the byte order of a text. (See *Section 2.13, Special Characters and Noncharacters*, and *Section 16.8, Specials.*)

Byte Serialization. The order of a series of bytes determined by a computer architecture.

Byte-Swapped. Reversal of the order of a sequence of bytes.

Canonical. (1) Conforming to the general rules for encoding—that is, not compressed, compacted, or in any other form specified by a higher protocol. (2) Characteristic of a normative mapping and form of equivalence specified in *Chapter 3, Conformance.*

Canonical Decomposable Character. A character that is not identical to its canonical decomposition. (See definition D69 in *Section 3.7, Decomposition.*)

Canonical Decomposition. Mapping to an inherently equivalent sequence—for example, mapping ä to a + ◌̈. (For a full, formal definition, see definition D68 in *Section 3.7, Decomposition.*)

Canonical Equivalent. Two character sequences are said to be canonical equivalents if their full canonical decompositions are identical. (See definition D70 in *Section 3.7, Decomposition.*)

Cantillation Mark. A mark that is used to indicate how a text is to be chanted or sung.

Capital Letter. Synonym for *uppercase letter.* (See *case.*)

Case. (1) Feature of certain alphabets where the letters have two distinct forms. These variants, which may differ markedly in shape and size, are called the *uppercase* letter (also known as *capital* or *majuscule*) and the *lowercase* letter (also known as *small* or *minuscule*). (2) Normative property of characters, consisting of uppercase, lowercase, and titlecase (Lu, Ll, and Lt). (See *Section 4.2, Case—Normative.*)

Case Mapping. The association of the uppercase, lowercase, and titlecase forms of a letter. (See *Section 5.18, Case Mappings.*)

Case-Ignorable. A character C is defined to be *case-ignorable* if C has the value MidLetter for the Word_Break property or its General_Category is one of Nonspacing_Mark (Mn), Enclosing_Mark (Me), Format (Cf), Modifier_Letter (Lm), or Modifier_Symbol (Sk). (See definition D121 in *Section 3.13, Default Case Algorithms.*)

Case-Ignorable Sequence. A sequence of zero or more case-ignorable characters. (See definition D122 in *Section 3.13, Default Case Algorithms.*)

CCS. Acronym for *coded character set.*

Cedilla. A mark originally placed beneath the letter *c* in French, Portuguese, and Spanish to indicate that the letter is to be pronounced as an *s*, as in *façade*. Obsolete Spanish diminutive of *ceda*, the letter *z*.

CEF. Acronym for *character encoding form.*

CES. Acronym for *character encoding scheme.*

Character. (1) The smallest component of written language that has semantic value; refers to the abstract meaning and/or shape, rather than a specific shape (see also *glyph*), though in code tables some form of visual representation is essential for the reader's understanding. (2) Synonym for *abstract character.* (3) The basic unit of encoding for the Unicode character encoding. (4) The English name for the ideographic written elements of Chinese origin. [See *ideograph* (2).]

Character Block. (See *block.*)

Character Class. A set of characters sharing a particular set of properties.

Character Encoding Form. Mapping from a character set definition to the actual code units used to represent the data.

Character Encoding Scheme. A *character encoding form* plus byte serialization. There are seven character encoding schemes in Unicode: UTF-8, UTF-16, UTF-16BE, UTF-16LE, UTF-32, UTF-32BE, and UTF-32LE.

Character Name. A unique string used to identify each abstract character encoded in the standard. (See definition D4 in *Section 3.3, Semantics.*)

Character Name Alias. An additional unique string identifier, other than the character name, associated with an encoded character in the standard. (See definition D5 in *Section 3.3, Semantics.*)

Character Properties. A set of property names and property values associated with individual characters. (See *Chapter 4, Character Properties.*)

Character Repertoire. The collection of characters included in a character set.

Character Sequence. Synonym for *abstract character sequence.*

Character Set. A collection of elements used to represent textual information.

Charset. (See *coded character set.*)

Chillu. Abbreviation for *chilaaksharam* (singular) (*cillakṣaram*). Refers to any of a set of sonorant consonants in Malayalam, when appearing in syllable-final position with no inherent vowel.

Choseong. A sequence of one or more leading consonants in Korean.

Chữ Hán. The name for Han characters used in Vietnam; derived from *hànzì.*

Chữ Nôm. A demotic script of Vietnam developed from components of Han characters. Its creators used methods similar to those used by the Chinese in creating Han characters.

CJK. Acronym for Chinese, Japanese, and Korean. A variant, *CJKV,* means Chinese, Japanese, Korean, and Vietnamese.

CLDR. (See *Common Locale Data Repository.*)

Coded Character. (See *encoded character.*)

Coded Character Sequence. An ordered sequence of one or more code points. Normally, this consists of a sequence of encoded characters, but it may also include noncharacters or reserved code points. (See definition D12 in *Section 3.4, Characters and Encoding.*)

Coded Character Representation. Synonym for *coded character sequence.*

Coded Character Set. A character set in which each character is assigned a numeric code point. Frequently abbreviated as *character set, charset,* or *code set.*

Code Page. A coded character set, often referring to a coded character set used by a personal computer—for example, PC code page 437, the default coded character set used by the U.S. English version of the DOS operating system.

Code Point. Any value in the Unicode codespace; that is, the range of integers from 0 to $10FFFF_{16}$. (See definition D10 in *Section 3.4, Characters and Encoding.*)

Code Position. Synonym for *code point.* Used in ISO character encoding standards.

Code Set. (See *coded character set.*)

Codespace. (1) A range of numerical values available for encoding characters. (2) For the Unicode Standard, a range of integers from 0 to $10FFFF_{16}$. (See definition D9 in *Section 3.4, Characters and Encoding.*)

Code Unit. The minimal bit combination that can represent a unit of encoded text for processing or interchange. The Unicode Standard uses 8-bit code units in the UTF-8 encoding form, 16-bit code units in the UTF-16 encoding form, and 32-bit code units in the UTF-32 encoding form. (See definition D77 in *Section 3.9, Unicode Encoding Forms.*)

Code Value. Obsolete synonym for *code unit.*

Collation. The process of ordering units of textual information. Collation is usually specific to a particular language. Also known as *alphabetizing* or *alphabetic sorting.* Unicode Technical Report #10, "Unicode Collation Algorithm," defines a complete, unambiguous, specified ordering for all characters in the Unicode Standard.

Combining Character. A character with the General Category of Combining Mark (M). (See definition D52 in *Section 3.6, Combination.*) (See also *nonspacing mark.*)

Combining Character Sequence. A maximal character sequence consisting of either a base character followed by a sequence of one or more characters where each is a combining character, ZERO WIDTH JOINER, or ZERO WIDTH NON-JOINER; or a sequence of one or more characters where each is a combining character, ZERO WIDTH JOINER, or ZERO WIDTH NON-JOINER. (See definition D56 in *Section 3.6, Combination.*)

Combining Class. A numeric value in the range 0..255 given to each Unicode code point, formally defined as the property Canonical_Combining_Class. (See definition D104 in *Section 3.11, Canonical Ordering Behavior.*)

Common Locale Data Repository. The repository of locale data in XML format maintained by the Unicode Consortium (http://www.unicode.org/cldr/). This repository provides information needed in the localization of software products into a wide variety of languages, supplying (among other things): date, time, number, and currency formats; sorting, searching, and matching information; and translated names for languages, territories, scripts, currencies, and time zones. (See also *Locale Data Markup Language.*)

Compatibility. (1) Consistency with existing practice or preexisting character encoding standards. (2) Characteristic of a normative mapping and form of equivalence specified in *Section 3.7, Decomposition.*

Compatibility Character. A character that would not have been encoded except for compatibility and round-trip convertibility with other standards. (See *Section 2.3, Compatibility Characters.*)

Compatibility Composite Character. Synonym for *compatibility decomposable character.*

Compatibility Decomposable Character. A character whose compatibility decomposition is not identical to its canonical decomposition. (See definition D66 in *Section 3.7, Decomposition.*)

Compatibility Decomposition. Mapping to a roughly equivalent sequence that may differ in style. (For a full, formal definition, see definition D65 in *Section 3.7, Decomposition.*)

Compatibility Equivalent. Two character sequences are said to be compatibility equivalents if their full compatibility decompositions are identical. (See definition D67 in *Section 3.7, Decomposition.*)

Compatibility Precomposed Character. Synonym for *compatibility decomposable character.*

Compatibility Variant. A character that generally can be remapped to another character without loss of information other than formatting.

Composite Character. (See *decomposable character.*)

Composite Character Sequence. (See *combining character sequence.*)

Conformance. Adherence to a specified set of criteria for use of a standard. (See *Chapter 3, Conformance.*)

Conjunct Form. A ligated form representing a *consonant conjunct.*

Consonant Cluster. A sequence of two or more consonantal sounds. Depending on the writing system, a consonant cluster may be represented by a single character or by a sequence of characters. (Contrast *digraph.*)

Consonant Conjunct. A sequence of two or more adjacent consonantal letterforms, consisting of a sequence of one or more dead consonants followed by a normal, live consonant letter. A consonant conjunct may be ligated into a single conjunct form, or it may be represented by graphically separable parts, such as subscripted forms of the consonant letters. Consonant conjuncts are associated with the Brahmi family of Indic scripts. (See *Section 9.1, Devanagari.*)

Contextual Variant. A text element can have a presentation form that depends on the textual context in which it is rendered. This presentation form is known as a *contextual variant.*

Control Codes. The 65 characters in the ranges U+0000..U+001F and U+007F..U+009F. Also known as *control characters.*

Cursive. Writing where the letters of a word are connected.

DBCS. Acronym for *double-byte character set.*

Dead Consonant. An Indic consonant character followed by a *virama* character. This sequence indicates that the consonant has lost its inherent vowel. (See *Section 9.1, Devanagari.*)

Decimal Digits. Digits that can be used to form decimal-radix numbers.

Decomposable Character. A character that is equivalent to a sequence of one or more other characters, according to the decomposition mappings found in the Unicode Character Database, and those described in *Section 3.12, Conjoining Jamo Behavior.* It may also be known as a *precomposed* character or a *composite* character. (See definition D63 in *Section 3.7, Decomposition.*)

Decomposition. (1) The process of separating or analyzing a text element into component units. These component units may not have any functional status, but may be simply formal units—that is, abstract shapes. (2) A sequence of one or more characters that is equivalent to a decomposable character. (See definition D64 in *Section 3.7, Decomposition.*)

Decomposition Mapping. A mapping from a character to a sequence of one or more characters that is a canonical or compatibility equivalent and that is listed in the character names list or described in *Section 3.12, Conjoining Jamo Behavior.* (See definition D62 in *Section 3.7, Decomposition.*)

Defective Combining Character Sequence. A combining character sequence that does not start with a base character. (See definition D57 in *Section 3.6, Combination.*)

Demotic Script. (1) A script or a form of a script used to write the vernacular or common speech of some language community. (2) A simplified form of the ancient Egyptian hieratic writing.

Dependent Vowel. A symbol or sign that represents a vowel and that is attached or combined with another symbol, usually one that represents a consonant. For example, in writing systems based on Arabic, Hebrew, and Indic scripts, vowels are normally represented as dependent vowel signs.

Deprecated. Of a coded character or a character property, strongly discouraged from use. (Not the same as *obsolete.*)

Deprecated Character. A coded character whose use is strongly discouraged. Such characters are retained in the standard, but should not be used. (See definition D13 in *Section 3.4, Characters and Encoding.*)

Designated Code Point. Any code point that has either been assigned to an abstract character (*assigned characters*) or that has otherwise been given a normative function by the standard (surrogate code points and noncharacters). This definition excludes reserved code points. Also known as *assigned code point.* (See *Section 2.4, Code Points and Characters.*)

Diacritic. (1) A mark applied or attached to a symbol to create a new symbol that represents a modified or new value. (2) A mark applied to a symbol irrespective of whether it changes the value of that symbol. In the latter case, the diacritic usually represents an independent value (for example, an accent, tone, or some other linguistic information). Also called *diacritical mark* or *diacritical.* (See also *combining character* and *nonspacing mark.*)

Diaeresis. Two horizontal dots over a letter, as in *naïve.* The diaeresis is not distinguished from the *umlaut* in the Unicode character encoding. (See *umlaut.*)

Digits. (See *Arabic digits*, *European digits*, and *Indic digits.*)

Digraph. A pair of signs or symbols (two graphs), which together represent a single sound or a single linguistic unit. The English writing system employs many digraphs (for example, *th*, *ch*, *sh*, *qu*, and so on). The same two symbols may not always be interpreted as a digraph (for example, *ca<u>th</u>ode* versus *ca<u>th</u>ouse*). When three signs are so combined, they are called a *trigraph.* More than three are usually called an *n-graph.*

Dingbats. Typographical symbols and ornaments.

Diphthong. A pair of vowels that are considered a single vowel for the purpose of phonemic distinction. One of the two vowels is more prominent than the other. In writing systems, diphthongs are sometimes written with one symbol and sometimes with more than one symbol (for example, with a *digraph*).

Direction. (See *paragraph direction.*)

Directionality Property. A property of every graphic character that determines its horizontal ordering as specified in Unicode Standard Annex #9, "The Bidirectional Algorithm." (See *Section 4.4, Directionality—Normative.*)

Display Cell. A rectangular region on a display device within which one or more glyphs are imaged.

Display Order. The order of glyphs presented in text rendering.

Double-Byte Character Set. One of a number of character sets defined for representing Chinese, Japanese, or Korean text (for example, JIS X 0208-1990). These character sets are often encoded in such a way as to allow double-byte character encodings to be mixed with single-byte character encodings. Abbreviated DBCS. (See also *multibyte character set.*)

Ductility. The ability of a cursive font to stretch or compress the connective baseline to effect text justification.

Dynamic Composition. Creation of composite forms such as accented letters or Hangul syllables from a sequence of characters.

EBCDIC. Acronym for Extended Binary-Coded Decimal Interchange Code. A group of coded character sets used on mainframes that consist of 8-bit coded characters. EBCDIC coded character sets reserve the first 64 code positions (x00 to x3F) for control codes, and reserve the range x41 to xFE for graphic characters. The English alphabetic characters are in discontinuous segments with uppercase at xC1 to xC9, xD1 to xD9, xE2 to xE9, and lowercase at x81 to x89, x91 to x99, xA2 to xA9.

Embedding. A concept relevant to bidirectional behavior. (See Unicode Standard Annex #9, "The Bidirectional Algorithm," for detailed terminology and definitions.)

Encapsulated Text. (1) Plain text surrounded by formatting information. (2) Text recoded to pass through narrow transmission channels or to match communication protocols.

Enclosing Mark. A nonspacing mark with the General Category of Enclosing Mark (Me). (See definition D54 in *Section 3.6, Combination.*) Enclosing marks are a subclass of nonspacing marks that surround a base character, rather than merely being placed over, under, or through it.

Encoded Character. An association (or mapping) between an *abstract character* and a *code point.* (See definition D11 in *Section 3.4, Characters and Encoding.*) By itself, an abstract character has no numerical value, but the process of "encoding a character" associates a particular code point with a particular abstract character, thereby resulting in an "encoded character."

Encoding Form. (See *character encoding form.*)

Encoding Scheme. (See *character encoding scheme.*)

Equivalence. In the context of text processing, the process or result of establishing whether two text elements are identical in some respect.

Equivalent Sequence. (See *canonical equivalent.*)

Escape Sequence. A sequence of bytes that is used for code extension. The first byte in the sequence is *escape* (hex 1B).

EUDC. Acronym for end-user defined character. A character defined by an end user, using a private-use code point, to represent a character missing in a particular character encoding. These are common in East Asian implementations.

European Digits. Forms of decimal digits first used in Europe and now used worldwide. Historically, these digits were derived from the Arabic digits; they are sometimes called "Arabic numerals," but this nomenclature leads to confusion with the real *Arabic digits.*

Fancy Text. (See *rich text.*)

Fixed Position Class. A subset of the range of numeric values for combining classes—specifically, any value in the range 10..199. (See definition D105 in *Section 3.11, Canonical Ordering Behavior.*)

Floating (*diacritic, accent, mark*). (See *nonspacing mark.*)

Folding. An operation that maps similar characters to a common target, such as uppercasing or lowercasing a string. Folding operations are most often used to temporarily ignore certain distinctions between characters.

Font. A collection of glyphs used for the visual depiction of character data. A font is often associated with a set of parameters (for example, size, posture, weight, and serifness), which, when set to particular values, generate a collection of imagable glyphs.

Format Character. A character that is inherently invisible but that has an effect on the surrounding characters.

Format Code. Synonym for *format character.*

Formatted Text. (See *rich text.*)

FSS-UTF. Acronym for *File System Safe UCS Transformation Format*, published by the X/Open Company Ltd., and intended for the UNIX environment. Now known as *UTF-8.*

Fullwidth. Characters of East Asian character sets whose glyph image extends across the entire character display cell. In legacy character sets, fullwidth characters are normally encoded in two or three bytes. The Japanese term for fullwidth characters is *zenkaku.*

GCGID. Acronym for Graphic Character Global Identifier. These are listed in the IBM document *Character Data Representation Architecture, Level 1, Registry SC09-1391.*

General Category (GC). Partition of the characters into major classes such as letters, punctuation, and symbols, and further subclasses for each of the major classes. (See *Section 4.5, General Category—Normative.*)

Generative. Synonym for *productive.*

Glyph. (1) An abstract form that represents one or more glyph images. (2) A synonym for *glyph image.* In displaying Unicode character data, one or more glyphs may be selected to depict a particular character. These glyphs are selected by a rendering engine during composition and layout processing. (See also *character.*)

Glyph Code. A numeric code that refers to a glyph. Usually, the glyphs contained in a font are referenced by their glyph code. Glyph codes may be local to a particular font; that is, a different font containing the same glyphs may use different codes.

Glyph Identifier. Similar to a glyph code, a glyph identifier is a label used to refer to a glyph within a font. A font may employ both local and global glyph identifiers.

Glyph Image. The actual, concrete image of a glyph representation having been rasterized or otherwise imaged onto some display surface.

Glyph Metrics. A collection of properties that specify the relative size and positioning along with other features of a glyph.

Grapheme. (1) A minimally distinctive unit of writing in the context of a particular writing system. For example, ‹b› and ‹d› are distinct graphemes in English writing systems because there exist distinct words like big and dig. Conversely, ‹*a*› and ‹a› are not distinct graphemes because no word is distinguished on the basis of these two different forms. (2) What a user thinks of as a character.

Grapheme Base. A character with the property Grapheme_Base, or any standard Korean syllable block. (See definition D58 in *Section 3.6, Combination.*)

Grapheme Cluster. A maximal character sequence consisting of a grapheme base followed by zero or more grapheme extenders or, alternatively, by the sequence <CR, LF>. (See definition D60 in *Section 3.6, Combination.*) A grapheme cluster represents a horizontally segmentable unit of text, consisting of some grapheme base (which may consist of a Korean syllable) together with any number of nonspacing marks applied to it.

Grapheme Extender. A character with the property Grapheme_Extend. (See definition D59 in *Section 3.6, Combination.*) Grapheme extender characters consist of all nonspacing marks, ZERO WIDTH JOINER, ZERO WIDTH NON-JOINER, and a small number of spacing marks.

Graphic Character. A character with the General Category of Letter (L), Combining Mark (M), Number (N), Punctuation (P), Symbol (S), or Space Separator (Zs). (See definition D50 in *Section 3.6, Combination.*)

Guillemet. Punctuation marks resembling small less-than and greater-than signs, used as quotation marks in French and other languages. (See "Language-Based Usage of Quotation Marks" in *Section 6.2, General Punctuation.*)

Halant. A preferred Hindi synonym for a *virama.* It literally means *killer,* referring to its function of *killing* the inherent vowel of a consonant letter. (See *virama.*)

Half-Consonant Form. In the Devanagari script and certain other scripts of the Brahmi family of Indic scripts, a dead consonant may be depicted in the so-called half-form. This form is composed of the distinctive part of a consonant letter symbol without its vertical stem. It may be used to create conjunct forms that follow a horizontal layout pattern. Also known as *half-form.*

Halfwidth. Characters of East Asian character sets whose glyph image occupies half of the character display cell. In legacy character sets, halfwidth characters are normally encoded in a single byte. The Japanese term for halfwidth characters is *hankaku.*

Han Characters. Ideographic characters of Chinese origin. (See *Section 12.1, Han.*)

Hangul. The name of the script used to write the Korean language.

Hangul Syllable. (1) Any of the 11,172 encoded characters of the Hangul Syllables character block, U+AC00..U+D7A3. Also called a *precomposed Hangul syllable* to clearly distinguish it from a Korean syllable block. (2) Loosely speaking, a *Korean syllable block.*

Hanja. The Korean name for Han characters; derived from the Chinese word *hànzì.*

Hankaku. (See *halfwidth.*)

Han Unification. The process of identifying Han characters that are in common among the writing systems of Chinese, Japanese, Korean, and Vietnamese.

Hànzì. The Mandarin Chinese name for Han characters.

Harakat. Marks that indicate vowels or other modifications of consonant letters in Arabic script.

Hasant. The Bangla name for *halant.* (See *virama.*)

Higher-Level Protocol. Any agreement on the interpretation of Unicode characters that extends beyond the scope of this standard. Note that such an agreement need not be formally announced in data; it may be implicit in the context. (See definition D16 in *Section 3.4, Characters and Encoding.*)

High-Surrogate Code Point. A Unicode code point in the range U+D800 to U+DBFF. (See definition D71 in *Section 3.8, Surrogates.*)

High-Surrogate Code Unit. A 16-bit code unit in the range $D800_{16}$ to $DBFF_{16}$, used in UTF-16 as the leading code unit of a surrogate pair. Also known as a *leading surrogate.* (See definition D72 in *Section 3.8, Surrogates.*)

Hiragana. One of two standard syllabaries associated with the Japanese writing system. Hiragana syllables are typically used in the representation of native Japanese words and grammatical particles.

HTML. HyperText Markup Language. A text description language related to SGML; it mixes text format markup with plain text content to describe formatted text. HTML is ubiquitous as the source language for Web pages on the Internet. Starting with HTML 4.0, the Unicode Standard functions as the reference character set for HTML content. (See also *SGML.*)

IANA. Acronym for Internet Assigned Numbers Authority.

ICU. Acronym for International Components for Unicode, an Open Source set of C/C++ and Java libraries for Unicode and software internationalization support. For information, see http://icu.sourceforge.net/

Ideograph. (1) Any symbol that primarily denotes an idea (or meaning) in contrast to a sound (or pronunciation)—for example, ☎ and 💣. (2) An English term commonly used to refer to Han characters, equivalent to the borrowings *hànzì*, *kanji*, and *hanja.*

Ideographic Property. Informative property of characters that are ideographs. (See *Section 4.10, Letters, Alphabetic, and Ideographic.*)

IICore. A subset of common-use CJK unified ideographs, defined as the fixed collection 370 IICore in ISO/IEC 10646. This subset contains 9,810 ideographs and is intended for common use in East Asian contexts, particularly for small devices that cannot support the full range of CJK unified ideographs encoded in the Unicode Standard.

Ill-Formed Code Unit Sequence. A code unit sequence that does not follow the specification of a Unicode encoding form. (See definition D84 in *Section 3.9, Unicode Encoding Forms.*)

In-Band. An in-band channel conveys information about text by embedding that information within the text itself, with special syntax to distinguish it. In-band information is encoded in the same character set as the text, and is interspersed with and carried along with the text data. Examples are XML and HTML markup.

Independent Vowel. In Indic scripts, certain vowels are depicted using independent letter symbols that stand on their own. This is often true when a word starts with a vowel or a word consists of only a vowel.

Indic Digits. Forms of decimal digits used in various Indic scripts (for example, Devanagari: U+0966 ०, U+0967 १, U+0968 २, U+0969 ३). Arabic digits (and, eventually, European digits) derive historically from these forms.

Informative. Information in this standard that is not normative but that contributes to the correct use and implementation of the standard.

Inherent Vowel. In writing systems based on a script in the Brahmi family of Indic scripts, a consonant letter symbol normally has an inherent vowel, unless otherwise indicated. The phonetic value of this vowel differs among the various languages written with these writing systems. An inherent vowel is overridden either by indicating another vowel with an explicit vowel sign or by using *virama* to create a dead consonant.

Inner Caps. Mixed case format where an uppercase letter is in a position other than first in the word—for example, "G" in the Name "McGowan."

IPA. (1) The International Phonetic Alphabet. (2) The International Phonetic Association, which defines and maintains the International Phonetic Alphabet.

IRG. Acronym for Ideographic Rapporteur Group, a subgroup of ISO/IEC JTC1/SC2/WG2. (See *Appendix E, Han Unification History.*)

ISCII. Acronym for Indian Script Code for Information Interchange.

Jamo. The Korean name for a single letter of the Hangul script. Jamos are used to form Hangul syllables.

Joiner. An invisible character that affects the joining behavior of surrounding characters. (See *Section 8.2, Arabic*, and "Cursive Connection" in *Section 16.2, Layout Controls.*)

Jongseong. A sequence of one or more trailing consonants in Korean.

JTC1. The Joint Technical Committee 1 of the International Organization for Standardization and the International Electrotechnical Commission responsible for information technology standardization.

Jungseong. A sequence of one or more vowels in Korean.

Kana. The name of a primarily syllabic script used by the Japanese writing system. It comes in two forms: *hiragana* and *katakana*. The former is used to write particles, grammatical affixes, and words that have no *kanji* form; the latter is used primarily to write foreign words.

Kanji. The Japanese name for Han characters; derived from the Chinese word *hànzì*. Also romanized as *kanzi*.

Katakana. One of two standard syllabaries associated with the Japanese writing system. Katakana syllables are typically used in representation of borrowed vocabulary (other than that of Chinese origin), sound-symbolic interjections, or phonetic representation of "difficult" kanji characters in Japanese.

Kerning. (1) Changing the space between certain pairs of letters to improve the appearance of the text. (2) The process of mapping from pairs of glyphs to a positioning offset used to change the space between letters.

Korean Syllable Block. A sequence of Korean jamos, consisting of one or more leading consonants followed by one or more vowels followed by zero or more trailing consonants, or any canonically equivalent sequence including a precomposed Hangul syllable. In regular expression notation: *L L* V V* T**. Also called a *standard Korean syllable block.* (See *Section 3.12, Conjoining Jamo Behavior.*)

LDML. (See *Locale Data Markup Language.*)

Leading Consonant. (1) In Korean, a jamo character with the Hangul_Syllable_Type property value Leading_Jamo (in the range U+1100..U+1159 or U+115F HANGUL CHOSEONG FILLER). Abbreviated as *L*. (See definition D107 in *Section 3.12, Conjoining Jamo Behavior.*) (2) Any initial consonant in a syllable.

Leading Surrogate. Synonym for *high-surrogate code unit.*

Letter. (1) An element of an alphabet. In a broad sense, it includes elements of syllabaries and ideographs. (2) Informative property of characters that are used to write words.

Ligature. A glyph representing a combination of two or more characters. In the Latin script, there are only a few in modern use, such as the ligatures between "f" and "i" (= ﬁ) or "f" and "l" (= ﬂ). Other scripts make use of many ligatures, depending on the font and style.

Little-endian. A computer architecture that stores multiple-byte numerical values with the least significant byte (LSB) values first.

Locale Data Markup Language. The XML specification for the exchange of locale data, defined by Unicode Technical Standard #35, "Locale Data Markup Language (LDML)." (See also *Common Locale Data Repository.*)

Logical Order. The order in which text is typed on a keyboard. For the most part, logical order corresponds to phonetic order. (See *Section 2.2, Unicode Design Principles.*)

Logical Store. Memory representation.

Logosyllabary. A writing system in which the units are used primarily to write words and/or morphemes of words, with some subsidiary usage to represent just syllabic sounds. The best example is the Han script.

Lowercase. (See *case.*)

Low-Surrogate Code Point. A Unicode code point in the range U+DC00 to U+DFFF. (See definition D73 in *Section 3.8, Surrogates.*)

Low-Surrogate Code Unit. A 16-bit code unit in the range $DC00_{16}$ to $DFFF_{16}$, used in UTF-16 as the trailing code unit of a surrogate pair. Also known as a *trailing surrogate.* (See definition D74 in *Section 3.8, Surrogates.*)

LSB. Acronym for *least significant byte.*

LZW. Acronym for *Lempel-Ziv-Welch,* a standard algorithm widely used for compression of data.

Majuscule. Synonym for *uppercase.* (See *case.*)

Mathematical Property. Informative property of characters that are used as operators in mathematical formulae.

Matra. A dependent vowel in an Indic script. It is the name for vowel letters that follow consonant letters in logical order. A matra often has a completely different letterform from that for the same phonological vowel used as an independent letter.

MBCS. Acronym for *multibyte character set.*

MIME. Multipurpose Internet Mail Extensions. MIME is a standard that allows the embedding of arbitrary documents and other binary data of known types (images, sound, video, and so on) into e-mail handled by ordinary Internet electronic mail interchange protocols.

Minuscule. Synonym for *lowercase.* (See *case.*)

Mirrored Property. The property of characters whose images are mirrored horizontally in text that is laid out from right to left (versus from left to right). (See *Section 4.7, Bidi Mirrored—Normative.*)

Missing Glyph. (See *replacement glyph.*)

Modifier Letter. A character with the Lm General Category in the Unicode Character Database. Modifier letters, which look like letters or punctuation, modify the pronunciation of other letters (similar to diacritics). (See *Section 7.8, Modifier Letters.*)

Monotonic. Modern Greek written with the basic accent, the *tonos.*

MSB. Acronym for *most significant byte.*

Multibyte Character Set. A character set encoded with a variable number of bytes per character, often abbreviated as MBCS. Many large character sets have been defined as MBCS so as to keep strict compatibility with the ASCII subset and/or ISO/IEC 2022.

Named Unicode Algorithm. A Unicode algorithm that is specified in the Unicode Standard or in other standards published by the Unicode Consortium and that is given an explicit name for ease of reference. (See definition D18 in *Section 3.4, Characters and Encoding.* See also *Table 3-1,* "Named Unicode Algorithms," for a list of named Unicode algorithms.)

Namespace. (1) A set of names, no two of which are identical. (2) A set of names together with name matching rules, so that all names are distinct under the matching rules. (See definition D6 in *Section 3.3, Semantics.*) Character names are distinct if they do not match under the name matching rules in effect for the standard.

Nekudot. Marks that indicate vowels or other modifications of consonantal letters in Hebrew.

Neutral Character. A character that can be written either right to left or left to right, depending on context. (See Unicode Standard Annex #9, "The Bidirectional Algorithm.")

NFC. (See *Normalization Form C.*)

NFD. (See *Normalization Form D.*)

NFKC. (See *Normalization Form KC.*)

NFKD. (See *Normalization Form KD.*)

Noncharacter. A code point that is permanently reserved for internal use and that should never be interchanged. Noncharacters consist of the values U+*n*FFFE and U+*n*FFFF (where *n* is from 0 to 10_{16}), and the values U+FDD0..U+FDEF.

Non-joiner. An invisible character that affects the joining behavior of surrounding characters. (See *Section 8.2, Arabic*, and "Cursive Connection" in *Section 16.2, Layout Controls.*)

Non-overridable. A characteristic of a Unicode character property that cannot be changed by a higher-level protocol.

Nonspacing Diacritic. A diacritic that is a nonspacing mark.

Nonspacing Mark. A combining character with the General Category of Nonspacing Mark (Mn) or Enclosing Mark (Me). (See definition D53 in *Section 3.6, Combination.*) The position of a nonspacing mark in presentation depends on its base character. It generally does not consume space along the visual baseline in and of itself. (See also *combining character.*)

Normalization. A process of removing alternate representations of equivalent sequences from textual data, to convert the data into a form that can be binary-compared for equivalence. In the Unicode Standard, normalization refers specifically to processing to ensure that canonical-equivalent (and/or compatibility-equivalent) strings have unique representations. For more information, see "Equivalent Sequences" in *Section 2.2, Unicode Design Principles*, and Unicode Standard Annex #15, "Unicode Normalization Forms."

Normalization Form. One of the four Unicode normalization forms defined in Unicode Standard Annex #15, "Unicode Normalization Forms"—namely, NFC, NFD, NFKC, and NFKD.

Normalization Form C (NFC). The normalization form that results from the canonical decomposition of a Unicode string, followed by the replacement of all decomposed sequences by primary composites where possible.

Normalization Form D (NFD). The normalization form that results from the canonical decomposition of a Unicode string.

Normalization Form KC (NFKC). The normalization form that results from the compatibility decomposition of a Unicode string, followed by the replacement of all decomposed sequences by primary composites where possible.

Normalization Form KD (NFKD). The normalization form that results from the compatibility decomposition of a Unicode string.

Normative. Required for conformance with the Unicode Standard.

NSM. Acronym for *nonspacing mark.*

Numeric Value Property. A property of characters used to represent numbers. (See *Section 4.6, Numeric Value—Normative.*)

Obsolete. Applies to a character that is no longer in current use, but that has been used historically. Whether a character is obsolete depends on context. For example, the Cyrillic letter *big yus* is obsolete for Russian, but is used in modern Bulgarian. (Not the same as *deprecated.*)

Octet. An ordered sequence of eight bits considered as a unit. The Unicode Standard follows current industry practice in referring to an octet as a *byte.* (See *byte.*)

Out-of-Band. An out-of-band channel conveys additional information about text in such a way that the textual content, as encoded, is completely untouched and unmodified. This is typically done by separate data structures that point into the text.

Overridable. A characteristic of a Unicode character property that may be changed by a higher-level protocol to create desired implementation effects.

Paragraph Direction. The default direction (*left* or *right*) of the text of a paragraph. This direction does not change the display order of characters within an Arabic or English word. However, it *does* change the display order of adjacent Arabic and English words and the display order of neutral characters, such as punctuation and spaces. For more details, see Unicode Standard Annex #9, "The Bidirectional Algorithm," especially definitions BD2–BD5.

Paragraph Embedding Level. The embedding level that determines the default bidirectional orientation of the text in that paragraph.

Phoneme. A minimally distinct sound in the context of a particular spoken language. For example, in American English, /p/ and /b/ are distinct phonemes because *pat* and *bat* are distinct; however, the two different sounds of /t/ in *tick* and *stick* are not distinct in English, even though they are distinct in other languages such as Thai.

Pinyin. Standard system for the romanization of Chinese on the basis of Mandarin pronunciation.

Pivot Conversion. The use of a third character encoding to serve as an intermediate step in the conversion between two other character encodings. The Unicode Standard is widely used to support pivot conversion, as its character repertoire is a superset of most other coded character sets.

Plain Text. Computer-encoded text that consists *only* of a sequence of code points from a given standard, with no other formatting or structural information. Plain text interchange is commonly used between computer systems that do not share higher-level protocols. (See also *rich text.*)

Plane. A range of 65,536 (10000_{16}) contiguous Unicode code points, where the first code point is an integer multiple of 65,636 (10000_{16}). Planes are numbered from 0 to 16, with the number being the first code point of the plane divided by 65,536. Thus Plane 0 is U+0000..U+FFFF, Plane 1 is U+10000..U+1FFFF, ..., and Plane 16 (10_{16}) is U+100000..10FFFF. (Note that ISO/IEC 10646 uses hexadecimal notation for the plane numbers—for example, Plane B instead of Plane 11.) (See *Basic Multilingual Plane* and *supplementary planes.*)

Points. (1) The nonspacing vowels and other signs of written Hebrew. (2) A unit of measurement in typography.

Polytonic. Ancient Greek written with several contrastive accents.

Precomposed Character. (See *decomposable character.*)

Presentation Form. A ligature or variant glyph that has been encoded as a character for compatibility. (See also *compatibility character* (1).)

Primary Composite. A character that has a canonical decomposition mapping in the Unicode Character Database (or is a canonical Hangul decomposition) but that is not in the Composition Exclusion Table. (See Unicode Standard Annex #15, "Unicode Normalization Forms.")

Private Use. Refers to designated code points in the Unicode Standard or other character encoding standards whose interpretations are not specified in those standards and whose use may be determined by private agreement among cooperating users.

Private Use Area (PUA). Any one of the three blocks of private-use code points in the Unicode Standard.

Private-Use Code Point. Code points in the ranges U+E000..U+F8FF, U+F0000..U+FFFFD, and U+100000..U+10FFFD. (See definition D49 in *Section 3.5, Properties.*) These code points are designated in the Unicode Standard for private use.

Productive. Said of a feature or rule that can be employed in novel combinations or circumstances, rather than being restricted to a fixed list. In the Unicode Standard, combining marks—particularly the accents—are productive. In contrast, variation selectors are deliberately not productive. Also known as *generative.*

Property. (See *character properties.*)

Property Alias. A unique identifier for a particular Unicode character property. (See definition D47 in *Section 3.5, Properties.*)

Property Value Alias. A unique identifier for a particular enumerated value for a particular Unicode character property. (See definition D48 in *Section 3.5, Properties.*)

Provisional. A property or feature that is unapproved and tentative and that may be incomplete or otherwise not in a usable state.

PUA. Acronym for *Private Use Area.*

Puḷḷi. The Tamil name for *virama.* (See *virama.*)

Radical. A structural component of a Han character conventionally used for indexing. The traditional number of such radicals is 214.

Rendering. (1) The process of selecting and laying out glyphs for the purpose of depicting characters. (2) The process of making glyphs visible on a display device.

Repertoire. (See *character repertoire.*)

Replacement Character. A character used as a substitute for an uninterpretable character from another encoding. The Unicode Standard uses U+FFFD REPLACEMENT CHARACTER for this function.

Replacement Glyph. A glyph used to render a character that cannot be rendered with the correct appearance in a particular font. It often is shown as an open □ or black ■ rectangle. Also known as a *missing glyph.* (See *Section 5.3, Unknown and Missing Characters.*)

Reserved Code Point. Any code point of the Unicode Standard that is reserved for future assignment. Also known as an *unassigned code point.* (See definition D15 in *Section 3.4, Characters and Encoding.*)

Rich Text. Also known as *styled text.* The result of adding information to plain text. Examples of information that can be added include font data, color, formatting information, phonetic annotations, interlinear text, and so on. The Unicode Standard does not address the representation of rich text. It is expected that systems and applications will implement proprietary forms of rich text. Some public forms of rich text are available (for example, ODA, HTML, and SGML). When everything except primary content is removed from rich text, only plain text should remain.

Row. A range of 256 contiguous Unicode code points, where the first code point is an integer multiple of 256. Two code points are in the same row if they share all but the last two hexadecimal digits. (See *plane.*)

SAM. Acronym for Syriac abbreviation mark.

SBCS. Acronym for *single-byte character set.* Any one-byte character encoding. This term is generally used in contrast with DBCS and/or MBCS.

Scalar Value. (See *Unicode scalar value.*)

Script. A collection of letters and other written signs used to represent textual information in one or more writing systems. For example, Russian is written with a subset of the Cyrillic script; Ukranian is written with a different subset. The Japanese writing system uses several scripts.

SCSU. Acronym for Standard Compression Scheme for Unicode. See Unicode Technical Standard #6, "A Standard Compression Scheme for Unicode."

SGML. Standard Generalized Markup Language. A standard framework, defined in ISO 8879, for defining particular text markup languages. The SGML framework allows for mixing structural tags that describe format with the plain text content of documents, so that fancy text can be fully described in a plain text stream of data. (See also *HTML*, *XML*, and *rich text*.)

Shaping Characters. Characters that assume different glyphic forms depending on the context.

Shift-JIS. A shifted encoding of the Japanese character encoding standard, JIS X 0208, that is widely deployed in PCs.

Signature. An optional code sequence at the beginning of a stream of coded characters that identifies the *character encoding scheme* used for the following text. (See *Unicode signature*.)

Sinogram. Chinese character. (See *ideograph*.)

SJIS. Acronym for *Shift-JIS*.

Small Letter. Synonym for *lowercase letter*. (See *case*.)

Sorting. (See *collation*.)

Spacing Mark. A combining character that is not a nonspacing mark. (See definition D55 in *Section 3.6, Combination*.) (See *nonspacing mark*.)

Standard Korean Syllable Block. (See *Korean syllable block*.)

Static Form. (See *decomposable character*.)

Styled Text. (See *rich text*.)

Subtending Mark. A format character whose graphic form extends under a sequence of following characters—for example, U+0600 ARABIC NUMBER SIGN.

Supplementary Character. A Unicode encoded character having a supplementary code point.

Supplementary Code Point. A Unicode code point between U+10000 and U+10FFFF.

Supplementary Planes. Planes 1 through 16, consisting of the supplementary code points.

Surrogate Character. A misnomer. It would be an encoded character having a surrogate code point, which is impossible. Do not use this term.

Surrogate Code Point. A Unicode code point in the range U+D800..U+DFFF. Reserved for use by UTF-16, where a pair of surrogate code units (a high surrogate followed by a low surrogate) "stand in" for a supplementary code point.

Surrogate Pair. A representation for a single abstract character that consists of a sequence of two 16-bit code units, where the first value of the pair is a *high-surrogate code unit* and the second value is a *low-surrogate code unit*. (See definition D75 in *Section 3.8, Surrogates*.)

Syllabary. A type of writing system in which each symbol typically represents both a consonant and a vowel, or in some instances more than one consonant and a vowel.

Syllable. (1) An element of a syllabary. (2) A basic unit of articulation that corresponds to a pulmonary pulse.

Syllable Block. A sequence of Korean characters that should be grouped into a single square cell for display. (See *Section 3.12, Conjoining Jamo Behavior.*)

Symmetric Swapping. The process of rendering a character with a mirrored glyph when its resolved directionality is right-to-left in a bidirectional context. (See *mirrored property* and Unicode Standard Annex #9, "The Bidirectional Algorithm.")

Tagging. The association of attributes of text with a point or range of the primary text. The value of a particular tag is not generally considered to be a part of the "content" of the text. A typical example of tagging is to mark the language or the font for a portion of text.

Tailorable. A characteristic of an algorithm for which a higher-level protocol may specify different results than those specified in the algorithm. A tailorable algorithm without actual tailoring is also known as a default algorithm, and the results of an algorithm without tailoring are known as the default results.

TES. Acronym for *transfer encoding syntax.*

TEX. Computer language designed for use in typesetting—in particular, for typesetting math and other technical material. (According to Knuth, TEX rhymes with the word *blecchhh.*)

Text Element. A minimum unit of text in relation to a particular text process, in the context of a given writing system. In general, the mapping between text elements and code points is many-to-many. (See *Chapter 2, General Structure.*)

Titlecase. Uppercased initial letter followed by lowercase letters in words. A casing convention often used in titles, headers, and entries, as exemplified in this glossary.

Tonal Sandhi. A phonological process whereby the tone associated with one syllable in a tonal language influences the realization of a tone associated with a neighboring syllable.

Tone Mark. A diacritic or nonspacing mark that represents a phonemic tone. Tone languages are common in Southeast Asia and Africa. Because tones always accompany vowels (the syllabic nucleus), they are most frequently written using functionally independent marks attached to a vowel symbol. However, some writing systems such as Thai place tone marks on consonant symbols; Chinese does not use tone marks (except when it is written phonemically).

Tonemic. Refers to the underlying, distinctive units of a tonal system in a language. Tones of a tonal language are often referred to by numbers ("tone 1," "tone 2," and so on), and each tone has an idealized, specific tone level or contour that is considered to be its tonemic value. The term was created by analogy with *phonemic.*

Tonetic. Refers to the surface, actual pitch realization of tones in a tonal system. Tonetic values are what can be directly measured by tracking pitch contours in actual speech recordings. The term was created by analogy with *phonetic.*

Tonos. The basic accent in modern Greek, having the form of an acute accent.

Trailing Consonant. (1) In Korean, a jamo character with the Hangul_Syllable_Type property value Vowel_Jamo (in the range U+11A8..U+11F9). Abbreviated as *T*. (See definition D113 in *Section 3.12, Conjoining Jamo Behavior.*) (2) Any final consonant in a syllable.

Trailing Surrogate. Synonym for *low-surrogate code unit.*

Transcoding. Conversion of character data between different character sets.

Transfer Encoding Syntax. A reversible transformation applied to text and other data to allow it to be transmitted—for example, Base64, uuencode.

Transformation Format. A mapping from a coded character sequence to a unique sequence of code units (typically bytes).

Triangulation. (See *pivot conversion.*)

Typographic Interaction. Graphical application of one nonspacing mark in a position relative to a grapheme base that is already occupied by another nonspacing mark, so that some rendering adjustment must be done (such as default stacking or side-by-side placement) to avoid illegible overprinting or crashing of glyphs. (See definition D106 in *Section 3.11, Canonical Ordering Behavior.*)

UAX. Acronym for *Unicode Standard Annex.*

UCA. Acronym for *Unicode Collation Algorithm.*

UCD. Acronym for *Unicode Character Database.* (See *Section 4.1, Unicode Character Database.*)

UCS. Acronym for Universal Character Set, which is specified by International Standard ISO/IEC 10646, which is equivalent in repertoire to the Unicode Standard.

UCS-2. ISO/IEC 10646 encoding form: Universal Character Set coded in 2 octets. (See *Appendix C, Relationship to ISO/IEC 10646.*)

UCS-4. ISO/IEC 10646 encoding form: Universal Character Set coded in 4 octets. (See *Appendix C, Relationship to ISO/IEC 10646.*)

Umlaut. Two horizontal dots over a letter, as in German *Köpfe*. The umlaut is not distinguished from the *diaeresis* in the Unicode character encoding. (See *diaeresis.*)

Unassigned. Code points that either are reserved for future use or are never to be used.

Unassigned Character. Synonym for *not assigned to an abstract character.* This refers to surrogate code points, noncharacters, and reserved code points. (See *Section 2.4, Code Points and Characters.*)

Unassigned Code Point. (See *undesignated code point.*)

Undesignated Code Point. Synonym for *reserved code point.* These code points are reserved for future assignment and have no other designated normative function in the standard. (See *Section 2.4, Code Points and Characters.*)

Unicameral. A script that has no *case* distinctions. Most often used in the context of European alphabets.

Unicode. The universal character encoding, maintained by the Unicode Consortium. This encoding standard provides the basis for processing, storage, and interchange of text data in any language in all modern software and information technology protocols.

Unicode Algorithm. The logical description of a process used to achieve a specified result involving Unicode characters. (See definition D17 in *Section 3.4, Characters and Encoding.*)

Unicode Collation Algorithm. Tailorable text comparison mechanism used for searching, sorting, and matching Unicode strings. See Unicode Technical Standard #10, "Unicode Collation Algorithm."

Unicode Character Database. A collection of files providing normative and informative Unicode character properties and mappings. (See *Chapter 4, Character Properties*, and the UnicodeCharacterDatabase.html documentation file.)

Unicode Encoding Form. A character encoding form that assigns each Unicode scalar value to a unique code unit sequence. The Unicode Standard defines three Unicode encoding forms: UTF-8, UTF-16, and UTF-32. (See definition D79 in *Section 3.9, Unicode Encoding Forms.*)

Unicode Encoding Scheme. A specified byte serialization for a Unicode encoding form, including the specification of the handling of a *byte order mark* (BOM), if allowed. (See definition D94 in *Section 3.10, Unicode Encoding Schemes.*)

Unicode Scalar Value. Any Unicode code point except high-surrogate and low-surrogate code points. In other words, the ranges of integers 0 to $D7FF_{16}$ and $E000_{16}$ to $10FFFF_{16}$, inclusive. (See definition D76 in *Section 3.9, Unicode Encoding Forms.*)

Unicode Signature. An implicit marker to identify a file as containing Unicode text in a particular encoding form. An initial *byte order mark* (BOM) may be used as a Unicode signature.

Unicode Standard Annex. An integral part of the Unicode Standard published as a separate document.

Unicode String. A code unit sequence containing code units of a particular Unicode encoding form. (See definition D80 in *Section 3.9, Unicode Encoding Forms.*)

Unicode Technical Note. Informative publication containing information of possible interest concerning the Unicode Standard or related topics.

Unicode Technical Report. Formally approved Unicode Consortium publication containing informative technical analysis of a topic related to the Unicode Standard.

Unicode Technical Standard. Formally approved specification published by the Unicode Consortium that is related to, but not part of, the Unicode Standard.

Unicode Transformation Format. An ambiguous synonym for either *Unicode encoding form* or *Unicode encoding scheme.* The latter terms are now preferred.

Unification. The process of identifying characters that are in common among writing systems.

UPA. Acronym for Uralic Phonetic Alphabet.

Uppercase. (See *case.*)

URO. Acronym for Unified Repertoire and Ordering, the original set of CJK unified ideographs used in the Unicode Standard.

User-Defined Character. (See *EUDC.*)

User-Perceived Character. What everyone thinks of as a character in their script.

UTF. Acronym for *Unicode* (or *UCS*) *Transformation Format.*

UTF-2. Obsolete name for *UTF-8.*

UTF-7. Unicode (or UCS) Transformation Format, 7-bit encoding form, specified by *RFC-2152.*

UTF-8. (1) The UTF-8 encoding form. (2) The UTF-8 encoding scheme. (3) "UCS Transformation Format 8," defined in Annex D of ISO/IEC 10646:2003; technically equivalent to the definitions in the Unicode Standard.

UTF-8 Encoding Form. The Unicode encoding form that assigns each Unicode scalar value to an unsigned byte sequence of one to four bytes in length, as specified in *Table 3-6.* (See definition D92 in *Section 3.9, Unicode Encoding Forms.*)

UTF-8 Encoding Scheme. The Unicode encoding scheme that serializes a UTF-8 code unit sequence in exactly the same order as the code unit sequence itself. (See definition D95 in *Section 3.10, Unicode Encoding Schemes.*)

UTF-16. (1) The UTF-16 encoding form. (2) The UTF-16 encoding scheme. (3) "Transformation format for 16 planes of Group 00," defined in Annex C of ISO/IEC 10646:2003; technically equivalent to the definitions in the Unicode Standard.

UTF-16 Encoding Form. The Unicode encoding form that assigns each Unicode scalar value in the ranges U+0000..U+D7FF and U+E000..U+FFFF to a single unsigned 16-bit code unit with the same numeric value as the Unicode scalar value, and that assigns each Unicode scalar value in the range U+10000..U+10FFFF to a surrogate pair, according to *Table 3-5,* "UTF-16 Bit Distribution." (See definition D91 in *Section 3.9, Unicode Encoding Forms.*)

UTF-16 Encoding Scheme. The UTF-16 encoding scheme that serializes a UTF-16 code unit sequence as a byte sequence in either big-endian or little-endian formats. (See definition D98 in *Section 3.10, Unicode Encoding Schemes.*)

UTF-16BE. The Unicode encoding scheme that serializes a UTF-16 code unit sequence as a byte sequence in big-endian format. (See definition D96 in *Section 3.10, Unicode Encoding Schemes.*)

UTF-16LE. The Unicode encoding scheme that serializes a UTF-16 code unit sequence as a byte sequence in little-endian format. (See definition D97 in *Section 3.10, Unicode Encoding Schemes.*)

UTF-32. (1) The UTF-32 encoding form. (2) The UTF-32 encoding scheme.

UTF-32 Encoding Form. The Unicode encoding form that assigns each Unicode scalar value to a single unsigned 32-bit code unit with the same numeric value as the Unicode scalar value. (See definition D90 in *Section 3.9, Unicode Encoding Forms.*)

UTF-32 Encoding Scheme. The Unicode encoding scheme that serializes a UTF-32 code unit sequence as a byte sequence in either big-endian or little-endian formats. (See definition D101 in *Section 3.10, Unicode Encoding Schemes.*)

UTF-32BE. The Unicode encoding scheme that serializes a UTF-32 code unit sequence as a byte sequence in big-endian format. (See definition D99 in *Section 3.10, Unicode Encoding Schemes.*)

UTF-32LE. The Unicode encoding scheme that serializes a UTF-32 code unit sequence as a byte sequence in little-endian format. (See definition D100 in *Section 3.10, Unicode Encoding Schemes.*)

UTN. Acronym for *Unicode Technical Note.*

UTR. Acronym for *Unicode Technical Report.*

UTS. Acronym for *Unicode Technical Standard.*

Virama. From Sanskrit *virāma.* The name of a sign used in many Indic and other Brahmi-derived scripts to suppress the inherent vowel of the consonant to which it is applied, thereby generating a *dead consonant.* (See *Section 9.1, Devanagari.*) The sign varies in shape from script to script and may be known by other names in various languages. For example, in Hindi it is known as *hal* or *halant*, in Bangla it is called *hasant*, and in Tamil it is called *puḷḷi.*

Visual Ambiguity. A situation arising from two characters (or sequences of characters) being rendered indistinguishably.

Visual Order. Characters ordered as they are presented for reading. (Contrast with *logical order.*)

Vocalization. Marks placed above, below, or within consonants to indicate vowels or other aspects of pronunciation. A feature of Middle Eastern scripts.

Vowel. In Korean, a jamo character with the Hangul_Syllable_Type property value Vowel_Jamo (in the range U+1161..U+11A2 or U+1160 HANGUL JUNGSEONG FILLER). Abbreviated as V. (See definition D110 in *Section 3.12, Conjoining Jamo Behavior.*)

Vowel Mark. In many scripts, a mark used to indicate a vowel or vowel quality.

W3C. Acronym for World Wide Web Consortium.

wchar_t. The ANSI C defined *wide character* type, usually implemented as either 16 or 32 bits. ANSI specifies that `wchar_t` be an integral type and that the C-language source character set be mappable by simple extension (zero- or sign-extension).

Writing Direction. The direction or orientation of writing characters within lines of text in a writing system. Three directions are common in modern writing systems: left to right, right to left, and top to bottom.

Writing System. A set of rules for using one or more scripts to write a particular language. Examples include the American English writing system, the British English writing system, the French writing system, and the Japanese writing system.

XML. eXtensible Markup Language. A subset of SGML constituting a particular text markup language for interchange of structured data. The Unicode Standard is the reference character set for XML content. (See also *SGML* and *rich text.*) XML is a trademark of the World Wide Web Consortium.

Y-variant. Two CJK unified ideographs with identical semantics and non-unifiable shapes—for example, U+732B and U+8C93. (See *Z-variant.*)

Z-variant. Two CJK unified ideographs with identical semantics and unifiable shapes—for example, U+8AAA and U+8AAC. (See *Y-variant.*)

Zenkaku. (See *fullwidth.*)

Zero Width. Characteristic of some spaces or format control characters that do not advance text along the horizontal baseline. (See *nonspacing mark.*)

References

Citations are given for the standards and dictionaries that were used as the actual resources for *The Unicode Standard*, primarily for Version 1.0. Where a Draft International Standard (DIS) is known to have progressed to International Standard status, the entry for the DIS has been revised. *A revised or reaffirmed edition, with a different date, may have been published subsequently.* For the current version of a standard, see the catalog issued by the standards organization. The Web site of the International Organization for Standardization (http://www.iso.org) includes the *ISO Catalogue* and links to the sites of member organizations. Many of the ISO character set standards were originally developed by ECMA and are also ECMA standards.

In general, American library practice has been followed for the romanization of titles and names written in non-Roman script. Exceptions are when information supplied by an author had to be used because the name or title in the original script was unavailable.

R.1 Source Standards and Specifications

This section identifies the standards and specifications used as sources for the Unicode Standard. The section also includes selected current standards and specifications relevant to the use of coded character sets.

AAT: "About Apple Advanced Typography Fonts." In *TrueType Reference Manual*, Chapter 6: *Font Files.* Apple Computer, ©1997–2002 (last updated 18 Dec 2002).

http://developer.apple.com/fonts/TTRefMan/RM06/Chap6AATIntro.html

ANSI X3.4: American National Standards Institute. *Coded character set—7-bit American national standard code for information interchange.* New York: 1986. (ANSI X3.4-1986).

ANSI X3.32: American National Standards Institute. *American national standard graphic representation of the control characters of American national standard code for information interchange.* New York: 1973. (ANSI X3.32-1973).

ANSI Y10.20: American National Standards Institute. *Mathematic signs and symbols for use in physical sciences and technology.* New York: 1988. (ANSI Y10.20-1975 (R1988)).

ANSI Z39.47: American National Standards Institute. *Extended Latin alphabet coded character set for bibliographic use.* New York: 1985. (ANSI Z39.47-1985).

ANSI Z39.64: American National Standards Institute. *East Asian character code for bibliographic use.* New Brunswick, NJ: Transaction, 1991. (ANSI Z39.64-1989).

ASMO 449: Arab Organization for Standardization and Metrology. *Data processing 7-bit coded character set for information interchange.* [s.l.]: 1983. (Arab standard specifications, 449-1982). Authorized English translation.

CCCII: *Zhongwen Zixun Jiaohuanma (Chinese Character Code for Information Interchange).* Revised edition. Taipei: Xingzhengyuan Wenhua Jianshe Xiaozu (Executive Yuan Committee for Cultural Construction), 1985.

CNS 11643-1986: *Tongyong hanzi biaozhun jiaohuanma (Han character standard interchange code for general use).* Taipei: Xingzhengyuan (Executive Yuan), 1986.

CNS 11643-1992: *Zhongwen biaozhun jiaohuanma (Chinese standard interchange code).* Taipei: 1992.

Obsoletes 1986 edition.

EACC: (See ANSI Z39.64.)

ECMA Registry: (See ISO Register.)

ELOT 1373: Hellenic Organization for Standardization (ELOT). *The Greek Byzantine musical notation system.* Athens: 1997.

GB 2312: *Xinxi jiaohuanyong hanzi bianmaji, jibenji (Code of Chinese graphic character set for information interchange, primary set).* Beijing: Jishu Biaozhun Chubanshe (Technical Standards Press), 1981. (GB 2312-1980).

GB 12345: *Xinxi jiaohuanyong hanzi bianmaji, fuzhuji (Code of Chinese ideogram set for information interchange, supplementary set).* Beijing: Jishu Biaozhun Chubanshe (Technical Standards Press), 1990. (GB 12345-1990).

GB 13000: *Xinxi jishu—Tongyong duobawei bianma zifuji (UCS)—Diyi bufen: Tixi jiegou yu jiben duowenzhong pingmian (Information technology—Universal multiple-octet coded character set (UCS)—Part 1: Architecture and basic multilingual plane).* Beijing: Jishu Biaozhun Chubanshe (Technical Standards Press), 1993. (GB 13000.1-93) (ISO/IEC 10646.1-1993).

GB 13134: *Xinxi jiaohuanyong yiwen bianma zifuji (Yi coded character set for information interchange)*, [prepared by] Sichuansheng Minzushiwu Weiyuanhui. Beijing: Jishu Biaozhun Chubanshe (Technical Standards Press), 1991. (GB 13134-1991).

GB 18030: *Xinxi jishu—Xinxi jiaohuan yong hanzi bianma zufuji—Jibenji de kuochong. (Information technology—Chinese ideograms coded character set for information interchange—Extension for the basic set).* Beijing: Guojiao zhiliang jishu jianduju, 2000. (GB 18030-2000).

GBK: *Xinxi jiaohuanyong hanzi bianma kuozhan guifan (Extended Code of Chinese graphic character set for information interchange).* Beijing: Zhongguo dianzi gongyebu [and] Guojiao jishu jianduju, 1995.

The Chinese-specific subset of GB 13000.1-93.

HKSCS-2001: *Hong Kong Supplementary Character Set – 2001.* Hong Kong: Information Technology Services Department & Official Languages Agency, Government of the Hong Kong Special Administrative Region, 2001.

English: http://www.info.gov.hk/digital21/eng/hkscs/download/e_hkscs.pdf

Chinese: http://www.info.gov.hk/digital21/chi/hkscs/download/c_hkscs.pdf

Irish Standard 434:1999. *Information technology—8-bit single-byte graphic coded character set for Ogham / Teicneolaíocht eolais—Tacar carachtar grafach Oghaim códaithe go haonbheartach le 8 ngiotán.*

ISCII-88: India. Department of Electronics. *Indian script code for information interchange.* New Delhi: 1988.

ISCII-91: India. Bureau of Indian Standards. *Indian script code for information interchange.* New Delhi: 1991.

ISIRI 3342: Institute of Standards and Industrial Research of Iran. *estaandaard-e tabaadol-e ettelaa'aat-e 8 biti-e faarsi = Farsi 8-bit coded character set for information interchange.* Tehran: 1372 [i.e. 1993]. (ISIRI 3342:1993).

ISO Register: International Organization for Standardization. *ISO international register of coded character sets to be used with escape sequences.*

Current register: http://www.itscj.ipsj.or.jp/ISO-IR/

ISO 639: International Organization for Standardization. *Code for the representation of names of languages.* [Geneva]: 1988. (ISO 639:1988).

ISO/IEC 646: International Organization for Standardization. *Information technology—ISO 7-bit coded character set for information interchange.* [Geneva]: 1991. (ISO/IEC 646:1991).

ISO/IEC 2022: International Organization for Standardization. *Information processing—ISO 7-bit and 8-bit coded character sets—Code extension techniques.* 3rd ed. [Geneva]: 1986. (ISO 2022:1994).

Edition 4 (ISO/IEC 2022:1994) has title: *Information technology—Character code structure and extension techniques.*

ISO 2033: International Organization for Standardization. *Information processing—Coding of machine-readable characters (MICR and OCR).* 2nd ed. [Geneva]: 1983. (ISO 2033:1983).

ISO 2047: International Organization for Standardization. *Information processing—Graphical representations for the control characters of the 7-bit coded character set.* [Geneva]: 1975. (ISO 2047:1975).

ISO/IEC 2375: International Organization for Standardization. *Information technology—Procedure for registration of escape sequences and coded character sets.* [Geneva]: 2003. (ISO/IEC 2375:2003).

ISO 3166: International Organization for Standardization. *Codes for the representation of names of countries and their subdivisions.* [Geneva]. Part 1: *Country Codes* (ISO 3166-1:1997). Part 2: *Country subdivision code* (ISO 3166-2:1998). Part 3: *Code for formerly used names of countries* (ISO 3166-3:1999).

ISO/IEC 4873: International Organization for Standardization. *Information technology—ISO 8-bit code for information interchange—Structure and rules for implementation.* [Geneva]: 1991. (ISO/IEC 4873:1991).

ISO 5426: International Organization for Standardization. *Extension of the Latin alphabet coded character set for bibliographic information interchange.* 2nd ed. [Geneva]: 1983. (ISO 5426:1983).

ISO 5426-2: International Organization for Standardization. Information and documentation—*Extension of the Latin alphabet coded character set for bibliographic information interchange—Part 2: Latin characters used in minor European languages and obsolete typography.* [Geneva]: 1996. (ISO 5426-2:1986).

ISO 5427: International Organization for Standardization. *Extension of the Cyrillic alphabet coded character set for bibliographic information interchange.* [Geneva]: 1984. (ISO 5427:1984).

ISO 5428: International Organization for Standardization. *Greek alphabet coded character set for bibliographic information interchange.* [Geneva]: 1984. (ISO 5428-1984).

ISO/IEC 6429: International Organization for Standardization. *Information technology—Control functions for coded character sets.* 3rd ed. [Geneva]: 1992. (ISO/IEC 6429:1992).

ISO 6438: International Organization for Standardization. *Documentation—African coded character set for bibliographic information interchange.* [Geneva]: 1983. (ISO 6438:1983).

ISO 6861:1996. International Organization for Standardization. Information and documentation—*Glagolitic alphabet coded character set for bibliographic information interchange.* [Geneva]: 1996. (ISO 6861:1996).

ISO 6862: International Organization for Standardization. *Information and documentation—Mathematics character set for bibliographic information interchange.* [Geneva]: 1996. (ISO 6862:1996).

ISO/IEC 6937: International Organization for Standardization. *Information processing—Coded character sets for text communication.* [Geneva]: 1984.

Edition 3 (ISO/IEC 6937:2001) has the following title: *Information technology—Coded graphic character set for text communication—Latin alphabet.*

ISO/IEC 8859: International Organization for Standardization. *Information processing—8-bit single-byte coded graphic character sets.* [Geneva]: 1987–.

These parts of ISO/IEC 8859 predate the Unicode Standard, Version 1.0, and were used as resources: Part 1, *Latin alphabet No. 1;* Part 2, *Latin alphabet No. 2;* Part 3, *Latin alphabet No. 3;* Part 4, *Latin alphabet No. 4;* Part 5, *Latin/Cyrillic alphabet;* Part 6, *Latin/Arabic alphabet;* Part 7, *Latin/Greek alphabet;* Part 8, *Latin/Hebrew alphabet;* and Part 9, *Latin alphabet No. 5.*

The other parts of ISO/IEC 8859 are Part 10, *Latin alphabet No. 6*; Part 11, *Latin/Thai alphabet*; Part 13, *Latin alphabet No. 7*; Part 14, *Latin alphabet No. 8 (Celtic)*; Part 15, *Latin alphabet No. 9*; and Part 16, *Latin alphabet No. 10*. There is no Part 12.

ISO 8879: International Organization for Standardization. *Information processing—Text and office systems—Standard generalized markup language (SGML)*. [Geneva]: 1986. (ISO 8879:1986).

ISO 8957: International Organization for Standardization. *Information and documentation—Hebrew alphabet coded character sets for bibliographic information interchange.* [Geneva]: 1996. (ISO 8957:1996).

ISO 9036: International Organization for Standardization. *Information processing—Arabic 7-bit coded character set for information interchange.* [Geneva]: 1987. (ISO 9036:1987).

ISO/IEC 9573-13: International Organization for Standardization. *Information technology—SGML support facilities—Techniques for using SGML—Part 13: Public entity sets for mathematics and science.* [Geneva]: 1991. (ISO/IEC TR 9573-13:1991).

ISO/IEC 9995-7: International Organization for Standardization. *Information technology—Keyboard layouts for text and office systems—Part 7: Symbols used to represent functions.* [Geneva]: 1994. (ISO/IEC 9995-7:1994).

ISO/IEC 10367: International Organization for Standardization. *Information technology—Standardized coded graphic character sets for use in 8-bit codes.* [Geneva]: 1991. (ISO/IEC 10367:1991).

ISO 10585: International Organization for Standardization. *Information and documentation—Armenian alphabet coded character set for bibliographic information interchange.* [Geneva]: 1996. (ISO 10585:1996).

ISO 10586: International Organization for Standardization. *Information and documentation—Georgian alphabet coded character set for bibliographic information interchange.* [Geneva]: 1996. (ISO 10586:1996).

ISO/IEC 10646: International Organization for Standardization. *Information Technology—Universal Multiple-Octet Coded Character Set (UCS).* [Geneva]: 2003. (ISO/IEC 10646:2003).

ISO/IEC 10646/Amd 1:2005: International Organization for Standardization. *Information Technology—Universal Multiple-Octet Coded Character Set (UCS). Glagolitic, Coptic, Georgian and other characters.* [Geneva]: 2005. (ISO/IEC 10646:2003/Amd 1:2005).

ISO/IEC 10646/Amd 2:2006: International Organization for Standardization. *Information Technology—Universal Multiple-Octet Coded Character Set (UCS). N'Ko, Phags-pa, Phoenician and other characters.* [Geneva]: 2006. (ISO/IEC 10646:2003/Amd 2:2006).

ISO 10754: International Organization for Standardization. *Information and documentation—Extension of the Cyrillic alphabet coded character set for non-Slavic languages for bibliographic information interchange.* [Geneva]: 1996. (ISO 10754:1996).

ISO/TR 11548-1: International Organization for Standardization. *Communication aids for blind persons—Identifiers, names and assignation to coded character sets for 8-dot Braille characters—Part 1: General guidelines for Braille identifiers and shift marks.* [Geneva]: 2001. (ISO/TR 11548-2001).

ISO/TR 11548-2: International Organization for Standardization. *Communication aids for blind persons—Identifiers, names and assignation to coded character sets for 8-dot Braille characters—Part 2: Latin alphabet based character sets.* [Geneva]: 2001. (ISO/TR 11548-2:2001).

ISO 11822: International Organization for Standardization. *Information and documentation—Extension of the Arabic coded character set for bibliographic information interchange.* [Geneva]: 1996. (ISO 11822:1996).

ISO/IEC 14651: International Organization for Standardization. *Information technology—International string ordering and comparison—Method for comparing character strings and description of the common template tailorable ordering.* [Geneva]: 2001. (ISO/IEC 14651:2001).

ISO 15919: International Organization for Standardization. *Information and documentation—Transliteration of Devanagari and related Indic scripts into Latin characters.* [Geneva]: 2001. (ISO 15919:2001).

ISO 15924: International Organization for Standardization. *Information and Documentation—Codes for the representation of names of scripts = Information et documentation—Codes pour la représentation des noms d'écritures.* Bilingual edition = Édition bilingue. [Geneva: in press]. (ISO 15924:2003).

ISO/IEC TR 19769: International Organization for Standardization. *Information technology—Programming languages, their environments and system software interfaces—Extensions for the programming language C to support new character data types.* [Geneva]: 2004. (ISO/IEC TR 19769:2004).

JIS X 0208: Japanese Industrial Standards Committee. *7 bitto oyobi 8 bitto no 2 baito jouhou koukan you fugouka kanji shuugou (7-bit and 8-bit double byte coded kanji sets for information interchange).* Tokyo: Japanese Standards Association, 1997. (JIS X 0208:1997).

Revision of the 1990 edition, which was the original source for the Unicode Standard.

JIS X 0212: Japanese Industrial Standards Committee. *Jouhou koukan you kanji fugou—hojo kanji (Code of the supplementary Japanese graphic character set for information interchange).* Tokyo: Japanese Standards Association, 1990. (JIS X 0212:1990).

JIS X 0213: Japanese Industrial Standards Committee. *7 bitto oyobi 8 bitto no 2 baito jouhou koukan you fugouka kakuchou kanji shuugou (7-bit and 8-bit double byte coded extended kanji sets for information interchange).* Tokyo: Japanese Standards Association, 2000. (JIS X 0213:2000).

JIS X 0221: Japanese Industrial Standards Committee. *Information Technology—Universal Multiple-Octet Coded Character Set (UCS)—Part 1: Architecture and Basic Multilingual Plane.* Tokyo: Japanese Standards Association, 2001. (JIS X 0221-1:2001).

Identical to ISO/IEC 10646-1:2000.

JIS X 4051-1995: *Line Composition Rules for Japanese Documents.* Japanese Standards Association, 1995.

JIS X 4051:2004: Japanese Industrial Standards Committee. *Nihongo Bunsho no Kumihan Houhou.* (*Formatting rules for Japanese documents*). Tokyo: Japanese Standards Association, 2004. (JIS X 4051:2004).

Revision of the 1995 edition, used in Unicode Standard Annex #14, *Line Breaking Properties.*

JIS X 4052:2000: Japanese Industrial Standards Committee. *Nihongo Bunsho no Kumihan Shitei Koukan Keishiki.* (*Exchange format for Japanese documents with composition markup*). Tokyo: Japanese Standards Association, 2000. (JIS X 4052:2000).

KPS 9566-97: Committee for Standardization of the Democratic People's Republic of Korea. (*Code of the Korean graphic character set for information interchange*). Pyongyang: 1997. (KPS 9566-97).

KPS 10721-2000: Committee for Standardization of the Democratic People's Republic of Korea. (*Code of the supplementary Korean hanja set for information interchange*). Pyongyang: 2000. (KPS 10721-2000).

KS C 5601: Korea Industrial Standards Association. *Chongbo kyohwanyong puho (Han'gul mit Hancha).* Seoul: 1989. (KS C 5601-1987).

KS X 1001: Korean Agency for Technology and Standards. *Chongbo kyohwanyong puho (Han'gul mit Hancha). (Code for information interchange (Hanguel and Hanja)).* Seoul: 1992. (KS X 1001-1992).

Last confirmed 1998. Originally designated as KS C 5601-1992.

KS X 1002: Korean Agency for Technology and Standards. *Chongbo kyohwanyong puho hwakchang set'u. (Extension code sets for information interchange.)* Seoul: 1991. (KS X 1002-1991).

Last confirmed 1996. Originally designated as KS C 5657-1991.

MIME: (See RFCs 2045-2049, 4648-4649.)

OpenType: *OpenType™ Specification*, version 1.4.

http://partners.adobe.com/asn/developer/opentype/main.html (Adobe Systems, ©2000–2003)

http://www.microsoft.com/typography/otspec/ (Microsoft, ©2001)

The RFCs listed below are available through the *Request for Comments* page of the IETF Web site (http://www.ietf.org/rfc.html). This page provides for retrieval by RFC number and includes a list of all RFCs in numerical order (*RFC Index*).

RFC 2045: *Multipurpose Internet Mail Extensions (MIME). Part One: Format of Internet message bodies*, by N. Freed and N. Borenstein. November 1996. (Status: DRAFT STANDARD).

Updated by RFC 2184, RFC 2231.

RFC 2046: *Multipurpose Internet Mail Extensions (MIME). Part Two: Media types*, by N. Freed and N. Borenstein. November 1996. (Status: DRAFT STANDARD).

Updated by RFC 2646, RFC 3798.

RFC 2047: *MIME (Multipurpose Internet Mail Extensions). Part Three: Message header extensions for non-ASCII text*, by K. Moore. November 1996. (Status: DRAFT STANDARD).

Updated by RFC 2184, RFC 2231.

RFC 2048: Obsoleted by RFC 4288, RFC 4289.

RFC 2049: *Multipurpose Internet Mail Extensions (MIME). Part Five: Conformance criteria and examples*, by N. Freed and N. Borenstein. November 1996. (Status: DRAFT STANDARD).

RFC 2152: *UTF-7: A mail-safe transformation format of Unicode*, by D. Goldsmith and M. Davis. May 1997. (Status: INFORMATIONAL).

RFC 3066: Obsoleted by RFC 4646, RFC 4647.

RFC 3629: *UTF-8: A transformation format of ISO 10646*, by F. Yergeau. November 2003. (Also STD0063). (Status: STANDARD).

RFC 4288: *Media type specifications and registration procedures*, by N. Freed and J. Klensin. December 2005. (Also BCP0013). (Status: BEST CURRENT PRACTICE).

RFC 4289: *Multipurpose Internet Mail Extensions (MIME). Part Four: Registration procedures*, by N. Freed and J. Klensin. December 2005. (Also BCP0013). (Status: BEST CURRENT PRACTICE).

RFC 4646: *Tags for identifying languages*, edited by A. Phillips and M. Davis. 2006. (Also BCP0047). (Status: BEST CURRENT PRACTICE).

RFC 4647: *Matching of language tags*, edited by A. Phillips and M. Davis. 2006. (Also BCP0047). (Status: BEST CURRENT PRACTICE).

SI 1311.1: Standards Institution of Israel. *Information technology: ISO 8-bit coded character set with Hebrew points.* [Tel Aviv: 1996] (SI 1311.1 (1996)).

SI 1311.2: Standards Institution of Israel. *Information technology: ISO 8-bit coded character set with Hebrew accents.* [Tel Aviv: 1996] (SI 1311.2 (1996)).

SLS 1134: Sri Lanka Standards Institution. *Sinhala character code for information interchange.* Colombo: 1996. (SLS 1134: 1996).

TIS 620-2529: Thai Industrial Standards Institute, Ministry of Industry. *Thai Industrial Standard for Thai character code for computer.* Bangkok: 1986. (TIS 620-2529–1986).

TIS 620-2533: Thai Industrial Standards Institute. *Standard for Thai character codes for computers.* Bangkok: 1990. (TIS 620-2533–1990). ISBN 974-606-153-4.

In Thai. Online version: http://www.nectec.or.th/it-standards/std620/std620.htm

Extensible Markup Language (XML) 1.0. 4th ed. (W3C Recommendation 16 August 2006). Editors: Tim Bray, Jean Paoli, C. M. Sperberg-McQueen, Eve Maler, [and] François Yergeau.

http://www.w3.org/TR/2006/REC-xml-20060816/

Extensible Markup Language (XML), 1.1. 2nd ed. (W3C Recommendation 16 August 2006). Editors: Tim Bray, Jean Paoli, C. M. Sperberg-McQueen, Eve Maler, François Yergeau, [and] John Cowan.

http://www.w3.org/TR/2006/REC-xml11-20060816/

R.2 Source Dictionaries for Han Unification

Dae Jaweon. Seoul: Samseong Publishing Co. Ltd., 1988.

Dai Kan-Wa Jiten / Morohashi Tetsuji cho. Shu teiban. Tokyo: Taishukan Shoten, Showa 59-61 [1984–86].

Hanyu Da Zidian. 1st ed. Chendu: Sichuan Cishu Publishing, 1986.

KangXi Zidian. 7th ed. Beijing: Zhonghua Bookstore, 1989.

R.3 Other Sources for the Unicode Standard

General

ALA-LC Romanization Tables: Transliteration Schemes for Non-Roman Scripts, Approved by the Library of Congress and the American Library Association. Tables compiled and edited by Randall K. Barry. Washington, DC: Library of Congress, 1997. ISBN 0-8444-0940-5.

Balinese

Medra, Nengah. *Pedoman Pasang Aksara Bali.* Denpasar: Dinas Kebudayaan Propinsi Bali, 2003.

Menaka, Made. *Kamus Kawi Bali* / olih, made Menaka. Singaraja: Yayasan Kawi Sastra Mandala, 1990.

Simpen, I Wayan. *Pasang Aksara Bali.* Denpasar: Upada Sastra, 1992.

Also published: Denpasar: Dinas Pengajaran Daerah Tingkat I Bali, 1979.

Canadian Aboriginal Syllabics

Canadian Aboriginal Syllabic Encoding Committee. *Repertoire of Unified Canadian Aboriginal Syllabics Proposed for Inclusion into ISO/IEC 10646: International Standard Universal Multiple-Octet Coded Character Set.* [Canada]: CASEC [1994].

Cherokee

Alexander, J. T. *A Dictionary of the Cherokee Indian Language.* [Sperry, Oklahoma?]: Published by the author, 1971.

Holmes, Ruth Bradley. *Beginning Cherokee*, by Ruth Bradley Holmes and Betty Sharp Smith. 2nd ed. Norman: University of Oklahoma Press, 1977. ISBN 0-8061-1464-9.

New Echota Letters: Contributions of Samuel A. Worcester to the Cherokee Phoenix, edited by Jack Frederick Kilpatrick and Anna Gritts Kilpatrick. Dallas: Southern Methodist University Press, [s.d.].

Includes reprint of an article by S. A. Worcester, which appeared in the *Cherokee Phoenix*, Feb. 21, 1828.

Coptic

Browne, Gerald M. *Old Nubian Grammar.* München: Lincom Europa, 2002. (*Languages of the world: Materials*, 330). ISBN 3-89586-893-0 (pbk.).

Kasser, Rodolphe. "La 'Genève 1986': une nouvelle série de caractères typographiques coptes, protocoptes et vieux-coptes créée à Genève." *Bulletin de la Société d'égyptologie de Genève*, 12 (1988): 59–60. ISSN 0255-6286.

Kasser, Rodolphe. "A standard system of sigla for referring to the dialects of Coptic." *Journal of Coptic Studies*, 1 (1990): 141–151. ISSN 1016-5584.

Cypriot *See* Linear B and Cypriot.

Deseret

Encyclopedia of Mormonism, entry for "Deseret Alphabet."

New York: Macmillan, 1992. ISBN 0-02-904040-X.

Monson, Samuel C. *Representative American Phonetic Alphabets.* New York: 1954.

Ph.D. dissertation—Columbia University.

Ethiopic

Armbruster, Carl Hubert. *Initia Amharica: An Introduction to Spoken Amharic.* Cambridge: Cambridge University Press, 1908–1920.

Launhardt, Johannes. *Guide to Learning the Oromo (Galla) Language.* Addis Ababa: Launhardt, [1973?].

Leslau, Wolf. *Amharic Textbook.* Weisbaden, Harrassowitz; Berkeley: University of California Press, 1968.

Glagolitic

Glagolitica: zum Ursprung der slavischen Schriftkultur, herausgegeben von Heinz Miklas, unter der Mitarbeit von Sylvia Richter und Velizar Sadovski. Wien: Verlag der Österreichischen Akademie der Wissenschaften, 2000. (*Schriften der Balkan-Kommission, Philologische Abteilung,* 41). ISBN 3-7001-2895-9.

Khaburgaev, Georgii Aleksandrovich. *Staroslavianskii iazyk.* Izd. 2-e, perer. i dop. Moskva: Prosveshchenie, 1986.

Žubrinic, Darko. *Hrvatska glagoljica: biti pismen—biti svoj.* Zagreb: Hrvatsko književno društvo sv. Jeronima (sv. Cirila i Metoda): Element, 1996. ISBN 953-6111-35-7.

Gothic

Ebbinghaus, Ernst. "The Gothic Alphabet." In *The World's Writing Systems,* edited by Peter T. Daniels and William Bright. New York: Oxford University Press, 1996. ISBN 0-19-507993-0.

Greek Editorial Marks

Austin, Colin. *Comicorum Graecorum Fragmenta in Papyris Reperta,* ed. Colinus Austin. Berolini [Berlin], Novi Eboraci [New York]: de Gruyter, 1973, p. 29. ISBN 3110024012.

Homer. *Iliad. Homeri Ilias,* edidit Thomas W. Allen. 3 vols. Oxonii [Oxford]: e typographeo Clarendoniano [Clarendon Press], 1931, vol. 2: pp. 39, 234.

The Oxyrhynchus Papyri, Part XV, edited with translations and notes by Bernard P. Grenfell and Arthur S. Hunt. London: Egypt Exploration Society, 1921, p. 56. (*Egypt Exploration Society, Graeco-Roman Memoirs,* 18).

International Phonetic Alphabet

Esling, John. "Computer Coding of the IPA: Supplementary Report." *Journal of the International Phonetic Association,* 20:1 (1990), 22–26.

International Phonetic Association. *Handbook of the International Phonetic Association: A Guide to the Use of the International Phonetic Alphabet.* Cambridge: Cambridge University Press, 1999. ISBN 0-521-65236-7; 0-521-63751-1 (pbk.).

International Phonetic Association.
http://www2.arts.gla.ac.uk/IPA/ipa.html

Journal of the International Phonetic Association, 24.2 (1994): 95–98, and 25.1 (1995): 21.

Pullum, Geoffrey K. "Remarks on the 1989 Revision of the International Phonetic Alphabet." *Journal of the International Phonetic Association,* 20:1 (1990), 33–40.

Pullum, Geoffrey K., and William A. Ladusaw. *Phonetic Symbol Guide.* 2nd ed. Chicago: University of Chicago Press, 1996. ISBN 0-226-68535-7; 0-226-68536-5 (pbk.).

Wells, John Christopher. *Accents of English*. Cambridge, New York: Cambridge University Press, 1982.

Vol. 1: *Introduction*. ISBN 0-521-22919-7; ISBN 0-521-29719-2 (pbk.); vol. 2: *The British Isles*. ISBN 0-521-24224-X, ISBN 0-521-28540-2 (pbk.); vol. 3: *Beyond the British Isles*. ISBN 0-521-24225-8, ISBN 0-521-28541-0 (pbk.).

Kharoshthi

Glass, Andrew. *A Preliminary Study of Kharosthi Manuscript Paleography*. 2000.

Thesis (M.A.), University of Washington, 2000.

Glass, Andrew. "Kharoṣṭhī Manuscripts: A Window on Gandhāran Buddhism." *Nagoya Studies in Indian Culture and Buddhism*, 24 (2004): 129–152. ISSN 0285-7154.

Salomon, Richard. *Ancient Buddhist Scrolls from Gandhāra: The British Library Kharosthi Fragments*. Seattle: University of Washington Press; London: British Library, 1999. ISBN 029597768X; 0295977698 (pbk).

Limbu

Bairagi Kaila, ed. *Limbu-Nepali-Angreji śabdakoś*. [Limbu-Nepali-English Dictionary.] Kathmandu: Royal Nepal Academy, [in press.]

Includes an introduction describing the Limbu script.

Cemjonga, Imana Simha. *Yakthun-Pene-Mikphula Pancheka. = Limbu-Nepali-Angareji śabdakoś. = Limbu-Nepali-English Dictionary.* [Lekhaka] Imanasimha Cemajon. [Kathamandu]: Nepala Ekedemi [2018 vi., i.e., 1962]

In Devanagari script. Author also known as Chemjong, Iman Singh.

Driem, George van. *A Grammar of Limbu*. Berlin, New York: Mouton de Gruyter, 1987. (Mouton grammar library, 4.) ISBN 0-89925-345-8.

Appendix: *Anthology of Kiranti scripts*, pp. 550–558.

Shafer, Robert. *Introduction to Sino-Tibetan*. Wiesbaden: Harrassowitz, 1966–1974.

Published in five parts with continuous pagination.

Sprigg, R. K. "Limbu Books in the Kiranti Script." In International Congress of Orientalists (24th: 1957: Munich). *Akten des Vierundzwanzigsten Internationalen Orientalisten-Kongresses München 28. August bis 4. September 1957*, hrsg. von Herbert Franke. Wiesbaden: Deutsche Morgenländische Gesellschaft, in Kommission bei Franz Steiner Verlag, 1959.

The modern script described in this work is now outdated.

Sprigg, R. K. [Review of van Driem (1987)]. *Bulletin of the School of Oriental and African Studies, University of London*, 52 (1989):1.163–165.

Subba, B. B. *Limbu, Nepali, English Dictionary*. Gangtok: Text Book Unit, Directorate of Education, Govt. of Sikkim, 1979 [i.e. 1980].

Cover title: Yakthun-Pene-Mikphula-panchekva. In Limbu and Devnagari scripts.

Subba, B. B. *Yakthuŋ huʔsiŋlam* ("Limbu self-teaching method") = *Limbu akṣar gāiḍ* ("Limbu letter guide"). Gangtok: Kwality Stores, 1991?

In Nepali and Limbu.

Yoṅhāṅ, Khel Rāj. *Limbū Nepālī śabdakoś.* [Lalitpur]: 2052 B.S. [i.e. 1995].

In Limbu script.

Linear B and Cypriot

Bennett, Emmett L. "Aegean Scripts." In *The World's Writing Systems*, edited by Peter T. Daniels and William Bright. New York: Oxford University Press, 1996. ISBN 0-19-507993-0.

Chadwick, John. *The Decipherment of Linear B.* 2nd ed. London: Cambridge University Press., 1967 [i.e. 1968].

Chadwick, John. *Linear B and Related Scripts.* Berkeley: University of California Press; [London]: British Museum, 1987. (*Reading the Past*, v. 1.) ISBN 0-520-06019-9.

Hooker, J. T. *Linear B: An Introduction.* Bristol: Bristol Classical Press, 1980. ISBN 0-906515-69-6.

Corrected printing published 1983. ISBN 0-906515-69-6; 0-906515-62-9 (pbk.).

International Colloquium on Mycenaean Studies (3rd: 1961: Racine, WI). *Mycenaean Studies: Proceedings of the Third International Colloquium for Mycenaean Studies held at "Wingspread," 4–8 September 1961*, edited by Emmett L. Bennett, Jr. Madison: University of Wisconsin Press, 1964.

Appendix: The Wingspread Convention for the Transcription of Mycenaean (Linear B) Texts: pp. 254–262.

Masson, Olivier. *Les Inscriptions chypriotes syllabiques: recueil critique et commenté.* Réimpr. augm. Paris: E. de Boccard, 1983.

Sampson, Geoffrey. *Writing Systems: A Linguistic Introduction.* Stanford, CA: Stanford University Press, 1985. ISBN 0-8047-1254-9.

Also published: London, Hutchinson. ISBN 0-09-156980-X; 0-09-173051-1 (pbk.).

Ventris, Michael. *Documents in Mycenaean Greek.* 1st ed. by Michael Ventris and John Chadwick with a foreword by Alan J. B. Wace. 2nd ed. by John Chadwick. Cambridge: Cambridge University Press, 1973. ISBN 0-521-08558-6.

Mathematics

Mathematical Markup Language (MathML) Version 2.0. (W3C Recommendation 21 February 2001). Editors: David Carlisle, Patrick Ion, Robert Miner, [and] Nico Poppolier.

Latest version: http://www.w3.org/TR/MathML2/

STIPub Consortium. STIX (Scientific and Technical Information Exchange) Project.

http://www.ams.org/STIX/

Swanson, Ellen. *Mathematics into Type*. Updated ed. by Arlene O'Sean and Antoinette Schleyer. Providence, RI: American Mathematical Society, 1999. ISBN 0-8218-1961-5.

Music

Catholic Church. *Graduale Sacrosanctae Romanae Ecclesiae de Tempore et de Sanctis SS. D. N. Pii X. Pontificis Maximi*. Parisiis: Desclée, 1961. (*Graduale Romanum*, no. 696.)

Gazimihal, Mahmut R. *Anadolu türküleri ve mûsikî istikbâlimiz* [by] Mahmut Ragip. [Istanbul]: Mârifet Matbaasi, 1928.

Heussenstamm, George. *Norton Manual of Music Notation*. New York: W.W. Norton, 1987. ISBN 0-393-95526-5 (pbk.).

Kennedy, Michael. *Oxford Dictionary of Music*. Oxford, New York: Oxford University Press, 1985. ISBN 0-19-311333-3.

Second ed. published 1994. ISBN 0-19-869162-9.

New Encyclopedia Britannica. 15th ed. Entry for "Music."

The New Harvard Dictionary of Music, edited by Don Michael Randel. Cambridge, MA: Belknap Press of Harvard University Press, 1986. ISBN 0-674-61525-5.

Ottman, Robert W. *Elementary Harmony: Theory and Practice*. 2nd ed. Englewood Cliffs, NJ: Prentice-Hall, 1970. ISBN 0-13-257451-9.

Fifth ed. published 1998. ISBN 0-13-281610-5.

Rastall, Richard. *The Notation of Western Music: An Introduction*. London: Dent, 1983. ISBN 0-460-04205-X.

Also published: New York: St. Martin's Press, 1982. ISBN 0-312-57963-2.

Read, Gardner. *Music Notation: A Manual of Modern Practice*. Boston: Allyn and Bacon, 1964.

Stone, Kurt. *Music Notation in the Twentieth Century: A Practical Guidebook*. New York: W.W. Norton, 1980. ISBN 0-393-95053-0.

Understanding Music with AI: Perspectives on Music Cognition, edited by Mira Balaban, Kemal Ebcioglu, and Otto Laske. Cambridge, MA: MIT Press; Menlo Park, CA: AAAI Press, 1992. ISBN 0-262-52170-9.

Myanmar

Mranmā–Aṅglip abhidhān = Myanmar–English Dictionary. Rankun: Dept. of Myanmar Language Commission, Ministry of Education, Union of Myanmar, 1993.

Compiled and edited by the Myanmar Language Commission.

Mranmā cālui:poṅg:satpui kyam: nhaṅ. khwaithā:. [Rankun]: 1996.

Translated title: Myanmar orthography treatise.

Roop, D. Haigh. *An Introduction to the Burmese Writing System.* [Honolulu]: Center for Southeast Asian Studies, University of Hawaii at Manoa, 1997. (*Southeast Asia Paper,* 11).

Originally published: New Haven: Yale University Press, 1972. (*Yale linguistic series*). ISBN 0-300-01528-3.

N'Ko

Introduction to N'Ko. http://home.gwu.edu/~cwme/Nko/Nkohome.htm

Kanté, Souleymane. *Méthode pratique d'écriture n'ko,* 1961. Kankan, Guinea: Association de traditherapeutes et pharmacologues, 1995.

N'Ko: The Common Language of Mandens. www.nkoinstitute.com

N'Ko: The Mandingo Language Site. www.kanjamadi.com

Ogham

McManus, Damian. *A Guide to Ogam.* Maynooth: An Sagart, 1991. (*Maynooth monographs,* 4). ISBN 1-87068-417-6.

Old Italic

Bonfante, Larissa. "The Scripts of Italy." In *The World's Writing Systems,* edited by Peter T. Daniels and William Bright. New York: Oxford University Press, 1996. ISBN 0-19-507993-0.

Cristofani, Mauro. "L'alfabeto etrusco." In *Lingue e dialetti dell'Italia antica,* a cura di Aldo Larosdocimi. Roma: Biblioteca di storia patria, a cura dell' Ente per la diffusione e l'educazione storia, 1978. (*Popoli e civiltà dell'Italia antica,* VI.)

Gordon, Arthur E. *Illustrated Introduction to Latin Epigraphy.* Berkeley: University of California Press, 1983. ISBN 0-520-03898-3.

Marinetti, Anna. *Le iscrizione sudpicene.* I. *Testi.* Firenze: Olschki, 1985. ISBN 88-222-3331-X (v. 1).

Parlangèli, Oronzo. *Studi Messapici.* Milano: Istituto lombardo di scienze e lettere, 1960.

Old Persian

Schmitt, Rüdiger. The Bisitun Inscriptions of Darius the Great, Old Persian Text. London, School of Oriental and African Studies, 1991 (*Corpus Inscriptionum Iranicarum,* Part I: *Inscriptions of ancient Iran,* v.1, Text 1). ISBN 0-7286-0181-8.

Schweiger, Günter. *Kritische Neuedition der achaemenidischen Keilinschriften.* Taimering: Schweiger VWT-Verlag, 1998. (*Studien zur Iranistik*). ISBN 3-934548-00-8.

Osmanya

Afkeenna iyo fartiisa: buug koowaad. Xamar: Goosanka afka iyo suugaanta Soomaalida, 1971.

Translated title: *Our language and its handwriting: book one.*

Cerulli, Enrico. "Tentativo indigeno di formare un alfabeta somalo." *Oriente moderno*, 12 (1932): 212–213. ISSN 0030-5472.

Gaur, Albertine. *A History of Writing*. London: British Library, 1992. ISBN 0-7123-0270-0.

Also published: Rev. ed. New York: Cross River Press, 1992. ISBN 1-558-59358-6.

Gregersen, Edgar A. *Language in Africa: An Introductory Survey.* New York: Gordon and Breach, 1977. (*Library of Anthropology*). ISBN: 0-677-04380-5; 0-677-04385-6 (pbk.).

Maino, Mario. "L'alfabeta 'Osmania' in Somalia." *Rassegna di studi etiopici*, 10 (1951): 108–121. ISSN 0390-3699.

Nakanishi, Akira. *Writing Systems of the World: Alphabets, Syllabaries, Pictograms.* Rutland, VT: Tuttle, 1980. ISBN 0-8048-1293-4; 0-8048-1654-9 (pbk.).

Revised translation of *Sekai no moji.*

Phags-pa

Luo, Changpei. *Basibazi yu Yuandai Hanyu [ziliao huibian]* / Luo Changpei, Cai Meibiao bian zhu. Beijing: Kexue chubanshe, 1959.

Poppe, Nikolai Nikolaevich. *The Mongolian Monuments in hP'ags-pa Script.* Translated and edited by John R. Krueger. 2nd ed. Wiesbaden: Harrassowitz, 1957. (*Göttinger asiatische Forschungen*, 8).

Zhaonasitu. *Menggu ziyun jiaoben* / Zhaonasitu, Yang Naisi bian zhu. [Beijing]: Min zu chu ban she, 1987.

Author Zhaonasitu also known as Jagunasutu or Junast.

Philippine Scripts

Doctrina Christiana: The First Book Printed in the Philippines, Manila 1593. A facsimile of the copy in the Lessing J. Rosenwald Collection, with an introductory essay by Edwin Wolf II. Washington, DC: Library of Congress, 1947.

Kuipers, Joel C., and Ray McDermott. "Insular Southeast Asian Scripts." In *The World's Writing Systems.* Edited by Peter T. Daniels and William Bright. New York: Oxford University Press, 1996. ISBN 0-19-507993-0.

Santos, Hector. *The Living Scripts.* Los Angeles: Sushi Dog Graphics, 1995. (*Ancient Philippine scripts series*, 2).

User's guide accompanying *Computer Fonts, Living Scripts* software.

Santos, Hector. *Our Living Scripts.* January 31, 1997.

http://www.bibingka.com/dahon/living/living.htm

Part of his *A Philippine Leaf.*

Santos, Hector. *The Tagalog Script.* Los Angeles: Sushi Dog Graphics, 1994. (*Ancient Philippine scripts series*, 1).

User's guide accompanying *Tagalog Script Fonts* software.

Santos, Hector. *The Tagalog Script*. October 26, 1996.
http://www.bibingka.com/dahon/tagalog/tagalog.htm
Part of his *A Philippine Leaf.*

Phoenician

Branden, Albertus van den. *Grammaire phénicienne*. Beyrouth: Librairie du Liban, 1969. (*Bibliothèque de l'Université Saint-Esprit*, 2).

McCarter, P. Kyle. *The Antiquity of the Greek Alphabet and the Early Phoenician Scripts*. Missoula, MT: Published by Scholars Press for Harvard Semitic Museum, 1975. (Harvard Semitic Monographs; 9.) ISBN 0-89130-066-X.

Noldeke, Theodor. *Beiträge zur semitischen Sprachwissenschaft*. Strassburg: Karl J. Trübner, 1904.

Reprinted as: vol. 1 of *Beiträge und Neue Beiträge zur semitischen Sprachwissenschaft: achtzehn Aufsätze und Studien*. Amsterdam: APA-Philo Press, [1982].

Also published on microfiche by the American Theological Library Association.

Powell, Barry B. *Homer and the Origin of the Greek Alphabet*. Cambridge, New York: Cambridge University Press, 1991. ISBN 0-521-37157-0.

Reprinted, 1996. ISBN 0-521-58907-X (pbk).

Runic

Friesen, Otto von. *Runorna*. Stockholm: A. Bonnier, [1933]. (*Nordisk kultur*, 6).

Haugen, Einar Ingvald. *The Scandinavian Languages: An Introduction to Their History*. London: Faber, 1976. ISBN 0-571-10423-1.

Also published: Cambridge, MA: Harvard University Press, 1976. ISBN 0-674-79002-2.

Musset, Lucien. *Introduction à la runologie*. Paris: Aubier-Montaigne, 1965.

Page, Raymond Ian. *Runes*. Berkeley: University of California Press; [London]: British Museum, 1987. (*Reading the Past*). ISBN 0-520-06114-4.

British Museum Publications edition has ISBN 0-7141-8065-3.

Shavian

ConScript Unicode Registry [by] John Cowan and Michael Everson. "E700–E72F Shavian."

Included in the ConScript Registry (http://www.evertype.com/standards/csur/index.html) in 1997. Shavian was withdrawn from the ConScript Registry in 2001, because of its addition to the Unicode Standard and ISO/IEC 10646.

Crystal, David. *The Cambridge Encyclopedia of Language*. Cambridge, New York: Cambridge University Press, 1987. ISBN 0-521-26438-3.

2nd ed. Cambridge, New York: Cambridge University Press, 1997. ISBN 0-521-55050-5; 0-521-55967-7.

DeMeyere, Ross. *About Shavian*. 1997. http://www.demeyere.com/Shavian/info.html.

Shaw, George Bernard. *Androcles and the Lion: An Old Fable Renovated, by Bernard Shaw, with a Parallel Text in Shaw's Alphabet to Be Read in Conjunction Showing Its Economies in Writing and Reading.* Harmondsworth: Penguin Books, 1962.

Sinhala

Gunasekara, Abraham Mendis. *A Comprehensive Grammar of the Sinhalese Language.* New Delhi: Asian Education Services, 1986.

Reprint of 1891 edition.

Syriac

Kefarnissy, Paul. *Grammaire de la langue Araméenne syriaque*. Beyrouth: 1962.

Nöldeke, Theodor. *Compendious Syriac Grammar.* With a table of characters by Julius Euting. Translated from the 2nd and improved German ed., by James A. Crichton. London: Williams & Norgate, 1904.

Reprinted: Tel Aviv: Zion Pub. Co. [1970].

Robinson, Theodore Henry. *Paradigms and Exercises in Syriac Grammar.* 4th ed. Rev. by L. H. Brockington. Oxford: Clarendon Press; New York: Oxford University Press, 1962. ISBN 0-19-815416-X, 0-19-815458-5 (pbk.).

Tai Le

Coulmas, Florian. *The Blackwell Encyclopedia of Writing Systems.* Oxford, Cambridge: Blackwell, 1996. ISBN 0-631-19446-0.

Dehong writing, pp. 118–119.

Lá ai^{2} maɯ^{3} lá ai^{2} ka va^{3} mi^{2} tse^{2} laɯ ya pa me na^{4} ka na: tá va ʔá na kó ma^{6} sá na^{2} teh ma^{6}. Yina^{5}lána^{5} mina^{5}su^{4} su^{4}pána^{2}se^{3} (Yunnan minzu chubanshe). 1988. ISBN 7-5367-1100-4.

Tsa va^{4} má^{3} hó va^{3}: la ta^{6} mé^{2} sá ai^{3} seh va^{2} xo ŋa^{3}. Yina^{5}lána^{5} mina^{5}su^{4} su^{4}pána^{2}se^{3} (Yunnan minzu chubanshe). 1997. ISBN 7-5367-1455-6.

Thaana

Geiger, Wilhelm. *Maldivian Linguistic Studies.* New Delhi: Asian Educational Services, 1996. ISBN 81-206-1201-9.

Originally published: Colombo: H. C. Cottle, Govt. Printer, 1919.

Maniku, Hassan Ahmed. *Say It in Maldivian (Dhivehi)*, [by] H. A. Maniku [and] J. B. Disanayaka. Colombo: Lake House Investments, 1990.

Ugaritic

O'Connor, M. "Epigraphic Semitic Scripts." In *The World's Writing Systems*, edited by Peter T. Daniels and William Bright. New York: Oxford University Press, 1996. ISBN 0-19-507993-0.

Walker, C. B. F. *Cuneiform*. London: British Museum Press, 1987. (*Reading the Past*, v. 3.) ISBN 0-7141-8059-9.

University of California Press edition has ISBN 0-520-06115-2 (pbk.).

Yi

Nuo-su bbur-ma shep jie zzit. = Yi wen jian zi ben. Chengdu: Sìchuan minzu chubanshe, 1984.

Nip huo bbur-ma ssix jie. = Yi Han zidian. Chengdu: Sìchuan minzu chubanshe, 1990. ISBN 7-5409-0128-4.

R.4 Selected Resources: Technical

American Mathematical Society. *TeX Resources.* http://www.ams.org/tex/tex-resources.html

For AMS TeX-related products, see *AMS TeX Resources.* http://www.ams.org/tex/

André, Jacques. *Unicode, écriture du monde?* / Jacques André, Henri Hudrisier. Paris: Lavoisier, 2002. (*Document numérique*, v. 6, no. 3–4.) ISBN 2-7426-0594-7.

Bringhurst, Robert. *The Elements of Typographic Style.* 3rd ed. Point Roberts, WA: Hartley & Marks, 2004. ISBN 0-88179-205-5; 0-88179-206-3 (pbk.).

Chaundy, Theodore William. *The Printing of Mathematics: Aids for Authors and Editors and Rules for Compositors and Readers at the University Press, Oxford.* By T. W. Chaundy, P. R. Barrett, and Charles Batey. London: Oxford University Press [1965].

Reprint of the second impression (revised) 1957.

Deitsch, Andrew. *Java Internationalization* [by] Andrew Deitsch and David Czarnecki. Beijing, Sebastopol, CA: O'Reilly, 2001. ISBN 0-596-00019-7.

Desgraupes, Bernard. *Passeport pour Unicode.* Paris: Vuibert, informatique, 2005. ISBN 2-7117-4827-8.

Developing International Software [by] Dr. International. 2nd ed. Redmond, WA: Microsoft, 2002. ISBN 0-7356-1583-7.

Also published: London: Chrysalis, 2002.

Esselink, Bert. *A Practical Guide to Localization*. Amsterdam, Philadelphia: John Benjamins, 2000. ISBN: 1-588-11006-0 (pbk.), 1-588-11005-2 (hardcover).

Rev. ed. of *A Practical Guide to Software Localization*.

Flanagan, David. *Java in a Nutshell.* 5th ed. Sebastopol, CA: O'Reilly, 2005. ISBN 0896007736.

Garneau, Denis. *Keys to Sort and Search for Culturally-Expected Results.* [s.l.] IBM, 1990. (IBM document number GG24-3516, June 1, 1990).

Gillam, Richard. *Unicode Demystified: A Practical Programmer's Guide to the Encoding Standard.* Boston: Addison-Wesley, 2002. ISBN 0-201-70052-2.

Graham, Tony. *Unicode: A Primer.* Foster City, CA: MIS Press, M&T Books, 2000. ISBN 0-7645-4625-2.

The Guide to Translation and Localization: Preparing Products for the Global Marketplace. [5th ed.] Portland, OR: Lingo Systems; [Sandpoint, ID]: Multilingual Computing, 2004. ISBN 0970394829 (pbk.).

IBM. *e-Business Globalization Solution Design Guide: Getting Started.* 2002, updated 2004. (*IBM Redbook*) (SG24-6851-00) ISBN 0738426563.

Available in PDF, HTML, or hardcopy from:
http://www.redbooks.ibm.com/abstracts/sg246851.html?Open

ICU User Guide. http://icu.sourceforge.net/userguide/

User guide for International Components for Unicode (ICU), a set of C/C++ and Java libraries for Unicode support.

International Organization for Standardization. *Information Technology—An Operational Model for Characters and Glyphs.* Geneva: 1998. (ISO/IEC TR 15285:1998).

International User Interfaces, edited by Elisa M. del Galdo and Jakob Nielsen. New York: Wiley, 1996. ISBN: 0-471-14965-9.

Knuth, Donald E. *TEX, the Program.* Reading, MA: Addison-Wesley, 1986. (*Computers & Typesetting*, B). ISBN 0-201-13437-3.

Knuth, Donald E. *The TEXbook.* 21st printing, rev. Reading, MA: Addison-Wesley, 1994. (*Computers & Typesetting*, A). ISBN 0-201-13448-9.

Korpela, Jukka K. *Unicode Explained.* Beijing, Sebastopol, CA: O'Reilly, 2006. ISBN: 0-596-10121-X.

Krantz, Steven G. *Handbook of Typography for the Mathematical Sciences.* Boca Raton: Chapman & Hall/CRC, 2001. ISBN 1584881496.

Lamport, Leslie. *LATEX, a Document Preparation System: User's Guide & Reference Manual.* 2nd ed. Reading, MA: Addison-Wesley, 1999, ©1994. ISBN 0-201-52983-1.

Updated for LATEX 2nd ed.

Language Culture Type: International Type Design in the Age of Unicode, edited by John D. Berry; with a special section showing the winners in Bukva:Raz!, the type design competition of the Association typographique internationale. New York: ATypI, Graphis, 2002. ISBN 1-932026-01-0.

Lunde, Ken. *CJKV Information Processing.* Beijing, Sebastopol, CA: O'Reilly, 1999. ISBN 1-56592-224-7.

Mathematics in Type. Richmond, VA: The William Byrd Press, [1954].

PAN Localization Project. *Survey of Language Computing in Asia 2005*, by Sarmad Hussain, Nadir Durrani, and Sana Gul. Lahore: Center for Research in Urdu Language Processing; Ottawa: International Development Research Center, 2005. ISBN 969-8961-00-3.

Available as a book and also in PDF from:
http://www.idrc.ca/uploads/user-S/11446781751Survey.pdf

Savourel, Yves. *XML Internationalization and Localization.* Indianapolis, IN: Sams, 2001. ISBN 0-672-32096-7.

Also published: Hemel Hempstead: Prentice-Hall, 2001.

Swanson, Ellen. *Mathematics into Type.* Updated ed. [by] Arlene O'Sean and Antoinette Schleyer. Providence, RI: American Mathematical Society, 1999. ISBN 0821819615.

Unicode Guide, [by] Joe Becker, Rich Gillam, Mark Davis, and the Unicode Consortium Editorial Committee. Boca Raton, FL: BarCharts, 2006. (QuickStudy: Computer). ISBN 978-14230-180-9.

Wick, Karel. *Rules for Type-setting Mathematics.* Prague: Publishing House of the Czechoslovak Academy of Sciences, 1965.

W3C Internationalization (I18n) Activity. http://www.w3.org/International/

W3C Web Internationalization Tutorials. http://www.w3.org/International/tutorials/

Tutorials include *Character sets & encodings in XHTML, HTML and CSS*, and *Using language information in XHTML, HTML and CSS*, both by Richard Ishida.

Yunikodo kanji joho jiten = Sanseido's Unicode Kanji Information Dictionary / Yunikodo Kanji Joho Jiten Henshu Iinkai hen. Tokyo: Sanseido, 2000. ISBN 4-385-13690-4.

R.5 Selected Resources: Scripts and Languages

Bibliographies

A Bibliography on Writing and Written Language, edited by Konrad Ehlich, Florian Coulmas, and Gabriele Graefen. Berlin, New York: Mouton de Gruyter, 1996. (*Trends in Linguistics. Studies and Monographs*, 89.) ISBN 3-11-010158-0.

Contains references to about 27,500 publications covering mainly 1930–1992.

Michael Everson's Cool Bibliography of Typography and Scripts.

http://www.evertype.com/scriptbib.html

Selected Works

Allworth, Edward. *Nationalities of the Soviet East: Publications and Writing Systems.* New York: Columbia University Press, 1971. ISBN 0-231-03274-9.

The Alphabet Makers: A Presentation from the Museum of the Alphabet, Waxhaw, North Carolina. 2nd ed. Huntington Beach, CA: Summer Institute of Linguistics, 1991. ISBN 0-938978-13-6.

Alphabete und Schriftzeichen des Morgen- und Abendlandes. 2. übearb, u. erw. Aufl. Berlin: Bundesdruckerei, 1969.

Bergsträsser, Gotthelf. *Introduction to the Semitic Languages: Text Specimens and Grammatical Sketches.* Translated with an appendix on the scripts by Peter T. Daniels. [2nd ed.] Winona Lake: Eisenbrauns, 1995. ISBN 0-931464-10-2.

Translation of *Einführung in die semitischen Sprachen*, 1928.

The Book of a Thousand Tongues, by Eugene A. Nida. Rev. ed. London: United Bible Society, 1972.

First ed. by Eric M. North, 1938.

The Cambridge Encyclopedia of the World's Ancient Languages, edited by Roger D. Woodard. Cambridge, New York: Cambridge University Press, 2004. ISBN: 0521562562.

Campbell, George L. *Compendium of the World's Languages.* London: Routledge, 1990. ISBN 0-415-06937-6 (set); 0-415-06978-5 (v.1); 0-415-06979-3 (v.2).

Cleator, Philip Ellaby. *Lost Languages*, by P. E. Cleator. London: Day, 1959.

Also published: London: R. Hale, [1959]; New York: John Day Co. [1961]; [New York]: New American Library [1962].

Comrie, Bernard, ed. *The Languages of the Soviet Union.* Cambridge: Cambridge University Press, 1981. ISBN 0-521-23230-9; 0-521-9877-6 (pbk.).

Comrie, Bernard, ed. *The World's Major Languages.* Oxford: Oxford University Press, 1987. ISBN 0-19-520521-9; 0-19-506511-5 (pbk.).

Coulmas, Florian. *The Blackwell Encyclopedia of Writing Systems.* Cambridge, MA: Blackwell, 1996. ISBN 0-631-19446-0.

Coulmas, Florian. *The Writing Systems of the World.* Oxford, New York: Blackwell, 1989.

Crystal, David. *The Cambridge Encyclopedia of Language.* 2nd ed. Cambridge, New York: Cambridge University Press, 1997. ISBN 0-521-55050-5; 0-521-55967-7 (pbk.).

Dalby, Andrew. *Dictionary of Languages: The Definitive Reference to More Than 400 Languages.* New York: Columbia University Press, 1998. ISBN 0231115687; 0231115695 (pbk.).

Daniels, Peter T. *The World's Writing Systems.* (See *World's Writing Systems.*)

DeFrancis, John. *Visible Speech: The Diverse Oneness of Writing Systems.* Honolulu: University of Hawaii Press, 1989. ISBN 0-8248-1207-7.

Diringer, David. *The Alphabet: A Key to the History of Mankind.* 3rd ed., completely rev. with the assistance of Reinhold Regensburger. New York: Funk and Wagnalls, 1968.

Also published: London: Hutchinson. ISBN 0-906764-0-8.

Diringer, David. *Writing*. London: Thames and Hudson, 1962.

Also published: New York: Praeger.

Dixon, Robert M. W. *The Languages of Australia*. Cambridge: Cambridge University Press, 1980. ISBN 0-521-22329-6.

Drucker, Johanna. *The Alphabetic Labyrinth: The Letters in History and Imagination*. London: Thames & Hudson, 1999. ISBN 0-500-28068-1.

Endo, Shotoku. *Hayawakari chugoku kantai-ji*. Tokyo: Kokusho Kankokai, Showa 61 [1986].

Faulmann, Carl. *Das Buch der Schrift: enthaltend die Schriftzeichen und Alphabete aller Zeiten und aller Völker.* 2. verm. und verb. Aufl. Wien: Kaiserlich-Königliche Hof- und Staatsdruckerei, 1880.

Reprinted as: *Schriftzeichen und Alphabete aller Zeiten und Völker.* Augsburg: Augustus Verlag, 1990. ISBN 3-8043-0142-8.

Reprinted as: *Das Buch der Schrift: enthaltend die Schriftzeichen und Alphabete aller Zeiten und aller Völker des Erdkreises.* Frankfurt am Main: Eichborn, 1990. ISBN 3-8218-1720-8.

Friedrich, Johannes. *Extinct Languages*. New York: Philosophical Library, 1957.

Translation of *Entzifferung Verschollener Schriften und Sprachen.* Berlin: Springer-Verlag, 1954.

Also published: London: Peter Owen [1962]; Westport, CT: Greenwood Press [1971, ©1957]. ISBN 0-8371-5748-X; New York: Dorset Press, 1989, ©1957. ISBN 0-88029-338-1.

Friedrich, Johannes. *Geschichte der Schrift*. Heidelberg: C. Winter, 1966.

Gaur, Albertine. *A History of Writing*. Rev. ed. New York: Cross River Press, 1992. ISBN 1-558-59358-6.

Also published: London: British Library. ISBN 0-7123-0270-0.

Gelb, Ignace J. *A Study of Writing*. Rev. ed. Chicago: University of Chicago Press, 1963. ISBN 0-226-28605-3; 0-226-28606-1 (pbk.).

Giliarevskii, Rudzhero Sergeevich. *Languages Identification Guide*, by Rudzhero S. Gilyarevsky and Vladimir S. Grivnin. Moscow: Nauka, 1970.

Gordon, Cyrus Herzl. *Forgotten Scripts: How They Were Deciphered and Their Impact on Contemporary Culture* [by] Cyrus H. Gordon. New York: Basic Books [1968].

The Gospel in Many Tongues: Specimens of 875 Languages ... London: British and Foreign Bible Society, 1965.

Haarmann, Harald. *Universalgeschichte der Schrift*. Frankfurt: Campus Verlag, 1990. ISBN 3-593-34346-0.

Habein, Yaeko Sato. *The History of the Japanese Written Language.* Tokyo: University of Tokyo Press, 1984. ISBN 0-86008-347-0; 4-13-087047-5.

Healey, John F. *The Early Alphabet*. Berkeley: University of California Press; [London]: British Museum, 1990. (*Reading the Past*, 9). ISBN 0-520-07309-6.

British Museum Publications edition has ISBN 0-7141-8073-4.

A History of Writing: From Hieroglyph to Multimedia, edited by Anne-Marie Christin. Paris: Flammarion; London: Thames & Hudson, 2002. ISBN 2-08-010887-5.

Ifrah, Georges. *From One to Zero, a Universal History of Numbers*. New York: Penguin, 1987. ISBN 0-14-009919-0.

Translation of *Histoire universelle des chiffres*. Also published: New York: Viking, 1985. ISBN 0-670-37395-8.

Isaev, Magomet Izmailovich. *Sto tridtsat' ravnopravnykh: o iazykakh narodov SSSR*. Moskva: Nauka, 1970.

Jensen, Hans. *Sign, Symbol and Script: An Account of Man's Efforts to Write*. New York: Putnam, 1969.

Translation of *Die Schrift in Vergangenheit und Gegenwart* (Berlin: Deutscher Verlag, 1969). Also published: London: Allen & Unwin. ISBN 0-04-400021-9.

Katzner, Kenneth. *The Languages of the World*. New ed. London: Routledge, 1995. ISBN 0-415-11809-3.

Lyovin, Anatole. *Introduction to the Languages of the World*. New York: Oxford University Press, 1997. ISBN 0-19-508115-3; ISBN 0-19-508116-1 (pbk.)

Malherbe, Michel. *Les Langages de l'humanité: une encyclopédie des 3000 langues parlées dans le monde*. Paris: Laffont, 1995. ISBN 2-221-05947-6.

Muller, Siegfried H. *The World's Living Languages: Basic Facts of Their Structure, Kinship, Location, and Number of Speakers*. New York: Ungar, 1964.

Musaev, Kenesbai Musaevich. *Alfavity iazykov narodov SSSR*. Moskva: Nauka, 1965.

Naik, Bapurao S. *Typography of Devanagari*. 1st ed., rev. Bombay: Directorate of Languages, Govt. of Maharashtra, 1971.

Nakanishi, Akira. *Writing Systems of the World: Alphabets, Syllabaries, Pictograms*. Rutland, VT: Tuttle, 1980. ISBN 0-8048-1293-4; 0-8048-1654-9 (pbk.).

Revised translation of *Sekai no moji*.

Nida, Eugene A. *The Book of a Thousand Tongues*. (See *Book of a Thousand Tongues*.)

Pavlenko, Nikolai Andreevich. *Istoria pis'ma*. 2. izd. Minsk: Vysshaia Shkola, 1987.

Ramsey, S. Robert. *The Languages of China*. 2nd printing with revisions. Princeton: Princeton University Press, 1989. ISBN 0-691-01468-X.

Second ed. published London: Gollancz, 1974. ISBN 0-575-01758-9.

Robinson, Andrew. *The Story of Writing*. London: Thames and Hudson, 1995. ISBN 0-500-01665-8.

Ruhlen, Merritt. *A Guide to the World's Languages, volume 1: Classification, with a Postscript on Recent Developments.* Stanford, CA: Stanford University Press, 1991. ISBN 0-8047-1894-6 (v. 1).

Also published: London: Arnold. ISBN 0-340-56186-6 (v.1).

Sampson, Geoffrey. *Writing Systems: A Linguistic Introduction.* Stanford, CA: Stanford University Press, 1985. ISBN 0-8047-1254-9.

Also published: London: Hutchinson. ISBN 0-09-156980-X; 0-09-173051-1 (pbk.).

Sekai moji jiten / Kono, Rokuro; Chino, Eiichi; Nishida, Tatsuo. Tokyo: Sanseido, 2001. (*Gengogaku daijiten = The Sanseido Encyclopaedia of Linguistics*, 7). ISBN 4-385-15177-6.

Senner, Wayne M. *The Origins of Writing.* Lincoln: University of Nebraska Press, 1989. ISBN 0-8032-4202-6; 0-8032-9167-1 (pbk.).

Shepherd, Walter. *Shepherd's Glossary of Graphic Signs and Symbols.* Compiled and classified for ready reference by Walter Shepherd. New York: Dover, 1971. ISBN 0-486-20700-5.

Also published: London: Dent. ISBN 0-460-03818-4.

Shinmura, Izuru. *Kojien* / Shinmura Izuru hen. Dai 4-han. Tokyo: Iwanami Shoten, 1991.

Stevens, John. *Sacred Calligraphy of the East.* 3rd ed., rev. and expanded. Boston: Shambala, 1995. ISBN 1-570-62122-5.

Suarez, Jorge A. *The Mesoamerican Indian Languages.* Cambridge: Cambridge University Press, 1983. ISBN 0-521-22834-4; 0-521-29669-2 (pbk.).

von Ostermann, Georg F. *Manual of Foreign Languages.* 4th ed., revised and enlarged. New York: Central Book Company, 1952.

Wemyss, Stanley. *The Languages of the World, Ancient and Modern: The Alphabets, Ideographs, and Other Written Characters of the World in Sound and Symbol.* Philadelphia: 1950.

The World's Writing Systems. Edited by Peter T. Daniels and William Bright. New York: Oxford University Press, 1996. ISBN 0-19-507993-0.

Indices

I.1 Unicode Names Index

The Unicode Names index contains three types of entries.

- Formal character names—all uppercase
- Alternative character names (aliases)—all lowercase
- Character group names—mixed case (titlecase)

Formal character names are unmodified from the character names lists, although the name strings may be indexed by different words in the names. Alternative character names and character group names are occasionally modified slightly to make them understandable out of context (for example, from "Hangul" to "Korean Hangul").

Not every character is indexed. Large groups of similar characters, including CJK ideographs, Korean Hangul syllables, and compatibility characters, are indexed by their character group names, such as block names, subblocks, alphabet names, relevant standards, or group summaries (for example, "Roman Numerals").

I.2 General Index

The General Index covers the contents of this book, excluding the annexes. To find topics in the Unicode Standard Annexes, Unicode Technical Standards, and Unicode Technical Reports, refer to their 5.0.0 versions on the CD-ROM accompanying this book, or use the search feature on the Unicode Web site for the latest versions.

For definitions of terms used in this book, see the *Glossary.* To find the code points for specific characters or the code ranges for particular scripts, see *Section I.1, Unicode Names Index.*

A

B

C

D

E

H

I

J

K

L

M

N

O

P

Q

R

S

V

Unicode Standard Annex #9

The Bidirectional Algorithm

Summary

This annex describes specifications for the positioning of characters flowing from right to left, such as Arabic or Hebrew.

Contents

X1 Introduction

The Unicode Standard prescribes a *memory* representation order known as logical order. When text is presented in horizontal lines, most scripts display characters from left to right. However, there are several scripts (such as Arabic or Hebrew) where the natural ordering of horizontal text in display is from right to left. If all of the text has the same horizontal direction, then the ordering of the display text is unambiguous. However, when bidirectional text (a mixture of left-to-right and right-to-left horizontal text) is present, some ambiguities can arise in determining the ordering of the displayed characters.

This annex describes the algorithm used to determine the directionality for bidirectional Unicode text. The algorithm extends the implicit model currently employed by a number of existing implementations and adds explicit format codes for special circumstances. In most cases, there is no need to include additional information with the text to obtain correct display ordering.

However, in the case of bidirectional text, there are circumstances where an implicit bidirectional ordering is not sufficient to produce comprehensible text. To deal with these cases, a minimal set of directional formatting codes is defined to control the ordering of characters when rendered. This allows exact control of the display ordering for legible interchange and ensures that plain text used for simple items like filenames or labels can always be correctly ordered for display.

The directional formatting codes are used *only* to influence the display ordering of text. In all other respects they should be ignored—they have no effect on the comparison of text or on word breaks, parsing, or numeric analysis.

When working with bidirectional text, the characters are still interpreted in logical order—only the display is affected. The display ordering of bidirectional text depends on the directional properties of the characters in the text.

X2 Directional Formatting Codes

Two types of explicit codes are used to modify the standard implicit Unicode Bidirectional Algorithm. In addition, there are implicit ordering codes, the *right-to-left* and *left-to-right* marks. All of these codes are limited to the current paragraph; thus their effects are terminated by a *paragraph separator*. The directional types left-to-right and right-to-left are called *strong types*, and characters of those types are called strong directional characters. The directional types associated with numbers are called *weak types*, and characters of those types are called weak directional characters.

Although the term *embedding* is used for some explicit codes, the text within the scope of the codes is not independent of the surrounding text. Characters within an embedding can affect the ordering of characters outside, and vice versa. The algorithm is designed so that the use of explicit codes can be equivalently represented by out-of-line information, such as stylesheet information. However, any alternative representation will be defined by reference to the behavior of the explicit codes in this algorithm.

X2.1 Explicit Directional Embedding

The following codes signal that a piece of text is to be treated as embedded. For example, an English quotation in the middle of an Arabic sentence could be marked as being embedded left-to-right text. If there were a Hebrew phrase in the middle of the English quotation, the that phrase could be marked as being embedded right-to-left. These codes allow for nested embeddings.

RLE	Right-to-Left Embedding	Treat the following text as embedded right-to-left.
LRE	Left-to-Right Embedding	Treat the following text as embedded left-to-right.

The precise meaning of these codes will be made clear in the discussion of the algorithm. The effect of right-left line direction, for example, can be accomplished by simply embedding the text with RLE...PDF.

X2.2 Explicit Directional Overrides

The following codes allow the bidirectional character types to be overridden when required for special cases, such as for part numbers. These codes allow for nested directional overrides.

RLO	Right-to-Left Override	Force following characters to be treated as strong right-to-left characters.
LRO	Left-to-Right Override	Force following characters to be treated as strong left-to-right characters.

The precise meaning of these codes will be made clear in the discussion of the algorithm. The right-to-left override, for example, can be used to force a part number made of mixed English, digits and Hebrew letters to be written from right to left.

X2.3 Terminating Explicit Directional Code

The following code terminates the effects of the last explicit code (either embedding or override) and restores the bidirectional state to what it was before that code was encountered.

PDF	Pop Directional Format	Restore the bidirectional state to what it was before the last LRE, RLE, RLO, or LRO.

X2.4 Implicit Directional Marks

These characters are very light-weight codes. They act exactly like right-to-left or left-to-right characters, except that they do not display or have any other semantic effect. Their use is more convenient than using explicit embeddings or overrides because their scope is much more local.

RLM	Right-to-Left Mark	Right-to-left zero-width character
LRM	Left-to-Right Mark	Left-to-right zero-width character

There is no special mention of the implicit directional marks in the following algorithm. That is because their effect on bidirectional ordering is exactly the same as a corresponding strong directional character; the only difference is that they do not appear in the display.

X3 Basic Display Algorithm

The Bidirectional Algorithm takes a stream of text as input and proceeds in three main phases:

- Separation of the input text into paragraphs. The rest of the algorithm affects only the text between paragraph separators.
- Resolution of the embedding levels of the text. In this phase, the directional character types, plus the explicit format codes, are used to produce resolved embedding levels.
- Reordering the text for display on a line-by-line basis using the resolved embedding levels, once the text has been broken into lines.

The algorithm reorders text only within a paragraph; characters in one paragraph have no effect on characters in a different paragraph. Paragraphs are divided by the Paragraph Separator or appropriate Newline Function (for guidelines on the handling of CR, LF, and CRLF, see *Section X4.4, Directionality*, and *Section 5.8, Newline Guidelines* of [Unicode]). Paragraphs may also be determined by higher-level protocols: for example, the text in two different cells of a table will be in different paragraphs.

Combining characters always attach to the preceding base character in the memory representation. Even after reordering for display and performing character shaping, the glyph representing a combining character will attach to the glyph representing its base character in memory. Depending on the line orientation and the placement direction of base letterform glyphs, it may, for example, attach to the glyph on the left, or on the right, or above.

This annex uses the numbering conventions for normative definitions and rules in *Table 1*.

Table 1. Normative Definitions and Rules

Numbering	Section
BDn	Definitions
Pn	Paragraph levels
Xn	Explicit levels and directions
Wn	Weak types
Nn	Neutral types
In	Implicit levels
Ln	Resolved levels

X3.1 Definitions

BD1. The *bidirectional characters types* are values assigned to each Unicode character, including unassigned characters.

BD2. *Embedding levels* are numbers that indicate how deeply the text is nested, and the default direction of text on that level. The minimum embedding level of text is zero, and the maximum explicit depth is level 61.

> Embedding levels are explicitly set by both override format codes and by embedding format codes; higher numbers mean the text is more deeply nested. The reason for having a limitation is to provide a precise stack limit for implementations to guarantee the same results. Sixty-one levels is far more than sufficient for ordering, even with mechanically generated formatting; the display becomes rather muddied with more than a small number of embeddings.

BD3. The default direction of the current embedding level (for the character in question) is called the *embedding direction*. It is **L** if the embedding level is even, and **R** if the embedding level is odd.

> For example, in a particular piece of text, Level 0 is plain English text. Level 1 is plain Arabic text, possibly embedded within English level 0 text. Level 2 is English text, possibly embedded within Arabic level 1 text, and so on. Unless their direction is overridden, English text and numbers will always be an even level; Arabic text (excluding numbers) will always be an odd level. The exact meaning of the embedding level will become clear when the reordering algorithm is discussed, but the following provides an example of how the algorithm works.

BD4. The *paragraph embedding level* is the embedding level that determines the default bidirectional orientation of the text in that paragraph.

BD5. The direction of the paragraph embedding level is called the *paragraph direction.*

- In some contexts the paragraph direction is also known as the *base direction.*

BD6. The *directional override status* determines whether the bidirectional type of characters is to be reset with explicit directional controls. This status has three states, as shown in *Table 2.*

Table 2. Directional Override Status

Status	Interpretation
Neutral	No override is currently active
Right-to-left	Characters are to be reset to **R**
Left-to-right	Characters are to be reset to **L**

BD7. A *level run* is a maximal substring of characters that have the same embedding level. It is maximal in that no character immediately before or after the substring has the same level (a level run is also known as a *directional run).*

Example

In this and the following examples, case is used to indicate different implicit character types for those unfamiliar with right-to-left letters. Uppercase letters stand for right-to-left characters (such as Arabic or Hebrew), and lowercase letters stand for left-to-right characters (such as

English or Russian).

Memory: `car is THE CAR in arabic`

Character types: `LLL-LL-RRR-RRR-LL-LLLLLL`

Resolved levels: `000000001111111000000000`

Notice that the neutral character (space) between THE and CAR gets the level of the surrounding characters. The level of the neutral characters can also be changed by inserting appropriate directional marks around neutral characters. These marks have no other effects.

Table 3 lists additional abbreviations used in the examples and internal character types used in the algorithm.

Table 3. Abbreviations for Examples and Internal Types

Symbol	Description
N	Neutral or Separator (B, S, WS, ON)
e	The text ordering type (L or R) that matches the embedding level direction (even or odd)
sor	The text ordering type (L or R) assigned to the position before a level run.
eor	The text ordering type (L or R) assigned to the position after a level run.

X3.2 Bidirectional Character Types

The normative bidirectional character types for each character are specified in the Unicode Character Database [UCD] and are summarized in *Table 4*. This is a summary only: there are exceptions to the general scope. For example, certain characters such as U+0CBF KANNADA VOWEL SIGN I are given Type L (instead of NSM) to preserve canonical equivalence.

- The term European digits is used to refer to decimal forms common in Europe and elsewhere, and Arabic-Indic digits to refer to the native Arabic forms. (See *Section 8.2, Arabic* of [Unicode], for more details on naming digits.)
- Unassigned characters are given strong types in the algorithm. This is an explicit exception to the general Unicode conformance requirements with respect to unassigned characters. As characters become assigned in the future, these bidirectional types may change. For assignments to character types, see DerivedBidiClass.txt [DerivedBIDI] in the [UCD].
- Private-use characters can be assigned different values by a conformant implementation.
- For the purpose of the Bidirectional Algorithm, inline objects (such as graphics) are treated as if they are an U+FFFC OBJECT REPLACEMENT CHARACTER.
- As of Unicode 4.0, the Bidirectional Character Types of a few Indic characters were altered so that the Bidirectional Algorithm preserves canonical equivalence. That is, two canonically equivalent strings will result in equivalent ordering after applying the algorithm. This invariant will be maintained in the future.

  Note: The Bidirectional Algorithm does *not* preserve compatibility equivalence.

Table 4. Bidirectional Character Types

Category	Type	Description	General Scope
Strong	**L**	Left-to-Right	LRM, most alphabetic, syllabic, Han ideographs, non-European or non-Arabic digits, ...
	LRE	Left-to-Right Embedding	LRE
	LRO	Left-to-Right Override	LRO
	R	Right-to-Left	RLM, Hebrew alphabet, and related punctuation
	AL	Right-to-Left Arabic	Arabic, Thaana, and Syriac alphabets, most punctuation specific to those scripts, ...
	RLE	Right-to-Left Embedding	RLE
	RLO	Right-to-Left Override	RLO
Weak	**PDF**	Pop Directional Format	PDF
	EN	European Number	European digits, Eastern Arabic-Indic digits, ...
	ES	European Number Separator	PLUS SIGN, MINUS SIGN
	ET	European Number Terminator	DEGREE SIGN, currency symbols, ...
	AN	Arabic Number	Arabic-Indic digits, Arabic decimal and thousands separators, ...
	CS	Common Number Separator	COLON, COMMA, FULL STOP (*period*), NO-BREAK SPACE, ...
	NSM	Nonspacing Mark	Characters marked Mn (Nonspacing_Mark) and Me (Enclosing_Mark) in the Unicode Character Database
	BN	Boundary Neutral	Most formatting and control characters, other than those explicitly given types above
Neutral	**B**	Paragraph Separator	PARAGRAPH SEPARATOR, appropriate Newline Functions, higher-level protocol paragraph determination
	S	Segment Separator	*Tab*
	WS	Whitespace	SPACE, FIGURE SPACE, LINE SEPARATOR, FORM FEED, General Punctuation spaces, ...
	ON	Other Neutrals	All other characters, including OBJECT REPLACEMENT CHARACTER

X3.3 Resolving Embedding Levels

The body of the Bidirectional Algorithm uses character types and explicit codes to produce a list of resolved levels. This resolution process consists of five steps: (1) determining the paragraph level; (2) determining explicit embedding levels and directions; (3) resolving weak types; (4) resolving neutral types; and (5) resolving implicit embedding levels.

X3.3.1 The Paragraph Level

P1. Split the text into separate paragraphs. A paragraph separator is kept with the previous paragraph. Within each paragraph, apply all the other rules of this algorithm.

P2. In each paragraph, find the first character of type L, AL, or R.

Because paragraph separators delimit text in this algorithm, this will generally be the first strong character after a paragraph separator or at the very beginning of the text. Note that the characters of type LRE, LRO, RLE, or RLO are ignored in this rule. This is because typically they are used to indicate that the embedded text is the *opposite* direction than the paragraph level.

P3. If a character is found in P2 and it is of type AL or R, then set the paragraph embedding level to one; otherwise, set it to zero.

Whenever a higher-level protocol specifies the paragraph level, rules P2 and P3 do not apply.

X3.3.2 Explicit Levels and Directions

All explicit embedding levels are determined from the embedding and override codes, by applying the explicit level rules X1 through X9. These rules are applied as part of the same logical pass over the input.

Explicit Embeddings

X1. Begin by setting the current embedding level to the paragraph embedding level. Set the directional override status to neutral. Process each character iteratively, applying rules X2 through X9. Only embedding levels from 0 to 61 are valid in this phase.

In the resolution of levels in rules I1 and I2, the maximum embedding level of 62 can be reached.

X2. With each RLE, compute the least greater ***odd*** *embedding level.*

> *a. If this new level would be valid, then this embedding code is valid. Remember (push) the current embedding level and override status. Reset the current level to this new level, and reset the override status to* ***neutral****.*
>
> *b. If the new level would not be valid, then this code is invalid. Do not change the current level or override status.*

For example, level 0 → 1; levels 1, 2 → 3; levels 3, 4 → 5; ...59, 60 → 61; above 60, no change (do not change levels with RLE if the new level would be invalid).

X3. With each LRE, compute the least greater ***even*** *embedding level.*

a. If this new level would be valid, then this embedding code is valid. Remember (push) the current embedding level and override status. Reset the current level to this new level, and reset the override status to ***neutral****.*

b. If the new level would not be valid, then this code is invalid. Do not change the current level or override status.

For example, levels 0, 1 → 2; levels 2, 3 → 4; levels 4, 5 → 6; ...58, 59 → 60; above 59, no change (do not change levels with LRE if the new level would be invalid).

Explicit Overrides

An explicit directional override sets the embedding level in the same way the explicit embedding codes do, but also changes the directional character type of affected characters to the override direction.

X4. With each RLO, compute the least greater ***odd*** *embedding level.*

a. If this new level would be valid, then this embedding code is valid. Remember (push) the current embedding level and override status. Reset the current level to this new level, and reset the override status to ***right-to-left****.*

b. If the new level would not be valid, then this code is invalid. Do not change the current level or override status.

X5. With each LRO, compute the least greater ***even*** *embedding level.*

a. If this new level would be valid, then this embedding code is valid. Remember (push) the current embedding level and override status. Reset the current level to this new level, and reset the override status to ***left-to-right****.*

b. If the new level would not be valid, then this code is invalid. Do not change the current level or override status.

X6. For all types besides RLE, LRE, RLO, LRO, and PDF:

a. Set the level of the current character to the current embedding level.

b. Whenever the directional override status is not neutral, reset the current character type to the directional override status.

If the directional override status is neutral, then characters retain their normal types: Arabic characters stay AL, Latin characters stay L, neutrals stay N, and so on. If the directional override status is R, then characters become R. If the directional override status is L, then characters become L.

Terminating Embeddings and Overrides

There is a single code to terminate the scope of the current explicit code, whether an embedding or a directional override. All codes and pushed states are completely popped at the end of paragraphs.

X7. With each PDF, determine the matching embedding or override code. If there was a valid matching code, restore (pop) the last remembered (pushed) embedding level and directional override.

X8. All explicit directional embeddings and overrides are completely terminated at the end of each paragraph. Paragraph separators are **not** *included in the embedding.*

X9. Remove all RLE, LRE, RLO, LRO, PDF, and BN codes.

- Note that an implementation does not have to actually remove the codes; it just has to behave as though the codes were not present for the remainder of the algorithm. Conformance does not require any particular placement of these codes as long as all other characters are ordered correctly.

  See *Section X5, Implementation Notes*, for information on implementing the algorithm without removing the formatting codes.

- The *zero width joiner* and *non-joiner* affect the shaping of the adjacent characters—those that are adjacent in the original backing-store order, even though those characters may end up being rearranged to be non-adjacent by the Bidirectional Algorithm. For more information, see *Section X5.3, Joiners.*

*X10. The remaining rules are applied to each run of characters at the same level. For each run, determine the start-of-level-run (**sor**) and end-of-level-run (**eor**) type, either L or R. This depends on the higher of the two levels on either side of the boundary (at the start or end of the paragraph, the level of the "other" run is the base embedding level). If the higher level is odd, the type is R; otherwise, it is L.*

For example:

```
Levels:  0   0   0   1   1   1   2

Runs:   <--- 1 ---> <--- 2 ---> <3>
```

Run 1 is at level 0, *sor* is L, *eor* is R.
Run 2 is at level 1, *sor* is R, *eor* is L.
Run 3 is at level 2, *sor* is L, *eor* is L.

For two adjacent runs, the *eor* of the first run is the same as the *sor* of the second.

X3.3.3 Resolving Weak Types

Weak types are now resolved one level run at a time. At level run boundaries where the type of the character on the other side of the boundary is required, the type assigned to *sor* or *eor* is used.

Nonspacing marks are now resolved based on the previous characters.

W1. Examine each nonspacing mark (NSM) in the level run, and change the type of the NSM to the type of the previous character. If the NSM is at the start of the level run, it will get the type of **sor**.

Assume in this example that *sor* is R:

```
AL   NSM NSM → AL   AL   AL
sor NSM      → sor R
```

The text is next parsed for numbers. This pass will change the directional types European Number Separator, European Number Terminator, and Common Number Separator to be European Number text, Arabic Number text, or Other Neutral text. The text to be scanned may have already had its type altered by directional overrides. If so, then it will not parse as numeric.

W2. Search backward from each instance of a European number until the first strong type (R, L, AL, or ***sor****) is found. If an AL is found, change the type of the European number to Arabic number.*

```
AL EN     → AL AN
AL N EN   → AL N AN
sor N EN  → sor N EN
L N EN    → L N EN
R N EN    → R N EN
```

W3. Change all ALs to R.

W4. A single European separator between two European numbers changes to a European number. A single common separator between two numbers of the same type changes to that type.

```
EN ES EN → EN EN EN
EN CS EN → EN EN EN
AN CS AN → AN AN AN
```

W5. A sequence of European terminators adjacent to European numbers changes to all European numbers.

```
ET ET EN → EN EN EN
EN ET ET → EN EN EN
AN ET EN → AN EN EN
```

W6. Otherwise, separators and terminators change to Other Neutral.

```
AN ET     → AN ON
L  ES EN → L  ON EN
EN CS AN → EN ON AN
ET AN     → ON AN
```

W7. Search backward from each instance of a European number until the first strong type (R, L, or ***sor****) is found. If an L is found, then change the type of the European number to L.*

```
L  N EN => L  N  L
R  N EN => R  N  EN
```

X3.3.4 Resolving Neutral Types

Neutral types are now resolved one level run at a time. At level run boundaries where the type of the character on the other side of the boundary is required, the type assigned to *sor* or *eor* is used.

The next phase resolves the direction of the neutrals. The results of this phase are that all neutrals become either **R** or **L**. Generally, neutrals take on the direction of the surrounding text. In case of a conflict, they take on the embedding direction.

*N1. A sequence of neutrals takes the direction of the surrounding strong text if the text on both sides has the same direction. European and Arabic numbers act as if they were R in terms of their influence on neutrals. Start-of-level-run (**sor**) and end-of-level-run (**eor**) are used at level run boundaries.*

```
R  N  R  → R  R  R
L  N  L  → L  L  L
R  N  AN → R  R  AN
AN N  R  → AN R  R
R  N  EN → R  R  EN
EN N  R  → EN R  R
```

Note that any AN or EN remaining after W7 will be in an right-to-left context.

N2. Any remaining neutrals take the embedding direction.

```
N → e
```

Assume in this example that *eor* is L and *sor* is R. Then an application of N1 and N2 yields the following:

```
L   N eor → L   L eor
R   N eor → R   e eor
sor N L   → sor e L
sor N R   → sor R R
```

Examples. A list of numbers separated by neutrals and embedded in a directional run will come out in the run's order.

```
Storage:    he said "THE VALUES ARE 123, 456, 789, OK".
Display:    he said "KO ,789 ,456 ,123 ERA SEULAV EHT".
```

In this case, both the comma and the space between the numbers take on the direction of the surrounding text (uppercase = right-to-left), ignoring the numbers. The commas are not considered part of the number because they are not surrounded on both sides (see *Section X3.3.3, Resolving Weak Types*). However, if there is an adjacent left-to-right sequence, then European numbers will adopt that direction:

```
Storage:    he said "IT IS A bmw 500, OK."
Display:    he said ".KO ,bmw 500 A SI TI"
```

X3.3.5 Resolving Implicit Levels

In the final phase, the embedding level of text may be increased, based on the resolved character type. Right-to-left text will always end up with an odd level, and left-to-right and numeric text will always end up with an even level. In addition, numeric text will always end up with a higher level than the paragraph level. (Note that it is possible for text to end up at levels higher than 61 as a result of this process.) This results in the following rules:

I1. For all characters with an even (left-to-right) embedding direction, those of type R go up one level and those of type AN or EN go up two levels.

I2. For all characters with an odd (right-to-left) embedding direction, those of type L, EN or AN go up one level.

Table 5 summarizes the results of the implicit algorithm.

Table 5. Resolving Implicit Levels

Type	Embedding Level	
	Even	**Odd**
L	EL	EL+1
R	EL+1	EL
AN	EL+2	EL+1
EN	EL+2	EL+1

X3.4 Reordering Resolved Levels

The following rules describe the logical process of finding the correct display order. As opposed to resolution phases, these rules act on a per-line basis *and are applied **after** any line wrapping is applied to the paragraph.*

Logically there are the following steps:

- The levels of the text are determined according to the previous rules.
- The characters are shaped into glyphs according to their context *(taking the embedding levels into account for mirroring).*
- The accumulated widths of those glyphs *(in logical order)* are used to determine line breaks.
- For each line, rules L1–L4 are used to reorder the characters on that line.
- The glyphs corresponding to the characters on the line are displayed in that order.

L1. On each line, reset the embedding level of the following characters to the paragraph embedding level:

1. *Segment separators,*
2. *Paragraph separators,*

3. *Any sequence of whitespace characters preceding a segment separator or paragraph separator, and*
4. *Any sequence of white space characters at the end of the line.*

- The types of characters used here are the *original* types, not those modified by the previous phase.
- Because a PARAGRAPH SEPARATOR breaks lines, there will be at most one per line, at the end of that line.

In combination with the following rule, this means that trailing whitespace will appear at the visual end of the line (in the paragraph direction). Tabulation will always have a consistent direction within a paragraph.

L2. From the highest level found in the text to the lowest odd level on each line, including intermediate levels not actually present in the text, reverse any contiguous sequence of characters that are at that level or higher.

This reverses a progressively larger series of substrings. The following four examples illustrate this. In these examples, the paragraph embedding level for the first and third examples is assumed to be 0 (left-to-right direction), and for the second and fourth examples is assumed to be 1 (right-to-left direction).

Example 1 (embedding level = 0)

Memory: car means CAR.

Resolved levels: 00000000001110

Reverse level 1: car means RAC.

Example 2 (embedding level = 1)

Memory: car MEANS CAR.

Resolved levels: 22211111111111

Reverse level 2: rac MEANS CAR.

Reverse levels 1-2: .RAC SNAEM car

Example 3 (embedding level = 0)

Memory: he said "car MEANS CAR."

Resolved levels: 000000000222111111111100

Reverse level 2: he said "rac MEANS CAR."

Reverse levels 1-2: he said "RAC SNAEM car."

Example 4 (embedding level = 1)

Memory: DID YOU SAY 'he said "car MEANS CAR"'?

Resolved levels: 11111111111112222222224443333333333211

Reverse level 4: DID YOU SAY 'he said "rac MEANS CAR"'?

Reverse levels 3-4: DID YOU SAY 'he said "RAC SNAEM car"'?

Reverse levels 2-4: `DID YOU SAY '"rac MEANS CAR" dias eh'?`

Reverse levels 1-4: `?'he said "RAC SNAEM car"' YAS UOY DID`

L3. Combining marks applied to a right-to-left base character will at this point precede their base character. If the rendering engine expects them to follow the base characters in the final display process, then the ordering of the marks and the base character must be reversed.

Many font designers provide default metrics for combining marks that support rendering by simple overhang. Because of the reordering for right-to-left characters, it is common practice to make the glyphs for most combining characters overhang to the left (thus assuming the characters will be applied to left-to-right base characters) and make the glyphs for combining characters in right-to-left scripts overhang to the right (thus assuming that the characters will be applied to right-to-left base characters). With such fonts, the display ordering of the marks and base glyphs may need to be adjusted when combining marks are applied to "unmatching" base characters. See *Section 5.13, Rendering Nonspacing Marks* of [Unicode], for more information.

L4. A character is depicted by a mirrored glyph if and only if (a) the resolved directionality of that character is R, and (b) the Bidi_Mirrored property value of that character is true.

- *The Bidi_Mirrored property is defined by Section 4.7, Bidi Mirrored—Normative of [Unicode]; the property values are specified in [UCD].*
- *This rule can be overridden in certain cases; see HL6.*

For example, U+0028 LEFT PARENTHESIS—which is interpreted in the Unicode Standard as an opening parenthesis—appears as "(" when its resolved level is even, and as the mirrored glyph ")" when its resolved level is odd. Note that for backward compatibility the characters U+FD3E (﴾) ORNATE LEFT PARENTHESIS and U+FD3F (﴿) ORNATE RIGHT PARENTHESIS are not mirrored.

X3.5 Shaping

Cursively connected scripts, such as Arabic or Syriac, require the selection of positional character shapes that depend on adjacent characters (see *Section 8.2, Arabic* of [Unicode]). Shaping is logically applied *after* the Bidirectional Algorithm is used and is limited to characters within the same directional run. Consider the following example string of Arabic characters, which is represented in memory as characters 1, 2, 3, and 4, and where the first two characters are overridden to be LTR. To show both paragraph directions, the next two are embedded, but with the normal RTL direction.

1	2	3	4
ج 062C JEEM	ع 0639 AIN	ل 0644 LAM	م 0645 MEEM
L	L	R	R

One can use embedding codes to achieve this effect in plain text or use markup in HTML, as in the examples below. (The **bold** text would be for the right-to-left paragraph direction.)

- LRM/**RLM** LRO *JEEM AIN* PDF RLO *LAM MEEM* PDF
- <p dir="ltr"/"**rtl**">LRO *JEEM AIN* PDF RLO *LAM MEEM* PDF</p>
- <p dir="ltr"/"**rtl**"><bdo dir="ltr">*JEEM AIN*</bdo>
  <bdo dir="rtl">*LAM MEEM*</bdo></p>

The resulting shapes will be the following, according to the paragraph direction:

Left-Right Paragraph				**Right-Left Paragraph**			
1	**2**	**4**	**3**	**4**	**3**	**1**	**2**
ج	عـ	م	لـ	م	لـ	ج	عـ
JEEM-F	AIN-I	MEEM-F	LAM-I	MEEM-F	LAM-I	JEEM-F	AIN-I

X3.5.1 Shaping and Line Breaking

The process of breaking a paragraph into one or more lines that fit within particular bounds is outside the scope of the Bidirectional Algorithm. Where character shaping is involved, the width calculations must be based on the shaped glyphs.

Note that the *soft-hyphen* (SHY) works in cursively connected scripts as it does in other scripts. That is, it indicates a point where the line could be broken in the middle of a word. If the rendering system breaks at that point, the display—including shaping—should be what is appropriate for the given language. For more information on this and other line breaking issues, see Unicode Standard Annex #14, "Line Breaking Properties" [UAX14].

X4 Bidirectional Conformance

A process that claims conformance to this specification shall satisfy the the following clauses:

UAX9-C1. *In the absence of a permissible higher-level protocol, a process that renders text shall display all visible representations of characters (excluding format characters) in the order described by Section X3, Basic Display Algorithm, of this annex. In particular, this includes definitions BD1–BD7 and steps P1–P3, X1–X10, W1–W7, N1–N2, I1–I2, and L1–L4.*

- As is the case for all other Unicode algorithms, this is a *logical* description—particular implementations can have more efficient mechanisms as long as they produce the same results. See C18 in *Chapter 3, Conformance* of [Unicode], and the notes following.
- The Bidirectional Algorithm specifies part of the intrinsic semantics of right-to-left characters and is thus required for conformance to the Unicode Standard where any such characters are displayed.

UAX9-C2. *The only permissible higher-level protocols are those listed in Section X4.3, Higher-Level Protocols. They are HL1, HL2, HL3, HL4, HL5, and HL6.*

Use of higher-level protocols is discouraged, because it introduces interchange problems and can lead to security problems. For more information, see Unicode Technical Report #36, "Unicode Security Considerations" [UTR36].

X4.1 Boundary Neutrals

The goal in marking a format or control character as BN is that it have no effect on the rest of the algorithm. (ZWJ and ZWNJ are exceptions; see X9). Because conformance does not require the precise ordering of format characters with respect to others, implementations can handle them in different ways as long as they preserve the ordering of the other characters.

X4.2 Explicit Formatting Codes

As with any Unicode characters, systems do not have to support any particular explicit directional formatting code (although it is not generally useful to include a terminating code without including the initiator). Generally, conforming systems will fall into three classes:

- *No bidirectional formatting.* This implies that the system does not visually interpret characters from right-to-left scripts.
- *Implicit bidirectionality.* The implicit Bidirectional Algorithm and the directional marks RLM and LRM are supported.
- *Full bidirectionality.* The implicit Bidirectional Algorithm, the implicit directional marks, and the explicit directional embedding codes are supported: RLM, LRM, LRE, RLE, LRO, RLO, PDF.

X4.3 Higher-Level Protocols

The following clauses are the only permissible ways for systems to apply higher-level protocols to the ordering of bidirectional text. Some of the clauses apply to *segments* of structured text. This refers to the situation where text is interpreted as being structured, whether with explicit markup such as XML or HTML, or internally structured such as in a word processor or spreadsheet. In such a case, a segment is span of text that is distinguished in some way by the structure.

HL1. Override P3, and set the paragraph embedding level explicitly.

- A higher-level protocol may set the paragraph level explicitly and ignore P3. This can be done on the basis of the context, such as on a table cell, paragraph, document, or system level.

HL2. Override W2, and set EN or AN explicitly.

- A higher-level process may reset characters of type EN to AN, or vice versa, and ignore W2. For example, style sheet or markup information can be used within a span of text to override the setting of EN text to be always be AN, or vice versa.

HL3. Emulate directional overrides or embedding codes.

- A higher-level protocol can impose a directional override or embedding on a segment of structured text. The behavior must always be defined by reference to what would happen if the equivalent explicit codes as defined in the algorithm were inserted into the text. For example, a style sheet or markup can set the embedding level on a span of text.

HL4. Apply the Bidirectional Algorithm to segments.

- The Bidirectional Algorithm can be applied independently to one or more segments of structured text. For example, when displaying a document consisting of textual data and visible markup in an editor, a higher-level process can handle syntactic elements in the markup separately from the textual data.

HL5. Provide artificial context.

- Text can be processed by the Bidirectional Algorithm as if it were preceded by a character of a given type and/or followed by a character of a given type. This allows a piece of text that is extracted from a longer sequence of text to behave as it did in the larger context.

HL6. Additional mirroring.

- Characters with a resolved directionality of R that do not have the Bidi_Mirrored property can also be depicted by a mirrored glyph in specialized contexts. Such contexts include, but are not limited to, historic scripts and associated punctuation, private-use characters, and characters in mathematical expressions. (See *Section X6, Mirroring.*)

Clauses HL1 and HL3 are not logically necessary; they are covered by applications of clauses HL4 and HL5. However, they are included for clarity because they are more common operations.

As an example of the application of HL4, suppose an XML document contains the following fragment. (Note: This is a simplified example for illustration: element names, attribute names, and attribute values could all be involved.)

```
ARABICenglishARABIC<e1 type='ab'>ARABICenglish<e2 type='cd'>english
```

This can be analyzed as being five different segments:

a. `ARABICenglishARABIC`

b. `<e1 type='ab'>`

c. `ARABICenglish`

d. `<e2 type='cd'>`

e. `english`

To make the XML file readable as source text, the display in an editor could order these elements all in a uniform direction (for example, all left-to-right) and apply the Bidirectional Algorithm to each field separately. It could also choose to order the element names, attribute names, and attribute values uniformly in the same direction (for example, all left-to-right). For final display, the markup could be ignored, allowing all of the text (segments a, c, and e) to be reordered together.

When text using a higher-level protocol is to be converted to Unicode plain text, for consistent appearance formatting codes should be inserted to ensure that the order matches that of the higher-level protocol.

X5 Implementation Notes

X5.1 Reference Code

There are two versions of BIDI reference code available. Both have been tested to produce identical results. One version is written in Java, and the other is written in C++. The Java version is designed to closely follow the steps of the algorithm as described below. The C++ code is designed to show one of the optimization methods that can be applied to the algorithm, using a state table for one phase.

One of the most effective optimizations is to first test for right-to-left characters and not invoke the Bidirectional Algorithm unless they are present.

There are two directories containing source code for reference implementations: BidiReferenceJava and BidiReferenceCpp [Code9]. Implementers are encouraged to use this resource to test their implementations.

X5.2 Retaining Format Codes

Some implementations may wish to retain the format codes when running the algorithm. The following provides a summary of how this may be done. Note that this summary is an informative implementation guideline; it should provide the same results as the explicit algorithm above, but in case of any deviation the explicit algorithm is the normative statement for conformance.

- In rule X9, instead of removing the format codes, assign the embedding level to each embedding character, and turn it into BN.
- In rule X10, assign L or R to the last of a sequence of adjacent BNs according to the *eor* / *sor*, and set the level to the higher of the two levels.
- In rule W1, search backward from each NSM to the first character in the level run whose type is not BN, and set the NSM to its type. If the NSM is the first non-BN character, it will get the type of *sor*.

- In rule W4, scan past BN types that are adjacent to ES or CS.
- In rule W5, change all appropriate sequences of ET and BN, not just ET.
- In rule W6, change all BN types adjacent to ET, ES, or CS to ON as well.
- In rule W7, scan past BN.
- In rules N1 and N2, treat BNs adjoining neutrals same as those neutrals.
- In rules I1 and I2, ignore BN.
- In rule L1, include format codes and BN together with whitespace characters in the sequences whose level gets reset before a separator or line break. Resolve any LRE, RLE, LRO, RLO, PDF, or BN to the level of the preceding character if there is one, and otherwise to the base level.

Implementations that display visible representations of format characters will want to adjust this process to position the format characters optimally for editing.

X5.3 Joiners

As described under X9, the *zero width joiner* and *non-joiner* affect the shaping of the adjacent characters—those that are adjacent in the original backing-store order—even though those characters may end up being rearranged to be non-adjacent by the Bidirectional Algorithm. To determine the joining behavior of a particular character after applying the Bidirectional Algorithm, there are two main strategies:

- When shaping, an implementation can refer back to the original backing store to see if there were adjacent ZWNJ or ZWJ characters.
- Alternatively, the implementation can replace ZWJ and ZWNJ by an out-of-band character property associated with those adjacent characters, so that the information does not interfere with the Bidirectional Algorithm and the information is preserved across rearrangement of those characters. Once the Bidirectional Algorithm has been applied, that out-of-band information can then be used for proper shaping.

X5.4 Vertical Text

In the case of vertical line orientation, the Bidirectional Algorithm is still used to determine the levels of the text. However, these levels are not used to reorder the text, because the characters are usually ordered uniformly from top to bottom. Instead, the levels are used to determine the rotation of the text. Sometimes vertical lines follow a vertical baseline in which each character is oriented as normal (with no rotation), with characters ordered from top to bottom whether they are Hebrew, numbers, or Latin. When setting text using the Arabic script in vertical lines, it is more common to employ a horizontal baseline that is rotated by 90° counterclockwise so that the characters are ordered from top to bottom. Latin text and numbers may be rotated 90° clockwise so that the characters are also ordered from top to bottom.

The Bidirectional Algorithm is used when some characters are ordered from bottom to top. For example, this happens with a mixture of Arabic and Latin glyphs when all the glyphs are rotated uniformly 90° clockwise. The Unicode Standard does not specify whether text is presented horizontally or vertically, or whether text is rotated. That is left up to higher-level protocols.

X5.5 Usage

Because of the implicit character types and the heuristics for resolving neutral and numeric directional behavior, the implicit bidirectional ordering will generally produce the correct display without any further work. However, problematic cases may occur when a right-to-left paragraph begins with left-to-right characters, or there are nested segments of different-direction text, or there are weak characters on directional boundaries. In these cases, embeddings or directional marks may be required to get the right display. Part numbers may also require directional overrides.

The most common problematic case is that of neutrals on the boundary of an embedded language. This can be addressed by setting the level of the embedded text correctly. For example, with all the text at level 0 the following occurs:

Memory: `he said "I NEED WATER!", and expired.`

Display: `he said "RETAW DEEN I!", and expired.`

If the exclamation mark is to be part of the Arabic quotation, then the user can select the text *I NEED WATER!* and explicitly mark it as embedded Arabic, which produces the following result:

Memory: `he said "`**<RLE>**`I NEED WATER!`**<PDF>**`", and expired.`

Display: `he said "!RETAW DEEN I", and expired.`

A simpler method of doing this is to place a right directional mark (RLM) after the exclamation mark. Because the exclamation mark is now not on a directional boundary, this produces the correct result.

Memory: `he said "I NEED WATER!`**<RLM>**`", and expired.`

Display: `he said "!RETAW DEEN I", and expired.`

This latter approach is preferred because it does not make use of the stateful format codes, which can easily get out of sync if not fully supported by editors and other string manipulation. The stateful format codes are generally needed only for more complex (and rare) cases such as double embeddings, as in the following:

Memory: `DID YOU SAY '`**<LRE>**`he said "I NEED WATER!`**<RLM>**`", and expired.`**<PDF>**`'?`

Display: `?'he said "!RETAW DEEN I", and expired.' YAS UOY DID`

Migrating from 2.0 to 3.0

In the Unicode Character Database for [Unicode3.0], new bidirectional character types were introduced to make the body of the Bidirectional Algorithm depend only on the types of characters, and not on the character values. The changes from the 2.0 bidirectional types are listed in *Table 6*.

Table 6. New Bidirectional Types in Unicode 3.0

Characters	New Bidirectional Type
All characters with General_Category Me, Mn	NSM
All characters of type R in the Arabic ranges (0600..06FF, FB50..FDFF, FE70..FEFE) (Letters in the Thaana and Syriac ranges also have this value.)	AL
The explicit embedding characters: LRO, RLO, LRE, RLE, PDF	LRO, RLO, LRE, RLE, PDF, respectively
Formatting characters and controls (General_Category Cf and Cc) that were of bidirectional type ON	BN
Zero Width Space	BN

Implementations that use older property tables can adjust to the modifications in the Bidirectional Algorithm by algorithmically remapping the characters in *Table 6* to the new types.

X6 Mirroring

The mirrored property is important to ensure that the correct character codes are used for the desired semantic. This is of particular importance where the name of a character does not indicate the intended semantic, such as with U+0028 "(" LEFT PARENTHESIS. While the name indicates that it is a left parenthesis, the character really expresses an *open parenthesis*—the *leading* character in a parenthetical phrase, not the trailing one.

Some of the characters that do not have the Bidi_Mirrored property may be rendered with mirrored glyphs, according to a higher level protocol that adds mirroring: see *Section X4.3, Higher-Level Protocols*, especially HL6. Except in such cases, mirroring must be done according to rule L4, to ensure that the correct character code is used to express the intended semantic of the character, and to avoid interoperability and security problems.

Implementing rule L4 calls for mirrored glyphs. These glyphs may not be exact *graphical* mirror images. For example, clearly an italic parenthesis is not an exact mirror image of another— "*(*" is not the mirror image of "*)*". Instead, mirror glyphs are those acceptable as mirrors within the normal parameters of the font in which they are represented.

In implementation, sometimes pairs of characters are acceptable mirrors for one another—for example, U+0028 "(" LEFT PARENTHESIS and U+0029 ")" RIGHT PARENTHESIS or U+22E0 "⋠" DOES NOT PRECEDE OR EQUAL and U+22E1 "⋡" DOES NOT SUCCEED OR EQUAL. Other characters such as U+2231 "∱" CLOCKWISE INTEGRAL do not have corresponding characters that can be used for acceptable mirrors. The informative Bidi Mirroring data file [Data9], lists the paired characters with acceptable mirror glyphs. A comment in the file indicates where the pairs are "best fit": they should be acceptable in rendering, although ideally the mirrored glyphs may have somewhat different shapes.

Acknowledgments

Mark Davis is the author of the initial version and has added to and maintained the text of this annex.

Thanks to the following people for their contributions to the Bidirectional Algorithm or for their feedback on earlier versions of this annex: Alaa Ghoneim (علاء غنيم), Ahmed Talaat (أحمد طلعت), Asmus Freytag, Avery Bishop, Behdad Esfahbod (بهداد اسفهبد), Doug Felt, Eric Mader, Ernest Cline, Gidi Shalom-Bendor (גידי שלום-בן דור), Isai Scheinberg, Israel Gidali (ישראל גידלי), Joe Becker, John McConnell, Jonathan Kew, Jonathan Rosenne (יונתן רוזן), Khaled Sherif (خالد شريف), Kamal Mansour (كمال منصور), Kenneth Whistler, Maha Hassan (مها حسن), Markus Scherer, Martin Dürst, Mati Allouche (מתתיהו אלוש), Michel Suignard, Mike Ksar (ميشيل قصار), Murray Sargent, Paul Nelson, Rick McGowan, Roozbeh Pournader (روزبه پورنادر), Steve Atkin, and Thomas Milo (تُومَاسْ مِيلُو).

References

For references for this annex, see Unicode Standard Annex #41, "Common References for Unicode Standard Annexes."

Modifications

For details of the change history, see the online copy of this annex at http://www.unicode.org/reports/tr9/.

Unicode Standard Annex #11

East Asian Width

Summary

This annex presents the specifications of an informative property for Unicode characters that is useful when interoperating with East Asian Legacy character sets.

Contents

X1 Overview

When dealing with East Asian text, there is the concept of an *inherent* width of a character. This width takes on either of two values: *narrow* or *wide*. For traditional mixed-width East Asian legacy character sets, this classification into narrow and wide corresponds with few exceptions directly to the storage size for each character: a few narrow characters use a single byte per character and all other characters (usually wide) use two or more bytes.

Layout and line breaking (to cite only two examples) in East Asian context show systematic variations depending on the value of this East_Asian_Width property. *Wide* characters behave like ideographs; they tend to allow line breaks after each character and remain upright in vertical text layout. *Narrow* characters are kept together in words or runs that are rotated sideways in vertical text layout.

For a traditional East Asian *fixed pitch* font, this width translates to a display width of either one half or a whole unit width. A common name for this unit width is “Em”. While an Em is customarily the *height* of the letter “M”, it is the same as the unit *width* in East Asian fonts, because in these fonts the standard character cell is square. In contrast, the character width for a fixed-pitch Latin font like Courier is generally 3/5 of an Em.

In modern practice, most alphabetic characters are rendered by variable-width fonts using narrow characters, even if their encoding in common legacy sets uses multiple bytes.

Except for a few characters, which are explicitly called out as *fullwidth* or *halfwidth* in the Unicode Standard, characters are not duplicated based on distinction in width. Some characters, such as the ideographs, are always wide; others are always narrow; and some can be narrow or wide, depending on the context. The Unicode character property *East_Asian_Width* provides a default classification of characters, which an implementation can use to decide at runtime whether to treat a character as narrow or wide.

X2 Scope

The East_Asian_Width is an informative property and provides a useful concept for implementations that

- Have to interwork with East Asian legacy character encodings
- Support both East Asian and Western typography and line layout
- Need to associate fonts with unmarked text runs containing East Asian characters

This annex gives general guidelines how to use this property. It does not provide rules or specifications of how this property might be used in font design or line layout, because, while a useful property for this purpose, it is only one of several character properties that would need to be considered. The specific assignments of property values for given characters may change over time to reflect evolving practice and should be considered recommendations that may be overridden by implementations.

X3 Description

By convention, 1/2 Em wide characters of East Asian legacy encodings are called “halfwidth” (or *hankaku* characters in Japanese); the others are called correspondingly “fullwidth” (or *zenkaku*) characters. Legacy encodings often use a single byte for the halfwidth characters and two bytes for the fullwidth characters. In the Unicode Standard, no such distinction is made, but understanding the distinction is often necessary when interchanging data with legacy systems, especially when fixed-size buffers are involved.

Some character blocks in the compatibility zone contain characters that are explicitly marked “halfwidth” and “fullwidth” in their character name, but for all other characters the width property must be implicitly derived. Some characters behave differently in an East Asian context than in a non-East Asian context. Their default width property is considered ambiguous and needs to be resolved into an actual width property based on context.

The Unicode Character Database [UCD] assigns to each Unicode character as its default width property one of six values: *Ambiguous, Fullwidth, Halfwidth, Narrow, Wide,* or *Neutral* (= *Not East Asian*). For any given operation, these six default property values resolve into only two property values, *narrow* and *wide,* depending on context.

X4 Definitions

All terms not defined here shall be as defined elsewhere in the Unicode Standard.

ED1. East_Asian_Width: In the context of interoperating with East Asian legacy character encodings and implementing East Asian typography, East_Asian_Width is a categorization of character. It can take on two abstract values, *narrow* and *wide*.

In legacy implementations, there is often a corresponding difference in encoding length (one or two bytes) as well as a difference in displayed width. However, the *actual* display width of a glyph is given by the font and may be further adjusted by layout. An important class of fixed-width legacy fonts contains glyphs of just two widths, with the wider glyphs twice as wide as the narrower glyphs.

> **Note**: For convenience, the classification further distinguishes between explicitly and implicitly wide and narrow characters.

ED2. East Asian Fullwidth (F): All characters that are defined as Fullwidth in the Unicode Standard [Unicode] by having a compatibility decomposition of type <wide> to characters elsewhere in the Unicode Standard that are implicitly narrow but unmarked.

> **Note:** The Unicode property value aliases drop the common prefix East Asian for this and the following property values.

ED3. East Asian Halfwidth (H): All characters that are explicitly defined as Halfwidth in the Unicode Standard by having a compatibility decomposition of type <narrow> to characters elsewhere in the Unicode Standard that are implicitly wide but unmarked, plus the WON SIGN.

ED4. East Asian Wide (W): All other characters that are *always* wide. These characters occur only in the context of East Asian typography where they are wide characters (such as the Unified Han Ideographs or Squared Katakana Symbols). This category includes characters that have explicit halfwidth counterparts.

ED5. East Asian Narrow (Na): All other characters that are *always* narrow and have explicit fullwidth or wide counterparts. These characters are implicitly narrow in East Asian typography and legacy character sets because they have explicit fullwidth or wide counterparts. All of ASCII is an example of East Asian Narrow characters.

> It is useful to distinguish characters explicitly defined as halfwidth from other narrow characters. In particular, halfwidth punctuation behaves in some important ways like ideographic punctuation, and knowing a character is a halfwidth character can aid in font selection when binding a font to unstyled text.

ED6. East Asian Ambiguous (A): All characters that can be sometimes wide and sometimes narrow. Ambiguous characters require additional information not contained in the character code to further resolve their width.

Ambiguous characters occur in East Asian legacy character sets as *wide* characters, but as *narrow* (i.e., normal-width) characters in non-East Asian usage. (Examples are the Greek and Cyrillic alphabet found in East Asian character sets, but also some of the mathematical symbols.) Private-use characters are considered ambiguous by default, because additional information is required to know whether they should be treated as wide or narrow.

Figure 1. Venn Diagram Showing the Set Relations for Five of the Six Categories

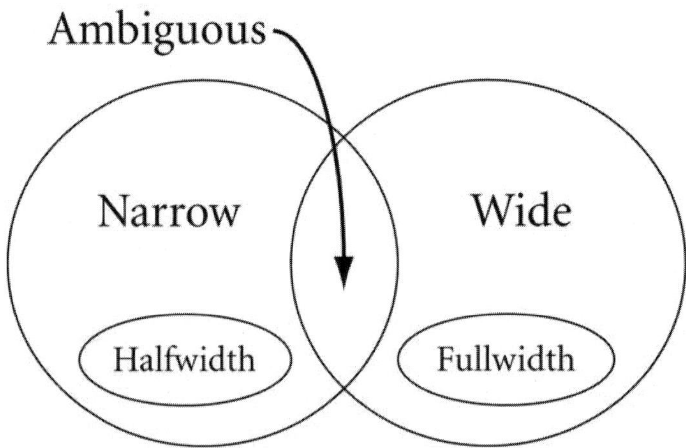

Because East Asian legacy character sets do not always include complete case pairs of Latin characters, two members of a case pair may have different East_Asian_Width properties:

```
Ambiguous:      01D4    LATIN SMALL LETTER U WITH CARON
NEA Neutral:    01D3    LATIN CAPITAL LETTER U WITH CARON
```

When they are treated as *wide* characters, ambiguous characters would typically be rendered upright in vertical text runs.

ED7. Neutral (Not East Asian): All other characters. Neutral characters do not occur in legacy East Asian character sets. By extension, they also do not occur in East Asian typography. For example, there is no traditional Japanese way of typesetting Devanagari.

Strictly speaking, it makes no sense to talk of narrow and wide for neutral characters, but because for all practical purposes they behave like Na, they are treated as narrow characters (the same as Na) under the recommendations below.

In a broad sense, *wide characters* include W, F, and A (when in East Asian context), and *narrow characters* include N, Na, H, and A (when not in East Asian context).

Figure 2. Examples for Each Character Class and Their Resolved Widths

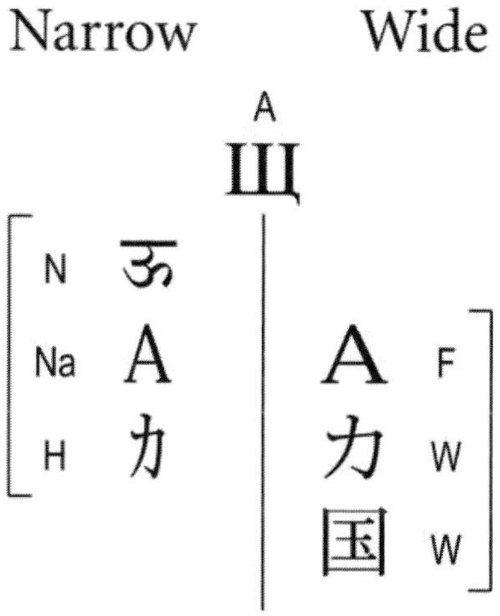

X4.1 Relation to the Terms "Fullwidth" and "Halfwidth"

When converting a DBCS mixed-width encoding to and from Unicode, the fullwidth characters in such a mixed-width encoding are mapped to the fullwidth compatibility characters in the FFxx block, whereas the corresponding halfwidth characters are mapped to ordinary Unicode characters (for example, ASCII in U+0021..U+007E, plus a few other scattered characters).

In the context of interoperability with DBCS character encodings, this restricted set of Unicode characters in the General Scripts area can be construed as halfwidth, rather than fullwidth. (This applies only to the restricted set of characters that can be paired with the fullwidth compatibility characters.)

In the context of interoperability with DBCS character encodings, all other Unicode characters that are not explicitly marked as halfwidth can be construed as fullwidth.

In any other context, Unicode characters not explicitly marked as being either fullwidth or halfwidth compatibility forms are neither halfwidth nor fullwidth.

Seen in this light, the "halfwidth" and "fullwidth" properties are not unitary character properties in the same sense as "space" or "combining" or "alphabetic." They are, instead, relational properties of a pair of characters, one of which is explicitly encoded as a halfwidth or fullwidth form for compatibility in mapping to DBCS mixed-width character encodings.

What is "fullwidth" by default today could in theory become "halfwidth" tomorrow by the introduction of another character on the SBCS part of a mixed-width code page somewhere, requiring the introduction of another fullwidth compatibility character to complete the mapping. However, because the single byte part of mixed-width character sets is limited, there are not going to be many candidates and neither the Unicode Technical Committee [UTC] nor WG2 has any intention to encode additional compatibility characters for this purpose.

X4.2 Ambiguous Characters

Ambiguous width characters are all those characters that can occur as fullwidth characters in any of a number of East Asian legacy character encodings. They have a "resolved" width of either narrow or wide depending on the context of their use. If they are not used in the context of the specific legacy encoding to which they belong, their width resolves to narrow. Otherwise, it resolves to fullwidth or halfwidth. The term *context* as used here includes extra information such as explicit markup, knowledge of the source code page, font information, or language and script identification. For example:

- Greek characters resolve to narrow when used with a standard Greek font, because there is no East Asian legacy context.
- Private-use character codes and the replacement character have ambiguous width, because they may stand in for characters of any width.
- Ambiguous quotation marks are generally resolved to wide when they enclose and are adjacent to a wide character, and to narrow otherwise.

Modern Rendering Practice. Modern practice is evolving toward rendering ever more of the ambiguous characters with proportionally spaced, narrow forms that rotate with the direction of writing, making a distinction within the legacy character set. In other words, context information beyond the choice of font or source character set is employed to resolve the width of the character. This annex does not attempt to track such changes in practice; therefore, the set of characters with mappings to legacy character sets that have been assigned ambiguous width constitute a superset of the set of such characters that may be rendered as wide characters in a given context. In particular, an application might find it useful to treat characters from alphabetic scripts as narrow by default. Conversely, many of the symbols in the Unicode Standard have no mappings to legacy character sets, yet they may be rendered as "wide" characters if they appear in an East Asian context. An implementation might therefore elect to treat them as ambiguous even though they are classified as *neutral* here.

X5 Recommendations

When mapping Unicode to East Asian legacy character encodings

- Wide Unicode characters *always* map to fullwidth characters.
- Narrow (and neutral) Unicode characters *always* map to halfwidth characters.
- Halfwidth Unicode characters *always* map to halfwidth characters.
- Ambiguous Unicode characters *always* map to fullwidth characters.

When mapping Unicode to non-East Asian legacy character encodings

- Wide Unicode characters *do not* map to *non*-East Asian legacy character encodings.
- Narrow (and neutral) Unicode characters *always* map to regular (narrow) characters.
- Halfwidth Unicode characters *do not* map.
- Ambiguous Unicode characters *always* map to regular (narrow) characters.

When processing or displaying data

- Wide characters behave like ideographs in important ways, such as layout. Except for certain punctuation characters, they are not rotated when appearing in vertical text runs. In fixed-pitch fonts, they take up one Em of space.
- Halfwidth characters behave like ideographs in some ways, however, they are rotated like narrow characters when appearing in vertical text runs. In fixed-pitch fonts, they take up 1/2 Em of space.
- Narrow characters behave like Western characters, for example, in line breaking. They are rotated sideways, when appearing in vertical text. In fixed-pitch East Asian fonts, they take up 1/2 Em of space, but in rendering, a non-East Asian, proportional font is often substituted.
- Ambiguous characters behave like wide or narrow characters depending on the context (language tag, script identification, associated font, source of data, or explicit markup; all can provide the context). If the context cannot be established reliably, they should be treated as narrow characters by default.

X6 Classifications

The classifications presented here are based on the most widely used mixed-width legacy character sets in use in East Asia as of this writing. In particular, the assignments of the Neutral or Ambiguous categories depend on the contents of these character sets. For example, an implementation that knows *a priori* that it needs to interchange data *only* with the Japanese Shift-JIS character set, but not with other East Asian character sets, could reduce the number of characters in the Ambiguous classification to those actually encoded in Shift-JIS. Alternatively, such a reduction could be done implicitly at runtime in the context of interoperating with Shift-JIS fonts or data sources. Conversely, if additional character sets are created and widely adopted for legacy purposes, more characters would need to be classified as ambiguous.

X6.1 Unassigned and Private-Use Characters

All private-use characters are by default classified as Ambiguous, because their definition depends on context. All unassigned characters are by default classified as Neutral, except for the ranges U+20000..U+2FFFD and U+30000..U+3FFFD—all code positions in these ranges are intended for CJK ideographs (W). For additional recommendations for handling the default property value for unassigned characters, see *Section 5.3, Unknown and Missing Characters,* in [Unicode].

X6.2 Combining Marks

Combining marks have been classified and are given a property assignment based on their typical applicability. For example, combining marks typically applied to characters of class **N**, **Na,** or **W** are classified as **A**. Combining marks for purely non-East Asian scripts are marked as **N**, and nonspacing marks used only with wide characters are given a **W**. Even more so than for other characters, the East_Asian_Width property for combining marks is not the same as their display width.

In particular, nonspacing marks do not possess actual advance width. Therefore, even when displaying combining marks, the East_Asian_Width property cannot be related to the advance width of these characters. However, it can be useful in determining the encoding length in a legacy encoding, or the choice of font for the range of characters including that nonspacing mark. The width of the glyph image of a nonspacing mark should always be chosen as the appropriate one for the width of the base character.

X6.3 Data File

The East_Asian_Width classification of all Unicode characters is listed in the file EastAsianWidth.txt [Data11] in the Unicode Character Database [UCD]. This is a tab-delimited, two-column, plain text file, with code position and East_Asian_Width designator. A comment at the end of each line indicates the character name. Ideographic, Hangul, Surrogate, and Private Use ranges are collapsed by giving a range in the first column.

X6.4 Adding Characters

As more characters are added to the Unicode Standard, or if additional character sets are created and widely adopted for legacy purposes, the assignment of East_Asian_Width may be changed for some characters. Implementations should not make any assumptions to the contrary. The sets of Narrow, Fullwidth, and Halfwidth characters are fixed for all practical purposes. New characters for most scripts will be Neutral characters; however, characters for East Asian scripts using wide characters will be classified as Wide. Symbol characters that are, or are expected to be, used both as wide characters in East Asian usage and as narrow characters in non-East Asian usage will be classified Ambiguous.

References

For references for this annex, see Unicode Standard Annex #41, "Common References for Unicode Standard Annexes."

Acknowledgments

Asmus Freytag is the author of the initial version and has added to and maintained the text of this annex.

Michel Suignard provided extensive input into the analysis and source material for the detail assignments of these properties. Mark Davis and Ken Whistler performed consistency checks on the data files at various times. Tomohiro Kubota reviewed the East_Asian_Width assignments against some common legacy encodings.

Modifications

For details of the change history, see the online copy of this annex at http://www.unicode.org/reports/tr11/.

Unicode Standard Annex #14

Line Breaking Properties

Summary

This annex presents the specification of line breaking properties for Unicode characters as well as a default algorithm for determining line break opportunities. A model implementation using pair tables is also provided.

Contents

X1 Overview and Scope

The text of The Unicode Standard [Unicode] presents a limited description of some of the characters with specific functions in line breaking, but does not give a complete specification of line breaking behavior. This annex provides more detailed information about default line breaking behavior reflecting best practices for the support of multilingual texts.

For most Unicode characters, considerable variation in line breaking behavior can be expected, including variation based on local or stylistic preferences. For that reason, the line breaking properties provided for these characters are informative. Some characters are intended to explicitly influence line breaking. Their line breaking behavior is therefore expected to be identical across all implementations. The Unicode Standard assigns normative line breaking properties to those characters. The Unicode Line Breaking Algorithm is a tailorable set of rules that uses these line breaking properties in context to determine line break opportunities.

This annex opens with formal definitions, a summary of the line breaking task and a brief section on conformance requirements. Three main sections follow:

- *Section X5, Line Breaking Properties*, contains a narrative description of the line breaking behavior of the characters of the Unicode Standard, grouping them in alphabetical order by line breaking class.
- *Section X6, Line Breaking Algorithm*, provides a set of rules listed in order of precedence that constitute a line breaking algorithm.
- *Section X7, Pair Table-Based Implementation*, describes an efficient pair table-based implementation of the algorithm.

The final two sections discuss issues of customization and implementation.

- *Section X8, Customization*, provides a discussion of how to tailor the algorithm.
- *Section X9, Implementation Notes*, provides additional information to implementers using regular expression-based techniques or requiring legacy support for combining marks.

X2 Definitions

All terms not defined here shall be as defined in the Unicode Standard [Unicode5.0]. The notation defined in this annex differs somewhat from the notation defined elsewhere in the Unicode Standard. All other notation used here without an explicit definition shall be as defined elsewhere in the Unicode Standard.

LD1 Line Fitting: The process of determining how much text will fit on a line of text, given the available space between the margins and the actual display width of the text.

LD2 Line Break: The position in the text where one line ends and the next one starts.

LD3 Line Break Opportunity: A place where a line is allowed to end.

- Whether a given position in the text is a valid line break opportunity depends on the context as well as the line breaking rules in force.

LD4 Line Breaking: The process of selecting one among several line break opportunities such that the resulting line is optimal or ends at a user-requested explicit line break.

LD5 Line Breaking Property: A character property with enumerated values, as listed in *Table 1*, and separated into normative and informative.

- Line breaking property values are used to classify characters and, taken in context, determine the type of break.

LD6 Line Breaking Class: A class of characters with the same line breaking property value.

The Line Breaking Classes are described in *Section X5.1, Description of Line Breaking Properties.*

LD7 Mandatory Break: A line must break following a character that has the mandatory break property.

Such a break is also known as a *forced* break and is indicated in the rules as **B** !, where **B** is the character with the mandatory break property.

LD8 Direct Break: A line break opportunity exists between two adjacent characters of the given line breaking classes.

A direct break is indicated in the rules below as **B** ÷ **A**, where **B** is the character class of the character *before* and **A** is the character class of the character *after* the break. If they are separated by one or more space characters, a break opportunity also exists after the last space. In the pair table, the optional space characters are not shown.

LD9 Indirect Break: A line break opportunity exists between two characters of the given line breaking classes *only* if they are separated by one or more spaces.

- For an indirect break, a break opportunity exists after the last space. No break opportunity exists if the characters are immediately adjacent.

An indirect break is indicated in the pair table in *Table 2* as **B** % **A**, where **B** is the character class of the character *before* and **A** is the character class of the character *after* the break. Even though space characters are not shown in the pair table, an indirect break can occur only if one or more spaces follow B. In the notation of the rules in *Section X6, Line Breaking Algorithm*, this would be represented as two rules: **B** × **A** *and* **B SP+** ÷ **A**.

LD10 Prohibited Break: No line break opportunity exists between two characters of the given line breaking classes, even if they are separated by one or more space characters.

A direct break is indicated in the pair table in *Table 2* as **B** ^ **A**, where **B** is the character class of the character *before* and **A* is the character class of the character *after* the break, and the optional space characters are not shown. In the notation of the rules in *Section X6, Line Breaking Algorithm*, this would be expressed as a rule of the form: **B SP*** × **A**.

LD11 Hyphenation: Hyphenation uses language-specific rules to provide additional line break opportunities *within* a word.

- Hyphenation improves the layout of narrow columns, especially for languages with many longer words, such as German or Finnish. For the purpose of this annex, it is assumed that hyphenation is equivalent to inserting *soft hyphen* characters. All other aspects of hyphenation are outside the scope of this annex.

Table 1 provides a summary listing of all line breaking classes while *Section X5.1, Description of Line Breaking Properties*, provides a detailed description of each line breaking class, including detailed overview of the line breaking behavior for characters of that class.

Table 1. Line Breaking Classes (* = non-tailorable)

Class	Descriptive Name	Examples	Characters with This Property...
		Non-tailorable Line Breaking Classes	
BK *	*Mandatory Break*	NL, PS	Cause a line break (after)
CR *	*Carriage Return*	CR	Cause a line break (after), except between CR and LF
LF *	*Line Feed*	LF	Cause a line break (after)
CM *	*Attached Characters and Combining Marks*	Combining marks, control codes	Prohibit a line break between the character and the preceding character
NL *	*Next Line*	NEL	Cause a line break (after)
SG *	*Surrogates*	Surrogates	Should not occur in well-formed text
WJ *	*Word Joiner*	WJ	Prohibit line breaks before or after
ZW *	*Zero Width Space*	ZWSP	Provide a break opportunity
GL *	*Non-breaking ("Glue")*	CGJ, NBSP, ZWNBSP	Prohibit line breaks before or after
SP *	*Space*	SPACE	Generally provide a line break opportunity after the character, enable indirect breaks
		Break Opportunities	
B2	*Break Opportunity Before and After*	Em dash	Provide a line break opportunity before and after the character
BA	*Break Opportunity After*	Spaces, hyphens	Generally provide a line break opportunity after the character
BB	*Break Opportunity Before*	Punctuation used in dictionaries	Generally provide a line break opportunity before the character
HY	*Hyphen*	HYPHEN-MINUS	Provide a line break opportunity after the character, except in numeric context
CB	*Contingent Break Opportunity*	Inline objects	Provide a line break opportunity contingent on additional information

		Characters Prohibiting Certain Breaks	
CL	*Closing Punctuation*	")", "]", "}", etc.	Prohibit line breaks before
EX	*Exclamation/ Interrogation*	"!", "?", etc.	Prohibit line breaks before
IN	*Inseparable*	Leaders	Allow only indirect line breaks between pairs
NS	*Nonstarter*	small kana	Allow only indirect line breaks before
OP	*Opening Punctuation*	"(", "[", "{", etc.	Prohibit line breaks after
QU	*Ambiguous Quotation*	Quotation marks	Act like they are both opening and closing
		Numeric Context	
IS	*Infix Separator (Numeric)*	. ,	Prevent breaks after any and before numeric
NU	*Numeric*	Digits	Form numeric expressions for line breaking purposes
PO	*Postfix (Numeric)*	%, ¢	Do not break following a numeric expression
PR	*Prefix (Numeric)*	$, £, ¥, etc.	Do not break in front of a numeric expression
SY	*Symbols Allowing Break After*	/	Prevent a break before, and allow a break after
		Other Characters	
AI	*Ambiguous (Alphabetic or Ideographic)*	Characters with Ambiguous East Asian Width	Act like **AL** when the resolved EAW is N; otherwise, act as **ID**
AL	*Ordinary Alphabetic and Symbol Characters*	Alphabets and regular symbols	Are alphabetic characters or symbols that are used with alphabetic characters
H2	*Hangul LV Syllable*	Hangul	Form Korean syllable blocks
H3	*Hangul LVT Syllable*	Hangul	Form Korean syllable blocks
ID	*Ideographic*	Ideographs	Break before or after, except in some numeric context
JL	*Hangul L Jamo*	Conjoining jamo	Form Korean syllable blocks
JV	*Hangul V Jamo*	Conjoining jamo	Form Korean syllable blocks
JT	*Hangul T Jamo*	Conjoining jamo	Form Korean syllable blocks
SA	*Complex Context Dependent (South East Asian)*	South East Asian: Thai, Lao, Khmer	Provide a line break opportunity contingent on additional, language-specific context analysis
XX	*Unknown*	Unassigned, private-use	Have as yet unknown line breaking behavior or unassigned code positions

X3 Introduction

Lines are broken as result of one of two conditions. The first condition is the presence of an explicit line breaking character. The second condition results from a formatting algorithm having selected among available line break opportunities; ideally the chosen line break results in the optimal layout of the text.

Different formatting algorithms may use different methods to determine an optimal line break. For example, simple implementations consider a single line at a time, trying to find a *locally optimal* line break. A basic, yet widely used approach is to allow no compression or expansion of the intercharacter and interword spaces and consider the longest line that fits. When compression or expansion is allowed, a locally optimal line break seeks to balance the relative merits of the resulting amounts of compression and expansion for different line break candidates.

When expanding or compressing interword space according to common typographical practice, only the spaces marked by U+0020 SPACE, U+00A0 NO-BREAK SPACE, and U+3000 IDEOGRAPHIC SPACE are subject to compression, and only spaces marked by U+0020 SPACE, U+00A0 NO-BREAK SPACE, and occasionally spaces marked by U+2009 THIN SPACE are subject to expansion. All other space characters normally have fixed width. When expanding or compressing intercharacter space, the presence of U+200B ZERO WIDTH SPACE or U+2060 WORD JOINER is always ignored.

Local custom or document style determines whether and to what degree expansion of intercharacter space is allowed in justifying a line. In languages, such as German, where intercharacter space is commonly used to mark e m p h a s i s (like this), allowing variable intercharacter spacing would have the unintended effect of adding random emphasis, and should therefore be avoided.

In table headings that use Han ideographs, even extreme amounts of intercharacter space commonly occur as short texts are spread out across the entire available space to distribute the characters evenly from end to end.

More complex formatting algorithms may take into account the interaction of line breaking decisions for the whole paragraph. The well-known text layout system [TEX] implements an example of such a *globally optimal* strategy that may make complex tradeoffs across an entire paragraph to avoid unnecessary hyphenation and other legal, but inferior breaks. For a description of this strategy, see [Knuth78].

The definition of optimal line breaks is outside the scope of this annex, as are methods for their selection. For the purpose of this annex, what is important is not so much what defines the optimal amount of text on the line, but how to determine all legal line break *opportunities*. Whether and how any given line break opportunity is actually used is up to the full layout system. Some layout systems will further evaluate the raw line break opportunities returned from the line breaking algorithm and apply additional rules. TEX, for example, uses line break opportunities based on hyphens only as a last resort.

Finally, most text layout systems will support an emergency mode that handles the case of an unusual line that contains no ordinary line break opportunities. In such line layout emergencies, line breaks are placed with no regard to the ordinary line breaking behavior of the characters involved.

X3.1 Determining Line Break Opportunities

Three principal styles of context analysis determine line break opportunities.

1. *Western*: spaces and hyphens are used to determine breaks
2. *East Asian:* lines can break anywhere, unless prohibited
3. *South East Asian*: line breaks require morphological analysis

The Western style is commonly used for scripts employing the space character. Hyphenation is often used with space-based line breaking to provide additional line break opportunities—however, it requires knowledge of the language and it may need user interaction or overrides.

The second style of context analysis is used with East Asian ideographic and syllabic scripts. In these scripts, lines can break anywhere, except before or after certain characters. The precise set of prohibited line breaks may depend on user preference or local custom and is commonly tailorable.

Korean makes use of both styles of line break. When Korean text is justified, the second style is commonly used, even for interspersed Latin letters. But when ragged margins are used, the Western style (relying on spaces) is commonly used instead, even for ideographs.

The third style is used for scripts such as Thai, which do not use spaces, but which restrict word breaks to syllable boundaries, the determination of which requires knowledge of the language comparable to that required by a hyphenation algorithm. Such an algorithm is beyond the scope of the Unicode Standard.

For multilingual text, the Western and East Asian styles can be unified into a single set of specifications, based on the information in this annex. Unicode characters have explicit line breaking properties assigned to them. These can be utilized with these two styles of context analysis for line break opportunities. Customization for user preferences or document style can then be achieved by tailoring that specification.

In bidirectional text, line breaks takes are determined before applying rule L1 of the Unicode Bidirectional Algorithm [Bidi]. However, line breaking is strictly independent of directional properties of the characters or of any auxiliary information determined by the application of rules of that algorithm.

X4 Conformance

There is no single method for determining line breaks; the rules may differ based on user preference and document layout. Therefore the information in this annex, including the specification of the line breaking algorithm, must allow for the necessary flexibility in determining line breaks according to different conventions. However, some characters have been encoded explicitly for their effect on line breaking. Users adding such characters to a text expect that they will have the desired effect. For that reason, these characters have been given non-tailorable line breaking behavior. The conformance requirements are spelled out in the following subsections.

At times, this specification recommends best practice. These recommendations are not normative and conformance with this specification does not depend on their realization. These recommendations contain the expression "This specification recommends ...", or some similar wording.

X4.1 Line Breaking Algorithm

UAX14-C1. *In the absence of a permissible higher-level protocol, a process that determines line breaks in Unicode text, and that purports to implement the Unicode Line Breaking Algorithm, shall do so in accordance with the specifications in this annex.*

- As is the case for all other Unicode algorithms, this specification is a *logical* description—particular implementations can have more efficient mechanisms as long as they produce the same results. See C18 in *Chapter 3, Conformance*, of [Unicode], and the notes following.
- The line breaking algorithm specifies part of the intrinsic semantics of characters specifically encoded for their line breaking behavior and, therefore, is required for conformance to the Unicode Standard where text containing such characters is broken into lines.

UAX14-C2. *The permissible higher-level protocols are described in Section X4.3, Higher-Level Protocols.*

X4.2 Line Breaking Properties

All line breaking classes are normative, but overridable, except for those line breaking classes marked with * in *Table 1*, which are not overridable.

X4.3 Higher-Level Protocols

There are many different ways to break lines of text, and the Unicode Standard does not intend to unnecessarily restrict the ways in which implementations can do this. However, for characters that are encoded solely or primarily for their line breaking behavior, interpretation of these characters must be consistent with their semantics as defined by their normative line breaking behavior. This leads to the following permissible higher-level protocols:

UAX14-HL1. *Override rule 2 and report a break at the start of text.*

- A higher-level protocol may report a break at the start of text (**sot**). As written, the rule is intended to ensure that the line breaking algorithm always produces lines that have at least one character in them. However, an analysis in terms of text boundaries would more naturally report a boundary at the **sot**, leaving it to any client to skip past that boundary in breaking lines.

UAX14-HL2. *Tailor any tailorable line break class.*

- A higher-level protocol may change the algorithm to produce results as if the membership of any tailorable line break class had been changed.

UAX14-HL3. *Override any rule in Section X6.2,Tailorable Line Breaking Rules, or add new rules to that section.*

- A higher-level protocol my change the algorithm to produce results as if any of the rules in *Section X6.2, Tailorable Line Breaking Rules*, had been deleted or amended, or as if new rules had been added.

Because of the way the specification is set up, HL2 and HL3 have no effect on the results for text containing only characters of the non-tailorable line breaking classes. However, they allow for unrestricted tailoring of the results for texts containing only characters from the tailorable line breaking classes as well as wide latitude in defining the behavior of mixed texts.

X5 Line Breaking Properties

This section provides detailed narrative descriptions of the line breaking behavior of many Unicode characters. In a few instances, the descriptions in this section provide additional detail about handling a given character at the end of a line, which goes beyond the simple determination of line breaks.

This section also summarizes the membership of character classes for each value of the line breaking property. Note that the mnemonic names for the line break classes are intended neither as exhaustive descriptions of their membership nor as indicators of their entire range of behaviors in the line breaking process. Instead, their main purpose is to serve as unique, yet broadly mnemonic labels. In other words, as long as their line break behavior is identical, otherwise unrelated characters will be found grouped together in the same line break class.

The classification by property values defined in this section and in the data file is used as input into two algorithms defined in *Section X6, Line Breaking Algorithm*, and *Section X7, Pair Table-Based Implementation*. These sections describe workable default line breaking methods. *Section X8, Customization*, discusses how the default line breaking behavior can be tailored to the needs of particular languages for particular document styles and user preferences.

Data File

The full classification of all Unicode characters by their line breaking properties is available in the file LineBreak.txt [Data14] in the Unicode Character Database [UCD]. This is a tab-delimited, two-column, plain text file, with code position and line breaking class. A comment at the end of each line indicates the character name. Ideographic, Hangul, Surrogate, and Private Use ranges are collapsed by giving a range in the first column.

Future Updates

As more scripts are added to the Unicode Standard and become more widely implemented and used on computers, more line breaking classes may be added or the assignment of line breaking class may be changed for some characters. Implementations should not make any assumptions to the contrary. Any future updates will be reflected in the latest version of the data file. (See the Unicode Character Database [UCD] for any specific version of the data file.)

X5.1 Description of Line Breaking Properties

Line breaking classes are listed alphabetically. Each line breaking class is marked with an annotation in parentheses with the following meanings:

(A)—the class allows a break opportunity *after* in specified contexts

(XA)—the class prevents a break opportunity *after* in specified contexts

(B)—the class allows a break opportunity *before* in specified contexts

(XB)—the class prevents a break opportunity *before* in specified contexts

(P)—the class allows a break opportunity for a *pair* of same characters

(XP)—the class prevents a break opportunity for a *pair* of same characters

Note: The use of the letters **B** and **A** in these annotations marks the position of the break opportunity relative to the character. It is not to be confused with the use of the same letters in the other parts of this annex, where they indicate the positions of the characters relative to the break opportunity.

AI: Ambiguous (Alphabetic or Ideograph)

Some characters that ordinarily act like alphabetic or symbol characters (which have the **AL** line breaking class) are treated like ideographs (line breaking class **ID**) in certain East Asian legacy contexts. Their line breaking behavior therefore depends on the context. In the absence of appropriate context information, they are treated as class **AL**, but see the note at the end of this description.

As originally defined, the line break class **AI** contained *all* characters with East Asian Width property A (ambiguous width) that would otherwise be **AL** in this classification. They take the **AL** line breaking class only when their *resolved* width is N (narrow) and take the line breaking class **ID** when their resolved width is W (wide). For more information on East Asian Width and how to resolve it, see Unicode Standard Annex #11, *East Asian Width* [EAW].

The original definition included many Latin, Greek, and Cyrillic characters. These characters are now classified by default as **AL** because use of the **AL** line breaking class better corresponds to modern practice. Where strict compatibility with older legacy implementations is desired, some of these characters need to be treated as **ID** in certain contexts. This can be done by always tailoring them to **ID** or by continuing to classify them as **AI** and resolving them to **ID** where required.

As part of the same revision, the set of ambiguous characters has been extended to completely encompass the enclosed alphanumeric characters used for numbering of bullets.

As updated, the **AI** line breaking class includes all characters with East Asian Width A that are outside the range U+0000..U+1FFF, plus the following characters:

24EA	CIRCLED DIGIT ZERO
2780..2793	DINGBAT CIRCLED SANS-SERIF DIGIT ONE..DINGBAT NEGATIVE CIRCLED SANS-SERIF NUMBER TEN

The line breaking rules in *Section X6, Line Breaking Algorithm*, and the pair table in *Section X7, Pair Table-Based Implementation*, assume that all ambiguous characters have been resolved appropriately as part of assigning line breaking classes to the input characters.

> **Note:** Normally characters with class **AI** are resolved to either **ID** or **AL**. However, the following two characters are used as punctuation marks in Spanish, where they would behave more like a character of class **OP**. Implementations might therefore wish to tailor these characters to class **OP** for use in Spanish.

00A1	INVERTED EXCLAMATION MARK
00BF	INVERTED QUESTION MARK

AL: Ordinary Alphabetic and Symbol Characters (XP)

Ordinary characters require other characters to provide break opportunities; otherwise, no line breaks are allowed between pairs of them. However, this behavior is tailorable. In some Far Eastern documents, it may be desirable to allow breaking between pairs of ordinary characters—particularly Latin characters and symbols.

> **Note:** Use ZWSP as a manual override to provide break opportunities around alphabetic or symbol characters.

Except as listed explicitly below as part of another line breaking class, and except as assigned class **AI** or **ID** based on East Asian Width, this class contains the following characters:

ALPHABETIC—all remaining characters of General Categories Lu, Ll, Lt, Lm, and Lo
SYMBOLS—all remaining characters of General Categories Sm, Sk, and So
NON-DECIMAL NUMBERS—all remaining characters of General Categories Nl, and No
PUNCTUATION—all remaining characters of General Categories Pc, Pd, and Po

Plus these characters:

0600..0603	ARABIC NUMBER SIGN..ARABIC SIGN SAFHA
06DD	ARABIC END OF AYAH
070F	SYRIAC ABBREVIATION MARK
2061..2063	FUNCTION APPLICATION..INVISIBLE SEPARATOR

These characters occur in the middle or at the beginning of words or alphanumeric or symbol sequences. However, when alphabetic characters are tailored to allow breaks, these characters should not allow breaks after.

BA: Break Opportunity After (A)

Like SPACE, the characters in this class provide a break opportunity; unlike SPACE, they do not take part in determining indirect breaks. They can be subdivided into several categories.

Breaking Spaces

Breaking spaces are the following subset of characters with General_Category Zs:

1680	OGHAM SPACE MARK
2000	EN QUAD
2001	EM QUAD
2002	EN SPACE
2003	EM SPACE
2004	THREE-PER-EM SPACE
2005	FOUR-PER-EM SPACE
2006	SIX-PER-EM SPACE
2008	PUNCTUATION SPACE
2009	THIN SPACE
200A	HAIR SPACE
205F	MEDIUM MATHEMATICAL SPACE

All of these space characters have a specific width, but otherwise behave as breaking spaces. In setting a justified line, none of these spaces normally changes in width, except for THIN SPACE when used in mathematical notation. See also the **SP** property.

The Ogham space mark is rendered visibly between words but should be elided at the end of a line.

See the **ID** property for U+3000 IDEOGRAPHIC SPACE. For a list of all space characters in the Unicode Standard, see *Section 6.2, General Punctuation,* in [Unicode5.0].

Tabs

0009	TAB

Except for the effect of the location of the tab stops, the tab character acts similarly to a space for the purpose of line breaking.

Conditional Hyphens

00AD	SOFT HYPHEN (SHY)

SHY marks an optional place where a line break may occur inside a word. It can be used with all scripts. SHY is rendered invisibly and has no width: it merely indicates an optional line break. The rendering of the optional line break depends on the script. For the Latin script, rendering the line break typically means displaying a hyphen at the end of the line; however, some languages require a change in spelling surrounding a line break. For examples, see *Section X5.3, Use of Soft Hyphen.*

Breaking Hyphens

Breaking hyphens establish explicit break opportunities immediately after each occurrence.

058A	ARMENIAN HYPHEN
2010	HYPHEN

2012 FIGURE DASH
2013 EN DASH

Hyphens are graphic characters with width. Because, unlike spaces, they print, they are included in the measured part of the preceding line, except where the layout style allows hyphens to hang into the margins.

Visible Word Dividers

The following are other forms of visible word dividers that provide break opportunities:

05BE	HEBREW PUNCTUATION MAQAF
0F0B	TIBETAN MARK INTERSYLLABIC TSHEG
1361	ETHIOPIC WORDSPACE
17D5	KHMER SIGN BARIYOOSAN
10100	AEGEAN WORD SEPARATOR LINE
10101	AEGEAN WORD SEPARATOR DOT
10102	AEGEAN CHECK MARK
1039F	UGARITIC WORD DIVIDER
103D0	OLD PERSIAN WORD DIVIDER
12470	CUNEIFORM PUNCTUATION SIGN OLD ASSYRIAN WORD DIVIDER

The Tibetan *tsheg* is a visible mark, but it functions effectively like a space to separate words (or other units) in Tibetan. It provides a break opportunity after itself. For additional information, see *Section X5.5, Tibetan Line Breaking*.

The *ethiopic word space* is a visible word delimiter and is kept on the previous line. In contrast, U+1360 ETHIOPIC SECTION MARK is typically used in a sequence of several such marks on a separate line, and separated by spaces. As such lines are typically marked with separate hard line breaks (**BK**), the section mark is treated like an ordinary symbol and given line break class **AL**.

2027 HYPHENATION POINT

A hyphenation point is a raised dot, which is mainly used in dictionaries and similar works to visibly indicate syllabification of words. Syllable breaks are potential line break opportunities in the middle of words. When an actual line break falls inside a word containing hyphenation point characters, the hyphenation point is rendered as a regular hyphen at the end of the line.

007C VERTICAL LINE

In some dictionaries, a vertical bar is used instead of a hyphenation point. In this usage, U+0323 COMBINING DOT BELOW is used to mark stressed syllables, so all breaks are marked by the vertical bar. For an actual break opportunity, the vertical bar is rendered as a hyphen.

Word Separators

Historic texts, especially ancient ones, often do not use spaces, even for scripts where modern use of spaces is standard. Special punctuation was used to mark word boundaries in such texts. For modern text processing these should be treated as line break opportunities by default. **WJ** can be used to override this default, where necessary.

16EB	RUNIC SINGLE DOT PUNCTUATION
16EC	RUNIC MULTIPLE DOT PUNCTUATION
16ED	RUNIC CROSS PUNCTUATION
2056	THREE DOT PUNCTUATION
2058	FOUR DOT PUNCTUATION
2059	FIVE DOT PUNCTUATION
205A	TWO DOT PUNCTUATION
205B	FOUR DOT MARK
205D	TRICOLON
205E	VERTICAL FOUR DOTS

Dandas

DEVANAGARI DANDA is similar to a full stop. The *danda* or historically related symbols are used with several other Indic scripts. Unlike a full stop, the *danda* is not used in number formatting. DEVANAGARI DOUBLE DANDA marks the end of a verse. It also has analogues in other scripts.

0964	DEVANAGARI DANDA
0965	DEVANAGARI DOUBLE DANDA
0E5A	THAI CHARACTER ANGKHANKHU
104A	MYANMAR SIGN LITTLE SECTION
104B	MYANMAR SIGN SECTION
1735	PHILIPPINE SINGLE PUNCTUATION
1736	PHILIPPINE DOUBLE PUNCTUATION
17D4	KHMER SIGN KHAN
17D5	KHMER SIGN BARIYOOSAN
17D8	KHMER SIGN BEYYAL
17DA	KHMER SIGN KOOMUUT
10A56	KHAROSHTHI PUNCTUATION DANDA
10A57	KHAROSHTHI PUNCTUATION DOUBLE DANDA

Tibetan

0F85	TIBETAN MARK PALUTA
0F34	TIBETAN MARK BSDUS RTAGS
0F7F	TIBETAN SIGN RNAM BCAD
0FBE	TIBETAN KU RU KHA
0FBF	TIBETAN KU RU KHA BZHI MIG CAN

For additional information, see *Section X5.5, Tibetan Line Breaking*.

Other Terminating Punctuation

Termination punctuation stays with the line, but otherwise allows a break after it. This is similar to **EX**, except that the latter may be separated by a space from the preceding word without allowing a break, whereas these marks are used without spaces.

1802	MONGOLIAN COMMA
1803	MONGOLIAN FULL STOP
1804	MONGOLIAN COLON

1805	MONGOLIAN FOUR DOTS
1808	MONGOLIAN MANCHU COMMA
1809	MONGOLIAN MANCHU FULL STOP
1A1E	BUGINESE PALLAWA
2CF9	COPTIC OLD NUBIAN FULL STOP
2CFA	COPTIC OLD NUBIAN DIRECT QUESTION MARK
2CFB	COPTIC OLD NUBIAN INDIRECT QUESTION MARK
2CFC	COPTIC OLD NUBIAN VERSE DIVIDER
2CFE	COPTIC FULL STOP
2CFF	COPTIC MORPHOLOGICAL DIVIDER
10A50	KHAROSHTHI PUNCTUATION DOT
10A51	KHAROSHTHI PUNCTUATION SMALL CIRCLE
10A52	KHAROSHTHI PUNCTUATION CIRCLE
10A53	KHAROSHTHI PUNCTUATION CRESCENT BAR
10A54	KHAROSHTHI PUNCTUATION MANGALAM
10A55	KHAROSHTHI PUNCTUATION LOTUS

BB: Break Opportunities Before (B)

Characters of this line break class move to the next line at a line break and thus provide a line break opportunity before.

Dictionary Use

00B4	ACUTE ACCENT

In some dictionaries, stressed syllables are indicated with a spacing acute accent instead of the hyphenation point. In this case the accent moves to the next line, and the preceding line ends with a hyphen.

02C8	MODIFIER LETTER VERTICAL LINE
02CC	MODIFIER LETTER LOW VERTICAL LINE

These characters are used in dictionaries to indicate stress and secondary stress when IPA is used. Both are prefixes to the stressed syllable in IPA. Breaking before them keeps them with the syllable.

> **Note:** It is hard to find actual examples in most dictionaries because the pronunciation fields usually occur right after the headword, and the columns are wide enough to prevent line breaks in most pronunciations.

Tibetan Head Letters

0F01	TIBETAN MARK GTER YIG MGO TRUNCATED A
0F02	TIBETAN MARK GTER YIG MGO -UM RNAM BCAD MA
0F03	TIBETAN MARK GTER YIG MGO -UM GTER TSHEG MA
0F04	TIBETAN MARK INITIAL YIG MGO MDUN MA
0F06	TIBETAN MARK CARET YIG MGO PHUR SHAD MA
0F07	TIBETAN MARK YIG MGO TSHEG SHAD MA
0F09	TIBETAN MARK BSKUR YIG MGO

0F0A	TIBETAN MARK BKA- SHOG YIG MGO
0FD0	TIBETAN MARK BSKA- SHOG GI MGO RGYAN
0FD1	TIBETAN MARK MNYAM YIG GI MGO RGYAN

Tibetan head letters allow a break before. For more information, see *Section X5.5, Tibetan Line Breaking.*

Mongolian

1806 MONGOLIAN TODO SOFT HYPHEN

Despite its name, this Mongolian character is not an invisible control like SOFT HYPHEN, but rather a visible character like a regular hyphen. Unlike the hyphen, MONGOLIAN TODO SOFT HYPHEN stays with the following line. Whenever optional line breaks are to be marked, SOFT HYPHEN should be used instead.

B2: Break Opportunity Before and After (B/A/XP)

2014 EM DASH

The EM DASH is used to set off parenthetical text. Normally, it is used without spaces. However, this is language dependent. For example, in Swedish, spaces are used around the EM DASH. Line breaks can occur before and after an EM DASH, but not between a pair of them. Such pairs are sometimes used instead of a single quotation dash. For that reason, the line should not be broken between EM DASHes even though not all fonts use connecting glyphs for the EM DASH.

BK: Mandatory Break (A) (Non-tailorable)

Explicit breaks act independently of the surrounding characters. No characters can be added to the **BK** class as part of tailoring, but implementations are not required to support the VT character.

000C	FORM FEED (FF)
000B	LINE TABULATION (VT)

FORM FEED separates pages. The text on the new page starts at the beginning of the line. No paragraph formatting is applied.

2028 LINE SEPARATOR (LS)

The text after the LINE SEPARATOR starts at the beginning of the line. No paragraph formatting is applied. This is similar to HTML <BR>.

2029 PARAGRAPH SEPARATOR (PS)

The text of the new paragraph starts at the beginning of the line. Paragraph formatting is applied.

Newline Function (NLF)

Newline Functions are defined in the Unicode Standard as providing additional explicit breaks. They are not individual characters, but are encoded as sequences of the control characters NEL,

LF, and CR. If a character sequence for a Newline Function contains more than one character, it is kept together. The particular sequences that form an NLF depend on the implementation and other circumstances as described in *Section 5.8, Newline Guidelines*, of [Unicode5.0].

This specification defines the NLF implicitly. It defines the three character classes **CR**, **LF**, and **NL**. Their line break behavior, defined in rule **LB5** in *Section X6.1, Non-tailorable Line Breaking Rules*, is to break after **NL**, **LF**, or **CR**, but not between **CR** and **LF**.

CB: Contingent Break Opportunity (B/A)

By default, there is a break opportunity both *before* and *after* any inline object. Object-specific line breaking behavior is implemented in the associated object itself, and where available can override the default to prevent either or both of the default break opportunities. Using U+FFFC OBJECT REPLACEMENT CHARACTER allows the object anchor to take a character position in the string.

FFFC	OBJECT REPLACEMENT CHARACTER

Object-specific line break behavior is best implemented by querying the object itself, not by replacing the **CB** line breaking class by another class.

CL: Closing Punctuation (XB)

The closing character of any set of paired punctuation must be kept with the preceding character, and the same applies to all forms of wide comma and full stop. This line break class contains the following characters plus any characters of General_Category Pe in the Unicode Character Database.

3001..3002	IDEOGRAPHIC COMMA..IDEOGRAPHIC FULL STOP
FE11	PRESENTATION FORM FOR VERTICAL IDEOGRAPHIC COMMA
FE12	PRESENTATION FORM FOR VERTICAL IDEOGRAPHIC FULL STOP
FE50	SMALL COMMA
FE52	SMALL FULL STOP
FF0C	FULLWIDTH COMMA
FF0E	FULLWIDTH FULL STOP
FF61	HALFWIDTH IDEOGRAPHIC FULL STOP
FF64	HALFWIDTH IDEOGRAPHIC COMMA

CM: Attached Characters and Combining Marks (XB)

Combining Characters

Combining character sequences are treated as units for the purpose of line breaking. The line breaking behavior of the sequence is that of the base character.

The preferred base character for showing combining marks in isolation is U+00A0 NO-BREAK SPACE. If a line break before or after the combining sequence is desired, U+200B ZERO WIDTH SPACE can be used. The use of U+0020 SPACE as a base character is deprecated.

For most purposes, combining characters take on the properties of their base characters, and that is how the **CM** class is treated in rule **LB9** of this specification. As a result, if the sequence <0021, 20E4> is used to represent a triangle enclosing an exclamation point, it is effectively treated as **EX**, the line break class of the exclamation mark. If U+2061 CAUTION SIGN had been used, which also looks like an exclamation point inside a triangle, it would have the line break class of **AL**. Only the latter corresponds to the line breaking behavior expected by users for this symbol. To avoid surprising behavior, always use a base character that is a symbol when using enclosing combining marks (General_Category Me).

The **CM** line break class includes all combining characters with General_Category Mc, Me, and Mn, unless listed explicitly elsewhere. This includes *viramas.*

Control and Formatting Characters

Most control and formatting characters are ignored in line breaking and do not contribute to the line width. By giving them class **CM**, the line breaking behavior of the last preceding character that is not of class **CM** affects the line breaking behavior.

> **Note:** When control codes and format characters are rendered visibly during editing, more graceful layout might be achieved by assigning them the **AL** or **ID** class instead.

The **CM** line break class includes all characters of General_Category Cc and Cf, unless listed explicitly elsewhere.

CR: Carriage Return (A) (Non-tailorable)

000D	CARRIAGE RETURN (CR)

A **CR** indicates a mandatory break after, unless followed by a **LF**. See also the discussion under **BK**.

> **Note:** On some platforms the character sequence <CR, CR, LF> is used to indicate the location of actual line breaks, whereas <CR, LF> is treated like a hard line break. As soon as a user edits the text, the location of all the <CR, CR, LF> sequences may change as the new text breaks differently, while the relative position of any <CR, LF> to the surrounding text stays the same. This convention allows an editor to return a buffer and the client to tell which text is displayed on which line by counting the number of <CR, CR, LF> and <CR, LF> sequences.

EX: Exclamation/Interrogation (XB)

Characters in this line break class behave like closing characters, except in relation to postfix (**PO**) and non-starter characters (**NS**).

0021	EXCLAMATION MARK
003F	QUESTION MARK
05C6	HEBREW PUNCTUATION NUN HAFUKHA
060C	ARABIC COMMA
061B	ARABIC SEMICOLON
061E	ARABIC TRIPLE DOT PUNCTUATION MARK

061F	ARABIC QUESTION MARK
066A	ARABIC PERCENT SIGN
06D4	ARABIC FULL STOP
07F9	NKO EXCLAMATION MARK
0F0D	TIBETAN MARK SHAD
0F0E	TIBETAN MARK NYIS SHAD
0F0F	TIBETAN MARK TSHEG SHAD
0F10	TIBETAN MARK NYIS TSHEG SHAD
0F11	TIBETAN MARK RIN CHEN SPUNGS SHAD
0F14	TIBETAN MARK GTER TSHEG
1944	LIMBU EXCLAMATION MARK
1945	LIMBU QUESTION MARK
2762	HEAVY EXCLAMATION MARK ORNAMENT
2763	HEAVY HEART EXCLAMATION MARK ORNAMENT
A876	PHAGS-PA MARK SHAD
A877	PHAGS-PA MARK DOUBLE SHAD
FE15	PRESENTATION FORM FOR VERTICAL EXCLAMATION MARK
FE16	PRESENTATION FORM FOR VERTICAL QUESTION MARK
FE56..FE57	SMALL QUESTION MARK..SMALL EXCLAMATION MARK
FF01	FULLWIDTH EXCLAMATION MARK
FF1F	FULLWIDTH QUESTION MARK

GL: Non-breaking ("Glue") (XB/XA) (Non-tailorable)

Non-breaking characters prohibit breaks on either side, but that prohibition can be overridden by **SP** or **ZW**. In particular, when NBSP follows SPACE, there is a break opportunity after the SPACE and NBSP will go as visible space onto the next line. See also **WJ**. The following lists the characters of line break class **GL** with additional description.

00A0	NO-BREAK SPACE (NBSP)
202F	NARROW NO-BREAK SPACE (NNBSP)
180E	MONGOLIAN VOWEL SEPARATOR (MVS)

NO-BREAK SPACE is the preferred character to use where two words should be visually separated but kept on the same line, as in the case of a title and a name "Dr.<NBSP>Joseph Becker". When SPACE follows NBSP, there is no break, because there never is a break in front of SPACE. NARROW NO-BREAK SPACE is used in Mongolian. The MONGOLIAN VOWEL SEPARATOR acts like a NNBSP in its line breaking behavior. It additionally affects the shaping of certain vowel characters as described in *Section 13.2, Mongolian*, of [Unicode5.0].

034F	COMBINING GRAPHEME JOINER

This character has no visible glyph and its presence indicates that adjoining characters are to be treated as a graphemic unit, therefore preventing line breaks between them.

2007	FIGURE SPACE

This is the preferred space to use in numbers. It has the same width as a digit and keeps the number together for the purpose of line breaking.

2011	NON-BREAKING HYPHEN (NBHY)

This is the preferred character to use where words must be hyphenated but may not be broken at the hyphen.

0F08	TIBETAN MARK SBRUL SHAD
0F0C	TIBETAN MARK DELIMITER TSHEG BSTAR
0F12	TIBETAN MARK RGYA GRAM SHAD

The TSHEG BSTAR looks exactly like a Tibetan *tsheg*, but can be used to prevent a break like *no-break space*. It inhibits breaking on either side. For more information, see *Section X5.5, Tibetan Line Breaking*.

035C..0362	COMBINING DOUBLE BREVE BELOW..COMBINING DOUBLE RIGHTWARDS ARROW BELOW

These diacritics span two characters, so no word or line breaks are possible on either side.

H2: Hangul LV Syllable (B/A)

This class includes all characters of Hangul Syllable Type LV.

Together with conjoining jamos, Hangul syllables form Korean Syllable Blocks, which are kept together; see [Boundaries]. Korean uses space-based line breaking in many styles of documents. To support these, Hangul syllables and conjoining jamo need to be tailored to use class **AL**, while the default in this specification is class **ID**, which supports the case of Korean documents not using space-based line breaking. See *Section X8.1, Types of Tailoring*. See also **JL**, **JT**, **JV**, and **H3**.

H3: Hangul LVT Syllable (B/A)

This class includes all characters of Hangul Syllable Type LVT. See also **JL**, **JT**, **JV**, and **H2**.

HY: Hyphen (XA)

002D	HYPHEN-MINUS

Some additional context analysis is required to distinguish usage of this character as a hyphen from its usage as a minus sign (or indicator of numerical range). If used as hyphen, it acts like HYPHEN.

> **Note:** Some typescript conventions use runs of HYPHEN-MINUS to stand in for longer dashes or horizontal rules. If actual character code conversion is not performed and it is desired to treat them like the characters or layout elements they stand for, line breaking needs to support these runs explicitly.

ID: Ideographic (B/A)

> **Note:** This class includes characters other than Han ideographs.

Characters with this property do not require other characters to provide break opportunities;

lines can ordinarily break before and after and between pairs of ideographic characters. The **ID** line break class consists of the following characters:

2E80..2FFF	CJK, KANGXI RADICALS, DESCRIPTION SYMBOLS
3000	IDEOGRAPHIC SPACE
3040..309F	*Hiragana* (except small characters)
30A0..30FF	*Katakana* (except small characters)
3400..4DBF	CJK UNIFIED IDEOGRAPHS EXTENSION A
4E00..9FAF	CJK UNIFIED IDEOGRAPHS
F900..FAFF	CJK COMPATIBILITY IDEOGRAPHS
A000..A48F	YI SYLLABLES
A490..A4CF	YI RADICALS
FE62..FE66	SMALL PLUS SIGN to SMALL EQUALS SIGN
FF10..FF19	WIDE DIGITS
20000..2A6D6	CJK UNIFIED IDEOGRAPHS EXTENSION B
2F800..2FA1D	CJK COMPATIBILITY IDEOGRAPHS SUPPLEMENT

It also includes all of the FULLWIDTH LATIN letters and all of the blocks in the range 3000..33FF not covered elsewhere.

> **Note:** Use U+2060 WORD JOINER as a manual override to prevent break opportunities around characters of class **ID**.

U+3000 IDEOGRAPHIC SPACE may be subject to expansion or compression during line justification.

Korean

Korean is encoded with conjoining jamo, Hangul syllables, or both. See also **JL**, **JT**, **JV**, **H2**, and **H3**. The following set of compatibility jamo is treated as **ID** by default.

3130..318F	HANGUL COMPATIBILITY JAMO

IN: Inseparable Characters (XP)

Leaders

These characters are intended to be used in consecutive sequence. There is never a line break between two character of this class.

2024	ONE DOT LEADER
2025	TWO DOT LEADER
2026	HORIZONTAL ELLIPSIS
FE19	PRESENTATION FORM FOR VERTICAL HORIZONTAL ELLIPSIS

HORIZONTAL ELLIPSIS can be used as a three-dot leader.

IS: Numeric Separator (Infix) (XB)

Characters that usually occur inside a numerical expression may not be separated from the numeric characters that follow, unless a space character intervenes. For example, there is no break in “100.00” or “10,000”, nor in “12:59”.

002C	COMMA
002E	FULL STOP
003A	COLON
003B	SEMICOLON
037E	GREEK QUESTION MARK (canonically equivalent to 003B)
0589	ARMENIAN FULL STOP
060D	ARABIC DATE SEPARATOR
07F8	NKO COMMA
2044	FRACTION SLASH
FE10	PRESENTATION FORM FOR VERTICAL COMMA
FE13	PRESENTATION FORM FOR VERTICAL COLON
FE14	PRESENTATION FORM FOR VERTICAL SEMICOLON

When not used in a numeric context, infix separators are sentence-ending punctuation. Therefore they always prevent breaks before.

JL: Hangul L Jamo (B)

The **JL** line break class consists of all characters of Hangul Syllable Type L.

Conjoining jamos form Korean Syllable Blocks, which are kept together; see [Boundaries]. Korean uses space-based line breaking in many styles of documents. To support these, Hangul syllables and conjoining jamo need to be tailored to use class **AL**, while the default in this specification is class **ID**, which supports the case of Korean documents not using space-based line breaking. See *Section X8.1, Types of Tailoring*. See also **JT**, **JV**, **H2**, and **H3**.

JT: Hangul T Jamo (A)

The **JT** line break class consists of all characters of Hangul Syllable Type T. See also **JL**, **JV**, **H2**, and **H3**.

JV: Hangul V Jamo (XA/XB)

The **JV** line break class consists of all characters of Hangul Syllable Type V. See also **JL**, **JT**, **H2**, and **H3**.

LF: Line Feed (A) (Non-tailorable)

000A	LINE FEED (LF)

There is a mandatory break after any LF character, but see the discussion under **BK**.

NL: Next Line (A) (Non-tailorable)

0085	NEXT LINE (NEL)

The **NL** class acts like **BK** in all respects (there is a mandatory break after any NEL character). It cannot be tailored, but implementations are not required to support the NEL character; see the discussion under **BK**.

NS: Nonstarters (XB)

Nonstarter characters cannot start a line, but unlike **CL** they may allow a break in some context when they follow one or more space characters. Nonstarters include

0E5A..0E5B	THAI CHARACTER ANGKHANKHU..THAI CHARACTER KHOMUT
17D4	KHMER SIGN KHAN
17D6	KHMER SIGN CAMNUC PII KUUH
203C	DOUBLE EXCLAMATION MARK
203D	INTERROBANG
2047	DOUBLE QUESTION MARK
2048	QUESTION EXCLAMATION MARK
2049	EXCLAMATION QUESTION MARK
3005	IDEOGRAPHIC ITERATION MARK
301C	WAVE DASH
303C	MASU MARK
303B	VERTICAL IDEOGRAPHIC ITERATION MARK
309B.. 309E	KATAKANA-HIRAGANA VOICED SOUND MARK..HIRAGANA VOICED ITERATION MARK
30A0	KATAKANA-HIRAGANA DOUBLE HYPHEN
30FB..30FE	KATAKANA MIDDLE DOT..KATAKANA VOICED ITERATION MARK
A015	YI SYLLABLE WU
FE54..FE55	SMALL SEMICOLON..SMALL COLON
FF1A..FF1B	FULLWIDTH COLON.. FULLWIDTH SEMICOLON
FF65	HALFWIDTH KATAKANA MIDDLE DOT
FF70	HALFWIDTH KATAKANA-HIRAGANA PROLONGED SOUND MARK
FF9E..FF9F	HALFWIDTH KATAKANA VOICED SOUND MARK..HALFWIDTH KATAKANA SEMI-VOICED SOUND MARK

plus all Hiragana, Katakana, and Halfwidth Katakana "small" characters.

> **Note:** Optionally, the **NS** restriction may be relaxed and characters treated like **ID** to achieve a more permissive style of line breaking, especially in some East Asian document styles.

NU: Numeric (XP)

These characters behave like ordinary characters in the context of ordinary characters but activate the prefix and postfix behavior of prefix and postfix characters.

Numeric characters consist of decimal digits (all characters of General_Category Nd), except those with East_Asian_Width F (Fullwidth), plus these characters:

066B	ARABIC DECIMAL SEPARATOR
066C	ARABIC THOUSANDS SEPARATOR

Unlike with **IS**, the Arabic numeric punctuation does not occur as sentence terminal punctuation outside numbers.

OP: Opening Punctuation (XA)

The opening character of any set of paired punctuation must be kept with the following character. The **OP** line break class consists of all characters of General_Category Ps in the Unicode Character Database.

PO: Postfix (Numeric) (XB)

Characters that usually follow a numerical expression may not be separated from preceding numeric characters or preceding closing characters, even if one or more space characters intervene. For example, there is no break in "(12.00) %".

Some of these characters—in particular, *degree sign* and *percent sign*—can appear on both sides of a numeric expression. Therefore the line breaking algorithm by default does not break between **PO** and numbers or letters on either side.

The list of postfix characters is

0025	PERCENT SIGN
00A2	CENT SIGN
00B0	DEGREE SIGN
060B	AFGHANI SIGN
20300	PER MILLE SIGN
2031	PER TEN THOUSAND SIGN
2032..2037	PRIME..REVERSED TRIPLE PRIME
20A7	PESETA SIGN
2103	DEGREE CELSIUS
2109	DEGREE FAHRENHEIT
FDFC	RIAL SIGN
FE6A	SMALL PERCENT SIGN
FF05	FULLWIDTH PERCENT SIGN
FFE0	FULLWIDTH CENT SIGN

Alphabetic characters are also widely used as unit designators in a postfix position. For purposes of line breaking, their classification as alphabetic is sufficient to keep them together with the preceding number.

PR: Prefix (Numeric) (XA)

Characters that usually precede a numerical expression may not be separated from following numeric characters or following opening characters, *even* if a space character intervenes. For example, there is no break in "$ (100.00)".

Many currency signs can appear on both sides, or even the middle, of a numeric expression. Therefore the line breaking algorithm, by default, does not break between **PR** and numbers or letters on either side.

The **PR** line break class consists of all currency symbols (General_Category Sc) except as listed explicitly in **PO**, as well as the following:

002B	PLUS SIGN
005C	REVERSE SOLIDUS
00B1	PLUS-MINUS
2116	NUMERO SIGN
2212	MINUS SIGN
2213	MINUS-OR-PLUS-SIGN

> **Note:** Many currency symbols may be used either as prefix or as postfix, depending on local convention. For details on the conventions used, see [CLDR].

QU: Ambiguous Quotation (XB/XA)

Some paired characters can be either opening or closing depending on usage. The default is to treat them as both opening and closing.

> **Note:** If language information is available, it can be used to determine which character is used as the opening quote and which as the closing quote. See the information in *Section 6.2, General Punctuation*, in [Unicode5.0].

The **QU** line break class consists of characters of General_Category Pf or Pi in the Unicode Character Database as well as

0022	QUOTATION MARK
0027	APOSTROPHE
275B	HEAVY SINGLE TURNED COMMA QUOTATION MARK ORNAMENT
275C	HEAVY SINGLE COMMA QUOTATION MARK ORNAMENT
275D	HEAVY DOUBLE TURNED COMMA QUOTATION MARK ORNAMENT
275E	HEAVY DOUBLE COMMA QUOTATION MARK ORNAMENT

U+23B6 BOTTOM SQUARE BRACKET OVER TOP SQUARE BRACKET is subtly different from the others in this class, in that it is *both* an opening and a closing punctuation character at the same time. However, its use is limited to certain vertical text modes in terminal emulation. Instead of creating a one-of-a-kind class for this rarely used character, assigning it to the **QU** class approximates the intended behavior.

SA: Complex-Context Dependent (South East Asian) (P)

Runs of these characters require morphological analysis to determine break opportunities. This is similar to, for example, a hyphenation algorithm. For the characters that have this property, **no** line breaks will be found otherwise. Therefore complex context analysis, often involving dictionary lookup of some form, is required to determine non-emergency line breaks.

If such analysis is not available, they should be treated as **AL**.

> **Note:** These characters can be mapped into their equivalent line breaking classes as the result of dictionary lookup, thus permitting a logical separation of this algorithm from the morphological analysis.

The class **SA** consists of all characters of General_Category Cf, Lo, Lm, Mn, or Mc in the following ranges, except as noted elsewhere:

0E00..0E7F	Thai
0E80..0EFF	Lao
1000..109F	Myanmar
1780..17FF	Khmer
1950..197F	Tai Le
1980..19DF	New Tai Lue

SG: Surrogates (XP) (Non-tailorable)

Line break class **SG** comprises all code points with General_Category Cs. The line breaking behavior of isolated surrogates is undefined.

> **Note:** The use of this line breaking class is deprecated. It was of limited usefulness for UTF-16 implementations that do not support characters beyond the BMP. The correct implementation is to resolve a *pair* of surrogates into a supplementary character before line breaking.

SP: Space (A) (Non-tailorable)

The space characters are explicit break opportunities; however, spaces at the end of a line are not measured for fit. If there is a sequence of space characters, and breaking after any of the space characters would result in the same visible line, then the line breaking position after the last space character in the sequence is the locally most optimal one. In other words, because the last character measured for fit is *before* the space character, any number of space characters are kept together invisibly on the previous line and the first non-space character starts the next line.

0020	SPACE (SP)

> **Note:** By default, SPACE, but none of the other breaking spaces, is used in determining an indirect break. For other breaking space characters, see **BA**.

SY: Symbols Allowing Break After (A)

URLs are now so common in regular plain text that they must be taken into account when assigning general-purpose line breaking properties. The **SY** line breaking property is intended to provide a break after, but not in front of, digits so as to not break "1/2" or "06/07/99".

002F	SOLIDUS

Slash (*solidus*) is allowed as an additional, limited break opportunity to improve layout of Web addresses. As a side effect, some common abbreviations such as "w/o" or "A/S", which normally would not be broken, acquire a line break opportunity. The recommendation in this case is for the layout system not to utilize a line break opportunity allowed by **SY** unless the distance between it and the next line break opportunity exceeds an implementation-defined minimal distance.

> **Note:** Normally, symbols are treated as **AL**. However, symbols can be added to this line breaking class or classes **BA**, **BB**, and **B2** by tailoring. This can be used to allow additional line breaks—for example, after "=". Mathematics requires additional specifications for line breaking, which are outside the scope of this annex.

WJ: Word Joiner (XB/XA) (Non-tailorable)

These characters glue together left and right neighbor characters such that they are kept on the same line.

2060	WORD JOINER (WJ)
FEFF	ZERO WIDTH NO-BREAK SPACE (ZWNBSP)

The word joiner character is the preferred choice for an invisible character to keep other characters together that would otherwise be split across the line at a direct break. The character FEFF has the same effect, but because it is also used in an unrelated way as a *byte order mark*, the use of the WJ as the preferred interword glue simplifies the handling of FEFF.

By definition, WJ and ZWNBSP take precedence over the action of **SP**, but not **ZW**.

XX: Unknown (XP)

The **XX** line break class consists of all characters with General_Category Co and all code points with General_Category Cn.

Unassigned code positions, private-use characters, and characters for which reliable line breaking information is not available are assigned this default line breaking property. The default behavior for this class is identical to class **AL**. Users can manually insert ZWSP or WORD JOINER around characters of class **XX** to allow or prevent breaks as needed.

In addition, implementations can override or tailor this default behavior—for example, by assigning characters the property **ID** or another class. Doing so may give better default behavior for their users. There are other possible means of determining the desired behavior of private-use characters. For example, one implementation might treat any private-use character in ideographic context as **ID**, while another implementation might support a method for assigning specific properties to specific definitions of private-use characters. The details of such use of private-use characters are outside the scope of this standard.

For supplementary characters, a useful default is to treat characters in the range 10000..1FFFD as **AL** and characters in the ranges 20000..2FFFD and 30000..3FFFD as **ID**, until the implementation can be revised to take into account the actual line breaking properties for these characters.

For more information on handling default property values for unassigned characters, see the discussion on default property values in *Section 5.3, Unknown and Missing Characters*, of [Unicode5.0].

The line breaking rules in *Section X6, Line Breaking Algorithm*, and the pair table in *Section X7, Pair Table-Based Implementation*, assume that all unknown characters have been assigned one of the other line breaking classes, such as **AL**, as part of assigning line breaking classes to the input characters.

ZW: Zero Width Space (A) (Non-tailorable)

200B ZERO WIDTH SPACE (ZWSP)

This character is used to enable additional (invisible) break opportunities wherever SPACE cannot be used. As its name implies, it normally has no width. However, its presence between two characters does not prevent increased letter spacing in justification.

X5.2 Dictionary Usage

Dictionaries follow specific conventions that guide their use of special characters to indicate features of the terms they list. Marks used for some of these conventions may occur near line break opportunities and therefore interact with line breaking. For example, in one dictionary a natural hyphen in a word becomes a tilde dash when the word is split.

Examples of conventions used in several dictionaries are briefly described in this subsection. Where possible, the default line breaking properties for characters commonly used in dictionaries have been assigned to accommodate these and similar conventions. However, implementing the full conventions in dictionaries requires special support.

Looking up the noun "syllable" in eight dictionaries yields eight different conventions:

Dictionary of the English Language (Samuel Johnson, 1843) **SYʹLLABLE** where ʹ is an oversized U+02B9 and follows the vowel of the main syllable (not the syllable itself).

Oxford English Dictionary (1st Edition) **si·lă'bl** where · is a slightly raised middle dot indicating the vowel of the stressed syllable (similar to Johnson's acute). The letter ă is U+0103. The ' is an apostrophe.

Oxford English Dictionary (2nd Edition) has gone to IPA **ˈsIləb(ə)l** where ˈ is U+02C8, I is U+026A, and ə is U+0259 (both times). The ˈ comes before the stressed syllable. The () indicate the *schwa* may be omitted.

Chambers English Dictionary (7th Edition) **silʹə-bl** where the stressed syllable is followed by ʹ U+02B9, ə is U+0259, and **-** is a hyphen. When splitting a word like **abateʹ- ment**, the stress mark ʹ goes after stressed syllable followed by the hyphen. No special convention is used when splitting at hyphen.

BBC English Dictionary **sIləbl̲** where I̲ is <U+026A, U+0332> and ə is U+0259. The vowel of the stressed syllable is underlined.

Collins Cobuild English Language Dictionary **sIləbə°l̲** where I̲ is <U+026A, U+0332> and has the same meaning as in the *BBC English Dictionary*. The ə is U+0259 (both times). The ° is a U+2070 and indicates the *schwa* may be omitted.

Readers Digest Great Illustrated Dictionary **syl·la·ble** (**sĭlləb'l**) The spelling of the word has hyphenation points (· is a U+2027) followed by phonetic spelling. The vowel of the stressed syllable is given an accent, rather than being followed by an accent. The ' is an apostrophe.

Webster's 3rd New International Dictionary **syl·la·ble** /**'siləbəl**/ The spelling of the word has hyphenation points (· is a U+2027) and is followed by phonetic spelling. The stressed syllable is preceded by ˈ U+02C8. The ə's are *schwas* as usual. *Webster's* splits words at the end of a line with a normal hyphen. A U+2E17 DOUBLE OBLIQUE HYPHEN indicates that a hyphenated word is split at the hyphen.

Some dictionaries use a character that looks like a vertical series of four dots to indicate places where there is a syllable, but no allowable break. This can be represented by a sequence of U+205E VERTICAL FOUR DOTS followed by U+2060 WORD JOINER.

X5.3 Use of Soft Hyphen

Unlike U+2010 HYPHEN, which always has a visible rendition, the character U+00AD SOFT HYPHEN (SHY) is an invisible format character that merely indicates a preferred intraword line break position. If the line is broken at that point, then whatever mechanism is appropriate for intraword line breaks should be invoked, just as if the line break had been triggered by another mechanism, such as a dictionary lookup. Depending on the language and the word, that may produce different visible results—for example

- Simply inserting a hyphen glyph
- Inserting a hyphen glyph and changing spelling in the divided word parts
- Not showing any visible change and simply breaking at that point
- Inserting a hyphen glyph at the beginning of the new line

The following are a few examples of spelling changes. Each example shows the line break as " / " and any inserted hyphens. There are many other cases.

- In pre-reform German orthography, a "c" before the hyphenation point can change into a "k": "Drucker" hyphenates into "Druk- / ker".
- In modern Dutch, an *e-diaeresis* after the hyphenation point can change into a simple "e": "geërfde" hyphenates into "ge- / erfde", and "geëerd" into "ge-/ eerd".
- In German and Swedish, a consonant is sometimes doubled: Swedish "tuggummi"; hyphenates into "tugg- / gummi".
- In Dutch, a letter can disappear: "opaatje" hyphenates into "opa- / tje".

The inserted hyphen glyph can take a wide variety of shapes, as appropriate for the situation. Examples include shapes like U+2010 HYPHEN, U+058A ARMENIAN HYPHEN, U+180A MONGOLIAN NIRUGU, or U+1806 MONGOLIAN TODO SOFT HYPHEN.

When a SHY is used to represent a possible hyphenation location, the spelling is that of the word without hyphenation: "tug<SHY>gummi". It is up to the line breaking implementation to make any necessary spelling changes when such a possible hyphenation is actually used.

Sometimes it is desirable to encode text that includes line breaking decisions and will not be further broken into lines. If such text includes hyphenations, the spelling must reflect the changes due to hyphenation: "tugg<U+2010>/ gummi", including the appropriate character for any inserted hyphen. For a list of dash-like characters in Unicode, see *Section 6.2, General Punctuation*, in [Unicode5.0].

Hyphenation, and therefore the SHY, can be used with the Arabic script. If the rendering system breaks at that point, the display—including shaping—should be what is appropriate for the given language. For example, sometimes a hyphen-like mark is placed on the end of the line. This mark looks like a *kashida*, but is not connected to the letter preceding it, looking as if the mark is placed and the line divided after the contextual shapes for the line have been determined. For more information on shaping, see [Bidi] and *Section 8.2, Arabic*, of [Unicode5.0].

There are three types of hyphens: explicit hyphens, conditional hyphens, and dictionary-inserted hyphens resulting from a hyphenation process. There is no character code for the third kind of hyphen. If a distinction is desired, the fact that a hyphen is dictionary-inserted must be represented out of band or by using another control code instead of SHY.

The action of a hyphenation algorithm is equivalent to the insertion of a SHY. However, when a word contains an explicit SHY, it is customarily treated as overriding the action of the hyphenator for that word.

X5.4 Use of Double Hyphen

In some fonts, noticeably Fraktur fonts, it is customary to use a double-stroke form of the hyphen, usually oblique. Such use is merely a font-based glyph variation and does not affect line breaking in any way. In texts using such a font, automatic hyphenation or SHY would also result in the display of a double-stroke, oblique hyphen.

In some dictionaries, such as *Webster's 3rd New International Dictionary*, double-stroke, oblique hyphens are used to indicate a hyphen at the end of the line that should be retained when the term shown is not line wrapped. It is not necessary to store a special character in the data; one merely needs to substitute the glyph of any ordinary hyphen that winds up at the end of a line. In such convention, automatic hyphenation or SHY would result in the display of an ordinary hyphen without further substitution.

Certain linguistic notations make use of a double-stroke, oblique hyphen to indicate specific features. The U+2E17 DOUBLE OBLIQUE HYPHEN character used in this case is not a hyphen and does not represent a line break opportunity. Automatic hyphenation or SHY would result in the display of an ordinary hyphen.

X5.5 Tibetan Line Breaking

The Tibetan script uses spaces sparingly, relying instead on the *tsheg*. There is no punctuation equivalent to a period in Tibetan; Tibetan *shad* characters indicate the end of a "phrase," not a sentence. "Phrases" are often metrical—that is, written after every *N* syllables—and a new sentence can often start within the middle of a phrase. Sentence boundaries need to be determined grammatically rather than by punctuation.

Traditionally there is nothing akin to a paragraph in Tibetan text. It is typical to have many pages of text without a paragraph break—that is, without an explicit line break. The closest thing to a paragraph in Tibetan is a new section or topic starting with U+0F12 or U+0F08. However, these occur inline: one section ends and a new one starts on the same line, and the new section is marked only by the presence of one of these characters.

Some modern books, newspapers, and magazines format text more like English with a break before each section or topic—and (often) the title of the section on a separate line. Where this is done, authors insert an explicit line break. Western punctuation (full stop, question mark, exclamation mark, comma, colon, semicolon, quotes) is starting to appear in Tibetan documents, particularly those published in India, Bhutan, and Nepal. Because there are no formal rules for their use in Tibetan, they get treated generically by default. In Tibetan documents published in China, CJK bracket and punctuation characters occur frequently; these should be treated as in Chinese written horizontally.

> **Note:** The detailed rules for formatting Tibetan texts are complex, and the original assignment of line break classes was found to be wholly insufficient for the purpose. In [Unicode4.1], the assignment of line break classes for Tibetan was revised significantly in an attempt to better model Tibetan line breaking behavior. No new rules or line break classes were added.

The set of line break classes for Tibetan should provide a good starting point, even though there is limited practical experience in their implementation. As more experience is gained, some modifications, possibly including new rules or additional line break classes, can be expected.

It is the stated intention of the Unicode Consortium to review these assignments in a future version and to furnish a more detailed and complete description of Tibetan line breaking and line formatting behavior.

X6 Line Breaking Algorithm

Unicode Standard Annex #29, "Text Boundaries" [Boundaries], describes a particular method for boundary detection. It is based on a set of hierarchical rules and character classifications. That method is well suited for implementation of some of the advanced heuristics for line breaking.

A slightly simplified implementation of such an algorithm can be devised that uses a two-dimensional table to resolve break opportunities between pairs or characters. It is described in *Section X7, Pair Table-Based Implementation*.

The line breaking algorithm presented in this section can be expressed in a series of rules that take line breaking classes defined in *Section X5.2, Description of Line Breaking Properties*, as input. The title of each rule contains a mnemonic summary of the main effect of the rule. The formal statement of each line breaking rules consists either of a remap rule or of one or more regular expressions containing one or more line breaking classes and one of three special symbols indicating the type of line break opportunity:

! Mandatory break at the indicated position

× No break allowed at the indicated position

÷ Break allowed at the indicated position

The rules are applied in order. That is, there is an implicit "otherwise" at the front of each rule following the first. It is possible to construct alternate sets of such rules that are fully equivalent. To be equivalent, an alternate set of rules must have the same effect.

The distinction between a direct break and an indirect break as defined in *Section X2, Definitions*, is handled in rule **LB18**, which explicitly considers the effect of **SP**. Because rules are applied in order, allowing breaks following **SP** in rule **LB18** implies that any prohibited break in rules **LB19**–**LB30** is equivalent to an indirect break.

The examples for each rule use representative characters, where 'H' stands for an ideographs, 'h' for small kana, and '9' for digits. Except where a rule contains no expressions, the italicized text of the rule is intended merely as a handy summary.

The algorithm consists of a part for which tailoring is prohibited and a freely tailorable part.

X6.1 Non-tailorable Line Breaking Rules

The rules in this subsection and the membership in the classes **BK**, **CM**, **CR**, **GL**, **LF**, **NL**, **WJ**, and **ZW** are not tailorable; see *Section X4, Conformance.*

Resolve line breaking classes:

*LB1 Assign a line breaking class to each code point of the input. Resolve **AI**, **CB**, **SA**, **SG**, and **XX** into other line breaking classes depending on criteria outside the scope of this algorithm.*

In the absence of such criteria, it is recommended that classes **AI**, **SA**, **SG**, and **XX** be resolved to **AL**, except that characters of class **SA** that have General_Category Mn or Mc be resolved to **CM** (see **SA**). Unresolved class **CB** is handled in rule **LB20**.

Start and end of text:

There are two special logical positions: **sot**, which occurs before the first character in the text, and **eot,** which occurs after the last character in the text. Thus an empty string would consist of **sot** followed immediately by **eot**. With these two definitions, the line break rules for start and end of text can be specified as follows:

LB2 Never break at the start of text.

sot ×

LB3 Always break at the end of text.

! eot

These two rules are designed to deal with degenerate cases, so that there is at least one character on each line, and at least one line break for the whole text. Emergency line breaking behavior usually also allows line breaks anywhere on the line if a legal line break cannot be found. This has the effect of preventing text from running into the margins.

Mandatory breaks:

A hard line break can consist of **BK** or a Newline Function (NLF) as described in *Section 5.8, Newline Guidelines*, of [Unicode5.0]. These three rules are designed to handle the line ending and line separating characters as described there.

*LB4 Always break after hard line breaks (but never between **CR** and **LF**).*

BK !

*LB5 Treat **CR** followed by **LF**, as well as **CR**, **LF**, and **NL** as hard line breaks.*

CR × LF

CR !

LF !

NL !

LB6 Do not break before hard line breaks.

× (BK | CR | LF | NL)

Explicit breaks and non-breaks:

LB7 Do not break before spaces or zero width space.

× SP

× ZW

LB8 Break after zero width space.

ZW ÷

Combining marks:

See also *Section X9.2, Legacy Support for Space Character as Base for Combining Marks.*

LB9 Do not break a combining character sequence; treat it as if it has the line breaking class of the base character in all of the following rules.

Treat X CM* as if it were X.

where X is any line break class except **BK**, **CR**, **LF**, **NL**, **SP**, or **ZW**.

At any possible break opportunity between **CM** and a following character, **CM** behaves as if it had the type of its base character. Note that despite the summary title of this rule it is not limited to standard combining character sequences. For the purposes of line breaking, sequences containing most of the control codes or layout control characters are treated like combining sequences.

LB10 Treat any remaining combining mark as ***AL****.*

Treat any remaining CM as it if were AL.

This catches the case where a **CM** is the first character on the line or follows **SP**, **BK**, **CR**, **LF**, **NL**, or **ZW**.

Word joiner:

LB11 Do not break before or after Word joiner and related characters.

× WJ

WJ ×

Non-breaking characters:

LB12 Do not break before or after NBSP and related characters.

[^SP] × GL

GL ×

Unlike the case for **WJ**, inserting a **SP** overrides the non-breaking nature of a **GL**. The expression [^SP] designates any line break class other than **SP**. The symbol ^ is used, instead of !, to avoid confusion with the use of ! to indicate an explicit break.

X6.2 Tailorable Line Breaking Rules

The following rules and classes referenced in them can be tailored by a conformant implementations; see *Section X4, Conformance.*

Opening and closing:

These have special behavior with respect to spaces, and therefore come before rule 19.

LB13 Do not break before ']' or '!' or ';' or '/', even after spaces.

× CL

× EX

× IS

× SY

LB14 Do not break after '[', even after spaces.

OP SP* ×

LB15 Do not break within '"[', even with intervening spaces.

QU SP* × OP

LB16 Do not break within ']h', even with intervening spaces.

CL SP* × NS

LB17 Do not break within '——', even with intervening spaces.

B2 SP* × B2

Spaces:

LB18 Break after spaces.

SP ÷

Special case rules:

LB19 Do not break before or after quotation marks, such as ' " '.

× QU

QU ×

*LB20 Break before and after unresolved **CB**.*

÷ CB

CB ÷

Conditional breaks should be resolved external to the line breaking rules. However, the default action is to treat unresolved **CB** as breaking before and after.

LB21 Do not break before hyphen-minus, other hyphens, fixed-width spaces, small kana, and other non-starters, or after acute accents.

× BA

× HY

× NS

BB ×

LB22 Do not break between two ellipses, or between letters or numbers and ellipsis.

AL × IN

ID × IN

IN × IN

NU × IN

Examples: '9...', 'a...', 'H...'

Numbers:

Do not break alphanumerics.

LB23 Do not break within 'a9', '3a', or 'H%'.

ID × PO

AL × NU

NU × AL

LB24 Do not break between prefix and letters or ideographs.

PR × ID

PR × AL

PO × AL

In general, lines should not be broken inside numbers of the form described by the following regular expression:

(**PR** | **PO**) ? (**OP** | **HY**) ? **NU** (**NU** | **SY** | **IS**) * **CL** ? (**PR** | **PO**) ?

Examples: $(12.35)   2,1234   (12)¢   12.54¢

The default line breaking algorithm approximates this with the following rule. Note that some cases have already been handled, such as '9,', '[9'. For a tailoring that supports the regular expression directly, see *Section X8.2, Examples of Customization.*

LB25 Do not break between the following pairs of classes relevant to numbers:

CL × PO

CL × PR

NU × PO

NU × PR

PO × OP

PO × NU

PR × OP

PR × NU

HY × NU

IS × NU

NU × NU

SY × NU

Example pairs: '$9', '$[', '$-', '-9', '/9', '99', ',9', '9%' ']%'

Korean syllable blocks

Conjoining jamo, Hangul syllables, or combinations of both form Korean Syllable Blocks. Such blocks are effectively treated as if they were Hangul syllables; no breaks can occur in the middle of a syllable block. See Unicode Standard Annex #29, "Text Boundaries" [Boundaries], for more information on Korean Syllable Blocks.

LB26 Do not break a Korean syllable.

JL × (JL | JV | H2 | H3)

(JV | H2) × (JV | JT)

(JT | H3) × JT

The effective line breaking class for the syllable block matches the line breaking class for Hangul syllables, which is **ID** by default. This is achieved by the following rule:

*LB27 Treat a Korean Syllable Block the same as **ID**.*

(JL | JV | JT | H2 | H3) × IN

(JL | JV | JT | H2 | H3) × PO

PR × (JL | JV | JT | H2 | H3)

When Korean uses SPACE for line breaking, these classes, as well as characters of class **ID**, are often tailored to **AL**; see *Section X8, Customization.*

Finally, join alphabetic letters into words and break everything else.

LB28 Do not break between alphabetics ("at").

AL × AL

LB29 Do not break between numeric punctuation and alphabetics ("e.g.").

IS × AL

LB30 Do not break between letters, numbers, or ordinary symbols and opening or closing punctuation.

(AL | NU) × OP

CL × (AL | NU)

The purpose of this rule is to prevent breaks in common cases where a part of a word appears between delimiters—for example, in "person(s)".

LB31 Break everywhere else.

ALL ÷

÷ ALL

X7 Pair Table-Based Implementation

A two-dimensional table can be used to resolve break opportunities between pairs of characters. The rows of the table are labeled with the possible values of the line breaking property of the leading character in the pair. The columns are labeled with the line breaking class for the following character of the pair. Each intersection is labeled with the resulting line break opportunity.

The Japanese standard JIS X 4051-1995 [JIS] provides an example of such a table-based definition. However, it uses line breaking classes whose membership is not solely determined by the line breaking property (as in this annex), but in some cases by heuristic analysis or markup of the text.

The implementation provided here directly uses the line breaking classes defined previously.

X7.1 Minimal Table

If two rows of the table have identical values and the corresponding columns also have identical values, then the two line breaking classes can be coalesced. For example, the JIS standard uses 20 classes, of which only 14 appear to be unique. Any minimal table representation is unique, except for trivial reordering of rows and columns.

X7.2 Extended Context

Most of the rules in *Section X6, Line Breaking Algorithm*, involve only pairs of characters, or they apply to a single line break class preceded or followed by any character. These rules can be represented directly in a pair table. However, rules **LB14–LB17** require extended context to handle spaces.

By broadening the definition of a pair from **B A**, where **B** is the line breaking class before a break and **A** the one after, to **B SP* A**, where **SP*** is an optional run of space characters, the same table can be used to distinguish between cases where **SP** can or cannot provide a line break opportunity (that is, direct and indirect breaks). Rules equivalent to the ones given in *Section X6, Line Breaking Algorithm*, can be formulated without explicit use of **SP** by using **%** to express indirect breaks instead. These rules can then be simplified to involve only pairs of classes—that is, only constructions of the form:

B ÷ A

B % A

B × A

where either **A** or **B** may be empty. These simplified rules can be automatically translated into a pair table, as in *Table 2*. Line breaking analysis then proceeds by pair table lookup as explained below. (For readability in table layout, the symbol ^ is used in the table instead of × and _ is used instead of ÷.)

Rule **LB9** requires extended context for handling combining marks. This extended context must also be built into the code that interprets the pair table. For convenience in detecting the condition where **A** = **CM**, the symbols # and @ are used in the pair table, instead of % and ^, respectively. See *Section X7.5, Combining Marks.*

X7.3 Example Pair Table

Table 2 implements the line breaking behavior described in this annex, with the limitation that only context of the form **B SP* A** is considered. **BK**, **CR**, **LF**, **NL**, and **SP** classes are handled explicitly in the outer loop, as given in the code sample below. Pair context of the form **B CM*** can be handled by handling the special entries @ and # in the driving loop, as explained in *Section X7.5, Combining Marks.* Conjoining jamos are considered separately in *Section X7.6, Conjoining Jamos.* In *Table 2,* the rows are labeled with the **B** class and the columns are labeled with the **A** class.

Table 2. Example Pair Table

	OP	CL	QU	GL	NS	EX	SY	IS	PR	PO	NU	AL	ID	IN	HY	BA	BB	B2	ZW	CM	WJ	H2	H3	JL	JV	JT
OP	^	^	^	^	^	^	^	^	^	^	^	^	^	^	^	^	^	^	^	@	^	^	^	^	^	^
CL	_	^	%	%	^	^	^	^	%	%	%	%	_	_	%	%	_	_	^	#	^	_	_	_	_	_
QU	^	^	%	%	%	^	^	^	%	%	%	%	%	%	%	%	%	%	^	#	^	%	%	%	%	%
GL	%	^	%	%	%	^	^	^	%	%	%	%	%	%	%	%	%	%	^	#	^	%	%	%	%	%
NS	_	^	%	%	%	^	^	^	_	_	_	_	_	_	%	%	_	_	^	#	^	_	_	_	_	_
EX	_	^	%	%	%	^	^	^	_	_	_	_	_	_	%	%	_	_	^	#	^	_	_	_	_	_
SY	_	^	%	%	%	^	^	^	_	_	%	_	_	_	%	%	_	_	^	#	^	_	_	_	_	_
IS	_	^	%	%	%	^	^	^	_	_	%	%	_	_	%	%	_	_	^	#	^	_	_	_	_	_
PR	%	^	%	%	%	^	^	^	_	_	%	%	%	_	%	%	_	_	^	#	^	%	%	%	%	%
PO	%	^	%	%	%	^	^	^	_	_	%	%	_	_	%	%	_	_	^	#	^	_	_	_	_	_
NU	%	^	%	%	%	^	^	^	%	%	%	%	_	%	%	%	_	_	^	#	^	_	_	_	_	_
AL	%	^	%	%	%	^	^	^	_	_	%	%	_	%	%	%	_	_	^	#	^	_	_	_	_	_
ID	_	^	%	%	%	^	^	^	_	%	_	_	_	%	%	%	_	_	^	#	^	_	_	_	_	_
IN	_	^	%	%	%	^	^	^	_	_	_	_	_	%	%	%	_	_	^	#	^	_	_	_	_	_
HY	_	^	%	%	%	^	^	^	_	_	%	_	_	_	%	%	_	_	^	#	^	_	_	_	_	_
BA	_	^	%	%	%	^	^	^	_	_	_	_	_	_	%	%	_	_	^	#	^	_	_	_	_	_
BB	%	^	%	%	%	^	^	^	%	%	%	%	%	%	%	%	%	%	^	#	^	%	%	%	%	%
B2	_	^	%	%	%	^	^	^	_	_	_	_	_	_	%	%	_	^	^	#	^	_	_	_	_	_
ZW	_	_	_	_	_	_	_	_	_	_	_	_	_	_	_	_	_	_	^	_	_	_	_	_	_	_
CM	_	^	%	%	%	^	^	^	_	_	%	%	_	%	%	%	_	_	^	#	^	_	_	_	_	_
WJ	%	^	%	%	%	^	^	^	%	%	%	%	%	%	%	%	%	%	^	#	^	%	%	%	%	%
H2	_	^	%	%	%	^	^	^	_	%	_	_	_	%	%	%	_	_	^	#	^	_	_	_	%	%
H3	_	^	%	%	%	^	^	^	_	%	_	_	_	%	%	%	_	_	^	#	^	_	_	_	_	%
JL	_	^	%	%	%	^	^	^	_	%	_	_	_	%	%	%	_	_	^	#	^	%	%	%	%	_
JV	_	^	%	%	%	^	^	^	_	%	_	_	_	%	%	%	_	_	^	#	^	_	_	_	%	%
JT	_	^	%	%	%	^	^	^	_	%	_	_	_	%	%	%	_	_	^	#	^	_	_	_	_	%

Resolved outside the pair table: **AI**, **BK**, **CB**, **CR**, **LF**, **NL**, **SA**, **SG**, **SP**, **XX**

Table 2 uses the following notation:

^ denotes a *prohibited break*: B ^ A is equivalent to **B SP* × A**; in other words, never break before A and after B, even if one or more spaces intervene.

% denotes an *indirect break opportunity:* B % A is equivalent to **B × A** *and* **B SP+ ÷ A**; in other words, do not break before A, unless one or more spaces follow B.

@ denotes a *prohibited break for combining marks:* B @ A is equivalent to **B SP* × A**, where A is of class **CM**. For more details, see *Section X7.5, Combining Marks.*

# denotes an *indirect break opportunity for combining marks following a space*: B # A is equivalent to (**B** × **A** *and* **B SP+** ÷ **A**), where A is of class **CM**.

_ denotes a *direct break opportunity* (equivalent to ÷ as defined above).

X7.4 Sample Code

The following two sections provide sample code [Code14] that demonstrates how the pair table is used. For a complete implementation of the line breaking algorithm, `if` statements to handle the line breaking classes **CR**, **LF**, and **NL** need to be added. They have been omitted here for brevity, but see *Section X7.7, Explicit Breaks.*

The sample code assumes that the line breaking classes **AI**, **CB**, **SG**, and **XX** have been resolved according to rule **LB1** as part of initializing the `pcls` array. The code further assumes that the complex line break analysis for characters with line break class **SA** is handled in function `findComplexBreak`, for which the following placeholder is given:

```
// placeholder function for complex break analysis
// cls - resolved line break class, may differ from pcls[0]
// pcls - pointer to array of line breaking classes (input)
// pbrk - pointer to array of line breaking opportunities (output)
// cch - remaining length of input
int
findComplexBreak(enum break_class cls, enum break_class *pcls,
                              enum break_action *pbrk, int cch)
{
        if (!cch)
            return 0;
        for (int ich = 1; ich < cch; ich++) {

            // .. do complex break analysis here
            // and report any break opportunities in pbrk ..

            pbrk[ich-1] = PROHIBITED_BRK; // by default, no break

            if (pcls[ich] != SA)
                break;
        }
        return ich;
}
```

The entries in the example pair table correspond to the following enumeration. For diagnostic purposes, the sample code returns these value to indicate not only the location but also the type of rule that triggered a given break opportunity.

```
enum break_action {
        DIRECT_BRK = 0,                 // _ in table
        INDIRECT_BRK,                   // % in table
        COMBINING_INDIRECT_BRK,         // # in table
        COMBINING_PROHIBITED_BRK,       // @ in table
        PROHIBITED_BRK,                 // ^ in table
        EXPLICTI_BRK };                 // ! in rules
```

Because the contexts involved in indirect breaks of the form **B SP* A** are of indefinite length, they need to be handled explicitly in the driver code. The sample implementation of a `findLineBrk` function below remembers the line break class for the last characters seen, but skips any occurrence of **SP** without resetting this value. Once character **A** is encountered, a simple lookback is used to see if it is preceded by a **SP**. This lookback is necessary only if **B** % **A**.

```
// handle spaces separately, all others by table
// pcls - pointer to array of line breaking classes (input)
// pbrk - pointer to array of line break opportunities (output)
// cch - number of elements in the arrays ("count of characters") (input)
// ich - current index into the arrays (variable) (returned value)
// cls - current resolved line break class for 'before' character (variable)

int
findLineBrk(enum break_class *pcls, enum break_action *pbrk, int cch)
{
    if (!cch) return 0;

    enum break_class cls = pcls[0];    // class of 'before' character

    // loop over all pairs in the string up to a hard break
    for (int ich = 1; (ich < cch) &amp;&amp; (cls != BK); ich++) {

        // handle explicit breaks here (see Section 7.7)

        // handle spaces explicitly
        if (pcls[ich] == SP) {
            pbrk[ich-1] = PROHIBITED_BRK;    // apply rule LB7: × SP
            continue;                        // do not update cls
        }

        // handle complex scripts in a separate function
        if (pcls[ich] == SA) {
            ich += findComplexBreak(cls, &pcls[ich-1], &pbrk[ich-1],
                        cch - (ich-1));
            if (ich < cch)
                cls = pcls[ich];
            continue;
        }

        // lookup pair table information in brkPairs[before, after];
        enum break_action brk = brkPairs[cls][pcls[ich]];

        pbrk[ich-1] = brk;                   // save break action in output array

        if (brk == INDIRECT_BRK) {           // resolve indirect break
            if (pcls[ich - 1] == SP)         // if context is A SP * B
                pbrk[ich-1] = INDIRECT_BRK;  //     break opportunity
            else                             // else
                pbrk[ich-1] = PROHIBITED_BRK; //    no break opportunity
        }

        // handle breaks involving a combining mark (see Section 7.5)

        // save cls of 'before' character (unless bypassed by 'continue')
        cls = pcls[ich];
    }
    pbrk[ich-1] = EXPLICIT_BRK;              // always break at the end

    return ich;
}
```

The function returns all of the break opportunities in the array pointed to by `pbrk`, using the values in the table. On return, `pbrk[ich]` is the type of break after the character at index `ich`.

A common optimization in implementation is to determine only the nearest line break opportunity prior to the position of the first character that would cause the line to become overfull. Such an optimization requires backward traversal of the string instead of forward traversal as shown in the sample code.

X7.5 Combining Marks

The implementation of combining marks in the pair table presents an additional complication because rule **LB9** defines a context **X CM*** that is of arbitrary length. There are some similarities to the way contexts of the form **B SP* A** that are involved in indirect breaks are evaluated. However, contexts of the form **SP CM*** or **CM* SP** also need to be handled, while rule **LB10** requires some **CM*** to be treated like **AL**.

Implementing LB10. This rule can be reflected directly in the example pair table in *Table 2* by assigning the same values in the row marked **CM** as in the row marked **AL**. Incidentally, this is equivalent to rewriting the rules **LB11–LB31** by duplicating any expression that contains an **AL** on its lefthand side with another expression that contains a **CM**. For example, in **LB22**

AL × IN

would become

AL × IN

CM × IN

Rewriting these rules as indicated here (and then deleting **LB10**) is fully equivalent to the original rules because rule **LB9** already accounts for all **CM**s that are not supposed to be treated like **AL**. For complete prescription see Example 9 in *Section X8.2, Examples of Customization.*

Implementing LB9. Rule **LB9** is implemented in the example pair table in *Table 2* by assigning a special # entry in the column marked **CM** for all rows referring to a line break class that allows a direct or indirect break after itself. (Note that the intersection between the row for class **ZW** and the column for class **CM** must be assigned "_" because of rule **LB8**.) The # corresponds to a `break_action` value of `COMBINING_INDIRECT_BREAK`, which triggers the following code in the sample implementation:

```
else if (brk == COMBINING_INDIRECT_BRK) {     // resolve combining mark break
    pbrk[ich-1] = PROHIBITED_BRK;              // do not break before CM
    if (pcls[ich-1] == SP){
        #ifndef LEGACY_CM                      // new: space is not a base
            pbrk[ich-1] = COMBINING_INDIRECT_BRK;     // apply rule SP ÷
        #else
            pbrk[ich-1] = PROHIBITED_BRK;      // legacy: keep SP CM together
            if (ich > 1)
                pbrk[ich-2] = ((pcls[ich - 2] == SP) ?
                                                INDIRECT_BRK : DIRECT_BRK);
        #endif
    } else                                     // apply rule LB9: X CM * -> X
        continue;                              // do not update cls
}
```

When handling a `COMBINING_INDIRECT_BREAK`, the last remembered line break class in variable `cls` is *not* updated, except for those cases covered by rule **LB10**. A *tailoring* of rule **LB9** that keeps the last SPACE character preceding a combining mark, if any, and therefore breaks before that SPACE character can easily be implemented as shown in the sample code. (See *Section X9.2, Legacy Support for Space Character as Base for Combining Marks.*)

Any rows in *Table 2* for line break classes that prohibit breaks after must be handled explicitly. In the example pair table, these are assigned a special entry "@", which corresponds to a special break action of COMBINING_PROHIBITED_BREAK that triggers the following code:

```
else if (brk == COMBINING_PROHIBITED_BRK) { // this is the case OP SP* CM
    pbrk[ich-1] = COMBINING_PROHIBITED_BRK;  // no break allowed
    if (pcls[ich-1] != SP)
        continue;                           // apply rule LB9: X CM* -> X
}
```

The only line break class that unconditionally prevents breaks across a following **SP** is **OP**. The preceding code fragment ensures that **OP CM** is handled according to rule **LB9** and **OP SP CM** is handled as **OP SP AL** according to rule **LB10**.

X7.6 Conjoining Jamos

For Korean Syllable Blocks, the information in rule **LB26** is represented by a simple pair table shown in *Table 3.*

Table 3. Korean Syllable Block Pair Table

	H2	H3	JL	JV	JT
H2	_	_	_	%	%
H3	_	_	_	_	%
JL	%	%	%	%	_
JV	_	_	_	%	%
JT	_	_	_	_	%

When constructing a pair table such as *Table 2*, this pair table for Korean syllable blocks in *Table 3* is merged with the main pair table for all other line break classes by adding the cells from *Table 3* beyond the lower-right corner of the main pair table. Next, according to rule **LB27**, any empty cells in the new rows are filled with the same values as in the existing row for class **ID**, and any empty cells for the new columns are filled with the same values as in the existing column for class **ID**. The resulting merged table is shown in *Table 2.*

X7.7 Explicit Breaks

Handling explicit breaks is straightforward in the driver code, although it does clutter up the loop condition and body of the loop a bit. For completeness, the following sample shows how to change the loop condition and add `if` statements to the loop that handle **BK**, **NL**, **CR**, and **LF**. Because **NL** and **BK** behave identically by default, this code can be simplified in implementations where the character classification is changed so that **BK** will always be substituted for **NL** when assigning the line break class. Because this optimization does not change the result, it is not considered a tailoring and does not affect conformance.

```
// handle case where input starts with an LF
if (cls == LF)
    cls = BK;

// treat NL like BK
if (cls == NL)
    cls = BK;
```

```
// loop over all pairs in the string up to a hard break or CRLF pair
for (int ich = 1; (ich < cch) && (cls != BK) && (cls != CR || pcls[ich] == LF); ich++) {

    // handle BK, NL and LF explicitly
    if (pcls[ich] == BK ||pcls[ich] == NL ||  pcls[ich] == LF)
    {
        pbrk[ich-1] = PROHIBITED_BRK;
        cls = BK;
        continue;
    }

    // handle CR explicitly
    if(pcls[ich] == CR)
    {
        pbrk[ich-1] = PROHIBITED_BRK;
        cls = CR;
        continue;
    }

    // handle spaces explicitly...
```

X8 Customization

A real-world line breaking algorithm must be tailorable to some degree to meet user or document requirements.

In Korean, for example, two distinct line breaking modes occur, which can be summarized as breaking after each character or breaking after spaces (as in Latin text). The former tends to occur when text is set justified; the latter, when ragged margins are used. In that case, even ideographs are broken only at space characters. In Japanese, for example, tighter and looser specifications of prohibited line breaks may be used.

Specialized text or specialized text constructs may need specific line breaking behavior that differs from the default line breaking rules given in this annex. This may require additional tailorings beyond those considered in this section. For example, the rules given here are insufficient for mathematical equations, whether inline or in display format. Likewise, text that commonly contains lengthy URLs might benefit from special tailoring that suppresses **SY** × **NU** from rule **LB25** within the scope of a URL to allow breaks after a "/" separated segment in the URL regardless of whether the next segment starts with a digit.

The remainder of this section gives an overview of common types of tailorings and examples of how to customize the pair table implementation of the line breaking algorithm for these tailorings.

X8.1 Types of Tailoring

There are three principal ways of tailoring the sample pair table implementation of the line breaking algorithm:

1. **Changing the line breaking class assignment for some characters**
   This is useful in cases where the line breaking properties of one class of characters are occasionally lumped together with the properties of another class to achieve a less restrictive line breaking behavior.

2. **Changing the table value assigned to a pair of character classes**
   This is particularly useful if the behavior can be expressed by a change at a limited number of pair intersections. This form of customization is equivalent to permanently overriding some of the rules in *Section X6, Line Breaking Algorithm*.
3. **Changing the interpretation of the line breaking actions**
   This is a dynamic equivalent of the preceding. Instead of changing the values for the pair intersection directly in the table, they are labeled with special values that cause different actions for different customizations. This is most suitable when customizations need to be enabled at run time.

Beyond these three straightforward customization steps, it is always possible to augment the algorithm itself—for example, by providing specialized rules to recognize and break common constructs, such as URLs, numeric expressions, and so on. Such open-ended customizations place no limits on possible changes, other than the requirement that characters with normative line breaking properties be correctly implemented.

Reference [Cedar97] reports on a real-world implementation of a pair table-based implementation of a line breaking algorithm substantially similar to the one presented here, and including the types of customizations presented in this section. That implementation was able to simultaneously meet the requirements of customers in many European and East Asian countries with a single implementation of the algorithm.

X8.2 Examples of Customization

Example 1. The exact method of resolving the line break class for characters with class **SA** is not specified in the default algorithm. One method of implementing line breaks for complex scripts is to invoke context-based classification for all runs of characters with class **SA**. For example, a dictionary-based algorithm could return different classes for Thai letters depending on their context: letters at the start of Thai words would become **BB** and other Thai letters would become **AL**. Alternatively, for text consisting of or predominantly containing characters with line breaking class **SA**, it may be useful to instead defer the determination of line breaks to a different algorithm entirely. *Section X7.4, Sample Code*, sketches such approach in which the interface to the dictionary-based algorithm directly reports break opportunities.

Example 2. To implement terminal style line breaks, it would be necessary to allow breaks inside a run of spaces. This requires a change in the way the driver loop handles spaces and, therefore, cannot be simply done by customizing the pair table. However, the additional task of line wrapping runs of spaces could also be performed after the fact at the layout system level while leaving unchanged the actual line breaking algorithm.

Example 3. Depending on the nature of the document, Korean either uses implicit breaking around characters (type 2 as defined above in *Section X3, Introduction*) or uses spaces (type 1). Space-based layout is common in magazines and other informal documents with ragged margins, while books, with both margins justified, use the other type, as it affords more line break opportunities and therefore leads to better justification. Reference [Suign98] shows how the necessary customizations can be elegantly handled by selectively altering the interpretation of the pair entries. Only the intersections of **ID/ID**, **AL/ID**, and **ID/AL** are affected. For alphabetic style line breaking, breaks for these cases require space; for ideographic style line breaking, these cases do not require spaces. Therefore, one defines a pseudo-action, which is then resolved into either direct or indirect break action based on user selection of the preferred behavior for a given text.

Example 4. Sometimes in a Far Eastern context it is necessary to allow alphabetic characters and digit strings to break anywhere. According to reference [Suign98], this can again be done in the same way as Korean. In this case the intersections of **NU/NU**, **NU/AL**, **AL/AL**, and **AL/NU** are affected.

Example 5. Some users prefer to relax the requirement that Kana syllables be kept together. For example, the syllable *kyu,* spelled with the two kanas *KI* and "small *yu*", would no longer be kept together as if *KI* and *yu* were atomic. This customization can be handled via the first method by changing the classification of the Kana small characters from **NS** to **ID** as needed.

Example 6. Some implementations may wish to tailor the line breaking algorithm to resolve grapheme clusters according to Unicode Standard Annex #29, "Text Boundaries" [Boundaries], as a first stage. Generally, the line breaking algorithm does not create line break opportunities within default grapheme clusters; therefore such a tailoring would be expected to produce results that for most practical cases are close to what are defined by the default algorithm. However, if such a tailoring is chosen, characters that are members of line break class **CM** but not part of the definition of default grapheme clusters must still be handled by rules **LB9** and **LB10**, or by some additional tailoring.

Example 7. Regular expression-based line breaking engines might get better results using a tailoring that directly implements the following regular expression for numeric expressions:

(**PR** | **PO**) ? (**OP** | **HY**) ? **NU** (**NU** | **SY** | **IS**) * **CL** ? (**PR** | **PO**) ?

This is equivalent to replacing the rule **LB25** by the following tailored rule:

Regex-Number: Do not break numbers.

(PR | PO) × (OP | HY)? NU

(OP | HY) × NU

NU × (NU | SY | IS)

NU (NU | SY | IS)* × (NU | SY | IS | CL)

NU (NU | SY | IS)* CL? × (PO | PR)

This customized rule uses extended contexts that cannot be represented in a pair table.

When the tailored rule is used, **LB13** must also be tailored as follows:

[^NU] × CL

× EX

[^NU] × IS

[^NU] × SY

Otherwise, single digits may be handled by rule **LB13** before being handled in the regular expression. In these tailored rules, [^NU] designates any line break class other than **NU**. The symbol ^ is used, instead of !, to avoid confusion with the use of ! to indicate an explicit break.

Example 8. For some implementations it may be difficult to implement **LB9** due to the added complexity of its indefinite length context. Because combining marks are most commonly applied to characters of class **AL**, rule **LB10** by itself generally produces acceptable results for such implementations, but such an approximation is not a conformant tailoring.

X9 Implementation Notes

This section provides additional notes on implementation issues.

X9.1 Combining Marks in Regular Expression-Based Implementations

For implementations that use regular expressions, it is not possible to directly express rules **LB9** and **LB10**. However, it is possible to make these rules unnecessary by rewriting *all* the rules from **LB11** on down so that the overall result of the algorithm is unchanged. This restatement of the rules is therefore not a tailoring, but rather an equivalent statement of the algorithm that can be directly expressed as regular expressions.

To replace rule **LB9**, terms of the form

B # **A**

B SP* # **A**

B #

B SP* #

are replaced by terms of the form

B CM* # **A**

B CM* SP* # **A**

B CM* #

B CM* SP* #

where **B** and **A** are any line break class or set of alternate line break classes, such as (X |Y), and where # is any of the three operators !, ÷, or ×.

Note that because **sot**, **BK**, **CR**, **LF**, **NL**, and **ZW** are all handled by rules above **LB9**, these classes cannot occur in position **B** in any rule that is rewritten as shown here.

Replace **LB10** by the following rule:

× CM

For each rule containing AL on its left side, add a rule that is identical except for the replacement of AL by CM, but taking care of correctly handling sets of alternate line break classes. For example, for rule

$$(AL \mid NU) \times OP$$

add another rule

$$CM \times OP.$$

These prescriptions for rewriting the rules are, in principle, valid even where the rules have been tailored as permitted in *Section X4, Conformance.* However, for extended context rules such as in Example 7, additional considerations apply. These are described in *Section X6.2, Replacing Ignore Rules*, of Unicode Standard Annex #29, "Text Boundaries" [Boundaries].

X9.2 Legacy Support for Space Character as Base for Combining Marks

As stated in [Unicode5.0], *Section 7.9, Combining Marks*, combining characters are shown in isolation by applying them to U+00A0 NO-BREAK SPACE (NBSP). In earlier versions, this recommendation included the use of U+0020 SPACE. This use of SPACE for this purpose is now deprecated because it has been found to lead to many complications in text processing. When using either NBSP or SPACE as the base character, the visual appearance is the same, but the line breaking behavior is different. Under the current rules, **SP CM*** will allow a break between **SP** and **CM***, which could result in a new line starting with a combining mark. Previously, whenever the base character was **SP**, the sequences **CM*** and **SP CM*** were defined to act like indivisible clusters, allowing breaks on either side like **ID**.

Where backward compatibility with documents created under the prior practice is desired, the following tailoring should be applied to those **CM** characters that have a General_Category value of Combining_Mark (M):

*Legacy-CM: In all of the rules following rule **LB8**, if a space is the base character for a combining mark, the space is changed to type **ID**. In other words, break before **SP** in the same cases as one would break before an **ID**.*

Treat **SP CM*** as if it were **ID**.

While this tailoring changes the location of the line break opportunities in the string, it should ordinarily not affect the display of the text. That is because spaces at the end of the line are normally invisible and the recommended display for isolated combining marks is the same as if they were applied to a preceding SPACE or NBSP.

References

For references for this annex, see Unicode Standard Annex #41, "Common References for Unicode Standard Annexes."

Acknowledgments

Asmus Freytag is the author of the initial version and has added to and maintained the text of this annex.

The initial assignments of properties are based on input by Michel Suignard. Mark Davis provided algorithmic verification and formulation of the rules, and detailed suggestions on the algorithm and text. Ken Whistler, Rick McGowan and other members of the editorial committee provided valuable feedback. Tim Partridge enlarged the information on dictionary usage. Sun Gi Hong reviewed the information on Korean and provided copious printed samples. Eric Muller reanalyzed the behavior of the soft hyphen and collected the samples. Christopher Fynn provided the background information on Tibetan line breaking. Andrew West, Kamal Mansour, Andrew Glass, Daniel Yacob, and Peter Kirk suggested improvements for Mongolian, Arabic, Kharoshthi, Ethiopic, and Hebrew punctuation characters, respectively. Kent Karlsson reviewed the line break properties for consistency. Andy Heninger reviewed the rules and provided input on regular expression-based implementations. Many others provided additional review of the rules and property assignments.

Modifications

Change History

For details of the change history, see the online copy of this annex at http://www.unicode.org/reports/tr14/.

Rule Numbering Across Versions

Table 4 documents changes in the numbering of line breaking rules. A duplicate number indicates that a rule was subsequently split. (In each version, the rules are applied in their numerical order, not in the order they appear in this table.) Versions prior to 3.0.1 are not documented here.

Table 4. Rule Numbering Across Versions

5.0.0	4.1.0	4.0.1	4.0.0	3.2.0	3.1.0	3.0.1
LB1	1	1	1	1	1	1
LB2	2a	2a	2a	2a	2a	2a
LB3	2b	2b	2b	2b	2b	3b
LB4	3a	3a	3a	3a	3a	3a
LB5	3b	3b	3b	3a	3a	3a
LB6	3c	3c	3c	3b	3b	3b
LB7	4	4	4	4	4	4
LB8	5	5	5	5	5	5
	deprecated	7a	7a	7	7	7
LB9	7b	7b	7b	6	6	6
LB10	7c	7c	7c			
LB11	11b	11b	11b	13	13	13
LB12	13	11b	11b	13	13	13
LB13	8	8	8	8	8	8
LB14	9	9	9	9	9	9
LB15	10	10	10	10	10	10
LB16	11	11	11	11	11	11
LB17	11a	11a	11a	11a	11a	
LB18	12	12	12	12	12	12
LB19	14	14	14	14	14	14
LB20	14a	14a	14a			
LB21	15	15	15	15	15	15
LB22	16	16	16	16	16	16
LB23	17	17	17	17	17	17
LB24	18	18	18	18	18	18
LB25	18	18	18	18	18	18
	removed	18b	18b	15b	15b	15b
LB26	18b	6	6	6	6	6
LB27	18c	6	6	6	6	6
LB28	19	19	19	19	19	19
LB29	19b	19b				
LB30						
LB31	20	20	20	20	20	20

Unicode Standard Annex #15

Unicode Normalization Forms

Summary

This annex describes specifications for four normalized forms of Unicode text. With these forms, equivalent text (canonical or compatibility) will have identical binary representations. When implementations keep strings in a normalized form, they can be assured that equivalent strings have a unique binary representation.

Contents

X1 Introduction

The Unicode Standard defines two equivalences between characters: canonical equivalence and compatibility equivalence. Canonical equivalence is a basic equivalency between characters or sequences of characters. *Figure 1* illustrates this equivalence.

Figure 1. Canonical Equivalence

Combining sequence	Ç	↔	C ◌̧
Hangul	가	↔	가
Singleton	Ω	↔	Ω

For round-trip compatibility with existing standards, Unicode has encoded many entities that are really variants of existing nominal characters. The visual representations of these characters are typically a subset of the possible visual representations of the nominal character. These are given compatibility decompositions in the standard. Because the characters are visually distinguished, replacing a character by a compatibility equivalent may mean this visual distinction is lost. If the visual distinction is stylistic, then markup or styling could be used to represent the formatting information. However, some characters with compatibility decompositions are used in mathematical notation to represent distinction of a semantic nature; replacing the use of distinct character codes by formatting may cause problems. See *Figure 2* for examples of compatibility equivalents.

Both canonical and compatibility equivalences are explained in more detail in *Chapter 2, General Structure*, and *Chapter 3, Conformance,* of *The Unicode Standard* in [Unicode]. In addition, the Unicode Standard describes several forms of normalization in *Section 5.6, Normalization.* These Normalization Forms are designed to produce a unique normalized form for any given string. Two of these forms are precisely specified in *Section 3.7, Decomposition*, in [Unicode]. In particular, the standard defines a *canonical decomposition* format, which can be used as a normalization for interchanging text. This format allows for binary comparison while maintaining canonical equivalence with the original unnormalized text.

The standard also defines a *compatibility decomposition* format, which allows for binary comparison while maintaining compatibility equivalence with the original unnormalized text. The latter can also be useful in many circumstances, because it folds the differences between characters that are inappropriate in those circumstances. For example, the halfwidth and fullwidth *katakana* characters will have the same compatibility decomposition and are thus compatibility equivalents; however, they are not canonical equivalents.

Figure 2. Compatibility Equivalence

Font variants	ℋ		ℍ	
Breaking differences	‑			
Cursive forms	ﻧ	ﻨ	ﻦ	ﻥ
Circled	①			
Width, size, rotated	ｶ	カ	︴	︷
Superscripts/subscripts	⁹		₉	
Squared characters	㌀			
Fractions	¼			
Others	ǆ			

Table 1. Normalization Forms

Title	Description	Specification
Normalization Form D (NFD)	Canonical Decomposition	*Sections 3.7*, *3.11*, and *3.12* [Unicode]; also summarized under *Section X10, Decomposition*
Normalization Form C (NFC)	Canonical Decomposition, followed by Canonical Composition	See *Section X5, Specification*
Normalization Form KD (NFKD)	Compatibility Decomposition	*Sections 3.7*, *3.11*, and *3.12* [Unicode]; also summarized under *Section X10, Decomposition*
Normalization Form KC (NFKC)	Compatibility Decomposition, followed by Canonical Composition	See *Section X5, Specification*

Both of these formats are normalizations to decomposed characters. While *Section 3.7, Decomposition*, in [Unicode] also discusses normalization to composite characters (also known as *decomposable* or *precomposed* characters), it does not precisely specify a format. Because of the nature of the precomposed forms in the Unicode Standard, there is more than one possible specification for a normalized form with composite characters. This annex provides a unique specification for normalization, and a label for each normalized form.

The four Normalization Forms are labeled as shown in *Table 1*.

As with decomposition, there are two forms of normalization that convert to composite characters: *Normalization Form C* and *Normalization Form KC*. The difference between these depends on whether the resulting text is to be a *canonical* equivalent to the original unnormalized text or a *compatibility* equivalent to the original unnormalized text. (In *NFKC* and *NFKD*, a *K* is used to stand for *compatibility* to avoid confusion with the *C* standing for *composition*.) Both types of normalization can be useful in different circumstances.

Figures 3–6 illustrate different ways in which source text can be normalized. In the first three figures, the NFKD form is always the same as the NFD form, and the NFKC form is always the same as the NFC form, so for simplicity those columns are omitted. For consistency, all of these examples use Latin characters, although similar examples are found in other scripts.

Figure 3. Singletons

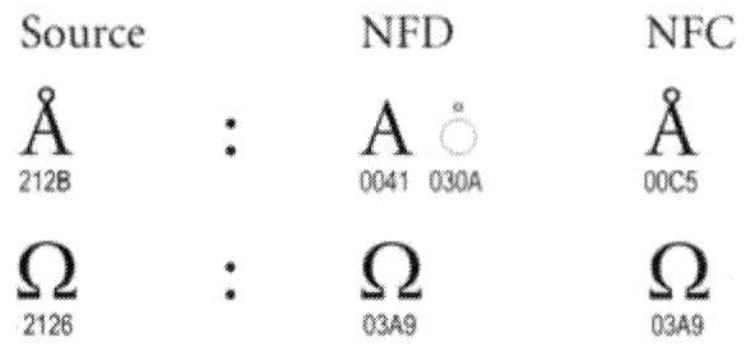

Source		NFD	NFC
Å 212B	:	A ̊ 0041 030A	Å 00C5
Ω 2126	:	Ω 03A9	Ω 03A9

Certain characters are known as singletons. They never remain in the text after normalization. Examples include the *angstrom* and *ohm* symbols, which map to their normal letter counterparts *a-with-ring* and *omega*, respectively.

Figure 4. Canonical Composites

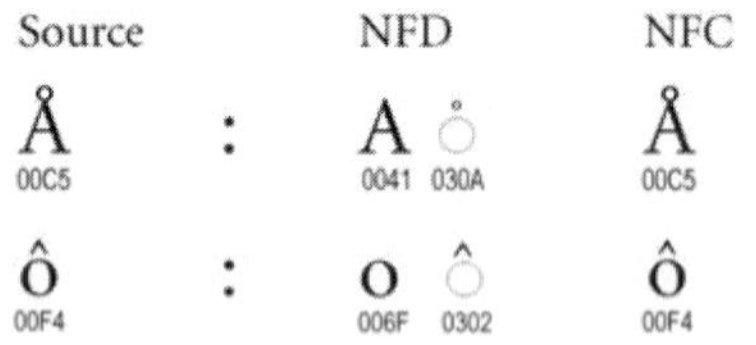

Source		NFD	NFC
Å 00C5	:	A ̊ 0041 030A	Å 00C5
ô 00F4	:	o ̂ 006F 0302	ô 00F4

Many characters are known as canonical composites, or precomposed characters. In the D forms, they are decomposed; in the C forms, they are *usually* precomposed. (For exceptions, see *Section X6, Composition Exclusion Table*.)

Normalization provides a unique order for combining marks, with a uniform order for all D and C forms. Even when there is no precomposed character, as with the “q” with accents in *Figure 5*, the ordering may be modified by normalization.

Figure 5. Multiple Combining Marks

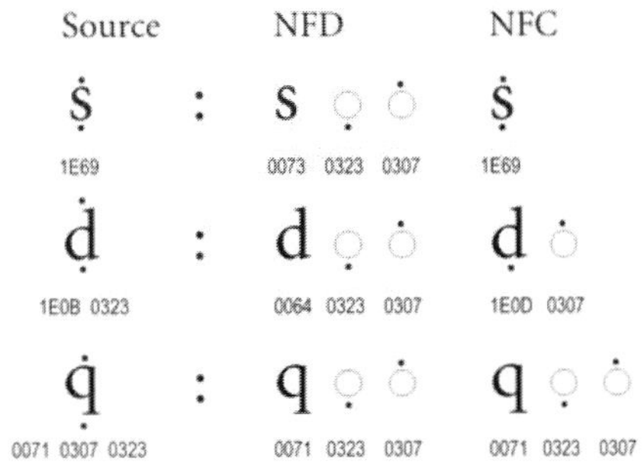

Source		NFD	NFC
ṩ 1E69	:	s ◌̣ ◌̇ 0073 0323 0307	ṩ 1E69
ḍ̇ 1E0B 0323	:	d ◌̣ ◌̇ 0064 0323 0307	ḍ ◌̇ 1E0D 0307
q̣̇ 0071 0307 0323	:	q ◌̣ ◌̇ 0071 0323 0307	q ◌̣ ◌̇ 0071 0323 0307

The example of the letter "d" with accents shows a situation where a precomposed character plus another accent changes in NF(K)C to a *different* precomposed character plus a different accent.

Figure 6. Compatibility Composites

Source		NFD	NFC	NFKD	NFKC
ﬁ FB01	:	ﬁ FB01	ﬁ FB01	f i 0066 0069	f i 0066 0069
2⁵ 0032 2075	:	2 ⁵ 0032 2075	2 ⁵ 0032 2075	2 5 0032 0035	2 5 0032 0035
ẛ̣ 1E9B 0323	:	ſ ◌̣ ◌̇ 017F 0323 0307	ẛ ◌̣ 1E9B 0323	s ◌̣ ◌̇ 0073 0323 0307	ṩ 1E69

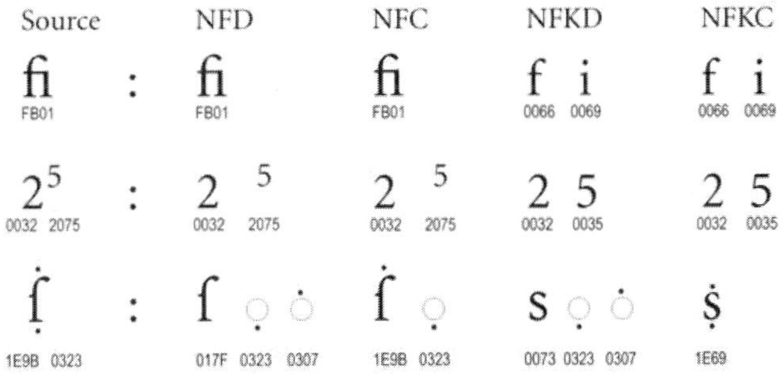

In the NFKC and NFKD forms, many formatting distinctions are removed, as shown in *Figure 6*. The "ﬁ" ligature changes into its components "f" and "i", the superscript formatting is removed from the "5", and the long "s" is changed into a normal "s".

Normalization Form KC does *not* attempt to map character sequences to compatibility composites. For example, a compatibility composition of "office" does *not* produce "o\uFB03ce", even though "\uFB03" is a character that is the compatibility equivalent of the sequence of three characters "ffi". In other words, the composition phase of NFC and NFKC are the same—only their decomposition phase differs, with NFKC applying compatibility decompositions.

All of the definitions in this annex depend on the rules for equivalence and decomposition found in *Chapter 3, Conformance*, of [Unicode] and the decomposition mappings in the Unicode Character Database [UCD].

> **Note:** Text exclusively containing only ASCII characters (U+0000..U+007F) is left unaffected by all of the Normalization Forms. This is particularly important for programming languages (see *Section X13, Programming Language Identifiers*).

Normalization Form C uses canonical composite characters where possible, and maintains the distinction between characters that are compatibility equivalents. Typical strings of composite accented Unicode characters are already in Normalization Form C. Implementations of Unicode that restrict themselves to a repertoire containing no combining marks (such as those that declare themselves to be implementations at level 1 as defined in ISO/IEC 10646-1) are already typically using Normalization Form C. (Implementations of later versions of 10646 need to be aware of the versioning issues—see *Section X3, Versioning and Stability.*)

The *W3C Character Model for the World Wide Web* [CharMod] uses Normalization Form C for XML and related standards (that document is not yet final, but this requirement is not expected to change). See the *W3C Requirements for String Identity, Matching, and String Indexing* [CharReq] for more background.

Normalization Form KC additionally folds the differences between compatibility-equivalent characters that are inappropriately distinguished in many circumstances. For example, the halfwidth and fullwidth *katakana* characters will normalize to the same strings, as will Roman numerals and their letter equivalents. More complete examples are provided in *Section X7, Examples and Charts.*

Normalization Forms KC and KD must *not* be blindly applied to arbitrary text. Because they erase many formatting distinctions, they will prevent round-trip conversion to and from many legacy character sets, and unless supplanted by formatting markup, they may remove distinctions that are important to the semantics of the text. It is best to think of these Normalization Forms as being like uppercase or lowercase mappings: useful in certain contexts for identifying core meanings, but also performing modifications to the text that may not always be appropriate. They can be applied more freely to domains with restricted character sets, such as in *Section X13, Programming Language Identifiers.*

To summarize the treatment of compatibility composites that were in the source text:

- Both NFD and NFC maintain compatibility composites.
- Neither NFKD nor NFKC maintains compatibility composites.
- None of the forms *generate* compatibility composites that were not in the source text.

For a list of all characters that may change in any of the Normalization Forms (aside from reordering), see Normalization Charts [Charts].

X1.1 Concatenation

In using normalization functions, it is important to realize that *none* of the Normalization Forms are closed under string concatenation. That is, even if two strings X and Y are normalized, their string concatenation X+Y is *not* guaranteed to be normalized. This even happens in NFD, because accents are canonically ordered, and may rearrange around the point where the strings are joined. Consider the string concatenation examples shown in *Table 2.*

However, it is possible to produce an optimized function that concatenates two normalized strings and *does* guarantee that the result is normalized. Internally, it only needs to normalize characters around the boundary of where the original strings were joined, within stable code points. For more information, see *Section X14.1, Stable Code Points.*

Table 2. String Concatenation

Form	String1	String2	Concatenation	Correct Normalization
NFD	a ^	. (dot under)	a ^ .	a . ^
NFC	a	^	a ^	â
NFC	ㄱ	ㅏ ㄱ	ㄱ ㅏ ㄱ	각

However, all of the Normalization Forms *are* closed under substringing. For example, if one takes a substring of a normalized string X, from offsets 5 to 10, one is guaranteed that the resulting string is still normalized.

X2 Notation

All of the definitions in this annex depend on the rules for equivalence and decomposition found in *Chapter 3, Conformance*, of [Unicode] and the Character Decomposition Mapping and Canonical Combining Class property in the Unicode Character Database [UCD]. Decomposition *must* be done in accordance with these rules. In particular, the decomposition mappings found in the Unicode Character Database must be applied recursively, and then the string put into canonical order based on the characters' combining classes.

Table 3 lists examples of the notational conventions used in this annex.

Table 3. Notation Examples

Example Notation	Description
combiningClass(X)	The combining class of a character X
"...\uXXXX..."	The Unicode character U+XXXX embedded within a string
"...\UXXXXXXXX..."	The Unicode character U+XXXXXXXX embedded within a string
B-C	A single character that is equivalent to the sequence of characters B + C
k_i, a_m, and k_f	Conjoining jamo types (initial, medial, final) represented by subscripts
"ç"	*c* followed by a *nonspacing cedilla:* spacing accents (without a dotted circle) may be used to represent nonspacing accents
NFX(S)	Any Normalization Form: NFD(S), NFKD(S), NFC(S), and NFKC(S) are the possibilities
toNFX(s)	A function that produces the the normalized form of a string s according to the definition of Normalization Form X
isNFC(s)	A binary property of a string s: isNFX(s) is true if and only if toNFX(s) is identical to s; see also *Section X14, Detecting Normalization Forms.*
X ≈ Y	X is canonically equivalent to Y
X[a, b]	The substring of X that includes all code units after offset a and before offset b; for example, if X is "abc", then X[1,2] is "b"

Additional conventions used in this annex:

1. A sequence of characters may be represented by using plus signs between the character names or by using string notation.
2. An *offset into a Unicode string* is a number from 0 to *n*, where *n* is the length of the string and indicates a position that is logically between Unicode code units (or at the very front or end in the case of 0 or *n*, respectively).
3. Unicode names may be shortened, as shown in *Table 4*.

Table 4. Character Abbreviation

Abbreviation	Full Unicode Name
E-grave	LATIN CAPITAL LETTER E WITH GRAVE
ka	KATAKANA LETTER KA
hw_ka	HALFWIDTH KATAKANA LETTER KA
ten	COMBINING KATAKANA-HIRAGANA VOICED SOUND MARK
hw_ten	HALFWIDTH KATAKANA VOICED SOUND MARK

X3 Versioning and Stability

It is crucial that Normalization Forms remain stable over time. That is, if a string that does not have any unassigned characters is normalized under one version of Unicode, it must remain normalized under all future versions of Unicode. This is the backward compatibility requirement. To meet this requirement, a fixed version for the composition process is specified, called the *composition version.* The composition version is defined to be **Version 3.1.0** of the Unicode Character Database. For more information, see

- Versions of the Unicode Standard [Versions]
- Unicode 3.1 [Unicode3.1]
- Unicode Character Database [UCD]

To see what difference the composition version makes, suppose that a future version of Unicode were to add the composite *Q-caron.* For an implementation that uses that future version of Unicode, strings in Normalization Form C or KC would continue to contain the sequence Q + *caron,* and *not* the new character *Q-caron,* because a canonical composition for *Q-caron* was not defined in the composition version. See *Section X6, Composition Exclusion Table,* for more information.

It would be possible to add more compositions in a future version of Unicode, as long as the backward compatibility requirement is met. It requires that for any new composition XY → Z, at most one of X or Y was defined in a previous version of Unicode. That is, Z must be a new character, and either X or Y must be a new character. However, the Unicode Consortium strongly discourages new compositions, even in such restricted cases.

In addition to fixing the composition version, future versions of Unicode must be restricted in terms of the kinds of changes that can be made to character properties. Because of this, the Unicode Consortium has a clear policy to guarantee the stability of Normalization Forms.

X3.1 Stability of Normalized Forms

A normalized string is guaranteed to be stable; that is, once normalized, a string is normalized according to all future versions of Unicode.

More precisely, if a string has been normalized according to a particular version of Unicode *and* contains only characters allocated in that version, it will qualify as normalized according to any future version of Unicode.

X3.2 Stability of the Normalization Process

The *process* of producing a normalized string from an unnormalized string has the same results under each version of Unicode, except for certain edge cases addressed in the following corrigenda:

- Three corrigenda correct certain data mappings for a total of seven characters:

Corrigendum #2, "U+FB1D Normalization" [Corrigendum2]
Corrigendum #3, "U+F951 Normalization" [Corrigendum3]
Corrigendum #4, "Five Unihan Canonical Mapping Errors" [Corrigendum4]

- Corrigendum #5, "Normalization Idempotency" [Corrigendum5], fixed a problem in the description of the normalization process for some instances of particular sequences. *Such instances never occur in meaningful text.*

X3.3 Guaranteeing Process Stability

Unicode provides a mechanism for those implementations that require not only normalized strings, *but also the normalization process,* to be absolutely stable between two versions (including the edge cases mentioned in *Section X3.2, Stability of the Normalization Process*). This, of course, is true only where the repertoire of characters is limited to those character present in the earlier version of Unicode.

To have the newer implementation produce the same results as the older version (for characters defined as of the older version):

1. Premap a maximum of seven (rare) characters according to whatever corrigenda came between the two versions (see [Errata]).
    - For example, for a Unicode 4.0 implementation to produce the same results as Unicode 3.2, the five characters mentioned in [Corrigendum4] are premapped to the *old* values given in version 4.0 of the UCD data file [Corrections].

2. If the earlier version is before Unicode 4.1 and the later version is 4.1 or later, reorder the sequences listed in *Table 11* of *Section X20, Corrigendum 5 Sequences*, as follows:

From:	first_character	intervening_character(s)	*last_character*
To:	first_character	*last_character*	intervening_character(s)

3. Apply the newer version of normalization.

Note: For step 2, in most implementations it is actually more efficient (and much simpler) to parameterize the code to provide for both pre- and post-Unicode 4.1 behavior. This typically takes only one additional conditional statement.

X3.4 Forbidding Characters

An alternative approach for certain protocols is to forbid characters that differ in normalization status across versions. The characters and sequences affected are not in any practical use, so this may be viable for some implementations. For example, when upgrading from Unicode 3.2 to Unicode 5.0, there are three relevant corrigenda:

- Corrigendum #3, "U+F951 Normalization" [Corrigendum3]
- Corrigendum #4, "Five Unihan Canonical Mapping Errors" [Corrigendum4]
  The five characters are U+2F868, U+2F874, U+2F91F, U+2F95F, and U+2F9BF.
- Corrigendum #5, "Normalization Idempotency" [Corrigendum5]

The characters in Corrigenda #3 and #4 are all extremely rare Han characters. They are compatibility characters included only for compatibility with a single East Asian character set standard each: U+F951 for a duplicate character in KS X 1001, and the other five for CNS 11643-1992. That's why they have canonical decomposition mappings in the first place.

The duplicate character in KS X 1001 is a rare character in Korean to begin with—in a South Korean standard, where the use of Han characters at all is uncommon in actual data. And this is a pronunciation duplicate, which even if it were used would very likely be inconsistently and incorrectly used by end users, because there is no visual way for them to make the correct distinctions.

The five characters from CNS 11643-1992 have even less utility. They are minor glyphic variants of unified characters—the kinds of distinctions that are subsumed already within all the unified Han ideographs in the Unicode Standard. They are from Planes 4–15 of CNS 11643-1992, which never saw any commercial implementation in Taiwan. The IT systems in Taiwan almost all implemented Big Five instead, which was a slight variant on Planes 1 and 2 of CNS 11643-1986, and which included none of the five glyph variants in question here.

As for Corrigendum #5, it is important to recognize that none of the affected sequences occur in any well-formed text in any language. See *Section X20, Corrigendum 5 Sequences.*

For more information, see *Section X18, Corrigenda.*

X4 Conformance

UAX15-C1. *A process that produces Unicode text that purports to be in a Normalization Form shall do so in accordance with the specifications in this annex.*

UAX15-C2. *A process that tests Unicode text to determine whether it is in a Normalization Form shall do so in accordance with the specifications in this annex.*

UAX15-C3. *A process that purports to transform text into a Normalization Form must be able to pass the conformance test described in Section X15, Conformance Testing.*

UAX15-C4. *A process that purports to transform text according to the Stream-Safe Text Format must do so in accordance with the specifications in this annex.*

The specifications for Normalization Forms are written in terms of a process for producing a decomposition or composition from an arbitrary Unicode string. This is a *logical* description—particular implementations can have more efficient mechanisms as long as they produce the same result. See C18 in *Chapter 3, Conformance*, of [Unicode] and the notes following. Similarly, testing for a particular Normalization Form does not require applying the process of normalization, so long as the result of the test is equivalent to applying normalization and then testing for binary identity.

X5 Specification

This section specifies the format for Normalization Forms C and KC. It uses four definitions D1, D2, D3, D4, and two rules R1 and R2. In these definitions and rules, and in explanatory text, the term "character" is used. It should be interpreted as meaning "code point," because the algorithm applies to any sequence of code points, including those containing code points that are not assigned characters.

All combining character sequences start with a character of combining class zero. For simplicity, the following term is defined for such characters:

D1. A character S is a *starter* if it has a combining class of zero in the Unicode Character Database. Any other character is a *non-starter.*

Because of the definition of canonical equivalence, the order of combining characters with the same combining class makes a difference. For example, *a-macron-breve* is not the same as *a-breve-macron*. Characters cannot be composed if that would change the canonical order of the combining characters.

D2. In any character sequence beginning with a starter S, a character C is *blocked* from S if and only if there is some character B between S and C, and either B is a starter or it has the same **or higher** combining class as C.

- This definition is to be applied only to strings that are already canonically decomposed.

When B blocks C, changing the order of B and C would result in a character sequence that is *not* canonically equivalent to the original. See *Section 3.11, Canonical Ordering Behavior* [Unicode].

If a combining character sequence is in canonical order, then testing whether a character is blocked requires looking at only the immediately preceding character.

The process of forming a composition in Normalization Form C or KC involves two steps:

1. Decomposing the string according to the canonical (or compatibility, respectively) mappings of the Unicode Character Database that correspond to the latest version of Unicode supported by the implementation.
2. Composing the resulting string according to the *canonical* mappings of the composition version of the Unicode Character Database by successively composing each unblocked character with the last starter.

Figure 7 shows a sample of the how the composition process works. The dark green cubes represent starters, and the light gray cubes represent non-starters. In the first step, the string is fully decomposed and reordered. In the second step, each character is checked against the last non-starter and starter, and combined if all the conditions are met. Examples are provided in *Section X 7, Examples and Charts,* and a code sample is provided in *Section X11, Code Sample.*

Figure 7. Composition Process

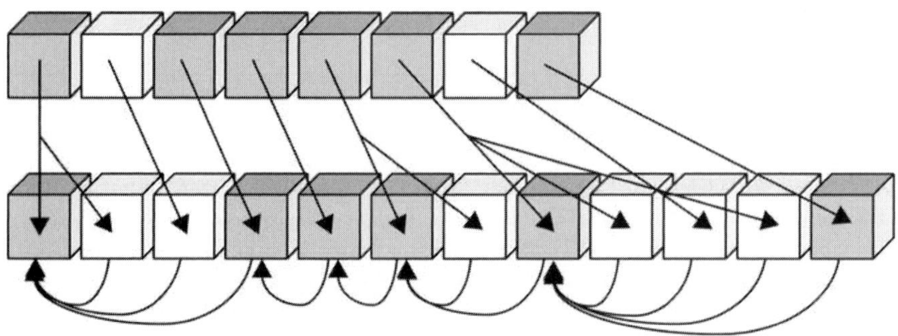

A precise notion is required for when an unblocked character can be composed with a starter. This uses the following two definitions.

D3. A *primary composite* is a character that has a canonical decomposition mapping in the Unicode Character Database (or has a canonical Hangul decomposition) but is not in the *Section X6, Composition Exclusion Table.*

Note: Hangul syllable decomposition is considered a canonical decomposition. See *[Unicode]* and *Section X16, Hangul.*

D4. A character X can be *primary combined* with a character Y if and only if there is a primary composite Z that is canonically equivalent to the sequence <X, Y>.

Based upon these definitions, the following rules specify the Normalization Forms C and KC.

R1. Normalization Form C

The Normalization Form C for a string S is obtained by applying the following process, or any other process that leads to the same result:

1. Generate the *canonical* decomposition for the source string S according to the decomposition mappings in the *latest supported* version of the Unicode Character Database.
2. Iterate through each character C in that decomposition, from first to last. If C is not blocked from the last starter L and it can be primary combined with L, then replace L by the composite L-C and remove C.

The result of this process is a new string S', which is in Normalization Form C.

R2. Normalization Form KC

The Normalization Form KC for a string S is obtained by applying the following process, or any other process that leads to the same result:

1. Generate the *compatibility* decomposition for the source string S according to the decomposition mappings in the *latest supported* version of the Unicode Character Database.
2. Iterate through each character C in that decomposition, from first to last. If C is not blocked from the last starter L and it can be primary combined with L, then replace L by the composite L-C and remove C.

The result of this process is a new string S', which is in Normalization Form KC.

X6 Composition Exclusion Table

There are four classes of characters that are excluded from composition:

1. **Script-specifics:** precomposed characters that are generally not the preferred form for particular scripts.
   - These *cannot* be computed from information in the Unicode Character Database.
   - An example is U+0958 (क़) DEVANAGARI LETTER QA.
2. **Post composition version:** precomposed characters that are added after Unicode 3.0 [Unicode3.0] and whose decompositions exist in prior versions of Unicode. This set will be updated with each subsequent version of Unicode. For more information, see *Section X3, Versioning and Stability.*
   - These *cannot* be computed from information in the Unicode Character Database.
   - An example is U+2ADC (⫝̸) FORKING.
3. **Singletons:** characters having decompositions that consist of single characters (as described below).
   - These *are* computed from information in the Unicode Character Database.
   - An example is U+2126 (Ω) OHM SIGN.

4. **Non-starter decompositions:** precomposed characters whose decompositions start with a non-starter.
    - These *are* computed from information in the Unicode Character Database.
    - An example is U+0344 (̈́) COMBINING GREEK DIALYTIKA TONOS.

Two characters may have the same canonical decomposition in the Unicode Character Database. *Table 5* shows an example.

Table 5. Same Canonical Decomposition

Source	Same Decomposition
212B (Å) ANGSTROM SIGN	0041 (A) LATIN CAPITAL LETTER A + 030A (˚) COMBINING RING ABOVE
00C5 (Å) LATIN CAPITAL LETTER A WITH RING ABOVE	

The Unicode Character Database will first decompose one of the characters to the other, and then decompose from there. That is, one of the characters (in this case, U+212B ANGSTROM SIGN) will have a singleton decomposition. Characters with singleton decompositions are included in Unicode for compatibility with certain preexisting standards. These singleton decompositions are excluded from primary composition.

Data File

The Composition Exclusion Table is available as machine-readable data file [Exclusions].

All four classes of characters are included in this file, although the singletons and non-starter decompositions are commented out, as they can be computed from the decomposition mappings in the Unicode Character Database.

A derived property containing the complete list of exclusions, `Comp_Ex`, is available separately in the Unicode Charactger Database [UCD] and is described in the UCD documentation [UCDDoc]. Implementations can avoid computing the singleton and non-starter decompositions from the Unicode Character Database by using the `Comp_Ex` property instead.

X7 Examples and Charts

This section provides some detailed examples of the results when each of the Normalization Forms is applied. The Normalization Charts [Charts] provide charts of all the characters in Unicode that differ from at least one of their Normalization Forms (NFC, NFD, NFKC, NFKD).

Basic Examples

The basic examples in *Table 6* do not involve compatibility decompositions. Therefore, in each case Normalization Forms NFD and NFKD are identical, and Normalization Forms NFC and NFKC are also identical.

Table 6. Basic Examples

	Original	NFD, NFKD	NFC, NFKC	Notes
a	D-dot_above	D + dot_above	D-dot_above	Both decomposed and precomposed canonical sequences produce the same result.
b	D + dot_above	D + dot_above	D-dot_above	
c	D-dot_below + dot_above	D + dot_below + dot_above	D-dot_below + dot_above	The *dot_above* cannot be combined with the D because the D has already combined with the intervening *dot_below*.
d	D-dot_above + dot_below	D + dot_below + dot_above	D-dot_below + dot_above	
e	D + dot_above + dot_below	D + dot_below + dot_above	D-dot_below + dot_above	
f	D + dot_above + horn + dot_below	D + horn + dot_below + dot_above	D-dot_below + horn + dot_above	There may be intervening combining marks, so long as the result of the combination is canonically equivalent.
g	E-macron-grave	E + macron + grave	E-macron-grave	Multiple combining characters are combined with the base character.
h	E-macron + grave	E + macron + grave	E-macron-grave	
i	E-grave + macron	E + grave + macron	E-grave + macron	Characters will *not* be combined if they would not be canonical equivalents because of their ordering.
j	angstrom_sign	A + ring	A-ring	Because Å (A-ring) is the preferred composite, it is the form produced for both characters.
k	A-ring	A + ring	A-ring	

Effect of Compatibility Decompositions

The examples in *Table 7* and *Table 8* illustrate the effect of compatibility decompositions. When text is normalized in forms NFD and NFC, as in *Table 7*, compatibility-equivalent strings do not result in the same strings. However, when the same strings are normalized in forms NFKD and NFKC, as shown in *Table 8*, they do result in the same strings. The tables also contain an entry showing that Hangul syllables are maintained under all Normalization Forms.

Table 7. NFD and NFC Applied to Compatibility-Equivalent Strings

	Original	NFD	NFC	Notes
l	"Äffin"	"A\u0308ffin"	"Äffin"	The *ffi_ligature* (U+FB03) is *not* decomposed, because it has a compatibility mapping, not a canonical mapping. (See Table 8.)
m	"Ä\uFB03n"	"A\u0308\uFB03n"	"Ä\uFB03n"	
n	"Henry IV"	"Henry IV"	"Henry IV"	Similarly, the ROMAN NUMERAL IV (U+2163) is *not* decomposed.
o	"Henry \u2163"	"Henry \u2163"	"Henry \u2163"	
p	ga	ka + ten	ga	Different compatibility equivalents of a single Japanese character will *not* result in the same string in NFC.
q	ka + ten	ka + ten	ga	
r	hw_ka + hw_ten	hw_ka + hw_ten	hw_ka + hw_ten	
s	ka + hw_ten	ka + hw_ten	ka + hw_ten	
t	hw_ka + ten	hw_ka + ten	hw_ka + ten	
u	kaks	$k_i + a_m + ks_f$	kaks	Hangul syllables are maintained under normalization.

Table 8. NFKD and NFKC Applied to Compatibility-Equivalent Strings

	Original	NFKD	NFKC	Notes
l'	"Äffin"	"A\u0308ffin"	"Äffin"	The *ffi_ligature* (U+FB03) *is* decomposed in NFKC (where it is not in NFC).
m'	"Ä\uFB03n"	"A\u0308ffin"	"Äffin"	
n'	"Henry IV"	"Henry IV"	"Henry IV"	Similarly, the resulting strings here are identical in NFKC.
o'	"Henry \u2163"	"Henry IV"	"Henry IV"	
p'	ga	ka + ten	ga	Different compatibility equivalents of a single Japanese character *will* result in the same string in NFKC.
q'	ka + ten	ka + ten	ga	
r'	hw_ka + hw_ten	ka + ten	ga	
s'	ka + hw_ten	ka + ten	ga	
t'	hw_ka + ten	ka + ten	ga	
u'	kaks	$k_i + a_m + ks_f$	kaks	Hangul syllables are maintained under normalization.*

*In earlier versions of Unicode, jamo characters like ks_f had compatibility mappings to $k_f + s_f$. These mappings were removed in Unicode 2.1.9 to ensure that Hangul syllables are maintained.

X8 Design Goals

The following are the design goals for the specification of the Normalization Forms and are presented here for reference. The first goal is a fundamental conformance feature of the design.

Goal 1: Uniqueness

The first, and by far the most important, design goal for the Normalization Forms is uniqueness. Two equivalent strings will have *precisely* the same normalized form. More explicitly,

1. If two strings x and y are canonical equivalents, then
   toNFC(x) = toNFC(y)
   toNFD(x) = toNFD(y)
2. If two strings are compatibility equivalents, then
   toNFKC(x) = toNFKC(y)
   toNFKD(x) = toNFKD(y)
3. All of the transformations are idempotent: that is,
   toNFC(toNFC(x)) = toNFC(x)
   toNFD(toNFD(x)) = toNFD(x)
   toNFKC(toNFKC(x)) = toNFKC(x)
   toNFKD(toNFKD(x)) = toNFKD(x)

Goal 1.3 is a consequence of Goals 1.2 and 1.1, but is stated here for clarity.

Goal 2: Stability

The second major design goal for the Normalization Forms is stability of characters that are not involved in the composition or decomposition process.

1. If X contains a character with a compatibility decomposition, then toNFD(X) and toNFC(X) still contain that character.
2. As much as possible, if there are no combining characters in X, then toNFC(X) = X.
   - The only characters for which this is not true are those in the *Section X6, Composition Exclusion Table.*
3. Irrelevant combining marks should not affect the results of composition. See example **f** in *Section X7, Examples and Charts,* where the *horn* character does not affect the results of composition.

Goal 3: Efficiency

The third major design goal for the Normalization Forms is to allow efficient implementations.

1. It is possible to implement efficient code for producing the Normalization Forms. In particular, it should be possible to produce Normalization Form C very quickly from strings that are already in Normalization Form C or are in Normalization Form D.

2. Normalization Forms that compose do not have to produce the shortest possible results, because that can be computationally expensive.

X9 Implementation Notes

There are a number of optimizations that can be made in programs that produce Normalization Form C. Rather than first decomposing the text fully, a quick check can be made on each character. If it is already in the proper precomposed form, then no work has to be done. Only if the current character is combining or in *Section X6, Composition Exclusion Table*, does a slower code path need to be invoked. (This code path will need to look at previous characters, back to the last starter. See *Section X14, Detecting Normalization Forms*, for more information.)

The majority of the cycles spent in doing composition are spent looking up the appropriate data. The data lookup for Normalization Form C can be very efficiently implemented, because it has to look up only pairs of characters, not arbitrary strings. First a multistage table (also known as *trie;* see [Unicode] *Chapter 5, Implementation Guidelines*) is used to map a character *c* to a small integer *i* in a contiguous range from 0 to *n*. The code for doing this looks like:

```
i = data[index[c >> BLOCKSHIFT] + (c & BLOCKMASK)];
```

Then a pair of these small integers are simply mapped through a two-dimensional array to get a resulting value. This yields much better performance than a general-purpose string lookup in a hash table.

Because the Hangul compositions and decompositions are algorithmic, memory storage can be significantly reduced if the corresponding operations are done in code. See *Section X16, Hangul*, for more information.

> **Note:** Any such optimizations must be carefully checked to ensure that they still produce conformant results. In particular, the code must still be able to pass the test described in *Section X15, Conformance Testing.*

For more information on useful implementation techniques, see *Section X14, Detecting Normalization Forms,* and [UTN5].

X10 Decomposition

For those reading this annex online, the following summarizes the canonical decomposition process. For a complete discussion, see *Sections 3.7, Decomposition* , and *3.11, Canonical Ordering Behavior* [Unicode].

Canonical decomposition is the process of taking a string, recursively replacing composite characters using the Unicode canonical decomposition mappings (including the algorithmic Hangul canonical decomposition mappings; see *Section X16, Hangul*), and putting the result in canonical order.

Compatibility decomposition is the process of taking a string, replacing composite characters using *both* the Unicode canonical decomposition mappings *and* the Unicode compatibility decomposition mappings, and putting the result in canonical order.

A string is put into *canonical order* by repeatedly replacing any exchangeable pair by the pair in reversed order. When there are no remaining exchangeable pairs, then the string is in canonical order. Note that the replacements can be done in any order.

A sequence of two adjacent characters in a string is an *exchangeable pair* if the combining class (from the Unicode Character Database) for the first character is greater than the combining class for the second, and the second is not a starter; that is, if `combiningClass(first) > combiningClass(second) > 0`. See *Table 9*.

Table 9. Examples of Exchangeable Pairs

Sequence	Combining Classes	Status
<acute, cedilla>	230, 202	exchangeable, because 230 > 202
<a, acute>	0, 230	not exchangeable, because 0 <= 230
<diaeresis, acute>	230, 230	not exchangeable, because 230 <= 230
<acute, a>	230, 0	not exchangeable, because the second class is zero

Example of Decomposition. The following three steps demonstrate the decomposition process for an example string containing the characters "ác´¸" *(a-acute, c, acute, cedilla).*

1. The data file contains the following relevant information:
   code; name; ... combining class; ... decomposition.

```
0061;LATIN SMALL LETTER A;...0;...
0063;LATIN SMALL LETTER C;...0;...
00E1;LATIN SMALL LETTER A WITH ACUTE;...0;...0061 0301;...
0107;LATIN SMALL LETTER C WITH ACUTE;...0;...0063 0301;...
0301;COMBINING ACUTE ACCENT;...230;...
0327;COMBINING CEDILLA;...202;...
```

2. Applying the canonical decomposition mappings results in "a´c´¸" *(a, acute, c, acute, cedilla).*
   - This is because `00E1` *(a-acute)* has a canonical decomposition mapping to `0061 0301` *(a, acute)*
3. Applying the canonical ordering results in "a´c¸´" *(a, acute, c, cedilla, acute).*
   - This is because *cedilla* has a lower combining class (202) than acute (230) does. The positions of 'a' and 'c' are not affected, because they are starters.

X11 Code Sample

A code sample is available for each of the four Normalization Forms. For clarity, this sample is not optimized. The implementations for NFKC and NFC transform a string in two passes: pass 1 decomposes, while pass 2 composes by successively composing each unblocked character with the last starter.

In some implementations, people may be working with streaming interfaces that read and write small amounts at a time. In those implementations, the text back to the last starter needs to be buffered. Whenever a second starter would be added to that buffer, the buffer can be flushed.

The sample is written in Java, although for accessibility it avoids the use of object-oriented techniques. For access to the code and for a live demonstration, see Normalizer.html [Sample]. Equivalent Perl code is available on the W3C site [CharLint].

X12 Legacy Encodings

While the Normalization Forms are specified for Unicode text, they can also be extended to non-Unicode (legacy) character encodings. This is based on mapping the legacy character set strings to and from Unicode using definitions D5 and D6.

D5. An *invertible transcoding* T for a legacy character set L is a one-to-one mapping from characters encoded in L to characters in Unicode with an associated mapping T^{-1} such that for any string S in L, $T^{-1}(T(S)) = S$.

Most legacy character sets have a single invertible transcoding in common use. In a few cases there may be multiple invertible transcodings. For example, Shift-JIS may have two different mappings used in different circumstances: one to preserve the '/' semantics of $5C_{16}$, and one to preserve the '¥' semantics.

The character indexes in the legacy character set string may be different from character indexes in the Unicode equivalent. For example, if a legacy string uses visual encoding for Hebrew, then its first character might be the last character in the Unicode string.

If transcoders are implemented for legacy character sets, it is recommended that the result be in Normalization Form C where possible. See Unicode Technical Report #22, "Character Mapping Tables," for more information.

D6. Given a string S encoded in L and an invertible transcoding T for L, the *Normalization Form X of S under T* is defined to be the result of mapping to Unicode, normalizing to Unicode Normalization Form X, and mapping back to the legacy character encoding—for example, $T^{-1}(NFX(T(S)))$. Where there is a single invertible transcoding for that character set in common use, one can simply speak of the Normalization Form X of S.

Legacy character sets are classified into three categories based on their normalization behavior with accepted transcoders.

1. *Prenormalized.* Any string in the character set is already in Normalization Form X.
    - For example, ISO 8859-1 is prenormalized in NFC.
2. *Normalizable.* Although the set is not prenormalized, any string in the set *can* be normalized to Normalization Form X.
    - For example, ISO 2022 (with a mixture of ISO 5426 and ISO 8859-1) is normalizable.
3. *Unnormalizable.* Some strings in the character set cannot be normalized into Normalization Form X.
    - For example, ISO 5426 is unnormalizable in NFC under common transcoders, because it contains combining marks but not composites.

X13 Programming Language Identifiers

This section has been moved to Unicode Standard Annex #31, "Identifier and Pattern Syntax" [UAX 31].

X14 Detecting Normalization Forms

The Unicode Character Database supplies properties that allow implementations to quickly determine whether a string x is in a particular Normalization Form—for example, isNFC(x). This is, in general, many times faster than normalizing and then comparing.

For each Normalization Form, the properties provide three possible values for each Unicode code point, as shown in *Table 10*.

Table 10. Description of Quick_Check Values

Valuee	Description
NO	The code point cannot occur in that Normalization Form.
YES	The code point is a starter and can occur in the Normalization Form. In addition, for NFKC and NFC, the character may compose with a following character, but it *never* composes with a previous character.
MAYBE	The code point can occur, subject to canonical ordering, but with constraints. In particular, the text may not be in the specified Normalization Form depending on the context in which the character occurs.

Code that uses this property can do a *very* fast first pass over a string to determine the Normalization Form. The result is also either NO, YES, or MAYBE. For NO or YES, the answer is definite. In the MAYBE case, a more thorough check must be made, typically by putting a copy of the string into the Normalization Form and checking for equality with the original.

- Even the slow case can be optimized, with a function that does not perform a complete normalization of the entire string, but instead works incrementally, only normalizing a limited area around the MAYBE character. See *Section X14.1, Stable Code Points*.

This check is much faster than simply running the normalization algorithm, because it avoids any memory allocation and copying. The vast majority of strings will return a definitive YES or NO answer, leaving only a small percentage that require more work. The sample below is written in Java, although for accessibility it avoids the use of object-oriented techniques.

```
public int quickCheck(String source) {
    short lastCanonicalClass = 0;
    int result = YES;
    for (int i = 0; i < source.length(); ++i) {
        char ch = source.charAt(i);
        short canonicalClass = getCanonicalClass(ch);
        if (lastCanonicalClass > canonicalClass && canonicalClass != 0) {
            return NO;        }
        int check = isAllowed(ch);
```

```
        if (check == NO) return NO;
        if (check == MAYBE) result = MAYBE;
        lastCanonicalClass = canonicalClass;
    }
    return result;
}

public static final int NO = 0, YES = 1, MAYBE = -1;
```

The `isAllowed()` call should access the data from Derived Normalization Properties file [NormProps] for the Normalization Form in question. (For more information, see the UCD documentation [UCDDoc].) For example, here is a segment of the data for NFC:

```
...

0338        ; NFC_MAYBE # Mn      COMBINING LONG SOLIDUS OVERLAY

...

F900..FA0D ; NFC_NO    # Lo [270] CJK COMPATIBILITY IDEOGRAPH-F900..CJK COMPATIBILITY IDEOGRAPH-FA0D

...
```

These lines assign the value NFC_MAYBE to the code point U+0338, and the value NFC_NO to the code points in the range U+F900..U+FA0D. There are no MAYBE values for NFD and NFKD: the `quickCheck` function will always produce a definite result for these Normalization Forms. All characters that are not specifically mentioned in the file have the values YES.

The data for the implementation of the `isAllowed()` call can be accessed in memory with a hash table or a trie (see *Section X9, Implementation Notes*); the latter will be the fastest.

There is also a Unicode Consortium stability policy that canonical mappings are always limited in all versions of Unicode, so that no string when decomposed with NFD expands to more than 3× in length (measured in code units). This is true whether the text is in UTF-8, UTF-16, or UTF-32. This guarantee also allows for certain optimizations in processing, especially in determining buffer sizes. See also *Section X21, Stream-Safe Text Format.*

X14.1 Stable Code Points

It is sometimes useful to distinguish the set of code points that are *stable* under a particular Normalization Form. They are the set of code points never affected by that particular normalization process. This property is very useful for skipping over text that does not need to be considered at all, either when normalizing or when testing normalization.

Formally, each stable code point CP fulfills *all* of the following conditions:

1. CP has canonical combining class 0.
2. CP is (as a single character) not changed by this Normalization Form.

In case of NFC or NFKC, each stable code point CP fulfills *all* of the following additional conditions:

3. CP can never compose with a previous character.
4. CP can never compose with a following character.
5. CP can never change if another character is added.

Example. In NFC, *a-breve* satisfies all but (5), but if one adds an *ogonek* it changes to *a-ogonek* plus *breve*. So *a-breve* is not stable in NFC. However, *a-ogonek* is stable in NFC, because it does satisfy (1–5).

Concatenation of normalized strings to produce a normalized result can be optimized using stable code points. An implementation can find the last stable code point L in the first string, and the first stable code point F in the second string. The implementation has to normalize only the range from (and including) L to the last code point before F. The result will then be normalized. This can be a very significant savings in performance when concatenating large strings.

Because characters with the Quick_Check=YES property value satisfy conditions 1–3, the optimization can also be performed using the Quick_Check property. In this case, the implementation finds the last code point L with Quick_Check=YES in the first string and the first code point F with Quick_Check=YES in the second string. It then normalizes the range of code points starting from (and including) L to the code point just before F.

X15 Conformance Testing

Implementations must be thoroughly tested for conformance to the normalization specification. The Normalization Conformance Test [Test15] file is available for testing conformance. This file consists of a series of fields. When Normalization Forms are applied to the different fields, the results shall be as specified in the header of that file.

X16 Hangul

Because the Hangul compositions and decompositions are algorithmic, memory storage can be significantly reduced if the corresponding operations are done in code rather than by simply storing the data in the general-purpose tables. Here is sample code illustrating algorithmic Hangul canonical decomposition and composition done according to the specification in *Section 3.12, Combining Jamo Behavior* [Unicode]. Although coded in Java, the same structure can be used in other programming languages.

The canonical Hangul decompositions specified here and in *Section 3.12, Combining Jamo Behavior*, in [Unicode] directly decompose precomposed Hangul syllable characters into two or three Hangul Jamo characters. This differs from all other canonical decompositions in two ways. First, they are arithmetically specified. Second, they directly map to more than two characters. The canonical decomposition *mapping* for all other characters maps each character to one or two others. A character may have a canonical *decomposition* to more than two characters, but it is expressed as the recursive application of mappings to at most a pair of characters at a time.

Hangul decomposition could also be expressed this way. All LVT syllables decompose into an LV syllable plus a T jamo. The LV syllables themselves decompose into an L jamo plus a T jamo. Thus the Hangul canonical decompositions are fundamentally the same as the other canonical decompositions in terms of the way they decompose. This analysis can also be used to produce more compact code than what is given below.

Common Constants

```
static final int
    SBase = 0xAC00, LBase = 0x1100, VBase = 0x1161, TBase = 0x11A7,
    LCount = 19, VCount = 21, TCount = 28,
    NCount = VCount * TCount,   // 588
    SCount = LCount * NCount;   // 11172
```

Hangul Decomposition

```
public static String decomposeHangul(char s) {
    int SIndex = s - SBase;
    if (SIndex < 0 || SIndex >= SCount) {
        return String.valueOf(s);
    }
    StringBuffer result = new StringBuffer();
    int L = LBase + SIndex / NCount;
    int V = VBase + (SIndex % NCount) / TCount;
    int T = TBase + SIndex % TCount;
    result.append((char)L);
    result.append((char)V);
    if (T != TBase) result.append((char)T);
    return result.toString();
}
```

Hangul Composition

Notice an important feature of Hangul composition: whenever the source string is not in Normalization Form D, one cannot just detect character sequences of the form <L, V> and <L, V, T>. It is also necessary to catch the sequences of the form <LV, T>. To guarantee uniqueness, these sequences must also be composed. This is illustrated in step 2.

```
public static String composeHangul(String source) {
    int len = source.length();
    if (len == 0) return "";
    StringBuffer result = new StringBuffer();
    char last = source.charAt(0);            // copy first char
    result.append(last);

    for (int i = 1; i < len; ++i) {
        char ch = source.charAt(i);

        // 1. check to see if two current characters are L and V

        int LIndex = last - LBase;
        if (0 <= LIndex && LIndex < LCount) {
            int VIndex = ch - VBase;
            if (0 <= VIndex && VIndex < VCount) {

                // make syllable of form LV

                last = (char)(SBase + (LIndex * VCount + VIndex) * TCount);

                result.setCharAt(result.length()-1, last); // reset last
                continue; // discard ch
            }
        }


        // 2. check to see if two current characters are LV and T

        int SIndex = last - SBase;
        if (0 <= SIndex && SIndex < SCount && (SIndex % TCount) == 0) {
            int TIndex = ch - TBase;
            if (0 < TIndex && TIndex < TCount) {
```

```
                    // make syllable of form LVT

                    last += TIndex;
                    result.setCharAt(result.length()-1, last); // reset last
                    continue; // discard ch
                }
            }
            // if neither case was true, just add the character
            last = ch;
            result.append(ch);
        }
        return result.toString();
    }
```

Additional transformations can be performed on sequences of Hangul jamo for various purposes. For example, to regularize sequences of Hangul jamo into standard syllables, the *choseong* and *jungseong* fillers can be inserted, as described in *Chapter 3, Conformance*, of [Unicode]. For keyboard input, additional compositions may be performed. For example, the trailing consonants $k_f + s_f$ may be combined into ks_f. In addition, some Hangul input methods do not require a distinction on input between initial and final consonants, and change between them on the basis of context. For example, in the keyboard sequence $m_i + e_m + n_i + s_i + a_m$, the consonant n_i would be reinterpreted as n_f, because there is no possible syllable *nsa*. This results in the two syllables *men* and *sa*.

However, none of these additional transformations are considered part of the Unicode Normalization Forms.

Hangul Character Names

Hangul decomposition is also used to form the character names for the Hangul syllables. While the sample code that illustrates this process is not directly related to normalization, it is worth including because it is so similar to the decomposition code.

```
public static String getHangulName(char s) {
    int SIndex = s - SBase;
    if (0 > SIndex || SIndex >= SCount) {
        throw new IllegalArgumentException("Not a Hangul Syllable: " + s);
    }
    StringBuffer result = new StringBuffer();
    int LIndex = SIndex / NCount;
    int VIndex = (SIndex % NCount) / TCount;
    int TIndex = SIndex % TCount;
    return "HANGUL SYLLABLE " + JAMO_L_TABLE[LIndex]
      + JAMO_V_TABLE[VIndex] + JAMO_T_TABLE[TIndex];
}

static private String[] JAMO_L_TABLE = {
    "G", "GG", "N", "D", "DD", "R", "M", "B", "BB",
    "S", "SS", "", "J", "JJ", "C", "K", "T", "P", "H"
};

static private String[] JAMO_V_TABLE = {
    "A", "AE", "YA", "YAE", "EO", "E", "YEO", "YE", "O",
    "WA", "WAE", "OE", "YO", "U", "WEO", "WE", "WI",
    "YU", "EU", "YI", "I"
};

static private String[] JAMO_T_TABLE = {
    "", "G", "GG", "GS", "N", "NJ", "NH", "D", "L", "LG", "LM",
    "LB", "LS", "LT", "LP", "LH", "M", "B", "BS",
    "S", "SS", "NG", "J", "C", "K", "T", "P", "H"
};
```

X17 Intellectual Property

Transcript of letter regarding disclosure of IBM Technology
(Hard copy is on file with the Chair of UTC and the Chair of NCITS/L2)
Transcribed on 1999-03-10

February 26, 1999

The Chair, Unicode Technical Committee

Subject: Disclosure of IBM Technology - Unicode Normalization Forms

The attached document entitled "Unicode Normalization Forms" does not require IBM technology, but may be implemented using IBM technology that has been filed for US Patent. However, IBM believes that the technology could be beneficial to the software community at large, especially with respect to usage on the Internet, allowing the community to derive the enormous benefits provided by Unicode.

This letter is to inform you that IBM is pleased to make the Unicode normalization technology that has been filed for patent freely available to anyone using them in implementing to the Unicode standard.

Sincerely,

W. J. Sullivan,
Acting Director of National Language Support
and Information Development

X18 Corrigenda

The Unicode Consortium has well-defined policies in place to govern changes that affect backward compatibility. For information on these stability policies, especially regarding normalization, see Unicode Policies [Policies]. In particular:

> *Once a character is encoded, its canonical combining class and decomposition mapping will not be changed in a way that will destabilize normalization.*

What this means is:

> *If a string contains only characters from a given version of the Unicode Standard (for example, Unicode 3.1.1), and it is put into a normalized form in accordance with that version of Unicode, then it will be in normalized form according to any future version of Unicode.*

This guarantee has been in place for Unicode 3.1 and after. It has been necessary to correct the decompositions of a small number of characters since Unicode 3.1, as listed in the Normalization Corrections data file [Corrections], but such corrections are in accordance with the above principles: all text normalized on old systems will test as normalized in future systems. All text normalized in future systems will test as normalized on past systems. What may change, for those few characters, is that *unnormalized* text may normalize differently on past and future systems.

It is straightforward for any implementation with a future version of Unicode to support all past versions of normalization. For an implementation of Unicode Version X to support a version of NFC that precisely matches a older Unicode Version Y, the following two steps are taken:

1. Before applying the normalization algorithm, map the characters that were corrected to their *old* values in Unicode Version Y.
    - Use the table in [Corrections] for this step, by including any code points that have a version later than Y and less than or equal to X.
    - For example, for a Unicode 4.0 implementation to duplicate Unicode 3.2 results, exactly five characters must be mapped.
2. In applying the normalization algorithm, handle any code points that were not defined in Unicode Version X as if they were unassigned.
    - That is, the code points will not decompose or compose, and their canonical combining class will be zero.
    - The Derived_Age property in the Unicode Character Database [UCD] can be used for the set of code points in question.

[Unicode4.1] corrected a definitional problem with D2.

X19 Canonical Equivalence

This section describes the relationship of normalization to respecting (or preserving) canonical equivalence. A process (or function) *respects* canonical equivalence when canonical-equivalent inputs always produce canonical-equivalent outputs. For a function that transforms one string into another, this may also be called *preserving* canonical equivalence. There are a number of important aspects to this concept:

1. The outputs are *not* required to be identical, only canonically equivalent.
2. *Not* all processes are required to respect canonical equivalence. For example:
    - A function that collects a set of the General_Category values present in a string will and should produce a different value for *<angstrom sign, semicolon>* than for *<A, combining ring above, greek question mark>*, even though they are canonically equivalent.
    - A function that does a binary comparison of strings will also find these two sequences different.
3. Higher-level processes that transform or compare strings, or that perform other higher-level functions, must respect canonical equivalence or problems will result.

The canonically equivalent inputs or outputs are not just limited to strings, but are also relevant to the *offsets* within strings, because those play a fundamental role in Unicode string processing.

> Offset P into string X is canonically equivalent to offset Q into string Y if and only if both of the following conditions are true:
>
> $X[0, P] \approx Y[0, Q]$, and
> $X[P, \text{len}(X)] \approx Y[Q, \text{len}(Y)]$

This can be written as $P_X \approx Q_Y$. Note that whenever X and Y are canonically equivalent, it follows that $0_X \approx 0_Y$ and $\text{len}(X)_X \approx \text{len}(Y)_Y$.

Example 1. Given X = *<angstrom sign, semicolon>* and Y = *<A, combining ring above, greek question mark>*,

$0_X \approx 0_Y$
$1_X \approx 2_Y$
$2_X \approx 3_Y$
1_Y has no canonically equivalent offset in X

The following are examples of processes that involve canonically equivalent strings *and/or* offsets.

Example 2. When `isWordBreak(string, offset)` respects canonical equivalence, then

`isWordBreak`(*<A-ring, semicolon>*, 1) = `isWordBreak`(*<A, ring, semicolon>*, 2)

Example 3. When `nextWordBreak(string, offset)` respects canonical equivalence, then

`nextWordBreak`(*<A-ring, semicolon>*, 0) = 1 if and only if `nextWordBreak`(*<A, ring, semicolon>*, 0) = 2

Respecting canonical equivalence is related to, but different from, preserving a canonical Normalization Form NFx (where NFx means either NFD or NFC). In a process that preserves a Normalization Form, whenever any input string is normalized according to that Normalization Form, then every output string is also normalized according to that form. A process that preserves a canonical Normalization Form respects canonical equivalence, but the reverse is not necessarily true.

In building a system that as a whole respects canonical equivalence, there are two basic strategies, with some variations on the second strategy.

A. Ensure that each system component respects canonical equivalence.
B. Ensure that each system component preserves NFx, and one of the following:
   1. Reject any non-NFx text on input to the whole system.
   2. Reject any non-NFx text on input to each component.
   3. Normalize to NFx all text on input to the whole system.
   4. Normalize to NFx all text on input to each component.

5. All three of the following:
    a. Allow text to be marked as NFx when generated.
    b. Normalize any unmarked text on input to each component to NFx.
    c. Reject any marked text that is not NFx.

There are trade-offs for each of these strategies. The best choice or mixture of strategies will depend on the structure of the components and their interrelations, and how fine-grained or low-level those components are. One key piece of information is that it is much faster to check that text is NFx than it is to convert it. This is especially true in the case of NFC. So even where it says "normalize" above, a good technique is to first check if normalization is required, and perform the extra processing only if necessary.

- Strategy A is the most robust, but may be less efficient.
- Strategies B1 and B2 are the most efficient, but would reject some data, including that converted 1:1 from some legacy code pages.
- Strategy B3 does not have the problem of rejecting data. It can be more efficient than A: because each component is assured that all of its input is in a particular Normalization Form, it does not need to normalize, except internally. But it is less robust: any component that fails can "leak" unnormalized text into the rest of the system.
- Strategy B4 is more robust than B1 but less efficient, because there are multiple points where text needs to be checked.
- Strategy B5 can be a reasonable compromise; it is robust but allows for all text input.

X20 Corrigendum 5 Sequences

Table 11 shows all of the problem sequences relevant to Corrigendum 5. *It is important to emphasize that none of these sequences will occur in any meaningful text, because none of the intervening characters shown in the sequences occur in the contexts shown in the table.*

Table 11. Problem Sequences

First Character	Intervening Character(s)	Last Character
09C7 BENGALI VOWEL SIGN E	One or more characters with a non-zero Canonical Combining Class property value—for example, an acute accent.	09BE BENGALI VOWEL SIGN AA **or** 09D7 BENGALI AU LENGTH MARK
0B47 ORIYA VOWEL SIGN E		0B3E ORIYA VOWEL SIGN AA **or** 0B56 ORIYA AI LENGTH MARK **or** 0B57 ORIYA AU LENGTH MARK
0BC6 TAMIL VOWEL SIGN E		0BBE TAMIL VOWEL SIGN AA **or** 0BD7 TAMIL AU LENGTH MARK
0BC7 TAMIL VOWEL SIGN EE		0BBE TAMIL VOWEL SIGN AA
0B92 TAMIL LETTER O		0BD7 TAMIL AU LENGTH MARK
0CC6 KANNADA VOWEL SIGN E		0CC2 KANNADA VOWEL SIGN UU **or** 0CD5 KANNADA LENGTH MARK **or** 0CD6 KANNADA AI LENGTH MARK
0CBF KANNADA VOWEL SIGN I OR 0CCA KANNADA VOWEL SIGN O		0CD5 KANNADA LENGTH MARK
0D47 MALAYALAM VOWEL SIGN EE		0D3E MALAYALAM VOWEL SIGN AA
0D46 MALAYALAM VOWEL SIGN E		0D3E MALAYALAM VOWEL SIGN AA **or** 0D57 MALAYALAM AU LENGTH MARK
1025 MYANMAR LETTER U		102E MYANMAR VOWEL SIGN II
0DD9 SINHALA VOWEL SIGN KOMBUVA		0DCF SINHALA VOWEL SIGN AELA-PILLA **or** 0DDF SINHALA VOWEL SIGN GAYANUKITTA
1100..1112 HANGUL CHOSEONG KIYEOK..HIEUH [19 instances]		1161..1175 HANGUL JUNGSEONG A..I [21 instances]
[:HangulSyllableType=LV:]		11A8..11C2 HANGUL JONGSEONG KIYEOK..HIEUH [27 instances]

X21 Stream-Safe Text Format

There are certain protocols that would benefit from using normalization, but that have implementation constraints. For example, a protocol may require buffered serialization, in which only a portion of a string may be available at a given time. Consider the extreme case of a string containing a *digit 2* followed by 10,000 *umlauts* followed by one *dot-below*, then a *digit 3*. As part of normalization, the *dot-below* at the end must be reordered to immediately after the *digit 2*, which means that 10,003 characters need to be considered before the result can be output.

Such extremely long sequences of combining marks are not illegal, even though for all practical purposes they are not meaningful. However, the possibility of encountering such sequences forces a conformant, serializing implementation to provide large buffer capacity or to provide a special exception mechanism just for such degenerate cases. The Stream-Safe Text Format specification addresses this situation.

D5. *Stream-Safe Text Format:* A Unicode string is said to be in Stream-Safe Text Format if it would not contain any sequences of non-starters longer than 30 characters in length when normalized to NFKD.

- Such a string can be normalized in buffered serialization with a buffer size of 32 characters, which would require no more than 128 bytes in any Unicode Encoding Form.
- Incorrect buffer handling can introduce subtle errors in the results. Any buffered implementation should be carefully checked against the normalization test data.
- The value of 30 is chosen to be significantly beyond what is required for any linguistic or technical usage. While it would have been feasible to chose a smaller number, this value provides a very wide margin, yet is well within the buffer size limits of practical implementations.

D6. *Stream-Safe Text Process* is the process of producing a Unicode string in Stream-Safe Text Format by processing that string from start to finish, inserting U+034F COMBINING GRAPHEME JOINER (CGJ) within long sequences of non-starters. The exact position of the inserted CGJs are determined according to the following algorithm, which describes the generation of an output string from an input string:

1. If the input string is empty, return an empty output string.
2. Set nonStarterCount to zero.
3. For each code point C in the input string:
    a. Produce the NFKD decomposition S.
    b. If nonStarterCount plus the number of initial non-starters in S is greater than 30, append a CGJ to the output string and set the nonStarterCount to zero.
    c. Append C to the output string.
    d. If there are no starters in S, increment nonStarterCount by the number of code points in S; otherwise, set nonStarterCount to the number of trailing non-starters in S (which may be zero).
4. Return the output string.

The Stream-Safe Text Process ensures not only that the resulting text is in Stream-Safe Text Format, but that any normalization of the result is also in Stream-Safe Text Format. This is true for any input string that does not contain unassigned code points.

It is important to realize that if the Stream-Safe Text Process modifies the input text by insertion of CGJs, the result will *not* be canonically equivalent to the original. The Stream-Safe Text

Format is designed for use in protocols and systems that accept the limitations on the text imposed by the format, just as they may impose their own limitations, such as removing certain control codes.

Implementations can optimize this specification as long as they produce the same results. In particular, the information used in Step 3 can be precomputed: it does not require the actual normalization of the character.

The Stream-Safe Text Format will not modify ordinary texts. Where it modifies an exceptional text, the resulting string would no longer be canonically equivalent to the original, but the modifications are minor and do not disturb any meaningful content. The modified text contains all of the content of the original, with the only difference being that reordering is blocked across long groups of non-starters. Any text in Stream-Safe Text Format can be normalized with very small buffers using any of the standard Normalization Forms.

For efficient processing, the Stream-Safe Text Process can be implemented in the same implementation pass as normalization. In such a case, the choice of whether to apply the Stream-Safe Text Process can be controlled by an input parameter.

Acknowledgments

Mark Davis and Martin Dürst created the initial versions of this annex. Mark Davis has added to and maintains the text.

Thanks to Kent Karlsson, Marcin Kowalczyk, Rick Kunst, Sadahiro Tomoyuki, Markus Scherer, Dick Sites, and Ken Whistler for feedback on this annex, including earlier versions. Asmus Freytag extensively reformatted the text for publication as part of the book.

References

For references for this annex, see Unicode Standard Annex #41, "Common References for Unicode Standard Annexes."

Modifications

For details of the change history, see the online copy of this annex at http://www.unicode.org/reports/tr9/.

Unicode Standard Annex #24

Script Names

Summary

This annex specifies an assignment of script names to all Unicode code points. This information is useful in mechanisms such as regular expressions and other text processing tasks.

Contents

X1 Introduction

> *Script*: A collection of symbols used to represent textual information in one or more writing systems.

The majority of characters encoded in the Unicode Standard [Unicode] are elements of collections called scripts. Exceptions include symbols, punctuation characters intended for use with multiple scripts, and characters that do not have a stand-alone script identity because they are intended to be used in combination with another character.

Therefore, a text in a given script is likely to consist of characters from that script, together with shared punctuation and characters whose script identity depends on the characters with which they are used.

X1.1 Classification of Text by Script Name

The Unicode Character Database [UCD] provides a mapping from Unicode characters to script name values. This information is useful for a variety of tasks that need to analyze a piece of text and determine what parts of it are in which script. Examples include regular expressions or assigning different fonts to parts of a plain text stream based on the prevailing script.

These processes are similar to the task of bibliographers in cataloging documents by their script. However, bibliographers often ignore small inclusions of other scripts in the form of quoted material in cataloging. Conversely, significant differences in the writing style for the same script may be reflected in the bibliographical classification—for example, Fraktur or Gaelic for the Latin script.

Script information is also taken into consideration in collation. The data in the Default Unicode Collation Element Table (DUCET) are grouped by script, so that letters of different script values have different primary sort weights. However, numbers, symbols, and punctuation are not grouped with the letters. For the purposes of ordering, therefore, script is most significant for the letters. For more information, see Unicode Technical Standard #10, "Unicode Collation Algorithm" [UCA].

These examples demonstrate that the definition of *script* depends on the intended purposes of the classification. *Table 1* summarizes some of the purposes for which text elements can be classified by script.

Table 1. Classification of Text by Script Name

Granularity	Classification	Purpose	Special Values
Document	Bibliographical	Record in which script a text is printed or published; subdivides some scripts—for example, Latin into normal, Fraktur, and Gaelic styles	**Unknown**
Character	Graphological/ typographical	Describe to which script a character belongs based on its origin	
	Orthographical	Describe with which script (or scripts) a character is used	**Common**, **Inherited**
	For collation	Group letters by script in collation element table	
Run	For font binding or search	Determine extent of run of like script in (potentially) mixed-script text	

Bibliographical, graphological, or historical classifications of scripts need different distinctions than the type of text-processing–related needs supported by Unicode script values. The requirements of the task not only affect how fine-grained the classification is, but also what kinds of special values are needed to make the system work. For example, when bibliographers are unable to determine the script of a document, they may classify it using a special value for **Unknown**. In text processing, the identities of all characters are normally known, but some characters may be shared across scripts or attached to any character, thus requiring special values for **Common** and **Inherited**.

Despite these differences, the vast majority of Unicode script values correspond more or less directly to the script identifiers used by bibliographers and others. Unicode script values are therefore mapped to their equivalents in the registry of script identifiers defined by [ISO15924].

X1.2 Scripts and Blocks

Unicode characters are also divided into non-overlapping ranges called blocks [Blocks]. Many of these blocks have the same name as one of the scripts because characters of that script are primarily encoded in that block. However, blocks and scripts differ in the following ways:

- Blocks are simply ranges, and often contain code points that are unassigned.
- Characters from the same script may be in several different blocks.
- Characters from different scripts may be in the same block.

As a result, for mechanisms such as regular expressions, using script values produces more meaningful results than simple matches based on block names.

For more information, see *Annex A, Character Blocks,* in Unicode Technical Standard #18, "Unicode Regular Expressions" [RegEx].

X2 Usage Model

The script values form a full partition of the codespace: every code point is assigned a single script value. This value either a specific script value, such as **Cyrillic,** or one of the following three special values:

- **Inherited**—for characters that may be used with multiple scripts, and inherit their script from the preceding characters. Includes nonspacing marks, enclosing marks, and the zero width joiner/non-joiner characters.
- **Common**—for other characters that may be used with multiple scripts.
- **Unknown**—for unassigned, private-use, and noncharacter code points.

As new scripts are added to the standard, more script values will be added. See *Section X3.2, Assignment of Script Values.*

A character is assigned a specific Unicode script value (as opposed to **Common** or **Inherited**) only when it is clearly not used with other scripts. This facilitates the use of the Script property for common tasks such as regular expressions, but means that some characters that are definite members of a given script by their graphology nevertheless are assigned one of the generic values. As more data on the usage of individual characters is collected, the script value assigned to a character may change. If it becomes established that a character is regularly used with more than one script, it will be assigned the **Common** value, where previously it would have had a more specific script value. However, the opposite type of change is possible as well.

X2.1 Handling Characters with the Common Script Property

In determining the boundaries of a run of text in a given script, programs must resolve any of the special script values, such as **Common,** based on the context of the surrounding characters. A simple heuristic uses the script of the preceding character, which works well in many cases. However, this may not always produce optimal results. For example, in the text "... gamma (γ) is ...", this heuristic would cause matching parentheses to be in different scripts.

Generally, paired punctuation, such as brackets or quotation marks, belongs to the enclosing or outer level of the text and should therefore match the script of the enclosing text. In addition, opening and closing elements of a pair resolve to the same script values, where possible. The use of quotation marks is language dependent; therefore it is not possible to tell from the character code alone whether a particular quotation mark is used as an opening or closing punctuation. For more information, see *Section 6.2, General Punctuation,* of [Unicode].

Some characters that are normally used as paired punctuation may also be used singly. An example is U+2019 RIGHT SINGLE QUOTATION MARK, which is also used as *apostrophe,* in which case it no longer acts as an enclosing punctuation. An example from physics would be <ψ| or |ψ>, where the enclosing punctuation characters may not form consistent pairs.

X2.2 Handling Nonspacing Marks

Implementations that determine the boundaries between characters of given scripts should never break between a nonspacing mark (a character with General_Category value of Mn or Me) and its base character. Thus, for boundary determinations and similar sorts of processing, a nonspacing mark—whatever its script value—should inherit the script value of its base character.

Normally, a nonspacing mark has the **Inherited** script value to reflect this. However, in cases where the best interpretation of a nonspacing mark *in isolation* would be a specific script, its script property value may be different from **Inherited**. For example, the Hebrew marks and accents are used only with Hebrew characters and are therefore assigned the **Hebrew** script value.

X2.3 Using Script Names in Regular Expressions

The script property is useful in regular expression syntax for easy specification of spans of text that consist of a single script or mixture of scripts. In general, regular expressions should use specific script values only in conjunction with both **Common** and **Inherited**. For example, to distinguish a sequence of characters appropriate for **Greek**, one would use

```
((Greek | Common) (Inherited | Me | Mn)?)*
```

The preceding expression matches all characters that are either in **Greek** or in **Common** and which are optionally followed by characters in **Inherited**. For completeness, the regular expression also allows any nonspacing or enclosing mark.

Some languages commonly use multiple scripts, so for **Japanese** one might use

```
((Hiragana | Katakana | Han | Latin | Common) (Inherited | Me |
Mn)?)*
```

Note that while it is necessary to include Latin in the preceding expression to ensure that it can cover the typical script use found in many Japanese texts, doing so would make it difficult to isolate a run of Japanese inside an English document, for example. For more information, see Unicode Technical Standard #18, "Unicode Regular Expressions" [RegEx].

X2.4 Limitations

The script values form a full partition of the Unicode codespace, but that partition does not exhaust the possibilities for useful and relevant script-like subsets of Unicode characters.

For example, a user might wish to define a regular expression to span typical mathematical expressions, but the subset of Unicode characters used in mathematics does not correspond to any particular script. Instead, it requires use of the **Math** property, other character properties, and particular subsets of Latin, Greek, and Cyrillic letters. For information on other character properties, see the [UCD].

In texts of an academic, scientific, or engineering nature, the use of isolated Greek characters is common—for example, Ω for ohm; α, β, and γ for types of radioactive decays or in names of chemical compounds; π for 3.1415..., and so on. It is generally undesirable to treat such usage the same as ordinary text in the Greek script. Some commonly used characters, such as µ, already exist twice in the Unicode Standard, but with different script values.

X2.5 Spoofing

The script property values may also be useful in providing users feedback to signal possible spoofing, where visually similar characters (*confusable characters*) are substituted in an attempt to mislead a user. For example, a domain name such as `macchiato.com` could be spoofed with `macchiatο.com` (using U+03BF GREEK LETTER SMALL LETTER OMICRON for the first "o") or `maссhiato.com` (using U+0441 CYRILLIC SMALL LETTER ES for the first two "c"s). The user can be alerted to odd cases by displaying mixed scripts with different colors, highlighting, or boundary marks: `macchiat|ο|.com` or `ma|сс|hiato.com`, for example.

Possible spoofing is not limited to mixtures of scripts. Even in ASCII, there are confusable characters such as 0 and O, or 1 and l. For a more complete approach, the use of script values needs to be augmented with other information such as General_Category values and lists of individual characters that are not distinguished by other Unicode properties. For additional information, see Unicode Technical Report #36, "Unicode Security Considerations" [Security].

X3 Values

Table 2 illustrates some of the script values used in the data file. The short name for the Unicode script value matches the ISO 15924 code. Further subdivisions of scripts by ISO 15924 into varieties are shown in parentheses. For a complete list of values and short names, see the Property Value Aliases [PropValue]. As with all property value aliases, the values in the file are not case sensitive, and the presence of hyphen or underscore is optional. The order in which the scripts are listed here or in the data file is not significant.

Table 2. Unicode Script Values and ISO 15924 Codes

Script Value	ISO 15924
Common	*Zyyy*
Inherited	*Qaai*
Unknown	Zzzz
LATIN	Latn (Latf, Latg)
CYRILLIC	Cyrl (Cyrs)
ARMENIAN	Armn
HEBREW	Hebr
ARABIC	Arab
SYRIAC	Syrc (Syrj, Syrn, Syre)
BRAILLE	Brai
...	...

Although Braille is not a script in the same sense as Latin or Greek, it is given a script value in [Data24]. This is useful for various applications for which these script values are intended, such as matching spans of similar characters in regular expressions.

X3.1 Relation to ISO 15924 Codes

ISO 15924: *Code for the Representation of Names of Scripts* [ISO15924] provides an enumeration of four-letter script codes. In the [UCD] file [PropValue], corresponding codes from [ISO15924] are provided as short names for the scripts.

In some cases the match between these script values and the ISO 15924 codes is not precise, because the goals are somewhat different. ISO 15924 is aimed primarily at the bibliographic identification of scripts; consequently, it occasionally identifies varieties of scripts that may be useful for book cataloging, but that are not considered distinct scripts in the Unicode Standard. For example, ISO 15924 has separate script codes for the Fraktur and Gaelic varieties of the Latin script.

Where there are no corresponding ISO 15924 codes, the private-use ones starting with Q are used. Such values are likely to change in the future. In such a case, the Q-names will be retained as aliases in the [PropValue] for backward compatibility.

X3.2 Assignment of Script Values

New characters and scripts are continually added to the Unicode Standard. The following methodology is used to assign script values when new characters are added to the Unicode Standard:

A. If a character is used in only one script, assign it to that script
B. Otherwise, nonspacing marks (Mn, Me) and zero width joiner/non-joiner are **Inherited**
C. Otherwise, use **Common**

Script values are not immutable. As more data on the usage of individual characters is collected, script values may be reassigned using the above methodology.

X3.3 New Script Names

The following methodology is used to create names for new scripts added to the Unicode Standard. Script names are limited to

A. Latin letters A–Z or a–z
B. Digits 0–9
C. SPACE and medial HYPHEN-MINUS

Script names are guaranteed to be unique, even when ignoring case differences and the presence of SPACE or HYPHEN-MINUS. Underscores are not used when assigning script names. Similar restrictions apply to block names.

X4 Data File

The Scripts.txt data file is available at [Data24]. The format of the file is similar to that of Blocks.txt [Blocks]. The fields are separated by semicolons. The first field contains either a single code point or the first and last code points in a range separated by "..". The second field provides the script value for that range. The comment (after a #) indicates the General_Category and the character name. For each range, it gives the character count in square brackets and uses the names for the first and last characters in the range. For example:

```
0B01;       ORIYA # Mn ORIYA SIGN CANDRABINDU
0B02..0B03; ORIYA # Mc [2] ORIYA SIGN ANUSVARA..ORIYA SIGN VISARGA
```

The value **Unknown** is the default value, given to all code points that are not explicitly mentioned in the data file.

Acknowledgments

Mark Davis authored the initial versions. Asmus Freytag has added to and maintains the text of this annex.

Thanks to Ken Whistler and Julie Allen for comments on this annex, including earlier versions.

References

For references for this annex, see Unicode Standard Annex #41, "Common References for Unicode Standard Annexes."

Modifications

For details of the change history, see the online copy of this annex at http://www.unicode.org/reports/tr24/.

Unicode Standard Annex #29

Text Boundaries

Summary

This annex describes guidelines for determining default boundaries between certain significant text elements: grapheme clusters ("user-perceived characters"), words, and sentences. For line break boundaries, see UAX #14, "Line Breaking Properties."

Contents

X1 Introduction

This annex describes guidelines for determining default boundaries between certain significant text elements: grapheme clusters ("user-perceived characters"), words, and sentences. The process of boundary determination is also called *segmentation*.

A string of Unicode-encoded text often needs to be broken up into text elements programmatically. Common examples of text elements include what users think of as characters, words, lines (more precisely, where line breaks are allowed), and sentences. The precise determination of text elements may vary according to orthographic conventions for a given script or language. The goal of matching user perceptions cannot always be met exactly because the text alone does not always contain enough information to unambiguously decide boundaries. For example, the *period* (U+002E FULL STOP) is used ambiguously, sometimes for end-of-sentence purposes, sometimes for abbreviations, and sometimes for numbers. In most cases, however, programmatic text boundaries can match user perceptions quite closely, although sometimes the best that can be done is not to surprise the user.

Rather than concentrate on algorithmically searching for text elements (often called *segments*), a simpler and more useful computation instead detects the *boundaries* (or *breaks*) between those text elements. The determination of those boundaries is often critical to performance, so it is important to be able to make such a determination as quickly as possible. (For a general discussion of text elements, see *Chapter 2, General Structure*, of [Unicode].)

The default boundary determination mechanism specified in this annex provides a straightforward and efficient way to determine some of the most significant boundaries in text: grapheme clusters (what end users usually think of as characters), words, and sentences. Boundaries used in line breaking (also called word wrapping) are to be found in [LineBreak].

The sheer number of characters in the Unicode Standard, together with its representational power, place requirements on both the specification of text element boundaries and the underlying implementation. The specification needs to allow for the designation of large sets of characters sharing the same characteristics (for example, uppercase letters), while the implementation must provide quick access and matches to those large sets. The mechanism also must handle special features of the Unicode Standard, such as nonspacing marks and conjoining jamo.

The default boundary determination builds upon the uniform character representation of the Unicode Standard, while handling the large number of characters and special features such as nonspacing marks and conjoining jamo in an effective manner. As this mechanism lends itself to a completely data-driven implementation, it can be tailored to particular orthographic conventions or user preferences without recoding.

As in other Unicode algorithms, these specifications provide a *logical* description of the processes: implementations can achieve the same results without using code or data that follows these rules step-by-step. In particular, many production-grade implementations will use a state-table approach. In that case, the performance does not depend on the complexity or number of rules. Rather, the only feature affecting performance is the number of characters that may match *after* the boundary position in a rule that applies.

X1.1 Notation

A boundary specification summarizes boundary property values used in that specification, then lists the rules for boundary determinations in terms of those property values. The summary is provided as a list, where each element of the list is one of the following:

- A literal character
- A range of literal characters
- All characters satisfying a given condition, using properties defined in the Unicode

Character Database [UCD]:

Non-Boolean property values are given as *<property>=<property value>*, such as General_Category = Titlecase_Letter.

Boolean properties are given as *<property>=true*, such as Uppercase = true.

Other conditions are specified textually in terms of UCD properties.

- Boolean combinations of the above
- The two special identifiers *sot* and *eot* stand for start and end of text, respectively

For example, the following is such a list:

General_Category = Line Separator (Zl), or
General_Category = Paragraph Separator (Zp), or
General_Category = Control (Cc), or
General_Category = Format (Cf)
and not `U+000D CARRIAGE RETURN (CR)<]`
and not `U+000A LINE FEED (LF)`
and not `U+200C ZERO WIDTH NON-JOINER (ZWNJ)`
and not `U+200D ZERO WIDTH JOINER (ZWJ)`

In the table assigning the boundary property values, all of the values are intended to be disjoint except for the special value **Any**. In case of conflict, rows higher in the table have precedence in terms of assigning property values to characters. Data files containing explicit assignments of the property values are found in [Props].

Boundary determination is specified in terms of an ordered list of rules, indicating the status of a boundary position. The rules are numbered for reference and are applied in sequence to determine whether there is a boundary at a given offset. That is, there is an implicit "otherwise" at the front of each rule following the first. The rules are processed from top to bottom. As soon as a rule matches and produces a boundary status (boundary or no boundary) for that offset, the process is terminated.

Each rule consists of a left side, a boundary symbol (see *Table 1*), and a right side. Either of the sides can be empty. The left and right sides use the boundary property values in regular expressions. The regular expression syntax used is a simplified version of the format supplied in Unicode Technical Standard #18, "Unicode Regular Expressions" [RegEx].

Table 1. Boundary Symbols

÷	Boundary (allow break here)
×	No boundary (do not allow break here)
→	Treat whatever on the left side as if it were what is on the right side

An *underscore* ("_") is used to indicate a space in examples.

These rules are constrained in three ways, to make implementations significantly simpler and more efficient. These constraints have not been found to be limitations for natural language use. In particular, the rules are formulated so that they can be efficiently implemented, such as with a deterministic finite-state machine based on a small number of property values.

1. *Single boundaries.* Each rule has exactly one boundary position. This restriction is more a limitation on the specification methods, because a rule with multiple boundaries could be expressed instead as multiple rules. For example:

   "a b ÷ c d ÷ e f" could be broken into two rules "a b ÷ c d e f" and "a b c d ÷ e f"

   "a b × c d × e f" could be broken into two rules "a b × c d e f" and "a b c d × e f"

2. *Ignore degenerates.* No special provisions are made to get marginally better behavior for degenerate cases that never occur in practice, such as an *A* followed by an Indic combining mark.
3. *Limited negation.* Negation of expressions is limited to instances that resolve to a match against single characters, such as "¬(OLetter | Upper | Lower | Sep)".

X2 Conformance

There are many different ways to divide text elements corresponding to grapheme clusters, words, and sentences, and the Unicode Standard does not restrict the ways in which implementations can produce these divisions.

This specification defines a *default* mechanism; more sophisticated implementations can *and should* tailor it for particular locales or environments. For example, reliable detection of Thai, Lao, Chinese, or Japanese word break boundaries requires the use of dictionary lookup, analogous to English hyphenation. An implementation therefore may need to provide means to override or subclass the default mechanism described in this annex. Note that tailoring can *either* add boundary positions *or* remove boundary positions, compared to the default specified here.

> **Note:** Locale-sensitive boundary specifications can be expressed in LDML [UTS35] and be contained in the Common Locale Data Repository [CLDR]. The repository already contains some tailorings, with more to follow.

To maintain canonical equivalence, all of the following specifications are defined on NFD text, as defined in Unicode Standard Annex #15, "Unicode Normalization Forms" [UAX15]. A boundary exists in non-NFD text if and only if it would occur at the corresponding position in NFD text. However, the default rules have been written to provide equivalent results for non-NFD text and can be applied directly. Even in the case of tailored rules, the requirement to use NFD is only a logical specification; in practice, implementations can avoid normalization and achieve the same results. For more information, see *Section X6, Implementation Notes.*

X3 Grapheme Cluster Boundaries

One or more Unicode characters may make up what the user thinks of as a character or basic unit of the language. To avoid ambiguity with the computer use of the term *character*, this is called a *grapheme cluster*. For example, "G" + *acute-accent* is a grapheme cluster: it is thought of as a single character by users, yet is actually represented by two Unicode code points.

There are many types of Grapheme clusters. Examples include: combining character sequences, such as (g + ring above); digraphs, such as Slovak "ch", and sequences with letter modifiers, such as k^w. Grapheme cluster boundaries are important for collation, regular expressions, and counting "character" positions within text. Word boundaries, line boundaries, and sentence boundaries do not occur within a grapheme cluster. In this section, the Unicode Standard provides a determination of where the default grapheme boundaries fall in a string of characters. This algorithm can be tailored for specific locales or other customizations, which is what is done in providing contracting characters in collation tailoring tables.

> **Note:** Default grapheme clusters have been referred to as "locale-independent graphemes." The term *cluster* is used to emphasize that the term *grapheme* is used differently in linguistics. For simplicity and to align terminology with Unicode Technical Standard #10, "Unicode Collation Algorithm" [UTS10], the terms *default* and *tailored* are used in preference to *locale-independent* and *locale-dependent*, respectively.

As far as a user is concerned, the underlying representation of text is not important, but it is important that an editing interface present a uniform implementation of what the user thinks of as characters. Grapheme clusters commonly behave as units in terms of mouse selection, arrow key movement, backspacing, and so on. For example, when an accented character is represented by a character sequence, then using the right arrow key would skip from the start of the base character to the end of the last character of the cluster.

However, in some cases editing a grapheme cluster element by element may be preferable. For example, on a given system the *backspace key* might delete by code point, while the *delete key* may delete an entire cluster. Moreover, there is not a one-to-one relationship between grapheme clusters and keys on a keyboard. A single key on a keyboard may correspond to a whole grapheme cluster, a part of a grapheme clusters, or a sequence of more than one grapheme clusters.

In those relatively rare circumstances where programmers need to supply end users with character counts, the counts should correspond to the number of segments delimited by grapheme cluster boundaries. Grapheme clusters are also used in searching and matching; for more information, see Unicode Technical Standard #10, "Unicode Collation Algorithm" [UTS10], and Unicode Technical Standard #18, "Unicode Regular Expressions" [UTS18].

The principal requirements for default grapheme cluster boundaries are the handling of nonspacing marks and Hangul conjoining jamo. Boundaries may be further tailored for requirements of different languages, such as the addition of Indic, Thai, or Tibetan character clusters.

A default grapheme cluster begins with a base character, except when a nonspacing mark is at the start of text, or when it is preceded by a control or format character. In place of a single base character, a Hangul syllable composed of one or more characters may serve as the base. For the rules defining the default boundaries, see *Table 2*. For more information on the composition of Hangul syllables, see *Chapter 3, Conformance*, of [Unicode].

> **Note:** The boundary between default grapheme clusters can be determined by just the two adjacent characters. See *Section X7, Testing*, for a chart showing the interactions of pairs of characters.

Degenerate Cases. These definitions are designed to be simple to implement. They need to provide an algorithmic determination of the valid, default grapheme clusters and to exclude sequences that are normally not considered default grapheme clusters. However, they do *not* have to cover edge cases that will not occur in practice.

The definition of default grapheme clusters is not meant to exclude the use of more sophisticated definitions of tailored grapheme clusters where appropriate: definitions that more precisely match the user expectations within individual languages for given processes. For example, “ch” may be considered a grapheme cluster in Slovak, for processes such as collation. The default definition is, however, designed to provide a much more accurate match to overall user expectations for what the user perceives of as *characters* than is provided by individual Unicode code points.

Display of Grapheme Clusters. Grapheme clusters are not the same as ligatures. For example, the grapheme cluster “ch” in Slovak is not normally a ligature and, conversely, the ligature “fi” is not a grapheme cluster. Default grapheme clusters do not necessarily reflect text display. For example, the sequence <f, i> may be displayed as a single glyph on the screen, but would still be two grapheme clusters.

For more information on the matching of grapheme clusters with regular expressions, see Unicode Techncial Standard #18, “Unicode Regular Expressions” [UTS18].

> **Note:** As with the other default specifications, implementations may override (tailor) the results to meet the requirements of different environments or particular languages.

X3.1 Default Grapheme Cluster Boundary Specification

The Grapheme_Cluster_Break property value assignments are explicitly listed in the corresponding data file; see [Props]. The contents of this data file are summarized in *Table 2.*

Table 2. Grapheme_Cluster_Break Property Values

Value	Summary List of Characters
CR	U+000D CARRIAGE RETURN (CR)
LF	U+000A LINE FEED (LF)
Control	General_Category = Line Separator (Zl), or General_Category = Paragraph Separator (Zp), or General_Category = Control (Cc), or General_Category = Format (Cf) *and not* U+000D CARRIAGE RETURN (CR) *and not* U+000A LINE FEED (LF) *and not* U+200C ZERO WIDTH NON-JOINER (ZWNJ) *and not* U+200D ZERO WIDTH JOINER (ZWJ)
Extend	Grapheme_Extend = true
L	Hangul_Syllable_Type=L, that is: U+1100 (ᄀ) HANGUL CHOSEONG KIYEOK ..U+1159 (ᅙ) HANGUL CHOSEONG YEORINHIEUH U+115F (ᅟ) HANGUL CHOSEONG FILLER

V	Hangul_Syllable_Type=V, that is:
	`U+1160 (>ᅠ) HANGUL JUNGSEONG FILLER`
	`..U+11A2 (ᆢ) HANGUL JUNGSEONG SSANGARAEA`

T	Hangul_Syllable_Type=T, that is:
	`U+11A8 (ᆨ) HANGUL JONGSEONG KIYEOK`
	`..U+11F9 (ᇹ) HANGUL JONGSEONG YEORINHIEUH`

LV	Hangul_Syllable_Type=LV, that is:
	`U+AC00 (가) HANGUL SYLLABLE GA`
	`U+AC1C (개) HANGUL SYLLABLE GAE`
	`U+AC38 (갸) HANGUL SYLLABLE GYA`
	`...`

LVT	Hangul_Syllable_Type=LVT, that is:
	`U+AC01 (각) HANGUL SYLLABLE GAG`
	`U+AC02 (갂) HANGUL SYLLABLE GAGG`
	`U+AC03 (갃) HANGUL SYLLABLE GAGS`
	`U+AC04 (간) HANGUL SYLLABLE GAN`
	`...`

Any	Any character (includes all of the above)

Grapheme Cluster Boundary Rules

Break at the start and end of text.

GB1.	sot	÷	
GB2.		÷	eot

Do not break between a CR and LF. Otherwise, break before and after controls.

GB3.	CR	×	LF
GB4.	(Control | CR | LF)	÷	
GB5.		÷	(Control | CR | LF)

Do not break Hangul syllable sequences.

GB6.	L	×	(L | V | LV | LVT)
GB7.	(LV | V)	×	(V | T)
GB8.	(LVT | T)	×	T

Do not break before extending characters.

GB9.		×	Extend

Otherwise, break everywhere.

GB10.	Any	÷	Any

X4 Word Boundaries

Word boundaries are used in a number of different contexts. The most familiar ones are selection (double-click mouse selection or "move to next word" control-arrow keys) and the dialog option "Whole Word Search" for search and replace. They are also used in database queries, to determine whether elements are within a certain number of words of one another.

Word boundaries can also be used in *intelligent cut and paste*. With this feature, if the user cuts a selection of text on word boundaries, adjacent spaces are collapsed to a single space. For example, cutting "quick" from "The_quick_fox" would leave "The_ _fox". Intelligent cut and paste collapses this text to "The_fox". *Figure 1* gives an example of word boundaries.

Figure 1. Word Boundaries

The		quick		(	"	brown	"	)		fox		can't		jump		32.3		feet	,		right	?

There is a boundary, for example, on either side of the word *brown*. These are the boundaries that users would expect, for example, if they chose Whole Word Search. Matching *brown* with Whole Word Search works because there is a boundary on either side. Matching *brow* does not. Matching *"brown"* also works because there are boundaries between the parentheses and the quotation marks.

Proximity tests in searching determines whether, for example, "quick" is within three words of "fox". That is done with the above boundaries by ignoring any words that do not contain a letter, as in *Figure 2*. Thus, for proximity, "fox" is within three words of "quick". This same technique can be used for "get next/previous word" commands or keyboard arrow keys. Letters are not the only characters that can be used to determine the "significant" words; different implementations may include other types of characters such as digits or perform other analysis of the characters.

Figure 2. Extracted Words

The	quick	brown	fox	can't	jump	32.3	feet	right

Word boundaries are related to line boundaries, but are distinct: there are some word break boundaries that are not line break boundaries, and vice versa. A line break boundary is usually a word break boundary, but there are exceptions such as a word containing a SHY (soft hyphen): it will break across lines, yet is a single word.

> **Note:** As with the other default specifications, implementations may override (tailor) the results to meet the requirements of different environments or particular languages. For some languages, it may also be necessary to have different tailored word break rules for selection versus Whole Word Search.
>
> In particular, the characters with the Line_Break property values of Contingent_Break (CB), Complex_Context (SA/South East Asian), and XX (Unknown) are assigned word boundary property values based on criteria outside of the scope of this annex.

X4.1 Default Word Boundary Specification

The Word_Break property value assignments are explicitly listed in the corresponding data file; see [Props]. The contents of this data file are summarized in *Table 3.*

Table 3. Word_Break Property Values

Value	Summary List of Characters
Format	General_Category = Format (Cf) *and not* U+200C ZERO WIDTH NON-JOINER (ZWNJ) *and not* U+200D ZERO WIDTH JOINER (ZWJ)
Katakana	Script = KATAKANA, *or* any of the following: U+3031 (〱) VERTICAL KANA REPEAT MARK U+3032 (〲) VERTICAL KANA REPEAT WITH VOICED SOUND MARK U+3033 (〳) VERTICAL KANA REPEAT MARK UPPER HALF U+3034 (〴) VERTICAL KANA REPEAT WITH VOICED SOUND MARK UPPER HALF U+3035 (〵) VERTICAL KANA REPEAT MARK LOWER HALF U+309B (゛) KATAKANA-HIRAGANA VOICED SOUND MARK U+309C (゜) KATAKANA-HIRAGANA SEMI-VOICED SOUND MARK U+30A0 (=?) KATAKANA-HIRAGANA DOUBLE HYPHEN U+30FC (ー) KATAKANA-HIRAGANA PROLONGED SOUND MARK U+FF70 (-) HALFWIDTH KATAKANA-HIRAGANA PROLONGED SOUND MARK U+FF9E (ﾞ) HALFWIDTH KATAKANA VOICED SOUND MARK U+FF9F (ﾟ) HALFWIDTH KATAKANA SEMI-VOICED SOUND MARK
ALetter	Alphabetic = true, *or* U+05F3 (') HEBREW PUNCTUATION GERESH *and* Ideographic = false *and* Word_Break ≠Katakana *and* LineBreak ≠Complex_Context (SA) *and* Script ≠ Hiragana *and* Grapheme_Extend = false
MidLetter	Any of the following: U+0027 (') APOSTROPHE U+00B7 (·) MIDDLE DOT U+05F4 (") HEBREW PUNCTUATION GERSHAYIM U+2019 (') RIGHT SINGLE QUOTATION MARK (curly apostrophe) U+2027 (‧) HYPHENATION POINT U+003A (:) COLON (used in Swedish)
MidNum	Line_Break = Infix_Numeric *and not* U+003A (:) COLON
Numeric	Line_Break = Numeric
ExtendNumLet	General_Category = Connector_Punctuation
Any	Any character (includes all of the above)

Word Boundary Rules

Break at the start and end of text.

WB1.	sot	÷	
WB2.		÷	eot

Do not break within CRLF.

WB3.	CR	×	LF

Ignore Format and Extend characters, except when they appear at the beginning of a region of text.
(See Section X6.2, Replacing Ignore Rules.)

WB4.	X (Extend | Format)*	→	X

Do not break between most letters.

WB5.	ALetter	×	ALetter

Do not break letters across certain punctuation.

WB6.	ALetter	×	MidLetter ALetter
WB7.	ALetter MidLetter	×	ALetter

Do not break within sequences of digits, or digits adjacent to letters ("3a", or "A3").

WB8.	Numeric	×	Numeric
WB9.	ALetter	×	Numeric
WB10.	Numeric	×	ALetter

Do not break within sequences, such as "3.2" or "3,456.789".

WB11.	Numeric MidNum	×	Numeric
WB12.	Numeric	×	MidNum Numeric

Do not break between Katakana.

WB13.	Katakana	×	Katakana

Do not break from extenders.

WB13a.	(ALetter | Numeric | Katakana | ExtendNumLet)	×	ExtendNumLet
WB13b.	ExtendNumLet	×	(ALetter | Numeric | Katakana)

Otherwise, break everywhere (including around ideographs).

WB14.	Any	÷	Any

Notes:

- It is not possible to provide a uniform set of rules that resolves all issues across languages or that handles all ambiguous situations within a given language. The goal for the specification presented in this annex is to provide a workable default; tailored implementations can be more sophisticated.
- For Thai, Lao, Khmer, Myanmar, and other scripts that do not use typically use spaces between words, a good implementation should not just depend on the default word boundary specification, but should use a more sophisticated mechanism, as is also required for line breaking. Ideographic scripts such as Japanese and Chinese are even more complex. Where Hangul text is written without spaces, the same applies. However, in the absence of such a more sophisticated mechanism, the rules specified in this annex at least supply a well-defined default.
- The correct interpretation of hyphens in the context of word boundaries is challenging. It is quite common for separate words to be connected with a hyphen: "out-of-the-box," "under-the-table," "Italian-American," and so on. A significant number are hyphenated names, such as "Smith-Hawkins." When doing a Whole Word Search or query, users expect to find the word within those hyphens. While there are some cases where they are separate words (usually to resolve some ambiguity such as "re-sort" as opposed to "resort"), it is better overall to keep the hyphen out of the default definition. Hyphens include U+002D HYPHEN-MINUS, U+2010 HYPHEN, possibly also U+058A (-) ARMENIAN HYPHEN, and U+30A0 KATAKANA-HIRAGANA DOUBLE HYPHEN.
- Implementations may, however, build on the information supplied by word boundaries. For example, a spell-checker would first check that each word according to the above definition was valid, checking four words in "out-of-the-box." However, if that failed, it could build the compound word and check if it as a whole was in the dictionary (even if all the components were not in the dictionary), such as with "re-iterate." Of course, spell-checkers for highly inflected or agglutinative languages will need much more sophisticated algorithms.
- The use of the apostrophe is ambiguous. It is usually considered part of one word ("can't" or "aujourd'hui") but it may also be considered as part of two words ("l'objectif"). A further complication is the use of the same character as an apostrophe and as a quotation mark. Therefore leading or trailing apostrophes are best excluded from the default definition of a word. In some languages, such as French and Italian, tailoring to break words when the character after the apostrophe is a vowel may yield better results in more cases. This can be done by adding a rule WB5a.

  Break between apostrophe and vowels (French, Italian).

WB5a.	*apostrophe* ÷ vowels

  and defining appropriate property values for apostrophe and vowels. Apostrophe includes U+0027 (') APOSTROPHE and U+2019 (') RIGHT SINGLE QUOTATION MARK (curly apostrophe). Finally, in some transliteration schemes, apostrophe is used at the beginning of words, requiring special tailoring.

- To allow acronyms like “U.S.A.”, a tailoring may include U+002E FULL STOP in ExtendNumLet.
- Certain cases such as colons in words (c:a) are included in the default even though they may be specific to relatively small user communities (Swedish) because they do not occur otherwise, in normal text, and so do not cause a problem for other languages.
- For Hebrew, a tailoring may include a double quotation mark between letters, because legacy data may contain that in place of `U+05F4 (״) gershayim`. This can be done by adding double quotation mark to MidLetter. `U+05F3 (׳)` HEBREW PUNCTUATION GERESH may also be included in a tailoring.
- Format characters are included if they are not initial. Thus <LRM><ALetter> will break before the <letter>, but there is no break in <ALetter><LRM><ALetter> or <ALetter><LRM>.
- Characters such as hyphens, apostrophes, quotation marks, and colon should be taken into account when using identifiers that are intended to represent words of one or more natural languages. See *Section X2.3, Specific Character Adjustments*, of [UAX31]. Treatment of hyphens, in particular, may be different in the case of processing identifiers than when using word break analysis for a Whole Word Search or query, because when handling identifiers the goal will be to parse maximal units corresponding to natural language “words,” rather than to find smaller word units within longer lexical units connected by hyphens.

X5 Sentence Boundaries

Sentence boundaries are often used for triple-click or some other method of selecting or iterating through blocks of text that are larger than single words. They are also used to determine whether words occur within the same sentence in database queries.

Plain text provides inadequate information for determining good sentence boundaries. Periods can signal the end of a sentence, indicate abbreviations, or be used for decimal points, for example. Without much more sophisticated analysis, one cannot distinguish between the two following examples of the sequence <?, ”, space, uppercase-letter>:

He said, “Are you going?”	John shook his head.

“Are you going?” John asked.

Without analyzing the text semantically, it is impossible to be certain which of these usages is intended (and sometimes ambiguities still remain). However, in most cases a straightforward mechanism works well.

> **Note:** As with the other default specifications, implementations are free to override (tailor) the results to meet the requirements of different environments or particular languages.

X5.1 Default Sentence Boundary Specification

The Sentence_Break property value assignments are explicitly listed in the corresponding data file; see [Props]. The contents of this data file are summarized in *Table 4*.

Table 4. Sentence_Break Property Values

Value	Summary List of Characters
Sep	Any of the following characters: U+000A LINE FEED (LF) U+000D CARRIAGE RETURN (CR) U+0085 NEXT LINE (NEL) U+2028 LINE SEPARATOR (LS) U+2029 PARAGRAPH SEPARATOR (PS)
Format	General_Category = Format (Cf) *and not* U+200C ZERO WIDTH NON-JOINER (ZWNJ) *and not* U+200D ZERO WIDTH JOINER (ZWJ)
Sp	Whitespace = true *and* Sentence_Break≠ Sep *and not* U+00A0 (NBSP) NO-BREAK SPACE (NBSP)
Lower	Lowercase = true *and* GRAPHEME EXTEND = false
Upper	General_Category = Titlecase_Letter (Lt), *or* Uppercase = true
OLetter	Alphabetic = true, *or* U+00A0 (NBSP) NO-BREAK SPACE (NBSP), *or* U+05F3 (׳) HEBREW PUNCTUATION GERESH *and* Lower = false *and* Upper = false *and* Grapheme_Extend = false
Numeric	Linebreak = Numeric (NU)
ATerm	U+002E (.) FULL STOP
STerm	STerm = true
Close	General_Category = Open_Punctuation (Po), *or* General_Category = Close_Punctuation (Pe), *or* Linebreak = Quotation (QU) *and not* U+05F3 (׳) HEBREW PUNCTUATION GERESH *and* ATerm = false *and* STerm = false
Any	Any character (includes all of the above)

Sentence Boundary Rules

Break at the start and end of text.

SB1.	sot	÷	
SB2.		÷	eot

Do not break within CRLF.

SB3.	CR	×	LF

Break after paragraph separators.

SB4.	Sep	÷	

Ignore Format and Extend characters, except when they appear at the beginning of a region of text. (See Section X6.2, Replacing Ignore Rules.)

SB5.	X (Extend | Format)*	→	X

Do not break after ambiguous terminators like period, if they are immediately followed by a number or lowercase letter, if they are between uppercase letters, or if the first following letter (optionally after certain punctuation) is lowercase. For example, a period may be an abbreviation or numeric period, and thus may not mark the end of a sentence.

SB6.	ATerm	×	Numeric
SB7.	Upper ATerm	×	Upper
SB8.	ATerm Close* Sp*	×	(¬(OLetter | Upper | Lower | Sep))* Lower
SB8a.	(STerm | ATerm) Close* Sp*	×	(STerm | ATerm)

Break after sentence terminators, but include closing punctuation, trailing spaces, and a paragraph separator (if present). [See note below.]

SB9.	(STerm | ATerm) Close*	×	(Close | Sp | Sep)
SB10.	(STerm | ATerm) Close* Sp*	×	(Sp | Sep)
SB11.	(STerm | ATerm) Close* Sp*	÷	

Otherwise, do not break.

SB12.	Any	×	Any

Notes:

- Note added in proof. NBSP should have been given the property Sp (to match the updated Word_Break). Implementations are encouraged to tailor Sp so as to include NBSP.
- Note added in proof: The context required for determining a break position should never extend beyond the surrounding break positions on either side. Implementations

are recommended to add Sterm and ATerm to the righthand side of Rule SB8, which then becomes:

SB8* ATerm Close* Sp* × (¬(OLetter | Upper | Lower | Sep | STerm | ATerm))* Lower

- Note added in proof: Rule SB11 has a typo. Implementations are recommended to implement the following corrected version which adds a Sep?:

SB11* (STerm | ATerm) Close* Sp* Sep? ÷

- Rules SB6-8 are designed to forbid breaks within strings like

c.d
3.4
U.S.
... the resp. leaders are ...
... etc.)' '(the ...

They permit breaks in strings like

She said "See spot run."	John shook his head. ...
... etc.	它们指...
...理数字.	它们指...

They cannot detect cases like "...Mr. Jones..."; more sophisticated tailoring would be required to detect such cases.

X6 Implementation Notes

X6.1 Normalization

The boundary specifications are stated in terms of text normalized according to Normalization Form NFD (see Unicode Standard Annex #15, "Unicode Normalization Forms" [UAX15]). In practice, normalization of the input is not required. To ensure that the same results are returned for canonically equivalent text (that is, the same boundary positions will be found, although those may be represented by different offsets), the grapheme cluster boundary specification has the following features:

a. There is never a break within a sequence of nonspacing marks.
b. There is never a break between a base character and subsequent nonspacing marks.

The specification also avoids certain problems by explicitly assigning the Extend property value to certain characters, such as U+09BE (া) BENGALI VOWEL SIGN AA, to deal with particular compositions.

The other default boundary specifications never break within grapheme clusters, and they always use a consistent property value for each grapheme cluster as a whole.

X6.2 Replacing Ignore Rules

An important rule for the default word and sentence specifications ignores Extend and Format characters. The main purpose of this rule is to always treat a grapheme cluster as a single character—that is, as if it were simply the first character of the cluster. Both word and sentence specifications do not distinguish between L, V, T, LV, and LVT: thus it does not matter whether there is a sequence of these or a single one. In addition, there is a specific rule to disallow breaking within CRLF. Thus ignoring Extend is sufficient to disallow breaking within a grapheme cluster. Format characters are also ignored by default, because these characters are normally irrelevant to such boundaries.

The "Ignore" rule is then equivalent to making the following changes in the rules:

Replace the "Ignore" rule by the following, to disallow breaks within sequences (except after CRLF and related characters):

Original	→	Modified
X (Extend | Format)*→X	→	(¬Sep) × (Extend | Format)

In all subsequent rules, insert (Extend | Format) after every boundary property value. (It is not necessary to do this after the final property, on the right side of the break symbol.) For example:*

Original	→	Modified
X Y × Z W	→	X (Extend | Format)* Y (Extend | Format)* × Z (Extend | Format)* W
X Y ×	→	X (Extend | Format)* Y (Extend | Format)* ×

An alternate expression that resolves to a single character is treated as a whole. For example:

Original	→	Modified
(STerm | ATerm)	→	(STerm | ATerm) (Extend | Format)*
not	→	(STerm (Extend | Format)* | ATerm (Extend | Format)*)

The Ignore rules should not be overridden by tailorings, with the possible exception of remapping some of the Format characters to other classes.

X6.3 Regular Expressions

The preceding rules can be converted into a regular expression that will produce the same results. The regular expression must be evaluated starting at a known boundary (such as the start of the text) and take the longest match (except in the case of sentence boundaries, where the shortest match needs to be used).

The conversion into a regular expression is fairly straightforward, although it takes a little thought. For example, the Default Grapheme Cluster Boundaries of *Table 1* can be transformed into the following regular expression:

```
  Control
| CR LF
| ( ¬Control? | L+ | T+ | L* ( LV? V+ | LV | LVT ) T* ) Extend*
```

Such a regular expression can also be turned into a fast deterministic finite-state machine. For more information on Unicode Regular Expressions, see Unicode Technical Standard #18, "Unicode Regular Expressions" [UTS18].

X6.4 Random Access

A further complication is introduced by random access. When iterating through a string from beginning to end, a regular expression or state machine works well. From each boundary to find the next boundary is very fast. By constructing a state table for the reverse direction from the same specification of the rules, reverse iteration is possible.

However, suppose that the user wants to iterate starting at a random point in the text, or detect whether a random point in the text is a boundary. If the starting point does not provide enough context to allow the correct set of rules to be applied, then one could fail to find a valid boundary point. For example, suppose a user clicked after the first space after the question mark in "Are_you_there? _ _ No,_I'm_not". On a forward iteration searching for a sentence boundary, one would fail to find the boundary before the "N", because the "?" had not been seen yet.

A second set of rules to determine a "safe" starting point provides a solution. Iterate backward with this second set of rules until a safe starting point is located, then iterate forward from there. Iterate forward to find boundaries that were located between the safe point and the starting point; discard these. The desired boundary is the first one that is not less than the starting point. The safe rules must be designed so that they function correctly no matter what the starting point is, so they have to be conservative in terms of finding boundaries, and only find those boundaries that can be determined by a small context (a few neighboring characters).

Figure 3. Random Access

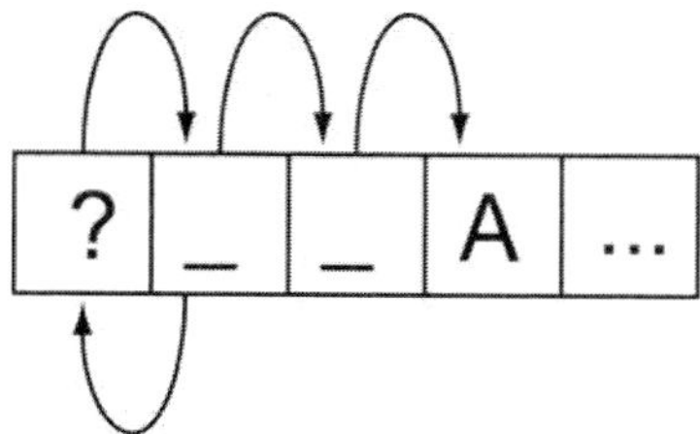

This process would represent a significant performance cost if it had to be performed on every search. However, this functionality can be wrapped up in an iterator object, which preserves the information regarding whether it currently is at a valid boundary point. Only if it is reset to an arbitrary location in the text is this extra backup processing performed. The iterator may even cache local values that it has already traversed.

X6.5 Tailoring

Rule-based implementation can also be combined with a code-based or table-based tailoring mechanism. For typical state machine implementations, for example, a Unicode character is typically passed to a mapping table that maps characters to boundary property values. This mapping can use an efficient mechanism such as a trie. Once a boundary property value is produced, it is passed to the state machine.

The simplest customization is to adjust the values coming out of the character mapping table. For example, to mark the appropriate quotation marks for a given language as having the sentence boundary property value Close, artificial property values can be introduced for different quotation marks. A table can be applied after the main mapping table to map those artificial character property values to the real ones. To change languages, a different small table is substituted. The only real cost is then an extra array lookup.

For code-based tailoring a different special range of property values can be added. The state machine is set up so that any special property value causes the state machine to halt and return a particular exception value. When this exception value is detected, the higher-level process can call specialized code according to whatever the exceptional value is. This can all be encapsulated so that it is transparent to the caller.

For example, Thai characters can be mapped to a special property value. When the state machine halts for one of these values, then a Thai word break implementation is invoked internally, to produce boundaries within the subsequent string of Thai characters. These boundaries can then be cached so that subsequent calls for next or previous boundaries merely return the cached values. Similarly Lao characters can be mapped to a different special property value, causing a different implementation to be invoked.

X7 Testing

There is no requirement that Unicode-conformant implementations implement these default boundaries. As with the other default specifications, implementations are also free to override (tailor) the results to meet the requirements of different environments or particular languages. For those who do implement the default boundaries as specified in this annex, and wish to check that that their implementation matches that specification, three test files have been made available in [Tests29].

These tests cannot be exhaustive, because of the large number of possible combinations; but they do provide samples that test all pairs of property values, using a representative character for each value, plus certain other sequences.

A sample HTML file is also available for each that shows various combinations in chart form, in [Charts29]. The header cells of the chart consist of a property value, followed by a representative code point number. The body cells in the chart show the *break status*: whether a break occurs between the row property value and the column property value. If the browser supports tool-tips, then hovering the mouse over the code point number will show the character name, General_Category, Line_Break, and Script property values. Hovering over the break status will display the number of the rule responsible for that status.

> **Note:** To determine a boundary it is *not* sufficient to just test the two adjacent characters, except for the case of the default grapheme clusters.

The chart may be followed by some test cases. These test cases consist of various strings with the break status between each pair of characters shown by blue lines for breaks and by whitespace for non-breaks. Hovering over each character (with tool-tips enabled) shows the character name and property value; hovering over the break status shows the number of the rule responsible for that status.

Due to the way they have been mechanically processed for generation, the test rules do not match the rules in this annex precisely. In particular:

1. The rules are cast into a more regex-style.
2. The rules "sot ÷", "÷ eot", and "÷ Any" are added mechanically and have artificial numbers.
3. The rules are given decimal numbers without prefix, so rules such as WB13a are given a number using tenths, such as 13.1.
4. Where a rule has multiple parts (lines), each one is numbered using hundredths, such as
   - 21.01) × $BA
   - 21.02) × $HY
   - ...
5. Any "treat as" or "ignore" rules are handled as discussed in this annex, and thus reflected in a transformation of the rules not visible in the tests.

The mapping from the rule numbering in this annex to the numbering for the test rules is summarized in *Table 5.*

Table 5. Numbering of Rules

<table>
<tr><th>Rule in This Annex</th><th>Test Rule</th><th>Comment</th></tr>
<tr><td>xx1</td><td>0.1</td><td>start of text</td></tr>
<tr><td>xx2</td><td>0.2</td><td>end of text</td></tr>
<tr><td>SB8a</td><td>8.1</td><td rowspan="3">letter style</td></tr>
<tr><td>WB13a</td><td>13.1</td></tr>
<tr><td>WB13b</td><td>13.2</td></tr>
<tr><td>GB10</td><td rowspan="2">999</td><td rowspan="2">any</td></tr>
<tr><td>WB14</td></tr>
</table>

Acknowledgments

Mark Davis is the author of the initial version and has added to and maintained the text of this annex.

Thanks to Julie Allen, Asmus Freytag, Ted Hopp, Andy Heninger, Michael Kaplan, Steve Tolkin, Ken Whistler, and Eric Mader for their feedback on this annex, including earlier versions.

References

For references for this annex, see Unicode Standard Annex #41, "Common References for Unicode Standard Annexes."

Modifications

For details of the change history, see the online copy of this annex at http://www.unicode.org/reports/tr29/.

Unicode Standard Annex #31

Identifier and Pattern Syntax

Summary

This annex describes specifications for recommended defaults for the use of Unicode in the definitions of identifiers and in pattern-based syntax. It also supplies guidelines for use of normalization with identifiers.

Contents

X1 Introduction

A common task facing an implementer of the Unicode Standard is the provision of a parsing and/or lexing engine for identifiers, such as programming language variables or domain names. To assist in the standard treatment of identifiers in Unicode character-based parsers and lexical analyzers, a set of specifications is provided here as a recommended default for the definition of identifier syntax. These guidelines are no more complex than current rules in the common programming languages, except that they include more characters of different types. This annex also provides guidelines for the user of normalization and case insensitivity with identifiers, expanding on a section that was originally in Unicode Standard Annex #15, "Unicode Normalization Forms" [UAX15].

The specification in this annex provide a definition of identifiers that is guaranteed to be backward compatible with each successive release of Unicode, but also allows any appropriate new Unicode characters to become available in identifiers. In addition, Unicode character properties for stable pattern syntax are provided. The resulting pattern syntax is stable over future versions of the Unicode Standard. These properties can either be used alone or in conjunction with the identifier characters.

Figure 1 shows the disjoint categories of code points defined in this annex (the sizes of the boxes are not to scale):

Figure 1. Code Point Categories for Identifier Parsing

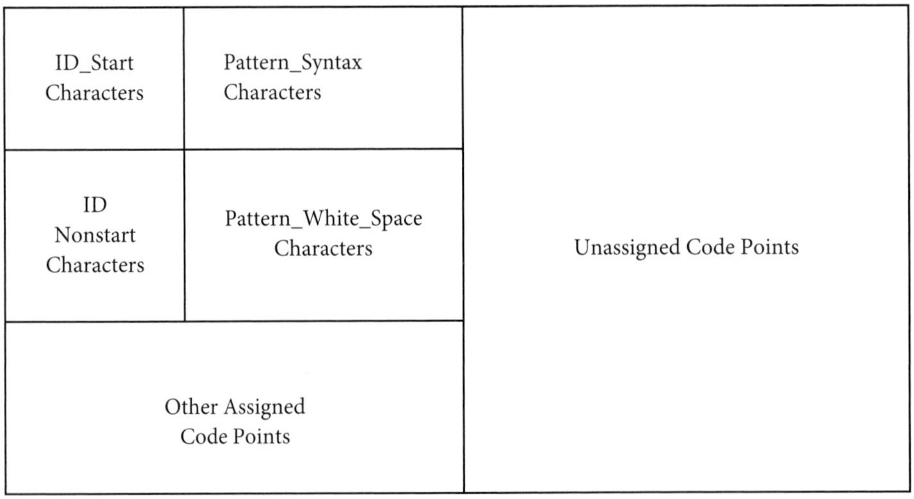

ID_Start Characters

Pattern_Syntax Characters

ID Nonstart Characters

Pattern_White_Space Characters

Other Assigned Code Points

Unassigned Code Points

The set consisting of the union of *ID_Start* and *ID Nonstart* characters is known as *Identifier Characters* and has the property *ID_Continue*. The *ID Nonstart* set is defined as the set difference *ID_Continue* minus *ID_Start*. While lexical rules are traditionally expressed in terms of the latter, the discussion here is simplified by referring to disjoint categories.

Stability. There are certain features that developers can depend on for stability:

- Identifier characters, Pattern_Syntax characters, and Pattern_White_Space are disjoint: they will never overlap.
- The Identifier characters are always a superset of the ID_Start characters.
- The Pattern_Syntax characters and Pattern_White_Space characters are immutable and will not change over successive versions of Unicode.
- The ID_Start and ID Nonstart characters may grow over time, either by the addition of new characters provided in a future version of Unicode or (in rare cases) by the addition of characters that were in Other. However, neither will ever decrease.

In successive versions of Unicode, the only allowed changes of characters from one of the above classes to another are those listed with a + sign in *Table 1.*

Table 1. Permitted Changes in Future Versions

	ID_Start	ID Nonstart	Other Assigned
Unassigned	+	+	+
Other Assigned	+	+	
ID Nonstart	+		

The Unicode Consortium has formally adopted a stability policy on identifiers. For more information, see [Stability].

Programming Languages. Each programming language standard has its own identifier syntax; different programming languages have different conventions for the use of certain characters such as $, @, #, and _ in identifiers. To extend such a syntax to cover the full behavior of a Unicode implementation, implementers may combine those specific rules with the syntax and properties provided here.

Each programming language can define its identifier syntax as *relative* to the Unicode identifier syntax, such as saying that identifiers are defined by the Unicode properties, with the addition of "$". By addition or subtraction of a small set of language specific characters, a programming language standard can easily track a growing repertoire of Unicode characters in a compatible way.

Similarly, each programming language can define its own whitespace characters or syntax characters relative to the Unicode Pattern_White_Space or Pattern_Syntax characters, with some specified set of additions or subtractions.

Systems that want to extend identifiers so as to encompass words used in natural languages may add characters identified in *Section X4, Word Boundaries,* of [UAX29] with the property values Katakana, ALetter, and MidLetter, plus characters described in the notes at the end of that section.

To preserve the disjoint nature of the categories illustrated in *Figure 1,* any character *added* to one of the categories must be *subtracted* from the others.

> **Note:** In many cases there are important security implications that may require additional constraints on identifiers. For more information, see [UTR36].

X1.1 Conformance

The following describes the possible ways that an implementation can claim conformance to this specification.

UAX31-C1. An implementation claiming conformance to this specification at any Level shall identify the version of this specification and the version of the Unicode Standard.

UAX31-C2. An implementation claiming conformance to Level 1 of this specification shall describe which of the following it observes:

- *R1 Default Identifiers*
- *R2 Alternative Identifiers*
- *R3 Pattern_White_Space and Pattern_Syntax Characters*
- *R4 Normalized Identifiers*
- *R5 Case-Insensitive Identifiers*

X2 Default Identifier Syntax

The formal syntax provided here captures the general intent that an identifier consists of a string of characters beginning with a letter or an ideograph, and following with any number of letters, ideographs, digits, or underscores. It provides a definition of identifiers that is guaranteed to be backward compatible with each successive release of Unicode, but also adds any appropriate new Unicode characters.

D1. Default Identifier Syntax

```
<identifier> := <ID_Start> <ID_Continue>*
```

Identifiers are defined by the sets of lexical classes defined as properties in the Unicode Character Database. These properties are shown in *Table 2.*

Table 2. Lexical Classes for Identifiers

Properties	Alternates	General Description of Coverage
`ID_Start`	`XID_Start`	Characters having the Unicode General_Category of uppercase letters, lowercase letters, titlecase letters, modifier letters, other letters, letter numbers, plus stability extensions. Note that "other letters" includes ideographs.
`ID_Continue`	`XID_Continue`	All of the above, plus characters having the Unicode General_Category of nonspacing marks (Mn), spacing combining marks (Mc), decimal nubmer (Nd), connector punctuations (Pc), plus stability extensions. These are also known simply as *Identifier Characters*, because they are a superset of the `ID_Start`.

The innovations in the identifier syntax to cover the Unicode Standard include the following:

- Incorporation of proper handling of combining marks.
- Allowance for layout and format control characters, which should be ignored when parsing identifiers.
- The XID_Start and XID_Continue properties are improved lexical classes that incorporate the changes described in *Section X5.1, NFKC Modifications.* They are

recommended for most purposes, especially for security, over the original ID_Start and ID_Continue properties.

X2.1 Combining Marks

Combining marks are accounted for in identifier syntax: a composed character sequence consisting of a base character followed by any number of combining marks is valid in an identifier. Combining marks are required in the representation of many languages, and the conformance rules in *Chapter 3, Conformance*, of [Unicode] require the interpretation of canonical-equivalent character sequences.

Enclosing combining marks (such as U+20DD..U+20E0) are excluded from the definition of the lexical class `ID_Continue`, because the composite characters that result from their composition with letters are themselves not normally considered valid constituents of these identifiers.

X2.2 Layout and Format Control Characters

Certain Unicode characters are used to control joining behavior, bidirectional ordering control, and alternative formats for display. These have the General_Category value of Cf. Unlike space characters or other delimiters, they do not indicate word, line, or other unit boundaries.

While it is possible to ignore these characters in determining identifiers, the recommendation is to not ignore them and to not permit them in identifiers except in special cases. This is because of the possibility for confusion between two visually identical strings; see [UTR36]. Some possible exceptions are the ZWJ and ZWNJ in certain contexts, such as between certain characters in Indic words.

X2.3 Specific Character Adjustments

Specific identifier syntaxes can be treated as tailorings (or *profiles*) of the generic syntax based on character properties. For example, SQL identifiers allow an underscore as an identifier continue, but not as an identifier start; C identifiers allow an underscore as either an identifier continue or an identifier start. Specific languages may also want to exclude the characters that have a Decomposition_Type other than Canonical or None, or to exclude some subset of those, such as those with a Decomposition_Type equal to Font.

There are circumstances in which identifers are expected to more fully encompass words or phrases used in natural languages. In these cases, a profile should consider whether the characters in *Table 3* should be allowed in identifiers, and perhaps others, depending on the languages in question. In some environments even spaces are allowed in identifiers, such as in SQL: *SELECT * FROM Employee Pension.*

Table 3. Characters for Natural Language Identifiers

0027 (') APOSTROPHE
002D (-) HYPHEN-MINUS
002E (.) FULL STOP
003A (:) COLON

00B7 (·) MIDDLE DOT
058A (֊) ARMENIAN HYPHEN
05F3 (׳) HEBREW PUNCTUATION GERESH
05F4 (״) HEBREW PUNCTUATION GERSHAYIM
200C (ZWNJ) ZERO WIDTH NON-JOINER
200D (ZWJ) ZERO WIDTH JOINER
2010 (‐) HYPHEN
2019 (’) RIGHT SINGLE QUOTATION MARK
2027 (‧) HYPHENATION POINT
30A0 (゠) KATAKANA-HIRAGANA DOUBLE HYPHEN

For more information on characters that may occur in words, see *Section X4, Word Boundaries*, in [UAX29].

For programming language identifiers, normalization and case have a number of important implications. For a discussion of these issues, see *Section X5, Normalization and Case.*

X2.4 Backward Compatibility

Unicode General_Category values are kept as stable as possible, but they can change across versions of the Unicode Standard. The bulk of the characters having a given value are determined by other properties, and the coverage expands in the future according to the assignment of those properties. In addition, the Other_ID_Start property adds a small list of characters that qualified as ID_Start characters in some previous version of Unicode solely on the basis of their General_Category properties, but that no longer qualify in the current version. This list consists of four characters:

U+2118 (℘) SCRIPT CAPITAL P
U+212E (℮) ESTIMATED SYMBOL
U+309B (゛) KATAKANA-HIRAGANA VOICED SOUND MARK
U+309C (゜) KATAKANA-HIRAGANA SEMI-VOICED SOUND MARK

Similarly, the Other_ID_Continue property adds a small list of characters that qualified as ID_Continue characters in some previous version of Unicode solely on the basis of their General_Category properties, but that no longer qualify in the current version. This list consists of nine characters:

U+1369 (፩) ETHIOPIC DIGIT ONE...U+1371 (፱) ETHIOPIC DIGIT NINE

The Other_ID_Start and Other_ID_Continue properties are thus designed to ensure that the Unicode identifier specification is backward compatible. Any sequence of characters that qualified as an identifier in some version of Unicode will continue to qualify as an identifier in future versions.

R1 Default Identifiers

To meet this requirement, an implementation shall use definition D1 and the properties ID_Start and ID_Continue (or XID_Start and XID_Continue) to determine whether a string is an identifier.

Alternatively, it shall declare that it uses a *profile* and define that profile with a precise list of characters that are added to or removed from the above properties and/or provide a list of additional constraints on identifiers.

X3 Alternative Identifier Syntax

The disadvantage of working with the lexical classes defined previously is the storage space needed for the detailed definitions, plus the fact that with each new version of the Unicode Standard new characters are added, which an existing parser would not be able to recognize. In other words, the recommendations based on that table are not upwardly compatible.

This problem can be addressed by turning the question around. Instead of defining the set of code points that are allowed, define a small, fixed set of code points that are reserved for syntactic use and allow everything else (including unassigned code points) as part of an identifier. All parsers written to this specification would behave the same way for all versions of the Unicode Standard, because the classification of code points is fixed forever.

The drawback of this method is that it allows "nonsense" to be part of identifiers because the concerns of lexical classification and of human intelligibility are separated. Human intelligibility can, however, be addressed by other means, such as usage guidelines that encourage a restriction to meaningful terms for identifiers. For an example of such guidelines, see the XML 1.1 specification by the W3C [XML1.1].

By increasing the set of disallowed characters, a reasonably intuitive recommendation for identifiers can be achieved. This approach uses the full specification of identifier classes, as of a particular version of the Unicode Standard, and permanently disallows any characters not recommended in that version for inclusion in identifiers. All code points unassigned as of that version would be allowed in identifiers, so that any future additions to the standard would already be accounted for. This approach ensures both upwardly compatible identifier stability and a reasonable division of characters into those that do and do not make human sense as part of identifiers.

With or without such fine-tuning, such a compromise approach still incurs the expense of implementing large lists of code points. While they no longer change over time, it is a matter of choice whether the benefit of enforcing somewhat word-like identifiers justifies their cost.

Alternatively, one can use the properties described below and allow all sequences of characters to be identifiers that are neither Pattern_Syntax nor Pattern_White_Space. This has the advantage of simplicity and small tables, but allows many more "unnatural" identifiers.

R2 Alternative Identifiers

To meet this requirement, an implementation shall define identifiers to be any string of characters that contains neither Pattern_White_Space nor Pattern_Syntax characters.

Alternatively, it shall declare that it uses a *profile* and define that profile with a precise list of characters that are added to or removed from the sets of code points defined by these properties.

X4 Pattern Syntax

There are many circumstances where software interprets patterns that are a mixture of literal characters, whitespace, and syntax characters. Examples include regular expressions, Java collation rules, Excel or ICU number formats, and many others. In the past, regular expressions and other formal languages have been forced to use clumsy combinations of ASCII characters for their syntax. As Unicode becomes ubiquitous, some of these will start to use non-ASCII characters for their syntax: first as more readable optional alternatives, then eventually as the standard syntax.

For forward and backward compatibility, it is advantageous to have a fixed set of whitespace and syntax code points for use in patterns. This follows the recommendations that the Unicode Consortium made regarding completely stable identifiers, and the practice that is seen in XML 1.1 [XML1.1]. (In particular, the Unicode Consortium is committed to not allocating characters suitable for identifiers in the range U+2190..U+2BFF, which is being used by XML 1.1.)

With a fixed set of whitespace and syntax code points, a pattern language can then have a policy requiring all possible syntax characters (even ones currently unused) to be quoted if they are literals. Using this policy preserves the freedom to extend the syntax in the future by using those characters. Past patterns on future systems will always work; future patterns on past systems will signal an error instead of silently producing the wrong results.

Example 1:

In version 1.0 of program X, '≈' is a reserved syntax character; that is, it does not perform an operation, and it needs to be quoted. In this example, '\' *quotes* the next character; that is, it causes it to be treated as a literal instead of a syntax character. In version 2.0 of program X, '≈' is given a real meaning—for example, "uppercase the subsequent characters".

- The pattern abc...\≈...xyz works on both versions 1.0 and 2.0, and refers to the literal character because it is quoted in both cases.
- The pattern abc...≈...xyz works on version 2.0 and uppercases the following characters. On version 1.0, the engine (rightfully) has no idea what to do with ≈. Rather than silently fail (by ignoring ≈ or turning it into a literal), it has the opportunity signal an error.

As of [Unicode4.1], two Unicode character properties can be used for for stable syntax: Pattern_White_Space and Pattern_Syntax. Particular pattern languages may, of course, override these recommendations (for example, adding or removing other characters for compatibility in ASCII).

For stability, the values of these properties are absolutely invariant, not changing with successive versions of Unicode. Of course, this does not limit the ability of the Unicode Standard to add more symbol or whitespace characters, but the syntax and whitespace characters recommended for use in patterns will not change.

When *generating* rules or patterns, all whitespace and syntax code points that are to be literals require quoting, using whatever quoting mechanism is available. For readability, it is recommended practice to quote or escape all literal whitespace and default ignorable code points as well.

Example 2:

Consider the following, where the items in angle brackets indicate literal characters:

a<SPACE>b => x<ZERO WIDTH SPACE>y + z;

Because <SPACE> is a Pattern_White_Space character, it requires quoting. Because <ZERO WIDTH SPACE> is a default ignorable character, it should also be quoted for readability. So if in this example \uXXXX is used for hex expression, but resolved before quoting, and single quotes are used for quoting, this might be expressed as

'a\u0020b' => 'x\u200By' + z;

R3 Pattern_White_Space and Pattern_Syntax Characters

To meet this requirement, an implementation shall use Pattern_White_Space characters as all and only those characters interpreted as whitespace in parsing, and shall use Pattern_Syntax characters as all and only those characters with syntactic use.

Alternatively, it shall declare that it uses a *profile* and define that profile with a precise list of characters that are added to or removed from the sets of code points defined by these properties.

- All characters other than those defined by these properties are available for use as identifiers or literals.

X5 Normalization and Case

R4 Normalized Identifiers

To meet this requirement, an implementation shall specify the Normalization Form and shall provide a precise list of any characters that are excluded from normalization. If the Normalization Form is NFKC, the implementation shall apply the modifications in *Section X5.1, NFKC Modifications*, given by the properties XID_Start and XID_Continue. Except for identifiers containing excluded characters, any two identifiers that have the same Normalization Form shall be treated as equivalent by the implementation.

R5 Case-Insensitive Identifiers

To meet this requirement, an implementation shall specify either simple or full case folding, and adhere to the Unicode specification for that folding. Any two identifiers that have the same case-folded form shall be treated as equivalent by the implementation.

This section discusses issues that must be taken into account when considering normalization and case folding of identifiers in programming languages or scripting languages. Using normalization avoids many problems where apparently identical identifiers are not treated equivalently. Such problems can appear both during compilation and during linking—in particular across different programming languages. To avoid such problems, programming languages can normalize identifiers before storing or comparing them. Generally if the programming language has case-sensitive identifiers, then Normalization Form C is appropriate; whereas, if the programming language has case-insensitive identifiers, then Normalization Form KC is more appropriate.

> **Note:** In mathematically oriented programming languages that make distinctive use of the Mathematical Alphanumeric Symbols, such as U+1D400 MATHEMATICAL BOLD CAPITAL A, an application of NFKC must filter characters to exclude characters with the property value Decomposition_Type=Font. For related information, see Unicode Technical Report #30, "Character Foldings."

X5.1 NFKC Modifications

Where programming languages are using NFKC to fold differences between characters, they need the following modifications of the identifier syntax from the Unicode Standard to deal with the idiosyncrasies of a small number of characters. These modifications are reflected in the XID_Start and XID_Continue properties.

1. ***Middle dot.*** Because most Catalan legacy data is encoded in Latin-1, U+00B7 MIDDLE DOT is allowed in ID_Continue. If the programming language is using a dot as an operator, then U+2219 BULLET OPERATOR or U+22C5 DOT OPERATOR should be used instead. However, care should be taken when dealing with U+00B7 MIDDLE DOT, as many processes will assume its use as punctuation, rather than as a letter extender.
2. ***Characters that behave like combining marks.*** Certain characters are not formally combining characters, although they behave in most respects as if they were. In most cases, the mismatch does not cause a problem, but when these characters have compatibility decompositions, they can cause identifiers not to be closed under Normalization Form KC. In particular, the following four characters are included in XID_Continue and not XID_Start:

   U+0E33 THAI CHARACTER SARA AM

   U+0EB3 LAO VOWEL SIGN AM

   U+FF9E HALFWIDTH KATAKANA VOICED SOUND MARK

   U+FF9F HALFWIDTH KATAKANA SEMI-VOICED SOUND MARK
3. ***Irregularly decomposing characters.*** U+037A GREEK YPOGEGRAMMENI and certain Arabic presentation forms have irregular compatibility decompositions and are excluded from both XID_Start and XID_Continue. It is recommended that all Arabic presentation forms be excluded from identifiers in any event, although only a few of them must be excluded for normalization to guarantee identifier closure.

With these amendments to the identifier syntax, all identifiers are closed under all four Normalization Forms. Identifiers are also closed under case operations (with one exception). This means that for any string S:

<table>
<tr><td rowspan="2"><code>isIdentifier(S)</code></td><td rowspan="2">implies</td><td><code>isIdentifier(toNFD(S))</code>
<code>isIdentifier(toNFC(S))</code>
<code>isIdentifier(toNFKD(S))</code>
<code>isIdentifier(toNFKC(S))</code></td><td>Normalization Closure</td></tr>
<tr><td><code>isIdentifier(toLowercase(S))</code>
<code>isIdentifier(toUppercase(S))</code>
<code>isIdentifier(toFoldedcase(S))</code></td><td>Case Closure</td></tr>
</table>

The one exception for casing is U+0345 COMBINING GREEK YPOGEGRAMMENI. In the very unusual case that U+0345 is at the start of S, U+0345 is not in XID_Start, but its uppercase and case-folded versions are. In practice, this is not a problem because of the way normalization is used with identifiers.

> **Note:** Those programming languages with case-insensitive identifiers should use the case foldings described in *Section 3.13, Default Case Algorithms*, of [Unicode] to produce a case-insensitive normalized form.

When source text is parsed for identifiers, the folding of distinctions (using case mapping or NFKC) must be delayed until after parsing has located the identifiers. Thus such folding of distinctions should not be applied to string literals or to comments in program source text.

The Unicode Character Database (UCD) provides support for handling case folding with normalization: the property FC_NFKC_Closure can be used in case folding, so that a case folding of an NFKC string is itself normalized. These properties, and the files containing them, are described in the UCD documentation [UCD].

Acknowledgments

Mark Davis is the author of the initial version and has added to and maintained the text of this annex.

Thanks to Eric Muller, Asmus Freytag, Julie Allen, Kenneth Whistler, and Martin Duerst for feedback on this annex.

References

For references for this annex, see Unicode Standard Annex #41, "Common References for Unicode Standard Annexes."

Modifications

For details of the change history, see the online copy of this annex at http://www.unicode.org/reports/tr31/.

Unicode Standard Annex #34

Unicode Named Character Sequences

Summary

This annex defines the concept of Unicode named character sequences, specifies a notational convention for them and a set of rules constraining possible names applied to character sequences.

Contents

X1 Overview

The Unicode Standard specifies notational conventions for referring to sequences of characters (or code points), using angle brackets surrounding a comma-delimited list of code points, code points plus character names, and so on. For example, both of the designations in *Table 1* refer to a combining character sequence consisting of the letter "a" with a circumflex and an acute accent applied to it.

Table 1. Example of a Combining Character Sequence

<U+0061, U+0302, U+0301>
<U+0061 LATIN SMALL LETTER A, U+0302 COMBINING CIRCUMFLEX ACCENT, U+0301 COMBINING ACUTE ACCENT>

See *Appendix A, Notational Conventions,* in [Unicode] for the description of the conventions for expression of code points and for the representation of sequences of code points.

The Unicode conventions for referring to a sequence of characters (or code points) are a generalization of the formal syntax specified in ISO/IEC 10646:2003 for UCS Sequence Identifiers, or USI. A USI has the form

<UID_1, UID_2, ... UID_n>

where the UID_i represent the short identifiers for code points—most commonly "U+0061" or "0061". A USI must contain at least two code points.

Table 2. Examples of Named Sequences

Sequence	Name	Notes on Usage
ī̀ 012B 0300	LATIN SMALL LETTER I WITH MACRON AND GRAVE	Livonian
˥˩ 02E5 02E9	MODIFIER LETTER EXTRA-HIGH EXTRA-LOW CONTOUR TONE BAR	Contour tone letter
ㇷ゚ 31F7 309A	KATAKANA LETTER AINU P	Ainu in kana transcription
◌ុំ 17BB 17C6	KHMER VOWEL SIGN SRAK OM	Khmer
◌ាំ 17B6 17C6	KHMER VOWEL SIGN SRAK AM	Khmer
◌្ក 17D2 1780	KHMER CONSONANT SIGN COENG KA	Khmer

Such a conventional notation for sequences of Unicode code points that are treated as a unit is often useful. For example, other standards may need to refer to entities that are represented in Unicode by sequences of characters. Mapping tables may map single characters in other standards to sequences of Unicode characters, and listings of repertoire coverage for fonts or keyboards may need to reference entities that do not correspond to single Unicode code points.

In some limited circumstances it is necessary to also provide a name for such sequences. The primary example is the need to have an identifier for a sequence to correlate with an identifier in another standard, for which a cross-mapping to Unicode is desired. To address this need, the Unicode Standard defines a mechanism for naming sequences and provides a short list of sequences that have been formally named. This list is deliberately selective: it is neither possible nor desirable to attempt to provide names for all possible sequences of Unicode characters that could be of interest.

This annex defines the concept of a *Unicode named character sequence*, specifies a notational convention for such sequences, and a set of rules constraining possible names applied to character sequences. *Section X5, Data Files*, identifies the data file containing the normative list of Unicode named character sequences. As is the case for character names, named character sequences are strictly synchronized with ISO/IEC 10646.

Table 2 provides some examples of Unicode named character sequences to illustrate the kinds of entities that have been formally named. The "Sequence" column illustrates the entity in question with a representative rendering above the sequence of encoded Unicode characters that represent that entity. The "Name" column shows the name that has been associated with that sequence.

X1.1 Relation to Variation Sequences

Unicode named character sequences differ from Unicode variation sequences. The latter are documented in *Section 16.4, Variation Selectors,* in [Unicode] and are listed exhaustively in the data file StandardizedVariants.txt in the Unicode Character Database [UCD].

Variation sequences always consist of a sequence of precisely defined code points, the second of which must be a variation selector. There are additional constraints on which types of characters they can start with. Variation sequences have a restricted range of glyphic shapes, but have no associated name.

Named character sequences can, in principle, consist of code point sequences of any length, without constraints on what types of characters are involved. They do not have a specifically defined glyphic shape, but they *do* have a formally specified name associated with them.

X2 Definitions and Notation

SD1 Unicode named character sequence: A specific sequence of two or more Unicode characters, together with a formal name designating that sequence.

The notation for a Unicode named character sequence consists of the general conventions for character sequences in *Appendix A, Notational Conventions,* of [Unicode], together with name conventions as specified in *Section X4, Names*. Thus a typical representation of a Unicode named character sequence would be

<U+012B, U+0300> LATIN SMALL LETTER I WITH MACRON AND GRAVE

In contexts that supply other clear means for delimitation, such as data files or tables, the bracketing and comma delimitation conventions for the sequences may be dropped, as in

012B 0300;LATIN SMALL LETTER I WITH MACRON AND GRAVE

X3 Conformance

Conformance to the Unicode Standard *requires* conformance to the specification in this annex. The relationship between conformance to the Unicode Standard and conformance to an individual Unicode Standard Annex (UAX) is described in more detail in *Section 3.2, Conformance Requirements,* in [Unicode].

UAX34-C1: *If a process purports to implement Unicode named character sequences, it shall use only those named character sequences defined in the file NamedSequences.txt in the Unicode Character Database.*

Only the named character sequences in NamedSequences.txt are named in this standard. No other Unicode character sequences are given names in this version of the Unicode Standard, although named character sequences may be added in the future. Only sequences that are in Normalization Form NFC are given names in the Unicode Standard.

Conformance to this clause should not be construed as preventing implementers from providing informal names of their choice to any entities or character sequences, as appropriate. However, such informal names are not specified in any way by this standard for use in interchange.

The use of unnamed sequences is not affected by the specifications in this annex.

X3.1 Provisional Process for Named Character Sequences

When named character sequences are first suggested for inclusion in the Unicode Standard, they may be accepted provisionally. In such cases, they are listed in the file NamedSequencesProv.txt. See [DataProv].

Character sequences and proposed names listed in NamedSequencesProv.txt are *provisional* only and have no other status. They become part of the standard itself only when approved for inclusion in NamedSequences.txt.

The use of a provisional list is meant to allow sufficient time for review and comment on proposed named character sequences before they are finally approved. This also enables the normative data file, NamedSequences.txt, to remain stable.

X4 Names

Names of Unicode named character sequences are unique. They are part of the same namespace as Unicode character names. As a result, where a name exists as a character name, a modified name must be assigned instead. The same applies to not-yet-encoded characters.

Where possible, the names for sequences are constructed by appending the names of the constituent elements together while eliding duplicate elements, and possibly introducing the words between elements for clarity. Where this process would result in a name that already exists, the name is modified suitably to guarantee uniqueness. *Table 3* gives some examples of names for hypothetical sequences constructed according in this manner.

Table 3. Examples of Hypothetical Sequence Names

USI	Alternate Representation of Sequence	Name
<0041, 0043, 0043>	<A, B, C>	LATIN CAPITAL LETTER A B C
<00CA, 0046>	<AE, F>	LATIN CAPITAL LETTER AE F
<0058, 030A>	<X, COMBINING RING ABOVE>	LATIN CAPITAL LETTER X WITH RING ABOVE

Where names are constructed other than by merging existing character names for the constituent characters of the sequence, convention restricts any additional items to the Latin capital letters A to Z, SPACE, HYPHEN-MINUS, and the digits 0 to 9, provided that a digit is not the first character in a word. This convention makes it possible to turn names into identifiers using straightforward transformations.

Names for named sequences are constructed according to the following rules:

R1: Only Latin capital letters A to Z, digits 0 to 9 (provided that a digit is not the first character in a word), SPACE, and HYPHEN-MINUS are used for writing the names.

R2: Only one name is given to each named sequence, and each named sequence must have a unique name within the namespace that named sequences share with character names.

R3: Like character names, names for sequences are unique if they are different even when SPACE and medial HYPHEN-MINUS characters are ignored, and when the strings "LETTER", "CHARACTER", and "DIGIT" are ignored in comparison of the names.

The following two character names are exceptions to this rule, because they were created before this rule was specified:

116C HANGUL JUNGSEONG OE
1180 HANGUL JUNGSEONG O-E

Examples of unacceptable names that are not unique:

SARATI LETTER AA
SARATI CHARACTER AA

These two names would not be unique if the strings "LETTER" and "CHARACTER" were ignored.

R4: Where possible, names for named sequences are constructed by appending the names of the constituent elements together while eliding duplicate elements, and possibly introducing the words "WITH" or "AND" between elements for clarity. Should this process result in a name that already exists, the name is modified suitably to guarantee uniqueness among character names and names for named sequences.

R5: Where applicable, the rules from Appendix L in ISO/IEC 10646:2003 apply.

> **Note:** Just like character names, the names for sequences may be translated, with the translated names for each language being unique with respect to each other and the

corresponding set of translated character names. However, translated names are not restricted to the same limited character set as the English names. Translated names may not be suitable as identifiers without modification.

X5 Data Files

A normative data file, NamedSequences.txt, is available consisting of those named sequences defined for this version of [Unicode]. The sequences are listed in the data file in an abbreviated format. For the location of the data file, see [Data34].

In addition, a provisional data file, NamedSequencesProv.txt, is available containing sequences and names proposed for the standard but not yet approved as part of the normative list of named character sequences. For the location of the data file, see [DataProv].

Acknowledgments

Ken Whistler authored the initial versions. Asmus Freytag has added to and maintains the text of this annex.

Thanks to Mark Davis and Julie Allen for comments on this annex, including earlier versions.

References

For references for this annex, see Unicode Standard Annex #41, "Common References for Unicode Standard Annexes."

Modifications

For details of the change history, see the online copy of this annex at http://www.unicode.org/reports/tr34/.

Unicode Standard Annex #41

Common References for Unicode Standard Annexes

Summary

This annex presents a common set of references for the Unicode Standard Annexes.

Contents

X1 References to Publications by the Unicode Consortium

Publications may be listed more than once under different headings.

[Bidi] UAX #9: *Unicode Bidirectional Algorithm*
http://www.unicode.org/reports/tr9/

[Blocks] Blocks data file
For the latest version, see:
http://www.unicode.org/Public/UNIDATA/Blocks.txt
For the 5.0.0 version, see:
http://www.unicode.org/Public/5.0.0/ucd/Blocks.txt

[Boundaries] UAX #29: *Text Boundaries*
http://www.unicode.org/reports/tr29/

[Charts] Online Code Charts
http://www.unicode.org/charts/
An index to character names with links to the corresponding chart is found at
http://www.unicode.org/charts/charindex.html

[Charts15] Normalization Charts
http://www.unicode.org/reports/tr15/charts

[Charts29] Charts for the test files
For the latest version, see:
http://www.unicode.org/Public/UNIDATA/auxiliary/GraphemeBreakTest.html
http://www.unicode.org/Public/UNIDATA/auxiliary/WordBreakTest.html
http://www.unicode.org/Public/UNIDATA/auxiliary/SentenceBreakTest.html
For the 5.0.0 version, see:
http://www.unicode.org/Public/5.0.0/ucd/auxiliary/GraphemeBreakTest.html
http://www.unicode.org/Public/5.0.0/ucd/auxiliary/WordBreakTest.html
http://www.unicode.org/Public/5.0.0/ucd/auxiliary/SentenceBreakTest.html

[CLDR] Common Locale Data Repository
http://www.unicode.org/cldr/

[Code9] Reference code implementing the Bidirectional Algorithm
For the original verified C/C++ reference implementation, see:
http://www.unicode.org/reports/tr9/BidiReferenceCpp/
For the original verified Java reference implementation, see:
http://www.unicode.org/reports/tr9/BidiReferenceJava/
For updates to the C/C++ sample code, see:
http://www.unicode.org/Public/PROGRAMS/BidiReferenceCpp/

[Code14] Sample code implementing the Line Break Algorithm using a pair table
http://www.unicode.org/Public/PROGRAMS/LineBreakSampleCpp/
Contains the code samples shown in UAX #14 together with driver code.

[Collation] UTS #10: *Unicode Collation Algorithm (UCA)*
http://www.unicode.org/reports/tr10/

[Corrections] Normalization Corrections
For the latest version, see:
http://www.unicode.org/Public/UNIDATA/NormalizationCorrections.txt
For the 5.0.0 version, see:
http://www.unicode.org/Public/5.0.0/ucd/NormalizationCorrections.txt

[Corrigendum1] Corrigendum #1: *UTF-8 Shortest Form*
http://www.unicode.org/versions/corrigendum1.html

[Corrigendum2] Corrigendum #2: *Yod with Hiriq Normalization*
http://www.unicode.org/versions/corrigendum2.html

[Corrigendum3] Corrigendum #3: *U+F951 Normalization*
http://www.unicode.org/versions/corrigendum3.html

[Corrigendum4] Corrigendum #4: *Five CJK Canonical Mapping Errors*
http://www.unicode.org/versions/corrigendum4.html

[Corrigendum5] Corrigendum #5: *Normalization Idempotency*
http://www.unicode.org/versions/corrigendum5.html

[Data9] Bidi Mirroring
For the latest version, see:
http://www.unicode.org/Public/UNIDATA/BidiMirroring.txt
For the 5.0.0 version, see:
http://www.unicode.org/Public/5.0.0/ucd/BidiMirroring.txt

[Data11] East Asian Width property data file
For the latest version, see:
http://www.unicode.org/Public/UNIDATA/EastAsianWidth.txt
For the 5.0.0 version, see:
http://www.unicode.org/Public/5.0.0/ucd/EastAsianWidth.txt

[Data14] Line Break property data file
For the latest version, see:
http://www.unicode.org/Public/UNIDATA/LineBreak.txt
For the 5.0.0 version, see:
http://www.unicode.org/Public/5.0.0/ucd/LineBreak.txt

[Data24] Scripts data file
For the latest version, see:
http://www.unicode.org/Public/UNIDATA/Scripts.txt
For the 5.0.0 version, see:
http://www.unicode.org/Public/5.0.0/ucd/Scripts.txt

[Data34] Named Sequences data file
For the latest version, see:
http://www.unicode.org/Public/UNIDATA/NamedSequences.txt
For the 5.0.0 version see:
http://www.unicode.org/Public/5.0.0/ucd/NamedSequences.txt

[DataProv] Provisional Named Sequences data file
For the latest version, see:
http://www.unicode.org/Public/UNIDATA/NamedSequencesProv.txt
For the 5.0.0 version see:
http://www.unicode.org/Public/5.0.0/ucd/NamedSequencesProv.txt

[DerivedBIDI] Derived Bidi Properties
For the latest version see:
http://www.unicode.org/Public/UNIDATA/extracted/DerivedBidiClass.txt
For the 5.0.0 version, see:
http://www.unicode.org/Public/5.0.0/ucd/extracted/DerivedBidiClass.txt

[EAW] UAX #11: *East Asian Width*
http://www.unicode.org/reports/tr11/

[Errata] Updates and Errata
http://www.unicode.org/errata

[Exclusions] Composition Exclusion Table
For the latest version, see:
http://www.unicode.org/Public/UNIDATA/CompositionExclusions.txt
For the 5.0.0 version, see:
http://www.unicode.org/Public/5.0.0/ucd/CompositionExclusions.txt

[FAQ] Unicode Frequently Asked Questions
http://www.unicode.org/faq/
For answers to common questions on technical issues.

[Feedback] Reporting Form
http://www.unicode.org/reporting.html
For reporting errors and requesting information online.

[Glossary] Unicode Glossary
http://www.unicode.org/glossary/
For explanations of terminology used in this and other documents.

[HangulST] Hangul Syllable Types
For the latest version, see:
http://www.unicode.org/Public/UNIDATA/HangulSyllableType.txt
For the 5.0.0 version, see:
http://www.unicode.org/Public/5.0.0/ucd/HangulSyllableType.txt

[LineBreak] UAX #14: *Line Breaking Properties*
http://www.unicode.org/reports/tr14/

[NormProps] Derived Normalization Properties
For the latest version, see:
http://www.unicode.org/Public/UNIDATA/DerivedNormalizationProps.txt
For the 5.0.0 version, see:
http://www.unicode.org/Public/5.0.0/ucd/DerivedNormalizationProps.txt

[Policies] Unicode Policies
http://www.unicode.org/policies/

[Props] Property Data:
For the latest version, see:
http://www.unicode.org/Public/UNIDATA/auxiliary/GraphemeBreakProperty.txt
http://www.unicode.org/Public/UNIDATA/auxiliary/WordBreakProperty.txt
http://www.unicode.org/Public/UNIDATA/auxiliary/SentenceBreakProperty.txt
For the 5.0.0 version, see:
http://www.unicode.org/Public/5.0.0/ucd/auxiliary/GraphemeBreakProperty.txt
http://www.unicode.org/Public/5.0.0/ucd/auxiliary/WordBreakProperty.txt
http://www.unicode.org/Public/5.0.0/ucd/auxiliary/SentenceBreakProperty.txt

[PropValue] Property Value Aliases data file
For the latest version, see:
http://www.unicode.org/Public/UNIDATA/PropertyValueAliases.txt
For the 5.0.0 version, see:
http://www.unicode.org/Public/5.0.0/ucd/PropertyValueAliases.txt

[RegEx] UTS #18: *Unicode Regular Expressions*
http://www.unicode.org/reports/tr18/

[Reports] Unicode Technical Reports
http://www.unicode.org/reports/
For information on the status and development process for technical reports, and for a list of technical reports.

[Sample] Sample Normalizer code
http://www.unicode.org/reports/tr15/Normalizer.html

[Security] UTR #36: *Security Considerations for the Implementation of Unicode and Related Technology*
http://www.unicode.org/reports/tr36/

[Stability] Unicode Consortium Stability Policies
http://www.unicode.org/standard/stability_policy.html

[Tests15] Normalization Conformance Test
For the latest version, see:
http://www.unicode.org/Public/UNIDATA/NormalizationTest.txt
For the 5.0.0 version, see:
http://www.unicode.org/Public/5.0.0/ucd/NormalizationTest.txt

[Tests29] Test data:
For the latest version, see:
http://www.unicode.org/Public/UNIDATA/auxiliary/GraphemeBreakTest.txt
http://www.unicode.org/Public/UNIDATA/auxiliary/WordBreakTest.txt
http://www.unicode.org/Public/UNIDATA/auxiliary/SentenceBreakTest.txt
For the 5.0.0 version, see:
http://www.unicode.org/Public/5.0.0/ucd/auxiliary/GraphemeBreakTest.txt
http://www.unicode.org/Public/5.0.0/ucd/auxiliary/WordBreakTest.txt
http://www.unicode.org/Public/5.0.0/ucd/auxiliary/SentenceBreakTest.txt

[UAX14] UAX #14: *Line Breaking Properties*
http://www.unicode.org/reports/tr14/

[UAX15] UAX #15: *Unicode Normalization Forms*
http://www.unicode.org/reports/tr15/

[UAX29] UAX #29: *Text Boundaries*
http://www.unicode.org/reports/tr29/

[UAX31] UAX #31: *Identifier and Pattern Syntax*
http://www.unicode.org/reports/tr31/

[UCA] UTS #10: *Unicode Collation Algorithm*
http://www.unicode.org/reports/tr10/

[UCD] Unicode Character Database
http://www.unicode.org/ucd/
For an overview of the Unicode Character Database and a list of its associated files, see:
http://www.unicode.org/Public/UNIDATA/UCD.html

[UCDDoc] Unicode Character Database Documentation
http://www.unicode.org/Public/UNIDATA/UCD.html

[Unicode] The Unicode Standard
For the latest version, see:
http://www.unicode.org/versions/latest/
For the 5.0.0 version, see:
http://www.unicode.org/versions/Unicode5.0.0/

[Unicode3.0] The Unicode Consortium. *The Unicode Standard, Version 3.0* (Reading, MA, Addison-Wesley, 2000. ISBN 0-201-61633-5).

[Unicode3.1] The Unicode Consortium. The Unicode Standard, Version 3.1.0, defined by: *The Unicode Standard, Version 3.0* (Reading, MA, Addison-Wesley, 2000. ISBN 0-201-61633-5), as amended by the *Unicode Standard Annex #27: Unicode 3.1*
http://www.unicode.org/reports/tr27/

[Unicode3.2] The Unicode Consortium. The Unicode Standard, Version 3.2.0, defined by: *The Unicode Standard, Version 3.0* (Reading, MA, Addison-Wesley, 2000. ISBN 0-201-61633-5), as amended by the *Unicode Standard Annex #27: Unicode 3.1* and the *Unicode Standard Annex #28: Unicode 3.2* http://www.unicode.org/reports/tr28/

[Unicode4.0] The Unicode Consortium. *The Unicode Standard, Version 4.0* (Boston, MA, Addison-Wesley, 2003. ISBN 0-321-18578-1).

[Unicode4.0.1] The Unicode Consortium. The Unicode Standard, Version 4.0.1, defined by: *The Unicode Standard, Version 4.0* (Boston, MA, Addison-Wesley, 2003. ISBN 0-321-18578-1), as amended by *Unicode 4.0.1* http://www.unicode.org/versions/Unicode4.0.1/

[Unicode4.1] The Unicode Consortium. The Unicode Standard, Version 4.1.0, defined by: *The Unicode Standard, Version 4.0* (Boston, MA, Addison-Wesley, 2003. ISBN 0-321-18578-1), as amended by *Unicode 4.0.1* and by *Unicode 4.1.0* http://www.unicode.org/versions/Unicode4.1.0/

[Unicode5.0] The Unicode Consortium. *The Unicode Standard, Version 5.0* (Boston, MA, Addison-Wesley, 2007. ISBN 0-321-48091-0).

[UTC] Unicode Technical Committee http://www.unicode.org/consortium/utc.html

[UTN5] UTN #5: *Canonical Equivalences in Applications* http://www.unicode.org/notes/tn5

[UTR36] UTR #36: *Unicode Security Considerations* http://www.unicode.org/reports/tr36/

[UTS35] UTS #35: *Locale Data Markup Language (LDML)* http://www.unicode.org/reports/tr35/

[UTS10] UTS #10: *Unicode Collation Algorithm (UCA)* *http://www.unicode.org/reports/tr10/*

[UTS18] UTS #18: *Unicode Regular Expressions* *http://www.unicode.org/reports/tr18/*

[UTS39] UTS #39: *Unicode Security Mechanisms* http://www.unicode.org/reports/tr39/

[Versions] Versions of the Unicode Standard http://www.unicode.org/versions/ *For information on version numbering, and citing and referencing the Unicode Standard, the Unicode Character Database, and Unicode Technical Reports.*

X2 References to Other Standards

[10646] International Organization for Standardization. *Information Technology*—Universal Multiple-Octet Coded Character Set (UCS). (ISO/IEC 10646:2003). *For availability, see:* http://www.iso.org

[ISO15924] ISO 15924: *Code for the Representation of Names of Scripts* http://www.unicode.org/iso15924/

[JIS] JIS X 4051-1995. *Line Composition Rules for Japanese Documents.* (『日本語文書の行組版方法』) Japanese Standards Association. 1995.

[XML1.1] Extensible Markup Language (XML) 1.1 http://www.w3.org/TR/xml11/

X3 Other References

[Cedar97] Cy Cedar, David Veintimilla, Michel Suignard, and Asmus Freytag, *Report from the Trenches: Microsoft Publisher goes Unicode.* Proceedings of the Eleventh International Unicode Conference, San Jose, CA, 1997.

[CharLint] Charlint—A Character Normalization Tool http://www.w3.org/International/charlint/

[CharMod] W3C Character Model for the World Wide Web http://www.w3.org/TR/charmod/

[CharReq] W3C Requirements for String Identity Matching and String Indexing http://www.w3.org/TR/WD-charreq

[Knuth78] Donald E. Knuth and Michael F. Plass, *Breaking Lines into Paragraphs*, republished in *Digital Typography*, CSLI 78 (Stanford, California: CLSI Publications 1997).

[Suign98] Michel Suignard, *Worldwide Typography and How to Apply JIS X 4051-1995 to Unicode.* Proceedings of the Twelfth International Unicode/ISO 10646 Conference, Tokyo, Japan, 1998.

[TEX] Donald E. Knuth, *TEX, the Program*, Volume B of *Computers & Typesetting* (Reading, MA, Addison-Wesley, 1986).

The main text of this book is set in Minion, designed by Rob Slimbach at Adobe Systems, Inc. The text of the character names list is set in Myriad, designed by Carol Twombly and Robert Slimbach at Adobe Systems, Inc. The main text was typeset using Adobe FrameMaker 7.2 running under Windows XP. Figures were created with Adobe Illustrator. The text of the annexes was edited in Microsoft FrontPage, and then printed from HTML using Mozilla FireFox. The code charts were produced with Unibook chart formatting software supplied by ASMUS, Inc. The PDFs for the code charts and annexes were post-processed with software from PDFLib GmbH. The Han radical-stroke index was typeset by Apple Computer, Inc.

The following companies and organizations supplied fonts both for the text and for the code charts:

Adobe Systems, Inc.
Apple Computer, Inc.
Atelier Fluxus Virus
Beijing Zhong Yi (Zheng Code) Electronics Company
DecoType, Inc.
Evertype
IBM Corporation
Microsoft Corporation
Monotype Imaging
Peking University Founder Group Corporation
Production First Software
SIL International
STAR–Sylheti Translation And Research

Additional fonts were supplied by individuals as listed in the Acknowledgments.